POPE & YOUNG CLUB

BOWHUNTING
BIG GAME RECORDS OF NORTH AMERICA

Fifth Edition
1999

The Second Official Pope and Young Club Conservation print, "Chip Shot," is a reproduction of the original Michael Sieve 24 x 36 inch oil painting.

Prepared and edited by the:
Book Editorial Committee

M. R. James, Editor
G. Fred Asbell
Roger Atwood
Dr. C. Randall Byers
Dave Coupland
Jim Dougherty
Harv Ebers

Billy Ellis III
Glenn Hisey
Dr. Donald Ace Morgan
Stan Rauch
Dr. David Samuel
Ron Sherer
Glenn St. Charles

Copyright© 1975, 1981, 1987, 1993 and 1999 by the Pope and Young Club. All rights reserved, including the right to reproduce the book or portions thereof in any form or by any means, electronic or mechanical, including photocopying, recording, or by any information storage and retrieval system, without permission in writing from the Pope and Young Club.

Libarary of Congress Catalog Card Number: 99-070403
ISBN Number: 0-9617966-2-6
Published in April, 1999

Produced and Published in the United States of America by:
    The Pope and Young Club
    P. O. Box 548
    Chatfield, MN 55923

Designed by Lisa M. Wayand

Dedication

Margaret and Glenn St. Charles

This fifth edition of the Pope and Young Club's record book is dedicated with deep respect and heartfelt appreciation to founder Glenn St. Charles and his wife, Margaret. Since the beginning it was Glenn's vision to establish an organization that would prove the effectiveness of the hunting bow by recording statistical data about North America's most outstanding big game animals harvested by broadhead-tipped arrows. His dream, fully supported by Margaret and the entire St. Charles family, is now a reality. Today the Pope and Young Club not only represents the highest ethical standards in fair chase bowhunting practices, it is the undisputed authority on this continent's exceptional big game bowhunting trophies. Further and perhaps equally important, it has evolved into one of America's most effective pro-hunting, pro-conservation organizations. None of this would have been possible without the foresight, the enduring faith, and guiding hand of Glenn and Margaret St. Charles. They helped to create and record the history of bowhunting in the twentieth century and for that we are eternally grateful.

CONTENTS

BOOK I

9	Acknowledgements
11	Foreword **by G. Fred Asbell**
14	Trophy Hunting, Fair Chase, History, Ethics and Hunter Image **by Glenn St. Charles**
20	Hunting in the Twenty-First Century **by Dr. David Samuel**
26	Big Game Records in the Twenty-First Century and Beyond **by Dr. C. Randall Byers**
32	Revisiting the Past, Working for the Future **by Stan Rauch**
38	Club Finances — Yesterday, Today and Tomorrow **by Dr. Donald Ace Morgan**
44	The Pope and Young/St. Charles Museum **by Joe St. Charles**
50	Saxton Temple Pope **by Doug Walker**
56	Bowhunting: It's Up To the Kids **by Jim Dougherty**
60	Thanks, Lord, for the Ladies! **by George Zanoni**
66	Bowhunting Equipment — and Restrictions **by Dave Holt**
74	Is Bowhunting Getting Too Easy? **by Dick Sage**
80	I've Learned I Still Have a Lot To Learn… **by M. R. James**
84	Some Tales of the Measurers' Tape **by Frank "Rit" Heller**
92	Pope and Young Club Q & A
96	Meet the Artist: Michael Sieve Profile and Paintings

BOOK II

THE RECORDS

Bears
- 130 Alaska Brown Bear
- 132 Black Bear
- 192 Grizzly Bear
- 194 Polar Bear

195 Bison

Caribou
- 196 Barren Ground Caribou (Including Velvet Entries)
- 203 Central Canada Caribou (Including Velvet Entries)
- 207 Mountain Caribou (Including Velvet Entries)
- 210 Quebec-Labrador Caribou (Including Velvet Entries)
- 218 Woodland Caribou

220 Cougar (Mountain Lion)

Elk
- 548 Roosevelt "Olympic" Elk
- 553 Yellowstone "American" Elk (Typical)
- 600 Yellowstone "American" Elk (Non-Typical)

Deer
- 238 Columbian Blacktail Deer (Typical Including Velvet Entries)
- 246 Columbian Blacktail Deer (Non-Typical Including Velvet Entries)
- 247 Sitka Blacktail Deer (Including Velvet Entries)
- 252 Coues Deer (Typical Including Velvet Entries)
- 256 Coues Deer (Non-Typical)
- 257 Mule Deer (Typical Including Velvet Entries)
- 285 Mule Deer (Non-Typical Including Velvet Entries)
- 291 Whitetail Deer (Typical Including Velvet Entries)
- 532 Whitetail Deer (Non-Typical Including Velvet Entries)

Moose
- 602 Alaska-Yukon Moose
- 608 Canada Moose
- 613 Shiras "Wyoming" Moose (Including Velvet Entries)

618 Muskox

621 Pronghorn Antelope

680 Rocky Mountain Goat

Sheep
- 687 Bighorn Sheep
- 691 Dall Sheep
- 695 Desert Sheep
- 697 Stone Sheep

Appendix

- 700 Big Game Minimum Score Requirements
- 701 How To Enter a Trophy
- 702 Official Scoring Charts of North American Big Game
- 736 Pope and Young History: Past and Present Club Officers
- 740 North American Fish & Game Departments
- 744 Pope and Young Official Measurers

Acknowledgements

THE LAST HALF of the twentieth century has been a period of steady and unprecedented bowhunting growth throughout North America. Not surprisingly, that surge has been directly reflected in the Pope and Young Club's record books. From a modest 1975 edition containing nearly 2,300 entries to this massive 1999 edition with more than 41,000 entries, the Club's hardcover books have become successively thicker with each respective printing. And, in each instance, the "meaty" quality of content found in every new edition has admirably complemented the record book's quantity.

Creating this mammoth new record book was both a costly and time-consuming venture for the Club. It required no small effort on the part of numerous individuals, most of whom volunteered their time and talents to this project. Also, considering the fact that much of the work was accomplished within a matter of months — with mere days between determining the final numerical rank of all entries following panel judging in mid-March and the April printing deadline necessary for an on-time May delivery — its creation can be considered something of a minor miracle. In truth, the book project would have proved to be an impossible undertaking without a unified and dedicated team effort.

As always, heading the team responsible for determining and approving book content was an Editorial Committee comprised of the Club's current Board of Directors and founder Glenn St. Charles. Led in its creative efforts by Editor M. R. James, the group included several key individuals who contributed thoughtful and timely chapters, commentary, and/or photos to the new book. Special thanks are due Dr. Dave Samuel, Dr. Randy Byers, Dr. Don Morgan, Stan Rauch, Jim Dougherty, Glenn St. Charles and G. Fred Asbell. Additional thanks go to Club members Joe St. Charles, Dave Holt, Dick Sage, George Zanoni, Rit Heller, and Doug Walker for their individual contributions. Finally, a note of heartfelt appreciation is due committeemen Dave Coupland, Ron Sherer, Billy Ellis III, Roger Atwood, and Harv Ebers for their helpful advice and constructive criticism.

Singular recognition is due Glenn Hisey, Executive Secretary, who promptly and efficiently coordinated behind the scenes book production efforts. Not only did he open and maintain lines of communication between Club headquarters and various contributors, suppliers, and the book's printer, Glenn provided complete and up-to-date computerized records for each species listed — assuring the correctness of all listings and accompanying illustrations — while he continued to capably run the routine daily business of the Club's Chatfield, Minnesota, office. Call him Pope and Young's "Answer Man" or "Miracle Man," either title fits Glenn perfectly. Kevin Hisey, too, deserves an official Club "attaboy" for his diligent efforts in tracking down book materials, proofreading copy, and generally assisting his father in keeping the Club — and the record book project — on track throughout this busy and hectic period.

Wildlife photographer Judd Cooney and artist Mike Sieve are to be commended for their contributions to this volume. Once again, Judd graciously donated numerous photos of big game and bowhunters to aptly illustrate various chapters and species listings. Mike, whose specially commissioned art graces this book's cover, not only created the Club's current Conservation Print but also painted the original art which is reproduced within the book's special color section, thanks to a licensing agreement with Wild Wings, Inc.

Freelance artist Lisa Wayand, who designed layouts for the Club's 1993 record book, again used her considerable creative talents to design this edition. Additionally, thanks are due Meg Colwell at Banta ISG/Viking Press for her work with the Club in this publishing venture.

Finally, a sincere thank you goes to the Boone and Crockett Club for granting permission to adapt its scoring methods and reproduce the B&C scoring forms for express use by the Pope and Young Club.

Foreword

THIS IS THE FIFTH EDITION of the Pope and Young Club record book. Within these pages are listings of the finest North American big game animals taken with bow and arrow over the last 41 years. I'm sure it can be said with certainty that in 1958, at the Club's very first awards banquet, no one present could possibly have foreseen such success. Consider that at the Grayling, Michigan, banquet 41 years ago, 41 heads were entered into the records, and that now, 41 years later, the program has accumulated in excess of *41,000 heads* — an increase of more than a thousandfold!

Increases of such proportions are easier to quantify than to fathom. Truly, who would have imagined this thousandfold growth? Yet there is no disputing the facts. The physical presence of this book alone says clearly that bowhunting and bowhunters are serious about big animals. And it says that the Pope and Young Club and trophy bowhunting have become a distinct part of the continually expanding cadre of hunters who favor the bow and arrow. Indeed, the Pope and Young Club and trophy bowhunting have settled comfortably into the pages of most every archery/bowhunting book and magazine available today. Trophy bowhunting, without question, has taken on gigantic significance within today's hunting community.

With growth, however, comes new challenges for tomorrow. Unlike a trophy taken in 1958, today's big trophy is sometimes accompanied by the potential for and/or illusion of some personal gain. It isn't how it's done in this organization, of course. Here, the dignity of the chase and the final moment without undue fanfare is our way, and we hope this is a way hunting will rediscover very soon. One of the Pope and Young Club's future challenges well may be keeping our eye on what we do best, maintaining the tradition and dignity in what we do and what we feel. The Pope and Young Club, like trophy bowhunting itself, has always been about pursuit of the very finest. Deciding exactly what you want to be, and then setting high standards and living by them, has always been the mark of the true hero and the strong organization.

This book represents the Pope and Young Club and 41 years of pursuit and conservation. From beginning to end, the Club's beliefs, ethics, and ideas are interwoven into this book's entries, commentary, and stories. Every line is a celebration of the hunter/conservation ethic. Simply stated, this book is about trophy bowhunting and the challenges inherent in pursuit of the finest and most difficult. It also speaks to the dedication of those within our Club who give of their time and energies to measure and record the successes of others. Without them this book would only be an idea, rather than a reality.

M. R. James, with assistance from others, assumed the responsibility for bringing this book to successful completion. For over a year he dedicated his time and editing efforts to our record book project. The immense size of this edition should tell you something of that effort — but only something. I don't know of any other Club volunteer who could have done it. The Pope and Young membership owes a huge debt of gratitude to M. R. James. By the way, this is the third record book M. R. has edited, and your compliments will be all the pay he ever receives.

May this Fifth Edition book inspire you to take to the woods and to protect and cherish them and their creatures — and to shoot an arrow just to see it fly.

G. Fred Asbell
President

BOWHUNTING: A Look Back, A Look Ahead...

TROPHY HUNTING, FAIR CHASE, HISTORY, ETHICS AND HUNTER IMAGE

by Glenn St. Charles

Editor's Note: In his 1998 book, **Bows on the Little Delta**, *Pope and Young founder Glenn St. Charles shared some of his memorable adventures and spoke his mind on a variety of timely topics. The following excerpts contain a few quotes which should be of special interest to today's hunters who seek a better understanding of bowhunting's past in order to help preserve its future.*

Trophy Hunting

"Emphasis on trophy hunting came into its own in February, 1958 when the NFAA/Pope and Young records came into being. Before that, if there was a choice, the bigger rack took the arrow, unless you were a meat hunter and liked the more tender steaks. Many hunters in the early days competed in the numbers game, 'Who killed the most?'

"Let it be known that the legends were not trophy hunters by today's standards. Art Young, Saxton Pope, Will Compton, Howard Hill, Fred Bear, Ben Pearson, and Chet Stevenson all shot and killed everything that came down the pike. They did it the old-fashioned way — no gimmicks or gadgets. The law of averages dictated that some of their kills would be trophies. Most of those that could meet the Pope and Young Club minimums and Fair Chase rules were eventually entered. Some were declared world records by their own standards — Pope and Young Club Fair Chase Rules be damned...

"These greats are not legends because of their exploits at killing game. They did much to bring bowhunting to the forefront as a sport. They carried the message to us with their appreciation of nature and man, their inventions, and their merchandising know-how. They were communicators, and more than anything else, they had one intangible ingredient that is common to legends — CHARISMA!

"They lived and hunted when legends were possible. They were pioneers and standouts when bowhunting was still considered a sport by all concerned parties. Simply getting the biggest and the most does not a legend make."

Fair Chase

"The accepted definition of Fair Chase by those who care is: *not taking unfair advantage of animals while hunting them in their native haunts*. Boone and Crockett Club and Pope and Young Club have Fair Chase rules for entry of trophy animals into their records.

"Fair Chase is a many-faceted concept — means different things to different people. Most hunters have their own agenda — 'fair chase' is whatever they feel comfortable with. Perhaps that is as it should be — to each his own. Those who hunt with concern for our image will be discreet in their hunt and in their stories that follow. The stuff-it-down-their-throats advocates will hunt with an entirely opposite look, and write the story phrased in blood and guts...

"The point of this is: *in today's world, anything we do that appears unsportsmanlike negatively affects our image; an image that is coming more and more under scrutiny.*"

History

"In the '30s, bowhunting was just the dream of a few. Between 1936 and 1940, bowhunting became a reality. However, we were reminded by our wildlife departments (DNR) and gun hunters that the Indians had abandoned the bow in favor of the rifle, which was a much better provider of meat for the tribe...

"At first we didn't kill many animals. We really didn't expect to. Bowhunting was new. Not much had been written about bowhunting. We were pioneers. We would write the books. Keep in mind that this was in the days before 'fair chase' and trophy hunting. We actually stalked and still-hunted. We weren't concerned about gender or size. We shot anything that was legal. Something was better than nothing. We shot lots of arrows and missed a lot. On those early hunts it seemed like the animals played games with us...

"Many bowhunters were making equipment in their basements and garages. Theirs was such a slow process they had very little impact on the growth of bowhunting. With the advent of plastics in the early '50s, the equipment picture changed. Now bows could be mass produced. New designs, recurves, became the latest trend. The archery industry really started rolling and so did bowhunting. With that, our demands for more areas and longer seasons grew. The gun hunters' concern changed to alarm. We were taking over their turf. Between them and the Humane Society (our main objector and the only anti-hunting group around at the time), we were beginning to have real problems...

"We were called on the carpet again and again by everybody concerned. The public demanded that the DNR get answers to the question: Was the bow really a viable hunting weapon?

"...the NFAA Hunting Activities Committee brought into being the bowhunter record system in February of 1958. The impressive trophy record is what DNR needed to get them off the hook with the public. Now they had proof that the bow was a viable hunting weapon. However, bowhunters would also have to change their ways. A set of Fair Chase Rules was put into place along with the record-keeping — all brought into being in the interest of perserving bowhunting.

"In 1960, the NFAA reluctantly, but graciously, turned over the valuable big game records to an avid group of bowhunters, who became the Pope and Young Club as we know it today. The records brought bowhunting to a new level. Now there was a new standard of measuring the size of the animals killed. The old way of gauging by weight, for the most part, disappeared. However, there are still those who judge a hunter by numbers of animals killed."

Ethics and Hunter Image

"My hunting began in the late '30s, the era that still adhered to the principles of Teddy Roosevelt: that hunting was good for the country, a manly sport that built character and sharpened the senses. The public felt comfortable in accepting that concept since most of their ancestors hunted to put meat on the table. The need for wild animal food gradually faded and hunting evolved into a sport. The DNRs managed wildlife for wildlife's sake and the hunter's sport. The public, at one time, was not into what sport hunting entailed — out of sight, out of mind.

"Times have changed. No longer are hunters out of sight, out of mind. TV has brought all of our hunting activities right into the living room in vivid color...We call hunting sport. The public sees it as killing for fun.

"...In my opinion, the voting public does not mind that we hunt. It is HOW we hunt that is causing the concern. This concern by the voting public makes them [non-hunters] very vulnerable to the views of the animal rights activists — thus the real root of our problems. Wouldn't it seem to make sense that we sacrifice some of our methods for the survival of hunting? Is that too much to ask?...

"Today, hunting is struggling for survival, especially bowhunting. It is human nature to react to trouble by pointing fingers — blame someone. The animal rights activists — yes, they are the ones. We anguish, wring our hands, and cry for someone to do something. The 'stuff it down their throats' and the 'don't let them get their foot in the door' advocates cry, 'They can't do this to us.'

"Oh, but they already have their foot in the door. However, the activists are only part of our problem — an 'in your face' problem. Perhaps they have distracted us so much that we have not seen the root of our trouble — our image — how the public perceives hunters. Isn't it possible that we hunters are our own worst enemies? In this light, part of the animal activist agenda would be to keep us distracted so that we don't recognize where we are failing.

"What Aldo Leopold wrote makes more sense today than it did fifty years ago:

I have the impression that the American sportsman is puzzled; he doesn't understand what's happening to him. Bigger and better gadgets are good for industry, so why not for outdoor recreation? ...The sportsman has no leaders to tell him what is wrong. The sporting press no longer represents sport; it has turned billboard for the gadgeteer. Wildlife administrators are too busy producing something to shoot at to worry much about the cultural value of shooting. Because everyone from Zenophon to Teddy Roosevelt said sport has value, it is assumed this value must be indestructible.

Advice and Wisdom

1. Credibility comes from firsthand knowledge, whether writing or speaking. Assumption, rumors, hearsay won't do it.

2. Don't search for a profound justification for hunting. You hunt because the animals are there where you want to be.

3. Hunt ethically and in fair chase. You'll know the feeling when you have done it right.

4. Don't let peer pressure make you a trophy hunter. Be a trophy hunter until something else comes along.

5. Respect the animals in life and death. A boot in the rump won't do it. A little humility is better. You may be alone, but remember there is a higher Presence.

6. If possible, find a home for all usable parts: the meat, hide, sinew, and hooves. It's called respect. A rack worthy of a mount deserves the best in taxidermy.

7. Do not get caught up in the numbers game. If asked how many animals you have killed, all you need to say is "enough."

8. Remember, everyone is a VIP.

9. You don't really know a person until you have hunted with him.

10. Leaders need credibility. Be an independent thinker. Never let anyone or any entity own you.

"Though the years, subtly we have gone from hunting, defined as 'a walk in the woods' in pursuit of animals to accepting under the heading of progress, every conceivable gadget and method that the shooting sports industry can devise to kill animals faster and farther. What they have done is compromise our sport by redefining the word 'hunting' to accommodate all the new stuff on the market… The question now is: Do we need it when the survival of hunting is at stake?…

"Industry will resist change. They will cite that the price of 'turning back the clock' is too high. That hunters are too ingrained in modern hunting concepts for change. Teddy Roosevelt's manly sport, Aldo Leopold's concern, and Howard Hill's hunting the hard way do not fit into today's concept of hunting…

"…As for the future — for what it's worth, I believe the animal rights folks will continue to get more offbeat and self-destruct when the non-hunting public, the voters, tell them to join the human race. As for hunting? Depends on how the public perceives us down the road. Animals are 'in.' Killing will not sell. Hunting will be a tough sell. I shudder to think of the alternative to change — 10 %, at best, of the population, hunters, trying to cram today's concept of hunting down the throats of 90% of the voting population, non-hunters."

Glenn St. Charles, founder of the Pope and Young Club, is recognized as a true bowhunting pioneer and legend. A member of the Archery Hall of Fame, he makes his home in Seattle, Washington.

HUNTING IN THE TWENTY-FIRST CENTURY

by Dr. Dave Samuel

FOR MOST OF THE 2 MILLION YEARS that humans have lived on this earth, they hunted in order to survive. Hunting led to cooperation, to the development of language and communication, to art forms, and to the invention of tools for hunting, skinning, and preparing wild game. One of these inventions was the bow and arrow. Playwright/author Robert Ardrey once wrote, "The invention of the bow and arrow, I believe, had as much significance to prehistoric man as the invention of the nuclear weapon to modern man." Obviously, hunting has played a major role in the evolution of the human race and some authors speculate that even our genetic makeup resulted, in part, from our evolution as a hunting animal.

One aspect of this evolution that is overlooked by modern day urbanites is the time frame of hunting. We've used cellular phones for 10 years, laptop computers for 15 years, television for 50 years, and sound movies for some 70 years. Your great grandparents used horses and buggies and non-Indians have lived in North America for about 500 years. Our ancestors domesticated animals and grains for human use a short 10,000 years ago, a brief one hundred centuries. *But humans have hunted for almost 2 million years — 20,000 centuries!* In that context, shouldn't people pause when a mere handful of critics charge that hunting is frivolous? Should we not harbor at least a few reservations about anti-hunters who say that because society has changed in the last 50 years, that an activity humans have practiced for well over a million years has no place in our modern world? When one looks at the long term context of hunting, of predator/prey cycles, of ecological communities, of man's position in the food chain, maybe the answers to some of our modern day problems can be found in the woods. One could make a good case, given the time frame of hunting, that getting back to our roots — the same roots that nourished us for some 2 million years — might be healthy for all mankind. But that is not happening. Instead of getting into the woods, we see modern man moving away from nature.

Fewer people go into the outdoors today. Almost all outdoor recreational activities — hiking, backpacking, canoeing, camping, fishing, and hunting with firearms

— have lost participants in recent years. There are several reasons for such waning interest. Most obvious is the growing urban society that separates us, and our children, from the realities of nature and the opportunities to get into the woods to experience nature for ourselves. Along with urban sprawl comes a loss of habitat and the pollution of waterways, factors which make it more difficult to recreate in the outdoors. Societal attitudes have also changed and today we have a more diverse population than ever before. This brings differing values and traditions along with less nature-related activity. Another reason for a decline in outdoor recreation is the fact that today's young people have all kinds of indoor activities to keep them busy and reduce their involvement in potential outdoor activities, including hunting.

At the same time all of these factors are causing reduced participation in outdoor sports, the anti-hunting strategy of state ballot referendums to eliminate hunting has been quite successful (also probably another spin-off of our urban society). Yes, there are many reasons for the decrease in hunting interest. We also are seeing a decrease in hunter numbers in some states. For example, there were 184,079 big game license sold in New York State in 1994; however, only 176,870 were sold in 1996. In California, hunting license sales have dropped thirty-one percent (134,000 hunters) since 1987. So while it's true that hunter numbers are stable or increasing in some states, decreases are becoming more common and these declining numbers — combined with added wildlife management responsibilities such as non-game and endangered species programs and little or no wildlife agency funding from general revenue accounts funded by all taxpayers, rather than just sportsmen — have led to a budget crisis in several states.

In 1998, the Washington Department of Fish and Wildlife experienced a shortfall of $19 million. This meant less wildlife and fish management and an adverse impact

on all state wildlife programs. The Oregon wildlife agency expects to trim one hundred jobs over the next six years to prepare for expected decreases in license sales. During 1996-97, the Idaho Department of Fish and Game made $6 million in budget cuts and eliminated 29 jobs. When license sales drop, revenues also drop. Because of the needs for more revenues, several states — namely Arizona, California, Florida, Pennsylvania, and West Virginia, among others — have created innovative ways to supplement income from hunting and fishing to pay for non-game and endangered species programs. They have implemented personalized conservation license plates and license plate renewal fees, lottery funds, wildlife print sales, and other methods to generate much-needed funds. These programs help but state agencies require more monies to do the best possible job. Agencies need more money from all taxpayers via general state revenues; however, that is not happening. In fact, many state wildlife agencies get no funds from general revenue accounts and in states that do those funding sources are decreasing payments. Thus, for most state wildlife and fisheries programs helping game and non-game species alike, it is still the hunters and fishermen who carry the load for everyone.

Other changes in hunting. Those individuals who do go into the woods are finding other notable changes. In the West, more and more ranchers faced with financial difficulties are charging hunters fees for access to their lands. Other landowners who once allowed locals to hunt now raise cash by leasing lands to outfitters. It is not uncommon today for ranchers and farmers from Montana to Texas to make more from selling hunting rights than from their livestock operations.

Western states are also becoming involved in programs that reduce access for the average hunter. In most instances the ranchers — or the guides and outfitters who lease the lands — had to carry out specific habitat programs designed to benefit wildlife. In exchange they often got a guaranteed number of hunting permits and other perks. In some areas, within limits, the ranchers could set dates for a hunting season that differed from general statewide hunting seasons. Ranchers used their political influence to force compromises that allowed them to gain these benefits. Landowners argued, and rightly so, that their crops fed wild animals so they deserved some kind of compensation.

Because leasing usually locks out the average hunter, some state wildlife agencies are getting into the leasing business themselves. In essence, the way it works is the wildlife agencies in states like Montana and Oklahoma, for example, pay farmers and ranchers to open their lands to public hunting. In most situations the cost to hunters is minimal and the better the wildlife management carried out by the landowner the more funds they receive. Montana's Block Managment Program is a good example of a state making an effort to keep the average hunter in the field.

There are also changes being generated by the antis. With our urban society, a withdrawal from the woods and the financial crunch faced by wildlife agencies, along with decreased contact with death in nature, it is easier for anti-hunting strategies to be successful. And the strategies are many. In recent years the most effective tactic has been state ballot referendums. Those referendums specifically have attacked trapping, hunting for mountain lions, and hunting for black bears using bait and dogs. Once those objectives are reached, such referendums certainly will expand to include other forms of hunting for other species.

Other anti-hunting strategies will gain in strength in the coming years. Various groups have resisted the efforts of state wildlife agencies to recruit new hunters. These vocal groups have publicly spoken against the Becoming An Outdoors Woman Program. They also oppose all efforts to recruit young people into hunting. Their attack has been bolstered by public school shootings in Arkansas, Mississippi, and Oregon. The Fund for Animals and other anti-hunting organizations used these tragedies to fuel their call for an end to youth hunting programs. In 1998 the Fund for Animals and actress Mary Tyler Moore formally objected to a proposed New

York State law to lower the minimum age for big game hunting from 16 to 12. Moore and other antis feel that hunting makes young people callous and insensitive to the suffering of animals. That particular value judgment would differ from the one held by those of us who grew up in hunting families. For us, and for thousands of generations over thousands of centuries, young people gained respect for and knowledge about animals through hunting. Many of us have strong, positive feelings about wildlife. We contribute money and time to many groups that work to benefit habitat protection programs and the resident birds and animals.

Sadly, our society — and our values — continue to change.

What is the future of hunting and what can you do? Some bowhunters may feel that we don't need to do anything because bowhunting is growing and healthy. And it is healthy. Even though gun hunting has shown decreases, bowhunting continues to expand both in interest and the number of participants. A 1997 study released by the Archery Manufacturers and Merchants Organization (AMO) noted there were

3.3 million bowhunters. Another study, conducted every five years by the National Shooting Sports Foundation (NSSF), surveys licensed hunters. It underscored the recent growth of bowhunting. In 1986 the percentage of all licensed hunters who had tried bowhunting was 19 percent; by 1991 that total had climbed to 33 percent; and by 1996 the number had reached 45 percent. Clearly, thoughts of Robin Hood, the appeal — the *fun* — of shooting bows and arrows and the challenges of bowhunting fascinate many Americans.

Even so, it is quite obvious that there is much work to be done to keep hunting alive. Hunters need to be aware of their roots, in evolution and in the conservation movement. As such, we must never tolerate unethical or illegal behavior in the field. The world is watching us. We must do good deeds and we must constantly guard against that one hunter who will cause others to look at us with disdain. We must become very pro-active in recruiting new hunters.

Our own "Discover the Outdoors Camp" is a prime example of what needs to be done on a larger scale. Why not take our how-to brochure and start a "Discover the Outdoors Camp" in your own neighborhood? Young people are hungry for outdoor experiences. Unfortunately, many have no real way to experience that need. But you can change that. Don't limit yourselves to grade and high schools. College and universities have many students enrolled in their fish and wildlife programs who do not hunt but want to learn. Go to area schools, meet with instructors and student leaders, and offer to do some simple archery instruction. Such gestures which introduce students to the bow and arrow can easily lead to expanded interest in the outdoors.

Many of us belong to state and local archery clubs. Why not make indoor and outdoor ranges and schedule shoots as places to attract and welcome women and youngsters? Clean up the grounds, encourage friends and children to attend — and have fun programs slanted to youngsters. Get them shooting bows and arrows and the kids will figure out ways to get out into the woods.

Hunting for wildlife management is necessary and the general public widely accepts that premise. But a slow erosion of your hunting rights will continue in the coming century unless you get involved. Many clubs and organizations — including our Pope and Young Club — are taking more interest in the conservation movement. But all of us who hunt — you, me, and our buddies — must do even more. Why not contribute to our Trust Fund in order to allow other Club monies to be directed to pro-wildlife activities? Why not consider our Club's Trust Fund in your will? Why not, as already suggested, get some of your hunting friends together and start your own "Discover the Outdoors Camp" right in your own backyard?

When we all are involved in such worthwhile activities, then and only then, will the future of hunting be assured.

Dr. Dave Samuel, a retired wildlife professor and one of the nation's foremost authorities on anti-hunting, heads the Club's Conservation Committee. He makes his home near Morgantown, West Virginia.

BIG GAME RECORDS IN THE TWENTY-FIRST CENTURY

by Dr. C. Randall Byers

A FEW SHORT YEARS AGO I hadn't even heard the term *millennia* often enough to know its meaning. Now, everyone is talking about how things are going to be in the next millennium, a period of one thousand years. No one can accurately predict what's going to happen over the next century or two, much less what lies beyond. But certainly the new millennium is going to bring countless changes. Will the Pope and Young Club's computer database operate as intended? For that matter, will the computer itself work?

Of more pressing concern will be the prospects for future hunting and the direction taken by the Pope and Young Club. In the spring of 1998, some Club members gathered in Omaha, Nebraska, for a strategic planning session. One purpose of this gathering of Club officers and guests was to envision and delineate the focus — the role, if you prefer — of our Club in the year 2020. One exercise in that planning process involved picking the three words which individuals in attendance felt best described his or her attitude toward our Club from among several dozen words contained in the Club's brochure. Five major themes emerged:

Ethics, records, conservation, leadership, and heritage.

Noteworthy is the fact that almost every one of the 18 individuals in attendance at the strategic planning session selected at least two of the first three themes. If one were to pick only three words to represent the ideals and images of the Pope and Young Club — now, in the past, or for the future — *ethics*, *records*, and *conservation* certainly are excellent choices.

Looking back, it is easy to see where we have been. In 1975, the Club published its First Edition of the **Bowhunting Big Game Records of North America**. M. R. James was editor of that initial book. Now you are reading from the Fifth Edition of the **Bowhunting Big Game Records**, a much larger, more comprehensive volume, also edited by M. R. James. But aside from these books' corresponding title and editor, they bear very little similarity in size or content. And while preparing both books also required a significant effort on the part of many Club members, Pope and Young fortunes changed considerably between 1975 and 1999. A six-figure book publishing budget was required for the '99 edition while the first edition cost the Club only one-tenth that amount. Of course, back in the 1970s Club finances were minimal. To provide some funding for the first book project, books from a special limited edition of two hundred leatherbound copies — each numbered with a gold stamp bearing the Club's official seal on the inside cover — were offered to members for the exorbitant price of $35.00 per copy. Clearly, if someone wants to offer me one of those orginal books for that same selling price today, please let me know.

That First Edition record book listed a grand total of 2,374 trophy-class animals. By contrast, approximately 6,000 entries had been received during the two-year recording period which ended December 31, 1998, the last day record book entries were accepted for inclusion in our Fifth Edition publication. Back in 1975 there were 592 typical whitetail deer entries topped by Mel Johnson's "Beanfield Buck" at 204 4/8. While Mel's Illinois buck still tops the all-time bowhunting records, some 3,000 whitetail entries were accepted during the last recording period alone. Put another way, more typical whitetails were listed in the Club's records during 1997-

98 than total entries for all species back in 1975! And only 104 bowhunters had Yellowstone elk listed in the '75 book while over 400 trophy bulls were entered during the 21st Recording Period, bringing the all-time total to 3,000-plus animals in this single big game category. In that same '75 book, the smallest elk listed scored 225 5/8 and the world record was 376 6/8; today the minimum stands at 260 0/8 and William Wright's 404 0/8 1992 Arizona bull tops the typical Yellowstone elk listings.

Among the hunting hints published in the First Edition was this comment: "By far the best method of bowhunting pronghorns is from blinds placed near watering holes." Apparently many bowhunters heeded this advice. In 1975 the pronghorn antelope minimum stood at 57 and the late Rolland Esterline's 57 0/8 buck occupied the bottom of the listing in 174th place. In the early 1980s, the pronghorn minimum was raised to 64 and as of January 1, 1999 the minimum became 67. Over 3,000 hunters have antelope listed in this latest edition of the ***Records***. The decades' old advice about hunting pronghorns "from blinds placed near watering holes" still holds as ever increasing numbers of bowhunters are successful in tagging these prairie speedsters.

In 1975 no one had yet entered a non-typical Coues' deer (minimum 68) or a desert bighorn sheep (minimum 115). Along with numerous one-time listings for velvet antlered trophies, hunters can and now do enter non-typical Columbian blacktail deer, Sitka blacktail deer, non-typical Yellowstone elk, central Canada barren ground caribou, Quebec/Labrador caribou, and muskox. The only category from the 1970s which is now closed to entries is jaguar. But perhaps one day in the new millennium hunting for these big cats from south of the Mexican border will resume. Who knows?

Minimum entries continue to inch upward, though more slowly now than in the past. The whitetail minimum was 115 in 1962; the desert bighorn standard was 115, too. Cougar stood at 12 and the black bear minimum was 17. Now these categories have minimums of 125, 140, 13 8/16, and 18, respectively. Along with the January 1, 1999 change to a 67 minimum for antelope, the minimum entry score for Shiras' moose rose to 125. Will the typical whitetail, black bear, and Yellowstone elk minimums rise during the next century?

Nobody knows. By the year 2020 we may well have in excess of 60,000 trophies in our records. In fact, it is not impossible to envision 60,000 typical whitetail entries by that time. Yet some of the early day trophies remain atop their respective categories today. Along with Mel Johnson's giant typical whitetail, Del Austin's huge non-typical whitetail that headed its category in '75 still ranks the best ever today at 279 7/8. The McIntyre polar bear, Dempsey Cape's woodland caribou, and Dr. Michael Cusack's Alaska-Yukon moose are likewise long-standing world records. Will they still stand atop the list two decades from now?

The First Edition of our record book contained a series of sketches by New York bowhunter, Club member and artist Wayne Trimm. Likewise, the works of Minnesota bowhunter, Club member and artist Michael Sieve provide the Fifth Edition with an artistic touch. Again, some things do not change. One only has to compare the Trimm and Sieve art, each presented in its own distinct style, to see the magnificence that these hunters see in the very creatures that they choose to hunt.

The introduction to the Records listing in the First Edition states: *The following section contains some very impressive records. And while it is important that each hunter's name be included as part of the listings, it should be understood that this importance is secondary to the magnificent animals themselves. True bowhunters have reverence for every hour of every day spent in the quest and realize that hunting success is measured in much more than the harvesting of a big game trophy. They also do everything in their power to conserve and perpetuate the delicate balance of nature in the hope that future generations of hunters*

may enjoy some part of what one day will be called the "good old days."

Those same words could serve to introduce the trophy listings in this edition published 24 years later. We can only hope they will be as true for the authors of the Club's Twenty-Second Edition of the ***Bowhunting Big Game Records of North America*** at the tail end of the next century.

As Club officers and members looked to the future during the Omaha strategic planning discussions, it became apparent that the key theme words — ethics, records, conservation, leadership, and heritage — continued to have a strong influence on this group's vision for the future. Key ideas, beliefs, and visions from each person were winnowed down, regrouped, and restated. Items were prioritzed, a difficult task since many good points had been brought forth. Ultimately, the three top priority statements, essentially the planning group's vision for the future, were:

1. The Pope and Young Club is a recognized leader in bowhunting.
2. The Pope and Young Club is fiscally strong and has financial goals.
3. The Pope and Young Club will promote trophy hunting and maintain the records of bowhunting.

Indeed, the Club is an established leader in bowhunting. The Club's early beginnings dictated the concept of ethical, fair chase hunting with the bow and arrow. The Club has evolved into a major force in the pro-hunting, pro-conservation movement. Our ***Bowhunting Big Game Records of North America*** books serve as a standard of achievement and a mark of the success of modern game management and the effectiveness of the bow and arrow, both as a hunting weapon and as a tool for game management. By the very activities we undertake, the Club provides a direct link to our hunting heritage through its records program.

Looking forward to this time a century from now, we can hope that the challenges of the twenty-first century are ones which once again concerned sportsmen and sportswomen can resolve. Issues such as population growth and loss of critical habitat certainly need to be faced. Public attitude toward hunting, especially influenced by the anti-hunting movement, is an issue today and will not go away unless we can somehow defuse the antis' arguments. More hunting will occur on private lands, making landholder/sportsmen's pacts even more essential. Game herds today stand, in many instances, at historic highs. Truly, the base exists for the continuance of our hunting heritage through the coming century if we maintain our due diligence in the protection and support of this resource.

The future is bright. New world records are certain to be taken in the twenty-second Recording Period (1999-2000), moving us one step further into the next millennium. And if we keep in mind those five key words which represent the Pope and Young Club — ethics, records, conservation, leadership, and heritage — they will continue to serve us well. Likewise, this admonishment from the 1975 record book should remain our challenge today and in the coming years:

True bowhunters have reverence for every hour of every day spent in the quest and realize that hunting success is measured in much more than the harvesting of a big game trophy. They also do everything in their power to conserve and perpetuate the delicate balance of nature in the hope that future generations of hunters may enjoy some part of what one day will be called the "good old days."

Senior member Dr. C. Randall Byers of Moscow, Idaho, is a college professor and Records Chairman of both the Pope and Young Club and the Boone and Crockett Club.

REVISITING THE PAST, WORKING FOR THE FUTURE

by Stan Rauch

THE BOW AND ARROW IS NOT *an effective means of harvesting big game animals.* As strange as that statement may seem to us today, that was precisely the opinion and attitude of many game agency employees and various segments of the public not so many years ago. In the late 1950s, there was an increased awareness by those hunting with the bow that a great deal needed to be done if better bowhunting opportunities were to become a reality. Proof was needed to convince doubters that bowhunting was indeed an efficient and humane method of harvesting big game animals. Game department professionals also wanted proof that bowhunters themselves were sincerely interested in the conservation policies that would ensure healthy wildlife populations for future generations to enjoy.

That situation was ultimately responsible for the Pope and Young Club being formed. Founder Glenn St. Charles and a small group of serious, dedicated bowhunters came to the conclusion that if they could document the nation's bowhunting successes, that information could be offered as proof positive that bowhunting was effective in taking all North American big game. The wheels were set in motion to establish a recording system to accomplish that goal. After extensive planning and effort, the Pope and Young Club officially came into being on January 27, 1961. The organization's records, patterned after the Boone and Crockett Club's proven scoring system, did in fact establish for all time that using the bow and arrow for big game was a legitimate hunting method. Moreover, it was consistent with and in fact supported conservation and wildlife management objectives.

Further, the primitive weapon status associated with the bow and arrow, with the corresponding difficulty in harvesting big game animals with short-range equipment, resulted in game agency officials recognizing the need to provide lengthy bow-only hunting seasons. The rest is history. Today over 3 million people across North America are enjoying the challenge and excitement of bowhunting.

Ask current bowhunters what the Pope and Young Club is and many will simply say that it is the organization that keeps bowhunting's records. This is true; however, the Club has evolved into so much more. From its very modest beginnings, the Club has grown to epitomize sportsmanship in hunting, emphasizing the fair chase philosophy while advocating and encouraging responsible bowhunting practices. The Club also has steadily solidified its respected leadership position within the hunting community. Today its active dedication to the protection of our bowhunting heritage and North America's wildlife are widely recognized.

As this Fifth Edition of **Bowhunting Big Game Records of North America** is published and distributed nationwide, it seems appropriate to take a look at some of the transitions that have taken place within the Club during the half dozen years since the Fourth Edition was printed in 1993. The central purpose and objectives of the Pope and Young Club, along with its membership structure, have been in place since its founding, defining the very character and identity of the organization. That solid foundation provides the strength and foresight for the Club to make steady progress in its work to preserve our rich bowhunting heritage in a rapidly changing world.

Pro-Conservation Efforts

Most certainly, the Club has stepped up its support of conservation, education, and pro-hunting initiatives and programs across the continent. Grants from the Club's Conservation Committee have provided increasingly strong, even phenomenal support of various conservation measures since the Fourth Edition book was published six short years ago. In fact, efforts during the 1990s have seen the Pope and Young Club become a true pro-conservation organization. For example, in 1991 a relatively modest $7,000 was available to fund approved conservation efforts; today the

Club grants over $50,000 annually with upwards of $300,000 in awards made over the last half dozen years. A few projects receiving monetary support include Judy Kovar's speaking program which introduces school children to our nation's hunting heritage, the Wildlife Legislative Fund of America, the Physically Challenged Bowhunters of America, National Shooting Sports Foundation, deer studies, bear studies, sheep studies, Project WILD, National Wildlife Conservation Officers, the Minnesota-based bow wounding study, Outdoor Education Foundation, National Forest Foundation's Center for Wildlife Information, Governors' Hunting Heritage Symposiums, and Orion, The Hunters' Institute.

The Club's conservation program is enthusiastically promoted by the membership and many others with multi-thousands of dollars raised in recent years to provide funds for an ever increasing number of grant requests. One hundred percent of the money raised for the Conservation Fund goes toward providing these grants. The majority of the funding is provided through the Club's hunt raffles and auctions of hunting trips and valuable archery-related items.

One additional, very special project that is funded by the Conservation Fund is the "Discover the Outdoors Camp." Created by the Pope and Young Club in 1995, the camp was established for the purpose of bringing together single parent families — mother or father and child — in an outdoor environment in the Colorado mountains where participants are taught to appreciate and enjoy the outdoors. There is no cost for parent/child pairs, with any transportation fees paid by a sponsoring group, often a state bowhunting organization, while camp staff and on-site costs are covered by the Pope and Young Club. Members are justifiably proud of the successful and highly acclaimed "Discover the Outdoors Camp." A current project goal is to establish a national model that state associations, clubs, or other groups can utilize to operate a similar camp in their region.

Membership Levels

The Club continues to be a progressive membership-based organization consisting of many of the most serious, dedicated, and involved bowhunters and conservationists to be found anywhere. The Club has three levels of membership: Associate,

Regular and Senior. All new members must join as an Associate. *A major misconception in the bowhunting community is a person must have taken and entered a record class animal to be eligible for Pope and Young Associate membership.* Actually, Club membership is completely separate from the Club's records, which is just one of the programs maintained by the Club. The only requirement is to be a bowhunter and to have pursued the challenge long enough to have taken at least one adult North American big game animal, under the rules of fair chase, with the bow and arrow. A whitetail doe, for example, readily fits that description.

Others wrongly think that anyone who has taken and entered a record class animal is automatically a member of the Pope and Young Club. This is not the case. Everyone, without exception, must apply for membership as an Associate. The Associate membership currently numbers some 3,000 bowhunters. By virtue of its numbers and a focus on working to guarantee bowhunting's future, the Associate membership provides a major, active part of support for the Club's various activities and goals.

Regular membership presently consists of no more than 100 persons and is open to any qualified applicant who has weathered the "test of time" by having greater seniority as an Associate than any other current applicant. He or she must also have taken with the bow and arrow at least one adult animal of each of three

of the various North American big game species, one of which meets the minimum qualifications of a trophy class animal and has been entered in the Pope and Young records. The potential Regular member must also demonstrate that he or she possesses those characteristics of good sportsmanship and a character consistent with the objectives and purposes of the Club.

Senior members are unlimited in number and move from the Regular ranks when the bowhunter has been a Regular member for at least five years and has taken at least one adult animal of each of four species, three of which must qualify for and be entered in the Club's records; or, he or she has been a Regular member for a period of 10 years. Currently there are approximately 175 Senior members.

In revisiting the early formative years of the Pope and Young Club, it is interesting to note the comments of founder Glenn St. Charles in a 1960 letter to the Advisory Board regarding the previously determined requirement for a maximum of 50 Regular members: "We must realize that perhaps our membership under this requirement will not fill up as fast and probably our objectives will not be met as quickly, such as publishing a book. We can, however, begin work on a modest book and start small. I believe in the overall picture we will be glad that we maintained a high level for membership requirements. We aren't trying to fool anyone with the idea that we will hold the membership at 50. We all want to see it get to 100; however, it is important that we get this Club really off the ground before it gets too large."

And off the ground it is. The continued formulation of new programs over the years, while also responding to the changes taking place in bowhunting, tell us that the membership structure has served the Club very well indeed. It is a special thing to be a member of the Pope and Young Club — at any membership level — as this is a unique organization consisting of individuals who actively care about the future of bowhunting, hunting ethics, and conservation in North America. Such membership is open to all bowhunters who have similar interests and dedication.

Due to a strong Canadian support base, we saw the Club take its biennial awards out of the United States for the first time in 1997, to Edmonton, Alberta. It was small surprise that the gathering in Edmonton was an immensely enjoyable and successful one.

In regard to Glenn St. Charles's comments from the early years about publishing a "modest book and start small," one only has to take note of the contents of this Fifth Edition record book to gain a large appreciation for how far the Club and bowhunting have come over the years. Who would have thought that we would have such widespread bowhunting opportunity that the vast number of record entries presented here in 1999 would represent literally thousands upon thousands of quality bowhunting experiences?

As we approach the twenty-first century, difficult challenges lie ahead for the Pope and Young Club. The human population explosion with its ever increasing demands on available space and resources pose serious problems for hunters and wildlife. The urbanization of the nation, along with changing societal values, will continue to have an adverse impact on hunting. Fortunately, the commitment of this Club in fostering fair chase bowhunting and sound bowhunter ethics, while working to preserve our bowhunting heritage, has been unfailingly strong over all years of the Club's existence. That solid foundation and commitment will undoubtedly continue to serve bowhunting well into the future.

Associate member Stan Rauch, a retired Air Force officer and current Pope and Young Second Vice President, is one of the Club's most active official measurers and supporters. He resides near Victor, Montana.

CLUB FINANCES THEN AND NOW— AND BEYOND

by Dr. Donald Ace Morgan

FINANCIALLY, THE POPE AND YOUNG CLUB has come a long, long way since its unheralded beginning almost 40 years ago. As is the case with any growing organization, finances have played a major part in the Club's expanding operations over the passing decades. Although the dollar amounts have changed rather dramatically, many of the basic ingredients have remained essentially unchanged. Over time, however, new financial resources have been added. This informal financial report takes a brief historic look at some past Club milestones, presents a brief summary of the organization's present financial health, and offers an educated guess regarding our Club's fiscal future.

In the Beginning...
Dues — At the first meeting of the proposed Pope and Young organization on June 29, 1960, dues were proposed for two groups. Members would pay "a $25 initiation fee and $10 per year dues. An Associate membership would be without initiation fee with $5 annual dues." Dues collected from that date through January 1962 totaled $1,160 (see illustration).

Obviously, membership dues have increased over the years. The first hike occurred in 1972 when dues for Regular members rose from $10 to $25 per year.

In 1974, the first change in Associate dues occurred, doubling from $5 to $10. The Board also hiked Regular/Senior dues to $50 at that time.

Associate dues were raised to $15 and Regular/Senior dues went from $50 to $75 in 1981.

The last dues change occurred in 1989 when annual Associate dues were increased to $25 and Regular/ Senior dues were raised to $100. Interestingly, the original initiation fee for Regular members has remained at $25 for nearly four decades now.

Entry Fees — In the beginning, trophy fees were not charged for entries because the Pope and Young Club was anxious to receive entries in order to prove hunting big game with a bow was viable. Even so, the number of entries grew slowly. By mid-1961, for example, only 243 entries had been submitted. Amazingly, in January 1962, with

POPE AND YOUNG CLUB

January 17, 1962
Box 887
Des Moines, Washington

24 regular memberships @ $35.00		$840.00
64 associate memberships @ $5.00		$320.00
	TOTAL INCOME	$1,160.00
Check No. 1	Letterheads and envelopes	$25.83
No. 2	Postage and stationery	$20.15
No. 3	Membership cards	$22.15
No. 4	Stationery	$25.22
No. 5	Promotional pictures for magazines and Pope and Young Book	$33.28
	TOTAL EXPENSES	$127.32
	BANK BALANCE	$1032.68

W.J. Brown

only some 300 total entries, the organization raised the minimum scores on five species! Obviously, the number of entries and changes in minimums had little impact on the Club's finances at that time.

The Board established the first entry fee ($10) in August of 1969. This fee was increased to $20 in 1976. The current entry fee of $25 was set in 1981, almost two decades ago.

During the recent 21st Recording Period which started January 1, 1997 and concluded on December 31, 1998, over 6,000 entries were received and processed. The money received from entry fees is a major source of revenue for the Club. Obviously, actions such as changes in minimum scores can have a direct — and negative — impact on entry fee revenues. Likewise, such changes can adversely affect proceeds from record book sales.

Banquet Costs — The first organizational meeting and banquet was held at Grayling, Michigan, in 1958. It had 35 members in attendance. Costs at that and subsequent meetings were not high. Still, founder Glenn St. Charles noted that members had to "pass the hat" at one banquet in order to pay the meal bill (it was either that or "wash dishes"). In truth, one of the main reasons for establishing two-year recording periods back in 1962 was to save the $350 cost of trophies and awards. By comparison, costs of the 1999 Pope and Young banquet in Omaha, Nebraska, are expected to exceed $60,000.

Directors' Expenses — Initially, temporary officers and later Board members had to pay their own expenses to attend banquets. According to Glenn St. Charles, some individuals chipped in to help pay the travel costs for officers who otherwise could not attend annual meetings. Today, travel and lodging fees are paid for Board members, although some Club officers elect to pay their own expenses.

Operating Revenues — As previously noted, initial revenues were limited to dues collected from members. The accompanying financial statement shows a total income of only $1,160 for a period of almost one and one-half years back in the early 1960s. Today, annual dues revenue are in the $100,000 range.

Operating Expenses — Expenses for 1960-62 totaled $127.32. That wouldn't cover the Club's monthly telephone bill today. In fact, in a non-banquet year, both revenues and expenses will exceed $250,000! For a banquet year, these figures will be much higher.

Record Books — The first printed record of trophies was the "pictoral printing" of all records up to and including the 1961 competitions. It was a poster sized sheet that listed all 243 animals recorded to date. In effect, this was the first "record book" produced by the Pope and Young Club. It cost $522 to print 5,000 copies, a rather hefty sum at the time. The actual first edition of ***Bowhunting Big Game Records of North America*** was printed in 1975 at a cost of about $12,000. Noteworthy is the fact the Club did not have the money to pay for the book! Various individuals loaned the Club the necessary funds, interest free, so that the book could be printed and sold. The loans were paid back out of the proceeds received from selling book copies. By comparison, this Fifth Edition record book cost approximately $125,000 to print. Best of all, the financially sound Club now has the ability to publish record books without borrowing the necessary money.

In Recent Years...
Based on information contained in this brief review, it should be obvious that the financial status of the Club has changed dramatically over the years. In addition, there are other financial activities in which the Club has become involved.

Trust Fund — The Pope and Young Trust Fund was a brilliant idea put forth by some farsighted Club members back in the mid-1980s. The fund was established as a vehicle for the organization to someday achieve total financial independence. Revenues from the Trust can eventually finance the operations of the Club. The first contributions were made in April of 1986 and totaled $650. By February of 1994, the Trust Fund had surpassed its initial goal of $100,000.

Conservation — Contributions for conservation activities did not really begin until the mid-1970s. Dollarwise, the amounts were relatively small in those days, amounting to only a few thousand dollars spent over a number of years. In fact, as late as 1990, the annual expenditure on Club conservation activities was only $7,000. Since that time, some dramatic changes have taken place. *The Club has spent almost $370,000 on conservation and pro-hunting programs during the past eight years.* Budgeted Club expenditures for the current fiscal year are $88,500.

Revenues — As noted earlier, the initial source of Club income was dues. Although dues are still a major source of funds, other sources now play a leading role. Entry fees for trophies and revenues from the sale of record books create an ongoing flow of revenue. Donations to the Club's Conservation and Trust Funds are steady and important, too. The biennial auctions and raffles are major income producers during banquet years, with monies raised used mainly to fund pro-conservation projects.

Communications — Initially, all Club communications were in the form of telephone calls and letters. Today, the Board continues to hold conference calls and to correspond on a regular basis. However, the two major sources of information, outside of Club press releases, are the quarterly *P&Y Newsletter* and the Club's website on the Internet. Both cost money. The website has a monthly fee in addition to costs involved when changes are made. And even though there are no editorial costs, printing and mailing fees for the *Newsletter* are substantial, now approaching $20,000 per year.

Museum — Acquisition of museum items has been ongoing for the past decade or more. Up to 1998, the Club had acquired, among other things, Art Young, Saxton Pope, Glenn St. Charles, and Howard Hill bows. These items had cost the Club only a few thousand dollars. However, in 1998, the Club acquired the extensive St. Charles collection of archery artifacts, valued at approximately half a million dollars. (For the immediate future, the collection will remain on display at the Pope and Young/St. Charles Museum in Seattle, Washington.) Purchase of such a valuable collection could not have taken place, financially, even as few as 10 short years ago.

And the Future...

Only time itself will accurately reveal the financial future of our Club. In May of 1998, the Board held its first strategic planning meeting and future sessions will likely be forthcoming. Outcomes of such events are difficult to predict. However, some of the following factors will have a financial impact on the Club's future:

Trust Fund — As already noted, the initial $100,000 goal for the Club's trust fund has been met and surpassed. In fact, as this is written we are well over half way to reaching the $200,000 mark. I suspect the next Trust Fund goal will be $1 million. And we can do it!

Board — The Board of Directors is made up of 13 highly motivated individuals from the United States and Canada, each with different backgrounds and skills. Except for the Executive Secretary, all serve on a volunteer basis, willingly donating their time and talents. This "free" service to the Club is immeasurable, from a financial perspective. Some of these individuals spend literally hundreds upon hundreds of hours each year working on Pope and Young Club business. Indeed, most current Board members have played a huge role in helping the Club achieve its current financial stability.

Professional Fund Raiser — At the 1998 meeting, the Board voted to try to hire a part-time Fund Raiser/Public Relations employee. Financial ramifications of this type of activity are speculative at best. However, the Board feels that the long term impact on the Club will be extremely positive — and profitable.

Membership — Since its beginnings with seven Regular and about 20 Associates in attendance, the Club has grown to more than 3,000 members. And the Club now is currently in the midst of a membership drive. Since dues continue to be a primary revenue source, the membership numbers will always have a financial impact on the Club.

Headquarters — The Club has had a variety of "homes" over the years. Today Club headquarters are situated in leased offices in Chatfield, Minnesota, but from time to time the idea of buying or building permanent headquarters is kicked around. Will this become a reality in the twenty-first century? Will a Club museum be part of the structure? Time alone will give us the answers.

The financial history of the Pope and Young Club has been fairly normal — meager beginnings, some rocky spots along the way, and finally financial stability. Hopefully, the Club's future will be sound. I know it certainly will be interesting.

Senior member Dr. Donald Ace Morgan is the Pope and Young Club Treasurer. He is a certified public accountant, a college professor, and a serious bowhunter who makes his home in Kearney, Nebraska.

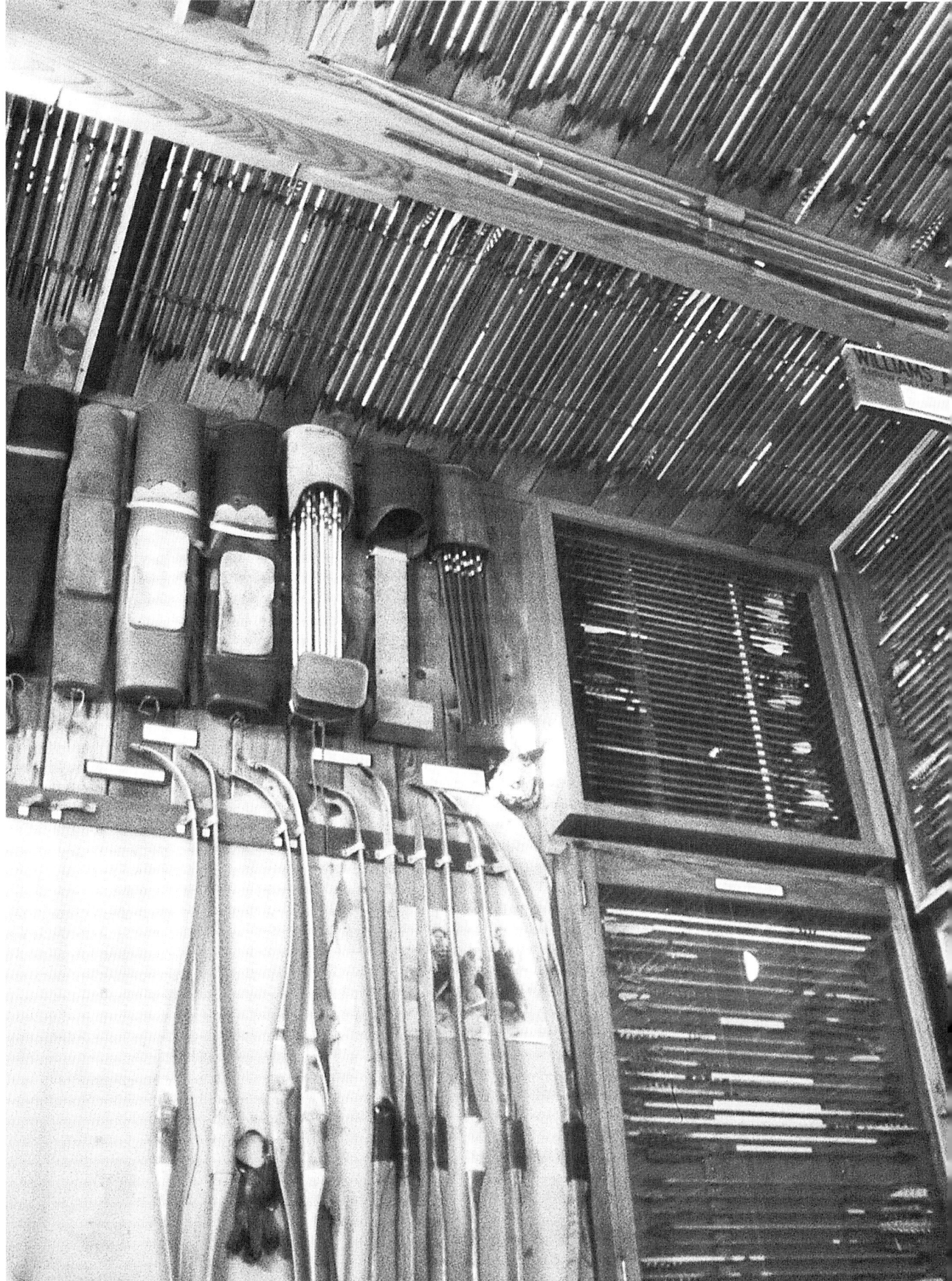

THE POPE AND YOUNG/ ST. CHARLES MUSEUM

by Joe St. Charles

MY FATHER GLENN ACQUIRED the shop contents of his mentor, Kore Duryee, in 1944. He ended up with several bows and many other older items. Over the many years since that initial acquisition, while running a retail archery store, dad occasionally would come across other interesting old tackle. Being the collector he is, Glenn accumulated quite a few items worth displaying in the small den next to our store, Northwest Archery Company, in Seattle, Washington. Soon after the Pope and Young Club was formed, several members discussed with dad the possibility of having a museum in the future.

In the January 28, 1963 Pope and Young Club newsletter, Glenn wrote the following words on the subject of a Club museum: "Early last year Fred Bear accepted the task of writing a biography on Art Young and Saxton Pope. In digging into some of the past history, he ran across a party who had been a very close associate of these two bowhunters. It was discovered that this party had some of Art Young's old equipment. Fred promptly purchased this equipment and donated it to the Pope & Young Club. Some of us had been thinking in terms of eventually starting some type of a museum with artifacts of Art Young and Saxton Pope and complementing it with hunting bows and other artifacts of some of our other old time bowhunters, both the past and present. This fine contribution from Fred will be a very nice start of these museum plans. Undoubtedly, there is someone in the organization who would like to spend the time and effort on furthering this project."

During 1977, after reading a copy of **Hunting with the Bow & Arrow** by Saxton Pope, I developed a keen interest in the history of our sport. I began to get involved with my father's pursuit of early bowhunting artifacts.

By 1983 we had accumulated so many items that we felt it was time to expand. Next to the orginal 15 x 30 foot den we opened up a wall and built a much larger room. It is 20 x 40 feet and has a 25 foot ceiling, lined with cedar. By 1985 we had completed many of the displays. As time passed, more items were found. The upgraded displays got better and better.

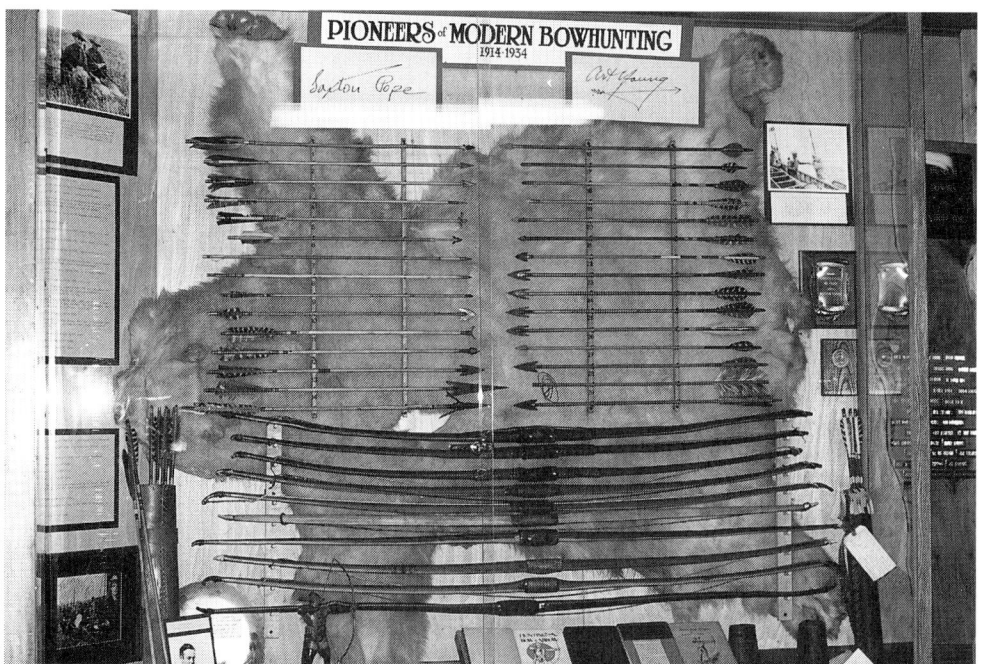

In 1990 the Pope and Young Club officers began discussions on how to preserve this lifelong collection. The desire was to keep it intact for the future. Finally, in July of 1998, the St. Charles collection became the property of the Pope and Young Club, thus assuring its preservation for all future generations of bowhunters.

Many of the Club's members already have visited our Seattle-based museum. But many have not. Following is a written tour of the highlights of a visit to the Pope and Young Club/St. Charles Museum.

The Library

Since most people's interest in bowhunting is sparked by reading, we start our tour at the museum library. The library informs us of the details of our heritage, telling us of the events, people, and innovations that have brought us to today. It also can identify many of the old items that we turn up. The library is a valuable research center and its contents are gladly shared with all visitors who desire to spend time paging through the collected materials.

The Club library consists of 60 feet of books, periodicals, catalogs, pamphlets, and photos. Some of the highlights include the 1792 classic "Essay on Archery" by Thomas Mosley from England, which is signed by the author. Next is a complete set of the first successful archery periodical to be published in the United States, **Ye Sylvan Archer**, printed from 1927 to 1943 and totaling 151 issues. Last is one of the nation's most complete collections of archery equipment catalogs and advertising materials, dating back to the 1880s.

Bows

Bows easily are the most popular items that collectors of archery equipment assemble. Each one represents many hours of time and effort by a skilled woodworker. Among the 200-plus wooden (pre-fiberglass) bows on display are longbows that date from 1879, crafted by Americans like E. I. Horsman, F. S. Barnes, Will Compton, Saxton Pope, James Duff, Doug Easton, Cassius Styles, Howard Hill, Gilman Keasey, and Glenn St. Charles. There are also classic English longbows by the British bowyers Ayres, Highfield, and Feltham, which date back to 1880.

We also have the most complete collections of American two-piece takedown bows available prior to 1960. These include bows by The Archers Company, Bear Archery, James Duff, Perry Mason Company, S. B. Hayden, Russ Willcox, Ron Robison, Frank Eicholtz, Ben Pearson, Stream-Exe, and True Temper.

Our display of all-wood static recurves holds works by Earl Hoyt, Jr., Nels Grumley, Damon Howatt, Glenn St. Charles, and the Ben Pearson Company. These date from 1935 to 1948.

Metal bows were popular at times both in the U.S. and England. Steel models by True Temper, Seefab, and Apollo are hanging next to aluminum creations by Par-X, Grimes, Ivanhoe, and the Jet Bow.

When mass produced fiberglass laminated bows were introduced in the late 1940s, a whole new list of names appeared on the market. With over 200 bows on display, there are models by Bear, Folberth, E. Bud Pierson, Eddings, Gordon, Sanders, Smithwick, United States, Tri-State, Mark, Root, Shakespeare, and Wing.

Arrows

Just like cartridges, arrows were meant to be spent. Those that survive the decades are worth collecting. As the years passed by, we accumulated over 600 different feathered shafts – and there is no end in sight. To conserve space, most of these collected shafts are mounted on the museum ceiling and most can be easily seen, though you may have to occasionally rest your neck while viewing them.

Many of the arrows are marked with the owner's name on them. Two of note are shafts from Howard Hill and Damon Howatt. Displayed along with this collection is a special bow that was left at his ranch by W. I. King. This bow is one of the two famous snake bows in a familiar photo that has been around for years, showing Chester Stevenson and W. I. King posing together with two of the snakiest character bows ever created.

Broadheads & Quivers

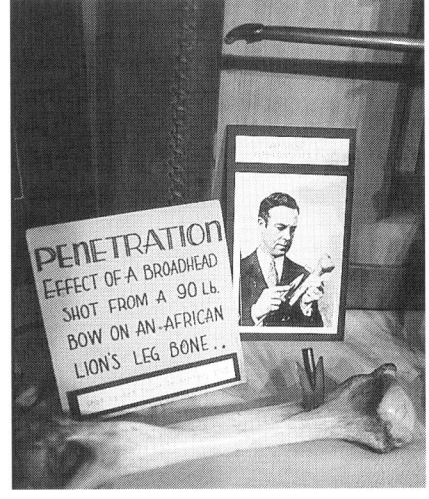

Broadheads are one of my passions. The museum's south wall is devoted to them. There are over 1,000 glue-on heads in our display cases. There are separate cases containing heads by Ace, Ben Pearson, and Cliff Zwickey.

The quivers are standing side by side in a row about 20 feet long and are stuffed with colorful arrows. The popular King back quiver, with nickel silver conchos, is displayed along with numerous Bear models. We have nice handmade quivers, too. Two of my personal favorites are a custom quiver made for my father by Lowell Roper, and a side quiver made for Howard Valentyne by Col. Milan Ellot. Both are beautifully tooled.

Miscellaneous Items

Some small items on display include national, state, and club patches, along with small awards medals and trophies. I have just completed a small museum exhibit of items made by Howard Hill. This display contains two bows – one of which was given to guide Ned Frost of Cody, Wyoming, in the 1930s. There also is an assortment of arrows Hill made during the 1930s and 1940s.

A Very Special Display

With donations from Fred Bear, Glenn St. Charles, Chuck Young (Art Young's grandson), Dr. Bert Grayson, and Bill Jardine, it is with great honor that we display much of the personal "artillery" of the two men most responsible for this century's interest in bowhunting. The Saxton Pope and Art Young exhibit is the museum's centerpiece. Labeled "Pioneers of Modern Bowhunting," it contains Pope and Young items used during all periods of these men's bowhunting careers.

Their adventures started when Ishi, the last Yana Indian, was brought to the University of California. Here Dr. Pope spent time with him and learned of his hunting skills with a bow. Four special arrows are near the top of this exhibit. These shafts represent all different styles Ishi made while living on the University campus.

We recently acquired an English yew longbow handcrafted by William "Chief" Compton. It was through Compton that Pope and Young first met. He instructed them in shooting, bow making, fletching, and arrowsmithing. Compton had them read Will Thompson's ***The Witchery of Archery*** for the first time. Then he further fired their imaginations by taking them hunting, where Dr. Pope took his first deer with the bow and arrow. These early day adventures produced two men who hunted together, handcrafted archery tackle together, and eventually wrote themselves into the hearts of many admiring sportsmen – and into bowhunting history.

We have on display six beautiful yew bows made by Dr. Pope. One is a handsome 68-inch, rawhide backed weapon that draws 72 pounds. It is named "Robin" and is dated 1924. This bow is one he used to down several African game animals on their eight-month safari in 1925. Another Pope bow was given to Ned Frost when they hunted grizzlies together during the well documented 1920 Yellowstone Park adventure.

Assembled in the museum is quite an assortment of Dr. Pope's feathered missiles, the oldest being one arrow he carried with him that may have dispatched a Yellowstone bruin. The unique crescent shaped bird head is also here. Also, there are three different flight arrows Pope made for testing the cast of bows mentioned in his treatise, ***A Study of Bows & Arrows.***

The most impressive of the Pope arrows is the 1,200-grain Rhino arrow which is mentioned in his tale of their African sojourn. It is one of 12 made and only two that made it back to the States. It sports a seven-inch long dagger-like broadhead. Standing below Pope's tackle is a full complement of the good doctor's early literary volumes, including a signed first edition of ***Hunting With the Bow and Arrow.***

If there is such a man as a "bowhunting super hero," Art Young would be that man. Tall, strong, and handsome, he possessed abilities as a bowhunter and trick shooter that lay mostly hidden by his personal modesty. Of his bows, we have three of yew and two of Osage orange. Young's 75-pound "Old Grizzly" bow was the productive yew of their Yellowstone adventures, as written by Dr. Pope. It is on display courtesy of Chuck Young and is a true treasure.

Following the example set by some Native Americans, Young realized the sheer ruggedness of bois d'arc. His 64-inch, 75 pound "Alaskan Brown" bow endured the rigors of the far north for months. Now 72 years old, worn and well used, it hangs in the museum as mute testimony to the hard yellow wood, having laid low most of Alaska's biggest game animals.

From the frigid north to the heated African plains near the Equator, Young traveled next. He whittled out "Alaska Brown's" bigger brother, "Simba Blood," finishing at 64 inches and 90 pounds of draw weight, also of bois d'arc. It successfully endured the heat of the Dark Continent, accounting for numerous animals. One lion's leg bone from this safari is on display in the museum, testimony to the penetrating power of Young's feathered shaft. Still embedded in the bone is a California By Products steel head, driven there by an arrow launched from "Simba Blood."

Also, one of the handmade Art Young shafts on our museum's wall successfully downed a Wyoming grizzly. It is armed with a fine work of steel, created by the hand of this accomplished arrowsmith. Another arrow has attached the manufactured "Art Young Signature Head" that was produced by popular demand for his style of broadhead during 1934.

Another piece of Young's bowhunting history is represented by two items used on his trip to the Northwest Territories off the coast of Baffin Island in 1926. They are the remains of an arrow which landed him a large walrus and another arrow that connected with a polar bear. The hide from that bear hangs as a backdrop for all the artifacts in this display case.

This Pope and Young exhibit, which pays homage to these two influential sportsmen, is alone worth the trip to Seattle. And if you ask, I will gladly open the display case and let you handle one of the bows either to absorb its magic or simply to snap a photo or two.

Museum Mounts

On the west side of the museum are many different mounts of North American game animals, all taken with a bow, many tagged by Glenn St. Charles. Included in this collection is his one time world record mule deer, which Glenn tagged in 1959.

The Pope and Young Club has been keeping the bowhunting records of North American big game animals for over 40 years. Now, along with the Club's big game records, we are preserving the rest of the bowhunting records in this collection. We now have a place to preserve the items that mean so much to us, so we can share with – and inspire – all future bowhunters.

Currently the museum exhibits can be viewed from 10:00 a.m. to 6:00 p.m., Tuesday through Friday, and from 10:00 a.m. to 5:00 p.m. on Saturday. The Pope and Young Club/St. Charles Museum is located only 10 minutes from Sea-Tac International Airport. Plan to stop by on your next trip to Seattle, setting aside three to four hours to view and absorb a part of our splendid bowhunting history.

For more information and answers to any questions regarding the museum, contact Joe St. Charles, 19807 1st Avenue South, Seattle, WA 98148; (206) 878-7361.

Joe St. Charles, himself a Regular member of the Pope and Young Club, serves the museum as its curator. He is one of the nation's most knowledgeable bowhunting historians.

DR. SAXTON TEMPLE POPE

by Doug Walker

I WAS HOLDING HISTORY in my hands. Saxton Pope's personal photo album contained his handwritten notes, drawings of his bows and sketches of arrowheads complete with penetration test results, various newspaper clippings, letters, snapshots, and much more. Pope's son, Lee, had made this special moment possible. Here, frozen in time, were this great man's unpublished thoughts and images, missing pieces that could add insight to his personal and professional life. And as I eagerly turned the ancient album's worn pages, I felt a special closeness to the bowhunting legend who in the first quarter of this century blazed a trail that millions of modern day hunting archers eventually would follow.

Incidentally, ever since the founding of the Pope and Young Club, I have searched diligently for any and all information about our Club's namesakes. After decades of fact-finding inquiry, I have no doubt it was Dr. Pope's friendship with Ishi, last of California's Yana (or Yahi) Indians, that sparked Pope's interest in archery. I am equally convinced that Saxton Pope was Art Young's mentor and inspiration. (Young's numerous letters and photographs with handwritten notations to Pope underscore his gratitude.) Consequently, although the exploits of this noted threesome are widely known and well documented, my research has uncovered certain fascinating facts about Dr. Pope that I now share here in hopes of adding historic perspective and depth to the story of a talented surgeon, writer, and archer deservedly recognized today as perhaps "the most influential bowhunter of this century."

The third of four children, Saxton Temple Pope was born September 4, 1875 in Fort Stockton, Texas. His father, Dr. Benjamin Franklin Pope, was a surgeon and Colonel in the U.S. Army. Young Pope's early days were spent in various army garrisons — from Long Island Sound to Fort Sully in the Dakota badlands to Fort McDowell on San Francisco's Angel Island — where he learned self reliance and craftsmanship from Army blacksmiths, saddlers, wheelwrights, and carpenters. He soon learned to ride, shoot, and hunt. Adept with his hands, he forged knives from old barrel hoops and crafted useful wood and leather goods from scraps salvaged

Saxton Pope's last picture prior to his death in 1926.

from army post trash heaps. And while his formal education on army posts was mostly a hit and miss process, there could be no mistaking the innate curiosity and intelligence that burned within the fertile mind of young Saxton Pope.

Although he enjoyed working with wood and tools and likely could have been a successful engineer, Pope ultimately decided to follow in his father's footsteps and enrolled in the University of California Medical School. Regardless, he just couldn't resist experimenting with various woodworking construction projects. He not only fashioned his own guitar and a Spinet piano, but it's a little known fact that eight years before two now famous brothers made aviation history at Kitty Hawk, North Carolina, Saxton Pope designed and constructed a glider, flying it briefly from the Angel Island hills. *A San Francisico Call Bulletin* news story dated January 23, 1895, was headlined "Flying Machine Tested Yesterday," and featured a photo of Saxton Pope standing beside his crashed glider. This early aeronautical adventure, while not entirely successful, nonetheless earned Pope admittance to the national flying fraternity and an eventual friendship with Wilbur and Orville Wright.

Pope, who truly excelled in his UC medical studies and was graduated with Sec-

Above: Ishi in his prime under the care of Saxton Pope, M.D.

Left: Ishi and Pope hunting on horseback, 1913.

Below left: Saxton's glider, 1895.

ond Honors in 1899, remained an independent thinker throughout his schooling. One day during his formal training as a surgeon he decided to correct a physical problem that had long bothered him. Afflicted since his youth with a painful deformity called hammer toe in which the main toe joint is bent upward like a claw, the self-reliant Pope simply administered some local anesthesia and quickly amputated the troublesome toe himself.

Following a one-year internship, Dr. Pope established a country practice in Watsonville, California, and specialized in surgery. He also married a classmate, Dr. Emma Wrightman, the daughter of a prominent seafaring merchant whose schooner plied a profitable trade between San Francisco and the South Pacific. It was his future wife who had won First Honors at the UC Medical School, and together they built a growing medical practice. Eventually Drs. Saxton and Emma Pope raised a family of four: Saxton, Jr., Elizabeth, Virginia, and Willard Lee Pope. The proud father introduced his youngsters to the outdoors during seasonal camping and hunting trips.

In 1912, the Pope family moved from Watsonville to San Francisco where Saxton Pope would eventually become Chief Surgeon for San Francisco's Emergency Hospital and a Professor of Surgery in the Medical School of the University of California. He published numerous scientific papers and soon became involved in the study of

Ishi, the primitive Indian captured August 29, 1911 in Oroville, California. Anthropology professors Alfred Kroeber and T. T. Waterman had arranged living quarters for Ishi in the Anthropology Museum on the UC campus. They later requested Dr. Pope conduct a complete physical examination on Ishi, and from this chance professional meeting evolved a strong personal friendship — and lasting inspiration. It is safe to speculate that without Ishi's influence, Saxton Pope and Arthur Young may never have become the "fathers of modern bowhunting."

By 1914, people strolling through San Francisco's Golden Gate Park often would see two men — one white and distinguished looking in a suit and tie, the other dark and stocky, clad in khaki work clothes with his hair pulled back in a ponytail — shooting their handcrafted bows and arrows. What the park visitors were witnessing, unknown to them, was the birth of modern day bowhunting. And what followed shooting practice in the park were initial forays afield for small game — rabbits and quail — and eventually bowhunts for blacktail deer. Over time Ishi, Pope, Young, and their friend Will "Chief" Compton, as well as anthropologists Waterman and Kroeber, all traveled into the northern California wilds, visiting Ishi's homeland bordering the rugged Deer and Mill Creek areas in the shadow of Mount Lassen.

On one trip, Ishi led his friends into a draw not far from a cave where the Yana Indians had lived, looked around to get his bearings, then kicked at the sandy earth. He next got down on his knees and scooped away enough soil to expose the skeleton of a bear he'd killed as a young brave and ceremoniously buried as a tribute to the gods. These visits to Ishi's homeland were both emotional and rewarding experiences for the last member of his tribe and his white friends alike.

Ishi commonly referred to Saxton Pope as "Popey" or "*Kuwi*," the latter term being the Indian's word for medicine man. Interestingly, the medicine man label may have had less to do with Dr. Pope's profession than his deftness performing sleight-of-hand tricks to the amazement of Ishi and other onlookers. Long fascinated with magic, Pope had learned how to palm coins as a youngster and frequently performed the tricks for any appreciative audience. He frequently visited children's hospital wards where he surprised and delighted the youngsters by drawing coins from their ears, noses, and clothing. And once, during a visit to Chinatown in San Francisco, Pope befuddled a Chinese merchant by picking a single egg from a basket, cracking it, producing a $5 gold piece, and handing it to the merchant to pay for his purchase. As Pope walked away, the merchant was busy breaking open the remaining eggs in a futile search for additional gold coins.

At the museum, Ishi helped construct an Indian village display. He also treated visitors to demonstrations of routine tribal tasks such as crafting bows and arrows, chipping obsidian into arrowheads, and starting fires by friction. Two of the most treasured items in my personal collection of archery artifacts are two obsidian arrowheads — one spear point and one deer point — that were given to me by Lee Pope. They were chipped by Ishi at the university's museum and personally given to Pope's son, Lee, by the last Yana Indian himself. Incidentally, the 1986 bronze sculpture of Pope and Young facing a charging grizzly, contains an exact copy of the deer point in my collection. It was cast by the Texas artist, Max Greiner, Jr., from my arrowhead.

Lee Pope proved to be a treasure trove of information. In addition to sharing his father's photo album, he showed me other family mementos. Among these items were Saxton Pope's hand-crafted mandolin — called the "Mosquito" — which was the perfect size to roll up inside a sleeping bag, and Art Young's handcrafted miniature violin. He noted his father and good friend enjoyed many evenings singing and playing these instruments around a flickering campfire.

Included in the old album was an archery score card dated June 20, 1915. Pope had noted "windy and cold" on the card and recorded the scores shot that day by himself and several friends. The archers each shot several groups of six arrows at

Saxton Pope and Art Young "resting at the rock."

targets placed at various intervals of 40, 50, and 60 yards. The card revealed he scored 59 hits for a total score 237 points, Will Compton had 71 hits and a score of 347, Art Young 77 hits for a score of 315, Dr. J. V. Cooke 67 hits for a score of 278, and Ishi 45 hits for 221 points. Ishi shot well at 40 yards but misses at longer distances pulled his total score down.

Ishi died of tuberculosis at 12:20 p.m. March 25, 1916, with Dr. Pope at his side. Following an autopsy performed by Dr. Cooke, Ishi was embalmed and placed in a coffin. Dr. Pope, Professor Waterman, and a few friends reverently added his bow, a quiver full of arrows, some Indian money, dried venison, acorn meal, his fire sticks, and a small amount of tobacco. They then accompanied the coffin bearing Ishi to Laurel Hill cemetary near San Francisco for cremation. The ashes were placed in a small Indian pottery jar bearing the simple inscription: "Ishi, the last Yahi Indian, died March 25, 1916."

Ten years later, after a full decade of well documented bowhunting adventures with Art Young, Saxton Pope contracted pneumonia soon after returning to California from a 1925 African safari. He never recovered and died in 1926. Art Young passed away in 1935. Today, decades later, their hunting adventures continue to live and inspire new generations of archers in Pope's two books **Hunting With the Bow and Arrow** and **The Adventurous Bowmen**, as well as Stewart Edward White's book, **Lions in the Path** and many outdoor magazine articles.

Speaking personally, I cannot think of two better namesakes for our Club than Saxton Pope and Arthur Young. Likewise, it is fitting indeed that our Club's highest honor, the Ishi Award, remembers their good friend and hunting companion. The spirit of these three great men resides within the fraternity of modern day bowhunters, and especially with the membership ranks of the Pope and Young Club, the greatest archery/bowhunting organization in the world. I for one am proud to be a small part of it all.

Senior member Doug Walker resides in California with his wife Betty. He served on our Club's very first Board of Directors and is a past Secretary and Big Game Chairman.

Each July the Pope and Young Club hosts a group of single parent families at a "Discover the Outdoors Camp" in the Colorado Rockies. Here young people and their mother or father enjoy a long weekend of planned activities which include basics in archery, woodsmanship, map reading and compass use, fishing, and a host of other outdoor activities which introduce them to nature. Club volunteers and guest instructors host the camp which was designed to serve as a model for state bowhunting organizations to follow in conducting their own camps for children who otherwise may never know the pleasures waiting in the great outdoors.

BOWHUNTING: IT'S UP TO THE KIDS

by Jim Dougherty

I T'S FREQUENTLY SAID that bowhunting today is "bigger and better" than ever, and by most any measurement that's certainly true. There are more of us bowhunting now than ever before — upwards of 3 million hunting archers in North America — and in a modern society that demands numbers to survive socially as well as politically, more is certainly better. Regardless, more bodies and votes will always be necessary for our survival.

We also have better and somewhat more user friendly bowhunting equipment than in the "old days." Quite likely this is the primary reason there are more of us today, notably more women and kids, than ever in our long and distinguished history. Unfortunately, some within the bowhunting community resent the intrusion of allegedly easier to use "newfangled" equipment, a perspective that sometimes interrupts our strong call for unity. In today's world of cockeyed and selfish causes — with so many people determined to destroy us — we must understand that no single persuasion is more important than bowhunting itself and that in the face of other more dangerous themes equipment choice should be a non-issue.

Change is inevitable and should be accepted. Mutual respect within our fraternity is an essential element in the catalyst of bowhunting's ultimate survival. We need no issues within bowhunting except synergy. Each of us should be free to choose what suits us best, practically and spiritually. It need go no further than that.

On the subject of change, it logically follows that the bowhunting industry is bigger, too. It's huge, in fact, which translates to political clout to be reckoned with, listened to and heard by people who matter since sales of our equipment generate millions of tax dollars. This money improves our wildlands and the well being of wildlife. It also helps to protect our sport.

Because we have grown, we have better and lengthier bowhunting seasons. We long ago proved the primary goal of our Pope and Young Club's founder, Glenn St. Charles, namely that using the hunting bow and arrow can be a viable, honest, and effective hunting method. Today the efficiency of bowhunting tackle is factually etched in stone. Today we are a factor to be reckoned with when game management policies are set. That's a far cry from the way bowhunters were once perceived. Back when I was a young man, I knew the bow and arrows with their razor-edged broadheads could be every bit as efficient as the old Winchester in my closet that I had no interest in using. Back then the best we had were short, token archery seasons that opened prior to gun season — and these seasons were given almost grudgingly to quiet us down. That was back when people laughed at me — at us. "Stick and feather guys" and "feather flingers." They called us those names and worse. We don't hear much of that anymore.

What we do hear is anti-hunting sentiment and animal rights diatribe. We're told that hunting is cruel, inhumane, and unnecessary, that a pig's life is as important as a child's, that the life of a laboratory rat is more important than finding a cure for cancer. We're also told that contraception — birth control for animals — is the simple solution to maintaining herd balance. We hear lukewarm acceptance of hunting and are told hunting for food is okay but hunting for trophies is not. We hunters know better, of course, but as our rural environment continues its collapse, it's unlikely these widely held perceptions are going to change.

Does that paint a grim picture for the future of hunting? Not necessarily, although it demands that we pay greater attention to our methods and manners. Equally important, it requires that we continue to grow, that hunting's positive message — not just that part which applies to bowhunting — be presented to the public in a way people will understand us and our values. We must prove that hunters have always given far more to wildlife than we've taken.

We hunters know the truth. We've talked about it for years, mostly among ourselves. Unfortunately, the facts of our positive pro-hunting, pro-conservation message often get lost amid media bias that seemingly is more interested in anti-hunting sensationalism than the truth. Only rarely does the actual value of hunting receive a kind word. Our movie and television screens are alive daily with scenes of murder, mayhem, and sex, yet even on popular outdoor shows the quick, clean taking of a whitetail buck onscreen is seldom permitted. And those of us who have appeared in broadcast hunting shows are not supposed to use the word "kill." Seems that's something reserved for people.

Still, bowhunting is strong, flourishing. Our challenge as we enter a new century is to maintain its strength in the face of

Judy Kovar signing photos for kids after seminar session.

PHOTO BY HERMAN KOVAR

a changing modern society. I'm convinced that hunting's future lies with our youth — the kids — and already we are involved in a great tug of war with their minds and emotions. Our enemies, the antis and animal rights extremists, know this. They can read our statistics, our demographics as well as we can. They know that hunters, as a group, are aging. They know that shaping the opinions of the kids is the way to win their war against hunting — and never doubt for a second that they consider this an all-out war. They are organized, well heeled, and committed. Their propaganda aimed at school children denounces hunting while preaching animal rights. Although emotionally based and factually flawed, it is offered in a convincing manner designed to sow seeds of anti-hunting bias in young minds.

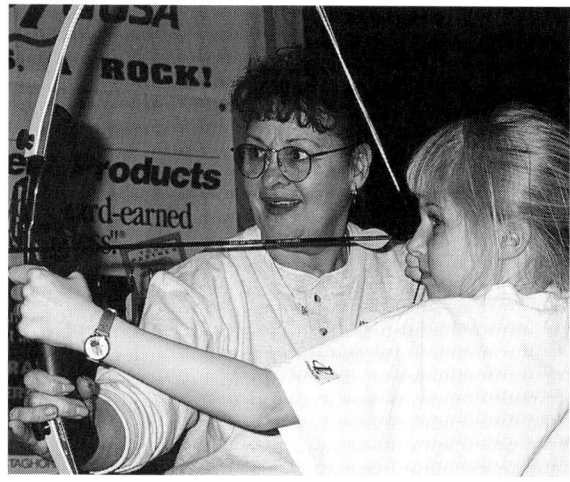

That's exactly what we're up against, that's what we're fighting. That's why the Pope and Young Club is so deeply committed to funding Judy Kovar's efforts (Judy's positive "Hunting Heritage" program reaches tens of thousands of school children each year). Additionally, our Club's "Discover the Outdoors Camp" for single parent families (held in Colorado each July) touches young lives and changes young minds where nature and hunting are concerned. Other valuable Club-sponsored projects help to educate and inform. In fact, Club dollars assigned by our Conservation Committee to various nationwide pro–hunting, pro-conservation efforts in recent years are fast approaching a grand total of $500,000!

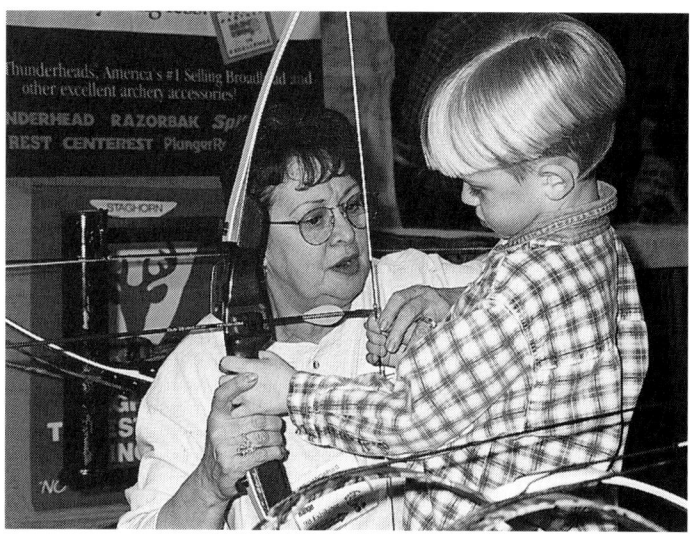

Obviously, the Pope and Young Club recognizes we must do more than merely maintain records of outstanding big game animals in order to protect and perpetuate our hunting heritage. But the future of hunting should not be left solely to organizations like ours. Individually, we must all do more. We must take it upon ourselves to introduce kids — not just our own children and grandchildren but all interested youngsters — to hiking, camping, fishing, and hunting. It's a great way to get kids off city sidewalks and into the outdoors. Rare is the child from either a rural or urban background that doesn't carry the seed of outdoor adventure within his mind and soul. All that's needed to make the seeds sprout and bloom is cultivating, nurturing by someone like you and me.

Hunting's future — our Club's future — lies in those dormant seeds. Each of us has the opportunity to make some of them grow. That knowledge should be incentive enough to stir us to action. It's the very least we can do on behalf of hunting.

Arlene Cianciarulo of Illinois and other volunteers help to introduce many youngsters to archery each year.

Senior member Jim Dougherty is a member of the Archery Hall of Fame and respected outdoor writer. He travels from his Tulsa, Oklahoma, home each year to speak at bowhunting seminars across North America.

THANKS, LORD, FOR THE LADIES!

by George Zanoni

I LOVE MY WIFE, CAROLYN, but I'll admit I also have special feelings for a number of other women — the special ladies of the Pope and Young Club. These women bowhunters are indeed special, not just because they may happen to be good wives or mothers or successful career-minded professionals. They're special to me because of the passion we share for hunting with the bow and arrow. They're special to me because of their determination to overcome all of the "it's-still-a-man's-world" obstacles and win hard-earned admiration and respect from their fellow bowhunters by proving themselves in the field. They're special to me because they set a good example for other women — and especially for today's children — by proving that bowhunting is for anyone, regardless of age or gender, who is interested and willing to accept the challenge. That's why I say, "God bless all of these special ladies!"

While it's true that more women are bowhunting today than ever before, their total number still represents a mere fraction — less than 3 percent, I've heard — of today's 3 million-plus bowhunters. In truth, we need more women bowhunters because the more we involve women and youngsters in our sport, the brighter our future will be. And thanks to widely popular gender-specific programs like Becoming an Outdoors Woman, more women are becoming involved in hunting, fishing, and other outdoor activities each year. Our Club's own annual "Discover the Outdoors Camp" plants additional seeds in the fertile minds of some eager women and children. Still, it's left mostly to the hunters — the fathers, husbands, and boyfriends — to introduce their interested daughters, wives, and sweethearts to bowhunting. And that's a shame.

Unfortunately, it's a fact some men simply

Suzy Sherer (upper left) poses with her big woodland caribou. Carolyn Siebrasse Zanoni (left and right) shows two record book animals taken decades apart, an Illinois whitetail and a Wyoming pronghorn.

61

Idaho bowhunter Pat Stewart used one arrow at 15 yards to stop this Alaskan black bear in 1986.

Midge Dandridge (below) poses with a California black bear that she arrowed in 1973.

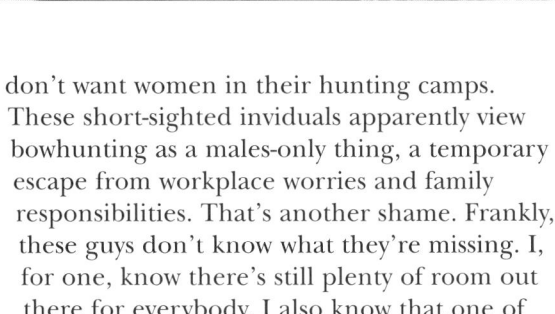

don't want women in their hunting camps. These short-sighted inviduals apparently view bowhunting as a males-only thing, a temporary escape from workplace worries and family responsibilities. That's another shame. Frankly, these guys don't know what they're missing. I, for one, know there's still plenty of room out there for everybody. I also know that one of the true joys of spending time in a hunting camp is sharing the experiences and stories with your fellow hunters. It doesn't make a bit of difference if the person sharing the day's bowhunting adventure around the campfire is a male or female.

On occasion I've been asked to compare my hunts with the guys and hunting with my wife. My answer is always the same. "There's no way to compare the two; they are both special to me." I've enjoyed both many times. But over the years I have come to learn one important fact: You don't have to tote the heaviest pack, draw the stoutest bow, climb the tallest peaks, or cuss and "chaw" tobacco to be a bowhunter. Bowhunting is for anyone and everyone who possesses the proper frame of mind. That certainly includes women.

Back in the late 1950s and early 1960s when my wife-to-be, Carolyn Siebrasse, a professional nurse, was getting started in bowhunting, relatively few women bowhunted. Most women archers seemed content to involve themselves in target archery competition. Those few who did take up the sport most likely were the wives of men who themselves were serious archers and bowhunters. Single women like Carolyn often were viewed with suspicion by male bowhunters and by the few

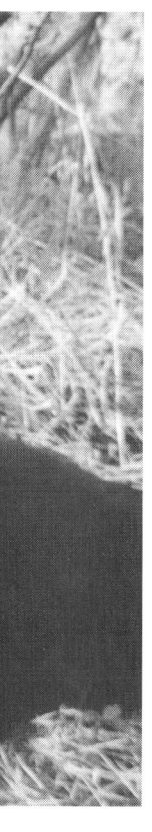

Californian Betty Gulman (left) shows her trophy pronghorn.

Iowa bowhunter Judy Grooms has good reason to smile. Check out her Alaskan moose.

guides and outfitters back then who catered to hunters armed only with bows and arrows. "A woman bowhunter? Come on! Really?"

Really! Carolyn and other determined women love bowhunting with the same passion we men feel. Yet once not so long ago they had to prove themselves and convince men that they just wanted to bowhunt, nothing more, and that they were little different than any male hunter. Through dogged determination and persistence, they made their point. Over time these women bowhunting "pioneers" became welcome in more and more hunting camps, both as clients and peers. Their combined efforts blazed a wide trail for other interested ladies to follow in ensuing years.

Carolyn already was a very successful bowhunter when we first met. This was one of the many attractions that drew me to her. Frankly, I was fascinated by a woman who not only had taken trophy class whitetails in Illinois but who more than once had traveled West — on her own — to take black bear and mountain lion. Once, during a 1966 bowhunt in the high country of Utah, Carolyn couldn't get a clear shot at the treed cat from ground level so she promptly climbed 90 feet into a Douglas fir across from the snarling lion and shot the cougar tree-to-tree. So much for the standard male image of a helpless woman. This was a bowhunter who just happened to be a woman.

Historically speaking, it was 1961 when Carolyn took her first big game trophy, a Pope and Young whitetail buck (reportedly the first record book buck shot by a female bowhunter). One arrow, complete penetration, using a 40 pound Joe Fries recurve bow, cedar arrow, and Hilbre two-blade broadhead. No man could have done it any better.

Despite being qualified, Carolyn didn't become a Regular member of the Pope and Young Club until January of 1967. In those early days, Regular membership was limited to 50 members (she was fifty-eighth on the list). When a 1966 by-laws change doubled the Regular membership ranks, she promptly moved up from Associate membership. By the way, in 1980 Carolyn became the Club's first female Senior member.

Margaret "Rick" Cooley, another Illinois bowhunter, was the Club's first female Regular member. She and her husband, Richard "Dick" Cooley, were among the original 50 Pope and Young Regular members. The names of only two women, Margaret Cooley and Carolyn Zanoni, were listed among the names of the 100 Regular members appearing in the Club's first record book published in 1975.

Today, decades later, only two other notable women bowhunters are listed on the Pope and Young Club's list of Senior members. They are Suzy Sherer of Idaho, who became a Regular member in 1983, and Californian Midge Dandridge who joined the Regular ranks in 1977.

Currently four women — Karen Brunner of Montana, Judy Grooms of Iowa, Betty Gulman of California, and Patricia Stewart of Idaho — are Regular members of the Pope and Young Club. Many more are Associate members who have been actively involved in both bowhunting and Club activities. These include, to name only a few, dedicated women such as Judy Clyncke of Colorado, Carol Mauch of Nebraska (who just happens to hold the current world record for Quebec-Labrador caribou), and Judy Kovar of Illinois. In all, there are about 70 female Associates.

No listing of past active Associates would be complete without mentioning Rosalyn "Rosie" Malinsoki, who was present at the very first official meeting of the Pope and Young Club in Seattle on January 27, 1961. Additionally, one of the most prominent Associates in Club history is Naomi Torrey-Simmons who served as Executive Secretary from 1976 until 1990 when she was elected Second Vice President, serving one two-year term in office. She also served as our Club's Treasurer between 1976 and 1987.

And when it comes to consistent bowhunting success, we must not overlook the accomplishments of women Associates like Carolyn Godfrey, Pam Baird and Kay Lang, Janet George, Connie Larson, Toni Lynde, Cindi Richardson, Kathy Strecker, Charlie White, and Vicki Cianciarulo, to mention a mere handful. Neither can we forget to recognize nationally known target archers/bowhunters like Ann Clark and Ann Hoyt, both longtime members of the Archery Hall of Fame, who continue to hunt well into the autumn of their lives. Each is proof positive of the fact that dedicated female bowhunters can be every bit as successful as their male counterparts. Each is a worthy role model for beginning women bowhunters.

Frankly, my own wife and favorite bowhunting partner does not know how many years she can continue to bowhunt. Rheumatoid arthritis has slowed her considerably in recent years. No longer can she walk woodland and mountain trails, still-hunting and stalking big game. In fact, Carolyn's time afield these days is limited to ground blinds, her favorite bow and nocked arrow clutched in misshapen, pain-stricken hands. Yet she has absolutely no regrets. Remembrances of past bowhunts are a constant comfort. Simply by closing her eyes she can once again be prowling some Utah or Colorado mountainside, sitting patiently in a midwestern deer stand or crouched in a Wyoming pit blind near some prairie waterhole, stalking across the vast Canadian tundra, or drifting the Mississippi River backwaters with bowfishing tackle in search of spawning roughfish. She has her special memories of mule deer and whitetails, black bears and mountain lions, pronghorns and caribou, and all of the other magnificent game animals she has hunted over the last half century.

And now as her lifelong hunting career nears its end, she does as she has always done. Carolyn constantly encourages all people she meets — especially women — to get outdoors, to give bowhunting a try. Among her most gratifying memories are the unsolicited comments she has received in return for her encouragement. More than one woman has said, "Thanks to you, I'm involved in archery. You inspired me. It's because of you that I'm now a bowhunter." This is her legacy. This is her just reward.

Carolyn, like other successful women bowhunters, has discovered an undeniable truism: *Bowhunting is not just a man's sport. It can and should be enjoyed by both sexes. Each bowhunter — man or woman, boy or girl — is truly unique. Each individual can contribute many wonderful personal experiences, stories, and unforgettable moments to the unfolding history of bowhunting.*

I'm convinced it is this sharing — no matter one's gender or age or physical ability — that makes bowhunting so very, very special. And without the many contributions that all women bowhunters have made and continue to make today, bowhunting would be a much poorer, much less satisfying outdoor pastime for all of us.

George Zanoni, himself a Senior member, has bowhunted across North America for decades. He and his wife, Carolyn, are one of the Club's best known couples. They make their home in Westchester, Illinois.

BOWHUNTING EQUIPMENT— AND RESTRICTIONS

by Dave Holt

THE YOUNG GIRL STARED CURIOUSLY as Tom and I released our first arrows on the practice range near my new house. Bow shooting is safe and legal in the suburban Colorado area where I live; however, my newly constructed archery course was quite visible and I couldn't help but wonder how my new neighbors would react when my friends and I began flinging arrows.

As we shot, the girl watched from the top of a gully about 75 yards away. Several times we waved and she waved back. And from that day on she was there watching almost every time anyone shot. In truth, it didn't take long for 10-year-old Dacia McPherson and her father, Richard, to join us on my practice range. Richard was quick to pick up on Dacia's intense interest in archery and he gave her all the parental support possible.

Soon Dacia had her own bow — a compound — and plenty of shooting lessons. She took to archery like few people I've seen. Before long she was asking us questions about bowhunting. By the time she was 11, she had earned her Bowhunter Education certificate. About the time she turned 12, after countless hours of shooting practice, she made her initial bowhunt. On that late December trip to south Texas she stalked and killed a javelina with the very first arrow she ever released at a game animal. It was a clean, one-shot kill, made from a distance of 18 yards. Before returning to Colorado, she also arrowed her first whitetail buck. And as a bonus, Dacia collected a fat feral hog on the final evening of her unforgettable adventure. Four shots — all made from less than 25 yards — resulted in three game animals on the camp meat pole. Not bad for a beginning bowhunter, no matter what his or her age.

Shortly after Dacia's first hunt, I received a call from a fellow wanting me to support the use of crossbows for able-bodied hunters in the archery season. Because

Dacia McPherson and Dave Holt

I'm known in archery circles as a technical person, he apparently had assumed I would be all for the idea. I kindly shared what my young neighbor had just accomplished in Texas using conventional bowhunting tackle. I also explained that I believe we need to keep a dramatic line between bowhunting and gun hunting equipment. He didn't agree but at least was gracious enough to hear me out.

Generally, the moment people begin to address modern bowhunting equipment issues from crossbows to compounds and all the available accessories, many challenges, differences of opinion and emotionally volatile issues rear their ugly heads. Following are a couple of the basic problems we face:

It is human nature for man to constantly search for something better — an easier way of doing things. This is what led people to develop the gun, the automobile, the airplane, the computer along with an almost endless list of other modern day items. Most of us now perceive many of these inventions as rather essential and I'm certainly not condemning any modern conveniences like cars, planes, and computers. But when it comes to our little corner of the world — bowhunting — I can see no need to try to reinvent the gun. If we want to spend more hunting days afield, there must be some truth to the claim that ours is a difficult pursuit which requires a higher degree of preparation and dedication than other forms of hunting.

And if today's available equipment allows the Dacias of the world —12-year-old girls — to participate in bowhunting with a reasonable chance for success, then we have already made our wonderful sport available to the vast majority of those who are willing to invest a moderate amount of effort and time. Moreover, if bowhunting didn't require considerably more time and effort, could we honestly look our rifle hunting counterparts in the eye and say we truly deserve a three month season while they need only one week?

Pro-technology critics argue that there is no good reason to stop the daily advancement of bowhunting equipment; some insist technology is self-limiting. True, advancements in modern bowhunting gear may have slowed somewhat, but I don't believe they have stopped — or will. For example, there is now a bow with a track attached that is capable of shooting a four-inch arrow. This arrow is nothing more than a long broadhead — the blades are located at the rear and double as the fletching. Although a recent ruling by the Pope and Young Club precludes the acceptance of trophy class animals taken with such futuristic hunting tackle, no one can say what the fertile mind of man will devise next. I have seen for myself certain prototype bows that are strikingly different in design and function from currently available models.

So at its 1998 Directors Meeting in Omaha, Nebraska, the Pope and Young Board voted to change Article IX, Section 9.2, of the Club's bylaws to include an expanded, more complete definition of hunting bows, arrows, and broadheads for the taking of record book big game animals (see the accompanying statement). As a Club member and bowhunter, I'm convinced the move was a wise one. Here's why.

Other popular outdoor pastimes such as golf, tennis, baseball, and bowling —

even sport fishing — long ago initiated certain equipment regulations to keep things reasonably equal and fair within their respective ranks. Meanwhile, many participants in bowhunting cannot agree on what action, if any, to take regarding acceptable equipment. I certainly don't claim to know the answers; however, I can tell you that if all bowhunting groups had waited for more advanced hunting tackle to arrive and then tried to stop its use, the challenge would prove far more difficult, maybe impossible, to overcome.

Currently, most serious bowhunters I know draw the line at using crossbows, primarily because they are aimed and shot like a gun. But from that single glimmer of agreement we find few exact points of unity arise. Disagreement abounds even within this great organization — the Pope and Young Club — let alone within the general bowhunting community.

I like to use a theoretical football field to explain why bowhunters have such a difficult time agreeing exactly where to stop the space age advancement of bowhunting equipment. On this imaginary field the home team's one yard line is painted solid white and the opponent's one yard line is painted solid black. From the all-black one yard line the color takes the remaining 98 yards to change slowly to solid white. Few onlookers would agree exactly where black stops and the white starts. Much of the area is gray.

Now think of the advancement of modern bowhunting equipment represented by a slow-moving turtle. Perhaps no single small step the turtle takes is worth noticing, but given enough time this slow-moving creature will reach the far end of the football field. And when we finally take the time to look around and check on the turtle's progress, it may be too late to change its course.

The Pope and Young Club took a truly bold step in 1988 by defining bowhunting equipment with regard to its record book entries. Actually, the first step toward equipment restrictions was taken when the Club was formed in 1961, because record book entries have always been limited to "bowhunting" tackle. But the 1988 action defined acceptable bowhunting gear in a more precise manner. The Club's Rules of Fair Chase initially defined an acceptable modern hunting bow and arrow as follows:

"For the purpose of entry of an animal into the Records a bow shall be defined as a longbow, recurve bow or compound bow that is hand-held and hand-drawn, and that has no mechanical device to enable the hunter to lock the bow at full or partial draw. No compound bow shall have a let-off of more than 65 percent. The arrow shall be propelled only by the energy stored by the drawn bow."

(Interestingly, at the time of this ruling only one short decade ago, compound bows with a 65 percent let-off were near the upper limit of what was being produced and sold by major bow companies. Today, compounds with let-offs of 75 to 80 percent or more are the norm. That turtle moves ahead, slowly but surely creeping toward the far end of the playing field.)

Further, with regard to electronics, the Club's updated Fair Chase rule specifically disallows animals taken: "By the use of electronic devices for attracting, locating or pursuing game, or guiding the hunter to such game or by the use of a bow or arrow to which any electronic device is attached."

The Club immediately took some criticism for placing restrictions on modern bowhunting gear. Some challenged the Club's "right" to declare electronics and high let-off compound bows — legal equipment in many states and provinces — a violation of fair chase rules. In reality, despite widespread grumbling, these two equipment restrictions were relatively minor ones and each was well reasoned:

First, *disallowing electronics on the hunting bow and arrows* was a simple black and white issue. It still is. Either you do or you don't have any electronic device attached to the bow and arrow. It's that simple. Club President G. Fred Asbell clearly explained the rationale behind this action:

"We simply drew a line in the sand. Club leaders felt that as modern technologies and product possibilities developed, the challenge to bowhunting's future would be continuous. Consequently, a decision was made to disallow the use of *all electronics* on the bow and arrow. This decision was not made to specifically eliminate the use of lighted sights, as some wrongly believe. This was not a ruling to prevent anyone from shooting better or recovering game, as some critics claim. Again, it applies to **all electronics** — past, present and future — on the bow and arrow and it only applies to those bowhunters seeking to enter animals into the record book. Incidentally, the Boone and Crockett Club has similar rules about the use of electronics."

Second, *limiting a compound bow's reduction in holding weight to a maximum of 65 percent* of the peak draw force — the so-called let-off rule — was, unfortunately, much more complex. Why? Really, there are two different methods of measuring let-off. And it is not easy for the average person to measure or compute a compound's let-off. In addition, it's a particularly difficult measurement to take in the field.

Recognizing the need to take subsequent action, in 1997 the Pope and Young Club further clarified how let-off is to be measured. At that time the Board approved the following language change to its Fair Chase statement: "A let-off of sixty-five (65) percent on a compound is the maximum allowed, *as defined by AMO's method of measuring let-off and allowing for a minor deviation due to rigging and manufacturing variables.*"

Unfortunately, compound let-off measurements will always be somewhat complex. But I for one don't believe these complexities make the Pope and Young let-off rule any less necessary. As a long time bowhunter, I'm convinced that understanding when to draw on a big game animal is one of the most crucial aspects of the sport. There certainly is a much shorter time window to work with when shooting a recurve or longbow than there is using a compound with even a 65 percent let-off. And if we imagine a compound with a 90 percent let-off, the shooter could draw and hold for several minutes ahead of the time to release an arrow. In my opinion compound bows with 100 percent let-off are little more than vertical crossbows, regardless of how they are aimed or how the arrows are released.

Some argue the benefits of let-off are self-limiting. And as long as it doesn't reach 100 percent or full-draw holding devices, that may be true. I'm not sure. This issue, nonetheless, reminds me of the football field and the turtle. Bowhunters simply need to agree where to draw the line — and we need to agree soon. That's where the Club's past action becomes increasingly important.

As previously mentioned, the Pope and Young Club made a decisive first move in '88 by placing a few minor restrictions on bowhunting equipment — which, it should be stressed, only affects entries for their own record book. Still, a few "anything goes" advocates question the wisdom of that Club decision. Certain manufacturers viewed the step as a threat to their bottom line. Consequently, the Club has taken and continues to take plenty of heat on this point, particularly from non-members.

Because of my deep involvement in bowhunting, I see all sides of the industry and there certainly are misunderstandings. The manufacturers are primarily interested in producing and marketing products the public wants to purchase, and the vast majority of bowhunters want bows with more let-off because such bows are physically easier to shoot.

Simply stated, a large number of bowhunters want all the bells and whistles. I'm afraid some people would use a gun in the bow season, if it were legal, just because it is easier — human nature, I guess. But the manufacturers either make what the majority of folks want to buy or they go out of business. Yet it's wrong to suggest the Club is attempting to dictate standards which apply to all archery hunters. Today, there are about 3 million bowhunters and less than 3,500 Pope and Young Club members. G. Fred Asbell put things in clear and proper perspective with the following explanation:

"The Pope and Young Club is basically a private organization. The standards it sets are for that organization only. The Club's Fair Chase standards only apply to what can be entered into the Club's own record system. They are not rules and regulations for the bowhunting world. They do not limit what can be manufactured, sold, or used.

"In many instances the Club has tighter restrictions than do various states and provinces. For example, hunting and taking trophy animals on game farms or high-fenced commercial hunting operations is legal in many areas, but Pope and Young does not accept these animals. Crossbows are legal in some areas, but Pope and Young does not accept animals taken with a crossbow. Party hunting is legal in some areas, but Pope and Young does not accept into its records any animal not legally tagged with a specific bowhunter's tag. The point is, just because it is legal to hunt in a certain manner within a state or province — or it is legal to use certain equipment there — this does not make it automatically acceptable for animals to be entered into the Pope and Young Club's record system."

Again, I doubt that the advance of modern bowhunting equipment has ceased. And I do feel that reasonable equipment restrictions will serve our sport well in the long run. The Club could have stood by and watched the turtle take one slow step at a time. Rather, it chose to dig a trench in the playing field and set standards for bowhunters wanting to enter their big game animals in the Pope and Young records. Only time will prove the wisdom of this decision; however, I for one feel better knowing the Club has made a reasonable effort to define and preserve fair chase bowhunting at a sensible place in time.

Many may argue that this is not a job for the Pope and Young Club and that may be true. But, unfortunately, no one else stepped forward. And if a 12-year-old Colorado girl can work hard and enjoy bowhunting success with today's conventional equipment, does it not make sense that Club leaders should define what this prominent organization feels is a reasonable definition of a bow and arrow?

"Clearly, it should be apparent it is not the purpose of the Pope and Young Club to set standards for equipment for all bowhunters," explains G. Fred Asbell. "Equipment issues should be handled by individual states and provinces if and when it is deemed necessary. Of course, restraint and good judgment on the part of the manufacturing and the bowhunting communities could negate the need for any such regulations. But history, which gives us some insight into our future, tells us that some regulation will, of necessity, happen.

"The future of bowhunting — the future of all hunting — cannot be thought to rest in the hands of any single organization or individual. It rests in *our* hands. And we must remember that we are all being observed more than ever before by the hunting, the non-hunting, the regulatory, and the anti-hunting communities. That fact — and a genuine concern about the future of bowhunting — gave the Pope and Young Club the motivation to impose certain requirements on its own record book entries."

Again, not everyone agrees with what the Pope and Young Club has already done in terms of restricting equipment. But the Club has taken several positive steps it considers in the best interests of its members and all of bowhunting. The Club's primary motive should be as clear as a mountain spring; it is acting decisively to protect the sport we all love.

Colorado-based bowhunter Dave Holt, an Associate member, is the Technical Editor of Bowhunter *magazine and one of the nation's leading authorities on modern archery equipment.*

POPE & YOUNG CLUB

Definition of a Hunting Bow, Arrow, and Broadhead for the Taking of Big Game Animals

HUNTING BOW
A hunting bow for big game shall be a longbow, flat bow, recurve bow, compound bow, or any combination of these designs meeting the following requirements and restrictions:

- A device for launching an arrow, which derives its propulsive energy solely from the bending and recovery of two limbs.
- The bow must be hand drawn by a single and direct, uninterrupted pulling action of the shooter. The bowstring must be moved from brace height to the full draw position by the muscle power of the shooter's body. The energy used to propel the arrow shall not be derived from any other source such as hydraulic, pneumatic, mechanical, or similar devices. These limitations shall not exclude the mechanical leverage advantage provided by eccentric wheels or cams so long as the available energy stored in the bent limbs of the bow is the sole result of a single, continuous, and direct pulling effort by the shooter.
- The bow must be hand-held. One hand shall hold the bow and the other hand draw the bowstring. The bowstring must be moved and/or held at all points in the draw cycle entirely by the muscle power of the shooter until release. The bowstring must be released as a direct and conscious action of the shooter's either relaxing the tension of the fingers or triggering the release action of a hand-held release.
- The bow shall be no shorter than 30 inches.

Exceptions
Physically handicapped bowhunters shall be excepted from the requirements of holding or shooting the bow with their hands.

Exclusions
The following shall not be considered a hunting bow:

- *A crossbow.*
- *Any device with a gun-type stock or incorporating any device or mechanism that holds the bowstring at partial or full draw without the shooter's muscle power.*

Also, electronic or battery-powered devices shall not be attached to the hunting bow.

No portion of the bow's riser (handle) or any track, trough, channel, or other device that attaches directly to the bow's riser shall contact, support, and/or guide the arrow from a point rearward of the bow's brace height.

Let-Off for Compound Bows

Definition of let-off: *That characteristic of a bow that results in a reduction of the force necessary to increase the draw length after the highest level of draw force has been reached.* This is a characteristic generally associated with, but not restricted to, compound bows.

The maximum let-off on a compound bow shall be measured at a point in the draw cycle after the peak draw weight has been attained. It shall be measured near the end of the draw cycle where the minimum holding force is reached. This point in the draw cycle of a compound bow is known as "the bottom of the valley."

Determination of the percent of let-off: The values of the peak draw force and the let-off force shall be used to calculate the percent of let-off. The peak force is the maximum force obtained during the draw cycle. The let-off force is the lowest force reached following the peak force during a single uninterrupted draw cycle. In all cases, both the highest and lowest force shall be read from a scale during a single and continual pull condition, without relaxation. This technique eliminates the introduction of hysteresis, which can distort the reading.

$$\text{Percent of let-off} = \frac{100 \times (\text{Peak Draw Force} - \text{Minimum Holding Force})}{\text{Peak Draw Force}}$$

The nominal percent of let-off for hunting bows shall be a maximum of 65 percent. It is recognized that variations in draw length and/or draw weight can affect the percent of let-off on compound bows. For these reasons minor variations in let-off are acceptable.

HUNTING ARROW

A hunting arrow shall have the following characteristics:

- It shall be a projectile of at least 20 inches overall length. The length of the arrow shall be measured from the rearward point of the nock to the tip of the broadhead.
- Fletching shall be attached to the aft end.
- A broadhead shall be mounted to the fore end.
- The arrow shall weigh no less than 300 grains with the broadhead attached.

Exclusions

No electronic or battery-powered devices shall be attached to the arrow.
No poison, drug, or explosives shall be attached to the arrow.

HUNTING BROADHEAD

The broadhead for big game shall meet the following requirements:

- Possess two or more sharp cutting edges, fixed or movable, that can be sharpened and/or replaced.
- Be at least 7/8 inches wide at the widest point of the sharp cutting edge.
- Weigh no less than 70 grains.

IS BOWHUNTING GETTING TOO EASY?

by Dick Sage

IF YOU'VE JUST RETURNED from a bowhunting adventure cold, wet, and skunked, you're probably muttering, "Easy? This guy has flipped out!" Perhaps, but these days a lot of people seem to be wondering aloud if the equipment revolution has excessively reduced the personal effort required to harvest a big game animal with a hunting bow. It's certainly a contention worth examination and comment.

Since I took up bowhunting in 1948, there certainly have been major changes not only in equipment but in every phase of archery/bowhunting. From handcrafted selfbows to manufactured hard cam compounds, from cedar or birch to graphite or aluminum shafts, and from Cascophen to space age expoxy glues, the changes have been dramatic. Field archery for fun and hunting practice in the '40s and '50s has given way to a sophisticated "field archery" game. Shooting realistic 3-D animal targets "in the woods at unknown ranges" has become the new kid on the block, only to take a competitive turn while many "fun and practice" shooters stand on the sidelines.

Equipment and games aren't the only changes. Bowhunting itself has undergone a major transformation. For example, I took my first deer in 1952 with a Bear longbow, a homemade cedar shaft, and MA-3 broadhead. I was hunting on a farm where the owner was reluctant to let "idiots" hunt. He eventually relented, commenting, "I guess you nuts won't hurt either the deer or yourselves." When I dragged my six-point whitetail into his yard that November day long ago, he still needed convincing I didn't use a gun. And he wasn't the only one who examined that buck's carcass for bullet holes! That particular year New Jersey bowhunters harvested just over 100 deer; in 1997 they took over 20,000 deer! Back in 1952 we hunted a special two-week season for bucks only; in '97 the New Jersey season extended over a four-month period for either bucks or does, and simply by applying and paying a small fee any bowhunter could qualify for licenses or permits which would allow the harvest in excess of a dozen deer! That is a very big change.

Bowhunting techniques have also evolved. Initially, many bowhunters were more

Sage arrowed this whitetail in 1989.

archers than hunters and their techniques were often zany. Usually, they hunted from ground blinds or stands. I don't recall hearing about treestands until the early '60s; my first treestand kill was in 1967 and it was the first time I ever hunted from an elevated stand. How things have changed. During the Pope and Young Club's 1995-96 recording period, 80 percent of the hunters reportedly took their trophy whitetails from treestands!

Practically all of my early whitetail hunts involved stalking and still-hunting, either alone or in the company of a partner. Today's bowhunters seldom use those time honored ground hunting methods (only one in ten of whitetail hunters in the 1995-96 Pope and Young data) and some even proclaim these hunting techniques "impossible" when using a bow. Even now when my increasingly clumsy feet have a mind of their own, it is still the way I prefer to hunt deer when conditions permit. It is the embodiment of the one-on-one experience that initially drew many of us afield with our bows.

And there's more. Back in the '50s if you wanted to hunt anything except local whitetails, you did the dog work yourself. Trying to convince outfitters that the bow was a legitimate weapon was a chore — and often unsuccessful. To a large extent Fred Bear's exploits and efforts started a major turnaround. If Howard Hill and Saxton Pope et al. invigorated the nation's bowhunters, Fred Bear finished the job by converting many within the gun hunting fraternity. Today if you want to hunt non-local species, pick up any bowhunting publication, make a call, and you're in business. And today's sophisticated archery/bowhunting publications weren't around back then, either. The NFAA's **Archery** magazine and Carl Hulbert's **National Bowhunter** were our primary sources of info on equipment and bowhunting. When my copy of **Archery** showed up, I read every word of it from cover to cover the day it arrived.

Left: Cliff Wiseman with Newfoundland caribou taken in 1962.

Far left: Cliff Wiseman and Jim Newhook with Newfoundland moose taken in 1960.

In the late 1950s, three of us from New Jersey's Watchung Bowmen got interested in hunting moose with our bows. About that time Lee Wulff (all fly fishermen will know that name) wrote an article about bowhunting moose and woodland caribou in Newfoundland where he maintained a salmon fishing camp. Since Lee then lived only a couple of dozen miles from my New York birthplace, I imposed on his hospitality and got some firsthand information. In the fall of 1960 my buddies and I left New Jersey and drove and ferried our way to Newfoundland. We returned a week later with three bull moose. None made the "book" and it doesn't sound like much of an accomplishment these days; however, it was a milestone hunt for us. The total bill for that bowhunt — including gas, licenses, outfitting fees and everything else — was $400 apiece! Today one hunting license costs more than that.

One member of that three-man team, Cliff Wiseman, returned in 1962 and harvested the then world record woodland caribou in the same hunting area. Len Cardinale, another Watchung Bowmen member, got his Colorado mountain lion about that same time. Things were changing.

Slow acceptance by a profession attuned to the gun was an important reason behind founding the Pope and Young Club. Outfitters, game departments, and a skeptical public needed to be shown we could make quick, humane kills with our bows and razor sharp broadheads. Eventually, even the so-called "big three" hunting/fishing magazines signed on, albeit reluctantly since they weren't above an occasional anti-bowhunting article.

The bottom line is there have been major changes in essentially every facet of bowhunting. But there is one thing that has not changed. It is still one hunter with a bow and a desire versus one animal with superior survival instincts. Bowhunting began as a one-on-one sport; it is still a one-on-one sport.

To which I say: "Thank God!"

So how do you assess whether bowhunting today is "too easy"? The percentage of bowhunters taking animals has certainly increased, but so have the deer populations and hunting seasons are often several times as long as they once were. Initial typical success rates of 1 to 5 percent now average 15 percent across the continent and in some states one of every three bowhunters harvests an animal. Hunters do have better equipment and pre-hunt training, such as hunter education programs, which is a plus. Those factors also have contributed to fewer wounding shots. But make no bones about it. In the "good old days" we lost animals because neither we nor our hunting equipment were as capable as we believed and because we had not yet learned to respect the shorter ranges at which our bows were most effective. We tried to emulate shots made by the legendary Howard Hill or Joe Dolan. And mostly we failed.

There can be no denying that better equipment in the hands of better trained and more responsible bowhunters has increased our success. But it is simplistic to overlook those other factors that have, at least in my opinion, been even more significant. Not to be ignored is the explosion of game animal populations (e.g., whitetails and pronghorns, to name only two) over the last five decades. In 1950 the New Jersey deer population was estimated at 50,000 animals. By 1997 it had increased threefold and hunters with shotguns, muzzleloaders, and bows harvested 59,551 deer!

"How should the Pope and Young Club react to the equipment issue?" That's a frequently asked question these days. To some bowhunters, the Club's current equipment specifications seem to be based on the idea that electronic aids and high let-off bows give hunters too much of an advantage. Of particular concern to other hunters is the concern if we continually "ease up" on equipment restrictions, won't we make a trophy animal less worthy of that designation? Well, here's my opinion. Back in 1971 I took a Quebec-Labrador caribou with my recurve that scored 296 4/8 (the minimum at that time was 265 0/8). My bull made the "book" then, but the minimum today is 325 0/8. While it was certainly tougher to take a book animal scoring 265 in 1971 than it is to get one today scoring over 325, I'm convinced that modern equipment is not the reason. Outfitters able and willing to handle bowhunters in '71 were relatively few and far between; today they are not quite a dime a dozen, but for sure, fifty cents will get you lots of invitations.

Some people wrongly believe the Club's electronics ban was based primarily on the concern that lighted sight pins would be perceived as allowing the hunter to shoot beyond legal hours. If this were true, it would be a valid restriction and would make a lot of sense to the non-hunter. And it's true in marginal situations the electronically lighted pin can help a shooter. Yet anyone who has ever tried to use a lighted sight pin after dark knows the brightness of the pin further dims the ability to see the target.

Admittedly, I may be a bit prejudiced on this particular point because at the age of 76 my eyes need all the help they can get. For me, the advent of non-electronic fiber-optic sights — which are perfectly legal under P&Y rules — has been a godsend. Although I have tried but never hunted with a lighted sight pin, Club President G. Fred Asbell spoke for multitudes when he said: "Electronics and bowhunting seem incompatible to many. When we speak of bowhunting as a more difficult and challenging method of hunting — which is the basis of our separate and lengthy archery-only seasons and the main reason why many of us began hunting with the bow and arrow — the use of electronics in bowhunting seems to stretch those basic principles."

Most bowhunters certainly would agree that it is easier to use a modern compound bow than the more traditional longbows and recurves. Also, it's true that as the let-off increases, it is easier to hold at full draw for the inevitable situation where you have to wait out an animal for an acceptable shot. This is a definite equipment plus. Consequently, the Club established its 65 percent let-off as the break point. At the time this rule was established years ago let-offs of 55 percent or so were the industry norm with maximum let-off of that time around 65 percent; however, in recent years the manufacturing trend has been to produce and promote high let-off compounds. Today, it is easy to buy compound bows with let-offs of 75 to 80 percent or more. Regardless, compound bows with let-offs of 65 percent or more are still being made and sold, and any compound user wanting to enter an animal in the Pope and Young record book must abide by the Club's equipment rules. No excuses. No exceptions.

Interestingly, there is one piece of modern mechanical equipment which is suspect when investigating the "too easy" charge. That is the treestand. Take treestands away from bowhunters and the rest of those so-called equipment "advantages" soon fade into obscurity. Conversely, take all those other so-called "advantages" away and allow the use of treestands and the success ratios would suffer far less. Probably fewer hunters would use the bow if compounds did not exist, but I doubt the success rates would change significantly. Consider this: With average shots at whitetails in the range of 15 to 25 yards *and made from tree stands*, how can arrow speed, fancy sights, hard cams, etc. really play a major role in success ratios? The only real plus in these cases is the ability to hold longer at full draw. What these things often do is allow bowhunters to use equipment to play other games during the off season and then use the same tackle when they go hunting.

Dick Sage with guide returning to camp after a successful hunt in British Columbia, 1973.

So how would I answer the question posed at the start of this chapter? I personally do not believe that bowhunting has gotten too easy, and I don't believe this conclusion is a result of me having moved into my "golden years." Equipment innovations, treestands, etc. have simply made it possible for a broader spectrum of hunters to enjoy a wonderful way of hunting game animals over a longer span of years. Having done it "the hard way" and "the easy way," I personally find very little difference in the challenge of the sport or the thrill of the hunt itself. Furthermore, I see minimal effect on my results. I honestly believe there is room between the extremes advocated by traditionalists and high techers to include most if not all would be bowhunters. This room helps maximize our numbers and today this is of paramount importance. With all hunting under daily attack, we can ill afford to thin our ranks except for clearly unacceptable practices.

Few people regard bowhunting as a competitive sport, and certainly the Pope and Young Club does not encourage competition. Consequently, should we be concerned if some bowhunters choose to use equipment that provides an "easier" way, even when these somewhat easier routes still present a true challenge for most bowhunters? I don't think so. In fact, I can sum up my view concerning the selection and use of bowhunting tackle by quoting the old lady's explanation after she kissed her cow on the rump: "Everybody to their own tastes."

Senior member Dick Sage has written for a wide variety of national archery and bowhunting publications for over four decades. He makes his home in Queensbury, New York.

"I'VE LEARNED I STILL HAVE A LOT TO LEARN..."

by M.R. James

HE'S ONE OF BOWHUNTING'S biggest boosters. He's also one of Pope and Young's most passionate promoters. He's Tom Hoffman of Albany, New York, an Associate Member whose unabashed love for our sport and heartfelt pride in our Club is evident in his every word and deed.

Forget the fact that in 1998 he made bowhunting history by becoming the first person to collect at least one Pope and Young record book animal representing all 28 species of North American big game. Forget the fact that in 1996 he became only the third bowhunter — after Chuck Adams and Jim Ryan — to ever collect all 28 species of North American big game. And forget the fact he was the first bowhunter to twice take all four species of North American wild sheep. Such hunting deeds speak for themselves; Tom Hoffman speaks for bowhunting in a clear, strong voice that is both articulate and persuasive.

"Because we fail more often than we succeed, we bowhunters should always be proud of our accomplishments," he states. "We're constantly making bowhunting memories, and we share our adventures with others through our photos, videos, and stories told around a campfire. These are all special memories of our outdoor adventures. They last a lifetime."

Life for Tom Hoffman began in Albany 55 years ago. By age 5 he was tagging along after his father, Jack, on family hunts for rabbits and pheasants. By 16 he'd collected his first New York whitetail, launching a long and well-traveled rifle hunting career that eventually spanned most of North America and continued nonstop until 1982 when he shot his first deer — a spikehorn — with a bow and arrow. Although he didn't realize it at the time, releasing that arrow changed his hunting life forever.

"My cousin, Doris Hoffman, owned an archery shop and she had set me up with bowhunting gear," Tom explains. "Dave Simpson, an Alberta sheep guide I'd rifle hunted with, kept urging me to try bowhunting and go for one of the giant rams in Canmore's bow-only bighorn sheep area. But on my very first out-of-state bowhunt in October of 1983 I hunted Alaska's Kajulik Bay for brown bear and caribou. The archery bug bit me hard during that trip."

Tom took both a record book brownie and barren ground bull on his initial non-resident bowhunt; however, it wasn't these exceptional trophies that converted him from rifleman to bowhunter: it was the total bowhunting experience.

"I found bowhunting to be an incredible thrill," admits the veteran hunter. "Getting close to game, remaining unseen, and getting off a good shot was more challenging than anything I'd ever imagined. I also felt closer to nature than ever before. I returned home knowing only one thing: I wanted more bowhunting experiences."

More bowhunting experiences quickly followed. Undeterred by blown stalks, missed shots, and trips ending with no game taken, Tom stubbornly persisted in his passionate pursuit of big game. As he honed his shooting and bowhunting skills, he began to experience consistent success. And Tom proudly submitted each of his largest trophies for recording in the Pope and Young Club listings.

"Some people think it's strictly an ego thing," Tom says. "It's not. Or it shouldn't be. The Pope and Young record book not only documents specific bowhunting accomplishments, but it recognizes outstanding animals taken ethically under the rules of fair chase. Collectively, it represents the accomplishments of thousands of people who have worked hard to excel despite daunting challenges. Further, it provides proof positive of bowhunting's effectiveness. So when you submit an animal for scoring, as you sign your name to the fair chase affidavit, you're helping to write a lasting history of our sport. It's something to be taken seriously. And the $25 entry fee isn't a payoff to the Club to get your name listed in the book; it's a long term investment in the future of hunting. The money collected by the Club goes to various projects benefiting hunters and wildlife alike."

Because of his unshaken faith in the Pope and Young Club and its work, Tom Hoffman constantly encourages bowhunters to join or enter their trophy animals — or both. He urges donating Club record books to schools and libraries to spread bowhunting's message to non-hunters. He also makes it a habit to give a copy of the lat-

Bowhunter Tom Hoffman has a special love for wild sheep.

est P&Y record book to archery shops and to guides or outfitters wherever he travels.

"People ask me what animal I like to hunt most. That's like asking what's my favorite food. Sometimes I prefer beef. At other times it's fish or chicken or pork. It's the same with bowhunting, but if you try to pin me down I'll admit I have a fondness for wild sheep. That's because of the beautiful country where they live, combined with the physical and mental challenge of sheep hunting. Believe me, you have to learn to live with defeat — and pain — when bowhunting sheep.

"There are times when you swear you'll never do it again. You're on some mountain. You're bone tired, footsore, wet, and cold. You think to yourself, for the same amount of money I could be over in Hawaii basking in the sun on some sandy beach. And yet if you're a serious bowhunter, the choice is a no-brainer. You pick up your bow and head up the mountain again. And again. And again."

One of Tom Hoffman's favorite books is a little publication titled **Live, Learn and Pass It On** by Jackson Brown. Its title page teaser notes what the book is about: "People ages 5 to 95 share what they've learned about life, love, and other good stuff." Tom's favorite quote was penned by a 92-year-old who said, "I've learned I still have a lot to learn."

"I've learned I still have a lot to learn about bowhunting," Tom admits.

Modest and unassuming despite his many hunting successes, Tom Hoffman delights in hearing and swapping stories with other bowhunters. And he's not above laughing at himself for some screw-up in the field. "Some people take themselves far too seriously," he says. "They won't admit missing a shot or blowing a chance at an animal. I think we should be honest about our mistakes as well as our successes. We should never get reckless with the facts, either. There's nothing ever wrong with telling the truth."

The truth is that between two successful bear hunts taken 15 years apart — one for Alaskan brown bear in 1983 and another for Arizona black bear in 1998 — Tom Hoffman arrowed one or more Pope and Young animals representing each of the 28 North American big game species. This is an unprecedented accomplishment which he acknowledges but refuses to dwell on. Far more important than personal accomplishments is working collectively with other concerned individuals to preserve the future of both bowhunting and the Pope and Young Club.

Motivated. Enthusiastic. Patient. Determined. Principled. Loyal. Each of these qualities can be used to accurately describe Tom Hoffman, man and bowhunter. "Some people say I'm awfully lucky — and certainly luck plays a part in any hunt. But what I am is blessed with good health, a good business that allows me to support my bowhunting habit, and a good wife of 35 years who completely supports my addiction." Tom and Carole Hoffman are the proud parents of three grown children and six grandchildren.

What does the future hold for Tom Hoffman? By now that answer should be obvious. "I'm very proud to be a bowhunter, and I'm looking forward to many more hunts for a variety of species. I want to go different places and meet different people. I want to revisit special camps and hunting areas and bowhunt with old friends. I want to help the Pope and Young Club and bowhunting itself continue to grow, and I'm very optimistic about our future. Lots of people who don't hunt themselves view bowhunters as individuals who aren't afraid of odds and who pursue wild game one-on-one in a challenging, ethical, and fair chase fashion. Lots of people I talk to respect what we're doing and how we do it. If we can continue to convince the non-hunters we're an important part of the modern wildlife conservation scene, we'll win the war and continue to enjoy hunting well into the new millennium."

Senior member M. R. James lives in Montana and has served on the Club's Board of Directors since 1986. He also has been Editor of three of the five P&Y record books.

SOME TALES OF THE MEASURERS' TAPE

by Frank "Rit" Heller
with contributions from fellow measurers
Len Cardinale, Clark Gallup, Stan Godfrey
and M.R. James

WHEN WE POPE AND YOUNG MEASURERS score big game trophies for our fellow bowhunters, we commonly hear stories of how these record book animals were taken. Most of the tales we hear describe routine hunting adventures; however, on occasion some successful hunter will pass along an unusual, memorable story or a yarn that's almost impossible to believe. Some of stories are funny. Others seemingly prove the timeworn adage that at times it's better to be lucky than good. All are uncommon and all involve the taking of trophy class animals.

Following is a mere sampling of such tales. No hunters' names or specific locations are used — for what should be obvious reasons:

Once a 12-year-old boy, his father, and his uncle showed up at my place to have the youngster's whitetail rack scored. I learned the father and boy's uncle had successfully bowhunted together for many years. When the boy was old enough to legally hunt deer, he obtained his first license and eagerly joined his father and uncle for some early season hunting. The adults promptly set him up in a treestand just inside a small woodlot, next to a standing cornfield, overlooking two well-used deer trails.

Since the youngster was in school and could only hunt weekends and evenings, they kept placing him in the well-located elevated stand. After several uneventful outings, the impatient boy started to complain that he couldn't see well enough from his pre-chosen ambush point. Seems the corn was too high and the leaves too thick for him to see any nearby deer. The father, quickly growing tired of his son's complaints, decided to let the boy choose his own ambush site. He figured this would teach a valuable lesson in patience as well as an appreciation for just how hard it is to select a good stand.

As the trio arrived early the following Saturday morning, they discovered the corn had been picked since their last hunt. Regardless, the boy promptly chose a spot on the ground about 10 rows into the harvested field where four or five stalks still stood. The father and uncle looked at each other knowingly, smiled, and said the choice was fine, the boy should try this spot if he liked it. Then they headed for their own carefully chosen stands.

Shortly after daybreak, three deer emerged from a far corner of the picked cornfield running as if the devil himself were chasing after them. And wouldn't you know it? They bounded within 20 yards of where the young bowhunter crouched, stopped broadside, and stood looking back. The youngster immediately shot the big buck through both lungs with the very first arrow he'd ever released at any animal.

THEN THERE'S THE STORY OF THE YOUNG MAN in his mid-twenties who booked his first out-of-state bowhunt, a black bear hunt in Canada. He'd diligently saved his money for two years while contacting outfitters and checking their references. Since none of his hunting buddies could be talked into joining in on the adventure, he ended up booking a hunt and going alone, anticipating the experience of his lifetime.

Arriving a day early, he absorbed advice from the camp's guides and veteran bear hunters. He was told to let the bear move to the bait and begin feeding before moving lest he spook the wary animal. He was told to pick a good spot on a broadside target and to listen and watch where the bear went after the shot, mentally marking the spot in his mind. There are lots of bears around, he was told. Be patient and wait for a big bruin, was the sage advice, a bear with a head that appears large in comparison to the rest of its body.

The following evening his guide walked him to his stand. And a rather long and winding walk it was, passing through dense timber, across two streams, and around a swampy bog. By the time they arrived at the treestand, the young man was completely turned around — although he was supposed to have remembered enough landmarks to be able to find his way back along the trail to the road in the dark. As the guide departed and he climbed into his elevated perch amid swarms of hungry black flies, the hunter noticed that he was hot, tired, and thirsty — and about this time he realized he'd left his canteen in camp. His head reeled with sudden doubts and concerns.

Time dragged. As dusk finally closed in, the bowhunter almost gave in to the temptation to climb down and try to find his way out to the distant roadway before full dark. Stubbornly, he stayed put, convinced that if he stuck it out everything

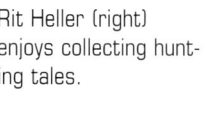

Rit Heller (right) enjoys collecting hunting tales.

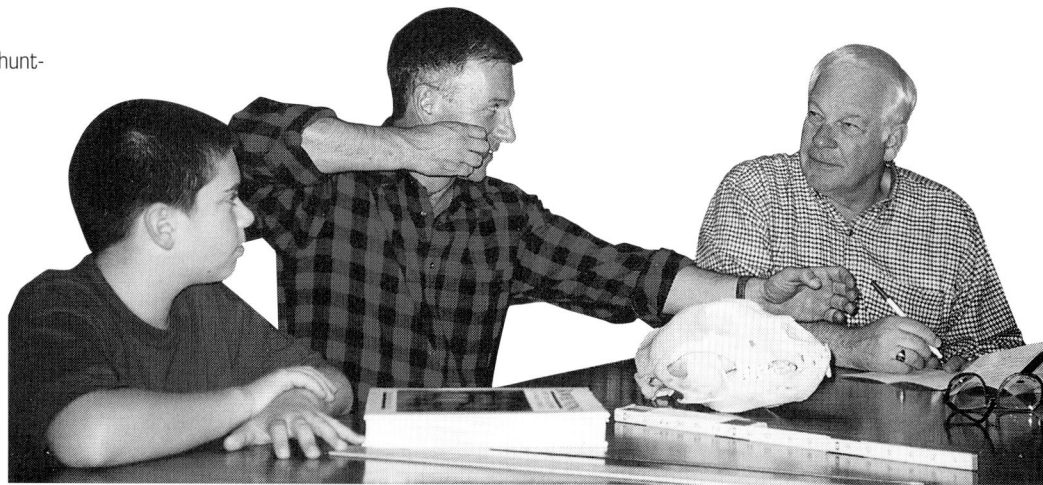

would turn out okay. Glancing down, he was shocked to see a big black bear moving toward the bait. Automatically, he reached for his bow, but as he turned a boot scraped the stand platform and the bear vanished. He'd just screwed up big time — and he knew it!

His heart was a thudding wildly. Long moments passed and shadows deepened. *What should I do now?* he wondered. He was trembling so badly the pine tree itself seemed to be shaking. It was shaking. He glanced down and his blood turned to ice. The big bear was down there, climbing up the trunk toward his stand!

Screaming, he stood and instinctively drew his bow, aiming at the center of the black blob in the branches below. He released his arrow. The bear thumped to earth in a shower of broken limbs, crashing headlong into the heavy brush. Then an ominous silence settled over the dark woodlands as the thoroughly shaken bowhunter found himself very much alone.

Soon darkness was complete. Despite trembling hands, he managed to retrieve his flashlight from his pack. But when he flipped the switch, nothing happened. The batteries were dead. *Now what?* Remembering his matches, he scratched one to flickering life but could not see beyond its meager circle of light. Lighting another match, he dropped it in hopes of seeing the bottom of the tree. It winked out before hitting the ground. Another followed and stayed lit — but nothing was visible in its meager light and soon it burned itself out. He thought about striking another match when a sudden thought stopped him cold. *What if I start a forest fire?* No, better to sit in the cooling darkness and wait for help that was sure to come.

It was nearly midnight when he finally heard shouts and saw lights moving his way through the inky blackness. His concerned guide and two helpful hunters had come to his assistance. And the following morning the shaken bear hunter and his guide returned to the stand where they soon found a very dead bear in the nearby brush. The tree-climbing bruin later qualified for the Pope and Young records.

The guide invited the young bowhunter back the following year to try for an even larger bruin. His offer was declined. Seems the bowhunter said he wanted to try for some other big game species. He'd apparently had enough of black bear hunting to last him for quite a while.

ANOTHER FELLOW PURCHASED A BOW and related tackle, got shooting instruction, and made friends at a local archery club. Some guys told him about a hunting trip for mule deer and mountain goats they had planned and invited him to fill the group's last opening. The guy agreed.

During the mule deer hunt, he was picked up by his buddies after a morning hunt and on the way back to the ranch house they spotted a large muley buck standing in a clear cut. The new bowhunter, who had never ever shot at a big game animal, was urged to leave the truck and try for the unsuspecting buck. The nervous novice moved into shooting position and attempted a rather long shot at the buck — missing so badly that the big mule deer didn't even react to the errant arrow.

The excited tyro decided to try another shot. This arrow landed short, glanced off a rock, and struck the muley in a rear leg. The broadhead sliced the buck's femoral artery, dropping it within 50 yards. Everyone in the bowhunting group — including the shooter — was astounded. Later in the same hunt the fortunate bowhunter also arrowed a goat, becoming the only person in the group of veteran hunters to take both species during the trip.

Ironically, he didn't understand or appreciate what he had just accomplished. When his buddies encouraged him to have both animals scored for the Pope and Young records, he didn't know anything about the Club or what it represented to

bowhunters. Although personally content to return from the hunt with two fine big game trophies, he finally had the animals officially scored — for his friends' sake. Each made the book.

WANT MORE "BEGINNER'S LUCK" STORIES? Okay, how about these two hard–to-believe tales.

Many years ago, another beginning bowhunter went deer hunting with some friends. He climbed into a tree over a well-tracked whitetail trail and waited. A huge buck eventually appeared and moved past below. As the hunter started to draw his bow and follow the moving target, his elbow accidentally bumped a tree limb. The jolt caused him to release the arrow although his bow was only half-drawn at the time.

To the hunter's complete surprise, the shaft smacked the buck in the hip. Penetration was minimal but his sharp broadhead did cut the femoral artery. The huge buck was recovered only a short distance away.

And then there was the mule deer hunter who slept in after a late night party celebrating a buddy's birthday. Groggy and red-eyed, his head splitting, the late rising bowhunter finally rolled out of his sleeping bag, picked up his bow, and staggered to a waterhole just behind camp where he plopped down to wait for the world to stop spinning.

Finally opening his aching eyes, he found himself staring at a big-racked buck curiously peering at him across the shimmering waterhole. Amazingly, the buck hung around long enough for the bowhunter to fit an arrow to the string and make a killing shot. The hungover hunter later joked that when he opened his eyes he saw a whole herd of big bucks — and simply shot at the deer standing in the middle of the group.

SPEAKING OF HUNTS FROM THE EARLY YEARS of bowhunting, a fellow went north to Quebec in the days when only one caribou was legal. The guy was determined to be selective and tag a good bull since the trip was quite expensive and he knew he likely wouldn't be able to afford a return hunt. His guide catered mostly to rifle hunters and knew little about clients armed with the bow and arrow.

"How far can you shoot a caribou with that thing?" he asked the bowhunter who promptly replied that he could shoot pretty well at longer ranges. The client went on to explain that it was likely even a mortally hit bull would run off after the arrow struck. "You shoot him and I'll find him," was the guide's confident response.

On the very first day of the hunt the bowhunter shot at a very good bull, but the arrow hit the antlers, its broadhead burying itself in one of the bez points. The huge caribou simply shook its head and took off running, disappearing across the vast tundra.

Rain and fog soon set in and the balance of the hunt was less than ideal. A few more caribou were sighted but none was close enough — or big enough — to shoot at. It wasn't until the last day that the sun finally broke through, dissipating the ground fog and revealing hundreds of migrating caribou on the move nearby. Several blown stalks later, the bowhunter and guide spotted a small herd with a good bull in the group.

The hunter eased close and made a killing shot on the big bull. As the guide checked out the bull's record book rack, he pointed to the broadhead and small piece of shaft imbedded in the bez point.

"Like I told you earlier," the guide remarked matter-of-factly, "you shoot him and I'll find him."

ANOTHER GUIDE AND BOWHUNTER, this pair chasing mountain caribou, spotted a lone bull bedded over 200 yards away in relatively open country. Only a few stunted spruce trees could be used for cover and consequently a conventional stalk seemed out of the question. The hunter was almost sure to be spotted before he could get close enough to loose a well-aimed arrow.

So why not try something different? After cutting down one of the small spruce trees, the bowhunter held it in front of him as he began a long and painfully slow crawl directly at the distant bull. Hours later, he was within 30 yards and delivered a killing shot. Apparently the giant caribou never realized the small spruce tree was getting closer. That big bull once ranked as the book's best mountain caribou.

ONE DAY A BOWHUNTER ON A PRE-SEASON SCOUTING TRIP found a deer lying near the railroad tracks cutting through a farm he often hunted. The small buck seemed uninjured but stunned. It allowed the hunter to walk right up to it without attempting to rise. Hurrying back to the farmhouse, he told the landowner what he'd found. The two men returned to where the buck lay unmoving. Had it been hit by a passing train? They simply couldn't tell. Using a blanket, the men carried the small deer away from the tracks into a nearby woods.

For nearly two weeks either the farmer or hunter tended to the buck, bringing it food and water each day. The deer stayed bedded or simply stood near its bed when the men approached. On a whim, the farmer — who raised hogs — clipped an orange and numbered ear tag to the buck's ear. Finally, the deer simply disappeared.

The farmer and hunter often spoke of the buck, wondering about its fate. As the years passed, the small deer was forgotten. Then, seven years later, one fall day the hunter killed a Pope and Young buck on the farm — a buck with a numbered ear tag still in place.

ONE EVENING ANOTHER DEER HUNTER took a 35-yard shot at a large whitetail. But as he released the arrow, the deer stepped ahead, causing the shaft to strike farther back than intended. The wounded buck bounded across a grassy field and quickly disappeared into a small woodlot.

After waiting 30 minutes, the hunter moved from his stand to look for blood sign. Only a few drops were visible. Knowing he'd need help, he enlisted the help of two hunting buddies. They searched well into the night, using flashlights and a Coleman lantern, finally calling off the search when no additional sign — or the buck — could be found.

The following morning was a work day and his friends couldn't continue their search until evening. The anxious hunter returned home and enlisted his wife and young daughter to lend a hand. Daybreak found them back in the hunting area. The couple made several circles, taking turns carrying the daughter. No sign of the wounded buck was found and all too soon it was time to return to town and head for work. As they arrived back at the truck, the little girl announced she had to "go potty." The mother directed her to go behind a clump of bushes. The daughter immediately let out a scream and started crying. "There's a big animal behind that bush," she sobbed. Sure enough. It was the father's buck, quite dead. It later qualified for the record book.

TWO HUNTING BUDDIES SAVED UP THEIR MONEY for a dream hunt of a lifetime, a trip to Alaska for moose and caribou. Each was quite proficient with his compound bow which was carefully tuned and fully equipped with sights, an overdraw, kisser button, and other assorted accessories. One fellow packed along a take-down recurve as his backup bow — just in case of some emergency.

After arriving in Alaska, the friend's bow case didn't show up. Time passed. Still no bow. Finally, the buddy said, "You can use my take-down bow. At least it's something."

The guy that borrowed the recurve hadn't shot a stickbow in years; however, he accepted his friend's offer and spent time shooting around camp before going hunting. The result of the dream hunt that almost turned into a nightmare? Today the recurve shooter has both a moose and caribou in our record book. His generous partner didn't fare quite as well.

FINALLY, SEVERAL YEARS AGO a fellow called me to measure a whitetail he had taken. When he and a hunting partner arrived, the bowhunter was quiet and unassuming. As the bowhunter handed me the rack, I knew it was going to be close to the minimum of 125 (typical). The antlers had 10 points but some of the tines were short, it didn't have much of a spread, and the main beams were a little thin.

I took extra time as I carefully measured the rack, finally tallying up the score. It came in at 125 3/8 inches. I congratulated the hunter and asked some routine questions about the hunt. He handed me some field photos he'd taken of the buck and at first I thought they were overexposed with too much bright sun and no shade at all. Then I looked more carefully.

"Was the buck white?" I asked.

"Yes," he said.

The bowhunter had never mentioned this fact. Talk about a trophy, a white 10-point whitetail that made our book! That deer still ranks as the rarest trophy I have ever scored.

Pennsylvania bowhunter Frank "Rit" Heller is a Senior Member who served on the Board of Directors from 1978 to 1990 and continues to serve our Club as an official measurer.

POPE AND YOUNG CLUB Q & A

Following are answers to a few of the most frequently asked questions bowhunters direct to Pope and Young Club headquarters, officers, and volunteer measurers:

I have an animal I want officially scored. How do I locate the measurer living closest to my home?
Contact Pope and Young Headquarters, P. O. Box 548, Chatfield, MN 55923; (507) 867-4144.

How much does it cost to have an animal measured?
There is no charge to have an animal measured. Our official scorers are all volunteers who provide this valuable service free of charge to the hunting public for the Pope and Young Club. There is a recording fee, currently $25.00, to submit an entry for possible acceptance into the Records. Once accepted, the score becomes official and the entry will remain in the Club's archives of big game records throughout history.

Do I have to be a member of the Pope and Young Club to enter an animal in the record book?
It is not necessary for a bowhunter to be a member of the Pope and Young Club in order to enter a trophy; the Records are open to anyone who legally takes an eligible animal. Final acceptance of an entry is at the discretion of the Board of Directions of the Club. The only requirement for bowhunters wanting to join the Club as an Associate member is to have harvested at least one big game animal with a bow. Membership application forms are printed in Club newsletters and are available upon request from the Club's Minnesota office. Presently, the membership fee for Pope and Young Club Associates is $25.00 per year.

I have an entry in the Records. Why am I not getting Club newsletters? Aren't I a member?
Honoring an animal with a listing in the Pope and Young Records does not constitute joining the Club. Each is entirely separate. As mentioned above, bowhunters wishing to join the Club must obtain, complete, and submit a membership application form.

I recently joined the Club as an Associate Member. How can I become a Regular Member?
The Club founders established a unique membership structure designed to reward longevity both as a bowhunter and as a supporter of the Pope and Young Club. The number of Regular Members is now limited to 100 persons at any given time. Associate Members may, at any time, request a Regular Membership application; however, to be considered the Associate must have harvested at least three different species of North American big game (e.g., whitetail deer, Yellowstone elk, and black bear) and have at least one animal which qualifies for, and is entered in, the Records. Once the application is received by the Club, the Associate Member's name is added to a "waiting list" for vacancies to open in the Regular Member ranks. This waiting list is ranked by seniority (based on when the individual joined the Club as an Associate Member). Whenever vacancies occur, an equivalent number of Associates from the top of the waiting list are reviewed for advancement to Regular Membership. A third membership designation, Senior Member, was established years ago to allow for a slow but steady influx of new members into the Regular Membership ranks.

How do I become an official measurer?
The first step in the appointment process is to request and complete a Measurer's Application form and return it to the Club's headquarters. Then, based on the information on the application and the need for additional measurers in the applicant's area, the applicant may receive an invitation to attend one of the Club's measurer training workshops. These three-day limited invitation workshops generally take place during the summer months.

I entered an animal last year and bought a book. Why wasn't my name in it?
New editions of the Club record book are published every six years. The first edition of **Bowhunting Big Game Records of North America** *was published in 1975; the second edition appeared in 1981, the third edition in 1987, the fourth edition in 1993, and this book, the fifth edition, in 1999. Entries received too late for inclusion in one record book will appear in the next edition. Recent entries are published in the Club's quarterly newsletter.*

I shot a deer on December 15. The deadline for this record book was December 31. Why isn't my deer listed in the Club records?
Deadlines concerning the Records are based on when the entry is submitted and accepted, not when an animal is shot. Given the manditory 60-day drying period, an animal shot in mid-December could not be measured until mid-February. Then the entry materials would have to be completed and submitted to the Club's national office for possible acceptance. After an entry is accepted, a certificate is mailed to the bowhunter and his name and the animal's official score appears in the next available Club newsletter. The same information will appear in the next edition of the Club's record book (published at six-year intervals).

I tagged a buck in 1983 but never considered entering it until now. Is it too late?
No, regardless of when an eligible animal was harvested, it can be entered in the Records by having it officially scored and submitting the necessary paperwork, photos, and recording fee. Each trophy class animal may only be submitted for acceptance once; however, there is no time limit on entering animals in the Club Records.

Can I have more than one official measurer score my trophy in order to obtain the best possible score?
"Score shopping" is the practice of a trophy owner contacting several measurers in an attempt to gain a larger score. The Club does not condone the practice of score shopping and will take appropriate action when such instances occur. Official scorers may ask the owner if a trophy has previously been officially measured and refuse to remeasure the animal if that is the case.

Are animals confined behind high fences eligible for the record book?
Some are and some aren't. For example, game living on fenced military reservations may be accepted while animals contained on game farms are not. All high fence situations are considered on a case by case basis. To expand its Fair Chase Affidavit statement which excludes all entries taken "while confined behind fences as on game farms," the Club Board of Directors changed the wording in 1996 to read: "While behind game-proof fences where introduced and/or confined animals are held for commercial hunting purposes (e.g., game farms, shooting preserves, or private hunting operations) where fees are charged for the animals harvested."

Can locked antler trophies be entered in the Club records?
Occasionally a bowhunter will take a trophy which has locked antlers with another animal. While the harvest of such animals may be legal, clearly the animals do not have an opportunity for normal escape. Hence, such animals are ineligible for entry into the Pope and Young records.

I shot a buck but didn't find it for several days. Can I still enter this animal in the Club Records?
It depends on the circumstances. Since the Pope and Young Club does not accept picked up or found trophies, we also carefully evaluate instances where wounded game was not recovered immediately. We ask bowhunters to provide a detailed account of the facts surrounding their search and ultimate recovery. Each incident is considered on a case by case basis before a ruling is made.

I know of a bowhunter who took an animal illegally and then entered the animal in the Pope and Young Records? What can I do about it?
The Club is vitally concerned with keeping its listings free of any and all illegally taken big game animals; however, entries are not removed based merely on hearsay or rumor. Concrete proof must be offered to the Club so an investigation may be conducted. People with knowledge of any illegal entries should submit their charges in writing to Club headquarters, supplying any available proof to support their allegations. Club officials routinely investigate questionable entries and take appropriate action, including the removal of illegally taken animals and publication of this action, when charges of wrongdoing are proved true.

How often does the Pope and Young Club meet?
Biennial conventions and awards banquets are convened in various cities across this continent. Recent meetings were in Omaha, Nebraska, in Edmonton, Alberta, in Traverse City, Michigan, in Minneapolis, Minnesota, and in Seattle, Washington. These gatherings coincide with the Club's two-year recording periods after which members and guests gather the following spring to recognize the top entries submitted and to enjoy a long weekend of good fellowship, educational seminars, entertainment, and fund-raising activities.

ARTIST
MICHAEL SIEVE

ONE OF AMERICA'S foremost big game artists, Minnesota-based sportsman Michael Sieve believes the best, most memorable wildlife art is inspired by actual experiences in the field. Consequently, he routinely depicts unforgettable scenes witnessed during hunts with bow or gun — or special sights captured on film during his photographic outings — and creates exceptionally realistic paintings that are both naturally accurate and artistically pleasing. A painstaking researcher of wildlife and natural history, he complements his artist's eye for detail with a hunter's sense of closeness to nature. The end result is a painting that shares a special outdoor moment, freezing action and firing the imagination of any man or woman with a love of wild places and wild creatures.

"Many hours spent deer hunting have increased my perception while in the woods," Sieve explains. "I have never had enough patience to sit in a tree, so I have always stalked deer. This technique makes you very aware of everything around you. The wind, noise levels, the direction of sunlight, plants, and branches on the ground — everything becomes critical when you are only 10 yards away from a wary buck."

An avid bowhunter for over a quarter of a century and a professional artist since 1979, Michael Sieve remains a dedicated conservationist who applies proven wildlife management practices on his own property and actively supports numerous conservation groups. Further, he has helped to generate millions of dollars for wildlife rehabilitation and habitat restoration through the design of over 20 conservation stamps and prints, donating original and limited edition artwork, and working on other pro-conservation efforts. "Chip Shot" is his second Pope and Young painting.

In all, over 100 of Sieve's original artworks have been chosen for limited edition prints and canvases. One painting, "Evening Stand," was commissioned by the Pope and Young Club in 1986 and a signed/numbered limited edition print series generated thousands of dollars for our Club. It also graced the cover of the 1987 edition of **Bowhunting Big Game Records of North America**. Today the original art hangs in the Pope and Young/St. Charles Museum in Seattle, Washington. Other original paintings are found in public and private collections throughout the world, and his images have been featured on the covers and within the pages of North America's finest hunting, wildlife, and nature publications.

Big Game Oil Paintings

PAGE

99	"One Chance Only," 16" x 24", 1995
101	"The Master of Intimidation—Elk," 15" x 28", 1995
103	"Adrenaline Surge—Whitetail Deer," 17" x 28", 1992
105	"Chip Shot," 24" x 36", oil
107	"Indian Summer—Mule Deer," 15" x 27", 1998
109	"The Black Ghost—Black Bear," 16 1/2" x 25", 1991
111	"Ladies First," 17" x 26 1/2", 1997
113	"Monarch of the North—Moose," 19" x 16", 1988
115	"Peak Experience—Mountain Goats," 24" x 16", 1989
117	"White Silence—Mule Deer," 15 1/2" x 25", 1988
119	"Water Rights—Pronghorns," 15" x 29", 1992
121	"The Passing Herd—Bison," 15" x 30", 1994
123	"Alaskan Classic—Dall Sheep," 17 1/2" x 24", 1982
125	"Tidal Flats—Brown Bear," 15 1/2" 25", 1988
127	"Athabasca River Challenge," 15" x 27 1/2", 1984

"One Chance Only"

"The Master of Intimidation—Elk"

"Adrenaline Surge—Whitetail Deer"

"Chip Shot"

"Indian Summer—Mule Deer"

"The Black Ghost—Black Bear"

"Ladies First"

"Monarch of the North—Moose"

"Peak Experience—Mountain Goats"

"White Silence—Mule Deer"

"Water Rights—Pronghorns"

"The Passing Herd—Bison"

"Alaskan Classic—Dall Sheep"

"Tidal Flats—Brown Bear"

"Athabasca River Challenge"

BRUCE FELKER PHOTO

THE RECORDS

LEN RUE, JR. PHOTO

World Record Alaskan Brown Bear (Tie)

Score: 28 7/16
Unimak Island, Alaska - 1985
Hunter: John D. "Jack" Frost

Score: 28 7/16
Ursus Cove, Alaska - 1995
Hunter: Monty Browning

ALASKAN BROWN BEAR

Minimum Score 20

Ursus arctos middendorffi and certain related subspecies

SCORE	GREATEST LENGTH	GREATEST WIDTH	SEX	AREA	STATE/ PROVINCE	HUNTER'S NAME	DATE	RANK
28 7/16	17 11/16	10 12/16	M	Unimak Island	AK	John D. 'Jack' Frost	1985	1
28 7/16	18 0/16	10 7/16	M	Ursus Cove	AK	Monty Browning	1995	1
28 0/16	17 15/16	10 1/16	M	Wide Bay, AK Pen.	AK	Fred Bear	1960	3
27 12/16	16 12/16	11 0/16	M	Kodiak Island	AK	Arthur Heinze	1993	4
27 8/16	16 6/16	11 2/16	M	Grayback Mtn.	AK	Scott Mileur	1997	5
27 5/16	16 10/16	10 11/16	M	Kodiak Island	AK	Bob Ameen	1994	6
27 1/16	16 15/16	10 2/16	M	Bear Bay	AK	Fred Bear	1962	7
27 1/16	17 2/16	9 15/16	M	Dog Salmon River	AK	Chuck Adams	1989	7
26 13/16	17 0/16	9 13/16	M	Wide Bay	AK	Archie Nesbitt	1991	9
26 6/16	16 12/16	9 10/16	M	Wide Bay	AK	David E. Snowden, Jr.	1997	10
26 4/16	16 14/16	9 6/16	M	Naknek River	AK	Gary M. Martin	1997	11
25 13/16	16 2/16	9 11/16	M	Meshik River	AK	Robert Edward Speegle, MD	1997	12
25 8/16	16 5/16	9 3/16	M	Kodiak Island	AK	Tim R. Dawson	1998	13
25 5/16	15 14/16	9 7/16	M	Lake Clark	AK	Richard L. Busk	1991	14
25 2/16	16 2/16	9 0/16	M	Chichagof Island	AK	Kenneth T. Wotring	1982	15
25 0/16	15 14/16	9 2/16	M	Kodiak Island	AK	Lloyd L. Garrels	1993	16
24 14/16	15 10/16	9 4/16	M	Naknek River	AK	Joseph D. Maddock	1998	17
24 12/16	16 3/16	8 9/16	M	Port Heiden	AK	Gardner Rowell	1995	18
24 12/16	15 14/16	8 14/16	M	Tsiu River	AK	Gary F. Bogner	1998	18
24 10/16	15 4/16	9 6/16	M	Kodiak Island	AK	Dean Stebner	1991	20
24 2/16	15 3/16	8 15/16	M	Admiralty Island	AK	Rick Kinmon	1992	21
24 2/16	15 11/16	8 7/16	M	Cold Bay	AK	George Krasinski	1997	21
24 1/16	14 12/16	9 5/16	M	Admiralty Island	AK	Richard J. Callahan	1991	23
23 14/16	15 11/16	8 3/16	M	Port Heiden	AK	H. Gale McKnight	1995	24
23 11/16	14 11/16	9 0/16	F	Olga Bay	AK	Richard E. Boggio	1993	25
23 10/16	15 2/16	8 8/16	F	Port Heiden	AK	George P. Mann	1989	26
23 6/16	14 6/16	9 0/16	M	Kodiak Island	AK	Gordon Longville	1961	27
23 4/16	14 11/16	8 9/16	M	Admiralty Island	AK	John R. Thiele	1984	28
23 4/16	15 3/16	8 1/16	F	Joshua Green River	AK	John Koldeway	1985	28
23 2/16	15 2/16	8 0/16	M	Sunflower Creek	AK	Bruce S. Richardson	1996	30
22 15/16	14 2/16	8 13/16	F	Sheepcreek-Valdez	AK	Gerald R. Gold	1966	31
22 8/16	15 1/16	7 7/16	M	Cinder River	AK	Ken Grosslight	1997	32
22 7/16	14 2/16	8 5/16	F	Merrill Pass	AK	Ralph Ertz	1975	33
22 6/16	14 4/16	8 2/16	M	Kodiak Island	AK	Buddy Watson	1965	34
22 5/16	14 9/16	7 12/16	M	Portage Creek	AK	John "Jack" C. Culpepper III	1991	35
22 3/16	14 0/16	8 3/16	M	Chichagof Island	AK	David Heller	1995	36
22 2/16	14 8/16	7 10/16	M	Chichagof Island	AK	John Gary Price	1995	37
22 0/16	14 8/16	7 8/16	M	Wide Bay	AK	Randy Lee Waddell	1995	38
22 0/16	14 5/16	7 11/16	M	Cooper Landing	AK	Kenneth D. Carvajal	1998	38
21 15/16	14 7/16	7 8/16	M	Kajulik Bay	AK	Thomas J. Hoffman	1983	40
21 13/16	13 15/16	7 14/16	F	Merrill Pass	AK	Dan Hollingsworth	1975	41
21 13/16	13 4/16	8 9/16	F	Dana Glacier	AK	Dan W. Morrison	1975	41
21 12/16	14 0/16	7 12/16	M	Afognak Island	AK	Dr. Chuck Leidheiser	1996	43
21 10/16	13 14/16	7 12/16	F	Alaska Peninsula	AK	Bill Van Houten	1961	44
21 10/16	13 9/16	8 1/16	F	Alphabet Hills	AK	Braun Kopsack	1996	44
21 9/16	14 4/16	7 5/16	M	Alaska Peninsula	AK	Kurt Lepping	1989	46
21 8/16	13 9/16	7 15/16	M	Hoonah	AK	Len Cardinale	1979	47
21 8/16	14 0/16	7 8/16	M	Wide Bay	AK	John Ribic	1993	47
21 8/16	13 9/16	7 15/16	M	Deadmans Bay	AK	Walter Palmer	1994	47
21 7/16	13 8/16	7 15/16	F	Fidalgo Bay	AK	Joseph West	1966	50
21 7/16	14 1/16	7 6/16	M	Chichagof Island	AK	Ray Keenan	1984	50
21 7/16	13 11/16	7 12/16	M	Clear Creek	AK	Eric Colledge	1992	50
21 6/16	13 13/16	7 9/16	F	Imuya Bay	AK	J. Dale Hale	1991	53
21 2/16	13 14/16	7 4/16	M	Anachuck River	AK	Martin Hanson	1958	54
21 1/16	13 12/16	7 5/16	F	Mat-Su Borough	AK	Rickie D. Snell	1985	55
20 15/16	13 4/16	7 11/16	M	Admiralty Island	AK	Allen L. Grierson	1985	56
20 14/16	13 10/16	7 4/16	M	Chulitna River	AK	Rick D. Snell	1997	57
20 12/16	13 8/16	7 4/16	F	King Salmon	AK	Rhonda Baker	1977	58
20 11/16	13 9/16	7 2/16	M	Talkeetna Mtns.	AK	L.M. Peppers	1983	59
20 8/16	13 3/16	7 5/16	M	Kichatna River	AK	Douglas W. Hill	1994	60
20 7/16	13 4/16	7 3/16	M	Wide Bay	AK	Keith Appel	1994	61
20 7/16	13 8/16	6 15/16	F	Wide Bay	AK	William Welton	1995	61
20 3/16	12 3/16	8 0/16	M	Sunday Creek	AK	Bob Ehle	1998	63
20 1/16	12 14/16	7 3/16	M	Fog Lakes	AK	Dennis L. Lattery	1984	64

JUDD COONEY PHOTO

World Record Black Bear
Score: 23 3/16
Mendocino County, California - 1993
Hunter: Robert J. Shuttleworth, Jr.

BLACK BEAR

Minimum Score 18

Ursus americanus americanus and certain related subspecies

SCORE	GREATEST LENGTH	GREATEST WIDTH	SEX	AREA	STATE/PROVINCE	HUNTER'S NAME	DATE	RANK
23 3/16	13 15/16	9 4/16	M	Mendocino County	CA	Robert J. Shuttleworth, Jr.	1993	1
22 8/16	14 1/16	8 7/16	M	Kanawha County	WV	G. Murphy / V. Ryan	1991	2
22 8/16	13 13/16	8 11/16	M	Rockingham County	VA	Roger O. Wyant	1994	2
22 6/16	13 12/16	8 10/16	M	Gronlid	SAS	Floyd Forster	1992	4
22 4/16	13 7/16	8 13/16	M	Sinbad Ridge	CO	Ray Cox	1978	5
22 3/16	14 2/16	8 1/16	M	Grahamdale	MAN	Collin P. Stone	1996	6
22 2/16	14 0/16	8 2/16	M	Olha	MAN	Carl Farler	1992	7
22 0/16	13 11/16	8 5/16	M	Lincoln County	WI	Bob Faufau	1981	8
22 0/16	13 12/16	8 4/16	M	Prince of Wales Island	AK	George P. Mann	1991	8
22 0/16	13 10/16	8 6/16	M	Bronson Lake	SAS	Roger Fournier	1992	8
22 0/16	13 10/16	8 6/16	M	Los Angeles County	CA	Joe Clay	1992	8
22 0/16	13 11/16	8 5/16	M	Graham County	AZ	Mark D. Morris	1995	8
22 0/16	13 11/16	8 5/16	M	Pine County	MN	Darrin Stream	1995	8
21 15/16	13 13/16	8 2/16	M	Prince of Wales Island	AK	Stanley L. Parkerson	1991	14
21 15/16	13 9/16	8 6/16	M	Poplarfield	MAN	Samuel Amodeo	1995	14
21 14/16	13 7/16	8 7/16	M	Prince of Wales Island	AK	Jim Ponciano	1990	16
21 14/16	13 14/16	8 0/16	M	Weldon	SAS	Ron S. Bodnarchuk	1998	16
21 13/16	13 9/16	8 4/16	M	Idaho County	ID	Harold Boyack	1976	18
21 13/16	13 1/16	8 12/16	M	Dog Lake	ONT	Larry Murray	1990	18
21 13/16	14 4/16	7 9/16	M	Rossburn	MAN	Barry Minshull	1990	18
21 13/16	13 12/16	8 1/16	M	White County	GA	John Wood	1995	18
21 13/16	13 5/16	8 8/16	M	Prince of Wales Island	AK	Dyrk Eddie	1996	18
21 13/16	13 5/16	8 8/16	M	Choiceland	SAS	John Foster	1998	18
21 12/16	13 5/16	8 7/16	M	Price County	WI	Robert Brotske	1981	24
21 12/16	13 6/16	8 6/16	M	Big River	SAS	Bill Dear	1985	24
21 12/16	13 3/16	8 9/16	M	Prince of Wales Island	AK	Mark Robecker	1991	24
21 12/16	13 10/16	8 2/16	M	Alonsa	MAN	Cory Mozdzen	1991	24
21 12/16	13 6/16	8 6/16	M	Peace River	ALB	Mike Scott	1992	24
21 12/16	13 10/16	8 2/16	M	Riding Mtn.	MAN	Mike Minshull	1998	24
21 11/16	13 9/16	8 2/16	M	Nipawin	SAS	Ray Mastel	1974	30
21 11/16	13 7/16	8 4/16	M	Sevier County	UT	Robert F. Fitzgerald	1984	30
21 11/16	13 9/16	8 2/16	M	Chelan	SAS	Ray Svennes	1995	30
21 11/16	13 13/16	7 14/16	M	Rusk County	WI	Gregory Baneck	1995	30
21 11/16	13 4/16	8 7/16	M	Olha	MAN	Gary G. Lex	1996	30
21 10/16	13 6/16	8 4/16	M	Hudson Bay	SAS	Craig Richardson	1985	35
21 10/16	13 5/16	8 5/16	M	Grande Prairie	ALB	Blair Trout	1989	35
21 10/16	13 10/16	8 0/16	M	Prince of Wales Island	AK	James E. Hodson	1991	35
21 10/16	13 4/16	8 6/16	M	North Battleford	SAS	John Leite	1993	35
21 10/16	13 8/16	8 2/16	M	Grant County	WV	Carnie Carr, Jr.	1993	35
21 9/16	13 5/16	8 4/16	M	Iron County	WI	Gary Johnson	1982	40
21 9/16	13 9/16	8 0/16	M	Bay Tree	ALB	David E. Samuel	1990	40
21 9/16	13 5/16	8 4/16	M	Duck Mtns.	MAN	Mark Braun	1997	40
21 8/16	13 6/16	8 2/16	M	Hudson Bay	SAS	Garry Benson	1976	43
21 8/16	13 2/16	8 6/16	M	Kern County	CA	Dean M. Lutge	1981	43
21 8/16	13 2/16	8 6/16	M	Shasta County	CA	Ed Woodring	1996	43
21 7/16	13 7/16	8 0/16	M	Nipawin	SAS	Don Adams	1975	46
21 7/16	13 7/16	8 0/16	M	Mendocino County	CA	Jim Oliver	1984	46
21 7/16	13 0/16	8 7/16	M	Garfield County	CO	Norman J. O'Bryan	1985	46
21 7/16	13 11/16	7 12/16	M	Gordondale	ALB	Zig Kertenis, Jr.	1993	46
21 7/16	13 2/16	8 5/16	M	Ellice	MAN	Jamie Poole	1994	46
21 7/16	13 8/16	7 15/16	M	Clinch County	GA	Danny Hinson	1997	46
21 6/16	13 6/16	8 0/16	M	Bayfield County	WI	Larry L. Frye	1975	52
21 6/16	13 6/16	8 0/16	M	Grant County	WV	Carnie Carr, Sr.	1988	52
21 6/16	13 4/16	8 2/16	M	North Hudson Bay	SAS	Malcolm Garratt	1991	52
21 6/16	13 2/16	8 4/16	M	York County	NBW	Kenneth J. Fluck	1991	52
21 6/16	12 15/16	8 7/16	M	Girouxville	ALB	Ed Spruyt	1996	52
21 6/16	13 15/16	7 7/16	M	Sawyer County	WI	Rolland Manthei	1998	52
21 5/16	13 5/16	8 0/16	M	Ministikwan	SAS	Gary Mutter	1985	58
21 5/16	13 0/16	8 5/16	M	Kenora	ONT	Robert Svoboda	1986	58
21 5/16	13 2/16	8 3/16	M	Swan River	MAN	Richard C. Weber	1991	58
21 5/16	12 14/16	8 7/16	M	Sawyer County	WI	Mark Heath	1991	58
21 5/16	13 4/16	8 1/16	M	Prince of Wales Island	AK	Rick Schikora	1992	58
21 5/16	12 12/16	8 9/16	M	Terrace	BC	Wayne Topolewski	1992	58
21 5/16	13 8/16	7 13/16	M	Sawyer County	WI	Steve Bouton	1992	58
21 5/16	13 4/16	8 1/16	M	Round Lake	SAS	Floyd Forster	1994	58
21 5/16	13 10/16	7 11/16	M	Bay Tree	ALB	Zig Kertenis, Jr.	1995	58
21 5/16	13 6/16	7 15/16	M	Horseshoe Lake	ALB	Darren Daniel	1995	58
21 5/16	13 5/16	8 0/16	M	Shawano County	WI	Scott Johnson	1995	58
21 5/16	13 2/16	8 3/16	M	Falher	ALB	Stephen L. Collins	1996	58
21 5/16	13 15/16	7 6/16	M	Usherville	SAS	John Stephen Williams	1997	58
21 5/16	13 2/16	8 3/16	M	Prince of Wales Island	AK	Steven R. Martin	1998	58
21 5/16	13 6/16	7 15/16	M	Wolf Lake	ALB	Thomas G. Lester III	1998	58
21 4/16	13 7/16	7 13/16	M	Tehama County	CA	Jim Cox	1980	73
21 4/16	13 5/16	7 15/16	M	Cass County	MN	Myles Keller	1980	73
21 4/16	13 4/16	8 0/16	M	Duck Mtn.	MAN	Dave Cordes	1984	73
21 4/16	13 8/16	7 12/16	M	Spiritwood	SAS	Ron Schira	1985	73
21 4/16	13 4/16	8 0/16	M	Mille Lacs County	MN	Timothy J. Dusbabek	1987	73
21 4/16	13 1/16	8 3/16	M	Catron County	NM	Gary L. Raney	1988	73

BLACK BEAR

Minimum Score 18 — Continued

SCORE	GREATEST LENGTH	GREATEST WIDTH	SEX	AREA	STATE/ PROVINCE	HUNTER'S NAME	DATE	RANK
21 4/16	13 0/16	8 4/16	M	Ketchikan	AK	Doug Miller	1989	73
21 4/16	13 5/16	7 15/16	M	Flatbush	ALB	Dave Falls	1990	73
21 4/16	13 4/16	8 0/16	M	Flotten Lake	SAS	Michael S. Meier	1991	73
21 4/16	13 4/16	8 0/16	M	Prince of Wales Island	AK	George P. Mann	1993	73
21 4/16	13 4/16	8 0/16	M	Prince of Wales Island	AK	Eric Lance Whary	1995	73
21 3/16	13 0/16	8 3/16	M	Eaglehead Lake	ONT	Ty Sweeney	1986	84
21 3/16	12 15/16	8 4/16	M	Lane County	OR	Ray Cross	1989	84
21 3/16	13 3/16	8 0/16	M	Prince of Wales Island	AK	George P. Mann	1990	84
21 3/16	13 7/16	7 12/16	M	Assinaboine River	SAS	Rodney S. Petrychyn	1991	84
21 3/16	13 1/16	8 2/16	M	Catron County	NM	John M. Burton, Jr.	1991	84
21 3/16	13 3/16	8 0/16	M	Prince of Wales Island	AK	Darren Emery	1993	84
21 3/16	12 12/16	8 7/16	M	Ulster County	NY	David Bell	1993	84
21 3/16	13 3/16	8 0/16	M	Kashawbowe	ONT	Kevin Wagner	1994	84
21 3/16	13 1/16	8 2/16	M	Sawyer County	WI	Robert Bernard Stushek	1996	84
21 3/16	12 12/16	8 7/16	M	Orange County	NY	David Bell	1997	84
21 3/16	12 14/16	8 5/16	M	Thunder Bay	ONT	Reg Begin, Jr.	1998	84
21 2/16	13 2/16	8 0/16	M	Madera County	CA	Clarke Merrill	1963	95
21 2/16	13 7/16	7 12/16	M	Hubbard County	MN	Dean Como	1974	95
21 2/16	13 4/16	7 14/16	M	Hudson Bay	SAS	Sam Qualls	1981	95
21 2/16	13 10/16	7 8/16	M	Langlade County	WI	Mike Steliga	1981	95
21 2/16	13 6/16	7 12/16	M	Rockingham County	VA	Roger O. Wyant	1984	95
21 2/16	13 1/16	8 1/16	M	Caribou County	ID	Ronald J. Thompson	1986	95
21 2/16	12 14/16	8 4/16	M	Herkimer County	NY	John Palmer	1986	95
21 2/16	13 4/16	7 14/16	M	Glaslyn	SAS	Tony L. Johnson	1989	95
21 2/16	13 0/16	8 2/16	M	Jackson County	OR	Brian Day	1989	95
21 2/16	13 9/16	7 9/16	M	Prairie River	SAS	Tom White	1991	95
21 2/16	13 3/16	7 15/16	M	Fort a la Corne	SAS	Gerald Gilmore	1994	95
21 2/16	13 10/16	7 8/16	M	Coos County	NH	Gary J. Russell	1996	95
21 2/16	13 5/16	7 13/16	M	St. Louis County	MN	Dale Long	1997	95
21 2/16	13 1/16	8 1/16	M	Choiceland	SAS	James Foster	1998	95
21 2/16	13 0/16	8 2/16	M	Aroostook County	ME	Linda Harlow	1998	95
21 1/16	13 1/16	8 0/16	M	Hubbard County	MN	Darrell Magnussen	1974	110
21 1/16	13 2/16	7 15/16	M	Quetico Provincial Park	ONT	Robert Filbrandt	1981	110
21 1/16	13 1/16	8 0/16	M	Cass County	MN	John Hughes	1987	110
21 1/16	13 1/16	8 0/16	M	Lincoln County	WI	Daniel Lemke	1987	110
21 1/16	12 13/16	8 4/16	M	Siskiyou County	CA	Jules Pacheco	1987	110
21 1/16	13 1/16	8 0/16	M	Charlevoix County	MI	Gerald L. Fuller	1988	110
21 1/16	13 0/16	8 1/16	M	Kanawha County	WV	Brian Petty	1991	110
21 1/16	13 4/16	7 13/16	M	Oconto County	WI	Patrick J. Gauthier	1995	110
21 1/16	13 1/16	8 0/16	M	Prince of Wales Island	AK	Shawn Price	1996	110
21 1/16	13 5/16	7 12/16	M	Hudson Bay	SAS	Arlan Dowiasch	1996	110
21 1/16	13 3/16	7 14/16	M	Round Lake	SAS	Floyd Forster	1997	110
21 1/16	13 2/16	7 15/16	M	Lincoln County	WI	Kraig M. See	1997	110
21 1/16	13 1/16	8 0/16	M	Polk County	AR	Donald Cost	1997	110
21 0/16	12 13/16	8 3/16	M	Sioux Narrows	ONT	R. B. Cooley	1960	123
21 0/16	12 14/16	8 2/16	M	Uncompahgre N.F.	CO	Dr. James Emerson	1974	123
21 0/16	13 3/16	7 13/16	M	Shasta County	CA	Norman Mallonee	1974	123
21 0/16	13 3/16	7 13/16	M	Ashland County	WI	Bryan C. Anderson	1980	123
21 0/16	13 2/16	7 14/16	M	Yavapai County	AZ	Mike Whelan	1981	123
21 0/16	13 2/16	7 14/16	M	Riding Mtn.	MAN	James A. Carson	1982	123
21 0/16	13 2/16	7 14/16	M	Sawyer County	WI	John G. Bohmann	1982	123
21 0/16	12 15/16	8 1/16	M	Kosciusko Island	AK	Michael C. Fezatte	1982	123
21 0/16	13 3/16	7 13/16	M	Langlade County	WI	Michael Steliga	1982	123
21 0/16	13 4/16	7 12/16	M	Hudson Bay	SAS	Archie Lovelace	1983	123
21 0/16	12 10/16	8 6/16	M	Echouani Lake	QUE	Collins F. Kellogg	1985	123
21 0/16	13 3/16	7 13/16	M	Debden	SAS	Allan Sykes	1986	123
21 0/16	13 1/16	7 15/16	M	Carrot River	SAS	Demetry Procyk	1987	123
21 0/16	13 0/16	8 0/16	M	Carbon County	UT	Lonnie K. Bell	1989	123
21 0/16	12 13/16	8 3/16	M	Iron County	WI	Todd J. Braver	1989	123
21 0/16	13 0/16	8 0/16	M	Le Domaine	QUE	Tony Beceiro	1990	123
21 0/16	12 14/16	8 2/16	M	Lake County	MT	Colin L. Andrews	1990	123
21 0/16	12 12/16	8 4/16	M	Herkimer County	NY	Glen Stedman	1990	123
21 0/16	13 0/16	8 0/16	M	Ventura County	CA	Jeff Prentice	1991	123
21 0/16	13 1/16	7 15/16	M	Peace River	ALB	Doug Walker	1991	123
21 0/16	13 1/16	7 15/16	M	Prince of Wales Island	AK	Rick M. Young	1992	123
21 0/16	12 14/16	8 2/16	M	Bay Tree	ALB	Sedgwick Bryant Loyd II	1994	123
21 0/16	12 13/16	8 3/16	M	Delay River	QUE	Brian Dayett	1994	123
21 0/16	12 14/16	8 2/16	M	Washburn County	WI	Sonjonae Setser	1995	123
21 0/16	13 3/16	7 13/16	M	Barron County	WI	Jeffrey P. Tomesh	1995	123
21 0/16	12 10/16	8 6/16	M	Ulster County	NY	Thomas Nolan	1995	123
21 0/16	12 14/16	8 2/16	M	Marathon County	WI	Orville Sazama	1996	123
21 0/16	13 3/16	7 13/16	M	Mineral County	WV	Rex D. Miller	1996	123
21 0/16	13 5/16	7 11/16	M	Crooked Creek	ALB	Ryan Poland	1997	123
21 0/16	13 13/16	7 3/16	M	Sidney Lake	SAS	Donald Wright	1998	123
20 15/16	13 4/16	7 11/16	M	Sequoia National Forest	CA	Robert Shilling	1971	153
20 15/16	12 12/16	8 3/16	M	Lincoln County	WI	Jay Manthei	1980	153
20 15/16	13 1/16	7 14/16	M	Nipawin	SAS	Glen Sellsted	1981	153
20 15/16	12 14/16	8 1/16	M	Goodsoil	SAS	Ralph Clarke	1982	153

BLACK BEAR

Minimum Score 18 — Continued

SCORE	GREATEST LENGTH	GREATEST WIDTH	SEX	AREA	STATE/ PROVINCE	HUNTER'S NAME	DATE	RANK
20 15/16	12 11/16	8 4/16	M	Routt County	CO	Mark A. Chapman	1982	153
20 15/16	13 0/16	7 15/16	M	Monominto	MAN	Erik Thienpondt	1983	153
20 15/16	12 15/16	8 0/16	M	Meadow Lake	SAS	Bruce Stieber	1986	153
20 15/16	12 11/16	8 4/16	M	Washago	ONT	Chris Marsh	1992	153
20 15/16	12 15/16	8 0/16	M	Makwa	SAS	Raymond Schediny	1995	153
20 15/16	13 0/16	7 15/16	M	Carswell Lake	SAS	Steve Rucinski	1995	153
20 14/16	12 10/16	8 6/16	M	Mesa County	CO	Richard A. Schreiber	1973	163
20 14/16	13 0/16	7 14/16	M	Prince of Wales Island	AK	Gary G. Smith	1978	163
20 14/16	12 8/16	8 6/16	M	Red Lake	ONT	George Law	1981	163
20 14/16	13 2/16	7 12/16	M	Cass County	MN	Craig Enervold	1982	163
20 14/16	13 6/16	7 8/16	M	Duck Mtn.	MAN	John 'Jack' Cordes	1984	163
20 14/16	12 9/16	8 5/16	M	Routt County	CO	Lonny Vanatta	1984	163
20 14/16	12 12/16	8 2/16	M	Thunder Bay	ONT	Tim Walters	1985	163
20 14/16	12 15/16	7 15/16	M	Camas County	ID	Ed Cushman	1986	163
20 14/16	12 13/16	8 1/16	M	Prince of Wales Island	AK	Kevin Robinson	1988	163
20 14/16	13 2/16	7 12/16	M	Edmonton	ALB	Bruce Nederveld	1990	163
20 14/16	13 0/16	7 14/16	M	Prince of Wales Island	AK	Thomas Chadwick	1991	163
20 14/16	12 11/16	8 3/16	M	Prince of Wales Island	AK	Robert A. Meister	1992	163
20 14/16	13 2/16	7 12/16	M	Ministikwan Lake	SAS	Brent Maxwell	1992	163
20 14/16	13 0/16	7 14/16	M	Venango County	PA	Larry Rossman	1992	163
20 14/16	12 8/16	8 6/16	M	Kamloops	BC	Mark Guglielmini	1995	163
20 14/16	12 14/16	8 0/16	M	Riding Mtn.	MAN	Dale E. Shoemaker	1995	163
20 14/16	12 14/16	8 0/16	M	Ministikwan Lake	SAS	Bud Nugent	1995	163
20 14/16	13 2/16	7 12/16	M	Missaukee County	MI	Larry Ritchie	1995	163
20 14/16	13 4/16	7 10/16	M	Pine County	MN	Kevin Kubat	1996	163
20 14/16	13 2/16	7 12/16	M	Bayfield County	WI	William R. See	1996	163
20 14/16	13 2/16	7 12/16	M	Prince of Wales Island	AK	Larry Daly	1997	163
20 14/16	12 13/16	8 1/16	M	St. Louis County	MN	David McKenzie	1997	163
20 14/16	13 4/16	7 10/16	M	Gila County	AZ	Thomas J. Hoffman	1998	163
20 14/16	13 1/16	7 13/16	M	Grande Prairie	ALB	Buck Horn	1998	163
20 13/16	12 12/16	8 1/16	M	Marrns Creek	ID	Joe Schreideler	1977	187
20 13/16	12 11/16	8 2/16	M	Langlade County	WI	Eugene Strong	1978	187
20 13/16	12 14/16	7 15/16	M	Humboldt County	CA	Calvin Farner	1983	187
20 13/16	13 4/16	7 9/16	M	Meadow Lake	SAS	D. Mitch Kottas	1988	187
20 13/16	12 15/16	7 14/16	M	Carrot River	SAS	Mike Palmer	1989	187
20 13/16	12 14/16	7 15/16	M	Pine County	MN	Steven J. Gardas	1989	187
20 13/16	12 15/16	7 14/16	M	Prince of Wales Island	AK	George P. Mann	1992	187
20 13/16	12 13/16	8 0/16	M	Davidson	QUE	Jack Satterfield, Jr.	1992	187
20 13/16	13 2/16	7 11/16	M	Prince of Wales Island	AK	Lon E. Lauber	1993	187
20 13/16	12 14/16	7 15/16	M	Prince of Wales Island	AK	Kirk Westervelt	1993	187
20 13/16	13 2/16	7 11/16	M	Spiritwood	SAS	Dewayne Mullins	1995	187
20 13/16	12 12/16	8 1/16	M	Kiui Island	AK	Joel J. Bickler, DDS	1995	187
20 13/16	12 14/16	7 15/16	M	Buffalo Narrows	SAS	Roland J. Quick	1997	187
20 13/16	12 14/16	7 15/16	M	Bernalillo County	NM	Chris Zamora	1997	187
20 13/16	13 1/16	7 12/16	M	Caribou County	ID	Eldon Richter	1998	187
20 12/16	12 12/16	8 0/16	M	Apache County	AZ	Dr. C. G. Clare	1967	202
20 12/16	12 5/16	8 7/16	M	Emmet County	MI	Hawley H. Rhew	1974	202
20 12/16	12 12/16	8 0/16	M	Douglas County	WI	Robert J. Schmidt	1975	202
20 12/16	12 15/16	7 13/16	M	Armstrong	ONT	Paul Mahaney	1977	202
20 12/16	13 0/16	7 12/16	M	San Miguel County	CO	John W. Rowe	1978	202
20 12/16	12 15/16	7 13/16	M	Bonneville County	ID	John Hill	1983	202
20 12/16	12 11/16	8 1/16	M	Prince of Wales Island	AK	Jack Williams	1985	202
20 12/16	12 12/16	8 0/16	M	Carbon County	WY	Steve Powell	1985	202
20 12/16	12 11/16	8 1/16	M	Plumas County	CA	Kevin Hull	1986	202
20 12/16	13 0/16	7 12/16	M	Aitkin County	MN	Merrill D. Holm	1986	202
20 12/16	12 14/16	7 14/16	M	Prince of Wales Island	AK	Kevin Robinson	1988	202
20 12/16	13 0/16	7 12/16	M	Douglas County	WI	Harold Halverson	1990	202
20 12/16	12 11/16	8 1/16	M	Ketchikan	AK	Greg Munther	1991	202
20 12/16	12 12/16	8 0/16	M	Lloydminster	SAS	Steve Preziosi	1991	202
20 12/16	13 0/16	7 12/16	M	Athabasca River	ALB	Larry Oppe	1992	202
20 12/16	12 14/16	7 14/16	M	Carswell Lake	SAS	Steven Rucinski	1992	202
20 12/16	12 7/16	8 5/16	M	Fort McMurray	ALB	Darrin West	1992	202
20 12/16	12 11/16	8 1/16	M	Torrance County	NM	Steve Alderete	1992	202
20 12/16	12 14/16	7 14/16	M	Preeceville	SAS	James D. Guess	1993	202
20 12/16	12 12/16	8 0/16	M	Hudson Bay	SAS	Paul Chinski	1994	202
20 12/16	12 13/16	7 15/16	M	Marquette County	MI	Darryl D. Ansel	1994	202
20 12/16	13 3/16	7 9/16	M	Slave Lake	ALB	Kay Shipley	1995	202
20 12/16	13 0/16	7 12/16	M	Darwell	ALB	John Saddoris	1995	202
20 12/16	12 13/16	7 15/16	M	Buffalo Narrows	SAS	Kenneth M. Asboth	1995	202
20 12/16	13 2/16	7 10/16	M	Apache County	AZ	Edward A. Petersen	1997	202
20 12/16	13 4/16	7 8/16	M	Steuben County	NY	Daniel Stambaugh	1997	202
20 12/16	12 14/16	7 14/16	M	Dipper Lake	SAS	Bryce Dillabough	1998	202
20 12/16	13 6/16	7 6/16	M	Peace River	ALB	Joe Coleman	1998	202
20 11/16	12 13/16	7 14/16	M	Thunder Bay	ONT	Mel Johnson	1974	230
20 11/16	12 14/16	7 13/16	M	Pitkin County	CO	Dale W. Gray	1975	230
20 11/16	13 2/16	7 9/16	M	Rio Blanco County	CO	Walter Krom	1976	230
20 11/16	13 2/16	7 9/16	M	Rockingham County	VA	Roger O. Wyant	1982	230
20 11/16	13 2/16	7 9/16	M	Quesnel	BC	Russell Thornberry	1987	230

BLACK BEAR

Minimum Score 18 — Continued

SCORE	GREATEST LENGTH	GREATEST WIDTH	SEX	AREA	STATE/PROVINCE	HUNTER'S NAME	DATE	RANK
20 11/16	12 10/16	8 1/16	M	Sunbury County	NBW	Raymond Faulknor	1987	230
20 11/16	12 14/16	7 13/16	M	Chuit River	AK	George P. Mann	1987	230
20 11/16	13 3/16	7 8/16	M	Rappahannock County	VA	Jeff S. Good	1987	230
20 11/16	13 2/16	7 9/16	M	Prince of Wales Island	AK	Tracy Lucas	1989	230
20 11/16	12 11/16	8 0/16	M	Prince of Wales Island	AK	Glen Berry	1990	230
20 11/16	13 0/16	7 11/16	M	Douglas County	WI	Roger W. Hansen	1990	230
20 11/16	13 2/16	7 9/16	M	Prince of Wales Island	AK	Ken A. Vorisek	1991	230
20 11/16	12 15/16	7 12/16	M	Douglas County	WI	Steve Wittke	1992	230
20 11/16	12 13/16	7 14/16	M	Thorne Bay	AK	Steve McCoy	1993	230
20 11/16	12 11/16	8 0/16	M	Prince Of Wales Island	AK	Miles A. Tanner	1994	230
20 11/16	12 11/16	8 0/16	M	Swan River	SAS	Donald L. Sagner	1994	230
20 11/16	12 10/16	8 1/16	M	Nipigon	ONT	Scott Beurkens	1995	230
20 11/16	12 14/16	7 13/16	M	William's Lake	ONT	Cathy Barnowsky	1995	230
20 11/16	12 13/16	7 14/16	M	Piney	MAN	Russell K. Mehling	1995	230
20 11/16	12 14/16	7 13/16	M	Debolt	ALB	Dave Jeffers	1996	230
20 11/16	13 3/16	7 8/16	M	Porcupine Plains	SAS	Dana Morezak	1996	230
20 11/16	13 0/16	7 11/16	M	Bayfield County	WI	Steven Henthorn	1997	230
20 10/16	13 1/16	7 9/16	M	Rio Blanco County	CO	Frank 'Rit' Heller	1969	252
20 10/16	12 10/16	8 0/16	M	Sierra County	CA	Ervin K. McMakin	1971	252
20 10/16	12 14/16	7 12/16	M	Ft. Francis	ONT	George Geisert	1973	252
20 10/16	12 10/16	8 0/16	M	Crawford Park	MAN	Brent Mills	1981	252
20 10/16	12 10/16	8 0/16	M	Tweed	ONT	John E. Lawson	1983	252
20 10/16	12 12/16	7 14/16	M	Lac La Ronge	SAS	Steve Hammond	1985	252
20 10/16	12 14/16	7 12/16	M	Cass County	MN	James D. Zahalka	1987	252
20 10/16	12 12/16	7 14/16	M	Prince of Wales Island	AK	Danny Moore	1990	252
20 10/16	12 8/16	8 2/16	M	Ravalli County	MT	John C. Locke	1990	252
20 10/16	12 11/16	7 15/16	M	Nairn Township	ONT	Ron Hergott	1990	252
20 10/16	12 13/16	7 13/16	M	Iron County	WI	Jeff Ott	1990	252
20 10/16	13 0/16	7 10/16	M	Stone Lake	ONT	Jack A. Vos	1991	252
20 10/16	12 15/16	7 11/16	M	Pine County	MN	Thomas Behrends	1991	252
20 10/16	12 15/16	7 11/16	M	Winifred Lake	ALB	Cornel Yarmoloy	1992	252
20 10/16	12 12/16	7 14/16	M	Green Lake	SAS	Randy K. McBroom	1995	252
20 10/16	13 2/16	7 8/16	M	Kirkland Lake	ONT	Jason Mazzocato	1995	252
20 10/16	13 0/16	7 10/16	M	Lake County	CA	Matt Schuler	1996	252
20 10/16	12 12/16	7 14/16	M	Kern County	CA	Gilbert R. Garcia	1996	252
20 10/16	12 12/16	7 14/16	M	Lewisporte	NFL	Francis Ogden	1996	252
20 10/16	12 9/16	8 1/16	M	Delta County	MI	Scott B. Merchant	1996	252
20 10/16	13 3/16	7 7/16	M	Reita Lake	ALB	Arliss McNalley	1997	252
20 10/16	13 6/16	7 4/16	M	Hudson Bay	SAS	Dairl Hicks	1997	252
20 10/16	12 14/16	7 12/16	M	Iron River	ALB	Michael K. Frank	1997	252
20 10/16	12 12/16	7 14/16	M	Dorion	ONT	Larry Paulsen	1997	252
20 10/16	12 10/16	8 0/16	M	Green Lake	SAS	Randy Zion	1998	252
20 9/16	12 12/16	7 13/16	M	Lake County	MN	Art A. Heinze	1970	277
20 9/16	12 12/16	7 13/16	M	Prince of Wales Island	AK	Roy C. Ewen	1973	277
20 9/16	12 7/16	8 2/16	M	Grand County	CO	Curt Lynn	1973	277
20 9/16	12 12/16	7 13/16	M	Wawa	ONT	Robert C. McGuire	1975	277
20 9/16	12 11/16	7 14/16	M	Aitkin County	MN	Myles Keller	1977	277
20 9/16	13 1/16	7 8/16	M	Thunder Bay	ONT	Lester W. Jass	1979	277
20 9/16	12 13/16	7 12/16	M	Delta County	CO	Steve McCarthy	1982	277
20 9/16	12 9/16	8 0/16	M	Franklin County	NY	Edward M. Odell	1982	277
20 9/16	12 11/16	7 14/16	M	Missaukee County	MI	Gregory Korkoske	1983	277
20 9/16	12 10/16	7 15/16	M	Northwest of Dryden	ONT	Larry Bauman	1984	277
20 9/16	13 1/16	7 8/16	M	Durban	MAN	David H. Boland	1985	277
20 9/16	12 7/16	8 2/16	M	Thunder Bay	ONT	Daniel Schuttler	1985	277
20 9/16	13 1/16	7 8/16	M	Florence County	WI	Daniel G. Villenauve	1986	277
20 9/16	12 9/16	8 0/16	M	Custer County	ID	Doug Burkman	1987	277
20 9/16	12 13/16	7 12/16	M	Prince of Wales Island	AK	Glen Berry	1988	277
20 9/16	12 10/16	7 15/16	M	Prince of Wales Island	AK	Richard L. Westervelt	1988	277
20 9/16	12 15/16	7 10/16	M	McAdams	NBW	David F. Baldwin	1988	277
20 9/16	12 13/16	7 12/16	M	Aroostook County	ME	Danny Corey	1988	277
20 9/16	13 3/16	7 6/16	M	Douglas County	WI	Steve Peterson	1988	277
20 9/16	12 10/16	7 15/16	M	Marinette County	WI	Perry Kosek	1988	277
20 9/16	13 1/16	7 8/16	M	Poplarfield	MAN	John C. Collins	1991	277
20 9/16	13 0/16	7 9/16	M	Catron County	NM	Patty Foley	1991	277
20 9/16	13 1/16	7 8/16	M	Summit County	UT	Maury Butterfield	1992	277
20 9/16	12 12/16	7 13/16	M	Ft. McMurray	ALB	Sammy J. Schrimsher	1992	277
20 9/16	13 6/16	7 3/16	M	Sudbury	ONT	Vinnie Pisani	1992	277
20 9/16	12 14/16	7 11/16	M	Smoky Lake	ALB	Cheryl Lane	1993	277
20 9/16	13 0/16	7 9/16	M	Arran	SAS	David G. Harmon	1994	277
20 9/16	12 10/16	7 15/16	M	Prince of Wales Island	AK	Michael Davis	1994	277
20 9/16	12 12/16	7 13/16	M	Catron County	NM	Robert W. Ricke	1994	277
20 9/16	12 10/16	7 15/16	M	Athabasca River	ALB	Steve Barnhill	1995	277
20 9/16	12 9/16	8 0/16	M	Besnard Lake	SAS	Carol Macaulay	1995	277
20 9/16	12 12/16	7 13/16	M	Mulchatna River	AK	Howard Olson	1996	277
20 9/16	12 13/16	7 12/16	M	Parry Sound	ONT	Jim C. DeHoey	1997	277
20 9/16	13 1/16	7 8/16	M	La Crete	ALB	Stanley Russell	1997	277
20 8/16	12 13/16	7 11/16	M	Queen Charlotte Islands	BC	Peter Halbig	1960	311
20 8/16	12 14/16	7 10/16	M	Shawano County	WI	Bud Wiesman	1974	311

BLACK BEAR

Minimum Score 18 — Continued

SCORE	GREATEST LENGTH	GREATEST WIDTH	SEX	AREA	STATE/PROVINCE	HUNTER'S NAME	DATE	RANK
20 8/16	12 14/16	7 10/16	M	Kamsack	SAS	Steve Boychuk	1977	311
20 8/16	12 14/16	7 10/16	M	Tehama County	CA	Anthony P. Davi	1980	311
20 8/16	12 11/16	7 13/16	M	Strathnaver	BC	Dan Wicks	1981	311
20 8/16	12 13/16	7 11/16	M	Valley County	ID	Dave Scott	1982	311
20 8/16	12 1/16	8 7/16	M	Ignace	ONT	Jerry Klinesmith	1983	311
20 8/16	13 2/16	7 6/16	M	Cass County	MN	Anne M. Zahalka	1988	311
20 8/16	12 15/16	7 9/16	M	Dryden	ONT	Robert J. Crane	1990	311
20 8/16	12 15/16	7 9/16	M	Nolalu	ONT	Billy Roy Leach	1991	311
20 8/16	12 8/16	8 0/16	M	Tehama County	CA	Kim Cooper	1991	311
20 8/16	12 11/16	7 13/16	M	Pitkin County	CO	Stanley E. Lauriski	1992	311
20 8/16	12 12/16	7 12/16	M	Prince of Wales Island	AK	Glen Berry	1992	311
20 8/16	12 10/16	7 14/16	M	Mendocino County	CA	James W. Rutledge	1992	311
20 8/16	12 8/16	8 0/16	M	Plumas County	CA	Mike Ellena	1993	311
20 8/16	13 0/16	7 8/16	M	Sherwood Park	ALB	Pat Morphy	1994	311
20 8/16	12 13/16	7 11/16	M	Endeavour	SAS	Wayne Arnson	1994	311
20 8/16	12 14/16	7 10/16	M	Peace River	ALB	Tom Lester	1994	311
20 8/16	12 10/16	7 14/16	M	Vermilion Bay	ONT	Larry Saunders	1995	311
20 8/16	12 9/16	7 15/16	M	Athabasca River	ALB	John Visscher	1995	311
20 8/16	12 10/16	7 14/16	M	File Lake	MAN	Robert Schulz	1995	311
20 8/16	12 15/16	7 9/16	M	Beltrami County	MN	Steve Young	1995	311
20 8/16	13 1/16	7 7/16	M	Pineshill Forest Reserve	SAS	Kenneth D. Wiers	1996	311
20 8/16	12 12/16	7 12/16	M	Langlade County	WI	Charles W. Drexler, Sr.	1996	311
20 8/16	12 12/16	7 12/16	M	Marinette County	WI	Andrew Semrad	1997	311
20 8/16	12 15/16	7 9/16	M	Mistatim	SAS	Scott L. Koelzer	1998	311
20 8/16	12 14/16	7 10/16	M	Lac La Biche	ALB	Jeffrey S. Weisswasser	1998	311
20 7/16	13 9/16	6 14/16	M	Nenana	AK	Robert Dunn	1968	338
20 7/16	12 10/16	7 13/16	M	Price County	WI	Bob Eckarot	1974	338
20 7/16	12 14/16	7 9/16	M	Montezuma County	CO	Bryan C. Neeley	1974	338
20 7/16	12 7/16	8 0/16	M	Whiteshell	MAN	Ken Warkentin	1978	338
20 7/16	12 11/16	7 12/16	M	Mille Lacs County	MN	Milt Zernechel	1980	338
20 7/16	12 6/16	8 1/16	M	Marquette County	MI	Thomas Benak	1982	338
20 7/16	12 11/16	7 12/16	M	Mat-Su Borough	AK	Jack V. Rouse	1983	338
20 7/16	12 10/16	7 13/16	M	St. Louis County	MN	Ken Lenk	1983	338
20 7/16	12 12/16	7 11/16	M	Garfield County	CO	Roger Bolander	1985	338
20 7/16	12 14/16	7 9/16	M	Arran	SAS	Bill Clink	1986	338
20 7/16	12 14/16	7 9/16	M	Valleyview	ALB	Stan Walchuk, Jr.	1986	338
20 7/16	12 11/16	7 12/16	M	Routt County	CO	Bill Grammer	1987	338
20 7/16	12 4/16	8 3/16	M	Atikokan	ONT	Kenny Stoner	1988	338
20 7/16	12 12/16	7 11/16	M	Iron County	WI	Brian Tessmann	1989	338
20 7/16	12 7/16	8 0/16	M	Rappahannock County	VA	Collis W. Dodson, Jr.	1989	338
20 7/16	12 11/16	7 12/16	M	Prince of Wales Island	AK	Dennis Brieske	1990	338
20 7/16	12 12/16	7 11/16	M	Madera County	CA	James Joseph Doherty, Jr.	1991	338
20 7/16	12 12/16	7 11/16	M	Spirit River	ALB	Jim Stinson	1992	338
20 7/16	12 11/16	7 12/16	M	Fort McMurray	ALB	James Pike	1992	338
20 7/16	12 7/16	8 0/16	M	San Bernardino County	CA	Allen Davis	1992	338
20 7/16	13 0/16	7 7/16	M	Douglas County	WI	Mark P. Haan	1992	338
20 7/16	13 0/16	7 7/16	M	Rockingham County	VA	Donald Bare	1992	338
20 7/16	12 12/16	7 11/16	M	Perrault Falls	ONT	Patrick D. Gaffney	1993	338
20 7/16	12 8/16	7 15/16	M	Becker County	MN	Joe Caron	1993	338
20 7/16	12 12/16	7 11/16	M	Bayfield County	WI	Edwin A. Koenigs	1993	338
20 7/16	12 15/16	7 8/16	M	Pine River	MAN	Peter McGillivray	1994	338
20 7/16	12 9/16	7 14/16	M	Graham County	AZ	Warren Strickland	1994	338
20 7/16	12 11/16	7 12/16	M	Minto	NBW	Joseph Maringo	1994	338
20 7/16	12 13/16	7 10/16	M	Utterson	ONT	Jeff Coleman	1996	338
20 7/16	12 10/16	7 13/16	M	Wawa	ONT	Brett Grams	1996	338
20 7/16	12 15/16	7 8/16	M	Bayfield County	WI	Glenn A. Klomsten	1996	338
20 7/16	12 13/16	7 10/16	M	Trinity County	CA	Bart Pontoni	1996	338
20 7/16	12 15/16	7 8/16	M	Kelwood	MAN	Doug J. Herman	1997	338
20 7/16	12 6/16	8 1/16	M	Whiteswan Lake	SAS	Terry Krahn	1997	338
20 7/16	12 11/16	7 12/16	M	Ft. McMurray	ALB	Rhonda Hunter	1997	338
20 7/16	13 0/16	7 7/16	M	Olha	MAN	Dana M. Draper	1997	338
20 7/16	12 9/16	7 14/16	M	Carswell Lake	SAS	Christopher J. Leitzke	1998	338
20 7/16	12 8/16	7 15/16	M	Peace River	ALB	Jerry W. Laton	1998	338
20 6/16	12 11/16	7 11/16	M	Tulare County	CA	Quentin M. Boutch	1967	376
20 6/16	12 11/16	7 11/16	M	Garfield County	CO	Steve Bergman	1970	376
20 6/16	12 15/16	7 7/16	M	Kern County	CA	Leo Farley	1973	376
20 6/16	12 8/16	7 14/16	M	Shasta County	CA	Susan Mallonee	1974	376
20 6/16	12 6/16	8 0/16	M	Saguache County	CO	Ed Wiseman	1975	376
20 6/16	12 11/16	7 11/16	M	Reindeer Lake	SAS	James Buchanan	1976	376
20 6/16	12 12/16	7 10/16	M	Flower Station	ONT	Richard H. Shoup	1977	376
20 6/16	12 9/16	7 13/16	M	Ear Falls	ONT	Terry R. Fletcher	1978	376
20 6/16	12 11/16	7 11/16	M	St. Louis County	MN	Russell Wimberly	1979	376
20 6/16	12 11/16	7 11/16	M	Reserve	SAS	Richard Loffler	1984	376
20 6/16	12 14/16	7 8/16	M	Bayfield County	WI	Paul Deckert	1984	376
20 6/16	12 9/16	7 13/16	M	Ignace	ONT	Randy J. Tylke	1985	376
20 6/16	13 2/16	7 4/16	M	Meadow Lake	SAS	Craig Larson	1986	376
20 6/16	12 5/16	8 1/16	M	Spiritwood	SAS	Robert W. Peet	1987	376
20 6/16	12 8/16	7 14/16	M	Wrangel Island	AK	Bob Smith	1987	376

BLACK BEAR

Minimum Score 18

Continued

SCORE	GREATEST LENGTH	GREATEST WIDTH	SEX	AREA	STATE/ PROVINCE	HUNTER'S NAME	DATE	RANK
20 6/16	12 13/16	7 9/16	M	Athabasca	ALB	John Visscher	1988	376
20 6/16	12 14/16	7 8/16	M	Hudson Bay	SAS	Kendall Haberstroh	1988	376
20 6/16	12 8/16	7 14/16	M	Rochester	ALB	Dave Gerber	1988	376
20 6/16	12 13/16	7 9/16	M	Wandering River	ALB	Warren Witherspoon	1988	376
20 6/16	12 10/16	7 12/16	M	Wallowa County	OR	Russell McCall	1989	376
20 6/16	12 15/16	7 7/16	M	Pine County	MN	Thomas Behrends	1989	376
20 6/16	12 14/16	7 8/16	M	Ashland County	WI	James A. Liermann	1989	376
20 6/16	12 9/16	7 13/16	M	Lac Forant	QUE	Harold Shepard	1990	376
20 6/16	12 10/16	7 12/16	M	La Plata County	CO	Paul Nichols	1991	376
20 6/16	12 10/16	7 12/16	M	Clearwater County	ID	Steve Stajkowski	1991	376
20 6/16	12 11/16	7 11/16	M	Iron County	MI	Jeff Fontecchio	1991	376
20 6/16	12 7/16	7 15/16	M	Missoula County	MT	Rick L. Stone	1991	376
20 6/16	12 6/16	8 0/16	M	Plumas County	CA	Bill Graves	1991	376
20 6/16	13 0/16	7 6/16	M	Hubbard County	MN	Hal Dickelman	1992	376
20 6/16	12 9/16	7 13/16	M	Wolf Lake	ALB	Tim Pardely	1993	376
20 6/16	13 0/16	7 6/16	M	Rio Arriba County	NM	Larson Panzy	1993	376
20 6/16	12 7/16	7 15/16	M	Clark County	WA	Michael T. Davis	1993	376
20 6/16	12 10/16	7 12/16	M	Fort Chimo	QUE	Jerry McNeal	1994	376
20 6/16	12 12/16	7 10/16	M	Orange County	NY	Richard Berger	1994	376
20 6/16	12 10/16	7 12/16	M	McKinley County	NM	Timothy T. Dwyer	1995	376
20 6/16	13 1/16	7 5/16	M	Mineral County	WV	Gary Wayne Evans	1995	376
20 6/16	12 8/16	7 14/16	M	Los Angeles County	CA	Jerry Maytum	1995	376
20 6/16	12 13/16	7 9/16	M	Qu'Appelle	SAS	Brad Thompson	1996	376
20 6/16	12 12/16	7 10/16	M	High Level	ALB	Charles H. Thatcher	1996	376
20 6/16	12 9/16	7 13/16	M	Sheridan County	WY	Dan Brockman	1996	376
20 6/16	12 12/16	7 10/16	M	Fort McMurray	ALB	Bob Ehle	1996	376
20 6/16	12 4/16	8 2/16	M	Falher	ALB	Vicki Cianciarulo	1996	376
20 6/16	13 1/16	7 5/16	M	Burnett County	WI	Jerry Strese	1996	376
20 6/16	12 1/16	8 5/16	M	Bobcaygeon	ONT	Giulio Calvelli	1997	376
20 6/16	12 10/16	7 12/16	M	Madison County	MT	Darryle "Pete" Otto	1997	376
20 6/16	13 2/16	7 4/16	M	Price County	WI	Douglas Erickson	1997	376
20 6/16	12 8/16	7 14/16	M	Tingley Creek	BC	Dave Schwemler	1998	376
20 5/16	12 14/16	7 7/16	M	Shasta County	CA	Harv Ebers	1964	423
20 5/16	12 12/16	7 9/16	M	St. Louis County	MN	Jay Deones	1970	423
20 5/16	12 13/16	7 8/16	M	Buncombe County	NC	Robert T. Austin	1971	423
20 5/16	13 0/16	7 5/16	M	Emma Lake	SAS	Ernie Johnston	1972	423
20 5/16	12 4/16	8 1/16	M	Montezuma County	CO	Stanley A. Coval	1975	423
20 5/16	12 11/16	7 10/16	M	Montrose County	CO	Jack Cassidy	1976	423
20 5/16	12 11/16	7 10/16	M	Lemhi County	ID	Richard R. Smith	1977	423
20 5/16	12 10/16	7 11/16	M	Lincoln County	NM	Tom Mitchell	1978	423
20 5/16	12 12/16	7 9/16	M	Marquette County	MI	Bernard E. Stiritz	1980	423
20 5/16	12 9/16	7 12/16	M	Hudson Bay	SAS	Sam Qualls	1981	423
20 5/16	12 13/16	7 8/16	M	Bonneville County	ID	Michael Ferraro	1981	423
20 5/16	12 3/16	8 2/16	M	Presque Isle County	MI	William C. Green III	1981	423
20 5/16	12 9/16	7 12/16	M	Deviin Lake	ONT	J. E. Abhold	1982	423
20 5/16	12 5/16	8 0/16	M	Meagher County	MT	Richard M. Campbell	1982	423
20 5/16	12 12/16	7 9/16	M	Otero County	NM	Michael Crabb	1984	423
20 5/16	12 7/16	7 14/16	M	Atikokan	ONT	Greg Morehead	1985	423
20 5/16	12 8/16	7 13/16	M	Archuleta County	CO	Ronald J. Murphy	1985	423
20 5/16	12 6/16	7 15/16	M	Jackson County	OR	David Greisen, Jr.	1985	423
20 5/16	12 10/16	7 11/16	M	Ontonagon County	MI	Dale W. Gray	1986	423
20 5/16	12 9/16	7 12/16	M	Siskiyou County	CA	Bob Jensen	1986	423
20 5/16	12 7/16	7 14/16	M	Gila County	AZ	Eric Pierce	1987	423
20 5/16	12 10/16	7 11/16	M	Douglas County	WI	William T. Solie	1987	423
20 5/16	12 12/16	7 9/16	M	Prince of Wales Island	AK	Mike Taylor	1989	423
20 5/16	12 4/16	8 1/16	M	Okanogan County	WA	D. Kirk Sapp	1989	423
20 5/16	12 10/16	7 11/16	M	Lincoln County	WI	Gerald O. Arndt	1989	423
20 5/16	13 0/16	7 5/16	M	Mesa County	CO	Paul Alan Seidelman	1989	423
20 5/16	12 14/16	7 7/16	M	Prince of Wales Island	AK	Glen Berry	1990	423
20 5/16	12 12/16	7 9/16	M	Lac La Biche	ALB	Ronald H. Haver	1990	423
20 5/16	12 9/16	7 12/16	M	Prince of Wales Island	AK	Timothy Putnam	1991	423
20 5/16	12 6/16	7 15/16	M	Shasta County	CA	Douglas Trouette	1991	423
20 5/16	12 7/16	7 14/16	M	Skownan	MAN	Walt Krom	1992	423
20 5/16	12 7/16	7 14/16	M	Wanless	MAN	Arley Paul Heer	1993	423
20 5/16	12 9/16	7 12/16	M	Stone Creek	BC	Joe Tschampa	1993	423
20 5/16	12 10/16	7 11/16	M	Ft. Vermilion	ALB	Brian Burnstad	1993	423
20 5/16	12 10/16	7 11/16	M	Prince of Wales Island	AK	Larry D. Jones	1993	423
20 5/16	12 12/16	7 9/16	M	Wallowa County	OR	Stephen Herrera	1994	423
20 5/16	12 12/16	7 9/16	M	Bissett	MAN	Richard Nevels	1994	423
20 5/16	12 5/16	8 0/16	M	Athabasca River	ALB	Billy Tillotson	1994	423
20 5/16	12 6/16	7 15/16	M	Smeaton	SAS	Don G. Scofield	1994	423
20 5/16	12 6/16	7 15/16	M	Calling Lake	ALB	Rich McGowan	1994	423
20 5/16	12 10/16	7 11/16	M	Pine County	MN	John Cardinal	1994	423
20 5/16	12 10/16	7 11/16	M	Bayfield County	WI	Douglas E. Callies	1994	423
20 5/16	13 1/16	7 4/16	M	Burnett County	WI	Steven Constant	1994	423
20 5/16	13 1/16	7 4/16	M	Beltrami County	MN	Gregory T. Ose	1994	423
20 5/16	12 13/16	7 8/16	M	Rio Arriba County	NM	Robert John Seeds	1994	423
20 5/16	12 7/16	7 14/16	M	Chibougamau	QUE	Brian Brochu	1995	423

BLACK BEAR

Minimum Score 18 — Continued

SCORE	GREATEST LENGTH	GREATEST WIDTH	SEX	AREA	STATE/ PROVINCE	HUNTER'S NAME	DATE	RANK
20 5/16	12 10/16	7 11/16	M	Cadillac	QUE	Ron Miller	1995	423
20 5/16	12 8/16	7 13/16	M	Plumas County	CA	Mark Nelson	1995	423
20 5/16	12 9/16	7 12/16	M	Hudson Bay	SAS	Glen Gulka	1995	423
20 5/16	12 6/16	7 15/16	M	St. Louis County	MN	Bill G. Koenig	1995	423
20 5/16	12 14/16	7 7/16	M	McDowell County	WV	Kevin P. Kelley	1995	423
20 5/16	12 11/16	7 10/16	M	Prince of Wales Island	AK	Jim Bauers	1996	423
20 5/16	12 12/16	7 9/16	M	Marathon County	WI	Dan Infalt	1997	423
20 5/16	12 11/16	7 10/16	M	Raleigh County	WV	Larry Murphy	1997	423
20 5/16	12 11/16	7 10/16	M	Spirit River	ALB	Michael Ambur	1998	423
20 5/16	12 9/16	7 12/16	M	Two Forks River	SAS	Don Mason	1998	423
20 5/16	12 12/16	7 9/16	M	Cibola County	NM	Michael A. Rendon	1998	423
20 4/16	12 6/16	7 14/16	M	Oceana County	MI	William Benson	1967	480
20 4/16	12 11/16	7 9/16	M	Somerset County	ME	Felix Nosewicz	1968	480
20 4/16	12 10/16	7 10/16	M	Mesa County	CO	M. R. James	1971	480
20 4/16	12 12/16	7 8/16	M	Los Alamos County	NM	Kenneth A. Meyer	1971	480
20 4/16	12 12/16	7 8/16	M	Sawyer County	WI	George Geisert	1972	480
20 4/16	12 7/16	7 13/16	M	Madison County	MT	Bob Savage	1977	480
20 4/16	12 5/16	7 15/16	M	Kashabowie	ONT	Hans C. Forssell	1978	480
20 4/16	12 7/16	7 13/16	M	Valora	ONT	Elmer R. Luse, Jr.	1981	480
20 4/16	12 8/16	7 12/16	M	Siskiyou County	CA	Bill Waters	1981	480
20 4/16	12 8/16	7 12/16	M	Mesa County	CO	Larry A. McIntosh	1982	480
20 4/16	12 5/16	7 15/16	M	Nez Perce County	ID	Hubert M. Sims, Jr.	1982	480
20 4/16	12 7/16	7 13/16	M	Trinity County	CA	Rodney A. York	1983	480
20 4/16	12 8/16	7 12/16	M	Rockingham County	VA	Charles Larry Danner	1984	480
20 4/16	12 12/16	7 8/16	M	Carrot River	SAS	William Jorgensen	1985	480
20 4/16	12 8/16	7 12/16	M	Swan River	MAN	Marc N. Shaft	1985	480
20 4/16	12 11/16	7 9/16	M	Waterhen River	SAS	Pink Atkins	1986	480
20 4/16	12 10/16	7 10/16	M	Mat-Su Valley	AK	Bill Parker	1987	480
20 4/16	12 6/16	7 14/16	M	Wrangel Island	AK	Bob Smith	1987	480
20 4/16	12 10/16	7 10/16	M	Canoe Lake	SAS	Richard Robert Ritzel	1988	480
20 4/16	12 7/16	7 13/16	M	Ft. McMurray	ALB	Tom C. Johnson	1988	480
20 4/16	12 10/16	7 10/16	M	Prince of Wales Island	AK	Danny Moore	1989	480
20 4/16	12 5/16	7 15/16	M	Cranberry Portage	MAN	Dean K. Reidt	1989	480
20 4/16	12 14/16	7 6/16	M	King County	WA	Greg Winters	1989	480
20 4/16	12 12/16	7 8/16	M	Olha	MAN	Tim Stahman	1990	480
20 4/16	12 12/16	7 8/16	M	Lanark	ONT	Ben Graham	1990	480
20 4/16	12 7/16	7 13/16	M	Caramat	ONT	Rick Stump	1990	480
20 4/16	12 4/16	8 0/16	M	Dorion	ONT	Bruce Hudalla	1991	480
20 4/16	12 8/16	7 12/16	M	Ignace	ONT	Thomas C. Klinesmith	1991	480
20 4/16	12 10/16	7 10/16	M	Howley	NFL	Roger Lewis	1991	480
20 4/16	12 9/16	7 11/16	M	Lewis County	WA	Kevin R. Amos	1991	480
20 4/16	12 11/16	7 9/16	M	Lane County	OR	Dave Smith	1991	480
20 4/16	12 13/16	7 7/16	M	Dubreuilville	ONT	Terry J. DeBlaay	1992	480
20 4/16	12 4/16	8 0/16	M	Ear Falls	ONT	Larry Foreman	1992	480
20 4/16	12 7/16	7 13/16	M	Madison County	MT	Larry Stackhouse	1992	480
20 4/16	12 11/16	7 9/16	M	Beauval	SAS	Alan Sims	1993	480
20 4/16	12 8/16	7 12/16	M	Rocky Lake	MAN	Tim Finley	1993	480
20 4/16	12 9/16	7 11/16	M	Wabigoon	ONT	Kermit L. Johnson	1993	480
20 4/16	12 11/16	7 9/16	M	Jackson County	OR	Mark G. Nouguier	1993	480
20 4/16	12 14/16	7 6/16	M	Price County	WI	William Peterson	1993	480
20 4/16	12 14/16	7 6/16	M	Essex County	NY	Paul Durling	1993	480
20 4/16	12 6/16	7 14/16	M	Clarke Lake	SAS	Steve Byerly	1994	480
20 4/16	12 7/16	7 13/16	M	Snow Lake	MAN	Craig Warren Barrows	1994	480
20 4/16	12 9/16	7 11/16	M	Christopher Lake	SAS	Scott G. Yeomans	1994	480
20 4/16	12 8/16	7 12/16	M	Prince of Wales Island	AK	Fred C. Church	1995	480
20 4/16	12 10/16	7 10/16	M	Carswell Lake	SAS	Dave Donahue	1995	480
20 4/16	12 10/16	7 10/16	M	Alpine County	CA	John H. Wiegel	1995	480
20 4/16	12 12/16	7 8/16	M	Thunder Bay	ONT	Marc Hellinghausen	1996	480
20 4/16	12 11/16	7 9/16	M	Tulare County	CA	Dennis Crew	1996	480
20 4/16	12 15/16	7 5/16	M	Orange County	NY	George E. Decker	1996	480
20 4/16	12 10/16	7 10/16	M	Farwell Canyon	BC	Daryl Buchholtz	1997	480
20 4/16	13 6/16	6 14/16	M	Athabasca River	ALB	Roger Wintle	1997	480
20 4/16	12 11/16	7 9/16	M	Prince of Wales Island	AK	E. Lance Whary	1997	480
20 4/16	12 12/16	7 8/16	M	Brunswick Lake	ONT	Jerome L. Schellinger	1997	480
20 4/16	13 4/16	7 0/16	M	Clearwater County	MN	Donnie Hutson	1997	480
20 4/16	12 10/16	7 10/16	M	Apache County	AZ	Clyde H. Gavin	1997	480
20 4/16	12 8/16	7 12/16	M	Carrot River	SAS	Mike Polich	1998	480
20 4/16	12 6/16	7 14/16	M	Ile-a-la-Crosse	SAS	Dennis Wademan	1998	480
20 4/16	12 8/16	7 12/16	M	Spirit River	ALB	Joseph E. Barno	1998	480
20 3/16	12 13/16	7 6/16	M	Prince Rupert	BC	Frank Huneck	1960	538
20 3/16	12 6/16	7 13/16	M	Ignace	ONT	Jerry Ulrich	1968	538
20 3/16	12 4/16	7 15/16	M	Adams County	ID	Joe Adams	1971	538
20 3/16	12 8/16	7 11/16	M	Coos County	OR	Robert L. Wegand	1971	538
20 3/16	12 3/16	8 0/16	M	Boise County	ID	Mark W. Powell	1975	538
20 3/16	12 12/16	7 7/16	M	Smoke Lake	ALB	Kenneth Szgatti	1975	538
20 3/16	12 6/16	7 13/16	M	Dolores County	CO	Randy E. Dossey	1979	538
20 3/16	12 5/16	7 14/16	M	Dolores County	CO	Marvin Reichenau	1979	538
20 3/16	12 10/16	7 9/16	M	Itasca County	MN	Gerald N. Rivetts, Jr.	1980	538

BLACK BEAR

Minimum Score 18 — Page 140 — Continued

SCORE	GREATEST LENGTH	GREATEST WIDTH	SEX	AREA	STATE/PROVINCE	HUNTER'S NAME	DATE	RANK
20 3/16	12 12/16	7 7/16	M	Burnett County	WI	Dan McElfresh	1982	538
20 3/16	12 8/16	7 11/16	M	Foxford	SAS	Brian Acton	1982	538
20 3/16	12 14/16	7 5/16	M	Loon Lake	SAS	Dennis Meyer	1984	538
20 3/16	12 13/16	7 6/16	M	Catron County	NM	John R. Caminiti	1984	538
20 3/16	12 3/16	8 0/16	M	Marquette County	MI	Kurt Funk	1985	538
20 3/16	12 13/16	7 6/16	M	Red Lake	ONT	Gerald Dykin	1986	538
20 3/16	12 12/16	7 7/16	M	Sioux Lookout	ONT	Tom Rosenthal	1986	538
20 3/16	12 12/16	7 7/16	M	McMunn	MAN	Rod Black	1987	538
20 3/16	12 11/16	7 8/16	M	Canterbury	NBW	David G. Cote	1987	538
20 3/16	12 4/16	7 15/16	M	Schefferville	QUE	Charles L. Buechel, Jr.	1987	538
20 3/16	12 7/16	7 12/16	M	Iron County	WI	Mike Lutz	1987	538
20 3/16	12 13/16	7 6/16	M	Ft. Assiniboine	ALB	Wes Skakun	1988	538
20 3/16	12 8/16	7 11/16	M	Pine County	MN	Ed Nielsen	1989	538
20 3/16	12 8/16	7 11/16	M	Houghton County	MI	Loren G. Baker	1989	538
20 3/16	13 2/16	7 1/16	M	Chisago County	MN	Dennis Jaworski	1989	538
20 3/16	12 8/16	7 11/16	M	Coconino County	AZ	William Bedlion	1989	538
20 3/16	12 10/16	7 9/16	M	Goodsoil	SAS	Larry H. Hoyt	1990	538
20 3/16	12 5/16	7 14/16	M	Lac La Biche	ALB	Jesse Meyer	1991	538
20 3/16	12 10/16	7 9/16	M	LaLoche	SAS	Robert Bramlett	1992	538
20 3/16	12 11/16	7 8/16	M	Wabasca River	ALB	Greg Duncan	1992	538
20 3/16	12 4/16	7 15/16	M	Chapleau	ONT	J. R. Mester	1992	538
20 3/16	12 9/16	7 10/16	M	Smoky Lake	ALB	Randy Ewen	1993	538
20 3/16	12 6/16	7 13/16	M	Ft. McMurray	ALB	David E. Stepp	1993	538
20 3/16	12 9/16	7 10/16	M	Hudson Bay	SAS	Dennis M. Dalan	1993	538
20 3/16	12 9/16	7 10/16	M	Cook County	MN	Rodney L. Tryon	1993	538
20 3/16	12 7/16	7 12/16	M	Rocky Mountain House	ALB	Steve Ouwerkerk	1994	538
20 3/16	12 10/16	7 9/16	M	Riding Mtn.	MAN	Gary L. Christensen	1994	538
20 3/16	12 10/16	7 9/16	M	Peace River	ALB	Zig Kertenis, Jr.	1994	538
20 3/16	13 3/16	7 0/16	M	Hudson Bay	SAS	Scott McCay	1994	538
20 3/16	12 6/16	7 13/16	M	Savant Lake	ONT	Brian Mark Winter	1994	538
20 3/16	12 10/16	7 9/16	M	Silver Lake	ONT	Walter Wright	1994	538
20 3/16	13 0/16	7 3/16	M	Timmins	ONT	Tony Muhich	1994	538
20 3/16	12 6/16	7 13/16	M	Catron County	NM	William F. Kern	1994	538
20 3/16	12 12/16	7 7/16	M	Clearwater County	ID	Dana L. Lott	1995	538
20 3/16	13 0/16	7 3/16	M	Mafeking	MAN	Kimberly J. Schwierking	1995	538
20 3/16	12 12/16	7 7/16	M	Nevada County	CA	Edward L. Tillotson	1995	538
20 3/16	12 5/16	7 14/16	M	Chinchaga	ALB	Dwayne Huggins	1996	538
20 3/16	12 12/16	7 7/16	M	Athabasca River	ALB	John Visscher	1996	538
20 3/16	12 9/16	7 10/16	M	Athabasca River	ALB	Ronald T. Morgan	1997	538
20 3/16	12 9/16	7 10/16	M	Kane Lake	SAS	Tim Lupia	1997	538
20 3/16	12 14/16	7 5/16	M	Aitkin County	MN	Keith Van Hale	1997	538
20 3/16	12 10/16	7 9/16	M	Peace River	ALB	Gary Day	1998	538
20 3/16	12 14/16	7 5/16	M	Duck Mtn.	SAS	Ron Vandermeulen	1998	538
20 2/16	12 9/16	7 9/16	M	St. Louis County	MN	James Harwood	1966	590
20 2/16	12 9/16	7 9/16	M	St. Louis County	MN	Ron Johnson	1968	590
20 2/16	12 6/16	7 12/16	M	Bayfield County	WI	Clarence J. Biddle	1973	590
20 2/16	12 6/16	7 12/16	M	Iron County	WI	Chuck Ramsay	1973	590
20 2/16	12 9/16	7 9/16	M	Delta County	CO	Bill Izon	1976	590
20 2/16	12 10/16	7 8/16	M	Montrose County	CO	John Brandt	1978	590
20 2/16	12 1/16	8 1/16	M	Del Norte County	CA	Fred D. Davis, Jr.	1978	590
20 2/16	12 12/16	7 6/16	M	Montezuma County	CO	Floyd H. Hicks	1978	590
20 2/16	12 8/16	7 10/16	M	Mesa County	CO	Dennis Behn	1979	590
20 2/16	12 9/16	7 9/16	M	Delta County	CO	Scott Dillon	1981	590
20 2/16	12 6/16	7 12/16	M	Mendocino County	CA	Kenneth Marquardt	1981	590
20 2/16	12 12/16	7 6/16	M	Tehama County	CA	Randy Rehse	1981	590
20 2/16	12 2/16	7 6/16	M	Hudson Bay	SAS	Randy Lorenz	1982	590
20 2/16	12 7/16	7 11/16	M	Iron County	MI	George J. Hronkin III	1982	590
20 2/16	12 10/16	7 8/16	M	Douglas County	WI	Ron Ekstrand	1983	590
20 2/16	12 6/16	7 12/16	M	Kuiu Island	AK	William F. Burgess	1984	590
20 2/16	12 7/16	7 11/16	M	Meadow Lake	SAS	Richard W. Theurer	1984	590
20 2/16	12 8/16	7 10/16	M	Nipigon	ONT	Richard Scorzafava	1985	590
20 2/16	12 4/16	7 14/16	M	Sudbury	ONT	Ben L. Staponski	1986	590
20 2/16	13 1/16	7 1/16	M	Sudbury	ONT	Frank Calabro	1986	590
20 2/16	12 13/16	7 5/16	M	Chisago County	MN	Mark Piel	1986	590
20 2/16	12 6/16	7 12/16	M	Mendocino County	CA	Patrick M. Griffin	1986	590
20 2/16	12 8/16	7 10/16	M	Lake of the Woods	ONT	Karen Raasch	1987	590
20 2/16	12 8/16	7 10/16	M	Duchesne County	UT	Kenneth M. Labrum	1988	590
20 2/16	12 6/16	7 12/16	M	El Paso County	CO	Russ Nily	1988	590
20 2/16	12 14/16	7 4/16	M	Pine County	MN	Brian D. Scarnegie	1988	590
20 2/16	12 7/16	7 11/16	M	Crawford County	MI	Jerry D. Pratt	1988	590
20 2/16	12 8/16	7 10/16	M	Meadow Lake	SAS	Ian Twidale	1989	590
20 2/16	13 0/16	7 2/16	M	Beltrami County	MN	James Luverne Johnson	1989	590
20 2/16	12 7/16	7 11/16	M	Marathon County	WI	Daniel Auner	1989	590
20 2/16	12 9/16	7 9/16	M	Sullivan County	NY	John P. Dise	1989	590
20 2/16	12 8/16	7 10/16	M	Rabun County	GA	Terry Tyler	1989	590
20 2/16	12 8/16	7 10/16	M	Catron County	NM	Larry Joe Cearley	1990	590
20 2/16	12 10/16	7 8/16	M	Latah County	ID	Mick McCullough	1990	590
20 2/16	12 7/16	7 11/16	M	Fort McMurray	ALB	Ron LeBreton	1990	590

BLACK BEAR

Minimum Score 18   Continued

SCORE	GREATEST LENGTH	GREATEST WIDTH	SEX	AREA	STATE/ PROVINCE	HUNTER'S NAME	DATE	RANK
20 2/16	12 11/16	7 7/16	M	Kuiu Island	AK	Joe Miguel	1991	590
20 2/16	12 8/16	7 10/16	M	Fort McMurray	ALB	Fred Joseph	1991	590
20 2/16	12 8/16	7 10/16	M	Fort McMurray	ALB	Margaret Whittle Hice	1991	590
20 2/16	12 8/16	7 10/16	M	Rabun County	GA	Chuck Conner	1991	590
20 2/16	12 10/16	7 8/16	M	Otero County	NM	Beto Gutierrez	1991	590
20 2/16	12 12/16	7 6/16	M	Monds Township	ONT	Jeff Standafer	1992	590
20 2/16	12 4/16	7 14/16	M	Square Lake	ALB	Dave Stull	1992	590
20 2/16	12 6/16	7 12/16	M	Peace River	ALB	John Lindell	1992	590
20 2/16	12 10/16	7 8/16	M	Sussex	NBW	Kamel K. Wozniak, Jr.	1993	590
20 2/16	12 7/16	7 11/16	M	Green Lake	SAS	Pat DeMeglio	1993	590
20 2/16	12 11/16	7 7/16	M	Emo	ONT	James R. Gabrick	1993	590
20 2/16	12 7/16	7 11/16	M	Lincoln County	NM	Dennis Holt	1993	590
20 2/16	12 4/16	7 14/16	M	Green Lake	SAS	John C."Jack" Culpepper III	1994	590
20 2/16	12 6/16	7 12/16	M	Lac Ile-a-la Crosse	SAS	Dr. D. Kirk Brown, MD	1994	590
20 2/16	12 10/16	7 8/16	M	Cranberry Portage	MAN	B. Duane Kropf	1994	590
20 2/16	12 6/16	7 12/16	M	Crow Wing County	MN	Tom Neu	1994	590
20 2/16	12 13/16	7 5/16	M	Otero County	NM	Earl McClaflin	1994	590
20 2/16	12 8/16	7 10/16	M	Red Lake	ONT	Arden L. Straw	1994	590
20 2/16	12 9/16	7 9/16	M	Usherville	SAS	James Scott Todd	1995	590
20 2/16	12 10/16	7 8/16	M	McNalley Lake	ALB	Donald A. Carpenter	1995	590
20 2/16	12 12/16	7 6/16	M	Rainbow Lake	ALB	Edward J. Roskopf	1995	590
20 2/16	12 2/16	8 0/16	M	Thunder Bay	ONT	Ian Robinson	1995	590
20 2/16	12 6/16	7 12/16	M	Besnard Lake	SAS	Andy Milam	1995	590
20 2/16	12 13/16	7 5/16	M	Marathon County	WI	David C. Arndt	1995	590
20 2/16	12 7/16	7 11/16	M	Alma	NBW	Ed Kiker, Jr.	1995	590
20 2/16	12 12/16	7 6/16	M	Kane Lake	SAS	Peeler G. Lacey, MD	1996	590
20 2/16	12 11/16	7 7/16	M	Iron River	ALB	Michael J. Madaj	1996	590
20 2/16	12 5/16	7 13/16	M	Mattawa	ONT	Brian Lafreniere	1996	590
20 2/16	12 8/16	7 10/16	M	Burnett County	WI	Dan Muchow	1996	590
20 2/16	12 7/16	7 11/16	M	Peace River	ALB	Cordie Schlomer	1997	590
20 2/16	12 6/16	7 12/16	M	Chibougamau	QUE	Seth Stevens	1997	590
20 2/16	12 8/16	7 10/16	M	Temiscaming	QUE	H. James Blamy	1997	590
20 1/16	12 9/16	7 8/16	M	Shasta County	CA	Robert G. Sinclair	1967	657
20 1/16	12 5/16	7 12/16	M	Nipigon	ONT	Wilfred J. Ritchie, Jr.	1968	657
20 1/16	12 6/16	7 11/16	M	Vilas County	WI	Ben Jones	1972	657
20 1/16	11 15/16	8 2/16	M	Deep Creek, Ruby	AK	Harry Copeland	1976	657
20 1/16	12 10/16	7 7/16	M	Cowlitz County	WA	Smokey Crews	1976	657
20 1/16	12 10/16	7 7/16	M	Kitsap County	WA	Bud Jones	1977	657
20 1/16	12 4/16	7 13/16	M	Montrose County	CO	Mike Barber	1978	657
20 1/16	12 10/16	7 7/16	M	E. Braintree	MAN	Ed Beamish	1979	657
20 1/16	12 0/16	8 1/16	M	Vilas County	WI	Peter J. Leder	1979	657
20 1/16	12 10/16	7 7/16	M	Grand County	UT	Thomas W. Newman	1979	657
20 1/16	12 4/16	7 13/16	M	Archuleta County	CO	Len Cardinale	1980	657
20 1/16	12 3/16	7 14/16	M	Archuleta County	CO	Judd Cooney	1980	657
20 1/16	12 10/16	7 7/16	M	Mistatim	SAS	Gregory Simoneau	1980	657
20 1/16	12 5/16	7 12/16	M	Fremont County	ID	Nancy Atwood	1981	657
20 1/16	12 6/16	7 11/16	M	Clark County	ID	Garry James Kite	1981	657
20 1/16	12 6/16	7 11/16	M	Hudson Bay	SAS	Jerry Bien	1982	657
20 1/16	12 9/16	7 8/16	M	Glenn County	CA	Ron Fonseca	1982	657
20 1/16	12 6/16	7 11/16	M	Hudson Bay	SAS	Craig Richardson	1982	657
20 1/16	13 0/16	7 1/16	M	Bladen County	NC	R. G. Harris	1983	657
20 1/16	12 8/16	7 9/16	M	Fergus County	MT	Tom Storm	1984	657
20 1/16	12 1/16	8 0/16	M	Powell County	MT	Gene Coughlin	1984	657
20 1/16	12 4/16	7 13/16	M	Lost Lake	ONT	Gunter Lemke	1985	657
20 1/16	12 7/16	7 10/16	M	Lewis County	WA	Keith Heldreth	1985	657
20 1/16	12 5/16	7 12/16	M	Siskiyou County	CA	Stan Allison	1985	657
20 1/16	12 10/16	7 7/16	M	Hudson Bay	SAS	Bill Zahradka	1987	657
20 1/16	12 5/16	7 12/16	M	Ft. McMurray	ALB	Reg Adair	1987	657
20 1/16	12 4/16	7 13/16	M	Sevier County	UT	Tom Dale Harrison	1988	657
20 1/16	12 7/16	7 10/16	M	Carbon County	WY	Bill McEwen	1988	657
20 1/16	12 8/16	7 9/16	M	Ft. McMurray	ALB	Darrin West	1989	657
20 1/16	12 3/16	7 14/16	M	Williams Lake	BC	Don Davidson	1989	657
20 1/16	12 8/16	7 9/16	M	Sioux Lookout	ONT	Jim Graf	1989	657
20 1/16	12 8/16	7 9/16	M	Dryden	ONT	Alan E. Forbes	1989	657
20 1/16	12 11/16	7 6/16	M	Clatsop County	OR	David Soyars	1989	657
20 1/16	12 11/16	7 6/16	M	Keweenaw County	MI	Fred Embry Pickett	1989	657
20 1/16	12 11/16	7 6/16	M	Flatbush	ALB	Steve Neuberger	1990	657
20 1/16	12 8/16	7 9/16	M	Glenfell	ONT	Lucien Fecteau	1990	657
20 1/16	12 9/16	7 8/16	M	Prince of Wales Island	AK	Dennis Sturgis, Jr.	1990	657
20 1/16	12 6/16	7 11/16	M	Aitkin County	MN	William Gene Kuhlman	1990	657
20 1/16	12 2/16	7 15/16	M	Bathurst	NBW	Norbert Legacy	1991	657
20 1/16	12 10/16	7 7/16	M	Tulare County	CA	Dean Grommet	1991	657
20 1/16	12 9/16	7 8/16	M	Union County	OR	Gregg Hargett	1991	657
20 1/16	12 2/16	7 15/16	M	Prince of Wales Island	AK	Don Davidson	1991	657
20 1/16	12 7/16	7 10/16	M	Harney County	OR	Marti Boatman	1991	657
20 1/16	12 15/16	7 2/16	M	Whitemouth Lake	MAN	Serge L. Proulx	1991	657
20 1/16	12 8/16	7 9/16	M	Lynn Lake	MAN	Bill Lilly, Jr.	1993	657
20 1/16	12 5/16	7 12/16	M	Zec Dumoine	QUE	John Ross	1993	657

BLACK BEAR

Minimum Score 18 — Continued

SCORE	GREATEST LENGTH	GREATEST WIDTH	SEX	AREA	STATE/PROVINCE	HUNTER'S NAME	DATE	RANK
20 1/16	12 5/16	7 12/16	M	Humboldt County	CA	Jonathan Owens	1993	657
20 1/16	12 10/16	7 7/16	M	Douglas County	WI	Bob Kaszynski	1993	657
20 1/16	12 6/16	7 11/16	M	Rock Island Lake	ALB	Gilles A. Blouin	1994	657
20 1/16	12 2/16	7 15/16	M	Nestor Falls	ONT	Mark S. Gerstein	1994	657
20 1/16	12 9/16	7 8/16	M	Echo Bay	ONT	William McDonald	1994	657
20 1/16	12 6/16	7 11/16	M	Price County	WI	Dale S. Karch	1994	657
20 1/16	12 8/16	7 9/16	M	Prince of Wales Island	AK	Craig D. Morrow	1995	657
20 1/16	12 8/16	7 9/16	M	Valleyview	ALB	Mark Kobe	1995	657
20 1/16	12 1/16	8 0/16	M	El Dorado County	CA	Michael Davis	1995	657
20 1/16	12 12/16	7 5/16	M	Oxford County	ME	Gary J. Russell	1997	657
20 1/16	12 3/16	7 14/16	M	Buffalo Narrows	SAS	Corey T. Williams	1998	657
20 1/16	12 5/16	7 12/16	M	Prince of Wales Island	AK	Bob Ameen	1998	657
20 1/16	12 14/16	7 3/16	M	Wabasca River	ALB	Mark Kronyak	1998	657
20 1/16	12 4/16	7 13/16	M	Sioux Narrows	ONT	Clint Arndt	1998	657
20 0/16	12 10/16	7 6/16	M	Oneida County	WI	Fred Felbab	1964	717
20 0/16	12 4/16	7 12/16	M	Shasta County	CA	Jim Dougherty	1970	717
20 0/16	13 4/16	6 12/16	M	Cumberland County	TN	Louis Wix	1970	717
20 0/16	12 11/16	7 5/16	M	Fremont County	ID	Earl Peterson	1978	717
20 0/16	12 4/16	7 12/16	M	Kalkaska County	MI	Doug Daniels	1978	717
20 0/16	12 9/16	7 7/16	M	Adams County	ID	Jack Arbaugh	1979	717
20 0/16	12 10/16	7 6/16	M	Tehama County	CA	Jim Dueval	1980	717
20 0/16	12 7/16	7 9/16	M	Prince George	BC	Ron F. McKay	1980	717
20 0/16	12 10/16	7 6/16	M	Ear Falls	ONT	Richard Eldridge	1981	717
20 0/16	12 6/16	7 10/16	M	Red Lake	ONT	Donald Schram	1981	717
20 0/16	12 5/16	7 11/16	M	Grand County	CO	Randy O. Vineyard	1981	717
20 0/16	12 6/16	7 10/16	M	Bobcaygeon	ONT	Arthur H. Whitney	1982	717
20 0/16	12 7/16	7 9/16	M	Sierra County	NM	Ray Hatfield	1983	717
20 0/16	12 5/16	7 11/16	M	Otter Lake	QUE	C. Roger Jerzerick	1983	717
20 0/16	12 3/16	7 13/16	M	Wallowa County	OR	Bill Lancaster	1983	717
20 0/16	12 7/16	7 9/16	M	Itasca County	MN	Roger Millard	1984	717
20 0/16	12 6/16	7 10/16	M	Apache County	AZ	Robert E. David	1984	717
20 0/16	12 8/16	7 8/16	M	Langlade County	WI	Jeff Traska	1984	717
20 0/16	12 2/16	7 14/16	M	Cowlitz County	WA	Annette Crews	1985	717
20 0/16	12 12/16	7 4/16	M	Meadow Lake	SAS	Robert Bain	1986	717
20 0/16	12 3/16	7 13/16	M	Thunder Bay	ONT	Bob Vrbsky	1986	717
20 0/16	12 8/16	7 8/16	M	Caribou County	ID	Coby Tigert	1986	717
20 0/16	12 15/16	7 1/16	M	Aitkin County	MN	Scott H. Mogen	1986	717
20 0/16	12 12/16	7 4/16	M	Rockingham County	VA	Roger Wyant	1986	717
20 0/16	12 8/16	7 8/16	M	Cold Lake	ALB	Glenn Moir	1987	717
20 0/16	12 6/16	7 10/16	M	Pinehurst Lake	ALB	Jay Stewart	1988	717
20 0/16	12 11/16	7 5/16	M	King County	WA	Brent R. Perschon	1988	717
20 0/16	12 11/16	7 5/16	M	Lake of the Woods County	MN	Dallas Vanden Einde	1988	717
20 0/16	12 5/16	7 11/16	M	Gogebic County	MI	Ted Nugent	1988	717
20 0/16	12 6/16	7 10/16	M	Elmore County	ID	Mark E. Zastrow	1989	717
20 0/16	12 5/16	7 11/16	M	Graham Area	ONT	Ian Robinson	1989	717
20 0/16	12 5/16	7 11/16	M	Carbon County	UT	Dave Scott	1989	717
20 0/16	12 4/16	7 12/16	M	Sudbury	ONT	Ray Hatfield	1989	717
20 0/16	12 8/16	7 8/16	M	High Prairie	ALB	Thomas Hlinka	1989	717
20 0/16	12 8/16	7 8/16	M	Wallowa County	OR	Terry Garbacik	1989	717
20 0/16	12 5/16	7 11/16	M	Iron County	WI	R. Joe Maciejewski	1989	717
20 0/16	12 9/16	7 7/16	M	Crawford County	MI	Jerry D. Pratt	1989	717
20 0/16	12 8/16	7 8/16	M	Catron County	NM	Dr. Dale Mansfield	1989	717
20 0/16	12 10/16	7 6/16	M	Ile-a-la-Crosse	SAS	Michael D Tofte	1990	717
20 0/16	12 6/16	7 10/16	M	Kenora	ONT	Steven G. Dennis	1990	717
20 0/16	12 0/16	8 0/16	M	Seibert Lake	ALB	Keith Dana	1990	717
20 0/16	12 6/16	7 10/16	M	Garfield County	CO	Gus Sexauer	1990	717
20 0/16	12 12/16	7 4/16	M	Fraser River	BC	Dave Hannas	1990	717
20 0/16	12 3/16	7 13/16	M	Cowlitz County	WA	Edward H. Soyars	1991	717
20 0/16	12 10/16	7 6/16	M	Pine County	MN	Tom Katt	1991	717
20 0/16	12 6/16	7 10/16	M	Catron County	NM	Bruce Carlisle	1991	717
20 0/16	12 12/16	7 4/16	M	Douglas County	WI	Philip Stener	1991	717
20 0/16	12 7/16	7 9/16	M	Bissett	MAN	David Harris	1992	717
20 0/16	12 12/16	7 4/16	M	Red Earth	ALB	Dave Bathke	1992	717
20 0/16	12 8/16	7 8/16	M	Thompson	MAN	Jack Baltz	1992	717
20 0/16	12 4/16	7 12/16	M	Robinson Township	ONT	Tom Harper	1992	717
20 0/16	12 9/16	7 7/16	M	Hudson Bay	SAS	Lawrence Gulka	1992	717
20 0/16	12 3/16	7 13/16	M	St. Calixte	QUE	Brian D. Hurd	1992	717
20 0/16	12 8/16	7 8/16	M	Dryden	ONT	Bryan Moorefield	1993	717
20 0/16	12 11/16	7 5/16	M	Itasca County	MN	Douglas Anderson	1993	717
20 0/16	12 8/16	7 8/16	M	Pine County	MN	Dean K. Reidt	1993	717
20 0/16	12 7/16	7 9/16	M	High Level	ALB	Keith Corporon	1994	717
20 0/16	12 9/16	7 7/16	M	Fort McMurray	ALB	David W. Stuhr	1994	717
20 0/16	12 7/16	7 9/16	M	Williamson Township	ONT	Maurice Benoit	1994	717
20 0/16	12 2/16	7 14/16	M	Lac Seul	ONT	James Kurth	1994	717
20 0/16	12 6/16	7 10/16	M	Crooked Creek	ALB	Rick Martin	1994	717
20 0/16	12 3/16	7 13/16	M	Carlton County	MN	Tom King	1994	717
20 0/16	12 0/16	8 0/16	M	Oneida County	WI	Chad Leal	1994	717
20 0/16	12 4/16	7 12/16	M	Hornepayne	ONT	Jeff Holland	1995	717

BLACK BEAR

Minimum Score 18 Continued

SCORE	GREATEST LENGTH	GREATEST WIDTH	SEX	AREA	STATE/ PROVINCE	HUNTER'S NAME	DATE	RANK
20 0/16	12 8/16	7 8/16	M	Vancouver Island	BC	Bruce Kuykendall	1995	717
20 0/16	12 0/16	8 0/16	M	Poplarfield	MAN	Edwin J. Smith	1995	717
20 0/16	12 9/16	7 7/16	M	Kahiltna River	AK	Danny J. Germany	1995	717
20 0/16	12 10/16	7 6/16	M	Laurier	MAN	Bobby Joe Furlow	1995	717
20 0/16	12 2/16	7 14/16	M	Rio Arriba County	NM	James Goss, Jr.	1995	717
20 0/16	12 4/16	7 12/16	M	Perrault Falls	ONT	Scott A. Cisewski	1995	717
20 0/16	12 11/16	7 5/16	M	Marquette County	MI	Gary Corlew	1995	717
20 0/16	12 9/16	7 7/16	F	Price County	WI	David Pepper	1995	717
20 0/16	12 5/16	7 11/16	M	Fresno County	CA	Alfredo Flores	1995	717
20 0/16	12 14/16	7 2/16	M	Besnard Lake	SAS	Scotty Reynolds	1996	717
20 0/16	12 7/16	7 9/16	M	Swan River	MAN	David A. Little	1996	717
20 0/16	12 10/16	7 6/16	M	Bayfield County	WI	Blaine Wollin	1996	717
20 0/16	12 15/16	7 1/16	M	Sawyer County	WI	Anthony R. Aaron	1996	717
20 0/16	12 10/16	7 6/16	M	Vermette Lake	SAS	Ronald F. Lax	1997	717
20 0/16	12 9/16	7 7/16	M	Kane Lake	SAS	Richard A. Jacobs	1997	717
20 0/16	12 8/16	7 8/16	M	Tulare County	CA	Frank Birtcher	1997	717
20 0/16	12 10/16	7 6/16	M	Barron County	WI	Kevin M. Giles	1997	717
20 0/16	12 11/16	7 5/16	M	Park County	MT	Larry Schwend	1997	717
20 0/16	12 4/16	7 12/16	M	Snow Lake	MAN	Mike J. Sutter	1998	717
20 0/16	12 7/16	7 9/16	M	Dauphin River	MAN	Reginald Robillard	1998	717
20 0/16	12 10/16	7 6/16	M	Greenlee County	AZ	Michael Wayne Spivey	1998	717
19 15/16	11 15/16	8 0/16	F	Iron County	WI	Robert W. Blair	1967	802
19 15/16	12 0/16	7 15/16	M	Bayfield County	WI	Gary P. Kalal	1973	802
19 15/16	12 7/16	7 8/16	M	Blind River	ONT	John Lee	1973	802
19 15/16	12 8/16	7 7/16	M	Dryden	ONT	Robert C. Kirschner	1974	802
19 15/16	12 3/16	7 12/16	M	Conejos County	CO	Joseph Strasser, Jr.	1978	802
19 15/16	12 4/16	7 11/16	M	Grande Prairie	ALB	Wolf Hoffman	1979	802
19 15/16	12 1/16	7 14/16	M	Gunnison County	CO	Arthur Pace	1980	802
19 15/16	12 8/16	7 7/16	M	Florence County	WI	Peter H. Kortenhorn	1981	802
19 15/16	12 7/16	7 8/16	M	Dolores County	CO	Stanley A. Coval	1981	802
19 15/16	12 2/16	7 13/16	M	Ear Falls	ONT	Mike Woolman	1981	802
19 15/16	11 14/16	8 1/16	M	Penobscot County	ME	Henry C. Williams III	1983	802
19 15/16	12 3/16	7 12/16	M	Sandoval County	NM	James M. Finn	1984	802
19 15/16	12 9/16	7 6/16	M	Burnett County	WI	Jerry Strese	1984	802
19 15/16	12 8/16	7 7/16	M	Baker County	OR	Steven E. Lewis	1986	802
19 15/16	12 0/16	7 15/16	M	Dryden	ONT	Lane Foshee	1987	802
19 15/16	12 4/16	7 11/16	M	Pine County	MN	Randy Broz	1987	802
19 15/16	12 7/16	7 8/16	M	Carrot River	SAS	Ron Gunwall	1988	802
19 15/16	12 1/16	7 14/16	M	Pickerel River	ONT	Walter L. Douglas	1988	802
19 15/16	12 10/16	7 5/16	M	Garfield County	CO	James Bowerman	1988	802
19 15/16	12 13/16	7 2/16	M	Douglas County	WI	Timothy E. Freid	1988	802
19 15/16	12 9/16	7 6/16	M	Chippewa County	MI	Edwin A. Armentrout	1988	802
19 15/16	12 5/16	7 10/16	M	Clearwater County	ID	John H. Dyche	1989	802
19 15/16	12 4/16	7 11/16	M	Grande Prairie	ALB	Ron Jungwirth	1990	802
19 15/16	12 9/16	7 6/16	M	Wahkiakum County	WA	Brandon Casey	1990	802
19 15/16	12 9/16	7 6/16	M	Jackson County	OR	Joe Holland	1990	802
19 15/16	12 9/16	7 6/16	M	Bayfield County	WI	Jeffrey Tuescher	1990	802
19 15/16	12 12/16	7 3/16	M	Rockingham County	VA	Roger O. Wyant	1990	802
19 15/16	12 4/16	7 11/16	M	Torrance County	NM	Eric Montoya	1990	802
19 15/16	12 7/16	7 8/16	M	Prince of Wales Island	AK	Chuck Lynde	1991	802
19 15/16	12 5/16	7 10/16	M	Kenora	ONT	Gary Liebsch	1991	802
19 15/16	12 3/16	7 12/16	M	La Ronge	SAS	James E. Hummel	1992	802
19 15/16	12 7/16	7 8/16	M	Prince of Wales Island	AK	Don Vernay	1992	802
19 15/16	12 2/16	7 13/16	M	Matagami	QUE	Jacques Harvey	1992	802
19 15/16	12 8/16	7 7/16	M	Riding Mtn.	MAN	Robert J. Wech	1992	802
19 15/16	12 5/16	7 10/16	M	Ear Falls	ONT	Fay Williams, Jr.	1992	802
19 15/16	12 8/16	7 7/16	M	Price County	WI	Gary L. Hintz	1992	802
19 15/16	12 3/16	7 12/16	M	Missaukee County	MI	Owen Anderson	1992	802
19 15/16	12 7/16	7 8/16	M	Wapawekka Lake	SAS	Douglas R. Peterson	1993	802
19 15/16	12 5/16	7 10/16	M	Price County	WI	Les Strunk	1993	802
19 15/16	12 2/16	7 13/16	M	Tulare County	CA	Gary W. Thurow	1993	802
19 15/16	12 7/16	7 8/16	M	Entwhistle	ALB	Andre Titley	1994	802
19 15/16	12 8/16	7 7/16	M	McNalley Lake	ALB	Jody Davis	1994	802
19 15/16	12 12/16	7 3/16	M	Carrot River	SAS	Craig Kaczmarek	1994	802
19 15/16	12 4/16	7 11/16	M	Aitkin County	MN	Dennis Winzenburg	1994	802
19 15/16	12 6/16	7 9/16	M	Crawford County	MI	Terry Bart Paladino	1994	802
19 15/16	12 3/16	7 12/16	M	Prince of Wales Island	AK	Bob Ameen	1995	802
19 15/16	12 10/16	7 5/16	M	Trapper Creek	AK	William Simmang	1995	802
19 15/16	12 14/16	7 1/16	M	Frenchman Butte	SAS	Donald Wayne Wright	1996	802
19 15/16	12 5/16	7 10/16	M	Sioux Lookout	ONT	Scott A. Johnson	1996	802
19 15/16	12 8/16	7 7/16	M	Hearst	ONT	Kenneth Neal Onken	1996	802
19 15/16	12 8/16	7 7/16	M	Atikokan	ONT	Lynn Reese	1996	802
19 15/16	12 6/16	7 9/16	M	Chilako River	BC	Emile Matte	1997	802
19 15/16	12 8/16	7 7/16	M	Navajo County	AZ	Alfred J. Gemrich	1997	802
19 15/16	12 4/16	7 11/16	M	Redditt	ONT	Don K. Petersen	1997	802
19 15/16	12 9/16	7 6/16	M	Lake Nipigon	ONT	Andrew Van Timmeren	1997	802
19 15/16	12 6/16	7 9/16	M	Biscotasing	ONT	Thomas Hlinka	1997	802
19 15/16	12 6/16	7 9/16	M	Parry Sound	ONT	Greg Peters	1997	802

BLACK BEAR

Minimum Score 18   Continued

SCORE	GREATEST LENGTH	GREATEST WIDTH	SEX	AREA	STATE/PROVINCE	HUNTER'S NAME	DATE	RANK
19 15/16	12 14/16	7 1/16	M	Grant County	NM	Mike Scarsella	1997	802
19 15/16	12 7/16	7 8/16	M	Elmore County	ID	Bill Magnusson	1997	802
19 15/16	12 8/16	7 7/16	M	Douglas County	WI	David Hudacek	1997	802
19 15/16	12 3/16	7 12/16	M	Missaukee County	MI	Dawn M. Adlen	1997	802
19 15/16	12 5/16	7 10/16	M	Athabasca River	ALB	Leonard Anglewitz	1998	802
19 15/16	12 5/16	7 10/16	M	High Level	ALB	Ray Farley	1998	802
19 15/16	12 5/16	7 10/16	M	Kelvington	SAS	Cameron Hayden	1998	802
19 14/16	12 2/16	7 12/16	M	Routt County	CO	Ronald C. Gravenkemper	1962	866
19 14/16	12 2/16	7 12/16	M	Colcord Mtn.	AZ	Hugh Pearson	1963	866
19 14/16	12 5/16	7 9/16	M	Rio Blanco County	CO	H. R. 'Dutch' Wambold	1969	866
19 14/16	12 4/16	7 10/16	M	La Plata County	CO	Wayne E. Knisley	1971	866
19 14/16	12 12/16	7 2/16	M	Tulare County	CA	Ronald J. Wade	1972	866
19 14/16	12 0/16	7 14/16	M	Mesa County	CO	Clint Johnston	1973	866
19 14/16	12 4/16	7 10/16	M	Ignace	ONT	Thomas Tietz	1977	866
19 14/16	12 6/16	7 8/16	M	Missoula County	MT	Dwayne Garner	1978	866
19 14/16	12 3/16	7 11/16	M	Thunder Bay	ONT	Lester W. Jass	1978	866
19 14/16	12 4/16	7 10/16	M	Routt County	CO	Mark Chapman	1979	866
19 14/16	12 2/16	7 12/16	M	Gunnison County	CO	Robert Feller	1979	866
19 14/16	12 5/16	7 9/16	M	Marinette County	WI	Paul B. Pelzek	1979	866
19 14/16	12 12/16	7 2/16	M	Hudson Bay	SAS	Jerry Bien	1980	866
19 14/16	12 7/16	7 7/16	M	Sandoval County	NM	Mark Johnson	1980	866
19 14/16	12 6/16	7 8/16	M	Baraga County	MI	Thomas G. Young	1981	866
19 14/16	12 6/16	7 8/16	M	Glenn County	CA	Guy W. Foster	1982	866
19 14/16	12 8/16	7 6/16	M	Duck Mtn.	MAN	John 'Jack' Cordes	1983	866
19 14/16	12 5/16	7 9/16	M	Mesa County	CO	Raymond Roussett, Jr.	1983	866
19 14/16	12 5/16	7 9/16	M	Ear Falls	ONT	Brent Allen Poindexter	1985	866
19 14/16	12 11/16	7 3/16	M	Kootenai County	ID	John S. Thomson, Jr.	1986	866
19 14/16	12 4/16	7 10/16	M	Boise County	ID	Scott Privette	1986	866
19 14/16	12 8/16	7 6/16	M	Little Susitna River	AK	Brett Blessing	1986	866
19 14/16	12 5/16	7 9/16	M	Elmore County	ID	Ed Sweet	1988	866
19 14/16	12 3/16	7 11/16	M	Dolores County	CO	Bill Corley	1988	866
19 14/16	12 5/16	7 9/16	M	Warren	ONT	Gary Lawrence Harding	1988	866
19 14/16	12 14/16	7 0/16	M	Douglas County	WI	Dale Jaworski	1988	866
19 14/16	12 4/16	7 10/16	M	Delta County	CO	Rick L. Gillenwater	1989	866
19 14/16	12 7/16	7 7/16	M	Dryden	ONT	Jeffrey R. Beilke	1989	866
19 14/16	12 4/16	7 10/16	M	Green Lake	SAS	Fortunato Cuevas	1989	866
19 14/16	12 7/16	7 7/16	M	Fredericton	NBW	Edward J. Bleau	1989	866
19 14/16	12 4/16	7 10/16	M	Deep River	ONT	Rand J. Moore	1989	866
19 14/16	12 1/16	7 13/16	M	Luce County	MI	Terry L. Cook	1989	866
19 14/16	12 10/16	7 4/16	M	Clearwater County	ID	John M. Ramsey	1990	866
19 14/16	12 7/16	7 7/16	M	Cumberland House	SAS	Jim Jarvis	1991	866
19 14/16	12 5/16	7 9/16	M	Ile-a-la Crosse	SAS	Gary Schwieters	1991	866
19 14/16	12 4/16	7 10/16	M	Grand County	UT	Royce Carroll	1991	866
19 14/16	12 7/16	7 7/16	M	Dryden	ONT	Bruce E. Crocker	1991	866
19 14/16	12 8/16	7 6/16	M	Peace River	ALB	Cal Clevenger	1992	866
19 14/16	12 7/16	7 7/16	M	Frog Lake	ALB	Mark Stevens	1992	866
19 14/16	12 9/16	7 5/16	M	Pine County	MN	Kirk D. Grupa	1992	866
19 14/16	12 10/16	7 4/16	M	Kitsap County	WA	Kenneth W. Holmes	1992	866
19 14/16	12 8/16	7 6/16	M	Sawyer County	WI	Daniel T. Seibert	1992	866
19 14/16	12 4/16	7 10/16	M	Zionville	NBW	Anthony Del Delmastro	1992	866
19 14/16	12 4/16	7 10/16	M	Red Lake	ONT	John W. Flies	1993	866
19 14/16	12 5/16	7 9/16	M	Christopher Lake	SAS	Dr. J. Richard Bland III	1994	866
19 14/16	12 10/16	7 4/16	M	St. Isadore	ALB	Charles R. Leidheiser	1994	866
19 14/16	12 8/16	7 6/16	M	St. Louis County	MN	Mark J. Haus	1994	866
19 14/16	12 6/16	7 8/16	M	Marshall County	MN	Tony Hoglo	1994	866
19 14/16	12 10/16	7 4/16	M	Riding Mtn.	MAN	Mike T. Berceau	1994	866
19 14/16	12 11/16	7 3/16	M	Creighton	SAS	Aaron Abaurrea	1995	866
19 14/16	12 12/16	7 2/16	M	Ear Falls	ONT	John W. Flies	1996	866
19 14/16	12 7/16	7 7/16	M	Carrot River	SAS	Kevin Kaczmarek	1996	866
19 14/16	12 7/16	7 7/16	M	Duck Mtns.	MAN	Al Kuntz	1996	866
19 14/16	12 6/16	7 8/16	M	Price County	WI	William T. Zeman	1996	866
19 14/16	12 12/16	7 2/16	M	Washburn County	WI	Jerre Lerum	1996	866
19 14/16	12 2/16	7 12/16	M	Sioux Lookout	ONT	Randall McPherson	1997	866
19 14/16	12 6/16	7 8/16	M	Kenora	ONT	Dick Schwab	1997	866
19 14/16	12 2/16	7 12/16	M	Falher	ALB	Jody Kellnhofer	1997	866
19 14/16	12 4/16	7 10/16	M	San Juan County	NM	Jim Willems	1997	866
19 14/16	12 5/16	7 9/16	M	Seamore Canal	AK	Jerry Karsky	1998	866
19 14/16	12 10/16	7 4/16	M	Navajo County	AZ	V. Randy Liljenquist	1998	866
19 14/16	12 8/16	7 6/16	M	Archuleta County	CO	Don J. Papczynski	1998	866
19 14/16	12 9/16	7 5/16	M	Shawano County	WI	Brett A. Olson	1998	866
19 13/16	12 7/16	7 6/16	M	Shasta County	CA	Stan L. McIntyre	1968	929
19 13/16	12 4/16	7 9/16	M	Dolores County	CO	Daryl Tieben	1976	929
19 13/16	12 11/16	7 2/16	M	Wawa	ONT	Robert C. McGuire	1977	929
19 13/16	12 7/16	7 6/16	M	Estaire	ONT	David L. Roose	1980	929
19 13/16	12 5/16	7 8/16	M	Bonneville County	ID	Tom Edwards	1981	929
19 13/16	12 6/16	7 7/16	M	Humboldt County	CA	Bill Hofferber	1981	929
19 13/16	12 7/16	7 6/16	M	Douglas County	WI	Richard Peterson	1982	929
19 13/16	12 9/16	7 4/16	M	Tucker County	WV	Robert B. Golightly	1982	929

BLACK BEAR

Minimum Score 18 — Continued — 145

SCORE	GREATEST LENGTH	GREATEST WIDTH	SEX	AREA	STATE/PROVINCE	HUNTER'S NAME	DATE	RANK
19 13/16	12 2/16	7 11/16	M	Beardmore	ONT	Mike Mooney	1984	929
19 13/16	12 11/16	7 2/16	M	Hudson Bay	SAS	Craig Richardson	1985	929
19 13/16	12 4/16	7 9/16	M	Graham	ONT	Todd Henck	1985	929
19 13/16	12 5/16	7 8/16	M	Gallatin County	MT	Lavern Rucker	1985	929
19 13/16	12 6/16	7 7/16	M	Calvin Twp.	ONT	Bob Foulkrod	1986	929
19 13/16	12 3/16	7 10/16	M	Snohomish County	WA	Greg Winters	1986	929
19 13/16	12 8/16	7 5/16	M	Revillagigedo Island	AK	Michael Edwards	1987	929
19 13/16	12 0/16	7 13/16	M	Adies Pond	NFL	Ernest Libby	1988	929
19 13/16	12 4/16	7 9/16	M	Ear Falls	ONT	Rickey L. Morley	1988	929
19 13/16	12 3/16	7 10/16	M	Sexsmith	ALB	Oral Murphy	1989	929
19 13/16	12 5/16	7 8/16	M	Cranberry Portage	MAN	Ron Rogers	1989	929
19 13/16	12 1/16	7 12/16	M	Caramat	ONT	Steven Fowler	1990	929
19 13/16	12 5/16	7 8/16	M	Rio Arriba County	NM	Dwayne Sargent	1990	929
19 13/16	12 8/16	7 5/16	M	Frog Lake	ALB	Darrell Pinske	1991	929
19 13/16	12 13/16	7 0/16	M	Riding Mtn.	MAN	Dean A. Toth	1991	929
19 13/16	12 9/16	7 4/16	M	Sioux Lookout	ONT	Wayne D. Kluver	1992	929
19 13/16	12 5/16	7 8/16	M	Utikamu	ALB	Donald L. DeLong	1992	929
19 13/16	11 15/16	7 14/16	M	Brace Bridge	ONT	David D. Williams	1992	929
19 13/16	12 8/16	7 5/16	M	Spokane County	WA	Rob Culp	1992	929
19 13/16	12 5/16	7 8/16	M	Fergus County	MT	Stephen G. Gilpatrick	1992	929
19 13/16	12 8/16	7 5/16	M	Ashland County	WI	Steven D. Pfaff	1992	929
19 13/16	12 6/16	7 7/16	M	Marinette County	WI	Rick Semrad	1992	929
19 13/16	12 5/16	7 8/16	M	Nakina	ONT	Harry Walker	1992	929
19 13/16	12 9/16	7 4/16	M	Caramat	ONT	John E. Hartwig	1993	929
19 13/16	12 2/16	7 11/16	M	Howley	NFL	Bill Vaznis	1993	929
19 13/16	12 0/16	7 13/16	M	Koochiching County	MN	Jeremy Scott Kalisch	1993	929
19 13/16	12 5/16	7 8/16	M	Green Lake	SAS	Robert B.J. Small	1994	929
19 13/16	12 4/16	7 9/16	M	Madera County	CA	James J. Doherty, Jr.	1994	929
19 13/16	12 5/16	7 8/16	M	Prince of Wales Island	AK	Randall F. Cooley	1994	929
19 13/16	12 1/16	7 12/16	M	The Pas	MAN	Joseph P. Oreskovich	1995	929
19 13/16	12 8/16	7 5/16	M	Sturgeon Landing	SAS	Corey Hugelen	1995	929
19 13/16	12 5/16	7 8/16	M	Snow Lake	MAN	Thomas S. Pierce	1995	929
19 13/16	12 4/16	7 9/16	M	Graham County	AZ	David Wolf	1995	929
19 13/16	12 2/16	7 11/16	M	Missanabie	ONT	Alan J. Shier	1995	929
19 13/16	12 8/16	7 5/16	M	Douglas County	WI	Michael Olsen	1995	929
19 13/16	11 15/16	7 14/16	M	Schoolcraft County	MI	Scott Butler	1995	929
19 13/16	12 7/16	7 6/16	M	Williams Lake	BC	Christopher R. Paquette	1996	929
19 13/16	12 10/16	7 3/16	M	Endeavour	SAS	Lynn R. Jerome	1996	929
19 13/16	12 1/16	7 12/16	M	Buffalo Narrows	SAS	Roland J. Quick	1996	929
19 13/16	12 7/16	7 6/16	M	Athabasca River	ALB	Doy Curtis	1996	929
19 13/16	12 9/16	7 4/16	M	Kearney	ONT	David W. Norton	1996	929
19 13/16	12 8/16	7 5/16	M	Loon Lake	SAS	Philip Muller	1996	929
19 13/16	12 5/16	7 8/16	M	Gander	NFL	John W. Shields	1996	929
19 13/16	12 2/16	7 11/16	M	Rainbow Lake	ALB	R. Lee Williams, M.D.	1996	929
19 13/16	12 4/16	7 9/16	M	Tulare County	CA	Bill Sweetser	1996	929
19 13/16	12 14/16	6 15/16	M	Price County	WI	Fred Grambort	1996	929
19 13/16	12 12/16	7 1/16	M	Ashland County	WI	Chris Gonyo	1996	929
19 13/16	12 5/16	7 8/16	M	Santa Barbara County	CA	Robert D. Snyder	1996	929
19 13/16	12 5/16	7 8/16	M	Prince of Wales Island	AK	Dyrk Eddie	1997	929
19 13/16	12 3/16	7 10/16	M	Bruce	ONT	Bob Phair	1997	929
19 13/16	12 3/16	7 10/16	M	Sioux Narrows	ONT	Phil Perry	1997	929
19 13/16	12 1/16	7 12/16	M	Saddle Hills	ALB	Brad Stewart	1997	929
19 13/16	12 7/16	7 6/16	M	Aroostook County	ME	Rocco Antonelli	1997	929
19 13/16	12 1/16	7 12/16	M	Thurston	ALB	Douglas M. Schalla	1997	929
19 13/16	12 4/16	7 9/16	M	Jackson County	CO	Thomas G. Kelley	1997	929
19 13/16	12 7/16	7 6/16	M	Otero County	NM	Dale E. Guseman	1997	929
19 13/16	12 5/16	7 8/16	M	Bissett	MAN	Michael A. Toncevich	1998	929
19 13/16	12 5/16	7 8/16	M	Madera County	CA	Keith Van Gilder	1998	929
19 12/16	12 2/16	7 10/16	M	Chapleau	ONT	Lawrence Gallagher	1966	995
19 12/16	11 14/16	7 14/16	M	Lake County	MT	Joe Lawrence	1966	995
19 12/16	12 7/16	7 5/16	M	Grand County	UT	Edmund H. Auffhammer	1968	995
19 12/16	12 3/16	7 9/16	M	Chapleau	ONT	Anne M. Fiaschetti	1971	995
19 12/16	12 7/16	7 5/16	M	Catron County	NM	Joe E. Stroube	1971	995
19 12/16	12 4/16	7 8/16	F	Colfax County	NM	Bill Conn, Jr.	1973	995
19 12/16	12 4/16	7 8/16	M	Itasca County	MN	James R. Kroupa	1973	995
19 12/16	12 2/16	7 10/16	M	Conejos County	CO	Michael Miller	1974	995
19 12/16	12 3/16	7 9/16	M	Siskiyou County	CA	Wayne Haley	1975	995
19 12/16	12 6/16	7 6/16	M	Garfield County	CO	David Freeman	1976	995
19 12/16	12 1/16	7 11/16	M	Killarney	ONT	Ken Barnhart	1979	995
19 12/16	12 13/16	6 15/16	M	Crow Wing County	MN	Dave A. Engholm	1980	995
19 12/16	12 8/16	7 4/16	M	Riding Mtn.	MAN	James Carson	1980	995
19 12/16	12 0/16	7 12/16	M	North Bay	ONT	Ronald Gerrits	1980	995
19 12/16	12 5/16	7 7/16	M	Lewis & Clark County	MT	James L. Marlen	1980	995
19 12/16	12 8/16	7 4/16	M	Beluga	AK	John Moline	1980	995
19 12/16	12 4/16	7 8/16	M	Caribou County	ID	Alan G. Smith	1981	995
19 12/16	11 14/16	7 14/16	M	San Juan County	UT	Rick Collard	1982	995
19 12/16	12 7/16	7 5/16	M	The Pas	MAN	Ken Evenson	1983	995
19 12/16	12 3/16	7 9/16	M	Koochiching County	MN	Mike Little	1983	995

BLACK BEAR

Minimum Score 18 — Continued

SCORE	GREATEST LENGTH	GREATEST WIDTH	SEX	AREA	STATE/ PROVINCE	HUNTER'S NAME	DATE	RANK
19 12/16	12 8/16	7 4/16	M	Gogebic County	MI	Steven D. Baker	1983	995
19 12/16	12 4/16	7 8/16	M	Madison County	MT	John Lantow	1984	995
19 12/16	12 10/16	7 2/16	M	Game Area #23	MAN	Gary Kaluzniak	1984	995
19 12/16	12 1/16	7 11/16	M	St. Louis County	MN	Clancy Lindvall	1984	995
19 12/16	12 8/16	7 4/16	M	Union County	OR	Brad Hathaway	1984	995
19 12/16	12 3/16	7 9/16	M	Roseau County	MN	Gregg L. Dirks	1985	995
19 12/16	12 5/16	7 7/16	M	Ignace	ONT	Raymond Nowak, Jr.	1986	995
19 12/16	12 5/16	7 7/16	M	Cass County	MN	Lauren Brorby	1986	995
19 12/16	12 4/16	7 8/16	M	Mesa County	CO	Larry Shoop	1987	995
19 12/16	12 6/16	7 6/16	M	Mesa County	CO	Stephen K. Meredith	1987	995
19 12/16	12 10/16	7 2/16	M	Swan River	MAN	Harrey Bergen	1987	995
19 12/16	12 4/16	7 8/16	M	Westbank	BC	Robert McCulley	1987	995
19 12/16	12 8/16	7 4/16	M	Tucker County	WV	Russell L. James	1987	995
19 12/16	12 8/16	7 4/16	M	Prince of Wales Island	AK	Glen Berry	1988	995
19 12/16	12 6/16	7 6/16	M	Chaffee County	CO	Bob Merciez	1988	995
19 12/16	12 6/16	7 6/16	M	Miles Bay	ONT	Kenneth Rader	1988	995
19 12/16	12 6/16	7 6/16	M	Bear Paw Landing	QUE	Lonnie Rumley	1988	995
19 12/16	12 5/16	7 7/16	M	St. Louis County	MN	Scott Gruhlke	1988	995
19 12/16	12 0/16	7 12/16	M	Amos	QUE	Simon Harvey	1989	995
19 12/16	12 0/16	7 12/16	M	Aitkin County	MN	Scott Dirkes	1989	995
19 12/16	12 1/16	7 11/16	M	Sioux Lookout	ONT	Daniel J. Riegelman	1989	995
19 12/16	12 10/16	7 2/16	M	St. Louis County	MN	Dr Eugene T. Altiere	1989	995
19 12/16	12 4/16	7 8/16	M	Coos County	OR	Russell McCall	1989	995
19 12/16	11 13/16	7 15/16	M	Vilas County	WI	Gary F. Robinson	1989	995
19 12/16	12 11/16	7 1/16	M	Langlade County	WI	Stanley William Janusiewicz	1989	995
19 12/16	12 9/16	7 3/16	M	Prince of Wales Island	AK	Dyrk Eddie	1990	995
19 12/16	12 6/16	7 6/16	M	Athabasca	ALB	Ryk Visscher	1990	995
19 12/16	12 6/16	7 6/16	M	Columbia County	WA	Kenneth Fuller	1990	995
19 12/16	12 4/16	7 8/16	M	Atikokan	ONT	Rick Grooms	1991	995
19 12/16	12 11/16	7 1/16	M	Iron County	MI	Michael A. Samuels	1991	995
19 12/16	12 10/16	7 2/16	M	Newton County	AR	Joel Phillips	1991	995
19 12/16	12 0/16	7 12/16	M	Harcourt Park	ONT	Henry Quittard	1991	995
19 12/16	12 1/16	7 11/16	M	Las Animas County	CO	Garry Woodman	1992	995
19 12/16	12 8/16	7 4/16	M	La Plata County	CO	John L. Gardner	1992	995
19 12/16	12 8/16	7 4/16	M	Vermette Lake	SAS	Eric Erickson	1992	995
19 12/16	12 3/16	7 9/16	M	Lac Kipawa	QUE	Ken H. Taylor	1992	995
19 12/16	12 6/16	7 6/16	M	Manitouwadge	ONT	Dolan D. Waters	1992	995
19 12/16	12 11/16	7 1/16	M	Sawyer County	WI	Rodney Pearson	1992	995
19 12/16	11 15/16	7 13/16	M	Clinton County	NY	Mark Wood	1992	995
19 12/16	12 10/16	7 2/16	M	Prince of Wales Island	AK	George E. Mann	1993	995
19 12/16	12 4/16	7 8/16	M	Prince of Wales Island	AK	Danny Moore	1994	995
19 12/16	12 6/16	7 6/16	M	Peace River	ALB	Peter F. Woeck	1994	995
19 12/16	12 5/16	7 7/16	M	Lynn Lake	MAN	Ernest Gilbert	1994	995
19 12/16	12 8/16	7 4/16	M	Keeley Lake	SAS	Paul J. Sisz	1994	995
19 12/16	12 4/16	7 8/16	M	Umatilla County	OR	Tom Huebner	1994	995
19 12/16	12 6/16	7 6/16	M	Roseau County	MN	Donald Roseen	1994	995
19 12/16	12 5/16	7 7/16	M	St. Louis County	MN	Richard C Ross	1994	995
19 12/16	12 4/16	7 8/16	M	Bissett	MAN	Keith L. Mark	1994	995
19 12/16	12 7/16	7 5/16	M	Brookfield	NS	Jeffrey H. Batula	1994	995
19 12/16	12 8/16	7 4/16	M	Falher	ALB	Stephen L. Collins	1995	995
19 12/16	12 11/16	7 1/16	M	Emo	ONT	Randy Loken	1995	995
19 12/16	12 8/16	7 4/16	M	Bissett	MAN	Mitchell D. Storm	1995	995
19 12/16	11 15/16	7 13/16	M	Bellecombe	QUE	Guy Roy	1995	995
19 12/16	12 9/16	7 3/16	M	Olha	MAN	Mike Lenz	1995	995
19 12/16	12 6/16	7 6/16	M	Athabasca River	ALB	Gerald Cavaliere, Jr.	1995	995
19 12/16	12 8/16	7 4/16	M	Catron County	NM	Lew Webb, Jr.	1995	995
19 12/16	12 4/16	7 8/16	M	Kinwow Bay	MAN	Baird R. Booth	1996	995
19 12/16	12 8/16	7 4/16	M	May Lake	ALB	Terry Ermel	1996	995
19 12/16	12 2/16	7 10/16	M	Longlac	ONT	Harley Krauss	1996	995
19 12/16	12 3/16	7 9/16	M	Dubreuilville	ONT	Randal L. Zorn	1996	995
19 12/16	12 14/16	6 14/16	M	Swan River	MAN	Archie J. Nesbitt	1996	995
19 12/16	12 7/16	7 5/16	M	King County	WA	Brad Thomsen	1996	995
19 12/16	12 6/16	7 6/16	M	Koochiching County	MN	Jesse Turck	1996	995
19 12/16	12 8/16	7 4/16	M	Nakina	ONT	Bob Wind	1996	995
19 12/16	12 1/16	7 11/16	M	Franklin County	NY	Walter Tanzini	1996	995
19 12/16	12 13/16	6 15/16	M	Douglas County	WI	Ken Bjorge	1996	995
19 12/16	12 9/16	7 3/16	M	Polk County	AR	Keith W. Brown	1996	995
19 12/16	12 8/16	7 4/16	M	Athabasca River	ALB	Robert B. Stryker	1997	995
19 12/16	12 9/16	7 3/16	M	Saddle Hills	ALB	Allen Avery	1997	995
19 12/16	12 5/16	7 7/16	M	Nicholas County	WV	Robert Trygstad	1997	995
19 12/16	12 7/16	7 5/16	M	Prince of Wales Island	AK	E. Lance Whary	1998	995
19 12/16	11 15/16	7 13/16	M	Pakwash Lake	ONT	Charles Dunn	1998	995
19 12/16	12 10/16	7 2/16	M	Wanless	MAN	Travis Tharp	1998	995
19 11/16	12 3/16	7 8/16	M	Atikokan	ONT	Dennis Gregory	1967	1,088
19 11/16	12 2/16	7 9/16	M	Montezuma County	CO	Marvin Reichenau	1972	1,088
19 11/16	12 3/16	7 8/16	M	La Plata County	CO	Robert L. Everett	1973	1,088
19 11/16	12 4/16	7 7/16	M	Larimer County	CO	Lee Kline	1974	1,088
19 11/16	11 15/16	7 12/16	M	Chapleau	ONT	Donald E. Meushaw	1975	1,088

BLACK BEAR

Minimum Score 18 — Continued

SCORE	GREATEST LENGTH	GREATEST WIDTH	SEX	AREA	STATE/PROVINCE	HUNTER'S NAME	DATE	RANK
19 11/16	12 9/16	7 2/16	M	Montezuma County	CO	Marvin Reichenau	1976	1,088
19 11/16	12 11/16	7 0/16	M	Garfield County	CO	C. David Wix	1976	1,088
19 11/16	12 4/16	7 7/16	M	Somerset County	ME	Anthony Carratura	1977	1,088
19 11/16	12 4/16	7 7/16	M	Washington County	ME	Charles Hardish	1977	1,088
19 11/16	12 0/16	7 11/16	M	Ignace	ONT	John Dmytryka	1978	1,088
19 11/16	12 6/16	7 5/16	M	Itasca County	MN	Daniel "Boone" Bell	1979	1,088
19 11/16	11 11/16	8 0/16	M	Washington County	ME	Gary Farquhar	1979	1,088
19 11/16	12 1/16	7 10/16	M	Boise County	ID	Michael Sherer	1981	1,088
19 11/16	11 14/16	7 13/16	M	Essex County	NY	Paul Durling	1981	1,088
19 11/16	12 5/16	7 6/16	M	Prince of Wales Island	AK	Doug Miller	1982	1,088
19 11/16	12 3/16	7 8/16	M	Gunflint Lake	ONT	Kelly Wilhelmi	1982	1,088
19 11/16	12 1/16	7 10/16	M	Routt County	CO	Guenter Hackl	1983	1,088
19 11/16	12 11/16	7 0/16	M	Boise County	ID	L. Dean Goodner	1983	1,088
19 11/16	12 5/16	7 6/16	M	Dickinson County	MI	Mike Vandeven	1983	1,088
19 11/16	12 0/16	7 11/16	M	Archuleta County	CO	Britton F. Kelley, Jr.	1984	1,088
19 11/16	12 0/16	7 11/16	M	Sioux Lookout	ONT	James E. Tiefenthaler	1984	1,088
19 11/16	11 7/16	8 4/16	M	Gogama	ONT	Frank E. Brinton IV	1985	1,088
19 11/16	11 15/16	7 12/16	M	Cascaden	ONT	Ronnie Long	1985	1,088
19 11/16	12 6/16	7 5/16	M	Garfield County	CO	Paul B. Walker	1986	1,088
19 11/16	12 0/16	7 11/16	M	Sudbury	ONT	Wendell L. DeWitt	1987	1,088
19 11/16	12 7/16	7 4/16	M	Nestor Falls	ONT	Martin J. Weber	1987	1,088
19 11/16	12 3/16	7 8/16	M	Valley County	ID	Jon Vanderhoef	1987	1,088
19 11/16	12 7/16	7 4/16	M	Marinette County	WI	Tim H. Boucher	1988	1,088
19 11/16	12 3/16	7 8/16	M	Forest County	WI	Tim B. Olk	1988	1,088
19 11/16	12 5/16	7 6/16	M	Carbon County	UT	Bill Mamales	1989	1,088
19 11/16	12 8/16	7 3/16	M	Ester Passage	AK	Don Williams	1989	1,088
19 11/16	12 6/16	7 5/16	M	Grand County	UT	Paul Ensz	1989	1,088
19 11/16	12 5/16	7 6/16	M	Dryden	ONT	Jack T. Wolf	1989	1,088
19 11/16	12 5/16	7 6/16	M	Blair	ONT	Douglass J. Street	1989	1,088
19 11/16	12 6/16	7 5/16	M	Alcona County	MI	Fred Eugene Upperstrom	1989	1,088
19 11/16	12 7/16	7 4/16	M	Cynthia	ALB	Bert Skulmoski	1990	1,088
19 11/16	12 1/16	7 10/16	M	Thaddeus Lake	ONT	Gary R. Ziesmer	1990	1,088
19 11/16	12 12/16	6 15/16	M	Green Lake	SAS	Richard P. Smith	1991	1,088
19 11/16	12 2/16	7 9/16	M	Fort McMurray	ALB	Edward Smith	1991	1,088
19 11/16	11 15/16	7 12/16	M	Madison County	MT	Larry Rather	1991	1,088
19 11/16	12 4/16	7 7/16	M	Prince of Wales Island	AK	Don Youngblood	1992	1,088
19 11/16	12 8/16	7 3/16	M	Lake of the Woods	ONT	Earl Fulkerson	1992	1,088
19 11/16	11 14/16	7 13/16	M	Vancouver Island	BC	Richard P. Smith	1992	1,088
19 11/16	12 7/16	7 4/16	M	Fort McMurray	ALB	Steve Swinhoe	1992	1,088
19 11/16	12 1/16	7 10/16	M	Harvey Station	NBW	Dennis Hayden	1992	1,088
19 11/16	12 2/16	7 9/16	M	Sideburn Lake	ONT	David Jerome Miller	1992	1,088
19 11/16	12 4/16	7 7/16	M	Lincoln County	MT	Gary C. Cargill	1992	1,088
19 11/16	12 5/16	7 6/16	M	Prince of Wales Island	AK	Joe K. Lilley	1993	1,088
19 11/16	12 9/16	7 2/16	M	Torch River	SAS	Floyd Forster	1993	1,088
19 11/16	12 2/16	7 9/16	M	McNulty Lake	ONT	Alexander (Sandy) MacPherson	1993	1,088
19 11/16	12 12/16	6 15/16	M	Pine County	MN	Roger Glenn Rarick	1993	1,088
19 11/16	12 11/16	7 0/16	M	Florence County	WI	William Schommer	1993	1,088
19 11/16	12 1/16	7 10/16	M	Carroll County	NH	Jack Smith	1993	1,088
19 11/16	12 8/16	7 3/16	M	Wood County	WI	Jack Rueth	1993	1,088
19 11/16	12 4/16	7 7/16	M	Shole Cove	AK	Jeffrey C. Kinney	1994	1,088
19 11/16	12 0/16	7 11/16	M	Hallam Township	ONT	Barry Vondette	1994	1,088
19 11/16	12 7/16	7 4/16	M	File Lake	MAN	Bobby Harrell	1994	1,088
19 11/16	12 0/16	7 11/16	M	Forestville	QUE	Marty Adams	1994	1,088
19 11/16	12 8/16	7 3/16	M	Waldo County	ME	Robert J. Amaral	1994	1,088
19 11/16	12 6/16	7 5/16	M	Polk County	MN	Dana C. Klos	1994	1,088
19 11/16	12 3/16	7 8/16	M	Chalk River	ONT	Kirk McCutcheon	1995	1,088
19 11/16	12 1/16	7 10/16	M	Weyackwin	SAS	Joseph L. Wright	1995	1,088
19 11/16	12 6/16	7 5/16	M	Oak Lake	ONT	Mike Guenther	1995	1,088
19 11/16	12 1/16	7 10/16	M	Smooth Stone Lake	SAS	Vance A. Fairhurst	1995	1,088
19 11/16	12 12/16	6 15/16	M	Rossburn	MAN	Barry Minshull	1995	1,088
19 11/16	12 5/16	7 6/16	M	Bayfield County	WI	Arthur E. Hyde	1995	1,088
19 11/16	12 10/16	7 1/16	M	Beaverdam	ALB	Randy Babey	1996	1,088
19 11/16	12 3/16	7 8/16	M	Wrangell	AK	Chris Staniar	1996	1,088
19 11/16	12 11/16	7 0/16	M	Olha	MAN	Thomas Blanchard	1996	1,088
19 11/16	12 9/16	7 2/16	M	Price County	WI	Scott Lewandowski	1996	1,088
19 11/16	12 6/16	7 5/16	M	Meagher County	MT	Billy Howard	1996	1,088
19 11/16	12 0/16	7 11/16	M	Iron County	WI	Tom Brewczynski	1997	1,088
19 11/16	12 5/16	7 6/16	M	Crawford County	MI	Christopher J. Scott	1997	1,088
19 11/16	12 5/16	7 6/16	M	Meadow Lake	SAS	Lyle Sheppard	1998	1,088
19 11/16	12 7/16	7 4/16	M	Fort McMurray	ALB	Terry C. Parkinson	1998	1,088
19 11/16	12 10/16	7 1/16	M	Stenen	SAS	David B. Cull	1998	1,088
19 11/16	12 4/16	7 7/16	M	Lakeville	NBW	Kevin Gallagher	1998	1,088
19 11/16	12 9/16	7 2/16	M	Fremont County	ID	Aaron Bateman	1998	1,088
19 11/16	12 6/16	7 5/16	M	Savant Lake	ONT	Ken Nelms	1998	1,088
19 11/16	12 8/16	7 3/16	M	Rossburn	MAN	Adam Bartsch	1998	1,088
19 10/16	12 0/16	7 10/16	M	Lincoln County	NM	David B. Terk	1964	1,168
19 10/16	12 6/16	7 4/16	M	Iron County	WI	William Tutt	1966	1,168
19 10/16	12 10/16	7 0/16	M	Madera County	CA	John D. Faulconer	1971	1,168

BLACK BEAR

Minimum Score 18 — Continued

SCORE	GREATEST LENGTH	GREATEST WIDTH	SEX	AREA	STATE/ PROVINCE	HUNTER'S NAME	DATE	RANK
19 10/16	12 2/16	7 8/16	M	Nez Perce County	ID	Bob Gulman	1972	1,168
19 10/16	12 4/16	7 6/16	M	Forest County	WI	James L. Rablin	1972	1,168
19 10/16	12 7/16	7 3/16	M	Boise County	ID	Jimmie DeSaro, Jr.	1975	1,168
19 10/16	12 4/16	7 6/16	M	LaRonge	SAS	David L. Miller	1976	1,168
19 10/16	11 13/16	7 13/16	M	El Paso County	CO	Billy Mulholland	1976	1,168
19 10/16	12 6/16	7 4/16	M	Sandilands	MAN	Jerry Parizek	1976	1,168
19 10/16	12 4/16	7 6/16	M	Gunnison County	CO	Travis L. Wakefield	1977	1,168
19 10/16	12 2/16	7 8/16	M	St. Louis County	MN	Richard G. Butters	1979	1,168
19 10/16	12 6/16	7 4/16	M	Grand County	UT	Sam Nesi, Jr.	1979	1,168
19 10/16	12 12/16	6 14/16	M	Itasca County	MN	Gordon Steffen	1979	1,168
19 10/16	12 3/16	7 7/16	M	Trinity County	CA	Willis Duhon	1981	1,168
19 10/16	11 12/16	7 14/16	M	Fort Frances	ONT	Ron Carlson	1982	1,168
19 10/16	12 2/16	7 8/16	M	Vermillion Bay	ONT	Dean Hamilton	1983	1,168
19 10/16	12 2/16	7 8/16	M	Siskiyou County	CA	Jerry Martinez	1983	1,168
19 10/16	12 11/16	6 15/16	M	Iron County	MI	Leslie Vorpahl	1983	1,168
19 10/16	12 9/16	7 1/16	M	Sioux Lookout	ONT	Larry J. Selzler	1984	1,168
19 10/16	12 6/16	7 4/16	M	Langlade County	WI	Thomas Radtke	1984	1,168
19 10/16	12 5/16	7 5/16	M	Archuleta County	CO	Joel L. Duncan	1986	1,168
19 10/16	12 1/16	7 9/16	M	Lanark	ONT	Elmer M. Hagood, Jr.	1986	1,168
19 10/16	12 4/16	7 6/16	M	Sudbury	ONT	Richard W. Dohm	1987	1,168
19 10/16	12 3/16	7 7/16	M	Woody Lake	SAS	L. 'Andy' Anderson	1987	1,168
19 10/16	12 2/16	7 8/16	M	Gallatin County	MT	Frank W. Holland	1987	1,168
19 10/16	12 4/16	7 6/16	M	Siskiyou County	CA	Jeff Buck	1987	1,168
19 10/16	13 1/16	6 9/16	M	Limestone Lake	ONT	Steve Schwarzkopf	1988	1,168
19 10/16	12 5/16	7 5/16	M	Squaw Rapids	SAS	Phillip M. Revering	1988	1,168
19 10/16	12 8/16	7 2/16	M	Oxford County	ME	Richard Grannis	1988	1,168
19 10/16	12 5/16	7 5/16	M	Clearwater River	BC	Michael H. Ritcey	1988	1,168
19 10/16	12 4/16	7 6/16	M	Valley County	ID	Robert Dowen	1989	1,168
19 10/16	12 9/16	7 1/16	M	Archuleta County	CO	Ron R. Maez	1989	1,168
19 10/16	12 4/16	7 6/16	M	Smeaton	SAS	Gene A. Welle	1990	1,168
19 10/16	12 2/16	7 8/16	M	Vivian	MAN	Erik Thienpondt	1990	1,168
19 10/16	12 4/16	7 6/16	M	Grande Prairie	ALB	Tom Zimmerman	1990	1,168
19 10/16	12 2/16	7 8/16	M	Wawa	ONT	Edwin L. DeYoung	1990	1,168
19 10/16	12 2/16	7 8/16	M	Troy Lake	MAN	Derek McCarthy	1990	1,168
19 10/16	12 5/16	7 5/16	M	Canterbury	NBW	Don Rahe	1990	1,168
19 10/16	12 2/16	7 8/16	M	Gila County	AZ	Amos Culbert	1990	1,168
19 10/16	12 2/16	7 8/16	M	La Plata County	CO	John L. Gardner	1990	1,168
19 10/16	12 6/16	7 4/16	M	Gila County	AZ	Warren Mark Smith	1990	1,168
19 10/16	12 8/16	7 2/16	M	Cordova	AK	Tony Casagrande	1990	1,168
19 10/16	12 2/16	7 8/16	M	Kosciusko Island	AK	Rob Seelye	1991	1,168
19 10/16	12 7/16	7 3/16	M	The Pas	MAN	Marvin Weible	1991	1,168
19 10/16	12 5/16	7 5/16	M	Thompson	MAN	Thomas P. Rabette	1991	1,168
19 10/16	12 1/16	7 9/16	M	Athabasca River	ALB	Bruce R. Schoeneweis	1991	1,168
19 10/16	12 3/16	7 7/16	M	Taylors Brook	NFL	Thomas Spero	1991	1,168
19 10/16	12 8/16	7 2/16	M	Clinton County	NY	Jim Provost	1991	1,168
19 10/16	12 5/16	7 5/16	M	Sechelt	BC	Ken Davidson	1992	1,168
19 10/16	12 8/16	7 2/16	M	Beluga River	AK	James R. Bussell	1992	1,168
19 10/16	12 6/16	7 4/16	M	Thurston County	WA	Curt L. Lake	1992	1,168
19 10/16	12 1/16	7 9/16	M	Ear Falls	ONT	Robert J. Skorupski	1992	1,168
19 10/16	12 8/16	7 2/16	M	Coos County	NH	Paul Michaud	1992	1,168
19 10/16	12 2/16	7 8/16	M	Dryden	ONT	Mike Barkac	1992	1,168
19 10/16	12 4/16	7 6/16	M	Swan River	MAN	Jeff Glaser	1992	1,168
19 10/16	12 2/16	7 8/16	M	St. Louis County	MN	Kenneth G. Larsen	1992	1,168
19 10/16	12 2/16	7 8/16	M	Las Animas County	CO	Lonny Stuht	1992	1,168
19 10/16	12 3/16	7 7/16	M	Delta County	MI	Ronald J. Sharkey	1992	1,168
19 10/16	12 2/16	7 8/16	M	Nestor Falls	ONT	Roy R. Loomis	1993	1,168
19 10/16	11 12/16	7 14/16	M	Wabowden	MAN	Ken Whitney	1993	1,168
19 10/16	11 15/16	7 11/16	M	Green Lake	SAS	Ray Murphy	1993	1,168
19 10/16	12 0/16	7 10/16	M	Besnard Lake	SAS	Travis Todd	1993	1,168
19 10/16	11 14/16	7 12/16	M	Hastings	ONT	Robert L. Moon, Jr.	1993	1,168
19 10/16	12 2/16	7 8/16	M	Thunder Bay	ONT	Joseph Scott Mandel	1993	1,168
19 10/16	12 5/16	7 5/16	M	Catron County	NM	Mark Rucker	1993	1,168
19 10/16	12 6/16	7 4/16	M	Sullivan County	NY	Theresa Henriksen	1993	1,168
19 10/16	11 9/16	8 1/16	M	Buffalo Narrows	SAS	Bill Rethage	1994	1,168
19 10/16	12 8/16	7 2/16	M	Sturgeon Landing	SAS	Ryan Hugelen	1994	1,168
19 10/16	12 1/16	7 9/16	M	Silver Valley	ALB	Walter Krom	1994	1,168
19 10/16	12 3/16	7 7/16	M	Lemhi County	ID	Michael Judas	1995	1,168
19 10/16	12 3/16	7 7/16	M	La Ronge	SAS	Steve Hammond	1995	1,168
19 10/16	12 5/16	7 5/16	M	Carrot River	SAS	Ronald Gullickson	1995	1,168
19 10/16	12 7/16	7 3/16	M	Tuolumne County	CA	David R. Krawchuk	1995	1,168
19 10/16	11 12/16	7 14/16	M	El Dorado County	CA	Rick L. Self	1995	1,168
19 10/16	12 4/16	7 6/16	M	Atikokan	ONT	Ted Bower	1995	1,168
19 10/16	12 8/16	7 2/16	M	Sioux Narrows	ONT	Gary W. Bishop	1995	1,168
19 10/16	12 2/16	7 8/16	M	Madera County	CA	Jim Doherty, Jr.	1995	1,168
19 10/16	12 4/16	7 6/16	M	Prince of Wales Island	AK	Danny Moore	1996	1,168
19 10/16	12 0/16	7 10/16	M	Birch Mtns.	ALB	John "Jack" Nothardt	1996	1,168
19 10/16	11 14/16	7 12/16	M	Jellicoe	ONT	Dale Long	1996	1,168
19 10/16	12 7/16	7 3/16	M	Sawyer County	WI	David Fetting	1996	1,168

BLACK BEAR

Minimum Score 18 — Continued

SCORE	GREATEST LENGTH	GREATEST WIDTH	SEX	AREA	STATE/PROVINCE	HUNTER'S NAME	DATE	RANK
19 10/16	12 8/16	7 2/16	M	Bayfield County	WI	Jerald Smith	1996	1,168
19 10/16	12 2/16	7 8/16	M	Los Angeles County	CA	David Whiteman	1996	1,168
19 10/16	12 3/16	7 7/16	M	Clarke Lake	SAS	Robert C. Braun	1997	1,168
19 10/16	12 15/16	6 11/16	M	Kelvington	SAS	Leamon Ferrell	1997	1,168
19 10/16	12 5/16	7 5/16	M	Woodcamp Creek	AK	George Grovhoug	1997	1,168
19 10/16	12 4/16	7 6/16	M	Peace River	ALB	Zig Kertenis, Jr.	1997	1,168
19 10/16	12 3/16	7 7/16	M	Peace River	ALB	Cordie Schlomer	1997	1,168
19 10/16	11 11/16	7 15/16	M	Wabigoon	ONT	Enoch S. Studley, Jr.	1997	1,168
19 10/16	12 11/16	6 15/16	M	Menominee County	MI	Dean R. Heath	1997	1,168
19 10/16	12 5/16	7 5/16	M	Clearwater County	ID	Kevin Schmid	1998	1,168
19 10/16	11 15/16	7 11/16	M	Black River	ONT	Jack Leggo	1998	1,168
19 9/16	12 10/16	6 15/16	M	Douglas County	WI	Edwin Fitzgerald	1966	1,260
19 9/16	12 6/16	7 3/16	M	Grand County	CO	Judd Cooney	1967	1,260
19 9/16	12 0/16	7 9/16	M	Ignace	ONT	Gordon Bentley	1968	1,260
19 9/16	11 15/16	7 10/16	M	Idaho County	ID	Kenneth Wallenberg	1970	1,260
19 9/16	11 9/16	8 0/16	M	Boise County	ID	Ronald L. Sherer	1971	1,260
19 9/16	12 1/16	7 8/16	M	Blount County	TN	Gary Jordan	1973	1,260
19 9/16	12 5/16	7 4/16	M	Franklin County	ME	Ralph Pfister	1977	1,260
19 9/16	11 9/16	8 0/16	M	Boise County	ID	Susan D. Sherer	1978	1,260
19 9/16	12 4/16	7 5/16	M	Idaho County	ID	Bob Jacobsen	1979	1,260
19 9/16	12 4/16	7 5/16	M	Valley County	ID	L. Dean Goodner	1979	1,260
19 9/16	11 11/16	7 14/16	M	Sandilands	MAN	Ron Derlago	1979	1,260
19 9/16	12 4/16	7 5/16	M	Grand County	CO	Leonard L. Kohan	1980	1,260
19 9/16	12 0/16	7 9/16	M	Pitkin County	CO	Judy Nielsen	1981	1,260
19 9/16	11 11/16	7 14/16	M	Bobcaygeon	ONT	Dale W. Gray	1982	1,260
19 9/16	12 4/16	7 5/16	M	Ear Falls	ONT	Grant A. Poindexter	1982	1,260
19 9/16	12 0/16	7 9/16	M	Ft. Wainwright	AK	Gregory Dean Royse	1983	1,260
19 9/16	12 4/16	7 5/16	M	Coconino County	AZ	Dale H. Long	1983	1,260
19 9/16	12 5/16	7 4/16	M	Sawyer County	WI	Richard Carolfi	1983	1,260
19 9/16	12 3/16	7 6/16	M	Mesa County	CO	Jeff Tedore	1984	1,260
19 9/16	12 8/16	7 1/16	M	Beluga River	AK	Chad Burris	1984	1,260
19 9/16	12 5/16	7 4/16	M	Itasca County	MN	Dennis K. Fideldy	1984	1,260
19 9/16	12 6/16	7 3/16	M	Uintah County	UT	John C. Matejov	1985	1,260
19 9/16	12 6/16	7 3/16	M	La Tuque	QUE	John C. Hutchinson	1986	1,260
19 9/16	12 5/16	7 4/16	M	Bonneville County	ID	Larry C Ross	1986	1,260
19 9/16	12 7/16	7 2/16	M	Washington County	ME	Cliff Wiseman	1986	1,260
19 9/16	12 7/16	7 2/16	M	Hudson Bay	SAS	Bill Zahradka	1987	1,260
19 9/16	12 1/16	7 8/16	M	Kenora	ONT	Scott A. Lamphier	1987	1,260
19 9/16	12 5/16	7 4/16	M	Atikokan	ONT	Lawrence A. Meyers	1987	1,260
19 9/16	12 5/16	7 4/16	M	Fort Coulonge	QUE	Harvey D. Garrett	1988	1,260
19 9/16	12 1/16	7 8/16	M	Barron County	WI	Dennis O. Freid	1988	1,260
19 9/16	12 10/16	6 15/16	M	Taylor County	WI	Rick Smith	1988	1,260
19 9/16	12 4/16	7 5/16	M	Emmet County	MI	Randall J. McCune	1988	1,260
19 9/16	12 2/16	7 7/16	M	Madison County	MT	Gary R. Petty	1988	1,260
19 9/16	12 1/16	7 8/16	M	Prince of Wales Island	AK	Carl E. Brent	1989	1,260
19 9/16	11 11/16	7 14/16	M	Las Animas County	CO	R. L. Erdmann	1989	1,260
19 9/16	12 4/16	7 5/16	M	Killala Lake	ONT	Orrin Malick	1989	1,260
19 9/16	12 9/16	7 0/16	M	Saint John	NBW	Mike L. LaVan	1989	1,260
19 9/16	11 15/16	7 10/16	M	Fort Coulonge	QUE	J. J. Fegan	1989	1,260
19 9/16	12 1/16	7 8/16	M	Carrot River	SAS	Quince Hale	1989	1,260
19 9/16	12 7/16	7 2/16	M	Prince of Wales Island	AK	Dan E. Hiltz	1989	1,260
19 9/16	12 11/16	6 14/16	M	Messines	QUE	Charles L. Hart III	1989	1,260
19 9/16	12 6/16	7 3/16	M	Kings County	NBW	Ernest Sperl	1989	1,260
19 9/16	12 5/16	7 4/16	M	Mowat Township	ONT	Ricky McDaniel	1990	1,260
19 9/16	12 1/16	7 8/16	M	Boise County	ID	James L. Sullivan	1990	1,260
19 9/16	12 5/16	7 4/16	M	Madison County	ID	Rita Harris	1990	1,260
19 9/16	11 15/16	7 10/16	M	Lac Flavrian	QUE	Eric Grandbois	1990	1,260
19 9/16	12 5/16	7 4/16	M	Somerset County	ME	Gregory A. Bonecutter, Sr.	1990	1,260
19 9/16	12 1/16	7 8/16	M	Lake of the Woods County	MN	Brian McGregor	1990	1,260
19 9/16	12 0/16	7 9/16	M	Sudbury	ONT	Jim Bratton	1991	1,260
19 9/16	12 0/16	7 9/16	M	High Level	ALB	R. E. Smith	1991	1,260
19 9/16	11 13/16	7 12/16	M	Leaf River	QUE	Gary Kjellander	1991	1,260
19 9/16	12 4/16	7 5/16	M	St. Louis County	MN	Edwin John Durushia	1991	1,260
19 9/16	12 4/16	7 5/16	M	Dolores County	CO	Jay Jaburg	1991	1,260
19 9/16	12 2/16	7 7/16	M	Routt County	CO	Bob Sanders	1991	1,260
19 9/16	12 9/16	7 0/16	M	Logan Lake	BC	Abe Dougan	1992	1,260
19 9/16	12 5/16	7 4/16	M	Remigny	QUE	Steve Reedy	1992	1,260
19 9/16	12 0/16	7 9/16	M	Lynn Lake	MAN	Ernest B. Gilbert	1993	1,260
19 9/16	12 3/16	7 6/16	M	Kipawa	QUE	John Mascellino	1993	1,260
19 9/16	12 6/16	7 3/16	M	Hector Lake	ONT	Dick Clark	1994	1,260
19 9/16	11 15/16	7 10/16	M	Ena Lake	SAS	John R. Burgher	1994	1,260
19 9/16	12 4/16	7 5/16	M	Holinshead Lake	ONT	Michael Kemp	1995	1,260
19 9/16	12 2/16	7 7/16	M	Lake Nameigos	ONT	Jeffrey T. Schwartz	1995	1,260
19 9/16	11 15/16	7 10/16	M	Mendocino County	CA	Michael J. Camp	1995	1,260
19 9/16	12 7/16	7 2/16	M	Bayfield County	WI	Roger Lemler	1995	1,260
19 9/16	12 6/16	7 3/16	M	Rio Arriba County	NM	Rick Thaden	1995	1,260
19 9/16	12 6/16	7 3/16	M	Slave Lake	ALB	Terry C. Parkinson	1996	1,260
19 9/16	12 5/16	7 4/16	M	Conklin	ALB	Tom Nelson	1996	1,260

BLACK BEAR

Minimum Score 18 — Continued

SCORE	GREATEST LENGTH	GREATEST WIDTH	SEX	AREA	STATE/PROVINCE	HUNTER'S NAME	DATE	RANK
19 9/16	12 1/16	7 8/16	M	Wawang Lake	ONT	Jeffrey J. Rhinehart	1996	1,260
19 9/16	12 2/16	7 7/16	M	Poplarfield	MAN	Jim Jepson	1996	1,260
19 9/16	12 6/16	7 3/16	M	Indian River	AK	Rick Schikora	1996	1,260
19 9/16	12 4/16	7 5/16	M	Aroostook County	ME	Mike Bacher	1996	1,260
19 9/16	12 4/16	7 5/16	M	Chippewa County	WI	Matthew T. Hussin	1996	1,260
19 9/16	12 4/16	7 5/16	M	Iron County	WI	Dennis J. Kaderavek	1996	1,260
19 9/16	12 3/16	7 6/16	M	Weymouth	NS	Paul I. Scott	1996	1,260
19 9/16	12 7/16	7 2/16	M	Burnett County	WI	Scott J. Strese	1996	1,260
19 9/16	12 5/16	7 4/16	M	Athabasca River	ALB	Russell Thornberry	1997	1,260
19 9/16	12 3/16	7 6/16	M	Jogues	ONT	Dennis L. Fulcer	1997	1,260
19 9/16	12 0/16	7 9/16	M	Lemhi County	ID	Brian Oestreich	1997	1,260
19 9/16	11 12/16	7 13/16	M	Preissac	QUE	Paul Sedera	1997	1,260
19 9/16	12 10/16	6 15/16	M	Kittitas County	WA	Dave Boothman	1997	1,260
19 9/16	11 15/16	7 10/16	M	Greenlee County	AZ	Woody Kazlo	1997	1,260
19 9/16	12 8/16	7 1/16	M	Duck Mtn.	MAN	Robert J. Fox	1998	1,260
19 9/16	12 7/16	7 2/16	M	Bissett	MAN	Robert W. Harris	1998	1,260
19 9/16	11 15/16	7 10/16	M	Chipewyan Lake	ALB	David D. Manuszak	1998	1,260
19 9/16	12 4/16	7 5/16	M	Sussex	NBW	Harold Croteau	1998	1,260
19 8/16	12 3/16	7 5/16	M	Chapleau	ONT	Bob Sharpe	1959	1,345
19 8/16	12 4/16	7 4/16	M	Presque Isle County	MI	Eugene W. McKechnie	1964	1,345
19 8/16	12 6/16	7 2/16	M	Forest County	WI	Jerad Dittrich	1965	1,345
19 8/16	12 1/16	7 7/16	M	Piscataquis County	ME	James Matulis	1967	1,345
19 8/16	12 6/16	7 2/16	M	Crow Wing County	MN	James L. Beard	1975	1,345
19 8/16	11 12/16	7 12/16	M	Boise County	ID	Jack Arbaugh	1976	1,345
19 8/16	11 11/16	7 13/16	M	Atikokan	ONT	David Graves	1978	1,345
19 8/16	12 2/16	7 6/16	M	Ear Falls	ONT	Grant Poindexter	1978	1,345
19 8/16	12 5/16	7 3/16	M	Archuleta County	CO	Robert Hoague	1981	1,345
19 8/16	12 3/16	7 5/16	M	Broadwater County	MT	Jan Hamer	1982	1,345
19 8/16	12 3/16	7 5/16	M	Remigny	QUE	Joe Hopwood	1982	1,345
19 8/16	11 15/16	7 9/16	M	Madison County	MT	Shep Lantow	1982	1,345
19 8/16	12 7/16	7 1/16	M	Loon Lake	SAS	Brian Acton	1984	1,345
19 8/16	12 6/16	7 2/16	M	Hudson Bay	SAS	Bill Zahradka	1984	1,345
19 8/16	12 0/16	7 8/16	M	Las Animas County	CO	Sam Durham	1984	1,345
19 8/16	11 11/16	7 13/16	M	Converse County	WY	Neil Hymas	1984	1,345
19 8/16	12 8/16	7 0/16	M	Sioux Narrows	ONT	Kenneth E. Krahn	1985	1,345
19 8/16	12 2/16	7 6/16	M	Grant County	OR	Mike E. Billman	1985	1,345
19 8/16	11 14/16	7 10/16	M	Siskiyou County	CA	Richard L. Westervelt	1985	1,345
19 8/16	12 6/16	7 2/16	M	One Portage Lake	MAN	Paolo Strapazzon	1986	1,345
19 8/16	12 4/16	7 4/16	M	Minden	ONT	William J. Davi	1986	1,345
19 8/16	12 8/16	7 0/16	M	Lincoln County	MT	Jim Eff	1986	1,345
19 8/16	12 4/16	7 4/16	M	Custer County	ID	Richard D. Stocking	1986	1,345
19 8/16	12 5/16	7 3/16	M	Huerfano County	CO	Randy Wright	1987	1,345
19 8/16	11 13/16	7 11/16	M	Essex County	NY	Paul Durling	1987	1,345
19 8/16	12 5/16	7 3/16	M	Hancock County	ME	John R. Mitchell	1987	1,345
19 8/16	12 0/16	7 8/16	M	Maniwaki	QUE	Aldo Bonacasta, Jr.	1989	1,345
19 8/16	12 10/16	6 14/16	M	Duchesne County	UT	Jerry B. Reynolds	1989	1,345
19 8/16	11 15/16	7 9/16	M	La Ronge	SAS	Robert D. Lingo	1989	1,345
19 8/16	12 1/16	7 7/16	M	San Fernando Island	AK	Kurt Goesch	1989	1,345
19 8/16	12 0/16	7 8/16	M	Zec Maganasipi	QUE	Stephen Kotz	1989	1,345
19 8/16	12 2/16	7 6/16	M	Bigoray River	ALB	Gunter Lemke	1990	1,345
19 8/16	12 11/16	6 13/16	M	Fort McMurray	ALB	Mike Menke	1990	1,345
19 8/16	12 5/16	7 3/16	M	Archuleta County	CO	Roger DeGroat	1990	1,345
19 8/16	12 4/16	7 4/16	M	Clackamas County	OR	Ben R. Cook	1990	1,345
19 8/16	11 14/16	7 10/16	M	Custer County	ID	David J. McPherson	1990	1,345
19 8/16	12 5/16	7 3/16	M	Forest County	WI	Mark Gaffke	1990	1,345
19 8/16	12 3/16	7 5/16	M	Rio Arriba County	NM	Robert J. Seeds	1990	1,345
19 8/16	12 7/16	7 1/16	M	Mons Township	ONT	Russell Trusty	1991	1,345
19 8/16	12 1/16	7 7/16	M	Atikokan	ONT	Jim Aebel	1991	1,345
19 8/16	11 14/16	7 10/16	M	Thunder Bay	ONT	Dave McKenzie	1991	1,345
19 8/16	12 4/16	7 4/16	M	Zec Dumoine	QUE	John K. Deveney	1991	1,345
19 8/16	12 0/16	7 8/16	M	Routt County	CO	Joel Anderson	1992	1,345
19 8/16	12 4/16	7 4/16	M	Fort McMurray	ALB	Mark A. Balavender	1992	1,345
19 8/16	12 0/16	7 8/16	M	Fort McMurray	ALB	Jim Trafford	1992	1,345
19 8/16	12 5/16	7 3/16	M	Zec St. Patrice	QUE	Ted Brilhart	1992	1,345
19 8/16	11 15/16	7 9/16	M	Snow Lake	MAN	Thomas C. Schnarre	1992	1,345
19 8/16	11 15/16	7 9/16	M	Lake Preissac	QUE	Bob Sands	1992	1,345
19 8/16	11 14/16	7 10/16	M	Obatogamau Lake	QUE	Zig Kertenis, Jr.	1992	1,345
19 8/16	12 1/16	7 7/16	M	Lac La Biche	ALB	Tom Nelson	1993	1,345
19 8/16	11 13/16	7 11/16	M	Besnard Lake	SAS	Tommy Mackey	1993	1,345
19 8/16	12 0/16	7 8/16	M	Matagami	QUE	Jacques Harvey	1993	1,345
19 8/16	12 8/16	7 0/16	M	Clearwater County	MN	Jon Drechsel	1993	1,345
19 8/16	12 1/16	7 7/16	M	Butte County	CA	Dr. Douglas R. Hahn	1993	1,345
19 8/16	12 4/16	7 4/16	M	Buffalo Narrows	SAS	Paul Kamenar, Jr.	1994	1,345
19 8/16	11 12/16	7 12/16	M	Hearst	ONT	Tom Schoenike	1994	1,345
19 8/16	12 3/16	7 5/16	M	Koochiching County	MN	Kenneth S. Turck	1994	1,345
19 8/16	12 2/16	7 6/16	M	Atikokan	ONT	Dr. John R. Thodos	1994	1,345
19 8/16	12 4/16	7 4/16	M	O'Sullivan Lake	ONT	Michael W. Ziembo	1994	1,345
19 8/16	12 2/16	7 6/16	M	Sandoval County	NM	Phillip K. Whatley	1994	1,345

BLACK BEAR

SCORE	GREATEST LENGTH	GREATEST WIDTH	SEX	AREA	STATE/ PROVINCE	HUNTER'S NAME	DATE	RANK
19 8/16	11 14/16	7 10/16	M	Valley County	ID	Robert Staudt, Jr.	1994	1,345
19 8/16	12 2/16	7 6/16	M	Boise County	ID	Scott Carlson	1995	1,345
19 8/16	11 14/16	7 10/16	M	Smoky Lake	ALB	Mark Johnson	1995	1,345
19 8/16	12 2/16	7 6/16	M	Athabasca River	ALB	Vince Migliorato	1995	1,345
19 8/16	12 4/16	7 4/16	M	Hudson Bay	SAS	Tawnya M. Lee	1995	1,345
19 8/16	12 2/16	7 6/16	M	Temiscaming	QUE	Tim Burris	1995	1,345
19 8/16	12 4/16	7 4/16	M	St. Louis County	MN	Craig Mitchell Robarge	1995	1,345
19 8/16	12 4/16	7 4/16	M	Grand Rapids	MAN	Dale Shove	1995	1,345
19 8/16	12 8/16	7 0/16	M	Carrot River	SAS	Christopher Germain	1995	1,345
19 8/16	12 6/16	7 2/16	M	Herkimer County	NY	Fran Madore	1995	1,345
19 8/16	12 1/16	7 7/16	M	Oxford County	ME	Gary J. Russell	1995	1,345
19 8/16	12 0/16	7 8/16	M	Anama Bay	MAN	Charles W. Haase	1995	1,345
19 8/16	12 4/16	7 4/16	M	Lassen County	CA	Thomas Devlin	1995	1,345
19 8/16	12 5/16	7 3/16	M	Kinwow Bay	MAN	Richard R. Sherman	1996	1,345
19 8/16	12 7/16	7 1/16	M	Steepbank River	ALB	Don Budd	1996	1,345
19 8/16	12 0/16	7 8/16	M	Fort McMurray	ALB	Joe Del Vecchio	1996	1,345
19 8/16	12 4/16	7 4/16	M	Long Lake	ONT	John Nordrum	1996	1,345
19 8/16	12 2/16	7 6/16	M	Candle Lake	SAS	David Clardy	1996	1,345
19 8/16	12 2/16	7 6/16	M	High Level	ALB	John T. Harrison	1996	1,345
19 8/16	12 5/16	7 3/16	M	Dorion	ONT	Bruce Hudalla	1996	1,345
19 8/16	12 2/16	7 6/16	M	Madison County	ID	Donald M. Sherick	1996	1,345
19 8/16	12 3/16	7 5/16	M	Big Sandy Lake	SAS	Renee Welle	1996	1,345
19 8/16	12 7/16	7 1/16	M	Hawkrock	SAS	Jacob Kuntz	1996	1,345
19 8/16	12 4/16	7 4/16	M	Menominee County	MI	Niles H. Amundsen	1996	1,345
19 8/16	12 4/16	7 4/16	M	Douglas County	WI	Gary M. Bay	1996	1,345
19 8/16	12 2/16	7 6/16	M	Iron County	WI	John R. Guillen	1996	1,345
19 8/16	12 4/16	7 4/16	M	Crooked Creek	ALB	Brent Watson	1997	1,345
19 8/16	12 4/16	7 4/16	M	Dryden	ONT	Penny J. Bowser	1997	1,345
19 8/16	11 12/16	7 12/16	M	Fort Vermilion	ALB	W. C. MacCarty III, MD	1997	1,345
19 8/16	11 13/16	7 11/16	M	Lake Manitowik	ONT	Chuck Webb	1997	1,345
19 8/16	12 5/16	7 3/16	M	English River	ONT	Lou Milanesi	1997	1,345
19 8/16	12 8/16	7 0/16	M	Peace River	ALB	Mark Titus	1997	1,345
19 8/16	12 1/16	7 7/16	M	Chelmsford	ONT	Kyle Geremesz	1997	1,345
19 8/16	12 1/16	7 7/16	M	Grand Lake	NFL	William L. Switzer	1997	1,345
19 8/16	11 12/16	7 12/16	M	Dryden	ONT	John R. Gegner	1997	1,345
19 8/16	12 0/16	7 8/16	M	Howell	ONT	Bryan Cripe	1997	1,345
19 8/16	12 3/16	7 5/16	M	Addison County	VT	Alan Rixon	1997	1,345
19 8/16	11 15/16	7 9/16	M	Grant County	WV	Terrence Weidman	1997	1,345
19 8/16	12 4/16	7 4/16	M	Athabasca River	ALB	Leonard Anglewitz	1998	1,345
19 8/16	12 1/16	7 7/16	M	Thunder Bay	ONT	Johnny Prewett	1998	1,345
19 8/16	11 13/16	7 11/16	M	Manitouwadge	ONT	Jim Dunigan	1998	1,345
19 8/16	11 15/16	7 9/16	M	Harvey Station	NBW	John D. Thomas, Jr.	1998	1,345
19 7/16	12 3/16	7 4/16	M	Kenora	ONT	Norman Pint	1964	1,447
19 7/16	12 5/16	7 2/16	M	Caribou County	ID	Ronald S. Curtis	1969	1,447
19 7/16	11 10/16	7 13/16	M	St. Louis County	MN	Don Dvoroznak	1970	1,447
19 7/16	11 15/16	7 8/16	M	Moffat County	CO	Louis Preba	1972	1,447
19 7/16	12 0/16	7 7/16	M	Nestor Falls	ONT	Dennis Bartness	1974	1,447
19 7/16	12 0/16	7 7/16	M	Haddo Township	ONT	Paul Sorke	1974	1,447
19 7/16	12 0/16	7 7/16	M	La Plata County	CO	Mike Dunaway	1975	1,447
19 7/16	12 7/16	7 0/16	M	Somme	SAS	Phil Patchin	1975	1,447
19 7/16	12 3/16	7 4/16	M	Garfield County	UT	Lee G. Stoddard	1975	1,447
19 7/16	12 7/16	7 0/16	M	Snohomish County	WA	Charles J. Bartlett	1976	1,447
19 7/16	12 1/16	7 6/16	M	Roscommon County	MI	Roger Maeder	1976	1,447
19 7/16	12 0/16	7 7/16	M	Larimer County	CO	Ron Breitsprecher	1977	1,447
19 7/16	12 2/16	7 5/16	M	Costilla County	CO	Dr. Thomas I. LaValle	1978	1,447
19 7/16	12 5/16	7 2/16	M	Byers Lake	AK	Eugene Smith, Jr.	1978	1,447
19 7/16	11 11/16	7 12/16	M	Fremont County	CO	Ronald E. Sniff	1978	1,447
19 7/16	12 4/16	7 3/16	M	Idaho County	ID	Ray Koenig	1979	1,447
19 7/16	12 11/16	6 12/16	M	Tehama County	CA	Roy B. Cartwright	1980	1,447
19 7/16	12 7/16	7 0/16	M	Cass County	MN	Wayne Enger	1980	1,447
19 7/16	12 2/16	7 5/16	M	Starkey Unit	OR	Bill Lancaster	1980	1,447
19 7/16	11 15/16	7 8/16	M	Wolf Lake Road	ONT	Gary Johnston	1981	1,447
19 7/16	12 0/16	7 7/16	M	Huerfano County	CO	Kent Connally	1983	1,447
19 7/16	11 14/16	7 9/16	M	Bayfield County	WI	Steve Finn	1983	1,447
19 7/16	12 0/16	7 7/16	M	Dryden	ONT	Alan Koester	1984	1,447
19 7/16	11 8/16	7 15/16	M	Caramat	ONT	Robert D. DuBois	1984	1,447
19 7/16	12 3/16	7 4/16	M	Hudson Bay	SAS	Bill Zahradka	1986	1,447
19 7/16	12 3/16	7 4/16	M	Archuleta County	CO	Richard M. Young, Jr.	1986	1,447
19 7/16	11 8/16	7 15/16	M	Sioux Narrows	ONT	Richard Sapp	1986	1,447
19 7/16	11 15/16	7 8/16	M	Mine Centre	ONT	Lonnie Johnson	1987	1,447
19 7/16	12 3/16	7 4/16	M	Siskiyou County	CA	John E. Koblos	1987	1,447
19 7/16	12 5/16	7 2/16	M	Lac La Biche	ALB	Daniel J. Hungle	1988	1,447
19 7/16	11 13/16	7 10/16	M	Vermilion Bay	ONT	John Gritmacker	1988	1,447
19 7/16	12 4/16	7 3/16	M	Marathon County	WI	Stanley J. Budleski	1988	1,447
19 7/16	12 3/16	7 4/16	M	Catron County	NM	Parris Nottingham	1988	1,447
19 7/16	12 0/16	7 7/16	M	Mayerthorpe	ALB	Dan Perez	1989	1,447
19 7/16	12 5/16	7 2/16	M	Kimowin Lake	ALB	Thomas Schneider	1989	1,447
19 7/16	12 4/16	7 3/16	M	Buffalo Narrows	SAS	Matt Curry	1990	1,447

BLACK BEAR

Minimum Score 18 — Continued

SCORE	GREATEST LENGTH	GREATEST WIDTH	SEX	AREA	STATE/PROVINCE	HUNTER'S NAME	DATE	RANK
19 7/16	12 3/16	7 4/16	M	Cadillac	QUE	Bob Drumm	1990	1,447
19 7/16	12 8/16	6 15/16	M	Prince of Wales Island	AK	Doy Curtis	1990	1,447
19 7/16	12 8/16	6 15/16	M	Bayfield County	WI	George Herold	1990	1,447
19 7/16	12 5/16	7 2/16	M	Baraga County	MI	Mark Savic	1990	1,447
19 7/16	12 3/16	7 4/16	M	Otter Creek	SAS	Les King	1991	1,447
19 7/16	12 1/16	7 6/16	M	Ear Falls	ONT	Joseph E. Church	1991	1,447
19 7/16	12 6/16	7 1/16	M	Goodsoil	SAS	Charles Ranua	1991	1,447
19 7/16	11 10/16	7 13/16	M	Apisko Lake	MAN	Karl Teitt	1991	1,447
19 7/16	12 5/16	7 2/16	M	Boise County	ID	Russ Meyer	1991	1,447
19 7/16	12 4/16	7 3/16	M	Menominee County	WI	Kurt L. Goodwill	1991	1,447
19 7/16	12 0/16	7 7/16	M	Roseau County	MN	Rick Hill	1991	1,447
19 7/16	12 1/16	7 6/16	M	Elk River	BC	Alan Williams	1991	1,447
19 7/16	12 0/16	7 7/16	M	Garfield County	CO	Stace Strouse	1991	1,447
19 7/16	12 5/16	7 2/16	M	Wallowa County	OR	Tony Piper	1991	1,447
19 7/16	12 4/16	7 3/16	M	Meadow Lake	SAS	Matthew Curry	1992	1,447
19 7/16	12 6/16	7 1/16	M	Peace River	ALB	Kevin A. Hayden	1992	1,447
19 7/16	11 11/16	7 12/16	M	Williams Lake	ONT	Eric Matheson	1992	1,447
19 7/16	11 9/16	7 14/16	M	Alpine County	CA	Kevin L. Hall	1992	1,447
19 7/16	12 0/16	7 7/16	M	Florence County	WI	Steven J. Woulf	1992	1,447
19 7/16	12 0/16	7 7/16	M	Houghton County	MI	Gary Lubinski	1992	1,447
19 7/16	12 3/16	7 4/16	M	Orange County	NY	Eric Puletti	1992	1,447
19 7/16	12 0/16	7 7/16	M	Clahome River	BC	Wayne L. Meyers	1993	1,447
19 7/16	12 5/16	7 2/16	M	Bissett	MAN	David Harris	1993	1,447
19 7/16	12 4/16	7 3/16	M	Wandering River	ALB	Chris Boscamp	1993	1,447
19 7/16	11 14/16	7 9/16	M	Christopher Lake	SAS	Watson T. Jackson	1993	1,447
19 7/16	12 5/16	7 2/16	M	Laurie Lake	SAS	Rene Suda	1993	1,447
19 7/16	11 14/16	7 9/16	M	Oxford County	ME	Mark Kronyak	1993	1,447
19 7/16	12 8/16	6 15/16	M	Augusta County	VA	Michael J. Sandy	1993	1,447
19 7/16	12 5/16	7 2/16	M	Randolph County	WV	James Rowan	1993	1,447
19 7/16	12 2/16	7 5/16	M	Athabasca River	ALB	George "Matt" Potts	1994	1,447
19 7/16	12 2/16	7 5/16	M	Carrot River	SAS	Ronny Stoy	1994	1,447
19 7/16	12 3/16	7 4/16	M	Livengood	AK	Ricky R. Janssen	1994	1,447
19 7/16	12 6/16	7 1/16	M	Minto Flats	AK	Harry M. Ronsman	1994	1,447
19 7/16	12 4/16	7 3/16	M	Oxford County	ME	Craig S. Anderson	1994	1,447
19 7/16	12 4/16	7 3/16	M	Atikokan	ONT	Dr. John R. Thodos	1994	1,447
19 7/16	12 2/16	7 5/16	M	Grafton County	NH	Darren Lee	1994	1,447
19 7/16	11 14/16	7 9/16	M	Mesomikenda Lake	ONT	William H. Osborne	1994	1,447
19 7/16	12 6/16	7 1/16	M	Bayfield County	WI	Jim Horneck	1994	1,447
19 7/16	12 5/16	7 2/16	M	Orange County	NY	Joseph W. Talasco	1994	1,447
19 7/16	12 5/16	7 2/16	M	Centre County	PA	Eric Anton Derugen	1994	1,447
19 7/16	11 8/16	7 15/16	M	Waweig	NBW	Joseph E. White, Jr.	1995	1,447
19 7/16	11 13/16	7 10/16	M	Lemhi County	ID	Bruce Carlisle	1995	1,447
19 7/16	12 0/16	7 7/16	M	Upshur County	WV	Walter K. Depoy	1995	1,447
19 7/16	12 5/16	7 2/16	M	Swastika	ONT	Mike Darlak	1996	1,447
19 7/16	12 5/16	7 2/16	M	Waterhen	MAN	Ken Vettel	1996	1,447
19 7/16	12 3/16	7 4/16	M	Camperville	MAN	Mark Vink	1996	1,447
19 7/16	12 0/16	7 7/16	M	Evain	QUE	Jacques Robichaud	1996	1,447
19 7/16	11 15/16	7 8/16	M	Ear Falls	ONT	Elmer Van Gheem	1996	1,447
19 7/16	12 7/16	7 0/16	M	Mesa County	CO	Eric A. Sawyer	1996	1,447
19 7/16	12 2/16	7 5/16	M	Summit County	CO	Kevin Brothers	1996	1,447
19 7/16	12 2/16	7 5/16	M	Clearwater County	ID	Charles J. Kager	1997	1,447
19 7/16	12 2/16	7 5/16	M	Carrot River	SAS	Mark P. Wagner	1997	1,447
19 7/16	12 2/16	7 5/16	M	Clarke Lake	SAS	Robert Wood	1997	1,447
19 7/16	12 7/16	7 0/16	M	Woodridge	MAN	Peter U. Funk	1997	1,447
19 7/16	12 0/16	7 7/16	M	Lac des Mille Lacs	ONT	John Glick	1997	1,447
19 7/16	12 3/16	7 4/16	M	Kaladar	ONT	James Deyo	1997	1,447
19 7/16	11 14/16	7 9/16	M	Carlton County	MN	Walter W. Trader	1997	1,447
19 7/16	12 1/16	7 6/16	M	Lake County	MN	Kevin Schmieg	1997	1,447
19 7/16	12 2/16	7 5/16	M	White County	GA	Jim Collins	1997	1,447
19 7/16	12 3/16	7 4/16	M	Athabasca River	ALB	Johnny Watson	1998	1,447
19 7/16	12 0/16	7 7/16	M	Siskiyou County	CA	Dan Kothgassner	1998	1,447
19 7/16	12 1/16	7 6/16	M	Ashland County	WI	Jeffrey L. Stezenski	1998	1,447
19 6/16	12 7/16	6 15/16	M	Shasta County	CA	L. Dale Towery	1965	1,545
19 6/16	11 14/16	7 8/16	M	Atikokan	ONT	Dennis Gregory	1969	1,545
19 6/16	11 14/16	7 8/16	M	Mesa County	CO	Charles Leidheiser	1971	1,545
19 6/16	12 2/16	7 4/16	M	Franklin County	ME	Walter Seville	1971	1,545
19 6/16	12 6/16	7 0/16	F	Sawyer County	WI	Ronald Curry, Jr.	1972	1,545
19 6/16	12 3/16	7 3/16	M	Uncompahgre N.F.	CO	Thomas J. Hentrick	1975	1,545
19 6/16	12 2/16	7 4/16	M	Ashland County	WI	Jim Keim	1977	1,545
19 6/16	12 2/16	7 4/16	M	Atikokan	ONT	Earle K. Gray	1979	1,545
19 6/16	11 14/16	7 8/16	M	Wabigoon Lake	ONT	Gary W. Shaffer	1979	1,545
19 6/16	11 13/16	7 9/16	M	Cascade County	MT	H. Richard Long	1981	1,545
19 6/16	12 4/16	7 2/16	M	Lewis & Clark County	MT	Donald K. MacCallum	1982	1,545
19 6/16	12 0/16	7 6/16	M	Aroostook County	ME	Frank 'Rit' Heller	1982	1,545
19 6/16	12 2/16	7 4/16	M	Hampshire County	MA	James 'Boomer' Hayden	1982	1,545
19 6/16	12 4/16	7 2/16	M	Hudson Bay	SAS	David Tofte	1983	1,545
19 6/16	12 4/16	7 2/16	M	Sioux Lookout	ONT	Ray Ryan	1983	1,545
19 6/16	12 2/16	7 4/16	M	Beluga River	AK	Christine Koldeway	1984	1,545

BLACK BEAR

Minimum Score 18 — Continued

SCORE	GREATEST LENGTH	GREATEST WIDTH	SEX	AREA	STATE/PROVINCE	HUNTER'S NAME	DATE	RANK
19 6/16	12 9/16	6 13/16	M	Kitsap County	WA	Betty Jones	1984	1,545
19 6/16	11 15/16	7 7/16	M	Lemhi County	ID	Ron Scherer	1985	1,545
19 6/16	11 14/16	7 8/16	M	Heathcote	ONT	Joseph A. Lasch	1985	1,545
19 6/16	11 14/16	7 8/16	M	Drury Twp.	ONT	John Wyszynski	1985	1,545
19 6/16	11 10/16	7 12/16	M	Kenora	ONT	Mark D. Moss	1985	1,545
19 6/16	12 1/16	7 5/16	M	Bighorn County	WY	Joel D. Prickett	1985	1,545
19 6/16	12 0/16	7 6/16	M	Shasta County	CA	Larry Mork	1985	1,545
19 6/16	12 1/16	7 5/16	M	Teton County	ID	Marc S. Johnson	1986	1,545
19 6/16	11 12/16	7 10/16	M	Herkimer County	NY	Patrick Niznik	1986	1,545
19 6/16	12 0/16	7 6/16	M	Trinity County	CA	Robert Pearce	1986	1,545
19 6/16	12 0/16	7 6/16	M	Washago	ONT	James E. Doberstein	1987	1,545
19 6/16	12 0/16	7 6/16	M	Clearwater County	ID	Dennis Blackford	1987	1,545
19 6/16	12 2/16	7 4/16	M	Graham County	AZ	Jeffrey Keith Volk	1987	1,545
19 6/16	12 3/16	7 3/16	M	Oneida County	WI	James J. Wallack	1987	1,545
19 6/16	11 14/16	7 8/16	M	Hillsport	ONT	Richard Shive	1988	1,545
19 6/16	11 15/16	7 7/16	M	Valley County	ID	William R. Vanderhoef	1988	1,545
19 6/16	12 4/16	7 2/16	M	Madera County	CA	Ken Woolsey	1988	1,545
19 6/16	11 14/16	7 8/16	M	Union County	OR	Jerry Cnossen	1988	1,545
19 6/16	12 4/16	7 2/16	M	Fresno County	CA	DeeAnn Robinson	1988	1,545
19 6/16	12 3/16	7 3/16	M	Bayfield County	WI	Daniel L Snider	1989	1,545
19 6/16	12 3/16	7 3/16	M	Colfax County	NM	Steven A. Leyh	1990	1,545
19 6/16	12 2/16	7 4/16	M	Fraser Lake	BC	Stanley D. Moore	1990	1,545
19 6/16	11 14/16	7 8/16	M	Aulneau Peninsula	ONT	Mike Koska	1990	1,545
19 6/16	12 3/16	7 3/16	M	Peace River	ALB	Mike Conroy	1990	1,545
19 6/16	11 12/16	7 10/16	M	Franklin County	ME	Peter L. Shippee	1990	1,545
19 6/16	12 1/16	7 5/16	M	Colfax County	NM	Daniel Hurd	1990	1,545
19 6/16	11 14/16	7 8/16	M	Prince of Wales Island	AK	Mark Robecker	1990	1,545
19 6/16	12 5/16	7 1/16	M	Prince of Wales Island	AK	David Rue	1991	1,545
19 6/16	12 2/16	7 4/16	F	Lac La Biche	ALB	Bruce Nederveld	1991	1,545
19 6/16	12 0/16	7 6/16	M	Fort McMurray	ALB	Galen F. Shinkle	1991	1,545
19 6/16	12 6/16	7 0/16	M	Bruce County	ONT	Dean Adams	1991	1,545
19 6/16	12 4/16	7 2/16	M	Minto Flats	AK	James Wayne Dillard	1991	1,545
19 6/16	11 15/16	7 7/16	M	Falconbridge	ONT	Daniel Ralich	1991	1,545
19 6/16	12 4/16	7 2/16	M	Darlens	QUE	Dennis L. Blankenship	1991	1,545
19 6/16	12 7/16	6 15/16	M	Leaf River	QUE	Joseph Testerman	1991	1,545
19 6/16	11 14/16	7 8/16	M	Lake County	MN	David Ruzek	1991	1,545
19 6/16	12 1/16	7 5/16	M	Bancroft	ONT	Jeffrey C. Fretz	1991	1,545
19 6/16	11 13/16	7 9/16	M	Iron County	MI	Craig A. Murdock	1991	1,545
19 6/16	12 2/16	7 4/16	M	Hood River County	OR	Michael L. Tollen	1991	1,545
19 6/16	12 1/16	7 5/16	M	Marathon County	WI	John J. Fischer	1991	1,545
19 6/16	12 3/16	7 3/16	M	Hearst	ONT	Russell V. Riese	1992	1,545
19 6/16	11 15/16	7 7/16	M	Sheridan County	WY	Lee Jernigan	1992	1,545
19 6/16	11 14/16	7 8/16	M	Koochiching County	MN	Doug Streit	1992	1,545
19 6/16	12 2/16	7 4/16	M	Rutland County	VT	Lawrence St. Pierre	1992	1,545
19 6/16	12 5/16	7 1/16	M	Hudson Bay	SAS	Mark K. Swallow	1993	1,545
19 6/16	11 12/16	7 10/16	M	Wanless	MAN	Leonard Rock	1993	1,545
19 6/16	12 3/16	7 3/16	M	Clearwater County	ID	Kevin Schmid	1993	1,545
19 6/16	12 2/16	7 4/16	M	Dryden	ONT	Ted Anderson	1993	1,545
19 6/16	11 12/16	7 10/16	M	Canterbury	NBW	Tom Taylor	1993	1,545
19 6/16	12 3/16	7 3/16	M	St. Louis County	MN	Vern Blonigen	1993	1,545
19 6/16	12 0/16	7 6/16	M	Mora County	NM	Glen A. Fuller	1993	1,545
19 6/16	12 0/16	7 6/16	M	Catron County	NM	Abe Dimas, Jr.	1993	1,545
19 6/16	12 5/16	7 1/16	M	Oxford County	ME	Daniel J. Smith	1993	1,545
19 6/16	12 0/16	7 6/16	M	Peace River	ALB	Peter C. Swenson	1994	1,545
19 6/16	12 3/16	7 3/16	M	McNalley Lake	ALB	Jody Davis	1994	1,545
19 6/16	12 9/16	6 13/16	M	Fisher Branch	MAN	James R. Weir	1994	1,545
19 6/16	12 1/16	7 5/16	M	Lynn Lake	MAN	G. Fred Asbell	1994	1,545
19 6/16	12 2/16	7 4/16	M	Larder Lake	ONT	Thomas R. Johnson	1994	1,545
19 6/16	12 2/16	7 4/16	M	Atikokan	ONT	David N. Andersen	1994	1,545
19 6/16	11 15/16	7 7/16	M	Washington County	ME	Perry H. Perkins	1994	1,545
19 6/16	11 14/16	7 8/16	M	Sudbury	ONT	Carl L. Ledford	1995	1,545
19 6/16	11 14/16	7 8/16	M	Thunder Hills	SAS	John J. Sestak	1995	1,545
19 6/16	12 1/16	7 5/16	M	Atikokan	ONT	Todd Schumacher	1995	1,545
19 6/16	12 5/16	7 1/16	M	North Bay	ONT	Marty Klemm	1995	1,545
19 6/16	12 0/16	7 6/16	M	Wawa	ONT	Richard L. Warren	1995	1,545
19 6/16	11 14/16	7 8/16	M	Holinshead Lake	ONT	Kenneth Beckel	1995	1,545
19 6/16	12 4/16	7 2/16	M	Lake of the Woods County	MN	Chad D. Hagen	1995	1,545
19 6/16	12 6/16	7 0/16	M	Klickitat County	WA	Gary Holwegner	1995	1,545
19 6/16	12 2/16	7 4/16	M	Idaho County	ID	Pat Hylton	1996	1,545
19 6/16	12 8/16	6 14/16	M	Bluffly Lake	ONT	Robb S. Thompson	1996	1,545
19 6/16	12 4/16	7 2/16	M	Woodridge	MAN	Peter U. Funk	1996	1,545
19 6/16	12 2/16	7 4/16	M	Raith	ONT	Paul E. Moore	1996	1,545
19 6/16	11 14/16	7 8/16	M	King County	WA	Ken Melton	1996	1,545
19 6/16	12 0/16	7 6/16	M	Somerset County	ME	Matthew Adamou	1996	1,545
19 6/16	12 8/16	6 14/16	M	Chisago County	MN	Richard Owen	1996	1,545
19 6/16	12 8/16	6 14/16	M	Douglas County	WI	James Wanner	1996	1,545
19 6/16	12 2/16	7 4/16	M	Mariposa County	CA	Arthur M. Cain	1996	1,545
19 6/16	12 4/16	7 2/16	M	Big Horn County	WY	Roger Coguill	1997	1,545

BLACK BEAR

Minimum Score 18 — Continued

SCORE	GREATEST LENGTH	GREATEST WIDTH	SEX	AREA	STATE/PROVINCE	HUNTER'S NAME	DATE	RANK
19 6/16	12 4/16	7 2/16	M	Prince of Wales Island	AK	Danny Moore	1997	1,545
19 6/16	12 3/16	7 3/16	M	Meadow Lake	SAS	Thomas Pigeon	1997	1,545
19 6/16	12 3/16	7 3/16	M	Lake Wabigoon	ONT	Dwayne H. Cushman	1997	1,545
19 6/16	11 14/16	7 8/16	M	Idaho County	ID	Don Polanski	1997	1,545
19 6/16	12 3/16	7 3/16	M	Gila County	AZ	Gary Mehaffey	1997	1,545
19 6/16	11 13/16	7 9/16	M	Rio Arriba County	NM	Zac Bryant	1997	1,545
19 6/16	12 2/16	7 4/16	M	Holinshead Lake	ONT	Kenneth A. Shattuck, Jr.	1998	1,545
19 6/16	11 14/16	7 8/16	M	Ignace	ONT	Wilmer Garlick	1998	1,545
19 6/16	12 4/16	7 2/16	M	Saddle Hills	ALB	David Watson	1998	1,545
19 6/16	12 1/16	7 5/16	M	Harney County	OR	Bill Andersen	1998	1,545
19 5/16	11 13/16	7 8/16	M	Clearwater County	ID	William R. Vanderhoef	1959	1,649
19 5/16	11 12/16	7 9/16	M	Upper Peninsula	MI	Donald Schram	1961	1,649
19 5/16	12 0/16	7 5/16	M	Gunnison County	CO	James Jarvis	1976	1,649
19 5/16	11 12/16	7 9/16	M	Las Animas County	CO	Barry Powell	1976	1,649
19 5/16	12 3/16	7 2/16	M	Raith	ONT	Jon K. Young	1976	1,649
19 5/16	12 1/16	7 4/16	M	Mesa County	CO	T. J. Colburn	1977	1,649
19 5/16	11 11/16	7 10/16	M	Franklin County	ME	Al Del Greco	1978	1,649
19 5/16	11 11/16	7 10/16	M	Ear Falls	ONT	Michael Mealey	1978	1,649
19 5/16	12 0/16	7 5/16	M	Washington County	ME	Dan Paugh	1978	1,649
19 5/16	12 6/16	6 15/16	M	Dolores County	CO	Marv Reichenau	1979	1,649
19 5/16	12 1/16	7 4/16	M	Oneida County	NY	Ronald J. Beerhalter	1980	1,649
19 5/16	12 2/16	7 3/16	M	Tulare County	CA	Fred R. Cisneros	1981	1,649
19 5/16	11 14/16	7 7/16	M	White Lake	ONT	Daniel B. Johnson	1981	1,649
19 5/16	11 15/16	7 6/16	M	Bonneville County	ID	Richard K. Russell	1981	1,649
19 5/16	12 2/16	7 3/16	M	Dryden	ONT	Craig A. Swenson	1982	1,649
19 5/16	12 1/16	7 4/16	M	Sudbury County	ONT	William Doczy	1983	1,649
19 5/16	12 4/16	7 1/16	M	St. Louis County	MN	Kimberley Anne McGurren	1983	1,649
19 5/16	12 1/16	7 4/16	M	King County	WA	Larry Jensen	1983	1,649
19 5/16	11 13/16	7 8/16	M	Smeaton	SAS	Gene Welle	1984	1,649
19 5/16	11 14/16	7 7/16	M	Caribou County	ID	Coby Tigert	1984	1,649
19 5/16	12 1/16	7 4/16	M	Snohomish County	WA	Mathew Hayvaz	1984	1,649
19 5/16	12 1/16	7 4/16	M	Plumas County	CA	Dr. Ronald H. Thole	1984	1,649
19 5/16	12 1/16	7 4/16	M	Parry Sound	ONT	Ronald D. Lundy	1985	1,649
19 5/16	12 4/16	7 1/16	M	Cass County	MN	Brad Blanchard	1985	1,649
19 5/16	12 8/16	6 13/16	M	Caldwell County	NC	Danny K. Adams	1986	1,649
19 5/16	12 8/16	6 13/16	M	Grand County	UT	David Snyder	1986	1,649
19 5/16	12 5/16	7 0/16	M	Valley County	ID	Brian Hunter Heck	1986	1,649
19 5/16	11 9/16	7 12/16	M	Flathead County	MT	Jay Vojta, Jr.	1987	1,649
19 5/16	12 1/16	7 4/16	M	Garfield County	WA	David Jansen	1987	1,649
19 5/16	12 3/16	7 2/16	M	Catron County	NM	Stan Rauch	1988	1,649
19 5/16	12 0/16	7 5/16	M	Rocky Lake	MAN	Cecil Tharp	1988	1,649
19 5/16	12 3/16	7 2/16	M	Rocky Lake	MAN	Tim Finley	1988	1,649
19 5/16	11 11/16	7 10/16	M	Fort Coulonge	QUE	David Keith Burchette	1988	1,649
19 5/16	11 14/16	7 7/16	M	North Bay	QUE	Jeff Anderson	1988	1,649
19 5/16	12 1/16	7 4/16	M	High Prairie	ALB	Joseph F. Petti	1989	1,649
19 5/16	12 4/16	7 1/16	M	Montrose County	CO	Clint Hovey	1989	1,649
19 5/16	11 15/16	7 6/16	M	Sioux Lookout	ONT	Stan Godfrey	1989	1,649
19 5/16	12 1/16	7 4/16	M	Zec Maganasipi	QUE	F.Edward Campbell	1989	1,649
19 5/16	11 14/16	7 7/16	M	Cold Lake	ALB	Glenn Moir	1989	1,649
19 5/16	11 10/16	7 11/16	M	Las Animas County	CO	David Brooks	1990	1,649
19 5/16	12 3/16	7 2/16	M	Fawcett	ALB	Garfield Vikse	1990	1,649
19 5/16	11 15/16	7 6/16	M	Stranger Lake	ONT	Mitchell S. Thorpe	1990	1,649
19 5/16	12 1/16	7 4/16	M	Oconto County	WI	James A. Krouse	1990	1,649
19 5/16	11 15/16	7 6/16	M	MacNeil Twp.	ONT	Ted Whittle	1990	1,649
19 5/16	12 9/16	6 12/16	M	Utah County	UT	Kevin D. Hatfield	1991	1,649
19 5/16	11 15/16	7 6/16	M	High Level	ALB	Bobby G. Williams	1991	1,649
19 5/16	12 1/16	7 4/16	M	Rio Arriba County	NM	Tim J. Mariner	1991	1,649
19 5/16	12 6/16	6 15/16	F	Boise County	ID	Scott T. Doxey	1991	1,649
19 5/16	12 2/16	7 3/16	M	Idaho County	ID	Charles R. Whitfield	1991	1,649
19 5/16	12 3/16	7 2/16	M	Pitkin County	CO	James P. Krasinski, Sr.	1991	1,649
19 5/16	12 0/16	7 5/16	M	Colfax County	NM	Stephen W. Long	1991	1,649
19 5/16	12 1/16	7 4/16	M	Athabasca River	ALB	Casmir S. Domurat, Jr.	1991	1,649
19 5/16	12 7/16	6 14/16	M	Cranberry Portage	MAN	John Beardslee	1992	1,649
19 5/16	11 12/16	7 9/16	M	Saguache County	CO	Dennis Reid	1992	1,649
19 5/16	11 12/16	7 9/16	M	Tanana Flats	AK	Tommy L. Ramsey	1992	1,649
19 5/16	11 15/16	7 6/16	M	Skagit County	WA	Rick W. Giles	1992	1,649
19 5/16	12 7/16	6 14/16	M	Rusk County	WI	James R. Williams	1992	1,649
19 5/16	12 5/16	7 0/16	M	Catron County	NM	David H. Boland	1992	1,649
19 5/16	12 0/16	7 5/16	M	Oxford County	ME	Lance A. Tyler	1992	1,649
19 5/16	12 5/16	7 0/16	M	Grande Prairie	ALB	Charles Markwood	1993	1,649
19 5/16	12 2/16	7 3/16	M	Webbwood	ONT	Michael J. Perry	1993	1,649
19 5/16	12 1/16	7 4/16	M	North Bay	ONT	Russell E. Steele	1993	1,649
19 5/16	12 5/16	7 0/16	M	Lac Ile-a-la Crosse	SAS	Dewayne Mullins	1993	1,649
19 5/16	12 2/16	7 3/16	M	Nolalu	ONT	John E. Sliger	1993	1,649
19 5/16	12 2/16	7 3/16	M	Kings	NBW	Amedeo Guglielmo	1993	1,649
19 5/16	12 0/16	7 5/16	M	Aulneau Peninsula	ONT	Michael Koska	1993	1,649
19 5/16	11 15/16	7 6/16	M	Bayfield County	WI	Richard S. Nemitz	1993	1,649
19 5/16	11 13/16	7 8/16	M	Athabasca River	ALB	Allen J. Miraglia	1994	1,649

BLACK BEAR

Minimum Score 18 — Continued

SCORE	GREATEST LENGTH	GREATEST WIDTH	SEX	AREA	STATE/ PROVINCE	HUNTER'S NAME	DATE	RANK
19 5/16	12 5/16	7 0/16	M	Carrot River	SAS	Andrew D. Pearson	1994	1,649
19 5/16	12 3/16	7 2/16	M	Bonanza	ALB	Kirk Rawnsley	1994	1,649
19 5/16	12 2/16	7 3/16	M	Sioux Narrows	ONT	Michael J. Goza	1994	1,649
19 5/16	11 15/16	7 6/16	M	Slave Lake	ALB	Greg Ogle	1994	1,649
19 5/16	12 6/16	6 15/16	M	Fort McMurray	ALB	Darlene J. Stansfield	1994	1,649
19 5/16	12 8/16	6 13/16	M	Hudson Bay	SAS	James D. Ray	1994	1,649
19 5/16	12 5/16	7 0/16	M	Carrot River	SAS	Larry T. Fischer	1994	1,649
19 5/16	12 0/16	7 5/16	M	Idaho County	ID	Timothy R. McGuffin	1994	1,649
19 5/16	12 3/16	7 2/16	M	Laurier	MAN	Clay Childress	1994	1,649
19 5/16	12 6/16	6 15/16	M	Aulneau Peninsula	ONT	Michael Koska	1994	1,649
19 5/16	11 9/16	7 12/16	M	McKinley County	NM	James Baumgardner	1994	1,649
19 5/16	11 13/16	7 8/16	M	Plumas County	CA	Robert Trujillo	1994	1,649
19 5/16	12 2/16	7 3/16	M	Nicholas County	WV	Harold Davis	1994	1,649
19 5/16	12 2/16	7 3/16	M	High Level	ALB	David Westmoreland	1995	1,649
19 5/16	11 13/16	7 8/16	M	Kenora District	ONT	Howard Gibbs	1995	1,649
19 5/16	12 1/16	7 4/16	M	Hearst	ONT	Thomas H. Meszler	1995	1,649
19 5/16	11 10/16	7 11/16	M	Hornepayne	ONT	Mitchell J. Genz	1995	1,649
19 5/16	11 10/16	7 11/16	M	Longlac	ONT	Thomas M. Stieg	1995	1,649
19 5/16	11 11/16	7 10/16	M	Missanabie	ONT	Todd D. Armstrong	1995	1,649
19 5/16	11 15/16	7 6/16	M	Clova	QUE	Nicolas Chrisovergis	1995	1,649
19 5/16	11 15/16	7 6/16	M	Carroll County	NH	John Bassi	1995	1,649
19 5/16	12 4/16	7 1/16	M	Chapleau	ONT	Gregory James Bishop	1995	1,649
19 5/16	12 2/16	7 3/16	M	Holinshead Lake	ONT	Jeffery R. Bloniarz	1996	1,649
19 5/16	11 15/16	7 6/16	M	Chelsea Township	ONT	Marty W. Atkinson	1996	1,649
19 5/16	12 5/16	7 0/16	M	Douglas County	WI	Tom Vengrin	1996	1,649
19 5/16	12 8/16	6 13/16	M	San Jose Creek	BC	Allan Tew	1997	1,649
19 5/16	12 1/16	7 4/16	M	Whiteswan Lake	SAS	Eugene Arndt	1997	1,649
19 5/16	12 2/16	7 3/16	M	Rosenberry	MAN	George Martinez	1997	1,649
19 5/16	12 3/16	7 2/16	M	Bissett	MAN	Curtis A. Summer	1997	1,649
19 5/16	11 11/16	7 10/16	M	Wawa	ONT	Eric Adams	1997	1,649
19 5/16	11 15/16	7 6/16	M	Carswell Lake	SAS	Dennis R. Allman	1997	1,649
19 5/16	11 13/16	7 8/16	M	Lynn Lake	MAN	Don Barry	1997	1,649
19 5/16	12 4/16	7 1/16	M	Vogar	MAN	Edward Antonacci	1997	1,649
19 5/16	12 4/16	7 1/16	M	Nenana River	AK	Brock E. Graziadei	1997	1,649
19 5/16	11 12/16	7 9/16	M	Bear Lake	BC	Lorenzo Bortolotto	1997	1,649
19 5/16	12 7/16	6 14/16	M	Prince of Wales Island	AK	Stephen Herrera	1998	1,649
19 5/16	12 6/16	6 15/16	M	Athabasca River	ALB	Frank S. Noska IV	1998	1,649
19 5/16	11 12/16	7 9/16	M	Guthrie Lake	MAN	John Beardslee	1998	1,649
19 5/16	12 1/16	7 4/16	M	Ft. Coulonge	QUE	James McCarthy	1998	1,649
19 5/16	11 15/16	7 6/16	M	Zec Capitachouane	QUE	Ken H. Taylor	1998	1,649
19 5/16	12 9/16	6 12/16	M	Kanabec County	MN	Dale Kane	1998	1,649
19 4/16	12 4/16	7 0/16	M	Ashland County	WI	Herbert H. Lange	1961	1,758
19 4/16	12 4/16	7 0/16	M	Murphy Dome	AK	Thomas Clark	1963	1,758
19 4/16	11 15/16	7 5/16	M	Jackson County	OR	Bob Jacobs	1964	1,758
19 4/16	12 0/16	7 4/16	M	Idaho County	ID	Dick Gulman	1967	1,758
19 4/16	12 3/16	7 1/16	M	L'Ascension	QUE	Michael L. Kaluszka	1971	1,758
19 4/16	11 8/16	7 12/16	M	Idaho County	ID	Harold Boyack	1973	1,758
19 4/16	11 12/16	7 8/16	M	Wasco County	OR	John Higgins	1974	1,758
19 4/16	11 11/16	7 9/16	M	Wanapitei River	ONT	Ken Barnhart	1976	1,758
19 4/16	11 11/16	7 9/16	M	Gunnison County	CO	Roger Reinbold	1976	1,758
19 4/16	12 1/16	7 3/16	M	Saguache County	CO	Richard Baumfalk	1977	1,758
19 4/16	11 14/16	7 6/16	M	Pigeon Mtn.	ALB	David R. Coupland	1977	1,758
19 4/16	12 4/16	7 0/16	M	Bayfield County	WI	Bruce Eggenberger	1977	1,758
19 4/16	11 15/16	7 5/16	M	Capreol	ONT	Bobby Clenney	1978	1,758
19 4/16	12 0/16	7 4/16	M	Franklin County	ME	Harry Feaster	1978	1,758
19 4/16	11 13/16	7 7/16	M	Thessalon	ONT	Robert R. Rider	1979	1,758
19 4/16	12 4/16	7 0/16	M	Ontonagon County	MI	Daniel F. Stiltner	1979	1,758
19 4/16	11 12/16	7 8/16	M	Bayfield County	WI	Dave Tabbert	1979	1,758
19 4/16	12 1/16	7 3/16	M	Price County	WI	Glenn E. Gaulke	1980	1,758
19 4/16	11 12/16	7 8/16	M	Shoshone County	ID	Bill Hoffman, Sr.	1980	1,758
19 4/16	11 14/16	7 6/16	M	Dryden	ONT	Gerald T. Flynn	1981	1,758
19 4/16	11 12/16	7 8/16	M	Idaho County	ID	Ray Koenig	1981	1,758
19 4/16	12 2/16	7 2/16	M	Archuleta County	CO	Denny Lane Williamson	1981	1,758
19 4/16	11 14/16	7 6/16	M	St. Lawrence County	NY	Henry P. Bouchard	1982	1,758
19 4/16	12 1/16	7 3/16	M	Park County	MT	Gary Hartman	1982	1,758
19 4/16	12 8/16	6 12/16	M	Burnett County	WI	David Hess	1982	1,758
19 4/16	12 4/16	7 0/16	M	Mackinac County	MI	Dale H. Betcher	1983	1,758
19 4/16	11 14/16	7 6/16	M	Emo	ONT	Hal McClelland	1983	1,758
19 4/16	12 5/16	6 15/16	M	Game Area #23	MAN	Gary Kaluzniak	1984	1,758
19 4/16	12 0/16	7 4/16	M	Susitna River	AK	Patricia A. Stewart	1984	1,758
19 4/16	11 14/16	7 6/16	M	Touchwood Lake	ALB	Warren Witherspoon	1984	1,758
19 4/16	12 0/16	7 4/16	M	Game Area #23	MAN	Gary Kaluzniak	1984	1,758
19 4/16	11 12/16	7 8/16	M	Rollet	QUE	George Ollert	1984	1,758
19 4/16	11 11/16	7 9/16	M	Siskiyou County	CA	Greg Nichols	1984	1,758
19 4/16	11 14/16	7 6/16	M	Wawa	ONT	James C. Hicks	1984	1,758
19 4/16	12 1/16	7 3/16	M	Archuleta County	CO	Lisa Cooney	1985	1,758
19 4/16	12 2/16	7 2/16	M	Cheboygan County	MI	Steve E. Hutchinson	1985	1,758
19 4/16	12 4/16	7 0/16	M	Madison County	MT	John Ralph	1985	1,758

BLACK BEAR

Minimum Score 18 — Continued

SCORE	GREATEST LENGTH	GREATEST WIDTH	SEX	AREA	STATE/PROVINCE	HUNTER'S NAME	DATE	RANK
19 4/16	12 2/16	7 2/16	M	Siskiyou County	CA	Bruce Kipley	1985	1,758
19 4/16	12 6/16	6 14/16	M	Turtle River	ONT	Al Haines	1986	1,758
19 4/16	12 2/16	7 2/16	M	Archuleta County	CO	David Swanson	1986	1,758
19 4/16	12 1/16	7 3/16	M	Keeley Lake	SAS	Bruce E. Menz	1986	1,758
19 4/16	12 0/16	7 4/16	M	Delay River	QUE	Benjamin O. Brookhart III	1986	1,758
19 4/16	11 13/16	7 7/16	M	La Plata County	CO	Karen Stevens	1987	1,758
19 4/16	12 3/16	7 1/16	M	Fort Coulonge	QUE	David W. Wachter	1987	1,758
19 4/16	12 0/16	7 4/16	M	Wawa	ONT	Bruce Waterman	1987	1,758
19 4/16	12 0/16	7 4/16	M	Shining Tree	ONT	Alan J. Skowron	1988	1,758
19 4/16	11 11/16	7 9/16	M	Canterbury	NBW	David G. Cote	1988	1,758
19 4/16	12 2/16	7 2/16	M	Iron County	MI	Douglas Wagner	1988	1,758
19 4/16	11 14/16	7 6/16	M	Iron County	WI	Roger Adamavich	1988	1,758
19 4/16	11 15/16	7 5/16	M	Herkimer County	NY	Paul Tomeo	1988	1,758
19 4/16	12 1/16	7 3/16	M	Grand County	UT	Jay Wick	1989	1,758
19 4/16	11 15/16	7 5/16	M	High Level	ALB	Stuart Sinclair-Smith	1989	1,758
19 4/16	12 0/16	7 4/16	M	Mitehell	QUE	Bruce D. Trapp	1989	1,758
19 4/16	11 14/16	7 6/16	M	San Fernando Island	AK	Kurt Goesch	1989	1,758
19 4/16	12 0/16	7 4/16	M	Dryden	ONT	Kreg A. Elmer	1989	1,758
19 4/16	12 2/16	7 2/16	M	Douglas County	WI	Dennis Nicholson	1989	1,758
19 4/16	11 14/16	7 6/16	M	Ravalli County	MT	Travis E. Proctor	1989	1,758
19 4/16	12 2/16	7 2/16	M	Sandoval County	NM	James O. Marquis	1989	1,758
19 4/16	12 0/16	7 4/16	M	Snow Lake	MAN	Jerry D. Heistan	1990	1,758
19 4/16	11 11/16	7 9/16	M	River Valley	ONT	Jim D. Mullins	1990	1,758
19 4/16	12 2/16	7 2/16	M	East Bull Lake	ONT	Gerald A. Dick II	1990	1,758
19 4/16	12 1/16	7 3/16	M	Sheridan County	WY	Dennis F. Craft	1990	1,758
19 4/16	12 2/16	7 2/16	M	Delta County	MI	Bob Bouck	1990	1,758
19 4/16	12 7/16	6 13/16	M	Schoolcraft County	MI	Dennis W. Kleeman	1990	1,758
19 4/16	11 12/16	7 8/16	M	Archuleta County	CO	Grant Adkisson	1991	1,758
19 4/16	12 0/16	7 4/16	M	Lincoln County	OR	Chad Fletcher	1991	1,758
19 4/16	11 11/16	7 9/16	M	Waldie Township	ONT	Richard C. Witt	1991	1,758
19 4/16	12 5/16	6 15/16	M	Chippewa County	WI	William E. Gladitsch	1991	1,758
19 4/16	12 0/16	7 4/16	M	Longlac	ONT	Steven R. Anderson	1992	1,758
19 4/16	12 0/16	7 4/16	M	Yukon River	AK	Bruce A. Haas	1992	1,758
19 4/16	12 2/16	7 2/16	M	Davidson	QUE	Brian I. King	1992	1,758
19 4/16	11 14/16	7 6/16	M	Merrimack County	NH	Thomas Thayer	1992	1,758
19 4/16	11 13/16	7 7/16	M	Bennington County	VT	Robert Marceau	1992	1,758
19 4/16	12 4/16	7 0/16	M	Pocahontas County	WV	David N. Herndon	1992	1,758
19 4/16	12 2/16	7 2/16	M	Blackhawk	ONT	Greg Wallace	1993	1,758
19 4/16	12 4/16	7 0/16	M	Prince of Wales Island	AK	James D. Cruz	1993	1,758
19 4/16	11 14/16	7 6/16	M	Kenora	ONT	Steven L. Ketelboeter	1993	1,758
19 4/16	11 14/16	7 6/16	M	La Ronge	SAS	Mark C. Petersen	1993	1,758
19 4/16	11 3/16	8 1/16	M	Cochrane	ONT	James De Luca, Jr.	1993	1,758
19 4/16	11 14/16	7 6/16	M	Ft. McMurray	ALB	Billy Tillotson	1993	1,758
19 4/16	12 0/16	7 4/16	M	Armstrong	ONT	Kenneth C. Schroeder	1993	1,758
19 4/16	11 14/16	7 6/16	M	Fredericton	NBW	John Zilinski	1993	1,758
19 4/16	11 6/16	7 14/16	M	Siskiyou County	CA	Roy E. Grace	1993	1,758
19 4/16	12 3/16	7 1/16	M	Ft. McMurray	ALB	Richard R. Strelow	1993	1,758
19 4/16	12 0/16	7 4/16	M	Webster	ONT	Kent Hare	1993	1,758
19 4/16	12 0/16	7 4/16	M	Carrot River	SAS	Udo Kerber	1993	1,758
19 4/16	11 15/16	7 5/16	M	Cleveland Peninsula	AK	William H. Welton	1994	1,758
19 4/16	12 4/16	7 0/16	M	Peace River	ALB	Roy D. Baird	1994	1,758
19 4/16	12 4/16	7 0/16	M	Wolf Lake	ALB	Greg Lumley	1994	1,758
19 4/16	12 2/16	7 2/16	M	Carrot River	SAS	Gary Wissmueller	1994	1,758
19 4/16	12 3/16	7 1/16	M	Buffalo Head Prairie	ALB	E. Josh Isbell	1994	1,758
19 4/16	11 14/16	7 6/16	M	Baie Comeau	QUE	Trevor W.G. McEntyre	1994	1,758
19 4/16	12 3/16	7 1/16	M	Fresno County	CA	Tony Williams	1994	1,758
19 4/16	12 6/16	6 14/16	M	Ontonagon County	MI	Gregory Schleusner	1994	1,758
19 4/16	11 10/16	7 10/16	M	Beaverhead County	MT	Kevin Hadley	1994	1,758
19 4/16	11 13/16	7 7/16	M	Carroll County	NH	Richard N. Kimball	1994	1,758
19 4/16	12 0/16	7 4/16	M	Kapuskasing	ONT	Floyd S. Kines	1995	1,758
19 4/16	12 2/16	7 2/16	M	Yaughn Lake	ONT	Dewayne Leming	1995	1,758
19 4/16	12 1/16	7 3/16	M	Chibougamau	QUE	Seth Stevens	1995	1,758
19 4/16	11 15/16	7 5/16	M	Lake Besnard	SAS	Eric J. Collier	1995	1,758
19 4/16	12 2/16	7 2/16	M	Horsefly	BC	Allan Tew	1995	1,758
19 4/16	11 9/16	7 11/16	M	Mono County	CA	John H. Klaasen	1995	1,758
19 4/16	12 2/16	7 2/16	M	Bissett	MAN	Glenn R. Daily	1995	1,758
19 4/16	11 10/16	7 10/16	M	Wawa	ONT	Tad H. Ralston	1995	1,758
19 4/16	11 13/16	7 7/16	M	Mendocino County	CA	Gerald E. Boelens	1995	1,758
19 4/16	12 3/16	7 1/16	M	Kittitas County	WA	James O. Whitlatch, Jr.	1995	1,758
19 4/16	11 14/16	7 6/16	M	Otero County	NM	Gene Foster	1995	1,758
19 4/16	12 11/16	6 9/16	M	Burnett County	WI	Chad A. Olson	1995	1,758
19 4/16	12 2/16	7 2/16	M	Snow Lake	MAN	Christopher Kaforski	1996	1,758
19 4/16	12 1/16	7 3/16	M	Minaki	ONT	Brian L. Grimes	1996	1,758
19 4/16	12 5/16	6 15/16	M	Rossburn	MAN	Barry Minshull	1996	1,758
19 4/16	12 1/16	7 3/16	M	Hawkrock	SAS	Al Kuntz	1996	1,758
19 4/16	11 15/16	7 5/16	M	Oxford County	ME	John R. Willhoyte	1996	1,758
19 4/16	12 2/16	7 2/16	M	Florence County	WI	Peter Meeuwsen	1996	1,758
19 4/16	11 12/16	7 8/16	M	Tulare County	CA	Clebio Leal Santos	1996	1,758

BLACK BEAR

Minimum Score 18   Continued   157

SCORE	GREATEST LENGTH	GREATEST WIDTH	SEX	AREA	STATE/ PROVINCE	HUNTER'S NAME	DATE	RANK
19 4/16	11 14/16	7 6/16	M	Athabasca River	ALB	Robert B. Stryker	1997	1,758
19 4/16	12 6/16	6 14/16	M	Meadow Lake	SAS	Tom Younger	1997	1,758
19 4/16	12 0/16	7 4/16	M	Shining Tree	ONT	John F. Belha, Jr.	1997	1,758
19 4/16	12 0/16	7 4/16	M	Lac des Mille Lacs	ONT	Doug Vislisel	1997	1,758
19 4/16	12 5/16	6 15/16	M	Crow Wing County	MN	Dan Berger	1997	1,758
19 4/16	11 15/16	7 5/16	M	Herkimer County	NY	Steve Balyszak	1997	1,758
19 4/16	12 3/16	7 1/16	M	Rio Arriba County	NM	Richard A. Smith	1998	1,758
19 4/16	11 14/16	7 6/16	M	Brunswick Lake	ONT	Thomas J. Kuehl	1998	1,758
19 4/16	12 6/16	6 14/16	M	Marchand	MAN	Don Reimer	1998	1,758
19 3/16	11 12/16	7 7/16	M	Mineral County	CO	Edward Wintz	1960	1,882
19 3/16	12 2/16	7 1/16	M	Rio Arriba County	NM	Dan Ward	1964	1,882
19 3/16	11 13/16	7 6/16	M	Iron Bridge	ONT	Philip L. Hawkins	1965	1,882
19 3/16	11 12/16	7 7/16	M	Shasta County	CA	Michael D. Combs	1967	1,882
19 3/16	11 11/16	7 8/16	M	Sudbury District	ONT	Floyd Eccleston	1970	1,882
19 3/16	11 13/16	7 6/16	M	Uncompahgre N.F.	CO	Charles Bojarski	1971	1,882
19 3/16	11 14/16	7 5/16	M	Sequoia National Forest	CA	Martin Szekeresh, Jr.	1973	1,882
19 3/16	11 11/16	7 8/16	M	Powell County	MT	Gary L. Wilson	1975	1,882
19 3/16	11 13/16	7 6/16	M	Fremont County	ID	Roger Atwood	1977	1,882
19 3/16	12 3/16	7 0/16	M	Dryden	ONT	Bill Rose	1978	1,882
19 3/16	11 14/16	7 5/16	M	Saguache County	CO	Ross M. Clark	1979	1,882
19 3/16	11 13/16	7 6/16	M	Roscommon County	MI	Roger J. Maeder	1979	1,882
19 3/16	11 15/16	7 4/16	M	Bonneville County	ID	Fred Huffman	1980	1,882
19 3/16	11 14/16	7 5/16	M	Conejos County	CO	Frank Scott	1980	1,882
19 3/16	12 1/16	7 2/16	M	Iron County	WI	Frank Rasch	1982	1,882
19 3/16	11 15/16	7 4/16	M	Las Animas County	CO	Tom Nelson	1983	1,882
19 3/16	12 1/16	7 2/16	M	Delta County	CO	Doug McCauley	1983	1,882
19 3/16	12 1/16	7 2/16	M	Graham	ONT	Michael Perrott	1983	1,882
19 3/16	11 12/16	7 7/16	M	Grand County	CO	Jim Williams	1983	1,882
19 3/16	11 14/16	7 5/16	M	Kenora	ONT	Kenneth Gilb	1983	1,882
19 3/16	12 3/16	7 0/16	M	Madison County	ID	Garry L. Bolinder	1983	1,882
19 3/16	12 2/16	7 1/16	M	Hubbard County	MN	Omar Maggard	1984	1,882
19 3/16	11 13/16	7 6/16	M	Black Sturgeon Lake	ONT	Clarence 'Bud' Mrozek	1985	1,882
19 3/16	12 2/16	7 1/16	M	Durban	MAN	Bill Clink	1985	1,882
19 3/16	12 6/16	6 13/16	M	Aitkin County	MN	Timothy J. Duffney	1985	1,882
19 3/16	12 2/16	7 1/16	M	Whitemud Creek	ALB	Paul St. Laurent	1986	1,882
19 3/16	11 11/16	7 8/16	M	Caramat	ONT	Burley Hall	1986	1,882
19 3/16	11 15/16	7 4/16	M	Thunder Bay	ONT	Ron K. Serwa	1986	1,882
19 3/16	11 15/16	7 4/16	M	Bending Lake	ONT	John Lamp	1986	1,882
19 3/16	11 12/16	7 7/16	M	Park County	CO	Robert Wright	1987	1,882
19 3/16	11 12/16	7 7/16	M	Sussex	NBW	Roger W. Kerry	1987	1,882
19 3/16	11 11/16	7 8/16	M	Sioux Narrows	ONT	Todd Gebert	1987	1,882
19 3/16	11 15/16	7 4/16	M	Clearwater County	ID	Don Larson	1987	1,882
19 3/16	11 9/16	7 10/16	M	Black River	ONT	E. L. Boyd III	1987	1,882
19 3/16	12 2/16	7 1/16	M	Custer County	CO	Rod Niles	1987	1,882
19 3/16	11 15/16	7 4/16	M	Boise County	ID	Curtis B. Wiker	1987	1,882
19 3/16	11 12/16	7 7/16	M	Franklin County	ME	Jim Roy	1987	1,882
19 3/16	12 4/16	6 15/16	M	Itasca County	MN	Cary Dalton	1987	1,882
19 3/16	12 1/16	7 2/16	M	Durban	MAN	Mike Delfino, Jr.	1987	1,882
19 3/16	12 3/16	7 0/16	M	Siskiyou County	CA	Clifford Mosley	1987	1,882
19 3/16	11 14/16	7 5/16	M	Boise County	ID	Dave Scott	1988	1,882
19 3/16	11 9/16	7 10/16	M	Siskiyou County	CA	William Payne	1988	1,882
19 3/16	11 15/16	7 4/16	M	High Prairie	ALB	Stephen Ebel	1989	1,882
19 3/16	12 0/16	7 3/16	M	Latah County	ID	Steve Krier	1989	1,882
19 3/16	11 11/16	7 8/16	M	Carbon County	UT	Hugh H. Hogle	1989	1,882
19 3/16	11 10/16	7 9/16	M	Lac Le Truite Territory	QUE	Brian Hendricks	1989	1,882
19 3/16	12 8/16	6 11/16	M	Extall River	BC	Larry H. Hill	1990	1,882
19 3/16	12 4/16	6 15/16	M	Wawang Lake	ONT	Todd A. Sturgul	1990	1,882
19 3/16	11 15/16	7 4/16	M	Manigotagan	MAN	Bruce Huewan	1990	1,882
19 3/16	12 2/16	7 1/16	M	High Level	ALB	David Petet	1990	1,882
19 3/16	11 12/16	7 7/16	M	Lane County	OR	Dave Elliott	1990	1,882
19 3/16	11 15/16	7 4/16	M	Prince of Wales Island	AK	Glen Berry	1991	1,882
19 3/16	12 2/16	7 1/16	M	Fort Chipwan	ALB	Patrick H. Aucoin	1991	1,882
19 3/16	12 6/16	6 13/16	M	Nancy Lake	AK	Mark R. Daum	1991	1,882
19 3/16	12 4/16	6 15/16	M	Beluga River	AK	Dr. Robert Edward Speegle	1991	1,882
19 3/16	12 2/16	7 1/16	M	High Level	ALB	Gino Giannetti	1991	1,882
19 3/16	12 4/16	6 15/16	M	Sheridan County	WY	Scott Runde	1991	1,882
19 3/16	12 5/16	6 14/16	M	Latuque	QUE	Bernard E. Beaudin	1991	1,882
19 3/16	12 1/16	7 2/16	M	Grand Rapids	MAN	James R. Kramp	1991	1,882
19 3/16	12 2/16	7 1/16	M	St. Louis County	MN	John Cardinal	1991	1,882
19 3/16	12 3/16	7 0/16	M	Montezuma County	CO	Paula R. Morton	1992	1,882
19 3/16	11 12/16	7 7/16	M	Edmonton	ALB	Keith Morris	1992	1,882
19 3/16	12 2/16	7 1/16	M	Idaho County	ID	Charles R. Whitfield	1992	1,882
19 3/16	12 3/16	7 0/16	M	Duchesne County	UT	Hal R. Stauff	1992	1,882
19 3/16	11 13/16	7 6/16	M	Raleigh Lake	ONT	Jeffrey Rueth	1992	1,882
19 3/16	11 15/16	7 4/16	M	Lemhi County	ID	Gary Sims	1992	1,882
19 3/16	12 4/16	6 15/16	M	Apache County	AZ	James S. Nelson IV	1993	1,882
19 3/16	12 3/16	7 0/16	M	Highland Valley	BC	Kenneth Arthur Brown	1993	1,882
19 3/16	12 0/16	7 3/16	M	Monds Township	ONT	John Standafer	1993	1,882

BLACK BEAR

Minimum Score 18 — Continued

SCORE	GREATEST LENGTH	GREATEST WIDTH	SEX	AREA	STATE/ PROVINCE	HUNTER'S NAME	DATE	RANK
19 3/16	11 11/16	7 8/16	M	Atikokan	ONT	Darrell J. Langan	1993	1,882
19 3/16	11 15/16	7 4/16	M	Archuleta County	CO	Tonnie Elwood Davis	1993	1,882
19 3/16	12 0/16	7 3/16	M	McBride	BC	Reg Meisner	1993	1,882
19 3/16	12 6/16	6 13/16	M	Oneida County	WI	Shawn Umland	1993	1,882
19 3/16	11 14/16	7 5/16	M	Wapawekka Lake	SAS	Gary Schwieters	1993	1,882
19 3/16	12 2/16	7 1/16	M	Kelowna	BC	Chris Partridge	1994	1,882
19 3/16	12 6/16	6 13/16	M	White Fox	SAS	Edward Toelken	1994	1,882
19 3/16	11 14/16	7 5/16	M	Fort McMurray	ALB	Mike Walker	1994	1,882
19 3/16	12 3/16	7 0/16	M	Prince of Wales Island	AK	Rick Schikora	1994	1,882
19 3/16	12 10/16	6 9/16	M	Fort Frances	ONT	Greg Wallace	1994	1,882
19 3/16	12 0/16	7 3/16	M	Wabasca River	ALB	Dave Holt	1994	1,882
19 3/16	11 15/16	7 4/16	M	Tucker County	WV	Charles R. Burks	1994	1,882
19 3/16	11 13/16	7 6/16	M	Tulare County	CA	Herb DeLong	1994	1,882
19 3/16	12 5/16	6 14/16	M	Riding Mtn.	MAN	Bill Clink	1995	1,882
19 3/16	11 12/16	7 7/16	M	Boise County	ID	Bruce A. Capes	1995	1,882
19 3/16	12 4/16	6 15/16	M	Spiritwood	SAS	Frank Jones	1995	1,882
19 3/16	11 13/16	7 6/16	M	La Ronge	SAS	Patrick Young	1995	1,882
19 3/16	12 0/16	7 3/16	M	Kapacasing	ONT	Lester W. Fraser	1995	1,882
19 3/16	12 4/16	6 15/16	M	Lodge Pole	ALB	Steve MacKenzie	1995	1,882
19 3/16	12 8/16	6 11/16	M	Cranberry Portage	MAN	Joseph F. Blazevich	1995	1,882
19 3/16	12 0/16	7 3/16	M	Vermilion Bay	ONT	Roy Legler	1995	1,882
19 3/16	12 0/16	7 3/16	M	Algoma	ONT	Todd Howard Parker	1995	1,882
19 3/16	11 13/16	7 6/16	M	Fort McMurray	ALB	J. A. Tyburczy	1996	1,882
19 3/16	12 0/16	7 3/16	M	Hudson	ONT	Steve Lehner	1996	1,882
19 3/16	12 1/16	7 2/16	M	Usherville	SAS	Jeff Stephenson	1996	1,882
19 3/16	11 12/16	7 7/16	M	Chibougamau	QUE	David Kretschmar	1996	1,882
19 3/16	12 6/16	6 13/16	M	Pine County	MN	Mike Sannan	1996	1,882
19 3/16	11 13/16	7 6/16	M	Aroostook County	ME	Daniel J. Dyer	1996	1,882
19 3/16	11 13/16	7 6/16	M	Sturgeon Lake	ONT	Steven A. Page	1996	1,882
19 3/16	11 14/16	7 5/16	M	Sawyer County	WI	Timothy Kelley	1996	1,882
19 3/16	12 7/16	6 12/16	M	Carrot River	SAS	Brad Hedke	1997	1,882
19 3/16	11 13/16	7 6/16	M	Howell	ONT	Donnie Hamby	1997	1,882
19 3/16	12 4/16	6 15/16	M	Whiteshell Provincial Park	MAN	Wendell Schatkowsky	1998	1,882
19 3/16	12 5/16	6 14/16	M	Prince of Wales Island	AK	Danny Moore	1998	1,882
19 3/16	12 2/16	7 1/16	M	Calabogie	ONT	Randy R. Martin	1998	1,882
19 2/16	11 9/16	7 9/16	M	Sudbury	ONT	Clarence Grandt	1963	1,986
19 2/16	11 12/16	7 6/16	M	Blount County	TN	Don Dvoroznak	1968	1,986
19 2/16	11 13/16	7 5/16	M	Chapleau	ONT	Gerald E. Taft	1968	1,986
19 2/16	11 12/16	7 6/16	M	Trinity County	CA	Fred M. Frakes	1970	1,986
19 2/16	12 3/16	6 15/16	M	Shasta County	CA	Gerald P. Doyle	1971	1,986
19 2/16	11 14/16	7 4/16	M	Vilas County	WI	William L. Yessa	1971	1,986
19 2/16	11 11/16	7 7/16	M	Kormak	ONT	Marvin E. Davis	1972	1,986
19 2/16	11 15/16	7 3/16	M	Uncompahgre N.F.	CO	Ed Bonardi	1973	1,986
19 2/16	11 13/16	7 5/16	M	Lemhi County	ID	Curley Keadle	1973	1,986
19 2/16	12 0/16	7 2/16	M	Dolores County	CO	Marvin Reichenau	1973	1,986
19 2/16	11 14/16	7 4/16	M	Archuleta County	CO	Judd Cooney	1974	1,986
19 2/16	11 13/16	7 5/16	M	Vancouver Island	BC	F. Guillon/A. Klopfenstein	1974	1,986
19 2/16	12 1/16	7 1/16	M	Dryden	ONT	Ken Horton	1977	1,986
19 2/16	12 4/16	6 14/16	M	Vilas County	WI	Michael Gapa	1979	1,986
19 2/16	11 14/16	7 4/16	M	Skamania County	WA	John H. Wahl	1979	1,986
19 2/16	11 11/16	7 7/16	M	Shasta County	CA	Mark David Broadhead	1980	1,986
19 2/16	11 14/16	7 4/16	M	Douglas County	CO	Thomas P. Grainger	1980	1,986
19 2/16	12 1/16	7 1/16	M	Chetwynd	BC	Ron F. McKay	1980	1,986
19 2/16	12 0/16	7 2/16	M	Bayfield County	WI	William F. Schutte	1980	1,986
19 2/16	11 15/16	7 3/16	M	Las Animas County	CO	David S. Bunce	1981	1,986
19 2/16	12 4/16	6 14/16	M	Whitecourt	ALB	Wade Johnson	1981	1,986
19 2/16	12 4/16	6 14/16	M	St. Louis County	MN	Charlie Paine	1981	1,986
19 2/16	12 2/16	7 0/16	M	Flathead County	MT	Owen Weaver	1981	1,986
19 2/16	12 0/16	7 2/16	M	Boise County	ID	Larry Hoff	1982	1,986
19 2/16	11 12/16	7 6/16	M	Las Animas County	CO	Bill R. Lopatta	1982	1,986
19 2/16	12 0/16	7 2/16	M	Moose Creek	AK	Robert T. Thomason, Jr.	1983	1,986
19 2/16	11 10/16	7 8/16	M	Gallatin County	MT	Pat Sinclair	1983	1,986
19 2/16	11 14/16	7 4/16	M	Savant Lake	ONT	Mark Milford	1983	1,986
19 2/16	12 4/16	6 14/16	M	Grassy Narrows	ONT	Mike Jacobs	1983	1,986
19 2/16	11 12/16	7 6/16	M	Caramat	ONT	Thomas Hlinka	1983	1,986
19 2/16	12 3/16	6 15/16	M	Aulneau Peninsula	ONT	Mike Koska	1984	1,986
19 2/16	11 14/16	7 4/16	M	Atikokan	ONT	Roger L. Hensley	1984	1,986
19 2/16	11 12/16	7 6/16	M	Mackinac County	MI	Carson D. McMullen	1984	1,986
19 2/16	12 2/16	7 0/16	M	Grand County	UT	Diane Snyder	1985	1,986
19 2/16	12 5/16	6 13/16	M	Hudson Bay	SAS	Floyd Forster	1985	1,986
19 2/16	11 11/16	7 7/16	M	Valley County	ID	Kenneth A. Hyde	1985	1,986
19 2/16	12 3/16	6 15/16	M	Sanpete County	UT	Terry Casper	1986	1,986
19 2/16	12 1/16	7 1/16	M	Rocky Lake	MAN	Dennis Jacobson	1986	1,986
19 2/16	12 0/16	7 2/16	M	French River	ONT	Mike Bishop	1986	1,986
19 2/16	11 14/16	7 4/16	M	Boise County	ID	Gary Titus	1986	1,986
19 2/16	12 0/16	7 2/16	M	Durban	MAN	David H. Boland	1986	1,986
19 2/16	12 2/16	7 0/16	M	Duck Mtn.	MAN	Chris Switzer	1987	1,986
19 2/16	12 0/16	7 2/16	M	Hearst	ONT	Paul David Forquer	1987	1,986

BLACK BEAR

Minimum Score 18 — Continued

SCORE	GREATEST LENGTH	GREATEST WIDTH	SEX	AREA	STATE/ PROVINCE	HUNTER'S NAME	DATE	RANK
19 2/16	12 0/16	7 2/16	M	King County	WA	Irvin E. Harris, Jr.	1987	1,986
19 2/16	12 0/16	7 2/16	M	Catron County	NM	Perry D. Harper	1987	1,986
19 2/16	12 7/16	6 11/16	M	Cass County	MN	Philip M. Scott	1987	1,986
19 2/16	12 2/16	7 0/16	M	Haywood County	NC	Michael Treadway	1987	1,986
19 2/16	11 15/16	7 3/16	M	Greenbrier County	WV	Billy J. Hutchinson	1987	1,986
19 2/16	12 6/16	6 12/16	M	Taylor County	WI	Allen K. Beard	1988	1,986
19 2/16	12 4/16	6 14/16	M	Price County	WI	Randall J. Johnson	1988	1,986
19 2/16	11 13/16	7 5/16	M	Rio Arriba County	NM	James H. Miller	1989	1,986
19 2/16	12 2/16	7 0/16	M	Knouff Lake	BC	Steve Zelisko	1989	1,986
19 2/16	11 10/16	7 8/16	M	Caramat	ONT	Chris Hile	1989	1,986
19 2/16	12 1/16	7 1/16	M	Starr Lake	MAN	Brian Gross	1989	1,986
19 2/16	11 14/16	7 4/16	M	Thunder Bay	ONT	E. Alex Gouthro	1989	1,986
19 2/16	11 15/16	7 3/16	M	Jim Lake	AK	Tom Hocking	1989	1,986
19 2/16	11 13/16	7 5/16	M	La Tuque	QUE	Ronald T. Kinnas	1989	1,986
19 2/16	11 12/16	7 6/16	M	Prince of Wales Island	AK	Steve Martin	1989	1,986
19 2/16	11 14/16	7 4/16	M	Thunder Bay	ONT	Dale Miller	1990	1,986
19 2/16	12 2/16	7 0/16	M	Christopher Lake	SAS	Lance W. McCrary	1990	1,986
19 2/16	11 15/16	7 3/16	M	Kenora	ONT	Jeffrey C. Dais	1991	1,986
19 2/16	12 0/16	7 2/16	M	Longlac	ONT	Steven R. Anderson	1991	1,986
19 2/16	11 13/16	7 5/16	M	High Level	ALB	R. E. Smith	1991	1,986
19 2/16	12 1/16	7 1/16	M	Bear Paw Landing	ONT	Paul Keil, Jr.	1991	1,986
19 2/16	11 12/16	7 6/16	M	Le Domaine	QUE	Steven J. Niedzielski	1991	1,986
19 2/16	12 2/16	7 0/16	M	Pine County	MN	Joseph M. Butler	1991	1,986
19 2/16	12 0/16	7 2/16	M	Cook County	MN	John Truebenbach	1991	1,986
19 2/16	11 14/16	7 4/16	M	Sullivan County	NY	Larry Micera	1991	1,986
19 2/16	12 0/16	7 2/16	M	Beauville	SAS	Don Lindsay	1992	1,986
19 2/16	12 2/16	7 0/16	M	Cranberry Lake	ALB	Terry C. Parkinson	1992	1,986
19 2/16	11 15/16	7 3/16	M	La Loche	SAS	Troy D. Huffman	1992	1,986
19 2/16	11 12/16	7 6/16	M	Oxford County	ME	Gary J. Russell	1992	1,986
19 2/16	11 15/16	7 3/16	M	Greene County	NY	Dean Close	1992	1,986
19 2/16	12 4/16	6 14/16	M	Emo	ONT	Paul Kolbeck	1993	1,986
19 2/16	11 12/16	7 6/16	M	Coal Creek	BC	Jim Helinger, Jr.	1993	1,986
19 2/16	11 13/16	7 5/16	M	Kelvington	SAS	Milan R. Liesener	1993	1,986
19 2/16	12 3/16	6 15/16	M	Susitna River	AK	Brian D. McJunkin	1993	1,986
19 2/16	12 4/16	6 14/16	M	San Juan County	NM	Perry Harper	1993	1,986
19 2/16	12 0/16	7 2/16	M	Bissett	MAN	Richard P. Smith	1993	1,986
19 2/16	12 2/16	7 0/16	M	Bissett	MAN	Dennis Wylie	1993	1,986
19 2/16	11 15/16	7 3/16	M	Remigny	QUE	Michael Bolin	1993	1,986
19 2/16	11 14/16	7 4/16	M	Beauval	SAS	M. R. James	1993	1,986
19 2/16	12 2/16	7 0/16	M	Marshall County	MN	Al Hugg	1993	1,986
19 2/16	12 1/16	7 1/16	M	Grays Harbor County	WA	Tom McManus	1993	1,986
19 2/16	12 0/16	7 2/16	M	French River	ONT	John Fredrick Orr	1994	1,986
19 2/16	12 1/16	7 1/16	M	Besnard Lake	SAS	Ronald J. Collier	1994	1,986
19 2/16	11 13/16	7 5/16	M	Evain	QUE	Jacques Robichaud	1994	1,986
19 2/16	11 15/16	7 3/16	M	St. Louis County	MN	Jim Leqve	1994	1,986
19 2/16	11 13/16	7 5/16	M	Penobscot County	ME	Norman Bisson	1994	1,986
19 2/16	11 11/16	7 7/16	M	Aroostook County	ME	Richard W. Higgins	1994	1,986
19 2/16	12 1/16	7 1/16	M	Steuben County	NY	Philip J. Pomeroy	1994	1,986
19 2/16	12 1/16	7 1/16	M	Tulare County	CA	John Garr	1994	1,986
19 2/16	12 3/16	6 15/16	M	Green Lake	SAS	Jeff Rouse	1995	1,986
19 2/16	12 2/16	7 0/16	M	Sioux Narrows	ONT	Jeff Ramthun	1995	1,986
19 2/16	12 0/16	7 2/16	M	High Level	ALB	Tracy Roy	1995	1,986
19 2/16	11 9/16	7 9/16	M	Adair Township	ONT	David G. Bockheim	1995	1,986
19 2/16	12 2/16	7 0/16	M	Mendocino County	CA	David W. Rickert II	1995	1,986
19 2/16	11 1/16	8 1/16	M	Pine County	MN	Jeff Lengsfeld	1995	1,986
19 2/16	12 0/16	7 2/16	M	Aroostook County	ME	Rudy Conley	1995	1,986
19 2/16	12 4/16	6 14/16	M	Green Lake	SAS	David L. Miller	1996	1,986
19 2/16	11 9/16	7 9/16	M	Mine Centre	ONT	Mike Wissink	1996	1,986
19 2/16	11 13/16	7 5/16	M	Bonanza	ALB	John L. Nelson, Sr.	1996	1,986
19 2/16	12 0/16	7 2/16	M	Snow Lake	MAN	Toby J. Williams	1996	1,986
19 2/16	12 4/16	6 14/16	M	Carrot River	SAS	Gary Greene	1996	1,986
19 2/16	12 2/16	7 0/16	M	Dryden	ONT	Dean Bergman	1996	1,986
19 2/16	11 14/16	7 4/16	M	Hearst	ONT	Bernie Kibbe	1996	1,986
19 2/16	11 9/16	7 9/16	M	Washago	ONT	David A. Hammer	1996	1,986
19 2/16	12 1/16	7 1/16	M	Algoma	ONT	Milford Ross	1996	1,986
19 2/16	12 6/16	6 12/16	M	Remigny	QUE	Raymonde Paquin	1996	1,986
19 2/16	11 14/16	7 4/16	M	Thompson	MAN	Chris Yaritz	1996	1,986
19 2/16	12 8/16	6 10/16	M	Newton County	AR	Eric R. Duncan	1996	1,986
19 2/16	12 1/16	7 1/16	M	Revillagigedo Island	AK	Roy L. Redifer	1997	1,986
19 2/16	12 0/16	7 2/16	M	Mossy River	SAS	Troy S. Johnson	1997	1,986
19 2/16	12 4/16	6 14/16	M	Athabasca River	ALB	Henry F. Trotter III	1997	1,986
19 2/16	12 4/16	6 14/16	M	Leoville	SAS	Compton Owens	1997	1,986
19 2/16	12 4/16	6 14/16	M	Clark County	ID	Aaron Bateman	1997	1,986
19 2/16	11 12/16	7 6/16	M	Falher	ALB	Jody Kellnhofer	1997	1,986
19 2/16	12 2/16	7 0/16	M	Carroll County	NH	Matt Troiano	1997	1,986
19 2/16	12 2/16	7 0/16	M	Delta County	CO	Kelly Brooks	1997	1,986
19 2/16	12 8/16	6 10/16	M	Ferry County	WA	Doug Kikendall	1997	1,986
19 2/16	12 2/16	7 0/16	M	San Jose Creek	BC	Allan Tew	1998	1,986

BLACK BEAR

Minimum Score 18 — Continued

SCORE	GREATEST LENGTH	GREATEST WIDTH	SEX	AREA	STATE/PROVINCE	HUNTER'S NAME	DATE	RANK
19 2/16	12 5/16	6 13/16	M	Olha	MAN	Bill Clink	1998	1,986
19 2/16	11 14/16	7 4/16	M	Lac La Biche	ALB	Patrick J. Rankin	1998	1,986
19 2/16	11 15/16	7 3/16	M	Tanana Flats	AK	Tommy L. Ramsey	1998	1,986
19 2/16	12 2/16	7 0/16	M	Nipawin	SAS	Jim Horneck	1998	1,986
19 1/16	11 1/16	8 0/16	M	Jackson County	OR	Leander Lowel	1959	2,111
19 1/16	11 12/16	7 5/16	M	Mineral County	CO	Ed Wintz	1959	2,111
19 1/16	11 15/16	7 2/16	M	Gogebic County	MI	Margaret R. Cooley	1961	2,111
19 1/16	11 5/16	7 12/16	M	Upper Peninsula	MI	Jerry D. Anderson	1967	2,111
19 1/16	12 1/16	7 0/16	M	Red Lake	ONT	Don Ellett	1969	2,111
19 1/16	11 15/16	7 2/16	M	Langlade County	WI	Roland Mantzke	1969	2,111
19 1/16	11 14/16	7 3/16	M	Archuleta County	CO	Maurice Chambers	1973	2,111
19 1/16	11 15/16	7 2/16	M	Marquette County	MI	Pete Hillesheim	1974	2,111
19 1/16	11 4/16	7 13/16	M	Vancouver Island	BC	Klaus Schultz	1974	2,111
19 1/16	12 1/16	7 0/16	M	Itasca County	MN	William Biggs	1976	2,111
19 1/16	12 3/16	6 14/16	M	Garfield County	CO	Michael D. Dickess	1976	2,111
19 1/16	11 11/16	7 6/16	M	St. Louis County	MN	Gerry Benson	1977	2,111
19 1/16	12 0/16	7 1/16	M	Kitsap County	WA	Larry A. Martin	1977	2,111
19 1/16	11 10/16	7 7/16	M	Oxford County	ME	James P. Wellever	1978	2,111
19 1/16	12 2/16	6 15/16	M	Oneida County	WI	Douglas A. Severson	1979	2,111
19 1/16	12 1/16	7 0/16	M	Lincoln County	WY	Ronell Skinner	1979	2,111
19 1/16	11 12/16	7 5/16	M	Marquette County	MI	Jeff Apel	1980	2,111
19 1/16	12 2/16	6 15/16	M	Cass County	MN	Robert M. Burtch	1980	2,111
19 1/16	11 13/16	7 4/16	M	Coos County	NH	James 'Boomer' Hayden	1980	2,111
19 1/16	12 0/16	7 1/16	M	Terrace	BC	Bill Coburn	1981	2,111
19 1/16	11 12/16	7 5/16	M	Caribou Snare Creek	AK	Bill Krenz	1981	2,111
19 1/16	11 14/16	7 3/16	M	Franklin County	ME	Albert J. Kolatac	1982	2,111
19 1/16	12 2/16	6 15/16	M	Bayfield County	WI	Larry Frye	1982	2,111
19 1/16	11 15/16	7 2/16	M	Kenora	ONT	Ray Hawver	1982	2,111
19 1/16	11 14/16	7 3/16	M	Nestor Falls	ONT	Larry Streiff	1982	2,111
19 1/16	11 12/16	7 5/16	M	Espanola	ONT	Donald W. Taylor	1982	2,111
19 1/16	11 15/16	7 2/16	M	Bonneville County	ID	Ronnel J. Stacey	1983	2,111
19 1/16	11 15/16	7 2/16	M	Jellicoe	ONT	Ed Herzog	1983	2,111
19 1/16	12 1/16	7 0/16	M	Pitkin County	CO	Perry Smith	1983	2,111
19 1/16	12 4/16	6 13/16	M	Rockingham County	VA	Roger O. Wyant	1983	2,111
19 1/16	12 3/16	6 14/16	M	Hudson Bay	SAS	Warren Buss	1984	2,111
19 1/16	12 0/16	7 1/16	M	Essex County	NY	Paul Durling	1984	2,111
19 1/16	11 15/16	7 2/16	M	Plumas County	CA	Mike Holley	1984	2,111
19 1/16	12 1/16	7 0/16	M	Coos County	OR	Rick Gabbard	1984	2,111
19 1/16	11 14/16	7 3/16	M	Redditt	ONT	Jim Christman	1985	2,111
19 1/16	11 15/16	7 2/16	M	Little Bear Lake	SAS	Michael J. Ward	1986	2,111
19 1/16	12 2/16	6 15/16	M	Terrance Lake	ONT	Jerry Krolik	1986	2,111
19 1/16	12 6/16	6 11/16	M	Nez Perce County	ID	Steve Marcell	1986	2,111
19 1/16	11 15/16	7 2/16	F	Sanpete County	UT	Judy Hallman	1986	2,111
19 1/16	12 2/16	6 15/16	M	Plumas County	CA	Mike Holley	1986	2,111
19 1/16	12 3/16	6 14/16	M	Alpine County	CA	Rick Lund	1986	2,111
19 1/16	12 2/16	6 15/16	M	Carbon County	UT	Hugh Hogle	1987	2,111
19 1/16	11 13/16	7 4/16	M	Fremont County	CO	Cheryl Ray	1987	2,111
19 1/16	11 15/16	7 2/16	M	Atikokan	ONT	Paul Maas	1987	2,111
19 1/16	11 15/16	7 2/16	M	Grand County	UT	O. Clair Adams	1988	2,111
19 1/16	11 15/16	7 2/16	M	Zone 67	SAS	Ivan Buss	1988	2,111
19 1/16	12 0/16	7 1/16	M	Dryden	ONT	Terry C. Arndt	1988	2,111
19 1/16	11 14/16	7 3/16	M	Bryson Lake	QUE	Stephen P. Pointer	1988	2,111
19 1/16	11 10/16	7 7/16	M	Inyo County	CA	Jim Voges	1988	2,111
19 1/16	11 15/16	7 2/16	M	Millville	NBW	Lamar M. Shafer	1988	2,111
19 1/16	12 0/16	7 1/16	M	Smokey Lake	ALB	Greg Reynolds	1989	2,111
19 1/16	11 14/16	7 3/16	M	Hornepayne	ONT	Paul R. Chaffee	1989	2,111
19 1/16	11 14/16	7 3/16	M	Larimer County	CO	Ed Bennett	1989	2,111
19 1/16	11 6/16	7 11/16	M	Dryden	ONT	Troy S. Lowrey	1989	2,111
19 1/16	12 2/16	6 15/16	M	Porcupine Mtns.	SAS	Dave McKenzie	1989	2,111
19 1/16	11 10/16	7 7/16	M	Warren	ONT	Gary Lawrence Harding	1989	2,111
19 1/16	11 13/16	7 4/16	M	Kenora	ONT	Chuck Harris	1989	2,111
19 1/16	11 15/16	7 2/16	M	Sudbury	ONT	Randolph J. Hempton	1989	2,111
19 1/16	11 14/16	7 3/16	M	Fort McMurray	ALB	Jim Trafford	1990	2,111
19 1/16	11 14/16	7 3/16	M	Kenora	ONT	Shawn A. Wahl	1990	2,111
19 1/16	12 1/16	7 0/16	M	Duchesne County	UT	Roger Cyfers	1990	2,111
19 1/16	11 15/16	7 2/16	M	Marathon	ONT	David Weerstra	1990	2,111
19 1/16	11 12/16	7 5/16	M	Stevens County	WA	Robert M. Larson	1990	2,111
19 1/16	12 1/16	7 0/16	M	Prince of Wales Island	AK	Bernie Weisgerber	1990	2,111
19 1/16	11 11/16	7 6/16	M	Wallowa County	OR	Dick Dohm	1990	2,111
19 1/16	12 1/16	7 0/16	M	Prince of Wales Island	AK	Dan Moore	1991	2,111
19 1/16	12 3/16	6 14/16	M	Lincoln County	OR	Richard S. Gaebel	1991	2,111
19 1/16	11 3/16	7 14/16	F	Riding Mtn.	MAN	Cory A. Pardon	1991	2,111
19 1/16	12 4/16	6 13/16	M	High Level	ALB	Gino Giannetti	1991	2,111
19 1/16	11 12/16	7 5/16	M	Sandoval County	NM	Wayne C. Wendel	1991	2,111
19 1/16	12 1/16	7 0/16	M	Beltrami County	MN	Charles W. Gahagan	1991	2,111
19 1/16	12 3/16	6 14/16	M	Smokey Lake	ALB	Andy Melnychuk	1991	2,111
19 1/16	12 0/16	7 1/16	M	Preston County	WV	Robert Peddicord	1991	2,111
19 1/16	11 15/16	7 2/16	M	Grand County	CO	Cary Laman	1992	2,111

BLACK BEAR

Minimum Score 18 — Continued

SCORE	GREATEST LENGTH	GREATEST WIDTH	SEX	AREA	STATE/ PROVINCE	HUNTER'S NAME	DATE	RANK
19 1/16	12 0/16	7 1/16	M	Montrose County	CO	Johnnie R. Walters	1992	2,111
19 1/16	11 15/16	7 2/16	M	Trinity County	CA	Edward Bianchi	1992	2,111
19 1/16	12 2/16	6 15/16	M	Prince of Wales Island	AK	Kelly Norskog	1992	2,111
19 1/16	11 13/16	7 4/16	M	Sioux Narrows	ONT	Steve Young	1992	2,111
19 1/16	11 15/16	7 2/16	M	Prince of Wales Island	AK	Monty Moravec	1993	2,111
19 1/16	12 1/16	7 0/16	M	Prince of Wales Island	AK	Danny Moore	1993	2,111
19 1/16	12 1/16	7 0/16	M	Fisher Branch	MAN	Michael Delfino, Sr.	1993	2,111
19 1/16	11 12/16	7 5/16	M	Kashabowie	ONT	Andrew Schweitzer	1993	2,111
19 1/16	12 0/16	7 1/16	M	Le Domaine	QUE	Nicholas J. Barone, Jr.	1993	2,111
19 1/16	11 15/16	7 2/16	M	Redditt	ONT	Gary Niesen	1993	2,111
19 1/16	12 5/16	6 12/16	M	Beltrami County	MN	Keith Dahl	1993	2,111
19 1/16	12 3/16	6 14/16	M	Atikokan	ONT	Mark A. Stephens	1993	2,111
19 1/16	12 4/16	6 13/16	M	Isanti County	MN	Bryan Becklin	1993	2,111
19 1/16	11 15/16	7 2/16	M	Alsek River	BC	Randy R. McGregor	1994	2,111
19 1/16	11 12/16	7 5/16	M	Blind River	ONT	Eugene Morgan	1994	2,111
19 1/16	12 3/16	6 14/16	M	Lake Brunswick	ONT	Kevin J. Benzschawel	1994	2,111
19 1/16	11 10/16	7 7/16	M	Stenen	SAS	Tim R. Dawson	1994	2,111
19 1/16	11 9/16	7 8/16	M	Thunder Bay	ONT	Skip Simpson	1994	2,111
19 1/16	12 1/16	7 0/16	M	Saddle Hills	ALB	Dale Collins	1994	2,111
19 1/16	12 1/16	7 0/16	M	Gogebic County	MI	Brian R. Hewitt	1994	2,111
19 1/16	12 2/16	6 15/16	M	Iron County	WI	Richard M. Kanzelberger	1994	2,111
19 1/16	12 3/16	6 14/16	M	Albemarle County	VA	John Patterson	1994	2,111
19 1/16	12 0/16	7 1/16	M	Tehama County	CA	Greg Carr	1994	2,111
19 1/16	11 11/16	7 6/16	M	La Ronge	SAS	Paul Wolf	1995	2,111
19 1/16	11 11/16	7 6/16	M	Ghost River	ONT	Roy L. Walk	1995	2,111
19 1/16	11 15/16	7 2/16	M	Elsas	ONT	William R. Hecker, Jr.	1995	2,111
19 1/16	12 1/16	7 0/16	M	Koochiching County	MN	Arnie Streit	1995	2,111
19 1/16	11 12/16	7 5/16	M	Sawyer County	WI	Bill Yoakum	1995	2,111
19 1/16	11 9/16	7 8/16	M	Sipiwesk Lake	MAN	Jeffrey Williams	1996	2,111
19 1/16	12 6/16	6 11/16	M	Nipawin	SAS	Gregory Bokash	1996	2,111
19 1/16	11 13/16	7 4/16	M	Candle Lake	SAS	Ed Anderson	1996	2,111
19 1/16	12 5/16	6 12/16	M	Beltrami County	MN	Brian Aune	1996	2,111
19 1/16	11 11/16	7 6/16	M	Swan River	MAN	Daniel M. Permanian	1996	2,111
19 1/16	12 2/16	6 15/16	M	Vermilion Bay	ONT	Sandy Schulz	1996	2,111
19 1/16	11 14/16	7 3/16	M	Blaine County	ID	Larry R. Newton	1997	2,111
19 1/16	11 15/16	7 2/16	M	Buffalo Narrows	SAS	Arnt A. Fossum	1997	2,111
19 1/16	11 12/16	7 5/16	M	Wawa	ONT	Wendall Matson	1997	2,111
19 1/16	12 1/16	7 0/16	M	Coconino County	AZ	Lynn E. DeSpain	1997	2,111
19 1/16	11 13/16	7 4/16	M	Fort McMurray	ALB	Mark Kuhn	1998	2,111
19 1/16	12 5/16	6 12/16	M	Lewis Lake	MAN	Jeff Celletti	1998	2,111
19 1/16	12 1/16	7 0/16	M	Lynn Lake	MAN	Terry Coward	1998	2,111
19 1/16	11 8/16	7 9/16	M	Skamania County	WA	Annette Crews	1998	2,111
19 0/16	12 6/16	6 10/16	M	Iron County	WI	Charles Kroll	1966	2,227
19 0/16	11 9/16	7 7/16	M	Sioux Narrows	ONT	Walter J. Sawicki	1967	2,227
19 0/16	11 13/16	7 3/16	M	Kamloops	BC	Terry J. Haines	1968	2,227
19 0/16	11 12/16	7 4/16	M	Chapleau	ONT	Kenneth R. Larson	1968	2,227
19 0/16	11 15/16	7 1/16	M	Ignace	ONT	Stanley Olson	1968	2,227
19 0/16	11 10/16	7 6/16	M	Kenora	ONT	Barry Englehardt	1969	2,227
19 0/16	11 12/16	7 4/16	M	Armstrong	ONT	James Mahoney	1969	2,227
19 0/16	11 8/16	7 8/16	M	Shasta County	CA	Patrick J. Marley	1969	2,227
19 0/16	11 11/16	7 5/16	M	Skamania County	WA	Dennis E. DesJardins	1970	2,227
19 0/16	11 11/16	7 5/16	M	Skamania County	WA	Dennis E. DesJardins	1970	2,227
19 0/16	11 7/16	7 9/16	M	Grand County	UT	C. Donald Lechner	1970	2,227
19 0/16	11 9/16	7 7/16	M	Lemhi County	ID	Douglas Kittredge	1971	2,227
19 0/16	11 11/16	7 5/16	M	Saguache County	CO	Gary Ginther	1973	2,227
19 0/16	11 14/16	7 2/16	M	Cloyne	ONT	Tom Erkinger	1976	2,227
19 0/16	11 14/16	7 2/16	M	Lanark	ONT	Guy Pointer	1977	2,227
19 0/16	11 14/16	7 2/16	M	St. Louis County	MN	Jimmy F. Rogers	1978	2,227
19 0/16	11 8/16	7 8/16	M	Wawa	ONT	Don LaDuke	1980	2,227
19 0/16	12 5/16	6 11/16	M	Sullivan County	NY	John Nasuta	1980	2,227
19 0/16	11 9/16	7 7/16	M	Boise County	ID	Richard C. Nichols	1981	2,227
19 0/16	11 14/16	7 2/16	M	North Bay	ONT	Grant R. Beattie	1981	2,227
19 0/16	12 1/16	6 15/16	M	Fort St. John	BC	Duane Hicks	1981	2,227
19 0/16	11 11/16	7 5/16	M	Ravalli County	MT	Rod Osburn	1981	2,227
19 0/16	11 8/16	7 8/16	M	Coos County	NH	Edward Silva	1981	2,227
19 0/16	11 14/16	7 2/16	F	San Juan County	UT	Sheldon Anderson	1982	2,227
19 0/16	12 1/16	6 15/16	M	Las Animas County	CO	Bob Lopatta	1982	2,227
19 0/16	11 14/16	7 2/16	M	Pacific County	WA	Annette Crews	1983	2,227
19 0/16	11 13/16	7 3/16	M	Siskiyou County	CA	Fred Searle	1983	2,227
19 0/16	11 14/16	7 2/16	M	Fort Frances	ONT	Kerry Ella	1984	2,227
19 0/16	11 9/16	7 7/16	M	Chapeau	QUE	Joseph D. Maddock	1984	2,227
19 0/16	11 13/16	7 3/16	M	Meadow Lake	SAS	Gary Bauer	1984	2,227
19 0/16	12 1/16	6 15/16	M	Fremont County	ID	Joe Bronson	1984	2,227
19 0/16	11 15/16	7 1/16	M	York County	NBW	Daniel L. Shaffer	1984	2,227
19 0/16	11 13/16	7 3/16	M	Bingham County	ID	Mike Lee Wohlschlegel	1984	2,227
19 0/16	12 1/16	6 15/16	M	Lincoln County	WI	Jim Wurster	1984	2,227
19 0/16	11 14/16	7 2/16	M	Vilas County	WI	Mike Eidson	1984	2,227
19 0/16	11 13/16	7 3/16	M	Mine Centre	ONT	Bob Roulet	1985	2,227

BLACK BEAR

Minimum Score 18 — Continued

SCORE	GREATEST LENGTH	GREATEST WIDTH	SEX	AREA	STATE/PROVINCE	HUNTER'S NAME	DATE	RANK
19 0/16	12 2/16	6 14/16	M	Ear Falls	ONT	Brent Allen Poindexter	1985	2,227
19 0/16	11 8/16	7 8/16	M	Chelan County	WA	Leroy E. House	1986	2,227
19 0/16	11 14/16	7 2/16	M	Ravalli County	MT	John Locke	1987	2,227
19 0/16	11 14/16	7 2/16	M	Grays Harbor County	WA	Mark Tupper	1987	2,227
19 0/16	12 0/16	7 0/16	M	Tulare County	CA	Don Reid	1987	2,227
19 0/16	12 0/16	7 0/16	M	Smeaton	SAS	Gene Welle	1988	2,227
19 0/16	12 7/16	6 9/16	M	Cranbrook	BC	Jasper Kenneth White, Jr.	1988	2,227
19 0/16	11 10/16	7 6/16	M	Sioux Lookout	ONT	Steve Schmidt	1988	2,227
19 0/16	12 4/16	6 12/16	M	Langlade County	WI	Jeff Traska	1988	2,227
19 0/16	11 13/16	7 3/16	M	Carroll County	NH	Brian Libby	1988	2,227
19 0/16	12 0/16	7 0/16	M	Hardy County	WV	Clarence W. Houck	1988	2,227
19 0/16	11 12/16	7 4/16	M	Cold Lake	ALB	Ron R. Dixon	1989	2,227
19 0/16	11 9/16	7 7/16	M	Cochrane	ONT	Ed Rogalski	1989	2,227
19 0/16	12 2/16	6 14/16	M	Ft. McMurray	ALB	James Pike	1989	2,227
19 0/16	12 0/16	7 0/16	M	Chapleau	ONT	Dennis D. Wentz	1989	2,227
19 0/16	11 14/16	7 2/16	M	Drury Twp.	ONT	Marty Masek	1989	2,227
19 0/16	11 13/16	7 3/16	M	Foleyet	ONT	Mike Schmidt	1989	2,227
19 0/16	11 10/16	7 6/16	M	Sandoval County	NM	Noble Sinclair	1989	2,227
19 0/16	11 12/16	7 4/16	M	Kitsap County	WA	Gary A. Bell	1989	2,227
19 0/16	11 11/16	7 5/16	M	Pierce County	WA	Warren L. Byrd	1989	2,227
19 0/16	11 15/16	7 1/16	M	Aroostook County	ME	Louis J. Lorenzo	1989	2,227
19 0/16	12 1/16	6 15/16	M	Langlade County	WI	Glen A. Rutten	1989	2,227
19 0/16	11 11/16	7 5/16	M	Bella Coola	BC	J. Dale Hale	1989	2,227
19 0/16	12 0/16	7 0/16	M	Sheridan County	WY	Larry O. Burtis	1990	2,227
19 0/16	11 8/16	7 8/16	M	Chelmsford	ONT	Timothy C. Shock	1990	2,227
19 0/16	11 13/16	7 3/16	M	Chapleau	ONT	Dennis Dawson	1990	2,227
19 0/16	12 2/16	6 14/16	M	Minaki	ONT	Carroll Cunningham	1990	2,227
19 0/16	11 12/16	7 4/16	M	Wallowa County	OR	Eugene Smith, Jr.	1990	2,227
19 0/16	12 1/16	6 15/16	M	Bayfield County	WI	Randall O. Nash	1990	2,227
19 0/16	12 0/16	7 0/16	M	Sawyer County	WI	Kim Lemke	1990	2,227
19 0/16	11 9/16	7 7/16	M	Manitouwadge	ONT	Rick Buchanan	1991	2,227
19 0/16	11 14/16	7 2/16	M	Hearst	ONT	Steven B. Karel	1991	2,227
19 0/16	11 15/16	7 1/16	M	Remigny	QUE	Max Reagin	1991	2,227
19 0/16	11 10/16	7 6/16	M	Matagami	QUE	Jacques Harvey	1991	2,227
19 0/16	12 5/16	6 11/16	M	Sevier County	UT	Dennis Nielsen	1991	2,227
19 0/16	12 4/16	6 12/16	M	Ft. McMurray	ALB	Floyd Forster	1991	2,227
19 0/16	12 0/16	7 0/16	M	Ontonagon County	MI	Carl R. Birely	1991	2,227
19 0/16	11 12/16	7 4/16	M	Oxford County	ME	Gary J. Russell	1991	2,227
19 0/16	12 0/16	7 0/16	M	Custer County	ID	Pascal Perrin	1992	2,227
19 0/16	11 14/16	7 2/16	M	Hudson Bay	SAS	Sheldon Poss	1992	2,227
19 0/16	11 9/16	7 7/16	M	Holinshead Lake	ONT	John E. Larsen	1992	2,227
19 0/16	11 10/16	7 6/16	M	Thompson	MAN	Jack Baltz	1992	2,227
19 0/16	11 9/16	7 7/16	M	Grande Prairie	ALB	Les Baird	1992	2,227
19 0/16	11 4/16	7 12/16	M	Wanless	MAN	Tim Finley	1992	2,227
19 0/16	11 9/16	7 7/16	M	Mammeville	QUE	George A. Kearns	1992	2,227
19 0/16	12 0/16	7 0/16	M	Goodsoil	SAS	Carol Hathaway	1992	2,227
19 0/16	12 2/16	6 14/16	M	Koochiching County	MN	Arnie Streit	1992	2,227
19 0/16	11 14/16	7 2/16	M	Houghton County	MI	Jeffrey D. Emanuel	1992	2,227
19 0/16	11 10/16	7 6/16	M	Zec Rapides des Joachims	QUE	Arthur E. Thibodeau, Jr.	1992	2,227
19 0/16	12 2/16	6 14/16	M	Blackhawk	ONT	Gary Marion	1993	2,227
19 0/16	11 11/16	7 5/16	M	White River	ONT	David A. Dusthimer	1993	2,227
19 0/16	11 14/16	7 2/16	M	Lac Ile-a-la Crosse	SAS	Rocky Drake	1993	2,227
19 0/16	11 11/16	7 5/16	M	Lake County	MN	Donald Van Meveren	1993	2,227
19 0/16	12 5/16	6 11/16	M	Aitkin County	MN	Pete Peterson	1993	2,227
19 0/16	11 9/16	7 7/16	M	Powell County	MT	Scott C. Godown	1993	2,227
19 0/16	11 12/16	7 4/16	M	Alpena County	MI	Brett Anderson	1993	2,227
19 0/16	11 14/16	7 2/16	M	Elmore County	ID	Kirk W. Reese	1994	2,227
19 0/16	12 3/16	6 13/16	M	Hudson Bay	SAS	Mike Adkins	1994	2,227
19 0/16	11 14/16	7 2/16	M	Slave Lake	ALB	Greg Ogle	1994	2,227
19 0/16	11 10/16	7 6/16	M	Nipawin	SAS	Robert H. Torstenson	1994	2,227
19 0/16	11 10/16	7 6/16	M	Baie Comeau	QUE	Louis J. Lorenzo	1994	2,227
19 0/16	12 0/16	7 0/16	M	Emo	ONT	Randy Loken	1994	2,227
19 0/16	12 2/16	6 14/16	M	Women River	ONT	Paul Borden	1994	2,227
19 0/16	11 13/16	7 3/16	M	Grand Falls	NFL	Dean Coppolella	1994	2,227
19 0/16	12 6/16	6 10/16	M	Aitkin County	MN	Michael Thorp	1994	2,227
19 0/16	11 12/16	7 4/16	M	Marinette County	WI	Kevin Sommers	1994	2,227
19 0/16	11 12/16	7 4/16	M	Clark County	WI	Richard Rinehart	1994	2,227
19 0/16	12 1/16	6 15/16	M	Lane County	OR	Rick Wayne Miller	1994	2,227
19 0/16	12 4/16	6 12/16	M	Spirit River	ALB	James R. Stinson	1995	2,227
19 0/16	12 4/16	6 12/16	M	Dryden	ONT	Richard J. Kain	1995	2,227
19 0/16	12 4/16	6 12/16	M	Creighton	SAS	Cory Smith	1995	2,227
19 0/16	12 0/16	7 0/16	M	Vancouver Island	BC	Guy Davis	1995	2,227
19 0/16	12 2/16	6 14/16	M	Wabigoon	ONT	Anita R. Daggett	1995	2,227
19 0/16	12 2/16	6 14/16	M	NorthMark	ALB	Phil Neiser	1995	2,227
19 0/16	12 6/16	6 10/16	M	Otero County	NM	George W. Semple	1995	2,227
19 0/16	11 13/16	7 3/16	M	Campbell River	BC	Gary F. Bogner	1996	2,227
19 0/16	12 8/16	6 8/16	M	Dryden	ONT	Christopher J. Dean	1996	2,227
19 0/16	11 15/16	7 1/16	M	Lynn Lake	MAN	Jeff Welhouse	1996	2,227

BLACK BEAR

Minimum Score 18 — Continued

SCORE	GREATEST LENGTH	GREATEST WIDTH	SEX	AREA	STATE/PROVINCE	HUNTER'S NAME	DATE	RANK
19 0/16	11 11/16	7 5/16	M	Cadillac	QUE	John McDonald	1996	2,227
19 0/16	11 14/16	7 2/16	M	Oba	ONT	William E. Haynes	1996	2,227
19 0/16	11 14/16	7 2/16	M	Greenlee County	AZ	Rick Forrest	1996	2,227
19 0/16	11 14/16	7 2/16	M	Baraga County	MI	Mike Holy	1996	2,227
19 0/16	11 15/16	7 1/16	M	Coos County	NH	Mark P. Lachapelle	1996	2,227
19 0/16	11 15/16	7 1/16	M	Athabasca River	ALB	Sonny Evans	1997	2,227
19 0/16	11 14/16	7 2/16	M	Bissett	MAN	David Harris	1997	2,227
19 0/16	12 4/16	6 12/16	M	Carrot River	SAS	Larry Peterson	1997	2,227
19 0/16	12 2/16	6 14/16	M	Theodore River	AK	H. Gale McKnight	1997	2,227
19 0/16	11 12/16	7 4/16	M	Woodstock	NBW	Frederick Winkelmann	1997	2,227
19 0/16	12 0/16	7 0/16	M	Cabonga Reservoir	QUE	Vincent Grasso	1997	2,227
19 0/16	12 3/16	6 13/16	M	Chibougamau	QUE	Brian Brochu	1997	2,227
19 0/16	11 7/16	7 9/16	M	Ignace	ONT	Chuck Harris	1997	2,227
19 0/16	11 11/16	7 5/16	M	Pinard	ONT	Gerald L. Cripe	1997	2,227
19 0/16	12 4/16	6 12/16	M	Price County	WI	Dennis L. Lemke	1997	2,227
19 0/16	11 14/16	7 2/16	M	Zama	ALB	Tom Jordan	1998	2,227
19 0/16	11 15/16	7 1/16	M	Nusatsum River	BC	Rick Paquette	1998	2,227
19 0/16	12 0/16	7 0/16	M	Oak Lake	ONT	Ronald A. Hall	1998	2,227
19 0/16	12 2/16	6 14/16	M	Theodore River	AK	H. Gale McKnight	1998	2,227
19 0/16	11 10/16	7 6/16	M	Belleterre	QUE	Robert Amaral	1998	2,227
19 0/16	11 13/16	7 3/16	M	Siskiyou County	CA	James Brent Kincaid	1998	2,227
19 0/16	12 0/16	7 0/16	M	Aroostook County	ME	Ken Lamb	1998	2,227
18 15/16	11 9/16	7 6/16	M	King George IV Lake	NFL	Frank M. Davis	1958	2,363
18 15/16	11 15/16	7 0/16	M	Flathead County	MT	Danny Moore	1976	2,363
18 15/16	12 1/16	6 14/16	M	Pitkin County	CO	Sharon Payne	1976	2,363
18 15/16	12 0/16	6 15/16	M	St. Louis County	MN	Roy Kahabka	1978	2,363
18 15/16	12 2/16	6 13/16	M	Hubbard County	MN	Dr. James Schubert	1978	2,363
18 15/16	11 14/16	7 1/16	M	Delta County	CO	Bob Gulman, Jr.	1979	2,363
18 15/16	11 4/16	7 11/16	M	Kalkaska County	MI	Gregory Korkoske	1979	2,363
18 15/16	12 0/16	6 15/16	M	Pough Lake	ONT	Jozset Vass	1979	2,363
18 15/16	11 11/16	7 4/16	M	Roscommon County	MI	Lloyd B. Beebe	1980	2,363
18 15/16	11 15/16	7 0/16	M	Sandilands	MAN	Fred Hay	1981	2,363
18 15/16	12 1/16	6 14/16	M	Boise County	ID	Jack Arbaugh	1981	2,363
18 15/16	12 0/16	6 15/16	M	San Miguel County	NM	Dick McClain	1981	2,363
18 15/16	12 1/16	6 14/16	M	Espanola	ONT	Martin Masek	1982	2,363
18 15/16	12 0/16	6 15/16	M	Valley County	ID	Bob Dawson	1982	2,363
18 15/16	11 15/16	7 0/16	M	Larimer County	CO	Douglas Beck	1982	2,363
18 15/16	11 9/16	7 6/16	M	Pontiac	QUE	Chuck Wade	1983	2,363
18 15/16	11 10/16	7 5/16	M	Warren	ONT	Clarence Keaton	1983	2,363
18 15/16	11 14/16	7 1/16	M	Coos County	NH	Greg White	1984	2,363
18 15/16	12 2/16	6 13/16	M	Little Sturge Lake	ONT	David F. Martinek	1985	2,363
18 15/16	11 15/16	7 0/16	M	Delta County	CO	Terry Bridgman	1985	2,363
18 15/16	11 9/16	7 6/16	M	Renfrew	ONT	Jeffrey Tucker	1985	2,363
18 15/16	11 14/16	7 1/16	M	Timiskaming	ONT	Gary F. Greene	1985	2,363
18 15/16	11 8/16	7 7/16	M	Poitras	ONT	Robert H. Pavlovic	1985	2,363
18 15/16	12 2/16	6 13/16	M	Mine Centre	ONT	Larry Looman	1986	2,363
18 15/16	11 12/16	7 3/16	M	Hudson Bay	SAS	Bruce Balerud	1986	2,363
18 15/16	12 4/16	6 11/16	M	Espanola	ONT	Terry J. Gerber	1986	2,363
18 15/16	11 14/16	7 1/16	M	Cygnet Lake	ONT	Greg Roufs	1986	2,363
18 15/16	12 0/16	6 15/16	M	Sioux Lookout	ONT	Dr. Joe Nilsson	1986	2,363
18 15/16	11 12/16	7 3/16	M	Findlay Lake	QUE	Paul Bertrand	1986	2,363
18 15/16	11 13/16	7 2/16	M	King County	WA	Steven Jackl	1986	2,363
18 15/16	11 11/16	7 4/16	M	Lincoln County	WY	Vaughn Ballard	1987	2,363
18 15/16	11 14/16	7 1/16	M	Coos County	OR	G. Julie Woodman	1987	2,363
18 15/16	11 7/16	7 8/16	M	Herkimer County	NY	Daniel R. Walters	1987	2,363
18 15/16	12 1/16	6 14/16	M	Rockingham County	VA	Donald G. Hodges	1987	2,363
18 15/16	11 12/16	7 3/16	M	Cold Lake	ALB	Joseph R. Weber	1988	2,363
18 15/16	11 12/16	7 3/16	M	Latah County	ID	David B. Silcock	1988	2,363
18 15/16	11 14/16	7 1/16	M	Iron County	WI	Henry J. Lindberg	1988	2,363
18 15/16	11 14/16	7 1/16	M	Lemhi County	ID	Randy Lee Davison	1988	2,363
18 15/16	11 6/16	7 9/16	M	Elmore County	ID	John Turner	1989	2,363
18 15/16	11 10/16	7 5/16	M	Caramat	ONT	Charles P. Morgan, Jr.	1989	2,363
18 15/16	11 8/16	7 7/16	M	Boise County	ID	Julian Salutregui	1989	2,363
18 15/16	11 7/16	7 8/16	M	Zec Restigo	QUE	Clade St. Amour	1989	2,363
18 15/16	12 1/16	6 14/16	M	Fayette County	WV	Michael D. King	1989	2,363
18 15/16	11 10/16	7 5/16	M	Tucker County	WV	Robert McGee	1989	2,363
18 15/16	12 6/16	6 9/16	M	Beltrami County	MN	Ronald Alan Lemire	1990	2,363
18 15/16	12 1/16	6 14/16	M	Otero County	NM	John F. Schultz	1990	2,363
18 15/16	11 14/16	7 1/16	M	Tucker County	WV	Randall Lee Marsh	1990	2,363
18 15/16	12 1/16	6 14/16	M	Lincoln County	NM	Jack Berger	1990	2,363
18 15/16	12 1/16	6 14/16	M	Kenora	ONT	David Johnson	1991	2,363
18 15/16	11 12/16	7 3/16	M	Valley County	ID	David R. Heck	1991	2,363
18 15/16	11 11/16	7 4/16	M	Fort McMurray	ALB	Wes Whenham	1992	2,363
18 15/16	11 13/16	7 2/16	M	Siebert Lake	ALB	Orest Popil	1992	2,363
18 15/16	11 13/16	7 2/16	M	Aroostook County	ME	Richard C. Tucker	1992	2,363
18 15/16	11 14/16	7 1/16	M	St. Louis County	MN	Clarence A. Plansky	1992	2,363
18 15/16	11 12/16	7 3/16	M	Baie Comeau	QUE	Richard J. Bombard	1993	2,363
18 15/16	12 1/16	6 14/16	M	Swan River	MAN	Jim Horneck	1993	2,363

BLACK BEAR

Minimum Score 18 — Continued

SCORE	GREATEST LENGTH	GREATEST WIDTH	SEX	AREA	STATE/PROVINCE	HUNTER'S NAME	DATE	RANK
18 15/16	11 14/16	7 1/16	M	Kenora	ONT	Dale R. Perreault	1993	2,363
18 15/16	11 15/16	7 0/16	M	High Level	ALB	Dean Yardley	1993	2,363
18 15/16	11 12/16	7 3/16	M	Thompson	MAN	Ralph Pfister	1993	2,363
18 15/16	11 11/16	7 4/16	M	Zec Dumoine	QUE	Richard Deveney	1993	2,363
18 15/16	11 12/16	7 3/16	M	Flathead County	MT	James Hershberger	1993	2,363
18 15/16	12 0/16	6 15/16	M	Fayette County	WV	Gordon L. Pugh	1993	2,363
18 15/16	11 15/16	7 0/16	M	Alsek River	BC	Randy R. McGregor	1994	2,363
18 15/16	11 12/16	7 3/16	M	Alsek River	BC	Scott Ebert	1994	2,363
18 15/16	12 1/16	6 14/16	M	Carswell Lake	SAS	Patrick C. Resch	1994	2,363
18 15/16	11 13/16	7 2/16	M	Green River	NBW	Larry E. Gardiner	1994	2,363
18 15/16	11 13/16	7 2/16	M	Cranberry Portage	MAN	Lee A. Hofer	1994	2,363
18 15/16	11 10/16	7 5/16	M	Thompson	MAN	Jeff Danielson	1994	2,363
18 15/16	11 15/16	7 0/16	M	Mono County	CA	Guy Taylor	1994	2,363
18 15/16	11 13/16	7 2/16	M	St. Louis County	MN	Kevin Murphy	1994	2,363
18 15/16	12 1/16	6 14/16	M	Catron County	NM	Jeffrey N. Englebert	1994	2,363
18 15/16	12 2/16	6 13/16	M	Mackinac County	MI	Jerry D. Pratt	1994	2,363
18 15/16	12 0/16	6 15/16	M	Richer	MAN	David A. Goertzen	1995	2,363
18 15/16	12 0/16	6 15/16	M	Prince of Wales Island	AK	Justin Westervelt	1995	2,363
18 15/16	11 15/16	7 0/16	M	Lesser Slave Lake	ALB	Robert "Grub" Matthews	1995	2,363
18 15/16	11 6/16	7 9/16	M	Marathon	ONT	Arnita Finch	1995	2,363
18 15/16	11 14/16	7 1/16	M	Cranberry Portage	MAN	Kevin Reid	1995	2,363
18 15/16	12 0/16	6 15/16	M	Prince of Wales Island	AK	Jerome J. Krier, Jr.	1995	2,363
18 15/16	11 12/16	7 3/16	M	Nipigon	ONT	Tim Walters	1995	2,363
18 15/16	11 11/16	7 4/16	M	Dryden	ONT	Al Smith	1995	2,363
18 15/16	11 14/16	7 1/16	M	Dryden	ONT	Kevin Bradley Mills	1995	2,363
18 15/16	12 6/16	6 9/16	M	Pine County	MN	John Cardinal	1995	2,363
18 15/16	12 2/16	6 13/16	M	Sublette County	WY	John Gedroez	1995	2,363
18 15/16	12 1/16	6 14/16	M	Price County	WI	Dale Grant	1995	2,363
18 15/16	11 12/16	7 3/16	M	Nestor Falls	ONT	Larry Burman	1996	2,363
18 15/16	11 13/16	7 2/16	M	Seibert Lake	ALB	Orest Popil	1996	2,363
18 15/16	11 9/16	7 6/16	M	Limestone Siding	NBW	Daniel Dyer	1996	2,363
18 15/16	11 15/16	7 0/16	M	Rocky Mountain House	ALB	Vern McPherson	1996	2,363
18 15/16	11 15/16	7 0/16	M	Mine Centre	ONT	Richard D. Friedrichsen	1996	2,363
18 15/16	11 10/16	7 5/16	M	Senneterre	QUE	Scott Schulze	1996	2,363
18 15/16	12 2/16	6 13/16	M	Wabigoon	ONT	Robert Barrie	1996	2,363
18 15/16	12 0/16	6 15/16	M	Koochiching County	MN	Charles Oslund	1996	2,363
18 15/16	11 10/16	7 5/16	M	Ashland County	WI	Greg Tarlton	1996	2,363
18 15/16	12 1/16	6 14/16	M	Athabasca River	ALB	M. R. James	1997	2,363
18 15/16	12 3/16	6 12/16	M	Olha	MAN	Paul K. Koslowski	1997	2,363
18 15/16	11 11/16	7 4/16	M	Clarke Lake	SAS	Gordon Braun	1997	2,363
18 15/16	12 0/16	6 15/16	M	Ear Falls	ONT	Randy Neukirch	1997	2,363
18 15/16	12 3/16	6 12/16	M	Bradbury River	MAN	Larry G. Lottman	1997	2,363
18 15/16	11 12/16	7 3/16	M	Prince William	NBW	Jeffrey Durham Thomas	1997	2,363
18 15/16	12 2/16	6 13/16	M	Skamania County	WA	Kevin Schmid	1997	2,363
18 15/16	11 8/16	7 7/16	M	Lewis County	NY	Ben Nellenback	1997	2,363
18 15/16	12 1/16	6 14/16	M	Beluga	AK	Lewis Ledlow	1998	2,363
18 15/16	11 8/16	7 7/16	M	Plaster Rock	NBW	Stephen Brecq	1998	2,363
18 15/16	11 15/16	7 0/16	M	Black Sturgeon Lake	ONT	Jim Case	1998	2,363
18 15/16	12 0/16	6 15/16	M	Teton County	ID	Rick Goodliffe	1998	2,363
18 15/16	11 15/16	7 0/16	M	Cranberry Portage	MAN	Gregory W. Palmer	1998	2,363
18 15/16	11 13/16	7 2/16	M	Lynn Lake	MAN	Kenneth M. Thompson	1998	2,363
18 14/16	11 6/16	7 8/16	M	Vermillion Bay	ONT	Wayne I. Munkel	1966	2,470
18 14/16	12 7/16	6 7/16	M	Vanderhoof	BC	Cecil Raphael	1967	2,470
18 14/16	11 2/16	7 12/16	M	Cranberry Portage	MAN	Carl Anderson	1968	2,470
18 14/16	11 11/16	7 3/16	M	Orleans County	VT	James Gilman	1969	2,470
18 14/16	11 12/16	7 2/16	M	Idaho County	ID	Peter Eremo	1970	2,470
18 14/16	12 2/16	6 12/16	M	Mesa County	CO	Jerry Cunningham	1972	2,470
18 14/16	12 3/16	6 11/16	M	Madera County	CA	Duane A. Whittle	1973	2,470
18 14/16	11 12/16	7 2/16	M	Lake County	MN	Art Heinze	1974	2,470
18 14/16	12 2/16	6 12/16	M	Vermillion Bay	ONT	Myles Keller	1974	2,470
18 14/16	11 13/16	7 1/16	M	Lincoln County	OR	Stanley D. Miles	1974	2,470
18 14/16	12 0/16	6 14/16	M	Wabigoon	ONT	Keith Olson	1975	2,470
18 14/16	11 14/16	7 0/16	M	Minaki	ONT	Greg Stezenski	1975	2,470
18 14/16	11 10/16	7 4/16	M	Nipigon	ONT	Vickery Frederick	1976	2,470
18 14/16	11 13/16	7 1/16	M	Prince George	BC	Jim Jackson	1976	2,470
18 14/16	11 14/16	7 0/16	M	Somerset County	ME	John J. Sweeney	1976	2,470
18 14/16	11 13/16	7 1/16	M	Custer County	CO	William Henderson	1978	2,470
18 14/16	11 12/16	7 2/16	M	Bighorn Mountains	WY	David M. Nahrgang	1978	2,470
18 14/16	12 0/16	6 14/16	M	Washington County	ME	Raymond Olson	1979	2,470
18 14/16	11 14/16	7 0/16	M	Bob Marshall Wilderness	MT	James Dean	1980	2,470
18 14/16	11 10/16	7 4/16	M	Sandilands	MAN	Larry Kraynyk	1980	2,470
18 14/16	11 11/16	7 3/16	M	Marquette County	MI	William Robert Baltrip	1981	2,470
18 14/16	11 9/16	7 5/16	M	Grant County	NM	Ross Johnson	1981	2,470
18 14/16	12 0/16	6 14/16	M	Ignace	ONT	Robert I. Mussey	1981	2,470
18 14/16	11 14/16	7 0/16	M	Dryden	ONT	Gary J. O'Donnell	1981	2,470
18 14/16	11 9/16	7 5/16	M	Kootenai County	ID	Stanley Leake	1982	2,470
18 14/16	11 12/16	7 2/16	M	Chapleau	ONT	Robert J. Davis	1982	2,470
18 14/16	11 15/16	6 15/16	M	Sioux Lookout	ONT	Michael R. Traub	1982	2,470

BLACK BEAR

Minimum Score 18 — Continued

SCORE	GREATEST LENGTH	GREATEST WIDTH	SEX	AREA	STATE/ PROVINCE	HUNTER'S NAME	DATE	RANK
18 14/16	11 14/16	7 0/16	M	Montezuma County	CO	William C. Shuster	1983	2,470
18 14/16	11 9/16	7 5/16	M	Aulneau Peninsula	ONT	Michael F. Koska	1983	2,470
18 14/16	11 13/16	7 1/16	M	Thunder Bay	ONT	Todd Gilb	1983	2,470
18 14/16	11 13/16	7 1/16	M	Park County	MT	Cecil Hendricks	1983	2,470
18 14/16	11 12/16	7 2/16	M	Mine Centre	ONT	Al Haines	1984	2,470
18 14/16	11 9/16	7 5/16	M	Jackson County	CO	Kurt Keskimaki	1984	2,470
18 14/16	11 12/16	7 2/16	M	Tatalina River	AK	Timothy J. Barber	1984	2,470
18 14/16	11 6/16	7 8/16	M	Fort Frances	ONT	Lloyd R. Branchcomb	1984	2,470
18 14/16	11 13/16	7 1/16	M	Wallowa County	OR	Jerry Jensen	1984	2,470
18 14/16	11 12/16	7 2/16	M	Scoop Lake	BC	Ronald Montross	1984	2,470
18 14/16	11 8/16	7 6/16	M	Mine Centre	ONT	Gary Schuler	1985	2,470
18 14/16	11 12/16	7 2/16	M	Fremont County	CO	LeRoy Miller	1985	2,470
18 14/16	12 1/16	6 13/16	M	Ignace	ONT	Ken Terry	1985	2,470
18 14/16	11 10/16	7 4/16	M	Atikokan	ONT	Eugene Francisco	1985	2,470
18 14/16	11 12/16	7 2/16	M	San Miguel County	NM	Dick McClain	1986	2,470
18 14/16	12 0/16	6 14/16	M	Grant County	OR	Don D. Litts	1986	2,470
18 14/16	11 15/16	6 15/16	M	Coos County	OR	Bruce B. Stamp	1986	2,470
18 14/16	11 10/16	7 4/16	M	Park County	CO	Mike Boland	1987	2,470
18 14/16	11 8/16	7 6/16	M	Ignace	ONT	Robert James Lewis	1987	2,470
18 14/16	12 2/16	6 12/16	M	Archuleta County	CO	H. Kitchener Layland, Jr.	1987	2,470
18 14/16	11 9/16	7 5/16	M	Ear Falls	ONT	Daniel J. Mercer	1988	2,470
18 14/16	11 11/16	7 3/16	M	Green Lake	SAS	Steven Kent Camburn	1988	2,470
18 14/16	12 0/16	6 14/16	M	Winefred Lake	ALB	Danny Moore	1988	2,470
18 14/16	11 11/16	7 3/16	M	Fort Coulonge	QUE	Hubert L. Norfleet, Jr.	1988	2,470
18 14/16	11 9/16	7 5/16	M	Idaho County	ID	Ron Smith	1988	2,470
18 14/16	11 13/16	7 1/16	M	Saddle Hills	ALB	Ben White	1988	2,470
18 14/16	11 12/16	7 2/16	M	Waterhen River	SAS	Pink Atkins	1988	2,470
18 14/16	12 0/16	6 14/16	M	Koochiching County	MN	Matt Barry	1988	2,470
18 14/16	12 1/16	6 13/16	M	Luce County	MI	Terry L. Cook	1988	2,470
18 14/16	11 12/16	7 2/16	M	Mann River	SAS	David P. Heinselman II	1989	2,470
18 14/16	11 10/16	7 4/16	M	Prince William Sound	AK	Richard Moran	1989	2,470
18 14/16	12 2/16	6 12/16	M	Espanola	ONT	Leonard Rock	1989	2,470
18 14/16	11 15/16	6 15/16	M	Sioux Lookout	ONT	Tom Nebbs	1989	2,470
18 14/16	11 13/16	7 1/16	M	Pelican Narrows	SAS	Doug Otte	1989	2,470
18 14/16	12 4/16	6 10/16	M	Rocky Lake	MAN	Cecil Tharp	1989	2,470
18 14/16	11 12/16	7 2/16	M	Fort Coulonge	QUE	Barry J. Horton	1989	2,470
18 14/16	11 8/16	7 6/16	M	Coos County	NH	Mark Milne	1989	2,470
18 14/16	11 15/16	6 15/16	M	Sanders County	MT	Greg L. Munther	1989	2,470
18 14/16	11 10/16	7 4/16	M	Le Club Trout Lake	QUE	Kenneth Augsburger	1990	2,470
18 14/16	11 15/16	6 15/16	M	Trois Rivers	QUE	Lee Libbey	1990	2,470
18 14/16	11 8/16	7 6/16	M	Boise County	ID	Julian Salutrequi	1990	2,470
18 14/16	11 11/16	7 3/16	M	Minaki	ONT	Joe Devlin	1990	2,470
18 14/16	11 5/16	7 9/16	M	Elmore County	ID	John Turner	1990	2,470
18 14/16	12 2/16	6 12/16	M	Chippewa County	WI	Donald J. Lunemann	1990	2,470
18 14/16	11 15/16	6 15/16	M	Forest County	WI	Douglas R. Oswald	1990	2,470
18 14/16	12 0/16	6 14/16	M	Lincoln County	NM	Rocky Drake	1991	2,470
18 14/16	11 7/16	7 7/16	M	Lynn Lake	MAN	Steve Gorr	1991	2,470
18 14/16	11 14/16	7 0/16	M	Grays Harbor County	WA	Alex Langbell	1991	2,470
18 14/16	11 12/16	7 2/16	M	Creston	BC	Robert Kuny	1991	2,470
18 14/16	12 0/16	6 14/16	M	Beltrami County	MN	Brian Aune	1991	2,470
18 14/16	11 14/16	7 0/16	M	Stevens County	WA	Michael R. Brunson	1991	2,470
18 14/16	11 12/16	7 2/16	M	Monds Township	ONT	Phillip H. Fisher	1992	2,470
18 14/16	11 12/16	7 2/16	M	Ignace	ONT	Tony Dickerson	1992	2,470
18 14/16	12 5/16	6 9/16	M	Linn County	OR	Alec Hansen	1992	2,470
18 14/16	11 12/16	7 2/16	M	Juniper	NBW	Ray Busch	1992	2,470
18 14/16	11 14/16	7 0/16	M	Randolph County	WV	Daniel R. Gillenwater	1992	2,470
18 14/16	11 11/16	7 3/16	M	Vancouver Island	BC	Ben Gibson	1993	2,470
18 14/16	11 9/16	7 5/16	M	Dryden	ONT	Dennis Hudek	1993	2,470
18 14/16	11 12/16	7 2/16	M	Dryden	ONT	Al Forbes	1993	2,470
18 14/16	12 1/16	6 13/16	M	Christopher Lake	SAS	Foster V. Yancey, Jr.	1993	2,470
18 14/16	11 13/16	7 1/16	M	Snow Lake	MAN	Dan Pitts	1993	2,470
18 14/16	12 0/16	6 14/16	M	Bayfield County	WI	Russ Fritsch	1993	2,470
18 14/16	12 1/16	6 13/16	M	Eau Claire County	WI	Mark R. Scholze	1993	2,470
18 14/16	11 15/16	6 15/16	M	Rabun County	GA	Kirk Perteet	1993	2,470
18 14/16	11 15/16	6 15/16	M	Athabasca River	ALB	William Wuerthele	1994	2,470
18 14/16	12 1/16	6 13/16	M	White River	ONT	Dennis J. Arnold	1994	2,470
18 14/16	11 14/16	7 0/16	M	Athabasca River	ALB	Billy Tillotson	1994	2,470
18 14/16	11 12/16	7 2/16	M	High Level	ALB	Todd Veal	1994	2,470
18 14/16	11 12/16	7 2/16	M	Armstrong	ONT	Kevin Daniels	1994	2,470
18 14/16	12 1/16	6 13/16	M	Ear Falls	ONT	Robert L. Bara	1994	2,470
18 14/16	11 12/16	7 2/16	M	Aroostook County	ME	Mike Collins	1994	2,470
18 14/16	11 10/16	7 4/16	M	Woodstock	NBW	Tom Smith	1994	2,470
18 14/16	12 0/16	6 14/16	M	Kapuskasing	ONT	Vaughn Wright	1995	2,470
18 14/16	12 0/16	6 14/16	M	High Level	ALB	Kevin Rousseau	1995	2,470
18 14/16	12 0/16	6 14/16	M	Oba	ONT	Robert J. Dunne, Jr.	1995	2,470
18 14/16	12 6/16	6 8/16	M	Aitkin County	MN	James Henriksen	1995	2,470
18 14/16	12 1/16	6 13/16	M	Oconto County	WI	Gregory A. Stingle	1995	2,470
18 14/16	11 14/16	7 0/16	M	Idaho County	ID	W. J. Lucas III	1995	2,470

BLACK BEAR

Minimum Score 18 — Continued

SCORE	GREATEST LENGTH	GREATEST WIDTH	SEX	AREA	STATE/PROVINCE	HUNTER'S NAME	DATE	RANK
18 14/16	12 0/16	6 14/16	M	Torch River	SAS	William S. Garner	1996	2,470
18 14/16	11 14/16	7 0/16	M	Sturgeon Landing	SAS	Joe Ness	1996	2,470
18 14/16	12 4/16	6 10/16	M	Athabasca River	ALB	Jewell Leadford	1996	2,470
18 14/16	12 1/16	6 13/16	M	Coconino County	AZ	John David Willis	1996	2,470
18 14/16	11 14/16	7 0/16	M	Page County	VA	Robert L. Cave	1996	2,470
18 14/16	11 14/16	7 0/16	M	Athabasca River	ALB	Roger Wintle	1997	2,470
18 14/16	12 0/16	6 14/16	M	Sturgeon Landing	SAS	Ryan Hugelen	1997	2,470
18 14/16	12 2/16	6 12/16	M	Garnier Lake	ALB	Greg Lumley	1997	2,470
18 14/16	12 0/16	6 14/16	M	Brunswick Lake	ONT	Mark H. Kulke	1997	2,470
18 14/16	11 10/16	7 4/16	M	Oneida County	NY	Ed Rosenburgh	1997	2,470
18 14/16	12 0/16	6 14/16	M	Carrot River	SAS	Larry T. Fischer	1998	2,470
18 14/16	11 12/16	7 2/16	M	Fort McMurray	ALB	Mark Kuhn	1998	2,470
18 14/16	12 0/16	6 14/16	M	Smeaton	SAS	Gene A. Welle	1998	2,470
18 14/16	11 9/16	7 5/16	M	Dryden	ONT	Robert A. Cuff	1998	2,470
18 14/16	12 1/16	6 13/16	M	Trinity County	CA	Terry J. Hunter	1998	2,470
18 14/16	11 14/16	7 0/16	M	Price County	WI	Gary L. Hintz	1998	2,470
18 13/16	11 11/16	7 2/16	M	Iron County	MI	John E. Lawson	1971	2,591
18 13/16	11 8/16	7 5/16	M	Washington County	ME	Norman Jolliffe	1973	2,591
18 13/16	11 6/16	7 7/16	M	Jefferson County	CO	Chuck Hutton	1974	2,591
18 13/16	11 11/16	7 2/16	M	Colfax County	NM	Jerry R. Wood	1974	2,591
18 13/16	11 10/16	7 3/16	M		ONT	Lee Murphy	1975	2,591
18 13/16	11 8/16	7 5/16	M	Pemberton	BC	Dr. Michael R. Cummings	1976	2,591
18 13/16	11 8/16	7 5/16	M	Sanders County	MT	Jay Gunter	1976	2,591
18 13/16	11 7/16	7 6/16	M	Messines	QUE	Larry R. Scott, Sr.	1977	2,591
18 13/16	11 12/16	7 1/16	M	Dryden	ONT	Dr. Bill Young	1977	2,591
18 13/16	12 0/16	6 13/16	M	Gem County	ID	DeLoy Desaro	1978	2,591
18 13/16	11 10/16	7 3/16	M	Somerset County	ME	Ray King	1978	2,591
18 13/16	11 14/16	6 15/16	M	Chapleau	ONT	Maurice Perrault	1978	2,591
18 13/16	11 13/16	7 0/16	M	Koochiching County	MN	Mark A. Andrist	1979	2,591
18 13/16	11 11/16	7 2/16	M	Smokey Mountain	WA	Ronald D. Hopkins	1979	2,591
18 13/16	11 12/16	7 1/16	M	Wawa	ONT	Robert C. McGuire	1979	2,591
18 13/16	12 4/16	6 9/16	M	Lincoln County	WI	Bob Faufau	1980	2,591
18 13/16	11 11/16	7 2/16	M	Thunder Bay	ONT	David Manthei	1980	2,591
18 13/16	11 14/16	6 15/16	M	Armistice Lake	ONT	Cliff Buland, Jr.	1982	2,591
18 13/16	12 4/16	6 9/16	M	Price County	WI	Gary Berg	1982	2,591
18 13/16	12 3/16	6 10/16	M	Tulare County	CA	Bill Sweetser	1982	2,591
18 13/16	11 15/16	6 14/16	M	Kenora	ONT	John L. Angel	1982	2,591
18 13/16	12 1/16	6 12/16	M	Hudson Bay	SAS	Mark Hughes	1982	2,591
18 13/16	12 0/16	6 13/16	M	The Pas	MAN	Scott Lang	1983	2,591
18 13/16	11 12/16	7 1/16	M	Iron County	MI	John O. Cowell	1983	2,591
18 13/16	11 5/16	7 8/16	M	Caramat	ONT	Robert A. Boyer	1984	2,591
18 13/16	12 1/16	6 12/16	M	Sunbury County	NBW	Burchel Blevins	1984	2,591
18 13/16	12 1/16	6 12/16	M	Dist. 21	ONT	Ron Harger	1985	2,591
18 13/16	11 7/16	7 6/16	M	Otter Lake	QUE	Dana P. Calhoun	1985	2,591
18 13/16	12 2/16	6 11/16	M	St. James Bay	AK	John Gary Price	1985	2,591
18 13/16	12 0/16	6 13/16	M	Sierra County	NM	Kendall Doyle	1985	2,591
18 13/16	11 11/16	7 2/16	M	Thunder Bay	ONT	Howard Leopold	1985	2,591
18 13/16	11 14/16	6 15/16	M	Kenora	ONT	Ron Books	1986	2,591
18 13/16	11 8/16	7 5/16	M	Gallatin County	MT	Stephen Lockington	1986	2,591
18 13/16	11 12/16	7 1/16	M	Nakina	ONT	Ronald Mifflin	1986	2,591
18 13/16	11 11/16	7 2/16	M	Archuleta County	CO	Lonnie Draper	1986	2,591
18 13/16	12 3/16	6 10/16	M	Wasilla	AK	Ted Grover	1986	2,591
18 13/16	12 0/16	6 13/16	M	Atikokan	ONT	Steve Weekly	1987	2,591
18 13/16	11 10/16	7 3/16	M	Sundridge	ONT	Abby Lape	1987	2,591
18 13/16	11 8/16	7 5/16	M	Archuleta County	CO	Mark Charles Petersen	1987	2,591
18 13/16	12 2/16	6 11/16	M	Fox Creek	ALB	Ryk Visscher	1987	2,591
18 13/16	11 14/16	6 15/16	M	Crook County	OR	Jeff Carver	1987	2,591
18 13/16	11 12/16	7 1/16	M	Teton County	MT	Ron Carpenter	1987	2,591
18 13/16	11 7/16	7 6/16	M	Hampshire County	MA	Raymond H. Moulton, Jr.	1987	2,591
18 13/16	11 14/16	6 15/16	M	Wawa	ONT	Dale Rohrbeck	1988	2,591
18 13/16	12 1/16	6 12/16	M	Pine County	MN	Arnold F. Ostgarden	1988	2,591
18 13/16	12 0/16	6 13/16	M	Iron County	WI	Gary G. Johnson	1988	2,591
18 13/16	11 15/16	6 14/16	M	Bayfield County	WI	William F. Schutte	1988	2,591
18 13/16	12 0/16	6 13/16	M	Las Animas County	CO	Richard J. Racioppi	1989	2,591
18 13/16	11 7/16	7 6/16	M	Mine Centre	ONT	Willard L. Voight	1989	2,591
18 13/16	11 12/16	7 1/16	M	Cowan	MAN	Vito Benedetto	1989	2,591
18 13/16	11 9/16	7 4/16	M	Nestor Falls	ONT	Robert E. Grainger	1989	2,591
18 13/16	11 10/16	7 3/16	M	La Tuque	QUE	Bernard E. Beaudin, Jr.	1989	2,591
18 13/16	11 12/16	7 1/16	M	Cadillac	QUE	Jerry Woodrum	1989	2,591
18 13/16	12 2/16	6 11/16	M	Aitkin County	MN	David Emmen	1989	2,591
18 13/16	11 10/16	7 3/16	M	Fayette County	WV	James E. Grey	1989	2,591
18 13/16	11 10/16	7 3/16	M	Grafton County	NH	Donald O. Goodwin	1989	2,591
18 13/16	11 14/16	6 15/16	M	Fawcett	ALB	Troy Dzioba	1990	2,591
18 13/16	11 14/16	6 15/16	M	Gowganda	ONT	Bob E. Collins	1990	2,591
18 13/16	11 11/16	7 2/16	M	Wawa	ONT	Pauly Paul	1990	2,591
18 13/16	11 15/16	6 14/16	M	Augusta County	VA	Raymond Leverock	1990	2,591
18 13/16	12 4/16	6 9/16	M	Apache County	AZ	Stephen D. Hornady	1991	2,591
18 13/16	12 0/16	6 13/16	M	Creston	BC	Robert Kuny	1991	2,591

BLACK BEAR

Minimum Score 18 — Continued

SCORE	GREATEST LENGTH	GREATEST WIDTH	SEX	AREA	STATE/ PROVINCE	HUNTER'S NAME	DATE	RANK
18 13/16	11 9/16	7 4/16	M	Fauquier	ONT	Bradley I. Anderson	1991	2,591
18 13/16	12 0/16	6 13/16	M	Hubbard County	MN	Loren Schoewe	1991	2,591
18 13/16	11 15/16	6 14/16	M	Asotin County	WA	Brady Olson	1991	2,591
18 13/16	11 11/16	7 2/16	M	St. Louis County	MN	Jeffrey C. Minske	1991	2,591
18 13/16	11 13/16	7 0/16	M	Baker County	OR	Tom Christakos	1991	2,591
18 13/16	10 14/16	7 15/16	M	Madison County	MT	Tom L. Miller	1991	2,591
18 13/16	12 0/16	6 13/16	M	Montezuma County	CO	Jerry Rush	1992	2,591
18 13/16	11 14/16	6 15/16	M	Camas County	ID	Dallas Smith	1992	2,591
18 13/16	11 10/16	7 3/16	M	Grand County	CO	Terry Sleppy	1992	2,591
18 13/16	12 0/16	6 13/16	M	Red Lake	ONT	Jeff Basco	1992	2,591
18 13/16	11 10/16	7 3/16	M	Kenora	ONT	Jerry Lee Andrews	1992	2,591
18 13/16	11 12/16	7 1/16	M	Kuiu Island	AK	Michael Speigle	1992	2,591
18 13/16	11 10/16	7 3/16	M	Schoolcraft County	MI	Delbert Franklin Steward	1992	2,591
18 13/16	12 0/16	6 13/16	M	Moffat County	CO	Rodney Lee Wilt	1992	2,591
18 13/16	11 15/16	6 14/16	M	Caribou County	ID	Russell Clark	1992	2,591
18 13/16	11 12/16	7 1/16	M	Fannin County	GA	Mac Gignilliat	1992	2,591
18 13/16	11 10/16	7 3/16	M	Lane County	OR	Vernon E. King, Jr.	1993	2,591
18 13/16	11 5/16	7 8/16	M	Loring	ONT	Douglas L. Buchler	1993	2,591
18 13/16	11 15/16	6 14/16	M	Minitonas	MAN	Gregory B. McPhillips	1993	2,591
18 13/16	11 15/16	6 14/16	M	Clam Lake	ONT	Dick Byers	1993	2,591
18 13/16	12 1/16	6 12/16	M	Milner Ridge	MAN	Daniel Chartrand	1993	2,591
18 13/16	11 10/16	7 3/16	M	Sublette County	WY	Justin J. Shirley	1993	2,591
18 13/16	11 14/16	6 15/16	M	Belleterre	QUE	Jerry Ashley	1993	2,591
18 13/16	12 3/16	6 10/16	M	Josephine County	OR	Steven Mazzola	1993	2,591
18 13/16	11 15/16	6 14/16	M	Koochiching County	MN	Scott Schultz	1993	2,591
18 13/16	12 1/16	6 12/16	M	Aitkin County	MN	Mike Smieja	1993	2,591
18 13/16	11 15/16	6 14/16	M	Itasca County	MN	Donald J. Bergstrom	1993	2,591
18 13/16	12 6/16	6 7/16	M	Alpena County	MI	Alan Dale Shepherd	1993	2,591
18 13/16	12 0/16	6 13/16	M	Pacific County	WA	Ricky Ray Foster	1993	2,591
18 13/16	11 9/16	7 4/16	M	Canterbury	NBW	Arthur W. Little	1994	2,591
18 13/16	12 3/16	6 10/16	M	Camas County	ID	David Sass	1994	2,591
18 13/16	11 13/16	7 0/16	M	Wabigoon Township	ONT	Ronnie Blewer	1994	2,591
18 13/16	12 1/16	6 12/16	M	High Level	ALB	Kenneth Kovar	1995	2,591
18 13/16	11 9/16	7 4/16	M	Minaki	ONT	Joe Krejci	1995	2,591
18 13/16	12 1/16	6 12/16	M	Prince of Wales Island	AK	Danny Moore	1995	2,591
18 13/16	12 5/16	6 8/16	M	Carrot River	SAS	Mark A. Johnson	1995	2,591
18 13/16	12 0/16	6 13/16	M	Red Earth	ALB	John Clark Fisher	1995	2,591
18 13/16	11 13/16	7 0/16	M	Prince of Wales Island	AK	Dyrk Eddie	1995	2,591
18 13/16	11 10/16	7 3/16	M	High Level	ALB	Earnie Banks	1995	2,591
18 13/16	11 11/16	7 2/16	M	Finleson Lake	ONT	Kevin Van Arsdale	1995	2,591
18 13/16	12 5/16	6 8/16	M	Ignace	ONT	Ray Redlin, Jr.	1995	2,591
18 13/16	11 13/16	7 0/16	M	Fort McMurray	ALB	Tom Bridenstine	1995	2,591
18 13/16	11 12/16	7 1/16	M	Larder Lake	ONT	Karl W. Lockwood	1995	2,591
18 13/16	11 14/16	6 15/16	M	Wawa	ONT	Mitchell R. Sitterding	1995	2,591
18 13/16	11 9/16	7 4/16	M	Wawa	ONT	William D. Brooks	1995	2,591
18 13/16	11 10/16	7 3/16	M	Tulare County	CA	Frank Steven Birtcher	1995	2,591
18 13/16	11 15/16	6 14/16	M	Kenora	ONT	Jeff Pals	1995	2,591
18 13/16	11 9/16	7 4/16	M	Missanabie	ONT	Robert L. Busch	1995	2,591
18 13/16	11 13/16	7 0/16	M	Keg River	ALB	Eric Rauhanen	1995	2,591
18 13/16	11 14/16	6 15/16	M	Fort a la Corne	SAS	Kevin Sean Schauenberg	1996	2,591
18 13/16	12 1/16	6 12/16	M	Big Sandy Lake	SAS	Brian Richard Trachsel	1996	2,591
18 13/16	11 7/16	7 6/16	M	Kirkland Lake	ONT	Shawn Rothrock	1996	2,591
18 13/16	11 11/16	7 2/16	M	Spring Creek	ALB	Douglas E. Erickson	1996	2,591
18 13/16	11 5/16	7 8/16	M	Snohomish County	WA	Christopher C. Hill	1996	2,591
18 13/16	11 11/16	7 2/16	M	Atikokan	ONT	Jim Saunoris, Jr.	1996	2,591
18 13/16	12 3/16	6 10/16	M	Itasca County	MN	Mark A. Slinger	1996	2,591
18 13/16	11 13/16	7 0/16	M	Douglas County	WI	Todd D. Sorenson	1996	2,591
18 13/16	12 0/16	6 13/16	M	Moffat County	CO	Scott Brasfield	1996	2,591
18 13/16	11 12/16	7 1/16	M	Red Lake	ONT	Janet M. King	1997	2,591
18 13/16	11 12/16	7 1/16	M	Kipawa	QUE	Bill Griffin	1997	2,591
18 13/16	12 0/16	6 13/16	M	The Pas	MAN	Bill Prigge	1997	2,591
18 13/16	11 6/16	7 7/16	M	Armstrong	ONT	Jim Patterson	1997	2,591
18 13/16	11 14/16	6 15/16	M	Livengood	AK	Tom Everett	1997	2,591
18 13/16	11 9/16	7 4/16	M	Thompson	MAN	Chris Yaritz	1997	2,591
18 13/16	11 7/16	7 6/16	M	Hawk River	SAS	Ricky Bullington	1997	2,591
18 13/16	12 0/16	6 13/16	M	Coconino County	AZ	Dave R. Goitia, Jr.	1997	2,591
18 13/16	12 0/16	6 13/16	M	Green Lake	SAS	John B. Mesics, Sr.	1998	2,591
18 13/16	11 9/16	7 4/16	M	Fredericton	NBW	Terry M. Phelps	1998	2,591
18 13/16	11 6/16	7 7/16	M	Hillsport	ONT	Andrew Rushing, Jr.	1998	2,591
18 12/16	12 1/16	6 11/16	M	Shasta County	CA	Harv Ebers	1964	2,722
18 12/16	11 11/16	7 1/16	M	Carbon County	UT	Marvin Tye	1965	2,722
18 12/16	11 9/16	7 3/16	M	Manowam Lake	QUE	Dennis H. Driscoll	1969	2,722
18 12/16	11 5/16	7 7/16	M	Siskiyou County	CA	W. E. Cates	1972	2,722
18 12/16	11 13/16	6 15/16	M	Franklin County	ME	Bob Kuhar	1973	2,722
18 12/16	11 14/16	6 14/16	M	Trinity County	CA	Daniel Higuera	1974	2,722
18 12/16	11 13/16	6 15/16	M	Uncompahgre N.F.	CO	Anthony Keeling	1975	2,722
18 12/16	12 1/16	6 11/16	M	Hubbard County	MN	Jack Smythe	1977	2,722
18 12/16	12 2/16	6 10/16	M	Lesser Slave Lake	ALB	Gene Solyntjes	1978	2,722

167

BLACK BEAR

Minimum Score 18 — Continued

SCORE	GREATEST LENGTH	GREATEST WIDTH	SEX	AREA	STATE/PROVINCE	HUNTER'S NAME	DATE	RANK
18 12/16	11 14/16	6 14/16	M	Fremont County	ID	Dennis L. Shirley	1979	2,722
18 12/16	11 10/16	7 2/16	M	Franklin County	ME	Len Cardinale	1980	2,722
18 12/16	12 2/16	6 10/16	M	Gunnison County	CO	James F. Dougherty	1980	2,722
18 12/16	11 3/16	7 9/16	M	Franklin County	ME	John Janelli	1980	2,722
18 12/16	11 14/16	6 14/16	M	Lake County	MN	Herbert O. Lundberg	1980	2,722
18 12/16	11 15/16	6 13/16	M	Sandy Bar Creek	CA	Dale H. BracKen	1981	2,722
18 12/16	11 12/16	7 0/16	M	Warren County	VA	Joseph A. Ramey	1981	2,722
18 12/16	11 12/16	7 0/16	M	Clear Creek County	CO	David L. Skiff	1981	2,722
18 12/16	12 0/16	6 12/16	M	Lemhi County	ID	Bob Ulshafer	1981	2,722
18 12/16	11 14/16	6 14/16	M	Remigny	QUE	Richard L. Jackson	1982	2,722
18 12/16	12 1/16	6 11/16	M	Idaho County	ID	Robert Dale Evans	1982	2,722
18 12/16	11 14/16	6 14/16	M	Madoc	ONT	Mel Johnson	1982	2,722
18 12/16	11 6/16	7 6/16	M	Archuleta County	CO	Steve Vittetow	1982	2,722
18 12/16	12 0/16	6 12/16	M	Kenmount	ONT	James D. Murray	1983	2,722
18 12/16	11 8/16	7 4/16	M	McAdam	NBW	David W. Peltier	1983	2,722
18 12/16	12 3/16	6 9/16	M	Langlade County	WI	Michael Steliga	1983	2,722
18 12/16	12 2/16	6 10/16	M	Langlade County	WI	Larry Petts	1983	2,722
18 12/16	11 13/16	6 15/16	M	Graham	ONT	Joe Neal Walters	1984	2,722
18 12/16	11 6/16	7 6/16	M	Boise County	ID	Gary Kinney	1984	2,722
18 12/16	11 14/16	6 14/16	M	Koochiching County	MN	Daniel Krasean	1984	2,722
18 12/16	11 12/16	7 0/16	M	Koochiching County	MN	Larry Hillman	1984	2,722
18 12/16	12 0/16	6 12/16	M	Dryden	ONT	Mark Guelzow	1985	2,722
18 12/16	12 0/16	6 12/16	M	Riverside County	CA	Paul Persano	1985	2,722
18 12/16	11 11/16	7 1/16	M	Capreol	ONT	Lawrence M. Sowders	1986	2,722
18 12/16	11 9/16	7 3/16	M	Pitkin County	CO	Gary B. McClure	1986	2,722
18 12/16	11 12/16	7 0/16	M	Wawa	ONT	Thomas May	1986	2,722
18 12/16	11 14/16	6 14/16	M	Savant Lake	ONT	Marlo G. Sloan	1987	2,722
18 12/16	11 14/16	6 14/16	M	Thunder Bay	ONT	Eugene M. Tonk II	1987	2,722
18 12/16	12 0/16	6 12/16	M	Cumberland House	SAS	Dave Kapanke	1987	2,722
18 12/16	11 6/16	7 6/16	M	Killaloe Station	ONT	Norman J. Roy	1987	2,722
18 12/16	12 1/16	6 11/16	M	Ft. McMurray	ALB	James Pike	1987	2,722
18 12/16	12 6/16	6 6/16	M	Otero County	NM	Ronnie B. Hall	1987	2,722
18 12/16	11 10/16	7 2/16	M	King County	WA	Curtis A. Geise	1987	2,722
18 12/16	11 5/16	7 7/16	M	Marquette County	MI	Alvin Meadows	1987	2,722
18 12/16	11 10/16	7 2/16	M	Spokane County	WA	Tracy Kenworthy	1987	2,722
18 12/16	11 15/16	6 13/16	M	Peers	ALB	Kevin Hehn	1988	2,722
18 12/16	11 13/16	6 15/16	M	Yaremko Twp.	ONT	Ed Oplinger	1988	2,722
18 12/16	11 13/16	6 15/16	M	Oxford County	ME	Robert Grannis	1988	2,722
18 12/16	11 10/16	7 2/16	M	Marquette County	MI	Dale B. Parish	1988	2,722
18 12/16	12 1/16	6 11/16	F	Rio Arriba County	NM	Kelley B. Ward	1989	2,722
18 12/16	11 10/16	7 2/16	M	Snow Lake	MAN	Dick Pugh	1989	2,722
18 12/16	11 9/16	7 3/16	M	Eagle Lake	ONT	Allan Marohn	1989	2,722
18 12/16	11 10/16	7 2/16	M	Rapides des Joachims	QUE	Ron Bice	1989	2,722
18 12/16	11 8/16	7 4/16	M	Zec Dumoine	QUE	Paul J. Sisz	1989	2,722
18 12/16	11 8/16	7 4/16	M	Aitkin County	MN	Dr. Ken Nordberg	1989	2,722
18 12/16	11 10/16	7 2/16	M	Shoshone County	ID	Randy Huber	1989	2,722
18 12/16	11 14/16	6 14/16	M	Ferry County	WA	Bob Conyers	1989	2,722
18 12/16	11 8/16	7 4/16	M	Mesa County	CO	Ricky R. Lowery	1990	2,722
18 12/16	11 9/16	7 3/16	M	Highwinds Lake	ONT	John E. Larsen	1990	2,722
18 12/16	11 15/16	6 13/16	M	Black River	ONT	James S. Nowakowski	1990	2,722
18 12/16	11 14/16	6 14/16	M	Lac La Ronge	SAS	Randy G. Cook	1990	2,722
18 12/16	11 11/16	7 1/16	M	Clearwater County	ID	Stan Bocian	1990	2,722
18 12/16	11 7/16	7 5/16	M	Atikokan	ONT	Roger Carpenter	1990	2,722
18 12/16	11 12/16	7 0/16	M	Mystery Lake	MAN	Lois Monteath	1991	2,722
18 12/16	11 11/16	7 1/16	M	Idaho County	ID	Dr. Andrew F. Jones	1991	2,722
18 12/16	11 9/16	7 3/16	M	Kapuskasing	ONT	Harold A. Eichorn	1991	2,722
18 12/16	11 10/16	7 2/16	M	Caramat	ONT	Rick Stump	1991	2,722
18 12/16	11 15/16	6 13/16	M	Wasilla	AK	Sam J. Smith	1991	2,722
18 12/16	11 4/16	7 8/16	M	Fredericton	NBW	Mark Clerici	1991	2,722
18 12/16	11 6/16	7 6/16	M	Bayfield County	WI	Cynthia G. Sotona	1991	2,722
18 12/16	12 0/16	6 12/16	M	Kootenai County	ID	Mark Jones	1992	2,722
18 12/16	12 0/16	6 12/16	M	Prince of Wales Island	AK	Dave Rue	1992	2,722
18 12/16	12 1/16	6 11/16	M	Shoshone County	ID	Craig R. Anderson	1992	2,722
18 12/16	11 15/16	6 13/16	M	Fort Assinobane	ALB	Brian R. Burrows	1992	2,722
18 12/16	11 13/16	6 15/16	M	Flatbush	ALB	Kevin Wilson	1992	2,722
18 12/16	11 10/16	7 2/16	M	Riverton	MAN	Richard D. Riesberg	1992	2,722
18 12/16	11 8/16	7 4/16	M	Butler	ONT	Robert H. Pavlovic	1992	2,722
18 12/16	11 9/16	7 3/16	M	Kashabowie	ONT	Chris Neumann	1992	2,722
18 12/16	11 9/16	7 3/16	M	Terrace Bay	ONT	Alvin Anderson	1992	2,722
18 12/16	11 11/16	7 1/16	M	Temiscaming	ONT	Jerry Boudreault	1992	2,722
18 12/16	11 7/16	7 5/16	M	Skamania County	WA	Larry E. Sides, Jr.	1992	2,722
18 12/16	11 12/16	7 0/16	M	Coconino County	AZ	James Q. Anderson	1992	2,722
18 12/16	11 10/16	7 2/16	M	Wawa	ONT	Peter G. Dykstra	1992	2,722
18 12/16	11 8/16	7 4/16	M	Cook County	MN	Arthur Heinze	1992	2,722
18 12/16	11 12/16	7 0/16	M	Stevens County	WA	Dan L. Moultrie	1992	2,722
18 12/16	11 13/16	6 15/16	M	Iron County	WI	Keith Skadahl	1992	2,722
18 12/16	11 9/16	7 3/16	M	Crooked Lake	ONT	Robert Hagan	1993	2,722
18 12/16	12 0/16	6 12/16	M	May Lake	ALB	Terry Ermel	1994	2,722

BLACK BEAR

Minimum Score 18 — Continued

SCORE	GREATEST LENGTH	GREATEST WIDTH	SEX	AREA	STATE/ PROVINCE	HUNTER'S NAME	DATE	RANK
18 12/16	11 5/16	7 7/16	M	Athabasca River	ALB	William Wuerthele	1994	2,722
18 12/16	11 11/16	7 1/16	M	Peace River	ALB	Mark Zimmermann	1994	2,722
18 12/16	12 0/16	6 12/16	M	Thompson	MAN	C. M. "Lucky" Lentz	1994	2,722
18 12/16	12 2/16	6 10/16	M	Prince of Wales Island	AK	Garry A. Thoms	1994	2,722
18 12/16	11 10/16	7 2/16	M	Athabasca River	ALB	Chris Davis	1994	2,722
18 12/16	11 7/16	7 5/16	M	Rio Arriba County	NM	Michael A. Sisneros	1994	2,722
18 12/16	11 7/16	7 5/16	M	White River	ONT	Dave Slager	1994	2,722
18 12/16	12 1/16	6 11/16	M	Anglin Lake	SAS	Alan Bzdel	1994	2,722
18 12/16	11 15/16	6 13/16	M	West Tree	ONT	Frances Higley	1994	2,722
18 12/16	11 7/16	7 5/16	M	Dryden	ONT	Paul Tuscher	1994	2,722
18 12/16	12 0/16	6 12/16	M	Notre-Dame	QUE	Richard J. Hale	1994	2,722
18 12/16	11 13/16	6 15/16	M	Lane County	OR	Rick Dealba	1994	2,722
18 12/16	11 14/16	6 14/16	M	Mahnomen County	MN	Mike Ahles	1994	2,722
18 12/16	11 14/16	6 14/16	M	High Level	ALB	Ben Catriz	1995	2,722
18 12/16	12 3/16	6 9/16	M	Prince Albert	SAS	Eldon Richter	1995	2,722
18 12/16	11 7/16	7 5/16	M	Baie Comeau	QUE	Stan Andriski, Jr.	1995	2,722
18 12/16	11 10/16	7 2/16	M	Baie Comeau	QUE	Michael Heywood	1995	2,722
18 12/16	11 10/16	7 2/16	M	Siskiyou County	CA	Lon E. Lauber	1995	2,722
18 12/16	11 10/16	7 2/16	M	Franklin County	ME	Jeffery S. Pillsbury	1995	2,722
18 12/16	11 12/16	7 0/16	M	Luce County	MI	Mark Alan Boulton	1995	2,722
18 12/16	12 1/16	6 11/16	M	Sublette County	WY	Ron Gunyan, Jr.	1995	2,722
18 12/16	11 12/16	7 0/16	M	Essex County	NY	Paul Durling	1995	2,722
18 12/16	11 9/16	7 3/16	M	Bathurst	NBW	Bill Lahue	1996	2,722
18 12/16	12 4/16	6 8/16	M	Swan River	MAN	Patrick Reeve	1996	2,722
18 12/16	11 14/16	6 14/16	M	Oak Lake	ONT	Thomas G. Vils	1996	2,722
18 12/16	11 11/16	7 1/16	M	Slave River	ALB	N. Carlton Baker, Jr.	1996	2,722
18 12/16	12 0/16	6 12/16	M	Clarke Lake	SAS	Tony Chirles	1996	2,722
18 12/16	11 8/16	7 4/16	M	Thaddeus Lake	ONT	Nick Martin	1996	2,722
18 12/16	11 15/16	6 13/16	M	Fort McMurray	ALB	Erik Danielsen	1996	2,722
18 12/16	11 10/16	7 2/16	M	La Tuque	QUE	T. Scott McKnight	1996	2,722
18 12/16	11 15/16	6 13/16	M	Prince of Wales Island	AK	Charles Wagner	1996	2,722
18 12/16	11 10/16	7 2/16	M	Sawtooth Mtns.	AK	Pete Buist	1996	2,722
18 12/16	11 12/16	7 0/16	M	Rusk County	WI	Duane Coates	1996	2,722
18 12/16	12 0/16	6 12/16	M	Sawyer County	WI	Timothy Schneider	1996	2,722
18 12/16	11 13/16	6 15/16	M	Rio Arriba County	NM	James E. Vance	1997	2,722
18 12/16	12 1/16	6 11/16	M	Buffalo Narrows	SAS	Christopher R. Beck	1997	2,722
18 12/16	11 8/16	7 4/16	M	Sioux Lookout	ONT	John G. Nelson	1997	2,722
18 12/16	12 0/16	6 12/16	M	La Crete	ALB	Ronald D. Rod	1997	2,722
18 12/16	11 15/16	6 13/16	M	Bradbury River	MAN	Steven W. Hartley	1997	2,722
18 12/16	11 10/16	7 2/16	M	Slave River	ALB	Owen Keeton, Jr.	1997	2,722
18 12/16	11 13/16	6 15/16	M	Thaddeus Lake	ONT	Nick Martin	1997	2,722
18 12/16	11 15/16	6 13/16	M	Hazel Dell	SAS	Ron Luthi	1998	2,722
18 12/16	11 14/16	6 14/16	M	Olha	MAN	Martin Stubstad	1998	2,722
18 12/16	11 9/16	7 3/16	M	Idaho County	ID	James R. Ball	1998	2,722
18 12/16	11 15/16	6 13/16	M	Oak Lake	ONT	Ole Braaten	1998	2,722
18 12/16	11 12/16	7 0/16	M	Mattice	ONT	Ed Pollock	1998	2,722
18 12/16	11 12/16	7 0/16	M	Brunswick Lake	ONT	Thomas E. Schoenike	1998	2,722
18 12/16	11 14/16	6 14/16	M	Christopher Lake	SAS	Ben W. Fitzgerald	1998	2,722
18 12/16	11 13/16	6 15/16	M	Chipewyan Lake	ALB	David D. Manuszak	1998	2,722
18 12/16	11 8/16	7 4/16	M	Clearwater County	ID	R. M. "Dick" Newell	1998	2,722
18 11/16	11 12/16	6 15/16	M	Presque Isle County	MI	Herbert Miller	1957	2,859
18 11/16	11 8/16	7 3/16	M	Chirvakum Creek	WA	Joe Zuend	1962	2,859
18 11/16	11 13/16	6 14/16	M	Iron County	MI	Donald Schram	1965	2,859
18 11/16	11 7/16	7 4/16	M	Shawano County	WI	Kenneth Karbon	1970	2,859
18 11/16	11 10/16	7 1/16	M	Lac Cayamant	QUE	Charles Shaffner	1971	2,859
18 11/16	11 9/16	7 2/16	M	Grand County	UT	Dennis Schoenick	1972	2,859
18 11/16	11 7/16	7 4/16	M	San Miguel County	NM	Dr. Rick H. Jackson	1975	2,859
18 11/16	11 12/16	6 15/16	M	Nestor Falls	ONT	Greg Roach	1977	2,859
18 11/16	11 11/16	7 0/16	M	Estaire	ONT	Donnie Evans	1978	2,859
18 11/16	11 10/16	7 1/16	M	Lake Nipigon	ONT	Gary L. Smith	1978	2,859
18 11/16	11 7/16	7 4/16	M	Clearwater County	ID	John Wagner	1978	2,859
18 11/16	11 15/16	6 12/16	M	Itasca County	MN	Harold Whitt	1979	2,859
18 11/16	11 9/16	7 2/16	M	Huerfano County	CO	Patricia J. Matarazzo	1980	2,859
18 11/16	11 10/16	7 1/16	M	Franklin County	ME	Jeff Roberts	1980	2,859
18 11/16	11 11/16	7 0/16	M	Gogebic County	MI	Edward Burley	1981	2,859
18 11/16	11 10/16	7 1/16	M	Itasca County	MN	Tom Brudeli	1981	2,859
18 11/16	11 11/16	7 0/16	M	Iron County	MI	Tom A. Longnecker	1981	2,859
18 11/16	11 12/16	6 15/16	M	Washington County	ME	Lincoln Michaud	1981	2,859
18 11/16	11 11/16	7 0/16	M	Dryden	ONT	Harry L. Stalter	1981	2,859
18 11/16	11 8/16	7 3/16	M	Franklin County	MA	George Holmes, Jr.	1982	2,859
18 11/16	11 9/16	7 2/16	M	Chapleau	ONT	Jim Grooters	1982	2,859
18 11/16	11 11/16	7 0/16	M	Atikokan	ONT	Al Taylor	1983	2,859
18 11/16	11 15/16	6 12/16	M	Dorset	ONT	Daryll E. Smith	1983	2,859
18 11/16	11 5/16	7 6/16	M	Lynn Lake	MAN	Gord Monteath	1983	2,859
18 11/16	11 12/16	6 15/16	M	Valley County	ID	George Wadsworth	1983	2,859
18 11/16	11 6/16	7 5/16	M	Klamath County	OR	Jeffery K. Russell	1983	2,859
18 11/16	11 13/16	6 14/16	M	Rio Arriba County	NM	William Rule	1983	2,859
18 11/16	11 10/16	7 1/16	M	North of Fort Frances	ONT	Kerry Ella	1984	2,859

BLACK BEAR

Minimum Score 18 — Continued

SCORE	GREATEST LENGTH	GREATEST WIDTH	SEX	AREA	STATE/PROVINCE	HUNTER'S NAME	DATE	RANK
18 11/16	11 7/16	7 4/16	M	Muskoka	ONT	Alexander Button	1984	2,859
18 11/16	11 9/16	7 2/16	M	Bonner County	ID	Brian T. Farley	1984	2,859
18 11/16	11 14/16	6 13/16	M	Franklin County	ME	Harold Osborne	1984	2,859
18 11/16	11 15/16	6 12/16	M	Spokane County	WA	David Lossett, Sr.	1984	2,859
18 11/16	11 11/16	7 0/16	M	Smeaton	SAS	Randy Modin	1985	2,859
18 11/16	11 9/16	7 2/16	M	Opasatika	ONT	Rob J. Smith	1985	2,859
18 11/16	11 12/16	6 15/16	M	Huerfano County	CO	Jerry Barth	1985	2,859
18 11/16	11 13/16	6 14/16	M	Sioux Lookout	ONT	Todd Koelzer	1986	2,859
18 11/16	11 15/16	6 12/16	M	Lost Lake	ONT	Richard Martin	1986	2,859
18 11/16	11 10/16	7 1/16	M	Fort Coulonge	QUE	Kevin Ball	1986	2,859
18 11/16	12 2/16	6 9/16	M	Duck Mtns.	MAN	Terry Schar	1986	2,859
18 11/16	12 0/16	6 11/16	M	Aroostook County	ME	Gilbert P. Verwey	1986	2,859
18 11/16	11 14/16	6 13/16	M	Oconto County	WI	James S. Nowakowski	1986	2,859
18 11/16	11 10/16	7 1/16	M	Routt County	CO	Lonny Vanatta	1987	2,859
18 11/16	11 12/16	6 15/16	M	Ear Falls	ONT	Jeff Knights	1987	2,859
18 11/16	11 5/16	7 6/16	M	Fremont County	WY	Pat Eastes	1987	2,859
18 11/16	11 12/16	6 15/16	M	Delay River	QUE	W. R. "Tony" Dukes	1987	2,859
18 11/16	11 14/16	6 13/16	M	Ashland County	WI	Joe VyVyan	1987	2,859
18 11/16	12 1/16	6 10/16	M	Catron County	NM	Nick Arnett	1987	2,859
18 11/16	11 12/16	6 15/16	M	Gila County	AZ	Paul Neill	1987	2,859
18 11/16	11 9/16	7 2/16	M	Boise County	ID	Troy M. Miller	1988	2,859
18 11/16	11 10/16	7 1/16	M	Zec Maganasipi	QUE	Shawn P. Harrington	1988	2,859
18 11/16	11 12/16	6 15/16	M	Valley County	ID	Jim Wilson	1988	2,859
18 11/16	11 9/16	7 2/16	M	Coos County	NH	Gerard D. Theriault	1988	2,859
18 11/16	11 7/16	7 4/16	M	Franklin County	ME	Jim Roy	1988	2,859
18 11/16	11 10/16	7 1/16	M	Madison County	MT	Ricky Huffstetler	1988	2,859
18 11/16	12 3/16	6 8/16	M	Carrot River	SAS	Kurt Schroeder	1988	2,859
18 11/16	11 15/16	6 12/16	M	Larimer County	CO	James Little	1989	2,859
18 11/16	11 11/16	7 0/16	M	Idaho County	ID	Ronald Smith	1989	2,859
18 11/16	11 7/16	7 4/16	M	McAdam	NBW	Joseph Khan	1989	2,859
18 11/16	11 11/16	7 0/16	M	Coos County	NH	David G. Cote	1989	2,859
18 11/16	11 5/16	7 6/16	M	Manitouwadge	ONT	Charles W. Haertel	1990	2,859
18 11/16	11 11/16	7 0/16	M	Owl River	ALB	Thomas J. Papoutsis	1990	2,859
18 11/16	12 2/16	6 9/16	M	Coos County	NH	Gary J. Russell	1990	2,859
18 11/16	11 15/16	6 12/16	M	Mesa County	CO	Ron A. Stover	1990	2,859
18 11/16	12 0/16	6 11/16	M	Luce County	MI	Owen Anderson	1990	2,859
18 11/16	11 12/16	6 15/16	M	Rocky Mountain House	ALB	Randy Bernier	1991	2,859
18 11/16	11 15/16	6 12/16	M	Remigny	QUE	Steve Reedy	1991	2,859
18 11/16	11 15/16	6 12/16	M	Wanless	MAN	Louis Raimondi	1991	2,859
18 11/16	11 15/16	6 12/16	M	Thompson	MAN	Richard E. Davis	1991	2,859
18 11/16	11 14/16	6 13/16	M	Chulitna River	AK	Karen L. Schwanke	1991	2,859
18 11/16	11 9/16	7 2/16	M	Essex County	NY	Paul Durling	1991	2,859
18 11/16	11 13/16	6 14/16	M	Maple Leaf	ONT	Kurt M. Zurawski	1992	2,859
18 11/16	11 8/16	7 3/16	M	Wabigoon	ONT	John H. Rosenstock	1992	2,859
18 11/16	11 10/16	7 1/16	M	Wanless	MAN	Damon Finley	1992	2,859
18 11/16	11 9/16	7 2/16	M	Nenana	AK	David E. Rankin	1992	2,859
18 11/16	11 6/16	7 5/16	M	Thunder Bay	ONT	Randy Adkins	1992	2,859
18 11/16	11 7/16	7 4/16	M	McNeil Township	ONT	Archie Mackinnon	1992	2,859
18 11/16	11 11/16	7 0/16	M	Zec Maganasipi	QUE	Thaddeus A. Tykarsky	1992	2,859
18 11/16	11 12/16	6 15/16	M	Carroll County	NH	Arthur E. Thibodeau, Jr.	1992	2,859
18 11/16	11 10/16	7 1/16	M	Houghton County	MI	Mitchell Bellamy	1992	2,859
18 11/16	12 0/16	6 11/16	M	Rusk County	WI	Douglas Bleecker	1992	2,859
18 11/16	12 4/16	6 7/16	M	Sawyer County	WI	Steve Johnson	1992	2,859
18 11/16	11 14/16	6 13/16	M	Charlevoix County	MI	Ronald E. Olund	1992	2,859
18 11/16	11 5/16	7 6/16	M	Cadotte Lake	ALB	Mitchell Morra	1993	2,859
18 11/16	11 13/16	6 14/16	M	Ravalli County	MT	Robert A. Bourne	1993	2,859
18 11/16	11 15/16	6 12/16	M	McBride Lake	SAS	Howard Beeson	1993	2,859
18 11/16	11 4/16	7 7/16	M	Terrace Bay	ONT	Larry L. Huffman	1993	2,859
18 11/16	11 6/16	7 5/16	M	Idaho County	ID	Michael G. Teff	1993	2,859
18 11/16	11 13/16	6 14/16	M	Itasca County	MN	Peter Q. Hill	1993	2,859
18 11/16	11 5/16	7 6/16	M	Nakina	ONT	Darren W. Wilson	1993	2,859
18 11/16	11 13/16	6 14/16	M	Fort St. John	BC	Scott Ebert	1994	2,859
18 11/16	11 8/16	7 3/16	M	Vasiloff Twp.	ONT	Michael L. Ritter	1994	2,859
18 11/16	11 15/16	6 12/16	M	Lake of the Woods County	MN	Bob Rippel	1994	2,859
18 11/16	11 14/16	6 13/16	M	Carlton County	MN	Donald Schleicher	1994	2,859
18 11/16	11 10/16	7 1/16	M	Umatilla County	OR	Jim Dunigan	1994	2,859
18 11/16	11 10/16	7 1/16	M	Ontonagon County	MI	Terry Riley	1994	2,859
18 11/16	11 15/16	6 12/16	M	Plumas County	CA	W. Kent Brown	1994	2,859
18 11/16	12 2/16	6 9/16	M	Icy Bay	AK	Wade Keatts	1995	2,859
18 11/16	11 13/16	6 14/16	M	Millville	NBW	Edward A. Hornberger	1995	2,859
18 11/16	11 6/16	7 5/16	M	Bryce Township	ONT	Joe Hassinger	1995	2,859
18 11/16	11 4/16	7 7/16	M	Penobscot County	ME	Robert Shannon Brewer	1995	2,859
18 11/16	11 9/16	7 2/16	M	St. Louis County	MN	Dave Cerise	1995	2,859
18 11/16	11 11/16	7 0/16	M	Aitkin County	MN	Bill Gratz	1995	2,859
18 11/16	11 6/16	7 5/16	M	Juniper	NBW	Frederick Donarummo	1995	2,859
18 11/16	11 10/16	7 1/16	M	Rio Arriba County	NM	Paul Voshell	1995	2,859
18 11/16	11 12/16	6 15/16	M	Worthington	ONT	Jack A. Wilson	1996	2,859
18 11/16	11 15/16	6 12/16	M	High Level	ALB	Bob Hudson, Jr.	1996	2,859

BLACK BEAR

Minimum Score 18 — Continued

SCORE	GREATEST LENGTH	GREATEST WIDTH	SEX	AREA	STATE/PROVINCE	HUNTER'S NAME	DATE	RANK
18 11/16	12 3/16	6 8/16	M	High Prairie	ALB	David Wesley Dickson	1996	2,859
18 11/16	11 13/16	6 14/16	M	Pierceland	SAS	Pat R. Potts	1996	2,859
18 11/16	11 14/16	6 13/16	M	Slave River	ALB	N. Carlton Baker, Jr.	1996	2,859
18 11/16	12 5/16	6 6/16	M	Carrot River	SAS	Marvin Pinkowski	1996	2,859
18 11/16	11 9/16	7 2/16	M	Atikokan	ONT	David Wolf	1996	2,859
18 11/16	12 0/16	6 11/16	M	Red Lake	ONT	Mike Koback	1996	2,859
18 11/16	11 11/16	7 0/16	M	Lake of the Woods	ONT	Jack Kelley	1996	2,859
18 11/16	11 11/16	7 0/16	M	Carrot River	SAS	Greg Hunter	1996	2,859
18 11/16	11 9/16	7 2/16	M	Bathurst	NBW	Bruce A. Grant	1996	2,859
18 11/16	12 0/16	6 11/16	M	Beltrami County	MN	Todd Hannon	1996	2,859
18 11/16	12 1/16	6 10/16	M	Forrest County	WI	Steve Daebler	1996	2,859
18 11/16	11 13/16	6 14/16	M	Forest County	WI	Alfred J. Keyser	1996	2,859
18 11/16	11 14/16	6 13/16	M	Calaveras County	CA	Darrel Sudduth	1996	2,859
18 11/16	11 14/16	6 13/16	M	Skownan	MAN	Nick Wegner	1997	2,859
18 11/16	11 10/16	7 1/16	M	Falher	ALB	Stephen L. Collins	1997	2,859
18 11/16	11 9/16	7 2/16	M	Sudbury	ONT	William J. Igo	1997	2,859
18 11/16	11 7/16	7 4/16	M	Fort Coulonge	QUE	Terry Lee Worley	1997	2,859
18 11/16	11 10/16	7 1/16	M	Rapides-des-Joachims	QUE	Don Delabbio	1997	2,859
18 11/16	11 6/16	7 5/16	M	Turtle Lake	QUE	Ricky D. McKinney	1997	2,859
18 11/16	11 8/16	7 3/16	M	Grafton County	NH	Dr. Michael G. Tveraas	1997	2,859
18 11/16	12 0/16	6 11/16	M	Eureka Peak Mtn.	BC	Byron LaFollette	1997	2,859
18 11/16	12 1/16	6 10/16	M	Fisher Branch	MAN	T. Noble II	1998	2,859
18 11/16	11 11/16	7 0/16	M	Maynard Falls	ONT	Scott G. Hettinger	1998	2,859
18 11/16	11 14/16	6 13/16	M	West Prairie River	ALB	Don Lind	1998	2,859
18 11/16	11 6/16	7 5/16	M	San Juan County	UT	David R. Lundberg	1998	2,859
18 11/16	12 1/16	6 10/16	M	Bayfield County	WI	Joseph C. Hinderman	1998	2,859
18 10/16	11 8/16	7 2/16	M	Iron County	WI	Carl Hulbert	1963	2,991
18 10/16	11 8/16	7 2/16	M	Montreal River	ONT	S. Robinson/J. Beach	1966	2,991
18 10/16	11 7/16	7 3/16	M	Rio Grande County	CO	Ron Wintz	1967	2,991
18 10/16	11 11/16	6 15/16	M	Vermillion Bay	ONT	Thomas L. A. Pucci	1968	2,991
18 10/16	11 12/16	6 14/16	M	Idaho County	ID	Randolph Coleman	1970	2,991
18 10/16	12 2/16	6 8/16	M	McLeod Lake	BC	Ron McKay	1973	2,991
18 10/16	11 8/16	7 2/16	M	Las Animas County	CO	Dr. John Adams	1974	2,991
18 10/16	11 5/16	7 5/16	M	Madison County	ID	Bruce W. Baird	1974	2,991
18 10/16	11 0/16	7 10/16	M	Marinette County	WI	Dan Stencel	1974	2,991
18 10/16	11 8/16	7 2/16	M	Franklin County	ME	Mark Checki	1976	2,991
18 10/16	11 13/16	6 13/16	M	Starkey Unit	OR	Timothy D. Palmore	1976	2,991
18 10/16	11 5/16	7 5/16	M	Grand County	CO	Lyle Willmarth	1976	2,991
18 10/16	11 10/16	7 0/16	M	Clearwater County	ID	Tom Cummings	1977	2,991
18 10/16	11 11/16	6 15/16	M	Lewis & Clark County	MT	Scott Koelzer	1977	2,991
18 10/16	12 1/16	6 9/16	M	Palmer	AK	John F. Sumrall	1977	2,991
18 10/16	11 8/16	7 2/16	M	Uncompahgre N.F.	CO	William Hendricks	1978	2,991
18 10/16	11 12/16	6 14/16	M	Stone Creek	BC	Larry McKay	1978	2,991
18 10/16	11 10/16	7 0/16	M	Chaffee County	CO	Frank A. Morminello	1978	2,991
18 10/16	11 10/16	7 0/16	M	Mendocino County	CA	Russell L. Browning	1979	2,991
18 10/16	11 14/16	6 12/16	M	Dolores County	CO	Stanley A. Coval	1979	2,991
18 10/16	11 14/16	6 12/16	M	Pipe Lake	ONT	Richard Colby	1980	2,991
18 10/16	11 5/16	7 5/16	M	Boise County	ID	Richard C. Nichols	1981	2,991
18 10/16	11 2/16	7 8/16	M	Judith Basin County	MT	Don Davidson	1981	2,991
18 10/16	11 7/16	7 3/16	M	Thunder Bay	ONT	Roberta Byerly	1982	2,991
18 10/16	11 7/16	7 3/16	M	Warren County	NY	Ernie Ahr	1982	2,991
18 10/16	12 0/16	6 10/16	M	Susitna Valley	AK	Matt Jones	1982	2,991
18 10/16	11 12/16	6 14/16	M	Gunnison County	CO	Mike Miller	1982	2,991
18 10/16	11 10/16	7 0/16	M	Meagher County	MT	John Levison	1983	2,991
18 10/16	11 14/16	6 12/16	M	Clearwater County	ID	Tim Newbold	1983	2,991
18 10/16	11 9/16	7 1/16	M	Ear Falls	ONT	Ron Marion	1983	2,991
18 10/16	11 14/16	6 12/16	M	Douglas County	OR	Ralph Burt	1983	2,991
18 10/16	11 2/16	7 8/16	M	Rouyn-Noranda	QUE	Claude St. Amour	1983	2,991
18 10/16	12 0/16	6 10/16	M	Mine Centre	ONT	Edwin John Durushia	1984	2,991
18 10/16	11 13/16	6 13/16	M	Lemhi County	ID	Clint Bevins	1984	2,991
18 10/16	11 13/16	6 13/16	M	Beluga River	AK	Dennis Redden	1984	2,991
18 10/16	12 2/16	6 8/16	M	Fremont County	WY	Jerry Bodar	1984	2,991
18 10/16	12 1/16	6 9/16	M	Valley County	ID	Gary Angell	1985	2,991
18 10/16	11 11/16	6 15/16	M	Hudson Bay	SAS	Warren Buss	1985	2,991
18 10/16	11 6/16	7 4/16	M	Huerfano County	CO	Michael Beckwith	1985	2,991
18 10/16	11 7/16	7 3/16	M	Jellicoe	ONT	John Paul McKown	1985	2,991
18 10/16	11 13/16	6 13/16	M	Las Animas County	CO	Tom Storr	1985	2,991
18 10/16	11 10/16	7 0/16	F	Sanpete County	UT	C. Danny Butler	1986	2,991
18 10/16	11 14/16	6 12/16	M	Nestor Falls	ONT	Byron Korby	1986	2,991
18 10/16	11 12/16	6 14/16	M	Fort Coulonge	QUE	Glenn R Noel	1986	2,991
18 10/16	11 4/16	7 6/16	M	Papineau Twp.	ONT	Fred Law	1986	2,991
18 10/16	11 10/16	7 0/16	M	Fort Coulonge	QUE	F. Edward Campbell	1986	2,991
18 10/16	11 6/16	7 4/16	M	Carlton County	MN	Donald Schleicher	1986	2,991
18 10/16	11 14/16	6 12/16	M	Long Lake	ALB	Dave Gerber	1987	2,991
18 10/16	11 14/16	6 12/16	M	Sturgeon Landing	SAS	Jeff Scherr	1987	2,991
18 10/16	11 13/16	6 13/16	M	Black River	QUE	Robert L. Brilhart	1987	2,991
18 10/16	12 0/16	6 10/16	M	Price Creek	ONT	Rick Candos	1987	2,991
18 10/16	11 10/16	7 0/16	M	Sudbury	ONT	William F. Boggess	1987	2,991

BLACK BEAR

Minimum Score 18 — Continued

SCORE	GREATEST LENGTH	GREATEST WIDTH	SEX	AREA	STATE/PROVINCE	HUNTER'S NAME	DATE	RANK
18 10/16	12 3/16	6 7/16	M	Ignace	ONT	Donald W. Goers	1987	2,991
18 10/16	11 13/16	6 13/16	M	Sioux Lookout	ONT	Mike Prokop	1987	2,991
18 10/16	11 11/16	6 15/16	M	Fort Coulonge	QUE	James E. Turner, Jr.	1987	2,991
18 10/16	11 12/16	6 14/16	M	Lemhi County	ID	Art C. Hrabec	1988	2,991
18 10/16	11 10/16	7 0/16	M	Dryden	ONT	Tony Mollus	1988	2,991
18 10/16	11 10/16	7 0/16	M	Perrault Falls	ONT	Ronald R. Mower	1988	2,991
18 10/16	11 12/16	6 14/16	M	Black River	QUE	Ronald E. Whitfield	1988	2,991
18 10/16	11 8/16	7 2/16	M	Bathurst	NBW	Thomas J. Liguori	1988	2,991
18 10/16	12 2/16	6 8/16	M	Tulare County	CA	Bill Sweetser	1988	2,991
18 10/16	11 12/16	6 14/16	M	Florence County	WI	Richard J. Gohr	1988	2,991
18 10/16	11 13/16	6 13/16	M	Coos County	OR	Rick Gabbard	1988	2,991
18 10/16	11 10/16	7 0/16	M	Bathurst	NBW	Larry D. Benedict	1989	2,991
18 10/16	11 15/16	6 11/16	M	King County	WA	David B. Young	1989	2,991
18 10/16	11 13/16	6 13/16	M	Ashland County	WI	Wilbur C. Kuecker	1989	2,991
18 10/16	11 6/16	7 4/16	M	Catron County	NM	Tracy G. Hardy	1989	2,991
18 10/16	11 12/16	6 14/16	M	Poplarfield	MAN	Karl Dunich	1990	2,991
18 10/16	11 12/16	6 14/16	M	Smokey River	ALB	Chris G. Sanford	1990	2,991
18 10/16	11 2/16	7 8/16	M	Boise County	ID	Gary C. Gapp	1990	2,991
18 10/16	11 9/16	7 1/16	M	Chibougamau	QUE	Brian R. Brochu	1990	2,991
18 10/16	11 12/16	6 14/16	M	King County	WA	Donald H. Hubble	1990	2,991
18 10/16	11 10/16	7 0/16	M	Blind River	ONT	Thomas M. Losiewski	1990	2,991
18 10/16	11 15/16	6 11/16	M	Perry Sound	ONT	Robert Hill, Jr.	1990	2,991
18 10/16	11 10/16	7 0/16	M	Page County	VA	Charles F. Cave	1990	2,991
18 10/16	12 1/16	6 9/16	M	Prince of Wales Island	AK	Ken A. Vorisek	1991	2,991
18 10/16	11 11/16	6 15/16	M	Zec Capitachouane	QUE	Jay A. Mengel	1991	2,991
18 10/16	11 11/16	6 15/16	M	Idaho County	ID	Stephan S. Jones	1991	2,991
18 10/16	11 6/16	7 4/16	M	Los Alamos County	NM	David R. Aikin	1991	2,991
18 10/16	11 11/16	6 15/16	M	Chapleau	ONT	Linda S. Schwochert	1991	2,991
18 10/16	11 13/16	6 13/16	M	Barrier Lake	SAS	Ray Fredin	1991	2,991
18 10/16	11 12/16	6 14/16	M	Coos County	NH	Harry Bodenrader	1991	2,991
18 10/16	11 10/16	7 0/16	M	Millville	NBW	Stephen Buck	1991	2,991
18 10/16	11 11/16	6 15/16	M	Wallowa County	OR	Brett Duane Monaghan	1991	2,991
18 10/16	11 12/16	6 14/16	M	Ontonagon County	MI	Bruce R. Bell	1991	2,991
18 10/16	11 6/16	7 4/16	M	French River	ONT	Kenneth E. Briggs	1992	2,991
18 10/16	11 11/16	6 15/16	M	Zec Maganasipi	QUE	Frank Luksa	1992	2,991
18 10/16	11 11/16	6 15/16	M	Sandilands	MAN	Jac D. Hiebert	1992	2,991
18 10/16	11 12/16	6 14/16	M	Terrace Bay	ONT	Paul J. Paiser	1992	2,991
18 10/16	11 10/16	7 0/16	M	Yukon River	AK	Timothy J. Barber	1992	2,991
18 10/16	11 14/16	6 12/16	M	Price County	WI	Daniel E. Kester	1992	2,991
18 10/16	11 13/16	6 13/16	M	Aitkin County	MN	Donald K. Olson	1992	2,991
18 10/16	11 11/16	6 15/16	M	Wallowa County	OR	Jeff Matson	1992	2,991
18 10/16	11 15/16	6 11/16	M	Grand Rapids	MAN	Robert L. Loveall	1993	2,991
18 10/16	11 12/16	6 14/16	M	Sioux Lookout	ONT	Marlene Odahlen-Hinz	1993	2,991
18 10/16	11 10/16	7 0/16	M	Lake Preissac	QUE	Brian Sands	1993	2,991
18 10/16	11 9/16	7 1/16	M	Kipawa	QUE	Carol Ference	1993	2,991
18 10/16	11 10/16	7 0/16	M	Houghton County	MI	Robert K. Benson	1993	2,991
18 10/16	11 11/16	6 15/16	M	La Loche	SAS	Brian E. Ronneberg	1994	2,991
18 10/16	11 12/16	6 14/16	M	Bonneville County	ID	Spencer P. Barnard	1994	2,991
18 10/16	11 14/16	6 12/16	M	Keeley Lake	SAS	Charles Niessner	1994	2,991
18 10/16	11 11/16	6 15/16	M	Armstrong	ONT	Scott J. Teigen	1994	2,991
18 10/16	11 15/16	6 11/16	M	Carrot River	SAS	Christopher Germain	1994	2,991
18 10/16	12 2/16	6 8/16	M	Coconino County	AZ	Donald Kenneth Baker	1994	2,991
18 10/16	11 14/16	6 12/16	M	Packwash Lake	ONT	Lou Edelis	1995	2,991
18 10/16	11 5/16	7 5/16	M	Boise County	ID	Terry Bennett	1995	2,991
18 10/16	11 14/16	6 12/16	M	Clarke Lake	SAS	Ron Tandy	1995	2,991
18 10/16	11 11/16	6 15/16	M	Lake Winnipegosis	MAN	Gerald Catterfeld	1995	2,991
18 10/16	11 12/16	6 14/16	M	Wabigoon	ONT	Allen S. Kenyon	1995	2,991
18 10/16	11 11/16	6 15/16	M	Blueberry River	ONT	Conway Marvin	1995	2,991
18 10/16	11 12/16	6 14/16	M	Lake Cowen	SAS	Richard A. Pippenger	1995	2,991
18 10/16	11 8/16	7 2/16	M	Fort Coulonge	QUE	Quinton E. Johnston	1995	2,991
18 10/16	11 6/16	7 4/16	M	Armstrong	ONT	Robert Terrance Hurley	1995	2,991
18 10/16	11 14/16	6 12/16	M	Iron County	WI	Christopher Gorenc	1995	2,991
18 10/16	11 14/16	6 12/16	M	Athabasca River	ALB	William Riley	1996	2,991
18 10/16	11 12/16	6 14/16	M	Kootenai County	ID	Shane Moyer	1996	2,991
18 10/16	11 10/16	7 0/16	M	Hearst	ONT	Kenyon W. Woods	1996	2,991
18 10/16	11 12/16	6 14/16	M	Hudson Bay	SAS	Gary Jensen	1996	2,991
18 10/16	11 10/16	7 0/16	M	Peace River	ALB	Daniel A. Kasprzyk	1996	2,991
18 10/16	11 12/16	6 14/16	M	High Level	ALB	Ken Whitney	1996	2,991
18 10/16	11 10/16	7 0/16	M	Lynn Lake	MAN	Dave Canfield	1996	2,991
18 10/16	11 11/16	6 15/16	M	Lemhi County	ID	Russell D. Kennedy	1996	2,991
18 10/16	11 7/16	7 3/16	M	Cook County	MN	Earl Lowell Goodman	1996	2,991
18 10/16	11 5/16	7 5/16	M	Coos County	NH	Mark Hakansson	1996	2,991
18 10/16	11 11/16	6 15/16	M	Boise County	ID	John F. Thomas	1997	2,991
18 10/16	11 7/16	7 3/16	M	Sheridan County	WY	Andrew D. Weisgerber	1997	2,991
18 10/16	11 14/16	6 12/16	M	Domaine Preissac	QUE	Jeanne Hughes	1997	2,991
18 10/16	11 14/16	6 12/16	M	Clearwater River	ALB	Darryl Quidort	1997	2,991
18 10/16	12 0/16	6 10/16	M	Lac des Mille Lacs	ONT	Thomas E. Rothrock	1997	2,991
18 10/16	11 10/16	7 0/16	M	Lynn Lake	MAN	Sean T. Barry	1997	2,991

BLACK BEAR

Minimum Score 18 — Continued

SCORE	GREATEST LENGTH	GREATEST WIDTH	SEX	AREA	STATE/ PROVINCE	HUNTER'S NAME	DATE	RANK
18 10/16	11 9/16	7 1/16	M	Riou Lake	SAS	Pat Reilly	1997	2,991
18 10/16	11 9/16	7 1/16	M	Ear Falls	ONT	Don Noonan	1997	2,991
18 10/16	11 10/16	7 0/16	M	Jackson County	OR	G. Pat Crisler	1997	2,991
18 10/16	11 14/16	6 12/16	M	Sawyer County	WI	Scott Tenold	1997	2,991
18 10/16	12 0/16	6 10/16	M	Oconto County	WI	Ronald F. Lax	1997	2,991
18 10/16	12 1/16	6 9/16	M	Webster County	WV	Scott Cochran	1997	2,991
18 10/16	11 12/16	6 14/16	M	Navajo County	AZ	Steve D. Munier	1997	2,991
18 10/16	11 9/16	7 1/16	M	La Ronge	SAS	Mike Maser	1998	2,991
18 10/16	11 13/16	6 13/16	M	Brunswick Lake	ONT	Mark H. Kulke	1998	2,991
18 10/16	11 12/16	6 14/16	M	Amisk Lake	SAS	Lee Wahlund	1998	2,991
18 10/16	11 12/16	6 14/16	M	Red Lake	ONT	Jon Lozzio	1998	2,991
18 10/16	11 8/16	7 2/16	M	Ear Falls	ONT	Dwight Hearing	1998	2,991
18 10/16	11 13/16	6 13/16	M	Marinette County	WI	Scott Dyer	1998	2,991
18 9/16	11 5/16	7 4/16	M	Chelan County	WA	Wayne Hathaway	1960	3,134
18 9/16	11 6/16	7 3/16	M	Olsen Bay	AK	Don Daniels	1963	3,134
18 9/16	11 10/16	6 15/16	M	Iron County	MI	Don Schram	1964	3,134
18 9/16	11 10/16	6 15/16	M	Mattawa	ONT	Dr. Max G. Menefee	1966	3,134
18 9/16	11 5/16	7 4/16	M	St. Louis County	MN	Ron Johnson	1967	3,134
18 9/16	11 5/16	7 4/16	M	Blue Jay Ridge	CA	Delbert Allmon	1972	3,134
18 9/16	11 6/16	7 3/16	M	Nez Perce County	ID	Betty Gulman	1972	3,134
18 9/16	11 12/16	6 13/16	M	Rio Arriba County	NM	Curtis W. McClahan	1973	3,134
18 9/16	12 0/16	6 9/16	M	Swan Hills	ALB	Gerald L. Egbert	1976	3,134
18 9/16	11 7/16	7 2/16	M	Franklin County	ME	John G. Morningstar	1977	3,134
18 9/16	11 9/16	7 0/16	M	Ottawa River	QUE	Roger D. Davis	1978	3,134
18 9/16	11 12/16	6 13/16	M	Fremont County	ID	Tom Savage	1979	3,134
18 9/16	11 13/16	6 12/16	M	Wabigoon	ONT	Jon Helgason	1979	3,134
18 9/16	11 4/16	7 5/16	M	Caramat	ONT	John LaForge	1979	3,134
18 9/16	11 5/16	7 4/16	M	Idaho County	ID	Darrel Howard	1980	3,134
18 9/16	11 13/16	6 12/16	M	Sawyer County	WI	Joe Gohres	1980	3,134
18 9/16	11 6/16	7 3/16	M	Catron County	NM	Cornie P. Intveld	1980	3,134
18 9/16	11 11/16	6 14/16	M	Ravalli County	MT	Mike F. Bartz	1981	3,134
18 9/16	11 9/16	7 0/16	M	Marquette County	MI	Gary Lohman	1981	3,134
18 9/16	11 7/16	7 2/16	M	Idaho County	ID	Darrell Howard	1982	3,134
18 9/16	11 11/16	6 14/16	M	Marquette County	MI	Keith B. Putnam	1982	3,134
18 9/16	11 13/16	6 12/16	M	Dryden	ONT	Dennis L. Havey	1982	3,134
18 9/16	11 7/16	7 2/16	M	Nipigon	ONT	James P. Kina	1982	3,134
18 9/16	11 8/16	7 1/16	M	Susitna Valley	AK	Patrick McKay	1982	3,134
18 9/16	12 3/16	6 6/16	M	Game Area #23	MAN	Gary Kaluzniak	1983	3,134
18 9/16	12 5/16	6 4/16	M	Carlton County	MN	Larry H. Hoyt	1983	3,134
18 9/16	11 10/16	6 15/16	M	Ear Falls	ONT	Scott J. Strook	1984	3,134
18 9/16	11 8/16	7 1/16	M	Temiscaminque	QUE	Joe G. Hopwood	1984	3,134
18 9/16	11 9/16	7 0/16	M	Cedar Lake	ONT	Brad Wiehr	1984	3,134
18 9/16	11 9/16	7 0/16	M	Idaho County	ID	Ronald J. Larson	1984	3,134
18 9/16	11 9/16	7 0/16	M	Shasta County	CA	Peter Esposito	1984	3,134
18 9/16	11 8/16	7 1/16	M	Sudbury	ONT	Vinnie Pisani	1985	3,134
18 9/16	11 9/16	7 0/16	M	Dryden	ONT	James F. Hendricks	1985	3,134
18 9/16	11 10/16	6 15/16	M	Pancake Bay	ONT	Brad L. Rogers	1985	3,134
18 9/16	11 10/16	6 15/16	M	Mendocino County	CA	Charles Verne	1985	3,134
18 9/16	11 7/16	7 2/16	M	Lemhi County	ID	Thomas Fuller	1985	3,134
18 9/16	11 12/16	6 13/16	M	Cass County	MN	Larry Fischer	1985	3,134
18 9/16	11 6/16	7 3/16	M	Missoula County	MT	Terry See	1985	3,134
18 9/16	11 12/16	6 13/16	M	Sudbury	ONT	David L. Willis	1986	3,134
18 9/16	11 11/16	6 14/16	M	Boundary County	ID	Walt Dinning	1986	3,134
18 9/16	11 11/16	6 14/16	M	Clearwater County	ID	Ronnie Larson	1986	3,134
18 9/16	11 2/16	7 7/16	M	Caramat	ONT	Scott A. Atton	1986	3,134
18 9/16	11 9/16	7 0/16	M	Fort Coulonge	QUE	Westley Keller	1986	3,134
18 9/16	11 10/16	6 15/16	M	Washington County	ME	Marty Kane	1986	3,134
18 9/16	12 2/16	6 7/16	M	Burnett County	WI	Duane Hoefs	1986	3,134
18 9/16	11 9/16	7 0/16	M	Mine Centre	ONT	Stan H. Myers	1987	3,134
18 9/16	11 13/16	6 12/16	M	Monominto	MAN	Erik Thienpondt	1987	3,134
18 9/16	11 10/16	6 15/16	M	Montreal River	ONT	Thomas Hlinka	1987	3,134
18 9/16	12 1/16	6 8/16	M	Clearwater County	MN	Kevin Anderson	1987	3,134
18 9/16	11 5/16	7 4/16	M	Puperville	ONT	John DeWyse	1987	3,134
18 9/16	11 8/16	7 1/16	M	Los Alamos County	NM	Robert Hand	1987	3,134
18 9/16	11 9/16	7 0/16	M	Jackson County	OR	Jeff S. Cleveland	1987	3,134
18 9/16	11 10/16	6 15/16	M	Kenora	ONT	James G. Aldrich	1988	3,134
18 9/16	11 10/16	6 15/16	M	Wanless	MAN	Jon P. Thomas	1988	3,134
18 9/16	11 9/16	7 0/16	M	Kenora	ONT	John E. Larsen	1988	3,134
18 9/16	11 6/16	7 3/16	M	Clearwater County	ID	Gregg Tanner	1988	3,134
18 9/16	11 8/16	7 1/16	M	Temiscaming	QUE	Daniel E. Wallace	1988	3,134
18 9/16	11 13/16	6 12/16	M	Oneida County	WI	Tim Johnson	1988	3,134
18 9/16	11 14/16	6 11/16	M	Oneida County	WI	Greg L. Reed	1988	3,134
18 9/16	11 11/16	6 14/16	M	Rockingham County	VA	Roger O. Wyant	1988	3,134
18 9/16	11 14/16	6 11/16	M	Prince of Wales Island	AK	Dyrk Eddie	1989	3,134
18 9/16	11 12/16	6 13/16	M	Lane County	OR	Steven T Jones	1989	3,134
18 9/16	11 6/16	7 3/16	M	Clericy	QUE	Roger Stricklen	1989	3,134
18 9/16	11 10/16	6 15/16	M	Swift Creek	BC	Dan Yalowega	1989	3,134
18 9/16	11 11/16	6 14/16	M	Waterhen Lake	MAN	Walt Krom	1989	3,134

BLACK BEAR

Minimum Score 18 — Continued

SCORE	GREATEST LENGTH	GREATEST WIDTH	SEX	AREA	STATE/PROVINCE	HUNTER'S NAME	DATE	RANK
18 9/16	11 8/16	7 1/16	M	San Miguel County	NM	Harold Wallace	1989	3,134
18 9/16	11 10/16	6 15/16	M	Idaho County	ID	Monty Moravec	1990	3,134
18 9/16	11 8/16	7 1/16	M	Campbell River	BC	Don Quackenbush	1990	3,134
18 9/16	11 9/16	7 0/16	M	Pluto Lake	ONT	John D. Schmidt	1990	3,134
18 9/16	11 10/16	6 15/16	M	King County	WA	G. Dan Feighner	1990	3,134
18 9/16	11 11/16	6 14/16	M	Lincoln County	NM	Charlie C. Bing	1990	3,134
18 9/16	11 15/16	6 10/16	M	Marinette County	WI	Jeffrey J. Zepnick	1990	3,134
18 9/16	11 12/16	6 13/16	M	Holinshead Lake	ONT	Jack Leschner	1991	3,134
18 9/16	11 5/16	7 4/16	M	Clearwater County	ID	Johnny Watson	1991	3,134
18 9/16	11 6/16	7 3/16	M	County #1	ALB	Douglas E. Erickson	1991	3,134
18 9/16	11 12/16	6 13/16	M	Grand County	UT	Kim Tatman	1991	3,134
18 9/16	11 3/16	7 6/16	M	Haileybury	ONT	Dean G. Bartolomucci	1991	3,134
18 9/16	11 13/16	6 12/16	M	Idaho County	ID	Monty Moravec	1991	3,134
18 9/16	12 2/16	6 7/16	M	Lewis County	WA	Ronald D. Amrine	1991	3,134
18 9/16	11 11/16	6 14/16	M	Somerset County	ME	Corey Sibbio	1991	3,134
18 9/16	11 13/16	6 12/16	M	Gallatin County	MT	Bruce A. Porisch	1991	3,134
18 9/16	11 12/16	6 13/16	M	Slave Lake	ALB	Bill Vaznis	1991	3,134
18 9/16	11 15/16	6 10/16	M	Roscommon County	MI	Elmer E. Clemson	1991	3,134
18 9/16	11 12/16	6 13/16	M	Gila County	AZ	Mark Ovitt	1991	3,134
18 9/16	12 2/16	6 7/16	M	Warren County	VA	John B. Stewart	1991	3,134
18 9/16	10 14/16	7 11/16	M	Nicholas County	WV	Steve A. Antoline	1991	3,134
18 9/16	11 13/16	6 12/16	M	Erickson	MAN	Glen Newton	1992	3,134
18 9/16	11 13/16	6 12/16	M	Emo	ONT	Steven J. Snyder	1992	3,134
18 9/16	11 12/16	6 13/16	M	Snohomish County	WA	John P. Hennessy	1992	3,134
18 9/16	11 13/16	6 12/16	M	Dalton Highway	AK	Ronald W. Lang, Jr.	1993	3,134
18 9/16	11 11/16	6 14/16	M	Prince of Wales Island	AK	Jim Young	1993	3,134
18 9/16	11 10/16	6 15/16	M	Highwinds Lake	ONT	Robert G. Carter	1993	3,134
18 9/16	11 9/16	7 0/16	M	McBride	BC	Richard Kopp	1993	3,134
18 9/16	11 10/16	6 15/16	M	Stenen	SAS	Tom Langford	1993	3,134
18 9/16	12 1/16	6 8/16	M	Upper Skeena River	BC	Kristen J. Mustad	1993	3,134
18 9/16	11 7/16	7 2/16	M	Ft. McMurray	ALB	Jim Miller, Jr.	1993	3,134
18 9/16	11 9/16	7 0/16	M	Idaho County	ID	K-Tal Johnson	1993	3,134
18 9/16	11 9/16	7 0/16	M	Baie Comeau	QUE	Trevor W.G. McEntyre	1993	3,134
18 9/16	11 6/16	7 3/16	M	Latuque	QUE	Daniel F. Walsh	1993	3,134
18 9/16	11 11/16	6 14/16	M	Bella Coola	BC	Lawrence Michalchuk	1993	3,134
18 9/16	11 9/16	7 0/16	M	Iron County	WI	Paul Jaeger	1993	3,134
18 9/16	12 0/16	6 9/16	M	Jackson County	OR	Brian Day	1993	3,134
18 9/16	12 2/16	6 7/16	M	Duck Mtns.	SAS	Jeff Jacob	1994	3,134
18 9/16	11 12/16	6 13/16	M	Lemhi County	ID	Mark A. Mathews	1994	3,134
18 9/16	11 11/16	6 14/16	M	Timmins	ONT	James F. Blanton	1994	3,134
18 9/16	11 5/16	7 4/16	M	Atikokan	ONT	Mark "Root" Gies	1994	3,134
18 9/16	11 10/16	6 15/16	M	Sioux Lookout	ONT	John P. Liska	1994	3,134
18 9/16	11 8/16	7 1/16	M	Zec Dumoine	QUE	Frederick Hendrickson	1994	3,134
18 9/16	12 1/16	6 8/16	M	Cass County	MN	Dorian Cornelius	1994	3,134
18 9/16	11 11/16	6 14/16	M	Union County	OR	Dave M. Seida	1994	3,134
18 9/16	11 7/16	7 2/16	M	Ravalli County	MT	Scott Lindsey	1994	3,134
18 9/16	12 0/16	6 9/16	M	Latah County	ID	Nicholas Orth	1994	3,134
18 9/16	11 10/16	6 15/16	M	Hudson Bay	SAS	Tag Reed	1995	3,134
18 9/16	11 9/16	7 0/16	M	Slave Lake	ALB	Gregory Noble Spickler	1995	3,134
18 9/16	11 11/16	6 14/16	M	Cabonga	QUE	Len Cardinale	1995	3,134
18 9/16	11 12/16	6 13/16	M	Upsala	ONT	Dale L. Toltzmann	1995	3,134
18 9/16	11 7/16	7 2/16	M	Washington County	ME	Brian D. Smith	1995	3,134
18 9/16	11 12/16	6 13/16	M	Ignace	ONT	Kevin Linton	1995	3,134
18 9/16	11 6/16	7 3/16	M	Kirkland Lake	ONT	Howard L. Nester	1995	3,134
18 9/16	12 3/16	6 6/16	M	Ontonagon County	MI	Troy A. Martinez	1995	3,134
18 9/16	11 14/16	6 11/16	M	Lincoln County	WI	James H. Dimpfl	1995	3,134
18 9/16	11 15/16	6 10/16	M	Kootenai County	ID	Cristina Lafrenz	1996	3,134
18 9/16	11 14/16	6 11/16	M	La Corey	ALB	Dawn Ollenberger	1996	3,134
18 9/16	11 11/16	6 14/16	M	Athabasca River	ALB	Doy Curtis	1996	3,134
18 9/16	11 14/16	6 11/16	M	Shoshone County	ID	Roger Stewart	1996	3,134
18 9/16	11 8/16	7 1/16	M	Wawang Lake	ONT	Frank Frye	1996	3,134
18 9/16	11 14/16	6 11/16	M	Franklin County	ME	Thomas R. Umlauf	1996	3,134
18 9/16	11 10/16	6 15/16	M	Grafton County	NH	Jeffrey D. Stout	1996	3,134
18 9/16	11 14/16	6 11/16	M	Sawyer County	WI	Gene Dehnhoff	1996	3,134
18 9/16	11 13/16	6 12/16	M	Orange County	NY	Joseph W. Talasco	1996	3,134
18 9/16	11 11/16	6 14/16	M	Tuolumne County	CA	Jef Lindenmayer	1996	3,134
18 9/16	12 0/16	6 9/16	M	High Level	ALB	Tom Russom	1997	3,134
18 9/16	11 14/16	6 11/16	M	High Level	ALB	Kevin Drysdale	1997	3,134
18 9/16	11 10/16	6 15/16	M	Lac La Ronge	SAS	Steve Hammond	1997	3,134
18 9/16	11 13/16	6 12/16	M	Big Sandy Lake	SAS	Duane Reitmeier	1997	3,134
18 9/16	11 13/16	6 12/16	M	Montreal River Harbour	ONT	Thomas J. Liguori	1997	3,134
18 9/16	11 13/16	6 12/16	M	Yavapai County	AZ	Chris J. Dunn	1997	3,134
18 9/16	11 12/16	6 13/16	M	Sandilands	MAN	Russell K. Mehling	1998	3,134
18 9/16	11 6/16	7 3/16	M	Carroll Inlet	AK	Larry Daly	1998	3,134
18 9/16	11 8/16	7 1/16	M	Ray River	AK	Michael Chadwick	1998	3,134
18 9/16	11 8/16	7 1/16	M	Swan Lake	ALB	Derrill Herman	1998	3,134
18 9/16	11 15/16	6 10/16	M	Wabigoon	ONT	Leon R. Meidam	1998	3,134
18 9/16	11 11/16	6 14/16	M	Nipawin	SAS	Michael E. Puhl	1998	3,134

BLACK BEAR

Minimum Score 18 — Continued — 175

SCORE	GREATEST LENGTH	GREATEST WIDTH	SEX	AREA	STATE/ PROVINCE	HUNTER'S NAME	DATE	RANK
18 8/16	11 8/16	7 0/16	M	Whatcom County	WA	Jack Fish	1961	3,277
18 8/16	11 13/16	6 11/16	M	Prince William Sound	AK	Bob Snelson	1962	3,277
18 8/16	11 8/16	7 0/16	M	Iron County	WI	Maynard Peck	1963	3,277
18 8/16	11 6/16	7 2/16	M	Clearwater County	ID	Robert J. Kreisher	1965	3,277
18 8/16	11 11/16	6 13/16	M	Sapawe	ONT	Dennis Gregory	1967	3,277
18 8/16	11 4/16	7 4/16	M	Mineral County	CO	Ron Wintz	1967	3,277
18 8/16	11 12/16	6 12/16	M	Siskiyou County	CA	Lyle L. Stroble	1968	3,277
18 8/16	11 7/16	7 1/16	M	Franklin County	ME	John Miterko	1970	3,277
18 8/16	12 0/16	6 8/16	M	Forest County	WI	Vilas Backhaus	1972	3,277
18 8/16	11 4/16	7 4/16	M	Messines	QUE	John W. Redmond	1973	3,277
18 8/16	11 10/16	6 14/16	M	Somerset County	ME	John D. Bonargo	1974	3,277
18 8/16	11 7/16	7 1/16	M	La Plata County	CO	Ronald C. Gaines	1975	3,277
18 8/16	11 0/16	7 8/16	M	Messines	QUE	Arthur R. Litschewski	1975	3,277
18 8/16	11 7/16	7 1/16	M	Hopetown	ONT	Dale Bailey	1976	3,277
18 8/16	11 6/16	7 2/16	M	Dryden	ONT	Jim Dyer	1977	3,277
18 8/16	11 6/16	7 2/16	M	Sioux Narrows	ONT	David Bailey	1978	3,277
18 8/16	11 8/16	7 0/16	M	Cook County	MN	Paul Smith	1978	3,277
18 8/16	11 6/16	7 2/16	M	Sandoval County	NM	Johnny R. Trujillo	1978	3,277
18 8/16	11 4/16	7 4/16	M	Franklin County	ME	John Janelli	1979	3,277
18 8/16	11 13/16	6 11/16	M	Lincoln County	WI	James Lechleitner	1981	3,277
18 8/16	12 0/16	6 8/16	M	Burnett County	WI	Gary K. Roholt	1981	3,277
18 8/16	11 6/16	7 2/16	M	Atikokan	ONT	Larry Stewart	1982	3,277
18 8/16	11 12/16	6 12/16	M	Kanabec County	MN	Raymond J. Altman	1982	3,277
18 8/16	11 10/16	6 14/16	M	Bancroft	ONT	Dean J. Farkas	1982	3,277
18 8/16	11 3/16	7 5/16	M	Love	SAS	David M. Tofte	1982	3,277
18 8/16	11 7/16	7 1/16	M	Terrace Bay	ONT	William J. Ernst	1983	3,277
18 8/16	11 7/16	7 1/16	M	McAdam	NBW	David Baldwin	1983	3,277
18 8/16	12 1/16	6 7/16	M	Ear Falls	ONT	Ernest C. Boser	1983	3,277
18 8/16	11 12/16	6 12/16	M	Langlade County	WI	Raymond Juedes	1983	3,277
18 8/16	11 11/16	6 13/16	M	Vilas County	WI	Alan L. Black	1983	3,277
18 8/16	11 8/16	7 0/16	M	Park County	CO	Larry A. Welchlen	1984	3,277
18 8/16	11 2/16	7 6/16	M	Carbon County	WY	Vaughn Ross	1984	3,277
18 8/16	11 10/16	6 14/16	M	Swan River	MAN	Kevin Hisey	1984	3,277
18 8/16	11 6/16	7 2/16	M	Spokane County	WA	Kenneth R. Wengert	1984	3,277
18 8/16	11 11/16	6 13/16	M	Iron County	WI	Gary Johnson	1984	3,277
18 8/16	11 9/16	6 15/16	M	Ft. McMurray	ALB	Darrin West	1985	3,277
18 8/16	11 12/16	6 12/16	M	Kootenai County	ID	Kenneth R. Wengert	1985	3,277
18 8/16	11 10/16	6 14/16	M	Susitna River	AK	Roger Stewart	1985	3,277
18 8/16	11 9/16	6 15/16	M	Fremont County	ID	Doug Burkman	1985	3,277
18 8/16	11 10/16	6 14/16	M	Penobscot County	ME	G. Kent Tableman	1985	3,277
18 8/16	11 14/16	6 10/16	M	Shasta County	CA	Larry Walkley	1985	3,277
18 8/16	11 6/16	7 2/16	M	Pitkin County	CO	Richard E. Davis	1986	3,277
18 8/16	11 4/16	7 4/16	M	Lemhi County	ID	Art Hrabec	1986	3,277
18 8/16	11 6/16	7 2/16	M	White River	ONT	Daniel B. Meece	1986	3,277
18 8/16	11 11/16	6 13/16	M	St. James Bay	AK	Ronald Callahan	1986	3,277
18 8/16	11 7/16	7 1/16	M	Jones	ONT	Hank Denowski	1986	3,277
18 8/16	11 5/16	7 3/16	M	Palfrey Lake	NBW	Lou Probo	1986	3,277
18 8/16	11 8/16	7 0/16	M	Cook County	MN	Kevin Cook	1986	3,277
18 8/16	11 10/16	6 14/16	M	Augusta County	VA	W. Thurman Hensley	1986	3,277
18 8/16	12 0/16	6 8/16	M	Siskiyou County	CA	Larry Holmes	1986	3,277
18 8/16	11 10/16	6 14/16	M	Rusagonis	NBW	Stephen Buckingham	1987	3,277
18 8/16	11 13/16	6 11/16	M	Savant Lake	ONT	Rod Brasel	1987	3,277
18 8/16	11 12/16	6 12/16	M	Atikokan	ONT	Dean M. Westby	1987	3,277
18 8/16	11 12/16	6 12/16	M	Mine Centre	ONT	Terry Hadd	1987	3,277
18 8/16	11 12/16	6 12/16	M	Hartland	NBW	Frank Cinquemani	1987	3,277
18 8/16	11 5/16	7 3/16	M	Oliver	BC	A. R. Bryant	1987	3,277
18 8/16	11 6/16	7 2/16	M	Caramat	ONT	William M. Long	1987	3,277
18 8/16	11 4/16	7 4/16	F	Grassy Narrows	ONT	Mike Jacobs	1987	3,277
18 8/16	11 9/16	6 15/16	M	Pennhorwood Twp.	ONT	Harry A. Weishaar	1987	3,277
18 8/16	12 4/16	6 4/16	M	National Mills	MAN	T. J. Kearns	1987	3,277
18 8/16	11 9/16	6 15/16	M	Lincoln County	NM	Jon R. Reid	1987	3,277
18 8/16	11 13/16	6 11/16	M	Iron County	MI	Andy Holinga	1987	3,277
18 8/16	11 11/16	6 13/16	M	Unit 66	SAS	Donald Goracke	1987	3,277
18 8/16	11 8/16	7 0/16	M	Dryden	ONT	Tommy M. Brown	1988	3,277
18 8/16	12 0/16	6 8/16	M	Wallowa County	OR	William Kevin McCadden	1988	3,277
18 8/16	11 14/16	6 10/16	M	Mesa County	CO	Ron A. Stover	1988	3,277
18 8/16	11 13/16	6 11/16	M	Houghton County	MI	Daniel Glinn	1988	3,277
18 8/16	11 6/16	7 2/16	M	Ravalli County	MT	John Locke	1988	3,277
18 8/16	11 6/16	7 2/16	M	Douglas County	OR	Tom E. Tipton	1988	3,277
18 8/16	11 11/16	6 13/16	M	Rocky Mtn. House	ALB	Andrew Wiese	1989	3,277
18 8/16	11 13/16	6 11/16	M	Wapawekka Hills	SAS	Ronald J. Collier	1989	3,277
18 8/16	11 12/16	6 12/16	M	Archuleta County	CO	Michael G. Morton	1989	3,277
18 8/16	11 1/16	7 7/16	M	Webbwood	ONT	Jim Norris	1989	3,277
18 8/16	11 6/16	6 13/16	M	Red Lake	ONT	Donald Tjader	1989	3,277
18 8/16	11 14/16	6 10/16	M	Felix	ONT	Scott Trelstad	1989	3,277
18 8/16	11 10/16	6 14/16	M	Shining Tree	ONT	Bernard J. Higley	1989	3,277
18 8/16	11 10/16	6 14/16	M	Las Animas County	CO	Joe Johnston	1989	3,277
18 8/16	11 9/16	6 15/16	M	Baraga County	MI	Randy I Lee	1989	3,277

BLACK BEAR

Minimum Score 18 — Continued

SCORE	GREATEST LENGTH	GREATEST WIDTH	SEX	AREA	STATE/ PROVINCE	HUNTER'S NAME	DATE	RANK
18 8/16	11 12/16	6 12/16	M	Douglas County	OR	Stephen Herrera	1989	3,277
18 8/16	11 6/16	7 2/16	M	Atikokan	ONT	Robert M. Jurica	1990	3,277
18 8/16	11 8/16	7 0/16	M	Ft. McMurray	ALB	James Pike	1990	3,277
18 8/16	11 12/16	6 12/16	M	Peace River	ALB	Roy M. Goodwin	1990	3,277
18 8/16	11 9/16	6 15/16	M	Highland Grove	ONT	Bob Capece	1990	3,277
18 8/16	11 9/16	6 15/16	M	Rocky Lake	MAN	Morris McManus	1990	3,277
18 8/16	11 14/16	6 10/16	M	Doaktown	NBW	Scott E. Komaridis	1990	3,277
18 8/16	11 10/16	6 14/16	M	St. Alexis Des Monts	QUE	Mike Hammond	1990	3,277
18 8/16	11 15/16	6 9/16	M	Swan River	MAN	Joseph S. Holiday	1990	3,277
18 8/16	11 2/16	7 6/16	M	Somerset County	ME	Bob Eisele	1990	3,277
18 8/16	11 9/16	6 15/16	M	Shawano County	WI	Ricky R. Kauffman	1990	3,277
18 8/16	11 6/16	7 2/16	M	Zec Rapides Des Joachins	QUE	Ken Dwyer	1990	3,277
18 8/16	11 10/16	6 14/16	M	Graham County	AZ	Dave Bushell	1991	3,277
18 8/16	11 14/16	6 10/16	M	Peace River	ALB	Bruce McRae	1991	3,277
18 8/16	11 13/16	6 11/16	M	Fawcett	ALB	James W. Thomson	1991	3,277
18 8/16	11 8/16	7 0/16	M	Braice Township	ONT	Timothy A. Salisbury	1991	3,277
18 8/16	11 10/16	6 14/16	M	Hythe	ALB	Rex Dacus	1991	3,277
18 8/16	11 9/16	6 15/16	M	Brown Bear Lake	ONT	Mark Kayser	1991	3,277
18 8/16	11 15/16	6 9/16	M	Lewis County	WA	Wayne A. Grasseth	1991	3,277
18 8/16	11 10/16	6 14/16	M	Grand County	UT	Pat Snyder	1991	3,277
18 8/16	11 14/16	6 10/16	M	Doaktown	NBW	George Louis	1991	3,277
18 8/16	11 14/16	6 10/16	M	Sioux Lookout	ONT	John Shields	1991	3,277
18 8/16	11 14/16	6 10/16	M	Remigny	QUE	Tom Mundy	1991	3,277
18 8/16	11 4/16	7 4/16	M	Ear Falls	ONT	Steve Jancar	1991	3,277
18 8/16	11 12/16	6 12/16	M	Pine County	MN	Brandon R. Johnson	1991	3,277
18 8/16	11 6/16	7 2/16	M	Forest County	WI	Steven W. Kluth	1991	3,277
18 8/16	11 8/16	7 0/16	M	Linn County	OR	Rick Kopf	1991	3,277
18 8/16	11 5/16	7 3/16	M	Pelican Lake	MAN	Douglas R. Buchler	1992	3,277
18 8/16	11 14/16	6 10/16	M	Cold Lake	ALB	Ron Dixon	1992	3,277
18 8/16	11 12/16	6 12/16	M	Barrier Lake	SAS	Ray Fredin	1992	3,277
18 8/16	11 12/16	6 12/16	M	Tanana Flats	AK	Tommy L. Ramsey	1992	3,277
18 8/16	11 14/16	6 10/16	M	Fisher Branch	MAN	Fred W. Lambley	1992	3,277
18 8/16	11 9/16	6 15/16	M	Wabigoon	ONT	Charles Drerup	1992	3,277
18 8/16	11 8/16	7 0/16	M	Cochrane	ONT	Stephen Ferris	1992	3,277
18 8/16	11 9/16	6 15/16	M	Klamath County	OR	Ronald Aubry	1992	3,277
18 8/16	11 5/16	7 3/16	M	Custer County	ID	Darrell Nunez	1993	3,277
18 8/16	11 6/16	7 2/16	M	Aulneau Peninsula	ONT	Michael Koska	1993	3,277
18 8/16	11 0/16	7 8/16	M	Christopher Lake	SAS	Harold Alka	1993	3,277
18 8/16	11 10/16	6 14/16	M	Armstrong	ONT	Jerome D. Larson	1993	3,277
18 8/16	12 0/16	6 8/16	M	Arntfield	QUE	Ken H. Taylor	1993	3,277
18 8/16	12 2/16	6 6/16	M	Pine County	MN	Adam Flod	1993	3,277
18 8/16	11 14/16	6 10/16	M	Baraga County	MI	Pat Barnett	1993	3,277
18 8/16	11 11/16	6 13/16	M	Trinity County	CA	Michael R. Geller	1993	3,277
18 8/16	12 0/16	6 8/16	M	Carrot River	SAS	Luke M. Fischer	1994	3,277
18 8/16	11 5/16	7 3/16	M	Wapawekka Lake	SAS	Jerry Bowen	1994	3,277
18 8/16	11 9/16	6 15/16	M	Patuanak	SAS	M. Robert DeLaney	1994	3,277
18 8/16	11 10/16	6 14/16	M	Sioux Lookout	ONT	Gregory G. Henan	1994	3,277
18 8/16	11 12/16	6 12/16	M	Rossburn	MAN	Barry Minshull	1994	3,277
18 8/16	11 10/16	6 14/16	M	Dryden	ONT	Mark Kendrick Williams	1994	3,277
18 8/16	11 12/16	6 12/16	M	Sawyer County	WI	Jay Girard	1994	3,277
18 8/16	11 12/16	6 12/16	M	Ontonagon County	MI	David A. Kasten	1994	3,277
18 8/16	11 13/16	6 11/16	M	Burnett County	WI	Tom McAlpine	1994	3,277
18 8/16	11 8/16	7 0/16	M	Fredericton	NBW	Tony DeMase	1994	3,277
18 8/16	12 0/16	6 8/16	M	Lane County	OR	Gary Nyden	1994	3,277
18 8/16	11 6/16	7 2/16	M	Mac Millan River	YUK	Ed DeYoung	1995	3,277
18 8/16	11 6/16	7 2/16	M	Poplarfield	MAN	Larry L. Helgerson	1995	3,277
18 8/16	11 6/16	7 2/16	M	Prince of Wales Island	AK	Garry A. Thoms	1995	3,277
18 8/16	11 15/16	6 9/16	M	Mistatim	SAS	John David Bryant	1995	3,277
18 8/16	11 5/16	7 3/16	M	Kearl Lake	ALB	Kenneth Hinke	1995	3,277
18 8/16	11 8/16	7 0/16	M	Thessalon	ONT	William Fry	1995	3,277
18 8/16	11 1/16	7 7/16	M	Searchmont	ONT	Edward Pylman	1995	3,277
18 8/16	11 14/16	6 10/16	M	Wawa	ONT	James J. Borg	1995	3,277
18 8/16	11 6/16	7 2/16	M	Kitsap County	WA	Roy L. Schultz	1995	3,277
18 8/16	11 8/16	7 0/16	M	Somerset County	ME	David Bilotti	1995	3,277
18 8/16	12 0/16	6 8/16	M	Pine County	MN	Scott Ketchmark	1995	3,277
18 8/16	11 9/16	6 15/16	M	Dryden	ONT	Brian Kendall	1995	3,277
18 8/16	12 0/16	6 8/16	M	Crook County	OR	Jim Merrill	1995	3,277
18 8/16	11 8/16	7 0/16	M	Oneida County	WI	Richard A. Klassa	1995	3,277
18 8/16	11 14/16	6 10/16	M	Big Sandy Lake	SAS	Gale Olsen	1996	3,277
18 8/16	11 8/16	7 0/16	M	English River	ONT	Paul Cox	1996	3,277
18 8/16	11 4/16	7 4/16	M	Matheson	ONT	Dr. Anthony Marrara	1996	3,277
18 8/16	11 10/16	6 14/16	M	Indian River	AK	Rick Schikora	1996	3,277
18 8/16	11 8/16	7 0/16	M	Rimouski	QUE	Chris Noack	1996	3,277
18 8/16	11 13/16	6 11/16	M	Price County	WI	David J. Kerkove	1996	3,277
18 8/16	11 14/16	6 10/16	M	Buffalo Narrows	SAS	Randy A. Shobe	1997	3,277
18 8/16	11 11/16	6 13/16	M	Pelican Lake	MAN	Kent George	1997	3,277
18 8/16	11 13/16	6 11/16	M	Love	SAS	Bruce Ott	1997	3,277
18 8/16	11 11/16	6 13/16	M	St. Mary's River	BC	Robert Faiers	1997	3,277

BLACK BEAR

Minimum Score 18 — Continued

SCORE	GREATEST LENGTH	GREATEST WIDTH	SEX	AREA	STATE/ PROVINCE	HUNTER'S NAME	DATE	RANK
18 8/16	11 14/16	6 10/16	M	Chapleau	ONT	Thomas LaCombe	1997	3,277
18 8/16	11 8/16	7 0/16	M	Mattice	ONT	Myron E. Jochmann	1997	3,277
18 8/16	11 12/16	6 12/16	M	Shoshone County	ID	Roger Stewart	1997	3,277
18 8/16	11 12/16	6 12/16	M	Teton County	ID	Thomas Thiel	1997	3,277
18 8/16	11 3/16	7 5/16	M	Cartie	ONT	Vernon Sowers	1997	3,277
18 8/16	11 8/16	7 0/16	M	La Tuque	QUE	John Mange, Jr.	1997	3,277
18 8/16	11 10/16	6 14/16	M	Grant County	WV	Jimmy Lucas, Jr.	1997	3,277
18 8/16	11 9/16	6 15/16	M	Athabasca River	ALB	Gene Mathias	1998	3,277
18 8/16	11 11/16	6 13/16	M	Hornepayne	ONT	Brian Stiglich	1998	3,277
18 8/16	11 12/16	6 12/16	M	Tulliby Lake	ALB	Larry Flaata	1998	3,277
18 8/16	11 9/16	6 15/16	M	Ile-a-la-Crosse	SAS	Drew McCartney	1998	3,277
18 8/16	11 9/16	6 15/16	M	Marathon	ONT	Robert Zabavski	1998	3,277
18 8/16	11 8/16	7 0/16	M	Savant Lake	ONT	Lee Nelms	1998	3,277
18 8/16	11 5/16	7 3/16	M	Lac Barriere	QUE	Dan Lindsey	1998	3,277
18 8/16	11 10/16	6 14/16	M	Piscataquis County	ME	Steven C. Gatling	1998	3,277
18 7/16	11 11/16	6 12/16	M	Oneida County	WI	Tim Johnson	1967	3,448
18 7/16	11 5/16	7 2/16	M	Franklin County	ME	Ed Hall	1968	3,448
18 7/16	11 11/16	6 12/16	M	Larimer County	CO	Ronald M. Breitsprecher	1975	3,448
18 7/16	11 8/16	6 15/16	M	Piscataquis County	ME	John Kuhar	1975	3,448
18 7/16	11 9/16	6 14/16	M	Clearwater County	ID	Edward Russell	1976	3,448
18 7/16	11 12/16	6 11/16	M	Cass County	MN	Walter L. Lash	1976	3,448
18 7/16	11 13/16	6 10/16	M	Albemarle County	VA	J. C. Locke	1976	3,448
18 7/16	11 11/16	6 12/16	M	Atikokan	ONT	John Carlson	1977	3,448
18 7/16	11 9/16	6 14/16	M	Lake County	MN	W. Dan Williams, Jr.	1977	3,448
18 7/16	11 7/16	7 0/16	M	English Bay	AK	Roger Stewart	1978	3,448
18 7/16	12 1/16	6 6/16	M	Iron County	WI	Douglas R. Parrott	1979	3,448
18 7/16	11 1/16	7 6/16	M	Phelps Twp.	ONT	Robert C. Precious	1979	3,448
18 7/16	11 10/16	6 13/16	M	Almonte	ONT	Thomas S. Gerstner	1980	3,448
18 7/16	11 9/16	6 14/16	M	Franklin County	ME	Bob Spano	1980	3,448
18 7/16	11 6/16	7 1/16	M	Meagher County	MT	Gary H. Thompson	1980	3,448
18 7/16	11 12/16	6 11/16	M	Beluga	AK	Tom Atkins	1981	3,448
18 7/16	11 4/16	7 3/16	M	El Paso County	CO	Max Tallent	1981	3,448
18 7/16	11 15/16	6 8/16	M	Archuleta County	CO	James P. Mitchell	1982	3,448
18 7/16	11 8/16	6 15/16	M	Kenora	ONT	Floyd McDanell	1982	3,448
18 7/16	11 10/16	6 13/16	M		ONT	Bill Stonebraker	1982	3,448
18 7/16	11 12/16	6 11/16	M	Sierra County	NM	James N. Amlong, Jr.	1983	3,448
18 7/16	11 10/16	6 13/16	M	Kirkland Lake	ONT	Michael Hogan	1983	3,448
18 7/16	11 7/16	7 0/16	M	Nipigon	ONT	Wayne Beltz, Jr.	1983	3,448
18 7/16	11 9/16	6 14/16	M	Timmins	ONT	Paul Eldridge	1983	3,448
18 7/16	11 10/16	6 13/16	M	Tatalina River	AK	Timothy J. Barber	1983	3,448
18 7/16	11 6/16	7 1/16	M	Clackamas County	OR	Robert L. Smitherman	1983	3,448
18 7/16	11 14/16	6 9/16	M	Pine County	MN	Alan C. Porter	1983	3,448
18 7/16	11 9/16	6 14/16	M	Sudbury	ONT	Terry William Polkinghorne	1984	3,448
18 7/16	11 1/16	7 6/16	M	Sioux Lookout	ONT	Steve Sherry	1984	3,448
18 7/16	11 9/16	6 14/16	M	Skeleton Lake	ALB	Dwayne Alton	1984	3,448
18 7/16	11 8/16	6 15/16	M	Devlin	ONT	Jim Leqve	1984	3,448
18 7/16	11 11/16	6 12/16	M	Luce County	MI	Terry L. Cook	1984	3,448
18 7/16	11 13/16	6 10/16	M	Marquette County	MI	Randy Clark	1984	3,448
18 7/16	11 2/16	7 5/16	M	Lemhi County	ID	Dennis Derrer	1985	3,448
18 7/16	11 7/16	7 0/16	M	Kenora	ONT	Steven Duerksen	1985	3,448
18 7/16	11 2/16	7 5/16	M	Adams County	ID	Rick Clinton	1985	3,448
18 7/16	11 13/16	6 10/16	M	Las Animas County	CO	Kelly Williams	1985	3,448
18 7/16	11 9/16	6 14/16	M	Douglas County	OR	Jim Nielsen	1985	3,448
18 7/16	11 7/16	7 0/16	M	Gallatin County	MT	Terry L. Anderson	1985	3,448
18 7/16	11 9/16	6 14/16	M	Mine Centre	ONT	Bob Roulet	1986	3,448
18 7/16	11 10/16	6 13/16	M	Emo	ONT	Bruce Eggenberger	1986	3,448
18 7/16	11 12/16	6 11/16	M	Savant Lake	ONT	Daniel J. Gartner	1986	3,448
18 7/16	11 9/16	6 14/16	F	Smith	ALB	Dave Gerber	1986	3,448
18 7/16	12 0/16	6 7/16	M	Porcupine Plain	SAS	Peter Reimer	1987	3,448
18 7/16	11 5/16	7 2/16	M	Perrault Falls	ONT	Larry Gohlke	1987	3,448
18 7/16	11 7/16	7 0/16	M	Thunder Bay	ONT	Larry H. Hoyt	1987	3,448
18 7/16	11 11/16	6 12/16	M	Victoria County	ONT	William H. Guile	1987	3,448
18 7/16	11 9/16	6 14/16	M	Dryden	ONT	Richard E. Kohles	1987	3,448
18 7/16	11 8/16	6 15/16	M	Halfway River	BC	Dave Hannas	1987	3,448
18 7/16	11 7/16	7 0/16	M	Highland Valley	BC	Kenneth A. Brown	1987	3,448
18 7/16	11 9/16	6 14/16	M	Chelmsford	ONT	Bernard Langhorne	1987	3,448
18 7/16	11 7/16	7 0/16	M	Manitouwadge	ONT	Robert Mitchell	1988	3,448
18 7/16	11 13/16	6 10/16	M	Ft. McMurray	ALB	James Pike	1988	3,448
18 7/16	11 7/16	7 0/16	M	Geraldton	ONT	Gary E. Mayle	1988	3,448
18 7/16	11 10/16	6 13/16	M	Kootenai County	ID	Linda Leake	1988	3,448
18 7/16	11 11/16	6 12/16	M	Sublette County	WY	Keith Dana	1988	3,448
18 7/16	11 11/16	6 12/16	M	Susitna River	AK	Dave Hyrb	1988	3,448
18 7/16	11 12/16	6 11/16	M	King County	WA	David A. Emery	1988	3,448
18 7/16	11 10/16	6 13/16	M	Somerset County	ME	David James Obuchowski	1988	3,448
18 7/16	11 10/16	6 13/16	M	Kenora	ONT	Joe Devlin	1989	3,448
18 7/16	11 15/16	6 8/16	M	Zec Restigo	QUE	Joseph Sabo	1989	3,448
18 7/16	11 4/16	7 3/16	M	Wawa	ONT	Michael J. Klaeser	1989	3,448
18 7/16	11 9/16	6 14/16	M	Esther Island	AK	Tim Fritzler	1989	3,448

BLACK BEAR

Minimum Score 18 — Continued

SCORE	GREATEST LENGTH	GREATEST WIDTH	SEX	AREA	STATE/PROVINCE	HUNTER'S NAME	DATE	RANK
18 7/16	11 10/16	6 13/16	M	Jefferson County	WA	Wayne Haag	1989	3,448
18 7/16	12 1/16	6 6/16	M	Sawyer County	WI	John H. Henriksen	1989	3,448
18 7/16	11 6/16	7 1/16	M	Rockingham County	VA	Roger O. Wyant	1989	3,448
18 7/16	11 11/16	6 12/16	M	Belleterre	QUE	Terry Gaudlip	1990	3,448
18 7/16	11 9/16	6 14/16	M	Ft. McMurray	ALB	Floyd Forster	1990	3,448
18 7/16	11 11/16	6 12/16	M	Lincoln County	WY	John Trout, Jr.	1990	3,448
18 7/16	11 4/16	7 3/16	M	Rollet	QUE	Claude St' Amour	1990	3,448
18 7/16	11 12/16	6 11/16	M	Cumberland House	SAS	Mike Lewandowski	1991	3,448
18 7/16	11 6/16	7 1/16	M	Latah County	ID	Daniel D. Davenport	1991	3,448
18 7/16	11 10/16	6 13/16	M	La Ronge	SAS	Brian Hummel	1991	3,448
18 7/16	11 6/16	7 1/16	M	Caramat	ONT	Kelly Russell	1991	3,448
18 7/16	11 8/16	6 15/16	M	Moon Beam	ONT	John Meyers	1991	3,448
18 7/16	11 3/16	7 4/16	M	Zec Dumoine	QUE	Joseph Arkuszeski	1991	3,448
18 7/16	11 11/16	6 12/16	M	Terrace Bay	ONT	Greg Huffman	1991	3,448
18 7/16	11 13/16	6 10/16	M	Lake of the Woods	ONT	Bob Wickler	1991	3,448
18 7/16	11 11/16	6 12/16	M	Livengood	AK	Todd A. Wolf	1991	3,448
18 7/16	11 12/16	6 11/16	M	Idaho County	ID	Dan Hiltz	1991	3,448
18 7/16	11 13/16	6 10/16	M	Carbon County	WY	Damon Handley	1991	3,448
18 7/16	11 9/16	6 14/16	M	Temiscaming	QUE	Louis Seville	1991	3,448
18 7/16	11 9/16	6 14/16	M	Delta County	MI	James S. Stankowski	1991	3,448
18 7/16	11 12/16	6 11/16	M	Houghton County	MI	Tony E. La Pratt	1991	3,448
18 7/16	11 8/16	6 15/16	M	Spirit River	ALB	Paul Deme	1992	3,448
18 7/16	11 2/16	7 5/16	M	Sudbury	ONT	Phillip Wilkinson	1992	3,448
18 7/16	11 10/16	6 13/16	M	Fort McMurray	ALB	Jon P. Thomas	1992	3,448
18 7/16	11 6/16	7 1/16	M	Lane County	OR	Charles A. Noe	1992	3,448
18 7/16	11 8/16	6 15/16	M	Piscataquis County	ME	Robert G. Poth	1992	3,448
18 7/16	11 8/16	6 15/16	M	Nemegauche	ONT	Lawrence Lee Wilbur	1992	3,448
18 7/16	11 6/16	7 1/16	M	Wallowa County	OR	Thompson Holmes	1992	3,448
18 7/16	11 12/16	6 11/16	M	Thunder Bay	ONT	Harry Domask	1993	3,448
18 7/16	11 11/16	6 12/16	M	Chinchaga River	ALB	Patrick R. Cahill	1993	3,448
18 7/16	11 11/16	6 12/16	M	Shorty Creek	AK	Roy Bartlett	1993	3,448
18 7/16	11 5/16	7 2/16	M	Armstrong	ONT	Dianne Daniels	1993	3,448
18 7/16	11 12/16	6 11/16	M	King County	WA	Garn J. Kennedy	1993	3,448
18 7/16	11 10/16	6 13/16	M	St. Louis County	MN	Jeff P. Peterson	1993	3,448
18 7/16	11 10/16	6 13/16	M	Caribou County	ID	Greg Blotter	1993	3,448
18 7/16	11 9/16	6 14/16	M	Nevada County	CA	Gerald E. Boelens	1993	3,448
18 7/16	11 10/16	6 13/16	M	Emo	ONT	Paul Kolbeck	1994	3,448
18 7/16	11 14/16	6 9/16	M	Carrot River	SAS	Mark P. Wagner	1994	3,448
18 7/16	11 9/16	6 14/16	M	Lac Ile-a-la Crosse	SAS	Dewayne Mullins	1994	3,448
18 7/16	11 10/16	6 13/16	M	Nestor Falls	ONT	Mark D. Bonneville	1994	3,448
18 7/16	11 10/16	6 13/16	M	Carrot River	SAS	Jan P. Herzfeldt	1994	3,448
18 7/16	11 10/16	6 13/16	M	Zec Labrieville	QUE	Ken H. Taylor	1994	3,448
18 7/16	11 11/16	6 12/16	M	Carlton County	MN	Eric Halverson	1994	3,448
18 7/16	11 13/16	6 10/16	M	Cook County	MN	Dale R. Goodman	1994	3,448
18 7/16	11 9/16	6 14/16	M	St. Louis County	MN	Daniel J. Weiss	1994	3,448
18 7/16	11 14/16	6 9/16	M	Catron County	NM	Adrian P. Lucero	1994	3,448
18 7/16	12 0/16	6 7/16	M	Rio Arriba County	NM	Nick Seifert	1994	3,448
18 7/16	11 13/16	6 10/16	M	Carroll County	NH	Billy Jack Smith	1994	3,448
18 7/16	11 5/16	7 2/16	M	Carroll County	NH	Paul Keyes	1994	3,448
18 7/16	11 15/16	6 8/16	M	Goat River	BC	Ken Taylor	1995	3,448
18 7/16	12 1/16	6 6/16	M	Hudson Bay	SAS	Norma J. Lee	1995	3,448
18 7/16	11 8/16	6 15/16	M	Gowganda	ONT	Bruce Fair	1995	3,448
18 7/16	11 12/16	6 11/16	M	Fredericton	NBW	Ronald Larsen	1995	3,448
18 7/16	11 6/16	7 1/16	M	Dryden	ONT	Michael A. Lago	1995	3,448
18 7/16	11 15/16	6 8/16	M	Lanark	ONT	Dave Glithero	1995	3,448
18 7/16	11 5/16	7 2/16	M	Zec Capitachouane	QUE	Ken H. Taylor	1995	3,448
18 7/16	11 12/16	6 11/16	M	Kern County	CA	Larry Quary	1995	3,448
18 7/16	11 8/16	6 15/16	M	Muldrew Lake	ONT	Jim Latour	1995	3,448
18 7/16	12 0/16	6 7/16	M	San Juan County	UT	Kurt Wood	1995	3,448
18 7/16	11 10/16	6 13/16	M	Chilako River	BC	Geoff Will	1996	3,448
18 7/16	11 10/16	6 13/16	M	Kaministiquia	ONT	La Moine Dohms	1996	3,448
18 7/16	11 7/16	7 0/16	M	Lac Leivesque	QUE	Laurier Therrien	1996	3,448
18 7/16	11 9/16	6 14/16	M	Swan River	MAN	Russell A. Nichols	1996	3,448
18 7/16	11 7/16	7 0/16	M	Thompson	MAN	Carm Bongiovanni	1996	3,448
18 7/16	11 6/16	7 1/16	M	Dinorwic	ONT	Dick Schuette	1996	3,448
18 7/16	12 4/16	6 3/16	M	Lac La Biche	ALB	John Alan Dormire	1997	3,448
18 7/16	12 1/16	6 6/16	M	Bissett	MAN	Paul D. Redden	1997	3,448
18 7/16	11 5/16	7 2/16	M	Ray River	AK	Amy Bothman	1997	3,448
18 7/16	11 7/16	7 0/16	M	Bathurst	NBW	Rodger Adydan	1997	3,448
18 7/16	11 12/16	6 11/16	M	Oliver Lake	ONT	John M. Knight	1997	3,448
18 7/16	11 6/16	7 1/16	M	Kane Lake	SAS	Dennis Dunn	1997	3,448
18 7/16	11 4/16	7 3/16	M	Cranberry Portage	MAN	John Emerson Stelmok	1997	3,448
18 7/16	11 6/16	7 1/16	M	Mendocino County	CA	Bart Pontoni	1997	3,448
18 7/16	11 8/16	6 15/16	M	Ignace	ONT	Paul Wenninger	1998	3,448
18 7/16	11 11/16	6 12/16	M	Vickers Lake	MAN	Mike Wendel	1998	3,448
18 7/16	11 13/16	6 10/16	M	Ray River	AK	Tom Chadwick	1998	3,448
18 6/16	11 9/16	6 13/16	M	Mariposa County	CA	Douglas Walker	1965	3,587
18 6/16	11 8/16	6 14/16	M	Fulton County	NY	Peter Mertens	1966	3,587

BLACK BEAR

Minimum Score 18 — Continued

SCORE	GREATEST LENGTH	GREATEST WIDTH	SEX	AREA	STATE/ PROVINCE	HUNTER'S NAME	DATE	RANK
18 6/16	11 8/16	6 14/16	M	Clear Creek County	CO	Jim Dougherty	1970	3,587
18 6/16	11 12/16	6 10/16	M	Franklin County	ME	Joe Melchiore	1970	3,587
18 6/16	11 10/16	6 12/16	M	Yancey County	NC	Jerry Rushing	1970	3,587
18 6/16	11 2/16	7 4/16	M	Chetwynd	BC	Lee E. Hansel	1973	3,587
18 6/16	11 4/16	7 2/16	M	Valley County	ID	Charles F. Maloney	1973	3,587
18 6/16	11 8/16	6 14/16	M	Becker County	MN	Gordon Swenson	1973	3,587
18 6/16	11 6/16	7 0/16	M	Dryden	ONT	John L. Dykes	1974	3,587
18 6/16	11 12/16	6 10/16	M	Flathead County	MT	Dr. Barry Wensel	1974	3,587
18 6/16	11 8/16	6 14/16	M	Archuleta County	CO	Judd Cooney	1975	3,587
18 6/16	12 0/16	6 6/16	M	Snohomish County	WA	Jim Gregory	1975	3,587
18 6/16	11 0/16	7 6/16	M	Larimer County	CO	Michael Lewis	1975	3,587
18 6/16	11 10/16	6 12/16	M	Saguache County	CO	Sandra Scheid	1975	3,587
18 6/16	11 6/16	7 0/16	M	Somerset County	ME	Anthony Ciletti	1976	3,587
18 6/16	11 12/16	6 10/16	M	Rio Blanco County	CO	Brad Cook	1978	3,587
18 6/16	11 5/16	7 1/16	M	Lemhi County	ID	Roy Auwen	1979	3,587
18 6/16	11 8/16	6 14/16	M	Marinette County	WI	William Brunette	1979	3,587
18 6/16	11 14/16	6 8/16	M	Thunder Bay	ONT	Neil E. Gilles	1980	3,587
18 6/16	11 10/16	6 12/16	M	Red Lake	ONT	Leon L. Miller	1981	3,587
18 6/16	11 4/16	7 2/16	M	Espanola	ONT	Ronald E. Hergott	1982	3,587
18 6/16	11 5/16	7 1/16	M	Siskiyou County	CA	Dave S. Semple	1982	3,587
18 6/16	11 7/16	6 15/16	M	Uintah County	UT	Bill Dunstan IV	1982	3,587
18 6/16	11 14/16	6 8/16	M	Game Area #23	MAN	Gary Kaluzniak	1983	3,587
18 6/16	11 8/16	6 14/16	M	McAdam	NBW	Donald R. Shipley	1983	3,587
18 6/16	11 5/16	7 1/16	M	Ramsey Twp.	ONT	Robert H. Pavlovic	1983	3,587
18 6/16	11 12/16	6 10/16	M	Cheboygan County	MI	Roger A. Greve	1983	3,587
18 6/16	11 15/16	6 7/16	M	Sawyer County	WI	Kevin Capelle	1983	3,587
18 6/16	11 8/16	6 14/16	M	Chelan County	WA	Edward M. Beitner	1983	3,587
18 6/16	11 15/16	6 7/16	M	Greene County	NY	Bob Spina	1983	3,587
18 6/16	11 4/16	7 2/16	M	Douglas County	OR	Tim O'Kelly	1984	3,587
18 6/16	11 15/16	6 7/16	M	Cass County	MN	James D. Zahalka	1984	3,587
18 6/16	11 8/16	6 14/16	M	Marquette County	MI	George M. Barosko	1984	3,587
18 6/16	11 10/16	6 12/16	M	Luce County	MI	Norman E. Bell	1984	3,587
18 6/16	11 2/16	7 4/16	M	Bathurst	NBW	Daryl Labarron	1985	3,587
18 6/16	11 4/16	7 2/16	M	Pontiac	QUE	Loren L. Fish	1985	3,587
18 6/16	11 3/16	7 3/16	M	Carroll County	NH	Donald W. Murdock	1985	3,587
18 6/16	11 8/16	6 14/16	F	Spiritwood	SAS	Kent W. Brigham	1986	3,587
18 6/16	11 10/16	6 12/16	M	Rio Arriba County	NM	Terry Sanders	1986	3,587
18 6/16	11 8/16	6 14/16	M	Thunder Bay	ONT	Gene Anderson	1986	3,587
18 6/16	11 3/16	7 3/16	M	Valley County	ID	Larry Hoff	1986	3,587
18 6/16	10 15/16	7 7/16	M	Fremont County	ID	Blair R. Jones	1986	3,587
18 6/16	11 14/16	6 8/16	M	Hudson Bay	SAS	C. Randall Byers	1987	3,587
18 6/16	11 3/16	7 3/16	M	Wabigoon	ONT	Robert Barrie	1987	3,587
18 6/16	11 10/16	6 12/16	M	St. Louis County	MN	Loren Slette	1987	3,587
18 6/16	11 9/16	6 13/16	M	Oxford County	ME	Patrick Ferrie	1987	3,587
18 6/16	11 15/16	6 7/16	M	Lincoln County	WI	James G. Gouger	1987	3,587
18 6/16	11 10/16	6 12/16	M	Wolf Lake	ALB	Keith Baker	1988	3,587
18 6/16	11 15/16	6 7/16	M	Hudson Bay	SAS	Kent Brandt	1988	3,587
18 6/16	11 15/16	6 7/16	M	Emo	ONT	Robert John Brown	1988	3,587
18 6/16	11 6/16	7 0/16	M	Gull River	ONT	Larry R. Brosamle	1988	3,587
18 6/16	11 7/16	6 15/16	M	Kenora	ONT	Dean M. Westby	1988	3,587
18 6/16	11 11/16	6 11/16	M	Chelsea	QUE	Jim Ray	1988	3,587
18 6/16	11 1/16	7 5/16	M	Jocko River	ONT	Gary Boals	1988	3,587
18 6/16	12 1/16	6 5/16	M	Susitna River	AK	Richmon R. Schumann	1988	3,587
18 6/16	11 8/16	6 14/16	M	La Plata County	CO	Dale Sunblom	1988	3,587
18 6/16	11 6/16	7 0/16	M	Chibougamau	QUE	Dale R. Walburger	1988	3,587
18 6/16	11 1/16	7 5/16	M	Okanogan County	WA	Duane N. Fink	1988	3,587
18 6/16	11 4/16	7 2/16	M	Delay River	QUE	Dennis N. Ballweg	1988	3,587
18 6/16	11 6/16	7 0/16	M	Ashland County	WI	Thomas J. Mischo	1988	3,587
18 6/16	11 12/16	6 10/16	M	Coconino County	AZ	Richard Dawe, Jr.	1988	3,587
18 6/16	11 11/16	6 11/16	M	Saguache County	CO	Sid Strzok	1989	3,587
18 6/16	11 10/16	6 12/16	M	Mens Twp.	ONT	Jon T. Wente	1989	3,587
18 6/16	11 7/16	6 15/16	M	Emo	ONT	Leo Hazelton	1989	3,587
18 6/16	11 7/16	6 15/16	M	Peace River	ALB	John Peruchini	1990	3,587
18 6/16	11 10/16	6 12/16	M	Dolores County	CO	Duain Morton	1990	3,587
18 6/16	12 0/16	6 6/16	M	Buffalo Narrows	SAS	David M Tofte	1990	3,587
18 6/16	11 4/16	7 2/16	M	Messines	QUE	Charles L. Hart III	1990	3,587
18 6/16	11 7/16	6 15/16	M	Meadow Lake	SAS	Tonnie Elwood Davis	1990	3,587
18 6/16	11 13/16	6 9/16	M	Bayfield County	WI	Gary J. Ader	1990	3,587
18 6/16	11 14/16	6 8/16	M	Iron County	WI	Thomas R. Hujet	1990	3,587
18 6/16	11 6/16	7 0/16	M	Clatsup County	OR	William H. Stevens	1991	3,587
18 6/16	11 13/16	6 9/16	F	Rainy River	ONT	Michael Judas	1991	3,587
18 6/16	11 12/16	6 10/16	M	Plevna	ONT	Brant Bergstrome	1991	3,587
18 6/16	11 12/16	6 10/16	M	Itasca County	MN	Shawn E. Eyre	1991	3,587
18 6/16	11 4/16	7 2/16	M	Colfax County	NM	Rodrigo Cruz	1991	3,587
18 6/16	11 12/16	6 10/16	M	Caribou County	ID	Trent McBride	1991	3,587
18 6/16	11 10/16	6 12/16	M	Savant Lake	ONT	Dean Wells	1992	3,587
18 6/16	11 6/16	7 0/16	M	Elma	MAN	David A. Goertzen	1992	3,587
18 6/16	11 12/16	6 10/16	M	Thunder Bay	ONT	Michael Kemp	1992	3,587

BLACK BEAR

Minimum Score 18 — Continued

SCORE	GREATEST LENGTH	GREATEST WIDTH	SEX	AREA	STATE/PROVINCE	HUNTER'S NAME	DATE	RANK
18 6/16	11 7/16	6 15/16	M	Vermillion Bay	ONT	Dennis Forstner	1992	3,587
18 6/16	11 12/16	6 10/16	M	Chippewa County	MI	William Pettett, Jr.	1992	3,587
18 6/16	11 8/16	6 14/16	M	Lake Besnard	SAS	Roger Brock	1992	3,587
18 6/16	11 9/16	6 13/16	M	Cascade County	MT	Mark Seabaugh	1992	3,587
18 6/16	11 10/16	6 12/16	M	Sioux Narrows	ONT	Fay Lloyd	1992	3,587
18 6/16	12 0/16	6 6/16	M	Fisher Branch	MAN	Robert G. Olafson	1993	3,587
18 6/16	11 12/16	6 10/16	M	La Ronge	SAS	Trent Findley	1993	3,587
18 6/16	11 15/16	6 7/16	M	Snohomish County	WA	John L. Campbell	1993	3,587
18 6/16	11 10/16	6 12/16	M	Houghton County	MI	Rick W. Demarr	1993	3,587
18 6/16	11 12/16	6 10/16	M	Lewis & Clark County	MT	Gerald Biresch	1993	3,587
18 6/16	11 9/16	6 13/16	M	Prince of Wales Island	AK	Dyrk Eddie	1994	3,587
18 6/16	11 11/16	6 11/16	M	Cadillac	QUE	Edward M. Wojtys	1994	3,587
18 6/16	11 6/16	7 0/16	M	Manitouwadge	ONT	Mike Losee	1994	3,587
18 6/16	11 9/16	6 13/16	M	Umatilla County	OR	Javier Garcia	1994	3,587
18 6/16	11 11/16	6 11/16	M	Aitkin County	MN	Brad Blanchard	1994	3,587
18 6/16	11 11/16	6 11/16	M	McMeekin Twp.	ONT	Roger Thompson	1994	3,587
18 6/16	11 4/16	7 2/16	M	Boarder Lake	BC	Tim R. Dawson	1994	3,587
18 6/16	11 15/16	6 7/16	M	Riding Mtn.	MAN	Steven M. Bins	1994	3,587
18 6/16	10 13/16	7 9/16	M	Beaverhead County	MT	Frank Russell	1994	3,587
18 6/16	11 9/16	6 13/16	M	Shoshone County	ID	Roger Stewart	1995	3,587
18 6/16	11 15/16	6 7/16	M	Aulneau Peninsula	ONT	Mr. Michael Koska	1995	3,587
18 6/16	11 12/16	6 10/16	M	Dryden	ONT	Rick Kroll	1995	3,587
18 6/16	11 11/16	6 11/16	M	Alford Lake	ALB	Derrill Herman	1995	3,587
18 6/16	11 7/16	6 15/16	M	Nestor Falls	ONT	Dale E. Springer	1995	3,587
18 6/16	11 9/16	6 13/16	M	Cygmet Lake	ONT	Kelvin W. Lancaster	1995	3,587
18 6/16	11 14/16	6 8/16	M	Red Lake	ONT	Doug Johnson	1995	3,587
18 6/16	11 7/16	6 15/16	M	Oba	ONT	Robert J. Guarnaccio	1995	3,587
18 6/16	11 13/16	6 9/16	M	Catron County	NM	Jason Ashcroft	1995	3,587
18 6/16	11 13/16	6 9/16	M	Savante	ONT	Martin Hug	1995	3,587
18 6/16	11 13/16	6 9/16	M	Uintah County	UT	Rick Copeland	1995	3,587
18 6/16	11 10/16	6 12/16	M	Falcon Lake	MAN	D. P. Domaszek	1996	3,587
18 6/16	11 7/16	6 15/16	M	Kenora	ONT	Dick Melka	1996	3,587
18 6/16	11 8/16	6 14/16	M	Red Lake	ONT	Rocky A. King	1996	3,587
18 6/16	11 14/16	6 8/16	M	Meadow Lake	SAS	Jerry W. Laton	1996	3,587
18 6/16	11 6/16	7 0/16	M	Kirkland Lake	ONT	Roy L. Walk	1996	3,587
18 6/16	11 9/16	6 13/16	M	Dryden	ONT	Richard Rogers	1996	3,587
18 6/16	11 6/16	7 0/16	M	Ear Falls	ONT	Duane R. Hearing	1996	3,587
18 6/16	11 8/16	6 14/16	M	Holinshead Lake	ONT	Don Davidson	1996	3,587
18 6/16	11 13/16	6 9/16	M	Calling Lake	ALB	Robert Bartoshesky	1996	3,587
18 6/16	11 9/16	6 13/16	M	Red Lake	ONT	Daniel G. Prusik	1996	3,587
18 6/16	11 11/16	6 11/16	M	Ontonagon County	MI	Paul Ranft	1996	3,587
18 6/16	11 10/16	6 12/16	M	Oconto County	WI	Richard Liebl	1996	3,587
18 6/16	11 10/16	6 12/16	M	Washburn County	WI	Michael Prehn	1996	3,587
18 6/16	11 12/16	6 10/16	M	Holokuk Mtns.	AK	Tom Crabill	1996	3,587
18 6/16	11 9/16	6 13/16	M	Grouard	ALB	Greg Ogle	1997	3,587
18 6/16	11 9/16	6 13/16	M	Woosey Lake	MAN	John Janke	1997	3,587
18 6/16	11 12/16	6 10/16	M	Aerobus Lake	ONT	Kirt Hoffmann	1997	3,587
18 6/16	11 8/16	6 14/16	M	French River	ONT	John Orr	1997	3,587
18 6/16	11 12/16	6 10/16	M	Shikag Lake	ONT	Robert L. Gardner	1997	3,587
18 6/16	11 8/16	6 14/16	M	Thessalon	ONT	Larry Cornett	1997	3,587
18 6/16	11 5/16	7 1/16	M	Dog Lake	ONT	Wayne S. Walden	1997	3,587
18 6/16	11 14/16	6 8/16	M	Ministikwan	SAS	Larry Hillis	1997	3,587
18 6/16	11 5/16	7 1/16	M	Clackamas County	OR	Dan Ellis	1997	3,587
18 6/16	11 10/16	6 12/16	M	Essex County	NY	Paul Durling	1997	3,587
18 6/16	11 7/16	6 15/16	F	Prince of Wales Island	AK	Peggy "Bailey" Whary	1998	3,587
18 6/16	11 11/16	6 11/16	M	Indian River	AK	Rick Schikora	1998	3,587
18 6/16	11 8/16	6 14/16	M	Dryden	ONT	Alan E. Forbes	1998	3,587
18 6/16	11 12/16	6 10/16	M	Apache County	AZ	Robert G. Petersen	1998	3,587
18 6/16	11 10/16	6 12/16	M	Apache County	AZ	Robert G. Petersen	1998	3,587
18 6/16	11 5/16	7 1/16	M	Marathon	ONT	Michael L. Ritter	1998	3,587
18 5/16	11 3/16	7 2/16	M	Iron Bridge	ONT	Philip L. Hawkins	1965	3,727
18 5/16	11 9/16	6 12/16	M	Gogebic County	MI	LaVern Miller	1971	3,727
18 5/16	11 6/16	6 15/16	M	Florence County	WI	Jim Thimmig	1971	3,727
18 5/16	11 3/16	7 2/16	M	Forest County	WI	Ernie V. Hutchinson	1972	3,727
18 5/16	11 4/16	7 1/16	M	St. Louis County	MN	Art Heinze	1973	3,727
18 5/16	11 9/16	6 12/16	M	Coconino County	AZ	Stan Nordell	1975	3,727
18 5/16	11 7/16	6 14/16	M	Gunnison County	CO	Rick Hunckler	1976	3,727
18 5/16	11 7/16	6 14/16	M	Montezuma County	CO	Stanley A. Coval	1977	3,727
18 5/16	11 7/16	6 14/16	M	Ear Falls	ONT	John Brandt	1980	3,727
18 5/16	11 9/16	6 12/16	M	Park County	MT	Charles Burdette	1980	3,727
18 5/16	11 3/16	7 2/16	M	E. Braintree	MAN	Chester Surma	1980	3,727
18 5/16	11 12/16	7 3/16	M	Douglas County	OR	Dan Viles	1980	3,727
18 5/16	11 5/16	7 0/16	M	Gogebic County	MI	Donald E. Thompson, Jr.	1981	3,727
18 5/16	11 7/16	6 14/16	M	Blind River	ONT	Cleve Roush	1982	3,727
18 5/16	11 11/16	6 10/16	M	Iron County	WI	Keith Kaat	1982	3,727
18 5/16	11 11/16	6 10/16	M	Alatna River	AK	John D. 'Jack' Frost	1982	3,727
18 5/16	11 4/16	7 1/16	M	Missoula County	MT	Tom Storm	1983	3,727
18 5/16	11 9/16	6 12/16	M	Sundridge	ONT	Abby Lape	1983	3,727

BLACK BEAR

Minimum Score 18 — Continued

SCORE	GREATEST LENGTH	GREATEST WIDTH	SEX	AREA	STATE/PROVINCE	HUNTER'S NAME	DATE	RANK
18 5/16	11 9/16	6 12/16	M	Kootenai County	ID	Larry M. Leake	1985	3,727
18 5/16	11 8/16	6 13/16	M	Thunder Bay	ONT	Bob Kraus	1985	3,727
18 5/16	11 11/16	6 10/16	M	Hudson Bay	SAS	Clark Jenner	1985	3,727
18 5/16	11 8/16	6 13/16	M	Cold Lake	ALB	Orest Popil	1985	3,727
18 5/16	11 6/16	6 15/16	M	Atikokan	ONT	Bruce Wynn	1985	3,727
18 5/16	11 12/16	6 9/16	M	Lake County	MT	Don Davidson	1986	3,727
18 5/16	11 14/16	6 7/16	M	Grand County	CO	Lyle Willmarth	1986	3,727
18 5/16	11 8/16	6 13/16	M	Massey	ONT	Jim Hunsaker	1986	3,727
18 5/16	11 11/16	6 10/16	M	Sudbury	ONT	Richard Dohm	1986	3,727
18 5/16	11 4/16	7 1/16	M	Park County	CO	Gary Christoffersen	1986	3,727
18 5/16	11 13/16	6 8/16	M	Rocky Lake	MAN	Tim Finley	1986	3,727
18 5/16	11 5/16	7 0/16	M	Blaine County	ID	Larry R. Newton	1986	3,727
18 5/16	11 11/16	6 10/16	M	Iron County	MI	Richard Seasword	1986	3,727
18 5/16	11 5/16	7 0/16	M	Kootenai County	ID	Linda Leake	1987	3,727
18 5/16	11 8/16	6 13/16	M	Algonquin	ONT	Stephen Michael Carroll	1987	3,727
18 5/16	11 11/16	6 10/16	M	Saint James Bay	AK	Richard J. Callahan	1987	3,727
18 5/16	11 7/16	6 14/16	M	Lemhi County	ID	Mike Lopez	1987	3,727
18 5/16	11 2/16	7 3/16	M	Plumas County	CA	Steven Demello	1987	3,727
18 5/16	11 5/16	7 0/16	M	Somerset County	ME	Al Cresci	1987	3,727
18 5/16	11 10/16	6 11/16	M	Placer County	CA	Kenneth Braden	1987	3,727
18 5/16	11 13/16	6 8/16	M	Athabasca River	ALB	Archie J. Nesbitt	1988	3,727
18 5/16	11 11/16	6 10/16	M	Sundre	ALB	David R. Coupland	1988	3,727
18 5/16	11 9/16	6 12/16	M	Ignace	ONT	Joel Breitung	1988	3,727
18 5/16	11 9/16	6 12/16	M	Bonneville County	ID	Terri L. Stephens	1988	3,727
18 5/16	11 12/16	6 9/16	M	San Miguel County	CO	LaJuan Hare	1989	3,727
18 5/16	11 11/16	6 10/16	M	Grand County	UT	Troy Olson	1989	3,727
18 5/16	11 10/16	6 11/16	M	Manitouwadge	ONT	Stuart Hazard III	1989	3,727
18 5/16	11 8/16	6 13/16	M	Boise Franc Rd.	QUE	August S. Gray	1989	3,727
18 5/16	11 6/16	6 15/16	M	Pierce County	WA	Howard L. Harding	1989	3,727
18 5/16	11 7/16	6 14/16	M	Aroostook County	ME	Tad David Proudlove	1989	3,727
18 5/16	11 3/16	7 2/16	M	Powell Lake	ONT	Michael J. Goza	1989	3,727
18 5/16	11 4/16	7 1/16	M	MacNeil Twp.	ONT	Ted Whittle	1989	3,727
18 5/16	11 14/16	6 7/16	M	Lemhi County	ID	Al Youman	1990	3,727
18 5/16	11 1/16	7 4/16	M	Gravel Lake Cabins	ONT	James D. Smith	1990	3,727
18 5/16	11 3/16	7 2/16	M	Prince of Wales Island	AK	Gordon Diehl	1990	3,727
18 5/16	11 10/16	6 11/16	M	Ashland County	WI	Kenneth A. Johnson	1990	3,727
18 5/16	11 11/16	6 10/16	M	Oconto County	WI	Chuck D. Peterson	1990	3,727
18 5/16	11 12/16	6 9/16	M	Telegraph Creek	BC	Rick Simonson	1990	3,727
18 5/16	11 6/16	6 15/16	M	Crimson Lake	ALB	Dale Peters	1991	3,727
18 5/16	11 2/16	7 3/16	M	Chipmunk Creek	BC	Ken Scheer	1991	3,727
18 5/16	11 8/16	6 13/16	M	Atikokan	ONT	Judy Grooms	1991	3,727
18 5/16	11 1/16	7 4/16	M	Clearwater County	ID	Gary L. Haynes	1991	3,727
18 5/16	11 6/16	6 15/16	M	Las Animas County	CO	H. Brian Jackson	1991	3,727
18 5/16	11 12/16	6 9/16	M	Poplarfield	MAN	Jim McHale	1991	3,727
18 5/16	11 10/16	6 11/16	M	Laure	MAN	Ted Hysell	1992	3,727
18 5/16	11 6/16	6 15/16	M	Sandoval County	NM	Noble Sinclair	1992	3,727
18 5/16	11 4/16	7 1/16	M	Idaho County	ID	Rex Summerfield	1992	3,727
18 5/16	11 5/16	7 0/16	M	Grafton County	NH	Dana E. Plourde	1992	3,727
18 5/16	11 8/16	6 13/16	M	Swan River	MAN	Richard C. Weber	1992	3,727
18 5/16	11 12/16	6 9/16	M	Chippewa County	WI	Anthony F. Grimme	1992	3,727
18 5/16	11 10/16	6 11/16	M	Clark County	WI	Dennis M. Oczachowski	1992	3,727
18 5/16	11 12/16	6 9/16	M	Towns County	GA	Willis Dyer	1992	3,727
18 5/16	11 7/16	6 14/16	M	Lac La Biche	ALB	Lewis Coker	1993	3,727
18 5/16	11 8/16	6 13/16	M	Bonneville County	ID	Ken Lumpkin	1993	3,727
18 5/16	11 9/16	6 12/16	M	Fort Coulonge	QUE	Russ Kay	1993	3,727
18 5/16	11 14/16	6 7/16	M	Longlac	ONT	Terry J. Smith	1993	3,727
18 5/16	11 6/16	6 15/16	M	Madison County	MT	David Moris	1993	3,727
18 5/16	11 9/16	6 12/16	M	Beaverhead County	MT	Lee Murphree	1993	3,727
18 5/16	11 5/16	7 0/16	M	Washington County	ME	Del Dinsmore	1993	3,727
18 5/16	11 8/16	6 13/16	M	Sup Lake	ONT	Scott Ellery	1993	3,727
18 5/16	12 4/16	6 1/16	M	La Corey	ALB	Dewain Ollenberger	1994	3,727
18 5/16	11 11/16	6 10/16	M	Slave Lake	ALB	Carl H. Breidegam	1994	3,727
18 5/16	11 9/16	6 12/16	M	Smeaton	SAS	Gene A. Welle	1994	3,727
18 5/16	11 9/16	6 12/16	M	High Level	ALB	Donny Roy	1994	3,727
18 5/16	11 8/16	6 13/16	M	High Level	ALB	Kenneth T. Blount	1994	3,727
18 5/16	11 5/16	7 0/16	M	Benton County	OR	Gary Champion	1994	3,727
18 5/16	11 5/16	7 0/16	M	Folyette	ONT	James Twork	1994	3,727
18 5/16	11 11/16	6 10/16	F	Olha	MAN	Mike W. Lenz	1994	3,727
18 5/16	11 3/16	7 2/16	M	Thunder Bay	ONT	James Sturz	1994	3,727
18 5/16	11 12/16	6 9/16	M	Itasca County	MN	John E. Tasker	1994	3,727
18 5/16	11 12/16	6 9/16	M	Prince of Wales Island	AK	Kirk Westervelt	1994	3,727
18 5/16	11 11/16	6 10/16	M	San Miguel County	CO	Anthony Scott Wagner	1994	3,727
18 5/16	11 6/16	6 15/16	M	Bridgeville	NS	Christopher M.W. Tobin	1994	3,727
18 5/16	11 13/16	6 8/16	M	Kootenai County	ID	D. V. Moyer	1995	3,727
18 5/16	11 7/16	6 14/16	M	Dryden	ONT	Paul Tuscher	1995	3,727
18 5/16	11 6/16	6 15/16	M	Elmore County	ID	Anthony L. Mudd	1995	3,727
18 5/16	11 10/16	6 11/16	M	Nipawin	SAS	Thomas J. Beissel	1995	3,727
18 5/16	11 11/16	6 10/16	M	Smeaton	SAS	Gene Welle	1995	3,727

BLACK BEAR

Minimum Score 18 — Continued

SCORE	GREATEST LENGTH	GREATEST WIDTH	SEX	AREA	STATE/ PROVINCE	HUNTER'S NAME	DATE	RANK
18 5/16	11 7/16	6 14/16	M	Fort McMurray	ALB	Wayne Palinckx	1995	3,727
18 5/16	11 5/16	7 0/16	M	Kenora	ONT	Matt Schwab	1995	3,727
18 5/16	11 6/16	6 15/16	M	Lake Manitowik	ONT	Chuck Webb	1995	3,727
18 5/16	11 15/16	6 6/16	M	St. George	NBW	Mike Steever	1995	3,727
18 5/16	11 11/16	6 10/16	M	Forest County	WI	Steven W. Jackson	1995	3,727
18 5/16	11 7/16	6 14/16	M	Snow Lake	MAN	George Massie	1996	3,727
18 5/16	11 8/16	6 13/16	M	Deux Rivers	QUE	Albert Gawet	1996	3,727
18 5/16	11 10/16	6 11/16	M	Caramat	ONT	A. Will Vander Ende	1996	3,727
18 5/16	11 6/16	6 15/16	M	High Level	ALB	Landon Koteskey	1996	3,727
18 5/16	11 10/16	6 11/16	M	Athabasca River	ALB	Michael Hilley	1997	3,727
18 5/16	11 5/16	7 0/16	M	High Level	ALB	Del Karnuth	1997	3,727
18 5/16	11 5/16	7 0/16	M	Marathon	ONT	Michael L. Ritter	1997	3,727
18 5/16	11 14/16	6 7/16	M	Tanana River	AK	George W. Pearson	1997	3,727
18 5/16	11 12/16	6 9/16	M	Beltrami County	MN	Todd Hannon	1997	3,727
18 5/16	11 10/16	6 11/16	M	Swan Lake	ALB	Derrill Herman	1998	3,727
18 5/16	11 11/16	6 10/16	M	Clarke Lake	SAS	Lori Goldade	1998	3,727
18 5/16	11 10/16	6 11/16	M	Smeaton	SAS	Nathan V. Schwartz	1998	3,727
18 5/16	11 12/16	6 9/16	M	Beluga	AK	Terry L. Kolich	1998	3,727
18 5/16	11 12/16	6 9/16	M	Lake County	MN	Steven S. Bruggeman	1998	3,727
18 4/16	10 14/16	7 6/16	M	Latah County	ID	Don Lawrence	1962	3,842
18 4/16	11 7/16	6 13/16	M	Curry County	OR	Gerald Rimbey	1962	3,842
18 4/16	11 4/16	7 0/16	M	Shawano County	WI	Peter Erickson	1967	3,842
18 4/16	11 12/16	6 8/16	M	Ft. Frances	ONT	Wayne Keefer	1968	3,842
18 4/16	11 6/16	6 14/16	M	Idaho County	ID	Larry W. Gehre	1972	3,842
18 4/16	11 12/16	6 8/16	M	Itasca County	MN	Lonny Herrick	1973	3,842
18 4/16	11 10/16	6 10/16	M	La Plata County	CO	Kenneth L. Biegel	1974	3,842
18 4/16	11 7/16	6 13/16	M	Tuolumne County	CA	Willis Chapman	1974	3,842
18 4/16	11 6/16	6 14/16	M	Harcourt	ONT	Robert M. Sweisthal	1977	3,842
18 4/16	11 7/16	6 13/16	M	Boise County	ID	Richard C. Nichols	1978	3,842
18 4/16	11 12/16	6 8/16	M	Caribou County	ID	Randy J. Stephens	1978	3,842
18 4/16	11 7/16	6 13/16	M	Vermillion Bay	ONT	Daniel D. Carlson	1979	3,842
18 4/16	11 6/16	6 14/16	M	Lily Lake	BC	Stanley Moore	1979	3,842
18 4/16	11 8/16	6 12/16	M	Mesa County	CO	David E. Samuel	1979	3,842
18 4/16	11 9/16	6 11/16	M	Beltrami County	MN	Greg Siekaniec	1979	3,842
18 4/16	11 7/16	6 13/16	M	Piscataquis County	ME	Mark Sutherly	1979	3,842
18 4/16	11 7/16	6 13/16	M	Essex County	VT	James 'Boomer' Hayden	1980	3,842
18 4/16	11 12/16	6 8/16	M	Tehama County	CA	Gerald McKenzie	1980	3,842
18 4/16	11 7/16	6 13/16	M	St. Louis County	MN	Mike Schullo	1981	3,842
18 4/16	11 8/16	6 12/16	M	Dryden	ONT	Alan E. Forbes	1982	3,842
18 4/16	11 12/16	6 8/16	M	Susitna River	AK	Mel Hein	1983	3,842
18 4/16	11 6/16	6 14/16	M	Seine River	ONT	George David Shelton	1983	3,842
18 4/16	11 4/16	7 0/16	M	Cloud Bay	ONT	Ronald C. Maikranz	1983	3,842
18 4/16	11 10/16	6 10/16	M	Iron County	MI	Jim Johnson	1983	3,842
18 4/16	11 10/16	6 10/16	M	Mistatim	SAS	Jeff Grewe	1984	3,842
18 4/16	11 8/16	6 12/16	M	Saguache County	CO	Jerry Barth	1984	3,842
18 4/16	10 14/16	7 6/16	M	Idaho County	ID	James Jay Hill	1984	3,842
18 4/16	11 4/16	7 0/16	M	Langlade County	WI	Edward R. Jenelewicz	1984	3,842
18 4/16	11 8/16	6 12/16	M	Oxford County	ME	Gary Russell	1984	3,842
18 4/16	11 12/16	6 8/16	M	Sudbury	ONT	Nancy A. Guisbert	1985	3,842
18 4/16	11 10/16	6 10/16	M	Fawcett Lake	ALB	David R. Coupland	1985	3,842
18 4/16	11 8/16	6 12/16	M	Bell Lake	ONT	Dale D. Conley	1985	3,842
18 4/16	11 8/16	6 12/16	M	Jellicoe	ONT	Mike Mooney	1985	3,842
18 4/16	11 0/16	7 4/16	M	Oxford County	ME	Allen Baker	1985	3,842
18 4/16	11 6/16	6 14/16	M	Lemhi County	ID	Mark Neer	1985	3,842
18 4/16	12 0/16	6 4/16	M	Ft. Assiniboine	ALB	Jim Dahlberg	1985	3,842
18 4/16	11 10/16	6 10/16	M	Siskiyou County	CA	Arthur M. Cain	1985	3,842
18 4/16	11 5/16	6 15/16	M	Smeaton	SAS	Renee Welle	1986	3,842
18 4/16	11 8/16	6 12/16	M	Standard Creek	AK	William B. Childress	1986	3,842
18 4/16	11 10/16	6 10/16	M	Fort Coulonge	QUE	Anthony G. Horrell	1986	3,842
18 4/16	11 2/16	7 2/16	M	Dryden	ONT	Gene Rokus	1986	3,842
18 4/16	11 10/16	6 10/16	M	Beaconsfield	NBW	William Clark	1986	3,842
18 4/16	11 8/16	6 12/16	M	Fergus	ONT	David L. Reeves	1986	3,842
18 4/16	11 11/16	6 9/16	M	Lac du Bonnet	MAN	Russell R. Popp	1987	3,842
18 4/16	11 3/16	7 1/16	M	Grand County	CO	Jerry L. Novak	1987	3,842
18 4/16	11 5/16	6 15/16	M	Boise County	ID	Jim Wilson	1987	3,842
18 4/16	11 15/16	6 5/16	M	Canoe Lake	SAS	Kim Steven Hussong	1988	3,842
18 4/16	11 12/16	6 8/16	M	Slave Lake	ALB	Kevin Hehn	1988	3,842
18 4/16	11 4/16	7 0/16	M	Felix	ONT	Bradley C. Chamberlain	1988	3,842
18 4/16	11 5/16	6 15/16	M	Kenora	ONT	Greg Zirbel	1988	3,842
18 4/16	11 14/16	6 6/16	M	Jackson County	OR	Jim Turcke	1988	3,842
18 4/16	11 7/16	6 13/16	M	Duchesne County	UT	Dirk B. Watrous	1989	3,842
18 4/16	11 11/16	6 9/16	M	Sioux Lookout	ONT	Manfred Gehrlein	1989	3,842
18 4/16	11 8/16	6 12/16	M	Lake Manitou	QUE	Keith Mitchell	1989	3,842
18 4/16	11 5/16	6 15/16	M	Lincoln County	MT	Robert W. "Bill" Armstrong, Jr	1989	3,842
18 4/16	11 2/16	7 2/16	M	Ravalli County	MT	James Patenaude	1989	3,842
18 4/16	11 4/16	7 0/16	M	Gallatin County	MT	Andy Locker	1989	3,842
18 4/16	11 10/16	6 10/16	M	Conejos County	CO	Rick Ivers	1990	3,842
18 4/16	11 7/16	6 13/16	M	Unit 9A	ONT	Dave Steinhorst	1990	3,842

BLACK BEAR

Minimum Score 18 — Continued

SCORE	GREATEST LENGTH	GREATEST WIDTH	SEX	AREA	STATE/PROVINCE	HUNTER'S NAME	DATE	RANK
18 4/16	11 12/16	6 8/16	M	Rainy River	ONT	Michael Judas	1990	3,842
18 4/16	11 7/16	6 13/16	M	Green Lake	SAS	Herb B. Merkert, Jr.	1990	3,842
18 4/16	11 2/16	7 2/16	M	Biscotasing	ONT	Thomas Hlinka	1990	3,842
18 4/16	11 8/16	6 12/16	M	Sultan	ONT	Daniel A. Phillips	1990	3,842
18 4/16	11 8/16	6 12/16	M	Chibougamau	QUE	Alfred Bergeron	1990	3,842
18 4/16	11 7/16	6 13/16	M	Wawa	ONT	Mark R. Sherman	1990	3,842
18 4/16	11 6/16	6 14/16	M	Border Lake	BC	Dean Stebner	1990	3,842
18 4/16	11 5/16	6 15/16	M	Moon Beam	ONT	Dick Clark	1991	3,842
18 4/16	11 6/16	6 14/16	M	Boise County	ID	Richard R. Larrivee	1991	3,842
18 4/16	11 10/16	6 10/16	M	Buffalo Narrows	SAS	Bernard J. Garcarz	1991	3,842
18 4/16	11 2/16	7 2/16	M	Kapuskasing	ONT	Jim Melton	1991	3,842
18 4/16	11 9/16	6 11/16	M	Longlac	ONT	Douglas C. Arnold	1991	3,842
18 4/16	11 6/16	6 14/16	M	Temiscaming	QUE	Fred Wallace	1991	3,842
18 4/16	11 5/16	6 15/16	M	La Plata County	CO	Perry Howell	1991	3,842
18 4/16	11 8/16	6 12/16	M	Kalkaska County	MI	David L. Roose	1991	3,842
18 4/16	11 9/16	6 11/16	M	Saddle Hills	ALB	Ken Baker	1992	3,842
18 4/16	11 5/16	6 15/16	M	Mink Lake	ONT	David Kennedy	1992	3,842
18 4/16	11 4/16	7 0/16	M	Rouyn-Noranda	QUE	Daniel K. Shivery	1992	3,842
18 4/16	11 11/16	6 9/16	M	Manitouwadge	ONT	Douglas E. McGuire	1992	3,842
18 4/16	11 8/16	6 12/16	M	Lac La Biche	ALB	Tom L. Nelson	1992	3,842
18 4/16	11 8/16	6 12/16	M	Fort McMurray	ALB	Bill Thompson	1992	3,842
18 4/16	11 10/16	6 10/16	M	Bird River	MAN	William Patrick McQuillen	1992	3,842
18 4/16	11 5/16	6 15/16	M	Mine Centre	ONT	David Wolf	1992	3,842
18 4/16	11 12/16	6 8/16	M	Boise County	ID	Bruce Capes	1992	3,842
18 4/16	11 2/16	7 2/16	M	Wawa	ONT	Sam J. Salem, DDS	1992	3,842
18 4/16	11 8/16	6 12/16	M	Kenora	ONT	Dick Schwab	1992	3,842
18 4/16	11 8/16	6 12/16	M	Hearst	ONT	David L. Gubine	1992	3,842
18 4/16	11 4/16	7 0/16	M	Valmont	QUE	Karlton Pinnix	1992	3,842
18 4/16	11 5/16	6 15/16	M	Clearwater County	ID	Jim Bradford	1992	3,842
18 4/16	11 4/16	7 0/16	M	Saguenay	QUE	Stan M. Hepler	1992	3,842
18 4/16	11 10/16	6 10/16	M	Zec Restigo	QUE	William E. Lockwood, Jr.	1992	3,842
18 4/16	11 11/16	6 9/16	M	Gogebic County	MI	Daniel Holtrop	1992	3,842
18 4/16	11 8/16	6 12/16	M	Sawyer County	WI	Paul Strong	1992	3,842
18 4/16	11 10/16	6 10/16	M	Valleyview	ALB	Bill Vaznis	1993	3,842
18 4/16	11 9/16	6 11/16	M	Pelly River	YUK	Steve Byerly	1993	3,842
18 4/16	11 6/16	6 14/16	M	Hastings	ONT	Donnie Covey	1993	3,842
18 4/16	11 11/16	6 9/16	M	Campbell River	BC	Gary F. Bogner	1993	3,842
18 4/16	11 5/16	6 15/16	M	King County	WA	Eric C. Laugen	1993	3,842
18 4/16	11 2/16	7 2/16	M	Thunder Bay	ONT	Mark E. Lindgren	1993	3,842
18 4/16	11 10/16	6 10/16	M	Boise County	ID	Tom D'Aquino	1993	3,842
18 4/16	11 10/16	6 10/16	M	Preston County	WV	Rob Peddicord	1993	3,842
18 4/16	11 6/16	6 14/16	M	East Bull Lake	ONT	Steven M. Best	1994	3,842
18 4/16	11 8/16	6 12/16	M	Kenora	ONT	David E. Johnson	1994	3,842
18 4/16	11 8/16	6 12/16	M	Carswell Lake	SAS	Steve Rucinski	1994	3,842
18 4/16	11 12/16	6 8/16	M	Ft. Vermilion	ALB	Johnnie R. Walters	1994	3,842
18 4/16	11 1/16	7 3/16	M	Sioux Narrows	ONT	Lincoln O. Stafslien	1994	3,842
18 4/16	11 8/16	6 12/16	M	Atikokan	ONT	Lynn Reese	1994	3,842
18 4/16	11 7/16	6 13/16	M	Chisholm Township	ONT	Dennis Durocher	1994	3,842
18 4/16	11 12/16	6 8/16	M	Koochiching County	MN	Gerald J. Gohman	1994	3,842
18 4/16	11 10/16	6 10/16	M	Koochiching County	MN	Howard L. Turck	1994	3,842
18 4/16	12 1/16	6 3/16	M	Craven County	NC	Tonnie Elwood Davis	1994	3,842
18 4/16	11 8/16	6 12/16	M	White Fox	SAS	Jeffrey J. Tobin	1995	3,842
18 4/16	11 13/16	6 7/16	M	Athabasca River	ALB	Steve Barnhill	1995	3,842
18 4/16	11 12/16	6 8/16	M	Egg Lake	MAN	Jack Evans	1995	3,842
18 4/16	11 14/16	6 6/16	M	Dryden	ONT	Dean Bergman	1995	3,842
18 4/16	11 9/16	6 11/16	M	Thunder Bay	ONT	Dan Nagel	1995	3,842
18 4/16	11 10/16	6 10/16	M	Fort McMurray	ALB	Wayne Palinckx	1995	3,842
18 4/16	11 3/16	7 1/16	M	Bissett	MAN	J. Greg Keck	1995	3,842
18 4/16	11 13/16	6 7/16	M	Atikokan	ONT	Travis Graves	1995	3,842
18 4/16	11 8/16	6 12/16	M	Lemon Lake	BC	Joe Webster	1995	3,842
18 4/16	11 10/16	6 10/16	M	St. Louis County	MN	Gregory Gall	1995	3,842
18 4/16	11 8/16	6 12/16	M	La Plata County	CO	Dennis L. Howell	1995	3,842
18 4/16	12 0/16	6 4/16	M	Carlton County	MN	Brent Larson	1995	3,842
18 4/16	11 4/16	7 0/16	M	Gilmer County	GA	Billy J. Wilson, Jr.	1995	3,842
18 4/16	11 2/16	7 2/16	M	Cold Lake	ALB	Glenn E. Moir	1996	3,842
18 4/16	11 6/16	6 14/16	M	Dryden	ONT	Paul Martin Zizelman	1996	3,842
18 4/16	11 7/16	6 13/16	M	Fort Vermilion	ALB	Stephen A. Hrycko	1996	3,842
18 4/16	11 5/16	6 15/16	M	Meadow Lake	SAS	David L. Duncan	1996	3,842
18 4/16	11 12/16	6 8/16	M	Bonanza	ALB	John L. Nelson, Sr.	1996	3,842
18 4/16	11 3/16	7 1/16	M	Manitouwadge	ONT	Joe Herold	1996	3,842
18 4/16	11 9/16	6 11/16	M	Ear Falls	ONT	Dwight Hearing	1996	3,842
18 4/16	11 6/16	6 14/16	M	Bissett	MAN	Wayne Nicholson	1996	3,842
18 4/16	11 8/16	6 12/16	M	Forest County	WI	Jackie Cook	1996	3,842
18 4/16	11 8/16	6 12/16	M	Spirit River	ALB	Jim Stinson	1997	3,842
18 4/16	11 11/16	6 9/16	M	Prince of Wales Island	AK	Rick Tobalsky	1997	3,842
18 4/16	11 12/16	6 8/16	M	Hudson Bay	SAS	Dale E. Mateer, DDS	1997	3,842
18 4/16	11 12/16	6 8/16	M	Sheridan County	WY	Robert A. Austin	1997	3,842
18 4/16	11 9/16	6 11/16	M	Nipawin	SAS	Jim Horneck	1997	3,842

BLACK BEAR

Minimum Score 18 — Continued

SCORE	GREATEST LENGTH	GREATEST WIDTH	SEX	AREA	STATE/PROVINCE	HUNTER'S NAME	DATE	RANK
18 4/16	11 11/16	6 9/16	M	Indian River	AK	Rick Schikora	1997	3,842
18 4/16	11 7/16	6 13/16	M	Dryden	ONT	Mark A. Ascheman	1997	3,842
18 4/16	11 9/16	6 11/16	M	Itasca County	MN	Ken Thorson	1997	3,842
18 4/16	11 8/16	6 12/16	M	Carroll Inlet	AK	Larry Daly	1998	3,842
18 4/16	11 8/16	6 12/16	M	McNalley Lake	ALB	Dallas Smith	1998	3,842
18 4/16	11 12/16	6 8/16	M	Slave River	ALB	William P. Woller	1998	3,842
18 4/16	11 13/16	6 7/16	M	Bissett	MAN	Glen P. Mertens	1998	3,842
18 4/16	11 4/16	7 0/16	M	White River	ONT	Stuart Wright, Jr.	1998	3,842
18 4/16	11 8/16	6 12/16	M	Nestor Falls	ONT	Nicholas Vezzi	1998	3,842
18 4/16	11 4/16	7 0/16	M	La Plata County	CO	Garth Schultheis	1998	3,842
18 3/16	11 1/16	7 2/16	M	Penobscot County	ME	Charles A. Kronyak	1965	3,989
18 3/16	11 0/16	7 3/16	M	Custer County	ID	C. Randall Byers	1966	3,989
18 3/16	11 4/16	6 15/16	M	Franklin County	ME	Philip Copp	1967	3,989
18 3/16	11 6/16	6 13/16	M	Florence County	WI	Elaine S. Peck	1967	3,989
18 3/16	11 15/16	6 4/16	M	Garfield County	CO	Bob Swinehart	1967	3,989
18 3/16	11 3/16	7 0/16	M	Douglas County	CO	Larry Baker	1975	3,989
18 3/16	11 8/16	6 11/16	M	Penobscot County	ME	Neil Zullo	1975	3,989
18 3/16	11 6/16	6 13/16	M	Slave Lake	ALB	Gordon Roline	1976	3,989
18 3/16	11 8/16	6 11/16	M	Targhee National Forest	ID	Thomas Pinkston	1978	3,989
18 3/16	11 3/16	7 0/16	M	Sudbury	ONT	Alvin Lybarger	1979	3,989
18 3/16	10 15/16	7 4/16	M	St. Louis County	MN	George Sheets	1979	3,989
18 3/16	11 9/16	6 10/16	M	Anchorage	AK	Ronald Arch	1980	3,989
18 3/16	11 10/16	6 9/16	M	Renfrew	ONT	Walter Cymbal	1980	3,989
18 3/16	11 11/16	6 8/16	M	Fremont County	ID	Doug M. Chase	1981	3,989
18 3/16	11 6/16	6 13/16	M	Thunder Bay	ONT	Sharon Larsen	1981	3,989
18 3/16	11 7/16	6 12/16	M	Fort Frances	ONT	Pam Baird	1982	3,989
18 3/16	11 3/16	7 0/16	M	Baraga County	MI	Jim Humber III	1982	3,989
18 3/16	11 2/16	7 1/16	M	Meagher County	MT	Chuck Adams	1982	3,989
18 3/16	11 6/16	6 13/16	M	Sierra County	CA	Robert Smith	1982	3,989
18 3/16	11 8/16	6 11/16	M	Dryden	ONT	Richard Stock	1983	3,989
18 3/16	11 6/16	6 13/16	M	Fremont County	CO	Al Weaver	1983	3,989
18 3/16	11 1/16	7 2/16	M	Echouani Lake	QUE	Collins F. Kellogg	1983	3,989
18 3/16	11 12/16	6 7/16	M	Burnett County	WI	Daniel D. Clayton	1983	3,989
18 3/16	11 10/16	6 9/16	M	Otter Lake	QUE	Dana P. Calhoun	1984	3,989
18 3/16	11 10/16	6 9/16	M	Moose River	ONT	Bob Duncan	1984	3,989
18 3/16	11 5/16	6 14/16	M	Standard Creek	AK	James A. Jones	1984	3,989
18 3/16	11 2/16	7 1/16	M	Idaho County	ID	David Gename	1984	3,989
18 3/16	11 11/16	6 8/16	M	Langlade County	WI	Dan Buss	1984	3,989
18 3/16	11 2/16	7 1/16	M	Wallowa County	OR	Mike Tyrholm	1984	3,989
18 3/16	11 3/16	7 0/16	M	Valley County	ID	Douglas Bunch	1984	3,989
18 3/16	11 6/16	6 13/16	M	Douglas County	WI	Dennis Plantenberg	1984	3,989
18 3/16	11 10/16	6 9/16	F	Augusta County	VA	W. Thurman Hensley	1984	3,989
18 3/16	11 6/16	6 13/16	M	Bear Paw Landing	ONT	Gordan Rabetski	1985	3,989
18 3/16	11 3/16	7 0/16	M	Larimer County	CO	Doug O'Herron	1985	3,989
18 3/16	11 7/16	6 12/16	M	English River	ONT	Richard Nielsen	1985	3,989
18 3/16	11 3/16	7 0/16	M	Ignace	ONT	Walter E. Hammerling	1985	3,989
18 3/16	12 1/16	6 2/16	M	Durban	MAN	Bill Wright, Jr.	1985	3,989
18 3/16	11 6/16	6 13/16	M	Ear Falls	ONT	James C. Gates	1986	3,989
18 3/16	11 15/16	6 4/16	M	Loon Lake	SAS	Harvey McNalley	1986	3,989
18 3/16	11 4/16	6 15/16	M	Idaho County	ID	David Gename	1986	3,989
18 3/16	11 6/16	6 13/16	M	King County	WA	Charles D. Singh	1986	3,989
18 3/16	11 12/16	6 7/16	M	Catron County	NM	Stan Rauch	1987	3,989
18 3/16	11 9/16	6 10/16	M	Minaki	ONT	Donald Schram	1987	3,989
18 3/16	11 9/16	6 10/16	M	Webbwood	ONT	Stephen P. Turay	1987	3,989
18 3/16	11 6/16	6 13/16	M	Gogama	ONT	Tom P. Kidwell	1987	3,989
18 3/16	11 6/16	6 13/16	M	Jims Lake	QUE	David A. Shepard	1987	3,989
18 3/16	11 5/16	6 14/16	M	Bonneville County	ID	Ron Stacey	1987	3,989
18 3/16	11 2/16	7 1/16	M	Washington County	ME	Norman R. Gulbransen	1987	3,989
18 3/16	11 11/16	6 8/16	M	Goodsoil	SAS	John Kalbfleisch	1987	3,989
18 3/16	11 3/16	7 0/16	M	Oxford County	ME	Patrick Abalsamo	1987	3,989
18 3/16	11 3/16	7 0/16	M	Ravalli County	MT	Shaun Twardoski	1987	3,989
18 3/16	11 6/16	6 13/16	M	Chippewa Falls	ONT	Christopher J. Hodyna	1988	3,989
18 3/16	11 13/16	6 6/16	M	Cordova	AK	Jack E. Lape	1988	3,989
18 3/16	11 6/16	6 13/16	M	Sled Lake	SAS	Thomas C. Phillips	1988	3,989
18 3/16	11 8/16	6 11/16	M	Dryden	ONT	Stanley M. Eddy	1988	3,989
18 3/16	11 8/16	6 11/16	M	Idaho County	ID	Howard Holmes	1988	3,989
18 3/16	11 1/16	7 2/16	M	Oxford County	ME	Jack Smith	1988	3,989
18 3/16	11 12/16	6 7/16	M	Washburn County	WI	Edward Peterson	1988	3,989
18 3/16	11 3/16	7 0/16	M	Lemhi County	ID	Dennis N. Minnich	1989	3,989
18 3/16	11 7/16	6 12/16	M	Keg River	ALB	David W. Williams	1989	3,989
18 3/16	11 5/16	6 14/16	M	Boise County	ID	Robert Barrow	1989	3,989
18 3/16	11 8/16	6 11/16	M	Cass County	MN	Mike Honek	1989	3,989
18 3/16	11 2/16	7 1/16	F	Prince of Wales Island	AK	Rickie D. Snell	1990	3,989
18 3/16	11 10/16	6 9/16	M	Elk Point	ALB	C. B. Farnsworth	1990	3,989
18 3/16	11 7/16	6 12/16	M	Long Lac	ONT	David L. Fuller	1990	3,989
18 3/16	11 11/16	6 8/16	M	Kenora	ONT	Wayne D. May	1990	3,989
18 3/16	12 2/16	6 1/16	M	Beltrami County	MN	Evelyn Johnson	1990	3,989
18 3/16	11 12/16	6 7/16	M	Bonnyville	ALB	Glen Garton	1991	3,989

BLACK BEAR

Minimum Score 18 — Continued

SCORE	GREATEST LENGTH	GREATEST WIDTH	SEX	AREA	STATE/PROVINCE	HUNTER'S NAME	DATE	RANK
18 3/16	11 2/16	7 1/16	M	Algoma	ONT	Patrick W. Farrow	1991	3,989
18 3/16	11 13/16	6 6/16	M	Peace River	ALB	James D. Caldwell	1991	3,989
18 3/16	11 6/16	6 13/16	M	Fairbanks	AK	Randolph M.S. Galloway	1991	3,989
18 3/16	11 10/16	6 9/16	M	Grand County	UT	Dave Justmann	1991	3,989
18 3/16	11 0/16	7 3/16	M	Dowling	ONT	Lawrence Fillhard	1991	3,989
18 3/16	11 10/16	6 9/16	M	La Ronge	SAS	Roger Wintle	1991	3,989
18 3/16	11 10/16	6 9/16	M	Fort McMurray	ALB	Len Cardinale	1991	3,989
18 3/16	11 5/16	6 14/16	M	Latuque	QUE	William R. Lewis	1991	3,989
18 3/16	11 10/16	6 9/16	M	Grand Rapids	MAN	Billy J. Waddell	1992	3,989
18 3/16	11 6/16	6 13/16	M	Conejos County	CO	Steve Brock	1992	3,989
18 3/16	11 5/16	6 14/16	M	Zec Rapides des Joachims	QUE	John Neal, Jr.	1992	3,989
18 3/16	11 7/16	6 12/16	M	Saddle Hills	ALB	Wilf Lehners	1992	3,989
18 3/16	11 10/16	6 9/16	M	Lake Besnard	SAS	Roger Wintle	1992	3,989
18 3/16	11 13/16	6 6/16	M	Zec Domion	QUE	James R. Battreall	1992	3,989
18 3/16	12 0/16	6 3/16	M	Bayfield County	WI	Gile Gibbons	1992	3,989
18 3/16	11 12/16	6 7/16	F	Forest County	WI	Scott P. Allen	1992	3,989
18 3/16	11 12/16	6 7/16	M	Lac La Biche	ALB	Russell Bertch	1993	3,989
18 3/16	11 8/16	6 11/16	M	Atikokan	ONT	Jim Kirkendall	1993	3,989
18 3/16	11 11/16	6 8/16	M	Bissett	MAN	Robert Harris	1993	3,989
18 3/16	11 11/16	6 8/16	M	Smeaton	SAS	Gene A. Welle	1993	3,989
18 3/16	11 10/16	6 9/16	M	Thunder Bay	ONT	Michael J. Kemp	1993	3,989
18 3/16	11 12/16	6 7/16	M	Lac La Biche	ALB	Bruce Nederveld	1993	3,989
18 3/16	11 13/16	6 6/16	M	Pine County	MN	Jeff Zormeier	1993	3,989
18 3/16	11 12/16	6 7/16	M	Itasca County	MN	Bob Stafford	1993	3,989
18 3/16	11 6/16	6 13/16	M	Thunder Bay	ONT	Mike Hudalla	1994	3,989
18 3/16	11 11/16	6 8/16	M	Exshaw	ALB	Mark Wuerthele	1994	3,989
18 3/16	11 10/16	6 9/16	M	Prince of Wales Island	AK	Robert N. Titus	1994	3,989
18 3/16	11 3/16	7 0/16	M	Strong Township	ONT	Roy A. Kelly	1994	3,989
18 3/16	11 8/16	6 11/16	M	Cold Lake	ALB	Eric Rauhanen	1994	3,989
18 3/16	11 9/16	6 10/16	M	Prince of Wales Island	AK	Gerald L. Egbert	1994	3,989
18 3/16	11 7/16	6 12/16	M	Webbwood	ONT	William A. Dickerson	1994	3,989
18 3/16	11 14/16	6 5/16	M	Hudson Bay	SAS	William E. Lee, Jr.	1994	3,989
18 3/16	11 8/16	6 11/16	M	Forest Area	SAS	Ginger Fausel	1994	3,989
18 3/16	11 12/16	6 7/16	M	Kelvington	SAS	Martin A. White	1994	3,989
18 3/16	11 10/16	6 9/16	M	Penobscot County	ME	Wade A. Paradis	1994	3,989
18 3/16	11 10/16	6 9/16	M	Otero County	NM	Kirk M. Folsom	1994	3,989
18 3/16	11 1/16	7 2/16	M	Missoula County	MT	Johnnie Wisnewski	1994	3,989
18 3/16	11 8/16	6 11/16	M	Lincoln County	NM	Chris Barrilleaux	1994	3,989
18 3/16	11 5/16	6 14/16	M	Yarmouth County	NS	Bill Terry, Sr.	1994	3,989
18 3/16	11 9/16	6 10/16	M	Red Earth	ALB	Philip Coulson	1995	3,989
18 3/16	11 8/16	6 11/16	M	Shining Tree	ONT	John F. Belha, Jr.	1995	3,989
18 3/16	11 7/16	6 12/16	M	Swanson River	AK	Keith Appel	1995	3,989
18 3/16	11 6/16	6 13/16	M	Smoky Lake	ALB	Mark Johnson	1995	3,989
18 3/16	11 5/16	6 14/16	M	Sioux Lookout	ONT	John Shields	1995	3,989
18 3/16	11 5/16	6 14/16	M	Lynn Lake	MAN	Sam J. Valore	1995	3,989
18 3/16	11 8/16	6 11/16	M	Ignace	ONT	Gaylord Winterberg	1995	3,989
18 3/16	11 8/16	6 11/16	M	Oak Lake	ONT	Ronald A. Hall	1995	3,989
18 3/16	11 7/16	6 12/16	M	Hearst	ONT	Russ Riese	1995	3,989
18 3/16	11 4/16	6 15/16	M	Dorion	ONT	Larry Paulsen	1995	3,989
18 3/16	10 15/16	7 4/16	M	Algoma	ONT	Robert V. Haley, Jr.	1995	3,989
18 3/16	11 8/16	6 11/16	M	Lynn Lake	MAN	Andrew W. Szczesniak	1995	3,989
18 3/16	11 14/16	6 5/16	M	Becker County	MN	Wayne Enger	1995	3,989
18 3/16	11 10/16	6 9/16	M	Douglas County	WI	Lane M. Henck	1995	3,989
18 3/16	11 11/16	6 8/16	M	Atikokan	ONT	Ted Kaczmarek	1996	3,989
18 3/16	11 3/16	7 0/16	M	Valley County	ID	Jason L. Angell	1996	3,989
18 3/16	11 12/16	6 7/16	M	Canton Township	ONT	Jeffery C. Weber	1996	3,989
18 3/16	11 11/16	6 8/16	M	Emo	ONT	Robert Kopp	1996	3,989
18 3/16	11 8/16	6 11/16	M	Wabigoon	ONT	Jay Peake	1996	3,989
18 3/16	11 11/16	6 8/16	M	Marathon	ONT	Michael L. Ritter, Jr.	1996	3,989
18 3/16	11 12/16	6 7/16	M	Fairbanks	AK	Robert G. Brown	1996	3,989
18 3/16	11 9/16	6 10/16	M	Bayfield County	WI	Craig Stinebrink	1996	3,989
18 3/16	11 8/16	6 11/16	M	Ellershouse	NS	Brian W. MacKenzie	1996	3,989
18 3/16	11 7/16	6 12/16	M	Saddle Hills	ALB	Dustin Brown	1997	3,989
18 3/16	11 7/16	6 12/16	M	Hawkrock River	SAS	Paul Rankin	1997	3,989
18 3/16	11 2/16	7 1/16	M	Fulton County	NY	Paul W. Graham	1997	3,989
18 3/16	11 11/16	6 8/16	M	Athabasca River	ALB	Steve Haufsk	1998	3,989
18 3/16	11 8/16	6 11/16	M	Idaho County	ID	Marlon J. Clapham	1998	3,989
18 3/16	11 6/16	6 13/16	M	Teton County	ID	Thomas Thiel	1998	3,989
18 3/16	11 7/16	6 12/16	M	Oxford County	ME	Roger M. Tyler	1998	3,989
18 2/16	11 8/16	6 10/16	M	Murphy Dome	AK	Richard Cooper	1955	4,126
18 2/16	11 2/16	7 0/16	M	Sudbury	ONT	Floyd Eccleston	1961	4,126
18 2/16	11 4/16	6 14/16	M	Penobscot County	ME	Bill L. Carlos	1963	4,126
18 2/16	11 8/16	6 10/16	M	Penobscot County	ME	Dennis H. Driscoll	1967	4,126
18 2/16	11 8/16	6 10/16	M	Franklin County	ME	Kenneth Rapp	1969	4,126
18 2/16	11 5/16	6 13/16	M	Chapleau	ONT	Ed Helgason	1970	4,126
18 2/16	11 6/16	6 12/16	M	Chetwynd	BC	Lee E. Hansel	1973	4,126
18 2/16	11 9/16	6 9/16	M	La Plata County	CO	Rose Neeley	1975	4,126
18 2/16	11 6/16	6 12/16	M	Waupaca County	WI	Neil Pietenpol	1975	4,126

BLACK BEAR

Minimum Score 18 — Continued

SCORE	GREATEST LENGTH	GREATEST WIDTH	SEX	AREA	STATE/PROVINCE	HUNTER'S NAME	DATE	RANK
18 2/16	11 10/16	6 8/16	M	Marinette County	WI	Jack Baxter	1976	4,126
18 2/16	10 14/16	7 4/16	M	Flathead County	MT	Paul P. Schafer	1976	4,126
18 2/16	11 12/16	6 6/16	M	Iron County	MI	Harry W. Squibb	1976	4,126
18 2/16	11 6/16	6 12/16	M	Madison County	ID	Paul Beesley	1977	4,126
18 2/16	11 10/16	6 8/16	M	King County	WA	Stephen C. Zabransky	1978	4,126
18 2/16	11 7/16	6 11/16	M	Kootenai County	ID	Stanley Leake	1979	4,126
18 2/16	11 8/16	6 10/16	M	Powell County	MT	Paul Brunner	1979	4,126
18 2/16	11 9/16	6 9/16	M	St. Louis County	MN	James D. Coakley	1979	4,126
18 2/16	11 4/16	6 14/16	M	Whitney	ONT	Doug Merkel	1979	4,126
18 2/16	11 11/16	6 7/16	F	Fremont County	ID	Paul Phillips	1979	4,126
18 2/16	11 7/16	6 11/16	M	Boise County	ID	Larry Spiva	1979	4,126
18 2/16	11 14/16	6 4/16	M	Boise County	ID	Larry Hoff	1980	4,126
18 2/16	11 10/16	6 8/16	M	Gunnison County	CO	Holt Dougherty	1980	4,126
18 2/16	11 11/16	6 7/16	M	Chichester	QUE	Don Marin	1981	4,126
18 2/16	11 4/16	6 14/16	M	Piscataquis County	ME	Daniel E. Reznik	1981	4,126
18 2/16	11 4/16	6 14/16	M	Ear Falls	ONT	Robert J. Roach	1981	4,126
18 2/16	10 15/16	7 3/16	M	Coos County	NH	Phillip E. Williams	1981	4,126
18 2/16	11 8/16	6 10/16	M	Ignace	ONT	Elmer R. Luce, Jr.	1982	4,126
18 2/16	11 4/16	6 14/16	M	Washington County	ME	Richard Manchur	1982	4,126
18 2/16	11 10/16	6 8/16	M	Clearwater County	ID	Dan J. Martin	1983	4,126
18 2/16	11 4/16	6 14/16	M	Longlac	ONT	Bill Zaepfel	1983	4,126
18 2/16	11 10/16	6 8/16	M	Algonquin	ONT	Walter F. Dotson, Jr.	1983	4,126
18 2/16	11 8/16	6 10/16	M	Dwight	ONT	Walt Krom	1983	4,126
18 2/16	11 5/16	6 13/16	M	Sundridge	ONT	Jack Lape	1983	4,126
18 2/16	11 2/16	7 0/16	M	Haliburton	ONT	John Dawson	1983	4,126
18 2/16	11 1/16	7 1/16	M	Boice County	ID	Larry Spiva	1983	4,126
18 2/16	11 8/16	6 10/16	M	Oneida County	WI	Don Ries	1983	4,126
18 2/16	11 7/16	6 11/16	M	Ontonagon County	MI	Greg M. Ebel	1983	4,126
18 2/16	11 4/16	6 14/16	M	Latah County	ID	Marcus B. Caudill	1984	4,126
18 2/16	11 2/16	7 0/16	M	Cumberland House	SAS	Wayne Muth	1984	4,126
18 2/16	11 6/16	6 12/16	M	Latah County	ID	Robert Walter Brooks	1984	4,126
18 2/16	11 10/16	6 8/16	M	Clearwater County	ID	Mark McMurray	1984	4,126
18 2/16	11 6/16	6 12/16	M	Pontiac	QUE	Russ Kay	1984	4,126
18 2/16	11 8/16	6 10/16	M	Fiddler Twp.	ONT	Mike Johnson	1984	4,126
18 2/16	11 9/16	6 9/16	M	Valley County	ID	Kenneth Hyde	1984	4,126
18 2/16	11 7/16	6 11/16	M	Sunbury County	NBW	Mike Lamade	1985	4,126
18 2/16	11 4/16	6 14/16	M	Fort Coulonge	QUE	Wm. Fred Stone	1985	4,126
18 2/16	11 6/16	6 12/16	M	Penobscot County	ME	Gary Thorne	1985	4,126
18 2/16	11 6/16	6 12/16	M	Riverside County	CA	Jim Wagner	1985	4,126
18 2/16	11 6/16	6 12/16	M	Jackson County	OR	Lou Probo	1985	4,126
18 2/16	11 8/16	6 10/16	M	Eagle Lake	ONT	Paul Sieg	1986	4,126
18 2/16	11 7/16	6 11/16	M	Fort Frances	ONT	Randy Durushia	1986	4,126
18 2/16	11 9/16	6 9/16	M	Wabigoon	ONT	Robert Barrie	1986	4,126
18 2/16	11 8/16	6 10/16	F	Hudson Bay	SAS	Floyd Forster	1986	4,126
18 2/16	11 15/16	6 3/16	M	Duck Mtn.	MAN	Bill Clink	1986	4,126
18 2/16	10 10/16	7 8/16	M	Thaddeus Lake	ONT	Robert Brodhagen	1986	4,126
18 2/16	11 10/16	6 8/16	M	Grant County	NM	Dr. Douglas R. Hahn	1986	4,126
18 2/16	11 1/16	7 1/16	M	Siskiyou County	CA	Kirk Westervelt	1986	4,126
18 2/16	11 6/16	6 12/16	M	Atikokan	ONT	Jim Holdenried	1987	4,126
18 2/16	11 12/16	6 6/16	M	Hudson Bay	SAS	Billy Ellis III	1987	4,126
18 2/16	11 5/16	6 13/16	M	Ignace	ONT	Richard Nielsen	1987	4,126
18 2/16	11 4/16	6 14/16	M	Clearwater County	ID	Timothy A. King	1987	4,126
18 2/16	11 7/16	6 11/16	M	Teton County	ID	Frank W. Sparkman	1987	4,126
18 2/16	11 6/16	6 12/16	M	Graham County	AZ	Michael E. Duperret	1987	4,126
18 2/16	11 11/16	6 7/16	F	Duck Mtn.	MAN	Richard W. Sage	1987	4,126
18 2/16	11 4/16	6 14/16	M	Marathon	ONT	Robert W. Russell	1987	4,126
18 2/16	11 2/16	7 0/16	M	Essex County	NY	John Douglas Durling	1987	4,126
18 2/16	11 15/16	6 3/16	M	King County	WA	Mark A. Graham	1987	4,126
18 2/16	11 2/16	7 0/16	M	Baker County	OR	Scott Reed	1988	4,126
18 2/16	11 7/16	6 11/16	M	Latah County	ID	Kirk T. Byers	1988	4,126
18 2/16	11 6/16	6 12/16	M	Wabigoon	ONT	Albert J. Smith	1988	4,126
18 2/16	11 6/16	6 12/16	M	Bear Lake County	ID	Rick Bergholm	1988	4,126
18 2/16	11 7/16	6 11/16	M	La Tuque	QUE	Tracey S. Goodrich	1988	4,126
18 2/16	11 6/16	6 12/16	M	Wawa	ONT	Donald L. Cox	1988	4,126
18 2/16	11 8/16	6 10/16	M	Valley County	ID	Phil Barton	1988	4,126
18 2/16	11 1/16	7 1/16	M	Sandoval County	NM	Derek A. Tierney	1988	4,126
18 2/16	11 5/16	6 13/16	M	Atikokan	ONT	Marc Headington	1988	4,126
18 2/16	11 13/16	6 5/16	M	Loon Lake	SAS	Daniel J. Robertson	1988	4,126
18 2/16	11 8/16	6 10/16	M	Whitefish Bay	ONT	Walter Skic	1989	4,126
18 2/16	11 7/16	6 11/16	M	Caviar Lake	ONT	Glen Bohl	1989	4,126
18 2/16	11 2/16	7 0/16	M	Clearwater County	ID	Dr Christopher L Allen	1989	4,126
18 2/16	11 8/16	6 10/16	M	Bernalillo County	NM	Joseph Strasser, Jr.	1989	4,126
18 2/16	11 8/16	6 10/16	M	King County	WA	Kenneth Bean	1989	4,126
18 2/16	11 12/16	6 6/16	M	Valley County	ID	Larry Hoff	1989	4,126
18 2/16	11 10/16	6 8/16	M	Lincoln County	WI	William J. Niehaus	1989	4,126
18 2/16	11 6/16	6 12/16	M	San Miguel County	NM	Dick McClain	1989	4,126
18 2/16	11 6/16	6 12/16	M	Lane County	OR	Jay P. Marcott	1989	4,126
18 2/16	11 8/16	6 10/16	M	Longlac	ONT	Steven R. Anderson	1990	4,126

BLACK BEAR

Minimum Score 18 — Continued

SCORE	GREATEST LENGTH	GREATEST WIDTH	SEX	AREA	STATE/PROVINCE	HUNTER'S NAME	DATE	RANK
18 2/16	11 2/16	7 0/16	M	Dryden	ONT	Robert J. Crane	1990	4,126
18 2/16	11 8/16	6 10/16	M	Cumberland House	SAS	Denny Raper	1990	4,126
18 2/16	11 2/16	7 0/16	M	Lake Ascension	QUE	Michael Stone	1990	4,126
18 2/16	11 4/16	6 14/16	M	Folette	ONT	Richard A. Bugher	1990	4,126
18 2/16	11 2/16	7 0/16	M	Zec Restigo	QUE	Michael P. Murphy	1990	4,126
18 2/16	11 8/16	6 10/16	M	Stevens County	WA	Allen J. Thrush	1990	4,126
18 2/16	11 15/16	6 3/16	M	Polk County	AR	Don Cost	1990	4,126
18 2/16	11 2/16	7 0/16	M	Lake Kipawa	QUE	Billy Feltman	1991	4,126
18 2/16	11 8/16	6 10/16	M	Holinshead Lake	ONT	Linda Turek	1991	4,126
18 2/16	11 8/16	6 10/16	M	Lebel Township	ONT	Mike Hartling	1991	4,126
18 2/16	11 2/16	7 0/16	M	Aroostook County	ME	Charles Stulz	1991	4,126
18 2/16	11 4/16	6 14/16	M	Gift Lake	ALB	Ronald C. Putzler	1992	4,126
18 2/16	11 8/16	6 10/16	M	Winefred Lake	ALB	Billy Tillotson	1992	4,126
18 2/16	11 11/16	6 7/16	M	Grand County	CO	Barry J. Smith	1992	4,126
18 2/16	11 9/16	6 9/16	M	Tyson's Lake	ONT	Gary L. Seabright	1992	4,126
18 2/16	11 9/16	6 9/16	M	Savant Lake	ONT	Jerry G. Marchant	1992	4,126
18 2/16	11 10/16	6 8/16	M	Spiritwood	SAS	Nick A. Mathews	1992	4,126
18 2/16	11 6/16	6 12/16	M	Margo Lake	ONT	Dean V. Ashton	1992	4,126
18 2/16	11 12/16	6 6/16	M	Huerfano County	CO	Ronny Stephens	1992	4,126
18 2/16	11 8/16	6 10/16	M	Archuleta County	CO	Kevin J. Fuksa	1992	4,126
18 2/16	11 7/16	6 11/16	M	Porcupine Mtns.	MAN	John Paul Schaffer	1992	4,126
18 2/16	11 4/16	6 14/16	M	Jogues	ONT	Robert J. Rinderknecht	1992	4,126
18 2/16	11 10/16	6 8/16	F	Aaron	SAS	Troy Cooper	1993	4,126
18 2/16	11 2/16	7 0/16	M	La Ronge	SAS	James Hummel	1993	4,126
18 2/16	11 8/16	6 10/16	M	Monds Township	ONT	Tim Standafer	1993	4,126
18 2/16	11 7/16	6 11/16	M	Porcupine Plain	SAS	Ross D. Meyer	1993	4,126
18 2/16	11 9/16	6 9/16	M	Candle Lake	SAS	Larry Kerschner	1993	4,126
18 2/16	11 4/16	6 14/16	M	Clearwater County	ID	Loy Dean Peters	1993	4,126
18 2/16	11 6/16	6 12/16	M	Sioux Lookout	ONT	Gary R. Shields	1993	4,126
18 2/16	11 12/16	6 6/16	M	Swan River	MAN	Robert Burdick	1993	4,126
18 2/16	11 4/16	6 14/16	M	Vermillion Bay	ONT	Dennis W. Tabor	1993	4,126
18 2/16	11 2/16	7 0/16	M	Sussex	NBW	Rene Arsenault	1993	4,126
18 2/16	11 9/16	6 9/16	M	Ile-a-la Crosse	SAS	Dennis M. Filipiak	1993	4,126
18 2/16	11 7/16	6 11/16	M	Zec Restigo	QUE	Frank J. Martin	1993	4,126
18 2/16	11 9/16	6 9/16	M	Iron County	WI	Ron Macak	1993	4,126
18 2/16	11 9/16	6 9/16	M	Sawyer County	WI	Dale A. Williquette	1993	4,126
18 2/16	11 12/16	6 6/16	M	Bayfield County	WI	Todd W. Henck	1993	4,126
18 2/16	11 8/16	6 10/16	M	Chisholm	ALB	Rob Kubicek	1994	4,126
18 2/16	11 10/16	6 8/16	M	Rocky Mountain House	ALB	Darrell Peters	1994	4,126
18 2/16	11 7/16	6 11/16	M	Canoe Lake	SAS	Stephen S. King	1994	4,126
18 2/16	11 4/16	6 14/16	M	Fort McMurray	ALB	Robert L. Stansfield	1994	4,126
18 2/16	11 14/16	6 4/16	M	Manitouwadge	ONT	Daniel Hoogerhyde	1994	4,126
18 2/16	11 8/16	6 10/16	M	Barclay	ONT	Thomas B. Reinke	1994	4,126
18 2/16	11 10/16	6 8/16	M	Lac Seul	ONT	Manfred Gehrlein	1994	4,126
18 2/16	11 9/16	6 9/16	M	Sheridan County	WY	Lyle R. Prell	1994	4,126
18 2/16	11 8/16	6 10/16	M	Fort Coulonge	QUE	Terry Lee Summey	1994	4,126
18 2/16	11 2/16	7 0/16	M	Washington County	ME	Dennis De Marco	1994	4,126
18 2/16	11 9/16	6 9/16	M	Harney County	OR	Brian K. Arndt	1994	4,126
18 2/16	11 10/16	6 8/16	M	Marathon County	WI	James D. Churchill	1994	4,126
18 2/16	11 0/16	7 2/16	M	Somerset County	ME	David W. Stanley	1994	4,126
18 2/16	11 10/16	6 8/16	M	Caramat	ONT	Daniel E. Tyburski	1995	4,126
18 2/16	11 6/16	6 12/16	M	Nobel	ONT	Peter N. Synyard	1995	4,126
18 2/16	11 2/16	7 0/16	M	Ear Falls	ONT	Thomas R. Walters	1995	4,126
18 2/16	11 5/16	6 13/16	M	Foleyet	ONT	Dennis R. Eynon	1995	4,126
18 2/16	11 12/16	6 6/16	M	Duck Mtns.	MAN	Sam Y. Perone	1995	4,126
18 2/16	11 5/16	6 13/16	M	Cowlitz County	WA	David H. Soyars	1995	4,126
18 2/16	11 6/16	6 12/16	M	Lake of the Woods	ONT	Bradley Hering	1995	4,126
18 2/16	11 12/16	6 6/16	M	Tehama County	CA	Doug Burgard	1995	4,126
18 2/16	11 7/16	6 11/16	M	Tehama County	CA	Scott Vick	1995	4,126
18 2/16	11 12/16	6 6/16	M	Garnier Lake	ALB	Vernon Goad	1996	4,126
18 2/16	11 9/16	6 9/16	M	Byne Township	ONT	Gerald F. Maas	1996	4,126
18 2/16	11 4/16	6 14/16	M	Rainbow Lake	ALB	Lorenzo Dow Utterback	1996	4,126
18 2/16	11 6/16	6 12/16	M	St. Louis County	MN	Michael Loesch	1996	4,126
18 2/16	11 4/16	6 14/16	M	Red Earth	ALB	Kevin Lamb	1997	4,126
18 2/16	11 6/16	6 12/16	M	Ft. McMurray	ALB	Jeffrey L. Thacker	1997	4,126
18 2/16	11 7/16	6 11/16	M	Rossburn	MAN	Barry Minshull	1997	4,126
18 2/16	10 15/16	7 3/16	M	Terrace Bay	ONT	Jim Peterleus	1997	4,126
18 2/16	11 7/16	6 11/16	M	Domaine Preissac	QUE	Joe Jackson	1997	4,126
18 2/16	11 5/16	6 13/16	M	Navajo County	AZ	Douglas McEvers	1997	4,126
18 2/16	11 5/16	6 13/16	M	Franklin County	MA	Vincent Paniczko	1997	4,126
18 2/16	10 14/16	7 4/16	M	Cheboygan County	MI	Joe A. La Haie	1997	4,126
18 2/16	11 11/16	6 7/16	M	Bayfield County	WI	Michael K. Paulcheck	1997	4,126
18 2/16	11 8/16	6 10/16	M	Sioux Lookout	ONT	John Shields	1998	4,126
18 2/16	11 8/16	6 10/16	M	Ray River	ALB	Tom Chadwick	1998	4,126
18 1/16	11 8/16	6 9/16	M	Chelan County	WA	Dick Smethvrst	1965	4,287
18 1/16	11 4/16	6 13/16	M	Clearwater County	ID	Jess Stinichcome	1965	4,287
18 1/16	11 0/16	7 1/16	M	Somerset County	ME	Raymond Benedetto	1970	4,287
18 1/16	11 7/16	6 10/16	M	Archuleta County	CO	A. H. Gutierrez, Jr.	1971	4,287

BLACK BEAR

Minimum Score 18 — Continued

SCORE	GREATEST LENGTH	GREATEST WIDTH	SEX	AREA	STATE/ PROVINCE	HUNTER'S NAME	DATE	RANK
18 1/16	11 7/16	6 10/16	M	Franklin County	ME	Walter Krom	1972	4,287
18 1/16	11 3/16	6 14/16	M	Blackwater River	BC	Ron McKay	1974	4,287
18 1/16	10 15/16	7 2/16	M	Chapleau	ONT	Kevin E. Murphy	1975	4,287
18 1/16	11 3/16	6 14/16	M	Delta County	MI	Rick Moudry	1975	4,287
18 1/16	11 12/16	6 5/16	M	Itasca County	MN	Chuck Schultz	1976	4,287
18 1/16	11 4/16	6 13/16	M	Franklin County	ME	Bernard Caruso	1977	4,287
18 1/16	11 1/16	7 0/16	M	Saguache County	CO	Robert Faris II	1977	4,287
18 1/16	11 8/16	6 9/16	M	Kalkaska County	MI	Jerome H. Lubbers	1978	4,287
18 1/16	11 3/16	6 14/16	M	Fremont County	CO	Robert Andrew	1978	4,287
18 1/16	11 9/16	6 8/16	M	Cooper Landing	AK	Richard A. Hoag	1979	4,287
18 1/16	11 6/16	6 11/16	M	Clearwater County	ID	George P. Mann	1980	4,287
18 1/16	11 0/16	7 1/16	M	Oxford County	ME	Michael Matoushek	1980	4,287
18 1/16	11 10/16	6 7/16	M	Kenora	ONT	Ervin Wagner	1980	4,287
18 1/16	11 8/16	6 9/16	M	Iron County	MI	George Hronkin III	1981	4,287
18 1/16	11 9/16	6 8/16	M	Dryden	ONT	Anne M. Fancher	1982	4,287
18 1/16	11 5/16	6 12/16	M	Idaho County	ID	Brad L. Johnson	1982	4,287
18 1/16	11 9/16	6 8/16	M	Archuleta County	CO	Stephen E. Kennedy	1982	4,287
18 1/16	11 8/16	6 9/16	M	Mineral County	MT	Greg L. Munther	1982	4,287
18 1/16	11 8/16	6 9/16	M	Dwight	ONT	Michael D. Moore	1983	4,287
18 1/16	10 10/16	7 7/16	M	Fort Coulonge	QUE	Curtis A. Peterman	1983	4,287
18 1/16	11 5/16	6 12/16	M	Park County	CO	Dan Tekavec	1983	4,287
18 1/16	11 2/16	6 15/16	M	Colfax County	NM	Dean Oatman	1983	4,287
18 1/16	11 10/16	6 7/16	M	Ignace	ONT	Kenneth C. Kaufmann	1984	4,287
18 1/16	11 13/16	6 4/16	M	Price County	WI	Tom Gouger	1984	4,287
18 1/16	11 5/16	6 12/16	M	Clackamas County	OR	Bob Smitherman	1984	4,287
18 1/16	11 8/16	6 9/10	M	Marinette County	WI	James L. Behn	1984	4,287
18 1/16	11 3/16	6 14/16	M	Ashland County	WI	Tony D. Snow	1984	4,287
18 1/16	11 9/16	6 8/16	M	McBride Lake	SAS	John Rook	1985	4,287
18 1/16	11 3/16	6 14/16	M	Clearwater County	ID	Gene Kiele	1985	4,287
18 1/16	11 11/16	6 6/16	M	Nass River	BC	John Jones	1985	4,287
18 1/16	11 9/16	6 8/16	M	King County	WA	Greg Winters	1985	4,287
18 1/16	11 6/16	6 11/16	M	Payette County	ID	Gary Kinney	1986	4,287
18 1/16	11 6/16	6 11/16	M	Lemhi County	ID	Anthony S. Winterer	1986	4,287
18 1/16	11 5/16	6 12/16	M	Bird River	MAN	Dale Selby	1986	4,287
18 1/16	11 2/16	6 15/16	M	Lemhi County	ID	Cathy Lee Jordan	1986	4,287
18 1/16	11 5/16	6 12/16	M	Josephine County	OR	Terry Garbacik	1986	4,287
18 1/16	11 9/16	6 8/16	M	Becker County	MN	Richard Enger	1986	4,287
18 1/16	11 9/16	6 8/16	M	Wallowa County	OR	Michael Crawford	1986	4,287
18 1/16	11 11/16	6 6/16	M	Delta County	CO	Jon P. Thomas	1986	4,287
18 1/16	10 13/16	7 4/16	M	Pitkin County	CO	T. Michael Casey	1987	4,287
18 1/16	11 6/16	6 11/16	M	Natal Twp.	ONT	Terry D. Colescott	1988	4,287
18 1/16	11 6/16	6 11/16	M	Maganasipi Lake	QUE	Gerard Mascellino	1988	4,287
18 1/16	11 3/16	6 14/16	M	Timmins	ONT	Allen G. Hughes	1988	4,287
18 1/16	11 4/16	6 13/16	M	Idaho County	ID	John Zawaski	1988	4,287
18 1/16	11 9/16	6 8/16	M	Lemhi County	ID	Tim Kanapeckas	1988	4,287
18 1/16	11 12/16	6 5/16	M	Houghton County	MI	John Knieper	1988	4,287
18 1/16	11 7/16	6 10/16	M	Skamania County	WA	Annette Crews	1988	4,287
18 1/16	11 11/16	6 6/16	M	Huerfano County	CO	Jim Witcombe	1989	4,287
18 1/16	11 11/16	6 6/16	M	Mayerthorpe	ALB	Rudy Wilkison	1989	4,287
18 1/16	11 7/16	6 10/16	M	Ignace	ONT	Gordan A. Etris	1989	4,287
18 1/16	11 7/16	6 10/16	M	Ear Falls	ONT	Larry Sparks	1989	4,287
18 1/16	11 8/16	6 9/16	M	Terrace Bay	ONT	Troy D. Huffman	1989	4,287
18 1/16	11 1/16	7 0/16	M	Idaho County	ID	Monty Moravec	1989	4,287
18 1/16	11 4/16	6 13/16	M	Rapides des Joachims	QUE	Pete Karels	1989	4,287
18 1/16	11 8/16	6 9/16	M	McKerrow	ONT	Terry Walton	1989	4,287
18 1/16	11 1/16	7 0/16	M	Dorion	ONT	Larry Paulsen	1989	4,287
18 1/16	11 0/16	7 1/16	M	Custer County	ID	Patrick Patterson	1989	4,287
18 1/16	11 3/16	6 14/16	M	Zec Dumoine	QUE	Richard E. Lockwood, Sr.	1989	4,287
18 1/16	11 3/16	6 14/16	M	Lewis & Clark County	MT	Ronald Parker	1989	4,287
18 1/16	11 9/16	6 8/16	M	Houston	BC	Michael Whited	1990	4,287
18 1/16	11 3/16	6 14/16	M	Apisko Lake	MAN	Jerry Stroot	1990	4,287
18 1/16	11 5/16	6 12/16	M	Ear Falls	ONT	Mark Zink	1990	4,287
18 1/16	11 7/16	6 10/16	M	Nipigon	ONT	Fred W. Achilles	1990	4,287
18 1/16	11 8/16	6 9/16	M	Green Lake	SAS	William Smith	1990	4,287
18 1/16	11 7/16	6 10/16	M	Huerfano County	CO	Robert L. Beckwith	1990	4,287
18 1/16	11 9/16	6 8/16	M	Lake of the Woods	ONT	Scott J. Simons	1991	4,287
18 1/16	11 9/16	6 8/16	M	Geraldton	ONT	Clark M. Vickers	1991	4,287
18 1/16	11 1/16	7 0/16	M	Pacific County	WA	Brandy Knight	1991	4,287
18 1/16	11 8/16	6 9/16	M	Riding Mtn.	MAN	Ryan J. Dorak	1991	4,287
18 1/16	11 6/16	6 11/16	M	Kelvington	SAS	Ross Meyer	1992	4,287
18 1/16	11 10/16	6 7/16	M	Poplarfield	MAN	Dan Dietrich	1992	4,287
18 1/16	11 9/16	6 8/16	M	Kelvington	SAS	Robert C. McCardell	1992	4,287
18 1/16	11 3/16	6 14/16	M	Hornepayne	ONT	David M. Lakich	1992	4,287
18 1/16	11 11/16	6 6/16	M	Buffalo Narrows	SAS	Dan Phenix	1992	4,287
18 1/16	11 8/16	6 9/16	M	Dalton Highway	AK	Thomas Chadwick	1992	4,287
18 1/16	11 5/16	6 12/16	M	Atikokan	ONT	Ron Smith	1992	4,287
18 1/16	11 2/16	6 15/16	M	Whatcom County	WA	Marc Walker	1992	4,287
18 1/16	11 12/16	6 5/16	M	Baraga County	MI	Roger Crosthwaite	1992	4,287

BLACK BEAR

Minimum Score 18 — Continued

SCORE	GREATEST LENGTH	GREATEST WIDTH	SEX	AREA	STATE/PROVINCE	HUNTER'S NAME	DATE	RANK
18 1/16	11 11/16	6 6/16	M	Pine County	MN	Greg Gulden	1992	4,287
18 1/16	11 7/16	6 10/16	M	Sawyer County	WI	Jeff Priest	1992	4,287
18 1/16	11 6/16	6 11/16	M	DeBolt	ALB	Jim Hillstead	1993	4,287
18 1/16	11 11/16	6 6/16	F	Apache County	AZ	Gregory A. Nixon	1993	4,287
18 1/16	11 8/16	6 9/16	M	Thaddeus Lake	ONT	Mel Gilbertson	1993	4,287
18 1/16	11 2/16	6 15/16	M	Whitefish Lake	ONT	John Matteson	1993	4,287
18 1/16	11 7/16	6 10/16	M	Meadow Lake	SAS	Jim Richards	1993	4,287
18 1/16	11 3/16	6 14/16	M	Bathurst	NBW	William LaHue	1993	4,287
18 1/16	11 5/16	6 12/16	M	Aroostook County	ME	Joe Layton	1993	4,287
18 1/16	11 4/16	6 13/16	M	Grant County	OR	Mike Slinkard	1993	4,287
18 1/16	11 1/16	7 0/16	F	Duck Mtns.	SAS	Kurt Heffel	1993	4,287
18 1/16	11 9/16	6 8/16	M	Candle Lake	SAS	Larry D. Kerschner	1994	4,287
18 1/16	11 1/16	7 0/16	M	Radisson	ONT	Rodney Carpenter	1994	4,287
18 1/16	11 4/16	6 13/16	M	Woodlands	MAN	Angelo Novelli	1994	4,287
18 1/16	11 8/16	6 9/16	M	Wabigoon	ONT	Charles Drerup	1994	4,287
18 1/16	11 8/16	6 9/16	M	Marathon County	WI	Jesse J. Arndt	1994	4,287
18 1/16	11 13/16	6 4/16	M	Catron County	NM	Brad Miller	1994	4,287
18 1/16	11 6/16	6 11/16	M	Halifax County	NS	Richard D. Russell	1994	4,287
18 1/16	11 12/16	6 5/16	M	Polk County	AR	Don Cost	1994	4,287
18 1/16	11 9/16	6 8/16	M	Poplarfield	MAN	Keith Boesel	1995	4,287
18 1/16	11 6/16	6 11/16	M	Dryden	ONT	Jerry Carr	1995	4,287
18 1/16	11 5/16	6 12/16	M	Copperfield	ONT	Thomas Lane	1995	4,287
18 1/16	11 12/16	6 5/16	M	Besnard Lake	SAS	Stephen McCarty	1995	4,287
18 1/16	11 8/16	6 9/16	M	San Juan County	UT	Gary A. Clum	1995	4,287
18 1/16	11 9/16	6 8/16	M	Sandilands	MAN	Lynn Plett	1995	4,287
18 1/16	11 0/16	7 1/16	F	Rio Arriba County	NM	Michael K. Fuller	1996	4,287
18 1/16	11 4/16	6 13/16	M	Juniper	NBW	Joseph Bartlette	1996	4,287
18 1/16	11 4/16	6 13/16	M	Searchmont	ONT	Michael J. Windemuller	1996	4,287
18 1/16	11 7/16	6 10/16	M	Piscataquis County	ME	James E. Favreau	1996	4,287
18 1/16	11 15/16	6 2/16	M	Polk County	WI	Craig Hedke	1996	4,287
18 1/16	11 9/16	6 8/16	M	Langlade County	WI	Joel Taylor	1996	4,287
18 1/16	11 10/16	6 7/16	M	Pacific County	WA	Dan Heasley	1996	4,287
18 1/16	11 13/16	6 4/16	M	Tuolumne County	CA	Ron Jarvis	1996	4,287
18 1/16	11 9/16	6 8/16	M	Carrot River	SAS	Chuck Riggenbach	1997	4,287
18 1/16	11 9/16	6 8/16	M	Hudson Bay	SAS	Max E. Hatfield	1997	4,287
18 1/16	11 4/16	6 13/16	M	Domaine Preissac	QUE	Clark M. Vickers	1997	4,287
18 1/16	11 3/16	6 14/16	M	Elk Lake	ONT	Chuck J. Chirrup, Jr.	1998	4,287
18 1/16	11 10/16	6 7/16	M	Sturgeon Landing	SAS	Nathaniel Schroeder	1998	4,287
18 1/16	11 5/16	6 12/16	M	Sioux Lookout	ONT	Allen E. Borgeson	1998	4,287
18 1/16	11 10/16	6 7/16	M	Threemile Creek	AK	Doug Ferry	1998	4,287
18 1/16	11 6/16	6 11/16	F	Sandilands	MAN	Shelley A. Mehling	1998	4,287
18 0/16	11 0/16	7 0/16	M	Polk County	OR	H. Dale Overholser	1959	4,410
18 0/16	11 9/16	6 7/16	M	Prince William Sound	AK	Bob Snelson	1962	4,410
18 0/16	11 12/16	6 4/16	M	Franklin County	ME	John Iannuzzo	1966	4,410
18 0/16	11 6/16	6 10/16	M	Jackson County	OR	Pat Mastan	1970	4,410
18 0/16	11 2/16	6 14/16	M	Franklin County	ME	Donald R. Pyne	1970	4,410
18 0/16	11 0/16	7 0/16	M	Franklin County	ME	John Fedor	1973	4,410
18 0/16	11 8/16	6 8/16	M	Igitna River	AK	George Faerber	1974	4,410
18 0/16	11 4/16	6 12/16	M		ONT	Larry Kuskie	1974	4,410
18 0/16	11 10/16	6 6/16	M	Franklin County	ME	Michael P. Murphy	1974	4,410
18 0/16	11 6/16	6 10/16	F	Taylor County	WI	Christopher A. Jeffords	1976	4,410
18 0/16	11 9/16	6 7/16	M	Marathon County	WI	Jay Schultz	1977	4,410
18 0/16	11 12/16	6 4/16	M	Boise County	ID	Clae Kress	1978	4,410
18 0/16	11 6/16	6 10/16	M	Franklin County	ME	James E. Roy	1978	4,410
18 0/16	11 8/16	6 8/16	F	Hubbard County	MN	George Arimond	1979	4,410
18 0/16	11 6/16	6 10/16	M	Siskiyou County	CA	John Grochowski, Jr.	1979	4,410
18 0/16	11 10/16	6 6/16	M	Bonneville County	ID	Paul M. Kniss	1980	4,410
18 0/16	11 1/16	6 15/16	M	Somerset County	ME	Albert Buonanno	1980	4,410
18 0/16	11 3/16	6 13/16	M	Almonte	ONT	Stephen Van Zile	1981	4,410
18 0/16	11 8/16	6 8/16	M	Red Lake	ONT	Bernie Pawlaser	1981	4,410
18 0/16	11 5/16	6 11/16	M	St. Lawrence County	NY	Richard Hurteau	1981	4,410
18 0/16	11 4/16	6 12/16	M	Custer County	CO	Leonard Moore	1981	4,410
18 0/16	11 7/16	6 9/16	M	Thunder Bay	ONT	Rob J. Smith	1981	4,410
18 0/16	11 8/16	6 8/16	M	Hatcher Pass	AK	Roger Stewart	1981	4,410
18 0/16	11 6/16	6 10/16	M	Susitna River	AK	Roger G. Stewart	1984	4,410
18 0/16	11 7/16	6 9/16	M	Archuleta County	CO	Roy S. Marlow III	1984	4,410
18 0/16	11 10/16	6 6/16	M	Little Susitna River	AK	Gary G. Wall	1984	4,410
18 0/16	11 5/16	6 11/16	M	Beluga Mtn.	AK	Dick Carlson	1984	4,410
18 0/16	11 6/16	6 10/16	M	Sublette County	WY	Randy Erye	1984	4,410
18 0/16	11 6/16	6 10/16	M	Messines	QUE	Howard 'Butch' Malone	1984	4,410
18 0/16	11 1/16	6 15/16	M	North Bay	ONT	John R. Rexroad	1984	4,410
18 0/16	11 2/16	6 14/16	M	Kechika Range	BC	Wade L. Carstens	1984	4,410
18 0/16	11 7/16	6 9/16	M	Iron County	WI	Floyd J. Vancil	1984	4,410
18 0/16	11 7/16	6 9/16	M	Gilpin County	CO	Bryon Scott Johnson	1985	4,410
18 0/16	11 3/16	6 13/16	M	Anchorage	AK	Ronald D. Mills	1985	4,410
18 0/16	11 5/16	6 11/16	M	Idaho County	ID	Ed Vallee	1985	4,410
18 0/16	11 9/16	6 7/16	M	Clearwater County	MN	Kyle Bauman	1985	4,410
18 0/16	11 7/16	6 9/16	M	Wayne County	PA	Mike B. Lamade	1985	4,410

BLACK BEAR

Minimum Score 18 — Continued

SCORE	GREATEST LENGTH	GREATEST WIDTH	SEX	AREA	STATE/PROVINCE	HUNTER'S NAME	DATE	RANK
18 0/16	11 10/16	6 6/16	M	Brandon	MAN	Gary Kaluzniak	1986	4,410
18 0/16	11 6/16	6 10/16	M	Pasguia Hills	SAS	Marcus Vogel	1986	4,410
18 0/16	11 1/16	6 15/16	M	Missoula County	MT	John L. Wozniak	1986	4,410
18 0/16	11 6/16	6 10/16	F	Rouyn-Noranda	QUE	Roy Cucuzza	1986	4,410
18 0/16	11 8/16	6 8/16	F	Duck Mtn.	MAN	Marty Stubstad	1986	4,410
18 0/16	11 5/16	6 11/16	M	Idaho County	ID	Jay J. Bowman	1986	4,410
18 0/16	11 8/16	6 8/16	M	Durban	MAN	Jerry V. Finley	1986	4,410
18 0/16	11 5/16	6 11/16	M	Oxford County	ME	Christopher Scott Harriman	1986	4,410
18 0/16	11 7/16	6 9/16	M	Cook County	MN	Richard P. Smith	1986	4,410
18 0/16	11 9/16	6 7/16	M	Dryden	ONT	Jeff Duhrkopf	1986	4,410
18 0/16	11 4/16	6 12/16	M	Clearwater County	ID	Christopher B. Holmes	1987	4,410
18 0/16	11 8/16	6 8/16	M	Vermillion Bay	ONT	Jerry Podratz	1987	4,410
18 0/16	11 5/16	6 11/16	M	Dryden	ONT	Kevin Smaby	1987	4,410
18 0/16	11 10/16	6 6/16	M	Capreol	ONT	Tony Willwerth	1987	4,410
18 0/16	11 8/16	6 8/16	M	Cowlitz County	WA	David Soyars	1987	4,410
18 0/16	11 4/16	6 12/16	M	Muldrew Township	ONT	Daniel P. Wieske	1987	4,410
18 0/16	11 11/16	6 5/16	M	Crow Wing County	MN	Ron Snyder	1987	4,410
18 0/16	11 5/16	6 11/16	M	Conejos County	CO	Joseph E. Marrinan, Jr.	1988	4,410
18 0/16	11 0/16	7 0/16	M	Dorion	ONT	Larry D. Paulsen	1988	4,410
18 0/16	11 12/16	6 4/16	M	Talkeetna	AK	Beverly Hajenga	1988	4,410
18 0/16	11 4/16	6 12/16	M	Fort Coulonge	QUE	Terry Lee Summey	1988	4,410
18 0/16	11 9/16	6 7/16	M	Susitna River	AK	Tom Orbison	1988	4,410
18 0/16	11 6/16	6 10/16	M	Valley County	ID	Julie E. Johnston	1988	4,410
18 0/16	10 14/16	7 2/16	M	Atikokan	ONT	Matthew Andersen	1988	4,410
18 0/16	11 11/16	6 5/16	M	Athabasca River	ALB	Grant Adkisson	1989	4,410
18 0/16	11 4/16	6 12/16	M	Algoma	ONT	Denis Belcourt	1989	4,410
18 0/16	11 6/16	6 10/16	M	Sexsmith	ALB	Ted Brown	1989	4,410
18 0/16	11 9/16	6 7/16	M	Dryden	ONT	Albert J. Smith	1989	4,410
18 0/16	11 6/16	6 10/16	M	Lac Nilgaut	QUE	John S. Ashe	1989	4,410
18 0/16	11 8/16	6 8/16	M	Flotten Lake	SAS	Paul Prochaska	1989	4,410
18 0/16	11 2/16	6 14/16	M	Rollet	QUE	Douglas E. Ott	1989	4,410
18 0/16	11 9/16	6 7/16	M	Zec Restigo	QUE	David Dibblee	1989	4,410
18 0/16	11 4/16	6 12/16	M	Beurling River	QUE	Philippe Galley	1989	4,410
18 0/16	11 7/16	6 9/16	M	Saddle Hills	ALB	Dr. Michael D. Pickering, O.D.	1990	4,410
18 0/16	11 4/16	6 12/16	M	Cranberry Portage	MAN	Bob Beardsley	1990	4,410
18 0/16	11 5/16	6 11/16	M	Sturgeon Landing	SAS	Kay Lang	1990	4,410
18 0/16	11 6/16	6 10/16	M	Red Lake	ONT	Fred Sprague	1990	4,410
18 0/16	11 4/16	6 12/16	M	Echo Bay	ONT	Ralph W. Fairbanks	1990	4,410
18 0/16	11 10/16	6 6/16	M	Latuque	QUE	Ronald T. Kinnas	1990	4,410
18 0/16	11 12/16	6 4/16	M	Lake County	MN	John Koschmeder	1990	4,410
18 0/16	11 6/16	6 10/16	M	Delta County	MI	Rob Horwitz	1990	4,410
18 0/16	11 6/16	6 10/16	M	Caldwell County	NC	Teddy Adams	1990	4,410
18 0/16	11 9/16	6 7/16	M	The Pas	MAN	George G. Wilson, Jr.	1991	4,410
18 0/16	11 10/16	6 6/16	M	Biscotasing	ONT	Everett W. Ayers	1991	4,410
18 0/16	11 8/16	6 8/16	M	Minitonas	MAN	Mark C. Dale	1991	4,410
18 0/16	11 2/16	6 14/16	M	Norman Wells	NWT	Lyndon Walker	1991	4,410
18 0/16	11 11/16	6 5/16	M	Gunnison County	CO	Robert Kuntz	1991	4,410
18 0/16	11 10/16	6 6/16	M	Tobin Lake	SAS	Kirk Winters	1991	4,410
18 0/16	11 1/16	6 15/16	M	Chippewa County	WI	Larry Paulsen	1991	4,410
18 0/16	11 5/16	6 11/16	M	Ravalli County	MT	David H. Stalling	1991	4,410
18 0/16	11 9/16	6 7/16	M	Mesa County	CO	Steven R. Hickok	1992	4,410
18 0/16	11 5/16	6 11/16	M	Lake Caviar	ONT	Roger E. Wendorf	1992	4,410
18 0/16	11 9/16	6 7/16	M	Lincoln County	WY	Jim Fowler	1992	4,410
18 0/16	11 0/16	7 0/16	M	Idaho County	ID	T. J. Conrads	1992	4,410
18 0/16	10 14/16	7 2/16	M	Widdifield Township	ONT	Cliff O'Donnell	1992	4,410
18 0/16	11 6/16	6 10/16	M	Dryden	ONT	Ollie Crow	1992	4,410
18 0/16	11 8/16	6 8/16	M	La Plata County	CO	Dennis L. Howell	1992	4,410
18 0/16	11 8/16	6 8/16	M	Swan River	MAN	Mark Barbee	1993	4,410
18 0/16	11 6/16	6 10/16	M	Mariana Lakes	ALB	Ryk Visscher	1993	4,410
18 0/16	11 14/16	6 2/16	M	Pine River	MAN	Jim Snyder	1993	4,410
18 0/16	11 3/16	6 13/16	M	Caramat	ONT	Donald J. Stratton	1993	4,410
18 0/16	11 3/16	6 13/16	M	Savant Lake	ONT	Brian Kent Foltz	1993	4,410
18 0/16	11 7/16	6 9/16	M	Baraga County	MI	Dean A. Pode	1993	4,410
18 0/16	11 4/16	6 12/16	M	Mackinac County	MI	David M. Cole	1993	4,410
18 0/16	11 7/16	6 9/16	M	Athabasca River	ALB	Witt Stephens	1994	4,410
18 0/16	11 11/16	6 5/16	M	Ile-a-la Crosse	SAS	Michael Turner	1994	4,410
18 0/16	11 5/16	6 11/16	M	Clearwater County	ID	Cory Schmid	1994	4,410
18 0/16	11 6/16	6 10/16	M	Marathon	ONT	Dennis S. Kelly	1994	4,410
18 0/16	11 8/16	6 8/16	M	Aitkin County	MN	Jason Bruestle	1994	4,410
18 0/16	11 13/16	6 3/16	M	Sawyer County	WI	William D. Baker	1994	4,410
18 0/16	11 9/16	6 7/16	M	Oconto County	WI	Gary Sigl	1994	4,410
18 0/16	11 10/16	6 6/16	M	Cass County	MN	Bill Krout	1994	4,410
18 0/16	11 7/16	6 9/16	M	Kirkland Lake	ONT	Nathan M. Lipsen	1995	4,410
18 0/16	11 5/16	6 11/16	M	Monds Township	ONT	Bob Coyle	1995	4,410
18 0/16	11 11/16	6 5/16	M	Rocky Lake	MAN	Scott D. Schmidt	1995	4,410
18 0/16	11 7/16	6 9/16	M	Prince of Wales Island	AK	Gerald L. Egbert	1995	4,410
18 0/16	11 8/16	6 8/16	M	Porcupine Hills	SAS	John Moorhouse	1995	4,410
18 0/16	11 5/16	6 11/16	M	Ignace	ONT	Perry D. Larson	1995	4,410

BLACK BEAR

Minimum Score 18 — Continued

SCORE	GREATEST LENGTH	GREATEST WIDTH	SEX	AREA	STATE/ PROVINCE	HUNTER'S NAME	DATE	RANK
18 0/16	11 5/16	6 11/16	M	Lake Wabigoon	ONT	Lowell L. Dupee	1995	4,410
18 0/16	11 3/16	6 13/16	M	Go Home Lake	ONT	Vito Palazzolo	1995	4,410
18 0/16	11 9/16	6 7/16	M	Lake Wabigoon	ONT	Gary M. Glunn	1995	4,410
18 0/16	11 6/16	6 10/16	M	La Tuque	QUE	Edward P. Bushey, Jr.	1995	4,410
18 0/16	11 3/16	6 13/16	M	Colfax County	NM	Kim Sevitts	1995	4,410
18 0/16	11 5/16	6 11/16	M	Brazeau Dam	ALB	Wayne Depperschmidt	1996	4,410
18 0/16	11 4/16	6 12/16	M	Smeaton	SAS	James M. Augustine	1996	4,410
18 0/16	11 6/16	6 10/16	M	Hearst	ONT	Jeff Phillips	1996	4,410
18 0/16	11 7/16	6 9/16	M	Dorion	ONT	Casey A. Blum	1996	4,410
18 0/16	11 13/16	6 3/16	M	High Level	ALB	Ronald R. Grenadier	1996	4,410
18 0/16	11 7/16	6 9/16	M	Hearst	ONT	Gregory D. Keeton	1996	4,410
18 0/16	11 8/16	6 8/16	M	San Juan County	UT	David B. Nielsen	1996	4,410
18 0/16	11 8/16	6 8/16	F	Apache County	AZ	Glen Johnson	1996	4,410
18 0/16	11 6/16	6 10/16	M	Rio Arriba County	NM	Blaine Underwood	1996	4,410
18 0/16	11 5/16	6 11/16	M	Douglas County	WI	Robert M. Zembo	1996	4,410
18 0/16	11 4/16	6 12/16	M	Athabasca River	ALB	Mark Calkins	1997	4,410
18 0/16	11 9/16	6 7/16	M	Candle Lake	SAS	Carl L. Biscontini	1997	4,410
18 0/16	11 7/16	6 9/16	M	Dorion	ONT	Bruce Hudalla	1997	4,410
18 0/16	11 10/16	6 6/16	M	Cranberry Portage	MAN	Richard E. Christian	1997	4,410
18 0/16	11 12/16	6 4/16	M	Ear Falls	ONT	Randy LeRoy Strong	1997	4,410
18 0/16	11 10/16	6 6/16	M	Prince Albert	SAS	Nathan Jones	1997	4,410
18 0/16	11 12/16	6 4/16	M	Valley County	ID	Larry Hoff	1997	4,410
18 0/16	11 11/16	6 5/16	M	Madera County	CA	Sandy Verlench	1997	4,410
18 0/16	11 6/16	6 10/16	M	Aroostook County	ME	Robert J. Murowsky	1997	4,410
18 0/16	11 11/16	6 5/16	M	Asotin County	WA	Gary Sciuchetti	1997	4,410
18 0/16	11 9/16	6 7/16	M	Jackson County	WI	Stewart B. Gilbertson	1997	4,410
18 0/16	11 8/16	6 8/16	M	Kitsap County	WA	Steve Simpson	1997	4,410
18 0/16	11 8/16	6 8/16	M	Hoyt	NBW	Nelson Graham	1997	4,410
18 0/16	11 8/16	6 8/16	M	Nicholas County	WV	Joseph Miller	1997	4,410
18 0/16	11 7/16	6 9/16	M	Carrot River	SAS	Joseph P. Furlong	1998	4,410
18 0/16	11 6/16	6 10/16	M	Cranberry Portage	MAN	David R. Rogers	1998	4,410
18 0/16	11 2/16	6 14/16	M	Mattice	ONT	Martin Larson	1998	4,410
18 0/16	11 6/16	6 10/16	M	Lac Kanasuta	QUE	Al Ferris	1998	4,410
18 0/16	11 4/16	6 12/16	M	Price County	WI	Matt Drossel	1998	4,410
18 0/16	11 8/16	6 8/16	M	Salt Prairie	ALB	John Tillotson	1998	4,410

LEN CLIFFORD PHOTO

World Record Grizzly Bear
Score: 25 13/16
Moose Lake, British Columbia - 1987
Hunter: Derril Lamb

(Tie)
Score 25 13/16
Gathto Creek, British Columbia - 1997
Hunter: Jim Boyer

GRIZZLY BEAR

Minimum Score 19

Ursus arctos horribilis

SCORE	GREATEST LENGTH	GREATEST WIDTH	SEX	AREA	STATE/ PROVINCE	HUNTER'S NAME	DATE	RANK
25 13/16	16 1/16	9 12/16	M	Moose Lake	BC	Derril Lamb	1987	1
25 13/16	16 0/16	9 13/16	M	Gathto Creek	BC	Jim Boyer	1997	1
25 6/16	16 0/16	9 6/16	M	Anzac River	BC	Harley Tison	1972	3
25 3/16	15 13/16	9 6/16	M	Stevens Lakes	BC	Dr. Rex Hancock	1968	4
25 2/16	16 0/16	9 2/16	M	Windy	AK	Rick D. Snell	1997	5
24 14/16	15 10/16	9 4/16	M	Yellowstone National Park	WY	Art Young	1920	6
24 13/16	15 6/16	9 7/16	M	Moose Lake	BC	Tony Di Giovanni	1993	7
24 11/16	15 2/16	9 9/16	M	Stevens Lakes	BC	Dr. R. L. Hambrick	1965	8
24 9/16	15 13/16	8 12/16	M	Bella Coola	BC	William P. Mastrangel	1956	9
24 5/16	14 13/16	9 8/16	M	Unalakleet River	AK	Thomas J. Hoffman	1993	10
24 4/16	14 10/16	9 10/16	M	Unalakleet River	AK	Stan Godfrey	1997	11
23 13/16	15 6/16	8 7/16	M	Gulkana River	AK	Art Kragness	1973	12
23 12/16	14 15/16	8 13/16	M	Kotzebue	AK	James P. Jacobson	1981	13
23 7/16	14 14/16	8 9/16	M	Kakwa River	ALB	Rick Michalski	1981	14
22 13/16	14 3/16	8 10/16	M	Kingcome Inlet	BC	Peter Halbig	1982	15
22 12/16	14 6/16	8 6/16	M	Brazeua River	ALB	Curt Lynn	1973	16
22 7/16	13 15/16	8 8/16	M	Earn Lake	YUK	Dr. R. D. Keeler	1986	17
22 1/16	14 0/16	8 1/16	M	Galena	AK	Larry Spiva	1992	18
22 1/16	13 14/16	8 3/16	M	Dalton Hwy	AK	Bruce Hakel	1996	18
21 11/16	14 2/16	7 9/16	M	Unalakleet River	AK	George P. Mann	1996	20
21 10/16	13 9/16	8 1/16	F	Council	AK	Mark Wayne Smith	1996	21
21 8/16	13 15/16	7 9/16	F	Bella Coola	BC	J. Dale Hale	1989	22
21 4/16	13 2/16	8 2/16	F	White River	YUK	Ray F. Daniels	1994	23
21 3/16	13 13/16	7 6/16	M	East Fork Jack River	AK	Rick Hayley	1997	24
21 1/16	13 3/16	7 14/16	F	Tolovana	AK	Larry Edward Townsend	1990	25
21 1/16	13 5/16	7 12/16	M	Atigun Pass	AK	J. R. Pederson	1996	25
21 0/16	13 11/16	7 5/16	M	Little Tok River	AK	Don Davidson, Jr.	1987	27
21 0/16	13 6/16	7 10/16	M	Bonnet Plume Range	YUK	Tim Good	1995	27
20 13/16	13 2/16	7 11/16	F	Chicken	AK	Larry Daly	1997	29
20 11/16	13 8/16	7 3/16	M	Knight Inlet	BC	Gary F. Bogner	1995	30

GRIZZLY BEAR

Minimum Score 19 — Continued

SCORE	GREATEST LENGTH	GREATEST WIDTH	SEX	AREA	STATE/PROVINCE	HUNTER'S NAME	DATE	RANK
20 10/16	13 3/16	7 7/16	F	Rivers Inlet	BC	Chuck Adams	1988	31
20 9/16	13 1/16	7 8/16	F	Meziadin Lake	BC	Glenn Hisey	1992	32
20 7/16	13 0/16	7 7/16	F	Kispiox	BC	Dr. Rex Hancock	1965	33
20 6/16	12 14/16	7 8/16	F	Scoop Lake	BC	Ronald Montross	1984	34
20 3/16	13 2/16	7 1/16	M	Galbraith Lake	AK	Maxallen D. Jackson	1981	35
20 1/16	13 1/16	7 0/16	M	Stevens Lakes	BC	Fred Bear	1961	36
20 1/16	12 15/16	7 2/16	F	Kakwa River	ALB	Herb Schmidt	1983	36
20 0/16	12 14/16	7 2/16	F	Yellowstone National Park	WY	Saxton T. Pope	1920	38
20 0/16	12 13/16	7 3/16	M	Ivishak River	AK	Jeff Lindeman	1988	38
19 15/16	12 11/16	7 4/16	M	Dalton Hwy.	AK	Thomas Chadwick	1984	40
19 14/16	12 8/16	7 6/16	F	Ptarmigan Creek	AK	Donald O. Smith	1964	41
19 14/16	13 0/16	6 14/16	M	Atigun Pass	AK	Alan Richey	1984	41
19 14/16	12 13/16	7 1/16	M	Caribou Mtn.	AK	Kenneth N. Liddle	1994	41
19 12/16	12 12/16	7 0/16	F	Morkill River	BC	Archie Nesbitt	1993	44
19 10/16	12 5/16	7 5/16	F	Stevens Lakes	BC	G. Fred Asbell	1969	45
19 8/16	12 8/16	7 0/16	M	Tangle Lakes	AK	John Musacchia	1972	46
19 8/16	12 10/16	6 14/16	M	Whitehorse	YUK	Scott Koelzer	1977	46
19 5/16	11 15/16	7 6/16	F	Stevens Lakes	BC	Walter Krom	1968	48
19 5/16	12 11/16	6 10/16	M	Pingston River	AK	John D. "Jack" Frost	1993	48
19 2/16	12 12/16	6 6/16	F	Nenana River	AK	Rick D. Snell	1993	50
19 0/16	12 10/16	6 6/16	M	Kispiox River	BC	Charles Kroll	1960	51
19 0/16	12 8/16	6 8/16	M	Brooks Range	AK	Ronald W. Lang, Jr.	1992	51
19 0/16	12 0/16	7 0/16	M	Logan Mtns.	YUK	Jon P. Thomas	1993	51
19 0/16	12 4/16	6 12/16	F	Sagavanirktok River	AK	Garry A. Thoms	1995	51

LEONARD LEE RUE III PHOTO

World Record Polar Bear
Score: 26 6/16
Cape Lisburne, Alaska - 1958
Hunter: Richard McIntyre

POLAR BEAR

Minimum Score 20   *Ursus maritimus*

SCORE	GREATEST LENGTH	GREATEST WIDTH	SEX	AREA	STATE/PROVINCE	HUNTER'S NAME	DATE	RANK
26 6/16	16 4/16	10 2/16	M	Cape Lisburne	AK	Richard McIntyre	1958	1
26 0/16	16 2/16	9 14/16	M	Resolute Bay	NWT	Gary F. Bogner	1989	2
25 14/16	16 3/16	9 11/16	M	Chukchi Sea	AK	Larry Jones	1965	3
25 4/16	16 3/16	9 1/16	M	Baffin Island	NWT	George P. Mann	1994	4
25 1/16	15 5/16	9 12/16	F	Baffin Island	NWT	Arthur Young	1926	5
25 0/16	15 12/16	9 4/16	M	Resolute Bay	NWT	George P. Mann	1991	6
24 15/16	15 3/16	9 12/16	M	Taloyoak	NWT	Ricardo Longoria	1998	7
24 14/16	15 11/16	9 3/16	M	Victoria Island	NWT	Archie Nesbitt	1993	8
24 4/16	15 5/16	8 15/16	F	Baffin Island	NWT	Arthur Young	1926	9
23 15/16	15 4/16	8 11/16	M	Resolute Bay	NWT	Gary F. Bogner	1989	10
23 13/16	14 13/16	8 14/16	M	Bathurst Island	NWT	Archie Nesbitt	1989	11
23 8/16	14 15/16	8 9/16	M	Gjoa Haven	NWT	Mark Connor	1998	12
23 0/16	14 12/16	8 4/16	M	Allan Island	NWT	Thomas J. Hoffman	1990	13
20 11/16	13 11/16	7 0/16	M	Agu Bay	NWT	Adrian L. Erickson	1994	14
20 10/16	13 6/16	7 4/16	M	Boothia Peninsula	NWT	Bruce R. Schoeneweis	1995	15

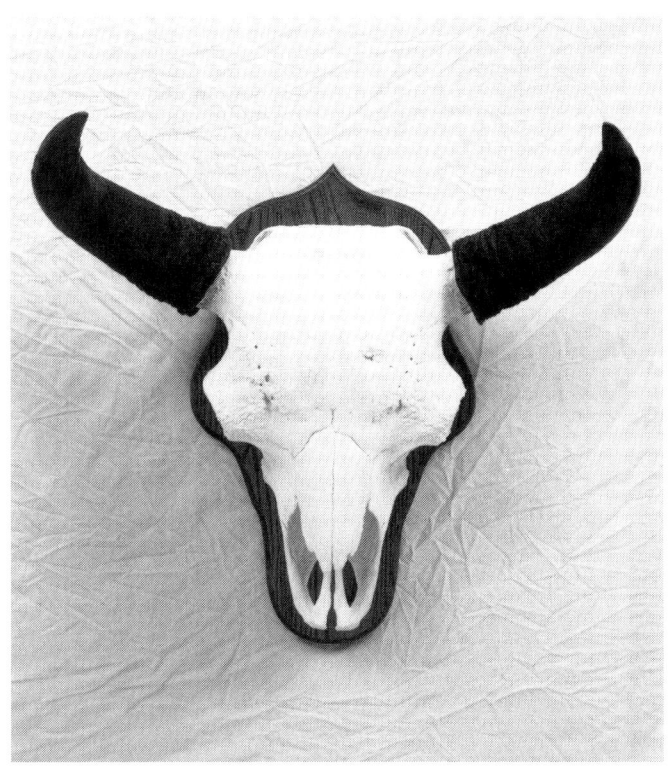

World Record Bison
Score: 115 6/8
Garfield County, Utah - 1991
Hunter: Pete Shepley

BISON

Minimum Score 100

Bison, bison, bison and Bison bison athabascae

SCORE	LENGTH OF R HORN	L	CIRCUMFERENCE R OF BASE	L	GREATEST SPREAD	AREA	STATE/ PROVINCE	HUNTER'S NAME	DATE	RANK
115 6/8	16 4/8	17 7/8	13 2/8	14 0/8	29 0/8	Garfield County	UT	Pete Shepley	1991	1
115 0/8	18 7/8	19 7/8	14 0/8	14 1/8	30 4/8	Coconino County	AZ	William B. Bedlion	1998	2
113 4/8	19 3/8	19 0/8	13 5/8	13 1/8	32 4/8	Coconino County	AZ	George Richardson	1996	3
112 2/8	18 4/8	18 0/8	14 1/8	14 1/8	29 6/8	Farewell Lake	AK	George A. Moerlein	1972	4
111 4/8	18 4/8	18 2/8	13 2/8	13 3/8	27 3/8	Wayne County	UT	Richie Bland	1996	5
111 0/8	18 0/8	17 6/8	13 3/8	13 4/8	27 2/8	Garfield County	UT	Craig Bonham	1983	6
110 6/8	19 0/8	18 7/8	12 7/8	12 6/8	27 2/8	Garfield County	UT	Jim Ryan	1989	7
110 6/8	17 4/8	17 2/8	13 5/8	13 4/8	26 4/8	Garfield County	UT	Archie J. Nesbitt	1996	7
110 4/8	16 2/8	15 2/8	14 1/8	14 1/8	26 7/8	Garfield County	UT	Paul B. Brunner	1979	9
110 2/8	14 4/8	14 5/8	13 4/8	13 4/8	23 7/8	Davis County	UT	Mike Ellena	1987	10
108 6/8	18 5/8	18 7/8	12 2/8	12 2/8	26 2/8	Garfield County	UT	Mike Poynor	1987	11
108 4/8	16 3/8	17 7/8	12 6/8	12 7/8	30 0/8	Davis County	UT	Troy M. Miller	1991	12
106 6/8	17 2/8	16 4/8	13 0/8	12 7/8	25 0/8	Garfield County	UT	Chuck Adams	1986	13
105 6/8	18 0/8	18 2/8	12 6/8	12 7/8	28 5/8	Delta Junction	AK	David Ray Western	1990	14
105 2/8	16 2/8	16 3/8	13 0/8	12 7/8	27 4/8	Delta Junction	AK	Scott Schultz	1986	15
105 0/8	17 4/8	17 4/8	12 2/8	12 3/8	23 0/8	Delta Junction	AK	Tony Russ	1992	16
104 4/8	17 2/8	17 7/8	13 1/8	12 4/8	24 4/8	Withrow Mtn.	BC	George P. Mann	1992	17
103 6/8	17 4/8	17 7/8	11 6/8	12 0/8	25 2/8	Garfield County	UT	Thomas J. Hoffman	1990	18
103 6/8	15 7/8	15 7/8	13 0/8	12 7/8	25 2/8	Garfield County	UT	Eldon Richter	1996	18
103 4/8	18 3/8	18 1/8	12 1/8	12 4/8	26 7/8	Farewell	AK	Carl E. Brent	1996	20
102 4/8	15 3/8	15 3/8	12 6/8	12 6/8	24 2/8	Garfield County	UT	Dale Drilling	1991	21
102 2/8	15 6/8	15 5/8	12 4/8	12 4/8	23 5/8	Garfield County	UT	Hugh H. Hogle	1992	22
101 4/8	16 7/8	16 6/8	12 4/8	12 4/8	25 0/8	Delta Junction	AK	John Sarvis	1991	23
100 6/8	16 1/8	16 1/8	12 1/8	12 0/8	24 1/8	Garfield County	UT	Max Park	1989	24

World Record Barren Ground Caribou
Score: 448 6/8
Lake Clark, Alaska - 1984
Hunter: Dennis Burdick

BARREN GROUND CARIBOU

Minimum Score 325

Rangifer tarandus granti, *Rangifer tarandus stonei* and *Rangifer tarandus arcticus*

SCORE	LENGTH OF MAIN BEAM R / L		INSIDE SPREAD	NUMBER OF POINTS R / L		AREA	STATE/ PROVINCE	HUNTER'S NAME	DATE	RANK
448 6/8	48 4/8	48 5/8	40 3/8	17	20	Lake Clark	AK	Dennis Burdick	1984	1
446 6/8	55 0/8	55 6/8	40 5/8	23	19	Meshik River	AK	Art Kragness	1970	2
424 4/8	50 1/8	49 7/8	45 2/8	15	13	Naknek River	AK	Jack Wood	1990	3
424 0/8	52 7/8	51 1/8	41 6/8	21	12	Delta River	AK	Bill Brown	1960	4
419 6/8	51 1/8	49 0/8	35 0/8	15	15	Pilot Point	AK	Scott Atton	1987	5
417 2/8	60 2/8	60 2/8	39 0/8	11	11	Dog Salmon River	AK	John S. Alley	1987	6
417 0/8	50 5/8	52 3/8	33 6/8	13	17	Little Delta River	AK	Fred Bear	1959	7
416 1/8	53 5/8	53 2/8	44 2/8	14	18	Kipchuk River	AK	Roy Humphires	1986	8
415 3/8	45 0/8	46 0/8	31 1/8	17	18	Ugashik River	AK	Ron Madsen	1987	9
414 6/8	48 3/8	47 1/8	39 7/8	13	12	Aleutian Range	AK	Robert Smith	1983	10
414 5/8	51 7/8	51 7/8	35 1/8	12	12	Shotgun Hills	AK	Doug Aikin	1995	11
414 3/8	62 1/8	63 6/8	51 7/8	14	10	King Salmon	AK	Larry Spiva	1983	12
412 5/8	53 3/8	54 3/8	37 3/8	15	21	Lake Iliamna	AK	Don Wells	1982	13
407 4/8	54 3/8	55 3/8	51 4/8	20	14	Lake Becharof	AK	Larry Jones	1969	14
407 4/8	57 3/8	52 6/8	29 3/8	10	15	White Fish Lake	AK	Ron Lehmann	1984	14
407 2/8	51 7/8	53 0/8	34 3/8	14	11	Squirrel River	AK	George A. Moerlein	1993	16
406 7/8	50 3/8	49 7/8	49 3/8	12	12	Salmon River	AK	Gary R. Haske	1987	17
406 4/8	52 0/8	53 2/8	36 7/8	9	7	Lake Iliamna	AK	Wright W. Allen	1993	18
406 2/8	56 5/8	58 2/8	37 3/8	11	23	Port Heiden	AK	Art Heinze	1973	19
405 3/8	47 2/8	48 3/8	38 4/8	15	14	Chanuk Creek	AK	Roger O. Wyant	1989	20
405 2/8	40 5/8	43 6/8	38 1/8	16	14	Iqiuqiq	AK	Ray Capp	1996	21
405 0/8	61 4/8	62 5/8	47 0/8	13	13	Bonanza Hills	AK	Dan Hollingsworth	1982	22
404 7/8	51 2/8	50 6/8	40 0/8	13	14	Franklin Bluffs	AK	Rickie D. Snell	1989	23
404 2/8	46 6/8	47 7/8	34 0/8	18	16	Mulchatna River	AK	Steven B Novy	1987	24
403 2/8	48 0/8	44 6/8	38 1/8	15	15	Shot Gun Creek	AK	Roger O. Wyant	1994	25
401 6/8	57 7/8	56 7/8	45 3/8	13	14	Purcell Mtn.	AK	Chris Sanford	1998	26
401 3/8	53 4/8	52 6/8	42 0/8	14	16	Glenn Highway	AK	Harv Ebers	1959	27
401 2/8	50 3/8	50 2/8	37 7/8	13	13	Lake Clark	AK	Pat Breen	1986	28
400 4/8	52 1/8	51 7/8	40 4/8	14	11	Otter Lake	AK	Jim Wondzell	1995	29
400 2/8	51 6/8	51 6/8	43 2/8	14	14	Upper Noatak River	AK	Patrick Campanella	1989	30
400 0/8	53 1/8	53 1/8	37 0/8	9	19	Lake Louise	AK	George Moerlein	1962	31
399 5/8	55 3/8	57 6/8	46 6/8	12	8	Swan River	AK	Dr. Steven G. Hammons	1992	32
399 2/8	51 2/8	51 5/8	41 6/8	15	14	Pilot Point	AK	Michael O'Brien	1996	33
399 0/8	50 5/8	51 2/8	40 2/8	16	14	Clemmons	AK	Bob Lee	1960	34
397 4/8	46 4/8	46 3/8	34 2/8	15	15	Telaquana Lake	AK	John Moline	1971	35
397 4/8	48 2/8	49 0/8	44 1/8	12	14	Muddy River	AK	Roger O. Wyant	1990	35
397 1/8	55 0/8	55 4/8	42 7/8	15	16	Ugashik River	AK	Jim McCain	1986	37
396 6/8	50 1/8	49 5/8	49 1/8	12	15	Aleutian Range	AK	Chuck Adams	1984	38
396 6/8	52 4/8	50 4/8	42 4/8	9	11	Fishtrap Lake	AK	Allen L. Dougal	1986	38
396 5/8	57 7/8	55 1/8	49 4/8	13	11	Tyone Lake	AK	James Moline	1961	40
396 5/8	50 0/8	46 6/8	40 5/8	13	16	Telaquana Lake	AK	Eldon W. Zeller	1972	40
396 2/8	55 3/8	53 0/8	33 3/8	18	19	Little Delta River	AK	Keith R. Clemmons	1958	42
395 7/8	41 7/8	44 0/8	34 6/8	15	14	Lake Clark	AK	Robert McCrum	1995	43
394 5/8	51 0/8	48 7/8	27 6/8	13	19	Susitna	AK	Ron Mason	1980	44
394 2/8	49 0/8	48 6/8	32 6/8	15	15	Big Bend	AK	Roger O. Wyant	1993	45
394 0/8	53 6/8	53 7/8	36 2/8	8	9	Port Alsworth	AK	Vince Shepherd	1989	46
392 8/8	51 3/8	55 4/8	32 6/8	13	15	Aleutian Range	AK	Chuck Adams	1983	47
391 7/8	53 6/8	50 5/8	45 6/8	11	14	Glenn Highway	AK	Joe West	1965	48
391 7/8	57 0/8	56 3/8	31 4/8	11	14	Lake Clark	AK	Jim Jarvis	1982	48
391 7/8	53 6/8	54 1/8	40 6/8	9	9	Nushagak Hills	AK	James C. Kelly	1995	48
391 0/8	49 3/8	53 0/8	41 6/8	11	13	Ugashik River	AK	Dr. Robert Roland-Smith	1986	51
391 0/8	56 0/8	53 7/8	53 0/8	12	10	Kenai	AK	David L. Hawkins	1988	51
390 5/8	53 2/8	52 7/8	42 0/8	11	10	Hook River	AK	William Elfland	1990	53
390 1/8	43 5/8	41 1/8	37 7/8	12	15	Lake Iliamna	AK	Kevin Anderson	1992	54
390 0/8	58 7/8	57 1/8	37 5/8	15	16	Whitefish Lake	AK	Charles C. Smith	1988	55
389 7/8	47 3/8	49 1/8	40 7/8	16	14	Mulchatna River	AK	Greg L. Munther	1987	56
389 4/8	48 0/8	49 2/8	34 0/8	22	19	Mother Goose Lake	AK	Dennis L. Smythe	1975	57
389 3/8	44 0/8	45 1/8	35 3/8	16	15	Galena	AK	Lon E. Lauber	1993	58
388 5/8	52 0/8	53 2/8	32 6/8	18	18	Delta River	AK	Dick Bolding	1957	59
388 2/8	56 5/8	57 1/8	47 2/8	18	16	Ugashik River	AK	George Moerlein	1972	60
388 2/8	50 7/8	55 7/8	30 5/8	14	15	Atigun Pass	AK	Alan Richey	1984	60
388 2/8	46 1/8	45 0/8	36 2/8	18	19	Mulchatna River	AK	John Joseph Carvajal	1994	60
387 7/8	42 0/8	40 6/8	31 5/8	23	25	McGrath	AK	Robert Barrie	1975	63
387 5/8	60 2/8	59 1/8	45 4/8	8	10	Atigun Pass	AK	David E. Rankin	1989	64
387 0/8	52 2/8	62 4/8	51 3/8	10	10	Lake Iliamna	AK	Jon Vanderhoef	1983	65
387 0/8	54 5/8	51 0/8	41 4/8	13	13	Becharof Lake	AK	Doug Fisher	1997	65
386 7/8	48 4/8	44 5/8	43 4/8	19	18	Little Delta	AK	Dale K. Marcy	1964	67
386 6/8	50 2/8	52 0/8	32 3/8	12	12	Nushagak River	AK	Richard Mazol	1991	68
386 0/8	47 3/8	45 6/8	35 1/8	16	12	Big Bend	AK	Roger O. Wyant	1993	69
385 3/8	51 2/8	53 5/8	40 0/8	13	11	King Salmon	AK	Tom Daley	1984	70
385 2/8	58 5/8	57 0/8	38 0/8	14	17	Talkeetna Mtns.	AK	Harvey Matz	1959	71
384 6/8	40 1/8	37 5/8	41 2/8	19	21	Yanert River	AK	E. Donnall Thomas, Jr.	1984	72
384 6/8	58 0/8	60 0/8	40 5/8	12	9	Cinder River	AK	Dean Stebner	1995	72
384 5/8	47 2/8	47 5/8	37 5/8	16	15	Talkeetna Mtns.	AK	Dr. Rex Hancock	1962	74
384 3/8	49 2/8	49 1/8	34 4/8	15	18	Alaska Peninsula	AK	Betty Gulman	1968	75
384 0/8	55 3/8	57 3/8	40 6/8	12	9	Mulchatna River	AK	Carl E. Brent	1990	76
384 0/8	60 0/8	56 0/8	45 0/8	7	6	Tidy Mtn.	AK	John (Jack) C. Culpepper III	1993	76
382 7/8	46 2/8	44 5/8	33 7/8	22	17	Wide Bay	AK	Archie Nesbitt	1991	78

BARREN GROUND CARIBOU

Minimum Score 325   Continued

SCORE	LENGTH OF MAIN BEAM R	LENGTH OF MAIN BEAM L	INSIDE SPREAD	NUMBER OF POINTS R	NUMBER OF POINTS L	AREA	STATE/PROVINCE	HUNTER'S NAME	DATE	RANK
382 4/8	50 2/8	51 3/8	39 2/8	17	27	King Salmon River	AK	Eugene Smith, Jr.	1978	79
382 3/8	57 6/8	58 6/8	41 7/8	11	12	Mulchatna River	AK	William C. Shuster	1993	80
381 6/8	41 7/8	40 7/8	31 4/8	12	11	Kuskokwim Mtns.	AK	Ted K. Jaycox	1995	81
381 5/8	51 1/8	47 1/8	39 1/8	14	19	Ugu River	AK	Stanley J. Rogers, Jr.	1974	82
381 2/8	51 4/8	53 2/8	41 1/8	11	13	Ugashik River	AK	Craig Richardson	1988	83
381 1/8	52 4/8	50 7/8	43 2/8	12	17	Galbraith Lake	AK	Edward L. Russell	1981	84
381 1/8	52 6/8	57 5/8	36 5/8	13	11	Lyme Village	AK	Don Nettum	1993	84
380 7/8	46 1/8	47 7/8	36 7/8	13	15	Delta Creek	AK	Wayne Trimm	1960	86
380 5/8	61 2/8	62 2/8	36 5/8	8	9	King Salmon	AK	Glenn Hisey	1984	87
380 4/8	52 4/8	50 1/8	44 4/8	17	16	Upper Ugashik Lake	AK	Kim Hussong	1992	88
380 0/8	48 1/8	49 1/8	30 2/8	14	18	Cutler River	AK	Jay Deones	1990	89
380 0/8	48 1/8	46 4/8	37 7/8	13	14	Mulchatna River	AK	Michael J. Spence	1998	89
379 6/8	49 5/8	53 0/8	39 1/8	13	12	Shotgun Hill	AK	Joe Ellithorpe	1987	91
379 6/8	57 4/8	59 0/8	45 3/8	10	11	Kotzebue	AK	Bill Barkley	1993	91
379 6/8	53 0/8	53 0/8	36 7/8	12	10	Cinder River	AK	D. Kevin Moore, DDS	1994	91
379 5/8	46 2/8	48 4/8	33 2/8	20	19	Alatna River	AK	Don D. Seward	1975	94
378 7/8	45 5/8	45 0/8	36 7/8	12	11	Moose Creek	AK	Richard Moran	1989	95
378 3/8	55 2/8	55 1/8	49 2/8	13	15	Taylor Mtns.	AK	George P. Mann	1997	96
378 1/8	47 3/8	47 3/8	40 4/8	10	10	Lake Clark	AK	Neil K. Hymas	1984	97
377 7/8	55 7/8	57 0/8	40 0/8	11	11	Ugashik River	AK	Douglas A. Smythe	1986	98
377 6/8	52 0/8	51 4/8	35 6/8	13	19	Dawn Lake	AK	Bob Kroll	1963	99
377 4/8	50 2/8	50 2/8	33 0/8	15	23	Kobuk River	AK	Mark Keiser	1994	100
376 7/8	50 2/8	45 4/8	40 2/8	14	13	Alaska Peninsula	AK	Bob Gulman	1968	101
376 7/8	52 6/8	50 5/8	49 4/8	16	14	Alaska Peninsula	AK	Roger O. Iveson	1976	101
376 6/8	63 5/8	63 7/8	44 6/8	11	10	Mulchatna River	AK	Nicholas Testi	1997	103
376 4/8	51 6/8	53 7/8	38 6/8	12	15	Little Underhill Creek	AK	Gary L. Stephens	1992	104
376 0/8	58 3/8	52 3/8	44 0/8	9	10	Lake Clark	AK	Joe Ball	1986	105
375 7/8	50 6/8	50 1/8	32 3/8	14	14	Cutler River	AK	Jay Deones	1997	106
375 5/8	54 0/8	56 1/8	39 3/8	14	13	Lake Iliamna	AK	Dr. Dale Schlehuber	1992	107
374 7/8	50 0/8	55 4/8	45 4/8	12	10	Nushagak Hills	AK	Steven J. Niedzielski	1995	108
374 4/8	51 2/8	50 4/8	38 3/8	13	11	Taylor Mtns.	AK	Bob Ehle	1998	109
374 3/8	57 2/8	51 4/8	33 4/8	11	12	Hohlitna River	AK	Rick Tollison	1978	110
374 0/8	48 0/8	49 7/8	40 5/8	10	8	Dog Salmon River	AK	Bob Holzberger	1991	111
373 6/8	47 5/8	47 5/8	40 2/8	11	17	Delta Creek	AK	Dwight Guynn	1980	112
373 5/8	46 6/8	46 7/8	39 5/8	18	15	Devil Creek	AK	Douglas Walker	1966	113
373 2/8	57 2/8	57 0/8	34 7/8	9	8	Kilbuck Mtns.	AK	Greg Munther	1998	114
372 5/8	44 6/8	44 6/8	25 5/8	11	11	Atigun River	AK	James W. Black, Jr.	1988	115
372 0/8	56 7/8	58 5/8	38 6/8	9	11	Lake Iliamna	AK	Gary Wright	1991	116
371 7/8	47 4/8	49 1/8	46 1/8	16	17	Prudhoe Bay	AK	Randy Richardson	1986	117
371 6/8	46 4/8	48 6/8	33 0/8	12	13	Cutler River	AK	Randy Doyle	1985	118
371 5/8	40 1/8	40 1/8	34 1/8	17	28	Maclaren River	AK	Dick Cooley	1962	119
371 5/8	48 5/8	49 1/8	41 6/8	20	15	Port Heiden	AK	Jim Dougherty	1968	119
371 4/8	46 4/8	45 2/8	31 2/8	11	13	Grayling Creek	AK	Carl H. Spaeth	1997	121
371 3/8	51 5/8	51 6/8	39 5/8	11	17	Cinder River	AK	Keith Pilz	1976	122
370 7/8	56 3/8	56 1/8	42 6/8	11	12	Arctic Coastal Plain	AK	Robin D. Johnson	1987	123
370 6/8	53 3/8	55 5/8	37 1/8	10	10	King Salmon River	AK	Ed Evans	1990	124
370 6/8	58 4/8	60 0/8	39 1/8	12	12	Lake Iliamna	AK	Glen Berry	1993	124
370 5/8	45 3/8	48 3/8	39 2/8	11	15	Lake Iliamna	AK	John Meschko	1981	126
370 4/8	46 4/8	47 7/8	34 5/8	12	11	Dog Salmon River	AK	Gary Thompson	1991	127
370 3/8	48 7/8	49 7/8	32 3/8	10	12	Shenjek Lake	AK	J. Keith Chastain	1984	128
370 2/8	55 3/8	54 5/8	38 5/8	9	9	Mulchatna River	AK	William A. Sheka, Jr.	1984	129
370 2/8	52 3/8	51 3/8	41 7/8	13	12	Mulchatna Drainage	AK	Matt Wood	1992	129
370 1/8	54 0/8	52 6/8	34 5/8	10	13	North Slope	AK	Ronald L. Sherer	1983	131
370 1/8	49 6/8	49 6/8	43 4/8	9	11	Lake Clark	AK	Ron Crouch	1989	131
370 1/8	50 0/8	50 2/8	38 5/8	12	14	Keefer Creek	AK	Mark Hockenberry	1994	131
370 0/8	54 0/8	51 6/8	42 1/8	12	12	Becharof Lake	AK	Bill B. Hobbins	1997	134
369 6/8	42 4/8	42 0/8	46 5/8	13	15	Lake Iliamna	AK	David L. Wolf	1988	135
369 5/8	44 0/8	44 4/8	34 4/8	13	14	Ugashik River	AK	William J. Stonebraker	1987	136
369 3/8	47 7/8	49 4/8	40 1/8	12	12	Mulchatna River	AK	Jeffrey L. Rentzel	1990	137
369 3/8	55 4/8	53 1/8	38 5/8	11	9	Wolf Lake	AK	Tim Cuthriell	1996	137
369 1/8	52 0/8	51 4/8	34 1/8	12	9	Fairbanks	AK	Keith Jensen	1986	139
368 7/8	46 6/8	47 1/8	40 7/8	16	17	Prudhoe Bay	AK	Calvin Farner	1985	140
368 5/8	43 4/8	45 4/8	30 1/8	16	14	Lower Talarik Creek	AK	John D. "Jack" Frost	1994	141
368 4/8	58 2/8	55 6/8	40 1/8	12	11	Ambler	AK	Rick Kinmon	1983	142
368 2/8	51 1/8	53 6/8	44 1/8	12	12	Swift River	AK	Rolf J. Sandberg	1986	143
368 2/8	49 7/8	49 7/8	41 1/8	10	12	King Salmon	AK	David Isom	1987	143
368 2/8	48 2/8	48 5/8	40 0/8	10	10	Mulchatna River	AK	Rick Albers	1994	143
368 0/8	51 5/8	46 4/8	36 3/8	14	19	Port Heiden	AK	John E. Lawson	1970	146
368 0/8	55 1/8	54 5/8	38 3/8	14	10	King Salmon River	AK	Rick Grooms	1979	146
367 4/8	50 2/8	52 1/8	49 7/8	12	13	Lake Iliamna	AK	David Niehaus	1991	148
367 4/8	47 1/8	47 1/8	35 0/8	12	12	Lake Iliamna	AK	Larry E. Sides, Jr.	1994	148
367 2/8	55 0/8	57 5/8	41 5/8	12	12	Tundra Lake	AK	Jim Garant	1988	150
366 5/8	49 5/8	48 0/8	28 7/8	13	14	Carlos Creek	AK	Braun Kopsack	1989	151
366 3/8	45 0/8	47 7/8	41 6/8	12	10	Hohlitna River	AK	Vance Henry	1988	152
366 2/8	47 6/8	47 3/8	35 3/8	12	17	Stoney River	AK	Craig E. Thomas	1989	153
366 1/8	45 4/8	45 7/8	37 1/8	12	13	Iliamna	AK	Grady A. Shelton	1994	154
366 0/8	54 1/8	53 5/8	47 2/8	10	12	Upper Stuyahok River	AK	Jim Bradford	1989	155
365 6/8	48 7/8	50 4/8	38 6/8	14	12	Shotgun Hills	AK	John L. Chase	1997	156

BARREN GROUND CARIBOU

Minimum Score 325 — Continued

SCORE	LENGTH OF MAIN BEAM R	LENGTH OF MAIN BEAM L	INSIDE SPREAD	NUMBER OF POINTS R	NUMBER OF POINTS L	AREA	STATE/PROVINCE	HUNTER'S NAME	DATE	RANK
365 4/8	47 3/8	45 7/8	27 0/8	12	12	Cutler River	AK	Larry Streiff	1990	157
365 3/8	51 6/8	53 6/8	40 7/8	9	8	Naknek	AK	Joe Keathley	1996	158
365 2/8	42 7/8	43 6/8	40 1/8	10	11	Ptarmigan Lake	AK	Dan Wolf	1997	159
364 6/8	53 5/8	51 5/8	26 3/8	12	19	Sagavanirktok River	AK	Judd Cooney	1982	160
364 5/8	45 6/8	45 5/8	32 7/8	14	11	Cantwell	AK	Rick D. Snell	1991	161
364 2/8	48 3/8	48 0/8	30 6/8	11	11	Cinder River	AK	Jack Dykstra	1991	162
363 6/8	52 0/8	53 4/8	39 3/8	13	14	Dillingham	AK	Glen Shatzer	1992	163
363 2/8	52 5/8	50 4/8	35 2/8	13	15	Squirrel River	AK	John J. Boland	1995	164
363 2/8	53 4/8	51 7/8	36 3/8	15	13	Lake Iliamna	AK	Richard S. Kinas	1997	164
363 0/8	53 4/8	52 6/8	37 5/8	10	9	King Salmon	AK	Kent D. Keenlyne	1982	166
363 0/8	47 0/8	47 0/8	39 5/8	8	10	Aleutian Range	AK	H. Richard Long	1984	166
363 0/8	36 3/8	38 3/8	28 3/8	15	14	Shot Gun Creek	AK	Roger O. Wyant	1994	166
362 7/8	50 6/8	49 6/8	42 4/8	10	12	Happy Valley	AK	Jeff Krienke	1995	169
362 6/8	54 3/8	52 0/8	37 6/8	7	9	Lake Clark	AK	John Thomas Cruger	1987	170
362 6/8	49 3/8	48 6/8	36 2/8	10	11	Ugashik Lake	AK	Kyle Culver	1989	170
362 4/8	44 3/8	47 2/8	34 4/8	17	18	Egegik River	AK	Walter Eslinger	1970	172
362 4/8	45 7/8	46 7/8	28 3/8	18	19	Healy River	AK	Ricky L. Mitchell	1988	172
362 3/8	44 0/8	47 2/8	35 2/8	10	9	Mulchatna River	AK	Ken Conley	1994	174
362 2/8	51 1/8	51 1/8	36 0/8	14	11	Sourdough	AK	Dan Jordan	1965	175
362 0/8	46 1/8	47 4/8	33 5/8	13	10	Swan River	AK	William C. Shuster	1993	176
361 7/8	57 4/8	57 0/8	34 1/8	13	13	White Hills	AK	Dick Carlson	1984	177
361 3/8	54 4/8	54 0/8	46 1/8	9	10	Kajulik Bay	AK	Thomas J. Hoffman	1983	178
361 3/8	51 6/8	52 5/8	44 2/8	13	12	Brooks Range	AK	John Ribic	1986	178
361 0/8	49 2/8	48 4/8	41 2/8	11	11	Mulchatna River	AK	James W. Southworth	1983	180
360 7/8	51 7/8	50 2/8	41 2/8	14	16	Iliamna	AK	Scott Halbert	1992	181
360 6/8	52 7/8	52 3/8	36 4/8	10	8	Lake Clark	AK	John W. Rose	1986	182
360 6/8	57 4/8	53 1/8	36 1/8	12	14	Cinnabar Creek	AK	James C. Davis	1994	182
360 4/8	56 3/8	53 4/8	41 2/8	12	14	Ugashik Lake	AK	Bruce B. Stamp	1992	184
360 2/8	54 7/8	53 6/8	41 2/8	10	11	Ptarmigan Lake	AK	Paul D. Wolf	1997	185
360 2/8	50 2/8	50 2/8	39 6/8	13	10	Shungnak	AK	Christofer Schultz	1998	185
360 0/8	52 3/8	52 2/8	32 6/8	8	8	Maclaren River	AK	Rick D. Snell	1994	187
359 6/8	45 5/8	46 3/8	43 7/8	17	16	Mulchatna River	AK	Ralph Ertz	1982	188
359 6/8	51 3/8	51 1/8	40 1/8	15	14	Kujulik Bay	AK	Norman Stahlman	1987	188
359 3/8	52 7/8	53 4/8	29 7/8	10	9	Lake Clark	AK	Mark Buehrer	1985	190
358 6/8	41 4/8	45 4/8	39 0/8	11	10	Aniakchak River	AK	Gary N. Moore, DDS	1994	191
358 6/8	55 6/8	53 6/8	31 5/8	8	9	Taylor Mtns.	AK	Rick A. Albers	1996	191
358 6/8	47 4/8	47 7/8	35 6/8	12	12	Nushagak River	AK	Jerry Nied	1998	191
358 5/8	49 2/8	34 6/8	40 5/8	13	14	Becharof Lake	AK	Joseph O. Fogleman	1986	194
358 4/8	50 0/8	51 0/8	34 1/8	13	12	Alaska Peninsula	AK	Chris Cassidy	1982	195
358 2/8	54 7/8	57 1/8	35 5/8	13	10	Tyone Lake	AK	Jake Sonnentag	1961	196
358 2/8	53 5/8	54 5/8	41 0/8	13	13	Maclaren River	AK	George Moerlein	1963	196
358 0/8	48 4/8	49 3/8	36 5/8	9	11	King Salmon	AK	Norm Epperson	1983	198
358 0/8	46 1/8	45 6/8	35 3/8	14	13	Aniak Lake	AK	Kevin L. Hall	1998	198
357 5/8	48 6/8	49 0/8	45 3/8	11	12	Deadhorse	AK	George P. Mann	1986	200
357 5/8	53 2/8	52 0/8	38 5/8	8	8	Maclaren River	AK	Debra A. Schaugaard	1994	200
357 4/8	57 0/8	57 5/8	35 5/8	11	10	Iliamna	AK	Mark Jensen	1994	202
357 3/8	48 0/8	48 3/8	39 7/8	11	13	King Salmon	AK	Gerry C. Stinski	1986	203
356 6/8	44 6/8	44 2/8	31 7/8	12	15	Dillingham	AK	Kurt M. Spencer	1996	204
356 6/8	52 1/8	52 4/8	38 0/8	10	9	Lake Selby	AK	Ricky Smith	1996	204
356 4/8	49 7/8	49 6/8	38 1/8	12	12	Mulchatna River	AK	Scott McDowell	1994	206
355 7/8	54 7/8	53 7/8	26 7/8	10	10	Mulchatna River	AK	Dan L. Carroll	1987	207
355 6/8	43 5/8	42 4/8	28 2/8	12	14	Deadhorse	AK	Jim Hodson	1985	208
355 6/8	49 3/8	50 0/8	33 3/8	14	14	Noatak River	AK	Roger A. Rasmussen	1990	208
355 5/8	57 0/8	56 0/8	44 0/8	15	16	Sagavanirktok River	AK	David D. Bestul	1986	210
354 7/8	46 0/8	46 0/8	36 0/8	10	10	Sagavanirktok River	AK	Kevin R. Wiley	1986	211
354 6/8	49 4/8	51 4/8	44 6/8	10	14	Kuktuli River	AK	Neil Summers	1982	212
354 6/8	47 1/8	45 0/8	44 1/8	12	13	Mulchatna River	AK	Richard LeBlond	1985	212
354 6/8	51 7/8	51 1/8	33 4/8	10	12	King Salmon	AK	Bruce A. Bouley	1987	212
354 4/8	49 0/8	47 1/8	42 4/8	13	13	Upnuk Lake	AK	Carl E. Garner	1997	215
354 1/8	49 0/8	50 6/8	39 4/8	10	9	Alaska Range	AK	Roger Wintle	1985	216
354 0/8	44 2/8	44 3/8	34 1/8	9	8	Lime Hills	AK	Bernard G. Norton	1990	217
353 6/8	52 5/8	52 4/8	47 1/8	12	10	Ugashik Lake	AK	Scott Lang	1988	218
353 5/8	48 1/8	46 7/8	37 4/8	14	12	Kotzebue	AK	Larry Welchlen	1988	219
353 3/8	48 2/8	46 6/8	36 7/8	17	13	Caribou Creek	AK	H. R. 'Dutch' Wambold	1964	220
353 3/8	54 4/8	53 3/8	43 2/8	11	12	Telaquana Lake	AK	Jake Sonnentag	1971	220
353 3/8	48 4/8	48 1/8	34 7/8	15	13	Galena	AK	Kenneth V. Butler	1995	220
353 1/8	45 4/8	46 2/8	37 4/8	13	14	Richardson Highway	AK	Donald O. Smith	1963	223
352 5/8	46 5/8	48 5/8	39 1/8	11	10	Carin Mtns.	AK	Wayne Haag	1997	224
352 4/8	49 4/8	45 6/8	31 6/8	8	10	Nushagak River	AK	Dwight Schuh	1993	225
352 3/8	48 2/8	46 5/8	30 2/8	14	14	Lacabana Lake	AK	O. Dale Porter	1986	226
352 2/8	54 1/8	54 0/8	45 1/8	9	10	Pilot Point	AK	John D. 'Jack' Frost	1980	227
351 5/8	48 4/8	52 6/8	38 5/8	10	11	Ugashik Lake	AK	Diane Snyder	1984	228
351 2/8	62 4/8	59 5/8	36 2/8	13	12	Ugashik Lake	AK	John Amundson	1986	229
351 2/8	46 1/8	48 6/8	38 1/8	14	14	Prudhoe Bay	AK	James R. Sanders, Jr.	1988	229
351 2/8	50 0/8	50 6/8	36 4/8	12	8	Ugashik River	AK	David A. Widby	1988	229
351 2/8	49 3/8	48 5/8	40 4/8	12	12	Port Heiden	AK	Mike Traub	1989	229
351 1/8	50 6/8	49 6/8	40 2/8	13	11	Lake Clark	AK	Bob Schwanke	1988	233
351 1/8	44 5/8	45 7/8	40 2/8	13	14	Ugashik River	AK	Joe P. Twitchell, Jr.	1988	233

199

BARREN GROUND CARIBOU

Minimum Score 325

SCORE	LENGTH OF MAIN BEAM R	LENGTH OF MAIN BEAM L	INSIDE SPREAD	NUMBER OF POINTS R	NUMBER OF POINTS L	AREA	STATE/PROVINCE	HUNTER'S NAME	DATE	RANK
350 7/8	51 3/8	49 0/8	27 2/8	20	21	Big Delta	AK	Bill Brown	1958	235
350 6/8	55 1/8	56 0/8	31 4/8	9	8	Lake Clark	AK	Stacy M. Tompkinson	1986	236
350 6/8	46 7/8	47 1/8	37 2/8	9	10	Lime Hills	AK	John Crum	1988	236
350 5/8	51 1/8	47 6/8	43 4/8	9	11	Selawik River	AK	Kirk Westervelt	1985	238
350 3/8	51 3/8	44 0/8	41 3/8	11	14	Meshik River	AK	Art Kragness	1970	239
350 3/8	47 5/8	47 1/8	25 5/8	12	12	40 Mile River	AK	Stan Parkerson	1984	239
350 3/8	42 0/8	45 6/8	38 6/8	9	11	Fish Lake	AK	Vikki Gross	1991	239
350 3/8	53 4/8	54 5/8	43 3/8	9	9	Franklin Bluff	AK	Matthew Dickson	1998	239
350 2/8	50 3/8	48 4/8	33 6/8	10	10	Tidy Mtn.	AK	John (Jack) C. Culpepper III	1993	243
350 1/8	58 6/8	57 2/8	31 0/8	9	9	Mulchatna River	AK	Daniel P. Fleming	1994	244
350 0/8	50 2/8	48 0/8	36 1/8	13	10	Sag River	AK	Guy Doyle	1991	245
349 7/8	52 2/8	45 3/8	35 1/8	15	11	Pilot Point	AK	Rolf J. Sandberg	1976	246
349 7/8	48 1/8	49 3/8	28 7/8	10	12	Franklin Bluffs	AK	Craig Kulchak	1982	246
349 6/8	51 2/8	53 0/8	43 5/8	9	10	Koktuli River	AK	Kristine Staffeldt	1992	248
349 5/8	47 7/8	47 3/8	44 6/8	11	8	Alaska Peninsula	AK	Vee F. Hanks	1990	249
349 5/8	50 0/8	50 0/8	46 6/8	11	8	Cutler River	AK	Jerry Notch	1997	249
349 4/8	55 7/8	57 3/8	39 2/8	9	11	Prudhoe Bay	AK	Rick Grooms	1986	251
349 4/8	46 2/8	48 0/8	34 5/8	12	13	Grayling Creek	AK	James C. Carlson	1997	251
349 2/8	52 4/8	51 5/8	36 4/8	13	8	Kobuk River	AK	Rick Kinmon	1986	253
349 2/8	49 7/8	48 7/8	41 1/8	8	10	Taylor Mtn.	AK	Mark A. McGillivray	1994	253
349 1/8	47 2/8	50 4/8	34 1/8	11	9	Deadhorse	AK	James M. Young	1980	255
348 3/8	43 6/8	44 6/8	42 0/8	13	14	Putilick Mt.	AK	Gary B. Gingerich	1986	256
348 2/8	50 2/8	48 3/8	42 4/8	10	11	Lower Mulchatna River	AK	Robert L. Atchley	1993	257
348 2/8	48 5/8	48 5/8	34 4/8	13	11	Franklin Bluffs	AK	Eric Colledge	1996	257
348 1/8	49 0/8	49 6/8	39 2/8	7	8	Mulchatna River	AK	LeRoy Hansen	1994	259
348 0/8	51 1/8	49 2/8	37 3/8	10	13	Alaska Range	AK	Salvatore J. Scaltrito	1983	260
348 0/8	48 3/8	49 6/8	43 7/8	10	8	Kaskanac Foothills	AK	Jeffrey S. Stevens	1988	260
348 0/8	50 4/8	50 0/8	29 0/8	13	12	Galbraith Lake	AK	Stan Parkerson	1990	260
348 0/8	47 4/8	46 0/8	32 7/8	16	18	Kotzabue	AK	Carl H. Spaeth	1991	260
348 0/8	51 1/8	53 0/8	34 4/8	12	13	Taylor Mtn.	AK	Edward A. Conkell	1994	260
347 7/8	48 1/8	48 7/8	30 4/8	9	7	Lake Iliamna	AK	Steve Bellis	1992	265
347 6/8	55 6/8	59 0/8	42 0/8	10	10	Stuyahok River	AK	Marlon Clapham	1989	266
347 5/8	46 4/8	47 6/8	37 6/8	20	16	Colville River	AK	John D. 'Jack' Frost	1982	267
347 4/8	46 2/8	45 2/8	41 7/8	12	14	Ogilvie Range	YUK	Emile Gele	1965	268
347 3/8	46 7/8	52 4/8	37 0/8	9	9	Mulchatna River	AK	Ray Roussett, Jr.	1986	269
347 1/8	52 0/8	50 1/8	39 0/8	14	13	Dog Salmon River	AK	Gary H. Thompson	1989	270
347 1/8	45 4/8	47 2/8	33 0/8	12	10	King Salmon River	AK	John "Rosey" Roseland	1991	270
346 7/8	50 4/8	50 2/8	32 0/8	10	19	Telaquana Lake	AK	Gary Wall	1974	272
346 5/8	50 0/8	48 6/8	36 5/8	10	12	Little Delta	AK	Herb Lindsay	1964	273
346 5/8	49 1/8	48 2/8	35 2/8	17	17	Sagavanirktok River	AK	Judd Cooney	1982	273
346 5/8	48 0/8	47 4/8	35 7/8	10	12	Porcupine River	AK	Mike Cummings	1994	273
346 1/8	43 6/8	45 0/8	35 0/8	18	13	Shotgun Hills	AK	Doug Aikin	1995	276
346 0/8	56 0/8	55 3/8	30 3/8	16	12	Franklin Bluffs	AK	Pete Trottier	1994	277
345 7/8	49 3/8	50 7/8	36 0/8	10	11	Mulchatna River	AK	Michael J. Spence	1998	278
345 5/8	49 5/8	49 5/8	35 6/8	12	12	Alaska Range	AK	Lon E. Lauber	1988	279
345 3/8	47 5/8	49 0/8	37 4/8	16	22	Kuskokwim Mtn.	AK	Robert K. Paulson	1977	280
345 3/8	54 0/8	48 1/8	36 5/8	12	14	Cutler River	AK	Doug Strecker	1985	280
345 3/8	51 0/8	50 4/8	41 2/8	8	8	Wood-Tikchik	AK	Richard Van Valkenburg	1994	280
345 2/8	47 3/8	48 6/8	32 4/8	11	10	Port Heiden	AK	Dennis G. Goldbach	1979	283
345 2/8	46 4/8	48 7/8	34 4/8	10	11	Alaska Peninsula	AK	Calvin Farner	1987	283
345 2/8	56 3/8	57 0/8	37 7/8	9	9	Lake Clark	AK	Mel Tenneson	1988	283
345 2/8	45 5/8	46 4/8	28 6/8	12	12	Koksetna River	AK	Steve Brockmann	1994	283
345 1/8	51 4/8	53 4/8	43 1/8	9	8	Lake Lach Buna	AK	Bob Ebert	1983	287
345 1/8	47 2/8	45 5/8	42 1/8	10	12	Mulchatna River	AK	E. Donnall Thomas, Jr.	1985	287
345 0/8	56 0/8	52 1/8	39 2/8	14	9	Wrench Creek	AK	Richard L. Westervelt	1991	289
344 7/8	51 4/8	50 4/8	34 0/8	13	12	Lake Clark	AK	Troy Hymas	1984	290
344 6/8	52 5/8	51 1/8	29 4/8	15	11	Susitna Valley	AK	Ronald D. Hopkins	1974	291
344 5/8	52 1/8	53 0/8	34 1/8	16	15	Squirrel River	AK	Gary Renfro	1998	292
344 4/8	49 7/8	51 6/8	38 6/8	13	16	Mirror Lake	AK	Robert E. Speegle, MD	1990	293
344 4/8	51 6/8	51 0/8	37 2/8	8	8	Ketok Mtn.	AK	Bob Koepsell	1992	293
344 2/8	46 1/8	43 6/8	27 7/8	11	13	Franklin Bluffs	AK	Matthew A. Jones	1987	295
344 2/8	49 1/8	49 7/8	34 2/8	11	12	Kiana	AK	Frank A. Johnson	1995	295
344 1/8	49 2/8	50 0/8	33 2/8	11	10	Happy Valley	AK	Tim J. Mariner	1991	297
344 1/8	50 7/8	50 4/8	43 1/8	10	11	Tagagawik River	AK	Doug Larsen	1993	297
343 6/8	45 2/8	46 3/8	30 6/8	14	14	Mulchatna Drainage	AK	Christopher G. Hixson	1990	299
343 6/8	53 3/8	51 7/8	33 1/8	13	11	Tagg River	AK	Gayland Jones	1991	299
343 6/8	52 6/8	54 1/8	30 3/8	10	9	Coleen River	AK	Marvin Whitehead	1997	299
343 5/8	50 6/8	53 6/8	41 0/8	8	12	Little Delta River	AK	Herman J. Griese	1980	302
343 4/8	48 0/8	50 1/8	28 6/8	16	13	Grayling Creek	AK	Carl G. Handyside	1997	303
343 3/8	54 6/8	52 7/8	46 4/8	9	10	Mulchatna River	AK	Donald Wagner	1993	304
343 2/8	45 6/8	47 7/8	35 6/8	9	8	Prudhoe Bay	AK	Victor Lee Littleton	1989	305
343 1/8	51 6/8	53 2/8	38 6/8	8	13	Taylor Highway	AK	Jae Beardon	1961	306
343 1/8	52 2/8	51 2/8	34 4/8	10	9	333 Dalton Highway	AK	Robert A. Chadwick	1987	306
343 0/8	49 4/8	48 2/8	40 7/8	9	14	Wrench Creek	AK	Kirk Westervelt	1991	308
342 5/8	44 0/8	45 1/8	32 0/8	11	12	Toolik Lake	AK	Blaine L. Thompson	1995	309
342 5/8	47 2/8	47 1/8	38 1/8	6	9	Purcell Mtn.	AK	Chris Sanford	1998	309
342 5/8	47 4/8	48 4/8	30 7/8	13	10	Squirrel River	AK	Mike Brezonick	1998	309
342 4/8	50 7/8	53 4/8	38 0/8	9	10	Dalton Highway	AK	Tom Chadwick	1991	312

BARREN GROUND CARIBOU

Minimum Score 325   Continued

SCORE	LENGTH OF MAIN BEAM R / L	INSIDE SPREAD	NUMBER OF POINTS R / L	AREA	STATE/PROVINCE	HUNTER'S NAME	DATE	RANK
342 0/8	45 7/8 / 49 3/8	40 7/8	13 / 16	Imuya Bay	AK	Archie Nesbitt	1989	313
341 6/8	58 2/8 / 56 3/8	39 6/8	11 / 14	McGrath	AK	Jim Holdenried	1982	314
341 6/8	50 1/8 / 50 3/8	34 3/8	14 / 13	Grayling Creek	AK	Daniel K. Carlson	1997	314
341 5/8	48 5/8 / 47 6/8	33 4/8	12 / 13	Alaska Peninsula	AK	Edward L. Russell	1980	316
341 4/8	53 3/8 / 52 2/8	43 4/8	14 / 12	Franklin Bluffs	AK	Dr. Jack Harvey	1984	317
341 4/8	43 3/8 / 45 0/8	30 4/8	14 / 11	Brooks Range	AK	Jeff Lindeman	1988	317
341 2/8	49 2/8 / 49 7/8	29 1/8	9 / 8	Toolik Lake	AK	Judy Watson	1988	319
341 1/8	46 6/8 / 48 1/8	41 0/8	9 / 9	Axburgh Lake	AK	Ryan J. Dorak	1994	320
341 0/8	49 2/8 / 49 0/8	37 2/8	14 / 13	King Salmon	AK	Reggie Callender	1971	321
340 7/8	46 1/8 / 46 7/8	30 6/8	8 / 8	Wolfe Lake	AK	Tracy G. Hardy	1990	322
340 6/8	49 2/8 / 49 3/8	27 1/8	12 / 13	Brooks Range	AK	Roger G. Stewart	1983	323
340 4/8	52 4/8 / 51 2/8	34 5/8	12 / 11	Sheenjek River	AK	Curtis Adams	1995	324
340 3/8	46 4/8 / 45 7/8	39 3/8	9 / 12	Mulchatna River	AK	Dr. Steven G. Hammons	1993	325
340 3/8	47 5/8 / 44 0/8	33 1/8	11 / 10	Kuparuk River	AK	Jeff Barnes, Sr.	1995	325
340 3/8	46 6/8 / 49 4/8	40 4/8	11 / 11	Lake Iliamna	AK	Dyrk Eddie	1995	325
340 0/8	49 0/8 / 51 0/8	36 2/8	14 / 14	Franklin Bluffs	AK	John T. Toenes	1985	328
339 7/8	48 3/8 / 43 4/8	36 3/8	14 / 12	Prudhoe Bay	AK	John Bilek	1986	329
339 7/8	51 4/8 / 52 0/8	32 4/8	15 / 12	Sagavanirktok River	AK	Ron Serwa	1987	329
339 7/8	50 0/8 / 48 5/8	40 4/8	9 / 14	Branch River	AK	Dale E. Christiansen	1995	329
339 6/8	44 4/8 / 47 4/8	32 4/8	12 / 9	Prudhoe Bay	AK	Wayne Piersol	1987	332
339 6/8	44 4/8 / 47 6/8	35 7/8	14 / 11	Mulchatna River	AK	Barbara Helm	1998	332
339 5/8	46 3/8 / 46 2/8	40 5/8	13 / 9	Becharof Lake	AK	Doug Fisher	1995	334
339 4/8	46 0/8 / 45 0/8	29 0/8	12 / 13	Port Heiden	AK	Dennis G. Goldbach	1980	335
339 4/8	49 5/8 / 51 7/8	41 0/8	12 / 10	Franklin Bluffs	AK	Roger E. Wheelock	1982	335
339 3/8	48 3/8 / 47 4/8	35 5/8	9 / 10	Sparvon Lake	AK	Brad Ham	1997	337
339 2/8	44 4/8 / 44 6/8	29 2/8	11 / 11	Mulchatna River	AK	Paul Voshell	1994	338
339 2/8	49 6/8 / 47 3/8	39 0/8	10 / 12	Grayling Creek	AK	Carl H. Spaeth	1997	338
339 1/8	52 5/8 / 53 4/8	38 4/8	10 / 12	Little Delta	AK	Dr. Judd Grindell	1959	340
339 0/8	45 3/8 / 51 5/8	34 4/8	18 / 13	Tyone Lake	AK	Jake Sonnentag	1963	341
338 7/8	47 2/8 / 48 1/8	29 6/8	8 / 9	Mulchatna Basin	AK	Brad C. Bryant	1993	342
338 4/8	49 4/8 / 47 7/8	35 1/8	11 / 16	Bonanza Hills	AK	Larry Langston	1974	343
338 4/8	46 6/8 / 47 2/8	30 7/8	14 / 12	Brooks Range	AK	Lyle Willmarth	1984	343
338 3/8	52 4/8 / 49 1/8	29 3/8	9 / 10	Tundra Lake	AK	Carl Handyside	1991	345
338 3/8	44 7/8 / 41 1/8	32 4/8	7 / 7	Deadman Lake	AK	Larry Daly	1996	345
338 0/8	53 3/8 / 55 4/8	40 0/8	12 / 10	Adak Island	AK	Lon E. Lauber	1984	347
338 0/8	48 7/8 / 48 7/8	38 6/8	13 / 14	Ugashik Lake	AK	Dave Scott	1989	347
337 7/8	50 7/8 / 51 7/8	39 6/8	16 / 11	Cold Bay	AK	John Sarvis	1985	349
337 5/8	49 7/8 / 49 1/8	41 6/8	12 / 14	Cinder River	AK	Francis Hosch	1966	350
337 3/8	47 4/8 / 47 3/8	32 2/8	13 / 14	Maclaren River	AK	George Moerlein	1963	351
337 1/8	50 6/8 / 51 2/8	29 1/8	19 / 18	Dry Creek	AK	Russell Kucinski	1983	352
337 1/8	49 3/8 / 50 2/8	37 7/8	9 / 9	Lime Hills	AK	Clifford R. Neville, Sr.	1990	352
337 1/8	49 0/8 / 51 6/8	32 6/8	10 / 11	Mulchatna River	AK	Kent Reierson	1996	352
337 1/8	45 4/8 / 43 1/8	37 7/8	8 / 10	Nishlik Lake	AK	Robert Bartoshesky	1996	352
336 7/8	48 3/8 / 48 2/8	39 2/8	11 / 9	Tag River	AK	Louis Strahler	1997	356
336 6/8	55 2/8 / 51 1/8	42 0/8	12 / 14	Featherly Pass	AK	Dale DeBoer	1987	357
336 0/8	42 7/8 / 45 2/8	35 0/8	13 / 9	Lake Iliamna	AK	Todd F. Lewis	1988	358
336 0/8	46 3/8 / 48 5/8	36 4/8	10 / 10	Mulchatna River	AK	Stan Rauch	1994	358
336 0/8	42 0/8 / 44 5/8	36 2/8	16 / 11	Whitefish Lake	AK	Paul St. John	1997	358
335 5/8	52 4/8 / 55 2/8	25 4/8	10 / 6	Chilikadrotna River	AK	Charles W. Rehor	1993	361
335 4/8	43 6/8 / 45 5/8	36 4/8	15 / 12	Sag River	AK	Stan Parkerson	1986	362
335 3/8	48 0/8 / 50 6/8	38 4/8	10 / 9	Lake Iliamna	AK	Steve Welch	1996	363
335 2/8	50 0/8 / 49 1/8	24 6/8	10 / 10	Nushagak River	AK	Bob Ameen	1998	364
335 1/8	47 3/8 / 48 3/8	22 5/8	9 / 10	Colville River	AK	Bob Gulman	1984	365
334 7/8	52 7/8 / 54 0/8	34 0/8	14 / 10	Squirrel River	AK	James Borron	1992	366
334 6/8	44 6/8 / 46 0/8	41 2/8	9 / 11	Sandy River	AK	Roger O. Wyant	1988	367
334 5/8	43 6/8 / 42 3/8	33 0/8	15 / 11	Carlos Creek	AK	Braun Kopsack	1988	368
334 5/8	51 1/8 / 50 1/8	32 7/8	12 / 14	Wrench Creek	AK	Kirk Westervelt	1991	368
334 4/8	43 1/8 / 45 3/8	33 6/8	13 / 9	Franklin's Bluffs	AK	John F. Gilmore	1991	370
334 1/8	45 7/8 / 50 0/8	35 1/8	7 / 10	Nikabuna Lake	AK	Timothy J. Conrads	1988	371
334 1/8	43 0/8 / 41 4/8	35 6/8	14 / 12	Pilot Point	AK	Joe W. Wright	1995	371
334 0/8	45 3/8 / 45 5/8	30 0/8	15 / 13	Happy Valley	AK	Michael Chadwick	1992	373
334 0/8	51 1/8 / 51 0/8	39 7/8	12 / 11	Kvnchak River	AK	Russell Hadley	1994	373
333 7/8	54 4/8 / 56 0/8	47 2/8	10 / 8	Selawik River	AK	Kirk Westervelt	1985	375
333 7/8	53 3/8 / 53 5/8	30 2/8	9 / 8	Nushagak River	AK	Bob Ameen	1998	375
333 5/8	47 2/8 / 47 2/8	32 5/8	15 / 11	Ugashik	AK	Stanley Winslow	1973	377
333 5/8	47 7/8 / 48 4/8	32 0/8	12 / 17	Happy Valley	AK	Troy Graziadei	1984	377
333 3/8	52 3/8 / 50 2/8	38 5/8	12 / 13	Nushagak River	AK	John M. Carbine	1998	379
333 1/8	44 0/8 / 44 6/8	35 0/8	12 / 13	Sagavanirktok River	AK	Steven M. Stroka	1991	380
333 0/8	44 6/8 / 44 7/8	35 4/8	11 / 13	Nicuhuna Lake	AK	Robert L. Atchley	1993	381
332 7/8	53 0/8 / 54 3/8	36 2/8	18 / 15	Denali Hwy.	AK	Junie Moll	1961	382
332 7/8	54 0/8 / 53 0/8	40 5/8	14 / 9	Mulchatna River	AK	Dan S. Frandsen	1993	382
332 6/8	49 5/8 / 50 7/8	30 4/8	12 / 9	Squirrel River	AK	Charles Kuss	1992	384
332 6/8	49 0/8 / 46 7/8	30 3/8	7 / 9	Mulchatna River	AK	Jeff DeCavitch	1997	384
332 5/8	48 1/8 / 47 2/8	35 7/8	18 / 13	Caribou River Drainage	AK	Al Reay	1981	386
332 4/8	47 2/8 / 47 3/8	40 3/8	10 / 11	Mulchatna River	AK	Skip Koske	1986	387
332 3/8	45 3/8 / 46 1/8	29 1/8	9 / 10	Mulchatna River	AK	Mike Barrett	1987	388
332 2/8	52 5/8 / 53 0/8	26 1/8	9 / 9	Kukaklek Lake	AK	Jay Kuhre	1989	389
332 2/8	42 0/8 / 46 1/8	34 7/8	9 / 9	Mulchatna River	AK	Rick Schack	1996	389

BARREN GROUND CARIBOU

Minimum Score 325   Continued

SCORE	LENGTH OF MAIN BEAM R	LENGTH OF MAIN BEAM L	INSIDE SPREAD	NUMBER OF POINTS R	NUMBER OF POINTS L	AREA	STATE/PROVINCE	HUNTER'S NAME	DATE	RANK
332 1/8	44 6/8	43 7/8	33 2/8	13	15	Mulchatna River	AK	Richard R. Schnell	1990	391
332 1/8	44 7/8	46 1/8	41 0/8	10	10	Non Dalton	AK	Gary L. Wilford	1992	391
332 1/8	46 2/8	46 3/8	35 5/8	12	10	Mulchatna River	AK	Rick Albers	1994	391
332 1/8	42 1/8	44 6/8	36 5/8	10	10	Kilbuck Mtns.	AK	Greg Munther	1998	391
331 7/8	54 3/8	55 0/8	35 6/8	9	16	Port Heiden	AK	John E. Lawson	1970	395
331 7/8	52 6/8	54 0/8	39 3/8	7	9	Mulchatna River	AK	Ray Heal	1997	395
331 5/8	45 5/8	48 1/8	35 6/8	12	11	High Lakes	AK	Doug Walker	1970	397
331 5/8	50 3/8	50 5/8	39 3/8	12	11	Ugashik River	AK	Terry Sanders	1988	397
331 5/8	48 1/8	47 6/8	37 1/8	14	16	Brooks Range	AK	James L. Behn	1991	397
331 1/8	47 6/8	46 1/8	28 7/8	12	14	Bonanza Hills	AK	Dan Klebenow	1990	400
330 5/8	51 1/8	51 5/8	35 6/8	15	10	Tangle Lakes	AK	R. Glen Williams	1966	401
330 4/8	50 2/8	49 3/8	26 7/8	12	10	Atigun Pass	AK	Tom Payer	1994	402
330 2/8	47 7/8	49 7/8	34 3/8	13	10	Franklin's Bluffs	AK	Eudane Vicenti	1991	403
330 2/8	41 4/8	40 4/8	29 4/8	11	10	Dillingham	AK	John Holt	1997	403
330 0/8	54 2/8	55 0/8	37 7/8	13	12	Atigun Pass	AK	Keith K. Appel	1984	405
329 7/8	47 4/8	47 3/8	31 0/8	10	15	Dawn Lake	AK	Chuck Kroll	1963	406
329 7/8	56 4/8	53 7/8	40 3/8	9	12	Little Delta	AK	Bill Tutt	1964	406
329 6/8	49 6/8	49 4/8	33 1/8	6	8	Sagavanirktok River	AK	Patricia A. Stewart	1983	408
329 4/8	57 6/8	53 2/8	41 3/8	8	9	Chandler River	AK	Chuck Roady	1986	409
329 4/8	46 0/8	46 1/8	37 7/8	15	12	Ugashik River	AK	Stan Rauch	1988	409
329 1/8	49 0/8	48 4/8	40 2/8	11	8	Ambler	AK	Dean Bergman	1986	411
329 0/8	46 4/8	46 4/8	40 4/8	9	6	Denali Hwy.	AK	Gordon Spidle	1988	412
328 7/8	49 3/8	48 7/8	37 6/8	10	7	Tutna Lake	AK	Gene Clark	1987	413
328 4/8	42 6/8	44 3/8	31 5/8	18	12	Little Delta	AK	Roy Bryan	1964	414
328 4/8	47 6/8	47 7/8	35 3/8	11	13	Sagavanirktok River	AK	Paul G. Barclay	1981	414
328 3/8	50 2/8	49 1/8	30 3/8	9	9	Prudhoe Bay	AK	Denver Perry	1981	416
328 2/8	42 0/8	39 7/8	27 2/8	8	9	Prudhoe Bay	AK	Gene Barcak	1985	417
328 1/8	47 0/8	47 5/8	32 7/8	7	10	Mulchatna	AK	Joaquin Macias	1992	418
327 7/8	45 4/8	43 5/8	36 2/8	8	11	Mulchatna River	AK	Barbara Helm	1998	419
327 7/8	47 1/8	49 0/8	25 5/8	13	11	Green Lake	AK	Troy McGinnis	1998	419
327 6/8	40 7/8	41 3/8	36 7/8	15	12	Galbraith Lake	AK	G. Stevens Abdoe	1983	421
327 6/8	39 7/8	40 0/8	37 3/8	12	11	Sagavanirktok River	AK	Roger Stewart	1989	421
327 5/8	47 3/8	49 3/8	40 0/8	13	13	North Slope	AK	Susan D. Sherer	1983	423
327 5/8	45 5/8	46 4/8	36 1/8	11	10	Prudhoe Bay	AK	Dennis Redden	1992	423
327 3/8	46 1/8	47 0/8	40 0/8	8	9	Selawik River	AK	Richard L. Westervelt	1985	425
327 2/8	45 6/8	48 5/8	35 6/8	12	12	Noatak River	AK	Donald R. Powers	1987	426
327 2/8	48 6/8	47 3/8	30 6/8	11	11	Kobuk River	AK	Niels Knudsen	1990	426
327 2/8	51 3/8	51 0/8	29 4/8	10	11	Dillingham	AK	John Holt	1997	426
326 7/8	47 6/8	51 2/8	27 3/8	15	13	Dago Creek	AK	Don Davidson	1980	429
326 6/8	49 1/8	47 3/8	41 0/8	12	18	Anchorage	AK	Roy Bryan	1964	430
326 5/8	43 0/8	45 0/8	38 3/8	12	12	Galena	AK	Larry Spiva	1992	431
326 5/8	52 7/8	52 3/8	47 2/8	9	8	Nuna River	AK	David Rue	1998	431
326 4/8	47 7/8	49 7/8	31 7/8	10	11	Brooks Range	AK	Roger Stewart	1985	433
326 4/8	54 7/8	54 0/8	39 0/8	8	7	Iliamna	AK	David Wolf	1994	433
326 4/8	48 6/8	47 0/8	33 3/8	9	8	Lake Iliamna	AK	Mike Craig	1997	433
326 3/8	47 6/8	49 0/8	39 0/8	11	13	King Salmon	AK	Glenn Hisey	1983	436
326 3/8	51 0/8	53 1/8	41 1/8	11	10	Yellow Creek Hill	AK	Don Poole	1992	436
326 0/8	54 5/8	52 6/8	19 0/8	11	12	Squirrel River	AK	Connie Renfro	1998	438
325 6/8	49 0/8	46 1/8	21 1/8	14	13	Atigun Pass	AK	Maxallen D. Jackson	1980	439
325 4/8	52 4/8	52 3/8	31 0/8	13	15	Galbraith Lake	AK	Maxallen D. Jackson	1981	440
325 3/8	45 5/8	48 1/8	33 0/8	15	16	Cerban Lake	AK	James F. Watson	1997	441
325 3/8	46 4/8	46 5/8	34 1/8	9	10	Grayling Creek	AK	Bill Cmiel	1997	441
325 1/8	55 7/8	55 6/8	32 3/8	8	9	Prudhoe Bay	AK	Garry A. Thoms	1986	443
325 0/8	46 6/8	48 5/8	30 5/8	8	9	Ugashik River	AK	Bob "Jake" Jacobsen	1988	444

BARREN GROUND CARIBOU (VELVET ANTLERS)

Minimum Score 325

SCORE	LENGTH OF MAIN BEAM R	LENGTH OF MAIN BEAM L	INSIDE SPREAD	NUMBER OF POINTS R	NUMBER OF POINTS L	AREA	STATE/PROVINCE	HUNTER'S NAME	DATE	RANK
439 3/8	56 2/8	55 6/8	35 1/8	13	11	Mulchatna River	AK	Rick Valdez	1995	*
372 3/8	52 7/8	52 5/8	33 1/8	9	8	Soldotna	AK	Donny Roy	1998	*
370 7/8	47 6/8	51 4/8	34 1/8	18	16	Nushagak River	AK	Gary Potter	1998	*
357 1/8	49 3/8	49 2/8	39 3/8	12	13	Cutler River	AK	Terry Krahn	1991	*
348 1/8	43 4/8	45 3/8	30 6/8	13	14	Clark Lake	AK	Brett Duane Monaghan	1994	*
348 0/8	44 0/8	44 0/8	40 2/8	9	9	Iliamna	AK	Jeff Barnett	1995	*
345 1/8	46 2/8	46 6/8	36 5/8	12	15	Atigun Pass	AK	Steven G. Miller	1993	*
343 3/8	48 7/8	49 0/8	34 2/8	8	6	Windy Creek	AK	Chris Reynolds	1996	*
341 3/8	45 3/8	44 6/8	32 5/8	15	14	Sagavanirktok River	AK	Kenneth J. Hardy	1997	*
341 1/8	43 5/8	45 0/8	40 0/8	9	9	Taylor Mtn.	AK	Dean A. Wetzel	1993	*

BARREN GROUND CARIBOU (VELVET ANTLERS)
Minimum Score 325   Continued

SCORE	LENGTH OF MAIN BEAM R / L	INSIDE SPREAD	NUMBER OF POINTS R / L	AREA	STATE/ PROVINCE	HUNTER'S NAME	DATE	RANK
340 7/8	59 6/8 60 6/8	35 6/8	7 5	Deadhorse	AK	Matt Moore	1998	*
340 0/8	48 4/8 46 6/8	33 0/8	12 12	Dalton Highway	AK	John McCullough	1991	*
339 4/8	53 6/8 56 0/8	35 4/8	11 12	Groundhog Mtn.	AK	Steve Hohensee	1996	*
339 0/8	50 2/8 50 2/8	28 5/8	10 10	Talkeetna Mtns.	AK	Charles A. Eisenhower	1996	*
337 4/8	48 3/8 47 1/8	28 0/8	12 10	Happy Valley	AK	Jeremiah Dickson	1995	*
326 4/8	44 0/8 42 5/8	33 2/8	11 9	Kobuk River	AK	Charles C. Ellithorpe, DVM	1997	*
326 0/8	47 1/8 46 0/8	29 7/8	9 9	Carin Mtn.	AK	David J. Barrow	1995	*

* Velvet entries will be listed in only one record book.

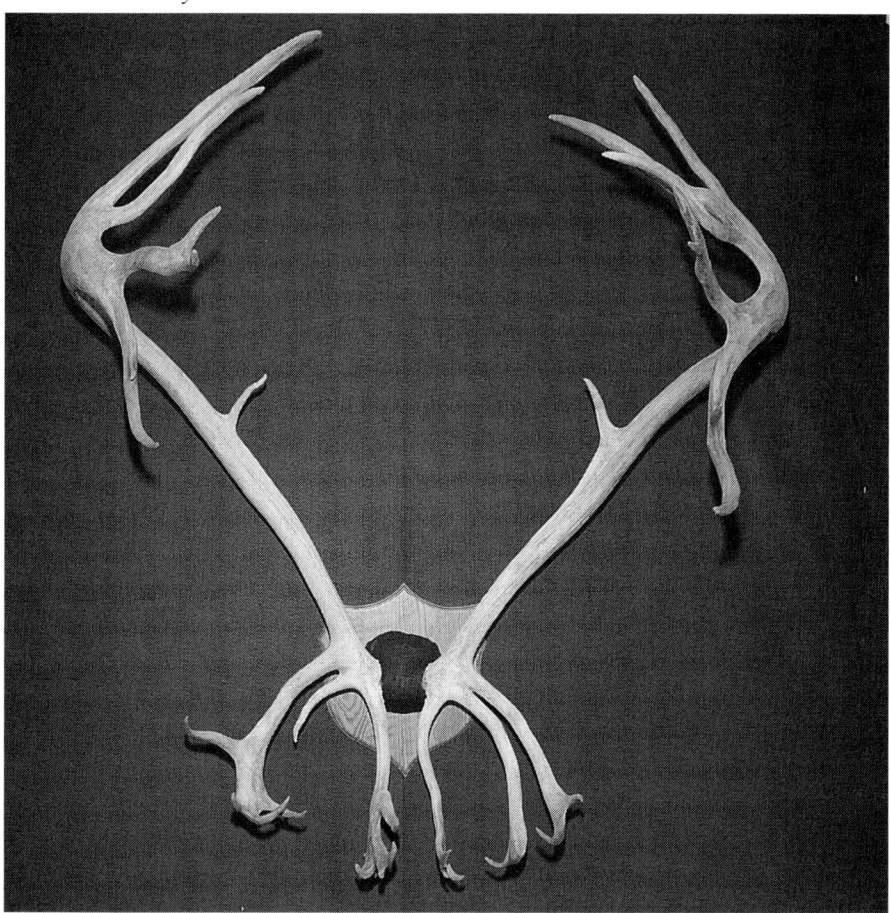

World Record Central Canada Caribou
Score: 420 6/8
Humpy Lake, Northwest Territories - 1994
Hunter: Al Kuntz

CENTRAL CANADA CARIBOU
Minimum Score 300   *Rangifer tarandus articus*

SCORE	LENGTH OF MAIN BEAM R / L	INSIDE SPREAD	NUMBER OF POINTS R / L	AREA	STATE/ PROVINCE	HUNTER'S NAME	DATE	RANK
420 6/8	55 1/8 57 0/8	39 0/8	12 12	Humpy Lake	NWT	Al Kuntz	1994	1
405 3/8	55 5/8 53 7/8	34 5/8	16 17	MacKay Lake	NWT	Dan Gartner	1997	2
388 4/8	42 3/8 43 2/8	29 7/8	20 19	Little Marten Lake	NWT	Adrian L. Erickson	1990	3
387 3/8	55 4/8 52 2/8	31 0/8	14 11	Little Marten Lake	NWT	James Gopffarth	1996	4
387 1/8	53 2/8 55 6/8	36 3/8	13 13	Baffin Island	NWT	Randall J. Kiessel	1986	5
385 5/8	52 7/8 51 3/8	36 7/8	14 18	Munroe Lake	MAN	Thomas A. Koepke, M.D.	1997	6
381 6/8	46 2/8 46 5/8	29 1/8	13 20	MacKay Lake	NWT	Tom Taylor	1995	7
374 3/8	51 1/8 51 1/8	32 6/8	15 13	Warburton Bay	NWT	Duane Hicks	1987	8
373 1/8	48 4/8 49 7/8	40 3/8	11 13	MacKay Lake	NWT	Richard Martin	1990	9
372 2/8	46 0/8 48 4/8	30 0/8	14 14	Area 1	MAN	Don McCrea	1992	10
371 6/8	47 7/8 46 5/8	30 2/8	12 12	MacKay Lake	NWT	Greg Leroux	1990	11

CENTRAL CANADA CARIBOU

Minimum Score 300

Continued

SCORE	LENGTH OF MAIN BEAM R	LENGTH OF MAIN BEAM L	INSIDE SPREAD	NUMBER OF POINTS R	NUMBER OF POINTS L	AREA	STATE/PROVINCE	HUNTER'S NAME	DATE	RANK
371 1/8	50 3/8	48 4/8	44 0/8	13	13	MacKay Lake	NWT	Dan Brockman	1990	12
370 7/8	53 0/8	51 3/8	32 4/8	10	13	Warburton Bay	NWT	John Campbell	1995	13
370 7/8	50 4/8	51 0/8	33 6/8	13	13	MacKay Lake	NWT	James D. Powless	1997	13
369 2/8	53 5/8	54 3/8	37 5/8	11	9	White Island	NWT	Curt Wells	1996	15
368 2/8	51 7/8	51 7/8	31 7/8	11	11	Warburton Bay	NWT	Patrick M. Condie	1995	16
366 0/8	53 0/8	53 0/8	31 7/8	14	12	MacKay Lake	NWT	John D. Totemeier	1990	17
365 7/8	45 4/8	46 6/8	40 0/8	11	10	Desteffany Lake	NWT	Doug Strecker	1996	18
365 3/8	49 4/8	50 6/8	30 5/8	14	13	Courageous Lake	NWT	Thomas J. Hoffman	1994	19
365 1/8	47 2/8	47 1/8	31 0/8	14	13	Artillery Lake	NWT	Kenneth A. Heinrichs	1997	20
364 6/8	46 3/8	47 2/8	28 2/8	11	8	Courageous Lake	NWT	Steve Crooks	1990	21
364 6/8	55 0/8	54 6/8	36 1/8	12	12	MacKay Lake	NWT	Michael J. Spence	1995	21
364 5/8	53 5/8	54 6/8	36 1/8	10	9	Warburton Bay	NWT	Lyle Sheppard	1997	23
364 3/8	49 7/8	51 4/8	24 6/8	12	12	Baffin Island	NWT	John C. Gall	1992	24
362 3/8	53 0/8	51 0/8	40 3/8	15	10	MacKay Lake	NWT	William A. Dreyer III	1995	25
360 7/8	55 0/8	54 2/8	39 4/8	13	14	Courageous Lake	NWT	Ron Hise	1997	26
360 5/8	50 3/8	51 5/8	39 7/8	10	13	Humpy Lake	NWT	Bill Vaznis	1994	27
359 7/8	47 2/8	47 6/8	32 1/8	13	9	Point Lake	NWT	James A. Brown	1990	28
359 6/8	53 6/8	54 4/8	33 3/8	8	9	MacKay Lake	NWT	Tom Taylor	1995	29
359 6/8	53 5/8	54 5/8	44 6/8	10	10	MacKay Lake	NWT	Scott R. Barefoot	1997	29
359 1/8	48 1/8	48 4/8	35 0/8	14	14	Courageous Lake	NWT	John D. "Jack" Frost	1994	31
358 2/8	50 4/8	53 6/8	30 0/8	13	10	Artillery Lake	NWT	Brian T. Butts	1998	32
358 1/8	51 6/8	51 7/8	34 2/8	9	11	Lake Providence	NWT	Gerry Backhaus	1988	33
358 0/8	46 4/8	46 5/8	34 6/8	14	13	MacKay Lake	NWT	Mike Wheeler	1991	34
357 4/8	51 5/8	50 5/8	30 2/8	12	12	MacKay Lake	NWT	Glenn Hisey	1997	35
357 1/8	43 3/8	45 0/8	34 1/8	11	15	Desteffany Lake	NWT	Kathy Strecker	1996	36
356 4/8	47 0/8	44 7/8	29 6/8	15	15	Warburton Bay	NWT	Patrick M. Condie	1995	37
356 0/8	53 1/8	50 2/8	33 1/8	12	10	Courageous Lake	NWT	Bob Dawson	1988	38
355 6/8	47 0/8	48 6/8	40 3/8	15	14	MacKay Lake	NWT	Stan Godfrey	1988	39
355 6/8	50 5/8	49 5/8	31 6/8	12	14	Artillery Lake	NWT	Dave Popp	1997	39
355 3/8	41 0/8	44 0/8	33 0/8	21	22	MacKay Lake	NWT	William E. Gerhardt	1997	41
353 2/8	55 7/8	56 6/8	39 5/8	13	12	MacKay Lake	NWT	Tom Taylor	1995	42
351 7/8	50 3/8	49 5/8	35 7/8	14	13	Warburton Bay	NWT	Reagan Dunn	1997	43
348 5/8	45 6/8	44 4/8	30 3/8	14	17	Desteffany Lake	NWT	Jay Deones	1996	44
348 1/8	44 0/8	44 0/8	39 1/8	16	15	Warburton Bay	NWT	David R. Coupland	1992	45
348 1/8	54 5/8	51 3/8	31 1/8	13	11	Warburton Bay	NWT	Tom Foss	1993	45
348 0/8	46 0/8	47 6/8	36 6/8	14	14	Lake Providence	NWT	Ron Books	1991	47
346 6/8	50 6/8	54 1/8	37 3/8	10	11	MacKay Lake	NWT	James D. Powless	1997	48
346 5/8	51 3/8	53 6/8	34 0/8	10	10	Glover Lake	MAN	Rick Hogg	1995	49
345 2/8	56 7/8	52 2/8	31 3/8	12	10	Yellowknife	NWT	Gil Gilbertson	1990	50
343 6/8	48 6/8	48 4/8	38 1/8	11	10	MacKay Lake	NWT	Christian Fourquet	1995	51
343 5/8	45 2/8	44 4/8	39 4/8	15	14	Desteffany Lake	NWT	Larry D. Jones	1994	52
343 3/8	53 2/8	52 0/8	37 5/8	9	10	MacKay Lake	NWT	Carolyn Godfrey	1990	53
343 3/8	44 0/8	44 3/8	35 4/8	16	13	Courageous Lake	NWT	Robert Edward Speegle, MD	1994	53
343 1/8	47 4/8	48 5/8	37 5/8	12	12	Lake Providence	NWT	Ron Books	1991	55
343 0/8	47 7/8	50 2/8	32 7/8	8	9	Nodinka Narrows	NWT	Gunter Lemke	1991	56
342 6/8	44 6/8	43 7/8	24 2/8	14	12	MacKay Lake	NWT	Chuck Kronenwetter	1994	57
342 6/8	44 4/8	44 6/8	27 6/8	11	11	Desteffany Lake	NWT	David Harris	1998	57
341 4/8	52 2/8	51 7/8	31 5/8	10	10	Desteffany Lake	NWT	Kevin Hisey	1996	59
341 0/8	53 4/8	50 6/8	27 5/8	11	10	Warburton Bay	NWT	Richard E. LaCrone	1997	60
340 2/8	48 2/8	46 4/8	30 4/8	14	14	Lake Providence	NWT	Doug Walker	1988	61
340 2/8	49 6/8	45 5/8	28 0/8	18	14	Lake Providence	NWT	Doug Walker	1988	61
340 0/8	45 0/8	44 6/8	32 6/8	13	14	Rendezvous Lake	NWT	Richard A. Hjort	1989	63
339 5/8	50 6/8	48 4/8	34 5/8	10	10	Humpy Lake	NWT	Johnnie R. Walters	1992	64
339 4/8	51 0/8	51 0/8	27 4/8	11	10	MacKay Lake	NWT	Steve Tice	1994	65
338 6/8	58 5/8	60 1/8	39 1/8	10	9	MacKay Lake	NWT	Stan Godfrey	1990	66
337 6/8	50 3/8	48 2/8	34 5/8	12	13	MacKay Lake	NWT	Michael J. Spence	1995	67
336 7/8	46 1/8	46 2/8	28 4/8	14	13	MacKay Lake	NWT	Mark Wuerthele	1995	68
336 3/8	47 0/8	48 2/8	31 7/8	12	11	Little Duck Lake	MAN	Rick Hogg	1993	69
336 2/8	45 5/8	47 1/8	27 3/8	13	9	MacKay Lake	NWT	Stan Godfrey	1990	70
336 0/8	50 0/8	49 4/8	31 0/8	11	11	MacKay Lake	NWT	William E. Terry, Sr.	1995	71
335 6/8	49 6/8	49 2/8	37 0/8	7	7	Nodinka Narrows	NWT	Marc Nyrose	1991	72
335 4/8	49 1/8	44 3/8	32 0/8	12	14	MacKay Lake	NWT	Dan Gartner	1997	73
335 2/8	42 3/8	43 4/8	27 3/8	14	17	MacKay Lake	NWT	R. E. Smith	1992	74
335 2/8	51 3/8	50 3/8	30 3/8	14	12	MacKay Lake	NWT	Mark Wuerthele	1995	74
335 2/8	45 2/8	46 5/8	22 5/8	16	15	Warburton Bay	NWT	Michael R. Westvang	1995	74
334 6/8	52 6/8	51 5/8	43 6/8	9	8	Jolly Lake	NWT	Mark Mathieson	1997	77
334 2/8	45 2/8	43 6/8	31 6/8	10	12	MacKay Lake	NWT	Michael J. Underhill	1990	78
333 0/8	41 5/8	43 1/8	22 1/8	13	13	MacKay Lake	NWT	Jay St. Charles	1992	79
332 4/8	51 7/8	51 1/8	36 0/8	11	10	Lake Providence	NWT	Jeff Fitts	1993	80
332 3/8	46 4/8	47 4/8	26 7/8	13	11	Yellowknife	NWT	Bruce R. Schoeneweis	1990	81
332 3/8	42 0/8	42 0/8	39 0/8	16	19	Caribou Bay	NWT	Richard A. Case	1994	81
331 4/8	53 2/8	54 0/8	29 0/8	11	11	Point Lake	NWT	Cam Wilson	1987	83
331 2/8	44 6/8	46 1/8	28 6/8	14	15	MacKay Lake	NWT	David Emken	1990	84
331 2/8	47 1/8	47 1/8	28 1/8	13	10	Rendezvous Lake	NWT	Lucas Osellame	1996	84
331 2/8	55 2/8	52 4/8	33 6/8	11	10	MacKay Lake	NWT	Robert Priem	1997	84
331 0/8	49 2/8	49 3/8	29 4/8	14	11	MacKay Lake	NWT	Charles L. Hunt	1990	87
330 3/8	46 6/8	47 0/8	32 0/8	11	11	MacKay Lake	NWT	Glenn Hisey	1997	88
330 0/8	52 0/8	50 6/8	31 6/8	9	9	MacKay Lake	NWT	Manfred Gehrlein	1990	89

CENTRAL CANADA CARIBOU

Minimum Score 300 — Continued

SCORE	LENGTH OF MAIN BEAM R	LENGTH OF MAIN BEAM L	INSIDE SPREAD	NUMBER OF POINTS R	NUMBER OF POINTS L	AREA	STATE/PROVINCE	HUNTER'S NAME	DATE	RANK
329 7/8	52 2/8	50 0/8	35 0/8	9	11	Jolly River	NWT	Jay St. Charles	1987	90
329 6/8	45 1/8	48 4/8	35 2/8	15	16	Humpy Lake	NWT	Randy Kottke	1997	91
329 4/8	49 3/8	50 2/8	36 0/8	17	14	MacKay Lake	NWT	Terry Tabor	1990	92
328 5/8	50 6/8	49 7/8	28 6/8	20	15	Little Marten Lake	NWT	Marc N. Shaft	1997	93
328 4/8	49 7/8	49 0/8	39 2/8	12	9	MacKay Lake	NWT	Ryk Visscher	1991	94
328 3/8	50 2/8	51 6/8	34 2/8	13	10	MacKay Lake	NWT	Tom Vanasche	1995	95
327 7/8	47 0/8	45 1/8	29 0/8	11	11	MacKay Lake	NWT	Charles L. Hunt	1990	96
327 7/8	49 0/8	46 5/8	30 2/8	18	14	MacKay Lake	NWT	Sheldon Showalter	1995	96
327 4/8	49 7/8	48 7/8	31 0/8	9	9	Warburton Bay	NWT	Dennis Dunn	1997	98
326 7/8	49 1/8	47 1/8	30 7/8	11	10	MacKay Lake	NWT	Tom Taylor	1992	99
326 6/8	50 7/8	50 5/8	35 1/8	8	11	Artillery Lake	NWT	Brian T. Butts	1998	100
325 5/8	48 6/8	49 0/8	19 0/8	11	11	MacKay Lake	NWT	Kevin Lyons	1997	101
324 6/8	45 0/8	42 1/8	30 4/8	13	12	Glover Lake	MAN	Rick Hogg	1998	102
324 6/8	44 7/8	45 5/8	23 7/8	10	9	Humpy Lake	NWT	Dewayne Mullins	1998	102
323 7/8	39 7/8	46 2/8	29 1/8	11	13	Desteffany Lake	NWT	Jay Deones	1996	104
323 6/8	49 3/8	46 4/8	31 2/8	12	10	MacKay Lake	NWT	Scott R. Barefoot	1997	105
323 5/8	44 4/8	45 0/8	26 4/8	12	16	Wejalini Lake	MAN	Gord Monteath	1991	106
322 4/8	44 6/8	43 5/8	26 4/8	13	12	MacKay Lake	NWT	Tom Taylor	1995	107
320 4/8	53 4/8	54 4/8	30 3/8	7	7	MacKay Lake	NWT	Ryk Visscher	1991	108
320 2/8	52 2/8	54 2/8	35 2/8	8	11	MacKay Lake	NWT	Manfred Gehrlein	1990	109
319 5/8	48 2/8	47 5/8	27 0/8	10	11	Desteffany Lake	NWT	Robert Harris	1998	110
319 2/8	47 6/8	46 3/8	23 6/8	12	11	MacKay Lake	NWT	Sheldon Showalter	1995	111
318 0/8	45 6/8	46 2/8	28 2/8	12	10	Humpy Lake	NWT	Johnnie R. Walters	1992	112
316 5/8	46 6/8	48 6/8	37 0/8	7	7	MacKay Lake	NWT	Howard L. Harding	1992	113
316 4/8	52 4/8	52 6/8	28 1/8	10	9	MacKay Lake	NWT	Bob Barden	1996	114
315 6/8	46 6/8	50 0/8	28 4/8	11	11	MacKay Lake	NWT	Jim Visscher	1990	115
315 6/8	43 2/8	46 5/8	35 1/8	9	8	Warburton Bay	NWT	David R. Coupland	1992	115
315 5/8	49 7/8	48 6/8	29 7/8	13	8	Nejanilini Lake	MAN	Jeffrey Schwartz	1996	117
315 4/8	38 2/8	40 0/8	28 6/8	12	13	Humpy Lake	NWT	Al Kuntz	1994	118
315 3/8	44 6/8	44 7/8	31 5/8	9	9	Nejanilini Lake	MAN	Russell K. Mehling	1994	119
315 3/8	46 6/8	45 1/8	21 0/8	15	15	MacKay Lake	NWT	Steve Hohensee	1994	119
315 0/8	43 3/8	42 5/8	27 5/8	13	17	Courageous Lake	NWT	Brad White	1997	121
313 7/8	49 2/8	50 5/8	31 6/8	6	8	MacKay Lake	NWT	Wade Carstens	1993	122
313 6/8	47 2/8	49 5/8	26 0/8	11	10	Jolly River	NWT	Ty Martin	1987	123
313 6/8	51 5/8	49 6/8	25 6/8	11	10	MacKay Lake	NWT	James Kelter	1992	123
313 5/8	45 6/8	47 0/8	23 6/8	14	11	Warburton Bay	NWT	Michael R. Westvang	1995	125
313 2/8	44 6/8	47 7/8	24 6/8	9	8	Desteffany Lake	NWT	Robert Harris	1998	126
312 6/8	50 0/8	50 4/8	30 4/8	13	11	MacKay Lake	NWT	Bret Estes	1996	127
312 3/8	44 2/8	45 0/8	31 3/8	13	11	Combo Lake	NWT	Thomas J. Hoffman	1997	128
312 2/8	47 0/8	46 0/8	38 6/8	10	10	MacKay Lake	NWT	Dennis G. Hicks	1990	129
312 1/8	51 4/8	44 5/8	24 4/8	14	17	MacKay Lake	NWT	Duane Hicks	1988	130
312 0/8	48 5/8	51 5/8	28 5/8	15	12	Rendezvous Lake	NWT	Albert Osellame	1996	130
312 0/8	43 2/8	43 0/8	32 4/8	13	12	Pellatt Lake	NWT	V. Randy Liljenquist	1997	130
311 4/8	50 1/8	48 3/8	28 0/8	8	11	MacKay Lake	NWT	Marc Nyrose	1991	133
311 3/8	43 7/8	43 1/8	27 3/8	10	10	MacKay Lake	NWT	Andy Carpenter	1997	134
311 0/8	48 2/8	47 4/8	40 7/8	10	10	MacKay Lake	NWT	John Visscher	1991	135
310 7/8	51 0/8	52 2/8	25 1/8	13	8	MacKay Lake	NWT	Ryk Visscher	1990	136
310 1/8	47 6/8	47 5/8	23 6/8	14	12	Warburton Bay	NWT	Richard E. LaCrone	1997	137
310 0/8	42 2/8	45 6/8	21 4/8	9	11	MacKay Lake	NWT	John Visscher	1990	138
309 5/8	44 4/8	45 4/8	14 7/8	12	12	MacKay Lake	NWT	Steve Tice	1994	139
309 2/8	45 7/8	46 2/8	32 2/8	11	12	Little Marten Lake	NWT	Drew Mouton	1992	140
309 1/8	45 6/8	47 1/8	31 4/8	7	6	MacKay Lake	NWT	Chuck Kronenwetter	1994	141
308 5/8	51 1/8	50 0/8	34 1/8	6	7	MacKay Lake	NWT	Greg Schleusner	1998	142
308 3/8	47 6/8	49 6/8	24 7/8	9	10	MacKay Lake	NWT	Roy Goodwin	1995	143
308 0/8	42 4/8	45 5/8	30 5/8	10	11	White Island	NWT	Kendall Bauer	1996	144
307 7/8	47 0/8	48 4/8	30 6/8	10	10	MacKay Lake	NWT	Tom Taylor	1994	145
307 6/8	43 5/8	43 5/8	35 0/8	7	8	Yellowknife	NWT	Jim Wondzell	1994	146
307 3/8	50 6/8	48 4/8	31 3/8	14	11	MacKay Lake	NWT	Warren Witherspoon	1993	147
307 2/8	48 6/8	48 6/8	35 0/8	8	9	MacKay Lake	NWT	Joseph R. St. Charles	1993	148
307 1/8	48 6/8	51 6/8	34 7/8	10	11	Humpy Lake	NWT	Chester Kottke, Jr.	1997	149
306 7/8	41 6/8	41 2/8	22 6/8	8	13	Desteffany Lake	NWT	Randy E. Doyle	1996	150
305 4/8	50 5/8	50 2/8	28 0/8	8	8	MacKay Lake	NWT	Dan Brockman	1990	151
304 7/8	48 1/8	48 3/8	29 7/8	9	8	MacKay Lake	NWT	David R. Coupland	1991	152
304 6/8	45 3/8	46 0/8	25 2/8	13	11	MacKay Lake	NWT	Howard L. Harding	1992	153
304 4/8	53 6/8	54 3/8	33 2/8	7	7	Humpy Lake	NWT	Dr. Chuck Leidheiser	1997	154
303 5/8	48 5/8	47 7/8	35 5/8	8	10	Desteffany Lake	NWT	Larry Streiff	1996	155
303 2/8	45 6/8	48 0/8	26 0/8	11	8	Jolly Lake	NWT	Greg Wadsworth	1996	156
302 6/8	44 6/8	44 2/8	29 0/8	11	9	MacKay Lake	NWT	Les Malsch	1990	157
302 4/8	46 1/8	46 2/8	33 5/8	9	14	Courageous Lake	NWT	Wm. R. Vanderhoef	1987	158
302 1/8	50 7/8	50 7/8	30 2/8	7	10	MacKay Lake	NWT	Russ Tye	1992	159
301 4/8	43 5/8	42 1/8	28 0/8	9	9	Little Marten Lake	NWT	Jerry Rush	1993	160
301 0/8	43 2/8	43 4/8	30 3/8	9	6	Jolly Lake	NWT	Greg Wadsworth	1996	161
300 6/8	40 4/8	39 7/8	30 4/8	10	15	MacKay Lake	NWT	Dale Holpainen	1992	162

CENTRAL CANADA CARIBOU (VELVET ANTLERS)

Minimum Score 300

SCORE	LENGTH OF MAIN BEAM R / L	INSIDE SPREAD	NUMBER OF POINTS R / L		AREA	STATE/PROVINCE	HUNTER'S NAME	DATE	RANK
375 3/8	57 2/8	52 6/8	30 6/8	8	10	MacKay Lake	NWT	Richard Thrasher	1996	*
372 0/8	53 5/8	56 4/8	40 7/8	8	11	MacKay Lake	NWT	John Sebert	1996	*
371 0/8	50 0/8	49 4/8	32 4/8	12	11	MacKay Lake	NWT	Geoff Sagen	1996	*
369 7/8	46 2/8	42 3/8	34 7/8	13	15	Snake River	NWT	Ray Fredin	1995	*
362 4/8	48 7/8	50 7/8	24 4/8	11	13	MacKay Lake	NWT	Dale Devlin	1997	*
361 6/8	49 4/8	50 0/8	34 5/8	11	10	MacKay Lake	NWT	Kent S. Ringheim	1995	*
360 0/8	50 7/8	49 0/8	27 1/8	8	8	MacKay Lake	NWT	Reagan Dunn	1994	*
359 6/8	47 4/8	46 6/8	38 3/8	12	9	Horton Lake	NWT	Dave Fowler	1993	*
356 6/8	52 2/8	54 4/8	43 5/8	11	10	Point Lake	NWT	Tim Dumbeck	1995	*
356 2/8	48 4/8	50 5/8	34 4/8	9	11	Humpy Lake	NWT	Gary F. Bogner	1997	*
355 1/8	45 4/8	45 4/8	30 2/8	14	16	Hillbilly Bay	NWT	Gregory B. McPhillips	1996	*
349 5/8	50 4/8	50 4/8	27 3/8	13	14	MacKay Lake	NWT	Dan Gartner	1996	*
348 2/8	48 4/8	50 4/8	22 6/8	11	11	MacKay Lake	NWT	Ronald Rockwell	1996	*
348 1/8	52 2/8	51 6/8	37 2/8	8	10	Jolly Lake	NWT	Ken Baker	1996	*
344 0/8	53 2/8	54 3/8	28 5/8	10	10	MacKay Lake	NWT	Richard Thrasher	1996	*
342 0/8	50 6/8	47 2/8	27 4/8	11	12	Point Lake	NWT	Robert J. Otto	1995	*
339 2/8	50 0/8	49 0/8	29 1/8	11	8	MacKay Lake	NWT	Dan Gartner	1996	*
337 4/8	43 6/8	47 1/8	31 5/8	12	10	Barelzon Lake	NWT	Conway Marvin	1993	*
337 1/8	50 7/8	51 3/8	32 1/8	10	11	MacKay Lake	NWT	John Sebert	1995	*
335 4/8	43 2/8	45 1/8	27 7/8	12	12	MacKay Lake	NWT	Bryant Dunn	1994	*
334 4/8	48 6/8	50 2/8	25 5/8	9	16	Little Marten Lake	NWT	Dave Justmann	1995	*
333 3/8	51 7/8	55 4/8	26 4/8	11	8	MacKay Lake	NWT	John Sebert	1995	*
329 5/8	49 4/8	46 5/8	30 2/8	13	13	MacKay Lake	NWT	Glenn Kuklick	1995	*
325 6/8	49 0/8	51 0/8	25 4/8	13	9	Lake Providence	NWT	Jeff Fitts	1993	*
325 3/8	50 5/8	48 1/8	36 2/8	8	10	MacKay Lake	NWT	John Looze	1996	*
320 1/8	44 0/8	44 1/8	22 1/8	8	9	Point Lake	NWT	Robert S. Barber	1995	*
317 0/8	46 3/8	46 3/8	37 7/8	9	9	Warburton Bay	NWT	Don Delabbio	1996	*
313 3/8	50 0/8	48 0/8	22 2/8	5	7	MacKay Lake	NWT	Ronald Rockwell	1996	*
305 6/8	37 6/8	37 5/8	22 6/8	22	18	Snake River	NWT	Gregory B. McPhillips	1996	*
303 7/8	47 0/8	49 1/8	28 6/8	7	9	Jolly Lake	NWT	Mark Mathieson	1997	*
301 4/8	45 3/8	45 5/8	26 2/8	12	11	MacKay Lake	NWT	Bradley Looze	1996	*

* *Velvet entries will be listed in only one record book.*

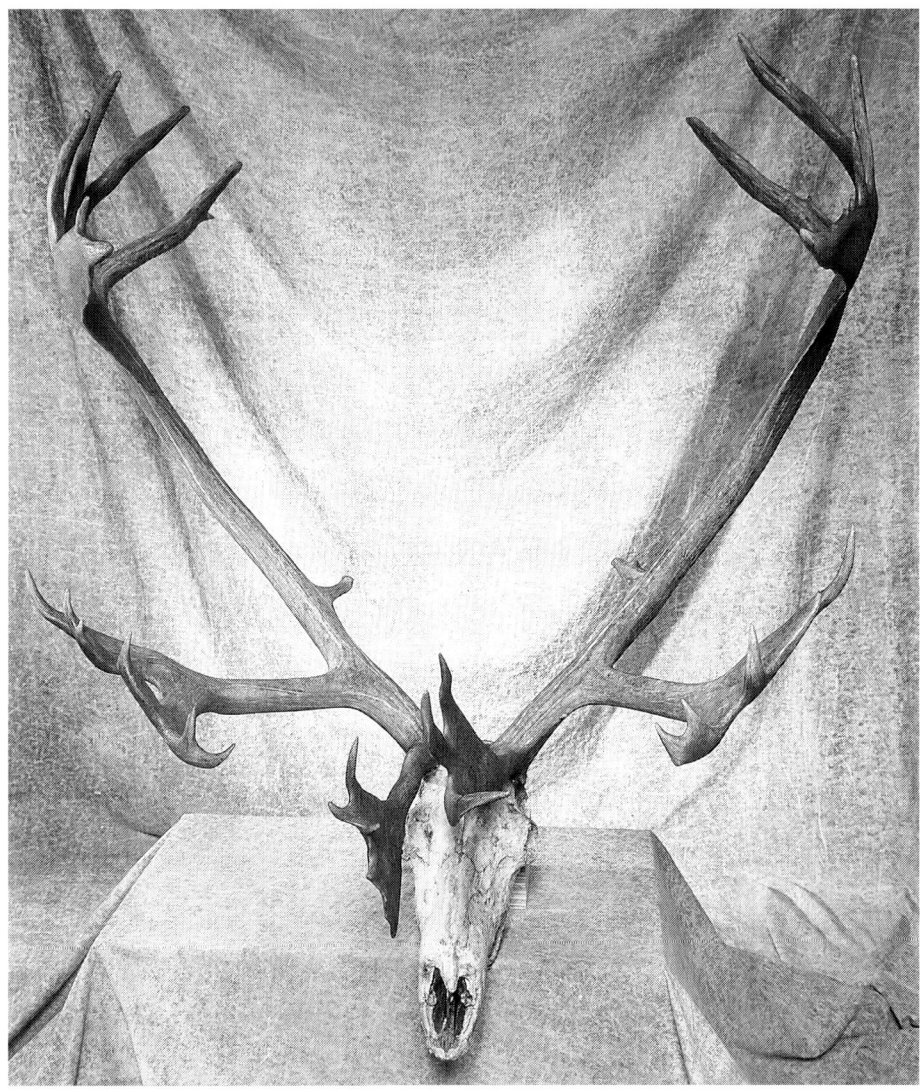

World Record Mountain Caribou
Score: 413 6/8
Divide Lake, Northwest Territories - 1995
Hunter: Chuck Adams

MOUNTAIN CARIBOU

Minimum Score 300

Rangifer tarandus osborni, Rangifer tarandus fortidens and *Rangifer tarandus montanus*

SCORE	LENGTH OF R MAIN BEAM L		INSIDE SPREAD	NUMBER R OF POINTS L		AREA	STATE/ PROVINCE	HUNTER'S NAME	DATE	RANK
413 6/8	47 2/8	46 0/8	39 1/8	14	12	Divide Lake	NWT	Chuck Adams	1995	1
410 2/8	54 0/8	55 6/8	46 0/8	15	12	Cassiar Mtns.	BC	Thomas B. Frye	1978	2
399 0/8	49 7/8	51 5/8	40 2/8	8	11	Cassiar Mtns.	BC	Joseph Hinderman	1997	3
396 4/8	44 0/8	45 1/8	42 4/8	18	15	Divide Lake	NWT	John E. Anderson	1995	4
391 3/8	53 3/8	54 1/8	36 6/8	13	15	Tuya Lake	BC	John D. "Jack" Frost	1995	5
390 1/8	55 2/8	51 6/8	34 1/8	15	11	Firesteel River	BC	Melvin K. Wolf	1970	6
387 6/8	44 3/8	42 7/8	36 0/8	15	14	Cold Fish Lake	BC	Steve Gorr	1976	7
378 2/8	49 3/8	47 4/8	37 0/8	11	10	O'Grady Lake	NWT	C. Randall Byers	1988	8
378 0/8	42 1/8	44 1/8	31 7/8	12	11	Tahltan River	BC	Arthur Harlow	1988	9
374 6/8	55 4/8	55 6/8	40 2/8	10	8	Thutade Lake	BC	Edward C. Pawinski	1984	10
374 1/8	43 6/8	47 1/8	35 0/8	16	16	Duti River	BC	Dr. Lowell Eddy	1967	11
373 3/8	45 5/8	43 7/8	31 0/8	13	17	June Lake	NWT	Dennis Palmer	1988	12
373 3/8	47 7/8	47 3/8	30 7/8	18	15	O'Grady Lake	NWT	Randall R. Giesey	1993	12
373 2/8	45 4/8	44 7/8	37 7/8	10	13	Natla River	NWT	Chuck Adams	1990	14
371 7/8	48 1/8	47 1/8	39 1/8	15	13	Tatlatui Lake	BC	Larry Alma	1979	15
371 7/8	46 0/8	46 0/8	36 4/8	14	12	Divide Lake	NWT	Mike Parsons	1988	15
371 3/8	38 7/8	39 3/8	30 3/8	16	15	Thutade Lake	BC	Bob Brill	1980	17

MOUNTAIN CARIBOU

Minimum Score 300 — Continued

SCORE	LENGTH OF MAIN BEAM R	LENGTH OF MAIN BEAM L	INSIDE SPREAD	NUMBER OF POINTS R	NUMBER OF POINTS L	AREA	STATE/ PROVINCE	HUNTER'S NAME	DATE	RANK
370 1/8	45 1/8	45 2/8	29 6/8	12	16	Cassiar Mtns.	BC	Ray Wilson	1988	18
370 1/8	45 5/8	48 4/8	40 6/8	8	10	Russell Lake	YUK	Bob Fromme	1990	18
370 0/8	46 4/8	44 5/8	30 4/8	14	14	Natla River	NWT	Janice J. Traub	1985	20
368 0/8	43 1/8	45 0/8	30 0/8	13	13	Keele River	NWT	Jay Brown	1991	21
367 4/8	47 0/8	45 4/8	29 7/8	17	13	June Lake	NWT	Nathan L. Andersohn	1995	22
365 7/8	49 0/8	49 6/8	34 0/8	12	12	O'Grady Lake	NWT	R. Brian Oates	1990	23
365 2/8	47 4/8	48 5/8	32 1/8	14	13	Horseshoe Lake	NWT	Mike Parsons	1989	24
361 2/8	49 4/8	53 2/8	31 7/8	12	10	O'Grady Lake	NWT	G. Fred Asbell	1988	25
357 6/8	39 2/8	38 5/8	27 4/8	12	12	McNeil Lake	YUK	Todd Zeuske	1994	26
357 5/8	46 0/8	45 2/8	31 6/8	11	11	Caribou Pass	NWT	Duane Hicks	1996	27
356 5/8	38 7/8	40 5/8	32 0/8	15	16	Horseshoe Lake	NWT	Don Davidson	1989	28
354 3/8	41 3/8	42 4/8	28 6/8	10	10	O'Grady Lake	NWT	C. Randall Byers	1991	29
352 1/8	44 7/8	43 7/8	36 5/8	13	15	June Lake	NWT	Garry Bolinder	1996	30
351 6/8	46 4/8	45 0/8	37 4/8	11	11	Watson Lake	YUK	Pete Shepley	1985	31
350 6/8	41 0/8	42 0/8	30 1/8	8	8	Caribou Lake	NWT	John W. Borlang	1989	32
350 5/8	46 7/8	46 5/8	33 7/8	12	13	Mountain River	NWT	Tom D. Slusser	1991	33
349 2/8	47 0/8	45 5/8	34 4/8	11	10	Nahanni Butte	NWT	William E. Terry, Sr.	1994	34
348 6/8	51 2/8	49 5/8	44 5/8	10	11	Ragged Range	NWT	Tom Taylor	1993	35
348 3/8	52 4/8	55 3/8	48 5/8	12	9	O'Grady Lake	NWT	Marc N. Shaft	1988	36
347 5/8	33 4/8	32 5/8	31 4/8	14	11	O'Grady Lake	NWT	Don Davidson	1991	37
347 1/8	44 6/8	46 6/8	37 6/8	14	12	Stikine River	BC	Claudio Canonica	1988	38
347 1/8	43 7/8	40 5/8	34 4/8	15	15	Divide Lake	NWT	Chuck Adams	1993	38
345 0/8	51 5/8	49 1/8	33 7/8	13	11	Divide Lake	NWT	Al Reay	1982	40
344 4/8	57 3/8	56 2/8	38 6/8	10	9	O'Grady Lake	NWT	Steven R. Hohensee	1992	41
343 3/8	48 2/8	50 6/8	35 4/8	15	11	Serpentine Mt.	BC	Randolph P. Wilson	1976	42
342 2/8	47 6/8	47 1/8	34 4/8	10	9	Divide Lake	NWT	Stanley Walchuk, Jr.	1984	43
342 0/8	40 6/8	36 4/8	32 0/8	18	17	Caribou Pass	NWT	Ryk Visscher	1996	44
340 7/8	46 4/8	45 3/8	37 3/8	9	12	Horseshoe Lake	NWT	Jerry Keller	1990	45
339 6/8	42 7/8	44 6/8	20 0/8	20	18	Tatlatui Lake	BC	G. Fred Asbell	1975	46
339 5/8	44 6/8	44 5/8	24 5/8	15	13	O'Grady Lake	NWT	Mark Wuerthele	1993	47
339 4/8	47 0/8	48 6/8	37 0/8	10	11	Divide Lake	NWT	Dan Brockman	1991	48
336 7/8	45 1/8	47 4/8	29 2/8	8	10	June Lake	NWT	Mike Zech	1989	49
336 1/8	46 6/8	47 2/8	36 3/8	7	9	Summit Lake	YUK	Gregory White	1989	50
336 1/8	42 7/8	40 5/8	36 6/8	12	15	Nacha Creek	BC	Scott L. Koelzer	1994	50
335 4/8	43 7/8	43 4/8	32 0/8	13	10	Divide Lake	NWT	Mark Zastrow	1991	52
334 2/8	40 7/8	40 0/8	36 5/8	15	11	Wolverine Creek	NWT	Stan Godfrey	1988	53
334 1/8	40 4/8	41 1/8	33 7/8	13	17	Firesteel River	BC	Walter Krom	1971	54
333 5/8	45 1/8	47 2/8	31 0/8	12	11	Firesteel River	BC	Jay Deones	1978	55
332 1/8	40 0/8	40 4/8	32 5/8	10	12	Firesteel River	BC	Larry Alma	1984	56
328 5/8	51 6/8	50 5/8	40 4/8	9	12	Kilgore Lake	BC	Mike Parsons	1998	57
328 3/8	41 2/8	40 6/8	26 5/8	12	10	Divide Lake	NWT	Chuck Adams	1992	58
327 0/8	41 2/8	40 1/8	31 4/8	15	15	Mountain River	NWT	Mike Barrett	1990	59
326 7/8	46 2/8	47 4/8	34 4/8	10	8	Tae Mtn.	YUK	Edwin L. DeYoung	1996	60
326 3/8	53 4/8	52 1/8	26 5/8	9	8	Tay Mtn.	YUK	Don Lind	1997	61
326 2/8	37 7/8	41 1/8	27 7/8	15	14	Divide Lake	NWT	John Baird	1994	62
324 1/8	35 3/8	36 3/8	32 1/8	15	18	Cassiar Mtns.	BC	Mike Parsons	1994	63
324 1/8	38 5/8	40 0/8	31 5/8	10	10	Ludwig Lake	BC	Guy Leibenguth	1997	63
323 5/8	42 3/8	44 2/8	36 2/8	11	9	O'Grady Lake	NWT	J. Dale Hale	1998	65
321 7/8	48 4/8	47 3/8	32 4/8	13	14	Kitchener Lake	BC	Stephen E. Mitchell	1970	66
320 6/8	43 6/8	44 4/8	31 7/8	11	12	Thutade Lake	BC	Jack W. Kriener	1974	67
319 4/8	45 0/8	45 2/8	40 5/8	10	12	Kitchener Lake	BC	Doug Strecker	1979	68
319 1/8	44 3/8	48 5/8	24 7/8	13	10	Cold Fish Lake	BC	Steve Gorr	1975	69
318 7/8	38 2/8	40 0/8	35 4/8	9	9	Mackenzie Mtns.	NWT	Steven Weekly	1987	70
317 4/8	43 1/8	42 6/8	34 1/8	10	8	Divide Lake	NWT	Jim Wondzell	1993	71
317 3/8	43 1/8	45 5/8	29 0/8	11	11	Keele River	NWT	Ron Serwa	1988	72
315 5/8	43 3/8	44 3/8	29 1/8	11	12	Kitchener Lake	BC	Dick Crowder	1976	73
314 7/8	42 6/8	46 0/8	33 5/8	10	10	Divide Lake	NWT	Dale Drilling	1989	74
314 5/8	44 7/8	47 6/8	32 7/8	10	9	Ittlemit Lake	YUK	Chuck Buchanan	1979	75
314 3/8	43 7/8	43 3/8	30 7/8	9	12	Divide Lake	NWT	Duane Zemliska	1991	76
314 2/8	42 7/8	44 0/8	28 3/8	10	10	O'Grady Lake	NWT	Don Davidson, Jr.	1988	77
313 4/8	40 2/8	45 1/8	32 7/8	10	8	Mackenzie Mtns.	NWT	John 'Jack' Cordes	1985	78
309 2/8	43 3/8	41 2/8	27 2/8	10	13	Thutade Lake	BC	Harold H. Vander Horst	1974	79
307 7/8	46 6/8	47 4/8	29 7/8	9	9	Thutade Lake	BC	Kim S. Ades	1984	80
306 2/8	43 4/8	43 2/8	29 2/8	11	10	Tatlatui Lake	BC	Robert Pitt	1975	81
304 2/8	37 2/8	40 7/8	27 1/8	10	10	O'Grady Lake	NWT	P. Tod Byers	1991	82
303 6/8	42 4/8	42 4/8	25 2/8	9	12	Tatlatui Lake	BC	Rick Gilley	1983	83

MOUNTAIN CARIBOU (VELVET ANTLERS)

Minimum Score 300

SCORE	LENGTH OF R MAIN BEAM L		INSIDE SPREAD	NUMBER R OF POINTS L		AREA	STATE/ PROVINCE	HUNTER'S NAME	DATE	RANK
432 2/8	46 6/8	46 3/8	43 0/8	15	15	O'Grady Lake	NWT	J. Dean Bodoh	1990	*
394 1/8	47 6/8	49 0/8	37 3/8	13	11	Godlin Lake	NWT	Thomas J. Hoffman	1990	*
377 6/8	45 1/8	45 6/8	27 2/8	18	13	O'Grady Lake	NWT	Don Davidson	1993	*
374 7/8	44 1/8	44 7/8	33 5/8	12	12	Mackenzie Mtns.	NWT	Chuck Adams	1985	*
364 2/8	41 4/8	46 0/8	29 6/8	14	14	Archie Lake	NWT	Dallas Smith	1997	*
363 1/8	48 1/8	48 7/8	38 3/8	9	10	Divide Lake	NWT	Pam Baird	1994	*
361 3/8	45 3/8	46 4/8	35 2/8	12	11	Horseshoe Lake	NWT	Dave Brummond	1991	*
360 7/8	45 0/8	44 0/8	39 1/8	12	11	O'Grady Lake	NWT	Dan Bertalan	1993	*
359 1/8	49 1/8	48 6/8	29 2/8	14	14	Hook Lake	NWT	Bob Wickler	1987	*
353 2/8	44 7/8	46 5/8	26 0/8	14	12	O'Grady Lake	NWT	Ron Rockwell	1993	*
348 4/8	48 2/8	48 5/8	31 6/8	9	10	Natla River	NWT	Kevin L. Reid	1995	*
330 4/8	49 4/8	48 4/8	37 2/8	9	7	O'Grady Lake	NWT	Sheldon Poss	1994	*
329 2/8	43 5/8	42 0/8	31 6/8	10	12	Divide Lake	NWT	Mike Traub	1984	*
328 6/8	45 0/8	46 6/8	25 3/8	10	11	Divide Lake	NWT	Cameron Hayden	1997	*
318 3/8	43 6/8	44 1/8	33 3/8	9	12	Divide Lake	NWT	Mike Honek	1995	*
316 2/8	41 4/8	41 0/8	29 6/8	9	12	Natla River	NWT	Richard A. Case	1990	*
305 0/8	44 0/8	44 5/8	35 4/8	9	9	O'Grady Lake	NWT	Corey Hugelen	1991	*
304 0/8	44 6/8	44 4/8	27 5/8	9	10	O'Grady Lake	NWT	Edwin Evans	1993	*
302 0/8	37 2/8	36 2/8	31 4/8	11	13	Keele River	NWT	Gregg Welch	1995	*
301 1/8	48 2/8	48 1/8	31 2/8	9	11	O'Grady Lake	NWT	Darin E. Pfingsten	1994	*

Velvet entries will be listed in only one record book.

World Record Quebec-Labrador Caribou
Score: 434 0/8
Tunulik River, Quebec - 1984
Hunter: Carol Ann Mauch

QUEBEC-LABRADOR CARIBOU

Minimum Score 325

Rangifer tarandus caboti from Quebec and Labrador

SCORE	LENGTH OF R MAIN BEAM L		INSIDE SPREAD	NUMBER R OF POINTS L		AREA	STATE/ PROVINCE	HUNTER'S NAME	DATE	RANK
434 0/8	53 6/8	56 1/8	46 1/8	17	12	Tunulik River	QUE	Carol Ann Mauch	1984	1
429 1/8	52 2/8	52 2/8	45 1/8	15	17	Delay River	QUE	Bob Foulkrod	1985	2
419 4/8	50 0/8	50 6/8	40 2/8	12	11	Natuak Lake	QUE	Patricio Sada Muguerza	1993	3
416 6/8	51 2/8	49 6/8	50 0/8	13	14	Lake Consigny	QUE	Ricardo L. Garza	1989	4
416 5/8	45 3/8	47 7/8	47 4/8	28	27	George River	QUE	Collins F. Kellogg	1978	5
415 7/8	51 5/8	55 3/8	53 0/8	16	16	Ungava Bay	QUE	Dr. Woodallen G. Snyder	1984	6
412 7/8	52 7/8	53 0/8	49 3/8	17	18	LG4	QUE	Gary Robbins	1990	7
412 2/8	50 2/8	53 1/8	43 0/8	18	19	Delay River	QUE	Leonard L. Campbell	1995	8
411 4/8	56 4/8	57 0/8	52 0/8	16	14	Ungava Region	QUE	Richard S. Neely	1977	9
410 2/8	52 4/8	51 6/8	48 4/8	15	16	Pons Island	QUE	Don Young	1988	10
410 0/8	56 0/8	55 6/8	52 1/8	13	11	Schefferville	QUE	Charles L. Buechel, Jr.	1987	11
407 5/8	50 3/8	50 0/8	45 3/8	13	15	Delay River	QUE	Jeff Baker	1988	12
403 7/8	51 3/8	50 3/8	43 5/8	14	16	Delay River	QUE	Dr. James J. Barnes	1987	13
403 2/8	48 2/8	47 2/8	35 2/8	16	16	Lake Droilland	QUE	Tom Johnson	1991	14
402 3/8	59 4/8	57 7/8	56 6/8	13	14	Ungava Bay	QUE	Leonard J. Letendre	1989	15
401 3/8	49 4/8	49 0/8	51 1/8	14	14	Lac Pon's	QUE	Gordon Demeritt	1988	16
399 7/8	52 3/8	53 1/8	49 6/8	12	12	Whiskey Lake	QUE	D.F.Baldwin & T. Barta	1985	17
398 5/8	52 2/8	54 2/8	51 1/8	20	17	George River	QUE	Richard Mielke	1981	18
398 5/8	54 4/8	54 5/8	52 4/8	10	11	Caniapiscau River	QUE	Henry O. Fromm	1987	18
398 1/8	51 4/8	52 2/8	48 3/8	11	11	Lac Otelnuk	QUE	Rudy Tremain	1989	20
396 1/8	51 6/8	51 2/8	48 1/8	14	15	Weymouth Inlet	QUE	Tink Nathan	1986	21
395 6/8	59 4/8	55 4/8	47 7/8	18	16	George River	QUE	Paul Brunner	1980	22
394 5/8	54 3/8	53 3/8	49 1/8	14	11	Deception Bay	QUE	Leo Neuls, Jr.	1998	23
392 4/8	52 4/8	53 4/8	44 7/8	15	13	Caniapiscau River	QUE	Mike Ingold	1988	24
392 2/8	53 4/8	59 2/8	42 2/8	13	11	Potier Bay	QUE	Donald L. Sagner	1995	25
392 0/8	51 4/8	50 6/8	48 2/8	18	27	Lac Cananee	QUE	Brad L. Johnson	1981	26
391 0/8	55 6/8	56 2/8	39 4/8	17	15	George River	QUE	Jim McCrory	1980	27
389 5/8	50 4/8	49 6/8	42 1/8	16	13	Ronalds Lake	QUE	Chris Kantianis	1993	28
388 3/8	49 2/8	51 6/8	40 5/8	12	12	Delay River	QUE	Richard E. Davis	1987	29
388 2/8	46 0/8	45 4/8	42 6/8	11	11	Delay River	QUE	William G. Mason	1988	30
387 6/8	62 1/8	60 7/8	53 7/8	12	11	Delay River	QUE	Roy M. Goodwin	1987	31
387 6/8	50 1/8	49 4/8	45 6/8	12	14	Pons River	QUE	Louis J. Lorenzo	1991	31
387 4/8	42 2/8	39 5/8	47 7/8	24	16	Delay River	QUE	Larry Smith	1987	33
387 1/8	52 0/8	53 5/8	48 4/8	9	12	Schefferville	QUE	Tom Kayser	1986	34
387 1/8	47 0/8	44 5/8	46 6/8	14	13	Weeks Lake	QUE	Donald L. Stout	1990	34
386 4/8	56 2/8	54 4/8	57 7/8	15	20	George River	QUE	John Kuhar	1972	36
385 5/8	50 2/8	52 2/8	50 7/8	16	18	Pons Island	QUE	James C. Walters	1987	37
385 1/8	47 0/8	49 2/8	43 3/8	12	15	Saglek Bay	LAB	Zig Kertenis, Jr.	1988	38
384 7/8	50 6/8	50 0/8	50 0/8	15	18	Whale River	QUE	David L. Willis	1986	39
384 7/8	46 1/8	45 7/8	57 6/8	12	11	Pons Lake	QUE	George P. Mann	1994	39
384 4/8	46 4/8	46 5/8	42 4/8	15	16	Schefferville	QUE	Elmer R. Luce, Jr.	1987	41
384 2/8	45 2/8	46 6/8	49 0/8	19	19	Schefferville	QUE	Elmer R. Luce, Jr.	1987	42
384 1/8	46 1/8	45 6/8	45 7/8	14	12	Caniapiscau River	QUE	Shaun R. Murphy	1994	43
384 0/8	46 0/8	44 3/8	43 0/8	17	13	Weymouth Inlet	QUE	Jules Pacheco	1986	44
383 7/8	47 3/8	49 5/8	46 7/8	14	17	Lake Loudin	QUE	Roger M. Schmitt	1988	45
383 6/8	49 6/8	48 3/8	46 1/8	26	18	Wayne Lake	QUE	Brian Preston	1993	46
383 4/8	49 6/8	50 0/8	46 0/8	14	12	Schefferville	QUE	Robert B. Stryker	1994	47
381 6/8	50 4/8	52 0/8	50 2/8	13	13	Delay River	QUE	Robert G. McCulley	1988	48
381 4/8	51 0/8	51 6/8	41 2/8	17	19	Wedge Hill Lodge	QUE	John Janelli	1980	49
381 3/8	52 0/8	49 2/8	48 0/8	13	14	Ungava Region	QUE	Wayne A. Vanstratten	1986	50
381 2/8	48 3/8	50 4/8	39 1/8	13	14	Caniapiscau River	QUE	David C. Arndt	1986	51
381 0/8	51 0/8	52 1/8	44 3/8	14	13	LG4	QUE	Stephen Kotz	1990	52
380 6/8	56 0/8	52 1/8	40 4/8	12	12	Oltanook Lake	QUE	Ken Mowerson	1986	53
380 6/8	53 6/8	54 0/8	46 2/8	12	13	Kuujjuaq	QUE	Steven L. Fair	1993	53
380 5/8	57 6/8	53 5/8	56 7/8	11	16	Ungava Region	QUE	Donald Schram	1982	55
379 7/8	49 0/8	50 2/8	51 2/8	15	13	Schefferville	QUE	Michael C. Dysh	1990	56
379 6/8	49 4/8	49 2/8	42 5/8	11	12	Schefferville	QUE	Ted Jaycox	1986	57
379 6/8	45 7/8	50 1/8	48 2/8	16	16	Pons River	QUE	Chris Cass	1993	57
379 4/8	45 0/8	47 3/8	46 0/8	17	14	Alubiack Fiord	QUE	Tim Finley	1994	59
379 0/8	55 6/8	55 4/8	48 2/8	12	13	Delay River	QUE	Paul Rigsby	1988	60
378 7/8	54 2/8	54 2/8	54 3/8	11	12	Tunulik River	QUE	Jay G. St. Charles	1986	61
378 4/8	49 5/8	49 0/8	44 3/8	14	15	Fort Chimo	QUE	Robert Pyne	1989	62
378 3/8	50 0/8	50 7/8	40 6/8	13	14	Fort Chimo	QUE	Nickoles J. Giannetti	1993	63
377 3/8	51 6/8	55 2/8	52 4/8	12	13	Schefferville	QUE	Frank 'Rit' Heller	1978	64
377 3/8	49 5/8	49 7/8	36 2/8	19	17	Lac Minto	QUE	Charles Nopper	1997	64
377 0/8	53 6/8	55 7/8	36 7/8	15	15	Delay River	QUE	Dale Underwood	1990	66
376 7/8	48 1/8	49 6/8	51 0/8	17	13	Lake Lac Hine	QUE	Edward A. Mertins	1990	67
376 7/8	43 6/8	44 1/8	44 0/8	14	14	Deception Bay	QUE	Leo Neuls, Sr.	1998	67
376 5/8	50 4/8	50 4/8	57 0/8	13	11	Ungava Bay	QUE	Ed Riley	1985	69
376 2/8	49 2/8	48 2/8	49 4/8	17	18	Fort Chimo	QUE	David Bailey	1985	70
376 2/8	51 7/8	54 1/8	44 1/8	16	17	Bolen Camp	QUE	John "Chip" Klass	1995	70
376 1/8	47 1/8	47 2/8	36 4/8	14	14	Deception Bay	QUE	Leo Neuls, Sr.	1998	72
376 0/8	51 0/8	50 4/8	42 0/8	11	13	Lac Bienville	QUE	L. Reed Breight	1997	73
375 7/8	46 5/8	47 6/8	37 2/8	24	25	Ungava Region	QUE	Jose Rivero	1979	74
375 5/8	51 4/8	52 2/8	50 2/8	14	16	Lac Minto	QUE	Jason D. Cook	1997	75
375 1/8	60 3/8	59 6/8	42 0/8	15	16	George River	QUE	Robert M. Sweisthal, Jr.	1980	76
374 7/8	49 5/8	52 1/8	59 2/8	11	15	Ungava Region	QUE	Bob Frank	1979	77
374 6/8	47 5/8	48 7/8	43 6/8	13	12	Weeks Lake	QUE	Raymond Villeneuve	1990	78

QUEBEC-LABRADOR CARIBOU

Minimum Score 325
Continued

SCORE	LENGTH OF MAIN BEAM R / L	INSIDE SPREAD	NUMBER OF POINTS R / L		AREA	STATE/ PROVINCE	HUNTER'S NAME	DATE	RANK
374 4/8	54 0/8	59 2/8	34 7/8	9 / 12	Schefferville	QUE	Brian L. Johnson	1988	79
374 4/8	51 0/8	47 4/8	39 1/8	14 / 13	George River	QUE	David A. Spacek	1990	79
374 3/8	60 2/8	59 0/8	52 5/8	14 / 13	Schefferville	QUE	Bill Heather	1979	81
373 6/8	48 1/8	47 0/8	36 3/8	6 / 6	Lippe Lake	QUE	Robert L. Goldsberry	1994	82
373 6/8	48 5/8	45 2/8	36 5/8	13 / 14	Pons River	QUE	Louis Kitcoff	1996	82
373 3/8	53 2/8	51 1/8	40 0/8	15 / 13	Fort Chimo	QUE	Scott M. Showalter	1982	84
373 2/8	49 2/8	44 4/8	43 0/8	15 / 13	LG 4	QUE	Christopher Germain	1992	85
373 0/8	45 3/8	44 2/8	39 2/8	20 / 10	Wolf Lake	QUE	Bruce A. Hopkins	1993	86
372 7/8	44 2/8	45 2/8	37 7/8	17 / 17	Delay River	QUE	Ray Moulton	1986	87
372 7/8	46 6/8	47 4/8	47 6/8	15 / 13	Henrys Lake	QUE	Kip Boten	1990	87
372 5/8	46 3/8	43 2/8	37 6/8	15 / 20	Ungava Bay	QUE	Si Pellow	1988	89
372 4/8	55 7/8	53 1/8	43 2/8	13 / 13	Ungava Bay	QUE	David Dunnigan	1984	90
372 4/8	53 0/8	58 7/8	43 4/8	11 / 10	Lac LeFrancois	QUE	Raymond W. Murray III	1990	90
372 4/8	45 6/8	45 5/8	41 1/8	16 / 16	LG4	QUE	Paul J. Sisz	1991	90
372 1/8	52 6/8	53 2/8	52 4/8	17 / 15	Ungava Bay	QUE	Roy M. Goodwin	1989	93
371 6/8	48 7/8	50 1/8	42 6/8	17 / 16	Fort Chimo	QUE	Robert Pyne	1989	94
371 5/8	48 6/8	47 3/8	42 4/8	16 / 13	Maricourt Lake	QUE	James Kingsley	1992	95
370 7/8	46 6/8	44 5/8	41 2/8	5 / 6	Schefferville	QUE	Elmer R. Luce, Jr.	1986	96
370 5/8	45 0/8	48 0/8	37 5/8	20 / 14	Caniapiscau River	QUE	Gregory White	1987	97
370 2/8	46 0/8	46 7/8	55 1/8	12 / 13	Delay River	QUE	Mike Iuzzolino	1991	98
369 1/8	53 6/8	52 4/8	50 5/8	14 / 12	Jack's Lake	QUE	Denis Weisensel	1989	99
368 6/8	51 3/8	52 6/8	51 7/8	11 / 14	Kuujjuak River	QUE	Glen Ogle	1988	100
368 5/8	52 0/8	46 1/8	44 4/8	21 / 15	Fort Chimo	QUE	Joseph A. Borgna	1989	101
368 5/8	47 2/8	46 2/8	46 0/8	15 / 16	LG4	QUE	Claude St' Amour	1990	101
368 4/8	53 0/8	51 4/8	43 4/8	13 / 12	Fort Chimo	QUE	Jerry Schauer	1990	103
368 0/8	46 0/8	47 6/8	44 1/8	15 / 15	Caniapiscau River	QUE	Gary Weckwerth	1994	104
367 4/8	54 7/8	52 0/8	43 3/8	11 / 14	George River	QUE	Lee Kline	1980	105
367 1/8	50 6/8	51 5/8	39 7/8	13 / 11	Schefferville	QUE	Raymond A. Guay	1988	106
367 0/8	47 0/8	48 0/8	44 7/8	12 / 12	Fort Chimo	QUE	James E. Doberstein	1989	107
367 0/8	55 3/8	53 4/8	47 4/8	11 / 15	LG 4	QUE	Anthony Pennimpede	1993	107
366 4/8	53 1/8	55 5/8	44 6/8	15 / 14	Fort Chimo	QUE	Larry DeVormer, Sr.	1988	109
366 2/8	54 7/8	52 3/8	55 0/8	20 / 16	Ungava Region	QUE	Joe Caruso	1979	110
366 1/8	48 0/8	48 2/8	38 2/8	21 / 14	Mistinibi Lake	QUE	Dieter Foerst	1981	111
365 7/8	53 5/8	53 1/8	46 4/8	16 / 14	Lac Minto	QUE	Greg Bonecutter, Sr.	1998	112
365 6/8	49 0/8	49 3/8	39 5/8	20 / 17	Pons River	QUE	Thomas Mathews	1988	113
364 5/8	49 0/8	51 0/8	34 4/8	13 / 11	George River	QUE	Gary L. Fritzler	1983	114
364 4/8	54 6/8	54 1/8	53 6/8	10 / 9	Delay River	QUE	W. R. "Tony" Dukes	1987	115
364 3/8	53 4/8	53 1/8	48 0/8	12 / 10	George River	QUE	Billy Ellis	1980	116
364 3/8	50 5/8	50 6/8	41 5/8	11 / 17	Ungava Bay	QUE	Stephen Michael Carroll	1988	116
364 2/8	49 5/8	47 3/8	41 0/8	16 / 16	Big Island Lake	QUE	Jim Ponciano	1985	118
364 2/8	57 7/8	58 5/8	55 2/8	13 / 14	Delay River	QUE	Bob Watkins	1987	118
363 7/8	50 3/8	50 1/8	49 1/8	12 / 11	Delay River	QUE	Robert Bain	1987	120
363 7/8	50 6/8	54 3/8	39 1/8	13 / 15	Lac Tasiataq	QUE	William J. Gleeson	1998	120
363 6/8	48 0/8	49 3/8	46 7/8	12 / 13	Fort Chimo	QUE	Chuck Adams	1996	122
363 4/8	52 6/8	52 2/8	34 2/8	14 / 15	Ungava Bay	QUE	Steve Bruggeman	1990	123
363 2/8	48 3/8	47 6/8	40 7/8	19 / 19	Tunulik River	QUE	Randal S. Maday	1992	124
363 0/8	48 6/8	47 5/8	48 6/8	13 / 14	Tunulik River	QUE	Rick Morgan	1986	125
363 0/8	45 5/8	48 0/8	44 3/8	10 / 14	Ungava Bay	QUE	James Norvell	1989	125
362 4/8	53 7/8	47 1/8	53 1/8	10 / 16	River De Paz	QUE	David F. Baldwin	1981	127
362 4/8	55 7/8	53 6/8	45 5/8	12 / 11	Fort Chimo	QUE	William H. Moyer	1988	127
362 3/8	47 6/8	48 3/8	41 4/8	13 / 12	Tunulik River	QUE	David J. Hell	1986	129
362 2/8	53 0/8	52 1/8	47 6/8	11 / 12	Saglek Bay	LAB	Charles Allen Poole	1990	130
362 2/8	53 1/8	56 2/8	44 0/8	11 / 13	LG 4	QUE	Kurt M. Zurawski	1994	130
362 0/8	60 2/8	57 5/8	49 4/8	11 / 14	Delay River	QUE	Richard V. McKeown	1990	132
361 4/8	48 2/8	47 2/8	40 4/8	11 / 14	Fort Chimo	QUE	Dave Seidelman	1985	133
361 4/8	54 6/8	55 0/8	53 4/8	11 / 11	Akuliak	QUE	Perry Merkes	1988	133
361 3/8	54 4/8	55 6/8	42 0/8	12 / 11	Schefferville	QUE	Elmer R. Luce, Jr.	1986	135
361 3/8	47 7/8	48 6/8	41 5/8	14 / 14	Delay River	QUE	John Akkerman	1990	135
361 0/8	52 2/8	51 1/8	36 5/8	15 / 12	Delay River	QUE	Jerry Costanza	1991	137
360 3/8	50 0/8	51 0/8	42 1/8	14 / 12	Schefferville	QUE	Robert M. Burtch	1988	138
360 1/8	46 3/8	48 4/8	53 0/8	14 / 11	Schefferville	QUE	Steven H. Byerly	1989	139
360 0/8	57 2/8	58 4/8	43 6/8	10 / 10	Fort Chimo	QUE	Linda Berkompas	1989	140
359 7/8	50 4/8	51 2/8	47 0/8	15 / 17	George River	QUE	Cecil Tharp	1982	141
359 7/8	50 0/8	50 1/8	42 2/8	11 / 11	Ribero Lake	QUE	Rick Bolin	1986	141
359 7/8	51 3/8	52 2/8	42 1/8	13 / 14	Delay River	QUE	Edward G. Gilkes	1988	141
359 7/8	53 6/8	53 6/8	40 7/8	13 / 20	Ungava Bay	QUE	Greg Strait	1989	141
359 6/8	49 6/8	50 5/8	35 4/8	13 / 12	Schefferville	QUE	Steven P. Salmieri	1989	145
359 4/8	53 7/8	54 0/8	42 0/8	13 / 17	Weymouth Inlet	QUE	David C. Smart	1988	146
359 4/8	48 2/8	52 2/8	50 7/8	12 / 14	Pons River	QUE	Mark J. Hendrickson	1997	146
359 3/8	44 7/8	46 5/8	37 1/8	18 / 15	Fort Chimo	QUE	Roger Schwarz	1988	148
359 3/8	49 1/8	47 5/8	51 6/8	9 / 11	Lake Sammy	QUE	Chuck Adams	1989	148
359 0/8	47 4/8	51 3/8	42 4/8	9 / 10	Maricourt River	QUE	Evan Steinhorst	1990	150
358 6/8	50 6/8	53 1/8	42 2/8	18 / 23	George River	QUE	Dale Selby	1980	151
358 2/8	41 6/8	42 1/8	34 7/8	15 / 18	Delay River	QUE	Ray Moulton	1986	152
358 1/8	52 1/8	50 4/8	48 0/8	14 / 17	Pons Island	QUE	Harold B. "Pat" Clark	1987	153
358 1/8	49 2/8	54 0/8	51 2/8	16 / 12	Jack's Lake	QUE	Raymond A. Luce	1989	153
358 0/8	52 4/8	52 0/8	41 7/8	15 / 17	Ungava Region	QUE	Carl G. Esterly	1983	155
358 0/8	45 2/8	44 4/8	43 6/8	14 / 16	Delay River	QUE	Joel Adam	1992	155

QUEBEC-LABRADOR CARIBOU

Minimum Score 325 — Continued

SCORE	LENGTH OF MAIN BEAM R	L	INSIDE SPREAD	NUMBER OF POINTS R	L	AREA	STATE/PROVINCE	HUNTER'S NAME	DATE	RANK
357 7/8	49 0/8	50 5/8	42 1/8	12	11	Caniapiscau River	QUE	Alexander C. Maven	1994	157
357 5/8	56 1/8	52 4/8	43 3/8	17	15	Delay River	QUE	Steve Beilgard	1989	158
357 2/8	50 3/8	50 5/8	47 5/8	15	14	Pons Lake	QUE	George P. Mann	1994	159
357 0/8	48 2/8	50 4/8	42 2/8	17	13	Lake Narcy	QUE	Roy Hampton	1988	160
356 6/8	49 1/8	49 3/8	41 6/8	13	13	Fort Chimo	QUE	Chris W. Taylor	1989	161
356 5/8	50 2/8	52 1/8	47 2/8	9	8	River aux Feuilles	QUE	Fred Krueger	1998	162
356 4/8	51 5/8	53 3/8	44 6/8	11	10	Ungava Bay	QUE	Larry Nirk	1983	163
356 4/8	46 0/8	47 5/8	42 0/8	17	20	Schefferville	QUE	William A.S. Heuer, Jr.	1987	163
356 4/8	54 2/8	53 2/8	38 6/8	9	12	Fort Chimo	QUE	Roy Javenkowski	1989	163
356 4/8	48 7/8	46 1/8	50 2/8	15	13	Jack's Lake	QUE	William F. Jackson	1989	163
356 1/8	47 3/8	47 2/8	45 0/8	16	12	Lake Cambrian	QUE	Clyde Doolittle	1988	167
356 0/8	55 4/8	56 4/8	49 4/8	17	23	Schefferville	QUE	Gregory G. Justus	1980	168
356 0/8	54 3/8	54 0/8	45 6/8	10	8	Schefferville	QUE	Dr. Nicholas J. Gray	1981	168
355 5/8	55 6/8	58 0/8	50 4/8	10	14	George River	QUE	Charles E. Spreeman	1985	170
355 5/8	44 7/8	47 4/8	41 0/8	15	13	Delay River	QUE	Robert Hoague	1993	170
355 4/8	47 0/8	47 2/8	36 3/8	17	18	Sixteen-Island-Lake	QUE	W. Bruce Nicolls	1987	172
355 4/8	50 4/8	52 3/8	40 3/8	20	16	Ungava Bay	QUE	Marc Augustin	1992	172
355 1/8	55 7/8	56 0/8	48 0/8	10	13	Tunulik River	QUE	Tom Paluso	1988	174
355 1/8	49 6/8	50 2/8	39 7/8	9	9	Schefferville	QUE	Jerry Keller	1991	174
355 0/8	58 3/8	54 1/8	35 4/8	9	10	Fort Chimo	QUE	Lewis Miller	1990	176
354 7/8	53 7/8	55 2/8	55 3/8	10	10	Bird Lake	QUE	Steve Draisey	1994	177
354 6/8	48 4/8	48 7/8	49 6/8	13	14	Schefferville	QUE	Tom Hlinka	1990	178
354 6/8	47 0/8	46 6/8	30 1/8	11	12	Lac Fremin	QUE	Richard G. Marshall	1995	178
354 5/8	56 2/8	55 7/8	40 2/8	13	13	Lac Minto	QUE	Charles Grubbs	1997	180
354 4/8	47 5/8	48 0/8	48 0/8	15	12	Lake Otelnuk	QUE	Steve Vanzile	1986	181
354 4/8	48 1/8	43 5/8	45 3/8	10	9	Doreen Lake	QUE	Eugene Arndt	1990	181
354 2/8	50 2/8	50 1/8	41 5/8	9	10	Big Island	QUE	Fred C. Church	1985	183
354 1/8	59 2/8	61 5/8	51 4/8	13	7	Ungava Bay	QUE	Joe Prinzi	1985	184
354 1/8	44 3/8	45 2/8	40 1/8	10	12	Schefferville	QUE	Robert Pyne	1985	184
354 0/8	50 3/8	50 1/8	48 2/8	13	13	Lake Des Bergere	QUE	Ronald L. Musser	1988	186
353 7/8	57 0/8	53 6/8	45 0/8	12	14	Fort Chimo	QUE	David Samuel	1991	187
353 4/8	52 7/8	51 2/8	39 6/8	14	12	Schefferville	QUE	Robert J. Lewis	1986	188
353 2/8	61 5/8	58 2/8	47 5/8	12	10	Tunulik River	QUE	Jon Vanderhoef	1984	189
353 0/8	50 4/8	49 2/8	46 2/8	13	9	Ungava Region	QUE	Casimir Leknius	1977	190
352 6/8	44 2/8	48 0/8	38 5/8	16	15	Delay River	QUE	Val S. Schmaus, Jr.	1989	191
352 4/8	50 2/8	47 1/8	48 4/8	11	11	Bear Lake	QUE	Glenn Schrempf	1994	192
352 3/8	51 1/8	48 2/8	40 4/8	11	12	Caniapiscau River	QUE	Jimmy J. Meadows	1990	193
352 0/8	55 4/8	54 6/8	44 3/8	11	11	Ungava Bay	QUE	Tink Nathan	1984	194
352 0/8	48 1/8	47 7/8	41 7/8	12	12	Mistinibi Lake	QUE	John Anthony Jerome	1987	194
351 6/8	44 0/8	43 6/8	35 1/8	20	20	Schefferville	QUE	Steven P. Salmieri	1989	196
351 6/8	48 3/8	48 0/8	36 2/8	14	10	Barrel Lake	QUE	Thomas Egnew	1994	196
351 5/8	51 4/8	49 1/8	48 1/8	15	14	George River	QUE	Frank Charette	1982	198
351 5/8	50 3/8	51 0/8	41 1/8	11	12	Loudin Lake	QUE	Steven J. Lepic	1988	198
351 3/8	44 2/8	41 5/8	39 3/8	15	16	Ricky Lake	QUE	William A.S. Heuer, Jr.	1987	200
351 2/8	48 5/8	48 3/8	42 2/8	10	10	Delay River	QUE	Fred J. Ward	1988	201
351 0/8	53 2/8	52 7/8	36 6/8	20	15	Dihourse Lake	QUE	Kenneth W. Lohr	1982	202
351 0/8	48 0/8	51 2/8	48 0/8	12	12	Delay River	QUE	Robert Bain	1987	202
350 6/8	55 5/8	56 2/8	45 3/8	14	12	Tunulik River	QUE	Henry F. Rauch	1982	204
350 6/8	38 3/8	38 2/8	31 7/8	12	13	Jack's Lake	QUE	Tony Odhner	1989	204
350 6/8	56 7/8	55 5/8	35 5/8	16	14	Schefferville	QUE	John W. Offord	1990	204
350 5/8	46 2/8	46 6/8	38 7/8	12	13	Schefferville	QUE	Greg Seymour	1986	207
350 5/8	43 6/8	46 6/8	44 6/8	14	12	Ungava Bay	QUE	Alan Niemeyer	1989	207
350 3/8	49 5/8	49 6/8	46 0/8	16	14	Desbergere	QUE	Lee Burnett	1989	209
350 2/8	55 7/8	52 0/8	46 6/8	13	14	Weymouth Inlet	QUE	Tom Taylor	1991	210
349 7/8	43 5/8	41 5/8	34 3/8	13	14	Kenny Lake	QUE	Ross Trujillo, Jr.	1991	211
349 6/8	47 0/8	44 1/8	37 4/8	20	15	George River	QUE	Charlie Kroll	1980	212
349 6/8	45 7/8	49 5/8	44 7/8	16	15	Ungava Peninsula	QUE	Bill VyVyan	1988	212
349 6/8	51 1/8	51 5/8	48 5/8	10	11	Lac Minto	QUE	Jack L. "Jackson" Ward	1997	212
349 4/8	51 0/8	51 3/8	37 0/8	12	13	Caniapiscau River	QUE	Henry O. Fromm	1987	215
349 4/8	46 5/8	46 2/8	43 2/8	17	13	Harold Lake	QUE	Don Davidson	1990	215
349 4/8	51 3/8	50 3/8	48 4/8	11	9	Delay River	QUE	Bob Mussey	1990	215
349 4/8	49 1/8	43 6/8	42 6/8	16	12	Ungava Bay	QUE	Steve Bruggeman	1990	215
349 3/8	48 6/8	52 4/8	44 0/8	8	11	Delay River	QUE	Roger Gipple	1988	219
349 3/8	49 2/8	53 2/8	45 6/8	17	16	Harold Lake	QUE	Craig Ambos	1992	219
349 2/8	49 5/8	49 0/8	37 5/8	10	11	Fort Chimo	QUE	James E. Doberstein	1989	221
349 0/8	49 3/8	49 1/8	35 7/8	12	9	Tunulik River	QUE	Ty Martin	1986	222
349 0/8	46 7/8	45 6/8	45 4/8	10	13	Pons River	QUE	Wayne A. Lamoreux	1991	222
349 0/8	51 4/8	51 5/8	35 6/8	10	10	Drummondville	QUE	Jim Gabrick	1994	222
348 7/8	46 6/8	49 4/8	31 4/8	17	20	Mulay River	QUE	Don Keady	1987	225
348 7/8	50 2/8	51 1/8	39 2/8	12	14	Boland Lake	QUE	Robert J. Pastor	1995	225
348 5/8	52 0/8	51 7/8	45 0/8	9	10	Lac Coulounge	QUE	John W. Borlang	1987	227
348 5/8	49 6/8	52 2/8	48 3/8	11	14	LG4	QUE	Donald W. Hoffman	1991	227
348 3/8	53 0/8	49 7/8	40 4/8	11	14	Jack's Lake	QUE	William F. Jackson	1989	229
348 3/8	41 6/8	44 5/8	46 1/8	12	16	Kuujjuaq	QUE	Al Potter	1996	229
348 1/8	52 4/8	55 1/8	28 7/8	18	14	George River	QUE	Bob Goodall	1980	231
348 1/8	49 0/8	50 2/8	44 2/8	14	9	George River	QUE	Phillip J. Taylor	1984	231
347 7/8	53 1/8	54 1/8	49 6/8	15	14	Wayne Lake	QUE	Jay J. Kaster	1988	233
347 5/8	52 3/8	52 2/8	49 0/8	12	12	Ungava Region	QUE	Charles R. Leidheiser	1977	234

QUEBEC-LABRADOR CARIBOU

Minimum Score 325 — Continued

SCORE	LENGTH OF MAIN BEAM R	L	INSIDE SPREAD	NUMBER OF POINTS R	L	AREA	STATE/PROVINCE	HUNTER'S NAME	DATE	RANK
347 5/8	44 6/8	45 3/8	41 7/8	13	12	Kenny Lake	QUE	Matt Lamoreux	1991	234
347 4/8	44 3/8	45 7/8	39 3/8	13	11	Delay River	QUE	Candace H. Roberts	1993	236
347 4/8	55 5/8	56 5/8	47 0/8	13	17	George River	QUE	Mark D. Thomson	1993	236
347 1/8	51 4/8	53 6/8	47 1/8	11	11	Schefferville	QUE	Ronnie Everett	1986	238
346 7/8	54 4/8	58 4/8	41 0/8	10	11	Akuliak	QUE	Lauri Johnson	1985	239
346 6/8	48 2/8	47 2/8	49 2/8	9	12	Delay River	QUE	Gregory J. Fries	1987	240
346 6/8	55 1/8	56 4/8	43 7/8	13	11	Delay River	QUE	Robert Pastor	1988	240
346 6/8	46 7/8	47 5/8	41 5/8	12	10	Jack's Lake	QUE	Curt Christensen	1989	240
346 6/8	41 4/8	43 3/8	40 6/8	18	17	Delay River	QUE	Michael L. Ritter	1994	240
346 6/8	50 2/8	47 5/8	43 4/8	14	10	Deception Bay	QUE	Tulsa Green	1998	240
346 3/8	47 5/8	47 3/8	40 6/8	11	10	Maricourt Lake	QUE	Jerry W. Huffaker	1990	245
346 2/8	50 5/8	49 1/8	44 3/8	11	13	Ungava Bay	QUE	Lou Kindred	1986	246
346 2/8	46 3/8	43 5/8	38 6/8	14	14	Lake Otelnuk	QUE	Eddie Cooper	1988	246
346 1/8	55 0/8	55 0/8	37 3/8	12	17	River Lac Cambrien	QUE	Kent W. Brigham	1987	248
346 1/8	41 0/8	42 5/8	39 5/8	17	15	Schefferville	QUE	Edward Faucher	1990	248
346 1/8	42 4/8	46 2/8	40 4/8	13	13	LG4	QUE	Mark D. Mishinski	1991	248
346 1/8	45 2/8	49 0/8	50 4/8	7	8	Lake Ikirtuuq	QUE	Dallas Smith	1996	248
346 0/8	48 6/8	50 6/8	45 7/8	13	14	George River	QUE	William E. Bullock	1982	252
346 0/8	51 6/8	52 4/8	43 2/8	12	10	Delay River	QUE	Dennis N. Ballweg	1988	252
345 7/8	52 6/8	54 1/8	45 2/8	11	13	Ungava Bay	QUE	John Musacchia	1978	254
345 7/8	52 3/8	51 7/8	44 2/8	13	17	Schefferville	QUE	Barry J. Smith	1988	254
345 6/8	49 6/8	43 6/8	48 0/8	12	17	Lake Ikirtuuq	QUE	Nicholas Barone, Jr.	1992	256
345 6/8	52 0/8	50 2/8	33 4/8	17	14	Delay River	QUE	William Elfland	1994	256
345 6/8	49 6/8	50 3/8	43 3/8	10	10	Ungava Bay	QUE	Bruce H. Sabaini	1996	256
345 6/8	43 5/8	45 5/8	36 5/8	13	13	Lac Minto	QUE	David M. Chauvet	1998	256
345 3/8	51 4/8	53 5/8	36 1/8	14	11	Maricourt River	QUE	Michael J. Churchill	1990	260
345 3/8	53 0/8	50 2/8	40 3/8	11	11	LG 4	QUE	Todd Fugate	1993	260
345 2/8	47 2/8	48 7/8	41 5/8	11	18	Fort Chimo	QUE	Bob Jensen	1982	262
345 2/8	43 2/8	48 0/8	48 0/8	10	12	Delay River	QUE	William "Ted" Bennett	1988	262
345 1/8	56 5/8	52 5/8	42 3/8	11	10	Ungava Bay	QUE	Richard Gamache	1988	264
345 1/8	50 3/8	53 1/8	41 4/8	16	14	Delay River	QUE	Steve Waible	1994	264
344 7/8	45 0/8	48 7/8	37 7/8	16	14	Mulay River	QUE	Don Keady	1987	266
344 6/8	51 0/8	50 5/8	38 6/8	10	11	Schefferville	QUE	Gregg Tanner	1985	267
344 6/8	53 6/8	55 3/8	41 5/8	15	18	16 Islands	QUE	Chris McDonnell	1990	267
344 4/8	45 6/8	46 7/8	45 0/8	12	10	Ungava Bay	QUE	David Baldwin	1986	269
344 4/8	44 4/8	47 6/8	41 4/8	14	12	Ungava Bay	QUE	James Norvell	1989	269
344 2/8	43 2/8	43 0/8	43 2/8	13	13	Melezes River	QUE	G. Fred Asbell	1990	271
343 7/8	54 2/8	51 1/8	39 3/8	13	13	Lake Nullualuk	QUE	Clifford White	1992	272
343 7/8	44 1/8	46 3/8	34 3/8	13	13	Delay River	QUE	Michael L. Ritter	1993	272
343 6/8	48 0/8	48 0/8	38 4/8	11	14	Akuliak	QUE	Barry Dyar	1985	274
343 6/8	52 2/8	51 1/8	48 3/8	12	12	Schefferville	QUE	Gregory V. Pilot	1992	274
343 6/8	43 6/8	44 6/8	48 7/8	11	9	Caniapiscau River	QUE	Gary Weckwerth	1994	274
343 3/8	48 0/8	47 0/8	44 7/8	14	12	George River	QUE	Leonard L. Kohan	1981	277
343 3/8	49 2/8	50 1/8	43 5/8	9	10	Ungava Bay	QUE	L. Dan Neebe	1988	277
343 3/8	47 0/8	45 5/8	40 5/8	8	11	Pons River	QUE	Martin R. Walls	1993	277
343 2/8	47 0/8	43 7/8	36 1/8	17	17	Delay River	QUE	Eric A. Voss	1993	280
343 2/8	45 0/8	46 1/8	43 3/8	13	13	Fort Chimo	QUE	Chuck Adams	1996	280
343 1/8	51 3/8	48 6/8	48 4/8	17	18	Kuujjuak River	QUE	Arthur J. Pelon	1985	282
342 7/8	53 4/8	52 6/8	39 5/8	14	14	George River	QUE	Frank Hogan	1980	263
342 7/8	54 4/8	54 2/8	41 4/8	11	10	Lac Minto Island	QUE	Greg Bonecutter, Sr.	1997	283
342 7/8	48 5/8	48 6/8	42 1/8	16	13	Deception Bay	QUE	Al Ferris	1997	283
342 6/8	43 3/8	47 1/8	40 7/8	17	17	Kuujjuak River	QUE	Steven Sendek	1985	286
342 5/8	47 4/8	50 3/8	46 1/8	15	10	Tuktu Camp	QUE	Martin G. Billeri	1977	287
342 5/8	50 5/8	51 0/8	46 4/8	14	14	LG4	QUE	Gregory A. Bonecutter, Sr.	1991	287
342 4/8	43 1/8	45 4/8	44 0/8	11	13	Delay River	QUE	William Bos	1990	289
342 2/8	47 5/8	50 3/8	42 0/8	13	10	Ungava Bay	QUE	Rayot A. DiFate	1988	290
342 1/8	48 4/8	51 2/8	34 6/8	9	11	Lac Minto	QUE	Kirk Munger	1998	291
341 7/8	48 0/8	49 1/8	37 1/8	14	15	Lac Minto	QUE	John Koschmeder	1997	292
341 6/8	47 4/8	47 5/8	44 1/8	10	13	Ungava Bay	QUE	Steve Crooks	1988	293
341 6/8	46 1/8	45 0/8	52 0/8	12	18	Delay River	QUE	Jim E. Roe	1988	293
341 5/8	53 7/8	53 5/8	41 6/8	7	11	Barrel Lake	QUE	John Hale	1994	295
341 3/8	48 5/8	48 6/8	47 4/8	14	15	George River	QUE	William B. Bullock, Jr.	1982	296
341 2/8	50 4/8	49 6/8	50 2/8	15	12	Pons River	QUE	Walter F. Dotson, Jr.	1987	297
341 2/8	49 3/8	44 6/8	48 6/8	13	11	Schefferville	QUE	Robert J. Lewis	1987	297
341 2/8	43 4/8	43 5/8	32 4/8	16	16	Caniapiscau River	QUE	Mike Klaeser	1994	297
341 0/8	51 3/8	45 7/8	44 4/8	14	12	Ungava Region	QUE	Glenn Reno	1980	300
341 0/8	45 0/8	43 5/8	35 0/8	14	16	May Lake	QUE	Larry M. Peterson	1990	300
340 5/8	54 7/8	57 7/8	51 0/8	14	13	Tunulik River	QUE	Jean-Claude Duff	1985	302
340 5/8	46 4/8	46 1/8	34 0/8	17	14	Schefferville	QUE	Pat Vincenti	1990	302
340 4/8	50 4/8	49 7/8	36 6/8	14	13	Lac D'Iberville	QUE	Stephen M. Kenworthy	1997	304
340 3/8	39 2/8	48 7/8	31 5/8	18	15	George River	QUE	Craig Richardson	1982	305
340 3/8	45 7/8	47 2/8	41 0/8	12	12	Lac Minto	QUE	Jeffrey G. Starcher	1997	305
340 2/8	41 6/8	44 6/8	46 7/8	16	12	Shirley Lake	QUE	Duane Zemliska	1990	307
340 1/8	46 4/8	47 3/8	37 7/8	17	13	LG4	QUE	Fred Johnston III	1991	308
339 7/8	49 1/8	49 0/8	44 3/8	17	15	Weymouth Inlet	QUE	Chuck Adams	1991	309
339 7/8	47 4/8	47 4/8	37 7/8	13	11	Lac Minto	QUE	Kenneth Wade Anderson	1997	309
339 6/8	45 4/8	47 3/8	43 3/8	15	13	Ungava Bay	QUE	Dean M. Westby	1986	311
339 6/8	50 3/8	49 5/8	42 5/8	12	12	Ungava Peninsula	QUE	Bill Vyvyan	1988	311

QUEBEC-LABRADOR CARIBOU

Minimum Score 325 — Continued — 215

SCORE	LENGTH OF MAIN BEAM R	L	INSIDE SPREAD	NUMBER OF POINTS R	L	AREA	STATE/ PROVINCE	HUNTER'S NAME	DATE	RANK
339 6/8	42 2/8	41 5/8	51 1/8	13	13	Delay River	QUE	Robert Hermann	1989	311
339 6/8	48 1/8	48 3/8	46 0/8	11	11	Martha's Lake	QUE	Mark Zastrow	1992	311
339 4/8	47 7/8	48 2/8	44 6/8	13	15	Audiepure Lake	QUE	Stan Godfrey	1983	315
339 3/8	46 0/8	46 1/8	44 2/8	14	16	Tunulik River	QUE	David Quong	1992	316
339 3/8	45 5/8	45 7/8	45 6/8	11	13	Lac Minto	QUE	David M. Chauvet/Jeff Scott	1998	316
339 1/8	41 0/8	45 0/8	33 1/8	10	16	Lake Gordon	QUE	Lee Jernigan	1995	318
339 0/8	56 4/8	55 0/8	45 5/8	12	11	Tuktu Camp	QUE	John C. Mitchell	1984	319
339 0/8	47 6/8	47 6/8	51 3/8	12	10	Long Lake	QUE	Mark Gerhard	1990	319
338 6/8	55 4/8	55 0/8	36 2/8	13	12	Maricourt River	QUE	Ronald S. Pulcine	1989	321
338 6/8	48 7/8	51 0/8	37 4/8	9	8	Ungava Bay	QUE	Michael R. Knight	1991	321
338 6/8	48 7/8	51 0/8	37 4/8	9	8	Ungava Bay	QUE	Michael R. Knight	1991	321
338 4/8	54 4/8	56 3/8	36 4/8	15	12	Potier River	QUE	Lawrence R. Gibbons	1990	324
338 3/8	47 1/8	46 1/8	38 0/8	19	20	George River	QUE	Len Cardinale	1971	325
338 3/8	54 0/8	53 3/8	32 0/8	13	16	Schefferville	QUE	Kenneth C. Kaufman	1987	325
338 2/8	44 2/8	42 5/8	39 2/8	18	22	Lac Fremin	QUE	Edwin W. Hoffacker	1995	327
338 1/8	48 4/8	47 4/8	40 6/8	17	13	Ungava Bay	QUE	Alan Niemeyer	1989	328
338 0/8	40 3/8	45 0/8	34 7/8	15	16	Echo Lake	QUE	Matthew J. Luxem	1989	329
338 0/8	46 7/8	44 1/8	31 4/8	11	12	LG 4	QUE	Bryant Shermoe	1995	329
337 7/8	48 3/8	47 2/8	45 5/8	14	12	De Pas & George River	QUE	Fred F. Potts	1974	331
337 7/8	44 0/8	45 3/8	42 3/8	13	11	Schefferville	QUE	Dale Drilling	1987	331
337 7/8	52 3/8	53 1/8	41 6/8	13	14	Whiskey Lake	QUE	Thomas Ippolito	1987	331
337 6/8	52 0/8	51 7/8	45 4/8	9	10	Tunulik River	QUE	Jay E. Johnson	1985	334
337 6/8	51 0/8	51 5/8	48 4/8	8	9	Pons River	QUE	Bradford Higson	1986	334
337 4/8	46 4/8	46 5/8	45 1/8	15	12	Wayne Lake	QUE	Randall L. Schoenly	1987	336
337 0/8	52 5/8	52 2/8	39 7/8	13	12	Jack's Lake	QUE	Greg Odhner	1989	337
337 0/8	49 6/8	50 2/8	45 5/8	12	14	Melezes River	QUE	Donald L. Clark	1993	337
336 6/8	48 2/8	46 5/8	34 7/8	17	16	Delay River	QUE	W.R. "Tony" Dukes	1987	339
336 6/8	48 0/8	47 3/8	38 5/8	10	9	George River	QUE	Pat Reilly	1993	339
336 6/8	45 4/8	44 7/8	44 5/8	12	11	Lac Minto	QUE	J. Ken Martin	1995	339
336 4/8	53 4/8	52 2/8	41 0/8	10	10	George River	QUE	David Tofte	1982	342
336 4/8	51 3/8	52 4/8	38 6/8	10	10	Schefferville	QUE	William L. Hall	1994	342
336 1/8	53 0/8	52 0/8	51 0/8	15	19	Twin Lake	QUE	Jon P. Thomas	1982	344
336 0/8	42 3/8	41 7/8	45 3/8	13	13	Lake Leopard	QUE	Robert B. Seger II	1989	345
335 5/8	51 7/8	52 1/8	41 3/8	10	12	Tunulik River	QUE	DeeAnn Robinson	1992	346
335 4/8	48 1/8	50 0/8	40 2/8	10	14	Pons River	QUE	Thomas Hopkins	1987	347
335 3/8	49 1/8	46 2/8	49 1/8	16	17	Ungava Peninsula	QUE	Tony Snow	1988	348
335 3/8	50 3/8	53 0/8	39 7/8	12	12	Caniapiscau River	QUE	Robert H. Van Alstyne	1992	348
335 3/8	53 4/8	53 1/8	39 0/8	14	13	Delay River	QUE	Ryk Visscher	1995	348
335 2/8	44 0/8	45 6/8	47 7/8	19	12	Lake Otelnuk	QUE	John L. Wagner	1989	351
335 0/8	51 2/8	50 2/8	42 4/8	9	12	Tunulik River	QUE	Robert A. Shank	1988	352
334 7/8	44 5/8	44 0/8	40 0/8	14	18	Pons River	QUE	Joe Hoffman	1991	353
334 6/8	49 5/8	47 7/8	41 4/8	13	14	Shirley Lake	QUE	Jerry E. Burt	1990	354
334 2/8	48 7/8	46 7/8	34 3/8	13	14	Dugue River	QUE	Lee A. Heath	1990	355
334 2/8	43 6/8	44 6/8	43 4/8	14	14	Ungava Bay	QUE	David Gillette	1992	355
334 1/8	40 5/8	43 3/8	38 4/8	17	13	Serigny River	QUE	Howard T. Isenberg, Jr.	1990	357
334 1/8	47 5/8	47 6/8	38 0/8	17	13	Lake Anonyme	QUE	Dennis Hayden	1992	357
333 7/8	44 0/8	41 7/8	47 2/8	13	12	Lake Gerido	QUE	Larry C. Reese	1996	359
333 6/8	47 1/8	45 4/8	43 6/8	10	11	Delay River	QUE	Steven Pfaff	1994	360
333 5/8	53 2/8	52 7/8	41 6/8	12	13	Tunulik River	QUE	Gregory G. Kilby	1985	361
333 5/8	43 2/8	45 0/8	48 6/8	8	8	Boland Lake	QUE	Rick L. Morley	1996	361
333 4/8	51 3/8	53 0/8	45 1/8	7	7	Delay River	QUE	Robert H. Pavlovic	1988	363
333 3/8	45 3/8	48 2/8	45 3/8	12	13	Lake Loudon	QUE	Jim Gompf	1990	364
333 2/8	55 4/8	52 6/8	47 5/8	13	15	Schefferville	QUE	Al Reay	1978	365
333 2/8	51 6/8	53 1/8	46 1/8	11	10	Whiskey Lake	QUE	Glenn R. Kuklick	1986	365
333 1/8	51 3/8	52 5/8	49 7/8	5	8	Schefferville	QUE	Robert James Lewis	1987	367
333 0/8	48 6/8	48 1/8	38 7/8	10	13	Lake Maricourt	QUE	Dale L. Hughes	1990	368
332 7/8	47 6/8	48 4/8	48 6/8	11	8	Schefferville	QUE	Darwin L. Damp	1988	369
332 6/8	49 1/8	46 2/8	40 4/8	10	12	Agnew Lake	QUE	James P Loughran	1989	370
332 5/8	45 1/8	45 4/8	46 7/8	16	14	Lac Minto	QUE	Terry Heckert	1997	371
332 4/8	51 6/8	51 1/8	36 3/8	10	11	Tunulik River	QUE	Glenn St. Charles	1984	372
332 3/8	56 2/8	51 2/8	39 6/8	9	12	Kuujjuak River	QUE	Mark Thompson	1987	373
332 3/8	48 3/8	48 4/8	43 4/8	12	12	Riviere aux Melezes	QUE	David R. Rogers	1987	373
332 3/8	45 1/8	41 6/8	38 4/8	16	16	Lac de Grasse	QUE	Dwaine S. Starr	1994	373
332 2/8	46 6/8	46 6/8	40 6/8	14	11	LG 4	QUE	Gregory Dodson	1993	376
332 2/8	46 7/8	46 4/8	43 0/8	11	14	Lac Minto	QUE	Millard Glen Starcher	1997	376
332 0/8	53 4/8	48 5/8	52 2/8	8	10	Ungava Bay	QUE	Richard J. Chobot, Jr.	1986	378
332 0/8	50 4/8	50 2/8	43 0/8	12	11	Weymouth Inlet	QUE	Kenneth M. Beno	1988	378
331 7/8	46 0/8	42 6/8	43 7/8	14	12	Fort Chimo	QUE	Harold Halverson	1991	380
331 6/8	52 0/8	52 6/8	45 4/8	15	14	Schefferville	QUE	Thomas E. Smith	1981	381
331 6/8	46 7/8	47 3/8	38 0/8	14	13	Cedar Lake	QUE	Anders J. Meyer	1989	381
331 5/8	55 5/8	55 6/8	39 1/8	14	9	Pons River	QUE	Robert Amaral	1986	383
331 3/8	47 1/8	47 1/8	47 1/8	9	9	Whiskey Lake	QUE	Peter L. Halbig	1986	384
331 3/8	45 3/8	47 1/8	35 4/8	14	16	Fort Chimo	QUE	Gene Culver	1989	384
331 3/8	45 7/8	48 0/8	50 4/8	10	9	Fort Chimo	QUE	John Leo Hojan	1990	384
331 0/8	48 0/8	56 3/8	58 5/8	9	7	Waymouth Inlet	QUE	Edwin DeYoung	1989	387
331 0/8	43 4/8	45 2/8	35 0/8	11	14	Lac Minto	QUE	J. Ken Martin	1995	387
330 7/8	49 4/8	48 0/8	42 4/8	12	10	LG 4	QUE	Frank Kozielec, Jr.	1992	389
330 7/8	48 7/8	50 4/8	47 6/8	10	11	Lac Minto	QUE	Billie Grogg	1997	389

QUEBEC-LABRADOR CARIBOU

Minimum Score 325

Continued

SCORE	LENGTH OF MAIN BEAM R / L	INSIDE SPREAD	NUMBER OF POINTS R / L		AREA	STATE/ PROVINCE	HUNTER'S NAME	DATE	RANK
330 7/8	45 3/8	46 4/8	36 1/8	15	12	Lac Tasiataq	QUE	Gilbert Hernandez	1998	389
330 6/8	45 5/8	47 1/8	36 0/8	13	14	Pons Island	QUE	Lou Edelis	1987	392
330 6/8	46 7/8	48 6/8	41 6/8	11	7	Caniapiscau River	QUE	John L. Gardner	1994	392
330 5/8	49 4/8	48 6/8	36 6/8	14	15	LG4	QUE	Charles Moore	1991	394
330 5/8	41 1/8	42 4/8	37 0/8	16	15	Delay River	QUE	William E. Terry, Sr.	1992	394
330 2/8	49 1/8	49 4/8	37 5/8	16	16	Delay River	QUE	Roy Goodwin	1986	396
330 2/8	46 0/8	48 7/8	37 0/8	14	11	Delay River	QUE	James Kingsley	1990	396
330 0/8	49 5/8	45 6/8	31 0/8	12	10	Fort Chimo	QUE	Larry Hayes	1986	398
330 0/8	48 3/8	49 4/8	39 5/8	13	12	Caniapiscau River	QUE	Ken Bruckner	1992	398
330 0/8	50 2/8	49 4/8	43 0/8	11	8	Harold Lake	QUE	Ron Haver	1992	398
329 4/8	44 2/8	47 2/8	39 2/8	12	10	Lac Minto	QUE	Gary W. Kelley	1997	401
329 2/8	47 0/8	48 0/8	42 3/8	14	10	Schefferville	QUE	Jerry W. Robertson	1988	402
329 1/8	52 5/8	48 7/8	43 7/8	16	13	George River	QUE	Jerry V. Finley	1981	403
329 0/8	42 6/8	39 5/8	40 2/8	13	15	Rogers Lake	QUE	Joe Powroznik	1988	404
329 0/8	51 5/8	55 2/8	37 7/8	8	7	Melaise River	QUE	A. Owen Shifflett	1989	404
328 7/8	43 3/8	47 6/8	40 4/8	16	14	Lac Minto	QUE	Greg Bonecutter, Sr.	1998	406
328 6/8	55 4/8	56 7/8	42 3/8	9	11	Ungava Region	QUE	David L. Cook	1982	407
328 6/8	43 0/8	42 4/8	38 5/8	17	13	Schefferville	QUE	Michael J. Kennedy	1992	407
328 5/8	49 1/8	52 4/8	45 2/8	13	12	Pons River	QUE	Jim Ellis	1986	409
328 5/8	44 5/8	44 3/8	33 0/8	16	14	Schefferville	QUE	Kenneth C. Kaufmann	1987	409
328 4/8	44 6/8	43 0/8	39 0/8	16	16	Long Lake	QUE	David J. Stanislawski	1990	411
328 2/8	49 6/8	49 1/8	48 1/8	8	9	Pons Island	QUE	Gary Reich	1987	412
328 2/8	42 2/8	43 3/8	49 5/8	13	8	Delay River	QUE	August S. Gray	1988	412
328 0/8	47 6/8	47 1/8	41 5/8	11	10	Big Island	QUE	Ralph Willits	1989	414
328 0/8	51 6/8	48 7/8	44 6/8	12	8	Melezes River	QUE	Peter L. Bucklin	1990	414
328 0/8	54 4/8	56 0/8	44 7/8	12	15	Maricourt Lake	QUE	Doug Kerska	1990	414
327 7/8	47 1/8	48 0/8	40 7/8	12	12	Lac Minto Island	QUE	Patrick Farrow	1997	417
327 6/8	52 0/8	53 0/8	45 3/8	15	19	Schefferville	QUE	Irv Plotz	1981	418
327 6/8	49 3/8	48 5/8	48 6/8	14	17	Weymouth Inlet	QUE	David L. Stull	1989	418
327 5/8	43 0/8	44 4/8	45 3/8	11	18	LG 4	QUE	Stephen Kotz	1992	420
327 4/8	51 5/8	50 4/8	33 6/8	8	7	Sir James Lake	QUE	Bryan Lee White	1993	421
327 4/8	48 5/8	49 0/8	37 6/8	8	9	Lac Minto	QUE	Gene Wilson	1997	421
327 0/8	47 3/8	47 0/8	44 3/8	12	15	Lake Martine	QUE	Tom Nelson	1990	423
326 7/8	45 7/8	45 6/8	50 2/8	11	6	Schefferville	QUE	Joseph Strasser, Jr.	1988	424
326 6/8	53 6/8	54 3/8	44 0/8	8	10	Tunulik River	QUE	Ty Martin	1986	425
326 6/8	44 0/8	47 0/8	34 1/8	12	13	Delay River	QUE	Douglas Kerska	1988	425
326 6/8	46 5/8	46 1/8	35 4/8	12	11	Pons Lake	QUE	George E. Mann	1995	425
326 6/8	50 3/8	50 2/8	39 4/8	12	11	Lac Minto Island	QUE	Greg Bonecutter, Sr.	1997	425
326 3/8	49 4/8	52 0/8	39 2/8	12	11	Drummondville	QUE	Leo Hazelton	1994	429
326 2/8	46 1/8	45 1/8	32 7/8	13	15	Lake Leopard	QUE	Wes Seaver	1989	430
326 2/8	45 0/8	46 6/8	47 7/8	7	7	Schefferville	QUE	Jerry Parsons	1990	430
326 2/8	48 2/8	46 3/8	45 5/8	6	5	Lac Fremin	QUE	Richard F. Wamboldt	1995	430
326 1/8	59 3/8	57 0/8	43 6/8	10	17	Ungava Region	QUE	Gary L. Snyder	1977	433
326 1/8	48 0/8	49 2/8	46 7/8	8	8	Delay River	QUE	Roger Gipple	1988	433
326 1/8	48 2/8	49 4/8	58 6/8	9	11	Lake Sabrina	QUE	David G. Anderson	1993	433
326 0/8	45 6/8	45 5/8	45 0/8	12	14	Delay River	QUE	Warren Strickland	1989	436
325 7/8	50 6/8	50 2/8	35 0/8	12	8	Lac Minto	QUE	Kenneth Wade Anderson	1997	437
325 5/8	49 4/8	48 3/8	53 0/8	8	9	Delay River	QUE	Paul Converse	1991	438
325 5/8	49 1/8	49 2/8	37 6/8	12	10	Gordon Lake	QUE	Bobby J. Jones	1995	438
325 4/8	46 7/8	50 4/8	41 2/8	8	9	Lake Riqouville	QUE	Paul M. Kniss	1990	440
325 3/8	45 3/8	47 5/8	48 4/8	9	7	Lac Louis	QUE	Alan J. Rhinerson	1991	441
325 3/8	39 4/8	42 3/8	36 1/8	15	12	Kuujjuaq	QUE	Joseph S. Duarte, Jr.	1996	441
325 1/8	60 1/8	60 5/8	49 3/8	7	4	Tunulik River	QUE	Ron Carpenter	1982	443
325 1/8	42 0/8	46 4/8	40 4/8	11	11	Lake Narcy	QUE	Kenny E. Leo	1988	443
325 1/8	49 5/8	49 7/8	51 1/8	16	13	LG 4	QUE	Bryant Shermoe	1995	443

QUEBEC-LABRADOR CARIBOU (VELVET ANTLERS)

Minimum Score 325

SCORE	LENGTH OF MAIN BEAM R / L	INSIDE SPREAD	NUMBER OF POINTS R / L		AREA	STATE/ PROVINCE	HUNTER'S NAME	DATE	RANK
378 0/8	48 2/8	50 3/8	42 7/8	10	10	Ungava Bay	QUE	Archie Nesbitt	1993	*
378 0/8	54 7/8	55 2/8	43 4/8	11	10	Lake Chappiteau	QUE	Kevin Schauenberg	1998	*
376 5/8	48 0/8	48 0/8	36 6/8	17	13	Schefferville	QUE	Jeffrey Fitz Maurice	1994	*
374 1/8	53 3/8	53 1/8	53 7/8	10	13	Delay River	QUE	Michael L. Ritter	1993	*
372 4/8	58 3/8	55 1/8	42 2/8	10	11	Trophy Lake	QUE	David Seifert	1995	*
367 7/8	55 0/8	57 2/8	46 3/8	12	10	Fort Chimo	QUE	Gene Culver	1989	*
363 7/8	42 3/8	43 5/8	32 0/8	13	16	Pons Island	QUE	Edward D. Dougherty	1995	*
360 1/8	53 4/8	53 7/8	48 4/8	10	9	Jupiter Lake	QUE	Dave Justmann	1997	*
358 3/8	50 6/8	50 7/8	44 1/8	14	10	Tunulik River	QUE	Jerry Robinson, Jr.	1992	*
357 3/8	50 3/8	50 1/8	45 4/8	14	20	Fort Chimo	QUE	Mark "Root" Gies	1994	*
356 5/8	51 3/8	51 2/8	39 7/8	14	13	Weymouth Inlet	QUE	Dr. Bruce Heare	1994	*
354 6/8	52 1/8	51 4/8	35 6/8	12	8	Potier River	QUE	Timothy Angelo	1995	*
352 7/8	53 6/8	54 4/8	45 6/8	12	14	Weymouth Inlet	QUE	Gregg Welch	1992	*

QUEBEC-LABRADOR CARIBOU (VELVET ANTLERS)

Minimum Score 325

SCORE	LENGTH OF R MAIN BEAM L		INSIDE SPREAD	NUMBER R OF POINTS L		AREA	STATE/ PROVINCE	HUNTER'S NAME	DATE	RANK
352 2/8	45 4/8	47 1/8	40 3/8	12	9	Pons Island	QUE	Edward D. Dougherty	1995	*
349 7/8	39 2/8	41 2/8	36 4/8	12	13	Delay River	QUE	Steve Neuberger	1993	*
346 2/8	51 2/8	50 5/8	36 2/8	12	13	Delay River	QUE	Ryk Visscher	1993	*
345 7/8	47 2/8	46 2/8	37 7/8	11	12	Delay River	QUE	John Lind	1993	*
345 4/8	46 3/8	49 0/8	41 4/8	15	9	Pons Island	QUE	Joseph C. Granitz, Jr.	1995	*
344 3/8	47 3/8	49 1/8	50 2/8	7	11	Delay River	QUE	Mike Ritter, Jr.	1992	*
342 6/8	47 1/8	46 2/8	42 3/8	13	15	Timber Lake	QUE	Thomas E. Rothrock	1994	*
342 4/8	49 0/8	47 2/8	42 3/8	14	15	Delay River	QUE	Wes Skakun	1993	*
342 1/8	55 0/8	55 1/8	39 1/8	14	14	Lac Minto	QUE	Randy Kerian	1997	*
341 4/8	48 6/8	53 7/8	50 1/8	10	10	Long Lake	QUE	Ted K. Jaycox	1986	*
339 7/8	49 4/8	49 0/8	45 6/8	8	12	Delay River	QUE	Duane Hicks	1993	*
338 6/8	49 2/8	50 5/8	41 1/8	11	11	Maricourt Lake	QUE	Dan Brockman	1989	*
337 0/8	50 2/8	48 1/8	39 2/8	11	12	Delay River	QUE	John Visscher	1993	*
336 2/8	50 2/8	47 0/8	42 1/8	8	7	Delay River	QUE	Ryk Visscher	1993	*
336 2/8	47 1/8	47 4/8	34 3/8	12	11	Potier River	QUE	Lewis E. Hartenstine	1995	*
335 4/8	36 3/8	37 7/8	32 4/8	13	12	Schefferville	QUE	Gerald D. Combs	1993	*
332 2/8	47 3/8	46 4/8	38 2/8	12	11	Timber Lake	QUE	Thomas E. Rothrock	1994	*
332 1/8	46 1/8	48 2/8	47 7/8	11	11	Delay River	QUE	Darryl Kublik	1993	*
332 0/8	47 0/8	49 2/8	35 3/8	14	10	Jacks Lake	QUE	Roger Rothhaar	1994	*
331 3/8	51 0/8	51 0/8	40 7/8	12	11	Pons River	QUE	Tom C. Siebeneck	1995	*
330 2/8	41 1/8	42 5/8	31 6/8	14	13	Boland Lake	QUE	Thomas J. Hoffman	1997	*
329 2/8	41 0/8	40 5/8	40 2/8	12	13	Melezes River	QUE	Mike Boyd	1992	*
328 0/8	49 6/8	50 3/8	41 0/8	14	10	Weymouth Inlet	QUE	Steve D. Munier	1993	*
326 3/8	41 3/8	44 4/8	39 0/8	11	14	Delay River	QUE	John Visscher	1994	*

* *Velvet entries will be listed in only one record book.*

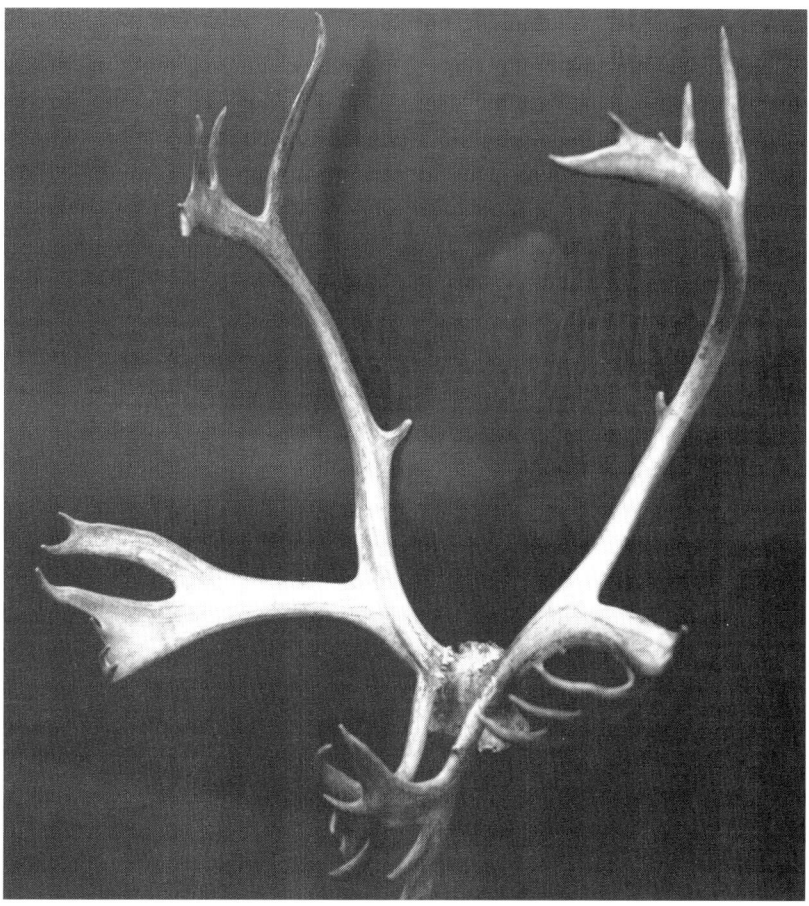

World Record Woodland Caribou
Score: 345 2/8
Victoria River, Newfoundland - 1966
Hunter: Dempsey Cape

WOODLAND CARIBOU

Minimum Score 220

Rangifer tarandus caribou from Nova Scotia, New Brunswick, and Newfoundland

SCORE	LENGTH OF MAIN BEAM R	L	INSIDE SPREAD	NUMBER OF POINTS R	L	AREA	STATE/ PROVINCE	HUNTER'S NAME	DATE	RANK
345 2/8	46 6/8	46 4/8	27 3/8	11	12	Victoria River	NFL	Dempsey Cape	1966	1
324 7/8	40 2/8	42 3/8	36 0/8	11	10	Deer Pond	NFL	Frank M. Monberger	1993	2
324 0/8	42 7/8	42 3/8	26 6/8	10	11	Sitdown Pond	NFL	Ed J. Bowser	1966	3
310 1/8	41 0/8	41 0/8	29 2/8	10	12	Millertown	NFL	Gerhart Huber	1966	4
309 3/8	46 1/8	49 1/8	38 4/8	9	12	St. Anthony	NFL	Stuart G. Hazard III	1998	5
301 4/8	38 5/8	36 3/8	30 0/8	7	9	Parsons Pond	NFL	Jeff Wingard	1997	6
287 4/8	35 0/8	34 1/8	27 6/8	9	10	Dashwood Pond	NFL	Kerry K. Kammer	1990	7
286 4/8	37 0/8	37 0/8	29 5/8	9	11	Rocky Pond	NFL	Chuck Adams	1988	8
284 5/8	39 0/8	41 1/8	37 0/8	14	10	Gander	NFL	Ron Timm	1997	9
284 0/8	38 5/8	34 6/8	24 2/8	12	9	Bishop's Falls	NFL	Michael E. Petkwitz	1997	10
280 7/8	34 2/8	33 7/8	28 0/8	7	8	Gander River	NFL	Ron Dunne	1997	11
280 4/8	37 5/8	34 6/8	28 7/8	11	12	Buchans Plateau	NFL	Gary Martin	1996	12
279 2/8	36 6/8	34 5/8	25 3/8	16	11	Stag Lake	NFL	Mike Traub	1993	13
276 7/8	42 3/8	43 0/8	25 2/8	10	9	King George IV Lake	NFL	Mark McCarty	1966	14
275 7/8	36 5/8	35 2/8	37 0/8	12	10	Deer Pond	NFL	John J.J. Rybinski	1998	15
275 6/8	35 4/8	33 4/8	25 6/8	10	9	Alex Pond	NFL	Paul Locey	1988	16
274 7/8	38 5/8	39 4/8	29 0/8	8	8	Caribou Creek	NFL	Dan Bertalan	1992	17
272 4/8	41 0/8	45 0/8	30 4/8	7	7	Cross Pond	NFL	Thomas J. Hoffman	1993	18
272 1/8	33 2/8	33 0/8	25 2/8	13	10	Buchans Plateau	NFL	Eddie Smith	1988	19
270 6/8	33 4/8	33 6/8	34 2/8	9	10	Atikonak Lake	NFL	Dr. James L. Emerson	1973	20
269 1/8	37 1/8	37 4/8	23 4/8	15	13	Corner Brook	NFL	Al Reay	1980	21

WOODLAND CARIBOU

Minimum Score 220 — Continued

SCORE	LENGTH OF MAIN BEAM R	L	INSIDE SPREAD	NUMBER OF POINTS R	L	AREA	STATE/PROVINCE	HUNTER'S NAME	DATE	RANK
267 7/8	29 3/8	31 4/8	27 4/8	12	11	Stag Lake	NFL	Richard A. Case	1993	22
267 6/8	40 6/8	42 1/8	32 1/8	10	8	Gaff Topsails	NFL	John D. "Jack" Frost	1997	23
267 4/8	37 1/8	35 2/8	23 2/8	8	10	Deer Pond	NFL	Neil Summers	1996	24
267 0/8	35 4/8	34 2/8	22 7/8	8	7	Alex Pond	NFL	James Pike	1991	25
265 7/8	39 1/8	38 5/8	32 0/8	9	11	Deer Pond	NFL	Dr. David Samuel	1998	26
265 1/8	36 2/8	36 0/8	28 3/8	8	9	Deer Pond	NFL	Tom D. Slusser	1993	27
263 2/8	35 5/8	35 3/8	34 5/8	7	9	Terra Nova	NFL	Glen Mertens	1995	28
262 6/8	39 4/8	41 6/8	34 4/8	6	7	Buchans Plateau	NFL	Fred A. Turner	1984	29
262 0/8	28 5/8	30 5/8	29 5/8	12	11	Grey River	NFL	Jack Dawe	1998	30
261 2/8	34 3/8	34 6/8	20 3/8	9	9	Cross Pond	NFL	Duane D. Zemliska	1994	31
261 0/8	29 4/8	31 4/8	29 6/8	11	12	Koskaecodde Lake	NFL	Bill Kotarski	1997	32
260 3/8	35 2/8	35 3/8	27 5/8	9	11	Buchans Plateau	NFL	William R. Vanderhoef	1986	33
259 5/8	37 6/8	32 2/8	34 7/8	10	11	Buchans Plateau	NFL	John 'Jack' Cordes	1982	34
259 0/8	31 1/8	27 4/8	27 0/8	12	16	Saddler Pond	NFL	Stan Godfrey	1989	35
259 0/8	37 0/8	37 6/8	29 6/8	8	8	Victoria River	NFL	J. D. Thomas	1996	35
258 7/8	40 4/8	37 6/8	33 1/8	6	7	Lloyds River	NFL	Harold A. Hill	1964	37
258 6/8	37 6/8	38 3/8	26 7/8	7	8	Stag Lake	NFL	R. Brian Oates	1993	38
258 5/8	33 6/8	33 0/8	25 6/8	10	9	Howley	NFL	Ken Mowerson	1989	39
258 5/8	37 1/8	38 4/8	26 7/8	9	9	Lapoile	NFL	Nicholas Misciagna	1992	39
258 1/8	36 7/8	33 6/8	25 4/8	10	11	Atikonak Lake	NFL	Bill L. Carlos	1972	41
257 0/8	33 7/8	35 2/8	32 0/8	8	9	Buchans Plateau	NFL	Walter J. Palmer	1993	42
256 5/8	31 5/8	36 0/8	15 7/8	8	8	Alex Pond	NFL	Jay Deones	1993	43
256 2/8	32 4/8	34 4/8	27 0/8	11	12	Alex Pond	NFL	Gary F. Bogner	1996	44
253 7/8	37 4/8	35 5/8	32 1/8	10	8	Buchans Plateau	NFL	Steve D. Munier	1990	45
253 2/8	39 1/8	38 4/8	30 7/8	7	9	Alex Pond	NFL	Michael J. Spence	1993	46
253 1/8	33 6/8	33 4/8	24 0/8	10	9	Buchans Plateau	NFL	Mark Zastrow	1995	47
252 2/8	36 1/8	33 1/8	24 7/8	7	9	Alex Pond	NFL	Karen J. Deones	1993	48
252 0/8	35 4/8	38 0/8	29 3/8	12	10	Portland Creek	NFL	Clarence Bowers	1998	49
250 1/8	33 0/8	32 1/8	26 4/8	10	12	Deer Pond	NFL	Warren Strickland	1994	50
249 4/8	37 6/8	33 4/8	31 0/8	9	11	13 Mile Bog	NFL	John D. Thomas, Jr.	1998	51
249 3/8	36 5/8	37 2/8	26 4/8	9	9	Millertown	NFL	Cliff Wiseman	1962	52
248 0/8	40 7/8	36 7/8	34 0/8	7	7	Sitdown Pond	NFL	Dr. Ed Bowser	1965	53
247 3/8	34 5/8	37 4/8	28 4/8	7	7	King George IV Lake	NFL	Bill Hirst	1966	54
246 3/8	35 6/8	35 7/8	21 0/8	9	8	Stag Lake	NFL	Susan D. Sherer	1996	55
246 2/8	32 4/8	29 0/8	27 0/8	10	9	Alex Pond	NFL	Darrin West	1991	56
245 4/8	33 2/8	35 5/8	29 1/8	8	8	Rogers River	NFL	Randy Petersburg	1998	57
243 6/8	34 6/8	34 6/8	27 7/8	7	6	Greys Island	NFL	Terry Krahn	1991	58
242 2/8	36 1/8	36 5/8	30 5/8	7	8	Moon Lake	NFL	Michael R. Deschamps	1996	59
241 6/8	33 2/8	30 6/8	29 2/8	9	11	Buchans Plateau	NFL	Glenn Hisey	1982	60
241 2/8	33 2/8	34 6/8	25 1/8	11	11	Interior District	NFL	Bill Goff	1965	61
239 1/8	35 3/8	34 0/8	26 6/8	10	12	Buchans Plateau	NFL	Mark Buehrer	1997	62
238 7/8	19 1/8	27 2/8	26 7/8	9	8	Stag Lake	NFL	G. Fred Asbell	1996	63
237 4/8	35 4/8	35 6/8	27 5/8	7	6	Stag Lake	NFL	Ron Sherer	1996	64
237 2/8	35 0/8	36 2/8	29 7/8	7	8	Saddler Pond	NFL	Carolyn Godfrey	1989	65
237 1/8	35 1/8	35 2/8	24 6/8	10	7	Buchans Plateau	NFL	Doug Strecker	1990	66
236 3/8	36 0/8	35 0/8	25 3/8	12	9	Princess Lake	NFL	John Musacchia	1967	67
235 3/8	32 3/8	34 2/8	24 4/8	8	8	Buchans Plateau	NFL	John Neal	1998	68
233 2/8	38 0/8	37 0/8	27 5/8	7	4	Gull Lake	NFL	M. W. Bowser	1958	69
232 6/8	34 2/8	31 2/8	32 7/8	7	5	Millertown	NFL	Tom Taylor	1992	70
232 5/8	33 3/8	35 0/8	24 5/8	6	7	Deer Lake	NFL	Douglas L. Buchler	1984	71
232 4/8	35 5/8	34 7/8	26 7/8	6	6	Buchans Plateau	NFL	Terrence H. Estes	1984	72
232 1/8	30 3/8	30 7/8	25 3/8	10	8	Victoria Lake	NFL	Robert Bartoshesky	1998	73
231 0/8	32 0/8	31 7/8	22 6/8	9	7	Grey River	NFL	Lou Kindred	1996	74
228 7/8	31 4/8	28 3/8	25 2/8	8	8	Buchans Plateau	NFL	Walter J. Palmer	1993	75
228 5/8	30 1/8	28 4/8	21 6/8	8	7	Stag Lake	NFL	Dr. Charles Leidheiser	1995	76
228 1/8	33 1/8	33 0/8	27 3/8	6	8	Ocean Pond	NFL	David J. Lamoreaux	1998	77
227 7/8	36 1/8	33 0/8	27 1/8	10	9	Princess Lake	NFL	Ken Rapp	1966	78
226 6/8	29 6/8	30 6/8	28 3/8	6	8	Buchans Plateau	NFL	Robert J. McCarthy	1997	79
225 4/8	34 2/8	34 5/8	27 6/8	7	8	Bruce's Pond	NFL	Randy Doyle	1990	80
225 0/8	38 0/8	40 3/8	25 1/8	5	8	Victoria River	NFL	Clarence Bowers, Jr.	1966	81
224 4/8	32 2/8	31 1/8	28 0/8	7	8	Rogers River	NFL	Duane C. Baumler	1998	82
224 1/8	36 0/8	35 0/8	27 4/8	8	9	Lloyds River	NFL	Harold A. Hill	1965	83
223 4/8	36 6/8	37 5/8	28 0/8	5	9	Andrews Pond	NFL	Gregory White	1993	84
222 1/8	31 2/8	30 4/8	29 7/8	7	7	Greys Island	NFL	William E. Terry, Sr.	1993	85
222 0/8	32 3/8	33 1/8	30 1/8	7	8	Buchans Plateau	NFL	Mark Connor	1998	86
221 0/8	32 6/8	30 2/8	27 2/8	11	8	Saddler Pond	NFL	Paul Locey	1982	87
220 2/8	37 6/8	40 7/8	24 0/8	7	14	Alex Pond	NFL	Dr. James J. Schubert	1980	88
220 1/8	33 6/8	31 3/8	24 2/8	8	8	Stony Lake	NFL	Larry Streiff	1995	89

World Record Cougar
Score: 16 1/16
Park County, Wyoming - 1993
Hunter: Scott M. Moore

JUDD COONEY PHOTO

COUGAR (MOUNTAIN LION)

Minimum Score 13 8/16

Felis concolor hippolestes

SCORE	GREATEST LENGTH	GREATEST WIDTH	SEX	AREA	STATE/ PROVINCE	HUNTER'S NAME	DATE	RANK
16 1/16	9 7/16	6 10/16	M	Park County	WY	Scott M. Moore	1993	1
15 11/16	9 2/16	6 9/16	M	Idaho County	ID	Jerry J. James	1982	2
15 11/16	9 4/16	6 7/16	M	Idaho County	ID	Mike McCall	1985	2
15 11/16	9 7/16	6 4/16	M	Ferry County	WA	Bill Buckingham	1986	2
15 11/16	9 3/16	6 8/16	M	Montrose County	CO	Randell Thompson	1992	2
15 10/16	9 0/16	6 10/16	M	Unit 5-5	BC	Harold J. Coult	1986	6
15 10/16	9 5/16	6 5/16	M	Kootenai County	ID	Thomas E. Bangs	1993	6
15 10/16	9 2/16	6 8/16	M	San Miguel County	CO	Robert D. Parker	1994	6
15 9/16	9 3/16	6 6/16	M	Rio Arriba County	NM	Robert John Seeds	1995	9
15 8/16	9 1/16	6 7/16	M	Lemhi County	ID	Doug Kittredge	1971	10

COUGAR (MOUNTAIN LION)

Minimum Score 13 8/16 — Continued

SCORE	GREATEST LENGTH	GREATEST WIDTH	SEX	AREA	STATE/PROVINCE	HUNTER'S NAME	DATE	RANK
15 8/16	8 15/16	6 9/16	M	Clearwater County	ID	John R. Bridwell	1988	10
15 8/16	8 15/16	6 9/16	M	Gila County	AZ	Stephen D. Hornady	1991	10
15 8/16	9 0/16	6 8/16	M	Sanders County	MT	Wayne M. Foley	1993	10
15 8/16	9 2/16	6 6/16	M	Lemhi County	ID	Ray F. Doskus	1994	10
15 8/16	9 3/16	6 5/16	M	Lemhi County	ID	Michael Judas	1995	10
15 8/16	9 4/16	6 4/16	M	Skinner Mtn.	BC	Jeff Ashe	1997	10
15 8/16	9 2/16	6 6/16	M	Garfield County	CO	Richard A. Mowles	1997	10
15 7/16	9 2/16	6 5/16	M	Huerfano County	CO	J. D. Dodge	1971	18
15 7/16	9 0/16	6 7/16	M	Idaho County	ID	William Egner	1972	18
15 7/16	9 4/16	6 3/16	M	Sandoval County	NM	Tom David	1980	18
15 7/16	9 2/16	6 5/16	M	Rio Arriba County	NM	Dick Ray	1985	18
15 7/16	9 2/16	6 5/16	M	Uintah County	UT	John M Mc Ateer	1985	18
15 7/16	9 0/16	6 7/16	M	Idaho County	ID	Steven Anderson	1986	18
15 7/16	8 15/16	6 8/16	M	Ferry County	WA	John Peruchini	1989	18
15 7/16	8 14/16	6 9/16	M	Shoshone County	ID	Eugene L. Lewis	1991	18
15 7/16	9 0/16	6 7/16	M	Clearwater County	ID	Dennis L. Butler	1992	18
15 7/16	9 3/16	6 4/16	M	Colfax County	NM	Donald Travis	1994	18
15 7/16	9 1/16	6 6/16	M	Clearwater County	ID	Mike Lewis	1997	18
15 6/16	9 4/16	6 2/16	M	Grand County	UT	Art Kragness	1969	29
15 6/16	8 11/16	6 11/16	M	Taos County	NM	George P. Mann	1981	29
15 6/16	9 2/16	6 4/16	M	Water Valley	ALB	Don Ferguson	1983	29
15 6/16	9 0/16	6 6/16	M	Idaho County	ID	Ralph L. Hatter	1987	29
15 6/16	8 14/16	6 8/16	M	Lavington	BC	Chris Barker	1992	29
15 6/16	9 0/16	6 6/16	M	Elmore County	ID	Kelly Dougherty	1993	29
15 6/16	8 14/16	6 8/16	M	Dolores County	CO	Thadius Countess	1998	29
15 5/16	8 15/16	6 6/16	M	Mesa County	CO	John Lamicq, Jr.	1969	36
15 5/16	8 15/16	6 6/16	M	Mineral County	MT	Dennis Moos	1976	36
15 5/16	8 15/16	6 6/16	M	Larimer County	CO	Glenn Schmidt	1976	36
15 5/16	8 13/16	6 8/16	M	Madison County	MT	Don Schaufler	1982	36
15 5/16	9 0/16	6 5/16	M	Idaho County	ID	A. M. Oakes, Jr.	1985	36
15 5/16	9 2/16	6 3/16	M	Rio Blanco County	CO	Rob Raley	1985	36
15 5/16	9 0/16	6 5/16	M	Clearwater County	ID	Daniel J. Greve	1985	36
15 5/16	9 0/16	6 5/16	M	Idaho County	ID	Drexel Schilling	1987	36
15 5/16	9 1/16	6 4/16	M	Clearwater County	ID	Rudy Marmelo, Jr.	1990	36
15 5/16	9 0/16	6 5/16	M	Lindsey Lake	BC	Harvey J. Surina	1991	36
15 5/16	9 3/16	6 2/16	M	Rio Arriba County	NM	Robert John Seeds	1992	36
15 5/16	9 0/16	6 5/16	M	Delta County	CO	William E. Kallister	1995	36
15 5/16	9 1/16	6 4/16	M	Custer County	ID	Mike Woltering	1995	36
15 5/16	9 0/16	6 5/16	M	Clearwater County	ID	Bob Bosshardt	1997	36
15 5/16	8 15/16	6 6/16	M	Mesa County	CO	Darryl Powell	1997	36
15 4/16	9 0/16	6 4/16	M	Gila County	AZ	Dr. James L. Smith	1958	51
15 4/16	8 15/16	6 5/16	M	Ogden County	UT	Royce Ross	1971	51
15 4/16	9 0/16	6 4/16	M	Uintah County	UT	Albert L. Farace	1986	51
15 4/16	9 2/16	6 2/16	M	San Juan County	UT	Diane Snyder	1986	51
15 4/16	9 0/16	6 4/16	M	Madison County	MT	Pat Connell	1986	51
15 4/16	8 14/16	6 6/16	M	Clearwater County	ID	Elwood Schultz	1986	51
15 4/16	9 1/16	6 3/16	M	San Miguel County	CO	G. Merrill Jones	1987	51
15 4/16	9 0/16	6 4/16	M	Porcupine Hills	ALB	John Visscher	1990	51
15 4/16	8 15/16	6 5/16	M	Carbon County	UT	Kenny E. Leo	1993	51
15 4/16	8 13/16	6 7/16	M	Lewis & Clark County	MT	Lee D. Laeupple	1993	51
15 4/16	9 0/16	6 4/16	M	Shoshone County	ID	Paul Schaumburg	1993	51
15 4/16	9 2/16	6 2/16	M	Rio Arriba County	NM	Robert John Seeds	1994	51
15 4/16	9 0/16	6 4/16	M	Beaver Valley	BC	Jim Dunigan	1996	51
15 4/16	8 14/16	6 6/16	M	Moyie Lake	BC	Robert Faiers	1997	51
15 4/16	9 1/16	6 3/16	M	Broadwater County	MT	Kevin Harms	1998	51
15 3/16	8 13/16	6 6/16	M	Ventura County	CA	Warren C. Johnston	1953	66
15 3/16	9 0/16	6 3/16	M	Fremont County	CO	Art Heinze	1976	66
15 3/16	8 14/16	6 5/16	M	Douglas County	CO	Donald R. Looper	1977	66
15 3/16	8 13/16	6 6/16	M	Rio Arriba County	NM	Anderson Bakewell, S.J.	1978	66
15 3/16	8 4/16	6 15/16	M	Cassia County	ID	Ronald C. Ward	1984	66
15 3/16	8 13/16	6 6/16	M	Clallam County	WA	Ron W. Cram	1984	66
15 3/16	8 14/16	6 5/16	M	Huerfano County	CO	Bob Sigman	1987	66
15 3/16	8 14/16	6 5/16	M	Clearwater County	ID	Mike T. McCain	1988	66
15 3/16	8 14/16	6 5/16	M	Lincoln County	MT	Jon Greeno Clark	1989	66
15 3/16	9 1/16	6 2/16	M	Ravalli County	MT	Mario Locatelli	1990	66
15 3/16	9 2/16	6 1/16	M	Archuleta County	CO	Charles T. Ames	1991	66
15 3/16	8 15/16	6 4/16	M	Idaho County	ID	Steve B. Schilling	1992	66
15 3/16	8 15/16	6 4/16	M	Daggett County	UT	John Richardson	1992	66
15 3/16	8 13/16	6 6/16	M	Bannock County	ID	Brad Hough	1992	66
15 3/16	8 14/16	6 5/16	M	Lincoln County	MT	Terry Krogstad	1993	66
15 3/16	9 0/16	6 3/16	M	Clear Creek County	CO	Mark Turner	1995	66
15 3/16	8 15/16	6 4/16	M	Judith Basin County	MT	John "Rosey" Roseland	1997	66
15 3/16	8 15/16	6 4/16	M	Idaho County	ID	Jesse Higgins	1998	66
15 2/16	8 15/16	6 3/16	M	Rio Blanco County	CO	Leonard Cardinale	1963	84
15 2/16	9 0/16	6 2/16	M	Grand County	UT	Richard Oakleaf	1967	84
15 2/16	8 12/16	6 6/16	M	Flathead County	MT	Jerry Almos	1971	84
15 2/16	8 14/16	6 4/16	M	Wallowa County	OR	Terrell Buchanan	1973	84
15 2/16	9 0/16	6 2/16	M	Utah County	UT	Max F. Park	1975	84

COUGAR (MOUNTAIN LION)

Minimum Score 13 8/16 — Continued

SCORE	GREATEST LENGTH	GREATEST WIDTH	SEX	AREA	STATE/PROVINCE	HUNTER'S NAME	DATE	RANK
15 2/16	8 14/16	6 4/16	M	Sanders County	MT	Conrad Anderson	1984	84
15 2/16	8 14/16	6 4/16	M	Meagher County	MT	Gene Clark	1985	84
15 2/16	8 12/16	6 6/16	M	Teton County	WY	Craig Richardson	1986	84
15 2/16	8 14/16	6 4/16	M	Wallowa County	OR	Thomas C. Ashcroft	1986	84
15 2/16	8 14/16	6 4/16	M	Daggett County	UT	Franco DiPietro	1987	84
15 2/16	8 14/16	6 4/16	M	Conejos County	CO	Wayne Miller	1987	84
15 2/16	9 0/16	6 2/16	M	Mesa County	CO	Frank P. Alameno	1987	84
15 2/16	8 15/16	6 3/16	M	Clearwater County	ID	Michael J. Kennedy	1987	84
15 2/16	8 13/16	6 5/16	M	Pincher Creek	ALB	Duane B. Schultz	1988	84
15 2/16	8 12/16	6 6/16	M	Iron County	UT	Bob Spina	1989	84
15 2/16	8 15/16	6 3/16	M	Park County	CO	Jack P. Van Vianen	1990	84
15 2/16	8 13/16	6 5/16	M	Shoshone County	ID	Pat D. Jerald	1991	84
15 2/16	8 15/16	6 3/16	M	Rio Arriba County	NM	Robert John Seeds	1991	84
15 2/16	8 9/16	6 9/16	M	Lincoln County	MT	Jim Eff	1992	84
15 2/16	8 11/16	6 7/16	M	Kootenay Lake	BC	Robert Kuny	1993	84
15 2/16	8 12/16	6 6/16	M	Park County	MT	Primo Scapin	1993	84
15 2/16	8 15/16	6 3/16	M	Kootenay River	BC	Brian Schuck	1993	84
15 2/16	9 0/16	6 2/16	M	Larimer County	CO	Don Watowa	1994	84
15 2/16	8 13/16	6 5/16	M	Porcupine Hills	ALB	Dan Croy	1995	84
15 2/16	9 1/16	6 1/16	M	Mesa County	CO	M. David Bennett, Jr.	1996	84
15 2/16	8 15/16	6 3/16	M	Delta County	CO	Ray Kennedy	1996	84
15 2/16	8 12/16	6 6/16	M	Rio Arriba County	NM	Robert John Seeds	1996	84
15 2/16	8 14/16	6 4/16	M	Madison County	MT	Cody Stemler	1996	84
15 2/16	8 14/16	6 4/16	M	Rocky Mountain House	ALB	Dennis Tucker	1997	84
15 2/16	8 14/16	6 4/16	M	Chain Lakes	ALB	Tom Foss	1998	84
15 1/16	8 13/16	6 4/16	M	Iron County	UT	William P. Mastrangel	1964	114
15 1/16	8 12/16	6 5/16	M	Nez Perce County	ID	Pete Baughman, Jr.	1979	114
15 1/16	8 15/16	6 2/16	M	Rio Arriba County	NM	Joe Strasser, Jr.	1980	114
15 1/16	8 14/16	6 3/16	M	San Juan County	UT	Shad D. Schmidt	1981	114
15 1/16	8 13/16	6 4/16	M	Archuleta County	CO	Judd Cooney	1982	114
15 1/16	9 1/16	6 0/16	M	Lincoln County	MT	Gary C. Cargill	1986	114
15 1/16	8 15/16	6 2/16	M	Clearwater County	ID	Charles "Smitty" Smith	1987	114
15 1/16	8 11/16	6 6/16	M	Sundre	ALB	Fred Houtstra	1987	114
15 1/16	9 1/16	6 0/16	M	Valley County	ID	Douglas L. Petty	1987	114
15 1/16	8 14/16	6 3/16	M	Ouray County	CO	Steven A. Rider	1989	114
15 1/16	9 0/16	6 1/16	M	Millard County	UT	Edwin A. Lewis	1990	114
15 1/16	8 14/16	6 3/16	M	Rio Blanco County	CO	Dr. Gerald L. Dowling	1990	114
15 1/16	9 0/16	6 1/16	M	Taos County	NM	Bill Porteous	1990	114
15 1/16	8 15/16	6 2/16	M	Mineral County	MT	Gerg Balzum	1990	114
15 1/16	8 12/16	6 5/16	M	Eagle County	CO	Richard E. Davis	1990	114
15 1/16	9 0/16	6 1/16	M	Sanders County	MT	Phillip J. Taylor	1992	114
15 1/16	8 10/16	6 7/16	M	Lincoln County	MT	William R. Vyvyan	1992	114
15 1/16	9 0/16	6 1/16	M	Carbon County	UT	Ray T. Bridge	1993	114
15 1/16	8 11/16	6 6/16	M	Boundary County	ID	Ron Frederickson	1994	114
15 1/16	8 14/16	6 3/16	M	Sanders County	MT	Dennis Gripp	1994	114
15 1/16	8 14/16	6 3/16	M	Flathead County	MT	Shawn P. Price	1994	114
15 1/16	8 14/16	6 3/16	M	Rio Blanco County	CO	Bruce R. Schoeneweis	1994	114
15 1/16	8 15/16	6 2/16	M	Grand County	CO	Rick Karbowski	1997	114
15 1/16	9 0/16	6 1/16	M	Eagle County	CO	David TerMaat	1997	114
15 1/16	8 12/16	6 5/16	M	Park County	MT	Michael R. Deschamps	1997	114
15 0/16	8 11/16	6 5/16	M	Elko County	NV	Earl Dudley	1959	139
15 0/16	8 13/16	6 3/16	M	Utah County	UT	Richard C. Smith	1968	139
15 0/16	8 11/16	6 5/16	M	Mizzezula Mtns.	BC	Bengt G. Bjalme	1969	139
15 0/16	8 12/16	6 4/16	M	Columbia Lake	BC	Ray Lundstrom	1979	139
15 0/16	8 14/16	6 2/16	M	Madison County	MT	George A. Dieruf	1980	139
15 0/16	8 12/16	6 4/16	M	Lemhi County	ID	Roy Auwen	1981	139
15 0/16	8 11/16	6 5/16	M	Sandoval County	NM	Ernest C. Torres	1981	139
15 0/16	8 11/16	6 5/16	M	Rio Arriba County	NM	Mike Ray	1982	139
15 0/16	8 11/16	6 5/16	M	Mineral County	MT	Grover L. Hedrick	1983	139
15 0/16	8 10/16	6 6/16	M	Sanders County	MT	Joe Schaefer	1984	139
15 0/16	8 10/16	6 6/16	M	Wallowa County	OR	Chuck Warner	1985	139
15 0/16	9 0/16	6 0/16	M	Rio Grande County	CO	Richard J. Dugas	1986	139
15 0/16	8 12/16	6 4/16	M	San Juan County	NM	Richard M. Young, Jr.	1987	139
15 0/16	8 10/16	6 6/16	M	Sanpete County	UT	Craig Adams	1988	139
15 0/16	9 0/16	6 0/16	M	Elmore County	ID	Ed Strayhorn	1989	139
15 0/16	8 14/16	6 2/16	M	Rio Arriba County	NM	Robert J. Seeds	1989	139
15 0/16	8 13/16	6 3/16	M	Pillar Lake	BC	Kent Michie/Terry Wasylyszyn	1989	139
15 0/16	8 12/16	6 4/16	M	Cache County	UT	Gino Giannetti	1990	139
15 0/16	8 14/16	6 2/16	M	Carbon County	UT	Roy Wheeler, Jr.	1990	139
15 0/16	8 12/16	6 4/16	M	Camas County	ID	Andy Moore	1990	139
15 0/16	8 12/16	6 4/16	M	Shoshone County	ID	Buster Karrer	1991	139
15 0/16	8 11/16	6 5/16	M	Fergus County	MT	Chuck Taylor	1991	139
15 0/16	8 12/16	6 4/16	M	Spokane County	WA	Colin McRae	1991	139
15 0/16	8 14/16	6 2/16	M	Garfield County	UT	Gregory Nixon	1992	139
15 0/16	8 13/16	6 3/16	M	Gallatin County	MT	Darrell Otteson	1992	139
15 0/16	8 14/16	6 2/16	M	Lemhi County	ID	Daniel R. Darrah	1992	139
15 0/16	8 13/16	6 3/16	M	Montezuma County	CO	John L. Gardner	1993	139
15 0/16	8 12/16	6 4/16	M	Montrose County	CO	Corey W. Murray	1993	139

COUGAR (MOUNTAIN LION)

Minimum Score 13 8/16   Continued

SCORE	GREATEST LENGTH	GREATEST WIDTH	SEX	AREA	STATE/ PROVINCE	HUNTER'S NAME	DATE	RANK
15 0/16	8 15/16	6 1/16	M	Montezuma County	CO	Robert D. Crask	1993	139
15 0/16	8 15/16	6 1/16	M	Boise County	ID	Mark W. Rose	1995	139
15 0/16	8 11/16	6 5/16	M	Battle Creek	BC	Glenn Dreger	1995	139
15 0/16	8 15/16	6 1/16	M	Valley County	ID	John Pyle	1995	139
15 0/16	9 0/16	6 0/16	M	Rio Arriba County	NM	K-Tal Johnson	1995	139
15 0/16	8 14/16	6 2/16	M	San Juan County	UT	David A. Bronson	1997	139
15 0/16	8 12/16	6 4/16	M	Bonner County	ID	Shawn Frederickson	1997	139
15 0/16	8 13/16	6 3/16	M	Benewah County	ID	Don Houk	1998	139
14 15/16	8 12/16	6 3/16	M	Lincoln County	MT	Allen Apling	1959	175
14 15/16	8 11/16	6 4/16	M	Boundary County	ID	Rick Furniss	1968	175
14 15/16	8 14/16	6 1/16	M	Rio Blanco County	CO	Jack Pawlak	1971	175
14 15/16	8 13/16	6 2/16	M	Rio Blanco County	CO	Stanley R. Winslow	1971	175
14 15/16	8 14/16	6 1/16	M	Carbon County	UT	Larry Wright	1975	175
14 15/16	8 11/16	6 4/16	M	Idaho County	ID	Dick Gulman	1976	175
14 15/16	8 12/16	6 3/16	M	Piute County	UT	Douglas Wagner	1976	175
14 15/16	8 11/16	6 4/16	M	Deer Lodge County	MT	Scott Koelzer	1979	175
14 15/16	8 15/16	6 0/16	M	Montezuma County	CO	Roy Keefer	1984	175
14 15/16	8 14/16	6 1/16	M	Cascade County	MT	Charles A. Vande Hei	1984	175
14 15/16	8 13/16	6 2/16	M	Sevier County	UT	Chuck Morger	1988	175
14 15/16	8 11/16	6 4/16	M	Park County	MT	Patrick Gilligan	1988	175
14 15/16	8 13/16	6 2/16	M	Ouray County	CO	Doug McCauley	1988	175
14 15/16	8 14/16	6 1/16	M	Garfield County	CO	Bruce R. Schoeneweis	1989	175
14 15/16	8 13/16	6 2/16	M	Bear Lake County	ID	Rick Berghelm	1990	175
14 15/16	8 12/16	6 3/16	M	Missoula County	MT	Mike Miller	1990	175
14 15/16	8 12/16	6 3/16	M	San Miguel County	CO	Monroe A. Hare	1991	175
14 15/16	8 12/16	6 3/16	M	Idaho County	ID	Mark Jacobson	1991	175
14 15/16	8 12/16	6 3/16	M	Missoula County	MT	Kenneth B. Scobie	1991	175
14 15/16	8 12/16	6 3/16	M	Ravalli County	MT	James A. Haase	1993	175
14 15/16	8 13/16	6 2/16	M	Elmore County	ID	Tony Mudd	1993	175
14 15/16	8 10/16	6 5/16	M	Kananaskis	ALB	Harry Schilling	1993	175
14 15/16	8 12/16	6 3/16	M	Sandoval County	NM	Rett Kelly	1993	175
14 15/16	8 15/16	6 0/16	M	Tatlayoka Lake	BC	Glenn Dreger	1994	175
14 15/16	8 13/16	6 2/16	M	Morgan County	UT	Claude Archuleta	1994	175
14 15/16	8 13/16	6 2/16	M	La Plata County	CO	Valerie Gardner	1994	175
14 15/16	8 13/16	6 2/16	M	Moffat County	CO	Rob Bathurst	1995	175
14 15/16	8 13/16	6 2/16	M	Caven Creek	BC	Brian Chittim	1996	175
14 15/16	8 11/16	6 4/16	M	Rio Blanco County	CO	Clare Streeter	1998	175
14 15/16	8 12/16	6 3/16	M	Kelowna	BC	Rick Pasutto	1998	175
14 14/16	8 14/16	6 0/16	M	Lincoln County	MT	Dr. B. L. Lundberg	1958	205
14 14/16	8 11/16	6 3/16	M	Flathead County	MT	Jack Whitney	1967	205
14 14/16	8 10/16	6 4/16	M	Lemhi County	ID	Ray Torrey	1969	205
14 14/16	8 10/16	6 4/16	M	Granite County	MT	John Lawler	1972	205
14 14/16	8 13/16	6 1/16	M	Elmore County	ID	Dan F. Hackney	1973	205
14 14/16	8 15/16	5 15/16	M	Lemhi County	ID	Jim Dougherty	1980	205
14 14/16	8 11/16	6 3/16	M	Utah County	UT	Kelly R. Clements	1981	205
14 14/16	8 12/16	6 2/16	M	Lemhi County	ID	Jay Meyers	1982	205
14 14/16	8 12/16	6 2/16	M	Iron County	UT	Craig R. White	1983	205
14 14/16	8 12/16	6 2/16	M	Montezuma County	CO	Ms. Charlie White	1983	205
14 14/16	8 12/16	6 2/16	M	Madison County	MT	Cecil I. Tharp	1984	205
14 14/16	8 14/16	6 0/16	M	Rio Blanco County	CO	Calvin Farner	1986	205
14 14/16	8 10/16	6 4/16	M	Flathead County	MT	Bruce Whitaker	1988	205
14 14/16	8 13/16	6 1/16	M	Utah County	UT	Daniel M. Taylor	1989	205
14 14/16	8 13/16	6 1/16	M	Clearwater County	ID	Reva Anne Hyde	1990	205
14 14/16	8 11/16	6 3/16	M	Grand County	UT	Joseph A. Segaria	1991	205
14 14/16	8 10/16	6 4/16	M	Fergus County	MT	Allen Fritz	1991	205
14 14/16	8 13/16	6 1/16	M	North Fork	ALB	Victor Lawson	1991	205
14 14/16	8 12/16	6 2/16	M	Moffat County	CO	Mike Camilletti, Sr.	1993	205
14 14/16	8 11/16	6 3/16	M	Bonner County	ID	Timothy J. Duffney	1993	205
14 14/16	8 11/16	6 3/16	M	Stevens County	WA	Thomas Patterson	1993	205
14 14/16	8 13/16	6 1/16	M	Millard County	UT	David Edwards	1994	205
14 14/16	8 12/16	6 2/16	M	Rio Blanco County	CO	Frank L. Fackovec	1994	205
14 14/16	8 12/16	6 2/16	M	Whatshau River	BC	Gary Atkins	1994	205
14 14/16	8 12/16	6 2/16	M	Ravalli County	MT	Anthony "Del" Del Mastro	1994	205
14 14/16	8 12/16	6 2/16	M	Lincoln County	MT	James Hershberger	1994	205
14 14/16	9 0/16	5 14/16	F	San Miguel County	CO	Wyatt C. Watson	1995	205
14 14/16	8 11/16	6 3/16	M	Toby Creek	BC	Kent G. Kebe	1995	205
14 14/16	8 12/16	6 2/16	M	Vaseux Creek	BC	Terry L. Bixler	1995	205
14 14/16	8 10/16	6 4/16	M	Teton County	WY	Craig A. Germond	1996	205
14 14/16	8 13/16	6 1/16	M	Montezuma County	CO	Ronald R. Grenadier	1998	205
14 13/16	8 11/16	6 2/16	M	Chelan County	WA	Dr. R.Congdon	1951	236
14 13/16	8 11/16	6 2/16	M	Ferry County	WA	R. O. Hilderbrant	1965	236
14 13/16	8 12/16	6 1/16	F	Duchesne County	UT	Larry Jones	1967	236
14 13/16	8 13/16	6 0/16	M	Garfield County	CO	Albert L. Heise	1971	236
14 13/16	8 13/16	6 0/16	M	Chaffee County	CO	Phillip B. Grable	1973	236
14 13/16	8 10/16	6 3/16	M	Huerfano County	CO	William F. Eikleberry	1974	236
14 13/16	8 12/16	6 1/16	M	Emery County	UT	Rex Peterson	1975	236
14 13/16	8 11/16	6 2/16	M	Uintah County	UT	Ronald D. Shank	1976	236
14 13/16	8 12/16	6 1/16	M	Warner	BC	John 'Jack' Cordes	1977	236

COUGAR (MOUNTAIN LION)

Minimum Score 13 8/16 — Continued

SCORE	GREATEST LENGTH	GREATEST WIDTH	SEX	AREA	STATE/PROVINCE	HUNTER'S NAME	DATE	RANK
14 13/16	8 10/16	6 3/16	M	Stevens County	WA	Tim C. Boyd	1979	236
14 13/16	8 10/16	6 3/16	M	Elmore County	ID	Dr. Robert T. Laughery	1979	236
14 13/16	8 14/16	5 15/16	M	Mesa County	CO	Jim R. Lewis	1981	236
14 13/16	8 13/16	6 0/16	M	Idaho County	ID	Ray Keenan	1982	236
14 13/16	8 12/16	6 1/16	M	Moffat County	CO	John A. Lee	1982	236
14 13/16	8 11/16	6 2/16	M	McGuire Creek	BC	William Morley	1983	236
14 13/16	8 12/16	6 1/16	M	Sanders County	MT	Gil Gilbertson	1984	236
14 13/16	8 11/16	6 2/16	M	San Miguel County	CO	David E. Smith	1985	236
14 13/16	8 12/16	6 1/16	M	Albany County	WY	R.D. Keeler, D.C.	1985	236
14 13/16	8 13/16	6 0/16	M	Camas County	ID	Larry R. Newton	1987	236
14 13/16	8 11/16	6 2/16	M	Fish Creek	ALB	Ken Maier	1987	236
14 13/16	8 9/16	6 4/16	M	Montezuma County	CO	Richard Kimball	1987	236
14 13/16	8 11/16	6 2/16	M	Clearwater County	ID	Thomas A. Kayser	1988	236
14 13/16	8 11/16	6 2/16	M	Clearwater County	ID	Ralph Albright	1989	236
14 13/16	8 12/16	6 1/16	M	Emery County	UT	Sam Raby	1989	236
14 13/16	8 12/16	6 1/16	M	Dolores County	CO	Robert R. Hoffa, Jr.	1990	236
14 13/16	8 10/16	6 3/16	M	Black Mtn.	ALB	Udo Kerber	1991	236
14 13/16	8 14/16	5 15/16	M	Powell County	MT	Todd Johnson	1991	236
14 13/16	8 10/16	6 3/16	M	Elko	BC	Gordon Mailey	1991	236
14 13/16	8 11/16	6 2/16	M	Carbon County	UT	Tracy Jacobsen	1992	236
14 13/16	8 13/16	6 0/16	M	Archuleta County	CO	Sam B. Ray	1992	236
14 13/16	8 12/16	6 1/16	M	Fremont County	CO	Robert W. Allen	1992	236
14 13/16	8 11/16	6 2/16	M	Sanders County	MT	Tony Naismith	1992	236
14 13/16	8 13/16	6 0/16	M	Shoshone County	ID	Kenneth L. Way	1992	236
14 13/16	8 11/16	6 2/16	M	Delta County	CO	Dennis Hayden	1993	236
14 13/16	8 9/16	6 4/16	M	Kittitas County	WA	Scott Kieser	1993	236
14 13/16	8 11/16	6 2/16	M	Gallatin County	MT	John Berger	1993	236
14 13/16	8 9/16	6 4/16	M	Sanders County	MT	Don E. Smith	1993	236
14 13/16	8 11/16	6 2/16	M	Boise County	ID	August S. Gray	1993	236
14 13/16	8 11/16	6 2/16	M	Las Animas County	CO	Dr. J. Richard Bland III	1994	236
14 13/16	8 12/16	6 1/16	M	Granite County	MT	Mickey E. Lotz	1994	236
14 13/16	8 10/16	6 3/16	M	Madison County	MT	Robert Maier	1994	236
14 13/16	8 10/16	6 3/16	M	Saguache County	CO	Mike Haynes	1995	236
14 13/16	8 13/16	6 0/16	M	Boise County	ID	Barry Gwin	1996	236
14 13/16	8 12/16	6 1/16	M	Sanders County	MT	Judy Kovar	1996	236
14 13/16	8 11/16	6 2/16	M	Rio Blanco County	CO	Roger C. Trout	1997	236
14 13/16	8 11/16	6 2/16	M	Cache County	UT	Monte Green	1997	236
14 12/16	8 14/16	5 14/16	M	Chelan County	WA	Dr. R. Congdon	1952	282
14 12/16	8 12/16	6 0/16	M	Clallam County	WA	Lloyd Beebe	1953	282
14 12/16	8 11/16	6 3/16	M	Rio Blanco County	CO	LeRoy Wood	1965	282
14 12/16	8 12/16	6 0/16	M		CO	Clyde Hector	1967	282
14 12/16	8 13/16	5 15/16	M	Garfield County	UT	Harold Boyack	1968	282
14 12/16	8 11/16	6 1/16	M	Valley County	ID	John Buford Reese	1976	282
14 12/16	8 10/16	6 2/16	M	Maguire Creek	BC	William Morley	1979	282
14 12/16	8 10/16	6 2/16	M	Boulder County	CO	Doug Beck	1984	282
14 12/16	8 10/16	6 2/16	M	Larimer County	CO	Jim Johnson	1985	282
14 12/16	8 14/16	5 14/16	M	Moffat County	CO	Michael B. Moline	1985	282
14 12/16	8 11/16	6 1/16	M	Cache County	UT	Ed Lawlor	1985	282
14 12/16	8 9/16	6 3/16	M	Madison County	MT	Ken Hoehn	1985	282
14 12/16	9 0/16	5 12/16	M	Custer County	CO	David Waldrop	1986	282
14 12/16	8 12/16	6 0/16	M	Emery County	UT	Ricky Schroder	1986	282
14 12/16	8 11/16	6 1/16	M	Rio Arriba County	NM	Robert John Seeds	1988	282
14 12/16	8 11/16	6 1/16	M	Utah County	UT	Blake A. Ryan	1988	282
14 12/16	8 12/16	6 0/16	M	Saguache County	CO	Mark Wuerthele	1988	282
14 12/16	8 9/16	6 3/16	M	Archuleta County	CO	Leo F. Neuls	1988	282
14 12/16	8 10/16	6 2/16	M	Wallowa County	OR	Paul Turcke	1988	282
14 12/16	8 10/16	6 2/16	M	Saguache County	CO	Roger Maurice Tyler	1989	282
14 12/16	8 8/16	6 4/16	M	San Juan County	UT	Henry Gilbertson	1989	282
14 12/16	8 11/16	6 1/16	M	Flathead County	MT	Gary A. Crowe	1989	282
14 12/16	8 10/16	6 2/16	M	Mesa County	CO	Kerry Kammer	1990	282
14 12/16	8 10/16	6 2/16	M	Sevier County	UT	James Schade	1991	282
14 12/16	8 13/16	5 15/16	M	Rio Blanco County	CO	Ross L. Talbott	1991	282
14 12/16	8 13/16	5 15/16	M	Elk River	BC	Doug Scott	1991	282
14 12/16	8 11/16	6 1/16	M	Duchesne County	UT	Kent E. Smith	1992	282
14 12/16	8 9/16	6 3/16	M	Lewis & Clark County	MT	Mike Knapstad	1992	282
14 12/16	8 10/16	6 2/16	M	Nakasp	BC	Edwin L. DeYoung	1992	282
14 12/16	8 11/16	6 1/16	M	Kootenay River	BC	Brian Schuck	1992	282
14 12/16	8 11/16	6 1/16	M	Lincoln County	NV	Stephen L. Geller	1992	282
14 12/16	8 8/16	6 4/16	M	Flathead County	MT	Ira S. Uradomo	1992	282
14 12/16	8 10/16	6 2/16	M	Princeton	BC	Dr. Peeler Grayson Lacey	1992	282
14 12/16	8 13/16	5 15/16	M	Carbon County	MT	Thomas E. Hart, Jr.	1993	282
14 12/16	8 12/16	6 0/16	M	Garfield County	CO	Jay R. Rasch	1993	282
14 12/16	8 11/16	6 1/16	M	La Plata County	CO	Michael Falcone	1993	282
14 12/16	8 14/16	5 14/16	M	Carbon County	UT	Hugh H. Hogle	1993	282
14 12/16	8 10/16	6 2/16	M	Ravalli County	MT	Mark Hoselton	1994	282
14 12/16	8 10/16	6 2/16	M	Huerfano County	CO	David Hinton	1994	282
14 12/16	8 13/16	5 15/16	M	Rio Blanco County	CO	Stephen W. Greer	1994	282
14 12/16	8 14/16	5 14/16	M	Wayne County	UT	Robert M. Daggett	1995	282

COUGAR (MOUNTAIN LION)

Minimum Score 13 8/16   Continued

SCORE	GREATEST LENGTH	GREATEST WIDTH	SEX	AREA	STATE/ PROVINCE	HUNTER'S NAME	DATE	RANK
14 12/16	8 10/16	6 2/16	M	Madison County	MT	Mark Kronyak	1995	282
14 12/16	8 10/16	6 2/16	M	Lemhi County	ID	Dick Wenger	1995	282
14 12/16	8 12/16	6 0/16	M	San Miguel County	CO	Fritz A. Brennecke	1995	282
14 12/16	8 9/16	6 3/16	M	Jefferson County	CO	Dan Eaton	1995	282
14 12/16	8 9/16	6 3/16	M	Robb	ALB	Dwayne Huggins	1996	282
14 12/16	8 9/16	6 3/16	M	Clark County	ID	Aaron Bateman	1997	282
14 12/16	8 12/16	6 0/16	M	Rio Grande County	CO	Tobias Dellamano	1997	282
14 12/16	8 12/16	6 0/16	M	Clearwater County	ID	Larry Davis	1997	282
14 12/16	8 10/16	6 2/16	M	Lewis & Clark County	MT	Grant M. Winn II	1998	282
14 12/16	8 11/16	6 1/16	M	Missoula County	MT	Rory Indreland	1998	282
14 11/16	8 10/16	6 1/16	M	Sundre	ALB	Tom Decker	1966	333
14 11/16	8 8/16	6 3/16	M	Custer County	ID	Ralph V. Pehrson	1969	333
14 11/16	8 9/16	6 2/16	M	Boise County	ID	Harlow D. Austad	1971	333
14 11/16	8 8/16	6 3/16	M	Kettle River	BC	Irvin Plotz	1976	333
14 11/16	8 12/16	5 15/16	M	Lincoln County	MT	Ronald J. Wade	1976	333
14 11/16	8 10/16	6 1/16	M	Garfield County	UT	Bradford L. Sheltrown	1977	333
14 11/16	8 10/16	6 1/16	M	Middle Fork	ID	Robert Frank	1978	333
14 11/16	8 10/16	6 1/16	M	Flathead County	MT	Dr. James J. Shubert	1978	333
14 11/16	8 14/16	5 13/16	M	Custer County	CO	Philip Stegenga	1979	333
14 11/16	8 12/16	5 15/16	M	Columbia County	WA	John Wahl	1979	333
14 11/16	8 9/16	6 2/16	M	Ravalli County	MT	Bill Mitchell	1980	333
14 11/16	8 10/16	6 1/16	M	San Miguel County	CO	Judd Cooney	1981	333
14 11/16	8 12/16	5 15/16	M	Utah County	UT	Fred Tarran	1982	333
14 11/16	8 8/16	6 3/16	M	Chaffee County	CO	Reggie Spiegelberg	1983	333
14 11/16	8 11/16	6 0/16	M	Lemhi County	ID	Stewart P. Fitzgerald	1985	333
14 11/16	8 10/16	6 1/16	M	Washakie County	WY	Nelson Scherrer	1986	333
14 11/16	8 7/16	6 4/16	M	Socorro County	NM	Chuck Sherwin	1986	333
14 11/16	8 11/16	6 0/16	M	Montezuma County	CO	Carla D. Coval	1987	333
14 11/16	8 7/16	6 4/16	M	Elko County	NV	Robert Pyne	1987	333
14 11/16	8 12/16	5 15/16	M	Owyhee County	ID	Gladwin F. Mills	1988	333
14 11/16	8 11/16	6 0/16	M	Valley County	ID	Tom Augustine	1988	333
14 11/16	8 10/16	6 1/16	M	Washakie County	WY	Ron Books	1989	333
14 11/16	8 12/16	5 15/16	M	Teton County	WY	Joseph P. Furlong	1989	333
14 11/16	8 10/16	6 1/16	M	Park County	MT	Patrick Gilligan	1989	333
14 11/16	8 12/16	5 15/16	M	Lemhi County	ID	Randy Lee Cooley	1989	333
14 11/16	8 12/16	5 15/16	M	Montezuma County	CO	Phil M. Elmore	1990	333
14 11/16	8 12/16	5 15/16	M	Humboldt County	NV	Dean Knoles	1990	333
14 11/16	8 8/16	6 3/16	M	Clearwater County	ID	Thomas Storr	1990	333
14 11/16	8 12/16	5 15/16	M	Lemhi County	ID	Bill Connors	1990	333
14 11/16	8 10/16	6 1/16	M	San Juan County	UT	Aaron Bronson	1991	333
14 11/16	8 12/16	5 15/16	M	Coconino County	AZ	George N. Davies	1991	333
14 11/16	8 12/16	5 15/16	M	Albany County	WY	Steven Perkins	1992	333
14 11/16	8 11/16	6 0/16	M	Lewis & Clark County	MT	Sonny Templeton	1993	333
14 11/16	8 8/16	6 3/16	M	Bragg Creek	ALB	Wayne Greene	1993	333
14 11/16	8 2/16	6 9/16	M	Shoshone County	ID	Scott Trelstad	1995	333
14 11/16	8 12/16	5 15/16	M	Uintah County	UT	Scott Anspaugh	1995	333
14 11/16	8 11/16	6 0/16	M	Wayne County	UT	Jerry J. Gilbertson	1996	333
14 11/16	8 9/16	6 2/16	M	Redburn Creek	BC	Gilles Rondeau	1996	333
14 11/16	8 11/16	6 0/16	M	Kane County	UT	Sean Crosby	1997	333
14 11/16	8 8/16	6 3/16	M	Wigwam River	BC	Tony Zielinski	1997	333
14 11/16	8 10/16	6 1/16	M	Carbon County	UT	Karen K. Jacobsen	1997	333
14 11/16	8 12/16	5 15/16	M	Corbin	BC	William T. Carroll, Jr.	1997	333
14 11/16	8 9/16	6 2/16	M	Custer County	ID	Scott C. Quinn	1998	333
14 11/16	8 12/16	5 15/16	M	Washington County	UT	Steve Letcher	1998	333
14 11/16	8 10/16	6 1/16	M	Wasatch County	UT	Ed Bitterman	1998	333
14 11/16	8 10/16	6 1/16	M	Nye County	NV	Ricardo Longoria	1998	333
14 10/16	8 10/16	6 0/16	M	Lincoln County	MT	Dr. Lowell L. Eddy	1967	379
14 10/16	8 10/16	6 0/16	M	Idaho County	ID	C. Bruce Peeples, Jr.	1970	379
14 10/16	8 9/16	6 1/16	M	Carbon County	UT	Paul E. Nottingham	1972	379
14 10/16	8 8/16	6 2/16	M	Rio Blanco County	CO	Paul Janke	1976	379
14 10/16	8 10/16	6 0/16	M	Flathead County	MT	Jerry Karsky	1976	379
14 10/16	8 10/16	6 0/16	M	Pincher Creek	ALB	Theo Mitchell	1977	379
14 10/16	8 8/16	6 2/16	M	Madison County	MT	Don Schaufler	1977	379
14 10/16	8 10/16	6 0/16	M	Sevier County	UT	Harold Hugelen	1979	379
14 10/16	8 10/16	6 0/16	M	Fremont County	CO	Pete J. Santi	1979	379
14 10/16	8 11/16	5 15/16	M	Las Animas County	CO	Glenn R. Kuklick	1980	379
14 10/16	8 9/16	6 1/16	M	Elmore County	ID	L. Dean Goodner	1981	379
14 10/16	8 10/16	6 0/16	M	Fremont County	CO	Johnny J. Lama	1981	379
14 10/16	8 13/16	5 13/16	M	Fremont County	CO	Carolyn E. Lama	1981	379
14 10/16	8 10/16	6 0/16	M	Carbon County	UT	Claude A. Flippin	1982	379
14 10/16	8 8/16	6 2/16	M	Sanders County	MT	Scott Lennard	1982	379
14 10/16	8 9/16	6 1/16	M	Box Elder County	UT	Jerry Mason	1982	379
14 10/16	8 13/16	5 13/16	M	San Miguel County	CO	James Yuds	1982	379
14 10/16	8 10/16	6 0/16	M	Montezuma County	CO	Mike Morgan	1983	379
14 10/16	8 10/16	6 0/16	M	Piute County	UT	James C. Hicks	1983	379
14 10/16	8 15/16	5 11/16	M	Chaffee County	CO	Tom Bowman	1983	379
14 10/16	8 9/16	6 1/16	M	San Juan County	NM	Gary Weber	1984	379
14 10/16	8 9/16	6 1/16	M	Douglas County	NV	Kirk Westervelt	1986	379

COUGAR (MOUNTAIN LION)

Minimum Score 13 8/16 Continued

SCORE	GREATEST LENGTH	GREATEST WIDTH	SEX	AREA	STATE/ PROVINCE	HUNTER'S NAME	DATE	RANK
14 10/16	8 8/16	6 2/16	M	Flathead County	MT	Dyrk Eddie	1986	379
14 10/16	8 9/16	6 1/16	M	Montrose County	CO	David Ernest Nesler	1987	379
14 10/16	8 11/16	5 15/16	M	Sevier County	UT	Kelly Poulsen	1987	379
14 10/16	8 13/16	5 13/16	M	Alamosa County	CO	Tim Walters	1987	379
14 10/16	8 10/16	6 0/16	M	Owyhee County	ID	Richard Fritz	1988	379
14 10/16	8 9/16	6 1/16	M	Nye County	NV	Arrah C. Curry	1988	379
14 10/16	8 10/16	6 0/16	M	Carbon County	UT	Dennis G. McElvain	1988	379
14 10/16	8 9/16	6 1/16	M	Gilpin County	CO	Garry V. Woodman	1988	379
14 10/16	8 12/16	5 14/16	M	Montezuma County	CO	Steven J. Vittetow	1989	379
14 10/16	8 9/16	6 1/16	M	Wheatland County	MT	Albert W. Winter	1989	379
14 10/16	8 10/16	6 0/16	M	Umatilla County	OR	Javier Garcia	1989	379
14 10/16	8 10/16	6 0/16	M	Judith Basin County	MT	John Rosey Roseland	1989	379
14 10/16	8 11/16	5 15/16	M	Clearwater County	ID	Bill Trescott	1989	379
14 10/16	8 7/16	6 3/16	M	Lander County	NV	Jack Dykstra	1990	379
14 10/16	8 11/16	5 15/16	M	Swan Lake	ALB	Dave Gerber	1990	379
14 10/16	8 10/16	6 0/16	M	Arrow Lake	BC	Jim Ryan	1990	379
14 10/16	8 10/16	6 0/16	M	Missoula County	MT	Monty Moravec	1990	379
14 10/16	8 12/16	5 14/16	M	Carbon County	UT	Paul Martinez	1991	379
14 10/16	8 12/16	5 14/16	M	Kane County	UT	Glen C. Ames	1991	379
14 10/16	8 9/16	6 1/16	M	Morgan County	UT	Brian Dam	1992	379
14 10/16	8 7/16	6 3/16	M	Lincoln County	MT	Tony Snow	1992	379
14 10/16	8 8/16	6 2/16	M	Missoula County	MT	Max G. Bauer, Jr.	1992	379
14 10/16	8 8/16	6 2/16	M	Gila County	AZ	John Novak	1993	379
14 10/16	8 8/16	6 2/16	M	La Plata County	CO	Edward A. Petersen	1993	379
14 10/16	8 11/16	5 15/16	M	Lewis & Clark County	MT	Carl A. Templeton	1993	379
14 10/16	8 10/16	6 0/16	M	Phillips County	MT	Alan Fedorenko	1993	379
14 10/16	8 10/16	6 0/16	M	Powder River County	MT	Jim Wilkins	1994	379
14 10/16	8 8/16	6 2/16	M	Clear Creek County	CO	Connie Renfro	1994	379
14 10/16	8 12/16	5 14/16	M	Sanpete County	UT	Bobby Olsen	1994	379
14 10/16	8 11/16	5 15/16	M	Pueblo County	CO	Tommy Chambliss	1994	379
14 10/16	8 11/16	5 15/16	M	Elmore County	ID	Robert E. Speegle, MD	1994	379
14 10/16	8 13/16	5 13/16	M	Moffat County	CO	Dave Burke	1995	379
14 10/16	8 10/16	6 0/16	M	West Kettle	BC	James Harold Simonds, Jr.	1995	379
14 10/16	8 9/16	6 1/16	M	Boise County	ID	Norman Henderson	1995	379
14 10/16	8 10/16	6 0/16	M	Larimer County	CO	Thomas H. Harris	1995	379
14 10/16	8 10/16	6 0/16	M	Moyie	BC	Phil Renney	1995	379
14 10/16	8 9/16	6 1/16	M	Madison County	MT	Mark E. Steingruber	1996	379
14 10/16	8 11/16	5 15/16	M	Montrose County	CO	Lisa A. West	1996	379
14 10/16	8 9/16	6 1/16	M	Clearwater County	ID	Eugene Lewis	1996	379
14 10/16	8 7/16	6 3/16	M	Boise County	ID	Rick Tribby	1996	379
14 10/16	8 12/16	5 14/16	M	Sullivan Creek	ALB	David A. Little	1997	379
14 10/16	8 8/16	6 2/16	M	Clear Creek County	CO	David L. Skiff	1997	379
14 10/16	8 7/16	6 3/16	M	Las Animas County	CO	Pat Powell	1998	379
14 10/16	8 10/16	6 0/16	M	Harold Creek	ALB	Terry Hagman	1998	379
14 9/16	8 5/16	6 4/16	M	Gila County	AZ	Ben Pearson	1958	445
14 9/16	8 10/16	5 15/16	M	Idaho County	ID	Keith N. Johnson	1966	445
14 9/16	8 8/16	6 1/16	M	Grand County	UT	Henry 'Hank' Frey	1974	445
14 9/16	8 8/16	6 1/16	M	Lemhi County	ID	Richard E. Vail	1974	445
14 9/16	8 8/16	6 1/16	M	Sandoval County	NM	John W. Rose	1979	445
14 9/16	8 11/16	5 14/16	M	Garfield County	UT	Al Schweitzer	1979	445
14 9/16	8 8/16	6 1/16	M	San Miguel County	NM	Richard McClain	1980	445
14 9/16	8 9/16	6 0/16	M	Jefferson County	CO	Lee Veldhouse	1984	445
14 9/16	8 6/16	6 3/16	M	Idaho County	ID	LeRoy West	1984	445
14 9/16	8 7/16	6 2/16	M	Elmore County	ID	Susan D. Sherer	1984	445
14 9/16	8 10/16	5 15/16	M	Rio Blanco County	CO	Don Waechtler	1984	445
14 9/16	8 9/16	6 0/16	M	Cherryville	BC	Al Breitkreutz	1985	445
14 9/16	8 9/16	6 0/16	M	Douglas County	CO	Wayne Kraft	1986	445
14 9/16	8 9/16	6 0/16	F	Wheatland County	MT	Jim Bouchard	1986	445
14 9/16	8 10/16	5 15/16	M	Fremont County	CO	Bill Goodspeed	1986	445
14 9/16	8 10/16	5 15/16	M	Clearwater County	ID	Jeffrey S. Stevens	1986	445
14 9/16	8 9/16	6 0/16	M	Asotin County	WA	Bill Meyers, Jr.	1987	445
14 9/16	8 9/16	6 0/16	M	Grand County	UT	Wes Walton	1987	445
14 9/16	8 10/16	5 15/16	M	Barnes Lake	BC	Kenneth Arthur Brown	1988	445
14 9/16	8 11/16	5 14/16	M	Chaffee County	CO	David Douty	1988	445
14 9/16	8 8/16	6 1/16	M	Jefferson County	CO	Steve Fausel	1989	445
14 9/16	8 10/16	5 15/16	M	Kane County	UT	Jeff Buck	1989	445
14 9/16	8 9/16	6 0/16	M	Owyhee County	ID	Bernard Langhorne	1990	445
14 9/16	8 10/16	5 15/16	M	Sanpete County	UT	Larry Mathis	1990	445
14 9/16	8 9/16	6 0/16	M	Duchesne County	UT	Don Keady	1991	445
14 9/16	8 8/16	6 1/16	M	Madison County	MT	Fred Richter	1991	445
14 9/16	8 9/16	6 0/16	M	Sanders County	MT	William A. Kaminski	1991	445
14 9/16	8 10/16	5 15/16	M	Valley County	ID	Bob Dawson	1991	445
14 9/16	8 9/16	6 0/16	M	Catron County	NM	Dwight E. Moser	1992	445
14 9/16	8 10/16	5 15/16	M	Water Valley	ALB	Steve Ouwerkerk	1992	445
14 9/16	8 9/16	6 0/16	M	Lemhi County	ID	Marc Williams	1992	445
14 9/16	8 11/16	5 14/16	M	Duchesne County	UT	Bruce J. Smith	1993	445
14 9/16	8 8/16	6 1/16	M	Clay Creek	BC	Glenn Dreger	1993	445
14 9/16	8 10/16	5 15/16	M	Hood River County	OR	Timothy R. McGuffin	1993	445

COUGAR (MOUNTAIN LION)

Minimum Score 13 8/16 — Continued

SCORE	GREATEST LENGTH	GREATEST WIDTH	SEX	AREA	STATE/PROVINCE	HUNTER'S NAME	DATE	RANK
14 9/16	8 9/16	6 0/16	M	Grand County	CO	Barry J. Smith	1993	445
14 9/16	8 11/16	5 14/16	M	Kootenai County	ID	Michael Christoforo	1993	445
14 9/16	8 12/16	5 13/16	M	Larimer County	CO	Jay Ervin	1994	445
14 9/16	8 11/16	5 14/16	M	Granite County	MT	Douglas P. Stein	1994	445
14 9/16	8 10/16	5 15/16	M	Uintah County	UT	Steven E. Sheehy	1995	445
14 9/16	8 9/16	6 0/16	M	Montezuma County	CO	Robert Hermann	1995	445
14 9/16	8 10/16	5 15/16	M	Uintah County	UT	Scott Kunz	1995	445
14 9/16	8 9/16	6 0/16	M	Chaffen Creek	ALB	James Pike	1995	445
14 9/16	8 9/16	6 0/16	M	Ravalli County	MT	Larry Dominquez	1995	445
14 9/16	8 11/16	5 14/16	M	Adams County	ID	Blake Owen Fischer	1995	445
14 9/16	8 10/16	5 15/16	M	Laird Lake	BC	Ryan J. Dorak	1996	445
14 9/16	8 11/16	5 14/16	M	Madison County	MT	Todd Hanson	1996	445
14 9/16	8 11/16	5 14/16	M	Lemhi County	ID	Michael Judas	1996	445
14 9/16	8 12/16	5 13/16	M	Custer County	ID	Steve Farrell	1996	445
14 9/16	8 11/16	5 14/16	M	Lemhi County	ID	John R. Koschmeder	1997	445
14 9/16	8 9/16	6 0/16	M	Fremont County	WY	Jeff Strangfeld	1997	445
14 9/16	8 10/16	5 15/16	M	Sevier County	UT	Daniel J. Kelly	1997	445
14 9/16	8 10/16	5 15/16	M	Delta County	CO	Scott Hargrove	1998	445
14 8/16	8 9/16	5 15/16	F	Latah County	ID	Charles Kelso	1965	497
14 8/16	8 8/16	6 0/16	M	Ventura County	CA	Betty Gulman	1967	497
14 8/16	8 10/16	5 14/16	M	Catron County	NM	Ed Schaub	1970	497
14 8/16	8 8/16	6 0/16	M	Weber County	UT	Norm Goodwin	1971	497
14 8/16	8 9/16	5 15/16	M	Lemhi County	ID	Dr. Henry C. McDonald	1971	497
14 8/16	8 9/16	5 15/16	M	Emery County	UT	Terry Molneux	1972	497
14 8/16	8 9/16	5 15/16	M	Kane County	UT	Charles F. Maloney, Jr.	1973	497
14 8/16	8 6/16	6 2/16	M	Lincoln County	MT	Jerry Brown	1975	497
14 8/16	8 6/16	6 2/16	M	Duchesne County	UT	Roland Mantzke	1976	497
14 8/16	8 10/16	5 14/16	M	Elmore County	ID	Ronald L. Sherer	1979	497
14 8/16	8 9/16	5 15/16	M	Boise County	ID	Richard C. Nichols	1981	497
14 8/16	8 12/16	5 12/16	M	Saguache County	CO	J. Keith Chastain	1982	497
14 8/16	8 7/16	6 1/16	M	Utah County	UT	Dell J. Christensen	1982	497
14 8/16	8 8/16	6 0/16	M	Eagle County	CO	Stephen W. Nottingham	1982	497
14 8/16	8 8/16	6 0/16	M	Sheep River	ALB	Bob Toothill	1984	497
14 8/16	8 10/16	5 14/16	M	Grand County	UT	Harold Lee Schuerman	1984	497
14 8/16	8 10/16	5 14/16	M	Washoe County	NV	Jerry Pennington	1984	497
14 8/16	8 8/16	6 0/16	M	Garfield County	CO	Douglas Starks	1984	497
14 8/16	8 10/16	5 14/16	M	Union County	OR	Ken Richter	1984	497
14 8/16	8 9/16	5 15/16	M	Archuleta County	CO	Howard Payne	1985	497
14 8/16	8 7/16	6 1/16	M	Idaho County	ID	William A.S. Hever, Sr.	1985	497
14 8/16	8 9/16	5 15/16	M	Fremont County	CO	Oney Cole	1985	497
14 8/16	8 9/16	5 15/16	M	Iron County	UT	Patrick Barwick	1985	497
14 8/16	8 7/16	6 1/16	M	Elmore County	ID	Chris Koldeway	1985	497
14 8/16	8 10/16	5 14/16	M	Larimer County	CO	David Skiff	1987	497
14 8/16	8 9/16	5 15/16	M	Sweet Grass County	MT	Dwight Wagner	1987	497
14 8/16	8 7/16	6 1/16	M	Flathead County	MT	Chris Switzer	1987	497
14 8/16	8 8/16	6 0/16	M	Lane County	OR	Larry D. Jones	1987	497
14 8/16	8 5/16	6 3/16	M	Caribou County	ID	Eric De Clark	1987	497
14 8/16	8 8/16	6 0/16	M	Chaffee County	CO	Scott Pelino	1987	497
14 8/16	8 8/16	6 0/16	M	Saguache County	CO	William Larry Wray	1987	497
14 8/16	8 9/16	5 15/16	M	Garfield County	CO	Roy M. Goodwin	1988	497
14 8/16	8 12/16	5 12/16	M	Webb County	TX	Daniel Juarez, Jr.	1988	497
14 8/16	8 7/16	6 1/16	M	Sheridan County	WY	Bill Roberts	1988	497
14 8/16	8 9/16	5 15/16	M	Elko County	NV	Donald Thompson	1988	497
14 8/16	8 9/16	5 15/16	M	Missoula County	MT	Bob Lussier	1988	497
14 8/16	8 10/16	5 14/16	M	Custer County	ID	Chip Palmer	1989	497
14 8/16	8 8/16	6 0/16	M	Boise County	ID	Curtis Wiker	1989	497
14 8/16	8 8/16	6 0/16	M	Larimer County	CO	John D. Lindell	1989	497
14 8/16	8 9/16	5 15/16	M	Montrose County	CO	Jimmy C. Garner	1990	497
14 8/16	8 6/16	6 2/16	M	Linn County	OR	Wayne Mathews	1990	497
14 8/16	8 11/16	5 13/16	M	Judith Basin County	MT	Kelly Norskog	1990	497
14 8/16	8 10/16	5 14/16	M	Montezuma County	CO	Mark D. Thomson	1991	497
14 8/16	8 9/16	5 15/16	M	Sevier County	UT	MayBen Crane	1991	497
14 8/16	8 9/16	5 15/16	M	San Miguel County	CO	DeWayne Mullins	1992	497
14 8/16	8 10/16	5 14/16	M	Garfield County	CO	Carroll Thomas Roach	1992	497
14 8/16	8 8/16	6 0/16	M	Eagle County	CO	Ron Janicki	1992	497
14 8/16	8 6/16	6 2/16	M	Idaho County	ID	Rick A. Albers	1992	497
14 8/16	8 7/16	6 1/16	M	Nakusp	BC	Dave Richardson	1992	497
14 8/16	8 9/16	5 15/16	M	Gallatin County	MT	Kevin Conners	1992	497
14 8/16	8 10/16	5 14/16	M	Terrell County	TX	E. Josh Isbell	1992	497
14 8/16	8 12/16	5 12/16	M	San Miguel County	CO	Steve Mazur	1993	497
14 8/16	8 11/16	5 13/16	M	Chaffee County	CO	Terry J. Krause	1993	497
14 8/16	8 8/16	6 0/16	M	Valley County	ID	Rick Addison	1994	497
14 8/16	8 6/16	6 2/16	M	Lemhi County	ID	Bob Johnson	1994	497
14 8/16	8 8/16	6 0/16	M	Ravalli County	MT	Scott L. Henriques	1994	497
14 8/16	8 8/16	6 0/16	M	Los Alamos County	NM	Kevin Reid	1995	497
14 8/16	8 6/16	6 2/16	M	Coconino County	AZ	Casey Robinson	1995	497
14 8/16	8 9/16	5 15/16	M	Albany County	WY	Tom Pindell	1995	497
14 8/16	8 9/16	5 15/16	M	Mesa County	CO	Mark Richards	1995	497

COUGAR (MOUNTAIN LION)

Minimum Score 13 8/16 — Continued

SCORE	GREATEST LENGTH	GREATEST WIDTH	SEX	AREA	STATE/PROVINCE	HUNTER'S NAME	DATE	RANK
14 8/16	8 10/16	5 14/16	M	Jefferson County	WA	Larry Keith Stauffer	1996	497
14 8/16	8 9/16	5 15/16	M	Moffat County	CO	Russell S. Overton	1996	497
14 8/16	8 8/16	6 0/16	M	Lemhi County	ID	William C. Shuster	1996	497
14 8/16	8 8/16	6 0/16	M	Sanders County	MT	Robert J. Kain	1996	497
14 8/16	8 8/16	6 0/16	M	Rio Blanco County	CO	Paul Chackan	1997	497
14 8/16	8 9/16	5 15/16	M	Owyhee County	ID	Bob Amaral	1997	497
14 8/16	8 11/16	5 13/16	M	Garfield County	UT	Randy Forsythe	1997	497
14 8/16	8 10/16	5 14/16	M	Boise County	ID	Jim Wilson	1998	497
14 8/16	8 8/16	6 0/16	M	Lincoln County	NV	Dale Cooley	1998	497
14 7/16	8 9/16	5 14/16	M	Elmore County	ID	William R. Vanderhoef	1966	566
14 7/16	8 11/16	5 12/16	M	Range Creek	UT	Gordy J. Longville	1967	566
14 7/16	8 6/16	6 1/16	M	White Pine County	NV	Barry L. May	1975	566
14 7/16	8 8/16	5 15/16	M	Lemhi County	ID	Wally Rueger	1975	566
14 7/16	8 9/16	5 14/16	M	Carbon County	UT	Rick Hunckler	1977	566
14 7/16	8 9/16	5 14/16	M	Duffy Lake	BC	Wilfred Klingsat	1977	566
14 7/16	8 9/16	5 14/16	M	Ravalli County	MT	Kim Engelbert	1978	566
14 7/16	8 6/16	6 1/16	M	Custer County	ID	Jim L. McCrory	1978	566
14 7/16	8 7/16	6 0/16	M	San Miguel County	CO	Bob Mays, Sr.	1979	566
14 7/16	8 6/16	6 1/16	M	Sevier County	UT	Lee Jernigan	1980	566
14 7/16	8 10/16	5 13/16	M	Lemhi County	ID	Daniel M. Alegre	1983	566
14 7/16	8 9/16	5 14/16	M	Sanders County	MT	Jerry V. Finley	1983	566
14 7/16	8 8/16	5 15/16	M	Franklin County	ID	Clair J. Buxton	1983	566
14 7/16	8 9/16	5 14/16	M	Judith Basin County	MT	Kay Davidson	1984	566
14 7/16	8 9/16	5 14/16	M	Duchesne County	UT	Jerry Ippolito	1984	566
14 7/16	8 8/16	5 15/16	M	Lemhi County	ID	Dennis N. Minnich	1984	566
14 7/16	8 6/16	6 1/16	M	Dolores County	CO	Ms. Charlie White	1984	566
14 7/16	8 8/16	5 15/16	M	Lander County	NV	David P. Lindman	1985	566
14 7/16	8 9/16	5 14/16	M	Catron County	NM	Stan Rauch	1986	566
14 7/16	8 8/16	5 15/16	M	Mesa County	CO	Sandy Vancourt	1987	566
14 7/16	8 7/16	6 0/16	M	Emery County	UT	Clark James Stokes	1987	566
14 7/16	8 8/16	5 15/16	M	Meagher County	MT	Sandra L. Gratz	1987	566
14 7/16	8 8/16	5 15/16	M	Skagit County	WA	Jerry Solie	1987	566
14 7/16	8 9/16	5 14/16	M	Sanpete County	UT	Don M. Markus	1988	566
14 7/16	8 6/16	6 1/16	M	Garfield County	CO	Doug Starks	1988	566
14 7/16	8 9/16	5 14/16	M	San Miguel County	CO	Robert Bain	1989	566
14 7/16	8 6/16	6 1/16	M	Cascade County	MT	Gene Henck	1989	566
14 7/16	8 12/16	5 11/16	M	Carbon County	UT	Stanley W. Biltz	1989	566
14 7/16	8 7/16	6 0/16	M	Lemhi County	ID	John Henry Smith	1989	566
14 7/16	8 4/16	6 3/16	M	Madison County	MT	Stephen P. (Pat) Connell	1990	566
14 7/16	8 9/16	5 14/16	M	Wasatch County	UT	E. Duane Park	1990	566
14 7/16	8 9/16	5 14/16	M	Rio Arriba County	NM	Jim Marquis	1990	566
14 7/16	8 6/16	6 1/16	M	Wallowa County	OR	William K. McCadden	1990	566
14 7/16	8 8/16	5 15/16	M	Fremont County	CO	Steve Sylvia	1991	566
14 7/16	8 9/16	5 14/16	M	Rio Arriba County	NM	Vito Benedetto	1991	566
14 7/16	8 7/16	6 0/16	M	Millard County	UT	Phillip R. Brown	1992	566
14 7/16	8 6/16	6 1/16	M	Idaho County	ID	Fred H. Simonton III	1992	566
14 7/16	8 9/16	5 14/16	M	Rio Blanco County	CO	Tim Cuthriell	1992	566
14 7/16	8 8/16	5 15/16	M	Valley County	ID	Jeffrey Winters	1992	566
14 7/16	8 8/16	5 15/16	M	Churchill County	NV	Dan Klebenow	1992	566
14 7/16	8 11/16	5 12/16	M	Sanpete County	UT	J. Seth Kunz	1992	566
14 7/16	8 6/16	6 1/16	M	Rio Grande County	CO	John Olson	1992	566
14 7/16	8 9/16	5 14/16	M	Gilpin County	CO	Steve Barnhill	1992	566
14 7/16	8 9/16	5 14/16	M	Granite County	MT	William J. Siebeneck	1992	566
14 7/16	8 9/16	5 14/16	M	Utah County	UT	Britton Ercanbrack	1993	566
14 7/16	8 9/16	5 14/16	M	Duchesne County	UT	Jason Williams	1993	566
14 7/16	8 9/16	5 14/16	M	White Pine County	NV	Wayne Long	1993	566
14 7/16	8 10/16	5 13/16	M	Montezuma County	CO	Doug Aiken	1993	566
14 7/16	8 10/16	5 13/16	M	Park County	CO	Ron Adamson	1993	566
14 7/16	8 9/16	5 14/16	M	Douglas County	CO	Duffy Daugherty	1993	566
14 7/16	8 6/16	6 1/16	M	Montezuma County	CO	David R. Hall	1993	566
14 7/16	8 10/16	5 13/16	M	Elmore County	ID	Richard Nemitz	1993	566
14 7/16	8 8/16	5 15/16	M	Valley County	ID	Randy A. Reeves	1994	566
14 7/16	8 10/16	5 13/16	M	Lemhi County	ID	Jason F. Lambley	1994	566
14 7/16	8 6/16	6 1/16	M	Rosebud County	MT	Jae Notti	1994	566
14 7/16	8 10/16	5 13/16	M	Duchesne County	UT	Tim R. Dawson	1994	566
14 7/16	8 8/16	5 15/16	M	Nye County	NV	Wayne Piersol	1994	566
14 7/16	8 8/16	5 15/16	M	San Juan County	UT	Brad D. Bunker	1994	566
14 7/16	8 8/16	5 15/16	M	Boise County	ID	Angus M. Brown	1994	566
14 7/16	8 7/16	6 0/16	M	Porcupine Hills	ALB	Nick Frederick	1995	566
14 7/16	8 10/16	5 13/16	M	Deer Lodge County	MT	John M. Rokisky	1995	566
14 7/16	8 7/16	6 0/16	M	Grand County	CO	Paul M. Martin	1995	566
14 7/16	8 7/16	6 0/16	M	Powell County	MT	Cody Pallister	1996	566
14 7/16	8 7/16	6 0/16	M	Rio Blanco County	CO	Bob Black	1996	566
14 7/16	8 7/16	6 0/16	M	Box Elder County	UT	Craig P. Mitton	1996	566
14 7/16	8 9/16	5 14/16	M	Morgan County	UT	Tim J. Misewicz	1996	566
14 7/16	8 9/16	5 14/16	M	Ravalli County	MT	Jack E. Williams	1996	566
14 7/16	8 9/16	5 14/16	M	Mohave County	AZ	John Garr	1996	566
14 7/16	8 8/16	5 15/16	M	Boise County	ID	Daniel J. Smith	1996	566

COUGAR (MOUNTAIN LION)

Minimum Score 13 8/16 — Continued

SCORE	GREATEST LENGTH	GREATEST WIDTH	SEX	AREA	STATE/PROVINCE	HUNTER'S NAME	DATE	RANK
14 7/16	8 9/16	5 14/16	M	Graham County	AZ	Joseph Barraza	1997	566
14 7/16	8 10/16	5 13/16	M	Millard County	UT	Kurt Wood	1997	566
14 7/16	8 9/16	5 14/16	M	Cochise County	AZ	Jame L. Todd	1998	566
14 6/16	8 7/16	5 15/16	M	Sequoia National Forest	CA	Douglas Walker	1960	638
14 6/16	8 7/16	5 15/16	M	Elmore County	ID	C. Randall Byers	1966	638
14 6/16	8 8/16	5 14/16	M	Missoula County	MT	John Hershey	1969	638
14 6/16	8 7/16	5 15/16	M	Lemhi County	ID	Ray Torrey	1971	638
14 6/16	8 6/16	6 0/16	M	Falkland	BC	W. Klingsat	1974	638
14 6/16	8 7/16	5 15/16	M	Colfax County	NM	Richard A. Meyer	1974	638
14 6/16	8 8/16	5 14/16	M	Huerfano County	CO	Douglas E. Miller	1974	638
14 6/16	8 7/16	5 15/16	M	Clearwater County	ID	Oscar Levingston	1975	638
14 6/16	8 7/16	5 15/16	M	Carbon County	UT	Thomas W. Pinkston	1977	638
14 6/16	8 8/16	5 14/16	M	Uintah County	UT	Donald Redfox	1978	638
14 6/16	8 5/16	6 1/16	M	Fremont County	CO	Russell Hull	1979	638
14 6/16	8 9/16	5 13/16	M	Dry Wash Creek	UT	Mark J. Checki	1981	638
14 6/16	8 6/16	6 0/16	M	Chaffee County	CO	Judy Clyncke	1981	638
14 6/16	8 8/16	5 14/16	M	Ravalli County	MT	Dean Irwin	1982	638
14 6/16	8 6/16	6 0/16	M	Colfax County	NM	Joseph Wambach	1982	638
14 6/16	8 8/16	5 14/16	M	San Juan County	NM	Mike Ray	1983	638
14 6/16	8 8/16	5 14/16	M	Wasatch County	UT	Kendall Julander	1983	638
14 6/16	8 7/16	5 15/16	M	Clearwater County	ID	Tim Newbold	1983	638
14 6/16	8 9/16	5 13/16	M	Walla Walla County	WA	Winford Bradford	1983	638
14 6/16	8 3/16	6 3/16	M	Caribou County	ID	Rhett Bradford	1984	638
14 6/16	8 6/16	6 0/16	M	Lemhi County	ID	Donald L. Minnich	1984	638
14 6/16	8 8/16	5 14/16	M	Lemhi County	ID	Phil R. Ginochio	1985	638
14 6/16	8 5/16	6 1/16	M	Boise County	ID	David W. Peltier	1985	638
14 6/16	8 8/16	5 14/16	M	Cochise County	AZ	John Holcomb	1985	638
14 6/16	8 6/16	6 0/16	M	Flathead County	MT	Earl W. Weaver	1986	638
14 6/16	8 8/16	5 14/16	M	Missoula County	MT	Vinnie Pisani	1987	638
14 6/16	8 8/16	5 14/16	M	Summit County	UT	Jeffrey W. Potter	1988	638
14 6/16	8 10/16	5 12/16	M	Fremont County	CO	Daniel Daly	1988	638
14 6/16	8 7/16	5 15/16	M	Sanders County	MT	Harold R. Anderson	1988	638
14 6/16	8 6/16	6 0/16	M	Lincoln County	MT	Rich Hjort	1989	638
14 6/16	8 11/16	5 11/16	M	Josephine County	OR	Brian Day	1990	638
14 6/16	8 9/16	5 13/16	M	Garfield County	CO	Johnnie R. Walters	1991	638
14 6/16	8 6/16	6 0/16	M	Oldman River	ALB	Tom Foss	1991	638
14 6/16	8 10/16	5 12/16	M	Beaver County	UT	Robert Barrie	1991	638
14 6/16	8 7/16	5 15/16	M	Elmore County	ID	Wm. "Bill" MacCarty III	1991	638
14 6/16	8 6/16	6 0/16	M	Mesa County	CO	James Bornman	1992	638
14 6/16	8 8/16	5 14/16	M	Flathead County	MT	M. R. James	1992	638
14 6/16	8 6/16	6 0/16	M	Greenlee County	AZ	Tom Taylor	1993	638
14 6/16	8 10/16	5 12/16	M	Carbon County	UT	Dina Wise	1993	638
14 6/16	8 7/16	5 15/16	M	Chaffee County	CO	Al Miller	1993	638
14 6/16	8 8/16	5 14/16	M	Rio Arriba County	NM	Marvin M. Maestas	1994	638
14 6/16	8 8/16	5 14/16	M	Montrose County	CO	Ron Baldwin	1994	638
14 6/16	8 6/16	6 0/16	M	Nakusp	BC	Gary J. Burns	1994	638
14 6/16	8 7/16	5 15/16	M	Silver Bow County	MT	Mike Perala	1994	638
14 6/16	8 8/16	5 14/16	M	Duchesne County	UT	Thomas Ostrander	1994	638
14 6/16	8 8/16	5 14/16	M	Sanpete County	UT	Burke Lyon	1995	638
14 6/16	8 8/16	5 14/16	M	Porcupine Hills	ALB	Warren Witherspoon	1995	638
14 6/16	8 9/16	5 13/16	F	Ferry County	WA	Joe Arcieri	1995	638
14 6/16	8 9/16	5 13/16	M	Fergus County	MT	Donny Roy	1996	638
14 6/16	8 7/16	5 15/16	M	Steamboat Mtn.	BC	Kent G. Kebe	1996	638
14 6/16	8 7/16	5 15/16	M	Nakusp	BC	John Mastroianni	1996	638
14 6/16	8 9/16	5 13/16	M	Madison County	MT	Scott Dell	1996	638
14 6/16	8 9/16	5 13/16	M	Boise County	ID	Todd Felt	1996	638
14 6/16	8 11/16	5 11/16	M	San Juan County	UT	Melinda K. Schmidt	1997	638
14 6/16	8 6/16	6 0/16	M	Rio Blanco County	CO	Roger Becker	1997	638
14 6/16	8 9/16	5 13/16	M	Clearwater County	ID	Eugene Lewis	1997	638
14 6/16	8 11/16	5 11/16	M	Garfield County	CO	Terry J. Gerber	1998	638
14 5/16	8 6/16	5 15/16	M	Esmeralda County	NV	Don Schram	1965	695
14 5/16	8 9/16	5 12/16	M	Tatla Lake	BC	William L. Nickerson	1966	695
14 5/16	8 8/16	5 13/16	M	Garfield County	UT	H. R. 'Dutch' Wambold	1966	695
14 5/16	8 8/16	5 13/16	M	Garfield County	UT	Robert K. Paulson	1968	695
14 5/16	8 10/16	5 11/16	M	Carbon County	UT	M. R. James	1970	695
14 5/16	8 8/16	5 13/16	M	Chaffee County	CO	Michael Ballard	1975	695
14 5/16	8 7/16	5 14/16	M	White Pine County	NV	James L. Beard	1975	695
14 5/16	8 8/16	5 13/16	M	Beaver County	UT	Bruce Post	1975	695
14 5/16	8 7/16	5 14/16	M	Las Animas County	CO	Barry L. Powell	1975	695
14 5/16	8 8/16	5 13/16	M	Daggett County	UT	Bob Butler	1976	695
14 5/16	8 9/16	5 12/16	M	Elmore County	ID	L. Dean Goodner	1978	695
14 5/16	8 10/16	5 11/16	M	Grand County	UT	Terry L. Benzine	1978	695
14 5/16	8 9/16	5 12/16	M	Fire Mtn.	BC	John 'Jack' Cordes	1978	695
14 5/16	8 7/16	5 14/16	M	Custer County	CO	William Henderson	1979	695
14 5/16	8 7/16	5 14/16	M	Judith Basin County	MT	Don Davidson	1981	695
14 5/16	8 7/16	5 14/16	M	Montezuma County	CO	Marvin Reichenau	1981	695
14 5/16	8 10/16	5 11/16	M	Dolores County	CO	Mike Gleason	1982	695
14 5/16	8 6/16	5 15/16	M	Lemhi County	ID	Stephen N. Bean	1983	695

COUGAR (MOUNTAIN LION)

Minimum Score 13 8/16   Continued

SCORE	GREATEST LENGTH	GREATEST WIDTH	SEX	AREA	STATE/PROVINCE	HUNTER'S NAME	DATE	RANK
14 5/16	8 8/16	5 13/16	M	Custer County	ID	Robert L. Hudman	1984	695
14 5/16	8 5/16	6 0/16	M	Jefferson County	CO	Jeff Fulkner	1984	695
14 5/16	8 8/16	5 13/16	M	Rio Blanco County	CO	Michael Ingold	1984	695
14 5/16	8 7/16	5 14/16	M	Sanders County	MT	Alan Gaston	1984	695
14 5/16	8 8/16	5 13/16	M	Sanpete County	UT	Judy Hallman	1985	695
14 5/16	8 5/16	6 0/16	M	Colfax County	NM	Jim Stauft	1985	695
14 5/16	8 7/16	5 14/16	M	Idaho County	ID	Jay D. Stringer	1985	695
14 5/16	8 8/16	5 13/16	M	Judith Basin County	MT	Joseph R. "Bob" Fabian	1986	695
14 5/16	8 9/16	5 12/16	M	Dona Ana County	NM	Larry M. Sellers	1986	695
14 5/16	8 9/16	5 12/16	M	Kane County	UT	Allan Dangerfield	1986	695
14 5/16	8 5/16	6 0/16	M	Sanders County	MT	Byron E. Wates, Jr.	1986	695
14 5/16	8 10/16	5 11/16	M	Pend Oreille County	WA	Leonard F. Rock	1986	695
14 5/16	8 8/16	5 13/16	M	Daggett County	UT	Jeff Schneider	1987	695
14 5/16	8 9/16	5 12/16	M	Grand County	UT	James S. Saunoris	1987	695
14 5/16	8 7/16	5 14/16	M	Elmore County	ID	Alfred John Gemrich	1988	695
14 5/16	8 5/16	6 0/16	M	Idaho County	ID	Daniel R. Hooper	1988	695
14 5/16	8 6/16	5 15/16	M	Lane County	OR	John Stone	1988	695
14 5/16	8 6/16	5 15/16	M	Madison County	MT	Scott T. Smolen	1988	695
14 5/16	8 8/16	5 13/16	M	Mesa County	CO	Richard Gerhart	1988	695
14 5/16	8 7/16	5 14/16	M	Idaho County	ID	Doug Hawkins	1989	695
14 5/16	8 8/16	5 13/16	M	Sanders County	MT	Charles R. Gallo	1990	695
14 5/16	8 8/16	5 13/16	M	Broadwater County	MT	Mike Parsons	1990	695
14 5/16	8 7/16	5 14/16	M	West Kettle River	BC	Lyndon Walker	1990	695
14 5/16	8 5/16	6 0/16	M	San Miguel County	CO	Roger Degroat	1991	695
14 5/16	8 6/16	5 15/16	M	Fisher Creek	ALB	Robin Arthurs	1991	695
14 5/16	8 7/16	5 14/16	M	Montezuma County	CO	Jerry Rush	1991	695
14 5/16	8 7/16	5 14/16	M	Garfield County	CO	Marvin Weible	1991	695
14 5/16	8 7/16	5 14/16	M	Garfield County	CO	Terry C. Parkinson	1992	695
14 5/16	8 5/16	6 0/16	M	Lake County	MT	Dave R. Daubenberger	1992	695
14 5/16	8 5/16	6 0/16	M	Edgewood	BC	Gerald V. Shields	1993	695
14 5/16	8 4/16	6 1/16	M	Sublette County	WY	Ron Couture	1993	695
14 5/16	8 8/16	5 13/16	M	Porcupine Hills	ALB	Ryk Visscher	1993	695
14 5/16	8 9/16	5 12/16	M	Duchesne County	UT	James L. Kelly III	1994	695
14 5/16	8 9/16	5 12/16	M	Grand County	CO	Dave Parri	1994	695
14 5/16	8 9/16	5 12/16	M	Custer County	ID	Scott Brower	1994	695
14 5/16	8 10/16	5 11/16	M	Sevier County	UT	Casey J. Cardwell	1994	695
14 5/16	8 10/16	5 11/16	M	Elko County	NV	Vincent D'Ascoli	1995	695
14 5/16	8 7/16	5 14/16	M	Lemhi County	ID	Mark A. Mathews	1995	695
14 5/16	8 7/16	5 14/16	M	Stevens County	WA	Avery L. Hansen	1995	695
14 5/16	8 6/16	5 15/16	M	Powell County	MT	Gene Meyer	1995	695
14 5/16	8 5/16	6 0/16	M	Madison County	MT	Ivan J. Muzljakovich	1995	695
14 5/16	8 8/16	5 13/16	M	Idaho County	ID	Matt March	1996	695
14 5/16	8 5/16	6 0/16	M	Larimer County	CO	Emilio Bonetti	1996	695
14 5/16	8 11/16	5 10/16	M	Elko County	NV	Wayne E. Testolin	1996	695
14 5/16	8 9/16	5 12/16	M	Moffat County	CO	Daniel L. Wells	1997	695
14 5/16	8 6/16	5 15/16	M	Cascade County	MT	Jim Winjum	1997	695
14 5/16	8 6/16	5 15/16	M	Albany County	WY	Jerry Bowen	1997	695
14 5/16	8 7/16	5 14/16	M	Idaho County	ID	Larry E. Sholly, Jr.	1997	695
14 5/16	8 5/16	6 0/16	M	Ravalli County	MT	Mike Coutu	1997	695
14 5/16	8 7/16	5 14/16	M	Fergus County	MT	D. Mitch Kottas	1997	695
14 5/16	8 6/16	5 15/16	M	Fergus County	MT	Kenneth Roy	1998	695
14 5/16	8 9/16	5 12/16	M	Wasatch County	UT	Larry Knight	1998	695
14 4/16	8 8/16	5 12/16	M	Stoneman Lake	AZ	Dr. C. L. Clare	1962	765
14 4/16	8 8/16	5 12/16	M	Lincoln County	MT	Dale McNutt	1964	765
14 4/16	8 10/16	5 10/16	M	Elmore County	ID	Don Bennett	1968	765
14 4/16	8 4/16	6 0/16	M	Missoula County	MT	Tony Dumay	1968	765
14 4/16	8 6/16	5 14/16	M	Elmore County	ID	John E. Anderson	1972	765
14 4/16	8 6/16	5 14/16	M	Lemhi County	ID	Kenneth Anselmi	1972	765
14 4/16	8 6/16	5 14/16	M	Nye County	NV	Ken Viles	1972	765
14 4/16	8 4/16	6 0/16	M	Salmon River	ID	Bob Tucker	1974	765
14 4/16	8 6/16	5 14/16	M	Lemhi County	ID	H. R. 'Rusty' Neely	1975	765
14 4/16	8 4/16	6 0/16	M	Mesa County	CO	Robert Tobias	1975	765
14 4/16	8 6/16	5 14/16	M	Custer County	ID	Gerald Conway	1978	765
14 4/16	8 8/16	5 12/16	M	McMullen County	TX	James E. Jordan	1978	765
14 4/16	8 4/16	6 0/16	M	Washington County	UT	Richard L. Mobilio	1979	765
14 4/16	8 8/16	5 12/16	M	Garfield County	UT	George Holfeltz	1980	765
14 4/16	8 3/16	6 1/16	M	Colfax County	NM	Stephen 'Don' Hornady	1980	765
14 4/16	8 4/16	6 0/16	M	Garfield County	CO	T. Michael Casey	1982	765
14 4/16	8 6/16	5 14/16	M	Salt Lake County	UT	William L. Randles	1982	765
14 4/16	8 8/16	5 12/16	M	Lincoln County	NV	David A. Widby	1982	765
14 4/16	8 6/16	5 14/16	M	Clearwater County	ID	Ralph Ertz	1983	765
14 4/16	8 5/16	5 15/16	M	Elmore County	ID	Brad L. Johnson	1983	765
14 4/16	8 6/16	5 14/16	M	Lemhi County	ID	Bob Hudson	1984	765
14 4/16	8 6/16	5 14/16	M	Spokane County	WA	Kenneth R. Wengert	1984	765
14 4/16	8 7/16	5 13/16	M	Lander County	NV	Peter Esposito	1984	765
14 4/16	8 8/16	5 12/16	M	Sanpete County	UT	C. Danny Butler	1985	765
14 4/16	8 7/16	5 13/16	M	Lander County	NV	Leonard Ruimveld	1985	765
14 4/16	8 5/16	5 15/16	M	Montrose County	CO	Tony Hoza	1986	765

COUGAR (MOUNTAIN LION)

Minimum Score 13 8/16 — Continued

SCORE	GREATEST LENGTH	GREATEST WIDTH	SEX	AREA	STATE/PROVINCE	HUNTER'S NAME	DATE	RANK
14 4/16	8 6/16	5 14/16	M	Colfax County	NM	John L. Chapman	1986	765
14 4/16	8 8/16	5 12/16	M	Eureka County	NV	Marty Pawelek	1986	765
14 4/16	8 6/16	5 14/16	M	Jackson County	OR	Jon Updegraff	1986	765
14 4/16	8 6/16	5 14/16	M	Coconino County	AZ	Todd Rice	1986	765
14 4/16	8 4/16	6 0/16	M	Nakusp	BC	Len Surina	1987	765
14 4/16	8 5/16	5 15/16	M	Benewah County	ID	William N. Latshaw	1988	765
14 4/16	8 8/16	5 12/16	M	Colfax County	NM	Robert L. Pagel	1988	765
14 4/16	8 6/16	5 14/16	M	Ravalli County	MT	Erik "Rick" Aslesen	1988	765
14 4/16	8 8/16	5 12/16	M	White Pine County	NV	Archie Nesbitt	1988	765
14 4/16	8 8/16	5 12/16	M	Iron County	UT	Bernie E. Belfrage	1988	765
14 4/16	8 5/16	5 15/16	M	Douglas County	OR	Stanley Myers	1988	765
14 4/16	8 7/16	5 13/16	M	Yavapai County	AZ	Roy Ruiz	1989	765
14 4/16	8 7/16	5 13/16	M	Carbon County	UT	Mike Hillis	1990	765
14 4/16	8 8/16	5 12/16	M	Converse County	WY	James P. Smith	1990	765
14 4/16	8 8/16	5 12/16	M	Sweet Grass County	MT	Roger A. Greve, Jr.	1990	765
14 4/16	8 5/16	5 15/16	M	Coconino County	AZ	H. Gordon Purl	1990	765
14 4/16	8 6/16	5 14/16	M	Rio Blanco County	CO	Kenton Meyers	1990	765
14 4/16	8 7/16	5 13/16	M	Ouray County	CO	Randy Caspersen	1991	765
14 4/16	8 9/16	5 11/16	M	Fremont County	CO	Bill Hartman	1991	765
14 4/16	8 4/16	6 0/16	M	Wasatch County	UT	Karl Hirst	1991	765
14 4/16	8 8/16	5 12/16	M	Boise County	ID	Larry Hoff	1991	765
14 4/16	8 7/16	5 13/16	M	Boise County	ID	William James Tuffield II	1991	765
14 4/16	8 8/16	5 12/16	M	Clearwater County	ID	Patrick L. Hovey	1992	765
14 4/16	8 9/16	5 11/16	M	Mesa County	CO	Alan Parkerson	1992	765
14 4/16	8 4/16	6 0/16	M	Judith Basin County	MT	Don Davidson	1992	765
14 4/16	8 6/16	5 14/16	M	Lake County	MT	Ken Vorisek	1992	765
14 4/16	8 7/16	5 13/16	M	Carbon County	WY	Robert E. Bergquist	1992	765
14 4/16	8 8/16	5 12/16	M	Ram Creek	BC	Tom Marshall	1993	765
14 4/16	8 6/16	5 14/16	M	Utah County	UT	Dusty Mitchell	1993	765
14 4/16	8 10/16	5 10/16	M	Rio Arriba County	NM	Nelson G. Martinez, Jr.	1993	765
14 4/16	8 5/16	5 15/16	M	Coconino County	AZ	Blaine "Bub" Mathews	1993	765
14 4/16	8 8/16	5 12/16	M	Lemhi County	ID	John Shaffer, Jr.	1993	765
14 4/16	8 8/16	5 12/16	M	Washington County	UT	Pat Abalsamo	1994	765
14 4/16	8 8/16	5 12/16	M	Lincoln County	NV	Tom Carter	1994	765
14 4/16	8 8/16	5 12/16	M	Garfield County	CO	Robert L. Moon, Jr.	1994	765
14 4/16	8 9/16	5 11/16	M	Idaho County	ID	Kevin Schmid	1994	765
14 4/16	8 7/16	5 13/16	M	Valley County	ID	Lewis Zane Abbott	1994	765
14 4/16	8 6/16	5 14/16	M	Archuleta County	CO	Dewey J. Mast	1995	765
14 4/16	8 6/16	5 14/16	M	San Juan County	UT	Adam Bronson	1995	765
14 4/16	8 6/16	5 14/16	M	Mohave County	AZ	Ward Villamor	1995	765
14 4/16	8 7/16	5 13/16	M	Emery County	UT	Richard A. Smith	1996	765
14 4/16	8 9/16	5 11/16	M	Fremont County	CO	Dave Vomela	1996	765
14 4/16	8 5/16	5 15/16	M	Platte County	WY	Mike Boughton	1996	765
14 4/16	8 5/16	5 15/16	M	Fergus County	MT	Brad Johnson	1996	765
14 4/16	8 8/16	5 12/16	M	Okanagan Valley	BC	James Schomberg	1997	765
14 4/16	8 4/16	6 0/16	M	Gunnison County	CO	Joe D. Belas	1998	765
14 3/16	8 6/16	5 13/16	M	Nye County	NV	Dick Gulman	1968	837
14 3/16	8 7/16	5 12/16	M	Ferry County	WA	Tom Smith	1968	837
14 3/16	8 5/16	5 14/16	M	Grand County	UT	John B. Baughman	1969	837
14 3/16	8 6/16	5 13/16	M	Douglas County	NV	Bill Fuller	1972	837
14 3/16	8 7/16	5 12/16	M	Huerfano County	CO	Marvin C. Clyncke	1973	837
14 3/16	8 9/16	5 10/16	M	Juab County	UT	Samuel McCarty	1975	837
14 3/16	8 7/16	5 12/16	M	Stevens County	WA	Ronald A. Carpenter	1977	837
14 3/16	8 8/16	5 11/16	M	Chaffee County	CO	John C. Dekker	1977	837
14 3/16	8 8/16	5 11/16	M	Sevier County	UT	Claude Flippin	1980	837
14 3/16	8 7/16	5 12/16	M	Adams County	ID	Rube Powell	1982	837
14 3/16	8 4/16	5 15/16	M	Mesa County	CO	William G. Padilla	1982	837
14 3/16	8 6/16	5 13/16	M	Judith Basin County	MT	Stan Colton	1983	837
14 3/16	8 5/16	5 14/16	M	Madison County	MT	Tony Schaufler	1983	837
14 3/16	8 4/16	5 15/16	M	Flathead County	MT	Gary A. Crowe	1983	837
14 3/16	8 6/16	5 13/16	M	Sierra County	NM	Kendall Doyle	1985	837
14 3/16	8 4/16	5 15/16	M	Montezuma County	CO	Duain Morton	1985	837
14 3/16	8 5/16	5 14/16	F	Shuswap River	BC	Mark Siegmueller	1985	837
14 3/16	8 5/16	5 14/16	M	Sanders County	MT	Jim Clark	1985	837
14 3/16	8 4/16	5 15/16	M	Clearwater County	ID	Dexter Siler	1986	837
14 3/16	8 7/16	5 12/16	M	Idaho County	ID	Tony E. Hyde	1986	837
14 3/16	8 5/16	5 14/16	M	Lemhi County	ID	Ben L. Fahnolz	1987	837
14 3/16	8 6/16	5 13/16	M	Idaho County	ID	G. Sam Cloninger	1987	837
14 3/16	8 8/16	5 11/16	M	Elko County	NV	Charles Lee Pemble	1989	837
14 3/16	8 8/16	5 11/16	M	Tooele County	UT	Dale G. Kelson	1989	837
14 3/16	8 6/16	5 13/16	M	Fremont County	CO	R. E. Smith	1989	837
14 3/16	8 5/16	5 14/16	M	Lemhi County	ID	Richard Smith	1990	837
14 3/16	8 7/16	5 12/16	M	Ravalli County	MT	Jim Loughran	1990	837
14 3/16	8 14/16	5 5/16	M	Grand County	CO	Cary Laman	1991	837
14 3/16	8 5/16	5 14/16	M	Sheridan County	WY	Tom Hlinka	1992	837
14 3/16	8 4/16	5 15/16	M	Duchesne County	UT	M. Tim McIntyre	1994	837
14 3/16	8 5/16	5 14/16	M	Fergus County	MT	Dan Gill	1994	837
14 3/16	8 6/16	5 13/16	M	Lemhi County	ID	Dale F. Slama	1994	837

COUGAR (MOUNTAIN LION)

Minimum Score 13 8/16 — Continued

SCORE	GREATEST LENGTH	GREATEST WIDTH	SEX	AREA	STATE/ PROVINCE	HUNTER'S NAME	DATE	RANK
14 3/16	8 7/16	5 12/16	M	Duchesne County	UT	William C. Bolt, Jr.	1994	837
14 3/16	8 7/16	5 12/16	M	Dolores County	CO	David M. Richards	1995	837
14 3/16	8 5/16	5 14/16	M	Uintah County	UT	Dennis Lee Ingram	1995	837
14 3/16	8 5/16	5 14/16	M	Moffat County	CO	Kenny E. Leo	1996	837
14 3/16	8 8/16	5 11/16	M	Las Animas County	CO	Rick East	1997	837
14 3/16	8 7/16	5 12/16	M	Moffat County	CO	Donald H. Corey	1997	837
14 3/16	8 7/16	5 12/16	M	Washington County	UT	Rick Sarkisian	1997	837
14 3/16	8 8/16	5 11/16	M	Piute County	UT	Robert Staudt, Jr.	1998	837
14 3/16	8 4/16	5 15/16	M	Madison County	MT	Brian Koelzer	1998	837
14 3/16	8 6/16	5 13/16	M	Black Cat Hills	ALB	Brent Watson	1998	837
14 2/16	8 6/16	5 12/16	M	Okanogan County	WA	Dr. Russell Congdon	1950	879
14 2/16	8 6/16	5 12/16	M	Kane County	UT	William P. Mastrangel	1957	879
14 2/16	8 4/16	5 14/16	M	Fresno County	CA	John Faulconer	1964	879
14 2/16	8 6/16	5 12/16	M	Garfield County	CO	Phillip C. Durr	1970	879
14 2/16	8 4/16	5 14/16	M	Uintah County	UT	Larry Jones	1970	879
14 2/16	8 6/16	5 12/16	M	Rio Blanco County	CO	James L. Emerson	1976	879
14 2/16	8 4/16	5 14/16	M	Lane County	OR	Eugene W. Gramzow	1978	879
14 2/16	8 5/16	5 13/16	M	Saguache County	CO	John T. Rauch	1979	879
14 2/16	8 4/16	5 14/16	M	Ravalli County	MT	Dean Irwin	1980	879
14 2/16	8 3/16	5 15/16	M	Montrose County	CO	Hoyte Driggers	1981	879
14 2/16	8 4/16	5 14/16	M	Greenlee County	AZ	Fred L. Smith	1982	879
14 2/16	8 8/16	5 10/16	M	Duchesne County	UT	Bill Painter	1982	879
14 2/16	8 9/16	5 9/16	M	Duchesne County	UT	Michael Wieck	1983	879
14 2/16	8 6/16	5 12/16	M	Garfield County	UT	Carl D. Winton	1984	879
14 2/16	8 4/16	5 14/16	M	Sweet Grass County	MT	David W. Sorensen	1984	879
14 2/16	8 2/16	6 0/16	M	Catron County	NM	Dean Hamilton	1985	879
14 2/16	8 8/16	5 10/16	M	Ravalli County	MT	John L Wozniak	1985	879
14 2/16	8 3/16	5 15/16	M	Mesa County	CO	David A. Schroeder	1986	879
14 2/16	8 6/16	5 12/16	M	Sanpete County	UT	Joe Johnston	1986	879
14 2/16	8 5/16	5 13/16	M	Larimer County	CO	Jerry L. Novak	1987	879
14 2/16	8 6/16	5 12/16	M	Mesa County	CO	Norm Stahlman	1987	879
14 2/16	8 6/16	5 12/16	M	Grand County	UT	J. Dale Hale	1988	879
14 2/16	8 4/16	5 14/16	M	Lemhi County	ID	Kent Brandt	1988	879
14 2/16	8 7/16	5 11/16	M	Dolores County	CO	Ernest N. Schroch	1988	879
14 2/16	8 6/16	5 12/16	M	Garfield County	CO	James "Boomer" Hayden	1988	879
14 2/16	8 4/16	5 14/16	M	Cranbrook	BC	Paul Deme	1989	879
14 2/16	8 6/16	5 12/16	M	Mesa County	CO	Tom Nelson	1989	879
14 2/16	8 9/16	5 9/16	M	Nye County	NV	Jesse Andrew Westby	1989	879
14 2/16	8 4/16	5 14/16	M	Greenlee County	AZ	Brian Davis	1989	879
14 2/16	8 1/16	6 1/16	M	Box Elder County	UT	Ellis Wall	1990	879
14 2/16	8 6/16	5 12/16	M	Mesa County	CO	Don Marascalco	1990	879
14 2/16	8 7/16	5 11/16	M	Custer County	ID	Trent Haberstroh	1990	879
14 2/16	8 6/16	5 12/16	M	Park County	CO	Bryon Scott Johnson	1991	879
14 2/16	8 6/16	5 12/16	M	Arrow Lakes	BC	Glenn Dreger	1991	879
14 2/16	8 11/16	5 7/16	M	Wayne County	UT	Charles M. Moore	1991	879
14 2/16	8 7/16	5 11/16	M	Sevier County	UT	Jack W. Powell	1991	879
14 2/16	8 4/16	5 14/16	M	Elmore County	ID	Jon Brockfeld	1992	879
14 2/16	8 8/16	5 10/16	M	Garfield County	UT	Steven R. Farr	1992	879
14 2/16	8 8/16	5 10/16	M	Beaver County	UT	Glen L. Mahlum	1993	879
14 2/16	8 5/16	5 13/16	M	Nye County	NV	Dave Steger	1993	879
14 2/16	8 4/16	5 14/16	M	Archuleta County	CO	Lester D. Hawkins, Jr.	1993	879
14 2/16	8 5/16	5 13/16	M	Lemhi County	ID	Rob Valnoski	1993	879
14 2/16	8 5/16	5 13/16	M	Mesa County	CO	Paul Kamps	1994	879
14 2/16	8 8/16	5 10/16	M	Wasatch County	UT	Dallas Smith	1994	879
14 2/16	8 5/16	5 13/16	M	Duchesne County	UT	Steve Statler	1995	879
14 2/16	8 5/16	5 13/16	M	Grand County	CO	Daniel Thomas Cresci	1995	879
14 2/16	8 7/16	5 11/16	M	Moffat County	CO	John T. Johnson	1996	879
14 2/16	8 6/16	5 12/16	M	Clearwater County	ID	Rod Simmer	1996	879
14 2/16	8 5/16	5 13/16	M	Mora County	NM	Wes McAdams	1997	879
14 2/16	8 4/16	5 14/16	M	Catron County	NM	William E. Webb	1997	879
14 2/16	8 4/16	5 14/16	M	Fremont County	CO	Fred Eichler	1997	879
14 2/16	8 4/16	5 14/16	M	Idaho County	ID	Glenn Burney	1997	879
14 2/16	8 4/16	5 14/16	M	Carbon County	MT	Mike O'Connor	1998	879
14 1/16	8 14/16	5 3/16	M	Garfield County	CO	Jack Peters	1964	932
14 1/16	8 7/16	5 10/16	M	Rio Blanco County	CO	Charles Kohler	1969	932
14 1/16	8 7/16	5 10/16	M	Chaffee County	CO	Frank B. Parrish	1969	932
14 1/16	8 6/16	5 11/16	M	Elmore County	ID	Jerry E. Burt	1971	932
14 1/16	8 3/16	5 14/16	M	Mesa County	CO	Cary E. Weldon	1972	932
14 1/16	8 5/16	5 12/16	M	Carbon County	UT	David K. Elliot	1973	932
14 1/16	8 5/16	5 12/16	M	Butte County	ID	Ken Anselmi	1975	932
14 1/16	8 5/16	5 12/16	M	Rio Blanco County	CO	Chris Christian	1976	932
14 1/16	8 5/16	5 12/16	M	Wayne County	UT	C. Duane Kerr	1979	932
14 1/16	8 5/16	5 12/16	M	Cache County	UT	Val D. Larsen	1980	932
14 1/16	8 5/16	5 12/16	M	Coconino County	AZ	Fred McDonald	1980	932
14 1/16	8 5/16	5 12/16	M	Elko County	NV	Don Tripp	1980	932
14 1/16	8 5/16	5 12/16	M	Lemhi County	ID	Jim Jungk	1981	932
14 1/16	8 4/16	5 13/16	M	Adams County	ID	Dennis Atwater	1982	932
14 1/16	8 9/16	5 8/16	M	Coconino County	AZ	Dale Tasa	1982	932

COUGAR (MOUNTAIN LION)

Minimum Score 13 8/16 — Continued — 233

SCORE	GREATEST LENGTH	GREATEST WIDTH	SEX	AREA	STATE/PROVINCE	HUNTER'S NAME	DATE	RANK
14 1/16	8 5/16	5 12/16	M	Douglas County	CO	Gary James Morrow	1982	932
14 1/16	8 4/16	5 13/16	M	Madison County	MT	Dick Curtis	1983	932
14 1/16	8 6/16	5 11/16	M	Madison County	MT	John E. Larsen	1984	932
14 1/16	8 5/16	5 12/16	M	Tooele County	UT	Dennis L. Shirley	1984	932
14 1/16	8 6/16	5 11/16	M	Flathead County	MT	Dean F. Bergman	1984	932
14 1/16	8 5/16	5 12/16	M	Lander County	NV	Louis Probo	1984	932
14 1/16	8 4/16	5 13/16	M	Gilpin County	CO	Kurt W. Keskimaki	1985	932
14 1/16	8 4/16	5 13/16	M	Idaho County	ID	William J. Bowen	1986	932
14 1/16	8 5/16	5 12/16	M	Lincoln County	MT	Ben Rossetto	1986	932
14 1/16	8 8/16	5 9/16	M	Millard County	UT	Dave Scott	1987	932
14 1/16	8 5/16	5 12/16	M	Lemhi County	ID	Bobby A. Berg	1987	932
14 1/16	8 2/16	5 15/16	M	White Pine County	NV	Perry W. Greene, Jr.	1987	932
14 1/16	8 5/16	5 12/16	M	Conejos County	CO	Mike Boland	1987	932
14 1/16	8 5/16	5 12/16	M	Elmore County	ID	Mark Zastrow	1988	932
14 1/16	8 5/16	5 12/16	M	Coconino County	AZ	Don Flagel	1988	932
14 1/16	8 6/16	5 11/16	M	Montrose County	CO	Joe Garvey	1988	932
14 1/16	8 5/16	5 12/16	M	Alamosa County	CO	Dan Call	1989	932
14 1/16	8 6/16	5 11/16	M	Sevier County	UT	William G. Cummard II	1989	932
14 1/16	8 5/16	5 12/16	M	Meagher County	MT	Michael A. Blase, Jr.	1990	932
14 1/16	8 4/16	5 13/16	M	Custer County	ID	David Hotten	1991	932
14 1/16	8 5/16	5 12/16	M	Eureka County	NV	Gilbert Hernandez	1991	932
14 1/16	8 4/16	5 13/16	M	Garfield County	CO	Roger Wintle	1992	932
14 1/16	8 4/16	5 13/16	M	Pueblo County	CO	Tim Rose	1992	932
14 1/16	8 6/16	5 11/16	M	Park County	CO	Jack P. Van Vianen	1992	932
14 1/16	8 6/16	5 11/16	M	Boise County	ID	Nelson Beane	1992	932
14 1/16	8 5/16	5 12/16	M	Lemhi County	ID	Charles R. Setter	1992	932
14 1/16	8 6/16	5 11/16	M	Custer County	ID	Charles G. Schibler	1993	932
14 1/16	8 7/16	5 10/16	M	Porcupine Hills	ALB	David R. Coupland	1993	932
14 1/16	8 5/16	5 12/16	M	Boise County	ID	Mike Carfello	1994	932
14 1/16	8 7/16	5 10/16	M	Colfax County	NM	Jack Dell	1994	932
14 1/16	8 4/16	5 13/16	M	Little Jumpingpound Creek	ALB	Michael F. Rijavec	1995	932
14 1/16	8 7/16	5 10/16	M	Gila County	AZ	Thomas J. Hoffman	1995	932
14 1/16	8 6/16	5 11/16	M	Boise County	ID	Mark Reimels	1995	932
14 1/16	8 5/16	5 12/16	M	Boundary County	ID	John Thomas	1995	932
14 1/16	8 5/16	5 12/16	M	Lemhi County	ID	L. Scot Jenkins	1995	932
14 1/16	8 2/16	5 15/16	M	Madison County	MT	D. Mitch Kottas	1995	932
14 1/16	8 8/16	5 9/16	M	White Pine County	NV	Marcos D. Alfaro	1996	932
14 1/16	8 7/16	5 10/16	M	Rio Arriba County	NM	Joe Silva, Sr.	1997	932
14 1/16	8 7/16	5 10/16	M	Sevier County	UT	Baird R. Booth	1997	932
14 1/16	8 5/16	5 12/16	M	Garfield County	CO	Rob Crawford	1997	932
14 1/16	8 5/16	5 12/16	M	Sanders County	MT	Ron Ruberstell	1997	932
14 1/16	8 3/16	5 14/16	M	Madison County	MT	Carl Hanson	1997	932
14 1/16	8 2/16	5 15/16	M	Sweet Grass County	MT	Bill Bryce	1998	932
14 0/16	8 4/16	5 12/16	M	Uintah County	UT	Dr. Quentin F. Mangion	1962	990
14 0/16	8 4/16	5 12/16	M	Gila County	AZ	Hugh Pearson	1963	990
14 0/16	8 4/16	5 12/16	M	Flathead County	MT	Dorn L. Brinker	1969	990
14 0/16	8 3/16	5 13/16	M	Valley County	ID	Ronald N. Kolpin	1972	990
14 0/16	8 1/16	5 15/16	M	Yavapai County	AZ	Louis A. Vohs	1973	990
14 0/16	8 5/16	5 11/16	M	Lemhi County	ID	T. A. Low IV	1977	990
14 0/16	8 2/16	5 14/16	M	Duchesne County	UT	James Sot	1977	990
14 0/16	8 4/16	5 12/16	M	Blacktail Mtn.	UT	Jerry Dittrich	1978	990
14 0/16	8 5/16	5 11/16	M	Fremont County	CO	Gary Fisher	1979	990
14 0/16	8 4/16	5 12/16	M	San Juan County	UT	Gary Paluszcyk	1979	990
14 0/16	8 4/16	5 12/16	M	Boise County	ID	Paul Anderson	1980	990
14 0/16	8 3/16	5 13/16	M	Coconino County	AZ	Larry Almaraz	1981	990
14 0/16	8 3/16	5 13/16	M	San Miguel County	CO	Robert Finelli	1981	990
14 0/16	8 5/16	5 11/16	M	Madison County	MT	Leland S. Speakes, Jr.	1984	990
14 0/16	8 4/16	5 12/16	M	Wasatch County	UT	Vicki Mamales	1985	990
14 0/16	8 2/16	5 14/16	M	Madison County	MT	Pat Sinclair	1985	990
14 0/16	8 8/16	5 8/16	M	Rio Grande County	CO	Tom Tietz	1985	990
14 0/16	8 2/16	5 14/16	M	Madison County	MT	Carl Spaeth	1986	990
14 0/16	8 3/16	5 13/16	M	Coconino County	AZ	George Richardson	1987	990
14 0/16	8 2/16	5 14/16	M	San Juan County	NM	Keith Hardy	1987	990
14 0/16	8 6/16	5 10/16	M	Judith Basin County	MT	Noel J. Poux	1988	990
14 0/16	8 4/16	5 12/16	M	San Miguel County	CO	Jack Downing	1988	990
14 0/16	8 4/16	5 12/16	M	Idaho County	ID	David A. Shupp	1989	990
14 0/16	8 7/16	5 9/16	M	Millard County	UT	Norman Bradley	1990	990
14 0/16	8 4/16	5 12/16	M	Tooele County	UT	Merrill Clarke	1990	990
14 0/16	8 6/16	5 10/16	M	Elmore County	ID	Julian Salutrequi	1990	990
14 0/16	8 7/16	5 9/16	M	Iron County	UT	Ken Wilson	1990	990
14 0/16	8 4/16	5 12/16	M	Lemhi County	ID	Larry Dockery	1990	990
14 0/16	8 6/16	5 10/16	M	Union County	OR	Jeff Carver	1990	990
14 0/16	8 5/16	5 11/16	M	Coconino County	AZ	Kenneth Meadors	1991	990
14 0/16	8 3/16	5 13/16	M	Stoney Lake	BC	Gregory White	1991	990
14 0/16	8 2/16	5 14/16	M	Granite County	MT	Richard E. LaCrone	1992	990
14 0/16	8 6/16	5 10/16	M	Routt County	CO	Gary F. Bogner	1992	990
14 0/16	8 3/16	5 13/16	M	Lewis & Clark County	MT	Jay Roberson	1992	990
14 0/16	8 6/16	5 10/16	M	Archuleta County	CO	Tony R. Stephens	1993	990

COUGAR (MOUNTAIN LION)

Minimum Score 13 8/16 — Continued

SCORE	GREATEST LENGTH	GREATEST WIDTH	SEX	AREA	STATE/ PROVINCE	HUNTER'S NAME	DATE	RANK
14 0/16	8 4/16	5 12/16	M	Carbon County	WY	Craig Boheler	1993	990
14 0/16	8 5/16	5 11/16	M	Routt County	CO	Glen Merica	1993	990
14 0/16	8 6/16	5 10/16	M	Wager Coulee	ALB	Archie Nesbitt	1993	990
14 0/16	8 8/16	5 8/16	M	Montezuma County	CO	Brian T. Myers	1993	990
14 0/16	8 4/16	5 12/16	M	Garfield County	CO	Michael Pratt	1994	990
14 0/16	8 5/16	5 11/16	M	Jefferson County	CO	Jason Adamson	1994	990
14 0/16	8 7/16	5 9/16	M	Chaffee County	CO	Ray Woods	1994	990
14 0/16	8 6/16	5 10/16	M	Longview	ALB	Lauren Hoover	1996	990
14 0/16	8 3/16	5 13/16	M	Powell County	MT	Michael A. Dunwell	1996	990
14 0/16	8 4/16	5 12/16	M	Fremont County	CO	Rick Wilson	1997	990
14 0/16	8 4/16	5 12/16	M	Moffat County	CO	Joe George	1997	990
14 0/16	8 2/16	5 14/16	M	Maricopa County	AZ	Ronald R. Lacy	1997	990
14 0/16	8 4/16	5 12/16	M	Mesa County	CO	Kerry N. Koning	1997	990
14 0/16	8 3/16	5 13/16	M	Grand County	CO	Bob Bodemann	1998	990
14 0/16	8 5/16	5 11/16	M	Humboldt County	NV	Mark Connor	1998	990
13 15/16	8 3/16	5 12/16	M	Gila County	AZ	Hugh Pearson	1963	1040
13 15/16	8 5/16	5 10/16	M	Rio Blanco County	CO	Joel Hogan	1967	1040
13 15/16	8 6/16	5 9/16	M	Okanogan County	WA	Stuart Irwin	1971	1040
13 15/16	8 5/16	5 10/16	M	Lemhi County	ID	John Mascellino	1972	1040
13 15/16	8 3/16	5 12/16	M	San Miguel County	CO	Ken Grandow	1979	1040
13 15/16	8 6/16	5 9/16	M	Elmore County	ID	Richard C. Nichols	1980	1040
13 15/16	8 3/16	5 12/16	M	Judith Basin County	MT	Ed Evans	1981	1040
13 15/16	8 5/16	5 10/16	M	Las Animas County	CO	David S. Bunce	1982	1040
13 15/16	8 5/16	5 10/16	M	Piute County	UT	Lynn Kuhlmann	1984	1040
13 15/16	8 3/16	5 12/16	M	Boise County	ID	William Atkinson, Jr.	1985	1040
13 15/16	8 4/16	5 11/16	M	Lemhi County	ID	James S. Disalvo	1985	1040
13 15/16	8 2/16	5 13/16	M	Elko County	NV	Donald Pyne	1987	1040
13 15/16	8 3/16	5 12/16	M	Elmore County	ID	Carolyn Godfrey	1987	1040
13 15/16	8 5/16	5 10/16	M	Sevier County	UT	Philippe Lantagne	1988	1040
13 15/16	8 6/16	5 9/16	M	Washington County	UT	Gerald Laurino	1988	1040
13 15/16	8 2/16	5 13/16	M	Carbon County	UT	Gail B. Raby	1989	1040
13 15/16	8 4/16	5 11/16	M	Nye County	NV	Charles Pat Walker, Jr.	1990	1040
13 15/16	8 4/16	5 11/16	M	Carbon County	UT	Roger Cyfers	1990	1040
13 15/16	8 5/16	5 10/16	M	Chaffee County	CO	Scott Pelino	1990	1040
13 15/16	8 5/16	5 10/16	M	Beaverhead County	MT	Lynn Lamphiear	1991	1040
13 15/16	8 4/16	5 11/16	M	Lincoln County	MT	Dennis L. Kari	1991	1040
13 15/16	8 2/16	5 13/16	M	Flathead County	MT	David D. Johnston	1992	1040
13 15/16	8 4/16	5 11/16	M	Washington County	UT	Henry C. Williams, Jr.	1993	1040
13 15/16	8 6/16	5 9/16	M	Coconino County	AZ	Robert Y. Childers	1993	1040
13 15/16	8 5/16	5 10/16	M	Routt County	CO	Mike E. Neilson	1993	1040
13 15/16	8 6/16	5 9/16	M	San Miguel County	CO	Pat Snyder	1994	1040
13 15/16	8 0/16	5 15/16	M	Catron County	NM	Gary L. Robertson	1994	1040
13 15/16	8 6/16	5 9/16	M	Rio Arriba County	NM	Vince Podnar	1994	1040
13 15/16	8 5/16	5 10/16	M	Porcupine Hills	ALB	Pete Dohrs	1994	1040
13 15/16	8 4/16	5 11/16	M	Shoshone County	ID	David J. Crownhart	1994	1040
13 15/16	8 2/16	5 13/16	M	Boise County	ID	Gene Hopkins	1995	1040
13 15/16	8 7/16	5 8/16	M	150 Mile House	BC	Daniel Kelly	1997	1040
13 15/16	8 4/16	5 11/16	M	Rio Blanco County	CO	James E. Corby	1998	1040
13 14/16	8 4/16	5 10/16	M	Flathead County	MT	Jerry Almos	1970	1073
13 14/16	8 6/16	5 8/16	F	Coconino County	AZ	Midge Dandridge	1972	1073
13 14/16	8 1/16	5 13/16	M	Mesa County	CO	Stan Bocian	1974	1073
13 14/16	8 5/16	5 9/16	M	Chaffee County	CO	Ben Cuadra	1975	1073
13 14/16	8 2/16	5 12/16	M	Boise County	ID	Robert L. Bevan	1976	1073
13 14/16	8 6/16	5 8/16	M	Lemhi County	ID	James C. Costopoulos	1976	1073
13 14/16	8 1/16	5 13/16	M	Garfield County	CO	Lou Kindred	1977	1073
13 14/16	8 4/16	5 10/16	M	Lemhi County	ID	Dan E. Hershberger	1979	1073
13 14/16	8 4/16	5 10/16	M	Rio Blanco County	CO	Wayne Watson, Sr.	1979	1073
13 14/16	8 3/16	5 11/16	M	Uintah County	UT	Dan Darrell Boy	1980	1073
13 14/16	8 9/16	5 5/16	M	Washington County	UT	Scott Petersen	1982	1073
13 14/16	8 3/16	5 11/16	M	Grand County	UT	Henry 'Hank' Frey	1982	1073
13 14/16	8 3/16	5 11/16	M	Archuleta County	CO	Ronald Murphy	1983	1073
13 14/16	8 1/16	5 13/16	M	Lemhi County	ID	Wendell L. Seelig	1983	1073
13 14/16	8 2/16	5 12/16	M	Sevier County	UT	John Alden Brown, Jr.	1984	1073
13 14/16	8 3/16	5 11/16	M	Sanpete County	UT	Bob Fitzgerald	1984	1073
13 14/16	8 5/16	5 9/16	M	Chaffee County	CO	Raymond Roussett, Jr.	1985	1073
13 14/16	8 5/16	5 9/16	M	Elmore County	ID	John Koldeway	1985	1073
13 14/16	8 2/16	5 12/16	M	Gilpin County	CO	Lyle Willmarth	1986	1073
13 14/16	8 6/16	5 8/16	M	San Miguel County	CO	Ronald J. Collier	1986	1073
13 14/16	8 2/16	5 12/16	M	Sheridan County	WY	Mike Pilch	1987	1073
13 14/16	8 4/16	5 10/16	M	Coconino County	AZ	Cindi Richardson	1987	1073
13 14/16	8 5/16	5 9/16	M	Lincoln County	MT	Kenneth Mamatz	1988	1073
13 14/16	7 15/16	5 15/16	M	Sheridan County	WY	Harold Carnell	1988	1073
13 14/16	8 4/16	5 10/16	M	White Pine County	NV	Randy Bennett	1989	1073
13 14/16	8 4/16	5 10/16	M	Idaho County	ID	Kenny Holliday	1990	1073
13 14/16	8 3/16	5 11/16	M	Elmore County	ID	Stan Godfrey	1991	1073
13 14/16	8 2/16	5 12/16	M	Grand County	UT	Dale Bigger	1991	1073
13 14/16	8 3/16	5 11/16	F	Clearwater County	ID	Russ A. Van Rite	1991	1073
13 14/16	8 3/16	5 11/16	M	Madison County	MT	Randall Brown	1991	1073

COUGAR (MOUNTAIN LION)

Minimum Score 13 8/16 — Continued

SCORE	GREATEST LENGTH	GREATEST WIDTH	SEX	AREA	STATE/ PROVINCE	HUNTER'S NAME	DATE	RANK
13 14/16	8 5/16	5 9/16	M	Elmore County	ID	Richard A. Schreiber	1991	1073
13 14/16	8 4/16	5 10/16	M	Tooele County	UT	Anthony E. Martinez II	1992	1073
13 14/16	8 3/16	5 11/16	M	Catron County	NM	G. David Moser	1992	1073
13 14/16	8 7/16	5 7/16	M	Washington County	UT	Edward X. Thompson	1992	1073
13 14/16	8 2/16	5 12/16	M	Judith Basin County	MT	John "Rosey" Roseland	1993	1073
13 14/16	8 4/16	5 10/16	M	Sevier County	UT	Randy P. Forsythe	1994	1073
13 14/16	8 3/16	5 11/16	M	Lemhi County	ID	Stewart P. Fitzgerald	1995	1073
13 14/16	8 2/16	5 12/16	M	White Pine County	NV	W. Scott Perry	1996	1073
13 14/16	8 3/16	5 11/16	M	Montrose County	CO	Richard Weaver	1997	1073
13 14/16	8 2/16	5 12/16	M	Broadwater County	MT	Guy Jette	1997	1073
13 14/16	8 2/16	5 12/16	M	Madison County	MT	Ken Southworth	1998	1073
13 14/16	8 4/16	5 10/16	M	Larimer County	CO	K. C. Heinrich	1998	1073
13 14/16	8 2/16	5 12/16	M	Summit County	CO	Bob Reedy	1998	1073
13 13/16	8 2/16	5 11/16	M	Esmeralda County	NV	George Hooker	1961	1116
13 13/16	7 15/16	5 14/16	M	Lemhi County	ID	Vern Herman	1969	1116
13 13/16	8 2/16	5 11/16	M	El Paso County	CO	L. Clark Kiser	1984	1116
13 13/16	8 4/16	5 9/16	M	Mesa County	CO	Edgar Bobo	1984	1116
13 13/16	8 1/16	5 12/16	M	Sandoval County	NM	David Taylor	1985	1116
13 13/16	8 1/16	5 12/16	M	San Juan County	UT	David Snyder	1985	1116
13 13/16	8 3/16	5 10/16	M	Johnson County	WY	Terry Krahn	1986	1116
13 13/16	8 3/16	5 10/16	M	Cochise County	AZ	Randy Hall	1987	1116
13 13/16	8 5/16	5 8/16	M	Boulder County	CO	Jerry Souders	1987	1116
13 13/16	8 0/16	5 13/16	M	Greenlee County	AZ	Eugene Fritsky	1989	1116
13 13/16	8 2/16	5 11/16	M	San Juan County	UT	Ronald D. Kirk	1990	1116
13 13/16	8 5/16	5 8/16	M	Garfield County	CO	Neil Smith	1990	1116
13 13/16	8 3/16	5 10/16	M	Chaffee County	CO	David Spacek	1990	1116
13 13/16	8 5/16	5 8/16	M	San Miguel County	CO	Evans V. Brewster	1991	1116
13 13/16	8 4/16	5 9/16	M	Coconino County	AZ	Stephen A. Kotz	1991	1116
13 13/16	8 1/16	5 12/16	M	San Juan County	UT	Daniel Willems	1992	1116
13 13/16	8 6/16	5 7/16	M	Chaffee County	CO	A. M. Salazar	1992	1116
13 13/16	8 2/16	5 11/16	M	Granite County	MT	Richard E. LaCrone	1994	1116
13 13/16	8 5/16	5 8/16	M	White Pine County	NV	Mark Shrewsbury	1994	1116
13 13/16	8 8/16	5 5/16	M	Ferry County	WA	Michael R. Land	1994	1116
13 13/16	8 4/16	5 9/16	M	Chaffee County	CO	Paul Bohochik	1994	1116
13 13/16	8 3/16	5 10/16	M	Box Elder County	UT	H. Douglas Herold	1994	1116
13 13/16	8 3/16	5 10/16	M	San Juan County	UT	Michael C. Parkinson	1995	1116
13 13/16	8 1/16	5 12/16	M	Montezuma County	CO	Dennis L. Howell	1996	1116
13 13/16	8 1/16	5 12/16	M	Park County	CO	John Colby	1996	1116
13 13/16	8 3/16	5 10/16	M	Elmore County	ID	Dawn Traub	1996	1116
13 13/16	8 3/16	5 10/16	M	Broadwater County	MT	Marc Brittain	1996	1116
13 13/16	8 5/16	5 8/16	M	Boundary County	ID	Rich Wynn	1996	1116
13 13/16	8 1/16	5 12/16	M	Coconino County	AZ	Lon Hadfield	1997	1116
13 13/16	8 2/16	5 11/16	M	Montezuma County	CO	Dean Brown	1997	1116
13 12/16	8 4/16	5 8/16	M	Shasta National Forest	CA	Harv Ebers	1963	1146
13 12/16	8 0/16	5 12/16	M	Swan R. Valley	MT	Joe Lawrence	1965	1146
13 12/16	7 11/16	6 1/16	M	Garfield County	UT	Robert E. Todd	1969	1146
13 12/16	8 2/16	5 10/16	M	Pima County	AZ	Sherwin Lipsitz	1976	1146
13 12/16	8 3/16	5 9/16	M	Lemhi County	ID	Ray Torrey	1978	1146
13 12/16	8 3/16	5 9/16	M	Custer County	ID	Larry Bonetti	1979	1146
13 12/16	8 4/16	5 8/16	M	Lemhi County	ID	Buck Farni	1979	1146
13 12/16	8 3/16	5 9/16	M	Carbon County	UT	Claude Flippin	1981	1146
13 12/16	8 4/16	5 8/16	M	Uintah County	UT	Ken Labrum	1985	1146
13 12/16	8 2/16	5 10/16	M	Grand County	UT	Robert Jacobsen	1986	1146
13 12/16	8 0/16	5 12/16	M	Gallatin County	MT	Carmine Agostinelli	1986	1146
13 12/16	8 4/16	5 8/16	M	Clearwater County	ID	George J. McCuster	1986	1146
13 12/16	8 2/16	5 10/16	M	San Miguel County	CO	Joe Wright	1987	1146
13 12/16	8 2/16	5 10/16	M	Powell County	MT	Thomas W. Moore	1987	1146
13 12/16	8 3/16	5 9/16	M	Carbon County	UT	Jim Saunoris, Jr.	1987	1146
13 12/16	8 3/16	5 9/16	M	Lemhi County	ID	Dan L. Moultrie	1988	1146
13 12/16	8 2/16	5 10/16	M	Douglas County	OR	Rick Gabbard	1988	1146
13 12/16	8 4/16	5 8/16	M	Garfield County	CO	Warren Strickland	1989	1146
13 12/16	8 3/16	5 9/16	M	Rio Blanco County	CO	Tom Brakke	1990	1146
13 12/16	8 3/16	5 9/16	M	Beaverhead County	MT	Jeff D. Wingard	1991	1146
13 12/16	8 3/16	5 9/16	M	St. Mary's River	BC	Richard Kirkvold	1991	1146
13 12/16	8 6/16	5 6/16	M	Sandoval County	NM	Thomas W. Dunn	1991	1146
13 12/16	8 3/16	5 9/16	M	Montrose County	CO	Gregory Hise	1992	1146
13 12/16	8 4/16	5 8/16	M	Summit County	UT	Tony Park	1992	1146
13 12/16	8 4/16	5 8/16	M	Washington County	UT	Norman J. Roy	1993	1146
13 12/16	8 2/16	5 10/16	M	Boundary County	ID	Dustin Myers	1993	1146
13 12/16	8 0/16	5 12/16	M	Natrona County	WY	Miles Bundy	1994	1146
13 12/16	8 1/16	5 11/16	M	Lemhi County	ID	Michael Judas	1994	1146
13 12/16	8 2/16	5 10/16	M	Wasatch County	UT	Will Stump	1995	1146
13 12/16	8 0/16	5 12/16	M	Grand County	UT	Daniel Day	1995	1146
13 12/16	8 3/16	5 9/16	M	Carbon County	UT	Michael J. DeCaro	1995	1146
13 12/16	8 5/16	5 7/16	M	Catron County	NM	Robert A. Dale	1996	1146
13 12/16	8 3/16	5 9/16	M	Elko County	NV	Aaron T. Hughes	1997	1146
13 12/16	8 2/16	5 10/16	M	Boundary County	ID	Richard M. Penn	1997	1146
13 12/16	8 3/16	5 9/16	M	Fremont County	CO	Ben L. Nelson	1997	1146

COUGAR (MOUNTAIN LION)

Minimum Score 13 8/16 — Continued

SCORE	GREATEST LENGTH	GREATEST WIDTH	SEX	AREA	STATE/PROVINCE	HUNTER'S NAME	DATE	RANK
13 12/16	8 4/16	5 8/16	M	Flathead County	MT	Shawn Price	1997	1146
13 11/16	8 3/16	5 8/16	M	Valley County	ID	Clarence Grandt	1972	1182
13 11/16	8 3/16	5 8/16	M	Mesa County	CO	William J. Vincent	1972	1182
13 11/16	8 2/16	5 9/16	M	Carbon County	UT	Bernard R. Giacoletto	1975	1182
13 11/16	8 6/16	5 5/16	M	San Juan County	UT	James Karlovec	1975	1182
13 11/16	7 15/16	5 12/16	M	Grand County	UT	David Seidelman	1975	1182
13 11/16	8 0/16	5 11/16	M	Garfield County	CO	Darlene Frye	1976	1182
13 11/16	8 4/16	5 7/16	M	Boise County	ID	Fred Sanders	1981	1182
13 11/16	7 15/16	5 12/16	M	Missoula County	MT	Blair Hamer	1983	1182
13 11/16	8 3/16	5 8/16	M	Gilpin County	CO	John Rhine	1984	1182
13 11/16	8 3/16	5 8/16	M	Clearwater County	ID	Mike I. Powers	1984	1182
13 11/16	8 3/16	5 8/16	F	Socorro County	NM	Paul Persano	1986	1182
13 11/16	8 3/16	5 8/16	M	Pima County	AZ	Ernest R. Allen	1987	1182
13 11/16	8 4/16	5 7/16	M	Boise County	ID	Raymond A. Guay	1987	1182
13 11/16	8 1/16	5 10/16	M	Nye County	NV	Ronald W. Lindquist	1987	1182
13 11/16	8 4/16	5 7/16	M	Washington County	UT	Jules Pacheco	1989	1182
13 11/16	8 0/16	5 11/16	F	Clearwater County	ID	Colin G. Crook	1989	1182
13 11/16	8 1/16	5 10/16	M	Asotin County	WA	Mark Kolowith	1990	1182
13 11/16	8 3/16	5 8/16	M	Fremont County	CO	Travis Todd	1990	1182
13 11/16	8 3/16	5 8/16	M	Jackson County	OR	Florian Davis	1990	1182
13 11/16	8 5/16	5 6/16	M	Uintah County	UT	Robert G. Petersen	1991	1182
13 11/16	8 4/16	5 7/16	M	Saguache County	CO	Roger M. Tyler	1992	1182
13 11/16	8 3/16	5 8/16	M	Fergus County	MT	Mike Bentler	1992	1182
13 11/16	8 2/16	5 9/16	M	Park County	WY	Rene Suda	1993	1182
13 11/16	8 3/16	5 8/16	M	Garfield County	CO	William Rasch	1993	1182
13 11/16	8 5/16	5 6/16	M	Garfield County	CO	Lee Bange	1993	1182
13 11/16	8 3/16	5 8/16	M	Los Alamos County	NM	Timothy F.H. Smith	1995	1182
13 11/16	8 1/16	5 10/16	M	White Pine County	NV	Thomas W. Fuller	1996	1182
13 11/16	8 2/16	5 9/16	M	Park County	MT	Mike O'Connor	1996	1182
13 11/16	8 1/16	5 10/16	M	Montrose County	CO	David C. Gordon, Jr.	1997	1182
13 11/16	8 5/16	5 6/16	M	Fremont County	CO	Stacy Hoeme	1997	1182
13 11/16	8 0/16	5 11/16	M	Elmore County	ID	George E. Mann	1997	1182
13 11/16	8 3/16	5 8/16	M	Sanpete County	UT	Don Noonan	1997	1182
13 11/16	8 1/16	5 10/16	F	Moffat County	CO	Wendell "Butch" Howes, Jr.	1998	1182
13 11/16	8 3/16	5 8/16	M	Humboldt County	NV	Donald Draper	1998	1182
13 11/16	8 3/16	5 8/16	M	Princeton	BC	Mark A. Jackson	1998	1182
13 10/16	8 2/16	5 8/16	F	Moffat County	CO	Roland C. Gravenkemper	1959	1217
13 10/16	8 0/16	5 10/16	F	Sana Arroya Canyon	UT	Edward Collins	1967	1217
13 10/16	7 14/16	5 12/16	M	Fremont County	CO	Jeffrey D. McKnight	1970	1217
13 10/16	7 15/16	5 11/16	M	Boise County	ID	Robert B. Braswell	1971	1217
13 10/16	7 12/16	5 14/16	M	Lemhi County	ID	Richard R. Smith	1976	1217
13 10/16	8 2/16	5 8/16	M	Grand County	UT	Karen Jacobsen	1980	1217
13 10/16	8 3/16	5 7/16	M	Sevier County	UT	Robert C. McGuire	1980	1217
13 10/16	8 0/16	5 10/16	M	Coconino County	AZ	Les Shelton	1981	1217
13 10/16	8 2/16	5 8/16	M	Garfield County	UT	William B. McGuire, Jr.	1983	1217
13 10/16	8 2/16	5 8/16	M	Sevier County	UT	Kenneth L. Jackson	1984	1217
13 10/16	8 0/16	5 10/16	M	Flathead County	MT	Charles J. Williams	1986	1217
13 10/16	8 4/16	5 6/16	M	Colfax County	NM	I. Lionel Kelley	1986	1217
13 10/16	7 15/16	5 11/16	M	Beaver County	UT	David L. Welch	1987	1217
13 10/16	8 2/16	5 8/16	M	Fergus County	MT	John "Rosey" Roseland	1987	1217
13 10/16	8 1/16	5 9/16	M	Millard County	UT	Roy Evans	1988	1217
13 10/16	8 1/16	5 9/16	M	Washington County	UT	Ken Mowerson	1988	1217
13 10/16	8 1/16	5 9/16	M	Lincoln County	NV	Glen R. Cousins	1988	1217
13 10/16	8 3/16	5 7/16	M	Blairmore	ALB	Larry Vayro	1990	1217
13 10/16	8 2/16	5 8/16	M	Elmore County	ID	Mike Ambur	1990	1217
13 10/16	8 1/16	5 9/16	M	Jackson County	OR	Randy D. Peyton	1990	1217
13 10/16	7 15/16	5 11/16	M	Iron County	UT	Jeryl F. Williams	1991	1217
13 10/16	8 1/16	5 9/16	M	Teller County	CO	Dennis R. Bader	1991	1217
13 10/16	8 0/16	5 10/16	M	Custer County	ID	Phil Sulllvan	1991	1217
13 10/16	7 14/16	5 12/16	F	Montrose County	CO	Dale Laird	1992	1217
13 10/16	8 0/16	5 10/16	M	Taos County	NM	Robert L. Pagel	1992	1217
13 10/16	8 1/16	5 9/16	M	Washakie County	WY	Warren Warmbold	1993	1217
13 10/16	8 3/16	5 7/16	M	Granite County	MT	Mike Boyd	1993	1217
13 10/16	8 3/16	5 7/16	M	Grand County	CO	Andrew C. Bair	1994	1217
13 10/16	8 4/16	5 6/16	M	Rio Arriba County	NM	Joe Cordonier	1994	1217
13 10/16	8 1/16	5 9/16	M	Eagle County	CO	Sheldon S. Showalter	1994	1217
13 10/16	8 0/16	5 10/16	M	Catron County	NM	Jorge Garcia-Segovia	1995	1217
13 10/16	8 1/16	5 9/16	M	Kootenay River	BC	Gilles Rondeau	1995	1217
13 10/16	8 2/16	5 8/16	M	Idaho County	ID	W. J. Lucas III	1995	1217
13 10/16	7 14/16	5 12/16	M	Larimer County	CO	John E. Hostetler	1995	1217
13 10/16	8 3/16	5 7/16	M	Granite County	MT	Mike H. Boyd	1995	1217
13 10/16	8 0/16	5 10/16	M	Yavapai County	AZ	Al Kuntz	1996	1217
13 10/16	8 1/16	5 9/16	M	Coconino County	AZ	Joe Miguel	1996	1217
13 10/16	8 2/16	5 8/16	M	Iron County	UT	Cindy L. Brush	1997	1217
13 10/16	8 0/16	5 10/16	M	White Pine County	NV	William C. Brewer	1997	1217
13 10/16	8 0/16	5 10/16	M	Carbon County	UT	Tommy D. Langston	1998	1217
13 10/16	8 3/16	5 7/16	M	Cow Lake	ALB	Jason J. Brown	1998	1217
13 9/16	8 0/16	5 9/16	M	Carbon County	UT	Tom Kludy	1965	1258

COUGAR (MOUNTAIN LION)

Minimum Score 13 8/16   Continued   237

SCORE	GREATEST LENGTH	GREATEST WIDTH	SEX	AREA	STATE/PROVINCE	HUNTER'S NAME	DATE	RANK
13 9/16	8 1/16	5 8/16	M	Elmore County	ID	Larry Bergmann	1972	1258
13 9/16	8 0/16	5 9/16	F	Custer County	ID	John Kuhar	1975	1258
13 9/16	8 1/16	5 8/16	M	Carbon County	UT	Michael Judas	1977	1258
13 9/16	7 15/16	5 10/16	M	Rio Blanco County	CO	John Horstman	1977	1258
13 9/16	8 0/16	5 9/16	M	Saguache County	CO	Ed R. Wiseman	1977	1258
13 9/16	8 3/16	5 6/16	M	Peachland	BC	Roger Gipple	1983	1258
13 9/16	7 15/16	5 10/16	M	Hot Springs County	WY	John Backs	1983	1258
13 9/16	8 5/16	5 4/16	M	Monroe County	UT	Peter Esposito	1984	1258
13 9/16	7 14/16	5 11/16	M	Sanders County	MT	Fred J. Hoppe	1984	1258
13 9/16	8 3/16	5 6/16	M	Beaver County	UT	Joseph Drover	1985	1258
13 9/16	8 2/16	5 7/16	M	San Juan County	UT	Charles R. Horvath	1985	1258
13 9/16	8 0/16	5 9/16	M	Lemhi County	ID	Ed Montouri	1985	1258
13 9/16	8 0/16	5 9/16	M	Sanders County	MT	Dr. Eugene T. Altiere	1985	1258
13 9/16	8 1/16	5 8/16	M	Juab County	UT	Kirt Prestwich	1986	1258
13 9/16	8 2/16	5 7/16	M	Clearwater County	ID	Terry L. Sochor	1987	1258
13 9/16	8 1/16	5 8/16	M	Garfield County	UT	George E. Wright	1987	1258
13 9/16	8 0/16	5 9/16	M	White Pine County	NV	Robert S. Price	1987	1258
13 9/16	8 3/16	5 6/16	M	Rio Blanco County	CO	Steven J. Lepic	1987	1258
13 9/16	8 0/16	5 9/16	M	Fremont County	CO	Chuck Anderson, Jr.	1987	1258
13 9/16	8 1/16	5 8/16	M	Garfield County	CO	Steven W. Kluth	1988	1258
13 9/16	8 2/16	5 7/16	M	Granite County	MT	Rocky Drake	1989	1258
13 9/16	8 4/16	5 5/16	M	Mesa County	CO	Steve Haberland	1990	1258
13 9/16	8 2/16	5 7/16	M	Mesa County	CO	Troy James	1991	1258
13 9/16	8 0/16	5 9/16	M	Duchesne County	UT	Roy Hampton	1992	1258
13 9/16	7 15/16	5 10/16	F	Chaffee County	CO	Dave Luko	1992	1258
13 9/16	8 4/16	5 5/16	F	Park County	CO	Howard D. Drummond	1992	1258
13 9/16	8 3/16	5 6/16	M	Elko County	NV	John F. Amerson	1993	1258
13 9/16	8 1/16	5 8/16	M	La Plata County	CO	Dr. S. Mark Rayburg	1994	1258
13 9/16	8 1/16	5 8/16	M	Fergus County	MT	D. Mitch Kottas	1994	1258
13 9/16	8 1/16	5 8/16	M	Duchesne County	UT	Don R. Gifford	1996	1258
13 9/16	8 2/16	5 7/16	M	Montrose County	CO	Rod Van Sickle	1997	1258
13 8/16	8 0/16	5 8/16	M	Uintah County	UT	CreetieKerr	1964	1290
13 8/16	8 2/16	5 6/16	M	Uintah County	UT	Dr. George A. Waldriff	1965	1290
13 8/16	7 12/16	5 12/16	F	Lincoln County	MT	G. H. Malinoski	1967	1290
13 8/16	8 8/16	5 0/16	F	Churchill County	NV	Quentin P. Nightingale	1971	1290
13 8/16	8 1/16	5 7/16	M	Coconino County	AZ	Tim Kennedy	1974	1290
13 8/16	8 2/16	5 6/16	M	Coconino County	AZ	Robert West	1974	1290
13 8/16	8 0/16	5 8/16	M	Carbon County	UT	John Brandt	1978	1290
13 8/16	8 0/16	5 8/16	M	Cassia County	ID	Leon Peterson	1978	1290
13 8/16	8 2/16	5 6/16	M	Penticton	BC	Dale W. Gray	1979	1290
13 8/16	8 0/16	5 8/16	M	Lemhi County	ID	John A. McCarthy	1979	1290
13 8/16	8 1/16	5 7/16	M	Fremont County	CO	Steve Byerly	1981	1290
13 8/16	8 2/16	5 6/16	M	Clearwater County	ID	Donita K. Powers	1982	1290
13 8/16	7 10/16	5 14/16	M	Park County	WY	David C. Gordon, Sr.	1983	1290
13 8/16	8 1/16	5 7/16	F	Wallowa County	OR	Jim Turcke	1983	1290
13 8/16	8 1/16	5 7/16	M	Washington County	UT	Nic Blake	1984	1290
13 8/16	8 1/16	5 7/16	M	Alamosa County	CO	Barry J. Smith	1985	1290
13 8/16	7 13/16	5 11/16	M	Madison County	MT	Jim Ellis	1985	1290
13 8/16	8 3/16	5 5/16	M	Sevier County	UT	Greg Strait	1986	1290
13 8/16	8 0/16	5 8/16	M	Coconino County	AZ	Mike T. Miller	1988	1290
13 8/16	7 15/16	5 9/16	M	Fergus County	MT	Lisa Roseland	1988	1290
13 8/16	8 0/16	5 8/16	M	Fergus County	MT	John Fleharty	1988	1290
13 8/16	8 0/16	5 8/16	M	Montrose County	CO	Gene Mathias	1988	1290
13 8/16	8 0/16	5 8/16	M	Graham County	AZ	Tracy G. Hardy	1989	1290
13 8/16	8 3/16	5 5/16	M	Boise County	ID	Gerard J. Gareri	1990	1290
13 8/16	8 0/16	5 8/16	M	Lincoln County	MT	Jon Clark	1991	1290
13 8/16	8 2/16	5 6/16	M	Sevier County	UT	Raymond J. Francingues, Jr.	1992	1290
13 8/16	8 1/16	5 7/16	M	Fremont County	CO	Tommy M. Brown	1992	1290
13 8/16	8 0/16	5 8/16	M	Idaho County	ID	Larry Campbell	1994	1290
13 8/16	8 3/16	5 5/16	M	Custer County	ID	Walter Palmer	1994	1290
13 8/16	8 1/16	5 7/16	M	Saguache County	CO	Michael C. Dysh	1994	1290
13 8/16	7 15/16	5 9/16	M	Coconino County	AZ	Tom Egnew	1994	1290
13 8/16	8 0/16	5 8/16	M	Wasatch County	UT	Timothy A. Presnell	1995	1290
13 8/16	8 0/16	5 8/16	M	Jefferson County	MT	Joseph R. Balyeat	1995	1290
13 8/16	8 0/16	5 8/16	M	Madison County	MT	Bob Morton	1995	1290
13 8/16	8 0/16	5 8/16	M	Custer County	ID	Brian Brockette	1996	1290
13 8/16	8 1/16	5 7/16	F	Delta County	CO	John "Jack" Nothardt	1997	1290
13 8/16	8 0/16	5 8/16	M	Garfield County	UT	Alan Scano	1997	1290
13 8/16	8 0/16	5 8/16	M	Montrose County	CO	Harry Seifred	1997	1290
13 8/16	8 1/16	5 7/16	M	Missoula County	MT	Rudy Lupp	1997	1290
13 8/16	8 0/16	5 8/16	M	Carbon County	UT	George Brandon Farish	1998	1290
13 8/16	8 0/16	5 8/16	M	Fergus County	MT	Larry Jensen	1998	1290

World Record Columbian Blacktail Deer (Typical Antlers)
Score: 172 2/8
Marion County, Oregon - 1969
Hunter: B.G. Shurtleff

COLUMBIAN BLACKTAIL DEER (TYPICAL ANTLERS)
Minimum Score 90 — *Odocoileus hemionus columnianus*

SCORE	LENGTH OF MAIN BEAM R	L	INSIDE SPREAD	NUMBER OF POINTS R	L	AREA	STATE/ PROVINCE	HUNTER'S NAME	DATE	RANK
172 2/8	26 3/8	25 7/8	20 4/8	7	7	Marion County	OR	B. G. Shurtleff	1969	1
172 0/8	26 4/8	25 5/8	22 6/8	4	4	Multnomah County	OR	Dave Brill	1985	2
171 4/8	24 3/8	24 4/8	21 0/8	5	5	Josephine County	OR	Marte Scheuffele	1978	3
169 2/8	25 6/8	26 2/8	19 7/8	9	8	Jackson County	OR	Randy Allen	1995	4
164 7/8	23 6/8	23 3/8	19 7/8	5	5	Marion County	OR	B. G. Shurtleff	1977	5
161 2/8	24 4/8	25 5/8	18 4/8	5	5	Josephine County	OR	Marte Scheuffele	1975	6
160 7/8	23 0/8	23 4/8	19 4/8	6	5	Jackson County	OR	Dr. G. Scott Jennings	1972	7
160 7/8	23 4/8	24 0/8	17 3/8	5	5	Jackson County	OR	David B. Baird	1991	7
156 7/8	23 5/8	24 1/8	23 1/8	5	5	Trinity County	CA	Steve Bradford	1986	9
152 6/8	22 2/8	22 2/8	18 0/8	5	5	Clackamas County	OR	Phillip L. Severson	1991	10
150 4/8	23 4/8	23 1/8	20 2/8	5	5	Jackson County	OR	E. C. Brittsan	1976	11
147 3/8	22 5/8	23 3/8	17 4/8	5	6	Jackson County	OR	Sam Burton	1996	12
146 6/8	20 0/8	20 0/8	17 6/8	5	5	Marion County	OR	Jim Brackenbury	1990	13
146 6/8	22 3/8	24 2/8	15 0/8	5	5	Lane County	OR	Bryan P. Kamahoahoa	1993	13
146 2/8	21 4/8	22 4/8	17 2/8	5	5	Lane County	OR	Robert Martell	1988	15
144 5/8	21 2/8	20 3/8	16 6/8	6	7	Jackson County	OR	LeRoy Bedingfield	1970	16
144 5/8	21 6/8	22 7/8	21 7/8	5	5	Contra Costa County	CA	Wayne Ortland	1993	16
143 7/8	21 0/8	20 6/8	21 0/8	5	5	Shasta County	CA	Dave Swenson	1968	18
142 4/8	21 4/8	21 5/8	17 4/8	5	5	Lane County	OR	Vernon King, Sr.	1988	19
142 2/8	19 1/8	19 7/8	19 0/8	5	5	Lake County	OR	Don Chandler	1968	20
141 7/8	20 7/8	21 0/8	17 3/8	5	5	Jackson County	OR	Chester Stevenson	1917	21
141 6/8	22 1/8	23 0/8	20 6/8	4	4	Trinity County	CA	Tod Hawkins	1993	22
141 2/8	20 2/8	21 3/8	18 6/8	5	5	Jackson County	OR	Robert L. Freeman	1991	23
140 6/8	21 3/8	20 4/8	16 2/8	3	3	Jackson County	OR	Art W. Lee	1965	24
140 6/8	22 6/8	22 5/8	15 4/8	4	5	Jackson County	OR	Dr. G. Scott Jennings	1973	24

COLUMBIAN BLACKTAIL DEER (TYPICAL ANTLERS)

Minimum Score 90 — Continued

SCORE	LENGTH OF MAIN BEAM R	LENGTH OF MAIN BEAM L	INSIDE SPREAD	NUMBER OF POINTS R	NUMBER OF POINTS L	AREA	STATE/ PROVINCE	HUNTER'S NAME	DATE	RANK
140 6/8	21 2/8	20 7/8	17 6/8	5	5	Jackson County	OR	Les Higinbotham	1992	24
140 3/8	19 6/8	21 0/8	16 7/8	5	6	Lewis County	WA	Nate Hamilton	1993	27
139 6/8	21 5/8	22 0/8	17 4/8	4	4	Lewis County	WA	Marte Scheuffele	1995	28
138 4/8	22 5/8	22 4/8	18 5/8	5	5	Siskiyou County	CA	John Bridgewater	1980	29
137 6/8	20 3/8	22 0/8	15 6/8	5	5	Jackson County	OR	John Schauble	1986	30
137 2/8	20 2/8	19 7/8	16 1/8	6	5	Jackson County	OR	Steve Wirth	1983	31
137 1/8	21 2/8	20 1/8	16 1/8	4	6	Linn County	OR	Scot E. Lafond	1991	32
137 0/8	20 3/8	20 1/8	14 5/8	4	4	Mendocino County	CA	Russell L. Browning	1980	33
137 0/8	21 1/8	21 2/8	15 7/8	4	5	Linn County	OR	Charlie Endicott	1985	33
136 7/8	21 0/8	20 7/8	15 3/8	6	6	Skamania County	WA	Melvin W. Berry	1991	35
136 6/8	21 0/8	21 1/8	18 2/8	5	5	Linn County	OR	Tom Nichols	1985	36
136 5/8	21 1/8	22 1/8	17 1/8	4	5	Linn County	OR	Rebecca Saunders	1986	37
136 4/8	21 4/8	21 6/8	16 4/8	4	6	Clackamas County	OR	Craig Hyatt	1990	38
135 2/8	19 5/8	20 1/8	16 0/8	6	5	Linn County	OR	Dave Evans	1995	39
135 0/8	22 0/8	21 2/8	18 7/8	6	4	Jackson County	OR	Bob Staten	1964	40
134 5/8	21 0/8	16 0/8	16 2/8	5	4	Jackson County	OR	Milton L. Cady	1968	41
134 5/8	21 7/8	21 7/8	17 0/8	7	5	Trinity County	CA	Bob Auser	1981	41
134 4/8	22 5/8	21 4/8	15 6/8	4	4	Glenn County	CA	Steve Bashaw	1989	43
133 7/8	20 6/8	20 6/8	18 7/8	4	4	Jackson County	OR	Donald R. Pritchett	1966	44
133 7/8	19 4/8	21 6/8	13 7/8	7	7	Linn County	OR	J. C. James	1984	44
133 2/8	20 1/8	20 2/8	17 0/8	5	5	Jackson County	OR	Chester Stevenson	1921	46
133 1/8	18 7/8	17 6/8	15 3/8	5	5	Lane County	OR	Matt Dodson	1990	47
133 0/8	20 5/8	21 0/8	14 6/8	5	5	Benton County	OR	Robert W. Worthean	1982	48
132 7/8	21 1/8	20 0/8	13 4/8	5	6	Lewis County	WA	Marte Scheuffele	1981	49
132 7/8	20 0/8	20 0/8	14 7/8	5	5	Lane County	OR	Clyde Romero, Jr.	1991	49
132 6/8	20 1/8	20 6/8	18 0/8	4	5	Jackson County	OR	Stanley Moore	1962	51
132 5/8	22 0/8	21 0/8	16 1/8	7	7	Clackamas County	OR	Charlie Medlicott	1983	52
132 3/8	18 6/8	19 4/8	16 7/8	5	5	Jackson County	OR	Donald R. Pritchett	1966	53
132 2/8	20 5/8	21 7/8	16 7/8	6	6	Josephine County	OR	Marte Scheuffele	1973	54
132 1/8	20 2/8	19 6/8	18 4/8	5	7	Jackson County	OR	John Schauble	1985	55
131 7/8	22 0/8	21 6/8	16 7/8	4	4	Douglas County	OR	Jim Hodson	1987	56
131 7/8	19 1/8	18 0/8	18 5/8	5	5	Josephine County	OR	Richard J. Darner	1993	56
131 4/8	21 5/8	22 0/8	17 3/8	6	4	Multnomah County	OR	Dennis Thorud	1985	58
131 3/8	20 0/8	20 0/8	15 5/8	5	5	Jackson County	OR	Joe Williamson	1965	59
131 3/8	20 1/8	20 2/8	17 3/8	5	5	Douglas County	OR	Ken French	1988	59
131 3/8	20 4/8	20 6/8	17 3/8	5	5	Jackson County	OR	Leonard Scharf	1993	59
131 2/8	19 6/8	19 3/8	22 2/8	5	5	Linn County	OR	David F. Scheid	1968	62
131 2/8	21 2/8	21 4/8	18 2/8	5	4	Clatsop County	OR	B. G. Shurtleff	1979	62
131 1/8	19 4/8	19 4/8	14 5/8	5	5	Kitsap County	WA	Dale Axtman	1983	64
130 7/8	22 2/8	21 4/8	15 2/8	6	7	Benton County	OR	Chuck Warner	1991	65
130 7/8	21 0/8	19 0/8	17 1/8	5	6	Marion County	OR	Loren A. McLaughlin	1993	65
130 7/8	18 7/8	18 5/8	14 1/8	5	5	Linn County	OR	Smokey Crews	1996	65
130 5/8	20 1/8	21 3/8	18 5/8	4	4	Mendocino County	CA	Carl Musto	1994	68
130 4/8	19 0/8	19 2/8	19 5/8	5	5	Humboldt County	CA	Jim Dervin	1992	69
130 3/8	21 4/8	22 2/8	17 6/8	5	4	Glenn County	CA	Buck Devlin	1993	70
130 2/8	19 6/8	19 4/8	14 6/8	5	5	Lane County	OR	Steve Rogers	1992	71
130 1/8	19 0/8	18 7/8	15 1/8	5	5	Linn County	OR	Duane Etherington	1983	72
129 5/8	18 7/8	18 5/8	17 7/8	5	5	Colusa County	CA	Jay Overholtzer	1988	73
129 4/8	19 0/8	18 3/8	19 5/8	4	5	Jackson County	OR	Bruce B. Stamp	1988	74
129 3/8	26 1/8	25 3/8	19 2/8	5	3	Klamath County	OR	Troy Fennel	1964	75
129 3/8	21 4/8	21 1/8	16 7/8	5	5	Siskiyou County	CA	Daniel Franks	1991	75
129 1/8	20 4/8	20 4/8	16 3/8	4	4	Douglas County	OR	Tom E. Tipton	1988	77
129 0/8	21 1/8	20 4/8	16 4/8	5	4	Lane County	OR	Scott P. Lawson	1994	78
128 7/8	18 2/8	18 2/8	16 3/8	5	5	Lane County	OR	Dave E. Jarrett	1982	79
128 5/8	19 1/8	18 7/8	15 7/8	5	5	Lake County	CA	Joe Emmons	1989	80
128 5/8	19 6/8	19 7/8	16 5/8	5	5	Mendocino County	CA	Rodney E. Carley	1993	80
128 5/8	23 1/8	23 4/8	17 7/8	4	5	Josephine County	OR	Lee Darrow	1995	80
128 3/8	19 3/8	19 7/8	14 5/8	4	5	Benton County	OR	Ray G. Kelton	1993	83
128 3/8	20 3/8	19 7/8	15 1/8	6	5	Humboldt County	CA	Dan Noga	1994	83
128 2/8	19 3/8	19 4/8	14 4/8	8	5	Clackamas County	OR	John Christiansen	1981	85
128 2/8	20 1/8	20 3/8	15 2/8	6	5	Linn County	OR	Steve Richards	1983	85
128 1/8	20 6/8	20 7/8	17 1/8	5	5	Mendocino County	CA	Charles C. Pacheco	1993	87
127 7/8	19 2/8	20 3/8	18 7/8	5	5	Linn County	OR	Chuck Warner	1987	88
127 5/8	22 0/8	22 1/8	16 3/8	6	5	Josephine County	OR	Frank Sanders	1991	89
127 5/8	21 1/8	20 1/8	16 1/8	5	5	Douglas County	OR	Joe Hulburt	1991	89
127 4/8	21 3/8	21 1/8	19 6/8	5	5	Linn County	OR	John Stone	1981	91
127 3/8	21 4/8	20 2/8	19 7/8	4	4	Mendocino County	CA	Lawrence Christensen	1991	92
127 2/8	20 2/8	19 6/8	14 6/8	5	5	Trinity County	CA	George Flournoy, Jr.	1986	93
127 1/8	18 7/8	19 5/8	16 1/8	6	5	Mendocino County	CA	James Buffum	1965	94
126 7/8	19 6/8	20 2/8	17 7/8	5	4	Snohomish County	WA	David Randolph	1997	95
126 5/8	18 2/8	17 4/8	13 7/8	5	5	Douglas County	OR	Kenneth A. French	1989	96
126 4/8	17 1/8	18 5/8	14 6/8	5	5	Linn County	OR	Dennis H. Wessels	1985	97
126 2/8	18 3/8	17 5/8	14 0/8	5	5	Lane County	OR	Phil Hunter	1995	98
125 7/8	19 1/8	19 4/8	13 7/8	5	5	Marion County	OR	Doug Harris	1985	99
125 6/8	19 3/8	18 5/8	14 2/8	4	4	Siskiyou County	CA	Cliff Dewell	1969	100
125 4/8	19 7/8	21 6/8	19 6/8	6	6	Josephine County	OR	Dave Hall	1983	101
125 3/8	18 1/8	18 6/8	16 1/8	5	5	Josephine County	OR	Lee Darrow	1973	102
125 3/8	22 0/8	23 4/8	19 3/8	5	4	Lane County	OR	Joe Lilley	1992	102

COLUMBIAN BLACKTAIL DEER (TYPICAL ANTLERS)

Minimum Score 90 — Continued

SCORE	LENGTH OF MAIN BEAM R	LENGTH OF MAIN BEAM L	INSIDE SPREAD	NUMBER OF POINTS R	NUMBER OF POINTS L	AREA	STATE/PROVINCE	HUNTER'S NAME	DATE	RANK
125 2/8	19 6/8	19 0/8	11 6/8	5	5	Douglas County	OR	Bruce B. Stamp	1990	104
125 0/8	18 5/8	17 2/8	14 4/8	4	4	Jackson County	OR	Robert J. Jensen	1994	105
124 7/8	19 2/8	19 2/8	14 1/8	4	4	Humboldt County	CA	Mike Taylor	1987	106
124 7/8	18 0/8	19 0/8	15 3/8	5	4	Alameda County	CA	Eugene Damron	1988	106
124 7/8	20 0/8	20 2/8	14 3/8	5	4	Jackson County	OR	Robert L. Freeman	1994	106
124 6/8	20 7/8	19 0/8	16 6/8	4	5	Clackamas County	OR	Joseph Suire	1983	109
124 4/8	22 4/8	22 3/8	20 0/8	5	3	Clackamas County	OR	Glen Berry	1995	110
124 2/8	20 0/8	20 6/8	16 4/8	4	5	Lewis County	WA	Sandy Tyler	1957	111
124 2/8	19 0/8	19 5/8	17 2/8	4	5	Lane County	OR	David Wright Bucknum	1989	111
124 0/8	19 0/8	19 2/8	19 7/8	4	4	Kitsap County	WA	Boyd Edward Shelby, Jr.	1995	113
123 7/8	17 3/8	17 4/8	15 1/8	5	5	Siskiyou County	CA	Bill Collinsworth	1983	114
123 7/8	19 0/8	19 5/8	14 3/8	5	5	Marion County	OR	Mike Miller	1996	114
123 6/8	19 5/8	20 0/8	16 2/8	5	5	Lane County	OR	Steve Rogers	1990	116
123 5/8	19 0/8	19 0/8	15 1/8	5	5	Lewis County	WA	Bob Eisele	1991	117
123 5/8	21 6/8	22 1/8	18 1/8	5	4	King County	WA	Kelly McGuinness	1992	117
123 4/8	21 3/8	21 7/8	16 2/8	4	4	Thurston County	WA	Al Kowalski	1978	119
123 4/8	19 0/8	20 0/8	14 4/8	4	5	Lewis County	WA	Randal E. White	1990	119
123 4/8	19 0/8	19 6/8	15 2/8	6	4	Linn County	OR	Tad Jones	1993	119
123 3/8	18 6/8	19 1/8	17 3/8	5	5	Trinity County	CA	Glen S. Ceccon	1987	122
123 1/8	20 0/8	20 3/8	16 1/8	5	6	Trinity County	CA	Gary Mayberry	1968	123
123 0/8	20 0/8	21 0/8	14 4/8	6	5	Klickitat County	WA	Larry Ramsey	1977	124
123 0/8	18 6/8	18 7/8	14 6/8	6	6	Jackson County	OR	Larry Frost	1984	124
123 0/8	21 0/8	20 6/8	15 0/8	5	5	Clackamas County	OR	Alan M. Taylor	1991	124
123 0/8	19 1/8	19 2/8	14 0/8	5	5	Jefferson County	WA	David Neault	1996	124
122 7/8	19 1/8	20 4/8	16 1/8	4	4	Trinity County	CA	Loran G. August	1981	128
122 5/8	17 7/8	18 1/8	15 3/8	5	5	Trinity County	CA	Ted Lohse	1985	129
122 5/8	19 0/8	19 1/8	15 1/8	5	4	Mendocino County	CA	Mark Masamori	1992	129
122 5/8	19 2/8	19 5/8	15 1/8	4	4	Linn County	OR	Mark Penninger	1993	129
122 3/8	19 1/8	18 6/8	17 1/8	6	6	Josephine County	OR	Grant McCarty	1994	132
122 1/8	19 5/8	19 5/8	17 4/8	5	6	Jackson County	OR	Richard G. Speer	1965	133
122 0/8	19 7/8	20 4/8	15 6/8	4	4	Contra Costa County	CA	Donald M. Graves	1990	134
121 7/8	20 5/8	20 6/8	15 7/8	5	5	Lewis County	WA	Robert E. Hill	1988	135
121 4/8	20 6/8	20 5/8	17 4/8	5	4	Lane County	OR	Bradley M. Dorsing	1991	136
121 4/8	17 7/8	16 5/8	15 0/8	4	4	Linn County	OR	Richard L. Rounds	1991	136
121 3/8	15 5/8	15 2/8	14 0/8	5	5	Humboldt County	CA	Doug Walker	1965	138
121 3/8	19 7/8	18 7/8	16 4/8	7	5	Trinity County	CA	Mark Greving	1982	138
121 2/8	22 4/8	22 4/8	22 2/8	4	4	Humboldt County	CA	Arthur Cain	1991	140
121 1/8	20 3/8	20 6/8	18 2/8	4	3	Yamhill County	OR	Ray Kelton	1981	141
121 0/8	18 0/8	17 0/8	14 4/8	5	5	Benton County	OR	Larry D. Jones	1966	142
120 6/8	18 5/8	19 0/8	15 4/8	5	5	Humboldt County	CA	Joe Henry	1980	143
120 6/8	20 0/8	19 6/8	18 2/8	4	3	Linn County	OR	Jim R. Brown	1987	143
120 3/8	17 1/8	18 1/8	12 7/8	5	5	Santa Cruz County	CA	Douglas G. Bonetti	1987	145
120 3/8	19 2/8	18 7/8	18 1/8	6	6	Glenn County	CA	Jim Alves	1987	145
120 3/8	20 5/8	21 1/8	14 2/8	5	6	Linn County	OR	Bob Sartini	1997	145
120 2/8	21 2/8	20 3/8	17 1/8	5	5	Linn County	OR	Steve L. Winterstein	1991	148
120 1/8	18 3/8	18 4/8	15 5/8	5	5	Lane County	OR	Dale Drilling	1990	149
120 0/8	21 4/8	22 0/8	19 6/8	4	4	Marion County	OR	Norman D. Arnold	1992	150
119 6/8	20 0/8	20 3/8	16 2/8	4	4	Pacific County	WA	John Higgins	1973	151
119 5/8	20 2/8	20 0/8	16 1/8	5	5	Marion County	OR	Ronald A. Bersin	1994	152
119 4/8	20 5/8	20 4/8	16 2/8	5	4	Mendocino County	CA	Edward V. Moore	1989	153
119 3/8	21 5/8	21 4/8	17 3/8	4	3	Humboldt County	CA	Art Young	1918	154
119 0/8	20 6/8	19 2/8	15 6/8	5	5	Kitsap County	WA	Bob Devine	1986	155
119 0/8	20 3/8	19 5/8	19 0/8	5	4	Mendocino County	CA	Matt Burke	1996	155
118 6/8	20 4/8	20 2/8	14 6/8	4	5	Skamania County	WA	Frank Adkins	1967	157
118 6/8	18 4/8	17 7/8	14 4/8	4	4	Santa Clara County	CA	Eugene Damron	1987	157
118 5/8	19 0/8	19 5/8	19 5/8	4	4	Sonoma County	CA	Paul Fiedorek	1987	159
118 4/8	20 3/8	19 7/8	19 2/8	4	5	Slesse Creek	BC	Ken Davidson	1987	160
118 4/8	20 0/8	20 3/8	14 4/8	4	4	Lincoln County	OR	Terry Smith	1992	160
118 4/8	20 6/8	19 4/8	14 0/8	5	5	Lane County	OR	Cameron Hanes	1994	160
118 4/8	18 1/8	18 2/8	17 0/8	5	5	Kitsap County	WA	Boyd E. Shelby, Jr.	1997	160
118 2/8	18 2/8	18 7/8	14 2/8	5	5	Linn County	OR	Kevin Christopher	1994	164
117 7/8	18 0/8	18 1/8	15 7/8	5	4	Benton County	OR	Chuck Warner	1992	165
117 6/8	19 4/8	18 4/8	14 2/8	4	5	Island County	WA	Robin Brigge	1996	166
117 4/8	18 0/8	18 2/8	14 1/8	5	5	Benton County	OR	Chris Reed	1970	167
117 4/8	18 4/8	18 4/8	15 6/8	4	4	Sonoma County	CA	Jerry Maytum	1994	167
117 3/8	18 5/8	19 4/8	15 1/8	4	4	Jackson County	OR	Duane A. Brentano	1972	169
117 3/8	18 1/8	18 3/8	16 3/8	4	4	Humboldt County	CA	Dennis A. McClelland	1989	169
117 3/8	18 3/8	19 7/8	16 3/8	4	4	Lincoln County	OR	Dianna Rorie	1991	169
117 2/8	18 3/8	18 6/8	13 2/8	5	4	Clackamas County	OR	Dan Sandberg	1992	172
117 0/8	17 0/8	17 4/8	16 4/8	5	5	Lane County	OR	Brad Dorsing	1992	173
116 7/8	18 6/8	18 2/8	13 7/8	5	5	Kitsap County	WA	Don D. Axtman	1990	174
116 5/8	19 5/8	20 3/8	12 5/8	4	5	Pacific County	WA	Smokey Crews	1969	175
116 5/8	20 1/8	20 7/8	17 3/8	4	4	Lincoln County	OR	Fred Rorie	1990	175
116 5/8	20 4/8	21 2/8	19 1/8	4	4	Snohomish County	WA	Jerry Solie	1995	175
116 3/8	16 4/8	16 4/8	14 5/8	5	5	Mission	BC	Albert Klimmer	1994	178
116 3/8	20 0/8	20 1/8	18 6/8	5	4	Humboldt County	CA	Robert C. Gregory	1996	178
116 2/8	18 7/8	19 7/8	19 0/8	4	4	Jackson County	OR	Ray Gibson	1962	180
116 2/8	18 6/8	18 4/8	16 6/8	5	4	Trinity County	CA	Mike Lindley	1983	180

COLUMBIAN BLACKTAIL DEER (TYPICAL ANTLERS)

Minimum Score 90 — Continued

SCORE	LENGTH OF MAIN BEAM R	L	INSIDE SPREAD	NUMBER OF POINTS R	L	AREA	STATE/PROVINCE	HUNTER'S NAME	DATE	RANK
116 2/8	17 4/8	17 2/8	14 0/8	5	4	Clackamas County	OR	W. Troy Stevens	1988	180
116 1/8	19 0/8	19 4/8	15 3/8	5	4	King County	WA	John Martin	1983	183
116 0/8	18 1/8	16 7/8	17 6/8	5	5	Jackson County	OR	Billy Mathews	1996	184
115 6/8	19 6/8	19 6/8	16 6/8	5	4	Clackamas County	OR	Jack Smith	1981	185
115 6/8	19 2/8	18 2/8	18 0/8	5	5	Siskiyou County	CA	Fred Searle	1983	185
115 6/8	22 0/8	22 3/8	15 0/8	4	5	Benton County	OR	Richard Rowen	1994	185
115 5/8	17 4/8	17 4/8	13 7/8	5	5	Siskiyou County	CA	Mike Garretson	1981	188
115 5/8	17 0/8	17 1/8	14 5/8	5	5	Polk County	OR	Randy Gunn	1981	188
115 4/8	22 2/8	21 7/8	19 2/8	5	3	Lane County	OR	Ken Holland	1988	190
115 2/8	19 4/8	19 4/8	16 2/8	4	4	Humboldt County	CA	J. E. Grundman	1963	191
115 2/8	16 6/8	16 4/8	15 4/8	5	5	Douglas County	OR	Kevin Dicke	1989	191
115 1/8	16 6/8	16 3/8	15 7/8	5	5	Sumas Mtn.	BC	Peter L. Halbig	1985	193
115 1/8	17 4/8	18 0/8	14 3/8	5	4	Marion County	OR	Ronald J. Miller	1989	193
115 0/8	21 2/8	21 0/8	17 1/8	6	4	Marion County	OR	Chuck Lynde	1989	195
115 0/8	20 6/8	21 5/8	20 4/8	4	4	Mendocino County	CA	Doug Burgard	1995	195
114 4/8	17 1/8	17 6/8	19 4/8	4	4	Clackamas County	OR	Darrell J. Scheffer	1995	197
114 1/8	20 1/8	19 3/8	15 5/8	5	4	Kitsap County	WA	Boyd Shelby	1989	198
114 0/8	17 3/8	16 6/8	16 0/8	5	4	Clackamas County	OR	Dave Showerman	1982	199
113 7/8	18 3/8	19 3/8	11 0/8	4	6	Siskiyou County	CA	William J. Bagdasarian	1993	200
113 7/8	17 6/8	17 2/8	14 3/8	6	4	Lane County	OR	Cameron Hanes	1994	200
113 6/8	17 3/8	15 6/8	15 0/8	5	5	Benton County	OR	Gregory M. McHuron	1966	202
113 5/8	18 7/8	19 1/8	18 3/8	4	4	Columbia County	OR	Cory Miller	1995	203
113 4/8	18 1/8	17 5/8	15 2/8	4	4	Mendocino County	CA	Jeff S. Spangler	1982	204
113 4/8	19 2/8	19 2/8	19 0/8	4	5	Linn County	OR	John Stone	1986	204
113 4/8	19 0/8	19 3/8	20 3/8	5	4	Sonoma County	CA	Jerry Giovannoni	1994	204
113 2/8	18 2/8	17 5/8	16 0/8	4	4	King County	WA	Vick Stevens	1984	207
113 2/8	17 0/8	16 7/8	12 2/8	4	4	Lane County	OR	Neil Summers	1991	207
113 0/8	17 2/8	17 3/8	13 4/8	5	5	Lewis County	WA	Don Kennedy	1989	209
112 7/8	19 1/8	17 6/8	14 1/8	4	5	Skagit County	WA	J. B. Bright	1986	210
112 7/8	18 3/8	19 1/8	21 2/8	4	3	King County	WA	Darin Evans Brandt	1995	210
112 5/8	21 2/8	20 4/8	14 1/8	5	5	King County	WA	Greg Tedlund	1984	212
112 5/8	18 2/8	18 5/8	13 5/8	5	5	Yamhill County	OR	Dean A. McMullen	1992	212
112 5/8	21 0/8	20 2/8	16 7/8	3	4	Pierce County	WA	Brandon J. White	1997	212
112 4/8	16 0/8	15 1/8	13 4/8	5	5	Trinity County	CA	Dennis Schroer	1982	215
112 4/8	18 6/8	17 6/8	14 2/8	5	5	Lane County	OR	Steve Rogers	1989	215
112 3/8	16 7/8	16 3/8	13 7/8	5	5	Snohomish County	WA	Jack Davis	1975	217
112 3/8	17 4/8	19 2/8	13 6/8	4	5	Douglas County	OR	Ken French	1980	217
112 3/8	20 5/8	15 7/8	18 1/8	5	5	Lane County	OR	Chad T. Montgomery	1994	217
112 2/8	18 5/8	19 1/8	15 2/8	4	4	Pacific County	WA	Leon Poindexter	1968	220
112 1/8	17 1/8	17 4/8	13 3/8	5	5	Benton County	OR	Gary Nyden	1986	221
112 0/8	18 4/8	19 2/8	16 4/8	4	4	Lane County	OR	Ken Kalinowski	1988	222
111 7/8	17 7/8	17 0/8	14 5/8	4	4	Pacific County	WA	Smokey Crews	1967	223
111 5/8	20 0/8	19 4/8	15 5/8	5	5	Pierce County	WA	Randy Cole	1989	224
111 5/8	16 4/8	15 5/8	12 3/8	5	5	Lincoln County	OR	Jeffrey D. Messmer	1989	224
111 3/8	16 0/8	17 3/8	17 4/8	5	4	Linn County	OR	Chuck Warner	1985	226
111 3/8	19 5/8	19 6/8	16 3/8	5	4	Lane County	OR	David Chapman	1986	226
111 2/8	21 1/8	20 5/8	15 6/8	3	6	Lane County	OR	Brad Dorsing	1994	228
111 0/8	19 2/8	18 4/8	14 4/8	4	3	Skagit County	WA	Sam Ingram	1988	229
111 0/8	18 3/8	18 2/8	14 7/8	5	5	Lane County	OR	Stuart Johnson	1994	229
111 0/8	21 0/8	20 6/8	17 6/8	4	5	Mendocino County	CA	Mark Masamori	1997	229
110 7/8	18 3/8	17 0/8	16 3/8	4	4	Jackson County	OR	Dale K. Marcy	1966	232
110 7/8	17 5/8	18 3/8	14 5/8	4	5	Marion County	OR	David Conway	1991	232
110 6/8	18 4/8	17 7/8	17 0/8	4	4	Del Norte County	CA	Michael Penn	1979	234
110 6/8	20 6/8	21 5/8	19 4/8	3	3	Contra Costa County	CA	Richard L. Westervelt	1987	234
110 6/8	21 1/8	21 4/8	22 0/8	2	2	Mendocino County	CA	Ken Bilstein	1995	234
110 5/8	19 7/8	20 3/8	13 4/8	4	6	Jackson County	OR	Dr. G. Scott Jennings	1979	237
110 4/8	17 1/8	17 3/8	13 6/8	4	4	Clark County	WA	Larry D. Nahrstedt	1968	238
110 4/8	17 0/8	18 7/8	17 4/8	4	4	Marin County	CA	Howard C. Gold	1976	238
110 4/8	18 4/8	18 4/8	15 6/8	4	4	Pierce County	WA	Greg Paige	1990	238
110 3/8	16 1/8	15 1/8	15 7/8	5	5	Wild Deer Lake	BC	Guy Anttila	1970	241
110 3/8	19 3/8	20 0/8	13 6/8	6	5	North Vancouver	BC	Fred Day	1970	241
110 2/8	19 6/8	20 0/8	17 4/8	5	5	Lane County	OR	Richard M. Cook	1982	243
109 7/8	22 0/8	21 3/8	14 5/8	5	5	Linn County	OR	Steve Gilbert	1982	244
109 6/8	21 1/8	20 7/8	16 4/8	3	4	Lewis County	WA	Barney Johnson	1974	245
109 6/8	17 4/8	18 2/8	18 2/8	4	4	Santa Cruz County	CA	Robert Alan Nottingham	1992	245
109 5/8	20 4/8	19 4/8	15 3/8	5	4	Douglas County	OR	Teddy Rainville	1980	247
109 5/8	19 1/8	21 0/8	14 5/8	3	3	Lake County	CA	Paul W. Farina	1983	247
109 5/8	16 2/8	16 2/8	14 5/8	4	4	Siskiyou County	CA	Ralph Atkinson	1984	247
109 5/8	17 1/8	17 2/8	15 7/8	4	4	Clackamas County	OR	Randy Teeney	1985	247
109 5/8	18 4/8	18 6/8	15 5/8	4	4	Lane County	OR	Wm E. Sweetland	1985	247
109 5/8	21 4/8	19 7/8	19 5/8	3	3	Santa Clara County	CA	Eugene Damron	1991	247
109 5/8	19 3/8	19 6/8	13 3/8	5	5	Trinity County	CA	Michael Chiera	1995	247
109 4/8	19 6/8	19 7/8	14 2/8	6	5	Pierce County	WA	Don Axtman	1989	254
109 4/8	16 5/8	16 4/8	12 6/8	5	5	Clackamas County	OR	Nick G. Kathrein	1991	254
109 3/8	17 0/8	17 5/8	14 4/8	6	5	Lane County	OR	Mark Klein	1982	256
109 3/8	18 3/8	17 2/8	16 7/8	4	4	Clackamas County	OR	Stanley P. Stagl	1989	256
109 3/8	17 0/8	17 7/8	17 5/8	4	4	Cowlitz County	WA	Tom Heltemes	1990	256
109 3/8	18 3/8	17 0/8	15 1/8	4	3	Alameda County	CA	William Young, Jr. DVM	1991	256

COLUMBIAN BLACKTAIL DEER (TYPICAL ANTLERS)

Minimum Score 90
Continued

SCORE	LENGTH OF MAIN BEAM R	LENGTH OF MAIN BEAM L	INSIDE SPREAD	NUMBER OF POINTS R	NUMBER OF POINTS L	AREA	STATE/PROVINCE	HUNTER'S NAME	DATE	RANK
109 2/8	17 5/8	16 5/8	14 2/8	5	5	Lane County	OR	Brandy Knight	1991	260
109 1/8	19 7/8	19 7/8	14 1/8	5	4	Lewis County	WA	Glen Marquis	1990	261
109 0/8	20 0/8	20 0/8	15 6/8	4	3	Josephine County	OR	Sam Burten	1987	262
109 0/8	18 0/8	18 4/8	15 4/8	4	4	Humboldt County	CA	John Roley	1996	262
108 7/8	17 6/8	19 1/8	13 7/8	5	5	Jackson County	OR	Joe Williamson	1963	264
108 7/8	16 7/8	17 0/8	13 5/8	5	5	Josephine County	OR	Michael Penn	1983	264
108 6/8	20 2/8	20 0/8	20 4/8	3	3	Linn County	OR	Gary S. Solberg	1994	266
108 5/8	19 2/8	18 4/8	16 3/8	3	3	Douglas County	OR	Rick Gabbard	1984	267
108 4/8	16 1/8	16 2/8	11 6/8	5	4	Clackamas County	OR	Ed Franzen	1985	268
108 4/8	18 0/8	17 7/8	16 2/8	5	4	Lane County	OR	Jim Howell	1988	268
108 3/8	19 1/8	19 2/8	13 1/8	4	3	Mendocino County	CA	Gaylen Kessel	1988	270
108 1/8	19 1/8	18 4/8	15 2/8	6	6	Skagit County	WA	Charles Kager	1988	271
108 1/8	18 0/8	17 5/8	17 5/8	4	4	Sonoma County	CA	Robert Larson	1992	271
108 1/8	21 2/8	19 2/8	12 6/8	5	5	King County	WA	Thomas E. Pugmire	1992	271
108 0/8	18 3/8	19 5/8	16 0/8	4	4	Trinity County	CA	Michael Hopper	1989	274
108 0/8	18 0/8	17 2/8	16 4/8	4	5	Lane County	OR	Dwight Schuh	1989	274
108 0/8	16 6/8	18 4/8	12 7/8	6	5	Douglas County	OR	Bruce B. Stamp	1994	274
107 7/8	17 2/8	17 7/8	16 1/8	4	4	Tehama County	CA	Ernie Owen	1992	277
107 7/8	20 6/8	20 7/8	19 7/8	3	3	Sonoma County	CA	Michael Bradeen	1992	277
107 6/8	18 2/8	18 4/8	19 3/8	3	4	Trinity County	CA	Dennis Alan Betts	1980	279
107 6/8	17 2/8	17 4/8	13 0/8	4	3	Lane County	OR	James A. Conway	1988	279
107 6/8	18 1/8	18 0/8	15 4/8	4	4	Douglas County	OR	Joe Cordonier	1989	279
107 5/8	17 5/8	18 5/8	14 1/8	5	4	Clackamas County	OR	Bob Manley	1982	282
107 5/8	21 2/8	20 2/8	16 7/8	3	3	Lane County	OR	Rick Willhite	1993	282
107 4/8	21 4/8	22 3/8	19 4/8	2	2	Trinity County	CA	John R. Sample	1989	284
107 4/8	17 7/8	18 6/8	14 1/8	5	5	Lane County	OR	Tad Jones	1995	284
107 3/8	18 2/8	19 0/8	17 5/8	4	4	Lane County	OR	Cameron Hanes	1993	286
107 3/8	18 2/8	19 2/8	12 3/8	5	5	Lewis County	WA	Michael E. Croft	1997	286
107 2/8	17 5/8	17 5/8	16 0/8	4	4	Mendocino County	CA	Edwin Thomas	1997	288
107 1/8	15 7/8	15 4/8	13 7/8	4	4	Lincoln County	OR	Ray Kelton	1982	289
107 1/8	19 3/8	19 3/8	17 5/8	3	4	Clackamas County	OR	Guy P. Hurlbert	1995	289
107 0/8	17 5/8	16 7/8	12 4/8	5	5	Lane County	OR	Neil Summers	1990	291
106 7/8	18 3/8	18 2/8	16 3/8	4	3	Skamania County	WA	Steve Shipp	1984	292
106 7/8	18 3/8	19 1/8	13 3/8	4	4	King County	WA	Mike Adkins	1995	292
106 6/8	19 3/8	20 0/8	19 6/8	4	3	Contra Costa County	CA	Frank Sanders	1990	294
106 6/8	17 6/8	17 4/8	16 4/8	4	5	Mendocino County	CA	Joseph N. Fowles	1995	294
106 5/8	18 2/8	18 7/8	18 1/8	4	4	Pierce County	WA	Kenneth Villines	1996	296
106 3/8	17 6/8	17 0/8	14 1/8	4	5	Pierce County	WA	Kenneth D. Villines	1995	297
106 2/8	17 1/8	16 3/8	13 6/8	5	4	Lewis County	WA	Mike Mussman	1984	298
106 1/8	19 4/8	19 0/8	12 7/8	3	4	Trinity County	CA	Mike Lindley	1981	299
106 0/8	17 4/8	17 6/8	17 7/8	4	5	Trinity County	CA	Chuck Adams	1982	300
106 0/8	17 5/8	17 5/8	14 2/8	4	4	Skamania County	WA	Jeffrey L. Kujala	1984	300
106 0/8	17 6/8	17 7/8	14 6/8	5	4	Lane County	OR	Dan Rogers	1989	300
105 7/8	19 0/8	19 0/8	14 5/8	6	6	Kitsap County	WA	Boyd E. Shelby, Jr.	1992	303
105 7/8	17 7/8	17 3/8	14 7/8	4	5	Mendocino County	CA	Michael Christensen	1995	303
105 5/8	17 5/8	18 5/8	15 7/8	5	5	Cowlitz County	WA	Jay Wall	1994	305
105 5/8	18 5/8	18 4/8	19 6/8	5	5	Trinity County	CA	John R. Sample	1996	305
105 4/8	16 6/8	15 4/8	14 6/8	4	4	Mendocino County	CA	Serge Engurasoff	1998	307
105 3/8	17 3/8	17 3/8	15 5/8	3	4	Coos County	OR	Gary Scorby	1971	308
105 3/8	19 3/8	19 2/8	15 6/8	7	5	Columbia County	OR	Leo E. Eickhoff	1995	308
105 1/8	18 6/8	19 2/8	15 7/8	3	3	Stanislaus County	CA	Harold Arnold	1970	310
105 1/8	18 1/8	18 1/8	18 4/8	3	3	San Mateo County	CA	John Grochowski	1985	310
104 6/8	17 3/8	17 2/8	13 6/8	5	4	Coos County	OR	Darryl S. Herndon	1989	312
104 5/8	16 2/8	16 2/8	12 7/8	4	4	King County	WA	Ken Gettman	1987	313
104 5/8	17 3/8	18 0/8	15 5/8	4	4	Jackson County	OR	Robon Evans	1992	313
104 5/8	16 5/8	17 3/8	11 5/8	4	4	Linn County	OR	Gary Johnston	1992	313
104 3/8	18 5/8	18 3/8	15 3/8	4	4	Polk County	OR	Tim Nolan	1987	316
104 3/8	17 4/8	18 2/8	16 5/8	4	4	Lane County	OR	Cameron Hanes	1990	316
104 3/8	19 7/8	20 0/8	12 1/8	4	4	Alameda County	CA	Wayne Piersol	1993	316
104 2/8	16 4/8	17 0/8	16 2/8	4	4	Lake County	CA	Phil Phillips	1991	319
104 2/8	17 2/8	17 4/8	16 2/8	5	4	Mendocino County	CA	Michael Christensen	1991	319
104 1/8	15 4/8	15 6/8	13 3/8	5	5	Clackamas County	OR	Ben Cook	1988	321
104 0/8	18 6/8	21 6/8	15 1/8	5	5	Trinity County	CA	Chuck Adams	1982	322
104 0/8	18 0/8	17 5/8	17 2/8	4	4	Tehama County	CA	Robert Stockton	1993	322
103 6/8	15 7/8	16 4/8	12 2/8	5	5	Linn County	OR	Doug Bashor	1986	324
103 5/8	17 7/8	18 3/8	15 5/8	3	3	Linn County	OR	Gary Burns	1981	325
103 4/8	19 0/8	19 5/8	13 2/8	3	3	Lane County	OR	Randy Cook	1988	326
103 4/8	16 6/8	17 1/8	13 7/8	5	4	Lane County	OR	Neil Summers	1989	326
103 3/8	16 7/8	16 6/8	17 0/8	3	4	Sonoma County	CA	Arnie Dado	1986	328
103 2/8	17 7/8	17 7/8	15 0/8	4	4	Lewis County	WA	Charles L. Hunt	1990	329
103 2/8	15 7/8	16 0/8	16 3/8	4	4	Polk County	OR	Jon Simonson	1995	329
103 2/8	16 6/8	16 5/8	13 6/8	4	4	Linn County	OR	Daniel L. Sommers	1997	329
103 1/8	18 5/8	18 5/8	18 1/8	3	3	Lake County	CA	Arnie Dado	1992	332
103 0/8	15 5/8	15 0/8	14 0/8	5	5	Mendocino County	CA	Gregg L. Welch	1982	333
103 0/8	19 2/8	19 0/8	14 4/8	5	3	Clark County	WA	W. R. "Rick" Hassler	1988	333
103 0/8	20 1/8	20 0/8	15 6/8	3	2	Tehama County	CA	Gary Shinn	1989	333
103 0/8	16 6/8	17 2/8	12 4/8	4	4	Santa Clara County	CA	Thomas L. Liston	1990	333
103 0/8	18 6/8	18 7/8	16 6/8	3	4	Josephine County	OR	Brain Day	1994	333

COLUMBIAN BLACKTAIL DEER (TYPICAL ANTLERS)

Minimum Score 90 — Continued

SCORE	LENGTH OF MAIN BEAM R	L	INSIDE SPREAD	NUMBER OF POINTS R	L	AREA	STATE/PROVINCE	HUNTER'S NAME	DATE	RANK
102 7/8	18 5/8	18 0/8	14 2/8	4	5	Lane County	OR	Larry D. Jones	1997	338
102 6/8	17 4/8	17 4/8	17 4/8	3	3	Polk County	OR	Robert L. Ball	1975	339
102 5/8	16 7/8	16 6/8	14 5/8	4	4	Deschutes County	OR	Steve L. Stilwell	1976	340
102 4/8	18 0/8	18 0/8	14 4/8	4	3	Mendocino County	CA	Doug Burgard	1995	341
102 3/8	18 4/8	19 1/8	16 5/8	4	4	Siskiyou County	CA	Terry Proctor	1988	342
102 2/8	17 7/8	16 5/8	12 0/8	3	4	Clackamas County	OR	A. Corey Heath	1980	343
102 0/8	17 2/8	17 0/8	13 6/8	4	4	Jackson County	OR	George Miller	1966	344
102 0/8	17 3/8	16 6/8	13 0/8	5	4	Lane County	OR	Bruce Stevens	1995	344
101 6/8	18 2/8	18 6/8	14 6/8	4	3	Josephine County	OR	Thomas J. Hoffman	1994	346
101 6/8	18 3/8	19 6/8	15 3/8	5	4	Josephine County	OR	Sam Burton	1995	346
101 4/8	18 5/8	17 5/8	15 1/8	5	5	King County	WA	Mike D. Dunham	1987	348
101 3/8	17 0/8	17 4/8	15 3/8	4	3	Jackson County	OR	Dr. G. Scott Jennings	1959	349
101 2/8	17 1/8	18 2/8	13 4/8	4	3	Lane County	OR	Michael J. Fuller	1996	350
101 0/8	13 3/8	17 1/8	15 0/8	4	5	Lincoln County	OR	Terry W. Smith	1996	351
100 7/8	17 1/8	17 2/8	14 7/8	4	4	Marshall Creek	BC	Ken Scheer	1988	352
100 6/8	15 6/8	15 5/8	15 4/8	4	5	Klamath County	OR	Dr. George Miller	1964	353
100 6/8	18 1/8	18 0/8	16 2/8	3	3	Humboldt County	CA	Steven Tisdale	1993	353
100 5/8	17 0/8	17 4/8	13 7/8	5	4	Clackamas County	OR	Stanley P. Stagl	1990	355
100 4/8	18 7/8	18 3/8	15 4/8	3	4	Washington County	OR	Everett A. Proctor	1992	356
100 1/8	16 7/8	16 6/8	13 7/8	4	4	Douglas County	OR	James F. Rayner	1988	357
100 1/8	18 4/8	18 5/8	11 5/8	4	5	Lane County	OR	Cameron Hanes	1992	357
100 1/8	16 7/8	16 7/8	13 3/8	4	4	Lincoln County	OR	Terry W. Smith	1994	357
100 1/8	19 0/8	18 5/8	11 5/8	3	3	Multnomah County	OR	Marc B. Caldwell	1996	357
100 0/8	18 2/8	18 5/8	14 2/8	3	4	Kitsap County	WA	Boyd E. Shelby, Jr.	1990	361
99 6/8	20 6/8	20 0/8	14 0/8	2	2	Pacific County	WA	Robert A. Brown	1965	362
99 6/8	17 1/8	17 2/8	14 6/8	5	4	Humboldt County	CA	Greg Gottschalk	1990	362
99 6/8	18 3/8	18 3/8	16 4/8	4	3	Linn County	OR	Keith Julien	1994	362
99 6/8	17 4/8	18 1/8	15 0/8	3	4	Sonoma County	CA	Ed Fanchin	1998	362
99 5/8	17 3/8	18 1/8	12 7/8	4	4	Lewis County	WA	Eric H. Ames	1989	366
99 5/8	16 5/8	17 0/8	13 7/8	5	4	Clackamas County	OR	Tim Streight	1990	366
99 3/8	17 5/8	18 0/8	15 1/8	3	3	Siskiyou County	CA	Dave S. Semple	1984	368
99 3/8	16 2/8	16 0/8	15 1/8	4	4	Clark County	WA	Jerry K. Wake	1992	368
99 1/8	19 2/8	18 5/8	11 3/8	4	3	Lincoln County	OR	Fred Rorie	1988	370
99 1/8	16 1/8	14 2/8	10 7/8	5	6	Durrance Lake	BC	Klaus Wolff	1996	370
99 1/8	17 7/8	18 3/8	13 1/8	3	4	King County	WA	Todd Bosnick	1997	370
99 0/8	16 3/8	16 5/8	14 0/8	5	5	Lincoln County	OR	Charles M. Roeser	1974	373
99 0/8	21 2/8	19 7/8	15 6/8	4	5	Santa Clara County	CA	Mike Walker	1979	373
99 0/8	16 6/8	16 6/8	12 6/8	4	4	Mendocino County	CA	Russell L. Browning	1983	373
99 0/8	17 0/8	16 3/8	13 2/8	4	4	Contra Costa County	CA	Richard L. Westervelt	1985	373
99 0/8	16 2/8	16 5/8	14 6/8	4	5	Kitsap County	WA	Cecil McConnell	1986	373
99 0/8	16 7/8	15 7/8	15 4/8	4	4	Clackamas County	OR	Darrell Scheffer	1991	373
98 7/8	20 2/8	19 4/8	14 1/8	3	2	Pacific County	WA	William V. Mishler	1968	379
98 7/8	16 1/8	16 5/8	12 5/8	4	3	Cowlitz County	WA	Neal Amos	1997	379
98 6/8	17 6/8	18 0/8	16 0/8	4	3	Skagit County	WA	Eric Olson	1994	381
98 6/8	17 4/8	18 1/8	14 2/8	4	4	Mendocino County	CA	Jerry Boelens	1996	381
98 5/8	19 2/8	19 2/8	14 5/8	3	3	Mendocino County	CA	Joseph A. Wyman	1990	383
98 3/8	16 1/8	16 3/8	14 3/8	4	4	Sonoma County	CA	Ray Torrey	1967	384
98 3/8	16 3/8	16 1/8	17 0/8	4	4	Lane County	OR	Gary R. Swan	1990	384
98 1/8	16 0/8	16 3/8	12 7/8	4	4	Rogue Unit	OR	Barbara Richardson	1964	386
98 1/8	17 3/8	17 1/8	17 1/8	4	4	Clackamas County	OR	Blake M. Bartley	1988	386
98 0/8	19 7/8	19 6/8	14 6/8	4	2	Pacific County	WA	Morris Wolters	1967	388
98 0/8	18 5/8	19 0/8	15 6/8	3	3	Sonoma County	CA	Mark Bonales	1996	388
97 7/8	16 3/8	15 5/8	16 1/8	5	5	Benton County	OR	Harold Stice	1957	390
97 6/8	16 2/8	16 2/8	14 2/8	4	4	Clallam County	WA	Joel Peterson	1996	391
97 5/8	20 2/8	19 7/8	16 7/8	3	3	Marin County	CA	Mike Taylor	1985	392
97 5/8	17 4/8	17 6/8	13 5/8	3	3	Siskiyou County	CA	Randy Root	1987	392
97 4/8	18 6/8	18 2/8	18 6/8	3	3	Whatcom County	WA	Steve Holland	1963	394
97 4/8	18 1/8	18 4/8	15 6/8	3	3	Marion County	OR	Ken Kalinowski	1981	394
97 4/8	20 3/8	19 7/8	15 4/8	4	3	Trinity County	CA	Rodney A. York	1987	394
97 4/8	17 2/8	18 0/8	17 0/8	3	3	Siskiyou County	CA	John Shuping	1994	394
97 3/8	19 1/8	18 4/8	20 0/8	3	3	Marin County	CA	Joe Checchio	1985	398
97 3/8	17 2/8	18 0/8	14 5/8	3	3	Linn County	OR	Michael A. Cramblit	1989	398
97 3/8	16 1/8	17 5/8	15 3/8	4	5	Marion County	OR	Craig Germond	1997	398
97 2/8	16 7/8	17 0/8	12 2/8	4	3	Pacific County	WA	Todd Hubble	1980	401
97 2/8	17 4/8	17 4/8	13 4/8	4	4	King County	WA	Jay E. Tinker	1986	401
97 1/8	16 5/8	16 7/8	13 7/8	3	3	Cowlitz County	WA	Jerry W. Adams	1994	403
97 0/8	16 7/8	16 4/8	12 0/8	4	4	Pacific County	WA	Lawrence Rogers	1972	404
97 0/8	18 0/8	18 3/8	14 4/8	3	2	Mendocino County	CA	Wayne Piersol	1991	404
97 0/8	18 1/8	16 5/8	18 0/8	4	4	Jackson County	OR	Tony Snow	1992	404
97 0/8	17 3/8	17 5/8	17 0/8	3	3	Linn County	OR	William M. Dupee, Jr.	1995	404
96 7/8	17 2/8	17 2/8	14 7/8	4	4	Glenn County	CA	Joe Williams	1977	408
96 7/8	16 2/8	16 6/8	14 5/8	3	3	Kitsap County	WA	Boyd E. Shelby, Jr.	1991	408
96 6/8	16 5/8	16 3/8	12 0/8	4	4	Benton County	OR	John W. Shipley	1991	410
96 6/8	17 1/8	17 0/8	13 0/8	3	3	Linn County	OR	Tom Vanasche	1994	410
96 6/8	17 6/8	17 6/8	16 6/8	3	2	King County	WA	Tim Gordan Wallis	1995	410
96 5/8	17 6/8	17 6/8	11 5/8	4	5	Clark County	WA	Lorie Lehman	1994	413
96 4/8	18 2/8	17 4/8	12 4/8	4	3	Benton County	OR	Jim Nielsen	1997	414
96 1/8	15 4/8	15 0/8	13 3/8	4	4	Pacific County	WA	Lynne Sharp	1965	415

COLUMBIAN BLACKTAIL DEER (TYPICAL ANTLERS)

Minimum Score 90   Continued

SCORE	LENGTH OF R MAIN BEAM L		INSIDE SPREAD	NUMBER OF R POINTS L		AREA	STATE/ PROVINCE	HUNTER'S NAME	DATE	RANK
96 0/8	16 0/8	15 7/8	12 6/8	4	4	Soda Springs	OR	Harold Benson	1961	416
96 0/8	15 5/8	16 2/8	13 6/8	4	5	Clackamas County	OR	Robert Oxley	1989	416
95 6/8	17 0/8	16 7/8	15 6/8	4	4	Mendocino County	CA	Gerald Boelens	1997	418
95 5/8	17 5/8	15 2/8	14 3/8	5	5	Siskiyou County	CA	Thomas V. Sieverding	1971	419
95 5/8	16 1/8	17 2/8	12 1/8	4	4	Humboldt County	CA	Calvin Farner	1983	419
95 4/8	14 0/8	16 6/8	16 0/8	4	4	Josephine County	OR	Lee Darrow	1997	421
95 3/8	17 1/8	18 1/8	13 3/8	4	4	Josephine County	OR	Sam Burton	1994	422
95 2/8	16 6/8	16 2/8	12 4/8	3	3	Trinity County	CA	Tim P. Kanapeckas	1995	423
94 7/8	17 7/8	18 2/8	16 3/8	2	2	Santa Cruz County	CA	Robert Alan Nottingham	1984	424
94 7/8	15 7/8	16 1/8	14 1/8	4	4	Shasta County	CA	Danny R. Shurtleff	1987	424
94 7/8	18 4/8	18 2/8	16 3/8	2	2	Sonoma County	CA	Wayne Piersol	1992	424
94 6/8	16 3/8	17 1/8	14 2/8	5	4	Lewis County	WA	Daniel A. Yirka	1987	427
94 6/8	18 7/8	19 3/8	17 2/8	3	2	Sonoma County	CA	Mike Taylor	1989	427
94 6/8	19 6/8	18 3/8	16 6/8	3	3	San Juan County	WA	Scott L. Buck	1998	427
94 5/8	15 6/8	15 3/8	10 7/8	4	4	Benton County	OR	Raymond E. Root	1970	430
94 5/8	15 7/8	15 5/8	16 1/8	4	4	Sonoma County	CA	Russell L. Browning	1980	430
94 5/8	15 3/8	15 2/8	12 5/8	4	4	Sonoma County	CA	Thomas K. Powell	1988	430
94 5/8	17 2/8	17 3/8	14 5/8	4	4	Sonoma County	CA	Mark Bonales	1995	430
94 4/8	18 0/8	17 5/8	13 2/8	4	3	Mendocino County	CA	Chuck Adams	1983	434
94 3/8	18 0/8	16 2/8	16 5/8	2	4	Klamath County	OR	Don Pritchett	1964	435
94 3/8	17 1/8	17 0/8	15 5/8	3	3	Siskiyou County	CA	William J. Bagdasarian	1993	435
94 0/8	16 7/8	18 4/8	12 0/8	4	4	Capitol Forest	WA	C. N. Pickle	1960	437
94 0/8	17 6/8	17 5/8	11 4/8	3	4	Benton County	OR	Edward U. Tobler	1970	437
94 0/8	16 6/8	16 5/8	18 0/8	3	3	Humboldt County	CA	Craig Coolahan	1989	437
93 7/8	18 2/8	16 4/8	16 5/8	4	5	Sonoma County	CA	Sean Dunn	1992	440
93 7/8	16 2/8	15 7/8	12 7/8	4	5	Douglas County	OR	Walter Phillips	1992	440
93 6/8	18 3/8	18 5/8	13 6/8	2	4	Lewis County	WA	Floyd Gregg	1962	442
93 6/8	15 6/8	15 5/8	12 6/8	4	4	Mendocino County	CA	Chuck Adams	1979	442
93 5/8	15 1/8	14 7/8	15 1/8	4	5	Jackson County	OR	Rodney Ness	1995	444
93 5/8	18 5/8	18 1/8	18 3/8	3	3	Alameda County	CA	Rodger M. Benadom	1996	444
93 3/8	16 4/8	15 6/8	15 3/8	3	3	Coos County	OR	Steve Simpson	1985	446
93 3/8	18 5/8	18 5/8	15 4/8	5	5	Clackamas County	OR	Randy Teeney	1987	446
93 2/8	17 0/8	16 7/8	12 4/8	4	3	Linn County	OR	Joe Mengore	1983	448
93 2/8	16 2/8	17 2/8	17 3/8	3	3	Humboldt County	CA	Monty Clemmer	1986	448
93 0/8	17 3/8	17 6/8	14 0/8	4	3	Clallam County	WA	Wayne Haag	1987	450
92 6/8	16 0/8	16 3/8	13 4/8	5	5	Marion County	OR	Larry Jones	1986	451
92 3/8	18 0/8	18 2/8	15 1/8	3	2	Mendocino County	CA	Wilfred Willis	1982	452
92 0/8	18 4/8	18 4/8	19 2/8	2	2	Josephine County	OR	Joe White	1986	453
92 0/8	16 4/8	16 5/8	16 0/8	3	3	Santa Cruz County	CA	H. Brian Malsbury	1987	453
91 5/8	15 1/8	15 2/8	13 1/8	5	5	King County	WA	Vic Stevens	1986	455
91 3/8	17 3/8	17 0/8	16 3/8	2	2	Mendocino County	CA	Joseph Wyman	1991	456
91 3/8	17 5/8	16 6/8	12 3/8	3	3	Pierce County	WA	Boyd Edward Shelby, Jr.	1996	456
91 2/8	18 0/8	17 4/8	13 4/8	5	3	Yamhill County	OR	R. Keith Potter	1990	458
91 1/8	17 1/8	18 0/8	13 1/8	3	3	Benton County	OR	Jim Nielsen	1981	459
91 1/8	15 3/8	16 5/8	13 1/8	3	4	Lane County	OR	Ken Kalinowski	1986	459
91 1/8	15 4/8	16 1/8	16 3/8	3	3	Sonoma County	CA	Ernie Fechter	1990	459
90 7/8	15 5/8	15 1/8	12 3/8	3	3	Clallam County	WA	Renny Mason	1989	462
90 5/8	16 7/8	17 1/8	15 1/8	2	2	Santa Clara County	CA	Sandee Cox	1989	463
90 5/8	19 5/8	17 3/8	14 7/8	3	2	Kitsap County	WA	Terry Ray Chapman	1992	463
90 5/8	15 4/8	16 1/8	9 7/8	4	4	Cowlitz County	WA	Ryan Davenport	1998	463
90 4/8	14 6/8	14 3/8	12 3/8	4	4	Whatcom County	WA	Jack Fish	1956	466
90 4/8	16 4/8	16 7/8	15 0/8	2	2	Merced County	CA	Jim Walton	1980	466
90 3/8	16 6/8	15 6/8	14 3/8	4	5	Mendocino County	CA	Chuck Adams	1977	468
90 2/8	14 5/8	15 1/8	12 0/8	4	4	Pacific County	WA	Leonard Bray	1965	469
90 1/8	16 5/8	15 6/8	11 5/8	3	3	King County	WA	Don D. Axtman	1997	470
90 0/8	15 0/8	14 6/8	12 6/8	4	4	Benton County	OR	Tom Ronchetti	1990	471

COLUMBIAN BLACKTAIL DEER (TYPICAL VELVET ANTLERS)

Minimum Score 90

SCORE	LENGTH OF R MAIN BEAM L		INSIDE SPREAD	NUMBER OF R POINTS L		AREA	STATE/ PROVINCE	HUNTER'S NAME	DATE	RANK
159 2/8	23 0/8	24 0/8	17 0/8	5	6	Humboldt County	CA	Stephen Oliberos	1996	*
148 5/8	20 0/8	20 5/8	19 1/8	5	5	Siskiyou County	CA	Wally Schwartz	1998	*
147 5/8	22 2/8	22 6/8	17 7/8	5	5	Shasta County	CA	Alan Weaver	1998	*
144 6/8	19 4/8	20 2/8	16 4/8	5	5	Trinity County	CA	Jim Schaafsma	1990	*
140 6/8	20 4/8	18 4/8	16 4/8	7	5	Trinity County	CA	Jim Schaafsma	1992	*
139 0/8	20 3/8	21 1/8	17 1/8	5	7	Shasta County	CA	Jason Montagner	1998	*
135 7/8	21 0/8	20 1/8	17 5/8	5	5	Mendocino County	CA	Robert Ward	1995	*
135 6/8	19 0/8	18 1/8	16 4/8	4	5	Mendocino County	CA	John R. Sample	1992	*
133 0/8	20 6/8	21 4/8	18 4/8	5	5	Humboldt County	CA	Tim Knutsen	1991	*
132 4/8	19 2/8	18 3/8	15 2/8	5	5	Sonoma County	CA	Timothy Peelen	1995	*
132 3/8	22 1/8	22 3/8	16 1/8	4	5	Trinity County	CA	Robert Dias	1995	*
131 3/8	20 3/8	20 1/8	17 4/8	5	6	Santa Cruz County	CA	Gregory R. Bonetti	1987	*

COLUMBIAN BLACKTAIL DEER (TYPICAL VELVET ANTLERS)

Minimum Score 90 — Continued

SCORE	LENGTH OF MAIN BEAM R	LENGTH OF MAIN BEAM L	INSIDE SPREAD	NUMBER OF POINTS R	NUMBER OF POINTS L	AREA	STATE/ PROVINCE	HUNTER'S NAME	DATE	RANK
131 2/8	18 5/8	18 5/8	16 6/8	5	5	Siskiyou County	CA	Wally Schwartz	1991	*
128 6/8	17 5/8	18 0/8	13 2/8	5	5	King County	WA	Larry Jensen	1984	*
128 5/8	20 5/8	20 2/8	15 5/8	4	4	Shasta County	CA	Jason Montagner	1998	*
127 3/8	20 7/8	20 6/8	18 7/8	4	4	Mendocino County	CA	Gregg Welch	1986	*
124 4/8	20 4/8	17 6/8	16 2/8	5	5	Humboldt County	CA	Phil Grunert	1997	*
123 5/8	18 2/8	18 7/8	13 1/8	5	5	Humboldt County	CA	Sean Campbell	1998	*
123 1/8	21 1/8	21 3/8	16 5/8	4	4	Trinity County	CA	Parrey Cremeans	1997	*
122 2/8	18 3/8	19 0/8	14 6/8	5	5	Trinity County	CA	Stefan Olsen	1990	*
121 5/8	19 6/8	19 1/8	16 1/8	4	4	Mendocino County	CA	Gregg Welch	1987	*
121 2/8	19 1/8	19 6/8	16 6/8	4	4	Santa Cruz County	CA	Douglas G. Bonetti	1987	*
120 1/8	19 4/8	19 2/8	15 3/8	5	5	Lane County	OR	James J. Dilworth	1996	*
119 4/8	19 6/8	19 3/8	18 2/8	5	3	Santa Clara County	CA	Darin Filice	1993	*
116 6/8	20 2/8	20 3/8	18 4/8	4	4	Trinity County	CA	Carolyn A. Godfrey	1998	*
114 2/8	19 2/8	17 6/8	12 4/8	3	4	Siskiyou County	CA	Doug Meeks	1998	*
113 2/8	22 4/8	21 2/8	21 2/8	4	4	Trinity County	CA	Mike Barsi	1993	*
110 5/8	17 0/8	17 0/8	15 5/8	4	4	Lake County	CA	Phil C. Phillips	1997	*
109 7/8	21 3/8	21 4/8	20 0/8	4	3	Trinity County	CA	Kyle Saunderson	1990	*
109 1/8	16 4/8	17 7/8	14 1/8	4	5	Mendocino County	CA	Chuck Adams	1977	*
107 4/8	17 3/8	18 3/8	15 6/8	4	4	Trinity County	CA	Mark Greving	1996	*
105 6/8	19 6/8	20 2/8	18 2/8	3	3	Colusa County	CA	Matt Schuler	1996	*
105 1/8	15 2/8	15 3/8	11 1/8	5	5	Mendocino County	CA	Ronald S. Fornesi	1995	*
104 0/8	16 5/8	18 2/8	18 2/8	4	4	Lake County	CA	Phil Phillips	1993	*
104 0/8	16 6/8	17 2/8	15 0/8	4	5	Trinity County	CA	Rick Pollard	1997	*
103 3/8	21 1/8	21 5/8	17 5/8	3	4	Lake County	CA	John R. Sample	1988	*
103 3/8	20 1/8	19 1/8	15 7/8	3	3	Humboldt County	CA	Jonathan Owens	1993	*
101 5/8	17 4/8	18 5/8	15 0/8	5	7	Trinity County	CA	Mark Greving	1985	*
101 2/8	18 6/8	19 1/8	15 6/8	3	4	Humboldt County	CA	Charles E. Nichol	1996	*
100 7/8	20 2/8	19 5/8	14 3/8	3	4	Mendocino County	CA	Alan Seymour	1995	*
100 7/8	19 3/8	18 6/8	19 5/8	3	4	Lake County	CA	John R. Sample	1998	*
99 0/8	16 2/8	16 6/8	17 1/8	4	4	Mendocino County	CA	Chuck Adams	1970	*
97 6/8	18 7/8	19 6/8	17 0/8	2	2	Sonoma County	CA	Will Willis	1995	*
95 0/8	18 6/8	18 2/8	17 2/8	3	3	Tehama County	CA	Dan McLearn	1998	*
92 2/8	16 6/8	16 4/8	9 4/8	2	2	Humboldt County	CA	Charles E. Nichol	1997	*
91 0/8	18 5/8	18 5/8	14 4/8	2	2	Mendocino County	CA	Ron Jarvis	1991	*
90 2/8	17 2/8	16 5/8	15 6/8	2	2	Mendocino County	CA	Lee Gualtieri	1997	*
90 0/8	18 7/8	17 0/8	13 1/8	8	6	Jefferson County	WA	Brent A. Hancock	1996	*

Velvet entries will be listed in only one record book.

World Record Columbian Blacktail Deer (Non-Typical Antlers)
Score: 194 4/8
Jackson County, Oregon - 1988
Hunter: James Decker

COLUMBIAN BLACKTAIL DEER (NON-TYPICAL ANTLERS)

Minimum Score 125 — *Odocoileus hemionus columnianus*

SCORE	LENGTH OF MAIN BEAM R	LENGTH OF MAIN BEAM L	INSIDE SPREAD	NUMBER OF POINTS R	NUMBER OF POINTS L	AREA	STATE/ PROVINCE	HUNTER'S NAME	DATE	RANK
194 4/8	23 3/8	23 4/8	19 1/8	8	10	Jackson County	OR	James Decker	1988	1
168 1/8	21 5/8	21 3/8	15 3/8	8	7	Jackson County	OR	Chuck Woolley	1991	2
167 0/8	23 0/8	24 6/8	20 2/8	6	6	Josephine County	OR	Marte Scheuffele	1988	3
166 4/8	22 3/8	23 0/8	19 4/8	6	8	Marion County	OR	Chad A. Richardson	1997	4
146 0/8	19 2/8	19 0/8	15 7/8	7	7	San Mateo County	CA	John Grochowski	1984	5
139 5/8	18 6/8	18 6/8	15 7/8	5	8	Siskiyou County	CA	Kurt Case	1980	6
133 4/8	18 0/8	18 4/8	13 2/8	6	6	Josephine County	OR	Robert K. Wood	1994	7
132 3/8	18 0/8	18 4/8	18 6/8	6	6	Trinity County	CA	Jim Schaafsma	1991	8
132 1/8	18 7/8	20 5/8	16 6/8	5	4	Snohomish County	WA	Allan Lyndsay Moro	1992	9
131 6/8	22 7/8	22 6/8	18 3/8	7	4	Douglas County	OR	Jerry R. De Loach	1975	10

COLUMBIAN BLACKTAIL DEER (NON-TYPICAL VELVET ANTLERS)

Minimum Score 125

SCORE	LENGTH OF MAIN BEAM R	LENGTH OF MAIN BEAM L	INSIDE SPREAD	NUMBER OF POINTS R	NUMBER OF POINTS L	AREA	STATE/ PROVINCE	HUNTER'S NAME	DATE	RANK
146 5/8	20 5/8	22 0/8	18 5/8	6	6	Mendocino County	CA	John R. Sample	1994	*
130 5/8	20 7/8	20 6/8	17 0/8	4	6	Mendocino County	CA	David W. Rickert II	1996	*

* Velvet entries will be listed in only one record book.

World Record Sitka Blacktail Deer
(Typical Antlers)
Score: 117 1/8
Ugak Bay, Alaska - 1985
Hunter: Marte Scheuffele

SITKA BLACKTAIL DEER (TYPICAL ANTLERS)

Minimum Score 75

Odocoileus hemionus sitkensis

SCORE	LENGTH OF MAIN BEAM R	LENGTH OF MAIN BEAM L	INSIDE SPREAD	NUMBER OF POINTS R	NUMBER OF POINTS L	AREA	STATE/ PROVINCE	HUNTER'S NAME	DATE	RANK
117 1/8	17 5/8	18 6/8	15 5/8	5	5	Ugak Bay	AK	Marte Scheuffele	1985	1
116 3/8	18 4/8	18 2/8	13 1/8	5	5	Prince of Wales Island	AK	Charles Hakari	1987	2
116 1/8	19 1/8	18 4/8	14 1/8	5	4	Prince of Wales Island	AK	Marte Scheuffele	1996	3
115 6/8	17 1/8	16 3/8	14 6/8	5	5	Prince of Wales Island	AK	Kirt O. Marsh	1988	4
114 3/8	18 5/8	18 7/8	18 1/8	5	5	Kodiak Island	AK	Jim Ryan	1986	5
112 2/8	19 0/8	19 2/8	16 4/8	4	4	Kodiak Island	AK	John D. "Jack" Frost	1987	6
110 5/8	17 3/8	17 1/8	15 5/8	6	5	Kodiak Island	AK	Bill Krenz	1988	7
109 1/8	17 2/8	16 0/8	15 5/8	5	5	Ugak Bay	AK	Marte Scheuffele	1996	8
108 4/8	16 4/8	15 6/8	15 0/8	5	5	Kodiak Island	AK	Chuck Adams	1986	9
107 6/8	17 2/8	16 2/8	14 2/8	5	5	Kodiak Island	AK	Chuck Adams	1986	10
107 4/8	17 3/8	17 4/8	14 4/8	5	5	Kodiak Island	AK	Chuck Adams	1987	11
107 4/8	17 3/8	17 1/8	14 4/8	5	5	Prince of Wales Island	AK	Danny Moore	1988	11
107 2/8	15 3/8	15 1/8	13 6/8	5	5	Kodiak Island	AK	Chris Dau	1986	13
106 4/8	17 3/8	16 6/8	16 5/8	5	6	Kodiak Island	AK	Douglas G. Bonetti	1985	14
106 3/8	17 1/8	16 6/8	13 3/8	5	5	Deadman's Bay	AK	Leon R. Meidam	1995	15
105 3/8	16 3/8	16 4/8	15 1/8	5	6	Kodiak Island	AK	John T. Toenes	1988	16
104 6/8	18 4/8	19 1/8	16 4/8	4	4	Kodiak Island	AK	Pat McCollum	1994	17
104 5/8	18 0/8	17 5/8	17 7/8	4	5	Kodiak Island	AK	Richard L. Westervelt	1987	18
103 5/8	18 4/8	17 2/8	15 7/8	4	5	Kodiak Island	AK	Chuck Adams	1987	19
103 2/8	18 3/8	17 5/8	17 4/8	4	5	Amook Island	AK	Garry A. Thoms	1989	20
103 0/8	17 7/8	17 1/8	12 6/8	5	4	Olga Bay	AK	John D. "Jack" Frost	1998	21

SITKA BLACKTAIL DEER (TYPICAL ANTLERS)

Minimum Score 75

SCORE	LENGTH OF MAIN BEAM R	LENGTH OF MAIN BEAM L	INSIDE SPREAD	NUMBER OF POINTS R	NUMBER OF POINTS L	AREA	STATE/PROVINCE	HUNTER'S NAME	DATE	RANK
102 7/8	16 4/8	16 0/8	14 2/8	6	5	Kodiak Island	AK	John D. "Jack" Frost	1994	22
102 2/8	18 4/8	16 6/8	13 4/8	4	5	Kodiak Island	AK	Brad H. Parker	1989	23
102 1/8	15 4/8	15 4/8	13 5/8	5	5	Kodiak Island	AK	Chuck Adams	1996	24
102 0/8	18 0/8	18 0/8	16 2/8	5	4	Kodiak Island	AK	John D. 'Jack' Frost	1986	25
101 6/8	15 4/8	16 2/8	13 6/8	5	5	Kodiak Island	Ak	Gary G. Wall	1986	26
101 5/8	16 6/8	15 6/8	14 1/8	5	5	Kodiak Island	AK	John D. "Jack" Frost	1997	27
101 3/8	15 6/8	16 3/8	14 3/8	5	5	Kodiak Island	AK	Lon E. Lauber	1991	28
101 3/8	16 5/8	16 3/8	14 1/8	5	5	Kodiak Island	AK	V. Randy Liljenquist	1993	28
101 0/8	19 0/8	19 0/8	17 0/8	5	5	Kodiak Island	AK	Gene Coughlin	1984	30
101 0/8	18 1/8	17 7/8	16 4/8	5	4	Kodiak Island	AK	Danny Moore	1986	30
100 5/8	17 7/8	17 0/8	16 3/8	4	5	Ugak Bay	AK	Thomas Chadwick	1987	32
99 4/8	17 4/8	17 7/8	16 0/8	4	5	Kodiak Island	AK	Danny Moore	1984	33
99 4/8	16 0/8	15 6/8	13 2/8	5	5	Kodiak Island	AK	E. Lance Whary	1998	33
99 3/8	15 4/8	16 2/8	15 1/8	4	5	Kodiak Island	AK	Thomas J. Hoffman	1988	35
99 2/8	16 6/8	16 2/8	13 6/8	4	5	Kodiak Island	AK	Chuck Adams	1995	36
99 0/8	14 1/8	15 5/8	13 4/8	5	5	Kodiak Island	AK	Al Besch	1984	37
98 7/8	16 6/8	16 6/8	14 5/8	5	4	Kodiak Island	AK	Danny Moore	1986	38
98 5/8	16 6/8	16 2/8	16 5/8	4	4	Kodiak Island	AK	Craig D. Morrow	1987	39
98 5/8	15 7/8	16 0/8	13 1/8	5	5	Kodiak Island	AK	Tim Moerlein	1992	39
98 5/8	16 6/8	16 1/8	13 7/8	5	5	Kodiak Island	AK	Chuck Adams	1998	39
98 4/8	16 4/8	14 2/8	14 0/8	4	5	Kodiak Island	AK	Michael L. Nunn	1984	42
98 4/8	14 4/8	17 0/8	17 1/8	5	4	Kodiak Island	AK	Tom Chadwick	1985	42
98 4/8	15 6/8	16 0/8	14 2/8	5	5	Prince of Wales Island	AK	Danny Moore	1993	42
98 2/8	14 7/8	14 7/8	13 4/8	5	5	Kodiak Island	AK	Philip F. Nuechterlein	1985	45
98 2/8	15 0/8	14 7/8	13 2/8	5	5	Kodiak Island	AK	Glenn Vandergaw	1988	45
97 7/8	18 2/8	18 4/8	14 1/8	4	4	Larson Bay	AK	Carol Kindred	1989	47
97 6/8	18 1/8	18 0/8	18 0/8	4	3	Kodiak Island	AK	Patricia A. Stewart	1983	48
97 5/8	16 4/8	17 4/8	16 7/8	4	5	Prince of Wales Island	AK	Marvin H. Walter	1987	49
97 5/8	16 7/8	17 2/8	16 3/8	4	4	Kodiak Island	AK	Roger Stewart	1988	50
97 2/8	15 0/8	13 6/8	13 0/8	5	5	Kodiak Island	AK	Chuck Adams	1986	51
96 6/8	15 4/8	15 1/8	14 0/8	4	5	Kodiak Island	AK	Bob Ameen	1983	52
96 4/8	18 1/8	18 2/8	15 6/8	4	5	Prince of Wales Island	AK	Glen R. Shepard	1987	53
96 3/8	16 1/8	16 6/8	15 5/8	4	4	Kodiak Island	AK	Gary G. Wall	1986	54
96 2/8	17 5/8	17 0/8	15 6/8	3	4	Kodiak Island	AK	Dick McClain	1990	55
96 1/8	17 1/8	16 3/8	13 7/8	4	4	Kodiak Island	AK	Don Rossiter	1985	56
95 6/8	17 5/8	17 4/8	17 0/8	3	3	Kodiak Island	AK	Paul Persano	1986	57
95 6/8	17 3/8	17 2/8	14 4/8	5	4	Kodiak Island	AK	Terry Krahn	1995	57
95 3/8	17 4/8	17 3/8	15 5/8	4	4	Kodiak Island	AK	John D. "Jack" Frost	1990	59
95 3/8	15 4/8	16 0/8	15 1/8	4	4	Kodiak Island	AK	Mike Traub	1992	59
95 3/8	16 1/8	15 7/8	14 5/8	4	4	Kodiak Island	AK	Bob Ameen	1995	59
95 1/8	18 0/8	17 6/8	16 4/8	4	5	Kodiak Island	AK	Thomas E. Rothrock	1997	62
94 7/8	16 7/8	16 7/8	13 1/8	5	6	Kodiak Island	AK	Chuck Adams	1984	63
94 6/8	16 0/8	15 2/8	13 6/8	4	4	Kodiak Island	AK	Bob Ameen	1993	64
94 5/8	18 2/8	17 7/8	14 7/8	4	4	Kodiak Island	AK	V. Randy Liljenquist	1993	65
94 3/8	16 1/8	15 5/8	16 1/8	4	4	Kodiak Island	AK	Dyrk Eddie	1986	66
94 3/8	16 4/8	16 1/8	15 5/8	4	4	Kodiak Island	AK	Doug Keller	1988	66
94 2/8	15 4/8	15 1/8	14 4/8	4	4	Kodiak Island	AK	F. Dan Dinelli	1996	68
94 2/8	15 3/8	16 6/8	14 4/8	4	5	Kodiak Island	AK	John D. "Jack" Frost	1997	68
94 1/8	16 5/8	17 2/8	14 5/8	4	4	Kodiak Island	AK	Chuck Adams	1997	70
94 1/8	16 4/8	16 7/8	13 5/8	6	4	Old Harbor	AK	Garry A. Thoms	1997	70
93 4/8	15 2/8	15 4/8	15 4/8	5	4	Kodiak Island	AK	Paul Persano	1986	72
93 4/8	15 7/8	15 0/8	14 0/8	4	4	Kodiak Island	AK	David A. Widby	1996	72
93 3/8	15 2/8	15 4/8	13 3/8	5	5	Kodiak Island	AK	Herman J. Griese	1982	74
93 3/8	17 4/8	15 4/8	13 5/8	4	4	Kodiak Island	AK	Chuck Adams	1987	74
93 2/8	16 0/8	15 6/8	15 0/8	4	4	Kodiak Island	AK	John Toenes	1987	76
93 2/8	18 0/8	17 1/8	14 0/8	4	4	Kodiak Island	AK	Russell M. Kucinski	1989	76
93 2/8	16 1/8	15 6/8	14 4/8	3	4	Kodiak Island	AK	Bob Ameen	1995	76
93 2/8	16 1/8	16 2/8	13 4/8	4	4	Kodiak Island	AK	Chuck Adams	1997	76
93 1/8	15 6/8	15 1/8	15 5/8	5	4	Kodiak Island	AK	Lon E. Lauber	1994	80
92 7/8	16 3/8	15 6/8	15 1/8	4	4	Kodiak Island	AK	John Sarvis	1987	81
92 7/8	15 3/8	14 5/8	16 3/8	5	4	Prince of Wales Island	AK	William H. Welton	1993	81
92 7/8	16 0/8	16 0/8	14 1/8	4	4	Kodiak Island	AK	Lon E. Lauber	1994	81
92 7/8	16 6/8	16 2/8	14 1/8	3	3	Kodiak Island	AK	Roy Whitford	1994	81
92 3/8	17 7/8	17 1/8	16 1/8	3	3	Kodiak Island	AK	William C. Shuster	1992	85
92 2/8	14 5/8	14 3/8	13 2/8	5	5	Kodiak Island	AK	Lon E. Lauber	1994	86
92 1/8	14 7/8	14 0/8	15 0/8	4	4	Kodiak Island	AK	Richard Moran	1988	87
92 0/8	16 5/8	16 0/8	13 4/8	4	4	Kodiak Island	AK	Chuck Adams	1986	88
92 0/8	15 2/8	16 2/8	13 4/8	6	5	Larson Bay	AK	Lou Kindred	1989	88
91 7/8	16 1/8	16 5/8	14 7/8	4	4	Afognak Island	AK	Edward L. Russell	1980	90
91 7/8	14 4/8	15 0/8	12 3/8	4	4	Queen Charlotte Islands	BC	Grant Janczyn	1991	90
91 5/8	14 2/8	14 2/8	14 5/8	4	4	Afognak Island	AK	Ray Ryan	1984	92
91 5/8	14 4/8	15 1/8	12 7/8	5	5	Kodiak Island	AK	Danny Moore	1986	92
91 4/8	14 6/8	14 4/8	13 0/8	5	5	Kodiak Island	AK	Chuck Adams	1986	94

SITKA BLACKTAIL DEER (TYPICAL ANTLERS)

Minimum Score 75 — Continued

SCORE	LENGTH OF MAIN BEAM R	LENGTH OF MAIN BEAM L	INSIDE SPREAD	NUMBER OF POINTS R	NUMBER OF POINTS L	AREA	STATE/PROVINCE	HUNTER'S NAME	DATE	RANK
91 2/8	12 4/8	16 2/8	13 2/8	5	4	Kodiak Island	AK	Randy Mannix	1984	95
91 2/8	15 2/8	16 0/8	14 4/8	4	4	Kodiak Island	AK	Tim Stelzer	1988	95
90 7/8	15 4/8	15 3/8	15 1/8	4	4	Kodiak Island	AK	Kirk Westervelt	1987	97
90 7/8	15 6/8	15 4/8	13 1/8	4	4	Kodiak Island	AK	John Sarvis	1987	97
90 7/8	15 5/8	15 6/8	14 3/8	4	4	Kodiak Island	AK	Jon Vanderhoef	1989	97
90 7/8	15 5/8	15 7/8	13 5/8	4	4	Kodiak Island	AK	John R. Hughes	1994	97
90 7/8	16 4/8	15 2/8	13 1/8	4	5	Kodiak Island	AK	Chris Reynolds	1996	97
90 6/8	18 2/8	16 6/8	16 4/8	3	3	Kodiak Island	AK	Lon E. Lauber	1993	102
90 6/8	14 3/8	14 0/8	12 2/8	5	5	Prince of Wales Island	AK	William H. Welton	1995	102
90 4/8	15 3/8	15 3/8	13 3/8	5	5	Kodiak Island	AK	Reggie Spiegelberg	1986	104
90 4/8	15 3/8	14 6/8	14 0/8	4	4	Kodiak Island	AK	Stan Parkerson	1992	104
90 2/8	16 4/8	16 5/8	15 6/8	5	3	Kodiak Island	AK	Mike Fenton	1988	106
90 2/8	14 2/8	15 2/8	12 2/8	4	5	Sturgeon Bay	AK	Richard A. Williams	1997	106
90 0/8	14 2/8	14 2/8	14 0/8	4	4	Kodiak Island	AK	Patricia Stewart	1989	108
89 7/8	17 1/8	16 7/8	15 7/8	4	3	Kodiak Island	AK	John Sarvis	1991	109
89 6/8	15 1/8	14 3/8	12 4/8	5	4	Kodiak Island	AK	John Sarvis	1984	110
89 6/8	16 0/8	15 4/8	14 2/8	4	5	Kodiak Island	AK	Lon E. Lauber	1993	110
89 6/8	18 4/8	17 6/8	15 2/8	3	4	Kodiak Island	AK	E. Lance Whary	1997	110
89 5/8	16 1/8	17 0/8	16 5/8	3	4	Kodiak Island	AK	Tony Russ	1992	113
89 4/8	16 0/8	15 2/8	14 6/8	3	4	Kodiak Island	AK	Bennett L. McMillian	1997	114
89 4/8	15 4/8	15 5/8	15 2/8	4	5	Kodiak Island	AK	Chuck Adams	1998	114
89 3/8	17 7/8	17 1/8	15 3/8	3	3	Kodiak Island	AK	Chuck Adams	1994	116
89 3/8	15 6/8	15 3/8	12 7/8	5	3	Kodiak Island	AK	Chuck Adams	1997	116
89 2/8	16 0/8	15 5/8	14 2/8	4	4	Kodiak Island	AK	Chuck Adams	1994	118
89 2/8	14 7/8	15 0/8	12 6/8	4	3	Kodiak Island	AK	Chuck Adams	1998	118
89 1/8	17 2/8	16 4/8	16 3/8	3	2	Kiliuda Bay	AK	Rick Tollison	1978	120
89 1/8	13 3/8	12 4/8	12 1/8	4	4	Kodiak Island	AK	Loren Flagg	1997	120
89 0/8	16 3/8	16 4/8	18 3/8	4	3	Kodiak Island	AK	Roger Stewart	1987	122
89 0/8	15 7/8	15 0/8	13 2/8	4	4	Kodiak Island	AK	George A. Moerlein	1990	122
89 0/8	15 5/8	13 0/8	11 6/8	4	4	Kodiak Island	AK	Bob Ameen	1994	122
89 0/8	16 1/8	15 6/8	14 6/8	5	4	Kodiak Island	AK	Chuck Adams	1996	122
89 0/8	15 4/8	15 3/8	12 6/8	5	3	Kodiak Island	AK	Chuck Adams	1996	122
88 7/8	15 7/8	15 5/8	16 4/8	3	4	Kodiak Island	AK	Kirk Westervelt	1987	127
88 6/8	14 7/8	15 0/8	12 6/8	5	4	Kodiak Island	AK	John Sarvis	1986	128
88 5/8	14 5/8	15 2/8	12 7/8	4	4	Queen Charlotte Islands	BC	Atley Lovelace	1984	129
88 5/8	17 0/8	16 4/8	15 5/8	3	4	Kodiak Island	AK	Larry Spiva	1986	129
88 5/8	14 1/8	14 2/8	13 3/8	5	4	Prince of Wales Island	AK	William H. Welton	1994	129
88 4/8	14 3/8	14 0/8	14 2/8	5	4	Afognak Island	AK	Edward L. Russell	1983	132
88 3/8	16 2/8	15 4/8	14 1/8	3	3	Kodiak Island	AK	Bob Ameen	1996	133
88 2/8	16 0/8	15 4/8	14 2/8	4	4	Kodiak Island	AK	Michael Menke	1986	134
88 2/8	16 0/8	16 0/8	15 2/8	3	3	Kodiak Island	AK	Reggie Spiegelberg	1986	134
88 0/8	16 7/8	16 0/8	15 0/8	3	4	Kodiak Island	AK	Richard L. Westervelt	1987	136
88 0/8	15 3/8	15 6/8	13 6/8	4	4	Kodiak Island	AK	Tony Russ	1992	136
88 0/8	16 0/8	15 5/8	15 4/8	4	4	Kodiak Island	AK	Neil J. Russell	1993	136
87 6/8	14 5/8	14 6/8	15 3/8	4	4	Kodiak Island	AK	Bob Ameen	1998	139
87 3/8	16 3/8	17 3/8	14 3/8	4	3	Kodiak Island	AK	Tom Payer	1988	140
87 2/8	16 6/8	16 5/8	17 1/8	4	2	Kodiak Island	AK	Lon E. Lauber	1990	141
87 2/8	16 0/8	16 4/8	16 0/8	4	3	Deadman's Bay	AK	Leon R. Meidam	1995	141
87 2/8	16 2/8	17 0/8	15 0/8	4	4	Kodiak Island	AK	Neil Russell	1996	141
86 7/8	15 0/8	14 4/8	14 3/8	4	4	Kodiak Island	AK	Jim Hodson	1985	144
86 7/8	15 1/8	15 2/8	14 3/8	4	4	Kodiak Island	AK	Stan Parkerson	1990	144
86 7/8	14 5/8	14 7/8	12 3/8	4	4	Kodiak Island	AK	Chuck Adams	1998	144
86 6/8	16 2/8	14 7/8	14 2/8	4	4	Kodiak Island	AK	Matt Jones	1985	147
86 6/8	15 5/8	15 2/8	15 4/8	4	4	Kodiak Island	AK	Bob Ameen	1991	147
86 5/8	16 1/8	15 5/8	16 3/8	4	3	Admiralty Island	AK	Charles R. Hakari	1983	149
86 4/8	13 7/8	15 0/8	14 0/8	5	5	Kodiak Island	AK	Emron A. Yancey	1986	150
86 4/8	15 2/8	14 4/8	15 2/8	4	4	Kodiak Island	AK	Bob Ameen	1995	150
86 4/8	15 2/8	15 5/8	14 6/8	4	3	Old Harbor	AK	David Rue	1997	150
86 2/8	16 0/8	15 1/8	14 0/8	4	4	Kodiak Island	AK	Troy Graziadei	1989	153
86 1/8	15 0/8	13 7/8	12 7/8	4	4	Kodiak Island	AK	John Toenes	1987	154
86 1/8	14 6/8	15 6/8	12 5/8	3	3	Kodiak Island	AK	Elmer R. Luce, Jr.	1994	154
86 1/8	15 1/8	14 5/8	11 5/8	4	4	Kodiak Island	AK	Chuck Adams	1997	154
85 6/8	15 6/8	15 2/8	13 6/8	4	3	Kodiak Island	Ak	Bob Hayes	1986	157
85 3/8	16 3/8	16 0/8	15 5/8	3	3	Afognak Island	AK	Roger Stewart	1980	158
85 2/8	15 4/8	15 0/8	14 0/8	3	4	Afognak Island	AK	Ralph Ertz	1983	159
85 2/8	15 7/8	14 6/8	13 4/8	4	4	Kodiak Island	AK	Marv Walter	1989	159
85 1/8	16 0/8	15 4/8	15 7/8	4	3	Kodiak Island	AK	Nathan L. Andersohn	1996	161
85 0/8	14 6/8	14 5/8	15 7/8	4	4	Kodiak Island	AK	John Sarvis	1985	162
85 0/8	13 1/8	14 4/8	15 1/8	4	4	Kodiak Island	AK	Roger Stewart	1987	162
85 0/8	14 6/8	16 2/8	14 0/8	3	5	Kosciusko Island	AK	Danny Moore	1992	162
84 7/8	14 3/8	16 1/8	16 1/8	3	4	Kodiak Island	AK	George P. Mann	1996	165
84 7/8	15 2/8	14 6/8	13 1/8	4	4	Kodiak Island	AK	Tony Russ	1996	165
84 5/8	14 1/8	13 5/8	13 3/8	4	4	Kodiak Island	AK	Lon E. Lauber	1992	167
84 5/8	14 6/8	14 2/8	12 3/8	4	4	Kodiak Island	AK	Dawn Traub	1992	167

SITKA BLACKTAIL DEER (TYPICAL ANTLERS)

Minimum Score 75

SCORE	LENGTH OF MAIN BEAM R	LENGTH OF MAIN BEAM L	INSIDE SPREAD	NUMBER OF POINTS R	NUMBER OF POINTS L	AREA	STATE/PROVINCE	HUNTER'S NAME	DATE	RANK
84 2/8	14 6/8	14 1/8	14 7/8	4	3	Kodiak Island	AK	Bill Krenz	1988	169
84 1/8	16 2/8	16 6/8	15 1/8	4	3	Kodiak Island	AK	Ralph Ertz	1984	170
84 1/8	14 4/8	14 6/8	13 1/8	3	4	Kodiak Island	AK	Elmer R. Luce, Jr.	1994	170
84 0/8	16 0/8	16 1/8	15 2/8	3	3	Kodiak Island	AK	Lon E. Lauber	1990	172
83 6/8	14 1/8	14 4/8	11 6/8	4	4	Kodiak Island	AK	Russell M. Kucinski	1989	173
83 6/8	15 4/8	15 0/8	15 2/8	4	3	Kodiak Island	AK	Elmer R. Luce, Jr.	1997	173
83 5/8	15 3/8	15 6/8	13 7/8	2	3	Kodiak Island	AK	Bob Ameen	1994	175
83 4/8	15 5/8	15 3/8	13 4/8	3	4	Kodiak Island	AK	Dale Holpainen	1997	176
83 3/8	14 6/8	14 4/8	12 5/8	4	3	Prince of Wales Island	AK	Danny Moore	1994	177
83 3/8	15 0/8	14 2/8	14 1/8	4	4	Kodiak Island	AK	John Sarvis	1996	177
83 2/8	15 4/8	15 2/8	15 4/8	3	3	Montague Island	AK	Ray Uhl	1978	179
83 2/8	14 4/8	14 0/8	13 2/8	6	6	Afognak Island	AK	Ralph Ertz	1981	179
83 2/8	15 0/8	14 3/8	13 4/8	4	4	Kodiak Island	AK	David A. Widby	1996	179
83 0/8	14 3/8	13 3/8	12 4/8	4	4	Kodiak Island	AK	Rich Biehl	1992	182
82 7/8	15 3/8	15 1/8	14 5/8	4	3	Kodiak Island	AK	John Sarvis	1991	183
82 6/8	15 0/8	14 4/8	13 2/8	5	4	Kodiak Island	AK	Bob Ameen	1997	184
82 6/8	14 6/8	15 0/8	15 1/8	4	3	Kodiak Island	AK	Bob Ameen	1998	184
82 4/8	12 6/8	14 0/8	12 6/8	5	5	Afognak Island	AK	Ralph Ertz	1980	186
82 4/8	14 4/8	13 7/8	14 5/8	4	4	Kodiak Island	AK	Richard L. Westervelt	1986	186
82 4/8	14 4/8	15 4/8	14 6/8	3	3	Kodiak Island	AK	Kirk Westervelt	1986	186
82 4/8	14 4/8	14 1/8	14 0/8	4	3	Kodiak Island	AK	Ken Vorisek	1996	186
82 4/8	12 6/8	13 0/8	13 0/8	5	5	Kodiak Island	AK	Cameron R. Hanes	1997	186
82 3/8	16 0/8	15 1/8	14 7/8	3	3	Kodiak Island	AK	Tony Russ	1992	191
82 3/8	14 0/8	14 5/8	13 1/8	4	4	Kodiak Island	AK	John Sarvis	1997	191
82 2/8	14 3/8	14 2/8	12 4/8	4	4	Kodiak Island	AK	Kurt Keskimaki	1986	193
82 2/8	15 7/8	14 5/8	15 2/8	3	4	Kodiak Island	AK	Barry J. Smith	1996	193
82 1/8	15 6/8	14 7/8	13 7/8	3	4	Kodiak Island	AK	Kevin Hisey	1993	195
82 0/8	15 4/8	15 7/8	15 0/8	3	3	Kodiak Island	AK	Bob Ameen	1993	196
82 0/8	15 2/8	14 7/8	13 6/8	3	3	Kodiak Island	AK	Stephen Kotz	1996	196
81 7/8	15 4/8	14 2/8	13 7/8	3	3	Kodiak Island	Ak	Dyrk Eddie	1986	198
81 7/8	15 2/8	14 4/8	11 7/8	4	4	Kodiak Island	AK	E. Lance Whary	1997	198
81 6/8	14 4/8	14 5/8	13 4/8	4	4	Kodiak Island	AK	Roger Stewart	1988	200
81 6/8	14 1/8	13 3/8	13 2/8	4	4	Kodiak Island	AK	George P. Mann	1996	200
81 5/8	16 3/8	15 6/8	15 7/8	2	2	Kodiak Island	AK	Thomas Chadwick	1997	202
81 4/8	14 5/8	15 4/8	13 2/8	4	3	Kodiak Island	AK	Ron Faust	1995	203
81 4/8	13 3/8	13 3/8	12 6/8	3	3	Kodiak Island	AK	Bob Ameen	1996	203
81 3/8	12 7/8	13 3/8	13 6/8	4	3	Kodiak Island	AK	Lon E. Lauber	1991	205
81 2/8	15 0/8	11 7/8	13 4/8	4	4	Kodiak Island	AK	Richard L. Westervelt	1986	206
81 2/8	14 2/8	14 2/8	15 5/8	2	2	Uyak Bay	AK	Herman Griese	1987	206
81 2/8	16 0/8	15 5/8	14 4/8	4	3	Amook Island	AK	Garry A. Thoms	1989	206
81 2/8	14 0/8	15 0/8	16 0/8	3	4	Kodiak Island	AK	Bob Ameen	1997	206
81 1/8	15 3/8	15 3/8	12 1/8	3	4	Sturgeon Bay	AK	Richard A. Williams	1997	210
81 1/8	14 0/8	14 6/8	13 5/8	5	4	Kodiak Island	AK	Bob Ameen	1997	210
80 7/8	14 4/8	14 5/8	12 1/8	4	4	Kodiak Island	AK	Chuck Adams	1996	212
80 7/8	16 0/8	15 7/8	12 3/8	3	3	Kodiak Island	AK	Bruce Bartenfelder	1997	212
80 6/8	14 2/8	13 0/8	13 0/8	4	4	Kodiak Island	AK	Roger Stewart	1988	214
80 5/8	16 2/8	15 5/8	14 1/8	3	2	Kodiak Island	AK	Bob Ameen	1994	215
80 4/8	14 2/8	15 7/8	13 2/8	4	3	Kodiak Island	AK	Steve Gorr	1989	216
80 2/8	15 1/8	14 6/8	14 2/8	4	4	Kodiak Island	AK	E. Lance Whary	1997	217
80 1/8	13 2/8	13 1/8	13 1/8	4	4	Kodiak Island	AK	Jim Hodson	1985	218
80 0/8	15 6/8	14 5/8	14 2/8	3	4	Afognak Island	AK	Charlie Kroll	1984	219
80 0/8	13 4/8	13 6/8	13 0/8	4	4	Kodiak Island	AK	Tony Russ	1990	219
79 7/8	15 0/8	12 6/8	13 7/8	4	4	Ugak Bay	AK	Carl E. Brent	1988	221
79 5/8	14 5/8	15 0/8	12 7/8	4	3	Kodiak Island	AK	Richard L. Westervelt	1988	222
79 4/8	15 0/8	13 5/8	14 0/8	3	3	Kodiak Island	AK	Jim Hodson	1986	223
79 4/8	13 7/8	14 0/8	15 4/8	3	3	Kodiak Island	AK	Richard Gibson	1988	223
79 4/8	13 6/8	13 7/8	13 6/8	4	4	Kodiak Island	AK	John Sarvis	1992	223
79 4/8	15 0/8	15 0/8	15 1/8	3	3	Kodiak Island	AK	Bob Ameen	1993	223
79 4/8	13 6/8	14 1/8	13 6/8	4	3	Kodiak Island	AK	Jim Hayes	1994	223
79 4/8	14 0/8	13 7/8	14 5/8	4	4	Kodiak Island	AK	Dean Stebner	1994	223
79 3/8	16 1/8	16 1/8	17 0/8	4	3	Kodiak Island	AK	Chad Doell	1991	229
79 3/8	14 0/8	13 7/8	12 3/8	4	4	Kodiak Island	AK	Louis Strahler	1995	229
79 2/8	14 7/8	15 1/8	14 4/8	4	3	Kodiak Island	AK	Lon E. Lauber	1990	231
79 2/8	15 0/8	14 4/8	12 2/8	3	4	Kodiak Island	AK	John Sarvis	1990	231
79 0/8	14 7/8	14 0/8	13 4/8	3	4	Kodiak Island	AK	Jim Hodson	1987	233
78 6/8	13 7/8	14 3/8	13 0/8	4	4	Kodiak Island	AK	John Sarvis	1990	234
78 6/8	14 1/8	15 1/8	11 2/8	4	3	Kodiak Island	AK	Shawn McCrosky	1991	234
78 6/8	14 6/8	14 6/8	16 1/8	3	3	Glass Peninsula	AK	Marvin H. Walter	1992	234
78 5/8	15 7/8	15 7/8	19 0/8	2	3	Kodiak Island	AK	Roger Stewart	1987	237
78 5/8	14 5/8	14 2/8	13 7/8	3	4	Kodiak Island	AK	Tim Moerlein	1988	237
78 5/8	14 2/8	13 2/8	13 5/8	3	3	Kodiak Island	AK	Bob Ameen	1997	237
78 4/8	14 2/8	13 4/8	13 0/8	3	4	Prince of Wales Island	AK	Danny Moore	1993	240
78 1/8	14 3/8	15 1/8	12 3/8	3	3	Kodiak Island	AK	Danny Moore	1984	241

Continued

SITKA BLACKTAIL DEER (TYPICAL ANTLERS)

Minimum Score 75

SCORE	LENGTH OF MAIN BEAM R	LENGTH OF MAIN BEAM L	INSIDE SPREAD	NUMBER OF POINTS R	NUMBER OF POINTS L	AREA	STATE/PROVINCE	HUNTER'S NAME	DATE	RANK
78 1/8	14 4/8	14 7/8	13 5/8	4	4	Kodiak Island	AK	Len Cardinale	1986	241
78 1/8	14 3/8	13 4/8	13 7/8	4	4	Kodiak Island	AK	Michael V. Frost	1990	241
78 1/8	14 1/8	14 0/8	11 3/8	3	3	Kodiak Island	AK	Alan Harris	1995	241
78 0/8	13 1/8	12 6/8	12 6/8	3	3	Kodiak Island	AK	David A. Widby	1988	245
78 0/8	16 3/8	15 3/8	16 4/8	4	3	Kodiak Island	AK	Lon E. Lauber	1992	245
78 0/8	14 7/8	15 3/8	13 2/8	2	4	Kodiak Island	AK	Joseph D. Pault	1992	245
77 7/8	14 4/8	14 0/8	14 3/8	3	3	Kodiak Island	AK	Stan Parkerson	1991	248
77 5/8	14 3/8	14 2/8	15 1/8	3	4	Kodiak Island	AK	Bob Ameen	1986	249
77 4/8	14 3/8	14 2/8	13 0/8	4	3	Kodiak Island	AK	Craig E. Scarbrough	1990	250
77 4/8	14 6/8	15 3/8	15 0/8	4	3	Kodiak Island	AK	David A. Widby	1990	250
77 4/8	15 0/8	13 6/8	13 2/8	4	2	Kodiak Island	AK	Bob Ameen	1994	250
77 3/8	13 4/8	13 0/8	12 1/8	4	4	Kodiak Island	AK	John Sarvis	1990	253
77 3/8	15 1/8	14 7/8	15 1/8	2	2	Prince of Wales Island	AK	Don Davidson	1991	253
77 2/8	15 2/8	15 2/8	13 2/8	3	3	Kodiak Island	AK	Chuck Adams	1984	255
77 2/8	13 3/8	14 2/8	16 3/8	4	3	Kodiak Island	AK	Neil Russell	1996	255
77 2/8	12 1/8	12 3/8	11 6/8	4	4	Kodiak Island	AK	John Sarvis	1996	255
77 2/8	14 7/8	14 6/8	12 6/8	3	3	Kodiak Island	AK	William C. Shuster	1997	255
76 7/8	14 0/8	13 3/8	10 7/8	4	4	Kodiak Island	AK	John Sarvis	1987	259
76 7/8	14 0/8	13 7/8	13 7/8	4	3	Kodiak Island	AK	Chuck Adams	1994	259
76 6/8	13 6/8	13 6/8	14 7/8	3	3	Kodiak Island	AK	Patricia Stewart	1988	261
76 6/8	13 6/8	12 3/8	13 2/8	3	3	Kodiak Island	AK	John Amerson	1994	261
76 5/8	12 7/8	13 1/8	13 5/8	4	3	Kodiak Island	AK	Tony Russ	1990	263
76 4/8	14 6/8	14 2/8	12 6/8	4	4	Sturgeon Bay	AK	Richard A. Williams	1997	264
76 2/8	14 7/8	13 7/8	14 4/8	2	2	Kodiak Island	AK	Bob Ameen	1996	265
76 0/8	15 4/8	14 6/8	14 2/8	3	3	Kodiak Island	AK	Lyle Willmarth	1986	266
76 0/8	14 0/8	14 4/8	14 7/8	2	3	Old Harbor	AK	Garry A. Thoms	1997	266
75 6/8	13 5/8	13 7/8	12 0/8	3	4	Afognak Island	AK	H. Richard Long	1984	268
75 6/8	14 2/8	14 3/8	11 6/8	4	3	Kodiak Island	AK	Rick A. Albers	1997	268
75 4/8	12 4/8	12 2/8	11 4/8	4	4	Kodiak Island	AK	John Sarvis	1987	270
75 4/8	13 0/8	12 5/8	12 4/8	4	4	Kodiak Island	AK	John Sarvis	1988	270
75 4/8	13 1/8	12 3/8	12 0/8	3	3	Kodiak Island	AK	Mark F. Vancas	1994	270
75 3/8	12 4/8	12 1/8	11 5/8	4	4	Kodiak Island	AK	John Sarvis	1994	273
75 3/8	12 3/8	13 1/8	14 0/8	4	4	Kodiak Island	AK	Bob Ameen	1996	273
75 2/8	13 5/8	13 1/8	12 6/8	3	4	Kodiak Island	AK	Gary G. Wall	1985	275
75 2/8	13 4/8	13 0/8	13 7/8	3	4	Kodiak Island	AK	Lon E. Lauber	1991	275
75 0/8	14 2/8	14 2/8	12 2/8	4	3	Kodiak Island	AK	Richard Moran	1988	277
75 0/8	14 0/8	14 0/8	15 1/8	4	3	Old Harbor	AK	Garry A. Thoms	1997	277

SITKA BLACKTAIL DEER (TYPICAL VELVET ANTLERS)

Minimum Score 75

SCORE	LENGTH OF MAIN BEAM R	LENGTH OF MAIN BEAM L	INSIDE SPREAD	NUMBER OF POINTS R	NUMBER OF POINTS L	AREA	STATE/PROVINCE	HUNTER'S NAME	DATE	RANK
92 4/8	16 0/8	16 0/8	16 0/8	4	4	Kosciusko Island	AK	Danny Moore	1992	*
86 0/8	14 1/8	14 0/8	13 2/8	4	4	Kodiak Island	AK	Dave Holt	1995	*

Velvet entries will be listed in only one record book.

World Record Coues Deer (Typical Antlers)
Score: 116 0/8
Grant County, New Mexico - 1997
Hunter: Edward J. Holguin

COUES DEER (TYPICAL ANTLERS)

Minimum Score 65 — *Odocoileus virginianus couesi*

SCORE	LENGTH OF MAIN BEAM R	L	INSIDE SPREAD	NUMBER OF POINTS R	L	AREA	STATE/ PROVINCE	HUNTER'S NAME	DATE	RANK
116 0/8	17 3/8	18 2/8	12 0/8	6	6	Grant County	NM	Edward J. Holguin	1997	1
113 0/8	19 2/8	19 2/8	15 6/8	4	4	Cochise County	AZ	Dennis Eaton	1991	2
110 5/8	19 5/8	19 2/8	16 1/8	4	4	Pinal County	AZ	Chuck Adams	1989	3
110 4/8	19 0/8	19 2/8	13 4/8	4	5	Pima County	AZ	Mike J. Frey	1991	4
107 1/8	17 3/8	17 3/8	16 1/8	5	4	Gila County	AZ	Paul J. Koren	1996	5
106 4/8	16 0/8	16 4/8	12 6/8	4	4	Greenlee County	AZ	Eddie Claypool	1994	6
106 1/8	17 5/8	18 5/8	14 3/8	5	5	Cochise County	AZ	Harlon Wilson	1982	7
105 7/8	17 5/8	17 2/8	11 7/8	4	6	Pima County	AZ	Harold Boyack	1985	8
105 6/8	16 2/8	16 6/8	14 4/8	5	4	Grant County	NM	Elmer R. Luce, Jr.	1998	9
104 2/8	18 2/8	17 7/8	15 0/8	4	4	Gila County	AZ	Larry Peterson	1978	10
103 5/8	17 7/8	17 5/8	16 1/8	5	5	Sonora	MEX	Jim Velazquez	1991	11
103 4/8	16 4/8	16 6/8	12 6/8	4	4	Pima County	AZ	Barry Sopher	1994	12
103 2/8	16 7/8	17 2/8	14 4/8	4	4	Grant County	NM	Daryl Tow	1990	13
103 2/8	18 1/8	19 3/8	17 2/8	4	4	Gila County	AZ	Michael P. Wanat	1997	13
102 7/8	17 1/8	15 5/8	13 3/8	5	5	Grant County	NM	Daniel Morningstar	1988	15
102 5/8	16 6/8	17 1/8	13 7/8	4	4	Graham County	AZ	Kirk Westervelt	1996	16
102 2/8	17 2/8	17 3/8	15 7/8	5	4	Coconino County	AZ	Michael Wanat	1996	17
101 7/8	15 6/8	17 0/8	15 6/8	5	4	Grant County	NM	Peter LaScala	1989	18
101 4/8	16 2/8	15 4/8	13 2/8	4	4	Pima County	AZ	Heath Hibbard	1997	19

COUES DEER (TYPICAL ANTLERS)

Minimum Score 65 Continued

SCORE	LENGTH OF MAIN BEAM R	LENGTH OF MAIN BEAM L	INSIDE SPREAD	NUMBER OF POINTS R	NUMBER OF POINTS L	AREA	STATE/PROVINCE	HUNTER'S NAME	DATE	RANK
101 3/8	17 0/8	18 3/8	14 3/8	4	4	Sierra County	NM	John D. "Jack" Frost	1994	20
100 6/8	16 6/8	16 3/8	12 6/8	4	4	Graham County	AZ	Hugh H. Hamman	1966	21
100 5/8	17 4/8	17 3/8	11 5/8	4	4	Cochise County	AZ	Mark Heller	1995	22
100 4/8	17 5/8	16 5/8	12 4/8	4	5	Cochise County	AZ	Dallas Scherck	1971	23
100 2/8	17 0/8	16 0/8	14 5/8	4	5	Cochise County	AZ	Ray Edwards	1984	24
100 1/8	17 7/8	17 1/8	11 7/8	5	5	Sonora	MEX	Marte Scheuffele	1974	25
100 1/8	16 6/8	17 7/8	14 1/8	4	5	Pima County	AZ	John D. "Jack" Frost	1993	25
100 0/8	16 2/8	17 2/8	12 2/8	4	4	Hidalgo County	NM	Eddie Claypool	1997	27
99 6/8	16 6/8	17 0/8	14 0/8	4	4	Pima County	AZ	Tracy Gene Hardy	1982	28
99 3/8	16 7/8	16 0/8	13 3/8	4	4	Gila County	AZ	David B. Hatch	1988	29
99 1/8	16 3/8	16 2/8	13 5/8	4	4	Pima County	AZ	Jim Walton	1992	30
98 7/8	15 7/8	15 5/8	14 5/8	4	5	Gila County	AZ	Darryl Kessler	1978	31
98 5/8	13 0/8	13 4/8	12 3/8	6	4	Graham County	AZ	John A. Holcomb	1983	32
98 5/8	16 6/8	16 2/8	14 3/8	4	5	Pima County	AZ	George G. Alcorta	1989	32
98 4/8	16 5/8	16 7/8	12 2/8	4	4	Santa Cruz County	AZ	Thomas J. Hoffman	1993	34
98 3/8	17 1/8	17 0/8	13 7/8	4	4	Cochise County	AZ	David Schied	1973	35
98 3/8	18 2/8	18 0/8	15 1/8	4	4	Grant County	NM	Duane Beenblossom	1993	35
98 2/8	16 5/8	16 5/8	14 0/8	4	4	Grant County	NM	Larry M. Looman	1991	37
98 0/8	17 1/8	16 7/8	15 0/8	4	4	Cochise County	AZ	Brian Palmer	1990	38
97 7/8	16 0/8	16 3/8	12 3/8	4	4	Cochise County	AZ	Randy Breland	1989	39
97 6/8	16 2/8	16 2/8	11 4/8	4	4	Santa Cruz County	AZ	Brian Ham	1992	40
97 4/8	16 0/8	15 0/8	14 1/8	4	5	Pima County	AZ	Steve Fossman	1989	41
97 2/8	16 5/8	16 5/8	13 4/8	4	4	Cochise County	AZ	Dave Burdick	1994	42
96 5/8	16 0/8	16 0/8	13 7/8	4	4	Pima County	AZ	Jay Black	1993	43
96 3/8	16 6/8	17 1/8	15 6/8	6	5	Graham County	AZ	Maurice Holthaus	1984	44
96 3/8	16 3/8	16 6/8	12 7/8	5	4	Grant County	NM	Duane Beenblossom	1992	44
95 5/8	15 7/8	16 2/8	13 5/8	4	4	Santa Cruz County	AZ	Bill Krenz	1984	46
95 3/8	17 2/8	17 6/8	15 3/8	5	4	Maricopa County	AZ	Bob Fromme	1986	47
95 0/8	14 6/8	14 7/8	10 6/8	4	4	Santa Cruz County	AZ	Ted N. McMillion	1996	48
94 3/8	15 6/8	15 4/8	12 3/8	4	4	Cochise County	AZ	Randy Breland	1987	49
94 1/8	15 0/8	16 0/8	13 6/8	5	4	Greenlee County	AZ	John T. Skeen	1975	50
94 1/8	14 3/8	15 2/8	13 3/8	4	4	Cochise County	AZ	Daniel Staples	1981	50
94 0/8	16 6/8	16 1/8	14 0/8	4	4	Greenlee County	AZ	Jack Sartain	1983	52
93 1/8	14 3/8	15 0/8	14 3/8	4	4	Pima County	AZ	Jerry Muir	1982	53
92 6/8	16 0/8	17 0/8	13 4/8	4	4	Pima County	AZ	Peter C. Knagge	1986	54
92 4/8	15 6/8	16 1/8	13 2/8	4	5	Pima County	AZ	Rick Forrest	1991	55
92 2/8	16 1/8	16 2/8	14 2/8	4	5	Santa Cruz County	AZ	Rowland J. Robinson	1985	56
92 2/8	17 5/8	17 4/8	12 6/8	4	5	Greenlee County	AZ	Tom Taylor	1993	56
91 7/8	18 4/8	17 7/8	14 1/8	4	4	Cochise County	AZ	Richard S. Barkley	1995	58
91 7/8	17 0/8	16 5/8	12 7/8	4	4	Grant County	NM	Jeff Campbell	1997	58
91 6/8	15 1/8	15 4/8	14 4/8	4	4	Cochise County	AZ	Randy Breland	1981	60
91 5/8	17 0/8	18 1/8	14 5/8	4	4	Pima County	AZ	Edward A. Chavez	1997	61
91 2/8	15 2/8	14 6/8	12 2/8	4	4	Santa Cruz County	AZ	Perry Schaal	1983	62
91 1/8	14 5/8	14 4/8	14 6/8	4	5	Yavapai County	AZ	Kyle Brock	1986	63
91 0/8	16 2/8	15 5/8	12 6/8	4	4	Gila County	AZ	John Radford	1972	64
90 6/8	17 0/8	17 5/8	14 6/8	4	4	Cochise County	AZ	Richard E. 'Dick' Johnson	1986	65
90 0/8	15 5/8	14 6/8	10 4/8	4	4	Cochise County	AZ	Bob Ramirez	1990	66
90 0/8	16 2/8	17 1/8	14 2/8	4	4	Catron County	NM	Eddie Claypool	1998	66
89 1/8	14 6/8	15 2/8	14 3/8	4	4	Gila County	AZ	Mark Ovitt	1994	68
89 0/8	15 3/8	16 5/8	13 2/8	4	4	Sierra County	NM	Perry Harper	1989	69
88 5/8	14 2/8	15 1/8	11 3/8	4	4	Gila County	AZ	Michael P. Wanat	1995	70
88 4/8	15 6/8	17 1/8	11 6/8	4	5	Cochise County	AZ	R. Ertz	1991	71
88 4/8	16 2/8	15 5/8	12 0/8	4	4	Cochise County	AZ	Walt Costello	1997	71
88 0/8	13 7/8	13 4/8	11 2/8	4	4	Grant County	NM	Al Haines	1991	73
87 7/8	15 4/8	13 1/8	12 7/8	4	4	Cochise County	AZ	Dan Gwaltney	1989	74
87 7/8	12 7/8	13 6/8	10 5/8	4	4	Apache County	AZ	Shaun Finch	1995	74
87 3/8	15 6/8	15 5/8	13 7/8	4	4	Gila County	AZ	V. Randy Liljenquist	1996	76
87 1/8	14 1/8	13 6/8	10 3/8	4	4	Grant County	NM	Stan Godfrey	1993	77
87 0/8	15 2/8	15 4/8	12 0/8	4	4	Santa Cruz County	AZ	Chris Warren	1998	78
86 5/8	14 5/8	14 3/8	8 5/8	4	4	Santa Cruz County	AZ	Richard D. Amado	1994	79
86 2/8	15 1/8	16 3/8	14 4/8	4	4	Grant County	NM	Bill Elmer	1992	80
86 2/8	15 5/8	16 3/8	12 0/8	4	4	Grant County	NM	Mike W. Leonard	1997	80
86 1/8	14 7/8	15 6/8	14 3/8	4	3	Pinal County	AZ	Steve E. Allen	1979	82
85 7/8	17 4/8	16 6/8	15 1/8	5	4	Pima County	AZ	Reid Rutherford	1997	83
85 5/8	13 4/8	13 3/8	12 7/8	4	4	Hidalgo County	NM	John D. "Jack" Frost	1992	84
85 4/8	13 6/8	16 0/8	12 2/8	5	4	Santa Cruz County	AZ	Brad Wedding	1990	85
85 1/8	14 7/8	14 7/8	11 3/8	4	4	Cochise County	AZ	Mark Escapule	1993	86
85 0/8	15 0/8	14 6/8	12 0/8	5	5	Graham County	AZ	Dennis L. Shirley	1991	87
84 7/8	13 0/8	12 2/8	10 3/8	4	4	Cochise County	AZ	Dave Rhodes	1976	88
84 6/8	14 4/8	14 5/8	12 6/8	4	4	Pima County	AZ	Bill Thompkins	1988	89
84 2/8	15 0/8	13 4/8	13 2/8	4	4	Pima County	AZ	Robert W. Ledbetter	1989	90
84 2/8	15 4/8	15 0/8	15 2/8	4	4	Greenlee County	AZ	Donald P. Travis	1998	90
84 1/8	13 4/8	13 7/8	12 5/8	4	4	Maricopa County	AZ	Ed Matteson	1963	92
83 1/8	14 4/8	13 6/8	11 7/8	4	4	Santa Cruz County	AZ	Kurt W. Keskimaki	1995	93

COUES DEER (TYPICAL ANTLERS)

Minimum Score 65 — Continued

SCORE	LENGTH OF MAIN BEAM R	LENGTH OF MAIN BEAM L	INSIDE SPREAD	NUMBER OF POINTS R	NUMBER OF POINTS L	AREA	STATE/PROVINCE	HUNTER'S NAME	DATE	RANK
82 6/8	15 3/8	15 7/8	13 3/8	4	4	Coconino County	AZ	Carl Vance	1973	94
82 6/8	14 7/8	14 2/8	10 2/8	4	4	Santa Cruz County	AZ	Thomas L. Wright	1993	94
82 5/8	14 3/8	15 2/8	13 1/8	4	4	Gila County	AZ	Mike Mahoney	1976	96
81 6/8	13 1/8	13 1/8	12 0/8	4	4	Pima County	AZ	Jack R. Frazier	1984	97
81 5/8	14 3/8	14 4/8	12 3/8	4	4	Greenlee County	AZ	David L. Willis	1992	98
81 2/8	12 4/8	12 1/8	13 0/8	4	4	Graham County	AZ	Bill Cross	1967	99
81 1/8	16 1/8	14 7/8	12 3/8	4	4	Pima County	AZ	Robert Forrest	1991	100
81 0/8	14 5/8	14 0/8	13 2/8	4	4	Grant County	NM	Bob J. Brown	1960	101
80 7/8	14 2/8	14 3/8	14 3/8	4	4	Gila County	AZ	Gary H. Mehaffey	1989	102
80 6/8	15 2/8	15 5/8	14 6/8	3	4	Grant County	NM	George M. Ratliff	1992	103
80 5/8	14 6/8	14 7/8	11 5/8	4	4	Greenlee County	AZ	Glenn W. Isler	1993	104
80 5/8	14 5/8	14 0/8	13 3/8	3	3	Gila County	AZ	Ronald Nuss, Jr.	1994	104
80 4/8	16 1/8	15 2/8	12 7/8	3	4	Grant County	NM	Mike Burroughs	1993	106
80 2/8	16 4/8	15 2/8	14 6/8	3	4	Gila County	AZ	Randy L. Hill	1996	107
80 1/8	13 4/8	13 4/8	10 3/8	4	4	Pima County	AZ	Dave Snyder	1983	108
79 7/8	13 5/8	13 7/8	11 3/8	4	4	Grant County	NM	Elmer R. Luce, Jr.	1996	109
79 5/8	12 7/8	13 7/8	10 7/8	4	4	Grant County	NM	Mike Burroughs	1995	110
79 2/8	16 0/8	13 7/8	13 5/8	4	4	Pima County	AZ	David C. Durkee	1987	111
78 2/8	14 0/8	14 1/8	12 4/8	4	4	Pima County	AZ	Jim Walton	1990	112
78 1/8	15 0/8	14 6/8	12 5/8	4	4	Santa Cruz County	AZ	Matt Mueller	1994	113
78 0/8	12 3/8	12 5/8	10 2/8	4	4	Gila County	AZ	Gary Mehaffey	1992	114
77 7/8	15 3/8	14 7/8	12 5/8	3	3	Gila County	AZ	Tom Hashem	1964	115
77 6/8	14 2/8	14 1/8	9 6/8	5	5	Pima County	AZ	Richard Dawe, Jr.	1964	116
77 4/8	14 4/8	13 7/8	10 4/8	4	5	Sierra County	NM	Charles E. Franzoy	1972	117
77 1/8	13 1/8	13 5/8	12 1/8	4	4	Gila County	AZ	Thomas J. Hoffman	1995	118
76 6/8	12 7/8	13 3/8	12 0/8	4	3	Cochise County	AZ	Robert G. Ables	1989	119
76 6/8	12 7/8	12 6/8	12 2/8	4	4	Santa Cruz County	AZ	Kurt W. Keskimaki	1994	119
76 4/8	14 7/8	14 3/8	12 0/8	3	3	Gila County	AZ	Monty Dyke	1989	121
75 4/8	13 1/8	12 7/8	12 0/8	4	4	Coconino County	AZ	Les Shelton	1987	122
75 2/8	13 2/8	13 7/8	10 2/8	4	4	Cochise County	AZ	Russell L. Gann	1987	123
75 2/8	14 4/8	14 6/8	12 0/8	4	4	Graham County	AZ	Chuck Adams	1989	123
75 2/8	12 7/8	13 0/8	10 6/8	4	4	Cochise County	AZ	R. Ertz	1990	123
75 2/8	13 4/8	13 5/8	11 6/8	4	3	Pima County	AZ	Tony Otte	1993	123
75 2/8	14 0/8	13 6/8	13 6/8	4	4	Cochise County	AZ	Stan Parkerson	1995	123
75 0/8	15 0/8	15 7/8	14 6/8	3	3	Grant County	NM	David H. Boland	1994	128
74 5/8	14 5/8	14 6/8	10 5/8	3	3	Sierra County	NM	Jim Ryan	1988	129
74 3/8	13 6/8	13 3/8	11 1/8	3	4	Greenlee County	AZ	Richard E. Bickley	1998	130
74 2/8	12 6/8	12 1/8	9 4/8	4	4	Grant County	NM	Mike W. Leonard	1992	131
73 6/8	12 6/8	13 1/8	10 4/8	4	4	Pima County	AZ	Howard Cooper	1980	132
73 6/8	12 2/8	13 5/8	11 2/8	4	3	Pima County	AZ	William E. Dickinson	1982	132
73 5/8	12 2/8	12 7/8	13 4/8	5	4	Hidalgo County	NM	Larry Behrends	1969	134
73 4/8	15 0/8	14 4/8	13 2/8	2	4	Pima County	AZ	Michael L. Henrikson	1979	135
73 4/8	9 2/8	13 3/8	11 0/8	4	4	Pima County	AZ	Dave Rue	1994	135
73 2/8	13 0/8	13 0/8	10 6/8	4	4	Gila County	AZ	Jim Mercer	1958	137
72 6/8	13 2/8	13 4/8	12 4/8	4	3	Sierra County	NM	Thomas J. Hoffman	1994	138
72 5/8	13 7/8	14 2/8	11 1/8	4	4	Grant County	NM	Bill L. Marek	1997	139
72 4/8	11 6/8	11 6/8	11 4/8	4	4	Gila County	AZ	Gary H. Behrends	1969	140
72 0/8	13 1/8	12 6/8	10 2/8	4	3	Greenlee County	AZ	Tom Taylor	1995	141
71 5/8	13 1/8	13 0/8	12 3/8	3	3	Santa Cruz County	AZ	Andrew J. Long	1996	142
71 4/8	15 1/8	14 7/8	14 0/8	3	2	Gila County	AZ	Gilbert Wiley	1996	143
71 2/8	13 2/8	12 7/8	13 2/8	4	3	Pima County	AZ	Stephen E. Johnson	1979	144
70 7/8	13 3/8	15 0/8	12 5/8	4	4	Grant County	NM	David H. Boland	1996	145
70 7/8	13 4/8	14 6/8	13 1/8	3	3	Cochise County	AZ	Thomas Chadwick	1996	145
68 6/8	13 2/8	12 7/8	10 0/8	3	4	Atasco Mtns.	AZ	Peter C. Knagge	1978	147
68 6/8	12 5/8	12 7/8	12 0/8	4	4	Cochise County	AZ	Daniel Staples	1980	147
68 5/8	12 0/8	12 2/8	11 7/8	3	3	Graham County	AZ	Matthew Liljenquist	1995	149
67 4/8	13 0/8	13 3/8	13 0/8	4	4	Graham County	AZ	Chuck Adams	1988	150
66 6/8	12 1/8	11 7/8	10 6/8	4	4	Pima County	AZ	Steve Neuberger	1989	151
66 4/8	12 3/8	12 4/8	8 6/8	3	3	Pima County	AZ	Larry Rogge	1984	152
66 3/8	12 1/8	12 5/8	9 7/8	4	4	Grant County	NM	Don Guber	1996	153
66 3/8	11 7/8	11 7/8	11 7/8	3	3	Cochise County	AZ	Joe Diedrich	1997	153
66 2/8	12 3/8	12 5/8	10 0/8	3	3	Grant County	NM	Chuck Schultz	1991	155
66 1/8	11 5/8	12 2/8	11 1/8	4	4	Graham County	AZ	Anna C. Ward	1997	156
65 3/8	11 7/8	12 0/8	6 4/8	5	5	Catron County	NM	Tim Wells	1997	157
65 0/8	14 3/8	11 0/8	7 2/8	4	3	Grant County	NM	Dr. Eugene T. Altiere	1998	158

COUES DEER (TYPICAL VELVET ANTLERS)

Minimum Score 65

SCORE	LENGTH OF MAIN BEAM R L		INSIDE SPREAD	NUMBER OF POINTS R L		AREA	STATE/ PROVINCE	HUNTER'S NAME	DATE	RANK
114 2/8	18 0/8	16 7/8	12 6/8	5	5	Pima County	AZ	Michael Sarapa	1996	*
108 3/8	16 7/8	17 6/8	14 1/8	5	5	Gila County	AZ	William C. Longenbaugh	1994	*
100 2/8	15 0/8	15 3/8	15 3/8	5	4	Gila County	AZ	Monty Dyke	1988	*
97 6/8	16 0/8	16 0/8	12 0/8	4	4	Greenlee County	AZ	Larry R. Marin	1996	*
95 0/8	15 2/8	15 3/8	13 4/8	4	4	Graham County	AZ	John A. Bierhaus	1997	*
93 7/8	16 1/8	16 2/8	14 1/8	4	4	Gila County	AZ	Kathy Trimble	1994	*
89 2/8	15 5/8	15 3/8	13 4/8	4	4	Gila County	AZ	Monte R. Watts	1994	*
85 7/8	14 6/8	13 4/8	13 0/8	4	5	Cochise County	AZ	Paul W. Olson	1994	*
85 4/8	13 3/8	13 3/8	12 2/8	4	4	Santa Cruz County	AZ	Robert Murphey	1997	*
83 3/8	14 1/8	13 4/8	14 3/8	4	3	Pima County	AZ	Patrick T. Lioy	1997	*
81 1/8	13 6/8	14 3/8	14 4/8	4	4	Cochise County	AZ	Shawn Preston	1989	*
76 6/8	12 2/8	12 4/8	9 2/8	4	4	Gila County	AZ	Lee Braudt	1996	*
76 1/8	11 2/8	11 3/8	11 6/8	4	4	Pima County	AZ	Derek McMurry	1995	*
68 2/8	12 0/8	12 3/8	11 4/8	3	4	Coconino County	AZ	Josh Epperson	1994	*

* *Velvet entries will be listed in only one record book.*

World Record Coues Deer (Non-Typical Antlers)
Score: 124 0/8
Coconino County, Arizona - 1987
Hunter: John George Evans

COUES DEER (NON-TYPICAL ANTLERS)

Minimum Score 95 — *Odocoileus virginianus couesi*

SCORE	LENGTH OF MAIN BEAM R	LENGTH OF MAIN BEAM L	INSIDE SPREAD	NUMBER OF POINTS R	NUMBER OF POINTS L	AREA	STATE/PROVINCE	HUNTER'S NAME	DATE	RANK
124 0/8	17 7/8	17 0/8	16 3/8	5	6	Coconino County	AZ	John George Evans	1987	1
119 5/8	19 3/8	18 6/8	13 0/8	6	6	Pima County	AZ	Art GonzaLes	1987	2
116 7/8	16 7/8	17 0/8	11 5/8	6	8	Santa Cruz County	AZ	John F. May	1991	3
112 4/8	18 4/8	18 6/8	13 2/8	5	5	Pima County	AZ	David G. Snyder	1984	4
110 5/8	18 1/8	18 5/8	14 1/8	5	5	Greenlee County	AZ	Roy Jimenez	1998	5
101 6/8	17 1/8	16 0/8	13 4/8	4	6	Grant County	NM	Daryl Tow	1993	6
96 4/8	15 4/8	13 2/8	15 5/8	6	7	Gila County	AZ	Larry Behrends	1989	7

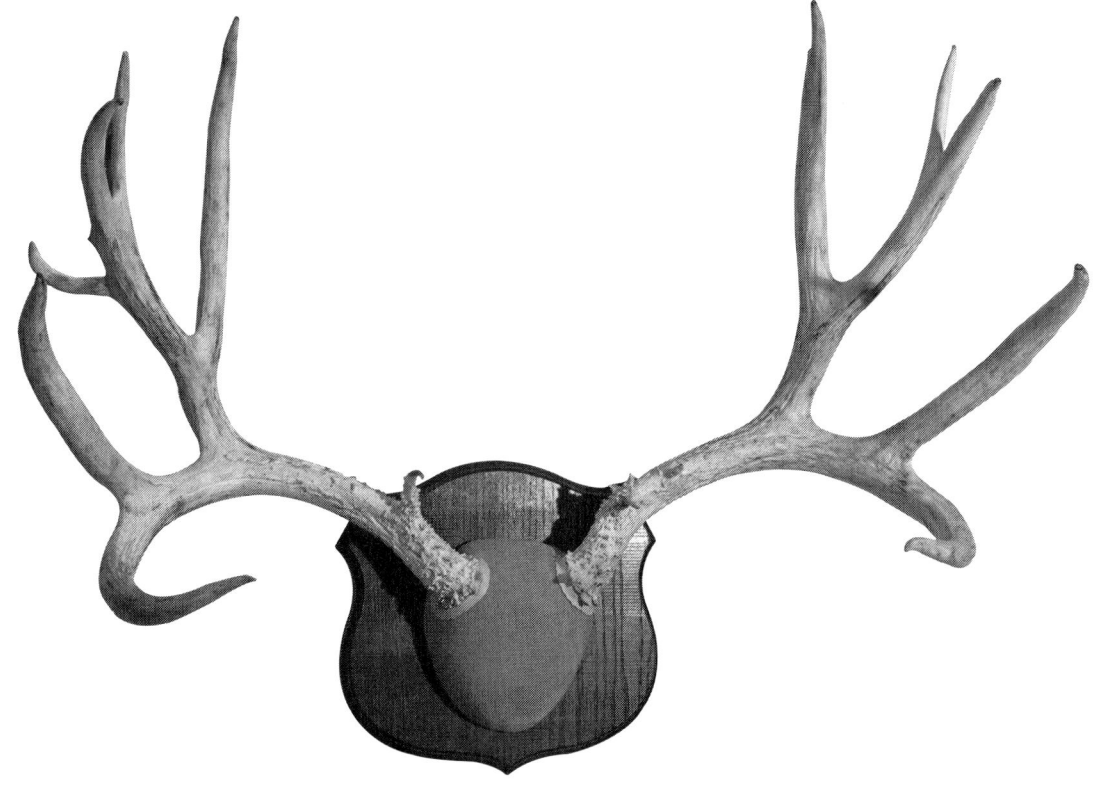

World Record Mule Deer (Typical Antlers)
Score: 203 1/8
White River National Forest, Colorado - 1979
Hunter: Bill Barcus

MULE DEER (TYPICAL ANTLERS)

Minimum Score 145 *Odocoileus hemionus* and certain related subspecies

SCORE	LENGTH OF MAIN BEAM R	LENGTH OF MAIN BEAM L	INSIDE SPREAD	NUMBER OF POINTS R	NUMBER OF POINTS L	AREA	STATE/PROVINCE	HUNTER'S NAME	DATE	RANK
203 1/8	28 5/8	27 6/8	30 2/8	7	7	White River N.F.	CO	Bill Barcus	1979	1
202 6/8	26 7/8	26 2/8	26 7/8	7	6	Gove County	KS	Carl Ghan, Jr.	1992	2
200 6/8	27 7/8	25 3/8	25 0/8	5	7	Eagle Creek	SAS	Ron Cordes	1998	3
200 0/8	24 7/8	26 2/8	25 1/8	6	5	Coconino County	AZ	Adam R. Kowalski, Jr.	1995	4
198 4/8	28 0/8	26 0/8	32 2/8	7	7	Apache County	AZ	William T. Rose	1985	5
197 6/8	24 1/8	24 7/8	23 3/8	5	6	Dolores County	CO	Jim Horneck	1988	6
197 1/8	24 2/8	22 4/8	21 4/8	6	6	Beaver County	UT	David Snyder	1982	7
197 0/8	24 6/8	27 7/8	23 6/8	5	5	Park County	CO	Ronald E. Sniff	1969	8
196 5/8	25 0/8	25 6/8	23 4/8	5	6	Coconino County	AZ	Jim Wagner	1986	9
195 7/8	29 7/8	29 7/8	30 2/8	6	7	Crook County	OR	Gidion "Hop" Jackson	1990	10
195 6/8	28 0/8	29 4/8	28 4/8	7	5	San Juan County	NM	David A. Brooks	1995	11
194 7/8	25 1/8	24 3/8	22 7/8	5	5	Sublette County	WY	Gil Winters	1998	12
194 1/8	22 6/8	22 4/8	19 1/8	5	5	Elmore County	ID	Roger W. Taylor	1994	13
193 5/8	27 0/8	30 1/8	23 1/8	6	5	Cibola County	NM	Kenny R. Bruton	1987	14
193 3/8	28 2/8	28 0/8	24 7/8	6	5	Baker County	OR	Anthony A. Myers	1996	15
193 1/8	25 2/8	25 6/8	23 5/8	6	7	Rawlins County	KS	Matt Park	1997	16
193 0/8	28 1/8	28 5/8	31 0/8	5	6	Weld County	CO	Lance Hockett	1996	17
192 7/8	24 6/8	23 3/8	23 0/8	6	5	San Isabel National Forest	CO	Donald D. Garrison	1972	18
192 1/8	25 3/8	26 2/8	23 0/8	6	5	Lemhi County	ID	Mike Nelson	1978	19
192 0/8	25 6/8	26 4/8	22 0/8	7	5	Uncompahgre Plateau	CO	Donald Click	1973	20
191 3/8	23 5/8	25 1/8	24 3/8	5	5	Rio Arriba County	NM	Ryan Turner	1995	21
190 6/8	27 4/8	27 4/8	25 7/8	9	8	Mesa County	CO	Allen Personious	1976	22

MULE DEER (TYPICAL ANTLERS)

Minimum Score 145
Continued

SCORE	LENGTH OF MAIN BEAM R / L	INSIDE SPREAD	NUMBER OF POINTS R / L		AREA	STATE/PROVINCE	HUNTER'S NAME	DATE	RANK
190 5/8	26 2/8 / 26 2/8	22 4/8	7	8	Teller County	CO	Dan Mersman	1982	23
190 2/8	21 3/8 / 23 3/8	21 7/8	6	5	Boise County	ID	Ricky D. Addison	1984	24
190 1/8	25 3/8 / 24 6/8	25 3/8	6	5	Moffat County	CO	Glenn Pritchard	1990	25
190 0/8	25 1/8 / 23 4/8	24 4/8	5	5	Utah County	UT	John Edwards	1967	26
190 0/8	24 6/8 / 27 2/8	25 2/8	6	5	Baker County	OR	Mike Raney	1996	26
189 5/8	22 5/8 / 23 1/8	23 4/8	5	5	Rosebud River	ALB	Douglas R. Lowen	1994	28
189 3/8	27 0/8 / 27 0/8	24 1/8	6	5	Tooele County	UT	Ken Davis	1963	29
189 2/8	26 4/8 / 26 0/8	26 6/8	5	5	Crook County	OR	John Nelson	1992	30
189 1/8	23 6/8 / 23 7/8	23 6/8	5	8	Chelan County	WA	R. Early/D. Davies, Jr.	1983	31
189 0/8	24 4/8 / 23 5/8	25 6/8	5	6	Montezuma County	CO	Al Newkirk	1983	32
188 7/8	25 2/8 / 26 3/8	21 1/8	6	6	Settlement Canyon	UT	Derald R. Evans	1965	33
188 6/8	24 5/8 / 24 6/8	21 2/8	5	5	Mesa County	CO	Bob Jensen	1974	34
188 4/8	25 6/8 / 26 6/8	24 3/8	6	5	Abbey	SAS	Barry Minor	1979	35
188 3/8	25 0/8 / 23 6/8	24 1/8	5	5	Lincoln County	CO	Windell Penton	1997	36
188 2/8	24 3/8 / 24 4/8	23 2/8	6	6	Mesa County	CO	John Lamicq, Jr.	1967	37
187 7/8	23 7/8 / 24 7/8	22 5/8	5	6	Duck Creek	UT	Gerald Clark	1966	38
187 6/8	28 3/8 / 28 1/8	32 3/8	6	6	Weld County	CO	Randy Henderson	1993	39
187 5/8	23 2/8 / 22 5/8	18 3/8	5	5	Moffat County	CO	Leonard Jefferson	1971	40
187 5/8	25 0/8 / 25 1/8	28 3/8	8	5	Boulder County	CO	Jeff Biemiller	1991	40
187 5/8	24 4/8 / 25 7/8	25 1/8	5	5	Billings County	ND	Dan Simerson	1995	40
187 5/8	27 5/8 / 28 4/8	23 2/8	6	6	Rio Arriba County	NM	Pat Lovato	1998	40
187 4/8	25 7/8 / 25 0/8	21 5/8	6	7	Lake County	OR	Marte Scheuffele	1984	44
187 2/8	24 3/8 / 22 3/8	22 2/8	5	5	Dawes County	NE	Kirk Peters	1989	45
187 2/8	23 3/8 / 22 7/8	23 2/8	5	5	Mohave County	AZ	Kyle Bundy	1992	45
187 2/8	25 4/8 / 25 4/8	22 0/8	7	6	Teton County	WY	Don Hoard	1995	45
187 1/8	23 6/8 / 25 6/8	25 2/8	7	7	Milk River	ALB	Robin Tremblay	1992	48
187 0/8	24 6/8 / 23 4/8	23 6/8	6	5	Rio Arriba County	NM	Doug Aikin	1995	49
186 7/8	25 3/8 / 25 0/8	20 1/8	5	6	Eagle County	CO	Dr. J. D. Jones	1963	50
186 7/8	26 3/8 / 26 0/8	22 0/8	6	8	Uncompahgre Plateau	CO	Jerry Click	1973	50
186 7/8	25 2/8 / 25 3/8	21 7/8	4	4	Piegan Creek	ALB	Dave Moore	1993	50
186 6/8	24 5/8 / 25 2/8	24 2/8	5	5	Cassia County	ID	Pat Miller	1965	53
186 5/8	25 1/8 / 25 6/8	19 2/8	5	6	Elbert County	CO	Loren Dellinger	1984	54
186 4/8	24 2/8 / 23 1/8	24 4/8	5	5	White River N.F.	CO	Walt Seville	1977	55
186 2/8	26 4/8 / 26 0/8	27 4/8	6	9	Gunnison County	CO	Don E. Lampert	1973	56
186 1/8	24 1/8 / 24 0/8	21 3/8	5	5	Cassia County	ID	Bill Shockey	1965	57
186 1/8	25 3/8 / 24 0/8	25 4/8	5	5	Humboldt County	NV	Tim Bray	1984	57
185 6/8	24 1/8 / 24 4/8	24 0/8	5	5	Imperial County	CA	Gilbert Clement	1982	59
185 5/8	24 2/8 / 25 4/8	27 0/8	7	6	Mesa County	CO	Art Cook	1962	60
185 4/8	22 0/8 / 22 3/8	20 4/8	5	5	Coconino County	AZ	Ronald Hollamon	1978	61
185 0/8	26 0/8 / 26 2/8	26 3/8	5	6	Larimer County	CO	Don Lampert	1969	62
185 0/8	26 1/8 / 25 1/8	24 0/8	5	5	Montrose County	CO	Darryl L. Coe	1988	62
185 0/8	23 5/8 / 25 0/8	21 0/8	5	4	Norton County	KS	Pete Killman	1993	62
185 0/8	24 0/8 / 24 3/8	23 2/8	5	5	Clear Creek County	CO	Bradley John Kuhn	1996	62
184 7/8	25 7/8 / 25 4/8	21 7/8	5	5	Mesa County	CO	James L. Peterson	1983	66
184 7/8	24 2/8 / 24 4/8	25 1/8	6	5	Maricopa County	AZ	Timothy Gibson	1987	66
184 6/8	23 0/8 / 23 2/8	23 3/8	5	5	Mesa County	CO	David L. Myers	1976	68
184 3/8	24 4/8 / 23 3/8	28 4/8	6	5	Caribou County	ID	Coby Tigert	1983	69
184 3/8	25 1/8 / 26 4/8	23 0/8	6	6	Teton County	WY	Kevin D. Marshall	1995	69
184 2/8	25 2/8 / 24 3/8	22 7/8	5	6	Teton County	WY	Donald R. Williamson	1991	71
184 2/8	26 4/8 / 25 2/8	21 2/8	5	5	Coconino County	AZ	Wally Schwartz	1998	71
184 1/8	24 3/8 / 24 6/8	24 6/8	5	6	Delta County	CO	Scott Kolb	1963	73
184 1/8	27 5/8 / 27 0/8	25 3/8	5	4	Bernalillo County	NM	Gregory A. Gwash	1970	73
184 1/8	24 6/8 / 25 2/8	24 2/8	6	5	Ravalli County	MT	Brett Neal	1994	73
184 0/8	24 1/8 / 25 1/8	24 2/8	5	6	Boise County	ID	Joseph Greenley	1984	76
183 7/8	25 0/8 / 24 3/8	23 7/8	5	5	Moffat County	CO	Joel Hogan	1966	77
183 7/8	24 2/8 / 24 4/8	23 1/8	6	5	Pima County	AZ	Jimmy Marsh	1994	77
183 6/8	26 4/8 / 27 3/8	27 0/8	5	4	Iron County	UT	Ted Garrett	1963	79
183 6/8	23 4/8 / 23 2/8	24 2/8	5	5	Billings County	ND	Daniel J. Erickstad	1992	79
183 5/8	26 6/8 / 25 7/8	25 5/8	5	5	Sanpete County	UT	Weldon Noland	1965	81
183 5/8	20 2/8 / 19 3/8	20 2/8	6	6	Rio Arriba County	NM	Billy Terrazas	1985	81
183 4/8	29 0/8 / 26 5/8	23 6/8	5	4	Kiowa County	CO	Dave Moyer	1988	83
183 3/8	25 7/8 / 26 1/8	22 4/8	7	5	Sevier County	UT	Kyle Johnson	1970	84
183 2/8	25 5/8 / 26 5/8	22 7/8	6	9	Wasatch County	UT	Blake Spencer	1963	85
183 1/8	25 0/8 / 25 1/8	24 5/8	5	6	White Pine County	NV	Robert Price	1986	86
183 0/8	25 1/8 / 25 5/8	25 2/8	5	6	Lincoln County	MT	John C. Bartlett	1982	87
182 7/8	23 3/8 / 22 0/8	21 7/8	5	5	Caribou County	ID	Neil Dursteler	1967	88
182 7/8	24 4/8 / 25 1/8	24 1/8	5	5	Cache County	UT	Robert Bronson	1985	88
182 6/8	22 0/8 / 22 2/8	20 2/8	5	7	Chelan County	WA	Glenn St. Charles	1959	90
182 6/8	23 3/8 / 23 4/8	20 3/8	7	5	Moffat County	CO	Glenn Pritchard	1987	90
182 5/8	26 4/8 / 25 4/8	21 5/8	5	5	Lincoln County	WY	Lael Eddins	1978	92
182 4/8	25 2/8 / 24 2/8	25 0/8	5	5	Humboldt County	NV	George Rajnus	1985	93
182 4/8	24 5/8 / 24 3/8	21 4/8	5	5	Mesa County	CO	Charles C. Perry	1985	93
182 4/8	25 0/8 / 25 5/8	21 2/8	5	5	Mesa County	CO	David M. Gant	1986	93
182 4/8	23 5/8 / 25 4/8	20 4/8	5	5	Cypress	ALB	James Drader	1992	93
182 2/8	25 6/8 / 24 2/8	25 2/8	6	5	Mesa County	CO	Robert C. Dawson	1974	97
182 2/8	25 1/8 / 25 2/8	24 0/8	6	5	Caribou County	ID	Eric Bowman	1983	97
182 2/8	25 4/8 / 26 1/8	23 6/8	7	9	Graham County	KS	Phillip L. Kirkland	1988	97
182 0/8	23 5/8 / 23 3/8	20 6/8	5	5	Elmore County	ID	Dallas R. Doty, Jr.	1992	100

MULE DEER (TYPICAL ANTLERS)

Minimum Score 145 Continued

SCORE	LENGTH OF MAIN BEAM R	LENGTH OF MAIN BEAM L	INSIDE SPREAD	NUMBER OF POINTS R	NUMBER OF POINTS L	AREA	STATE/PROVINCE	HUNTER'S NAME	DATE	RANK
181 7/8	21 7/8	21 1/8	22 6/8	5	5	Power County	ID	Austin Cummins	1970	101
181 5/8	24 3/8	24 0/8	21 5/8	5	5	Wakely	CO	Lynn Grace	1964	102
181 4/8	24 4/8	23 2/8	25 6/8	5	5	Garfield County	CO	Henry Wichers	1967	103
181 4/8	23 6/8	23 3/8	24 7/8	5	5	Butte County	ID	Richard A. Southwell	1980	103
181 4/8	23 0/8	23 1/8	23 7/8	6	5	El Paso County	CO	Craig E. Kimball	1998	103
181 3/8	26 0/8	26 5/8	26 3/8	5	5	Montrose County	CO	John Lamb	1981	106
181 2/8	22 1/8	22 6/8	20 5/8	5	6	Larimer County	CO	Wayne Eberhard	1972	107
181 1/8	24 3/8	25 4/8	19 3/8	6	6	Union County	OR	Thomas Mussatto	1968	108
181 0/8	24 7/8	22 7/8	23 0/8	6	6	Rio Arriba County	NM	Charles Tapia	1965	109
181 0/8	26 0/8	25 5/8	24 4/8	5	5	Boise County	ID	Tom D'Aquino	1991	109
180 7/8	25 2/8	24 7/8	22 7/8	5	5	Washoe County	NV	Donald E. Callen	1984	111
180 6/8	23 6/8	24 6/8	20 4/8	5	5	La Plata County	CO	Ralph RePola	1988	112
180 6/8	23 0/8	23 7/8	24 4/8	6	6	Harney County	OR	John F. Nelson	1997	112
180 5/8	24 2/8	23 3/8	23 5/8	5	5	Cochise County	AZ	Wendell Miles	1992	114
180 4/8	24 1/8	25 1/8	21 6/8	4	4	Mesa County	CO	Jack Kruckenburg	1958	115
180 4/8	24 0/8	24 7/8	21 0/8	6	6	Fremont County	ID	Steven M. Jones	1979	115
180 4/8	24 6/8	25 3/8	24 0/8	6	5	Ravalli County	MT	Gary Habeck	1984	115
180 4/8	22 6/8	22 2/8	21 7/8	7	6	Montezuma County	CO	Marvin Reichenau	1987	115
180 3/8	24 0/8	25 5/8	27 5/8	5	5	Boise County	ID	Benton K. Wetzel	1970	119
180 3/8	25 1/8	25 2/8	23 5/8	5	5	Kiowa County	CO	Jeff Barber	1994	119
180 3/8	26 2/8	25 7/8	24 7/8	6	5	Millarville	ALB	Gary Duet	1995	119
180 2/8	24 5/8	24 7/8	25 7/8	8	5	Garfield County	CO	Michael R. Allen	1967	122
180 2/8	23 1/8	24 0/8	23 2/8	5	5	Lincoln County	NV	Fred B. Allen III	1974	122
180 2/8	23 2/8	24 2/8	24 0/8	5	5	Humboldt County	NV	Robert A. Ashby	1980	122
180 1/8	22 0/8	22 4/8	19 3/8	5	5	Dawson County	MT	Gordon M. Quilling	1957	125
180 1/8	24 6/8	24 4/8	21 5/8	5	5	Grant County	OR	Kim C. Thiele	1989	125
180 1/8	25 2/8	25 7/8	23 3/8	6	5	Cibola County	NM	Gary Patterson	1995	125
179 7/8	23 7/8	22 5/8	23 7/8	5	5	Yuma County	CO	Michael Trujillo	1997	128
179 6/8	25 0/8	25 7/8	20 0/8	5	5	Umatilla County	OR	Dannie W. Crawley	1991	129
179 6/8	25 2/8	25 3/8	22 2/8	5	5	Whiskey Gap	ALB	Don B. Yuill	1991	129
179 6/8	22 7/8	24 5/8	21 1/8	6	6	Okotoks	ALB	Harvey Paddock	1991	129
179 5/8	26 4/8	27 1/8	27 2/8	5	7	Union County	NM	Ronnie Williams	1984	132
179 4/8	24 3/8	23 0/8	21 4/8	5	8	Ada County	ID	Vance Gardner	1971	133
179 4/8	22 2/8	24 3/8	19 6/8	5	5	Garfield County	CO	Ed Downard	1984	133
179 4/8	27 2/8	27 5/8	23 4/8	6	5	Crook County	OR	Mark Quant	1995	133
179 3/8	26 2/8	24 2/8	20 0/8	5	4	San Miguel County	NM	Robert Montoya	1993	136
179 3/8	23 2/8	25 2/8	20 7/8	5	5	Lane County	KS	Elwin L. Schwartz	1994	136
179 2/8	24 2/8	24 1/8	24 6/8	5	4	Illinois Creek Drainage	unk	Gordon E. Scott	1964	138
179 0/8	19 1/8	19 4/8	21 4/8	5	6	Sandoval County	NM	D. J. Heckler, Jr.	1969	139
179 0/8	23 6/8	23 4/8	24 1/8	5	5	Lake County	CO	Sam E. Adkins	1978	139
179 0/8	23 5/8	24 4/8	22 4/8	5	5	Elko County	NV	Jerry Vega	1986	139
179 0/8	23 0/8	23 0/8	21 4/8	6	5	Harney County	OR	Cameron Hanes	1991	139
179 0/8	22 6/8	23 0/8	20 4/8	5	5	Lincoln County	WY	Mike Barrett	1991	139
178 6/8	24 2/8	23 4/8	19 0/8	5	5	Sublette County	WY	Marte Scheuffele	1984	144
178 5/8	24 2/8	23 2/8	24 7/8	6	6	Rio Blanco County	CO	Rex Schmude	1968	145
178 4/8	24 6/8	25 0/8	23 1/8	5	5	Carter County	MT	R. C. Tucker	1958	146
178 4/8	24 0/8	23 6/8	18 2/8	5	5	Sandoval County	NM	Doug Aikin	1990	146
178 4/8	25 5/8	26 2/8	21 6/8	6	7	Boise County	ID	Thomas M. Szurgot	1990	146
178 4/8	24 7/8	26 1/8	21 5/8	5	6	Klamath County	OR	Jim Harmon	1997	146
178 3/8	28 3/8	27 3/8	28 3/8	5	5	Finney County	KS	Larry Ochs	1968	150
178 3/8	21 3/8	22 2/8	19 5/8	5	5	San Juan County	UT	Shane Barr	1992	150
178 3/8	27 4/8	27 3/8	26 5/8	5	5	Okanogan County	WA	Douglas Duane Kikendall	1992	150
178 3/8	26 2/8	25 7/8	22 5/8	6	5	Taber	ALB	Darcy Miller	1994	150
178 2/8	24 0/8	24 2/8	20 4/8	5	5	Delta County	CO	Larry Bishop	1992	154
178 0/8	23 4/8	23 7/8	23 4/8	5	6	Lake County	OR	Ronald C. Halpin	1966	155
178 0/8	24 4/8	23 6/8	24 6/8	5	5	Garfield County	CO	Larry Santek	1985	155
178 0/8	25 0/8	24 4/8	24 6/8	7	6	Lincoln County	MT	Jerry Brown	1986	155
178 0/8	25 1/8	23 2/8	21 4/8	5	5	Ada County	ID	Thomas M. Szurgot	1992	155
178 0/8	21 1/8	22 0/8	18 2/8	5	4	Natrona County	WY	Brian L. Wagner	1993	155
177 7/8	23 2/8	23 7/8	23 2/8	4	4	Routt County	CO	Richard M. Hansen	1964	160
177 7/8	26 1/8	26 2/8	23 1/8	4	4	Gunnison County	CO	Glen Farnum	1978	160
177 7/8	23 6/8	23 0/8	19 3/8	6	6	Mesa County	CO	John D Wood	1984	160
177 7/8	24 3/8	26 4/8	23 1/8	6	5	Coconino County	AZ	James Miner	1987	160
177 7/8	26 1/8	25 3/8	26 7/8	5	5	Elbert County	CO	Robert Nelson	1990	160
177 6/8	27 2/8	26 0/8	32 2/8	6	7	McKinley County	NM	Eloy Salaz	1987	165
177 6/8	22 2/8	22 4/8	24 6/8	5	6	Sublette County	WY	Dana Patrick Furgason	1992	165
177 6/8	25 3/8	24 7/8	20 7/8	6	6	Drumheller	ALB	Tyler Colberg	1994	165
177 6/8	24 5/8	25 0/8	20 6/8	5	5	Grant County	OR	David D. Chapman	1995	165
177 6/8	24 7/8	24 2/8	17 1/8	4	5	Linn County	OR	Jeff Baker	1997	165
177 4/8	25 6/8	26 0/8	22 4/8	5	4	Fremont County	WY	Walter Millhollin	1960	170
177 4/8	23 0/8	22 5/8	22 2/8	5	5	Oneida County	ID	J. L. Shelton	1980	170
177 4/8	24 4/8	22 1/8	23 4/8	5	5	Oldman River	ALB	Kevin Wiebe	1991	170
177 4/8	23 2/8	22 6/8	21 4/8	6	7	Sherman County	KS	Brian K. Somers	1994	170
177 4/8	24 4/8	23 0/8	23 0/8	5	4	Ada County	ID	Neil J. Russell	1994	170
177 4/8	24 4/8	25 6/8	22 2/8	4	5	Natrona County	WY	Brian D. Balfour	1996	170
177 3/8	25 5/8	26 4/8	20 7/8	6	6	Caribou County	ID	Jack Daniels	1990	176
177 2/8	22 6/8	23 6/8	28 6/8	6	6	Pima County	AZ	Sherwin Lipsitz	1977	177
177 2/8	21 5/8	23 2/8	20 6/8	6	5	Malheur County	OR	Bennie B. Simpson	1986	177

MULE DEER (TYPICAL ANTLERS)

Minimum Score 145 — Continued

SCORE	LENGTH OF MAIN BEAM R	LENGTH OF MAIN BEAM L	INSIDE SPREAD	NUMBER OF POINTS R	NUMBER OF POINTS L	AREA	STATE/PROVINCE	HUNTER'S NAME	DATE	RANK
177 1/8	23 3/8	23 3/8	26 2/8	5	6	Logan County	KS	Thomas Standard	1967	179
177 1/8	23 7/8	24 4/8	22 0/8	4	6	Meagher County	MT	Mike Weitz	1981	179
177 1/8	23 4/8	23 7/8	22 1/8	6	5	La Plata County	CO	James N. Hinson	1987	179
177 1/8	23 5/8	24 4/8	21 3/8	5	5	Albany County	WY	Jerry Bowen	1988	179
177 1/8	23 1/8	23 1/8	22 7/8	5	5	Harney County	OR	Robert Reed	1991	179
177 1/8	25 2/8	26 1/8	25 1/8	5	5	Boulder County	CO	Greg Allen Nichols	1992	179
177 1/8	21 3/8	21 1/8	23 0/8	6	6	Franklin County	ID	Kerry L. Payne	1993	179
177 0/8	22 0/8	23 6/8	24 4/8	6	5	White Pine County	NV	Dr. Donald Wicher	1961	186
177 0/8	24 4/8	25 5/8	21 4/8	7	6	Garfield County	CO	Steve U'Selis	1967	186
176 7/8	20 7/8	21 5/8	20 7/8	5	5	Ada County	ID	Neil Russell	1996	188
176 7/8	22 5/8	23 5/8	20 3/8	5	6	Eagle Hill	ALB	Dallas Kaiser	1997	188
176 7/8	23 7/8	25 2/8	20 6/8	6	5	Mankota	SAS	Barry Hanson	1998	188
176 6/8	26 3/8	25 1/8	26 0/8	4	5	Yuma County	CO	Mark Sievers	1985	191
176 6/8	27 4/8	26 6/8	22 4/8	5	5	Wasatch County	UT	Doug Strecker	1987	191
176 6/8	25 7/8	24 7/8	25 6/8	5	5	Humboldt County	NV	Robert G. Hopper	1990	191
176 6/8	24 6/8	24 2/8	24 0/8	4	4	Carbon County	WY	Donald A. Carpenter	1990	191
176 5/8	22 5/8	22 2/8	20 6/8	5	6	Lincoln County	WY	Bart DeCora	1989	195
176 5/8	28 0/8	27 6/8	29 7/8	6	6	Weld County	CO	Tim Bradley	1989	195
176 4/8	23 4/8	23 5/8	20 0/8	5	5	Ada County	ID	Edward Keeton	1983	197
176 4/8	21 5/8	21 7/8	19 0/8	6	7	Conejos County	CO	Rick Gabbard	1987	197
176 4/8	22 2/8	22 7/8	21 4/8	5	5	Union County	OR	Kevin S. Robins	1994	197
176 3/8	20 0/8	21 1/8	26 3/8	5	5	Torrance County	NM	Frank Johnson	1989	200
176 3/8	21 3/8	21 5/8	22 3/8	5	5	Yuma County	CO	Chad Rockwell	1997	200
176 2/8	22 1/8	24 0/8	20 4/8	5	6	Lincoln County	NE	M. R. Buchtel	1959	202
176 2/8	24 1/8	24 3/8	23 2/8	5	5	Russell County	KS	Duane Mai	1982	202
176 2/8	21 4/8	23 1/8	21 5/8	5	6	Meade County	KS	Roger Davis	1986	202
176 1/8	24 3/8	24 3/8	23 1/8	7	6	Duchesne County	UT	M.H. 'Bill' Wilkinson, Jr.	1964	205
176 1/8	24 2/8	24 2/8	23 1/8	5	5	Treasure County	MT	Christopher Downs	1993	205
176 0/8	23 6/8	23 7/8	21 2/8	6	5	San Juan County	UT	Charles Farmer	1964	207
176 0/8	22 3/8	21 5/8	18 6/8	5	5	Coconino County	AZ	Tom Dennis	1972	207
176 0/8	24 7/8	24 7/8	23 6/8	5	6	Cassia County	ID	Earl Peterson	1981	207
176 0/8	22 1/8	23 4/8	21 0/8	6	6	Bingham County	ID	Doug Burkman	1994	207
175 7/8	24 5/8	24 1/8	18 0/8	6	9	Presidio County	TX	Neal Bouldin	1987	211
175 7/8	27 7/8	26 6/8	27 0/8	4	7	Cypress Hills	ALB	Russell Gregory Meidinger	1990	211
175 7/8	24 6/8	24 1/8	19 6/8	6	5	Salt Lake County	UT	Scott Fritsch	1997	211
175 7/8	23 0/8	24 2/8	21 6/8	5	5	Scott County	KS	Stacy Hoeme	1998	211
175 6/8	22 6/8	22 5/8	22 6/8	5	5	Uintah County	UT	Merlin L. Killpack	1957	215
175 6/8	24 4/8	24 4/8	25 4/8	6	6	Mesa County	CO	Joe Egner	1965	215
175 6/8	24 3/8	25 0/8	22 1/8	4	6	Larimer County	CO	Kevin Vinzant	1986	215
175 6/8	22 4/8	23 1/8	26 7/8	6	5	Flathead County	MT	Kory McGavin	1992	215
175 5/8	23 6/8	25 0/8	21 1/8	4	4	Grant County	OR	Larry Saunders	1985	219
175 5/8	23 4/8	25 3/8	24 7/8	5	5	San Miguel County	NM	Dick McClain	1989	219
175 5/8	25 5/8	24 1/8	24 0/8	6	7	Weld County	CO	Jerry Joseph	1993	219
175 5/8	22 3/8	22 2/8	24 4/8	5	5	Scott County	KS	John C. Walker	1995	219
175 5/8	24 1/8	23 3/8	24 5/8	6	6	Santa Cruz County	AZ	Milton Sommerfeld, Jr.	1997	219
175 4/8	24 6/8	24 7/8	21 7/8	6	9	Colfax County	NM	Max Crocker	1981	224
175 4/8	21 2/8	20 3/8	21 0/8	5	6	San Juan County	CO	Stan Overstreet	1989	224
175 4/8	25 5/8	23 0/8	21 0/8	5	5	Cheyenne County	CO	Ronald R. Smith	1991	224
175 3/8	21 5/8	23 1/8	19 5/8	6	7	Park County	CO	Marvin Clyncke	1981	227
175 3/8	24 4/8	24 0/8	23 1/8	5	5	Billings County	ND	Joe Kytoichuk	1983	227
175 2/8	24 1/8	24 4/8	24 4/8	7	6	Emery County	UT	Ron Myers	1958	229
175 2/8	24 6/8	25 3/8	23 6/8	6	7	Garfield County	CO	Robert Pitt	1978	229
175 1/8	24 6/8	27 1/8	27 5/8	5	5	Sawlog Creek	KS	Merle Schulte	1974	231
175 1/8	21 7/8	22 2/8	19 7/8	4	4	Lincoln County	NV	Fred B. Allen III	1975	231
175 1/8	24 1/8	25 4/8	21 5/8	7	8	Delta County	CO	Michael Sturm	1977	231
175 1/8	21 4/8	22 7/8	21 6/8	6	6	Millard County	UT	Jason Woodland	1985	231
175 1/8	23 1/8	23 3/8	25 3/8	5	5	Jefferson County	ID	Brian Rhead	1997	231
175 1/8	23 2/8	25 2/8	19 2/8	5	7	Colfax County	NM	Mark Sulllvan	1997	231
175 0/8	23 1/8	22 4/8	20 6/8	5	6	Deschutes County	OR	Marte Scheuffele	1987	237
175 0/8	22 6/8	23 4/8	19 5/8	5	6	Manyberries	ALB	Carl A. Miller	1996	237
174 7/8	23 7/8	23 7/8	18 3/8	5	6	Delta County	CO	Paul Dickson	1969	239
174 7/8	22 5/8	21 7/8	23 0/8	5	5	Gallatin County	MT	Bob Savage	1970	239
174 7/8	21 5/8	22 1/8	23 7/8	5	5	Garfield County	CO	Norman L. Richerson	1978	239
174 7/8	25 5/8	23 0/8	28 2/8	5	5	Elbert County	CO	Robert D. Olivier	1981	239
174 7/8	22 5/8	21 2/8	20 3/8	5	5	Rio Arriba County	NM	Nelson Martinez, Jr.	1995	239
174 6/8	26 2/8	26 0/8	26 2/8	5	5	Lake County	OR	Gene Lyons	1969	244
174 6/8	24 0/8	20 5/8	21 2/8	5	6	Garfield County	CO	Jewell Petz	1970	244
174 6/8	26 4/8	25 5/8	24 6/8	5	5	Lea County	NM	Eddie Carpenter	1993	244
174 6/8	22 4/8	23 6/8	23 2/8	5	4	Endiang	ALB	Ron McLellan	1997	244
174 5/8	25 0/8	25 0/8	23 1/8	4	4	Moffat County	CO	Roland C. Gravenkemper	1961	248
174 5/8	23 6/8	22 6/8	19 4/8	6	6	Sevier County	UT	Kenneth L. Shirley	1968	248
174 5/8	22 7/8	23 1/8	20 5/8	7	5	Wichita County	KS	Stacy Hoeme	1990	248
174 5/8	22 5/8	22 5/8	21 1/8	5	5	Pennington County	SD	Ed Heeb	1993	248
174 5/8	23 7/8	24 7/8	16 7/8	5	7	Flagstaff County	ALB	Pride Benson	1997	248
174 4/8	26 0/8	23 5/8	26 4/8	6	5	Mesa County	CO	Douglas D. Watts	1976	253
174 4/8	24 3/8	24 1/8	22 6/8	4	5	Mesa County	CO	Jay Verzuh	1983	253
174 4/8	25 0/8	24 5/8	19 6/8	5	5	Consort	ALB	Trevor J. Wignall	1997	253
174 3/8	21 0/8	23 7/8	23 1/8	6	5	Pima County	AZ	Robert A. Edgar	1982	256

MULE DEER (TYPICAL ANTLERS)

Minimum Score 145

SCORE	LENGTH OF MAIN BEAM R	LENGTH OF MAIN BEAM L	INSIDE SPREAD	NUMBER OF POINTS R	NUMBER OF POINTS L	AREA	STATE/PROVINCE	HUNTER'S NAME	DATE	RANK
174 3/8	22 5/8	22 6/8	21 5/8	5	5	Lassen County	CA	Rick Pollard	1994	256
174 3/8	24 3/8	24 6/8	23 4/8	6	6	Coconino County	AZ	Eric Vielhauer	1996	256
174 2/8	22 7/8	22 6/8	21 2/8	5	5	Natrona County	WY	Pat McAteer	1982	259
174 2/8	23 0/8	22 5/8	23 1/8	5	5	Billings County	ND	Mark Lothspeich	1984	259
174 2/8	25 3/8	23 7/8	25 0/8	6	6	Douglas County	CO	Daniel G. Weippert	1986	259
174 2/8	24 7/8	24 6/8	21 0/8	5	6	Umatilla County	OR	Clifford W. Widel	1991	259
174 2/8	24 1/8	24 6/8	25 6/8	5	5	Catron County	NM	Eddie Claypool	1996	259
174 1/8	21 5/8	23 0/8	22 0/8	6	5	Gray County	KS	Jim Sobba	1994	264
174 0/8	25 0/8	25 1/8	20 6/8	5	5	Ravalli County	MT	John Schulz	1976	265
173 7/8	25 3/8	25 2/8	26 0/8	4	4	Uintah County	UT	Hal Wallentine	1962	266
173 7/8	25 4/8	25 4/8	21 0/8	5	5	Garfield County	CO	Danny C. Lloyd	1969	266
173 7/8	24 2/8	24 1/8	22 6/8	7	6	Eagle County	CO	Edward L. Berlier	1970	266
173 7/8	25 0/8	24 5/8	23 5/8	7	7	Okotoks	ALB	Dave Demeter	1981	266
173 7/8	22 5/8	22 4/8	20 3/8	6	5	Fraser River	BC	Don Sankey	1995	266
173 6/8	25 3/8	24 4/8	23 5/8	7	6	Sevier County	UT	Morris Stuart	1972	271
173 6/8	23 6/8	24 0/8	20 4/8	6	5	Boulder County	CO	Floyd Sulllvan	1982	271
173 6/8	21 4/8	22 0/8	22 4/8	6	5	Humboldt County	NV	Joel C. Lenz	1984	271
173 6/8	25 4/8	20 3/8	27 4/8	5	6	Meadow Lake	BC	Chip Young	1987	271
173 6/8	24 6/8	22 5/8	18 6/8	5	5	Boise County	ID	Thomas M. Szurgot	1991	271
173 5/8	24 6/8	24 7/8	23 7/8	5	5	Morton County	ND	Pat Sulllvan	1957	276
173 5/8	25 1/8	25 5/8	25 2/8	7	5	Pima County	AZ	Joe Nochta	1959	276
173 5/8	21 4/8	21 1/8	21 0/8	6	7	Chaffee County	CO	Lee Rowe	1966	276
173 5/8	23 3/8	23 7/8	24 5/8	5	5	San Juan County	UT	Robert G. Hester	1972	276
173 5/8	23 5/8	22 7/8	22 7/8	5	6	Natrona County	WY	M. Robert DeLaney	1995	276
173 4/8	24 3/8	24 2/8	27 2/8	5	6	Garfield County	CO	Don Mayen	1966	281
173 4/8	22 1/8	22 1/8	20 4/8	6	7	Ada County	ID	David D. Howard	1971	281
173 4/8	23 5/8	24 4/8	21 0/8	4	6	Mesa County	CO	G. Fred Asbell	1974	281
173 4/8	21 5/8	20 4/8	21 2/8	5	5	Montrose County	CO	Chip Greene	1978	281
173 4/8	23 6/8	23 3/8	20 4/8	5	5	Eagle County	CO	Donald R. Hoard	1992	281
173 4/8	24 0/8	22 4/8	20 4/8	5	6	Larimer County	CO	Eric Vance	1995	281
173 3/8	22 4/8	24 1/8	24 7/8	5	5	Coconino County	AZ	Jack Richards	1958	287
173 3/8	23 0/8	23 5/8	23 5/8	5	5	Sevier County	UT	Robert J. Shumway	1969	287
173 3/8	21 5/8	22 6/8	22 0/8	6	5	Caribou County	ID	Jim Walton	1983	287
173 2/8	22 6/8	23 1/8	22 6/8	6	6	Millard County	UT	George Kendall	1959	290
173 2/8	25 6/8	25 1/8	22 4/8	5	5	Dolores County	CO	Jack Acree	1969	290
173 2/8	24 0/8	24 0/8	21 4/8	5	7	Bernalillo County	NM	Rolland Hanna	1972	290
173 2/8	25 1/8	24 3/8	24 3/8	6	5	Carbon County	UT	Demar Guymon	1982	290
173 2/8	27 6/8	27 2/8	25 6/8	7	7	Norton County	KS	Mark S. Myers	1991	290
173 2/8	25 6/8	24 4/8	26 4/8	5	5	Socorro County	NM	Anthony J. Turrietta	1995	290
173 2/8	23 0/8	21 7/8	18 2/8	6	5	Logan County	KS	Walter E. Lovins	1997	290
173 1/8	26 3/8	25 0/8	21 3/8	5	5	Coconino County	AZ	H. H. Harter	1961	297
173 1/8	23 3/8	24 1/8	20 5/8	5	5	Teton County	ID	Paul Beesley	1976	297
173 1/8	22 1/8	22 5/8	21 6/8	5	6	Bear Lake County	ID	Steven A. Dewey	1985	297
173 1/8	23 3/8	22 2/8	23 0/8	5	7	Deschutes County	OR	Jonathan Roy Manbeck	1987	297
173 0/8	23 4/8	24 0/8	24 1/8	5	5	Gray County	KS	Bob Barnes	1966	301
173 0/8	21 5/8	22 2/8	24 5/8	4	5	Mesa County	CO	Floyd Kendall	1966	301
173 0/8	26 6/8	26 5/8	23 5/8	6	6	Edmonton	ALB	Brian Berrecloth	1981	301
173 0/8	25 4/8	25 4/8	26 7/8	6	5	Carbon County	UT	Tom Riebe	1983	301
173 0/8	22 2/8	22 2/8	18 2/8	5	5	Caribou County	ID	Larry Jaeger	1985	301
173 0/8	24 3/8	22 4/8	22 2/8	5	5	Boise County	ID	Kenneth A. Hyde	1988	301
172 7/8	22 6/8	22 2/8	20 2/8	6	5	Boise County	ID	Marlin Tullis	1982	307
172 7/8	22 2/8	22 5/8	22 7/8	5	5	Cabri	SAS	Clarence R. Hughes	1989	307
172 7/8	22 5/8	23 3/8	18 7/8	6	5	Colfax County	NM	Joe Amador	1991	307
172 7/8	22 5/8	22 5/8	21 1/8	4	5	Cache County	UT	David Teuscher	1992	307
172 7/8	26 0/8	25 0/8	21 1/8	5	6	Scott County	KS	Brett Eisenhour	1995	307
172 6/8	21 5/8	21 6/8	16 7/8	6	5	Bowman County	ND	LeRoy Brandenburger	1967	312
172 6/8	28 7/8	26 3/8	28 7/8	6	6	Rio Arriba County	NM	Kerino H. Revel	1968	312
172 6/8	21 7/8	22 4/8	19 4/8	5	4	Ada County	ID	Ronald B. Jones	1971	312
172 6/8	23 4/8	24 0/8	20 7/8	7	5	San Juan County	UT	Harold Boyack	1975	312
172 6/8	22 3/8	23 0/8	20 6/8	4	5	Mabel Lake	BC	Mark Siegmueller	1984	312
172 6/8	23 1/8	22 5/8	22 0/8	4	4	Rio Blanco County	CO	Brad Murray	1985	312
172 6/8	23 3/8	23 1/8	20 4/8	5	5	Franklin County	ID	Lance Henderson	1992	312
172 6/8	23 2/8	22 2/8	23 6/8	6	6	Coconino County	AZ	David Baldwin	1996	312
172 5/8	23 6/8	24 2/8	22 3/8	5	5	Bernalillo County	NM	Noble Sinclair	1982	320
172 5/8	22 4/8	20 7/8	20 4/8	5	6	Lincoln County	WY	Mike Barrett	1990	320
172 4/8	24 3/8	22 7/8	24 3/8	6	5	Malheur County	OR	Carl R. Stone	1957	322
172 4/8	25 3/8	25 4/8	24 2/8	5	5	Owyhee County	ID	Don Rosenvall	1961	322
172 4/8	25 6/8	23 6/8	20 3/8	5	5	Chelan County	WA	Timothy E Pflugh	1984	322
172 4/8	25 4/8	25 7/8	22 2/8	6	6	Mesa County	CO	Dewayne Young	1986	322
172 4/8	21 3/8	22 2/8	22 4/8	5	7	Union County	OR	Carl M. Nelson	1992	322
172 4/8	25 7/8	24 4/8	16 1/8	6	7	Teton County	WY	Dallas Smith	1995	322
172 4/8	24 7/8	25 2/8	28 1/8	5	5	Montezuma County	CO	Bryon D. Long	1996	322
172 3/8	23 3/8	22 6/8	21 6/8	5	7	Garfield County	CO	Kenneth Rapp	1974	329
172 3/8	22 0/8	22 0/8	20 3/8	5	5	Ouray County	CO	Don Castrup	1975	329
172 3/8	25 3/8	25 4/8	23 0/8	6	6	Shasta County	CA	Russell Browning	1983	329
172 3/8	24 5/8	24 1/8	23 0/8	5	6	Norton County	KS	Greg J. McCall	1985	329
172 3/8	23 7/8	22 5/8	24 4/8	5	5	Montrose County	CO	Greg Blackburn	1986	329
172 2/8	24 4/8	25 3/8	21 0/8	6	7	Rock Creek	CO	Louis Prestridge	1961	334

MULE DEER (TYPICAL ANTLERS)

Minimum Score 145 — Continued

SCORE	LENGTH OF MAIN BEAM R	LENGTH OF MAIN BEAM L	INSIDE SPREAD	NUMBER OF POINTS R	NUMBER OF POINTS L	AREA	STATE/ PROVINCE	HUNTER'S NAME	DATE	RANK
172 2/8	26 0/8	26 0/8	25 6/8	5	5	Wasatch County	UT	Bill Dean	1965	334
172 2/8	21 4/8	22 3/8	19 2/8	5	5	Caribou County	ID	Bret Davis	1991	334
172 2/8	24 1/8	25 0/8	23 2/8	5	5	Sheridan County	WY	Charles F. Neisess	1995	334
172 1/8	24 1/8	24 6/8	24 5/8	5	5	Rio Grande County	CO	Marvin Tompkins	1960	338
172 1/8	22 3/8	22 3/8	18 1/8	4	4	Lake County	OR	Ralph Hoover	1964	338
172 1/8	24 0/8	24 4/8	23 7/8	5	6	Sevier County	UT	Bob Covington	1965	338
172 1/8	21 1/8	22 2/8	20 7/8	5	5	Saguache County	CO	Rick Duggan	1984	338
172 1/8	20 3/8	20 6/8	20 6/8	5	6	Perkins County	SD	Travis Bies	1988	338
172 1/8	22 4/8	23 3/8	21 0/8	6	5	Bowman County	ND	Scott P. Bradac	1992	338
172 1/8	23 7/8	24 6/8	23 5/8	6	5	Salt Lake County	UT	Mike Raetz	1997	338
172 0/8	26 1/8	26 3/8	26 1/8	4	5	Baker County	OR	James D. Hanley	1960	345
172 0/8	25 6/8	26 0/8	21 4/8	4	5	Beechy	SAS	Terry Carruthers	1987	345
172 0/8	22 3/8	22 4/8	22 2/8	5	5	Gunnison County	CO	Darrell Jones	1995	345
171 7/8	23 4/8	23 5/8	27 2/8	5	5	Uintah County	UT	Alvin Sisam	1966	348
171 7/8	26 4/8	24 5/8	24 5/8	4	5	Lancer	SAS	Del Erickson	1976	348
171 7/8	20 3/8	20 5/8	17 7/8	5	5	Larimer County	CO	Mike Kolano	1985	348
171 7/8	23 1/8	24 1/8	25 5/8	9	5	Scott County	KS	Mike Stoppel	1986	348
171 6/8	23 0/8	22 7/8	22 2/8	5	5	Carbon County	WY	Steve Parker	1974	352
171 6/8	22 7/8	21 6/8	23 3/8	8	8	Teton County	MT	James Dean	1977	352
171 6/8	24 7/8	25 4/8	21 6/8	5	6	Delta County	CO	Louis A. Brunett	1983	352
171 6/8	24 2/8	23 3/8	24 4/8	5	5	Teton County	WY	Guy Williamson	1992	352
171 6/8	25 6/8	24 6/8	25 1/8	6	5	Maricopa County	AZ	Larry Drake	1995	352
171 6/8	25 7/8	25 5/8	27 0/8	6	7	San Juan County	NM	Mark Teahan	1998	352
171 5/8	24 3/8	24 3/8	23 2/8	6	5	Harney County	OR	Chuck Warner	1977	358
171 5/8	23 5/8	24 0/8	19 1/8	4	5	Sweetwater County	WY	Keith Dana	1983	358
171 5/8	24 0/8	24 0/8	25 3/8	5	7	Las Animas County	CO	Gary Lehnherr	1995	358
171 4/8	21 6/8	23 3/8	25 2/8	5	6	Uncompahgre N.F.	CO	Vito Benedetto	1976	361
171 4/8	24 4/8	24 3/8	21 2/8	5	5	Stutsman County	ND	Harold Hugelen	1977	361
171 4/8	23 0/8	22 6/8	22 3/8	6	5	Clark County	KS	Dan Fenton	1980	361
171 4/8	24 7/8	25 6/8	23 6/8	4	4	Baker County	OR	Mike Raney	1987	361
171 3/8	23 4/8	23 5/8	22 5/8	6	5	Ravalli County	MT	Joe Wandstrath	1980	365
171 3/8	24 5/8	25 5/8	26 5/8	5	5	Chaffee County	CO	Bruce Fish	1981	365
171 3/8	26 6/8	24 2/8	20 3/8	4	4	Lake County	OR	Michael Wright	1991	365
171 3/8	24 1/8	22 3/8	23 1/8	6	7	Scott County	KS	Dean Hamilton	1993	365
171 2/8	23 2/8	23 6/8	20 2/8	4	5	Summit County	UT	Kent Garfield	1959	369
171 2/8	24 0/8	23 7/8	19 2/8	5	5	Richland County	MT	Dennis Engle	1966	369
171 2/8	21 5/8	22 0/8	16 2/8	5	6	Routt County	CO	Joe Mucka	1975	369
171 2/8	22 6/8	24 2/8	24 7/8	5	5	McKenzie County	ND	Andrew Johnson	1992	369
171 2/8	23 3/8	21 4/8	18 3/8	5	6	Teton County	WY	Deon F. Heiner	1993	369
171 1/8	28 0/8	26 4/8	22 4/8	8	7	Wasatch County	UT	Frank Snyder	1959	374
171 1/8	25 4/8	25 3/8	24 7/8	7	6	Millard County	UT	Shirley B. Pace	1962	374
171 1/8	23 3/8	23 2/8	22 7/8	5	5	Juab County	UT	Farren Anderson	1964	374
171 1/8	20 7/8	22 7/8	22 2/8	6	7	Mesa County	CO	Curtis Bateman	1983	374
171 1/8	22 7/8	23 2/8	21 5/8	5	5	Garden County	NE	Monte Shaul	1985	374
171 0/8	21 7/8	23 0/8	21 6/8	5	6	Meade County	KS	Keith Whitney	1986	379
171 0/8	25 1/8	23 0/8	25 4/8	5	8	Adams County	ID	Alan Dehlin	1992	379
171 0/8	23 3/8	23 0/8	21 4/8	4	4	Weld County	CO	Chet Trivette	1997	379
170 7/8	21 1/8	22 7/8	19 3/8	4	4	Beaver County	UT	Richard L. Anderson	1960	382
170 7/8	22 7/8	21 5/8	24 4/8	5	5	Bernalillo County	NM	Dr. E. J. Bowser	1971	382
170 7/8	23 4/8	22 1/8	19 6/8	6	5	Uncompahgre N.F.	CO	Allen G. Hughes	1974	382
170 7/8	23 3/8	22 6/8	17 6/8	5	7	Red Willow County	NE	William E. Peck, Jr.	1992	382
170 7/8	22 5/8	23 1/8	20 7/8	4	5	Boise County	ID	Doug Hawker	1992	382
170 7/8	23 4/8	24 4/8	22 7/8	6	5	Garfield County	CO	William S. Drake	1995	382
170 6/8	22 7/8	22 4/8	22 6/8	5	6	Chelan County	WA	Gerald Weiss	1967	388
170 6/8	25 2/8	24 5/8	25 0/8	5	5	Uintah County	UT	Eugene Damron	1974	388
170 6/8	24 4/8	24 5/8	21 7/8	5	7	Baker County	OR	Luke Maher	1994	388
170 6/8	23 2/8	23 1/8	21 4/8	5	6	Elmore County	ID	Rod Bradley	1996	388
170 6/8	24 1/8	24 3/8	20 6/8	5	4	Salt Lake County	UT	Darin N. Miller	1996	388
170 6/8	25 5/8	24 1/8	21 6/8	5	5	Manyberries	ALB	Carl A. Miller	1997	388
170 5/8	24 7/8	25 6/8	19 7/8	5	6	Garfield County	CO	Robert H. Pitt	1971	394
170 4/8	23 2/8	23 0/8	22 0/8	5	5	Carbon County	WY	James E. Lawrence	1971	395
170 4/8	21 1/8	21 5/8	20 1/8	6	5	Humboldt County	NV	Vic Christison	1982	395
170 4/8	26 0/8	24 4/8	25 0/8	5	5	Torrance County	NM	Henry Montoya	1988	395
170 4/8	24 3/8	23 3/8	18 1/8	6	6	Camas County	ID	Bruce McStay	1988	395
170 4/8	23 0/8	23 1/8	19 6/8	5	5	Brunson Lake	BC	Daryl Buchholtz	1991	395
170 3/8	20 7/8	19 4/8	21 4/8	5	5	Ada County	ID	Jim Spearman	1970	400
170 3/8	23 6/8	24 5/8	19 7/8	5	5	Chelan County	WA	Dave Johnson	1977	400
170 3/8	21 0/8	21 0/8	20 0/8	5	5	Harney County	OR	Chuck Warner	1979	400
170 3/8	23 4/8	23 3/8	19 6/8	6	6	Caribou County	ID	Gregg Welch	1988	400
170 3/8	23 2/8	23 2/8	21 6/8	5	6	Chelan County	WA	Wayne Pippin	1991	400
170 3/8	23 4/8	24 2/8	20 3/8	5	5	Meagher County	MT	Michael L. McHugh	1993	400
170 2/8	24 7/8	23 7/8	24 2/8	6	6	Slope County	ND	Jim Peters	1954	406
170 2/8	23 1/8	23 1/8	20 1/8	5	7	Fishlake National Forest	UT	Stan Rock	1961	406
170 2/8	23 0/8	23 3/8	20 1/8	7	5	Rio Arriba County	NM	Robert H. Keadle	1966	406
170 2/8	21 3/8	20 4/8	20 4/8	7	7	McKenzie County	ND	Don Davidson	1982	406
170 2/8	23 7/8	25 0/8	24 4/8	4	5	Colfax County	NM	Michael A. Sisneros	1991	406
170 2/8	22 5/8	22 4/8	19 2/8	5	5	Bernalillo County	NM	Barron Freeman	1992	406
170 2/8	24 4/8	24 6/8	26 5/8	5	5	Teton County	WY	Donald R. Williamson	1995	406

MULE DEER (TYPICAL ANTLERS)

Minimum Score 145 — Continued

SCORE	LENGTH OF MAIN BEAM R	LENGTH OF MAIN BEAM L	INSIDE SPREAD	NUMBER OF POINTS R	NUMBER OF POINTS L	AREA	STATE/PROVINCE	HUNTER'S NAME	DATE	RANK
170 2/8	24 2/8	24 0/8	24 6/8	4	5	Pima County	AZ	James H. Caves III	1997	406
170 1/8	23 3/8	24 0/8	19 7/8	5	5	Gray County	KS	Dick Masters	1968	414
170 1/8	22 7/8	22 7/8	20 3/8	5	5	Thomas County	KS	Gerald Paxton	1987	414
170 0/8	23 3/8	22 2/8	23 6/8	7	7	Pima County	AZ	James M. Fry	1975	416
170 0/8	22 4/8	23 0/8	20 6/8	4	5	Routt County	CO	Robert Syvertson, Jr.	1975	416
170 0/8	23 3/8	23 7/8	24 2/8	5	6	Uncompahgre N.F.	CO	Robert Meyler IV	1976	416
170 0/8	23 5/8	22 7/8	19 7/8	5	6	Grant County	OR	Timothy D. Palmore	1976	416
170 0/8	24 2/8	24 0/8	26 3/8	5	5	Saguache County	CO	Pat Schambow	1985	416
170 0/8	21 4/8	22 2/8	19 6/8	5	5	Norton County	KS	David Bainter	1988	416
170 0/8	26 0/8	24 6/8	25 2/8	6	4	Klamath County	OR	Jeffrey A. Eder	1992	416
170 0/8	25 0/8	25 3/8	23 2/8	5	5	Lake County	OR	Jim DeCaire	1994	416
170 0/8	24 0/8	22 4/8	22 7/8	5	6	Johnson County	WY	John C. Yoder	1997	416
169 7/8	23 3/8	22 7/8	24 3/8	4	5	Caribou County	ID	Chet Hopkins	1968	425
169 7/8	24 1/8	24 1/8	21 1/8	5	5	Larimer County	CO	Ron Morgan	1993	425
169 7/8	23 4/8	22 2/8	22 7/8	4	4	Lane County	KS	Dean Hamilton	1996	425
169 6/8	23 0/8	23 3/8	23 0/8	5	5	Garfield County	CO	C. W. Gilbreath	1967	428
169 6/8	25 0/8	23 0/8	22 2/8	4	4	Platte County	WY	Jerry Bowen	1976	428
169 6/8	22 0/8	23 0/8	22 2/8	5	5	Elbert County	CO	Mike Amendt	1981	428
169 6/8	21 7/8	22 2/8	20 0/8	5	5	Garfield County	CO	Eddy Oliger	1986	428
169 6/8	22 3/8	22 3/8	20 4/8	5	6	Camas County	ID	Jim Walters	1988	428
169 6/8	20 6/8	19 7/8	17 2/8	5	5	Valley County	ID	Neil Thagard	1992	428
169 6/8	22 0/8	20 7/8	20 2/8	5	6	Elkwater	ALB	Bruce R. Schoeneweis	1995	428
169 6/8	23 3/8	22 7/8	23 1/8	6	6	Edmonton	ALB	Marven Fehlauer	1996	428
169 5/8	24 3/8	24 3/8	22 0/8	5	7	Lincoln County	MT	Harold Leslie	1980	436
169 5/8	26 0/8	25 5/8	19 5/8	9	8	Garfield County	CO	Jay A. Keeler	1984	436
169 5/8	22 6/8	22 2/8	20 5/8	5	4	Eagle County	CO	Michael Dziekan	1988	436
169 4/8	23 0/8	23 3/8	26 7/8	5	5	Owyhee County	ID	Dwane Marler	1955	439
169 4/8	21 3/8	22 1/8	19 6/8	5	5	Bowman County	ND	Scott Bradac	1994	439
169 3/8	21 4/8	22 3/8	19 5/8	5	5	McKinley County	NM	Hayden Lambson	1979	441
169 3/8	22 5/8	22 2/8	26 2/8	5	5	Norton County	KS	Joseph E. Schroeder	1979	441
169 3/8	20 4/8	22 3/8	22 3/8	5	5	Elmore County	ID	Steve Bresnahan	1980	441
169 3/8	22 3/8	22 0/8	19 3/8	5	5	Box Elder County	UT	Bob Doutre	1981	441
169 3/8	20 1/8	20 5/8	19 5/8	5	5	Park County	WY	William D. Rhodes	1992	441
169 2/8	22 3/8	21 6/8	23 4/8	6	5	Chelan County	WA	Larry Lockhart	1966	446
169 2/8	26 0/8	26 0/8	20 6/8	5	5	Umatilla County	OR	Dennis Hernley	1987	446
169 2/8	24 6/8	23 6/8	21 1/8	6	5	Pinal County	AZ	Robert Wakefield	1991	446
169 2/8	25 3/8	26 4/8	26 0/8	6	6	Comanche County	KS	Greg Hill	1996	446
169 1/8	24 2/8	23 4/8	21 1/8	7	6	San Juan County	UT	Dean Wolf	1970	450
169 1/8	23 2/8	24 7/8	21 4/8	6	7	Elmore County	ID	Champ Church	1986	450
169 1/8	25 1/8	24 0/8	23 2/8	5	5	Dolores County	CO	Eugene Davenport	1990	450
169 1/8	23 7/8	24 1/8	20 3/8	4	5	Hand County	SD	Fred Kober	1991	450
169 1/8	23 4/8	22 3/8	21 1/8	5	6	Bingham County	ID	Todd F. Lewis	1992	450
169 1/8	22 6/8	23 5/8	17 3/8	5	5	Elko County	NV	John V. Bottari	1995	450
169 1/8	19 6/8	20 5/8	22 0/8	5	6	Barrhead	ALB	Phil Wierenga	1995	450
169 1/8	22 1/8	22 2/8	20 3/8	5	5	Natrona County	WY	Mark Miller	1997	450
169 0/8	22 0/8	21 5/8	20 0/8	5	4	Colfax County	NM	Gary Ginther	1973	458
169 0/8	23 5/8	24 6/8	22 6/8	5	5	Fremont County	CO	Bill W. Canterbury	1975	458
169 0/8	23 2/8	24 6/8	24 3/8	6	5	San Juan County	UT	Harold Boyack	1978	458
169 0/8	25 1/8	24 7/8	21 2/8	7	7	Bernalillo County	NM	John L. Padilla	1989	458
169 0/8	24 1/8	20 3/8	22 4/8	5	5	Elmore County	ID	David E. Sass	1991	458
169 0/8	23 3/8	24 1/8	20 6/8	5	4	Deschutes County	OR	Marte Scheuffele	1992	458
169 0/8	22 5/8	23 2/8	24 4/8	5	5	Hanna	ALB	Glen Hutton	1994	458
169 0/8	21 6/8	21 4/8	19 7/8	7	5	Caribou County	ID	Randy K. Guinn	1994	458
168 7/8	21 1/8	21 1/8	24 2/8	5	5	Cache County	UT	Carl Roush	1979	466
168 7/8	21 6/8	24 3/8	22 7/8	5	6	Park County	CO	Jim Johnson	1980	466
168 7/8	21 3/8	22 3/8	21 5/8	5	5	Union County	OR	Jerry W. Simmons	1982	466
168 7/8	24 6/8	25 3/8	22 6/8	6	5	Boise County	ID	Champ Church	1992	466
168 6/8	23 1/8	24 2/8	20 6/8	5	4	Baker County	OR	Joe Williamsen	1959	470
168 6/8	24 7/8	24 3/8	23 4/8	5	5	Little Belt Mtns.	MT	James Ployhar	1969	470
168 6/8	21 5/8	21 5/8	17 6/8	6	5	Ravalli County	MT	Bob Brill	1977	470
168 6/8	20 5/8	19 0/8	19 2/8	5	6	Umatilla County	OR	Donald E. Durland	1983	470
168 6/8	22 4/8	23 0/8	17 4/8	6	5	Mesa County	CO	J.D. 'Butch' Shivers	1985	470
168 6/8	23 7/8	24 5/8	21 4/8	6	6	San Miguel County	CO	Jay Scott	1986	470
168 6/8	24 2/8	24 4/8	25 3/8	5	5	Boulder County	CO	Craig Archer	1996	470
168 5/8	20 6/8	21 5/8	18 3/8	5	5	Gunnison County	CO	Edward Maxfield Vanderslice	1991	477
168 5/8	20 5/8	22 7/8	22 3/8	5	4	Stillwater County	MT	Dr. Dale Schlehuber	1992	477
168 5/8	23 7/8	25 5/8	25 6/8	4	5	Columbia County	WA	David Kent	1993	477
168 4/8	24 6/8	24 7/8	21 6/8	5	5	Utah County	UT	Garland Bray	1970	480
168 4/8	23 4/8	22 4/8	23 7/8	5	5	Uncompahgre N.F.	CO	Paul R. Holmes	1974	480
168 4/8	22 2/8	21 6/8	22 5/8	4	4	Carbon County	WY	David Paskett	1990	480
168 4/8	21 3/8	22 2/8	20 4/8	5	5	Pennington County	SD	Douglas E. McDonald	1994	480
168 3/8	23 5/8	23 3/8	17 5/8	5	5	Chelan County	WA	George Wells	1960	484
168 3/8	22 7/8	22 0/8	19 6/8	5	6	Mineral County	CO	Richard Kolish	1961	484
168 3/8	21 7/8	22 5/8	22 7/8	5	5	Weber County	UT	Dennis L. Shirley	1972	484
168 3/8	24 1/8	23 2/8	22 1/8	5	6	Eureka County	NV	Joel C. Lenz	1986	484
168 2/8	28 6/8	26 5/8	26 0/8	4	5	Uintah County	UT	S. K. Daniels	1908	488
168 2/8	25 0/8	24 0/8	21 7/8	5	5	Mesa County	CO	Jack Kenyon	1965	488
168 2/8	22 6/8	24 0/8	22 6/8	5	5	La Plata County	CO	Don Putterbaugh	1966	488

MULE DEER (TYPICAL ANTLERS)

Minimum Score 145 — Continued

SCORE	LENGTH OF MAIN BEAM R	LENGTH OF MAIN BEAM L	INSIDE SPREAD	NUMBER OF POINTS R	NUMBER OF POINTS L	AREA	STATE/PROVINCE	HUNTER'S NAME	DATE	RANK
168 2/8	22 0/8	22 6/8	21 4/8	5	5	Mesa County	CO	Joseph Sverak	1968	488
168 2/8	24 1/8	22 1/8	21 4/8	4	4	Chaffee County	CO	Frank A. Morminello	1977	488
168 2/8	25 0/8	24 3/8	20 6/8	5	5	Humboldt County	NV	James A. Dallimore	1983	488
168 2/8	22 0/8	21 4/8	18 6/8	6	5	Caribou County	ID	Gene Keller	1985	488
168 2/8	25 3/8	24 2/8	25 0/8	6	5	Lincoln County	MT	Alan L. Davis	1992	488
168 2/8	22 0/8	22 4/8	17 6/8	4	4	Gilpin County	CO	Bart Thompson	1996	488
168 1/8	21 4/8	21 5/8	19 7/8	5	5	Grand County	CO	Lenard Boughton	1968	497
168 1/8	21 3/8	22 2/8	19 7/8	6	6	McKenzie County	ND	Craig A. Ross	1983	497
168 1/8	24 3/8	25 5/8	25 4/8	6	4	Cochrane	ALB	Larry Collins	1990	497
168 1/8	22 6/8	23 0/8	19 5/8	5	5	Okotoks	ALB	Wayne Porterfield	1996	497
168 0/8	25 3/8	24 3/8	23 0/8	4	6	Uncompahgre N.F.	CO	Dick Gulman	1976	501
168 0/8	23 0/8	22 7/8	24 2/8	5	4	Elko County	NV	James A. Algerio	1980	501
168 0/8	24 0/8	22 7/8	23 2/8	5	5	Jefferson County	CO	Robert Anderson	1980	501
168 0/8	23 4/8	24 1/8	20 4/8	5	5	Ada County	ID	Ed Davidson	1994	501
167 7/8	24 3/8	24 0/8	27 2/8	6	6	Grand County	UT	Bob Paulson	1967	505
167 7/8	23 1/8	22 1/8	22 6/8	6	6	Routt County	CO	Edwin W. Foerster	1987	505
167 7/8	25 1/8	25 1/8	29 0/8	5	6	Pima County	AZ	Carnie R. Marks	1993	505
167 7/8	22 2/8	22 5/8	18 7/8	5	5	Ada County	ID	Trevor Bonfiglio	1995	505
167 6/8	21 4/8	20 6/8	18 5/8	5	5	Wallowa County	OR	Leonard Brooks	1967	509
167 6/8	22 7/8	23 5/8	23 0/8	5	5	Boise County	ID	Ed Moser	1982	509
167 6/8	23 5/8	24 5/8	20 2/8	5	6	Okotoks	ALB	Grant Hill	1989	509
167 6/8	23 0/8	23 0/8	21 0/8	5	5	Jerome County	ID	Guy G. Fitzgerald	1992	509
167 6/8	23 6/8	24 7/8	20 4/8	5	5	Dawson County	NE	Monte Koch	1993	509
167 6/8	24 1/8	23 4/8	22 0/8	6	5	Kathyrn	ALB	Dominic Barbario	1996	509
167 6/8	24 4/8	24 5/8	22 0/8	5	5	Graham County	KS	Randy Wilson	1997	509
167 5/8	21 2/8	22 1/8	26 0/8	5	5	Grand County	CO	Michael A. Contreras	1978	516
167 5/8	24 0/8	23 2/8	21 4/8	5	6	Greenlee County	AZ	Eddie Claypool	1995	516
167 4/8	20 2/8	20 5/8	19 0/8	5	5	Cascade County	MT	Ron Johnson	1987	518
167 4/8	22 7/8	20 4/8	21 2/8	5	5	Sweet Grass County	MT	Dr. Dale Schlehuber	1990	518
167 4/8	23 4/8	22 6/8	24 0/8	5	5	Wichita County	KS	Jack D. Kuhlmann	1990	518
167 4/8	22 4/8	23 3/8	19 1/8	6	6	Pinal County	AZ	Sonny Nieto	1991	518
167 4/8	22 2/8	22 1/8	17 2/8	4	5	Abbey	SAS	Floyd Forster	1992	518
167 4/8	24 6/8	25 2/8	19 2/8	5	5	Klickitat County	WA	Leon Wells	1992	518
167 3/8	21 4/8	21 3/8	19 3/8	5	5	Owyhee County	ID	Eugene R. Mallard	1963	524
167 3/8	25 0/8	25 0/8	19 3/8	7	5	Klamath County	OR	V. Kenneth Murdock	1978	524
167 3/8	21 6/8	22 7/8	19 0/8	5	7	Mesa County	CO	Paul H. Dickson	1984	524
167 3/8	18 7/8	23 0/8	22 1/8	5	5	Baker County	OR	Kevin Kennedy	1987	524
167 3/8	22 5/8	23 7/8	25 3/8	5	5	Washoe County	NV	Ralph L. Albright	1988	524
167 3/8	23 7/8	24 1/8	20 7/8	5	5	Baker County	OR	Jeff McCrary	1991	524
167 3/8	24 0/8	24 2/8	20 5/8	5	5	West Lake	BC	Bob Dunlop	1991	524
167 3/8	24 7/8	24 6/8	22 5/8	7	8	Gunnison County	CO	Duane Lyerly	1992	524
167 2/8	20 7/8	21 5/8	20 3/8	5	4	Lincoln County	WY	Ronell Skinner	1980	532
167 2/8	23 0/8	23 0/8	20 6/8	6	5	Mesa County	CO	Jim Bennett	1981	532
167 2/8	22 6/8	22 4/8	18 0/8	5	4	Sublette County	WY	Marte Scheuffele	1989	532
167 2/8	25 0/8	24 7/8	23 2/8	5	7	La Plata County	CO	Michael B. Mitchell	1994	532
167 2/8	22 5/8	22 1/8	21 4/8	5	6	Norton County	KS	George J. Campbell	1996	532
167 2/8	21 4/8	22 0/8	20 2/8	5	5	Dundy County	NE	Matt Gideon	1998	532
167 1/8	21 1/8	19 3/8	18 2/8	6	6	Anahim Lake	BC	Guy Antilla	1965	538
167 1/8	26 3/8	24 4/8	21 2/8	5	4	Humboldt County	NV	Jerry Stout	1965	538
167 1/8	24 1/8	24 2/8	23 7/8	6	7	Gunnison County	CO	Richard L. Geissler	1983	538
167 1/8	22 0/8	21 3/8	19 3/8	5	5	Converse County	WY	Barry J. Smith	1991	538
167 1/8	24 4/8	25 0/8	23 3/8	5	5	Lake County	OR	Mike Slinkard	1996	538
167 3/8	23 3/8	24 2/8	22 2/8	4	4	Eagle County	CO	Arvine Routh	1965	543
167 0/8	23 3/8	24 4/8	22 0/8	5	5	Mesa County	CO	Mike Gilbert	1973	543
167 0/8	23 2/8	23 1/8	22 1/8	7	8	Grand County	CO	Michael K. Ward	1973	543
167 0/8	21 2/8	19 7/8	18 4/8	5	5	Mesa County	CO	Glen Hitt	1975	543
167 0/8	23 5/8	22 5/8	20 4/8	5	6	Garfield County	CO	Randy Edwards	1987	543
167 0/8	22 0/8	22 4/8	22 0/8	7	7	Warner	ALB	Gary Erickson	1991	543
167 0/8	22 7/8	24 1/8	20 0/8	5	5	Calgary	ALB	Dave Browne	1994	543
166 7/8	21 2/8	22 0/8	20 5/8	5	5	Uintah County	UT	Orson Stilson	1964	550
166 7/8	21 6/8	22 5/8	19 5/8	5	5	Phillips County	MT	Mark Kostecki	1994	550
166 7/8	22 2/8	23 5/8	23 1/8	5	5	Pima County	AZ	James Dale Casady	1996	550
166 6/8	25 1/8	25 3/8	24 4/8	5	6	Uintah County	UT	Doug Walker	1967	553
166 6/8	24 3/8	23 4/8	23 4/8	5	4	Mesa County	CO	David E. Samuel	1974	553
166 6/8	23 4/8	30 0/8	20 2/8	5	5	Adams County	CO	John C. Schmidt	1974	553
166 6/8	24 0/8	23 1/8	21 2/8	5	5	Grant County	OR	Paul J. Zink	1998	553
166 5/8	22 6/8	23 0/8	20 1/8	5	5	Baker County	OR	Lloyd V. Christensen	1959	557
166 5/8	23 4/8	23 6/8	23 5/8	5	5	Montezuma County	CO	Marvin Reichenau	1983	557
166 5/8	22 0/8	22 1/8	19 7/8	5	5	Grant County	OR	Ray Kelton	1985	557
166 5/8	24 5/8	24 5/8	22 0/8	5	6	Milk River Ridge	ALB	Brian Carriere	1990	557
166 5/8	23 6/8	22 4/8	22 3/8	5	5	Bernalillo County	NM	Ruben E. Chavez	1992	557
166 4/8	23 2/8	24 0/8	22 2/8	7	7	Owyhee County	ID	Bill Payne	1958	562
166 4/8	23 5/8	22 6/8	21 6/8	5	5	Owyhee County	ID	Blake Murphy	1961	562
166 4/8	20 3/8	20 5/8	16 6/8	5	5	Adams County	ID	Jack St. Germain	1986	562
166 4/8	23 6/8	23 3/8	20 0/8	5	4	Morrow County	OR	Phil Jackson	1992	562
166 3/8	21 7/8	22 5/8	21 0/8	6	7	Butte County	SD	L. G. Braun	1957	566
166 3/8	24 6/8	24 3/8	20 1/8	5	6	Lane County	KS	Dean Hamilton	1988	566
166 3/8	21 4/8	22 1/8	20 1/8	5	5	Ada County	ID	Brian Krebbs	1992	566

MULE DEER (TYPICAL ANTLERS)

Minimum Score 145   Continued

SCORE	LENGTH OF MAIN BEAM R	LENGTH OF MAIN BEAM L	INSIDE SPREAD	NUMBER OF POINTS R	NUMBER OF POINTS L	AREA	STATE/ PROVINCE	HUNTER'S NAME	DATE	RANK
166 3/8	20 5/8	22 3/8	20 1/8	5	5	Jefferson County	CO	Larry J. Jones	1998	566
166 2/8	25 2/8	23 1/8	18 0/8	5	5	Mesa County	CO	Lloyd Kell	1967	570
166 2/8	21 3/8	22 2/8	23 6/8	5	5	Garfield County	CO	Jim Walters	1975	570
166 2/8	22 3/8	22 4/8	23 2/8	5	5	Scott County	KS	Mel Jamison	1986	570
166 2/8	24 2/8	25 2/8	20 4/8	5	5	Platte County	WY	Terry Brown	1992	570
166 2/8	22 3/8	21 3/8	17 6/8	5	6	Exshaw	ALB	David Stecker	1992	570
166 2/8	22 3/8	24 7/8	21 0/8	6	5	Billings County	ND	Larry Ellis	1994	570
166 2/8	19 0/8	19 4/8	16 7/8	7	5	Caribou County	ID	Randy K. Guinn	1997	570
166 1/8	21 4/8	22 1/8	18 1/8	5	5	Carbon County	WY	Duncan G. Weibel	1955	577
166 1/8	20 6/8	21 4/8	19 5/8	5	5	Ada County	ID	M. F. Smith	1968	577
166 1/8	20 4/8	22 4/8	21 3/8	5	5	Calgary	ALB	Dean Reed	1981	577
166 0/8	20 0/8	20 7/8	19 5/8	6	5	Lincoln County	NE	M. R. Buchtel	1958	580
166 0/8	19 7/8	21 1/8	17 6/8	5	5	Mohave County	AZ	Norman J. Brown	1966	580
166 0/8	24 4/8	23 0/8	21 6/8	4	4	Garfield County	CO	Robert G. Kuper	1966	580
166 0/8	24 6/8	24 4/8	26 0/8	5	5	Cassia County	ID	Jack B. Watts	1968	580
166 0/8	23 4/8	24 0/8	24 2/8	5	4	Lewis & Clark County	MT	Donald Davidson, Jr.	1980	580
166 0/8	22 2/8	23 1/8	17 6/8	6	6	Elbert County	CO	Billy Tillotson	1986	580
166 0/8	22 0/8	23 0/8	22 4/8	5	5	Maricopa County	AZ	Daniel Whitaker	1988	580
166 0/8	21 7/8	22 2/8	22 4/8	6	5	El Paso County	CO	Freeman Howard	1989	580
166 0/8	22 0/8	21 3/8	17 0/8	5	5	Coconino County	AZ	John Coats	1998	580
165 7/8	23 4/8	25 0/8	25 0/8	9	6	Owyhee County	ID	Thomas Eld	1964	589
165 7/8	23 6/8	25 6/8	20 3/8	5	5	Moffat County	CO	Albert A. Adams	1982	589
165 7/8	22 6/8	22 4/8	25 6/8	6	7	Gray County	KS	Allen D. Bailey	1985	589
165 7/8	25 3/8	25 1/8	20 5/8	5	6	Mesa County	CO	James C. Snortum	1991	589
165 7/8	23 6/8	23 4/8	21 5/8	6	5	Hilda	ALB	Larry Hoffman	1993	589
165 7/8	22 5/8	24 4/8	22 0/8	6	6	Coconino County	AZ	Jack Hightower	1993	589
165 6/8	24 0/8	23 2/8	19 2/8	6	6	Garfield County	CO	John Richard	1972	595
165 6/8	23 6/8	23 4/8	17 2/8	5	5	Grand County	CO	Burt Thompson	1983	595
165 6/8	23 0/8	21 5/8	16 6/8	4	5	Graham County	KS	Randy Wilson	1989	595
165 5/8	21 1/8	21 0/8	20 5/8	5	5	Utah County	UT	Frank Eicholt	1964	598
165 5/8	21 0/8	21 2/8	18 5/8	5	5	Zone 5	SAS	Ward Minifie	1985	598
165 5/8	21 7/8	21 0/8	23 3/8	5	5	McKinley County	NM	Richard W. Eustace, Jr.	1988	598
165 5/8	22 4/8	24 0/8	17 7/8	5	5	Rich County	UT	Colby Steffen Hagen	1992	598
165 5/8	21 5/8	22 5/8	20 7/8	5	5	San Juan County	NM	Steven J. Vittetow	1997	598
165 4/8	23 1/8	23 6/8	24 1/8	6	5	Mesa County	CO	Bob Woodhouse	1978	603
165 4/8	22 4/8	23 4/8	19 0/8	5	5	San Miguel County	NM	Louis Baca	1985	603
165 4/8	21 6/8	22 6/8	25 7/8	5	5	Hodgeman County	KS	Charles Fuller	1985	603
165 4/8	24 1/8	24 7/8	19 3/8	7	6	Kane County	UT	Richard Jolley	1986	603
165 4/8	21 0/8	21 5/8	18 3/8	6	5	Billings County	ND	Harold Hugelen	1990	603
165 4/8	25 2/8	25 6/8	28 2/8	4	4	Las Animas County	CO	J. Keith Chastain	1995	603
165 4/8	23 0/8	23 5/8	18 0/8	5	6	Gilpin County	CO	Mark Kaufman	1996	603
165 4/8	24 6/8	23 3/8	22 1/8	6	6	Lincoln County	MT	Sandy Colville	1996	603
165 3/8	27 0/8	26 0/8	19 1/8	7	5	Mesa County	CO	Kent Stumpf	1973	611
165 3/8	24 4/8	25 0/8	18 3/8	7	7	Duchesne County	UT	Everett Burson	1984	611
165 3/8	23 2/8	21 2/8	20 0/8	5	6	Boise County	ID	Peter Cintorino	1985	611
165 3/8	22 2/8	22 0/8	17 0/8	6	5	Bonner County	ID	Bob Driggars	1991	611
165 3/8	19 3/8	20 4/8	17 5/8	4	4	Rio Blanco County	CO	Tom L. Buchholz	1993	611
165 3/8	21 5/8	21 4/8	21 6/8	5	5	Jefferson County	CO	Steve Smith	1998	611
165 2/8	26 5/8	27 0/8	25 2/8	5	5	Mesa County	CO	Ray Carpenter	1960	617
165 2/8	20 6/8	20 1/8	18 4/8	5	5	Clear Creek County	CO	John Marolt III	1967	617
165 2/8	22 0/8	21 5/8	19 4/8	5	5	Cassia County	ID	John Wells	1989	617
165 1/8	20 5/8	22 3/8	20 2/8	5	6	Sevier County	UT	Severin Jensen	1959	620
165 1/8	23 2/8	24 0/8	27 3/8	6	6	Douglas County	CO	Dale Slade	1967	620
165 1/8	23 4/8	25 4/8	26 0/8	5	7	Mesa County	CO	George J. Hronkin III	1982	620
165 1/8	21 3/8	22 2/8	20 1/8	5	5	Valley County	ID	Charles "Chuck" Boatman	1985	620
165 1/8	25 6/8	24 2/8	24 3/8	6	6	Fremont County	WY	Jerry A. Bodar	1988	620
165 0/8	24 3/8	25 0/8	19 7/8	5	6	Rio Arriba County	NM	David L. Chandler	1967	625
165 0/8	23 4/8	22 6/8	23 5/8	5	6	Cochise County	AZ	Richard Dawe, Jr.	1976	625
165 0/8	22 2/8	22 1/8	22 0/8	5	5	Saguache County	CO	Michael Snodgrass	1977	625
165 0/8	26 4/8	25 2/8	25 0/8	4	5	Lake County	OR	Wayne Lamson, Jr.	1981	625
165 0/8	24 6/8	25 6/8	21 4/8	5	5	Los Alamos County	NM	Doug Aikin	1985	625
165 0/8	22 1/8	21 7/8	21 2/8	5	5	Sanders County	MT	Craig Phillips	1990	625
165 0/8	23 3/8	24 4/8	17 2/8	4	4	Larimer County	CO	Mitch Brown	1992	625
165 0/8	24 2/8	24 2/8	18 1/8	5	6	Franklin County	WA	Bill Barnett	1994	625
165 0/8	22 4/8	22 5/8	21 6/8	5	5	Scott County	KS	D. Larry Potts	1994	625
165 0/8	24 0/8	23 3/8	23 6/8	5	6	Pima County	AZ	Carnie R. Marks	1995	625
165 0/8	21 0/8	21 1/8	17 6/8	5	5	Red Deer River	ALB	Richard Milder	1998	625
164 7/8	24 0/8	22 7/8	23 5/8	4	4	Mesa County	CO	Richard Rounds	1973	636
164 7/8	22 3/8	21 7/8	19 5/8	5	5	Routt County	CO	Paul Blotz	1974	636
164 7/8	24 3/8	23 0/8	25 5/8	5	5	Piute County	UT	Art Whitby	1992	636
164 7/8	23 3/8	21 6/8	21 4/8	7	5	Luna County	NM	Gary Shiflett	1993	636
164 7/8	21 5/8	23 3/8	19 1/8	4	5	Elbert County	CO	Matt Burrows	1994	636
164 6/8	22 4/8	21 3/8	18 2/8	5	5	Skyline Drive	UT	George Heath	1964	641
164 6/8	20 3/8	22 0/8	22 1/8	4	4	White Pine County	NV	Larry T. Gilbertson	1984	641
164 5/8	25 6/8	26 1/8	24 4/8	5	5	Fox Valley	SAS	Doug Findlay	1977	643
164 5/8	20 4/8	21 3/8	20 3/8	4	5	Grand County	UT	Don Dvoroznak	1979	643
164 5/8	22 2/8	23 2/8	19 4/8	5	6	Cassia County	ID	Richard Ponciano	1985	643
164 5/8	19 5/8	20 7/8	16 6/8	6	5	Mesa County	CO	Don Walsh	1986	643

MULE DEER (TYPICAL ANTLERS)

Minimum Score 145
Continued

SCORE	LENGTH OF MAIN BEAM R	LENGTH OF MAIN BEAM L	INSIDE SPREAD	NUMBER OF POINTS R	NUMBER OF POINTS L	AREA	STATE/PROVINCE	HUNTER'S NAME	DATE	RANK
164 5/8	23 6/8	24 2/8	21 0/8	6	5	Scott County	KS	Lynn Freese	1987	643
164 4/8	23 2/8	23 6/8	25 4/8	5	5	Calgary	ALB	David Lovo	1979	648
164 4/8	21 4/8	21 7/8	20 4/8	5	5	Fergus County	MT	Michael B. Bryson	1986	648
164 4/8	21 4/8	21 6/8	19 2/8	6	6	Lincoln County	WY	Mike Barrett	1989	648
164 4/8	21 5/8	22 2/8	22 3/8	6	6	Red Deer Lake	ALB	Larry Mandseth	1989	648
164 4/8	23 6/8	22 4/8	19 0/8	6	6	Adams County	CO	Mike Crites	1992	648
164 4/8	21 4/8	21 4/8	19 0/8	5	5	Wallowa County	OR	Michael J. Bishop	1994	648
164 4/8	23 0/8	22 3/8	19 4/8	5	5	Powder River County	MT	Don G. Scofield	1994	648
164 3/8	21 7/8	23 0/8	19 7/8	5	5	Siskiyou County	CA	Dale Gatlin	1959	655
164 3/8	24 6/8	23 4/8	24 6/8	8	8	Elko County	NV	Dick Woltering	1960	655
164 3/8	22 3/8	22 3/8	23 2/8	5	5	Sheridan County	KS	Kevin J. Ryan	1974	655
164 3/8	20 1/8	21 4/8	19 0/8	7	7	Conejos County	CO	Frank Holloway	1983	655
164 3/8	22 5/8	22 3/8	20 1/8	5	5	Routt County	CO	Richard L. Charles, Sr.	1990	655
164 3/8	23 6/8	22 4/8	19 5/8	5	5	Carbon County	WY	Dean P. Reed	1991	655
164 3/8	20 7/8	20 7/8	18 3/8	5	5	Lincoln County	WY	Mike Barrett	1992	655
164 2/8	23 2/8	24 0/8	19 4/8	7	9	Garfield County	CO	D. H. Nolting	1956	662
164 2/8	22 6/8	21 6/8	22 0/8	6	5	Routt County	CO	John Hale	1975	662
164 2/8	20 6/8	23 1/8	18 4/8	7	6	Dolores County	CO	Tommy C. Jeffcoat	1977	662
164 2/8	21 7/8	22 0/8	21 6/8	5	5	Greenlee County	AZ	Steve E. Allen	1980	662
164 2/8	24 4/8	24 3/8	23 7/8	6	6	Stafford County	KS	Rob Ginest	1982	662
164 2/8	22 0/8	20 4/8	18 4/8	4	4	Cassia County	ID	Bryan Sprauge	1984	662
164 2/8	26 6/8	24 1/8	25 7/8	5	4	San Juan County	NM	Ronnie H. Begay	1988	662
164 2/8	22 7/8	24 1/8	19 2/8	6	5	Kyle	SAS	Terry Chornomud	1995	662
164 2/8	22 3/8	23 2/8	24 0/8	5	5	Vermilion	ALB	Glenn Moir	1997	662
164 2/8	24 4/8	24 4/8	22 0/8	5	5	Humboldt County	NV	Sean Shea	1998	662
164 1/8	25 3/8	25 6/8	23 6/8	8	7	Owyhee County	ID	Merlie Hampton	1962	672
164 1/8	24 0/8	24 6/8	24 6/8	6	5	Summit County	CO	Russell F. Rider	1964	672
164 1/8	24 4/8	23 1/8	22 7/8	4	4	Garfield County	CO	Roy Hoff	1968	672
164 1/8	22 3/8	22 1/8	19 3/8	5	5	Columbia County	WA	Wayne Dickhaut	1983	672
164 1/8	23 4/8	23 1/8	20 7/8	5	5	Kananaskis	ALB	Don Warner	1992	672
164 1/8	20 5/8	20 6/8	19 0/8	6	5	Albany County	WY	Jerry Bowen	1992	672
164 1/8	17 3/8	16 7/8	22 2/8	5	5	Boise County	ID	Ken Gettman	1994	672
164 1/8	22 5/8	23 2/8	20 1/8	5	5	Bear Lake County	ID	Matthew Denning	1996	672
164 1/8	23 1/8	22 4/8	20 3/8	5	5	Weld County	CO	Casey J. Hatch	1998	672
164 0/8	19 4/8	20 1/8	19 6/8	5	5	Garfield County	CO	Dr. Lowell L. Eddy	1968	681
164 0/8	20 7/8	22 0/8	23 3/8	4	4	West Desert	UT	Myron Adams	1969	681
164 0/8	21 3/8	21 3/8	18 0/8	4	4	Ada County	ID	Richard C. Nichols	1971	681
164 0/8	24 6/8	25 3/8	23 7/8	7	6	White Pine County	NV	Robert Davie	1983	681
164 0/8	25 1/8	24 3/8	22 4/8	4	4	Yakima County	WA	Earl Prentice	1990	681
164 0/8	23 4/8	24 4/8	24 2/8	5	5	Elbert County	CO	Kim Cooper	1992	681
163 7/8	20 1/8	21 3/8	17 6/8	5	6	Frontier County	NE	Keene Hueftle	1961	687
163 7/8	19 0/8	20 6/8	18 1/8	5	5	Phillips County	KS	Phillip Pfortmiller	1986	687
163 7/8	24 1/8	25 7/8	27 3/8	5	5	McKinley County	NM	Dois Chesshir	1989	687
163 7/8	20 4/8	22 1/8	19 6/8	6	5	Maricopa County	AZ	Richard S. Jones	1990	687
163 7/8	23 0/8	20 3/8	17 7/8	5	5	Fergus County	MT	Paul L. Reese	1991	687
163 7/8	24 2/8	23 7/8	23 5/8	6	5	El Paso County	CO	Clyde A. Bayne	1997	687
163 6/8	22 2/8	21 2/8	21 4/8	5	5	Pima County	AZ	Tom Bylina	1988	693
163 6/8	26 2/8	26 6/8	27 4/8	3	5	Bella Coola	BC	Lawrence Michalchuk	1995	693
163 5/8	23 3/8	23 2/8	22 3/8	5	5	White Pine County	NV	Joe Marich	1978	695
163 5/8	19 0/8	19 0/8	17 7/8	5	5	Gallatin County	MT	Jim Diercks	1981	695
163 5/8	21 2/8	21 0/8	18 1/8	5	5	Mesa County	CO	Edwin L. Porter	1983	695
163 5/8	20 6/8	20 6/8	22 6/8	6	5	Bear Lake County	ID	Terry Davis	1984	695
163 5/8	21 6/8	24 3/8	18 7/8	5	5	Eagle Hill	ALB	Ian Kaiser	1994	695
163 5/8	23 3/8	19 5/8	18 0/8	6	5	Spring Coulee	ALB	Gary Erickson	1996	695
163 5/8	18 7/8	19 7/8	18 7/8	5	5	Leduc	ALB	Dean Busat	1997	695
163 4/8	23 1/8	23 2/8	20 4/8	5	5		UT	Darwin Crawford	1964	702
163 4/8	24 1/8	24 1/8	25 0/8	5	5	Lake County	OR	William P. Petredis	1972	702
163 4/8	24 4/8	24 0/8	22 2/8	9	5	Osborne County	KS	Gary Krier	1984	702
163 3/8	22 5/8	25 4/8	17 6/8	8	7	Coconino County	AZ	Jake Price	1963	705
163 3/8	21 6/8	22 1/8	17 5/8	5	5	Gunnison County	CO	Clark Gallup	1970	705
163 3/8	23 3/8	23 7/8	21 7/8	5	5	Val Marie	SAS	John Vinge	1992	705
163 2/8	22 6/8	22 6/8	23 4/8	5	5	Mesa County	CO	Larry D. Tillett	1972	708
163 2/8	21 5/8	20 1/8	19 7/8	6	6	Chaffee County	CO	J. Melvin Rose	1973	708
163 2/8	23 7/8	24 3/8	21 2/8	5	4	Coconino County	AZ	Edward R. Allen, Sr.	1974	708
163 2/8	20 6/8	21 2/8	22 0/8	5	5	Calgary	ALB	Richard P. King	1987	708
163 2/8	22 0/8	22 7/8	17 2/8	5	5	Kyle	SAS	Brian W. Johns	1991	708
163 2/8	23 0/8	23 6/8	21 2/8	5	5	Baker County	OR	T. Blaine McKnight	1992	708
163 1/8	20 0/8	22 6/8	19 5/8	4	4	Routt County	CO	Robert H. Blue	1983	714
163 1/8	21 6/8	21 6/8	20 7/8	4	4	McKenzie County	ND	Mike 'Myron' Rosemore	1986	714
163 1/8	23 1/8	22 4/8	24 0/8	5	5	Seward County	KS	Travis Leonard	1993	714
163 1/8	22 3/8	22 0/8	21 5/8	5	5	Milk River	ALB	Craig Chandler	1997	714
163 0/8	24 2/8	23 4/8	24 2/8	5	7	La Plata County	CO	Bryan B. Owen	1964	718
163 0/8	23 3/8	25 3/8	20 6/8	5	5	Coconino County	AZ	Larry Hayden	1983	718
163 0/8	21 3/8	22 5/8	18 2/8	5	5	Teton County	WY	Al Nelson	1985	718
163 0/8	20 7/8	20 0/8	17 6/8	5	5	Mesa County	CO	Jim Hall	1987	718
163 0/8	22 3/8	23 0/8	21 6/8	5	5	Culberson County	TX	Kyle Johnson	1992	718
163 0/8	22 3/8	22 3/8	19 0/8	4	4	Yuma County	CO	Garry Neuschwanger	1992	718
163 0/8	20 6/8	21 2/8	20 6/8	5	5	Hall County	NE	Jason A. Hettler	1994	718

MULE DEER (TYPICAL ANTLERS)

Minimum Score 145

SCORE	LENGTH OF MAIN BEAM R	LENGTH OF MAIN BEAM L	INSIDE SPREAD	NUMBER OF POINTS R	NUMBER OF POINTS L	AREA	STATE/ PROVINCE	HUNTER'S NAME	DATE	RANK
163 0/8	22 2/8	23 1/8	18 6/8	5	5	Calgary	ALB	Fred V. Kugler	1997	718
162 7/8	23 6/8	23 7/8	24 1/8	5	4	Elko County	NV	Orrin M. Owens	1966	726
162 7/8	23 1/8	22 7/8	20 1/8	5	5	Billings County	ND	Allan R. Bottolfson	1981	726
162 7/8	23 5/8	21 6/8	20 5/8	5	5	Fremont County	CO	Jerry Tiemeyer	1981	726
162 7/8	24 0/8	23 6/8	23 5/8	5	5	Umatilla County	OR	Rick L. Evans	1985	726
162 7/8	23 1/8	21 6/8	23 1/8	5	4	San Juan County	NM	Rick Mace	1995	726
162 7/8	20 7/8	22 3/8	19 5/8	6	5	Cochrane	ALB	Tom Foss	1996	726
162 7/8	20 4/8	21 4/8	15 5/8	5	5	Coconino County	AZ	Lynn D. Nelson	1996	726
162 6/8	21 1/8	23 4/8	23 2/8	5	5	Chelan County	WA	Les Eide	1954	733
162 6/8	23 5/8	24 2/8	18 5/8	5	6	Chelan County	WA	Brian Kayler	1984	733
162 6/8	22 4/8	24 0/8	19 6/8	5	5	Larimer County	CO	Ron Morgan	1986	733
162 6/8	22 1/8	23 1/8	22 2/8	5	5	Chelan County	WA	Rod Courter	1986	733
162 6/8	22 2/8	22 6/8	23 5/8	5	5	Weld County	CO	Dan Wacker	1988	733
162 6/8	21 7/8	22 6/8	18 2/8	5	5	Uinta County	WY	Frank W. Sheets	1992	733
162 6/8	22 6/8	22 5/8	21 6/8	5	5	Cheyenne County	KS	David Hamilton	1992	733
162 6/8	22 7/8	23 6/8	22 3/8	6	5	Coconino County	AZ	David J. Dettorre	1997	733
162 5/8	19 6/8	20 1/8	22 0/8	5	5	Pima County	AZ	Jerry Clarno	1978	741
162 5/8	22 4/8	21 0/8	21 2/8	7	6	Washoe County	NV	Ed Fuller	1984	741
162 5/8	21 4/8	21 1/8	20 7/8	5	5	Las Animas County	CO	Chris J. Furia	1986	741
162 5/8	20 2/8	21 6/8	19 2/8	7	5	Ada County	ID	Ronald L. Cash	1990	741
162 5/8	22 4/8	23 3/8	19 1/8	6	5	Montrose County	CO	Thomas D. Thompson	1991	741
162 5/8	24 3/8	24 7/8	21 3/8	5	5	Sheridan County	WY	Butch West	1992	741
162 5/8	21 7/8	23 4/8	18 1/8	5	5	Highwood River	ALB	Troy W. Clark	1995	741
162 5/8	18 2/8	21 7/8	22 4/8	4	5	Yuma County	CO	Tobias Dellamano	1996	741
162 5/8	20 2/8	19 3/8	19 1/8	5	5	Yuma County	CO	Tom Pindell	1997	741
162 4/8	21 3/8	21 0/8	19 2/8	5	5	Emery County	UT	Kerry Ware	1964	750
162 4/8	24 5/8	25 7/8	27 6/8	5	8	Leader	SAS	Don Tourand	1982	750
162 4/8	21 0/8	21 7/8	17 2/8	5	5	Slope County	ND	Todd Seymonski	1983	750
162 4/8	21 2/8	20 7/8	23 0/8	5	5	Hooker County	NE	Will Boyer	1991	750
162 4/8	23 0/8	25 0/8	25 6/8	4	5	Yuma County	CO	Jerry Bowen	1997	750
162 3/8	25 2/8	25 0/8	22 6/8	7	7	Bear Lake County	ID	Marriner Jensen	1957	755
162 3/8	25 6/8	26 3/8	27 5/8	4	5	Pima County	AZ	Steve Mikitish	1983	755
162 3/8	23 0/8	22 7/8	24 3/8	5	6	Mesa County	CO	Billy T. Edwards	1988	755
162 2/8	23 3/8	26 2/8	25 0/8	4	5	Owyhee County	ID	Ralph Collins	1960	758
162 2/8	20 7/8	20 2/8	22 3/8	6	5	Park County	WY	Jim Patterson	1968	758
162 2/8	22 5/8	23 0/8	17 0/8	5	5	Eureka County	NV	Gordon Diehl	1980	758
162 2/8	23 5/8	23 2/8	19 6/8	5	5	Lassen County	CA	Chuck Mazza	1984	758
162 2/8	23 4/8	23 5/8	21 4/8	5	5	Park County	CO	Randy W. Gorby, Jr.	1988	758
162 2/8	22 3/8	26 4/8	20 0/8	6	5	Bernalillo County	NM	William A. Brandon	1988	758
162 2/8	22 7/8	22 3/8	19 4/8	5	7	Camas County	ID	James C. O'Connor	1991	758
162 1/8	23 7/8	23 6/8	18 1/8	5	5	Fishlake National Forest	UT	R. E. Kerr	1957	765
162 1/8	23 2/8	22 5/8	22 1/8	5	5	Range Creek	UT	Frank Turner	1965	765
162 1/8	22 4/8	22 5/8	17 2/8	5	6	Mesa County	CO	Joel Prickett	1973	765
162 1/8	20 3/8	22 0/8	23 0/8	7	5	Mora County	NM	Michael J. Maes	1977	765
162 1/8	21 7/8	21 7/8	23 1/8	6	6	Dundy County	NE	Jim Lutz	1980	765
162 1/8	24 2/8	21 2/8	21 5/8	6	5	Logan County	KS	Mel Jamison	1985	765
162 0/8	22 3/8	23 1/8	21 2/8	5	5	Elko County	NV	Larry D Jones	1985	771
162 0/8	21 5/8	20 7/8	21 0/8	6	6	Rawlins County	KS	Ken Krien	1988	771
162 0/8	22 3/8	22 4/8	16 4/8	4	5	Lumby	BC	Owen Schoenberger	1990	771
161 7/8	21 4/8	21 7/8	20 3/8	4	5	Rio Blanco County	CO	Douglas Kenyon	1964	774
161 7/8	22 6/8	21 6/8	21 5/8	5	5	Sevier County	UT	Clark Richards	1967	774
161 7/8	23 0/8	22 1/8	20 0/8	5	5	Rio Blanco County	CO	Leonard Conley	1973	774
161 7/8	20 4/8	22 5/8	20 7/8	6	6	Beaver County	UT	Joe Cordonier	1975	774
161 7/8	21 1/8	20 3/8	18 5/8	5	5	Plumas County	CA	John Grochowski, Jr.	1976	774
161 7/8	24 3/8	24 1/8	20 7/8	5	4	Maricopa County	AZ	Paul N. Rambeau	1981	774
161 7/8	25 4/8	23 6/8	22 5/8	8	5	Catron County	NM	Richard D. Trapp	1986	774
161 7/8	24 6/8	25 1/8	22 3/8	4	3	Grant County	WA	Daniel A. Whitmus	1994	774
161 7/8	21 4/8	21 4/8	22 6/8	5	6	Ada County	ID	Rory Clinton	1994	774
161 7/8	23 7/8	22 5/8	19 5/8	6	6	Weyburn	SAS	Paul Chinski	1996	774
161 6/8	21 3/8	21 3/8	21 6/8	5	5	Garfield County	CO	Warren Buss	1978	784
161 6/8	20 5/8	21 5/8	21 2/8	5	5	Elko County	NV	Gregory Higgins	1988	784
161 6/8	21 2/8	22 2/8	21 2/8	5	5	Campbell County	WY	Loy Peters	1990	784
161 6/8	22 2/8	22 6/8	21 2/8	6	7	Lincoln County	CO	James Hipps	1992	784
161 5/8	22 0/8	22 4/8	19 3/8	5	5	Lander County	NV	Paul Q. Lenz	1984	788
161 5/8	22 5/8	22 5/8	21 7/8	5	5	Rio Arriba County	NM	Craig A. Pilley	1987	788
161 5/8	23 5/8	22 3/8	21 6/8	5	6	Ford County	KS	Jeff Cuer	1988	788
161 5/8	23 5/8	22 5/8	22 6/8	6	5	Converse County	WY	Jeff Reynolds	1990	788
161 5/8	23 3/8	23 5/8	21 3/8	4	5	Boise County	ID	David Gallegos	1991	788
161 4/8	24 5/8	24 6/8	24 2/8	7	7	Salt Lake County	UT	Frank M. Davis	1957	793
161 4/8	24 4/8	24 2/8	23 6/8	4	3	Owyhee County	ID	William R. Vanderhoef	1958	793
161 4/8	22 5/8	23 5/8	19 2/8	5	5	Sheridan County	WY	Mike Barrett	1985	793
161 4/8	25 6/8	24 1/8	24 6/8	5	7	Apache County	AZ	Robert A. Wood	1987	793
161 4/8	21 6/8	20 2/8	18 4/8	5	6	Grant County	OR	Jeff McCrary	1990	793
161 4/8	21 4/8	22 0/8	21 2/8	5	5	Elbert County	CO	Patrick V. Mulhern, Jr.	1990	793
161 4/8	21 6/8	21 6/8	16 6/8	5	5	Lincoln County	WY	Delmar Bright	1992	793
161 4/8	21 4/8	21 3/8	19 5/8	6	5	Campbell County	WY	Art Cain	1994	793
161 3/8	22 5/8	21 7/8	19 1/8	5	5	Elko County	NV	Bert W. Fox	1961	801
161 3/8	23 2/8	21 6/8	22 3/8	4	4	Box Butte County	NE	Fred H. D. Krueger	1970	801

MULE DEER (TYPICAL ANTLERS)

Minimum Score 145 — Continued

SCORE	LENGTH OF MAIN BEAM R	LENGTH OF MAIN BEAM L	INSIDE SPREAD	NUMBER OF POINTS R	NUMBER OF POINTS L	AREA	STATE/PROVINCE	HUNTER'S NAME	DATE	RANK
161 3/8	18 5/8	21 1/8	22 1/8	6	5	Cochrane	ALB	Colby Robison	1982	801
161 3/8	22 5/8	22 7/8	22 1/8	5	5	Rush County	KS	Clarence Tuzicka	1990	801
161 3/8	22 3/8	22 4/8	18 2/8	5	6	Stanislaus County	CA	Ron Crouch	1992	801
161 2/8	21 0/8	20 6/8	16 7/8	5	6	Ada County	ID	Ed Moser	1971	806
161 2/8	24 6/8	23 5/8	20 4/8	3	3	Mesa County	CO	Billy Ellis	1976	806
161 2/8	23 6/8	25 2/8	25 4/8	5	5	San Juan County	UT	Todd Hurst	1984	806
161 2/8	23 4/8	22 3/8	17 6/8	5	5	Big Horn County	MT	Mike Barrett	1984	806
161 2/8	23 7/8	23 0/8	22 4/8	5	5	Billings County	ND	Cally G Marsh	1989	806
161 2/8	23 0/8	23 1/8	22 4/8	5	5	Apache County	AZ	Johnny C. Parsons	1992	806
161 2/8	24 4/8	23 4/8	20 6/8	5	5	Apache County	AZ	Bruce Kallenberger	1993	806
161 2/8	24 0/8	22 0/8	22 2/8	5	5	Colfax County	NM	Stacy Hoeme	1994	806
161 2/8	22 1/8	21 4/8	19 6/8	6	5	La Plata County	CO	Pat Palmer	1996	806
161 1/8	25 0/8	24 0/8	25 0/8	5	5	Los Alamos County	NM	J. R. McDaniels	1960	815
161 1/8	20 5/8	20 4/8	15 5/8	5	5	Garfield County	CO	John Murray	1963	815
161 1/8	23 1/8	21 7/8	18 1/8	5	5	San Juan County	CO	Eddie Claypool	1984	815
161 1/8	24 6/8	25 6/8	20 3/8	5	4	Kittitas County	WA	Sam Grant	1988	815
161 1/8	19 4/8	20 5/8	16 7/8	5	5	Coconino County	AZ	Richard S. Brown	1998	815
161 0/8	23 0/8	23 4/8	19 2/8	4	5	Milk River	ALB	Archie Nesbitt	1992	820
161 0/8	22 4/8	23 3/8	25 2/8	5	6	Colfax County	NM	Mark Sullivan	1995	820
161 0/8	22 5/8	22 3/8	18 2/8	6	5	Coconino County	AZ	William C. Rhodes	1996	820
161 0/8	22 1/8	23 0/8	16 0/8	5	6	Niobrara County	WY	Gary Morse	1998	820
160 7/8	24 0/8	23 5/8	22 3/8	4	5	Teton County	ID	Gary S. Paynter	1987	824
160 7/8	21 4/8	21 6/8	18 7/8	5	5	Haakon County	SD	Melvin Buchheim	1993	824
160 7/8	21 3/8	21 3/8	21 6/8	5	6	Teton County	WY	Arron J. Wagner	1993	824
160 7/8	20 5/8	21 3/8	16 1/8	5	5	Colfax County	NM	Bruce Imig	1995	824
160 7/8	25 3/8	24 2/8	22 1/8	5	5	Rio Arriba County	NM	Wally Schwartz	1996	824
160 6/8	20 6/8	21 4/8	21 5/8	5	5	Colfax County	NM	Carl Osborne	1965	829
160 6/8	22 6/8	22 4/8	21 1/8	7	6	Chelan County	WA	Paul Cohoon	1967	829
160 6/8	21 3/8	22 2/8	26 7/8	6	6	San Juan County	UT	Dale Warren	1972	829
160 6/8	22 4/8	22 6/8	15 4/8	5	4	Washoe County	NV	Lawrence Heward	1974	829
160 6/8	20 5/8	20 3/8	19 4/8	5	5	Boise County	ID	Mike McCollum	1975	829
160 6/8	21 0/8	22 4/8	21 4/8	5	5	Grand County	CO	Terry J. Kramer	1978	829
160 6/8	21 7/8	23 2/8	19 2/8	6	5	Thomas County	KS	Darren Andrews	1986	829
160 6/8	22 2/8	21 1/8	19 6/8	6	7	Archuleta County	CO	James Daugherty	1987	829
160 6/8	24 6/8	25 0/8	28 2/8	5	7	Washoe County	NV	Tom Hauptman	1988	829
160 6/8	23 4/8	21 6/8	24 3/8	7	9	Cheyenne County	CO	Monte Baker	1990	829
160 6/8	23 0/8	23 3/8	18 0/8	6	5	Baker County	OR	Mike Raney	1992	829
160 6/8	22 0/8	22 0/8	20 3/8	5	7	Finney County	KS	Eddie Rojas, Jr.	1996	829
160 6/8	21 6/8	22 5/8	18 6/8	5	5	Otero County	NM	Jerry Bales	1997	829
160 6/8	22 6/8	21 6/8	20 6/8	5	5	Rio Arriba County	NM	Patrick Lovato	1997	829
160 5/8	20 5/8	20 5/8	19 7/8	4	4	Humboldt County	NV	Mike Toone	1961	843
160 5/8	22 3/8	22 1/8	24 7/8	5	5	San Juan County	UT	Russell Smith	1971	843
160 5/8	21 1/8	21 2/8	20 7/8	5	5	Routt County	CO	Mark Chapman	1975	843
160 5/8	21 1/8	21 6/8	17 7/8	4	4	Moffat County	CO	Glenn Pritchard	1985	843
160 5/8	23 5/8	23 3/8	21 5/8	5	5	Nevada County	CA	Richard L. Westervelt	1992	843
160 5/8	24 0/8	25 2/8	27 0/8	5	6	Teton County	WY	Ronell Skinner	1992	843
160 5/8	22 6/8	22 6/8	25 4/8	5	6	Park County	MT	Nathan Broell	1993	843
160 4/8	23 6/8	23 1/8	20 0/8	7	8	Elko County	NV	Robert Narrimore	1963	850
160 4/8	23 5/8	23 5/8	18 0/8	5	5	Lemhi County	ID	Robert J. Eckardt	1978	850
160 4/8	24 4/8	23 2/8	24 4/8	4	5	Coconino County	AZ	Bruce McIntyre	1979	850
160 4/8	23 0/8	22 2/8	23 6/8	5	5	Washoe County	NV	Robert L. Brooks, Jr.	1983	850
160 4/8	23 3/8	24 1/8	16 6/8	6	6	Platte County	WY	Dennis Crew	1995	850
160 3/8	22 7/8	22 3/8	18 0/8	5	5	Tooele County	UT	Clair Adams	1958	855
160 3/8	22 4/8	22 4/8	18 2/8	6	6	Mesa County	CO	Ed Adkins	1974	855
160 3/8	20 6/8	22 1/8	20 1/8	4	4	Mesa County	CO	Ralph Ertz	1980	855
160 3/8	22 0/8	23 4/8	19 1/8	6	6	Jefferson County	CO	Steve Rehm	1984	855
160 3/8	24 4/8	22 2/8	22 0/8	6	6	Pima County	AZ	Ronald J. Hover	1987	855
160 3/8	23 3/8	23 5/8	20 3/8	5	5	Lake County	OR	Carl E. Garner	1991	855
160 3/8	22 1/8	21 5/8	23 7/8	5	5	Cochrane	ALB	Tom Foss	1994	855
160 2/8	19 2/8	21 2/8	19 0/8	5	5	Millard County	UT	Scott Chesley	1962	862
160 2/8	19 6/8	21 2/8	20 6/8	5	5	Lemhi County	ID	Kemper McMaster	1978	862
160 2/8	20 5/8	21 1/8	17 0/8	5	5	Mesa County	CO	Bill Dunbar	1984	862
160 2/8	25 6/8	24 6/8	23 3/8	6	6	Scott County	KS	Michael E. Woodard	1984	862
160 2/8	21 4/8	20 5/8	20 6/8	5	5	Gooding County	ID	Robert Dowen	1986	862
160 2/8	21 6/8	22 6/8	18 0/8	4	4	Sioux County	NE	Wayne Depperschmidt	1989	862
160 2/8	23 7/8	22 2/8	18 2/8	6	6	Montrose County	CO	Jackie Wright	1995	862
160 2/8	23 3/8	23 1/8	19 0/8	6	6	Lake Diefenbaker	SAS	Darren Breckner	1995	862
160 2/8	22 0/8	22 6/8	18 2/8	4	4	Boise County	ID	Dwayne Sturbaum	1995	862
160 2/8	22 2/8	22 1/8	25 0/8	5	5	Jefferson County	OR	Travis Williams	1997	862
160 1/8	20 2/8	20 7/8	19 7/8	5	5	Meagher County	MT	Mickey Anderson, Jr.	1966	872
160 1/8	23 6/8	22 2/8	24 0/8	5	5	Moffat County	CO	Ron Hopkins	1970	872
160 1/8	22 7/8	22 7/8	23 3/8	5	5	Mesa County	CO	Gary J. Oden	1988	872
160 1/8	22 1/8	22 6/8	20 1/8	5	5	Deschutes County	OR	R. Sean Glaab	1992	872
160 1/8	19 0/8	18 6/8	15 5/8	5	5	Ravalli County	MT	Michael A. Dunwell	1994	872
160 1/8	24 0/8	23 6/8	27 0/8	5	5	Malheur County	OR	Steven Nichols	1996	872
160 1/8	22 3/8	21 3/8	18 1/8	5	6	Weld County	CO	Reggie Spiegelberg	1996	872
160 0/8	22 4/8	21 7/8	20 2/8	5	5	Chaffee County	CO	Paul J. Zeisler	1964	879
160 0/8	23 0/8	22 7/8	20 3/8	6	5	Gunnison County	CO	Wayne Depperschmidt	1973	879

MULE DEER (TYPICAL ANTLERS)

Minimum Score 145 — Continued

SCORE	LENGTH OF MAIN BEAM R	LENGTH OF MAIN BEAM L	INSIDE SPREAD	NUMBER OF POINTS R	NUMBER OF POINTS L	AREA	STATE/ PROVINCE	HUNTER'S NAME	DATE	RANK
160 0/8	21 4/8	21 7/8	19 2/8	5	5	Linn County	OR	Mary Cook	1980	879
160 0/8	23 3/8	24 2/8	20 2/8	5	5	Saguache County	CO	Russell Hull	1980	879
160 0/8	26 2/8	25 1/8	25 0/8	5	5	La Plata County	CO	Michael R. Hinson	1986	879
160 0/8	21 7/8	22 5/8	17 6/8	5	5	Cherry County	NE	Lloyd C. Smith	1990	879
159 7/8	24 2/8	25 0/8	19 4/8	5	6	Colfax County	NM	James Kelly	1957	885
159 7/8	20 7/8	21 6/8	21 6/8	5	5	Liberty County	MT	Kenneth Aaberge	1960	885
159 7/8	22 5/8	23 0/8	18 7/8	5	5	Sanders County	MT	Walt Borgmann	1968	885
159 7/8	23 1/8	21 3/8	17 3/8	5	5	Bernalillo County	NM	Lee Burnett	1972	885
159 7/8	25 4/8	22 4/8	21 0/8	6	6	Mesa County	CO	Ronald E. Stull	1974	885
159 7/8	21 5/8	22 3/8	20 1/8	5	5	Okotoks	ALB	Cam Cook	1990	885
159 7/8	19 7/8	20 6/8	19 2/8	6	6	Ellsworth County	KS	Rod Buchholz	1997	885
159 6/8	23 4/8	22 7/8	22 3/8	7	7	Owyhee County	ID	Gilbert Martin	1960	892
159 6/8	22 2/8	21 4/8	19 4/8	5	5	Beaver County	UT	Joe Cordonier	1974	892
159 6/8	22 0/8	22 0/8	20 6/8	4	4	Kamloops	BC	Barry Anderson	1982	892
159 6/8	21 2/8	21 3/8	18 6/8	5	5	Albany County	WY	Jerry Bowen	1984	892
159 6/8	22 6/8	23 2/8	20 6/8	5	5	Labette County	KS	Steve Cooper	1986	892
159 6/8	21 3/8	22 0/8	22 0/8	5	4	Caribou County	ID	Paul Persano	1986	892
159 6/8	23 7/8	24 2/8	20 6/8	8	6	Norton County	KS	Eldon L. Myers	1991	892
159 6/8	25 7/8	26 6/8	20 4/8	5	5	Kane County	UT	William D. Hofeling	1993	892
159 6/8	21 1/8	22 5/8	22 2/8	5	5	Sheridan County	WY	Bruce Kramer	1993	892
159 6/8	21 4/8	20 4/8	16 2/8	6	5	Gove County	KS	Carl L. Ghan, Jr.	1993	892
159 6/8	22 2/8	21 6/8	18 6/8	5	5	Garfield County	MT	Corey Hugelen	1994	892
159 6/8	23 0/8	22 0/8	19 2/8	5	5	Carbon County	WY	Glen H. Burns	1995	892
159 5/8	22 7/8	22 5/8	25 3/8	5	5	Gove County	KS	Alan Kaiser	1986	904
159 5/8	24 5/8	23 6/8	20 1/8	7	6	Crook County	OR	Kent Gutches	1991	904
159 4/8	20 5/8	21 0/8	17 6/8	5	5	Franklin County	ID	Curtis Henderson	1992	906
159 4/8	21 7/8	21 1/8	22 0/8	5	6	Grant County	OR	Bill Hueckman	1993	906
159 4/8	23 1/8	23 6/8	21 6/8	5	5	Elbert County	CO	Jason Dirscherl	1995	906
159 3/8	21 1/8	20 4/8	16 5/8	4	4	Millard County	UT	Dean Todd	1956	909
159 3/8	22 4/8	22 7/8	18 4/8	5	5	Wasco County	OR	Bill Neary	1966	909
159 3/8	22 2/8	22 1/8	20 3/8	5	4	Kiowa County	CO	Mike Edwards	1996	909
159 3/8	22 3/8	22 5/8	20 7/8	5	5	Johnson County	WY	Richard A. Tesch	1997	909
159 2/8	21 1/8	20 4/8	17 2/8	5	5	Garfield County	CO	Robert Pitt	1978	913
159 2/8	19 6/8	20 0/8	17 6/8	4	4	Crook County	WY	Mark L. Shumate	1986	913
159 2/8	22 2/8	22 7/8	18 0/8	6	6	Converse County	WY	Rick L. Morley	1996	913
159 1/8	22 6/8	21 6/8	20 5/8	5	7	Garfield County	CO	Jack Peters	1963	916
159 1/8	23 0/8	23 2/8	18 7/8	4	5	Garfield County	CO	Donald J. Walsh	1977	916
159 1/8	21 1/8	22 0/8	20 7/8	5	5	White Pine County	NV	Steve Wood	1978	916
159 1/8	25 6/8	26 2/8	27 5/8	5	7	Maricopa County	AZ	George Toot	1980	916
159 1/8	24 0/8	22 7/8	20 5/8	5	5	Clear Creek County	CO	Dave Skiff	1982	916
159 1/8	17 1/8	19 3/8	19 4/8	4	4	Jefferson County	CO	Calvin Farner	1986	916
159 0/8	22 3/8	21 2/8	25 2/8	5	6	Ada County	ID	Deloy Desaro	1973	922
159 0/8	20 6/8	21 1/8	17 1/8	5	6	Montrose County	CO	David M. Gant	1977	922
159 0/8	21 3/8	22 7/8	22 2/8	6	5	San Juan County	CO	Dennis Atwater	1978	922
159 0/8	22 4/8	22 6/8	19 6/8	5	5	Lincoln County	MT	Christopher C. Crooks	1991	922
159 0/8	22 7/8	23 3/8	19 2/8	5	5	Rio Arriba County	NM	Matthew Quintana	1994	922
158 7/8	20 1/8	19 7/8	22 1/8	5	5	Sevier County	UT	Mike Otten	1973	927
158 7/8	21 2/8	22 6/8	21 7/8	5	5	Elmore County	ID	Peter J Cintorino	1981	927
158 7/8	20 1/8	19 4/8	21 4/8	5	6	Carbon County	WY	Daniel S. Christie	1982	927
158 7/8	22 7/8	22 2/8	17 0/8	5	5	Klamath County	OR	Harold McCraven	1986	927
158 7/8	21 7/8	22 0/8	17 5/8	5	5	Chase County	NE	John F. Burke	1987	927
158 7/8	24 6/8	26 3/8	24 0/8	5	5	Yavapai County	AZ	Wally Schwartz	1989	927
158 7/8	22 2/8	21 4/8	21 5/8	6	5	La Plata County	CO	Michael R. Hinson	1989	927
158 7/8	20 0/8	21 4/8	18 1/8	5	6	Logan County	KS	James Beougher	1989	927
158 7/8	23 2/8	23 5/8	22 3/8	6	6	Crystal Springs	ALB	James R. Godlonton	1993	927
158 6/8	21 3/8	22 3/8	22 0/8	5	5	Lake County	OR	Lyle Reeder	1954	936
158 6/8	21 6/8	20 7/8	17 0/8	6	4	Stacy	MT	Dewey Olsen	1960	936
158 6/8	21 1/8	22 2/8	22 0/8	4	5	Platte County	WY	Jerry Bowen	1987	936
158 6/8	22 3/8	23 3/8	20 4/8	4	4	Lassen County	CA	David Gallegos	1988	936
158 6/8	19 5/8	19 1/8	19 0/8	5	5	Campbell County	WY	Richard Hettinga	1990	936
158 6/8	21 5/8	20 7/8	21 2/8	5	5	Malheur County	OR	Steve C. Scott	1992	936
158 6/8	20 5/8	20 2/8	17 0/8	5	5	Cypress	ALB	Dan David	1993	936
158 6/8	22 1/8	23 0/8	19 6/8	4	5	Albany County	WY	Jerry Bowen	1994	936
158 6/8	21 1/8	22 1/8	20 3/8	6	5	Prowers County	CO	Randy Wright	1994	936
158 5/8	22 2/8	22 5/8	18 1/8	6	6	Weber County	UT	Bruce N. Moss	1974	945
158 5/8	22 1/8	22 3/8	18 5/8	6	5	Hodgeman County	KS	Ron Adams	1985	945
158 5/8	21 7/8	20 7/8	17 6/8	6	5	Morton County	KS	Kevin E. White	1987	945
158 5/8	21 3/8	22 5/8	21 5/8	5	5	Rio Arriba County	NM	Eudane Vicenti	1995	945
158 5/8	27 2/8	25 5/8	21 3/8	6	5	Mesa County	CO	Mark Boarman	1996	945
158 4/8	23 3/8	23 6/8	22 6/8	4	4	Albany County	WY	Nelson W. Brower	1979	950
158 4/8	21 0/8	19 6/8	18 2/8	5	5	Greeley County	KS	Keith Foster	1981	950
158 4/8	20 0/8	20 3/8	15 4/8	5	5	Lane County	KS	Hurley T. Smith	1982	950
158 4/8	24 2/8	23 2/8	18 4/8	5	4	Garfield County	CO	Orvie E. Linsin	1989	950
158 4/8	19 5/8	18 5/8	18 4/8	6	6	Maricopa County	AZ	Lawrence Drake	1992	950
158 4/8	22 1/8	20 2/8	19 2/8	5	5	Douglas County	CO	Kenneth H. Karbon	1992	950
158 4/8	24 0/8	22 7/8	30 2/8	5	5	Ada County	ID	Robert D. Dowen	1992	950
158 4/8	20 7/8	23 0/8	16 4/8	5	4	Lincoln County	WA	Chris Lesher	1995	950
158 3/8	25 1/8	21 1/8	20 1/8	6	5	Sheridan County	NE	Gerald J. McKinney	1974	958

MULE DEER (TYPICAL ANTLERS)

Minimum Score 145

Continued

SCORE	LENGTH OF MAIN BEAM R / L	INSIDE SPREAD	NUMBER OF POINTS R / L		AREA	STATE/ PROVINCE	HUNTER'S NAME	DATE	RANK
158 3/8	24 5/8 / 24 2/8	21 3/8	4	6	Ada County	ID	Robert E. Stauts	1979	958
158 3/8	22 6/8 / 23 6/8	20 1/8	4	5	Mesa County	CO	James C. Kennedy	1995	958
158 2/8	23 4/8 / 19 3/8	21 4/8	6	4	Caribou County	ID	Gary L. Vaughn	1969	961
158 2/8	23 4/8 / 22 1/8	20 0/8	6	7	Gosper County	NE	Johnny Hemelstrand	1972	961
158 2/8	19 7/8 / 20 1/8	19 2/8	5	5	Las Animas County	CO	Byron E. Brown	1984	961
158 2/8	21 2/8 / 21 2/8	20 0/8	6	5	Butte County	ID	Gene Fitzgerald	1985	961
158 2/8	22 6/8 / 22 6/8	19 5/8	6	5	Pinal County	AZ	Mark Ovitt	1990	961
158 2/8	23 0/8 / 22 4/8	23 0/8	5	5	Billings County	ND	Mark Buehrer	1990	961
158 2/8	20 4/8 / 22 3/8	19 4/8	5	4	McKenzie County	ND	Terry Sivertson	1991	961
158 2/8	23 2/8 / 23 0/8	15 7/8	6	5	Washington County	CO	Larry Wagner	1993	961
158 2/8	24 2/8 / 23 1/8	23 7/8	6	8	Caribou County	ID	Ronald Dye	1994	961
158 1/8	20 7/8 / 20 0/8	18 3/8	5	5		UT	Gordon Young	1963	970
158 1/8	21 0/8 / 22 3/8	24 0/8	6	6	Rio Blanco County	CO	Jerry R. Bowen	1970	970
158 1/8	20 6/8 / 20 3/8	17 7/8	5	4	Texas County	OK	J. Alva Hammond	1981	970
158 1/8	21 4/8 / 21 6/8	18 5/8	5	5	Boulder County	CO	Mike Miller	1987	970
158 1/8	21 5/8 / 21 7/8	21 3/8	5	5	Osborne County	KS	Blaine Parrott	1989	970
158 1/8	21 5/8 / 21 1/8	18 2/8	5	5	Converse County	WY	James Saunoris	1991	970
158 1/8	23 5/8 / 23 0/8	18 5/8	5	5	Moffat County	CO	Kieth Hardy	1991	970
158 1/8	22 6/8 / 24 4/8	28 0/8	8	5	Lane County	KS	Dean Hamilton	1991	970
158 1/8	21 0/8 / 22 0/8	21 5/8	5	5	Jefferson County	CO	Jerry L. Grueneberg	1992	970
158 1/8	21 7/8 / 21 0/8	19 1/8	5	6	Culberson County	TX	Gary J. Oden	1992	970
158 0/8	21 4/8 / 21 0/8	21 4/8	7	7	Golden Valley County	ND	Bob Ross	1959	980
158 0/8	22 2/8 / 23 3/8	21 2/8	5	5	Owyhee County	ID	R. W. McIntire	1961	980
158 0/8	25 4/8 / 24 4/8	24 4/8	3	3	Garfield County	CO	Jimmy R. Speer	1970	980
158 0/8	21 7/8 / 22 6/8	19 2/8	5	5	Mesa County	CO	Matt Spohnhauer	1975	980
158 0/8	24 7/8 / 24 1/8	21 0/8	6	7	Elbert County	CO	Quince Hale	1989	980
158 0/8	23 5/8 / 23 0/8	22 6/8	5	5	Rosebud County	MT	Irvin May	1990	980
158 0/8	21 3/8 / 21 1/8	17 0/8	6	5	Rosebud County	MT	Chuck Adams	1996	980
158 0/8	20 6/8 / 22 1/8	18 5/8	6	5	Sheridan County	WY	Chris Apel	1997	980
158 0/8	22 5/8 / 23 6/8	21 6/8	4	4	Harney County	OR	Paul G. Okita	1998	980
157 7/8	23 6/8 / 24 0/8	21 3/8	4	5	Rio Arriba County	NM	Larry Wright	1972	989
157 7/8	20 2/8 / 22 2/8	22 5/8	5	6	Owyhee County	ID	Duane Zemliska	1985	989
157 7/8	21 6/8 / 22 0/8	21 4/8	5	6	Mesa County	CO	Jerol W. Vaughn	1985	989
157 7/8	20 7/8 / 21 2/8	19 2/8	6	7	Jackson County	CO	Vance E Phelps,II	1989	989
157 7/8	22 6/8 / 22 6/8	21 3/8	5	5	Culberson County	TX	Gary J. Oden	1989	989
157 7/8	19 7/8 / 19 6/8	18 3/8	5	5	Billings County	ND	Terry Buechler	1991	989
157 7/8	21 0/8 / 22 5/8	16 5/8	7	6	Harris	SAS	Joe Schmidt	1994	989
157 7/8	21 6/8 / 21 6/8	24 1/8	5	5	Coaldale	ALB	Doug Doram	1994	989
157 7/8	21 5/8 / 22 3/8	21 0/8	6	5	Trego County	KS	Kent Hensley	1994	989
157 7/8	22 4/8 / 23 0/8	23 7/8	7	7	La Plata County	CO	Larry D. Mead	1998	989
157 6/8	23 7/8 / 23 4/8	23 7/8	6	5	Owyhee County	ID	Roland Duram	1964	999
157 6/8	22 5/8 / 23 3/8	21 0/8	5	5	Mesa County	CO	Terry J. Gerber	1976	999
157 6/8	21 6/8 / 21 4/8	22 6/8	5	5	Elmore County	ID	Harold Lefler	1981	999
157 6/8	20 4/8 / 23 2/8	19 0/8	4	4	Archuleta County	CO	Bryan Rumbo	1989	999
157 6/8	19 0/8 / 19 3/8	19 3/8	6	5	Converse County	WY	Jerry Miller	1992	999
157 6/8	22 0/8 / 20 6/8	18 4/8	5	6	Grant County	OR	Phil Grunert	1995	999
157 6/8	22 6/8 / 22 3/8	21 0/8	5	6	Manyberries	ALB	Michael R. Deschamps	1995	999
157 6/8	19 0/8 / 19 5/8	16 4/8	5	5	Natrona County	WY	Casey Middleton	1998	999
157 5/8	19 6/8 / 21 5/8	24 4/8	5	5	Owyhee County	ID	Fred Audette	1960	1,007
157 5/8	19 6/8 / 20 0/8	18 3/8	5	5	Montezuma County	CO	Marvin Reichenau	1973	1,007
157 5/8	24 1/8 / 23 4/8	21 7/8	5	5	Washoe County	NV	Donald J. Taysom	1984	1,007
157 5/8	23 6/8 / 24 1/8	20 3/8	9	6	Cheyenne County	KS	Chet Gardner	1984	1,007
157 5/8	23 0/8 / 22 3/8	20 5/8	4	4	McKinley County	NM	Frank Hausner	1991	1,007
157 5/8	23 6/8 / 24 5/8	26 5/8	5	5	Maricopa County	AZ	William L. Tuvell	1992	1,007
157 5/8	21 0/8 / 21 6/8	19 4/8	6	6	Elko County	NV	Bob Sneed	1997	1,007
157 4/8	23 1/8 / 23 2/8	23 2/8	5	6	Grand County	UT	Dean Caldwell	1960	1,014
157 4/8	22 2/8 / 22 4/8	19 4/8	5	5	Garfield County	CO	Bob Gulman	1966	1,014
157 4/8	18 5/8 / 19 2/8	16 0/8	4	4	Bernalillo County	NM	William R. Johnson	1969	1,014
157 4/8	22 1/8 / 20 2/8	21 0/8	5	6	Carter County	MT	Edward Susa	1983	1,014
157 4/8	22 3/8 / 23 5/8	20 6/8	5	5	Mesa County	CO	Paul H. Dickson	1986	1,014
157 4/8	21 4/8 / 21 0/8	19 2/8	5	5	Powder River County	MT	Mark L. Frank	1989	1,014
157 4/8	22 0/8 / 23 7/8	21 7/8	5	6	Yavapai County	AZ	Greg Allen Huyett	1993	1,014
157 4/8	22 4/8 / 21 1/8	21 0/8	5	5	Pennington County	SD	Gary Buckley	1993	1,014
157 4/8	21 4/8 / 22 0/8	18 4/8	5	5	Powell County	MT	Marlon Clapham	1995	1,014
157 3/8	26 2/8 / 26 0/8	21 2/8	7	6	Sevier County	UT	Dale Gardner	1958	1,023
157 3/8	21 6/8 / 20 0/8	20 0/8	6	6	Routt County	CO	Bing Kemp	1966	1,023
157 3/8	24 1/8 / 24 1/8	23 3/8	6	7	Montrose County	CO	James A. Davison	1984	1,023
157 3/8	17 4/8 / 19 0/8	16 3/8	5	5	Albany County	WY	Paul Ayotte	1985	1,023
157 3/8	21 0/8 / 21 0/8	20 5/8	5	5	Caribou County	ID	Gary Hunt	1986	1,023
157 3/8	22 1/8 / 22 7/8	17 7/8	6	5	Cypress	ALB	Mike Maloney	1991	1,023
157 3/8	23 5/8 / 23 2/8	25 6/8	4	5	Rawlins County	KS	Craig Doll	1994	1,023
157 2/8	22 5/8 / 21 4/8	20 6/8	6	6	McKenzie County	ND	Roy Mitten	1956	1,030
157 2/8	21 5/8 / 21 4/8	16 4/8	5	5	Bernalillo County	NM	Robert F. Knight	1970	1,030
157 2/8	24 4/8 / 24 2/8	20 1/8	6	5	Wheeler County	OR	Darrell J. Scheffer	1990	1,030
157 2/8	20 2/8 / 22 3/8	22 6/8	4	5	Bear Lake County	ID	Daved E. English	1991	1,030
157 2/8	22 5/8 / 22 7/8	18 0/8	7	5	Sioux County	NE	Jerry Overstreet	1993	1,030
157 1/8	22 0/8 / 23 4/8	23 3/8	6	4	Harney County	OR	Gary Soeth	1980	1,035
157 1/8	23 6/8 / 23 3/8	20 7/8	6	7	Boise County	ID	Gary Kinney	1981	1,035

MULE DEER (TYPICAL ANTLERS)

Minimum Score 145 — Continued

SCORE	LENGTH OF MAIN BEAM R	LENGTH OF MAIN BEAM L	INSIDE SPREAD	NUMBER OF POINTS R	NUMBER OF POINTS L	AREA	STATE/PROVINCE	HUNTER'S NAME	DATE	RANK
157 1/8	21 4/8	21 6/8	20 5/8	5	5	Clear Creek County	CO	Janet Schreur	1987	1,035
157 1/8	21 5/8	21 1/8	19 0/8	5	7	Calgary	ALB	Stuart Sinclair-Smith	1987	1,035
157 1/8	23 0/8	20 7/8	21 6/8	5	6	Meade County	KS	Randy Blehm	1989	1,035
157 1/8	21 1/8	20 4/8	16 3/8	5	5	Boyd County	NE	Glenn T. Zink	1990	1,035
157 1/8	22 2/8	21 7/8	19 5/8	5	5	Campbell County	WY	David Westmoreland	1994	1,035
157 1/8	23 4/8	23 5/8	20 2/8	5	6	Gove County	KS	Joshua Hoeme	1997	1,035
157 0/8	21 4/8	21 5/8	18 0/8	5	5	Mesa County	CO	Robert O. Bash	1976	1,043
157 0/8	22 6/8	21 4/8	16 0/8	5	5	Lassen County	CA	Tom McMurphy	1977	1,043
157 0/8	21 6/8	20 3/8	18 6/8	5	5	Lane County	KS	Dean Hamilton	1978	1,043
157 0/8	21 4/8	20 7/8	16 5/8	6	6	Deer Lodge County	MT	Mike Softich	1981	1,043
157 0/8	23 7/8	23 7/8	18 6/8	4	4	Clackamas County	OR	Thomas L. Carter	1984	1,043
157 0/8	21 4/8	21 1/8	23 3/8	5	6	Baker County	OR	Chuck Warner	1988	1,043
157 0/8	22 4/8	23 1/8	20 0/8	5	6	Pennington County	SD	Tim J. Hoeck	1990	1,043
157 0/8	20 5/8	22 3/8	21 6/8	5	5	Ada County	ID	Robert Dowen	1994	1,043
157 0/8	23 3/8	22 7/8	23 0/8	5	5	Rosebud County	MT	Chuck Adams	1998	1,043
156 7/8	24 3/8	24 0/8	23 4/8	4	4	Garfield County	CO	John Lamicq, Jr.	1966	1,052
156 7/8	21 2/8	20 6/8	18 3/8	5	5	Mesa County	CO	David H. Boland	1978	1,052
156 7/8	20 2/8	20 2/8	19 2/8	4	4	Rio Blanco County	CO	George David Epperson	1983	1,052
156 7/8	23 5/8	21 6/8	21 7/8	5	5	McKenzie County	ND	Steve Rehak	1985	1,052
156 7/8	21 4/8	20 2/8	15 7/8	5	5	Teller County	CO	Butch Smerkonich	1985	1,052
156 7/8	23 2/8	22 3/8	21 2/8	6	5	Chelan County	WA	Brian Kayler	1985	1,052
156 7/8	25 3/8	22 7/8	22 3/8	5	5	Laramie County	WY	Duane Christensen	1991	1,052
156 7/8	22 1/8	21 4/8	20 7/8	4	5	Fort St. John	BC	Steven W. Hiebert	1992	1,052
156 7/8	25 2/8	23 4/8	19 3/8	6	5	Harney County	OR	Terry D. Brumley	1994	1,052
156 7/8	24 3/8	25 1/8	26 2/8	4	4	Brooks	ALB	Bruce T. Saunders	1995	1,052
156 7/8	21 3/8	22 0/8	16 7/8	5	5	Slope County	ND	Jon Brewer	1996	1,052
156 7/8	21 7/8	22 1/8	19 5/8	6	6	Converse County	WY	Jack Dilts	1996	1,052
156 6/8	23 6/8	24 2/8	20 0/8	6	5	Uintah County	UT	Terry Peck	1964	1,064
156 6/8	22 5/8	22 6/8	19 4/8	5	5	Mesa County	CO	Ed Meyer	1967	1,064
156 6/8	21 6/8	22 6/8	23 4/8	6	6	Wallowa County	OR	Randy Hopp	1979	1,064
156 6/8	22 0/8	22 0/8	22 1/8	5	6	Routt County	CO	Moulton Larmay	1981	1,064
156 6/8	24 0/8	22 7/8	25 0/8	6	6	Lane County	KS	Dean Hamilton	1982	1,064
156 6/8	23 2/8	22 2/8	18 4/8	4	5	Kittitas County	WA	Rich Carnahan	1982	1,064
156 6/8	23 7/8	22 6/8	22 0/8	4	4	Lemhi County	ID	Glen Palmer	1988	1,064
156 6/8	20 5/8	20 6/8	19 2/8	5	5	Weld County	CO	Dale Elliott	1991	1,064
156 6/8	23 1/8	25 0/8	20 6/8	4	5	Nevada County	CA	Stan Boyer	1995	1,064
156 6/8	19 7/8	20 2/8	21 5/8	5	5	Greenlee County	AZ	Eddie Claypool	1996	1,064
156 6/8	20 6/8	20 6/8	23 2/8	5	5	Siskiyou County	CA	Brian E. Neuschafer	1997	1,064
156 5/8	21 2/8	21 3/8	20 3/8	5	5	Slope County	ND	Vern R. Keim	1959	1,075
156 5/8	20 1/8	21 1/8	22 3/8	5	5	Rio Blanco County	CO	Jim Pickering	1966	1,075
156 5/8	20 0/8	21 6/8	18 6/8	6	6	Larimer County	CO	Leslie McKenzie	1970	1,075
156 5/8	21 7/8	21 0/8	19 3/8	7	6	Lower Arrow Lake	BC	Gerald Bond	1983	1,075
156 5/8	20 7/8	18 5/8	18 6/8	6	6	Caribou County	ID	Michael Aldrich	1984	1,075
156 5/8	23 5/8	24 2/8	20 6/8	6	6	Deschutes County	OR	Marte Scheuffele	1989	1,075
156 5/8	23 4/8	23 5/8	20 4/8	5	6	Writting On Stone Park	ALB	Ryan Krampl/John Krampl	1994	1,075
156 5/8	21 1/8	21 2/8	17 1/8	4	5	Lemhi County	ID	John Bennett	1995	1,075
156 4/8	21 7/8	22 1/8	20 0/8	5	4	Weston County	WY	Thomas L. A. Pucci	1956	1,083
156 4/8	20 0/8	20 0/8	19 2/8	5	5	Owyhee County	ID	Bill Leisi	1961	1,083
156 4/8	22 2/8	24 2/8	20 3/8	4	5	Summit County	UT	Richard Douglass	1964	1,083
156 4/8	23 1/8	21 4/8	20 4/8	4	4	Elko County	NV	Paul Dinan	1968	1,083
156 4/8	23 1/8	20 7/8	19 2/8	4	4	Chouteau County	MT	Michael R. Buesseler	1971	1,083
156 4/8	20 7/8	21 3/8	22 5/8	5	6	Gunnison County	CO	Jim Jarvis	1974	1,083
156 4/8	22 5/8	23 6/8	21 4/8	4	5	Campbell County	WY	James P. Smith	1983	1,083
156 4/8	20 1/8	20 6/8	18 4/8	5	5	Grant County	OR	Jeffrey A. Young	1986	1,083
156 4/8	22 2/8	22 7/8	17 6/8	4	5	Humboldt County	NV	Monte D. Fuller	1988	1,083
156 4/8	25 1/8	23 3/8	19 6/8	5	5	Boise County	ID	Kevin J.P. Stephenson	1988	1,083
156 4/8	22 0/8	21 1/8	22 5/8	5	6	Coconino County	AZ	Michael Chase	1994	1,083
156 4/8	25 2/8	25 0/8	21 4/8	4	4	Powder River County	MT	Paul T. Shore	1996	1,083
156 3/8	21 6/8	22 6/8	25 0/8	5	6	Owyhee County	ID	Bill Kerr	1962	1,095
156 3/8	25 5/8	24 6/8	23 5/8	3	3	Mohave County	AZ	Bill Cross	1963	1,095
156 3/8	21 2/8	24 5/8	25 3/8	7	6	Lake County	OR	Orvil Winters	1965	1,095
156 3/8	24 5/8	24 2/8	23 4/8	5	7	Cottle County	TX	Mike Ramage	1991	1,095
156 3/8	21 2/8	21 5/8	20 5/8	5	5	Converse County	WY	Steve Williams	1993	1,095
156 3/8	23 5/8	24 1/8	21 7/8	5	5	Colfax County	NM	Jerry Gallegos	1996	1,095
156 2/8	21 5/8	20 6/8	20 0/8	5	5	Mesa County	CO	Donald Aaron	1971	1,101
156 2/8	20 5/8	20 2/8	19 2/8	5	5	Clark County	KS	Rod Lies	1976	1,101
156 2/8	22 6/8	21 2/8	21 2/8	5	5	Eureka County	NV	David Sharpe	1990	1,101
156 2/8	22 0/8	21 3/8	19 2/8	5	5	Monidoka County	ID	Steven Lee Morrison	1994	1,101
156 2/8	23 1/8	23 0/8	19 4/8	4	4	Salt Lake County	UT	Jerry Dee Slaugh	1997	1,101
156 2/8	25 2/8	26 0/8	21 1/8	7	6	Coconino County	AZ	Jim Machac	1997	1,101
156 1/8	20 6/8	20 7/8	20 2/8	5	6	Millard County	UT	Jerry White	1962	1,107
156 1/8	25 1/8	25 6/8	18 5/8	5	5	Rio Arriba County	NM	Gary Isom	1985	1,107
156 1/8	22 4/8	22 3/8	18 7/8	4	5	Billings County	ND	Tom Fitch	1998	1,107
156 0/8	21 4/8	21 0/8	18 2/8	5	5	Iron County	UT	Ken McKnight	1966	1,110
156 0/8	20 0/8	20 1/8	18 2/8	5	6	Chelan County	WA	Steve Gorr	1975	1,110
156 0/8	22 1/8	20 7/8	18 6/8	5	5	Powder River County	MT	Dan Brockman	1986	1,110
156 0/8	21 4/8	21 6/8	19 2/8	4	4	Powder River County	MT	Eugene Arndt	1996	1,110
155 7/8	21 3/8	21 6/8	21 0/8	5	6	McKenzie County	ND	Mark E. Ferry	1981	1,114

MULE DEER (TYPICAL ANTLERS)

Minimum Score 145 — Continued

SCORE	LENGTH OF MAIN BEAM R	L	INSIDE SPREAD	NUMBER OF POINTS R	L	AREA	STATE/ PROVINCE	HUNTER'S NAME	DATE	RANK
155 7/8	22 5/8	23 1/8	22 3/8	5	5	Caribou County	ID	Randy J. Stephens	1988	1,114
155 7/8	24 1/8	21 0/8	27 4/8	5	5	San Juan County	NM	Curtis K. Owen	1994	1,114
155 7/8	23 3/8	23 1/8	23 3/8	5	4	Powder River County	MT	Don G. Scofield	1996	1,114
155 6/8	24 1/8	24 1/8	22 0/8	3	4	Owyhee County	ID	Lynn Thomas	1960	1,118
155 6/8	22 2/8	21 3/8	18 4/8	4	5	Garfield County	CO	Henery Jaman	1966	1,118
155 6/8	21 7/8	21 4/8	20 0/8	5	6	White Pine County	NV	Roger A. Picchi	1986	1,118
155 6/8	22 0/8	21 1/8	19 0/8	6	5	Sheridan County	WY	Stan Chiras	1988	1,118
155 6/8	22 5/8	21 5/8	17 6/8	5	7	Hitchcock	SAS	Gerald Steinke	1993	1,118
155 6/8	22 2/8	22 6/8	21 2/8	5	6	Springbank	ALB	David R. Coupland	1994	1,118
155 5/8	23 2/8	23 3/8	22 3/8	5	6	Chelan County	WA	R. F. Kelly	1960	1,124
155 5/8	20 7/8	20 4/8	21 6/8	5	5	Elko County	NV	Frank M. Davis	1967	1,124
155 5/8	23 3/8	23 1/8	17 5/8	6	6	Albany County	WY	Jerry Bowen	1974	1,124
155 5/8	22 4/8	22 3/8	19 5/8	5	5	Dolores County	CO	Jay Jaburg	1975	1,124
155 5/8	24 0/8	25 6/8	22 0/8	7	5	Coconino County	AZ	Robert G. Arcieri	1977	1,124
155 5/8	21 0/8	20 5/8	18 1/8	4	4	Carbon County	WY	Robert K. Paulson	1979	1,124
155 5/8	21 0/8	20 4/8	18 7/8	5	5	Garfield County	CO	Joe Wiater	1982	1,124
155 5/8	21 4/8	20 4/8	17 7/8	5	5	Platte County	WY	James D. Wagner	1982	1,124
155 5/8	20 5/8	20 5/8	19 1/8	5	5	Carbon County	WY	Andy Lindahl	1984	1,124
155 5/8	19 5/8	19 7/8	20 4/8	5	4	Dunn County	ND	Todd Boechler	1989	1,124
155 5/8	20 2/8	20 0/8	19 5/8	4	4	Powder River County	MT	Dewey R. Woodall	1993	1,124
155 5/8	22 3/8	21 7/8	17 1/8	5	5	Colfax County	NM	Robert H. Torstenson	1994	1,124
155 5/8	20 5/8	21 1/8	17 5/8	5	5	Arapahoe County	CO	Ivan Littlejohn	1995	1,124
155 5/8	24 3/8	21 4/8	22 3/8	4	4	Converse County	WY	Kim Pruitt	1998	1,124
155 4/8	22 2/8	23 6/8	23 2/8	5	4	Millard County	UT	Shirl Pace	1966	1,138
155 4/8	19 4/8	21 0/8	19 6/8	5	5	Wayne County	UT	Harold Boyack	1968	1,138
155 4/8	21 0/8	21 6/8	22 4/8	5	5	Lake County	OR	Wayne Lamson, Jr.	1980	1,138
155 4/8	21 7/8	22 0/8	19 0/8	5	5	Albany County	WY	Jerry Bowen	1985	1,138
155 4/8	21 6/8	20 4/8	21 0/8	5	5	Los Alamos County	NM	Doug Aikin	1987	1,138
155 4/8	22 7/8	21 4/8	17 4/8	5	6	Chelan County	WA	Danny Kohlman	1991	1,138
155 4/8	25 2/8	25 0/8	26 4/8	4	4	Walla Walla County	WA	Lance R. Rea	1992	1,138
155 4/8	22 1/8	21 0/8	18 2/8	5	5	Crook County	WY	Dean Ransbottom	1994	1,138
155 4/8	22 2/8	20 0/8	22 2/8	5	5	Campbell County	WY	Kevin D. O'Brien	1997	1,138
155 4/8	25 6/8	24 7/8	19 0/8	3	5	Jefferson County	CO	Dennis Modlin	1997	1,138
155 3/8	22 4/8	22 2/8	25 2/8	5	6	Bow River	ALB	Michael D. Coupland	1986	1,148
155 3/8	21 1/8	20 5/8	19 7/8	5	5	Teller County	CO	James L. Anderson	1987	1,148
155 3/8	21 0/8	20 7/8	16 4/8	6	6	Routt County	CO	Gary Halbritter	1995	1,148
155 2/8	20 2/8	19 4/8	19 2/8	5	5	Owyhee County	ID	Ralph O. Collins	1957	1,151
155 2/8	23 6/8	24 2/8	22 4/8	6	5	Ada County	ID	Ronald K. White	1971	1,151
155 2/8	20 7/8	21 3/8	22 7/8	6	5	Uncompahgre N.F.	CO	Donald Click	1979	1,151
155 2/8	21 3/8	22 0/8	24 1/8	6	4	Box Elder County	UT	Richard Hess	1981	1,151
155 2/8	22 0/8	22 6/8	19 4/8	5	5	Lake County	OR	Chuck Warner	1981	1,151
155 2/8	21 7/8	22 1/8	17 6/8	5	5	Mesa County	CO	Rudy Wilkison	1984	1,151
155 2/8	19 1/8	20 6/8	18 5/8	6	5	Colfax County	NM	Dean K. Oatman	1985	1,151
155 2/8	21 0/8	22 4/8	19 6/8	5	5	Eagle County	CO	Tom Tietz	1985	1,151
155 2/8	23 5/8	24 0/8	24 7/8	5	4	Elbert County	CO	Billy Tillotson	1985	1,151
155 2/8	24 1/8	22 5/8	20 0/8	6	7	Hitchcock County	NE	Roger Lewis	1986	1,151
155 2/8	20 4/8	21 4/8	16 0/8	6	5	Payette County	ID	Jon Skinner	1994	1,151
155 2/8	24 1/8	23 2/8	19 6/8	5	5	Lethbridge	ALB	Doug Doram	1996	1,151
155 2/8	22 5/8	21 4/8	16 2/8	5	5	Wasco County	OR	Michael K. Miller	1997	1,151
155 2/8	20 5/8	21 4/8	17 6/8	5	5	Blackfalds	ALB	Colin Campbell	1997	1,151
155 1/8	21 2/8	21 3/8	17 7/8	6	5	Sevier County	UT	Ray Shepard	1965	1,165
155 1/8	22 0/8	22 6/8	22 5/8	5	7	Lane County	KS	Dean Hamilton	1983	1,165
155 1/8	21 5/8	22 0/8	21 1/8	5	6	Custer County	NE	John Slack	1988	1,165
155 1/8	19 0/8	20 4/8	18 3/8	5	5	Powder River County	MT	Gene Smith	1991	1,165
155 1/8	21 6/8	22 2/8	21 3/8	5	5	Osborne County	KS	Dennis Fisk	1992	1,165
155 1/8	22 3/8	22 2/8	16 5/8	5	5	Harney County	OR	Edward Reed	1994	1,165
155 1/8	21 6/8	21 5/8	16 3/8	5	5	Manyberries	ALB	Bob Barden	1997	1,165
155 0/8	23 2/8	21 4/8	22 0/8	5	4	Lake County	OR	Bill Chahon	1967	1,172
155 0/8	23 4/8	23 0/8	22 0/8	6	5	Broadwater County	MT	Larry P. Stevens	1968	1,172
155 0/8	19 7/8	22 4/8	17 6/8	4	4	Summit County	CO	Harley Smith	1976	1,172
155 0/8	22 6/8	23 0/8	21 2/8	6	6	Rio Blanco County	CO	Larry Streiff	1978	1,172
155 0/8	24 2/8	24 4/8	26 0/8	4	3	Mesa County	CO	Duane Beenblossom	1979	1,172
155 0/8	21 7/8	22 0/8	20 1/8	5	5	Mesa County	CO	Clarence Bowers, Jr.	1979	1,172
155 0/8	21 2/8	22 6/8	21 6/8	4	4	Slope County	ND	Bill Schwendinger	1982	1,172
155 0/8	20 5/8	19 3/8	18 4/8	5	5	Bernalillo County	NM	Doug Aikin	1983	1,172
155 0/8	21 2/8	21 6/8	21 4/8	5	5	Boise County	ID	Larry S. Zurgot	1985	1,172
155 0/8	22 6/8	23 2/8	18 6/8	5	5	Bernalillo County	NM	Joseph L. Moyer	1988	1,172
155 0/8	21 4/8	21 4/8	20 2/8	5	5	Sundre	ALB	Larry K. Nielsen	1989	1,172
155 0/8	18 3/8	19 0/8	20 6/8	4	5	Wallace County	KS	Dave Hale	1992	1,172
155 0/8	22 3/8	21 3/8	23 2/8	5	6	Weld County	CO	John P. Johnson	1994	1,172
155 0/8	24 0/8	22 4/8	23 2/8	5	5	Calgary	ALB	Bill A. Riel	1995	1,172
155 0/8	22 5/8	22 2/8	22 0/8	5	5	Sheridan County	WY	Jerry Shatek	1998	1,172
154 7/8	22 3/8	23 4/8	23 3/8	5	5	Dolores County	CO	Oscar A. Harden	1957	1,187
154 7/8	19 4/8	21 2/8	19 2/8	5	6	Millard County	UT	Dale Moore	1961	1,187
154 7/8	21 6/8	21 7/8	16 7/8	4	4	Elko County	NV	Jim Cox	1974	1,187
154 7/8	21 5/8	22 3/8	18 3/8	5	6	Elko County	NV	John S. Chace, Jr.	1982	1,187
154 7/8	20 4/8	21 0/8	18 7/8	5	5	Pinal County	AZ	Gary D. Rancher	1994	1,187
154 7/8	21 1/8	21 1/8	18 1/8	5	5	Larimer County	CO	Patrick Wensman	1994	1,187

MULE DEER (TYPICAL ANTLERS)

Minimum Score 145

SCORE	LENGTH OF MAIN BEAM R	LENGTH OF MAIN BEAM L	INSIDE SPREAD	NUMBER OF POINTS R	NUMBER OF POINTS L	AREA	STATE/PROVINCE	HUNTER'S NAME	DATE	RANK
154 7/8	21 1/8	19 6/8	20 7/8	5	5	Jefferson County	CO	Larry J. Jones	1996	1,187
154 6/8	23 1/8	22 7/8	20 2/8	4	5	Montrose County	CO	Dave Reitz	1983	1,194
154 6/8	17 5/8	20 1/8	13 4/8	5	5	El Paso County	CO	Michael Thompson	1984	1,194
154 6/8	20 3/8	20 4/8	22 4/8	5	5	Mesa County	CO	R. L. Harrison III	1985	1,194
154 6/8	22 5/8	22 7/8	17 7/8	5	5	Elbert County	CO	Randy Kendrick	1998	1,194
154 5/8	20 3/8	21 7/8	21 7/8	5	5	Lincoln County	NV	Larry Gehre	1963	1,198
154 5/8	21 3/8	19 3/8	16 7/8	4	5	Garfield County	CO	Tommy Biffle	1975	1,198
154 5/8	23 6/8	23 2/8	20 0/8	5	8	San Juan County	UT	Bruce Gordon	1980	1,198
154 5/8	20 1/8	19 5/8	19 5/8	5	5	Lake County	OR	Dale A. Bolin	1983	1,198
154 5/8	19 6/8	21 1/8	18 7/8	5	5	Pennington County	SD	Scott Lindgren	1986	1,198
154 5/8	20 1/8	19 4/8	21 3/8	5	5	Crook County	WY	Calvin Farner	1986	1,198
154 5/8	22 3/8	21 3/8	19 3/8	5	6	Montrose County	CO	Eugene Roesler	1989	1,198
154 5/8	21 5/8	22 6/8	21 1/8	5	5	Garfield County	WA	Lee Campbell	1990	1,198
154 5/8	19 1/8	20 0/8	17 1/8	5	5	Pima County	AZ	Jeff Ferri	1990	1,198
154 5/8	21 6/8	21 3/8	17 7/8	6	6	Millarville	ALB	Joel Bickler	1991	1,198
154 5/8	24 4/8	24 0/8	19 7/8	5	6	Washington County	UT	Neil Stratton	1992	1,198
154 5/8	20 2/8	20 3/8	25 1/8	7	5	Converse County	WY	Ron Miller	1994	1,198
154 5/8	18 3/8	18 2/8	19 6/8	5	5	Montezuma County	CO	Bryon D. Long	1998	1,198
154 4/8	22 3/8	22 0/8	22 2/8	5	5	Washoe County	NV	Gary Van Ness	1959	1,211
154 4/8	22 3/8	22 5/8	21 0/8	6	6	Routt County	CO	Douglas J. Peterson	1965	1,211
154 4/8	22 5/8	24 0/8	18 1/8	6	6	Frontier County	NE	Mark Stencel	1986	1,211
154 4/8	20 2/8	20 0/8	22 3/8	6	7	Pima County	AZ	Rick Forrest	1992	1,211
154 4/8	19 6/8	19 6/8	21 7/8	5	5	Weld County	CO	Gerald Rasmussen, Jr.	1995	1,211
154 4/8	19 1/8	19 6/8	18 0/8	5	5	Weston County	WY	Bill Snodgrass	1997	1,211
154 3/8	21 7/8	23 1/8	20 5/8	4	5	Pawnee County	KS	Robert E. Lagree	1970	1,217
154 3/8	18 0/8	18 1/8	17 5/8	5	5	Yavapai County	AZ	James R. Reckas	1989	1,217
154 3/8	25 6/8	26 1/8	27 0/8	3	4	Elbert County	CO	Douglas Cringan	1991	1,217
154 3/8	23 7/8	23 4/8	21 3/8	6	6	San Juan County	NM	Randy Sweetland	1997	1,217
154 2/8	21 7/8	21 5/8	17 4/8	8	8	Grant County	OR	Lloyd V. Christensen	1960	1,221
154 2/8	22 5/8	22 3/8	19 5/8	4	4	Mesa County	CO	Jimmy E. Ash	1966	1,221
154 2/8	22 2/8	21 2/8	21 0/8	7	8	Kirby	WY	Steve Gorr	1970	1,221
154 2/8	20 5/8	20 0/8	19 2/8	5	5	Moffat County	CO	Mary E. Nussberger	1978	1,221
154 2/8	21 2/8	23 7/8	22 4/8	5	5	Blaine County	ID	Dean Muchow	1979	1,221
154 2/8	21 2/8	21 5/8	18 6/8	5	5	Mesa County	CO	Carl Phillips	1980	1,221
154 2/8	23 4/8	23 0/8	19 1/8	5	6	Chelan County	WA	Daniel S Nelson	1984	1,221
154 1/8	18 3/8	16 6/8	16 1/8	5	7	Carbon County	UT	Lieb D. Miller	1959	1,228
154 1/8	19 6/8	20 5/8	18 1/8	5	6	Jefferson County	OR	Doris T. Barden	1960	1,228
154 1/8	21 4/8	21 4/8	20 4/8	4	4	Rio Grande County	CO	Kenneth G. McCombs	1969	1,228
154 1/8	20 3/8	21 0/8	16 0/8	5	6	Montrose County	CO	Arthur L. Pace	1974	1,228
154 1/8	23 5/8	21 6/8	23 6/8	4	4	Montrose County	CO	Don Allen, Jr.	1979	1,228
154 1/8	22 6/8	22 5/8	22 5/8	5	4	Malheur County	OR	Jim Nielsen	1988	1,228
154 1/8	22 1/8	21 0/8	19 3/8	5	4	Albany County	WY	Jerry Bowen	1990	1,228
154 1/8	21 0/8	21 3/8	20 5/8	5	4	Converse County	WY	Herb Mielke	1992	1,228
154 1/8	19 1/8	18 1/8	18 0/8	6	5	Teller County	CO	Rodney W. Purvis	1995	1,228
154 0/8	22 7/8	22 6/8	20 6/8	7	6	Coconino County	AZ	Stuart Diehl	1962	1,237
154 0/8	22 0/8	22 2/8	19 4/8	5	5	Mesa County	CO	Al Dawson	1964	1,237
154 0/8	24 6/8	24 4/8	29 0/8	5	4	Grant County	OR	Chuck Lynde	1972	1,237
154 0/8	25 2/8	24 4/8	21 2/8	5	4	Mesa County	CO	Dale Anderson	1973	1,237
154 0/8	20 4/8	21 4/8	19 3/8	6	5	Calgary	ALB	Manfred Grewe	1981	1,237
154 0/8	22 7/8	23 6/8	22 5/8	9	7	Lake County	OR	Charles F. Brown	1985	1,237
154 0/8	20 3/8	20 2/8	17 2/8	5	4	Converse County	WY	Lee Jernigan	1987	1,237
154 0/8	22 1/8	22 1/8	18 0/8	5	4	Elmore County	ID	Timothy J. Conrads	1988	1,237
154 0/8	18 5/8	18 5/8	16 4/8	5	4	Baker County	OR	John A. Eyers	1990	1,237
154 0/8	22 0/8	22 5/8	20 0/8	6	5	Sublette County	WY	Nelson J. Capestany	1991	1,237
154 0/8	21 3/8	22 3/8	19 0/8	5	5	Weld County	CO	Gary L. Clancy	1991	1,237
154 0/8	24 2/8	25 2/8	21 6/8	5	4	Converse County	WY	G. Lowe Morrison	1995	1,237
153 7/8	19 5/8	19 2/8	19 1/8	6	5	Meagher County	MT	LeRoy Dukes	1972	1,249
153 7/8	22 6/8	21 7/8	16 6/8	6	6	Rio Blanco County	CO	Kevin Jackson	1973	1,249
153 7/8	22 4/8	19 6/8	17 7/8	5	5	Uintah County	UT	Matt Brooks	1974	1,249
153 7/8	23 3/8	22 4/8	23 1/8	6	6	Baker County	OR	Randy Jennings	1981	1,249
153 7/8	22 5/8	23 3/8	19 2/8	6	6	Pinal County	AZ	Jesse Pena	1988	1,249
153 7/8	20 5/8	20 0/8	19 3/8	5	5	Oneida County	ID	Dave Scott	1990	1,249
153 7/8	23 1/8	23 1/8	21 7/8	6	5	Billings County	ND	Steve Schaper	1990	1,249
153 7/8	24 2/8	23 4/8	22 6/8	5	5	Lincoln County	CO	Michael B. Lamade	1992	1,249
153 7/8	20 7/8	21 2/8	19 7/8	5	5	Garfield County	CO	Kelly P. Bowe	1993	1,249
153 7/8	19 6/8	19 7/8	16 1/8	5	5	Powder River County	MT	Rich Driscoll	1994	1,249
153 7/8	20 5/8	21 2/8	20 5/8	5	5	Bannock County	ID	BracKen Henderson	1994	1,249
153 7/8	20 3/8	21 4/8	15 3/8	5	5	Sheridan County	WY	Gary Challoner	1997	1,249
153 7/8	20 0/8	20 1/8	20 2/8	5	5	Natrona County	WY	Jim Van Norman	1998	1,249
153 6/8	23 0/8	21 7/8	18 0/8	5	5	Dawes County	NE	William W. Plooster	1958	1,262
153 6/8	22 5/8	22 7/8	24 5/8	6	6	Cherry County	NE	Albert Selk	1995	1,262
153 6/8	20 0/8	20 6/8	18 0/8	5	5	Bonneville County	ID	Thomas Thiel	1997	1,262
153 5/8	22 0/8	22 4/8	20 7/8	4	4	Billings County	ND	Ed Bry, Jr.	1957	1,265
153 5/8	21 0/8	20 7/8	17 7/8	6	7	Moffat County	CO	Zenus E. Cozart	1962	1,265
153 5/8	21 4/8	21 4/8	18 7/8	5	6	Moffat County	CO	Hugh Cox	1971	1,265
153 5/8	22 3/8	22 7/8	23 4/8	5	5	Pinal County	AZ	James M. Fry	1974	1,265
153 5/8	22 6/8	23 1/8	24 0/8	5	5	Routt County	CO	Lee R. Hoxit	1978	1,265
153 5/8	21 4/8	21 1/8	19 7/8	4	4	Milk River Ridge	ALB	Don Gibb	1992	1,265

MULE DEER (TYPICAL ANTLERS)

Minimum Score 145 — Continued

SCORE	LENGTH OF MAIN BEAM R	LENGTH OF MAIN BEAM L	INSIDE SPREAD	NUMBER OF POINTS R	NUMBER OF POINTS L	AREA	STATE/PROVINCE	HUNTER'S NAME	DATE	RANK
153 5/8	21 5/8	23 1/8	20 1/8	5	5	Grant County	WA	J. G. "Rusty" Watson	1997	1,265
153 4/8	22 5/8	21 7/8	22 4/8	5	5	San Juan County	UT	Roy D. Chesley	1963	1,272
153 4/8	23 0/8	23 0/8	17 4/8	6	5	Brown County	NE	Seth Fritzler	1965	1,272
153 4/8	20 1/8	22 1/8	20 2/8	6	5	Wasatch County	UT	Don Callister	1967	1,272
153 4/8	21 2/8	22 0/8	22 2/8	4	4	Slope County	ND	Todd Seymanski	1991	1,272
153 4/8	21 7/8	22 1/8	17 4/8	5	5	Mesa County	CO	Joseph M. Schmidt	1992	1,272
153 4/8	23 3/8	22 2/8	20 2/8	5	5	Yavapai County	AZ	Patrick M. Kirby	1993	1,272
153 3/8	22 1/8	21 1/8	21 1/8	4	5	Garfield County	CO	John Nottingham	1974	1,278
153 3/8	19 6/8	21 1/8	22 5/8	5	5	Meagher County	MT	Chuck Adams	1979	1,278
153 3/8	22 0/8	23 1/8	21 2/8	5	6	Weld County	CO	Gary Thurow	1988	1,278
153 3/8	20 1/8	19 3/8	18 1/8	5	5	Carbon County	WY	Peter Schinke	1989	1,278
153 3/8	21 3/8	21 6/8	21 1/8	4	3	Rio Arriba County	NM	James Michael Bridges	1989	1,278
153 3/8	24 5/8	24 5/8	21 4/8	4	5	Sheridan County	WY	Ron Niziolek	1993	1,278
153 3/8	18 7/8	19 2/8	17 7/8	4	5	Nevada County	CA	Kevil Pelton	1997	1,278
153 2/8	21 0/8	21 0/8	20 0/8	5	5	Custer County	MT	Gene T. Buck	1961	1,285
153 2/8	21 4/8	21 3/8	17 6/8	5	5	Garfield County	CO	Randy Gilmore	1982	1,285
153 2/8	21 2/8	20 3/8	20 0/8	6	6	Coconino County	AZ	Richard S Jones	1985	1,285
153 2/8	19 4/8	20 0/8	15 6/8	5	5	Gregory County	SD	Terry Marcukaitis	1985	1,285
153 2/8	20 1/8	20 6/8	14 6/8	6	5	Washoe County	NV	Ronald W. Lindquist	1986	1,285
153 2/8	20 3/8	22 3/8	20 0/8	5	5	Billings County	ND	Gary J. Peters	1987	1,285
153 2/8	21 6/8	22 0/8	23 0/8	5	5	Campbell County	WY	David A. O'Brien	1993	1,285
153 2/8	22 5/8	22 2/8	20 5/8	7	6	Turin	ALB	Raymond Bahr	1994	1,285
153 2/8	21 2/8	22 1/8	16 4/8	5	5	Converse County	WY	Bill Randles	1995	1,285
153 2/8	23 6/8	24 5/8	26 0/8	5	5	Cochise County	AZ	Louie Herrera	1995	1,285
153 2/8	22 3/8	23 3/8	18 6/8	5	5	Chelan County	WA	Leroy E. House	1996	1,285
153 1/8	22 0/8	22 3/8	24 0/8	5	4	Millard County	UT	Milton F. McQueary	1961	1,296
153 1/8	23 5/8	25 2/8	20 2/8	5	4	Rio Blanco County	CO	Thomas Nicholls	1967	1,296
153 1/8	22 0/8	21 5/8	21 5/8	5	4	Garfield County	CO	Lester Meredith	1974	1,296
153 1/8	21 5/8	22 3/8	22 3/8	5	5	Park County	WY	Jim Dinkins	1978	1,296
153 1/8	21 0/8	22 7/8	18 7/8	7	5	Converse County	WY	Ted Jaycox	1982	1,296
153 1/8	21 6/8	21 4/8	19 7/8	4	5	Chelan County	WA	Don McNees, Jr.	1983	1,296
153 1/8	19 5/8	19 7/8	19 1/8	5	5	Dolores County	CO	Mark Beeler	1992	1,296
153 1/8	23 5/8	21 4/8	21 1/8	6	5	Delia	ALB	Brian Kakuk	1996	1,296
153 1/8	22 1/8	23 0/8	18 7/8	5	6	Hays	ALB	David R. Coupland	1996	1,296
153 0/8	21 1/8	22 1/8	23 2/8	5	6	Golden Valley County	MT	Tim Ford	1979	1,305
153 0/8	21 7/8	22 6/8	20 2/8	6	5	Valley County	ID	James J. Akenson	1988	1,305
153 0/8	22 0/8	21 6/8	19 0/8	5	6	Vertigris Lake	ALB	Keith Heppler	1989	1,305
153 0/8	21 5/8	24 0/8	21 6/8	5	5	Lake County	OR	Mike Benton	1990	1,305
153 0/8	17 6/8	20 0/8	20 2/8	6	5	Colfax County	NM	Justin L. Sanchez	1990	1,305
153 0/8	26 5/8	26 1/8	25 6/8	3	3	Hartley County	TX	Todd Hodnett	1992	1,305
153 0/8	24 0/8	24 0/8	21 6/8	4	4	Billings County	ND	John Holdorf	1995	1,305
153 0/8	21 5/8	22 4/8	13 6/8	6	6	Catron County	NM	Richard V. Gray	1997	1,305
153 0/8	22 1/8	22 4/8	21 6/8	5	5	Luna County	NM	Kevin Schmid/Diane Schmid	1998	1,305
152 7/8	20 7/8	21 7/8	20 1/8	6	6	Gove County	KS	Alan D. Beougher	1970	1,314
152 7/8	20 4/8	21 7/8	15 3/8	4	4	White River N.F.	CO	Leonard Steiner	1978	1,314
152 7/8	22 1/8	23 0/8	21 3/8	5	5	Gila County	AZ	Steven Weekley	1985	1,314
152 7/8	22 0/8	22 7/8	21 7/8	5	4	Custer County	ID	Kevin Pearce	1994	1,314
152 7/8	23 1/8	20 7/8	21 3/8	6	7	Trego County	KS	Ryan Hagans	1995	1,314
152 6/8	21 6/8	21 0/8	21 6/8	6	5	Graham County	AZ	Herbert Tom	1981	1,319
152 6/8	22 0/8	21 4/8	22 0/8	5	4	Delta County	CO	Timothy L. McKay	1990	1,319
152 6/8	24 0/8	22 6/8	21 2/8	5	5	Converse County	WY	M. R. James	1991	1,319
152 6/8	19 5/8	19 1/8	18 0/8	4	4	Billings County	ND	William E. Lee, Jr.	1991	1,319
152 6/8	19 7/8	21 1/8	17 0/8	5	6	Albany County	WY	Tom Pindell	1994	1,319
152 6/8	19 6/8	21 1/8	18 1/8	5	4	Laramie County	WY	Brian Rhead	1995	1,319
152 6/8	21 6/8	21 2/8	20 0/8	4	4	Dolores County	CO	Richard C. Johnston	1996	1,319
152 6/8	19 2/8	19 2/8	17 0/8	5	5	Elk River	ALB	Dave Bathke	1996	1,319
152 6/8	20 2/8	21 6/8	19 6/8	5	5	Cochise County	AZ	Rick Forrest	1998	1,319
152 6/8	19 6/8	19 3/8	20 0/8	5	5	Maricopa County	AZ	Matthew Liljenquist	1998	1,319
152 5/8	21 3/8	21 5/8	20 3/8	4	4	Elko County	NV	Bill Freeman	1961	1,329
152 5/8	22 0/8	22 3/8	22 3/8	5	5	Fremont County	WY	Gene Farley	1964	1,329
152 5/8	23 3/8	23 4/8	19 4/8	7	5	Valley County	ID	James J. Akenson	1984	1,329
152 5/8	22 4/8	22 1/8	21 6/8	6	6	Mesa County	CO	Don Rogers	1986	1,329
152 5/8	19 5/8	16 4/8	22 6/8	5	4	Wichita County	KS	Jack D. Kuhlmann	1986	1,329
152 5/8	20 2/8	19 7/8	19 1/8	5	5	Graham County	KS	Danny G. Coday	1989	1,329
152 5/8	20 7/8	22 1/8	20 3/8	4	4	Humboldt County	NV	Rob Fletcher	1991	1,329
152 5/8	22 3/8	23 0/8	20 7/8	5	5	San Juan County	CO	Joseph Testerman	1993	1,329
152 4/8	28 7/8	27 7/8	24 4/8	4	3	Montrose County	CO	John A. Wilk	1978	1,337
152 4/8	21 1/8	20 7/8	17 5/8	5	6	Madison County	MT	Tony Rebich	1982	1,337
152 4/8	21 6/8	21 7/8	16 6/8	5	5	Harney County	OR	Jim Hodson	1988	1,337
152 4/8	21 6/8	21 2/8	20 4/8	5	5	Harney County	OR	Michael J. Bradeen	1989	1,337
152 4/8	22 4/8	22 1/8	23 3/8	5	5	Calgary	ALB	Dave Browne	1991	1,337
152 4/8	21 7/8	24 1/8	22 0/8	5	5	Greenlee County	AZ	Dan Martin	1994	1,337
152 4/8	23 0/8	22 3/8	18 6/8	4	4	Converse County	WY	Lee Jernigan	1997	1,337
152 4/8	24 0/8	23 0/8	22 2/8	4	5	Jefferson County	OR	Jay Roth	1998	1,337
152 3/8	20 6/8	20 7/8	20 2/8	5	6	Carbon County	UT	John C. Culpepper	1969	1,345
152 3/8	23 0/8	21 7/8	22 4/8	4	4	Montrose County	CO	Viron Barbay	1985	1,345
152 3/8	20 7/8	21 3/8	19 3/8	5	5	Cochise County	AZ	Stan Wacker	1989	1,345
152 3/8	22 7/8	23 0/8	19 5/8	6	6	Mesa County	CO	Jeffrey M. Davis	1994	1,345

MULE DEER (TYPICAL ANTLERS)

Minimum Score 145

SCORE	LENGTH OF MAIN BEAM R	LENGTH OF MAIN BEAM L	INSIDE SPREAD	NUMBER OF POINTS R	NUMBER OF POINTS L	AREA	STATE/ PROVINCE	HUNTER'S NAME	DATE	RANK
152 3/8	24 1/8	22 0/8	20 7/8	5	5	Larimer County	CO	Gene DeVore, Jr.	1997	1,345
152 2/8	21 0/8	21 0/8	19 0/8	5	6	Grand County	UT	Roger Smith	1962	1,350
152 2/8	19 3/8	20 4/8	20 4/8	5	5	Elko County	NV	Jack Konvalin	1963	1,350
152 2/8	26 0/8	26 0/8	22 0/8	4	4	Garfield County	CO	Jim Dougherty	1968	1,350
152 2/8	21 5/8	21 7/8	21 5/8	5	5	Millard County	UT	David G. Snyder	1968	1,350
152 2/8	21 0/8	21 0/8	24 6/8	6	6	Madison County	MT	Dave Bonczyk	1972	1,350
152 2/8	20 1/8	20 2/8	18 0/8	4	4	Billings County	ND	Harold Hugelen	1995	1,350
152 2/8	23 5/8	22 6/8	22 2/8	5	5	Yuma County	CO	Jerry Bowen	1996	1,350
152 2/8	22 3/8	23 4/8	24 1/8	5	5	Eagle County	CO	Greg Close	1997	1,350
152 2/8	21 7/8	22 6/8	23 1/8	5	5	Ellis County	KS	Rick Cunningham	1997	1,350
152 1/8	20 1/8	20 1/8	18 1/8	5	5	Cochise County	AZ	John Behrends	1969	1,359
152 1/8	23 4/8	22 5/8	23 6/8	6	6	Ross Lake	ALB	Darcy Barrett	1988	1,359
152 1/8	21 2/8	21 1/8	16 1/8	5	5	White Pine County	NV	Larry D. Draper	1994	1,359
152 1/8	20 7/8	21 2/8	18 4/8	6	5	Twin Falls County	ID	Darrell Nunez	1994	1,359
152 1/8	21 6/8	22 1/8	18 5/8	5	5	Garfield County	UT	L. Grant Foster	1996	1,359
152 0/8	20 0/8	20 6/8	17 3/8	8	7	Garfield County	UT	Bob Mackinnon	1970	1,364
152 0/8	19 3/8	19 5/8	18 0/8	5	5	Bowman County	ND	Mark Loutzenhiser	1985	1,364
152 0/8	20 2/8	22 7/8	18 6/8	6	6	Elko County	NV	LeRoy McQueen	1986	1,364
152 0/8	21 2/8	21 2/8	22 1/8	5	5	Harney County	OR	Billy Jack Elbert	1989	1,364
152 0/8	19 6/8	20 6/8	21 4/8	5	4	Yavapai County	AZ	Nick Arnett	1994	1,364
151 7/8	22 0/8	22 2/8	20 0/8	6	8	Duchesne County	UT	Rowland S. Enomoto	1965	1,369
151 7/8	22 0/8	21 2/8	21 7/8	5	4	Chelan County	WA	L. James Bailey	1977	1,369
151 7/8	22 1/8	22 7/8	21 5/8	7	5	Pima County	AZ	Douglas L. Sweepe	1988	1,369
151 7/8	21 2/8	21 2/8	18 3/8	5	5	Bergen	ALB	Sandy Watt	1990	1,369
151 7/8	25 1/8	25 4/8	23 1/8	4	4	Powder River County	MT	Keith Furgerson	1992	1,369
151 7/8	21 6/8	22 4/8	18 1/8	5	5	Powder River County	MT	Richard Driscoll	1995	1,369
151 7/8	23 3/8	23 2/8	19 2/8	5	7	Elbert County	CO	Bobby D. Benison	1996	1,369
151 6/8	20 3/8	20 2/8	21 4/8	4	5	Garfield County	MT	Herman Hass	1961	1,376
151 6/8	18 7/8	21 7/8	21 7/8	6	6	Rio Blanco County	CO	Doug Kenyon	1967	1,376
151 6/8	17 5/8	15 4/8	14 4/8	5	5	Garfield County	CO	Roger Smith	1973	1,376
151 6/8	22 5/8	21 0/8	20 0/8	5	5	Mesa County	CO	Steve Fossen	1974	1,376
151 6/8	19 3/8	21 6/8	16 5/8	5	5	Grand County	CO	Mark Chapman	1978	1,376
151 6/8	20 3/8	20 4/8	15 7/8	7	7	Mesa County	CO	Jack O. Rothwell	1979	1,376
151 6/8	20 0/8	20 4/8	19 0/8	5	5	Lane County	KS	Dean Hamilton	1985	1,376
151 6/8	21 0/8	20 2/8	18 2/8	7	6	Carbon County	WY	Rene Suda	1990	1,376
151 6/8	19 7/8	20 2/8	19 7/8	6	5	Platte County	WY	Jason W. Dirscherl	1994	1,376
151 6/8	23 0/8	21 6/8	21 5/8	4	6	Osborne County	KS	Robert Grabast	1994	1,376
151 6/8	19 6/8	20 2/8	20 5/8	5	5	San Juan County	NM	Bert Poulton	1996	1,376
151 5/8	21 5/8	20 5/8	20 5/8	5	5	Garfield County	UT	Dick Gulman	1968	1,387
151 5/8	20 2/8	18 7/8	18 1/8	6	6	Chaffee County	CO	Eugene K. Post	1971	1,387
151 5/8	20 5/8	20 5/8	18 1/8	5	5	Mesa County	CO	Richard E. Davis, Jr.	1977	1,387
151 5/8	19 4/8	20 3/8	16 3/8	6	5	Phillips County	KS	Michael L. Hoft	1985	1,387
151 5/8	20 0/8	20 1/8	20 2/8	5	5	Billings County	ND	Greg Obrigewitch	1987	1,387
151 5/8	22 4/8	22 2/8	21 1/8	5	5	Caribou County	ID	Roger Wright	1990	1,387
151 5/8	21 4/8	21 4/8	18 3/8	5	5	Medicine Hat	ALB	John Carber, Jr.	1997	1,387
151 5/8	21 4/8	21 0/8	17 1/8	5	6	Campbell County	WY	Leon R. Nyreen	1997	1,387
151 5/8	20 3/8	21 6/8	17 7/8	7	5	Cochrane	ALB	Tom Foss	1997	1,387
151 4/8	24 5/8	24 5/8	26 2/8	4	6	Bingham County	ID	Craig A. Young	1982	1,396
151 4/8	21 7/8	22 0/8	18 6/8	5	5	Grant County	OR	Karl Geaney	1994	1,396
151 4/8	23 0/8	21 3/8	18 3/8	5	4	Carter County	MT	Larry L. Lawman	1995	1,396
151 4/8	24 2/8	24 5/8	22 6/8	4	5	Jefferson County	OR	Steve Davis	1995	1,396
151 4/8	22 4/8	22 7/8	21 2/8	4	5	Modoc County	CA	Wayne Wood	1997	1,396
151 4/8	21 1/8	18 7/8	19 2/8	5	6	Hawks Creek	BC	Allan Tew	1997	1,396
151 4/8	20 0/8	18 3/8	21 4/8	5	5	Weld County	CO	Nathan L. Andersohn	1998	1,396
151 3/8	22 4/8	19 2/8	19 1/8	5	5	Dolores County	CO	Dennis Atwater	1979	1,403
151 3/8	22 0/8	21 5/8	21 7/8	5	5	Washoe County	NV	David J. Fujii	1981	1,403
151 3/8	19 0/8	20 5/8	21 4/8	5	5	Lane County	KS	Dean Hamilton	1986	1,403
151 3/8	22 7/8	22 1/8	17 1/8	4	4	Mesa County	CO	Dennis Kelly	1991	1,403
151 3/8	21 0/8	22 0/8	18 3/8	4	6	Caribou County	ID	RanDon Wright	1991	1,403
151 3/8	22 2/8	21 6/8	20 6/8	6	5	Sheridan County	WY	David L. Willis	1992	1,403
151 2/8	22 7/8	19 2/8	16 4/8	5	5	Chelan County	WA	G. H. Malinoski	1959	1,409
151 2/8	24 5/8	23 1/8	24 5/8	7	6	Bear Lake County	ID	Keith V. Hymos	1961	1,409
151 2/8	23 2/8	22 7/8	22 4/8	5	4	Chelan County	WA	Ron Carpenter	1973	1,409
151 2/8	20 6/8	22 6/8	22 0/8	7	5	Uncompahgre N.F.	CO	Clifford Patterson	1976	1,409
151 2/8	21 4/8	21 3/8	20 0/8	5	5	Phillips County	MT	Brian Roness	1984	1,409
151 2/8	21 0/8	20 6/8	17 0/8	7	5	Stanley County	SD	Dale DeBoer	1985	1,409
151 2/8	24 5/8	25 7/8	19 1/8	7	5	Dundy County	NE	Michael C. Dysh	1988	1,409
151 2/8	22 5/8	21 3/8	19 2/8	4	4	Black Diamond	ALB	Marc Nyrose	1989	1,409
151 2/8	22 4/8	21 0/8	22 6/8	5	5	County of 40 Mile	ALB	Tammy Glass	1992	1,409
151 2/8	21 7/8	21 5/8	19 6/8	6	5	Otero County	NM	Frank Rodriguez	1993	1,409
151 1/8	21 4/8	22 2/8	20 2/8	6	7	Butte County	SD	John Kirk	1958	1,419
151 1/8	23 7/8	22 7/8	20 1/8	4	5	Mesa County	CO	Bill Martens	1984	1,419
151 1/8	20 3/8	20 6/8	16 7/8	5	5	McKenzie County	ND	Kurt T. Hovet	1988	1,419
151 1/8	19 0/8	19 2/8	13 7/8	5	5	Boise County	ID	Ken Dory	1989	1,419
151 1/8	20 6/8	21 1/8	19 3/8	7	6	Valmarie	SAS	Steve Von Hagen	1992	1,419
151 1/8	20 7/8	21 0/8	20 5/8	5	5	Stillwater County	MT	Gary F. Bogner	1994	1,419
151 1/8	20 3/8	21 2/8	22 1/8	5	5	El Paso County	CO	Ed Ruroede	1996	1,419
151 0/8	22 1/8	22 0/8	20 6/8	5	7	Chelan County	WA	Deryl E. Bland	1964	1,426

MULE DEER (TYPICAL ANTLERS)

Minimum Score 145 — Continued

SCORE	LENGTH OF MAIN BEAM R	LENGTH OF MAIN BEAM L	INSIDE SPREAD	NUMBER OF POINTS R	NUMBER OF POINTS L	AREA	STATE/PROVINCE	HUNTER'S NAME	DATE	RANK
151 0/8	18 4/8	21 2/8	17 4/8	5	5	Moffat County	CO	Wayne Liskey	1966	1,426
151 0/8	22 0/8	19 1/8	23 2/8	5	4	Uncompahgre N.F.	CO	Roy Miller	1972	1,426
151 0/8	21 1/8	21 0/8	22 2/8	6	5	Rio Arriba County	NM	Howard Payne	1984	1,426
151 0/8	20 3/8	21 4/8	19 0/8	5	5	Platte County	WY	Jody Nordin	1984	1,426
151 0/8	19 0/8	18 4/8	19 4/8	5	5	Maricopa County	AZ	Dave Barnhart	1986	1,426
151 0/8	22 4/8	20 6/8	20 2/8	5	5	Coconino County	AZ	Randy Barnes	1986	1,426
151 0/8	25 1/8	24 7/8	23 1/8	4	6	Cochrane	ALB	Denny Williamson	1989	1,426
151 0/8	19 4/8	19 2/8	20 1/8	5	5	Abbey	SAS	Clarence Hughes	1990	1,426
151 0/8	20 6/8	20 4/8	21 6/8	6	5	Humboldt County	NV	Fred C. Church	1992	1,426
151 0/8	18 0/8	18 4/8	22 2/8	5	5	Elbert County	CO	Kim Cooper	1993	1,426
151 0/8	20 6/8	21 2/8	19 6/8	5	5	Pennington County	SD	Scott R. Marsich	1994	1,426
151 0/8	22 2/8	22 6/8	23 3/8	5	5	Harris	SAS	Joe Schmidt	1995	1,426
151 0/8	23 3/8	24 1/8	19 4/8	4	4	Empress	ALB	Dave Holt	1995	1,426
150 7/8	22 3/8	23 4/8	20 0/8	6	6	Hockberry Creek	KS	Dale Redmond	1967	1,440
150 7/8	22 5/8	19 3/8	25 3/8	5	4	San Juan County	UT	Ken Ciarelli	1968	1,440
150 7/8	22 6/8	22 6/8	20 1/8	6	6	Fremont County	CO	Dave Elliott	1976	1,440
150 7/8	20 4/8	20 2/8	19 1/8	5	5	Idaho County	ID	Gary Belvoir	1981	1,440
150 7/8	20 1/8	21 1/8	16 1/8	5	5	Coconino County	AZ	Les Shelton	1984	1,440
150 7/8	20 3/8	20 7/8	17 5/8	4	4	Washington County	UT	E. Kip Fowler	1993	1,440
150 6/8	20 5/8	20 3/8	20 5/8	5	6	Washington County	UT	Jack Richards	1960	1,446
150 6/8	20 2/8	20 0/8	18 2/8	5	5	Bernalillo County	NM	Lee Braudt	1968	1,446
150 6/8	21 6/8	22 1/8	22 4/8	4	5	Hamilton County	KS	Mike Gilbert	1976	1,446
150 6/8	22 5/8	21 2/8	23 2/8	5	6	Box Elder County	UT	Steven B. Perry	1980	1,446
150 6/8	21 2/8	20 6/8	18 4/8	5	5	Grant County	OR	Rodney Keenon	1982	1,446
150 6/8	22 4/8	22 6/8	19 0/8	5	4	County of Warner	ALB	Giuliano Coslovi	1987	1,446
150 6/8	25 7/8	23 2/8	25 0/8	4	5	Lassen County	CA	Rick Pollard	1992	1,446
150 6/8	20 1/8	20 6/8	16 6/8	5	5	Boise County	ID	Jeff L. Varner	1994	1,446
150 5/8	24 2/8	24 7/8	19 6/8	6	5	Bernalillo County	NM	Alan Spitznagle	1982	1,454
150 5/8	22 3/8	22 4/8	16 1/8	5	5	Grant County	NM	Mark Garrison	1989	1,454
150 5/8	20 1/8	19 5/8	21 0/8	5	5	Boise County	ID	David R. Heck	1991	1,454
150 4/8	21 6/8	22 0/8	21 5/8	5	6	Pima County	AZ	Tony Don	1980	1,457
150 4/8	21 4/8	21 4/8	19 4/8	5	4	Garfield County	CO	Keith Backhaus	1981	1,457
150 4/8	22 0/8	21 6/8	22 5/8	5	5	Carbon County	UT	C. J. Coleman	1987	1,457
150 4/8	21 3/8	20 6/8	18 0/8	6	5	Wallowa County	OR	Billy L. Moores	1996	1,457
150 3/8	22 6/8	22 7/8	15 5/8	4	5	Summit County	UT	Clifton Rees	1962	1,461
150 3/8	19 6/8	20 3/8	19 7/8	4	5	Grand County	UT	Lowell W. Dobson	1968	1,461
150 3/8	21 0/8	21 0/8	15 7/8	5	5	Bernalillo County	NM	Michael M. Emery	1973	1,461
150 3/8	21 6/8	21 1/8	19 7/8	5	5	Washoe County	NV	Fred C. Church	1983	1,461
150 3/8	20 0/8	20 1/8	21 1/8	5	5	Lane County	KS	Dean Hamilton	1984	1,461
150 3/8	20 5/8	20 1/8	22 7/8	5	4	Cascade County	MT	Bennie J. Rossetto	1990	1,461
150 3/8	22 1/8	20 6/8	20 1/8	5	5	Boise County	ID	Russ Meyer	1991	1,461
150 3/8	19 7/8	19 4/8	23 7/8	4	4	Chouteau County	MT	Dwight P. Martin	1992	1,461
150 3/8	19 2/8	18 6/8	16 1/8	5	5	McKenzie County	ND	Brent Smith	1993	1,461
150 3/8	20 7/8	21 2/8	19 6/8	5	6	Ford County	KS	J. C. Falco	1993	1,461
150 3/8	21 1/8	21 2/8	19 7/8	5	5	Harney County	OR	Tyler Saunders	1996	1,461
150 2/8	13 0/8	19 7/8	15 3/8	3	6	Boise County	ID	Ralph Hoobing	1964	1,472
150 2/8	21 3/8	22 1/8	23 7/8	4	4	Valley County	MT	Andy Hicks	1981	1,472
150 2/8	22 1/8	22 0/8	20 4/8	6	5	Maricopa County	AZ	Mike Ottenbacher	1987	1,472
150 2/8	22 1/8	22 0/8	15 6/8	5	5	Wasatch County	UT	Ronald Whaley	1987	1,472
150 2/8	22 2/8	22 4/8	22 0/8	4	5	Union County	OR	Brian J. Scott	1990	1,472
150 2/8	21 4/8	24 3/8	24 0/8	4	3	Bow River	ALB	Bob Gruszecki	1991	1,472
150 2/8	22 1/8	19 2/8	20 7/8	5	6	Bernalillo County	NM	Anthony Ortega	1992	1,472
150 2/8	20 3/8	21 7/8	19 6/8	5	5	Rio Blanco County	CO	Chris Hofer	1994	1,472
150 2/8	20 5/8	21 2/8	18 6/8	5	5	Huerfano County	CO	Alan Blair	1996	1,472
150 2/8	20 3/8	21 7/8	19 4/8	5	5	Campbell County	SD	Douglas A. Goehring	1996	1,472
150 2/8	19 6/8	21 4/8	21 2/8	4	5	Salt Lake County	UT	Norman Kevin Davis	1996	1,472
150 1/8	18 3/8	18 5/8	17 3/8	6	7	Garfield County	CO	J. B. Hogan	1961	1,483
150 1/8	24 7/8	26 2/8	24 0/8	5	5	Deschutes County	OR	Walter M. Graham	1963	1,483
150 1/8	22 3/8	22 2/8	18 3/8	5	5	Jackson County	CO	William B. Tutt	1964	1,483
150 1/8	22 6/8	22 7/8	22 3/8	4	4	Gove County	KS	Merton Ikenberry	1966	1,483
150 1/8	21 3/8	21 4/8	20 1/8	5	5	Washoe County	NV	Felton Hickman	1970	1,483
150 1/8	21 4/8	22 5/8	24 1/8	4	4	Cochrane	ALB	Jim Hillstead	1989	1,483
150 1/8	23 2/8	24 2/8	20 5/8	5	5	Campbell County	WY	John Keenan	1993	1,483
150 1/8	24 7/8	23 4/8	17 1/8	5	4	Oldman River	ALB	Doug Doram	1993	1,483
150 1/8	25 7/8	25 0/8	20 7/8	5	4	Empress	ALB	Michael E. Kessler	1993	1,483
150 1/8	20 1/8	20 5/8	19 4/8	5	6	Lincoln County	NE	Tyron Lenz	1994	1,483
150 1/8	21 6/8	22 7/8	15 1/8	5	5	Rosebud County	MT	Chuck Adams	1997	1,483
150 1/8	21 2/8	22 1/8	19 4/8	5	6	Rio Arriba County	NM	Richard W. Eustace, Jr.	1998	1,483
150 0/8	21 2/8	22 4/8	24 4/8	4	4	Eureka County	NV	B. Verlyn Ownes	1963	1,495
150 0/8	18 7/8	18 6/8	16 3/8	5	6	Garfield County	UT	Dick Gulman	1966	1,495
150 0/8	19 3/8	21 4/8	20 4/8	5	5	Elko County	NV	Dick Woltering	1968	1,495
150 0/8	20 0/8	20 1/8	18 1/8	6	6	Larimer County	CO	Tom Tietz	1979	1,495
150 0/8	22 4/8	21 7/8	18 4/8	5	4	White Pine County	NV	Scott Faiman	1987	1,495
150 0/8	24 2/8	23 2/8	20 4/8	6	4	Pima County	AZ	Rick Betten	1991	1,495
150 0/8	19 3/8	17 2/8	16 0/8	4	4	Weber County	UT	Robert G. Petersen	1992	1,495
149 7/8	21 2/8	23 0/8	20 5/8	4	4	Sevier County	UT	Milt McQueary	1964	1,502
149 7/8	20 1/8	20 1/8	17 3/8	5	5	Trego County	KS	Larry Pearson	1974	1,502
149 7/8	23 5/8	22 6/8	26 2/8	4	5	Pima County	AZ	Michael B. Cachero	1985	1,502

MULE DEER (TYPICAL ANTLERS)

Minimum Score 145

SCORE	LENGTH OF MAIN BEAM R	LENGTH OF MAIN BEAM L	INSIDE SPREAD	NUMBER OF POINTS R	NUMBER OF POINTS L	AREA	STATE/PROVINCE	HUNTER'S NAME	DATE	RANK
149 7/8	20 0/8	22 2/8	19 2/8	6	4	Platte County	WY	G. Fred Asbell	1988	1,502
149 7/8	21 0/8	20 7/8	19 7/8	4	5	Billings County	ND	Kevin Clyde	1989	1,502
149 7/8	21 4/8	21 5/8	19 5/8	5	4	McKenzie County	ND	Wade Leer	1990	1,502
149 7/8	20 4/8	22 0/8	18 3/8	5	5	Furnas County	NE	Walter S. Wright	1991	1,502
149 7/8	22 7/8	22 7/8	21 5/8	4	3	Campbell County	WY	Steve Boster	1991	1,502
149 7/8	22 1/8	20 5/8	17 7/8	5	5	Boise County	ID	Jerry E. Burt	1992	1,502
149 6/8	21 3/8	21 1/8	19 6/8	4	4	Garfield County	CO	Skip Candahl	1966	1,511
149 6/8	26 5/8	27 5/8	25 0/8	7	4	Uncompahgre Plateau	CO	Jim Moan	1976	1,511
149 6/8	20 6/8	21 1/8	22 1/8	6	6	Mesa County	CO	Parker Leon	1984	1,511
149 6/8	21 1/8	21 6/8	19 5/8	5	5	Baker County	OR	Chuck Warner	1986	1,511
149 6/8	23 6/8	23 6/8	24 2/8	5	4	Armstrong	BC	Tim Meissner	1992	1,511
149 6/8	26 2/8	26 3/8	26 6/8	5	5	Fall River County	SD	Bruce Briesemeister	1993	1,511
149 6/8	18 2/8	19 4/8	19 6/8	5	5	Elko County	NV	Jay A. Doke	1995	1,511
149 5/8	18 1/8	20 7/8	17 7/8	5	5	Rio Blanco County	CO	Joseph H. French	1972	1,518
149 5/8	21 2/8	20 2/8	19 1/8	6	8	Canmore	ALB	Karl Pachonik	1982	1,518
149 5/8	21 6/8	22 0/8	18 3/8	6	4	Boise County	ID	Tom Weston	1984	1,518
149 5/8	20 6/8	22 1/8	18 7/8	5	5	Nye County	NV	Ed Fuller	1986	1,518
149 5/8	22 3/8	21 4/8	22 5/8	5	5	Johnson County	WY	Edward H. Carmichael	1989	1,518
149 5/8	22 3/8	22 7/8	22 7/8	5	5	Garfield County	CO	John W. Borlang	1990	1,518
149 5/8	24 5/8	20 5/8	23 0/8	4	6	Gallatin County	MT	Doug Stackhouse	1992	1,518
149 5/8	22 7/8	24 2/8	25 6/8	4	5	Rosebud County	MT	Jack Ferguson	1998	1,518
149 5/8	20 3/8	20 7/8	19 1/8	6	5	Platte County	WY	Jerry Bowen	1998	1,518
149 4/8	22 4/8	22 4/8	19 2/8	4	4	Colfax County	NM	Ed Foster	1966	1,527
149 4/8	22 2/8	22 4/8	22 4/8	4	5	Montrose County	CO	John A. Wilk	1977	1,527
149 4/8	21 1/8	20 5/8	20 0/8	6	5	Valencia County	NM	Frank Johnson	1985	1,527
149 4/8	21 4/8	20 7/8	23 0/8	5	5	Delta County	CO	Larry Tiner	1986	1,527
149 4/8	21 0/8	21 3/8	18 4/8	5	5	Valencia County	NM	Frank Johnson	1987	1,527
149 4/8	19 0/8	20 4/8	21 2/8	5	5	Meade County	KS	Randy Blehm	1988	1,527
149 4/8	21 3/8	23 4/8	22 0/8	5	6	Pinal County	AZ	John R. Villegas	1993	1,527
149 3/8	22 4/8	21 6/8	17 1/8	4	4	Okanogan County	WA	Irl Stamps	1939	1,534
149 3/8	22 4/8	20 4/8	19 1/8	5	7	Baker County	OR	Chuck Brackin	1964	1,534
149 3/8	21 5/8	22 5/8	20 7/8	5	4	Mesa County	CO	John Smith	1964	1,534
149 3/8	23 0/8	24 0/8	22 4/8	4	4	White Pine County	NV	Milo W. Burt	1971	1,534
149 3/8	22 6/8	22 1/8	19 2/8	6	4	San Juan County	UT	Randy Radant	1984	1,534
149 3/8	20 7/8	21 6/8	20 6/8	6	5	Jackson County	OR	Greg Chakarun	1985	1,534
149 3/8	22 4/8	21 2/8	20 7/8	5	6	Coconino County	AZ	Duane R. Richardson	1987	1,534
149 3/8	21 2/8	21 7/8	17 7/8	5	5	Jackson County	OR	Jason Tarrant	1988	1,534
149 3/8	20 2/8	20 0/8	17 1/8	5	5	Slope County	ND	Todd Seymanski	1990	1,534
149 3/8	22 3/8	22 5/8	20 1/8	6	5	Morrill County	NE	R. Matthew Bilby	1990	1,534
149 3/8	21 2/8	22 3/8	21 5/8	4	5	Pima County	AZ	Samuel Fatovich	1995	1,534
149 2/8	22 6/8	22 5/8	21 4/8	4	4	Lake County	CO	Thomas V. Sieverding	1972	1,545
149 2/8	25 5/8	25 2/8	25 0/8	6	4	Lincoln County	WY	Mike Barrett	1984	1,545
149 2/8	22 3/8	22 5/8	21 4/8	5	5	Garfield County	CO	James P. Speck	1984	1,545
149 2/8	19 5/8	19 2/8	17 2/8	5	5	San Juan County	NM	Michael R. Hinson	1987	1,545
149 2/8	19 4/8	20 4/8	19 0/8	5	5	Grant County	OR	Gary Kiepert	1990	1,545
149 2/8	21 0/8	21 2/8	21 4/8	4	5	Billings County	ND	Dale R. Zietz	1993	1,545
149 2/8	22 1/8	22 1/8	22 0/8	4	4	Jefferson County	CO	Larry J. Jones	1995	1,545
149 1/8	24 4/8	24 0/8	18 1/8	6	4	Washoe County	NV	Cecil D. Martin	1987	1,552
149 0/8	24 0/8	22 5/8	22 4/8	4	4	Mesa County	CO	Tom Hentrick	1974	1,553
149 0/8	20 4/8	19 6/8	23 4/8	5	5	Lincoln County	WY	Vaughn Cross	1978	1,553
149 0/8	25 3/8	24 3/8	22 4/8	5	5	Beaver County	UT	William H. Chilvers	1987	1,553
149 0/8	24 2/8	22 7/8	22 7/8	5	7	Elmore County	ID	Brian J. Brewster	1998	1,553
148 7/8	19 4/8	19 6/8	20 2/8	5	4	Garfield County	CO	Charles E. Whaley	1974	1,557
148 7/8	22 3/8	23 5/8	20 3/8	6	4	Hodgeman County	KS	James Wiggins	1978	1,557
148 7/8	22 3/8	23 3/8	21 3/8	4	4	Crook County	OR	Vernon Simpson	1982	1,557
148 7/8	24 1/8	24 3/8	20 7/8	5	5	Gunnison County	CO	Mike Reedy	1992	1,557
148 7/8	21 7/8	22 1/8	21 6/8	6	4	Boise County	ID	Edward Keeton	1994	1,557
148 6/8	20 7/8	20 6/8	13 2/8	5	4	Okanogan County	WA	Dennis N. Johnson	1971	1,562
148 6/8	21 3/8	20 5/8	15 7/8	5	7	Lane County	KS	Vernon L. McBee	1971	1,562
148 6/8	21 0/8	22 3/8	21 3/8	5	6	Umatilla County	OR	Loren R. Olsen	1981	1,562
148 6/8	19 4/8	20 7/8	19 4/8	5	5	Converse County	WY	Greg Popie	1982	1,562
148 6/8	22 6/8	23 4/8	19 6/8	5	4	Siskiyou County	CA	Jim Langley	1984	1,562
148 6/8	21 2/8	20 0/8	17 6/8	5	5	Sioux County	NE	Jeffrey Sales	1985	1,562
148 6/8	25 0/8	23 7/8	20 2/8	4	5	Garfield County	CO	Tom Urbenek	1988	1,562
148 6/8	21 2/8	21 1/8	20 6/8	5	4	Gove County	KS	Joel Beougher	1989	1,562
148 6/8	21 1/8	19 1/8	18 4/8	5	5	Campbell County	WY	Paul E. Korn	1997	1,562
148 5/8	21 3/8	18 7/8	23 6/8	5	5	Park County	CO	Ed Zehner	1972	1,571
148 5/8	24 4/8	23 7/8	23 2/8	6	6	Chelan County	WA	Ted A. Kinsey	1983	1,571
148 5/8	22 0/8	22 0/8	21 1/8	5	5	Albany County	WY	Kevin Anderson	1988	1,571
148 5/8	21 7/8	21 3/8	23 1/8	5	7	Harney County	OR	Patrick E. Wheeler	1990	1,571
148 5/8	22 5/8	22 5/8	18 7/8	4	5	Moffat County	CO	Larry Dean Bicknase	1992	1,571
148 5/8	20 5/8	21 0/8	15 5/8	5	5	Crook County	OR	Frank Sanders	1992	1,571
148 5/8	25 7/8	25 1/8	23 3/8	4	5	Bernalillo County	NM	Alex Jaramillo, Jr.	1996	1,571
148 4/8	19 4/8	19 0/8	17 0/8	5	5	Boise County	ID	Floyd Audette	1964	1,578
148 4/8	21 7/8	19 7/8	19 2/8	7	6	Perkins County	SD	Dr. David W. Schrody	1979	1,578
148 4/8	21 7/8	22 4/8	20 4/8	5	5	Campbell County	WY	Carrol D. Wert	1979	1,578
148 4/8	22 2/8	22 6/8	20 4/8	5	5	Converse County	WY	James D. Miller	1980	1,578
148 4/8	22 0/8	21 7/8	19 6/8	5	4	San Juan County	UT	Bill Clink	1985	1,578

MULE DEER (TYPICAL ANTLERS)

Minimum Score 145
Continued

SCORE	LENGTH OF MAIN BEAM R	LENGTH OF MAIN BEAM L	INSIDE SPREAD	NUMBER OF POINTS R	NUMBER OF POINTS L	AREA	STATE/PROVINCE	HUNTER'S NAME	DATE	RANK
148 4/8	20 7/8	22 2/8	20 2/8	5	5	Harney County	OR	Douglas Modey	1993	1,578
148 4/8	19 5/8	21 0/8	19 4/8	5	5	Springbank	ALB	Bry Loyd	1994	1,578
148 4/8	20 6/8	21 2/8	17 2/8	4	4	Lake County	OR	Tim Larocco	1996	1,578
148 3/8	22 5/8	23 5/8	18 5/8	5	4	Huerfano County	CO	Loren Johnson	1966	1,586
148 3/8	21 1/8	20 4/8	21 5/8	5	5	Carbon County	WY	Rod Schmidt	1984	1,586
148 3/8	23 2/8	24 2/8	28 5/8	6	4	Pueblo County	CO	Dean Aggson	1992	1,586
148 3/8	20 5/8	19 6/8	17 3/8	5	5	Colfax County	NM	Robert J. Sedlacko	1996	1,586
148 3/8	21 0/8	19 1/8	17 3/8	5	6	Teton County	WY	Justin Bliss	1996	1,586
148 3/8	20 3/8	19 5/8	17 5/8	5	5	Grant County	OR	Paul J. Zink	1997	1,586
148 2/8	20 3/8	21 0/8	17 6/8	5	5	Fergus County	MT	Bob Wanner	1977	1,592
148 2/8	20 1/8	20 6/8	20 4/8	5	5	Billings County	ND	Thomas Treto	1982	1,592
148 2/8	21 0/8	23 1/8	21 1/8	4	5	Cochrane	ALB	David Richardson	1983	1,592
148 2/8	21 5/8	21 2/8	20 4/8	4	5	Chelan County	WA	Joe Lilley	1988	1,592
148 2/8	19 2/8	21 0/8	20 4/8	5	5	Cassia County	ID	Monte B. Carlson	1989	1,592
148 2/8	22 5/8	21 1/8	21 0/8	6	5	Pima County	AZ	Daniel C. Hicks	1991	1,592
148 2/8	23 5/8	23 3/8	20 4/8	5	4	Baker County	OR	Mike Raney	1994	1,592
148 2/8	20 0/8	19 2/8	16 6/8	5	5	Beaverhead County	MT	Robert C. Howard	1995	1,592
148 2/8	18 7/8	19 1/8	17 6/8	5	5	Elko County	NV	Felton Hickman	1996	1,592
148 1/8	20 4/8	21 7/8	22 7/8	9	4	Emery County	UT	Bob Jacobsen	1961	1,601
148 1/8	23 0/8	22 3/8	19 5/8	4	4	Pitkin County	CO	William F. Havel	1962	1,601
148 1/8	21 7/8	21 7/8	21 5/8	4	5	Lake County	OR	Richard G. Speer	1964	1,601
148 1/8	20 0/8	21 0/8	21 0/8	4	5	Ford County	KS	Aubrey Ballard	1966	1,601
148 1/8	20 7/8	20 1/8	18 5/8	5	4	Grand County	CO	Judd Cooney	1969	1,601
148 1/8	19 0/8	19 3/8	18 5/8	5	5	Carbon County	UT	Leonard Thompson	1973	1,601
148 1/8	20 3/8	21 5/8	21 2/8	6	5	Sheridan County	KS	Tom Reedy	1980	1,601
148 1/8	21 4/8	19 6/8	18 5/8	4	5	Mesa County	CO	Jay Verzuh	1982	1,601
148 1/8	21 4/8	22 1/8	19 3/8	5	4	Sheridan County	WY	Mike Barrett	1983	1,601
148 1/8	21 5/8	21 0/8	21 0/8	6	6	Michichi	ALB	Rodney Dyck	1991	1,601
148 1/8	20 4/8	20 1/8	21 2/8	7	7	Hettinger County	ND	Scott Wiseman	1991	1,601
148 1/8	23 6/8	23 0/8	18 0/8	6	6	Fraser River	BC	Rick Paquette	1991	1,601
148 1/8	20 5/8	21 0/8	17 5/8	7	7	Red Deer Lake	ALB	J. Linley Biblow	1991	1,601
148 1/8	23 0/8	23 1/8	23 7/8	5	5	Dundy County	NE	Clay Burrell	1993	1,601
148 1/8	19 6/8	19 5/8	17 3/8	5	5	Golden Valley County	MT	Ronald G. Junkert	1994	1,601
148 1/8	26 0/8	25 6/8	24 1/8	4	4	Nevada County	CA	Harry Pelton	1995	1,601
148 1/8	24 6/8	24 4/8	21 7/8	6	5	Jefferson County	OR	Guy P. Hurlbert	1996	1,601
148 0/8	21 7/8	21 4/8	21 1/8	6	6	White River N.F.	CO	Paul M. Ramsey	1959	1,618
148 0/8	20 5/8	20 7/8	16 6/8	6	6	Jones County	SD	Gene M. Hove	1990	1,618
148 0/8	23 6/8	23 0/8	26 6/8	5	4	Colfax County	NM	Ray Valerio	1994	1,618
148 0/8	23 6/8	23 0/8	21 2/8	3	3	Billings County	ND	Gary Fleishauer	1996	1,618
147 7/8	22 3/8	24 0/8	23 3/8	3	4	Millard County	UT	Milton F. McQueary	1958	1,622
147 7/8	21 2/8	21 0/8	18 0/8	5	6	Deschutes County	OR	Joe Reynolds	1967	1,622
147 7/8	21 5/8	22 0/8	21 5/8	5	5	Johnson County	WY	Scott L. Koelzer	1978	1,622
147 7/8	23 3/8	23 7/8	24 0/8	5	4	Mesa County	CO	Garvin H. Gibbins	1984	1,622
147 7/8	23 7/8	22 7/8	20 7/8	5	4	Mesa County	CO	Richard Kunevicius	1985	1,622
147 7/8	22 2/8	21 0/8	21 5/8	5	4	Washoe County	NV	Cecil D. Martin	1986	1,622
147 7/8	22 1/8	21 4/8	19 7/8	5	5	Bernalillo County	NM	Chett Britton	1992	1,622
147 7/8	21 7/8	21 7/8	21 7/8	4	5	McGrath	ALB	CameRon Cook	1993	1,622
147 6/8	20 0/8	20 2/8	20 2/8	5	4	Garfield County	CO	Steve Love	1972	1,631
147 6/8	19 4/8	21 0/8	21 0/8	5	5	Routt County	CO	John P. Hale	1974	1,631
147 6/8	20 5/8	21 6/8	15 6/8	7	5	Garfield County	CO	Edwin Hurt	1980	1,631
147 6/8	22 5/8	22 2/8	20 5/8	5	5	Boise County	ID	Matt March, Jr.	1983	1,631
147 6/8	17 6/8	22 0/8	20 0/8	4	4	Malheur County	OR	Steve Savage	1985	1,631
147 6/8	24 1/8	22 3/8	22 6/8	5	4	McKenzie County	ND	Bryan R. Stein	1988	1,631
147 6/8	21 1/8	22 0/8	20 0/8	5	5	Innisfail	ALB	Derrill Herman	1997	1,631
147 5/8	21 6/8	21 4/8	20 1/8	5	5	Sevier County	UT	Rowland Enomoto	1963	1,638
147 5/8	23 0/8	23 0/8	24 2/8	5	6	San Juan County	UT	Jack Howard	1966	1,638
147 5/8	19 1/8	17 0/8	21 0/8	6	5	Grant County	OR	Arthur Redinger	1972	1,638
147 5/8	21 1/8	18 7/8	17 5/8	5	4	Sevier County	UT	Robert W. Shilling	1974	1,638
147 5/8	25 2/8	24 2/8	22 1/8	7	5	Garfield County	CO	Terry Bridgman	1978	1,638
147 5/8	18 6/8	18 7/8	21 0/8	5	4	Elbert County	CO	Calvin Farner	1984	1,638
147 5/8	21 7/8	22 7/8	25 2/8	3	3	Butte County	SD	Glenn D Priebe	1984	1,638
147 5/8	22 7/8	23 2/8	18 5/8	6	4	Rio Arriba County	NM	Craig Sanchez	1996	1,638
147 4/8	22 1/8	22 2/8	19 4/8	5	5	Bernalillo County	NM	Larry W. Johnson	1969	1,646
147 4/8	21 2/8	22 1/8	19 0/8	5	5	Boulder County	CO	Jack Frank	1970	1,646
147 4/8	21 0/8	21 0/8	18 5/8	5	5	Garfield County	CO	Paul R. Shannon	1975	1,646
147 4/8	22 3/8	21 5/8	17 4/8	5	5	Maricopa County	AZ	Stephen C. Christensen	1976	1,646
147 4/8	20 1/8	20 5/8	19 6/8	5	5	Routt County	CO	Tom N. Garvin	1983	1,646
147 4/8	23 0/8	24 0/8	24 0/8	6	6	Sweetwater County	WY	Vic Dana	1983	1,646
147 4/8	24 2/8	22 2/8	20 4/8	4	5	Harney County	OR	Gary D. Nyden	1985	1,646
147 4/8	19 5/8	19 5/8	16 6/8	5	5	Coconino County	AZ	Steven H. Cook	1989	1,646
147 4/8	22 4/8	23 0/8	21 2/8	5	5	Converse County	WY	George A. Zanoni	1991	1,646
147 4/8	19 4/8	20 6/8	17 2/8	5	6	Converse County	WY	Harry Cerutti	1991	1,646
147 4/8	20 5/8	21 3/8	14 6/8	7	5	Lumby	BC	Owen Schoenberger	1991	1,646
147 4/8	22 2/8	24 1/8	24 0/8	5	4	Modoc County	CA	Wayne Wood	1993	1,646
147 3/8	23 4/8	23 2/8	20 3/8	5	6	Cherry County	NE	Jack E. Joseph	1961	1,658
147 3/8	19 4/8	20 4/8	16 5/8	4	5	Latah County	ID	Chas. A. McDonald	1965	1,658
147 3/8	19 0/8	21 0/8	18 1/8	5	5	Johnson County	WY	Mike E. Neilson	1994	1,658

MULE DEER (TYPICAL ANTLERS)

Minimum Score 145 — Continued

SCORE	LENGTH OF MAIN BEAM R	LENGTH OF MAIN BEAM L	INSIDE SPREAD	NUMBER OF POINTS R	NUMBER OF POINTS L	AREA	STATE/PROVINCE	HUNTER'S NAME	DATE	RANK
147 3/8	22 0/8	22 0/8	20 5/8	5	5	Campbell County	WY	Leon R. Nyreen	1996	1,658
147 3/8	19 5/8	19 6/8	17 7/8	5	5	Big Horn County	WY	Donald J. Kane	1997	1,658
147 2/8	22 7/8	23 2/8	17 0/8	6	6	Cherry County	NE	Ken Hollpeter	1979	1,663
147 2/8	21 4/8	21 3/8	19 4/8	4	5	El Paso County	CO	Rick C. Wilson	1996	1,663
147 1/8	20 5/8	20 1/8	16 7/8	5	5	Uintah County	UT	Rolland Esterline	1967	1,665
147 1/8	19 6/8	23 6/8	17 0/8	6	5	Baker County	OR	Larry Garoutte	1970	1,665
147 1/8	22 6/8	21 2/8	19 5/8	5	5	Moffat County	CO	Larry Bicknase	1991	1,665
147 1/8	20 1/8	19 6/8	19 7/8	5	5	Esther	ALB	Steven J. Parkin	1996	1,665
147 0/8	20 3/8	20 7/8	20 2/8	5	5	Uintah County	UT	Merlin L. Killpack	1958	1,669
147 0/8	25 4/8	25 0/8	23 5/8	7	5	Grand County	UT	William W. Selby	1974	1,669
147 0/8	21 6/8	21 7/8	20 6/8	5	5	Dawson County	MT	Smucky Mann	1975	1,669
147 0/8	20 5/8	21 6/8	19 2/8	5	5	Laramie County	WY	Ronald J. Wedge	1978	1,669
147 0/8	20 4/8	20 4/8	17 2/8	5	5	Stanley County	SD	George Hipple	1982	1,669
147 0/8	21 6/8	21 3/8	18 2/8	5	5	Powder River County	MT	Max Miller	1990	1,669
147 0/8	22 6/8	22 3/8	20 2/8	6	6	Franklin County	ID	Dale Holpainen	1991	1,669
147 0/8	23 0/8	23 0/8	24 5/8	5	4	Sioux County	ND	James Red Tomahawk	1995	1,669
147 0/8	21 1/8	20 6/8	19 2/8	6	5	Rimbey	ALB	Gary Bruns	1996	1,669
147 0/8	22 1/8	22 6/8	23 3/8	5	5	Rawlins County	KS	Todd Fugate	1997	1,669
146 7/8	19 5/8	20 1/8	20 1/8	5	5	Grand County	UT	Norm Goodwin	1960	1,679
146 7/8	23 4/8	23 1/8	23 4/8	5	4	Emery County	UT	Bruce Ware	1961	1,679
146 7/8	19 2/8	20 0/8	18 5/8	5	5	Baker County	OR	James E. Hodson	1966	1,679
146 7/8	21 3/8	20 7/8	21 2/8	4	4	Carbon County	WY	John Swanson	1966	1,679
146 7/8	20 7/8	21 2/8	21 3/8	5	5	Meade County	SD	Kenneth McNenny	1967	1,679
146 7/8	21 2/8	21 4/8	18 7/8	5	5	Saguache County	CO	Skip Mulso	1974	1,679
146 7/8	21 0/8	20 2/8	18 3/8	4	4	Routt County	CO	Bob Stevens	1975	1,679
146 7/8	21 4/8	21 6/8	19 3/8	3	3	Clark County	ID	Robert Daniels	1978	1,679
146 7/8	20 3/8	21 5/8	20 3/8	6	5	Sheridan County	WY	David Shoop	1980	1,679
146 7/8	23 6/8	21 6/8	24 1/8	5	9	Pima County	AZ	Stacy Tompkinson	1984	1,679
146 7/8	19 7/8	20 4/8	17 3/8	5	5	Mesa County	CO	Gary L. Hoekman	1986	1,679
146 7/8	20 3/8	20 2/8	17 7/8	5	5	Orion	ALB	Kent Hillard	1990	1,679
146 7/8	22 0/8	23 1/8	26 7/8	6	5	Calgary	ALB	Archie Nesbitt	1991	1,679
146 7/8	24 7/8	22 6/8	18 5/8	5	8	Routt County	CO	Richard Gjerde	1993	1,679
146 7/8	21 7/8	21 7/8	17 7/8	5	5	Placer County	CA	Doug Burgard	1993	1,679
146 7/8	19 7/8	21 6/8	15 5/8	5	5	Raymond	ALB	Dr. Chuck Leidheiser	1996	1,679
146 6/8	19 6/8	20 3/8	15 7/8	4	4	Owyhee County	ID	Seneth Ward	1960	1,695
146 6/8	21 1/8	20 2/8	20 3/8	6	5	Mesa County	CO	Dennis Kelly	1981	1,695
146 6/8	20 4/8	19 7/8	19 0/8	6	7	Elbert County	CO	Donald Ace Morgan	1983	1,695
146 6/8	23 3/8	24 2/8	22 2/8	4	4	Pitkin County	CO	Bill Krenz	1983	1,695
146 6/8	18 7/8	20 1/8	19 6/8	5	4	Carbon County	WY	Rod Schmidt	1988	1,695
146 6/8	21 5/8	22 4/8	16 2/8	6	5	Meade County	KS	Mike Heinson	1989	1,695
146 6/8	21 6/8	21 0/8	22 5/8	6	5	Culberson County	TX	Curtis W. Mathis	1992	1,695
146 6/8	22 6/8	22 6/8	24 1/8	4	5	Pima County	AZ	Fred Slone	1992	1,695
146 6/8	19 1/8	18 2/8	16 4/8	5	5	Stillwater County	MT	Gary F. Bogner	1993	1,695
146 6/8	20 3/8	21 0/8	17 4/8	4	5	Archuleta County	CO	Donald B. Myers	1996	1,695
146 6/8	19 6/8	21 3/8	19 1/8	5	6	Rosalind	ALB	Sylvester "Sly" Baier	1997	1,695
146 6/8	23 3/8	24 4/8	19 2/8	5	5	Tehama County	CA	Richard Hall	1998	1,695
146 5/8	22 0/8	22 6/8	18 7/8	5	5	Chelan County	WA	Gerald King	1963	1,707
146 5/8	20 5/8	20 3/8	20 6/8	5	5	Johnson County	WY	Gary Olsen	1979	1,707
146 5/8	20 6/8	21 0/8	20 7/8	5	5	Uintah County	UT	Dave Lund	1987	1,707
146 5/8	21 2/8	22 2/8	15 7/8	4	5	Lemhi County	ID	Mike Muguira	1988	1,707
146 5/8	20 1/8	21 1/8	20 3/8	5	5	Sheridan County	WY	Mark Frank	1990	1,707
146 5/8	19 2/8	19 0/8	18 1/8	6	8	Wheatland County	MT	Jim Winjum	1992	1,707
146 5/8	20 4/8	19 2/8	17 5/8	4	4	Gunnison County	CO	Robert H. Johnson	1997	1,707
146 4/8	23 3/8	23 0/8	21 0/8	4	4	Wayne County	UT	Harold Boyack	1968	1,714
146 4/8	20 0/8	20 7/8	19 4/8	5	4	Mesa County	CO	Kaye B. McCrory	1978	1,714
146 4/8	24 0/8	26 5/8	23 0/8	7	6	Eagle County	CO	Dave Mendoza	1983	1,714
146 4/8	22 4/8	22 3/8	20 4/8	5	5	Piute County	UT	Tim Sayer	1984	1,714
146 4/8	22 3/8	22 1/8	19 6/8	5	4	Rio Grande County	CO	Jerry Woodland	1984	1,714
146 4/8	21 0/8	23 2/8	22 4/8	5	5	Bowman County	ND	Dwight Eckart	1984	1,714
146 4/8	21 7/8	22 4/8	16 7/8	5	8	Cache County	UT	Robert Bronson	1985	1,714
146 4/8	21 4/8	21 2/8	18 0/8	5	5	Mesa County	CO	John Papenfuss	1988	1,714
146 4/8	18 6/8	19 2/8	19 3/8	5	5	Warner	ALB	Keith Heppler	1991	1,714
146 3/8	19 0/8	19 0/8	17 3/8	5	5	Mohave County	AZ	George Kili	1964	1,723
146 3/8	20 2/8	21 1/8	19 1/8	5	5	Grand County	UT	Bob Paulson	1967	1,723
146 3/8	21 0/8	21 2/8	19 5/8	5	5	Mesa County	CO	Curtis W. Dorroh	1979	1,723
146 3/8	22 1/8	22 2/8	22 5/8	7	6	Lane County	KS	Dean Hamilton	1980	1,723
146 3/8	19 2/8	21 2/8	19 3/8	4	4	Boulder County	CO	Al Miller	1983	1,723
146 3/8	20 4/8	21 3/8	19 5/8	5	6	San Miguel County	NM	Ricardo Roybal	1984	1,723
146 3/8	21 1/8	19 4/8	21 4/8	5	5	Billings County	ND	Roy Boots	1985	1,723
146 3/8	24 7/8	24 6/8	24 3/8	4	4	Fall River County	SD	Michael A. Judas	1990	1,723
146 3/8	19 5/8	21 1/8	26 0/8	4	5	Salt Lake County	UT	Lance Brown	1996	1,723
146 2/8	25 4/8	23 6/8	23 4/8	5	5	Las Animas County	CO	Tom Valamdro	1967	1,732
146 2/8	21 0/8	20 2/8	19 1/8	7	6	Gallatin County	MT	Scott Koelzer	1969	1,732
146 2/8	21 4/8	21 4/8	20 0/8	5	5	Powder River County	MT	Charles R. Maloney	1973	1,732
146 2/8	22 4/8	22 0/8	19 0/8	4	5	Powder River County	MT	Mike Barrett	1985	1,732
146 2/8	18 6/8	18 4/8	18 2/8	5	5	Cache County	UT	John A. Bogucki	1988	1,732
146 2/8	21 6/8	21 4/8	18 4/8	4	5	Sublette County	WY	Roger O. Wyant	1990	1,732
146 2/8	22 6/8	21 7/8	25 5/8	5	5	Hidalgo County	NM	Steven Tisdale	1992	1,732

MULE DEER (TYPICAL ANTLERS)

Minimum Score 145

Continued

SCORE	LENGTH OF MAIN BEAM R	LENGTH OF MAIN BEAM L	INSIDE SPREAD	NUMBER OF POINTS R	NUMBER OF POINTS L	AREA	STATE/PROVINCE	HUNTER'S NAME	DATE	RANK
146 1/8	20 6/8	19 0/8	15 7/8	5	5	Ada County	ID	Jim Wenzel	1971	1,739
146 1/8	21 0/8	20 3/8	16 5/8	5	5	Clark County	ID	Max Heberling	1989	1,739
146 1/8	20 6/8	22 2/8	22 1/8	5	5	Graham County	KS	Jim Kerbaugh	1989	1,739
146 1/8	19 6/8	20 6/8	18 5/8	6	5	Morgan County	CO	Laszlo Nobi	1991	1,739
146 1/8	20 5/8	22 2/8	17 7/8	5	5	Otero County	NM	Roger Schoolcraft	1992	1,739
146 1/8	23 0/8	21 7/8	19 1/8	5	4	Bernalillo County	NM	Kennith Jaramillo, Sr.	1995	1,739
146 1/8	23 3/8	24 0/8	20 3/8	4	4	Morrow County	OR	Jeffrey H. Edwards	1996	1,739
146 0/8	20 4/8	20 2/8	18 2/8	5	5	Elko County	NV	Howard Hill	1944	1,746
146 0/8	21 2/8	21 3/8	20 2/8	5	5	Mesa County	CO	William F. DeEsch	1966	1,746
146 0/8	18 6/8	19 7/8	17 0/8	5	5	Decatur County	KS	A. E. 'Butch' Whelchel	1977	1,746
146 0/8	19 6/8	19 2/8	20 6/8	5	5	Converse County	WY	David A. Widby	1990	1,746
146 0/8	22 0/8	19 2/8	23 3/8	5	5	Niobrara County	WY	John H. Williams	1991	1,746
146 0/8	19 0/8	20 0/8	16 6/8	4	4	Fergus County	MT	Josef Rud	1998	1,746
145 7/8	21 1/8	20 4/8	20 5/8	5	6	Madera County	CA	Rodney York	1978	1,752
145 7/8	20 1/8	20 3/8	19 5/8	4	4	Chelan County	WA	Rick Morgan	1984	1,752
145 7/8	20 0/8	20 0/8	17 7/8	5	5	Valley County	ID	Robert Bruno	1988	1,752
145 7/8	21 5/8	22 0/8	19 1/8	5	4	Billings County	ND	Tom Schills	1988	1,752
145 7/8	20 1/8	19 1/8	15 1/8	5	5	Carbon County	WY	Joseph Parziale	1992	1,752
145 7/8	22 2/8	23 1/8	17 7/8	5	5	Lake County	OR	Claude Babb	1993	1,752
145 7/8	21 4/8	20 0/8	17 0/8	6	5	Ravalli County	MT	W. "Red" Chavez	1993	1,752
145 7/8	20 2/8	20 2/8	18 1/8	5	4	Meade County	SD	Mike Weyer	1993	1,752
145 6/8	17 0/8	18 3/8	16 0/8	5	5	Lake County	OR	George Rajnus	1961	1,760
145 6/8	22 2/8	24 3/8	21 4/8	5	3	Sevier County	UT	James R. Bell	1964	1,760
145 6/8	24 1/8	21 2/8	24 2/8	6	6	Chaffee County	CO	Gary Ginther	1973	1,760
145 6/8	22 3/8	22 0/8	20 2/8	5	5	Pecos County	TX	Butch Floyd	1975	1,760
145 6/8	21 3/8	19 4/8	17 0/8	5	4	Albany County	WY	Jerry Bowen	1980	1,760
145 6/8	20 6/8	22 0/8	21 0/8	6	5	Cheyenne County	KS	Kendall Helton	1988	1,760
145 6/8	22 5/8	24 2/8	17 3/8	6	5	Bernalillo County	NM	Alvin Chewiwi	1990	1,760
145 6/8	22 0/8	20 3/8	22 6/8	5	5	Wasco County	OR	Sean Corbin	1991	1,760
145 6/8	19 4/8	23 4/8	21 7/8	5	6	Estevan	SAS	Myron Duff	1992	1,760
145 6/8	19 4/8	19 2/8	17 2/8	5	5	Otero County	NM	Greg Perkins	1995	1,760
145 6/8	19 4/8	18 4/8	18 2/8	5	5	Sheridan County	WY	Gary L. Challoner	1995	1,760
145 6/8	21 4/8	21 2/8	16 6/8	5	5	Devon	ALB	Steve MacKenzie	1997	1,760
145 5/8	21 0/8	20 4/8	17 5/8	4	4	Grant County	OR	Charlie Endicott	1979	1,772
145 5/8	22 5/8	21 2/8	21 7/8	4	5	Ellis County	KS	Mark A. Murphey	1983	1,772
145 5/8	22 0/8	22 5/8	20 3/8	7	6	Rich County	UT	Wade Steffenhagen	1992	1,772
145 5/8	21 1/8	21 5/8	19 5/8	5	5	Larimer County	CO	Steve Banowetz	1998	1,772
145 4/8	20 5/8	18 4/8	19 4/8	6	6	Boulder County	CO	Bob Byerly	1967	1,776
145 4/8	19 6/8	14 2/8	18 4/8	7	4	Pima County	AZ	Peter C. Knagge	1976	1,776
145 4/8	21 5/8	21 6/8	19 6/8	5	5	Sioux County	NE	Steve Woitaszewski	1983	1,776
145 4/8	21 7/8	22 4/8	20 4/8	5	4	Converse County	WY	Frank N. Moore	1984	1,776
145 4/8	18 4/8	19 4/8	16 6/8	4	4	Platte County	WY	Dave Hiiva	1985	1,776
145 4/8	23 3/8	23 5/8	22 4/8	5	5	Lassen County	CA	Wayne Wood	1985	1,776
145 4/8	21 2/8	20 5/8	21 5/8	4	4	Jackson County	OR	Ron Schmelzer	1991	1,776
145 4/8	17 1/8	20 1/8	14 4/8	6	6	Sioux County	NE	Mike A. Ellingson	1992	1,776
145 4/8	22 2/8	21 7/8	20 6/8	4	4	McKenzie County	ND	Ryan Ferrell	1996	1,776
145 3/8	27 2/8	26 5/8	26 2/8	5	4	Moffat County	CO	Scott Showalter	1971	1,785
145 3/8	21 1/8	20 4/8	19 7/8	4	4	Sioux County	NE	William A. Voor Vart	1978	1,785
145 3/8	21 6/8	22 0/8	21 7/8	4	4	Summit County	UT	Larry Dickerson	1985	1,785
145 3/8	19 7/8	19 4/8	20 6/8	5	5	Larimer County	CO	Dane Dutrisac	1992	1,785
145 3/8	19 7/8	19 6/8	20 1/8	4	4	Caribou County	ID	Michael Sparks	1992	1,785
145 3/8	22 0/8	22 1/8	22 1/8	5	4	Pennington County	SD	Gary English	1992	1,785
145 3/8	21 5/8	22 2/8	19 1/8	5	5	Dundy County	NE	Matt Gideon	1993	1,785
145 3/8	23 1/8	22 1/8	20 5/8	5	4	Weld County	CO	Nathan L. Andersohn	1996	1,785
145 2/8	24 0/8	24 4/8	19 6/8	4	4	Bernalillo County	NM	Robert Bulcock, Jr.	1969	1,793
145 2/8	20 1/8	20 2/8	16 2/8	5	5	Uncompahgre N.F.	CO	Larry Holak	1979	1,793
145 2/8	22 4/8	23 1/8	17 4/8	5	5	Mesa County	CO	Paul T Brown	1985	1,793
145 2/8	22 2/8	22 7/8	19 7/8	6	7	Norton County	KS	Gary Long	1987	1,793
145 2/8	21 4/8	21 4/8	18 2/8	5	5	Natrona County	WY	Larry Nelson	1989	1,793
145 2/8	20 4/8	20 2/8	20 5/8	5	5	Sandy Point	ALB	Tim Sailer	1990	1,793
145 2/8	17 4/8	21 1/8	18 3/8	6	5	Bernalillo County	NM	Mark Sulllvan	1994	1,793
145 2/8	23 5/8	21 7/8	21 6/8	5	5	Columbia County	WA	Robert C. Allan	1995	1,793
145 1/8	23 0/8	23 3/8	22 7/8	5	4	Natrona County	WY	Bill Wade	1970	1,801
145 1/8	21 6/8	19 3/8	19 1/8	4	5	Eagle County	CO	Rick Duggan	1981	1,801
145 1/8	19 4/8	20 3/8	17 5/8	5	4	Coconino County	AZ	Dick Tone	1981	1,801
145 1/8	23 4/8	21 3/8	20 7/8	4	4	Summit County	CO	Mark Anderson	1982	1,801
145 1/8	18 5/8	19 4/8	17 5/8	5	5	Routt County	CO	Ronald P. Kelley, Sr.	1985	1,801
145 1/8	22 5/8	21 7/8	21 5/8	3	4	Baker County	OR	Arthur Marc Whisler	1986	1,801
145 1/8	22 2/8	22 3/8	17 7/8	4	4	Yakima County	WA	Robt. "Andy" Anderson	1986	1,801
145 1/8	21 3/8	20 6/8	19 1/8	4	5	Calgary	ALB	Jim Chapman	1991	1,801
145 1/8	20 5/8	22 5/8	21 1/8	6	6	Grant County	OR	Ken Arveson, Jr.	1992	1,801
145 0/8	22 1/8	21 6/8	17 6/8	5	5	El Paso County	CO	Thomas M. Farmer	1961	1,810
145 0/8	22 1/8	22 2/8	21 0/8	5	6	Trego County	KS	Don Howard	1966	1,810
145 0/8	22 3/8	22 4/8	21 2/8	5	5	Plumas County	CA	Wayne Ghidossi	1977	1,810
145 0/8	22 7/8	24 2/8	27 1/8	5	5	Cochise County	AZ	Joe F. Acosta	1986	1,810
145 0/8	20 5/8	20 4/8	19 4/8	4	5	Salt Lake County	UT	Lance Dalton	1989	1,810
145 0/8	19 7/8	19 7/8	17 4/8	5	5	Fremont County	WY	Gary Nyman	1990	1,810
145 0/8	22 2/8	20 7/8	19 2/8	6	5	Saguache County	CO	Mike Chatin	1991	1,810

MULE DEER (TYPICAL ANTLERS)

Minimum Score 145 — Continued

SCORE	LENGTH OF MAIN BEAM R	L	INSIDE SPREAD	NUMBER OF POINTS R	L	AREA	STATE/ PROVINCE	HUNTER'S NAME	DATE	RANK
145 0/8	17 4/8	19 0/8	19 6/8	5	5	Union County	OR	Russ Hultberg	1991	1,810
145 0/8	24 4/8	23 4/8	22 0/8	4	4	Vermilion	ALB	Graydon Bishop	1992	1,810
145 0/8	20 0/8	20 6/8	17 2/8	5	5	Gallatin County	MT	Craig L. Newman	1995	1,810
145 0/8	20 5/8	21 5/8	22 2/8	6	5	Jefferson County	OR	Jim Merrill	1997	1,810

MULE DEER (TYPICAL VELVET ANTLERS)

Minimum Score 145

SCORE	LENGTH OF MAIN BEAM R	L	INSIDE SPREAD	NUMBER OF POINTS R	L	AREA	STATE/ PROVINCE	HUNTER'S NAME	DATE	RANK
201 2/8	31 0/8	29 5/8	27 7/8	9	5	Maple Creek	SAS	Darcy Bowyer	1994	*
199 5/8	26 5/8	26 7/8	28 2/8	5	5	Coconino County	AZ	Mark Gehrig	1993	*
197 1/8	25 4/8	24 5/8	20 6/8	6	5	Mesa County	CO	Roger Auman	1993	*
189 0/8	26 2/8	26 4/8	23 4/8	4	4	Garfield County	CO	Robert L. Harvey	1979	*
188 5/8	26 5/8	26 4/8	20 4/8	6	5	Washoe County	NV	Fred C. Church	1997	*
188 3/8	25 2/8	25 7/8	21 3/8	5	5	Swift Current Creek	SAS	Bruce Louma	1998	*
187 5/8	22 2/8	25 1/8	19 7/8	5	5	Tooele County	UT	Shane Perkins	1993	*
187 2/8	27 1/8	26 2/8	21 7/8	6	7	Montezuma County	CO	Tom Kochanski	1994	*
186 5/8	25 2/8	25 5/8	23 6/8	6	5	Kane County	UT	Jan R. Gorringe	1994	*
186 4/8	26 6/8	24 6/8	19 0/8	5	6	Elko County	NV	Bob Sneed	1996	*
186 4/8	25 4/8	24 7/8	25 0/8	5	5	Grant County	OR	Richard Marks	1995	*
185 5/8	27 3/8	27 7/8	25 0/8	7	7	San Juan County	UT	Gary Nordgran	1993	*
185 4/8	26 5/8	28 2/8	24 7/8	6	5	San Juan County	UT	Todd Hurst	1998	*
185 3/8	23 2/8	26 2/8	25 1/8	5	6	Coconino County	AZ	Donald Volopich	1993	*
185 0/8	21 6/8	23 0/8	16 6/8	5	5	Park County	CO	Mike Mueller	1998	*
184 2/8	24 2/8	23 1/8	22 4/8	7	6	Lake Diefenbaker	SAS	Darren Breckner	1996	*
182 7/8	23 5/8	24 4/8	28 3/8	8	7	Kane County	UT	Klint Glover	1994	*
182 4/8	26 3/8	26 6/8	26 2/8	6	5	Mesa County	CO	John Alters	1997	*
182 3/8	23 1/8	21 3/8	23 6/8	5	5	Humboldt County	NV	Roger David Vanderhoff	1998	*
182 1/8	24 2/8	23 3/8	20 3/8	4	5	La Plata County	CO	Brian Myers	1995	*
181 7/8	24 2/8	25 0/8	20 0/8	7	6	Duchesne County	UT	Howard D. Van Wagoner, Jr.	1993	*
181 5/8	23 4/8	24 1/8	20 3/8	5	5	La Plata County	CO	Kenneth D. Canterbury	1995	*
181 5/8	24 0/8	24 4/8	18 2/8	5	6	Coconino County	AZ	Bob Nahmens	1998	*
181 4/8	23 5/8	25 3/8	29 1/8	6	6	Grand County	UT	Paul Anthony	1993	*
181 2/8	25 1/8	27 1/8	27 7/8	6	5	Garfield County	CO	Tommy Stokes	1995	*
181 1/8	24 5/8	24 5/8	16 7/8	5	6	Mesa County	CO	Ryan Bartholomew	1996	*
181 0/8	23 0/8	22 7/8	21 6/8	6	5	Garfield County	CO	Marv Meyers	1996	*
180 6/8	25 6/8	26 3/8	23 6/8	5	5	Washoe County	NV	Fred Slatin	1997	*
180 4/8	23 7/8	25 3/8	24 6/8	5	5	Lincoln County	NV	Troy T. Truman	1991	*
180 3/8	23 4/8	23 5/8	22 3/8	5	5	Elko County	NV	Kenneth J. Wilkinson	1995	*
180 0/8	23 5/8	23 1/8	22 4/8	5	5	Calgary	ALB	Dave Browne	1996	*
179 2/8	25 1/8	24 7/8	23 4/8	5	6	Washington County	UT	Tracy Pitcher	1992	*
179 2/8	22 4/8	24 4/8	21 4/8	5	5	Huerfano County	CO	Jeff Elem	1993	*
179 1/8	24 6/8	24 6/8	23 7/8	5	5	Moose Jaw	SAS	Kevin Schauenberg	1995	*
179 0/8	25 4/8	24 1/8	23 6/8	5	5	Chaffee County	CO	David Morgan	1996	*
179 0/8	26 2/8	25 0/8	20 4/8	5	5	Coconino County	AZ	Ciriaco Joran Gramajo	1998	*
178 7/8	23 2/8	23 5/8	16 3/8	7	5	Jefferson County	CO	Dennis Modlin	1998	*
178 2/8	23 7/8	24 2/8	22 2/8	5	5	Garfield County	CO	Dale Jenkins	1994	*
177 6/8	25 7/8	25 7/8	22 7/8	6	6	San Juan County	UT	Clark A. Moss	1997	*
177 5/8	25 2/8	24 4/8	19 7/8	6	5	Kane County	UT	Brian Valdez	1997	*
177 5/8	25 3/8	26 5/8	28 5/8	7	6	Gunnison County	CO	Chris Johnson	1998	*
177 4/8	21 2/8	21 5/8	17 4/8	7	5	Elko County	NV	Rick Lund	1995	*
177 3/8	22 4/8	22 5/8	20 5/8	5	5	Elko County	NV	Kenneth R. Moores	1996	*
177 1/8	23 1/8	23 6/8	23 1/8	5	6	Grand County	UT	John E. Burton	1962	*
177 1/8	23 7/8	23 4/8	21 5/8	5	5	Converse County	WY	Erv Wagner	1995	*
176 6/8	24 4/8	23 6/8	22 4/8	5	5	Gunnison County	CO	Larry Zach	1996	*
175 5/8	24 2/8	24 1/8	20 1/8	5	5	Maple Creek	SAS	Dave Atamanchuk	1997	*
175 3/8	24 6/8	24 3/8	24 1/8	4	6	Harney County	OR	Patrick E. Wheeler	1992	*
174 3/8	24 1/8	23 0/8	24 2/8	5	5	La Plata County	CO	Paul Nichols	1998	*
173 6/8	24 1/8	24 2/8	21 2/8	5	5	McKinley County	NM	Richard W. Eustace, Jr.	1995	*
173 6/8	23 3/8	23 4/8	21 5/8	5	7	La Plata County	CO	Steven H. Byerly	1996	*
173 6/8	24 3/8	24 4/8	21 1/8	5	5	Sanpete County	UT	Steve Searle	1997	*
173 2/8	24 2/8	24 1/8	25 0/8	5	5	Colfax County	NM	Ronald G. Ralston	1993	*
173 2/8	24 6/8	23 7/8	21 4/8	5	5	Archuleta County	CO	Jerry R. Huff	1994	*
172 4/8	22 5/8	22 4/8	17 4/8	6	5	Garfield County	CO	Bob Kostecki	1973	*
172 4/8	22 3/8	22 4/8	23 5/8	5	5	Chaffee County	CO	Troy Long	1993	*
172 4/8	21 4/8	20 4/8	17 1/8	6	5	Lake County	CO	Raul E. Martinez	1995	*
172 4/8	25 4/8	24 5/8	20 6/8	5	6	McKinley County	NM	Frank Hausner	1996	*
172 3/8	24 4/8	24 7/8	23 7/8	5	5	San Juan County	UT	Jeff Cisneros	1997	*
172 2/8	23 4/8	24 3/8	22 6/8	5	5	Kane County	UT	Gregory A. Strait	1995	*
171 7/8	22 6/8	21 3/8	17 7/8	5	7	Adams County	ID	Kevin P. Stephenson	1991	*

MULE DEER (TYPICAL VELVET ANTLERS)

Minimum Score 145   Continued

SCORE	LENGTH OF R MAIN BEAM L		INSIDE SPREAD	NUMBER OF R POINTS L		AREA	STATE/ PROVINCE	HUNTER'S NAME	DATE	RANK
171 7/8	24 4/8	23 2/8	22 0/8	6	6	Douglas County	CO	Philip E. Gage	1995	*
171 6/8	24 4/8	25 2/8	20 6/8	6	6	Dolores County	CO	Ronny Stephens	1992	*
171 2/8	23 5/8	24 1/8	19 6/8	5	5	Elko County	NV	Jerry Giovannoni	1993	*
171 1/8	25 2/8	23 5/8	21 7/8	6	5	Humboldt County	NV	Carl Erquiaga	1997	*
170 3/8	22 6/8	23 5/8	21 5/8	5	5	Mesa County	CO	Richard Sandoz	1995	*
169 6/8	22 6/8	22 2/8	20 6/8	5	5	Franklin County	ID	Steven A. Dewey	1991	*
169 1/8	24 4/8	24 3/8	24 7/8	5	6	Garfield County	UT	Chester Hughes	1996	*
169 0/8	22 0/8	20 4/8	21 0/8	6	6	Mohave County	AZ	Kyle Bundy	1995	*
168 6/8	23 0/8	23 0/8	24 2/8	5	5	Delta County	CO	Lee McAdams	1997	*
168 5/8	23 0/8	24 1/8	22 7/8	5	5	Bernalillo County	NM	Chuck Thomas	1991	*
168 2/8	21 4/8	21 4/8	17 0/8	5	6	Morgan County	UT	Jeffery J. Petersen	1994	*
168 0/8	22 4/8	21 6/8	20 0/8	5	5	Boulder County	CO	Mike Delamater	1987	*
168 0/8	21 5/8	20 5/8	22 4/8	6	5	Coconino County	AZ	Charles Canterbury	1993	*
167 7/8	24 0/8	24 2/8	22 1/8	5	5	Gunnison County	CO	Mike Basso	1995	*
167 7/8	23 1/8	23 5/8	21 1/8	5	5	Grant County	OR	Allen Branch	1996	*
167 7/8	23 5/8	25 2/8	21 5/8	5	5	Elko County	NV	Mike Benton	1997	*
167 4/8	19 3/8	20 3/8	17 1/8	6	6	La Glace	ALB	Terrance McNally	1997	*
167 3/8	23 0/8	24 0/8	23 3/8	5	5	Kane County	UT	V. Randy Liljenquist	1990	*
167 3/8	24 5/8	24 0/8	24 3/8	5	5	Jefferson County	CO	Pete Stanton	1995	*
167 2/8	25 2/8	25 0/8	22 2/8	5	5	San Juan County	UT	Scott Staley	1989	*
167 2/8	23 2/8	23 2/8	21 0/8	5	5	Mesa County	CO	Darrell Springer	1995	*
167 0/8	22 7/8	22 1/8	18 0/8	5	5	Millard County	UT	Layne Foxley	1978	*
167 0/8	23 4/8	23 2/8	19 6/8	4	5	Rio Arriba County	NM	Dennis A. Muirhead	1991	*
167 0/8	24 3/8	23 2/8	23 4/8	5	5	La Plata County	CO	Christian Dean	1998	*
166 7/8	22 0/8	23 4/8	19 3/8	8	5	Kane County	UT	Joe Barker	1993	*
166 4/8	22 2/8	22 0/8	21 4/8	6	5	Coconino County	AZ	Dan Bohlen	1993	*
166 4/8	22 7/8	23 3/8	19 0/8	5	5	La Plata County	CO	Randy M. Riebe	1997	*
166 3/8	22 7/8	23 3/8	18 4/8	6	6	Morgan County	UT	Robert G. Petersen	1994	*
166 2/8	21 5/8	21 5/8	20 0/8	5	5	Coconino County	AZ	Gilbert Federico	1993	*
166 2/8	21 1/8	21 6/8	18 2/8	5	5	Emery County	UT	Stewart B. Jones	1998	*
166 0/8	21 7/8	19 1/8	20 2/8	5	5	Coconino County	AZ	John D. Carpenter	1994	*
166 0/8	24 6/8	23 7/8	22 6/8	5	5	Oyen	ALB	Ryk Visscher	1996	*
165 5/8	22 5/8	23 2/8	20 5/8	6	6	Grand County	UT	Jim Gunderson	1994	*
165 3/8	25 4/8	24 7/8	20 3/8	5	5	Kane County	UT	Monte Green	1995	*
164 7/8	22 1/8	21 4/8	22 1/8	5	5	Boulder County	CO	N. T. Bloomingdale	1996	*
164 5/8	24 4/8	23 2/8	21 0/8	4	6	La Plata County	CO	E. J. Hale	1995	*
164 4/8	22 0/8	21 3/8	17 2/8	5	5	Elko County	NV	Ron Anderson	1995	*
164 3/8	21 0/8	21 2/8	20 5/8	5	5	Coconino County	AZ	Roy E. Grace	1997	*
164 2/8	23 0/8	22 2/8	21 2/8	5	5	Carbon County	UT	Alex Cole	1995	*
164 0/8	23 0/8	21 5/8	22 2/8	5	5	Washoe County	NV	Cecil Martin	1997	*
163 5/8	24 6/8	22 4/8	20 6/8	5	7	Rio Blanco County	CO	Edward Meiter	1993	*
163 4/8	19 7/8	20 3/8	14 2/8	5	5	Sanpete County	UT	Robert Jensen	1986	*
163 4/8	24 0/8	23 6/8	24 4/8	4	5	San Juan County	UT	Jesse L. Keison	1993	*
163 4/8	21 3/8	20 7/8	18 2/8	5	5	San Juan County	UT	David W. Lemmens	1995	*
163 4/8	25 7/8	23 4/8	22 0/8	5	6	Montrose County	CO	James K. Harney	1996	*
163 3/8	21 7/8	22 3/8	19 6/8	6	8	Coconino County	AZ	Edward J. Whitworth	1991	*
163 2/8	22 2/8	21 2/8	20 4/8	5	5	Utah County	UT	Alex Fisher	1993	*
163 1/8	25 5/8	25 3/8	22 5/8	4	5	Harney County	OR	Patrick E. Wheeler	1995	*
163 1/8	21 1/8	21 5/8	18 7/8	5	5	Sevier County	UT	Darren Camblin	1997	*
163 0/8	23 4/8	23 7/8	20 6/8	5	5	Garfield County	CO	Dale Jenkins	1995	*
162 7/8	22 3/8	21 5/8	22 6/8	5	5	Washoe County	NV	Ralph L. Albright	1996	*
162 6/8	22 4/8	22 6/8	21 6/8	5	5	McKenzie County	ND	Scott Heit	1994	*
162 4/8	23 7/8	23 0/8	21 6/8	4	5	Sandoval County	NM	Robert L. Pagel	1991	*
162 4/8	21 6/8	20 7/8	22 0/8	4	4	San Juan County	UT	Tad Jones	1995	*
162 3/8	24 5/8	24 0/8	20 7/8	5	5	Montrose County	CO	Thomas G. Sprouse	1995	*
162 2/8	22 7/8	25 5/8	20 5/8	5	6	Grand County	UT	Ken Arveson, Jr.	1996	*
162 1/8	22 1/8	21 2/8	19 7/8	5	5	Kane County	UT	Donald Bergantz	1992	*
162 0/8	21 1/8	22 5/8	18 3/8	6	5	Mesa County	CO	Loran D. Nowlin	1987	*
161 6/8	22 2/8	22 0/8	18 0/8	5	5	Colfax County	NM	Ralph E. Johnson, Jr.	1996	*
161 4/8	22 6/8	22 3/8	20 2/8	4	4	La Plata County	CO	Brian T. Myers	1993	*
161 4/8	22 2/8	22 2/8	25 4/8	6	5	Humboldt County	NV	Jerry J. Jessee	1995	*
161 4/8	23 4/8	23 1/8	27 2/8	5	5	Lake County	OR	Parrey Cremeans	1997	*
161 3/8	24 6/8	24 2/8	22 4/8	5	5	Mesa County	CO	David G. Anderson	1976	*
161 3/8	21 3/8	22 2/8	19 7/8	4	5	Modoc County	CA	Matthew Haslett	1992	*
161 3/8	21 1/8	21 3/8	19 6/8	5	6	Dolores County	CO	Donald B. Howell	1993	*
161 1/8	21 0/8	22 0/8	20 3/8	5	5	Mesa County	CO	Art Rayner	1994	*
160 7/8	25 0/8	23 5/8	21 1/8	4	5	Humboldt County	NV	John F. Dow	1995	*
160 6/8	22 7/8	21 4/8	17 7/8	4	5	Rich County	UT	Patrick Hogle	1994	*
160 6/8	20 2/8	21 0/8	23 4/8	4	4	Catron County	NM	Ron Madsen	1998	*
160 5/8	20 5/8	21 3/8	18 7/8	5	4	Archuleta County	CO	Alan R. Gibbs	1995	*
160 4/8	23 6/8	22 2/8	20 5/8	5	7	Campbell County	WY	David Westmoreland	1993	*
160 4/8	20 0/8	21 1/8	19 2/8	5	5	Morgan County	UT	Justin Bliss	1997	*
160 3/8	22 4/8	22 0/8	19 3/8	5	5	Drumheller	ALB	Gary Gillett	1995	*
160 0/8	22 3/8	23 0/8	21 2/8	6	6	Union County	OR	Lane Arthur Geertz	1992	*
159 7/8	24 1/8	24 4/8	19 5/8	5	5	San Juan County	UT	Dino Perry	1992	*
159 7/8	22 4/8	21 1/8	19 5/8	5	5	Wasatch County	UT	Jesse Sugden	1994	*
159 6/8	23 2/8	23 4/8	20 6/8	6	4	Bonneville County	ID	Craig Keele	1975	*

MULE DEER (TYPICAL VELVET ANTLERS)

Minimum Score 145

SCORE	LENGTH OF MAIN BEAM R	LENGTH OF MAIN BEAM L	INSIDE SPREAD	NUMBER OF POINTS R	NUMBER OF POINTS L	AREA	STATE/ PROVINCE	HUNTER'S NAME	DATE	RANK
159 5/8	22 6/8	23 0/8	18 5/8	4	5	Mesa County	CO	Dan Ratchford	1993	*
159 4/8	20 1/8	21 6/8	19 2/8	5	5	Grand County	UT	Art Jordan	1996	*
159 0/8	23 1/8	24 1/8	20 4/8	5	5	Colfax County	NM	Charles Dooner	1993	*
159 0/8	22 2/8	22 2/8	24 3/8	5	6	Chouteau County	MT	Gus Smith	1996	*
159 0/8	23 1/8	22 6/8	20 0/8	5	4	Elko County	NV	John V. Bottari	1997	*
158 6/8	21 5/8	21 4/8	20 4/8	5	5	Montrose County	CO	David Westmoreland	1994	*
158 4/8	23 7/8	25 4/8	21 0/8	4	4	Morgan County	UT	Jeffery J. Petersen	1996	*
158 3/8	19 6/8	19 5/8	18 3/8	5	7	Sheridan County	WY	Mitch Cangiamilla	1993	*
158 3/8	22 7/8	22 0/8	18 0/8	6	5	Hinsdale County	CO	Shad D. Schmidt	1998	*
158 2/8	23 7/8	24 6/8	21 6/8	5	4	Mesa County	CO	Kevin R. Yineman	1994	*
158 1/8	23 5/8	23 0/8	20 2/8	7	6	Elko County	NV	Garner R. Reynolds	1996	*
158 0/8	22 3/8	22 0/8	22 5/8	6	5	Beaver County	UT	Jim Emerson	1996	*
157 7/8	23 1/8	21 2/8	19 2/8	7	6	Coconino County	AZ	Dennis Myer	1993	*
157 7/8	19 6/8	19 3/8	18 5/8	5	4	Summit County	UT	Dallas Smith	1996	*
157 6/8	21 1/8	20 0/8	16 4/8	5	5	Routt County	CO	Keith R. Bedenbaugh	1997	*
157 4/8	24 0/8	23 2/8	20 3/8	5	5	Rio Blanco County	CO	Nathan Van Risseghem	1995	*
157 2/8	22 3/8	21 3/8	17 6/8	5	5	Elko County	NV	Scott Meshefski	1995	*
157 2/8	23 4/8	22 1/8	20 6/8	5	5	Kane County	UT	Kenny E. Leo	1998	*
157 1/8	24 2/8	24 6/8	19 1/8	5	4	Elko County	NV	Jerry Vega	1995	*
157 0/8	21 3/8	20 4/8	16 2/8	5	5	Mesa County	CO	Frank Rutledge	1992	*
157 0/8	19 7/8	19 7/8	16 0/8	5	5	Garfield County	UT	David R. Whittle	1994	*
156 6/8	23 7/8	24 3/8	21 0/8	5	5	Uintah County	UT	Leon E. Caldwell	1996	*
156 2/8	20 4/8	18 2/8	18 6/8	5	5	Saguache County	CO	Joseph R. Wilhelm	1987	*
156 2/8	24 4/8	24 2/8	24 2/8	6	6	Kane County	UT	Blair Maxfield	1994	*
156 2/8	22 4/8	21 1/8	20 4/8	5	5	Elko County	NV	Rob Sampley	1997	*
156 1/8	23 7/8	23 4/8	21 1/8	8	6	Harney County	OR	Patrick E. Wheeler	1993	*
156 1/8	21 0/8	20 5/8	20 3/8	4	5	Powder River County	MT	Gene Smith	1996	*
155 7/8	24 6/8	23 1/8	18 6/8	8	5	White Pine County	NV	Wally Behrenz	1997	*
155 6/8	22 0/8	23 1/8	20 4/8	5	6	Montrose County	CO	David Westmoreland	1993	*
155 4/8	18 7/8	19 1/8	18 4/8	4	4	Mesa County	CO	Jim Bennett	1995	*
155 2/8	20 3/8	21 3/8	19 2/8	5	5	Nevada County	CA	Michael J. Bradeen	1993	*
155 2/8	21 6/8	23 3/8	19 4/8	5	4	Apache County	AZ	Aaron Scott	1997	*
155 1/8	24 6/8	25 0/8	19 5/8	4	5	Harney County	OR	Ken Brown	1992	*
155 1/8	21 2/8	22 6/8	19 1/8	5	5	San Juan County	UT	Jerome Hansmann	1993	*
155 0/8	21 3/8	21 4/8	23 2/8	4	4	Kane County	UT	Thomas J. Hoffman	1990	*
154 6/8	20 5/8	19 7/8	17 0/8	5	5	Nye County	NV	Ken Tavener	1993	*
154 6/8	20 5/8	21 2/8	18 2/8	5	5	Washakie County	WY	Richard Wormington	1993	*
154 3/8	24 1/8	22 4/8	19 3/8	5	5	Moffat County	CO	Scott Jankowski	1998	*
154 2/8	23 6/8	24 1/8	22 0/8	5	5	Washington County	UT	Sheila Hunt	1995	*
154 2/8	23 3/8	24 0/8	25 4/8	5	4	Archuleta County	CO	Beau J. Pack	1997	*
154 1/8	22 1/8	22 5/8	22 7/8	4	4	San Juan County	UT	Shane Stratton	1995	*
154 0/8	23 2/8	24 0/8	24 3/8	5	6	Mesa County	CO	Lenard Thomas	1990	*
154 0/8	21 2/8	19 7/8	17 2/8	4	4	Washington County	UT	Wayne Wittwer	1993	*
154 0/8	21 1/8	19 6/8	19 6/8	6	5	Coconino County	AZ	Travis Lubinski	1994	*
154 0/8	20 1/8	20 4/8	19 0/8	5	5	Wallowa County	OR	Dan LaPlaca	1996	*
153 7/8	23 7/8	24 0/8	24 5/8	5	5	Kane County	UT	Monte Mecham	1994	*
153 7/8	21 2/8	22 2/8	19 3/8	5	5	Mesa County	CO	Stephen C. Rogers	1994	*
153 6/8	23 0/8	22 6/8	22 2/8	4	5	Emery County	UT	Doug Luke	1998	*
153 5/8	23 5/8	21 5/8	20 1/8	6	5	Buffalo	ALB	Glenn E. Moir	1994	*
153 4/8	20 4/8	19 4/8	17 0/8	5	5	Mesa County	CO	Jeffrey M. Davis	1992	*
153 3/8	22 4/8	22 3/8	21 1/8	5	5	La Plata County	CO	Blake Snowden	1996	*
153 2/8	23 2/8	22 6/8	19 6/8	5	5	Durango County	CO	Mike Staton	1992	*
153 2/8	21 5/8	21 4/8	20 0/8	4	4	Moffat County	CO	Denis V. Joiner	1993	*
153 2/8	21 1/8	21 7/8	17 5/8	5	6	Millard County	UT	Daniel R. Thompson	1996	*
153 1/8	22 0/8	21 6/8	20 7/8	6	5	Crook County	OR	Michael R. Nelson	1998	*
153 0/8	21 6/8	21 2/8	20 6/8	5	5	Elko County	NV	Susan E. Dorsa	1996	*
153 0/8	23 3/8	24 7/8	20 6/8	4	5	Salt Lake County	UT	Dwight Neilson	1998	*
152 6/8	21 2/8	21 0/8	21 0/8	6	5	Mesa County	CO	Michael Berry	1992	*
152 6/8	20 1/8	19 7/8	17 2/8	4	4	Morgan County	UT	Jeffery J. Petersen	1997	*
152 5/8	23 4/8	23 6/8	22 3/8	5	4	Mesa County	CO	Todd Bennett	1997	*
152 4/8	19 1/8	20 0/8	16 7/8	7	6	Mesa County	CO	James Emmons	1995	*
152 4/8	21 0/8	20 6/8	23 0/8	7	6	Montrose County	CO	Amy A. Sunn	1996	*
152 3/8	21 1/8	21 2/8	20 6/8	4	5	Custer County	CO	Leon V. Evans	1996	*
152 2/8	20 2/8	21 3/8	19 6/8	5	5	Lincoln County	NV	Leonard T. Anderson, Jr.	1993	*
152 2/8	20 3/8	20 4/8	21 5/8	5	5	Washoe County	NV	Felton Hickman	1994	*
151 6/8	22 4/8	22 0/8	23 3/8	4	4	Elko County	NV	Larry D. Skinner	1995	*
151 6/8	24 1/8	25 4/8	22 0/8	3	4	Elko County	NV	Bob Sneed	1995	*
151 6/8	21 6/8	21 6/8	22 0/8	5	5	Fresno County	CA	Steven K. Pickens	1998	*
151 4/8	21 7/8	21 7/8	19 0/8	5	5	Elko County	NV	Greg Silva	1993	*
151 3/8	21 1/8	21 3/8	23 4/8	5	5	Iron County	UT	Terry Proctor	1992	*
151 2/8	22 1/8	23 0/8	16 7/8	4	5	Coconino County	AZ	Philip Rippey	1994	*
150 7/8	20 5/8	20 2/8	18 5/8	5	5	Mesa County	CO	Tod Bennett	1995	*
150 6/8	26 1/8	26 4/8	23 3/8	6	5	Grant County	OR	Reid Murphy	1993	*
150 6/8	24 0/8	23 7/8	20 2/8	5	7	Elko County	NV	Troy Paxton	1994	*
150 6/8	21 7/8	22 3/8	19 2/8	5	4	Humboldt County	NV	Mario L. Pereira	1996	*
150 4/8	22 5/8	22 0/8	21 0/8	5	5	Nevada County	CA	John R. Sample	1996	*
150 2/8	21 7/8	22 5/8	22 4/8	5	4	Kane County	UT	Michael Littleford	1994	*

MULE DEER (TYPICAL VELVET ANTLERS)

Minimum Score 145

SCORE	LENGTH OF MAIN BEAM R	LENGTH OF MAIN BEAM L	INSIDE SPREAD	NUMBER OF POINTS R	NUMBER OF POINTS L	AREA	STATE/PROVINCE	HUNTER'S NAME	DATE	RANK
150 1/8	21 0/8	20 0/8	16 1/8	5	5	Sanpete County	UT	Rod Frazier	1990	*
150 1/8	20 1/8	21 0/8	16 5/8	5	5	Columbia County	WA	Jeanie E. Robanske	1994	*
149 7/8	20 5/8	20 5/8	19 3/8	5	5	Mono County	CA	Stan Voss	1995	*
149 6/8	17 6/8	18 0/8	18 2/8	6	5	Mesa County	CO	Andrew Slocum	1992	*
149 4/8	20 3/8	20 6/8	22 2/8	5	6	Routt County	CO	Roger Niewiadomski, Jr.	1997	*
149 3/8	21 6/8	21 6/8	19 1/8	5	5	Colfax County	NM	Richard I. Albright	1995	*
149 2/8	22 4/8	21 6/8	20 4/8	5	5	Huerfano County	CO	R. Kirk Ehren	1993	*
149 2/8	20 6/8	21 4/8	22 4/8	5	4	Chouteau County	MT	Tom Wilson	1994	*
148 7/8	24 0/8	24 2/8	19 7/8	6	5	San Juan County	UT	Dustin Hackney	1997	*
148 7/8	25 4/8	26 0/8	25 1/8	4	5	Washoe County	NV	Dyrk Eddie	1998	*
148 6/8	20 6/8	19 3/8	16 0/8	5	5	Jefferson County	CO	Donald E. Griffin	1997	*
148 5/8	25 3/8	24 3/8	21 3/8	5	5	Modoc County	CA	William Vernon	1996	*
148 2/8	21 2/8	21 2/8	21 7/8	6	5	La Plata County	CO	Travis James Brookshire	1995	*
148 1/8	19 4/8	20 0/8	14 7/8	5	4	Uintah County	UT	M. Brett Miller	1985	*
148 0/8	24 1/8	23 2/8	22 4/8	4	5	Gunnison County	CO	Randy Scott Wendt	1994	*
147 6/8	23 4/8	23 4/8	23 0/8	4	4	Campbell County	WY	Richard E. LaCrone	1996	*
147 4/8	18 4/8	18 1/8	15 6/8	5	5	Eagle County	CO	Brian Soucie	1994	*
147 4/8	22 3/8	21 6/8	18 4/8	5	5	Mesa County	CO	Jack Davis	1994	*
147 3/8	21 4/8	22 0/8	18 5/8	5	5	Grand County	UT	John Labrum	1993	*
147 3/8	21 4/8	21 4/8	19 4/8	7	5	Coconino County	AZ	Ken Moore	1993	*
147 3/8	22 0/8	19 5/8	17 7/8	5	4	Big Horn County	WY	Joseph Liska	1995	*
147 1/8	21 1/8	21 1/8	17 5/8	5	5	Piute County	UT	Larry Soeltz	1994	*
147 1/8	22 7/8	21 5/8	21 5/8	5	5	Mono County	CA	Joel Wahlenmaier	1995	*
147 1/8	22 5/8	23 0/8	18 5/8	5	4	Elko County	NV	Timothy D. Park	1998	*
147 0/8	22 1/8	20 7/8	20 4/8	7	6	La Plata County	CO	Cody L. Abernathy	1996	*
146 7/8	25 5/8	21 4/8	17 1/8	6	5	Sheridan County	WY	Gary L. Shinn	1995	*
146 7/8	22 2/8	22 1/8	20 1/8	4	4	Elko County	NV	Taron Grant	1998	*
146 6/8	18 4/8	20 0/8	17 0/8	5	4	Colfax County	NM	Robert Torstenson	1995	*
146 5/8	26 2/8	26 5/8	20 1/8	5	5	San Juan County	UT	Judy F. Hallman	1985	*
146 3/8	22 2/8	20 5/8	15 7/8	4	4	Boulder County	CO	Dennis Modlin	1994	*
146 2/8	20 3/8	21 1/8	19 2/8	5	5	Morgan County	UT	Hal R. Stauff	1996	*
146 0/8	22 4/8	22 0/8	22 0/8	4	5	Catron County	NM	David Gardner	1995	*
146 0/8	20 1/8	21 7/8	17 4/8	5	4	White Pine County	NV	Roy K. Keefer	1998	*
145 5/8	21 5/8	19 7/8	16 4/8	6	5	Morgan County	UT	Justin Bliss	1992	*
145 5/8	22 1/8	22 2/8	19 3/8	4	5	San Juan County	UT	Mark S. Farr	1993	*
145 3/8	24 5/8	23 3/8	18 4/8	5	5	Piute County	UT	Larry Soeltz	1993	*
145 3/8	24 0/8	24 4/8	23 5/8	3	3	Fremont County	WY	Shane A. Pugh	1993	*
145 3/8	20 3/8	18 4/8	18 1/8	5	5	White Pine County	NV	Roy Keefer	1995	*
145 2/8	22 2/8	21 6/8	18 4/8	6	7	Bernalillo County	NM	Alvin Harris	1993	*
145 2/8	22 2/8	22 2/8	24 4/8	5	5	Grant County	WA	Dan A. Whitmus	1997	*
145 1/8	19 4/8	19 0/8	16 5/8	5	5	Chaffee County	CO	Alex Walker III	1994	*
145 0/8	22 2/8	22 0/8	24 5/8	4	4	Gunnison County	CO	Scott Hargrove	1995	*
145 0/8	18 4/8	19 0/8	17 2/8	4	4	Powder River County	MT	Charles M. Fogarty	1995	*

Velvet entries will be listed in only one record book.

World Record Mule Deer (Non-Typical Antlers)
Score: 274 7/8
Morgan County, Colorado - 1987
Hunter: Kenneth W. Plank

MULE DEER (NON-TYPICAL ANTLERS)

Minimum Score 170

Odocoileus hemionus and certain related subspecies

SCORE	LENGTH OF MAIN BEAM R	LENGTH OF MAIN BEAM L	INSIDE SPREAD	NUMBER OF POINTS R	NUMBER OF POINTS L	AREA	STATE/ PROVINCE	HUNTER'S NAME	DATE	RANK
274 7/8	23 7/8	26 2/8	27 0/8	23	12	Morgan County	CO	Kenneth W. Plank	1987	1
274 4/8	28 6/8	29 0/8	21 1/8	12	12	Lincoln County	MT	Andrew Keim	1978	2
269 0/8	24 7/8	24 0/8	23 6/8	10	14	Lane County	KS	Dean Hamilton	1989	3
258 2/8	26 6/8	26 7/8	24 0/8	13	11	Mesa County	CO	David Glick	1976	4
257 7/8	25 6/8	25 0/8	19 1/8	18	14	Klamath County	OR	Brad Smith	1992	5
250 2/8	24 4/8	25 2/8	23 7/8	9	10	Jefferson County	CO	Larry J. Jones	1994	6
246 6/8	25 1/8	27 4/8	24 6/8	12	11	Mesa County	CO	Dean Derby II	1976	7
236 1/8	25 5/8	25 2/8	18 3/8	10	11	Coconino County	AZ	Stanley L. McIntyre	1965	8
235 1/8	24 1/8	23 6/8	20 6/8	13	13	Garfield County	CO	Mark Martin	1997	9
234 4/8	26 4/8	27 2/8	23 7/8	10	8	Juab County	UT	Dennis M. Hickman	1972	11
232 5/8	26 3/8	24 7/8	20 3/8	11	10	Rio Blanco County	CO	Harold Boyack	1979	12
232 3/8	23 2/8	21 2/8	23 0/8	12	14	Arapahoe County	CO	James P. Verney	1974	13
229 7/8	27 5/8	28 0/8	25 7/8	6	7	Lambs Canyon	UT	Lee Lindley	1942	14
228 0/8	25 0/8	25 1/8	25 2/8	10	8	Garfield County	CO	Leo W. Bange	1994	15
227 4/8	20 0/8	20 0/8	21 6/8	13	14	Decatur County	KS	David Bainter	1993	16
226 5/8	24 0/8	23 6/8	22 4/8	12	8	Crook County	WY	Charles Lee Smith	1987	17
226 4/8	23 5/8	27 6/8	19 2/8	9	11	Iron County	UT	Neil "Bud" Rhodes	1959	18
226 2/8	19 1/8	22 1/8	19 5/8	12	11	Wichita County	KS	Stacy Hoeme	1992	19
225 4/8	23 4/8	23 2/8	22 0/8	10	13	Herd Unit 54	UT	John C. Balch	1965	20
225 2/8	24 2/8	24 2/8	23 1/8	12	7	Garfield County	CO	Dennis Quinn	1972	21
224 6/8	25 5/8	25 5/8	22 4/8	9	9	Ferry County	WA	Romie Hilderbrant	1963	22
224 1/8	25 7/8	24 6/8	24 2/8	10	9	Washakie County	WY	William T. Ivey	1987	23
224 0/8	25 6/8	23 6/8	25 6/8	8	12	Lake County	OR	Jeff Eggleston	1986	24
224 0/8	24 2/8	23 1/8	25 4/8	10	10	Rio Arriba County	NM	Donald Cost	1993	24
223 7/8	27 5/8	26 4/8	24 4/8	12	9	Uncompahgre Mtns.	CO	Steve Haynes	1972	26
222 6/8	21 0/8	22 4/8	21 2/8	13	8	Lane County	KS	Dean Hamilton	1990	27
222 4/8	24 6/8	23 7/8	25 3/8	9	8	Barber County	KS	Perry Smith	1990	28
222 3/8	27 1/8	27 4/8	22 5/8	11	11	DeWinton	ALB	Blaine Southgate	1991	29
222 3/8	26 5/8	25 5/8	24 4/8	7	15	Harris	SAS	Anne Schmidt	1994	29
222 1/8	23 2/8	23 7/8	19 4/8	8	7	San Juan County	UT	Louie Arko	1972	31
222 1/8	25 5/8	24 5/8	20 4/8	8	10	Montrose County	CO	Lavern Rucker	1975	31
221 1/8	26 4/8	26 1/8	22 6/8	11	11	Bernalillo County	NM	Timothy Dwyer	1985	33
221 1/8	24 2/8	26 0/8	24 5/8	11	13	Jefferson County	OR	Michael Barden	1993	33
220 6/8	20 4/8	18 4/8	19 0/8	15	12	Coconino County	AZ	Placido Alderette	1978	35
220 3/8	27 3/8	27 1/8	23 1/8	11	7	Sanpete County	UT	I. B. 'Blackie' Owen	1964	36
220 2/8	26 6/8	26 0/8	24 7/8	8	9	Uncompahgre Plateau	CO	Michael T. Schwitters	1971	37
220 1/8	27 6/8	26 5/8	26 2/8	5	6	Delbert County	CO	Jim Early	1992	38
220 0/8	24 0/8	22 7/8	20 3/8	14	9	Union County	OR	Jon D. Silver	1995	38
219 6/8	24 2/8	25 2/8	20 5/8	9	9	Trego County	KS	Robert Walt	1993	40
219 5/8	21 2/8	23 1/8	26 0/8	9	8	Mesa County	CO	Roger Lewis	1980	41
219 5/8	25 6/8	26 3/8	24 0/8	7	9	Yuma County	CO	Garry Neuschwanger	1993	41
218 5/8	25 4/8	24 0/8	19 1/8	9	8	Rio Arriba County	NM	Kyle G. Woffinden	1993	43
218 1/8	22 0/8	24 1/8	16 5/8	9	8	Lincoln County	WY	Mike Barrett	1987	44
218 0/8	27 0/8	27 5/8	27 0/8	7	9	San Juan County	UT	Harold Boyack	1974	45
218 0/8	26 1/8	25 0/8	25 0/8	8	9	Garfield County	CO	Bob Hill	1979	45
217 6/8	25 6/8	26 4/8	23 6/8	8	10	Caribou County	ID	James C. Ashley	1977	47
217 6/8	25 5/8	24 5/8	22 5/8	12	13	White Pine County	NV	Russell Suminski	1981	47
217 4/8	27 2/8	25 6/8	23 2/8	10	9	Jefferson County	OR	Bryan Clifton Piper	1995	49
217 2/8	23 5/8	23 7/8	21 0/8	14	7	Beaverhead County	MT	Bob L. Walker	1992	50
216 6/8	23 4/8	24 4/8	22 0/8	9	12	Garfield County	CO	Richard Lepak	1975	51
216 2/8	21 7/8	22 5/8	19 4/8	8	9	Mohave County	AZ	William Cross	1965	52
216 2/8	21 7/8	23 1/8	18 5/8	12	7	Harney County	OR	Glen Shelley	1994	52
215 7/8	23 5/8	24 5/8	20 7/8	9	8	Clark County	KS	Dan Fenton	1988	54
215 7/8	23 5/8	24 2/8	21 6/8	10	14	Weld County	CO	Jon Brodie	1993	54
215 5/8	21 3/8	23 0/8	16 6/8	7	10	Uintah County	UT	Jon E Bingham	1969	56
214 6/8	25 7/8	27 3/8	31 3/8	9	7	McKinley County	NM	R. Grant Clawson	1987	57
214 0/8	25 3/8	25 4/8	22 3/8	8	9	McCone County	MT	James F. Kosi	1974	58
213 5/8	26 0/8	26 0/8	24 2/8	7	9	Scott County	KS	Edward Stewart	1993	59
213 0/8	22 2/8	23 3/8	18 7/8	10	9	Caribou County	ID	Bob McAteer	1966	60
212 6/8	23 4/8	23 3/8	24 4/8	8	8	Ness County	KS	Ralph Stum	1966	61
212 6/8	25 4/8	22 6/8	20 5/8	8	11	Logan County	CO	Dan Fox	1997	61
212 2/8	25 1/8	24 0/8	24 4/8	8	9	Sherman County	KS	Wayne Luckert	1987	63
212 2/8	24 3/8	25 1/8	24 7/8	8	7	Dundy County	NE	Matt Gideon	1996	63
212 0/8	21 0/8	20 5/8	19 5/8	10	9	Calgary	ALB	Bert Frelink	1985	65
211 1/8	23 5/8	24 4/8	20 6/8	7	7	Uintah County	UT	Vern Hatch	1962	66
210 4/8	24 3/8	25 0/8	27 5/8	7	8	Montrose County	CO	Thomas Gloden	1963	67
210 2/8	22 2/8	27 6/8	27 2/8	4	7	Mesa County	CO	Art Cook	1972	68
209 7/8	25 4/8	22 6/8	23 0/8	10	9	Caribou County	ID	Ray Kagel	1992	69
209 5/8	26 0/8	24 0/8	26 2/8	10	7	Caribou County	ID	Mike Barrett	1994	70
209 1/8	26 1/8	26 1/8	28 1/8	8	8	Garfield County	CO	Mark Martin	1995	71
208 7/8	26 6/8	27 1/8	22 7/8	10	8	Duchesne County	UT	Smiley Arrowchis	1989	72
208 7/8	25 3/8	26 5/8	24 3/8	6	8	Dundurn	SAS	Christopher A. Thurlow	1997	72
208 3/8	23 6/8	26 7/8	23 6/8	10	8	Adams County	ID	Donnie Lee Voss	1986	74
208 2/8	25 6/8	25 1/8	25 5/8	9	7	Gove County	KS	Dean Hamilton	1992	75
208 1/8	25 6/8	25 5/8	21 7/8	8	8	Grand County	UT	Charles Denver	1986	76
207 7/8	25 4/8	25 4/8	22 4/8	7	7	Osborne County	KS	Bill Wilson	1997	77
207 4/8	24 3/8	25 1/8	22 7/8	8	7	Montrose County	CO	Barry Kerley	1980	78
207 0/8	24 2/8	23 0/8	20 6/8	7	5	Elmore County	ID	Deloy Desaro	1972	79

MULE DEER (NON-TYPICAL ANTLERS)

Minimum Score 170 — Continued

SCORE	LENGTH OF MAIN BEAM R	LENGTH OF MAIN BEAM L	INSIDE SPREAD	NUMBER OF POINTS R	NUMBER OF POINTS L	AREA	STATE/ PROVINCE	HUNTER'S NAME	DATE	RANK
206 7/8	22 2/8	24 1/8	22 1/8	7	9	Lemhi County	ID	A. Laverne Hokanson	1967	80
205 3/8	24 2/8	24 0/8	22 0/8	8	8	Grand County	UT	C. B. 'John' Olsen	1958	81
205 2/8	26 4/8	26 0/8	20 3/8	5	8	Elbert County	CO	Matt Burrows	1996	82
205 1/8	22 7/8	20 7/8	20 6/8	7	8	Cabri	SAS	Gene Andreas	1987	83
204 7/8	24 4/8	24 5/8	25 4/8	8	10	Washoe County	NV	Sean Shea	1997	84
204 4/8	26 2/8	22 6/8	17 5/8	7	9	Fishlake National Forest	UT	Dick Kerr	1955	85
204 3/8	23 6/8	25 3/8	18 1/8	8	8	Mesa County	CO	Don Zanow	1976	86
204 1/8	25 3/8	26 2/8	17 2/8	11	10	Umatilla County	OR	Dan Follett	1982	87
204 1/8	26 0/8	26 1/8	25 2/8	8	8	Routt County	CO	Dennis Rowley	1987	87
203 0/8	25 1/8	23 6/8	25 2/8	9	7	Brooks	ALB	Chuck Adams	1998	89
202 5/8	26 0/8	25 3/8	23 3/8	6	7	Garfield County	CO	A. H. Sandidge	1972	90
202 4/8	22 0/8	21 5/8	16 4/8	9	8	Sioux County	NE	Douglas Buckley	1982	91
202 3/8	21 7/8	21 5/8	20 3/8	7	9	Summit County	UT	Lynn C. Maxfield	1986	92
202 1/8	23 7/8	23 6/8	18 1/8	9	8	Lane County	KS	Dean Hamilton	1994	93
201 6/8	21 4/8	22 5/8	22 0/8	9	8	Caribou County	ID	Dennis Dockstader	1969	94
201 5/8	21 5/8	23 4/8	21 4/8	10	9	Gunnison County	CO	Mark Martin	1994	95
200 6/8	25 3/8	24 1/8	22 4/8	7	6	Caribou County	ID	Shawn Stockton	1992	96
200 4/8	22 6/8	23 4/8	20 5/8	8	10	Cochrane	ALB	Dave Carles	1991	97
200 3/8	24 4/8	24 3/8	19 4/8	8	9	Farm Creek	UT	Tex Ross	1966	98
200 2/8	27 5/8	26 2/8	19 1/8	9	8	Montezuma County	CO	Bryon C. Neeley	1971	99
200 1/8	23 7/8	22 1/8	20 2/8	7	8	Pima County	AZ	Jim Johnson	1981	100
199 6/8	25 4/8	24 7/8	24 4/8	9	7	Twin Falls County	ID	Marvin Hedberg	1995	101
199 1/8	22 6/8	23 4/8	19 1/8	9	10	Mesa County	CO	James R. Boyles	1971	102
198 5/8	21 6/8	22 6/8	23 4/8	9	8	Franklin County	KS	John R. Coblentz	1966	103
198 5/8	24 1/8	23 3/8	19 2/8	5	11	Teller County	CO	Robert Runkles	1986	103
198 3/8	23 7/8	27 1/8	24 6/8	7	9	Pueblo County	CO	Daniel Wyberg	1993	105
198 3/8	23 0/8	21 1/8	22 6/8	8	8	Pima County	AZ	Tracy G. Hardy	1994	105
198 1/8	25 3/8	25 1/8	26 7/8	9	6	Eagle County	CO	Mark Martin	1996	107
198 0/8	21 5/8	22 0/8	19 0/8	8	9	Routt County	CO	Bruce F. Davison	1968	108
197 7/8	26 5/8	26 3/8	25 0/8	9	7	Lincoln County	MT	Gary Weber	1978	109
197 5/8	22 0/8	21 1/8	20 5/8	10	8	Elmore County	ID	Jerry G. Fetters	1970	110
197 5/8	23 0/8	23 1/8	20 0/8	8	7	Eagle County	CO	Donald R. Hoard	1989	110
197 4/8	24 6/8	24 4/8	25 5/8	9	7	Morton County	KS	Kevin White	1982	112
197 2/8	23 6/8	23 0/8	29 4/8	7	6	Pima County	AZ	Adam Pence	1998	113
196 5/8	23 0/8	22 7/8	19 7/8	9	8	Eureka County	NV	Randy Buffington	1993	114
196 3/8	28 6/8	27 2/8	25 5/8	6	7	Campbell County	SD	Troy Hanson	1996	115
195 7/8	25 0/8	24 6/8	22 6/8	6	7	Lemhi County	ID	James Stuart	1982	116
195 6/8	21 2/8	22 6/8	19 3/8	9	9	Weld County	CO	Densel Bolin	1974	117
195 6/8	23 7/8	26 7/8	18 1/8	8	7	Sanders County	MT	Jerry V Finley	1989	117
195 4/8	25 2/8	23 2/8	22 3/8	9	14	Garfield County	CO	Douglas Kenyon	1964	119
195 1/8	24 5/8	24 0/8	24 2/8	8	8	Eagle County	CO	Mark Martin	1998	120
195 0/8	23 4/8	22 3/8	18 7/8	7	10	County of Taber	ALB	Quincy Jensen	1990	121
194 7/8	23 0/8	22 7/8	19 7/8	6	7	Finney County	KS	Jay Sloan	1967	122
194 7/8	26 5/8	25 3/8	22 3/8	6	7	Duchesne County	UT	Frank Warburton	1969	122
194 5/8	27 0/8	25 2/8	25 0/8	7	7	Bonneville County	ID	Robert A. Balser	1998	124
194 1/8	25 6/8	24 4/8	22 4/8	7	6	Dolores County	CO	Richard Hasler	1996	125
193 7/8	23 4/8	24 0/8	22 1/8	9	7	Baker County	OR	B. G. Shurtleff	1980	126
193 7/8	22 4/8	23 5/8	23 2/8	8	5	Kearny County	KS	Robert J. Price	1985	126
193 7/8	27 3/8	26 3/8	27 2/8	12	10	Yakima County	WA	James R. Lucas	1990	126
193 6/8	22 5/8	22 6/8	20 0/8	9	9	Utah County	UT	Ivan B. Henderson, Jr.	1959	129
193 4/8	25 1/8	25 0/8	23 0/8	6	6	Owyhee County	ID	Marte Scheuffele	1995	130
193 3/8	22 3/8	22 1/8	19 1/8	7	7	Adams County	CO	Dale Harrington	1992	131
193 2/8	22 3/8	22 3/8	19 4/8	12	14	Franklin County	ID	Jason Vogel	1996	132
192 7/8	19 7/8	20 4/8	16 5/8	12	11	Scott County	KS	Stacy Hoeme	1994	133
192 5/8	25 0/8	26 6/8	19 0/8	7	10	Modoc County	CA	Scott Young	1996	134
192 4/8	24 4/8	25 0/8	21 3/8	6	7	Caribou County	ID	Mack Tigert	1985	135
192 4/8	24 2/8	22 3/8	17 7/8	6	6	Delta County	CO	Larick F. Spencer	1996	135
191 7/8	22 2/8	19 1/8	17 6/8	7	12	Bell Marsh Canyon	ID	Loren H. Dunn	1965	137
191 7/8	22 4/8	21 1/8	18 6/8	8	6	Sublette County	WY	Marte Scheuffele	1985	137
191 4/8	23 2/8	24 3/8	17 1/8	5	10	Garfield County	CO	J. D. Jones	1971	139
191 4/8	23 6/8	23 6/8	20 6/8	7	8	Grant County	OR	Joe Mengore	1981	139
191 4/8	23 4/8	23 6/8	19 4/8	8	9	Grant County	NM	John H. Trewern	1997	139
191 1/8	23 1/8	24 3/8	22 0/8	7	9	Smith County	KS	Linton Haresnape	1981	142
191 0/8	23 6/8	21 2/8	16 2/8	8	9	Imperial County	CA	Michael S. Flynn	1986	143
190 6/8	23 5/8	22 4/8	21 3/8	6	7	Huerfano County	CO	Ron Johnson	1970	144
189 4/8	23 4/8	23 4/8	17 2/8	7	8	Johnson County	WY	Charles Jahnke	1979	145
189 3/8	26 2/8	25 4/8	16 7/8	11	16	Lincoln County	MT	Darryl L. Lyght	1992	146
189 1/8	20 1/8	22 2/8	19 3/8	6	8	Garfield County	CO	Robert C. McCardell	1974	147
189 0/8	25 1/8	24 6/8	25 2/8	12	11	Dawson County	MT	Monte Dassinger	1973	148
189 0/8	20 0/8	22 3/8	16 7/8	8	6	Garfield County	CO	Stephen Kennedy	1975	148
187 7/8	17 1/8	22 1/8	16 3/8	12	8	Grand County	UT	Lee Allred	1958	150
187 6/8	23 3/8	23 1/8	20 3/8	9	6	Routt County	CO	Thane Anderson	1993	151
187 5/8	22 3/8	24 7/8	23 0/8	7	6	Leduc	ALB	Mike Pewarchuk	1996	152
187 3/8	25 0/8	25 1/8	21 4/8	8	7	Albany County	WY	Larry Hudson	1996	153
187 2/8	22 0/8	22 0/8	21 2/8	6	6	Eagle County	CO	Gary O. Glenn	1978	154
187 2/8	23 2/8	23 7/8	20 6/8	9	7	Ouray County	CO	Roger Wyant	1984	154
187 2/8	24 1/8	23 3/8	22 0/8	7	10	Dundy County	NE	Matt Gideon	1995	154
187 2/8	26 4/8	27 1/8	21 2/8	6	6	Rio Arriba County	NM	Robert J. Seeds	1998	154

MULE DEER (NON-TYPICAL ANTLERS)

Minimum Score 170

Continued

SCORE	LENGTH OF MAIN BEAM R	LENGTH OF MAIN BEAM L	INSIDE SPREAD	NUMBER OF POINTS R	NUMBER OF POINTS L	AREA	STATE/PROVINCE	HUNTER'S NAME	DATE	RANK
187 1/8	23 1/8	22 1/8	20 4/8	8	6	Calgary	ALB	Dave Browne	1995	158
186 6/8	25 6/8	22 1/8	24 6/8	8	6	Dolores County	CO	Michael W. Forth	1978	159
186 6/8	24 3/8	22 0/8	23 7/8	7	7	Platte County	WY	Jerry Bowen	1996	159
186 5/8	23 0/8	23 6/8	22 6/8	8	9	Pin Horn Range	ALB	Giuliano Coslovi	1988	161
186 4/8	25 5/8	24 2/8	27 0/8	6	5	Pueblo County	CO	Dale Norman Bigger	1994	162
186 0/8	23 3/8	24 2/8	21 4/8	8	8	Chaffee County	CO	John D. Hambleton	1975	163
186 0/8	23 1/8	21 5/8	21 0/8	8	7	Ravalli County	MT	Ed Barrett	1983	163
185 7/8	22 7/8	22 3/8	18 0/8	11	8	Klamath County	OR	Charles A. Warner	1975	165
185 4/8	21 0/8	21 4/8	18 5/8	9	9	Hanna	ALB	Dale Drummond	1992	166
185 2/8	22 5/8	20 5/8	23 6/8	8	7	Scott County	KS	Richard B. Spencer	1986	167
184 3/8	22 2/8	23 0/8	20 6/8	8	7	Culberson County	TX	Joe Montoya	1996	168
184 2/8	20 5/8	21 5/8	19 3/8	8	6	Duchesne County	UT	Dean Reynolds	1961	169
184 0/8	23 0/8	22 3/8	17 2/8	7	11	Rosebud County	MT	Rick Miller	1997	170
183 5/8	20 3/8	20 0/8	15 3/8	7	9	Didsbury	ALB	Paul Boody	1993	171
183 3/8	25 5/8	25 1/8	25 0/8	6	7	Franklin County	ID	Doug Ransom	1985	172
183 3/8	20 2/8	19 6/8	17 7/8	6	6	Laramie County	WY	Brian Rhead	1998	172
183 2/8	22 7/8	23 4/8	20 2/8	7	6	Scott County	KS	Stacy Hoeme	1995	174
182 5/8	19 5/8	19 5/8	16 3/8	7	7	Valley County	ID	Charles "Chuck" Boatman	1986	175
182 0/8	25 0/8	24 4/8	23 7/8	7	8	Kootenai County	ID	Rodney W. Willis	1977	176
181 7/8	22 7/8	23 5/8	19 5/8	7	6	Russell County	KS	Drew McCartney	1993	177
181 7/8	25 0/8	23 1/8	25 2/8	6	7	Scott County	KS	John C. Walker	1996	177
181 6/8	25 3/8	24 5/8	20 7/8	7	10	Red Deer Lake	ALB	Jeff Thomson	1996	179
181 5/8	27 0/8	24 3/8	23 4/8	7	9	Chelan County	WA	David M. Bartholemew	1967	180
181 4/8	27 5/8	26 3/8	27 4/8	5	7	Park County	CO	John Cliff	1967	181
181 3/8	23 1/8	22 6/8	23 0/8	9	8	Wichita County	KS	Stacy C. Hoeme	1986	182
181 2/8	25 6/8	26 2/8	25 2/8	6	7	Lane County	KS	Dean Hamilton	1995	183
181 0/8	22 1/8	20 7/8	19 3/8	8	9	McKenzie County	ND	Harvey K. Schlosser	1996	184
180 7/8	22 5/8	23 3/8	21 0/8	6	6	Gray County	KS	James R. Sobba	1991	185
180 7/8	22 1/8	24 3/8	19 5/8	6	5	Twin Falls County	ID	Ernie Owen	1995	185
180 7/8	23 2/8	24 1/8	22 0/8	5	9	Dona Ana County	NM	Kyle Traylor	1998	185
180 4/8	21 1/8	22 5/8	21 3/8	7	5	Utah County	UT	Frank Warburton	1972	188
180 2/8	23 4/8	24 4/8	27 5/8	9	7	Ness County	KS	Jed Bain	1992	189
180 1/8	22 4/8	24 4/8	19 4/8	9	7	Caribou County	ID	Ronald L. Owens	1998	190
180 0/8	23 5/8	25 1/8	23 1/8	7	8	Lassen County	CA	Jeff Gravano	1994	191
180 0/8	21 7/8	21 6/8	24 5/8	9	8	Baker County	OR	Richard Condos	1998	191
179 6/8	26 1/8	25 4/8	24 4/8	6	6	Converse County	WY	Lee Jernigan	1998	193
179 3/8	23 7/8	24 0/8	22 7/8	6	7	Morrow County	OR	Russ Brannon	1997	194
179 0/8	23 4/8	23 4/8	19 5/8	7	6	Jefferson County	OR	Brett Henderson	1995	195
179 0/8	20 0/8	20 0/8	18 2/8	6	7	Coconino County	AZ	James E. Riner	1998	195
178 5/8	25 3/8	24 6/8	31 0/8	6	7	San Juan County	UT	Guy Gates	1970	197
178 3/8	22 4/8	20 6/8	18 5/8	5	7	Boulder County	CO	Heath Dillon	1997	198
178 2/8	22 3/8	23 7/8	24 6/8	8	4	Calgary	ALB	Lindsey Paterson	1990	199
178 0/8	20 2/8	20 7/8	18 3/8	8	8	Las Animas County	CO	Michael A. Mattorano	1989	200
177 7/8	21 2/8	18 6/8	20 2/8	6	7	Garfield County	CO	Steve Byerly	1980	201
177 4/8	24 4/8	22 2/8	26 1/8	9	7	Rio Arriba County	NM	Michael D. Bruce	1986	202
177 4/8	22 2/8	20 2/8	19 0/8	6	7	Billings County	ND	Douglas Kerska	1993	202
177 4/8	22 2/8	21 2/8	20 2/8	9	6	Elko County	NV	Tim Pruitt	1996	202
177 3/8	21 1/8	22 4/8	23 3/8	9	8	Dawson County	MT	Gerald Polesky	1970	205
177 0/8	23 4/8	23 0/8	19 3/8	6	5	Calgary	ALB	Dave Browne	1997	206
176 7/8	20 5/8	22 5/8	21 2/8	7	7	Rock Creek	CO	Adolph Kuhns	1961	207
176 6/8	25 1/8	22 4/8	27 0/8	6	5	Grant County	OR	Chuck Warner	1983	208
176 0/8	23 3/8	23 5/8	20 4/8	6	6	Scott County	KS	Vince Strickler	1975	209
176 0/8	22 1/8	23 0/8	17 4/8	7	7	Gove County	KS	Rick Kreuter	1991	209
176 0/8	22 3/8	22 2/8	20 5/8	6	6	Park County	WY	Tracy A. LaFollette	1994	209
175 7/8	19 4/8	20 7/8	18 6/8	6	6	Routt County	CO	Chuck Nemec	1974	212
175 7/8	25 0/8	24 6/8	25 1/8	6	7	Jackson County	CO	Timothy Lee Nichols	1994	212
175 3/8	20 6/8	24 2/8	29 0/8	9	9	Ness County	KS	Pete McBee	1969	214
175 3/8	24 2/8	23 2/8	17 3/8	7	8	Culberson County	TX	Gary Oden	1985	214
174 6/8	22 5/8	21 2/8	24 0/8	6	9	Custer County	CO	Kurt Keskimaki	1981	216
174 5/8	22 4/8	23 3/8	19 6/8	6	8	Milk River	ALB	Stan Godfrey	1997	217
174 3/8	23 4/8	24 3/8	23 5/8	7	8	Dawson County	MT	Richard Harms	1972	218
174 3/8	21 1/8	21 2/8	22 1/8	6	7	Platte County	WY	Jerry Bowen	1995	218
174 2/8	23 6/8	23 1/8	22 0/8	9	10	Mesa County	CO	Art Cook	1958	220
174 1/8	25 7/8	24 5/8	18 7/8	7	5	Carbon County	UT	B. E. Epperson	1971	221
173 7/8	20 7/8	21 0/8	20 3/8	7	5	Lane County	KS	Dean Hamilton	1997	222
173 3/8	20 4/8	26 6/8	20 3/8	6	5	Morrow County	OR	Ray Kelton	1976	223
173 2/8	21 3/8	21 3/8	21 4/8	8	8	Elmore County	ID	Peter J. Cintorino	1980	224
173 1/8	19 7/8	22 1/8	17 1/8	8	7	Dawes County	NE	LaVerne J. Weber	1975	225
173 0/8	22 1/8	21 3/8	16 1/8	7	6	Culberson County	TX	Gary J. Oden	1988	226
173 0/8	23 2/8	23 3/8	20 3/8	8	6	Campbell County	SD	Douglas Goehring	1995	226
172 7/8	25 6/8	26 4/8	29 0/8	6	6	Grant County	OR	Ray Kelton	1980	228
172 7/8	23 4/8	24 3/8	22 2/8	8	5	Slope County	ND	Todd Seymanski	1982	228
172 7/8	24 0/8	24 6/8	20 6/8	9	7	Chouteau County	MT	Mike Chouinard	1995	228
172 4/8	20 5/8	22 4/8	20 7/8	7	10	Taber	ALB	Gary Peters	1997	231
171 7/8	24 0/8	23 4/8	20 4/8	5	7	Campbell County	WY	Paul Vomela	1992	232
171 5/8	22 0/8	20 6/8	20 1/8	6	6	Douglas County	CO	Bruce Hoover	1994	233
171 4/8	22 2/8	20 1/8	16 3/8	5	12	Mesa County	CO	Paul H. Dickson	1985	234
171 3/8	21 1/8	22 1/8	21 1/8	8	6	Meade County	KS	Richard A. Nordyke	1971	235

MULE DEER (NON-TYPICAL ANTLERS)

Minimum Score 170 — Continued

SCORE	LENGTH OF MAIN BEAM R	LENGTH OF MAIN BEAM L	INSIDE SPREAD	NUMBER OF POINTS R	NUMBER OF POINTS L	AREA	STATE/PROVINCE	HUNTER'S NAME	DATE	RANK
171 3/8	18 7/8	21 3/8	18 3/8	8	6	Magrath	ALB	Cameron Cook	1994	235
171 1/8	23 0/8	23 7/8	20 2/8	7	5	Niobrara County	WY	Rickey E. Morse	1998	237
171 0/8	23 5/8	24 0/8	21 5/8	5	8	Billings County	ND	Michael H. Cummings	1996	238
170 7/8	18 4/8	20 0/8	17 1/8	6	6	Wallowa County	OR	Wayne Van Zwoll	1977	239
170 6/8	23 6/8	24 1/8	21 2/8	7	7	Valley County	ID	John Pyle	1978	240
170 5/8	22 0/8	22 1/8	16 3/8	6	5	Lake County	OR	Bill Hendrick	1964	241
170 5/8	20 3/8	19 5/8	20 4/8	5	7	McCone County	MT	David Tofte	1985	241
170 3/8	19 0/8	22 6/8	19 3/8	8	6	Cardston	ALB	Bob W. Ehle	1996	243
170 0/8	19 5/8	17 5/8	19 5/8	7	5	Finney County	KS	Rod Lies	1968	244
170 0/8	25 6/8	15 5/8	21 0/8	6	6	Bingham County	ID	Tim Moon	1996	244

MULE DEER (NON-TYPICAL VELVET ANTLERS)

Minimum Score 170

SCORE	LENGTH OF MAIN BEAM R	LENGTH OF MAIN BEAM L	INSIDE SPREAD	NUMBER OF POINTS R	NUMBER OF POINTS L	AREA	STATE/PROVINCE	HUNTER'S NAME	DATE	RANK
264 6/8	23 7/8	23 6/8	22 7/8	12	16	Coconino County	AZ	Bruce Felker	1993	*
233 5/8	29 5/8	27 4/8	26 7/8	7	9	Montrose County	CO	Doug Aikin	1988	*
228 6/8	25 2/8	27 2/8	19 3/8	12	8	Utah County	UT	Maurice T. Patterson	1971	*
227 3/8	26 4/8	26 5/8	20 7/8	8	7	White Pine County	NV	Tony Angelopoulos	1968	*
223 5/8	25 7/8	27 1/8	24 1/8	10	9	Jefferson County	CO	Daved English	1991	*
219 6/8	22 3/8	22 4/8	21 6/8	11	8	La Plata County	CO	Terry Grimes	1997	*
219 5/8	22 6/8	23 3/8	22 3/8	9	7	Garfield County	UT	Todd Shakespeare	1992	*
217 6/8	25 0/8	23 7/8	26 2/8	6	8	Coconino County	AZ	Lance D. Robinson	1992	*
214 3/8	25 4/8	26 0/8	24 3/8	11	9	Caribou County	ID	Royce Brown	1984	*
214 3/8	22 1/8	21 3/8	21 7/8	12	9	Boise County	ID	Dan Higgs	1992	*
210 3/8	26 6/8	23 3/8	22 0/8	10	9	Mesa County	CO	Larry Stewart	1975	*
209 7/8	26 7/8	25 4/8	28 1/8	12	8	Humboldt County	NV	Mike Nuttall	1995	*
209 4/8	24 0/8	24 0/8	22 1/8	8	7	Kane County	UT	Marvin Thayn	1987	*
208 4/8	26 5/8	25 2/8	19 1/8	8	10	Box Elder County	UT	Peter D. Garcia III	1988	*
207 6/8	22 5/8	21 7/8	20 3/8	7	8	Sanpete County	UT	L. Boyd Brewer	1967	*
207 5/8	25 5/8	24 6/8	20 7/8	7	10	San Juan County	UT	David Snyder	1993	*
207 0/8	25 0/8	24 1/8	21 6/8	11	9	Coconino County	AZ	Shawn Migacz	1992	*
206 5/8	26 2/8	25 6/8	21 1/8	8	7	Elko County	NV	Anthony "Tony" A. Waidell	1967	*
206 5/8	22 7/8	23 5/8	21 0/8	7	10	La Plata County	CO	Darrell D. Paulek	1994	*
206 0/8	23 1/8	24 0/8	16 5/8	10	6	Sheridan County	WY	Stan Chiras	1989	*
205 5/8	23 5/8	24 6/8	21 2/8	9	9	Washoe County	NV	Benjamin Mull	1992	*
205 4/8	23 5/8	24 1/8	18 4/8	7	8	Humboldt County	NV	Neil J. Russell	1996	*
204 7/8	24 5/8	24 4/8	21 2/8	10	6	Washoe County	NV	Michael Ellena	1992	*
204 2/8	26 2/8	24 5/8	20 0/8	7	6	Garfield County	CO	Van T. Gray	1978	*
203 3/8	23 0/8	25 1/8	25 4/8	13	8	Sheridan County	WY	Mike Barrett	1981	*
203 1/8	23 2/8	23 1/8	19 7/8	7	9	Pershing County	NV	Patrick R. Michael	1995	*
202 5/8	23 0/8	22 6/8	17 7/8	9	9	Mesa County	CO	Charles Wehmeyer	1964	*
202 3/8	23 1/8	24 5/8	18 0/8	9	8	Eagle County	CO	Rudy Meyers	1974	*
202 3/8	21 3/8	22 4/8	20 0/8	8	8	Millard County	UT	Dennis Staley	1983	*
202 1/8	24 0/8	23 3/8	19 6/8	8	8	Colfax County	NM	Robert Torstenson	1996	*
202 0/8	26 4/8	27 0/8	26 2/8	5	6	Coconino County	AZ	Lee Braudt	1994	*
201 5/8	22 7/8	22 0/8	20 2/8	8	8	Coconino County	AZ	Michael Wood Magee	1992	*
201 0/8	22 6/8	22 0/8	16 7/8	6	9	Coconino County	AZ	Kevin Button	1994	*
200 7/8	27 2/8	26 3/8	25 5/8	6	7	Kane County	UT	Stewart B. Jones	1993	*
200 6/8	24 5/8	23 3/8	19 0/8	8	10	Duchesne County	UT	Randy Quick	1987	*
200 6/8	23 3/8	22 4/8	21 2/8	9	9	San Juan County	UT	Jeremy Harness	1991	*
200 2/8	22 7/8	22 3/8	18 3/8	7	8	Coconino County	AZ	Reggie Curry	1993	*
199 6/8	25 6/8	24 5/8	20 2/8	6	9	Vulcan	ALB	Randall G. Forsyth	1993	*
199 1/8	25 3/8	25 6/8	23 2/8	5	5	Kyle	SAS	Ed Medl	1996	*
199 0/8	24 5/8	24 5/8	18 6/8	7	10	Millarville	ALB	Joel Bickler	1996	*
197 4/8	22 2/8	22 5/8	23 1/8	9	8	Washoe County	NV	Thomas C. McMillan	1992	*
194 3/8	23 2/8	24 7/8	18 4/8	6	6	La Plata County	CO	Steve Vittetow	1998	*
193 4/8	23 2/8	23 5/8	21 6/8	7	6	Saguache County	CO	Barry J. Smith	1987	*
193 2/8	23 1/8	23 4/8	19 0/8	5	6	Salt Lake County	UT	Tim J. Misewicz	1995	*
193 1/8	23 3/8	23 2/8	19 7/8	8	7	Morgan County	UT	Dennis L. Shirley	1992	*
192 3/8	27 3/8	25 7/8	22 7/8	8	6	Montrose County	CO	Michael E. Ray	1996	*
191 5/8	23 4/8	23 1/8	22 3/8	8	7	Pitkin County	CO	Glen L. Mahlum	1990	*
189 3/8	20 0/8	23 3/8	20 5/8	6	8	Eagle County	CO	Coy W. Ford II	1995	*
188 4/8	26 4/8	25 5/8	30 6/8	5	6	Kane County	UT	Thomas J. Hoffman	1991	*
188 0/8	24 3/8	23 7/8	22 3/8	6	7	Coconino County	AZ	Dwayne Oberhoff	1994	*
186 0/8	23 2/8	23 7/8	20 3/8	10	10	Jefferson County	OR	Keith A. Mayor	1996	*
184 4/8	24 0/8	23 3/8	21 0/8	6	4	Lincoln County	NV	Rocky Chisholm	1988	*
184 4/8	22 3/8	23 3/8	17 3/8	6	6	Penticton	BC	Ernest Testani/Nick Testani	1993	*
183 2/8	24 0/8	22 7/8	23 0/8	10	7	Churchill County	NV	Gregg Tanner	1989	*
179 4/8	24 1/8	24 1/8	18 5/8	7	7	Baker County	OR	Chuck Warner	1989	*

MULE DEER (NON-TYPICAL VELVET ANTLERS)

Minimum Score 170

SCORE	LENGTH OF MAIN BEAM R	LENGTH OF MAIN BEAM L	INSIDE SPREAD	NUMBER OF POINTS R	NUMBER OF POINTS L	AREA	STATE/PROVINCE	HUNTER'S NAME	DATE	RANK
179 1/8	26 4/8	27 3/8	20 6/8	6	6	Coconino County	AZ	James L. Denham	1993	*
178 1/8	23 1/8	23 5/8	17 3/8	7	6	Natrona County	WY	Brian L. Wagner	1996	*
178 0/8	21 0/8	22 3/8	17 4/8	7	7	Sheridan County	WY	David Alde	1996	*
177 6/8	25 7/8	25 5/8	22 1/8	8	6	Mesa County	CO	Thomas J. Hentrick	1972	*
176 3/8	22 1/8	19 0/8	23 4/8	6	11	Coconino County	AZ	Carl J. Pugliese	1991	*
175 6/8	24 6/8	26 6/8	20 1/8	4	9	Jackson County	CO	Rick Hatter	1986	*
175 1/8	24 5/8	23 2/8	20 2/8	7	7	Park County	CO	Marvin Clyncke	1996	*
172 5/8	22 7/8	23 2/8	18 1/8	7	5	Delta County	CO	Gary Parker	1995	*
170 1/8	19 6/8	19 7/8	15 4/8	8	6	Garfield County	UT	E. Kip Fowler	1998	*

* *Velvet entries will be listed in only one record book.*

World Record Whitetail Deer (Typical Antlers)
Score: 204 4/8
Peoria County, Illinois - 1965
Hunter: Mel Johnson

WHITETAIL DEER (TYPICAL ANTLERS)

Minimum Score 125

Odocoileus virginianus and certain related subspecies

SCORE	LENGTH OF MAIN BEAM R	LENGTH OF MAIN BEAM L	INSIDE SPREAD	NUMBER OF POINTS R	NUMBER OF POINTS L	AREA	STATE/PROVINCE	HUNTER'S NAME	DATE	RANK
204 4/8	27 5/8	26 6/8	23 3/8	7	6	Peoria County	IL	M. J. Johnson	1965	1
197 6/8	25 6/8	26 4/8	18 6/8	7	7	Monroe County	IA	Lloyd Goad	1962	2
197 6/8	29 1/8	30 2/8	20 4/8	6	5	Wright County	MN	Curt Van Lith	1986	2
197 1/8	30 0/8	27 7/8	29 0/8	6	7	Edmonton	ALB	Don McGarvey	1991	4
195 7/8	26 1/8	27 7/8	20 5/8	6	6	Anoka County	MN	Barry Peterson	1995	5
194 2/8	26 5/8	25 0/8	21 0/8	6	6	Jones County	IA	Robert L. Miller	1977	6
194 0/8	25 6/8	25 3/8	23 6/8	6	7	Logan County	CO	Stuart Clodfelder	1981	7
194 0/8	27 4/8	27 1/8	19 0/8	5	5	Johnson County	IA	Steven E. Tyer	1994	7
193 5/8	29 4/8	29 0/8	19 6/8	7	7	Monroe County	IA	Roy Allison	1995	9
193 3/8	28 4/8	27 3/8	21 0/8	8	6	Henry County	IA	Sam Collora	1996	10
193 2/8	28 3/8	27 7/8	22 2/8	8	6	Jackson County	MI	Craig Calderone	1986	11
191 0/8	28 1/8	27 1/8	20 2/8	5	5	Scott County	IA	Jeffery L. Whisker	1993	12
190 5/8	27 0/8	27 1/8	18 0/8	5	7	Warren County	IA	Richard Swim	1981	13
190 4/8	28 6/8	28 3/8	20 0/8	5	6	Parke County	IN	B. Dodd Porter	1985	14
189 4/8	25 4/8	24 7/8	20 0/8	6	7	Monmouth County	NJ	Scott William Borden	1995	15
189 1/8	27 3/8	28 6/8	20 1/8	8	7	Kearney County	NE	Robert Vrbsky	1978	16
189 1/8	27 6/8	28 3/8	20 1/8	6	6	Allamakee County	IA	Randy Petersburg	1996	16
188 7/8	28 2/8	27 3/8	19 2/8	6	7	Shelby County	IL	James M. Holley	1995	18
188 2/8	25 3/8	26 2/8	17 7/8	8	10	Marion County	KY	Tim Raikes	1996	19
188 1/8	28 6/8	27 3/8	22 2/8	8	8	Des Moines County	IA	Kevin Peterson	1989	20
187 7/8	26 6/8	27 4/8	18 0/8	7	7	Neosho County	KS	Gary C. Freeman	1995	21
187 2/8	28 6/8	29 4/8	20 4/8	5	7	Nemaha County	KS	Doug Selbe	1995	22
187 0/8	29 5/8	29 0/8	18 0/8	7	6	Warren County	IL	John K. Poole	1994	23
186 5/8	24 4/8	24 7/8	16 7/8	7	10	Langlade County	WI	Fred J. Hofmann	1994	24
186 1/8	25 3/8	24 0/8	16 7/8	6	8	Sumner County	KS	Greg Hill	1988	25
186 1/8	31 2/8	30 5/8	24 0/8	5	8	Morris County	KS	Craig Johnson	1991	25
186 1/8	27 6/8	27 3/8	20 1/8	5	5	Buchanan County	IA	Garry W. Rasmussen	1994	25
185 6/8	26 3/8	26 2/8	20 7/8	8	8	Bryan County	OK	Larry Luman	1997	28
185 1/8	25 7/8	26 6/8	20 3/8	9	7	Jackson County	IL	Mark Guetersloh	1990	29
184 3/8	26 5/8	26 0/8	19 0/8	6	6	Keokuk County	IA	Randy Schmidt	1995	30
184 1/8	31 2/8	32 0/8	20 0/8	6	7	Marshall County	KS	Roger D. Seematter	1994	31
183 4/8	26 4/8	27 2/8	16 2/8	5	5	Monona County	IA	Dave Zima	1996	32
183 3/8	27 5/8	27 1/8	20 1/8	5	5	Talbot County	MD	Petey Councell	1994	33
183 2/8	29 1/8	28 3/8	20 4/8	5	6	Shawnee County	KS	Mark W. Young	1990	34
182 5/8	27 6/8	28 5/8	19 2/8	7	5	Republic County	KS	Jody Hadachek	1995	35
182 4/8	29 0/8	29 0/8	19 0/8	6	7	Bremer County	IA	Dave Elmore	1992	36
182 4/8	27 0/8	28 4/8	19 2/8	6	6	Franklin County	IL	Tim Broy	1997	36
182 2/8	27 2/8	28 3/8	21 1/8	8	6	Jefferson County	KS	John Welborn	1982	38
182 0/8	26 5/8	28 6/8	22 1/8	6	7	Jefferson County	KS	Michael J. Rose	1982	39
181 7/8	28 6/8	27 0/8	21 6/8	5	7	Greenwood County	KS	Boyd Schneider	1984	40
181 7/8	26 6/8	26 5/8	21 7/8	7	6	Dakota County	MN	Eugene Lengsfeld	1985	40
181 7/8	25 3/8	27 3/8	21 3/8	5	5	Logan County	IL	Terry Lee Rich	1986	40
181 7/8	27 2/8	26 5/8	19 6/8	6	7	Jefferson County	OH	Brad L. Eibel	1988	40
181 7/8	27 7/8	26 3/8	20 3/8	7	8	Phillips County	KS	GLen Eller	1993	40
181 7/8	27 4/8	26 5/8	20 5/8	6	6	Van Buren County	IA	Michael C. Mott	1995	40
181 6/8	26 1/8	26 4/8	17 6/8	5	5	Wabasha County	MN	Lee G. Partington	1971	46
181 6/8	27 5/8	27 7/8	21 4/8	5	5	Sussex County	DE	Donald Betts	1989	46
181 6/8	27 5/8	28 3/8	21 2/8	6	6	Bourbon County	KS	Larry Daly	1990	46
181 5/8	24 7/8	25 6/8	24 1/8	6	5	Racine County	WI	Andrae D'Acquisto	1996	49
181 4/8	29 6/8	29 5/8	24 2/8	6	5	Keya Paha County	NE	Steve R. Pecsenye	1966	50
181 4/8	26 0/8	28 5/8	18 6/8	9	7	Fulton County	IL	Arnold Hegele	1968	50
181 4/8	26 5/8	26 7/8	24 4/8	5	6	North Norfolk	MAN	Lloyd Lintott	1986	50
181 4/8	25 7/8	26 7/8	19 0/8	8	5	Reno County	KS	Charles McHaley, Jr.	1994	50
181 2/8	26 2/8	25 2/8	22 2/8	5	6	Will County	IL	Joseph Skubisz	1996	54
181 2/8	29 5/8	28 7/8	22 7/8	6	6	McHenry County	IL	Gary E. Konopasek	1997	54
180 5/8	26 6/8	26 4/8	20 5/8	5	5	Jefferson County	KS	Ron Artzer	1987	56
180 4/8	24 7/8	26 4/8	21 0/8	5	5	Henry County	IA	Jeff L. Weigert	1991	57
180 4/8	29 4/8	27 7/8	21 4/8	8	5	Ross County	OH	Gerald F. Hamm	1991	57
180 4/8	26 1/8	25 6/8	18 5/8	6	6	Perry County	IL	Mike Schneider	1991	57
180 3/8	26 5/8	27 5/8	19 5/8	7	8	Dakota County	MN	Bill Urbaniak	1996	60
180 2/8	25 3/8	25 6/8	20 1/8	8	6	Jefferson County	WI	Randy Latsch	1995	61
180 1/8	25 4/8	24 2/8	17 5/8	6	6	Winona County	MN	Kenneth W. Schreiber	1980	62
180 1/8	30 6/8	30 6/8	21 2/8	7	5	Mahoning County	OH	Robert A. Haney	1987	62
179 5/8	26 6/8	25 7/8	20 7/8	7	8	Lac qui Parle County	MN	Mary A. Barvels	1978	64
179 5/8	25 4/8	25 3/8	21 6/8	7	6	Van Buren County	IA	Blane A. Frey	1993	64
179 4/8	28 1/8	28 3/8	19 6/8	6	6	Clarke County	IA	Rodney D. Hommer	1990	66
179 4/8	25 2/8	25 2/8	19 4/8	5	5	Macoupin County	IL	Kurt A. Bohl	1997	66
179 3/8	26 2/8	26 5/8	17 3/8	5	5	Marshall County	SD	Phyllis Roehr	1976	68
179 3/8	26 1/8	26 6/8	22 0/8	8	6	Anoka County	MN	Tom Evertz	1996	68
179 1/8	28 1/8	27 7/8	24 6/8	5	6	Osage County	KS	Ralph Batchelor, Jr.	1985	70
179 1/8	25 6/8	25 6/8	16 3/8	6	5	Macoupin County	IL	William T. Wiser, Sr.	1994	70
179 0/8	25 7/8	25 7/8	22 1/8	6	6	Scotland County	MO	David Smith	1985	72
179 0/8	27 2/8	26 1/8	19 2/8	6	5	Wapello County	IA	Robert L. McDowell	1985	72
179 0/8	26 6/8	26 6/8	17 6/8	6	6	Edgar County	IL	Edward A. Inman	1985	72
179 0/8	27 3/8	27 7/8	19 3/8	7	7	Des Moines County	IA	Glen M. Thompson	1987	72
179 0/8	27 7/8	29 1/8	21 4/8	6	6	Union County	IA	Richard Reed	1996	72
178 7/8	26 3/8	28 0/8	21 0/8	7	8	Washington County	IA	Ronald A. Murphy	1990	77
178 7/8	30 0/8	29 4/8	18 1/8	5	5	Whiteside County	IL	Bernard Higley, Jr.	1990	77

WHITETAIL DEER (TYPICAL ANTLERS)

Minimum Score 125

SCORE	R MAIN BEAM L		INSIDE SPREAD	R POINTS L		AREA	STATE/PROVINCE	HUNTER'S NAME	DATE	RANK
178 7/8	29 4/8	28 4/8	21 2/8	6	7	Butler County	KS	Don Williamson	1993	77
178 5/8	26 4/8	26 1/8	20 7/8	7	7	La Salle County	IL	Larry G. Simmons	1995	80
178 4/8	26 2/8	25 0/8	21 2/8	5	6	Meade County	KS	Tim Ross	1985	81
178 4/8	25 1/8	25 0/8	18 4/8	5	5	Fulton County	IL	Locie L. Murphy	1985	81
178 4/8	25 1/8	25 4/8	19 4/8	5	5	Firdale	MAN	Randy Bean	1988	81
178 3/8	25 6/8	26 4/8	21 2/8	7	8	McPherson County	KS	Larry Daniels	1967	84
178 1/8	26 5/8	27 0/8	22 0/8	6	5	Lucas County	OH	Jim Carpenter	1997	85
178 0/8	27 5/8	27 3/8	21 4/8	5	5	Carroll County	IL	Art Heinze	1988	86
178 0/8	25 6/8	25 2/8	22 4/8	6	7	Ford County	KS	Scott Evans	1997	86
177 7/8	24 3/8	24 0/8	18 5/8	5	6	Harper County	OK	Scott Davis	1993	88
177 4/8	26 3/8	26 2/8	20 4/8	6	5	Swan River	MAN	Myles Keller	1994	89
177 3/8	27 1/8	26 3/8	20 3/8	6	5	Greene County	IA	Roger V. Carlson	1973	90
177 3/8	28 3/8	28 1/8	18 6/8	6	6	Wayne County	OH	Gary E. Landry	1975	90
177 3/8	27 3/8	26 5/8	20 7/8	5	7	Jones County	IA	Ken Dausener	1984	90
177 3/8	25 2/8	25 1/8	16 4/8	8	6	Miami County	KS	Keith L. Groshong	1991	90
177 3/8	26 5/8	27 2/8	20 3/8	6	6	Isanti County	MN	Jay Patchen	1994	90
177 2/8	27 5/8	26 3/8	17 3/8	8	7	Montgomery County	KY	Bobby M. Dale	1986	95
177 2/8	29 7/8	29 0/8	22 4/8	9	6	Miami County	KS	Carl C. Hughes	1995	95
177 1/8	28 4/8	26 6/8	20 2/8	6	7	Washington County	IA	Ernie Aronson	1985	97
177 1/8	27 1/8	28 6/8	21 2/8	7	5	St. Croix County	WI	Phillip R. Hovde	1990	97
177 0/8	28 2/8	28 1/8	18 3/8	8	6	Baltimore County	MD	Richard B. Traband	1990	99
177 0/8	25 7/8	27 3/8	19 0/8	6	6	Muscatine County	IA	Gary Stauffer	1995	99
176 7/8	27 5/8	27 0/8	18 4/8	5	7	Will County	IL	David Davis	1990	101
176 7/8	25 7/8	25 3/8	17 4/8	6	5	Sullivan County	IN	Larry A. Nash	1995	101
176 6/8	25 2/8	25 0/8	23 4/8	6	6	Marshall County	KS	Ray A. Mosher	1966	103
176 6/8	26 4/8	25 6/8	20 2/8	6	6	Muscatine County	IA	Don McCullough	1980	103
176 6/8	27 4/8	26 0/8	22 7/8	7	5	McHenry County	IL	Gene Melby	1988	103
176 6/8	25 7/8	25 1/8	21 4/8	6	6	Kane County	IL	Mark DuLong	1991	103
176 6/8	26 4/8	25 2/8	18 6/8	5	5	Clay County	KS	Randy Schumock	1997	103
176 4/8	28 3/8	28 1/8	21 6/8	9	6	Morgan County	OH	John Hite	1991	108
176 4/8	25 7/8	25 3/8	21 4/8	10	10	Davis County	IA	Jeffrey A. Getz	1991	108
176 4/8	25 5/8	24 3/8	20 2/8	5	5	Lincoln County	MT	James Hershberger	1994	108
176 4/8	27 2/8	26 6/8	20 3/8	6	5	Linn County	IA	David Heck	1994	108
176 4/8	25 6/8	26 1/8	17 7/8	8	6	Phillips County	KS	James D. Helget	1995	108
176 4/8	28 3/8	28 0/8	18 3/8	7	10	Muscatine County	IA	Tim Kroul	1997	108
176 3/8	24 6/8	26 4/8	18 3/8	6	6	Edmonton	ALB	Kevin D. Curry	1995	114
176 2/8	28 2/8	27 5/8	21 0/8	7	5	Houston County	MN	John Zahrte	1981	115
176 2/8	28 0/8	28 6/8	21 2/8	5	6	Kingman County	KS	Gerald Stroot	1981	115
176 2/8	23 6/8	23 3/8	19 4/8	8	7	Walworth County	WI	Tom Senft	1993	115
176 1/8	25 1/8	26 1/8	21 0/8	7	5	Lewis County	KY	Alfred Simms	1985	118
176 1/8	28 3/8	27 4/8	25 1/8	7	7	Clay County	KS	Larry L. Thompson	1988	118
176 1/8	27 1/8	27 4/8	23 5/8	6	5	Johnson County	MO	James Stephens	1990	118
176 0/8	25 5/8	23 6/8	25 5/8	6	5	Clay County	KS	Rayford W. Willingham	1985	121
176 0/8	30 0/8	29 5/8	20 7/8	4	6	Butler County	OH	Chris AlLen	1994	121
175 7/8	27 3/8	26 4/8	24 4/8	7	6	Kandiyohi County	MN	Eldon Hauser	1969	123
175 6/8	26 2/8	27 4/8	17 4/8	7	6	Clay County	IL	Scott Fritschle	1991	124
175 6/8	29 5/8	28 6/8	21 0/8	5	5	Kent County	MI	Ron Visser	1992	124
175 5/8	29 0/8	28 6/8	21 3/8	4	4	Burnett County	WI	Myles Keller	1977	126
175 5/8	25 4/8	25 2/8	22 2/8	7	7	Pratt County	KS	Gary Brehm	1984	126
175 5/8	26 0/8	25 6/8	22 2/8	5	6	Dickinson County	KS	Gary Stroda	1985	126
175 5/8	24 1/8	23 4/8	17 3/8	7	7	Woodbury County	IA	Paul Feddersen	1988	126
175 5/8	25 5/8	25 6/8	19 3/8	7	7	Lucas County	IA	Dean Chandler	1991	126
175 5/8	30 5/8	28 6/8	23 3/8	5	5	Bucks County	PA	Albert J. Muntz	1995	126
175 5/8	27 6/8	28 3/8	21 7/8	5	5	Knox County	IL	Dick DeMay	1996	126
175 4/8	26 0/8	25 4/8	17 7/8	9	5	Murray County	MN	Steven Wynia	1973	133
175 4/8	27 5/8	27 3/8	22 6/8	5	5	Jo Daviess County	IL	Richard McCartin	1991	133
175 3/8	25 7/8	26 5/8	19 7/8	5	5	Ottawa County	KS	Gary Gans	1985	135
175 3/8	28 4/8	29 0/8	19 0/8	5	6	Pottawatomie County	KS	Doug Selbe	1997	135
175 3/8	28 2/8	28 0/8	19 2/8	8	6	Mills County	IA	Robert Brewer	1997	135
175 2/8	28 5/8	27 2/8	23 5/8	6	6	Sangamon County	IL	Wm. Richard Olsen	1978	138
175 2/8	26 1/8	25 7/8	20 0/8	6	6	St. Mary Parish	LA	Shannon Presley	1981	138
175 1/8	24 4/8	24 4/8	21 5/8	5	6	Marion County	IA	Gordon Hayes	1973	140
175 1/8	26 3/8	28 0/8	21 3/8	7	9	Dodge County	MN	Bill Chase	1976	140
175 1/8	26 5/8	26 4/8	22 7/8	7	9	Bayfield County	WI	Bob Jaskowiak	1994	140
175 1/8	27 0/8	26 7/8	20 1/8	6	6	Scott County	IA	Jeffrey R. Coonts	1996	140
175 0/8	27 6/8	28 6/8	19 0/8	6	6	Lee County	IA	Stephen Douglas McKeehan, Jr.	1989	144
175 0/8	28 4/8	27 7/8	19 2/8	7	9	Jefferson County	IL	Curtis L. Rapp	1993	144
175 0/8	28 3/8	28 5/8	21 0/8	5	7	Schuyler County	IL	Marc S. Anthony	1995	144
174 6/8	24 0/8	25 2/8	20 7/8	7	6	Randolph County	IL	Jack D. Carter	1988	147
174 5/8	25 1/8	25 7/8	18 7/8	5	5	Pickaway County	OH	Hunter R. Certain	1985	148
174 5/8	25 1/8	25 0/8	16 5/8	5	5	Livingston County	MI	Nicholas Scott Converse	1987	148
174 4/8	25 4/8	24 7/8	17 2/8	7	5	Toole County	MT	Dale Farnes	1979	150
174 4/8	25 6/8	25 6/8	19 6/8	5	5	Chariton County	MO	Roger D. Guilford	1988	150
174 3/8	25 5/8	24 3/8	18 3/8	5	5	Taylor County	KY	Barry Eastridge	1987	152
174 3/8	28 4/8	27 6/8	20 3/8	7	7	Grant County	WI	Charles P. Fralick	1996	152
174 3/8	27 6/8	27 3/8	22 3/8	5	5	Osage County	KS	Evans Woehlecke	1997	152
174 2/8	27 7/8	27 0/8	21 2/8	5	5	Ashland County	WI	Kelly McClaire	1986	155
174 2/8	24 2/8	24 6/8	18 2/8	5	5	Mower County	MN	Jason Blom	1987	155

Continued

WHITETAIL DEER (TYPICAL ANTLERS)

Minimum Score 125 — Continued

SCORE	LENGTH OF MAIN BEAM R	LENGTH OF MAIN BEAM L	INSIDE SPREAD	NUMBER OF POINTS R	NUMBER OF POINTS L	AREA	STATE/ PROVINCE	HUNTER'S NAME	DATE	RANK
174 2/8	25 5/8	25 5/8	18 6/8	6	6	Wabaunsee County	KS	Henry C. Boss II	1991	155
174 2/8	30 0/8	30 5/8	21 5/8	6	6	Miami County	OH	Mike Newman	1996	155
174 1/8	23 2/8	23 5/8	18 6/8	9	7	Logan County	IL	Gregory C. Gobleman	1981	159
174 0/8	26 3/8	26 2/8	17 6/8	6	6	Harrison County	IA	Ricky G. Seydel	1989	160
174 0/8	28 0/8	27 4/8	22 4/8	6	5	Cuyahoga County	OH	Charles E. Suk	1994	160
174 0/8	25 7/8	26 3/8	23 0/8	8	5	Vermilion County	IL	Alex L. Ramm	1995	160
174 0/8	29 3/8	29 7/8	19 0/8	4	4	Johnson County	KS	Kevin Hancock	1996	160
174 0/8	26 4/8	26 4/8	18 0/8	5	5	La Salle County	IL	Mike Armstrong	1996	160
173 7/8	24 0/8	24 2/8	19 1/8	5	5	Noble County	OK	Danny McCants	1968	165
173 7/8	27 4/8	25 5/8	16 3/8	5	6	Pike County	MO	Jim Holdenried	1982	165
173 7/8	26 3/8	27 7/8	21 4/8	6	6	Will County	IL	Harry Hammock	1995	165
173 7/8	24 6/8	25 7/8	16 5/8	6	6	Clay County	MO	David Ruth	1995	165
173 7/8	25 3/8	26 2/8	20 2/8	7	6	Blue Earth County	MN	Jeffery Lee Zimmerman	1995	165
173 7/8	27 6/8	26 6/8	18 4/8	4	6	Wilbarger County	TX	John T. Wright	1998	165
173 6/8	26 6/8	27 1/8	19 7/8	7	5	Mercer County	IL	Floyd A. Clark	1961	171
173 6/8	26 1/8	25 0/8	21 5/8	6	5	Winneshiek County	IA	Herbert Amundson	1985	171
173 6/8	25 3/8	26 0/8	18 2/8	5	5	Crawford County	IA	Ed Willroth	1991	171
173 6/8	25 0/8	23 6/8	22 3/8	7	5	Haskell County	KS	Neal Heaton	1993	171
173 6/8	30 6/8	31 2/8	19 6/8	7	7	Union County	KY	Robert C. Caudill	1995	171
173 6/8	27 4/8	26 4/8	21 2/8	6	5	Brown County	IL	Michael Postema	1997	171
173 5/8	26 2/8	26 0/8	22 3/8	6	7	Muskingum County	OH	David R. Hatfield	1980	177
173 5/8	30 1/8	30 0/8	25 3/8	6	6	Jackson County	MO	Mike Sytkowski	1995	177
173 5/8	25 3/8	25 1/8	19 4/8	8	7	Buffalo County	WI	James R. Gabrick	1996	177
173 5/8	24 3/8	23 6/8	20 5/8	5	5	Pottawattamie County	IA	Steve Stuart	1997	177
173 4/8	26 2/8	27 1/8	23 4/8	6	5	Lac qui Parle County	MN	Dale W. Shackelford	1981	181
173 4/8	25 7/8	27 0/8	23 0/8	5	5	McHenry County	IL	Gordon Sunderlage	1987	181
173 4/8	29 6/8	29 2/8	17 6/8	6	5	Pike County	IL	Wayne S. Jones	1996	181
173 4/8	25 3/8	23 6/8	17 6/8	6	6	Louisa County	IA	Todd Goss	1997	181
173 3/8	26 4/8	26 5/8	20 1/8	5	6	Warren County	IL	Larry C. Harding	1974	185
173 3/8	26 3/8	24 6/8	16 5/8	6	5	Bent County	CO	Rick J. Tokarski	1994	185
173 3/8	27 2/8	27 0/8	28 7/8	5	6	Kane County	IL	James Meyer	1995	185
173 3/8	24 5/8	24 5/8	21 3/8	6	5	Sauk County	WI	Eric R. Sorge	1996	185
173 2/8	26 0/8	26 3/8	22 5/8	5	6	Miami County	KS	Dan R. Moore	1982	189
173 2/8	27 6/8	28 1/8	18 0/8	7	7	Monroe County	IN	Jake Wineinger	1990	189
173 2/8	24 2/8	25 0/8	19 0/8	5	5	Butler County	MO	Marcus O. Milligan	1997	189
173 2/8	26 5/8	26 5/8	24 6/8	5	5	Pickaway County	OH	Tim Ritchie	1997	189
173 1/8	28 0/8	28 2/8	21 5/8	7	7	Dunn County	WI	Jack K. Dodge	1987	193
173 1/8	28 1/8	28 6/8	21 1/8	5	6	Morrison County	MN	John McDonald	1993	193
173 1/8	28 6/8	27 6/8	19 3/8	4	4	Nemaha County	KS	Edward E. Daily	1994	193
173 1/8	25 5/8	24 2/8	23 3/8	5	5	Buffalo County	WI	Tom Johnson	1997	193
173 0/8	25 6/8	25 5/8	19 4/8	5	5	White County	IN	Eric L. Mohler	1978	197
173 0/8	25 4/8	26 1/8	15 2/8	6	5	Russell County	KS	Michael J. Pasek	1990	197
173 0/8	25 4/8	27 1/8	19 4/8	9	8	Clay County	MO	Neal B. Breshears	1996	197
172 7/8	27 6/8	27 1/8	18 5/8	5	6	Vermilion County	IL	Ed Gudgel	1988	200
172 7/8	27 2/8	27 7/8	19 7/8	5	5	Walworth County	WI	Robert Peterson	1988	200
172 6/8	26 7/8	27 6/8	19 4/8	5	5	Ripley County	IN	Steve A. Allen	1982	202
172 6/8	25 4/8	25 1/8	19 4/8	5	5	Sullivan County	TN	C. Alan Altizer	1984	202
172 6/8	26 4/8	25 5/8	16 4/8	5	5	Saline County	KS	Bruce Brown	1986	202
172 6/8	25 1/8	24 7/8	18 6/8	6	5	Fairfield County	OH	James Carmichael	1988	202
172 6/8	27 6/8	28 5/8	18 7/8	7	5	Pike County	IL	Jimmy Howard	1989	202
172 6/8	28 0/8	28 7/8	19 2/8	6	5	Moultrie County	IL	Joe Nelson	1991	202
172 6/8	25 4/8	25 4/8	17 4/8	6	7	Keokuk County	IA	Michael A. Veres	1995	202
172 6/8	24 5/8	27 5/8	21 1/8	6	6	Union County	SD	Scott Staum	1997	202
172 5/8	26 7/8	27 1/8	18 7/8	5	5	Rosebud County	MT	Michael E Gayheart	1989	210
172 4/8	26 0/8	26 0/8	18 2/8	7	6	Lucas County	IA	Jim Barlow	1985	211
172 4/8	26 4/8	26 4/8	15 2/8	5	5	Scotland County	MO	Charlie L. Smith	1985	211
172 4/8	27 3/8	27 3/8	18 2/8	5	6	Shelby County	IL	Gene E. Thoele	1991	211
172 4/8	24 5/8	26 2/8	16 6/8	5	5	Bond County	IL	Bill Brown	1995	211
172 4/8	24 7/8	24 6/8	21 0/8	5	5	Knox County	IL	Dan Courtright	1997	211
172 3/8	26 3/8	24 0/8	18 6/8	6	7	Clinton County	IL	James D. Rueter	1984	216
172 3/8	26 6/8	26 4/8	21 3/8	5	5	Marshall County	IA	Dale E. Smith	1988	216
172 3/8	27 0/8	26 7/8	19 1/8	5	5	Johnson County	KS	David Reed	1990	216
172 3/8	29 6/8	30 2/8	21 2/8	4	6	Prince Georges County	MD	Lance D. Canter	1993	216
172 2/8	26 1/8	25 3/8	19 2/8	5	5	Iowa County	IA	Ardith Lockridge	1965	220
172 2/8	27 3/8	25 1/8	18 4/8	5	5	Clinton County	IA	Robert S. Stankee	1985	220
172 2/8	27 6/8	26 5/8	19 4/8	5	5	Butler County	PA	Ralph W. Stoltenberg, Jr.	1986	220
172 2/8	26 7/8	27 6/8	26 2/8	6	5	Saunders County	NE	John I. Kunert	1986	220
172 2/8	25 1/8	26 4/8	19 6/8	5	5	Clay County	KS	Scott Otto	1989	220
172 2/8	25 0/8	25 2/8	17 4/8	9	6	Delaware County	OK	Bruce Hicks	1990	220
172 2/8	28 1/8	28 4/8	22 0/8	4	5	Champaign County	IL	Justin Park	1992	220
172 2/8	25 0/8	25 7/8	19 0/8	6	5	Des Moines County	IA	James E. Howie	1996	220
172 2/8	27 4/8	27 4/8	19 0/8	6	6	Green County	WI	Tom Cisewski	1998	220
172 1/8	26 4/8	26 3/8	19 5/8	7	6	Rice County	MN	Mike Sannan	1989	229
172 1/8	27 6/8	26 6/8	17 7/8	7	7	Russell County	KS	James H. Skucius	1990	229
172 1/8	25 1/8	24 6/8	22 5/8	8	8	Lake County	IL	Mark J. Kramer	1990	229
172 1/8	24 2/8	24 7/8	19 5/8	5	6	Wyandotte County	KS	Earl A. Cooksey	1992	229
172 1/8	29 3/8	30 2/8	21 0/8	7	8	Rock County	WI	Steven Kravick	1996	229
172 1/8	28 6/8	27 4/8	22 4/8	5	6	Greene County	OH	Jay M. Skrabacz	1997	229

WHITETAIL DEER (TYPICAL ANTLERS)

Minimum Score 125
Continued

SCORE	LENGTH OF MAIN BEAM R	LENGTH OF MAIN BEAM L	INSIDE SPREAD	NUMBER OF POINTS R	NUMBER OF POINTS L	AREA	STATE/ PROVINCE	HUNTER'S NAME	DATE	RANK
172 0/8	27 0/8	26 6/8	21 2/8	5	5	Greene County	IN	Jason Anderson	1991	235
172 0/8	25 6/8	25 2/8	17 7/8	5	6	Nicollet County	MN	Bruce Kramer	1991	235
172 0/8	25 4/8	23 4/8	16 6/8	6	6	McMullen County	TX	Steve Best	1991	235
172 0/8	28 1/8	28 1/8	21 1/8	5	6	Greene County	IL	Kenny Tally, Jr.	1995	235
172 0/8	26 3/8	26 4/8	20 2/8	7	7	Pottawatomie County	KS	Dale R. Larson	1995	235
172 0/8	26 6/8	25 3/8	22 1/8	6	6	Shawnee County	KS	Richard Matyak	1997	235
172 0/8	26 2/8	26 2/8	19 2/8	5	5	Delaware County	IA	Chuck Fessler	1997	235
171 7/8	26 2/8	26 4/8	24 1/8	5	5	Scotland County	MO	David Smith	1984	242
171 7/8	28 5/8	28 0/8	20 7/8	8	7	Linn County	IA	Charles Bemer	1985	242
171 7/8	27 5/8	26 6/8	21 5/8	6	6	Lucas County	IA	Tim M. Whitlatch	1989	242
171 7/8	26 3/8	25 4/8	21 3/8	5	5	Henderson County	KY	Aaron D. Parrish	1995	242
171 6/8	26 7/8	26 6/8	25 2/8	7	8	Richland County	ND	Todd Funfar	1982	246
171 6/8	28 1/8	27 1/8	17 6/8	7	6	Carroll County	OH	Randy S Mulheim	1983	246
171 6/8	24 6/8	23 4/8	20 6/8	5	5	Dunn County	WI	James W. Belmore	1991	246
171 6/8	28 0/8	28 0/8	20 6/8	7	8	Edmonton	ALB	Warren Witherspoon	1991	246
171 6/8	25 7/8	26 5/8	18 6/8	6	9	Todd County	MN	Chead D. Wessel	1993	246
171 6/8	26 4/8	26 5/8	19 0/8	5	5	Osage County	OK	Don Gaddis	1995	246
171 5/8	24 6/8	24 0/8	17 3/8	6	6	Calgary	ALB	Scott Simi	1979	252
171 5/8	25 3/8	25 2/8	20 3/8	8	6	Cowley County	KS	Michael L. Snyder	1985	252
171 5/8	26 3/8	25 5/8	19 3/8	5	5	Logan County	KY	Alan Scott	1987	252
171 5/8	25 0/8	25 4/8	21 3/8	5	5	Linn County	KS	Robert R. Goodwin	1994	252
171 5/8	23 6/8	23 4/8	19 7/8	6	6	Fergus County	MT	D. Mitch Kottas	1995	252
171 5/8	26 0/8	26 5/8	19 5/8	5	5	Grundy County	IL	Joseph Gray	1997	252
171 5/8	25 0/8	25 0/8	20 3/8	6	6	Douglas County	NE	Bryan Kindler	1997	252
171 5/8	26 5/8	24 5/8	18 4/8	7	6	Clayton County	IA	Chris Borcherding	1997	252
171 4/8	24 3/8	23 2/8	16 6/8	6	6	Ellsworth County	KS	Jim Willems	1985	260
171 4/8	24 4/8	25 4/8	19 6/8	6	6	Vermilion County	IL	Ken Becicka	1991	260
171 4/8	26 2/8	26 0/8	21 4/8	6	6	Louisa County	IA	Mike Noble	1992	260
171 4/8	22 5/8	22 2/8	16 1/8	6	7	Kleberg County	TX	Mike Lemker	1997	260
171 3/8	22 4/8	23 7/8	24 7/8	6	6	Cass County	ND	Warren Buss	1966	264
171 3/8	23 7/8	24 5/8	18 7/8	5	5	Harrison County	IA	R. A. Cronk	1985	264
171 3/8	27 4/8	27 6/8	21 3/8	7	6	Washington County	IL	Robert Schneider	1985	264
171 3/8	27 3/8	26 5/8	26 0/8	8	8	Jefferson County	WI	Gary Moyer	1987	264
171 3/8	24 1/8	24 7/8	18 5/8	6	6	Sangamon County	IL	Michael R. Vincent	1991	264
171 3/8	23 7/8	24 2/8	15 5/8	6	5	Johnson County	KS	Dave Ward	1993	264
171 3/8	27 2/8	27 0/8	17 7/8	5	5	Charles County	MD	Patrick E. Langley	1997	264
171 3/8	28 2/8	27 5/8	18 5/8	8	5	Logan County	WV	Terry McGrady	1997	264
171 2/8	25 1/8	23 2/8	20 6/8	5	6	Adams County	IA	Gary D. Maatsch	1990	272
171 2/8	25 0/8	25 5/8	20 2/8	5	5	Bartholomew County	IN	Gary Owsley	1995	272
171 2/8	25 0/8	25 7/8	19 2/8	5	5	Sedgwick County	KS	Julio C. Lazcano	1995	272
171 2/8	25 5/8	25 7/8	21 7/8	5	6	Jefferson County	WI	Fred Koehn	1996	272
171 2/8	25 6/8	24 5/8	18 2/8	5	5	Benton County	IA	Tim McLaud	1997	272
171 1/8	26 3/8	26 4/8	20 5/8	5	5	Itasca County	MN	John Parmeter	1964	277
171 1/8	23 5/8	24 0/8	16 7/8	6	6	Piatt County	IL	Ronald E. Waugh	1971	277
171 1/8	24 3/8	23 2/8	17 4/8	8	7	Morton County	ND	Tony Schatz	1974	277
171 1/8	25 2/8	24 2/8	21 1/8	6	6	Tazewell County	IL	John P. Condis	1987	277
171 1/8	27 0/8	25 6/8	18 3/8	5	6	Bourbon County	KS	Larry Daly	1988	277
171 1/8	25 3/8	25 2/8	20 1/8	5	5	Clark County	OH	Lafayette Boggs III	1991	277
171 1/8	25 7/8	25 3/8	20 3/8	5	5	McHenry County	IL	Mike Fischer	1993	277
171 0/8	30 0/8	27 5/8	19 5/8	5	8	Belmont County	OH	Charles J. Wilson	1979	284
171 0/8	27 4/8	27 4/8	22 2/8	5	5	Parke County	IN	Fred Sills	1985	284
171 0/8	24 7/8	24 7/8	21 1/8	7	7	Kleberg County	TX	Darwin D. Baucum	1994	284
171 0/8	26 5/8	26 5/8	18 4/8	5	5	Minnehaha County	SD	Carl L. Murra	1996	284
171 0/8	26 4/8	27 0/8	19 0/8	6	7	Becker County	MN	Jeff Holmer	1998	284
170 7/8	27 6/8	27 5/8	18 4/8	6	8	Republic County	KS	Carroll Couture	1986	289
170 7/8	27 4/8	28 4/8	21 4/8	7	8	Leavenworth County	KS	Jacob W. Dragieff	1987	289
170 7/8	25 6/8	25 7/8	22 1/8	6	6	Bureau County	IL	Steve W. Hayes	1990	289
170 6/8	26 1/8	25 3/8	17 4/8	5	5	Mitchell County	IA	Dan Block	1981	292
170 6/8	26 7/8	28 1/8	19 6/8	5	5	Racine County	WI	Anthony J Wozniak	1985	292
170 6/8	24 5/8	23 5/8	14 6/8	6	7	Jackson County	MI	Richard J. Galicki	1991	292
170 6/8	28 4/8	26 7/8	18 7/8	5	6	Tazewell County	IL	Steve R. Larimore	1995	292
170 6/8	24 6/8	25 3/8	15 4/8	6	5	Decatur County	IA	Mark Boswell	1996	292
170 5/8	26 3/8	25 5/8	18 3/8	5	6	Vermilion County	IL	Mark Pittman	1980	297
170 5/8	23 6/8	23 4/8	16 5/8	6	6	Teton County	MT	James R. Dean	1983	297
170 5/8	26 1/8	26 2/8	18 5/8	7	5	Schuyler County	MO	Mike Meinhardt	1989	297
170 5/8	25 7/8	25 5/8	22 4/8	6	5	Brown County	IL	Timothy I. Burkins	1992	297
170 5/8	24 7/8	25 7/8	17 1/8	5	5	Ogle County	IL	Dick V. Lalowski	1992	297
170 5/8	26 5/8	28 0/8	17 4/8	7	5	Montgomery County	MD	Scott Wilson	1995	297
170 5/8	26 4/8	25 3/8	18 2/8	6	6	Spruce Lake	SAS	Shaun Bleakney	1996	297
170 4/8	25 1/8	25 4/8	20 2/8	5	4	Des Moines County	IA	Bob Fudge	1966	304
170 4/8	25 3/8	24 7/8	20 0/8	6	6	Vilas County	WI	Rick R. Lax	1990	304
170 4/8	26 3/8	26 0/8	19 6/8	5	5	Rock Island County	IL	Joseph V. De Schepper	1991	304
170 4/8	29 0/8	29 3/8	19 1/8	6	5	Cerro Gordo County	IA	Chuck Harris	1991	304
170 4/8	24 6/8	24 5/8	18 0/8	7	7	Pawnee County	NE	Kenneth C. Mort	1991	304
170 4/8	26 1/8	26 5/8	21 5/8	6	8	Livingston County	IL	Alan Gray	1994	304
170 4/8	25 6/8	26 0/8	25 0/8	5	5	Marion County	IA	Henry Moore	1994	304
170 3/8	28 5/8	28 2/8	21 6/8	6	4	Hall County	NE	Gust Bergman	1965	311
170 3/8	25 5/8	26 3/8	17 7/8	6	5	Decatur County	IA	Julian Toney	1982	311

WHITETAIL DEER (TYPICAL ANTLERS)

Minimum Score 125 — Continued

SCORE	LENGTH OF MAIN BEAM R	LENGTH OF MAIN BEAM L	INSIDE SPREAD	NUMBER OF POINTS R	NUMBER OF POINTS L	AREA	STATE/ PROVINCE	HUNTER'S NAME	DATE	RANK
170 3/8	27 0/8	26 1/8	20 3/8	5	5	Ogle County	IL	John E. Lawson	1985	311
170 3/8	27 3/8	28 4/8	18 5/8	7	6	Howard County	IA	Clarence Mincks	1991	311
170 3/8	27 4/8	27 6/8	22 2/8	6	7	Crawford County	KS	Dave E. Onelio	1994	311
170 3/8	26 3/8	26 2/8	20 1/8	5	6	Pierce County	WI	Timothy B. Hasty	1994	311
170 3/8	25 4/8	24 7/8	16 7/8	6	7	Pulaski County	IL	Andrew French III	1995	311
170 3/8	23 0/8	23 2/8	17 3/8	6	6	McHenry County	IL	Donald E. Hoey	1996	311
170 3/8	26 6/8	27 2/8	22 4/8	6	6	Jo Daviess County	IL	Cliff Perry	1998	311
170 2/8	27 1/8	27 2/8	21 0/8	4	4	Lee County	AL	George P. Mann	1980	320
170 2/8	25 4/8	26 1/8	19 1/8	5	6	Clayton County	IA	Myles Keller	1989	320
170 2/8	26 0/8	25 4/8	19 1/8	8	8	Hocking County	OH	Kim Stevelt	1992	320
170 2/8	24 2/8	24 1/8	19 5/8	6	7	Crowley County	CO	Judy F. Hallman	1993	320
170 2/8	24 0/8	24 6/8	18 6/8	6	6	Davis County	IA	Chuck Riggenbach	1997	320
170 2/8	26 3/8	26 1/8	18 4/8	8	8	Hubbard County	MN	Michael E. Greetan	1998	320
170 1/8	26 1/8	27 1/8	22 1/8	5	5	Edwards County	KS	Jay Schaller	1968	326
170 1/8	25 4/8	25 7/8	22 2/8	6	7	Winona County	MN	Roger Traxler	1980	326
170 1/8	25 6/8	25 2/8	21 3/8	5	5	Mower County	MN	Robert D. Plumb	1984	326
170 1/8	26 7/8	26 0/8	20 7/8	5	6	Harford County	MD	Ed Garrison	1987	326
170 1/8	25 4/8	26 4/8	17 4/8	10	8	Washington County	IA	Marlin Derby	1987	326
170 1/8	26 0/8	26 4/8	18 1/8	7	6	Miami County	KS	Keith Groshong	1988	326
170 1/8	23 3/8	27 4/8	20 5/8	5	5	Racine County	WI	Michael H. Poeschel	1989	326
170 1/8	25 0/8	27 0/8	19 3/8	5	5	Winnebago County	IA	Matthew Modeland	1990	326
170 1/8	26 6/8	26 4/8	24 2/8	6	6	La Crosse County	WI	Scott R. Waura	1991	326
170 1/8	28 2/8	27 4/8	22 3/8	6	5	Lake County	IL	John W. Schnider	1992	326
170 1/8	27 1/8	26 0/8	21 7/8	6	6	Henry County	IL	Dave Oleson	1994	326
170 1/8	25 3/8	27 2/8	17 0/8	5	6	Dunn County	WI	Clarence Janota	1995	326
170 1/8	24 6/8	24 2/8	21 3/8	6	7	Otter Tail County	MN	Randy Litke	1995	326
170 1/8	25 4/8	24 3/8	19 5/8	6	6	Ashland County	OH	Steve Orchard	1996	326
170 1/8	24 0/8	24 2/8	19 7/8	7	5	Monona County	IA	John Marinaccio	1997	326
170 1/8	27 2/8	26 5/8	19 2/8	7	7	Kleberg County	TX	Robert Nichols	1997	326
170 1/8	24 6/8	23 6/8	18 1/8	6	6	Kenedy County	TX	Jarred W. PeepLes	1998	326
170 0/8	26 1/8	26 6/8	20 0/8	5	5	Scott County	KS	Monte L. Barker	1973	343
170 0/8	29 4/8	29 0/8	20 4/8	6	6	Puslinch Twp.	ONT	Richard Foss	1980	343
170 0/8	28 0/8	28 6/8	19 5/8	6	5	Jo Daviess County	IL	Bart Blocklinger	1982	343
170 0/8	25 1/8	24 7/8	19 1/8	8	8	Plymouth County	IA	David Erdmann	1987	343
170 0/8	25 1/8	25 5/8	19 6/8	5	5	Battle River	SAS	Gordon Stefanuk	1989	343
170 0/8	26 0/8	27 0/8	19 4/8	6	5	Jackson County	MI	Michael D. Fitzgerald	1990	343
170 0/8	25 4/8	23 4/8	21 0/8	5	5	Harvey County	KS	Dan Stahl	1991	343
170 0/8	28 7/8	27 3/8	23 1/8	5	6	McHenry County	IL	Daniel Doherty	1992	343
170 0/8	25 4/8	26 7/8	25 1/8	5	8	Wabaunsee County	KS	Henry C. Boss II	1995	343
170 0/8	28 4/8	27 2/8	21 6/8	5	5	Cross County	AR	Clay Bassham	1996	343
169 7/8	25 7/8	25 3/8	17 2/8	6	7	Neosho County	KS	Matt R. Morgan	1992	353
169 7/8	24 4/8	24 4/8	22 3/8	5	5	Walworth County	WI	James W. May	1995	353
169 6/8	26 0/8	27 3/8	20 6/8	4	4	Decatur County	IA	Bruce Jermyn	1979	355
169 6/8	29 6/8	29 2/8	27 0/8	6	6	Coffey County	KS	Jack McCullough	1984	355
169 6/8	26 7/8	26 7/8	24 3/8	7	6	Wyoming County	WV	James Blankenship	1994	355
169 6/8	25 5/8	26 4/8	22 3/8	6	6	Monroe County	WI	Timothy E. Slonka	1994	355
169 6/8	23 5/8	23 2/8	16 4/8	5	6	Warren County	IA	Nicholas Romano	1997	355
169 5/8	24 0/8	23 4/8	22 1/8	6	7	Neosho County	KS	Jeff Friederich	1992	360
169 4/8	23 7/8	25 2/8	17 7/8	6	7	Charles Mix County	SD	Don Carda	1974	361
169 4/8	24 6/8	24 6/8	18 7/8	7	7	Hennepin County	MN	Mark Kirkwold	1989	361
169 4/8	23 6/8	24 6/8	17 2/8	6	6	Harvey County	KS	Ron Hershberger	1989	361
169 4/8	26 0/8	25 4/8	22 4/8	7	6	Rock Island County	IL	Leo Hoogerwerf	1990	361
169 4/8	24 6/8	24 6/8	19 2/8	5	5	Lafayette County	WI	E. Michael Kitral	1991	361
169 4/8	26 3/8	26 3/8	20 0/8	7	7	Grundy County	IL	Robert Alfonso, Jr.	1996	361
169 3/8	27 1/8	27 5/8	22 1/8	5	5	Hamilton County	OH	Christopher J. Ludwig	1990	367
169 3/8	27 5/8	27 2/8	20 5/8	6	6	Knox County	IL	Robert J. Hinckley	1991	367
169 3/8	25 2/8	24 7/8	20 5/8	6	5	Niagara Twp.	ONT	Andre' Secco	1992	367
169 3/8	25 5/8	24 2/8	17 5/8	7	7	Dakota County	MN	Tom Leach	1993	367
169 3/8	27 7/8	28 4/8	19 5/8	5	7	Jefferson County	WI	Mark S. Chesney	1994	367
169 3/8	28 1/8	26 1/8	20 7/8	5	5	Goodhue County	MN	Marv Betcher	1996	367
169 2/8	26 1/8	27 2/8	21 6/8	6	6	Ashland County	OH	Darrell Huff	1985	373
169 2/8	25 4/8	25 2/8	19 7/8	6	5	McLean County	IL	Arthur L. Garrison	1992	373
169 2/8	25 1/8	24 6/8	21 4/8	5	5	Lee County	IL	Paul Harmon	1995	373
169 2/8	28 1/8	26 7/8	20 2/8	5	5	Woodson County	KS	Clint Shockley	1997	373
169 1/8	28 6/8	28 2/8	19 3/8	6	6	La Salle County	IL	Dave Mrowicki	1985	377
169 1/8	26 7/8	27 2/8	19 2/8	7	7	Parkland	ALB	Allan Gates	1995	377
169 0/8	25 6/8	26 0/8	18 0/8	7	5	Warren County	IA	Brad Vonk	1980	379
169 0/8	25 5/8	25 2/8	20 5/8	5	6	Marion County	KS	Max Williams	1985	379
169 0/8	27 2/8	26 7/8	22 2/8	5	5	Grant County	WI	Richard Hein	1986	379
169 0/8	24 5/8	25 6/8	20 3/8	6	7	Lyon County	KS	Steve Coe	1996	379
169 0/8	28 3/8	28 2/8	20 1/8	6	7	Metcalfe County	KY	Buddy Gentry	1997	379
168 7/8	24 3/8	24 4/8	20 7/8	5	5	Jackson County	IA	Al Weidenbacher	1984	384
168 7/8	27 4/8	27 0/8	19 0/8	5	6	Washington County	MN	Ronald Jacobson	1985	384
168 7/8	22 1/8	22 5/8	22 1/8	6	5	Jefferson County	IL	Rudy Moore	1987	384
168 7/8	23 4/8	23 4/8	18 3/8	6	6	Allamakee County	IA	Patrick Schellsmidt	1993	384
168 6/8	27 7/8	27 0/8	16 6/8	7	7	Muskingum County	OH	Gerald Shepler	1988	388
168 6/8	24 5/8	23 6/8	18 6/8	5	5	Fulton County	IL	Alan Miller	1996	388
168 5/8	26 2/8	26 0/8	18 5/8	5	6	Des Moines County	IA	Michael P. Anderson	1977	390

WHITETAIL DEER (TYPICAL ANTLERS)

Minimum Score 125

Continued

SCORE	LENGTH OF MAIN BEAM R	L	INSIDE SPREAD	NUMBER OF POINTS R	L	AREA	STATE/ PROVINCE	HUNTER'S NAME	DATE	RANK
168 5/8	26 3/8	26 1/8	20 6/8	5	6	Mahoning County	OH	Jeff J Hartman	1984	390
168 5/8	25 0/8	24 5/8	17 1/8	7	7	Calhoun County	IL	Dennis A. Kendall	1985	390
168 5/8	25 7/8	25 7/8	22 1/8	5	5	Taylor County	WI	Bradley Cornell	1986	390
168 5/8	26 7/8	27 6/8	20 6/8	6	6	Hancock County	OH	Robert E. Ebert	1988	390
168 5/8	25 6/8	25 6/8	19 5/8	5	5	Winnebago County	IA	Jim Orthel	1990	390
168 5/8	26 0/8	26 1/8	18 3/8	8	7	Harrison County	KY	Sam Blackburn	1991	390
168 5/8	24 7/8	25 4/8	21 6/8	6	7	Delaware County	OH	Steve Downey	1994	390
168 4/8	24 0/8	24 7/8	18 6/8	5	5	Lincoln County	KS	Gerald Huehl	1985	398
168 4/8	23 7/8	23 4/8	16 6/8	6	5	Grayson County	KY	John David Johnson	1989	398
168 4/8	23 0/8	22 0/8	21 6/8	5	5	Carroll County	MD	Mark A. Robinson	1993	398
168 4/8	24 7/8	25 1/8	20 2/8	5	5	Buffalo County	WI	Jeffrey Fisher	1997	398
168 3/8	25 1/8	26 1/8	19 5/8	5	5	Jefferson County	IL	Ben Howard	1988	402
168 3/8	25 0/8	24 6/8	19 3/8	5	5	Kingsbury County	SD	Donald B. Johnson	1989	402
168 3/8	24 6/8	25 2/8	21 3/8	6	7	Oconto County	WI	Peter M. Meeuwsen	1993	402
168 3/8	26 2/8	25 2/8	19 2/8	8	8	Shelby County	IL	Robert W. Bowman, Jr.	1993	402
168 3/8	26 1/8	25 6/8	22 6/8	6	5	Houston County	MN	Bruce C. Norton	1995	402
168 2/8	27 0/8	26 5/8	19 2/8	5	7	Cowley County	KS	Larry G. Gann	1975	407
168 2/8	25 0/8	24 4/8	21 2/8	5	5	Macon County	IL	Larry D. Smith	1985	407
168 2/8	27 2/8	26 7/8	20 4/8	5	6	Lyon County	KS	John R. Clifton	1985	407
168 2/8	25 4/8	25 1/8	20 3/8	7	5	Mercer County	KY	Steve Baxter	1989	407
168 2/8	24 1/8	25 0/8	17 4/8	5	5	Knox County	IL	Gale Harriman	1991	407
168 2/8	24 4/8	24 6/8	22 0/8	5	5	Piatt County	IL	Michael F. Bily	1996	407
168 1/8	24 6/8	24 6/8	20 1/8	6	5	Murray County	MN	Marvin Brouwer	1971	413
168 1/8	27 0/8	27 7/8	20 1/8	6	6	Blue Earth County	MN	Rich Detjen	1984	413
168 1/8	26 6/8	26 0/8	18 0/8	6	6	Clearwater County	ID	Emerald Hutchins	1994	413
168 1/8	25 3/8	25 4/8	18 3/8	5	5	Dakota County	MN	Craig Gill	1996	413
168 1/8	25 3/8	26 0/8	19 0/8	7	7	Houston County	MN	Jay M. Randall	1998	413
168 0/8	27 2/8	25 7/8	19 0/8	5	5	Vinton County	OH	Ronald E. Morgan	1978	418
168 0/8	26 0/8	25 6/8	19 1/8	10	5	Amherst County	VA	William Dixon Morgan	1980	418
168 0/8	25 4/8	23 7/8	15 6/8	7	7	De Witt County	IL	William R. Henson	1982	418
168 0/8	24 5/8	24 5/8	21 4/8	6	7	Jo Daviess County	IL	Dick Tasch	1989	418
168 0/8	25 1/8	26 1/8	18 2/8	5	5	Lincoln County	SD	Floyd McElroy	1996	418
167 7/8	27 6/8	27 7/8	21 2/8	6	6	Brown County	OH	David Grayson	1976	423
167 7/8	26 0/8	25 5/8	20 3/8	5	6	Clay County	IL	Tom Corry	1985	423
167 7/8	27 5/8	27 4/8	24 0/8	8	7	Clark County	IA	Gregory A. Torode	1992	423
167 7/8	26 2/8	26 5/8	27 7/8	5	5	Mercer County	IL	Neil A. Hamerlinck	1993	423
167 7/8	23 7/8	23 3/8	20 5/8	6	6	Washington County	MN	John Bronk	1994	423
167 7/8	25 5/8	26 0/8	21 4/8	5	6	Tompkins County	NY	Paul F. Stone	1996	423
167 7/8	25 2/8	25 3/8	21 1/8	5	5	Bureau County	IL	Edward Joiner	1997	423
167 6/8	26 4/8	26 2/8	19 6/8	5	5	Monona County	IA	Douglas M. Bonine	1985	430
167 6/8	27 2/8	27 1/8	21 2/8	5	5	Coffey County	KS	Edward L. Bess	1985	430
167 6/8	25 0/8	25 4/8	21 3/8	6	5	Nelson County	KY	Wayne Bodine	1994	430
167 6/8	28 4/8	28 4/8	20 0/8	6	6	Auglaize County	OH	Gary L. Hughes	1994	430
167 6/8	25 5/8	23 7/8	19 0/8	6	6	Christian County	KY	Tommy Clark	1997	430
167 5/8	27 7/8	26 6/8	20 7/8	7	7	Chase County	KS	William E. Drummond	1984	435
167 5/8	23 6/8	23 1/8	15 0/8	7	7	Meigs County	OH	Rick Bolin	1987	435
167 5/8	24 0/8	24 1/8	17 7/8	5	5	Leavenworth County	KS	John W. Garrison	1990	435
167 5/8	22 4/8	23 0/8	18 7/8	5	5	Washita County	OK	Alan Cooper	1991	435
167 5/8	28 1/8	27 7/8	20 6/8	6	4	Macoupin County	IL	Justin Bonnell	1991	435
167 5/8	29 0/8	29 0/8	19 2/8	7	5	Fulton County	IL	Robert A. Hammerich	1991	435
167 5/8	25 2/8	24 2/8	17 6/8	5	6	Boone County	MO	Hosie E. Roberts, Jr.	1993	435
167 5/8	27 6/8	28 2/8	18 6/8	5	6	Amherst Island	ONT	Bill Fenwick	1993	435
167 5/8	26 6/8	26 7/8	18 1/8	7	7	Pittsburg County	OK	Brett Foster	1994	435
167 5/8	23 4/8	24 5/8	24 1/8	6	5	Perry County	IL	Wilbur Engelhardt	1994	435
167 5/8	26 2/8	29 4/8	20 2/8	6	7	Richland County	IL	Dennis Graves	1995	435
167 5/8	26 2/8	27 2/8	19 5/8	5	5	Gallia County	OH	Dwane Rees	1995	435
167 4/8	22 4/8	23 1/8	18 4/8	5	5	Washington County	KS	Bill R. Mallean	1974	447
167 4/8	23 6/8	24 0/8	21 4/8	6	6	Coffey County	KS	Glen Stohs	1987	447
167 4/8	26 4/8	26 0/8	21 0/8	7	7	Sawyer County	WI	Gary R. Christman	1989	447
167 4/8	26 6/8	26 0/8	19 4/8	6	5	Winneshiek County	IA	Tom Gossman	1990	447
167 4/8	26 1/8	26 7/8	21 2/8	5	6	Pike County	IL	Timothy Fulmer	1990	447
167 4/8	27 0/8	26 5/8	18 7/8	5	6	Montgomery County	VA	Edward R. Sowers	1991	447
167 4/8	23 3/8	23 2/8	17 2/8	5	6	Linn County	KS	Willard W. Wills III	1992	447
167 4/8	26 7/8	26 7/8	17 7/8	7	8	Morgan County	IN	Steve Long	1995	447
167 4/8	26 0/8	24 3/8	18 6/8	5	5	St. Clair County	IL	Joe Little	1997	447
167 4/8	27 5/8	26 2/8	18 4/8	7	6	Dubuque County	IA	Doug Biermann	1997	447
167 3/8	25 1/8	25 0/8	20 5/8	5	7	Sauk County	WI	Daniel Kaczmar	1985	457
167 3/8	28 5/8	28 4/8	19 2/8	6	6	Sumner County	KS	Don Braddy	1986	457
167 3/8	28 6/8	26 1/8	20 1/8	5	6	Coshocton County	OH	Harold E. Frank	1989	457
167 3/8	24 6/8	24 2/8	19 3/8	5	5	Dawson County	MT	Jerry Fevold	1992	457
167 3/8	25 7/8	26 2/8	23 1/8	5	5	Waukesha County	WI	Kelvin E. Sandel	1992	457
167 3/8	25 7/8	26 6/8	18 3/8	6	6	Dakota County	NE	Kevin Hohenstein	1997	457
167 2/8	25 2/8	26 2/8	17 2/8	7	6	Todd County	KY	Glendeal Sigers	1987	463
167 2/8	24 3/8	24 3/8	21 4/8	5	6	Marion County	IA	Brad Van Dusseldorp	1992	463
167 2/8	25 7/8	26 0/8	21 6/8	5	6	Grundy County	IL	Michael Dunbar	1995	463
167 1/8	24 5/8	24 7/8	18 6/8	5	6	Chase County	KS	Ronald E. Rhodes	1985	466
167 1/8	22 5/8	22 6/8	25 2/8	5	7	Dodge County	MN	Myles Keller	1985	466
167 1/8	25 1/8	25 6/8	20 3/8	6	6	Reno County	KS	R. D. Loudenback	1987	466

WHITETAIL DEER (TYPICAL ANTLERS)

Minimum Score 125 — Continued

SCORE	LENGTH OF R MAIN BEAM L		INSIDE SPREAD	NUMBER OF R POINTS L		AREA	STATE/ PROVINCE	HUNTER'S NAME	DATE	RANK
167 1/8	23 4/8	24 0/8	18 5/8	6	5	McHenry County	IL	Charlie Rand	1989	466
167 1/8	25 2/8	25 4/8	18 7/8	6	5	Fulton County	IL	Michael Taff	1991	466
167 0/8	28 0/8	27 6/8	19 0/8	6	5	Clay County	MN	Ryan Hines	1986	471
167 0/8	26 0/8	26 1/8	18 2/8	5	5	Montgomery County	IN	Joe W. Woodrow	1988	471
167 0/8	25 5/8	24 6/8	18 2/8	5	5	Montgomery County	TN	Larry Lee Murphy	1989	471
167 0/8	26 3/8	25 7/8	18 3/8	6	6	Fountain County	IN	Steve McQueen	1991	471
167 0/8	27 0/8	26 6/8	22 4/8	6	5	Wilson County	KS	Ed Barton	1994	471
167 0/8	26 4/8	25 6/8	21 4/8	6	5	Otoe County	NE	Tom Tomes	1995	471
166 7/8	26 4/8	26 4/8	20 1/8	7	5	Saline County	NE	Scott Theis	1982	477
166 7/8	25 2/8	24 5/8	21 1/8	6	6	Geary County	KS	Dennis L. Gillam	1986	477
166 7/8	26 6/8	26 2/8	19 5/8	6	5	Jackson County	OH	Charles E. Cogdill	1990	477
166 7/8	23 7/8	24 2/8	19 4/8	8	6	Lake County	MN	Mark Hal Tucker	1991	477
166 7/8	27 4/8	27 1/8	20 5/8	4	4	Douglas County	WI	James N. Johnson	1992	477
166 7/8	27 5/8	27 1/8	22 4/8	5	4	St. Marys County	MD	Ricky D. Menard	1993	477
166 7/8	24 1/8	23 0/8	20 7/8	5	5	Parkland	ALB	Mark Williams	1994	477
166 7/8	26 5/8	26 1/8	22 5/8	7	6	Maverick County	TX	Gary Miller	1995	477
166 6/8	24 3/8	24 0/8	21 6/8	6	7	Lanigan	SAS	Bob Tempel	1985	485
166 6/8	27 3/8	26 6/8	17 6/8	5	5	Allegan County	MI	Larry Deater	1989	485
166 6/8	28 0/8	28 3/8	18 6/8	6	7	Monroe County	IN	Jeff A. Long	1992	485
166 6/8	23 0/8	23 4/8	17 2/8	7	7	Dubois County	IN	Edward Helming	1993	485
166 6/8	24 2/8	23 6/8	16 2/8	5	6	Pike County	IL	Gregory S. Guerrieri	1994	485
166 5/8	26 7/8	27 4/8	19 5/8	5	5	Lyon County	MN	Gene Gustafson	1982	490
166 5/8	25 2/8	25 0/8	17 5/8	6	7	Meade County	KS	Tim Ross	1987	490
166 5/8	26 4/8	25 0/8	17 2/8	6	8	Johnson County	IN	Joe F. Heath, Jr.	1989	490
166 5/8	25 0/8	25 2/8	21 3/8	8	6	Sarpy County	NE	Roy Symanietz	1990	490
166 5/8	25 5/8	25 5/8	21 5/8	7	8	Mills County	IA	Ted Love	1996	490
166 4/8	27 6/8	28 4/8	21 4/8	5	5	Juniper	NBW	Ron Peterson	1989	495
166 4/8	26 0/8	26 6/8	19 0/8	5	4	Pierce County	WI	Garrett "Gary" L. Fleishauer	1991	495
166 4/8	24 6/8	24 4/8	19 0/8	7	7	Buffalo County	WI	Dale Frost	1992	495
166 4/8	27 2/8	27 0/8	19 6/8	5	5	Gallia County	OH	Mike Wellman	1993	495
166 4/8	26 7/8	25 4/8	19 4/8	5	5	Hand County	SD	Kevin Bertsch	1993	495
166 4/8	25 6/8	26 1/8	18 2/8	5	5	Pottawatomie County	KS	Scott Hadsall	1994	495
166 4/8	26 2/8	26 5/8	17 2/8	6	6	Wayne County	IA	Scott Bunnell	1994	495
166 4/8	27 4/8	27 1/8	23 0/8	7	6	Marion County	IA	LeRoy Hansaker	1995	495
166 4/8	26 2/8	25 5/8	22 3/8	4	5	Winneshiek County	IA	Jeff Berns	1996	495
166 3/8	26 6/8	26 4/8	17 1/8	6	6	Clarke County	IA	Dwight E. Green	1965	504
166 3/8	26 3/8	26 0/8	18 2/8	8	5	Yankton County	SD	Roger Irwin	1985	504
166 3/8	25 2/8	25 1/8	17 6/8	9	7	Lake County	MN	Daniel H. Hall	1991	504
166 3/8	25 6/8	25 4/8	19 7/8	8	5	Suffolk County	NY	John Bennett	1993	504
166 3/8	27 4/8	25 4/8	18 1/8	5	5	Waupaca County	WI	Steven D. Breaker	1994	504
166 3/8	25 6/8	25 6/8	18 7/8	5	5	Rockingham County	VA	Thomas R. Keener	1995	504
166 3/8	27 1/8	26 5/8	21 1/8	5	7	Linn County	IA	Chad Huschka	1995	504
166 3/8	27 1/8	27 0/8	18 7/8	5	7	Clayton County	IA	David L. White	1995	504
166 2/8	29 3/8	29 4/8	21 5/8	6	4	Monona County	IA	G. K. Tuttle	1967	512
166 2/8	27 4/8	27 1/8	20 2/8	9	6	Republic County	KS	Virgil Graham	1986	512
166 2/8	25 1/8	26 7/8	19 1/8	6	6	Monroe County	IA	Cliff VanZee	1987	512
166 2/8	26 2/8	27 2/8	19 2/8	7	7	Mower County	MN	Kerry Schroeder	1988	512
166 2/8	24 5/8	24 7/8	19 2/8	6	7	Kane County	IL	Roy Howard	1991	512
166 2/8	25 7/8	26 4/8	18 4/8	6	5	Hancock County	IL	Doug Huls	1992	512
166 2/8	24 0/8	23 7/8	17 2/8	6	6	Piscataquis County	ME	Kelly D. Easler	1996	512
166 2/8	23 3/8	25 0/8	18 5/8	9	7	Vermilion County	IL	Jerry M. Courson	1997	512
166 1/8	23 2/8	23 5/8	19 3/8	5	5	Morrison County	MN	Corey Loney	1963	520
166 1/8	27 0/8	27 1/8	18 0/8	5	6	Stearns County	MN	Bruce C. Meade	1978	520
166 1/8	25 6/8	25 2/8	21 2/8	5	4	Texas County	OK	Max Crocker	1986	520
166 1/8	25 4/8	25 0/8	19 5/8	4	5	Chase County	KS	Lee Ayers	1987	520
166 1/8	24 5/8	24 5/8	17 1/8	5	6	Bartholomew County	IN	Bryan D. Cook	1989	520
166 1/8	23 4/8	23 2/8	17 2/8	7	6	White County	IN	Kerry Dean Morton	1989	520
166 1/8	27 3/8	28 7/8	20 2/8	8	5	Wayne County	IL	Ronald Riley	1990	520
166 1/8	25 4/8	26 0/8	18 4/8	7	6	Ross County	OH	Keith W. Orr	1991	520
166 1/8	24 2/8	25 2/8	21 1/8	6	6	Sibley County	MN	Robert M. Boettcher	1993	520
166 1/8	27 7/8	27 7/8	19 5/8	5	6	Jo Daviess County	IL	Dick V. Lalowski	1995	520
166 1/8	25 5/8	26 6/8	19 1/8	6	5	Washington County	IA	Al Chapman	1995	520
166 0/8	27 5/8	26 7/8	23 4/8	5	5	Clinton County	IA	Loy J. Brooker	1964	531
166 0/8	23 4/8	23 5/8	18 0/8	5	5	Bon Homme County	SD	Delbert Newman	1964	531
166 0/8	26 1/8	28 4/8	21 6/8	7	6	Shelby County	IL	Ernest D. Richardson	1977	531
166 0/8	26 6/8	24 2/8	22 7/8	6	6	Anoka County	MN	John A. Cardinal	1979	531
166 0/8	24 5/8	25 2/8	20 4/8	6	5	Tazewell County	IL	Jerry W. Kammerer	1981	531
166 0/8	24 4/8	25 5/8	19 2/8	5	5	Sedgwick County	KS	Louis Turner	1988	531
166 0/8	26 1/8	26 4/8	19 0/8	5	5	Martin County	IN	Terry L. McCrary	1988	531
166 0/8	25 2/8	26 1/8	18 6/8	5	5	McHenry County	IL	Brent A. Smith	1994	531
165 7/8	23 4/8	23 4/8	16 3/8	5	5	Wapello County	IA	Richard L. Larsen	1976	539
165 7/8	25 4/8	26 1/8	17 5/8	7	6	Licking County	OH	Pat Walker	1978	539
165 7/8	27 2/8	27 0/8	19 5/8	5	5	Prowers County	CO	Edward Henson	1980	539
165 7/8	23 0/8	26 0/8	18 1/8	5	5	Vermilion County	IL	Dick Bayer	1987	539
165 7/8	26 2/8	25 6/8	20 0/8	7	5	Weld County	CO	Mark Houtchens	1991	539
165 7/8	27 7/8	27 6/8	16 5/8	6	4	Madison County	IL	Tom Wieseman	1993	539
165 7/8	24 0/8	25 1/8	17 6/8	7	8	Fisher Branch	MAN	Frank Hall	1994	539
165 7/8	24 5/8	24 4/8	20 1/8	6	5	Madison County	MO	Tony Joe Helm	1994	539

WHITETAIL DEER (TYPICAL ANTLERS)

Minimum Score 125

SCORE	LENGTH OF MAIN BEAM R	L	INSIDE SPREAD	NUMBER OF POINTS R	L	AREA	STATE/ PROVINCE	HUNTER'S NAME	DATE	RANK
165 6/8	27 0/8	26 1/8	19 0/8	7	6	Pottawattamie County	IA	Dan Bowen	1968	547
165 6/8	28 1/8	25 7/8	18 4/8	5	6	Darke County	OH	Dean Neff	1988	547
165 6/8	25 1/8	25 1/8	19 0/8	7	6	Morrison County	MN	Rodney Mysliwiec	1988	547
165 6/8	25 1/8	26 2/8	18 3/8	5	6	Ottawa County	KS	Patrick E. Helget	1988	547
165 6/8	25 4/8	25 2/8	21 3/8	5	6	Randolph County	IL	David Uchtmann	1992	547
165 6/8	25 0/8	24 3/8	19 4/8	5	5	Vigo County	IN	Tim Jones	1994	547
165 6/8	25 7/8	24 3/8	16 4/8	7	6	Pike County	IL	Huston Martin III	1994	547
165 6/8	24 1/8	23 6/8	18 0/8	6	6	Shawnee County	KS	Willie Konrade	1995	547
165 5/8	29 0/8	29 2/8	20 2/8	7	8	Preble County	OH	Alan W. Risner	1992	555
165 4/8	25 6/8	25 1/8	21 0/8	5	5	Kent County	MD	Kent Price	1962	556
165 4/8	23 2/8	22 5/8	19 4/8	6	6	Peoria County	IL	Larry Toppe	1984	556
165 4/8	29 1/8	28 3/8	18 1/8	7	8	Buffalo County	WI	Patrick Ryan	1985	556
165 4/8	27 6/8	27 5/8	21 0/8	6	5	Will County	IL	Donald R. Spence	1988	556
165 4/8	25 6/8	27 2/8	22 0/8	5	5	Cherry County	NE	Jack Joseph	1990	556
165 4/8	26 1/8	25 2/8	20 0/8	5	5	Ohio County	KY	Dwight Keith	1994	556
165 4/8	27 0/8	25 5/8	16 2/8	7	7	Rockingham County	NC	Jerry Garland Chilton	1995	556
165 4/8	25 7/8	27 0/8	21 6/8	5	5	Guthrie County	IA	Larry Alexander	1995	556
165 4/8	23 3/8	23 3/8	17 2/8	6	6	Cochrane	ALB	Rob Valnoski	1996	556
165 4/8	27 0/8	26 7/8	21 1/8	6	5	Van Buren County	IA	Alan Andrews	1996	556
165 4/8	25 0/8	24 7/8	19 4/8	6	7	Ogle County	IL	James L. Morgan	1996	556
165 4/8	23 6/8	25 2/8	20 1/8	6	7	Dallas County	IA	Bret Renshaw	1997	556
165 3/8	23 7/8	25 6/8	17 1/8	5	7	Owen County	KY	Joseph Caruso	1977	568
165 3/8	27 0/8	27 2/8	22 5/8	7	7	Grundy County	IL	Gary R. Kuriger	1978	568
165 3/8	27 5/8	28 1/8	21 3/8	5	5	Marshall County	KS	Theodore J. Martin	1979	568
165 3/8	26 2/8	26 0/8	20 0/8	5	8	Victoria	MAN	David Wiklund	1984	568
165 3/8	26 1/8	24 1/8	20 3/8	5	5	Guthrie County	IA	Scott C. Kemble	1989	568
165 3/8	25 2/8	26 0/8	17 7/8	5	6	Hancock County	IN	Gary Dusang	1991	568
165 3/8	25 6/8	24 7/8	16 5/8	6	7	Rock Island County	IL	Roman H. Atnip	1991	568
165 3/8	25 6/8	25 6/8	20 1/8	5	5	Baca County	CO	Eddie Claypool	1991	568
165 3/8	26 4/8	25 6/8	18 6/8	5	6	Monroe County	MO	Larry Meier	1993	568
165 3/8	23 2/8	24 0/8	15 7/8	6	6	Coffey County	KS	Max A. Nichols	1993	568
165 3/8	26 0/8	26 1/8	19 7/8	7	6	Vermilion County	IL	Keith Downing	1993	568
165 3/8	27 0/8	27 4/8	20 1/8	5	5	Cass County	MI	Jim Hollingsworth	1995	568
165 2/8	26 5/8	24 6/8	18 1/8	6	6	McPherson County	KS	Daniel Willems	1981	580
165 2/8	25 6/8	24 2/8	18 2/8	5	5	Clermont County	OH	Nick Lung	1985	580
165 2/8	25 6/8	25 6/8	21 5/8	5	6	Dubuque County	IA	Paul J. Kluesner	1988	580
165 2/8	26 0/8	25 1/8	19 3/8	6	6	Wapello County	IA	Robert L. McDowell	1988	580
165 2/8	25 0/8	24 7/8	18 6/8	7	7	Dunn County	WI	Lamoine Roatch	1989	580
165 2/8	24 4/8	25 2/8	19 0/8	6	6	Harvey County	KS	Bob Stroble	1989	580
165 2/8	26 7/8	25 1/8	22 2/8	7	4	Mercer County	NJ	William E. Baker	1993	580
165 2/8	26 2/8	26 4/8	18 4/8	8	5	Sangamon County	IL	Daran Harn	1996	580
165 1/8	25 3/8	25 5/8	21 7/8	5	5	Barry County	MI	Jim Birmingham	1977	588
165 1/8	24 0/8	24 2/8	20 1/8	6	6	Sawyer County	WI	Robert N. Dale	1980	588
165 1/8	22 1/8	18 1/8	21 7/8	6	6	Iowa County	IA	David Roberts	1980	588
165 1/8	25 4/8	25 7/8	22 4/8	9	7	Wilson County	KS	Dr. Steven G. Mitchell	1987	588
165 1/8	25 6/8	25 3/8	17 5/8	5	5	Berrien County	MI	Ronald E. Aalfs	1989	588
165 1/8	24 4/8	23 2/8	16 7/8	6	5	Franklin County	IL	Terry Killgrove	1993	588
165 1/8	26 2/8	25 0/8	18 4/8	6	7	Jennings County	IN	Jerry W. St. John	1997	588
165 1/8	25 5/8	24 5/8	17 7/8	5	5	Bay County	MI	Terry L. Horner	1997	588
165 1/8	25 5/8	25 7/8	18 1/8	7	6	Brown County	IL	Dennis Cloninger	1997	588
165 0/8	26 0/8	24 6/8	18 3/8	6	5	Vilas County	WI	Jonothon Kostreva	1975	597
165 0/8	25 2/8	23 5/8	19 0/8	6	6	Stony Plain	ALB	Wayne C. Prier	1983	597
165 0/8	24 1/8	24 2/8	17 6/8	5	5	Doniphan County	KS	Richard Williams	1983	597
165 0/8	25 6/8	25 4/8	20 4/8	5	5	Jefferson County	KS	Emmet Copeland	1989	597
165 0/8	25 2/8	25 4/8	18 4/8	5	5	Montgomery County	IL	Steven L. Traylor	1989	597
165 0/8	27 2/8	28 1/8	19 6/8	5	5	Crawford County	IL	Charles E. Guyer	1990	597
165 0/8	29 0/8	30 1/8	23 5/8	6	6	Randolph County	IL	Bob Theobald	1990	597
165 0/8	25 1/8	25 3/8	19 4/8	5	5	Geary County	KS	Philip J. Palmer	1991	597
165 0/8	27 0/8	25 7/8	20 2/8	6	5	Stewart County	TN	Alan Coope	1992	597
165 0/8	23 7/8	25 0/8	19 0/8	7	6	Cook County	IL	Mark Stanley	1994	597
165 0/8	26 0/8	25 1/8	15 3/8	5	7	Jefferson County	WI	Robert N. Miller	1996	597
164 7/8	28 0/8	25 1/8	20 1/8	4	5	Kane County	IL	James A. Anderson	1980	608
164 7/8	25 4/8	26 2/8	19 3/8	5	5	Peoria County	IL	Joe R. McCord	1983	608
164 7/8	24 7/8	25 0/8	17 1/8	5	5	Elkhart County	IN	Joe Leszczynski	1984	608
164 7/8	25 0/8	25 4/8	19 3/8	6	6	Gray County	KS	Ralph W. Herron	1984	608
164 7/8	26 1/8	25 6/8	21 7/8	6	6	Madison County	MT	Gordan Sampson	1986	608
164 7/8	25 4/8	26 0/8	21 3/8	6	7	Coles County	IL	Ralph Garland	1988	608
164 7/8	26 5/8	27 3/8	18 7/8	6	5	Richland County	OH	Erwin Merkli	1988	608
164 7/8	27 5/8	27 6/8	23 1/8	7	7	Butler County	OH	Will McQueen	1989	608
164 7/8	26 4/8	25 4/8	17 7/8	6	5	Osage County	OK	Joe Admire, Sr.	1993	608
164 7/8	26 2/8	27 6/8	20 7/8	6	7	Anne Arundel County	MD	William Gabriel III	1996	608
164 6/8	28 1/8	26 5/8	20 7/8	8	6	Shelby County	OH	Jerry Atkinson	1975	618
164 6/8	26 4/8	28 2/8	22 2/8	5	6	Highland County	OH	Daniel L. Henges	1976	618
164 6/8	25 7/8	26 0/8	15 6/8	5	5	Sanilac County	MI	Michael J. Wines	1981	618
164 6/8	26 0/8	26 2/8	20 6/8	5	5	Macoupin County	IL	John E. Eldred	1985	618
164 6/8	26 5/8	26 5/8	26 4/8	8	5	Sullivan County	IN	John W. Hale	1988	618
164 6/8	23 6/8	22 3/8	20 2/8	5	5	La Salle County	IL	Randy Hooper	1988	618
164 6/8	24 5/8	24 5/8	17 0/8	5	5	Macon County	IL	Cal Heseman	1988	618

Continued 299

WHITETAIL DEER (TYPICAL ANTLERS)

Minimum Score 125 — Continued

SCORE	LENGTH OF R MAIN BEAM L		INSIDE SPREAD	NUMBER OF R POINTS L		AREA	STATE/ PROVINCE	HUNTER'S NAME	DATE	RANK
164 6/8	24 2/8	24 4/8	15 2/8	5	5	Emmet County	IA	Steven L. Reighard, Sr.	1990	618
164 6/8	27 7/8	26 6/8	19 5/8	6	7	Lincoln County	NE	Steve Stumbo	1996	618
164 6/8	26 1/8	25 1/8	17 6/8	5	5	Waukesha County	WI	Christopher E. Toutant	1997	618
164 6/8	25 1/8	26 0/8	18 4/8	5	5	Clay County	IL	Richard Stock	1997	618
164 5/8	25 2/8	23 5/8	18 5/8	8	6	Sumner County	KS	Archie A. Stralow	1967	629
164 5/8	26 3/8	24 6/8	20 6/8	5	6	Sedgwick County	CO	Brad Ham	1973	629
164 5/8	25 7/8	25 7/8	19 3/8	6	6	Fayette County	IA	Jerry Brown	1989	629
164 5/8	26 5/8	25 4/8	20 4/8	6	6	Saginaw County	MI	William J. Twarog	1990	629
164 5/8	25 6/8	26 1/8	18 0/8	8	7	McDonough County	IL	Scott Schauble	1994	629
164 5/8	26 3/8	26 5/8	22 4/8	6	6	Clark County	IL	Jason D. Wallace	1994	629
164 5/8	22 6/8	22 6/8	17 2/8	6	5	Rock County	WI	David R. Dummer, Jr.	1995	629
164 5/8	26 0/8	25 5/8	21 1/8	5	6	Portage County	WI	Jonah Reese	1995	629
164 5/8	25 4/8	24 5/8	20 6/8	6	5	Edgar County	IL	Joe Schmitt	1995	629
164 5/8	25 6/8	25 3/8	22 4/8	6	7	Ogle County	IL	Matt A. Mlsna	1996	629
164 5/8	26 5/8	24 6/8	19 1/8	5	5	Pottawattamie County	IA	Rodney P. Stahlnecker	1996	629
164 4/8	23 7/8	24 3/8	18 6/8	5	5	Morton County	ND	Butch Sammons	1985	640
164 4/8	27 5/8	27 0/8	19 3/8	5	6	Trempealeau County	WI	Keith Lynch	1985	640
164 4/8	23 5/8	23 5/8	20 7/8	6	6	Bond County	IL	Roger Munie	1987	640
164 4/8	26 6/8	26 4/8	18 6/8	7	6	Montgomery County	OH	Michael L. Mrusek	1990	640
164 4/8	26 7/8	26 6/8	17 0/8	5	5	Anoka County	MN	Paul Landberg	1991	640
164 4/8	26 0/8	27 1/8	18 2/8	6	5	Iroquois County	IL	Troy Gullquist	1992	640
164 3/8	25 4/8	25 4/8	19 6/8	8	7	Norman County	MN	Gilbert Guttormson	1953	646
164 3/8	21 4/8	21 6/8	16 5/8	6	6	Wibaux County	MT	Gerald Polesky	1959	646
164 3/8	28 4/8	28 0/8	20 4/8	7	8	Trigg County	KY	Charles Stahl	1965	646
164 3/8	25 1/8	25 2/8	18 3/8	5	5	Cottonwood County	MN	Jim Hansen	1972	646
164 3/8	26 4/8	25 5/8	17 3/8	7	8	Madison County	MT	Jim Schilke	1978	646
164 3/8	25 6/8	25 4/8	20 1/8	5	7	Saginaw County	MI	Larry Steinley	1979	646
164 3/8	27 1/8	27 5/8	20 7/8	4	4	Hardin County	OH	Anthony A. Krummrey	1982	646
164 3/8	28 0/8	27 5/8	21 1/8	6	8	Fayette County	OH	Steven J. Guess	1984	646
164 3/8	26 7/8	27 0/8	20 7/8	4	4	Louisa County	IA	Roger Gipple	1984	646
164 3/8	26 6/8	27 7/8	21 3/8	5	6	Perth	ONT	Michael Burwell	1986	646
164 3/8	26 7/8	25 5/8	18 7/8	5	5	Colfax County	NE	Dennis Indra	1987	646
164 3/8	25 2/8	24 6/8	20 5/8	5	5	Rock Island County	IL	Mike Mitten	1989	646
164 3/8	26 2/8	26 2/8	15 7/8	5	5	Scotland County	MO	David Westmoreland	1991	646
164 3/8	29 5/8	26 5/8	17 7/8	5	4	Van Buren County	MI	Kenneth J. Gillan	1991	646
164 3/8	24 7/8	25 2/8	16 4/8	6	6	Iron County	WI	Tom Brye	1992	646
164 3/8	25 6/8	24 6/8	22 0/8	6	5	Sturgeon	ALB	Neal Heaton	1992	646
164 3/8	25 2/8	26 1/8	17 3/8	5	6	Clark County	IL	Alan Lee	1992	646
164 3/8	25 6/8	24 7/8	18 0/8	5	8	Breckinridge County	KY	Richard P. Bagley	1994	646
164 3/8	25 4/8	25 0/8	17 6/8	6	6	Jefferson County	KS	Douglas J. Dee	1994	646
164 3/8	23 6/8	23 7/8	17 1/8	5	5	White County	IL	Bruce Hillyard	1994	646
164 3/8	26 5/8	26 3/8	18 7/8	6	5	Henry County	KY	Tom Jenkins	1995	646
164 2/8	27 2/8	26 2/8	21 0/8	11	7	Grundy County	IL	Jerome M. Fris	1972	667
164 2/8	26 7/8	26 2/8	17 5/8	6	6	Buffalo County	WI	Mark Busch	1986	667
164 2/8	26 0/8	25 6/8	19 0/8	5	5	Morrison County	MN	Tim Steinhoff	1987	667
164 2/8	26 6/8	27 1/8	19 6/8	6	5	Pike County	IL	Roger Pepper	1987	667
164 2/8	25 1/8	24 2/8	17 0/8	5	5	Mason County	IL	Richard J. "Buck" Fuller	1988	667
164 2/8	23 6/8	22 3/8	22 0/8	8	9	Kendall County	IL	Christopher Kiernan	1989	667
164 2/8	22 0/8	22 5/8	17 4/8	6	6	Lake County	IL	Steven Tjader	1989	667
164 2/8	26 7/8	27 5/8	20 6/8	5	7	Clark County	IL	Cole Lee	1990	667
164 2/8	23 4/8	24 4/8	19 0/8	6	5	Guthrie County	IA	Joe Dowell	1991	667
164 2/8	25 0/8	27 1/8	22 3/8	6	5	Montgomery County	IA	Dick Paul	1993	667
164 2/8	24 3/8	25 2/8	21 0/8	5	5	St. Croix County	WI	Tony Rizzo	1994	667
164 2/8	26 3/8	26 4/8	21 0/8	4	5	Ringgold County	IA	Steve Snow	1996	667
164 2/8	26 1/8	25 4/8	18 4/8	8	6	Jefferson County	KS	Lyle Beers	1997	667
164 1/8	26 5/8	26 3/8	18 2/8	6	5	Morrison County	MN	Lloyd Neuman	1971	680
164 1/8	26 2/8	26 4/8	22 5/8	5	5	Washington County	OH	Roger Pape	1980	680
164 1/8	24 6/8	24 5/8	16 5/8	5	5	Dundy County	NE	John Crump	1983	680
164 1/8	26 6/8	27 4/8	20 1/8	6	4	Adams County	IL	John Shaffer	1985	680
164 1/8	26 5/8	26 3/8	18 3/8	6	6	Otoe County	NE	Dale A. Hall	1989	680
164 1/8	25 4/8	26 1/8	20 5/8	6	5	Lawrence County	IN	Michael R. Davidson	1992	680
164 1/8	24 6/8	24 5/8	19 5/8	5	5	Spokane County	WA	Mike Ambach	1992	680
164 1/8	23 2/8	22 6/8	20 7/8	9	6	Nodaway County	MO	Lanny Guthrie	1993	680
164 1/8	24 2/8	24 2/8	19 3/8	7	6	Logan County	WV	Terry J. Cline	1993	680
164 1/8	24 6/8	24 5/8	17 6/8	5	6	Adair County	MO	Rodney Baumgartner	1993	680
164 1/8	24 5/8	25 4/8	17 1/8	5	6	Monroe County	WI	Gary Wright	1994	680
164 1/8	25 0/8	24 4/8	21 5/8	5	5	Republic County	KS	Gary Dahl	1997	680
164 0/8	24 3/8	25 0/8	16 6/8	5	5	Olmsted County	MN	Robert Meyer	1969	692
164 0/8	25 1/8	25 5/8	23 3/8	5	7	Morrison County	MN	Bruce Edberg	1977	692
164 0/8	28 0/8	26 4/8	22 6/8	5	5	Buffalo County	WI	Gerald Palmer	1986	692
164 0/8	25 5/8	26 5/8	19 6/8	6	5	Burnett County	WI	Gary A. Johnson	1989	692
164 0/8	25 4/8	25 2/8	22 2/8	7	6	Lawrence County	IL	Tom Childress	1992	692
164 0/8	23 5/8	24 1/8	17 4/8	7	7	Harlan County	KY	Gilbert E. Hensley	1992	692
164 0/8	24 0/8	24 6/8	19 2/8	6	5	Dallas County	IA	Iner Joelson	1994	692
164 0/8	26 4/8	26 1/8	19 2/8	4	5	Steuben County	IN	Kevin Smith	1995	692
164 0/8	26 4/8	26 0/8	19 6/8	5	5	Hennepin County	MN	Douglas Leo Moore	1997	692
164 0/8	25 2/8	25 3/8	15 4/8	5	5	Morrill County	NE	Tim Ray	1997	692
164 0/8	25 4/8	25 2/8	21 3/8	6	5	Jefferson County	IA	Robin Giebel	1997	692

WHITETAIL DEER (TYPICAL ANTLERS)

Minimum Score 125 — Continued

SCORE	LENGTH OF MAIN BEAM R	LENGTH OF MAIN BEAM L	INSIDE SPREAD	NUMBER OF POINTS R	NUMBER OF POINTS L	AREA	STATE/ PROVINCE	HUNTER'S NAME	DATE	RANK
163 7/8	26 3/8	26 4/8	19 3/8	9	10	Caldwell County	KY	Daniel R. Keith	1988	703
163 7/8	27 1/8	27 3/8	22 1/8	6	7	Cass County	IL	Richard Chase/Henry Susong	1993	703
163 7/8	23 4/8	24 6/8	18 3/8	5	5	Craig County	OK	Kelly Dougherty	1995	703
163 7/8	25 3/8	25 5/8	18 5/8	5	6	Wayne County	NY	Rick Martin	1997	703
163 7/8	24 1/8	24 5/8	18 6/8	5	6	Comanche County	KS	Darrell Allen	1997	703
163 7/8	23 4/8	25 0/8	19 1/8	5	5	Adams County	WI	Eric Johnson	1997	703
163 6/8	23 6/8	26 5/8	19 2/8	5	5	Fayette County	IA	Bob Nicolay	1981	709
163 6/8	23 5/8	25 4/8	19 4/8	7	8	Porter County	IN	Raymond T. Satterblom	1983	709
163 6/8	23 5/8	24 7/8	17 5/8	6	5	Graham County	KS	Russell Hull	1987	709
163 6/8	27 4/8	27 6/8	20 2/8	5	6	Clark County	IL	Gerald Shaffner	1991	709
163 6/8	23 0/8	23 7/8	18 3/8	7	5	Cook County	IL	Mike Ryan	1992	709
163 6/8	24 3/8	24 0/8	17 0/8	5	6	Cowley County	KS	Larry J. McKean	1992	709
163 6/8	24 4/8	25 1/8	17 6/8	5	5	Lee County	IA	Troy Matter	1994	709
163 6/8	26 4/8	27 1/8	18 7/8	6	5	Schuyler County	IL	Bruce Clements	1995	709
163 6/8	24 6/8	26 4/8	19 7/8	6	6	Page County	IA	Justin Blake	1997	709
163 5/8	25 6/8	25 4/8	21 6/8	5	5	Phillips County	KS	Bill Duncan	1969	718
163 5/8	26 5/8	26 1/8	21 3/8	6	6	Lawrence County	IL	Larry K. Karns	1975	718
163 5/8	25 5/8	25 1/8	19 3/8	5	5	Wright County	MN	Rick Heberling	1978	718
163 5/8	26 4/8	25 1/8	19 2/8	6	7	Fulton County	IL	Mike Reatherford	1982	718
163 5/8	25 1/8	25 4/8	19 4/8	6	8	Jackson County	MO	Chris Shotton	1985	718
163 5/8	25 4/8	26 2/8	19 0/8	6	7	Franklin County	IN	Roger Mullins	1987	718
163 5/8	23 4/8	23 1/8	19 3/8	5	6	Carver County	MN	Ryan Jopp	1991	718
163 5/8	21 3/8	21 2/8	15 1/8	6	5	Somerset County	MD	Mike Nichols	1992	718
163 5/8	26 3/8	29 0/8	21 0/8	8	6	Vermilion County	IL	James D. Rueter	1992	718
163 5/8	25 0/8	25 4/8	17 1/8	4	6	Billings County	ND	Ohne L. Raasch	1994	718
163 5/8	26 3/8	27 0/8	19 1/8	5	5	Henry County	MO	Keith Lawson	1996	718
163 5/8	26 2/8	26 5/8	22 1/8	8	6	Ramsey County	MN	Robert Meyer	1998	718
163 4/8	25 4/8	25 5/8	18 0/8	5	7	Renville County	ND	Bobby Triplett	1958	730
163 4/8	23 4/8	23 0/8	17 6/8	5	5	Wright County	MN	Dale Guetzkow	1978	730
163 4/8	28 1/8	30 0/8	23 2/8	5	5	Lawrence County	OH	Berkley Pennington, Sr.	1981	730
163 4/8	24 7/8	23 6/8	21 6/8	8	6	Racine County	WI	Greg A. Hanson	1991	730
163 4/8	24 1/8	24 2/8	20 7/8	7	7	Will County	IL	Clark Davis	1992	730
163 4/8	25 1/8	25 0/8	20 4/8	5	5	Macon County	AL	George P. Mann	1994	730
163 4/8	22 7/8	23 3/8	17 2/8	8	6	Otter Tail County	MN	Kurt Melancon	1994	730
163 4/8	27 0/8	26 6/8	18 2/8	4	4	Lapeer County	MI	Bruce R. Byrnes	1994	730
163 4/8	21 7/8	21 2/8	16 5/8	6	7	Waupaca County	WI	Jeffrey F. Hietpas	1994	730
163 4/8	26 0/8	25 1/8	19 4/8	6	6	Guthrie County	IA	Regi Goodale	1994	730
163 4/8	26 2/8	25 2/8	19 1/8	6	6	Seward County	KS	Josh Leonard	1994	730
163 4/8	25 3/8	26 6/8	19 0/8	5	5	Davis County	IA	Neil A. Adams	1995	730
163 4/8	28 6/8	27 7/8	21 2/8	4	5	Guthrie County	IA	Matthew J. Ewing	1996	730
163 4/8	26 6/8	26 7/8	21 4/8	6	6	Washtenaw County	MI	Troy J. Satterthwaite	1996	730
163 4/8	24 1/8	23 0/8	14 0/8	5	5	Pike County	IL	Jim Morgan	1997	730
163 3/8	24 4/8	22 7/8	22 1/8	5	5	Linn County	IA	Delmar Phillips	1960	745
163 3/8	24 3/8	23 7/8	17 5/8	8	7	Morrison County	MN	Alvin A. Diemert	1973	745
163 3/8	26 4/8	26 2/8	20 5/8	5	5	Scott County	KY	Garry Hoffman	1982	745
163 3/8	26 1/8	26 7/8	15 3/8	6	7	Chase County	KS	John Moore	1983	745
163 3/8	24 4/8	25 0/8	19 0/8	8	8	Winnebago County	IL	Bradley S. Conrad	1984	745
163 3/8	27 2/8	26 1/8	19 1/8	5	5	Eaton County	MI	Dennis Orr	1987	745
163 3/8	24 7/8	24 7/8	19 1/8	6	8	Jefferson County	IL	Ray Leneave	1993	745
163 3/8	25 5/8	26 5/8	14 5/8	5	5	Barrhead	ALB	Ryan Bielert	1995	745
163 3/8	25 0/8	25 7/8	18 5/8	5	5	Polk County	MN	Jim Ross	1995	745
163 3/8	27 6/8	26 1/8	22 2/8	6	7	Baltimore County	MD	Christian M. Phillips	1995	745
163 3/8	24 2/8	24 0/8	16 7/8	5	5	Republic County	KS	Lonnie Boman	1996	745
163 3/8	26 0/8	25 3/8	23 4/8	6	5	Page County	IA	Bob Hilton, Jr.	1996	745
163 3/8	24 5/8	26 3/8	20 4/8	7	6	Jackson County	IL	Mark Bennett	1997	745
163 2/8	28 2/8	27 3/8	23 7/8	6	5	Brown County	IL	Keith E. Meiser	1981	758
163 2/8	25 7/8	29 2/8	22 6/8	8	5	Drew County	AR	Larry Standley	1982	758
163 2/8	25 4/8	25 5/8	19 6/8	5	5	Mason County	KY	R. Kenton Ring	1982	758
163 2/8	26 1/8	24 6/8	16 3/8	5	7	Licking County	OH	Don Conrad	1985	758
163 2/8	24 1/8	24 4/8	21 2/8	5	5	Sumner County	KS	Kevin Disney	1985	758
163 2/8	23 3/8	23 7/8	19 0/8	5	7	Carroll County	MD	Jason Carder	1988	758
163 2/8	26 4/8	27 2/8	21 5/8	7	5	Kiowa County	KS	Jesse Zook	1989	758
163 2/8	25 4/8	26 7/8	19 2/8	5	4	Crawford County	KS	Melinda S. Nutt	1991	758
163 2/8	24 2/8	24 3/8	20 4/8	5	5	Hennepin County	MN	Larry Watson	1991	758
163 2/8	27 1/8	28 3/8	20 4/8	5	5	Ross County	OH	Sam Detty	1992	758
163 2/8	23 0/8	22 7/8	17 0/8	7	7	Houston County	MN	Aaron Augedahl	1992	758
163 2/8	24 2/8	24 2/8	17 4/8	5	5	Rock County	WI	Richard T. Hall	1993	758
163 2/8	25 1/8	23 3/8	19 4/8	5	6	Linn County	IA	Randy Gardner	1994	758
163 2/8	28 2/8	27 3/8	22 4/8	4	4	Sangamon County	IL	Robert N. Kirk	1995	758
163 2/8	25 1/8	24 7/8	17 6/8	5	6	Boone County	WV	Harold McCoy	1996	758
163 2/8	25 6/8	24 1/8	20 2/8	5	5	Hardin County	OH	Nathan King	1996	758
163 1/8	24 2/8	26 0/8	16 4/8	7	7	Logan County	WV	Gilbert Sexton	1963	774
163 1/8	27 6/8	27 5/8	18 6/8	8	5	Knox County	OH	Robert L. Hammond	1983	774
163 1/8	25 3/8	25 0/8	20 0/8	6	6	Lake County	IL	Andrew Holst	1987	774
163 1/8	25 1/8	25 6/8	21 3/8	6	5	Logan County	OH	Jerrod Pooler	1988	774
163 1/8	22 5/8	24 3/8	18 7/8	5	7	Clayton County	IA	Daniel J. Brady	1988	774
163 1/8	25 6/8	25 2/8	18 5/8	5	5	Wright County	MN	Jerry Goodale	1990	774
163 1/8	24 6/8	26 4/8	18 0/8	6	6	Bayfield County	WI	Steve Polkoski	1992	774

WHITETAIL DEER (TYPICAL ANTLERS)

Minimum Score 125   Continued

SCORE	LENGTH OF MAIN BEAM R	LENGTH OF MAIN BEAM L	INSIDE SPREAD	NUMBER OF POINTS R	NUMBER OF POINTS L	AREA	STATE/PROVINCE	HUNTER'S NAME	DATE	RANK
163 1/8	26 2/8	26 2/8	20 1/8	6	5	Edwards County	IL	Roger D. Shelby	1992	774
163 1/8	25 3/8	24 0/8	19 7/8	8	8	La Salle County	TX	Francis D. Elias	1992	774
163 1/8	27 2/8	26 7/8	23 3/8	4	5	Peoria County	IL	Larry Pollack	1995	774
163 0/8	24 0/8	24 6/8	20 0/8	5	5	Dickinson County	IA	Harold Ehrp	1959	784
163 0/8	25 2/8	25 0/8	15 1/8	6	6	Texas County	OK	Edward F. Bryan, Jr.	1976	784
163 0/8	26 3/8	25 3/8	22 0/8	7	8	Switzerland County	IN	Richard W. Keebler	1977	784
163 0/8	25 1/8	24 3/8	16 4/8	5	5	Ashland County	WI	Sid Kilger	1982	784
163 0/8	27 5/8	26 6/8	21 0/8	8	8	Gibson County	IN	Phil Scott	1986	784
163 0/8	25 6/8	24 2/8	20 0/8	5	6	Marshall County	KS	Tim Wanklyn	1986	784
163 0/8	24 6/8	24 0/8	19 2/8	6	6	Jefferson County	IN	Don Field	1987	784
163 0/8	27 4/8	27 2/8	19 3/8	6	8	Clarke County	IA	Gary Cobb	1988	784
163 0/8	24 4/8	24 1/8	20 4/8	5	6	Clermont County	OH	Larry W. Van	1990	784
163 0/8	20 7/8	19 6/8	15 0/8	6	7	Macoupin County	IL	Rick Tigo	1992	784
163 0/8	21 6/8	22 2/8	17 4/8	6	6	Will County	IL	Ray T. Guzak	1993	784
163 0/8	25 1/8	25 5/8	20 4/8	6	6	Will County	IL	Steve Connors	1994	784
163 0/8	23 4/8	23 7/8	21 4/8	5	5	Lincoln County	CO	Dennis Goody	1994	784
163 0/8	25 5/8	26 4/8	18 1/8	6	5	Fayette County	IL	Terry L. Jones	1996	784
163 0/8	25 5/8	26 1/8	19 2/8	6	5	Putnam County	MO	James W. Ross	1996	784
162 7/8	29 0/8	30 4/8	19 0/8	6	8	Queen Annes County	MD	L. P. Stephens, Jr.	1962	799
162 7/8	24 6/8	24 6/8	22 4/8	6	7	Cowley County	KS	Kenneth Highfill	1968	799
162 7/8	26 6/8	26 7/8	19 5/8	5	5	Lee County	IA	Mike Bentler	1983	799
162 7/8	24 0/8	23 5/8	22 3/8	5	5	Perry County	IL	Kevin Tate	1989	799
162 7/8	25 0/8	25 0/8	18 5/8	5	5	Baltimore County	MD	Bruce Hoover	1991	799
162 7/8	26 7/8	27 3/8	18 6/8	5	6	Edmonton	ALB	Mark Daniel Stanley	1991	799
162 7/8	23 1/8	24 2/8	16 5/8	5	5	Cuyahoga County	OH	Brett A. Hahner	1994	799
162 7/8	27 2/8	26 1/8	18 3/8	6	5	Sawyer County	WI	Tim Wozniak	1994	799
162 7/8	23 7/8	24 4/8	20 5/8	5	5	Chippewa County	WI	Terry Geist	1994	799
162 7/8	25 7/8	25 6/8	18 5/8	6	6	Outagamie County	WI	Pat Vande Hei	1995	799
162 7/8	25 4/8	25 0/8	16 3/8	4	4	Mason County	IL	David C. Session	1995	799
162 7/8	23 4/8	23 3/8	18 0/8	8	6	Scott County	MN	Rob Sieh	1996	799
162 7/8	27 3/8	27 0/8	21 7/8	4	5	McHenry County	IL	Troy Erckfritz	1996	799
162 7/8	22 0/8	22 4/8	19 3/8	6	5	Jackson County	IL	John Joiner	1996	799
162 7/8	22 7/8	24 0/8	17 7/8	6	5	Pike County	IL	Dan Perez	1997	799
162 7/8	25 4/8	26 3/8	14 7/8	5	6	Waukesha County	WI	Kevin Pavloski	1997	799
162 7/8	24 5/8	24 7/8	18 7/8	6	5	Jefferson County	MO	David Keith Wiley	1997	799
162 6/8	24 2/8	26 2/8	20 6/8	6	7	Rice County	MN	Ken Bakken	1957	816
162 6/8	26 2/8	26 2/8	19 4/8	5	6	Clayton County	IA	Dale Kartman	1984	816
162 6/8	24 1/8	24 7/8	17 4/8	5	5	Ozaukee County	WI	Joe Seaman	1989	816
162 6/8	24 2/8	25 2/8	18 5/8	6	5	Cedar County	IA	John Shepherd	1994	816
162 6/8	26 4/8	25 7/8	21 4/8	6	6	Parke County	IN	Tim Wilson	1997	816
162 6/8	26 2/8	26 7/8	17 6/8	9	6	Dallas County	IA	Robert Sulllvan	1997	816
162 5/8	26 2/8	24 0/8	20 7/8	8	7	Marshall County	KS	Gary W. Tobin	1966	822
162 5/8	26 4/8	27 5/8	20 3/8	4	4	Saunders County	NE	Robert Parkins	1967	822
162 5/8	26 6/8	26 6/8	21 5/8	5	7	Henry County	IL	Lewis E. Burson	1976	822
162 5/8	25 2/8	24 7/8	20 1/8	4	5	Lucas County	IA	Bill Brown	1979	822
162 5/8	25 2/8	25 3/8	15 7/8	5	8	Crawford County	KS	Fred Geier	1981	822
162 5/8	27 2/8	27 4/8	19 7/8	5	5	St. Charles County	MO	Roland Heiliger	1985	822
162 5/8	25 3/8	24 3/8	16 4/8	7	5	Buffalo County	WI	Paul Schultz	1986	822
162 5/8	25 4/8	25 3/8	16 3/8	7	6	Hubbard County	MN	Nick J. Thill, Jr.	1987	822
162 5/8	24 4/8	23 1/8	19 0/8	6	6	Pike County	IL	LeRoy Leonard	1987	822
162 5/8	25 0/8	25 1/8	20 3/8	6	6	Cerro Gordo County	IA	R. C. Field	1989	822
162 5/8	26 3/8	26 7/8	17 7/8	5	7	Wyandot County	OH	David Weininger	1991	822
162 5/8	25 6/8	25 7/8	18 2/8	6	6	Jennings County	IN	Guy F. Euler	1992	822
162 5/8	24 1/8	23 0/8	18 7/8	5	6	Jefferson County	IL	Edgar Knaus	1993	822
162 5/8	25 4/8	25 7/8	20 7/8	5	5	Washington County	WI	Edwin M. Ruege	1996	822
162 5/8	23 6/8	24 7/8	20 0/8	6	5	Suffolk County	NY	Rob Catalano	1997	822
162 5/8	31 3/8	29 4/8	18 1/8	5	5	Lake County	IL	Scott A. Strickfaden	1997	822
162 4/8	23 6/8	23 6/8	21 0/8	7	6	Branch County	MI	Randy Massey	1981	838
162 4/8	25 2/8	25 1/8	19 6/8	6	8	Louisa County	IA	Michael Bell	1983	838
162 4/8	25 4/8	27 0/8	18 6/8	5	5	Allegheny County	PA	Christopher T. Joyce	1985	838
162 4/8	26 0/8	26 4/8	22 0/8	5	5	Dundy County	NE	Bradley Wiese	1985	838
162 4/8	24 3/8	24 4/8	21 1/8	5	6	Stearns County	MN	Pat Gross	1986	838
162 4/8	23 1/8	24 1/8	18 0/8	5	6	Vermilion County	IL	Sandra Downing	1986	838
162 4/8	25 5/8	24 6/8	21 0/8	6	7	Will County	IL	Joseph R. Franco	1986	838
162 4/8	25 5/8	25 5/8	17 1/8	5	6	Anoka County	MN	Kim Van Tassel	1987	838
162 4/8	24 1/8	24 7/8	19 4/8	5	5	Champaign County	OH	Alan Shafer, Jr.	1993	838
162 4/8	24 5/8	24 0/8	18 2/8	5	8	Cass County	MI	Bruce Woodill	1995	838
162 3/8	24 2/8	24 6/8	19 7/8	5	6	Barber County	KS	GLen Snell	1982	848
162 3/8	27 2/8	27 2/8	19 6/8	5	6	Lake County	IL	Donald M. Hewkin	1986	848
162 3/8	25 3/8	25 6/8	21 6/8	5	6	Menard County	IL	Mitchell Coffey	1987	848
162 3/8	23 4/8	23 4/8	20 5/8	5	5	Ogle County	IL	Jeffrey S. Burke	1989	848
162 3/8	24 7/8	24 4/8	14 7/8	5	5	Morrison County	MN	Edward J. Kastner	1989	848
162 3/8	27 7/8	28 0/8	19 4/8	8	7	Edmonton	ALB	Dale Spooner	1992	848
162 3/8	25 5/8	25 5/8	17 2/8	5	7	Whiteside County	IL	Clint Walker	1995	848
162 3/8	26 6/8	25 3/8	21 5/8	5	5	Washington County	IA	James Cluney	1995	848
162 3/8	25 5/8	24 3/8	19 3/8	6	6	Dane County	WI	Ronald E. Goodrich	1997	848
162 3/8	24 0/8	24 7/8	17 2/8	5	6	Oakland County	MI	Matthew A. Jameson	1997	848
162 3/8	24 5/8	23 7/8	17 5/8	6	8	Bourbon County	KS	Don Slinkard	1997	848

WHITETAIL DEER (TYPICAL ANTLERS)

Minimum Score 125

SCORE	LENGTH OF MAIN BEAM R	LENGTH OF MAIN BEAM L	INSIDE SPREAD	NUMBER OF POINTS R	NUMBER OF POINTS L	AREA	STATE/PROVINCE	HUNTER'S NAME	DATE	RANK
162 2/8	22 2/8	24 7/8	17 6/8	6	5	Kingsbury County	SD	Dale Peterson	1972	859
162 2/8	24 6/8	24 0/8	16 2/8	5	5	Plymouth County	IA	Gary Mitchell	1980	859
162 2/8	24 1/8	24 2/8	20 4/8	6	5	Le Sueur County	MN	Joe Rybus	1981	859
162 2/8	24 7/8	24 2/8	19 0/8	5	5	Marion County	KS	Leslie Lalouette	1983	859
162 2/8	25 3/8	24 7/8	17 6/8	5	5	Trego County	KS	Craig Doll	1985	859
162 2/8	24 0/8	23 4/8	16 6/8	5	5	Hendricks County	IN	Leon Smith	1986	859
162 2/8	26 2/8	25 7/8	16 4/8	8	6	Litchfield County	CT	Warren Hensel	1988	859
162 2/8	21 4/8	23 7/8	21 2/8	6	5	Miller County	MO	Steve Wyrick	1990	859
162 2/8	25 5/8	26 0/8	16 2/8	6	6	Will County	IL	Mike O'Connor	1991	859
162 2/8	25 1/8	23 7/8	19 6/8	6	6	Henry County	IA	Myles Keller	1991	859
162 2/8	27 0/8	27 0/8	21 3/8	6	8	Vermilion County	IL	Alan Colwell	1995	859
162 2/8	26 0/8	25 2/8	22 0/8	6	5	Douglas County	KS	Keith Jones	1996	859
162 1/8	23 6/8	24 7/8	17 6/8	6	6	Buffalo County	WI	Bruce Curtis	1983	871
162 1/8	23 4/8	24 2/8	20 4/8	6	5	Winnebago County	IL	Jeffrey A. Saxby	1984	871
162 1/8	25 2/8	26 0/8	16 4/8	8	6	Monroe County	IA	Larry Whitson	1985	871
162 1/8	27 5/8	24 7/8	18 1/8	6	7	Lafayette County	WI	Charles D. Potter	1986	871
162 1/8	25 6/8	26 4/8	21 4/8	7	7	Clinton County	OH	Mark A. Ross	1988	871
162 1/8	26 7/8	27 0/8	18 7/8	5	5	Adams County	IL	Randall Lummer	1990	871
162 1/8	27 0/8	25 0/8	22 4/8	5	5	Newbrook	ALB	Jim Helling	1994	871
162 1/8	25 1/8	25 7/8	18 1/8	5	5	Buffalo County	WI	Terry Krahn	1994	871
162 1/8	26 4/8	25 5/8	21 5/8	6	6	Bureau County	IL	Ned L. Thompson	1994	871
162 1/8	26 2/8	26 1/8	17 6/8	5	6	Fulton County	IL	C. Wayne Miller	1995	871
162 1/8	24 0/8	24 6/8	17 4/8	7	6	Cole County	MO	Carl Rackers	1996	871
162 1/8	26 6/8	27 0/8	21 6/8	6	6	Rooks County	KS	Marc D. Gray	1997	871
162 0/8	25 0/8	27 1/8	20 4/8	8	6	Bond County	IL	Larry Nelson	1976	883
162 0/8	24 2/8	24 2/8	17 2/8	5	5	Wabash County	IL	Ron Hawf	1978	883
162 0/8	24 3/8	27 2/8	19 2/8	6	6	Edgar County	IL	John J. Dillon	1985	883
162 0/8	25 7/8	24 7/8	23 7/8	5	7	Marion County	KS	Don Bredemeier	1987	883
162 0/8	26 0/8	27 7/8	19 2/8	6	5	Mahoning County	OH	Mark A. Brooks	1988	883
162 0/8	28 0/8	28 6/8	19 0/8	6	5	Anoka County	MN	Dean Smith	1990	883
162 0/8	25 7/8	26 2/8	20 5/8	6	6	Tolland County	CT	Bruce Moore	1990	883
162 0/8	23 1/8	24 4/8	17 0/8	6	7	Richland County	ND	Tim Poehls	1992	883
162 0/8	25 4/8	25 0/8	17 7/8	6	7	Morrison County	MN	Kevin Windschitl	1993	883
162 0/8	25 1/8	28 0/8	23 4/8	7	5	Ashland County	OH	Larry G. Hammon	1993	883
162 0/8	24 5/8	24 2/8	18 2/8	5	6	Dane County	WI	Richard Graf, Jr.	1994	883
162 0/8	28 6/8	27 1/8	21 4/8	5	5	Hancock County	OH	Bradley D. DePuy	1994	883
162 0/8	28 1/8	27 6/8	18 0/8	4	5	Hancock County	IL	Frank Hanks	1995	883
162 0/8	24 7/8	24 7/8	17 0/8	5	5	Marathon County	WI	Gregg Danke	1996	883
162 0/8	25 0/8	25 0/8	20 4/8	5	5	Prince Georges County	MD	Charles Figgins	1996	883
161 7/8	23 4/8	25 4/8	18 3/8	5	5	Saunders County	NE	David Strimple	1961	898
161 7/8	24 2/8	24 1/8	20 7/8	5	5	Douglas County	NE	Noel Miller	1970	898
161 7/8	23 5/8	24 0/8	17 6/8	7	7	Fulton County	IL	Bob Neal	1981	898
161 7/8	26 0/8	27 2/8	20 7/8	5	5	Greene County	OH	Charles O. Hill	1982	898
161 7/8	25 3/8	26 0/8	20 6/8	7	7	Tuscarawas County	OH	Gary Stevens	1982	898
161 7/8	23 3/8	22 2/8	16 0/8	6	6	Brandon	MAN	Gary Kaluzniak	1985	898
161 7/8	26 5/8	25 6/8	18 3/8	6	6	Winona County	MN	Tim Rislow	1986	898
161 7/8	24 2/8	24 7/8	17 6/8	8	5	Jones County	IA	Paul Johnson	1986	898
161 7/8	23 4/8	24 4/8	16 5/8	5	5	Marion County	MO	James Schaefer	1987	898
161 7/8	23 1/8	23 2/8	18 3/8	5	5	Jefferson County	WI	Adam Achilli	1988	898
161 7/8	21 5/8	24 4/8	17 5/8	7	6	Ontario County	NY	Adam T. Kupis	1989	898
161 7/8	27 0/8	27 7/8	18 0/8	9	6	Mahoning County	OH	Nicholas Young	1990	898
161 7/8	25 6/8	25 6/8	21 1/8	5	4	Stark County	IL	Adam Shane	1995	898
161 7/8	28 2/8	27 5/8	19 0/8	9	6	Union County	IL	Gary Towell	1995	898
161 7/8	27 4/8	27 1/8	19 1/8	5	5	Webster County	MO	Jack J. Hubbell	1997	898
161 6/8	27 3/8	26 0/8	27 1/8	4	5	Lake County	IL	David Mitten	1987	913
161 6/8	22 6/8	23 6/8	17 6/8	5	6	Jo Daviess County	IL	Timothy T. Westemeier	1987	913
161 6/8	27 7/8	26 7/8	21 2/8	6	6	Pike County	IL	Brad Stamp	1988	913
161 6/8	26 2/8	24 0/8	19 0/8	6	5	Montgomery County	TN	Zane Mason	1991	913
161 6/8	23 6/8	23 7/8	21 5/8	7	5	Hancock County	IL	Jerry Pryor	1992	913
161 6/8	25 0/8	24 7/8	20 0/8	5	5	La Grange County	IN	Mark Robbins	1993	913
161 6/8	23 4/8	23 1/8	16 2/8	5	5	Clark County	IL	Paul Baird	1994	913
161 6/8	24 3/8	23 5/8	18 4/8	5	5	Westchester County	NY	Robert Olivier	1994	913
161 6/8	26 6/8	26 2/8	18 3/8	5	6	Starbuck	MAN	Greg Shirtliff	1996	913
161 5/8	23 3/8	23 1/8	14 5/8	6	6	Dunn County	WI	Leonard Hines	1970	922
161 5/8	22 6/8	22 5/8	18 6/8	5	6	Juneau County	WI	Harlan Steindl	1971	922
161 5/8	25 0/8	25 5/8	19 1/8	6	6	Jefferson County	IL	Rick Osborn	1982	922
161 5/8	22 5/8	24 3/8	17 7/8	5	5	Butler County	KS	Mike Turner	1982	922
161 5/8	26 3/8	24 4/8	16 4/8	5	6	Butler County	KS	Ronald Tilson	1983	922
161 5/8	27 2/8	27 4/8	18 1/8	7	8	Franklin County	KS	Dennis Ballweg	1987	922
161 5/8	25 4/8	24 2/8	19 1/8	5	5	Woodford County	IL	Lynn Roseman	1989	922
161 5/8	24 4/8	24 1/8	17 1/8	5	6	Forest County	WI	Daniel G. Van Hoosen	1990	922
161 5/8	26 3/8	26 1/8	20 0/8	6	6	Buffalo County	WI	Gerald Todd, Jr.	1992	922
161 5/8	24 0/8	24 0/8	16 3/8	5	5	East Carroll Parish	LA	F. Lane Mitchell	1993	922
161 5/8	25 3/8	25 4/8	21 5/8	5	5	Comanche County	KS	Jack Brannan	1993	922
161 5/8	24 0/8	24 3/8	19 1/8	7	7	Hamilton County	OH	Robert E. Plasters	1995	922
161 5/8	23 3/8	25 0/8	15 7/8	6	6	Logan County	WV	Robert Lee Adams, Jr.	1995	922
161 5/8	26 2/8	26 1/8	19 1/8	6	5	Franklin County	OH	Craig Bonham	1996	922
161 5/8	24 6/8	26 5/8	20 1/8	5	5	Guthrie County	IA	Kenneth E. Briggs	1996	922

WHITETAIL DEER (TYPICAL ANTLERS)

Minimum Score 125

SCORE	LENGTH OF MAIN BEAM R	LENGTH OF MAIN BEAM L	INSIDE SPREAD	NUMBER OF POINTS R	NUMBER OF POINTS L	AREA	STATE/PROVINCE	HUNTER'S NAME	DATE	RANK
161 5/8	23 6/8	23 6/8	18 1/8	5	5	Shawnee County	KS	Dwight Streeter	1997	922
161 4/8	26 1/8	26 1/8	19 2/8	5	4	Bond County	IL	Sam White	1974	938
161 4/8	26 0/8	25 6/8	17 4/8	8	6	East Feliciana Parish	LA	James K. Morgan	1977	938
161 4/8	25 2/8	27 0/8	20 2/8	5	5	Sumner County	KS	Phill Allton	1983	938
161 4/8	28 4/8	28 3/8	22 1/8	5	5	Jones County	IA	David A. Leuchs	1984	938
161 4/8	23 3/8	24 1/8	18 4/8	6	5	Cass County	NE	Ray Brock	1985	938
161 4/8	27 1/8	26 5/8	18 5/8	4	5	Crawford County	KS	Fred Geier	1988	938
161 4/8	26 1/8	26 6/8	16 7/8	5	6	Oconto County	WI	Jeffery J. Brabant	1989	938
161 4/8	25 0/8	25 1/8	18 7/8	6	7	Clinton County	IL	Tracy Hawes	1989	938
161 4/8	26 1/8	26 4/8	18 6/8	5	5	Dane County	WI	Greg Berndt	1990	938
161 4/8	24 6/8	25 3/8	19 6/8	5	5	Van Buren County	IA	Jim Francois	1990	938
161 4/8	25 2/8	25 5/8	18 0/8	6	6	Washburn County	WI	Larry Allen Blaylock	1991	938
161 4/8	25 1/8	24 0/8	19 0/8	6	5	McLean County	IL	Larry Alvis	1993	938
161 4/8	25 2/8	26 0/8	19 2/8	6	7	Henderson County	IL	Bob K. Agans	1994	938
161 4/8	22 7/8	23 1/8	16 6/8	5	5	Ripley County	IN	Steve A. Allen	1995	938
161 4/8	25 5/8	26 5/8	22 6/8	6	7	Anoka County	MN	Walter Slowikowski	1996	938
161 4/8	24 4/8	24 4/8	18 2/8	5	5	Hocking County	OH	Dave Hanson	1997	938
161 4/8	27 0/8	27 5/8	24 2/8	6	7	Clay County	KS	Tom E. Bowman	1997	938
161 3/8	25 0/8	23 6/8	16 6/8	8	7	Wyandotte County	KS	George F. Bigelow	1967	955
161 3/8	26 4/8	25 4/8	19 1/8	6	6	Sumner County	KS	Larry Wycoff	1980	955
161 3/8	29 1/8	27 2/8	23 4/8	7	8	Clark County	OH	Kenneth Preston	1982	955
161 3/8	27 2/8	25 4/8	22 3/8	4	6	Fayette County	IL	Bill Holman	1983	955
161 3/8	23 1/8	23 0/8	19 1/8	6	5	Auglaize County	OH	Lee Atha	1983	955
161 3/8	23 0/8	24 1/8	14 5/8	5	5	Butler County	KS	David R. Rogers	1985	955
161 3/8	27 7/8	27 1/8	19 3/8	4	4	Grant County	WI	Chris Nelson	1986	955
161 3/8	25 1/8	27 2/8	15 7/8	7	5	Anderson County	TN	John Johnson	1987	955
161 3/8	24 6/8	24 6/8	19 6/8	5	7	Lake County	IN	David R. Turbin	1988	955
161 3/8	26 4/8	25 1/8	19 0/8	6	6	Waukesha County	WI	Dirk Stolz	1989	955
161 3/8	25 1/8	25 3/8	19 1/8	5	5	McPherson County	KS	Daniel Willems	1990	955
161 3/8	27 0/8	26 7/8	19 4/8	6	6	Buffalo County	WI	Jason Windsor	1993	955
161 3/8	26 4/8	26 1/8	16 2/8	5	7	Switzerland County	IN	Rick Bogue	1994	955
161 3/8	25 2/8	25 5/8	20 7/8	5	5	Refugio County	TX	Terry George Arnim	1995	955
161 3/8	24 3/8	25 0/8	18 4/8	7	8	Lane County	KS	Dean Hamilton	1997	955
161 3/8	23 7/8	25 0/8	17 2/8	6	5	Spokane County	WA	Steve Mitchell	1997	955
161 2/8	24 2/8	24 0/8	20 0/8	5	5	Muskingum County	OH	Lee E Wilson	1984	971
161 2/8	23 3/8	24 7/8	18 7/8	6	6	Graham County	KS	Chris Jolly	1984	971
161 2/8	24 2/8	24 6/8	17 6/8	5	5	Sauk County	WI	Hank Loncki	1989	971
161 2/8	27 1/8	25 6/8	19 2/8	8	10	Cowley County	KS	Dwayne Graham	1990	971
161 2/8	24 6/8	24 7/8	16 7/8	6	5	Knox County	IL	Fred E. Miller	1992	971
161 2/8	24 6/8	24 3/8	19 0/8	6	5	Linn County	KS	Phil Dawson	1994	971
161 2/8	25 3/8	25 2/8	18 4/8	5	5	Shelby County	IL	Mike Cauble	1994	971
161 2/8	24 7/8	23 2/8	20 5/8	6	5	Lancaster County	NE	Clint Burge	1996	971
161 2/8	24 0/8	23 0/8	15 2/8	5	5	St. Walburg	SAS	Murray Davidson	1998	971
161 2/8	25 1/8	25 3/8	21 0/8	6	6	Coshocton County	OH	Norman M. Mast	1998	971
161 1/8	26 0/8	27 1/8	18 6/8	6	5	Clark County	IN	Frank Mauk, Jr.	1966	981
161 1/8	24 2/8	25 1/8	16 7/8	5	5	Marinette County	WI	Dale J. Hanson	1985	981
161 1/8	24 3/8	25 4/8	21 5/8	5	5	Lake County	IL	John Schnider	1987	981
161 1/8	23 6/8	23 6/8	17 6/8	5	6	Polk County	IA	Jim Garton, Jr.	1989	981
161 1/8	24 2/8	24 5/8	18 5/8	5	5	Wayne County	IL	Will Sapia	1990	981
161 1/8	26 0/8	24 0/8	20 3/8	5	5	Butler County	OH	Dale Gross	1990	981
161 1/8	25 4/8	25 1/8	20 5/8	5	5	Missoula County	MT	Vinnie Pisani	1993	981
161 1/8	27 6/8	27 6/8	19 7/8	4	6	Paulding County	OH	Tim Lamb	1994	981
161 1/8	23 3/8	24 1/8	16 1/8	5	9	Eau Claire County	WI	Anthony Johnson	1994	981
161 1/8	22 5/8	22 2/8	18 4/8	6	5	Rawlins County	KS	James Koggie	1994	981
161 1/8	25 4/8	26 2/8	16 4/8	5	6	Geary County	KS	Tim Stephens	1995	981
161 1/8	26 4/8	26 5/8	20 0/8	9	6	Iron County	WI	Bryan Bellows	1995	981
161 1/8	25 0/8	25 4/8	16 7/8	5	6	Goodhue County	MN	Bill Prigge	1997	981
161 0/8	26 2/8	25 1/8	19 4/8	5	5	La Crosse County	WI	Ray Howell	1977	994
161 0/8	28 0/8	27 3/8	23 4/8	4	4	Jefferson County	IN	Donnie Ball	1984	994
161 0/8	27 7/8	26 4/8	21 3/8	6	5	Morris County	KS	Craig Johnson	1985	994
161 0/8	27 2/8	27 1/8	19 2/8	5	5	Orange County	NC	R. J. Hickman	1987	994
161 0/8	27 1/8	26 0/8	22 2/8	4	4	Lucas County	IA	Gary Goering	1987	994
161 0/8	24 1/8	23 4/8	18 5/8	7	6	Butler County	OH	Fred S Spurlin	1987	994
161 0/8	25 0/8	24 4/8	16 4/8	5	6	Fond du Lac County	WI	David E. Stubbe	1988	994
161 0/8	24 5/8	24 0/8	15 3/8	6	6	Lawrence County	IN	Dale Waldbieser	1988	994
161 0/8	22 5/8	24 1/8	19 2/8	5	5	Dakota County	MN	Dave Vomela	1988	994
161 0/8	26 0/8	25 4/8	16 0/8	6	5	Day County	SD	Jim Madsen	1990	994
161 0/8	26 3/8	27 4/8	21 4/8	4	4	McHenry County	IL	Richard A. Houge	1991	994
161 0/8	22 0/8	22 0/8	15 4/8	5	5	Marion County	IA	Dwight T. Robuck	1991	994
161 0/8	23 3/8	23 7/8	20 6/8	5	5	Peoria County	IL	Robert E. Grainger	1991	994
161 0/8	27 4/8	26 7/8	19 7/8	6	4	Pottawatomie County	KS	Stan Mangas	1992	994
161 0/8	25 4/8	24 5/8	18 2/8	5	5	Knox County	IL	John S. Barrett	1993	994
161 0/8	25 1/8	25 1/8	19 4/8	5	5	Geary County	KS	Kevin Foerschler	1995	994
161 0/8	25 6/8	25 7/8	16 6/8	7	6	Buffalo County	WI	Dennis Palmer	1995	994
161 0/8	24 0/8	24 4/8	17 2/8	5	5	Butler County	PA	David Craig Snyder	1996	994
161 0/8	25 1/8	24 4/8	19 0/8	5	5	Jackson County	IL	Carl Vandeloo	1996	994
160 7/8	20 5/8	24 0/8	24 3/8	7	5	Frontier County	NE	Vernon Laverack	1959	1,013
160 7/8	25 5/8	27 3/8	21 4/8	5	6		IA	Everett Reid	1962	1,013

WHITETAIL DEER (TYPICAL ANTLERS)

Minimum Score 125

SCORE	LENGTH OF MAIN BEAM R	LENGTH OF MAIN BEAM L	INSIDE SPREAD	NUMBER OF POINTS R	NUMBER OF POINTS L	AREA	STATE/PROVINCE	HUNTER'S NAME	DATE	RANK
160 7/8	24 2/8	23 4/8	17 6/8	7	5	Smith County	KS	Ron Sturgeon	1965	1,013
160 7/8	24 4/8	24 2/8	17 1/8	5	5	Wayne County	WV	Willard Brown	1967	1,013
160 7/8	22 6/8	23 1/8	21 1/8	5	5	Lincoln County	MN	Bernie Ahlberg	1974	1,013
160 7/8	25 5/8	25 1/8	16 7/8	5	5	Clark County	IL	Wes Romines	1977	1,013
160 7/8	24 2/8	23 5/8	19 3/8	5	5	Saline County	KS	Ray Peterman	1979	1,013
160 7/8	25 1/8	26 7/8	18 5/8	4	4	Pike County	IL	Richard Dewey	1981	1,013
160 7/8	24 5/8	23 4/8	15 3/8	5	6	Leavenworth County	KS	Albert Lyle Karl	1982	1,013
160 7/8	25 2/8	25 6/8	19 5/8	7	7	Rockingham County	VA	Jim Burtner	1989	1,013
160 7/8	27 7/8	27 6/8	22 4/8	5	7	Clark County	OH	Ron McGuire	1989	1,013
160 7/8	28 1/8	28 6/8	21 5/8	4	4	Bond County	IL	James Coleman	1989	1,013
160 7/8	23 4/8	23 7/8	21 7/8	5	5	Sangamon County	IL	David C. Jostes	1990	1,013
160 7/8	25 2/8	24 1/8	17 1/8	5	5	Butler County	OH	Norman R. Sampson	1991	1,013
160 7/8	25 6/8	25 0/8	17 3/8	6	7	Parkland County	ALB	Sam Halabi	1991	1,013
160 7/8	27 2/8	25 4/8	18 0/8	5	6	Monroe County	IA	Robert L. McDowell	1992	1,013
160 7/8	23 6/8	23 3/8	21 0/8	6	6	Pueblo County	CO	Kenneth H. Karbon	1993	1,013
160 7/8	24 3/8	23 6/8	17 5/8	5	5	Ashland County	WI	Joe Bradle	1994	1,013
160 7/8	23 5/8	24 0/8	20 3/8	5	5	Fairfield County	OH	Roy Chestnut	1994	1,013
160 7/8	24 1/8	23 5/8	23 3/8	5	5	Polk County	AR	Donald Cost	1995	1,013
160 7/8	26 0/8	25 5/8	19 6/8	5	7	Dakota County	MN	Gerald Huntington	1995	1,013
160 6/8	25 4/8	25 7/8	17 0/8	6	5	Sarpy County	NE	Lawrence A. Klabunde	1968	1,034
160 6/8	26 2/8	25 7/8	19 2/8	6	4	Fillmore County	MN	Doyle Tarrence	1974	1,034
160 6/8	26 2/8	27 0/8	21 5/8	5	6	Alleghany County	VA	Roger O. Wyant	1984	1,034
160 6/8	26 5/8	26 0/8	19 2/8	4	4	Lake County	IL	Charles R. Zradicka	1986	1,034
160 6/8	24 0/8	25 0/8	17 2/8	4	4	Webster County	IA	Dave W. Hainzinger	1987	1,034
160 6/8	24 3/8	24 2/8	18 6/8	5	7	Muskegon County	MI	Dave Haack	1988	1,034
160 6/8	25 4/8	25 2/8	21 6/8	5	5	Bayfield County	WI	Jim Peters	1989	1,034
160 6/8	26 0/8	26 7/8	19 0/8	6	5	Franklin County	OH	Lacie Waller	1993	1,034
160 6/8	24 3/8	24 4/8	20 4/8	5	5	Edmonton	ALB	Ian Barclay	1993	1,034
160 6/8	25 2/8	25 0/8	18 2/8	7	6	Winneshiek County	IA	James Ryant	1994	1,034
160 6/8	24 6/8	26 0/8	16 5/8	6	7	Adams County	WI	Steve Paluszynski	1994	1,034
160 6/8	28 3/8	27 3/8	20 6/8	5	5	Queen Annes County	MD	Robert Radford	1994	1,034
160 6/8	25 7/8	27 0/8	16 7/8	6	5	Macoupin County	IL	Mike Nichols	1994	1,034
160 6/8	24 6/8	23 6/8	23 4/8	6	7	Wood County	WI	Daniel J. Lila	1995	1,034
160 6/8	23 7/8	24 0/8	18 5/8	6	6	Monroe County	WI	Charles Frederick	1995	1,034
160 6/8	26 3/8	27 5/8	18 4/8	8	6	Belmont County	OH	Mike Huber	1995	1,034
160 6/8	27 0/8	27 1/8	20 6/8	4	6	Mason County	IL	George Buck	1996	1,034
160 6/8	24 6/8	24 6/8	21 2/8	5	5	Knox County	MO	Jim Baker	1997	1,034
160 5/8	22 3/8	23 4/8	16 4/8	7	8	Lawrence County	IL	Bob Brian	1971	1,052
160 5/8	24 4/8	25 5/8	23 4/8	5	6	Murray County	MN	Paul Beech	1974	1,052
160 5/8	22 2/8	21 4/8	15 5/8	5	5	Montcalm County	MI	Rodney Snyder	1980	1,052
160 5/8	25 2/8	25 3/8	14 3/8	6	5	Hubbard County	MN	Myles Keller	1982	1,052
160 5/8	23 7/8	23 3/8	16 6/8	6	7	Morrison County	MN	Randy Johnson	1986	1,052
160 5/8	21 2/8	21 4/8	14 7/8	6	6	Kenedy County	TX	Cal Adger	1987	1,052
160 5/8	25 2/8	25 7/8	19 1/8	7	6	Waukesha County	WI	Dick Harris	1988	1,052
160 5/8	26 2/8	26 6/8	18 5/8	5	5	Van Buren County	IA	Noel E. Harlan	1988	1,052
160 5/8	27 3/8	24 4/8	18 5/8	5	5	Scott County	MN	Kris Huber	1988	1,052
160 5/8	26 2/8	24 6/8	19 5/8	5	6	Christian County	IL	Richard Krider	1988	1,052
160 5/8	25 1/8	25 6/8	16 6/8	5	6	Allamakee County	IA	Warren W. Woods	1991	1,052
160 5/8	26 1/8	27 5/8	19 5/8	7	7	Jefferson County	IL	Lanny Shaw	1995	1,052
160 5/8	22 6/8	22 4/8	15 1/8	6	6	Schuyler County	IL	Edd Clack	1995	1,052
160 5/8	23 4/8	25 4/8	18 2/8	7	6	Cook County	IL	Jason Gomez	1995	1,052
160 5/8	26 7/8	24 7/8	20 5/8	5	5	Jackson County	MO	Scott Liebenguth	1997	1,052
160 5/8	28 6/8	28 1/8	21 7/8	5	5	Knox County	OH	Tom Moxley	1997	1,052
160 4/8	26 6/8	25 4/8	20 7/8	7	7	Williams County	ND	John Bloom	1963	1,068
160 4/8	27 2/8	28 0/8	21 4/8	5	7	Lyon County	IA	Marvin H. Peterson	1970	1,068
160 4/8	23 1/8	22 4/8	19 0/8	6	7	Keith County	NE	Gil Wilkinson	1970	1,068
160 4/8	28 5/8	28 2/8	24 2/8	7	7	Fairfield County	OH	Robert A. Fletcher	1977	1,068
160 4/8	24 2/8	24 7/8	17 6/8	5	6	Dawson County	MT	Frank Legato	1978	1,068
160 4/8	26 0/8	26 2/8	19 2/8	5	5	Trempealeau County	WI	Duane Kupietz	1981	1,068
160 4/8	24 2/8	24 7/8	19 2/8	6	5	Waukesha County	WI	Donald T. Lurvey	1982	1,068
160 4/8	24 4/8	25 0/8	21 0/8	5	5	Daviess County	MO	Sam Boyd	1987	1,068
160 4/8	23 7/8	23 7/8	18 0/8	5	5	Jefferson County	OH	Robert E. Howell	1987	1,068
160 4/8	21 7/8	21 4/8	17 0/8	6	6	Fremont County	IA	Larry Zach	1987	1,068
160 4/8	24 2/8	25 0/8	19 0/8	5	5	Coles County	IL	Randy Rodebaugh	1988	1,068
160 4/8	27 3/8	27 2/8	19 1/8	6	4	Wayne County	MO	Carl Roach	1988	1,068
160 4/8	26 2/8	26 7/8	18 6/8	5	5	Schuyler County	IL	Tom Grover	1991	1,068
160 4/8	25 6/8	23 7/8	17 1/8	5	7	Pike County	IL	Tim Fulmer	1991	1,068
160 4/8	26 4/8	25 3/8	19 4/8	9	7	Putnam County	IL	Tony Day	1992	1,068
160 4/8	25 7/8	24 7/8	19 6/8	4	5	Olmsted County	MN	Jim Hanson	1992	1,068
160 4/8	25 1/8	24 3/8	18 2/8	5	5	Osage County	MO	Leon Luecke	1992	1,068
160 4/8	25 1/8	25 0/8	16 0/8	6	7	Lake County	IL	Kirk Short	1993	1,068
160 4/8	24 4/8	24 3/8	17 0/8	5	5	Montgomery County	PA	Donald D. Epprecht	1993	1,068
160 4/8	25 3/8	25 3/8	22 2/8	5	5	McHenry County	IL	Kenneth G. Wilson	1994	1,068
160 4/8	27 0/8	26 6/8	21 0/8	7	5	Price County	WI	Timothy Engel	1995	1,068
160 4/8	22 4/8	22 5/8	17 2/8	6	5	Decatur County	IA	Steve Snow	1995	1,068
160 4/8	27 0/8	26 5/8	19 0/8	5	5	Providence County	RI	Stephen Burchett	1996	1,068
160 4/8	24 0/8	25 0/8	18 6/8	6	6	Dallas County	IA	Tim Lockner	1997	1,068
160 4/8	25 3/8	23 6/8	18 5/8	7	5	Porter County	IN	Donald M. Dolph	1997	1,068

WHITETAIL DEER (TYPICAL ANTLERS)

Minimum Score 125

Continued

SCORE	LENGTH OF MAIN BEAM R	LENGTH OF MAIN BEAM L	INSIDE SPREAD	NUMBER OF POINTS R	NUMBER OF POINTS L	AREA	STATE/ PROVINCE	HUNTER'S NAME	DATE	RANK
160 3/8	22 2/8	22 4/8	20 7/8	6	6	Sheridan County	NE	Wayne Krotz	1975	1,093
160 3/8	24 3/8	24 2/8	17 1/8	5	5	St. Charles County	MO	Dan Schulte	1976	1,093
160 3/8	23 6/8	24 7/8	20 1/8	7	6	Barber County	KS	Herbie M. Landwehr, Jr.	1980	1,093
160 3/8	27 5/8	26 0/8	19 7/8	4	4	Clark County	IL	Gerald Shaffner	1983	1,093
160 3/8	26 4/8	26 5/8	18 3/8	6	5	Hamilton County	IL	Clifford R. Schoolman	1984	1,093
160 3/8	23 4/8	25 2/8	19 1/8	6	6	Jefferson County	IL	Jerry Newell	1986	1,093
160 3/8	24 2/8	23 5/8	20 3/8	7	5	Saskatoon	SAS	Maurice Parent	1987	1,093
160 3/8	23 4/8	23 2/8	19 1/8	6	6	Murray County	MN	Del Determan	1987	1,093
160 3/8	23 2/8	23 3/8	19 5/8	5	5	Rock County	WI	Ronald A. Vike, Jr.	1989	1,093
160 3/8	25 5/8	25 7/8	18 5/8	5	7	Clay County	MO	James Wollard	1991	1,093
160 3/8	24 6/8	25 6/8	19 6/8	5	6	Washita County	OK	Larry Snider	1991	1,093
160 3/8	28 5/8	28 6/8	21 2/8	6	5	Jay County	IN	Avery O. Coleman	1992	1,093
160 3/8	26 1/8	26 4/8	18 5/8	5	5	Montgomery County	MD	Joel I. Bullard	1993	1,093
160 3/8	23 3/8	23 3/8	18 1/8	5	5	Geary County	KS	William Ahlers	1993	1,093
160 3/8	26 2/8	26 1/8	17 3/8	5	6	Alamance County	NC	M. Todd Ramsey	1994	1,093
160 3/8	23 6/8	23 5/8	17 7/8	5	6	Jay County	IN	Robert Lingo	1994	1,093
160 3/8	25 4/8	24 4/8	16 7/8	5	5	Delaware County	IA	Jason N. Nolz	1994	1,093
160 3/8	23 1/8	23 3/8	18 3/8	5	6	Polk County	IA	John Flies	1994	1,093
160 3/8	25 0/8	24 4/8	15 0/8	6	5	Lincoln County	MO	Scott Creech	1995	1,093
160 3/8	26 4/8	27 1/8	19 7/8	5	4	Shelby County	IL	Steve A. Tripp	1995	1,093
160 3/8	26 6/8	27 0/8	21 1/8	5	5	Cherokee County	KS	Doug Walden	1995	1,093
160 3/8	23 4/8	23 0/8	15 5/8	5	5	Manitowoc County	WI	Wayne "Gaffer" Blaha	1997	1,093
160 3/8	25 2/8	25 2/8	16 5/8	7	5	Ness County	KS	Ron Stoecklein	1997	1,093
160 3/8	27 4/8	26 0/8	19 6/8	5	5	Vermilion County	IL	John Hubbard	1997	1,093
160 3/8	27 2/8	26 4/8	22 2/8	7	6	Jefferson County	OH	Tom Bateman	1997	1,093
160 2/8	25 6/8	26 3/8	19 2/8	5	5	Nance County	NE	Ralph I. Hansen	1963	1,118
160 2/8	25 7/8	26 0/8	21 4/8	4	4	Cherokee County	IA	Jerry L. Smith	1969	1,118
160 2/8	22 6/8	23 3/8	19 4/8	5	5	Valley County	MT	John "Rosey" Roseland	1981	1,118
160 2/8	23 1/8	23 1/8	18 0/8	6	6	Mills County	IA	Dale R. Clayton	1983	1,118
160 2/8	24 5/8	24 6/8	18 1/8	6	6	Phelps County	NE	Bruce Nielsen	1984	1,118
160 2/8	24 4/8	24 5/8	18 0/8	5	5	La Salle County	IL	John Thomas	1987	1,118
160 2/8	25 2/8	25 6/8	25 1/8	7	6	Lake County	IL	Woody Scruggs	1987	1,118
160 2/8	27 0/8	26 4/8	17 5/8	5	6	Ashland County	WI	Steven Roginske	1988	1,118
160 2/8	24 0/8	25 7/8	19 0/8	5	5	Rusk County	WI	Shawn Harris	1991	1,118
160 2/8	26 0/8	26 5/8	22 6/8	6	5	Winnebago County	IL	Douglas R. Greensides	1991	1,118
160 2/8	25 2/8	25 3/8	18 0/8	5	5	Jessamine County	KY	Roger Drury	1992	1,118
160 2/8	26 7/8	26 7/8	20 4/8	5	6	Comanche County	KS	Greg Hill	1992	1,118
160 2/8	27 1/8	28 0/8	17 4/8	5	6	Macoupin County	IL	Kenny Tate	1992	1,118
160 2/8	23 7/8	23 7/8	19 7/8	6	5	Stevens County	WA	Jay Baker	1992	1,118
160 2/8	25 2/8	25 6/8	18 4/8	7	7	Kalamazoo County	MI	Tom G. Ahrens	1993	1,118
160 2/8	22 6/8	23 0/8	16 6/8	6	6	St. Croix County	WI	Thomas E. Dulon	1993	1,118
160 2/8	24 7/8	22 4/8	19 3/8	5	6	Garden County	NE	Tim Heckenlively	1993	1,118
160 2/8	25 3/8	25 6/8	21 0/8	5	5	Wayne County	WV	Alex Spaulding	1994	1,118
160 2/8	24 5/8	24 7/8	19 0/8	6	7	St. Marys County	MD	Casey W. Moore	1994	1,118
160 2/8	27 4/8	27 5/8	19 0/8	5	5	McHenry County	IL	Kevin Lunde	1995	1,118
160 2/8	25 6/8	26 2/8	18 6/8	5	5	Kleberg County	TX	Warren Strickland	1995	1,118
160 2/8	25 4/8	24 6/8	18 4/8	5	6	Waukesha County	WI	John Morrison	1998	1,118
160 1/8	25 7/8	26 2/8	18 5/8	5	6	Polk County	MN	Scott Gullickson	1985	1,140
160 1/8	25 3/8	25 6/8	17 3/8	6	6	Blue Earth County	MN	Darwin Arndt	1985	1,140
160 1/8	27 5/8	26 4/8	19 1/8	4	4	Ross County	OH	Randall W. Haines	1986	1,140
160 1/8	27 5/8	27 6/8	21 7/8	5	5	Powell County	KY	Orville Fugate	1987	1,140
160 1/8	27 2/8	25 5/8	17 3/8	6	7	Coles County	IL	Jim Eveland	1987	1,140
160 1/8	28 6/8	29 7/8	21 3/8	5	4	Lafayette County	WI	Jeff J. Kahle	1988	1,140
160 1/8	22 3/8	23 0/8	19 1/8	5	5	Clayton County	IA	Wayne M. Lau	1989	1,140
160 1/8	23 7/8	25 0/8	21 1/8	5	5	Washington County	MS	Odis Hill, Jr.	1990	1,140
160 1/8	25 3/8	26 6/8	18 4/8	7	10	Huntington County	IN	Troy Harris	1991	1,140
160 1/8	24 1/8	23 1/8	17 1/8	6	6	Fergus County	MT	John Fleharty	1992	1,140
160 1/8	22 4/8	22 6/8	14 7/8	5	5	Hamiota	MAN	Terry Lee	1993	1,140
160 1/8	25 1/8	24 3/8	18 7/8	5	5	Keith County	NE	Gale Subbert	1994	1,140
160 1/8	21 5/8	25 2/8	15 5/8	6	5	Putnam County	MO	Jerry Williams	1994	1,140
160 1/8	26 5/8	25 2/8	19 3/8	5	5	Pierce County	WI	Dan Meixner	1994	1,140
160 1/8	27 4/8	27 0/8	19 2/8	7	5	Clark County	IL	Jared Hupp	1995	1,140
160 1/8	29 1/8	28 3/8	19 2/8	6	7	Allegheny County	PA	Wallace E. Carr	1996	1,140
160 1/8	26 4/8	26 3/8	17 5/8	5	5	Effingham County	IL	Michael E. Lee, Sr.	1997	1,140
160 1/8	25 0/8	25 4/8	21 3/8	5	5	Clay County	SD	Jeffrey J. Olson	1997	1,140
160 0/8	24 6/8	24 5/8	21 3/8	6	6	Worth County	IA	Terry Lynch	1972	1,158
160 0/8	26 3/8	24 7/8	21 6/8	8	5	Winona County	MN	James Enderson	1973	1,158
160 0/8	23 0/8	22 3/8	20 0/8	5	5	Cooper County	MO	Nancy Smith	1984	1,158
160 0/8	25 4/8	26 0/8	18 2/8	4	5	Stephenson County	IL	Richard K. Kerr	1985	1,158
160 0/8	22 7/8	23 0/8	17 2/8	6	5	Morrill County	NE	Michael A. Brening	1985	1,158
160 0/8	25 2/8	25 4/8	25 2/8	5	5	Ellsworth County	KS	Dave Fisher	1986	1,158
160 0/8	24 6/8	23 4/8	16 5/8	5	8	Charles County	MD	William J. Kovach	1990	1,158
160 0/8	23 5/8	25 1/8	20 4/8	5	5	Sawyer County	WI	Todd Carlson	1990	1,158
160 0/8	24 2/8	24 2/8	15 2/8	6	5	Buffalo County	WI	Scott Duellman	1990	1,158
160 0/8	27 3/8	26 5/8	20 4/8	5	5	Clermont County	OH	John Fischer	1991	1,158
160 0/8	23 6/8	23 5/8	18 7/8	5	6	Becker County	MN	Kurt Holland	1992	1,158
160 0/8	24 2/8	23 6/8	17 2/8	5	5	Butler County	KS	George Schuttler	1992	1,158
160 0/8	27 4/8	28 1/8	19 6/8	5	5	Clarke County	IA	Alan Shields	1993	1,158

WHITETAIL DEER (TYPICAL ANTLERS)

Minimum Score 125 — Continued

SCORE	LENGTH OF MAIN BEAM R	LENGTH OF MAIN BEAM L	INSIDE SPREAD	NUMBER OF POINTS R	NUMBER OF POINTS L	AREA	STATE/PROVINCE	HUNTER'S NAME	DATE	RANK
160 0/8	26 2/8	25 4/8	22 0/8	9	8	Jefferson County	KY	William S. Finney, Jr.	1993	1,158
160 0/8	23 3/8	23 7/8	19 2/8	5	5	Mower County	MN	Randy Hegge	1994	1,158
160 0/8	25 0/8	25 1/8	17 2/8	5	5	Weld County	CO	Michael Yeary	1994	1,158
160 0/8	23 6/8	23 2/8	17 3/8	7	6	Dane County	WI	Mark McCaulley	1994	1,158
160 0/8	21 4/8	22 4/8	17 2/8	5	5	Pontotoc County	OK	Bruce A. Hall	1995	1,158
160 0/8	26 0/8	25 7/8	18 4/8	5	5	Jefferson County	OH	Chuck Keenan	1995	1,158
160 0/8	27 6/8	27 7/8	23 7/8	6	7	Otero County	CO	Troy Cunningham	1995	1,158
160 0/8	24 4/8	25 3/8	18 2/8	5	6	Pulaski County	IL	Paul Landewee	1996	1,158
160 0/8	26 0/8	27 4/8	22 4/8	6	6	Shannon County	MO	Edward Thomas	1996	1,158
160 0/8	26 3/8	26 3/8	18 2/8	7	7	Noble County	OH	Mark A. Hudak	1997	1,158
160 0/8	27 1/8	26 6/8	21 3/8	6	5	Mercer County	IL	Dan Bergen	1997	1,158
160 0/8	23 4/8	22 1/8	19 0/8	5	6	Monona County	IA	Dr. David Samuel	1998	1,158
159 7/8	22 7/8	22 5/8	18 2/8	5	6	Clark County	KS	William Rule	1983	1,183
159 7/8	24 4/8	25 4/8	20 1/8	6	5	Garden County	NE	Wynn Fontenot	1984	1,183
159 7/8	25 7/8	25 2/8	19 5/8	5	5	Brown County	NE	Lorne Allen	1988	1,183
159 7/8	22 1/8	22 2/8	18 2/8	6	7	Alberta Beach	ALB	Joe Hanson	1991	1,183
159 7/8	24 6/8	25 1/8	19 5/8	6	5	Will County	IL	Gene Hagberg	1991	1,183
159 7/8	24 4/8	23 4/8	17 5/8	5	6	Webster County	KS	Ronald G. Nicholson	1991	1,183
159 7/8	27 3/8	28 1/8	18 5/8	5	5	Shawano County	WI	John Anderson, Jr.	1992	1,183
159 7/8	27 7/8	27 4/8	25 7/8	4	6	Ross County	OH	Robert Williams	1995	1,183
159 7/8	24 2/8	24 1/8	18 5/8	5	5	Linn County	KS	James D. Johnson	1995	1,183
159 7/8	24 6/8	24 7/8	18 0/8	6	8	Grayson County	VA	Ralph Haga, Jr.	1997	1,183
159 7/8	26 0/8	26 2/8	22 2/8	5	6	Wyoming County	WV	Blake Luce	1997	1,183
159 6/8	26 5/8	26 6/8	20 0/8	5	5	Winona County	MN	Arlie Herber	1977	1,194
159 6/8	21 2/8	21 2/8	17 0/8	5	5	Vanderburgh County	IN	Floyd Jackson	1977	1,194
159 6/8	24 1/8	23 2/8	19 6/8	5	6	Sherburne County	MN	Allen Hugget	1981	1,194
159 6/8	26 7/8	25 6/8	17 6/8	6	6	Buffalo County	WI	Bill Peterson	1981	1,194
159 6/8	25 0/8	25 0/8	18 2/8	5	5	Miami County	KS	Tom Wiggin	1982	1,194
159 6/8	25 6/8	25 1/8	20 6/8	4	4	Washington County	MS	Steve Nichols	1986	1,194
159 6/8	24 6/8	24 7/8	19 5/8	6	5	Page County	IA	Dave Bayless	1986	1,194
159 6/8	24 5/8	23 6/8	18 4/8	5	6	Rock Island County	IL	Russ Courter	1988	1,194
159 6/8	26 7/8	27 2/8	17 2/8	4	5	Greenwood County	KS	John Porubski	1989	1,194
159 6/8	26 7/8	26 0/8	19 7/8	7	7	Crawford County	WI	Mitch Staszak	1993	1,194
159 6/8	22 7/8	24 0/8	18 6/8	6	5	Stevens County	MN	Nic Magnuson	1994	1,194
159 6/8	26 7/8	25 4/8	18 4/8	5	5	Trumbull County	OH	Gregory D. Spano	1994	1,194
159 6/8	23 2/8	23 4/8	18 2/8	5	5	Ferry County	WA	Leroy Day/George Schernitzki	1995	1,194
159 6/8	24 4/8	24 7/8	18 4/8	5	6	Pike County	IL	Bill Westlake	1996	1,194
159 6/8	24 4/8	23 2/8	19 6/8	5	5	Saline County	IL	Marty Stokich	1996	1,194
159 6/8	22 7/8	19 5/8	17 6/8	5	5	Dunn County	WI	Eric Huseboe	1997	1,194
159 5/8	26 3/8	25 5/8	21 5/8	5	5	Des Moines County	IA	Richard Howard	1964	1,210
159 5/8	22 4/8	22 3/8	18 1/8	5	5	Pittsburg County	OK	John Baumann	1977	1,210
159 5/8	23 7/8	23 7/8	15 5/8	6	6	Reno County	KS	Richard A. Swisher	1978	1,210
159 5/8	24 6/8	23 1/8	18 1/8	5	5	Madison County	IL	Barry Ash	1980	1,210
159 5/8	24 5/8	26 1/8	18 5/8	6	5	Muskingum County	OH	Brent L. Taylor	1981	1,210
159 5/8	25 4/8	24 7/8	17 7/8	4	4	Ogle County	IL	Charles L. Martoglio	1982	1,210
159 5/8	24 6/8	24 6/8	20 7/8	6	5	Watonwan County	MN	Richard Enger	1983	1,210
159 5/8	26 2/8	26 2/8	23 6/8	6	6	Cochrane	ALB	Edward Defrancesco	1984	1,210
159 5/8	23 2/8	24 4/8	16 1/8	6	5	Hamilton County	IA	Stephen L. Cink	1987	1,210
159 5/8	23 3/8	23 6/8	15 7/8	6	7	Hennepin County	MN	John Earl Ford	1988	1,210
159 5/8	26 2/8	25 7/8	18 0/8	7	6	Sangamon County	IL	Hobart E. Watson	1992	1,210
159 5/8	26 6/8	26 6/8	24 2/8	5	4	La Porte County	IN	Drake Matovich	1993	1,210
159 5/8	26 4/8	25 7/8	19 7/8	5	6	Kiowa County	KS	Greg Hill	1993	1,210
159 5/8	25 6/8	24 4/8	21 7/8	5	5	Columbia County	WI	Patrick W. Jahn	1995	1,210
159 5/8	22 0/8	24 1/8	20 7/8	5	5	Page County	VA	Terry Lee Dorman	1995	1,210
159 5/8	25 2/8	24 5/8	19 5/8	5	5	Pendleton County	KY	Philip W. Fox	1996	1,210
159 5/8	28 0/8	27 7/8	22 2/8	7	6	Boone County	IA	Chuck Stotts	1996	1,210
159 4/8	27 6/8	27 6/8	25 4/8	4	4	Blue Earth County	MN	Harold Tow	1963	1,227
159 4/8	22 6/8	21 5/8	17 5/8	6	5	Wabash County	IL	Tom J. McRaven	1967	1,227
159 4/8	24 5/8	24 6/8	21 2/8	5	5	Hocking County	OH	James Allen Downs	1980	1,227
159 4/8	22 5/8	22 6/8	18 0/8	5	4	Morris County	KS	Kenneth R. Bryant	1983	1,227
159 4/8	24 4/8	24 6/8	18 0/8	5	6	Dade County	MO	Charles A. Myers	1985	1,227
159 4/8	24 7/8	27 3/8	18 0/8	6	6	Scott County	IA	Albert Perreault	1985	1,227
159 4/8	26 0/8	25 2/8	19 0/8	5	4	Goodhue County	MN	Brad C. Nesseth	1986	1,227
159 4/8	24 4/8	25 1/8	18 4/8	5	5	Will County	IL	Larry Elumbaugh	1987	1,227
159 4/8	26 6/8	25 7/8	19 0/8	4	4	Linn County	IA	Jim Arp	1989	1,227
159 4/8	24 2/8	24 2/8	16 4/8	5	5	Buffalo County	WI	Ronald Brenner	1990	1,227
159 4/8	25 2/8	23 4/8	18 3/8	5	6	Foster County	ND	Bryon Hallwachs	1990	1,227
159 4/8	24 5/8	24 2/8	18 0/8	5	5	Pike County	IL	Kevin McCallister	1991	1,227
159 4/8	25 4/8	25 4/8	20 2/8	5	5	Randolph County	IN	Roy Patterson	1991	1,227
159 4/8	25 7/8	24 4/8	24 4/8	5	5	Morgan County	IL	Jon A. Whalen	1993	1,227
159 4/8	24 6/8	23 1/8	23 4/8	5	5	Lyon County	IA	Mike Judas	1993	1,227
159 4/8	22 7/8	23 5/8	21 2/8	6	5	Butler County	KS	Robert Faris II	1994	1,227
159 4/8	27 3/8	27 1/8	21 4/8	6	6	Wyandot County	OH	Mike Saam	1995	1,227
159 4/8	25 0/8	25 3/8	20 2/8	5	5	Macon County	IL	Doug Key	1995	1,227
159 4/8	25 2/8	26 0/8	19 0/8	5	6	Des Moines County	IA	James L. Reiser	1996	1,227
159 4/8	23 6/8	23 3/8	22 2/8	6	6	Will County	IL	Ken Palmer	1997	1,227
159 3/8	27 6/8	27 1/8	22 3/8	4	4	Pike County	OH	Ray C. Pritchett, Jr.	1977	1,247
159 3/8	25 5/8	25 4/8	18 5/8	4	4	Washington County	KS	Tony Mann	1985	1,247

WHITETAIL DEER (TYPICAL ANTLERS)

Minimum Score 125

SCORE	LENGTH OF MAIN BEAM R	LENGTH OF MAIN BEAM L	INSIDE SPREAD	NUMBER OF POINTS R	NUMBER OF POINTS L	AREA	STATE/ PROVINCE	HUNTER'S NAME	DATE	RANK
159 3/8	24 6/8	23 6/8	18 3/8	6	6	Rock Island County	IL	Mike W. Greeno	1988	1,247
159 3/8	25 6/8	25 6/8	17 7/8	5	5	Pike County	IL	Phil McEuen	1988	1,247
159 3/8	28 0/8	26 2/8	21 3/8	5	5	Houston County	MN	Steve Bjerke	1989	1,247
159 3/8	26 0/8	26 0/8	19 1/8	8	5	Hillsdale County	MI	Dennis L. Burlew	1989	1,247
159 3/8	26 7/8	26 3/8	18 3/8	4	4	Washtenaw County	MI	Gregory Kuhn	1990	1,247
159 3/8	28 0/8	28 0/8	18 5/8	5	4	Chase County	KS	Dave Ward	1992	1,247
159 3/8	25 7/8	24 6/8	19 6/8	5	7	Westchester County	NY	Claude "Kenny" Pylant	1994	1,247
159 3/8	25 3/8	25 6/8	20 1/8	5	5	Ozaukee County	WI	Jeff Eder	1994	1,247
159 3/8	21 7/8	22 0/8	15 3/8	5	5	Van Buren County	IA	David Thornsberry	1995	1,247
159 3/8	25 5/8	25 6/8	17 6/8	6	6	Chippewa County	WI	Brian Starck	1997	1,247
159 2/8	22 4/8	24 0/8	20 2/8	6	7	Hamlin County	SD	John R. Gregory	1975	1,259
159 2/8	25 1/8	27 6/8	20 6/8	4	4	Yankton County	SD	Michael L. Tacke	1983	1,259
159 2/8	23 2/8	23 0/8	16 2/8	5	5	Anne Arundel County	MD	Jim Roy	1985	1,259
159 2/8	23 3/8	24 7/8	18 2/8	8	5	Madison County	IA	Tom Arpy	1987	1,259
159 2/8	24 2/8	24 3/8	18 2/8	5	5	Cass County	IA	Dan E. Mikkelsen	1988	1,259
159 2/8	24 1/8	24 3/8	18 0/8	5	6	Milwaukee County	WI	Terry R. Brandenburg	1989	1,259
159 2/8	31 2/8	31 0/8	21 2/8	4	6	Williamson County	IL	Lowell Mausey	1990	1,259
159 2/8	25 7/8	25 4/8	16 0/8	5	5	Buffalo County	WI	Larry Bloom	1994	1,259
159 2/8	23 6/8	22 4/8	19 0/8	5	5	Fulton County	IN	Dennis L. Kamp	1994	1,259
159 2/8	26 4/8	24 4/8	18 1/8	7	8	Dakota County	MN	Steve Huettl	1994	1,259
159 2/8	26 5/8	26 2/8	21 2/8	4	5	McLean County	IL	Gayland McKinnerney	1994	1,259
159 2/8	26 1/8	25 0/8	17 3/8	7	5	Osborne County	KS	Gary Ozias	1995	1,259
159 2/8	24 6/8	24 1/8	17 0/8	5	5	Dane County	WI	Ty Hauden	1995	1,259
159 2/8	24 4/8	24 4/8	17 5/8	6	7	Will County	IL	Frank Grigus	1996	1,259
159 2/8	27 6/8	27 3/8	20 4/8	5	5	Calhoun County	IL	Richard Graham	1997	1,259
159 2/8	24 3/8	23 2/8	17 4/8	6	6	Clark County	IL	Trey Downing	1997	1,259
159 2/8	22 3/8	22 0/8	16 4/8	5	5	Wayne County	IL	Jerry Gifford	1997	1,259
159 1/8	23 7/8	23 0/8	20 1/8	6	6	Lucas County	OH	Martin Higley	1962	1,276
159 1/8	22 4/8	24 2/8	16 5/8	7	6	Clayton County	IA	Gary Troester	1978	1,276
159 1/8	26 2/8	25 6/8	17 4/8	6	6	Heard County	GA	Howard E. Taylor	1980	1,276
159 1/8	24 7/8	25 7/8	21 5/8	8	6	Saline County	KS	Raymond Peterman	1984	1,276
159 1/8	25 0/8	25 1/8	18 1/8	5	5	Winona County	MN	Vernon Zachariason	1986	1,276
159 1/8	25 1/8	23 5/8	19 7/8	5	5	Allamakee County	IA	Daniel R. Kennedy	1987	1,276
159 1/8	23 1/8	23 6/8	18 5/8	5	5	Livingston County	MI	Keith Joseph Daniels	1988	1,276
159 1/8	23 2/8	24 2/8	16 5/8	5	5	Vermilion County	IL	Horace E. Marsh	1990	1,276
159 1/8	25 5/8	24 5/8	19 1/8	5	6	Stark County	IL	Kevin Heaton	1990	1,276
159 1/8	27 2/8	27 5/8	19 2/8	7	5	Douglas County	KS	Paul Gordon	1991	1,276
159 1/8	25 1/8	25 2/8	21 7/8	5	5	Clay County	MN	Randy Nelson	1992	1,276
159 1/8	22 0/8	22 0/8	18 5/8	5	5	Butler County	KS	David R. Rogers	1992	1,276
159 1/8	25 4/8	24 4/8	21 3/8	7	8	Harrison County	OH	Donald A. Gore	1994	1,276
159 1/8	25 4/8	25 0/8	20 1/8	5	5	Walworth County	WI	Bob Gallup	1994	1,276
159 1/8	25 5/8	26 6/8	22 1/8	4	4	Milwaukee County	WI	Jason Geschke	1997	1,276
159 0/8	25 7/8	26 1/8	17 6/8	5	5	Shelby County	IL	Gary E. Sievers	1971	1,291
159 0/8	22 6/8	22 6/8	18 4/8	5	5	Pulaski County	IN	William F. Bean	1977	1,291
159 0/8	23 3/8	23 7/8	18 3/8	7	7	Sarpy County	NE	Todd W. Steward	1985	1,291
159 0/8	26 0/8	25 6/8	20 0/8	5	5	Switzerland County	IN	Donald R. Barker	1986	1,291
159 0/8	24 0/8	24 2/8	16 6/8	5	5	Lawrence County	OH	Kevin Whitt	1986	1,291
159 0/8	25 6/8	25 2/8	14 4/8	5	5	Jackson County	MN	Ken Bute	1987	1,291
159 0/8	25 2/8	25 4/8	22 2/8	5	7	Pike County	IL	Steven R. Tice	1989	1,291
159 0/8	26 6/8	28 2/8	21 3/8	8	7	Clark County	IL	Ronald E. Pender	1989	1,291
159 0/8	23 6/8	23 6/8	18 4/8	5	6	Adair County	OK	Dan Mallory	1990	1,291
159 0/8	24 4/8	25 1/8	17 4/8	5	5	Davis County	IA	Gilbert H. Paulsen	1992	1,291
159 0/8	23 7/8	23 1/8	19 4/8	6	7	Clark County	IL	Stewart Lee	1992	1,291
159 0/8	24 4/8	24 2/8	18 2/8	6	5	Douglas County	WI	Russell E. Harvey	1993	1,291
159 0/8	24 0/8	23 6/8	19 3/8	7	7	Peoria County	IL	Jonathan Sarver	1994	1,291
159 0/8	26 3/8	26 1/8	19 7/8	7	6	Pike County	IL	Buzz Puterbaugh	1994	1,291
159 0/8	27 4/8	27 1/8	18 4/8	5	5	Ray County	MO	Kelly D. Holder	1994	1,291
159 0/8	23 5/8	22 6/8	17 6/8	5	7	Ottawa County	MI	Ken Melvin	1995	1,291
159 0/8	25 4/8	23 7/8	19 5/8	6	5	Refugio County	TX	Matt W. Mayo	1995	1,291
159 0/8	25 0/8	26 3/8	19 6/8	5	5	Anderson County	KS	Clifford Spencer	1995	1,291
159 0/8	24 6/8	24 3/8	18 2/8	5	5	Cedar County	IA	Rick Regennitter	1997	1,291
159 0/8	24 4/8	22 5/8	17 2/8	5	5	Cedar County	IA	Leland P. Kober	1997	1,291
159 0/8	24 4/8	25 3/8	19 2/8	5	6	Steuben County	NY	Bill Makitra	1997	1,291
159 0/8	22 3/8	23 5/8	15 0/8	5	5	Gainsborough Creek	MAN	Danny Maffenbeier	1998	1,291
158 7/8	24 7/8	22 4/8	20 3/8	5	6	Pope County	IL	Gary Thomas	1964	1,313
158 7/8	27 4/8	25 7/8	18 3/8	8	8	Blue Earth County	MN	Gordon F. Kopischke	1968	1,313
158 7/8	24 7/8	24 2/8	18 1/8	6	5	Owen County	IN	Steven Collins	1973	1,313
158 7/8	23 1/8	22 4/8	19 7/8	5	5	Sedgwick County	KS	Marion A. Crumm	1974	1,313
158 7/8	24 1/8	24 1/8	20 6/8	5	6	Putnam County	IL	David A. Heath	1975	1,313
158 7/8	27 2/8	26 7/8	19 4/8	7	8	Crawford County	OH	Charles Ellis	1977	1,313
158 7/8	24 4/8	24 1/8	17 7/8	5	5	Charles County	MD	Jim Wright	1986	1,313
158 7/8	25 2/8	25 2/8	20 3/8	6	7	Paulding County	OH	Karl A. Langham	1988	1,313
158 7/8	26 7/8	26 1/8	22 1/8	6	5	Henry County	MO	Lavern Rucker	1988	1,313
158 7/8	23 1/8	23 2/8	17 5/8	5	5	Pottawattamie County	IA	Mike L. Smith	1989	1,313
158 7/8	25 2/8	24 3/8	20 0/8	7	7	Marshall County	IA	Mark A. Hedum	1990	1,313
158 7/8	27 4/8	27 1/8	17 3/8	6	6	Chippewa County	WI	Dennis Johnson	1990	1,313
158 7/8	26 5/8	26 7/8	19 7/8	4	5	Westchester County	NY	Gregg Della Rocca	1991	1,313
158 7/8	26 7/8	26 6/8	18 7/8	4	4	Williamson County	IL	Mark Donahue	1993	1,313

Continued

WHITETAIL DEER (TYPICAL ANTLERS)

Minimum Score 125 — Continued

SCORE	LENGTH OF MAIN BEAM R	LENGTH OF MAIN BEAM L	INSIDE SPREAD	NUMBER OF POINTS R	NUMBER OF POINTS L	AREA	STATE/PROVINCE	HUNTER'S NAME	DATE	RANK
158 7/8	27 3/8	26 0/8	16 7/8	7	5	Greene County	OH	Mike Kennedy	1993	1,313
158 7/8	28 0/8	27 6/8	20 5/8	4	4	Knox County	IL	Todd A. Clayton	1995	1,313
158 7/8	26 0/8	25 6/8	17 5/8	6	6	Ross County	OH	John Virgin, Jr.	1995	1,313
158 7/8	24 2/8	24 4/8	18 1/8	4	4	Doniphan County	KS	Dennis R. Wisler	1995	1,313
158 6/8	22 5/8	22 7/8	15 6/8	7	7	Irion County	TX	John K. Watson	1977	1,331
158 6/8	26 5/8	26 5/8	18 6/8	6	6	Dodge County	MN	Mark A. Lenz	1986	1,331
158 6/8	25 0/8	25 4/8	19 2/8	5	6	Vernon County	WI	Dan Morrison	1988	1,331
158 6/8	25 1/8	24 0/8	20 2/8	5	5	Brooks County	TX	Billy Ellis III	1989	1,331
158 6/8	25 6/8	26 2/8	18 6/8	6	7	Howard County	IA	Mike Grube	1992	1,331
158 6/8	24 1/8	24 0/8	18 4/8	7	6	Geary County	KS	Mike Fraser	1992	1,331
158 6/8	25 1/8	25 3/8	18 6/8	6	6	Nemaha County	KS	Carol Hartter	1992	1,331
158 6/8	23 7/8	24 0/8	18 0/8	5	5	Jo Daviess County	IL	Jeff Dais	1994	1,331
158 6/8	26 0/8	26 1/8	16 7/8	7	6	Wright County	MN	Travis Drahota	1994	1,331
158 6/8	24 4/8	23 3/8	18 7/8	5	6	Fayette County	IL	Kent Goodin	1996	1,331
158 6/8	21 3/8	21 3/8	19 4/8	5	5	Louisa County	IA	Kevin Meyer	1996	1,331
158 6/8	25 6/8	25 6/8	26 7/8	5	5	Suffolk County	NY	Robert DeMarco	1997	1,331
158 6/8	23 2/8	24 2/8	18 0/8	6	5	Richland County	MT	Todd Dehner	1998	1,331
158 5/8	24 3/8	25 3/8	15 6/8	5	9	Marinette County	WI	Valerie P. Williams	1966	1,344
158 5/8	24 4/8	23 6/8	18 5/8	5	5	Shelby County	IL	Jim Helm	1977	1,344
158 5/8	25 5/8	26 1/8	18 1/8	4	4	Chariton County	MO	Brian Argetsinger	1986	1,344
158 5/8	22 7/8	23 3/8	17 1/8	5	5	Lee County	IA	Jeff Horsey	1989	1,344
158 5/8	23 4/8	23 1/8	20 1/8	7	7	Burlington County	NJ	Thomas A. Stevenson, Sr.	1989	1,344
158 5/8	26 5/8	27 6/8	19 1/8	5	5	Dane County	WI	Keith Matush	1990	1,344
158 5/8	25 2/8	26 0/8	21 4/8	6	5	La Salle County	IL	John Baunach	1992	1,344
158 5/8	24 4/8	23 4/8	19 7/8	5	5	Manitowoc County	WI	Jeff Wittmus	1993	1,344
158 5/8	26 2/8	26 0/8	19 3/8	4	4	Gallatin County	IL	Kenneth W. Sharp	1995	1,344
158 5/8	24 7/8	25 2/8	16 1/8	6	6	Webster County	NE	Bruce Vahlkamp	1995	1,344
158 5/8	24 5/8	24 5/8	17 7/8	6	6	Vernon County	WI	Daniel Hyatt	1995	1,344
158 5/8	21 4/8	21 1/8	15 1/8	6	6	Brown County	IL	Robert Anderson	1997	1,344
158 4/8	23 5/8	22 3/8	20 0/8	5	6	Cedar	KS	Gordon Reneberg	1965	1,356
158 4/8	26 4/8	25 2/8	22 6/8	5	5	Des Moines County	IA	Michael P. Anderson	1978	1,356
158 4/8	23 7/8	24 1/8	16 7/8	6	6	Boone County	IA	Chris W. Doran	1984	1,356
158 4/8	25 3/8	25 0/8	17 0/8	9	6	Adair County	MO	Terry Clay	1987	1,356
158 4/8	27 4/8	26 4/8	19 2/8	5	5	Adams County	MS	John Harvey	1989	1,356
158 4/8	25 3/8	25 0/8	20 6/8	6	6	Douglas County	WI	John Lawler	1991	1,356
158 4/8	26 3/8	26 7/8	18 6/8	5	5	Adams County	OH	Larry D. Napier	1991	1,356
158 4/8	25 2/8	23 7/8	19 2/8	6	5	Parke County	IN	Greg Spears	1992	1,356
158 4/8	22 6/8	23 2/8	19 2/8	5	5	Washington County	MN	Wayne A. Nicholson	1994	1,356
158 4/8	24 6/8	25 3/8	22 0/8	5	5	Shawano County	WI	Richard F. Onesti	1994	1,356
158 4/8	23 7/8	24 3/8	19 0/8	6	7	Lawrence County	OH	Greg Riggs	1995	1,356
158 4/8	24 1/8	24 1/8	19 4/8	5	5	Manitowoc County	WI	Timothy W. Garceau	1995	1,356
158 4/8	24 5/8	24 2/8	17 0/8	6	6	Jackson County	IL	Mark Frankford	1996	1,356
158 4/8	25 4/8	24 7/8	21 2/8	6	7	Fayette County	IA	Tim Nuss	1997	1,356
158 4/8	24 7/8	25 4/8	20 4/8	5	5	Rock Island County	IL	Don Thomsen	1997	1,356
158 4/8	24 3/8	24 6/8	18 2/8	5	5	Preble County	OH	Jim Lipps	1997	1,356
158 3/8	22 5/8	23 1/8	15 3/8	6	6	Texas County	OK	Edward F. Bryan, Jr.	1980	1,372
158 3/8	23 2/8	23 3/8	19 5/8	5	5	Jackson County	MI	Donald L. O'Dell	1984	1,372
158 3/8	27 5/8	28 6/8	23 4/8	8	4	Douglas County	WI	Gerald Berg	1988	1,372
158 3/8	24 4/8	24 4/8	19 3/8	5	7	Hennepin County	MN	Robert J. Evans, Jr.	1988	1,372
158 3/8	24 2/8	24 6/8	20 1/8	5	5	La Porte County	IN	Scott Saliwanchik	1988	1,372
158 3/8	25 4/8	24 6/8	19 3/8	5	7	Logan County	IL	Douglas A. Hullinger	1989	1,372
158 3/8	26 5/8	26 6/8	20 3/8	7	7	Jo Daviess County	IL	Michael P. Pickel	1990	1,372
158 3/8	27 3/8	26 5/8	22 6/8	5	6	Euphrasia	ONT	Tom Perks	1990	1,372
158 3/8	25 3/8	26 0/8	16 4/8	7	7	Lake County	IL	James C. Carlson	1991	1,372
158 3/8	24 5/8	24 5/8	18 5/8	5	5	Ferry County	WA	Shaun L. Henderson	1992	1,372
158 3/8	23 1/8	22 0/8	19 1/8	5	6	Treasure County	MT	John Moorhouse	1993	1,372
158 3/8	25 0/8	26 0/8	19 0/8	6	5	Newton County	IN	George G. Bogie	1995	1,372
158 3/8	27 1/8	27 7/8	18 6/8	5	6	Allamakee County	IA	Gary L. Mezera	1995	1,372
158 3/8	26 4/8	26 5/8	18 0/8	7	6	Marinette County	WI	Steve Jones	1997	1,372
158 2/8	26 4/8	24 6/8	22 7/8	5	7	Lee County	IA	Gary Frost	1965	1,386
158 2/8	25 0/8	26 4/8	21 2/8	5	6	Barron County	WI	Gary Kohlmeyer	1989	1,386
158 2/8	26 7/8	27 2/8	24 4/8	6	5	Carroll County	IL	David Kerr, Jr.	1992	1,386
158 2/8	23 4/8	22 4/8	17 0/8	7	5	La Salle County	IL	Lorin D. Gabehart	1993	1,386
158 2/8	23 7/8	24 2/8	17 4/8	5	5	Jackson County	IA	David Charles Horst	1994	1,386
158 2/8	25 1/8	26 0/8	20 2/8	5	4	Trumbull County	OH	Chuck Taninecz, Jr.	1994	1,386
158 2/8	25 2/8	25 6/8	17 6/8	5	5	Warren County	OH	Jeff Smith	1995	1,386
158 2/8	23 4/8	24 0/8	18 2/8	5	5	Peoria County	IL	Joel Pollack	1997	1,386
158 2/8	24 0/8	24 4/8	18 6/8	5	5	Marquette County	WI	Philip A. Manthey	1998	1,386
158 1/8	25 2/8	25 4/8	16 5/8	5	4	Randolph County	IN	Ron J. Carlin	1973	1,395
158 1/8	22 4/8	22 5/8	17 6/8	6	5	Kossuth County	IA	Steve Rochleau	1981	1,395
158 1/8	25 1/8	24 2/8	21 5/8	5	4	King George County	VA	L. M. "Ted" Williams	1981	1,395
158 1/8	21 6/8	22 7/8	18 7/8	7	5	Monona County	IA	Gary Mitchell	1983	1,395
158 1/8	25 2/8	25 4/8	17 7/8	6	6	Jackson County	IA	Jeff W. Ernst	1984	1,395
158 1/8	25 5/8	24 7/8	18 2/8	6	6	Brown County	OH	Michael W. Babcock	1985	1,395
158 1/8	26 4/8	26 4/8	18 1/8	6	6	Wyandot County	OH	Michael D Saam	1985	1,395
158 1/8	25 1/8	25 6/8	15 7/8	5	5	Columbiana County	OH	David S. Landsberger	1986	1,395
158 1/8	25 4/8	25 6/8	18 6/8	7	6	Rock Island County	IL	Donald G. Jones	1986	1,395
158 1/8	24 1/8	23 3/8	18 5/8	8	9	Racine County	WI	Joe Spang	1987	1,395

WHITETAIL DEER (TYPICAL ANTLERS)

Minimum Score 125 — Continued

SCORE	LENGTH OF MAIN BEAM R	LENGTH OF MAIN BEAM L	INSIDE SPREAD	NUMBER OF POINTS R	NUMBER OF POINTS L	AREA	STATE/PROVINCE	HUNTER'S NAME	DATE	RANK
158 1/8	25 5/8	25 0/8	20 6/8	6	7	Allamakee County	IA	Joe Lieb	1988	1,395
158 1/8	26 1/8	27 0/8	20 5/8	4	4	Adams County	IL	Jim Vahle	1988	1,395
158 1/8	22 2/8	21 5/8	17 2/8	6	5	Berkeley County	WV	Robert W. Deeds	1990	1,395
158 1/8	23 4/8	26 4/8	20 1/8	5	5	Bullitt County	KY	Tim Williams	1991	1,395
158 1/8	27 2/8	26 2/8	19 5/8	4	5	Pike County	OH	Robert Irwin Bazell	1993	1,395
158 1/8	25 3/8	24 1/8	17 5/8	6	6	Allen County	KS	Mark Spencer	1994	1,395
158 1/8	25 1/8	24 4/8	20 1/8	6	5	McDonough County	IL	Brian Sears	1995	1,395
158 1/8	25 2/8	25 1/8	20 6/8	8	5	Stark County	OH	Thomas M. Nelson	1996	1,395
158 1/8	26 4/8	26 0/8	18 5/8	9	6	Grundy County	IL	Mark Ermer	1996	1,395
158 1/8	23 2/8	23 7/8	19 7/8	8	6	Dodge County	WI	Ben Beine	1997	1,395
158 1/8	24 0/8	21 6/8	18 7/8	5	5	Lafayette County	WI	Daniel Popp	1997	1,395
158 1/8	26 3/8	26 1/8	18 5/8	5	5	Walworth County	WI	Michael Stelske	1997	1,395
158 1/8	24 1/8	24 4/8	17 5/8	5	5	Oldham County	KY	Jerry L. Wade	1997	1,395
158 0/8	24 0/8	23 5/8	18 6/8	6	6	Wayne County	IL	Bill Naney	1981	1,418
158 0/8	24 0/8	24 0/8	19 1/8	6	6	Lancaster County	NE	Martin Erickson	1983	1,418
158 0/8	26 5/8	26 1/8	19 6/8	4	5	Jackson County	OH	Jim Ridge	1986	1,418
158 0/8	24 2/8	23 6/8	19 2/8	5	5	Jackson County	IA	Terry Amling	1988	1,418
158 0/8	24 5/8	23 0/8	20 0/8	6	6	Houston County	MN	Michael Val Stevens	1989	1,418
158 0/8	24 6/8	24 5/8	20 6/8	5	6	Webster County	IA	Mike Jones	1989	1,418
158 0/8	24 1/8	24 7/8	17 6/8	5	7	Ogle County	IL	Art Heinze	1990	1,418
158 0/8	27 4/8	26 3/8	17 4/8	5	5	Van Buren County	IA	Gerald Palmer	1990	1,418
158 0/8	25 6/8	25 7/8	16 0/8	5	5	Bremer County	IA	Virgil Marlette	1991	1,418
158 0/8	22 2/8	22 1/8	18 4/8	6	5	Lincoln County	MO	Mark Gnade	1993	1,418
158 0/8	25 6/8	24 0/8	20 6/8	8	8	Jackson County	OH	Jordan R. Spyker	1993	1,418
158 0/8	25 4/8	24 7/8	16 0/8	6	5	Price County	WI	David L. Sanborn	1993	1,418
158 0/8	23 6/8	21 4/8	17 6/8	7	6	Stony Plain	ALB	David Swanson	1993	1,418
158 0/8	25 4/8	24 5/8	19 7/8	6	7	Mercer County	PA	Louis A. Nogay	1994	1,418
158 0/8	23 4/8	22 7/8	18 0/8	5	5	Keokuk County	IA	Barry Ledger	1994	1,418
158 0/8	24 0/8	23 7/8	20 0/8	5	5	Waukesha County	WI	Chris Gorecki	1994	1,418
158 0/8	24 4/8	23 6/8	16 0/8	7	6	Franklin County	PA	John E. Heckman	1995	1,418
158 0/8	23 4/8	24 2/8	22 0/8	5	5	Butler County	KS	Larry D. Walker, Jr.	1996	1,418
158 0/8	23 1/8	23 0/8	18 0/8	6	6	Douglas County	NE	Rodney Sigel	1997	1,418
157 7/8	23 0/8	25 0/8	19 5/8	5	5	Meeker County	MN	Russell T. Nelson	1974	1,437
157 7/8	28 5/8	28 6/8	25 7/8	4	4	Goodhue County	MN	John "Jack" Cordes	1975	1,437
157 7/8	23 7/8	24 1/8	16 4/8	5	7	Harvey County	KS	P. Bruce Mosiman	1984	1,437
157 7/8	26 5/8	27 2/8	19 1/8	5	6	Boone County	MO	Robert Hagans	1986	1,437
157 7/8	27 2/8	25 6/8	17 2/8	6	7	Calhoun County	MI	Jeff Edward Titus	1986	1,437
157 7/8	26 6/8	26 7/8	21 1/8	5	5	Vermilion County	IL	James D. Rueter	1987	1,437
157 7/8	21 2/8	22 6/8	16 5/8	5	7	Butler County	KS	Jim P. Smith	1987	1,437
157 7/8	24 2/8	24 2/8	19 7/8	5	5	Sedgwick County	KS	Jim Molitor	1988	1,437
157 7/8	23 3/8	22 6/8	18 2/8	6	5	Boone County	IA	Jim Humberg	1988	1,437
157 7/8	24 0/8	23 7/8	14 6/8	5	7	Simpson County	KY	Mike Stovall	1990	1,437
157 7/8	22 4/8	25 2/8	17 5/8	5	5	Sherburne County	MN	Ron Makarrall	1993	1,437
157 7/8	24 6/8	24 7/8	17 5/8	5	5	Smoky Lake	ALB	Brendle S. Daugherty	1994	1,437
157 7/8	26 4/8	26 5/8	21 1/8	4	4	Jackson County	MI	Gerald A. Slusarczyk	1994	1,437
157 7/8	25 6/8	25 7/8	20 3/8	7	5	Vigo County	IN	Ryan Howard	1994	1,437
157 7/8	26 0/8	26 2/8	21 3/8	7	5	Richardson County	NE	Donald J. Wickham, Jr.	1995	1,437
157 7/8	24 5/8	24 5/8	20 0/8	6	5	Fayette County	IL	Paul McConkey	1995	1,437
157 7/8	23 7/8	24 1/8	20 7/8	6	7	Benton County	IA	Mike Miner	1996	1,437
157 7/8	23 0/8	23 3/8	18 3/8	5	5	Somerset County	PA	Lynn A. Henry	1996	1,437
157 7/8	25 1/8	25 6/8	20 5/8	5	6	Miami County	OH	Terry L. Brower	1996	1,437
157 7/8	25 7/8	26 7/8	20 3/8	5	4	Waukesha County	WI	Paul A. Samuelson	1997	1,437
157 7/8	24 3/8	23 1/8	19 5/8	5	5	Buffalo County	WI	Marty Mattes	1997	1,437
157 6/8	23 7/8	24 2/8	15 4/8	5	5	Lyon County	MN	M. Dean Holm	1976	1,458
157 6/8	23 4/8	23 3/8	18 4/8	5	5	Phillips County	KS	Lavern A. Wheaton	1978	1,458
157 6/8	25 3/8	26 1/8	19 5/8	6	6	Des Moines County	IA	David Bollei	1979	1,458
157 6/8	24 7/8	25 2/8	21 4/8	4	6	Geauga County	OH	John A. Suszynski	1981	1,458
157 6/8	24 4/8	24 4/8	16 4/8	4	5	Oconto County	WI	Richard E. Liss	1983	1,458
157 6/8	23 3/8	23 6/8	17 1/8	6	6	Leavenworth County	KS	John Garrison	1983	1,458
157 6/8	23 6/8	23 6/8	17 5/8	8	6	Des Moines County	IA	Ken Thorndyke	1984	1,458
157 6/8	26 6/8	25 3/8	19 4/8	5	5	Genesee County	MI	Alfred L. Allen 1	987	1,458
157 6/8	25 1/8	25 4/8	18 4/8	4	5	Martin County	IN	Terry Kirkman	1987	1,458
157 6/8	27 2/8	28 6/8	19 2/8	5	5	Shawnee County	KS	Steven E. Deever	1988	1,458
157 6/8	23 4/8	22 7/8	18 2/8	7	5	Yankton County	SD	Alan Peterson	1988	1,458
157 6/8	25 4/8	25 4/8	21 4/8	4	4	McLean County	IL	Jim Dicken	1991	1,458
157 6/8	23 0/8	25 4/8	21 2/8	4	4	Vermilion	ALB	Glenn Moir	1992	1,458
157 6/8	25 5/8	25 1/8	18 5/8	6	5	Oakland County	MI	Bryan K. Malone	1992	1,458
157 6/8	25 2/8	25 1/8	16 1/8	7	5	Winneshiek County	IA	Gerald M. Hunter	1992	1,458
157 6/8	23 5/8	23 2/8	16 0/8	7	8	Benton County	MO	Rodney Owen	1992	1,458
157 6/8	26 0/8	26 0/8	18 6/8	5	5	Kalamazoo County	MI	Jeffrey A. Wisser	1993	1,458
157 6/8	24 1/8	25 2/8	15 2/8	4	4	Green County	WI	Timothy J. Scott	1993	1,458
157 6/8	26 5/8	25 2/8	19 2/8	6	5	Jefferson County	IN	Andrew W. Pickett	1994	1,458
157 6/8	25 1/8	24 6/8	17 5/8	7	5	Dodge County	MN	Dan Rendler	1994	1,458
157 6/8	23 0/8	23 7/8	21 5/8	7	7	Grant County	KS	Brandon D. Henson	1995	1,458
157 6/8	24 0/8	22 7/8	17 2/8	6	6	Pike County	IL	Buzz Puterbaugh	1995	1,458
157 6/8	26 3/8	26 5/8	18 2/8	5	4	Genesee County	NY	Richard C. Cooper	1996	1,458
157 6/8	24 0/8	23 2/8	18 4/8	5	5	Allamakee County	IA	Duane C. Baumler	1996	1,458
157 6/8	24 4/8	24 4/8	19 0/8	7	7	Warren County	IA	Bruce Hupke	1997	1,458

WHITETAIL DEER (TYPICAL ANTLERS)

Minimum Score 125   Continued

SCORE	LENGTH OF R MAIN BEAM L		INSIDE SPREAD	NUMBER OF R POINTS L		AREA	STATE/PROVINCE	HUNTER'S NAME	DATE	RANK
157 6/8	25 6/8	24 5/8	18 6/8	5	6	Lawrence County	OH	Denny Tieman	1998	1,458
157 5/8	22 4/8	23 2/8	16 5/8	6	7	Marion County	KS	Ron Hershberger	1982	1,484
157 5/8	22 7/8	24 2/8	18 7/8	5	6	Fulton County	AR	Lynn Luther	1983	1,484
157 5/8	27 4/8	27 2/8	21 1/8	5	6	Saline County	KS	Richard Cockroft	1985	1,484
157 5/8	24 3/8	23 7/8	19 5/8	6	5	Bartholomew County	IN	Jean E. Sneed	1986	1,484
157 5/8	24 1/8	24 0/8	15 7/8	6	6	Atoka County	OK	Patrick C. Patton	1988	1,484
157 5/8	25 5/8	26 0/8	21 1/8	5	5	Morgan County	IL	Roger Smith	1989	1,484
157 5/8	26 0/8	26 1/8	21 3/8	5	6	Wayne County	MO	Rod Bowling	1989	1,484
157 5/8	24 4/8	25 3/8	22 2/8	4	7	McHenry County	IL	Dennis Huhn	1990	1,484
157 5/8	27 2/8	25 7/8	19 7/8	4	4	Howard County	MD	William H. Ingram	1991	1,484
157 5/8	25 0/8	24 7/8	19 1/8	6	6	Wood County	WI	Michael L. Hewitt	1991	1,484
157 5/8	24 3/8	25 3/8	20 6/8	5	6	Du Page County	IL	Ron Knebel	1991	1,484
157 5/8	24 3/8	24 5/8	18 0/8	6	7	Washington County	IA	Chris Davies	1991	1,484
157 5/8	23 3/8	23 5/8	20 5/8	5	5	Ozaukee County	WI	Richard Kropp	1992	1,484
157 5/8	23 4/8	23 4/8	17 1/8	6	6	Brooks County	TX	Tom Buckner	1993	1,484
157 5/8	24 2/8	23 1/8	16 5/8	6	6	Noble County	IN	Glen Steele	1993	1,484
157 5/8	26 7/8	27 0/8	22 1/8	4	4	Montgomery County	MD	Donald R. Nycum	1994	1,484
157 5/8	24 2/8	24 4/8	16 7/8	7	9	Woodford County	IL	Bobby J. Evans	1994	1,484
157 5/8	22 1/8	25 4/8	16 6/8	5	7	Louisa County	IA	Dan Brauns	1994	1,484
157 5/8	23 7/8	23 7/8	19 3/8	5	5	Burnett County	WI	William L. LaPage	1994	1,484
157 5/8	28 3/8	26 0/8	18 3/8	5	5	Waukesha County	WI	Joe Loterbauer	1995	1,484
157 5/8	24 6/8	24 0/8	16 4/8	5	5	Lee County	IA	Brian J. Mehaffy	1996	1,484
157 5/8	21 7/8	22 0/8	15 7/8	5	5	Saline County	NE	Neil Formanek	1996	1,484
157 5/8	25 1/8	26 0/8	18 2/8	6	6	Harrison County	IA	Ben McDonald	1996	1,484
157 5/8	23 7/8	24 2/8	21 3/8	5	5	Kankakee County	IL	Joseph R. Pergram	1997	1,484
157 4/8	25 7/8	25 7/8	17 2/8	4	4	Marion County	IA	Charles H. Walter	1967	1,508
157 4/8	22 7/8	23 5/8	18 0/8	5	5	Kalamazoo County	MI	Guy Stutzman	1979	1,508
157 4/8	24 2/8	24 4/8	13 6/8	5	5	Webster County	IA	Larry K. Fossen	1980	1,508
157 4/8	23 1/8	22 4/8	20 4/8	4	6	Henry County	VA	Mike Weaver	1986	1,508
157 4/8	23 5/8	22 6/8	21 1/8	5	6	Jackson County	OH	Steven L. Roe	1987	1,508
157 4/8	23 5/8	23 4/8	19 2/8	5	5	Hardin County	IL	Larry Hall	1988	1,508
157 4/8	22 6/8	21 1/8	16 2/8	6	6	Grundy County	IL	Brian Bergmann	1988	1,508
157 4/8	24 7/8	24 3/8	18 4/8	4	5	Hennepin County	MN	Mike Hintzen	1990	1,508
157 4/8	21 3/8	27 3/8	21 4/8	5	5	Crawford County	IL	Steve Parker	1990	1,508
157 4/8	24 1/8	24 3/8	19 2/8	6	5	Sawyer County	WI	Gary Haus	1991	1,508
157 4/8	25 4/8	25 7/8	20 0/8	4	4	Lake County	IL	Russ Tallman	1992	1,508
157 4/8	23 4/8	23 6/8	17 6/8	6	5	Boone County	IA	Bart Bollie	1992	1,508
157 4/8	24 4/8	23 1/8	15 0/8	5	5	Chase County	KS	Gregory G. Windler	1992	1,508
157 4/8	27 1/8	27 3/8	20 2/8	4	5	Champaign County	IL	Joe Stark	1995	1,508
157 4/8	26 5/8	26 4/8	18 6/8	5	6	Wyandotte County	KS	William Danyale McDonald	1996	1,508
157 4/8	25 7/8	24 7/8	23 7/8	7	7	Jackson County	IL	Tim Cobin	1996	1,508
157 4/8	23 7/8	23 1/8	16 6/8	5	5	Steuben County	NY	Michael Dutcher	1997	1,508
157 4/8	26 4/8	26 2/8	19 7/8	5	4	Lake County	OH	Al DiLiberto	1997	1,508
157 4/8	24 6/8	25 6/8	20 6/8	4	4	Cedar County	IA	Keith Roszell	1997	1,508
157 3/8	23 0/8	23 2/8	22 7/8	5	5	Adams County	IL	John Musolino	1966	1,527
157 3/8	23 5/8	23 2/8	16 3/8	5	5	Harrison County	KY	Kevin Poe	1984	1,527
157 3/8	24 4/8	23 1/8	16 1/8	6	5	Yuma County	CO	Chuck Anderson, Sr.	1985	1,527
157 3/8	24 4/8	24 4/8	19 1/8	4	5	Vermilion County	IL	Russell A. Sill	1989	1,527
157 3/8	24 6/8	24 2/8	17 7/8	6	6	Price County	WI	Mike Case	1990	1,527
157 3/8	24 7/8	25 2/8	15 3/8	6	5	Pickaway County	OH	Willard Dean Clemmons	1992	1,527
157 3/8	24 7/8	25 5/8	19 7/8	5	5	Worcester County	MA	Roberta Davis	1992	1,527
157 3/8	24 6/8	23 6/8	18 1/8	5	5	Jefferson County	WI	Dale Schilt	1993	1,527
157 3/8	26 4/8	26 4/8	19 2/8	6	5	Cloud County	KS	Robert H. Gilbert	1994	1,527
157 3/8	24 5/8	24 1/8	18 7/8	6	6	Seneca County	OH	Shawn P. Bradner	1995	1,527
157 3/8	23 3/8	22 7/8	15 0/8	5	6	Reno County	KS	Michael L. Murphy	1995	1,527
157 3/8	27 5/8	26 7/8	20 2/8	7	5	Columbia County	WI	Kent Kirn	1995	1,527
157 3/8	25 4/8	25 1/8	18 1/8	5	5	Clermont County	OH	Todd M. Whitmer	1997	1,527
157 3/8	23 1/8	22 5/8	16 7/8	5	5	Sauk County	WI	Dave Malecki	1997	1,527
157 2/8	23 1/8	22 6/8	16 2/8	6	6	Johnson County	IL	Jim Casey	1963	1,541
157 2/8	22 3/8	23 2/8	16 4/8	5	5	Mountrail County	ND	Dean A. Rehak	1963	1,541
157 2/8	22 3/8	22 2/8	21 1/8	8	6	Cottonwood County	MN	Brian Grothe	1978	1,541
157 2/8	27 6/8	27 6/8	22 3/8	5	6	Jessamine County	KY	David Cartwright	1979	1,541
157 2/8	21 1/8	22 4/8	19 7/8	6	5	Lenawee County	MI	Rodney Lee Wilt	1980	1,541
157 2/8	25 4/8	25 0/8	17 6/8	5	5	Argyle	MAN	Russ Snell	1982	1,541
157 2/8	26 2/8	28 0/8	20 4/8	8	5	Westchester County	NY	Ralph Finacchiaro	1983	1,541
157 2/8	25 5/8	26 2/8	17 0/8	5	5	Chickasaw County	IA	Theodore J. Steege IV	1987	1,541
157 2/8	25 2/8	25 0/8	20 4/8	5	5	Ashland County	OH	Bert P. Reynolds	1989	1,541
157 2/8	23 5/8	23 6/8	19 7/8	7	6	Elbert County	CO	Tom Kelley	1990	1,541
157 2/8	24 5/8	23 4/8	22 0/8	6	7	Allegheny County	PA	James K. Stewart	1990	1,541
157 2/8	23 6/8	23 3/8	18 0/8	5	5	Houston County	MN	Rob Larson	1991	1,541
157 2/8	25 0/8	24 5/8	17 4/8	6	6	Chisago County	MN	Chris Peterson	1991	1,541
157 2/8	26 0/8	26 5/8	23 2/8	5	5	Priddis	ALB	Rennie F. Sherman	1992	1,541
157 2/8	25 7/8	24 4/8	18 2/8	5	5	Brown County	KS	Tony French	1992	1,541
157 2/8	25 1/8	24 4/8	17 4/8	5	5	Winnebago County	IL	Pat Van Barriger	1993	1,541
157 2/8	23 1/8	24 2/8	17 0/8	5	5	Washington County	KS	Doug Kruse	1994	1,541
157 2/8	23 5/8	23 1/8	17 2/8	7	6	Van Buren County	IA	Jeff Propst	1995	1,541
157 2/8	25 2/8	24 7/8	20 6/8	6	5	Cass County	IL	James Deppe	1996	1,541
157 2/8	28 3/8	27 4/8	18 2/8	5	5	Patrick County	VA	Jimmy Hall	1996	1,541

WHITETAIL DEER (TYPICAL ANTLERS)

Minimum Score 125 — Continued

SCORE	LENGTH OF MAIN BEAM R	L	INSIDE SPREAD	NUMBER OF POINTS R	L	AREA	STATE/PROVINCE	HUNTER'S NAME	DATE	RANK
157 2/8	24 1/8	26 1/8	21 5/8	5	6	Jones County	IA	Chad R. Machart	1997	1,541
157 1/8	25 3/8	26 1/8	18 5/8	6	6	Puslinch Twp.	ONT	Jeff Sinclair	1977	1,562
157 1/8	25 4/8	24 4/8	23 3/8	6	5	Fairfax County	VA	Chris Jackson	1986	1,562
157 1/8	25 7/8	22 4/8	16 4/8	7	5	Eaton County	MI	Bryan Coburn	1990	1,562
157 1/8	23 5/8	22 4/8	18 5/8	5	5	McHenry County	IL	Rich Matras	1991	1,562
157 1/8	25 6/8	25 7/8	18 7/8	6	4	Dakota County	MN	Vince LaCroix	1992	1,562
157 1/8	24 5/8	23 0/8	18 7/8	5	5	Buffalo County	WI	Doug Kensmoe	1992	1,562
157 1/8	26 4/8	25 5/8	19 7/8	4	4	Hennepin County	MN	Tony Welch	1993	1,562
157 1/8	26 3/8	24 4/8	18 0/8	6	6	Forest County	WI	Anthony J. Swiontek	1993	1,562
157 1/8	25 2/8	26 0/8	20 3/8	7	7	Adams County	WI	Michael S. Stammen	1994	1,562
157 1/8	26 0/8	26 1/8	19 2/8	6	6	Clayton County	IA	Randy R. Mack	1994	1,562
157 1/8	27 3/8	26 5/8	19 4/8	6	5	Beadle County	SD	Brian W. Diede	1994	1,562
157 1/8	22 4/8	21 7/8	17 5/8	5	5	Chariton County	MO	Tim Groves	1994	1,562
157 1/8	21 4/8	22 6/8	18 3/8	6	5	Jackson County	MN	John Jacobson	1995	1,562
157 1/8	25 7/8	25 5/8	19 7/8	6	6	Parke County	IN	Jeff Foster	1996	1,562
157 0/8	25 7/8	26 0/8	16 5/8	6	7	Watonwan County	MN	Dave Ellertson	1973	1,576
157 0/8	25 3/8	26 0/8	15 6/8	7	8	McKenzie County	ND	Donald Olson	1974	1,576
157 0/8	24 3/8	26 0/8	18 6/8	8	6	Ashland County	OH	William Kucic	1985	1,576
157 0/8	23 6/8	23 7/8	20 7/8	7	6	McLean County	IL	Daryle W. Tipsord	1985	1,576
157 0/8	24 5/8	23 4/8	17 5/8	5	6	Kiowa County	KS	Royce E. Frazier	1986	1,576
157 0/8	25 3/8	25 7/8	21 4/8	5	4	Blue Earth County	MN	Tom Lacina	1987	1,576
157 0/8	24 7/8	26 7/8	18 0/8	5	5	Roane County	TN	Larry T. Cook	1988	1,576
157 0/8	24 6/8	23 0/8	20 3/8	8	9	Lake County	IL	Mike Mitten	1988	1,576
157 0/8	23 6/8	23 4/8	18 2/8	6	7	Parke County	IN	Jeff Myers	1989	1,576
157 0/8	27 0/8	27 0/8	19 7/8	6	5	Clayton County	IA	Curt Ferguson	1989	1,576
157 0/8	25 6/8	26 1/8	19 4/8	7	6	Brown County	IL	Larry Grant	1992	1,576
157 0/8	22 4/8	22 2/8	18 0/8	6	7	Fayette County	WV	Jeff Stephenson	1993	1,576
157 0/8	27 3/8	27 5/8	18 6/8	7	8	Richland County	OH	Russ Winkler	1994	1,576
157 0/8	23 1/8	22 4/8	19 4/8	5	6	Nemaha County	KS	Darryl Becker	1994	1,576
157 0/8	27 1/8	25 4/8	19 4/8	7	8	Morgan County	KY	Glenn Hance	1996	1,576
157 0/8	25 5/8	26 4/8	17 4/8	5	5	Edmonton	ALB	Clay Wilson	1996	1,576
157 0/8	22 6/8	22 7/8	15 3/8	6	6	Clark County	IL	James P. Weisheit	1996	1,576
157 0/8	23 2/8	22 7/8	21 0/8	5	5	Carrot Creek	ALB	Curtis Dennis, Jr.	1997	1,576
156 7/8	28 7/8	26 6/8	19 7/8	5	5	Chippewa County	MN	Paul D. Lundgren	1969	1,594
156 7/8	25 2/8	24 5/8	19 7/8	6	5	Johnson County	KS	Jim Laybourne	1979	1,594
156 7/8	25 6/8	25 4/8	19 7/8	6	5	Lake County	IL	Dennis P. Schor	1979	1,594
156 7/8	27 1/8	25 0/8	21 3/8	5	6	Clearwater County	MN	Dennis Engerbretson	1980	1,594
156 7/8	23 7/8	23 7/8	19 5/8	5	5	Cherokee County	IA	Dan Roberts	1982	1,594
156 7/8	24 0/8	23 7/8	18 0/8	6	6	Butler County	KS	William D. George	1986	1,594
156 7/8	23 6/8	24 4/8	19 6/8	5	6	Atoka County	OK	Kevin W. Guinn	1987	1,594
156 7/8	26 6/8	26 4/8	20 1/8	5	5	Eugenia	ONT	Ron Lusher	1987	1,594
156 7/8	25 1/8	24 1/8	20 2/8	6	5	Franklin County	IA	Ron Hansen	1990	1,594
156 7/8	28 4/8	28 2/8	18 5/8	8	8	Talbot County	MD	Ray Kinsey	1992	1,594
156 7/8	24 5/8	23 4/8	19 1/8	6	5	Morrison County	MN	Stephan Felix	1992	1,594
156 7/8	26 0/8	26 0/8	21 3/8	4	4	Harrison County	IA	Albert Selk	1994	1,594
156 7/8	25 0/8	24 6/8	19 5/8	5	5	Suffolk County	NY	Tim Connor	1994	1,594
156 7/8	24 5/8	24 1/8	19 3/8	5	6	Dodge County	WI	Don Gourlie	1996	1,594
156 7/8	25 0/8	24 4/8	18 1/8	5	5	Dodge County	MN	Myles Keller	1996	1,594
156 7/8	25 4/8	25 4/8	20 7/8	5	6	Lawrence County	OH	Burnard Gibson	1997	1,594
156 7/8	23 3/8	23 7/8	19 7/8	5	5	McHenry County	IL	Scott Wulf	1997	1,594
156 7/8	26 0/8	25 7/8	17 3/8	5	5	Gallia County	OH	Gary C. Casto	1997	1,594
156 7/8	26 3/8	26 1/8	20 7/8	4	4	Jo Daviess County	IL	Joseph C. Hinderman	1998	1,594
156 6/8	27 1/8	26 5/8	20 5/8	5	5	Lincoln County	WV	Gary Smith	1970	1,613
156 6/8	24 1/8	24 0/8	16 6/8	5	5	Meigs County	OH	Brian Kelley	1982	1,613
156 6/8	26 7/8	26 4/8	20 0/8	6	5	Des Moines County	IA	Don Smith	1986	1,613
156 6/8	24 4/8	24 2/8	16 2/8	6	7	Clark County	IL	Gary Taylor	1986	1,613
156 6/8	24 4/8	24 4/8	20 2/8	5	4	Howard County	IA	Terry Larson	1987	1,613
156 6/8	25 4/8	24 6/8	19 2/8	5	5	Washington County	IL	Bruce Diedrich	1987	1,613
156 6/8	23 0/8	24 0/8	16 7/8	7	5	Walworth County	WI	Brian Strickler	1988	1,613
156 6/8	22 6/8	23 5/8	18 2/8	5	5	Miami County	OH	Gary L. Tipps	1988	1,613
156 6/8	26 4/8	26 5/8	18 4/8	6	5	Lapeer County	MI	Wayne Coulman	1990	1,613
156 6/8	23 7/8	24 2/8	15 6/8	5	5	County of Parkland	ALB	Rob Kubicek	1992	1,613
156 6/8	26 1/8	25 5/8	23 2/8	6	6	Suffolk County	NY	Herbert F. DeArmitt III	1992	1,613
156 6/8	25 4/8	25 1/8	18 0/8	5	5	Isabella County	MI	Robert J. Warner	1993	1,613
156 6/8	25 4/8	25 4/8	19 2/8	5	5	Sawyer County	WI	Alan A. Meyers	1993	1,613
156 6/8	23 6/8	25 6/8	20 6/8	5	5	Brown County	OH	James K. Kuntz	1993	1,613
156 6/8	25 3/8	24 7/8	19 5/8	5	6	Ozaukee County	WI	Greg Highstrom	1994	1,613
156 6/8	25 4/8	24 5/8	19 2/8	6	6	Price County	WI	Frank Plyer	1994	1,613
156 6/8	24 0/8	24 6/8	17 2/8	5	5	Hennepin County	MN	Rodney Jansen	1994	1,613
156 6/8	22 6/8	23 5/8	20 3/8	7	7	Pope County	IL	Richard Riddle	1995	1,613
156 6/8	24 5/8	25 0/8	21 4/8	5	5	Allegany County	NY	Stephen J. Lewandowski	1995	1,613
156 6/8	22 4/8	23 1/8	18 0/8	5	5	Jasper County	IN	Peter J. Kohne	1996	1,613
156 5/8	26 1/8	25 2/8	20 2/8	6	6	Grant County	WI	Walter Edge	1957	1,633
156 5/8	24 6/8	26 3/8	19 5/8	5	4	Traverse County	MN	Roland L. Hausmann	1960	1,633
156 5/8	22 7/8	25 0/8	19 6/8	7	7	Des Moines County	IA	E. E. Smith	1965	1,633
156 5/8	23 7/8	24 1/8	18 7/8	7	7	Nicollet County	MN	Thomas J. Merkley	1967	1,633
156 5/8	27 3/8	26 2/8	21 5/8	5	5	Queen Annes County	MD	Charles Milford Squires	1969	1,633
156 5/8	24 7/8	24 3/8	21 1/8	6	5	Wabaunsee County	KS	Tom Willard	1983	1,633

WHITETAIL DEER (TYPICAL ANTLERS)

Minimum Score 125

SCORE	LENGTH OF R MAIN BEAM L		INSIDE SPREAD	NUMBER OF R POINTS L		AREA	STATE/ PROVINCE	HUNTER'S NAME	DATE	RANK
156 5/8	22 0/8	22 2/8	16 1/8	6	8	Kossuth County	IA	Ron Burton	1985	1,633
156 5/8	24 3/8	24 3/8	19 3/8	5	5	Johnson County	IA	Larry Hermanstorfer	1987	1,633
156 5/8	22 6/8	23 3/8	20 7/8	5	5	Price County	WI	Larry Halvorson	1990	1,633
156 5/8	24 5/8	24 4/8	18 7/8	5	5	Eaton County	MI	Dudley Miller, Jr.	1990	1,633
156 5/8	25 3/8	25 6/8	16 3/8	6	6	Chariton County	MO	Nathan Leonard	1991	1,633
156 5/8	23 0/8	23 0/8	16 7/8	11	5	Leavenworth County	KS	Michael Paul	1994	1,633
156 5/8	25 6/8	25 7/8	22 3/8	8	7	Dekalb County	IL	Josef K. Rud	1994	1,633
156 5/8	23 6/8	21 7/8	14 6/8	6	5	Lee County	IL	Cory J. Zimmerly	1994	1,633
156 5/8	25 0/8	24 2/8	17 6/8	6	5	Monroe County	WI	Tim J. Cabasos	1995	1,633
156 5/8	25 5/8	25 6/8	18 5/8	5	5	Polk County	WI	David R. Daniels	1996	1,633
156 4/8	26 4/8	25 7/8	22 5/8	4	5	Williamson County	IL	Roy Williams	1960	1,649
156 4/8	26 3/8	24 4/8	17 4/8	5	5	Forest County	WI	Daniel Radder	1968	1,649
156 4/8	24 1/8	23 3/8	15 0/8	6	5	Jones County	IA	Gary McCormick	1977	1,649
156 4/8	23 7/8	24 1/8	18 3/8	6	6	Graham County	KS	Russell Hull	1979	1,649
156 4/8	24 4/8	23 6/8	21 4/8	5	5	Waukesha County	WI	Steve Hoelz	1987	1,649
156 4/8	27 0/8	27 5/8	19 1/8	6	6	McLeod County	MN	Craig Hrkal	1988	1,649
156 4/8	24 3/8	21 0/8	19 4/8	5	5	Jackson County	OH	Michael L. Cornett	1988	1,649
156 4/8	25 4/8	25 5/8	17 6/8	7	7	Osage County	KS	Gerald Britschge	1988	1,649
156 4/8	22 0/8	24 0/8	19 3/8	6	8	Macoupin County	IL	Rick D. Tigo	1990	1,649
156 4/8	23 6/8	24 1/8	18 0/8	5	5	Clarke County	IA	Mark G. Backstrom	1992	1,649
156 4/8	25 3/8	24 6/8	18 2/8	5	5	Nemaha County	KS	Steven L. Hanzlik	1992	1,649
156 4/8	24 2/8	23 4/8	18 7/8	6	8	Clark County	IL	Paul Baird	1993	1,649
156 4/8	26 7/8	28 0/8	23 4/8	4	4	Macon County	AL	Craig G. Shook	1995	1,649
156 4/8	22 2/8	23 5/8	18 6/8	5	6	Stafford County	KS	Bill Duncan	1995	1,649
156 4/8	27 5/8	27 5/8	19 4/8	4	4	Coshocton County	OH	John Zaayer	1996	1,649
156 4/8	24 6/8	26 0/8	18 4/8	6	5	Lawrence County	IL	David Fleming	1996	1,649
156 4/8	25 1/8	23 3/8	18 4/8	6	5	Clay County	IL	Rusty Windle	1997	1,649
156 4/8	24 7/8	24 1/8	15 6/8	5	5	Waupaca County	WI	Jason J. Firkus	1997	1,649
156 4/8	26 2/8	25 0/8	20 6/8	5	5	Osborne County	KS	Blake Grabast	1997	1,649
156 4/8	25 4/8	24 7/8	20 7/8	6	5	Jefferson County	WI	Charles E. Kiupelis	1997	1,649
156 4/8	25 4/8	25 1/8	19 3/8	5	6	Barton County	KS	Don Herter	1997	1,649
156 4/8	24 7/8	25 4/8	18 2/8	4	5	Marquette County	WI	Thomas J. Roll	1998	1,649
156 3/8	27 0/8	25 5/8	20 0/8	8	6	Hamilton County	KS	Mike Gilbert	1977	1,671
156 3/8	25 0/8	25 2/8	18 4/8	6	8	Russell County	KS	John W. Frost	1983	1,671
156 3/8	24 4/8	24 3/8	21 5/8	6	6	Mills County	IA	Douglas R. Roll	1986	1,671
156 3/8	25 4/8	25 2/8	16 7/8	6	5	Vernon County	WI	David Penchi	1987	1,671
156 3/8	22 1/8	23 4/8	17 1/8	6	7	Trempealeau County	WI	Ginger Molitor	1988	1,671
156 3/8	22 4/8	23 4/8	14 7/8	6	7	Polk County	WI	Jon Mattson	1989	1,671
156 3/8	25 0/8	24 5/8	20 5/8	5	4	Effingham County	IL	Tim Dillow	1989	1,671
156 3/8	24 4/8	24 2/8	19 7/8	5	7	Sioux County	IA	Owen Sandbulte	1991	1,671
156 3/8	27 4/8	26 4/8	21 4/8	6	6	Lawrence County	OH	Richard L. Carte	1991	1,671
156 3/8	22 6/8	21 6/8	17 6/8	5	6	Parke County	IN	Louis Murphy	1992	1,671
156 3/8	24 5/8	24 1/8	18 3/8	6	7	Strathcona	ALB	Mark Johnson	1992	1,671
156 3/8	26 2/8	27 2/8	19 1/8	5	5	Brown County	IL	Thomas J. Lavery	1993	1,671
156 3/8	23 3/8	22 5/8	18 3/8	5	6	Menard County	TX	Steve Cocanower	1995	1,671
156 3/8	22 2/8	22 2/8	17 1/8	6	6	Buchanan County	MO	Randy Clinton	1996	1,671
156 3/8	24 1/8	24 1/8	18 5/8	5	5	Clark County	WI	Tom Brown	1997	1,671
156 2/8	26 1/8	26 4/8	21 0/8	6	6	Butler County	KS	Ralph R. Belt	1967	1,686
156 2/8	25 0/8	23 2/8	18 0/8	9	6	Palo Alto County	IA	Earl J. Gustafson	1972	1,686
156 2/8	23 3/8	23 6/8	16 6/8	5	5	Fulton County	IL	Sam Smith	1973	1,686
156 2/8	25 3/8	25 3/8	23 6/8	5	6	Winona County	MN	Daniel McIntire	1979	1,686
156 2/8	22 2/8	22 7/8	16 6/8	5	5	Garfield County	MT	Larry H. Hoyt	1982	1,686
156 2/8	25 2/8	26 2/8	18 6/8	6	5	Stevens County	WA	Tom Duffey	1983	1,686
156 2/8	25 5/8	26 1/8	19 0/8	4	5	Ogle County	IL	Gary D. Shaw	1984	1,686
156 2/8	25 1/8	26 0/8	19 4/8	5	5	Oakland County	MI	David B. Tater	1984	1,686
156 2/8	24 2/8	24 6/8	21 0/8	5	4	Cass County	IL	Dale Milstead	1985	1,686
156 2/8	26 2/8	27 0/8	20 0/8	5	5	Washington County	IA	Carl Stogdill	1986	1,686
156 2/8	24 5/8	24 3/8	20 6/8	8	5	Kankakee County	IL	Al Weissbohn	1988	1,686
156 2/8	26 4/8	26 1/8	16 0/8	4	4	Washburn County	WI	Cullan Hanacek	1989	1,686
156 2/8	27 0/8	26 6/8	22 2/8	5	7	Lafayette County	WI	Mike Sigafus	1989	1,686
156 2/8	25 1/8	25 0/8	20 6/8	5	5	La Salle County	TX	Dr. F. D. Elias	1990	1,686
156 2/8	25 5/8	24 5/8	18 6/8	6	5	Mitchell County	IA	Don Weber	1990	1,686
156 2/8	25 6/8	25 3/8	18 4/8	5	5	Wilbarger County	TX	Kenneth W. Baker	1992	1,686
156 2/8	23 6/8	23 6/8	17 6/8	5	7	Johnston County	OK	Barbara L. Bray	1993	1,686
156 2/8	23 0/8	23 4/8	18 4/8	5	5	Allamakee County	IA	Jerry Custer	1994	1,686
156 2/8	25 3/8	24 2/8	16 1/8	5	6	Spencer County	IN	Jim Durlauf	1995	1,686
156 2/8	23 5/8	22 6/8	17 0/8	5	5	Pottawattamie County	IA	Robert Copenhaver	1996	1,686
156 2/8	27 6/8	28 4/8	22 1/8	6	7	Brown County	OH	Ronald J. Ballein	1996	1,686
156 2/8	26 1/8	25 6/8	20 6/8	5	5	De Soto County	MS	Chris Cordell	1997	1,686
156 2/8	23 4/8	23 5/8	20 2/8	6	5	Rice County	MN	Jerome D. Larson	1997	1,686
156 2/8	25 2/8	25 6/8	20 2/8	5	5	Madison County	KY	Gary W. Langford	1997	1,686
156 1/8	25 4/8	25 2/8	19 1/8	5	5	Crawford County	IL	Mickie D. Purcell	1972	1,710
156 1/8	24 3/8	23 7/8	19 7/8	5	5	Ravalli County	MT	Vernon L. Cooper	1977	1,710
156 1/8	25 4/8	25 6/8	19 1/8	5	5	Tompkins County	NY	Alan C. Boda	1981	1,710
156 1/8	22 6/8	23 2/8	17 7/8	5	5	Monroe County	OH	Wendell Newhouse	1982	1,710
156 1/8	24 3/8	25 0/8	19 7/8	7	8	Douglas County	NE	Oran L. Foxworthy	1984	1,710
156 1/8	25 5/8	24 6/8	22 1/8	4	4	Sumner County	KS	Ralph Shaver	1984	1,710
156 1/8	22 1/8	25 7/8	17 1/8	7	5	Cloud County	KS	Richard Bieker	1985	1,710

WHITETAIL DEER (TYPICAL ANTLERS)

Minimum Score 125

SCORE	LENGTH OF MAIN BEAM R	LENGTH OF MAIN BEAM L	INSIDE SPREAD	NUMBER OF POINTS R	NUMBER OF POINTS L	AREA	STATE/ PROVINCE	HUNTER'S NAME	DATE	RANK
156 1/8	24 5/8	24 4/8	18 1/8	5	5	Prowers County	CO	Lynn Leonard	1988	1,710
156 1/8	24 5/8	26 0/8	17 5/8	7	5	Osage County	KS	Daniel Beavers	1989	1,710
156 1/8	25 3/8	26 3/8	21 4/8	6	6	Sarpy County	NE	Gregg E. Lind	1990	1,710
156 1/8	25 4/8	27 0/8	19 4/8	6	6	Jackson County	IA	David Shepherd	1990	1,710
156 1/8	25 6/8	25 0/8	23 3/8	6	6	Hamilton County	OH	Dave Brackett	1990	1,710
156 1/8	27 6/8	28 1/8	20 1/8	7	5	Wayne County	IL	James Isles	1990	1,710
156 1/8	24 7/8	25 0/8	18 1/8	5	5	Jo Daviess County	IL	Brian Smith	1991	1,710
156 1/8	21 5/8	20 7/8	17 1/8	6	6	Morrison County	MN	Craig Haupt	1993	1,710
156 1/8	24 1/8	24 2/8	17 7/8	5	5	Fillmore County	MN	Justin R. Brown	1993	1,710
156 1/8	22 1/8	21 0/8	17 7/8	5	5	Lee County	IL	Dennis Staats	1993	1,710
156 1/8	24 7/8	25 2/8	20 7/8	5	6	Lake County	IL	Wayne K. Johnson	1994	1,710
156 1/8	22 6/8	22 2/8	16 3/8	5	5	Bottineau County	ND	Larry Tooke	1994	1,710
156 1/8	25 1/8	25 3/8	19 0/8	4	6	Sawyer County	WI	James R. Pollak	1995	1,710
156 1/8	23 4/8	24 0/8	15 7/8	5	5	Nemaha County	KS	Monty G. Noland	1995	1,710
156 1/8	23 6/8	24 2/8	21 1/8	5	5	Anoka County	MN	Robert Feigum	1995	1,710
156 1/8	24 5/8	24 3/8	18 7/8	4	4	Scott County	IA	Rodney Stalder	1995	1,710
156 1/8	23 3/8	24 0/8	19 5/8	8	6	Comanche County	KS	Greg Hill	1995	1,710
156 0/8	26 0/8	27 1/8	16 4/8	4	5	Bertie County	NC	Gordon Gardner	1975	1,734
156 0/8	23 4/8	23 7/8	19 6/8	5	5	Stark County	OH	Don Cerosky	1979	1,734
156 0/8	25 1/8	24 4/8	20 3/8	6	8	Brown County	IL	Lowell Leslie, Jr.	1980	1,734
156 0/8	25 5/8	25 6/8	19 6/8	4	4	Louisa County	IA	Roger Gipple	1982	1,734
156 0/8	22 2/8	22 5/8	19 6/8	7	7	Perry County	IL	Terry Queen	1983	1,734
156 0/8	24 0/8	24 2/8	17 6/8	5	7	Owen County	IN	Michael A. Miller	1986	1,734
156 0/8	26 5/8	25 2/8	18 4/8	7	6	Licking County	OH	Robert R. Hutchison	1989	1,734
156 0/8	24 1/8	23 3/8	18 0/8	5	5	Alpena County	MI	Samuel Lee Freese	1989	1,734
156 0/8	23 1/8	22 7/8	18 2/8	5	5	Trempealeau County	WI	Dane Zielke	1989	1,734
156 0/8	22 7/8	24 5/8	16 7/8	6	7	Butler County	KS	Dave Cornish	1989	1,734
156 0/8	25 2/8	25 0/8	20 2/8	5	6	Carver County	MN	Brian Klingelhutz	1990	1,734
156 0/8	24 6/8	24 4/8	18 0/8	8	8	Oklahoma County	OK	Greg Boydston	1990	1,734
156 0/8	24 0/8	25 5/8	18 5/8	5	7	Warren County	IL	Brian P. Monroe	1990	1,734
156 0/8	25 3/8	25 2/8	19 0/8	4	5	Clearwater County	ID	Robert Willkas	1990	1,734
156 0/8	26 1/8	24 6/8	22 0/8	7	6	Jasper County	IL	Dan Songer	1991	1,734
156 0/8	24 7/8	23 7/8	20 4/8	5	5	Macon County	IL	Charlie DeBose, Jr.	1991	1,734
156 0/8	23 3/8	24 4/8	18 2/8	5	5	Will County	IL	Larry G. Koerner	1991	1,734
156 0/8	27 3/8	26 1/8	18 1/8	6	5	Wright County	MN	Dave Herzan	1992	1,734
156 0/8	23 2/8	23 3/8	17 4/8	7	6	Grayson County	TX	Johnny Haddad	1992	1,734
156 0/8	26 7/8	26 7/8	19 0/8	5	5	Allamakee County	IA	Gene A. Hall	1993	1,734
156 0/8	25 3/8	25 7/8	21 0/8	6	5	Hamilton County	IL	Mark Snow	1993	1,734
156 0/8	27 4/8	27 0/8	21 0/8	6	6	Dane County	WI	Andy Maier	1993	1,734
156 0/8	25 3/8	24 0/8	15 6/8	5	6	Edwards County	IL	Walter W. Troyer	1993	1,734
156 0/8	25 6/8	25 6/8	20 4/8	6	4	Montgomery County	IL	Larry D. Whitley	1993	1,734
156 0/8	24 7/8	25 2/8	17 6/8	4	4	Saline County	IL	Rick Carr	1993	1,734
156 0/8	25 2/8	25 5/8	17 0/8	5	5	Woodbury County	IA	Douglas Sweeney	1994	1,734
156 0/8	24 1/8	23 4/8	21 3/8	7	6	Lenawee County	MI	Ronald E. Cross	1995	1,734
156 0/8	22 6/8	23 4/8	18 4/8	5	5	Hillsdale County	MI	Cora J. Fink	1995	1,734
156 0/8	23 4/8	23 6/8	17 6/8	7	5	Beltrami County	MN	Scott La Coursiere	1995	1,734
156 0/8	24 2/8	24 4/8	19 2/8	5	5	Vermilion County	IL	Mark Lourance	1996	1,734
156 0/8	23 6/8	24 7/8	20 0/8	7	7	Buffalo County	WI	Joseph Potter	1996	1,734
156 0/8	22 6/8	23 4/8	18 2/8	5	5	Dane County	WI	Rory Rossman	1996	1,734
156 0/8	27 3/8	26 6/8	21 1/8	4	5	Henderson County	KY	Edward Croft	1997	1,734
156 0/8	25 5/8	26 3/8	19 0/8	4	5	Greene County	PA	R. Adrian Whipkey	1998	1,734
155 7/8	24 7/8	24 4/8	19 7/8	5	5	Frontier County	NE	Charles Druse	1963	1,768
155 7/8	24 3/8	24 5/8	15 5/8	5	5	Harrison County	IA	Clarence N. Jackson, Jr.	1963	1,768
155 7/8	26 0/8	24 5/8	17 3/8	6	8	Neosho County	KS	Jeff Friederich	1983	1,768
155 7/8	25 4/8	25 1/8	16 7/8	5	5	Macon County	IL	Mike Nickell	1985	1,768
155 7/8	24 7/8	24 5/8	20 4/8	6	7	Becker County	MN	Paul Adams	1988	1,768
155 7/8	22 5/8	22 7/8	18 1/8	5	5	Bremer County	IA	John W. Breitbach	1989	1,768
155 7/8	26 7/8	26 5/8	23 1/8	5	5	Charles County	MD	Scott Bressler	1990	1,768
155 7/8	26 6/8	25 6/8	16 2/8	7	6	Anderson County	KS	Kurt A. Sayers	1990	1,768
155 7/8	22 1/8	23 5/8	21 5/8	6	5	Hardin County	IA	Tom Catlin	1990	1,768
155 7/8	22 1/8	20 6/8	21 5/8	5	5	Jackson County	WI	Calvin J. Haag	1991	1,768
155 7/8	26 0/8	25 3/8	18 7/8	5	5	Carroll County	IA	Cory Hulsing	1991	1,768
155 7/8	23 3/8	22 7/8	20 3/8	5	5	Tippecanoe County	IN	Steve Rider	1992	1,768
155 7/8	25 4/8	25 0/8	19 0/8	6	7	Trempealeau County	WI	Duane Dubiel	1992	1,768
155 7/8	25 1/8	24 1/8	18 1/8	5	5	Kankakee County	IL	Charles Gaidamavice	1992	1,768
155 7/8	24 7/8	24 6/8	22 5/8	5	5	Coahoma County	MS	Charles B. Neely	1994	1,768
155 7/8	25 7/8	27 0/8	20 7/8	5	6	Warren County	IA	Scott Messamaker	1994	1,768
155 7/8	24 5/8	24 2/8	17 5/8	6	6	Cass County	IL	Ron McCarthy	1994	1,768
155 7/8	22 7/8	23 6/8	22 3/8	5	5	Fulton County	IL	Bret L. Epkins	1995	1,768
155 7/8	24 2/8	23 6/8	19 7/8	6	5	Seward County	KS	Lynn Leonard	1995	1,768
155 7/8	25 7/8	25 4/8	21 5/8	5	5	Hopkins County	KY	Ben Hudson	1996	1,768
155 7/8	25 2/8	26 0/8	18 1/8	4	5	Treasure County	MT	Rob Seelye	1996	1,768
155 7/8	25 0/8	24 7/8	19 3/8	5	5	Jefferson County	MS	John A. Windham	1997	1,768
155 7/8	24 4/8	23 1/8	15 5/8	6	5	Muskingum County	OH	Dan Jennings	1997	1,768
155 6/8	25 1/8	24 4/8	18 4/8	4	5	Madison County	NE	Dick Gambill	1967	1,791
155 6/8	23 0/8	23 6/8	19 2/8	5	6	Monroe County	IA	John Vollmer	1982	1,791
155 6/8	24 0/8	23 6/8	16 7/8	5	6	Area 28	MAN	Gary Kaluzniak	1983	1,791
155 6/8	21 6/8	20 5/8	16 4/8	6	6	McHenry County	IL	Michael D. Patrick	1984	1,791

WHITETAIL DEER (TYPICAL ANTLERS)

Minimum Score 125 — Continued

SCORE	LENGTH OF MAIN BEAM R	LENGTH OF MAIN BEAM L	INSIDE SPREAD	NUMBER OF POINTS R	NUMBER OF POINTS L	AREA	STATE/PROVINCE	HUNTER'S NAME	DATE	RANK
155 6/8	25 2/8	24 1/8	20 2/8	5	5	Lawrence County	MO	David T. Kail	1984	1,791
155 6/8	23 7/8	23 5/8	18 2/8	5	5	Morrison County	MN	Thomas Barron, Jr.	1987	1,791
155 6/8	24 5/8	24 6/8	16 2/8	5	6	Des Moines County	IA	Pat Stallman	1988	1,791
155 6/8	26 0/8	26 2/8	16 6/8	5	5	Allamakee County	IA	Dan Brimeyer	1988	1,791
155 6/8	23 4/8	23 1/8	18 4/8	5	5	Marion County	IA	Thomas L. Tucker	1988	1,791
155 6/8	22 2/8	22 2/8	16 0/8	5	6	Troup County	GA	James E. Hogan	1989	1,791
155 6/8	24 0/8	24 0/8	14 4/8	5	5	Shelby County	IL	Brian Herzog	1991	1,791
155 6/8	22 7/8	24 0/8	17 1/8	6	5	Allamakee County	IA	Ernie Burroughs	1992	1,791
155 6/8	24 6/8	25 5/8	17 5/8	6	5	Laclede County	MO	Roy McCann	1992	1,791
155 6/8	24 6/8	24 1/8	18 6/8	5	5	Washington County	WI	Terry Farnham	1993	1,791
155 6/8	24 1/8	23 5/8	20 4/8	5	6	Gogebic County	MI	R. J. Spang	1993	1,791
155 6/8	26 1/8	26 6/8	20 6/8	5	5	Jefferson County	WI	Eddie Spiegelhoff	1994	1,791
155 6/8	27 1/8	26 5/8	19 2/8	6	5	Calvert County	MD	Bruce Williams	1995	1,791
155 6/8	26 2/8	26 0/8	21 4/8	4	4	Edgar County	IL	Joe Schmitt	1995	1,791
155 6/8	22 7/8	23 0/8	20 0/8	5	6	Rockingham County	NC	Martin E. Mabe	1996	1,791
155 6/8	23 2/8	24 5/8	18 5/8	7	7	Richland County	IL	Tony Prosser	1996	1,791
155 6/8	26 6/8	25 7/8	20 0/8	4	4	White County	IL	Bob Curtis	1996	1,791
155 6/8	26 6/8	26 6/8	20 6/8	4	4	Edgar County	IL	Greg Stuck	1997	1,791
155 5/8	25 5/8	26 0/8	19 1/8	5	6	Rice County	KS	Gordon Leo Rayl	1967	1,813
155 5/8	22 5/8	23 0/8	18 5/8	5	5	Anne Arundel County	MD	Gene Hyatt	1976	1,813
155 5/8	23 7/8	22 5/8	19 1/8	7	5	Harrison County	IA	Alfred S. Foster	1978	1,813
155 5/8	25 2/8	23 7/8	17 1/8	5	5	Trempealeau County	WI	Greg Halpern	1982	1,813
155 5/8	25 7/8	25 3/8	20 5/8	4	4	Clayton County	IA	Gerald W. Kluesner	1986	1,813
155 5/8	24 5/8	23 3/8	18 7/8	5	5	Chase County	KS	Jerry Keller	1986	1,813
155 5/8	25 6/8	27 3/8	20 4/8	9	7	Perry County	IL	Jerry M. Smith	1987	1,813
155 5/8	26 6/8	28 0/8	18 5/8	5	5	Logan County	OH	Dan Jergens	1987	1,813
155 5/8	23 6/8	25 0/8	17 5/8	5	5	Pierce County	WI	Greg Koehler	1988	1,813
155 5/8	23 3/8	23 0/8	18 5/8	6	6	Kane County	IL	James A. Anderson	1989	1,813
155 5/8	23 6/8	23 7/8	15 2/8	6	5	Brown County	IN	Frank Cross	1989	1,813
155 5/8	25 1/8	24 1/8	18 3/8	4	4	Fairfield County	CT	Stephen M. Ruttkamp	1989	1,813
155 5/8	24 3/8	24 5/8	19 3/8	5	5	Morrison County	MN	James Anderson	1990	1,813
155 5/8	23 3/8	22 7/8	18 1/8	5	5	Kingman County	KS	Ed Laverentz	1991	1,813
155 5/8	25 1/8	24 7/8	15 7/8	5	5	Cook County	MN	Richard D. Nelson	1991	1,813
155 5/8	25 6/8	25 7/8	18 5/8	6	7	Union County	KY	Charles E. Hobbs	1992	1,813
155 5/8	22 3/8	21 6/8	16 3/8	5	5	Willowbrook	SAS	John W. Makowetski	1993	1,813
155 5/8	24 2/8	23 3/8	16 1/8	6	6	Jackson County	WI	Glen R. Loppnow	1993	1,813
155 5/8	24 5/8	23 2/8	18 1/8	6	5	Grundy County	MO	Gary Vernon	1993	1,813
155 5/8	22 7/8	23 2/8	17 3/8	5	5	Winnebago County	WI	John H. Hay	1994	1,813
155 5/8	26 1/8	26 2/8	17 3/8	5	6	Cass County	MI	FrEd Kruger	1995	1,813
155 5/8	24 6/8	23 6/8	17 3/8	5	5	Mercer County	NJ	Richard E. Cincilla	1996	1,813
155 5/8	24 3/8	25 2/8	18 2/8	8	7	Waukesha County	WI	Sid Hennekens	1997	1,813
155 4/8	23 2/8	25 4/8	18 6/8	7	7	Westchester County	NY	Bernard J. Crescione	1960	1,836
155 4/8	25 5/8	25 5/8	16 4/8	5	5	Marion County	IA	Thomas L. Tucker	1967	1,836
155 4/8	26 2/8	25 4/8	22 3/8	5	6	Dubuque County	IA	Kurt Cable	1973	1,836
155 4/8	23 6/8	25 2/8	19 5/8	7	7	Flathead County	MT	Ralph Ertz	1977	1,836
155 4/8	22 3/8	22 3/8	18 1/8	5	6	Lucas County	IA	Lance Brauer	1980	1,836
155 4/8	23 2/8	23 6/8	16 6/8	5	5	Lyon County	KS	Ronald E. Rhodes	1981	1,836
155 4/8	27 0/8	26 2/8	20 0/8	4	4	Houston County	MN	Gary L. Maier	1985	1,836
155 4/8	23 4/8	24 0/8	20 0/8	5	5	Posey County	IN	Duane Daws	1985	1,836
155 4/8	24 1/8	24 0/8	19 4/8	5	5	Marinette County	WI	John Floriano	1985	1,836
155 4/8	25 1/8	24 6/8	18 0/8	5	6	Washburn County	WI	Wayne Dahlstrom	1986	1,836
155 4/8	25 7/8	26 3/8	22 0/8	7	6	Winnebago County	IL	Vaughn Zimmerman	1986	1,836
155 4/8	23 7/8	25 6/8	16 4/8	5	5	Forest County	WI	Robert R. Rost	1987	1,836
155 4/8	25 1/8	24 4/8	16 4/8	6	5	Jackson County	MO	Charles C. Shotton	1987	1,836
155 4/8	23 3/8	24 1/8	16 2/8	5	6	Hennepin County	MN	Delmer Bentz	1988	1,836
155 4/8	25 1/8	24 2/8	19 7/8	8	7	Meeker County	MN	Pete Roeser	1990	1,836
155 4/8	24 7/8	25 6/8	22 4/8	4	4	Morgan County	IL	Gerald L. Stone	1990	1,836
155 4/8	27 4/8	24 4/8	22 2/8	6	6	Rush County	IN	Daniel D. Drysdale	1991	1,836
155 4/8	24 3/8	24 1/8	18 3/8	7	8	Jefferson County	OH	Michael W. Brown	1991	1,836
155 4/8	26 3/8	26 2/8	22 0/8	4	4	Montgomery County	OH	Kim Hammontree	1991	1,836
155 4/8	23 5/8	24 6/8	16 6/8	6	6	Waupaca County	WI	James H. Dimpfl	1992	1,836
155 4/8	23 2/8	24 2/8	17 6/8	7	6	Bon Homme County	SD	Mike Peterson	1993	1,836
155 4/8	24 2/8	25 6/8	16 1/8	6	6	Pike County	IL	Paul Barry Salmon	1995	1,836
155 4/8	25 0/8	25 6/8	20 4/8	6	6	Van Buren County	IA	Jim Chambers	1996	1,836
155 4/8	23 3/8	23 6/8	18 6/8	6	5	Spokane County	WA	Skip March	1996	1,836
155 4/8	25 1/8	24 4/8	16 4/8	5	5	Blackford County	IN	Dennis K. Decker	1997	1,836
155 4/8	25 1/8	25 3/8	17 4/8	4	7	Union County	IL	Ronald Ury	1997	1,836
155 3/8	23 5/8	24 0/8	18 4/8	6	7	Finney County	KS	Wray Decker	1966	1,862
155 3/8	26 0/8	26 3/8	21 1/8	5	6	Chickasaw County	IA	William A. Harris	1978	1,862
155 3/8	23 3/8	24 2/8	16 0/8	6	5	Union County	OH	Jerry Faine	1982	1,862
155 3/8	26 2/8	25 5/8	19 6/8	5	4	Dodge County	MN	Jimmie Donald Hanna	1983	1,862
155 3/8	29 2/8	28 2/8	19 7/8	6	8	McDonough County	IL	Locie L. Murphy	1983	1,862
155 3/8	24 6/8	24 3/8	20 3/8	5	6	Codington County	SD	Mark Beutow	1983	1,862
155 3/8	24 4/8	24 5/8	21 3/8	5	5	Suffolk County	NY	John C. Wehrs	1984	1,862
155 3/8	21 4/8	22 0/8	15 5/8	5	6	McKenzie County	ND	Brent Smith	1985	1,862
155 3/8	23 7/8	23 6/8	16 5/8	5	5	Cherry County	NE	Gary Galloway	1985	1,862
155 3/8	25 4/8	25 6/8	20 3/8	7	5	Pulaski County	MO	Bruce Agee	1986	1,862
155 3/8	25 2/8	26 2/8	23 1/8	5	5	Sabine County	TX	Bobby Brundidge	1986	1,862

WHITETAIL DEER (TYPICAL ANTLERS)

Minimum Score 125 — Continued

SCORE	LENGTH OF MAIN BEAM R	LENGTH OF MAIN BEAM L	INSIDE SPREAD	NUMBER OF POINTS R	NUMBER OF POINTS L	AREA	STATE/ PROVINCE	HUNTER'S NAME	DATE	RANK
155 3/8	29 6/8	28 7/8	20 7/8	5	6	Highland County	OH	William E. Lee, Jr.	1987	1,862
155 3/8	24 6/8	24 5/8	18 1/8	5	5	Vermilion County	IL	Gary L. Wilford	1988	1,862
155 3/8	26 3/8	25 4/8	20 0/8	4	5	Butler County	KS	Mike Demel	1990	1,862
155 3/8	22 6/8	23 0/8	15 0/8	5	8	Menard County	IL	Norman Horn	1991	1,862
155 3/8	24 0/8	24 1/8	16 5/8	5	5	Fillmore County	MN	Danny L. Cole	1991	1,862
155 3/8	25 0/8	24 6/8	19 3/8	5	5	Dakota County	MN	Gene Lorentz	1992	1,862
155 3/8	23 5/8	23 4/8	16 7/8	5	7	Breckinridge County	KY	John Goins	1993	1,862
155 3/8	28 2/8	26 6/8	19 3/8	4	5	Stark County	OH	Bill Hall	1993	1,862
155 3/8	24 4/8	24 0/8	17 1/8	7	6	Bates County	MO	Mike Wheeler	1996	1,862
155 3/8	25 7/8	25 0/8	18 0/8	6	5	Ashland County	WI	Curt Walker	1996	1,862
155 3/8	25 3/8	26 2/8	18 6/8	6	5	Tuscarawas County	OH	Ronnie L. Duplain, Sr.	1996	1,862
155 3/8	26 2/8	26 1/8	17 5/8	4	4	Washington County	MN	Tony Joseph	1996	1,862
155 3/8	25 4/8	24 0/8	18 4/8	6	5	Coshocton County	OH	Mario Costanzo	1997	1,862
155 3/8	25 2/8	25 6/8	21 0/8	5	5	Mercer County	IL	Dan Bergen	1997	1,862
155 3/8	25 4/8	24 5/8	16 7/8	5	5	Howell County	MO	Carl Hicks	1997	1,862
155 3/8	24 5/8	25 3/8	16 1/8	5	5	Nodaway County	MO	Tony Flora	1997	1,862
155 3/8	27 5/8	26 4/8	18 7/8	4	5	Jersey County	IL	Jeff Dugger	1998	1,862
155 2/8	22 0/8	21 6/8	17 4/8	6	5	Benton County	IA	Gene Pollock	1958	1,890
155 2/8	25 0/8	25 5/8	18 3/8	5	6	Floyd County	IA	Richard G. Long	1967	1,890
155 2/8	26 4/8	25 4/8	15 2/8	6	6	Scott County	VA	Hugh McConnell	1978	1,890
155 2/8	21 6/8	21 7/8	20 0/8	5	5	Des Moines County	IA	Brad Entsminger	1980	1,890
155 2/8	24 5/8	24 2/8	15 4/8	5	6	Knox County	OH	Robert Hammond	1980	1,890
155 2/8	23 7/8	24 3/8	17 1/8	5	6	Richland County	MT	Wynn Privratsky	1980	1,890
155 2/8	25 3/8	25 4/8	18 4/8	5	5	Licking County	OH	Richard E Pipes	1984	1,890
155 2/8	24 4/8	24 1/8	18 0/8	6	6	Lake County	MI	John Mudrovich	1984	1,890
155 2/8	26 6/8	27 4/8	17 0/8	4	6	Allamakee County	IA	Ernie Burroughs	1985	1,890
155 2/8	27 0/8	25 4/8	21 6/8	4	5	Ogle County	IL	Vernon Rasmussen	1986	1,890
155 2/8	26 4/8	26 7/8	17 2/8	5	5	Holmes County	OH	Wanda L. Horwath	1988	1,890
155 2/8	27 0/8	26 0/8	18 6/8	5	5	Buffalo County	WI	Gary R. Stutz	1988	1,890
155 2/8	28 2/8	27 5/8	20 4/8	5	4	Parke County	IN	Charles Paxton	1989	1,890
155 2/8	23 7/8	25 2/8	18 0/8	6	5	Jefferson County	KS	Leon Lemons	1989	1,890
155 2/8	24 5/8	24 4/8	15 4/8	5	5	Burnett County	WI	William F. Hurley	1990	1,890
155 2/8	24 7/8	24 6/8	20 2/8	5	6	Appanoose County	IA	Steven P. Salmieri	1990	1,890
155 2/8	25 6/8	26 4/8	19 2/8	5	5	Monroe County	KY	Joyneta Wilkerson	1993	1,890
155 2/8	23 7/8	23 4/8	16 6/8	5	5	Lawrence County	IL	Vergil Jerrell	1993	1,890
155 2/8	26 7/8	26 5/8	17 0/8	6	6	Coles County	IL	Bill Davis	1994	1,890
155 2/8	27 5/8	26 5/8	17 2/8	5	6	Beaver County	PA	Eric Kasunic	1994	1,890
155 2/8	25 2/8	25 2/8	17 6/8	5	5	Waukesha County	WI	Donald Wehr	1994	1,890
155 2/8	23 5/8	26 0/8	21 0/8	6	5	Franklin County	KY	Larry B. Goode	1995	1,890
155 2/8	29 0/8	28 0/8	18 6/8	5	6	Warren County	IA	Mike Metz	1995	1,890
155 2/8	23 5/8	23 6/8	15 6/8	6	6	Fayette County	IN	Chris L. Mustin	1995	1,890
155 2/8	25 4/8	25 3/8	16 0/8	5	5	Northampton County	VA	D. Richard Felker II	1995	1,890
155 2/8	23 6/8	24 4/8	19 4/8	5	4	McPherson County	KS	Kendall Shaw	1995	1,890
155 2/8	26 4/8	25 4/8	18 6/8	5	5	Scott County	IA	Don Brunning	1996	1,890
155 2/8	24 3/8	24 5/8	16 7/8	6	9	Osage County	KS	Mike Vandevord	1997	1,890
155 2/8	24 6/8	24 7/8	17 4/8	5	5	Douglas County	WI	Kenneth W. Moen	1998	1,890
155 1/8	24 7/8	24 7/8	17 3/8	5	5	Roberts County	SD	Roland L. Hausmann	1959	1,919
155 1/8	25 2/8	24 7/8	19 3/8	6	6	Madison County	KY	Sonny Barker	1965	1,919
155 1/8	25 6/8	25 0/8	19 7/8	5	5	Morrison County	MN	Timothy L. Kampa	1984	1,919
155 1/8	24 7/8	25 7/8	19 7/8	5	5	Calhoun County	MI	Steve D. Munier	1985	1,919
155 1/8	29 0/8	26 6/8	22 0/8	5	4	Vermilion County	IL	Allen Walker	1986	1,919
155 1/8	25 7/8	25 4/8	17 3/8	5	5	Pawnee County	KS	Carol Moffatt	1986	1,919
155 1/8	24 4/8	24 7/8	16 7/8	5	5	Barron County	WI	Tom Lindquist	1987	1,919
155 1/8	25 4/8	26 7/8	19 7/8	6	5	Allegan County	MI	Craig S. Blank	1989	1,919
155 1/8	24 1/8	23 2/8	14 6/8	8	6	Chisago County	MN	James Lehman	1990	1,919
155 1/8	24 2/8	23 7/8	22 7/8	5	5	Clermont County	OH	Paul L. Voshell	1992	1,919
155 1/8	25 0/8	25 3/8	21 2/8	7	5	Will County	IL	Mike D. Francus	1992	1,919
155 1/8	23 5/8	23 2/8	15 3/8	5	5	Allamakee County	IA	Brian Keuning	1992	1,919
155 1/8	25 0/8	24 5/8	19 3/8	4	4	Sherburne County	MN	Cary Larson	1994	1,919
155 1/8	28 4/8	27 0/8	19 3/8	5	6	Linn County	IA	Dan Andrews	1994	1,919
155 1/8	26 1/8	27 3/8	18 3/8	7	5	Columbia County	WI	Douglas A. Jarzynski	1995	1,919
155 1/8	24 0/8	23 2/8	17 1/8	6	5	Coles County	IL	Cliff Campbell	1995	1,919
155 1/8	25 5/8	26 6/8	20 4/8	6	5	Charles Mix County	SD	Justin Plooster	1995	1,919
155 1/8	26 6/8	25 7/8	19 3/8	5	5	Butler County	KS	Jeffrey Howington	1995	1,919
155 1/8	24 0/8	24 2/8	18 7/8	5	6	Pipestone County	MN	Jim Lorenzen	1995	1,919
155 1/8	24 6/8	24 7/8	21 4/8	6	5	Plymouth County	IA	Guy H. Hempey	1997	1,919
155 1/8	23 7/8	23 6/8	20 4/8	6	6	Dane County	WI	Mike Padrutt	1997	1,919
155 1/8	21 7/8	21 7/8	19 6/8	6	5	Outagamie County	WI	Neil P. Merkes	1998	1,919
155 0/8	23 7/8	24 5/8	18 6/8	7	7	Pope County	MN	John Myhre	1982	1,941
155 0/8	24 6/8	24 1/8	22 7/8	6	7	Montgomery County	IL	Keith Pierce	1983	1,941
155 0/8	20 5/8	24 0/8	15 7/8	9	7	Lee County	IA	Ralph D. Zaehringer	1985	1,941
155 0/8	23 5/8	22 2/8	18 5/8	8	7	Clayton County	IA	Daniel L. Parker	1986	1,941
155 0/8	25 2/8	26 6/8	17 1/8	6	5	Barber County	KS	Robert Ricke	1987	1,941
155 0/8	24 7/8	24 6/8	16 4/8	6	5	Wayne County	MO	Steve Rueck	1988	1,941
155 0/8	25 3/8	25 1/8	18 6/8	7	8	Sawyer County	WI	Greg Peterson	1989	1,941
155 0/8	24 0/8	24 5/8	17 7/8	7	5	Jefferson County	WI	Scott Bolson	1989	1,941
155 0/8	27 1/8	26 2/8	21 2/8	5	7	St. Clair County	IL	Andy T. Contratto	1989	1,941
155 0/8	22 2/8	24 3/8	17 4/8	4	4	Wapello County	IA	Larry Johns	1990	1,941

WHITETAIL DEER (TYPICAL ANTLERS)

Minimum Score 125 Continued

SCORE	LENGTH OF MAIN BEAM R	LENGTH OF MAIN BEAM L	INSIDE SPREAD	NUMBER OF POINTS R	NUMBER OF POINTS L	AREA	STATE/PROVINCE	HUNTER'S NAME	DATE	RANK
155 0/8	23 6/8	23 1/8	18 4/8	6	6	Coffey County	KS	David W. Bess	1990	1,941
155 0/8	25 0/8	25 4/8	16 6/8	5	4	Marion County	KS	Ron Hershberger	1990	1,941
155 0/8	25 1/8	25 0/8	18 6/8	6	5	Polk County	MN	Steven Cornell	1990	1,941
155 0/8	25 7/8	25 4/8	18 0/8	5	5	Pope County	MN	Bradley D. Rosten	1991	1,941
155 0/8	27 4/8	27 3/8	23 6/8	5	6	Bent County	CO	Jay Waring	1991	1,941
155 0/8	26 4/8	25 1/8	19 4/8	7	4	Caroline County	MD	Jeff Towers	1991	1,941
155 0/8	22 2/8	21 6/8	23 1/8	5	6	Codington County	SD	Marty Lukonen	1993	1,941
155 0/8	24 0/8	24 1/8	18 4/8	5	6	Ogle County	IL	Douglas McNames	1994	1,941
155 0/8	23 2/8	22 4/8	19 4/8	5	5	Union County	KY	Tony Noe	1994	1,941
155 0/8	26 0/8	24 2/8	19 0/8	5	5	Jefferson County	KY	John Gutterman	1995	1,941
155 0/8	25 6/8	26 7/8	20 4/8	5	5	Washington County	WI	Jeffrey R. Gall	1996	1,941
155 0/8	22 6/8	22 4/8	17 6/8	7	6	Scott County	IA	John S. Carlin	1996	1,941
155 0/8	25 0/8	24 3/8	20 0/8	6	5	Montgomery County	IL	Marty Leitschuh	1996	1,941
155 0/8	25 1/8	24 0/8	15 2/8	4	4	Garfield County	NE	Jeff Breitkreutz	1997	1,941
155 0/8	24 1/8	24 5/8	17 5/8	7	7	Decatur County	IA	Richard Panke	1997	1,941
155 0/8	24 3/8	24 2/8	17 2/8	5	6	Washington County	IA	John Sabel	1997	1,941
155 0/8	26 1/8	26 3/8	21 5/8	6	8	Logan County	WV	Harold Sayers	1997	1,941
154 7/8	26 7/8	25 7/8	18 2/8	5	5	Murray County	MN	Craig Cohrs	1968	1,968
154 7/8	26 5/8	25 6/8	17 6/8	7	8	Pendleton County	KY	Thomas P. Jones	1969	1,968
154 7/8	22 5/8	23 2/8	23 1/8	6	6	Auglaize County	OH	Gary L. Dues	1979	1,968
154 7/8	23 4/8	23 5/8	16 4/8	5	4	Kingsbury County	SD	Dan R. Limmer	1981	1,968
154 7/8	23 0/8	24 0/8	19 5/8	5	6	Hennepin County	MN	Harold Greseth	1983	1,968
154 7/8	23 4/8	23 7/8	16 4/8	10	6	Lincoln County	MN	Paul Erickson	1983	1,968
154 7/8	24 2/8	23 6/8	19 1/8	4	5	Blue Earth County	MN	Rory Deutchman	1984	1,968
154 7/8	24 1/8	24 5/8	19 5/8	6	5	Dane County	WI	Casey A. Blum	1986	1,968
154 7/8	25 3/8	24 5/8	23 5/8	5	5	Nelson County	KY	Tom Blincoe	1987	1,968
154 7/8	26 7/8	26 2/8	15 4/8	4	7	Mason County	IL	Mark Meyer	1988	1,968
154 7/8	24 4/8	25 7/8	18 4/8	7	6	Washtenaw County	MI	William G. Knight	1988	1,968
154 7/8	24 7/8	26 4/8	21 7/8	7	5	Morris County	NJ	Craig Werder	1989	1,968
154 7/8	23 3/8	24 4/8	16 1/8	6	5	Traill County	ND	Paul Teegarden	1990	1,968
154 7/8	24 4/8	24 2/8	17 1/8	7	7	Brown County	WI	Michael J. Rasmussen	1990	1,968
154 7/8	24 4/8	24 6/8	21 5/8	5	4	Champaign County	IL	Robert A. Bryant	1990	1,968
154 7/8	25 5/8	25 0/8	19 7/8	5	5	Massac County	IL	Terry B. Lewis	1990	1,968
154 7/8	23 5/8	24 2/8	17 6/8	6	5	Dakota County	MN	Thomas Leach, Jr.	1991	1,968
154 7/8	23 0/8	23 3/8	20 5/8	6	6	Bureau County	IL	Gregory A. Bowers	1991	1,968
154 7/8	25 3/8	24 1/8	15 6/8	5	6	McLean County	IL	Daniel Rogers	1991	1,968
154 7/8	25 2/8	25 4/8	18 5/8	7	6	Edmunds County	SD	Russell D. Leair	1992	1,968
154 7/8	24 0/8	24 2/8	18 5/8	5	5	Cass County	MI	Scott E. Grice	1993	1,968
154 7/8	25 2/8	25 3/8	18 7/8	5	5	Hancock County	IL	Tim Hiland	1994	1,968
154 7/8	24 0/8	23 5/8	18 1/8	5	5	Webster County	IA	Dennis Vulgamott	1994	1,968
154 7/8	26 0/8	24 6/8	20 7/8	4	5	Lake County	IL	Alvin Roberts	1994	1,968
154 7/8	25 2/8	26 1/8	20 5/8	5	4	Johnson County	IA	Darrel Ballantyne	1995	1,968
154 7/8	26 0/8	26 0/8	18 3/8	5	5	Page County	IA	Bob Athen	1996	1,968
154 7/8	28 4/8	26 4/8	18 7/8	6	5	Madison County	MS	Rusty Crawford	1997	1,968
154 6/8	24 1/8	22 5/8	17 2/8	5	5	Minnehaha County	SD	Clifford Sudenga	1962	1,995
154 6/8	25 1/8	25 1/8	21 0/8	5	4	Cottonwood County	MN	Rodney Bailey	1975	1,995
154 6/8	24 7/8	25 6/8	20 0/8	5	5	Gray County	KS	Allen D. Bailey	1980	1,995
154 6/8	24 0/8	23 0/8	18 4/8	5	5	Van Buren County	MI	Rick Reese	1980	1,995
154 6/8	25 1/8	21 7/8	18 4/8	6	4	Mills County	IA	Doug Roll	1985	1,995
154 6/8	24 6/8	24 6/8	19 4/8	6	6	Seward County	KS	Lynn Leonard	1987	1,995
154 6/8	23 1/8	23 4/8	16 2/8	5	5	Wright County	MN	Rob Johnson	1987	1,995
154 6/8	24 5/8	24 4/8	18 3/8	6	5	Lincoln County	NE	Timothy M. Budin	1990	1,995
154 6/8	25 6/8	26 5/8	16 2/8	9	7	Pike County	IL	Stan Chamberlain	1990	1,995
154 6/8	24 2/8	24 7/8	18 2/8	8	6	Taylor County	WI	Barry Kappel	1991	1,995
154 6/8	24 0/8	24 4/8	17 3/8	7	5	Des Moines County	IA	Daniel W. Wegener	1991	1,995
154 6/8	25 0/8	25 5/8	20 4/8	5	5	Lewis County	KY	Alfred Lee Simms	1992	1,995
154 6/8	26 2/8	25 6/8	19 4/8	5	5	Anoka County	MN	Randy Gajeski	1993	1,995
154 6/8	24 4/8	23 6/8	23 0/8	5	5	Macoupin County	IL	Michael Dalton	1994	1,995
154 6/8	24 2/8	26 2/8	18 2/8	5	5	Marinette County	WI	Mitch Vincent	1994	1,995
154 6/8	24 6/8	24 3/8	18 0/8	6	5	Carroll County	IL	Harry R. Charneski	1994	1,995
154 6/8	24 3/8	25 0/8	20 6/8	5	5	Jackson County	IA	David W. Schrody	1994	1,995
154 6/8	25 7/8	26 2/8	20 7/8	4	5	Somerset County	NJ	Vincent Mancini	1995	1,995
154 6/8	26 3/8	25 7/8	18 7/8	5	6	Ross County	OH	Brian Sowers	1995	1,995
154 6/8	26 0/8	25 7/8	20 4/8	4	4	Marshall County	IL	Jeff Neuhalfen	1996	1,995
154 6/8	26 6/8	26 3/8	18 4/8	5	5	Cedar County	NE	David B. Cull	1997	1,995
154 6/8	24 7/8	24 7/8	21 5/8	6	5	Waukesha County	WI	Mike Scaff	1997	1,995
154 6/8	22 6/8	23 4/8	18 2/8	5	5	Dakota County	MN	Brian T. Lemay	1998	1,995
154 5/8	25 4/8	26 2/8	18 6/8	5	6	Jackson County	MN	Eugene C. La Maack	1955	2,018
154 5/8	23 7/8	24 0/8	20 7/8	4	4	Buchanan County	IA	Frank Sanderson	1983	2,018
154 5/8	25 4/8	24 5/8	21 3/8	4	4	Anne Arundel County	MD	Jim Roy	1984	2,018
154 5/8	24 3/8	25 4/8	17 2/8	7	8	Miami County	KS	Gary Wurdack	1985	2,018
154 5/8	26 1/8	25 4/8	21 3/8	4	4	Dunnville	ONT	Randy Robins	1985	2,018
154 5/8	26 2/8	26 3/8	18 3/8	5	5	Kingman County	KS	Dan J. Jacobs	1985	2,018
154 5/8	25 3/8	26 0/8	19 2/8	5	5	Scott County	IA	Howard A. Goettsch	1987	2,018
154 5/8	25 6/8	25 6/8	19 3/8	5	5	Pierce County	WI	Greg Koehler	1987	2,018
154 5/8	22 0/8	25 0/8	19 1/8	5	5	Henderson County	IL	Timothy H. Allaman	1989	2,018
154 5/8	25 3/8	23 0/8	22 6/8	8	6	McLean County	IL	Marvin Rexroat	1990	2,018
154 5/8	26 3/8	25 5/8	19 3/8	7	6	Gallia County	OH	Darres Craig	1990	2,018

WHITETAIL DEER (TYPICAL ANTLERS)

Minimum Score 125 — Continued

SCORE	LENGTH OF MAIN BEAM R	LENGTH OF MAIN BEAM L	INSIDE SPREAD	NUMBER OF POINTS R	NUMBER OF POINTS L	AREA	STATE/ PROVINCE	HUNTER'S NAME	DATE	RANK
154 5/8	23 6/8	24 5/8	16 2/8	7	5	Lincoln County	MO	Scott Hager	1991	2,018
154 5/8	24 4/8	24 7/8	17 5/8	5	5	Will County	IL	Rick Johns	1991	2,018
154 5/8	22 4/8	22 2/8	19 0/8	7	9	La Salle County	TX	Francis D. Elias	1992	2,018
154 5/8	24 0/8	22 1/8	20 5/8	6	7	Wyandotte County	KS	Earl A. Cooksey	1992	2,018
154 5/8	27 7/8	27 4/8	21 7/8	5	5	Charles County	MD	Frank J. Furr	1993	2,018
154 5/8	24 4/8	23 0/8	16 6/8	6	6	Stewart County	TN	Barry A. Elkins	1994	2,018
154 5/8	23 6/8	23 5/8	18 5/8	5	5	Nodaway County	MO	Max Harden	1996	2,018
154 5/8	22 4/8	22 0/8	19 0/8	6	6	Union County	KY	Jason Wooldridge	1997	2,018
154 4/8	24 0/8	24 3/8	23 2/8	5	5	Allamakee County	IA	Dayton Jones	1968	2,037
154 4/8	23 6/8	24 5/8	18 6/8	5	5	Davis County	IA	Ronald L. Simmons	1970	2,037
154 4/8	22 6/8	22 6/8	16 6/8	6	5	Fillmore County	MN	James J. Johnston	1974	2,037
154 4/8	24 4/8	24 0/8	19 3/8	7	8	Waupaca County	WI	Gary L. Hintz	1978	2,037
154 4/8	25 3/8	24 1/8	18 0/8	5	5	Will County	IL	Fred Lukanc	1978	2,037
154 4/8	24 4/8	23 6/8	20 0/8	5	5	Phillips County	KS	Dennis Fredrickson	1983	2,037
154 4/8	24 3/8	25 4/8	20 6/8	5	7	Monona County	IA	Bob Reitan	1986	2,037
154 4/8	25 1/8	25 6/8	23 0/8	4	4	Washington County	MN	Kenneth Brandl	1987	2,037
154 4/8	23 4/8	23 5/8	18 4/8	6	7	Kent County	MD	Donald P. Travis	1987	2,037
154 4/8	25 0/8	25 7/8	21 0/8	6	6	Fairfax County	VA	Michael E. Bury	1989	2,037
154 4/8	26 1/8	25 0/8	22 6/8	6	6	Litchfield County	CT	Eugene J. Wrabel, Jr.	1990	2,037
154 4/8	26 4/8	25 4/8	16 7/8	5	4	Adams County	OH	David W. Gilbert	1990	2,037
154 4/8	22 7/8	22 5/8	20 4/8	5	5	Letellier	MAN	Todd Amenrud	1991	2,037
154 4/8	24 6/8	25 5/8	18 0/8	4	5	Jefferson County	WI	Mark Stinebrink	1991	2,037
154 4/8	22 6/8	22 4/8	17 3/8	6	5	Geary County	KS	Dallas A. Pane	1992	2,037
154 4/8	23 4/8	23 1/8	18 2/8	5	6	Iron County	WI	Bruce Dianich	1992	2,037
154 4/8	24 4/8	24 1/8	19 4/8	6	5	Hennepin County	MN	Robert J. Evans, Jr.	1994	2,037
154 4/8	24 2/8	24 4/8	17 2/8	6	6	Lake County	IL	Joseph G. Wicinski	1995	2,037
154 4/8	23 1/8	21 4/8	17 6/8	5	5	Livingston County	IL	Donnie Griswold	1996	2,037
154 4/8	23 3/8	23 4/8	19 2/8	7	5	Mercer County	NJ	Marty H. Beekman, Jr.	1996	2,037
154 3/8	23 4/8	24 3/8	18 5/8	7	7	Wythe County	VA	C. D. Tarter	1961	2,057
154 3/8	27 2/8	26 0/8	21 5/8	4	4	Martin County	IN	Bill Clark	1967	2,057
154 3/8	25 3/8	25 2/8	19 1/8	4	4	Jefferson County	IL	Kirby Laur	1981	2,057
154 3/8	23 1/8	24 0/8	21 1/8	5	5	Sherman County	KS	Keith A. Foster	1984	2,057
154 3/8	24 2/8	23 5/8	17 1/8	5	5	Polk County	WI	Doug Greene	1986	2,057
154 3/8	24 3/8	24 2/8	18 5/8	5	5	Darke County	OH	Roy W. Ditty	1986	2,057
154 3/8	23 5/8	22 2/8	17 7/8	5	5	Highland County	OH	Martin Bullock	1986	2,057
154 3/8	24 3/8	23 7/8	20 5/8	5	5	Jackson County	WI	Daryl Lanphere	1987	2,057
154 3/8	23 3/8	22 7/8	17 5/8	6	5	Lake County	IL	James W. Smith	1988	2,057
154 3/8	24 4/8	24 4/8	19 5/8	6	6	St. Clair County	MI	Randy Shaffer	1988	2,057
154 3/8	25 3/8	25 3/8	17 5/8	4	4	Clay County	IL	Mike Fry	1988	2,057
154 3/8	25 1/8	25 4/8	17 2/8	6	6	Ottawa County	KS	James Helget	1990	2,057
154 3/8	23 5/8	25 1/8	18 5/8	4	4	Weld County	CO	Larry Gann	1991	2,057
154 3/8	25 0/8	25 0/8	20 6/8	5	6	Logan County	WV	Jimmy Diamond	1991	2,057
154 3/8	24 7/8	25 1/8	18 7/8	6	7	Howard County	IA	Roger Meirick	1992	2,057
154 3/8	25 0/8	24 1/8	20 3/8	6	4	Chester County	PA	Daniel Haines	1993	2,057
154 3/8	26 4/8	23 5/8	18 7/8	5	6	Clark County	OH	Ronnie Todd Cochran	1994	2,057
154 3/8	24 7/8	24 7/8	20 6/8	7	6	Ingham County	MI	Craig Prether	1994	2,057
154 3/8	26 7/8	25 7/8	18 1/8	5	5	Montgomery County	VA	Curtis L. Coleman	1995	2,057
154 3/8	23 7/8	24 2/8	16 5/8	5	5	Martin County	IN	Steven W. Sargent	1996	2,057
154 3/8	24 2/8	22 5/8	16 2/8	5	6	Spokane County	WA	Joel Enevold	1996	2,057
154 3/8	23 0/8	23 3/8	17 5/8	5	5	Battle River	ALB	Harley Rea	1997	2,057
154 3/8	24 7/8	24 4/8	18 1/8	5	5	Warren County	IA	Jeff Hoover	1997	2,057
154 3/8	24 1/8	23 4/8	19 3/8	6	7	Decatur County	IA	Dave J. Lamberts	1997	2,057
154 2/8	25 4/8	27 0/8	16 6/8	6	6	Waupaca County	WI	Carl Schoenike	1948	2,081
154 2/8	26 2/8	26 0/8	15 4/8	4	5	Aitkin County	MN	Ervin A. Buck	1959	2,081
154 2/8	25 1/8	25 7/8	17 6/8	5	6	Cloud County	KS	Jerrold L. Istas	1981	2,081
154 2/8	22 3/8	21 7/8	16 6/8	6	6	Clark County	MO	Myles Keller	1981	2,081
154 2/8	22 6/8	22 6/8	17 4/8	5	5	Burleigh County	ND	Tony Niemann	1984	2,081
154 2/8	24 6/8	25 1/8	17 0/8	5	5	Pendleton County	WV	Roger O. Wyant	1984	2,081
154 2/8	23 6/8	23 1/8	17 6/8	6	6	White County	IL	Bruce Masser	1984	2,081
154 2/8	24 6/8	23 1/8	18 0/8	8	7	Comanche County	KS	Tommie A. Berger	1985	2,081
154 2/8	24 3/8	23 7/8	18 3/8	5	6	Dane County	WI	Eric L. Hamele	1987	2,081
154 2/8	26 5/8	26 4/8	18 2/8	8	7	Coles County	IL	Rob King	1987	2,081
154 2/8	23 2/8	23 1/8	18 4/8	5	5	Millarville	ALB	Stuart Sinclair-Smith	1989	2,081
154 2/8	21 7/8	21 5/8	15 2/8	6	6	Fulton County	IL	Bruce A. Flynn	1989	2,081
154 2/8	23 6/8	23 0/8	19 2/8	6	5	Ashland County	WI	Joseph A. Schutte	1990	2,081
154 2/8	25 7/8	25 0/8	16 6/8	5	5	Washington County	MN	Lance Edward Vandeberg	1990	2,081
154 2/8	24 0/8	24 7/8	20 7/8	5	6	Highland County	OH	David Doyle	1991	2,081
154 2/8	25 0/8	25 2/8	15 1/8	7	5	Fayette County	IL	Mike Myers	1991	2,081
154 2/8	25 7/8	24 5/8	18 6/8	4	4	Anoka County	MN	Dan Kluth	1992	2,081
154 2/8	23 0/8	24 0/8	17 2/8	6	5	Louisa County	IA	Rick Stroud	1992	2,081
154 2/8	25 7/8	24 3/8	20 4/8	7	7	Montgomery County	IL	Steve Barricklow	1992	2,081
154 2/8	25 7/8	25 2/8	21 0/8	5	6	Ashland County	WI	Dave Matis	1993	2,081
154 2/8	25 1/8	26 2/8	19 6/8	5	5	Cecil County	MD	Wallace Pleasanton	1993	2,081
154 2/8	22 5/8	21 6/8	19 2/8	5	5	Van Buren County	IA	Deric Saunders	1993	2,081
154 2/8	23 1/8	22 4/8	19 6/8	5	5	Strathcona	ALB	Mark Irla	1993	2,081
154 2/8	23 2/8	24 1/8	19 2/8	5	5	Marathon County	WI	Mark Jon Miller	1994	2,081
154 2/8	27 6/8	26 3/8	21 6/8	6	5	Bucks County	PA	Richard A. McCurdy, Jr.	1994	2,081
154 2/8	23 6/8	24 2/8	17 6/8	5	5	Worth County	IA	Larry Porter	1995	2,081

WHITETAIL DEER (TYPICAL ANTLERS)

Minimum Score 125 — Continued

SCORE	LENGTH OF MAIN BEAM R	LENGTH OF MAIN BEAM L	INSIDE SPREAD	NUMBER OF POINTS R	NUMBER OF POINTS L	AREA	STATE/ PROVINCE	HUNTER'S NAME	DATE	RANK
154 2/8	27 6/8	27 4/8	18 4/8	4	4	St. Louis County	MO	Jesse Wiggins	1996	2,081
154 2/8	26 3/8	25 6/8	18 2/8	5	5	Ripley County	IN	Dan Castner	1996	2,081
154 2/8	25 4/8	25 6/8	18 7/8	7	6	Spokane County	WA	Phil Monroe	1997	2,081
154 2/8	23 6/8	24 2/8	21 0/8	4	4	Stark County	IL	Ronald Ellington	1997	2,081
154 1/8	24 6/8	23 7/8	15 5/8	5	5	Brown County	IN	Glen E. Parton	1970	2,111
154 1/8	24 6/8	25 5/8	20 4/8	5	7	Noble County	OH	Donald J. Mace	1973	2,111
154 1/8	23 5/8	23 7/8	19 5/8	5	6	Stoddard County	MO	Gary Barton	1980	2,111
154 1/8	24 6/8	23 4/8	19 6/8	5	7	Shawano County	WI	John Popp	1980	2,111
154 1/8	23 0/8	23 1/8	18 7/8	6	7	Faribault County	MN	Carlton Eastvold, Jr.	1982	2,111
154 1/8	26 5/8	26 2/8	20 1/8	6	7	Nelson County	KY	Tom Bullock	1983	2,111
154 1/8	23 7/8	23 4/8	18 3/8	5	5	Merrick County	NE	Lauren N Erickson	1985	2,111
154 1/8	22 6/8	24 7/8	17 5/8	5	5	Miami County	IN	Charles Wecht	1986	2,111
154 1/8	28 0/8	27 1/8	25 1/8	4	4	Buffalo County	WI	Frank Frost	1987	2,111
154 1/8	22 5/8	21 2/8	19 5/8	5	5	Poinsett County	AR	Barry Deckelman	1988	2,111
154 1/8	26 4/8	26 1/8	17 5/8	6	7	Saline County	KS	Shane Roberts	1989	2,111
154 1/8	24 4/8	24 1/8	19 5/8	5	4	Phillips County	KS	Gary Fritzler	1990	2,111
154 1/8	24 0/8	24 0/8	16 1/8	5	5	Marion County	IA	Frank M. Hashman	1991	2,111
154 1/8	25 2/8	25 6/8	20 5/8	5	7	Harrison County	IA	Gerald D. Dickman	1991	2,111
154 1/8	26 1/8	25 7/8	21 4/8	5	5	Calhoun County	MI	Hershel Brown	1992	2,111
154 1/8	26 7/8	28 7/8	19 1/8	7	5	Jefferson County	IN	Frank McClain	1992	2,111
154 1/8	24 1/8	23 0/8	18 0/8	5	6	Cheyenne County	CO	Travis Leonard	1992	2,111
154 1/8	23 0/8	22 2/8	16 5/8	5	5	Osage County	OK	Dan Gaston	1993	2,111
154 1/8	24 4/8	25 0/8	22 5/8	5	4	McHenry County	IL	Gary Pfaffinger	1993	2,111
154 1/8	24 5/8	25 2/8	17 7/8	6	6	Todd County	MN	Scott Swanson	1994	2,111
154 1/8	24 6/8	25 3/8	15 7/8	6	6	Portage County	OH	Timothy Scott Fitzgerald	1995	2,111
154 1/8	25 6/8	27 4/8	20 3/8	5	5	Shelby County	OH	Stephen A. Davis	1995	2,111
154 1/8	21 6/8	21 5/8	17 1/8	5	4	Frontier County	NE	Donald Bergantz	1995	2,111
154 1/8	21 3/8	22 7/8	16 6/8	6	5	Brown County	IN	Alan D. Baxter	1995	2,111
154 1/8	23 7/8	23 1/8	20 5/8	5	5	Cass County	IA	Mark Armstrong	1995	2,111
154 1/8	28 4/8	27 5/8	19 4/8	7	7	McHenry County	IL	Gary T. Lackhouse	1996	2,111
154 1/8	24 3/8	24 0/8	18 7/8	5	4	Kane County	IL	Dean V. Ashton	1997	2,111
154 1/8	25 7/8	25 6/8	19 3/8	5	5	Knox County	KY	Rickey C. Bates	1997	2,111
154 1/8	22 7/8	23 3/8	19 1/8	5	5	Johnson County	IL	Roger Dubson	1997	2,111
154 0/8	26 2/8	26 1/8	17 6/8	5	5	Marshall County	KS	Tim Wanklyn	1976	2,140
154 0/8	26 5/8	26 5/8	19 1/8	4	5	Guthrie County	IA	Gordon Headlee	1977	2,140
154 0/8	27 0/8	26 7/8	19 2/8	6	6	Kosciusko County	IN	Charles L. Baker	1979	2,140
154 0/8	27 2/8	25 7/8	18 4/8	6	4	Knox County	IL	James C. Drake	1979	2,140
154 0/8	22 4/8	22 1/8	18 2/8	5	5	Price County	WI	Jim Sorensen	1982	2,140
154 0/8	24 4/8	24 5/8	17 4/8	5	5	Monroe County	MO	Dallas L. Miller	1985	2,140
154 0/8	24 6/8	24 3/8	15 4/8	5	5	Clay County	IN	Terry L. Dewey	1985	2,140
154 0/8	25 1/8	24 1/8	19 2/8	5	5	Kent County	MD	J. Richard Herr	1985	2,140
154 0/8	25 1/8	23 1/8	21 1/8	6	6	Tuscarawas County	OH	Stephen Hinkley	1986	2,140
154 0/8	27 1/8	27 2/8	17 4/8	5	5	Waukesha County	WI	Duane Turinske	1989	2,140
154 0/8	22 3/8	23 4/8	21 0/8	7	8	Jones County	GA	John Bragg	1990	2,140
154 0/8	25 0/8	25 7/8	20 4/8	5	4	Henry County	MO	Matt Hull	1991	2,140
154 0/8	25 2/8	26 1/8	18 6/8	4	4	Sarpy County	NE	Timothy R. Mathewson	1992	2,140
154 0/8	24 3/8	25 4/8	20 1/8	6	7	Oakland County	MI	William Lacy	1993	2,140
154 0/8	23 2/8	24 2/8	18 6/8	5	6	Spokane County	WA	Luke Clausen	1993	2,140
154 0/8	24 4/8	23 3/8	20 6/8	5	5	Hamilton County	OH	Charlie Bledsoe	1994	2,140
154 0/8	22 7/8	23 7/8	15 5/8	6	7	Woodbury County	IA	Dennis Weisz	1995	2,140
154 0/8	23 1/8	23 2/8	23 0/8	5	5	Boundary County	ID	Damon Severson	1996	2,140
154 0/8	25 6/8	25 3/8	18 0/8	5	6	Dane County	WI	Scott Moran	1996	2,140
154 0/8	22 7/8	22 0/8	18 6/8	5	5	Wabasha County	MN	Gene Hippe	1997	2,140
154 0/8	25 2/8	24 7/8	22 0/8	4	5	Kent County	DE	D. Jeremy Henderson	1998	2,140
153 7/8	25 5/8	24 5/8	23 4/8	5	6	Lee County	IA	Chris Fowler	1980	2,161
153 7/8	22 6/8	22 2/8	17 5/8	5	5	McLean County	ND	Terry Cossette	1983	2,161
153 7/8	25 6/8	26 0/8	17 1/8	7	7	Black Hawk County	IA	Gary Schoeberl	1985	2,161
153 7/8	25 7/8	26 0/8	20 5/8	4	5	Bedford County	VA	Julian A. McFaden III	1986	2,161
153 7/8	24 2/8	24 6/8	18 7/8	5	5	Franklin County	IL	Dave Freeman	1987	2,161
153 7/8	24 4/8	25 4/8	19 7/8	6	6	Chase County	KS	Jerry Keller	1988	2,161
153 7/8	25 3/8	25 1/8	17 1/8	4	4	Stephenson County	IL	Richard Wickersham	1989	2,161
153 7/8	22 2/8	22 7/8	20 2/8	5	6	Cass County	ND	Dean Honrud	1991	2,161
153 7/8	23 5/8	23 5/8	16 3/8	6	6	Wallowa County	OR	Marte Scheuffele	1993	2,161
153 7/8	23 6/8	23 1/8	17 5/8	6	6	Mason County	IL	Christopher Thomas Novak	1993	2,161
153 7/8	22 0/8	22 6/8	16 7/8	6	6	Washington County	WI	Gary Bell	1993	2,161
153 7/8	27 1/8	26 1/8	20 7/8	5	5	Pike County	IL	Eddie Claypool	1994	2,161
153 7/8	23 5/8	24 4/8	17 5/8	5	5	St. Croix County	WI	Don Bock	1994	2,161
153 7/8	22 6/8	22 6/8	17 0/8	5	6	Appanoose County	IA	Richard Doll	1994	2,161
153 7/8	24 1/8	24 6/8	18 7/8	5	5	Ogle County	IL	Jeff Wiedel	1996	2,161
153 7/8	26 2/8	23 3/8	18 2/8	7	6	Rock Island County	IL	Oscar Ellis	1996	2,161
153 7/8	23 6/8	23 4/8	16 3/8	6	6	Rock County	WI	Matt Wellenkotter	1996	2,161
153 7/8	25 0/8	24 4/8	19 3/8	5	5	Eau Claire County	WI	Joel Stuttgen	1997	2,161
153 7/8	22 6/8	23 4/8	18 7/8	5	6	Randolph County	MO	Don Whitefield	1997	2,161
153 7/8	22 5/8	23 3/8	23 6/8	5	5	Delaware County	IA	Kevin Dempster	1997	2,161
153 7/8	23 7/8	23 4/8	19 5/8	6	5	Columbia County	WI	Stephen A. Heiman	1998	2,161
153 6/8	22 1/8	22 7/8	17 0/8	5	5	Kent County	MD	S. Russell Edie	1966	2,182
153 6/8	24 5/8	25 1/8	18 2/8	6	5	Lee County	IL	George Nevins	1976	2,182
153 6/8	23 3/8	24 3/8	18 0/8	5	5	Lincoln County	SD	Mike Pederson	1979	2,182

WHITETAIL DEER (TYPICAL ANTLERS)

Minimum Score 125 — Continued

SCORE	LENGTH OF MAIN BEAM R	LENGTH OF MAIN BEAM L	INSIDE SPREAD	NUMBER OF POINTS R	NUMBER OF POINTS L	AREA	STATE/PROVINCE	HUNTER'S NAME	DATE	RANK
153 6/8	24 1/8	23 7/8	16 0/8	5	5	Jasper County	MO	Steve Lewis	1983	2,182
153 6/8	24 5/8	23 6/8	18 0/8	5	5	Kenosha County	WI	John Schnider, Jr.	1984	2,182
153 6/8	25 1/8	24 7/8	18 4/8	5	5	Morrison County	MN	John Erdrich	1984	2,182
153 6/8	24 2/8	23 3/8	19 4/8	5	5	Chisago County	MN	Blair Rawlings	1985	2,182
153 6/8	22 7/8	23 0/8	17 7/8	5	6	Crook County	WY	Steven Blair	1986	2,182
153 6/8	25 5/8	25 0/8	19 5/8	6	6	Adair County	MO	Roger Roberts	1986	2,182
153 6/8	23 2/8	23 6/8	20 6/8	6	6	Hennepin County	MN	Steve Clark	1987	2,182
153 6/8	24 2/8	23 2/8	22 4/8	5	5	Idaho County	ID	Ron Beitelspacher	1988	2,182
153 6/8	24 2/8	24 2/8	17 0/8	7	6	St. Croix County	WI	Steve Huppert	1988	2,182
153 6/8	24 0/8	23 2/8	23 2/8	4	4	Fulton County	IL	John Koster	1989	2,182
153 6/8	21 6/8	21 5/8	17 1/8	6	5	Lucas County	IA	Orval W. Bedell	1990	2,182
153 6/8	22 4/8	23 2/8	16 2/8	5	5	Winnebago County	IL	Mark P. Stock	1991	2,182
153 6/8	24 4/8	25 3/8	20 3/8	4	5	Priddis	ALB	Lorne D. Rinkel	1991	2,182
153 6/8	25 7/8	26 4/8	22 0/8	5	4	Baraga County	MI	David C. Sikorsky	1991	2,182
153 6/8	24 0/8	25 7/8	16 5/8	7	7	Atchison County	MO	Tom Nauman	1991	2,182
153 6/8	24 4/8	24 0/8	22 4/8	5	7	Suffolk County	NY	Richard Supinsky	1991	2,182
153 6/8	23 5/8	23 5/8	21 2/8	6	5	Jackson County	IL	Sharen Oliver	1993	2,182
153 6/8	23 4/8	24 2/8	21 4/8	7	7	Chippewa County	WI	Steve L. Craker	1994	2,182
153 6/8	23 7/8	22 6/8	17 0/8	6	6	Saline County	KS	Stan E. Cox	1994	2,182
153 6/8	24 0/8	24 6/8	16 6/8	5	5	Pike County	IL	Gregory S. Guerrieri	1995	2,182
153 6/8	29 6/8	27 7/8	20 6/8	5	4	Warren County	OH	Scot Weyrauch	1995	2,182
153 6/8	24 2/8	23 7/8	18 2/8	5	6	Brown County	OH	Richard Schmalz	1996	2,182
153 6/8	28 6/8	29 1/8	19 2/8	6	5	Miami County	OH	Richard M. Harvey, Sr.	1996	2,182
153 6/8	24 6/8	23 4/8	18 2/8	6	5	Buffalo County	NE	Gary Mike Hubbard	1996	2,182
153 6/8	24 6/8	23 5/8	21 4/8	5	5	La Crosse County	WI	Michael Herde	1998	2,182
153 5/8	23 4/8	23 0/8	22 4/8	5	7	Harris	SAS	Garry Benson	1966	2,210
153 5/8	26 5/8	26 6/8	18 5/8	7	5	Hamilton County	IA	Harold Brown	1971	2,210
153 5/8	26 0/8	25 2/8	18 1/8	7	5	Halton Hills	ONT	Don Lewis	1978	2,210
153 5/8	23 4/8	24 0/8	18 7/8	5	5	Dorchester County	MD	David Logan White	1983	2,210
153 5/8	26 0/8	25 5/8	21 1/8	6	5	Will County	IL	John Madonis	1984	2,210
153 5/8	25 4/8	25 7/8	20 5/8	5	5	Stephenson County	IL	Clarence E. Hille, Jr.	1984	2,210
153 5/8	23 0/8	23 0/8	19 5/8	5	5	Sauk County	WI	Michael H. Smith	1986	2,210
153 5/8	24 0/8	24 4/8	19 6/8	5	6	Butler County	KS	Robert VanDeventer	1987	2,210
153 5/8	25 2/8	24 6/8	18 0/8	6	8	Lorain County	OH	Daniel T. Fortney	1988	2,210
153 5/8	25 0/8	25 0/8	17 5/8	5	5	Marathon County	WI	Paul Tuttle	1989	2,210
153 5/8	27 4/8	26 7/8	20 6/8	6	4	Allamakee County	IA	Raymond Boland	1989	2,210
153 5/8	25 7/8	24 7/8	17 5/8	5	6	Madison County	IA	Fred "Bud" Allen	1991	2,210
153 5/8	26 1/8	25 5/8	19 1/8	6	6	Boone County	IA	Dave Rimathe	1992	2,210
153 5/8	24 7/8	24 3/8	18 6/8	4	6	Outagamie County	WI	Scott M. Snortum	1992	2,210
153 5/8	26 5/8	26 1/8	22 5/8	5	5	Logan County	CO	Robert L. Syvertson, Jr.	1992	2,210
153 5/8	24 1/8	23 7/8	21 7/8	5	5	Howe Island	ONT	Nick Milonas	1993	2,210
153 5/8	25 0/8	25 3/8	17 3/8	5	5	Monroe County	WI	Aaron Seielstad	1994	2,210
153 5/8	23 1/8	23 4/8	17 1/8	5	5	Jackson County	MI	Randall J. Job	1995	2,210
153 5/8	24 3/8	24 0/8	24 6/8	5	5	Renville County	ND	Dan Marler	1995	2,210
153 5/8	31 2/8	30 2/8	23 0/8	8	6	McDonough County	IL	Max Wike	1996	2,210
153 5/8	24 6/8	24 5/8	20 5/8	5	5	Kane County	IL	Bob Perkins	1996	2,210
153 5/8	25 7/8	25 7/8	20 1/8	5	5	Keokuk County	IA	Kenneth P. Martin	1996	2,210
153 5/8	22 2/8	21 5/8	17 3/8	5	6	Pike County	IL	Keith K. Klink	1996	2,210
153 5/8	24 3/8	24 6/8	17 2/8	5	5	Highland County	OH	Klay Maynard	1996	2,210
153 5/8	23 3/8	22 7/8	14 1/8	5	7	Lyon County	IA	Scott Hanson	1997	2,210
153 5/8	26 3/8	26 7/8	18 5/8	5	5	Sawyer County	WI	Mike Freismuth	1997	2,210
153 4/8	25 7/8	25 2/8	19 3/8	7	6	Jackson County	MN	Lyle Babcock	1973	2,236
153 4/8	25 1/8	23 6/8	22 0/8	6	5	Knox County	OH	John L. Yarman, Jr.	1975	2,236
153 4/8	23 5/8	24 1/8	20 6/8	6	5	Billings County	ND	David L. Torkelson	1976	2,236
153 4/8	26 2/8	26 0/8	23 2/8	6	6	Douglas County	KS	Richard D. Brown	1979	2,236
153 4/8	25 5/8	25 7/8	23 4/8	6	5	Logan County	KY	Milton O. Gaddie	1979	2,236
153 4/8	24 4/8	24 2/8	16 2/8	5	6	Columbia County	FL	Robert Ballard	1980	2,236
153 4/8	22 5/8	22 4/8	14 6/8	5	5	Callaway County	MO	Marvin Giboney	1980	2,236
153 4/8	24 7/8	24 6/8	17 4/8	5	5	Vinton County	OH	Mike Laferty	1982	2,236
153 4/8	25 3/8	25 2/8	17 6/8	6	6	Morrison County	MN	Dennis Midas	1983	2,236
153 4/8	22 5/8	22 5/8	17 0/8	6	7	Licking County	OH	Jeff Fowls	1986	2,236
153 4/8	24 6/8	25 3/8	16 2/8	5	4	Trempealeau County	WI	David A. Stegemeyer	1987	2,236
153 4/8	24 6/8	24 1/8	19 0/8	5	5	Dubuque County	IA	Patrick J. McAndrew	1988	2,236
153 4/8	24 5/8	24 2/8	17 4/8	5	5	Ashland County	WI	Dennis A. Schmitt	1990	2,236
153 4/8	24 1/8	23 5/8	18 4/8	6	6	Montgomery County	MS	John M. Johnson	1991	2,236
153 4/8	23 5/8	24 1/8	17 2/8	5	7	Randolph County	MO	Harold Montgomery	1991	2,236
153 4/8	25 1/8	24 2/8	17 7/8	6	6	Lee County	IA	Dale Clark	1991	2,236
153 4/8	26 2/8	26 6/8	17 7/8	5	5	Knox County	IL	James Schmidt	1991	2,236
153 4/8	24 5/8	24 7/8	22 4/8	5	5	Iroquois County	IL	Randy Hiltz	1992	2,236
153 4/8	25 4/8	24 6/8	22 4/8	5	4	Peoria County	IL	Lee Lewis	1993	2,236
153 4/8	23 0/8	22 4/8	15 0/8	6	6	Mason County	WV	Larry McCarty	1993	2,236
153 4/8	22 1/8	22 6/8	17 2/8	5	5	Seward County	KS	Lynn Leonard	1994	2,236
153 4/8	25 4/8	25 0/8	18 0/8	4	5	Morris County	KS	Roy De Hoff	1995	2,236
153 4/8	25 5/8	25 1/8	17 6/8	5	5	Guthrie County	IA	Todd E. Castle	1995	2,236
153 4/8	22 6/8	23 1/8	18 4/8	5	7	Lonoke County	AR	Billy L. Gilliam	1995	2,236
153 4/8	26 1/8	25 3/8	17 2/8	5	4	Franklin County	IL	Darrell Roberts	1995	2,236
153 4/8	26 7/8	26 6/8	20 0/8	4	4	Edgar County	IL	Darrell Bozarth	1996	2,236
153 4/8	24 7/8	23 5/8	20 1/8	4	6	Winnebago County	IL	James R. Petersen	1996	2,236

WHITETAIL DEER (TYPICAL ANTLERS)

Minimum Score 125
Continued

SCORE	LENGTH OF MAIN BEAM R	LENGTH OF MAIN BEAM L	INSIDE SPREAD	NUMBER OF POINTS R	NUMBER OF POINTS L	AREA	STATE/ PROVINCE	HUNTER'S NAME	DATE	RANK
153 4/8	25 4/8	24 3/8	19 4/8	5	4	Carroll County	IL	John Tomczak	1996	2,236
153 4/8	30 1/8	31 2/8	21 3/8	5	7	Knox County	IL	Larry C. Harding	1996	2,236
153 4/8	23 4/8	26 0/8	18 0/8	8	5	Lenawee County	MI	Michael A. Urbanczyk	1997	2,236
153 4/8	24 4/8	24 5/8	23 0/8	5	5	Kleberg County	TX	Andy Milam	1997	2,236
153 4/8	23 0/8	22 5/8	17 2/8	5	5	Brown County	SD	Bryan B. Aaron	1997	2,236
153 4/8	24 5/8	24 7/8	22 0/8	7	6	Adams County	OH	Andy F. Yutzy	1997	2,236
153 4/8	23 6/8	23 4/8	17 6/8	6	5	Yuma County	CO	Jeff Lee	1998	2,236
153 3/8	25 5/8	24 7/8	19 4/8	5	6	Grundy County	IL	Ed Vitko, Jr.	1972	2,270
153 3/8	21 2/8	22 3/8	19 0/8	7	6	Morrison County	MN	Robert R. Ganzer	1973	2,270
153 3/8	25 5/8	27 6/8	21 1/8	4	4	Knox County	IL	Bill Richards	1981	2,270
153 3/8	25 1/8	24 3/8	19 3/8	4	4	Webster County	WV	Charles P. Green	1982	2,270
153 3/8	22 7/8	22 7/8	20 6/8	7	7	Macoupin County	IL	Charles M. Woolfolk	1983	2,270
153 3/8	24 7/8	24 7/8	17 7/8	6	7	Calumet County	WI	Matt Fuchs	1986	2,270
153 3/8	24 2/8	26 1/8	18 6/8	6	6	McHenry County	IL	Lenny Vohasek	1987	2,270
153 3/8	28 4/8	29 4/8	21 7/8	4	5	Dakota County	NE	Keith R. Claypool	1987	2,270
153 3/8	28 4/8	27 6/8	21 3/8	4	4	Howard County	MD	Chris Apostolakos	1987	2,270
153 3/8	23 1/8	22 7/8	20 3/8	5	5	Morgan County	CO	Michael Paul Hansen	1988	2,270
153 3/8	25 2/8	24 6/8	17 5/8	5	5	Suffolk County	NY	Ronald W. Tybaert	1988	2,270
153 3/8	25 5/8	24 2/8	19 1/8	6	5	Greene County	MO	Don M. Andrews	1988	2,270
153 3/8	24 4/8	24 4/8	18 2/8	5	6	Webb County	TX	Gilberto Guajardo, Jr.	1989	2,270
153 3/8	24 4/8	25 4/8	20 4/8	5	6	Lake County	IL	Mark Nelsen	1990	2,270
153 3/8	25 4/8	25 3/8	20 3/8	5	5	Racine County	WI	Dave L. Krupp	1990	2,270
153 3/8	23 1/8	22 7/8	19 7/8	5	5	Westchester County	NY	Michael A. Chirico	1990	2,270
153 3/8	25 4/8	25 3/8	16 1/8	5	5	Jefferson County	IA	Robin L. Geibel	1990	2,270
153 3/8	28 4/8	26 4/8	18 3/8	4	5	Bracken County	KY	George Clark	1990	2,270
153 3/8	24 2/8	24 6/8	18 0/8	5	7	Tazewell County	IL	Charles F. Estes	1991	2,270
153 3/8	25 1/8	25 2/8	19 1/8	4	4	McHenry County	IL	Roger A. Bacon	1992	2,270
153 3/8	23 5/8	22 7/8	20 3/8	6	6	Macon County	IL	Joe Sapp	1993	2,270
153 3/8	26 1/8	26 4/8	19 3/8	5	4	Scott County	IL	Gene E. Meier	1993	2,270
153 3/8	26 4/8	27 0/8	18 7/8	6	5	Linn County	IA	Hunter B. Techau	1993	2,270
153 3/8	24 6/8	25 2/8	15 3/8	5	6	Turner County	SD	Tony Waltner	1994	2,270
153 3/8	25 0/8	25 2/8	20 4/8	6	7	Macoupin County	IL	Joe Clements	1995	2,270
153 3/8	25 6/8	25 5/8	21 5/8	5	6	Butler County	KS	Kirk Kelly	1995	2,270
153 3/8	24 0/8	23 4/8	17 7/8	5	5	Logan County	WV	William L.T. Pack	1996	2,270
153 3/8	23 6/8	23 4/8	19 7/8	6	6	Van Buren County	IA	Mark Story	1996	2,270
153 3/8	24 3/8	23 6/8	20 1/8	5	5	Winnebago County	IL	Randy K. Thompson	1997	2,270
153 2/8	24 4/8	24 3/8	24 4/8	5	5	Burt County	NE	Harold W. Hawkins	1966	2,299
153 2/8	26 0/8	26 7/8	20 6/8	6	6	Winnebago County	IA	Ronald Gordon	1972	2,299
153 2/8	22 5/8	22 3/8	20 4/8	5	5	Lincoln County	NE	Greg Wingfield	1978	2,299
153 2/8	21 6/8	21 7/8	15 0/8	5	5	Wood County	WI	James Wilke	1984	2,299
153 2/8	26 3/8	25 2/8	18 4/8	7	5	Butler County	KS	Larry Womack	1984	2,299
153 2/8	24 3/8	23 6/8	20 2/8	5	5	Jackson County	MN	Bill Vangsness	1985	2,299
153 2/8	22 1/8	23 3/8	17 1/8	9	8	Seminole County	OK	James V. Flowers III	1986	2,299
153 2/8	24 4/8	24 7/8	19 0/8	5	5	Frederick County	MD	Grayson Mercer, Jr.	1986	2,299
153 2/8	25 0/8	25 5/8	19 5/8	9	6	Morgan County	IL	Sam Alfand	1986	2,299
153 2/8	23 0/8	24 2/8	19 0/8	5	6	Wapello County	IA	Jim Smith	1987	2,299
153 2/8	23 4/8	24 7/8	17 0/8	7	5	Pulaski County	IN	Steve Knebel	1988	2,299
153 2/8	25 1/8	25 1/8	21 6/8	4	4	Stephenson County	IL	Robert J. Schiffman	1989	2,299
153 2/8	24 6/8	24 4/8	20 4/8	7	5	Edmonton	ALB	Dale Spooner	1991	2,299
153 2/8	23 7/8	23 4/8	18 2/8	5	5	Coffey County	KS	Douglas Gilkison	1992	2,299
153 2/8	25 1/8	24 3/8	21 7/8	5	6	Carroll County	IL	Ed Smetana	1993	2,299
153 2/8	26 3/8	26 2/8	19 1/8	5	6	Kent County	MD	Robert G. Griffin	1994	2,299
153 2/8	24 3/8	23 6/8	14 4/8	6	8	Boone County	IA	James Perkins	1994	2,299
153 2/8	24 1/8	23 2/8	18 2/8	5	5	Piatt County	IL	Robert W. James	1995	2,299
153 2/8	24 2/8	23 7/8	24 0/8	6	7	Will County	IL	Timothy A. Butler	1995	2,299
153 2/8	24 0/8	23 5/8	20 3/8	6	5	Fayette County	IA	David Kemmerer	1995	2,299
153 2/8	23 1/8	23 4/8	17 3/8	8	5	Buffalo County	WI	David J. Brion	1995	2,299
153 2/8	23 3/8	23 5/8	19 2/8	5	6	Page County	IA	Chris Barton	1996	2,299
153 1/8	25 2/8	25 0/8	18 5/8	4	5	Lincoln County	NE	Rich Birch	1965	2,321
153 1/8	25 6/8	25 1/8	19 1/8	6	5	Christian County	IL	Michael Miloncus	1983	2,321
153 1/8	25 6/8	25 1/8	17 1/8	7	6	Moody County	SD	Paul Schlobohm	1983	2,321
153 1/8	27 2/8	27 1/8	27 2/8	6	5	Lee County	IA	Ronald Elbe	1986	2,321
153 1/8	22 5/8	21 3/8	18 1/8	5	5	White County	AR	Harold Dwain Marlin	1987	2,321
153 1/8	20 4/8	21 6/8	18 5/8	5	5	St. Clair County	IL	Jim Fetters	1987	2,321
153 1/8	24 3/8	24 3/8	16 5/8	5	6	Lake County	IL	Steve Andrews	1988	2,321
153 1/8	22 6/8	23 1/8	17 3/8	7	8	Walworth County	WI	Charles Palmer	1990	2,321
153 1/8	25 4/8	25 2/8	19 3/8	5	5	Monroe County	NY	Dan Scorza	1990	2,321
153 1/8	23 7/8	22 7/8	17 6/8	7	5	Washington County	OH	Scott J. Cogar	1992	2,321
153 1/8	24 3/8	24 1/8	20 4/8	6	5	Henry County	IA	William J. Wilson	1992	2,321
153 1/8	25 7/8	25 2/8	18 3/8	5	4	Wood County	OH	Mark Kubacki	1994	2,321
153 1/8	22 5/8	22 7/8	18 1/8	5	5	York County	PA	Joseph Kingston	1994	2,321
153 1/8	23 1/8	23 5/8	15 7/8	5	5	Livingston County	MI	Ted Thomas Ford	1994	2,321
153 1/8	24 0/8	24 2/8	17 7/8	5	5	Litchfield County	CT	Antonio E. Cacela	1995	2,321
153 1/8	25 0/8	24 2/8	20 3/8	5	6	Shelby County	MO	Glen Mertens	1995	2,321
153 0/8	25 0/8	25 2/8	17 4/8	5	5	Cambria County	PA	Andrew J. Getsy	1965	2,337
153 0/8	21 3/8	21 1/8	16 4/8	5	5	Burleigh County	ND	Jim Balzer	1977	2,337
153 0/8	24 7/8	25 1/8	16 3/8	5	6	Koochiching County	MN	Dr. Thomas Zbaracki	1980	2,337
153 0/8	23 2/8	23 6/8	16 0/8	5	5	Lawrence County	PA	Wayne Edwards	1981	2,337

WHITETAIL DEER (TYPICAL ANTLERS)

Minimum Score 125

SCORE	LENGTH OF MAIN BEAM R	LENGTH OF MAIN BEAM L	INSIDE SPREAD	NUMBER OF POINTS R	NUMBER OF POINTS L	AREA	STATE/PROVINCE	HUNTER'S NAME	DATE	RANK
153 0/8	23 5/8	23 6/8	15 7/8	6	6	Shelby County	IL	Bill D. Pesch	1983	2,337
153 0/8	23 7/8	24 3/8	18 4/8	5	5	Trumbull County	OH	Art Stanton	1985	2,337
153 0/8	25 3/8	25 2/8	19 4/8	4	5	Dane County	WI	Joe Eugster	1986	2,337
153 0/8	26 1/8	26 5/8	19 3/8	4	5	Mason County	IL	Gregory B. Snider	1986	2,337
153 0/8	24 2/8	24 2/8	21 6/8	5	6	Lake County	IL	Roger A. Bacon	1987	2,337
153 0/8	24 0/8	25 4/8	23 1/8	5	5	Lake County	IL	Kris Laho	1987	2,337
153 0/8	26 1/8	26 3/8	22 2/8	5	4	Craig County	OK	Eddie Claypool	1988	2,337
153 0/8	26 0/8	26 3/8	18 4/8	5	4	Sangamon County	IL	Randy Black	1988	2,337
153 0/8	26 2/8	25 5/8	15 1/8	5	5	Saline County	NE	Don Kohout	1990	2,337
153 0/8	26 1/8	24 4/8	15 5/8	6	5	Kay County	OK	Guy L. LeMonnier, Jr.	1990	2,337
153 0/8	22 3/8	22 1/8	15 0/8	5	5	Henry County	IA	Paul Ginkens	1990	2,337
153 0/8	22 0/8	21 5/8	17 7/8	8	7	Washburn County	WI	Dennis Regenauer	1990	2,337
153 0/8	26 0/8	25 4/8	19 0/8	4	4	Vinton County	OH	Randy Boggs	1991	2,337
153 0/8	25 3/8	26 4/8	18 3/8	6	6	Buffalo County	WI	Brad Johnson	1992	2,337
153 0/8	24 0/8	25 2/8	17 3/8	5	5	Edwards County	KS	Sheila Wood	1992	2,337
153 0/8	23 0/8	22 5/8	16 2/8	6	5	Casey County	KY	Carroll Gibson	1993	2,337
153 0/8	23 6/8	23 1/8	16 6/8	6	5	McLean County	IL	Robert F. Keith	1993	2,337
153 0/8	23 6/8	23 6/8	16 4/8	5	5	Racine County	WI	Calvin Kamrath	1994	2,337
153 0/8	23 6/8	22 5/8	18 4/8	5	5	Fond du Lac County	WI	Tim Frank	1995	2,337
153 0/8	27 3/8	26 4/8	21 3/8	6	5	Vernon County	WI	Tim Hoeth	1995	2,337
153 0/8	22 0/8	21 2/8	17 6/8	5	5	Washington County	WI	Rick Bertoni	1995	2,337
153 0/8	23 5/8	24 5/8	15 4/8	6	7	Meigs County	OH	Tim Smith	1995	2,337
153 0/8	24 3/8	23 3/8	21 7/8	7	6	Edmonton	ALB	Lynn R. Parrish	1995	2,337
153 0/8	27 2/8	28 0/8	21 0/8	4	4	Monroe County	NY	Robert Ferrarone	1995	2,337
153 0/8	25 3/8	25 0/8	19 0/8	5	4	Jefferson County	IA	Dennis Douthart	1996	2,337
153 0/8	25 5/8	24 1/8	22 4/8	6	5	Lincoln County	NE	Jason K. Swanson	1996	2,337
153 0/8	27 0/8	25 7/8	23 2/8	4	4	Somerset County	NJ	Andrew A. Confortini	1997	2,337
153 0/8	24 5/8	25 0/8	18 2/8	5	5	Waukesha County	WI	Doug Kennedy	1997	2,337
152 7/8	21 4/8	22 0/8	18 7/8	5	5	Polk County	WI	Wendle Johnson	1969	2,369
152 7/8	23 2/8	22 2/8	18 4/8	7	5	Morgan County	CO	Dr. Stuart Clodfelder	1974	2,369
152 7/8	22 1/8	23 0/8	17 0/8	6	5	Sullivan County	IN	Kenny Pirtle	1975	2,369
152 7/8	24 3/8	24 4/8	20 7/8	5	6	Missoula County	MT	Rick L. Stone	1981	2,369
152 7/8	23 2/8	23 4/8	19 1/8	6	5	Delaware County	PA	John A. Lashinsky	1984	2,369
152 7/8	24 2/8	24 2/8	20 3/8	5	5	Washington County	WI	Lee A. Richard	1984	2,369
152 7/8	21 6/8	22 2/8	19 7/8	5	5	Henry County	IL	Willard "Woody" Moore	1986	2,369
152 7/8	25 1/8	26 1/8	16 7/8	5	5	Highland County	OH	Jeffrey A. Swerlein	1988	2,369
152 7/8	23 2/8	23 0/8	20 1/8	6	6	Wayne County	WV	Larry Sarver	1988	2,369
152 7/8	23 3/8	23 6/8	19 2/8	5	8	Guthrie County	IA	Leonard H. Mussell	1989	2,369
152 7/8	23 7/8	23 7/8	20 5/8	5	6	Olmsted County	MN	Chris A. Valli	1989	2,369
152 7/8	22 6/8	22 2/8	18 1/8	5	5	Sauk County	WI	Hank Lee	1989	2,369
152 7/8	22 2/8	22 3/8	16 2/8	5	6	Chisago County	MN	John R. Palmer	1989	2,369
152 7/8	24 3/8	24 4/8	17 1/8	4	4	Oconto County	WI	Gary DeBauch	1990	2,369
152 7/8	26 0/8	25 7/8	20 2/8	6	5	Strafford County	NH	William S. Carlsen	1990	2,369
152 7/8	23 3/8	21 0/8	17 5/8	6	6	McHenry County	IL	William D. Lilly	1990	2,369
152 7/8	23 1/8	23 6/8	21 6/8	6	5	Creek County	OK	Carmon G. Romine, Jr.	1991	2,369
152 7/8	25 0/8	25 1/8	17 1/8	6	6	Loudoun County	VA	Michael R. Mutkus	1992	2,369
152 7/8	24 1/8	23 4/8	16 6/8	5	6	Langlade County	WI	Thomas H. Kubiaczyk	1993	2,369
152 7/8	22 4/8	22 5/8	17 0/8	5	7	Bullitt County	KY	Andy Cox	1994	2,369
152 7/8	25 1/8	24 6/8	21 7/8	5	5	Allegheny County	PA	Daniel A. Urbas	1995	2,369
152 7/8	24 6/8	24 4/8	20 1/8	5	5	Jefferson County	IA	D. Greiffendorf	1995	2,369
152 7/8	24 3/8	23 5/8	18 5/8	5	5	Grayson County	TX	Lynn Burkhead	1996	2,369
152 7/8	25 1/8	26 6/8	19 7/8	7	7	Marion County	KS	Michael Sowell	1996	2,369
152 7/8	26 6/8	26 3/8	21 5/8	4	5	Hamilton County	KS	Bill Kreie	1997	2,369
152 7/8	23 0/8	21 3/8	18 1/8	5	5	Kossuth County	IA	Charles Greg Arnold	1998	2,369
152 6/8	25 6/8	25 1/8	21 2/8	4	5	Jefferson County	IN	Robert Schmidt	1959	2,395
152 6/8	24 6/8	23 2/8	17 7/8	7	7	Winona County	MN	Donald M. Bzoskie	1978	2,395
152 6/8	24 7/8	24 1/8	21 0/8	4	4	Randolph County	IL	Steven Wydeck	1979	2,395
152 6/8	25 2/8	24 3/8	18 4/8	5	5	Saginaw County	MI	Jack W. Bare	1981	2,395
152 6/8	23 3/8	23 0/8	20 0/8	5	5	Morrison County	MN	Floyd Foslien	1981	2,395
152 6/8	25 0/8	25 2/8	17 6/8	6	6	Holt County	MO	Frank Berkemeier	1984	2,395
152 6/8	22 6/8	22 2/8	14 2/8	6	5	Rogers County	OK	Byron Jasper	1984	2,395
152 6/8	27 0/8	27 2/8	16 4/8	4	5	Roane County	TN	Rod Brown	1986	2,395
152 6/8	25 4/8	26 2/8	18 2/8	5	5	Texas County	OK	Don Callaway	1986	2,395
152 6/8	23 2/8	23 6/8	18 2/8	5	6	Logan County	OH	Richard D. Fullerton	1988	2,395
152 6/8	26 3/8	28 3/8	22 3/8	4	5	Vermilion County	IL	John E. Fry	1989	2,395
152 6/8	26 1/8	25 5/8	17 0/8	6	5	Lawrence County	IL	Ron Wells	1989	2,395
152 6/8	22 3/8	21 4/8	17 4/8	6	5	Winnebago County	IL	Drake R. Branca	1990	2,395
152 6/8	23 4/8	23 2/8	17 7/8	5	5	Ohio County	IN	Gary Copeland	1991	2,395
152 6/8	25 0/8	24 0/8	18 0/8	5	6	Cass County	MI	Kim C. Deda	1991	2,395
152 6/8	24 4/8	24 7/8	20 3/8	6	7	Worcester County	MA	Peter J. Warakomski	1991	2,395
152 6/8	24 6/8	24 4/8	20 4/8	5	5	Morrison County	MN	Ward Fiebiger	1992	2,395
152 6/8	22 2/8	22 4/8	18 3/8	6	6	Rock County	MN	Jim Lorenzen	1993	2,395
152 6/8	25 0/8	25 7/8	19 0/8	5	5	Greene County	OH	Mark A. Marsh	1994	2,395
152 6/8	27 2/8	26 4/8	21 2/8	5	4	Allamakee County	IA	Robyn Henderson	1996	2,395
152 5/8	23 5/8	24 5/8	19 7/8	6	5	Ralls County	MO	Donald Curless	1959	2,415
152 5/8	23 2/8	23 0/8	17 2/8	5	6	Monroe County	MO	Carl T. Peak	1968	2,415
152 5/8	25 6/8	25 3/8	17 7/8	5	5	McLean County	IL	Mike Turner	1981	2,415
152 5/8	23 1/8	24 0/8	16 1/8	6	6	Roseau County	MN	Dave Hovda	1982	2,415

WHITETAIL DEER (TYPICAL ANTLERS)

Minimum Score 125

SCORE	LENGTH OF MAIN BEAM R L		INSIDE SPREAD	NUMBER OF POINTS R L		AREA	STATE/ PROVINCE	HUNTER'S NAME	DATE	RANK
152 5/8	24 5/8	24 0/8	19 4/8	7	7	Delaware County	IA	Chet Goldsberry	1982	2,415
152 5/8	22 7/8	22 5/8	16 3/8	5	5	Lyon County	MN	Dwight A. Hemme	1984	2,415
152 5/8	25 2/8	22 2/8	17 1/8	5	5	Marathon County	WI	Marcell Wieloch	1986	2,415
152 5/8	22 6/8	24 2/8	17 7/8	7	6	Carver County	MN	Steve Polston	1986	2,415
152 5/8	26 0/8	25 0/8	20 5/8	4	4	Marion County	IA	Steven F. Donnelly, Jr.	1986	2,415
152 5/8	26 2/8	25 7/8	17 1/8	4	4	Forest County	WI	Greg Lenz	1988	2,415
152 5/8	23 0/8	21 2/8	17 3/8	5	5	Crawford County	IL	Steve Newkirk	1989	2,415
152 5/8	23 6/8	22 5/8	19 3/8	5	5	Winnebago County	IL	Tom Sanderson	1990	2,415
152 5/8	21 4/8	21 1/8	17 1/8	6	6	Hennepin County	MN	Dan Kittok	1990	2,415
152 5/8	21 0/8	21 1/8	15 1/8	5	5	Leavenworth County	KS	Thomas H. Rendall	1990	2,415
152 5/8	26 4/8	26 1/8	23 1/8	6	7	Pike County	IL	Rick Conrad	1991	2,415
152 5/8	25 3/8	26 0/8	18 2/8	6	6	Clinton County	IA	Shawn Petersen	1991	2,415
152 5/8	23 3/8	24 1/8	19 7/8	5	5	Guthrie County	IA	Gary D. Stewart	1994	2,415
152 5/8	23 0/8	23 1/8	18 7/8	7	6	Whiteside County	IL	Abraham Wuebben	1994	2,415
152 5/8	22 0/8	23 2/8	15 3/8	6	6	Maverick County	TX	Gary Miller	1995	2,415
152 5/8	22 1/8	23 0/8	15 7/8	6	5	Buffalo County	WI	Jesse D. Bloom	1995	2,415
152 5/8	24 2/8	24 5/8	16 5/8	5	6	Jackson County	MI	Mark Douglas Kelley	1995	2,415
152 5/8	23 2/8	22 4/8	17 7/8	4	4	Wilson County	KS	Roy L. Walk	1995	2,415
152 5/8	23 4/8	22 6/8	20 7/8	8	7	Will County	IL	Mark Anderson	1995	2,415
152 5/8	25 5/8	24 4/8	23 5/8	5	5	Kendall County	IL	Jim Childs	1996	2,415
152 5/8	23 5/8	24 0/8	20 5/8	5	5	Delaware County	OH	Tim Stamm	1996	2,415
152 4/8	24 6/8	24 0/8	19 2/8	8	6	Hardin County	KY	Jimmy D. Neal	1973	2,440
152 4/8	28 7/8	26 2/8	19 2/8	5	5	Somerset County	MD	Burgess Blevins	1974	2,440
152 4/8	24 3/8	24 0/8	19 2/8	5	5	Scott County	MN	Dean Jansen	1976	2,440
152 4/8	25 6/8	27 4/8	18 3/8	7	5	Westchester County	NY	Jack Dykstra	1986	2,440
152 4/8	21 5/8	21 3/8	18 6/8	5	5	Provost	ALB	Harvey McNalley	1987	2,440
152 4/8	24 5/8	25 5/8	20 4/8	7	7	Lake County	IL	Ted Bellefeuille	1987	2,440
152 4/8	23 6/8	24 6/8	17 6/8	5	5	Harris County	TX	John Hall	1987	2,440
152 4/8	23 0/8	22 7/8	19 0/8	6	6	Pike County	OH	Raymond McComas	1988	2,440
152 4/8	23 3/8	23 5/8	17 7/8	5	6	Lehigh County	PA	Steve C. Metzger	1989	2,440
152 4/8	26 1/8	27 4/8	21 6/8	5	5	Hocking County	OH	Chad Krahel	1990	2,440
152 4/8	25 6/8	25 5/8	20 3/8	5	6	St. Francois County	MO	Adam Ashby	1991	2,440
152 4/8	25 1/8	25 0/8	19 4/8	4	4	Wilkes County	NC	Joe Butcher	1992	2,440
152 4/8	23 1/8	23 2/8	16 5/8	7	6	Starke County	IN	Michael Palm	1992	2,440
152 4/8	24 1/8	23 1/8	15 2/8	5	5	Taylor County	WI	Dave Gebert	1992	2,440
152 4/8	26 0/8	25 5/8	18 2/8	5	4	Washington County	WI	Tony Snow	1992	2,440
152 4/8	23 6/8	24 3/8	19 4/8	4	4	Marion County	IL	Gary Rose	1992	2,440
152 4/8	26 3/8	27 0/8	22 5/8	5	5	Licking County	OH	Thomas E. Lott	1992	2,440
152 4/8	24 7/8	24 5/8	18 6/8	4	4	Ogle County	IL	Thomas W. Johnson	1992	2,440
152 4/8	22 7/8	23 6/8	15 6/8	5	5	Jay County	IN	Danny M. Bost	1993	2,440
152 4/8	23 4/8	23 4/8	18 0/8	5	5	Harrison County	OH	Ron Fishel	1994	2,440
152 4/8	25 1/8	25 2/8	22 6/8	4	5	Pulaski County	IL	Lawrence Helton	1994	2,440
152 4/8	25 4/8	25 4/8	16 0/8	6	6	Butler County	OH	Adam E. Wurzelbacher	1995	2,440
152 4/8	22 7/8	21 0/8	16 6/8	5	5	Ford County	IL	Gail Reiners	1995	2,440
152 4/8	22 4/8	22 3/8	20 6/8	5	5	Burleigh County	ND	Wes Berg	1995	2,440
152 4/8	25 0/8	25 1/8	21 4/8	5	5	East Carroll Parish	LA	Mike Edwards	1995	2,440
152 4/8	27 7/8	26 2/8	22 2/8	4	4	Tensas Parish	LA	Kenney Dunham	1996	2,440
152 4/8	23 5/8	23 3/8	21 2/8	5	5	Van Buren County	MI	Eric Vollrath	1996	2,440
152 4/8	25 0/8	24 5/8	17 6/8	5	5	Fayette County	OH	Whitlow Wyatt	1996	2,440
152 4/8	22 6/8	23 2/8	19 0/8	5	5	Fremont County	IA	Dave Holt	1997	2,440
152 4/8	25 2/8	24 7/8	19 4/8	4	4	Coweta County	GA	Rick Harris	1997	2,440
152 3/8	24 7/8	24 7/8	18 5/8	8	6	Pope County	IL	Dr. H. Neil Becker	1968	2,470
152 3/8	25 4/8	25 4/8	17 6/8	8	7	Jasper County	IA	Edward L. Stevens	1976	2,470
152 3/8	24 5/8	24 3/8	19 1/8	4	4	Guthrie County	IA	Barry Chalfant	1979	2,470
152 3/8	23 2/8	24 7/8	18 3/8	6	5	Schuyler County	IL	Stephen J. McCoy	1979	2,470
152 3/8	22 5/8	21 6/8	17 3/8	5	5	Butler County	KS	John Schwartz	1981	2,470
152 3/8	24 6/8	24 6/8	16 3/8	5	5	Oceana County	MI	J. C. Ingram	1982	2,470
152 3/8	24 7/8	25 3/8	19 7/8	4	4	Yorkton	SAS	Ron Vandermeulen	1983	2,470
152 3/8	24 0/8	24 4/8	19 5/8	5	5	Jewell County	KS	Rod Rose	1984	2,470
152 3/8	22 3/8	23 2/8	18 5/8	6	5	Kenosha County	WI	Howard Moore	1984	2,470
152 3/8	24 3/8	25 0/8	19 7/8	5	5	Logan County	IL	Charles E. Dumire	1984	2,470
152 3/8	25 0/8	24 3/8	17 2/8	5	8	Franklin County	KS	Joe Maloney	1985	2,470
152 3/8	23 0/8	22 5/8	17 7/8	5	6	Gasconade County	MO	John R Hawkins	1985	2,470
152 3/8	25 6/8	24 7/8	17 2/8	8	5	Washington County	KS	Stan Brustowicz	1985	2,470
152 3/8	26 6/8	29 1/8	21 1/8	6	5	Bullitt County	KY	Todd A. Edwards	1990	2,470
152 3/8	23 7/8	24 7/8	19 3/8	6	6	Pueblo County	CO	Steve Mayo	1990	2,470
152 3/8	23 1/8	23 4/8	19 5/8	5	5	Porter County	IN	William Dials	1991	2,470
152 3/8	26 1/8	25 2/8	18 5/8	5	7	Belmont County	OH	Chad Krahel	1991	2,470
152 3/8	22 4/8	21 5/8	17 7/8	5	5	Codington County	SD	Jerry Redlin	1991	2,470
152 3/8	26 0/8	25 2/8	20 7/8	5	7	Macomb County	MI	Paul L. Carabelli	1993	2,470
152 3/8	23 7/8	24 3/8	19 7/8	5	5	Poinsett County	AR	William Tyler	1993	2,470
152 3/8	25 6/8	25 7/8	19 7/8	5	4	Crawford County	IL	Charlie Guyer	1994	2,470
152 3/8	23 6/8	23 2/8	19 0/8	6	5	Adams County	IL	Larry D. Grant	1994	2,470
152 3/8	24 5/8	23 4/8	17 3/8	5	5	Chisago County	MN	Mike Shanahan	1994	2,470
152 3/8	24 4/8	25 2/8	17 3/8	5	5	McLean County	KY	Joseph A. Rhodes	1996	2,470
152 3/8	21 6/8	21 6/8	14 3/8	6	5	Duck Mtns.	MAN	Keith L. Vandever	1996	2,470
152 3/8	21 5/8	21 6/8	16 3/8	5	6	Pawnee County	NE	Gary R. Dowse	1996	2,470
152 3/8	26 6/8	26 5/8	18 7/8	4	4	Fulton County	IL	Dave Voorhees	1996	2,470

WHITETAIL DEER (TYPICAL ANTLERS)

Minimum Score 125

Continued

SCORE	LENGTH OF MAIN BEAM R	LENGTH OF MAIN BEAM L	INSIDE SPREAD	NUMBER OF POINTS R	NUMBER OF POINTS L	AREA	STATE/ PROVINCE	HUNTER'S NAME	DATE	RANK
152 3/8	24 1/8	25 1/8	16 6/8	5	5	Adams County	WI	Clifford W. Krentz	1997	2,470
152 3/8	25 2/8	23 2/8	20 5/8	6	5	Houston County	MN	Daniel W. Strasser	1997	2,470
152 3/8	25 6/8	26 1/8	17 1/8	6	7	Knox County	IN	Marcie Arnold	1997	2,470
152 3/8	24 7/8	25 2/8	14 7/8	7	6	Morgan County	IL	Shaun Nickel	1997	2,470
152 3/8	27 1/8	26 5/8	18 3/8	6	5	Harvey County	KS	John Wiebe	1997	2,470
152 3/8	24 1/8	25 3/8	17 7/8	4	4	Mason County	WV	Larry W. McCarty	1997	2,470
152 2/8	24 6/8	24 4/8	18 4/8	5	5	Cowley County	KS	Michael L. Snyder	1978	2,503
152 2/8	28 4/8	27 4/8	20 2/8	4	4	Winona County	MN	Leonard Anglewitz	1978	2,503
152 2/8	24 5/8	24 4/8	20 2/8	6	7	Miami County	KS	Brian J. Hammond	1982	2,503
152 2/8	24 2/8	23 5/8	17 4/8	6	4	Marshall County	KS	Dean C. Bookwalter	1982	2,503
152 2/8	22 2/8	21 7/8	19 5/8	5	7	Morrison County	MN	Willard L. Voight, Jr.	1984	2,503
152 2/8	24 3/8	23 4/8	16 6/8	6	5	Highland County	OH	James Stephens	1984	2,503
152 2/8	25 6/8	24 2/8	19 2/8	8	7	La Crosse County	WI	Kenne A. Happel	1985	2,503
152 2/8	25 3/8	25 3/8	21 6/8	5	5	Middlesex County	CT	Felix Nosewicz	1985	2,503
152 2/8	24 4/8	25 0/8	18 6/8	4	4	Marathon County	WI	Mark Schneider	1985	2,503
152 2/8	23 3/8	25 3/8	19 7/8	6	5	Columbia County	WI	Jeff A. Obrion	1986	2,503
152 2/8	25 6/8	25 6/8	18 6/8	5	4	Dubuque County	IA	Randy Miller	1989	2,503
152 2/8	25 4/8	25 1/8	18 6/8	7	5	Jasper County	IL	Eric Brooks	1989	2,503
152 2/8	26 4/8	25 7/8	19 1/8	7	5	Schuyler County	MO	Jim Pierceall	1990	2,503
152 2/8	24 4/8	24 1/8	15 2/8	5	6	Putnam County	OH	Pat Will	1990	2,503
152 2/8	24 4/8	24 1/8	17 6/8	5	5	Allamakee County	IA	Dennis L. Weber	1990	2,503
152 2/8	22 2/8	21 6/8	18 6/8	6	5	Spencer County	IN	Allen Kramer	1991	2,503
152 2/8	22 6/8	22 7/8	18 0/8	6	6	Winneshiek County	IA	David G. Baumler	1991	2,503
152 2/8	23 5/8	22 7/8	16 3/8	5	6	Rush County	KS	John Denk	1991	2,503
152 2/8	26 1/8	26 2/8	18 2/8	4	4	Sumner County	KS	Warren C. Townsend	1991	2,503
152 2/8	23 1/8	22 7/8	20 2/8	5	5	Kleberg County	TX	Wayne Peeples	1992	2,503
152 2/8	26 0/8	27 0/8	18 1/8	5	7	Tama County	IA	Tim Rowden	1994	2,503
152 2/8	22 6/8	22 7/8	17 6/8	5	5	Wayne County	MO	Carl Watkins	1995	2,503
152 2/8	24 4/8	24 2/8	17 6/8	6	6	Kane County	IL	Richard Hight	1995	2,503
152 2/8	24 3/8	24 2/8	22 6/8	6	5	Vermilion County	IL	Harvey Dove	1996	2,503
152 2/8	24 5/8	25 7/8	19 5/8	6	6	Adams County	IL	Tim Walmsley	1996	2,503
152 2/8	23 1/8	23 1/8	18 4/8	5	6	Carroll County	IL	Allen G. Comstock	1997	2,503
152 1/8	21 4/8	24 2/8	21 3/8	5	4	Owen County	IN	Edward L. Armstrong	1967	2,529
152 1/8	25 6/8	26 1/8	20 3/8	6	4	Watonwan County	MN	David Raney	1972	2,529
152 1/8	22 4/8	22 3/8	18 3/8	5	6	Ogle County	IL	Chuck Bowman	1974	2,529
152 1/8	25 1/8	25 3/8	17 1/8	6	6	Louisa County	IA	Duane O'Donnell	1979	2,529
152 1/8	24 1/8	24 5/8	19 3/8	5	5	Schuyler County	NY	Steve Herforth	1981	2,529
152 1/8	24 4/8	24 4/8	20 7/8	4	4	Iowa County	IA	Rick Ransom	1985	2,529
152 1/8	23 6/8	24 1/8	16 4/8	7	6	Pawnee County	KS	Karl E. Elmore	1987	2,529
152 1/8	24 7/8	22 7/8	18 1/8	5	6	Brooks County	TX	Jim L. McCrory	1988	2,529
152 1/8	24 2/8	24 0/8	17 1/8	6	5	Mercer County	ND	William F. Jensen	1989	2,529
152 1/8	23 1/8	23 2/8	19 5/8	5	6	Washington County	WI	Glenn E. Becker	1989	2,529
152 1/8	20 0/8	21 5/8	17 2/8	6	6	Pike County	IN	Keith M. Witte	1989	2,529
152 1/8	24 5/8	25 3/8	22 7/8	4	5	Monona County	IA	Rick Archer	1989	2,529
152 1/8	25 1/8	25 3/8	18 7/8	4	4	Scott County	IA	Gary Faley	1989	2,529
152 1/8	22 4/8	22 6/8	17 3/8	5	5	Powder River County	MT	Rich Driscoll	1990	2,529
152 1/8	24 4/8	24 0/8	17 3/8	4	4	Bond County	IL	James Grider	1990	2,529
152 1/8	24 3/8	24 0/8	20 7/8	4	5	Will County	IL	Robert L. Kamenjarin	1990	2,529
152 1/8	25 4/8	25 2/8	17 5/8	4	4	Kandiyohi County	MN	Elroy Thorson	1991	2,529
152 1/8	23 5/8	23 0/8	16 6/8	8	8	Clark County	MO	Duane Wilson	1991	2,529
152 1/8	22 4/8	23 7/8	16 1/8	4	4	Henry County	VA	Mike Weaver	1991	2,529
152 1/8	26 2/8	25 7/8	19 2/8	4	6	Franklin County	IL	Tom Haag	1991	2,529
152 1/8	25 3/8	25 3/8	19 0/8	5	7	Wabash County	IN	Mike Rees	1992	2,529
152 1/8	23 7/8	23 6/8	20 5/8	5	5	Todd County	MN	Bruce Hudalla	1992	2,529
152 1/8	25 3/8	25 4/8	20 1/8	5	5	Warren County	IA	Ken Sharp	1992	2,529
152 1/8	23 3/8	22 7/8	18 2/8	5	7	Oneida County	WI	David Simon	1993	2,529
152 1/8	23 0/8	23 2/8	16 3/8	5	5	Greenwood County	KS	Danny Linnebur	1993	2,529
152 1/8	23 3/8	23 2/8	19 7/8	5	5	St. Croix County	WI	Chad Olsen	1994	2,529
152 1/8	25 1/8	26 0/8	19 1/8	5	5	Porter County	IN	Robert E. Ford, Jr.	1994	2,529
152 1/8	25 1/8	24 4/8	18 5/8	6	5	Harford County	MD	Bruce W. Summers	1994	2,529
152 1/8	25 2/8	25 6/8	15 7/8	7	6	Pike County	IL	Dave Webel	1994	2,529
152 1/8	22 4/8	22 4/8	22 1/8	7	6	Lincoln County	MO	Steve Dietiker	1995	2,529
152 1/8	23 5/8	22 7/8	17 6/8	8	5	Worcester County	MD	Randall M. Hastings	1995	2,529
152 1/8	24 1/8	25 2/8	18 2/8	4	5	Scott County	IA	Daniel Hosaflook	1995	2,529
152 1/8	24 7/8	24 7/8	21 5/8	5	5	Pulaski County	VA	Michael P. Miller	1996	2,529
152 1/8	25 5/8	26 2/8	16 7/8	5	5	Aiken County	SC	Allan Gilbert	1997	2,529
152 1/8	24 4/8	24 3/8	21 5/8	4	4	Appanoose County	IA	Ronnie Everett	1997	2,529
152 0/8	24 0/8	24 6/8	20 2/8	5	5	Finney County	KS	Howard Haug, Jr.	1973	2,564
152 0/8	23 0/8	23 0/8	16 0/8	5	5	Allen County	KY	Johnny Upton	1976	2,564
152 0/8	22 1/8	22 1/8	16 2/8	5	6	Marshall County	SD	Merle Funston	1982	2,564
152 0/8	26 6/8	26 3/8	17 6/8	5	4	Clay County	MN	Anthony Laddusaw	1985	2,564
152 0/8	24 6/8	25 6/8	17 6/8	7	6	Dakota County	MN	Tom Esslinger	1985	2,564
152 0/8	24 6/8	24 3/8	17 6/8	5	5	Itasca County	MN	Thomas A. Leedham	1985	2,564
152 0/8	22 7/8	23 1/8	17 0/8	5	5	Champaign County	IL	John W. Chumbley	1985	2,564
152 0/8	24 6/8	24 6/8	20 4/8	4	5	Winnebago County	IL	Ronald R. Demus	1986	2,564
152 0/8	27 0/8	26 3/8	17 4/8	5	5	Lincoln County	MO	Donald E. Thompson, Jr.	1989	2,564
152 0/8	22 6/8	22 0/8	18 4/8	6	4	Cass County	NE	Mike Wright	1989	2,564
152 0/8	22 6/8	23 0/8	20 4/8	5	5	Iron County	WI	John A. Franke	1990	2,564

WHITETAIL DEER (TYPICAL ANTLERS)

Minimum Score 125

SCORE	LENGTH OF MAIN BEAM R	LENGTH OF MAIN BEAM L	INSIDE SPREAD	NUMBER OF POINTS R	NUMBER OF POINTS L	AREA	STATE/ PROVINCE	HUNTER'S NAME	DATE	RANK
152 0/8	23 0/8	22 0/8	17 0/8	5	5	Yankton County	SD	Daryl Miller	1990	2,564
152 0/8	24 2/8	24 3/8	19 6/8	5	4	Logan County	IL	James Booth	1991	2,564
152 0/8	26 3/8	26 3/8	20 2/8	7	6	Jackson County	MI	Robert J. Riddle	1992	2,564
152 0/8	22 2/8	22 0/8	17 2/8	6	6	Buffalo County	WI	Barry Ritscher	1992	2,564
152 0/8	24 5/8	24 6/8	18 4/8	5	6	Mercer County	IL	Richard D. Dochterman	1992	2,564
152 0/8	23 5/8	24 3/8	18 0/8	4	6	McHenry County	IL	Richard G. Hoey	1992	2,564
152 0/8	24 0/8	22 4/8	17 6/8	5	5	Columbia County	WI	Robert A. Williams	1992	2,564
152 0/8	27 6/8	27 4/8	20 4/8	4	4	Will County	IL	John Kamarauskas	1992	2,564
152 0/8	21 2/8	22 6/8	18 2/8	6	5	Ionia County	MI	Steve Jancar	1993	2,564
152 0/8	22 7/8	22 6/8	16 0/8	6	6	Kleberg County	TX	W. J. Lucas III	1993	2,564
152 0/8	22 5/8	22 2/8	18 3/8	5	6	Douglas County	MN	John P. Herd	1993	2,564
152 0/8	24 5/8	24 5/8	19 4/8	5	5	Buffalo County	WI	Edmund Smieja	1993	2,564
152 0/8	23 7/8	24 7/8	16 2/8	6	6	Montgomery County	PA	Tom Killoran	1993	2,564
152 0/8	25 2/8	24 4/8	19 2/8	5	8	Ellis County	KS	Dan Cross	1993	2,564
152 0/8	24 0/8	25 4/8	18 4/8	4	4	Christian County	KY	Barry Gant	1993	2,564
152 0/8	24 0/8	26 2/8	16 0/8	5	7	Seneca County	NY	Scott C. Smith	1993	2,564
152 0/8	24 0/8	23 1/8	16 6/8	5	5	Crawford County	PA	Angelo S. Lavarone, Jr.	1994	2,564
152 0/8	25 1/8	26 1/8	19 2/8	5	5	Athens County	OH	David A. Hawk	1994	2,564
152 0/8	21 2/8	22 0/8	16 6/8	5	5	Kerr County	TX	Robert L. Parker, Jr.	1994	2,564
152 0/8	26 5/8	26 3/8	20 0/8	4	5	Linn County	IA	Randal J. Willey	1994	2,564
152 0/8	24 2/8	26 0/8	19 0/8	4	4	Hennepin County	MN	Joe Bilek	1994	2,564
152 0/8	26 6/8	26 0/8	19 5/8	6	7	St. Louis County	MN	Nathan M. Samarzia	1995	2,564
152 0/8	23 5/8	24 1/8	21 0/8	6	5	Prince Georges County	MD	Tracy Ford	1995	2,564
152 0/8	23 2/8	22 4/8	16 2/8	5	5	Cavalier County	ND	James B. Sondeland	1995	2,564
152 0/8	26 6/8	24 3/8	19 6/8	5	5	Will County	IL	Brian Smith	1996	2,564
152 0/8	24 1/8	24 1/8	18 0/8	5	7	Scott County	IA	Patrick C. Lucas	1996	2,564
152 0/8	24 2/8	23 6/8	15 0/8	5	5	Taylor County	WI	Dave Gebert	1996	2,564
152 0/8	24 4/8	23 6/8	17 3/8	6	7	Rocky Rapids	ALB	Harvey Seguin	1997	2,564
152 0/8	24 6/8	24 7/8	20 0/8	5	6	Shawnee County	KS	Eldon Johnson	1997	2,564
152 0/8	25 0/8	25 4/8	15 6/8	5	6	Atchison County	KS	Richard Morgan	1997	2,564
152 0/8	24 5/8	23 0/8	19 0/8	6	5	Jo Daviess County	IL	Jack Rife	1997	2,564
152 0/8	24 4/8	23 1/8	18 3/8	5	6	Chippewa County	WI	Scott Steinmetz	1997	2,564
152 0/8	25 1/8	25 1/8	20 0/8	5	4	Knox County	IL	Roger A. Sheetz	1997	2,564
151 7/8	27 1/8	28 0/8	18 6/8	5	5	Morrison County	MN	Steve Smythe	1968	2,608
151 7/8	24 3/8	24 7/8	18 3/8	5	5	Davis County	IA	George C. Francis	1979	2,608
151 7/8	23 7/8	23 7/8	17 6/8	6	6	Tama County	IA	Kirk Lundberg	1980	2,608
151 7/8	26 1/8	25 6/8	18 0/8	5	7	Brown County	SD	Jan Hinrichs	1981	2,608
151 7/8	24 6/8	24 4/8	19 1/8	5	5	Will County	IL	Ike Rhodes	1984	2,608
151 7/8	24 6/8	25 4/8	18 1/8	6	6	McCook County	SD	James C. Perkins	1984	2,608
151 7/8	24 4/8	23 6/8	15 5/8	5	5	Grant County	WI	William Stetler	1985	2,608
151 7/8	25 1/8	24 5/8	16 7/8	7	6	Waukesha County	WI	Perry Scott Brummer	1986	2,608
151 7/8	24 1/8	22 3/8	17 2/8	6	5	Lewis County	MO	Sam Smith	1986	2,608
151 7/8	26 3/8	26 3/8	24 3/8	4	5	Peoria County	IL	Dick McKown	1986	2,608
151 7/8	23 7/8	23 4/8	19 7/8	5	5	Livingston County	MI	Charles D. Lemay	1987	2,608
151 7/8	21 6/8	21 5/8	17 3/8	6	6	Laurel County	KY	Jerry Hubbard	1987	2,608
151 7/8	25 3/8	24 5/8	17 0/8	5	8	Kingman County	KS	Terry Morisse	1988	2,608
151 7/8	25 4/8	25 5/8	22 7/8	6	5	Whitley County	IN	Frank J. Yaquinto	1990	2,608
151 7/8	22 1/8	22 2/8	16 1/8	5	6	Edmonton	ALB	Rick Bell	1991	2,608
151 7/8	24 0/8	22 4/8	15 3/8	5	5	Rock County	WI	Fred J. Townsend	1992	2,608
151 7/8	25 0/8	25 4/8	19 2/8	7	8	Graham County	KS	Russell Hull	1992	2,608
151 7/8	22 4/8	23 5/8	18 5/8	5	5	Allamakee County	IA	Mark A. Kamm	1993	2,608
151 7/8	23 4/8	23 7/8	19 7/8	5	5	Graves County	KY	Jamie Mason	1993	2,608
151 7/8	24 5/8	24 1/8	16 5/8	5	5	Dunn County	WI	Dan Wolf	1993	2,608
151 7/8	26 0/8	26 0/8	18 7/8	6	5	Morrison County	MN	Ross Engstran	1993	2,608
151 7/8	27 6/8	27 5/8	25 5/8	6	4	Washington County	MS	Frank Greenlee	1994	2,608
151 7/8	24 6/8	23 6/8	20 3/8	5	6	Union County	KY	Jimmy Vaught	1994	2,608
151 7/8	24 2/8	23 0/8	17 3/8	5	5	Strathcona	ALB	Tom Chadwick	1994	2,608
151 7/8	24 7/8	24 6/8	17 0/8	7	6	Douglas County	KS	John Hackathorn	1994	2,608
151 7/8	22 2/8	21 4/8	14 0/8	6	5	Kerr County	TX	Bobbie E. Kimbro	1995	2,608
151 7/8	22 1/8	22 1/8	21 0/8	7	6	Sherburne County	MN	Phil Hinkemeyer	1995	2,608
151 7/8	24 1/8	24 2/8	19 7/8	4	4	Jefferson County	WI	Dennis Messmann	1996	2,608
151 7/8	22 5/8	23 4/8	16 7/8	6	6	Wayne County	NY	Thomas A. Mitchell	1996	2,608
151 7/8	25 4/8	24 2/8	20 7/8	4	4	Issaquena County	MS	Chris Malinowski	1997	2,608
151 7/8	23 7/8	24 0/8	20 3/8	5	5	Meigs County	OH	Phillip R. King	1997	2,608
151 7/8	24 0/8	25 4/8	18 7/8	5	5	Allamakee County	IA	Jeffrey R. Paulus	1997	2,608
151 7/8	24 4/8	24 4/8	17 5/8	5	5	Shawnee County	KS	Frank Brennan	1997	2,608
151 7/8	22 6/8	23 0/8	18 7/8	6	6	Edmonton	ALB	Robert A. Mochilar	1997	2,608
151 7/8	24 1/8	23 0/8	20 4/8	7	6	Dakota County	MN	Todd Grieger	1997	2,608
151 6/8	22 1/8	23 2/8	15 4/8	6	5	Flathead County	MT	Jerry D. Almos	1970	2,643
151 6/8	25 4/8	24 7/8	21 0/8	8	6	Warren County	OH	Lundy Lewis	1981	2,643
151 6/8	25 0/8	24 7/8	17 4/8	5	5	Murray County	MN	Dennis Lunderborg	1982	2,643
151 6/8	25 7/8	22 1/8	20 1/8	5	9	Columbiana County	OH	Bill Lawrence	1983	2,643
151 6/8	23 7/8	24 0/8	21 4/8	4	4	Beaver County	OK	Max Crocker	1984	2,643
151 6/8	27 6/8	26 6/8	19 7/8	5	5	Champaign County	OH	Thomas R. Weaver	1984	2,643
151 6/8	24 2/8	24 0/8	21 5/8	5	6	Madison County	IA	Todd L. Fuson	1986	2,643
151 6/8	27 2/8	26 0/8	21 4/8	4	5	Greenwood County	KS	Jerry Ramshaw	1986	2,643
151 6/8	23 5/8	23 4/8	16 3/8	6	7	Wabasha County	MN	Wayne Techaw, Jr.	1987	2,643
151 6/8	25 4/8	26 6/8	18 2/8	6	5	Ogle County	IL	Jim Hill	1987	2,643

WHITETAIL DEER (TYPICAL ANTLERS)

Minimum Score 125 — Continued

SCORE	LENGTH OF MAIN BEAM R	L	INSIDE SPREAD	NUMBER OF POINTS R	L	AREA	STATE/PROVINCE	HUNTER'S NAME	DATE	RANK
151 6/8	24 1/8	23 4/8	20 4/8	4	4	Bond County	IL	Allen D. Ellsworth	1987	2,643
151 6/8	25 6/8	24 1/8	17 0/8	4	5	Albany County	NY	Bob Boyd	1988	2,643
151 6/8	25 5/8	26 1/8	18 6/8	6	9	Pulaski County	IL	Garrett Wilson	1988	2,643
151 6/8	25 5/8	24 6/8	21 4/8	4	5	Christian County	IL	Lee Penn	1988	2,643
151 6/8	23 3/8	23 6/8	17 0/8	5	5	Greene County	IA	GLen Garnett	1990	2,643
151 6/8	25 4/8	24 3/8	16 1/8	7	5	Ross County	OH	Randy Johnson	1990	2,643
151 6/8	24 7/8	25 0/8	19 6/8	4	4	St. Clair County	MI	Lawrence S. Cowhy	1991	2,643
151 6/8	24 1/8	23 6/8	17 6/8	6	5	Pottawattamie County	IA	Allan T. Carmichael	1992	2,643
151 6/8	25 5/8	23 7/8	19 4/8	5	7	Hocking County	OH	Chris R. Cetone	1992	2,643
151 6/8	24 0/8	23 4/8	18 2/8	5	5	Lancaster County	PA	Douglas D. Shiffler	1992	2,643
151 6/8	23 1/8	22 5/8	16 4/8	5	5	Cherry Lake	BC	Anthony P. Zielinski	1992	2,643
151 6/8	24 1/8	23 7/8	20 4/8	5	5	Shawano County	WI	Todd M. Krause	1992	2,643
151 6/8	24 1/8	22 5/8	19 7/8	6	5	McHenry County	IL	Zach Dagel	1992	2,643
151 6/8	24 2/8	24 0/8	19 5/8	6	5	Washington County	MN	Dave Vadnais	1993	2,643
151 6/8	25 5/8	25 5/8	18 6/8	4	4	Jersey County	IL	David Bailey, Jr.	1994	2,643
151 6/8	23 0/8	23 3/8	21 2/8	5	5	Nowata County	OK	Jeff Fitts	1994	2,643
151 6/8	24 1/8	23 3/8	20 4/8	5	6	Gratiot County	MI	Jeff Watson	1995	2,643
151 6/8	23 7/8	24 1/8	17 4/8	5	6	Keya Paha County	NE	John H. Smith	1995	2,643
151 6/8	22 3/8	22 0/8	20 2/8	5	5	Monroe County	IL	Dan Young	1995	2,643
151 6/8	23 1/8	23 2/8	18 3/8	5	6	Fayette County	IA	Steve Stern	1996	2,643
151 6/8	27 5/8	26 6/8	22 1/8	8	6	Morgan County	IL	Ray Rabon	1996	2,643
151 6/8	23 1/8	25 6/8	16 4/8	6	6	Vigo County	IN	Eric W. Corbin	1997	2,643
151 6/8	25 7/8	26 3/8	18 5/8	6	6	Milwaukee County	WI	Jeremy Meyer	1997	2,643
151 6/8	25 0/8	24 0/8	19 3/8	5	7	Des Moines County	IA	Robin Schneider	1997	2,643
151 5/8	26 2/8	24 7/8	20 6/8	6	6	Franklin County	KS	Kenneth Heinitz	1966	2,677
151 5/8	24 2/8	24 3/8	18 7/8	4	4	Douglas County	WI	Larry Allen Blaylock	1978	2,677
151 5/8	26 0/8	24 3/8	18 3/8	6	6	Reno County	KS	Dan Ropp	1981	2,677
151 5/8	26 6/8	26 1/8	17 3/8	4	4	Carter County	KY	Herbie Jackson	1982	2,677
151 5/8	25 6/8	25 4/8	21 5/8	6	7	Green County	WI	Alex Elkins	1982	2,677
151 5/8	26 6/8	26 5/8	17 5/8	4	4	Jackson County	OH	Jeffrey L. Walters	1984	2,677
151 5/8	24 7/8	25 2/8	20 7/8	5	5	Vermilion County	IL	Bill Fitton	1984	2,677
151 5/8	22 2/8	23 2/8	16 5/8	6	5	Fremont County	IA	Mike Laughlin	1989	2,677
151 5/8	25 7/8	25 3/8	21 7/8	4	4	Ringgold County	IA	Dale L. Clark	1989	2,677
151 5/8	25 1/8	25 3/8	20 3/8	5	5	St. Louis County	MO	Michael T. Horn	1989	2,677
151 5/8	23 4/8	22 2/8	20 1/8	5	5	Jefferson County	ID	Brent D. Barber	1990	2,677
151 5/8	24 5/8	24 4/8	20 4/8	6	6	Hunterdon County	NJ	Jack Baker	1990	2,677
151 5/8	26 0/8	24 2/8	16 0/8	6	5	Lee County	IA	Larry Galliart	1991	2,677
151 5/8	22 6/8	24 4/8	17 4/8	8	5	Wyandotte County	KS	Bruce McComb	1991	2,677
151 5/8	24 0/8	23 2/8	18 1/8	4	4	Fulton County	IL	Tim Wells	1992	2,677
151 5/8	21 4/8	21 6/8	19 7/8	5	7	Pike County	IL	Robert Sacher	1993	2,677
151 5/8	22 3/8	22 4/8	18 1/8	5	5	Millarville	ALB	Leo Comeau	1993	2,677
151 5/8	23 6/8	23 4/8	16 7/8	5	5	Highland County	OH	Paul A. Eldridge	1993	2,677
151 5/8	23 4/8	23 3/8	20 1/8	7	5	Clay County	AR	Stephen E. White	1993	2,677
151 5/8	24 1/8	24 2/8	18 1/8	5	5	Chester County	PA	Robert J. Dupoldt	1994	2,677
151 5/8	24 0/8	27 0/8	18 7/8	5	5	Caledon	ONT	Robert Urquhart	1995	2,677
151 5/8	23 5/8	23 7/8	17 5/8	5	8	Jones County	IA	Tim McDonough	1995	2,677
151 5/8	21 6/8	21 6/8	19 7/8	5	5	La Salle County	IL	Paul Garrison	1996	2,677
151 5/8	22 1/8	22 2/8	19 7/8	5	5	Allamakee County	IA	Steven W. Amann	1996	2,677
151 5/8	26 2/8	27 2/8	17 5/8	5	4	Clinton County	IL	Mike Timmons	1997	2,677
151 5/8	22 0/8	21 3/8	16 6/8	5	6	Morrison County	MN	Ben Brazil	1997	2,677
151 5/8	23 1/8	23 4/8	17 7/8	5	4	Brown County	IL	Erich Elendt	1997	2,677
151 4/8	23 2/8	22 5/8	16 0/8	6	6	Gogebic County	MI	Fred Felbab	1959	2,704
151 4/8	23 2/8	22 7/8	16 2/8	5	5	Murray County	MN	Jim F. Wyffels	1968	2,704
151 4/8	21 1/8	21 7/8	18 6/8	6	5	Brown County	SD	Duane Trost	1973	2,704
151 4/8	24 2/8	24 3/8	19 4/8	5	5	Marshall County	IL	William J. McNutt	1979	2,704
151 4/8	23 6/8	22 5/8	17 3/8	6	5	Pittsburg County	OK	Harry Milican	1983	2,704
151 4/8	26 4/8	26 0/8	20 2/8	4	4	Mason County	IL	David C. Gillespie	1984	2,704
151 4/8	21 3/8	21 5/8	19 0/8	5	6	Lincoln County	MT	Glenn W. Gibson	1985	2,704
151 4/8	22 7/8	22 4/8	17 0/8	5	5	Buffalo County	WI	Gerald Palmer	1985	2,704
151 4/8	24 4/8	24 7/8	23 0/8	5	5	Riley County	KS	L. F. Howerton	1985	2,704
151 4/8	25 1/8	25 1/8	21 2/8	5	4	Pierce County	WI	Dave Clare	1985	2,704
151 4/8	26 3/8	25 0/8	18 2/8	5	5	Polk County	WI	Todd C. Swenson	1986	2,704
151 4/8	22 4/8	21 4/8	18 0/8	6	5	McLeod County	MN	Ed Homan	1986	2,704
151 4/8	21 5/8	23 0/8	17 6/8	8	6	Day County	SD	Sandy Heuer	1987	2,704
151 4/8	24 4/8	25 2/8	17 5/8	4	6	Morrison County	MN	Troy Brown	1988	2,704
151 4/8	26 7/8	27 2/8	19 0/8	4	4	Pierce County	WI	Victor Howe	1988	2,704
151 4/8	24 2/8	23 3/8	17 4/8	5	5	Sumner County	KS	Lynn Reed	1988	2,704
151 4/8	25 6/8	23 5/8	18 0/8	5	5	Fayette County	IA	Jim Smith	1989	2,704
151 4/8	24 7/8	25 0/8	19 6/8	5	5	Lewis County	MO	Blaine Emrick	1990	2,704
151 4/8	23 7/8	23 2/8	16 0/8	5	5	Otero County	CO	Ron Rockwell	1990	2,704
151 4/8	26 1/8	25 1/8	16 4/8	5	5	Tuscarawas County	OH	Karl Paulik	1991	2,704
151 4/8	22 1/8	21 3/8	17 2/8	5	5	Steuben County	IN	Barry Bowers	1991	2,704
151 4/8	25 3/8	25 4/8	15 2/8	5	5	Lake County	IL	Steven Hysell	1992	2,704
151 4/8	23 0/8	25 2/8	20 4/8	7	6	Hamilton County	OH	Ronnie L. Smith	1992	2,704
151 4/8	26 6/8	25 5/8	22 0/8	4	5	Pike County	OH	Jim Borchelt	1993	2,704
151 4/8	24 0/8	24 0/8	17 0/8	6	6	Burnett County	WI	Steven R. Brink	1994	2,704
151 4/8	24 3/8	25 3/8	17 6/8	5	5	Kanawha County	WV	David Roberts	1994	2,704
151 4/8	26 0/8	26 1/8	19 3/8	7	5	Decatur County	IA	Richard D. Panke	1994	2,704

WHITETAIL DEER (TYPICAL ANTLERS)

Minimum Score 125 Continued

SCORE	LENGTH OF MAIN BEAM R	L	INSIDE SPREAD	NUMBER OF POINTS R	L	AREA	STATE/PROVINCE	HUNTER'S NAME	DATE	RANK
151 4/8	26 1/8	24 6/8	15 4/8	9	6	Douglas County	KS	Steven W. Stumbo	1994	2,704
151 4/8	26 5/8	26 1/8	17 0/8	4	5	Benton County	MO	Jim Pennington, Jr.	1995	2,704
151 4/8	25 7/8	25 7/8	19 3/8	6	6	Jefferson County	WI	Aaron Persinger	1995	2,704
151 4/8	23 1/8	25 6/8	17 6/8	6	5	Knox County	IL	Gale Harriman	1995	2,704
151 4/8	24 1/8	23 7/8	17 4/8	5	5	Chester County	PA	Steve Mihalcik	1995	2,704
151 4/8	25 3/8	23 7/8	19 0/8	5	5	Dane County	WI	Robert A. Ebert	1997	2,704
151 4/8	21 6/8	22 5/8	17 2/8	5	6	Morrison County	MN	Bill Bosaaen	1997	2,704
151 3/8	26 3/8	25 4/8	15 6/8	6	7	Martin County	IN	Robert E. Sloan	1968	2,738
151 3/8	23 2/8	23 7/8	19 1/8	5	5	Amherst County	VA	Jerry Armes	1975	2,738
151 3/8	23 4/8	24 0/8	18 3/8	5	6	Morris County	NJ	Phil D'Ottavio	1980	2,738
151 3/8	23 4/8	23 1/8	17 7/8	5	5	Langlade County	WI	Larry Petts	1983	2,738
151 3/8	26 1/8	26 1/8	18 0/8	5	7	Clay County	MN	Randy Swanson	1984	2,738
151 3/8	26 2/8	26 4/8	17 7/8	5	5	Osage County	KS	Gene Beam	1984	2,738
151 3/8	22 3/8	22 4/8	18 5/8	5	5	Trempealeau County	WI	Michael Baer	1984	2,738
151 3/8	25 2/8	25 4/8	17 3/8	6	5	Sauk County	WI	Casey A. Blum	1985	2,738
151 3/8	25 5/8	25 0/8	17 7/8	5	6	Posey County	IN	Donald R. Koester	1986	2,738
151 3/8	22 0/8	22 6/8	15 7/8	7	6	Stearns County	MN	Chuck Thies	1987	2,738
151 3/8	26 3/8	26 3/8	20 3/8	4	4	Roberts County	SD	Myles Keller	1987	2,738
151 3/8	24 1/8	23 5/8	17 3/8	4	4	Eaton County	MI	John A. Lee	1988	2,738
151 3/8	21 4/8	22 5/8	18 7/8	6	5	Logan County	IL	Eldon R. Broster	1989	2,738
151 3/8	23 5/8	23 5/8	17 5/8	5	5	Prince Georges County	MD	Sam Lyon	1989	2,738
151 3/8	25 6/8	24 1/8	17 7/8	5	5	Lake County	IL	Jeffery L. Allard	1989	2,738
151 3/8	22 5/8	22 5/8	17 7/8	5	5	Clayton County	IA	Robert C. Ungs	1990	2,738
151 3/8	25 7/8	24 7/8	20 7/8	6	5	Knox County	OH	Stan Tyson	1990	2,738
151 3/8	23 0/8	23 4/8	19 0/8	7	5	Cook County	IL	Dean Assink	1990	2,738
151 3/8	26 3/8	25 0/8	18 5/8	5	5	Dakota County	MN	Jeff Kamrud	1991	2,738
151 3/8	25 5/8	24 5/8	20 7/8	4	4	McHenry County	IL	Dave Pederson	1992	2,738
151 3/8	24 1/8	23 5/8	17 5/8	5	5	Morrison County	MN	Joe Adrian	1993	2,738
151 3/8	24 6/8	25 7/8	19 2/8	5	6	Chautauqua County	KS	Roy Urban	1993	2,738
151 3/8	26 2/8	26 3/8	18 1/8	4	4	Bayfield County	WI	Larry Fischer	1993	2,738
151 3/8	23 7/8	23 2/8	17 6/8	6	7	Rockland County	NY	Ben Risley	1993	2,738
151 3/8	26 5/8	27 0/8	22 6/8	5	7	Seneca County	OH	Dennis J. Heilman	1993	2,738
151 3/8	24 7/8	24 7/8	19 0/8	5	4	Johnson County	IL	Randall L. Steinmetz, Jr.	1993	2,738
151 3/8	27 0/8	26 6/8	20 1/8	4	4	Southampton County	VA	John B. Mitchell	1994	2,738
151 3/8	25 3/8	26 6/8	21 4/8	7	5	Boone County	IL	Dwight Gunderson	1994	2,738
151 3/8	26 1/8	25 3/8	19 7/8	6	7	Pope County	IL	Dale Cain	1994	2,738
151 3/8	21 2/8	21 0/8	15 1/8	5	6	Hudson Bay	SAS	Ted K. Jaycox	1994	2,738
151 3/8	24 3/8	24 1/8	20 5/8	4	4	Fayette County	IA	Dennis Welsh	1994	2,738
151 3/8	20 6/8	21 6/8	19 3/8	6	6	Du Page County	IL	Paul Tikusis	1995	2,738
151 3/8	23 1/8	24 2/8	15 1/8	6	5	Warren County	KY	Greg Green	1995	2,738
151 3/8	24 0/8	24 0/8	18 0/8	7	7	Lincoln County	KY	Randy Yocum	1995	2,738
151 3/8	25 2/8	25 6/8	20 3/8	5	4	Peoria County	IL	Paul Clay	1995	2,738
151 3/8	25 3/8	24 0/8	18 3/8	4	5	Winona County	MN	Dustin N. Luedtke	1996	2,738
151 3/8	23 6/8	23 4/8	18 0/8	7	6	Davis County	IA	Ben Cox	1996	2,738
151 3/8	22 6/8	23 0/8	19 1/8	5	5	Trumbull County	OH	Jerry McConahy	1996	2,738
151 3/8	23 0/8	23 1/8	19 7/8	5	5	Somerset County	ME	Mark T. Thomas	1997	2,738
151 3/8	25 6/8	26 2/8	18 4/8	6	6	Floyd County	IA	Darwin B. Goddard	1997	2,738
151 3/8	25 5/8	26 0/8	17 6/8	6	6	Monroe County	IA	Larry Zach	1997	2,738
151 3/8	26 3/8	25 1/8	20 3/8	4	4	Steuben County	IN	Rick A. Roemke	1998	2,738
151 2/8	25 5/8	25 6/8	17 2/8	4	4	Fillmore County	MN	David Carson	1967	2,780
151 2/8	24 1/8	23 4/8	14 1/8	7	5	Blue Earth County	MN	Rory Duetchman	1974	2,780
151 2/8	22 1/8	22 4/8	18 2/8	6	6	Clark County	SD	Dean L. Myers	1975	2,780
151 2/8	25 0/8	24 4/8	18 0/8	5	5	La Salle County	IL	John Sullivan	1977	2,780
151 2/8	25 3/8	24 6/8	18 6/8	4	5	Litchfield County	CT	Donald R. Groody	1982	2,780
151 2/8	23 4/8	24 4/8	17 6/8	7	6	Warrick County	IN	Thomas Scheucher	1982	2,780
151 2/8	26 2/8	25 3/8	18 0/8	5	5	Cowley County	KS	Michael L. Snyder	1984	2,780
151 2/8	22 4/8	22 3/8	13 7/8	6	5	Livingston County	IL	Tom Roe	1987	2,780
151 2/8	24 7/8	21 4/8	16 4/8	5	5	Benton County	IA	Jeff L. Jacobi	1987	2,780
151 2/8	24 1/8	23 5/8	17 0/8	5	6	Clarke County	GA	Terry Pahl	1988	2,780
151 2/8	23 4/8	22 5/8	20 1/8	7	5	Washburn County	WI	John Galvin	1988	2,780
151 2/8	22 6/8	23 7/8	20 2/8	5	5	Iroquois County	IL	Eric Edwards	1988	2,780
151 2/8	24 5/8	24 3/8	20 5/8	5	4	Fulton County	GA	John Brooks	1989	2,780
151 2/8	24 4/8	25 4/8	19 0/8	5	8	Fulton County	IL	Don DeRenzy	1990	2,780
151 2/8	26 1/8	26 0/8	15 0/8	5	6	Franklin County	VA	S. Gregory Venning	1990	2,780
151 2/8	24 5/8	25 1/8	17 6/8	5	5	Will County	IL	Ty Orgas	1990	2,780
151 2/8	25 0/8	25 2/8	15 6/8	5	5	Burlington County	NJ	Elliston M. Jacobs	1991	2,780
151 2/8	22 3/8	24 2/8	18 4/8	8	6	Tazewell County	IL	Ronald J. Ghighi	1992	2,780
151 2/8	20 0/8	21 1/8	18 6/8	5	5	McHenry County	IL	Michael F. Riske	1992	2,780
151 2/8	25 3/8	24 7/8	18 2/8	4	4	Coles County	IL	Alan Batson	1992	2,780
151 2/8	24 6/8	23 1/8	21 6/8	5	5	Waukesha County	WI	James Sackett	1993	2,780
151 2/8	22 7/8	24 4/8	19 2/8	5	6	Warren County	IA	Philip Martin	1993	2,780
151 2/8	21 4/8	20 4/8	15 0/8	6	6	Shoshone County	ID	Dana D. Atwood, Jr.	1993	2,780
151 2/8	22 2/8	22 0/8	14 0/8	5	5	Wayne County	MI	John K. Anderson	1994	2,780
151 2/8	25 7/8	24 7/8	18 1/8	7	6	Polk County	WI	Larry E. Carlson	1995	2,780
151 2/8	23 7/8	24 5/8	21 2/8	4	5	Lee County	IL	John Friel	1995	2,780
151 2/8	23 3/8	22 6/8	19 4/8	5	6	McLean County	IL	Kelly Spence	1995	2,780
151 2/8	23 3/8	23 2/8	18 7/8	5	6	Washburn County	WI	Tim Clare	1996	2,780
151 2/8	27 3/8	27 6/8	17 4/8	5	5	Portage County	WI	Alan R. Ruechel	1997	2,780

WHITETAIL DEER (TYPICAL ANTLERS)

Minimum Score 125   Continued

SCORE	LENGTH OF MAIN BEAM R L		INSIDE SPREAD	NUMBER OF POINTS R L		AREA	STATE/PROVINCE	HUNTER'S NAME	DATE	RANK
151 2/8	23 7/8	23 4/8	16 6/8	7	6	Pittsburg County	OK	Joe G. Arms	1997	2,780
151 2/8	24 0/8	25 0/8	16 0/8	6	5	Plymouth County	IA	Todd M. Laughton	1997	2,780
151 1/8	27 4/8	24 7/8	16 2/8	6	5	Adams County	IL	John C. Robinson	1967	2,811
151 1/8	22 3/8	23 4/8	18 4/8	7	5	Adair County	MO	Dr. Eddy Transano	1971	2,811
151 1/8	25 6/8	24 4/8	19 3/8	5	5	Lucas County	OH	Gail A. Rice	1978	2,811
151 1/8	22 6/8	22 6/8	17 4/8	7	6	Wood County	WI	Scott Arneson	1979	2,811
151 1/8	23 4/8	21 4/8	18 3/8	5	5	Minnehaha County	SD	Bradley D. Swier	1982	2,811
151 1/8	23 1/8	23 2/8	17 1/8	5	5	Barren County	KY	Steve England	1983	2,811
151 1/8	25 2/8	24 0/8	20 7/8	4	5	Franklin County	KS	Don Hrabe	1985	2,811
151 1/8	24 2/8	26 5/8	17 3/8	5	5	Bond County	IL	Gary Netzler	1987	2,811
151 1/8	24 5/8	23 4/8	17 7/8	5	5	Grant County	WI	Joe Devlin	1987	2,811
151 1/8	22 0/8	23 2/8	16 3/8	5	5	Jefferson County	MO	Steve North	1988	2,811
151 1/8	23 3/8	23 6/8	19 5/8	5	6	Okotoks	ALB	Dave Richardson	1989	2,811
151 1/8	25 1/8	24 7/8	19 1/8	5	5	Hamilton County	OH	Keith Casey	1989	2,811
151 1/8	22 2/8	21 0/8	17 1/8	5	5	Saline County	KS	James R. Weldy	1990	2,811
151 1/8	23 1/8	23 5/8	17 5/8	7	9	De Kalb County	MO	Jim W. Martin	1990	2,811
151 1/8	24 0/8	23 7/8	18 6/8	7	6	Stearns County	MN	Paul M. Froseth	1991	2,811
151 1/8	23 3/8	23 1/8	17 7/8	6	7	Duval County	TX	Dean Oatman	1992	2,811
151 1/8	25 6/8	26 0/8	18 0/8	6	4	Jackson County	IA	Dick Barker	1992	2,811
151 1/8	22 6/8	23 2/8	14 1/8	5	5	Coles County	IL	Mark Cooper	1992	2,811
151 1/8	22 5/8	22 5/8	17 7/8	6	5	Allamakee County	IA	Thomas J. Brimeyer	1992	2,811
151 1/8	26 4/8	25 4/8	20 1/8	4	4	Mason County	IL	Gregory B. Snider	1992	2,811
151 1/8	23 3/8	23 7/8	17 7/8	6	6	Kenedy County	TX	James Hill	1992	2,811
151 1/8	27 4/8	27 4/8	18 4/8	5	4	Prairie County	AR	Ed Smith	1992	2,811
151 1/8	25 2/8	24 2/8	15 5/8	6	5	Dane County	WI	Trevor J. Neuman	1993	2,811
151 1/8	22 7/8	23 3/8	22 5/8	4	5	Johnson County	IA	Thomas Jensen	1994	2,811
151 1/8	23 6/8	23 6/8	16 5/8	5	5	Monroe County	IA	Ed McDaniel	1994	2,811
151 1/8	23 0/8	23 0/8	16 7/8	5	5	Breckinridge County	KY	James Bowles	1994	2,811
151 1/8	25 1/8	25 1/8	16 7/8	7	6	Hamilton County	OH	Randall E. Sanders	1994	2,811
151 1/8	22 2/8	22 2/8	17 7/8	5	5	Winnebago County	IL	John Duggan	1995	2,811
151 1/8	21 6/8	20 7/8	18 7/8	5	6	Marshall County	KS	Robert Thompson	1996	2,811
151 1/8	24 4/8	24 2/8	15 5/8	4	4	Hampden County	MA	Stanley Marko	1996	2,811
151 1/8	25 5/8	24 6/8	18 5/8	4	5	Wyoming County	WV	Brian Janutolo	1997	2,811
151 1/8	24 0/8	23 1/8	19 0/8	6	6	Moultrie County	IL	Bret Guin	1997	2,811
151 1/8	23 4/8	23 7/8	16 7/8	5	5	Buchanan County	IA	Scott Smith	1997	2,811
151 1/8	23 2/8	22 7/8	18 1/8	5	5	Webster County	MO	Scott Stevens	1997	2,811
151 1/8	23 2/8	23 3/8	17 5/8	6	5	Vilas County	WI	Jay Kidd	1998	2,811
151 0/8	25 0/8	26 0/8	16 6/8	5	5	Warrick County	IN	Gerald G. Taylor	1970	2,846
151 0/8	23 6/8	24 5/8	19 6/8	5	5	Polk County	WI	Bryan Anderson	1976	2,846
151 0/8	30 1/8	29 0/8	20 2/8	7	5	Gray County	KS	Paul Meininger	1980	2,846
151 0/8	23 2/8	23 5/8	21 2/8	5	5	Grant County	WI	Doug J. Leibfried	1981	2,846
151 0/8	25 3/8	24 0/8	17 4/8	5	5	Columbia County	WI	Jeffrey M. Ballweg	1984	2,846
151 0/8	23 7/8	23 3/8	20 0/8	5	5	White County	IL	Eric D. Devore	1985	2,846
151 0/8	26 5/8	27 1/8	20 4/8	4	4	Appanoose County	IA	Steven P. Widmar	1986	2,846
151 0/8	26 7/8	24 5/8	18 0/8	5	4	Marshall County	IL	Bryan Blair	1987	2,846
151 0/8	24 4/8	24 6/8	18 2/8	5	5	Jefferson County	WI	Gary Goldbeck	1987	2,846
151 0/8	27 2/8	25 2/8	18 6/8	5	6	Northampton County	VA	Stanley I. Long	1988	2,846
151 0/8	26 0/8	25 4/8	19 0/8	6	6	Woodford County	IL	Stan Bocian	1988	2,846
151 0/8	25 6/8	23 6/8	21 2/8	5	5	Davis County	IA	Clayton Eakins	1990	2,846
151 0/8	23 3/8	24 4/8	19 6/8	5	5	Kosciusko County	IN	Ronald D. Newcomer	1990	2,846
151 0/8	24 5/8	25 0/8	18 4/8	6	6	Fayette County	IL	Kelly Tarter	1990	2,846
151 0/8	23 6/8	22 4/8	18 4/8	7	7	Pope County	MN	David Strickler	1991	2,846
151 0/8	24 6/8	23 3/8	24 6/8	6	5	Kenedy County	TX	Carl Walker	1991	2,846
151 0/8	24 7/8	25 5/8	17 6/8	6	6	Jasper County	IL	David Staley	1991	2,846
151 0/8	23 7/8	24 1/8	20 1/8	6	6	Price County	WI	Myron Sales	1993	2,846
151 0/8	24 1/8	23 6/8	19 4/8	7	5	Clark County	OH	David L. Stull	1993	2,846
151 0/8	24 3/8	24 2/8	17 0/8	4	6	Morgan County	IL	Kevin Mitchell	1993	2,846
151 0/8	24 1/8	25 0/8	18 0/8	5	5	Fond du Lac County	WI	Brian Grade	1994	2,846
151 0/8	24 1/8	22 7/8	19 4/8	5	5	Milwaukee County	WI	Joseph Banach	1995	2,846
151 0/8	24 1/8	24 6/8	17 0/8	5	5	Morgan County	OH	Richard Newsom	1995	2,846
151 0/8	21 4/8	22 2/8	18 2/8	6	6	Iowa County	IA	Karey Garringer	1995	2,846
151 0/8	26 2/8	26 3/8	19 6/8	5	6	Decatur County	IA	Corey A. Christopherson	1995	2,846
151 0/8	24 7/8	23 0/8	16 6/8	5	5	Morgan County	MO	Bob Sutton	1996	2,846
151 0/8	25 2/8	26 7/8	20 7/8	6	6	Suffolk County	NY	John Bennett	1996	2,846
151 0/8	25 0/8	25 4/8	18 2/8	6	6	Laurel County	KY	Mark Fields	1997	2,846
151 0/8	23 7/8	22 1/8	16 4/8	5	5	Dawson County	MT	Ray E. Peters	1997	2,846
151 0/8	26 6/8	27 4/8	21 4/8	4	4	McHenry County	IL	Donald R. Hanrahan	1997	2,846
151 0/8	21 5/8	22 0/8	16 4/8	5	5	Pike County	IL	Stan Chamberlain	1997	2,846
151 0/8	24 3/8	24 2/8	16 6/8	4	4	Edmonton	ALB	John Young	1997	2,846
151 0/8	25 4/8	25 6/8	20 0/8	4	5	Morrison County	MN	Daniel Kremers	1998	2,846
150 7/8	23 2/8	22 2/8	18 1/8	5	5	Trempealeau County	WI	Phillip Lunde	1969	2,879
150 7/8	22 6/8	22 5/8	20 1/8	5	5	Harlan County	NE	Edwin Witte	1973	2,879
150 7/8	24 3/8	22 5/8	17 5/8	7	6	Lancaster County	PA	J. John Buhay	1980	2,879
150 7/8	26 0/8	26 0/8	21 1/8	5	5	Kent County	MI	Robert Ten Eyck	1980	2,879
150 7/8	22 5/8	23 1/8	18 3/8	6	6	Cumberland County	ME	David C. Smart	1984	2,879
150 7/8	23 2/8	22 7/8	17 6/8	6	6	Washington County	IA	David Greenlee	1986	2,879
150 7/8	23 0/8	22 2/8	20 5/8	6	6	Becker County	MN	Arnold F. Ostgarden	1987	2,879
150 7/8	24 0/8	23 6/8	20 3/8	6	7	Butler County	KS	Rodney Koehn	1987	2,879

WHITETAIL DEER (TYPICAL ANTLERS)

Minimum Score 125 — Continued

SCORE	LENGTH OF MAIN BEAM R	LENGTH OF MAIN BEAM L	INSIDE SPREAD	NUMBER OF POINTS R	NUMBER OF POINTS L	AREA	STATE/PROVINCE	HUNTER'S NAME	DATE	RANK
150 7/8	24 4/8	23 2/8	20 5/8	5	5	Hopkins County	KY	Albert Hargis	1987	2,879
150 7/8	27 5/8	27 3/8	18 0/8	6	6	Menard County	IL	Darrell Holliday	1987	2,879
150 7/8	23 6/8	24 3/8	17 5/8	7	6	De Kalb County	IN	Eric L. Ditmars	1988	2,879
150 7/8	26 1/8	24 7/8	21 3/8	4	4	Black Hawk County	IA	Craig Cornelius	1989	2,879
150 7/8	28 6/8	27 4/8	19 4/8	5	6	Lawrence County	IL	Roger D. Wallace	1989	2,879
150 7/8	22 0/8	22 0/8	18 3/8	6	5	Brown County	IL	Lowell Leslie, Jr.	1991	2,879
150 7/8	24 5/8	24 2/8	17 5/8	5	5	Dickinson County	KS	George M. Havice	1991	2,879
150 7/8	24 4/8	23 6/8	17 0/8	5	6	Butler County	OH	Michael L. Gibbs	1992	2,879
150 7/8	26 1/8	27 2/8	21 6/8	5	6	Iron County	WI	Roger "Bucky" Adamovich	1992	2,879
150 7/8	24 2/8	23 3/8	17 3/8	5	5	Ellis County	KS	Stan Honas	1993	2,879
150 7/8	24 7/8	24 7/8	16 0/8	7	6	Clark County	WI	Darin E. Degenhardt	1993	2,879
150 7/8	25 1/8	24 6/8	18 6/8	5	5	Branch County	MI	Arthur L. Shirey, Sr.	1994	2,879
150 7/8	22 4/8	22 3/8	16 3/8	7	7	Letellier	MAN	Todd Amenrud	1994	2,879
150 7/8	23 6/8	24 6/8	18 3/8	5	6	Okanogan County	WA	Kevin P. Skirko	1994	2,879
150 7/8	26 4/8	26 5/8	17 7/8	7	7	Iron County	WI	Dave Matis	1995	2,879
150 7/8	23 3/8	23 3/8	15 4/8	7	5	Putnam County	MO	P. Mike O'Reilly	1995	2,879
150 7/8	22 6/8	23 4/8	19 1/8	5	6	Pike County	IL	Jay Verzuh	1995	2,879
150 7/8	25 7/8	26 0/8	19 5/8	6	5	Webster County	IA	Darle Myers	1995	2,879
150 7/8	24 6/8	24 7/8	19 7/8	5	5	Mitchell County	IA	Jerry Lee Mead	1996	2,879
150 7/8	24 1/8	23 5/8	16 1/8	6	6	Putnam County	IL	Gene Koehler	1996	2,879
150 6/8	22 3/8	22 0/8	16 4/8	5	5	Redwood County	MN	Irvin Plotz	1975	2,907
150 6/8	22 2/8	21 7/8	19 0/8	5	6	Allegan County	MI	Lane Humphreys	1979	2,907
150 6/8	24 4/8	23 7/8	18 6/8	6	6	Columbia County	WI	Jerry Ulrich	1980	2,907
150 6/8	25 2/8	24 6/8	19 6/8	5	6	Jo Daviess County	IL	Michael Muehleip	1981	2,907
150 6/8	25 3/8	25 3/8	20 1/8	4	6	Winnebago County	IL	Fred L. Smith	1985	2,907
150 6/8	24 6/8	24 6/8	16 4/8	5	5	Wayne County	IL	Ginger Harvey	1986	2,907
150 6/8	22 5/8	23 3/8	19 2/8	6	5	Floyd County	IA	Mark Koenigsfeld	1986	2,907
150 6/8	24 6/8	24 5/8	27 1/8	5	5	Greenwood County	KS	Ray Penner	1986	2,907
150 6/8	21 2/8	21 4/8	21 6/8	5	5	Clearwater County	ID	Gordon Fout	1987	2,907
150 6/8	24 6/8	25 1/8	21 4/8	4	4	Boone County	IA	Dave Rimathe	1988	2,907
150 6/8	22 6/8	21 6/8	15 6/8	5	5	Hocking County	OH	James Earl Roberts, Jr.	1988	2,907
150 6/8	25 4/8	25 1/8	17 2/8	4	4	Suffolk County	NY	Ed Viola	1988	2,907
150 6/8	21 5/8	21 7/8	17 0/8	6	5	Prince William County	VA	Jeff Redding	1990	2,907
150 6/8	25 3/8	24 0/8	18 7/8	5	6	Webster County	IA	Darrell Promes	1990	2,907
150 6/8	24 1/8	24 0/8	16 6/8	4	4	Linn County	IA	David Hotz	1990	2,907
150 6/8	24 3/8	23 0/8	19 2/8	5	6	Wapello County	IA	Joseph Mayhew	1991	2,907
150 6/8	24 0/8	24 4/8	20 2/8	5	5	Price County	WI	Michael J. Lobner	1991	2,907
150 6/8	24 5/8	24 7/8	18 6/8	6	6	Shawano County	WI	David M. Zachow	1993	2,907
150 6/8	23 1/8	23 0/8	21 2/8	5	5	Henry County	VA	Mike Weaver	1993	2,907
150 6/8	22 6/8	23 7/8	19 0/8	5	5	Knox County	IL	Robert J. Hinckley	1993	2,907
150 6/8	24 4/8	24 0/8	19 2/8	4	6	Sheboygan County	WI	Dennis P. Walter	1994	2,907
150 6/8	25 2/8	25 5/8	18 6/8	4	4	Kendall County	IL	David Musser	1994	2,907
150 6/8	27 2/8	27 5/8	20 2/8	5	7	Will County	IL	Rick Buchmeier	1994	2,907
150 6/8	23 4/8	23 6/8	19 2/8	5	5	Sauk County	WI	Chad Price	1996	2,907
150 6/8	21 7/8	21 4/8	18 0/8	5	5	Dane County	WI	Dean E. Goecks	1996	2,907
150 6/8	24 7/8	23 2/8	19 0/8	5	5	Jackson County	IL	Ron Braun	1996	2,907
150 6/8	24 5/8	24 0/8	19 0/8	5	5	Buffalo County	WI	Gerald Palmer	1997	2,907
150 6/8	23 7/8	25 2/8	18 0/8	5	5	Union County	IL	Mark Landewee	1997	2,907
150 5/8	21 0/8	22 7/8	19 3/8	6	5	Madison County	NE	Darwin Heppner	1967	2,935
150 5/8	22 7/8	22 6/8	22 1/8	5	6	Eaton County	MI	Greg Hoefler	1982	2,935
150 5/8	22 7/8	22 5/8	18 5/8	5	5	Ashland County	OH	Lyle Bennett	1984	2,935
150 5/8	24 4/8	23 4/8	18 1/8	7	5	Pratt County	KS	Scott Haworth	1984	2,935
150 5/8	22 3/8	22 3/8	17 3/8	5	5	Chippewa County	WI	Tim Walters	1985	2,935
150 5/8	25 6/8	24 5/8	21 7/8	5	5	Randolph County	IL	Loren Eggemeyer	1987	2,935
150 5/8	27 3/8	27 5/8	21 1/8	5	5	Adams County	IL	James A. Stupavsky	1988	2,935
150 5/8	26 2/8	26 1/8	18 5/8	5	5	Randolph County	AR	Joey White	1990	2,935
150 5/8	25 0/8	23 4/8	18 1/8	7	6	Randolph County	IL	Gary Vanpelt	1991	2,935
150 5/8	24 5/8	23 6/8	18 5/8	5	5	Comanche County	KS	Randy Eddy	1992	2,935
150 5/8	23 3/8	22 5/8	18 3/8	5	5	Elnora	ALB	Barry Mitchell	1993	2,935
150 5/8	24 6/8	24 0/8	20 5/8	5	6	Manitoulin Island	ONT	Greg Clark	1993	2,935
150 5/8	20 0/8	22 3/8	18 3/8	7	6	Montgomery County	IA	Buzz Dicks	1993	2,935
150 5/8	24 0/8	24 0/8	18 2/8	6	7	Livingston County	NY	Alan Tubbs	1994	2,935
150 5/8	22 7/8	21 6/8	14 6/8	7	6	Anoka County	MN	Larry Cooke	1996	2,935
150 5/8	23 7/8	24 4/8	17 3/8	6	6	Kleberg County	TX	Mike Lemker	1996	2,935
150 5/8	23 4/8	24 0/8	18 7/8	5	5	Stony Plain	ALB	David Paplawski	1997	2,935
150 5/8	24 3/8	25 4/8	19 1/8	4	4	Shelby County	KY	James L. Jamison	1998	2,935
150 4/8	24 4/8	24 4/8	18 6/8	5	4	Scott County	IA	Howard A. Goettsch	1974	2,953
150 4/8	22 5/8	22 3/8	14 7/8	6	7	Wabasha County	MN	Lee Partington	1975	2,953
150 4/8	21 4/8	21 6/8	15 6/8	6	6	Dunn County	WI	Mary Nussberger	1976	2,953
150 4/8	24 7/8	24 7/8	17 6/8	5	5	Guernsey County	OH	Miltos Stefanitais	1979	2,953
150 4/8	23 6/8	23 4/8	19 0/8	5	5	Schuyler County	NY	Donald L. Lane	1980	2,953
150 4/8	22 1/8	22 0/8	20 4/8	5	5	Woodford County	IL	Roger Miller	1980	2,953
150 4/8	24 2/8	25 1/8	19 4/8	4	4	Monroe County	WI	Dirk Gillette	1981	2,953
150 4/8	26 3/8	25 0/8	18 4/8	5	4	Miami County	OH	Richard G. Williamson	1981	2,953
150 4/8	24 7/8	27 2/8	28 1/8	5	4	Greenwood County	KS	Ray Penner	1984	2,953
150 4/8	23 6/8	22 3/8	16 0/8	4	4	Osage County	KS	Bill Senne	1985	2,953
150 4/8	26 2/8	26 2/8	18 2/8	4	4	Pepin County	WI	Myles Keller	1985	2,953
150 4/8	23 4/8	23 2/8	17 1/8	5	7	Florence County	WI	Carolyn Lemanski	1986	2,953

329

WHITETAIL DEER (TYPICAL ANTLERS)

Minimum Score 125 — Continued

SCORE	LENGTH OF MAIN BEAM R	LENGTH OF MAIN BEAM L	INSIDE SPREAD	NUMBER OF POINTS R	NUMBER OF POINTS L	AREA	STATE/ PROVINCE	HUNTER'S NAME	DATE	RANK
150 4/8	26 0/8	26 1/8	20 3/8	7	6	Knox County	MO	Roger Gipple	1986	2,953
150 4/8	24 4/8	25 6/8	19 2/8	5	5	La Salle County	IL	James Pierson	1989	2,953
150 4/8	23 5/8	24 6/8	18 0/8	5	5	Gregory County	SD	Dan Swiler	1990	2,953
150 4/8	24 6/8	24 7/8	17 4/8	5	5	Stoddard County	MO	Ken Heuer	1990	2,953
150 4/8	23 1/8	22 5/8	17 2/8	5	5	Ravalli County	MT	Mark Moreland	1991	2,953
150 4/8	22 7/8	23 1/8	17 0/8	5	5	Jackson County	WI	Scott R. Hanson	1991	2,953
150 4/8	25 0/8	24 4/8	19 6/8	5	4	Prowers County	CO	Neal Heaton	1991	2,953
150 4/8	23 6/8	22 4/8	18 1/8	6	6	Comanche County	KS	Randall Eddy	1991	2,953
150 4/8	21 6/8	22 0/8	17 6/8	5	5	Saginaw County	MI	Jerry D. Pratt	1991	2,953
150 4/8	24 1/8	25 2/8	18 6/8	5	4	Claiborne County	MS	Tripp Stennett	1992	2,953
150 4/8	27 4/8	18 5/8	18 6/8	7	7	Randolph County	IN	Ted Mooneyhan	1992	2,953
150 4/8	21 3/8	21 6/8	16 0/8	5	5	Clarke County	IA	William L. Tuttle	1992	2,953
150 4/8	22 7/8	22 6/8	20 4/8	5	5	Anoka County	MN	Paul Landberg	1993	2,953
150 4/8	23 0/8	24 2/8	18 0/8	5	5	Montgomery County	MD	Dewayne A. Leslie	1993	2,953
150 4/8	23 3/8	23 3/8	18 2/8	7	7	McDonough County	IL	Dane Metcalf	1993	2,953
150 4/8	24 5/8	26 2/8	15 5/8	7	6	Todd County	KY	Thomas Allen Haley	1994	2,953
150 4/8	22 4/8	22 0/8	20 2/8	5	5	Champaign County	IL	James Smith	1994	2,953
150 4/8	23 4/8	22 7/8	19 4/8	6	7	Jasper County	IA	Randy Taylor	1994	2,953
150 4/8	23 2/8	23 4/8	17 0/8	5	5	Hunterdon County	NJ	Charles Reinhart	1994	2,953
150 4/8	22 6/8	22 4/8	18 6/8	5	5	Lake County	IL	Brent A. Nelson	1995	2,953
150 4/8	25 7/8	22 5/8	18 1/8	5	6	Peoria County	IL	Denny Masching	1995	2,953
150 4/8	23 2/8	23 4/8	17 4/8	5	5	Bourbon County	KS	Chad Holt	1995	2,953
150 4/8	25 2/8	26 5/8	16 4/8	5	4	Washington County	KS	Doug Kruse	1996	2,953
150 4/8	24 6/8	25 0/8	17 4/8	7	7	Montgomery County	IL	Kevin Seely	1996	2,953
150 4/8	25 0/8	26 2/8	20 7/8	5	6	Webster County	WV	Jeff Bowman	1996	2,953
150 4/8	21 7/8	22 0/8	18 0/8	7	5	McDonald County	MO	Brian K. Sharp	1997	2,953
150 4/8	23 2/8	23 2/8	15 2/8	5	5	Chautauqua County	KS	Daniel L. Hubert	1997	2,953
150 4/8	24 4/8	25 1/8	21 6/8	5	5	Winneshiek County	IA	Shawn Bartz	1997	2,953
150 4/8	23 7/8	24 4/8	17 3/8	6	5	Highland County	OH	Jason Sowders	1997	2,953
150 3/8	24 5/8	24 5/8	22 5/8	4	4	Oneida County	WI	Philip Hildebrand	1967	2,994
150 3/8	28 0/8	27 4/8	20 5/8	4	5	Jones County	GA	Sid Hester	1969	2,994
150 3/8	20 4/8	21 2/8	16 7/8	5	5	Langlade County	WI	Herbert Buettner	1970	2,994
150 3/8	23 3/8	23 5/8	18 3/8	6	7	Graham County	KS	Russell Hull	1977	2,994
150 3/8	24 0/8	23 4/8	15 4/8	5	6	Juneau County	WI	Anthony Wulin	1977	2,994
150 3/8	22 2/8	22 3/8	15 3/8	5	5	Souris River	MAN	Garry William Kaluzniak	1980	2,994
150 3/8	26 0/8	24 4/8	16 4/8	9	8	Oakland County	MI	Donald J. Fisher	1981	2,994
150 3/8	25 1/8	25 0/8	17 2/8	5	5	Jackson County	MO	Marvin Thomey	1983	2,994
150 3/8	23 1/8	22 3/8	16 4/8	5	6	Dakota County	MN	Dave Vomela	1985	2,994
150 3/8	23 1/8	23 5/8	19 5/8	7	7	Yuma County	CO	Richard King	1985	2,994
150 3/8	24 0/8	24 2/8	16 4/8	6	6	Benton County	IA	Okee Walker	1986	2,994
150 3/8	26 1/8	26 1/8	16 6/8	7	5	Jackson County	OH	Robert E. Thomas, Jr.	1987	2,994
150 3/8	24 2/8	23 2/8	18 5/8	4	5	Clark County	IL	Max M. LeCrone	1988	2,994
150 3/8	24 0/8	25 2/8	15 4/8	5	7	Clark County	OH	Rick Rounds	1988	2,994
150 3/8	23 4/8	24 0/8	16 7/8	5	7	Branch County	MI	James E. Marvin	1990	2,994
150 3/8	23 0/8	22 5/8	20 1/8	5	5	Mason County	IL	Jeff Heilman	1990	2,994
150 3/8	24 0/8	24 4/8	20 7/8	5	5	Suffolk County	NY	Bruce R. Dickerson	1990	2,994
150 3/8	25 3/8	25 6/8	19 1/8	5	5	Greene County	OH	Rodney Curtis Bailey	1990	2,994
150 3/8	23 6/8	25 3/8	17 5/8	4	4	Vinton County	OH	Burl Keesee	1991	2,994
150 3/8	24 3/8	24 3/8	17 5/8	5	5	Throckmorton County	TX	Darrel Bewley	1992	2,994
150 3/8	23 2/8	23 4/8	19 7/8	5	5	Stearns County	MN	Brent Helgeson	1992	2,994
150 3/8	24 7/8	24 6/8	21 1/8	5	4	Roberts County	SD	Myles Keller	1992	2,994
150 3/8	23 0/8	24 0/8	17 3/8	5	5	Washington County	IA	James Cluney	1994	2,994
150 3/8	27 1/8	26 1/8	17 1/8	5	5	Cheshire County	NH	Bud Croteau	1994	2,994
150 3/8	23 4/8	22 4/8	15 7/8	6	6	Callaway County	MO	Gene Cogorno	1994	2,994
150 3/8	24 4/8	25 0/8	19 5/8	5	5	La Salle County	IL	Eduardo Rojas	1994	2,994
150 3/8	20 4/8	21 3/8	16 3/8	7	6	Douglas County	KS	Mark Young	1996	2,994
150 3/8	24 3/8	25 1/8	19 7/8	5	5	Green County	WI	Jamie Grinder	1997	2,994
150 2/8	23 5/8	23 3/8	17 2/8	6	6	Jackson County	WI	Roger Reinart	1972	3,022
150 2/8	26 0/8	24 2/8	19 0/8	4	5	Spink County	SD	Gerald A. Kettering	1978	3,022
150 2/8	23 3/8	23 5/8	14 0/8	5	5	Cottonwood County	MN	Leonard P. Thiner	1978	3,022
150 2/8	25 2/8	27 1/8	19 4/8	4	4	Fulton County	IL	William L. Beaird	1984	3,022
150 2/8	23 3/8	22 7/8	17 2/8	5	5	Marathon County	WI	Kevin Denzine	1985	3,022
150 2/8	25 1/8	25 2/8	16 7/8	7	5	Dodge County	WI	Fran Hallmeyer	1986	3,022
150 2/8	23 1/8	24 0/8	16 2/8	5	5	Price County	WI	Ben Grapa	1987	3,022
150 2/8	24 4/8	24 5/8	18 4/8	5	5	Wyoming	ONT	Pierre Parent	1987	3,022
150 2/8	24 4/8	25 3/8	17 1/8	7	5	Lawrence County	IL	James R. Griggs	1987	3,022
150 2/8	25 5/8	26 6/8	23 2/8	6	6	Meigs County	OH	Earl M. Johnson	1987	3,022
150 2/8	23 1/8	24 4/8	15 2/8	5	6	Crowley County	CO	Chuck Anderson, Sr.	1987	3,022
150 2/8	26 3/8	26 6/8	19 4/8	5	5	Howard County	MD	David Wilson	1988	3,022
150 2/8	24 0/8	23 7/8	20 3/8	4	7	Webster County	IA	Scott L. Powers	1988	3,022
150 2/8	22 4/8	23 1/8	18 1/8	6	7	Butler County	KS	Jack Evans	1988	3,022
150 2/8	25 3/8	24 1/8	19 2/8	4	4	Webster County	IA	Curtis Martens	1988	3,022
150 2/8	23 6/8	24 2/8	16 6/8	5	5	Cass County	MI	Donald Zehrung	1988	3,022
150 2/8	24 6/8	24 6/8	19 3/8	6	6	Lawrence County	OH	Scott Johnson	1989	3,022
150 2/8	24 1/8	24 0/8	17 1/8	6	8	Douglas County	WI	Steve Wittke	1990	3,022
150 2/8	21 4/8	21 5/8	15 2/8	5	5	Bremer County	IA	Rod Heidemann	1990	3,022
150 2/8	28 4/8	27 4/8	24 2/8	6	4	Napanee	ONT	Tim McCabe	1990	3,022
150 2/8	23 2/8	22 2/8	24 0/8	5	7	Kleberg County	TX	Wayne Peeples	1991	3,022

WHITETAIL DEER (TYPICAL ANTLERS)

Minimum Score 125 Continued

SCORE	LENGTH OF MAIN BEAM R	L	INSIDE SPREAD	NUMBER OF POINTS R	L	AREA	STATE/ PROVINCE	HUNTER'S NAME	DATE	RANK
150 2/8	23 4/8	23 0/8	15 6/8	5	5	Monroe County	MO	Montie R. Haupt	1991	3,022
150 2/8	23 4/8	23 5/8	16 0/8	6	6	Sauk County	WI	Fred Hess	1991	3,022
150 2/8	25 0/8	24 7/8	21 2/8	4	4	Lincoln County	WI	Mark Wimmer	1992	3,022
150 2/8	26 4/8	26 0/8	17 2/8	5	6	Wyandot County	OH	James D. Herring	1992	3,022
150 2/8	23 4/8	22 6/8	17 6/8	5	5	Mahaska County	IA	Greg Springer	1992	3,022
150 2/8	24 0/8	24 3/8	18 4/8	5	5	Uvalde County	TX	Michael R. Geller	1993	3,022
150 2/8	25 6/8	25 2/8	16 3/8	7	6	Plymouth County	IA	Jon T. Saunders	1994	3,022
150 2/8	23 1/8	22 7/8	20 4/8	5	5	Sawyer County	WI	Eugene J. Fleming	1995	3,022
150 2/8	26 1/8	26 6/8	21 4/8	5	5	Effingham County	IL	Gary Miller	1995	3,022
150 2/8	25 3/8	23 3/8	21 4/8	5	5	Marshall County	IL	Rich Shanklin	1995	3,022
150 2/8	24 1/8	22 6/8	16 7/8	5	6	Livingston County	IL	David Hoerner	1996	3,022
150 2/8	25 5/8	24 5/8	20 6/8	4	4	Shelby County	IL	Kris E. Knox	1996	3,022
150 2/8	23 4/8	22 7/8	19 4/8	5	5	Marquette County	WI	Charles Weyh	1996	3,022
150 2/8	23 7/8	24 5/8	16 5/8	7	6	Trempealeau County	WI	Sam D. Severson	1997	3,022
150 2/8	23 2/8	23 1/8	18 4/8	5	5	Christian County	KY	Chester Stewart	1997	3,022
150 2/8	20 5/8	20 7/8	14 4/8	7	7	Fremont County	WY	Scott Foster	1998	3,022
150 1/8	24 3/8	23 4/8	21 1/8	6	6	Luzerne County	PA	Edward Prutzman	1953	3,059
150 1/8	23 5/8	23 0/8	16 7/8	5	6	Johnson County	IA	Jim Keefer	1969	3,059
150 1/8	22 5/8	23 7/8	16 1/8	5	5	Guthrie County	IA	Bill Barringen	1975	3,059
150 1/8	24 2/8	24 5/8	16 7/8	5	5	Freeborn County	MN	Robert Haney	1977	3,059
150 1/8	20 6/8	20 2/8	18 1/8	6	6	Spencer County	ND	Lyle Fritz	1978	3,059
150 1/8	26 0/8	26 2/8	19 0/8	4	5	Butler County	OH	Roger S. Trigg	1979	3,059
150 1/8	24 7/8	26 2/8	19 7/8	5	6	Anoka County	MN	Patricia Barry	1980	3,059
150 1/8	22 1/8	22 4/8	17 7/8	5	5	Dearborn County	IN	Mike Serio	1982	3,059
150 1/8	22 7/8	22 5/8	17 1/8	5	4	Oldham County	KY	Phillip Burba	1985	3,059
150 1/8	23 4/8	24 2/8	17 3/8	4	5	Jefferson County	WI	Patrick Thiede	1985	3,059
150 1/8	24 4/8	24 3/8	20 1/8	7	8	Lake County	IL	James C. Carlson	1985	3,059
150 1/8	23 3/8	22 2/8	17 1/8	6	6	Guthrie County	IA	John D. Hambleton	1989	3,059
150 1/8	25 6/8	25 2/8	19 3/8	7	4	Leavenworth County	KS	Travis McGraw	1990	3,059
150 1/8	25 7/8	25 1/8	22 3/8	5	4	Perry County	IL	Roger D. Pyron	1990	3,059
150 1/8	22 6/8	22 4/8	21 1/8	5	6	Louisa County	IA	Larry H. Thumann, Sr.	1990	3,059
150 1/8	24 3/8	22 4/8	20 1/8	6	5	Fulton County	IL	Tim Wells	1991	3,059
150 1/8	23 3/8	22 2/8	18 6/8	7	6	Marion County	IL	R. Andrew Read	1991	3,059
150 1/8	26 2/8	24 6/8	20 7/8	4	5	Henry County	VA	Mike Weaver	1992	3,059
150 1/8	25 6/8	26 2/8	20 1/8	6	6	Iowa County	WI	Bob Washa	1992	3,059
150 1/8	25 3/8	25 2/8	23 0/8	5	5	Stephenson County	IL	George N. Miller	1992	3,059
150 1/8	26 7/8	27 2/8	23 5/8	6	6	McCreary County	KY	Eddie Howard	1992	3,059
150 1/8	23 3/8	24 1/8	17 1/8	5	5	Sedgwick County	KS	Ronnie Helsel	1992	3,059
150 1/8	24 1/8	23 1/8	16 5/8	5	5	Ashland County	WI	Jason Lawver	1992	3,059
150 1/8	27 1/8	27 2/8	21 1/8	4	4	Trempealeau County	WI	John Geske	1993	3,059
150 1/8	25 3/8	26 6/8	17 5/8	5	6	Clark County	OH	Lafayette Boggs III	1993	3,059
150 1/8	23 1/8	22 2/8	19 3/8	5	5	Lincoln County	WI	Marty Sosnovske	1993	3,059
150 1/8	23 3/8	23 4/8	15 2/8	7	5	De Witt County	IL	Joe Burzinski	1993	3,059
150 1/8	23 4/8	20 1/8	19 3/8	7	6	Brooke County	WV	Russell L. James	1993	3,059
150 1/8	26 3/8	25 5/8	18 0/8	4	6	Calhoun County	IL	Jeffery B. Foiles	1994	3,059
150 1/8	23 1/8	23 0/8	14 7/8	5	5	Forest County	WI	Donald J. Goffard	1994	3,059
150 1/8	22 5/8	23 3/8	16 7/8	5	5	Dimmit County	TX	Bob George	1994	3,059
150 1/8	25 6/8	25 4/8	21 6/8	5	4	Schuyler County	IL	John Johnston	1994	3,059
150 1/8	23 1/8	23 3/8	16 5/8	5	6	Jackson County	MI	Terry J. Filipek	1994	3,059
150 1/8	25 4/8	25 6/8	23 7/8	6	5	McIntosh County	OK	Brad Lanham	1995	3,059
150 1/8	22 7/8	22 5/8	19 7/8	5	5	Lee County	IL	Andy McCoy	1995	3,059
150 1/8	25 0/8	24 2/8	21 3/8	4	4	Montgomery County	IL	Dale H. Lessman	1995	3,059
150 1/8	23 7/8	24 6/8	20 1/8	7	6	Grant County	WI	Wayne A. Willkomm	1995	3,059
150 1/8	24 7/8	25 5/8	19 7/8	5	4	Montgomery County	IN	Chad M. Neukam	1995	3,059
150 1/8	25 7/8	25 6/8	23 1/8	4	6	Carroll County	IL	James C. Carlson	1997	3,059
150 1/8	24 4/8	25 7/8	19 7/8	5	5	Walworth County	WI	Jeffery Nelson	1997	3,059
150 1/8	24 3/8	25 0/8	18 7/8	6	5	Greene County	OH	Bob Galloway	1997	3,059
150 0/8	25 3/8	24 3/8	15 6/8	5	6	Adams County	WI	Daniel Becker	1957	3,100
150 0/8	26 6/8	27 1/8	17 6/8	5	4	Benton County	IA	Robert L. Walker	1961	3,100
150 0/8	26 4/8	26 4/8	18 4/8	5	5	Shelby County	IA	Einar Leistad	1970	3,100
150 0/8	22 0/8	23 2/8	17 2/8	5	6	Ozaukee County	WI	Rand Krueger	1980	3,100
150 0/8	24 5/8	23 0/8	17 4/8	5	5	Kosciusko County	IN	Gil Reed	1981	3,100
150 0/8	22 1/8	22 0/8	17 2/8	5	5	Lake County	IL	Daniel M. Bott	1983	3,100
150 0/8	22 3/8	22 4/8	17 1/8	6	6	Carroll County	AR	Larry Gasaway	1984	3,100
150 0/8	24 4/8	24 1/8	18 1/8	4	6	Penobscot County	ME	Kris T. Saunders	1985	3,100
150 0/8	21 0/8	21 4/8	15 7/8	4	5	Wabash County	IL	Paul Benham	1985	3,100
150 0/8	22 5/8	23 4/8	16 5/8	5	7	Tazewell County	IL	William H. Ray	1985	3,100
150 0/8	25 4/8	24 7/8	17 5/8	6	6	Livingston County	IL	James B. Smith	1985	3,100
150 0/8	23 7/8	23 3/8	20 0/8	5	5	White County	IL	Eric D. Devare	1985	3,100
150 0/8	23 6/8	24 2/8	17 0/8	5	5	Chase County	KS	Dan McClure	1985	3,100
150 0/8	22 2/8	21 4/8	16 4/8	5	6	Berkshire County	MA	Alan Ziegler	1986	3,100
150 0/8	25 1/8	25 3/8	20 0/8	4	4	Champaign County	OH	Douglas L. Hudson	1987	3,100
150 0/8	24 2/8	23 3/8	19 2/8	5	5	Ashtabula County	OH	Mike Morehouse	1988	3,100
150 0/8	25 4/8	26 2/8	18 4/8	5	5	Coles County	IL	Ron Osborne	1988	3,100
150 0/8	24 0/8	23 6/8	18 1/8	5	7	Lake County	IL	James D. Maricle	1989	3,100
150 0/8	22 3/8	22 5/8	15 0/8	6	6	Dane County	WI	Rick Krause	1990	3,100
150 0/8	23 5/8	23 0/8	18 2/8	5	5	Cedar County	IA	George R. Briggs	1990	3,100
150 0/8	24 4/8	25 2/8	20 2/8	6	5	Inglewood	ONT	Jack Leggo	1990	3,100

WHITETAIL DEER (TYPICAL ANTLERS)

Minimum Score 125 — Continued

SCORE	LENGTH OF MAIN BEAM R	LENGTH OF MAIN BEAM L	INSIDE SPREAD	NUMBER OF POINTS R	NUMBER OF POINTS L	AREA	STATE/PROVINCE	HUNTER'S NAME	DATE	RANK
150 0/8	23 4/8	23 3/8	15 4/8	5	5	Allamakee County	IA	Rodney Smed	1991	3,100
150 0/8	24 6/8	24 4/8	19 0/8	4	4	Mercer County	NJ	Scott Lysenko	1991	3,100
150 0/8	25 6/8	26 2/8	20 0/8	4	4	Todd County	MN	Brad G. Lorentz	1991	3,100
150 0/8	24 6/8	25 7/8	20 6/8	6	6	Buffalo County	WI	John W. Zahrte	1991	3,100
150 0/8	26 0/8	26 2/8	17 2/8	4	4	Portage County	WI	Robert J. Karnowski	1992	3,100
150 0/8	24 6/8	24 4/8	16 6/8	5	5	Fremont County	IA	Dave Holt	1992	3,100
150 0/8	24 4/8	24 3/8	18 6/8	5	5	Brown County	IL	Kevin Weeks	1992	3,100
150 0/8	22 1/8	23 5/8	19 4/8	5	5	Tuscarawas County	OH	Josh Deubner	1993	3,100
150 0/8	25 7/8	24 4/8	21 2/8	5	4	Jo Daviess County	IL	Jeff Parks	1993	3,100
150 0/8	24 4/8	24 0/8	18 4/8	5	6	Shawano County	WI	Brian M. Buckarma	1993	3,100
150 0/8	22 2/8	21 4/8	17 4/8	5	5	Goodhue County	MN	Steve Puppe	1994	3,100
150 0/8	25 3/8	26 2/8	17 0/8	6	6	Dodge County	WI	Larry Spittel	1994	3,100
150 0/8	23 4/8	23 0/8	18 6/8	5	5	Wayne County	MI	Gregory Kuhn	1994	3,100
150 0/8	23 6/8	24 3/8	15 0/8	5	5	St. Marys County	MD	Shawn Day	1995	3,100
150 0/8	22 0/8	21 7/8	17 4/8	7	8	Kent County	MI	Jason Leslie Eaton	1995	3,100
150 0/8	24 0/8	22 7/8	15 7/8	5	6	Harrison County	IA	Bob Siech	1995	3,100
150 0/8	23 3/8	22 1/8	20 4/8	5	5	Black Hawk County	IA	Bill Glenny	1996	3,100
150 0/8	22 6/8	23 1/8	18 6/8	5	5	Des Moines County	IA	Tim Wallin	1996	3,100
150 0/8	24 2/8	24 3/8	22 0/8	5	5	Cook County	IL	F. Dan Dinelli	1997	3,100
150 0/8	21 4/8	21 3/8	19 6/8	6	6	Saginaw County	MI	William R. Jerome	1997	3,100
150 0/8	24 3/8	24 0/8	17 4/8	4	4	Dane County	WI	Mike Grosse	1997	3,100
150 0/8	23 6/8	23 7/8	15 0/8	5	6	Holt County	MO	Juston W. Carr	1997	3,100
150 0/8	23 7/8	24 6/8	16 4/8	5	5	Morgan County	IN	Mike G. Graber	1997	3,100
150 0/8	24 1/8	24 4/8	20 6/8	4	4	Buffalo County	WI	Dennis Palmer	1997	3,100
149 7/8	26 0/8	25 6/8	20 3/8	4	4	Pulaski County	VA	Ray S. Carter	1962	3,145
149 7/8	21 6/8	21 1/8	17 3/8	5	5	Adams County	IL	Lyndall W. Heyen	1967	3,145
149 7/8	24 6/8	24 1/8	20 1/8	6	6	Will County	IL	Jerry Yost	1978	3,145
149 7/8	23 5/8	23 5/8	17 1/8	5	5	Scott County	KY	Mike Northcut	1980	3,145
149 7/8	25 1/8	24 1/8	18 7/8	6	6	Dauphin County	PA	Larry D. Wiestling	1983	3,145
149 7/8	25 0/8	25 0/8	17 5/8	5	5	Pittsburg County	OK	Doug Larimer	1985	3,145
149 7/8	22 0/8	22 1/8	17 0/8	7	6	Cumberland County	NJ	Bob Eisele	1986	3,145
149 7/8	24 6/8	25 4/8	16 4/8	6	6	Madison County	IL	Frank W. Gavillet	1986	3,145
149 7/8	24 7/8	24 4/8	17 7/8	6	5	Allegheny County	PA	George M. Conway	1987	3,145
149 7/8	25 0/8	24 2/8	19 6/8	6	4	Nicollet County	MN	Neil Treml	1987	3,145
149 7/8	25 1/8	24 3/8	20 7/8	5	4	Meade County	KS	Keith Whitney	1987	3,145
149 7/8	23 0/8	23 5/8	17 3/8	6	5	Jackson County	MO	Ty Easley	1988	3,145
149 7/8	24 4/8	24 1/8	16 4/8	6	5	Arenac County	MI	Jim Gall	1989	3,145
149 7/8	23 3/8	23 2/8	18 4/8	5	6	Kenosha County	WI	Thomas C. Zeihen	1989	3,145
149 7/8	26 0/8	26 3/8	21 7/8	4	6	Dodge County	WI	Steve Moritz	1991	3,145
149 7/8	23 1/8	24 2/8	17 6/8	5	6	Graham County	KS	Jim Kerbaugh	1991	3,145
149 7/8	25 4/8	26 1/8	16 5/8	5	5	Edgar County	IL	Dale Good	1992	3,145
149 7/8	22 5/8	23 2/8	17 4/8	5	6	De Witt County	IL	Charlie DeBose	1992	3,145
149 7/8	26 1/8	27 0/8	19 5/8	6	7	Washington County	KS	Ronald Montague	1993	3,145
149 7/8	23 2/8	23 6/8	18 3/8	5	5	Boone County	MO	Bruce Richardson	1994	3,145
149 7/8	26 5/8	26 1/8	18 4/8	5	6	Allegany County	NY	Christopher Enders	1994	3,145
149 7/8	24 3/8	24 3/8	23 3/8	6	4	Clarke County	IA	David C. Curnes	1994	3,145
149 7/8	26 0/8	25 0/8	18 3/8	5	8	Allegan County	MI	David L. Delpiere	1995	3,145
149 7/8	27 0/8	26 4/8	23 3/8	5	4	Greene County	OH	Joe Wright	1995	3,145
149 7/8	24 2/8	24 7/8	21 1/8	5	5	Anderson County	KS	Dennis L. Dahlke	1995	3,145
149 7/8	22 0/8	21 4/8	19 6/8	5	6	Sawyer County	WI	Timothy J. Drover	1996	3,145
149 7/8	25 2/8	25 4/8	19 1/8	5	5	Ross County	OH	Alan Parsons	1996	3,145
149 7/8	25 5/8	25 3/8	20 5/8	5	5	Hillsdale County	MI	Bruce J. Pearson	1997	3,145
149 7/8	25 0/8	25 4/8	21 7/8	5	4	Warren County	IA	Jacob Schuler	1997	3,145
149 6/8	23 4/8	23 5/8	17 1/8	7	6	Gull Lake	SAS	Keith Roney	1978	3,174
149 6/8	23 6/8	24 7/8	21 6/8	4	4	Branch County	MI	Howard W. Loehr	1983	3,174
149 6/8	25 1/8	26 0/8	20 6/8	4	5	Piatt County	IL	Marvin R. Salmon	1983	3,174
149 6/8	25 0/8	24 5/8	17 4/8	5	5	La Salle County	IL	Gary Tabor	1984	3,174
149 6/8	26 1/8	25 7/8	21 5/8	6	6	Anderson County	TN	Daniel W. Chase	1985	3,174
149 6/8	25 6/8	23 3/8	18 1/8	6	6	Douglas County	KS	Samuel J. Tunget	1985	3,174
149 6/8	23 7/8	23 2/8	19 2/8	5	7	Hocking County	OH	John E Furderer	1987	3,174
149 6/8	24 3/8	25 2/8	18 3/8	5	6	Kane County	IL	Steven J. Kamp	1988	3,174
149 6/8	25 6/8	24 7/8	19 4/8	6	7	Adams County	OH	Richard O. Ramsey	1990	3,174
149 6/8	21 5/8	21 7/8	18 5/8	5	8	Sangamon County	IL	Matthew W. Cloyd	1990	3,174
149 6/8	23 4/8	23 7/8	20 4/8	6	5	Waukesha County	WI	Mike Scaff	1991	3,174
149 6/8	24 1/8	23 5/8	20 0/8	5	5	Macoupin County	IL	James Olroyd	1992	3,174
149 6/8	23 4/8	24 3/8	17 5/8	6	5	Upson County	GA	Tony O. Chapman	1992	3,174
149 6/8	24 4/8	24 7/8	16 7/8	6	5	Iron County	MO	Teresa L. Campbell	1992	3,174
149 6/8	24 0/8	24 2/8	18 4/8	6	7	Yuma County	CO	Kevin Shively	1993	3,174
149 6/8	23 2/8	22 0/8	19 1/8	5	5	Millarville	ALB	Joel Bickler	1993	3,174
149 6/8	24 3/8	24 1/8	21 6/8	5	4	Pike County	MO	Cordell Queathem, Jr.	1993	3,174
149 6/8	23 1/8	22 3/8	19 1/8	6	6	Crawford County	PA	Richard W. Marks	1994	3,174
149 6/8	24 0/8	22 6/8	17 4/8	6	5	Walworth County	WI	Ernie Meinen	1995	3,174
149 6/8	24 2/8	24 7/8	17 0/8	7	5	Sawyer County	WI	Ed Schimke	1995	3,174
149 6/8	23 5/8	24 6/8	15 4/8	7	7	Vinton County	OH	Mark Meadows	1995	3,174
149 6/8	23 4/8	23 4/8	16 6/8	5	5	La Salle County	IL	Michael Elbrecht	1995	3,174
149 6/8	25 2/8	25 3/8	19 0/8	6	5	McHenry County	IL	Joe Florent	1995	3,174
149 6/8	25 3/8	25 4/8	19 6/8	4	4	McLean County	IL	Dale McKinnerney	1995	3,174
149 6/8	26 5/8	27 0/8	19 0/8	5	4	Boone County	NE	Jeff Beckwith	1997	3,174

WHITETAIL DEER (TYPICAL ANTLERS)

Minimum Score 125   Continued

SCORE	LENGTH OF MAIN BEAM R	LENGTH OF MAIN BEAM L	INSIDE SPREAD	NUMBER OF POINTS R	NUMBER OF POINTS L	AREA	STATE/PROVINCE	HUNTER'S NAME	DATE	RANK
149 6/8	27 3/8	26 7/8	19 0/8	4	4	Livingston County	IL	Richard D. Green	1997	3,174
149 6/8	26 2/8	27 6/8	21 4/8	5	6	Logan County	WV	James D. Collins II	1997	3,174
149 6/8	25 4/8	25 2/8	19 6/8	5	8	Ozaukee County	WI	Joseph V. Spata	1997	3,174
149 6/8	24 1/8	25 1/8	21 6/8	6	4	Cerro Gordo County	IA	Corey Martin	1997	3,174
149 6/8	22 6/8	24 0/8	18 4/8	5	5	Howard County	MD	Robert W. Evans, Jr.	1998	3,174
149 5/8	25 6/8	25 3/8	18 5/8	6	6	La Salle County	IL	Timothy L. Kakara	1975	3,204
149 5/8	25 4/8	25 2/8	20 1/8	6	5	Chase County	KS	John Moore	1981	3,204
149 5/8	24 5/8	25 2/8	20 1/8	5	7	Sheboygan County	WI	Leon Schultz	1983	3,204
149 5/8	24 4/8	23 5/8	20 1/8	5	5	Johnson County	NE	Brad Seitz	1984	3,204
149 5/8	22 4/8	23 1/8	16 5/8	6	5	York County	NE	Harold Bowman	1985	3,204
149 5/8	25 1/8	23 2/8	17 5/8	6	6	Livingston County	NY	John J. Valle	1985	3,204
149 5/8	22 7/8	23 3/8	21 1/8	5	5	Osage	SAS	Fred Paslawski	1986	3,204
149 5/8	25 1/8	25 0/8	16 7/8	5	4	McPherson County	KS	George E. Hoke	1986	3,204
149 5/8	27 3/8	28 6/8	20 3/8	5	6	Delaware County	IA	Robert J. Becker	1987	3,204
149 5/8	24 3/8	24 3/8	19 1/8	5	4	Kiowa County	KS	Karl L. Ballard	1987	3,204
149 5/8	26 4/8	26 1/8	20 7/8	4	4	Montgomery County	IL	Martin L. Leitschuh	1987	3,204
149 5/8	26 4/8	26 4/8	21 0/8	7	6	Jefferson County	IL	Terry Storey	1988	3,204
149 5/8	23 4/8	24 3/8	18 6/8	6	6	Fayette County	IA	Mike Barker	1989	3,204
149 5/8	23 4/8	22 3/8	17 1/8	5	5	Ripley County	IN	Kevin D. Hall	1989	3,204
149 5/8	24 3/8	25 3/8	18 2/8	7	6	Carroll County	IL	Art Heinze	1989	3,204
149 5/8	23 2/8	22 4/8	18 3/8	5	5	Crow Wing County	MN	Mike Brandes	1989	3,204
149 5/8	24 4/8	24 2/8	19 4/8	6	5	Macon County	IL	Gary Wayne Scheland, Sr.	1990	3,204
149 5/8	26 2/8	27 3/8	19 4/8	5	4	Jo Daviess County	IL	Ronald J. Blauwkamp	1990	3,204
149 5/8	24 5/8	24 5/8	20 2/8	6	5	Barber County	KS	Jim F. Shadid	1991	3,204
149 5/8	24 1/8	23 7/8	17 7/8	5	5	Otter Tail County	MN	Craig Smith	1991	3,204
149 5/8	24 4/8	24 7/8	15 5/8	6	6	Pottawatomie County	KS	Nathan Figge	1992	3,204
149 5/8	24 7/8	25 2/8	15 4/8	7	5	Howell County	MO	Thomas E. French	1992	3,204
149 5/8	26 0/8	26 0/8	16 0/8	6	7	Strathcona	ALB	Gord MacDonald	1992	3,204
149 5/8	21 3/8	21 4/8	15 5/8	6	5	Boone County	IA	Kevin L. Holm	1992	3,204
149 5/8	26 6/8	26 2/8	20 5/8	7	6	Hancock County	IL	Ryan D. Biery	1993	3,204
149 5/8	22 4/8	21 7/8	16 4/8	5	5	Winnebago County	WI	John Hay	1993	3,204
149 5/8	27 0/8	25 7/8	24 1/8	4	4	Clinton County	IN	Donny L. Pickell	1993	3,204
149 5/8	20 4/8	19 1/8	15 5/8	5	6	Iroquois County	IL	Doug Post	1993	3,204
149 5/8	24 3/8	24 2/8	18 0/8	7	6	Woodbury County	IA	Todd T. Carr	1993	3,204
149 5/8	23 3/8	22 4/8	18 7/8	5	5	Boone County	WV	Mark Summers	1994	3,204
149 5/8	26 0/8	24 2/8	21 2/8	5	5	Monroe County	IA	Bob McDowell	1994	3,204
149 5/8	24 4/8	24 3/8	16 5/8	5	5	Clinton County	IL	Jim Lohman	1994	3,204
149 5/8	24 6/8	24 6/8	20 7/8	7	5	Brooke	ONT	Bill Majovsky	1995	3,204
149 5/8	24 0/8	23 6/8	19 3/8	5	5	Kent County	MD	Charles W. Smith, Jr.	1995	3,204
149 5/8	25 0/8	25 5/8	21 0/8	7	5	Kankakee County	IL	Calvin R. Cox	1995	3,204
149 5/8	26 2/8	27 6/8	21 6/8	8	5	Dekalb County	IL	James G. Tippitt	1995	3,204
149 5/8	22 4/8	22 2/8	16 3/8	5	5	Madison Parish	LA	Jason Elrod	1996	3,204
149 5/8	26 6/8	26 7/8	18 7/8	5	5	Osborne County	KS	Blake Grabast	1996	3,204
149 5/8	22 4/8	23 2/8	17 6/8	5	6	Lyon County	IA	Paul E. Blotz	1996	3,204
149 5/8	25 6/8	27 4/8	24 4/8	4	6	Winneshiek County	IA	Gary L. Mezera	1996	3,204
149 5/8	25 0/8	25 0/8	17 3/8	5	5	Tensas Parish	LA	Robert T. Buller	1997	3,204
149 5/8	25 7/8	25 7/8	18 1/8	5	5	Wyoming County	WV	Robert Adams	1997	3,204
149 5/8	24 2/8	22 6/8	20 6/8	4	6	Scott County	IA	Ric Bishop	1997	3,204
149 5/8	24 1/8	24 1/8	20 3/8	6	5	Dane County	WI	Mark Gerhardt	1997	3,204
149 4/8	23 3/8	26 0/8	20 2/8	5	5	Woodbury County	IA	Don Gothier	1962	3,248
149 4/8	23 2/8	23 2/8	17 1/8	6	5	Newton County	IN	Gerald R. Metros	1973	3,248
149 4/8	22 5/8	22 3/8	17 4/8	7	5	Ogle County	IL	Jerome Bruns	1983	3,248
149 4/8	24 5/8	25 2/8	17 0/8	5	5	Sedgwick County	KS	Bob Shull	1984	3,248
149 4/8	25 3/8	25 0/8	21 4/8	4	4	Shawnee County	KS	Jim Dultmeier	1985	3,248
149 4/8	23 4/8	23 7/8	16 3/8	7	6	Platte County	WY	Jerry Bowen	1986	3,248
149 4/8	25 4/8	25 7/8	17 4/8	6	5	Dane County	WI	John Podebradsky	1986	3,248
149 4/8	23 5/8	24 5/8	22 0/8	5	5	Keokuk County	IA	Mike Krier	1986	3,248
149 4/8	22 6/8	22 3/8	16 7/8	6	6	Polk County	WI	Blaine Mortimer	1987	3,248
149 4/8	26 1/8	25 5/8	22 6/8	5	4	Lee County	IL	Rick Hornung	1988	3,248
149 4/8	23 1/8	21 6/8	19 6/8	5	7	Kossuth County	IA	Bruce K. Leeck	1989	3,248
149 4/8	28 2/8	25 2/8	19 0/8	5	6	Lancaster County	NE	Bog Spicha	1990	3,248
149 4/8	24 2/8	19 0/8	20 7/8	5	7	Buffalo County	WI	Matthew J. Gorniak	1990	3,248
149 4/8	25 0/8	24 4/8	18 4/8	6	5	Champaign County	IL	Bud Barnes	1991	3,248
149 4/8	24 2/8	23 6/8	18 6/8	5	4	Clayton County	IA	Joseph C. Hinderman	1991	3,248
149 4/8	23 1/8	24 0/8	16 7/8	6	5	Ravalli County	MT	Michael R. Lindquist	1993	3,248
149 4/8	23 6/8	23 0/8	16 1/8	6	6	Morrison County	MN	Terry F. Much	1993	3,248
149 4/8	24 6/8	24 6/8	17 4/8	4	4	Lake County	IL	Dr. John R. Thodos	1993	3,248
149 4/8	23 1/8	23 1/8	16 2/8	5	5	Marathon County	WI	Dean J. Novitzke	1993	3,248
149 4/8	21 5/8	23 2/8	16 4/8	5	5	McKenzie County	ND	Dennis Carns	1994	3,248
149 4/8	25 0/8	25 2/8	20 2/8	6	5	Dakota County	MN	Keith A. Klingborg	1995	3,248
149 4/8	24 3/8	23 7/8	16 2/8	5	6	Preble County	OH	Jason Hines	1995	3,248
149 4/8	21 1/8	26 2/8	19 1/8	6	5	Pierceland	SAS	Bruce A. Hatch	1995	3,248
149 4/8	25 2/8	26 0/8	16 5/8	6	6	Ross County	OH	David L. Buckler	1996	3,248
149 4/8	24 4/8	24 6/8	18 4/8	5	4	Logan County	CO	Janet L. George	1996	3,248
149 4/8	22 3/8	24 0/8	17 0/8	5	5	Deschaillons	QUE	Bruno Martin L'Herault	1996	3,248
149 4/8	22 5/8	24 1/8	16 2/8	5	5	Buffalo County	WI	Christopher S. Dellger	1996	3,248
149 4/8	25 3/8	24 5/8	17 6/8	6	5	Mills County	IA	Elaine D. Brown	1996	3,248
149 4/8	26 1/8	24 7/8	19 7/8	6	5	Marion County	IA	Lowdell Taylor	1997	3,248

WHITETAIL DEER (TYPICAL ANTLERS)

Minimum Score 125 — Continued

SCORE	LENGTH OF MAIN BEAM R	L	INSIDE SPREAD	NUMBER OF POINTS R	L	AREA	STATE/ PROVINCE	HUNTER'S NAME	DATE	RANK
149 4/8	22 4/8	21 3/8	17 6/8	5	5	Jackson County	WI	Todd Herrington	1997	3,248
149 3/8	26 6/8	25 4/8	22 1/8	4	4	Westchester County	NY	George Ferber	1957	3,278
149 3/8	23 4/8	23 3/8	15 7/8	5	5	Madison County	KY	Robert Young	1963	3,278
149 3/8	23 4/8	24 4/8	19 3/8	5	5	Newton County	IN	Philip Kozlowski	1968	3,278
149 3/8	23 7/8	23 2/8	15 7/8	5	5	Buffalo County	WI	Daniel J. Brunner	1969	3,278
149 3/8	24 1/8	24 2/8	19 3/8	5	5	Lawrence County	OH	Ronald E. Burnette	1971	3,278
149 3/8	23 7/8	23 4/8	17 5/8	5	5	Waushara County	WI	Ronald Anunson	1974	3,278
149 3/8	22 2/8	23 1/8	15 7/8	6	6	Lac qui Parle County	MN	Ron Patzer	1980	3,278
149 3/8	24 1/8	25 3/8	19 7/8	5	6	Perry County	IL	Vern Quillman	1981	3,278
149 3/8	24 2/8	23 3/8	19 3/8	6	7	Charles County	MD	Frank A. Rankin	1981	3,278
149 3/8	24 0/8	25 2/8	17 4/8	5	4	Washington County	OH	Charles E. Vaughan	1983	3,278
149 3/8	25 5/8	25 0/8	20 4/8	4	5	Noble County	OK	Bill Hughes	1984	3,278
149 3/8	22 5/8	22 6/8	15 5/8	5	5	Morgan County	CO	Stan Kingcade	1985	3,278
149 3/8	24 2/8	23 5/8	21 3/8	6	6	Iroquois County	IL	Dale W. Duits	1986	3,278
149 3/8	24 7/8	26 5/8	16 5/8	6	6	Athens County	OH	Ron Sallee	1986	3,278
149 3/8	26 6/8	24 7/8	17 7/8	5	4	Marshall County	IL	Bryan Blair	1987	3,278
149 3/8	21 7/8	23 4/8	18 7/8	6	6	Ozaukee County	WI	Mark Hoelz	1987	3,278
149 3/8	23 5/8	24 0/8	17 2/8	4	6	Sandusky County	OH	James Moll	1988	3,278
149 3/8	21 5/8	21 1/8	17 3/8	5	5	Morden	MAN	Allen K. Martens	1988	3,278
149 3/8	25 3/8	25 1/8	19 5/8	5	5	Muskingum County	OH	John W. Keefe	1988	3,278
149 3/8	23 1/8	22 5/8	18 7/8	4	5	Somerset County	NJ	Peter Paradise	1989	3,278
149 3/8	24 1/8	24 5/8	18 7/8	5	5	Buffalo County	WI	Randall Martin	1990	3,278
149 3/8	24 4/8	24 4/8	19 0/8	7	7	Johnson County	IA	Kevin Deets	1990	3,278
149 3/8	26 0/8	25 5/8	19 6/8	5	6	Monona County	IA	Richard Kelly	1990	3,278
149 3/8	27 0/8	25 4/8	21 1/8	5	4	Burt County	NE	Michael L. Johnson	1990	3,278
149 3/8	24 1/8	23 5/8	19 3/8	5	5	Stearns County	MN	Jeff Skinner	1991	3,278
149 3/8	24 6/8	26 2/8	20 7/8	6	6	McHenry County	IL	Brian Witte	1991	3,278
149 3/8	25 1/8	25 2/8	15 2/8	6	6	Owen County	KY	Robert C. Long, Jr.	1991	3,278
149 3/8	22 1/8	21 5/8	19 7/8	5	5	Grand Forks County	ND	Kendall J. Allgaier	1992	3,278
149 3/8	27 2/8	26 4/8	19 1/8	4	6	Johnson County	IL	Mike Stafford	1992	3,278
149 3/8	24 4/8	24 7/8	20 4/8	5	5	Crawford County	KS	William F. Nauyok III	1992	3,278
149 3/8	23 7/8	24 2/8	17 5/8	5	5	Hitchcock County	NE	Rob Seybold	1993	3,278
149 3/8	25 2/8	23 5/8	18 6/8	6	5	Ozaukee County	WI	William J. Ferguson	1993	3,278
149 3/8	27 4/8	25 4/8	17 5/8	4	5	Queen Annes County	MD	Charles M. Pierson	1994	3,278
149 3/8	26 2/8	25 1/8	21 5/8	4	4	Trempealeau County	WI	Jim P. Konkel	1994	3,278
149 3/8	23 7/8	23 6/8	19 3/8	5	5	Jefferson County	WI	Karen Raasch	1994	3,278
149 3/8	29 0/8	28 6/8	25 1/8	6	6	Wayne County	MI	Mark E. Oprisiu	1994	3,278
149 3/8	23 7/8	23 2/8	18 3/8	5	5	Winnebago County	IL	Dave Fisher	1994	3,278
149 3/8	24 4/8	25 2/8	18 2/8	5	7	Shelby County	IN	Dan Cord	1995	3,278
149 3/8	25 4/8	24 2/8	22 1/8	5	4	Allegan County	MI	William D. Brooks	1995	3,278
149 3/8	25 0/8	23 0/8	18 5/8	4	6	Buffalo County	WI	Dan Lee	1995	3,278
149 3/8	25 4/8	25 2/8	19 1/8	5	5	Grundy County	MO	Keith Vandevender	1995	3,278
149 3/8	24 4/8	24 7/8	18 7/8	4	5	Linn County	IA	Jamie Washburn	1995	3,278
149 3/8	24 3/8	24 0/8	19 1/8	5	6	Morrison County	MN	Jim Klassen	1996	3,278
149 3/8	26 3/8	24 7/8	18 7/8	5	5	Marquette County	WI	Arthur J. Gruner	1996	3,278
149 3/8	23 4/8	23 5/8	17 3/8	6	7	Neosho County	KS	Roger L. Barriger	1996	3,278
149 3/8	26 5/8	27 3/8	17 5/8	5	5	Clark County	IL	Todd Murphy	1996	3,278
149 3/8	23 1/8	23 5/8	21 7/8	6	5	Kanawha County	WV	Rick Boggess	1997	3,278
149 3/8	23 0/8	22 5/8	15 7/8	5	5	Blue Earth County	MN	Dan Friedrichs	1997	3,278
149 3/8	24 0/8	24 0/8	19 5/8	4	4	Iowa County	IA	Tim Krauss	1997	3,278
149 3/8	24 3/8	24 6/8	18 2/8	7	5	Wayne County	NY	Angus Hopkins	1997	3,278
149 3/8	23 0/8	23 0/8	18 5/8	5	5	Irion County	TX	David L. Duncan	1997	3,278
149 3/8	23 1/8	23 0/8	16 3/8	6	5	Washington County	PA	Dennis Gondella	1998	3,278
149 2/8	25 3/8	24 6/8	20 4/8	5	5	Westchester County	NY	Joseph H. Keeler	1957	3,330
149 2/8	22 0/8	22 1/8	16 6/8	5	5	Will County	IL	Daniel R. Altiery	1973	3,330
149 2/8	22 7/8	22 6/8	20 6/8	4	5	Auglaize County	OH	Fred Rostorfer	1980	3,330
149 2/8	23 3/8	23 4/8	15 3/8	5	7	Livingston County	MI	John Richmond	1981	3,330
149 2/8	23 4/8	22 6/8	18 6/8	6	6	Columbia County	WI	Gene R. Elsing	1981	3,330
149 2/8	24 0/8	22 1/8	17 4/8	5	5	Washtenaw County	MI	Fred Johnson	1984	3,330
149 2/8	27 4/8	26 6/8	20 2/8	7	7	Fulton County	IL	Locie L Murphy	1984	3,330
149 2/8	23 6/8	23 4/8	18 0/8	5	5	Jackson County	MO	Marvin Thomey	1984	3,330
149 2/8	23 4/8	23 2/8	19 4/8	6	5	Otter Tail County	MN	Kelly Shannon	1987	3,330
149 2/8	24 2/8	24 2/8	16 7/8	6	5	Warren County	KY	Jerry Sympson	1987	3,330
149 2/8	26 2/8	25 1/8	19 6/8	6	6	Tama County	IA	Travis Hansen	1988	3,330
149 2/8	23 1/8	23 7/8	17 0/8	5	4	Vinton County	OH	Brian D. Ehrhart	1989	3,330
149 2/8	21 6/8	19 7/8	15 6/8	5	5	Ashe County	NC	Marshall "Footsie" Eller	1991	3,330
149 2/8	24 2/8	24 1/8	18 2/8	5	5	Rusk County	WI	Ed Madlon	1992	3,330
149 2/8	23 5/8	22 6/8	20 2/8	5	5	East Carroll Parish	LA	Robert H. Jarvis	1993	3,330
149 2/8	23 3/8	23 6/8	15 4/8	5	5	Adams County	OH	Kenneth Ashcraft, Jr.	1993	3,330
149 2/8	20 5/8	26 0/8	18 6/8	5	4	Morrison County	MN	Kirt M. Dotzler	1993	3,330
149 2/8	24 4/8	24 6/8	15 7/8	6	5	Oconto County	WI	Wade Kempka	1993	3,330
149 2/8	24 4/8	24 2/8	18 7/8	6	6	Cass County	ND	Rob Dooley	1993	3,330
149 2/8	24 0/8	23 6/8	16 2/8	5	5	Brown County	MN	Paul Berg	1994	3,330
149 2/8	22 0/8	23 2/8	19 6/8	5	5	Muscatine County	IA	James E. Quinn	1994	3,330
149 2/8	24 1/8	24 2/8	17 6/8	5	5	Allamakee County	IA	Joe Lieb	1994	3,330
149 2/8	26 2/8	26 0/8	18 0/8	5	6	Pierce County	WI	Jeff Schoeder	1994	3,330
149 2/8	23 2/8	24 1/8	18 6/8	7	5	Washington County	IL	Kevin Woker	1995	3,330
149 2/8	24 5/8	24 5/8	17 4/8	5	5	Montgomery County	NC	Ricky E. Jennings	1995	3,330

WHITETAIL DEER (TYPICAL ANTLERS)

Minimum Score 125
Continued 335

SCORE	LENGTH OF MAIN BEAM R	L	INSIDE SPREAD	NUMBER OF POINTS R	L	AREA	STATE/ PROVINCE	HUNTER'S NAME	DATE	RANK
149 2/8	23 3/8	24 5/8	22 4/8	5	6	Plymouth County	MA	Daniel E. Chisholm	1995	3,330
149 2/8	21 7/8	22 0/8	19 2/8	6	5	Peoria County	IL	Joe Cooper	1995	3,330
149 2/8	24 5/8	24 6/8	19 7/8	7	5	Delaware County	IA	Daniel G. Putz	1995	3,330
149 2/8	24 5/8	26 6/8	19 0/8	5	6	Howe Island	ONT	Nick Milonas	1995	3,330
149 2/8	26 1/8	25 0/8	20 0/8	5	5	Henry County	IL	Robert Aldred	1996	3,330
149 2/8	24 7/8	25 3/8	17 2/8	4	4	Newton County	TX	Brian Babin	1996	3,330
149 2/8	25 6/8	25 7/8	17 2/8	5	4	Allamakee County	IA	Justin Grove	1996	3,330
149 2/8	23 4/8	22 7/8	20 0/8	5	5	La Salle County	IL	Dennis Brown	1996	3,330
149 2/8	25 7/8	25 0/8	20 1/8	4	6	Buena Vista County	IA	Dan D. Soellner	1996	3,330
149 2/8	26 2/8	26 2/8	21 5/8	6	5	Branch County	MI	Gregory J. Raatz	1997	3,330
149 2/8	23 3/8	25 4/8	20 3/8	5	4	Wicomico County	MD	Michael Pilchard	1997	3,330
149 2/8	26 3/8	26 2/8	22 4/8	4	7	McHenry County	IL	Darrell J. Prielipp	1997	3,330
149 2/8	29 0/8	28 4/8	22 6/8	4	4	Knox County	OH	Bill Banner	1997	3,330
149 2/8	24 2/8	24 1/8	18 6/8	5	5	Graves County	KY	Casey Kuppart	1998	3,330
149 1/8	25 4/8	25 0/8	17 0/8	5	7	Bon Homme County	SD	Terry Gretschman	1974	3,369
149 1/8	23 3/8	22 0/8	19 6/8	6	5	Coles County	IL	Bill Spaniol	1976	3,369
149 1/8	25 7/8	23 2/8	19 7/8	5	5	Clark County	IL	Gerald D. Shaffner	1984	3,369
149 1/8	24 0/8	24 6/8	19 4/8	6	6	Phillips County	KS	Bryan Henry	1984	3,369
149 1/8	22 3/8	24 2/8	17 2/8	6	5	Traill County	ND	Dale Grindeland	1986	3,369
149 1/8	26 1/8	27 3/8	19 5/8	7	7	Morrison County	MN	Jeff Moris	1987	3,369
149 1/8	25 6/8	24 7/8	16 3/8	5	4	Union County	KY	Joseph K. "Bo" Girten	1988	3,369
149 1/8	25 7/8	26 3/8	20 5/8	4	4	Washington County	MN	Scott Ralidak	1989	3,369
149 1/8	25 1/8	24 1/8	16 7/8	6	5	Vilas County	WI	Craig Hanson	1989	3,369
149 1/8	22 3/8	22 6/8	15 5/8	5	5	Stearns County	MN	Duane Gertken	1989	3,369
149 1/8	21 5/8	23 0/8	20 7/8	5	5	Peoria County	IL	Tom Missen	1989	3,369
149 1/8	23 1/8	23 0/8	17 1/8	11	8	Clinton County	IL	Tracy Hawes	1990	3,369
149 1/8	23 6/8	24 4/8	18 3/8	5	6	Crow Wing County	MN	Shane Gunderson	1991	3,369
149 1/8	24 2/8	25 4/8	16 3/8	7	7	Sarpy County	NE	Bernard J. Kubat, Jr.	1991	3,369
149 1/8	23 7/8	24 3/8	20 3/8	5	5	Iron County	WI	Kevin J. Genisot	1991	3,369
149 1/8	22 2/8	23 0/8	16 3/8	5	5	Neosho County	KS	Scotty Manbeck	1992	3,369
149 1/8	23 3/8	24 1/8	15 3/8	6	5	Hancock County	OH	Bruce O'Rear	1992	3,369
149 1/8	26 4/8	25 4/8	19 5/8	5	5	Noxubee County	MS	Chuck Allen	1993	3,369
149 1/8	26 1/8	24 2/8	18 7/8	4	5	Guilford County	NC	Wanda L. Peeples	1993	3,369
149 1/8	26 1/8	25 3/8	21 7/8	6	4	Peoria County	IL	Tom Missen	1993	3,369
149 1/8	22 0/8	23 1/8	17 7/8	5	5	Stevens County	WA	Greg Sorensen	1994	3,369
149 1/8	24 0/8	25 0/8	21 1/8	5	5	Kenosha County	WI	Jamie Boyd	1994	3,369
149 1/8	25 0/8	25 2/8	18 1/8	5	4	Scott County	MN	Norman J. Williams	1994	3,369
149 1/8	25 3/8	24 3/8	17 7/8	5	6	Whiteside County	IL	Clint Walker	1995	3,369
149 1/8	22 7/8	23 2/8	20 3/8	5	5	Waukesha County	WI	Tom Gorski	1995	3,369
149 1/8	26 0/8	24 7/8	20 4/8	4	5	Sangamon County	IL	Kent J. Sturhahn	1995	3,369
149 1/8	26 6/8	27 0/8	21 1/8	5	5	Brown County	IL	Bill Cross	1995	3,369
149 1/8	23 3/8	23 2/8	18 1/8	4	7	Linn County	MO	Marc Amer	1995	3,369
149 1/8	22 0/8	21 6/8	17 5/8	5	5	Lake County	IL	Gary Hannigan	1996	3,369
149 1/8	23 2/8	23 2/8	18 4/8	5	7	Grayson County	TX	Shane Wilson	1996	3,369
149 1/8	25 2/8	25 3/8	18 7/8	5	5	Worth County	GA	Ian Wolfgang Hindle	1997	3,369
149 1/8	23 6/8	23 2/8	17 5/8	5	5	Montgomery County	MD	Steven Nocket	1998	3,369
149 0/8	25 7/8	23 5/8	19 4/8	6	5	Mitchell County	IA	Elmer Krueger	1961	3,401
149 0/8	25 0/8	25 0/8	19 4/8	5	4	Black Hawk County	IA	Robert Riggle	1975	3,401
149 0/8	24 4/8	23 4/8	19 6/8	5	5	Marion County	KS	David C. Hett	1980	3,401
149 0/8	23 4/8	22 5/8	15 4/8	5	5	Pickaway County	OH	Weldon R. Snyder	1980	3,401
149 0/8	24 6/8	25 1/8	19 2/8	6	5	Warren County	IA	Grant Poindexter	1981	3,401
149 0/8	25 5/8	24 5/8	18 6/8	4	5	Kiowa County	KS	Dan Manwarren	1984	3,401
149 0/8	25 1/8	24 6/8	17 7/8	6	5	Calhoun County	MI	Larry C. Holcomb	1984	3,401
149 0/8	21 5/8	21 6/8	20 0/8	5	5	Atchison County	KS	Larry Bleier	1985	3,401
149 0/8	26 0/8	26 2/8	18 3/8	4	5	Morrison County	MN	Craig Krafthefer	1986	3,401
149 0/8	27 1/8	27 6/8	20 6/8	4	4	Dunn County	WI	Mark Sokup	1987	3,401
149 0/8	23 3/8	24 6/8	17 6/8	6	5	Marinette County	WI	Philip E. Bretl	1987	3,401
149 0/8	23 4/8	22 4/8	15 2/8	7	6	Kenosha County	WI	Alois Jeske, Sr.	1987	3,401
149 0/8	23 5/8	23 4/8	21 1/8	6	7	Washtenaw County	MI	Frank Schmidt, Jr.	1987	3,401
149 0/8	23 7/8	24 7/8	20 0/8	5	5	Clay County	IL	David Thompson	1987	3,401
149 0/8	23 0/8	22 7/8	17 4/8	5	6	Ozaukee County	WI	Jack Klotz	1988	3,401
149 0/8	24 1/8	24 4/8	19 1/8	6	7	San Augustine County	TX	Ed Gunter	1988	3,401
149 0/8	25 7/8	24 4/8	19 6/8	5	5	Hardin County	IA	William Stonebraker	1988	3,401
149 0/8	22 0/8	22 2/8	17 2/8	5	5	Kane County	IL	Bill Yoakum	1988	3,401
149 0/8	26 3/8	25 2/8	19 2/8	6	6	Dubuque County	IA	James A. Deckert	1990	3,401
149 0/8	23 3/8	22 6/8	18 6/8	5	5	Greene County	AR	Mike Croy	1990	3,401
149 0/8	23 0/8	22 4/8	17 7/8	6	6	Brown County	IN	Dale Snyder	1991	3,401
149 0/8	24 0/8	24 0/8	19 2/8	5	4	Schuyler County	IL	Bill Daugherty	1991	3,401
149 0/8	24 4/8	26 2/8	15 4/8	5	5	Bledsoe County	TN	Marty N. Swafford	1991	3,401
149 0/8	21 5/8	22 5/8	17 2/8	5	5	Du Page County	IL	Peter Schumacher	1991	3,401
149 0/8	25 3/8	25 0/8	19 0/8	5	5	Racine County	WI	Brek M. Zortman	1991	3,401
149 0/8	24 3/8	24 1/8	19 2/8	5	5	Taylor County	WI	Logan W. Winger	1992	3,401
149 0/8	24 5/8	25 1/8	21 2/8	5	5	Surry County	VA	Jeff S. Davis	1992	3,401
149 0/8	24 1/8	24 7/8	20 6/8	5	5	Lake County	IL	Wayne Johnson	1992	3,401
149 0/8	22 5/8	22 1/8	17 6/8	5	5	Menard County	IL	Ronald J. Wadsworth	1992	3,401
149 0/8	21 7/8	20 7/8	18 4/8	6	6	Livingston County	IL	Rick DeFauw	1993	3,401
149 0/8	22 4/8	24 3/8	20 3/8	5	6	Butler County	OH	James W. Burnes	1994	3,401
149 0/8	24 1/8	23 6/8	18 0/8	5	5	Dawes County	NE	Gary L. Mason	1994	3,401

WHITETAIL DEER (TYPICAL ANTLERS)

Minimum Score 125 — Continued

SCORE	LENGTH OF MAIN BEAM R	L	INSIDE SPREAD	NUMBER OF POINTS R	L	AREA	STATE/ PROVINCE	HUNTER'S NAME	DATE	RANK
149 0/8	21 5/8	21 3/8	14 6/8	6	6	Worcester County	MD	Kip Melson	1994	3,401
149 0/8	24 7/8	24 7/8	17 2/8	6	6	Houston County	MN	Bob Borowiak	1995	3,401
149 0/8	22 3/8	22 4/8	14 6/8	5	5	Livingston County	MI	Mark L. Klett	1995	3,401
149 0/8	24 7/8	25 0/8	17 2/8	5	5	Louisa County	IA	Robert McCulley	1995	3,401
149 0/8	24 0/8	22 4/8	16 0/8	8	6	Jackson County	MO	Stephen D. Vincent	1995	3,401
149 0/8	21 3/8	21 1/8	17 4/8	5	5	Dodge County	MN	Kerry Webster	1996	3,401
149 0/8	26 1/8	26 6/8	19 1/8	6	5	Kenedy County	TX	Richard M. Ley	1996	3,401
149 0/8	25 2/8	23 6/8	17 2/8	5	6	Walworth County	WI	James May	1997	3,401
149 0/8	20 2/8	20 4/8	14 0/8	7	7	Montgomery County	KS	Dr. Daniel J. Gray	1997	3,401
149 0/8	24 1/8	23 0/8	16 2/8	5	5	Athens County	OH	Charles Thompson	1997	3,401
149 0/8	23 3/8	22 3/8	16 4/8	5	5	Duval County	TX	F. H. Becker	1997	3,401
149 0/8	24 4/8	25 4/8	17 2/8	4	5	Linn County	IA	Christopher J. Swanke	1998	3,401
148 7/8	15 4/8	26 0/8	19 4/8	5	7	Lincoln County	WI	Ronald Pond	1961	3,445
148 7/8	24 6/8	24 0/8	18 7/8	4	5	Grant County	SD	Larry Turbak	1964	3,445
148 7/8	23 1/8	23 1/8	18 4/8	6	6	Knox County	OH	John E. Bumpus	1971	3,445
148 7/8	23 1/8	23 1/8	19 3/8	5	4	Clayton County	IA	Ralph Edward Livingston	1984	3,445
148 7/8	24 2/8	22 7/8	17 2/8	6	5	Clay County	KS	Larry Reed	1985	3,445
148 7/8	23 0/8	23 1/8	16 5/8	5	5	Erie County	NY	Martin Dollard	1986	3,445
148 7/8	24 3/8	22 7/8	20 3/8	6	6	Caledon Twp.	ONT	Jack Leggo	1988	3,445
148 7/8	24 4/8	26 2/8	18 5/8	4	4	Iroquois County	IL	Andrew C. McTaggart	1989	3,445
148 7/8	22 3/8	20 0/8	16 1/8	6	6	Lee County	IL	Marcus Nettz	1990	3,445
148 7/8	23 0/8	23 0/8	17 1/8	5	5	Fillmore County	MN	Brad Sutton	1990	3,445
148 7/8	24 6/8	25 0/8	21 1/8	5	5	Anoka County	MN	Bob Ross	1990	3,445
148 7/8	26 1/8	27 6/8	18 5/8	5	5	Heard County	GA	Jeffery T. Jackson	1990	3,445
148 7/8	22 0/8	22 7/8	18 5/8	5	5	Burleigh County	ND	Don Bieber	1991	3,445
148 7/8	24 1/8	24 6/8	19 7/8	6	6	Dane County	WI	Matthew A. Shimniok	1991	3,445
148 7/8	24 5/8	24 2/8	19 2/8	6	6	Stafford County	KS	Dan Schaad	1991	3,445
148 7/8	26 3/8	26 5/8	19 0/8	7	6	Buffalo County	WI	Ron Books	1992	3,445
148 7/8	24 7/8	24 5/8	18 3/8	5	4	Cass County	MI	William L. Bethard, Jr.	1992	3,445
148 7/8	24 3/8	23 6/8	20 1/8	4	4	Knox County	IL	Dennis Landon	1992	3,445
148 7/8	23 4/8	23 4/8	17 1/8	7	6	Brown County	SD	Brad Dinger	1993	3,445
148 7/8	24 2/8	25 3/8	20 1/8	6	5	Harding Township	ONT	Larry Ferguson	1993	3,445
148 7/8	24 6/8	24 5/8	19 3/8	4	5	Hillsdale County	MI	Terry J. Gerber	1994	3,445
148 7/8	26 0/8	25 6/8	20 7/8	5	4	Preble County	OH	Dean Ketring	1994	3,445
148 7/8	23 0/8	23 4/8	15 3/8	5	5	Shelby County	IL	Jonathan L. Gifford	1994	3,445
148 7/8	23 0/8	22 6/8	17 5/8	5	5	Osage County	KS	Tim Sparks	1994	3,445
148 7/8	24 5/8	25 4/8	18 5/8	5	5	Adams County	WI	Russell Scoville	1995	3,445
148 7/8	23 2/8	23 0/8	15 2/8	6	6	Clark County	IL	Gerald "Gabe" Shaffner	1995	3,445
148 7/8	23 3/8	22 4/8	19 4/8	7	5	Parke County	IN	Tom James	1996	3,445
148 7/8	22 6/8	22 2/8	17 5/8	5	5	Hendricks County	IN	James W. Thompson	1996	3,445
148 7/8	24 1/8	24 1/8	15 7/8	5	5	Winona County	MN	Steven Krage	1996	3,445
148 7/8	24 1/8	23 1/8	19 7/8	5	5	Morris County	NJ	David Barth	1996	3,445
148 7/8	21 7/8	22 0/8	17 5/8	5	5	Buffalo County	WI	John Larson	1996	3,445
148 7/8	23 6/8	25 2/8	21 3/8	6	5	Polk County	WI	Larry Selzler	1996	3,445
148 7/8	25 4/8	25 4/8	17 7/8	12	10	Grant County	IN	Kevin Kidwell	1997	3,445
148 7/8	23 6/8	24 2/8	18 3/8	7	6	Des Moines County	IA	Eric S. Rankin	1997	3,445
148 7/8	27 7/8	28 0/8	20 5/8	5	6	Richland County	OH	Craig Hallabrin	1997	3,445
148 7/8	24 1/8	25 0/8	17 5/8	6	5	Waukesha County	WI	Brad Lenhardt	1997	3,445
148 7/8	27 4/8	27 5/8	21 5/8	4	5	Montgomery County	PA	Jeff Steigelmann	1998	3,445
148 6/8	25 2/8	25 2/8	19 6/8	5	5	Iowa County	IA	Russ Sill	1967	3,482
148 6/8	23 0/8	23 0/8	18 4/8	5	5	Jefferson County	IN	Jim Coldiron	1969	3,482
148 6/8	21 3/8	21 1/8	19 1/8	6	6	Brown County	SD	Bill Franklin	1972	3,482
148 6/8	22 0/8	21 7/8	16 5/8	7	5	Schuylkill County	PA	Scott Bond	1979	3,482
148 6/8	24 2/8	23 4/8	22 6/8	6	7	Brookings County	SD	Larry Bohls	1982	3,482
148 6/8	24 1/8	23 6/8	17 2/8	5	5	Boone County	IA	Earl Taylor	1982	3,482
148 6/8	22 6/8	22 6/8	16 6/8	5	6	Reno County	KS	Davis J. Ediger	1982	3,482
148 6/8	22 6/8	22 3/8	15 2/8	5	4	Pierce County	ND	James Olson	1983	3,482
148 6/8	23 2/8	23 3/8	18 0/8	6	6	Kingsbury County	SD	Scott L. Laudenslager	1984	3,482
148 6/8	23 2/8	23 0/8	16 5/8	7	6	Jefferson County	WI	Steve Behm	1985	3,482
148 6/8	22 0/8	22 0/8	17 0/8	5	5	Monroe County	IN	Dene Snoddy	1986	3,482
148 6/8	23 1/8	25 3/8	18 7/8	6	5	Morgan County	IL	Steve North	1986	3,482
148 6/8	25 0/8	25 0/8	22 0/8	8	5	Jasper County	IA	William E. Webster	1987	3,482
148 6/8	25 0/8	23 4/8	17 5/8	5	6	Clermont County	OH	Timothy M. Singler	1988	3,482
148 6/8	24 0/8	23 0/8	17 0/8	5	5	Muscatine County	IA	Lyle Sindt	1988	3,482
148 6/8	25 1/8	25 0/8	18 6/8	5	5	Middlesex County	MA	Joe R. Shepard	1988	3,482
148 6/8	24 1/8	24 1/8	16 2/8	6	6	Chippewa County	MN	Paul D. Gill	1988	3,482
148 6/8	22 2/8	22 2/8	16 5/8	8	6	Edmonton	ALB	Dave Dickson	1990	3,482
148 6/8	23 1/8	23 3/8	16 6/8	5	5	Bon Homme County	SD	Leonard J. Magee	1990	3,482
148 6/8	24 6/8	25 2/8	24 3/8	5	5	Anne Arundel County	MD	Jim Roy	1990	3,482
148 6/8	23 4/8	23 5/8	18 2/8	5	5	Champaign County	IL	Terry Evans	1991	3,482
148 6/8	25 1/8	24 4/8	21 1/8	6	5	Bourbon County	KS	Larry Daly	1991	3,482
148 6/8	24 7/8	23 6/8	22 0/8	4	4	Zavala County	TX	Barry Powell	1992	3,482
148 6/8	23 5/8	22 2/8	17 2/8	5	5	Seward County	KS	Lynn Leonard	1992	3,482
148 6/8	26 1/8	25 2/8	18 5/8	7	7	Manitowoc County	WI	Daniel J. Kleiber	1992	3,482
148 6/8	24 4/8	24 3/8	22 4/8	4	4	Fairfield County	CT	Stephen Rohaly	1992	3,482
148 6/8	22 2/8	21 3/8	16 2/8	6	8	Holt County	MO	Jim Zawodny	1992	3,482
148 6/8	23 6/8	26 4/8	18 3/8	8	5	Iroquois County	IL	Dennis Clark	1993	3,482
148 6/8	25 1/8	24 5/8	21 0/8	5	5	Kenosha County	WI	Timothy Cox	1994	3,482

WHITETAIL DEER (TYPICAL ANTLERS)

Minimum Score 125 — Continued

SCORE	LENGTH OF R MAIN BEAM L		INSIDE SPREAD	NUMBER OF R POINTS L		AREA	STATE/ PROVINCE	HUNTER'S NAME	DATE	RANK
148 6/8	24 4/8	24 7/8	18 4/8	5	5	Henry County	IA	Mark Weber	1994	3,482
148 6/8	24 4/8	24 4/8	17 2/8	5	5	Dunn County	WI	Brian R. Bonesteel	1994	3,482
148 6/8	26 4/8	24 6/8	19 4/8	5	6	Montgomery County	IA	Dick Paul	1994	3,482
148 6/8	22 4/8	22 1/8	17 3/8	5	6	Granby River	BC	Randy Workman	1994	3,482
148 6/8	24 0/8	24 0/8	17 4/8	5	6	Knox County	IL	Frank T. Cain	1994	3,482
148 6/8	23 7/8	23 5/8	18 2/8	5	5	Oneida County	WI	David Klotzbuecher	1995	3,482
148 6/8	22 7/8	22 2/8	19 2/8	6	5	Walworth County	WI	Randy Vinge	1995	3,482
148 6/8	26 4/8	26 7/8	18 2/8	5	6	Athens County	OH	Charlie Grubbs	1995	3,482
148 6/8	22 1/8	23 1/8	19 0/8	5	5	Pottawattamie County	IA	Donald Combs	1996	3,482
148 6/8	24 2/8	24 2/8	21 0/8	6	6	Marshall County	IL	Timothy Myers	1997	3,482
148 6/8	29 5/8	28 1/8	21 0/8	4	6	Calhoun County	MI	Toby M. Wendt	1997	3,482
148 6/8	20 6/8	21 3/8	15 6/8	5	5	Kane County	IL	Fred Lehman	1997	3,482
148 6/8	22 4/8	22 4/8	16 2/8	6	6	Webster County	MS	Kenny May	1998	3,482
148 5/8	25 2/8	25 3/8	17 7/8	5	5	Newton County	IN	Larry Boezeman	1971	3,524
148 5/8	21 7/8	22 0/8	14 7/8	5	6	Pulaski County	MO	Ron Poston	1972	3,524
148 5/8	26 7/8	26 6/8	23 1/8	6	5	Coshocton County	OH	Charles H. Vlasek, Jr.	1979	3,524
148 5/8	23 0/8	22 6/8	22 1/8	5	5	Marion County	IA	Leonard Grimes	1981	3,524
148 5/8	23 1/8	24 5/8	18 6/8	5	5	Tuscola County	MI	Patrick C. Lewis	1983	3,524
148 5/8	25 6/8	25 6/8	19 6/8	6	5	Niobrara County	WY	Kenneth Fluck	1985	3,524
148 5/8	19 3/8	21 7/8	20 5/8	6	6	Dunn County	WI	Richard Urbaniak	1985	3,524
148 5/8	25 5/8	25 0/8	19 2/8	5	5	Piatt County	IL	David E. DeMoss	1985	3,524
148 5/8	22 1/8	24 1/8	20 5/8	5	5	Hancock County	WV	William Gary Rusinovich	1986	3,524
148 5/8	24 0/8	25 1/8	21 3/8	6	6	Houston County	MN	Bruce Norton	1987	3,524
148 5/8	23 3/8	23 5/8	17 7/8	5	5	Price County	WI	Dave A. Radosta	1987	3,524
148 5/8	26 4/8	25 7/8	18 5/8	4	5	Wabasha County	MN	Keith A. Ramthun	1988	3,524
148 5/8	20 3/8	21 3/8	16 7/8	5	5	Somerset County	PA	Brian Jones	1988	3,524
148 5/8	24 1/8	24 4/8	19 5/8	5	5	Sedgwick County	KS	Kent Lawson	1988	3,524
148 5/8	24 4/8	24 4/8	17 5/8	7	7	Chippewa County	MN	Gary Laughlin	1988	3,524
148 5/8	25 2/8	24 7/8	16 7/8	5	5	Crawford County	KS	Jim W. Heardt	1988	3,524
148 5/8	26 6/8	25 3/8	19 5/8	4	6	Hardin County	IL	Charles E. Spear	1989	3,524
148 5/8	23 1/8	24 2/8	19 5/8	4	5	Bureau County	IL	Gregory A. Bowers	1989	3,524
148 5/8	22 7/8	23 3/8	16 3/8	5	5	Rock County	WI	R. Wayne Douglas	1989	3,524
148 5/8	22 3/8	22 0/8	15 4/8	6	7	Licking County	OH	Randy Marcum	1990	3,524
148 5/8	23 2/8	23 1/8	18 5/8	5	5	Oneida County	WI	John L. Mueller	1990	3,524
148 5/8	23 4/8	22 6/8	18 5/8	5	7	Jackson County	MO	Donald Dutton	1991	3,524
148 5/8	24 1/8	23 5/8	18 5/8	5	5	Ogle County	IL	Thomas W. Sharkey	1991	3,524
148 5/8	20 7/8	21 3/8	19 1/8	6	8	Clinton County	OH	Vaughn Wright	1991	3,524
148 5/8	23 3/8	23 7/8	19 0/8	5	6	Warren County	IA	Mark Motsinger	1991	3,524
148 5/8	24 6/8	25 0/8	17 0/8	6	5	Price County	WI	Charles Pasewald	1992	3,524
148 5/8	24 3/8	23 2/8	19 1/8	5	5	Hamilton County	IA	Steve Doering	1992	3,524
148 5/8	23 5/8	23 0/8	19 3/8	4	4	Dallas County	IA	John Flies	1992	3,524
148 5/8	24 7/8	25 0/8	20 3/8	6	5	La Salle County	IL	Phill Pulfer	1993	3,524
148 5/8	24 2/8	24 4/8	18 6/8	5	6	Sauk County	WI	Rick Krumenauer	1993	3,524
148 5/8	23 3/8	23 6/8	16 3/8	6	6	Iroquois County	IL	Howard Brady	1994	3,524
148 5/8	26 2/8	23 3/8	15 4/8	5	6	Wapello County	IA	David Meyer	1994	3,524
148 5/8	24 4/8	25 4/8	19 4/8	5	7	Jackson County	WI	Michael Coleman	1995	3,524
148 5/8	25 3/8	24 0/8	19 5/8	5	5	Pepin County	WI	Kirk Peterson	1995	3,524
148 5/8	25 3/8	24 7/8	18 3/8	4	4	Knox County	IL	Gerald Duane Smith	1995	3,524
148 5/8	24 5/8	23 5/8	16 5/8	5	5	Louisa County	IA	Rick Stroud	1995	3,524
148 5/8	25 5/8	23 6/8	18 5/8	5	5	Starke County	IN	F. James Harris	1995	3,524
148 5/8	23 3/8	23 5/8	19 1/8	5	6	Kenosha County	WI	Thomas T. King	1995	3,524
148 5/8	25 0/8	24 5/8	21 1/8	5	5	Champaign County	OH	Roland A. Chamberlin	1995	3,524
148 5/8	25 4/8	24 7/8	20 3/8	6	5	Orange County	NC	Bob Arnao	1996	3,524
148 5/8	23 1/8	23 7/8	17 2/8	6	6	Benton County	IA	Chris Swanke	1996	3,524
148 5/8	22 6/8	22 7/8	17 5/8	7	7	Cotton County	OK	Scott Crew	1997	3,524
148 4/8	23 0/8	22 4/8	20 1/8	4	5	Murray County	MN	Mike Molitor	1968	3,566
148 4/8	20 7/8	21 4/8	16 6/8	5	5	Rock County	WI	Bruce Douglas	1978	3,566
148 4/8	26 0/8	22 0/8	18 0/8	5	5	Woodford County	IL	James M. Bill, Jr.	1982	3,566
148 4/8	24 2/8	24 5/8	21 5/8	5	5	Martin County	MN	Dean Roben	1982	3,566
148 4/8	25 1/8	24 4/8	16 6/8	5	5	Grant County	WI	William P Rodenkirch	1983	3,566
148 4/8	23 0/8	23 6/8	17 7/8	5	6	Pepin County	WI	Roger Anderson	1984	3,566
148 4/8	23 7/8	25 2/8	19 4/8	5	4	Jefferson County	OH	Larry C. Riggle	1984	3,566
148 4/8	25 5/8	24 2/8	18 4/8	5	5	Randolph County	IL	Conel H. Rogers, Jr.	1985	3,566
148 4/8	24 3/8	24 5/8	20 6/8	7	6	Meade County	KS	Randall J. VanDegrift	1985	3,566
148 4/8	22 2/8	22 2/8	19 6/8	5	5	Seward County	KS	Stuart G. Hazard III	1985	3,566
148 4/8	25 6/8	22 0/8	19 1/8	8	7	Kings County	NBW	Ken Kirkpatrick	1986	3,566
148 4/8	23 6/8	25 0/8	19 0/8	5	5	Edmonson County	KY	Marvin T. Pate	1987	3,566
148 4/8	26 2/8	26 1/8	18 6/8	6	6	Waukesha County	WI	Ron V. Schneider	1987	3,566
148 4/8	26 0/8	27 5/8	19 0/8	4	4	Orange County	NC	Todd McDonald	1988	3,566
148 4/8	27 3/8	27 1/8	20 2/8	4	4	Lawrence County	IL	Russell Morris	1988	3,566
148 4/8	21 6/8	21 4/8	17 6/8	5	5	Scott County	MN	Donald T. Turner	1989	3,566
148 4/8	22 1/8	23 1/8	15 2/8	5	6	Burleigh County	ND	Robert Matzke	1989	3,566
148 4/8	23 1/8	23 4/8	18 4/8	5	5	Woodford County	IL	Larry Messer	1989	3,566
148 4/8	24 3/8	24 2/8	16 4/8	6	5	Polk County	WI	Daniel Carlson	1989	3,566
148 4/8	22 5/8	22 7/8	17 2/8	5	5	Caldwell County	KY	Boyd Smith	1990	3,566
148 4/8	26 0/8	25 5/8	21 4/8	7	6	Cedar County	IA	Brian Barclay	1990	3,566
148 4/8	22 6/8	22 3/8	18 6/8	5	5	Oneida County	WI	Jeff Aulik	1990	3,566
148 4/8	25 2/8	26 0/8	16 7/8	5	5	Cumberland County	ME	Chester L. Brooks	1991	3,566

WHITETAIL DEER (TYPICAL ANTLERS)

Minimum Score 125 — Continued

SCORE	LENGTH OF MAIN BEAM R	LENGTH OF MAIN BEAM L	INSIDE SPREAD	NUMBER OF POINTS R	NUMBER OF POINTS L	AREA	STATE/ PROVINCE	HUNTER'S NAME	DATE	RANK
148 4/8	21 5/8	23 5/8	17 4/8	5	5	Warren County	IA	Dan Mork	1991	3,566
148 4/8	22 4/8	22 4/8	19 2/8	5	5	Baltimore County	MD	Bruce Hoover	1992	3,566
148 4/8	20 4/8	21 1/8	16 6/8	6	5	Hardin County	OH	Kevin Stahler	1992	3,566
148 4/8	23 6/8	23 3/8	17 6/8	5	5	Eau Claire County	WI	Jack T. Lawler	1992	3,566
148 4/8	23 5/8	22 2/8	18 4/8	5	5	Wayne County	MI	Ronald A. Stolberg	1992	3,566
148 4/8	26 3/8	25 7/8	19 4/8	5	7	Oneida County	WI	Jeffrey Roell	1993	3,566
148 4/8	22 7/8	23 3/8	18 4/8	5	5	Iowa County	WI	Dennis Cliff	1993	3,566
148 4/8	27 0/8	26 3/8	15 4/8	4	4	Iron County	WI	Gerold Schaff	1994	3,566
148 4/8	24 7/8	24 5/8	18 2/8	4	4	Outagamie County	WI	Gerald A. Snortum	1994	3,566
148 4/8	23 4/8	24 4/8	16 0/8	5	5	Lawrence County	OH	Robert Sturgill	1994	3,566
148 4/8	24 4/8	24 3/8	18 0/8	6	5	Pike County	IL	Mark Beeler	1994	3,566
148 4/8	23 6/8	25 5/8	19 4/8	6	5	Hunterdon County	NJ	Jeff Farr	1996	3,566
148 4/8	25 1/8	25 1/8	16 2/8	5	5	Lake County	IL	Jim Tahaney	1996	3,566
148 4/8	25 5/8	25 4/8	19 5/8	4	6	Allamakee County	IA	Jeff Wirth	1996	3,566
148 4/8	22 2/8	22 3/8	16 0/8	5	5	Dubuque County	IA	Doug Westhoff	1996	3,566
148 4/8	24 2/8	21 6/8	18 1/8	7	6	Ramsey County	MN	Robert Meyer, Jr.	1997	3,566
148 4/8	24 6/8	26 2/8	19 0/8	5	5	Martin County	IN	Kevin Olinger	1997	3,566
148 4/8	23 6/8	24 2/8	18 6/8	5	5	Allen County	IN	Randy Zion	1997	3,566
148 4/8	24 3/8	24 3/8	19 0/8	5	5	Kewaunee County	WI	Joe J. Dax	1997	3,566
148 4/8	23 2/8	24 2/8	22 2/8	4	4	Somerset County	NJ	James C. Kelly	1998	3,566
148 3/8	25 6/8	26 7/8	22 2/8	9	5	Scott County	MN	Bob Gregory	1967	3,609
148 3/8	23 5/8	23 7/8	17 5/8	5	5	Monroe County	NY	Robert J. Ranalletta	1976	3,609
148 3/8	23 0/8	23 4/8	18 0/8	6	7	Ballard County	KY	Gregory Joles	1978	3,609
148 3/8	22 5/8	22 1/8	17 5/8	6	6	Watonwan County	MN	Joe Graif	1981	3,609
148 3/8	23 5/8	23 7/8	24 1/8	6	5	Fairfield County	OH	Jim Jordan	1982	3,609
148 3/8	22 1/8	22 6/8	18 1/8	5	5	Morrison County	MN	Robert Redmann	1984	3,609
148 3/8	23 7/8	22 7/8	17 0/8	7	5	Fayette County	IN	Chris L. Mustin	1984	3,609
148 3/8	24 6/8	25 5/8	19 1/8	5	5	Baltimore County	MD	Donald Layne	1985	3,609
148 3/8	24 3/8	24 2/8	18 1/8	6	6	Phillips County	KS	Julius E. Schoenberger	1985	3,609
148 3/8	22 2/8	23 6/8	16 7/8	5	5	Ottawa County	KS	Wayne E. Smith	1985	3,609
148 3/8	22 0/8	21 7/8	17 5/8	7	7	Carter County	OK	Charles W. Chatham	1986	3,609
148 3/8	23 0/8	22 4/8	19 3/8	5	5	Macoupin County	IL	Don Snyder	1986	3,609
148 3/8	25 3/8	25 0/8	16 7/8	6	5	Noble County	IN	Daniel J. Bidwell	1987	3,609
148 3/8	24 5/8	24 2/8	22 0/8	5	4	Wright County	IA	Mark D. Slining	1987	3,609
148 3/8	23 2/8	23 0/8	20 1/8	5	6	Grant County	KY	Richard L. Koors	1988	3,609
148 3/8	23 4/8	23 4/8	19 3/8	5	6	Ionia County	MI	James E. Allen	1988	3,609
148 3/8	22 5/8	22 5/8	17 3/8	4	5	Morgan County	OH	Stacey Triplet	1989	3,609
148 3/8	22 5/8	24 4/8	18 3/8	5	5	Lewis & Clark County	MT	Sonny Templeton	1989	3,609
148 3/8	25 5/8	24 5/8	18 7/8	4	5	Stoddard County	MO	Clint Barnfield	1990	3,609
148 3/8	24 4/8	24 2/8	20 5/8	5	5	Boone County	IL	Wilmer V. Garlick	1990	3,609
148 3/8	27 0/8	23 6/8	18 3/8	4	4	Middlesex County	CT	Fredrick J. Massini	1990	3,609
148 3/8	26 1/8	25 6/8	19 1/8	4	6	Tama County	IA	Harold Cox	1990	3,609
148 3/8	27 3/8	27 5/8	18 5/8	5	4	Barton County	MO	Gregory W. Benander	1990	3,609
148 3/8	22 6/8	22 1/8	20 1/8	5	5	Kandiyohi County	MN	Bob Sampson	1991	3,609
148 3/8	27 0/8	26 0/8	18 1/8	9	6	Webster County	IA	Terry Rial	1992	3,609
148 3/8	26 4/8	25 6/8	21 2/8	6	4	Washington County	MN	Keith Johnson	1992	3,609
148 3/8	24 3/8	23 0/8	16 3/8	7	7	La Salle County	IL	Pete Stoneberg	1993	3,609
148 3/8	21 1/8	20 4/8	15 7/8	5	5	Roseau County	MN	Dillon Janousek	1993	3,609
148 3/8	22 1/8	23 2/8	17 6/8	6	6	Washington County	KS	Bob Funke	1993	3,609
148 3/8	24 2/8	24 2/8	16 2/8	7	5	Buffalo County	WI	John Charles	1994	3,609
148 3/8	23 0/8	22 7/8	17 1/8	5	5	Columbia County	WI	Ryan Traut	1994	3,609
148 3/8	26 2/8	27 7/8	20 5/8	4	4	Westchester County	NY	William J. Evans	1994	3,609
148 3/8	24 1/8	24 5/8	22 4/8	6	5	Chautauqua County	KS	Eddie Claypool	1994	3,609
148 3/8	24 2/8	24 1/8	18 1/8	5	5	Scotland County	MO	Steve Stoltz	1994	3,609
148 3/8	24 7/8	23 1/8	17 4/8	6	5	Winona County	MN	Roger Merchlewitz	1994	3,609
148 3/8	23 7/8	24 2/8	19 2/8	5	6	Sullivan County	NH	Don Goodwin	1995	3,609
148 3/8	24 6/8	24 4/8	16 7/8	4	5	Madison County	IL	Leo N. Brinson, Jr.	1995	3,609
148 3/8	23 4/8	24 4/8	19 7/8	5	5	Marshall County	KS	Terry Gunn	1995	3,609
148 3/8	26 1/8	26 0/8	19 3/8	4	4	Nemaha County	KS	Darryl Becker	1995	3,609
148 3/8	23 4/8	23 4/8	18 7/8	5	6	Lincoln County	WI	Trevor Sorce	1995	3,609
148 3/8	20 6/8	20 7/8	15 5/8	5	5	Okanogan County	WA	Kirk Sapp	1996	3,609
148 3/8	26 5/8	24 0/8	15 7/8	8	6	Butler County	IA	Curt J. Chase	1996	3,609
148 3/8	24 5/8	23 1/8	19 4/8	5	5	Clinton County	IL	Trey Johnson	1996	3,609
148 3/8	23 4/8	23 3/8	17 5/8	5	5	Kalamazoo County	MI	Mark S. Vlietstra	1997	3,609
148 2/8	22 3/8	21 6/8	16 2/8	5	5	Walworth County	SD	Irvin Guthmiller	1956	3,653
148 2/8	22 7/8	21 5/8	18 2/8	5	5	Harrison County	IA	James W. Glasscock	1968	3,653
148 2/8	25 1/8	24 1/8	15 4/8	5	5	Woodbury County	IA	Guy Hempey	1969	3,653
148 2/8	24 5/8	24 7/8	24 0/8	5	5	Jackson County	IL	Darrell Fritsche	1973	3,653
148 2/8	20 7/8	22 2/8	16 4/8	5	5	Pittsburg County	OK	Bill Hisle	1975	3,653
148 2/8	24 2/8	23 4/8	18 0/8	5	7	Latah County	ID	Don A. West	1976	3,653
148 2/8	26 5/8	24 3/8	19 7/8	6	8	Coshocton County	OH	Charles N. McDonald	1977	3,653
148 2/8	23 0/8	22 2/8	20 7/8	4	5	Sanford	MAN	Wayne Rodgers	1979	3,653
148 2/8	24 7/8	25 1/8	18 0/8	5	5	Winnebago County	IL	Fred Kelley	1981	3,653
148 2/8	24 6/8	23 3/8	16 5/8	4	6	Clark County	KS	Casey V. Rudd	1981	3,653
148 2/8	23 4/8	23 1/8	22 6/8	6	10	Marion County	IL	Paul Duncan	1982	3,653
148 2/8	27 3/8	27 0/8	20 7/8	5	6	Washington County	WI	Steve Karoses	1983	3,653
148 2/8	26 0/8	26 2/8	17 5/8	8	6	Adair County	MO	Tim Richardson	1983	3,653
148 2/8	23 0/8	23 6/8	17 0/8	5	5	Pierce County	WI	Mitchell C. Nelson	1984	3,653

WHITETAIL DEER (TYPICAL ANTLERS)

Minimum Score 125 — Continued

SCORE	R MAIN BEAM L		INSIDE SPREAD	R POINTS L		AREA	STATE/PROVINCE	HUNTER'S NAME	DATE	RANK
148 2/8	21 2/8	21 6/8	18 4/8	5	5	Kenosha County	WI	Marty Daniels	1985	3,653
148 2/8	25 7/8	26 0/8	20 0/8	4	4	Polk County	MN	Warren Nelson	1986	3,653
148 2/8	20 7/8	21 5/8	18 6/8	5	6	Butler County	KS	David R. Rogers	1986	3,653
148 2/8	24 2/8	23 6/8	16 3/8	6	5	Polk County	IA	Robert E. Morterud	1987	3,653
148 2/8	23 0/8	24 1/8	21 4/8	6	5	Clay County	MN	James F. Thompson	1987	3,653
148 2/8	25 7/8	26 4/8	18 2/8	5	5	Cross County	AR	Rickey W. Proctor	1987	3,653
148 2/8	22 7/8	24 1/8	19 5/8	6	6	Allen County	KS	Curt Stahl	1988	3,653
148 2/8	24 7/8	25 7/8	19 6/8	4	4	Belmont County	OH	Chad Krahel	1989	3,653
148 2/8	26 0/8	26 4/8	19 4/8	6	6	Will County	IL	Dennis J. Lake	1990	3,653
148 2/8	23 5/8	23 0/8	20 4/8	5	7	Jersey County	IL	Judy Kovar	1990	3,653
148 2/8	23 2/8	23 3/8	17 0/8	7	5	Marshall County	OK	James B. Evans, Jr.	1990	3,653
148 2/8	26 0/8	26 3/8	18 3/8	4	5	Lake County	IL	Donald R. Powers	1990	3,653
148 2/8	25 3/8	23 3/8	19 6/8	6	8	Phillips County	KS	Charles Bockhorn	1991	3,653
148 2/8	23 4/8	23 7/8	19 0/8	5	5	Steuben County	NY	Mark S. O'Donal	1991	3,653
148 2/8	27 6/8	27 2/8	17 6/8	5	6	Howard County	MO	Bodie Beach	1991	3,653
148 2/8	22 5/8	22 0/8	17 4/8	5	5	Vermilion County	IL	Jeffery Parkerson	1991	3,653
148 2/8	25 1/8	24 4/8	17 5/8	7	6	Fayette County	IL	Mike Ziemba	1991	3,653
148 2/8	25 0/8	24 4/8	18 0/8	5	5	Pike County	IL	Jerry Pennock	1991	3,653
148 2/8	24 3/8	25 0/8	16 7/8	9	8	Hennepin County	MN	Todd J. Zwak	1991	3,653
148 2/8	24 5/8	24 5/8	18 0/8	6	7	Dane County	WI	Alan Corlett	1991	3,653
148 2/8	24 0/8	24 7/8	19 4/8	4	5	Houston County	MN	Travis Peterson	1992	3,653
148 2/8	23 7/8	23 5/8	17 4/8	4	4	Knox County	IL	Gregg E. Moore	1993	3,653
148 2/8	24 7/8	25 3/8	17 4/8	5	8	Pembina County	ND	Myles Keller	1993	3,653
148 2/8	25 5/8	24 7/8	16 4/8	7	6	Butler County	KS	Frank Boyer	1994	3,653
148 2/8	21 2/8	22 0/8	16 4/8	5	6	Noble County	OH	Charles D. Bennethum, Jr.	1995	3,653
148 2/8	24 4/8	23 2/8	19 6/8	5	5	Ogle County	IL	Jeff Blascoe	1995	3,653
148 2/8	24 4/8	23 5/8	16 5/8	6	5	Coles County	IL	Jim Eveland	1995	3,653
148 2/8	23 7/8	23 5/8	16 2/8	5	5	Clermont County	OH	Zachary J. Watkins	1995	3,653
148 2/8	22 0/8	22 1/8	19 0/8	6	5	Jackson County	IA	David H. Lincoln	1995	3,653
148 2/8	24 6/8	24 6/8	19 4/8	5	5	Marion County	IA	Kyle Goodwin	1995	3,653
148 2/8	23 4/8	24 4/8	19 4/8	5	5	Bon Homme County	SD	Todd Hornstra	1995	3,653
148 2/8	25 0/8	25 0/8	17 2/8	5	5	Pike County	IL	Don Dye, Jr.	1995	3,653
148 2/8	24 5/8	24 0/8	17 4/8	5	5	Casey County	KY	Carroll Gibson	1996	3,653
148 2/8	25 1/8	24 5/8	17 4/8	5	5	Woods County	OK	Lloyd Mark Evans	1996	3,653
148 2/8	22 1/8	22 2/8	19 2/8	6	5	Dane County	WI	Joe Hoff	1997	3,653
148 2/8	23 4/8	24 0/8	16 4/8	6	5	Sauk County	WI	Scott E. Kotlowski	1997	3,653
148 2/8	20 7/8	20 5/8	19 4/8	6	6	Huron County	MI	David Charles Wille	1997	3,653
148 2/8	21 0/8	20 6/8	16 4/8	5	5	Treasure County	MT	Steve Trimble	1998	3,653
148 1/8	24 2/8	24 2/8	20 5/8	4	4	Erie County	NY	William R. Helmich	1975	3,705
148 1/8	23 0/8	22 5/8	17 2/8	5	6	Wellington County	ONT	Barry Marshall	1975	3,705
148 1/8	27 3/8	27 5/8	21 6/8	6	6	Tazewell County	IL	David Huser	1980	3,705
148 1/8	24 2/8	22 5/8	19 3/8	5	5	Uvalde County	TX	Jim Jordan	1986	3,705
148 1/8	23 3/8	22 7/8	18 5/8	5	5	Calumet County	WI	Joseph R. Mader	1986	3,705
148 1/8	23 6/8	24 5/8	17 6/8	5	8	Cass County	ND	Rodney P. Mathison	1986	3,705
148 1/8	23 2/8	24 0/8	19 5/8	6	5	Brown County	WI	Andy Dobesh	1987	3,705
148 1/8	22 6/8	22 3/8	18 2/8	6	5	Hickory County	MO	David Langton	1987	3,705
148 1/8	23 7/8	23 6/8	20 3/8	5	5	Crow Wing County	MN	Bob Brown	1988	3,705
148 1/8	24 4/8	25 0/8	19 5/8	5	6	Pike County	IL	Ray Hatfield	1988	3,705
148 1/8	22 4/8	22 7/8	20 1/8	5	5	Sawyer County	WI	Brad B. Christensen	1989	3,705
148 1/8	25 2/8	25 5/8	18 2/8	5	6	Iron County	WI	D. J. Sullivan	1990	3,705
148 1/8	23 0/8	22 4/8	21 1/8	5	6	Burnett County	WI	Sheldon Wendorf	1990	3,705
148 1/8	25 0/8	24 5/8	20 5/8	4	5	McHenry County	IL	Dennis E. Straumann	1990	3,705
148 1/8	24 2/8	23 5/8	14 1/8	6	6	Whiteside County	IL	Abraham Wuebben	1991	3,705
148 1/8	25 3/8	25 0/8	17 7/8	8	6	Stoddard County	MO	Ken Heuer	1991	3,705
148 1/8	24 0/8	24 6/8	20 5/8	4	5	Somerset County	MD	Mark Labo	1992	3,705
148 1/8	23 2/8	23 7/8	17 7/8	5	5	Laclede County	MO	Richard Blackman	1992	3,705
148 1/8	24 1/8	24 0/8	18 2/8	4	5	De Witt County	IL	James L. Nicholson	1992	3,705
148 1/8	22 7/8	22 4/8	22 1/8	5	5	Lake County	IL	Jeff Miller	1993	3,705
148 1/8	21 2/8	23 0/8	13 6/8	6	5	Platte County	MO	Clint Woods	1994	3,705
148 1/8	24 7/8	24 5/8	17 5/8	5	4	Macon County	IL	Mark Cecil Sutton	1994	3,705
148 1/8	23 3/8	23 7/8	19 3/8	6	5	Waukesha County	WI	Dana Hoppe	1994	3,705
148 1/8	25 1/8	24 6/8	17 7/8	4	4	Huron County	OH	Rodney L. Gribble	1994	3,705
148 1/8	25 7/8	26 3/8	20 2/8	5	4	McDowell County	WV	Roger Wolfe, Jr.	1994	3,705
148 1/8	24 6/8	24 7/8	19 3/8	5	4	Montgomery County	MO	Arthur Bader	1994	3,705
148 1/8	24 7/8	25 4/8	20 5/8	5	5	Kleberg County	TX	Robert Nichols	1995	3,705
148 1/8	23 0/8	23 2/8	18 3/8	5	5	Wright County	MN	Michael Halberg	1995	3,705
148 1/8	23 5/8	24 3/8	18 6/8	4	5	Porter County	IN	James S. Friday	1996	3,705
148 1/8	27 6/8	26 3/8	17 5/8	7	5	Seneca County	OH	Ronald Bivens	1996	3,705
148 1/8	21 6/8	21 4/8	15 7/8	5	6	Holmes County	MS	Billy Ellis III	1997	3,705
148 1/8	24 4/8	24 3/8	18 7/8	5	5	Washington Parish	LA	Hunter Lewis	1997	3,705
148 1/8	22 4/8	22 0/8	17 3/8	5	5	Douglas County	WI	Charles R. Pattee	1997	3,705
148 1/8	22 4/8	23 6/8	16 7/8	5	5	Wayne County	IL	Andy Schlichting	1997	3,705
148 1/8	24 6/8	24 4/8	21 1/8	5	5	Vilas County	WI	Gary Thomson	1997	3,705
148 0/8	22 1/8	22 2/8	14 6/8	5	5	Stanley County	SD	Brad Taylor	1979	3,740
148 0/8	23 5/8	23 1/8	18 6/8	5	6	Uvalde County	TX	M.H. "Bill" Wilkinson, Jr.	1980	3,740
148 0/8	22 6/8	23 1/8	17 6/8	5	5	Green County	WI	E. Dussault	1983	3,740
148 0/8	25 2/8	25 2/8	18 3/8	5	5	Buffalo County	WI	Daniel Folkedahl	1984	3,740
148 0/8	24 6/8	25 5/8	23 6/8	4	5	Clay County	MN	Keith J Fischer	1984	3,740

WHITETAIL DEER (TYPICAL ANTLERS)

Minimum Score 125   Continued

SCORE	LENGTH OF MAIN BEAM R	LENGTH OF MAIN BEAM L	INSIDE SPREAD	NUMBER OF POINTS R	NUMBER OF POINTS L	AREA	STATE/PROVINCE	HUNTER'S NAME	DATE	RANK
148 0/8	24 3/8	25 0/8	18 3/8	6	8	McIntosh County	ND	Garnes Ruff	1985	3,740
148 0/8	22 4/8	22 0/8	15 3/8	5	6	Norman County	MN	Les Krogstad	1985	3,740
148 0/8	25 7/8	27 7/8	16 7/8	7	6	Madison County	NY	Lloyd Weigel	1985	3,740
148 0/8	20 0/8	23 1/8	22 4/8	6	5	Dorchester County	MD	Bob Reinert	1985	3,740
148 0/8	24 2/8	24 3/8	19 5/8	6	5	Kittson County	MN	Steve Lindberg	1986	3,740
148 0/8	24 1/8	24 4/8	15 6/8	5	6	Vernon County	WI	Harry J. Curtis	1986	3,740
148 0/8	27 3/8	28 1/8	19 0/8	5	5	Putnam County	IN	Kevin W. Jones	1986	3,740
148 0/8	22 1/8	22 6/8	21 0/8	5	5	Suffolk County	NY	Steven Schoen	1987	3,740
148 0/8	23 6/8	23 6/8	18 4/8	6	6	Bremer County	IA	Leroy Matthias	1988	3,740
148 0/8	23 6/8	25 4/8	21 0/8	4	4	Marathon County	WI	Steven Marvin	1989	3,740
148 0/8	25 3/8	24 2/8	20 2/8	5	5	Shelby County	IL	David E. Varvil	1989	3,740
148 0/8	26 2/8	26 1/8	23 1/8	6	6	De Witt County	IL	Chris Dilks	1989	3,740
148 0/8	24 0/8	24 0/8	18 5/8	7	6	Williamson County	IL	Charles Tessone	1989	3,740
148 0/8	24 2/8	23 0/8	19 2/8	7	6	Allamakee County	IA	Tim Waid	1990	3,740
148 0/8	23 1/8	22 7/8	17 4/8	4	4	Boundary County	ID	Mike Hittle	1991	3,740
148 0/8	22 0/8	22 4/8	16 4/8	6	6	Deuel County	NE	Dirk Gosnell	1991	3,740
148 0/8	25 4/8	26 5/8	18 6/8	4	4	Vermilion County	IL	Darin Duitsman	1991	3,740
148 0/8	22 7/8	23 1/8	15 2/8	5	5	Chisago County	MN	Bill Barzydlo	1991	3,740
148 0/8	24 5/8	24 5/8	15 3/8	6	5	Clayton County	IA	Thomas Schremser	1991	3,740
148 0/8	24 1/8	23 5/8	16 6/8	7	6	Gallia County	OH	Gary Griffith	1991	3,740
148 0/8	25 1/8	23 2/8	16 4/8	5	5	Van Buren County	IA	Dan Brockman	1991	3,740
148 0/8	22 5/8	22 3/8	19 0/8	5	5	Jackson County	WI	Glen R. Loppnow	1992	3,740
148 0/8	23 4/8	24 5/8	18 4/8	5	5	Powell County	MT	George Croft	1992	3,740
148 0/8	25 2/8	25 5/8	17 1/8	7	7	Spokane County	WA	Dan E. Kersey	1992	3,740
148 0/8	24 4/8	25 4/8	20 6/8	5	5	Cuyahoga County	OH	Mark R. Johnson	1993	3,740
148 0/8	24 2/8	24 1/8	19 6/8	5	4	Steuben County	IN	Michael L. Osborne	1994	3,740
148 0/8	24 0/8	24 2/8	18 1/8	7	6	Jefferson County	WI	Craig Wetterling	1994	3,740
148 0/8	24 5/8	24 5/8	20 2/8	5	5	Jackson County	IN	Ray A. Strong	1994	3,740
148 0/8	26 3/8	26 1/8	21 4/8	4	6	Clayton County	IA	Daniel J. Brimeyer	1995	3,740
148 0/8	23 6/8	23 5/8	19 4/8	4	5	Pulaski County	IN	Daniel A. Beal	1995	3,740
148 0/8	24 0/8	24 3/8	21 6/8	4	4	Woodford County	KY	Daniel E. Jackson II	1995	3,740
148 0/8	23 0/8	24 1/8	17 4/8	6	5	Sussex County	DE	Don Fiedler	1997	3,740
148 0/8	22 2/8	23 1/8	21 2/8	5	6	Randolph County	IL	Mark Bradley	1997	3,740
148 0/8	24 0/8	26 1/8	19 2/8	4	4	Calhoun County	IL	Robert G. Fulton	1998	3,740
148 0/8	23 4/8	23 5/8	17 2/8	5	6	Jefferson County	WI	Ben Sikhart	1998	3,740
147 7/8	21 7/8	22 2/8	18 5/8	5	5	Green Lake County	WI	Al Hubbell	1974	3,780
147 7/8	25 6/8	24 7/8	21 7/8	4	4	Anne Arundel County	MD	James E. Roy	1977	3,780
147 7/8	22 2/8	22 3/8	18 5/8	5	5	Iron County	MI	David C. Tarsi	1978	3,780
147 7/8	26 3/8	25 6/8	17 5/8	4	4	Lafayette County	WI	Kim D. Gruenberg	1979	3,780
147 7/8	20 6/8	21 6/8	18 4/8	6	6	Cass County	NE	David R. Kempnich	1981	3,780
147 7/8	27 0/8	26 0/8	23 2/8	4	6	Cowley County	KS	Virgil Dwayne Graham	1982	3,780
147 7/8	25 1/8	26 1/8	21 6/8	5	5	McHenry County	IL	Greg Herdrich	1983	3,780
147 7/8	24 5/8	24 0/8	19 5/8	5	5	Guthrie County	IA	Vernie W. Grasty	1983	3,780
147 7/8	23 4/8	24 2/8	15 2/8	5	6	Harris County	TX	John Hall	1985	3,780
147 7/8	21 7/8	22 2/8	17 7/8	5	5	Butler County	OH	James Lynch	1985	3,780
147 7/8	21 2/8	21 1/8	19 6/8	6	5	Rice County	KS	David L. Boedeker	1986	3,780
147 7/8	23 6/8	23 3/8	18 2/8	6	6	Wabaunsee County	KS	Jim Hagan	1986	3,780
147 7/8	23 4/8	23 0/8	14 5/8	5	5	Langlade County	WI	Mark Helgeson	1986	3,780
147 7/8	23 4/8	23 4/8	20 3/8	5	5	Lake County	IL	David Mitten	1987	3,780
147 7/8	23 3/8	24 3/8	18 5/8	5	5	Dakota County	MN	Fred Kober	1988	3,780
147 7/8	22 1/8	22 3/8	15 5/8	6	6	Scott County	IA	Gary W. Gilkison	1988	3,780
147 7/8	25 0/8	24 3/8	15 7/8	6	6	Chippewa County	WI	Joseph L. Couey	1989	3,780
147 7/8	22 1/8	22 6/8	17 1/8	5	5	Macon County	IL	Earl Nelson	1989	3,780
147 7/8	24 5/8	25 1/8	19 5/8	4	4	Eau Claire County	WI	Robert W. Hall	1990	3,780
147 7/8	26 0/8	25 5/8	23 3/8	4	4	Allamakee County	IA	Kevin Sweeney	1990	3,780
147 7/8	25 7/8	26 3/8	19 5/8	4	4	Lake County	IL	Allen G. Comstock	1990	3,780
147 7/8	23 3/8	23 1/8	16 2/8	5	6	Waukesha County	WI	Andrae D'Acquisto	1991	3,780
147 7/8	24 1/8	22 4/8	16 4/8	6	6	Redwood County	MN	Gary Schunk	1992	3,780
147 7/8	23 2/8	23 0/8	17 0/8	7	7	La Salle County	TX	Jeremy Elias	1992	3,780
147 7/8	26 6/8	26 5/8	18 1/8	4	4	Calvert County	MD	Charles J. Wade	1993	3,780
147 7/8	22 6/8	23 2/8	17 5/8	5	6	Jackson County	OH	Edsel D. Duty	1993	3,780
147 7/8	25 0/8	25 0/8	18 0/8	5	8	Schuyler County	IL	Gregory Runkle	1993	3,780
147 7/8	24 7/8	25 2/8	18 7/8	4	5	Sauk County	WI	Michael J. McGann	1994	3,780
147 7/8	26 2/8	26 4/8	19 5/8	4	5	Knox County	IL	Kevin Engels	1994	3,780
147 7/8	24 4/8	24 2/8	17 1/8	6	5	Wapello County	IA	Ralph McConaughey	1995	3,780
147 7/8	26 5/8	26 1/8	14 6/8	7	6	Buffalo County	WI	Daniel H. Folkedahl	1995	3,780
147 7/8	26 2/8	25 7/8	19 2/8	4	6	Shelby County	IL	Joseph Hoene	1996	3,780
147 7/8	24 2/8	24 5/8	17 5/8	6	6	Jackson County	MI	Clare C. Butler	1996	3,780
147 7/8	24 1/8	24 7/8	18 6/8	7	6	Pike County	IL	Pat Davis	1996	3,780
147 7/8	24 7/8	24 7/8	16 4/8	5	5	Clay County	IL	Richard Stock	1996	3,780
147 7/8	22 5/8	22 4/8	21 5/8	5	5	Minnehaha County	SD	Tim Zoellner	1996	3,780
147 7/8	21 3/8	21 7/8	14 5/8	5	5	St. Clair County	MI	Jeffrey Curtis Vargo	1997	3,780
147 7/8	22 7/8	22 5/8	19 3/8	5	6	Missoula County	MT	Karl E. Evans	1997	3,780
147 7/8	21 5/8	20 7/8	15 3/8	5	6	Waupaca County	WI	Ronald L. Lutzewitz	1997	3,780
147 7/8	22 7/8	23 6/8	20 1/8	6	5	Bayfield County	WI	Jeff Ottman	1997	3,780
147 7/8	22 4/8	21 6/8	17 7/8	5	5	St. Charles County	MO	Daniel Gentz	1997	3,780
147 6/8	23 4/8	23 2/8	16 0/8	5	5	Morrison County	MN	John Zwickey	1955	3,821
147 6/8	23 5/8	24 3/8	16 6/8	6	7	Morrison County	MN	Allen E. Farmes	1957	3,821

WHITETAIL DEER (TYPICAL ANTLERS)

Minimum Score 125 Continued

SCORE	LENGTH OF MAIN BEAM R	LENGTH OF MAIN BEAM L	INSIDE SPREAD	NUMBER OF POINTS R	NUMBER OF POINTS L	AREA	STATE/ PROVINCE	HUNTER'S NAME	DATE	RANK
147 6/8	25 3/8	24 5/8	19 7/8	6	5	Jo Daviess County	IL	Jerry Fritz	1971	3,821
147 6/8	24 1/8	25 6/8	19 0/8	5	5	Dickinson County	MI	Myles Keller	1976	3,821
147 6/8	24 6/8	23 0/8	17 6/8	6	6	Butler County	KY	O. D. Phelps	1977	3,821
147 6/8	24 0/8	24 2/8	17 2/8	6	5	Harlan County	NE	Ron Breitsprecher	1978	3,821
147 6/8	22 1/8	22 2/8	19 6/8	5	5	Union County	IL	Karen Mason	1980	3,821
147 6/8	22 3/8	22 1/8	17 4/8	4	4	Mercer County	ND	Steven J. Prock	1980	3,821
147 6/8	25 6/8	24 6/8	18 0/8	5	5	Jackson County	IA	Carl Severson	1982	3,821
147 6/8	23 2/8	23 1/8	18 0/8	5	5	Sumner County	KS	Danny S. Holden	1982	3,821
147 6/8	22 3/8	22 4/8	21 2/8	4	4	Kingsbury County	SD	Mack Butler	1984	3,821
147 6/8	22 5/8	23 2/8	19 2/8	5	6	Stafford County	KS	Larry Bowser	1985	3,821
147 6/8	21 2/8	21 7/8	16 0/8	8	8	Macoupin County	IL	Leonard Koniak	1987	3,821
147 6/8	23 7/8	23 6/8	17 2/8	6	6	Crawford County	IL	Gary Bickers	1987	3,821
147 6/8	24 0/8	24 0/8	20 0/8	5	5	Iroquois County	IL	Gregory A. Hiser	1989	3,821
147 6/8	23 7/8	24 2/8	18 3/8	6	7	Monroe County	NY	Tim Bumbarger	1990	3,821
147 6/8	25 2/8	25 6/8	22 2/8	4	4	Delaware County	OH	Doug Fuller	1991	3,821
147 6/8	26 4/8	26 2/8	19 5/8	6	7	Clinton County	OH	Kevin L. Wilson	1991	3,821
147 6/8	22 1/8	21 6/8	18 4/8	8	7	Cedar County	IA	Paul Dykstra	1991	3,821
147 6/8	22 7/8	23 7/8	17 3/8	8	9	Marshall County	MN	Jeremy Beck	1992	3,821
147 6/8	24 3/8	23 2/8	21 5/8	6	6	Knox County	IL	Lee Murray	1992	3,821
147 6/8	24 0/8	24 4/8	16 6/8	5	5	Pittsburg County	OK	Roy Ward	1992	3,821
147 6/8	24 3/8	24 4/8	18 2/8	5	5	Calhoun County	IL	Randy Watters	1992	3,821
147 6/8	24 0/8	23 1/8	17 6/8	5	6	Wabaunsee County	KS	Ron Arand	1992	3,821
147 6/8	24 4/8	21 4/8	16 7/8	7	5	Harrison County	IA	Jamen Cates	1993	3,821
147 6/8	22 2/8	22 5/8	16 6/8	5	5	Morrison County	MN	Richard Asp	1994	3,821
147 6/8	25 4/8	25 5/8	19 6/8	6	4	Dane County	WI	Jeffrey Lee Zanow	1994	3,821
147 6/8	23 7/8	23 4/8	19 4/8	5	5	Ogle County	IL	Roy Nichols	1994	3,821
147 6/8	23 3/8	23 4/8	20 6/8	5	5	Washtenaw County	MI	Richard N. Lane	1995	3,821
147 6/8	24 7/8	24 3/8	19 1/8	7	7	Allegheny County	PA	Richard J. Blauser	1995	3,821
147 6/8	22 2/8	23 2/8	16 2/8	5	5	Kenosha County	WI	Joseph C. Albright	1995	3,821
147 6/8	23 5/8	24 4/8	18 1/8	6	5	Delaware County	IN	Steve Minard	1995	3,821
147 6/8	25 2/8	24 2/8	17 2/8	5	5	Appanoose County	IA	Dennis Palmer	1996	3,821
147 6/8	21 4/8	21 4/8	16 0/8	5	5	Jackson County	MO	Dennis W. Patrick	1996	3,821
147 6/8	23 1/8	23 2/8	19 0/8	6	7	Licking County	OH	Kerry Proctor	1996	3,821
147 6/8	24 0/8	24 6/8	20 2/8	7	5	Butler County	KY	David Whitehouse	1996	3,821
147 6/8	23 4/8	24 3/8	18 7/8	6	6	Ferry County	WA	Doug Kikendall	1997	3,821
147 6/8	25 0/8	25 6/8	18 0/8	4	4	Harford County	MD	Andrew Hacke	1997	3,821
147 6/8	21 6/8	21 5/8	19 2/8	5	5	Clay County	IA	Thomas Ray Gross	1997	3,821
147 6/8	25 2/8	25 2/8	18 2/8	5	5	Putnam County	NY	Jesse Jaycox	1998	3,821
147 5/8	23 7/8	23 5/8	19 1/8	5	5	Fillmore County	MN	Dale Honsey	1951	3,861
147 5/8	24 2/8	26 0/8	20 2/8	6	6	Nicollet County	MN	Thomas J. Merkley	1970	3,861
147 5/8	22 7/8	23 2/8	18 1/8	4	4	Wilkin County	MN	Darrel G. Montieth	1978	3,861
147 5/8	23 5/8	23 4/8	18 3/8	4	5	Morrison County	MN	Leon Fuchs	1981	3,861
147 5/8	22 2/8	22 7/8	16 6/8	6	5	Merrimack County	NH	Jerry Smith	1982	3,861
147 5/8	24 7/8	25 3/8	19 5/8	5	5	Peoria County	IL	Joe Shryock, Jr.	1983	3,861
147 5/8	24 6/8	25 2/8	17 2/8	5	6	Koochiching County	MN	Terrance L. Jaeger	1983	3,861
147 5/8	23 5/8	22 7/8	18 3/8	5	5	De Witt County	IL	John H. Piatt	1983	3,861
147 5/8	25 3/8	24 7/8	17 7/8	5	5	Butler County	PA	David L. Travaglio	1986	3,861
147 5/8	26 0/8	25 3/8	18 3/8	5	6	Morgan County	OH	Ron Newsom	1986	3,861
147 5/8	25 0/8	24 3/8	21 4/8	5	5	Winona County	MN	Rodney Blake	1986	3,861
147 5/8	23 1/8	25 6/8	18 7/8	5	5	Rock County	WI	John G. Donstad	1986	3,861
147 5/8	24 3/8	24 3/8	18 3/8	6	5	Washington County	MN	Scott Moncur	1987	3,861
147 5/8	24 7/8	24 5/8	17 5/8	5	5	Shelby County	IL	Dennis J. Lynch	1987	3,861
147 5/8	23 2/8	25 2/8	16 1/8	5	6	Perry County	IL	Scott Rice	1987	3,861
147 5/8	27 0/8	26 6/8	21 3/8	4	5	Baltimore County	MD	Kevin Vogt	1990	3,861
147 5/8	24 2/8	24 5/8	15 3/8	5	5	Walton County	GA	Kenny Starnes	1991	3,861
147 5/8	23 6/8	22 2/8	15 3/8	5	5	Lipscomb County	TX	Rick C. McDowell	1991	3,861
147 5/8	25 2/8	25 0/8	17 3/8	7	5	Union County	IL	Donald S. Blakley	1991	3,861
147 5/8	23 2/8	23 5/8	20 6/8	4	5	Marion County	KS	Dennis N. Ballweg	1991	3,861
147 5/8	23 7/8	22 1/8	18 2/8	5	5	Des Moines County	IA	Harold Lingenfelter	1992	3,861
147 5/8	24 7/8	24 6/8	19 5/8	8	8	Guernsey County	OH	Reuben W. Miller	1993	3,861
147 5/8	25 5/8	24 7/8	16 6/8	5	5	Washington County	KS	Scott A. Wilkens	1993	3,861
147 5/8	24 3/8	25 3/8	18 7/8	5	5	Rusk County	WI	Irving Schneiderwent	1993	3,861
147 5/8	22 7/8	23 4/8	15 7/8	5	5	Knox County	OH	Gary Sparks	1994	3,861
147 5/8	22 3/8	22 3/8	17 3/8	6	5	Dunn County	WI	John S. Fassbinder	1994	3,861
147 5/8	23 3/8	24 6/8	18 1/8	5	5	Belmont County	OH	Lewis R. Holcomb	1994	3,861
147 5/8	22 5/8	24 1/8	16 5/8	6	6	Marion County	IL	James W. Norman	1994	3,861
147 5/8	26 4/8	27 2/8	21 0/8	6	6	Pottawattamie County	IA	Forrest Brown	1994	3,861
147 5/8	25 7/8	26 4/8	21 7/8	5	4	Richland County	MT	Brad Hayward	1995	3,861
147 5/8	23 6/8	24 2/8	16 5/8	5	5	Dimmit County	TX	Marty Woods	1995	3,861
147 5/8	22 7/8	23 3/8	17 2/8	6	5	Van Buren County	IA	Elmer Luce, Jr.	1995	3,861
147 5/8	24 5/8	22 6/8	21 7/8	5	5	Woodford County	IL	Shawn Meyer	1995	3,861
147 5/8	22 6/8	24 6/8	18 7/8	5	6	Grafton County	NH	Jeff Stout	1995	3,861
147 5/8	23 7/8	24 1/8	18 3/8	6	6	Decatur County	IA	Larry Richard	1996	3,861
147 5/8	24 0/8	23 6/8	17 7/8	4	4	Butler County	KS	Shiloh Thomas	1996	3,861
147 5/8	25 2/8	25 6/8	20 0/8	6	6	Weld County	CO	Kevin Yerian	1996	3,861
147 5/8	24 3/8	22 4/8	20 0/8	6	7	Dakota County	MN	Bobby Johnson	1996	3,861
147 5/8	23 5/8	23 5/8	17 6/8	6	6	Iowa County	WI	Leslie Ladd	1997	3,861
147 5/8	26 7/8	25 0/8	17 5/8	5	4	Monroe County	NY	Christopher Consler	1997	3,861

WHITETAIL DEER (TYPICAL ANTLERS)

Minimum Score 125 — Continued

SCORE	LENGTH OF MAIN BEAM R	LENGTH OF MAIN BEAM L	INSIDE SPREAD	NUMBER OF POINTS R	NUMBER OF POINTS L	AREA	STATE/ PROVINCE	HUNTER'S NAME	DATE	RANK
147 5/8	26 3/8	24 4/8	21 5/8	5	5	Fairfax County	VA	Mike Nyalko	1997	3,861
147 5/8	24 3/8	24 6/8	16 7/8	5	5	Fairfield County	OH	David E. Jenkins	1997	3,861
147 5/8	25 4/8	23 5/8	17 1/8	4	5	Eau Claire County	WI	Dave Strassman	1998	3,861
147 4/8	22 2/8	22 6/8	18 4/8	4	4	Shawano County	WI	John Schoenike	1960	3,904
147 4/8	23 7/8	23 2/8	16 4/8	7	5	Darke County	OH	Jim Duvall	1977	3,904
147 4/8	24 0/8	23 3/8	20 6/8	6	6	Fulton County	OH	Gary R. Bailey	1980	3,904
147 4/8	22 6/8	22 2/8	16 6/8	5	5	Burleigh County	ND	James A. Sauvageau	1980	3,904
147 4/8	25 3/8	25 6/8	19 0/8	4	5	Blue Earth County	MN	Aaron L. Urke	1981	3,904
147 4/8	23 7/8	23 7/8	16 5/8	7	5	Trempealeau County	WI	Donald Skaar	1982	3,904
147 4/8	21 0/8	20 5/8	17 6/8	5	5	Cloud County	KS	Jeff Gerard	1982	3,904
147 4/8	23 0/8	23 1/8	18 4/8	5	5	St. Charles County	MO	Harry L. Smith	1983	3,904
147 4/8	24 1/8	26 0/8	18 6/8	4	4	Prairie County	AR	Joe Moody	1984	3,904
147 4/8	25 0/8	25 1/8	19 4/8	5	5	Dane County	WI	John M. Welke, Jr.	1985	3,904
147 4/8	23 6/8	23 0/8	14 6/8	5	5	Leader	SAS	Clifton Schneider	1986	3,904
147 4/8	26 1/8	26 2/8	19 6/8	6	4	Lincoln County	MO	Terry F. Fry	1986	3,904
147 4/8	22 5/8	22 3/8	16 2/8	5	5	Henry County	MO	Cary Dennis	1987	3,904
147 4/8	25 6/8	25 0/8	20 7/8	5	7	Jackson County	MI	Scot E. Gazlay	1987	3,904
147 4/8	24 3/8	24 3/8	16 4/8	4	5	Woodbury County	IA	Ron Frahm	1987	3,904
147 4/8	24 2/8	24 0/8	19 0/8	6	5	Hardin County	IA	William Stonebraker	1987	3,904
147 4/8	23 1/8	23 3/8	20 4/8	5	5	Pepin County	WI	Duane Peterson	1988	3,904
147 4/8	23 4/8	23 7/8	17 4/8	5	5	Sawyer County	WI	Mike Haegele	1988	3,904
147 4/8	24 2/8	24 1/8	17 4/8	5	5	Mahaska County	IA	Larry Smith	1989	3,904
147 4/8	26 5/8	22 6/8	19 2/8	5	5	Jersey County	IL	Judy Kovar	1989	3,904
147 4/8	23 2/8	23 2/8	20 0/8	5	5	Dickens County	TX	Jim Eppler	1990	3,904
147 4/8	25 4/8	25 1/8	18 0/8	5	5	Pulaski County	GA	Chris Cornelius	1990	3,904
147 4/8	25 4/8	25 4/8	23 6/8	4	4	Wayne County	IA	Connie Pherigo	1990	3,904
147 4/8	24 0/8	22 7/8	18 3/8	4	6	Clinton County	OH	Robert L. Sargent	1990	3,904
147 4/8	23 6/8	24 4/8	17 4/8	5	5	Henry County	IA	Bruce Barrie	1990	3,904
147 4/8	25 2/8	24 7/8	17 2/8	5	5	Lawrence County	IN	Gary L. Brown	1991	3,904
147 4/8	25 3/8	25 5/8	17 2/8	5	5	Eau Claire County	WI	Wayne R. Brixen	1991	3,904
147 4/8	28 0/8	26 3/8	22 3/8	5	5	Bayfield County	WI	Clifton D. Louis	1991	3,904
147 4/8	24 0/8	24 7/8	16 0/8	8	7	Muscatine County	IA	Craig A. Owens	1991	3,904
147 4/8	22 7/8	23 1/8	14 6/8	5	6	Dubuque County	IA	Curtis G. Steffen	1991	3,904
147 4/8	23 5/8	23 0/8	19 5/8	4	5	Henry County	IA	Troy Ailey	1991	3,904
147 4/8	21 2/8	20 3/8	16 0/8	5	5	Cochrane	ALB	Tom Foss	1992	3,904
147 4/8	22 2/8	22 2/8	15 4/8	5	7	Chautauqua County	KS	William Wilmeth	1992	3,904
147 4/8	22 3/8	23 3/8	20 4/8	4	4	Hunterdon County	NJ	Jeff Farr	1993	3,904
147 4/8	21 6/8	21 5/8	20 4/8	6	6	Greene County	IN	Zaldy Advincula	1993	3,904
147 4/8	25 6/8	24 3/8	18 5/8	5	6	Woodford County	IL	Joseph C. Jerse	1993	3,904
147 4/8	22 7/8	22 5/8	15 6/8	4	4	Wayne County	NY	Scott M. Aman	1993	3,904
147 4/8	23 4/8	24 2/8	18 2/8	5	5	Fayette County	IA	Marvin Buckmaster	1993	3,904
147 4/8	23 4/8	23 1/8	16 2/8	5	6	Cole County	MO	Anthony Norbert Boessen	1994	3,904
147 4/8	23 3/8	25 7/8	17 6/8	5	5	Macoupin County	IL	Brad Bellm	1995	3,904
147 4/8	23 5/8	24 2/8	18 4/8	5	5	Kane County	IL	George Moeller, Jr.	1995	3,904
147 4/8	23 3/8	22 6/8	23 7/8	5	7	Spink County	SD	Mike Hoesing	1995	3,904
147 4/8	23 6/8	23 4/8	16 6/8	5	4	Waukesha County	WI	Peter J. Purdy	1995	3,904
147 4/8	24 5/8	24 5/8	19 2/8	4	5	Delaware County	IA	William J. Gadient	1996	3,904
147 4/8	23 0/8	23 6/8	21 2/8	5	5	Knox County	MO	Tim Wells	1996	3,904
147 4/8	24 2/8	22 2/8	17 4/8	5	5	Hopkins County	KY	Darrin Eaton	1997	3,904
147 4/8	21 4/8	21 4/8	17 6/8	5	5	St. Croix County	WI	Steve Huppert	1997	3,904
147 4/8	23 7/8	22 6/8	18 4/8	5	5	Pike County	IL	Jeffrey R. Van Varick	1997	3,904
147 4/8	26 0/8	24 6/8	18 1/8	4	5	Jennings County	IN	Kevin D. Hall	1997	3,904
147 4/8	23 0/8	22 1/8	16 4/8	5	5	Humboldt County	IA	Dennis Evans	1997	3,904
147 4/8	26 5/8	27 2/8	18 3/8	5	5	McLean County	IL	David Grizzle	1997	3,904
147 4/8	26 2/8	25 5/8	20 0/8	5	5	La Salle County	TX	George W. Semple	1997	3,904
147 3/8	22 4/8	22 4/8	17 7/8	5	6	Waushara County	WI	Mike Barth	1977	3,956
147 3/8	21 5/8	21 5/8	16 3/8	6	5	Lee County	IA	Mark Clemens	1978	3,956
147 3/8	28 1/8	28 1/8	19 7/8	5	4	Huntingdon County	PA	John A. Williams	1979	3,956
147 3/8	23 5/8	23 7/8	18 3/8	5	5	Guthrie County	IA	Steve Hunerdosse	1982	3,956
147 3/8	22 0/8	22 3/8	12 7/8	7	5	Jackson County	MO	Marvin Thomey	1984	3,956
147 3/8	21 1/8	20 2/8	15 7/8	6	6	Troup County	GA	Eddie D. Martin	1984	3,956
147 3/8	22 4/8	24 2/8	16 5/8	6	5	Union County	IL	Ronald L. Kosydor	1985	3,956
147 3/8	22 6/8	23 0/8	18 3/8	5	5	Lee County	IA	Glenn E. Wagner	1985	3,956
147 3/8	23 1/8	23 2/8	15 7/8	6	5	Buffalo County	WI	Bill R. Berg	1986	3,956
147 3/8	25 6/8	25 1/8	19 5/8	5	4	McHenry County	IL	William R. Bishop, Jr.	1988	3,956
147 3/8	23 1/8	22 3/8	19 5/8	5	5	Vermilion County	IL	Dr H. Neil Becker	1988	3,956
147 3/8	23 5/8	25 3/8	19 1/8	4	4	Ellsworth County	KS	Rick Kirkpatrick	1989	3,956
147 3/8	27 0/8	25 7/8	19 1/8	4	4	Shelby County	IL	Terry Jo Anderson	1989	3,956
147 3/8	23 3/8	24 0/8	17 7/8	6	5	Warren County	IL	Bryan E. DeJaynes	1989	3,956
147 3/8	23 7/8	22 6/8	18 0/8	5	6	Sussex County	VA	Frank Patterson	1989	3,956
147 3/8	22 7/8	21 4/8	16 3/8	5	5	Marathon County	WI	Mark J. Duerr	1989	3,956
147 3/8	23 0/8	22 4/8	18 2/8	7	5	Davis County	IA	Robert L. McDowell	1990	3,956
147 3/8	22 4/8	23 2/8	19 1/8	4	4	Webb County	TX	Alvin Levy	1991	3,956
147 3/8	24 0/8	24 5/8	19 3/8	5	5	Westmoreland County	PA	David Bish	1992	3,956
147 3/8	22 6/8	22 3/8	20 0/8	5	6	Price County	WI	Stanley P. Mindock	1992	3,956
147 3/8	21 0/8	21 2/8	17 3/8	6	5	Vermilion County	IL	Robert Dave Mitchell	1992	3,956
147 3/8	23 7/8	23 5/8	18 3/8	5	5	Reno County	KS	Doug Chapman	1992	3,956
147 3/8	22 1/8	23 0/8	18 1/8	5	5	Sullivan County	IN	Joe Rehmel	1993	3,956

WHITETAIL DEER (TYPICAL ANTLERS)

Minimum Score 125   Continued

SCORE	LENGTH OF MAIN BEAM R	LENGTH OF MAIN BEAM L	INSIDE SPREAD	NUMBER OF POINTS R	NUMBER OF POINTS L	AREA	STATE/ PROVINCE	HUNTER'S NAME	DATE	RANK
147 3/8	24 5/8	25 0/8	19 5/8	5	4	Lee County	IL	Craig B. Walter	1993	3,956
147 3/8	21 3/8	21 4/8	17 1/8	6	5	Kerr County	TX	Chuck Adams	1993	3,956
147 3/8	25 4/8	26 4/8	18 2/8	5	5	Hillsdale County	MI	Matthew C. Sommers	1994	3,956
147 3/8	25 6/8	26 1/8	20 1/8	5	5	Cuyahoga County	OH	Mark Johnson	1994	3,956
147 3/8	22 6/8	22 4/8	17 5/8	6	6	Walworth County	WI	Bradley Wilson	1994	3,956
147 3/8	22 1/8	22 5/8	15 1/8	5	6	Woodbury County	IA	Mark R. Huntley	1994	3,956
147 3/8	21 2/8	21 4/8	17 5/8	6	5	Pottawatomie County	KS	James E. Kelty	1995	3,956
147 3/8	23 2/8	23 1/8	17 3/8	5	5	Brown County	OH	Troy Conley	1995	3,956
147 3/8	24 1/8	24 4/8	17 3/8	6	7	Rock County	WI	Dennis Krueger	1995	3,956
147 3/8	26 1/8	27 7/8	14 5/8	4	4	Douglas County	KS	Denzil L. Hackathorn	1996	3,956
147 3/8	24 0/8	21 2/8	19 7/8	5	5	Blackford County	IN	Mark Garrison	1996	3,956
147 3/8	24 4/8	24 6/8	17 2/8	8	6	Grundy County	IL	Brian L. Crawford	1996	3,956
147 3/8	25 7/8	25 7/8	20 7/8	4	4	McHenry County	IL	Jody Kellnhofer	1996	3,956
147 2/8	23 2/8	25 1/8	20 4/8	9	8	Clay County	IA	Uriah M. Hostetler	1964	3,992
147 2/8	23 2/8	22 4/8	19 2/8	5	5	Madison County	IN	Pat Moreland	1969	3,992
147 2/8	23 1/8	23 1/8	15 6/8	5	5	Green Lake County	WI	Don Chier	1973	3,992
147 2/8	25 2/8	25 2/8	20 6/8	5	5	Fayette County	IA	Terry Cannady	1976	3,992
147 2/8	21 3/8	20 6/8	17 4/8	5	5	Iroquois County	IL	Scott L. Mohler	1979	3,992
147 2/8	25 7/8	24 3/8	25 4/8	4	4	Parke County	IN	Alan W. Brannan	1980	3,992
147 2/8	24 6/8	22 7/8	18 4/8	5	6	Waushara County	WI	Tim J. Terrell	1980	3,992
147 2/8	23 2/8	22 6/8	19 2/8	5	7	Pembina County	ND	Roger Furstenau	1983	3,992
147 2/8	24 7/8	25 0/8	18 7/8	7	8	Clay County	MN	John Randash	1984	3,992
147 2/8	21 5/8	21 6/8	18 2/8	6	5	Grant County	MN	Harold Forcier	1984	3,992
147 2/8	24 5/8	24 3/8	18 2/8	6	5	Jackson County	OH	Keith Kuhn	1984	3,992
147 2/8	25 1/8	25 6/8	23 2/8	4	4	Gage County	NE	Jerry Miller	1987	3,992
147 2/8	25 0/8	23 0/8	14 4/8	7	6	Blue Earth County	MN	Bruce Kramer	1987	3,992
147 2/8	20 2/8	21 5/8	20 6/8	5	5	Somerset County	NJ	Harold J. Tallett	1987	3,992
147 2/8	24 0/8	22 6/8	20 6/8	5	5	Monroe County	GA	Patrick Carter	1988	3,992
147 2/8	23 1/8	24 6/8	19 7/8	7	7	Vermilion County	IL	Robert G. Downing	1988	3,992
147 2/8	24 4/8	22 1/8	21 2/8	6	7	Meigs County	OH	Patrick D. Kearns	1988	3,992
147 2/8	25 0/8	25 5/8	23 6/8	4	5	Cook County	IL	Charles Gaidamavice	1989	3,992
147 2/8	23 0/8	22 6/8	16 0/8	6	5	Morgan County	CO	Dean Procunier	1990	3,992
147 2/8	22 5/8	23 4/8	17 7/8	5	6	Allamakee County	IA	Mark D. Christopherson	1991	3,992
147 2/8	29 1/8	28 5/8	22 0/8	4	4	Lawrence County	OH	Randy Boggs	1991	3,992
147 2/8	25 1/8	24 1/8	18 6/8	4	5	Flathead County	MT	John C. Bartlett	1992	3,992
147 2/8	22 2/8	22 0/8	17 4/8	5	5	Lincoln County	MO	Larry Crouch	1992	3,992
147 2/8	23 3/8	21 1/8	21 0/8	5	5	Rock County	WI	Monica A. Freeman	1992	3,992
147 2/8	22 7/8	22 7/8	16 6/8	5	5	Cold Lake	ALB	Martin Belisle	1992	3,992
147 2/8	24 0/8	23 7/8	17 6/8	4	4	Eau Claire County	WI	Mike Payne	1992	3,992
147 2/8	21 5/8	21 5/8	18 6/8	5	5	Fergus County	MT	Mike Sweeney	1992	3,992
147 2/8	25 3/8	26 1/8	19 4/8	5	4	Daviess County	IN	Mark Moeller	1993	3,992
147 2/8	22 4/8	21 1/8	16 6/8	5	5	Washington County	OH	Ryan Fullenkamp	1994	3,992
147 2/8	25 4/8	24 5/8	16 6/8	5	5	Lake County	IL	David Shumway	1994	3,992
147 2/8	25 1/8	25 2/8	19 0/8	5	4	Lyon County	KS	Aaron Lazzers	1994	3,992
147 2/8	22 6/8	23 6/8	20 6/8	4	6	Lincoln County	SD	Collin C. Benson	1994	3,992
147 2/8	25 1/8	24 6/8	17 6/8	5	4	Lawrence County	MO	Jason Graff	1994	3,992
147 2/8	24 6/8	24 7/8	21 4/8	5	4	Davis County	IA	Gary Biles	1995	3,992
147 2/8	22 0/8	22 3/8	17 4/8	5	5	Dane County	WI	Darren Culles	1995	3,992
147 2/8	24 7/8	24 4/8	18 7/8	6	6	Brown County	IL	David Crooks	1995	3,992
147 2/8	23 5/8	24 0/8	18 0/8	5	5	Clay County	KS	Dan Ayers	1995	3,992
147 2/8	23 6/8	22 6/8	18 3/8	11	8	Dakota County	MN	John J. Boland	1995	3,992
147 2/8	21 3/8	20 7/8	16 4/8	5	5	Trempealeau County	WI	John P. Simerson	1996	3,992
147 2/8	22 6/8	22 4/8	16 3/8	6	5	Kingsbury County	SD	Jerry Ellingson	1996	3,992
147 2/8	22 4/8	22 2/8	16 2/8	6	5	Richardson County	NE	Ted Younker	1996	3,992
147 2/8	23 1/8	23 3/8	16 6/8	6	5	Todd County	KY	David D. Haley	1997	3,992
147 2/8	22 1/8	22 2/8	19 2/8	6	4	Hardin County	KY	Ricky J. Rankin	1997	3,992
147 2/8	20 5/8	21 7/8	18 0/8	6	6	Livingston County	MI	Joseph Metivier	1997	3,992
147 2/8	26 2/8	24 2/8	16 4/8	5	5	Waukesha County	WI	Louis Kimball	1997	3,992
147 2/8	23 2/8	22 2/8	18 6/8	5	5	Henry County	VA	Mike Weaver	1997	3,992
147 1/8	25 1/8	25 3/8	16 7/8	5	5	Delaware County	IA	Blair Berens	1963	4,038
147 1/8	24 7/8	24 4/8	18 4/8	7	7	Red Willow County	NE	Gary Ginther	1967	4,038
147 1/8	22 6/8	23 1/8	17 5/8	5	6	Iron County	WI	Dr. C. J. Rainaldo	1967	4,038
147 1/8	21 0/8	21 5/8	16 3/8	6	6	Vilas County	WI	Anthony J. Sahulcik, Jr.	1969	4,038
147 1/8	25 0/8	24 0/8	18 3/8	4	4	Dodge County	MN	Clark Gallup	1974	4,038
147 1/8	24 3/8	25 7/8	18 5/8	4	4	Coffey County	KS	Joyce Wilhite	1974	4,038
147 1/8	20 5/8	20 0/8	19 5/8	5	5	Redwood County	MN	Dennis Groebner	1975	4,038
147 1/8	22 1/8	22 1/8	19 3/8	5	5	Kiowa County	KS	Ralph A. Brown	1981	4,038
147 1/8	25 2/8	24 3/8	18 1/8	5	5	Hancock County	OH	Robert E. Ebert	1981	4,038
147 1/8	23 2/8	23 6/8	18 1/8	5	5	Teton County	MT	James R. Toms	1984	4,038
147 1/8	27 5/8	27 5/8	21 1/8	4	5	Highland County	OH	Larry K. Snoddy	1984	4,038
147 1/8	24 2/8	25 4/8	15 7/8	4	5	Wallace County	KS	Gerry Nix	1985	4,038
147 1/8	24 5/8	24 5/8	18 2/8	7	5	Burleigh County	ND	Chuck Welch	1986	4,038
147 1/8	24 1/8	24 5/8	15 3/8	6	5	Highland County	OH	Roger Dale Burton	1987	4,038
147 1/8	22 4/8	22 7/8	17 3/8	5	5	Vigo County	IN	Bob Miller	1987	4,038
147 1/8	23 6/8	23 5/8	19 6/8	6	8	Carroll County	IL	Edward Pannell	1987	4,038
147 1/8	24 2/8	23 1/8	17 0/8	5	4	Butler County	KS	Mike Schwelgert	1987	4,038
147 1/8	23 1/8	22 4/8	18 6/8	5	6	Phillips County	KS	Phillip Cromwell	1987	4,038
147 1/8	22 6/8	23 1/8	19 1/8	4	4	Hardin County	KY	Steve Crabtree	1987	4,038

WHITETAIL DEER (TYPICAL ANTLERS)

Minimum Score 125   Continued

SCORE	LENGTH OF MAIN BEAM R	LENGTH OF MAIN BEAM L	INSIDE SPREAD	NUMBER OF POINTS R	NUMBER OF POINTS L	AREA	STATE/PROVINCE	HUNTER'S NAME	DATE	RANK
147 1/8	23 3/8	24 0/8	19 5/8	5	4	Lake County	IL	Robert A. Turner	1989	4,038
147 1/8	21 1/8	22 0/8	17 5/8	5	5	Codington County	SD	Bryan Monteith	1989	4,038
147 1/8	25 4/8	23 6/8	17 4/8	6	5	Worcester County	MA	Terry D. Atwater	1990	4,038
147 1/8	25 1/8	23 3/8	18 4/8	7	5	Goodhue County	MN	Scott Johnson	1990	4,038
147 1/8	24 4/8	24 0/8	18 1/8	5	5	Marinette County	WI	Robert J. Randerson	1990	4,038
147 1/8	22 2/8	22 0/8	17 1/8	5	5	Union County	PA	Matthew McGinnis	1991	4,038
147 1/8	24 1/8	25 3/8	23 3/8	5	5	Missoula County	MT	Matthew J. Stout	1992	4,038
147 1/8	23 4/8	23 5/8	18 3/8	4	4	Tompkins County	NY	Don Zifchock	1992	4,038
147 1/8	26 7/8	26 1/8	18 3/8	5	4	Rush County	IN	Brock Cross	1993	4,038
147 1/8	22 3/8	21 4/8	16 1/8	6	6	Daviess County	KY	George Stuart	1993	4,038
147 1/8	22 6/8	24 0/8	16 5/8	5	5	Vernon County	MO	Larry D. Bogart	1993	4,038
147 1/8	23 5/8	23 1/8	21 1/8	4	5	Sheboygan County	WI	Jim Ziegler, Jr.	1993	4,038
147 1/8	23 7/8	23 3/8	19 1/8	5	5	Trempealeau County	WI	Jim Jessessky	1994	4,038
147 1/8	22 7/8	22 2/8	17 1/8	5	5	Washtenaw County	MI	Gary Young	1994	4,038
147 1/8	25 3/8	23 7/8	18 3/8	4	5	Iowa County	IA	Kevin Kuester	1994	4,038
147 1/8	24 0/8	23 3/8	20 1/8	4	6	Rolette County	ND	Doug Stewart	1994	4,038
147 1/8	25 2/8	25 6/8	22 1/8	4	5	St. Charles County	MO	Mark J. Shea	1995	4,038
147 1/8	26 4/8	26 4/8	18 7/8	7	4	Brown County	IL	Ronald Hanna	1995	4,038
147 1/8	23 0/8	21 7/8	17 3/8	6	5	Du Page County	IL	Larry L. Border	1995	4,038
147 1/8	22 2/8	22 2/8	18 5/8	4	4	Marion County	IL	Russell Leboff	1995	4,038
147 1/8	23 3/8	22 5/8	16 0/8	5	6	Page County	VA	Mark W. Richards, Sr.	1996	4,038
147 1/8	26 1/8	25 6/8	20 6/8	6	6	Dane County	WI	Phillip E. Oinonen	1996	4,038
147 1/8	22 7/8	23 0/8	16 7/8	4	4	Edgar County	IL	Frank C. Vail III	1996	4,038
147 1/8	22 2/8	22 2/8	18 7/8	5	6	Des Moines County	IA	Michael Graham	1996	4,038
147 1/8	21 2/8	21 6/8	16 6/8	5	6	Jackson County	AL	Eddie Bolt	1997	4,038
147 1/8	26 5/8	27 7/8	18 7/8	4	5	Menard County	IL	Brent Davis	1997	4,038
147 1/8	23 1/8	22 6/8	16 7/8	7	7	Eau Claire County	WI	Jim Simon	1997	4,038
147 1/8	25 3/8	25 3/8	17 7/8	4	4	Columbia County	WI	Richard A. Schreiber	1997	4,038
147 1/8	21 5/8	22 1/8	18 6/8	7	8	Wilson County	KS	Warren C. Townsend	1997	4,038
147 1/8	23 4/8	23 6/8	15 7/8	7	7	Sawyer County	WI	Fran E. Eilbes	1998	4,038
147 1/8	25 4/8	23 5/8	16 5/8	5	5	Vernon County	MO	Lawrence Mark Guthrie	1998	4,038
147 0/8	24 6/8	25 5/8	17 4/8	5	7	Dodge County	WI	Alex B. Feucht	1963	4,088
147 0/8	23 6/8	24 0/8	20 3/8	6	5	Hancock County	IL	Ron Paul	1974	4,088
147 0/8	24 3/8	24 7/8	19 2/8	7	7	Dodge County	NE	Donald W. Robinson	1974	4,088
147 0/8	28 5/8	26 2/8	19 0/8	5	4	Fulton County	IL	Bernard Smith	1974	4,088
147 0/8	19 1/8	20 1/8	19 2/8	5	5	Platte County	WY	Robert V. Kiser	1978	4,088
147 0/8	25 4/8	24 1/8	21 2/8	6	7	Morrison County	MN	Gordon Bayerkohler	1979	4,088
147 0/8	23 5/8	23 5/8	20 0/8	5	5	Allamakee County	IA	Don Kieler	1979	4,088
147 0/8	25 2/8	25 1/8	19 4/8	4	4	Iroquois County	IL	Bruce Courville	1980	4,088
147 0/8	26 4/8	26 2/8	16 0/8	5	7	Gage County	NE	Eldon C. Wellman	1981	4,088
147 0/8	24 4/8	23 7/8	18 6/8	4	5	Osborne County	KS	Mike Kidwell	1981	4,088
147 0/8	25 1/8	25 2/8	19 6/8	7	6	Charles County	MD	David G. Wilson	1981	4,088
147 0/8	22 3/8	22 2/8	18 4/8	5	5	Outagamie County	WI	Jim Vorland	1983	4,088
147 0/8	26 1/8	24 2/8	22 0/8	4	4	Dorchester County	MD	Michael F. Blair	1983	4,088
147 0/8	23 6/8	24 4/8	17 2/8	5	6	Lee County	IL	Donald E. Moore	1983	4,088
147 0/8	26 2/8	25 4/8	17 6/8	5	5	Vernon County	MO	Roger L. Hensley	1985	4,088
147 0/8	22 5/8	24 0/8	19 2/8	6	8	Cedar County	MO	David Barnard	1986	4,088
147 0/8	23 3/8	22 7/8	15 2/8	6	6	Bradley County	AR	Granville Pankey	1987	4,088
147 0/8	24 6/8	24 0/8	18 6/8	4	4	Wright County	MN	Dale Florek	1987	4,088
147 0/8	23 2/8	24 4/8	15 2/8	5	5	Washington County	MN	Richard Eisinger	1988	4,088
147 0/8	23 6/8	24 2/8	17 0/8	5	4	Livingston County	MI	Elmer DePlanche	1988	4,088
147 0/8	22 1/8	22 0/8	17 2/8	5	5	Winnebago County	IL	Timothy J. Stuebs	1988	4,088
147 0/8	24 6/8	24 6/8	18 0/8	8	7	Richland County	IL	Bill Taylor	1989	4,088
147 0/8	23 7/8	23 2/8	16 1/8	6	8	Jefferson County	OH	James Zink	1989	4,088
147 0/8	25 4/8	23 7/8	22 5/8	6	5	Woodford County	IL	Stan Bocian	1989	4,088
147 0/8	23 3/8	21 6/8	18 2/8	5	5	Warren County	IA	Larry Caldwell	1989	4,088
147 0/8	23 1/8	23 2/8	19 4/8	5	4	Boone County	IL	Michael A. Beasley	1989	4,088
147 0/8	22 7/8	24 3/8	16 2/8	5	5	Walsh County	ND	Dayton Larson	1990	4,088
147 0/8	25 2/8	25 6/8	17 6/8	5	5	Vermilion County	IL	Alexander Ramm	1990	4,088
147 0/8	22 3/8	23 1/8	18 6/8	6	5	Waupaca County	WI	Brian Shambeau	1991	4,088
147 0/8	24 7/8	24 5/8	18 1/8	6	6	Harrison County	OH	Robert M. Mensinger	1991	4,088
147 0/8	24 4/8	25 1/8	23 0/8	4	5	Ernestown	ONT	Detlef Udo Fischer	1991	4,088
147 0/8	27 4/8	27 1/8	23 0/8	4	5	Cape May County	NJ	Joseph C. Byrd	1992	4,088
147 0/8	25 7/8	27 2/8	19 4/8	5	5	Allen County	IN	Chad E. Nicodemus	1992	4,088
147 0/8	24 6/8	25 0/8	17 3/8	6	6	Wright County	MN	Greg Lavallee	1992	4,088
147 0/8	25 3/8	25 6/8	20 0/8	4	4	Edgar County	IL	Frank Vail, III	1992	4,088
147 0/8	23 2/8	24 1/8	16 6/8	5	7	Iroquois County	IL	Terry Doehring	1993	4,088
147 0/8	23 6/8	23 7/8	17 0/8	5	5	Vinton County	OH	Tom Dishong, Jr.	1993	4,088
147 0/8	22 6/8	22 3/8	17 4/8	5	5	Worth County	IA	Larry B. Porter	1993	4,088
147 0/8	23 0/8	22 6/8	18 2/8	5	6	Buffalo County	WI	Ronald Brenner	1993	4,088
147 0/8	26 6/8	25 3/8	20 2/8	6	5	Green Lake County	WI	Dale Dallman	1994	4,088
147 0/8	23 1/8	23 1/8	15 7/8	5	6	Richland County	MT	Scott Sundheim	1994	4,088
147 0/8	25 3/8	24 6/8	16 6/8	5	5	Waldo County	ME	Carol D. Macaulay	1994	4,088
147 0/8	25 5/8	26 0/8	18 4/8	5	6	Jo Daviess County	IL	Daniel Keppen	1994	4,088
147 0/8	23 4/8	24 5/8	18 4/8	5	5	Pike County	OH	Perry A. Cantrell	1994	4,088
147 0/8	23 2/8	23 2/8	18 0/8	5	5	Muskingum County	OH	James Barbour	1994	4,088
147 0/8	24 2/8	24 3/8	20 3/8	4	5	Baraga County	MI	Frank J. Kassuba	1995	4,088
147 0/8	24 0/8	23 2/8	15 4/8	5	5	Lake County	IL	Robert H. Fugett	1995	4,088

WHITETAIL DEER (TYPICAL ANTLERS)

Minimum Score 125

Continued

SCORE	LENGTH OF R MAIN BEAM L		INSIDE SPREAD	NUMBER OF R POINTS L		AREA	STATE/ PROVINCE	HUNTER'S NAME	DATE	RANK
147 0/8	22 5/8	21 3/8	16 4/8	5	5	Ogle County	IL	Roy Nichols	1996	4,088
147 0/8	23 3/8	23 4/8	15 4/8	5	5	Fulton County	IL	Tim Wells	1996	4,088
147 0/8	21 6/8	22 5/8	15 4/8	5	5	Osage County	KS	Gerald Britschge	1996	4,088
147 0/8	23 1/8	23 4/8	15 2/8	6	6	Des Moines County	IA	Robert J. Lewis	1996	4,088
147 0/8	23 1/8	23 0/8	17 6/8	5	5	Cecil County	MD	Robert Allen Shelley	1996	4,088
147 0/8	25 2/8	25 0/8	20 0/8	5	5	Buffalo County	WI	Wayne L. Olson	1997	4,088
147 0/8	23 5/8	24 0/8	18 6/8	6	6	Kalamazoo County	MI	Cameron Russell Cudney	1997	4,088
147 0/8	23 4/8	23 6/8	21 0/8	4	4	Jackson County	IA	Kevin A. Schmidt	1997	4,088
147 0/8	21 4/8	21 5/8	15 3/8	6	7	Doniphan County	KS	Stephen D. Wolfram	1997	4,088
147 0/8	22 7/8	22 5/8	14 7/8	6	5	Polk County	IA	Robert Howard	1997	4,088
147 0/8	23 7/8	23 5/8	19 4/8	5	5	Prowers County	CO	Neal Heaton	1997	4,088
147 0/8	24 4/8	23 3/8	19 4/8	5	5	Allegheny County	PA	Wayne Paul Neyman	1998	4,088
147 0/8	24 7/8	24 1/8	21 2/8	5	5	Dane County	WI	Bruce Lowrey	1998	4,088
146 7/8	24 0/8	24 3/8	22 1/8	5	7	Cass County	ND	Duane H. Olsen	1959	4,148
146 7/8	21 5/8	21 0/8	16 3/8	5	5	Buffalo County	NE	Dwight Bond	1970	4,148
146 7/8	23 5/8	22 6/8	16 6/8	6	6	Osceola County	IA	Roger Rehborg	1973	4,148
146 7/8	24 2/8	24 2/8	15 5/8	4	4	Martin County	IN	Clarence McIntosh	1976	4,148
146 7/8	22 2/8	21 2/8	19 7/8	5	5	Waushara County	WI	Norman A. Moss	1976	4,148
146 7/8	21 1/8	20 7/8	22 4/8	5	5	Ogle County	IL	Art Heinze	1981	4,148
146 7/8	23 1/8	21 6/8	16 1/8	5	5	Day County	SD	Cary Gill	1982	4,148
146 7/8	22 6/8	21 6/8	16 1/8	5	5	Jasper County	IA	Mike Needham	1982	4,148
146 7/8	25 3/8	25 0/8	18 7/8	5	4	Powhatan County	VA	W. Scott Thorpe	1985	4,148
146 7/8	24 7/8	23 5/8	18 3/8	6	6	Jackson County	MI	Randy R. Peck	1986	4,148
146 7/8	22 6/8	22 3/8	18 5/8	4	5	Jackson County	IL	Wayne Watt	1986	4,148
146 7/8	24 4/8	23 5/8	18 6/8	6	6	Florence County	WI	Mark S. Becker	1987	4,148
146 7/8	22 1/8	23 1/8	18 5/8	6	5	Le Flore County	OK	Bill Brannon	1988	4,148
146 7/8	23 2/8	25 2/8	17 1/8	6	7	Houston County	MN	James Roth	1988	4,148
146 7/8	24 2/8	24 0/8	19 3/8	4	5	Calvert County	MD	David Herbert	1989	4,148
146 7/8	23 2/8	22 7/8	15 1/8	5	6	Mercer County	MO	David Gentry	1989	4,148
146 7/8	24 5/8	24 2/8	17 4/8	5	7	Jackson County	IL	Steven W. Mifflin	1989	4,148
146 7/8	25 3/8	25 6/8	20 5/8	5	4	Queen Annes County	MD	Raymie J. Williams III	1990	4,148
146 7/8	23 5/8	20 0/8	18 3/8	6	5	Washington County	IL	Morris Lingle	1990	4,148
146 7/8	25 1/8	25 1/8	18 3/8	5	5	Berkshire County	MA	William Drumm	1990	4,148
146 7/8	21 6/8	21 6/8	16 5/8	5	5	Coke County	TX	Jack Mark Stone	1990	4,148
146 7/8	25 6/8	25 7/8	18 5/8	7	5	Keokuk County	IA	Roger Dekok	1991	4,148
146 7/8	22 5/8	22 0/8	17 1/8	6	5	Madison County	IL	Ronald Newby	1991	4,148
146 7/8	22 6/8	22 4/8	20 3/8	4	6	Fairfield County	OH	Kevin Blackstone	1991	4,148
146 7/8	23 4/8	24 4/8	17 1/8	5	6	Augusta Township	ONT	Henry P. Bouchard	1991	4,148
146 7/8	23 4/8	25 5/8	22 6/8	5	5	Guilford County	NC	David L. Hendrix	1992	4,148
146 7/8	24 7/8	24 7/8	21 3/8	4	4	Pepin County	WI	David L. Fayerweather	1993	4,148
146 7/8	24 2/8	24 2/8	15 4/8	7	5	Cumberland County	IL	Larry Thompson	1993	4,148
146 7/8	20 2/8	20 3/8	16 4/8	8	9	Genesee County	MI	Linda F. Luna	1993	4,148
146 7/8	23 4/8	23 7/8	21 2/8	6	4	Morgan County	CO	Mike Crites	1993	4,148
146 7/8	21 4/8	22 2/8	17 0/8	6	5	Seward County	KS	Lynn Leonard	1993	4,148
146 7/8	23 6/8	24 6/8	18 6/8	5	6	Coshocton County	OH	Gary Lynn Fischer	1994	4,148
146 7/8	23 2/8	23 1/8	17 6/8	6	7	Park County	WY	Larry Hicks	1994	4,148
146 7/8	25 1/8	24 2/8	18 7/8	5	5	Pierce County	WI	Ron Sarnstrom	1994	4,148
146 7/8	24 1/8	24 4/8	16 7/8	5	5	Hardin County	IA	William Stonebraker	1994	4,148
146 7/8	23 0/8	23 0/8	19 3/8	4	4	Fulton County	IL	Butch Sulteen	1994	4,148
146 7/8	27 5/8	28 5/8	17 7/8	4	4	Clermont County	OH	Lee Bumgardner	1994	4,148
146 7/8	27 1/8	28 1/8	19 3/8	5	5	McHenry County	IL	Mark Wagner	1994	4,148
146 7/8	22 7/8	21 4/8	19 7/8	5	5	Kleberg County	TX	Johnnie R. Walters	1994	4,148
146 7/8	19 4/8	20 2/8	16 6/8	5	6	Jackson County	KS	Rick Hummel	1995	4,148
146 7/8	26 1/8	27 5/8	21 5/8	5	4	New Haven County	CT	Jeffrey R. Corbett	1995	4,148
146 7/8	23 3/8	23 7/8	17 3/8	6	5	Menard County	IL	Mark Singleton	1995	4,148
146 7/8	24 3/8	24 1/8	20 2/8	6	6	McHenry County	IL	Rich Swanson	1995	4,148
146 7/8	24 7/8	24 7/8	17 5/8	5	5	Morgan County	OH	Ron Newsom	1996	4,148
146 7/8	25 0/8	22 7/8	19 7/8	5	5	Walworth County	WI	Jeffrey Nettesheim	1996	4,148
146 7/8	26 0/8	26 0/8	18 5/8	5	5	New Haven County	CT	Real J. Masse	1996	4,148
146 7/8	25 4/8	25 6/8	20 5/8	4	5	Portage County	OH	Dale A. Holmberg	1996	4,148
146 7/8	22 1/8	21 4/8	17 3/8	5	5	Elbert County	CO	Daniel F. Dirscherl	1996	4,148
146 7/8	22 2/8	22 6/8	15 3/8	6	5	Kankakee County	IL	Christopher Druckrey	1997	4,148
146 7/8	20 0/8	23 4/8	17 5/8	7	5	Brown County	WI	Gregory P. Clabots	1997	4,148
146 7/8	24 6/8	23 5/8	17 3/8	5	5	Dunn County	WI	Brian P. Knutson	1997	4,148
146 6/8	23 3/8	23 1/8	17 6/8	7	8	Roberts County	SD	Robert Hendren	1967	4,199
146 6/8	24 6/8	27 0/8	20 2/8	5	4	Neosho County	KS	Carl Walker	1968	4,199
146 6/8	26 1/8	25 3/8	18 1/8	4	5	Lee County	IA	Jim Bohenkamp	1970	4,199
146 6/8	25 6/8	25 5/8	18 0/8	5	5	Shelby County	IL	Gary E. Sievers	1972	4,199
146 6/8	21 5/8	21 5/8	18 3/8	6	7	Will County	IL	Richard Manegold	1976	4,199
146 6/8	23 0/8	25 6/8	16 3/8	6	5	Lafayette County	WI	Greg Penniston	1977	4,199
146 6/8	25 4/8	25 6/8	17 3/8	5	5	Tuscarawas County	OH	Tracy Sheaffer	1980	4,199
146 6/8	26 1/8	25 3/8	16 0/8	5	4	Waushara County	WI	James L. Reiff, Jr.	1981	4,199
146 6/8	24 7/8	25 0/8	18 6/8	5	6	Cedar County	IA	Mike Rummells	1982	4,199
146 6/8	25 2/8	24 3/8	18 0/8	5	5	Logan County	OH	David Katterheinrich	1984	4,199
146 6/8	21 6/8	22 5/8	22 4/8	5	5	Lincoln County	MO	Jerry Davis, Jr.	1987	4,199
146 6/8	26 6/8	25 6/8	24 4/8	5	5	Suffolk County	NY	Joe Barbato	1988	4,199
146 6/8	27 0/8	27 3/8	19 0/8	4	5	Noth Dumphries Twp.	ONT	Jeff Bendig	1988	4,199
146 6/8	24 0/8	23 1/8	17 2/8	5	4	Howard County	IA	Terry Lee Larson	1988	4,199

WHITETAIL DEER (TYPICAL ANTLERS)

Minimum Score 125 — Continued

SCORE	LENGTH OF MAIN BEAM R	L	INSIDE SPREAD	NUMBER OF POINTS R	L	AREA	STATE/ PROVINCE	HUNTER'S NAME	DATE	RANK
146 6/8	21 4/8	22 1/8	16 3/8	6	6	Richland County	ND	Allen Perlenfein	1989	4,199
146 6/8	22 7/8	22 4/8	18 6/8	5	5	Powell County	MT	Dan D. Boy	1989	4,199
146 6/8	24 7/8	25 3/8	18 2/8	4	4	Montgomery County	TN	Julia C. Davidson	1989	4,199
146 6/8	23 2/8	23 1/8	19 4/8	5	5	Fergus County	MT	Stan Chiras	1989	4,199
146 6/8	20 2/8	20 4/8	15 1/8	6	5	Pulaski County	GA	Dan B. Clifton	1989	4,199
146 6/8	26 3/8	26 0/8	19 4/8	5	5	Rusk County	WI	Gordon Bohochik	1990	4,199
146 6/8	26 1/8	23 2/8	19 6/8	6	6	Vermilion County	IL	Jack Toms, Jr.	1990	4,199
146 6/8	26 0/8	20 2/8	23 1/8	6	6	Osborne County	KS	Cary L. Sommerla	1990	4,199
146 6/8	24 2/8	23 2/8	18 0/8	5	5	Morgan County	OH	Mark Donnally	1991	4,199
146 6/8	23 6/8	23 0/8	16 6/8	6	5	De Kalb County	MO	Dennis Collins	1991	4,199
146 6/8	21 6/8	21 5/8	16 4/8	6	6	Waupaca County	WI	Thomas Conradt	1992	4,199
146 6/8	23 7/8	22 7/8	19 0/8	6	5	Cumberland County	IL	Pete Sweitzer	1992	4,199
146 6/8	22 1/8	22 0/8	16 0/8	5	5	Waukesha County	WI	Jane Nelson	1992	4,199
146 6/8	21 7/8	22 2/8	17 0/8	5	5	Sterling County	TX	Mike Belanger	1992	4,199
146 6/8	23 5/8	23 2/8	18 4/8	5	4	Breckinridge County	KY	R. Ray Wix	1993	4,199
146 6/8	26 0/8	25 6/8	17 6/8	8	5	Jackson County	IL	Gregg Tucker	1993	4,199
146 6/8	25 0/8	25 6/8	21 1/8	7	6	St. Francis County	AR	Tom Thompson	1993	4,199
146 6/8	25 5/8	24 6/8	19 0/8	5	4	Adams County	IA	Kenny Vaill	1993	4,199
146 6/8	27 0/8	25 2/8	19 0/8	6	8	Bourbon County	KS	Kevin G. Asbury	1993	4,199
146 6/8	20 5/8	21 2/8	17 0/8	5	5	Sheridan County	WY	George K. Warner	1994	4,199
146 6/8	24 2/8	24 4/8	23 7/8	5	4	Belknap County	NH	Tom Sleeper	1994	4,199
146 6/8	26 5/8	25 7/8	20 0/8	4	5	McHenry County	IL	Roger W. Gates	1994	4,199
146 6/8	23 6/8	24 0/8	19 0/8	5	7	Clay County	IA	Thomas Ray Gross	1994	4,199
146 6/8	25 0/8	24 6/8	18 6/8	5	6	Rice County	MN	Mike Johnson	1995	4,199
146 6/8	24 3/8	23 3/8	18 0/8	5	5	Pike County	IL	Troy Richart	1995	4,199
146 6/8	25 3/8	22 7/8	19 0/8	6	5	Anne Arundel County	MD	Hillory Dean	1995	4,199
146 6/8	23 3/8	23 5/8	19 0/8	4	4	Kankakee County	IL	Bryan Hays	1995	4,199
146 6/8	21 4/8	22 3/8	15 4/8	4	4	Van Buren County	IA	James Bohnenkamp	1995	4,199
146 6/8	25 6/8	25 4/8	20 2/8	6	4	Mills County	IA	David D. Greenwood	1995	4,199
146 6/8	25 6/8	24 7/8	18 0/8	5	5	Hillsdale County	MI	Gale E. Pauken	1996	4,199
146 6/8	24 1/8	24 1/8	14 5/8	5	6	Pike County	IL	Nelson Sherman, Jr.	1996	4,199
146 6/8	25 7/8	26 7/8	19 4/8	4	4	Pike County	IL	Mike Dixon	1996	4,199
146 6/8	23 3/8	22 6/8	20 2/8	5	5	Stoddard County	MO	Don Reynolds	1996	4,199
146 6/8	23 1/8	23 6/8	15 6/8	6	7	Kenedy County	TX	Thomas J. Hoffman	1997	4,199
146 6/8	24 4/8	24 7/8	21 4/8	4	4	Douglas County	WI	Donald Lietha, Jr.	1997	4,199
146 6/8	23 6/8	23 7/8	18 2/8	5	6	Iowa County	WI	Robert A. Ramsden	1997	4,199
146 6/8	25 5/8	25 4/8	19 4/8	4	4	Somerset County	NJ	Joseph Stavola	1997	4,199
146 6/8	23 0/8	22 1/8	20 6/8	5	6	Marathon County	WI	Bill Heil	1998	4,199
146 5/8	22 5/8	22 5/8	18 7/8	4	3	Brown County	SD	Donald Grote	1963	4,251
146 5/8	23 2/8	24 1/8	17 3/8	5	6	Buckingham County	VA	Larry D. Baker	1974	4,251
146 5/8	25 2/8	25 6/8	18 7/8	4	5	Carroll County	IL	Art Heinze	1978	4,251
146 5/8	24 2/8	24 1/8	18 7/8	6	7	Des Moines County	IA	Larry R. Booth	1979	4,251
146 5/8	20 6/8	22 1/8	19 4/8	7	7	Clinton County	IN	Sheldon H. Stoops	1979	4,251
146 5/8	23 4/8	24 0/8	19 1/8	5	5	Morrison County	MN	Bart Brodt	1984	4,251
146 5/8	24 3/8	24 4/8	16 5/8	6	5	Cole County	MO	Norman P. Stucky	1984	4,251
146 5/8	24 3/8	24 3/8	16 2/8	8	8	Clark County	MO	Allen L. Courtney	1986	4,251
146 5/8	23 6/8	23 4/8	20 3/8	4	5	Kent County	MI	Benjamin V. Lapus, Jr.	1986	4,251
146 5/8	24 7/8	24 1/8	17 7/8	5	5	Hartford County	CT	Peter J.M. Kiendzoir	1986	4,251
146 5/8	22 4/8	22 0/8	16 1/8	5	6	Wabash County	IL	Robert E. Campbell	1987	4,251
146 5/8	24 7/8	25 5/8	20 4/8	5	7	Washington County	WI	Tony Snow	1988	4,251
146 5/8	21 7/8	21 2/8	15 5/8	5	5	Nueces County	TX	Wayne Peeples	1989	4,251
146 5/8	24 5/8	24 7/8	18 6/8	5	6	Crawford County	KS	Cary R. Rybnick	1989	4,251
146 5/8	24 7/8	24 4/8	19 6/8	6	7	Forest County	WI	Jim Sot	1990	4,251
146 5/8	22 7/8	23 1/8	17 7/8	5	5	Cecil County	MD	Steven D. Flanagan	1990	4,251
146 5/8	24 0/8	24 7/8	16 1/8	5	6	Macomb County	MI	Frank M. Malik, Jr.	1990	4,251
146 5/8	25 6/8	25 6/8	19 3/8	5	5	Polk County	IA	Steve Dilling	1990	4,251
146 5/8	21 3/8	21 4/8	16 3/8	4	4	Dodge County	MN	Myles Keller	1990	4,251
146 5/8	24 0/8	23 1/8	16 3/8	6	6	Giles County	TN	Jerry Case	1991	4,251
146 5/8	21 0/8	21 1/8	16 5/8	5	5	Shawnee County	KS	Dan McConnell	1991	4,251
146 5/8	25 5/8	23 6/8	18 1/8	6	5	Ontario County	NY	Robert D. Koutras	1992	4,251
146 5/8	23 4/8	22 6/8	16 5/8	5	5	Roane County	WV	Edward Osborne	1992	4,251
146 5/8	22 6/8	22 4/8	16 1/8	6	5	Cocke County	TN	Terry Finchum	1993	4,251
146 5/8	22 6/8	22 4/8	20 7/8	6	9	Lac qui Parle County	MN	Wade Schmidt	1993	4,251
146 5/8	24 1/8	24 6/8	20 6/8	4	5	Morris County	NJ	Russell Davidson	1993	4,251
146 5/8	23 1/8	23 1/8	16 5/8	5	5	Dane County	WI	Jeffrey R. DeLaura	1994	4,251
146 5/8	24 1/8	23 1/8	18 5/8	5	6	Adams County	IL	Larry D. Grant	1994	4,251
146 5/8	24 3/8	23 5/8	16 7/8	6	5	Greene County	IL	Robert Neff	1994	4,251
146 5/8	25 2/8	26 2/8	22 5/8	5	4	Warren County	IL	Bryan E. DeJaynes	1994	4,251
146 5/8	22 6/8	23 0/8	18 3/8	5	5	Trempealeau County	WI	David Mikrut	1994	4,251
146 5/8	23 0/8	23 0/8	18 3/8	5	6	Sawyer County	WI	Greg Biskup	1994	4,251
146 5/8	24 0/8	23 5/8	16 1/8	5	5	Miami County	KS	Chuck Buckley	1994	4,251
146 5/8	22 3/8	21 7/8	17 5/8	5	5	Sedgwick County	CO	Everett Tarrell	1994	4,251
146 5/8	23 2/8	23 0/8	18 7/8	5	5	Berrien County	MI	Craig Miller	1995	4,251
146 5/8	25 5/8	24 5/8	22 1/8	4	4	Ogle County	IL	Scott Relien	1995	4,251
146 5/8	23 4/8	23 3/8	17 5/8	5	5	Hamilton County	IA	Chad M. Foster	1996	4,251
146 5/8	24 0/8	24 4/8	17 2/8	6	5	Grant County	WI	Glen Stangl	1996	4,251
146 5/8	22 5/8	21 3/8	16 2/8	6	7	Van Buren County	IA	Russ Miller	1996	4,251
146 5/8	24 6/8	23 7/8	20 3/8	5	4	Vilas County	WI	Roger A. Turner	1997	4,251

WHITETAIL DEER (TYPICAL ANTLERS)

Minimum Score 125 — Continued

SCORE	LENGTH OF MAIN BEAM R	LENGTH OF MAIN BEAM L	INSIDE SPREAD	NUMBER OF POINTS R	NUMBER OF POINTS L	AREA	STATE/ PROVINCE	HUNTER'S NAME	DATE	RANK
146 5/8	22 7/8	24 1/8	17 1/8	5	5	Crawford County	WI	Chuck Bender	1997	4,251
146 5/8	25 4/8	26 3/8	22 2/8	5	6	Montgomery County	OH	Dale Shepard	1997	4,251
146 5/8	24 2/8	23 5/8	22 1/8	5	5	Floyd County	IA	Dennis Noling	1997	4,251
146 4/8	22 0/8	22 1/8	17 4/8	5	5	Wood County	WI	George Davis	1967	4,294
146 4/8	24 4/8	24 0/8	15 0/8	5	5	Amherst County	VA	Garry B. Pruitt	1972	4,294
146 4/8	22 0/8	23 3/8	18 0/8	5	5	Vigo County	IN	Richard E. Smith	1973	4,294
146 4/8	25 0/8	24 7/8	18 6/8	5	5	Cayuga County	NY	John Andrews, Sr.	1974	4,294
146 4/8	24 2/8	25 2/8	17 6/8	6	5	Christian County	IL	Camron Fitzsimmons	1980	4,294
146 4/8	23 0/8	24 6/8	19 1/8	6	6	Ashland County	WI	Chris Westlund	1982	4,294
146 4/8	26 4/8	25 2/8	17 4/8	4	5	Polk County	MO	James Scott Hogan	1982	4,294
146 4/8	24 3/8	24 5/8	18 6/8	4	4	Greene County	IL	Daniel E. Kalaal	1983	4,294
146 4/8	21 5/8	21 2/8	15 0/8	5	5	Forest County	WI	Eugene A. Pribek	1985	4,294
146 4/8	22 3/8	22 7/8	16 0/8	5	5	Ritchie County	WV	Tim Jividen	1985	4,294
146 4/8	24 0/8	23 6/8	16 2/8	4	4	Randolph County	IL	Edward J. Lannon	1985	4,294
146 4/8	23 0/8	22 5/8	13 4/8	6	6	Trempealeau County	WI	Greg J. Halama	1986	4,294
146 4/8	23 4/8	25 3/8	17 0/8	7	7	Washington County	WI	Eric Handeland	1986	4,294
146 4/8	26 2/8	26 4/8	18 2/8	5	5	Jackson County	AR	Doug C. Cockrill	1986	4,294
146 4/8	22 3/8	22 3/8	17 0/8	4	4	Dunn County	ND	Todd W. Boechler	1986	4,294
146 4/8	24 4/8	24 4/8	19 4/8	4	5	Pulaski County	KY	Bobbie Ryan	1986	4,294
146 4/8	23 3/8	24 1/8	17 4/8	5	5	Le Sueur County	MN	Joe Rybus	1987	4,294
146 4/8	24 6/8	23 4/8	19 4/8	5	5	Rock County	WI	Gary Hookstead	1987	4,294
146 4/8	23 3/8	23 2/8	17 7/8	6	5	Cottonwood County	MN	Steven L. Erickson	1987	4,294
146 4/8	25 0/8	24 1/8	19 2/8	5	5	Mercer County	NJ	Robert Pazdan	1988	4,294
146 4/8	23 1/8	23 4/8	16 6/8	5	5	Langlade County	WI	Dale G. Kemp	1988	4,294
146 4/8	22 0/8	21 5/8	17 3/8	6	5	Randolph County	IL	Dale Scherle	1988	4,294
146 4/8	24 2/8	23 1/8	19 0/8	5	5	Benton County	IA	Norm Madison	1988	4,294
146 4/8	23 0/8	23 4/8	19 0/8	5	4	Waukesha County	WI	Steven Hamme	1989	4,294
146 4/8	25 0/8	25 6/8	16 4/8	5	5	Nelson County	VA	Larry W. Toms	1989	4,294
146 4/8	23 0/8	23 4/8	16 0/8	5	5	Boone County	AR	Phillip Vanderpool	1990	4,294
146 4/8	25 0/8	24 1/8	21 2/8	5	4	Putnam County	IN	Randy Nippe	1990	4,294
146 4/8	27 6/8	25 6/8	18 2/8	5	6	Middlesex County	MA	Jared Apostolakes	1990	4,294
146 4/8	23 5/8	23 3/8	18 4/8	5	5	Okotoks	ALB	Randy Brown	1991	4,294
146 4/8	23 4/8	24 0/8	24 1/8	5	5	Randolph County	AR	Darrell Hagood	1992	4,294
146 4/8	23 5/8	23 6/8	19 7/8	5	5	Union County	KY	Richard Mehlbauer	1992	4,294
146 4/8	24 4/8	23 5/8	18 6/8	5	5	Henry County	OH	Doug Michaelis	1992	4,294
146 4/8	23 0/8	22 6/8	18 4/8	5	5	Henry County	IA	Jack Bates	1992	4,294
146 4/8	24 6/8	25 2/8	22 0/8	5	5	Cass County	IL	Carl H. Musch	1992	4,294
146 4/8	23 3/8	22 4/8	19 6/8	5	5	Decatur County	KS	Dave Wilson	1992	4,294
146 4/8	26 4/8	24 5/8	18 7/8	8	6	Cass County	MO	John Gardner	1994	4,294
146 4/8	23 6/8	23 5/8	19 2/8	4	5	Vilas County	WI	Eugene A. Pribek	1994	4,294
146 4/8	23 1/8	23 0/8	18 4/8	5	5	Brown County	OH	Bernard J. Waters	1994	4,294
146 4/8	23 4/8	24 0/8	19 6/8	6	5	Cook County	IL	Daniel H. Albaugh	1994	4,294
146 4/8	23 0/8	21 2/8	16 0/8	6	5	Macon County	MO	Dean Mayfield	1994	4,294
146 4/8	24 5/8	23 6/8	18 4/8	4	4	Coles County	IL	Mike Finney	1995	4,294
146 4/8	24 1/8	24 7/8	15 6/8	4	4	Thurston County	NE	Mike Lutt	1995	4,294
146 4/8	24 1/8	23 0/8	21 7/8	6	5	Van Buren County	IA	Jim Chambers	1995	4,294
146 4/8	21 6/8	22 7/8	15 5/8	6	5	Chippewa County	WI	Dale Helland	1995	4,294
146 4/8	20 0/8	20 2/8	16 4/8	5	6	Brown County	SD	Brad Dinger	1995	4,294
146 4/8	23 7/8	23 4/8	20 6/8	4	4	Jefferson County	PA	James Kotch	1997	4,294
146 4/8	23 3/8	22 3/8	18 4/8	5	5	Eau Claire County	WI	Riley Fletschock	1997	4,294
146 4/8	24 2/8	21 7/8	17 2/8	5	6	Menard County	IL	Ron Wadsworth	1997	4,294
146 4/8	25 2/8	23 7/8	19 2/8	5	5	Hennepin County	MN	David A. Mundahl	1997	4,294
146 4/8	24 4/8	22 3/8	20 0/8	5	5	Allamakee County	IA	Rich Buchli	1997	4,294
146 4/8	24 2/8	24 7/8	18 4/8	4	4	Adams County	OH	George P. Hehr	1997	4,294
146 4/8	23 4/8	23 6/8	17 6/8	6	8	Muskingum County	OH	Bryan Cooper	1997	4,294
146 3/8	23 5/8	23 1/8	27 1/8	5	5	De Kalb County	IN	Stanley Bremer	1969	4,346
146 3/8	24 6/8	24 5/8	15 3/8	5	5	Palo Alto County	IA	Kim E. Gustafson	1972	4,346
146 3/8	22 7/8	22 4/8	17 1/8	5	5	Shiawassee County	MI	David Asberry	1978	4,346
146 3/8	23 1/8	23 6/8	19 2/8	6	6	Chase County	KS	Jim Wilson	1980	4,346
146 3/8	23 5/8	23 5/8	20 1/8	5	5	Hamilton County	OH	Jerome R. Buschle, Jr.	1981	4,346
146 3/8	23 1/8	23 1/8	17 5/8	4	5	Cecil County	MD	John M. Martino	1981	4,346
146 3/8	23 5/8	23 1/8	16 1/8	5	6	Jo Daviess County	IL	David R. Kammerude	1983	4,346
146 3/8	22 5/8	22 1/8	16 7/8	6	6	Floyd County	IA	Mike Bull	1983	4,346
146 3/8	24 0/8	22 2/8	19 1/8	5	5	Perry County	IL	Richard Kuhnert	1984	4,346
146 3/8	24 6/8	25 7/8	20 7/8	5	5	Hamilton County	OH	Bob Miller	1985	4,346
146 3/8	21 0/8	22 0/8	16 1/8	5	5	Wilson County	KS	Kevin D. O'Neill	1986	4,346
146 3/8	22 1/8	22 1/8	16 5/8	5	5	Blue Earth County	MN	Paul Busse	1987	4,346
146 3/8	23 2/8	24 3/8	17 7/8	4	4	Montgomery County	IL	John Snoddy	1987	4,346
146 3/8	23 5/8	23 5/8	19 4/8	5	5	Van Buren County	IA	Clint O'Day	1988	4,346
146 3/8	22 6/8	22 2/8	16 3/8	5	5	St. Francis County	AR	Johnny Smith	1989	4,346
146 3/8	24 0/8	24 0/8	20 3/8	4	4	Isanti County	MN	Kevin Caldwell	1990	4,346
146 3/8	24 0/8	23 2/8	17 3/8	6	5	Brown County	WI	Robert M. McLellan	1990	4,346
146 3/8	22 6/8	22 7/8	14 7/8	6	6	Polk County	WI	Barry Peterson	1991	4,346
146 3/8	25 4/8	25 0/8	15 4/8	7	6	Shelby County	MO	William P. McQuillen	1991	4,346
146 3/8	22 5/8	21 5/8	15 5/8	5	5	Hennepin County	MN	Greg Wermerskirchen	1991	4,346
146 3/8	22 4/8	23 4/8	17 5/8	5	5	McHenry County	IL	Donald E. Hoey	1991	4,346
146 3/8	24 0/8	24 2/8	19 1/8	4	4	Kane County	IL	Richard Hight	1993	4,346
146 3/8	22 6/8	22 4/8	16 4/8	5	6	Sauk County	WI	Bill H. Overson	1993	4,346

WHITETAIL DEER (TYPICAL ANTLERS)

Minimum Score 125 — Continued

SCORE	LENGTH OF MAIN BEAM R	LENGTH OF MAIN BEAM L	INSIDE SPREAD	NUMBER OF POINTS R	NUMBER OF POINTS L	AREA	STATE/ PROVINCE	HUNTER'S NAME	DATE	RANK
146 3/8	21 1/8	21 6/8	17 5/8	6	6	Adams County	IA	Bryant Shermoe	1993	4,346
146 3/8	20 0/8	21 4/8	15 5/8	5	7	Kenedy County	TX	John W. Wallace	1993	4,346
146 3/8	23 4/8	23 7/8	20 0/8	6	5	Cass County	ND	Mark R. Thompson	1993	4,346
146 3/8	22 7/8	23 0/8	18 7/8	7	6	Morrison County	MN	John Teschendorf	1994	4,346
146 3/8	23 7/8	23 5/8	19 5/8	5	5	Logan County	IL	William Bruner	1994	4,346
146 3/8	24 4/8	24 4/8	16 2/8	9	7	Stewart County	TN	John C. Hults	1995	4,346
146 3/8	24 3/8	24 6/8	19 1/8	5	6	Clay County	SD	Richard Brown	1995	4,346
146 3/8	25 7/8	26 4/8	19 0/8	6	6	Columbia County	WI	Larry Owens	1995	4,346
146 3/8	24 4/8	24 0/8	19 3/8	5	5	Waupaca County	WI	Phil T. Knutzen	1996	4,346
146 3/8	24 4/8	25 0/8	18 7/8	4	4	Auglaize County	OH	Ron Wireman	1996	4,346
146 3/8	23 2/8	23 1/8	19 1/8	5	6	Sanilac County	MI	William B. Thrash III	1997	4,346
146 3/8	21 4/8	22 2/8	15 4/8	6	5	Oakland County	MI	Dwight D. Paslean	1997	4,346
146 3/8	26 5/8	26 2/8	20 3/8	5	5	Peoria County	IL	Steven W. Nelson	1997	4,346
146 3/8	26 7/8	26 0/8	16 1/8	4	4	Knox County	IN	Virgil Lane	1997	4,346
146 3/8	23 3/8	23 0/8	16 3/8	5	6	Iowa County	WI	Larry G. Fesenfeld	1998	4,346
146 3/8	24 5/8	24 4/8	17 1/8	5	5	Wayne County	NY	Mark C. Meyer	1998	4,346
146 3/8	26 6/8	26 5/8	22 3/8	4	4	Jo Daviess County	IL	James G. Harkness	1998	4,346
146 2/8	24 3/8	24 1/8	18 2/8	5	5	Stearns County	MN	Mike Beuning	1945	4,386
146 2/8	26 5/8	25 6/8	20 6/8	5	5	Plymouth County	IA	Cash N. Howe	1974	4,386
146 2/8	24 6/8	24 1/8	18 2/8	5	5	Butler County	KS	David R. Rogers	1976	4,386
146 2/8	21 2/8	21 7/8	21 2/8	5	5	Clark County	KS	Danny R. Fenton	1977	4,386
146 2/8	22 7/8	23 5/8	16 5/8	6	6	Lafayette County	WI	Wayne Gassman	1977	4,386
146 2/8	24 4/8	24 6/8	15 6/8	4	4	Clark County	IL	Gerald Shaffner	1978	4,386
146 2/8	24 6/8	24 0/8	19 1/8	5	7	Berkeley County	SC	Hugh Gaskins	1980	4,386
146 2/8	25 1/8	24 2/8	20 2/8	6	4	Union County	OH	Charles Yoakum	1980	4,386
146 2/8	25 2/8	25 0/8	17 2/8	5	6	Graham County	KS	Russell Hull	1982	4,386
146 2/8	23 6/8	22 5/8	18 0/8	5	5	Brown County	OH	Ronald Akins	1982	4,386
146 2/8	24 4/8	24 3/8	19 4/8	5	4	Washington County	WI	J.J. Ziegler	1983	4,386
146 2/8	24 6/8	24 5/8	19 4/8	5	5	Lafayette County	WI	Roger Wand	1983	4,386
146 2/8	24 0/8	24 0/8	18 2/8	6	6	Dane County	WI	Roland G. Lettman	1983	4,386
146 2/8	26 7/8	26 3/8	16 5/8	7	6	Granville County	NC	Bradley Brann	1984	4,386
146 2/8	22 2/8	21 6/8	16 5/8	5	5	Parkland County	ALB	Michel Carigan	1984	4,386
146 2/8	26 1/8	25 0/8	18 6/8	5	5	St. Lawrence County	NY	Joseph W. Pudney	1985	4,386
146 2/8	25 0/8	22 7/8	14 4/8	4	4	Van Buren County	IA	Tom Weigand	1985	4,386
146 2/8	22 6/8	22 0/8	17 5/8	5	6	Dodge County	MN	David Lyke	1985	4,386
146 2/8	22 5/8	23 6/8	17 6/8	6	6	Ontonagon County	MI	Paul M. Kilpela	1986	4,386
146 2/8	24 3/8	24 5/8	19 1/8	5	6	Redwood County	MN	R. Tetrick/M. Tetrick	1986	4,386
146 2/8	24 1/8	25 6/8	20 6/8	6	5	Lake County	IL	Kenneth D. Staples	1986	4,386
146 2/8	25 5/8	25 0/8	17 6/8	6	4	Pike County	OH	John Ribic	1987	4,386
146 2/8	20 5/8	21 6/8	15 2/8	5	5	Jackson County	MI	Dale M. Leach	1987	4,386
146 2/8	24 0/8	22 7/8	19 6/8	4	4	Greenwood County	KS	Brian Deer	1987	4,386
146 2/8	21 4/8	22 2/8	18 2/8	6	6	Livingston County	IL	Tom Roe	1989	4,386
146 2/8	22 3/8	22 3/8	19 1/8	6	6	Fayette County	IA	Thomas D. Joyner, Jr.	1990	4,386
146 2/8	26 6/8	26 6/8	19 4/8	6	5	Pike County	IL	Robert L. Cox	1991	4,386
146 2/8	22 4/8	22 2/8	15 1/8	5	6	Sedgwick County	KS	Larry Buchholz	1991	4,386
146 2/8	25 0/8	24 3/8	18 4/8	9	7	Cowley County	KS	Larry J. McKean	1991	4,386
146 2/8	22 7/8	22 1/8	16 1/8	6	6	Morrison County	MN	Randy Loken	1991	4,386
146 2/8	21 2/8	21 4/8	15 3/8	7	6	Eau Claire County	WI	Terry Mueller	1993	4,386
146 2/8	22 6/8	23 1/8	20 4/8	5	5	Belmont County	OH	William P. Koval	1993	4,386
146 2/8	24 4/8	24 4/8	20 6/8	5	6	Webb County	TX	Norman Speer	1993	4,386
146 2/8	21 3/8	21 3/8	17 7/8	7	8	Cascade County	MT	Bruce Davidson	1994	4,386
146 2/8	22 0/8	21 3/8	16 5/8	6	7	Jefferson County	WI	Jeff McKenzie	1994	4,386
146 2/8	22 3/8	22 2/8	19 2/8	6	6	St. Joseph County	IN	Michael R. Ebersole	1994	4,386
146 2/8	25 1/8	24 2/8	19 6/8	6	5	Kankakee County	IL	Jim Brandt	1994	4,386
146 2/8	23 6/8	23 0/8	19 0/8	5	5	Douglas County	WI	Travis D. Hicks	1994	4,386
146 2/8	26 5/8	24 4/8	20 0/8	6	7	Stearns County	MN	Steven H. Moon	1994	4,386
146 2/8	22 3/8	21 5/8	17 2/8	5	7	Louisa County	IA	Robert Walker	1994	4,386
146 2/8	23 0/8	24 6/8	20 1/8	6	6	Cross County	AR	Aaron W. Curtis III	1995	4,386
146 2/8	25 4/8	25 0/8	19 0/8	5	4	Grant County	WI	Charles P. Fralick	1995	4,386
146 2/8	22 7/8	23 3/8	19 7/8	5	6	Massac County	IL	Thomas L. Adkins	1995	4,386
146 2/8	23 1/8	23 7/8	15 4/8	5	6	Oneida County	WI	Don Psenicka	1995	4,386
146 2/8	24 4/8	24 3/8	16 6/8	5	5	Kent County	MI	Frederick H. Syswerda	1995	4,386
146 2/8	21 7/8	22 0/8	15 2/8	5	5	Rock County	WI	Robert W. Doerr	1995	4,386
146 2/8	21 1/8	22 3/8	20 0/8	6	5	Logan County	WV	Danny Lee Bourne	1995	4,386
146 2/8	26 0/8	25 4/8	19 1/8	6	6	Chester County	PA	Joe Joyce	1996	4,386
146 2/8	22 4/8	22 4/8	17 2/8	7	6	Buffalo County	WI	Brian Potter	1996	4,386
146 2/8	20 6/8	19 5/8	20 3/8	6	5	Fulton County	IL	Greg Pauli	1996	4,386
146 2/8	21 4/8	21 3/8	16 6/8	6	6	Bayfield County	WI	Eric Carlson	1996	4,386
146 2/8	22 4/8	23 1/8	18 2/8	4	5	Queen Annes County	MD	Marc D. Weiss	1998	4,386
146 1/8	23 5/8	24 5/8	17 7/8	6	5	Delaware County	IA	Douglas G. Dabroski	1975	4,438
146 1/8	25 2/8	25 6/8	21 2/8	6	8	Jefferson County	WI	Neil L. Lindemann	1977	4,438
146 1/8	24 1/8	25 0/8	18 3/8	5	5	Lamar County	GA	Joe A. Medcalf	1977	4,438
146 1/8	24 2/8	24 2/8	19 3/8	4	4	Chisago County	MN	Richard Brown	1980	4,438
146 1/8	25 2/8	23 3/8	18 2/8	6	5	Dickinson County	MI	Edward J. Henkel	1980	4,438
146 1/8	25 3/8	25 2/8	19 1/8	5	5	Darke County	OH	Larry Moore	1980	4,438
146 1/8	25 2/8	25 5/8	17 6/8	5	6	Morrison County	MN	John Strait	1981	4,438
146 1/8	24 3/8	23 4/8	14 7/8	6	5	Chisago County	MN	Clancy Lindvall	1982	4,438
146 1/8	24 3/8	23 2/8	17 2/8	5	7	Waseca County	MN	Mark Williams	1982	4,438

WHITETAIL DEER (TYPICAL ANTLERS)

Minimum Score 125 Continued

SCORE	LENGTH OF MAIN BEAM R	L	INSIDE SPREAD	NUMBER OF POINTS R	L	AREA	STATE/ PROVINCE	HUNTER'S NAME	DATE	RANK
146 1/8	24 6/8	24 2/8	19 7/8	4	5	Douglas County	NE	Ralph Joos, Jr.	1984	4,438
146 1/8	23 4/8	21 5/8	16 1/8	5	5	Montcalm County	MI	David Tompsett	1985	4,438
146 1/8	25 5/8	25 7/8	20 0/8	5	4	Albert County	NBW	Mike Pugh	1986	4,438
146 1/8	23 4/8	23 4/8	15 1/8	6	6	Carlton County	MN	Rick Nelson	1986	4,438
146 1/8	23 1/8	23 0/8	14 5/8	5	5	Lucas County	IA	Bill Brown	1986	4,438
146 1/8	26 0/8	25 6/8	15 5/8	4	4	Buffalo County	WI	Dale E. Tenner	1987	4,438
146 1/8	23 4/8	22 3/8	21 1/8	5	5	Huntington County	IN	R.D. Tessmer /R.S. Tessmer	1988	4,438
146 1/8	24 4/8	24 2/8	18 5/8	5	4	Guernsey County	OH	Kerry Mora	1988	4,438
146 1/8	25 0/8	23 5/8	16 6/8	7	6	Coshocton County	OH	David M. Croft	1989	4,438
146 1/8	23 2/8	23 2/8	19 4/8	6	4	Gibson County	IN	Robert Bump	1990	4,438
146 1/8	25 0/8	24 0/8	22 3/8	5	6	Queen Annes County	MD	Ross F. Mills	1990	4,438
146 1/8	25 7/8	25 1/8	19 5/8	4	4	Medina County	OH	Chris Postle	1991	4,438
146 1/8	22 5/8	20 3/8	17 6/8	6	6	Oceana County	MI	Mark Rollenhagen	1991	4,438
146 1/8	21 7/8	21 5/8	15 5/8	5	5	Jo Daviess County	IL	Stan Godfrey	1992	4,438
146 1/8	23 1/8	25 1/8	17 7/8	4	4	Poinsett County	AR	Steve Anderson	1992	4,438
146 1/8	25 3/8	24 5/8	20 6/8	6	5	Adams County	WI	Douglas R. Shomperlen	1993	4,438
146 1/8	24 0/8	24 0/8	16 3/8	4	5	Chester County	PA	Bruce Skipper	1993	4,438
146 1/8	22 0/8	21 3/8	17 3/8	5	5	Cumberland County	IL	Gary Jones	1993	4,438
146 1/8	26 3/8	24 7/8	17 7/8	5	4	Jefferson County	IN	Terry R. Nelson	1993	4,438
146 1/8	24 0/8	23 0/8	19 5/8	6	6	Edmonton	ALB	Gunther Tondeleir	1993	4,438
146 1/8	23 0/8	24 1/8	16 7/8	6	5	La Crosse County	WI	Dean Tschumper	1993	4,438
146 1/8	23 3/8	23 2/8	20 1/8	7	6	Hardin County	IA	Ronald A. Sunken	1993	4,438
146 1/8	23 1/8	23 2/8	17 3/8	5	5	Ransom County	ND	Clyde Williamson	1993	4,438
146 1/8	24 6/8	25 0/8	17 3/8	5	5	Buffalo County	WI	Michael J. Barstad	1994	4,438
146 1/8	24 2/8	23 1/8	17 3/8	5	5	Scott County	IL	Donald W. Slater	1994	4,438
146 1/8	23 7/8	24 6/8	17 3/8	5	5	Washington County	WI	Brian Strachota	1994	4,438
146 1/8	22 6/8	22 1/8	16 7/8	5	5	Washtenaw County	MI	Tom Homer	1994	4,438
146 1/8	28 1/8	26 2/8	20 4/8	5	7	Monona County	IA	Douglas V. Johnston	1994	4,438
146 1/8	25 2/8	24 3/8	18 2/8	5	5	Fayette County	IA	David Bond	1994	4,438
146 1/8	26 7/8	27 7/8	21 0/8	6	4	Dubuque County	IA	Ron Johnson	1994	4,438
146 1/8	23 1/8	23 5/8	14 7/8	5	5	Ferry County	WA	Shawn Henderson	1995	4,438
146 1/8	24 6/8	24 5/8	15 7/8	5	7	Monroe County	IN	Clarence S. Dawson	1995	4,438
146 1/8	26 0/8	25 6/8	21 3/8	4	4	Kenosha County	WI	Daniel K. Halladay	1995	4,438
146 1/8	24 4/8	24 4/8	17 6/8	4	6	McMullen County	TX	Rick Daab	1996	4,438
146 1/8	23 0/8	23 6/8	17 5/8	6	6	Kent County	MD	John A. Price, Jr.	1996	4,438
146 1/8	24 5/8	25 5/8	18 4/8	6	7	Otero County	CO	George Bock	1996	4,438
146 1/8	22 0/8	21 7/8	16 3/8	5	5	Manitowoc County	WI	Scott Endries	1996	4,438
146 1/8	25 3/8	24 1/8	19 7/8	4	4	Rapides Parish	LA	Roy M. Snow	1996	4,438
146 1/8	23 4/8	23 3/8	18 1/8	6	6	Souris	MAN	Bryan Klein	1997	4,438
146 1/8	25 7/8	26 6/8	20 1/8	4	4	Linn County	IA	Duane D. Long	1997	4,438
146 1/8	23 4/8	23 5/8	19 0/8	5	4	McKenzie County	ND	Corey Hugelen	1997	4,438
146 1/8	25 4/8	23 6/8	21 5/8	5	5	Cochrane	ALB	Tom Foss	1997	4,438
146 1/8	23 3/8	23 4/8	20 3/8	5	5	Wyoming County	WV	Perry Tilley	1997	4,438
146 0/8	22 1/8	22 2/8	19 2/8	6	6	Richland County	MT	James L. Kelly	1958	4,490
146 0/8	21 1/8	20 6/8	17 5/8	5	6	Cass County	IN	William D. Finks	1967	4,490
146 0/8	24 0/8	25 0/8	18 4/8	5	5	Will County	IL	Terry Marcukaitis	1971	4,490
146 0/8	25 0/8	24 0/8	22 0/8	5	5	Winona County	MN	Henry Scharmack, Jr.	1973	4,490
146 0/8	20 5/8	20 5/8	14 3/8	7	8	Murray County	MN	John Stenke	1973	4,490
146 0/8	24 1/8	24 4/8	16 0/8	6	5	Keith County	NE	Gerald Spurgin	1975	4,490
146 0/8	23 0/8	22 4/8	18 1/8	6	5	Calgary	ALB	Fred Walker	1981	4,490
146 0/8	21 6/8	21 5/8	16 2/8	5	5	Saline County	NE	Donald D. Matejka	1982	4,490
146 0/8	22 0/8	23 0/8	18 2/8	6	6	Kewaunee County	WI	Harold Blahnik	1982	4,490
146 0/8	21 5/8	22 1/8	18 2/8	5	5	Roberts County	SD	John Fridgen	1984	4,490
146 0/8	27 0/8	27 2/8	21 6/8	4	4	Morrison County	MN	John Sobaski	1985	4,490
146 0/8	24 2/8	23 2/8	15 6/8	5	6	Fulton County	IL	John I. Briggs	1986	4,490
146 0/8	23 4/8	22 6/8	19 4/8	5	5	Clayton County	IA	Joe Lieb	1986	4,490
146 0/8	24 4/8	24 4/8	19 7/8	6	6	Jo Daviess County	IL	William Stephanopoulos	1986	4,490
146 0/8	25 2/8	24 0/8	18 2/8	4	4	Saunders County	NE	Gary Frerichs	1988	4,490
146 0/8	25 0/8	23 2/8	21 2/8	5	6	Clay County	MN	Patrick Cox	1989	4,490
146 0/8	22 1/8	23 2/8	17 0/8	5	5	Allamakee County	IA	Casey A. Blum	1989	4,490
146 0/8	22 0/8	22 3/8	16 4/8	5	5	Robertson County	KY	Jim Whisman	1989	4,490
146 0/8	22 0/8	21 0/8	17 0/8	5	5	Heard County	GA	Ray Hand	1990	4,490
146 0/8	23 7/8	23 3/8	18 1/8	6	5	Fillmore County	MN	Dean C. Irish	1990	4,490
146 0/8	23 3/8	22 6/8	16 0/8	4	5	Westchester County	NY	Ronald Moore	1991	4,490
146 0/8	26 3/8	26 4/8	16 2/8	7	5	St. Charles County	MO	Benjamin F. Hamrick	1992	4,490
146 0/8	24 1/8	23 0/8	19 2/8	5	5	Winnebago County	IL	David L. Miller	1992	4,490
146 0/8	26 1/8	26 1/8	18 4/8	7	5	Newton County	IN	Ralph G. Bogie	1992	4,490
146 0/8	26 5/8	27 6/8	17 0/8	4	6	Worcester County	MA	Michael P. Duffy	1992	4,490
146 0/8	24 0/8	23 6/8	17 6/8	6	5	Eau Claire County	WI	Tony Aaron	1992	4,490
146 0/8	25 2/8	25 2/8	21 6/8	4	4	Baltimore County	MD	Timothy Whitehead	1993	4,490
146 0/8	24 0/8	23 7/8	17 4/8	5	5	Door County	WI	Mark K. Bauldry	1993	4,490
146 0/8	20 2/8	23 1/8	18 0/8	5	5	Grundy County	IL	Leonard Erschen	1993	4,490
146 0/8	21 6/8	21 4/8	17 6/8	5	5	Henry County	VA	Mike Weaver	1993	4,490
146 0/8	21 4/8	22 2/8	18 0/8	6	5	Ottawa County	KS	Robert A. Stegmaier	1993	4,490
146 0/8	21 3/8	23 7/8	17 2/8	6	6	Harper County	KS	Scott Lagers	1994	4,490
146 0/8	21 3/8	21 3/8	20 4/8	5	5	Kane County	IL	Art P. Toney	1994	4,490
146 0/8	24 0/8	24 2/8	19 0/8	5	4	La Salle County	IL	Dewayne Mullins	1995	4,490
146 0/8	22 5/8	23 5/8	19 2/8	5	4	Osage County	KS	Gerald Britschge	1995	4,490

WHITETAIL DEER (TYPICAL ANTLERS)

Minimum Score 125

SCORE	LENGTH OF MAIN BEAM R	LENGTH OF MAIN BEAM L	INSIDE SPREAD	NUMBER OF POINTS R	NUMBER OF POINTS L	AREA	STATE/ PROVINCE	HUNTER'S NAME	DATE	RANK
146 0/8	23 2/8	23 0/8	17 0/8	4	5	Richland County	MT	Kurt A. Bensinger	1996	4,490
146 0/8	23 5/8	23 7/8	21 5/8	6	5	Clark County	WI	Michael A. Ruzic	1996	4,490
146 0/8	22 1/8	21 5/8	17 6/8	5	5	Winona County	MN	Steve R. Strike	1997	4,490
146 0/8	24 0/8	23 7/8	18 4/8	5	5	Knox County	IL	Jeff Nelson	1997	4,490
146 0/8	24 2/8	24 0/8	18 0/8	5	5	Suffolk County	NY	Neal Heaton	1997	4,490
146 0/8	25 1/8	25 2/8	19 6/8	6	5	Tuscarawas County	OH	William C. Gintz	1997	4,490
146 0/8	23 5/8	25 0/8	17 4/8	5	5	Buffalo County	WI	John W. Zahrte	1998	4,490
145 7/8	25 1/8	25 0/8	16 3/8	4	5	Wood County	WI	Laddimere Beranek	1959	4,532
145 7/8	25 4/8	24 4/8	19 1/8	4	5	Greeley County	NE	Bill W. Surface	1962	4,532
145 7/8	22 4/8	22 7/8	20 7/8	4	8	Lafayette County	WI	James Goetzke	1972	4,532
145 7/8	23 3/8	23 1/8	16 1/8	7	8	Polk County	MN	Willie Johnson/Tim Amuinson	1981	4,532
145 7/8	21 4/8	22 0/8	15 2/8	5	6	Chase County	KS	John L. Moore	1982	4,532
145 7/8	22 6/8	24 4/8	18 7/8	6	5	Lewis & Clark County	MT	Royce Dake	1982	4,532
145 7/8	23 5/8	24 0/8	16 5/8	8	5	Manitowoc County	WI	Thomas L. Alfson	1983	4,532
145 7/8	22 4/8	22 3/8	20 1/8	5	5	Harvey County	KS	Gregory K. Dirksen	1983	4,532
145 7/8	25 1/8	25 2/8	19 1/8	5	5	Monroe County	NY	Pat M. Moore	1987	4,532
145 7/8	24 1/8	23 0/8	18 5/8	5	5	Kent County	MD	Steve J. Grabowski, Jr.	1987	4,532
145 7/8	25 2/8	27 2/8	17 4/8	5	6	Brown County	IL	Ron Hanna	1988	4,532
145 7/8	26 4/8	24 4/8	17 0/8	5	7	Republic County	KS	Gary Dahl	1988	4,532
145 7/8	22 7/8	23 1/8	15 0/8	8	5	Shawnee County	KS	Bradley D Porubsky	1989	4,532
145 7/8	23 5/8	23 7/8	18 7/8	6	5	Lake County	IL	Mike Serwa	1990	4,532
145 7/8	23 7/8	23 5/8	17 1/8	6	5	Barry County	MO	Donald L. Randolph	1990	4,532
145 7/8	23 4/8	22 4/8	17 5/8	5	6	Republic County	KS	Jerry A. Thomas	1990	4,532
145 7/8	23 0/8	22 6/8	16 5/8	5	5	Arenac County	MI	Daryl Russell	1991	4,532
145 7/8	24 6/8	25 5/8	18 1/8	5	5	Aitkin County	MN	Daniel Picht	1991	4,532
145 7/8	25 2/8	25 1/8	19 1/8	5	4	Madison County	IA	Gary Knoll	1991	4,532
145 7/8	22 7/8	22 4/8	16 3/8	5	5	Washington County	IL	Stanley F. Musial	1991	4,532
145 7/8	22 2/8	22 3/8	18 4/8	7	7	Carroll County	IL	Paul Shipman	1991	4,532
145 7/8	24 0/8	24 0/8	19 3/8	5	6	Johnson County	IA	Bruce Charipar	1992	4,532
145 7/8	25 1/8	26 3/8	22 1/8	3	3	Steuben County	IN	Jim Loughran	1992	4,532
145 7/8	21 1/8	22 6/8	16 7/8	5	5	Henry County	VA	Mike Weaver	1992	4,532
145 7/8	25 0/8	24 4/8	18 0/8	6	7	Dane County	WI	Bennie P. Larson	1993	4,532
145 7/8	22 5/8	23 2/8	17 5/8	5	5	Dane County	WI	Stuart Smith	1994	4,532
145 7/8	22 0/8	22 6/8	17 5/8	5	5	Noble County	OH	John W. Denny	1994	4,532
145 7/8	22 4/8	23 0/8	16 3/8	5	5	McHenry County	IL	Troy D. Erckfritz	1995	4,532
145 7/8	23 1/8	24 5/8	16 3/8	5	5	Columbia County	WI	Perry L. Dahl	1996	4,532
145 7/8	24 5/8	24 3/8	22 4/8	5	5	Waupaca County	WI	Adam J. Lorge	1996	4,532
145 7/8	27 0/8	26 5/8	17 5/8	5	5	Dane County	WI	Lawrence O. Bushey	1996	4,532
145 7/8	24 4/8	24 6/8	19 1/8	5	5	Buffalo County	WI	Jack R. Dieckman	1996	4,532
145 7/8	22 1/8	23 5/8	16 2/8	7	6	Slope County	ND	Dennis Palmer	1996	4,532
145 7/8	26 5/8	27 0/8	20 3/8	5	4	La Salle County	IL	Wayne Riebe	1997	4,532
145 7/8	25 4/8	26 0/8	20 1/8	5	4	Montgomery County	OH	Christopher L. Lutz	1997	4,532
145 7/8	21 5/8	21 7/8	14 7/8	5	5	Martin County	IN	Jay Davis	1997	4,532
145 7/8	19 4/8	21 3/8	15 5/8	5	5	Oldham County	KY	Daniel Klingenfus	1997	4,532
145 7/8	23 2/8	24 1/8	14 3/8	5	4	Erie County	OH	Kent Hamilton	1997	4,532
145 6/8	20 0/8	20 5/8	17 0/8	5	6	Okmulgee County	OK	Pat Giulioli	1973	4,570
145 6/8	21 5/8	22 4/8	17 0/8	5	5	Monroe County	WI	Bob Besch	1980	4,570
145 6/8	22 0/8	22 0/8	17 2/8	5	5	Millarville	ALB	Richard Freudenberg	1982	4,570
145 6/8	23 2/8	23 4/8	15 5/8	6	5	Ravalli County	MT	Arden R. Cowan	1983	4,570
145 6/8	23 0/8	23 1/8	20 0/8	4	5	Aransas County	TX	Dr. Tip Coleman	1985	4,570
145 6/8	21 3/8	21 3/8	17 0/8	6	5	Clay County	MN	Darwin Cihak	1986	4,570
145 6/8	22 5/8	22 2/8	17 2/8	5	7	Jefferson County	WI	Randy Latsch	1986	4,570
145 6/8	23 1/8	22 2/8	15 2/8	6	6	Kenedy County	TX	George Cooper	1987	4,570
145 6/8	23 3/8	24 0/8	18 0/8	7	6	Van Buren County	IA	Don Kieler	1987	4,570
145 6/8	23 7/8	23 6/8	17 0/8	4	4	Polk County	WI	Andy Bollant	1988	4,570
145 6/8	21 4/8	21 7/8	15 2/8	5	5	Jefferson County	WI	Brad Hering	1989	4,570
145 6/8	23 3/8	24 1/8	17 6/8	5	7	St. Croix County	WI	David Saltness	1989	4,570
145 6/8	24 3/8	23 7/8	16 3/8	6	6	Linn County	IA	Darryl W. Martin	1989	4,570
145 6/8	24 3/8	24 7/8	21 0/8	4	4	Cecil County	MD	Earl McSorley	1989	4,570
145 6/8	22 3/8	22 3/8	14 0/8	5	5	Iron County	WI	Scott Hultman	1989	4,570
145 6/8	22 3/8	23 5/8	18 4/8	5	5	Meade County	KY	Kevin Anderson	1989	4,570
145 6/8	23 4/8	23 4/8	18 2/8	5	6	Worcester County	MA	Mark Doucimo	1990	4,570
145 6/8	25 3/8	25 6/8	19 4/8	7	9	Florence County	WI	Steven C. Gevaert	1991	4,570
145 6/8	21 5/8	22 2/8	18 4/8	5	4	Mercer County	IL	Dennis Nelson	1991	4,570
145 6/8	23 4/8	24 0/8	17 0/8	6	5	Jasper County	IL	Elmer R. Luce, Jr.	1991	4,570
145 6/8	21 4/8	21 4/8	17 2/8	5	5	Plymouth County	IA	Cash N. Howe	1991	4,570
145 6/8	26 7/8	27 4/8	19 6/8	4	4	Middlesex County	MA	Joe R. Shepard	1991	4,570
145 6/8	22 6/8	21 7/8	17 2/8	5	5	Pickett County	TN	Robert E. Lee	1993	4,570
145 6/8	24 2/8	25 4/8	20 6/8	6	6	Douglas County	WI	Jens Gregerson III	1993	4,570
145 6/8	21 6/8	23 1/8	17 0/8	6	8	Kewaunee County	WI	Phil J. Romdenne	1993	4,570
145 6/8	25 6/8	27 5/8	19 6/8	5	4	Knox County	OH	David B. Fowls	1993	4,570
145 6/8	24 6/8	24 4/8	18 6/8	5	5	Bayfield County	WI	Joseph Beedlow	1994	4,570
145 6/8	23 5/8	22 7/8	21 0/8	4	4	Coles County	IL	Matt Smith	1994	4,570
145 6/8	24 7/8	23 3/8	19 7/8	6	6	Rice County	MN	Howard L. Wolf	1994	4,570
145 6/8	21 1/8	21 7/8	15 4/8	5	5	Henry County	VA	Mike Weaver	1995	4,570
145 6/8	24 7/8	24 2/8	18 2/8	4	4	Franklin County	OH	Gregory J. Rustemeyer	1995	4,570
145 6/8	23 0/8	22 2/8	17 6/8	5	5	Jackson County	IN	Max E. Gambrel	1995	4,570
145 6/8	23 6/8	25 7/8	21 0/8	6	5	Walworth County	WI	Chuck Palmer	1995	4,570

Continued

WHITETAIL DEER (TYPICAL ANTLERS)

Minimum Score 125 Continued

SCORE	LENGTH OF MAIN BEAM R	L	INSIDE SPREAD	NUMBER OF POINTS R	L	AREA	STATE/ PROVINCE	HUNTER'S NAME	DATE	RANK
145 6/8	22 3/8	23 0/8	17 0/8	6	5	Putnam County	IN	Chris Nichols	1996	4,570
145 6/8	26 7/8	26 5/8	19 3/8	7	4	Jasper County	IL	Brian Collins	1996	4,570
145 6/8	24 7/8	25 6/8	15 4/8	5	5	Adams County	OH	Lonnie Shattuck, Jr.	1997	4,570
145 6/8	21 6/8	22 3/8	15 6/8	5	5	Harrison County	IA	Tracy Liddell	1997	4,570
145 6/8	25 0/8	25 2/8	19 6/8	6	7	Grant County	WI	Randy Hochhausen	1997	4,570
145 6/8	23 0/8	24 5/8	16 6/8	7	5	Cherokee County	IA	Curtis Otto	1997	4,570
145 5/8	25 1/8	24 4/8	19 7/8	6	5	Waseca County	MN	Robert Barrie	1971	4,609
145 5/8	23 7/8	24 0/8	21 2/8	4	6	Montgomery County	AL	Rett Kelly	1974	4,609
145 5/8	22 5/8	21 5/8	17 4/8	6	6	Moody County	SD	Harvey R. Benton	1976	4,609
145 5/8	23 5/8	23 0/8	18 4/8	6	7	Stearns County	MN	Larry Schwarze	1979	4,609
145 5/8	23 0/8	23 6/8	17 3/8	5	5	Rich Valley	ALB	Eric Teege	1980	4,609
145 5/8	23 2/8	23 4/8	18 1/8	5	5	St. Croix County	WI	Keith Andrea	1981	4,609
145 5/8	24 0/8	24 4/8	18 5/8	6	5	Athens County	OH	Steve Wilkes	1983	4,609
145 5/8	26 1/8	25 7/8	18 2/8	5	5	Houston County	GA	Issac W. Horne	1985	4,609
145 5/8	22 2/8	22 7/8	15 5/8	6	6	Isanti County	MN	Tim Dugas	1985	4,609
145 5/8	24 1/8	23 4/8	19 2/8	5	6	Black Hawk County	IA	John L. Derifield	1985	4,609
145 5/8	26 2/8	25 1/8	20 6/8	5	7	Christian County	IL	Carl Tucker	1985	4,609
145 5/8	23 2/8	24 3/8	20 4/8	6	5	Coffey County	KS	James Bowman	1985	4,609
145 5/8	25 5/8	24 5/8	16 7/8	5	4	Hancock County	OH	Dennis J. Morris	1986	4,609
145 5/8	23 3/8	24 2/8	17 5/8	5	5	Isanti County	MN	Jon Anderson	1986	4,609
145 5/8	26 5/8	24 3/8	19 7/8	4	5	Johnson County	IL	Jack D. Lambert	1986	4,609
145 5/8	24 7/8	25 7/8	23 7/8	6	4	Lake County	IL	Robert Henry Torstenson	1986	4,609
145 5/8	27 3/8	27 4/8	20 5/8	4	4	Marion County	IA	Leonard Grimes	1986	4,609
145 5/8	24 1/8	22 5/8	18 7/8	4	4	Sawyer County	WI	Dan Sours	1989	4,609
145 5/8	22 1/8	22 2/8	19 1/8	6	6	Calgary	ALB	Brent Brown	1989	4,609
145 5/8	23 5/8	24 1/8	18 1/8	5	4	Platte County	WY	Jerry Bowen	1991	4,609
145 5/8	22 6/8	21 6/8	19 7/8	6	6	Lake County	IL	William A. Murphy	1991	4,609
145 5/8	23 0/8	22 6/8	18 1/8	5	5	Lake County	IL	Matt Porter	1991	4,609
145 5/8	24 2/8	25 3/8	19 7/8	4	4	McHenry County	IL	Joe Roos	1991	4,609
145 5/8	26 5/8	26 0/8	19 4/8	5	6	Kendall County	IL	Douglas W. Musser	1992	4,609
145 5/8	24 6/8	26 4/8	17 4/8	4	5	Carbon County	MT	Mike Booke	1992	4,609
145 5/8	24 3/8	24 2/8	21 3/8	5	6	Highland County	OH	Rickey M. Davis	1994	4,609
145 5/8	25 5/8	25 6/8	16 1/8	5	5	Anoka County	MN	Robert Christensen	1994	4,609
145 5/8	21 7/8	21 5/8	15 6/8	5	6	Riley County	KS	Ron Phillips	1994	4,609
145 5/8	23 4/8	23 3/8	19 3/8	5	5	Ogle County	IL	Mickey D. Badertscher, Jr.	1994	4,609
145 5/8	23 6/8	23 2/8	14 1/8	5	5	Ashland County	WI	James Wilbur	1994	4,609
145 5/8	23 6/8	23 5/8	19 7/8	5	5	Chester County	PA	Randy D. Coyle	1994	4,609
145 5/8	25 0/8	25 4/8	18 2/8	5	5	Fulton County	IL	Patrick Cebuhar	1994	4,609
145 5/8	28 7/8	26 1/8	22 3/8	4	5	Miami County	OH	Richard Hunt	1994	4,609
145 5/8	25 0/8	24 5/8	17 1/8	7	5	Barry County	MO	R. Steven Crain	1995	4,609
145 5/8	22 6/8	23 2/8	18 5/8	5	6	Olmsted County	MN	John G. Wooldridge	1995	4,609
145 5/8	23 4/8	23 1/8	17 3/8	5	5	Berks County	PA	Robert J. Entler, Jr.	1995	4,609
145 5/8	23 6/8	22 6/8	18 1/8	5	5	Richland County	WI	Joe Bavlnka	1995	4,609
145 5/8	22 4/8	22 2/8	18 1/8	5	5	Buffalo County	WI	Carl Wermeling	1995	4,609
145 5/8	24 1/8	24 2/8	15 7/8	5	5	Codington County	SD	Troy A. Richardson	1995	4,609
145 5/8	26 3/8	25 3/8	17 7/8	4	4	Vermilion County	IL	Kenneth Roy	1995	4,609
145 5/8	24 2/8	23 0/8	20 7/8	5	5	Cape Girardeau County	MO	Darrell Hobbs	1995	4,609
145 5/8	24 0/8	24 6/8	19 1/8	4	4	Haskell County	OK	Johnny Traylor	1995	4,609
145 5/8	20 6/8	18 7/8	16 1/8	6	6	Monroe County	IN	David Smith	1996	4,609
145 5/8	22 4/8	22 6/8	17 1/8	5	5	Winona County	MN	Terrence Wobig	1997	4,609
145 5/8	24 2/8	24 2/8	17 6/8	5	6	Williamson County	TN	John Rutledge	1997	4,609
145 5/8	21 3/8	21 7/8	17 4/8	5	7	Marquette County	WI	Michael V. Marshall	1997	4,609
145 5/8	23 3/8	22 7/8	17 0/8	8	6	Mahaska County	IA	Robert Spoelstra	1997	4,609
145 5/8	21 4/8	23 2/8	21 1/8	5	5	Monona County	IA	Mark Jost	1997	4,609
145 5/8	24 4/8	23 2/8	15 1/8	5	5	Kent County	MD	Joseph Flanagan	1998	4,609
145 4/8	23 3/8	24 0/8	17 2/8	6	7	Morton County	ND	Eddy Wallery	1959	4,658
145 4/8	25 2/8	24 1/8	18 6/8	5	5	Waupaca County	WI	Craig Shambeau	1968	4,658
145 4/8	25 5/8	24 4/8	19 0/8	4	5	Monroe County	WI	Larry Arentz	1977	4,658
145 4/8	23 2/8	22 0/8	18 2/8	7	6	Mower County	MN	Walter E. Bauer	1977	4,658
145 4/8	24 3/8	23 0/8	20 4/8	5	4	Marion County	IA	Donald Bennett	1977	4,658
145 4/8	22 1/8	21 6/8	17 2/8	5	5	Van Buren County	MI	Bob Zedeck	1979	4,658
145 4/8	24 3/8	22 7/8	18 1/8	5	6	Lawrence County	AL	Richard McClanahan	1980	4,658
145 4/8	23 7/8	24 3/8	20 2/8	4	4	Kent County	MI	Peter Champnoise	1981	4,658
145 4/8	24 1/8	24 3/8	21 4/8	7	6	Hamilton County	OH	Jack Ranz	1982	4,658
145 4/8	24 0/8	24 1/8	18 7/8	5	4	Scott County	KY	Park Tackett	1984	4,658
145 4/8	23 0/8	24 0/8	19 4/8	4	5	Cass County	MI	Lee Davis	1985	4,658
145 4/8	24 0/8	22 6/8	18 0/8	6	6	Delaware County	OH	Ronald E. Murphy	1986	4,658
145 4/8	23 0/8	24 3/8	18 2/8	6	6	Trego County	KS	Morris Crisler	1986	4,658
145 4/8	24 0/8	25 1/8	21 3/8	6	6	Houston County	MN	Bruce Norton	1987	4,658
145 4/8	24 6/8	22 2/8	17 0/8	5	5	Jefferson County	MO	Steve North	1987	4,658
145 4/8	23 2/8	24 4/8	18 2/8	4	4	Adams County	IL	Gary Nebe	1987	4,658
145 4/8	23 6/8	23 7/8	18 4/8	4	4	Chester County	PA	Randy R. Caspersen	1988	4,658
145 4/8	24 4/8	24 6/8	17 2/8	4	4	Ravalli County	MT	Chris Landstrom	1988	4,658
145 4/8	23 5/8	23 3/8	17 0/8	7	6	Kankakee County	IL	Stanley Gawlinski	1990	4,658
145 4/8	25 5/8	25 5/8	18 1/8	5	5	Coles County	IL	Gary Jones	1990	4,658
145 4/8	22 3/8	22 4/8	17 4/8	5	5	Price County	WI	Phil Socwell	1990	4,658
145 4/8	23 4/8	23 4/8	19 0/8	5	6	Buffalo County	WI	Edward Brannen	1991	4,658
145 4/8	22 5/8	23 4/8	16 3/8	5	6	Appanoose County	IA	Steven P. Salmieri	1991	4,658

WHITETAIL DEER (TYPICAL ANTLERS)

Minimum Score 125   Continued

SCORE	LENGTH OF MAIN BEAM R	LENGTH OF MAIN BEAM L	INSIDE SPREAD	NUMBER OF POINTS R	NUMBER OF POINTS L	AREA	STATE/PROVINCE	HUNTER'S NAME	DATE	RANK
145 4/8	24 3/8	23 2/8	19 4/8	5	6	Baca County	CO	Kurt W. Keskimaki	1991	4,658
145 4/8	21 0/8	20 4/8	16 5/8	6	7	Osborne County	KS	Dennis Fisk	1991	4,658
145 4/8	25 6/8	25 5/8	16 2/8	5	5	Meade County	KY	Aaron H. Pierce	1992	4,658
145 4/8	21 3/8	21 6/8	17 2/8	5	6	Brooks County	TX	Jimmy W. McBee	1992	4,658
145 4/8	23 0/8	22 2/8	18 6/8	5	5	Will County	IL	Bob Ourth	1992	4,658
145 4/8	24 6/8	24 4/8	17 0/8	5	5	Braxton County	WV	Jeffrey Styers	1992	4,658
145 4/8	25 1/8	23 5/8	18 5/8	6	5	Edgar County	IL	Darrell Higgins	1993	4,658
145 4/8	26 1/8	25 5/8	18 4/8	5	5	Webb County	TX	David M. Richards	1993	4,658
145 4/8	26 0/8	25 5/8	19 0/8	5	4	Williamson County	IL	Tim Flowers	1994	4,658
145 4/8	22 1/8	22 5/8	18 2/8	7	7	Outagamie County	WI	Donald J. Calmes	1994	4,658
145 4/8	27 6/8	27 0/8	19 4/8	5	4	Brown County	IL	Tom Lavery	1994	4,658
145 4/8	23 0/8	23 5/8	17 6/8	5	5	Clay County	WV	Rodney Neal	1994	4,658
145 4/8	22 1/8	23 1/8	14 6/8	6	7	Aurora County	SD	Troy Kirsch	1994	4,658
145 4/8	24 0/8	22 6/8	18 4/8	4	4	Tazewell County	IL	Steven D. Kroll	1994	4,658
145 4/8	23 1/8	22 7/8	20 2/8	6	5	Livingston County	IL	Kurt Hobart	1995	4,658
145 4/8	23 4/8	23 3/8	20 2/8	4	4	Barron County	WI	Todd W. Bailey	1995	4,658
145 4/8	23 6/8	25 6/8	19 4/8	4	4	Greenwood County	KS	Jon Burgdorf	1995	4,658
145 4/8	24 2/8	25 5/8	16 0/8	5	5	Olmsted County	MN	Dave Frost	1995	4,658
145 4/8	23 3/8	23 7/8	17 2/8	5	5	Dorchester County	MD	Norman L. Eckels, Jr.	1995	4,658
145 4/8	24 4/8	24 2/8	17 2/8	6	9	Carroll County	MO	Larry Cochenour	1995	4,658
145 4/8	21 3/8	21 1/8	18 4/8	5	7	Todd County	KY	William E. Page	1996	4,658
145 4/8	25 0/8	24 6/8	20 6/8	4	4	Fairfield County	CT	Chris Look III	1997	4,658
145 4/8	22 6/8	22 4/8	16 2/8	5	5	Howard County	IA	Scott E. Runde	1997	4,658
145 4/8	24 4/8	25 7/8	17 7/8	5	5	Iroquois County	IL	Cary Pence	1997	4,658
145 4/8	23 4/8	23 4/8	16 0/8	5	6	Chase County	KS	Tony Cassity	1997	4,658
145 4/8	24 0/8	24 4/8	16 5/8	7	7	Steuben County	IN	Troy R. Portner	1998	4,658
145 3/8	24 3/8	25 1/8	20 5/8	5	5	Lyon County	KS	Edward Bess	1967	4,707
145 3/8	22 4/8	22 5/8	18 1/8	5	5	Morrison County	MN	Gerald A. Young	1971	4,707
145 3/8	23 4/8	23 4/8	18 6/8	5	5	Kanawha County	WV	Luther McClure	1973	4,707
145 3/8	24 5/8	25 5/8	22 1/8	4	5	Will County	IL	Philip J. Gariboldi	1977	4,707
145 3/8	26 7/8	26 3/8	20 2/8	4	4	Jackson County	MI	Scot Gazlay	1977	4,707
145 3/8	22 7/8	23 0/8	19 1/8	4	5	Des Moines County	IA	John Jindrich	1979	4,707
145 3/8	22 6/8	21 3/8	17 4/8	6	6	Marshall County	SD	Tim Johnson	1980	4,707
145 3/8	23 7/8	23 7/8	17 5/8	4	4	Pike County	OH	William H. Koehler	1981	4,707
145 3/8	23 3/8	23 6/8	17 2/8	5	4	Jackson County	OH	Joe W. Wright	1982	4,707
145 3/8	23 4/8	22 2/8	18 1/8	5	4	Osage County	KS	Gary Hunsicker	1985	4,707
145 3/8	22 0/8	21 6/8	17 5/8	5	5	Otter Tail County	MN	Walter Rieckman	1986	4,707
145 3/8	23 0/8	23 4/8	17 1/8	6	5	Delaware County	OH	Mark Yarnell	1986	4,707
145 3/8	20 4/8	21 0/8	15 1/8	6	6	Bayfield County	WI	James Rohr	1986	4,707
145 3/8	24 3/8	24 4/8	18 7/8	4	4	Vilas County	WI	Bruce Jacobson	1987	4,707
145 3/8	24 6/8	24 6/8	17 4/8	5	6	Le Sueur County	MN	Donald Attenberger	1988	4,707
145 3/8	22 4/8	22 0/8	16 3/8	5	6	McHenry County	IL	Bill Gilstead	1988	4,707
145 3/8	25 4/8	24 0/8	19 2/8	5	4	Peoria County	IL	Donald R. Ragain	1988	4,707
145 3/8	21 5/8	22 5/8	18 1/8	5	5	Osborne County	KS	Craig E. Pottberg	1988	4,707
145 3/8	22 7/8	22 3/8	18 1/8	6	5	Tuscarawas County	OH	Emery Schlabach	1988	4,707
145 3/8	23 4/8	24 5/8	16 3/8	7	5	Montgomery County	MD	James C. Dalrymple, Jr.	1988	4,707
145 3/8	25 7/8	25 7/8	19 3/8	4	4	Langlade County	WI	David Nelson	1989	4,707
145 3/8	24 1/8	23 5/8	18 4/8	5	5	Scott County	KY	Darrell Sharp	1990	4,707
145 3/8	23 7/8	23 5/8	16 5/8	5	5	Jennings County	IN	Gregory Dean Tucker	1990	4,707
145 3/8	24 2/8	24 2/8	17 7/8	6	7	Cherokee County	IA	Dennis Vaudt	1992	4,707
145 3/8	23 5/8	26 0/8	16 4/8	5	9	Crawford County	KS	Kim A. Ryan	1992	4,707
145 3/8	23 4/8	22 6/8	17 0/8	7	5	Daviess County	IN	Bob C. Graber	1992	4,707
145 3/8	22 6/8	22 2/8	18 3/8	5	7	Scott County	MN	Jason Sorenson	1992	4,707
145 3/8	22 2/8	22 3/8	20 1/8	5	5	Cook County	IL	David Daly	1992	4,707
145 3/8	22 0/8	22 6/8	19 7/8	4	4	Douglas County	MN	Ryan Augeson	1993	4,707
145 3/8	22 5/8	22 0/8	18 4/8	7	7	Du Page County	IL	Gerald Allison	1993	4,707
145 3/8	26 0/8	27 6/8	18 5/8	5	5	Milwaukee County	WI	Dennis Napreilla	1993	4,707
145 3/8	24 4/8	25 5/8	16 6/8	5	7	Saline County	MO	Brandon E. Isbell	1994	4,707
145 3/8	24 6/8	24 7/8	17 1/8	5	5	Wabasha County	MN	Tim L. Hansen	1994	4,707
145 3/8	21 7/8	23 1/8	19 3/8	4	5	Dane County	WI	Brad Madigan	1994	4,707
145 3/8	24 5/8	24 6/8	14 4/8	5	5	Clark County	SD	Don Aarstad	1994	4,707
145 3/8	24 6/8	26 3/8	20 3/8	5	5	Suffolk County	NY	Vincent Passero	1995	4,707
145 3/8	21 1/8	22 4/8	16 7/8	5	5	Appanoose County	IA	Lynn Moeller	1995	4,707
145 3/8	26 0/8	25 6/8	19 5/8	4	4	Plymouth County	IA	Jon T. Saunders	1996	4,707
145 3/8	25 0/8	23 7/8	16 7/8	5	5	Kenosha County	WI	Brian Koldeway	1996	4,707
145 3/8	23 4/8	22 7/8	20 1/8	5	5	St. Louis County	MO	Dave McConnell	1996	4,707
145 3/8	23 1/8	23 4/8	18 6/8	6	6	Sutton County	TX	Sherri K. Dean	1997	4,707
145 3/8	24 7/8	25 5/8	22 3/8	4	5	Edgar County	IL	Dana R. Cawthon	1997	4,707
145 3/8	24 0/8	25 0/8	22 4/8	4	5	Cloud County	KS	Gerald Dockins	1997	4,707
145 3/8	25 1/8	25 2/8	19 3/8	7	5	Yorkton	SAS	Al Mehling	1998	4,707
145 2/8	21 6/8	21 3/8	18 2/8	5	5	Des Moines County	IA	Gary Biles	1973	4,751
145 2/8	22 5/8	22 7/8	17 2/8	5	5	Yankton County	SD	Gordon Orton	1976	4,751
145 2/8	23 0/8	22 4/8	15 4/8	7	6	Douglas County	KS	Richard D. Brown	1978	4,751
145 2/8	23 3/8	23 0/8	16 2/8	5	5	Polk County	IA	Jim Young	1978	4,751
145 2/8	23 7/8	24 4/8	17 5/8	5	5	Livingston County	MI	Alan K. Newberry	1979	4,751
145 2/8	21 5/8	21 1/8	19 4/8	5	6	Clark County	AR	Thomas E. Taylor	1982	4,751
145 2/8	22 7/8	23 6/8	18 6/8	5	5	Madison County	IA	Stephen W. Kent	1982	4,751
145 2/8	26 2/8	25 7/8	22 1/8	6	6	Grant County	WI	Gary Wiest	1982	4,751

WHITETAIL DEER (TYPICAL ANTLERS)

Minimum Score 125 — Continued

SCORE	LENGTH OF MAIN BEAM R	LENGTH OF MAIN BEAM L	INSIDE SPREAD	NUMBER OF POINTS R	NUMBER OF POINTS L	AREA	STATE/PROVINCE	HUNTER'S NAME	DATE	RANK
145 2/8	24 1/8	24 2/8	18 6/8	4	4	Vernon County	WI	David Penchi	1982	4,751
145 2/8	24 2/8	22 0/8	22 0/8	5	6	Stephenson County	IL	Dwight Pickard	1983	4,751
145 2/8	26 6/8	25 6/8	21 2/8	4	4	Mercer County	NJ	James E. McCloskey, Jr.	1984	4,751
145 2/8	22 6/8	21 0/8	16 4/8	5	5	Hennepin County	MN	Robert L. Halverson	1985	4,751
145 2/8	23 0/8	23 0/8	15 6/8	5	5	Holt County	NE	Thomas D. Lanz	1986	4,751
145 2/8	22 5/8	22 1/8	17 0/8	5	5	Cloud County	KS	Mark Copple	1986	4,751
145 2/8	24 6/8	23 5/8	18 6/8	4	4	Issaquena County	MS	Charles A. Peeples	1988	4,751
145 2/8	23 2/8	24 0/8	17 2/8	5	5	Peoria County	IL	Lenny Asbell	1988	4,751
145 2/8	25 6/8	25 3/8	19 2/8	5	6	Du Page County	IL	Gregg Weck	1988	4,751
145 2/8	23 1/8	23 6/8	16 3/8	6	4	Lawrence County	IL	Lary Caddell	1988	4,751
145 2/8	25 7/8	25 4/8	21 0/8	4	4	Daviess County	IN	John H. Kenworthy	1989	4,751
145 2/8	23 0/8	22 5/8	16 6/8	6	4	Delaware County	IA	Dean Dempster	1989	4,751
145 2/8	24 5/8	24 0/8	18 4/8	4	6	Clearwater County	ID	Michael L. McCabe	1990	4,751
145 2/8	24 0/8	24 2/8	17 4/8	4	4	Columbia County	PA	Robert Markle	1990	4,751
145 2/8	23 1/8	22 0/8	17 2/8	5	5	Seward County	KS	Lynn Leonard	1990	4,751
145 2/8	24 4/8	24 6/8	18 0/8	4	4	Rock Island County	IL	Tim Pressly	1990	4,751
145 2/8	23 4/8	23 4/8	20 5/8	5	5	Belmont County	OH	Aaron Wiley	1990	4,751
145 2/8	22 2/8	22 0/8	17 4/8	5	5	Davis County	IA	Roy Glosser	1990	4,751
145 2/8	21 1/8	21 7/8	18 0/8	5	5	Chester County	PA	Stephen Daniels Raeburn	1991	4,751
145 2/8	24 0/8	23 5/8	18 0/8	9	6	Wyandotte County	KS	Earl A. Cooksey	1991	4,751
145 2/8	23 0/8	23 4/8	19 0/8	7	6	Webster County	IA	Steven W. Hiveley	1992	4,751
145 2/8	22 7/8	22 3/8	16 2/8	5	5	Pottawattamie County	IA	Jeffery L. Hodges	1992	4,751
145 2/8	22 2/8	22 0/8	16 2/8	5	6	Logan County	WV	Kevin A. Stone	1992	4,751
145 2/8	23 4/8	23 2/8	18 0/8	7	7	Cook County	IL	Daniel H. Albaugh	1993	4,751
145 2/8	22 1/8	23 2/8	19 6/8	5	5	Somerset County	MD	Michael Alan Pilchard	1993	4,751
145 2/8	22 1/8	22 1/8	21 0/8	5	5	Carroll County	IL	Mike Gibson	1993	4,751
145 2/8	20 4/8	21 2/8	14 4/8	5	5	Emmet County	IA	Timothy S. McCarthy	1993	4,751
145 2/8	24 0/8	23 4/8	17 6/8	5	5	Chippewa County	WI	Loren J. Roth	1994	4,751
145 2/8	21 0/8	22 4/8	17 1/8	7	5	Calhoun County	IL	David Triplo	1994	4,751
145 2/8	23 0/8	23 4/8	17 2/8	6	5	Lee County	IL	Gary Miller	1994	4,751
145 2/8	23 6/8	22 7/8	16 2/8	4	4	Brooks County	TX	Craig Weiland	1994	4,751
145 2/8	25 1/8	23 5/8	19 0/8	5	5	Issaquena County	MS	Robert H. Jarvis	1994	4,751
145 2/8	23 4/8	23 6/8	19 2/8	6	6	Dunn County	WI	Dave Lieffort	1994	4,751
145 2/8	23 0/8	22 2/8	15 6/8	6	5	Lancaster County	NE	Jim Ryan	1994	4,751
145 2/8	24 2/8	24 6/8	16 3/8	5	4	Calloway County	KY	Roger Moredock	1995	4,751
145 2/8	24 1/8	22 6/8	17 6/8	5	5	Lawrence County	IN	Kevin Luallen	1996	4,751
145 2/8	23 0/8	22 1/8	15 3/8	6	6	La Salle County	IL	John P. Hartman	1997	4,751
145 2/8	21 2/8	21 1/8	16 0/8	5	5	Marinette County	WI	Brian Wieting	1997	4,751
145 2/8	23 3/8	23 1/8	20 0/8	5	5	Calhoun County	MI	John P. Walters II	1997	4,751
145 2/8	26 1/8	24 2/8	17 4/8	7	5	Pike County	IL	Eddie Claypool	1997	4,751
145 2/8	26 0/8	24 6/8	20 0/8	6	5	Monona County	IA	Kyle Corey	1997	4,751
145 2/8	24 7/8	25 4/8	17 6/8	5	5	Raleigh County	WV	Robert Jarrell	1997	4,751
145 1/8	24 7/8	25 2/8	22 0/8	5	6	Grundy County	IL	Tony Muhich	1975	4,801
145 1/8	23 1/8	22 7/8	17 2/8	7	7	Dearborn County	IN	David Goodwin	1978	4,801
145 1/8	22 3/8	22 5/8	15 5/8	5	5	Kent County	MI	Virgil G. Baker, Jr.	1979	4,801
145 1/8	23 6/8	23 2/8	18 5/8	5	6	Green County	WI	Dan Behring	1979	4,801
145 1/8	24 6/8	24 0/8	18 5/8	6	5	Leavenworth County	KS	Chris Calovich	1982	4,801
145 1/8	23 0/8	23 0/8	17 3/8	5	5	Berkshire County	MA	Richard Scorzafava	1984	4,801
145 1/8	21 7/8	21 6/8	17 1/8	5	5	Calgary	ALB	Dwayne Andrus	1986	4,801
145 1/8	22 6/8	23 0/8	20 5/8	6	6	Floyd County	VA	Jeffery Weddle	1987	4,801
145 1/8	23 6/8	23 6/8	21 1/8	4	4	Montgomery County	OH	Sam Dycus	1987	4,801
145 1/8	23 0/8	22 0/8	16 1/8	4	5	Warren County	OH	Jeffery W. Combs	1987	4,801
145 1/8	23 6/8	23 4/8	18 6/8	5	7	Livingston County	NY	Gary Hartford	1988	4,801
145 1/8	23 2/8	24 3/8	20 3/8	4	5	Stanton County	NE	Gary Frowick	1989	4,801
145 1/8	25 4/8	25 6/8	18 7/8	4	4	Monroe County	IA	Tom Starns	1989	4,801
145 1/8	25 3/8	24 0/8	19 7/8	4	5	Buffalo County	WI	Mark E. Fetting	1990	4,801
145 1/8	22 6/8	22 2/8	18 1/8	5	5	Jones County	IA	Ronald W. Post	1990	4,801
145 1/8	24 2/8	22 7/8	20 1/8	5	5	Carroll County	MD	Bill Roach	1990	4,801
145 1/8	22 3/8	23 3/8	14 3/8	5	5	Cadogan	ALB	Judd Cooney	1991	4,801
145 1/8	23 5/8	23 5/8	20 7/8	4	5	Platte County	MO	Francisco Escobar	1991	4,801
145 1/8	22 2/8	21 7/8	16 5/8	5	5	Crawford County	IL	Charlie Guyer	1991	4,801
145 1/8	22 6/8	22 3/8	19 3/8	5	6	Weslock	ALB	Trevor Edwards	1992	4,801
145 1/8	22 2/8	22 4/8	18 7/8	4	4	Middlesex County	NJ	George A. Costantini	1993	4,801
145 1/8	21 1/8	21 0/8	13 7/8	5	6	Lincoln County	MO	Christopher Scoggins	1993	4,801
145 1/8	23 0/8	23 4/8	18 1/8	5	5	Perry County	IL	Charlie Korte	1993	4,801
145 1/8	24 7/8	23 7/8	18 3/8	5	5	Monroe County	IA	Fred "Bud" Allen	1993	4,801
145 1/8	24 7/8	25 4/8	20 5/8	4	4	Lawrence County	IL	Dan Deisher	1993	4,801
145 1/8	21 4/8	21 4/8	19 7/8	5	5	Valley County	MT	Gene Henck	1993	4,801
145 1/8	23 0/8	21 5/8	16 5/8	5	5	Edgar County	IL	Kenneth Wiehe	1993	4,801
145 1/8	24 0/8	23 4/8	18 7/8	6	5	Pike County	IL	William R. Graham	1993	4,801
145 1/8	25 1/8	24 7/8	17 5/8	5	5	Sullivan County	IN	Mike Crist	1994	4,801
145 1/8	24 0/8	23 2/8	16 1/8	5	6	Licking County	OH	Ron Engstrom	1994	4,801
145 1/8	21 4/8	24 1/8	17 1/8	6	6	Shiawassee County	MI	Chris A. Adolf	1994	4,801
145 1/8	21 6/8	21 7/8	15 5/8	6	6	Parke County	IN	Rick Marshall	1995	4,801
145 1/8	21 1/8	20 6/8	17 1/8	5	5	Edmonton	ALB	Steve MacKenzie	1996	4,801
145 1/8	24 1/8	23 5/8	18 0/8	4	5	Arkansas County	AR	Joe D. Milloway	1996	4,801
145 1/8	24 0/8	24 1/8	16 6/8	8	6	Livingston County	MI	Dave Kasbohm	1996	4,801
145 1/8	25 7/8	24 0/8	18 3/8	4	4	Spencer County	KY	Nathan D. Tucker	1996	4,801

WHITETAIL DEER (TYPICAL ANTLERS)

Minimum Score 125 — Continued

SCORE	LENGTH OF MAIN BEAM R	LENGTH OF MAIN BEAM L	INSIDE SPREAD	NUMBER OF POINTS R	NUMBER OF POINTS L	AREA	STATE/PROVINCE	HUNTER'S NAME	DATE	RANK
145 1/8	24 3/8	23 1/8	19 5/8	5	5	Waukesha County	WI	Kris Droegkamp	1996	4,801
145 1/8	22 5/8	22 7/8	18 3/8	5	5	Delaware County	IA	Kelly Salow	1996	4,801
145 1/8	25 1/8	25 3/8	19 3/8	5	6	Vermilion County	IL	Jack A. Miller	1996	4,801
145 1/8	26 2/8	27 1/8	20 4/8	4	5	Des Moines County	IA	Jeff Wilson	1997	4,801
145 1/8	23 1/8	23 3/8	19 2/8	6	6	Price County	WI	David Pepper	1997	4,801
145 1/8	23 1/8	24 1/8	16 5/8	5	5	Pike County	IL	Gregory S. Guerrieri	1997	4,801
145 1/8	23 5/8	23 4/8	17 7/8	5	5	Clermont County	OH	Mark D. Wolfson	1997	4,801
145 1/8	25 0/8	24 3/8	17 7/8	4	5	Coles County	IL	John H. Hoxmeier	1997	4,801
145 0/8	22 5/8	21 2/8	14 2/8	6	6	Washington County	IA	Doron Whitlock	1966	4,845
145 0/8	24 0/8	24 5/8	20 0/8	4	4	Grant County	SD	Kevin Bronson	1973	4,845
145 0/8	24 0/8	22 2/8	15 2/8	6	6	Trigg County	KY	Donald Powell	1974	4,845
145 0/8	23 1/8	22 6/8	15 2/8	5	5	Mahaska County	IA	Randy Randall	1978	4,845
145 0/8	21 5/8	22 4/8	15 4/8	5	5	Jones County	IA	Jim H. Dougherty	1979	4,845
145 0/8	24 2/8	22 1/8	14 1/8	8	6	Ste. Genevieve County	MO	Dr. Dennis Diaz	1980	4,845
145 0/8	23 6/8	24 2/8	19 6/8	5	5	Huntingdon County	PA	John A. Williams	1983	4,845
145 0/8	20 4/8	21 4/8	16 4/8	5	5	Polk County	MN	Grant Schultz	1984	4,845
145 0/8	23 0/8	23 4/8	19 1/8	9	5	St. Joseph County	IN	Monty Layne	1984	4,845
145 0/8	24 3/8	24 5/8	16 2/8	5	5	Peoria County	IL	Earl Evans	1985	4,845
145 0/8	23 3/8	24 4/8	18 2/8	4	4	Sumter County	AL	Denis Waldrop	1986	4,845
145 0/8	22 0/8	23 4/8	19 4/8	5	5	Champaign County	IL	David Teneyck	1986	4,845
145 0/8	22 4/8	22 3/8	17 6/8	6	6	Craighead County	AR	Rob Veach	1986	4,845
145 0/8	23 7/8	24 4/8	18 0/8	4	4	Bee County	TX	Gary Kraatz	1987	4,845
145 0/8	21 4/8	21 4/8	15 6/8	5	4	Traill County	ND	Chuck E. Spicer	1987	4,845
145 0/8	21 3/8	22 5/8	20 4/8	5	6	Bexar County	TX	Ben Wallace	1990	4,845
145 0/8	26 0/8	26 4/8	18 2/8	4	4	Milwaukee County	WI	Tony Snow	1990	4,845
145 0/8	24 5/8	23 2/8	16 6/8	5	5	Dougherty County	GA	Michael L. Layfield	1990	4,845
145 0/8	24 1/8	23 5/8	19 0/8	5	4	Allamakee County	IA	Timothy E. Lodermeier	1990	4,845
145 0/8	21 6/8	21 6/8	17 0/8	5	5	Sumner County	KS	Greg Hill	1990	4,845
145 0/8	21 6/8	21 4/8	16 2/8	5	5	Washburn County	WI	Leonard L. Schneider	1991	4,845
145 0/8	22 0/8	21 6/8	14 2/8	5	5	Ohio County	IN	Richard English	1991	4,845
145 0/8	22 4/8	23 1/8	18 0/8	5	6	Polk County	WI	Vernon H. Simon	1992	4,845
145 0/8	24 2/8	24 5/8	17 4/8	4	5	Darke County	OH	Bernard Grillot	1992	4,845
145 0/8	21 6/8	23 0/8	16 6/8	5	6	Waushara County	WI	Dean Frater	1992	4,845
145 0/8	22 1/8	21 6/8	19 3/8	6	6	Goodhue County	MN	John "Jack" Cordes	1993	4,845
145 0/8	23 2/8	23 0/8	19 6/8	5	6	Kankakee County	IL	Kirk Redenius	1993	4,845
145 0/8	21 1/8	22 4/8	17 7/8	6	6	Talbot County	MD	Jack Dell	1993	4,845
145 0/8	22 3/8	22 2/8	19 0/8	5	5	Williamson County	IL	Mark Frey	1994	4,845
145 0/8	23 2/8	24 4/8	19 0/8	5	5	Whiteside County	IL	William S. Milby	1994	4,845
145 0/8	21 4/8	16 3/8	17 7/8	6	5	Coles County	IL	Mike Cline	1994	4,845
145 0/8	25 2/8	24 6/8	17 0/8	5	5	Appanoose County	IA	Dennis Palmer	1994	4,845
145 0/8	23 2/8	24 0/8	20 3/8	5	5	Hardin County	KY	Lewis Graham	1994	4,845
145 0/8	23 7/8	23 7/8	16 0/8	5	5	Marathon County	WI	Scott Czerwonka	1995	4,845
145 0/8	25 3/8	25 7/8	19 4/8	4	5	Union County	IN	Mike McCabe	1995	4,845
145 0/8	24 1/8	25 2/8	19 6/8	5	4	Linn County	IA	Steven S. Millius	1995	4,845
145 0/8	24 2/8	24 0/8	15 4/8	5	6	Scott County	IL	Gene Meier	1995	4,845
145 0/8	22 4/8	22 6/8	16 4/8	4	4	Jackson County	WV	Robert Buckalew II	1995	4,845
145 0/8	25 7/8	26 4/8	21 4/8	6	5	Garden County	NE	Dan Schmid	1995	4,845
145 0/8	23 5/8	22 6/8	16 5/8	7	5	Grant County	WI	Josh Kreul	1996	4,845
145 0/8	24 0/8	23 2/8	16 2/8	5	5	Hart County	KY	Albert Grimes	1996	4,845
145 0/8	21 5/8	21 4/8	17 1/8	6	5	Olmsted County	MN	Bruce R. Long	1996	4,845
145 0/8	26 7/8	26 4/8	17 5/8	5	6	Phelps County	MO	Dwayne La Barge	1996	4,845
145 0/8	22 1/8	22 3/8	17 4/8	5	5	La Porte County	IN	Christopher M. Beck	1996	4,845
145 0/8	23 5/8	23 7/8	18 4/8	5	5	Cook County	IL	Dan Boss	1996	4,845
145 0/8	21 7/8	22 0/8	14 4/8	5	6	Wayne County	WV	Emery Dotson	1997	4,845
145 0/8	24 5/8	23 6/8	17 0/8	4	4	Union County	SD	Bradley R. Bertrand	1997	4,845
145 0/8	23 4/8	23 4/8	17 5/8	5	5	Clarke County	IA	Jeff Jorgensen	1997	4,845
145 0/8	24 2/8	25 0/8	18 6/8	5	4	Scott County	IA	Jeffrey R. Coonts	1997	4,845
145 0/8	22 4/8	22 0/8	17 6/8	5	5	Pike County	IL	Arnie Boccafogli	1997	4,845
145 0/8	22 4/8	24 6/8	16 6/8	5	5	Macoupin County	IL	Brad Bellm	1998	4,845
145 0/8	23 7/8	23 5/8	14 6/8	5	4	Richland County	MT	Kurt Bensinger	1998	4,845
144 7/8	23 0/8	23 4/8	19 7/8	6	6	Wyandotte County	KS	George F. Bigelow	1966	4,897
144 7/8	21 7/8	22 3/8	17 1/8	5	6	Sussex County	VA	Alvin D. Skinner	1972	4,897
144 7/8	25 1/8	25 0/8	18 3/8	5	6	Louisa County	IA	Harold E. Boysen	1978	4,897
144 7/8	25 7/8	25 4/8	21 7/8	4	5	Dallas County	IA	John M. Bascom	1979	4,897
144 7/8	20 2/8	20 1/8	15 2/8	6	5	Richland County	MT	Garth N. Kallevig	1980	4,897
144 7/8	25 7/8	25 4/8	19 3/8	4	4	Sumner County	KS	Dave Baldwin	1982	4,897
144 7/8	23 7/8	22 0/8	18 3/8	4	4	Cerro Gordo County	IA	Earl L. Goodman	1983	4,897
144 7/8	22 4/8	22 2/8	20 7/8	4	5	Perry County	IL	Greg Thompson	1985	4,897
144 7/8	22 3/8	22 1/8	17 5/8	5	5	Onondaga County	NY	Kim A. Schneider	1985	4,897
144 7/8	25 4/8	25 2/8	16 3/8	5	6	Mayes County	OK	John W. Madlock	1985	4,897
144 7/8	21 7/8	21 2/8	18 7/8	6	5	Texas County	OK	Max Crocker	1985	4,897
144 7/8	21 2/8	21 1/8	18 7/8	5	5	Osborne County	KS	Gary L. Ozias	1985	4,897
144 7/8	25 7/8	25 6/8	18 7/8	7	7	Washburn County	WI	William "Mike" Johnson	1987	4,897
144 7/8	22 4/8	21 4/8	16 6/8	6	5	Lake County	IL	Carl H. Spaeth	1987	4,897
144 7/8	24 6/8	24 4/8	16 2/8	5	6	Dearborn County	IN	Jerry O. Kent	1988	4,897
144 7/8	22 4/8	23 4/8	19 5/8	5	4	Buffalo County	WI	Gary Dorn	1988	4,897
144 7/8	26 4/8	26 0/8	15 7/8	6	5	Chambers County	AL	Craig Reynolds	1988	4,897
144 7/8	22 6/8	22 7/8	17 5/8	5	5	Kossuth County	IA	Robert Barslou	1989	4,897

WHITETAIL DEER (TYPICAL ANTLERS)

Minimum Score 125 — Continued

SCORE	LENGTH OF MAIN BEAM R	LENGTH OF MAIN BEAM L	INSIDE SPREAD	NUMBER OF POINTS R	NUMBER OF POINTS L	AREA	STATE/PROVINCE	HUNTER'S NAME	DATE	RANK
144 7/8	23 3/8	24 1/8	16 5/8	4	5	Mower County	MN	Robert Frost	1989	4,897
144 7/8	21 5/8	21 0/8	15 7/8	5	6	Kleberg County	TX	Wayne Peeples	1990	4,897
144 7/8	26 4/8	25 1/8	20 7/8	5	5	Berrien County	MI	Larry McLaughlin	1990	4,897
144 7/8	23 4/8	23 6/8	18 1/8	4	5	Worcester County	MD	David Johnson	1990	4,897
144 7/8	22 7/8	22 5/8	16 6/8	5	6	Pike County	IL	James Kerr	1990	4,897
144 7/8	22 7/8	23 7/8	16 1/8	4	4	Union County	IL	Doug Edwards	1990	4,897
144 7/8	24 4/8	23 0/8	21 1/8	4	5	Mills County	IA	John Bantz	1990	4,897
144 7/8	19 3/8	20 1/8	17 7/8	6	6	Anson County	NC	Tommy Michael Gilmore	1991	4,897
144 7/8	23 6/8	25 2/8	17 3/8	4	5	Allamakee County	IA	Bill Saddler	1991	4,897
144 7/8	25 3/8	25 6/8	18 1/8	5	4	Ardrossan	ALB	Terry Alan Myroniuk	1991	4,897
144 7/8	23 2/8	23 6/8	19 1/8	5	5	Berks County	PA	Frank P. Dattala	1992	4,897
144 7/8	24 4/8	23 3/8	17 2/8	5	6	Iroquois County	IL	Dennis Clark	1992	4,897
144 7/8	23 4/8	23 5/8	17 6/8	6	5	Jefferson County	WI	Ernie Turpin	1993	4,897
144 7/8	22 2/8	24 0/8	15 3/8	6	7	Lake County	IL	Alvin Roberts	1993	4,897
144 7/8	22 6/8	22 4/8	14 7/8	5	5	Waupaca County	WI	Scott Wolfe	1994	4,897
144 7/8	23 4/8	25 3/8	20 5/8	5	6	Douglas County	WI	Steven J. Cadotte	1995	4,897
144 7/8	23 0/8	20 5/8	17 6/8	7	8	Marion County	IL	Shawn Lowery	1995	4,897
144 7/8	24 2/8	24 2/8	19 7/8	5	4	Lac St. Anne	ALB	Dwayne Miller	1996	4,897
144 7/8	24 2/8	24 3/8	15 7/8	6	5	Jackson County	MO	Jim Moss	1996	4,897
144 7/8	23 7/8	24 7/8	16 7/8	5	5	Trempealeau County	WI	Dan Smith	1996	4,897
144 7/8	23 1/8	22 6/8	16 3/8	5	5	Kanawha County	WV	Gregory S. King	1996	4,897
144 7/8	21 6/8	21 3/8	19 3/8	7	6	Cook County	IL	Len Kamp	1996	4,897
144 7/8	24 3/8	24 3/8	18 7/8	4	4	Pepin County	WI	Larry Gruber	1997	4,897
144 7/8	23 5/8	24 4/8	20 6/8	5	6	Christian County	IL	Dwight Rorie	1997	4,897
144 7/8	21 3/8	21 6/8	18 3/8	5	5	Kenosha County	WI	Craig Bobula	1997	4,897
144 7/8	23 0/8	23 6/8	17 5/8	4	4	Boone County	IA	Gary Steel	1997	4,897
144 7/8	25 3/8	26 1/8	17 3/8	6	5	Washington County	OH	Eric Scott Estes	1997	4,897
144 7/8	24 7/8	25 4/8	16 6/8	5	4	Montgomery County	IA	Dick Paul	1997	4,897
144 7/8	21 5/8	20 6/8	18 3/8	5	5	Rusk County	WI	George Olivo	1997	4,897
144 6/8	19 6/8	20 0/8	15 2/8	6	7	Powell County	MT	Danny Moore	1974	4,944
144 6/8	21 7/8	22 1/8	17 4/8	6	7	Christian County	IL	Scott M. Cassidy	1983	4,944
144 6/8	25 2/8	24 6/8	19 2/8	4	5	Delaware County	PA	James Taylor	1984	4,944
144 6/8	21 0/8	21 4/8	17 0/8	5	5	Sumner County	KS	Jeffrey L. Nash	1984	4,944
144 6/8	23 4/8	23 0/8	16 2/8	5	4	Powell County	MT	Sonny Templeton	1986	4,944
144 6/8	25 7/8	25 4/8	19 0/8	4	4	Lake County	IL	Carl H. Spaeth	1986	4,944
144 6/8	24 1/8	25 4/8	18 0/8	4	5	Hancock County	MS	Alan J. Guess	1987	4,944
144 6/8	26 4/8	25 2/8	21 4/8	5	4	Lincoln County	ME	Darryl Flagg	1988	4,944
144 6/8	24 5/8	23 3/8	18 0/8	5	5	Bent County	CO	Kurt W. Keskimaki	1988	4,944
144 6/8	24 7/8	24 6/8	20 4/8	6	4	Clayton County	IA	Jim Kerns	1989	4,944
144 6/8	23 0/8	22 2/8	18 6/8	5	5	Fairfield County	OH	John W. Todhunter, Jr.	1989	4,944
144 6/8	26 0/8	25 7/8	14 3/8	6	5	Tazewell County	IL	Kevin Eggen	1989	4,944
144 6/8	23 7/8	23 7/8	15 6/8	4	5	Lee County	IA	Mark Webb	1989	4,944
144 6/8	22 3/8	21 0/8	16 4/8	5	5	Irion County	TX	William Jay Wilson	1989	4,944
144 6/8	24 3/8	23 6/8	16 6/8	6	5	Portage County	WI	Mike Kurzinski	1990	4,944
144 6/8	21 0/8	21 4/8	17 4/8	5	5	Middlesex	ONT	Kim Slobojin	1990	4,944
144 6/8	24 6/8	24 3/8	20 6/8	4	4	La Salle County	IL	Bart Pals	1991	4,944
144 6/8	25 7/8	26 2/8	18 2/8	5	5	Door County	WI	Larry Page	1991	4,944
144 6/8	22 3/8	22 1/8	18 6/8	5	4	County of St. Hyacinthe	QUE	Guy Turcotte	1991	4,944
144 6/8	24 1/8	23 5/8	19 2/8	5	5	Livingston County	IL	Tom Roe	1991	4,944
144 6/8	25 0/8	24 1/8	18 2/8	6	5	Waukesha County	WI	Ed Rahberger, Jr.	1992	4,944
144 6/8	23 4/8	23 1/8	16 6/8	5	5	Parke County	IN	Kyle Laney	1992	4,944
144 6/8	22 6/8	23 2/8	17 0/8	6	6	Eau Claire County	WI	Bob J. Grunewald	1993	4,944
144 6/8	23 3/8	23 4/8	16 2/8	5	5	Tompkins County	NY	Allen E. Cobane	1993	4,944
144 6/8	21 3/8	22 2/8	18 4/8	6	5	Logan County	KY	Timmy Shackelford	1993	4,944
144 6/8	25 3/8	25 3/8	19 4/8	6	5	Henry County	IA	Ben Moore	1993	4,944
144 6/8	23 7/8	24 3/8	17 3/8	6	6	Tillman County	OK	Edward Wayne Roach	1993	4,944
144 6/8	21 5/8	20 7/8	16 4/8	5	5	Flathead County	MT	Dennis Brieske	1994	4,944
144 6/8	24 0/8	24 3/8	18 4/8	7	5	Rock County	WI	Keith Hackett II	1994	4,944
144 6/8	24 6/8	23 5/8	18 0/8	4	7	Dubuque County	IA	Daniel C. Mehrl	1994	4,944
144 6/8	25 5/8	26 0/8	16 2/8	5	5	Limestone County	AL	Neal Baker	1994	4,944
144 6/8	24 0/8	24 3/8	17 3/8	6	6	Sawyer County	WI	Bernard Gavre	1994	4,944
144 6/8	24 1/8	22 5/8	19 6/8	6	6	Macon County	IL	Norman L. Mathias	1994	4,944
144 6/8	23 2/8	22 1/8	19 4/8	5	5	Webb County	TX	Matthew W. Howard	1995	4,944
144 6/8	26 1/8	25 5/8	16 5/8	5	6	Marathon County	WI	Dean Hanke	1995	4,944
144 6/8	22 7/8	22 4/8	18 4/8	5	5	Mecosta County	MI	Jake Neal	1995	4,944
144 6/8	23 5/8	24 4/8	18 4/8	4	4	Washtenaw County	MI	Phil Maly	1995	4,944
144 6/8	25 4/8	25 2/8	18 0/8	4	6	Allen County	OH	Mark Spallinger	1995	4,944
144 6/8	26 1/8	25 4/8	19 0/8	4	4	Cass County	NE	Roger Maxon	1995	4,944
144 6/8	23 3/8	23 7/8	18 0/8	6	5	Carroll County	MS	Tucker Miller III	1995	4,944
144 6/8	24 0/8	24 2/8	17 6/8	4	4	Dunn County	WI	Mike Lenz	1996	4,944
144 6/8	23 1/8	23 5/8	18 0/8	6	6	Allamakee County	IA	Robert Thornley	1997	4,944
144 5/8	24 0/8	24 4/8	21 3/8	4	4	Spink County	SD	Jerald Shantz	1959	4,986
144 5/8	22 1/8	22 1/8	15 7/8	5	5	Rock County	WI	T. Lawrence Hesgard	1966	4,986
144 5/8	23 6/8	23 6/8	19 7/8	4	4	Geauga County	OH	Rudy Grecar	1970	4,986
144 5/8	24 7/8	26 3/8	21 7/8	5	6	Valley County	MT	Leith Wimmer	1971	4,986
144 5/8	22 2/8	22 7/8	17 7/8	5	6	Vermillion County	IN	Robert McClara	1972	4,986
144 5/8	23 6/8	24 2/8	16 5/8	5	5	Will County	IL	Joseph Wyer	1978	4,986
144 5/8	23 2/8	23 6/8	18 3/8	5	5	Huntingdon County	PA	John A. Williams	1980	4,986

WHITETAIL DEER (TYPICAL ANTLERS)

Minimum Score 125

SCORE	LENGTH OF MAIN BEAM R	LENGTH OF MAIN BEAM L	INSIDE SPREAD	NUMBER OF POINTS R	NUMBER OF POINTS L	AREA	STATE/ PROVINCE	HUNTER'S NAME	DATE	RANK
144 5/8	24 4/8	22 7/8	16 3/8	5	5	Douglas County	WI	Oren Hanson	1982	4,986
144 5/8	22 2/8	21 2/8	18 1/8	4	5	Oconto County	WI	David Nelsen	1982	4,986
144 5/8	24 2/8	23 4/8	15 1/8	5	6	Traill County	ND	Arlin Ingebretson	1983	4,986
144 5/8	23 0/8	22 1/8	14 5/8	5	5	Price County	WI	Peter Koenig	1983	4,986
144 5/8	22 5/8	21 5/8	16 3/8	6	6	Stanley County	SD	Randy Kleinschmidt	1985	4,986
144 5/8	24 5/8	25 0/8	19 3/8	4	4	Calvert County	MD	Tom Hosselrode	1986	4,986
144 5/8	24 2/8	25 1/8	16 5/8	4	4	Washburn County	WI	Tom Elliot	1987	4,986
144 5/8	28 1/8	25 6/8	20 1/8	5	5	Howard County	MD	David Wilson	1988	4,986
144 5/8	22 2/8	22 3/8	15 1/8	6	6	Cherokee County	KS	David B. Price	1988	4,986
144 5/8	22 7/8	22 4/8	15 5/8	6	5	Pike County	IL	Jim Murphy	1988	4,986
144 5/8	23 0/8	23 6/8	17 5/8	5	5	Ramsey County	MN	Rick Westberg	1989	4,986
144 5/8	25 3/8	24 0/8	20 7/8	6	5	Lenawee County	MI	Melvin D. Hoffman	1989	4,986
144 5/8	22 7/8	23 1/8	19 3/8	6	7	Hopkins County	KY	Tracy Daves	1989	4,986
144 5/8	24 6/8	23 5/8	16 7/8	5	5	Prowers County	CO	Daniel Kavalunas	1989	4,986
144 5/8	22 7/8	25 0/8	20 5/8	5	6	Jasper County	IA	Brian Vander Velden	1989	4,986
144 5/8	25 3/8	26 0/8	22 1/8	5	5	Jo Daviess County	IL	Scott R. Jackson	1989	4,986
144 5/8	25 7/8	24 5/8	21 5/8	4	5	Chase County	KS	Rod Koehn	1989	4,986
144 5/8	26 0/8	26 3/8	20 1/8	4	4	Fayette County	IL	Dean Harrison	1990	4,986
144 5/8	25 3/8	25 3/8	21 6/8	5	6	Montgomery County	MD	Bret Giuliani	1991	4,986
144 5/8	23 0/8	23 3/8	20 5/8	4	4	Kankakee County	IL	Jim Wetmore	1991	4,986
144 5/8	27 6/8	27 1/8	22 3/8	5	4	Sauk County	WI	Mark A. Parrott	1991	4,986
144 5/8	22 0/8	22 2/8	15 1/8	5	5	Carroll County	MS	Jim L. McCrory	1991	4,986
144 5/8	22 1/8	21 7/8	19 1/8	4	5	Polk County	WI	Jerry Larsen	1992	4,986
144 5/8	24 0/8	24 2/8	16 5/8	6	5	Jay County	IN	Chuck Caster	1993	4,986
144 5/8	23 2/8	22 7/8	15 5/8	5	5	Prince William County	VA	Ted Falce	1993	4,986
144 5/8	22 5/8	23 5/8	17 1/8	5	4	Lake County	OH	David N. Russell, Jr.	1993	4,986
144 5/8	23 0/8	22 3/8	18 1/8	5	5	Chippewa County	WI	Casey Copas	1993	4,986
144 5/8	25 0/8	24 6/8	19 1/8	5	6	Buffalo County	WI	John J. Mack	1993	4,986
144 5/8	19 6/8	19 6/8	15 3/8	5	5	Livingston County	MI	Richard Powell	1993	4,986
144 5/8	20 6/8	23 2/8	16 6/8	6	5	Adair County	MO	Eddie Schmitz	1994	4,986
144 5/8	24 7/8	24 7/8	18 4/8	6	5	Chase County	KS	Clayton Shively	1994	4,986
144 5/8	26 2/8	25 1/8	16 7/8	4	5	Williamson County	IL	Gerald K. Brueggemann	1995	4,986
144 5/8	25 1/8	26 2/8	19 2/8	4	7	Delaware County	OH	Mitch Cole	1995	4,986
144 5/8	24 5/8	25 0/8	20 1/8	5	5	De Kalb County	GA	Craig Sears	1996	4,986
144 5/8	21 2/8	21 3/8	16 3/8	5	4	Lee County	IL	Mark G. Kaleel	1996	4,986
144 5/8	27 5/8	27 0/8	19 7/8	5	5	Grant County	WI	Wayne A. Willkomm	1996	4,986
144 5/8	22 3/8	24 5/8	15 6/8	5	6	Portage County	WI	Bob F. Jastromski	1996	4,986
144 5/8	24 0/8	26 1/8	18 2/8	5	7	Portage County	WI	Ralph L. Gagas	1997	4,986
144 5/8	21 6/8	22 0/8	18 7/8	5	6	Iowa County	WI	Ken Yerges	1997	4,986
144 5/8	22 3/8	22 2/8	14 5/8	7	5	Hardin County	KY	Roland C. Menton	1997	4,986
144 5/8	19 6/8	20 6/8	18 6/8	5	6	Namao	ALB	Randy Tellier	1997	4,986
144 5/8	23 2/8	23 2/8	19 3/8	6	5	Calhoun County	IL	Paul Holland	1997	4,986
144 5/8	25 5/8	25 1/8	20 5/8	4	4	Westchester County	NY	Robert Evans	1997	4,986
144 5/8	24 1/8	24 6/8	16 5/8	5	5	Douglas County	NE	Scott K. Reed	1997	4,986
144 4/8	22 6/8	22 6/8	16 3/8	5	7	Hall County	NE	Verne Skow	1958	5,037
144 4/8	23 2/8	23 6/8	16 3/8	5	6	Day County	SD	John E. Sigdestad	1963	5,037
144 4/8	25 3/8	26 1/8	16 4/8	5	4	Montgomery County	MD	Victor Ezerski	1975	5,037
144 4/8	23 0/8	24 5/8	14 5/8	6	8	Scott County	MN	Charlie Abeln	1977	5,037
144 4/8	23 1/8	22 2/8	17 2/8	5	5	Winnebago County	IA	Ronald Gorden	1977	5,037
144 4/8	23 2/8	22 5/8	18 4/8	5	6	Greene County	OH	Don F. Necina	1981	5,037
144 4/8	26 2/8	26 1/8	18 3/8	5	6	Jo Daviess County	IL	Kenneth Pluym	1985	5,037
144 4/8	25 6/8	26 4/8	19 7/8	7	7	Madison County	NY	John Loveday	1985	5,037
144 4/8	21 7/8	22 0/8	17 0/8	5	5	Morrison County	MN	Will Carlson	1986	5,037
144 4/8	25 1/8	24 5/8	19 2/8	4	4	Montgomery County	OH	Anthony W. Miller	1986	5,037
144 4/8	21 6/8	22 2/8	15 5/8	7	7	Peoria County	IL	Kevin Walsh	1986	5,037
144 4/8	22 3/8	23 3/8	16 4/8	5	5	Lincoln County	MO	Denton C. Raymond	1988	5,037
144 4/8	22 4/8	22 2/8	15 1/8	6	5	Howard County	IA	John R. Koschmeder	1988	5,037
144 4/8	24 7/8	24 5/8	22 6/8	5	4	Ravalli County	MT	Tom Storm	1988	5,037
144 4/8	25 1/8	24 0/8	21 0/8	5	6	Westchester County	NY	Frank Reindl	1988	5,037
144 4/8	22 2/8	23 0/8	18 6/8	5	5	Allegheny County	PA	John H. Matthews	1989	5,037
144 4/8	24 3/8	23 2/8	21 3/8	5	7	Jefferson County	WI	Mark A. Meyer	1989	5,037
144 4/8	23 7/8	24 3/8	21 2/8	6	6	Vermilion County	IL	Robert G. Downing	1989	5,037
144 4/8	24 2/8	25 0/8	17 0/8	5	5	Geauga County	OH	Joe Galfidi, Jr.	1990	5,037
144 4/8	24 4/8	24 5/8	22 6/8	4	4	Appanoose County	IA	Frank Delouis	1990	5,037
144 4/8	23 0/8	23 1/8	18 6/8	4	4	Lewis & Clark County	MT	Sonny Templeton	1990	5,037
144 4/8	25 4/8	25 1/8	20 1/8	6	6	Clark County	OH	Randy McConnaughey	1990	5,037
144 4/8	26 4/8	26 2/8	20 2/8	5	4	Colchester Township	ONT	Leo Potvin	1990	5,037
144 4/8	25 2/8	25 0/8	19 4/8	7	5	Pottawattamie County	IA	Mark E. Raney	1991	5,037
144 4/8	24 3/8	23 5/8	19 6/8	5	5	Iowa County	WI	Troy K. Koelzer	1991	5,037
144 4/8	22 6/8	23 0/8	18 7/8	5	4	Edgar County	IL	Jerry Lee Watters	1992	5,037
144 4/8	22 6/8	23 4/8	15 6/8	5	5	Juneau County	WI	Mark Marcinkowski	1993	5,037
144 4/8	25 7/8	24 3/8	20 5/8	5	5	Winneshiek County	IA	Wayne Lamoreux	1993	5,037
144 4/8	24 2/8	24 0/8	18 6/8	4	4	Cass County	NE	Bill Cox	1993	5,037
144 4/8	24 6/8	23 5/8	14 0/8	6	5	Wilkinson County	MS	Ronnie G. Richardson	1994	5,037
144 4/8	23 6/8	23 5/8	20 1/8	6	5	Kankakee County	IL	Rick Renzi	1994	5,037
144 4/8	23 6/8	24 1/8	17 0/8	5	5	Jay County	IN	Steve Hammond	1995	5,037
144 4/8	23 4/8	24 3/8	16 5/8	6	7	Lawrence County	OH	Richard P. Lynch	1995	5,037
144 4/8	24 4/8	23 6/8	17 4/8	5	5	Olmsted County	MN	Charlie L. Flicek	1995	5,037

WHITETAIL DEER (TYPICAL ANTLERS)

Minimum Score 125 — Continued

SCORE	LENGTH OF R MAIN BEAM L		INSIDE SPREAD	NUMBER OF R POINTS L		AREA	STATE/ PROVINCE	HUNTER'S NAME	DATE	RANK
144 4/8	22 6/8	22 5/8	14 6/8	5	5	Bright Sand Lake	SAS	Darren Feist	1996	5,037
144 4/8	22 7/8	22 6/8	16 6/8	6	5	Anoka County	MN	Tom Brunner	1996	5,037
144 4/8	24 1/8	24 0/8	21 6/8	4	4	Dane County	WI	Dan DiMaggio	1996	5,037
144 4/8	24 4/8	23 4/8	18 6/8	6	6	Morgan County	CO	Tony Burmester	1996	5,037
144 4/8	23 6/8	22 1/8	20 4/8	5	4	E. Carroll Parish	LA	John Poindexter	1997	5,037
144 4/8	25 0/8	24 5/8	14 6/8	4	7	Knox County	OH	Robert Fowler	1997	5,037
144 4/8	24 2/8	24 6/8	17 4/8	6	6	Clay County	IA	Jim R. Montgomery	1997	5,037
144 4/8	25 6/8	25 2/8	18 2/8	5	4	Lee County	IL	Gordon C. Gabelmann	1997	5,037
144 4/8	25 4/8	22 6/8	17 0/8	6	7	Lake County	IL	Richard W. Good, Jr.	1997	5,037
144 4/8	24 4/8	26 2/8	16 0/8	5	5	Chester County	PA	Steve Schmeusser	1998	5,037
144 3/8	23 7/8	23 5/8	17 2/8	6	7	Rock County	NE	Dick Mauch	1963	5,081
144 3/8	23 7/8	24 5/8	19 5/8	6	4	Delaware County	OH	Jack R. Hecker	1975	5,081
144 3/8	23 6/8	23 6/8	16 4/8	4	5	Columbia County	WI	Ronald Bordson	1976	5,081
144 3/8	22 5/8	23 7/8	16 5/8	5	6	Sawyer County	WI	Dave Phillips	1981	5,081
144 3/8	22 4/8	23 5/8	16 6/8	6	5	Murray County	MN	John Laundre	1981	5,081
144 3/8	23 1/8	22 7/8	17 7/8	6	6	Kingman County	KS	Scott Helmke	1982	5,081
144 3/8	23 0/8	23 6/8	19 7/8	5	5	Clayton County	IA	Kenneth Clayton	1982	5,081
144 3/8	22 6/8	22 4/8	18 7/8	6	5	Columbia County	WI	Jerry Ulrich	1984	5,081
144 3/8	24 1/8	24 4/8	19 5/8	5	6	Morrison County	MN	Rick Hayner	1984	5,081
144 3/8	21 6/8	22 1/8	18 3/8	5	5	Ripley County	IN	Dick Gambrel	1984	5,081
144 3/8	23 7/8	24 1/8	17 1/8	4	5	Anderson County	TN	Johnny Wayne Jobe	1985	5,081
144 3/8	21 1/8	21 5/8	19 7/8	6	5	Sussex County	NJ	Frank Tropona	1987	5,081
144 3/8	26 4/8	25 6/8	19 4/8	6	6	Decatur County	IA	Julian Toney	1987	5,081
144 3/8	23 5/8	23 1/8	15 3/8	5	6	Blue Earth County	MN	John Chatleain	1987	5,081
144 3/8	25 7/8	24 6/8	17 7/8	4	4	Lambton County	ONT	Robert B. Kennedy	1988	5,081
144 3/8	24 7/8	25 5/8	19 1/8	4	4	Polk County	IA	Todd Collins	1988	5,081
144 3/8	22 3/8	22 0/8	20 7/8	6	5	Anoka County	MN	Greg Seymour	1990	5,081
144 3/8	23 1/8	22 2/8	15 6/8	7	6	Beausejour	MAN	Dave DeLeeuw	1991	5,081
144 3/8	22 5/8	22 2/8	16 2/8	5	8	Norman County	MN	Joel Gwin	1991	5,081
144 3/8	23 1/8	24 0/8	19 1/8	5	6	Goodhue County	MN	John "Jack" Cordes	1991	5,081
144 3/8	22 2/8	22 7/8	15 7/8	5	6	Rockdale County	GA	Jim Conway	1991	5,081
144 3/8	25 4/8	25 0/8	19 5/8	5	6	Madison County	AR	Gary R. Catron	1991	5,081
144 3/8	21 5/8	21 6/8	16 7/8	5	6	Sauk County	WI	Timothy J. Terbilcox	1992	5,081
144 3/8	26 1/8	25 3/8	19 3/8	4	4	Lawrence County	IN	William Deaton	1992	5,081
144 3/8	22 4/8	23 2/8	17 2/8	7	6	Dane County	WI	Mark Orvick	1992	5,081
144 3/8	23 7/8	24 0/8	19 2/8	8	8	Logan County	KY	Marty Wilkins	1992	5,081
144 3/8	21 6/8	22 2/8	16 3/8	5	6	Waushara County	WI	Duane Apps	1992	5,081
144 3/8	22 4/8	21 4/8	18 5/8	5	5	Crawford County	IL	Kyle Mann	1992	5,081
144 3/8	22 3/8	22 6/8	18 5/8	5	5	Sauk County	WI	Rollin W. Sorge	1992	5,081
144 3/8	20 5/8	21 7/8	17 7/8	5	5	Leduc	ALB	Gerald P. Wrubleski	1993	5,081
144 3/8	24 2/8	24 4/8	18 5/8	4	4	Dakota County	MN	Tim Gaughan	1993	5,081
144 3/8	20 7/8	25 1/8	18 4/8	5	5	Harvey County	KS	Ron Hershberger	1993	5,081
144 3/8	21 5/8	21 7/8	15 7/8	5	5	Ashland County	WI	Augie Boehm	1993	5,081
144 3/8	25 3/8	23 6/8	15 5/8	5	6	Harrison County	MO	Sam Blackburn	1994	5,081
144 3/8	24 6/8	24 4/8	20 1/8	4	4	Lake County	IL	John F. Isaacson	1994	5,081
144 3/8	22 5/8	23 1/8	18 5/8	4	5	Darke County	OH	Ron Fansler	1994	5,081
144 3/8	22 2/8	23 4/8	20 1/8	5	5	Muskingum County	OH	Greg Morehead	1994	5,081
144 3/8	20 4/8	21 3/8	17 3/8	6	5	Oconto County	WI	Jeff Nowak	1994	5,081
144 3/8	24 4/8	23 3/8	19 7/8	5	5	Logan County	KY	David L. Yoder	1995	5,081
144 3/8	24 4/8	24 5/8	18 3/8	5	5	Caldwell County	MO	Jason Jedlicka	1995	5,081
144 3/8	22 2/8	25 0/8	17 1/8	4	6	Ross County	OH	Keith Orr	1995	5,081
144 3/8	22 7/8	22 5/8	17 1/8	6	5	Harrison County	OH	Walter Luikart	1995	5,081
144 3/8	21 5/8	21 1/8	20 1/8	5	5	Nemaha County	KS	Darryl Becker	1996	5,081
144 3/8	24 2/8	25 3/8	16 6/8	5	4	Hale County	AL	Patrick Suchey	1996	5,081
144 3/8	24 5/8	24 0/8	20 0/8	6	5	La Salle County	IL	Albert W. Marshall	1996	5,081
144 3/8	25 5/8	25 4/8	20 3/8	5	5	Sauk County	WI	Adam Lawinger	1996	5,081
144 3/8	22 5/8	22 3/8	16 5/8	5	5	Meigs County	OH	William T. Peneston	1996	5,081
144 3/8	20 1/8	20 5/8	16 3/8	5	5	Ferry County	WA	Jerry Solie	1996	5,081
144 3/8	22 5/8	23 1/8	20 7/8	5	4	Missoula County	MT	Rory J. Zarling	1996	5,081
144 3/8	22 3/8	22 5/8	18 6/8	7	6	Pulaski County	KY	Wayne Padgett	1997	5,081
144 3/8	25 2/8	25 4/8	17 5/8	4	5	Clark County	IL	Kevin Boyer	1997	5,081
144 3/8	24 0/8	23 6/8	19 5/8	5	4	Hocking County	OH	Harold L. Briedenbaugh	1997	5,081
144 3/8	24 2/8	23 0/8	17 5/8	5	5	Washington County	WI	Robert Naylor	1997	5,081
144 3/8	25 0/8	25 1/8	18 7/8	4	4	Knox County	IL	David EmKen	1997	5,081
144 3/8	24 5/8	25 1/8	20 5/8	4	5	Logan County	IL	Danny P. Boward	1997	5,081
144 3/8	23 4/8	24 0/8	19 1/8	5	5	Lake County	IL	Myron Hayes	1997	5,081
144 2/8	25 7/8	26 2/8	23 0/8	4	4	Bucks County	PA	Robert Weaver	1923	5,137
144 2/8	21 5/8	21 4/8	17 2/8	5	5	Miner County	SD	William Hueners	1965	5,137
144 2/8	21 7/8	21 7/8	14 2/8	5	5	Brown County	SD	Harold Larson	1966	5,137
144 2/8	20 6/8	20 7/8	15 4/8	5	5	Juneau County	WI	Gordon Stittleburg	1966	5,137
144 2/8	22 4/8	23 4/8	17 6/8	5	5	Steele County	MN	Maynard Bauer	1977	5,137
144 2/8	24 2/8	22 6/8	19 6/8	5	5	Miami County	OH	Dale Stull	1980	5,137
144 2/8	22 7/8	23 2/8	17 0/8	5	5	Coffey County	KS	Marc Chester	1983	5,137
144 2/8	20 3/8	20 1/8	15 4/8	5	5	Brown County	KS	Ken Spencer	1983	5,137
144 2/8	25 1/8	24 2/8	20 6/8	5	4	Hamilton County	IL	Paul Sebby	1984	5,137
144 2/8	24 0/8	24 3/8	19 3/8	7	6	Fairfield County	OH	Merle D. Strope	1986	5,137
144 2/8	21 5/8	20 6/8	20 4/8	5	6	Lake County	IL	Mike Mitten	1986	5,137
144 2/8	24 5/8	23 6/8	16 5/8	5	6	Clay County	IL	William Brummer	1988	5,137

WHITETAIL DEER (TYPICAL ANTLERS)

Minimum Score 125 — Continued

SCORE	LENGTH OF MAIN BEAM R / L		INSIDE SPREAD	NUMBER OF POINTS R / L		AREA	STATE/PROVINCE	HUNTER'S NAME	DATE	RANK
144 2/8	23 6/8	23 0/8	16 4/8	6	6	Christian County	IL	David Loyd	1988	5,137
144 2/8	29 0/8	28 2/8	19 1/8	5	5	Charles County	MD	Mel Wolfe	1989	5,137
144 2/8	22 4/8	22 6/8	14 0/8	5	5	Kenosha County	WI	John R. Griffin	1991	5,137
144 2/8	24 6/8	24 7/8	21 4/8	6	5	Beltrami County	MN	Scott LaCoursiere	1992	5,137
144 2/8	24 2/8	24 1/8	20 0/8	4	5	Crawford County	IL	John Hale	1992	5,137
144 2/8	24 0/8	24 3/8	16 7/8	6	4	Washington County	PA	Terry L. Kubacka	1993	5,137
144 2/8	24 5/8	23 5/8	20 4/8	6	5	Madison County	IA	Roy Mikesell	1993	5,137
144 2/8	23 5/8	21 0/8	18 2/8	5	6	Ashland County	WI	Mark Francis Ellias	1994	5,137
144 2/8	24 1/8	25 1/8	20 6/8	5	5	Douglas County	NE	Ron Nordell	1994	5,137
144 2/8	23 3/8	23 1/8	20 0/8	5	5	Lake County	IL	Mark Nelsen	1994	5,137
144 2/8	23 3/8	23 4/8	18 4/8	6	5	Slope County	ND	Jeremy Brockman	1994	5,137
144 2/8	21 6/8	22 6/8	16 0/8	6	5	Crawford County	KS	Dave E. Onelio	1995	5,137
144 2/8	23 3/8	24 0/8	16 4/8	6	6	Steuben County	IN	Michael R. Chambers	1995	5,137
144 2/8	24 3/8	24 4/8	20 2/8	4	5	Ingham County	MI	Paul Wygant	1995	5,137
144 2/8	23 1/8	23 2/8	16 0/8	4	4	Henderson County	IL	Steven Hartney	1995	5,137
144 2/8	26 2/8	24 6/8	19 6/8	5	5	Bayfield County	WI	Robert DeMars	1995	5,137
144 2/8	22 7/8	22 3/8	19 0/8	6	5	Raleigh County	WV	Mark Aliff	1995	5,137
144 2/8	23 0/8	23 5/8	16 6/8	6	5	Chitek Lake	SAS	Ken Brock	1995	5,137
144 2/8	25 7/8	26 1/8	17 6/8	6	4	Des Moines County	IA	Tyler Messer	1995	5,137
144 2/8	25 1/8	25 4/8	20 0/8	4	4	Chautauqua County	NY	Clarence Corbett	1995	5,137
144 2/8	23 5/8	22 5/8	19 1/8	6	6	Madison County	ID	Todd Kauer	1996	5,137
144 2/8	20 5/8	21 2/8	17 2/8	6	5	Kleberg County	TX	Roderick E. Nutter	1996	5,137
144 2/8	24 3/8	23 5/8	17 4/8	6	7	Lee County	IA	Dan E. Glasgow, Sr.	1996	5,137
144 2/8	24 6/8	24 6/8	17 5/8	6	5	Furnas County	NE	Gordon R. Smith	1996	5,137
144 2/8	22 4/8	21 2/8	14 4/8	7	6	Chariton County	MO	Scott Brooks	1996	5,137
144 2/8	22 1/8	23 5/8	18 2/8	4	5	Suffolk County	NY	Steve Kelly	1996	5,137
144 2/8	24 0/8	19 0/8	21 6/8	6	5	Suffolk County	NY	Lou Cannizzo	1996	5,137
144 2/8	21 7/8	24 1/8	21 5/8	5	4	Vermilion County	IL	Harvey Dove	1996	5,137
144 2/8	21 4/8	22 1/8	18 6/8	5	5	Scotland County	MO	James M. Slowinski	1997	5,137
144 2/8	24 7/8	25 1/8	20 6/8	4	4	Bucks County	PA	Tom Hooven	1997	5,137
144 2/8	22 6/8	21 7/8	15 4/8	8	5	Weld County	CO	Kevin Yerian	1997	5,137
144 2/8	22 5/8	21 7/8	17 2/8	5	5	Rock County	WI	Frank A. Cagney	1997	5,137
144 2/8	23 6/8	23 7/8	18 2/8	5	5	Boone County	IA	Kevin M. Christensen	1997	5,137
144 2/8	22 2/8	23 6/8	18 0/8	5	5	Union County	IA	Roy Mikesell	1997	5,137
144 2/8	23 6/8	23 6/8	17 0/8	5	5	Webb County	TX	Norman E. Speer	1997	5,137
144 1/8	21 3/8	21 2/8	17 2/8	5	7	Marshall County	KS	Jack Thornton	1965	5,184
144 1/8	25 0/8	24 0/8	17 7/8	5	4	Union County	IL	Pat Mitchell	1974	5,184
144 1/8	21 6/8	22 1/8	17 5/8	5	5	Jackson County	IL	Dave Yearian	1979	5,184
144 1/8	25 0/8	25 7/8	16 0/8	4	5	Vinton County	OH	Randy Fee	1981	5,184
144 1/8	23 7/8	23 1/8	19 1/8	4	4	Defiance County	OH	Alan Stark	1981	5,184
144 1/8	21 1/8	21 0/8	17 1/8	5	5	Maverick County	TX	Dean Oatman	1982	5,184
144 1/8	22 3/8	21 6/8	14 7/8	7	7	Calumet County	WI	Myron E. Jochmann	1982	5,184
144 1/8	26 3/8	26 0/8	20 3/8	3	4	Charles County	MD	Fred Dolinger	1982	5,184
144 1/8	21 1/8	21 6/8	17 0/8	7	7	Pittsburg County	OK	Brett Jones	1984	5,184
144 1/8	23 1/8	22 7/8	19 4/8	5	4	Des Moines County	IA	Ray Waschkat	1985	5,184
144 1/8	22 6/8	22 4/8	17 1/8	5	5	Woodbury County	IA	Ritch A. Stolpe	1985	5,184
144 1/8	24 7/8	24 3/8	20 3/8	4	4	Berkeley County	SC	Hugh Gaskins	1986	5,184
144 1/8	25 3/8	25 1/8	19 5/8	5	4	Shawnee County	KS	Steve Deever	1986	5,184
144 1/8	20 7/8	20 2/8	16 2/8	6	5	Hampshire County	MA	Larry Davis	1986	5,184
144 1/8	22 2/8	23 2/8	17 2/8	6	7	Hughes County	OK	Randy Fletcher	1987	5,184
144 1/8	21 6/8	22 1/8	17 0/8	5	6	Pepin County	WI	Joe Weiss	1987	5,184
144 1/8	24 4/8	22 0/8	17 3/8	6	6	Benton County	MO	Curtis A. Powell	1988	5,184
144 1/8	23 1/8	23 7/8	19 3/8	5	5	Montgomery County	IL	Mark Everett	1988	5,184
144 1/8	21 7/8	22 2/8	17 5/8	5	6	Kenedy County	TX	Pink Atkins	1988	5,184
144 1/8	26 2/8	26 0/8	16 6/8	4	5	Surry County	VA	William Allen Rickmond	1989	5,184
144 1/8	22 1/8	23 4/8	19 7/8	5	5	Marinette County	WI	Chuck Gerbenskey	1989	5,184
144 1/8	25 3/8	24 4/8	19 3/8	5	4	Hennepin County	MN	Ken Fluck	1989	5,184
144 1/8	23 4/8	23 7/8	16 1/8	7	7	Blue Earth County	MN	Terry R. Wehr	1989	5,184
144 1/8	23 1/8	22 7/8	13 3/8	5	5	Hood County	TX	Mike Searles	1990	5,184
144 1/8	25 0/8	24 1/8	20 7/8	4	4	Ferry County	WA	Don Ohman, Jr.	1990	5,184
144 1/8	24 1/8	23 7/8	17 1/8	6	5	Benton County	MO	Kelly Collins	1990	5,184
144 1/8	22 7/8	23 1/8	15 1/8	6	6	Cedar County	IA	Ron Petersen	1991	5,184
144 1/8	24 0/8	24 2/8	16 6/8	6	6	Hopkins County	KY	Randy Slinger	1991	5,184
144 1/8	21 6/8	22 2/8	14 5/8	5	5	Hendricks County	IN	Chester D. Aiduks	1991	5,184
144 1/8	25 1/8	25 5/8	16 5/8	4	4	Iron County	WI	Daniel J. Van Oss	1991	5,184
144 1/8	25 4/8	26 3/8	17 4/8	6	5	Scotland County	MO	Jim Johnson	1991	5,184
144 1/8	25 6/8	25 6/8	19 7/8	6	5	Leduc	ALB	Floyd Brunes	1992	5,184
144 1/8	22 7/8	19 2/8	21 5/8	5	5	Marquette County	WI	Dennis P. Gohlke	1992	5,184
144 1/8	25 2/8	25 1/8	18 1/8	4	4	Racine County	WI	Tim Steinke	1992	5,184
144 1/8	21 1/8	20 4/8	15 7/8	5	5	Livingston County	NY	Jeffrey C. Meredith	1993	5,184
144 1/8	23 4/8	23 1/8	18 0/8	5	7	Chester County	PA	Edwin Forteza	1993	5,184
144 1/8	24 0/8	23 7/8	18 0/8	6	6	Knox County	OH	Tim Meier	1994	5,184
144 1/8	22 3/8	22 3/8	19 7/8	6	5	Ozaukee County	WI	Rick Kropp, Jr.	1994	5,184
144 1/8	23 0/8	24 0/8	19 3/8	5	7	Hancock County	IL	Robert Bara	1994	5,184
144 1/8	23 4/8	24 2/8	17 4/8	6	6	Pocahontas County	WV	Everette McKinney	1994	5,184
144 1/8	20 7/8	20 7/8	16 4/8	7	6	Pottawatomie County	KS	Greg DeVader	1994	5,184
144 1/8	27 0/8	25 6/8	23 1/8	5	4	Brown County	IL	Sylvan Purcell, Jr.	1994	5,184
144 1/8	23 0/8	23 2/8	20 3/8	4	4	Tazewell County	IL	Jim Querciagrossa	1995	5,184

WHITETAIL DEER (TYPICAL ANTLERS)

Minimum Score 125

SCORE	LENGTH OF MAIN BEAM R	LENGTH OF MAIN BEAM L	INSIDE SPREAD	NUMBER OF POINTS R	NUMBER OF POINTS L	AREA	STATE/PROVINCE	HUNTER'S NAME	DATE	RANK
144 1/8	23 2/8	23 7/8	15 7/8	4	5	Calgary	ALB	Bill Riel	1996	5,184
144 1/8	23 6/8	23 6/8	18 7/8	5	5	Rock County	WI	Bob Miller	1996	5,184
144 1/8	23 1/8	23 5/8	16 4/8	6	5	Dubuque County	IA	Jim Boxleiter	1996	5,184
144 1/8	23 5/8	24 4/8	19 3/8	5	5	Washington County	OH	Michael R. Moore	1996	5,184
144 1/8	23 4/8	23 7/8	18 4/8	5	4	Cerro Gordo County	IA	Tom S. Hyde	1996	5,184
144 1/8	21 6/8	22 2/8	18 3/8	6	6	Braxton County	WV	Edward Clifton	1997	5,184
144 1/8	24 6/8	25 3/8	18 0/8	5	6	Pike County	IL	Mike Hogan	1997	5,184
144 1/8	25 4/8	24 6/8	18 1/8	5	5	Stark County	IL	Gerald Schaff	1997	5,184
144 1/8	20 7/8	20 5/8	17 4/8	6	5	Montcalm County	MI	John Sobie	1997	5,184
144 1/8	22 1/8	22 6/8	18 5/8	5	5	Morgan County	IL	Terry Day	1997	5,184
144 0/8	21 4/8	22 0/8	16 6/8	5	5	Adams County	IL	Gerald Morton	1963	5,237
144 0/8	22 4/8	23 0/8	18 6/8	5	5	Fayette County	IA	Kenneth Durnin	1971	5,237
144 0/8	24 4/8	23 5/8	17 6/8	5	4	Wayne County	WV	Eddie Mullins	1976	5,237
144 0/8	23 4/8	24 0/8	17 2/8	5	5	Hocking County	OH	Greg Bonecutter, Sr.	1979	5,237
144 0/8	23 2/8	23 3/8	18 4/8	5	5	Lee County	AL	George P. Mann	1979	5,237
144 0/8	24 2/8	24 4/8	18 4/8	5	4	Murray County	MN	Alan Metz	1979	5,237
144 0/8	23 5/8	24 4/8	18 6/8	4	4	Juneau County	WI	Kelly Urban	1980	5,237
144 0/8	25 6/8	25 6/8	17 5/8	4	5	Jackson County	OH	Thomas Hart	1981	5,237
144 0/8	22 4/8	22 3/8	18 2/8	5	5	Logan County	OH	Mark A. Payne	1981	5,237
144 0/8	22 0/8	22 1/8	21 7/8	7	8	Hennepin County	MN	Clarence D. Huls	1984	5,237
144 0/8	19 5/8	20 6/8	17 6/8	5	5	Fremont County	IA	Larry Zach	1984	5,237
144 0/8	23 5/8	23 6/8	19 2/8	6	4	Franklin County	KS	J. R. Oshel	1985	5,237
144 0/8	23 6/8	24 2/8	18 4/8	5	6	Monmouth County	NJ	Cliff Underwood	1985	5,237
144 0/8	23 7/8	23 2/8	19 0/8	5	5	Lewis & Clark County	MT	Sonny Templeton	1985	5,237
144 0/8	23 7/8	23 0/8	18 0/8	5	5	Hubbard County	MN	Tim Leeseberg	1985	5,237
144 0/8	24 1/8	23 5/8	16 5/8	7	8	Henderson County	KY	Michael Embry	1986	5,237
144 0/8	25 7/8	24 7/8	17 6/8	4	4	Union County	SD	Derrall Minor	1987	5,237
144 0/8	22 4/8	22 0/8	17 3/8	5	7	Mercer County	ND	Chris S. Hadland	1988	5,237
144 0/8	24 0/8	23 6/8	18 4/8	4	5	Lycoming County	PA	Peter Salamone	1988	5,237
144 0/8	22 4/8	24 7/8	17 2/8	5	5	Kane County	IL	Kurt J. Bird	1988	5,237
144 0/8	22 4/8	23 6/8	16 6/8	4	4	Starke County	IN	Daniel H. Chaney	1989	5,237
144 0/8	23 4/8	23 6/8	17 4/8	5	5	Du Page County	IL	Richard Maish	1989	5,237
144 0/8	25 6/8	26 2/8	16 0/8	6	6	Kankakee County	IL	Al Weissbohn	1989	5,237
144 0/8	24 7/8	24 6/8	17 2/8	4	5	Yellow Medicine County	MN	Brent Hassel	1990	5,237
144 0/8	22 5/8	22 5/8	16 7/8	7	6	Stark County	ND	Howard Sharpe	1990	5,237
144 0/8	24 1/8	25 0/8	18 6/8	5	4	Fulton County	OH	Mike Krasny	1990	5,237
144 0/8	24 5/8	24 0/8	19 0/8	4	5	Wapello County	IA	Dave D. Young	1990	5,237
144 0/8	26 4/8	25 2/8	17 1/8	6	5	Stokes County	NC	Phillip D. Ring	1991	5,237
144 0/8	24 5/8	24 6/8	18 0/8	5	5	McHenry County	IL	Ray Kraeplin	1991	5,237
144 0/8	22 4/8	22 4/8	15 0/8	5	5	Patrick County	VA	Ricky D. Boyd	1991	5,237
144 0/8	20 3/8	21 5/8	20 4/8	6	6	Cochrane	ALB	Tom Foss	1991	5,237
144 0/8	24 3/8	25 3/8	20 1/8	5	5	Lake County	IL	Richard Battaglia	1992	5,237
144 0/8	24 0/8	24 2/8	19 6/8	4	4	Black Hawk County	IA	Gregory E. Lough	1992	5,237
144 0/8	24 1/8	23 5/8	23 1/8	4	5	Cecil County	MD	Jerry T. Hewitt	1993	5,237
144 0/8	23 6/8	24 7/8	17 2/8	6	8	Portage County	WI	Jerry W. Irwin	1993	5,237
144 0/8	22 6/8	24 2/8	18 0/8	5	5	Hancock County	IN	Jim Moore	1993	5,237
144 0/8	22 1/8	22 7/8	19 2/8	6	6	Tippecanoe County	IN	Mitchell Tuinstra	1993	5,237
144 0/8	23 6/8	23 6/8	20 0/8	5	6	McHenry County	IL	David J. Binz	1994	5,237
144 0/8	22 1/8	21 3/8	18 3/8	6	5	Manitowoc County	WI	Dennis Waniger	1994	5,237
144 0/8	24 6/8	23 5/8	15 2/8	6	5	Wayne County	KY	Jeff Keith	1994	5,237
144 0/8	24 1/8	24 1/8	19 4/8	4	4	Peoria County	IL	Michael H. Reatherford	1994	5,237
144 0/8	22 7/8	23 5/8	16 2/8	5	4	Wood County	WI	Eugene "Toby" Keen	1995	5,237
144 0/8	22 6/8	22 6/8	17 0/8	6	6	Livingston County	MI	Kenneth Roy	1995	5,237
144 0/8	23 2/8	22 5/8	17 0/8	4	4	Irion County	TX	Ronnie L. Whitt	1995	5,237
144 0/8	23 2/8	23 3/8	17 2/8	4	4	Grundy County	IL	Russell Robak	1995	5,237
144 0/8	23 2/8	23 2/8	17 3/8	6	7	Anoka County	MN	Dennis Hoveland	1995	5,237
144 0/8	22 5/8	22 2/8	16 4/8	5	6	Lafayette County	MO	Troy McNeel	1995	5,237
144 0/8	24 2/8	24 7/8	17 0/8	5	5	Calhoun County	MI	Danny W. Murphy	1996	5,237
144 0/8	21 3/8	22 0/8	18 6/8	5	5	Atlantic County	NJ	Edgar Reinhardt	1996	5,237
144 0/8	23 6/8	24 0/8	17 6/8	5	5	Jackson County	MO	David A. Vestal	1996	5,237
144 0/8	23 2/8	23 0/8	18 0/8	5	5	Guernsey County	OH	James E. McMasters	1996	5,237
144 0/8	21 7/8	23 4/8	18 2/8	5	5	Tensas Parish	LA	Lynn Honeycutt	1997	5,237
144 0/8	23 0/8	22 1/8	16 0/8	5	5	Marathon County	WI	Constance M. Welch	1997	5,237
144 0/8	24 2/8	23 1/8	17 0/8	5	5	Buffalo County	WI	Chad M. Much	1997	5,237
144 0/8	22 2/8	22 0/8	17 1/8	6	7	Grant County	WI	Jeff A. Landon	1997	5,237
144 0/8	23 7/8	23 2/8	15 0/8	5	5	Winneshiek County	IA	Scott V. Stewart	1997	5,237
144 0/8	23 0/8	22 1/8	18 4/8	5	5	Kandiyohi County	MN	Jesse Vlaminck	1997	5,237
144 0/8	23 4/8	24 4/8	17 2/8	4	4	Winona County	MN	Terry C. Miller	1998	5,237
143 7/8	21 5/8	22 2/8	15 7/8	5	5	Oktibbeha County	MS	Frank Cascio, Jr.	1978	5,295
143 7/8	22 5/8	21 6/8	14 7/8	6	5	Traverse County	MN	Gary Anderson	1980	5,295
143 7/8	23 1/8	23 0/8	19 1/8	4	5	White County	IN	Richard Zaring	1980	5,295
143 7/8	27 3/8	26 2/8	19 0/8	5	6	Erie County	NY	Mark A. Bennett	1981	5,295
143 7/8	22 1/8	23 1/8	17 3/8	5	5	Taylor County	WI	Tony Kliscz	1981	5,295
143 7/8	28 6/8	26 3/8	21 1/8	4	5	Ross County	OH	Jack F. Hatton	1982	5,295
143 7/8	24 1/8	23 0/8	17 7/8	6	5	Morrill County	NE	Gerry Hrasky	1983	5,295
143 7/8	20 4/8	20 3/8	15 3/8	5	5	Macon County	AL	George P. Mann	1984	5,295
143 7/8	24 3/8	23 2/8	19 1/8	7	7	Allegheny County	PA	Richard J. Kudranski	1985	5,295
143 7/8	23 4/8	23 5/8	17 5/8	5	5	Ashland County	WI	Neal Turney	1987	5,295

WHITETAIL DEER (TYPICAL ANTLERS)

Minimum Score 125 — Continued

SCORE	LENGTH OF MAIN BEAM R	LENGTH OF MAIN BEAM L	INSIDE SPREAD	NUMBER OF POINTS R	NUMBER OF POINTS L	AREA	STATE/ PROVINCE	HUNTER'S NAME	DATE	RANK
143 7/8	26 0/8	26 3/8	21 4/8	7	7	Clinton County	MI	Louie Mrazek	1987	5,295
143 7/8	25 5/8	24 2/8	15 7/8	4	4	St. Croix County	WI	Robert K. Weaver	1987	5,295
143 7/8	21 2/8	21 6/8	15 5/8	5	5	Allamakee County	IA	Gary P. Cole	1987	5,295
143 7/8	23 6/8	23 5/8	21 5/8	5	5	La Salle County	IL	Gary Tabor	1987	5,295
143 7/8	21 4/8	22 4/8	18 3/8	5	5	Iroquois County	IL	Jerry Putnam	1987	5,295
143 7/8	23 4/8	24 5/8	17 4/8	5	8	Camden County	MO	John Cartwright	1989	5,295
143 7/8	22 7/8	22 5/8	18 3/8	6	6	Monroe County	WI	Chuck Underberg	1989	5,295
143 7/8	22 6/8	22 2/8	16 3/8	5	5	Hamilton County	IN	Scott Griffin	1990	5,295
143 7/8	23 5/8	22 0/8	17 7/8	5	5	Olmsted County	MN	Steven Laudon	1990	5,295
143 7/8	27 4/8	26 6/8	21 1/8	5	4	Bartholomew County	IN	James W. Smith	1990	5,295
143 7/8	26 2/8	24 6/8	17 5/8	6	4	Winnebago County	IL	Mark P. Stock	1990	5,295
143 7/8	24 3/8	24 5/8	16 3/8	5	5	Custer County	NE	Dan Dowse	1991	5,295
143 7/8	25 6/8	25 4/8	22 5/8	4	4	Calhoun County	MI	Greg H. St. John	1991	5,295
143 7/8	24 0/8	24 2/8	17 7/8	4	4	Porter County	IN	James Frahm	1991	5,295
143 7/8	23 7/8	23 0/8	14 5/8	5	5	McKenzie County	ND	Steve Rehak	1991	5,295
143 7/8	23 7/8	25 3/8	17 7/8	4	5	Marinette County	WI	Mark W. Johnson	1992	5,295
143 7/8	24 5/8	23 4/8	17 2/8	6	7	Dekalb County	IL	Jim Zielinski	1992	5,295
143 7/8	25 7/8	26 3/8	17 7/8	4	4	Adams County	IL	Edward Leach	1992	5,295
143 7/8	23 7/8	24 4/8	16 7/8	6	5	Shelby County	IL	Jim Harbert	1992	5,295
143 7/8	22 3/8	22 6/8	16 5/8	5	5	Kankakee County	IL	Tom Campbell	1992	5,295
143 7/8	23 5/8	23 4/8	17 2/8	6	4	Muskingum County	OH	Randy Pennell	1993	5,295
143 7/8	19 4/8	20 4/8	15 7/8	5	6	Daviess County	MO	Daniel Terry	1993	5,295
143 7/8	23 1/8	23 2/8	15 7/8	5	5	Cape Girardeau County	MO	Martin Blumenthal	1993	5,295
143 7/8	21 7/8	22 2/8	15 1/8	5	5	Tazewell County	IL	Thomas Watson	1993	5,295
143 7/8	23 4/8	23 7/8	20 3/8	4	4	Hennepin County	MN	Daniel Kittok	1993	5,295
143 7/8	22 6/8	22 7/8	18 1/8	4	5	La Salle County	IL	Ray F. Daniels	1993	5,295
143 7/8	22 2/8	23 3/8	18 5/8	5	5	Washington County	MN	Tim Dornseif	1994	5,295
143 7/8	21 7/8	21 2/8	18 3/8	4	4	Ingham County	MI	Daniel J. Briggs	1994	5,295
143 7/8	22 7/8	23 2/8	20 3/8	5	5	St. Croix County	WI	Steve J. Ball	1995	5,295
143 7/8	23 3/8	23 2/8	18 3/8	5	5	Mercer County	WV	Dwayne E. Repass	1995	5,295
143 7/8	25 0/8	23 6/8	18 4/8	4	6	Greene County	OH	George R. Fischer	1995	5,295
143 7/8	25 1/8	24 7/8	19 6/8	5	4	Jefferson County	WI	Matt Grischow	1996	5,295
143 7/8	23 4/8	24 0/8	18 1/8	5	5	Juneau County	WI	David W. Reynolds	1996	5,295
143 7/8	21 4/8	21 2/8	18 7/8	5	5	Logan County	KY	Russell D. Johnson	1996	5,295
143 7/8	24 3/8	24 4/8	20 1/8	4	4	Grant County	SD	Steve Snow	1996	5,295
143 7/8	26 3/8	24 6/8	18 7/8	7	6	Chisago County	MN	Buckley Smith	1996	5,295
143 7/8	24 1/8	24 0/8	19 1/8	6	5	Dubuque County	IA	Timothy J. Harle	1996	5,295
143 7/8	24 3/8	23 5/8	19 4/8	6	5	Calvert County	MD	James "Skip" Edwards	1997	5,295
143 7/8	23 5/8	23 0/8	24 4/8	5	5	Fairfax County	VA	James Robert Jones	1997	5,295
143 7/8	25 1/8	25 7/8	17 7/8	4	5	Perry County	IL	Ron Pyron	1997	5,295
143 7/8	24 6/8	23 6/8	17 7/8	5	5	Muscatine County	IA	Michael A. Owens	1997	5,295
143 6/8	22 3/8	21 0/8	18 6/8	6	10	Ionia County	MI	Bob Jones	1966	5,346
143 6/8	23 7/8	23 4/8	19 0/8	4	5	Iron County	WI	Lee C. Dix	1968	5,346
143 6/8	21 1/8	21 1/8	17 2/8	7	6	McHenry County	ND	William J. Berg	1978	5,346
143 6/8	20 7/8	21 2/8	15 2/8	6	5	Sabine County	TX	Max L. Turner	1982	5,346
143 6/8	23 0/8	21 3/8	17 4/8	5	5	Oneida County	WI	Pat Abraham	1983	5,346
143 6/8	24 6/8	26 1/8	24 1/8	4	6	Isanti County	MN	Donald Vandermey	1985	5,346
143 6/8	24 4/8	25 2/8	21 2/8	6	4	Shawnee County	KS	Kevin Hogan	1985	5,346
143 6/8	23 3/8	23 2/8	18 6/8	5	5	Ottawa County	OK	Ed Hammons	1986	5,346
143 6/8	24 7/8	25 4/8	19 2/8	5	5	Belmont County	OH	Tony Abranovic, Jr.	1986	5,346
143 6/8	23 1/8	23 1/8	17 0/8	5	5	Jackson County	OH	Randy Moore	1986	5,346
143 6/8	22 2/8	23 2/8	15 4/8	5	6	Platte County	NE	Brad Marler	1987	5,346
143 6/8	25 0/8	24 5/8	18 6/8	5	8	Washington County	MN	Scott Gerry	1987	5,346
143 6/8	25 0/8	24 4/8	18 2/8	7	7	Butler County	KS	Claude Allen	1987	5,346
143 6/8	24 5/8	23 6/8	18 0/8	6	6	Chester County	PA	Steve Thais	1987	5,346
143 6/8	24 1/8	24 2/8	19 4/8	5	5	Cowley County	KS	Warren C. Townsend	1988	5,346
143 6/8	22 7/8	24 7/8	18 2/8	4	5	Cloud County	KS	Gerald Dockins	1991	5,346
143 6/8	23 7/8	23 2/8	21 5/8	5	5	Clay County	MN	Bill Lunden	1992	5,346
143 6/8	24 4/8	23 7/8	18 1/8	6	5	Kleberg County	TX	Tom Winn	1992	5,346
143 6/8	25 0/8	26 1/8	16 4/8	6	4	Morgan County	IL	Ed Ward	1992	5,346
143 6/8	25 0/8	24 7/8	17 0/8	4	4	Chambers County	AL	Emory E. Lynn	1993	5,346
143 6/8	23 1/8	23 0/8	17 0/8	5	5	Iron County	WI	Chris F. Tuszke	1993	5,346
143 6/8	23 5/8	23 5/8	18 4/8	4	4	Knox County	IL	Kevin J. Engels	1993	5,346
143 6/8	23 0/8	23 0/8	16 0/8	5	5	Brooks County	TX	Ronnie Howard	1993	5,346
143 6/8	25 3/8	25 2/8	21 5/8	6	5	Pike County	IL	Jimmy Howard	1993	5,346
143 6/8	26 7/8	27 5/8	17 6/8	6	5	Anoka County	MN	Charlie Grove	1993	5,346
143 6/8	20 1/8	21 4/8	16 7/8	6	5	Manitowoc County	WI	Roger "Bucky" Wagner	1994	5,346
143 6/8	24 3/8	23 7/8	21 0/8	5	5	Sauk County	WI	Jeffrey D. Jensen	1994	5,346
143 6/8	24 5/8	25 1/8	17 4/8	4	4	Wayne County	IA	Dennis M. Jones	1994	5,346
143 6/8	25 1/8	23 5/8	20 3/8	8	7	Champaign County	IL	Michael R. Melvin	1994	5,346
143 6/8	23 2/8	23 1/8	17 0/8	5	5	Polk County	WI	Ron Kantola	1994	5,346
143 6/8	24 3/8	24 3/8	19 2/8	6	5	Lake County	OH	Bradley E. Nicholson	1994	5,346
143 6/8	23 1/8	22 4/8	16 4/8	5	5	Monroe County	WI	Spyder Akright	1995	5,346
143 6/8	23 2/8	23 0/8	16 6/8	5	6	Tazewell County	IL	Dan Gustafson	1995	5,346
143 6/8	22 4/8	22 6/8	16 6/8	5	5	Johnson County	IA	Brian J. Bourgeois	1995	5,346
143 6/8	24 1/8	24 5/8	16 5/8	4	5	Suffolk County	NY	Neal Heaton	1995	5,346
143 6/8	26 0/8	26 0/8	19 0/8	4	4	Douglas County	WI	Glen D. Hope	1995	5,346
143 6/8	23 2/8	23 4/8	15 4/8	4	4	Coles County	IL	Rick Campbell	1996	5,346

WHITETAIL DEER (TYPICAL ANTLERS)

Minimum Score 125   Continued

SCORE	LENGTH OF MAIN BEAM R	LENGTH OF MAIN BEAM L	INSIDE SPREAD	NUMBER OF POINTS R	NUMBER OF POINTS L	AREA	STATE/PROVINCE	HUNTER'S NAME	DATE	RANK
143 6/8	23 0/8	23 0/8	18 2/8	5	4	Marion County	IA	David L. Klobnak	1996	5,346
143 6/8	23 4/8	22 0/8	21 4/8	5	5	Oregon County	MO	Johnny Ray Bennett	1996	5,346
143 6/8	22 7/8	23 4/8	14 2/8	5	5	Osage County	OK	Bryan Jackson	1996	5,346
143 6/8	22 6/8	21 6/8	15 6/8	5	6	La Crosse County	WI	Bob Dearman	1996	5,346
143 6/8	22 0/8	22 0/8	16 2/8	5	5	Wood County	OH	Kenneth E. Greulich	1997	5,346
143 6/8	21 0/8	21 1/8	15 5/8	5	7	St. Croix County	WI	Justin Stahl	1997	5,346
143 6/8	22 5/8	22 7/8	18 2/8	5	5	Oakland County	MI	Michael Feeny	1997	5,346
143 6/8	21 5/8	21 1/8	17 0/8	5	5	Taylor County	WI	Roger Gebauer	1997	5,346
143 6/8	23 3/8	23 3/8	18 7/8	5	4	Mason County	IL	William B. Russell	1997	5,346
143 6/8	23 1/8	23 2/8	19 2/8	5	7	Story County	IA	Aaron Scharf	1997	5,346
143 5/8	22 5/8	23 4/8	17 4/8	6	4	Washington County	MN	Keith Christensen	1975	5,393
143 5/8	23 5/8	23 5/8	17 3/8	5	6	Neosha County	KS	Hugh B. Woolard	1976	5,393
143 5/8	23 2/8	23 5/8	15 7/8	5	6	Polk County	WI	Ron Simmons	1977	5,393
143 5/8	23 3/8	22 4/8	18 6/8	6	8	Houston County	MN	Arden M. Schock	1980	5,393
143 5/8	25 0/8	24 7/8	17 5/8	5	4	Miami County	OH	Philip C. Gudorf	1982	5,393
143 5/8	24 5/8	24 5/8	19 5/8	4	4	Vinton County	OH	Robert Irwin Bazell	1982	5,393
143 5/8	23 7/8	22 7/8	19 7/8	5	5	Randolph County	WV	Charles Byrd	1982	5,393
143 5/8	23 6/8	23 4/8	15 3/8	5	5	Union County	OR	Kim Tameris	1983	5,393
143 5/8	23 7/8	23 5/8	18 3/8	6	5	Blue Earth County	MN	Leroy Urban	1983	5,393
143 5/8	23 2/8	24 0/8	19 0/8	5	8	Morrison County	MN	Doug Heath	1984	5,393
143 5/8	22 1/8	22 7/8	20 1/8	5	5	Carroll County	IL	Art Heinze	1984	5,393
143 5/8	20 1/8	20 6/8	16 4/8	6	6	Pine County	MN	Mike Stauty	1984	5,393
143 5/8	25 1/8	23 6/8	16 3/8	7	8	Fayette County	IA	Roger DeKok	1985	5,393
143 5/8	23 4/8	24 4/8	20 1/8	4	4	Pike County	IL	Rick L. Rodhouse	1986	5,393
143 5/8	23 4/8	23 7/8	18 3/8	6	5	Bremer County	IA	Tom Markussen	1986	5,393
143 5/8	23 4/8	22 2/8	17 1/8	5	6	Itasca County	MN	Tom Meyer	1987	5,393
143 5/8	22 4/8	23 6/8	17 1/8	5	5	Dane County	WI	Tom Isaac	1987	5,393
143 5/8	23 1/8	23 1/8	19 5/8	5	5	Crow Wing County	MN	Tom Aspros	1987	5,393
143 5/8	24 5/8	25 1/8	17 2/8	6	6	Van Buren County	IA	Jim Francois	1988	5,393
143 5/8	23 0/8	23 0/8	19 7/8	4	5	Mahaska County	IA	David Walker, Sr.	1988	5,393
143 5/8	22 3/8	22 0/8	18 5/8	6	5	Mingo County	WV	Jerry W. Sammons	1988	5,393
143 5/8	23 4/8	23 5/8	17 3/8	5	5	Tompkins	SAS	Clarence R Hughes	1989	5,393
143 5/8	21 6/8	21 4/8	17 1/8	4	4	Reno County	KS	Robert Williams	1989	5,393
143 5/8	22 5/8	22 3/8	15 3/8	5	5	Isanti County	MN	Greg Seymour	1989	5,393
143 5/8	24 4/8	24 1/8	20 1/8	4	4	Henry County	IL	Neal Nelson	1990	5,393
143 5/8	24 2/8	24 2/8	17 2/8	5	6	Grand Traverse County	MI	Bill Alpers	1990	5,393
143 5/8	23 5/8	24 2/8	19 7/8	5	5	Wright County	MN	Nick Daleiden	1991	5,393
143 5/8	22 3/8	22 3/8	20 3/8	4	4	Harrison County	OH	Brent Heavilin	1991	5,393
143 5/8	21 0/8	21 1/8	19 6/8	6	6	Monroe County	OH	Darby A. Bender, Jr.	1991	5,393
143 5/8	19 4/8	19 6/8	17 3/8	5	5	Tazewell County	IL	Jim Plemmons	1991	5,393
143 5/8	21 5/8	21 5/8	16 5/8	7	7	Lewis & Clark County	MT	Scott Shanklin	1992	5,393
143 5/8	25 7/8	25 6/8	20 4/8	5	5	Bucks County	PA	Stephen Kollar	1992	5,393
143 5/8	25 0/8	24 4/8	17 5/8	6	5	St. Croix County	WI	Tom Jensen	1992	5,393
143 5/8	24 0/8	23 3/8	17 5/8	5	5	Price County	WI	Gene Puckhaber	1992	5,393
143 5/8	22 3/8	22 5/8	17 0/8	7	5	Jackson County	IA	Elmer E. Kemp	1992	5,393
143 5/8	21 1/8	21 4/8	16 7/8	5	6	Dickey County	ND	Mark Wonders	1993	5,393
143 5/8	21 5/8	20 4/8	17 7/8	5	5	Marathon County	WI	Daniel W. Pelot	1993	5,393
143 5/8	21 2/8	22 0/8	16 3/8	5	5	Latimer County	OK	Bob Ketcher	1993	5,393
143 5/8	23 6/8	24 0/8	19 3/8	5	5	Price County	WI	Dan Gotz	1993	5,393
143 5/8	23 5/8	22 5/8	18 3/8	5	5	Washington County	NE	Douglas Fiala	1993	5,393
143 5/8	22 7/8	23 1/8	16 7/8	5	5	Eaton County	MI	Patrick J. Rankin	1994	5,393
143 5/8	25 7/8	25 4/8	17 2/8	5	6	Douglas County	WI	Bradley Olson	1994	5,393
143 5/8	23 7/8	25 1/8	21 5/8	7	5	Putnam County	IL	Eric Jeppson	1994	5,393
143 5/8	24 1/8	25 4/8	17 7/8	4	4	Reno County	KS	John R. Richardson	1994	5,393
143 5/8	24 3/8	24 4/8	18 6/8	5	5	Macoupin County	IL	Frank T. Link	1994	5,393
143 5/8	20 6/8	22 7/8	25 2/8	5	6	Fairfield County	CT	Keith Dibble	1994	5,393
143 5/8	24 4/8	23 7/8	18 3/8	5	5	Walworth County	WI	Mark Aleckson	1995	5,393
143 5/8	24 2/8	24 2/8	16 7/8	4	5	Henry County	IL	Joe DeSchepper	1995	5,393
143 5/8	24 0/8	23 4/8	18 7/8	7	6	Lake County	IL	Kevin Dahm	1995	5,393
143 5/8	22 6/8	22 2/8	18 1/8	5	5	Delta County	MI	Gerald F. MacKenzie	1995	5,393
143 5/8	24 6/8	24 2/8	17 7/8	5	5	Oswego County	NY	Corey Moore	1995	5,393
143 5/8	25 6/8	27 2/8	19 4/8	7	7	Hamilton County	OH	David J. Olding	1995	5,393
143 5/8	23 7/8	23 4/8	19 0/8	6	5	Lake County	IL	Gregory Homola	1995	5,393
143 5/8	22 4/8	22 7/8	16 7/8	5	5	Butler County	IA	Howard Thompson	1996	5,393
143 5/8	23 1/8	23 6/8	18 7/8	4	4	Fentress County	TN	Edgar F. Parker III	1996	5,393
143 5/8	21 6/8	22 3/8	17 0/8	7	8	Blue Earth County	MN	Dick Sobtzak	1996	5,393
143 5/8	24 0/8	22 4/8	16 5/8	5	5	Chester County	PA	Herbert M. Evans	1996	5,393
143 5/8	24 4/8	24 4/8	19 4/8	7	5	Franklin County	OH	Mark M. Browning	1997	5,393
143 5/8	26 1/8	25 7/8	20 1/8	5	4	Hancock County	WV	Shane B. Murphy	1997	5,393
143 5/8	23 3/8	23 6/8	17 1/8	6	5	Tippecanoe County	IN	Frank J. Wolf II	1997	5,393
143 5/8	21 5/8	20 3/8	19 1/8	6	5	Vinton County	OH	Carlos J. Blackburn	1997	5,393
143 5/8	26 1/8	27 1/8	21 7/8	4	4	Sauk County	WI	Dennis D. Connors	1997	5,393
143 5/8	22 3/8	22 5/8	20 1/8	6	6	Dodge County	WI	Jeffrey M. Bahls	1997	5,393
143 5/8	22 4/8	22 4/8	16 3/8	4	5	Peoria County	IL	Bill Draper	1997	5,393
143 5/8	23 1/8	23 0/8	21 1/8	5	5	Arkansas County	AR	Danny Clark	1997	5,393
143 5/8	21 3/8	22 1/8	21 3/8	5	5	Kenedy County	TX	M. R. James	1997	5,393
143 4/8	23 7/8	23 0/8	20 0/8	5	7	Traverse County	MN	Roland L. Hausmann	1958	5,459
143 4/8	22 5/8	22 7/8	21 4/8	6	6	Ellis County	KS	Lee Couture	1969	5,459

WHITETAIL DEER (TYPICAL ANTLERS)

Minimum Score 125 — Continued

SCORE	LENGTH OF MAIN BEAM R	L	INSIDE SPREAD	NUMBER OF POINTS R	L	AREA	STATE/ PROVINCE	HUNTER'S NAME	DATE	RANK
143 4/8	24 3/8	25 0/8	17 2/8	5	5	Miami County	KS	Fred Supulver	1969	5,459
143 4/8	23 0/8	22 4/8	16 6/8	5	6	Sheboygan County	WI	Gary Mueller	1971	5,459
143 4/8	23 4/8	22 1/8	18 4/8	5	5	Saginaw County	MI	Dorm Haskins	1978	5,459
143 4/8	23 5/8	22 7/8	19 2/8	4	5	Belmont County	OH	Fred Holub	1980	5,459
143 4/8	23 4/8	24 0/8	17 2/8	6	5	Cherokee County	KS	Brett Thomas	1981	5,459
143 4/8	24 5/8	23 3/8	17 0/8	5	5	St. Clair County	MI	Art Brown	1981	5,459
143 4/8	24 2/8	24 4/8	17 6/8	5	6	Pike County	OH	Billy Ray Jenkins	1981	5,459
143 4/8	24 0/8	23 5/8	17 6/8	4	4	Finney County	KS	Wilferd Nichols	1981	5,459
143 4/8	23 6/8	23 1/8	18 2/8	7	5	Winona County	MN	Jim Keim	1982	5,459
143 4/8	23 6/8	23 1/8	18 6/8	4	4	Stafford County	KS	Larry Hoffman	1982	5,459
143 4/8	22 4/8	22 5/8	18 4/8	6	5	Huntingdon County	PA	John A. Williams	1984	5,459
143 4/8	24 4/8	23 7/8	17 6/8	5	5	Otter Tail County	MN	Ross R Grothe	1984	5,459
143 4/8	25 5/8	25 6/8	17 2/8	7	6	Sheboygan County	WI	Randy Mavis	1985	5,459
143 4/8	24 6/8	24 7/8	21 0/8	4	5	Logan County	IL	Mark E. Humbert	1985	5,459
143 4/8	23 3/8	25 4/8	19 0/8	6	4	Clayton County	IA	Paul "Buck" Farni, Jr.	1986	5,459
143 4/8	24 6/8	24 4/8	18 2/8	5	5	Henderson County	IL	Steve Fausel	1986	5,459
143 4/8	23 1/8	23 5/8	18 0/8	5	5	Lafayette County	WI	James D. Beau	1987	5,459
143 4/8	21 1/8	22 6/8	18 6/8	5	5	Blue Earth County	MN	Larry Tapper	1987	5,459
143 4/8	26 2/8	27 2/8	18 4/8	4	4	Anoka County	MN	Dean Leshovsky	1988	5,459
143 4/8	23 3/8	23 2/8	17 4/8	5	4	La Salle County	IL	Gene Brandolino	1988	5,459
143 4/8	22 4/8	22 7/8	16 3/8	7	7	Clay County	IA	Charles Norgaard	1988	5,459
143 4/8	22 6/8	22 6/8	16 0/8	5	5	Lewis County	WV	Clyde Moses	1988	5,459
143 4/8	24 4/8	24 3/8	19 2/8	5	5	Westchester County	NY	George R. Newman	1988	5,459
143 4/8	24 2/8	22 5/8	18 2/8	5	5	Greene County	IL	Leonard R. Walters	1988	5,459
143 4/8	22 6/8	22 3/8	19 0/8	6	5	Elk County	KS	Lance McIntosh	1988	5,459
143 4/8	24 2/8	23 3/8	17 5/8	6	5	Pottawatomie County	OK	Jerry Braziel	1988	5,459
143 4/8	21 6/8	22 6/8	20 4/8	4	5	Baltimore County	MD	William F. Smeltzer	1989	5,459
143 4/8	24 5/8	26 0/8	19 6/8	5	5	Winnebago County	IL	Andy L. Ballinger	1989	5,459
143 4/8	23 5/8	24 0/8	20 2/8	6	5	Andrew County	MO	Bill Wolf, Jr.	1990	5,459
143 4/8	21 3/8	22 3/8	16 2/8	5	6	Will County	IL	James Kamenjarin	1991	5,459
143 4/8	23 6/8	23 3/8	17 2/8	4	4	Pike County	MO	Henry F. Benson, Jr.	1991	5,459
143 4/8	25 1/8	23 6/8	19 0/8	6	6	Rusk County	WI	Ron Welch	1991	5,459
143 4/8	25 0/8	25 6/8	17 6/8	4	6	Macoupin County	IL	Ernie Gagnor	1991	5,459
143 4/8	22 4/8	22 4/8	15 0/8	6	6	Madison County	IA	Scott Creger	1991	5,459
143 4/8	21 6/8	21 5/8	19 2/8	5	6	Houghton County	MI	Randy Hinton	1992	5,459
143 4/8	25 6/8	25 0/8	20 0/8	6	5	Crawford County	WI	Tom Gainor	1992	5,459
143 4/8	22 6/8	21 5/8	20 3/8	6	7	Holmes County	OH	Derrick Columbo	1992	5,459
143 4/8	25 1/8	25 0/8	19 4/8	8	9	Winona County	MN	Douglas Kerska	1992	5,459
143 4/8	22 1/8	23 4/8	24 3/8	5	5	Jefferson County	OH	Bob Uyselt	1992	5,459
143 4/8	24 2/8	25 2/8	16 0/8	6	6	Ward County	ND	Lyle Helmers	1993	5,459
143 4/8	24 5/8	24 5/8	18 6/8	4	5	Missoula County	MT	James R. Clapham	1993	5,459
143 4/8	23 1/8	24 0/8	17 5/8	5	6	Dane County	WI	Rob Anderson	1993	5,459
143 4/8	21 5/8	22 1/8	16 4/8	5	5	Vilas County	WI	Dick Schmidt	1993	5,459
143 4/8	26 0/8	25 2/8	18 4/8	6	7	Martin County	IN	Charles A. Hamstra	1993	5,459
143 4/8	22 5/8	22 4/8	17 7/8	5	6	Sauk County	WI	Dale R. Dahlke	1993	5,459
143 4/8	22 7/8	22 1/8	17 3/8	6	5	Owen County	KY	Gary A. Bruewer	1993	5,459
143 4/8	23 6/8	24 3/8	17 5/8	6	6	Grundy County	IL	Steven Blanton	1993	5,459
143 4/8	21 7/8	22 1/8	18 0/8	6	5	Owen County	IN	Billy J. Beaman	1994	5,459
143 4/8	26 4/8	26 0/8	20 2/8	4	4	Oneida County	WI	David Groose	1994	5,459
143 4/8	23 5/8	23 1/8	20 0/8	5	5	Jackson County	IA	Ronald G. Hellweg	1994	5,459
143 4/8	21 6/8	22 2/8	19 2/8	5	5	Peoria County	IL	David A. Goodwin	1994	5,459
143 4/8	22 1/8	23 2/8	15 4/8	4	4	Iowa County	WI	Dick A. Scoville	1994	5,459
143 4/8	24 2/8	24 6/8	18 0/8	5	5	Peoria County	IL	Brad Christopherson	1994	5,459
143 4/8	24 2/8	24 0/8	18 4/8	5	5	Winneshiek County	IA	Randy E. Doyle	1994	5,459
143 4/8	25 0/8	26 4/8	17 2/8	6	5	Highland County	OH	Roger Dale Burton	1996	5,459
143 4/8	25 0/8	25 3/8	16 6/8	7	4	Martin County	IN	Glen Scott Akles	1996	5,459
143 4/8	23 6/8	24 0/8	18 4/8	5	5	Ohio County	KY	Scott Young	1997	5,459
143 4/8	23 7/8	23 2/8	16 2/8	4	5	Ottawa County	KS	John G. Nelson	1997	5,459
143 4/8	26 1/8	25 7/8	17 0/8	5	4	Pope County	IL	Fred A. Andalora	1997	5,459
143 3/8	25 0/8	23 6/8	16 3/8	6	5	Otter Tail County	MN	J. P. Maurins	1956	5,520
143 3/8	23 0/8	23 1/8	15 7/8	5	5	Comanche County	OK	Kenneth D. Cook	1971	5,520
143 3/8	22 2/8	22 0/8	17 2/8	7	7	Morrison County	MN	GLen Marklowitz	1972	5,520
143 3/8	22 3/8	22 4/8	20 1/8	4	6	Allamakee County	IA	Jim Schmidt	1974	5,520
143 3/8	24 1/8	25 2/8	17 1/8	5	5	Cass County	MN	Richard J. Schabert	1977	5,520
143 3/8	27 0/8	26 0/8	20 1/8	4	4	Charles County	MD	John Allen Williams	1980	5,520
143 3/8	24 1/8	24 0/8	15 5/8	4	5	Saginaw County	MI	Paul Mickey	1981	5,520
143 3/8	22 0/8	23 4/8	19 0/8	8	8	Pike County	IL	Steve Carlen	1982	5,520
143 3/8	24 1/8	23 7/8	17 5/8	5	5	Green County	WI	B. Duane Byrne	1984	5,520
143 3/8	23 6/8	24 3/8	17 4/8	4	4	Ogle County	IL	Dr. Juanito E. Delfinado	1984	5,520
143 3/8	25 3/8	24 7/8	19 1/8	4	4	Norman County	MN	Bryan Mickelson	1985	5,520
143 3/8	22 7/8	24 2/8	17 7/8	4	4	Walworth County	WI	Gary Jordan	1985	5,520
143 3/8	18 6/8	21 0/8	16 3/8	5	5	Slope County	ND	Jack Lefor	1985	5,520
143 3/8	24 0/8	23 6/8	22 2/8	5	6	Pennington County	MN	John A. Monroe	1986	5,520
143 3/8	22 6/8	22 2/8	20 6/8	6	4	Clayton County	IA	Francis Winter	1986	5,520
143 3/8	23 0/8	23 6/8	20 1/8	5	5	Green County	WI	Ernie V. Hutchinson	1986	5,520
143 3/8	22 1/8	22 2/8	15 7/8	5	6	Adams County	WI	Danny C. Winchester	1988	5,520
143 3/8	23 2/8	22 3/8	19 1/8	5	6	Du Page County	IL	Joseph Keim	1988	5,520
143 3/8	24 6/8	25 0/8	17 3/8	7	5	Pierce County	WI	Daniel D. Kern	1988	5,520

WHITETAIL DEER (TYPICAL ANTLERS)

Minimum Score 125 — Continued

SCORE	LENGTH OF MAIN BEAM R	LENGTH OF MAIN BEAM L	INSIDE SPREAD	NUMBER OF POINTS R	NUMBER OF POINTS L	AREA	STATE/ PROVINCE	HUNTER'S NAME	DATE	RANK
143 3/8	22 0/8	22 5/8	18 3/8	5	5	Greene County	IL	Mark Petersen	1988	5,520
143 3/8	21 3/8	22 3/8	17 1/8	5	7	Dodge County	WI	Jim Bauer	1989	5,520
143 3/8	22 5/8	22 1/8	18 1/8	5	5	Burlington County	NJ	Raymond Woodruff	1989	5,520
143 3/8	24 4/8	25 0/8	19 3/8	4	4	Mills County	IA	John Bantz	1989	5,520
143 3/8	23 6/8	23 5/8	20 1/8	5	4	Lake County	IL	John Roscop	1989	5,520
143 3/8	25 4/8	27 4/8	19 5/8	4	4	Montgomery County	PA	Charlie Haydt	1990	5,520
143 3/8	23 4/8	24 4/8	17 4/8	4	5	Gibson County	IN	Steve Feller	1990	5,520
143 3/8	24 6/8	25 2/8	20 2/8	6	5	Jackson County	OH	Gordon Gibbs	1990	5,520
143 3/8	25 2/8	25 1/8	20 5/8	4	6	Caledon Township	ONT	Carl Whittier	1990	5,520
143 3/8	24 5/8	24 3/8	16 7/8	4	4	Morris County	NJ	Geoffrey Stewart	1991	5,520
143 3/8	22 7/8	23 4/8	19 5/8	4	5	Adams County	WI	Michael E. Rykiel	1991	5,520
143 3/8	21 7/8	20 6/8	15 7/8	5	5	Burleigh County	ND	Ron Geffre	1991	5,520
143 3/8	23 6/8	23 4/8	17 1/8	5	5	Buckingham County	VA	Barry D. Warner	1992	5,520
143 3/8	21 5/8	22 2/8	16 3/8	5	5	Dakota County	NE	Nick Larsen	1992	5,520
143 3/8	24 0/8	23 4/8	21 1/8	5	5	Hardin County	IA	Jason P. Jedele	1992	5,520
143 3/8	24 6/8	23 6/8	18 1/8	6	5	Green County	WI	Ross D. Daniels	1992	5,520
143 3/8	24 1/8	24 0/8	18 2/8	7	6	Dane County	WI	Rick J. Miyagawa	1992	5,520
143 3/8	21 7/8	22 5/8	14 1/8	5	5	Will County	IL	Don Oswald	1993	5,520
143 3/8	23 2/8	24 0/8	17 1/8	5	5	La Salle County	TX	Gary Pitts	1993	5,520
143 3/8	24 2/8	24 2/8	19 3/8	6	5	Rock County	WI	James W. Keller	1993	5,520
143 3/8	22 7/8	22 7/8	20 2/8	4	6	Richland County	WI	Bob Wagner	1993	5,520
143 3/8	23 0/8	23 3/8	17 1/8	5	5	Nuevo Leon	MEX	Michael T. Thrasher	1993	5,520
143 3/8	22 2/8	20 0/8	15 6/8	5	6	Burleigh County	ND	Matthew J. Meidinger	1994	5,520
143 3/8	22 7/8	23 3/8	17 4/8	5	6	Shelby County	KY	Larry Duncan	1994	5,520
143 3/8	23 5/8	23 1/8	17 5/8	5	5	McHenry County	IL	Ed Fitzgerald	1994	5,520
143 3/8	25 3/8	25 2/8	16 7/8	4	5	Fillmore County	MN	Kyle Rosedahl	1994	5,520
143 3/8	22 6/8	22 2/8	16 0/8	6	5	Waushara County	WI	Bob Collins	1994	5,520
143 3/8	22 5/8	22 4/8	18 3/8	5	6	Marquette County	WI	Michael Vilkoski	1994	5,520
143 3/8	24 3/8	24 7/8	20 5/8	5	4	Franklin County	IL	Cathy DeNeal	1994	5,520
143 3/8	27 0/8	26 6/8	17 3/8	4	4	Baltimore County	MD	David A. Buchta	1995	5,520
143 3/8	22 5/8	23 0/8	15 6/8	6	5	Pike County	IL	Eddie Claypool	1995	5,520
143 3/8	25 3/8	25 4/8	19 1/8	4	4	Darke County	OH	Wally Harder	1995	5,520
143 3/8	22 4/8	23 4/8	20 1/8	6	6	Goodhue County	MN	Rex Novek	1996	5,520
143 3/8	21 3/8	20 6/8	19 3/8	5	5	Branch County	MI	Bret R. Cary	1996	5,520
143 3/8	24 1/8	22 3/8	17 7/8	4	4	Kent County	MD	Delmas Foster	1996	5,520
143 3/8	24 3/8	26 1/8	20 5/8	4	4	Washington County	MN	Steve Rosa	1996	5,520
143 3/8	24 7/8	24 4/8	19 6/8	6	6	Green Lake County	WI	Clarence E. Miller	1996	5,520
143 3/8	21 4/8	21 2/8	13 3/8	6	5	Wright County	IA	Steve Claude	1997	5,520
143 3/8	22 7/8	23 7/8	18 1/8	5	5	Pike County	MO	Gary Johnston	1997	5,520
143 3/8	24 0/8	23 1/8	19 3/8	5	6	Waukesha County	WI	Philip "Nicky" Holland	1997	5,520
143 3/8	20 6/8	20 4/8	18 3/8	7	6	Perry County	IL	Jeff Buchler	1997	5,520
143 2/8	25 0/8	24 0/8	16 6/8	5	6	Phillips County	AR	Stanley Zellner	1964	5,580
143 2/8	25 0/8	23 7/8	19 4/8	5	5	Geauga County	OH	Rudy Grecar	1971	5,580
143 2/8	26 0/8	25 0/8	17 4/8	8	7	Comanche County	OK	Lloyd Payne III	1976	5,580
143 2/8	25 2/8	26 1/8	18 4/8	4	4	Monroe County	IN	Mike Webb	1977	5,580
143 2/8	22 0/8	23 1/8	16 0/8	5	5	Fond du Lac County	WI	Jim Rickmeyer	1979	5,580
143 2/8	25 4/8	25 0/8	19 2/8	5	5	Price County	WI	Todd R. Sorensen	1981	5,580
143 2/8	24 6/8	25 0/8	18 4/8	5	5	Marion County	TN	Larry Gravitt	1981	5,580
143 2/8	21 7/8	21 6/8	18 4/8	5	5	Jefferson County	MT	Bob Peterson	1983	5,580
143 2/8	24 2/8	24 6/8	16 2/8	5	6	Green County	WI	Wellington W. Wert	1983	5,580
143 2/8	24 3/8	24 3/8	20 0/8	4	4	Edgar County	IL	Benton B. Caldwell	1983	5,580
143 2/8	23 2/8	23 3/8	13 4/8	5	5	Hardin County	IA	Rick McDowell	1983	5,580
143 2/8	24 5/8	23 4/8	19 0/8	5	4	Fairfield County	OH	Gary Lockwood	1984	5,580
143 2/8	23 2/8	22 4/8	18 7/8	5	6	Winona County	MN	Bill Clink	1984	5,580
143 2/8	24 3/8	24 6/8	15 6/8	6	6	Cooper County	MO	Vaughn Sell	1985	5,580
143 2/8	26 0/8	25 6/8	21 4/8	5	4	Montgomery County	MD	Bobby Ray Waters	1985	5,580
143 2/8	23 4/8	23 3/8	16 6/8	5	5	Warren County	IA	Lanny Caligiuri	1985	5,580
143 2/8	22 3/8	22 4/8	19 0/8	5	5	Washington County	MN	Ronald H. Krienke	1986	5,580
143 2/8	24 3/8	24 2/8	20 6/8	4	4	Greene County	AR	Danny J. Walker	1986	5,580
143 2/8	23 5/8	25 1/8	16 4/8	4	4	Sumner County	KS	Robert E. Daley	1986	5,580
143 2/8	23 1/8	23 5/8	18 6/8	6	5	Union County	SD	Larry Minter	1987	5,580
143 2/8	26 6/8	25 0/8	18 6/8	5	6	Spokane County	WA	Paul Fisher	1988	5,580
143 2/8	23 3/8	23 2/8	15 4/8	6	6	Butler County	OH	Robert G. Banks, Jr.	1988	5,580
143 2/8	23 1/8	22 5/8	16 6/8	5	5	Jackson County	MI	John R. Ahrens	1988	5,580
143 2/8	23 0/8	23 2/8	17 0/8	5	5	Lawrence County	KY	Michael Hatfield	1988	5,580
143 2/8	24 0/8	24 1/8	21 0/8	5	4	Hamilton County	OH	George Robert Freudiger	1988	5,580
143 2/8	21 7/8	22 2/8	17 2/8	5	5	Hancock County	IL	David Lee Sanderson	1988	5,580
143 2/8	24 2/8	25 2/8	21 4/8	5	5	Hamilton County	OH	John L. Cox	1989	5,580
143 2/8	24 4/8	23 4/8	22 2/8	4	4	Montcalm County	MI	Rickey P. Allen	1989	5,580
143 2/8	21 4/8	21 4/8	16 5/8	6	6	Defiance County	OH	Stanley Knittle	1989	5,580
143 2/8	22 5/8	22 4/8	18 0/8	5	4	Goodhue County	MN	Michael Schmidt	1990	5,580
143 2/8	22 4/8	21 2/8	17 0/8	6	6	Norton County	KS	Larry R. Hillman	1990	5,580
143 2/8	23 0/8	23 1/8	17 6/8	5	5	Greene County	OH	Richard McClelland	1990	5,580
143 2/8	26 5/8	26 6/8	19 6/8	6	6	Will County	IL	Chad Elumbaugh	1990	5,580
143 2/8	23 6/8	22 6/8	14 0/8	6	5	Licking County	OH	Thomas E. Lott	1991	5,580
143 2/8	21 1/8	22 0/8	16 4/8	5	5	Kleberg County	TX	Johnnie R. Walters	1991	5,580
143 2/8	22 5/8	23 4/8	17 3/8	8	7	Richland County	WI	Ronald S. Pulcine	1991	5,580
143 2/8	22 1/8	24 3/8	17 7/8	6	5	Iowa County	IA	Thomas Dvorak	1991	5,580

WHITETAIL DEER (TYPICAL ANTLERS)

Minimum Score 125 — Continued

SCORE	LENGTH OF MAIN BEAM R	LENGTH OF MAIN BEAM L	INSIDE SPREAD	NUMBER OF POINTS R	NUMBER OF POINTS L	AREA	STATE/PROVINCE	HUNTER'S NAME	DATE	RANK
143 2/8	24 5/8	25 4/8	18 4/8	5	4	Dakota County	MN	Tim L. Gaughan	1991	5,580
143 2/8	22 0/8	22 7/8	15 6/8	5	5	Barnes County	ND	Dean Klein	1992	5,580
143 2/8	24 1/8	23 7/8	17 6/8	4	4	Trimble County	KY	Todd Calvert	1992	5,580
143 2/8	24 6/8	24 5/8	17 6/8	4	5	Adams County	IL	David St. John	1992	5,580
143 2/8	22 6/8	22 4/8	17 0/8	5	6	Langlade County	WI	Lonnie Gene Eick	1992	5,580
143 2/8	23 6/8	23 7/8	17 4/8	4	6	Lake County	IL	Carl H. Spaeth	1992	5,580
143 2/8	23 5/8	24 2/8	21 2/8	4	5	Preble County	OH	Robert A. Worley	1992	5,580
143 2/8	24 4/8	23 7/8	19 2/8	4	6	Northumberland County	PA	Chuck Beaver	1993	5,580
143 2/8	23 5/8	24 6/8	15 4/8	4	5	Ohio County	IN	Troy Courtney	1993	5,580
143 2/8	23 6/8	23 2/8	20 0/8	5	4	Yankton County	SD	David B. Cull	1993	5,580
143 2/8	22 4/8	24 0/8	20 6/8	5	6	Walworth County	WI	Charles Palmer	1993	5,580
143 2/8	21 6/8	21 6/8	20 4/8	5	5	Marinette County	WI	Michael C. Kramer	1994	5,580
143 2/8	24 2/8	23 1/8	17 2/8	5	5	Burlington County	NJ	Louis J. Palfy, Jr.	1994	5,580
143 2/8	24 3/8	24 5/8	16 4/8	5	4	Jackson County	MI	Andrew D. Cook	1994	5,580
143 2/8	22 7/8	24 0/8	17 2/8	5	5	Green Lake County	WI	Craig A. Rohde	1994	5,580
143 2/8	24 4/8	25 6/8	20 6/8	4	4	Walworth County	WI	Steve Jacobson	1994	5,580
143 2/8	23 1/8	23 3/8	18 2/8	4	5	La Crosse County	WI	Ron Lichtie	1994	5,580
143 2/8	24 2/8	25 3/8	16 6/8	4	5	Harford County	MD	Matthew J. Reheard	1995	5,580
143 2/8	22 2/8	22 4/8	20 6/8	5	6	Lee County	IL	Steven Jacobs	1995	5,580
143 2/8	25 0/8	24 5/8	21 2/8	8	6	Dallas County	IA	Mike Prince	1995	5,580
143 2/8	23 3/8	23 7/8	21 4/8	5	6	Vernon County	MO	Paul Reedy	1995	5,580
143 2/8	25 0/8	26 5/8	18 3/8	4	7	Perry County	OH	Butch Samson	1995	5,580
143 2/8	24 6/8	24 0/8	19 2/8	4	4	Yazoo County	MS	Glenn Rose	1996	5,580
143 2/8	22 4/8	22 4/8	16 4/8	4	5	Jefferson County	WI	Paul Alane	1996	5,580
143 2/8	21 5/8	21 4/8	21 2/8	5	5	Chester County	PA	Skip Boyd	1996	5,580
143 2/8	25 0/8	24 4/8	18 0/8	4	4	Lake County	IL	Steven Hysell	1996	5,580
143 2/8	22 6/8	22 6/8	19 2/8	3	3	Piatt County	IL	Rusty Hunt	1997	5,580
143 2/8	19 7/8	22 5/8	18 2/8	6	5	Jefferson County	WV	James L. Jenkins	1997	5,580
143 2/8	23 4/8	24 5/8	19 4/8	4	5	Perry County	PA	Mark Mayberry	1997	5,580
143 2/8	23 0/8	23 4/8	15 6/8	5	4	Blackford County	IN	Mike Hatfield	1997	5,580
143 1/8	23 0/8	23 2/8	17 1/8	5	4	Graham County	KS	Russell Hull	1965	5,647
143 1/8	21 7/8	23 2/8	21 5/8	5	5	Linn County	IA	Tom Postel	1979	5,647
143 1/8	21 2/8	22 7/8	18 3/8	6	7	Lincoln County	MN	David J. Rouge	1981	5,647
143 1/8	22 6/8	22 1/8	18 6/8	6	5	Barry County	MI	Jay W. Gaston	1981	5,647
143 1/8	21 6/8	21 2/8	19 5/8	6	6	Holmes County	OH	Dale R. Kaufman	1983	5,647
143 1/8	22 5/8	22 4/8	19 5/8	5	5	Missoula County	MT	Greg Munther	1983	5,647
143 1/8	20 6/8	20 3/8	18 7/8	6	6	Olmsted County	MN	Brian Veloske	1984	5,647
143 1/8	24 6/8	25 4/8	17 7/8	6	7	Riley County	KS	Kenneth W. Lynch	1985	5,647
143 1/8	22 2/8	22 1/8	15 7/8	5	5	Washburn County	WI	Michael Elliot	1986	5,647
143 1/8	23 0/8	23 2/8	20 0/8	7	5	Iowa County	WI	Brad Burbach	1986	5,647
143 1/8	25 0/8	22 2/8	20 1/8	6	5	Crawford County	WI	John Becwar	1987	5,647
143 1/8	24 1/8	23 2/8	19 2/8	6	5	Cherry County	NE	Gary Galloway	1987	5,647
143 1/8	24 0/8	23 2/8	17 3/8	7	5	Shawnee County	KS	William A. Konrade	1987	5,647
143 1/8	24 1/8	22 2/8	22 5/8	4	4	Montcalm County	MI	A. Gene Higginson	1987	5,647
143 1/8	24 3/8	24 2/8	20 3/8	5	5	Clayton County	IA	Albert A. Weidenbacher	1987	5,647
143 1/8	23 6/8	24 6/8	21 1/8	4	4	Le Sueur County	MN	Randall Mathwig	1988	5,647
143 1/8	23 0/8	21 7/8	14 7/8	5	5	Ripley County	IN	Van R. Craft	1988	5,647
143 1/8	24 7/8	24 6/8	19 7/8	5	4	Fairfax County	VA	Kevin R. Lake	1989	5,647
143 1/8	22 7/8	23 5/8	17 5/8	5	4	Piatt County	IL	David M. James	1991	5,647
143 1/8	25 5/8	25 7/8	19 3/8	7	6	Schuyler County	IL	John Johnston	1991	5,647
143 1/8	22 0/8	22 4/8	18 5/8	5	5	Crawford County	IL	Charlie Guyer	1991	5,647
143 1/8	22 5/8	22 2/8	16 0/8	6	6	Vilas County	WI	Frank E. Caroselli	1991	5,647
143 1/8	24 1/8	21 2/8	17 0/8	5	6	Lafayette County	WI	Todd Hanson	1991	5,647
143 1/8	22 4/8	23 0/8	19 5/8	5	5	Carter County	MT	Keith L. Folk	1992	5,647
143 1/8	21 0/8	22 5/8	16 3/8	5	5	Chester County	PA	Vincent J. Mento	1992	5,647
143 1/8	24 0/8	23 2/8	18 7/8	4	4	Iroquois County	IL	Terry Doehring	1992	5,647
143 1/8	23 7/8	22 7/8	20 1/8	5	5	Delaware County	IA	Eric Klaren	1992	5,647
143 1/8	24 1/8	23 4/8	18 1/8	4	5	Muskingum County	OH	Danny Pyle	1993	5,647
143 1/8	22 7/8	21 4/8	19 1/8	5	6	Calhoun County	IL	Randy Cress	1993	5,647
143 1/8	25 1/8	24 7/8	18 3/8	4	5	Calhoun County	IL	David E. Willis	1993	5,647
143 1/8	22 6/8	22 4/8	17 6/8	5	4	Wilcox County	AL	Scott M. Ware	1994	5,647
143 1/8	23 2/8	23 0/8	17 0/8	4	6	Winnebago County	WI	Kenneth C. Walter	1994	5,647
143 1/8	25 7/8	24 0/8	18 7/8	4	5	Vermilion County	IL	Terry Everingham	1994	5,647
143 1/8	23 6/8	23 1/8	18 6/8	7	5	Langlade County	WI	David A. Nelson	1995	5,647
143 1/8	22 3/8	21 2/8	14 2/8	6	6	Muscogee County	GA	Dr. Garland K. "Crow" Gudger	1995	5,647
143 1/8	22 3/8	22 7/8	17 5/8	5	5	Polk County	WI	Aaron D. Baillargeon	1995	5,647
143 1/8	23 2/8	23 0/8	20 0/8	7	4	Butler County	KS	David R. Rogers	1995	5,647
143 1/8	27 4/8	26 6/8	20 5/8	3	4	Bond County	IL	Cory Holcmann	1995	5,647
143 1/8	23 7/8	24 3/8	16 1/8	4	4	Hamilton County	IA	Matthew R. Lewis	1996	5,647
143 1/8	23 1/8	23 0/8	17 1/8	5	5	Butler County	KS	Rodney Hommertzheim	1996	5,647
143 1/8	23 6/8	25 6/8	18 2/8	4	6	Vermilion County	IL	Donald Sollars	1996	5,647
143 1/8	23 1/8	24 1/8	17 7/8	5	6	Fond du Lac County	WI	Greg Schleusner	1996	5,647
143 1/8	25 6/8	25 5/8	19 2/8	4	6	Allamakee County	IA	Gary Charipar	1996	5,647
143 1/8	25 3/8	25 0/8	20 1/8	4	6	Will County	IL	Nick Ginnetti	1997	5,647
143 1/8	25 7/8	25 2/8	19 1/8	5	5	Parke County	IN	Chuck Paddock	1997	5,647
143 1/8	23 2/8	24 3/8	15 0/8	8	6	Yazoo County	MS	Jimmy Hilderbrand	1997	5,647
143 1/8	22 1/8	22 1/8	16 5/8	5	6	Polk County	WI	Rick Heintz	1997	5,647
143 1/8	25 1/8	26 1/8	18 3/8	5	6	Meigs County	OH	Patrick D. Kearns	1997	5,647

WHITETAIL DEER (TYPICAL ANTLERS)

Minimum Score 125 — Continued

SCORE	LENGTH OF MAIN BEAM R	LENGTH OF MAIN BEAM L	INSIDE SPREAD	NUMBER OF POINTS R	NUMBER OF POINTS L	AREA	STATE/ PROVINCE	HUNTER'S NAME	DATE	RANK
143 1/8	22 1/8	21 6/8	22 2/8	5	5	Trempealeau County	WI	Jeffery Stoll	1997	5,647
143 1/8	23 6/8	23 1/8	19 6/8	4	5	Peoria County	IL	Scott Turner	1997	5,647
143 1/8	19 7/8	19 7/8	16 1/8	6	6	Lyon County	KS	Michael Esch	1997	5,647
143 1/8	20 6/8	20 6/8	17 5/8	5	6	Wright County	IA	Ron Hansen	1997	5,647
143 0/8	23 5/8	22 0/8	19 4/8	5	5	Wright County	IA	Ronald Gorden	1958	5,699
143 0/8	25 1/8	25 6/8	18 4/8	6	7	Aitkin County	MN	Ervin A. Buck	1961	5,699
143 0/8	24 0/8	24 5/8	20 5/8	5	5	Pope County	IL	Bob E. Sims	1964	5,699
143 0/8	25 4/8	21 0/8	14 6/8	5	6	Ottawa County	KS	Scotty Baugh	1967	5,699
143 0/8	22 7/8	21 7/8	16 2/8	5	5	Edwards County	KS	Gerald L. Schaller	1972	5,699
143 0/8	20 2/8	19 6/8	15 4/8	5	5	Madison County	IA	Larry L. Cavanaugh	1979	5,699
143 0/8	24 3/8	24 4/8	18 1/8	6	5	Black Hawk County	IA	Richard Minahan	1980	5,699
143 0/8	24 3/8	25 0/8	18 2/8	4	4	Sawyer County	WI	Steve Olson	1981	5,699
143 0/8	22 6/8	22 0/8	19 2/8	5	6	Henry County	VA	Mike Weaver	1981	5,699
143 0/8	20 5/8	20 5/8	15 4/8	5	5	Seward County	KS	Lynn Leonard	1983	5,699
143 0/8	22 1/8	23 0/8	17 4/8	5	6	Montgomery County	PA	Robert J. Bochnak	1983	5,699
143 0/8	24 6/8	23 1/8	22 0/8	6	5	Kankakee County	IL	Rick Renzi	1983	5,699
143 0/8	21 0/8	21 4/8	17 6/8	6	7	Des Moines County	IA	Tom Delaney	1985	5,699
143 0/8	23 2/8	23 5/8	19 5/8	5	4	La Salle County	IL	Leroy W. Buckley, Jr.	1986	5,699
143 0/8	23 5/8	24 6/8	17 4/8	5	5	Alfalfa County	OK	David W. Dowell	1986	5,699
143 0/8	23 1/8	23 4/8	17 0/8	5	6	Sauk County	WI	Richard L. Kirkland	1987	5,699
143 0/8	20 3/8	21 1/8	18 2/8	6	5	Columbia County	WI	Howard H. Hill	1987	5,699
143 0/8	22 3/8	21 3/8	18 0/8	5	5	Missoula County	MT	Jon Cusker	1987	5,699
143 0/8	23 5/8	23 3/8	17 2/8	5	5	Fairfax County	VA	Harry R. Husch, Jr.	1988	5,699
143 0/8	22 6/8	24 0/8	18 0/8	5	5	Marathon County	WI	Mark Timken	1988	5,699
143 0/8	22 7/8	23 4/8	18 4/8	4	5	Bayfield County	WI	Wayne Zirn	1988	5,699
143 0/8	22 5/8	21 4/8	18 2/8	6	5	Licking County	OH	Stoney May	1988	5,699
143 0/8	24 4/8	25 0/8	17 2/8	5	5	Beltrami County	MN	Ross Campbell	1988	5,699
143 0/8	22 6/8	23 5/8	20 4/8	5	5	Montgomery County	MD	Richard H. Stabler	1989	5,699
143 0/8	23 1/8	24 1/8	17 4/8	4	4	Allen County	IN	Randy McIntosh	1989	5,699
143 0/8	23 6/8	22 2/8	17 2/8	6	6	Lee County	IA	Russell "Rusty" Robbins	1990	5,699
143 0/8	25 2/8	23 4/8	17 6/8	5	5	Christian County	KY	Gary Holbrook	1990	5,699
143 0/8	23 5/8	24 0/8	16 0/8	6	9	Wabash County	IL	Troy A. Hinderliter	1990	5,699
143 0/8	23 1/8	23 7/8	17 4/8	5	5	Watauga County	NC	Chris Carlton	1991	5,699
143 0/8	24 7/8	23 1/8	16 4/8	5	5	Dodge County	MN	Myles Keller	1991	5,699
143 0/8	24 6/8	24 3/8	17 0/8	5	5	Lincoln County	MO	Hugh Steavenson	1991	5,699
143 0/8	23 1/8	24 5/8	19 4/8	4	4	Jefferson County	OH	Joseph Daniel Nemitt	1991	5,699
143 0/8	23 1/8	23 2/8	19 0/8	5	5	Lafayette County	WI	Bradley D. Phillips	1991	5,699
143 0/8	22 3/8	22 1/8	17 6/8	5	5	Sebastian County	AR	Jim Garner	1992	5,699
143 0/8	24 3/8	24 6/8	17 0/8	4	4	Lake County	IL	Andrew D. Orals	1992	5,699
143 0/8	24 3/8	25 1/8	23 6/8	5	4	McHenry County	IL	Kory Lang	1993	5,699
143 0/8	23 6/8	23 5/8	18 0/8	4	4	Hendricks County	IN	Aaron Wesley Hamstra	1993	5,699
143 0/8	22 1/8	22 4/8	19 2/8	5	5	Berks County	PA	Mark L. Breidegam	1993	5,699
143 0/8	26 7/8	27 0/8	18 0/8	5	5	Allegheny County	PA	John M. Stankowski	1993	5,699
143 0/8	25 3/8	23 1/8	20 5/8	5	6	Jo Daviess County	IL	Jim Horneck	1993	5,699
143 0/8	24 6/8	25 2/8	17 6/8	5	5	Buffalo County	WI	Dave Fredrickson	1993	5,699
143 0/8	22 4/8	22 2/8	15 4/8	6	5	Wyoming County	WV	David K. Cox	1993	5,699
143 0/8	26 0/8	25 2/8	26 1/8	4	3	Edmonton	ALB	Warren Witherspoon	1993	5,699
143 0/8	23 5/8	22 5/8	19 0/8	5	5	Trempealeau County	WI	Rusty Severson	1994	5,699
143 0/8	21 6/8	23 4/8	20 0/8	5	5	Fulton County	IL	Barbara Briggs	1994	5,699
143 0/8	25 6/8	25 6/8	19 6/8	4	5	Scott County	IA	Gary Kiefer	1994	5,699
143 0/8	24 1/8	24 1/8	19 2/8	5	5	Poweshiek County	IA	Keven Gibson	1994	5,699
143 0/8	20 0/8	20 2/8	16 4/8	5	5	San Patricio County	TX	William Lee Emmons	1994	5,699
143 0/8	22 1/8	21 7/8	19 0/8	5	5	Valley County	MT	Anthony Swiontek	1995	5,699
143 0/8	24 1/8	25 0/8	18 2/8	5	5	Screven County	GA	Thomas W. Hughes	1995	5,699
143 0/8	23 2/8	22 6/8	20 6/8	4	4	Daviess County	MO	Daniel P. Minor	1995	5,699
143 0/8	22 1/8	23 4/8	13 4/8	5	6	Live Oak County	TX	Henry Tucker	1995	5,699
143 0/8	22 4/8	23 3/8	20 0/8	6	5	Geauga County	OH	John P. Ross	1995	5,699
143 0/8	25 0/8	25 3/8	17 2/8	5	4	Dakota County	MN	Derrick L. Bennett	1995	5,699
143 0/8	23 6/8	23 2/8	18 6/8	7	6	Davis County	IA	Jeffrey A. Getz	1995	5,699
143 0/8	21 6/8	25 3/8	20 2/8	7	4	Buffalo County	WI	Brian Potter	1995	5,699
143 0/8	24 2/8	24 3/8	17 4/8	5	5	Lawrence County	OH	Bob Fruda	1995	5,699
143 0/8	24 0/8	22 4/8	18 0/8	5	5	Boone County	MO	Jim Norden	1995	5,699
143 0/8	25 2/8	25 0/8	18 5/8	5	4	Dakota County	MN	Edwin J. Schneider	1995	5,699
143 0/8	26 1/8	26 1/8	16 4/8	5	5	Wayne County	KY	Adrian Bell	1995	5,699
143 0/8	25 3/8	25 4/8	20 6/8	5	4	Morris County	NJ	Dr. Dennis M. Noonan	1996	5,699
143 0/8	24 6/8	24 7/8	19 5/8	5	5	Trempealeau County	WI	Gary Kupka	1996	5,699
143 0/8	24 3/8	24 3/8	20 2/8	5	5	Athens County	OH	Curtis R. Rutter	1996	5,699
143 0/8	20 6/8	21 4/8	16 6/8	6	6	Tazewell County	IL	Matthew J. Wells	1996	5,699
143 0/8	26 0/8	24 5/8	20 0/8	4	4	Dodge County	WI	Earl Zimmerman	1997	5,699
143 0/8	24 5/8	25 5/8	20 5/8	4	5	Gasconade County	MO	Arvel L. Schneider	1997	5,699
143 0/8	24 3/8	24 2/8	20 6/8	4	4	Tompkins County	NY	Raymond G. Woods	1997	5,699
143 0/8	26 6/8	26 4/8	21 4/8	6	6	Gloucester County	NJ	Richard W. Etschman	1997	5,699
143 0/8	24 4/8	26 7/8	22 1/8	5	4	McPherson County	KS	Jay Bullinger	1997	5,699
143 0/8	24 6/8	22 2/8	18 6/8	5	5	Oconto County	WI	James F. Belongia	1997	5,699
142 7/8	20 4/8	20 6/8	16 3/8	5	5	Brown County	SD	Wayne Miller	1971	5,769
142 7/8	21 3/8	21 7/8	16 1/8	6	5	Becker County	MN	Kurt Lepping	1972	5,769
142 7/8	21 1/8	22 4/8	16 1/8	5	5	Jackson County	WI	Clark Gallup	1972	5,769
142 7/8	24 1/8	24 2/8	20 1/8	4	5	Douglas County	NE	Walter Ruff, Jr.	1973	5,769

WHITETAIL DEER (TYPICAL ANTLERS)

Minimum Score 125   Continued

SCORE	LENGTH OF R MAIN BEAM L		INSIDE SPREAD	NUMBER OF R POINTS L		AREA	STATE/ PROVINCE	HUNTER'S NAME	DATE	RANK
142 7/8	26 2/8	25 6/8	22 7/8	4	4	Carroll County	IL	Donald Lauer	1978	5,769
142 7/8	21 0/8	23 5/8	19 6/8	6	5	Teton County	MT	Richard C. Semrad	1979	5,769
142 7/8	22 2/8	21 5/8	13 7/8	4	4	St. Louis County	MN	Dan Tanner	1979	5,769
142 7/8	22 7/8	23 0/8	17 1/8	5	6	Redwood County	MN	Kenneth A. Gilb	1980	5,769
142 7/8	22 0/8	23 2/8	18 1/8	4	5	Warren County	IA	Charly Stills	1980	5,769
142 7/8	25 2/8	25 2/8	18 3/8	5	6	Freeborn County	MN	Kermit Askland	1982	5,769
142 7/8	21 2/8	21 2/8	16 7/8	5	5	Richland County	MT	Dave McGough	1983	5,769
142 7/8	21 0/8	20 4/8	18 0/8	5	6	Jefferson County	NE	Bob Funke	1983	5,769
142 7/8	22 3/8	23 1/8	17 7/8	5	4	Shelby County	IL	David Russell	1983	5,769
142 7/8	22 3/8	22 0/8	18 7/8	5	5	Winneshiek County	IA	Gary Baumler	1984	5,769
142 7/8	23 6/8	23 1/8	16 3/8	5	5	Webster County	IA	Edward E. Ulicki	1984	5,769
142 7/8	24 4/8	25 5/8	21 1/8	4	4	Will County	IL	Terry Marcukaitis	1984	5,769
142 7/8	24 4/8	24 5/8	20 1/8	5	5	Marshall County	KS	Steve Johnson	1984	5,769
142 7/8	24 5/8	24 6/8	20 3/8	6	4	Lafayette County	WI	Larry Rose	1985	5,769
142 7/8	25 0/8	26 1/8	15 5/8	4	5	Clark County	IN	Steve Bower	1986	5,769
142 7/8	25 5/8	26 6/8	19 2/8	6	5	Florence County	WI	Dale T. Nixon	1988	5,769
142 7/8	22 3/8	24 1/8	19 2/8	7	9	Murray County	OK	Charles R. Sanford	1988	5,769
142 7/8	24 0/8	24 0/8	17 7/8	6	6	Cass County	MI	Randall Smith	1988	5,769
142 7/8	23 4/8	23 2/8	15 1/8	4	4	Atascosa County	TX	Gene Lasseter	1989	5,769
142 7/8	23 6/8	23 2/8	20 1/8	4	5	Jo Daviess County	IL	James F. Delaney	1989	5,769
142 7/8	23 1/8	24 3/8	17 3/8	5	6	Hardin County	OH	Mark Preston	1989	5,769
142 7/8	26 7/8	24 3/8	21 2/8	7	5	White County	IL	Peter P. Fiala	1990	5,769
142 7/8	22 3/8	22 4/8	16 5/8	5	5	Cedar County	NE	Cathy M. Tramp	1990	5,769
142 7/8	23 6/8	24 5/8	18 1/8	5	4	Crawford County	KS	Shawn Pipkin	1991	5,769
142 7/8	25 2/8	24 5/8	20 3/8	5	5	Holmes County	OH	Charles Larue	1991	5,769
142 7/8	24 1/8	23 1/8	17 5/8	8	5	Adams County	IL	Steve Cornwell	1991	5,769
142 7/8	24 3/8	24 3/8	18 2/8	7	6	Green County	WI	Steve J. Gobeli	1992	5,769
142 7/8	21 3/8	22 0/8	16 4/8	6	5	Hennepin County	MN	Michael Mulcare	1992	5,769
142 7/8	24 4/8	25 4/8	18 1/8	5	5	Zavala County	TX	Joseph D. Krout, III	1992	5,769
142 7/8	25 1/8	26 2/8	19 3/8	4	6	East Carroll Parish	LA	George R. Bryant	1993	5,769
142 7/8	21 1/8	21 5/8	17 0/8	6	6	Bryan County	OK	Randy Cheshier	1993	5,769
142 7/8	21 5/8	22 1/8	15 3/8	5	7	Fayette County	WV	Thomas Stevens	1993	5,769
142 7/8	21 7/8	22 5/8	15 7/8	5	5	Marquette County	WI	Jay A. Severson	1994	5,769
142 7/8	22 6/8	24 7/8	22 2/8	8	8	Stearns County	MN	David Kloeppner	1994	5,769
142 7/8	24 0/8	23 3/8	18 3/8	5	5	Jo Daviess County	IL	Bob Bruss	1994	5,769
142 7/8	24 4/8	24 4/8	21 0/8	5	5	Warren County	IL	Rodney Retherford	1995	5,769
142 7/8	23 4/8	23 6/8	17 3/8	5	5	Des Moines County	IA	Craig A. Owens	1995	5,769
142 7/8	23 7/8	24 1/8	16 7/8	5	5	Schuyler County	IL	John Johnston	1995	5,769
142 7/8	24 6/8	24 3/8	15 7/8	5	4	Caldwell County	KY	Keith Westfall	1995	5,769
142 7/8	20 7/8	20 7/8	17 2/8	5	6	Mower County	MN	Ben Williams	1995	5,769
142 7/8	23 5/8	23 1/8	17 7/8	5	5	Trempealeau County	WI	Mike Engen	1996	5,769
142 7/8	24 6/8	25 5/8	20 7/8	5	4	Elgin	ONT	Mike Renaud	1996	5,769
142 7/8	22 4/8	21 5/8	21 1/8	6	6	Mitchell County	IA	Michael D. Rehnelt	1996	5,769
142 7/8	22 7/8	23 1/8	20 7/8	5	5	Worcester County	MA	Ronald Rosenlund	1996	5,769
142 7/8	23 1/8	23 0/8	17 1/8	5	4	Pike County	IL	Merlyn Winchell	1996	5,769
142 7/8	24 4/8	24 0/8	20 1/8	4	4	Rockingham County	NH	Richard Bourdelais	1996	5,769
142 7/8	21 6/8	21 7/8	14 7/8	5	5	Buffalo County	WI	Lynn Moeller	1996	5,769
142 7/8	23 4/8	23 5/8	16 5/8	5	5	Richland County	WI	Craig Fairbert	1997	5,769
142 7/8	21 2/8	21 3/8	16 6/8	5	6	Hand County	SD	Kevin Bertsch	1997	5,769
142 7/8	24 6/8	24 4/8	19 3/8	5	5	Pawnee County	KS	Jason Reece	1997	5,769
142 7/8	24 6/8	25 7/8	22 5/8	5	4	Chester County	PA	Jim Connor	1998	5,769
142 6/8	23 5/8	23 0/8	19 5/8	4	5	Green Lake County	WI	Mark Novitske	1969	5,824
142 6/8	22 2/8	21 7/8	18 7/8	6	4	Douglas County	MN	David Koenen	1973	5,824
142 6/8	25 3/8	25 4/8	16 6/8	4	4	Darke County	OH	Wayne Goubeaux	1974	5,824
142 6/8	25 6/8	25 7/8	16 6/8	4	4	Prairie County	AR	John W. Hogue	1978	5,824
142 6/8	21 3/8	21 3/8	18 6/8	5	6	Empress	ALB	Alan R. Francis	1980	5,824
142 6/8	22 4/8	21 1/8	19 4/8	4	4	De Kalb County	MO	Mark Garr	1982	5,824
142 6/8	25 3/8	25 5/8	19 0/8	7	5	Wallowa County	OR	Marte Scheuffele	1983	5,824
142 6/8	23 6/8	24 0/8	19 5/8	6	5	Jefferson County	WI	Jed Kottwitz	1983	5,824
142 6/8	24 2/8	23 7/8	19 2/8	6	5	Madison County	AL	Rocky Drake	1983	5,824
142 6/8	22 3/8	23 1/8	17 6/8	5	4	Clay County	KS	Larry Reed	1984	5,824
142 6/8	21 7/8	22 5/8	15 4/8	5	6	Lycoming County	PA	Kelly J. Cooper	1985	5,824
142 6/8	14 4/8	22 0/8	17 4/8	6	6	Waukesha County	WI	John Riehle	1985	5,824
142 6/8	22 0/8	22 1/8	17 2/8	5	5	Hamilton County	KS	Scott Showalter	1985	5,824
142 6/8	22 1/8	21 6/8	16 0/8	5	6	Cherokee County	TX	John Hall	1986	5,824
142 6/8	22 3/8	22 4/8	18 2/8	7	7	Lincoln County	MT	David R. Erickson	1987	5,824
142 6/8	23 5/8	23 3/8	15 4/8	6	6	Clayton County	IA	Scott W. Miller	1988	5,824
142 6/8	24 6/8	26 1/8	24 4/8	5	5	Oneida County	WI	Joseph Kwaterski	1988	5,824
142 6/8	20 5/8	21 0/8	16 4/8	6	5	Dodge County	NE	Mike Diers	1988	5,824
142 6/8	21 5/8	22 5/8	19 0/8	5	5	Woodford County	IL	Sid Schertz	1988	5,824
142 6/8	20 0/8	21 0/8	18 1/8	5	6	New Castle County	DE	Earl McSorley	1988	5,824
142 6/8	24 3/8	23 5/8	16 6/8	4	4	Saunders County	NE	Richard Cherovsky	1989	5,824
142 6/8	22 3/8	22 5/8	15 0/8	8	7	Cherokee County	OK	Monte Reid	1989	5,824
142 6/8	22 1/8	22 7/8	18 4/8	7	7	Price County	WI	Tom G. Verkilen	1989	5,824
142 6/8	23 5/8	23 5/8	16 6/8	5	5	Hancock County	IL	William T. Kirby	1989	5,824
142 6/8	21 3/8	22 0/8	20 6/8	7	9	Linn County	IA	Craig Cutts	1989	5,824
142 6/8	23 0/8	24 1/8	15 0/8	6	5	Tom Green County	TX	Ronnie Parsons	1990	5,824
142 6/8	23 2/8	24 3/8	15 4/8	5	5	Allegheny County	PA	David C. Williams	1990	5,824

WHITETAIL DEER (TYPICAL ANTLERS)

Minimum Score 125   Continued

SCORE	LENGTH OF R MAIN BEAM L		INSIDE SPREAD	NUMBER OF R POINTS L		AREA	STATE/ PROVINCE	HUNTER'S NAME	DATE	RANK
142 6/8	24 1/8	23 6/8	16 2/8	5	5	Eau Claire County	WI	Riley Allen Fletschock	1990	5,824
142 6/8	23 4/8	24 5/8	19 2/8	5	5	Effingham County	IL	Roger Loy	1990	5,824
142 6/8	23 1/8	23 2/8	18 6/8	6	5	Warren County	OH	Bruce Woods	1991	5,824
142 6/8	23 3/8	23 5/8	20 4/8	5	5	Outagamie County	WI	Joe P. DeBruin	1991	5,824
142 6/8	23 6/8	23 0/8	18 0/8	4	6	McLean County	IL	Eric B. Hill	1991	5,824
142 6/8	22 6/8	22 2/8	17 4/8	5	5	Cavan Township	ONT	Mark J. Dymond	1991	5,824
142 6/8	21 4/8	22 1/8	16 7/8	6	8	Ravalli County	MT	Melvin Harold Monson	1992	5,824
142 6/8	24 3/8	24 7/8	19 6/8	4	5	Saunders County	NE	William D. Meyers	1992	5,824
142 6/8	23 6/8	21 7/8	19 2/8	5	6	McLeod River	ALB	Shayne Wadlow	1992	5,824
142 6/8	22 6/8	22 4/8	16 0/8	5	5	McCulloch County	TX	Cecil Carder	1992	5,824
142 6/8	23 3/8	23 3/8	18 2/8	5	5	Licking County	OH	Orin Noyes	1992	5,824
142 6/8	22 2/8	23 1/8	16 4/8	5	5	La Crosse County	WI	Barry Christenson	1993	5,824
142 6/8	23 2/8	23 6/8	19 2/8	5	5	Darke County	OH	Dale L. Detro	1993	5,824
142 6/8	23 0/8	23 6/8	18 2/8	4	5	Green County	WI	Doug Cupp	1993	5,824
142 6/8	21 1/8	23 5/8	17 2/8	5	5	New Castle County	DE	Bruce Pyle	1993	5,824
142 6/8	24 4/8	25 5/8	17 6/8	4	6	St. Louis County	MO	Scott Leuthauser	1994	5,824
142 6/8	25 1/8	25 6/8	22 2/8	4	4	Bucks County	PA	William A. Car	1994	5,824
142 6/8	21 4/8	21 3/8	17 4/8	5	5	Franklin County	KS	Steven M. Hale	1994	5,824
142 6/8	22 5/8	22 5/8	18 6/8	4	4	McHenry County	IL	Kenneth A. Spence	1994	5,824
142 6/8	21 0/8	22 2/8	14 2/8	5	6	Portage County	WI	John Lane	1995	5,824
142 6/8	15 4/8	27 6/8	20 2/8	7	7	Marion County	IA	James D. Pendroy	1995	5,824
142 6/8	25 2/8	25 4/8	16 6/8	6	5	Franklin County	PA	Phares B. Witmer III	1995	5,824
142 6/8	22 0/8	21 6/8	16 2/8	5	5	Polk County	IA	Nick Hildreth	1995	5,824
142 6/8	22 1/8	22 1/8	17 4/8	5	5	Alexander County	IL	Brian Bard	1995	5,824
142 6/8	22 5/8	22 5/8	17 7/8	6	6	Waukesha County	WI	Richard M. Wasielewski	1995	5,824
142 6/8	24 1/8	23 3/8	20 2/8	5	4	Adair County	MO	Tom Drury	1996	5,824
142 6/8	22 1/8	22 6/8	16 7/8	4	6	Stephenson County	IL	Calvin B. Hanson	1996	5,824
142 6/8	27 1/8	26 3/8	23 5/8	5	5	Vinton County	OH	John Oberschlake	1996	5,824
142 6/8	24 5/8	25 2/8	16 2/8	5	5	Fairfax County	VA	Bobby J. Gray	1996	5,824
142 6/8	24 2/8	25 4/8	19 4/8	5	4	Jackson County	WI	Kenneth A. Olson	1996	5,824
142 6/8	23 7/8	23 7/8	17 7/8	7	7	Brown County	IL	Ricky Bishop	1996	5,824
142 6/8	24 0/8	22 4/8	15 2/8	5	5	Washington County	WI	David E. Witte	1996	5,824
142 6/8	23 1/8	22 6/8	15 6/8	6	5	Columbia County	WI	Eric R. De Venecia	1997	5,824
142 6/8	23 7/8	24 2/8	17 4/8	5	5	Ashtabula County	OH	Michael A. Candela	1997	5,824
142 6/8	25 6/8	24 4/8	18 6/8	6	5	Johnson County	IA	Jeff Jensen	1997	5,824
142 6/8	23 3/8	22 5/8	20 1/8	5	5	Appanoose County	IA	Ralph Lane, Jr.	1997	5,824
142 6/8	25 4/8	25 2/8	19 0/8	3	4	Howard County	MD	Mike Dunsmore	1998	5,824
142 6/8	26 6/8	26 0/8	23 6/8	5	4	Lucas County	OH	Michael S. Pasztor	1998	5,824
142 5/8	24 2/8	22 7/8	15 5/8	5	5	Fleming County	KY	Dewey Miller	1976	5,889
142 5/8	22 2/8	22 3/8	18 5/8	5	5	Richland County	OH	Joey A. Garcia	1980	5,889
142 5/8	22 0/8	22 2/8	16 7/8	5	5	Chase County	KS	Lanny Deering	1981	5,889
142 5/8	25 6/8	25 4/8	16 4/8	4	6	Darke County	OH	Norbert D. Schlecty	1981	5,889
142 5/8	22 5/8	22 2/8	18 1/8	6	6	Waukesha County	WI	Mike Edlebeck	1982	5,889
142 5/8	24 7/8	24 1/8	18 1/8	5	5	Dane County	WI	Dean Stolen	1982	5,889
142 5/8	24 0/8	24 2/8	20 3/8	5	5	Cochrane	ALB	Kenneth Bills	1982	5,889
142 5/8	20 1/8	20 6/8	16 4/8	6	5	Simpson County	KY	Murrell Ray Knight	1984	5,889
142 5/8	21 4/8	22 3/8	15 7/8	7	5	Pepin County	WI	James D. Williams	1984	5,889
142 5/8	22 6/8	22 5/8	20 3/8	5	4	Berkshire County	MA	Richard Scorzafava	1985	5,889
142 5/8	23 6/8	23 0/8	16 7/8	6	7	Stafford County	KS	Larry Hamby	1986	5,889
142 5/8	24 0/8	24 0/8	20 0/8	6	5	Page County	IA	Chris Barton	1987	5,889
142 5/8	22 5/8	23 6/8	16 3/8	6	8	Kossuth County	IA	Roger M. Batt	1987	5,889
142 5/8	25 1/8	24 1/8	18 5/8	4	4	Westchester County	NY	Kenneth Martin	1987	5,889
142 5/8	21 5/8	22 0/8	15 1/8	5	5	Will County	IL	Thomas J. Suggs	1987	5,889
142 5/8	22 3/8	23 0/8	17 0/8	7	6	Fairfield County	OH	Dean J. Kiourtsis	1988	5,889
142 5/8	23 1/8	20 4/8	18 7/8	5	5	Kalamazoo County	MI	Vern Kuipers	1988	5,889
142 5/8	25 4/8	25 3/8	17 7/8	4	4	Jackson County	IL	Dan Young	1988	5,889
142 5/8	25 3/8	24 5/8	19 1/8	5	5	Chickasaw County	IA	T. J. Colburn	1989	5,889
142 5/8	26 6/8	26 4/8	20 5/8	4	3	Scotland County	MO	John Emerson	1989	5,889
142 5/8	23 1/8	23 4/8	18 5/8	4	4	Parkland County	ALB	Sam Halabi	1990	5,889
142 5/8	26 7/8	26 2/8	17 6/8	8	7	Martin County	KY	James W. Howard	1990	5,889
142 5/8	23 6/8	23 3/8	19 0/8	5	5	Clark County	IL	Kenneth G. Geibel	1990	5,889
142 5/8	22 0/8	23 0/8	16 0/8	6	5	Buffalo County	WI	Eric Matheson	1990	5,889
142 5/8	22 6/8	22 4/8	16 7/8	6	7	Will County	IL	Joseph E. Voltolina	1990	5,889
142 5/8	24 0/8	25 2/8	18 7/8	5	6	St. Joesph County	IN	Mike Ritter	1991	5,889
142 5/8	23 3/8	23 1/8	18 0/8	6	5	Vilas County	WI	Phil Dreger	1991	5,889
142 5/8	23 5/8	24 5/8	18 0/8	6	5	Mission Creek	BC	Colin L. Fazan	1991	5,889
142 5/8	26 3/8	26 1/8	18 7/8	5	5	Louisa County	IA	Jeff Sindt	1991	5,889
142 5/8	24 1/8	27 1/8	19 2/8	6	5	Cumberland County	IL	Lonnie Finks	1992	5,889
142 5/8	22 4/8	23 1/8	16 1/8	5	5	Traill County	ND	Don Kluck	1992	5,889
142 5/8	25 1/8	25 5/8	20 4/8	5	5	Pike County	OH	Lynn A. Henry	1992	5,889
142 5/8	24 1/8	24 7/8	20 1/8	6	6	Allegheny County	PA	Paul W. Zoller	1993	5,889
142 5/8	24 6/8	24 5/8	22 7/8	4	4	Sauk County	WI	Tim Trebilcox	1993	5,889
142 5/8	22 5/8	22 3/8	16 7/8	5	5	La Crosse County	WI	James Pike	1993	5,889
142 5/8	23 5/8	23 5/8	16 7/8	4	4	Goshen County	WY	Eddie Claypool	1993	5,889
142 5/8	24 4/8	24 1/8	16 1/8	5	5	New Castle County	DE	Jeff Flanagan	1993	5,889
142 5/8	22 4/8	21 6/8	18 6/8	6	5	Ross County	OH	Charles A. Hawkins	1994	5,889
142 5/8	20 5/8	21 1/8	17 2/8	6	6	Clay County	IN	Doug Myers	1994	5,889
142 5/8	24 0/8	23 3/8	17 6/8	7	6	Spokane County	WA	Mike Ambach	1994	5,889

WHITETAIL DEER (TYPICAL ANTLERS)

Minimum Score 125 — Continued

SCORE	LENGTH OF MAIN BEAM R	LENGTH OF MAIN BEAM L	INSIDE SPREAD	NUMBER OF POINTS R	NUMBER OF POINTS L	AREA	STATE/PROVINCE	HUNTER'S NAME	DATE	RANK
142 5/8	21 4/8	21 6/8	16 5/8	5	5	Pittsburg County	OK	Rick Pingleton	1995	5,889
142 5/8	25 3/8	24 5/8	18 6/8	5	5	Bayfield County	WI	Gene Huettl	1995	5,889
142 5/8	23 3/8	23 2/8	15 7/8	5	4	Nemaha County	KS	David Shumaker	1995	5,889
142 5/8	23 4/8	22 0/8	19 5/8	5	5	Suffolk County	NY	John J. Gattuso	1995	5,889
142 5/8	22 4/8	21 1/8	19 1/8	4	4	Worcester County	MA	Brian Archambeault	1995	5,889
142 5/8	24 6/8	27 3/8	19 7/8	5	5	Jo Daviess County	IL	Jerry J. Smith	1995	5,889
142 5/8	23 6/8	23 6/8	18 3/8	5	5	Shelby County	IL	Stephan Tripp	1996	5,889
142 5/8	22 1/8	22 5/8	18 5/8	5	5	Montgomery County	AL	Price Bishop	1996	5,889
142 5/8	25 5/8	24 6/8	19 5/8	6	6	Allegheny County	PA	Dale Fleck	1996	5,889
142 5/8	23 1/8	24 0/8	18 7/8	5	5	Jackson County	MI	Roger A. Dodt	1997	5,889
142 5/8	24 4/8	23 4/8	18 3/8	4	5	Pike County	IL	Michael Mitale	1997	5,889
142 5/8	25 2/8	24 4/8	16 3/8	4	4	Jackson County	MO	Jonathan McGinness	1997	5,889
142 5/8	24 2/8	23 6/8	16 6/8	4	5	Appanoose County	IA	Bill Breeding	1997	5,889
142 5/8	23 7/8	23 1/8	20 3/8	7	5	Hughes County	OK	Will F. Tobey	1997	5,889
142 5/8	22 5/8	23 5/8	18 1/8	4	4	Winneshiek County	IA	Dean Miller	1997	5,889
142 4/8	22 5/8	22 4/8	19 0/8	5	5	Newton County	IN	Jim Manes	1963	5,944
142 4/8	23 3/8	23 4/8	18 4/8	4	5	Winnebago County	IA	Duane Peterson	1966	5,944
142 4/8	22 0/8	21 1/8	14 6/8	6	6	Dunn County	WI	John J. Logan	1970	5,944
142 4/8	24 7/8	24 0/8	19 6/8	4	4	Ballard County	KY	Archie Jacobs	1977	5,944
142 4/8	24 7/8	24 3/8	19 3/8	6	5	Jackson County	IL	Mark A. Bollman	1979	5,944
142 4/8	23 3/8	22 6/8	17 0/8	5	5	Musselshell County	MT	Larry W. Ostermiller	1979	5,944
142 4/8	21 0/8	21 5/8	18 4/8	6	5	Jo Daviess County	IL	Kelly John Arnold	1981	5,944
142 4/8	24 2/8	24 3/8	20 6/8	5	5	Robertson County	KY	Glen Arnold	1981	5,944
142 4/8	23 5/8	24 1/8	15 6/8	5	5	Treasure County	MT	Scott Brockway	1981	5,944
142 4/8	21 0/8	20 6/8	16 3/8	5	6	Winona County	MN	Ron J. Parks	1981	5,944
142 4/8	22 5/8	23 2/8	20 1/8	5	6	Murray County	MN	David Swanson	1983	5,944
142 4/8	22 0/8	22 2/8	14 6/8	5	5	McKenzie County	ND	David Tofte	1983	5,944
142 4/8	23 7/8	23 6/8	18 2/8	4	4	Bon Homme County	SD	Leon Somsen	1984	5,944
142 4/8	20 4/8	20 4/8	16 0/8	5	5	McLean County	ND	Curt Radke	1985	5,944
142 4/8	22 6/8	24 4/8	19 3/8	4	5	Lyon County	KS	Frank Mowdey	1986	5,944
142 4/8	24 7/8	25 0/8	19 3/8	5	5	Vilas County	WI	David Jablonski	1987	5,944
142 4/8	24 2/8	23 5/8	19 2/8	4	5	Jo Daviess County	IL	Brian Spillane	1988	5,944
142 4/8	20 4/8	20 3/8	16 6/8	5	5	Camrose	ALB	Dave Gerber	1988	5,944
142 4/8	25 4/8	25 6/8	17 5/8	5	5	Gallia County	OH	Alan Runyon	1988	5,944
142 4/8	23 0/8	24 6/8	18 3/8	6	6	Kingman County	KS	Ed Laverentz	1988	5,944
142 4/8	25 0/8	25 2/8	18 5/8	6	7	Bowman County	ND	Stan Chiras	1988	5,944
142 4/8	24 0/8	24 2/8	20 4/8	5	7	Shawnee County	KS	Randy Hildreth	1989	5,944
142 4/8	22 5/8	23 1/8	17 0/8	4	4	Crawford County	IL	Jim Sexton	1989	5,944
142 4/8	22 4/8	21 4/8	17 0/8	4	6	Dakota County	MN	Joseph Butler	1989	5,944
142 4/8	21 1/8	20 5/8	14 5/8	5	6	Hardin County	KY	Eugene Cotton	1990	5,944
142 4/8	23 7/8	23 0/8	17 4/8	5	5	Vilas County	WI	Dick Mutsch	1990	5,944
142 4/8	22 0/8	21 6/8	17 5/8	6	6	Adams County	WI	Mark Hoffman	1990	5,944
142 4/8	22 6/8	23 7/8	18 0/8	4	4	De Kalb County	GA	Michael Flowers	1990	5,944
142 4/8	24 3/8	24 5/8	18 6/8	5	5	Lincoln County	MO	Greg Grooms	1990	5,944
142 4/8	21 2/8	22 6/8	16 6/8	6	5	Wilkin County	MN	Brad Buth	1991	5,944
142 4/8	21 5/8	22 5/8	16 0/8	5	5	Mason County	IL	Jeff Heilman	1991	5,944
142 4/8	25 0/8	26 0/8	20 6/8	4	5	Charlevoix County	MI	Thomas B. Bacon	1991	5,944
142 4/8	23 2/8	21 6/8	16 4/8	5	5	Des Moines County	IA	Tom Lingenfelter	1991	5,944
142 4/8	21 0/8	21 4/8	17 5/8	5	5	Shawnee County	KS	Daniel L. Amspacker	1991	5,944
142 4/8	21 0/8	21 1/8	16 6/8	5	5	McHenry County	IL	Richard Tudor	1992	5,944
142 4/8	25 0/8	24 0/8	19 4/8	4	4	Harrison County	MO	Scott Shoemate	1993	5,944
142 4/8	24 6/8	24 2/8	14 5/8	6	6	Monroe County	MO	Todd Martens	1993	5,944
142 4/8	23 3/8	22 0/8	14 4/8	5	5	Logan County	CO	Pete Lauer	1993	5,944
142 4/8	22 6/8	22 7/8	15 6/8	5	5	Cottonwood County	MN	Jeff Radtke	1993	5,944
142 4/8	21 2/8	22 2/8	16 2/8	5	5	Will County	IL	Jack Haviland	1994	5,944
142 4/8	21 5/8	20 7/8	17 0/8	5	5	Polk County	WI	Kevin Jones	1994	5,944
142 4/8	21 6/8	21 6/8	16 4/8	5	5	Rockland County	NY	Scott Sahlstrom	1994	5,944
142 4/8	22 0/8	22 0/8	19 4/8	5	5	Passaic County	NJ	Erich Reuter	1995	5,944
142 4/8	25 2/8	23 2/8	18 6/8	4	6	Fremont County	IA	Richard Delanty	1995	5,944
142 4/8	21 5/8	21 1/8	16 2/8	5	5	Hand County	SD	Craig E. "Curly" Hargens	1995	5,944
142 4/8	21 6/8	22 4/8	17 6/8	5	5	Lee County	IA	Robert Lane	1995	5,944
142 4/8	23 4/8	23 5/8	16 6/8	5	5	Montgomery County	MS	Tony Arnold	1995	5,944
142 4/8	23 6/8	23 6/8	16 4/8	7	6	Ross County	OH	Paggie Peters	1996	5,944
142 4/8	23 6/8	23 7/8	18 2/8	4	4	Coffee County	GA	Scott Miller	1996	5,944
142 4/8	22 5/8	22 5/8	16 3/8	7	6	Gallia County	OH	Robert E. Lee	1996	5,944
142 4/8	21 2/8	21 2/8	18 0/8	6	6	Winneshiek County	IA	Duane C. Baumler	1996	5,944
142 4/8	23 5/8	24 3/8	17 4/8	4	4	Peoria County	IL	Stan Parkerson	1996	5,944
142 4/8	25 1/8	25 6/8	21 6/8	5	4	Buffalo County	WI	Tony Heil	1996	5,944
142 4/8	23 6/8	24 4/8	20 3/8	5	5	Dimmit County	TX	Chuck Adams	1997	5,944
142 4/8	24 3/8	24 6/8	17 6/8	5	5	Jackson County	MO	George Dusselier	1997	5,944
142 4/8	23 6/8	24 5/8	22 1/8	6	6	Bucks County	PA	Richard Franklin	1997	5,944
142 4/8	26 4/8	27 0/8	20 4/8	4	4	Cowley County	KS	Loy D. Peters	1997	5,944
142 4/8	21 4/8	21 5/8	18 0/8	5	5	Logan County	NE	James B. Meador	1997	5,944
142 4/8	21 7/8	22 1/8	16 4/8	6	6	Wayne County	MI	Dennis A. Schramm	1997	5,944
142 4/8	22 2/8	22 1/8	17 0/8	4	4	Prince Georges County	MD	Donald A. Molnar, Jr.	1997	5,944
142 4/8	22 4/8	24 4/8	18 3/8	5	4	Scott County	IA	John Sailor	1997	5,944
142 3/8	25 4/8	24 3/8	20 7/8	4	5	Mercer County	NJ	John K. Deveney	1975	6,005
142 3/8	21 5/8	21 5/8	15 1/8	5	5	Wapello County	IA	Larry Terrell	1977	6,005

WHITETAIL DEER (TYPICAL ANTLERS)

Minimum Score 125

SCORE	LENGTH OF MAIN BEAM R	LENGTH OF MAIN BEAM L	INSIDE SPREAD	NUMBER OF POINTS R	NUMBER OF POINTS L	AREA	STATE/PROVINCE	HUNTER'S NAME	DATE	RANK
142 3/8	23 4/8	22 4/8	18 1/8	5	5	Jersey County	IL	Jerry Cover	1979	6,005
142 3/8	22 0/8	21 6/8	16 7/8	5	4	Henry County	VA	Mike Weaver	1980	6,005
142 3/8	21 1/8	24 4/8	20 4/8	6	6	St. Charles County	MO	Edward J. Davidson	1980	6,005
142 3/8	22 5/8	22 0/8	18 1/8	5	5	Washtenaw County	MI	Philip John Maly	1983	6,005
142 3/8	21 4/8	22 5/8	17 5/8	6	7	Barton County	KS	Craig Doll	1984	6,005
142 3/8	20 6/8	21 0/8	17 5/8	5	5	Hardin County	TX	Mike Allen	1985	6,005
142 3/8	24 2/8	26 5/8	16 1/8	4	4	Wright County	MN	Donald J. Emons	1985	6,005
142 3/8	20 0/8	19 5/8	19 3/8	5	5	Shelby County	MO	Willard Otto	1985	6,005
142 3/8	24 6/8	23 5/8	19 1/8	4	4	Bremer County	IA	Dave Sullivan	1986	6,005
142 3/8	22 2/8	22 4/8	16 1/8	7	5	Wilson County	KS	Keith Jabben	1986	6,005
142 3/8	25 5/8	26 4/8	19 7/8	4	4	Benton County	IA	Ted Walton	1986	6,005
142 3/8	23 2/8	24 5/8	17 1/8	5	6	Muhlenberg County	KY	Kent Rhoads	1987	6,005
142 3/8	24 3/8	24 6/8	17 3/8	4	4	Kent County	MI	Frank J. Tusch	1987	6,005
142 3/8	22 6/8	25 2/8	15 6/8	5	6	Cumberland County	KY	Michael Groce	1987	6,005
142 3/8	20 4/8	20 3/8	17 0/8	6	6	Kenedy County	TX	Cal Adger	1988	6,005
142 3/8	22 4/8	22 4/8	17 3/8	5	5	St. Charles County	MO	Marty Marler	1988	6,005
142 3/8	23 0/8	24 2/8	16 5/8	5	6	Iron County	WI	Robert Peltonen	1988	6,005
142 3/8	23 2/8	23 2/8	17 2/8	8	6	Peoria County	IL	Larry Oppe	1988	6,005
142 3/8	22 6/8	24 6/8	18 2/8	6	6	Fairfield County	CT	Mitchell R. Ziemba	1988	6,005
142 3/8	23 3/8	23 2/8	16 1/8	4	4	Meade County	SD	Frank E. Virchow	1989	6,005
142 3/8	21 6/8	21 5/8	16 3/8	8	6	Osage County	KS	Mike VandeVord	1989	6,005
142 3/8	24 4/8	25 1/8	18 3/8	5	5	Knox County	IL	Brad Wunder	1990	6,005
142 3/8	22 5/8	23 2/8	16 3/8	5	5	Henderson County	TN	Pat Davis	1990	6,005
142 3/8	21 4/8	22 3/8	19 1/8	4	5	Monona County	IA	Patrick Salmen	1990	6,005
142 3/8	23 2/8	23 5/8	13 2/8	7	9	Allegheny County	PA	Paul W. Zoller	1991	6,005
142 3/8	24 5/8	24 4/8	16 6/8	7	7	De Witt County	IL	Jack Bray	1991	6,005
142 3/8	25 5/8	25 5/8	19 7/8	4	4	Hampshire County	MA	Eric Jalque	1991	6,005
142 3/8	22 4/8	22 7/8	16 7/8	4	5	Comal County	TX	Jim Butcher	1991	6,005
142 3/8	25 0/8	25 7/8	14 6/8	5	5	Cumberland County	NJ	Bob Eisele	1992	6,005
142 3/8	22 2/8	21 4/8	15 5/8	6	6	Kenosha County	WI	John R. Griffin	1992	6,005
142 3/8	23 6/8	24 2/8	15 2/8	5	6	Fulton County	IL	Tim Wells	1993	6,005
142 3/8	22 1/8	22 0/8	16 7/8	6	5	Lincoln County	NE	Dave Hinton	1993	6,005
142 3/8	24 3/8	25 2/8	21 6/8	6	8	Wilkin County	MN	Dave Balken	1993	6,005
142 3/8	23 1/8	23 3/8	17 3/8	3	4	Yuma County	CO	Alan White	1993	6,005
142 3/8	23 2/8	23 2/8	18 7/8	5	5	McHenry County	IL	Norton Baum	1993	6,005
142 3/8	20 7/8	21 3/8	16 2/8	6	6	Fayette County	WV	Bryan Berry	1993	6,005
142 3/8	27 5/8	27 1/8	20 1/8	9	6	Guernsey County	OH	D. Keith Kinney	1994	6,005
142 3/8	22 7/8	22 2/8	14 7/8	7	6	Marion County	MO	John Boskovich	1994	6,005
142 3/8	21 4/8	21 7/8	17 1/8	5	5	La Salle County	IL	Brian G. Dobberke	1994	6,005
142 3/8	21 4/8	22 6/8	18 5/8	5	5	Jackson County	MO	Jeff Estes	1994	6,005
142 3/8	24 5/8	24 0/8	22 3/8	4	5	Hillsborough County	NH	Bill Helstein	1994	6,005
142 3/8	23 6/8	25 3/8	18 3/8	4	4	Logan County	WV	Tom Green	1994	6,005
142 3/8	24 2/8	24 2/8	18 1/8	5	5	Stark County	IL	Gary Krause	1995	6,005
142 3/8	21 1/8	22 4/8	20 5/8	6	6	Osage County	OK	Donnie Gabbard	1995	6,005
142 3/8	22 4/8	22 6/8	16 3/8	5	5	Cayuga County	NY	Terry Van Wie	1995	6,005
142 3/8	23 6/8	24 0/8	18 6/8	4	5	Tazewell County	IL	Andy Payne	1996	6,005
142 3/8	23 1/8	24 1/8	18 5/8	5	5	Warren County	IA	Mike Schaefer	1996	6,005
142 3/8	22 3/8	23 0/8	20 5/8	5	5	McHenry County	IL	Donald R. Hanrahan	1996	6,005
142 3/8	25 3/8	25 1/8	20 3/8	5	4	Clark County	WI	Curt D. Zielke	1996	6,005
142 3/8	23 3/8	24 6/8	16 5/8	4	4	Marion County	IN	Dan Esterline	1996	6,005
142 3/8	22 0/8	21 6/8	17 3/8	4	5	McHenry County	IL	Brent A. Smith	1996	6,005
142 3/8	22 4/8	23 0/8	18 7/8	6	5	Buffalo County	WI	Bradley H. Goulet	1997	6,005
142 3/8	24 0/8	22 7/8	22 5/8	5	7	Spiritwood	SAS	Lizette Lohan	1997	6,005
142 3/8	22 4/8	22 3/8	16 3/8	5	5	Burnett County	WI	Michael G. Washburn	1997	6,005
142 3/8	24 4/8	25 2/8	18 2/8	6	6	Putnam County	MO	John Freihaut	1997	6,005
142 3/8	21 3/8	20 5/8	18 4/8	6	6	Allegheny County	PA	Charles LaBernz	1997	6,005
142 2/8	23 3/8	24 0/8	20 0/8	4	5	McLean County	ND	Robert Loftin	1959	6,063
142 2/8	23 2/8	22 6/8	17 6/8	5	6	Grant County	WI	Bob Woods	1962	6,063
142 2/8	21 1/8	22 2/8	18 1/8	6	4	Morrison County	MN	Dale Nieters	1971	6,063
142 2/8	21 2/8	21 1/8	17 1/8	6	5	Sabine County	TX	Norman D. Davis	1972	6,063
142 2/8	27 3/8	28 5/8	19 6/8	4	5	Harrison County	OH	Joe Cola	1976	6,063
142 2/8	24 3/8	23 7/8	19 6/8	4	4	Gallatin County	KY	Thomas W. Roberts	1976	6,063
142 2/8	24 1/8	24 1/8	17 0/8	6	5	Le Sueur County	MN	Gene Solyntjes	1976	6,063
142 2/8	22 4/8	23 6/8	19 0/8	7	5	Jones County	IA	Donald Bohlken	1978	6,063
142 2/8	21 7/8	21 0/8	17 0/8	6	6	Dodge County	MN	Myles Keller	1980	6,063
142 2/8	21 1/8	20 3/8	18 2/8	5	5	Edgar County	IL	Rory Steidl	1983	6,063
142 2/8	24 7/8	24 3/8	21 4/8	5	5	Jackson County	MI	Russell P. Blair	1983	6,063
142 2/8	22 7/8	24 5/8	18 0/8	5	5	Buffalo County	WI	Patrick Myers	1985	6,063
142 2/8	23 5/8	26 1/8	18 3/8	5	6	Eau Claire County	WI	Kenneth A. Sweeny	1985	6,063
142 2/8	21 4/8	22 0/8	18 4/8	5	5	Lake County	IL	Robert K. Lapacek	1986	6,063
142 2/8	22 5/8	22 2/8	17 2/8	5	5	Crawford County	IL	Robert L. Harvey	1987	6,063
142 2/8	24 0/8	25 0/8	17 2/8	6	4	Licking County	OH	Robert H. Wise	1987	6,063
142 2/8	22 6/8	23 3/8	16 1/8	7	6	Roberts County	SD	Myles Keller	1988	6,063
142 2/8	22 2/8	22 4/8	16 4/8	5	5	Cherokee County	IA	Brad Husman	1988	6,063
142 2/8	25 2/8	23 2/8	18 2/8	6	6	Jackson County	WI	Glen R. Loppnow	1989	6,063
142 2/8	20 7/8	20 7/8	15 4/8	5	5	Miller County	MO	John Patterson	1989	6,063
142 2/8	25 7/8	24 6/8	19 2/8	4	5	Dunn County	WI	Michael E. Suckow	1989	6,063
142 2/8	25 3/8	26 5/8	18 3/8	5	5	Hamilton County	IA	Larry Haren	1989	6,063

WHITETAIL DEER (TYPICAL ANTLERS)

Minimum Score 125 — Continued

SCORE	LENGTH OF MAIN BEAM R	LENGTH OF MAIN BEAM L	INSIDE SPREAD	NUMBER OF POINTS R	NUMBER OF POINTS L	AREA	STATE/PROVINCE	HUNTER'S NAME	DATE	RANK
142 2/8	25 0/8	23 3/8	17 4/8	6	4	Leavenworth County	KS	Jacob W. Dragieff	1989	6,063
142 2/8	24 4/8	25 1/8	19 2/8	5	5	Madison County	OH	Timothy A. Chenoweth	1990	6,063
142 2/8	22 3/8	23 4/8	16 4/8	5	5	Wetzel County	WV	Paul Pichardo	1990	6,063
142 2/8	23 5/8	24 1/8	16 4/8	4	4	Ashland County	WI	Lawrence D. Wollock	1990	6,063
142 2/8	25 2/8	25 6/8	22 6/8	5	5	Burlington County	NJ	Frank R. Buckman	1990	6,063
142 2/8	25 2/8	25 2/8	19 6/8	4	4	Clayton County	IA	Richard A. Preston	1990	6,063
142 2/8	25 5/8	26 3/8	21 2/8	4	4	Livingston County	IL	Tom Roe	1991	6,063
142 2/8	21 0/8	22 1/8	16 4/8	5	5	Cross County	AR	Wilburn Holt	1992	6,063
142 2/8	24 3/8	23 0/8	15 6/8	4	5	Towner County	ND	Troy Peterson	1992	6,063
142 2/8	24 4/8	23 4/8	15 3/8	5	6	Cecil County	MD	Michael L. Boyle	1992	6,063
142 2/8	20 4/8	22 2/8	19 0/8	5	4	Knox County	IL	Troy D. Huffman	1992	6,063
142 2/8	24 2/8	24 2/8	18 0/8	5	6	Pierce County	WI	Steve Borton	1992	6,063
142 2/8	24 2/8	23 5/8	19 5/8	5	6	Cass County	ND	Shane Kautzman	1993	6,063
142 2/8	21 0/8	21 3/8	16 2/8	5	5	Wood County	WI	Tom Krutzik	1993	6,063
142 2/8	22 7/8	22 5/8	15 4/8	6	6	Marathon County	WI	Shawn G. Stubbe	1993	6,063
142 2/8	22 4/8	21 5/8	19 2/8	5	5	Fairfield County	CT	Stephen T. Shay	1993	6,063
142 2/8	24 5/8	24 0/8	22 0/8	5	5	Mason County	MI	Brian Petersen	1994	6,063
142 2/8	24 7/8	25 4/8	19 6/8	6	5	Warren County	IA	James M. Engle	1994	6,063
142 2/8	23 1/8	22 0/8	17 4/8	4	4	Ross County	OH	Ben Fout	1994	6,063
142 2/8	23 4/8	23 4/8	18 5/8	5	6	Worcester County	MA	Russell Gray	1994	6,063
142 2/8	23 4/8	25 0/8	19 4/8	4	4	Hardin County	OH	Ray Davis	1994	6,063
142 2/8	27 2/8	26 1/8	19 3/8	4	5	Perry County	OH	Thomas E. Kunkler	1994	6,063
142 2/8	26 2/8	27 2/8	21 0/8	5	4	Jefferson County	IA	Chris E. Dodds	1994	6,063
142 2/8	22 7/8	22 0/8	16 6/8	5	5	Uvalde County	TX	Todd Alexander	1995	6,063
142 2/8	24 5/8	26 3/8	17 4/8	6	4	Montgomery County	AL	Zane Caudill	1995	6,063
142 2/8	24 1/8	24 0/8	16 2/8	4	4	Barron County	WI	Dwight Stuart	1995	6,063
142 2/8	24 2/8	23 7/8	19 4/8	4	4	Baltimore County	MD	Robert Coffman	1995	6,063
142 2/8	23 7/8	24 3/8	20 2/8	5	4	Milwaukee County	WI	Jeff Gricar	1996	6,063
142 2/8	21 0/8	20 5/8	15 6/8	5	5	Montgomery County	TN	Brandan Ty Motsinger	1996	6,063
142 2/8	23 4/8	21 5/8	18 4/8	5	7	Monmouth County	NJ	Lido D. Panfili	1996	6,063
142 2/8	24 4/8	22 3/8	18 6/8	5	4	Perry County	OH	Butch Samson	1996	6,063
142 2/8	21 4/8	21 4/8	18 0/8	5	5	Washington County	MN	Scott R. Nelson	1996	6,063
142 2/8	22 4/8	23 0/8	16 2/8	5	7	Winneshiek County	IA	Paul Styve	1997	6,063
142 2/8	22 0/8	21 7/8	20 2/8	4	4	Butler County	KS	Kent Wartick	1997	6,063
142 2/8	23 6/8	22 2/8	14 6/8	6	5	Hand County	SD	Jason D. Resel	1997	6,063
142 2/8	25 4/8	25 4/8	21 0/8	5	4	Tazewell County	IL	Richard Frederick	1997	6,063
142 2/8	21 5/8	21 7/8	16 0/8	5	5	Osage County	KS	Walter S. Church IV	1997	6,063
142 2/8	22 3/8	23 5/8	16 2/8	5	5	Randolph County	IL	Rob Boyd	1997	6,063
142 2/8	23 6/8	23 6/8	23 0/8	5	5	Harper County	KS	Frederick Koehn	1997	6,063
142 2/8	24 0/8	23 4/8	19 2/8	4	4	Concordia Parish	LA	Bill Dondero	1997	6,063
142 2/8	22 1/8	22 5/8	19 2/8	5	4	Maverick County	TX	Dennis J. Marbach	1997	6,063
142 2/8	22 4/8	22 2/8	13 6/8	6	5	Upton County	TX	Dean Titsworth	1997	6,063
142 2/8	23 2/8	23 2/8	17 6/8	4	6	Jackson County	WI	Leo J. George	1998	6,063
142 1/8	23 1/8	22 7/8	18 6/8	5	5	Huron County	OH	Thomas Sheldon	1956	6,128
142 1/8	23 6/8	23 1/8	15 3/8	6	6	Morgan County	GA	Jerry Wall	1966	6,128
142 1/8	25 1/8	25 2/8	20 3/8	6	6	Faribault County	MN	Timothy Anderson	1970	6,128
142 1/8	24 2/8	25 7/8	22 1/8	5	4	Pope County	AR	Danny L. Mathis	1971	6,128
142 1/8	24 2/8	24 0/8	18 3/8	6	5	Buffalo County	WI	Myles Keller	1973	6,128
142 1/8	23 7/8	23 7/8	17 5/8	5	5	Port Perry	ONT	Ken Steele	1979	6,128
142 1/8	23 4/8	23 4/8	16 7/8	4	4	Ripley County	IN	Dick Gambrel	1981	6,128
142 1/8	22 7/8	22 2/8	16 3/8	5	5	McPherson County	KS	James Willems	1981	6,128
142 1/8	22 1/8	21 6/8	14 5/8	5	5	Charles County	MD	John L. Penny	1982	6,128
142 1/8	20 1/8	20 5/8	13 7/8	5	5	Juneau County	WI	Dennis Dreischmeier	1982	6,128
142 1/8	24 6/8	25 3/8	18 1/8	4	4	Lawrence County	OH	Carl G. Coburn	1982	6,128
142 1/8	26 0/8	25 0/8	22 1/8	6	6	Medina County	OH	Bruce Hamilton	1983	6,128
142 1/8	21 2/8	21 4/8	16 5/8	6	6	Washington County	MD	David M. Kumsher	1985	6,128
142 1/8	25 0/8	24 2/8	18 3/8	6	7	Ohio County	IN	Ernest Frady	1985	6,128
142 1/8	20 2/8	20 7/8	17 0/8	6	5	Trego County	KS	William R. Whitworth	1985	6,128
142 1/8	25 0/8	24 6/8	17 7/8	4	4	Logan County	CO	Kent Sump	1985	6,128
142 1/8	24 4/8	25 2/8	19 1/8	4	5	Waushara County	WI	Lester W. Lant, Jr.	1986	6,128
142 1/8	23 3/8	22 3/8	18 5/8	4	5	Somerset County	NJ	John Maddaluna	1986	6,128
142 1/8	22 3/8	22 1/8	17 5/8	5	5	Pope County	AR	Todd Fountain	1987	6,128
142 1/8	24 0/8	24 3/8	16 2/8	5	6	Winnebago County	IA	Jerry Reynolds	1987	6,128
142 1/8	25 0/8	24 5/8	19 1/8	5	5	Rock County	WI	Gary Schiefelbein	1987	6,128
142 1/8	24 6/8	25 4/8	19 5/8	5	5	Jackson County	KS	Dayton R. Wright	1987	6,128
142 1/8	26 3/8	26 1/8	19 1/8	4	4	Charles County	MD	Douglas M. Garcia	1988	6,128
142 1/8	21 6/8	22 2/8	17 5/8	5	5	Noble County	IN	Frank M. McDonald	1989	6,128
142 1/8	25 7/8	25 5/8	22 7/8	7	6	Dubuque County	IA	Ken Treanor	1989	6,128
142 1/8	22 1/8	23 0/8	17 5/8	7	5	Saline County	MO	Jerry Underwood	1989	6,128
142 1/8	23 3/8	24 5/8	16 4/8	5	6	Logan County	IL	Donald D. Stiner	1989	6,128
142 1/8	23 2/8	23 6/8	17 7/8	5	5	Langlade County	WI	Robert A. Winkler	1990	6,128
142 1/8	25 3/8	24 5/8	20 7/8	4	4	Renville County	MN	Tom Neubauer	1990	6,128
142 1/8	23 4/8	24 1/8	17 3/8	5	5	Cass County	MO	Mike R. Wheeler	1990	6,128
142 1/8	25 4/8	23 3/8	17 1/8	4	4	Crawford County	IL	Steve L. Hobbs	1990	6,128
142 1/8	19 3/8	19 6/8	18 7/8	5	5	Weld County	CO	Dave Culter	1990	6,128
142 1/8	22 3/8	21 7/8	18 3/8	5	5	Winneshiek County	IA	Lonnie Tiedt	1990	6,128
142 1/8	24 0/8	22 6/8	17 3/8	5	6	Bucks County	PA	Michael J. Mullin	1991	6,128
142 1/8	21 1/8	21 5/8	18 7/8	5	5	Kendall County	IL	John D. Rogers II	1991	6,128

WHITETAIL DEER (TYPICAL ANTLERS)

Minimum Score 125 — Continued

SCORE	LENGTH OF MAIN BEAM R	LENGTH OF MAIN BEAM L	INSIDE SPREAD	NUMBER OF POINTS R	NUMBER OF POINTS L	AREA	STATE/PROVINCE	HUNTER'S NAME	DATE	RANK
142 1/8	24 4/8	24 1/8	16 7/8	5	5	Lawrence County	OH	Jerry L. Scythes	1991	6,128
142 1/8	23 0/8	22 3/8	16 7/8	5	5	Chariton County	MO	Dennis Meyers	1991	6,128
142 1/8	22 0/8	22 0/8	17 3/8	6	5	Crawford County	IL	Jim Liffick	1991	6,128
142 1/8	22 2/8	22 4/8	20 3/8	4	5	La Salle County	IL	Robert L. McAtee	1992	6,128
142 1/8	24 0/8	23 6/8	18 7/8	5	5	Buffalo County	WI	Michael J. Barstad	1993	6,128
142 1/8	23 5/8	22 5/8	14 0/8	6	5	Richland County	IL	Troy A. Hinderliter	1993	6,128
142 1/8	22 2/8	21 5/8	17 7/8	5	5	Forest County	WI	Randy R. Lepak	1993	6,128
142 1/8	20 2/8	20 2/8	19 7/8	6	7	Montcalm County	MI	Christopher Fedewa	1993	6,128
142 1/8	22 4/8	21 5/8	16 5/8	7	7	Okanogan County	WA	Fred Zissel	1994	6,128
142 1/8	24 1/8	22 5/8	16 4/8	6	5	Laclede County	MO	Gary Lemery	1994	6,128
142 1/8	25 0/8	23 4/8	15 5/8	5	5	Cedar County	MO	Mark A. Frieze	1994	6,128
142 1/8	23 5/8	24 0/8	19 5/8	6	5	Weld County	CO	Tim Mangina	1994	6,128
142 1/8	22 3/8	24 1/8	18 5/8	5	6	Worth County	IA	Mark Johnson	1994	6,128
142 1/8	24 1/8	23 4/8	19 1/8	6	5	Jefferson County	WI	Jack Findlay	1994	6,128
142 1/8	20 0/8	21 1/8	15 3/8	5	5	Chautauqua County	KS	John C. Ford	1994	6,128
142 1/8	21 5/8	24 4/8	15 5/8	5	5	Cass County	MI	Calvin Percy	1994	6,128
142 1/8	24 1/8	23 5/8	15 7/8	5	7	Waupaca County	WI	Merlin Reinke	1995	6,128
142 1/8	21 5/8	22 2/8	15 7/8	5	5	Hopkins County	KY	Greg Belk	1995	6,128
142 1/8	23 5/8	23 3/8	15 5/8	5	5	Franklin County	MO	Dennis Ross	1995	6,128
142 1/8	24 0/8	23 6/8	17 1/8	6	7	St. Louis County	MO	Robert O. Werges	1995	6,128
142 1/8	23 3/8	23 3/8	17 3/8	5	5	Delaware County	OH	Jeff Daily	1995	6,128
142 1/8	23 7/8	24 0/8	19 5/8	4	5	Charles Mix County	SD	Larry Hansum	1995	6,128
142 1/8	23 7/8	23 0/8	18 5/8	5	5	Webster County	KY	Robert Tatro, Jr.	1996	6,128
142 1/8	22 1/8	22 4/8	15 7/8	5	5	Seneca County	OH	Tom Weimerskirch	1996	6,128
142 1/8	26 2/8	24 3/8	19 7/8	4	4	Trempealeau County	WI	John Sobczak	1997	6,128
142 1/8	23 0/8	24 4/8	17 2/8	5	5	Pierce County	WI	Perry Goetsch	1997	6,128
142 1/8	21 5/8	20 5/8	18 3/8	6	5	Henry County	IA	Tracy C. Krebsbach	1997	6,128
142 1/8	21 3/8	20 6/8	16 7/8	5	5	Comanche County	OK	William Early Wilkins	1997	6,128
142 1/8	22 3/8	22 4/8	16 3/8	5	5	Douglas County	WI	Jeffrey N. Breitzmann	1997	6,128
142 1/8	23 1/8	24 7/8	23 3/8	8	5	Ogle County	IL	Danny Nichols	1997	6,128
142 0/8	22 4/8	23 0/8	17 2/8	6	5	Logan County	IL	Irwin L. Miller	1976	6,193
142 0/8	24 1/8	24 1/8	17 6/8	5	6	Winona County	MN	Clayton Bentson	1977	6,193
142 0/8	24 0/8	23 7/8	15 5/8	5	6	Bayfield County	WI	James J. Messerschmidt	1979	6,193
142 0/8	24 5/8	24 4/8	18 6/8	4	4	Woodford County	IL	Byron L. Davenport	1980	6,193
142 0/8	20 7/8	19 5/8	18 2/8	5	5	Shelby County	IL	Richard W. Neumann	1982	6,193
142 0/8	23 4/8	21 6/8	19 6/8	5	7	Union County	IL	Randy Cronk	1983	6,193
142 0/8	27 0/8	27 0/8	20 0/8	4	4	Ravalli County	MT	Harry Potton	1983	6,193
142 0/8	22 2/8	22 5/8	18 5/8	5	7	Will County	IL	Joseph R. Pergram	1983	6,193
142 0/8	21 5/8	20 5/8	17 6/8	5	5	Dubuque County	IA	Joe Lieb	1984	6,193
142 0/8	23 1/8	23 3/8	16 6/8	5	5	Dane County	WI	Joseph A. Radecki	1984	6,193
142 0/8	20 6/8	20 6/8	17 0/8	5	5	Shawnee County	KS	Eldon Johnson	1985	6,193
142 0/8	24 5/8	24 4/8	15 2/8	5	5	Morrison County	MN	Stan Spychalla	1986	6,193
142 0/8	22 6/8	23 2/8	16 0/8	5	5	Fergus County	MT	Mike Sweeney	1986	6,193
142 0/8	21 3/8	21 0/8	15 6/8	5	5	Burnett County	WI	Doug Anderson	1987	6,193
142 0/8	21 6/8	23 3/8	16 4/8	5	5	La Salle County	IL	William Weygand	1988	6,193
142 0/8	22 0/8	22 5/8	16 4/8	5	5	Buffalo County	WI	Jeff Wendorf	1988	6,193
142 0/8	23 0/8	22 7/8	16 6/8	5	5	Creek County	OK	Larry V Fears	1988	6,193
142 0/8	21 6/8	22 3/8	17 4/8	6	5	Pierce County	WI	Robert Barrie	1989	6,193
142 0/8	25 0/8	24 2/8	16 4/8	4	5	St. Croix County	WI	Keith Andrea	1990	6,193
142 0/8	23 0/8	23 6/8	19 0/8	4	4	Putnam County	WV	Forrest R. Woodard	1990	6,193
142 0/8	24 4/8	24 6/8	18 1/8	5	5	Suffolk County	NY	John Jeff Pfeifer	1990	6,193
142 0/8	21 0/8	20 6/8	18 0/8	5	5	Cooper County	MO	Fred Storozyszyn	1990	6,193
142 0/8	22 4/8	22 5/8	17 2/8	5	7	Winona County	MN	Dennis Marg	1991	6,193
142 0/8	23 3/8	24 0/8	18 6/8	5	5	Madison County	KY	Gary W. Langford	1991	6,193
142 0/8	24 5/8	23 4/8	20 0/8	6	5	Henderson County	KY	Lawrence F. Smithhart	1991	6,193
142 0/8	22 1/8	21 7/8	17 2/8	6	5	Poweshiek County	IA	Kevin Kudart	1991	6,193
142 0/8	24 2/8	24 3/8	17 0/8	7	6	Cook County	MN	Bruce Zimpel	1991	6,193
142 0/8	22 6/8	21 3/8	19 2/8	5	5	Sharkey County	MS	Kirby Deer, Jr.	1992	6,193
142 0/8	23 5/8	23 6/8	21 0/8	4	4	Chester County	PA	William J. Combs, Jr.	1992	6,193
142 0/8	24 7/8	24 6/8	19 0/8	8	6	Jefferson County	WI	Mike Leslie	1992	6,193
142 0/8	24 3/8	21 5/8	22 1/8	5	6	Summit County	OH	Tim E. Gall	1992	6,193
142 0/8	22 6/8	23 3/8	19 6/8	5	5	Adams County	IL	Timothy D. Walmsley	1992	6,193
142 0/8	20 2/8	20 6/8	14 2/8	5	5	McKenzie County	ND	Shawn A. Koosman	1993	6,193
142 0/8	23 7/8	23 5/8	19 4/8	4	5	Jo Daviess County	IL	Ronald R. Gawlik	1993	6,193
142 0/8	24 2/8	22 6/8	18 4/8	5	5	Hennepin County	MN	Greg A. Maciej	1993	6,193
142 0/8	22 3/8	21 6/8	18 6/8	5	5	Ottawa County	MI	Kurtis C. Boeve	1994	6,193
142 0/8	25 6/8	26 3/8	18 0/8	5	5	Orange County	NC	Derek J. Green	1994	6,193
142 0/8	22 7/8	23 0/8	17 0/8	5	5	Buffalo County	WI	Robert J. Seckora	1994	6,193
142 0/8	24 4/8	24 2/8	17 6/8	4	4	Polk County	WI	Dave Miller	1994	6,193
142 0/8	24 5/8	23 2/8	19 0/8	5	5	Shawnee County	KS	James Creviston II	1994	6,193
142 0/8	24 4/8	23 5/8	17 1/8	5	6	Anoka County	MN	Stanley Grygelko	1994	6,193
142 0/8	25 5/8	25 2/8	17 4/8	4	4	Cuyahoga County	OH	Kenneth D. Walter	1994	6,193
142 0/8	21 4/8	21 1/8	15 4/8	5	5	Spink County	SD	Randy Schultz	1994	6,193
142 0/8	25 1/8	24 6/8	17 4/8	4	4	St. Clair County	MI	James Glombowski	1995	6,193
142 0/8	22 6/8	22 4/8	17 0/8	5	5	Lapeer County	MI	Russell Martin	1995	6,193
142 0/8	23 6/8	25 3/8	19 7/8	5	6	Will County	IL	Nathan A. Teske	1995	6,193
142 0/8	23 4/8	22 6/8	17 2/8	5	5	Jackson County	MI	Richard Quentin Walker	1995	6,193
142 0/8	23 4/8	22 4/8	17 4/8	5	5	Buffalo County	WI	Bob Kostecki	1995	6,193

WHITETAIL DEER (TYPICAL ANTLERS)

Minimum Score 125 — Continued

SCORE	LENGTH OF MAIN BEAM R	LENGTH OF MAIN BEAM L	INSIDE SPREAD	NUMBER OF POINTS R	NUMBER OF POINTS L	AREA	STATE/PROVINCE	HUNTER'S NAME	DATE	RANK
142 0/8	22 4/8	19 6/8	19 6/8	5	5	New Haven County	CT	Jason Cuda	1995	6,193
142 0/8	24 0/8	24 2/8	18 4/8	4	4	Baltimore County	MD	Jack Schatz	1995	6,193
142 0/8	24 3/8	23 4/8	17 6/8	5	5	Marion County	KS	Dennis N. Ballweg	1995	6,193
142 0/8	22 4/8	23 0/8	18 0/8	5	5	Marshall County	IN	Jeff A. Ellinger	1995	6,193
142 0/8	23 6/8	23 3/8	16 5/8	7	9	Douglas County	KS	Mark Young	1995	6,193
142 0/8	23 3/8	22 0/8	16 4/8	5	5	Oakland County	MI	Gary Allen	1996	6,193
142 0/8	24 6/8	24 6/8	15 0/8	5	5	Coles County	IL	Bob Weber	1996	6,193
142 0/8	25 0/8	24 5/8	17 6/8	4	4	Marion County	IA	Merle Schulz	1996	6,193
142 0/8	23 4/8	23 1/8	17 2/8	5	4	Clarke County	IA	Don Mealey	1996	6,193
142 0/8	21 5/8	21 3/8	15 4/8	5	5	E. Carroll Parish	LA	Robert Songin	1996	6,193
142 0/8	25 0/8	25 0/8	20 3/8	6	6	Walworth County	WI	Mike Brady	1997	6,193
142 0/8	22 2/8	22 6/8	17 4/8	5	5	Gwinnett County	GA	Jeff Crowell	1997	6,193
142 0/8	24 5/8	23 2/8	18 6/8	5	5	Hardin County	OH	Lori Podhorsky	1997	6,193
142 0/8	22 7/8	22 3/8	16 7/8	6	5	Belmont County	OH	Rick Dufford	1997	6,193
142 0/8	24 4/8	24 7/8	18 2/8	6	6	Macoupin County	IL	Kevin Fones	1997	6,193
142 0/8	23 1/8	22 6/8	18 4/8	5	5	Benton County	IA	Kevin Nolan	1997	6,193
142 0/8	24 3/8	24 5/8	17 4/8	5	5	Westchester County	NY	Carl Colasacco	1997	6,193
141 7/8	24 2/8	24 5/8	23 3/8	4	6	Jackson County	IA	Thomas L. Berkley	1959	6,258
141 7/8	23 0/8	22 0/8	20 1/8	5	4	Pottawattamie County	IA	Gary A. Green	1968	6,258
141 7/8	20 0/8	19 6/8	15 7/8	5	5	Lincoln County	SD	Kai R. Anderson	1972	6,258
141 7/8	23 6/8	22 1/8	17 1/8	5	5	Stony Plain	ALB	Barry A. Olsen	1979	6,258
141 7/8	26 0/8	26 2/8	20 5/8	4	4	Hocking County	OH	Paul T. Sater	1979	6,258
141 7/8	23 7/8	23 3/8	17 3/8	5	5	Pine County	MN	Jack Pichotta	1980	6,258
141 7/8	25 5/8	26 2/8	18 3/8	4	4	Shelby County	OH	Kenneth E. Huffman	1982	6,258
141 7/8	26 2/8	26 3/8	21 0/8	5	6	Coshocton County	OH	Mike Stumph	1983	6,258
141 7/8	21 2/8	20 6/8	18 3/8	5	5	Dunn County	WI	Bruce Olson	1983	6,258
141 7/8	25 1/8	24 7/8	20 5/8	5	5	Kent County	ONT	John McGuigan	1984	6,258
141 7/8	25 7/8	24 4/8	19 5/8	4	4	Muskingum County	OH	Rick A. Goodin	1984	6,258
141 7/8	23 6/8	23 6/8	17 3/8	4	5	Camden County	MO	Steve West	1985	6,258
141 7/8	24 7/8	24 4/8	16 1/8	5	5	Anderson County	SC	J. Alan Wilson, Jr.	1985	6,258
141 7/8	25 3/8	24 6/8	20 0/8	5	5	Seneca County	NY	Dominic D'Amico	1985	6,258
141 7/8	22 6/8	21 1/8	18 3/8	5	5	Richland County	WI	Jerry L. Gander	1986	6,258
141 7/8	24 1/8	23 3/8	14 3/8	5	4	Waushara County	WI	Douglas F. Kornel	1987	6,258
141 7/8	24 6/8	25 2/8	21 3/8	5	8	Carroll County	IL	Art Heinze	1987	6,258
141 7/8	23 5/8	22 2/8	19 6/8	5	4	Kane County	IL	Carl S. Diesel	1987	6,258
141 7/8	20 6/8	21 7/8	17 5/8	6	6	Hunterdon County	NJ	Bob Petner	1987	6,258
141 7/8	23 6/8	25 0/8	22 5/8	4	5	Suffolk County	NY	Dennis Marinuzzi	1987	6,258
141 7/8	23 7/8	23 5/8	15 7/8	5	5	Kane County	IL	Bruce R. Cummins	1988	6,258
141 7/8	19 7/8	19 2/8	15 6/8	5	6	Burleigh County	ND	Gordon Smith	1988	6,258
141 7/8	21 4/8	21 4/8	18 7/8	5	5	Kittson County	MN	James B Frederick	1989	6,258
141 7/8	23 0/8	23 7/8	17 2/8	5	6	Calhoun County	MI	Edward A. Conkell	1989	6,258
141 7/8	24 2/8	22 7/8	18 3/8	4	4	Fulton County	IL	Tim Wells	1990	6,258
141 7/8	24 2/8	24 6/8	22 3/8	4	4	Somerset County	NJ	Bob Santiago	1990	6,258
141 7/8	21 7/8	22 1/8	17 3/8	5	5	Schuyler County	IL	John Johnston	1990	6,258
141 7/8	23 3/8	24 1/8	22 3/8	4	5	Crawford County	WI	Ivan Heisz	1991	6,258
141 7/8	24 4/8	25 1/8	19 3/8	5	6	Allegheny County	PA	Michael Barberich	1991	6,258
141 7/8	24 2/8	23 6/8	18 7/8	4	5	Massac County	IL	David T. Harris	1991	6,258
141 7/8	24 0/8	24 0/8	18 5/8	4	4	Webster County	IA	Edward E. Ulicki	1991	6,258
141 7/8	26 1/8	26 1/8	18 1/8	4	4	Marion County	OH	Sam M. Derugen	1991	6,258
141 7/8	26 5/8	26 5/8	17 5/8	4	4	Hamilton County	TX	David Parrish	1992	6,258
141 7/8	23 2/8	23 3/8	19 0/8	7	6	Douglas County	WI	Charles A. Wright	1992	6,258
141 7/8	22 4/8	23 6/8	16 1/8	4	4	Burleigh County	ND	Mike Sahli	1992	6,258
141 7/8	21 2/8	21 3/8	18 1/8	5	5	St. Charles County	MO	Mark Gutermuth	1992	6,258
141 7/8	23 0/8	23 1/8	19 1/8	4	4	Dawson County	NE	Jim McConathy, Jr.	1993	6,258
141 7/8	25 1/8	25 5/8	16 0/8	5	5	Scott County	MN	Mike Genty	1993	6,258
141 7/8	25 5/8	25 1/8	18 1/8	5	4	Montgomery County	MD	Mark A. Coletta	1993	6,258
141 7/8	23 3/8	23 6/8	19 1/8	6	6	Dunn County	WI	James W. Suckow	1994	6,258
141 7/8	23 6/8	23 4/8	17 4/8	4	4	Madison County	MO	Junior Shy	1994	6,258
141 7/8	21 5/8	21 5/8	23 0/8	4	4	Fremont County	IA	Curtis L. Athen	1995	6,258
141 7/8	28 6/8	28 0/8	20 1/8	5	4	La Salle County	IL	David Both	1995	6,258
141 7/8	23 3/8	22 3/8	19 3/8	7	5	Allegheny County	PA	Scott E. Walters	1995	6,258
141 7/8	24 7/8	24 7/8	15 7/8	5	5	Vinton County	OH	Robert J. Smith	1995	6,258
141 7/8	26 4/8	23 2/8	19 3/8	5	7	La Salle County	IL	Donald Greathouse	1995	6,258
141 7/8	24 2/8	24 2/8	17 4/8	5	6	Logan County	WV	Roger D. Maynard	1995	6,258
141 7/8	21 1/8	21 0/8	20 4/8	5	6	Talbot County	MD	J. Matthew Getsinger	1995	6,258
141 7/8	21 5/8	20 6/8	17 5/8	5	6	Carroll County	KY	Tim Dermon	1996	6,258
141 7/8	23 2/8	23 0/8	16 3/8	5	5	Becker County	MN	Joe Skarie	1996	6,258
141 7/8	26 3/8	27 4/8	23 3/8	4	4	Fairfax County	VA	Jack B. Yeager	1996	6,258
141 7/8	20 5/8	20 5/8	17 5/8	5	6	Des Moines County	IA	Gary Grassi	1996	6,258
141 7/8	22 4/8	23 2/8	18 5/8	5	5	Clayton County	IA	Wayne Salow	1996	6,258
141 7/8	21 7/8	23 0/8	16 7/8	5	4	Shackelford County	TX	Randy Rifenburgh	1997	6,258
141 7/8	22 5/8	22 5/8	17 7/8	5	5	Cass County	MI	Fred Kruger	1997	6,258
141 7/8	25 4/8	25 5/8	15 5/8	4	4	Monroe County	WI	Mark Jacobson	1997	6,258
141 7/8	24 6/8	25 2/8	22 4/8	6	5	E. Carroll Parish	LA	Randy Duncan	1997	6,258
141 7/8	23 4/8	23 4/8	17 5/8	5	5	Dimmit County	TX	Rodney E. Bellett	1997	6,258
141 6/8	24 3/8	24 2/8	20 0/8	4	4	Morrison County	MN	Rodney W. Olson	1958	6,316
141 6/8	21 6/8	22 2/8	15 2/8	5	5	Eau Claire County	WI	Gordy Robinson	1962	6,316
141 6/8	23 6/8	23 7/8	17 4/8	5	4	Dodge County	MN	Cy Champa	1969	6,316

WHITETAIL DEER (TYPICAL ANTLERS)

Minimum Score 125   Continued

SCORE	LENGTH OF MAIN BEAM R / L	INSIDE SPREAD	NUMBER OF POINTS R / L		AREA	STATE/PROVINCE	HUNTER'S NAME	DATE	RANK
141 6/8	23 6/8	24 4/8	24 0/8	4	4	Newton County	IN	Denny Raper	1980	6,316
141 6/8	26 2/8	25 2/8	22 6/8	4	4	Johnson County	NE	Ronald G. Filip	1981	6,316
141 6/8	20 5/8	22 6/8	17 2/8	5	5	Alpena County	MI	Michael E. Kaiser	1981	6,316
141 6/8	24 7/8	24 2/8	20 2/8	4	4	Todd County	MN	Ted Pilgrim	1981	6,316
141 6/8	24 4/8	23 2/8	17 2/8	5	6	Pittsburg County	OK	Richard H. Gill	1984	6,316
141 6/8	21 4/8	21 4/8	17 2/8	5	7	Hughes County	SD	Kent D. Keenlyne	1984	6,316
141 6/8	21 4/8	21 2/8	16 1/8	5	6	Lyon County	MN	Randy S Van Overbeke	1985	6,316
141 6/8	24 1/8	24 3/8	19 2/8	5	5	Strathcona	ALB	Jack Kempf	1985	6,316
141 6/8	20 6/8	21 2/8	16 4/8	5	5	Jefferson County	WI	Mike Leslie	1986	6,316
141 6/8	21 7/8	22 1/8	16 2/8	6	5	Audrain County	MO	Darrell Miller	1986	6,316
141 6/8	25 5/8	25 7/8	18 5/8	7	5	Meigs County	OH	James J. Vitale, Jr.	1987	6,316
141 6/8	23 1/8	23 7/8	17 1/8	6	6	Mower County	MN	Jeffrey L. Boucher	1987	6,316
141 6/8	25 2/8	25 1/8	18 2/8	4	4	Chisago County	MN	Patrick Smith	1988	6,316
141 6/8	23 1/8	23 5/8	19 4/8	5	6	Lee County	IL	Tim Robinson	1988	6,316
141 6/8	22 7/8	21 1/8	18 0/8	5	5	Highland County	OH	Roger O. Wyant	1988	6,316
141 6/8	25 0/8	25 0/8	16 5/8	4	5	York	ONT	Dave Barnacal	1989	6,316
141 6/8	22 3/8	22 3/8	15 4/8	5	5	Caldwell County	MO	Michael C. Burr	1989	6,316
141 6/8	23 3/8	23 1/8	19 2/8	6	5	Will County	IL	Ronald R. Henson	1990	6,316
141 6/8	23 1/8	23 1/8	17 2/8	4	4	Brazos County	TX	John Dury	1990	6,316
141 6/8	27 4/8	26 3/8	18 3/8	5	8	Ross County	OH	Don Rawn	1990	6,316
141 6/8	22 2/8	22 6/8	16 0/8	5	5	Clay County	MO	John Godfrey	1991	6,316
141 6/8	22 6/8	23 0/8	19 2/8	5	5	Columbia County	WI	Richard A. Prescott	1991	6,316
141 6/8	21 7/8	21 5/8	17 0/8	5	5	New Castle County	DE	Earl McSorley	1991	6,316
141 6/8	22 0/8	22 1/8	15 1/8	7	6	Oneida County	WI	David J. Hoppe	1991	6,316
141 6/8	23 5/8	22 3/8	17 0/8	4	4	Mercer County	IL	Charles L. Winston	1991	6,316
141 6/8	21 2/8	22 0/8	16 0/8	6	6	Buffalo County	WI	James K. Kraft	1992	6,316
141 6/8	24 1/8	25 5/8	20 1/8	6	8	Berrien County	MI	David Kennedy	1992	6,316
141 6/8	25 5/8	25 4/8	17 3/8	5	6	Lawrence County	OH	Brian Massie	1992	6,316
141 6/8	23 4/8	24 1/8	14 4/8	8	6	Oneida County	WI	Jeff A. Fehrenbach	1992	6,316
141 6/8	23 1/8	22 3/8	19 0/8	4	5	La Salle County	IL	James D. Lockhart	1992	6,316
141 6/8	24 7/8	24 7/8	19 6/8	4	4	Chase County	KS	Ron Smith	1992	6,316
141 6/8	21 3/8	21 4/8	16 6/8	5	5	Edmonson County	KY	Vernon Decker	1993	6,316
141 6/8	21 5/8	21 5/8	16 3/8	6	5	Hennepin County	MN	Richard Williams	1993	6,316
141 6/8	20 5/8	20 0/8	15 4/8	7	5	Hubbard County	MN	Bob Ness	1993	6,316
141 6/8	21 7/8	23 2/8	16 6/8	4	4	Butler County	KY	Ricky L. Harper	1993	6,316
141 6/8	24 1/8	23 6/8	16 3/8	5	6	Appanoose County	IA	Jeff Van Tress	1993	6,316
141 6/8	24 5/8	23 4/8	17 5/8	6	5	Hopkins County	KY	W. G. Hayden, Jr.	1993	6,316
141 6/8	27 4/8	28 2/8	22 2/8	6	4	Todd County	KY	Jerald Tabb	1993	6,316
141 6/8	25 0/8	24 4/8	22 0/8	4	4	Menard County	IL	Russ Dixon	1993	6,316
141 6/8	23 4/8	24 3/8	18 2/8	5	6	Tallapoosa County	AL	Wesley Ashcraft	1994	6,316
141 6/8	25 1/8	24 6/8	19 1/8	7	5	Crawford County	WI	Russ Gillitzer	1994	6,316
141 6/8	25 0/8	25 3/8	15 2/8	4	5	Monroe County	WI	Robert C. Stout	1994	6,316
141 6/8	23 0/8	23 1/8	19 4/8	4	4	Haskell County	KS	Neal Heaton	1994	6,316
141 6/8	23 4/8	23 4/8	19 6/8	4	5	Union County	KY	Huey K. Long	1994	6,316
141 6/8	20 2/8	21 2/8	17 4/8	5	5	Will County	IL	James A. Wetmore	1994	6,316
141 6/8	21 7/8	21 6/8	17 4/8	5	5	Jackson County	WI	Dan R. Merritt	1995	6,316
141 6/8	21 6/8	21 4/8	16 6/8	5	5	Crook County	WY	Scott Fullerton	1995	6,316
141 6/8	20 7/8	20 6/8	16 3/8	6	4	Washington County	NE	Don Sundell	1995	6,316
141 6/8	23 3/8	23 2/8	19 6/8	6	5	Brown County	SD	Jon Russell	1995	6,316
141 6/8	24 0/8	25 3/8	20 2/8	5	5	Westchester County	NY	Carl G. Schuster	1995	6,316
141 6/8	21 0/8	22 1/8	17 4/8	5	5	Manitowoc County	WI	Randy Flentje	1995	6,316
141 6/8	25 3/8	24 2/8	19 0/8	4	4	De Witt County	IL	Terry Poppe	1995	6,316
141 6/8	26 6/8	26 0/8	19 3/8	5	6	Knox County	OH	Jason Elliott	1995	6,316
141 6/8	22 7/8	21 7/8	18 2/8	4	4	Rock County	WI	Christopher A. Leach	1996	6,316
141 6/8	23 6/8	24 4/8	19 3/8	5	5	Wayne County	NY	Jim Mourey	1996	6,316
141 6/8	24 0/8	22 3/8	18 6/8	5	4	Morris County	NJ	John G. Belanger	1996	6,316
141 6/8	23 6/8	22 7/8	20 6/8	6	6	St. Charles County	MO	Jeff Narzinski	1996	6,316
141 6/8	21 4/8	21 5/8	18 2/8	4	4	Marshall County	KS	Roger Seematter	1996	6,316
141 6/8	22 7/8	23 3/8	19 6/8	5	5	Millarville	ALB	Joel Bickler	1996	6,316
141 6/8	24 6/8	24 6/8	20 2/8	5	4	Vermillion County	IN	John Moore	1996	6,316
141 6/8	20 2/8	20 6/8	17 0/8	5	6	Fond du Lac County	WI	Kenneth E. Fischer	1996	6,316
141 6/8	24 5/8	24 6/8	18 2/8	4	5	Steuben County	NY	Raymond Nisbet	1997	6,316
141 6/8	22 6/8	22 7/8	18 2/8	5	5	Genesee County	NY	Bill Nicoll	1997	6,316
141 6/8	23 7/8	23 5/8	18 4/8	5	5	Olmsted County	MN	Chad Powell	1997	6,316
141 5/8	24 0/8	24 3/8	21 6/8	6	3	Allegan County	MI	Stan Skorch	1967	6,383
141 5/8	23 3/8	23 5/8	19 5/8	4	5	Crawford County	IL	Jim Earleywine	1978	6,383
141 5/8	21 7/8	23 0/8	19 7/8	4	5	Shelby County	IL	Ed Ikemire	1979	6,383
141 5/8	24 5/8	24 6/8	17 2/8	5	6	Gallia County	OH	Buck Blankenship	1981	6,383
141 5/8	24 7/8	23 7/8	20 1/8	5	4	Roane County	TN	Thomas K. Grause	1981	6,383
141 5/8	25 2/8	26 0/8	18 1/8	4	4	Highland County	OH	Douglas Ambroza	1982	6,383
141 5/8	23 3/8	22 3/8	19 2/8	5	6	Missoula County	MT	Bob Jacobsen	1982	6,383
141 5/8	25 5/8	26 0/8	18 3/8	5	4	Dane County	WI	Don Magnuson	1983	6,383
141 5/8	22 2/8	23 2/8	18 1/8	5	5	Grant County	WI	Randy Dressler	1984	6,383
141 5/8	22 0/8	22 1/8	17 1/8	5	5	Yellow Medicine County	MN	Harold Greseth	1985	6,383
141 5/8	21 7/8	22 4/8	15 5/8	4	4	Sedgwick County	KS	Vince Albert	1986	6,383
141 5/8	22 4/8	22 4/8	17 1/8	6	7	Slope County	ND	Dick Cheatley	1987	6,383
141 5/8	22 3/8	22 4/8	16 3/8	5	5	Fillmore County	MN	Jim Vagts	1987	6,383
141 5/8	23 2/8	22 3/8	17 1/8	5	5	Ozaukee County	WI	Michael Karrels	1988	6,383

WHITETAIL DEER (TYPICAL ANTLERS)

Minimum Score 125

SCORE	LENGTH OF MAIN BEAM R	LENGTH OF MAIN BEAM L	INSIDE SPREAD	NUMBER OF POINTS R	NUMBER OF POINTS L	AREA	STATE/ PROVINCE	HUNTER'S NAME	DATE	RANK
141 5/8	23 5/8	26 2/8	19 0/8	7	7	Rock County	WI	Dale Snyder	1988	6,383
141 5/8	22 3/8	23 2/8	18 1/8	5	5	Wagoner County	OK	Terry Moody	1988	6,383
141 5/8	22 7/8	22 6/8	17 1/8	4	4	Strathcona	ALB	Ryk Visscher	1989	6,383
141 5/8	24 4/8	23 2/8	17 3/8	7	7	Butler County	KS	Mike Demel	1989	6,383
141 5/8	23 4/8	23 7/8	15 4/8	7	8	Sawyer County	WI	Dan Pleoger	1990	6,383
141 5/8	22 7/8	22 6/8	18 5/8	6	4	Washington County	MN	Rodney P. Bailey	1990	6,383
141 5/8	25 7/8	25 5/8	18 4/8	7	5	Tama County	IA	Dan Yuska	1990	6,383
141 5/8	23 4/8	23 6/8	16 6/8	6	5	Wyandot County	OH	Richard V. Ebert	1990	6,383
141 5/8	22 6/8	22 0/8	21 1/8	5	5	Boone County	IL	Anthony T. Smith	1990	6,383
141 5/8	25 1/8	26 1/8	18 0/8	5	6	Vermilion County	IL	Lonnie D. Massengale	1991	6,383
141 5/8	22 3/8	23 0/8	19 6/8	5	6	Athens County	OH	Michael A. Rex	1991	6,383
141 5/8	21 5/8	22 0/8	18 5/8	5	5	Pearl River County	MS	Tommy L. Rose	1993	6,383
141 5/8	22 3/8	23 4/8	15 6/8	7	6	Poplar Field	MAN	Richard Schweitzer	1993	6,383
141 5/8	23 0/8	22 6/8	17 1/8	5	6	Buffalo County	WI	Glenn Vinton	1993	6,383
141 5/8	22 4/8	23 1/8	16 7/8	5	5	Crowley County	CO	Frank G. Hallman	1993	6,383
141 5/8	23 6/8	23 0/8	15 1/8	5	6	La Salle County	TX	Kirk M. Folsom	1994	6,383
141 5/8	26 0/8	25 6/8	21 6/8	4	6	McHenry County	IL	Ernie Meinen	1994	6,383
141 5/8	24 6/8	25 2/8	16 5/8	4	5	Harrison County	MO	Mark Gann	1994	6,383
141 5/8	23 5/8	23 0/8	14 3/8	5	6	Logan County	AR	William Campbell	1994	6,383
141 5/8	24 1/8	23 1/8	20 3/8	4	5	Parke County	IN	Chuck Paddock	1994	6,383
141 5/8	25 4/8	25 6/8	18 3/8	4	4	Darke County	OH	Thomas E. Warner	1994	6,383
141 5/8	24 1/8	22 5/8	16 7/8	5	6	Crawford County	WI	Emerald A. Faulkner, Jr.	1994	6,383
141 5/8	21 2/8	21 1/8	16 4/8	5	6	Travis County	TX	Jerrell GreenWalt	1994	6,383
141 5/8	24 6/8	26 0/8	16 7/8	4	5	Kent County	MD	Bruce Fair	1994	6,383
141 5/8	24 4/8	24 1/8	18 5/8	5	5	Pope County	MN	Leroy Olson	1994	6,383
141 5/8	20 1/8	21 5/8	15 5/8	5	5	Buffalo County	WI	Joe J. Meinerz	1995	6,383
141 5/8	25 1/8	22 6/8	17 1/8	5	5	Bracken County	KY	Tony Schumann	1995	6,383
141 5/8	23 4/8	24 0/8	18 4/8	6	4	Marion County	IA	Gerald T. Dowell	1995	6,383
141 5/8	22 7/8	23 1/8	20 4/8	6	5	Winnebago County	IL	Dave Judy	1995	6,383
141 5/8	22 5/8	22 6/8	15 1/8	5	5	Waupaca County	WI	James J. Hlaban	1996	6,383
141 5/8	22 2/8	22 2/8	15 0/8	7	5	Lee County	IA	J. D. White	1996	6,383
141 5/8	25 0/8	25 4/8	19 7/8	6	6	Bayfield County	WI	Roger Lemler	1996	6,383
141 5/8	26 1/8	26 0/8	20 1/8	5	4	Creek County	OK	Dan R. Massey	1996	6,383
141 5/8	24 2/8	24 1/8	17 7/8	6	5	Crawford County	WI	Mark N. Livingston	1997	6,383
141 5/8	22 4/8	23 3/8	16 1/8	5	5	Hamilton County	OH	Josh Hamilton	1997	6,383
141 5/8	22 4/8	22 3/8	15 6/8	5	4	Washington County	MN	Jason Bellomy	1997	6,383
141 5/8	21 5/8	20 0/8	16 3/8	5	5	Manitowoc County	WI	Fran Nellis	1997	6,383
141 5/8	22 2/8	23 4/8	18 5/8	4	4	Wapello County	IA	Arnold E. Vest	1997	6,383
141 5/8	21 1/8	21 5/8	15 3/8	5	5	Powder River County	MT	Tom Detrick	1998	6,383
141 4/8	21 1/8	21 4/8	19 6/8	5	5	Hyde County	SD	Gordon Sampson	1974	6,436
141 4/8	22 3/8	22 3/8	17 4/8	5	5	Richland County	OH	Walter A. Bartashus	1976	6,436
141 4/8	23 3/8	22 7/8	17 3/8	5	7	Trigg County	KY	Wayne R. Brooks	1978	6,436
141 4/8	23 6/8	24 4/8	19 0/8	5	5	Jackson County	IA	Thomas E. Maas	1979	6,436
141 4/8	22 2/8	22 1/8	16 0/8	5	4	Stephenson County	IL	John Miller	1983	6,436
141 4/8	20 6/8	20 7/8	17 0/8	5	5	Cowley County	KS	George B. Smith	1983	6,436
141 4/8	22 2/8	22 2/8	20 0/8	6	5	Pepin County	WI	Brian Berger	1984	6,436
141 4/8	24 0/8	24 4/8	15 2/8	5	5	Jackson County	IA	Todd Simmons	1984	6,436
141 4/8	25 4/8	21 0/8	21 0/8	10	9	Wyandotte County	KS	Robert A. Bentz	1984	6,436
141 4/8	27 4/8	25 3/8	20 4/8	6	5	McNairy County	TN	Arlus Ray Burney	1985	6,436
141 4/8	22 2/8	22 7/8	17 3/8	7	6	Osborne County	KS	Craig Pottberg	1986	6,436
141 4/8	25 5/8	25 6/8	16 4/8	7	6	Knox County	IN	Keith Richard Bosecker	1988	6,436
141 4/8	22 4/8	22 7/8	17 4/8	5	6	Texas County	OK	Max Crocker	1988	6,436
141 4/8	21 7/8	20 6/8	13 2/8	5	6	Langlade County	WI	Mike Sheldon	1988	6,436
141 4/8	21 5/8	22 1/8	17 2/8	5	5	Westchester County	NY	Rayot A. DiFate	1988	6,436
141 4/8	24 7/8	24 0/8	20 2/8	5	5	Shawano County	WI	Jeffrey J. Gipp	1988	6,436
141 4/8	21 3/8	21 0/8	15 0/8	5	6	McHenry County	IL	James Coley	1989	6,436
141 4/8	26 5/8	26 6/8	21 0/8	5	4	Warren County	OH	Russell L. Wiessinger	1989	6,436
141 4/8	23 0/8	22 6/8	17 6/8	4	4	Sullivan County	IN	David Ridge	1989	6,436
141 4/8	21 6/8	21 4/8	18 4/8	5	5	Monona County	IA	Pat Boyle	1989	6,436
141 4/8	23 6/8	23 0/8	18 0/8	4	4	Knox County	OH	Gregg A. Melfe	1989	6,436
141 4/8	24 0/8	23 7/8	17 7/8	6	5	Prairie County	AR	Doug Casey	1990	6,436
141 4/8	21 5/8	21 7/8	13 6/8	5	7	Powell County	MT	Julian Proctor	1990	6,436
141 4/8	22 2/8	21 4/8	16 6/8	6	5	La Porte County	IN	Wayne Wood	1990	6,436
141 4/8	22 1/8	22 3/8	18 6/8	5	4	Jo Daviess County	IL	David W. Seas	1990	6,436
141 4/8	23 4/8	23 4/8	19 6/8	4	6	McHenry County	IL	Russ Tallman	1990	6,436
141 4/8	25 6/8	24 7/8	18 4/8	4	4	Oconto County	WI	John Pashek	1990	6,436
141 4/8	22 7/8	22 5/8	15 2/8	5	5	Waupaca County	WI	Jeff Behrens	1991	6,436
141 4/8	20 7/8	22 3/8	14 6/8	5	5	Loudoun County	VA	Roger Lane Pearce	1991	6,436
141 4/8	22 2/8	22 6/8	22 0/8	5	5	Hocking County	OH	Ernie Glason, Jr.	1991	6,436
141 4/8	23 3/8	22 7/8	15 4/8	6	6	Loudoun County	VA	Stephen L. George	1991	6,436
141 4/8	22 1/8	20 4/8	18 2/8	5	5	Anderson County	KS	Robert G. Coplen	1991	6,436
141 4/8	26 3/8	25 1/8	17 3/8	6	5	Jefferson County	IL	Ron Leek	1991	6,436
141 4/8	20 7/8	21 0/8	16 2/8	5	5	Kenedy County	TX	Peeler G. Lacey, MD	1992	6,436
141 4/8	22 5/8	22 7/8	15 4/8	5	5	Muskingum County	OH	Mike Wilson	1992	6,436
141 4/8	24 2/8	23 4/8	17 2/8	4	5	Richland County	ND	Robert Kapaun, Jr.	1992	6,436
141 4/8	24 1/8	24 0/8	18 0/8	4	4	Brown County	OH	Robert T. Walker	1992	6,436
141 4/8	22 0/8	22 0/8	19 0/8	5	5	Kiowa County	KS	Karl Ballard	1992	6,436
141 4/8	22 2/8	22 7/8	17 3/8	5	6	Calhoun County	IL	Dewaine Slinkard	1992	6,436

Continued

WHITETAIL DEER (TYPICAL ANTLERS)

Minimum Score 125 — Continued

SCORE	LENGTH OF MAIN BEAM R	L	INSIDE SPREAD	NUMBER OF POINTS R	L	AREA	STATE/ PROVINCE	HUNTER'S NAME	DATE	RANK
141 4/8	22 1/8	22 5/8	16 4/8	4	4	Jackson County	WI	Dave Eckel	1992	6,436
141 4/8	22 6/8	23 4/8	19 4/8	5	5	Kankakee County	IL	Jeffery J. Schneider	1993	6,436
141 4/8	22 1/8	23 5/8	20 3/8	7	8	Hawkins County	TN	Mark S. Rogers	1993	6,436
141 4/8	23 4/8	23 6/8	16 5/8	6	5	Schoharie County	NY	Bill Clapper, Jr.	1993	6,436
141 4/8	24 7/8	25 0/8	20 6/8	5	4	Bureau County	IL	Ronald L. Smith	1993	6,436
141 4/8	24 2/8	25 0/8	16 6/8	4	5	Pembina County	ND	Roger Furstenau	1993	6,436
141 4/8	21 0/8	21 2/8	17 2/8	5	6	Chautauqua County	NY	John J. Burkholder	1994	6,436
141 4/8	22 6/8	23 4/8	17 2/8	5	5	Dallas County	IA	Patrick J. Riley	1994	6,436
141 4/8	23 3/8	22 3/8	17 0/8	5	4	Worth County	IA	Larry Porter	1994	6,436
141 4/8	25 6/8	27 5/8	20 4/8	8	6	Jasper County	IL	Kenneth Huss	1995	6,436
141 4/8	19 4/8	19 2/8	14 2/8	6	5	Cherry County	NE	Paul Brakhage	1995	6,436
141 4/8	24 6/8	23 0/8	18 4/8	4	4	Tolland County	CT	Raymond Bienia	1995	6,436
141 4/8	21 3/8	21 1/8	17 0/8	5	6	Wapello County	IA	Dennis Bradley	1995	6,436
141 4/8	22 3/8	21 6/8	15 6/8	6	6	Pike County	IL	Dan Perez	1995	6,436
141 4/8	25 2/8	25 1/8	17 0/8	4	4	Lawrence County	IN	Arter V. Thompson	1995	6,436
141 4/8	25 4/8	23 7/8	21 7/8	5	5	Baltimore County	MD	Robert E. Roberts	1995	6,436
141 4/8	21 5/8	22 1/8	15 2/8	6	6	Madison County	MT	J. Dudley Ottley, Sr.	1995	6,436
141 4/8	21 6/8	21 7/8	19 2/8	6	5	Washington County	KS	Colby Manley	1995	6,436
141 4/8	22 2/8	22 3/8	17 0/8	5	5	Columbia County	WI	Michael K. Paulcheck	1996	6,436
141 4/8	20 7/8	20 6/8	15 6/8	6	6	Pike County	IL	Robert Sacher	1996	6,436
141 4/8	22 3/8	22 2/8	18 4/8	4	4	Fond du Lac County	WI	Devin Hill	1996	6,436
141 4/8	23 0/8	23 6/8	15 4/8	5	5	Washington County	MN	Patrick J. Ellias	1997	6,436
141 4/8	22 0/8	21 6/8	17 2/8	5	5	Appanoose County	IA	Paul Cockriel	1997	6,436
141 4/8	22 6/8	23 0/8	16 2/8	4	4	Broome County	NY	Dan Blanchard	1997	6,436
141 4/8	22 6/8	22 0/8	18 6/8	6	5	Logan County	OH	Mike Anderson	1997	6,436
141 4/8	25 2/8	25 0/8	19 6/8	5	4	Schuylkill County	PA	Terry Schwalm	1997	6,436
141 4/8	21 3/8	21 0/8	18 4/8	6	6	Bureau County	IL	Gregory A. Bowers	1997	6,436
141 4/8	24 5/8	24 0/8	17 0/8	5	4	Licking County	OH	Thomas L. Derugen	1997	6,436
141 4/8	22 3/8	23 4/8	22 4/8	4	4	Hanover County	VA	David Wayne Hardiman	1997	6,436
141 3/8	23 3/8	22 4/8	17 1/8	7	6	Hughes County	SD	Ross Krull	1969	6,504
141 3/8	24 5/8	26 3/8	16 3/8	5	6	Vilas County	WI	Dennis W. Essers	1976	6,504
141 3/8	24 6/8	24 5/8	18 2/8	6	10	Seneca County	OH	Bruce R. Stover	1980	6,504
141 3/8	24 0/8	23 1/8	19 7/8	5	5	Mitchell County	KS	Charlie Stevens	1981	6,504
141 3/8	23 5/8	23 3/8	17 4/8	7	5	Warren County	VA	Ronnie Wines	1981	6,504
141 3/8	22 3/8	21 5/8	15 1/8	5	5	Eau Claire County	WI	Terry R. Zich	1982	6,504
141 3/8	24 7/8	24 0/8	16 7/8	5	4	Burleigh County	ND	Andrew M. Schneider	1982	6,504
141 3/8	24 6/8	24 6/8	19 2/8	5	7	Putnam County	WV	James H. Myers	1983	6,504
141 3/8	25 1/8	25 0/8	19 7/8	5	4	Fayette County	IL	Mike Kistler	1983	6,504
141 3/8	22 2/8	22 1/8	18 5/8	4	5	Clermont County	OH	Harold A. Thompson, Jr.	1983	6,504
141 3/8	27 7/8	26 2/8	18 5/8	7	5	Boone County	IA	Dan A. Dillavou	1984	6,504
141 3/8	23 5/8	23 4/8	18 5/8	5	5	Dakota County	MN	Brad Bieber	1984	6,504
141 3/8	21 2/8	23 0/8	19 5/8	6	9	Louisa County	IA	Jay Schmelzer	1985	6,504
141 3/8	23 5/8	23 2/8	15 2/8	6	5	Kay County	OK	Guy LeMonnier	1985	6,504
141 3/8	25 5/8	25 3/8	19 5/8	4	5	Jackson County	MN	Merlin Jurgens	1985	6,504
141 3/8	18 6/8	23 1/8	15 5/8	5	5	Lake County	IL	Robert H. Fugett	1985	6,504
141 3/8	21 7/8	23 0/8	16 2/8	5	7	Jackson County	IA	David Schrody	1985	6,504
141 3/8	24 5/8	22 7/8	17 5/8	5	5	Howard Twp.	ONT	Wm. K. Jamieson	1985	6,504
141 3/8	22 6/8	23 1/8	19 3/8	5	5	Greene County	OH	Daniel J. Gereg	1987	6,504
141 3/8	23 5/8	23 1/8	16 1/8	5	5	Langlade County	WI	Bernhardt Behlke	1987	6,504
141 3/8	26 1/8	26 1/8	18 5/8	5	5	Fairfield County	OH	Thomas Moore	1988	6,504
141 3/8	23 6/8	22 3/8	18 2/8	5	6	Douglas County	WI	Perry Cunningham	1988	6,504
141 3/8	23 1/8	22 3/8	16 3/8	5	4	Licking County	OH	Ron Lohrman, Sr.	1988	6,504
141 3/8	19 7/8	21 4/8	15 3/8	4	5	Wapello County	IA	Stephen A. Cullinan	1989	6,504
141 3/8	25 3/8	25 6/8	18 3/8	5	5	Racine County	WI	Mark Wilcox	1989	6,504
141 3/8	25 4/8	26 4/8	18 7/8	5	4	Grant County	WI	Clifford T. Bailey	1990	6,504
141 3/8	23 1/8	23 0/8	17 0/8	7	6	Douglas County	WI	William James Back	1991	6,504
141 3/8	22 6/8	22 6/8	18 5/8	5	6	Douglas County	WI	Jeff Paulus	1991	6,504
141 3/8	21 3/8	21 2/8	15 5/8	5	5	Jackson County	MO	Wendell Hood	1991	6,504
141 3/8	23 2/8	23 2/8	18 3/8	5	6	Bayfield County	WI	Arthur E. Hyde	1992	6,504
141 3/8	20 3/8	20 3/8	15 7/8	5	5	St. Joseph County	IN	Michael L. Ritter	1992	6,504
141 3/8	23 5/8	23 4/8	20 3/8	5	5	Olmsted County	MN	Kyle T. Hutchinson	1992	6,504
141 3/8	22 4/8	22 5/8	20 1/8	6	6	Letellier	MAN	John Haspel	1992	6,504
141 3/8	20 6/8	20 5/8	16 2/8	6	6	Jasper County	IA	Gary W. Vasseau	1992	6,504
141 3/8	23 0/8	22 0/8	17 3/8	5	5	Duval County	TX	Ray Hinojosa	1992	6,504
141 3/8	22 3/8	23 4/8	14 1/8	7	6	Pettis County	MO	Travis G. Lorenz	1992	6,504
141 3/8	22 1/8	21 6/8	16 7/8	6	6	Iroquois County	IL	Daniel Marzano	1993	6,504
141 3/8	24 1/8	23 3/8	19 3/8	5	5	La Salle County	IL	Gary L. Tabor, Sr.	1993	6,504
141 3/8	21 4/8	21 4/8	16 1/8	5	5	Langlade County	WI	Jeffrey C. Mishler	1993	6,504
141 3/8	23 1/8	23 0/8	18 1/8	5	5	Mercer County	IL	Lonnie Dickey	1993	6,504
141 3/8	23 1/8	22 0/8	17 3/8	6	6	Real County	TX	Ben B. Wallace	1994	6,504
141 3/8	23 5/8	23 2/8	17 3/8	6	6	Vinton County	OH	Les Loranzan, Jr.	1994	6,504
141 3/8	23 6/8	22 3/8	19 0/8	6	6	La Grange County	IN	David V. Chupp	1994	6,504
141 3/8	26 0/8	25 4/8	19 1/8	4	5	Edgar County	IL	Dale Bozarth	1994	6,504
141 3/8	21 7/8	19 7/8	17 5/8	5	5	Pottawattamie County	IA	Doug Clayton	1994	6,504
141 3/8	23 1/8	23 5/8	18 7/8	5	5	Lehigh County	PA	Dale F. Arner	1995	6,504
141 3/8	24 0/8	22 7/8	16 7/8	5	5	Ionia County	MI	Jeff L. Fidler	1995	6,504
141 3/8	21 1/8	22 4/8	20 0/8	6	5	Bayfield County	WI	Stephen M. Sorenson	1995	6,504
141 3/8	23 7/8	23 0/8	15 2/8	5	7	Lapeer County	MI	Jeff Douglas	1995	6,504

WHITETAIL DEER (TYPICAL ANTLERS)

Minimum Score 125

Continued

SCORE	LENGTH OF MAIN BEAM R	LENGTH OF MAIN BEAM L	INSIDE SPREAD	NUMBER OF POINTS R	NUMBER OF POINTS L	AREA	STATE/PROVINCE	HUNTER'S NAME	DATE	RANK
141 3/8	24 0/8	24 3/8	19 1/8	4	4	Charles County	MD	Billy Moore	1995	6,504
141 3/8	24 0/8	24 3/8	17 3/8	5	5	Kingman County	KS	Terry Morisse	1995	6,504
141 3/8	22 7/8	23 5/8	17 1/8	4	5	Washington County	MO	Jimmy J. O'Neal, Jr.	1995	6,504
141 3/8	20 4/8	21 0/8	13 5/8	5	5	Montgomery County	MD	Richard L. Latimer, Jr.	1995	6,504
141 3/8	22 5/8	23 3/8	22 2/8	4	6	Major County	OK	Mike Hein	1996	6,504
141 3/8	25 1/8	24 7/8	20 2/8	4	6	Iowa County	WI	Sheldon Ward	1996	6,504
141 3/8	23 1/8	23 3/8	17 3/8	4	5	Jefferson County	KS	Jeff Dunn	1996	6,504
141 3/8	23 6/8	25 1/8	18 1/8	4	4	Sumner County	KS	Roger L. Emley	1996	6,504
141 3/8	21 3/8	21 3/8	17 1/8	5	5	Lee County	IL	Mike Burrs	1996	6,504
141 3/8	21 7/8	22 1/8	17 3/8	5	5	Racine County	WI	Thomas C. Berczyk	1997	6,504
141 3/8	21 6/8	22 5/8	16 7/8	6	5	Pike County	IL	David W. Reese	1997	6,504
141 3/8	23 3/8	24 5/8	20 4/8	6	5	Alexander County	IL	Donnie Blaney	1997	6,504
141 3/8	22 1/8	22 3/8	18 6/8	6	5	Des Moines County	IA	Craig A. Owens	1997	6,504
141 3/8	23 2/8	23 4/8	17 1/8	6	6	Sawyer County	WI	Jeffrey P. Tomesh	1997	6,504
141 3/8	23 5/8	22 7/8	19 1/8	5	6	Monroe County	IA	Larry Zach	1997	6,504
141 3/8	22 2/8	22 5/8	17 3/8	6	6	Breckinridge County	KY	Kevin Vessels	1997	6,504
141 3/8	24 3/8	24 6/8	18 7/8	5	5	Isanti County	MN	Robert Michaletz	1997	6,504
141 3/8	25 1/8	24 6/8	19 0/8	7	6	La Crosse County	WI	Greg Mueller	1997	6,504
141 3/8	24 0/8	23 4/8	17 7/8	4	4	St. Clair County	MI	Todd D. Louks	1998	6,504
141 2/8	24 4/8	23 1/8	16 6/8	5	5	Lee County	IA	Terry E. Woodworth	1973	6,572
141 2/8	22 5/8	23 1/8	22 2/8	4	5	Bon Homme County	SD	Jeff Miedema	1978	6,572
141 2/8	25 7/8	25 7/8	20 4/8	5	4	Douglas County	KS	Russell Stevens	1978	6,572
141 2/8	23 3/8	23 2/8	17 2/8	5	5	Cottonwood County	MN	Robert K. Vincent	1978	6,572
141 2/8	24 2/8	23 4/8	20 2/8	4	5	Dekalb County	IL	Bob Broos	1980	6,572
141 2/8	21 6/8	20 2/8	16 0/8	7	6	Grant County	WI	Thomas A. Franseen	1982	6,572
141 2/8	22 4/8	22 4/8	20 3/8	5	6	Allamakee County	IA	Glen A. Jones	1983	6,572
141 2/8	24 4/8	25 7/8	20 6/8	6	5	Powell County	MT	Steve Pocha	1984	6,572
141 2/8	21 6/8	20 5/8	19 2/8	6	5	Green County	WI	Randall A. Schupbach	1984	6,572
141 2/8	24 4/8	23 2/8	21 0/8	4	6	Fayette County	IL	Charlie Gelsinger, Jr.	1985	6,572
141 2/8	26 1/8	26 1/8	18 4/8	5	4	Lawrence County	OH	Don Nickles	1985	6,572
141 2/8	24 5/8	24 3/8	20 2/8	5	6	Pike County	OH	Harry R. Fite	1985	6,572
141 2/8	23 3/8	23 3/8	16 2/8	4	4	Kandiyohi County	MN	Jeffrey L. Danielson	1986	6,572
141 2/8	23 7/8	23 1/8	15 6/8	4	4	Green County	WI	Michael J. Beckwith	1986	6,572
141 2/8	21 4/8	20 7/8	19 6/8	5	5	Mercer County	OH	Rick Kaud, Sr.	1986	6,572
141 2/8	23 0/8	23 0/8	19 5/8	5	6	Portage County	WI	Philip P. Kalata	1987	6,572
141 2/8	21 1/8	21 5/8	19 6/8	5	6	Weld County	CO	Dale A. Elliott	1988	6,572
141 2/8	22 3/8	22 1/8	18 0/8	6	6	Price County	WI	Gerald Kozey	1988	6,572
141 2/8	22 7/8	23 3/8	18 4/8	5	4	La Salle County	TX	Dr. F. D. Elias	1989	6,572
141 2/8	23 0/8	23 1/8	16 2/8	5	6	Brown County	WI	David J. Schauer	1989	6,572
141 2/8	24 2/8	23 7/8	17 5/8	6	6	Berrien County	MI	Michael Holy	1989	6,572
141 2/8	20 0/8	21 4/8	16 4/8	5	5	Osborne County	KS	Craig E. Pottberg	1989	6,572
141 2/8	24 3/8	25 4/8	17 4/8	6	7	Hennepin County	MN	Robert Nash	1990	6,572
141 2/8	23 5/8	24 3/8	15 2/8	5	5	Screven County	GA	Don L. Allex	1990	6,572
141 2/8	23 4/8	23 6/8	20 3/8	6	6	Calgary	ALB	David R. Coupland	1990	6,572
141 2/8	24 2/8	25 4/8	21 7/8	5	5	Monroe County	NY	Dane R. Edwards	1990	6,572
141 2/8	22 5/8	22 3/8	18 0/8	5	5	Walworth County	WI	Ernie Meinen	1990	6,572
141 2/8	22 1/8	22 1/8	17 0/8	10	9	Delaware County	IA	Jeffrey J. Tobin	1991	6,572
141 2/8	23 5/8	22 3/8	18 0/8	5	5	Walworth County	WI	Robert R. Friend	1991	6,572
141 2/8	24 2/8	22 7/8	18 2/8	8	6	Holt County	MO	Collis Bosworth	1991	6,572
141 2/8	21 0/8	21 7/8	16 1/8	7	5	McHenry County	IL	Scott Kunzie	1992	6,572
141 2/8	24 4/8	21 5/8	20 0/8	6	6	Wapello County	IA	Ronald L. Simmons	1992	6,572
141 2/8	20 5/8	22 0/8	17 0/8	5	5	Douglas County	WI	Steve Wittke	1992	6,572
141 2/8	22 2/8	22 0/8	15 2/8	5	5	Carter County	MO	Bob Benedick	1992	6,572
141 2/8	24 0/8	23 4/8	19 2/8	5	4	Whiteside County	IL	Bernard J. Higley, Sr.	1992	6,572
141 2/8	22 2/8	23 1/8	18 4/8	4	4	Coles County	IL	James G. Aldrich	1992	6,572
141 2/8	24 4/8	23 4/8	20 0/8	4	4	Buffalo County	WI	Daniel Brockman	1993	6,572
141 2/8	23 2/8	24 4/8	18 2/8	4	5	Cass County	IL	Neal Kellam	1993	6,572
141 2/8	21 0/8	20 6/8	18 3/8	7	6	Oldham County	KY	Irv Turpen	1993	6,572
141 2/8	25 1/8	24 3/8	19 0/8	4	4	Allegheny County	PA	Thomas W. Eiler	1994	6,572
141 2/8	24 6/8	25 1/8	19 4/8	4	4	Logan County	IL	Michael C. Geskey	1994	6,572
141 2/8	21 2/8	21 2/8	23 5/8	5	5	Ontario County	NY	Timothy E. Serviss	1995	6,572
141 2/8	21 7/8	22 4/8	15 2/8	5	5	Douglas County	KS	Danzil L. Hackathorn	1995	6,572
141 2/8	23 0/8	21 5/8	17 6/8	5	6	Allamakee County	IA	Jim J. Oberfoell	1995	6,572
141 2/8	24 0/8	24 4/8	18 2/8	4	5	Waupaca County	WI	Marlin Stapleton, Jr.	1995	6,572
141 2/8	24 2/8	24 0/8	20 4/8	4	4	Eau Claire County	WI	Arnie Roytek	1995	6,572
141 2/8	23 7/8	23 7/8	16 5/8	6	6	Jefferson County	KY	Kent Stroud	1995	6,572
141 2/8	22 6/8	22 4/8	19 5/8	5	6	San Patricio County	TX	Lane Feazell	1995	6,572
141 2/8	25 0/8	24 7/8	17 0/8	4	5	Berks County	PA	Frank M. Maddona	1996	6,572
141 2/8	22 5/8	23 5/8	20 4/8	6	6	Oktibbeha County	MS	Kim Vickers	1996	6,572
141 2/8	22 2/8	21 1/8	15 1/8	8	6	Grundy County	MO	Ethan Griffin	1996	6,572
141 2/8	26 2/8	25 5/8	20 0/8	4	5	Berks County	PA	John A. Weir	1996	6,572
141 2/8	22 2/8	21 1/8	16 6/8	5	5	Meigs County	OH	Matt Wilson	1996	6,572
141 2/8	25 1/8	25 3/8	21 0/8	8	5	Jersey County	IL	John Mueller	1996	6,572
141 2/8	22 7/8	22 2/8	15 6/8	6	6	Ogle County	IL	Robert D. Bradley	1996	6,572
141 2/8	24 2/8	24 4/8	16 6/8	5	5	Marathon County	WI	Kurt Schreiner	1996	6,572
141 2/8	25 4/8	25 6/8	17 3/8	5	5	Queen Annes County	MD	Eric Miller	1997	6,572
141 2/8	24 1/8	23 6/8	22 0/8	4	5	Clark County	OH	Brian Loveless	1997	6,572
141 2/8	25 6/8	25 1/8	20 1/8	5	6	Dubuque County	IA	Joey Sarazin	1997	6,572

WHITETAIL DEER (TYPICAL ANTLERS)

Minimum Score 125 — Continued

SCORE	LENGTH OF MAIN BEAM R	L	INSIDE SPREAD	NUMBER OF POINTS R	L	AREA	STATE/ PROVINCE	HUNTER'S NAME	DATE	RANK
141 2/8	24 7/8	24 7/8	18 0/8	5	6	Anderson County	KS	Windell R. Johnson	1997	6,572
141 2/8	22 5/8	22 1/8	16 6/8	5	5	Olmsted County	MN	Mark W. Karppi	1998	6,572
141 1/8	26 2/8	27 6/8	19 0/8	4	5	Dodge County	NE	Gary Trost	1961	6,633
141 1/8	22 0/8	24 2/8	18 1/8	4	6	Shelby County	IL	Ron Ragan	1979	6,633
141 1/8	21 5/8	22 2/8	17 5/8	5	6	Talbot County	MD	Gary W. Sommers	1979	6,633
141 1/8	25 0/8	25 0/8	17 2/8	6	6	Jefferson County	OH	William J. Fedor	1981	6,633
141 1/8	24 2/8	24 6/8	17 1/8	5	4	Tuscaloosa County	AL	Bobby Hemphill	1981	6,633
141 1/8	24 0/8	23 1/8	23 3/8	5	5	Pittsburg County	OK	Dave Jilge	1981	6,633
141 1/8	22 1/8	22 7/8	19 0/8	6	5	Des Moines County	IA	David R. Bessine	1982	6,633
141 1/8	23 7/8	22 1/8	17 7/8	5	5	Stanley County	SD	Jim P. Hallock	1983	6,633
141 1/8	22 5/8	21 7/8	15 4/8	8	7	Boone County	MO	Craig S Gemming	1984	6,633
141 1/8	27 1/8	26 6/8	18 0/8	4	5	Boone County	MO	Dale Robb	1984	6,633
141 1/8	22 4/8	22 2/8	21 0/8	6	6	Wabaunsee County	KS	Charles Bisnette	1985	6,633
141 1/8	24 3/8	24 2/8	19 1/8	4	5	Kit Carson County	CO	Kenneth Assmus	1986	6,633
141 1/8	22 4/8	23 2/8	15 6/8	7	6	Texas County	OK	Max Crocker	1986	6,633
141 1/8	23 3/8	21 1/8	18 4/8	5	6	Jefferson County	IN	Dan Oliver	1986	6,633
141 1/8	24 1/8	23 3/8	17 5/8	5	5	Oneida County	WI	Rollie H. Bessett	1986	6,633
141 1/8	22 3/8	22 4/8	16 7/8	5	6	Harvey County	KS	Mark M. Jones	1987	6,633
141 1/8	22 5/8	21 7/8	17 5/8	4	4	Jasper County	MO	Roger Lindsey	1988	6,633
141 1/8	21 6/8	22 6/8	17 1/8	5	5	Buffalo County	WI	Bruce B. Pronschinske	1988	6,633
141 1/8	25 0/8	25 4/8	22 7/8	6	5	Randolph County	IL	Ron Dunker	1988	6,633
141 1/8	22 2/8	23 1/8	18 5/8	5	5	Madison County	IL	Roger Downer	1988	6,633
141 1/8	23 3/8	23 4/8	18 1/8	4	5	Plymouth County	IA	Timm M. Banks	1989	6,633
141 1/8	20 7/8	21 3/8	19 1/8	5	5	Indiana County	PA	David W. Magiera	1990	6,633
141 1/8	25 1/8	24 2/8	17 1/8	6	5	Anoka County	MN	Tim Dugas	1990	6,633
141 1/8	22 2/8	22 6/8	16 5/8	5	5	St. Charles County	MO	Carlis Stephens	1991	6,633
141 1/8	22 4/8	22 4/8	15 5/8	5	5	Kandiyohi County	MN	David Rannestad	1991	6,633
141 1/8	24 0/8	23 7/8	21 1/8	5	5	Allamakee County	IA	Cody Hawkins	1991	6,633
141 1/8	23 5/8	23 0/8	20 1/8	5	5	Anne Arundel County	MD	J. J. Fegan	1991	6,633
141 1/8	24 7/8	24 2/8	17 3/8	4	5	McHenry County	IL	Ernie Meinen	1991	6,633
141 1/8	26 1/8	25 2/8	20 6/8	4	5	Letcher County	KY	Terry Mullins	1992	6,633
141 1/8	21 5/8	21 3/8	18 5/8	5	5	Burleigh County	ND	Terry Lee Johnson	1992	6,633
141 1/8	23 2/8	24 1/8	18 3/8	5	6	Waushara County	WI	Ben Sullivan	1992	6,633
141 1/8	23 0/8	22 0/8	16 5/8	5	4	Flathead County	MT	Dan Perez	1993	6,633
141 1/8	21 6/8	21 7/8	17 2/8	6	5	Beltrami County	MN	Jon H. Becker	1993	6,633
141 1/8	22 6/8	22 7/8	17 3/8	4	4	Monroe County	IN	Russell L. Edwards	1993	6,633
141 1/8	21 4/8	21 6/8	16 3/8	6	5	Goodhue County	MN	Richard W. Rolls	1993	6,633
141 1/8	22 1/8	22 0/8	19 7/8	5	5	Green County	WI	John W. Elsner	1993	6,633
141 1/8	23 1/8	23 6/8	16 3/8	4	5	Chester County	PA	Edward F. McConnell	1993	6,633
141 1/8	23 5/8	22 6/8	17 3/8	5	5	La Porte County	IN	Dwayne E. Wireman	1994	6,633
141 1/8	25 5/8	26 2/8	17 1/8	6	7	Ripley County	IN	Eric Sampson	1994	6,633
141 1/8	19 7/8	20 4/8	14 3/8	5	5	Morrison County	MN	Duane E. Eilbes	1994	6,633
141 1/8	23 2/8	22 2/8	15 7/8	6	5	Dane County	WI	Steve Mulcahy	1994	6,633
141 1/8	26 2/8	25 4/8	21 7/8	4	5	Anne Arundel County	MD	Joseph W. Keller, Jr.	1994	6,633
141 1/8	22 6/8	24 1/8	16 7/8	5	5	Ashland County	WI	Leland Wertepny	1994	6,633
141 1/8	22 4/8	22 0/8	17 5/8	4	4	Scotland County	MO	Jay Smith	1994	6,633
141 1/8	22 5/8	22 4/8	16 1/8	5	6	Ashland County	WI	Patrick Mohr	1995	6,633
141 1/8	21 7/8	22 6/8	16 1/8	4	5	Crawford County	IA	Dick Frazier	1995	6,633
141 1/8	23 3/8	22 7/8	18 1/8	5	5	Forest County	WI	Daniel Brezinski	1995	6,633
141 1/8	24 4/8	23 4/8	16 5/8	5	5	Jackson County	WI	Michael R. Abel	1995	6,633
141 1/8	25 4/8	25 2/8	20 3/8	5	5	Perry County	OH	Todd J. Krieg	1996	6,633
141 1/8	24 0/8	22 0/8	15 3/8	9	6	Hale County	AL	Tim Kohlenberg	1996	6,633
141 1/8	22 0/8	22 3/8	15 7/8	5	5	Goshen County	WY	Reggie Theus	1996	6,633
141 1/8	23 3/8	23 1/8	18 1/8	4	4	Harper County	KS	Bryan Naccarato	1996	6,633
141 1/8	23 5/8	24 1/8	18 5/8	5	5	Macon County	IL	Dave M. Elliott	1996	6,633
141 1/8	24 1/8	23 5/8	17 7/8	4	4	Henry County	GA	Rocky Thompson	1997	6,633
141 1/8	24 5/8	25 1/8	19 5/8	5	5	Sullivan County	NH	Rick Eaton	1997	6,633
141 1/8	22 4/8	24 0/8	20 6/8	5	6	Waukesha County	WI	Douglas S. Giesen	1997	6,633
141 1/8	26 7/8	24 5/8	19 0/8	6	6	Chatham County	NC	William Phillips	1997	6,633
141 0/8	22 2/8	21 7/8	16 0/8	4	5	Hand County	SD	Robert Werdel	1963	6,690
141 0/8	21 5/8	22 0/8	16 0/8	4	5	Nobles County	MN	Rod McNab	1974	6,690
141 0/8	24 2/8	24 4/8	18 0/8	5	4	Vermilion County	IL	Larry Mollet	1974	6,690
141 0/8	24 2/8	24 1/8	18 3/8	4	5	Ohio County	IN	Mike Meyer	1979	6,690
141 0/8	22 4/8	22 4/8	16 2/8	5	5	Marion County	IA	Steven F. Donnelly, Jr.	1982	6,690
141 0/8	22 5/8	23 1/8	15 4/8	6	5	Marion County	WV	Samuel E. Clingan	1983	6,690
141 0/8	21 2/8	22 0/8	17 1/8	6	5	Floyd County	IA	Dennis Grauerholz	1983	6,690
141 0/8	24 3/8	23 5/8	18 1/8	5	4	Pine County	MN	Dave Hartl	1984	6,690
141 0/8	23 4/8	23 3/8	21 2/8	5	5	Flathead County	MT	Wes Plummer	1984	6,690
141 0/8	23 4/8	23 4/8	19 4/8	5	6	Douglas County	KS	Russell Stevens	1984	6,690
141 0/8	24 3/8	24 1/8	17 2/8	4	4	Pottawatomie County	KS	Loyd C. Flowers, Sr.	1984	6,690
141 0/8	24 5/8	23 7/8	17 4/8	5	4	Chatham County	NC	James T. Noonan III	1984	6,690
141 0/8	22 3/8	21 5/8	18 6/8	4	4	Cass County	NE	Roger E. Buck	1985	6,690
141 0/8	25 1/8	25 1/8	20 6/8	4	4	Prince Georges County	MD	Robert O. Turner II	1985	6,690
141 0/8	21 4/8	17 2/8	17 0/8	5	5	Guernsey County	OH	Todd E. Feichter	1986	6,690
141 0/8	25 0/8	24 5/8	17 6/8	5	5	Waterloo	ONT	John Wyszynski	1986	6,690
141 0/8	25 0/8	24 2/8	19 2/8	4	4	Williams County	OH	Timothy L. Garber	1987	6,690
141 0/8	23 1/8	23 6/8	18 4/8	5	4	Forest County	WI	Robert DuFek	1987	6,690
141 0/8	24 1/8	25 4/8	19 1/8	6	6	Westchester County	NY	Wayne Alan Simko	1987	6,690

WHITETAIL DEER (TYPICAL ANTLERS)

Minimum Score 125 — Continued

SCORE	LENGTH OF MAIN BEAM R	LENGTH OF MAIN BEAM L	INSIDE SPREAD	NUMBER OF POINTS R	NUMBER OF POINTS L	AREA	STATE/PROVINCE	HUNTER'S NAME	DATE	RANK
141 0/8	23 0/8	23 0/8	15 2/8	4	4	Grundy County	IL	Jim W. Zientek	1987	6,690
141 0/8	24 5/8	23 3/8	22 0/8	5	5	Warren County	IL	Jim M. Bratkovic	1988	6,690
141 0/8	24 0/8	23 1/8	18 0/8	5	5	Chemung County	NY	Kim E. Womer	1988	6,690
141 0/8	23 6/8	24 3/8	18 5/8	5	5	Wayne County	IL	Paul Fearn	1988	6,690
141 0/8	21 3/8	21 4/8	15 4/8	6	5	Livingston County	IL	Michael G. Keesee	1989	6,690
141 0/8	24 7/8	24 7/8	18 0/8	5	4	Riley County	KS	Robert L. Gardner	1989	6,690
141 0/8	21 4/8	22 2/8	15 0/8	6	6	Thorsby	ALB	John Trout, Jr.	1989	6,690
141 0/8	23 0/8	23 0/8	17 2/8	4	4	Burleigh County	ND	Jim Domaskin	1989	6,690
141 0/8	25 4/8	25 2/8	16 0/8	4	4	Anderdon Twp.	ONT	Leo Potvin	1989	6,690
141 0/8	26 6/8	26 2/8	19 0/8	5	5	La Salle County	TX	Dr. F. D. Elias	1990	6,690
141 0/8	23 6/8	23 3/8	20 5/8	5	5	Mercer County	NJ	Frank Prato	1990	6,690
141 0/8	23 2/8	22 7/8	17 0/8	5	5	Guthrie County	IA	John D. Hambleton	1990	6,690
141 0/8	22 2/8	22 4/8	15 2/8	5	5	Franklin County	IA	Arlynn Ahrens	1990	6,690
141 0/8	23 0/8	24 1/8	17 0/8	5	6	Weld County	CO	Chuck Brewer	1990	6,690
141 0/8	23 4/8	22 5/8	17 0/8	5	6	Gallia County	OH	Bobby Clenney	1991	6,690
141 0/8	22 7/8	23 3/8	17 3/8	5	5	Woodson County	KS	Joe Chippeaux	1991	6,690
141 0/8	29 4/8	29 0/8	19 0/8	4	4	Richardson County	NE	Perry Oates	1991	6,690
141 0/8	23 4/8	21 6/8	17 2/8	4	4	Ontario County	NY	Neil R. Ross	1991	6,690
141 0/8	21 6/8	20 2/8	15 0/8	5	5	McHenry County	IL	William D. Weiss	1991	6,690
141 0/8	25 3/8	25 1/8	18 4/8	5	5	Warren County	OH	W. H. "Billy" Brock III	1991	6,690
141 0/8	22 4/8	22 6/8	17 0/8	5	5	Lake County	MN	Larry Antonich	1991	6,690
141 0/8	22 1/8	21 0/8	15 2/8	6	6	Wood Mtn.	SAS	A. Jeff Best	1992	6,690
141 0/8	27 0/8	27 5/8	18 4/8	5	4	Geauga County	OH	Richard W. Rudnay	1992	6,690
141 0/8	24 1/8	22 3/8	15 7/8	4	5	Brown County	IL	Charles R. Figge	1992	6,690
141 0/8	23 0/8	22 4/8	17 5/8	6	6	Christian County	IL	Philip Estell	1992	6,690
141 0/8	23 0/8	23 6/8	15 4/8	6	6	Boone County	IL	Thomas C. Baker	1992	6,690
141 0/8	22 6/8	23 6/8	18 1/8	6	4	Linn County	IA	David Elsbury	1993	6,690
141 0/8	22 4/8	23 3/8	13 4/8	6	5	Buffalo County	WI	Ron Schultz	1993	6,690
141 0/8	25 3/8	23 1/8	19 2/8	4	4	Suffolk County	NY	Neal Heaton	1993	6,690
141 0/8	22 5/8	22 3/8	17 6/8	5	5	Henry County	VA	Mike Weaver	1993	6,690
141 0/8	23 4/8	23 4/8	16 6/8	5	5	Dubuque County	IA	Mark W. Breitsprecker	1993	6,690
141 0/8	24 5/8	25 0/8	18 2/8	4	5	Dallas County	IA	Joe Uedelhofen	1993	6,690
141 0/8	22 7/8	23 7/8	20 2/8	4	4	Vermilion County	IL	David A. Downing	1993	6,690
141 0/8	27 4/8	26 6/8	22 6/8	4	3	Saline County	IL	Mark L. Maynard	1993	6,690
141 0/8	24 2/8	24 2/8	16 4/8	6	5	Macoupin County	IL	John Wesbrook	1993	6,690
141 0/8	24 1/8	23 1/8	19 0/8	5	6	Sauk County	WI	Jerry Groth	1994	6,690
141 0/8	23 3/8	23 0/8	15 4/8	5	6	Kent County	MD	Tom Scilipoti	1994	6,690
141 0/8	21 0/8	20 6/8	15 2/8	6	5	Dodge County	MN	Terry Krahn	1994	6,690
141 0/8	23 6/8	22 3/8	17 2/8	6	5	Cecil County	MD	Raymond M. Cook	1994	6,690
141 0/8	23 5/8	22 6/8	16 2/8	5	4	Washington County	KS	Toby M. Bruna	1994	6,690
141 0/8	23 2/8	23 4/8	16 0/8	5	5	Jasper County	IL	Marty Draves	1994	6,690
141 0/8	25 5/8	23 4/8	19 3/8	6	6	Kennebec County	ME	Sue D. LaRue	1995	6,690
141 0/8	25 4/8	25 1/8	19 2/8	4	4	Tazewell County	IL	Tom McClary, Jr.	1995	6,690
141 0/8	23 1/8	21 7/8	19 6/8	5	5	Edgar County	IL	Dale Good	1995	6,690
141 0/8	23 7/8	24 0/8	19 0/8	5	6	Sawyer County	WI	Steven J. Olson	1995	6,690
141 0/8	24 4/8	24 2/8	18 0/8	4	4	Cumberland County	IL	Randy Rodebaugh	1995	6,690
141 0/8	23 1/8	23 2/8	17 2/8	5	5	Van Buren County	TN	Dwight Bottoms	1995	6,690
141 0/8	24 4/8	24 6/8	17 4/8	4	5	Mingo County	WV	Clifford Hall	1995	6,690
141 0/8	22 2/8	22 2/8	16 2/8	5	5	Goodhue County	MN	Peter Collins	1996	6,690
141 0/8	27 2/8	26 0/8	20 6/8	4	5	McHenry County	IL	Gary T. Lackhouse	1996	6,690
141 0/8	22 7/8	24 0/8	17 6/8	5	5	St. Louis County	MN	Brad Ronning	1996	6,690
141 0/8	22 4/8	23 5/8	18 4/8	5	5	Polk County	IA	John W. Flies	1996	6,690
141 0/8	22 6/8	23 0/8	20 5/8	6	8	Butler County	OH	Michael Rumpler	1996	6,690
141 0/8	23 1/8	22 2/8	18 0/8	5	5	Montcalm County	MI	Duane Keeler	1997	6,690
141 0/8	23 0/8	23 0/8	17 0/8	5	5	Trempealeau County	WI	Adam James Jarozewski	1997	6,690
141 0/8	22 2/8	22 0/8	18 0/8	5	5	Waushara County	WI	Brett C. Larsen	1997	6,690
141 0/8	21 4/8	21 6/8	16 4/8	4	5	Winona County	MN	Shawn E. Eyre	1997	6,690
141 0/8	22 4/8	22 3/8	15 4/8	7	5	Chautauqua County	KS	Foster V. Yancey, Jr.	1997	6,690
141 0/8	21 7/8	21 7/8	16 6/8	5	6	Walsh County	ND	Darrell W. Deutz	1998	6,690
141 0/8	23 7/8	24 2/8	16 4/8	4	4	Price County	WI	Roger A. Niewiadomski	1998	6,690
140 7/8	27 1/8	26 4/8	21 7/8	4	6	Dodge County	NE	Ivan T. Ross	1960	6,769
140 7/8	21 7/8	21 1/8	16 7/8	5	6	Hughes County	SD	Gerald Snyder	1962	6,769
140 7/8	24 5/8	24 5/8	17 1/8	4	4	Ripley County	IN	Melvin M. Weddell	1968	6,769
140 7/8	24 7/8	24 6/8	17 5/8	5	5	Jackson County	OH	Bob McGuire	1975	6,769
140 7/8	21 1/8	21 4/8	16 2/8	5	7	Guthrie County	IA	Dennis Rote	1977	6,769
140 7/8	21 7/8	21 6/8	14 3/8	5	6	Dunn County	WI	Douglas G. Clements	1981	6,769
140 7/8	22 0/8	21 7/8	19 7/8	6	5	St. Louis County	MO	Jack Repp	1982	6,769
140 7/8	21 7/8	23 1/8	17 3/8	4	4	Scott County	KS	Lynn Freese	1983	6,769
140 7/8	25 2/8	25 5/8	16 3/8	4	5	Morrison County	MN	Bob Woodhouse	1984	6,769
140 7/8	20 2/8	21 5/8	16 1/8	5	5	Saunders County	NE	David L Prochaska	1984	6,769
140 7/8	22 7/8	23 2/8	16 2/8	5	6	Sauk County	WI	Brad J. Luce	1984	6,769
140 7/8	22 3/8	22 3/8	16 7/8	5	5	Monroe County	WI	John W. Zahrte	1984	6,769
140 7/8	21 1/8	19 7/8	16 3/8	6	6	Claiborne County	MS	John Robert Moon	1985	6,769
140 7/8	26 5/8	26 2/8	12 3/8	5	6	Jefferson County	KY	William J. Paul III	1986	6,769
140 7/8	21 7/8	20 4/8	17 5/8	5	5	Macoupin County	IL	Richard E. Carter	1986	6,769
140 7/8	23 4/8	24 2/8	21 0/8	6	6	McHenry County	IL	John Totemeier	1986	6,769
140 7/8	22 5/8	23 2/8	19 1/8	4	4	Kleberg County	TX	William M. Wheless III	1986	6,769
140 7/8	21 4/8	21 1/8	17 3/8	5	4	Des Moines County	IA	Ronald L. Mott	1987	6,769

WHITETAIL DEER (TYPICAL ANTLERS)

Minimum Score 125 Continued

SCORE	LENGTH OF R MAIN BEAM L		INSIDE SPREAD	NUMBER OF R POINTS L		AREA	STATE/ PROVINCE	HUNTER'S NAME	DATE	RANK
140 7/8	22 1/8	21 5/8	19 1/8	5	5	Lake County	IL	Robert Tropple	1987	6,769
140 7/8	23 2/8	21 5/8	18 5/8	5	4	Stearns County	MN	Mike Beuning	1988	6,769
140 7/8	24 7/8	24 3/8	18 3/8	5	6	Harrison County	IA	Marvin Purcell	1988	6,769
140 7/8	23 5/8	23 3/8	17 1/8	4	5	Houston County	MN	Ronald Ehlers	1989	6,769
140 7/8	23 6/8	23 1/8	21 7/8	4	4	Winnebago County	WI	Tom Otto	1989	6,769
140 7/8	23 1/8	20 7/8	19 1/8	5	5	Waupaca County	WI	Dan Bauman	1989	6,769
140 7/8	22 2/8	23 1/8	17 1/8	4	5	Allegheny County	PA	James E. Lambert	1989	6,769
140 7/8	22 2/8	22 2/8	21 7/8	5	4	Walworth County	WI	Dale Sjoerdsma	1989	6,769
140 7/8	22 1/8	23 0/8	17 1/8	5	6	Wright County	MN	Ronald Dircks	1989	6,769
140 7/8	25 4/8	25 2/8	19 3/8	4	4	Clark County	IL	Mark Johnson	1989	6,769
140 7/8	23 2/8	24 5/8	16 7/8	4	4	Westchester County	NY	Curt Jorgenson	1989	6,769
140 7/8	22 6/8	23 2/8	23 2/8	8	5	La Salle County	IL	Gary L. Tabor, Sr.	1990	6,769
140 7/8	23 0/8	22 2/8	15 5/8	4	5	Maverick County	TX	F. H. Becker III	1990	6,769
140 7/8	25 2/8	25 2/8	14 7/8	8	7	Kossuth County	IA	Michael J. Miller	1991	6,769
140 7/8	24 5/8	24 3/8	18 6/8	6	5	Oklahoma County	OK	Tim Reid	1991	6,769
140 7/8	24 7/8	26 7/8	20 1/8	4	4	Butler County	OH	Kenny Butler	1991	6,769
140 7/8	22 3/8	23 4/8	20 3/8	5	6	Waukesha County	WI	Dan Infalt	1992	6,769
140 7/8	23 3/8	23 0/8	17 1/8	5	6	Gallia County	OH	Steven Ray Prince	1992	6,769
140 7/8	23 1/8	23 6/8	21 1/8	6	4	Clarke County	IA	Gary Cobb	1992	6,769
140 7/8	25 2/8	24 6/8	16 5/8	5	7	Chase County	KS	Jim Bob Watkins	1992	6,769
140 7/8	23 2/8	24 0/8	15 3/8	5	5	Sarpy County	NE	Robert J. Baratta	1993	6,769
140 7/8	24 1/8	24 0/8	15 1/8	5	6	Franklin County	VT	Mathew Raftery	1993	6,769
140 7/8	22 0/8	22 1/8	16 5/8	5	5	Douglas County	MN	Dave Faber	1993	6,769
140 7/8	21 4/8	21 4/8	16 1/8	7	6	Boone County	MO	Donald N. Schindler	1993	6,769
140 7/8	23 5/8	24 2/8	22 6/8	7	6	Hot Springs County	WY	Larry Dickerson	1993	6,769
140 7/8	21 7/8	21 6/8	15 3/8	5	5	Marquette County	WI	Randy J. Strehlow	1993	6,769
140 7/8	24 7/8	24 0/8	17 3/8	4	5	De Soto Parish	LA	Mark Fisher	1993	6,769
140 7/8	23 4/8	22 5/8	17 1/8	5	6	Boone County	MO	J. Ryan McCann	1993	6,769
140 7/8	25 3/8	25 2/8	21 7/8	4	4	Morrison County	MN	Tony Rasmussen	1994	6,769
140 7/8	23 0/8	22 4/8	19 1/8	5	4	Washington County	MN	Tom J. Nielsen	1994	6,769
140 7/8	21 6/8	21 6/8	17 6/8	5	6	Madison County	IL	Brion Boeshans	1994	6,769
140 7/8	22 3/8	22 7/8	17 1/8	5	6	Tompkins County	NY	John N. Wilson	1994	6,769
140 7/8	23 4/8	25 0/8	18 4/8	7	9	Greene County	MO	Doug Kyle	1994	6,769
140 7/8	22 5/8	22 4/8	16 1/8	6	6	Price County	WI	Roger G. Niewiadomski, Jr.	1995	6,769
140 7/8	24 0/8	23 7/8	16 5/8	5	6	Kerr County	TX	Gregory Scott Smith	1995	6,769
140 7/8	23 3/8	23 6/8	16 5/8	6	4	Harrison County	KY	Kevin Poe	1995	6,769
140 7/8	23 2/8	22 7/8	16 0/8	6	6	Pulaski County	KY	Rusty Wilson	1995	6,769
140 7/8	22 5/8	22 7/8	18 1/8	5	5	Berkshire County	MA	Jay and Joe D'Ambrosio	1995	6,769
140 7/8	21 5/8	23 7/8	16 0/8	6	5	Republic County	KS	Jim Snyder	1995	6,769
140 7/8	23 2/8	23 5/8	18 2/8	4	5	Peoria County	IL	William T. Trainor	1995	6,769
140 7/8	25 0/8	23 6/8	17 5/8	5	5	Morrison County	MN	Duane Fischbach	1996	6,769
140 7/8	22 4/8	22 1/8	16 3/8	5	5	Van Buren County	MI	Stephen Ryno	1997	6,769
140 7/8	21 0/8	21 7/8	16 7/8	5	6	Pope County	AR	David Edwards	1997	6,769
140 7/8	22 3/8	22 3/8	15 7/8	5	5	Lawrence County	OH	Tim Gormican	1997	6,769
140 6/8	24 2/8	24 6/8	19 5/8	5	6	Blue Earth County	MN	Earl D. Kopischke	1967	6,831
140 6/8	24 0/8	23 3/8	20 0/8	4	4	Cottonwood County	MN	Kerry Ella	1973	6,831
140 6/8	22 6/8	23 3/8	18 0/8	5	5	Morrison County	MN	Galen Miller	1973	6,831
140 6/8	21 4/8	22 1/8	18 0/8	7	5	Weld County	CO	Roger Bechler	1974	6,831
140 6/8	23 6/8	24 2/8	19 6/8	6	5	Grant County	MN	Ronald W. Johnson	1974	6,831
140 6/8	24 2/8	24 6/8	16 4/8	5	5	Brant Twp.	ONT	Kent Callen	1979	6,831
140 6/8	21 5/8	21 1/8	18 4/8	5	5	Kossuth County	IA	Larry M. Johnson	1979	6,831
140 6/8	21 5/8	22 2/8	18 2/8	6	6	Redwood County	MN	Todd Gilb	1981	6,831
140 6/8	20 0/8	19 2/8	16 7/8	6	9	Gregory County	SD	Leroy Lamp	1983	6,831
140 6/8	23 0/8	24 2/8	18 0/8	6	7	Putnam County	IN	E. Duyane Tucker	1984	6,831
140 6/8	23 0/8	23 5/8	18 0/8	4	4	Vinton County	OH	Randy Boggs	1984	6,831
140 6/8	23 6/8	24 1/8	18 3/8	5	6	Hancock County	WV	Daniel Salatino	1985	6,831
140 6/8	21 1/8	21 1/8	17 2/8	5	5	Hamlin County	SD	Ronald Schoffelman	1985	6,831
140 6/8	26 0/8	25 1/8	20 6/8	5	4	Lake County	IL	Carl H. Spaeth	1985	6,831
140 6/8	24 6/8	25 1/8	19 2/8	5	5	Dearborn County	IN	John B. Gosney	1986	6,831
140 6/8	22 6/8	22 7/8	16 4/8	6	5	Adams County	WI	Richardo L. Garza	1986	6,831
140 6/8	25 2/8	25 2/8	22 1/8	4	5	Carroll County	IL	Art Heinze	1986	6,831
140 6/8	24 7/8	23 3/8	18 2/8	5	4	Morgan County	CO	Gary Stampka	1986	6,831
140 6/8	24 6/8	24 6/8	18 2/8	6	5	Anoka County	MN	Byron Thomas	1986	6,831
140 6/8	23 0/8	23 3/8	18 6/8	4	4	Roberts County	SD	Myles Keller	1986	6,831
140 6/8	21 4/8	21 7/8	18 0/8	5	6	Morris County	NJ	Frank DeFilippis, Jr.	1987	6,831
140 6/8	25 2/8	24 7/8	21 2/8	4	5	Fairfield County	CT	Robert Bain	1987	6,831
140 6/8	20 7/8	21 5/8	15 5/8	5	6	Lyon County	MN	Charles Obler	1987	6,831
140 6/8	22 6/8	23 5/8	17 6/8	5	6	Jersey County	IL	Judy Kovar	1987	6,831
140 6/8	23 5/8	24 0/8	19 2/8	6	5	Ohio County	WV	Mike Pompeo	1987	6,831
140 6/8	24 5/8	24 0/8	17 4/8	4	4	Fairfax County	VA	Patrick Patterson	1987	6,831
140 6/8	25 6/8	24 7/8	21 3/8	4	5	Coles County	IL	Brad Sloat	1987	6,831
140 6/8	21 5/8	22 7/8	18 0/8	5	5	Monroe County	KY	Darrell Butler	1988	6,831
140 6/8	23 3/8	21 6/8	21 4/8	5	6	Du Page County	IL	Ronald Knebel	1989	6,831
140 6/8	22 7/8	23 1/8	15 7/8	5	5	Dane County	WI	Dennis L. Stiklestad	1989	6,831
140 6/8	22 2/8	21 7/8	17 4/8	6	5	Hennepin County	MN	Thomas Michael Knox	1989	6,831
140 6/8	21 7/8	20 4/8	17 6/8	4	4	Las Animas County	CO	Patrick E. Powell	1989	6,831
140 6/8	24 0/8	24 2/8	18 6/8	4	4	Union County	IL	Robert DuBois	1990	6,831
140 6/8	22 3/8	23 2/8	20 0/8	5	4	Scott County	KS	Brett Eisenhour	1990	6,831

WHITETAIL DEER (TYPICAL ANTLERS)

Minimum Score 125

Continued

SCORE	LENGTH OF MAIN BEAM R	LENGTH OF MAIN BEAM L	INSIDE SPREAD	NUMBER OF POINTS R	NUMBER OF POINTS L	AREA	STATE/ PROVINCE	HUNTER'S NAME	DATE	RANK
140 6/8	20 0/8	21 1/8	16 0/8	5	5	Creek County	OK	Don Peterson	1990	6,831
140 6/8	22 6/8	23 1/8	22 7/8	5	4	Dodge County	WI	Larry Unertl	1990	6,831
140 6/8	23 5/8	24 1/8	20 0/8	4	4	Chisago County	MN	Bill Stringer	1991	6,831
140 6/8	24 3/8	24 7/8	17 5/8	6	5	Carter County	OK	Bob Boone	1991	6,831
140 6/8	22 0/8	22 7/8	20 2/8	7	6	St. Marys County	MD	Marvin J. Edwards, Jr.	1992	6,831
140 6/8	25 2/8	25 4/8	17 2/8	8	5	Lawrence County	OH	Eddie Ray Belville, Jr.	1992	6,831
140 6/8	24 1/8	25 0/8	15 4/8	4	4	Fayette County	IL	Bruce Boaz, Jr.	1992	6,831
140 6/8	24 3/8	25 0/8	17 0/8	5	4	Lehigh County	PA	Douglas C. Neustadter	1993	6,831
140 6/8	24 2/8	24 5/8	16 1/8	5	7	Champaign County	IL	Richard Walden	1993	6,831
140 6/8	24 6/8	24 3/8	20 6/8	5	4	Rock County	WI	Mark Pierce	1994	6,831
140 6/8	23 3/8	23 4/8	16 2/8	4	5	Monroe County	IL	Joseph M. Hobbs	1994	6,831
140 6/8	25 0/8	23 6/8	16 0/8	4	5	Vermillion County	IN	Todd Wickens	1994	6,831
140 6/8	24 0/8	23 7/8	17 4/8	4	4	Lafayette County	WI	Michael T. Trapino	1994	6,831
140 6/8	28 6/8	27 0/8	22 6/8	4	5	Johnson County	IL	David Adamson	1994	6,831
140 6/8	21 6/8	21 4/8	18 0/8	5	5	Buffalo County	WI	Ed Brannen	1994	6,831
140 6/8	23 4/8	23 2/8	23 5/8	5	5	Clinton County	IA	Dennis L. Henningsen	1994	6,831
140 6/8	24 1/8	24 0/8	17 0/8	5	5	Kane County	IL	James Meyer	1994	6,831
140 6/8	22 0/8	22 0/8	14 4/8	7	5	Powell County	MT	Aaron DeMeyere	1995	6,831
140 6/8	23 4/8	23 3/8	18 6/8	5	5	Price County	WI	Mark Edwards	1995	6,831
140 6/8	23 2/8	23 3/8	19 6/8	4	4	Cape Girardeau County	MO	Robert Reed	1995	6,831
140 6/8	24 1/8	23 0/8	20 0/8	5	4	Kent County	MI	Todd Daily	1995	6,831
140 6/8	23 6/8	23 0/8	18 0/8	5	5	Goodhue County	MN	John "Jack" Cordes	1995	6,831
140 6/8	23 4/8	22 0/8	17 2/8	6	5	Washington County	OH	Rich Wynn	1996	6,831
140 6/8	21 7/8	22 3/8	17 6/8	5	5	Columbia County	WI	Kevin Wiesshoff	1996	6,831
140 6/8	22 6/8	22 5/8	16 3/8	5	5	Shawnee County	KS	Robert J. Sachs	1996	6,831
140 6/8	26 7/8	25 5/8	21 4/8	4	4	Buffalo County	WI	John Charles	1996	6,831
140 6/8	23 0/8	22 6/8	17 1/8	7	5	Dearborn County	IN	Tom Koch	1996	6,831
140 6/8	21 7/8	22 2/8	17 2/8	5	5	Pepin County	WI	Randy Marcks	1996	6,831
140 6/8	19 5/8	19 3/8	14 6/8	6	6	Kenedy County	TX	Chad Clark	1996	6,831
140 6/8	21 3/8	24 3/8	19 4/8	6	6	Perry County	AL	Kenneth Vining	1996	6,831
140 6/8	19 7/8	21 1/8	17 2/8	5	5	Furnas County	NE	Rick A. Collins	1997	6,831
140 6/8	25 1/8	26 4/8	19 7/8	5	5	Pike County	IL	Dennis George	1997	6,831
140 6/8	22 3/8	22 7/8	14 0/8	5	5	Butler County	KY	Jeff Waldrop	1997	6,831
140 6/8	22 7/8	22 0/8	17 1/8	5	4	Schuyler County	IL	Ronald W. Markle	1997	6,831
140 6/8	23 5/8	23 2/8	17 0/8	6	6	St. Charles County	MO	Tim Mackenberg	1997	6,831
140 6/8	24 7/8	25 0/8	19 7/8	6	4	Chisago County	MN	Len Butler	1998	6,831
140 5/8	20 7/8	21 0/8	14 2/8	5	5	Dodge County	WI	Donald D. Voss	1960	6,901
140 5/8	22 7/8	23 1/8	17 4/8	6	5	Fremont County	IA	Scott Morris	1972	6,901
140 5/8	25 0/8	26 0/8	19 4/8	6	5	Edgar County	IL	Richard Griffin	1973	6,901
140 5/8	25 5/8	25 0/8	19 2/8	5	5	Lewis County	WV	David A. Hill	1978	6,901
140 5/8	23 5/8	23 1/8	15 6/8	7	6	Morrison County	MN	Joan Morris	1979	6,901
140 5/8	23 4/8	23 3/8	19 4/8	6	6	Sargent County	ND	Richard Williams	1980	6,901
140 5/8	23 6/8	23 6/8	20 1/8	4	4	Hardin County	IA	Bill Stonebraker	1981	6,901
140 5/8	22 4/8	22 6/8	17 1/8	6	6	Kandiyohi County	MN	Mike Hannemann	1982	6,901
140 5/8	22 0/8	23 7/8	20 4/8	5	4	Christian County	IL	Richard E. Davis	1983	6,901
140 5/8	23 6/8	25 0/8	13 5/8	5	5	Surry County	VA	David W. Huffman	1983	6,901
140 5/8	21 2/8	21 6/8	17 5/8	5	6	Jefferson County	IA	Victor Stickels	1983	6,901
140 5/8	22 0/8	22 4/8	17 3/8	4	5	Oconto County	WI	Ron Thompson	1986	6,901
140 5/8	22 3/8	22 4/8	16 5/8	4	4	Marion County	IL	Ivan W. Barnett	1986	6,901
140 5/8	26 2/8	25 7/8	18 7/8	4	4	Roberts County	SD	Kevin Saxton	1986	6,901
140 5/8	24 4/8	24 2/8	17 4/8	5	6	Waushara County	WI	Mark D. Miller	1987	6,901
140 5/8	22 0/8	21 4/8	20 7/8	5	5	Burnett County	WI	Michael D. Roberts	1987	6,901
140 5/8	22 1/8	21 7/8	19 1/8	4	5	Macoupin County	IL	Don Koniak	1988	6,901
140 5/8	27 1/8	27 4/8	20 6/8	8	8	Franklin County	OH	Lloyd E Evans	1988	6,901
140 5/8	22 3/8	22 4/8	19 7/8	5	5	Llano County	TX	Larry Rodolph	1989	6,901
140 5/8	23 6/8	24 0/8	18 1/8	5	5	Buchanan County	IA	Larry Chesmore	1989	6,901
140 5/8	22 5/8	21 7/8	18 3/8	5	4	Washington County	MN	Kenneth Brandl	1989	6,901
140 5/8	20 4/8	20 4/8	15 1/8	4	4	Montgomery County	IN	John Foster	1989	6,901
140 5/8	22 2/8	22 4/8	19 7/8	4	5	Keya Paha County	NE	Terry Marcukaitis	1989	6,901
140 5/8	23 4/8	25 1/8	17 0/8	5	5	Zavala County	TX	Dan Lansford	1990	6,901
140 5/8	20 3/8	20 3/8	16 3/8	5	5	Waupaca County	WI	Chester Cychosz	1990	6,901
140 5/8	27 2/8	25 3/8	18 7/8	5	5	St. Charles County	MO	Gordon Stilwell	1990	6,901
140 5/8	24 3/8	24 2/8	20 1/8	5	6	Fulton County	IL	Mark Watkins	1990	6,901
140 5/8	23 3/8	23 7/8	17 1/8	5	4	Vernon County	WI	Louis Larry Franks	1991	6,901
140 5/8	22 1/8	21 6/8	18 1/8	5	6	Laurens County	SC	Galen F. Shinkle	1991	6,901
140 5/8	27 6/8	26 4/8	17 6/8	6	6	Jo Daviess County	IL	Jim Horneck	1991	6,901
140 5/8	21 6/8	22 1/8	17 5/8	4	4	Grovedale	ALB	Brent Watson	1991	6,901
140 5/8	22 7/8	23 1/8	16 6/8	6	6	Harrison County	IA	Marvin Purcell	1991	6,901
140 5/8	22 0/8	22 2/8	17 3/8	5	5	Arkansas County	AR	Johnnie Wages	1991	6,901
140 5/8	26 1/8	26 2/8	19 6/8	6	7	Suffolk County	NY	Chester Berry, Jr.	1991	6,901
140 5/8	25 0/8	26 0/8	18 4/8	5	6	E. Carroll Parish	LA	Dr. Trellis G. Green	1992	6,901
140 5/8	24 5/8	24 7/8	17 1/8	4	4	Randolph County	NC	Dr. Raymond E. Pifer	1992	6,901
140 5/8	24 1/8	24 4/8	17 5/8	4	4	Kalamazoo County	MI	Ronald L. Sagers	1992	6,901
140 5/8	23 6/8	23 0/8	19 1/8	4	4	Tazewell County	IL	Bill Mantle	1992	6,901
140 5/8	24 6/8	26 5/8	22 6/8	5	6	Webster County	IA	Edward E. Ulicki	1992	6,901
140 5/8	20 1/8	20 2/8	16 5/8	4	4	Fauquier County	VA	Marvin Breeden	1992	6,901
140 5/8	23 6/8	24 2/8	21 5/8	4	5	Suffolk County	NY	Walter C. Visco	1992	6,901
140 5/8	21 3/8	20 6/8	17 5/8	5	5	Ogle County	IL	Larry L. Anderson	1993	6,901

WHITETAIL DEER (TYPICAL ANTLERS)

Minimum Score 125

SCORE	LENGTH OF MAIN BEAM R	L	INSIDE SPREAD	NUMBER OF POINTS R	L	AREA	STATE/ PROVINCE	HUNTER'S NAME	DATE	RANK
140 5/8	22 2/8	22 6/8	18 1/8	5	6	Osceola County	MI	Randy Mast	1993	6,901
140 5/8	21 1/8	21 3/8	16 3/8	5	5	Waukesha County	WI	Robert Henry Christiansen	1993	6,901
140 5/8	22 4/8	22 1/8	16 3/8	5	5	Fayette County	IN	Timothy B. Selby	1993	6,901
140 5/8	21 7/8	21 5/8	17 3/8	5	5	Wood County	WI	Bruce F. Jordan	1993	6,901
140 5/8	23 5/8	25 2/8	16 5/8	4	4	Dakota County	MN	Michael Siebenaler	1993	6,901
140 5/8	22 6/8	22 5/8	19 1/8	5	5	Franklin County	PA	Dustin A. Sites	1994	6,901
140 5/8	22 7/8	23 0/8	15 5/8	6	5	Shelby County	IL	Gene Wooters	1994	6,901
140 5/8	25 3/8	26 0/8	17 7/8	4	4	Washtenaw County	MI	Donald L. Cox	1994	6,901
140 5/8	24 0/8	22 6/8	14 3/8	5	5	Menard County	IL	Robert Sampson	1994	6,901
140 5/8	21 4/8	21 5/8	16 5/8	5	5	Pottawatomie County	KS	Robert D. Beckley	1994	6,901
140 5/8	24 6/8	24 6/8	19 3/8	4	4	McDowell County	WV	Patrick Sopsher	1994	6,901
140 5/8	23 0/8	24 2/8	14 2/8	6	6	Wyoming County	WV	Robert McGee	1994	6,901
140 5/8	21 6/8	22 1/8	19 1/8	5	5	Hartford County	CT	Donald B. Ducor	1994	6,901
140 5/8	25 5/8	25 1/8	18 7/8	4	4	Lenawee County	MI	Keith Conklin II	1994	6,901
140 5/8	20 6/8	20 5/8	16 3/8	6	6	Douglas County	MN	Brian Loch	1995	6,901
140 5/8	25 6/8	25 1/8	17 0/8	5	7	Allegan County	MI	Ken Morris	1995	6,901
140 5/8	25 3/8	25 1/8	18 7/8	4	4	New Madrid County	MO	Bill R. Glaus	1995	6,901
140 5/8	23 4/8	22 7/8	15 3/8	5	5	Wright County	MO	Dean Bray	1996	6,901
140 5/8	26 4/8	27 2/8	17 1/8	4	4	Claiborne County	MS	Mike R. Hutchins	1996	6,901
140 5/8	22 2/8	22 5/8	17 3/8	5	5	Berks County	PA	Darren W. Franks	1996	6,901
140 5/8	22 0/8	22 3/8	15 1/8	7	5	Park County	WY	Marion O. DeBusk	1997	6,901
140 5/8	22 4/8	21 6/8	16 1/8	4	4	Ripley County	IN	Dick Gambrel	1997	6,901
140 5/8	23 1/8	22 4/8	16 3/8	7	6	Jefferson County	OH	Guy Agin	1997	6,901
140 5/8	23 4/8	24 6/8	17 1/8	6	6	Owen County	IN	Rick Inman	1997	6,901
140 5/8	22 2/8	23 2/8	18 1/8	5	5	Walworth County	WI	David W. Freitag	1997	6,901
140 5/8	21 6/8	21 5/8	17 7/8	5	6	Ashland County	WI	William F. Schutte	1997	6,901
140 5/8	23 5/8	23 2/8	16 1/8	6	5	Suffolk County	NY	Robert S. Marshall	1997	6,901
140 5/8	24 0/8	24 2/8	21 3/8	4	4	Montgomery County	PA	Dave McCoach	1998	6,901
140 4/8	24 5/8	22 7/8	18 2/8	7	6	Guthrie County	IA	Dale Kromrie	1964	6,971
140 4/8	21 1/8	21 1/8	15 5/8	5	5	Dickinson County	MI	Bernard Schmidt	1964	6,971
140 4/8	22 4/8	22 4/8	17 2/8	6	6	Pendleton County	KY	Gerald Bezold	1971	6,971
140 4/8	24 2/8	24 1/8	20 2/8	5	5	Fairfax County	VA	Daniel C. Holtz	1971	6,971
140 4/8	24 2/8	24 4/8	17 0/8	5	6	Waupaca County	WI	Allen D. Blum	1973	6,971
140 4/8	25 4/8	24 7/8	17 0/8	6	5	Berks County	PA	John R. Intelisano	1975	6,971
140 4/8	20 0/8	20 0/8	16 2/8	5	5	Osage County	KS	Mike Vandevord	1977	6,971
140 4/8	23 3/8	23 7/8	20 2/8	5	5	Clayton County	IA	Dave White	1977	6,971
140 4/8	26 1/8	24 5/8	17 5/8	7	5	Calhoun County	MI	Roger L. Sims	1979	6,971
140 4/8	22 2/8	22 1/8	18 4/8	5	5	Bradley County	AR	Barnard Smith	1979	6,971
140 4/8	25 0/8	23 5/8	19 0/8	5	4	Marquette County	WI	Ed Shields	1980	6,971
140 4/8	23 6/8	24 3/8	18 6/8	5	7	Marion County	KS	Max Williams	1980	6,971
140 4/8	21 7/8	22 0/8	17 7/8	6	5	Berkeley County	SC	Hugh Gaskins	1981	6,971
140 4/8	21 6/8	22 0/8	16 6/8	5	5	Hempstead County	AR	Dan Moore	1982	6,971
140 4/8	24 1/8	23 4/8	17 6/8	6	6	Oconto County	WI	Richard L. Roth	1982	6,971
140 4/8	24 3/8	24 6/8	19 0/8	5	4	Logan County	IL	William Edwards	1983	6,971
140 4/8	22 2/8	22 3/8	17 4/8	5	5	Jackson County	KY	David A. Cornett	1984	6,971
140 4/8	24 2/8	24 0/8	16 6/8	4	4	Waukesha County	WI	Paul B. Kressin	1984	6,971
140 4/8	23 3/8	22 5/8	15 6/8	4	5	Pike County	IL	Joseph M. Cerny	1984	6,971
140 4/8	22 3/8	21 5/8	17 6/8	5	5	Harford County	MD	Hank Voigt	1984	6,971
140 4/8	22 4/8	22 0/8	16 2/8	5	5	McPherson County	KS	Jon Crouse	1986	6,971
140 4/8	24 3/8	24 2/8	17 4/8	5	4	Morrison County	MN	Brian Busch	1986	6,971
140 4/8	25 6/8	26 1/8	19 5/8	4	6	Monroe County	MO	Rick Schwieter	1987	6,971
140 4/8	24 2/8	24 6/8	17 5/8	6	6	Greenup County	KY	Bill Fraley	1987	6,971
140 4/8	22 0/8	21 7/8	16 3/8	6	6	Iron County	MI	Gary Schnicke	1988	6,971
140 4/8	22 1/8	21 7/8	15 4/8	5	5	Jefferson County	WI	Ernie Turpin	1988	6,971
140 4/8	25 0/8	23 7/8	17 1/8	6	6	Greene County	IL	Michael E. Newingham	1988	6,971
140 4/8	23 4/8	23 5/8	17 2/8	7	5	Mitchell County	IA	Kevin West	1989	6,971
140 4/8	21 0/8	21 1/8	13 7/8	7	5	Kane County	IL	William Wishon, Jr.	1989	6,971
140 4/8	23 3/8	22 1/8	17 4/8	4	4	Washington County	MS	Bob Bruss	1989	6,971
140 4/8	21 6/8	22 2/8	16 2/8	5	5	Washtenaw County	MI	Donald Clarke	1989	6,971
140 4/8	25 0/8	24 5/8	17 6/8	5	5	Logan County	KY	Mike K. Kirby	1989	6,971
140 4/8	22 1/8	23 0/8	20 5/8	4	6	Caldwell County	KY	Mickey Mason	1989	6,971
140 4/8	23 5/8	22 4/8	23 4/8	6	7	Coffey County	KS	Russell W. Terry	1989	6,971
140 4/8	24 0/8	22 5/8	18 4/8	5	5	Jackson County	OK	Bill Akins	1989	6,971
140 4/8	22 3/8	22 1/8	14 5/8	5	6	Washington County	KS	Bob Funke	1990	6,971
140 4/8	23 5/8	23 6/8	17 2/8	5	5	Carlton County	MN	Scott Fredrickson	1990	6,971
140 4/8	25 4/8	23 6/8	17 4/8	5	5	Dane County	WI	Greg McGraw	1990	6,971
140 4/8	24 0/8	24 2/8	16 4/8	4	4	Hardin County	KY	John Standafer	1990	6,971
140 4/8	23 0/8	23 0/8	16 6/8	4	4	Jasper County	IA	Ed Stevens	1990	6,971
140 4/8	25 0/8	23 3/8	19 6/8	5	5	McHenry County	IL	David A. Bauman	1990	6,971
140 4/8	26 3/8	25 7/8	22 5/8	4	6	Lake County	IL	Kenneth J. Pratt	1990	6,971
140 4/8	24 2/8	25 4/8	21 4/8	4	5	La Salle County	TX	Francis D. Elias	1991	6,971
140 4/8	23 1/8	21 2/8	19 2/8	5	5	Chariton County	MO	Ben Gibson	1991	6,971
140 4/8	25 6/8	25 2/8	18 4/8	5	4	Carroll County	OH	Martin Vincent Joliat	1991	6,971
140 4/8	22 2/8	21 0/8	19 2/8	5	5	Suffolk County	NY	William Marvin	1991	6,971
140 4/8	23 0/8	22 1/8	16 0/8	5	5	Allamakee County	IA	Todd Zeuske	1991	6,971
140 4/8	21 5/8	22 5/8	17 6/8	4	4	Vermilion County	IL	Timothy T. Welker	1991	6,971
140 4/8	22 0/8	21 5/8	12 6/8	5	5	Boone County	KY	Ted Wyan	1992	6,971
140 4/8	22 1/8	16 6/8	16 4/8	5	5	Ontonagon County	MI	Dean K. Gomoll	1992	6,971

Continued

381

WHITETAIL DEER (TYPICAL ANTLERS)

Minimum Score 125 Continued

SCORE	LENGTH OF MAIN BEAM R	LENGTH OF MAIN BEAM L	INSIDE SPREAD	NUMBER OF POINTS R	NUMBER OF POINTS L	AREA	STATE/ PROVINCE	HUNTER'S NAME	DATE	RANK
140 4/8	21 3/8	21 1/8	15 2/8	5	5	Traill County	ND	Jerome Hertwig	1993	6,971
140 4/8	24 6/8	24 6/8	17 6/8	8	7	McDonough County	IL	David J. Graham	1993	6,971
140 4/8	22 5/8	22 5/8	15 4/8	5	5	Clinton County	MO	David Eads	1993	6,971
140 4/8	23 4/8	24 0/8	19 2/8	6	6	Adams County	WI	Steve Dallmann	1993	6,971
140 4/8	25 5/8	23 5/8	16 6/8	4	4	McLean County	IL	Steven Hysell	1993	6,971
140 4/8	23 1/8	23 2/8	17 2/8	5	6	Douglas County	MN	Rodney McClellan	1994	6,971
140 4/8	22 1/8	23 7/8	16 6/8	5	5	Hancock County	WV	Michael Clark	1994	6,971
140 4/8	25 6/8	26 4/8	18 6/8	5	4	Wayne County	OH	David W. Huffman	1994	6,971
140 4/8	22 1/8	21 6/8	14 4/8	6	5	Yuma County	CO	Jason Massey	1994	6,971
140 4/8	25 2/8	24 4/8	18 2/8	4	5	Douglas County	WI	Steve Wittke	1994	6,971
140 4/8	22 6/8	22 3/8	17 2/8	5	6	Montgomery County	OH	Mike Miller	1994	6,971
140 4/8	25 2/8	24 4/8	17 2/8	6	6	Rockingham County	NH	Michael Deschambeault	1995	6,971
140 4/8	21 7/8	22 0/8	17 0/8	5	5	Butler County	MO	Randal L. Norman	1995	6,971
140 4/8	23 5/8	22 4/8	17 0/8	4	5	Peoria County	IL	Larry Pollack	1995	6,971
140 4/8	23 6/8	24 0/8	16 2/8	6	5	Crow Wing County	MN	Larry Angrimson	1995	6,971
140 4/8	22 6/8	21 7/8	18 4/8	5	5	Des Moines County	IA	Michael C. Dysh	1995	6,971
140 4/8	22 6/8	23 1/8	20 6/8	5	5	Westchester County	NY	Marc Niad	1995	6,971
140 4/8	23 3/8	23 0/8	18 0/8	5	6	Clarke County	IA	Don Mealey	1996	6,971
140 4/8	22 4/8	22 2/8	17 0/8	5	6	Sauk County	WI	James L. Litscher	1996	6,971
140 4/8	24 0/8	24 3/8	14 2/8	6	5	Texas County	MO	Terry Cavaness	1996	6,971
140 4/8	24 6/8	24 6/8	18 6/8	4	4	Henry County	OH	Matthew E. Bilow	1996	6,971
140 4/8	23 6/8	23 6/8	19 6/8	5	4	Marion County	IA	Gerald T. Dowell	1996	6,971
140 4/8	24 6/8	22 5/8	21 0/8	4	5	Iowa County	WI	Jeff Ladd	1996	6,971
140 4/8	20 5/8	20 7/8	15 6/8	5	5	Sanders County	MT	Greg L. Munther	1996	6,971
140 4/8	23 2/8	22 4/8	19 0/8	5	6	Washington County	WI	Scott Jacobson	1996	6,971
140 4/8	21 1/8	22 1/8	19 0/8	5	5	Jasper County	IL	Kris Kocher	1996	6,971
140 4/8	23 2/8	22 1/8	17 6/8	5	5	Montgomery County	IA	Travis Paul	1997	6,971
140 4/8	22 1/8	21 6/8	17 4/8	5	5	Kane County	IL	Richard Hight	1997	6,971
140 4/8	24 0/8	25 1/8	16 0/8	4	4	Anoka County	MN	Willard Layland	1997	6,971
140 4/8	25 5/8	25 0/8	17 6/8	5	4	Chester County	PA	William E. Gerhardt	1998	6,971
140 4/8	22 4/8	22 0/8	14 5/8	4	6	La Crosse County	WI	Craig Hunter Rieber	1998	6,971
140 3/8	23 5/8	23 6/8	16 4/8	6	7	Guthrie County	IA	Leland Purviance	1964	7,052
140 3/8	27 0/8	26 1/8	19 5/8	0	0	Pulaski County	VA	Harold M. Peters	1965	7,052
140 3/8	22 6/8	23 5/8	19 0/8	5	4	Morrison County	MN	Gary D. Wells	1972	7,052
140 3/8	23 7/8	23 6/8	19 4/8	7	4	Goodhue County	MN	Dwight Dankers	1975	7,052
140 3/8	20 5/8	22 0/8	20 1/8	5	5	Rusk County	WI	Mark A. Rufledt	1977	7,052
140 3/8	21 3/8	21 4/8	15 1/8	5	5	Essex County	NY	Donald Frazier	1979	7,052
140 3/8	21 4/8	22 2/8	17 5/8	5	5	Washington County	NE	John Christopher	1981	7,052
140 3/8	23 6/8	23 0/8	20 3/8	5	4	Aitkin County	MN	Lloyd Boelter	1981	7,052
140 3/8	27 0/8	27 0/8	21 2/8	5	5	Hardin County	OH	Devere Sams	1984	7,052
140 3/8	24 0/8	24 0/8	19 2/8	5	4	Union County	IL	Steve Wilhite	1984	7,052
140 3/8	21 6/8	22 1/8	17 6/8	5	5	Chester County	PA	Jess A. Hassinger	1986	7,052
140 3/8	20 1/8	20 2/8	15 1/8	5	5	Pennington County	SD	Glenn Delabarre	1989	7,052
140 3/8	22 7/8	22 6/8	17 5/8	5	5	Butler County	KY	Brad Cardwell	1989	7,052
140 3/8	23 0/8	22 7/8	19 1/8	4	5	McHenry County	IL	Donald Kerns	1989	7,052
140 3/8	22 3/8	23 0/8	16 6/8	7	9	Montgomery County	IA	Dick Davis	1989	7,052
140 3/8	21 4/8	21 3/8	15 7/8	5	5	Logan County	KY	Russell Johnson	1989	7,052
140 3/8	22 6/8	23 5/8	17 7/8	4	4	Meeker County	MN	Lee Peterson	1989	7,052
140 3/8	22 4/8	24 4/8	14 4/8	6	4	Ripley County	IN	Kevin D. Hall	1990	7,052
140 3/8	25 2/8	25 4/8	19 1/8	4	5	Fairfax County	VA	Mark A. Palmer	1990	7,052
140 3/8	22 3/8	24 0/8	16 7/8	4	4	Fulton County	IL	Ronald R. Bahnsen	1990	7,052
140 3/8	21 6/8	22 6/8	16 3/8	5	5	Jo Daviess County	IL	Jack T. Wolf	1990	7,052
140 3/8	25 3/8	23 7/8	17 7/8	5	4	Chippewa County	WI	Allen Larson	1990	7,052
140 3/8	25 2/8	25 3/8	19 5/8	5	4	Jo Daviess County	IL	Thomas J. Smith	1990	7,052
140 3/8	24 2/8	24 4/8	17 7/8	5	6	Kenosha County	WI	Robin L. Schuirmann	1991	7,052
140 3/8	23 1/8	23 6/8	18 6/8	6	8	Sawyer County	WI	Christopher J. Radtke	1991	7,052
140 3/8	22 4/8	22 0/8	16 5/8	5	5	Fairfield County	CT	Robert P. McCarty	1991	7,052
140 3/8	23 7/8	23 0/8	19 5/8	6	6	Dunn County	WI	Scott Johnson	1992	7,052
140 3/8	22 6/8	23 1/8	20 3/8	4	4	Lebanon County	PA	Larry Shifflet	1992	7,052
140 3/8	24 4/8	24 7/8	20 6/8	4	6	Warren County	NJ	James Christopher Hausamann	1992	7,052
140 3/8	22 4/8	22 4/8	16 1/8	5	5	Tom Green County	TX	Ronnie Parsons	1992	7,052
140 3/8	22 4/8	22 1/8	18 1/8	6	5	Brown County	SD	Brian Griebenow	1993	7,052
140 3/8	22 5/8	22 5/8	14 3/8	4	4	Pike County	IL	Doug Cantrall	1993	7,052
140 3/8	22 7/8	22 2/8	19 5/8	4	4	Suffolk County	NY	Jeffrey Asendorf	1993	7,052
140 3/8	23 4/8	24 0/8	16 4/8	4	5	La Salle County	TX	Jerald Carter	1993	7,052
140 3/8	22 7/8	24 6/8	17 3/8	4	4	Marion County	IL	David Whitford	1994	7,052
140 3/8	23 5/8	24 7/8	17 1/8	4	4	Wayne County	NY	Kenneth Gene Van Koevering, Jr	1994	7,052
140 3/8	23 0/8	23 4/8	19 5/8	5	5	Waukesha County	WI	Michael Klermund	1994	7,052
140 3/8	23 0/8	23 0/8	19 7/8	5	4	Anderson County	KS	Dennis L. Dahlke	1994	7,052
140 3/8	23 5/8	24 2/8	20 2/8	6	6	Waukesha County	WI	Ken Johnson	1994	7,052
140 3/8	22 2/8	21 7/8	18 1/8	7	6	Suffolk County	NY	David Sacks	1994	7,052
140 3/8	23 7/8	24 0/8	15 3/8	5	5	Otter Tail County	MN	Steven Thoennes	1994	7,052
140 3/8	21 3/8	21 5/8	16 2/8	6	5	Lake County	IL	John Zradicka	1994	7,052
140 3/8	25 3/8	25 6/8	15 3/8	7	7	Macon County	MO	Tom Mixen	1994	7,052
140 3/8	21 5/8	22 1/8	15 3/8	5	5	Sterling County	TX	Randy Brewer	1995	7,052
140 3/8	23 1/8	23 3/8	16 5/8	5	6	Greene County	IL	Dixie Garner	1995	7,052
140 3/8	23 6/8	24 4/8	16 7/8	4	4	Cherokee County	KS	Gene R. Hamilton	1995	7,052
140 3/8	23 0/8	22 5/8	16 2/8	6	8	Winneshiek County	IA	Terry Schar	1995	7,052

WHITETAIL DEER (TYPICAL ANTLERS)

Minimum Score 125 — Continued

SCORE	LENGTH OF MAIN BEAM R	LENGTH OF MAIN BEAM L	INSIDE SPREAD	NUMBER OF POINTS R	NUMBER OF POINTS L	AREA	STATE/ PROVINCE	HUNTER'S NAME	DATE	RANK
140 3/8	23 4/8	23 0/8	19 4/8	6	6	Washington County	WI	Judy Staedler	1995	7,052
140 3/8	23 2/8	22 7/8	17 5/8	5	5	Preble County	OH	Jay "Snuffy" Combs	1995	7,052
140 3/8	24 3/8	20 4/8	22 7/8	6	5	Will County	IL	Jim Ehrhardt	1995	7,052
140 3/8	23 3/8	22 1/8	18 1/8	4	5	Dunn County	WI	Rick J. Brantner	1995	7,052
140 3/8	23 5/8	23 0/8	16 5/8	5	4	Macomb County	MI	Raymond B. Dault	1995	7,052
140 3/8	24 5/8	24 7/8	19 5/8	5	5	Dundurn	SAS	Sean Russell	1996	7,052
140 3/8	22 7/8	24 2/8	17 6/8	6	5	Warren County	MS	Armond Duval	1996	7,052
140 3/8	25 2/8	25 3/8	21 3/8	5	5	Rock County	WI	Jeromy Hatlevig	1996	7,052
140 3/8	22 4/8	21 2/8	17 3/8	5	5	Washington County	MN	Wayne A. Nicholson	1996	7,052
140 3/8	21 7/8	22 6/8	18 3/8	5	5	Green Lake County	WI	Michael "Mickey" Becker	1996	7,052
140 3/8	24 6/8	24 2/8	15 3/8	5	5	Claiborne County	MS	Chris Toney	1996	7,052
140 3/8	24 4/8	23 5/8	18 1/8	4	5	Summit County	OH	Michael P. Cirignano	1996	7,052
140 3/8	24 4/8	23 7/8	17 5/8	4	4	Henry County	IA	Joe McSorley	1996	7,052
140 3/8	22 0/8	24 2/8	19 3/8	5	4	Tuscaloosa County	AL	Keith McKnight	1996	7,052
140 3/8	22 5/8	23 1/8	16 3/8	5	5	Allegheny County	PA	Jeff Sefchik	1997	7,052
140 3/8	24 3/8	24 1/8	18 2/8	6	5	Allamakee County	IA	Les Smith	1997	7,052
140 3/8	22 2/8	23 0/8	16 5/8	7	6	Ohio County	KY	Jeff Leach	1997	7,052
140 3/8	23 1/8	23 1/8	19 5/8	6	6	Kosciusko County	IN	Eric E. Coburn	1997	7,052
140 3/8	23 4/8	24 2/8	22 7/8	5	6	Jackson County	IA	Milo F. Brown, Jr.	1997	7,052
140 3/8	25 7/8	25 4/8	18 7/8	4	4	Ottawa County	KS	Patrick E. Helget	1997	7,052
140 3/8	21 7/8	22 1/8	17 5/8	5	5	Houston County	MN	Bill Clink	1997	7,052
140 3/8	20 6/8	20 2/8	16 3/8	5	5	Washington County	WI	Steven Schultz	1997	7,052
140 3/8	23 2/8	22 7/8	19 1/8	4	4	Logan County	IL	Wayne Clark	1997	7,052
140 3/8	23 3/8	23 5/8	16 7/8	6	5	Brooks	ALB	Mark Nelson	1998	7,052
140 3/8	24 5/8	23 5/8	17 0/8	4	5	Winneshiek County	IA	Steve Daughtin	1998	7,052
140 3/8	23 1/8	23 0/8	16 7/8	5	5	Winnebago County	WI	Michael Zimmer	1998	7,052
140 2/8	20 5/8	21 5/8	25 0/8	6	6	Harrison County	IA	Larry Vaughn	1961	7,125
140 2/8	23 7/8	23 1/8	18 4/8	4	4	Redwood County	MN	Irvin Plotz	1967	7,125
140 2/8	25 1/8	25 2/8	16 2/8	8	9	Big Stone County	MN	Peter Behlen	1972	7,125
140 2/8	20 4/8	20 7/8	19 4/8	5	5	Morrison County	MN	Gary Sutherland	1973	7,125
140 2/8	21 2/8	20 4/8	18 0/8	5	5	Walworth County	WI	Michael Stang	1975	7,125
140 2/8	22 2/8	21 6/8	12 4/8	5	5	Platte County	MO	Edward D. Johnson	1977	7,125
140 2/8	24 5/8	24 2/8	21 4/8	4	4	Buffalo County	WI	Brent Bauer	1978	7,125
140 2/8	23 1/8	23 1/8	18 2/8	5	4	Cochrane	ALB	Warren McInenly	1980	7,125
140 2/8	23 5/8	23 2/8	17 6/8	6	5	Dunn County	WI	Terry W. Stallman	1981	7,125
140 2/8	22 6/8	23 7/8	17 2/8	4	5	Tazewell County	IL	Jim Plemmons	1982	7,125
140 2/8	21 2/8	20 6/8	16 2/8	7	8	Jackson County	WI	Gary L. Barneson	1985	7,125
140 2/8	24 1/8	24 6/8	17 4/8	5	4	Pike County	OH	Edwin H. Lynch	1985	7,125
140 2/8	21 7/8	22 5/8	16 6/8	5	4	Morrison County	MN	Jeffrey J. Moris	1985	7,125
140 2/8	23 1/8	22 3/8	15 6/8	4	4	Saline County	KS	Barry Miller	1985	7,125
140 2/8	26 3/8	27 2/8	21 2/8	4	3	Highland County	OH	Floyd Wagers, Jr.	1985	7,125
140 2/8	23 7/8	27 1/8	15 4/8	6	5	Butler County	KS	Mark Scott	1985	7,125
140 2/8	24 7/8	24 7/8	22 1/8	5	5	Dodge County	WI	Ron Tiedt	1986	7,125
140 2/8	23 4/8	23 0/8	18 4/8	5	4	Logan County	KY	Terry Baldwin	1987	7,125
140 2/8	23 0/8	23 2/8	20 2/8	4	5	Dubois County	IN	Glen J. Uebelhor	1987	7,125
140 2/8	23 1/8	23 2/8	15 6/8	8	8	Johnson County	IA	Shawn Smith	1988	7,125
140 2/8	23 5/8	24 4/8	21 4/8	4	5	Greenup County	KY	Dale Brown	1988	7,125
140 2/8	22 4/8	22 2/8	16 7/8	8	5	Kandiyohi County	MN	Gene Retka	1988	7,125
140 2/8	24 7/8	25 0/8	17 6/8	4	4	New Castle County	DE	Mike Smith	1988	7,125
140 2/8	21 5/8	21 5/8	21 0/8	5	5	Buffalo County	WI	David Baum	1988	7,125
140 2/8	24 0/8	24 2/8	17 2/8	6	7	Kit Carson County	CO	Dave Holt	1988	7,125
140 2/8	23 6/8	25 0/8	19 4/8	5	6	Baltimore County	MD	Wayne R. McElwain	1988	7,125
140 2/8	24 4/8	26 0/8	18 5/8	4	5	Pike County	OH	Stephen C. Miller	1988	7,125
140 2/8	22 0/8	22 7/8	18 6/8	5	5	Buffalo County	WI	David Stuhr	1989	7,125
140 2/8	21 0/8	22 2/8	15 2/8	4	5	Thurston County	NE	Scott R. Urbanec	1989	7,125
140 2/8	20 6/8	20 3/8	17 2/8	5	5	Tama County	IA	Loren W. Knoop	1989	7,125
140 2/8	23 7/8	24 2/8	18 3/8	6	5	Isanti County	MN	Craig Dugas	1989	7,125
140 2/8	25 2/8	26 0/8	17 0/8	4	4	Bennington County	VT	William Werner	1990	7,125
140 2/8	24 4/8	24 6/8	17 6/8	5	4	Jackson County	IL	Jim Rickhoff	1990	7,125
140 2/8	22 5/8	22 6/8	22 6/8	5	5	Lawrence County	PA	Kevin James Barber	1990	7,125
140 2/8	23 7/8	23 1/8	19 4/8	5	5	Monroe County	NY	Tony Casciani	1990	7,125
140 2/8	24 0/8	23 1/8	16 2/8	4	4	McHenry County	IL	Tom Pigott	1990	7,125
140 2/8	25 7/8	25 4/8	20 0/8	4	5	Ralls County	MO	Mike Hardy	1990	7,125
140 2/8	25 5/8	24 4/8	19 4/8	5	5	Highland County	OH	James Landrum	1991	7,125
140 2/8	23 5/8	23 4/8	18 2/8	4	4	Douglas County	MO	Charlie Johnston	1991	7,125
140 2/8	20 6/8	21 2/8	16 0/8	5	5	Richland County	MT	Sam McCorkel, Jr.	1992	7,125
140 2/8	21 6/8	21 7/8	19 4/8	5	5	McHenry County	IL	Mark N. Moore	1992	7,125
140 2/8	23 2/8	22 6/8	15 0/8	5	6	Val Verde County	TX	A. T. Coleman	1992	7,125
140 2/8	22 4/8	23 4/8	18 1/8	5	4	Jersey County	IL	Judy Kovar	1993	7,125
140 2/8	22 0/8	20 7/8	18 2/8	5	5	Lincoln County	WI	Keene Robl	1994	7,125
140 2/8	22 0/8	20 2/8	13 6/8	5	5	Noble County	IN	Jack W. Hostetler	1994	7,125
140 2/8	24 3/8	23 2/8	14 2/8	5	6	Chautauqua County	KS	Dean Walden	1994	7,125
140 2/8	19 0/8	20 1/8	17 2/8	4	5	Valley County	MT	Cory Kelm	1995	7,125
140 2/8	23 2/8	23 1/8	17 6/8	4	4	Moniteau County	MO	Steve Blank	1995	7,125
140 2/8	22 6/8	22 5/8	15 4/8	5	5	Tensas Parish	LA	Preston Walker	1995	7,125
140 1/8	23 3/8	24 4/8	18 5/8	5	5	Pike County	IL	Kenneth E. Carter	1991	7,193
140 1/8	21 3/8	21 7/8	15 5/8	5	5	Barry County	MI	Arthur P. Hayward, Jr.	1991	7,193
140 1/8	21 4/8	21 7/8	17 0/8	5	5	Marion County	IA	Chris Pendroy	1991	7,193

WHITETAIL DEER (TYPICAL ANTLERS)

Minimum Score 125 — Continued

SCORE	LENGTH OF MAIN BEAM R	LENGTH OF MAIN BEAM L	INSIDE SPREAD	NUMBER OF POINTS R	NUMBER OF POINTS L	AREA	STATE/ PROVINCE	HUNTER'S NAME	DATE	RANK
140 1/8	22 4/8	22 5/8	17 3/8	5	5	Fulton County	IL	Rex Lavin	1991	7,193
140 1/8	24 3/8	23 5/8	16 5/8	5	5	Marshall County	IA	Dale Smith	1991	7,193
140 1/8	22 0/8	20 7/8	15 1/8	5	5	Burnett County	WI	Michael Wynn	1991	7,193
140 1/8	22 2/8	21 6/8	17 5/8	7	6	Kit Carson County	CO	Dave Holt	1991	7,193
140 1/8	23 0/8	22 5/8	16 0/8	5	6	Kleberg County	TX	Chad Clark	1991	7,193
140 1/8	23 6/8	24 0/8	18 7/8	6	6	Duval County	TX	Ed Strayhorn	1991	7,193
140 1/8	21 7/8	21 1/8	15 5/8	5	5	Green Lake County	WI	David D. Casper	1992	7,193
140 1/8	21 2/8	21 0/8	17 3/8	5	6	Becker County	MN	Arnold F. Ostgarden	1992	7,193
140 1/8	24 4/8	24 5/8	20 3/8	4	4	Macomb County	MI	Tim M. Orebaugh	1992	7,193
140 1/8	22 3/8	23 1/8	19 5/8	4	4	Morrison County	MN	Randy Zinniel	1992	7,193
140 1/8	20 0/8	20 2/8	16 5/8	5	6	Crook County	WY	Jeff A. Broeckel	1993	7,193
140 1/8	20 5/8	20 3/8	18 0/8	6	5	Cook County	IL	F. Dan Dinelli	1993	7,193
140 1/8	22 2/8	22 6/8	16 5/8	5	5	Price County	WI	Bradley Dragovich	1993	7,193
140 1/8	20 2/8	21 4/8	19 7/8	5	6	Greene County	IL	Robert Neff	1993	7,193
140 1/8	25 0/8	24 0/8	16 5/8	5	6	Duck Mtns.	MAN	Myles Keller	1993	7,193
140 1/8	25 3/8	25 5/8	17 5/8	4	4	Ross County	OH	Robert Brown	1994	7,193
140 1/8	23 6/8	23 0/8	16 1/8	6	6	Buffalo County	WI	Troy Muche	1994	7,193
140 1/8	24 3/8	24 6/8	19 1/8	4	4	Carroll County	IL	Keith Holly	1994	7,193
140 1/8	22 0/8	22 7/8	17 6/8	6	6	Golden Valley County	ND	Michael Lingo	1994	7,193
140 1/8	24 3/8	24 7/8	18 7/8	5	5	Merrimack County	NH	David Wilson	1995	7,193
140 1/8	24 2/8	23 7/8	20 2/8	5	5	Franklin County	OH	Tim Davidheiser	1995	7,193
140 1/8	23 5/8	22 6/8	16 7/8	5	6	Sauk County	WI	Adam Klitzke	1995	7,193
140 1/8	21 5/8	22 2/8	18 5/8	4	4	Washington County	WI	Dan Infalt	1995	7,193
140 1/8	24 2/8	26 0/8	17 5/8	4	4	Buffalo County	WI	David L. Larson	1995	7,193
140 1/8	23 2/8	23 7/8	18 1/8	5	5	Dodge County	WI	Gary L. Boomsma	1995	7,193
140 1/8	23 3/8	23 3/8	17 5/8	5	5	Jasper County	IL	Michael Hewing	1995	7,193
140 1/8	22 7/8	22 7/8	17 7/8	5	4	Delaware County	IA	Mary Leonard	1995	7,193
140 1/8	23 3/8	22 4/8	17 1/8	5	5	Buffalo County	WI	John W. Zahrte	1995	7,193
140 1/8	20 7/8	20 6/8	20 5/8	5	6	Ferry County	WA	Doug Kikendall	1996	7,193
140 1/8	22 1/8	21 7/8	16 5/8	5	5	Gladwin County	MI	Richard E. Lindberg	1996	7,193
140 1/8	22 4/8	24 2/8	17 3/8	5	5	Monroe County	WI	C. Ron Hornburger	1996	7,193
140 1/8	21 3/8	21 1/8	17 1/8	6	5	Vernon County	WI	Ole Braaten	1996	7,193
140 1/8	24 2/8	24 4/8	21 2/8	4	5	Kane County	IL	Dean V. Ashton	1996	7,193
140 1/8	25 0/8	26 1/8	21 1/8	4	4	McLean County	IL	Scott Darnall	1996	7,193
140 1/8	21 4/8	23 0/8	17 1/8	5	5	Kleberg County	TX	John C. "Jack" Culpepper III	1996	7,193
140 1/8	23 0/8	22 4/8	17 7/8	4	4	Ravalli County	MT	Garret Decker	1996	7,193
140 1/8	22 4/8	21 6/8	18 1/8	6	5	Clark County	WI	Scott Baehr	1997	7,193
140 1/8	22 0/8	22 3/8	13 3/8	8	8	Burnet County	TX	Dennis Jowers	1997	7,193
140 1/8	24 1/8	23 0/8	17 1/8	5	6	Livingston County	NY	Jim Spencer	1997	7,193
140 1/8	25 6/8	26 1/8	19 7/8	5	5	Forsyth County	NC	Buck Horn	1997	7,193
140 1/8	23 3/8	23 1/8	17 1/8	4	4	Lake County	IL	Kevin Dahm	1997	7,193
140 1/8	22 6/8	22 0/8	18 7/8	5	5	La Crosse County	WI	Don Viner	1997	7,193
140 1/8	23 3/8	23 3/8	17 5/8	6	5	Randolph County	IL	Roy Brockmeyer	1997	7,193
140 1/8	22 7/8	23 2/8	16 3/8	5	5	Noble County	OH	Jody D. Laughery	1997	7,193
140 1/8	23 6/8	22 5/8	17 7/8	6	5	Lenawee County	MI	Jeff L. Bird	1997	7,193
140 1/8	24 6/8	24 1/8	17 5/8	4	4	Oakland County	MI	Dan Brooks	1997	7,193
140 1/8	24 2/8	23 5/8	14 6/8	6	5	Prairie County	AR	Greg London	1997	7,193
140 0/8	25 3/8	24 7/8	20 0/8	4	4	Houghton County	MI	Dr. V. R. Graber	1957	7,278
140 0/8	27 7/8	27 6/8	19 0/8	6	5	Ford County	KS	Melvin Miller	1973	7,278
140 0/8	23 1/8	22 0/8	19 2/8	6	6	Winona County	MN	Robert Fratzke	1974	7,278
140 0/8	22 0/8	22 1/8	15 5/8	8	6	Ottawa County	KS	Edward L. Wright	1974	7,278
140 0/8	23 3/8	22 3/8	15 0/8	5	5	Jackson County	MO	Marvin Thomey	1977	7,278
140 0/8	23 5/8	22 6/8	15 6/8	4	4	Rock County	WI	Bob Boden	1979	7,278
140 0/8	22 6/8	22 3/8	17 4/8	5	5	Macoupin County	IL	Terry Jenkins	1979	7,278
140 0/8	22 1/8	21 7/8	16 0/8	5	5	Brown County	SD	Todd T. Tunby	1980	7,278
140 0/8	22 3/8	22 7/8	16 4/8	5	5	Clay County	MN	Joe Lahlum	1981	7,278
140 0/8	20 6/8	21 2/8	16 2/8	5	5	Burleigh County	ND	Doran D. Alfstad	1982	7,278
140 0/8	23 3/8	21 7/8	19 2/8	5	5	Lucas County	IA	Bill Brown	1983	7,278
140 0/8	22 4/8	22 4/8	17 0/8	4	4	Washington County	KS	Stanley Brustowicz	1983	7,278
140 0/8	22 4/8	22 2/8	18 1/8	7	5	Starke County	IN	Connie N. McKee	1984	7,278
140 0/8	21 3/8	21 7/8	14 4/8	5	5	Hill County	MT	Steve Gorr	1984	7,278
140 0/8	25 3/8	26 2/8	20 6/8	5	5	Adams County	OH	Harry Tudor, Jr.	1984	7,278
140 0/8	21 5/8	21 7/8	16 4/8	5	5	Lake County	IL	Steve M. Andrews	1985	7,278
140 0/8	24 6/8	25 2/8	17 2/8	5	4	Pratt County	KS	Shawn M. James	1985	7,278
140 0/8	23 6/8	23 1/8	20 0/8	5	7	Brown County	MN	Hap Raabe	1986	7,278
140 0/8	20 2/8	21 6/8	14 6/8	5	5	Waupaca County	WI	Brian D. Korb	1986	7,278
140 0/8	27 4/8	23 1/8	20 0/8	5	5	Jackson County	OH	Dennis Crabtree	1986	7,278
140 0/8	22 7/8	22 4/8	18 2/8	5	4	Wabasha County	MN	Dan Rettmann	1986	7,278
140 0/8	24 7/8	22 2/8	18 4/8	5	6	Floyd County	IA	Scott Ginther	1987	7,278
140 0/8	25 0/8	24 6/8	20 0/8	3	3	Mahoning County	OH	Ronald K. Osborne	1987	7,278
140 0/8	22 4/8	23 1/8	19 0/8	4	4	Oceana County	MI	Robin Howard	1988	7,278
140 0/8	23 1/8	23 3/8	16 0/8	4	4	Monroe County	WI	Denis D. Haugrud	1988	7,278
140 0/8	22 5/8	22 0/8	16 2/8	5	6	Clearwater County	ID	Bob Carlson	1988	7,278
140 0/8	20 4/8	22 1/8	19 0/8	5	5	Nemaha County	NE	Keith Williams	1988	7,278
140 0/8	20 6/8	20 6/8	18 0/8	5	5	Washington County	MN	Douglas Wilson	1989	7,278
140 0/8	24 7/8	25 1/8	20 2/8	5	4	Jennings County	IN	Billy Neal	1989	7,278
140 0/8	22 0/8	22 7/8	17 2/8	5	5	Highland County	OH	Martin H. Bullock	1989	7,278

WHITETAIL DEER (TYPICAL ANTLERS) Continued

SCORE	LENGTH OF MAIN BEAM R	LENGTH OF MAIN BEAM L	INSIDE SPREAD	NUMBER OF POINTS R	NUMBER OF POINTS L	AREA	STATE/PROVINCE	HUNTER'S NAME	DATE	RANK
140 0/8	24 2/8	25 3/8	19 5/8	5	4	Livingston County	MO	Ron D. Easley	1989	7,278
140 0/8	23 7/8	23 6/8	16 1/8	6	6	Blue Earth County	MN	Dave Lobb	1989	7,278
140 0/8	24 5/8	24 5/8	20 2/8	6	6	Flathead River	BC	John P. Shannon	1990	7,278
140 0/8	25 1/8	24 7/8	18 6/8	6	5	Butler County	KS	Tim Ridder	1990	7,278
140 0/8	22 7/8	23 5/8	18 6/8	4	4	Todd County	MN	Steven R. Maack	1990	7,278
140 0/8	22 2/8	22 5/8	15 6/8	5	5	Ashland County	WI	David A. Stacey	1991	7,278
140 0/8	23 7/8	25 4/8	17 7/8	5	6	Lawrence County	IN	Arter Thompson	1991	7,278
140 0/8	22 2/8	23 0/8	17 0/8	6	5	Vinton County	OH	Tom Dishong, Jr.	1991	7,278
140 0/8	23 6/8	23 2/8	15 2/8	5	5	Franklin County	MO	William O. Schatz, Jr.	1991	7,278
140 0/8	23 7/8	23 4/8	17 0/8	4	5	Will County	IL	Richard L. Andre	1991	7,278
140 0/8	24 7/8	25 0/8	21 2/8	6	5	Monroe County	NY	Warren C. Bloom	1991	7,278
140 0/8	24 6/8	24 4/8	18 4/8	4	5	Humphreys County	TN	Ralph Bohannon	1992	7,278
140 0/8	21 7/8	21 3/8	17 6/8	5	5	Keya Paha County	NE	Rick Schack	1992	7,278
140 0/8	24 4/8	22 2/8	19 2/8	5	9	Hancock County	OH	Craig W. Sherman	1992	7,278
140 0/8	24 3/8	27 7/8	18 4/8	10	6	Livingston County	IL	David Diller	1992	7,278
140 0/8	25 6/8	25 4/8	18 0/8	4	4	Riley County	KS	Rob Gordon	1992	7,278
140 0/8	23 3/8	25 1/8	16 2/8	6	5	La Crosse County	WI	Mark Chrisinger	1992	7,278
140 0/8	23 5/8	23 2/8	18 2/8	4	4	Richland County	OH	Dan Root	1992	7,278
140 0/8	21 1/8	20 6/8	16 7/8	6	7	Anne Arundel County	MD	Andy Long	1992	7,278
140 0/8	23 4/8	22 6/8	16 6/8	5	6	Sullivan County	IN	John Hale	1992	7,278
140 0/8	24 2/8	23 1/8	22 2/8	5	4	Kenedy County	TX	Gene Scoggin	1992	7,278
140 0/8	24 6/8	25 6/8	23 4/8	7	6	Dane County	WI	Daryl A. Good	1993	7,278
140 0/8	22 6/8	22 0/8	19 2/8	5	5	Waukesha County	WI	Timothy J. Kuzmic	1993	7,278
140 0/8	23 0/8	24 1/8	17 0/8	5	5	Crawford County	PA	Carl M. Hazen	1993	7,278
140 0/8	23 2/8	23 3/8	15 4/8	5	5	Cattaraugus County	NY	Norris Luther	1993	7,278
140 0/8	25 0/8	24 3/8	18 6/8	4	4	Scott County	IA	Jeffrey R. Coonts	1993	7,278
140 0/8	23 4/8	23 7/8	18 6/8	4	4	Marinette County	WI	Mark W. Leipold	1993	7,278
140 0/8	25 3/8	24 6/8	20 0/8	6	4	Will County	IL	Ben Campbell	1993	7,278
140 0/8	23 2/8	23 5/8	17 6/8	5	6	Forest County	WI	Jim Sot	1993	7,278
140 0/8	23 4/8	25 1/8	19 2/8	7	6	Montgomery County	IL	Clifton C. Cange	1994	7,278
140 0/8	22 6/8	22 6/8	18 4/8	5	5	Rock County	WI	Larry D. Stangl	1994	7,278
140 0/8	21 5/8	21 1/8	16 0/8	5	5	Clark County	IL	Don Knoll	1994	7,278
140 0/8	22 2/8	21 1/8	18 6/8	7	5	Brooke County	WV	John Jay Irey	1994	7,278
140 0/8	25 2/8	16 3/8	22 0/8	5	5	Montgomery County	PA	William C. Fehon	1994	7,278
140 0/8	21 2/8	20 4/8	18 0/8	5	5	Mower County	MN	Mark Tindal	1994	7,278
140 0/8	21 5/8	21 3/8	16 0/8	5	5	Coles County	IL	Fred Hartbank	1994	7,278
140 0/8	25 5/8	24 7/8	20 6/8	7	5	Preble County	OH	Robert A. Worley	1994	7,278
140 0/8	23 7/8	22 7/8	20 2/8	5	6	Cass County	MI	Paul D. Papczynski	1994	7,278
140 0/8	22 3/8	22 6/8	20 2/8	5	5	Bucks County	PA	Michael C. Worrell	1995	7,278
140 0/8	22 4/8	22 1/8	16 6/8	4	4	Winona County	MN	Shawn Eyre	1995	7,278
140 0/8	22 5/8	22 7/8	15 2/8	4	4	Johnson County	MO	Mel Wright	1995	7,278
140 0/8	24 2/8	24 0/8	17 7/8	5	4	Christian County	IL	Jacky Chandler	1995	7,278
140 0/8	22 4/8	21 5/8	16 2/8	5	5	Sangamon County	IL	William E. Rohdeman	1995	7,278
140 0/8	25 4/8	24 4/8	16 4/8	4	4	Southampton County	VA	Kenneth G. Porter	1995	7,278
140 0/8	24 1/8	25 3/8	18 0/8	4	4	Westchester County	NY	Stephen L. Cook	1995	7,278
140 0/8	22 7/8	22 6/8	18 0/8	5	5	Rock County	WI	Cory Brown	1996	7,278
140 0/8	22 7/8	24 3/8	16 6/8	4	6	Oakland County	MI	Ronald Moses	1996	7,278
140 0/8	23 2/8	23 6/8	16 1/8	6	5	Highland County	OH	James Landrum	1996	7,278
140 0/8	22 0/8	22 2/8	17 6/8	5	5	Jefferson County	WI	Kurt Wegner	1996	7,278
140 0/8	22 4/8	22 6/8	16 4/8	4	4	Miami County	OH	Rick Wright	1996	7,278
140 0/8	22 6/8	21 6/8	17 0/8	5	6	Waseca County	MN	Robert Barrie	1997	7,278
140 0/8	23 5/8	22 5/8	17 4/8	4	4	Price County	WI	Rick Scanlon	1997	7,278
140 0/8	24 5/8	25 0/8	19 0/8	5	5	McHenry County	IL	Jacob Muench	1997	7,278
140 0/8	24 5/8	23 4/8	19 0/8	5	5	Montgomery County	MD	Darren Francis	1997	7,278
140 0/8	24 3/8	23 7/8	15 0/8	6	7	Montgomery County	KS	Greg Harris	1997	7,278
140 0/8	20 2/8	20 5/8	14 5/8	5	6	Brown County	WI	Quincy Koltz	1998	7,278
140 0/8	22 3/8	22 6/8	16 2/8	6	4	Door County	WI	Scott Klotz	1998	7,278
140 0/8	23 5/8	20 5/8	16 2/8	6	7	Pike County	IL	Hugh P. Riley	1998	7,278
140 0/8	25 0/8	24 2/8	16 6/8	4	5	Dane County	WI	Timothy J. Malec	1998	7,278
139 7/8	22 6/8	23 3/8	16 3/8	5	5	Martin County	IN	Warren Trinkle	1968	7,367
139 7/8	24 2/8	23 1/8	18 2/8	6	7	Jackson County	MI	Alfred A. Brenner	1973	7,367
139 7/8	23 0/8	23 4/8	18 0/8	8	5	St. Charles County	MO	Jerry D. Dale	1975	7,367
139 7/8	24 3/8	23 0/8	19 3/8	5	6	Woodford County	IL	Byron L. Davenport	1977	7,367
139 7/8	22 3/8	22 7/8	16 2/8	6	6	Lee County	IL	Charles L. Osborne	1977	7,367
139 7/8	23 6/8	22 0/8	14 0/8	5	6	Lyon County	KY	Denny Eubanks	1978	7,367
139 7/8	24 6/8	22 1/8	21 5/8	4	4	Perry County	IL	Dennis Vancil	1981	7,367
139 7/8	21 4/8	21 1/8	17 5/8	5	5	Roberts County	SD	Brian Sand	1983	7,367
139 7/8	23 1/8	23 6/8	18 5/8	4	4	Pike County	IL	Frank Dolbeare	1984	7,367
139 7/8	22 7/8	23 3/8	17 5/8	5	5	Walworth County	WI	James Kurth	1986	7,367
139 7/8	23 0/8	22 5/8	17 3/8	4	4	Allamakee County	IA	Ernie Burroughs	1986	7,367
139 7/8	23 4/8	24 7/8	18 7/8	4	4	Cowley County	KS	Steve Owen	1986	7,367
139 7/8	23 4/8	23 5/8	16 7/8	4	4	La Crosse County	WI	Rodney P. Schroeder	1987	7,367
139 7/8	23 1/8	24 5/8	18 3/8	5	4	Taylor County	WI	Diamond Dean	1988	7,367
139 7/8	22 6/8	22 0/8	18 7/8	4	4	Walworth County	WI	Eli Nieuwenhuis	1988	7,367
139 7/8	22 7/8	22 5/8	19 5/8	4	4	Prince Georges County	MD	Kevin Ball	1988	7,367
139 7/8	21 7/8	23 0/8	19 7/8	4	4	Washington County	MS	Richard Matthews	1989	7,367
139 7/8	24 6/8	25 1/8	19 7/8	5	5	Knox County	IL	Don Owen	1990	7,367
139 7/8	26 1/8	25 5/8	19 3/8	5	5	Waldo County	ME	Paul C. Hatch, Jr.	1990	7,367

385

WHITETAIL DEER (TYPICAL ANTLERS)

Minimum Score 125 — Continued

SCORE	LENGTH OF MAIN BEAM R	LENGTH OF MAIN BEAM L	INSIDE SPREAD	NUMBER OF POINTS R	NUMBER OF POINTS L	AREA	STATE/PROVINCE	HUNTER'S NAME	DATE	RANK
139 7/8	23 5/8	23 2/8	16 3/8	5	5	Heard County	GA	Dennis Ray Graham	1990	7,367
139 7/8	23 1/8	24 0/8	13 1/8	4	5	Price County	WI	Kyle Graf	1991	7,367
139 7/8	22 5/8	22 6/8	16 3/8	5	5	Manitowoc County	WI	Alan M. Rodewald	1991	7,367
139 7/8	22 6/8	21 0/8	17 2/8	6	5	Putnam County	OH	Jeffrey L. Kosch	1991	7,367
139 7/8	20 0/8	22 2/8	17 6/8	6	7	Lafayette County	WI	Mark E. Piper	1991	7,367
139 7/8	23 4/8	24 0/8	18 1/8	4	5	Clark County	IL	Kevin Boyer	1991	7,367
139 7/8	23 2/8	23 6/8	18 7/8	4	4	McLean County	IL	Daryle Tipsord	1992	7,367
139 7/8	21 5/8	22 3/8	16 0/8	6	6	Jerauld County	SD	Curtis L. Meylor	1992	7,367
139 7/8	24 3/8	24 5/8	18 1/8	5	5	Jersey County	IL	John Grounds	1992	7,367
139 7/8	23 2/8	23 3/8	16 3/8	5	4	Cloud County	KS	Greg Dockins	1992	7,367
139 7/8	20 4/8	22 1/8	17 6/8	6	5	Letellier	MAN	Randy Amenrud	1992	7,367
139 7/8	22 0/8	22 1/8	16 2/8	5	5	Polk County	MN	Kent Hollands	1992	7,367
139 7/8	25 7/8	25 3/8	19 7/8	4	5	Pueblo County	CO	Dale Bigger	1992	7,367
139 7/8	22 0/8	22 3/8	17 3/8	5	5	Langlade County	WI	James R. LeVeque	1993	7,367
139 7/8	26 4/8	25 1/8	19 0/8	5	5	Sumner County	KS	Lynn Reed	1993	7,367
139 7/8	22 3/8	22 3/8	16 5/8	5	5	La Salle County	IL	Todd Yeager	1993	7,367
139 7/8	22 7/8	23 4/8	19 3/8	5	6	Coles County	IL	Jon Willoughby	1993	7,367
139 7/8	23 1/8	23 4/8	18 3/8	4	4	Butler County	IA	Kelly Murray	1993	7,367
139 7/8	20 2/8	21 3/8	17 0/8	6	5	Audrain County	MO	Richard Bagley	1993	7,367
139 7/8	24 2/8	24 2/8	20 7/8	4	4	Washington County	MN	James Ralidak	1994	7,367
139 7/8	22 6/8	23 1/8	18 5/8	5	5	Lake County	IL	Ron Meverden	1994	7,367
139 7/8	22 6/8	22 2/8	15 1/8	5	5	Pike County	OH	William Koehler	1994	7,367
139 7/8	23 5/8	24 5/8	19 5/8	4	4	Pope County	IL	Ed Whitted	1994	7,367
139 7/8	22 7/8	23 7/8	17 2/8	5	5	Pottawatomie County	KS	Ray Burford	1994	7,367
139 7/8	24 2/8	23 2/8	21 0/8	4	6	Fayette County	IL	Charlie Gelsinger, Jr.	1995	7,367
139 7/8	22 7/8	22 6/8	15 7/8	4	4	Worcester County	MD	David L. Swift	1995	7,367
139 7/8	23 2/8	23 5/8	15 1/8	5	4	Kosciusko County	IN	Tracy Brookins	1995	7,367
139 7/8	23 7/8	23 4/8	22 1/8	5	6	Warren County	IA	Shane Marvelli	1995	7,367
139 7/8	23 7/8	24 2/8	17 6/8	7	6	Macoupin County	IL	Dave Burcham	1995	7,367
139 7/8	23 3/8	22 5/8	20 1/8	5	6	Westchester County	NY	Salvatore D'Amato	1995	7,367
139 7/8	23 3/8	23 6/8	20 1/8	7	6	Fulton County	IL	Bryan Anderson	1995	7,367
139 7/8	22 1/8	22 1/8	14 3/8	5	5	Knox County	IL	Gale Harriman	1996	7,367
139 7/8	22 7/8	23 0/8	19 0/8	6	4	Chester County	PA	Charles H. Chalfant	1996	7,367
139 7/8	24 2/8	24 2/8	19 1/8	5	5	Jones County	IA	Tracy Lee Meyers	1996	7,367
139 7/8	23 2/8	21 6/8	16 7/8	6	5	Warren County	OH	Steve Gerspacher	1997	7,367
139 7/8	25 4/8	22 7/8	17 7/8	4	6	Muscatine County	IA	James E. Quinn	1998	7,367
139 6/8	22 5/8	23 2/8	20 6/8	5	5	Barton County	KS	Charles Batman	1968	7,422
139 6/8	20 1/8	21 2/8	15 0/8	5	6	Macoupin County	IL	Mike Pirok	1978	7,422
139 6/8	23 4/8	23 0/8	20 4/8	5	5	Morgan County	OH	Marion Reed	1978	7,422
139 6/8	23 1/8	23 0/8	16 3/8	5	7	Ozaukee County	WI	Steven J. Baumann	1980	7,422
139 6/8	21 6/8	20 6/8	16 4/8	5	5	Clark County	AR	David McLemore	1980	7,422
139 6/8	28 0/8	27 4/8	21 3/8	3	5	Buffalo County	WI	Dean Sankey	1981	7,422
139 6/8	21 4/8	20 4/8	15 2/8	5	5	Idaho County	ID	Jim Sherman	1981	7,422
139 6/8	22 7/8	22 6/8	16 6/8	8	6	Pierce County	WI	Lee Langer	1982	7,422
139 6/8	24 1/8	22 4/8	16 6/8	5	5	Union County	IL	Leon Lane	1983	7,422
139 6/8	21 4/8	20 0/8	17 0/8	5	5	McLean County	IL	Willie Martin	1983	7,422
139 6/8	25 3/8	25 6/8	22 5/8	5	4	Reno County	KS	Wayne Finch	1983	7,422
139 6/8	22 5/8	22 3/8	19 0/8	4	4	Richland County	IL	Billy Joe Hicks	1983	7,422
139 6/8	23 2/8	23 5/8	19 0/8	4	4	Wabasha County	MN	Myles Keller	1983	7,422
139 6/8	22 6/8	22 4/8	16 1/8	6	6	Columbia County	WI	Steve Deminsky	1985	7,422
139 6/8	20 0/8	20 5/8	18 2/8	5	5	Campbell County	TN	Harold D. Tackett	1985	7,422
139 6/8	23 1/8	23 5/8	16 4/8	4	4	Kankakee County	IL	Dan Loyd	1986	7,422
139 6/8	24 4/8	25 6/8	20 0/8	5	5	Montgomery County	TN	Jim Asbury	1986	7,422
139 6/8	24 1/8	22 6/8	20 2/8	4	5	Harford County	MD	Mike Garrett	1987	7,422
139 6/8	26 2/8	25 3/8	17 7/8	5	5	Dane County	WI	Jeffrey P. Schultz	1987	7,422
139 6/8	25 2/8	23 6/8	19 2/8	4	4	Knox County	MO	Roger Gipple	1987	7,422
139 6/8	22 6/8	23 2/8	16 0/8	5	5	Iron County	MI	Dennis Schnicke	1988	7,422
139 6/8	25 1/8	25 4/8	15 6/8	4	4	Barber County	KS	Mark Asplund	1988	7,422
139 6/8	22 6/8	23 3/8	17 6/8	5	5	Dane County	WI	Donald K. Isaacson	1988	7,422
139 6/8	20 5/8	19 4/8	16 2/8	5	5	Webster County	IA	Terry D. Parker	1989	7,422
139 6/8	21 4/8	22 4/8	17 0/8	6	4	Southampton County	VA	John W. Alligood	1989	7,422
139 6/8	22 0/8	20 5/8	16 6/8	8	7	Washington County	OH	Brad Biehl	1989	7,422
139 6/8	24 0/8	22 7/8	17 3/8	6	5	Harrison County	IN	Paul Barker	1990	7,422
139 6/8	22 5/8	23 0/8	18 2/8	4	4	Logan County	WV	Jerry Sammons	1990	7,422
139 6/8	25 0/8	25 5/8	17 4/8	5	4	Chester County	PA	Blake S. Gibson	1990	7,422
139 6/8	23 4/8	23 4/8	16 5/8	6	5	Dodge County	WI	Randy Firari	1990	7,422
139 6/8	25 3/8	25 1/8	17 4/8	4	4	Montgomery County	AL	Nathan Lester	1990	7,422
139 6/8	23 3/8	23 2/8	16 4/8	6	7	Clarendon County	SC	James H. Smoak, Jr.	1991	7,422
139 6/8	21 0/8	21 6/8	16 0/8	5	5	Livingston County	MI	Thomas P. James	1991	7,422
139 6/8	24 1/8	24 1/8	17 0/8	5	4	Effingham County	IL	James Dirks	1991	7,422
139 6/8	21 6/8	21 5/8	18 4/8	5	6	Lincoln County	CO	Mel Hein	1991	7,422
139 6/8	23 3/8	24 7/8	18 6/8	4	5	Rock County	WI	Lee Crum	1992	7,422
139 6/8	22 7/8	23 0/8	15 6/8	4	5	Ashland County	WI	Dave Matis	1992	7,422
139 6/8	23 4/8	22 3/8	17 0/8	4	5	Washington County	MN	Mark Pelletier	1992	7,422
139 6/8	26 4/8	24 7/8	20 4/8	4	5	Westchester County	NY	Stephen L. Cook	1992	7,422
139 6/8	21 3/8	21 2/8	16 0/8	5	5	Marshall County	SD	Rick Stone	1992	7,422
139 6/8	23 0/8	24 0/8	18 0/8	6	5	Sauk County	WI	Brent Steinhorst	1992	7,422
139 6/8	23 0/8	22 3/8	16 2/8	5	5	Charlevoix County	MI	Larry Drost	1993	7,422

WHITETAIL DEER (TYPICAL ANTLERS)

Minimum Score 125 — Continued

SCORE	LENGTH OF MAIN BEAM R	LENGTH OF MAIN BEAM L	INSIDE SPREAD	NUMBER OF POINTS R	NUMBER OF POINTS L	AREA	STATE/PROVINCE	HUNTER'S NAME	DATE	RANK
139 6/8	21 6/8	22 3/8	17 4/8	5	6	McPherson County	KS	Darrell E. Kearns	1993	7,422
139 6/8	21 0/8	21 6/8	15 4/8	5	5	Crittenden County	KY	Darrell Townsend	1993	7,422
139 6/8	19 4/8	26 0/8	19 2/8	7	5	Lake County	IL	Ron E. Cox	1994	7,422
139 6/8	22 2/8	23 7/8	14 3/8	7	8	Yankton County	SD	Kevin R. DeJong	1994	7,422
139 6/8	19 7/8	20 3/8	14 5/8	5	6	Rawlins County	KS	Danny Carmen	1994	7,422
139 6/8	24 5/8	24 2/8	20 2/8	4	4	Leake County	MS	Eddie Chapman	1994	7,422
139 6/8	21 5/8	22 4/8	18 0/8	4	4	Linn County	KS	James D. Johnson	1994	7,422
139 6/8	21 5/8	22 4/8	18 1/8	5	4	Osage County	KS	Scotty Patton	1994	7,422
139 6/8	23 6/8	24 2/8	16 4/8	4	4	Calhoun County	IL	Bob Marshall	1994	7,422
139 6/8	21 3/8	22 1/8	16 5/8	6	6	Ravalli County	MT	Lyle S. Bainbridge	1995	7,422
139 6/8	26 0/8	25 0/8	18 2/8	4	5	Walworth County	WI	Randy Hackbarth	1995	7,422
139 6/8	23 4/8	23 2/8	15 7/8	6	5	Scott County	IA	Fred H. Smith, Jr.	1995	7,422
139 6/8	22 4/8	23 0/8	19 1/8	7	5	Randolph County	IL	Tom Cowell	1996	7,422
139 6/8	21 5/8	21 1/8	16 0/8	5	5	Jackson County	WI	Jeff L. German	1996	7,422
139 6/8	23 1/8	22 0/8	18 0/8	5	5	Jackson County	IN	Allan Branaman	1996	7,422
139 6/8	23 5/8	23 4/8	17 0/8	6	6	Berks County	PA	Frank W. Pitsko	1996	7,422
139 6/8	24 3/8	24 0/8	17 0/8	5	5	Rockingham County	NC	Dale L. Robbins	1997	7,422
139 6/8	23 7/8	24 2/8	21 0/8	4	4	Otter Tail County	MN	Kevin Kratzke	1997	7,422
139 6/8	23 1/8	22 7/8	18 2/8	4	5	Holt County	NE	Ralph Zeisler	1997	7,422
139 6/8	22 6/8	21 7/8	18 2/8	5	5	Clark County	WI	Jason Nuetzel	1997	7,422
139 6/8	23 3/8	23 6/8	13 6/8	4	4	Edgar County	IL	Jeremy A. Walters	1997	7,422
139 6/8	27 3/8	27 0/8	19 4/8	6	5	Racine County	WI	Michael A. Lietke	1997	7,422
139 6/8	20 2/8	21 1/8	15 4/8	5	5	Clark County	IN	Jeff Bailey	1997	7,422
139 6/8	25 5/8	27 2/8	19 0/8	4	4	Worcester County	MA	John J. Neri	1997	7,422
139 6/8	22 7/8	23 4/8	19 4/8	4	5	Marion County	KS	Dennis N. Ballweg	1997	7,422
139 6/8	23 2/8	23 6/8	20 1/8	8	7	Bracken County	KY	Tony Schumann	1998	7,422
139 5/8	22 0/8	22 3/8	18 6/8	6	6	Johnson County	IN	Howard VanSweringer	1961	7,490
139 5/8	24 4/8	24 6/8	19 1/8	5	4	Custer County	NE	Paul Ekberg	1974	7,490
139 5/8	27 3/8	28 1/8	20 0/8	4	7	Nicollet County	MN	Steve Suess	1976	7,490
139 5/8	22 2/8	23 3/8	18 5/8	5	5	Custer County	MT	Dale Drilling	1980	7,490
139 5/8	26 7/8	25 1/8	21 7/8	5	6	Westchester County	NY	Michael Iuzzolino	1980	7,490
139 5/8	23 2/8	22 3/8	16 5/8	5	5	La Salle County	IL	Jack Tabor	1983	7,490
139 5/8	22 4/8	22 2/8	16 5/8	4	5	Dickinson County	IA	Eldon L. Kraninger	1983	7,490
139 5/8	21 5/8	23 3/8	17 1/8	5	5	Dawson County	MT	Martin P. Weiske	1985	7,490
139 5/8	21 3/8	19 0/8	19 7/8	5	7	Ottawa County	MI	Thomas A. Dennis	1986	7,490
139 5/8	23 3/8	22 5/8	19 1/8	5	5	Fairfield County	CT	James A. McFadden, Sr.	1988	7,490
139 5/8	21 4/8	21 7/8	15 1/8	5	5	Clark County	IL	Gerald Shaffner	1988	7,490
139 5/8	24 2/8	23 3/8	19 0/8	4	5	Union County	IL	Jerry Koerkenmeier	1988	7,490
139 5/8	24 1/8	23 3/8	18 5/8	5	4	Suffolk County	NY	Carlos Squires	1988	7,490
139 5/8	21 5/8	21 0/8	14 0/8	5	6	Burleigh County	ND	Marcus Vogel	1989	7,490
139 5/8	24 1/8	23 4/8	18 1/8	4	5	Sabine County	TX	William Allen Duvall, Jr.	1989	7,490
139 5/8	21 2/8	22 6/8	18 5/8	5	5	St. Croix County	WI	Roger Ruelin	1989	7,490
139 5/8	26 1/8	25 7/8	19 7/8	3	5	Lac qui Parle County	MN	Mark Graham	1989	7,490
139 5/8	21 6/8	21 3/8	16 7/8	5	6	Blue Earth County	MN	Jim Wakefield	1989	7,490
139 5/8	23 5/8	22 4/8	17 7/8	4	4	Clay County	MO	Jeff Utz	1989	7,490
139 5/8	20 1/8	19 6/8	15 4/8	7	6	Lincoln County	WA	Monty K. Thomas	1991	7,490
139 5/8	24 4/8	23 4/8	18 2/8	4	5	La Crosse County	WI	Steve Tauscher	1991	7,490
139 5/8	22 4/8	18 6/8	15 7/8	5	7	Dane County	WI	Paul O. Jorstad	1991	7,490
139 5/8	25 3/8	24 0/8	18 1/8	4	4	Franklin County	IL	Ronald Jackson	1991	7,490
139 5/8	22 1/8	21 5/8	17 5/8	6	6	Coleman County	TX	J. Paul Ellis	1991	7,490
139 5/8	24 4/8	24 1/8	19 4/8	6	5	Tazewell County	IL	John P. Condis	1992	7,490
139 5/8	20 6/8	21 7/8	17 5/8	4	4	Pulaski County	MO	Marvin T. Wigley, Jr.	1992	7,490
139 5/8	25 0/8	22 0/8	18 1/8	5	5	Tompkins County	NY	Ray D. Knuutila	1992	7,490
139 5/8	22 7/8	23 2/8	17 5/8	6	6	Henry County	VA	Mike Weaver	1992	7,490
139 5/8	24 5/8	25 7/8	19 7/8	5	4	St. Joseph County	IN	Jerry White	1992	7,490
139 5/8	23 2/8	23 7/8	19 3/8	5	4	Montgomery County	MD	Randy Stockman	1992	7,490
139 5/8	22 4/8	22 6/8	17 4/8	6	6	La Crosse County	WI	Merlin Larson	1993	7,490
139 5/8	23 2/8	23 1/8	17 7/8	5	6	Rock County	WI	John G. Donstad	1993	7,490
139 5/8	21 2/8	23 3/8	19 6/8	6	8	Grayson County	TX	Grady Chambers	1993	7,490
139 5/8	23 1/8	23 1/8	16 0/8	5	7	Waupaca County	WI	Terryl Newton	1993	7,490
139 5/8	22 5/8	22 6/8	17 7/8	5	4	Tippecanoe County	IN	Brian Blankenship	1993	7,490
139 5/8	22 2/8	22 3/8	17 1/8	4	5	Langlade County	WI	David W. West	1994	7,490
139 5/8	24 7/8	23 4/8	17 1/8	4	5	Lee County	IL	Bill Heppler	1994	7,490
139 5/8	20 2/8	21 3/8	17 7/8	5	5	Marshall County	IN	Jonathan R. Fulmer	1994	7,490
139 5/8	24 3/8	24 7/8	18 7/8	4	5	Pottawattamie County	IA	Rodney Stahlnecker	1994	7,490
139 5/8	21 5/8	21 7/8	18 1/8	4	4	Fayette County	IL	Steve Garrison	1994	7,490
139 5/8	24 2/8	23 5/8	17 5/8	5	4	Grant County	WI	Jim Vosberg	1994	7,490
139 5/8	22 3/8	22 3/8	18 2/8	6	5	Marion County	KS	Stephen Kotz	1994	7,490
139 5/8	22 5/8	23 2/8	18 3/8	5	5	Winnebago County	IL	Mark D. Lester	1994	7,490
139 5/8	25 1/8	23 7/8	21 7/8	5	5	Geauga County	OH	Bill P. Stinchcomb	1994	7,490
139 5/8	22 1/8	22 1/8	16 0/8	6	5	Buffalo County	WI	Tony Hibbard	1995	7,490
139 5/8	23 6/8	25 1/8	16 7/8	4	4	Nemaha County	NE	Jason A. Swanson	1995	7,490
139 5/8	22 0/8	21 4/8	18 5/8	7	5	Marshall County	IL	Joe A. Newell	1995	7,490
139 5/8	26 3/8	26 2/8	20 6/8	7	6	Anoka County	MN	Todd Amenrud	1995	7,490
139 5/8	23 5/8	22 1/8	21 3/8	5	5	Kane County	IL	Tom Cousland	1995	7,490
139 5/8	23 4/8	24 5/8	18 0/8	4	5	Jim Hogg County	TX	H. C. Weil	1995	7,490
139 5/8	23 3/8	22 4/8	16 5/8	4	5	Sauk County	WI	Scott E. Sprecher	1996	7,490
139 5/8	22 1/8	21 5/8	19 5/8	4	4	Daviess County	MO	Ken Whithaus	1996	7,490

WHITETAIL DEER (TYPICAL ANTLERS)

Minimum Score 125

SCORE	LENGTH OF MAIN BEAM R	LENGTH OF MAIN BEAM L	INSIDE SPREAD	NUMBER OF POINTS R	NUMBER OF POINTS L	AREA	STATE/PROVINCE	HUNTER'S NAME	DATE	RANK
139 5/8	22 6/8	22 6/8	14 3/8	5	5	Berkshire County	MA	Darryl Darby	1996	7,490
139 5/8	22 5/8	21 7/8	21 3/8	4	4	Pratt County	KS	Greg Windler	1996	7,490
139 5/8	23 4/8	22 5/8	19 2/8	6	5	McDowell County	WV	Gary Rasnake	1996	7,490
139 5/8	23 4/8	22 7/8	17 5/8	5	5	Ozaukee County	WI	A. Matthew Albright	1997	7,490
139 5/8	22 6/8	22 5/8	16 7/8	4	6	St. Croix County	WI	Dave Iverson	1997	7,490
139 5/8	21 7/8	22 2/8	17 2/8	5	6	Cortland County	NY	Thomas Walden	1997	7,490
139 5/8	22 4/8	22 3/8	16 1/8	5	5	Decatur County	IA	Tom Lodovico	1997	7,490
139 5/8	23 0/8	22 2/8	17 5/8	5	5	Lawrence County	MO	Travis Ross	1997	7,490
139 5/8	25 4/8	25 5/8	17 7/8	5	4	Marion County	KS	Travis R. Sargent	1997	7,490
139 5/8	24 2/8	23 7/8	16 6/8	5	5	Windham County	CT	Mark A. Fortin	1998	7,490
139 4/8	23 5/8	23 0/8	20 0/8	5	4	Hart County	KY	Robert L. Galloway	1967	7,552
139 4/8	20 1/8	19 3/8	17 4/8	5	5	Clinton County	MI	Richard H. Wilt	1968	7,552
139 4/8	22 4/8	23 4/8	19 0/8	5	5	Fillmore County	MN	Orvis J. Dahl	1971	7,552
139 4/8	25 5/8	27 1/8	20 2/8	4	5	Jack County	TX	Ray Brewster	1975	7,552
139 4/8	22 2/8	23 2/8	17 5/8	5	4	Marshall County	KS	Tim Wanklyn	1978	7,552
139 4/8	22 0/8	21 5/8	16 4/8	6	7	Dane County	WI	Mike Schoenbeck	1981	7,552
139 4/8	21 6/8	22 0/8	17 4/8	5	5	Idaho County	ID	Dwight Schuh	1981	7,552
139 4/8	23 5/8	23 2/8	20 3/8	6	6	Rock County	WI	Dennis L. Meyer	1981	7,552
139 4/8	23 4/8	22 0/8	18 0/8	5	5	Licking County	OH	Richard E Pipes	1983	7,552
139 4/8	22 0/8	21 3/8	17 4/8	6	6	Jackson County	IN	Michael D. Clark	1984	7,552
139 4/8	21 0/8	21 0/8	16 6/8	4	4	Marion County	IA	Tim Pottorff	1985	7,552
139 4/8	23 1/8	23 4/8	17 4/8	5	5	Kittson County	MN	Stephen P. Skjold	1986	7,552
139 4/8	24 3/8	25 2/8	18 6/8	4	4	Jackson County	IL	David P. Beer	1986	7,552
139 4/8	24 0/8	23 1/8	21 0/8	6	4	Trego County	KS	Brian Miller	1986	7,552
139 4/8	23 2/8	24 4/8	16 7/8	5	7	Jersey County	IL	Herman Kovar	1986	7,552
139 4/8	22 4/8	21 5/8	15 6/8	5	5	Kenedy County	TX	Harold R. Arve, Jr.	1987	7,552
139 4/8	22 7/8	22 6/8	17 2/8	5	5	Waushara County	WI	Russell Marks	1987	7,552
139 4/8	25 4/8	26 2/8	18 1/8	6	7	Morrison County	MN	Martin Husnik	1987	7,552
139 4/8	24 6/8	24 4/8	18 4/8	6	5	Dukes County	MA	Louis Ashley	1987	7,552
139 4/8	24 3/8	23 4/8	17 0/8	5	5	Lowndes County	MS	Tim Graber	1987	7,552
139 4/8	22 7/8	22 2/8	19 2/8	5	5	Rooks County	KS	Michael Jirak	1987	7,552
139 4/8	22 5/8	22 7/8	18 4/8	5	5	Claiborne County	MS	Bill Cassell	1988	7,552
139 4/8	24 0/8	24 5/8	17 4/8	7	6	Rock County	MN	Jim Lorenzen	1988	7,552
139 4/8	21 0/8	21 5/8	14 0/8	5	5	Jackson County	WI	Aaron Dow	1988	7,552
139 4/8	25 5/8	26 3/8	17 0/8	6	6	Atlantic County	NJ	Bob Eisele	1988	7,552
139 4/8	24 5/8	25 3/8	20 0/8	6	6	Dubuque County	IA	Thomas Schwendinger	1988	7,552
139 4/8	24 7/8	24 4/8	18 2/8	4	5	Butler County	PA	David Penn	1990	7,552
139 4/8	24 1/8	25 0/8	17 2/8	5	7	Washington County	WI	Fred Geidel	1990	7,552
139 4/8	21 5/8	20 6/8	17 4/8	5	5	Barron County	WI	Al Jensen	1990	7,552
139 4/8	20 3/8	20 0/8	15 4/8	5	5	Florence County	WI	James W. Ernst	1991	7,552
139 4/8	22 6/8	23 2/8	19 4/8	5	5	Douglas County	WI	Dr. Michael R. Lawler	1991	7,552
139 4/8	19 4/8	22 1/8	17 2/8	5	5	Gogebic County	MI	Robert L. Peterson	1991	7,552
139 4/8	22 4/8	22 1/8	15 6/8	5	5	Berkshire County	MA	Jerry A. Shampang	1991	7,552
139 4/8	21 4/8	22 1/8	16 6/8	4	5	Whiteside County	IL	Trent McKenna	1991	7,552
139 4/8	21 4/8	22 3/8	15 4/8	6	5	Lincoln County	MT	Bart McCully	1992	7,552
139 4/8	23 0/8	23 5/8	14 4/8	4	4	Harford County	MD	William David Nelson	1992	7,552
139 4/8	18 6/8	19 6/8	15 0/8	6	7	De Kalb County	MO	Garry Pierson	1992	7,552
139 4/8	21 5/8	22 7/8	14 6/8	6	5	Christian County	KY	Bruce Pyle	1992	7,552
139 4/8	23 6/8	25 4/8	19 2/8	5	4	Franklin County	IN	Michael J. Peters	1992	7,552
139 4/8	22 2/8	23 5/8	17 7/8	4	5	Ontario County	NY	Nick Castiglia, Jr.	1993	7,552
139 4/8	22 6/8	24 3/8	20 6/8	5	5	McDowell County	WV	John Wolfe	1993	7,552
139 4/8	21 3/8	22 1/8	15 4/8	5	5	Dauphin County	PA	Duane Vragovich	1994	7,552
139 4/8	24 3/8	25 6/8	17 0/8	4	5	Crawford County	WI	Kenneth Fenske	1994	7,552
139 4/8	22 0/8	22 0/8	22 2/8	5	6	Pike County	IL	Gary Goldasich	1994	7,552
139 4/8	25 6/8	26 1/8	21 2/8	4	5	Clark County	OH	Richard Lyall	1994	7,552
139 4/8	24 2/8	24 2/8	17 4/8	5	5	Kankakee County	IL	Scott Olthoff	1994	7,552
139 4/8	23 5/8	24 6/8	18 1/8	6	5	Johnson County	IL	William Phillip Foreman	1994	7,552
139 4/8	23 1/8	22 6/8	17 1/8	6	5	Muskingum County	OH	Jerry Johnson	1994	7,552
139 4/8	22 4/8	22 1/8	19 2/8	4	4	Clarke County	IA	William L. Tuttle	1994	7,552
139 4/8	24 3/8	24 0/8	17 6/8	5	4	De Witt County	IL	John Martone	1994	7,552
139 4/8	23 6/8	26 2/8	19 0/8	4	4	Kent County	MD	Jim Samis	1994	7,552
139 4/8	23 0/8	22 5/8	19 3/8	6	5	Jefferson County	WI	Jeff Kruse	1995	7,552
139 4/8	22 4/8	22 3/8	15 3/8	6	5	Kerr County	TX	Lee Moore	1995	7,552
139 4/8	23 7/8	23 1/8	17 6/8	5	4	Richland County	ND	Jeff Bornong	1995	7,552
139 4/8	24 1/8	24 1/8	17 6/8	4	5	Tazewell County	IL	Dean E. Ingram	1996	7,552
139 4/8	21 3/8	22 4/8	19 2/8	5	5	Winnebago County	WI	Mike Sorensen	1996	7,552
139 4/8	23 2/8	23 3/8	18 0/8	4	4	Medina County	TX	Patrick R. Hughes	1997	7,552
139 4/8	23 3/8	22 7/8	18 0/8	6	5	Russell	MAN	Jeff Glasman	1997	7,552
139 4/8	21 0/8	20 5/8	17 5/8	5	6	Butler County	IA	Greg Cuvelier	1997	7,552
139 4/8	24 1/8	23 6/8	18 1/8	6	6	Beltrami County	MN	Steve Baltes	1997	7,552
139 4/8	22 1/8	22 3/8	17 0/8	6	5	Jefferson County	WI	Gregory Counter	1997	7,552
139 4/8	24 3/8	23 4/8	18 0/8	5	5	Kane County	IL	Jim Lutz	1997	7,552
139 4/8	24 2/8	23 1/8	17 2/8	5	4	Esterhazy	SAS	Murry Junek	1997	7,552
139 4/8	23 5/8	23 4/8	17 2/8	5	6	Price County	WI	Randy D. Niewiadomski	1998	7,552
139 4/8	20 4/8	20 4/8	23 6/8	5	5	Ste-Sophie d'Halifax	QUE	Raynald Groleau	1998	7,552
139 4/8	21 1/8	22 0/8	17 4/8	4	4	Johnson County	NE	Russell Topp	1998	7,552
139 3/8	24 0/8	27 0/8	18 2/8	5	5	Fulton County	IL	Raymond Rumler	1968	7,618
139 3/8	21 1/8	21 6/8	17 1/8	5	5	Outagamie County	WI	Thomas L. Haber	1975	7,618

WHITETAIL DEER (TYPICAL ANTLERS)

Minimum Score 125

SCORE	LENGTH OF MAIN BEAM R	LENGTH OF MAIN BEAM L	INSIDE SPREAD	NUMBER OF POINTS R	NUMBER OF POINTS L	AREA	STATE/PROVINCE	HUNTER'S NAME	DATE	RANK
139 3/8	21 1/8	21 1/8	16 3/8	6	6	Kalamazoo County	MI	Walter Myers	1977	7,618
139 3/8	24 7/8	22 5/8	16 3/8	5	6	Cumberland County	NJ	Winfield Cassaboon	1978	7,618
139 3/8	23 0/8	22 2/8	17 5/8	5	4	Des Moines County	IA	Ronald L. Cover	1978	7,618
139 3/8	23 0/8	21 2/8	14 7/8	5	5	Chatham County	NC	James Noonan III	1981	7,618
139 3/8	22 3/8	21 6/8	16 1/8	6	6	Jackson County	TN	Michael Mitchell	1983	7,618
139 3/8	24 3/8	24 5/8	20 3/8	7	7	Spokane County	WA	Mark Jones	1984	7,618
139 3/8	20 1/8	20 3/8	15 5/8	6	6	Dodge County	WI	Lester C. Neuman	1985	7,618
139 3/8	23 6/8	23 2/8	16 7/8	4	5	Guthrie County	IA	Larry Bryan	1985	7,618
139 3/8	23 0/8	21 7/8	17 7/8	5	6	Jefferson County	KS	Robert Ulmer	1985	7,618
139 3/8	24 1/8	23 4/8	17 7/8	5	5	Clayton County	IA	Ralph Livingston	1985	7,618
139 3/8	21 0/8	21 0/8	15 3/8	5	5	Morrison County	MN	Timothy Droher	1986	7,618
139 3/8	25 0/8	24 4/8	20 0/8	5	5	Lake County	IL	Kris A. Laho	1986	7,618
139 3/8	23 5/8	23 5/8	16 3/8	4	4	Ogle County	IL	Leo Pastuska, Jr.	1986	7,618
139 3/8	23 2/8	23 6/8	19 5/8	5	5	Rock County	WI	Ricky W. Peil	1986	7,618
139 3/8	23 6/8	23 5/8	16 7/8	6	5	Morgan County	OH	Jerry Beale	1986	7,618
139 3/8	23 5/8	23 2/8	17 7/8	5	5	McLeod County	MN	Don Ranzau	1986	7,618
139 3/8	20 4/8	22 0/8	17 3/8	5	5	Medina County	TX	Jimmy Glass	1987	7,618
139 3/8	22 4/8	23 0/8	14 3/8	5	5	Darke County	OH	Bruce Knick	1987	7,618
139 3/8	24 6/8	25 4/8	21 3/8	4	4	Brooke	ONT	Bill Majovsky	1987	7,618
139 3/8	21 1/8	21 2/8	15 4/8	7	6	Adams County	WI	John W. Faber	1988	7,618
139 3/8	22 0/8	22 3/8	15 1/8	5	5	Oconto County	WI	Gary L. Christensen	1988	7,618
139 3/8	24 4/8	24 2/8	18 4/8	5	4	Westchester County	NY	Morgan Seymour, Jr.	1988	7,618
139 3/8	21 2/8	22 1/8	16 2/8	7	5	Winnebago County	IL	Larry D. Stangl	1988	7,618
139 3/8	21 7/8	21 4/8	17 3/8	7	5	Columbia County	WI	Jerome Benisch	1989	7,618
139 3/8	21 2/8	21 2/8	17 1/8	6	5	Allen County	IN	Randy McCombs	1989	7,618
139 3/8	23 5/8	24 2/8	17 5/8	4	4	Wilkenson County	MS	Bruce Saale	1990	7,618
139 3/8	22 5/8	21 0/8	18 5/8	5	5	St. Joseph County	IN	Eric Erickson	1990	7,618
139 3/8	23 2/8	23 2/8	15 1/8	4	4	Boone County	AR	Phillip Vanderpool	1991	7,618
139 3/8	24 3/8	23 1/8	19 5/8	5	6	Waukesha County	WI	Michael T. McCann	1991	7,618
139 3/8	24 5/8	25 2/8	19 7/8	4	5	Jefferson County	IL	Lloyd Sweetin	1991	7,618
139 3/8	23 0/8	22 1/8	16 2/8	6	7	Carroll County	MO	Stanley L. Cooksey	1991	7,618
139 3/8	25 0/8	25 4/8	18 3/8	7	6	Rush County	IN	Brock Cross	1991	7,618
139 3/8	23 4/8	22 1/8	16 7/8	5	5	Langlade County	WI	David W. Nelsen	1992	7,618
139 3/8	21 6/8	22 0/8	16 7/8	5	5	Jones County	IA	Gary S. Grassi	1992	7,618
139 3/8	24 0/8	24 0/8	16 0/8	6	6	Marion County	IA	Mike Lanser	1992	7,618
139 3/8	22 3/8	23 0/8	17 1/8	4	4	Sangamon County	IL	Jason T. Musgrave	1993	7,618
139 3/8	22 0/8	22 1/8	14 1/8	6	5	Stevens County	WA	Kent Sipes	1993	7,618
139 3/8	22 0/8	21 7/8	22 4/8	8	5	Outagamie County	WI	Wayne E. Glatz	1993	7,618
139 3/8	23 3/8	23 3/8	17 3/8	5	5	Oakland County	MI	James M. Mauro	1993	7,618
139 3/8	22 7/8	21 5/8	15 6/8	5	6	Leavenworth County	KS	H. Burdett Rollins	1993	7,618
139 3/8	21 1/8	20 6/8	17 1/8	6	5	Caldwell County	KY	Chris Goodwin	1993	7,618
139 3/8	24 0/8	24 4/8	19 1/8	4	5	Suffolk County	NY	Gerald D. Higgins	1993	7,618
139 3/8	23 6/8	23 2/8	19 1/8	4	5	Monona County	IA	David L. Willis	1993	7,618
139 3/8	21 2/8	21 4/8	15 1/8	5	5	San Patricio County	TX	Domingo Lopez	1993	7,618
139 3/8	24 3/8	26 0/8	17 5/8	6	4	Wayne County	MI	Ronald R. Tillett	1994	7,618
139 3/8	23 2/8	22 5/8	16 5/8	8	4	Vermilion County	IL	Alex Kedas	1994	7,618
139 3/8	24 1/8	23 0/8	17 1/8	4	5	Anne Arundel County	MD	George L. Kane, Jr.	1994	7,618
139 3/8	22 5/8	22 7/8	16 1/8	5	6	Morrison County	MN	Ron Zahorski	1994	7,618
139 3/8	22 5/8	23 1/8	17 3/8	5	5	Dodge County	WI	Robert N. Webster IV	1994	7,618
139 3/8	22 4/8	23 1/8	18 2/8	6	7	Peoria County	IL	Larry T. Schmitt	1994	7,618
139 3/8	22 0/8	21 5/8	14 5/8	5	5	Walworth County	WI	Dale Wilson	1995	7,618
139 3/8	23 1/8	24 5/8	16 5/8	4	4	Oconto County	WI	Greg M. Wierzba	1995	7,618
139 3/8	23 4/8	23 3/8	15 0/8	6	5	Estill County	KY	Bobby G. Dawes	1995	7,618
139 3/8	24 1/8	23 4/8	18 3/8	7	6	Richland County	WI	Michael Wixom	1995	7,618
139 3/8	22 2/8	22 2/8	13 7/8	5	6	Buffalo County	WI	Thad W. Henderson	1995	7,618
139 3/8	22 0/8	22 2/8	20 1/8	5	5	Vernon County	WI	Randie O. Jorgensen	1995	7,618
139 3/8	23 5/8	23 6/8	18 7/8	4	4	La Salle County	IL	Dale Senica	1995	7,618
139 3/8	23 6/8	24 5/8	18 1/8	5	5	Anoka County	MN	Tom Evertz	1995	7,618
139 3/8	24 1/8	24 4/8	17 0/8	5	5	Crawford County	WI	Randall O. Nash	1996	7,618
139 3/8	22 5/8	24 7/8	19 5/8	4	4	Jo Daviess County	IL	Michael J. Bergles	1996	7,618
139 3/8	23 1/8	22 3/8	18 5/8	5	6	Dakota County	MN	Troy Franklin	1996	7,618
139 3/8	21 7/8	21 2/8	18 6/8	7	6	Cayuga County	NY	Alan Patrick	1996	7,618
139 3/8	19 7/8	20 4/8	15 5/8	6	5	Williams County	ND	Dean Halseth	1997	7,618
139 3/8	25 4/8	25 7/8	19 1/8	4	5	Dane County	WI	Mark A. Fay	1997	7,618
139 3/8	22 4/8	22 3/8	16 1/8	5	5	Dodge County	WI	Gary D. Naylor	1997	7,618
139 3/8	23 0/8	22 6/8	19 7/8	5	5	Stephenson County	IL	Wayne Crackenberger	1997	7,618
139 3/8	25 1/8	24 7/8	18 7/8	5	6	Madison County	OH	John Piccione	1998	7,618
139 2/8	21 6/8	22 6/8	16 4/8	6	6	Shelby County	IL	David McSchooler	1968	7,687
139 2/8	20 2/8	20 7/8	15 2/8	5	5	Burleigh County	ND	Burnell F. Paul	1971	7,687
139 2/8	22 1/8	23 2/8	17 2/8	5	5	Buffalo County	WI	Leonard Anglewitz	1972	7,687
139 2/8	24 2/8	23 4/8	17 6/8	4	4	McPherson County	KS	Glenn Waggoner	1977	7,687
139 2/8	23 1/8	23 1/8	18 2/8	4	4	Bayfield County	WI	Thomas E. Smith	1979	7,687
139 2/8	22 3/8	23 6/8	15 6/8	4	5	O'Brien County	IA	Ted Bruning	1980	7,687
139 2/8	21 3/8	21 6/8	17 1/8	6	5	Dodge County	NE	Dave Hain	1981	7,687
139 2/8	22 3/8	22 3/8	22 2/8	4	5	Whiteside County	IL	B. J. Higley	1981	7,687
139 2/8	24 6/8	23 7/8	17 2/8	5	6	Greenwood County	KS	Ed Tarver	1981	7,687
139 2/8	22 7/8	24 3/8	18 4/8	4	4	Richland County	WI	Dennis Kaderavek	1985	7,687
139 2/8	21 6/8	22 1/8	18 0/8	6	6	St. Charles County	MO	John Yacup	1985	7,687

WHITETAIL DEER (TYPICAL ANTLERS)

Minimum Score 125

SCORE	LENGTH OF MAIN BEAM R	LENGTH OF MAIN BEAM L	INSIDE SPREAD	NUMBER OF POINTS R	NUMBER OF POINTS L	AREA	STATE/PROVINCE	HUNTER'S NAME	DATE	RANK
139 2/8	23 5/8	25 0/8	14 6/8	6	5	Camden County	MO	Dewayne Holloway	1986	7,687
139 2/8	23 3/8	22 7/8	19 0/8	6	4	Saline County	KS	Hal Morris	1986	7,687
139 2/8	23 2/8	22 4/8	20 2/8	4	4	Delaware County	OH	David Orndorf	1986	7,687
139 2/8	24 3/8	23 6/8	17 6/8	5	4	Hennepin County	MN	Gary Gregg	1986	7,687
139 2/8	21 3/8	21 5/8	15 0/8	5	5	Dallas County	IA	Dave Rimathe	1987	7,687
139 2/8	25 2/8	23 6/8	19 6/8	5	4	Kenosha County	WI	William J. Raboine	1987	7,687
139 2/8	22 5/8	22 5/8	18 6/8	4	4	Hennepin County	MN	Paul H. Schutte	1987	7,687
139 2/8	21 1/8	22 0/8	22 3/8	4	4	Marion County	KS	Bret Lindsey	1988	7,687
139 2/8	22 7/8	23 3/8	16 6/8	4	4	Jersey County	IL	Larry W. Cornett	1989	7,687
139 2/8	20 5/8	21 4/8	17 6/8	5	5	Pepin County	WI	Ben Manor	1989	7,687
139 2/8	21 4/8	22 6/8	17 2/8	5	5	Atascosa County	TX	Joe Braun	1989	7,687
139 2/8	25 7/8	25 6/8	22 2/8	4	4	Kershaw County	SC	Wayne R. Gainey	1989	7,687
139 2/8	22 5/8	23 0/8	19 4/8	6	7	Livingston County	IL	Richard Halko	1990	7,687
139 2/8	18 1/8	20 7/8	14 2/8	6	6	Schuyler County	NY	Michael C. Voorheis	1990	7,687
139 2/8	21 2/8	20 5/8	15 7/8	5	5	Blue Earth County	MN	Darwin D. Arndt	1990	7,687
139 2/8	25 7/8	25 6/8	16 3/8	5	7	Polk County	IA	Carlis Stephens	1991	7,687
139 2/8	24 0/8	24 0/8	15 0/8	6	7	Montgomery County	AL	William R. "Bill" Henderson	1991	7,687
139 2/8	22 1/8	22 4/8	18 5/8	7	5	Iroquois County	IL	Robert G. Tammen	1991	7,687
139 2/8	21 7/8	21 2/8	19 2/8	6	7	Houston County	MN	Scott Forsyth	1992	7,687
139 2/8	25 4/8	25 3/8	18 3/8	5	4	New Castle County	DE	Joseph Jakonczuk	1992	7,687
139 2/8	22 7/8	22 7/8	18 4/8	4	4	Pike County	IL	Merlin Foltz	1992	7,687
139 2/8	22 0/8	21 7/8	18 0/8	5	5	Brooks County	TX	Tom Buckner	1993	7,687
139 2/8	20 1/8	21 1/8	15 0/8	5	7	St. Croix County	WI	Bruce Hatch	1993	7,687
139 2/8	23 0/8	23 0/8	16 4/8	5	5	Buffalo County	WI	Jeff Wendorf	1993	7,687
139 2/8	21 5/8	21 3/8	16 4/8	5	6	Cumberland County	IL	Michael D. Kutch	1993	7,687
139 2/8	21 5/8	22 4/8	17 0/8	5	5	Sawyer County	WI	Steven J. Olson	1994	7,687
139 2/8	22 3/8	23 0/8	18 0/8	4	4	Cross County	AR	Chris Sills	1994	7,687
139 2/8	24 4/8	25 2/8	17 2/8	5	6	Washington County	MN	Joe Thill	1994	7,687
139 2/8	23 4/8	25 0/8	17 2/8	5	6	Montgomery County	MD	Ronald L. Kuipers	1994	7,687
139 2/8	20 7/8	20 5/8	17 2/8	4	4	White County	IN	Firman D. Thompson	1994	7,687
139 2/8	21 6/8	22 6/8	20 1/8	6	6	Bureau County	IL	Gregory A. Bowers	1994	7,687
139 2/8	21 7/8	21 7/8	18 2/8	4	4	Washington County	IA	Ronald Ruth	1994	7,687
139 2/8	24 6/8	25 7/8	19 0/8	4	5	McLean County	IL	Todd Eades	1994	7,687
139 2/8	23 3/8	24 1/8	19 5/8	8	7	Vilas County	WI	Dan Herson	1995	7,687
139 2/8	25 2/8	23 0/8	15 6/8	6	5	Jackson County	OH	Carl Treadway	1995	7,687
139 2/8	20 4/8	21 3/8	16 1/8	5	6	Guthrie County	IA	Verner J. Lash, Jr.	1995	7,687
139 2/8	23 7/8	22 6/8	16 2/8	5	5	Pike County	IL	Troy Richart	1995	7,687
139 2/8	21 7/8	22 0/8	17 6/8	5	5	Seward County	NE	Daniel F. Hejl	1996	7,687
139 2/8	21 7/8	21 7/8	18 7/8	6	5	Wood County	WI	Clarence Arnold	1996	7,687
139 2/8	23 1/8	24 1/8	19 2/8	6	4	Hunterdon County	NJ	David Bodine	1996	7,687
139 2/8	20 1/8	20 3/8	15 2/8	5	5	Kalamazoo County	MI	Tyren Russell Cudney	1996	7,687
139 2/8	22 3/8	23 4/8	16 6/8	5	5	Pike County	OH	Dr. John Ribic	1996	7,687
139 2/8	22 7/8	23 2/8	17 3/8	5	5	Caroline County	MD	William Shull	1996	7,687
139 2/8	21 1/8	20 4/8	16 2/8	6	5	Dane County	WI	Mark Vils	1997	7,687
139 2/8	23 3/8	21 5/8	17 0/8	5	5	Iowa County	WI	Jerry Wagner	1997	7,687
139 2/8	23 6/8	24 0/8	18 1/8	9	8	Jefferson County	WI	Mark R. Kewan	1997	7,687
139 2/8	21 7/8	21 6/8	20 0/8	5	5	Parke County	IN	Craig Boyd	1997	7,687
139 2/8	20 3/8	20 6/8	12 4/8	6	6	Dearborn County	IN	Blake D. Hamilton	1997	7,687
139 2/8	23 4/8	23 6/8	19 7/8	6	6	Knox County	IL	Ryan Stafford	1997	7,687
139 2/8	21 7/8	22 7/8	16 0/8	4	4	Vernon County	WI	Jeffrey C. Schroeder	1997	7,687
139 2/8	21 1/8	22 0/8	16 3/8	6	5	Portage County	WI	Perry D. Larson	1997	7,687
139 2/8	23 3/8	23 3/8	18 2/8	5	4	Hughes County	OK	Tom Cartwright	1997	7,687
139 2/8	21 1/8	20 3/8	16 2/8	5	5	Priddis	ALB	Lorne D. Rinkel	1998	7,687
139 2/8	22 2/8	21 4/8	19 6/8	5	5	Lafayette County	WI	James Kingsley	1998	7,687
139 1/8	24 0/8	24 0/8	20 7/8	4	4	Pottawattamie County	IA	James R. Kirlin	1968	7,752
139 1/8	21 0/8	20 5/8	17 7/8	6	5	Calumet County	WI	Leo A. Broeckel	1969	7,752
139 1/8	20 3/8	21 7/8	18 1/8	5	5	Kalamazoo County	MI	Dr. Ronald L. Mahan	1975	7,752
139 1/8	23 2/8	22 4/8	19 7/8	5	5	Johnson County	IL	Billy J. Hillebrand	1977	7,752
139 1/8	23 1/8	20 0/8	16 3/8	5	5	Switzerland County	IN	James T. Brent	1979	7,752
139 1/8	22 2/8	22 4/8	20 1/8	5	5	Milton	ONT	Ernest Groh	1979	7,752
139 1/8	23 0/8	22 6/8	18 2/8	5	5	Montgomery County	PA	Joseph Maddock	1980	7,752
139 1/8	22 4/8	20 1/8	17 3/8	7	5	Green County	WI	Ora Howard	1980	7,752
139 1/8	21 4/8	21 3/8	16 4/8	6	5	Finney County	KS	Rodney Stapleton	1980	7,752
139 1/8	19 4/8	20 1/8	14 2/8	6	5	Shelby County	MO	Jamie McWilliams	1981	7,752
139 1/8	23 6/8	23 3/8	19 1/8	5	5	Boone County	IN	James L. Schenck	1981	7,752
139 1/8	22 4/8	23 2/8	18 7/8	5	5	Franklin County	MO	Tom Mitchell	1982	7,752
139 1/8	25 1/8	25 4/8	17 7/8	5	5	Tazewell County	IL	Scott A. Knight	1983	7,752
139 1/8	23 0/8	23 3/8	18 2/8	6	4	Douglas County	WI	Paul Ashley	1984	7,752
139 1/8	22 4/8	22 2/8	19 3/8	5	5	Ogle County	IL	Earl B. Thomas, Jr.	1984	7,752
139 1/8	23 4/8	24 7/8	18 1/8	4	5	McLean County	KY	Earl R. Smith	1985	7,752
139 1/8	22 4/8	22 2/8	16 4/8	6	5	Montgomery County	MD	Steve Hoffman	1985	7,752
139 1/8	22 1/8	23 5/8	18 7/8	4	4	Brown County	KS	Pat Bauman	1985	7,752
139 1/8	21 5/8	23 6/8	16 7/8	6	4	Preble County	OH	Jerrol L. Meredith	1985	7,752
139 1/8	19 5/8	23 6/8	17 1/8	5	5	Dakota County	NE	Michael W. McKenna	1986	7,752
139 1/8	20 7/8	20 5/8	14 1/8	5	5	Goodhue County	MN	Deick Bridley	1986	7,752
139 1/8	24 1/8	24 6/8	19 5/8	4	5	Clay County	MN	Terry Leach	1986	7,752
139 1/8	24 4/8	23 6/8	19 4/8	4	5	Webb County	TX	Mike Palmer	1986	7,752
139 1/8	25 5/8	24 7/8	20 3/8	4	5	Pike County	IL	Steve North	1987	7,752

WHITETAIL DEER (TYPICAL ANTLERS)

Minimum Score 125

SCORE	LENGTH OF MAIN BEAM R	LENGTH OF MAIN BEAM L	INSIDE SPREAD	NUMBER OF POINTS R	NUMBER OF POINTS L	AREA	STATE/PROVINCE	HUNTER'S NAME	DATE	RANK
139 1/8	25 7/8	24 2/8	19 5/8	5	6	Plymouth County	IA	Ed Fowler	1987	7,752
139 1/8	22 1/8	22 0/8	14 7/8	6	5	Langlade County	WI	Douglas L. Below	1988	7,752
139 1/8	21 1/8	21 6/8	16 0/8	7	5	Linn County	IA	Jeff Vanourney	1989	7,752
139 1/8	23 5/8	23 2/8	17 3/8	5	5	Jackson County	WI	Gary Barneson	1989	7,752
139 1/8	25 3/8	23 2/8	19 5/8	6	6	McHenry County	IL	Dennis E. Straumann	1989	7,752
139 1/8	21 3/8	21 4/8	16 3/8	5	5	Tippecanoe County	IN	Jim Foster	1989	7,752
139 1/8	23 0/8	22 4/8	16 3/8	5	5	Hocking County	OH	Jose M. Medina, Jr.	1990	7,752
139 1/8	26 6/8	23 1/8	14 1/8	6	5	Chase County	KS	Gregory G. Windler	1990	7,752
139 1/8	25 0/8	24 2/8	19 4/8	5	6	Hamilton County	OH	Matthew J. Smith	1990	7,752
139 1/8	24 2/8	23 4/8	20 3/8	6	5	Macoupin County	IL	Daniel Brown	1991	7,752
139 1/8	22 2/8	22 3/8	16 0/8	9	6	Oglethorpe County	GA	Vernon Segars	1991	7,752
139 1/8	25 6/8	24 3/8	20 5/8	4	4	Monmouth County	NJ	James A. Pavlisko	1992	7,752
139 1/8	21 7/8	22 6/8	15 3/8	5	5	Vernon County	MO	Edward L. Hyde, Sr.	1992	7,752
139 1/8	22 6/8	22 7/8	19 5/8	7	7	Hamilton County	IA	Gary Westrum	1992	7,752
139 1/8	22 0/8	23 7/8	19 5/8	4	4	Concordia Parish	LA	John Wood	1992	7,752
139 1/8	19 7/8	20 3/8	16 7/8	5	5	Terrell County	TX	Casey J. Carroll	1992	7,752
139 1/8	22 2/8	22 1/8	16 7/8	5	5	Chester County	PA	Roger Aughenbaugh	1993	7,752
139 1/8	26 7/8	27 3/8	19 3/8	5	4	Jefferson County	WI	Mike Fischer	1993	7,752
139 1/8	22 1/8	20 7/8	15 3/8	5	5	St. Louis County	MO	Karl Miller	1993	7,752
139 1/8	20 4/8	20 1/8	18 3/8	6	5	Adams County	IL	Bernie Andrew	1993	7,752
139 1/8	23 3/8	23 0/8	18 7/8	5	4	Columbia County	WI	Jon Lehrmann	1993	7,752
139 1/8	22 4/8	21 6/8	19 6/8	7	6	Granby River	BC	Craig R. Reichmuth	1993	7,752
139 1/8	23 1/8	22 4/8	18 1/8	5	5	Fairfield County	CT	Stephen W. Sumple	1994	7,752
139 1/8	20 3/8	21 0/8	20 7/8	5	5	Mason County	MI	Stanley Gajeski	1994	7,752
139 1/8	24 4/8	24 0/8	20 3/8	4	4	Washington County	PA	Kevin Klimas	1994	7,752
139 1/8	25 1/8	26 2/8	19 4/8	7	5	Winneshiek County	IA	Steve Weber	1994	7,752
139 1/8	22 4/8	23 6/8	18 7/8	5	5	Darke County	OH	Greg Knick	1994	7,752
139 1/8	25 1/8	25 1/8	20 5/8	4	5	Des Moines County	IA	Duane R. Mabry	1994	7,752
139 1/8	23 6/8	24 5/8	19 7/8	5	7	Hennepin County	MN	Keith Jacobsen	1994	7,752
139 1/8	23 1/8	23 0/8	20 0/8	5	4	Richland County	MT	William Nankivel	1995	7,752
139 1/8	21 3/8	21 6/8	19 6/8	5	6	Langdon	ALB	David Heinley	1995	7,752
139 1/8	22 6/8	22 5/8	16 4/8	5	6	Dane County	WI	Tory Martinson	1995	7,752
139 1/8	23 7/8	24 0/8	19 2/8	6	5	Washington County	KY	Mitch Glenn	1995	7,752
139 1/8	24 6/8	24 0/8	19 1/8	5	5	Geauga County	OH	Gregory A. Anderson	1995	7,752
139 1/8	23 7/8	24 4/8	16 4/8	4	6	Hillsdale County	MI	Thurlo Rodgers	1995	7,752
139 1/8	23 0/8	22 7/8	15 6/8	4	5	Charles Mix County	SD	Donald DeHaan	1995	7,752
139 1/8	22 3/8	21 3/8	16 1/8	5	6	Iowa County	WI	David B. Myhre	1996	7,752
139 1/8	23 6/8	25 1/8	18 3/8	4	4	Jennings County	IN	Jim Vierling	1996	7,752
139 1/8	24 6/8	23 6/8	16 5/8	5	5	Wake County	NC	Jay Adcock	1997	7,752
139 1/8	20 0/8	20 3/8	14 7/8	5	5	Coles County	IL	Mark Cooper	1997	7,752
139 1/8	22 6/8	22 6/8	15 5/8	5	5	Wyandot County	OH	Rocky A. Row	1997	7,752
139 1/8	20 1/8	21 2/8	17 7/8	5	5	Sawyer County	WI	Norm Hasenfang	1997	7,752
139 1/8	22 0/8	22 6/8	17 1/8	5	5	Prairie County	AR	Tommy L. Thrift, Jr.	1997	7,752
139 0/8	23 2/8	23 5/8	18 5/8	5	4	Warren County	IA	Grant A. Poindexter	1964	7,819
139 0/8	21 6/8	20 4/8	19 0/8	7	5	Butler County	KS	John Holzrechtes	1967	7,819
139 0/8	25 0/8	25 2/8	19 2/8	4	4	Mower County	MN	Ronald Grothe	1971	7,819
139 0/8	20 4/8	20 1/8	16 0/8	5	5	Fillmore County	MN	Richard Fryar	1972	7,819
139 0/8	24 2/8	24 5/8	15 7/8	7	6	Lewis County	WV	James Cogar	1976	7,819
139 0/8	21 3/8	21 0/8	14 2/8	5	5	Phillips County	MT	Bill Beede	1980	7,819
139 0/8	22 3/8	23 1/8	18 6/8	5	5	Grundy County	IL	Ronald A. Thompson	1980	7,819
139 0/8	25 4/8	25 5/8	19 4/8	5	5	Shelby County	OH	Richard A. Havenar	1981	7,819
139 0/8	18 7/8	23 2/8	17 4/8	6	5	Martin County	IN	Jan J. Armour	1981	7,819
139 0/8	22 1/8	20 7/8	16 2/8	8	8	Moultrie County	IL	Jim Dallefeld	1981	7,819
139 0/8	22 2/8	22 1/8	15 2/8	6	5	Linn County	MO	Robert L. "Bob" Schultz	1981	7,819
139 0/8	23 0/8	22 0/8	16 2/8	5	5	Cass County	MI	Allen Welburn	1981	7,819
139 0/8	24 2/8	25 1/8	18 2/8	5	6	Dawson County	NE	Randy Wilson	1982	7,819
139 0/8	25 1/8	25 7/8	21 1/8	4	5	Morrison County	MN	Pat Mckenzie	1982	7,819
139 0/8	20 4/8	23 4/8	18 0/8	5	5	Lake County	IL	Gary S. Rogers	1982	7,819
139 0/8	23 4/8	22 5/8	22 4/8	6	4	Clark County	IN	Noble E. McCutcheon	1985	7,819
139 0/8	23 2/8	22 4/8	16 2/8	4	4	Morrison County	MN	Doug Schmode	1985	7,819
139 0/8	21 4/8	22 1/8	17 6/8	4	4	Racine County	WI	Mark Nelsen	1985	7,819
139 0/8	22 7/8	23 1/8	17 0/8	5	6	Monroe County	NY	David Smith	1985	7,819
139 0/8	22 4/8	24 0/8	17 2/8	5	5	Adams County	IN	Rick A. Goldner	1985	7,819
139 0/8	25 4/8	25 4/8	17 6/8	4	4	Baltimore County	MD	Danny Stivers	1985	7,819
139 0/8	21 2/8	23 2/8	16 4/8	5	4	Morgan County	OH	Lynn A. Weingart	1985	7,819
139 0/8	28 3/8	27 0/8	21 2/8	6	6	Ashtabula County	OH	Brian G. Dingle	1986	7,819
139 0/8	21 5/8	21 3/8	19 4/8	4	5	Clay County	IL	William Brummer	1987	7,819
139 0/8	22 5/8	21 6/8	17 4/8	5	5	Carroll County	OH	Bill Hall	1987	7,819
139 0/8	24 4/8	24 6/8	19 7/8	5	5	Minnehaha County	SD	Jeffrey W. Satter	1987	7,819
139 0/8	24 2/8	23 3/8	18 4/8	6	4	Fairfield County	CT	Stephen M. Ruttkamp	1988	7,819
139 0/8	23 1/8	22 3/8	16 6/8	6	5	Ottawa County	KS	Rod Ponton	1988	7,819
139 0/8	24 0/8	24 6/8	18 7/8	5	5	Greenwood County	KS	Rod Dankert	1988	7,819
139 0/8	22 6/8	23 4/8	18 4/8	4	4	Jackson County	IL	Tim Cobin	1988	7,819
139 0/8	22 4/8	23 6/8	16 4/8	5	5	Renfrew	ONT	Glen McCutcheon	1989	7,819
139 0/8	22 4/8	23 1/8	17 1/8	7	5	Lake County	IL	Daniel Frey	1990	7,819
139 0/8	23 3/8	22 7/8	19 2/8	4	4	Calumet County	WI	Jeff Morgen	1990	7,819
139 0/8	20 7/8	20 4/8	14 6/8	5	5	Sawyer County	WI	John W. Olson	1990	7,819
139 0/8	21 4/8	21 3/8	15 4/8	5	5	Wilson County	KS	Sterling Bruce Collins	1990	7,819

WHITETAIL DEER (TYPICAL ANTLERS)

Minimum Score 125   Continued

SCORE	LENGTH OF MAIN BEAM R	LENGTH OF MAIN BEAM L	INSIDE SPREAD	NUMBER OF POINTS R	NUMBER OF POINTS L	AREA	STATE/PROVINCE	HUNTER'S NAME	DATE	RANK
139 0/8	24 2/8	26 2/8	18 0/8	4	4	Caroline County	MD	Jay Downes, Jr.	1991	7,819
139 0/8	21 7/8	22 1/8	16 2/8	5	4	Wabash County	IN	Danny Ray	1991	7,819
139 0/8	21 5/8	20 5/8	16 4/8	5	5	Winnebago County	IL	Dennis Frichtl	1991	7,819
139 0/8	24 5/8	24 2/8	18 5/8	6	5	Marshall County	WV	Jerry Smith	1991	7,819
139 0/8	22 7/8	23 5/8	22 0/8	5	4	Noble County	OH	Darrell E. Crum	1992	7,819
139 0/8	22 2/8	23 2/8	17 2/8	5	5	Van Buren County	IA	Jim Holdenried	1992	7,819
139 0/8	21 0/8	20 7/8	16 2/8	5	5	Burleigh County	ND	Matthew White	1993	7,819
139 0/8	22 1/8	22 6/8	18 6/8	5	4	Marquette County	MI	Frank E. Brogger	1993	7,819
139 0/8	22 7/8	23 4/8	20 4/8	9	7	Waukesha County	WI	Douglas Schroeder	1993	7,819
139 0/8	22 7/8	23 3/8	16 6/8	4	6	Breckinridge County	KY	Fred J. Pape, Jr.	1993	7,819
139 0/8	25 6/8	24 3/8	16 4/8	4	4	Kankakee County	IL	Frank Williams	1993	7,819
139 0/8	21 4/8	21 1/8	16 6/8	4	4	Pelly	SAS	Myles Keller	1993	7,819
139 0/8	22 7/8	21 7/8	18 4/8	5	5	Worcester County	MA	George S. Shosey	1993	7,819
139 0/8	23 1/8	23 3/8	19 4/8	5	4	Barron County	WI	Duane Marion	1994	7,819
139 0/8	24 6/8	23 2/8	18 6/8	4	5	Washington County	PA	David Manko	1994	7,819
139 0/8	23 5/8	23 1/8	16 4/8	5	4	De Kalb County	IN	Douglas A. Lucher	1994	7,819
139 0/8	23 5/8	24 3/8	16 4/8	5	5	Tazewell County	IL	Bret Epkins	1994	7,819
139 0/8	21 3/8	21 2/8	18 0/8	7	5	Grundy County	IL	Mike O'Connor	1994	7,819
139 0/8	22 4/8	23 0/8	17 0/8	5	4	Hendricks County	IN	William Mobley	1994	7,819
139 0/8	21 2/8	21 5/8	14 4/8	5	5	Vernon County	WI	Heath A. Tschumper	1994	7,819
139 0/8	24 4/8	24 3/8	21 6/8	5	4	Hunterdon County	NJ	Jeff Farr	1994	7,819
139 0/8	21 6/8	21 6/8	17 6/8	5	5	Beaver County	PA	Russell Nixon	1995	7,819
139 0/8	24 7/8	24 5/8	17 3/8	5	5	Platte County	WY	Jerry Bowen	1995	7,819
139 0/8	21 6/8	23 0/8	15 7/8	8	7	Nelson County	KY	Joe Mayfield	1995	7,819
139 0/8	23 3/8	23 6/8	15 7/8	5	4	Mills County	IA	Dave Messner	1995	7,819
139 0/8	24 4/8	24 0/8	18 4/8	4	4	Douglas County	MN	Paul Aufenkamp	1996	7,819
139 0/8	24 6/8	25 6/8	18 2/8	4	5	Cass County	MI	Gregory Crowel	1996	7,819
139 0/8	25 3/8	24 2/8	19 4/8	4	4	Macon County	IL	Michael P. Schollmeier	1996	7,819
139 0/8	23 1/8	22 6/8	17 6/8	6	5	Meeker County	MN	Jason Dudley Schultz	1996	7,819
139 0/8	21 4/8	21 4/8	18 4/8	5	6	Dakota County	NE	Mike Lutt	1997	7,819
139 0/8	22 2/8	22 0/8	17 0/8	5	5	Waupaca County	WI	Kirt Hoffmann	1997	7,819
139 0/8	24 1/8	24 7/8	15 6/8	4	4	Providence County	RI	Todd Brown	1997	7,819
139 0/8	21 1/8	22 0/8	18 0/8	5	5	Columbia County	WI	Chris DeLapp	1997	7,819
139 0/8	22 0/8	23 0/8	17 6/8	5	5	Walworth County	WI	Richard Herwald	1997	7,819
139 0/8	21 3/8	21 6/8	16 6/8	4	4	Whiteside County	IL	Clint Walker	1997	7,819
139 0/8	23 3/8	21 1/8	19 4/8	5	5	Pike County	IL	Roy L. Walk	1997	7,819
139 0/8	23 5/8	23 1/8	18 1/8	5	5	Wicomico County	MD	Brian L. Wolfe	1997	7,819
139 0/8	23 0/8	22 4/8	15 6/8	5	5	Des Moines County	IA	Stacy Fox	1997	7,819
139 0/8	20 4/8	21 1/8	16 0/8	5	5	Walworth County	WI	Kurt Schulz	1997	7,819
138 7/8	22 5/8	21 4/8	16 1/8	5	6	Sullivan County	IN	Mike Burch	1976	7,893
138 7/8	24 4/8	23 0/8	18 6/8	6	7	Cedar County	IA	Tom Foley	1978	7,893
138 7/8	22 5/8	24 1/8	19 3/8	4	6	Williams County	OH	Gary Bowles	1978	7,893
138 7/8	24 1/8	26 1/8	17 3/8	5	4	Delaware County	IA	Tom Wilhelm	1978	7,893
138 7/8	23 0/8	23 0/8	15 1/8	5	4	Hamilton County	OH	Donald R. Buehler	1980	7,893
138 7/8	27 6/8	25 4/8	21 2/8	4	4	Cowley County	KS	Maloy Rollins	1981	7,893
138 7/8	23 5/8	24 1/8	17 1/8	5	4	Clark County	SD	Jerry Comes	1982	7,893
138 7/8	23 1/8	26 3/8	19 1/8	6	4	Crawford County	MO	Bill Kaltenbach	1985	7,893
138 7/8	21 5/8	19 2/8	18 1/8	5	5	Jackson County	KS	Jimmy Braden	1985	7,893
138 7/8	20 3/8	20 7/8	18 1/8	5	6	Trigg County	KY	Ronnie Fox	1986	7,893
138 7/8	23 5/8	22 6/8	17 0/8	5	4	Sarpy County	NE	Richard L. Chandler	1986	7,893
138 7/8	22 6/8	22 4/8	19 1/8	4	4	Barber County	KS	Bob A. Christensen	1986	7,893
138 7/8	23 4/8	22 6/8	18 5/8	4	4	Charles County	MD	Florentino B. Garcia, Jr.	1986	7,893
138 7/8	22 5/8	22 6/8	17 6/8	5	5	Harlan County	NE	Bill Blincow	1987	7,893
138 7/8	23 3/8	23 5/8	14 7/8	5	5	Price County	WI	Howard Briske	1987	7,893
138 7/8	23 1/8	22 5/8	20 1/8	6	5	Seneca County	OH	Larry Farson	1987	7,893
138 7/8	25 0/8	25 0/8	17 7/8	5	4	Freeborn County	MN	Robert S. Mullenbach	1987	7,893
138 7/8	20 0/8	21 4/8	16 7/8	5	5	McMullen County	TX	Kevin Hilbig	1987	7,893
138 7/8	24 7/8	24 5/8	18 7/8	4	5	Onondaga County	NY	Paul A. Douglass	1988	7,893
138 7/8	21 7/8	23 1/8	17 5/8	5	5	Fayette County	IA	Scott Golberg	1988	7,893
138 7/8	23 6/8	23 7/8	20 5/8	5	4	Cecil County	MD	Daniel K. Shivery	1988	7,893
138 7/8	22 3/8	20 6/8	18 2/8	7	6	Henderson County	KY	Aubrey C. Hazelwood	1989	7,893
138 7/8	24 0/8	25 0/8	17 3/8	6	5	Woodson County	KS	Jerry Ramshaw	1989	7,893
138 7/8	23 5/8	23 3/8	23 1/8	4	4	Hillsdale County	MI	John Stadler	1989	7,893
138 7/8	22 0/8	22 4/8	19 3/8	5	5	Garrett County	MD	Donald C. Hade, Jr.	1990	7,893
138 7/8	23 2/8	23 6/8	18 3/8	5	4	Juneau County	WI	David Magnussen	1990	7,893
138 7/8	24 1/8	24 1/8	17 7/8	4	5	Vigo County	IN	Tom Mundy	1990	7,893
138 7/8	22 3/8	22 5/8	19 0/8	7	6	Oswego County	NY	Rodney G. Wallace	1990	7,893
138 7/8	22 1/8	21 0/8	16 1/8	5	6	Lee County	IL	Timothy W. Broos	1990	7,893
138 7/8	21 3/8	22 3/8	16 3/8	5	6	Dryden	ONT	Robert J. Brodhagen	1990	7,893
138 7/8	24 1/8	23 3/8	18 1/8	4	5	Racine County	WI	John S. Burrows	1990	7,893
138 7/8	19 6/8	20 3/8	19 3/8	5	7	Marinette County	WI	Douglas A. Nelson	1990	7,893
138 7/8	23 5/8	22 3/8	17 7/8	5	5	Kent County	MD	Bruce F. Bartenfelder	1990	7,893
138 7/8	24 1/8	22 6/8	19 5/8	4	4	Anderson County	TN	Alan Brown	1991	7,893
138 7/8	22 6/8	23 1/8	18 5/8	5	5	Winona County	MN	Lonnie W. Virnig	1991	7,893
138 7/8	24 1/8	22 1/8	16 7/8	4	4	Crawford County	IL	Cecil Brassfield	1991	7,893
138 7/8	24 7/8	25 2/8	20 1/8	5	4	Waukesha County	WI	Steven Crandell	1992	7,893
138 7/8	23 4/8	23 6/8	19 1/8	6	6	Charles County	MD	William D. Wyland	1992	7,893
138 7/8	24 0/8	24 4/8	16 7/8	4	4	Greene County	IL	Todd McGill	1992	7,893

WHITETAIL DEER (TYPICAL ANTLERS)

Minimum Score 125   Continued

SCORE	LENGTH OF MAIN BEAM R / L	INSIDE SPREAD	NUMBER OF POINTS R / L	AREA	STATE/ PROVINCE	HUNTER'S NAME	DATE	RANK
138 7/8	21 0/8 / 22 0/8	18 4/8	6 / 5	Winnebago County	WI	Paul G. Christman	1992	7,893
138 7/8	22 1/8 / 21 4/8	15 4/8	7 / 5	Kittson County	MN	Jeff LaBaron	1992	7,893
138 7/8	19 3/8 / 20 4/8	15 6/8	6 / 6	Cass County	MI	Thomas J. Williamson	1992	7,893
138 7/8	23 4/8 / 23 5/8	26 1/8	4 / 5	Stephenson County	IL	Dwight Peterson	1992	7,893
138 7/8	22 1/8 / 21 1/8	15 2/8	6 / 7	Pike County	IL	Brad Stamp	1992	7,893
138 7/8	21 3/8 / 21 6/8	19 3/8	5 / 5	Webb County	TX	Hack Berry	1992	7,893
138 7/8	22 0/8 / 22 3/8	13 5/8	5 / 5	Newton County	MO	Bill R. Harvill	1993	7,893
138 7/8	20 5/8 / 21 2/8	16 3/8	5 / 5	Buffalo County	WI	Herb R. Simek	1993	7,893
138 7/8	23 6/8 / 23 7/8	18 7/8	4 / 5	Van Buren County	IA	Melvin T. Digman	1993	7,893
138 7/8	20 4/8 / 21 3/8	16 1/8	5 / 5	Brown County	WI	Jason M. Wegand	1993	7,893
138 7/8	23 2/8 / 23 1/8	17 0/8	5 / 5	Lafayette County	WI	Daniel F. Palzkill	1993	7,893
138 7/8	19 6/8 / 20 4/8	17 7/8	5 / 5	Jackson County	WI	Matt Jessie	1994	7,893
138 7/8	23 3/8 / 23 1/8	19 1/8	5 / 5	Pierce County	WI	Douglas L. Hines	1994	7,893
138 7/8	22 6/8 / 23 6/8	20 5/8	5 / 5	Wayne County	OH	Winston L. Wycoff III	1994	7,893
138 7/8	23 4/8 / 25 0/8	16 7/8	6 / 5	Alachua County	FL	Craig C. Carpenter	1994	7,893
138 7/8	20 2/8 / 20 6/8	19 5/8	5 / 5	Meadow Lake	SAS	Ian Twidale	1994	7,893
138 7/8	21 6/8 / 21 1/8	17 3/8	5 / 5	Shawano County	WI	Raymond E. Creapeau, Jr.	1994	7,893
138 7/8	23 1/8 / 23 7/8	20 7/8	6 / 5	Charles County	MD	David Glessner	1994	7,893
138 7/8	23 1/8 / 23 5/8	19 7/8	4 / 4	Bartholomew County	IN	Craig Bolte	1994	7,893
138 7/8	21 5/8 / 21 3/8	14 3/8	5 / 5	Washington County	PA	Ron Kujawa	1994	7,893
138 7/8	23 4/8 / 24 6/8	19 6/8	7 / 5	Lake County	IL	Gene F. Mather, Jr.	1994	7,893
138 7/8	21 3/8 / 24 1/8	19 7/8	6 / 5	Lake County	IL	Ed G. Delli, Jr.	1994	7,893
138 7/8	21 5/8 / 22 7/8	15 5/8	5 / 6	Richland County	MT	Todd Dooley	1995	7,893
138 7/8	25 0/8 / 23 7/8	19 7/8	5 / 4	Dubuque County	IA	Mike Theis	1995	7,893
138 7/8	23 4/8 / 23 7/8	18 1/8	4 / 4	Brown County	WI	Jeff Walenski	1995	7,893
138 7/8	22 4/8 / 22 5/8	19 5/8	5 / 4	Harrison County	IA	Bill Vaznis	1995	7,893
138 7/8	22 0/8 / 22 1/8	18 5/8	5 / 5	Winnebago County	IL	David W. Grider	1995	7,893
138 7/8	22 1/8 / 21 5/8	15 6/8	6 / 8	McKenzie County	ND	David Tofte	1996	7,893
138 7/8	21 3/8 / 21 3/8	15 7/8	5 / 5	Pike County	IL	Steven M. King	1996	7,893
138 7/8	21 4/8 / 22 2/8	16 5/8	6 / 5	Clayton County	IA	Gerald M. Hunter	1996	7,893
138 7/8	25 2/8 / 25 6/8	19 1/8	4 / 4	Bon Homme County	SD	Ronald N. Ream	1996	7,893
138 7/8	23 5/8 / 24 3/8	18 3/8	4 / 5	Yankton County	SD	Kenny Kuchta	1996	7,893
138 7/8	27 0/8 / 25 0/8	21 4/8	6 / 5	Adams County	OH	Ken Dobbins, Jr.	1997	7,893
138 7/8	20 5/8 / 20 3/8	16 7/8	5 / 5	Richland County	WI	Michael Kieler	1997	7,893
138 7/8	20 5/8 / 21 4/8	16 1/8	5 / 6	Walworth County	WI	Eric Nokes	1997	7,893
138 7/8	23 0/8 / 22 6/8	17 1/8	5 / 5	Summit County	OH	Buzzy Papalia	1997	7,893
138 7/8	21 4/8 / 22 3/8	16 7/8	7 / 6	Palo Pinto County	TX	Mike C. Handy	1998	7,893
138 6/8	25 0/8 / 23 7/8	20 4/8	4 / 4	Phillips County	AR	Everett Foley	1968	7,969
138 6/8	22 0/8 / 20 7/8	20 3/8	6 / 5	Leavenworth County	KS	Michael Pearce	1977	7,969
138 6/8	21 5/8 / 21 5/8	15 2/8	5 / 5	Putnam County	GA	Tim S. Doxsey	1978	7,969
138 6/8	23 0/8 / 22 5/8	18 0/8	5 / 5	Des Moines County	IA	Dennis R. Morgan	1978	7,969
138 6/8	23 5/8 / 23 4/8	18 6/8	4 / 4	St. Joseph County	MI	Jack R. Menges	1979	7,969
138 6/8	26 6/8 / 26 5/8	17 5/8	5 / 5	Crawford County	IL	James R. Griggs	1980	7,969
138 6/8	24 3/8 / 24 1/8	17 6/8	6 / 4	Latah County	ID	Dolan McLean	1980	7,969
138 6/8	23 4/8 / 23 4/8	18 4/8	5 / 4	Chase County	KS	Jerry D. Keller	1982	7,969
138 6/8	25 1/8 / 24 2/8	18 5/8	5 / 3	Calgary	ALB	Keith Riddell	1983	7,969
138 6/8	23 0/8 / 22 7/8	17 2/8	5 / 6	Dane County	WI	Walter S. Jankowski	1985	7,969
138 6/8	22 3/8 / 23 3/8	18 2/8	5 / 5	Jefferson County	MT	Jeff Nathan	1986	7,969
138 6/8	21 3/8 / 20 6/8	17 2/8	4 / 4	Scott County	KS	Travess Funk	1986	7,969
138 6/8	23 1/8 / 23 1/8	21 4/8	4 / 4	Wyandotte County	KS	Dave Crockett	1986	7,969
138 6/8	20 1/8 / 20 1/8	18 3/8	7 / 6	Mercer County	MO	David N. Clark	1987	7,969
138 6/8	21 6/8 / 22 0/8	17 0/8	6 / 5	Elkhart County	IN	Jeffrey B. Isnogle	1987	7,969
138 6/8	23 5/8 / 22 2/8	20 2/8	5 / 5	Christian County	KY	Dwight Good	1987	7,969
138 6/8	21 4/8 / 22 3/8	19 3/8	4 / 5	Waukesha County	WI	Steve J. Cull	1987	7,969
138 6/8	22 7/8 / 23 2/8	19 2/8	4 / 4	Macoupin County	IL	Ernie Gagnor	1987	7,969
138 6/8	22 5/8 / 21 7/8	16 2/8	5 / 5	Menominee County	MI	Craig S. Haglund	1988	7,969
138 6/8	23 4/8 / 23 2/8	20 6/8	5 / 4	Winnebago County	IL	James R. Petersen	1988	7,969
138 6/8	24 4/8 / 23 1/8	16 0/8	5 / 4	Hardin County	OH	Ray Davis	1988	7,969
138 6/8	26 4/8 / 27 2/8	18 0/8	4 / 4	Jo Daviess County	IL	Pat Schambow	1990	7,969
138 6/8	23 0/8 / 23 2/8	18 4/8	4 / 5	Jasper County	IL	Elmer R. Luce, Jr.	1990	7,969
138 6/8	23 6/8 / 24 2/8	19 2/8	5 / 6	Jasper County	IL	David Roepke	1990	7,969
138 6/8	20 4/8 / 21 6/8	18 0/8	6 / 6	Shawano County	WI	Bradley D. Resch	1991	7,969
138 6/8	25 6/8 / 25 1/8	15 3/8	3 / 6	Vernon County	WI	Roger Ferries	1991	7,969
138 6/8	22 2/8 / 22 5/8	15 0/8	5 / 5	Knox County	OH	Dave Palmer	1991	7,969
138 6/8	23 4/8 / 24 2/8	16 6/8	4 / 4	Champaign County	OH	Kenny Pond	1991	7,969
138 6/8	23 6/8 / 23 1/8	20 6/8	4 / 5	Vilas County	WI	Jeff Reeves	1991	7,969
138 6/8	22 4/8 / 22 2/8	16 0/8	5 / 5	Licking County	OH	Jack L. Church	1992	7,969
138 6/8	24 0/8 / 22 7/8	18 2/8	5 / 4	Panola County	MS	R. Clay Moore	1992	7,969
138 6/8	20 0/8 / 21 4/8	18 0/8	4 / 4	De Witt County	IL	Jim Prawl	1992	7,969
138 6/8	23 6/8 / 23 5/8	19 0/8	4 / 6	Effingham County	IL	Rollin Wilson	1992	7,969
138 6/8	21 3/8 / 21 4/8	17 2/8	5 / 5	Will County	IL	Dan Baro	1993	7,969
138 6/8	24 6/8 / 24 3/8	23 0/8	6 / 5	Morrison County	MN	Ron Zahorski	1993	7,969
138 6/8	23 5/8 / 26 0/8	22 0/8	5 / 6	Cook County	IL	Bryon Tuscher	1993	7,969
138 6/8	23 7/8 / 23 4/8	17 6/8	4 / 4	Dubois County	IN	Tony Vogler	1993	7,969
138 6/8	22 5/8 / 23 1/8	16 2/8	4 / 4	Pike County	IL	Brad Stamp	1993	7,969
138 6/8	25 0/8 / 24 7/8	16 0/8	5 / 4	Belknap County	NH	Robert Daniels	1994	7,969
138 6/8	22 2/8 / 22 1/8	16 2/8	5 / 4	Platte County	WY	Jerry Bowen	1994	7,969
138 6/8	21 6/8 / 21 7/8	17 6/8	5 / 5	Adams County	OH	William G. Baker	1994	7,969

WHITETAIL DEER (TYPICAL ANTLERS)

Minimum Score 125   Continued

SCORE	LENGTH OF MAIN BEAM R / L	INSIDE SPREAD	NUMBER OF POINTS R / L		AREA	STATE/ PROVINCE	HUNTER'S NAME	DATE	RANK
138 6/8	24 3/8	24 0/8	20 4/8	4	4	Douglas County	WI	Keith G. Olson	1994	7,969
138 6/8	22 5/8	23 4/8	16 4/8	6	6	Knox County	IL	Michael J. McCall	1994	7,969
138 6/8	21 7/8	21 2/8	15 2/8	5	5	McHenry County	IL	Ernie Meinen	1994	7,969
138 6/8	19 7/8	20 0/8	14 5/8	6	6	San Patricio County	TX	Rodolfo T. Liserio	1994	7,969
138 6/8	22 0/8	22 0/8	15 4/8	4	5	Logan County	WV	Chad Perry	1994	7,969
138 6/8	23 2/8	23 2/8	18 6/8	4	4	Screven County	GA	Darryl W. Baker	1995	7,969
138 6/8	22 4/8	21 7/8	17 2/8	5	5	Smyth County	VA	Jimmy W. Castle	1995	7,969
138 6/8	23 4/8	23 7/8	17 6/8	5	4	Waukesha County	WI	Patrick Barwick	1995	7,969
138 6/8	23 6/8	23 5/8	19 4/8	4	4	La Salle County	IL	Fred Centko	1995	7,969
138 6/8	22 7/8	22 1/8	19 4/8	4	5	Washtenaw County	MI	Charles H. Birchmeier	1996	7,969
138 6/8	26 7/8	25 3/8	18 2/8	5	4	Charlotte County	VA	Robert L. Hall, Jr.	1996	7,969
138 6/8	22 6/8	22 6/8	19 5/8	5	6	Dane County	WI	Kevin Moreland	1996	7,969
138 6/8	24 0/8	23 4/8	17 1/8	5	5	Sangamon County	IL	Brian T. Bergmann	1996	7,969
138 6/8	20 6/8	21 3/8	16 4/8	5	5	Paulding County	OH	Kevin J. Howell, Sr.	1996	7,969
138 6/8	20 7/8	21 4/8	16 3/8	5	5	Blue Earth County	MN	Darwin Arndt	1996	7,969
138 6/8	23 6/8	24 1/8	15 7/8	4	5	St. Marys County	MD	Pete Ropshaw	1997	7,969
138 6/8	23 0/8	23 4/8	16 2/8	5	5	Hardin County	KY	Ricky Lowe	1997	7,969
138 6/8	23 2/8	22 5/8	17 0/8	5	5	Washington County	KS	Stan Brustowicz	1997	7,969
138 6/8	23 1/8	23 1/8	18 2/8	5	5	Portage County	WI	Thomas J. Mocadlo, Jr.	1997	7,969
138 6/8	22 6/8	22 7/8	17 2/8	4	4	Massac County	IL	Mike Mathes	1997	7,969
138 6/8	23 7/8	23 0/8	16 2/8	5	4	Fayette County	IL	Lynn Wollerman	1997	7,969
138 6/8	23 4/8	23 5/8	18 4/8	4	4	Livingston County	NY	Steven C. Farrell	1997	7,969
138 6/8	23 5/8	23 7/8	19 2/8	5	5	Major County	OK	L. Dale Adkins	1997	7,969
138 6/8	24 1/8	23 5/8	19 2/8	6	6	Dane County	WI	Daryl Thompson	1998	7,969
138 5/8	23 1/8	21 3/8	16 3/8	5	5	Washington County	KS	Stan Brustowicz	1923	8,034
138 5/8	24 6/8	23 3/8	17 3/8	5	5	Vilas County	WI	B. C. Roemer	1963	8,034
138 5/8	21 0/8	21 3/8	16 7/8	5	5	Martin County	IN	Tom Vieke	1967	8,034
138 5/8	24 0/8	24 3/8	17 3/8	4	6	Logan County	IL	Lee Miller	1971	8,034
138 5/8	25 0/8	25 1/8	16 7/8	4	4	Clinton County	IL	James D. Rueter	1973	8,034
138 5/8	23 0/8	23 4/8	16 2/8	4	5	Hennepin County	MN	Thomas F. Rose	1973	8,034
138 5/8	24 0/8	24 0/8	17 7/8	4	4	Chippewa County	WI	Patrick Kohls	1980	8,034
138 5/8	25 7/8	24 3/8	19 5/8	4	4	Auglaize County	OH	Bob Moser	1980	8,034
138 5/8	23 2/8	23 5/8	16 5/8	5	5	Colquitt County	GA	David A. Carmichael	1981	8,034
138 5/8	22 6/8	22 7/8	18 5/8	5	5	Woodford County	KY	Gary Hatton	1985	8,034
138 5/8	22 3/8	21 7/8	20 6/8	4	5	Greenwood County	KS	Gary Hughes	1985	8,034
138 5/8	25 3/8	24 5/8	18 0/8	6	6	Pickaway County	OH	John Walker	1986	8,034
138 5/8	25 1/8	24 3/8	19 0/8	6	5	Allen County	KY	Mark Lambert	1986	8,034
138 5/8	24 1/8	21 4/8	18 2/8	7	6	Wabasha County	MN	George Thomforde	1987	8,034
138 5/8	21 4/8	21 7/8	18 3/8	5	8	Sandridge	MAN	Bruce Huewan	1987	8,034
138 5/8	24 5/8	24 4/8	22 1/8	6	6	La Salle County	IL	Bill Goodin	1987	8,034
138 5/8	22 2/8	21 3/8	16 3/8	5	5	Maries County	MO	Wade Hicks, Jr.	1987	8,034
138 5/8	26 4/8	25 6/8	20 5/8	4	4	Ashtabula County	OH	Bob Wodzisz	1988	8,034
138 5/8	22 6/8	24 2/8	17 2/8	5	6	Kiowa County	KS	Karl Ballard	1988	8,034
138 5/8	20 5/8	20 4/8	13 3/8	5	5	Lincoln County	SD	Duane Larson	1988	8,034
138 5/8	23 0/8	23 1/8	16 3/8	5	5	Bremer County	IA	Jon Wolter	1988	8,034
138 5/8	26 0/8	25 6/8	17 7/8	5	4	McHenry County	IL	Tim Henn	1989	8,034
138 5/8	24 6/8	26 1/8	14 1/8	6	6	Texas County	MO	Victor Ray Wood	1989	8,034
138 5/8	22 5/8	22 4/8	17 7/8	4	5	Jasper County	IA	Russell Allspach	1989	8,034
138 5/8	24 3/8	22 7/8	16 2/8	4	5	Hancock County	IL	Marte McKee	1989	8,034
138 5/8	23 1/8	23 2/8	15 5/8	4	4	Buffalo County	WI	Donald R. Fox	1990	8,034
138 5/8	25 7/8	25 5/8	19 5/8	4	4	Richland County	OH	Chris Wilcox	1990	8,034
138 5/8	25 4/8	24 4/8	17 7/8	5	4	Fairfield County	CT	Warren C. Hensel	1990	8,034
138 5/8	21 7/8	21 3/8	14 7/8	5	5	Douglas County	MN	Milton Brede	1991	8,034
138 5/8	24 1/8	24 3/8	18 5/8	5	4	Columbia County	WI	Robert A. Schmitt	1991	8,034
138 5/8	22 5/8	22 5/8	16 1/8	5	5	Cherry County	NE	Lloyd C. Smith	1991	8,034
138 5/8	22 7/8	24 4/8	19 5/8	6	4	Grundy County	IL	Lindell Dorrough	1991	8,034
138 5/8	24 3/8	24 3/8	17 3/8	5	4	Jackson County	IN	Jeff Montgomery	1991	8,034
138 5/8	24 5/8	24 2/8	17 7/8	4	5	Woodbury County	IA	David A. Rodman	1992	8,034
138 5/8	24 5/8	24 1/8	17 5/8	4	5	Van Buren County	MI	Mark A. Anderson	1992	8,034
138 5/8	21 7/8	20 0/8	16 7/8	5	5	Sauk County	WI	Terry R. Neises	1992	8,034
138 5/8	21 0/8	22 0/8	16 7/8	5	6	St. Croix County	WI	Larry Quale	1992	8,034
138 5/8	25 0/8	24 7/8	14 5/8	4	5	Hancock County	OH	Robert E. Ebert	1992	8,034
138 5/8	22 0/8	21 5/8	20 3/8	5	4	Saginaw County	MI	Todd D. Shelly	1992	8,034
138 5/8	24 0/8	24 2/8	19 3/8	4	4	McLeod County	MN	Paul Skarvan	1992	8,034
138 5/8	22 5/8	22 1/8	17 0/8	6	5	Appanoose County	IA	David J. Westmoreland	1992	8,034
138 5/8	24 3/8	23 7/8	17 4/8	5	4	Crawford County	IA	Allan Hulsebus	1992	8,034
138 5/8	20 4/8	20 4/8	16 5/8	5	5	Putnam County	MO	Carl G. Allman	1993	8,034
138 5/8	23 6/8	24 2/8	18 6/8	6	5	Sedgwick County	KS	Joseph R. Althoff III	1993	8,034
138 5/8	22 4/8	24 6/8	17 7/8	6	6	Columbia County	WI	Wayne Buckley	1993	8,034
138 5/8	24 0/8	23 2/8	16 3/8	5	5	Beaver County	PA	Francis Szymoniak	1993	8,034
138 5/8	24 2/8	23 6/8	18 1/8	4	4	Walworth County	WI	Jeffrey J. Nettesheim	1993	8,034
138 5/8	22 5/8	22 5/8	17 7/8	5	5	Vilas County	WI	David Falkowski	1994	8,034
138 5/8	23 0/8	22 2/8	16 1/8	4	4	Morrison County	MN	Glen L. Mahlum	1994	8,034
138 5/8	24 6/8	24 4/8	15 3/8	4	4	Montgomery County	IN	Larry A. Culley	1994	8,034
138 5/8	22 2/8	22 5/8	15 7/8	6	6	Trempealeau County	WI	Robert J. Bandoli	1994	8,034
138 5/8	24 4/8	26 1/8	19 4/8	5	5	Morris County	NJ	Russ Davidson	1994	8,034
138 5/8	22 5/8	23 1/8	19 3/8	5	5	Sebastian County	AR	John Scott	1994	8,034
138 5/8	22 3/8	23 4/8	20 3/8	5	5	Sibley County	MN	William Greer	1994	8,034

WHITETAIL DEER (TYPICAL ANTLERS)

Minimum Score 125

SCORE	LENGTH OF MAIN BEAM R	LENGTH OF MAIN BEAM L	INSIDE SPREAD	NUMBER OF POINTS R	NUMBER OF POINTS L	AREA	STATE/ PROVINCE	HUNTER'S NAME	DATE	RANK
138 5/8	22 5/8	22 6/8	21 1/8	4	4	Cecil County	MD	Erik R. Johnson	1996	8,034
138 5/8	24 0/8	24 0/8	16 3/8	4	4	Lawrence County	AR	Dwight Milgrim	1996	8,034
138 5/8	24 2/8	24 2/8	18 5/8	6	6	Sawyer County	WI	Robert Thidemann	1996	8,034
138 5/8	20 6/8	19 4/8	16 1/8	5	5	Carroll County	MO	Wes Ford	1996	8,034
138 5/8	23 0/8	21 4/8	15 3/8	5	5	Wyoming County	WV	Mike Clay	1996	8,034
138 5/8	21 1/8	23 2/8	18 1/8	5	5	Knox County	IL	Robert D. Gardner	1996	8,034
138 5/8	21 1/8	21 7/8	18 1/8	7	6	La Crosse County	WI	Chad S. Blank	1996	8,034
138 5/8	22 4/8	21 4/8	16 7/8	6	5	La Salle County	IL	Gary L. Tabor	1996	8,034
138 5/8	23 0/8	21 0/8	19 2/8	5	4	Washington County	IA	Tony Batcheller	1996	8,034
138 5/8	22 1/8	23 4/8	16 3/8	4	4	Sauk County	WI	Brian J. Bellefeuil	1997	8,034
138 5/8	21 2/8	21 7/8	15 3/8	5	5	Douglas County	WI	Douglas S. Nelson	1997	8,034
138 5/8	22 7/8	23 7/8	17 5/8	5	5	Putnam County	IL	Stephen Sona	1997	8,034
138 5/8	20 6/8	20 6/8	17 1/8	5	5	Holt County	NE	Terry L. Schaaf	1997	8,034
138 5/8	23 2/8	22 3/8	13 5/8	5	5	Price County	WI	Tim J. Fritz	1997	8,034
138 5/8	23 4/8	23 1/8	18 5/8	7	5	Macon County	IL	Alan M. Easter	1997	8,034
138 5/8	23 0/8	23 4/8	16 6/8	5	4	McCurtain County	OK	Stanley Compton	1997	8,034
138 5/8	21 7/8	22 2/8	16 5/8	5	5	Lake County	IL	David J. Randall	1997	8,034
138 5/8	24 0/8	24 1/8	17 5/8	5	4	Allamakee County	IA	Arnie Crum	1997	8,034
138 5/8	23 5/8	24 2/8	17 5/8	5	5	Pennington County	MN	Todd Hannon	1997	8,034
138 5/8	21 3/8	22 3/8	18 6/8	7	7	Scott County	MN	Douglas Wilson	1998	8,034
138 5/8	24 1/8	23 3/8	17 3/8	4	4	Lincoln County	WI	Gary L. Crowell	1998	8,034
138 4/8	24 4/8	25 4/8	18 1/8	5	7	Emmet County	IA	Dr. Jerald T. Waite	1966	8,109
138 4/8	21 4/8	21 3/8	18 4/8	5	6	Mackinac County	MI	Terry Konle	1977	8,109
138 4/8	20 4/8	20 0/8	19 0/8	5	6	Jefferson County	WI	Edwin C. Wollin	1978	8,109
138 4/8	24 4/8	25 2/8	18 6/8	6	4	Pulaski County	KY	Eddie Howard	1979	8,109
138 4/8	24 0/8	23 7/8	21 0/8	4	4	Reno County	KS	Carl L. Gaston	1981	8,109
138 4/8	24 1/8	24 0/8	21 6/8	10	6	Lake County	IN	Horace Weaver	1981	8,109
138 4/8	24 4/8	23 4/8	19 0/8	5	5	Darke County	OH	Jim H. Duvall	1982	8,109
138 4/8	22 2/8	23 0/8	16 4/8	6	6	Hennepin County	MN	Raymen Peterson	1982	8,109
138 4/8	22 7/8	23 7/8	21 6/8	5	4	Jones County	IA	Hugh Shaw	1984	8,109
138 4/8	21 2/8	21 7/8	15 0/8	5	5	Des Moines County	IA	Brad Entsminger	1984	8,109
138 4/8	27 0/8	26 1/8	18 0/8	4	4	Anson County	NC	John Harris	1985	8,109
138 4/8	22 7/8	23 5/8	18 1/8	5	7	Greene County	IN	John W. Burks	1985	8,109
138 4/8	21 1/8	22 0/8	18 4/8	4	4	Adair County	OK	Fred Storozyszyn	1986	8,109
138 4/8	22 1/8	22 1/8	15 4/8	5	5	Sauk County	WI	Dale L. Luther	1986	8,109
138 4/8	26 0/8	25 0/8	19 6/8	6	6	Hancock County	OH	Leedwin C. Smith	1986	8,109
138 4/8	22 6/8	22 2/8	15 6/8	5	5	Tompkins County	NY	John A. Nichol	1987	8,109
138 4/8	19 3/8	21 4/8	18 7/8	5	6	Gray County	KS	Carl D. Christensen	1987	8,109
138 4/8	23 6/8	25 3/8	19 2/8	5	4	Lee County	AL	George P. Mann	1987	8,109
138 4/8	21 6/8	22 5/8	17 0/8	6	5	Jennings County	IN	Kevin D. Hall	1988	8,109
138 4/8	20 7/8	20 6/8	17 5/8	6	5	Genesee County	NY	Brian E. Wardell	1988	8,109
138 4/8	24 3/8	24 2/8	17 0/8	5	6	Pike County	IL	Dallas L. Miller	1988	8,109
138 4/8	24 6/8	23 5/8	16 6/8	4	4	Pike County	OH	Todd Frazier	1988	8,109
138 4/8	24 0/8	22 6/8	17 2/8	6	5	Page County	IA	Chris Barton	1988	8,109
138 4/8	23 0/8	21 7/8	19 1/8	5	6	Blue Earth County	MN	Rick Thompson	1989	8,109
138 4/8	23 1/8	23 1/8	21 0/8	4	4	Worcester County	MA	Dana Hanna	1989	8,109
138 4/8	23 1/8	23 2/8	19 2/8	7	5	Fairfax County	VA	Michael P. Hayes, Jr.	1989	8,109
138 4/8	24 2/8	25 0/8	16 2/8	6	5	Day County	SD	Joe George	1990	8,109
138 4/8	24 6/8	25 6/8	18 1/8	5	5	Jasper County	IL	James Meinhart	1990	8,109
138 4/8	23 3/8	22 6/8	19 4/8	6	5	Des Moines County	IA	John Bruckert	1990	8,109
138 4/8	23 4/8	24 0/8	15 0/8	4	4	Cochrane	ALB	Ed Look	1991	8,109
138 4/8	22 6/8	23 2/8	15 2/8	4	4	Claiborne County	MS	Hubert KleinPeter	1991	8,109
138 4/8	22 1/8	22 1/8	17 0/8	4	5	Wood County	WI	Joel Binder	1991	8,109
138 4/8	24 0/8	24 2/8	19 6/8	4	4	Sebastian County	AR	Donald L. Kendrick	1991	8,109
138 4/8	23 4/8	22 5/8	17 1/8	6	6	Columbia County	WI	Dale R. Peterson	1992	8,109
138 4/8	25 2/8	26 3/8	15 4/8	5	5	Jones County	IA	Darrell Schuman	1992	8,109
138 4/8	24 6/8	24 7/8	22 4/8	4	4	Muscatine County	IA	Todd A. Bermel	1992	8,109
138 4/8	25 3/8	23 6/8	16 2/8	4	5	Schuyler County	IL	Willey Basham	1992	8,109
138 4/8	25 6/8	25 1/8	20 0/8	5	5	Iroquois County	IL	Tod A. Fletcher	1992	8,109
138 4/8	24 2/8	25 1/8	20 2/8	4	4	Washington County	KS	Keith A. Beikman	1992	8,109
138 4/8	23 3/8	23 0/8	17 2/8	4	4	Swan Plain	SAS	Archie Nesbitt	1992	8,109
138 4/8	22 0/8	21 6/8	17 2/8	4	4	Morrison County	MN	Dennis Eickhoff	1993	8,109
138 4/8	23 0/8	22 6/8	16 2/8	5	5	Douglas County	KS	Ronnie D. Barnhardt	1993	8,109
138 4/8	25 7/8	24 6/8	21 4/8	5	4	Dearborn County	IN	Keith Casey	1993	8,109
138 4/8	22 5/8	22 0/8	19 2/8	4	4	Vinton County	OH	Mike Laferty	1993	8,109
138 4/8	25 1/8	24 4/8	21 6/8	3	4	Tazewell County	IL	Dusty Whitaker	1994	8,109
138 4/8	23 0/8	23 6/8	19 4/8	5	5	Sawyer County	WI	Daniel Kolberg	1994	8,109
138 4/8	24 6/8	24 3/8	17 4/8	4	4	Shiawassee County	MI	Jerry Hoy	1994	8,109
138 4/8	22 4/8	23 2/8	18 0/8	5	5	Lamar County	GA	Matthew Kramer	1994	8,109
138 4/8	23 6/8	23 5/8	17 0/8	4	4	Maries County	MO	Dick Wilde	1994	8,109
138 4/8	20 5/8	19 4/8	15 7/8	7	6	Mingo County	WV	Craig Branham	1994	8,109
138 4/8	22 3/8	23 0/8	15 6/8	5	5	Brown County	IL	Tim Purcell	1994	8,109
138 4/8	24 0/8	25 2/8	20 2/8	6	5	Columbia County	WI	Kent Kirn	1994	8,109
138 4/8	22 6/8	21 5/8	18 4/8	5	4	Steuben County	IN	Johnnie R. Kauffman	1995	8,109
138 4/8	23 2/8	23 5/8	18 2/8	6	6	Woodford County	IL	Stan Bocian	1995	8,109
138 4/8	25 2/8	27 6/8	20 4/8	4	4	Clayton County	IA	Kenny Etringer	1995	8,109
138 4/8	21 7/8	21 7/8	14 7/8	5	6	Dubuque County	IA	Larry W. Miller	1995	8,109
138 4/8	22 6/8	22 3/8	17 0/8	5	5	Douglas County	WI	Roger W. Hansen	1995	8,109

WHITETAIL DEER (TYPICAL ANTLERS)

Minimum Score 125   Continued

SCORE	LENGTH OF MAIN BEAM R	LENGTH OF MAIN BEAM L	INSIDE SPREAD	NUMBER OF POINTS R	NUMBER OF POINTS L	AREA	STATE/ PROVINCE	HUNTER'S NAME	DATE	RANK
138 4/8	21 3/8	22 0/8	18 0/8	5	5	San Patricio County	TX	Victor Muniz	1995	8,109
138 4/8	24 7/8	24 3/8	15 4/8	4	5	Berrien County	MI	Rian Huff	1996	8,109
138 4/8	23 0/8	22 7/8	19 0/8	5	5	Grant County	WI	Emerald A. Faulkner, Jr.	1996	8,109
138 4/8	23 0/8	24 4/8	17 4/8	6	5	Crawford County	OH	John T. Wright	1996	8,109
138 4/8	23 4/8	23 3/8	16 4/8	5	5	Jasper County	IA	George Lee Wells	1996	8,109
138 4/8	23 6/8	24 7/8	21 6/8	4	4	La Salle County	TX	Todd P. Wojtowecz	1997	8,109
138 4/8	24 7/8	23 2/8	20 0/8	4	4	Jo Daviess County	IL	Gabe McKee	1997	8,109
138 4/8	24 2/8	22 6/8	18 4/8	5	4	Walworth County	WI	Dennis Rucks	1997	8,109
138 4/8	22 5/8	24 1/8	17 1/8	5	4	Comanche County	KS	Bill Moreton, Sr.	1997	8,109
138 4/8	23 2/8	22 2/8	17 6/8	4	4	Cook County	IL	Tim Harkness	1998	8,109
138 3/8	20 1/8	20 2/8	18 3/8	6	6	Marshall County	SD	Robert Peterson	1962	8,176
138 3/8	22 4/8	20 3/8	16 7/8	6	5	Adams County	IL	David DeMoss	1967	8,176
138 3/8	20 0/8	21 3/8	16 5/8	5	5	Chase County	KS	Larry Krom	1971	8,176
138 3/8	22 1/8	22 7/8	16 7/8	4	4	O'Brien County	IA	Chuck Pemble	1973	8,176
138 3/8	20 4/8	21 4/8	17 6/8	5	6	Ferry County	WA	Robert Lantiegne	1980	8,176
138 3/8	21 4/8	21 5/8	19 1/8	7	5	Screven County	GA	John Frankhouser	1982	8,176
138 3/8	22 3/8	22 2/8	17 7/8	4	4	Republic County	KS	Carroll W. Couture	1982	8,176
138 3/8	22 4/8	22 1/8	16 5/8	6	5	Wilcox County	GA	George L. Haynie	1983	8,176
138 3/8	22 4/8	21 5/8	19 5/8	6	5	St. Clair County	MO	Lavern Rucker	1983	8,176
138 3/8	25 2/8	25 5/8	16 2/8	5	5	Vernon County	WI	Stan Getter	1984	8,176
138 3/8	24 4/8	23 2/8	17 7/8	5	5	Allen County	IN	Robert M. Wallin	1984	8,176
138 3/8	21 6/8	22 5/8	16 3/8	5	6	Marquette County	WI	David M. Borzick	1985	8,176
138 3/8	22 6/8	22 7/8	17 7/8	5	5	Clark County	WI	James F. Baker	1985	8,176
138 3/8	23 2/8	23 3/8	16 7/8	6	5	Fayette County	IA	Brad Volker	1986	8,176
138 3/8	23 4/8	26 5/8	18 5/8	4	5	McHenry County	IL	Edward Koenig	1986	8,176
138 3/8	24 0/8	23 4/8	17 5/8	4	4	Barton County	KS	Dan Byers	1986	8,176
138 3/8	22 6/8	22 1/8	17 3/8	4	4	Marshall County	KS	Frank Cornelison	1986	8,176
138 3/8	24 4/8	25 0/8	16 7/8	4	4	Fillmore County	MN	Neil Fishbaugher	1986	8,176
138 3/8	20 0/8	21 3/8	15 5/8	5	5	Ontario County	NY	Harry F. Voss	1987	8,176
138 3/8	22 7/8	22 0/8	19 7/8	5	5	Weld County	CO	Roger Bechler	1987	8,176
138 3/8	19 4/8	20 7/8	14 1/8	6	6	Crook County	WY	Glen R. Shrewsbury	1988	8,176
138 3/8	22 5/8	24 1/8	15 4/8	7	8	Cerro Gordo County	IA	Danny D. Ruiter	1988	8,176
138 3/8	22 0/8	22 5/8	20 7/8	4	4	Champaign County	IL	Rich Schrock	1988	8,176
138 3/8	21 7/8	22 7/8	14 6/8	4	6	Monona County	IA	Duane R. Miller	1988	8,176
138 3/8	25 3/8	25 1/8	16 5/8	4	7	Crawford County	IL	Robert Loveall	1988	8,176
138 3/8	24 0/8	24 0/8	16 7/8	5	5	Bremer County	IA	Tom Bluhm	1988	8,176
138 3/8	22 5/8	22 4/8	15 3/8	5	5	Saunders County	NE	Randy Banghart	1988	8,176
138 3/8	22 4/8	22 4/8	16 7/8	5	5	Dodge County	WI	Ben Beine	1989	8,176
138 3/8	22 3/8	23 5/8	18 3/8	5	5	Polk County	WI	Terry A. Sveback	1989	8,176
138 3/8	21 6/8	22 2/8	15 3/8	5	5	Nueces County	TX	Tom Winn	1989	8,176
138 3/8	23 2/8	25 0/8	20 0/8	6	6	Lake County	IL	James R. Swan	1989	8,176
138 3/8	24 0/8	24 4/8	22 5/8	5	5	Meigs County	OH	Jeff Russell	1990	8,176
138 3/8	24 3/8	24 5/8	15 7/8	4	4	Ogle County	IL	Charlie Nestrojil	1990	8,176
138 3/8	26 1/8	25 1/8	18 6/8	4	6	Pope County	IL	Gordon Beal	1990	8,176
138 3/8	22 6/8	22 3/8	16 1/8	4	5	Minnehaha County	SD	Arnie Sudenga	1991	8,176
138 3/8	24 4/8	24 5/8	17 1/8	4	4	Nicholas County	WV	David A. Moore	1991	8,176
138 3/8	24 0/8	23 5/8	19 3/8	4	5	Winnebago County	WI	Daniel R. Platta	1991	8,176
138 3/8	23 3/8	22 5/8	19 5/8	4	4	Polk County	IA	Ed Rice	1992	8,176
138 3/8	22 6/8	22 3/8	17 5/8	4	4	Hamilton County	IA	Mike Tempel	1992	8,176
138 3/8	21 7/8	23 0/8	18 0/8	6	5	Worcester County	MD	Robert Bryan Simms	1992	8,176
138 3/8	23 2/8	22 7/8	17 2/8	6	6	Anne Arundel County	MD	Gene Willsey	1992	8,176
138 3/8	22 3/8	22 0/8	19 0/8	5	6	Ingham County	MI	Shaun E. Morgan	1993	8,176
138 3/8	23 1/8	23 2/8	22 7/8	4	4	Juneau County	WI	Jerome P. Shere	1993	8,176
138 3/8	27 0/8	27 3/8	19 5/8	4	4	Snyder County	PA	Gene Wagner, Jr.	1993	8,176
138 3/8	20 5/8	22 1/8	15 5/8	5	5	Dakota County	NE	Mike Murphy	1993	8,176
138 3/8	26 2/8	25 0/8	20 4/8	5	4	Lake County	IL	Vincent J. Cassiani III	1993	8,176
138 3/8	23 4/8	24 1/8	18 5/8	4	4	Jefferson County	OH	Jim "Reabo" Rea	1993	8,176
138 3/8	23 7/8	24 2/8	17 5/8	4	5	Guthrie County	IA	Vernie W. Grasty	1993	8,176
138 3/8	20 7/8	21 4/8	13 5/8	5	5	Brooks County	TX	Craig Galloway	1993	8,176
138 3/8	22 4/8	21 4/8	16 7/8	5	5	Franklin County	VA	Mike Weaver	1994	8,176
138 3/8	21 4/8	22 2/8	18 7/8	5	5	Macon County	IL	Quintin Puckett	1994	8,176
138 3/8	25 5/8	25 6/8	22 6/8	4	5	Hickory County	MO	Tim R. Ott	1994	8,176
138 3/8	20 7/8	20 6/8	15 7/8	5	5	Polk County	WI	John B. Larson	1994	8,176
138 3/8	23 4/8	22 3/8	17 0/8	9	5	Sawyer County	WI	Jay Weidman	1994	8,176
138 3/8	22 5/8	24 0/8	19 7/8	7	6	Union County	SD	Larry Rosenbaum	1994	8,176
138 3/8	23 2/8	24 1/8	17 7/8	5	7	Blackfalds	ALB	Colin Campbell	1995	8,176
138 3/8	21 1/8	21 7/8	18 3/8	5	7	Iowa County	WI	Glenn Greene	1995	8,176
138 3/8	22 7/8	22 4/8	18 1/8	6	5	Dane County	WI	Mark Kruchten	1995	8,176
138 3/8	22 1/8	21 7/8	16 7/8	5	5	Columbia County	WI	Scott M. Hazard	1995	8,176
138 3/8	24 3/8	25 4/8	19 5/8	6	5	Harrison County	OH	John Lee Meyer	1995	8,176
138 3/8	22 4/8	21 4/8	16 7/8	4	4	Cumberland County	IL	Brian Banovz	1995	8,176
138 3/8	21 7/8	21 2/8	19 1/8	5	5	Du Page County	IL	James A. Wetmore	1995	8,176
138 3/8	24 3/8	24 2/8	17 5/8	4	4	Wilbarger County	TX	Randy Smith	1995	8,176
138 3/8	22 6/8	23 3/8	18 3/8	4	4	Noble County	OK	Steven R. Scott	1995	8,176
138 3/8	25 0/8	24 2/8	19 5/8	5	5	Fairfield County	OH	Kirk Smith	1996	8,176
138 3/8	20 0/8	20 6/8	14 3/8	5	5	Davis County	IA	John Bender	1996	8,176
138 3/8	22 4/8	22 7/8	16 0/8	4	5	Screven County	GA	Rodney Becton	1996	8,176
138 3/8	23 2/8	22 0/8	19 1/8	6	8	Walworth County	WI	Jeffrey L. Turbett	1996	8,176

WHITETAIL DEER (TYPICAL ANTLERS)

Minimum Score 125 · Continued

SCORE	LENGTH OF MAIN BEAM R	LENGTH OF MAIN BEAM L	INSIDE SPREAD	NUMBER OF POINTS R	NUMBER OF POINTS L	AREA	STATE/ PROVINCE	HUNTER'S NAME	DATE	RANK
138 3/8	24 1/8	24 0/8	21 5/8	4	4	Morgan County	IL	Steve Hartman	1996	8,176
138 3/8	20 5/8	21 0/8	17 7/8	6	5	Carroll County	IL	Roman Cirignani	1996	8,176
138 3/8	23 4/8	24 1/8	19 1/8	4	4	Monroe County	IL	Tommy Hefflinger	1996	8,176
138 3/8	22 7/8	22 7/8	18 3/8	5	5	Vernon County	WI	Bruce R. Youngbauer	1996	8,176
138 3/8	24 1/8	23 5/8	23 6/8	6	5	Mercer County	NJ	Ario George Thomas	1996	8,176
138 3/8	23 6/8	23 4/8	20 3/8	5	5	Forest County	WI	Gene Schmechel	1997	8,176
138 3/8	21 6/8	22 2/8	16 1/8	5	5	Oakland County	MI	Walter Arsenault	1997	8,176
138 3/8	20 7/8	22 3/8	16 7/8	5	5	Waupaca County	WI	Frank Radtke	1997	8,176
138 3/8	21 1/8	19 6/8	16 1/8	5	5	Allamakee County	IA	Richard D. Tenute	1997	8,176
138 3/8	21 5/8	21 6/8	16 1/8	4	4	Chautauqua County	KS	Gregory C. Bokash	1997	8,176
138 3/8	24 5/8	25 0/8	20 1/8	5	4	Tuscarawas County	OH	Jerry Hershberger	1997	8,176
138 3/8	25 5/8	26 3/8	19 5/8	5	4	Ozaukee County	WI	Ray Schultz	1997	8,176
138 2/8	20 6/8	20 6/8	17 0/8	5	5	Kent County	MD	Paul W. Broadhurst	1962	8,256
138 2/8	20 4/8	20 2/8	13 6/8	5	5	Adams County	IL	Russ Griffin	1970	8,256
138 2/8	23 3/8	21 3/8	18 4/8	5	5	Ripley County	IN	Pat Wolf	1971	8,256
138 2/8	23 3/8	22 0/8	16 4/8	5	4	Des Moines County	IA	Cory Dalton	1973	8,256
138 2/8	23 5/8	22 1/8	20 2/8	5	6	Crawford County	WI	Jim Ferebee	1976	8,256
138 2/8	21 2/8	21 2/8	16 3/8	5	7	Edmonton	ALB	Wilf Hunter	1978	8,256
138 2/8	23 4/8	23 2/8	17 2/8	5	5	Huron Twp.	ONT	Jim McAuley	1980	8,256
138 2/8	21 4/8	23 0/8	16 2/8	5	5	La Salle County	IL	Leonard Cochran	1981	8,256
138 2/8	21 6/8	22 4/8	17 4/8	5	6	Johnson County	AR	Jeff Adams	1981	8,256
138 2/8	25 2/8	25 1/8	19 7/8	4	5	Preble County	OH	William J. Hahn	1981	8,256
138 2/8	24 3/8	24 3/8	18 6/8	4	4	Cass County	IA	Reggie Schuler	1982	8,256
138 2/8	22 7/8	23 2/8	17 6/8	4	4	Clark County	OH	David Parrott	1983	8,256
138 2/8	24 7/8	26 0/8	16 0/8	7	6	Morgan County	GA	Rod Ayers	1983	8,256
138 2/8	22 4/8	23 3/8	20 4/8	4	5	Lenawee County	MI	Kevin S. Zalecki	1983	8,256
138 2/8	22 3/8	22 2/8	17 4/8	5	5	Washburn County	WI	Russell Worman	1983	8,256
138 2/8	22 1/8	22 5/8	17 4/8	5	5	Chippewa County	WI	Ty Sweeney	1984	8,256
138 2/8	24 6/8	25 4/8	18 4/8	5	4	Berks County	PA	Joseph W. Ruppe	1984	8,256
138 2/8	23 1/8	23 0/8	17 4/8	4	5	Waushara County	WI	Michael A. Hale	1984	8,256
138 2/8	23 4/8	23 6/8	16 6/8	5	5	Houston County	MN	Richard Crabtree	1985	8,256
138 2/8	22 6/8	21 7/8	17 2/8	5	5	Cass County	MO	Rusty Murry	1985	8,256
138 2/8	22 4/8	23 1/8	16 2/8	4	4	Morgan County	CO	Rodney Washburn	1985	8,256
138 2/8	22 5/8	22 1/8	18 2/8	6	6	Tazewell County	IL	Gary D. Stamm	1985	8,256
138 2/8	21 3/8	20 7/8	15 6/8	6	6	Hubbard County	MN	Jerry Lemke	1986	8,256
138 2/8	22 1/8	22 2/8	21 0/8	5	5	Will County	IL	William A. Spreitzer	1986	8,256
138 2/8	22 6/8	21 0/8	16 3/8	6	7	Brown County	IN	Roger D. Eads	1986	8,256
138 2/8	24 2/8	23 3/8	14 6/8	6	6	McLean County	IL	Roger D. List	1986	8,256
138 2/8	24 1/8	26 1/8	22 4/8	7	7	Jo Daviess County	IL	Mike Traub	1987	8,256
138 2/8	21 3/8	22 6/8	17 0/8	4	4	Oneida County	WI	Steve Graceffa	1988	8,256
138 2/8	24 5/8	23 4/8	16 5/8	5	6	Southampton County	VA	Alan Kee	1988	8,256
138 2/8	21 7/8	22 7/8	16 5/8	7	6	Plymouth County	IA	Jason J. Dannenberg	1988	8,256
138 2/8	24 0/8	23 1/8	20 2/8	5	6	Peoria County	IL	Henry Kirkham	1988	8,256
138 2/8	21 6/8	23 1/8	18 5/8	6	5	Warren County	IA	Bruce Hupke	1988	8,256
138 2/8	25 7/8	26 6/8	19 6/8	5	4	Howard County	MD	Dave Wilson	1989	8,256
138 2/8	23 6/8	24 1/8	15 6/8	5	5	Mingo County	WV	Shelia Sammons	1989	8,256
138 2/8	23 5/8	23 0/8	18 2/8	4	4	Pearl Lake	MAN	Michael N. Hust	1989	8,256
138 2/8	22 3/8	22 6/8	16 0/8	5	5	Jackson County	MI	James E. Plumb	1989	8,256
138 2/8	21 1/8	21 0/8	17 2/8	5	5	Bayfield County	WI	Frank A. Goodwin, Jr.	1989	8,256
138 2/8	23 3/8	23 0/8	18 6/8	5	5	Cape Girardeau County	MO	Timothy E. Bender	1989	8,256
138 2/8	22 6/8	23 1/8	16 6/8	4	5	Mercer County	MO	Henry Houk	1989	8,256
138 2/8	22 2/8	23 5/8	16 3/8	5	6	Polk County	WI	Warren P. Prellwitz	1990	8,256
138 2/8	25 2/8	23 3/8	17 3/8	6	6	Fairfield County	OH	Larry Sharp	1990	8,256
138 2/8	25 7/8	24 5/8	21 2/8	5	5	Marathon County	WI	Gary Heckendorf	1990	8,256
138 2/8	23 3/8	22 0/8	18 2/8	4	4	Belmont County	OH	Jerry Smith	1991	8,256
138 2/8	26 0/8	26 7/8	19 4/8	5	5	Allen County	OH	Gregory J. McMillen	1991	8,256
138 2/8	22 0/8	22 0/8	16 4/8	5	5	Cook County	MN	Dennis Gary Schlienz	1991	8,256
138 2/8	26 2/8	24 2/8	16 5/8	6	7	Parker County	TX	Ralph C. Wiggins, Jr.	1991	8,256
138 2/8	23 5/8	23 2/8	15 4/8	4	5	Hall County	GA	Kevin Williamson	1992	8,256
138 2/8	22 2/8	22 1/8	15 6/8	4	4	Crawford County	IA	Dan Hollingsworth	1992	8,256
138 2/8	22 3/8	22 6/8	18 4/8	6	6	Hennepin County	MN	Paul Kielb	1992	8,256
138 2/8	22 3/8	22 6/8	17 3/8	6	5	Meeker County	MN	Larry M. Looman	1992	8,256
138 2/8	25 7/8	25 1/8	17 0/8	6	5	Hocking County	OH	Jeffery A. Reid	1992	8,256
138 2/8	21 0/8	20 4/8	15 6/8	5	5	Florence County	WI	Dean J. Smaney	1992	8,256
138 2/8	23 7/8	24 0/8	18 2/8	4	5	Dakota County	MN	Bill R. Simek	1993	8,256
138 2/8	25 0/8	24 7/8	18 6/8	5	5	Story County	IA	Chris Hand	1993	8,256
138 2/8	22 0/8	22 6/8	18 3/8	5	6	Pottawattamie County	IA	Tim Hackett	1993	8,256
138 2/8	24 3/8	23 1/8	18 1/8	5	5	McHenry County	IL	Brent A. Smith	1993	8,256
138 2/8	23 6/8	23 5/8	16 6/8	6	5	Cheshire County	NH	John Aubuchont	1993	8,256
138 2/8	22 7/8	22 2/8	17 2/8	5	6	Monroe County	WI	Andy Pierce	1994	8,256
138 2/8	23 4/8	24 1/8	18 4/8	6	5	Iron County	WI	John H. Klopatek	1994	8,256
138 2/8	23 1/8	23 1/8	21 2/8	5	5	Plymouth County	IA	David A. Treft	1994	8,256
138 2/8	21 6/8	20 7/8	17 0/8	5	5	Gage County	NE	Donald Ball	1995	8,256
138 2/8	23 7/8	23 3/8	19 6/8	5	6	Lowndes County	MS	Danny B. Studdard	1995	8,256
138 2/8	24 4/8	23 1/8	23 4/8	4	4	Green Lake County	WI	Daniel J. Zodrow	1995	8,256
138 2/8	20 7/8	21 3/8	16 4/8	5	6	McDonough County	IL	Burt Volker	1995	8,256
138 2/8	26 2/8	26 3/8	15 7/8	7	5	Bayfield County	WI	Kevin Fennell	1995	8,256
138 2/8	19 3/8	21 5/8	15 0/8	6	6	Buffalo County	WI	John Stemper	1995	8,256

WHITETAIL DEER (TYPICAL ANTLERS)

Minimum Score 125 — Continued

SCORE	LENGTH OF MAIN BEAM R	L	INSIDE SPREAD	NUMBER OF POINTS R	L	AREA	STATE/ PROVINCE	HUNTER'S NAME	DATE	RANK
138 2/8	22 7/8	21 2/8	18 0/8	5	5	Sullivan County	IN	Steve Hobbs	1995	8,256
138 2/8	22 5/8	21 3/8	16 0/8	6	5	Hardin County	KY	Eric Dulin	1996	8,256
138 2/8	23 3/8	22 6/8	18 6/8	5	4	Eaton County	MI	Michael T. Austin	1996	8,256
138 2/8	22 6/8	22 1/8	17 2/8	5	5	Pike County	IL	John Gamberine	1996	8,256
138 2/8	21 7/8	21 3/8	15 2/8	5	5	Bibb County	GA	Chris McClellan	1996	8,256
138 2/8	23 3/8	22 4/8	16 0/8	4	4	Cherokee County	IA	Bruce H. Johnson	1996	8,256
138 2/8	20 4/8	20 3/8	17 2/8	5	5	Ransom County	ND	Steven Ackerland	1997	8,256
138 2/8	21 5/8	22 6/8	18 3/8	6	7	Irion County	TX	Brett McCown	1997	8,256
138 2/8	23 5/8	24 3/8	18 2/8	4	5	La Salle County	TX	Ricardo Longoria	1997	8,256
138 2/8	24 5/8	25 0/8	18 3/8	5	6	Taylor County	IA	Jim Hinson	1997	8,256
138 2/8	22 0/8	21 7/8	19 0/8	4	4	Dane County	WI	James Schulz	1997	8,256
138 2/8	23 5/8	23 7/8	18 6/8	5	5	Waukesha County	WI	Jim Gutenberger	1997	8,256
138 2/8	24 0/8	22 6/8	16 0/8	5	4	Cass County	IN	Donald R. Singley	1997	8,256
138 2/8	22 2/8	23 0/8	15 4/8	5	6	Langlade County	WI	Jay C. Schroepfer	1997	8,256
138 2/8	22 6/8	23 1/8	15 2/8	5	5	Kleberg County	TX	Greg Stockard	1997	8,256
138 2/8	22 5/8	21 3/8	13 5/8	6	5	Parker County	TX	Tom J. Davidson	1998	8,256
138 1/8	25 4/8	24 0/8	17 2/8	4	5	Cottonwood County	MN	Rodney Ella	1971	8,338
138 1/8	23 1/8	22 5/8	19 7/8	5	5	Pocahontas County	WV	Jim Manley II	1971	8,338
138 1/8	23 0/8	22 4/8	18 3/8	4	4	Anoka County	MN	Johnny E. Boatner	1978	8,338
138 1/8	22 1/8	21 0/8	19 3/8	5	5	Kalamazoo County	MI	Dale Gray	1978	8,338
138 1/8	22 5/8	24 6/8	20 1/8	6	7	Goodhue County	MN	Victor Lopresto	1979	8,338
138 1/8	24 0/8	25 4/8	17 3/8	4	5	Grand Traverse County	MI	Roger Kirby	1980	8,338
138 1/8	22 4/8	22 5/8	17 1/8	5	5	Huron County	OH	Larry Smith	1980	8,338
138 1/8	23 4/8	23 3/8	18 4/8	6	5	Bond County	IL	Donald E. Cruse, Jr.	1981	8,338
138 1/8	23 4/8	23 2/8	16 3/8	4	5	Jackson County	MO	Marvin Thomey	1982	8,338
138 1/8	24 1/8	23 4/8	15 7/8	5	4	Allamakee County	IA	Frank Saddler	1982	8,338
138 1/8	20 6/8	20 6/8	18 0/8	5	6	San Augustine County	TX	Billy E. Corley	1982	8,338
138 1/8	22 5/8	24 3/8	15 7/8	5	5	Price County	WI	Allen F. Feltz	1983	8,338
138 1/8	23 6/8	23 1/8	19 7/8	4	4	Allegan County	MI	Tim Leslie	1983	8,338
138 1/8	24 1/8	23 3/8	17 1/8	5	5	Jersey County	IL	Herman W. Kovar	1983	8,338
138 1/8	22 0/8	21 7/8	17 7/8	5	6	Franklin County	IN	Pearl Houston	1986	8,338
138 1/8	22 4/8	21 4/8	15 5/8	5	5	Greene County	MO	Jackie Davis	1986	8,338
138 1/8	22 5/8	22 3/8	17 3/8	4	5	Allamakee County	IA	Dan Brimeyer	1987	8,338
138 1/8	22 3/8	22 3/8	17 5/8	8	5	Jackson County	WI	Todd D. Reichert	1988	8,338
138 1/8	21 1/8	19 2/8	15 7/8	5	5	Dane County	WI	Mark Overland	1988	8,338
138 1/8	22 0/8	20 7/8	15 5/8	8	6	Nelson County	ND	Douglas Magnus	1989	8,338
138 1/8	21 1/8	21 6/8	18 5/8	5	5	Knox County	IL	C. F. Peterson	1989	8,338
138 1/8	23 7/8	23 0/8	19 5/8	5	5	Morris County	NJ	David Bright	1989	8,338
138 1/8	22 2/8	22 2/8	16 5/8	5	5	Oneida County	WI	Trygve Solberg	1989	8,338
138 1/8	19 1/8	21 7/8	20 5/8	5	5	Butler County	KS	Ron Shipman	1989	8,338
138 1/8	24 1/8	23 7/8	18 5/8	4	4	Webster County	IA	Tim Bacon	1990	8,338
138 1/8	20 3/8	20 2/8	15 7/8	6	7	Grant County	WI	Glen A. Klais	1990	8,338
138 1/8	21 4/8	21 3/8	19 3/8	5	6	Pike County	IL	William W. Singer	1990	8,338
138 1/8	21 6/8	22 2/8	19 5/8	5	5	Canadian County	OK	Keith Darrow	1990	8,338
138 1/8	23 1/8	22 6/8	21 1/8	6	6	Lucas County	IA	Bruce Elrod	1991	8,338
138 1/8	26 6/8	25 3/8	16 4/8	6	7	Sedgwick County	KS	Bob Campbell	1991	8,338
138 1/8	24 1/8	23 6/8	21 7/8	4	4	Pike County	IL	Wayne B. Puterbaugh	1991	8,338
138 1/8	23 0/8	21 7/8	17 1/8	8	5	Marathon County	WI	Floyd D. Matteson	1992	8,338
138 1/8	23 0/8	21 5/8	18 1/8	5	5	Warren County	IN	Mark Eminger	1992	8,338
138 1/8	24 0/8	23 0/8	18 5/8	4	4	Issaquena County	MS	Albert Tucker Hossley	1992	8,338
138 1/8	23 0/8	22 2/8	14 3/8	5	5	Fayette County	IL	Steve Hosick	1992	8,338
138 1/8	24 3/8	24 2/8	18 3/8	4	4	Bayham Township	ONT	Calvin Riddell	1992	8,338
138 1/8	22 0/8	22 0/8	16 6/8	6	7	Trempealeau County	WI	David A. Stegemeyer	1993	8,338
138 1/8	22 0/8	21 0/8	18 7/8	5	5	Kosciusko County	IN	Jim Nichols	1993	8,338
138 1/8	23 1/8	23 5/8	20 1/8	5	5	Calhoun County	MI	Richard Coon	1993	8,338
138 1/8	23 4/8	23 3/8	19 7/8	5	5	Wood County	OH	Fred Ault	1993	8,338
138 1/8	24 4/8	24 4/8	18 7/8	5	5	Morrison County	MN	Gary Sigafoos	1993	8,338
138 1/8	20 4/8	19 7/8	15 2/8	6	6	Vermillion County	IN	Don Guess	1993	8,338
138 1/8	27 0/8	28 4/8	23 2/8	5	3	Macoupin County	IL	Rick Tigo	1993	8,338
138 1/8	24 0/8	23 6/8	16 3/8	5	4	Eau Claire County	WI	Wayne Price	1993	8,338
138 1/8	21 6/8	20 0/8	15 7/8	6	5	Montgomery County	IA	Steve Philby	1993	8,338
138 1/8	24 2/8	23 0/8	20 3/8	4	5	Spink County	SD	R. Craig Oberle	1993	8,338
138 1/8	25 7/8	23 6/8	18 5/8	5	4	Wood County	WI	Darwin B. Keding	1993	8,338
138 1/8	20 7/8	21 7/8	16 7/8	5	5	McMullen County	TX	Scotty Reynolds	1993	8,338
138 1/8	23 1/8	22 5/8	17 7/8	5	5	Ripley County	IN	Chris Salyer	1994	8,338
138 1/8	24 0/8	23 3/8	17 5/8	5	5	Barron County	WI	Glenn E. Kolb	1994	8,338
138 1/8	23 1/8	22 6/8	20 3/8	5	4	Hancock County	IL	Roger Jackson	1994	8,338
138 1/8	20 2/8	18 7/8	14 7/8	6	7	La Salle County	TX	Stephen McCarty	1995	8,338
138 1/8	23 5/8	24 4/8	17 5/8	4	4	Linn County	KS	Gary Robertson	1995	8,338
138 1/8	23 1/8	23 1/8	15 3/8	5	5	Berrien County	MI	David Brelowski	1995	8,338
138 1/8	23 7/8	24 7/8	18 1/8	5	5	Adams County	OH	Jeffrey S. Smith	1995	8,338
138 1/8	22 2/8	22 6/8	18 7/8	5	5	Dallas County	IA	Nathan Hasty	1996	8,338
138 1/8	23 4/8	22 7/8	19 3/8	4	4	Lake County	IL	Brad Baley	1996	8,338
138 1/8	23 4/8	23 2/8	22 1/8	5	5	Jefferson County	NE	Robert W. Peperkorn	1997	8,338
138 1/8	22 3/8	20 3/8	15 1/8	6	3	Winnebago County	WI	David Heise	1997	8,338
138 1/8	25 6/8	26 3/8	22 3/8	5	4	Montgomery County	IA	Mike Philby	1997	8,338
138 1/8	21 6/8	21 4/8	18 5/8	5	5	Oakland County	MI	Steven C. Elliott	1997	8,338
138 1/8	23 3/8	22 4/8	15 7/8	5	5	Worcester County	MD	Wayne J. Zimmerer, Jr.	1997	8,338

WHITETAIL DEER (TYPICAL ANTLERS)

Minimum Score 125 — Continued

SCORE	LENGTH OF MAIN BEAM R	LENGTH OF MAIN BEAM L	INSIDE SPREAD	NUMBER OF POINTS R	NUMBER OF POINTS L	AREA	STATE/PROVINCE	HUNTER'S NAME	DATE	RANK
138 0/8	24 1/8	23 7/8	19 1/8	8	6	Frederick County	MD	Donald R. Shipley	1962	8,400
138 0/8	22 2/8	22 3/8	18 4/8	4	4	Dane County	WI	Ernest Kalar	1966	8,400
138 0/8	21 3/8	21 7/8	19 4/8	5	6	Washburn County	WI	John C. Gehlen	1971	8,400
138 0/8	21 4/8	21 6/8	13 0/8	5	5	Taylor County	KY	James Hedgespeth	1978	8,400
138 0/8	23 0/8	23 4/8	14 0/8	5	5	Jefferson County	WI	Dennis Roberts	1980	8,400
138 0/8	22 6/8	23 6/8	20 4/8	4	5	Traverse County	MN	Danny Hormann	1981	8,400
138 0/8	23 1/8	23 7/8	18 4/8	5	5	Langlade County	WI	Mike Plzak	1982	8,400
138 0/8	20 3/8	21 6/8	15 5/8	5	7	Payne County	OK	David Ray Beene	1983	8,400
138 0/8	22 6/8	22 5/8	16 6/8	5	5	Tyler County	WV	John S McMulley	1984	8,400
138 0/8	23 6/8	23 1/8	17 2/8	5	5	Lake County	IL	John R. Love	1984	8,400
138 0/8	22 1/8	21 2/8	14 4/8	5	5	De Kalb County	MO	Daniel E. Terry	1985	8,400
138 0/8	23 1/8	23 3/8	15 4/8	5	5	Marquette County	WI	Dennis J. Buchholz	1986	8,400
138 0/8	22 7/8	23 5/8	19 0/8	5	4	Waukesha County	WI	Steve Pease	1986	8,400
138 0/8	22 3/8	22 4/8	16 4/8	5	4	Waukesha County	WI	Edward P. Papp, Jr.	1986	8,400
138 0/8	24 4/8	26 2/8	16 2/8	7	7	Iroquois County	IL	Terry Doehring	1986	8,400
138 0/8	22 3/8	22 4/8	16 6/8	4	4	Harrison County	OH	Andy Staneart	1986	8,400
138 0/8	22 3/8	21 2/8	17 4/8	5	5	Vermilion County	IL	Carl Cornwell	1986	8,400
138 0/8	23 4/8	23 4/8	14 1/8	6	6	Price County	WI	Brent M. Zierer	1986	8,400
138 0/8	24 2/8	23 4/8	18 2/8	4	4	Campbell County	KY	Thomas A. Bezold	1987	8,400
138 0/8	24 0/8	24 0/8	17 6/8	4	5	Kent County	MI	Daniel K. Hall	1987	8,400
138 0/8	22 4/8	18 4/8	20 0/8	6	6	Rock County	NE	Doug Otte	1987	8,400
138 0/8	23 3/8	23 4/8	19 0/8	5	5	Outagamie County	WI	Bill Sulllvan	1987	8,400
138 0/8	24 7/8	26 1/8	20 0/8	5	7	Washington County	MN	Rodney P. Bailey	1987	8,400
138 0/8	21 1/8	20 7/8	15 4/8	5	5	Marshall County	MN	Leland J. Bratlie	1987	8,400
138 0/8	23 4/8	23 1/8	15 4/8	4	4	Linn County	MO	Earl Jones	1987	8,400
138 0/8	23 0/8	21 2/8	15 5/8	5	6	Shelby County	IL	Charlie V. DeBose, Jr.	1987	8,400
138 0/8	25 1/8	25 0/8	17 6/8	6	6	Scott County	MN	Jay M. Scherer	1988	8,400
138 0/8	22 6/8	23 2/8	18 4/8	5	5	Wright County	IA	Jack Jenkins	1988	8,400
138 0/8	23 0/8	23 1/8	21 6/8	5	4	Sioux County	NE	Dan Coffee	1988	8,400
138 0/8	25 0/8	25 0/8	18 4/8	4	5	Highland County	OH	Chris Dopel	1988	8,400
138 0/8	20 1/8	20 5/8	15 6/8	4	5	Todd County	MN	David Puetz	1989	8,400
138 0/8	25 5/8	26 5/8	21 0/8	4	4	Jefferson County	OH	Mike Sauer	1989	8,400
138 0/8	22 6/8	23 2/8	16 4/8	5	5	Meeker County	MN	Susan Barrick-Smith	1990	8,400
138 0/8	23 4/8	23 3/8	16 2/8	5	5	Tazewell County	IL	David A. Cufaude	1990	8,400
138 0/8	24 5/8	23 2/8	16 6/8	5	5	Geary County	KS	Ilija P. Milovanovic	1990	8,400
138 0/8	22 6/8	21 5/8	13 6/8	5	6	Pittsburg County	OK	Joe G. Arms	1991	8,400
138 0/8	21 2/8	20 4/8	15 2/8	5	5	Keokuk County	IA	Randy Schmidt	1991	8,400
138 0/8	22 6/8	21 6/8	16 0/8	6	6	Kingman County	KS	Terry Morisse	1991	8,400
138 0/8	23 7/8	24 3/8	18 2/8	5	5	Morgan County	IL	Steve Barfield	1991	8,400
138 0/8	19 7/8	21 3/8	15 0/8	5	5	Washington County	WI	Duane Duorak	1992	8,400
138 0/8	22 0/8	22 0/8	14 0/8	5	5	Polk County	WI	Kevin Thaemert	1992	8,400
138 0/8	23 2/8	22 6/8	16 4/8	4	4	Morrison County	MN	Jim Schwendinger	1992	8,400
138 0/8	20 7/8	21 6/8	18 7/8	5	6	Powell County	MT	Grant Richards	1992	8,400
138 0/8	20 0/8	24 5/8	17 4/8	4	6	Racine County	WI	Tom T. King	1992	8,400
138 0/8	22 6/8	23 0/8	17 7/8	6	5	Champaign County	OH	Dave Perdue	1992	8,400
138 0/8	19 6/8	19 4/8	19 2/8	5	5	Lewis & Clark County	MT	Sonny Templeton	1992	8,400
138 0/8	20 6/8	20 3/8	14 2/8	5	5	Sauk County	WI	Roger G. Weyh, Jr.	1992	8,400
138 0/8	23 2/8	23 4/8	16 5/8	7	5	Waupaca County	WI	Lee L. Genskow	1992	8,400
138 0/8	24 7/8	24 2/8	18 0/8	4	4	Baltimore County	MD	Rodney Collison	1993	8,400
138 0/8	24 5/8	24 7/8	18 4/8	4	4	Butler County	KY	Willie Durbin	1993	8,400
138 0/8	24 2/8	23 0/8	20 5/8	8	8	Kane County	IL	Jay A. Ervin	1993	8,400
138 0/8	23 3/8	22 5/8	20 6/8	6	4	Saginaw County	MI	Charles Michael Latty	1993	8,400
138 0/8	23 7/8	23 1/8	18 5/8	4	4	Will County	IL	Gary Tyranski	1993	8,400
138 0/8	24 0/8	23 4/8	16 1/8	5	6	Crawford County	PA	Dale A. Bohman	1993	8,400
138 0/8	22 2/8	21 7/8	18 0/8	5	5	Manitowoc County	WI	Anthony J. Bonde	1993	8,400
138 0/8	24 2/8	23 4/8	20 2/8	5	4	Anoka County	MN	Robert Feigum III	1993	8,400
138 0/8	21 1/8	21 4/8	16 0/8	6	6	Pontotoc County	OK	Robby Bailey	1994	8,400
138 0/8	22 6/8	22 4/8	15 4/8	5	5	Goodhue County	MN	William Steigauf	1994	8,400
138 0/8	23 2/8	23 3/8	17 4/8	4	5	Greene County	IN	Adam Bucher/Paul Bucher	1994	8,400
138 0/8	23 3/8	23 4/8	16 4/8	5	4	Holmes County	OH	Aaron Dillon	1994	8,400
138 0/8	23 2/8	23 3/8	17 7/8	5	5	Sawyer County	WI	John Stamper	1994	8,400
138 0/8	21 3/8	21 3/8	16 6/8	5	5	Trempealeau County	WI	Wayne Stalheim	1994	8,400
138 0/8	22 7/8	24 0/8	17 6/8	5	5	McLean County	IL	Stanley E. Camp	1995	8,400
138 0/8	21 4/8	22 3/8	17 2/8	5	5	Washburn County	WI	John M. Weber	1995	8,400
138 0/8	23 4/8	23 2/8	17 4/8	6	5	Waushara County	WI	Tim Soda	1995	8,400
138 0/8	23 1/8	22 4/8	17 6/8	5	6	Stevens County	WA	Nicholas Orth	1995	8,400
138 0/8	21 4/8	21 7/8	17 4/8	5	5	Dakota County	MN	Mike Pistulka	1996	8,400
138 0/8	22 0/8	22 7/8	18 2/8	5	5	Hardin County	IA	Matthew A. Tapken	1996	8,400
138 0/8	26 2/8	25 5/8	18 0/8	4	5	Allamakee County	IA	Ernie Burroughs	1996	8,400
138 0/8	24 4/8	24 5/8	19 6/8	5	5	Cass County	MI	Fred Kruger	1996	8,400
138 0/8	23 2/8	23 2/8	18 7/8	6	7	Allamakee County	IA	Tony M. Millius	1996	8,400
138 0/8	24 6/8	23 6/8	20 1/8	5	5	Eau Claire County	WI	Nick Wampole	1996	8,400
138 0/8	20 6/8	20 6/8	15 4/8	5	5	Vinton County	OH	Mike Williams	1996	8,400
138 0/8	20 6/8	21 3/8	17 0/8	5	5	Pope County	IL	John Hunt	1996	8,400
138 0/8	25 0/8	25 0/8	18 0/8	4	4	Harrison County	IA	Brian Kehrli	1997	8,400
138 0/8	21 5/8	21 7/8	17 2/8	4	5	Shawano County	WI	Ron Bystol	1997	8,400
138 0/8	22 3/8	22 1/8	14 7/8	5	8	Pike County	MO	Guy Young	1997	8,400
138 0/8	23 5/8	23 5/8	16 5/8	5	6	Dakota County	MN	Andy Lee Bohlen	1997	8,400

WHITETAIL DEER (TYPICAL ANTLERS)

Minimum Score 125
Continued

SCORE	LENGTH OF R MAIN BEAM L		INSIDE SPREAD	NUMBER OF R POINTS L		AREA	STATE/ PROVINCE	HUNTER'S NAME	DATE	RANK
138 0/8	23 4/8	22 7/8	21 2/8	6	6	La Salle County	TX	Bobby J. Jones	1997	8,400
138 0/8	23 5/8	24 0/8	16 0/8	5	5	Cook County	IL	Jason Brown	1997	8,400
138 0/8	25 3/8	24 5/8	19 5/8	5	7	Crittenden County	KY	Bob Pearson	1998	8,400
138 0/8	25 2/8	23 5/8	17 2/8	4	4	Bayfield County	WI	Gary Kane	1998	8,400
138 0/8	24 3/8	24 3/8	18 0/8	5	5	Calhoun County	MI	Ron E. Taig	1998	8,400
137 7/8	23 3/8	25 4/8	19 7/8	4	4	Hardin County	KY	Ancil Fields	1959	8,483
137 7/8	22 3/8	22 7/8	21 1/8	6	8	Williams County	ND	Ray Hoveskeland	1959	8,483
137 7/8	20 0/8	21 2/8	17 1/8	4	4	Platte County	NE	Lee Rupp	1968	8,483
137 7/8	21 5/8	21 3/8	16 3/8	5	5	Roseau County	MN	Terry Wilson	1977	8,483
137 7/8	23 0/8	23 4/8	17 5/8	5	5	Chippewa County	MN	Layton Albrecht	1978	8,483
137 7/8	21 6/8	22 2/8	19 0/8	5	4	Kay County	OK	Guy L. LeMonnier, Jr.	1979	8,483
137 7/8	20 6/8	20 1/8	14 5/8	5	5	Macon County	AL	George P. Mann	1981	8,483
137 7/8	21 7/8	21 3/8	14 0/8	5	6	Adams County	OH	Ronald L. Myers	1984	8,483
137 7/8	21 7/8	22 4/8	19 0/8	6	6	Labette County	KS	Rick R. Williamson	1986	8,483
137 7/8	23 3/8	23 2/8	19 0/8	5	5	Prince William County	VA	Franklin A. Siwik	1986	8,483
137 7/8	24 2/8	24 0/8	14 7/8	5	6	Waseca County	MN	Paul Hauck	1986	8,483
137 7/8	23 0/8	21 2/8	18 3/8	4	4	Williamson County	IL	Charles Zeigler	1986	8,483
137 7/8	22 3/8	21 7/8	22 2/8	5	7	Rock Island County	IL	Steve Holmgren	1986	8,483
137 7/8	23 4/8	23 5/8	17 2/8	6	6	Jo Daviess County	IL	Richard Geyer	1987	8,483
137 7/8	22 4/8	22 7/8	15 3/8	4	4	Osborne County	KS	Byron G. Siemiller	1987	8,483
137 7/8	23 0/8	24 0/8	19 6/8	5	6	Carroll County	MD	Daniel Peters	1988	8,483
137 7/8	24 0/8	24 1/8	19 7/8	5	6	Sangamon County	IL	Mike Capranica	1988	8,483
137 7/8	25 1/8	24 6/8	20 1/8	4	5	Orange County	NY	Scott Fairchild	1988	8,483
137 7/8	25 1/8	25 4/8	18 1/8	5	4	Hampden County	MA	Richard Bissaillon	1988	8,483
137 7/8	24 2/8	24 1/8	19 7/8	4	4	McLean County	IL	Larry Messer	1988	8,483
137 7/8	22 0/8	21 6/8	15 5/8	6	5	Prince Georges County	MD	Lance Canter	1989	8,483
137 7/8	21 6/8	21 0/8	20 5/8	6	5	Beltrami County	MN	Matt Stone	1989	8,483
137 7/8	22 6/8	24 4/8	17 2/8	7	6	Brooks County	TX	Jim L. McCrory	1989	8,483
137 7/8	23 0/8	23 2/8	19 0/8	6	6	Fulton County	IL	John I. Briggs	1989	8,483
137 7/8	21 7/8	23 1/8	16 7/8	4	6	Morris County	KS	Jeff L. Newbury	1989	8,483
137 7/8	23 1/8	23 4/8	21 1/8	4	5	Morris County	NJ	Tom LaMantia	1989	8,483
137 7/8	24 1/8	23 6/8	17 4/8	6	6	Anoka County	MN	Bruce Krinkie	1990	8,483
137 7/8	23 1/8	23 7/8	16 4/8	4	6	Holmes County	OH	Ronald S. Kline	1990	8,483
137 7/8	21 3/8	21 3/8	16 7/8	5	5	Ravalli County	MT	Charles Dooner	1990	8,483
137 7/8	23 1/8	24 0/8	15 5/8	4	4	Pike County	OH	Larry Cornett	1991	8,483
137 7/8	22 5/8	23 5/8	20 5/8	6	6	McHenry County	IL	Thomas A. Berthold	1991	8,483
137 7/8	22 7/8	23 1/8	15 5/8	4	4	Creek County	OK	Pat Murphy	1991	8,483
137 7/8	24 6/8	26 2/8	19 0/8	6	4	Prince Georges County	MD	Rob Clark	1991	8,483
137 7/8	22 5/8	23 5/8	16 0/8	5	5	Washington County	IA	Brent J. Graber	1991	8,483
137 7/8	21 6/8	22 0/8	15 5/8	5	5	Vilas County	WI	Dale Mayo	1991	8,483
137 7/8	22 3/8	22 2/8	18 1/8	5	5	Clermont County	OH	Tom McMonigle	1992	8,483
137 7/8	21 0/8	21 1/8	15 4/8	5	6	Madison County	IA	Gary Knoll	1992	8,483
137 7/8	21 3/8	22 0/8	19 3/8	5	5	Clark County	SD	Travis Young	1992	8,483
137 7/8	22 4/8	22 3/8	17 1/8	5	5	Dunn County	WI	Robert J. Constantine	1992	8,483
137 7/8	22 2/8	20 7/8	17 5/8	5	5	Montgomery County	MD	Victor S. Ezerski	1993	8,483
137 7/8	24 5/8	24 2/8	17 4/8	4	6	Calvert County	MD	Shawn A. Garren	1993	8,483
137 7/8	22 2/8	23 6/8	16 1/8	6	5	Clay County	MO	Joel Kimrey	1993	8,483
137 7/8	24 4/8	24 3/8	15 6/8	6	6	Butler County	KS	Kirk Kelly	1993	8,483
137 7/8	23 3/8	23 3/8	15 5/8	6	5	Douglas County	MN	Carl Steen	1993	8,483
137 7/8	21 5/8	23 1/8	18 1/8	4	5	Logan County	IL	Donald D. Stiner	1994	8,483
137 7/8	22 3/8	22 2/8	15 7/8	5	6	Eau Claire County	WI	Roger J. Mrdutt	1994	8,483
137 7/8	24 1/8	23 3/8	17 0/8	5	5	Monroe County	NY	Tim W. Briner	1994	8,483
137 7/8	23 7/8	23 4/8	17 0/8	6	6	Morrison County	MN	Bob Woodhouse	1994	8,483
137 7/8	22 7/8	22 3/8	19 1/8	4	4	Buffalo County	WI	Darin J. Pape	1994	8,483
137 7/8	22 7/8	21 6/8	15 7/8	4	5	Roane County	WV	David W. Heeter	1994	8,483
137 7/8	24 0/8	23 6/8	15 3/8	5	5	Gage County	NE	Dale T. Thornburg	1994	8,483
137 7/8	23 4/8	23 3/8	17 7/8	5	5	Winnebago County	WI	Jon P. Swanson	1994	8,483
137 7/8	22 5/8	22 1/8	20 5/8	5	5	Clayton County	IA	Harry Bries	1994	8,483
137 7/8	24 4/8	24 3/8	17 3/8	4	5	Jackson County	MI	Jerry A. Mitchell	1994	8,483
137 7/8	24 2/8	24 3/8	19 5/8	5	5	Redwood County	MN	Todd Gilb	1994	8,483
137 7/8	22 0/8	21 4/8	17 5/8	5	5	Howard County	MD	Mark Frye	1995	8,483
137 7/8	23 3/8	24 7/8	15 2/8	4	5	Gage County	NE	Russell Topp	1995	8,483
137 7/8	22 1/8	21 3/8	15 5/8	5	5	Kenedy County	TX	Randy Stafford	1995	8,483
137 7/8	21 5/8	21 3/8	15 5/8	5	5	Jackson County	WI	Dan Sorenson	1995	8,483
137 7/8	24 7/8	26 1/8	20 1/8	4	4	Clayton County	IA	Mark R. Klemm	1995	8,483
137 7/8	22 7/8	23 0/8	17 3/8	8	5	Kankakee County	IL	Al Messier	1995	8,483
137 7/8	24 4/8	23 6/8	16 4/8	5	6	Duck Mtns.	MAN	Myles Keller	1995	8,483
137 7/8	21 6/8	21 2/8	17 5/8	5	5	Clark County	IL	James Gilbert	1995	8,483
137 7/8	23 4/8	23 2/8	15 2/8	6	6	Dimmit County	TX	George W. Semple	1995	8,483
137 7/8	21 3/8	21 5/8	15 3/8	5	6	Fillmore County	MN	Dean Irish	1996	8,483
137 7/8	24 4/8	25 1/8	17 1/8	5	4	Copiah County	MS	James Barnett	1996	8,483
137 7/8	22 2/8	22 5/8	17 1/8	6	5	Washtenaw County	MI	Michael J. Spence	1996	8,483
137 7/8	22 0/8	21 3/8	20 4/8	5	6	Suffolk County	NY	Michael Fenezia	1996	8,483
137 7/8	23 4/8	24 3/8	19 0/8	6	6	McLean County	ND	Alan Howard	1996	8,483
137 7/8	24 0/8	24 1/8	17 7/8	4	4	Outagamie County	WI	Dennis Coenen, Jr.	1997	8,483
137 7/8	23 6/8	24 4/8	19 0/8	6	4	Clay County	KS	James Richmond	1997	8,483
137 7/8	25 1/8	24 2/8	18 2/8	5	5	Lake County	IL	Curt Leafblad	1997	8,483
137 7/8	20 7/8	23 5/8	15 7/8	4	5	Warren County	OH	Bob Johnstone	1997	8,483

WHITETAIL DEER (TYPICAL ANTLERS)

Minimum Score 125 — Continued

SCORE	LENGTH OF MAIN BEAM R	LENGTH OF MAIN BEAM L	INSIDE SPREAD	NUMBER OF POINTS R	NUMBER OF POINTS L	AREA	STATE/ PROVINCE	HUNTER'S NAME	DATE	RANK
137 7/8	24 2/8	24 6/8	20 0/8	5	5	Dakota County	MN	Jeff Lengsfeld	1997	8,483
137 7/8	25 2/8	25 3/8	18 5/8	4	4	Buffalo County	WI	Leonard Moeller	1997	8,483
137 7/8	22 1/8	23 0/8	13 2/8	5	6	Ralls County	MO	Michael Kamrowski	1998	8,483
137 7/8	22 4/8	21 2/8	18 5/8	4	4	Huron	ONT	Jim C. DeHoey	1998	8,483
137 6/8	24 5/8	23 7/8	19 2/8	4	5	Adams County	IL	William D. Force	1970	8,560
137 6/8	22 1/8	20 1/8	18 1/8	6	5	Watonwan County	MN	Thomas E. Isley	1972	8,560
137 6/8	20 7/8	21 1/8	16 4/8	5	5	Polk County	IA	John Dykes	1973	8,560
137 6/8	22 7/8	23 6/8	18 4/8	4	5	Roscommon County	MI	James J. Osentoski	1978	8,560
137 6/8	21 2/8	21 2/8	18 2/8	5	5	Goodhue County	MN	Tom Nesseth	1979	8,560
137 6/8	23 6/8	23 0/8	16 1/8	5	5	Middlesex County	CT	James Matulis	1980	8,560
137 6/8	22 0/8	22 6/8	17 6/8	5	5	Walkworth	ONT	Ken McGarrity	1982	8,560
137 6/8	20 4/8	21 5/8	26 2/8	4	6	Suffolk County	NY	Glenn L. Neuschwender	1982	8,560
137 6/8	21 2/8	21 7/8	19 6/8	5	5	Cowley County	KS	Michael R. Bowlin	1983	8,560
137 6/8	23 6/8	24 5/8	20 3/8	6	6	McHenry County	IL	Al Stroh	1983	8,560
137 6/8	21 7/8	22 6/8	16 4/8	5	5	Pine County	MN	Pat Riley	1984	8,560
137 6/8	23 1/8	23 2/8	16 2/8	4	4	Vernon County	WI	Gary Holcombe	1984	8,560
137 6/8	20 7/8	21 4/8	18 4/8	5	5	Crawford County	IL	Todd McDaniel	1985	8,560
137 6/8	22 4/8	21 7/8	17 0/8	5	5	Jefferson County	NE	Bob Funke	1985	8,560
137 6/8	25 1/8	26 1/8	16 7/8	5	4	Cumberland County	NS	P. Jeff Comeau	1985	8,560
137 6/8	23 7/8	23 3/8	17 6/8	5	4	Grand Forks County	ND	Dan M. Finnie	1986	8,560
137 6/8	23 5/8	22 4/8	19 6/8	5	4	Sauk County	WI	Kevin Pavelka	1986	8,560
137 6/8	19 0/8	20 4/8	14 4/8	5	5	Buffalo County	WI	John Kerhin	1986	8,560
137 6/8	20 7/8	19 6/8	17 2/8	5	5	Fulton County	IN	Bart Dauenhauer	1986	8,560
137 6/8	20 6/8	19 4/8	15 0/8	5	6	Russell County	KS	Terry W. Maier	1986	8,560
137 6/8	23 3/8	22 4/8	18 0/8	5	5	Morgan County	IL	Michael Cors	1987	8,560
137 6/8	24 1/8	23 0/8	20 3/8	6	5	Willow Creek	ALB	Randy Biegler	1988	8,560
137 6/8	23 2/8	23 6/8	19 4/8	6	5	Jo Daviess County	IL	John A. Basten	1988	8,560
137 6/8	22 5/8	23 1/8	16 3/8	4	7	Stearns County	MN	Pete Feider	1989	8,560
137 6/8	23 2/8	23 2/8	21 2/8	5	5	Shawano County	WI	Don Armstrong	1989	8,560
137 6/8	23 0/8	23 1/8	17 6/8	4	4	Day County	SD	Jim Cooper	1989	8,560
137 6/8	25 2/8	24 4/8	18 4/8	5	5	Cherokee County	KS	Darren Collins	1989	8,560
137 6/8	22 1/8	22 1/8	15 7/8	8	6	Reno County	KS	Greig Sims	1989	8,560
137 6/8	22 6/8	22 6/8	17 4/8	4	5	Washington County	MN	John Bailey	1989	8,560
137 6/8	21 0/8	20 6/8	14 0/8	5	5	Kenedy County	TX	Romulo Rangel, Jr.	1990	8,560
137 6/8	23 5/8	24 6/8	21 0/8	4	5	Mahaska County	IA	James E. Roe	1990	8,560
137 6/8	21 1/8	21 5/8	16 4/8	5	4	Des Moines County	IA	Mike Carter	1990	8,560
137 6/8	22 7/8	23 0/8	19 6/8	4	4	St. Croix County	WI	Phil Hovde	1991	8,560
137 6/8	24 5/8	23 2/8	17 6/8	5	4	Vermilion County	IL	Michael Olson	1991	8,560
137 6/8	21 4/8	21 6/8	16 0/8	5	5	Davis County	IA	Gary Biles	1991	8,560
137 6/8	24 0/8	24 6/8	18 0/8	4	4	Caldwell County	KY	Bobby Joe Morse	1992	8,560
137 6/8	24 5/8	23 2/8	20 2/8	4	4	Ashtabula County	OH	W. John Gaul, Jr.	1992	8,560
137 6/8	24 6/8	25 5/8	18 0/8	4	5	Washington County	MS	Wade Stephen Crenshaw	1993	8,560
137 6/8	23 2/8	23 3/8	17 2/8	5	5	Coahoma County	MS	Wayne Strider, Jr.	1993	8,560
137 6/8	21 1/8	21 1/8	17 0/8	5	5	Ontario County	NY	William M. Beck	1993	8,560
137 6/8	23 4/8	22 2/8	19 6/8	6	5	Wichita County	KS	Stacy Hoeme	1993	8,560
137 6/8	23 5/8	24 0/8	16 0/8	5	5	Richland County	IL	Frank Anderson	1993	8,560
137 6/8	22 7/8	22 4/8	20 0/8	5	5	Ashland County	WI	Michael A. Zacharias	1993	8,560
137 6/8	23 0/8	21 7/8	13 5/8	6	5	Marion County	IL	Bob Fabick	1993	8,560
137 6/8	20 6/8	20 3/8	19 0/8	5	5	Buffalo County	WI	Thad W. Henderson	1993	8,560
137 6/8	24 1/8	22 3/8	18 2/8	4	4	Greenwood County	KS	David R. Rogers	1993	8,560
137 6/8	21 2/8	21 0/8	17 6/8	5	5	McMullen County	TX	Daniel D. Countiss	1993	8,560
137 6/8	21 2/8	21 5/8	15 0/8	5	5	Langlade County	WI	Jerry Aulik	1994	8,560
137 6/8	22 4/8	22 4/8	18 4/8	6	5	Carter County	MO	Kevin Bonney	1994	8,560
137 6/8	20 0/8	22 2/8	24 1/8	5	5	Nicholas County	WV	Larry Derberry	1994	8,560
137 6/8	20 7/8	20 5/8	15 6/8	5	5	Pike County	IL	Jimmy Howard	1994	8,560
137 6/8	25 5/8	25 5/8	19 2/8	4	4	Hardin County	IL	Thomas Gebel	1994	8,560
137 6/8	21 6/8	22 6/8	15 2/8	5	5	Potter County	PA	Norm Lewis	1995	8,560
137 6/8	20 2/8	19 6/8	15 7/8	6	7	Bucks County	PA	John K. Sverha	1995	8,560
137 6/8	22 6/8	23 0/8	16 6/8	6	4	Vigo County	IN	Thomas E. Rothrock	1995	8,560
137 6/8	21 2/8	21 6/8	17 4/8	6	5	Buffalo County	WI	Jeff Ginder	1995	8,560
137 6/8	24 2/8	24 7/8	15 4/8	6	4	Warren County	MO	Edward A. Dowdy	1995	8,560
137 6/8	22 1/8	22 3/8	17 6/8	4	4	Wayne County	IA	Scott Bunnell	1995	8,560
137 6/8	25 4/8	25 2/8	15 4/8	4	4	Rock County	WI	J. Mitchel Rowley	1995	8,560
137 6/8	21 7/8	23 6/8	17 4/8	5	5	Wilson County	KS	Garry A. Thoms	1995	8,560
137 6/8	23 3/8	22 0/8	17 0/8	5	5	Washington County	OH	Clark Kendle Barrows	1995	8,560
137 6/8	22 0/8	21 7/8	14 2/8	4	4	Johnson County	KS	Donald F. Gibson, Jr.	1995	8,560
137 6/8	23 1/8	23 5/8	14 6/8	5	5	Sussex County	NJ	Jose Colon	1996	8,560
137 6/8	22 1/8	20 5/8	17 2/8	5	5	Fergus County	MT	D. Mitch Kottas	1996	8,560
137 6/8	24 3/8	25 1/8	18 6/8	4	4	Dane County	WI	Ron Mussehl	1996	8,560
137 6/8	23 3/8	22 3/8	17 4/8	5	9	Yuma County	CO	Matt Gideon	1996	8,560
137 6/8	22 0/8	22 2/8	17 0/8	4	4	Menard County	IL	George E. Hypke	1996	8,560
137 6/8	23 7/8	23 4/8	16 4/8	4	4	Franklin County	MO	Mark Kemper	1996	8,560
137 6/8	23 2/8	22 7/8	20 2/8	4	4	Athens County	OH	Tim Frei	1996	8,560
137 6/8	22 5/8	21 7/8	18 4/8	5	5	La Salle County	IL	Michael Elbrecht	1996	8,560
137 6/8	21 7/8	21 1/8	19 6/8	5	5	Chute St. Phillip	QUE	Normand Fortin	1997	8,560
137 6/8	22 0/8	22 4/8	16 2/8	4	4	Richland County	IL	Emery Blank	1997	8,560
137 6/8	22 1/8	22 7/8	16 0/8	5	6	Edgar County	IL	Ryan Neil Koenig	1997	8,560
137 6/8	21 4/8	20 5/8	16 0/8	5	5	Columbia County	WI	Christopher R. Love	1997	8,560

WHITETAIL DEER (TYPICAL ANTLERS)

Minimum Score 125 Continued

SCORE	LENGTH OF MAIN BEAM R	LENGTH OF MAIN BEAM L	INSIDE SPREAD	NUMBER OF POINTS R	NUMBER OF POINTS L	AREA	STATE/ PROVINCE	HUNTER'S NAME	DATE	RANK
137 6/8	22 0/8	22 0/8	16 4/8	5	5	Sawyer County	WI	Joel McVinnie	1997	8,560
137 6/8	21 4/8	21 2/8	16 2/8	6	5	Wilkes County	GA	Bob White	1997	8,560
137 6/8	24 1/8	24 5/8	21 4/8	6	5	Bolivar County	MS	Kevin Rogers	1997	8,560
137 6/8	23 6/8	23 7/8	18 0/8	4	5	Gallatin County	IL	Robert Maynard	1997	8,560
137 5/8	20 4/8	19 7/8	15 5/8	5	5	Clark County	SD	Delmar Tobey	1959	8,638
137 5/8	26 4/8	26 4/8	14 7/8	4	4	Rock County	NE	William Tutt	1963	8,638
137 5/8	20 4/8	20 4/8	17 1/8	4	4	Custer County	MT	Dale Drilling	1976	8,638
137 5/8	23 3/8	23 6/8	16 5/8	5	5	Crow Wing County	MN	Robert Woods	1979	8,638
137 5/8	23 3/8	24 1/8	21 5/8	4	4	Hardin County	KY	Thomas R. Abner	1979	8,638
137 5/8	21 6/8	22 6/8	16 5/8	5	5	Pittsburg County	OK	John Badger	1979	8,638
137 5/8	21 1/8	21 1/8	14 5/8	5	6	Hamilton County	OH	Jack McConnell	1979	8,638
137 5/8	23 3/8	22 5/8	15 5/8	4	4	Cloud County	KS	Don Watowa	1982	8,638
137 5/8	17 7/8	20 5/8	15 7/8	5	6	Waukesha County	WI	Tom Millane	1982	8,638
137 5/8	23 1/8	23 0/8	20 5/8	4	4	Prince Georges County	MD	Dave Williams	1982	8,638
137 5/8	22 5/8	22 2/8	15 3/8	5	5	Chippewa County	MN	Douglas Mittag	1983	8,638
137 5/8	24 5/8	24 0/8	16 5/8	6	5	Suffolk County	VA	Mark T. Smith	1984	8,638
137 5/8	20 3/8	20 0/8	16 7/8	5	5	Parke County	IN	Leonard Outcalt	1986	8,638
137 5/8	22 6/8	23 1/8	18 7/8	5	5	Rogers County	OK	Jimmy Wilson	1986	8,638
137 5/8	22 3/8	22 1/8	17 6/8	7	7	Fayette County	OH	Jeff Sheridan	1986	8,638
137 5/8	22 7/8	23 2/8	15 3/8	5	5	St. Croix County	WI	Doug Severude	1987	8,638
137 5/8	23 3/8	22 6/8	19 7/8	5	5	Schoolcraft County	MI	Dennis W. Kleeman	1987	8,638
137 5/8	21 5/8	20 6/8	18 1/8	4	4	Clarke County	IA	Doyle Curnes	1988	8,638
137 5/8	21 7/8	21 6/8	14 7/8	5	5	Hardin County	IA	Terry Portz	1988	8,638
137 5/8	21 7/8	20 7/8	15 1/8	5	5	Sheboygan County	WI	Wayne Ustby	1988	8,638
137 5/8	23 1/8	23 3/8	15 4/8	7	7	Shawnee County	KS	Mark Broxterman	1988	8,638
137 5/8	24 6/8	23 5/8	15 6/8	6	4	Washington County	IL	Paul Graves, Jr.	1988	8,638
137 5/8	24 1/8	23 2/8	18 7/8	4	5	Mason County	IL	Gregory B. Snider	1988	8,638
137 5/8	21 5/8	22 2/8	17 1/8	5	4	Hancock County	MS	Clifford E. Chauvin	1989	8,638
137 5/8	21 1/8	22 5/8	17 7/8	5	5	Switzerland County	IN	Rick Ritz	1989	8,638
137 5/8	24 1/8	23 3/8	15 2/8	5	5	Calhoun County	MI	Steven F. Collier	1989	8,638
137 5/8	20 1/8	21 3/8	15 0/8	6	5	Woodbury County	IA	John W. Beeson	1989	8,638
137 5/8	23 7/8	24 6/8	18 3/8	5	4	Fairfield County	CT	Gary W. Liljengren	1990	8,638
137 5/8	22 2/8	21 2/8	15 7/8	5	5	La Salle County	IL	Dirk Foltynewicz	1990	8,638
137 5/8	24 5/8	25 0/8	22 1/8	4	4	Caroline County	MD	J. Eric Wise	1991	8,638
137 5/8	22 1/8	21 3/8	19 3/8	5	5	Peoria County	IL	David Emken	1991	8,638
137 5/8	23 6/8	22 0/8	18 2/8	7	7	Mason County	MI	Luke Hoffman	1991	8,638
137 5/8	22 6/8	22 7/8	16 7/8	5	5	Miami County	KS	David L. Scott	1991	8,638
137 5/8	22 2/8	23 0/8	15 7/8	5	5	Missoula County	MT	Tom Kiesel	1992	8,638
137 5/8	19 2/8	20 3/8	16 3/8	6	7	Marquette County	WI	John W. Steuck	1992	8,638
137 5/8	20 3/8	21 6/8	17 7/8	5	5	Harding County	SD	Kim Smith	1992	8,638
137 5/8	23 1/8	23 4/8	15 3/8	5	5	Fulton County	IL	Patrick A. Cebuhar	1992	8,638
137 5/8	23 5/8	23 3/8	18 1/8	4	4	Harvey County	KS	Ron Hershberger	1992	8,638
137 5/8	21 3/8	21 3/8	20 7/8	5	4	Peoria County	IL	Denny Patterson	1992	8,638
137 5/8	24 2/8	24 5/8	17 7/8	6	5	Ferry County	WA	Leroy J. Day	1992	8,638
137 5/8	20 6/8	20 7/8	15 7/8	5	5	Stearns County	MN	Chuck McGannon	1993	8,638
137 5/8	21 7/8	21 7/8	16 3/8	6	5	Montgomery County	MD	Charles Riley III	1993	8,638
137 5/8	23 3/8	24 0/8	19 0/8	6	4	Outagamie County	WI	Rodney Barkholtz	1993	8,638
137 5/8	19 5/8	22 5/8	21 6/8	6	6	Marshall County	IN	Richard A. Fites	1993	8,638
137 5/8	23 7/8	23 7/8	17 1/8	4	4	New Haven County	CT	Kevin Conroy	1993	8,638
137 5/8	23 5/8	22 3/8	15 3/8	4	4	Union County	AR	S. Charles Rhodes	1993	8,638
137 5/8	22 5/8	23 0/8	20 0/8	6	7	Harding County	SD	Richard G. Cordell	1993	8,638
137 5/8	24 3/8	22 2/8	17 7/8	7	6	Williams County	OH	Jeff Hibbard	1993	8,638
137 5/8	22 2/8	21 2/8	15 6/8	6	5	Wapello County	IA	Dennis M. Bradley	1993	8,638
137 5/8	22 2/8	21 4/8	16 5/8	5	5	Buffalo County	WI	Nordahl E. Fleming	1994	8,638
137 5/8	20 6/8	21 2/8	17 3/8	6	5	Sauk County	WI	William L. Schaefer	1994	8,638
137 5/8	22 6/8	23 3/8	15 7/8	5	5	Marquette County	WI	Dennis A. Cossman	1994	8,638
137 5/8	23 6/8	23 4/8	18 1/8	5	5	Delaware County	IA	Daniel G. Putz	1994	8,638
137 5/8	21 2/8	21 4/8	17 3/8	6	6	Grant County	WI	Richard C. Weber	1994	8,638
137 5/8	25 4/8	25 2/8	19 4/8	4	5	Delaware County	OH	Jeff Daily	1994	8,638
137 5/8	22 5/8	24 2/8	16 4/8	5	7	Morris County	NJ	John Terhune	1994	8,638
137 5/8	23 6/8	25 3/8	19 0/8	5	4	Licking County	OH	Mike Wesley	1994	8,638
137 5/8	21 2/8	19 4/8	19 1/8	5	5	Queen Annes County	MD	Mike Chirico	1995	8,638
137 5/8	23 3/8	23 0/8	19 1/8	4	6	Buffalo County	WI	Steve Bertram	1995	8,638
137 5/8	25 6/8	23 4/8	18 3/8	5	5	Crow Wing County	MN	James Miller	1995	8,638
137 5/8	24 3/8	23 0/8	15 0/8	5	6	Ozaukee County	WI	Gene Swatek	1995	8,638
137 5/8	24 0/8	23 7/8	15 3/8	4	4	Hardin County	KY	Mike Green	1995	8,638
137 5/8	21 7/8	21 4/8	16 7/8	5	5	Saratoga County	NY	Jim DiScipio	1995	8,638
137 5/8	21 5/8	22 2/8	20 1/8	5	5	Franklin County	VA	Mike Weaver	1995	8,638
137 5/8	21 0/8	20 3/8	17 3/8	5	5	Clay County	MN	Bradley Burnside	1996	8,638
137 5/8	22 4/8	22 1/8	17 2/8	6	7	Warren County	MS	Walt Mitchell	1996	8,638
137 5/8	20 1/8	21 1/8	16 1/8	5	5	Pottawatomie County	KS	Ronald D. Artzer	1996	8,638
137 5/8	23 6/8	22 6/8	14 4/8	5	6	Grant County	WI	Robert J. Lewis	1996	8,638
137 5/8	23 3/8	23 5/8	16 5/8	5	4	Newport County	RI	James E. Hitchen	1996	8,638
137 5/8	22 4/8	22 5/8	16 5/8	5	5	Westchester County	NY	Joe Hewitt	1996	8,638
137 5/8	22 6/8	20 5/8	15 5/8	5	5	McKenzie County	ND	Scotty A. Rehak	1996	8,638
137 5/8	23 5/8	23 4/8	19 3/8	5	5	Oakland County	MI	James J. Scharf	1997	8,638
137 5/8	24 0/8	23 0/8	18 5/8	5	4	Shawnee County	KS	Mark Wittenburg	1997	8,638
137 5/8	22 4/8	21 5/8	16 3/8	5	4	Davis County	IA	Tracy Templeton	1997	8,638

WHITETAIL DEER (TYPICAL ANTLERS)

Minimum Score 125   Continued

SCORE	LENGTH OF MAIN BEAM R	LENGTH OF MAIN BEAM L	INSIDE SPREAD	NUMBER OF POINTS R	NUMBER OF POINTS L	AREA	STATE/PROVINCE	HUNTER'S NAME	DATE	RANK
137 5/8	21 3/8	21 5/8	16 5/8	5	5	Burnett County	WI	Justin Imme	1997	8,638
137 5/8	23 4/8	22 4/8	17 5/8	5	5	Monmouth County	NJ	John R. Rose	1997	8,638
137 5/8	23 3/8	23 6/8	16 3/8	4	4	Macon County	IL	Brad Morr	1997	8,638
137 5/8	22 7/8	23 5/8	16 3/8	5	4	Washburn County	WI	Ron Pierce	1997	8,638
137 5/8	23 0/8	22 5/8	18 3/8	5	5	De Kalb County	GA	Jimmy Jones	1998	8,638
137 4/8	23 4/8	23 6/8	18 2/8	5	4	Rice County	MN	Robert W. Berg	1965	8,717
137 4/8	23 6/8	22 0/8	21 4/8	5	5	Spink County	SD	Ray McIntyre	1967	8,717
137 4/8	25 4/8	24 0/8	18 6/8	4	4	Berrien County	MI	Lawrence C. Ford	1981	8,717
137 4/8	21 5/8	20 7/8	14 2/8	5	6	Pope County	MN	Roger Tollefson	1982	8,717
137 4/8	22 6/8	22 6/8	18 2/8	4	4	Newaygo County	MI	David Davis	1982	8,717
137 4/8	23 3/8	23 0/8	16 4/8	4	5	Vernon County	WI	Jerry Willer	1983	8,717
137 4/8	21 2/8	20 3/8	15 4/8	6	5	Pierson	MAN	Brad Minshull	1984	8,717
137 4/8	23 5/8	23 1/8	18 6/8	5	5	Nelson County	KY	James H. Stiles	1984	8,717
137 4/8	21 2/8	20 4/8	19 0/8	5	5	Sauk County	WI	Jimmie S Gluth	1984	8,717
137 4/8	22 5/8	20 4/8	16 4/8	5	5	Albany County	NY	James O'Connor	1984	8,717
137 4/8	22 3/8	22 7/8	16 6/8	5	5	Rogers County	OK	Ernie Merydith	1986	8,717
137 4/8	23 3/8	20 0/8	22 0/8	7	7	Union County	IL	Louis Biggs	1986	8,717
137 4/8	23 3/8	23 2/8	19 0/8	4	5	Lyon County	KS	Johnny Drake	1986	8,717
137 4/8	22 2/8	21 4/8	17 0/8	5	5	Crittenden County	KY	Karl W. Brantley	1986	8,717
137 4/8	22 3/8	22 0/8	19 6/8	4	4	Chilton County	AL	James White	1986	8,717
137 4/8	24 7/8	23 7/8	18 3/8	5	6	Waukesha County	WI	Max Mollgaard	1987	8,717
137 4/8	24 0/8	23 2/8	17 0/8	5	5	Forest County	WI	Ron H. Vander Kelen	1987	8,717
137 4/8	23 3/8	22 5/8	17 2/8	5	5	Garrett County	MD	Albert Schrock	1987	8,717
137 4/8	20 0/8	21 2/8	16 0/8	6	6	St. Joseph County	IN	Michael L. Ritter	1988	8,717
137 4/8	23 3/8	23 3/8	15 0/8	4	4	Racine County	WI	Robert Zortman	1988	8,717
137 4/8	21 4/8	21 5/8	19 0/8	5	5	Brooks County	TX	J. Dale Hale	1988	8,717
137 4/8	22 7/8	24 4/8	17 4/8	5	4	Forest County	WI	Duwayne C. Schneider	1988	8,717
137 4/8	25 4/8	24 7/8	17 6/8	4	4	Webster County	IA	Gary Forkner	1988	8,717
137 4/8	22 2/8	21 6/8	16 4/8	5	6	Sauk County	WI	Ronald VanSwol	1988	8,717
137 4/8	21 6/8	23 7/8	19 7/8	5	4	Stearns County	MN	Mike Poss	1989	8,717
137 4/8	21 1/8	21 3/8	15 0/8	6	5	Dubuque County	IA	Jim Hedley	1989	8,717
137 4/8	24 3/8	24 4/8	17 0/8	4	4	Choctaw County	MS	Charles B. Box	1990	8,717
137 4/8	22 7/8	24 2/8	14 3/8	6	8	St. Croix County	WI	Robert H. Olson	1990	8,717
137 4/8	24 1/8	24 1/8	18 4/8	4	4	Waushara County	WI	Jeffry J. Paulus	1990	8,717
137 4/8	25 0/8	24 4/8	19 2/8	5	5	Lunenburg County	VA	Thomas M. Hicks, Jr.	1990	8,717
137 4/8	22 2/8	23 0/8	18 4/8	5	5	Waukesha County	WI	Kevin Anderson	1990	8,717
137 4/8	22 0/8	22 5/8	18 0/8	5	5	Beltrami County	MN	Arnold Christanson	1990	8,717
137 4/8	22 0/8	21 5/8	15 6/8	5	5	Adams County	WI	Gary L. Ackerman	1990	8,717
137 4/8	23 7/8	22 7/8	17 5/8	7	8	Baca County	CO	Eddie Claypool	1990	8,717
137 4/8	23 3/8	23 7/8	18 3/8	6	5	Ogle County	IL	Lyle Bonnell	1990	8,717
137 4/8	25 1/8	26 1/8	23 3/8	5	5	Washtenaw County	MI	Brenda J. Brown	1991	8,717
137 4/8	20 5/8	20 2/8	16 2/8	6	5	Walsh County	ND	John Schlieman	1991	8,717
137 4/8	21 1/8	21 4/8	17 2/8	5	5	Bureau County	IL	Mark E. Michael	1991	8,717
137 4/8	22 1/8	21 7/8	17 7/8	5	6	Brown County	IL	Kevin Weeks	1991	8,717
137 4/8	24 4/8	22 5/8	14 5/8	5	5	Washington County	KS	Stan Brustowicz	1991	8,717
137 4/8	21 7/8	21 4/8	17 3/8	4	5	Berks County	PA	Paul S. Strunk, Jr.	1992	8,717
137 4/8	19 4/8	21 6/8	16 0/8	5	6	La Porte County	IN	Troy Schlarp	1992	8,717
137 4/8	21 7/8	21 7/8	17 4/8	5	5	Kenedy County	TX	Danny R. Sefcik	1992	8,717
137 4/8	25 4/8	25 4/8	18 2/8	4	4	Westchester County	NY	Stephen L. Cook	1993	8,717
137 4/8	23 3/8	23 5/8	16 6/8	4	5	Milwaukee County	WI	Tony Snow	1993	8,717
137 4/8	24 4/8	23 0/8	17 4/8	5	5	Ashtabula County	OH	Tim Cusano	1994	8,717
137 4/8	21 6/8	21 6/8	15 1/8	6	6	Wabasha County	MN	Jerry E. Hippe	1994	8,717
137 4/8	22 1/8	22 0/8	15 6/8	5	5	Winneshiek County	IA	Carol Mincks, Jr.	1994	8,717
137 4/8	22 5/8	22 1/8	17 2/8	6	6	Swan River	MAN	Terry Garmon	1994	8,717
137 4/8	23 0/8	22 7/8	21 6/8	4	4	Pulaski County	KY	Chuck Waters	1995	8,717
137 4/8	23 1/8	23 1/8	15 4/8	6	5	Meigs County	OH	David Findley	1995	8,717
137 4/8	26 4/8	25 2/8	18 6/8	5	4	Preble County	OH	Les Loranzan, Jr.	1995	8,717
137 4/8	22 2/8	22 4/8	18 6/8	5	5	Columbia County	WI	Kevin John Raimer	1995	8,717
137 4/8	25 1/8	24 1/8	21 0/8	5	5	Fulton County	IN	Jim Pearcy	1995	8,717
137 4/8	23 1/8	23 0/8	19 0/8	5	6	Logan County	OH	Kim Sevitts	1995	8,717
137 4/8	21 5/8	21 5/8	18 4/8	6	6	Muscatine County	IA	Larry H. Thumann, Sr.	1995	8,717
137 4/8	24 3/8	23 6/8	17 5/8	6	6	Lawrence County	OH	Jeff Wheeler	1996	8,717
137 4/8	22 3/8	22 7/8	15 2/8	5	5	Sauk County	WI	Gene Draper	1996	8,717
137 4/8	23 5/8	22 7/8	21 6/8	5	5	Hunterdon County	NJ	Dwayne Pedrick	1996	8,717
137 4/8	21 7/8	21 4/8	18 0/8	5	5	Brown County	SD	Craig R. Sommers	1996	8,717
137 4/8	23 3/8	23 6/8	18 0/8	4	4	Forest County	WI	Jim Sot	1996	8,717
137 4/8	21 4/8	20 1/8	16 1/8	5	6	Lapeer County	MI	William Randal Bailey	1998	8,717
137 3/8	22 0/8	21 4/8	19 7/8	5	4	Comanche County	OK	Edward J. Baumlin, Jr.	1960	8,779
137 3/8	20 6/8	20 2/8	12 6/8	5	10	Kootenai County	ID	John Ruthuen	1961	8,779
137 3/8	23 5/8	23 3/8	16 6/8	4	5	Allegan County	MI	Clayton Foster	1964	8,779
137 3/8	25 6/8	23 1/8	15 7/8	4	4	Madison County	IN	Lee Middleton	1966	8,779
137 3/8	25 1/8	24 4/8	20 7/8	4	4	Trempealeau County	WI	Randall J. Van Vleet	1966	8,779
137 3/8	20 2/8	19 7/8	16 5/8	5	5	Stone County	MO	Charles A. Myers	1974	8,779
137 3/8	22 3/8	22 3/8	19 1/8	4	4	Guthrie County	IA	John D. Hambleton	1974	8,779
137 3/8	23 2/8	20 2/8	17 0/8	5	6	Wood County	OH	Othon E. Katakis	1980	8,779
137 3/8	22 2/8	23 3/8	19 7/8	4	5	Dane County	WI	Donald W. Pache	1980	8,779
137 3/8	20 7/8	21 2/8	15 4/8	6	5	Jo Daviess County	IL	Herb Imbus	1981	8,779
137 3/8	21 4/8	20 6/8	15 3/8	5	5	St. Croix County	WI	Daniel A. Score	1982	8,779

403

WHITETAIL DEER (TYPICAL ANTLERS)

Minimum Score 125 — Continued

SCORE	LENGTH OF MAIN BEAM R	LENGTH OF MAIN BEAM L	INSIDE SPREAD	NUMBER OF POINTS R	NUMBER OF POINTS L	AREA	STATE/ PROVINCE	HUNTER'S NAME	DATE	RANK
137 3/8	23 4/8	23 2/8	15 5/8	4	5	Kootenai County	ID	David R. Oliver	1983	8,779
137 3/8	23 1/8	25 2/8	20 3/8	4	5	Meeker County	MN	Thomas Wylie	1983	8,779
137 3/8	22 5/8	22 5/8	16 6/8	6	4	Marion County	IL	Joseph B. Smith III	1983	8,779
137 3/8	21 0/8	19 7/8	15 7/8	5	5	Henry County	VA	Mike Weaver	1985	8,779
137 3/8	23 6/8	23 5/8	17 7/8	4	4	Green County	WI	Steve Bergemann	1986	8,779
137 3/8	23 6/8	20 7/8	19 7/8	5	5	Stephenson County	IL	Jeff S. Olsen	1986	8,779
137 3/8	23 7/8	23 6/8	16 4/8	5	6	Vinton County	OH	Daniel E. Kaiser	1986	8,779
137 3/8	24 5/8	23 6/8	21 3/8	4	4	Monroe County	PA	Terry R. Schneck	1987	8,779
137 3/8	25 5/8	24 3/8	17 3/8	5	5	Clay County	IL	Gary D. Cornell	1988	8,779
137 3/8	24 6/8	25 2/8	17 3/8	6	7	Pulaski County	KY	Bobbie Ryan	1988	8,779
137 3/8	21 5/8	21 2/8	14 1/8	6	6	Waushara County	WI	Chad Kropp	1989	8,779
137 3/8	25 3/8	25 3/8	19 7/8	4	5	Dane County	WI	James S. Obrecht	1989	8,779
137 3/8	24 6/8	20 7/8	17 2/8	5	7	Yankton County	SD	Gary Sejnohn	1989	8,779
137 3/8	24 1/8	23 5/8	19 7/8	4	4	Lancaster County	PA	J. John Buhay	1990	8,779
137 3/8	23 6/8	23 6/8	16 1/8	4	4	Delaware County	IA	Robert Becker	1990	8,779
137 3/8	20 2/8	20 1/8	17 3/8	6	5	Athens County	OH	Bruce Hann	1990	8,779
137 3/8	24 1/8	24 7/8	18 3/8	4	4	Jefferson County	WI	Rodney A. Sheldon	1990	8,779
137 3/8	23 2/8	23 3/8	19 5/8	7	7	Suffolk County	NY	Richard Berger	1990	8,779
137 3/8	19 5/8	20 3/8	17 1/8	5	5	Oconto County	WI	Keith M. Goodwill	1990	8,779
137 3/8	21 7/8	22 0/8	16 3/8	6	5	Henry County	MO	W. Chapman Spangler	1991	8,779
137 3/8	25 2/8	26 4/8	18 2/8	8	7	Tuscarawas County	OH	Daniel A. Mozena	1991	8,779
137 3/8	23 1/8	21 6/8	17 3/8	5	5	Early County	GA	Bobby G. Holmes	1991	8,779
137 3/8	23 6/8	23 2/8	16 7/8	4	5	McKenzie County	ND	James Raymond Legdre	1991	8,779
137 3/8	23 2/8	23 7/8	17 6/8	6	4	Hardin County	KY	John Standafer	1991	8,779
137 3/8	23 4/8	22 7/8	17 5/8	4	4	Calhoun County	MI	Peter R. Grevers	1992	8,779
137 3/8	19 0/8	20 1/8	18 3/8	5	5	Hickman County	KY	Kenny Evans	1992	8,779
137 3/8	23 1/8	23 3/8	16 1/8	5	5	Washtenaw County	MI	James A. West	1992	8,779
137 3/8	25 1/8	26 0/8	20 3/8	4	5	Lyon County	KS	Larry J. Holden	1992	8,779
137 3/8	25 5/8	25 3/8	18 1/8	4	4	Marinette County	WI	Ron Truckey	1993	8,779
137 3/8	23 4/8	23 2/8	15 1/8	4	5	Butler County	IA	Kody Kramer	1993	8,779
137 3/8	22 3/8	22 4/8	20 5/8	4	4	Johnson County	IA	Joseph C. Behr	1993	8,779
137 3/8	24 0/8	24 0/8	20 4/8	6	6	Fairfield County	CT	Carl Hornbecker	1993	8,779
137 3/8	24 1/8	22 2/8	19 3/8	4	5	Duval County	TX	Shirley Oatman	1993	8,779
137 3/8	24 0/8	23 4/8	16 7/8	5	5	Bayfield County	WI	Valerie A. Pumala	1994	8,779
137 3/8	23 2/8	23 4/8	20 2/8	4	5	Lehigh County	PA	Daniel R. Bachman	1994	8,779
137 3/8	21 6/8	20 5/8	17 1/8	8	7	Pike County	IL	Eddie Claypool	1994	8,779
137 3/8	23 0/8	23 6/8	18 4/8	6	7	Delaware County	IA	Mark A. Haight	1994	8,779
137 3/8	23 3/8	23 3/8	18 1/8	4	4	Sheboygan County	WI	Steve Roe	1994	8,779
137 3/8	24 0/8	22 6/8	18 0/8	5	5	Fulton County	IN	Troy Cowles	1995	8,779
137 3/8	21 6/8	22 3/8	16 5/8	6	7	Winnebago County	WI	David E. Koplien	1995	8,779
137 3/8	22 7/8	23 6/8	19 4/8	6	6	Pike County	MS	Michael Stevens	1995	8,779
137 3/8	22 6/8	23 2/8	16 3/8	5	4	Union County	IL	Billie McKee	1995	8,779
137 3/8	22 6/8	23 2/8	18 1/8	5	5	Crawford County	WI	David Sather	1995	8,779
137 3/8	22 3/8	20 2/8	16 6/8	5	6	Freeborn County	MN	Bradley R. Van Ryswyk	1995	8,779
137 3/8	21 5/8	21 7/8	17 3/8	5	5	Jackson County	WI	Brad Zimbauer	1995	8,779
137 3/8	23 3/8	23 1/8	15 7/8	7	5	Pike County	IL	Huston Martin III	1995	8,779
137 3/8	24 0/8	22 1/8	17 7/8	4	5	Kane County	IL	Raymond Boro	1995	8,779
137 3/8	25 6/8	25 4/8	22 1/8	4	4	Summit County	OH	Ron Lance	1995	8,779
137 3/8	25 2/8	24 2/8	18 1/8	6	4	Logan County	IL	Jeff E. Litterly	1995	8,779
137 3/8	21 2/8	21 2/8	14 3/8	5	5	Minnehaha County	SD	La Verne Boer	1996	8,779
137 3/8	22 2/8	23 4/8	18 5/8	4	4	Harrison County	IA	Scott D. Scharf	1996	8,779
137 3/8	21 6/8	23 2/8	23 1/8	6	5	Wilcox County	AL	Forrest J. Ware	1997	8,779
137 3/8	25 0/8	25 3/8	17 3/8	5	4	Vance County	NC	Jay Cohron	1997	8,779
137 3/8	25 3/8	24 3/8	19 3/8	6	6	Posey County	IN	Greg Waldbieser	1997	8,779
137 3/8	25 6/8	23 6/8	16 7/8	5	4	Todd County	KY	Jamie Lee Addison	1997	8,779
137 3/8	21 2/8	20 1/8	18 5/8	5	5	Crittenden County	KY	Marty Garrett	1997	8,779
137 3/8	22 5/8	23 0/8	19 5/8	4	4	Columbia County	WI	Jeff Gorman	1997	8,779
137 3/8	21 1/8	20 1/8	18 5/8	6	6	Green Lake County	WI	Tom Sulllvan	1997	8,779
137 3/8	23 1/8	23 3/8	15 0/8	6	6	Adair County	OK	Kevin J. Shawver	1997	8,779
137 3/8	20 4/8	20 2/8	17 1/8	7	7	Hampden County	MA	Aaron Gates	1997	8,779
137 3/8	23 5/8	23 4/8	18 1/8	6	5	Vinton County	OH	Dave Couch	1997	8,779
137 3/8	25 6/8	26 7/8	21 0/8	4	5	Warren County	MS	Gary Butler	1997	8,779
137 3/8	20 0/8	20 5/8	15 7/8	5	5	Powell County	MT	Paul R. Tremblay	1998	8,779
137 3/8	21 4/8	21 0/8	18 3/8	4	5	Columbia County	WI	Jack R. Sulllvan	1998	8,779
137 2/8	23 2/8	24 7/8	18 5/8	8	5	Phelps County	NE	Dick Cepel	1959	8,854
137 2/8	21 1/8	20 0/8	17 4/8	6	5	Brown County	SD	Richard Felch	1966	8,854
137 2/8	23 1/8	24 1/8	16 4/8	5	5	Marion County	IA	David Hedgecock	1973	8,854
137 2/8	22 7/8	23 2/8	17 2/8	5	4	Murray County	MN	Dale Florek	1976	8,854
137 2/8	21 4/8	21 1/8	17 2/8	7	7	Laramie River	WY	Mark A. Brant	1976	8,854
137 2/8	23 2/8	23 6/8	17 4/8	5	5	Brown County	OH	Howard Ayers	1977	8,854
137 2/8	22 4/8	22 6/8	19 0/8	5	5	Sanders County	MT	Dyrk Eddie	1980	8,854
137 2/8	25 0/8	24 4/8	16 6/8	4	4	Putnam County	TN	Doyle B. Wilmoth	1980	8,854
137 2/8	20 6/8	20 7/8	15 2/8	5	5	Rock County	WI	Ronald S. Pulcine	1981	8,854
137 2/8	21 4/8	22 5/8	16 6/8	5	5	Teton County	MT	William McRae	1982	8,854
137 2/8	21 7/8	18 5/8	16 4/8	7	6	St. Charles County	MO	Donald L. Hauser	1982	8,854
137 2/8	21 6/8	21 4/8	17 6/8	7	5	Linn County	IA	Dennis W. Frye	1983	8,854
137 2/8	23 6/8	23 5/8	20 0/8	4	4	Jo Daviess County	IL	Kenneth Scharfenorth	1983	8,854
137 2/8	23 1/8	22 4/8	16 2/8	4	5	Hughes County	SD	Alvin Truax	1983	8,854

WHITETAIL DEER (TYPICAL ANTLERS)

Minimum Score 125 Continued

SCORE	LENGTH OF MAIN BEAM R	LENGTH OF MAIN BEAM L	INSIDE SPREAD	NUMBER OF POINTS R	NUMBER OF POINTS L	AREA	STATE/PROVINCE	HUNTER'S NAME	DATE	RANK
137 2/8	22 1/8	20 2/8	17 0/8	5	5	Delaware County	OH	David Orndorf	1983	8,854
137 2/8	24 1/8	24 2/8	17 0/8	5	4	Arkansas County	AR	Sam Snowden	1984	8,854
137 2/8	22 1/8	21 7/8	18 0/8	4	4	Belmont County	OH	Walter Kapiskovsky	1984	8,854
137 2/8	22 0/8	21 4/8	17 0/8	5	5	Rock County	WI	Ronald S. Pulcine	1984	8,854
137 2/8	25 4/8	25 1/8	18 6/8	5	5	Sauk County	WI	Daniel A. Mundth	1985	8,854
137 2/8	22 4/8	23 0/8	17 4/8	5	4	Jewell County	KS	Mahlon McDill	1985	8,854
137 2/8	23 0/8	23 5/8	19 0/8	4	5	Outagamie County	WI	Greg D. Haese	1986	8,854
137 2/8	23 7/8	23 6/8	20 6/8	4	4	St. Joseph County	MI	Eric Roberts	1986	8,854
137 2/8	22 4/8	22 0/8	17 4/8	6	4	Benson County	ND	Clarence Toso, Jr.	1986	8,854
137 2/8	22 1/8	21 1/8	17 4/8	5	6	Allen County	KS	John C. Cleaver	1986	8,854
137 2/8	23 1/8	22 6/8	16 3/8	7	5	Jo Daviess County	IL	Thomas J. Smith	1986	8,854
137 2/8	22 4/8	22 0/8	16 0/8	5	5	Vermilion County	IL	David Downing	1986	8,854
137 2/8	23 4/8	23 5/8	18 2/8	6	6	Jefferson County	IN	George E Yazel	1988	8,854
137 2/8	21 3/8	21 6/8	15 7/8	7	6	Iron County	WI	Steve Innes	1988	8,854
137 2/8	21 5/8	20 4/8	16 0/8	5	5	Wright County	MN	Gregory T. Krieger	1988	8,854
137 2/8	23 1/8	22 0/8	17 0/8	4	4	Dakota County	NE	Michael W. McKenna	1988	8,854
137 2/8	24 5/8	24 4/8	24 5/8	5	4	Lehigh County	PA	Scott J. Schrader	1989	8,854
137 2/8	21 3/8	21 6/8	19 4/8	5	6	Huntingdon County	PA	Carl Zimmerman	1989	8,854
137 2/8	25 4/8	24 4/8	16 6/8	5	4	Hot Springs County	AR	Johnny L. Fryar	1989	8,854
137 2/8	21 2/8	20 5/8	16 2/8	4	4	Champaign County	IL	Bud Barnes	1989	8,854
137 2/8	23 7/8	24 0/8	18 1/8	6	6	Hamilton County	IA	Arlin Dickinson	1989	8,854
137 2/8	22 5/8	22 6/8	18 6/8	5	4	Kingman County	KS	Dan Jacobs	1989	8,854
137 2/8	22 3/8	22 7/8	15 7/8	5	4	Kidder County	ND	Steven L. Weisenburger	1990	8,854
137 2/8	23 0/8	23 3/8	16 4/8	5	4	Pepin County	WI	Leonard Schneider	1990	8,854
137 2/8	22 3/8	22 3/8	18 2/8	5	5	Buffalo County	WI	Steve Rucinski	1990	8,854
137 2/8	22 3/8	21 6/8	17 1/8	7	7	Jo Daviess County	IL	Steve Cole	1990	8,854
137 2/8	22 6/8	22 2/8	18 0/8	6	5	Wright County	IA	Jeff Nelson	1990	8,854
137 2/8	23 6/8	23 1/8	16 1/8	5	5	Marquette County	MI	John Carl Clark	1990	8,854
137 2/8	20 6/8	21 4/8	17 2/8	5	5	Somerset County	PA	Sheldon Barron	1991	8,854
137 2/8	23 3/8	22 1/8	21 2/8	6	6	Madison County	IA	Kent McMillen	1991	8,854
137 2/8	21 1/8	23 0/8	18 2/8	6	5	Jasper County	IL	Jack Houser	1991	8,854
137 2/8	23 0/8	21 6/8	18 6/8	5	5	Hillsborough County	NH	Bruce A. Thibodeau	1991	8,854
137 2/8	22 4/8	22 0/8	17 4/8	5	6	Anoka County	MN	Tim Dugas	1991	8,854
137 2/8	20 0/8	23 4/8	16 4/8	4	5	Langlade County	WI	Bob Schmidt	1992	8,854
137 2/8	22 4/8	21 5/8	17 6/8	5	5	Buffalo County	WI	Donald R. Fox	1992	8,854
137 2/8	23 4/8	24 2/8	15 6/8	5	5	McMullen County	TX	Frank Neill	1992	8,854
137 2/8	24 1/8	24 7/8	19 6/8	5	4	Isanti County	MN	Thomas C. DeCorsey	1992	8,854
137 2/8	22 5/8	22 6/8	20 4/8	5	5	Vermilion County	IL	Ken Pavlick	1992	8,854
137 2/8	19 3/8	19 4/8	16 4/8	5	5	Washington County	OH	D. Michael Taylor	1992	8,854
137 2/8	23 0/8	24 6/8	18 4/8	5	6	Kane County	IL	Jim Harner	1992	8,854
137 2/8	23 4/8	22 2/8	16 4/8	5	5	Noble County	OH	Mark Rossiter	1993	8,854
137 2/8	23 5/8	23 2/8	15 2/8	5	5	Delaware County	OH	Jimmie J. Dixon	1993	8,854
137 2/8	21 0/8	21 3/8	15 4/8	5	5	Hudson Bay	SAS	Ted K. Jaycox	1993	8,854
137 2/8	21 4/8	21 7/8	15 7/8	4	5	Jackson County	IL	Dale Shaw	1993	8,854
137 2/8	21 4/8	21 0/8	14 4/8	5	5	Maverick County	TX	F. H. Becker III	1994	8,854
137 2/8	23 2/8	22 0/8	16 0/8	5	5	Lincoln County	WI	Brian Schiltz	1994	8,854
137 2/8	22 2/8	23 4/8	17 2/8	5	6	Ontario County	NY	Thomas A. Simmons	1994	8,854
137 2/8	22 7/8	22 4/8	19 1/8	5	6	Muscatine County	IA	Tim Cox	1994	8,854
137 2/8	23 0/8	22 6/8	17 0/8	4	4	Sullivan County	NY	Andrew Conway	1994	8,854
137 2/8	21 3/8	22 2/8	15 6/8	5	5	Waukesha County	WI	Terry Moore	1994	8,854
137 2/8	25 4/8	26 2/8	14 7/8	5	6	Darke County	OH	Thomas E. Warner	1995	8,854
137 2/8	23 1/8	21 6/8	20 6/8	7	5	Franklin County	PA	Kenneth W. Weikel	1995	8,854
137 2/8	22 4/8	23 1/8	18 0/8	5	5	Clay County	NE	Lonnie Goble	1995	8,854
137 2/8	22 6/8	21 6/8	15 6/8	5	5	Clay County	SD	Jeffrey J. Olson	1995	8,854
137 2/8	20 4/8	22 4/8	16 2/8	6	5	Beaver County	PA	Tom Kirkpatrick II	1995	8,854
137 2/8	21 6/8	20 6/8	17 1/8	6	5	Waupaca County	WI	Randy W. Zietlow	1996	8,854
137 2/8	20 6/8	22 0/8	16 2/8	6	5	Adams County	IL	Steve Deck	1996	8,854
137 2/8	23 6/8	23 5/8	18 4/8	4	5	Morris County	NJ	James C. Kelly	1996	8,854
137 2/8	20 4/8	21 0/8	17 6/8	5	5	Brown County	WI	Gary Adkins	1997	8,854
137 2/8	24 7/8	25 0/8	17 2/8	4	4	Keya Paha County	NE	Joel Barrow	1997	8,854
137 2/8	23 1/8	22 4/8	16 7/8	5	6	Iowa County	WI	Jim Van Fossen	1997	8,854
137 2/8	22 6/8	22 6/8	19 2/8	5	5	St. Croix County	WI	Lamoine E. Roatch	1997	8,854
137 2/8	22 2/8	22 2/8	19 2/8	4	4	Armstrong County	PA	Gary M. Mrock	1997	8,854
137 1/8	26 5/8	24 7/8	18 5/8	4	4	Bartholomew County	IN	Jimmy Middleton	1963	8,931
137 1/8	22 4/8	21 4/8	19 7/8	5	5	Rock County	MN	Orville Hamm	1976	8,931
137 1/8	26 6/8	24 2/8	17 3/8	4	5	Muskingum County	OH	William H. Archer	1976	8,931
137 1/8	25 2/8	24 2/8	19 7/8	5	5	Newton County	IN	James Manes	1976	8,931
137 1/8	22 6/8	22 4/8	16 1/8	5	5	Itasca County	MN	Donald Kenneth Kress	1977	8,931
137 1/8	21 0/8	21 5/8	16 1/8	6	5	Tompkins County	NY	Carlo Troise	1978	8,931
137 1/8	23 7/8	23 3/8	18 0/8	6	6	Grant County	WI	Lloyd J. Hach	1982	8,931
137 1/8	21 6/8	20 0/8	18 2/8	6	6	Fairfield County	OH	Paul R. Baker	1982	8,931
137 1/8	24 0/8	23 4/8	18 7/8	5	4	Hardin County	IA	Tom Herold	1982	8,931
137 1/8	26 4/8	24 1/8	22 1/8	4	4	Christian County	IL	Daniel Hinds	1983	8,931
137 1/8	21 7/8	22 1/8	14 7/8	4	5	Rhea County	TN	Leland H. Rothwell, Sr.	1983	8,931
137 1/8	22 5/8	22 7/8	18 7/8	4	4	Carroll County	IL	Gary R. Schneider	1983	8,931
137 1/8	24 3/8	23 7/8	17 5/8	5	4	Allamakee County	IA	Craig Riechmann	1983	8,931
137 1/8	20 7/8	20 5/8	16 3/8	5	6	Jasper County	IA	Kevin Lynn Patterson	1984	8,931
137 1/8	24 4/8	24 0/8	19 3/8	6	5	Barbour County	AL	Bobby Dale Holmes	1985	8,931

WHITETAIL DEER (TYPICAL ANTLERS)

Minimum Score 125   Continued

SCORE	LENGTH OF MAIN BEAM R	LENGTH OF MAIN BEAM L	INSIDE SPREAD	NUMBER OF POINTS R	NUMBER OF POINTS L	AREA	STATE/PROVINCE	HUNTER'S NAME	DATE	RANK
137 1/8	21 3/8	22 1/8	17 7/8	4	4	Union County	IL	Kevin G. Bach	1985	8,931
137 1/8	20 6/8	21 7/8	14 7/8	6	5	Rock Island County	IL	Dr. Tom Brozovich	1987	8,931
137 1/8	22 1/8	23 0/8	18 1/8	5	4	Warren County	IA	Dale Smith	1987	8,931
137 1/8	23 2/8	22 7/8	16 3/8	4	4	Muskegon County	MI	Dan Thompson	1987	8,931
137 1/8	21 3/8	21 0/8	15 6/8	6	5	La Salle County	IL	Fran Klaas	1987	8,931
137 1/8	22 0/8	22 0/8	17 5/8	5	5	Putnam County	IN	Steve Buckallew	1987	8,931
137 1/8	22 5/8	23 3/8	15 2/8	4	5	Langlade County	WI	Jerry Aulik	1988	8,931
137 1/8	21 2/8	21 3/8	16 3/8	5	5	Columbia County	WI	Daniel L. Kaehne	1988	8,931
137 1/8	22 7/8	22 7/8	13 2/8	7	5	Pittsburg County	OK	Jeff Beach	1988	8,931
137 1/8	20 0/8	20 3/8	17 5/8	5	6	Ogle County	IL	Russell Robak	1988	8,931
137 1/8	24 0/8	23 7/8	17 0/8	7	4	Southampton County	VA	Jerry Vick	1988	8,931
137 1/8	20 3/8	19 6/8	18 1/8	5	5	Barron County	WI	Albert Fox	1989	8,931
137 1/8	21 6/8	22 1/8	20 7/8	5	5	Lake County	IN	James C. Gates	1989	8,931
137 1/8	26 0/8	24 4/8	19 5/8	4	4	Queen Annes County	MD	Mervin Lee Beiler	1989	8,931
137 1/8	24 6/8	26 6/8	21 6/8	6	6	Washington County	MN	Robert Wild	1989	8,931
137 1/8	25 1/8	24 6/8	18 1/8	6	6	Baltimore County	MD	Rick Thompson	1990	8,931
137 1/8	21 6/8	24 0/8	15 6/8	4	5	Woodbury County	IA	Mike McBride	1990	8,931
137 1/8	20 7/8	21 1/8	15 7/8	5	6	Saline County	IL	John Choate	1990	8,931
137 1/8	24 2/8	25 6/8	15 6/8	5	5	Harford County	MD	Mark McGovern	1991	8,931
137 1/8	22 2/8	22 3/8	16 3/8	5	6	Buffalo County	WI	Mike Chelf	1991	8,931
137 1/8	23 6/8	23 3/8	18 5/8	5	4	Clayton County	IA	Eugene Arndt	1991	8,931
137 1/8	22 2/8	23 0/8	16 5/8	5	5	Perry County	IL	Carl Gladson	1991	8,931
137 1/8	20 3/8	20 2/8	19 1/8	5	5	Irion County	TX	William Jay Wilson	1992	8,931
137 1/8	21 7/8	21 6/8	14 1/8	7	6	McMullen County	TX	Wes O'Rear	1992	8,931
137 1/8	23 1/8	23 0/8	20 5/8	6	7	Cass County	NE	James L. Johnson	1993	8,931
137 1/8	24 5/8	24 2/8	20 1/8	6	5	Frio County	TX	Andy Milam	1993	8,931
137 1/8	22 5/8	22 3/8	15 1/8	5	5	Schuyler County	NY	James Curatolo	1994	8,931
137 1/8	23 3/8	22 7/8	19 0/8	5	4	Montgomery County	MD	Jeffrey L. Harrison	1994	8,931
137 1/8	23 7/8	23 1/8	15 7/8	5	5	Calhoun County	MI	Charles "Brett" Mauk	1994	8,931
137 1/8	23 1/8	23 3/8	19 3/8	4	4	Van Buren County	IA	John R. Gegner	1994	8,931
137 1/8	21 7/8	22 3/8	18 6/8	5	6	Goshen County	WY	Jeff Fitts	1994	8,931
137 1/8	24 2/8	22 4/8	17 7/8	4	5	Westchester County	NY	Joseph DeCarlo	1994	8,931
137 1/8	23 3/8	22 6/8	17 5/8	5	5	Green County	WI	Pat Bushert	1995	8,931
137 1/8	21 2/8	22 2/8	15 7/8	5	5	Penobscot County	ME	Richard A. Jacobs	1995	8,931
137 1/8	23 0/8	24 7/8	17 7/8	5	4	Monroe County	WI	Jeffrey D. Zelley	1995	8,931
137 1/8	24 3/8	24 2/8	17 5/8	4	6	Eaton County	MI	Richard Allen Dimond	1995	8,931
137 1/8	25 0/8	23 2/8	19 0/8	8	7	Coles County	IL	Rich Eaton	1995	8,931
137 1/8	20 1/8	20 4/8	18 2/8	5	7	Goodhue County	MN	Ron Meyer	1995	8,931
137 1/8	21 6/8	21 3/8	19 6/8	5	7	Sarpy County	NE	James Redler	1996	8,931
137 1/8	25 3/8	24 3/8	15 5/8	5	5	Jackson County	IA	Dick Barker	1996	8,931
137 1/8	21 5/8	22 7/8	14 5/8	5	5	Washington County	OH	William G. Mason	1996	8,931
137 1/8	22 7/8	22 2/8	17 2/8	5	6	Eau Claire County	WI	Jim Simon	1996	8,931
137 1/8	26 1/8	24 7/8	17 7/8	7	6	Fayette County	IL	Jerry D. Miller	1996	8,931
137 1/8	25 0/8	26 0/8	17 2/8	6	5	Knox County	OH	Gary Sparks	1996	8,931
137 1/8	23 2/8	22 7/8	16 1/8	5	5	Butler County	KS	Robert O. Faris II	1996	8,931
137 1/8	21 3/8	21 5/8	18 7/8	6	6	Sullivan County	NH	Scott Griffin	1997	8,931
137 1/8	23 6/8	24 1/8	18 3/8	4	6	Rock County	WI	Jeff M. McCallum	1997	8,931
137 1/8	23 7/8	24 4/8	17 3/8	5	5	McHenry County	IL	Darrell J. Prielipp	1997	8,931
137 1/8	22 7/8	24 0/8	16 3/8	4	5	Noble County	OH	Terry L. Graves	1997	8,931
137 1/8	21 7/8	21 3/8	16 3/8	6	6	Edmonton	ALB	Steve MacKenzie	1997	8,931
137 1/8	23 1/8	23 5/8	18 5/8	4	5	Rice County	MN	Al Lozano	1997	8,931
137 1/8	26 4/8	25 3/8	18 5/8	5	5	Dubuque County	IA	John Duggan	1997	8,931
137 1/8	21 4/8	20 3/8	15 7/8	5	5	Green County	WI	Steve Gobeli	1998	8,931
137 0/8	26 0/8	24 0/8	19 6/8	5	4	Hughes County	SD	Gerald Snyder	1963	8,999
137 0/8	22 0/8	22 3/8	20 4/8	4	5	Berks County	PA	Frank "Rit" Heller	1971	8,999
137 0/8	21 4/8	22 3/8	18 2/8	4	7	Black Hawk County	IA	Bob Wood	1971	8,999
137 0/8	23 5/8	23 6/8	22 4/8	4	4	Freeborn County	MN	Brian Johnson	1978	8,999
137 0/8	24 5/8	25 7/8	20 2/8	5	4	Iroquois County	IL	Terry D. McDaniel	1978	8,999
137 0/8	22 1/8	22 3/8	17 0/8	5	4	Custer County	MT	Jim Walters	1978	8,999
137 0/8	21 5/8	22 2/8	14 6/8	4	4	Blue Earth County	MN	Stanley Defries	1980	8,999
137 0/8	22 2/8	23 1/8	15 5/8	5	6	Drew County	AR	Herman S. Fleming	1980	8,999
137 0/8	23 3/8	22 7/8	16 4/8	4	4	Walworth County	WI	Robert Mereness	1980	8,999
137 0/8	21 5/8	21 6/8	16 6/8	5	5	Scott County	KY	Milton Lee Pribble	1980	8,999
137 0/8	22 4/8	21 7/8	14 6/8	6	8	Pope County	MN	Pete Feider	1981	8,999
137 0/8	26 3/8	25 7/8	20 4/8	3	3	Cumberland County	ME	Richard L. Cote	1981	8,999
137 0/8	21 5/8	20 3/8	17 2/8	5	5	Randolph County	MO	Ronald Chirillo	1982	8,999
137 0/8	20 0/8	20 3/8	17 0/8	5	5	Douglas County	WI	Carl Ellison	1983	8,999
137 0/8	24 0/8	23 3/8	18 0/8	5	5	Crawford County	WI	Ken Fernette	1984	8,999
137 0/8	21 7/8	22 1/8	17 3/8	5	7	La Crosse County	WI	Steve Puent	1984	8,999
137 0/8	22 3/8	24 1/8	15 0/8	4	5	Green County	WI	William H. Holt	1986	8,999
137 0/8	22 3/8	20 7/8	17 6/8	5	5	Litchfield County	CT	John C. Murphy, Sr.	1986	8,999
137 0/8	23 1/8	24 7/8	12 4/8	6	7	Shawano County	WI	William E. Stoltenberg	1986	8,999
137 0/8	22 4/8	23 1/8	17 6/8	4	5	Pierce County	WI	Jim Klein	1986	8,999
137 0/8	21 5/8	22 1/8	18 2/8	4	4	Sauk County	WI	Randy Neises	1986	8,999
137 0/8	22 2/8	22 2/8	15 7/8	6	6	Reno County	KS	John R. Richardson	1986	8,999
137 0/8	21 3/8	23 2/8	15 6/8	5	5	Bucks County	PA	Harold E. Smith	1987	8,999
137 0/8	20 1/8	20 4/8	14 6/8	5	5	Kosciusko County	IN	Dave Shively	1987	8,999
137 0/8	22 7/8	22 6/8	18 6/8	4	4	Fillmore County	MN	John W. Zahrte	1987	8,999

WHITETAIL DEER (TYPICAL ANTLERS)

Minimum Score 125 — Continued

SCORE	LENGTH OF MAIN BEAM R	LENGTH OF MAIN BEAM L	INSIDE SPREAD	NUMBER OF POINTS R	NUMBER OF POINTS L	AREA	STATE/PROVINCE	HUNTER'S NAME	DATE	RANK
137 0/8	24 5/8	24 1/8	19 0/8	4	4	Hancock County	IN	Kent L. Fisk	1987	8,999
137 0/8	22 0/8	22 1/8	17 4/8	5	5	Wyoming County	WV	Lloyd Whitt	1987	8,999
137 0/8	22 6/8	21 4/8	19 4/8	5	4	Medina County	TX	Mike Palmer	1988	8,999
137 0/8	23 0/8	23 3/8	16 4/8	5	7	Macon County	MO	Harlan Deboer	1988	8,999
137 0/8	20 1/8	19 6/8	15 5/8	6	5	Des Moines County	IA	Duane Smith	1988	8,999
137 0/8	26 6/8	26 0/8	17 6/8	5	4	Nelson County	VA	Larry W. Toms	1988	8,999
137 0/8	24 0/8	23 6/8	17 0/8	4	5	Wabasha County	MN	Dale Hoffman	1989	8,999
137 0/8	23 6/8	23 2/8	19 0/8	5	5	Somerset County	NJ	Anthony Beceiro	1989	8,999
137 0/8	23 1/8	23 4/8	18 5/8	5	4	Greene County	IN	Quince Hale	1989	8,999
137 0/8	26 1/8	24 2/8	18 0/8	5	4	Baltimore County	MD	Richard B. Traband	1989	8,999
137 0/8	24 0/8	23 4/8	16 4/8	4	4	Cass County	NE	Tommy M. Brown	1990	8,999
137 0/8	27 4/8	25 7/8	21 0/8	6	4	Lake County	IL	Steven Hysell	1990	8,999
137 0/8	22 7/8	24 0/8	17 4/8	5	5	Bedford County	VA	Rocky Lee Williams	1990	8,999
137 0/8	20 3/8	20 5/8	15 3/8	6	5	Price County	WI	Rubert Retzlaff	1991	8,999
137 0/8	22 6/8	23 3/8	16 4/8	6	5	Plymouth County	IA	Jason J. Dannenberg	1991	8,999
137 0/8	21 4/8	24 3/8	18 4/8	6	5	Knox County	KY	Tony Morris	1991	8,999
137 0/8	22 0/8	22 0/8	19 2/8	5	5	Rush County	KS	Lanny Morgan	1991	8,999
137 0/8	22 4/8	21 4/8	17 4/8	5	5	Martin County	IN	Steven W. Sargent	1991	8,999
137 0/8	23 4/8	23 4/8	20 2/8	4	5	Dunn County	WI	Scott Stuart	1991	8,999
137 0/8	22 5/8	23 4/8	18 4/8	4	4	Fayette County	IL	Jon Washburn	1991	8,999
137 0/8	22 0/8	23 2/8	19 0/8	6	5	Meigs County	OH	Mike Whitley	1991	8,999
137 0/8	23 0/8	23 7/8	19 6/8	4	4	Allegheny County	PA	Paul W. Zoller	1992	8,999
137 0/8	23 0/8	22 4/8	18 4/8	8	5	Harvey County	KS	Dan Stahl	1992	8,999
137 0/8	23 5/8	24 4/8	21 0/8	4	4	Cherokee County	OK	Ronald Lynn Gibson	1992	8,999
137 0/8	23 7/8	23 4/8	16 6/8	5	5	Somerset County	ME	Clarence L. Ayotte	1993	8,999
137 0/8	21 1/8	21 6/8	16 5/8	5	6	East Feliciana Parish	LA	Guy Bergeron	1993	8,999
137 0/8	23 1/8	22 0/8	16 6/8	5	5	Butler County	PA	Richard C. Burkley	1993	8,999
137 0/8	24 0/8	24 5/8	18 1/8	6	6	Pine County	MN	Paul Anderberg	1994	8,999
137 0/8	21 7/8	21 7/8	18 0/8	5	5	Latimer County	OK	Robert J. Deela	1994	8,999
137 0/8	21 6/8	21 2/8	18 4/8	4	4	Grant County	WI	Kirk D. Hamann	1994	8,999
137 0/8	23 1/8	23 0/8	17 0/8	4	5	Pipestone County	MN	Douglas Schulze	1994	8,999
137 0/8	22 1/8	22 0/8	15 7/8	6	5	Bourbon County	KS	Kevin G. Asbury	1994	8,999
137 0/8	22 1/8	22 3/8	18 4/8	4	4	Clayton County	IA	Dale Kartman	1994	8,999
137 0/8	26 3/8	25 7/8	22 2/8	6	4	Kent County	MD	Jim Samis	1994	8,999
137 0/8	22 6/8	22 0/8	18 2/8	5	5	Granby River	BC	Al Bressanutti	1994	8,999
137 0/8	22 3/8	21 6/8	15 7/8	6	6	Fergus County	MT	Vince Luparell	1995	8,999
137 0/8	21 3/8	20 7/8	15 5/8	6	6	Bayfield County	WI	Rodney Hipsher	1995	8,999
137 0/8	22 1/8	21 4/8	15 6/8	4	4	Concordia Parish	LA	Hank Kizer	1996	8,999
137 0/8	20 7/8	20 5/8	15 6/8	5	5	Morden	MAN	Mario Maynard	1996	8,999
137 0/8	22 2/8	21 3/8	19 4/8	5	6	Jackson County	MI	Mark A. Wilson	1996	8,999
137 0/8	21 4/8	21 1/8	17 6/8	5	5	Burnett County	WI	Bill Johnson	1996	8,999
137 0/8	24 3/8	24 7/8	17 6/8	5	4	Mingo County	WV	Danny White	1996	8,999
137 0/8	22 3/8	22 4/8	17 2/8	6	10	St. Louis County	MN	Bruce A. Christopherson	1996	8,999
137 0/8	23 3/8	24 4/8	20 4/8	4	4	Rock County	WI	Richard Blackburn	1996	8,999
137 0/8	22 7/8	24 7/8	18 5/8	6	6	Yuma County	CO	Alan White	1996	8,999
137 0/8	25 0/8	25 2/8	19 2/8	4	4	Franklin County	VA	Mike Weaver	1996	8,999
137 0/8	26 0/8	24 7/8	18 0/8	5	4	Warren County	MO	Jim McCormick	1997	8,999
137 0/8	21 6/8	21 5/8	19 6/8	5	5	Delaware County	OH	James H. McCann	1997	8,999
137 0/8	23 0/8	22 5/8	18 0/8	7	6	Livingston County	MI	Christopher Karl Stawara	1997	8,999
137 0/8	20 4/8	20 4/8	17 2/8	6	6	Johnston County	OK	Daniel Parker	1997	8,999
137 0/8	23 5/8	24 6/8	20 6/8	5	5	Clark County	WI	Greg D. Opelt	1997	8,999
137 0/8	23 2/8	22 6/8	17 4/8	4	5	Buffalo County	WI	Timothy Weber	1997	8,999
137 0/8	23 3/8	22 3/8	17 2/8	4	4	Pulaski County	AR	Lyle K. Sinkey	1997	8,999
137 0/8	24 0/8	24 0/8	18 3/8	5	5	St. Louis County	MN	Nathan Samarzia	1997	8,999
137 0/8	23 6/8	23 0/8	17 4/8	5	4	Webb County	TX	Todd B. Swiedom	1997	8,999
137 0/8	22 5/8	21 6/8	18 4/8	5	5	Monroe County	PA	Christopher Boheim	1998	8,999
137 0/8	25 4/8	24 5/8	17 4/8	5	5	Simcoe	ONT	Allan W. Cook	1998	8,999
136 7/8	20 2/8	19 1/8	15 2/8	8	7	Ashland County	WI	Jim McGarvey	1965	9,081
136 7/8	23 5/8	23 6/8	18 1/8	4	5	Jefferson County	IN	James Coldiron	1972	9,081
136 7/8	22 3/8	22 6/8	17 0/8	6	5	Sullivan County	IN	John Chesterfield	1977	9,081
136 7/8	21 2/8	21 4/8	18 7/8	5	5	Fulton County	IL	Jeffrey L. Keefauver	1979	9,081
136 7/8	23 2/8	23 7/8	20 1/8	5	4	Muskingum County	OH	Larry Shoop	1979	9,081
136 7/8	23 5/8	24 0/8	19 3/8	5	5	Montgomery County	IN	Derrick Kidd	1980	9,081
136 7/8	24 6/8	23 7/8	21 1/8	4	4	Union County	IL	Carl E. Cronk	1983	9,081
136 7/8	20 7/8	19 5/8	15 3/8	5	5	Ozaukee County	WI	Scott T. Frank	1983	9,081
136 7/8	19 7/8	20 1/8	17 5/8	5	5	Kingsbury County	SD	Joe Jensen	1983	9,081
136 7/8	22 5/8	22 2/8	16 4/8	9	6	Washington County	KS	Randy Wilson	1983	9,081
136 7/8	22 3/8	22 2/8	18 3/8	4	5	Montgomery County	PA	Robert Pyne	1985	9,081
136 7/8	22 4/8	21 4/8	17 7/8	5	5	Woodson County	KS	Jerry Ramshaw	1985	9,081
136 7/8	25 1/8	25 1/8	17 6/8	6	5	Coshocton County	OH	Keith Duncan	1985	9,081
136 7/8	21 5/8	22 3/8	16 1/8	5	5	Lake County	IL	Steven Hysell	1985	9,081
136 7/8	23 6/8	24 0/8	16 2/8	7	7	Door County	WI	Daniel W. Herrbold	1986	9,081
136 7/8	24 5/8	24 6/8	21 7/8	4	4	Pike County	MO	Robert Frank	1986	9,081
136 7/8	22 3/8	22 3/8	20 1/8	4	4	Iron County	MI	Gene Luttrull	1986	9,081
136 7/8	23 3/8	24 0/8	21 7/8	5	5	Somerset County	NJ	Dave Cutting	1987	9,081
136 7/8	21 0/8	21 1/8	15 1/8	7	5	Green Lake County	WI	Michael D. Price	1987	9,081
136 7/8	19 2/8	18 2/8	15 7/8	5	5	Jefferson County	KS	Steve Gomel	1987	9,081
136 7/8	21 2/8	20 6/8	16 4/8	6	6	Jo Daviess County	IL	Thomas J. Smith	1987	9,081

WHITETAIL DEER (TYPICAL ANTLERS)

Minimum Score 125 — Continued

SCORE	LENGTH OF MAIN BEAM R	LENGTH OF MAIN BEAM L	INSIDE SPREAD	NUMBER OF POINTS R	NUMBER OF POINTS L	AREA	STATE/PROVINCE	HUNTER'S NAME	DATE	RANK
136 7/8	24 4/8	24 5/8	17 5/8	4	4	Monroe County	WI	Bill Hurst	1988	9,081
136 7/8	23 6/8	23 4/8	16 5/8	4	5	McCreary County	KY	Eddie Howard	1988	9,081
136 7/8	21 1/8	20 1/8	21 1/8	5	5	Monona County	IA	Dennis Rush	1988	9,081
136 7/8	23 7/8	23 7/8	16 1/8	5	5	Adams County	OH	J. Dale Gaffin	1988	9,081
136 7/8	24 1/8	25 1/8	21 1/8	5	4	Alleghany County	NC	Todd Evans	1989	9,081
136 7/8	23 7/8	23 2/8	17 3/8	5	5	New Haven County	CT	Thomas C Ravizza	1989	9,081
136 7/8	22 5/8	23 0/8	15 3/8	5	5	Lawrence County	KY	Alfred Adkins	1989	9,081
136 7/8	21 6/8	22 0/8	16 5/8	5	5	Dunn County	WI	Mark Gardow	1989	9,081
136 7/8	25 4/8	24 7/8	17 5/8	4	5	Story County	IA	Richard T. Lange	1989	9,081
136 7/8	21 6/8	21 3/8	19 1/8	4	4	Madison County	IL	Leroy Shea	1990	9,081
136 7/8	22 4/8	22 2/8	16 6/8	6	5	Randolph County	MO	Kenneth R. Wenger	1991	9,081
136 7/8	23 5/8	23 1/8	16 1/8	5	5	Macon County	MO	James A. Skyles	1991	9,081
136 7/8	22 3/8	23 1/8	17 3/8	5	5	Sawyer County	WI	David Jacobson	1991	9,081
136 7/8	23 5/8	24 4/8	18 3/8	5	5	Trempealeau County	WI	Todd Nelson	1991	9,081
136 7/8	25 2/8	23 7/8	20 5/8	5	4	Montgomery County	MD	Roger D. Stewart	1992	9,081
136 7/8	22 7/8	23 0/8	19 5/8	5	5	Marathon County	WI	Paul D. Waliczek	1992	9,081
136 7/8	22 5/8	23 3/8	18 3/8	4	4	McLean County	IL	Alison L. Darnall	1992	9,081
136 7/8	22 1/8	21 6/8	16 5/8	5	6	Waushara County	WI	Jesse W. Lange	1992	9,081
136 7/8	24 1/8	24 0/8	16 3/8	4	4	Johnson County	AR	Dave Lay	1992	9,081
136 7/8	19 3/8	18 6/8	16 7/8	6	6	La Salle County	TX	Dale R. Sanford	1992	9,081
136 7/8	23 4/8	23 2/8	19 7/8	4	4	East Carroll Parish	LA	David M. Marretta	1993	9,081
136 7/8	21 5/8	20 5/8	18 4/8	6	4	St. Joseph County	IN	Thomas S. Estes	1993	9,081
136 7/8	23 5/8	22 6/8	16 5/8	4	5	Penobscot County	ME	Robert Lucius	1993	9,081
136 7/8	21 6/8	21 4/8	17 1/8	6	5	Morgan County	GA	M. Scott Danner	1993	9,081
136 7/8	24 4/8	25 0/8	17 7/8	4	4	Ontonagon County	MI	Michael W. Heiss	1993	9,081
136 7/8	21 7/8	19 7/8	18 0/8	6	6	Leduc	ALB	Morris Moskal	1993	9,081
136 7/8	23 3/8	23 2/8	15 5/8	4	5	Brooks County	TX	Johnny L. Harrell	1993	9,081
136 7/8	22 7/8	22 7/8	18 3/8	5	4	Ozaukee County	WI	Mark D. Goodwin	1994	9,081
136 7/8	22 3/8	22 0/8	16 5/8	5	5	McLean County	IL	Tony Stolfa	1994	9,081
136 7/8	25 5/8	24 5/8	18 3/8	6	5	St. Louis County	MN	Jon Dahl	1994	9,081
136 7/8	22 2/8	22 1/8	16 7/8	4	5	Merrick County	NE	Richard Clark	1994	9,081
136 7/8	20 2/8	20 6/8	19 6/8	8	7	Weld County	CO	Dale Elliott	1994	9,081
136 7/8	23 5/8	24 4/8	17 6/8	5	4	Harvey County	KS	John Wiebe	1994	9,081
136 7/8	23 3/8	23 1/8	22 3/8	5	5	Hutchinson County	SD	Craig Roth	1994	9,081
136 7/8	22 2/8	22 5/8	17 2/8	5	6	Louisa County	IA	Wade Walker	1994	9,081
136 7/8	21 1/8	20 6/8	19 3/8	5	5	Edwards County	TX	Ronnie Juenke	1995	9,081
136 7/8	22 3/8	23 7/8	19 4/8	6	4	Eaton County	MI	Jack Hopkins	1995	9,081
136 7/8	23 0/8	22 2/8	17 5/8	4	4	Black Hawk County	IA	Todd Fischels	1995	9,081
136 7/8	22 6/8	23 1/8	17 0/8	6	5	Licking County	OH	Thomas E. Mewshaw	1995	9,081
136 7/8	21 7/8	21 6/8	15 3/8	5	5	Kenedy County	TX	Bert Kennedy	1996	9,081
136 7/8	20 7/8	22 2/8	14 3/8	4	6	Montgomery County	PA	Bill Woerner	1996	9,081
136 7/8	20 2/8	20 2/8	17 3/8	5	5	Jefferson County	WI	Jerry Coy	1996	9,081
136 7/8	25 4/8	23 7/8	16 7/8	4	4	Athens County	OH	Derrick Van Der Sluys	1996	9,081
136 7/8	22 2/8	22 7/8	17 5/8	5	5	Jim Wells County	TX	Rene Marroquin, Jr.	1997	9,081
136 7/8	25 7/8	26 3/8	20 3/8	6	6	Lincoln County	NE	John Croghan	1997	9,081
136 7/8	23 7/8	24 6/8	17 3/8	4	4	Lawrence County	PA	Ricky Joel Cameron	1997	9,081
136 7/8	22 6/8	22 7/8	14 7/8	5	5	Waukesha County	WI	Tim Husk	1997	9,081
136 7/8	25 3/8	25 4/8	17 5/8	4	4	Gilmer County	GA	Craig Sisson	1997	9,081
136 7/8	22 0/8	22 0/8	19 2/8	7	4	Allamakee County	IA	Ty Orgas	1997	9,081
136 7/8	22 7/8	22 3/8	17 1/8	5	4	Crawford County	IL	Roy Treece	1997	9,081
136 7/8	20 5/8	20 0/8	15 5/8	5	6	Shelby County	IL	James L. Harbert	1997	9,081
136 7/8	23 1/8	22 6/8	20 3/8	4	4	Mason County	IL	Mark Wagle	1997	9,081
136 7/8	20 5/8	19 7/8	18 5/8	5	5	Dane County	WI	John Donstad	1997	9,081
136 7/8	23 0/8	22 1/8	17 2/8	5	6	Coahuila	MEX	William A. Sheka, Jr.	1998	9,081
136 6/8	23 2/8	22 4/8	15 4/8	4	5	Ogle County	IL	Edwin Fitzgerald	1963	9,156
136 6/8	22 0/8	20 6/8	16 5/8	5	6	Hamlin County	SD	James Larson	1963	9,156
136 6/8	23 5/8	24 2/8	17 4/8	4	4	Mower County	MN	Robert Meyer	1965	9,156
136 6/8	21 4/8	20 6/8	18 2/8	5	6	Watonwan County	MN	Gary G. Miest	1969	9,156
136 6/8	22 1/8	20 6/8	17 4/8	5	5	Lake County	SD	Dennis DeBoer	1974	9,156
136 6/8	23 3/8	24 5/8	21 1/8	5	5	Whiteside County	IL	Art Heinze	1975	9,156
136 6/8	22 4/8	21 2/8	20 5/8	4	5	Queen Annes County	MD	Norman C. Herdegen	1977	9,156
136 6/8	27 4/8	24 0/8	18 4/8	6	6	Livingston County	MI	Peter Bolen	1979	9,156
136 6/8	22 4/8	23 5/8	17 0/8	6	5	Coahoma County	MS	David Holcomb	1979	9,156
136 6/8	22 0/8	20 6/8	16 0/8	5	4	Houston County	MN	Howard Lampert	1979	9,156
136 6/8	21 7/8	22 3/8	17 2/8	4	4	Waukesha County	WI	Jeff Dickenson	1984	9,156
136 6/8	22 0/8	22 3/8	17 6/8	5	5	Chippewa County	MI	James R. Dreves	1985	9,156
136 6/8	23 2/8	23 3/8	17 0/8	4	4	Sequoyah County	OK	Kyle Holt	1986	9,156
136 6/8	24 2/8	24 3/8	15 5/8	5	4	Dane County	WI	Jack Schulenberg	1986	9,156
136 6/8	22 3/8	23 2/8	17 0/8	5	5	Des Moines County	IA	Thomas E. Knoll	1986	9,156
136 6/8	19 3/8	21 3/8	14 2/8	5	5	Coffey County	KS	Dennis DeForest	1986	9,156
136 6/8	23 5/8	23 5/8	16 4/8	4	4	Anoka County	MN	Anthony J. Emmerich	1987	9,156
136 6/8	29 6/8	28 2/8	18 6/8	8	8	Perry County	IL	Danny Dauksch	1987	9,156
136 6/8	22 0/8	21 3/8	16 6/8	5	5	Athens County	OH	Alan W. Shafer	1987	9,156
136 6/8	19 0/8	21 4/8	15 2/8	5	5	Rock Island County	IL	Mikel D. Angel	1987	9,156
136 6/8	21 2/8	20 6/8	15 0/8	5	5	Grant County	SD	Russel L. Christensen	1987	9,156
136 6/8	23 5/8	22 7/8	19 7/8	4	5	Fayette County	IA	Paul C. Crawford	1987	9,156
136 6/8	25 3/8	26 4/8	22 1/8	5	4	Shelby County	IL	Bret Guin	1987	9,156
136 6/8	22 6/8	22 2/8	19 2/8	6	6	Sangamon County	IL	Steve Tice	1987	9,156

WHITETAIL DEER (TYPICAL ANTLERS)

Minimum Score 125

SCORE	LENGTH OF R MAIN BEAM L		INSIDE SPREAD	NUMBER OF R POINTS L		AREA	STATE/ PROVINCE	HUNTER'S NAME	DATE	RANK
136 6/8	22 6/8	23 1/8	16 6/8	5	5	Buffalo County	WI	Rodney Peterson	1988	9,156
136 6/8	22 5/8	23 1/8	17 6/8	4	5	Bayfield County	WI	Steven Schillinger	1988	9,156
136 6/8	23 5/8	22 3/8	14 0/8	5	5	Fayette County	IA	Darin Brincks	1988	9,156
136 6/8	22 2/8	22 7/8	17 4/8	6	7	Clark County	WI	Larry Davel	1988	9,156
136 6/8	27 3/8	25 3/8	20 4/8	4	4	Knox County	IL	Rod Combs	1988	9,156
136 6/8	22 5/8	22 3/8	14 6/8	5	4	Putnam County	IL	Jerome Sampson	1988	9,156
136 6/8	21 7/8	22 4/8	20 0/8	4	4	Kiowa County	KS	Karl Ballard	1988	9,156
136 6/8	21 3/8	21 0/8	20 6/8	4	4	Langlade County	WI	John Woltman	1989	9,156
136 6/8	21 4/8	22 5/8	16 4/8	6	5	Boone County	MO	Dale York	1989	9,156
136 6/8	21 3/8	19 7/8	15 4/8	6	5	Polk County	IA	Richard Roberts	1990	9,156
136 6/8	23 1/8	23 2/8	17 6/8	4	4	Hillsdale County	MI	Fred Abbas	1990	9,156
136 6/8	22 5/8	21 2/8	14 6/8	6	7	Waupaca County	WI	Charles Edminster	1990	9,156
136 6/8	23 4/8	23 4/8	19 2/8	4	4	Du Page County	IL	Richard B. Maish	1990	9,156
136 6/8	24 0/8	25 0/8	16 0/8	4	5	Macon County	GA	Ricky L. Gibbs	1991	9,156
136 6/8	22 7/8	22 5/8	18 2/8	5	5	Dodge County	MN	James Kuasnicka	1991	9,156
136 6/8	21 3/8	20 6/8	17 0/8	6	6	Spruce Grove	ALB	Lawrence Huot	1991	9,156
136 6/8	23 3/8	23 1/8	16 2/8	4	7	Oakland County	MI	Walter Poplawski	1991	9,156
136 6/8	23 1/8	23 1/8	19 6/8	6	6	Van Buren County	IA	Bill Grahlherr	1991	9,156
136 6/8	24 4/8	23 2/8	18 6/8	5	4	Jefferson County	NE	Norman Tedrow	1991	9,156
136 6/8	19 6/8	19 6/8	15 4/8	5	4	Uvalde County	TX	Wyatt Birkner	1992	9,156
136 6/8	22 0/8	23 0/8	17 2/8	4	4	Bond County	IL	William T. Rench	1992	9,156
136 6/8	20 6/8	21 0/8	16 2/8	5	5	Trempealeau County	WI	Tom Matchey	1992	9,156
136 6/8	24 3/8	23 2/8	17 0/8	5	5	Schoharie County	NY	Bill Clapper, Jr.	1992	9,156
136 6/8	23 0/8	22 7/8	19 0/8	4	4	Lee County	IL	Thomas F. Sawyer	1992	9,156
136 6/8	24 4/8	23 6/8	14 7/8	6	6	Ravalli County	MT	Chris W. Dix	1992	9,156
136 6/8	22 6/8	22 4/8	17 0/8	4	4	Ashtabula County	OH	Randy B. Nichols	1993	9,156
136 6/8	22 6/8	22 3/8	14 6/8	5	5	Warren County	NC	Douglas M. Branch	1993	9,156
136 6/8	24 0/8	22 3/8	18 4/8	6	9	Van Buren County	IA	Randy R. Peitz	1993	9,156
136 6/8	21 7/8	22 1/8	15 0/8	5	5	Langlade County	WI	Daniel Houdek	1993	9,156
136 6/8	22 7/8	23 0/8	17 4/8	5	4	Ashtabula County	OH	Ray Youngs	1993	9,156
136 6/8	23 1/8	22 4/8	17 0/8	5	4	Grant County	WI	Charles P. Fralick	1993	9,156
136 6/8	23 3/8	23 2/8	16 2/8	4	4	Crawford County	IA	Terry Pullen	1993	9,156
136 6/8	21 4/8	21 6/8	18 6/8	5	5	La Salle County	TX	Franklin Marker III	1994	9,156
136 6/8	22 1/8	22 7/8	21 2/8	5	6	Sauk County	WI	Todd J. Horkan	1994	9,156
136 6/8	21 2/8	20 5/8	16 2/8	6	6	Racine County	WI	Blane S. Schneider	1994	9,156
136 6/8	24 1/8	24 7/8	17 6/8	4	6	Sedgwick County	KS	Bryan Brimer	1994	9,156
136 6/8	25 3/8	25 6/8	17 4/8	4	4	Spotsylvania County	VA	James G. Colvin	1994	9,156
136 6/8	23 4/8	23 6/8	18 4/8	5	4	Grant County	WI	Galen Bremmer	1994	9,156
136 6/8	22 6/8	23 2/8	17 2/8	5	7	Delaware County	OH	Nick Wise	1994	9,156
136 6/8	22 5/8	22 1/8	16 6/8	4	4	Athens County	OH	Mitchell W. Bobo	1994	9,156
136 6/8	22 3/8	22 5/8	16 0/8	5	5	Hitchcock County	NE	Rob Seybold	1994	9,156
136 6/8	24 6/8	25 4/8	18 2/8	4	5	Waukesha County	WI	Glenn Oleston	1995	9,156
136 6/8	21 2/8	21 5/8	17 4/8	5	5	Livingston County	NY	Warren P. Heintz	1995	9,156
136 6/8	23 5/8	22 7/8	16 4/8	5	4	Anne Arundel County	MD	Shawn Bewley	1995	9,156
136 6/8	24 1/8	24 0/8	19 2/8	6	6	Pike County	IL	Ronnie Cannon	1995	9,156
136 6/8	24 2/8	25 0/8	18 0/8	4	4	Noble County	IN	John H. Taylor	1995	9,156
136 6/8	21 5/8	22 2/8	15 0/8	4	5	Slope County	ND	Steve Schroeder	1995	9,156
136 6/8	22 2/8	22 5/8	14 4/8	5	4	Howard County	NE	Glen Harvey	1996	9,156
136 6/8	23 6/8	22 5/8	15 5/8	5	6	Bedford County	VA	Jon F. Hannell	1996	9,156
136 6/8	24 5/8	24 6/8	18 1/8	6	4	Ross County	OH	Phillip Andrews	1996	9,156
136 6/8	22 6/8	23 3/8	18 1/8	5	5	Shelby County	MO	Chris Murphy	1996	9,156
136 6/8	20 4/8	20 7/8	19 3/8	6	6	Bayfield County	WI	Arthur E. Hyde	1996	9,156
136 6/8	24 5/8	23 6/8	17 4/8	6	5	Dodge County	WI	Glen Thompson	1996	9,156
136 6/8	23 7/8	24 4/8	16 2/8	4	4	Trempealeau County	WI	Scott Gunderson	1996	9,156
136 6/8	20 7/8	21 4/8	17 4/8	5	5	Powell County	MT	Rob Seelye	1996	9,156
136 6/8	24 1/8	24 1/8	18 6/8	4	4	Morris County	NJ	Steven J. Niedzielski	1997	9,156
136 6/8	23 7/8	23 2/8	18 4/8	4	4	Bucks County	PA	Joe Jablonski	1997	9,156
136 6/8	24 4/8	23 6/8	16 6/8	5	5	Allamakee County	IA	Gary Charipar	1997	9,156
136 6/8	23 2/8	23 2/8	16 5/8	5	5	McHenry County	IL	Kory Lang	1997	9,156
136 6/8	23 5/8	23 5/8	17 1/8	5	4	Frederick County	MD	Christopher F. Knott	1997	9,156
136 6/8	23 6/8	23 4/8	13 0/8	6	7	Baltimore County	MD	Craig E. Barnhart	1997	9,156
136 5/8	24 6/8	24 6/8	18 5/8	4	4	Braxton County	WV	John M. Friend	1965	9,241
136 5/8	23 4/8	22 5/8	16 5/8	4	4	Marathon County	WI	Leroy Kazmierczak	1966	9,241
136 5/8	23 7/8	23 4/8	17 2/8	5	7	Vinton County	OH	John Grigsby	1979	9,241
136 5/8	20 0/8	22 0/8	18 6/8	5	5	Perry County	IL	Robert P. Berry	1980	9,241
136 5/8	21 4/8	20 6/8	14 7/8	5	5	Huron County	MI	John F. Deroche	1981	9,241
136 5/8	22 1/8	22 0/8	16 3/8	5	5	Phillips County	AR	Larry Scott	1981	9,241
136 5/8	23 1/8	22 0/8	16 1/8	4	4	Crawford County	IL	Brentley D. Smith	1981	9,241
136 5/8	21 3/8	20 7/8	17 3/8	5	5	Jackson County	AL	Rocky Drake	1982	9,241
136 5/8	25 2/8	26 1/8	22 2/8	8	4	Champaign County	IL	Carl Park	1982	9,241
136 5/8	21 6/8	21 4/8	16 7/8	5	5	Jackson County	IA	Gregory L. Schulte	1982	9,241
136 5/8	23 5/8	23 1/8	20 1/8	4	4	Ripley County	IN	Steve A. Allen	1983	9,241
136 5/8	21 1/8	22 0/8	14 6/8	6	6	Oneida County	WI	Jeff Aulik	1983	9,241
136 5/8	22 0/8	22 2/8	18 1/8	5	5	Montgomery County	PA	Glenn Kuklick	1983	9,241
136 5/8	22 1/8	22 1/8	18 7/8	4	4	Cowley County	KS	Don Smith	1984	9,241
136 5/8	20 4/8	20 4/8	16 1/8	5	5	Pierce County	WI	Lester Clare	1985	9,241
136 5/8	21 4/8	21 1/8	18 7/8	5	4	Pine County	MN	Ron Ekstrand	1986	9,241
136 5/8	21 6/8	20 6/8	17 2/8	6	7	Hillsdale County	MI	Kim Cinglie	1986	9,241

Continued

WHITETAIL DEER (TYPICAL ANTLERS)

Minimum Score 125 — Continued

SCORE	LENGTH OF MAIN BEAM R	LENGTH OF MAIN BEAM L	INSIDE SPREAD	NUMBER OF POINTS R	NUMBER OF POINTS L	AREA	STATE/PROVINCE	HUNTER'S NAME	DATE	RANK
136 5/8	22 3/8	22 3/8	16 3/8	4	4	Anoka County	MN	Jarrod Fondie	1986	9,241
136 5/8	22 1/8	21 3/8	14 7/8	5	4	Meagher County	MT	William R. Asevica	1987	9,241
136 5/8	21 4/8	21 3/8	16 7/8	5	7	La Salle County	IL	Kevin R. Mallie	1987	9,241
136 5/8	24 2/8	23 4/8	18 4/8	5	5	Washington County	WI	Jack Brugger	1988	9,241
136 5/8	24 5/8	23 6/8	20 3/8	5	4	Effingham County	IL	Tony Hille	1988	9,241
136 5/8	21 6/8	21 7/8	15 3/8	4	4	Sedgwick County	KS	Gary Voth	1988	9,241
136 5/8	21 1/8	21 6/8	16 3/8	5	4	Huntington County	IN	Rusty Egolf	1988	9,241
136 5/8	23 6/8	24 7/8	17 5/8	4	4	Montgomery County	IL	Floyd Dennis Scheifer	1989	9,241
136 5/8	23 0/8	23 3/8	18 7/8	5	5	McCurtain County	OK	Jody Metcalf	1989	9,241
136 5/8	23 4/8	23 3/8	19 7/8	4	5	Fairfax County	VA	James E. Chabreck	1989	9,241
136 5/8	25 7/8	20 7/8	19 3/8	5	5	Effingham County	IL	Terry Westendorf	1989	9,241
136 5/8	22 4/8	22 2/8	18 1/8	5	5	Wabaunsee County	KS	Michael J. Rose	1989	9,241
136 5/8	23 1/8	23 0/8	17 7/8	4	4	Trinity County	TX	Blake Carlton Muirhead	1990	9,241
136 5/8	23 2/8	23 0/8	15 2/8	4	5	Williams County	ND	Corey Moen	1990	9,241
136 5/8	23 5/8	24 4/8	18 4/8	5	5	Stoddard County	MO	Ken Heuer	1990	9,241
136 5/8	24 5/8	22 7/8	20 5/8	5	5	Westchester County	NY	Gary Mammana	1990	9,241
136 5/8	23 3/8	23 3/8	15 0/8	6	6	Pike County	IL	Gary Wombles	1990	9,241
136 5/8	24 6/8	25 3/8	17 6/8	6	5	Marinette County	WI	Scott Dyer	1990	9,241
136 5/8	24 5/8	24 7/8	23 3/8	5	4	Washington County	MS	Frank H. Dallas	1991	9,241
136 5/8	21 3/8	22 6/8	14 2/8	6	5	Morgan County	GA	Scott Baldwin	1991	9,241
136 5/8	21 2/8	21 4/8	16 1/8	5	5	Price County	WI	Ronald Spatz	1991	9,241
136 5/8	21 7/8	23 2/8	20 7/8	5	5	Frio County	TX	Marc Knight	1991	9,241
136 5/8	23 1/8	22 3/8	21 1/8	5	5	E. Carroll Parish	LA	Alan T. Howard	1991	9,241
136 5/8	21 6/8	22 5/8	16 1/8	5	5	Jefferson County	KY	Jan Wheatley	1992	9,241
136 5/8	20 6/8	21 0/8	18 3/8	6	7	Chippewa County	MI	William A. Seppala	1992	9,241
136 5/8	22 1/8	22 1/8	15 5/8	4	4	Saginaw County	MI	William J. Twarog	1992	9,241
136 5/8	25 2/8	23 7/8	20 1/8	6	5	Winona County	MN	Mark Jertson	1993	9,241
136 5/8	22 6/8	22 7/8	17 1/8	6	6	Green County	WI	Dennis Hoesly	1993	9,241
136 5/8	22 3/8	22 4/8	17 5/8	5	5	Ottawa County	MI	Robert Bruursema	1994	9,241
136 5/8	23 0/8	23 4/8	18 5/8	4	4	Isabella County	MI	Brian F. Quillen	1994	9,241
136 5/8	21 3/8	22 3/8	16 3/8	4	5	Dunn County	WI	Tim Christopher	1994	9,241
136 5/8	24 3/8	25 2/8	20 1/8	5	4	Trempealeau County	WI	Jeffery Larson	1994	9,241
136 5/8	26 2/8	26 0/8	18 7/8	3	3	Peoria County	IL	Tony Pudik	1994	9,241
136 5/8	22 6/8	23 2/8	15 7/8	5	5	Knox County	IL	David Emken	1994	9,241
136 5/8	23 2/8	24 0/8	15 0/8	5	4	Webb County	TX	Andy Milam	1994	9,241
136 5/8	21 4/8	21 2/8	15 0/8	6	5	Oneida County	WI	John Botwinski	1995	9,241
136 5/8	21 2/8	20 6/8	17 2/8	8	6	Winnebago County	WI	Tom Panske	1995	9,241
136 5/8	21 7/8	22 1/8	16 1/8	5	7	Rusk County	WI	Steven G. Douglas	1995	9,241
136 5/8	21 2/8	20 4/8	16 7/8	4	4	Dodge County	WI	Gene Sitzman	1995	9,241
136 5/8	20 1/8	22 2/8	20 5/8	4	4	Cook County	IL	Edward Scott Evans	1995	9,241
136 5/8	22 1/8	22 4/8	17 5/8	4	5	Salem County	NJ	Donald J. Suchora	1995	9,241
136 5/8	24 3/8	24 6/8	19 5/8	5	5	Anoka County	MN	William J. Courteau	1995	9,241
136 5/8	23 3/8	23 1/8	18 6/8	5	5	Buffalo County	WI	Robert J. Decker	1996	9,241
136 5/8	20 4/8	20 6/8	15 3/8	5	5	Becker County	MN	Jeff Holmer	1996	9,241
136 5/8	19 1/8	19 4/8	16 3/8	5	5	Osage County	OK	Jim Weaver	1996	9,241
136 5/8	21 7/8	20 7/8	16 6/8	6	5	Rock County	WI	Jeff Lloyd	1996	9,241
136 5/8	23 3/8	22 6/8	19 1/8	4	4	Eau Claire County	WI	David A. Christianson	1996	9,241
136 5/8	23 2/8	23 3/8	19 1/8	5	4	New Kent County	VA	Allen Wray Austin	1996	9,241
136 5/8	22 4/8	22 3/8	16 5/8	5	5	Goodhue County	MN	Dean Bridley	1996	9,241
136 5/8	22 2/8	22 5/8	15 1/8	6	5	Madison County	IL	Nick Stilwell	1996	9,241
136 5/8	21 7/8	21 6/8	14 7/8	5	5	Howard County	IA	Scott V. Stewart	1996	9,241
136 5/8	24 7/8	23 3/8	17 2/8	4	5	Franklin County	MA	David M. Underwood	1996	9,241
136 5/8	22 0/8	22 6/8	17 7/8	6	5	Wirt County	WV	Timothy Baldrige	1997	9,241
136 5/8	21 3/8	21 0/8	16 7/8	5	5	Schuylkill County	PA	Jeff Pormann	1997	9,241
136 5/8	23 6/8	24 1/8	19 5/8	4	4	Queen Annes County	MD	Kevin L. Clark	1997	9,241
136 5/8	20 5/8	20 1/8	17 3/8	5	5	Henry County	VA	Mike Weaver	1997	9,241
136 5/8	22 5/8	21 2/8	23 3/8	4	5	Refugio County	TX	Kyle Metting	1997	9,241
136 5/8	22 0/8	21 1/8	19 1/8	5	6	McMullen County	TX	Lannie B. Philley	1998	9,241
136 5/8	22 1/8	22 6/8	19 7/8	5	5	Dimmit County	TX	Chuck Adams	1998	9,241
136 4/8	25 3/8	24 4/8	20 4/8	4	4	Roberts County	SD	ByRon Siegel	1963	9,317
136 4/8	24 6/8	23 6/8	21 6/8	4	4	Jo Daviess County	IL	Todd Muehleip	1975	9,317
136 4/8	27 4/8	26 2/8	17 3/8	6	6	Wake County	NC	Robert E. Butler	1977	9,317
136 4/8	23 1/8	22 3/8	17 0/8	5	5	Brevard County	FL	Mike Field	1979	9,317
136 4/8	22 0/8	23 7/8	18 4/8	5	5	Clark County	IL	Gerald Shaffner	1980	9,317
136 4/8	21 7/8	22 1/8	17 2/8	5	5	Coweta County	GA	Bobby Edwards	1981	9,317
136 4/8	22 4/8	22 4/8	18 2/8	5	5	Richardson County	NE	Don J. Wickham	1981	9,317
136 4/8	23 2/8	22 2/8	17 0/8	4	4	Boone County	IA	Michael Rolling	1982	9,317
136 4/8	24 0/8	24 0/8	18 3/8	6	7	Hancock County	IN	Paul E. Williams	1982	9,317
136 4/8	21 6/8	22 3/8	18 4/8	4	4	Oneida County	WI	Dennis Steinberger	1983	9,317
136 4/8	23 2/8	22 6/8	16 4/8	5	5	Cottonwood County	MN	Leonard P. Thiner	1983	9,317
136 4/8	22 0/8	22 0/8	17 6/8	6	5	Livingston County	MI	Thomas E. Shay	1984	9,317
136 4/8	22 5/8	22 4/8	16 4/8	5	5	Wyoming County	NY	Ray Minnick	1985	9,317
136 4/8	22 3/8	21 7/8	14 4/8	5	5	Clayton County	IA	Betty Jane Jungk	1985	9,317
136 4/8	21 7/8	22 7/8	17 2/8	4	4	Washington County	TN	Bobby Davis	1985	9,317
136 4/8	21 6/8	21 2/8	17 0/8	5	5	Marshall County	IA	Ed Albee	1985	9,317
136 4/8	23 3/8	23 2/8	17 2/8	4	5	Larue County	KY	Steve Crabtree	1986	9,317
136 4/8	23 0/8	22 5/8	19 0/8	4	5	Plymouth County	IA	Gary G. Bentley	1986	9,317
136 4/8	20 7/8	21 0/8	16 2/8	5	5	Buffalo County	WI	Peter Sehrbrock	1987	9,317

WHITETAIL DEER (TYPICAL ANTLERS)

Minimum Score 125 — Continued

SCORE	LENGTH OF MAIN BEAM R	L	INSIDE SPREAD	NUMBER OF POINTS R	L	AREA	STATE/ PROVINCE	HUNTER'S NAME	DATE	RANK
136 4/8	21 2/8	21 1/8	18 0/8	8	5	Montcalm County	MI	Byron J. Burton	1988	9,317
136 4/8	20 0/8	21 4/8	12 0/8	4	5	Wayne County	MO	Jeff Daves	1988	9,317
136 4/8	21 5/8	22 2/8	13 6/8	5	6	Vermillion County	IN	Lewis Peery	1988	9,317
136 4/8	22 3/8	21 2/8	16 6/8	4	4	Macon County	MO	Robert Brundage	1988	9,317
136 4/8	22 6/8	22 6/8	15 0/8	5	6	Adams County	OH	Joseph D. Gaffin	1988	9,317
136 4/8	22 3/8	22 6/8	20 0/8	5	5	Madison Parish	LA	Carl Childress	1988	9,317
136 4/8	24 6/8	25 5/8	16 4/8	4	4	Callaway County	MO	Bryan K. Coursey	1989	9,317
136 4/8	22 2/8	19 7/8	16 1/8	6	5	Kalamazoo County	MI	Michael E. McNaughton	1989	9,317
136 4/8	23 3/8	20 5/8	15 0/8	4	6	Waushara County	WI	Terry Flesch	1989	9,317
136 4/8	22 0/8	21 6/8	18 2/8	5	5	Cullman County	AL	James Trakel	1989	9,317
136 4/8	22 6/8	21 3/8	21 0/8	4	4	Harlan County	NE	Robert Elias	1989	9,317
136 4/8	25 4/8	25 0/8	18 6/8	4	6	Rockingham County	VA	Roger O. Wyant	1989	9,317
136 4/8	23 3/8	22 6/8	19 3/8	5	6	Beltrami County	MN	Denise Wiebolt	1989	9,317
136 4/8	21 5/8	22 1/8	18 5/8	7	7	Clark County	WI	David W. Calkins	1990	9,317
136 4/8	21 4/8	22 0/8	15 4/8	5	5	Vernon County	MO	Jerry M. Worley	1990	9,317
136 4/8	25 0/8	24 7/8	17 0/8	4	4	Saline County	IL	Ronald Phelps	1990	9,317
136 4/8	21 3/8	23 1/8	18 2/8	5	4	Buffalo County	WI	Lynn R. Moeller	1990	9,317
136 4/8	22 6/8	23 6/8	16 1/8	4	5	Madison Parish	LA	Martin B. Harthcock III	1990	9,317
136 4/8	24 4/8	24 2/8	19 1/8	6	7	Union County	NC	Westley Keller	1990	9,317
136 4/8	22 7/8	22 6/8	19 2/8	5	5	Delta County	MI	Eugene Percy Robinson	1991	9,317
136 4/8	25 4/8	23 2/8	17 4/8	4	4	Macon County	IL	Ricky Park	1991	9,317
136 4/8	22 1/8	21 5/8	17 0/8	4	4	Dunn County	WI	Steve Johnson	1991	9,317
136 4/8	21 3/8	21 5/8	17 6/8	4	4	Henry County	IL	Gary Felske	1991	9,317
136 4/8	21 1/8	20 7/8	16 4/8	5	5	La Crosse County	WI	Lee J. Keim	1992	9,317
136 4/8	24 7/8	26 4/8	16 6/8	4	4	Waukesha County	WI	Robin L. Casper	1992	9,317
136 4/8	21 6/8	22 0/8	16 4/8	5	5	Henry County	IA	Marvin Foster	1992	9,317
136 4/8	20 4/8	20 4/8	15 4/8	5	6	Putnam County	MO	Charles R. Gauch	1992	9,317
136 4/8	23 2/8	23 4/8	17 4/8	4	4	Anne Arundel County	MD	Brandon L. Dunaway	1993	9,317
136 4/8	23 4/8	19 3/8	18 2/8	5	5	Shawano County	WI	Theresa J. Carrow	1994	9,317
136 4/8	22 4/8	22 6/8	18 1/8	4	5	Shelby County	IL	Gary Arthur	1994	9,317
136 4/8	21 0/8	19 4/8	15 2/8	5	5	Grant County	WI	Brent McDonald	1994	9,317
136 4/8	23 4/8	23 4/8	20 4/8	4	4	Waukesha County	WI	Rick Schaefer	1994	9,317
136 4/8	23 2/8	23 1/8	19 1/8	6	4	Washington County	MN	Ben Bailey	1994	9,317
136 4/8	22 3/8	21 2/8	18 0/8	6	6	Juniata County	PA	Brent E. Musser	1994	9,317
136 4/8	23 2/8	23 5/8	18 4/8	6	4	Outagamie County	WI	Keith "Kip" Willems	1994	9,317
136 4/8	22 2/8	21 4/8	18 4/8	5	5	Pulaski County	IL	Garrett Wilson	1994	9,317
136 4/8	26 3/8	24 7/8	18 6/8	4	5	Lake County	IL	Carl Spaeth	1994	9,317
136 4/8	23 4/8	21 1/8	19 5/8	6	4	Harford County	MD	Donald Cutlip	1994	9,317
136 4/8	23 0/8	23 4/8	18 6/8	4	5	Putnam County	IN	Dave Ranard	1995	9,317
136 4/8	24 1/8	24 6/8	14 7/8	6	4	Green Lake County	WI	Rick Culver	1995	9,317
136 4/8	25 3/8	26 1/8	19 4/8	4	4	Berkshire County	MA	Frank "Buck" Kendall	1995	9,317
136 4/8	20 5/8	21 2/8	16 2/8	5	5	Berkshire County	MA	Peter M. Derby	1995	9,317
136 4/8	22 1/8	23 5/8	17 4/8	5	5	Cass County	MI	Brian Singleton	1995	9,317
136 4/8	26 0/8	26 2/8	22 6/8	3	4	Jackson County	MO	Wade Marler	1996	9,317
136 4/8	23 1/8	22 2/8	16 2/8	5	5	Cook County	IL	Jim Kocik	1996	9,317
136 4/8	21 5/8	22 1/8	16 2/8	5	5	Pottawatomie County	KS	Rod Simmer	1996	9,317
136 4/8	26 0/8	25 2/8	17 4/8	4	6	Berks County	PA	Tony J. Zawada	1996	9,317
136 4/8	24 1/8	23 3/8	20 6/8	5	5	Dane County	WI	Duane D. Broughton	1997	9,317
136 4/8	22 5/8	22 5/8	18 5/8	4	5	Ohio County	IN	Jeff Chase	1997	9,317
136 4/8	24 6/8	24 2/8	20 4/8	5	4	Monroe County	NY	Christopher Brower	1997	9,317
136 4/8	24 5/8	23 4/8	13 4/8	5	4	Charles County	MD	Joseph Goldsborough	1997	9,317
136 4/8	21 3/8	22 3/8	16 6/8	5	5	Webster County	IA	Douglas P. Haverkamp	1997	9,317
136 4/8	21 3/8	21 6/8	17 2/8	4	5	Fremont County	IA	Bow Steedly	1997	9,317
136 4/8	24 1/8	22 7/8	16 6/8	6	5	Madison County	KY	Eric Culver	1997	9,317
136 4/8	23 7/8	24 2/8	19 0/8	5	4	Ottawa County	MI	Mark E. Anderle	1998	9,317
136 3/8	23 5/8	24 2/8	17 6/8	4	5	Pope County	IL	Murray Schuchardt	1973	9,391
136 3/8	23 6/8	23 6/8	18 5/8	5	7	Pope County	MN	Ernie Janish	1976	9,391
136 3/8	24 4/8	24 3/8	18 5/8	5	5	Delaware County	OH	Ron E. Murphy	1979	9,391
136 3/8	22 7/8	22 1/8	16 3/8	4	5	Des Moines County	IA	John Thompson	1982	9,391
136 3/8	21 1/8	21 1/8	15 1/8	5	5	Iron County	WI	John W. Schulz	1983	9,391
136 3/8	22 2/8	22 2/8	18 1/8	4	4	Clay County	MO	Kent Robb Waters	1983	9,391
136 3/8	22 0/8	22 4/8	18 7/8	4	4	Webster County	KY	John Wayne Elkins	1983	9,391
136 3/8	25 0/8	24 3/8	18 1/8	5	4	Jackson County	MI	Johnny Lee Fry	1984	9,391
136 3/8	25 0/8	25 6/8	21 3/8	4	4	McPherson County	KS	Dan Koons	1985	9,391
136 3/8	22 4/8	20 7/8	15 6/8	6	5	Sedgwick County	KS	Gary Voth	1986	9,391
136 3/8	24 7/8	24 2/8	17 3/8	4	4	Antrim County	MI	Clifford L. Tulpa	1987	9,391
136 3/8	21 7/8	20 2/8	14 7/8	6	7	Rowan County	KY	Danny Mabry	1987	9,391
136 3/8	20 7/8	21 1/8	16 3/8	7	5	Clearwater County	MN	Christopher Kuam	1987	9,391
136 3/8	21 7/8	22 4/8	17 5/8	7	7	Wabaunsee County	KS	Charles Bisnette	1987	9,391
136 3/8	24 4/8	22 3/8	18 3/8	5	5	Waukesha County	WI	Dirk Stolz	1988	9,391
136 3/8	23 1/8	22 4/8	17 3/8	5	4	Vermilion County	IL	David E. Demoss	1988	9,391
136 3/8	20 0/8	19 7/8	15 1/8	5	5	Noxubee County	MS	Wayne Stewart, Jr.	1989	9,391
136 3/8	22 2/8	22 0/8	18 3/8	5	5	Washtenaw County	MI	Michael R. Sheats	1989	9,391
136 3/8	23 4/8	23 3/8	15 3/8	5	5	Linn County	KS	Loren J. Sayers	1989	9,391
136 3/8	21 3/8	22 2/8	16 5/8	5	5	Faribault County	MN	Randy Boettcher	1989	9,391
136 3/8	22 6/8	22 0/8	17 3/8	4	4	Walworth County	WI	Jim Janz	1989	9,391
136 3/8	24 7/8	23 2/8	19 4/8	4	5	Litchfield County	CT	Michael S. Camarota	1990	9,391
136 3/8	21 5/8	22 1/8	17 1/8	5	5	Mower County	MN	Gary Landherr	1990	9,391

WHITETAIL DEER (TYPICAL ANTLERS)

Minimum Score 125

SCORE	LENGTH OF MAIN BEAM R	LENGTH OF MAIN BEAM L	INSIDE SPREAD	NUMBER OF POINTS R	NUMBER OF POINTS L	AREA	STATE/ PROVINCE	HUNTER'S NAME	DATE	RANK
136 3/8	21 6/8	21 5/8	15 7/8	5	5	Bayfield County	WI	Glenn Sotona	1990	9,391
136 3/8	20 3/8	21 7/8	19 7/8	5	5	Madison County	IL	Steve Bell	1990	9,391
136 3/8	21 7/8	21 3/8	16 3/8	7	5	Shelby County	MO	Dwaine Totten	1990	9,391
136 3/8	22 3/8	22 0/8	17 5/8	5	4	Price County	WI	Kenneth L. Cork	1990	9,391
136 3/8	25 5/8	24 2/8	19 5/8	4	4	Tensas Parish	LA	James D. Vinson	1990	9,391
136 3/8	21 6/8	22 4/8	16 5/8	6	6	Sarpy County	NE	Gary W. Dillon	1990	9,391
136 3/8	19 3/8	19 6/8	15 1/8	5	5	Richland County	MT	Michael Barbula	1991	9,391
136 3/8	22 0/8	22 2/8	15 3/8	5	5	Sawyer County	WI	Randy Patko	1991	9,391
136 3/8	19 5/8	19 1/8	19 4/8	5	8	Panola County	TX	Robert David Fulgium	1991	9,391
136 3/8	21 6/8	22 1/8	19 7/8	5	5	Saginaw County	MI	Bill Holden	1991	9,391
136 3/8	23 5/8	25 0/8	18 4/8	6	8	Richland County	OH	Lon Greer	1991	9,391
136 3/8	23 6/8	22 7/8	18 1/8	4	4	Waukesha County	WI	Craig Markham	1991	9,391
136 3/8	23 2/8	23 0/8	16 0/8	5	4	Jackson County	OH	Les Barto	1991	9,391
136 3/8	22 0/8	21 4/8	21 5/8	5	5	Trempealeau County	WI	Bobby E. Lince	1991	9,391
136 3/8	25 1/8	25 1/8	19 0/8	4	5	McHenry County	IL	Dan Englund	1991	9,391
136 3/8	20 7/8	22 4/8	18 3/8	5	5	Webster County	IA	Tim Michehl	1991	9,391
136 3/8	23 1/8	24 3/8	17 7/8	5	5	Crow Wing County	MN	Kevin Smedbron	1991	9,391
136 3/8	21 2/8	21 7/8	16 5/8	5	5	Monroe County	WI	Art Richardson	1992	9,391
136 3/8	24 1/8	24 7/8	14 2/8	7	7	Green Lake County	WI	Bruce L. Schulz	1992	9,391
136 3/8	23 6/8	23 3/8	18 1/8	4	4	Jersey County	IL	Casey W. Jones	1992	9,391
136 3/8	22 3/8	23 4/8	18 3/8	5	4	Maverick County	TX	Steve Warner	1993	9,391
136 3/8	20 6/8	21 5/8	17 2/8	7	5	Lake County	IL	Doug R. Knigge	1993	9,391
136 3/8	24 1/8	22 4/8	19 5/8	4	4	Racine County	WI	Greg A. Hanson	1993	9,391
136 3/8	21 4/8	21 4/8	16 3/8	5	5	Lake County	IL	Erich Elendt	1993	9,391
136 3/8	24 1/8	24 1/8	17 7/8	4	5	Shelby County	OH	Steve Sherman	1993	9,391
136 3/8	23 6/8	23 5/8	16 3/8	5	5	Sanilac County	MI	Edward Thomas Conniff	1993	9,391
136 3/8	23 1/8	24 2/8	17 5/8	7	5	McHenry County	IL	Brad Wiehr	1994	9,391
136 3/8	22 1/8	22 1/8	19 3/8	5	5	Umatilla County	OR	Keith Burns	1994	9,391
136 3/8	23 4/8	23 6/8	16 3/8	4	4	Gasconade County	MO	Chris Lewis	1994	9,391
136 3/8	22 2/8	22 2/8	19 3/8	4	4	Brown County	IL	Keith Bennett	1994	9,391
136 3/8	22 4/8	22 1/8	17 5/8	7	6	Van Buren County	IA	Jim Chambers	1994	9,391
136 3/8	22 4/8	22 1/8	18 2/8	6	5	Beaverdam	ALB	Randy Babey	1994	9,391
136 3/8	23 1/8	22 0/8	18 1/8	5	5	Dodge County	MN	Steve Snow	1994	9,391
136 3/8	23 6/8	21 2/8	16 5/8	5	5	Columbia County	WI	William H. Basil	1995	9,391
136 3/8	23 6/8	20 1/8	20 4/8	5	5	Buffalo County	WI	Darren Muche	1995	9,391
136 3/8	23 0/8	23 2/8	19 7/8	4	4	Dubuque County	IA	Mark Oberfoell	1995	9,391
136 3/8	21 4/8	21 4/8	13 4/8	6	7	Webb County	TX	Bodie Colwell	1995	9,391
136 3/8	23 5/8	23 5/8	16 5/8	5	4	Waupaca County	WI	Wayne Krueger	1996	9,391
136 3/8	23 7/8	24 3/8	17 5/8	4	4	Van Buren County	MI	Mick Charron	1996	9,391
136 3/8	24 2/8	23 5/8	17 7/8	5	5	Monroe County	WI	William W. Wissestad	1996	9,391
136 3/8	21 5/8	21 6/8	19 3/8	6	5	Schuyler County	IL	Steve McCoy	1996	9,391
136 3/8	28 3/8	27 1/8	16 7/8	6	4	Montgomery County	MD	Sean Etchison	1996	9,391
136 3/8	22 2/8	23 0/8	18 5/8	5	6	Greenwood County	KS	Craig Gehring	1996	9,391
136 3/8	20 6/8	22 4/8	14 3/8	6	5	Refugio County	TX	Brent A. Tucker	1997	9,391
136 3/8	24 0/8	23 7/8	15 1/8	4	5	Houston County	MN	Chanc L. Vogel	1997	9,391
136 3/8	23 4/8	23 0/8	19 1/8	4	4	Iowa County	WI	Keith Peetz	1997	9,391
136 3/8	25 1/8	24 7/8	20 7/8	5	7	Pierce County	WI	Michelle M. Shafer	1997	9,391
136 3/8	25 6/8	24 2/8	15 1/8	5	5	Macomb County	MI	Christopher Kohsman	1997	9,391
136 3/8	23 1/8	23 2/8	15 1/8	8	5	Erie County	NY	Paul J. Herkey	1997	9,391
136 3/8	22 3/8	22 5/8	16 3/8	5	5	Waupaca County	WI	Steven W. Baitinger	1997	9,391
136 3/8	22 7/8	22 5/8	16 1/8	5	4	Grant County	OK	Kevin L. Dupus	1997	9,391
136 2/8	21 2/8	21 2/8	17 0/8	5	5	Sheridan County	ND	Robert Conklin	1967	9,465
136 2/8	20 0/8	22 4/8	17 4/8	5	4	Taylor County	WI	Roger Williams	1968	9,465
136 2/8	22 3/8	22 0/8	14 2/8	4	5	Lucas County	IA	Cynthia Squibb	1973	9,465
136 2/8	24 2/8	23 6/8	16 2/8	4	4	Lucas County	OH	John W. Wood	1975	9,465
136 2/8	21 1/8	20 6/8	16 4/8	5	5	Mercer County	NJ	John K. Deveney	1977	9,465
136 2/8	21 7/8	21 7/8	14 0/8	5	6	Jefferson County	IA	Scott Dillon	1980	9,465
136 2/8	21 4/8	22 0/8	15 3/8	4	7	Cass County	MI	Clark A. Baugher	1981	9,465
136 2/8	22 4/8	22 6/8	18 0/8	4	5	Nelson County	KY	Mark Gies	1982	9,465
136 2/8	21 6/8	21 6/8	16 5/8	6	5	McKenzie County	ND	David Tofte	1982	9,465
136 2/8	23 0/8	23 2/8	16 4/8	5	5	Loudoun County	VA	Larry C. Sherertz	1983	9,465
136 2/8	22 2/8	23 2/8	18 2/8	4	4	Fairfax County	VA	Frederick Alf, Jr.	1983	9,465
136 2/8	22 3/8	22 7/8	16 6/8	5	6	Fairfield County	CT	Paul Fitzgerald	1984	9,465
136 2/8	22 7/8	22 4/8	18 5/8	5	5	Crawford County	KS	Don Garritson	1984	9,465
136 2/8	22 1/8	22 3/8	15 0/8	6	5	Isabella County	MI	Donald E. Carlson	1985	9,465
136 2/8	21 0/8	23 0/8	20 0/8	6	5	Howard County	NE	Dwayne Berggren	1985	9,465
136 2/8	24 5/8	24 4/8	17 2/8	6	6	Gray County	KS	Melvin L. Weber	1985	9,465
136 2/8	21 0/8	21 5/8	15 0/8	5	5	Shawano County	WI	Dick Schardt	1985	9,465
136 2/8	22 0/8	22 2/8	18 4/8	5	5	Otter Tail County	MN	Lyle Tabbut	1986	9,465
136 2/8	20 5/8	20 4/8	15 3/8	6	6	Clay County	IN	Tom Yaraschefski	1986	9,465
136 2/8	22 7/8	22 4/8	19 7/8	7	6	Columbia County	WI	Troy M. McReath	1986	9,465
136 2/8	21 4/8	21 1/8	16 3/8	7	6	Goodhue County	MN	Terry Krahn	1987	9,465
136 2/8	26 2/8	24 6/8	16 4/8	5	6	Peoria County	IL	Robert Hammerich	1987	9,465
136 2/8	23 6/8	22 6/8	20 6/8	5	4	Vinton County	OH	Greg Bonecutter, Sr.	1988	9,465
136 2/8	22 3/8	22 3/8	18 6/8	4	4	Dakota County	MN	Michael Kennedy, Jr.	1989	9,465
136 2/8	23 2/8	23 4/8	20 2/8	4	4	Livingston County	IL	Alan E. Gray	1989	9,465
136 2/8	20 5/8	20 1/8	17 0/8	5	5	Livingston County	IL	Michael Horning	1989	9,465
136 2/8	24 1/8	23 7/8	16 3/8	5	5	Vigo County	IN	Mike Mundy	1989	9,465

WHITETAIL DEER (TYPICAL ANTLERS)

Minimum Score 125 — Continued

SCORE	LENGTH OF R MAIN BEAM L		INSIDE SPREAD	NUMBER OF R POINTS L		AREA	STATE/ PROVINCE	HUNTER'S NAME	DATE	RANK
136 2/8	23 3/8	23 4/8	20 2/8	4	5	St. Joseph County	IN	Bruce E. Thompson	1989	9,465
136 2/8	22 7/8	21 3/8	18 6/8	5	5	Oneida County	WI	Russell Ostermann	1989	9,465
136 2/8	23 1/8	22 6/8	21 6/8	4	4	Wayne County	IL	Pee Wee Hall	1989	9,465
136 2/8	23 6/8	23 2/8	16 2/8	5	4	Johnson County	MO	Roy A. Simpson	1989	9,465
136 2/8	23 2/8	24 0/8	18 0/8	4	4	Baltimore County	MD	Bruce D. Hoover	1989	9,465
136 2/8	23 3/8	22 6/8	16 0/8	5	4	Evans County	GA	Michael H. Clark, Sr.	1990	9,465
136 2/8	20 2/8	20 3/8	16 2/8	5	5	Bond County	IL	Len Hall	1990	9,465
136 2/8	22 3/8	22 5/8	18 0/8	5	5	Morrison County	MN	Jeff Schwartz	1990	9,465
136 2/8	22 7/8	22 7/8	18 6/8	5	6	Winnebago County	IL	Richard Van Wambeke	1990	9,465
136 2/8	23 6/8	24 3/8	19 2/8	4	4	Ballard County	KY	Scott Allen Drummond	1990	9,465
136 2/8	22 2/8	21 4/8	15 3/8	5	6	Jefferson County	WV	John K. Holliday	1991	9,465
136 2/8	21 4/8	22 4/8	18 6/8	4	4	Meigs County	OH	Ronnie Plemmons, Jr.	1991	9,465
136 2/8	21 3/8	21 6/8	15 2/8	4	4	Johnson County	KS	Brian McNamee	1992	9,465
136 2/8	24 2/8	23 4/8	19 0/8	8	6	Jackson County	IL	Grant C. Guthman	1992	9,465
136 2/8	22 1/8	22 3/8	18 2/8	5	5	Rimbey	ALB	Jim Bruns	1992	9,465
136 2/8	24 2/8	24 2/8	17 2/8	5	5	Bond County	IL	Paul D. Kinworthy	1992	9,465
136 2/8	24 6/8	24 1/8	15 6/8	4	6	Webster County	MO	Allen Davidson	1992	9,465
136 2/8	27 0/8	26 2/8	21 4/8	5	3	Athens County	OH	Mark A. Cross	1992	9,465
136 2/8	22 6/8	23 1/8	15 5/8	5	5	Queen Annes County	MD	Larry Morris	1992	9,465
136 2/8	24 0/8	23 5/8	15 4/8	4	4	Carroll County	IL	Art Heinze	1992	9,465
136 2/8	22 1/8	22 2/8	17 2/8	4	5	Woodford County	IL	Herb Beer	1992	9,465
136 2/8	22 6/8	22 3/8	18 4/8	6	6	St. Francois County	MO	Scott Aubuchon	1992	9,465
136 2/8	24 0/8	23 0/8	18 0/8	7	5	Alexander County	IL	Larry McHughs	1993	9,465
136 2/8	21 7/8	22 6/8	17 2/8	5	5	Hall County	GA	Bobby D. Standridge	1993	9,465
136 2/8	23 4/8	22 3/8	15 0/8	4	5	Green County	WI	Paul T. Ovadal	1993	9,465
136 2/8	25 3/8	25 2/8	21 6/8	6	4	Cheatham County	TN	Chris Hunt	1993	9,465
136 2/8	22 0/8	22 4/8	13 4/8	5	5	Buffalo County	WI	Donald R. Fox	1993	9,465
136 2/8	22 4/8	21 6/8	18 0/8	6	5	DeKalb County	IL	Corey R. Iversen	1993	9,465
136 2/8	22 1/8	22 1/8	19 4/8	4	5	Wayne County	NY	Michael J. Pastore	1993	9,465
136 2/8	22 6/8	22 4/8	16 2/8	6	6	Outagamie County	WI	Patrick J. Vande Hei	1993	9,465
136 2/8	20 4/8	21 6/8	19 7/8	6	6	Mercer County	NJ	Marcel Veenstra	1993	9,465
136 2/8	22 4/8	22 0/8	17 2/8	4	5	Van Buren County	MI	Michael Hughes	1993	9,465
136 2/8	21 2/8	21 0/8	15 7/8	6	5	St. Joseph County	IN	Charles A. White	1994	9,465
136 2/8	22 0/8	22 0/8	18 2/8	4	6	Jasper County	IA	Don Morris	1994	9,465
136 2/8	20 4/8	21 4/8	16 6/8	5	5	Saunders County	NE	Geoffrey Gloeb	1995	9,465
136 2/8	22 0/8	21 0/8	17 2/8	5	5	Todd County	KY	Ryan Sanders	1995	9,465
136 2/8	23 4/8	23 0/8	16 6/8	5	7	Copiah County	MS	Steven R. Pope	1995	9,465
136 2/8	22 5/8	21 6/8	17 0/8	5	5	Vigo County	IN	Dale Ferguson	1995	9,465
136 2/8	20 4/8	21 4/8	14 6/8	5	5	Douglas County	MO	Steve Moody	1995	9,465
136 2/8	22 1/8	20 0/8	18 2/8	5	6	Rock County	WI	Brian Shumway	1995	9,465
136 2/8	22 6/8	21 7/8	21 0/8	5	5	Tioga County	NY	Arleigh Reynolds	1995	9,465
136 2/8	22 0/8	22 5/8	15 6/8	4	4	Allamakee County	IA	Duane Baumler	1995	9,465
136 2/8	25 0/8	24 5/8	19 0/8	4	5	Providence County	RI	Steve Zira	1996	9,465
136 2/8	20 6/8	20 7/8	18 2/8	5	5	Goodhue County	MN	John "Jack" Cordes	1996	9,465
136 2/8	21 6/8	22 2/8	18 0/8	5	5	Dorchester County	MD	John N. Polizos	1996	9,465
136 2/8	24 4/8	24 4/8	18 4/8	6	7	Northumberland County	PA	Paul G. Hornberger	1996	9,465
136 2/8	22 5/8	23 2/8	17 3/8	5	6	Suffolk County	NY	Richard S. Gates	1996	9,465
136 2/8	20 4/8	21 1/8	17 3/8	7	5	Buffalo County	WI	Ron Schultz	1996	9,465
136 2/8	22 7/8	23 6/8	16 2/8	5	4	Dane County	WI	Daniel K. Kaiser	1996	9,465
136 2/8	22 2/8	21 0/8	15 1/8	7	7	Williams County	ND	Ron Borgeson	1997	9,465
136 2/8	22 6/8	23 3/8	16 0/8	4	4	Shawano County	WI	Joe Neumeier	1997	9,465
136 2/8	23 2/8	22 5/8	19 2/8	5	5	Iron County	WI	Mark Manzanares	1997	9,465
136 2/8	22 3/8	22 2/8	15 4/8	5	5	Trempealeau County	WI	Steve L. Bryn	1997	9,465
136 2/8	22 0/8	23 0/8	19 7/8	5	5	Tazewell County	IL	Jerry Manning	1997	9,465
136 2/8	21 2/8	20 7/8	18 2/8	4	4	Adams County	MS	Ben McDonald	1997	9,465
136 2/8	22 7/8	23 5/8	18 1/8	5	6	Wood County	WI	Mark G. Guse	1997	9,465
136 2/8	21 5/8	21 3/8	17 4/8	5	5	Houston County	MN	Travis Vick	1997	9,465
136 2/8	23 6/8	21 6/8	16 2/8	5	4	Dubuque County	IA	Michael J. Pitzen	1997	9,465
136 2/8	22 2/8	21 6/8	17 0/8	5	5	Peoria County	IL	Joseph Ronk	1997	9,465
136 2/8	24 1/8	22 2/8	18 0/8	5	5	Washington County	IL	Robert Schobert	1997	9,465
136 2/8	22 0/8	21 4/8	16 2/8	5	5	Muskingum County	OH	Harold Ansel	1997	9,465
136 2/8	20 2/8	20 4/8	14 1/8	6	6	Wyoming County	WV	Mike Clay	1997	9,465
136 2/8	21 1/8	21 6/8	19 0/8	4	5	Marathon County	WI	Rob Woytasik	1998	9,465
136 2/8	21 0/8	21 0/8	16 0/8	5	5	Macon County	MO	David Reese	1998	9,465
136 2/8	22 3/8	21 5/8	18 2/8	5	7	Mercer County	ND	Byron W. Borlaug	1998	9,465
136 2/8	21 6/8	17 5/8	19 0/8	4	5	Muskegon County	MI	Keven Stafford	1998	9,465
136 1/8	21 5/8	21 2/8	18 0/8	5	4	Spink County	SD	Louis Smith	1963	9,558
136 1/8	23 3/8	23 4/8	19 7/8	6	6	Litchfield County	CT	Eugene Clini, Jr.	1970	9,558
136 1/8	20 0/8	20 6/8	17 7/8	4	4	Meigs County	OH	Marlin L. Wolfe	1981	9,558
136 1/8	21 1/8	23 2/8	19 1/8	5	5	Morrison County	MN	Raymond G. Fair	1981	9,558
136 1/8	21 7/8	23 6/8	18 5/8	5	5	Mason County	WV	Darrell C. Hoffman	1982	9,558
136 1/8	23 2/8	23 5/8	19 1/8	5	5	Jefferson County	IL	Kevin Lisenby	1982	9,558
136 1/8	22 2/8	21 6/8	17 3/8	5	4	El Paso County	CO	Michael Thompson	1983	9,558
136 1/8	21 4/8	22 1/8	17 3/8	4	4	Fillmore County	MN	Glenn Hisey	1983	9,558
136 1/8	20 5/8	21 1/8	15 0/8	8	6	Atchison County	MO	Orville L. Chaslain	1983	9,558
136 1/8	23 3/8	23 3/8	18 1/8	5	6	Franklin County	OH	Richard J. Ferguson	1983	9,558
136 1/8	24 7/8	23 5/8	19 7/8	4	5	Wayne County	IA	Gary Purvis	1983	9,558
136 1/8	26 1/8	24 7/8	21 3/8	4	4	Claiborne Parish	LA	Joe M. Tuggle	1985	9,558

WHITETAIL DEER (TYPICAL ANTLERS)

Minimum Score 125 — Continued

SCORE	LENGTH OF MAIN BEAM R	LENGTH OF MAIN BEAM L	INSIDE SPREAD	NUMBER OF POINTS R	NUMBER OF POINTS L	AREA	STATE/PROVINCE	HUNTER'S NAME	DATE	RANK
136 1/8	24 4/8	22 4/8	16 7/8	4	4	Washington County	IA	Marc Phelps	1985	9,558
136 1/8	20 0/8	21 1/8	17 1/8	5	5	Dickinson County	KS	Donald L. Ackerman	1985	9,558
136 1/8	20 1/8	20 1/8	18 5/8	5	5	Lincoln County	MT	Michael F. Shepard	1985	9,558
136 1/8	21 3/8	21 5/8	15 3/8	5	6	Adams County	WI	Brad A. Bauer	1986	9,558
136 1/8	21 3/8	21 0/8	15 7/8	5	5	Duval County	TX	Peggy Barcak	1986	9,558
136 1/8	22 6/8	23 3/8	23 6/8	5	5	Oneida County	WI	Donald Strum	1986	9,558
136 1/8	24 2/8	23 5/8	17 7/8	5	5	Idaho County	ID	Art Christensen	1986	9,558
136 1/8	20 0/8	21 0/8	16 3/8	5	5	Petroleum County	MT	Todd Vogl	1987	9,558
136 1/8	18 4/8	18 2/8	15 7/8	6	6	Morrison County	MN	Matt Goethel	1987	9,558
136 1/8	20 0/8	19 7/8	14 3/8	6	6	Fairfax County	VA	Brian K. McCormick	1987	9,558
136 1/8	23 3/8	23 7/8	18 5/8	4	4	Dane County	WI	Scott Dahlk	1987	9,558
136 1/8	22 7/8	22 3/8	18 5/8	5	5	Bucks County	PA	Neil D. Adams	1988	9,558
136 1/8	26 0/8	24 6/8	20 4/8	6	6	Dane County	WI	Clyde J. Carpenter	1988	9,558
136 1/8	21 7/8	22 0/8	19 7/8	5	5	Vermilion County	IL	Floyd Lee Walton	1988	9,558
136 1/8	22 0/8	23 0/8	18 5/8	4	4	Meade County	KS	Mike Heinson	1988	9,558
136 1/8	24 4/8	23 1/8	19 5/8	4	6	Henry County	VA	Mike Weaver	1989	9,558
136 1/8	23 2/8	22 5/8	20 1/8	5	4	Osgoode Township	ONT	Andy Girard	1989	9,558
136 1/8	21 1/8	21 7/8	17 1/8	5	5	Brooke County	WV	Brian Johnston	1990	9,558
136 1/8	23 6/8	24 3/8	20 1/8	4	4	Des Moines County	IA	Randy Russell	1990	9,558
136 1/8	21 0/8	21 4/8	16 1/8	7	6	St. Louis County	MO	Donald Meissner	1990	9,558
136 1/8	21 7/8	21 4/8	16 5/8	6	6	Sussex County	NJ	Greg Coughlin	1991	9,558
136 1/8	20 4/8	21 4/8	16 3/8	5	5	La Salle County	TX	Dennis Faulkenberry	1991	9,558
136 1/8	23 0/8	23 5/8	19 1/8	4	4	Logan County	WV	Richard Breton	1991	9,558
136 1/8	24 4/8	25 2/8	19 1/8	4	4	Will County	IL	Richard T. Ginnetti	1991	9,558
136 1/8	24 3/8	23 7/8	17 1/8	4	4	Giles County	VA	Scotty Dean Perdue	1991	9,558
136 1/8	23 3/8	23 0/8	18 3/8	6	7	Kossuth County	IA	Rick E. Bauer	1991	9,558
136 1/8	18 7/8	19 2/8	18 0/8	7	7	Green Lake County	WI	Michael "Mickey" Becker	1991	9,558
136 1/8	23 4/8	23 4/8	18 5/8	5	5	Dubuque County	IA	Mike Strader	1991	9,558
136 1/8	24 0/8	23 7/8	16 1/8	5	4	Jackson County	IA	Aaron Lincoln	1991	9,558
136 1/8	21 4/8	22 1/8	18 1/8	4	5	Taylor County	WI	Mark A. Deml	1991	9,558
136 1/8	21 6/8	22 4/8	14 1/8	4	5	Dane County	WI	Marion W. Moore	1992	9,558
136 1/8	23 0/8	23 1/8	20 5/8	4	4	Sandusky County	OH	Mike Sarns	1992	9,558
136 1/8	22 0/8	21 6/8	17 3/8	5	5	Macon County	AL	Jerome Turner	1992	9,558
136 1/8	21 2/8	21 3/8	17 1/8	6	8	Adams County	IL	Harry Large, Jr.	1992	9,558
136 1/8	22 5/8	21 4/8	16 3/8	4	4	Marion County	KY	Clayton Denny	1993	9,558
136 1/8	23 3/8	23 3/8	16 3/8	5	5	Cass County	MI	Michael L. Ritter	1993	9,558
136 1/8	20 2/8	19 2/8	15 3/8	5	5	Allegan County	MI	Burt Thurston	1993	9,558
136 1/8	22 5/8	23 0/8	16 5/8	5	4	Gogebic County	MI	Chad Longhini	1993	9,558
136 1/8	21 0/8	20 6/8	13 2/8	5	6	McMullen County	TX	Robert R. Corder IV	1994	9,558
136 1/8	23 6/8	23 4/8	17 5/8	4	4	Oneida County	WI	Gary G. Lex	1995	9,558
136 1/8	21 7/8	22 3/8	16 7/8	4	4	Greene County	IN	Bruce A. Swafford	1995	9,558
136 1/8	22 6/8	24 4/8	16 7/8	5	5	Sangamon County	IL	Bill Boyle, Jr.	1995	9,558
136 1/8	24 1/8	24 4/8	18 3/8	4	5	Monroe County	IA	Tim Baird	1995	9,558
136 1/8	22 0/8	23 0/8	15 7/8	5	4	Midland County	MI	Jeff Doede	1995	9,558
136 1/8	20 2/8	20 2/8	14 6/8	6	5	Warren County	IA	Mark D. Moen	1995	9,558
136 1/8	21 2/8	21 1/8	18 4/8	6	7	Calgary	ALB	Walter L. Seville, Jr.	1995	9,558
136 1/8	22 7/8	23 1/8	16 3/8	5	5	Jo Daviess County	IL	Brian L. Williams	1996	9,558
136 1/8	22 6/8	22 7/8	15 1/8	5	5	Cass County	IL	Dwayne Curtis	1996	9,558
136 1/8	21 6/8	20 7/8	14 1/8	6	5	Guthrie County	IA	Regi Goodale	1996	9,558
136 1/8	24 5/8	22 6/8	15 2/8	5	6	Washington County	IA	Brad Gardner	1997	9,558
136 1/8	21 6/8	22 3/8	20 1/8	4	4	Brown County	SD	Brad Dinger	1997	9,558
136 1/8	22 2/8	23 0/8	15 3/8	5	5	Ottawa County	MI	Ken Melvin	1997	9,558
136 1/8	27 0/8	25 4/8	18 7/8	4	5	Marshall County	KS	R. Casey Kallenbach	1997	9,558
136 1/8	22 3/8	23 0/8	14 5/8	5	5	Washington County	WI	Mike Ramos	1997	9,558
136 1/8	20 7/8	21 5/8	18 7/8	5	5	Refugio County	TX	John Brower	1997	9,558
136 1/8	20 7/8	21 3/8	16 3/8	6	6	Trempealeau County	WI	Jamie L. Back	1998	9,558
136 1/8	22 7/8	22 2/8	15 3/8	5	5	Arkansas County	AR	David E. Snowden, Jr.	1998	9,558
136 0/8	22 7/8	23 0/8	17 1/8	5	6	Aitkin County	MN	Ervin A. Buck	1956	9,627
136 0/8	19 6/8	19 5/8	19 4/8	4	4	Jackson County	IL	Henry Mika	1962	9,627
136 0/8	23 2/8	23 4/8	17 2/8	5	5	Brookings County	SD	Douglas Tschetter	1964	9,627
136 0/8	23 6/8	23 0/8	18 0/8	4	4	Hamilton County	IN	Sondra K. Scifres	1975	9,627
136 0/8	23 3/8	23 2/8	18 2/8	4	4	Greene County	IN	Guy Aldrich	1977	9,627
136 0/8	22 2/8	22 2/8	18 0/8	5	5	Morris County	NJ	Len Cardinale	1980	9,627
136 0/8	22 7/8	23 3/8	19 4/8	4	4	Delaware County	IA	David Becker	1981	9,627
136 0/8	23 3/8	23 1/8	18 4/8	5	5	Houston County	MN	Roger Giese	1981	9,627
136 0/8	20 1/8	20 6/8	16 6/8	5	5	Ottawa County	KS	Rodney Ponton	1981	9,627
136 0/8	21 3/8	21 5/8	16 4/8	5	5	Juneau County	WI	Terry Taft	1981	9,627
136 0/8	22 1/8	23 5/8	17 2/8	5	5	Berkeley County	SC	Hugh Gaskins	1982	9,627
136 0/8	22 5/8	22 0/8	18 0/8	5	5	Red Willow County	NE	Dudley Jackson	1983	9,627
136 0/8	23 4/8	21 4/8	18 6/8	4	4	Hancock County	IL	Tim Lee	1983	9,627
136 0/8	24 0/8	23 5/8	17 1/8	7	5	Cherokee County	KS	Darren Collins	1983	9,627
136 0/8	21 5/8	21 1/8	18 0/8	5	5	Johnson County	IA	Danny Steggall	1983	9,627
136 0/8	23 2/8	22 5/8	18 4/8	4	4	Clark County	KS	William Rule	1984	9,627
136 0/8	22 4/8	21 6/8	17 4/8	5	5	Wayne County	NY	Eugene Vincent	1984	9,627
136 0/8	21 5/8	20 5/8	17 2/8	6	5	Flathead County	MT	Carter Jensen	1985	9,627
136 0/8	21 3/8	21 6/8	16 4/8	6	5	Winona County	MN	George McIntire	1985	9,627
136 0/8	23 3/8	23 6/8	13 6/8	6	5	Fayette County	OH	Ronnie L. Jenkins	1985	9,627
136 0/8	22 0/8	23 0/8	19 0/8	5	5	Jackson County	MI	William D. Burgess	1985	9,627

WHITETAIL DEER (TYPICAL ANTLERS)

Minimum Score 125   Continued

SCORE	LENGTH OF MAIN BEAM R	LENGTH OF MAIN BEAM L	INSIDE SPREAD	NUMBER OF POINTS R	NUMBER OF POINTS L	AREA	STATE/PROVINCE	HUNTER'S NAME	DATE	RANK
136 0/8	21 3/8	20 2/8	15 1/8	6	5	Jefferson County	MT	Mike Davis	1986	9,627
136 0/8	20 4/8	20 3/8	14 2/8	6	5	Clinton County	IA	Tom Wing	1986	9,627
136 0/8	23 1/8	22 5/8	17 0/8	5	5	Cortland County	NY	Ted W. Renninger	1986	9,627
136 0/8	23 0/8	23 0/8	16 4/8	5	5	Pike County	IN	Chris Schmitt	1986	9,627
136 0/8	22 7/8	23 4/8	17 6/8	5	5	Litchfield County	CT	Henry B. Church	1986	9,627
136 0/8	24 0/8	24 6/8	15 6/8	4	5	Hancock County	OH	Steven E. Smith	1987	9,627
136 0/8	20 3/8	19 4/8	18 3/8	6	6	Ogle County	IL	Jeffrey S. Burke	1987	9,627
136 0/8	25 1/8	25 4/8	21 0/8	4	4	Green County	WI	Will Pick	1987	9,627
136 0/8	22 7/8	22 5/8	21 1/8	5	6	Dane County	WI	Deane H. Brabender	1988	9,627
136 0/8	23 3/8	22 3/8	17 2/8	4	4	Meigs County	OH	Earl M. Johnson	1988	9,627
136 0/8	22 5/8	21 5/8	18 4/8	7	5	Dane County	WI	John Podebradsky	1989	9,627
136 0/8	21 1/8	21 4/8	16 6/8	4	4	La Salle County	IL	J. R. Price	1989	9,627
136 0/8	21 5/8	21 7/8	15 4/8	5	5	Otoe County	NE	Michael E. Rush	1989	9,627
136 0/8	24 0/8	25 0/8	17 4/8	5	4	Steuben County	IN	William A. Regadanz	1990	9,627
136 0/8	24 4/8	24 6/8	16 1/8	5	5	Buffalo County	WI	Daniel Motszko	1990	9,627
136 0/8	24 6/8	25 1/8	18 2/8	4	4	Pottawattamie County	IA	David M. Flenker	1990	9,627
136 0/8	25 4/8	25 0/8	21 2/8	5	4	Penobscot County	ME	Benjamin C. Brown	1991	9,627
136 0/8	24 5/8	25 0/8	19 3/8	5	6	Todd County	KY	Darrell Monroe	1991	9,627
136 0/8	22 5/8	23 5/8	19 0/8	5	4	Doniphan County	KS	John Meisenheimer	1991	9,627
136 0/8	20 4/8	22 0/8	17 6/8	6	5	Bayfield County	WI	Jeffrey R. Krawczyk	1991	9,627
136 0/8	24 5/8	24 7/8	14 4/8	4	4	Racine County	WI	Steve Holterman	1991	9,627
136 0/8	23 5/8	23 1/8	15 6/8	4	5	Muskegon County	MI	John Hansen	1991	9,627
136 0/8	22 0/8	21 7/8	17 6/8	5	4	Fairfield County	OH	Ron Perdew	1991	9,627
136 0/8	21 2/8	22 3/8	18 0/8	7	6	Ontonagon County	MI	Lawrence Nuyen	1991	9,627
136 0/8	23 0/8	25 1/8	19 6/8	3	5	Dorchester County	MD	Clint Walker	1992	9,627
136 0/8	24 3/8	23 7/8	14 7/8	6	5	Morrison County	MN	Terrance Elliot	1992	9,627
136 0/8	20 6/8	20 4/8	17 7/8	5	5	Richland County	ND	Jim Hicks	1992	9,627
136 0/8	22 6/8	22 1/8	18 4/8	7	7	Cherryville	BC	Tim Meissner	1992	9,627
136 0/8	24 3/8	23 6/8	15 3/8	5	6	Heard County	GA	Johnny Smith	1992	9,627
136 0/8	21 5/8	21 5/8	18 4/8	5	5	Oakland County	MI	James L. Mapletoft	1993	9,627
136 0/8	23 3/8	24 1/8	20 7/8	6	6	Waukesha County	WI	Jim Suchocki	1993	9,627
136 0/8	21 0/8	22 0/8	16 4/8	5	6	Carter County	OK	Wesley Cohea	1993	9,627
136 0/8	25 1/8	25 6/8	19 5/8	6	4	McHenry County	IL	Randy Bittner	1993	9,627
136 0/8	25 5/8	23 7/8	16 2/8	5	5	Pratt County	KS	Greg Windler	1993	9,627
136 0/8	22 3/8	23 0/8	18 0/8	4	5	Cumberland County	ME	Kurt Christensen	1993	9,627
136 0/8	24 0/8	24 4/8	18 4/8	5	6	St. Croix County	WI	Vaughn Voeltz	1994	9,627
136 0/8	21 6/8	21 2/8	16 0/8	5	5	Edmonton	ALB	Neil Johnson	1994	9,627
136 0/8	23 5/8	23 4/8	16 2/8	4	4	Brown County	IL	Jerry Sarver	1994	9,627
136 0/8	23 0/8	24 7/8	17 6/8	4	4	Jefferson County	IL	Charles Lusby	1994	9,627
136 0/8	22 5/8	21 6/8	16 2/8	5	6	Treasure County	MT	Jeff M. Reiter	1995	9,627
136 0/8	21 1/8	21 4/8	18 2/8	6	6	Monroe County	WI	Stefan J. Hagen	1995	9,627
136 0/8	21 5/8	21 6/8	17 0/8	5	4	De Kalb County	MO	Darren Turner	1995	9,627
136 0/8	24 2/8	23 5/8	18 1/8	4	5	Jackson County	WI	Bryan Staff	1995	9,627
136 0/8	22 3/8	22 5/8	17 6/8	5	6	Oneida County	WI	G. L. Conner	1995	9,627
136 0/8	21 2/8	21 2/8	16 2/8	5	4	Marion County	IA	Charles H. Walter	1995	9,627
136 0/8	24 1/8	23 6/8	17 6/8	5	4	Rock County	WI	Jeff Jerome	1996	9,627
136 0/8	26 0/8	26 0/8	18 2/8	4	5	Jefferson County	IA	Chad Cooper	1996	9,627
136 0/8	23 5/8	22 7/8	18 4/8	5	4	Macon County	GA	Gary Edward Campbell	1996	9,627
136 0/8	21 7/8	21 6/8	16 2/8	4	4	Clinton County	MI	Thomas E. Osborne	1996	9,627
136 0/8	19 6/8	19 7/8	15 6/8	5	5	Licking County	OH	Brian Meade	1996	9,627
136 0/8	22 6/8	22 3/8	18 3/8	4	5	Johnson County	IA	Douglas Middle	1996	9,627
136 0/8	19 3/8	20 7/8	15 6/8	6	5	Pike County	IL	Roderick Gillis	1996	9,627
136 0/8	21 3/8	22 0/8	22 3/8	6	4	Kane County	IL	Richard Hight	1997	9,627
136 0/8	22 6/8	22 3/8	20 0/8	6	7	Madison County	MT	Jim Kennedy	1997	9,627
136 0/8	22 3/8	22 4/8	22 2/8	5	5	Irion County	TX	Ronnie L. Whitt	1997	9,627
136 0/8	23 3/8	23 0/8	15 6/8	4	4	Jackson County	IN	Tony Lambert	1997	9,627
136 0/8	21 7/8	24 1/8	16 0/8	5	5	Nodaway County	MO	Mark DeMott	1997	9,627
136 0/8	19 4/8	19 3/8	14 6/8	5	5	Hendricks County	IN	Brent Cunningham	1997	9,627
136 0/8	20 0/8	20 1/8	16 4/8	5	5	Bee County	TX	Vance Meischen	1997	9,627
136 0/8	21 1/8	22 2/8	15 0/8	4	4	Pepin County	WI	Myles Keller	1997	9,627
136 0/8	20 1/8	19 0/8	15 4/8	5	5	Bexar County	TX	Deno Poulos	1998	9,627
135 7/8	23 6/8	22 2/8	16 7/8	6	8	Adams County	IL	Joe Johnson	1967	9,709
135 7/8	24 6/8	21 6/8	20 1/8	4	5	Westchester County	NY	Colin M. Pierson	1967	9,709
135 7/8	22 5/8	22 3/8	15 3/8	4	5	Brown County	IN	Junior R. Hutchings	1974	9,709
135 7/8	21 4/8	21 6/8	16 3/8	5	5	Sumner County	KS	Len Sanders	1980	9,709
135 7/8	24 6/8	24 3/8	15 5/8	5	5	Elgin	ONT	Mike Rusnak	1982	9,709
135 7/8	24 0/8	25 0/8	23 4/8	6	5	Suffolk County	NY	Richard W. Geminski	1982	9,709
135 7/8	24 1/8	23 0/8	21 1/8	4	4	Vermilion County	IL	Frank Palmer	1983	9,709
135 7/8	19 7/8	20 0/8	15 7/8	5	5	Renville County	MN	Daniel J. Scharba	1983	9,709
135 7/8	20 2/8	20 6/8	16 3/8	5	5	Duval County	TX	John Clinton Manges	1984	9,709
135 7/8	23 1/8	23 0/8	19 5/8	5	6	Monroe County	OH	Mark A. Landefeld	1984	9,709
135 7/8	22 4/8	22 2/8	18 3/8	4	4	Sauk County	WI	Dan Bauer	1985	9,709
135 7/8	21 5/8	21 5/8	14 6/8	8	8	Bibb County	GA	Robbie Whalen	1986	9,709
135 7/8	23 2/8	23 2/8	18 7/8	5	4	Burke County	GA	O. Jack Barrett, Jr.	1986	9,709
135 7/8	21 0/8	21 3/8	17 5/8	5	5	Greene County	OH	Charles W. Shoemaker	1986	9,709
135 7/8	25 5/8	26 5/8	18 7/8	3	3	Effingham County	IL	Don Thoele	1987	9,709
135 7/8	22 3/8	22 6/8	20 5/8	5	5	La Salle County	TX	Dr. F. D. Elias	1987	9,709
135 7/8	20 3/8	20 4/8	15 1/8	5	5	Greene County	IN	Jan J. Armour	1987	9,709

WHITETAIL DEER (TYPICAL ANTLERS)

Minimum Score 125   Continued

SCORE	LENGTH OF MAIN BEAM R / L	INSIDE SPREAD	NUMBER OF POINTS R / L		AREA	STATE/ PROVINCE	HUNTER'S NAME	DATE	RANK
135 7/8	21 5/8 / 24 1/8	17 3/8	8	6	La Salle County	IL	Winston Parkinson	1987	9,709
135 7/8	21 0/8 / 22 2/8	16 7/8	4	4	Henry County	VA	Mike Weaver	1987	9,709
135 7/8	23 6/8 / 22 7/8	20 7/8	6	7	Jasper County	MO	Bob Lambeth	1987	9,709
135 7/8	18 4/8 / 20 0/8	19 6/8	7	5	Calgary	ALB	Dwight Liliedahl	1987	9,709
135 7/8	22 3/8 / 22 0/8	16 5/8	5	5	Sheboygan County	WI	Earl J. Halbach	1988	9,709
135 7/8	21 0/8 / 21 1/8	16 7/8	4	5	Todd County	MN	Don Wienhold	1988	9,709
135 7/8	22 4/8 / 23 0/8	17 4/8	5	7	Stillwater County	MT	William A. Hever, Jr.	1988	9,709
135 7/8	22 6/8 / 22 2/8	17 7/8	5	5	Meigs County	OH	Mike Reynolds	1989	9,709
135 7/8	17 4/8 / 21 4/8	16 5/8	6	5	Ringgold County	IA	Jerry Sickels	1989	9,709
135 7/8	21 5/8 / 22 2/8	15 5/8	5	5	Cumberland County	IL	Gary D. Hanley	1989	9,709
135 7/8	24 4/8 / 25 2/8	18 3/8	4	6	Langlade County	WI	Douglas L. Below	1989	9,709
135 7/8	21 5/8 / 21 7/8	17 5/8	4	4	Dane County	WI	Ed Emberson	1989	9,709
135 7/8	21 1/8 / 20 7/8	15 5/8	5	5	Muskogee County	OK	Gary L. Peterson	1989	9,709
135 7/8	21 7/8 / 22 0/8	20 1/8	6	7	Marshall County	OK	Joel A. Trammell	1989	9,709
135 7/8	22 4/8 / 23 2/8	19 5/8	4	4	Sagadahoc County	ME	Robert Harper	1990	9,709
135 7/8	22 4/8 / 23 2/8	16 7/8	4	4	Cortland County	NY	Charles Streeter	1990	9,709
135 7/8	21 3/8 / 21 2/8	15 7/8	5	5	Kenosha County	WI	Jeffery A. Kloet	1990	9,709
135 7/8	24 3/8 / 22 6/8	17 7/8	4	4	Shawano County	WI	Brett A. Olson	1990	9,709
135 7/8	21 3/8 / 22 6/8	18 5/8	4	5	Shelby County	IL	Mel J. Johnson	1990	9,709
135 7/8	22 5/8 / 22 7/8	18 7/8	4	4	Marathon County	WI	Terry Nikolai	1991	9,709
135 7/8	22 1/8 / 20 6/8	13 7/8	5	5	Waukesha County	WI	Richard Anderson	1991	9,709
135 7/8	20 6/8 / 21 1/8	16 1/8	5	5	Lorain County	OH	Clyde E. Strader	1991	9,709
135 7/8	23 3/8 / 23 2/8	16 1/8	5	5	Woodford County	IL	Dan Schoolman	1991	9,709
135 7/8	22 1/8 / 22 0/8	19 1/8	5	4	Winnebago County	IL	James R. Petersen	1991	9,709
135 7/8	23 1/8 / 21 5/8	15 0/8	6	6	Sauk County	WI	Russell T. Reimer	1991	9,709
135 7/8	23 4/8 / 22 4/8	21 5/8	5	5	Whiteside County	IL	Art Heinze	1991	9,709
135 7/8	24 6/8 / 23 4/8	21 1/8	4	5	St. Louis County	MO	Scott Leuthauser	1992	9,709
135 7/8	24 6/8 / 23 7/8	19 5/8	4	4	Iroquois County	IL	Delbert C. Street	1992	9,709
135 7/8	21 6/8 / 23 2/8	17 4/8	6	7	Lee County	IA	Bruce W. Geltz	1992	9,709
135 7/8	24 7/8 / 24 7/8	17 3/8	6	5	Ashtabula County	OH	Mark R. Johnson	1992	9,709
135 7/8	20 5/8 / 20 5/8	15 3/8	5	5	Dane County	WI	Jeff R. Lange	1992	9,709
135 7/8	23 0/8 / 25 2/8	19 1/8	8	5	Monroe County	MO	James O. McMurdo	1992	9,709
135 7/8	22 3/8 / 23 6/8	18 5/8	5	5	St. Croix County	WI	Robert J. Sobieck	1993	9,709
135 7/8	22 1/8 / 22 0/8	19 5/8	6	5	Buffalo County	WI	Lynn R. Moeller	1993	9,709
135 7/8	20 4/8 / 20 6/8	16 1/8	5	5	Harris County	TX	Tim Dihman	1993	9,709
135 7/8	23 6/8 / 23 6/8	18 7/8	4	4	Bolivar County	MS	Fred Cooke III	1993	9,709
135 7/8	26 0/8 / 27 0/8	22 4/8	7	5	Coshocton County	OH	David Miktuk	1993	9,709
135 7/8	23 3/8 / 22 7/8	17 1/8	6	5	Menard County	IL	Roger Bramer II	1993	9,709
135 7/8	23 2/8 / 22 2/8	16 1/8	4	4	Jefferson County	OH	Gregory A. Capers	1993	9,709
135 7/8	21 6/8 / 21 4/8	16 3/8	5	5	Mercer County	IL	Cindy Short-Nelson	1993	9,709
135 7/8	21 6/8 / 21 2/8	16 4/8	6	6	West Feliciana Parish	LA	James "Jay" W. McCleary, Jr.	1993	9,709
135 7/8	20 1/8 / 20 1/8	14 3/8	6	5	Brule County	SD	Dennis Carlson	1993	9,709
135 7/8	23 3/8 / 23 5/8	18 3/8	4	4	Washington County	MS	Bobby R. Woods	1993	9,709
135 7/8	23 0/8 / 21 7/8	14 2/8	6	7	Wright County	MN	James Robert Dean	1994	9,709
135 7/8	21 0/8 / 21 0/8	18 7/8	6	5	Hennepin County	MN	Tad Morris	1994	9,709
135 7/8	23 0/8 / 22 3/8	18 3/8	5	5	Ogle County	IL	Mike Groom	1994	9,709
135 7/8	21 1/8 / 21 4/8	18 0/8	5	5	Delaware County	OK	Darren Rich	1994	9,709
135 7/8	21 3/8 / 21 4/8	17 5/8	5	5	Ozaukee County	WI	Daniel J. Weyker	1994	9,709
135 7/8	24 2/8 / 24 6/8	19 7/8	6	6	Oneida County	WI	Gary Knapp	1995	9,709
135 7/8	23 4/8 / 23 3/8	17 3/8	5	4	Nemaha County	KS	Kelly R. Girton	1995	9,709
135 7/8	22 4/8 / 23 0/8	15 3/8	5	5	Butler County	KS	David Kuttler, Jr.	1995	9,709
135 7/8	23 5/8 / 23 3/8	16 1/8	4	4	Adams County	OH	Jeffery S. Frieszell	1995	9,709
135 7/8	20 6/8 / 21 3/8	19 7/8	5	6	Cook County	IL	Kenneth S. Koeneman	1996	9,709
135 7/8	22 4/8 / 22 1/8	19 3/8	5	5	Ogle County	IL	Jeff M. Blascoe	1996	9,709
135 7/8	20 1/8 / 19 3/8	14 7/8	5	5	Gallatin County	KY	Harry Due	1996	9,709
135 7/8	22 1/8 / 20 5/8	19 1/8	5	5	Dorchester County	MD	Kevin Meagher, Sr.	1996	9,709
135 7/8	23 2/8 / 23 2/8	16 6/8	4	5	Crawford County	WI	Bob Woodhouse	1996	9,709
135 7/8	21 4/8 / 21 5/8	17 7/8	4	5	De Witt County	IL	Bob Black	1996	9,709
135 7/8	21 7/8 / 22 4/8	16 1/8	5	6	Ramsey County	MN	Nicholas Arrigo	1996	9,709
135 7/8	23 3/8 / 23 1/8	18 5/8	4	5	Minnehaha County	SD	Casey Weisser	1996	9,709
135 7/8	24 0/8 / 24 5/8	16 7/8	5	5	Harrison County	KY	John A. White	1997	9,709
135 7/8	22 6/8 / 21 3/8	18 3/8	5	5	Strafford County	NH	Scott Miller	1997	9,709
135 7/8	21 5/8 / 22 5/8	16 1/8	4	5	Pierce County	WI	Andrew P. Callow	1997	9,709
135 7/8	21 5/8 / 20 5/8	15 5/8	5	5	DeKalb County	IL	James V. Woodward	1997	9,709
135 7/8	23 6/8 / 23 6/8	18 1/8	5	5	Ohio County	KY	Robbie Hinton	1997	9,709
135 7/8	24 2/8 / 22 1/8	17 5/8	4	5	Boone County	MO	Gene Simmerman	1997	9,709
135 7/8	23 7/8 / 24 1/8	18 5/8	5	5	Henry County	VA	Mike Weaver	1997	9,709
135 7/8	20 6/8 / 21 1/8	18 3/8	5	5	Pierce County	WI	Jeffrey Schoeder	1997	9,709
135 7/8	22 1/8 / 22 2/8	17 3/8	4	4	Webster County	IA	Edward E. Ulicki	1997	9,709
135 7/8	25 2/8 / 24 5/8	20 1/8	4	4	Bent County	CO	Kurt W. Keskimaki	1997	9,709
135 7/8	24 6/8 / 24 6/8	18 1/8	8	6	Clayton County	IA	Scott Butters	1997	9,709
135 7/8	23 3/8 / 24 6/8	20 5/8	5	5	La Salle County	TX	Brad C. Bryant	1997	9,709
135 6/8	24 4/8 / 22 7/8	19 2/8	5	5	Winnebago County	IL	Edward Fuller	1963	9,798
135 6/8	22 6/8 / 23 2/8	20 6/8	4	4	Shawano County	WI	Darryl Erdman	1968	9,798
135 6/8	25 5/8 / 24 4/8	19 7/8	6	4	Knox County	IL	Fred E. Miller	1968	9,798
135 6/8	22 3/8 / 22 5/8	15 2/8	6	7	Dodge County	MN	Bradley Blanchard	1973	9,798
135 6/8	24 0/8 / 24 0/8	20 2/8	5	5	Parke County	IN	Charles Loomis	1978	9,798
135 6/8	23 0/8 / 24 1/8	16 0/8	4	4	Pine County	MN	Paul L. Videen	1979	9,798

WHITETAIL DEER (TYPICAL ANTLERS)

Minimum Score 125 — Continued

SCORE	LENGTH OF MAIN BEAM R	LENGTH OF MAIN BEAM L	INSIDE SPREAD	NUMBER OF POINTS R	NUMBER OF POINTS L	AREA	STATE/ PROVINCE	HUNTER'S NAME	DATE	RANK
135 6/8	20 7/8	22 7/8	15 0/8	6	6	Fayette County	GA	Tom Mann, Jr.	1980	9,798
135 6/8	20 2/8	20 2/8	16 0/8	5	5	Fulton County	IN	James L. Kerr	1981	9,798
135 6/8	22 0/8	23 0/8	15 2/8	5	6	Ozark County	MO	Bruce Webb	1981	9,798
135 6/8	20 3/8	21 0/8	15 2/8	5	5	Dubuque County	IA	Harry Bries	1982	9,798
135 6/8	22 5/8	21 1/8	15 6/8	5	5	Saline County	KS	Kenneth D. Sterling	1982	9,798
135 6/8	23 0/8	22 0/8	18 0/8	5	5	Shawano County	WI	Ron Vander Kelen	1982	9,798
135 6/8	22 1/8	22 5/8	16 6/8	5	5	Tompkins County	NY	Michael R. Deschamps	1982	9,798
135 6/8	21 4/8	21 6/8	14 2/8	4	4	Watonwan County	MN	Brad Nielsen	1984	9,798
135 6/8	21 1/8	21 2/8	15 3/8	7	6	Pope County	IL	Roy L. Arnold	1984	9,798
135 6/8	21 5/8	22 4/8	16 4/8	5	4	Oldham County	KY	Garnett B. Morgan, Jr.	1985	9,798
135 6/8	23 4/8	23 2/8	19 4/8	6	6	Allamakee County	IA	Mark E. Walleser	1985	9,798
135 6/8	25 1/8	26 3/8	19 4/8	4	4	Clarion County	PA	Gary D. Miller	1986	9,798
135 6/8	22 2/8	21 5/8	16 0/8	4	4	Crawford County	WI	James Yatzeck	1986	9,798
135 6/8	22 1/8	21 1/8	17 0/8	5	6	Warrick County	IN	Jim H. Sullenger	1987	9,798
135 6/8	22 3/8	22 4/8	17 6/8	5	5	Jackson County	MI	Garland Paul Ring	1988	9,798
135 6/8	19 5/8	19 2/8	15 4/8	5	5	Waukesha County	WI	Brian Tweeden	1988	9,798
135 6/8	21 0/8	21 7/8	17 6/8	4	5	Madison County	IA	Chuck Jordan	1988	9,798
135 6/8	21 6/8	21 4/8	16 2/8	6	7	Shelby County	MO	Jim Belt	1989	9,798
135 6/8	23 0/8	23 2/8	21 2/8	5	5	Will County	IL	Terry Adams	1989	9,798
135 6/8	20 7/8	21 1/8	16 4/8	5	5	Kankakee County	IL	Paul Karwoski	1989	9,798
135 6/8	25 5/8	25 4/8	19 6/8	5	5	Washington County	MD	Larry Stouffer	1989	9,798
135 6/8	23 3/8	23 2/8	16 6/8	5	4	Rockingham County	NH	Dana Standley	1990	9,798
135 6/8	23 4/8	24 6/8	15 4/8	4	5	Dakota County	MN	Mike Nowack	1990	9,798
135 6/8	24 4/8	23 5/8	19 7/8	6	6	Hart County	KY	Larry Baldwin	1990	9,798
135 6/8	25 1/8	24 6/8	17 2/8	4	4	Jackson County	OH	Keith Kauk	1990	9,798
135 6/8	23 7/8	22 6/8	18 0/8	5	5	Marshall County	IN	Michael A. Splix	1990	9,798
135 6/8	20 1/8	20 5/8	16 0/8	5	5	La Salle County	IL	John Liles	1990	9,798
135 6/8	22 5/8	21 7/8	15 6/8	4	4	Douglas County	NE	Jeff Christoffersen	1991	9,798
135 6/8	21 5/8	21 2/8	14 4/8	5	4	Buffalo County	WI	Curt Rotering	1991	9,798
135 6/8	20 5/8	19 7/8	16 4/8	5	6	Washburn County	WI	Mike Barrett	1991	9,798
135 6/8	22 2/8	21 2/8	16 2/8	5	6	Clay County	IN	Ted Froderman	1991	9,798
135 6/8	20 4/8	20 5/8	12 4/8	6	6	Hamilton County	OH	Kim S. Brockhoff	1991	9,798
135 6/8	23 2/8	22 6/8	18 0/8	5	5	Hampshire County	MA	Steve Drumm	1991	9,798
135 6/8	23 3/8	23 3/8	18 2/8	6	4	Chippewa County	WI	Alan Kohls	1991	9,798
135 6/8	24 3/8	25 4/8	20 0/8	8	6	Mahaska County	IA	Kelly Gordon	1991	9,798
135 6/8	23 6/8	23 4/8	16 2/8	4	5	Stokes County	NC	Jonathan Lee Brewer	1992	9,798
135 6/8	24 1/8	24 5/8	20 4/8	4	4	Lenawee County	MI	Todd S. Osborne	1992	9,798
135 6/8	21 4/8	23 1/8	17 0/8	5	5	La Crosse County	WI	Tim Cavadini	1992	9,798
135 6/8	22 1/8	22 5/8	17 6/8	4	4	Ottawa County	KS	D. Charles Towner	1992	9,798
135 6/8	22 6/8	22 0/8	17 4/8	4	5	Ogle County	IL	Marty R. Hobby	1992	9,798
135 6/8	25 0/8	26 1/8	15 3/8	6	5	Madison County	IL	Richard Kurtzeborn	1992	9,798
135 6/8	25 7/8	24 4/8	21 2/8	5	8	La Salle County	TX	Danny J. Carter	1992	9,798
135 6/8	23 6/8	24 4/8	18 4/8	4	4	Union County	KY	Dennis Padgett	1992	9,798
135 6/8	23 7/8	24 1/8	15 0/8	4	4	Bollinger County	MO	Andie McClain	1992	9,798
135 6/8	21 3/8	21 1/8	15 4/8	5	5	Juneau County	WI	Gary W. Pope	1993	9,798
135 6/8	20 0/8	21 1/8	15 2/8	5	5	Grundy County	MO	Tommy Graham	1993	9,798
135 6/8	22 0/8	22 6/8	18 4/8	5	5	Dodge County	WI	Robert C. Haseleu	1993	9,798
135 6/8	23 0/8	22 1/8	16 6/8	5	5	Buffalo County	WI	Walt Legge	1993	9,798
135 6/8	21 1/8	22 2/8	15 2/8	5	5	Clinton County	MO	Steve E. "Rusty" Chaney	1993	9,798
135 6/8	23 3/8	25 0/8	16 4/8	4	5	Bates County	MO	Michael W. Sheppard	1993	9,798
135 6/8	21 6/8	22 0/8	13 6/8	5	5	La Salle County	TX	Bobby Flanagan	1993	9,798
135 6/8	22 0/8	22 3/8	16 2/8	5	5	Irion County	TX	Rita Jean Whitt	1994	9,798
135 6/8	21 1/8	21 2/8	17 2/8	4	4	Sheboygan County	WI	Andy Pevonka	1994	9,798
135 6/8	24 7/8	24 4/8	18 3/8	6	4	Wyoming County	WV	Walter Lane, Jr.	1994	9,798
135 6/8	23 1/8	23 5/8	16 2/8	5	5	Waupaca County	WI	Howard H. Bestul	1994	9,798
135 6/8	22 4/8	22 3/8	15 2/8	5	6	Autauga County	AL	Kenny Diaz	1994	9,798
135 6/8	22 2/8	20 6/8	15 4/8	7	6	Waupaca County	WI	Jeff S. Gagnow	1994	9,798
135 6/8	23 3/8	21 4/8	18 4/8	4	4	Crawford County	WI	Bill F. McCann	1994	9,798
135 6/8	23 3/8	24 3/8	18 2/8	4	4	Walworth County	WI	James W. Boyd	1994	9,798
135 6/8	24 5/8	26 3/8	20 4/8	3	4	Jackson County	MI	Douglas I. Weeks	1994	9,798
135 6/8	25 5/8	24 2/8	15 4/8	4	5	Comanche County	KS	Roger Shelley	1994	9,798
135 6/8	23 6/8	24 1/8	19 6/8	6	4	Grant County	WI	Brian Nichols	1994	9,798
135 6/8	20 3/8	21 0/8	15 2/8	5	5	Adams County	WI	David R. Ehlke	1995	9,798
135 6/8	22 3/8	22 1/8	20 3/8	6	5	Sangamon County	IL	Bill Hood	1995	9,798
135 6/8	20 6/8	20 5/8	15 2/8	5	5	Menominee County	MI	Ken Marklein	1995	9,798
135 6/8	20 6/8	21 3/8	19 2/8	5	5	Adams County	WI	Michael E. Rykiel	1995	9,798
135 6/8	22 3/8	23 1/8	18 0/8	5	5	Rock County	WI	Ricky Greene	1995	9,798
135 6/8	22 4/8	22 0/8	15 4/8	5	5	Hardin County	KY	James R. Riley	1995	9,798
135 6/8	21 6/8	21 0/8	19 4/8	5	6	Walsh County	ND	Kent Trontvet	1996	9,798
135 6/8	24 6/8	24 1/8	18 6/8	5	4	Westchester County	NY	John Lewis	1996	9,798
135 6/8	23 4/8	24 3/8	20 0/8	4	4	Fulton County	IL	Michael S. Hinds	1996	9,798
135 6/8	24 4/8	24 0/8	22 2/8	4	4	Macoupin County	IL	Donald L. Sherwood	1996	9,798
135 6/8	21 5/8	22 0/8	18 2/8	4	5	DeKalb County	IL	Richard W. Haseman	1996	9,798
135 6/8	25 1/8	26 0/8	17 5/8	5	4	Lee County	GA	Stoney Grayson	1997	9,798
135 6/8	22 6/8	22 4/8	15 6/8	5	5	Winneshiek County	IA	Andy Ludeking	1997	9,798
135 6/8	23 2/8	22 7/8	19 4/8	5	6	Jasper County	IL	Brian Collins	1997	9,798
135 6/8	21 3/8	21 2/8	14 0/8	5	6	Winona County	MN	John W. Zahrte	1997	9,798
135 6/8	26 0/8	23 7/8	19 0/8	4	5	Fremont County	IA	Dan Spoelman	1997	9,798

WHITETAIL DEER (TYPICAL ANTLERS)

Minimum Score 125 Continued

SCORE	LENGTH OF MAIN BEAM R / L	INSIDE SPREAD	NUMBER OF POINTS R / L		AREA	STATE/ PROVINCE	HUNTER'S NAME	DATE	RANK
135 6/8	24 2/8	24 0/8	16 2/8	7	5	Jefferson County	MO	John Haaser	1997	9,798
135 6/8	23 2/8	24 7/8	17 2/8	4	4	Cattaraugus County	NY	Michael A. Pochron	1997	9,798
135 6/8	26 0/8	27 3/8	18 2/8	4	4	Vernon County	WI	Dan Starr	1997	9,798
135 6/8	21 6/8	22 1/8	19 0/8	4	5	Henry County	IL	Bradley De May	1997	9,798
135 6/8	21 0/8	20 3/8	14 6/8	5	6	Dearborn County	IN	Ken Spears	1997	9,798
135 6/8	23 2/8	24 1/8	18 6/8	4	4	Musselshell County	MT	Art Smith	1998	9,798
135 6/8	23 7/8	24 1/8	20 4/8	5	5	Sauk County	WI	Jeremy P. Pickarts	1998	9,798
135 6/8	20 2/8	20 0/8	18 2/8	6	5	Adams County	IL	Raymond L. Voss	1998	9,798
135 5/8	21 4/8	20 0/8	16 1/8	5	5	Sheboygan County	WI	Earl Uhl	1960	9,890
135 5/8	22 7/8	21 6/8	21 1/8	4	4	Union County	KY	Randy Joe Duncan	1965	9,890
135 5/8	22 1/8	22 1/8	19 3/8	5	5	Ringgold County	IA	William K. Seitz	1973	9,890
135 5/8	23 4/8	23 2/8	14 7/8	4	4	Jasper County	IN	Gary L. Hepler	1980	9,890
135 5/8	23 7/8	22 6/8	14 3/8	5	5	Allegheny County	PA	John Camillo	1980	9,890
135 5/8	23 5/8	21 2/8	17 5/8	4	5	Winona County	MN	Hank Scharmach	1981	9,890
135 5/8	22 6/8	22 0/8	18 3/8	4	4	Dodge County	MN	Robert Rhodes, Jr.	1982	9,890
135 5/8	21 4/8	21 4/8	16 5/8	5	5	Adams County	IN	Randy Johnson	1983	9,890
135 5/8	22 1/8	23 6/8	19 1/8	6	4	Montgomery County	IN	Derrick W. Kidd	1983	9,890
135 5/8	22 4/8	23 2/8	14 0/8	4	7	Anderson County	KS	Steve Spangler	1983	9,890
135 5/8	22 6/8	23 7/8	20 5/8	4	4	Jones County	IA	Donald Stuefen	1984	9,890
135 5/8	24 2/8	23 2/8	17 3/8	4	4	Buffalo County	WI	Edward Brannen	1984	9,890
135 5/8	21 3/8	22 2/8	19 7/8	4	4	Tama County	IA	Clyde Bearden	1985	9,890
135 5/8	23 7/8	25 4/8	21 5/8	4	4	Charles Mix County	SD	Frank Mingo	1985	9,890
135 5/8	22 1/8	22 2/8	17 7/8	4	4	Price County	WI	Leonard J. Stein	1985	9,890
135 5/8	19 7/8	20 1/8	15 7/8	7	6	Morrison County	MN	Kevin Hagstron	1986	9,890
135 5/8	23 0/8	24 2/8	16 3/8	5	5	Delaware County	PA	Earl McSorley	1986	9,890
135 5/8	22 2/8	22 2/8	15 7/8	4	5	Texas County	OK	Max Crocker	1986	9,890
135 5/8	19 6/8	19 3/8	15 7/8	5	4	Brown County	KS	Robert L. Hodge	1986	9,890
135 5/8	23 2/8	23 4/8	16 5/8	4	4	Price County	WI	Bill Fischer	1987	9,890
135 5/8	19 5/8	19 0/8	13 4/8	6	6	Pope County	IL	John F. Perso	1987	9,890
135 5/8	21 6/8	21 2/8	17 1/8	5	5	Madison County	IL	Jon Schmalz	1987	9,890
135 5/8	22 6/8	23 0/8	19 0/8	6	4	Crawford County	WI	Robert McCann	1987	9,890
135 5/8	23 0/8	22 1/8	18 5/8	5	6	Wabash County	IN	Tim Roberts	1987	9,890
135 5/8	23 0/8	22 2/8	21 7/8	4	5	Suffolk County	NY	Bret Jayne	1987	9,890
135 5/8	23 3/8	23 3/8	17 5/8	6	5	Cass County	IN	Roger Whitehead	1988	9,890
135 5/8	22 6/8	22 6/8	18 5/8	5	4	Steuben County	NY	John E. Steen, Sr.	1988	9,890
135 5/8	21 2/8	21 6/8	14 7/8	5	5	Kalamazoo County	MI	Mike Ovens	1988	9,890
135 5/8	22 3/8	22 2/8	19 1/8	4	4	Phillips County	KS	Monty Mai	1988	9,890
135 5/8	24 3/8	24 1/8	17 1/8	4	4	Guernsey County	OH	Thomas J. Hentrick	1989	9,890
135 5/8	22 1/8	23 1/8	20 7/8	5	5	Sharkey County	MS	Terry Murrell	1990	9,890
135 5/8	23 2/8	22 6/8	17 7/8	6	5	Ozaukee County	WI	Raymond Schultz	1990	9,890
135 5/8	21 4/8	21 4/8	16 6/8	6	6	Winona County	MN	Dan Pettersen	1990	9,890
135 5/8	23 2/8	23 4/8	17 3/8	4	4	Richland County	IL	Terry L. Mehl	1990	9,890
135 5/8	23 1/8	24 0/8	16 5/8	4	5	Forest County	WI	Elmer H. Van Gheem	1991	9,890
135 5/8	23 1/8	23 0/8	18 5/8	4	4	Coshocton County	OH	Gene Mathias	1991	9,890
135 5/8	23 0/8	22 6/8	16 7/8	4	4	Vermilion County	IL	Bob Gravely	1991	9,890
135 5/8	23 3/8	23 2/8	16 5/8	5	5	Dearborn County	IN	Tom Koch	1991	9,890
135 5/8	20 5/8	20 2/8	16 1/8	5	5	Spokane County	WA	Ronald J. Olmstead	1991	9,890
135 5/8	24 5/8	23 6/8	15 3/8	5	4	Kleberg County	TX	Dr. Terry W. Brandt	1991	9,890
135 5/8	22 1/8	22 6/8	16 1/8	6	4	Ravalli County	MT	Tom Wetherby	1992	9,890
135 5/8	22 4/8	22 0/8	12 7/8	5	5	Crawford County	AR	Tim Clemmons	1992	9,890
135 5/8	25 0/8	24 4/8	19 3/8	5	5	Macoupin County	IL	Dallas Ward	1992	9,890
135 5/8	22 6/8	23 0/8	19 7/8	4	4	Douglas County	WI	Kenneth G. Adams	1992	9,890
135 5/8	21 7/8	20 3/8	19 7/8	5	5	Winnebago County	IL	Tom Kingsbury	1992	9,890
135 5/8	24 0/8	23 2/8	17 1/8	5	5	Creek County	OK	Mark Stephens	1992	9,890
135 5/8	24 5/8	24 5/8	18 3/8	4	4	Niagara	ONT	Harry Walker	1992	9,890
135 5/8	23 5/8	22 4/8	16 5/8	5	5	Vernon County	WI	Gene Taylor	1993	9,890
135 5/8	22 7/8	22 4/8	16 7/8	4	4	Parke County	IN	Gary Lasure	1993	9,890
135 5/8	22 4/8	21 6/8	15 1/8	5	5	Kerr County	TX	Ronald G. Ralston	1993	9,890
135 5/8	23 4/8	23 5/8	17 3/8	4	4	Westchester County	NY	Stephen L. Cook	1993	9,890
135 5/8	22 1/8	21 6/8	18 3/8	5	6	Ravalli County	MT	Don Parsons	1993	9,890
135 5/8	22 0/8	22 3/8	15 6/8	6	5	Christian County	KY	Tom Patterson	1994	9,890
135 5/8	23 1/8	23 5/8	17 6/8	4	5	Norman County	MN	John A. Proznik	1994	9,890
135 5/8	23 3/8	23 1/8	20 3/8	5	5	Clay County	MO	Joel Kimrey	1994	9,890
135 5/8	25 1/8	25 2/8	18 4/8	5	10	Miami County	IN	Jeremy Crowder	1994	9,890
135 5/8	21 5/8	22 2/8	15 0/8	6	5	Green County	WI	Claude Leach	1994	9,890
135 5/8	23 6/8	23 3/8	15 7/8	5	5	Kenosha County	WI	Greg J. Gilliland	1994	9,890
135 5/8	24 3/8	24 0/8	20 3/8	6	5	Warren County	OH	Jim Agnew	1994	9,890
135 5/8	22 5/8	22 4/8	18 5/8	5	5	Belknap County	NH	Mark Lachapelle	1995	9,890
135 5/8	23 5/8	24 0/8	16 5/8	4	5	Allegan County	MI	Kevin R. Mohrland	1995	9,890
135 5/8	21 6/8	22 3/8	18 3/8	5	5	Mercer County	NJ	Jeffrey E. Tarrant	1995	9,890
135 5/8	22 5/8	22 4/8	18 3/8	4	4	Green County	WI	Kyle Allen	1995	9,890
135 5/8	18 6/8	19 4/8	15 5/8	6	5	Allegan County	MI	Russell A. Bertch	1995	9,890
135 5/8	23 6/8	23 2/8	19 4/8	5	6	Shawnee County	KS	Michael Troth	1995	9,890
135 5/8	22 3/8	22 1/8	19 1/8	4	4	Sawyer County	WI	Greg Biskup	1996	9,890
135 5/8	21 4/8	21 2/8	19 1/8	5	5	Chautauqua County	NY	Gale Sauer	1996	9,890
135 5/8	22 5/8	22 1/8	16 5/8	5	5	Adair County	MO	Charles M. Zeman	1996	9,890
135 5/8	25 0/8	26 7/8	18 1/8	4	4	Union County	NC	Albert Austin Gaddy	1996	9,890
135 5/8	20 6/8	19 7/8	18 0/8	5	7	Calgary	ALB	Dave Browne	1997	9,890

WHITETAIL DEER (TYPICAL ANTLERS)

Minimum Score 125

SCORE	LENGTH OF MAIN BEAM R	LENGTH OF MAIN BEAM L	INSIDE SPREAD	NUMBER OF POINTS R	NUMBER OF POINTS L	AREA	STATE/ PROVINCE	HUNTER'S NAME	DATE	RANK
135 5/8	23 3/8	22 5/8	17 3/8	5	6	Waukesha County	WI	John M. Plese	1997	9,890
135 5/8	22 6/8	21 5/8	21 7/8	4	4	Warren County	NJ	Robert L. Armstrong	1997	9,890
135 5/8	23 0/8	23 6/8	19 3/8	4	4	Putnam County	IN	Randy Kennedy	1997	9,890
135 5/8	24 4/8	23 6/8	19 1/8	6	4	Sanders County	MT	Donald S. Dvoroznak	1998	9,890
135 4/8	21 0/8	23 0/8	18 6/8	6	5	Mitchell County	IA	Arthur Cepeda	1962	9,964
135 4/8	23 4/8	23 4/8	18 6/8	4	4	Dodge County	WI	Daniel J. Rozek	1966	9,964
135 4/8	21 6/8	21 4/8	19 4/8	5	5	Mower County	MN	Arthur McKenzie	1972	9,964
135 4/8	21 3/8	23 0/8	18 0/8	5	5	Ripley County	IN	G. Fred Asbell	1973	9,964
135 4/8	20 5/8	20 5/8	13 2/8	5	5	Dickinson County	MI	Dave Bath	1973	9,964
135 4/8	23 0/8	23 6/8	18 0/8	5	5	Lyon County	KY	Kenneth McKay	1973	9,964
135 4/8	21 7/8	21 6/8	18 0/8	5	5	Mower County	MN	Clark Gallup	1975	9,964
135 4/8	22 7/8	22 6/8	19 0/8	6	5	Pittsburg County	OK	Bill Nelson	1977	9,964
135 4/8	23 4/8	23 2/8	17 3/8	5	4	Lincoln County	SD	Merle A. Henry	1980	9,964
135 4/8	21 3/8	22 2/8	16 6/8	5	4	Lincoln County	SD	Eldon D. Hagen	1981	9,964
135 4/8	19 0/8	19 0/8	14 3/8	6	8	Lee County	IA	Glenn E. Wagner	1981	9,964
135 4/8	22 5/8	22 1/8	14 6/8	5	5	Richland County	WI	Terry Yanske	1982	9,964
135 4/8	24 3/8	25 7/8	18 4/8	5	4	Freeborn County	MN	Richard Rippentrap	1982	9,964
135 4/8	25 2/8	23 3/8	19 3/8	5	6	Mercer County	IL	David McCaw	1983	9,964
135 4/8	22 0/8	22 4/8	14 3/8	7	6	Adams County	WI	David A. Schmitt	1984	9,964
135 4/8	25 0/8	20 5/8	18 0/8	5	6	Tazewell County	IL	Darrell A Lee	1984	9,964
135 4/8	23 1/8	22 5/8	17 4/8	5	5	Muskegon County	MI	R. Lawrence Meyers	1985	9,964
135 4/8	22 5/8	22 5/8	19 0/8	4	6	Meeker County	MN	Dan Winter	1986	9,964
135 4/8	23 0/8	23 1/8	16 2/8	5	5	Dane County	WI	Dave H. Klaas	1986	9,964
135 4/8	22 1/8	22 4/8	17 5/8	5	6	Breckinridge County	KY	Steve Drake	1986	9,964
135 4/8	21 4/8	23 1/8	18 2/8	5	6	Wright County	MN	Ed Rudenburg	1987	9,964
135 4/8	24 6/8	24 7/8	18 2/8	4	4	Pope County	MN	David A. Thompson	1987	9,964
135 4/8	24 2/8	23 6/8	17 4/8	4	4	Pulaski County	IL	Keith Wilson	1988	9,964
135 4/8	22 0/8	21 4/8	15 4/8	5	8	Jefferson County	IN	Roman C.E. Lawson	1988	9,964
135 4/8	22 7/8	23 3/8	15 6/8	4	4	Leavenworth County	KS	Richard L. Jackson	1988	9,964
135 4/8	23 1/8	23 2/8	18 0/8	4	4	Dunn County	WI	Joseph Gessner	1989	9,964
135 4/8	22 1/8	21 5/8	16 0/8	5	5	Dallas County	IA	Duane Albrecht	1989	9,964
135 4/8	22 3/8	24 1/8	17 5/8	4	6	Fayette County	IL	Jeff Fulk	1989	9,964
135 4/8	24 4/8	25 4/8	19 0/8	5	5	Suffolk County	NY	John Kowalski	1989	9,964
135 4/8	22 1/8	23 6/8	17 6/8	4	4	Buffalo County	WI	Robyn Lowenhagen	1990	9,964
135 4/8	21 5/8	21 7/8	18 3/8	6	5	Washington County	KS	Andy T. Bruna	1990	9,964
135 4/8	22 4/8	22 1/8	17 2/8	5	5	Waushara County	WI	Lewis J. Lewis	1990	9,964
135 4/8	21 4/8	21 3/8	16 2/8	5	6	Woodbury County	IA	Terry Guffy	1990	9,964
135 4/8	22 0/8	22 2/8	18 4/8	6	6	Wayne County	IA	Andy Merritt	1990	9,964
135 4/8	21 7/8	22 1/8	18 6/8	4	4	Boone County	IA	Bill Wiebe	1990	9,964
135 4/8	21 1/8	20 7/8	16 2/8	5	5	Jim Wells County	TX	Gary G. McKinny	1990	9,964
135 4/8	20 5/8	19 4/8	15 0/8	5	5	Columbia County	WA	Lyle C. Laughery	1991	9,964
135 4/8	21 4/8	20 5/8	16 6/8	5	5	Dodge County	MN	Mark Symes	1991	9,964
135 4/8	23 3/8	23 0/8	18 4/8	5	9	Madison County	IA	David Falke	1991	9,964
135 4/8	20 6/8	21 2/8	15 6/8	5	5	Walworth County	WI	Chuck Palmer	1991	9,964
135 4/8	21 7/8	21 2/8	17 2/8	5	5	McMullen County	TX	Jerry B. Bogle	1991	9,964
135 4/8	22 3/8	22 2/8	19 0/8	5	5	Ferry County	WA	David D. Gillespie	1991	9,964
135 4/8	23 6/8	23 2/8	19 4/8	5	5	La Salle County	TX	Howard Scott Reynolds	1991	9,964
135 4/8	24 0/8	22 4/8	17 0/8	4	5	Iron County	WI	James Pagel	1992	9,964
135 4/8	20 4/8	20 5/8	17 0/8	4	4	Livingston County	NY	Edwin W. Candie	1992	9,964
135 4/8	22 3/8	23 4/8	19 2/8	4	4	Westchester County	NY	Larry R. Bertuccelli	1992	9,964
135 4/8	23 4/8	23 3/8	19 6/8	4	4	Wayne County	MO	Donald P. Roper	1992	9,964
135 4/8	23 4/8	23 3/8	18 2/8	4	4	Ransom County	ND	Steve Kleefeld	1993	9,964
135 4/8	23 6/8	22 2/8	20 0/8	5	4	Albemarle County	VA	Herbert T. Brown	1993	9,964
135 4/8	24 6/8	23 2/8	16 6/8	4	5	Harrison County	IA	Mark Shamblen	1993	9,964
135 4/8	25 5/8	24 1/8	22 5/8	5	4	McMullen County	TX	Peter Swenson	1993	9,964
135 4/8	22 4/8	23 0/8	14 7/8	6	5	Cherokee County	OK	Stanley McKinney	1993	9,964
135 4/8	23 6/8	24 1/8	18 0/8	4	4	Montgomery County	IN	Larry Culley	1993	9,964
135 4/8	24 2/8	25 1/8	20 3/8	5	6	Kankakee County	IL	Frank Williams	1994	9,964
135 4/8	23 3/8	23 3/8	17 0/8	5	4	Cass County	NE	Jeffery A. Gunnels	1994	9,964
135 4/8	22 7/8	22 5/8	19 4/8	4	4	Kent County	MD	Kevin T. Payne	1994	9,964
135 4/8	21 5/8	22 7/8	17 2/8	6	6	Ozaukee County	WI	Cliff Janiak	1994	9,964
135 4/8	21 4/8	20 2/8	18 6/8	5	7	Sauk County	WI	Robert Figge	1994	9,964
135 4/8	25 0/8	25 4/8	16 3/8	4	6	Edgar County	IL	Larry Hoult	1994	9,964
135 4/8	23 6/8	23 4/8	19 0/8	4	4	Kane County	IL	Dean Ashton, Sr.	1994	9,964
135 4/8	23 0/8	22 6/8	20 0/8	4	4	Cuyahoga County	OH	Richard A. Douglas	1994	9,964
135 4/8	22 6/8	23 2/8	18 0/8	5	4	Hennepin County	MN	Jerome D. Larson	1994	9,964
135 4/8	23 0/8	23 7/8	18 2/8	7	6	Clay County	NE	David J. Hamik	1994	9,964
135 4/8	22 7/8	22 7/8	16 1/8	5	4	Marathon County	WI	Benjamin Benaszeski	1995	9,964
135 4/8	20 3/8	22 2/8	15 7/8	6	5	Burnet County	TX	Allen Spelce	1995	9,964
135 4/8	22 4/8	24 0/8	18 0/8	5	6	Franklin County	OH	Jeff Ross	1995	9,964
135 4/8	20 6/8	21 3/8	17 6/8	6	5	Tioga County	PA	Kenneth M. Walker, Jr.	1995	9,964
135 4/8	23 7/8	23 6/8	18 7/8	4	7	Shiawassee County	MI	Roger A. Montague	1995	9,964
135 4/8	23 1/8	23 0/8	20 2/8	5	5	Oneida County	WI	Rick Reed	1995	9,964
135 4/8	23 3/8	23 1/8	17 6/8	4	4	Lawrence County	OH	Steve Mays	1995	9,964
135 4/8	24 3/8	25 2/8	16 2/8	4	4	Cecil County	MD	Matthew Todd Willey	1995	9,964
135 4/8	24 5/8	23 4/8	19 0/8	6	5	Price County	WI	Michael W. Ullenbrauck	1995	9,964
135 4/8	24 5/8	23 6/8	17 4/8	6	6	Talbot County	MD	Rick Davis	1995	9,964
135 4/8	23 7/8	21 4/8	19 4/8	5	5	Logan County	CO	Pat Norris	1995	9,964

WHITETAIL DEER (TYPICAL ANTLERS)

Minimum Score 125

SCORE	LENGTH OF MAIN BEAM R	LENGTH OF MAIN BEAM L	INSIDE SPREAD	NUMBER OF POINTS R	NUMBER OF POINTS L	AREA	STATE/PROVINCE	HUNTER'S NAME	DATE	RANK
135 4/8	20 2/8	20 2/8	18 2/8	5	5	Worth County	IA	Larry B. Porter	1996	9,964
135 4/8	22 7/8	22 3/8	16 4/8	4	4	Eau Claire County	WI	Andrew T. Tyler	1996	9,964
135 4/8	23 6/8	24 5/8	15 6/8	5	4	Brunswick County	VA	Clinton D. Osterbind	1996	9,964
135 4/8	22 4/8	22 6/8	20 2/8	5	4	Crawford County	WI	Gary Becwar, Jr.	1996	9,964
135 4/8	23 3/8	23 1/8	19 3/8	6	5	Calhoun County	MI	Mitchell R. Aldrich	1996	9,964
135 4/8	24 1/8	23 0/8	17 4/8	5	4	Coshocton County	OH	Lyle Bennett	1996	9,964
135 4/8	21 3/8	21 2/8	15 7/8	6	5	Jefferson County	IN	Tom Bean	1996	9,964
135 4/8	20 4/8	20 2/8	20 0/8	7	7	Dimmit County	TX	Sonny Evans	1996	9,964
135 4/8	24 0/8	23 4/8	17 2/8	6	5	Portage County	WI	James E. Law	1997	9,964
135 4/8	21 1/8	20 2/8	15 6/8	5	5	Scott County	MN	Ron Lambrecht	1997	9,964
135 4/8	22 5/8	22 6/8	16 4/8	5	5	Peoria County	IL	William Streitmatter	1997	9,964
135 4/8	25 0/8	23 7/8	20 2/8	5	4	Marion County	IL	Mark Stinson	1997	9,964
135 4/8	22 7/8	24 0/8	18 0/8	5	5	Clayton County	IA	Dennis Ulbrich	1997	9,964
135 4/8	23 6/8	24 1/8	16 6/8	5	4	Jackson County	IA	Terry W. Amling	1997	9,964
135 4/8	23 7/8	23 0/8	18 1/8	7	4	Fulton County	IL	Steve Miller	1997	9,964
135 4/8	23 3/8	23 0/8	19 4/8	4	4	Miami County	KS	Scott Rogers	1997	9,964
135 4/8	21 1/8	22 6/8	16 4/8	6	6	Jasper County	IA	Jim Matthews	1997	9,964
135 4/8	23 1/8	24 4/8	15 2/8	4	5	Morrison County	MN	Bill Marchel	1998	9,964
135 3/8	22 0/8	22 2/8	17 1/8	5	5	Columbia County	WI	Chester Sroka	1936	10,056
135 3/8	23 2/8	23 0/8	21 0/8	6	6	Sully County	SD	R. L. Marso	1965	10,056
135 3/8	21 6/8	23 2/8	19 1/8	4	5	Brown County	SD	Arnie Goldade	1974	10,056
135 3/8	22 6/8	22 6/8	16 5/8	4	4	Iowa County	WI	Jerry Statz	1977	10,056
135 3/8	21 0/8	21 0/8	14 7/8	4	4	Richland County	MT	Dan Sturgis	1977	10,056
135 3/8	23 7/8	23 0/8	17 5/8	4	4	Iowa County	WI	Paul Klingelhoets	1978	10,056
135 3/8	22 3/8	21 5/8	15 5/8	5	5	Clark County	IN	Robert W. Thompson	1979	10,056
135 3/8	23 5/8	24 6/8	16 1/8	5	5	Burnett County	WI	Gene Hill	1980	10,056
135 3/8	22 7/8	23 0/8	19 1/8	4	4	Washington County	MN	Rodney P. Bailey	1981	10,056
135 3/8	24 1/8	24 1/8	19 7/8	4	4	Warren County	NJ	Bill L. Raub	1982	10,056
135 3/8	22 6/8	22 4/8	16 3/8	5	5	Dodge County	WI	George Warden	1983	10,056
135 3/8	20 7/8	21 3/8	16 3/8	5	5	Olmsted County	MN	Robert J. Constantine, Jr.	1983	10,056
135 3/8	21 2/8	21 1/8	16 1/8	5	5	Latah County	ID	Jim Frazier	1983	10,056
135 3/8	21 7/8	21 4/8	18 2/8	5	4	Champaign County	IL	Gary Ray Varner	1984	10,056
135 3/8	23 3/8	23 3/8	21 1/8	4	5	Ottawa County	MI	Ed Diemer	1984	10,056
135 3/8	21 7/8	21 3/8	15 3/8	5	5	Strathcona	ALB	Ryk Visscher	1985	10,056
135 3/8	22 5/8	22 5/8	18 3/8	4	4	Jones County	IA	William Janssen	1986	10,056
135 3/8	24 0/8	23 3/8	20 5/8	4	4	Harford County	MD	Eugene Sinar	1987	10,056
135 3/8	24 0/8	22 3/8	22 7/8	4	4	Geauga County	OH	Chris A. Waldron	1988	10,056
135 3/8	21 6/8	22 3/8	16 7/8	5	5	Trempealeau County	WI	Glen L. Mahlum	1989	10,056
135 3/8	22 5/8	22 6/8	18 5/8	4	4	Montgomery County	IL	Lonnie Ragland	1989	10,056
135 3/8	20 4/8	20 1/8	14 1/8	6	5	Dane County	WI	Edward M. Cleven	1989	10,056
135 3/8	23 1/8	21 4/8	19 7/8	4	5	Keokuk County	IA	Mike Krier	1989	10,056
135 3/8	23 4/8	23 2/8	20 5/8	4	5	Jo Daviess County	IL	Richard P. Geyer	1990	10,056
135 3/8	23 6/8	22 6/8	18 5/8	5	5	Ogle County	IL	Charlie Nestrojil	1990	10,056
135 3/8	22 5/8	22 5/8	17 4/8	6	5	Scott County	MN	Terry Regnier	1990	10,056
135 3/8	25 6/8	25 6/8	19 0/8	7	9	Jo Daviess County	IL	Jerry J. Smith	1990	10,056
135 3/8	23 5/8	23 6/8	19 7/8	4	4	Fairfax County	VA	James E. Chabreck	1990	10,056
135 3/8	22 2/8	22 5/8	18 5/8	5	5	Webster County	KY	E. Bert Combs	1991	10,056
135 3/8	23 3/8	23 4/8	19 7/8	3	4	Kane County	IL	Earl Sirchia	1991	10,056
135 3/8	22 2/8	24 0/8	17 4/8	5	4	Lapeer County	MI	Robert Fiore	1991	10,056
135 3/8	21 3/8	21 3/8	15 7/8	6	7	Sullivan County	IN	Steve Eastham	1991	10,056
135 3/8	21 6/8	20 6/8	16 4/8	6	6	Mower County	MN	Pat Johnson	1991	10,056
135 3/8	20 5/8	21 5/8	17 7/8	5	5	Dane County	WI	John Podebradsky	1991	10,056
135 3/8	23 0/8	21 3/8	18 5/8	5	5	Lincoln County	MN	David Rouge	1991	10,056
135 3/8	22 2/8	23 0/8	17 3/8	5	5	Champaign County	IL	Greg Burr	1991	10,056
135 3/8	20 3/8	21 1/8	15 1/8	6	5	Parker County	TX	John L. Chapman	1991	10,056
135 3/8	23 3/8	22 4/8	16 7/8	5	5	Clearwater County	ID	Len Young	1992	10,056
135 3/8	23 1/8	21 2/8	14 7/8	5	5	Pine County	MN	Gary Distler, Jr.	1992	10,056
135 3/8	22 4/8	22 4/8	16 7/8	5	5	Macoupin County	IL	John P. Clark	1992	10,056
135 3/8	23 3/8	22 6/8	15 1/8	4	4	Iowa County	IA	Don Murtha	1992	10,056
135 3/8	20 7/8	20 3/8	21 2/8	4	6	Bragg Creek	ALB	Lorne D. Rinkel	1993	10,056
135 3/8	20 0/8	19 5/8	16 1/8	5	5	Wayne County	MI	Gary A. Kaminski	1993	10,056
135 3/8	24 5/8	24 6/8	18 3/8	4	4	Mercer County	IL	Lane M. Whitehall	1993	10,056
135 3/8	20 1/8	19 6/8	15 3/8	5	6	Flathead County	MT	Ronny L. Nail	1994	10,056
135 3/8	20 3/8	20 6/8	15 3/8	7	5	Converse County	WY	Ricky L. Morley	1994	10,056
135 3/8	22 4/8	22 1/8	19 1/8	5	5	Saginaw County	MI	Francis Albert Turnwald	1994	10,056
135 3/8	24 5/8	24 1/8	20 0/8	4	4	Seneca County	NY	Craig D. Adam	1994	10,056
135 3/8	25 4/8	25 1/8	17 1/8	4	5	Kalamazoo County	MI	Ronald L. Sagers	1994	10,056
135 3/8	22 5/8	22 4/8	19 6/8	5	6	Steele County	MN	Darren Wagner	1994	10,056
135 3/8	22 0/8	21 5/8	15 7/8	6	6	Marshall County	IL	Dan McFarlin	1994	10,056
135 3/8	23 1/8	22 7/8	16 7/8	6	7	Shelby County	IA	Kelly Kobold	1994	10,056
135 3/8	21 7/8	21 7/8	18 1/8	5	5	Logan County	WV	Ed Jones	1994	10,056
135 3/8	21 2/8	22 0/8	19 3/8	5	5	Garden County	NE	Reggie Spiegelberg	1994	10,056
135 3/8	23 4/8	22 5/8	15 7/8	5	5	Oconto County	WI	Mac R. Rhode	1995	10,056
135 3/8	24 7/8	24 4/8	20 0/8	4	5	Chester County	PA	Robert N. Cooney	1995	10,056
135 3/8	22 1/8	21 6/8	16 7/8	4	6	Belmont County	OH	Scott Kull	1995	10,056
135 3/8	22 5/8	22 5/8	15 2/8	6	8	Lawrence County	OH	Dwayne Lewis	1995	10,056
135 3/8	24 2/8	23 5/8	16 3/8	4	5	Cole County	MO	John Schroer	1995	10,056
135 3/8	21 6/8	21 6/8	22 6/8	5	6	Leduc	ALB	Conrad Fennema	1996	10,056

Continued

WHITETAIL DEER (TYPICAL ANTLERS)

Minimum Score 125   Continued

SCORE	LENGTH OF MAIN BEAM R	LENGTH OF MAIN BEAM L	INSIDE SPREAD	NUMBER OF POINTS R	NUMBER OF POINTS L	AREA	STATE/PROVINCE	HUNTER'S NAME	DATE	RANK
135 3/8	22 1/8	21 7/8	16 1/8	4	4	Vernon County	WI	Daniel M. FLynn	1996	10,056
135 3/8	26 2/8	24 4/8	18 5/8	4	6	Geauga County	OH	Randal R. Hollis	1996	10,056
135 3/8	23 3/8	23 0/8	17 3/8	5	4	Vilas County	WI	Robert Berken	1996	10,056
135 3/8	21 5/8	23 3/8	19 3/8	4	4	Allegheny County	PA	Lawrence E. Pine	1996	10,056
135 3/8	22 0/8	21 6/8	19 5/8	5	5	Polk County	WI	Bradley K. Williamson	1996	10,056
135 3/8	23 0/8	23 0/8	17 5/8	4	4	Trempealeau County	WI	Mike Baer	1997	10,056
135 3/8	22 3/8	22 1/8	14 7/8	9	6	Pontotoc County	OK	Mike Scates	1997	10,056
135 3/8	22 5/8	21 4/8	20 1/8	5	5	Barrow County	GA	Glenn Jackson	1997	10,056
135 3/8	21 4/8	21 4/8	15 4/8	7	5	Madison County	KY	Joe Burton	1997	10,056
135 3/8	22 0/8	22 6/8	15 1/8	5	5	Linn County	IA	Charles White	1997	10,056
135 3/8	24 2/8	23 3/8	19 5/8	5	5	Suffolk County	NY	Ken Homan	1997	10,056
135 3/8	25 2/8	25 6/8	16 5/8	4	5	Albany County	NY	Jim Wunderlich	1997	10,056
135 3/8	24 1/8	23 7/8	19 1/8	5	4	Saunders County	NE	Mark Jost	1997	10,056
135 3/8	20 7/8	21 3/8	15 5/8	5	5	Powder River County	MT	Gene Smith	1997	10,056
135 3/8	21 6/8	21 6/8	17 4/8	5	5	Rock County	WI	Anthony "Tony" Peters	1997	10,056
135 3/8	20 2/8	21 0/8	16 4/8	6	6	Page County	IA	Dick Paul	1997	10,056
135 2/8	25 0/8	24 0/8	18 2/8	5	4	Lucas County	IA	Everett Parsons	1964	10,132
135 2/8	21 3/8	22 7/8	16 0/8	5	8	Brown County	SD	Jack Eagleson	1966	10,132
135 2/8	23 0/8	23 2/8	20 2/8	4	4	Cedar County	IA	Fred Wesselink	1971	10,132
135 2/8	20 6/8	21 2/8	18 0/8	5	5	Johnson County	IN	Thomas J. Brown	1978	10,132
135 2/8	17 4/8	16 5/8	13 1/8	7	7	Marshall County	IA	Mike Thomas	1978	10,132
135 2/8	24 0/8	23 2/8	17 4/8	5	6	Winona County	MN	Jim Keim	1979	10,132
135 2/8	22 2/8	21 0/8	15 4/8	4	4	Wood County	WI	Gordon Steidl	1982	10,132
135 2/8	21 5/8	22 5/8	16 6/8	5	6	Juneau County	WI	Steven Hysell	1983	10,132
135 2/8	21 3/8	22 0/8	17 6/8	4	4	Hocking County	OH	Rex Wollett	1983	10,132
135 2/8	22 0/8	21 6/8	16 0/8	5	5	Green Lake County	WI	Arwin Moldenhauer	1984	10,132
135 2/8	25 5/8	24 5/8	16 7/8	6	4	Polk County	MN	Warren Nelson	1984	10,132
135 2/8	22 0/8	21 7/8	17 6/8	4	4	Reno County	KS	Gary D. Walker	1985	10,132
135 2/8	23 4/8	23 7/8	14 6/8	4	4	Lincoln County	WI	Ken Rasmussen	1986	10,132
135 2/8	23 7/8	24 1/8	18 2/8	4	5	Clinton County	IA	Larry A. Lind	1986	10,132
135 2/8	20 3/8	21 6/8	17 1/8	5	5	Beaver County	PA	Ted Kramer	1987	10,132
135 2/8	20 4/8	21 2/8	13 6/8	5	5	Waupaca County	WI	Eugene K. Nuernberger	1987	10,132
135 2/8	21 0/8	21 2/8	17 5/8	6	10	Sedgwick County	CO	Dennis Myer	1987	10,132
135 2/8	23 4/8	23 0/8	21 4/8	4	5	Winneshiek County	IA	Sam Sexton	1987	10,132
135 2/8	25 1/8	25 1/8	17 5/8	5	6	Texas County	OK	Max Crocker	1987	10,132
135 2/8	22 0/8	22 0/8	16 0/8	4	4	Poweshiek County	IA	Robert Rotherham	1988	10,132
135 2/8	25 1/8	25 3/8	16 6/8	7	5	Forest County	WI	Ron H. Vander Kelen	1988	10,132
135 2/8	20 0/8	20 0/8	15 5/8	6	7	Jasper County	IA	Don Morris, Jr.	1988	10,132
135 2/8	21 1/8	20 2/8	15 6/8	5	6	Somerset County	PA	Lynn A. Henry	1989	10,132
135 2/8	22 3/8	22 1/8	15 6/8	8	7	Orange County	IN	Harold L. Lamb	1989	10,132
135 2/8	20 0/8	19 7/8	14 0/8	5	5	Mercer County	NJ	Glenn R. Kuklick	1990	10,132
135 2/8	22 0/8	21 5/8	15 6/8	5	5	Waushara County	WI	Richard J. Tokarski	1990	10,132
135 2/8	23 5/8	24 1/8	18 4/8	5	5	Vernon County	WI	Ron J. Zeihen	1990	10,132
135 2/8	22 6/8	22 4/8	17 6/8	5	5	Morris County	NJ	Theodore Cameron	1990	10,132
135 2/8	22 4/8	22 5/8	18 0/8	4	4	Kiowa County	CO	Lynn Leonard	1990	10,132
135 2/8	22 1/8	22 4/8	13 6/8	5	6	Osage County	OK	George Bennett	1990	10,132
135 2/8	23 1/8	23 2/8	16 4/8	4	4	Clarke County	IA	Jeff Jorgensen	1990	10,132
135 2/8	21 7/8	22 3/8	14 4/8	5	5	Sutton County	TX	Greg Howard	1991	10,132
135 2/8	22 5/8	23 6/8	16 2/8	5	5	Clay County	IL	Jay Lee Newby	1991	10,132
135 2/8	21 0/8	21 3/8	17 7/8	5	7	St. Louis County	MO	Michael W. Overstreet	1991	10,132
135 2/8	23 4/8	23 7/8	21 4/8	6	6	Waukesha County	WI	Bob Loepfe	1991	10,132
135 2/8	23 4/8	23 4/8	20 2/8	5	5	Will County	IL	Jim DeSmidt	1991	10,132
135 2/8	23 4/8	23 7/8	16 0/8	5	5	Marshall County	KS	Tim Wanklyn	1991	10,132
135 2/8	21 6/8	21 1/8	18 6/8	4	5	Webster County	KY	Ricky Blanford	1992	10,132
135 2/8	25 5/8	25 2/8	19 6/8	4	3	Clinton County	MO	John E. Harter, Jr.	1992	10,132
135 2/8	21 7/8	22 6/8	23 5/8	6	6	Morrison County	MN	Dale C. Roisum	1992	10,132
135 2/8	20 7/8	21 0/8	16 5/8	5	6	Hamilton County	IA	Gary L. Jensen	1992	10,132
135 2/8	21 5/8	22 2/8	17 0/8	5	5	Hennepin County	MN	Mike Knox	1992	10,132
135 2/8	20 7/8	20 1/8	17 1/8	5	4	Ocean County	NJ	Chuck R. Debow	1992	10,132
135 2/8	21 4/8	20 4/8	20 2/8	5	4	East Carroll Parish	LA	Joe Morelli	1992	10,132
135 2/8	20 6/8	20 6/8	16 4/8	4	4	Livingston County	MI	Steven K. Cheston	1993	10,132
135 2/8	20 1/8	21 3/8	14 2/8	6	5	Vigo County	IN	Curt Jones	1993	10,132
135 2/8	22 3/8	22 2/8	17 2/8	5	5	Vernon County	WI	David A. Van Dyke	1993	10,132
135 2/8	21 4/8	22 4/8	18 6/8	6	6	Chase County	KS	Tom Scott	1993	10,132
135 2/8	21 7/8	22 4/8	17 2/8	4	4	Jackson County	IA	Tom Hines	1993	10,132
135 2/8	21 4/8	22 0/8	17 2/8	5	5	Jackson County	OH	Keith Kuhn	1993	10,132
135 2/8	21 1/8	20 6/8	17 4/8	5	5	Armstrong County	PA	Robert Smith, Jr.	1993	10,132
135 2/8	20 5/8	20 1/8	13 4/8	5	5	Brooks County	TX	Keith Latimer	1993	10,132
135 2/8	23 0/8	24 0/8	26 3/8	4	6	San Patricio County	TX	Clyde Miller	1993	10,132
135 2/8	24 4/8	23 7/8	17 1/8	4	6	Berks County	PA	Mark I. Lesher	1994	10,132
135 2/8	23 5/8	24 0/8	15 2/8	4	4	Buffalo County	WI	Jeff Fisher	1994	10,132
135 2/8	23 1/8	22 7/8	18 2/8	4	4	Morgan County	OH	Steve Hill	1994	10,132
135 2/8	29 0/8	28 3/8	21 5/8	6	3	Du Page County	IL	Bruce R. Cifelli	1994	10,132
135 2/8	23 0/8	22 6/8	19 6/8	4	4	Prince Georges County	MD	Douglas S. Greenfield	1994	10,132
135 2/8	22 2/8	23 4/8	20 0/8	4	4	Yazoo County	MS	Thomas E. Lofton	1994	10,132
135 2/8	23 0/8	24 0/8	18 0/8	4	4	Parke County	IN	Todd Givens	1995	10,132
135 2/8	20 6/8	20 7/8	18 2/8	5	5	Walworth County	WI	Randy J. Fiesbeck	1995	10,132
135 2/8	22 2/8	22 2/8	16 2/8	4	4	Beltrami County	MN	John Mathweg	1995	10,132

WHITETAIL DEER (TYPICAL ANTLERS)

Minimum Score 125

Continued

SCORE	LENGTH OF MAIN BEAM R	LENGTH OF MAIN BEAM L	INSIDE SPREAD	NUMBER OF POINTS R	NUMBER OF POINTS L	AREA	STATE/ PROVINCE	HUNTER'S NAME	DATE	RANK
135 2/8	21 5/8	22 0/8	14 6/8	5	6	Pittsburg County	OK	Larry Gibson	1995	10,132
135 2/8	24 0/8	22 7/8	22 4/8	6	4	St. Joseph County	IN	Michael L. Ritter, Jr.	1995	10,132
135 2/8	23 2/8	22 3/8	17 0/8	4	4	Otsego County	NY	Brian C. Mabie	1995	10,132
135 2/8	19 3/8	20 3/8	14 6/8	5	5	Seward County	KS	Richard A. "Dick" Nordyke	1995	10,132
135 2/8	22 3/8	23 2/8	15 1/8	5	4	Miami County	KS	Rex Eastwood	1995	10,132
135 2/8	21 5/8	21 7/8	17 6/8	5	4	Humboldt County	IA	Jeff L. Warden	1995	10,132
135 2/8	23 2/8	23 2/8	17 7/8	6	5	Wayne County	KY	Roy Allen Bridgeman	1996	10,132
135 2/8	20 4/8	20 4/8	16 4/8	5	5	McKenzie County	ND	Murray Kline	1996	10,132
135 2/8	23 4/8	24 0/8	18 0/8	4	4	Vigo County	IN	John Davis	1996	10,132
135 2/8	22 5/8	21 6/8	20 0/8	4	4	Clark County	WI	Kevin J. Langreck	1996	10,132
135 2/8	22 0/8	22 0/8	19 3/8	5	6	Pike County	IL	Tim Farniok	1996	10,132
135 2/8	23 1/8	22 2/8	17 0/8	5	5	Jefferson County	IN	Dale Featherstone	1996	10,132
135 2/8	25 4/8	25 1/8	20 3/8	4	5	Summit County	OH	Michael A. Lutes	1996	10,132
135 2/8	23 0/8	22 4/8	16 4/8	6	6	Buffalo County	WI	Joseph P. Kabus	1997	10,132
135 2/8	21 5/8	21 7/8	14 6/8	5	5	Beadle County	SD	Bradley Borah	1997	10,132
135 2/8	22 7/8	22 5/8	17 4/8	4	4	Clinton County	IA	Donald D. Hall	1997	10,132
135 2/8	23 2/8	23 5/8	17 2/8	4	4	Anoka County	MN	Luke Darsow	1997	10,132
135 2/8	23 6/8	23 4/8	16 4/8	5	5	Fairfield County	CT	Truman M. Curtis	1997	10,132
135 2/8	26 3/8	25 5/8	17 5/8	8	6	Montgomery County	IL	Scott Paden	1997	10,132
135 2/8	24 2/8	23 3/8	14 2/8	4	5	Boone County	WV	Kevin Kimbler	1997	10,132
135 2/8	21 7/8	23 2/8	19 0/8	5	4	Brooks County	TX	B. J. Sumrall, Jr.	1997	10,132
135 2/8	24 6/8	25 5/8	21 2/8	4	5	Edwards County	IL	Mike Harness	1998	10,132
135 2/8	22 4/8	22 5/8	16 6/8	4	4	Claiborne County	MS	Lance Stroud	1998	10,132
135 2/8	21 6/8	18 5/8	17 2/8	5	5	Greene County	GA	Damen Braswell	1998	10,132
135 1/8	21 0/8	20 4/8	17 3/8	5	5	Westchester County	NY	Francis E. Hill	1958	10,218
135 1/8	21 6/8	21 3/8	19 7/8	6	5	Brookings County	SD	Ray Buckley	1961	10,218
135 1/8	21 5/8	21 5/8	17 7/8	4	4	Clark County	SD	Jack D. Chesmore	1971	10,218
135 1/8	21 5/8	21 6/8	18 0/8	5	6	Edmonson County	KY	Steve England	1974	10,218
135 1/8	21 7/8	22 0/8	16 3/8	4	4	Greene County	IN	Jan J. Armour	1976	10,218
135 1/8	22 2/8	22 7/8	17 3/8	4	5	Nodaway County	MO	Larry Davison	1982	10,218
135 1/8	23 4/8	22 7/8	18 3/8	5	4	Hamilton County	OH	Jerome Buschle, Jr.	1983	10,218
135 1/8	19 4/8	20 1/8	16 1/8	5	4	McLean County	IL	Robert P. Ryburn	1984	10,218
135 1/8	22 3/8	21 4/8	16 5/8	5	5	Missoula County	MT	Monty Moravec	1985	10,218
135 1/8	20 1/8	19 0/8	15 4/8	6	6	Dawes County	NE	Allen Mintken	1985	10,218
135 1/8	23 4/8	22 0/8	19 3/8	5	5	Eaton County	MI	Dr. Daniel C. Gulick	1985	10,218
135 1/8	23 1/8	23 6/8	18 3/8	6	5	Iowa County	WI	Joe Esser	1985	10,218
135 1/8	22 0/8	22 6/8	17 3/8	5	5	Maries County	MO	Darrel C. Littrell	1986	10,218
135 1/8	24 4/8	23 4/8	17 7/8	4	4	Arkansas County	AR	Wade D. Sweetin	1987	10,218
135 1/8	22 3/8	22 2/8	15 7/8	4	4	Lee County	IL	James R. Bonnell	1987	10,218
135 1/8	20 5/8	20 2/8	17 0/8	7	6	Buena Vista County	IA	Dale F. Kraft	1988	10,218
135 1/8	23 6/8	24 2/8	17 3/8	5	4	Juneau County	WI	Bennie L. Voigt	1988	10,218
135 1/8	23 0/8	22 5/8	16 2/8	4	5	Knox County	IL	Richard Carr	1988	10,218
135 1/8	24 7/8	24 1/8	16 1/8	5	5	Marshall County	KS	Jon Gunn	1988	10,218
135 1/8	22 0/8	22 4/8	20 2/8	6	5	Johnson County	IA	Dallas Eakes	1988	10,218
135 1/8	24 2/8	24 2/8	19 7/8	4	5	McHenry County	IL	Richard Martin	1988	10,218
135 1/8	23 1/8	21 7/8	17 5/8	7	5	Freeborn County	MN	Marvin Thompson	1989	10,218
135 1/8	24 3/8	24 3/8	19 5/8	4	4	Menard County	IL	George E. Hypke	1989	10,218
135 1/8	21 2/8	21 3/8	15 3/8	6	5	Columbia County	WI	Robert J. Lenz	1989	10,218
135 1/8	21 2/8	22 0/8	16 7/8	5	5	Jo Daviess County	IL	Raymond H. Bradt	1989	10,218
135 1/8	19 5/8	21 1/8	15 0/8	8	8	Reno County	KS	Doug Williams	1989	10,218
135 1/8	21 3/8	21 2/8	18 0/8	8	7	Brooks County	TX	Bear Brewer	1990	10,218
135 1/8	23 6/8	24 4/8	18 4/8	7	6	Pike County	IL	Richard Dewey	1990	10,218
135 1/8	23 4/8	22 6/8	16 1/8	5	5	Floyd County	VA	Jeffery Dale Weddle	1990	10,218
135 1/8	23 5/8	23 0/8	16 7/8	4	4	Oldham County	KY	Edwynn Burckle	1990	10,218
135 1/8	23 4/8	22 7/8	17 5/8	5	5	Starke County	IN	Morris Teague	1990	10,218
135 1/8	22 7/8	22 6/8	15 1/8	5	5	Marinette County	WI	James R. Vickman	1990	10,218
135 1/8	24 4/8	24 2/8	20 6/8	7	9	Athens County	OH	Ron M. Hawk	1990	10,218
135 1/8	23 0/8	23 0/8	20 1/8	5	5	Emmet County	IA	Richard D. Berry	1990	10,218
135 1/8	23 1/8	22 6/8	18 1/8	5	5	Olmsted County	MN	SKip Danewick	1991	10,218
135 1/8	19 4/8	19 6/8	15 7/8	5	5	Price County	WI	Jerry Timm	1991	10,218
135 1/8	23 5/8	24 4/8	18 1/8	4	4	Gogebic County	MI	Eugene A. Pribek	1991	10,218
135 1/8	21 4/8	21 4/8	16 3/8	4	4	Adams County	WI	Ronald R. Manz	1991	10,218
135 1/8	25 6/8	25 0/8	18 1/8	4	4	Upson County	GA	Tony Chapman	1991	10,218
135 1/8	20 1/8	21 6/8	15 5/8	5	5	Lafayette County	WI	Roger W. Davis	1991	10,218
135 1/8	21 0/8	20 0/8	16 7/8	5	5	Jackson County	IN	Paul Vice	1991	10,218
135 1/8	25 6/8	25 3/8	16 6/8	6	5	Orange County	IN	Terry Kirkman	1992	10,218
135 1/8	22 0/8	20 7/8	14 5/8	6	5	Pawnee County	OK	Travis Roberts	1992	10,218
135 1/8	22 5/8	22 6/8	17 2/8	6	5	Sawyer County	WI	John Weber	1992	10,218
135 1/8	22 6/8	24 0/8	17 4/8	5	7	Ottawa County	OH	Mike Lacer	1992	10,218
135 1/8	21 5/8	20 0/8	17 7/8	7	6	Alexander County	IL	Stacy Ice	1992	10,218
135 1/8	21 0/8	22 0/8	15 3/8	5	5	Randolph County	WV	Daniel R. Gillenwater	1992	10,218
135 1/8	21 5/8	21 0/8	15 3/8	5	5	Walsh County	ND	Jon Hanson	1993	10,218
135 1/8	20 5/8	20 2/8	14 1/8	5	5	Morton County	ND	Charles Boger	1993	10,218
135 1/8	22 2/8	21 4/8	16 5/8	5	5	Pepin County	WI	Randy Fleisbauer	1993	10,218
135 1/8	24 4/8	25 4/8	22 1/8	3	3	Marshall County	IL	Doug Gudat	1993	10,218
135 1/8	22 2/8	22 2/8	17 7/8	5	5	Shelby County	IL	Kenny Watson	1993	10,218
135 1/8	25 1/8	26 6/8	20 3/8	4	4	Vinton County	OH	John R. Thompson	1993	10,218
135 1/8	22 6/8	22 7/8	17 7/8	5	4	Clark County	KS	Wes Craig	1993	10,218

WHITETAIL DEER (TYPICAL ANTLERS)

Minimum Score 125 — Continued

SCORE	LENGTH OF MAIN BEAM R	LENGTH OF MAIN BEAM L	INSIDE SPREAD	NUMBER OF POINTS R	NUMBER OF POINTS L	AREA	STATE/PROVINCE	HUNTER'S NAME	DATE	RANK
135 1/8	21 7/8	20 5/8	17 2/8	5	6	Kossuth County	IA	Kent D. Berte	1993	10,218
135 1/8	21 2/8	21 1/8	16 5/8	6	5	Charlevoix County	MI	Denis Keehn	1993	10,218
135 1/8	23 3/8	23 5/8	15 3/8	4	5	Carroll County	IL	Daniel K. Carlson	1993	10,218
135 1/8	23 1/8	24 0/8	18 5/8	4	4	Montgomery County	PA	Lance Maleski	1994	10,218
135 1/8	20 7/8	21 3/8	15 1/8	5	5	Grundy County	MO	Jerry Harris	1994	10,218
135 1/8	22 6/8	22 1/8	19 5/8	5	5	Kenosha County	WI	Jim McCarville	1994	10,218
135 1/8	25 0/8	23 5/8	16 5/8	4	4	La Porte County	IN	Richard A. Kimmel	1994	10,218
135 1/8	19 3/8	20 6/8	14 1/8	5	5	West Feliciana Parish	LA	James C. Davis	1995	10,218
135 1/8	22 6/8	22 7/8	17 3/8	6	7	Richland County	WI	Ken Klumb	1995	10,218
135 1/8	21 7/8	22 2/8	16 7/8	4	4	Jackson County	WI	David A. Whitford	1995	10,218
135 1/8	24 6/8	24 1/8	21 1/8	6	5	Garrard County	KY	Mark Cain	1995	10,218
135 1/8	21 5/8	21 6/8	16 7/8	5	5	Marion County	IL	Chris Rose	1995	10,218
135 1/8	22 7/8	23 3/8	16 7/8	5	4	Williamson County	IL	Paul E. Lannom, Jr.	1995	10,218
135 1/8	22 3/8	22 0/8	16 1/8	4	4	Newton County	TX	Roger A. Humphrey	1996	10,218
135 1/8	21 3/8	21 1/8	16 1/8	5	6	Franklin County	VA	Carroll W. Weaver	1996	10,218
135 1/8	24 3/8	22 5/8	15 5/8	4	4	Vinton County	OH	Dan Durst	1996	10,218
135 1/8	22 5/8	21 6/8	17 6/8	6	7	Delaware County	IA	Dean Dempster	1996	10,218
135 1/8	22 3/8	22 6/8	18 0/8	4	6	Houston County	MN	Bill Clink	1996	10,218
135 1/8	22 2/8	23 4/8	21 6/8	4	6	Calhoun County	MI	George I. Swan, Jr.	1996	10,218
135 1/8	23 6/8	23 0/8	19 2/8	7	6	Sumner County	KS	Lyle Dockter	1996	10,218
135 1/8	22 0/8	22 4/8	16 7/8	4	4	Ashland County	WI	Daniel Bodinger	1996	10,218
135 1/8	24 0/8	24 4/8	17 3/8	4	4	Greene County	AL	Charles Thomas Howton	1997	10,218
135 1/8	24 1/8	23 2/8	14 2/8	7	5	Calvert County	MD	Steve E. Willsey	1997	10,218
135 1/8	19 4/8	23 0/8	19 3/8	6	7	Sauk County	WI	Dean R. Blum	1997	10,218
135 1/8	22 4/8	22 0/8	16 3/8	5	5	Tom Green County	TX	Kevin Reed	1997	10,218
135 1/8	20 7/8	21 3/8	16 3/8	5	5	Patrick County	VA	James L. Thompson	1997	10,218
135 1/8	22 4/8	23 4/8	18 2/8	6	6	Kerr County	TX	James C. Markovitz	1997	10,218
135 1/8	22 2/8	21 6/8	16 5/8	5	5	Houston County	MN	Ben Spanjers	1997	10,218
135 1/8	24 1/8	24 0/8	17 1/8	5	4	Iowa County	WI	Dean Fitzsimons	1997	10,218
135 1/8	20 4/8	20 4/8	17 4/8	6	6	Isabella County	MI	Byron Kortman	1997	10,218
135 1/8	24 3/8	24 0/8	19 1/8	5	5	Waukesha County	WI	Gary Heath	1997	10,218
135 1/8	23 0/8	23 6/8	20 4/8	6	6	Grayson County	TX	Ricky Pollan	1997	10,218
135 1/8	22 7/8	21 1/8	16 5/8	5	5	Shackelford County	TX	Christopher Jordan	1997	10,218
135 1/8	21 7/8	21 0/8	17 3/8	7	7	Bourbon County	KS	Mike Shrum	1998	10,218
135 0/8	22 0/8	20 6/8	17 0/8	4	4	Grant County	MN	Stanley D. Miles	1963	10,306
135 0/8	20 1/8	20 2/8	15 4/8	5	5	Dodge County	MN	Clark Gallup	1973	10,306
135 0/8	22 6/8	17 7/8	15 6/8	6	6	Butler County	KS	Phil Hamilton	1974	10,306
135 0/8	20 7/8	19 2/8	17 3/8	8	7	Peoria County	IL	Harry L. Stalter	1975	10,306
135 0/8	24 4/8	24 3/8	14 0/8	5	4	Buffalo County	WI	Steve Segerstrom	1978	10,306
135 0/8	20 5/8	20 7/8	18 0/8	6	6	Morrison County	MN	Larry Hochmayr	1979	10,306
135 0/8	23 6/8	24 0/8	19 6/8	4	4	Lafayette County	WI	Daniel H. Webster	1981	10,306
135 0/8	22 0/8	22 4/8	17 0/8	5	5	Noble County	OK	Glen Elliott	1981	10,306
135 0/8	25 7/8	26 6/8	22 4/8	7	6	Pickaway County	OH	Mouse Bailey	1982	10,306
135 0/8	24 2/8	24 2/8	20 6/8	8	6	Whiteside County	IL	Art Heinze	1983	10,306
135 0/8	23 4/8	24 0/8	17 4/8	5	4	Jackson County	MN	Kerry Ella	1984	10,306
135 0/8	22 3/8	22 1/8	19 4/8	5	5	Linn County	IA	David Padget	1985	10,306
135 0/8	23 6/8	23 6/8	17 0/8	4	5	Bayfield County	WI	Charles Wallisch	1985	10,306
135 0/8	21 2/8	22 5/8	20 2/8	6	5	Union County	IL	Robert Gordon	1985	10,306
135 0/8	22 2/8	22 1/8	17 4/8	5	5	Cherry County	NE	J. Philip Fuchs	1986	10,306
135 0/8	27 0/8	25 2/8	20 6/8	7	5	Waukesha County	WI	Jean Keller	1986	10,306
135 0/8	22 0/8	24 1/8	14 2/8	8	6	Putnam County	MO	William A. Knight	1986	10,306
135 0/8	22 3/8	22 1/8	16 4/8	5	6	Will County	IL	Ken Ericksen	1987	10,306
135 0/8	21 4/8	21 5/8	16 1/8	7	7	Waupaca County	WI	Jim Fauske	1988	10,306
135 0/8	23 4/8	21 4/8	15 4/8	5	6	Columbia County	WI	Stephen Schwarz	1988	10,306
135 0/8	21 0/8	20 3/8	15 2/8	5	5	Dixon County	NE	Tim Nelson	1988	10,306
135 0/8	22 0/8	22 0/8	14 4/8	4	5	Douglas County	WI	Gordon L. Retka	1988	10,306
135 0/8	22 1/8	20 7/8	18 0/8	5	5	Furnas County	NE	Robert Elias	1988	10,306
135 0/8	24 7/8	25 2/8	18 0/8	4	4	Douglas County	NE	Norman Armstrong	1988	10,306
135 0/8	23 0/8	21 0/8	18 0/8	6	5	Warren County	IL	Scott Johnson	1989	10,306
135 0/8	23 1/8	22 4/8	17 1/8	6	5	Bourbon County	KS	Larry Daly	1989	10,306
135 0/8	20 7/8	21 6/8	15 6/8	5	5	Indiana County	PA	Bernard E. Lazor	1990	10,306
135 0/8	20 3/8	20 2/8	16 0/8	5	5	Atascosa County	TX	Steven W. Self	1990	10,306
135 0/8	22 2/8	21 6/8	18 4/8	5	5	Guthrie County	IA	Dean Jackson	1990	10,306
135 0/8	22 0/8	22 2/8	16 2/8	5	5	Brooks County	TX	John W. Fullilove	1990	10,306
135 0/8	24 2/8	23 2/8	20 2/8	4	4	Champaign County	IL	Charles Flora	1990	10,306
135 0/8	21 3/8	22 7/8	15 7/8	4	6	Clinton County	IA	George D. Aurand	1990	10,306
135 0/8	24 0/8	23 6/8	20 2/8	4	4	Powell County	MT	Cary Gee	1990	10,306
135 0/8	24 0/8	24 2/8	15 4/8	4	5	Warren County	IA	Jim Baker	1991	10,306
135 0/8	24 3/8	24 0/8	15 6/8	5	4	Grenada County	MS	Larry G. West	1991	10,306
135 0/8	22 2/8	21 7/8	17 0/8	5	5	Berkshire County	MA	Steve McCartney	1991	10,306
135 0/8	22 2/8	22 0/8	17 4/8	4	4	Clark County	IL	Thomas E. Rothrock	1991	10,306
135 0/8	23 0/8	24 3/8	19 4/8	6	5	Crow Wing County	MN	Danny G. O'Neil	1992	10,306
135 0/8	18 7/8	19 3/8	14 4/8	6	6	Kay County	OK	Greggory D. Frederick	1992	10,306
135 0/8	24 1/8	23 3/8	17 2/8	5	6	Milwaukee County	WI	David Klosiewski	1992	10,306
135 0/8	21 1/8	19 0/8	17 0/8	5	4	Pike County	IL	Rick Kroencke	1992	10,306
135 0/8	22 0/8	22 0/8	18 2/8	5	5	Meeker County	MN	Chuck Schultz	1992	10,306
135 0/8	22 2/8	22 3/8	18 1/8	4	5	Washington County	MN	Cary Holter	1992	10,306
135 0/8	22 5/8	23 0/8	16 1/8	7	6	Vermillion County	IN	Tony Payton	1992	10,306

WHITETAIL DEER (TYPICAL ANTLERS)

Minimum Score 125   Continued

SCORE	LENGTH OF MAIN BEAM R / L	INSIDE SPREAD	NUMBER OF POINTS R / L	AREA	STATE/ PROVINCE	HUNTER'S NAME	DATE	RANK
135 0/8	21 4/8 21 5/8	15 6/8	6 5	Morgan County	IL	Mark D. Lowder	1992	10,306
135 0/8	25 7/8 26 0/8	21 0/8	4 4	Charles County	MD	David R. Spitzer	1992	10,306
135 0/8	22 6/8 23 4/8	19 2/8	4 4	Tuscarawas County	OH	Mark Mozena	1992	10,306
135 0/8	21 7/8 21 7/8	16 6/8	5 4	Ravalli County	MT	Ned Coorough	1993	10,306
135 0/8	23 2/8 23 4/8	18 0/8	4 4	Delaware County	PA	Rob Profitt	1993	10,306
135 0/8	20 6/8 21 3/8	16 6/8	5 5	Suffolk County	NY	Richard Kent	1993	10,306
135 0/8	23 6/8 22 6/8	16 2/8	4 4	Delaware County	IA	John D. Cooke	1993	10,306
135 0/8	24 0/8 24 3/8	18 6/8	4 5	Douglas County	WI	Rodney Olaf	1994	10,306
135 0/8	20 4/8 19 3/8	16 2/8	5 5	Stearns County	MN	Jeffrey J. Pauls	1994	10,306
135 0/8	21 7/8 22 7/8	16 0/8	5 5	Sherburne County	MN	Duane Michael Siekkinen	1994	10,306
135 0/8	22 6/8 19 5/8	14 0/8	5 5	Dane County	WI	Rodney A. Peterson	1994	10,306
135 0/8	23 1/8 22 7/8	16 4/8	4 4	Bayfield County	WI	Robert Carlson	1994	10,306
135 0/8	22 6/8 23 1/8	14 0/8	4 4	Buffalo County	WI	Jerry C. Moser	1994	10,306
135 0/8	23 7/8 23 6/8	21 0/8	7 6	Deville	ALB	Kevin Satterlee	1994	10,306
135 0/8	23 1/8 22 7/8	17 1/8	5 4	Pierson	MAN	Barry Minshull	1995	10,306
135 0/8	22 2/8 23 3/8	18 5/8	5 6	Woodford County	KY	Glen Burnett	1995	10,306
135 0/8	22 3/8 23 1/8	16 2/8	5 5	Ontario County	NY	Matt Fritz	1995	10,306
135 0/8	22 4/8 21 2/8	18 0/8	4 4	Dodge County	MN	Myles Keller	1995	10,306
135 0/8	22 3/8 21 0/8	14 4/8	4 5	Hancock County	OH	John Fenimore	1995	10,306
135 0/8	22 0/8 22 6/8	17 4/8	6 5	Duck Mtns.	MAN	Gary M. Martin	1995	10,306
135 0/8	25 4/8 23 1/8	16 0/8	4 5	Kent County	MI	John M. Quillan	1995	10,306
135 0/8	22 4/8 23 4/8	18 0/8	5 5	Portage County	OH	Ernest E. Woodby	1995	10,306
135 0/8	21 3/8 21 1/8	15 6/8	5 5	Iowa County	WI	Richard R. Kraemer	1995	10,306
135 0/8	22 4/8 21 7/8	19 0/8	6 7	Worcester County	MD	Charles Cooke	1995	10,306
135 0/8	20 6/8 20 4/8	17 2/8	4 5	Creek County	OK	Richard R. Morgan	1995	10,306
135 0/8	19 7/8 20 2/8	20 2/8	6 6	Will County	IL	Bryan P. Tuscher	1996	10,306
135 0/8	22 4/8 22 5/8	17 7/8	5 6	Montgomery County	TN	Kevin Sears	1996	10,306
135 0/8	21 3/8 22 0/8	17 4/8	4 4	Woodford County	IL	Bobby J. Evans	1996	10,306
135 0/8	20 6/8 21 2/8	15 6/8	5 6	Clark County	WI	Dan Sebold	1996	10,306
135 0/8	21 7/8 21 4/8	15 1/8	5 5	Hood County	TX	Bob Kagy	1996	10,306
135 0/8	21 3/8 22 4/8	17 7/8	5 6	Butler County	KS	Mike Schweigert	1997	10,306
135 0/8	21 6/8 21 6/8	18 4/8	4 6	Roberts County	SD	Myles Keller	1997	10,306
135 0/8	20 2/8 20 7/8	16 0/8	5 5	Jackson County	WI	Justin Smothers	1997	10,306
135 0/8	19 6/8 21 6/8	15 6/8	8 5	Cowley County	KS	Michael W. Peters	1997	10,306
135 0/8	20 6/8 19 2/8	16 2/8	5 5	Waukesha County	WI	Eric G. Nelson	1997	10,306
135 0/8	22 3/8 22 4/8	16 4/8	5 5	Queen Annes County	MD	Charley Downs, Jr.	1997	10,306
135 0/8	25 0/8 24 3/8	17 4/8	5 5	Lake County	IL	James Slosser	1997	10,306
135 0/8	21 4/8 22 3/8	16 6/8	5 5	Price County	WI	Bob Wolfe	1997	10,306
135 0/8	20 7/8 21 4/8	15 0/8	5 5	Buffalo County	WI	David L. Bathke	1998	10,306
134 7/8	20 1/8 21 4/8	16 3/8	5 5	Spokane County	WA	Harold Bratlie	1960	10,389
134 7/8	20 6/8 20 6/8	16 7/8	4 4	Lawrence County	SD	Oliver Lewis	1960	10,389
134 7/8	20 4/8 21 0/8	17 2/8	6 6	Cherokee County	OK	Addison Harrison	1965	10,389
134 7/8	20 7/8 21 6/8	17 7/8	5 5	Morrison County	MN	Thomas Ackerman	1971	10,389
134 7/8	24 5/8 24 1/8	21 3/8	7 6	Washington County	OH	Lyle W. Townson, Sr.	1974	10,389
134 7/8	19 3/8 20 3/8	14 0/8	7 5	Ottawa County	KS	Michael D. Patterson	1975	10,389
134 7/8	21 7/8 20 7/8	21 3/8	4 4	Mercer County	NJ	Jim Vandermark	1978	10,389
134 7/8	22 6/8 23 5/8	17 3/8	6 5	Dawson County	NE	Randy Wilson	1978	10,389
134 7/8	22 1/8 21 0/8	16 1/8	4 4	Morrison County	MN	James G. Hurrle	1980	10,389
134 7/8	21 0/8 21 2/8	16 5/8	5 5	Jackson County	MO	Marvin Thomey	1981	10,389
134 7/8	22 0/8 22 3/8	18 4/8	5 4	St. Marys County	MD	Samuel H. Wilson, Jr.	1981	10,389
134 7/8	24 4/8 23 4/8	20 4/8	4 5	St. Charles County	MO	T. J. Sorenson	1983	10,389
134 7/8	21 3/8 21 1/8	14 5/8	4 4	Polk County	WI	Larry Nicholas	1983	10,389
134 7/8	25 3/8 27 4/8	20 1/8	4 4	Morrow County	OH	Tony Burns	1983	10,389
134 7/8	24 1/8 22 0/8	16 7/8	5 5	Alcona County	MI	Galen M. Vernon	1983	10,389
134 7/8	24 3/8 24 4/8	17 1/8	5 5	Itasca County	MN	Karen L. Spotts	1984	10,389
134 7/8	22 1/8 19 5/8	17 1/8	4 4	Cass County	ND	David Skjei	1984	10,389
134 7/8	21 4/8 20 6/8	17 7/8	5 5	Bayham Twp.	ONT	Max Ward	1984	10,389
134 7/8	20 4/8 20 4/8	15 5/8	5 5	McKenzie County	ND	Wade Larmer	1985	10,389
134 7/8	21 5/8 22 5/8	18 5/8	5 5	Owen County	KY	James B Bevins	1985	10,389
134 7/8	22 6/8 22 7/8	17 7/8	4 4	Washington County	PA	Thomas W. Eiler	1986	10,389
134 7/8	21 4/8 22 6/8	15 6/8	4 5	Morrow County	OH	Jerry West	1986	10,389
134 7/8	21 2/8 20 6/8	16 5/8	5 5	Kit Carson County	CO	Dave Holt	1986	10,389
134 7/8	23 2/8 23 3/8	19 1/8	4 4	Clinton County	IA	John Sander	1986	10,389
134 7/8	23 0/8 23 0/8	18 3/8	4 4	Howard County	MD	Ron Thomas	1986	10,389
134 7/8	25 4/8 26 5/8	16 6/8	5 5	Anderson County	TN	Robert Allen Hendren	1987	10,389
134 7/8	22 4/8 22 5/8	16 7/8	6 6	Dodge County	WI	Roger Steger	1987	10,389
134 7/8	24 1/8 24 1/8	15 5/8	4 5	Dane County	WI	Dennis W. Brown	1987	10,389
134 7/8	20 4/8 21 0/8	11 3/8	5 5	Johnson County	KS	William A. Logue	1987	10,389
134 7/8	21 2/8 21 6/8	14 7/8	7 6	Texas County	OK	David Pennington	1988	10,389
134 7/8	22 3/8 22 5/8	20 3/8	5 5	Mower County	MN	Jeffrey L. Boucher	1988	10,389
134 7/8	24 4/8 24 3/8	19 4/8	4 4	Pope County	IL	Ed Hoke	1988	10,389
134 7/8	21 6/8 22 3/8	16 5/8	4 4	Morgan County	IL	John Conklin	1988	10,389
134 7/8	24 3/8 24 7/8	21 7/8	4 4	Suffolk County	NY	Richard Jensen	1988	10,389
134 7/8	23 3/8 23 1/8	18 4/8	5 6	Dawes County	NE	Stan Chiras	1988	10,389
134 7/8	21 0/8 21 5/8	16 3/8	5 5	Burnett County	WI	Ron Stellrecht	1989	10,389
134 7/8	24 5/8 24 1/8	17 1/8	4 4	Fayette County	PA	Spurgeon Kent	1989	10,389
134 7/8	21 6/8 20 6/8	13 7/8	5 6	Dane County	WI	Dave Dilley	1989	10,389
134 7/8	24 4/8 24 3/8	19 1/8	4 4	Cumberland County	NS	Richard Russell	1989	10,389

WHITETAIL DEER (TYPICAL ANTLERS)

Minimum Score 125 — Continued

SCORE	LENGTH OF MAIN BEAM R	LENGTH OF MAIN BEAM L	INSIDE SPREAD	NUMBER OF POINTS R	NUMBER OF POINTS L	AREA	STATE/ PROVINCE	HUNTER'S NAME	DATE	RANK
134 7/8	20 3/8	21 2/8	18 7/8	5	5	Bond County	IL	Steve Gower	1989	10,389
134 7/8	21 5/8	20 0/8	16 5/8	5	5	Morton County	ND	Art Dunn	1990	10,389
134 7/8	22 3/8	24 0/8	21 3/8	4	5	Langlade County	WI	John Sanger	1990	10,389
134 7/8	22 4/8	22 3/8	15 1/8	4	5	Steuben County	IN	Scott Feller	1990	10,389
134 7/8	22 5/8	22 3/8	17 7/8	5	5	Buffalo County	WI	Bob Kriesel	1990	10,389
134 7/8	21 6/8	22 5/8	19 3/8	5	5	Berks County	PA	Randall L. Schoenly	1990	10,389
134 7/8	22 2/8	22 1/8	14 1/8	5	5	Pike County	IL	Jimmy F. Howard	1990	10,389
134 7/8	20 7/8	21 0/8	15 2/8	5	6	Douglas County	WI	Mark J. Bergren	1990	10,389
134 7/8	24 4/8	23 7/8	15 7/8	4	4	Woolwrich	ONT	Peter Hartley	1990	10,389
134 7/8	22 5/8	22 3/8	19 3/8	4	5	Woodford County	IL	Steve M. Crisp	1990	10,389
134 7/8	22 6/8	22 1/8	18 1/8	4	4	Iron County	WI	William T. Scheels	1990	10,389
134 7/8	21 6/8	22 0/8	16 1/8	5	5	Langlade County	WI	Gerald McGee	1991	10,389
134 7/8	19 3/8	19 3/8	16 3/8	5	5	Lincoln County	SD	Dave Krier	1991	10,389
134 7/8	23 7/8	22 5/8	18 2/8	5	6	Sumner County	KS	Lynn Reed	1991	10,389
134 7/8	22 4/8	22 0/8	17 3/8	5	4	Holmes County	MS	Clarence C. Steelman	1991	10,389
134 7/8	22 3/8	21 2/8	18 3/8	4	4	Sangamon County	IL	David C. Jostes	1991	10,389
134 7/8	25 1/8	23 3/8	17 3/8	4	4	Licking County	OH	Dave Novotny	1991	10,389
134 7/8	23 1/8	23 7/8	18 1/8	5	5	Hennepin County	MN	Tom Schottenbauer	1991	10,389
134 7/8	21 5/8	21 0/8	18 5/8	4	4	Goshen County	WY	Mac Spaulding	1992	10,389
134 7/8	22 2/8	21 3/8	17 3/8	5	5	Henry County	IA	Bruce Krause	1992	10,389
134 7/8	21 4/8	21 7/8	16 5/8	5	5	Oneida County	NY	Thomas Dutcher	1992	10,389
134 7/8	24 7/8	24 4/8	17 2/8	5	6	Jefferson County	WI	Harlan R. Krull	1993	10,389
134 7/8	25 3/8	25 6/8	18 5/8	6	4	Washington County	IL	Kevin Woker	1993	10,389
134 7/8	22 0/8	22 1/8	17 3/8	4	5	Sawyer County	WI	Greg Biskup	1993	10,389
134 7/8	24 5/8	22 7/8	18 7/8	5	5	San Patricio County	TX	Edwin N. Goodman	1993	10,389
134 7/8	21 6/8	21 7/8	16 5/8	5	4	Kerr County	TX	Dan Perez	1994	10,389
134 7/8	23 7/8	24 0/8	18 6/8	4	6	Buffalo County	WI	Jeff Owen	1994	10,389
134 7/8	23 0/8	23 5/8	20 7/8	4	4	Dane County	WI	Jeff Berner	1994	10,389
134 7/8	24 4/8	24 2/8	20 1/8	4	4	Owen County	IN	Travis Cheeseman	1994	10,389
134 7/8	25 3/8	26 3/8	18 0/8	5	6	Fairfield County	OH	Hobert Payne	1994	10,389
134 7/8	23 1/8	23 0/8	19 7/8	4	5	Allegheny County	PA	David J. Butter	1994	10,389
134 7/8	23 3/8	23 0/8	21 5/8	5	5	Marion County	IA	Frank M. Hashman	1995	10,389
134 7/8	24 2/8	24 7/8	17 7/8	6	5	Tuscarawas County	OH	Matt Phillips	1995	10,389
134 7/8	23 6/8	24 1/8	20 1/8	4	4	Franklin County	OH	Robert W. McCarley	1995	10,389
134 7/8	20 4/8	20 5/8	19 1/8	5	5	Linn County	IA	Scott C. Novotny	1995	10,389
134 7/8	21 7/8	22 2/8	17 3/8	5	4	Clark County	IL	Jeff Haltom	1995	10,389
134 7/8	25 3/8	24 7/8	17 3/8	4	4	Cross County	AR	Robert C. Vanaman	1995	10,389
134 7/8	23 0/8	23 1/8	16 1/8	4	5	Wapello County	IA	Bill Gilstrap	1995	10,389
134 7/8	20 6/8	20 4/8	18 0/8	6	5	Pottawatomie County	KS	Terry Coward	1995	10,389
134 7/8	21 1/8	22 0/8	14 1/8	7	5	Platte County	WY	Jerry Bowen	1996	10,389
134 7/8	20 5/8	21 5/8	15 3/8	5	5	Billings County	ND	Dan Schramm	1996	10,389
134 7/8	23 4/8	24 4/8	18 2/8	5	6	Midland County	MI	Michael Moceri	1996	10,389
134 7/8	24 6/8	23 5/8	21 5/8	6	5	Monroe County	NY	Salvatore J. Condello	1996	10,389
134 7/8	22 3/8	22 0/8	18 1/8	5	4	Buffalo County	SD	Rob Knippling	1996	10,389
134 7/8	20 4/8	19 6/8	18 3/8	5	5	Kent County	MD	Glenn Martin Davis, Jr.	1996	10,389
134 7/8	22 0/8	20 7/8	17 1/8	5	5	Brown County	WI	Jon H. Mincheski	1996	10,389
134 7/8	22 1/8	20 6/8	17 3/8	5	4	Marshall County	IN	Richard A. Fites	1996	10,389
134 7/8	21 0/8	20 0/8	16 0/8	6	7	Pike County	IL	Eddie Claypool	1996	10,389
134 7/8	20 2/8	22 6/8	18 3/8	5	5	Pontotoc County	OK	Bill Snyder	1996	10,389
134 7/8	18 3/8	18 0/8	15 3/8	6	6	McCulloch County	TX	Scott Chesley	1997	10,389
134 7/8	23 6/8	22 6/8	19 1/8	5	5	Boone County	IL	Brett R. Alfors	1997	10,389
134 7/8	22 4/8	22 2/8	17 7/8	5	4	Pittsburg County	OK	Rodney Alexander	1997	10,389
134 7/8	22 2/8	22 3/8	17 4/8	5	6	Waukesha County	WI	Robert Rajnicek	1997	10,389
134 7/8	23 6/8	24 1/8	15 3/8	5	4	Jennings County	IN	Curtis Haines	1997	10,389
134 7/8	25 3/8	25 4/8	16 7/8	4	4	Webb County	TX	Roger Wintle	1997	10,389
134 6/8	25 2/8	24 7/8	15 6/8	4	4	Newton County	IN	Charles Oliver, Sr.	1967	10,483
134 6/8	20 0/8	20 0/8	16 5/8	5	6	Hughes County	SD	Dean Gretschmann	1970	10,483
134 6/8	20 7/8	20 6/8	17 2/8	5	5	St. Charles County	MO	James Ronquest	1979	10,483
134 6/8	20 3/8	20 5/8	16 4/8	5	5	Ionia County	MI	Barry Jackson	1980	10,483
134 6/8	22 6/8	22 1/8	15 4/8	8	5	Johnson County	KS	Richard J. Seidel	1980	10,483
134 6/8	21 1/8	20 3/8	15 4/8	5	6	Goodhue County	MN	Dennis Wille	1981	10,483
134 6/8	24 3/8	24 3/8	19 6/8	4	4	Vinton County	OH	Patrick D. Kearns	1982	10,483
134 6/8	24 4/8	24 1/8	20 2/8	4	4	Johnson County	NE	Michael G. Remund	1982	10,483
134 6/8	24 0/8	22 7/8	18 2/8	4	5	Dane County	WI	Daniel J. Gartner	1983	10,483
134 6/8	26 0/8	26 3/8	13 5/8	7	5	De Kalb County	MO	J. W. Martin	1984	10,483
134 6/8	25 6/8	25 7/8	17 3/8	6	4	Killam	ALB	Tim Colwell	1985	10,483
134 6/8	23 6/8	24 7/8	19 6/8	5	4	Summit County	OH	Dave Cvelbar	1985	10,483
134 6/8	21 5/8	22 2/8	14 0/8	5	5	Waukesha County	WI	John Fonslow	1985	10,483
134 6/8	23 0/8	23 0/8	19 2/8	6	6	Guernsey County	OH	Marty L. Matthews	1986	10,483
134 6/8	21 5/8	22 6/8	15 6/8	5	5	Republic County	KS	Paul Hill	1986	10,483
134 6/8	24 0/8	25 1/8	15 6/8	4	4	Anoka County	MN	Don Strozyk	1986	10,483
134 6/8	20 4/8	20 7/8	18 1/8	6	5	Rock Island County	IL	Alan L. Black	1986	10,483
134 6/8	19 5/8	21 6/8	14 6/8	5	5	Nemaha County	NE	Lonnie Wing	1987	10,483
134 6/8	20 7/8	21 1/8	15 0/8	5	5	Jefferson County	WI	Mark Beaudoin	1987	10,483
134 6/8	22 5/8	23 4/8	21 4/8	5	5	Washington County	MS	Bobby R. Woods	1987	10,483
134 6/8	24 2/8	23 5/8	15 7/8	5	4	Shelby County	IL	Michael E. Vest	1987	10,483
134 6/8	22 4/8	21 3/8	18 2/8	8	7	Kenedy County	TX	Miguel Mireles	1987	10,483
134 6/8	21 1/8	22 1/8	17 0/8	6	6	Adams County	WI	Dale Mueller	1988	10,483

WHITETAIL DEER (TYPICAL ANTLERS)

Minimum Score 125 — Continued

SCORE	LENGTH OF R MAIN BEAM L		INSIDE SPREAD	NUMBER OF R POINTS L		AREA	STATE/ PROVINCE	HUNTER'S NAME	DATE	RANK
134 6/8	20 1/8	20 2/8	16 6/8	5	5	Jackson County	OH	Earl Ireland	1988	10,483
134 6/8	27 1/8	25 1/8	21 0/8	3	4	Spotsylvania County	VA	Michael Richards	1988	10,483
134 6/8	22 5/8	22 3/8	19 4/8	5	5	Jefferson County	WI	Dean Evenson	1989	10,483
134 6/8	21 0/8	21 2/8	18 2/8	4	4	St. Clair County	MO	Ray Lochridge	1989	10,483
134 6/8	22 7/8	23 1/8	16 2/8	4	4	Warren County	IA	Michael T. Olson	1989	10,483
134 6/8	23 3/8	22 5/8	17 4/8	5	4	Washington County	WI	Ken Zimmer	1989	10,483
134 6/8	22 2/8	22 1/8	18 6/8	5	5	Madison County	IL	Kirby Knackstedt	1989	10,483
134 6/8	22 0/8	22 2/8	16 2/8	5	5	Athens County	OH	Mark A. Cross	1989	10,483
134 6/8	22 3/8	22 6/8	17 0/8	5	5	Phillips County	KS	Julius E. Schoenberger	1989	10,483
134 6/8	22 5/8	22 1/8	17 6/8	5	5	Westmoreland County	PA	Mark Martini	1990	10,483
134 6/8	22 7/8	23 4/8	17 4/8	5	5	Forest County	WI	Daniel J. Brezinski	1990	10,483
134 6/8	21 4/8	21 2/8	15 0/8	4	4	Racine County	WI	Ronald H. Coates	1990	10,483
134 6/8	21 7/8	23 0/8	16 2/8	4	5	Des Moines County	IA	Dave Bailey	1990	10,483
134 6/8	21 4/8	22 6/8	15 2/8	4	5	Mercer County	IL	Neil Hamerlinck	1990	10,483
134 6/8	21 2/8	22 2/8	16 0/8	5	4	Cass County	ND	Tim Poehls	1991	10,483
134 6/8	21 6/8	21 5/8	16 2/8	5	5	La Salle County	IL	MicheAl Underhill	1991	10,483
134 6/8	24 0/8	23 2/8	15 4/8	6	6	Laurens County	GA	Timothy S. Knight	1991	10,483
134 6/8	21 7/8	23 0/8	17 2/8	6	4	McLean County	IL	David Grizzle	1991	10,483
134 6/8	21 6/8	21 6/8	15 2/8	5	5	Jackson County	IL	Tim Cobin	1991	10,483
134 6/8	22 6/8	22 4/8	16 0/8	4	4	Morgan County	IL	Bob DuRocher	1991	10,483
134 6/8	22 2/8	23 4/8	21 0/8	5	4	Lake County	IL	Lee C. Papendorf	1991	10,483
134 6/8	21 7/8	22 5/8	17 4/8	5	4	Scott County	IN	Reggie Helton	1992	10,483
134 6/8	23 3/8	23 0/8	15 4/8	4	4	Monroe County	IN	Wes Giles	1992	10,483
134 6/8	23 6/8	24 2/8	20 6/8	5	5	Oktibbeha County	MS	Michael D. Malone	1992	10,483
134 6/8	23 1/8	22 6/8	17 2/8	5	5	Lincoln County	NE	Dave Hinton	1992	10,483
134 6/8	21 3/8	21 4/8	16 1/8	5	6	Ferry County	WA	Glen Berry	1992	10,483
134 6/8	20 2/8	21 2/8	16 6/8	4	4	Clay County	NE	George F. Hoffmeister, Jr.	1992	10,483
134 6/8	25 0/8	27 2/8	16 4/8	6	6	Allegheny County	PA	Mark Kowalski	1992	10,483
134 6/8	22 0/8	21 7/8	15 0/8	5	5	Green County	WI	Robert Mahlkuch	1993	10,483
134 6/8	23 3/8	23 0/8	15 4/8	6	6	Marathon County	WI	Kurt A. Evje	1993	10,483
134 6/8	21 3/8	21 2/8	17 0/8	5	5	Nicholas County	WV	William A. Young	1993	10,483
134 6/8	21 0/8	20 7/8	12 6/8	5	5	Grant County	NE	Ben Brandt	1993	10,483
134 6/8	23 4/8	22 7/8	19 1/8	4	5	Berkshire County	MA	David M. Gingras	1993	10,483
134 6/8	20 4/8	20 2/8	15 4/8	5	5	Wyandotte County	KS	Wayne Moody	1993	10,483
134 6/8	22 4/8	22 6/8	16 2/8	8	7	Spokane County	WA	Todd W. Steward	1994	10,483
134 6/8	23 5/8	24 1/8	17 0/8	4	4	Adams County	IL	David Wedding	1994	10,483
134 6/8	23 0/8	23 2/8	18 2/8	4	4	Union County	KY	Jackson Ball	1994	10,483
134 6/8	21 5/8	22 2/8	15 6/8	5	4	Clark County	SD	Kevin Wolf	1994	10,483
134 6/8	21 1/8	22 1/8	17 2/8	4	4	Eau Claire County	WI	Wesley H. Krueger	1994	10,483
134 6/8	21 2/8	20 5/8	17 6/8	5	6	Anne Arundel County	MD	Ronnie R. Hall	1994	10,483
134 6/8	21 2/8	21 2/8	15 0/8	5	5	Fairfax County	VA	Elton Polen, Jr.	1994	10,483
134 6/8	21 1/8	20 6/8	20 0/8	7	6	Kerr County	TX	Chuck Adams	1994	10,483
134 6/8	23 2/8	22 6/8	19 4/8	5	5	Livingston County	MI	Ron Brockmiller	1995	10,483
134 6/8	25 3/8	24 5/8	21 2/8	4	4	Patrick County	VA	Gary L. Scott	1995	10,483
134 6/8	23 0/8	23 2/8	18 2/8	6	6	Morrison County	MN	James J. Willard	1995	10,483
134 6/8	23 5/8	22 7/8	17 3/8	5	5	Montgomery County	PA	James Grinstead	1995	10,483
134 6/8	23 1/8	22 3/8	17 6/8	4	4	Buffalo County	WI	Dave Fredrickson	1995	10,483
134 6/8	20 3/8	20 6/8	18 2/8	4	5	Manitowoc County	WI	Michael Steffen	1995	10,483
134 6/8	22 0/8	21 5/8	17 6/8	6	6	Winnebago County	IL	Dan Belanger	1995	10,483
134 6/8	22 0/8	22 3/8	16 4/8	4	5	Baltimore County	MD	Michael E. Chronister	1995	10,483
134 6/8	24 0/8	24 1/8	19 2/8	6	5	La Crosse County	WI	Daniel R. Brown	1995	10,483
134 6/8	21 7/8	22 4/8	17 6/8	6	5	Wallowa County	OR	Randy Greenshields	1996	10,483
134 6/8	24 0/8	23 2/8	17 0/8	6	6	McHenry County	IL	Darrell J. Prielipp	1996	10,483
134 6/8	23 7/8	23 2/8	20 2/8	4	4	McDowell County	WV	Odis Orell	1996	10,483
134 6/8	22 3/8	24 3/8	16 6/8	4	4	Christian County	MO	Roger Satterfield	1996	10,483
134 6/8	24 5/8	25 2/8	17 6/8	5	4	Buffalo County	WI	Jesse Bloom	1996	10,483
134 6/8	25 0/8	24 6/8	22 2/8	6	6	Starke County	IN	Eric L. Shipp	1996	10,483
134 6/8	24 0/8	24 0/8	18 0/8	4	5	Otter Tail County	MN	Cameron Davis	1996	10,483
134 6/8	24 2/8	24 1/8	17 0/8	4	5	Saunders County	NE	Joseph F. Sloup	1996	10,483
134 6/8	22 5/8	24 1/8	18 4/8	5	5	Jefferson County	WI	David Mueller	1996	10,483
134 6/8	23 4/8	23 3/8	16 6/8	4	4	Seward County	NE	Jeff Jones	1996	10,483
134 6/8	23 2/8	21 3/8	24 7/8	4	4	James City County	VA	Rex Bowen	1997	10,483
134 6/8	22 0/8	23 4/8	17 0/8	4	4	Chatham County	NC	William Phillips	1997	10,483
134 6/8	21 5/8	22 3/8	17 2/8	5	6	Otoe County	NE	Bow Steedly	1997	10,483
134 6/8	23 0/8	24 6/8	17 6/8	5	5	Brown County	IL	Kevin J. Gustafson	1997	10,483
134 6/8	20 6/8	21 4/8	14 6/8	6	6	Lewis & Clark County	MT	Jay Sherley	1997	10,483
134 6/8	22 7/8	22 1/8	18 4/8	4	4	Charles County	MD	David Boyden	1998	10,483
134 5/8	20 6/8	22 4/8	18 7/8	7	6	Floyd County	IA	James K. Harris	1972	10,573
134 5/8	22 7/8	23 0/8	17 5/8	5	5	Brown County	WI	Michael J. Goza	1976	10,573
134 5/8	21 4/8	22 2/8	17 1/8	5	6	Republic County	KS	Don R. Dejmal	1978	10,573
134 5/8	24 1/8	24 3/8	18 1/8	5	5	Jasper County	IL	William Dowland	1979	10,573
134 5/8	22 2/8	22 0/8	16 2/8	7	6	Randolph County	WV	Robert E. Nace	1979	10,573
134 5/8	24 5/8	24 7/8	18 3/8	4	5	Dodge County	WI	Ken Bialoszynski	1980	10,573
134 5/8	22 1/8	22 2/8	17 3/8	4	4	Vinton County	OH	Paul Ingram	1980	10,573
134 5/8	22 2/8	21 5/8	19 6/8	5	5	Fulton County	IL	Cliff C. Conover	1982	10,573
134 5/8	23 0/8	22 3/8	18 0/8	6	6	Clark County	KS	William A. Rule	1982	10,573
134 5/8	24 0/8	24 4/8	15 5/8	4	5	Marion County	TN	Paul E. Worley	1983	10,573
134 5/8	23 0/8	22 2/8	17 2/8	7	8	Morrison County	MN	Harold "Nook" Blank	1983	10,573

WHITETAIL DEER (TYPICAL ANTLERS)

Minimum Score 125 Continued

SCORE	LENGTH OF MAIN BEAM R	L	INSIDE SPREAD	NUMBER OF POINTS R	L	AREA	STATE/ PROVINCE	HUNTER'S NAME	DATE	RANK
134 5/8	22 0/8	22 4/8	14 5/8	5	5	Bedford County	VA	Robert Sutton	1983	10,573
134 5/8	21 7/8	21 5/8	17 5/8	5	5	Russell County	AL	Jesse Waldrop	1983	10,573
134 5/8	22 7/8	23 4/8	14 1/8	4	5	Brooke County	WV	Myron Rees	1983	10,573
134 5/8	21 2/8	22 2/8	17 3/8	6	5	Pulaski County	KY	Glen Whitis, Jr.	1985	10,573
134 5/8	19 4/8	19 0/8	18 0/8	5	6	Brown County	KS	Ray Kirk	1985	10,573
134 5/8	25 7/8	23 6/8	19 1/8	6	5	Fairfield County	CT	Milan G. Bull	1985	10,573
134 5/8	20 7/8	21 5/8	15 2/8	5	6	Bremer County	IA	Tom Bluhm	1986	10,573
134 5/8	19 2/8	19 3/8	15 3/8	5	5	Ford County	KS	Brent Whitaker	1986	10,573
134 5/8	23 7/8	24 5/8	20 4/8	5	4	Meigs County	OH	Randie Lawson	1987	10,573
134 5/8	21 1/8	21 1/8	17 3/8	5	5	Sauk County	WI	Gregory D. Wilson	1987	10,573
134 5/8	23 1/8	21 4/8	16 7/8	4	4	Morrison County	MN	Mike Gulbrandson	1988	10,573
134 5/8	22 1/8	23 1/8	15 3/8	5	5	Knox County	IL	David Emken	1988	10,573
134 5/8	22 5/8	22 4/8	15 4/8	4	6	Dane County	WI	Aaron Halverson	1988	10,573
134 5/8	22 4/8	21 2/8	20 1/8	4	5	Athens County	OH	John P. Lavelle	1988	10,573
134 5/8	24 1/8	24 0/8	17 2/8	6	7	Douglas County	MN	James Dykema	1988	10,573
134 5/8	25 3/8	25 6/8	17 1/8	4	5	Stokes County	NC	Harold Teague	1989	10,573
134 5/8	22 2/8	22 0/8	18 3/8	4	4	Tunica County	MS	Beau Gregory	1989	10,573
134 5/8	20 2/8	20 0/8	16 3/8	5	5	Stephenson County	IL	Dwight Peterson	1990	10,573
134 5/8	20 6/8	21 5/8	16 5/8	6	5	Hancock County	WV	Terry A. Markle	1990	10,573
134 5/8	22 5/8	22 4/8	16 7/8	4	5	Racine County	WI	Michael Habrat	1990	10,573
134 5/8	24 0/8	23 7/8	16 5/8	5	5	Orange County	IN	Jan J. Armour	1990	10,573
134 5/8	24 0/8	23 7/8	19 7/8	6	5	Allamakee County	IA	Don Heim	1990	10,573
134 5/8	23 3/8	23 6/8	17 1/8	4	5	Delaware County	IA	N. Sperfslage	1990	10,573
134 5/8	21 0/8	20 6/8	16 1/8	5	5	Kenosha County	WI	Stephen Scheibl	1990	10,573
134 5/8	24 4/8	21 4/8	19 5/8	6	6	Sussex County	DE	Randall Johnson	1990	10,573
134 5/8	23 7/8	23 2/8	18 3/8	4	4	New Kent County	VA	Daryl Eubank	1991	10,573
134 5/8	18 0/8	18 4/8	13 1/8	5	5	Kandiyohi County	MN	Jerry Johnson	1991	10,573
134 5/8	22 0/8	22 2/8	18 1/8	5	4	Kit Carson County	CO	Stephen Kotz	1991	10,573
134 5/8	23 3/8	23 4/8	18 5/8	6	5	Washington County	MN	Joe Ugro III	1991	10,573
134 5/8	22 7/8	21 7/8	17 5/8	5	4	Morrison County	MN	Scott R. Kiekow	1992	10,573
134 5/8	23 2/8	23 6/8	19 1/8	4	4	Muskingum County	OH	Rob Browning	1992	10,573
134 5/8	26 7/8	27 6/8	18 5/8	4	4	Vinton County	OH	Vernon Rogers	1992	10,573
134 5/8	24 2/8	24 0/8	17 5/8	4	3	Kane County	IL	Jody Kellnhofer	1992	10,573
134 5/8	22 6/8	22 1/8	15 3/8	5	5	Howard County	MD	Kirk D. Souder	1992	10,573
134 5/8	21 4/8	21 2/8	15 5/8	4	4	McMullen County	TX	Daniel D. Countiss	1992	10,573
134 5/8	22 4/8	23 1/8	15 1/8	5	5	Clay County	TN	David A. Allred	1993	10,573
134 5/8	20 3/8	20 3/8	21 5/8	5	5	Hardin County	KY	Donald J. Vittitow, Jr.	1993	10,573
134 5/8	21 4/8	21 3/8	16 1/8	5	5	Jefferson County	IN	James Wildman	1993	10,573
134 5/8	21 6/8	22 1/8	18 7/8	5	5	Forest County	WI	Tad P. Dachelet	1993	10,573
134 5/8	21 4/8	21 4/8	17 1/8	5	5	Sawyer County	WI	Bradley Lyberg	1993	10,573
134 5/8	23 7/8	23 2/8	19 7/8	5	5	Hancock County	OH	Robert E. Ebert	1993	10,573
134 5/8	24 0/8	24 4/8	18 5/8	5	7	Washington County	MN	Lee Lakosky	1994	10,573
134 5/8	20 2/8	21 0/8	17 7/8	4	5	Saginaw County	MI	Terry C. Bishop	1994	10,573
134 5/8	21 3/8	21 6/8	15 1/8	5	5	Brown County	IL	Art Dirindin, Jr.	1994	10,573
134 5/8	19 1/8	19 1/8	14 3/8	5	5	Kenedy County	TX	Chad Clark	1994	10,573
134 5/8	25 1/8	23 3/8	15 3/8	6	8	Kingsbury County	SD	Gordon Skyberg	1994	10,573
134 5/8	22 0/8	22 0/8	16 5/8	5	5	Oneida County	WI	Tom Van Harpen	1995	10,573
134 5/8	22 7/8	22 1/8	16 5/8	6	8	Washington County	MN	Pat Forliti	1995	10,573
134 5/8	23 3/8	23 2/8	16 1/8	4	4	Dane County	WI	Doug S. Neath	1995	10,573
134 5/8	21 1/8	19 5/8	17 3/8	5	7	Kane County	IL	Carl Kwak	1995	10,573
134 5/8	23 0/8	22 3/8	16 1/8	4	4	Juneau County	WI	Aki Theoharis	1995	10,573
134 5/8	21 2/8	21 4/8	15 3/8	5	5	Gloucester County	NJ	Anthony J. Branda II	1996	10,573
134 5/8	22 2/8	21 2/8	16 5/8	5	4	Troup County	GA	Brandon L. Brooks	1996	10,573
134 5/8	21 3/8	20 6/8	14 7/8	5	5	Marquette County	WI	Jeffrey Goralski	1996	10,573
134 5/8	20 0/8	21 1/8	19 1/8	4	4	Delaware County	IN	Gary L. Beal	1996	10,573
134 5/8	21 6/8	21 5/8	16 3/8	4	4	Fond du Lac County	WI	Randy Roehl	1996	10,573
134 5/8	21 1/8	20 5/8	14 7/8	5	5	Buffalo County	WI	Todd Hangartner	1996	10,573
134 5/8	20 6/8	19 7/8	18 5/8	4	5	Washtenaw County	MI	Robert E. Macek	1996	10,573
134 5/8	24 5/8	23 6/8	18 3/8	5	4	Lake County	IL	Carl H. Spaeth	1996	10,573
134 5/8	23 7/8	22 6/8	17 5/8	4	4	Price County	WI	Troy W. Henderson	1997	10,573
134 5/8	19 7/8	21 4/8	14 7/8	5	5	Crow Wing County	MN	Kenneth Beckel	1997	10,573
134 5/8	22 5/8	22 6/8	14 7/8	4	5	Sedalia	ALB	Quinn Wagstaff	1997	10,573
134 5/8	20 2/8	23 1/8	21 3/8	5	5	Hunterdon County	NJ	Joe Rizzo	1997	10,573
134 5/8	20 6/8	20 7/8	14 2/8	5	7	Wyoming County	WV	Larry Bailey	1997	10,573
134 5/8	23 4/8	23 6/8	17 5/8	4	6	La Crosse County	WI	Jim Rogala	1997	10,573
134 5/8	24 3/8	23 6/8	18 2/8	6	5	Decatur County	IA	Myles Keller	1997	10,573
134 4/8	23 5/8	21 1/8	17 2/8	4	4	Faribault County	MN	Sherwood F. Krosch	1969	10,650
134 4/8	19 0/8	20 4/8	20 5/8	5	5	Morrison County	MN	Harold A. Walsh	1971	10,650
134 4/8	19 7/8	19 5/8	17 6/8	5	5	Ripley County	IN	Robert Pitt	1974	10,650
134 4/8	22 2/8	21 2/8	18 6/8	5	5	Des Moines County	IA	Ron Cover	1975	10,650
134 4/8	23 1/8	23 1/8	18 2/8	4	4	Carroll County	OH	Thomas E. Geibel	1978	10,650
134 4/8	25 0/8	24 0/8	15 6/8	4	4	Dane County	WI	Douglas E. Seals	1980	10,650
134 4/8	22 3/8	20 7/8	17 6/8	5	5	Carroll County	MD	Thomas Creech	1980	10,650
134 4/8	20 7/8	20 2/8	17 6/8	5	5	Lincoln County	MT	Sonny Templeton	1980	10,650
134 4/8	21 6/8	21 4/8	15 2/8	4	5	Vernon County	MO	Roger Hensley	1981	10,650
134 4/8	21 2/8	24 4/8	21 2/8	5	4	Wagoner County	OK	Harold Clay	1982	10,650
134 4/8	24 3/8	24 2/8	16 5/8	5	5	Yell County	AR	Gary Worm	1983	10,650
134 4/8	22 4/8	21 6/8	14 4/8	4	5	Crow Wing County	MN	Tom Aspros	1983	10,650

WHITETAIL DEER (TYPICAL ANTLERS)

Minimum Score 125   Continued

SCORE	LENGTH OF R MAIN BEAM L		INSIDE SPREAD	NUMBER OF R POINTS L		AREA	STATE/PROVINCE	HUNTER'S NAME	DATE	RANK
134 4/8	19 2/8	23 4/8	17 6/8	5	5	Somerset County	MD	Clint Kelbel	1983	10,650
134 4/8	22 6/8	23 0/8	16 6/8	4	5	Chippewa County	WI	Larry Paulsen	1984	10,650
134 4/8	21 2/8	24 2/8	22 0/8	4	4	Morris County	NJ	David Paddock	1984	10,650
134 4/8	22 7/8	23 5/8	15 6/8	5	5	Morgan County	OH	Dean Spears	1984	10,650
134 4/8	21 1/8	21 1/8	17 6/8	4	4	Monroe County	WV	Clarence J Burns	1984	10,650
134 4/8	19 4/8	19 6/8	16 4/8	6	5	Kingsbury County	SD	Reginald E. Faber, Jr.	1984	10,650
134 4/8	24 2/8	22 5/8	15 7/8	6	6	Hickman County	TN	Stanley Hunt	1985	10,650
134 4/8	23 1/8	24 2/8	18 0/8	5	4	Marshall County	MN	Bruce Becklund	1985	10,650
134 4/8	24 0/8	23 1/8	17 2/8	5	6	Clay County	IL	Myron Woomer	1985	10,650
134 4/8	21 3/8	19 7/8	18 0/8	5	5	McCulloch County	TX	Richard R. Curry	1986	10,650
134 4/8	22 0/8	22 3/8	14 2/8	5	5	Buffalo County	WI	Douglas Henderson	1986	10,650
134 4/8	25 3/8	24 6/8	20 1/8	5	5	Coffey County	KS	Glen Neilson	1986	10,650
134 4/8	24 5/8	23 7/8	16 6/8	4	4	Delta County	MI	Ronald E. Quick	1986	10,650
134 4/8	24 5/8	25 0/8	18 2/8	4	4	Morrison County	MN	Scott Bruber	1987	10,650
134 4/8	21 6/8	21 1/8	15 6/8	4	5	Preble County	OH	Robert B. Lickliter	1987	10,650
134 4/8	22 7/8	23 2/8	14 6/8	5	5	Claiborne County	TN	Glen Montgomery	1987	10,650
134 4/8	20 0/8	20 1/8	17 2/8	5	4	Lee County	IL	Gordon Gableman	1987	10,650
134 4/8	21 0/8	21 0/8	16 2/8	5	5	Lambton County	ONT	J. Barry Lugsdin	1987	10,650
134 4/8	24 6/8	22 6/8	19 3/8	7	6	Suffolk County	NY	John W. Wobst	1987	10,650
134 4/8	21 0/8	18 1/8	17 0/8	6	6	Charles County	MD	Scott Cutter	1987	10,650
134 4/8	22 7/8	25 2/8	20 2/8	4	5	Peoria County	IL	Steve Watts	1987	10,650
134 4/8	20 4/8	20 7/8	14 5/8	5	6	Bosque County	TX	Charles E. Rushing	1987	10,650
134 4/8	20 0/8	21 5/8	16 2/8	5	5	Clark County	IL	Thomas E. Rothrock	1988	10,650
134 4/8	22 2/8	21 4/8	17 0/8	5	5	Door County	WI	Daniel W. Herrbold	1988	10,650
134 4/8	23 4/8	23 4/8	19 0/8	4	5	Lake County	OH	Kenneth Udovic	1988	10,650
134 4/8	24 6/8	19 2/8	19 2/8	4	5	Winnebago County	IA	Tom Brakke	1988	10,650
134 4/8	20 4/8	20 5/8	14 0/8	6	6	Atascosa County	TX	Russell Janek	1989	10,650
134 4/8	26 0/8	24 7/8	19 2/8	7	7	Jefferson County	IN	Ronnie L. Fiesbeck	1989	10,650
134 4/8	23 5/8	23 3/8	18 0/8	4	4	Taylor County	WI	Paul A. Biederman	1989	10,650
134 4/8	24 5/8	24 3/8	16 0/8	5	5	Price County	WI	David Kelnhofer	1989	10,650
134 4/8	22 4/8	21 1/8	16 2/8	6	6	Grant County	WI	Ronald D. Olson	1989	10,650
134 4/8	22 4/8	22 7/8	17 0/8	5	5	Roberts County	SD	Ronnie Bucklin	1989	10,650
134 4/8	22 4/8	23 3/8	17 0/8	4	5	Traill County	ND	Michael Toomey	1990	10,650
134 4/8	24 4/8	23 5/8	20 2/8	4	4	Montgomery County	PA	Joseph A. Rizzo	1990	10,650
134 4/8	21 5/8	21 2/8	15 4/8	5	5	Goliad County	TX	Roy M. Goodwin	1990	10,650
134 4/8	22 6/8	22 3/8	13 6/8	5	5	Jefferson County	OH	James C. Riggle	1990	10,650
134 4/8	22 1/8	22 2/8	18 0/8	5	5	Beltrami County	MN	Irving Strom	1990	10,650
134 4/8	20 6/8	20 7/8	14 4/8	6	6	Hitchcock County	NE	William Elfland	1990	10,650
134 4/8	23 5/8	22 7/8	16 6/8	5	5	Waukesha County	WI	Henry Tilidetzke	1990	10,650
134 4/8	25 2/8	25 5/8	16 6/8	5	7	Clay County	MO	Joe Zuber	1990	10,650
134 4/8	21 1/8	21 0/8	18 4/8	5	5	Calhoun County	MI	John Eldridge	1991	10,650
134 4/8	22 7/8	23 7/8	14 0/8	5	5	Douglas County	WI	John L. Schnell	1991	10,650
134 4/8	20 2/8	22 3/8	11 6/8	5	5	Hillsdale County	MI	Jim Thiel	1991	10,650
134 4/8	22 6/8	21 2/8	13 6/8	6	6	Lee County	IA	Glenn E. Wagner	1991	10,650
134 4/8	23 6/8	23 6/8	17 1/8	5	5	Live Oak County	TX	Beau Walker	1991	10,650
134 4/8	23 3/8	23 4/8	14 0/8	4	4	Clinton County	MO	Jeremy Ingraham	1992	10,650
134 4/8	21 1/8	21 5/8	19 2/8	6	6	Dodge County	WI	Jeremy Schraufnagel	1992	10,650
134 4/8	23 2/8	22 4/8	15 4/8	5	5	Hocking County	OH	Norman Campbell	1992	10,650
134 4/8	22 4/8	22 3/8	19 7/8	4	5	Lyon County	IA	Owen Sandbulte	1992	10,650
134 4/8	20 4/8	20 2/8	23 4/8	5	7	Talbot County	MD	David Lighty	1992	10,650
134 4/8	23 7/8	21 5/8	16 1/8	6	5	Rusk County	WI	Gene Waeltz	1993	10,650
134 4/8	24 0/8	23 3/8	17 2/8	5	5	Worcester County	MD	Robert C. Taylor	1993	10,650
134 4/8	21 6/8	22 2/8	17 5/8	5	6	Cecil County	MD	Doug Willard	1993	10,650
134 4/8	22 3/8	22 4/8	17 6/8	5	5	Litchfield County	CT	Richard Rogers	1993	10,650
134 4/8	23 3/8	23 2/8	16 6/8	5	5	Macoupin County	IL	Brad Bellm	1994	10,650
134 4/8	21 6/8	21 6/8	13 6/8	5	5	Valley County	MT	Ricky Morris	1994	10,650
134 4/8	22 1/8	22 0/8	15 4/8	5	5	Hubbard County	MN	Donald L. Dehart	1994	10,650
134 4/8	20 2/8	20 4/8	16 2/8	5	4	Cheboygan County	MI	John Thomas Godek	1994	10,650
134 4/8	20 7/8	21 7/8	14 1/8	6	5	Tom Green County	TX	Mike Bewley	1994	10,650
134 4/8	23 6/8	23 6/8	18 2/8	5	5	Lehigh County	PA	Charles E. Mount, III	1994	10,650
134 4/8	22 6/8	23 4/8	17 6/8	4	4	Walworth County	WI	Jeffrey Litwin	1994	10,650
134 4/8	21 5/8	22 3/8	18 6/8	5	5	Shawano County	WI	Todd Schmidt	1994	10,650
134 4/8	21 4/8	22 4/8	15 6/8	5	5	Roscommon County	MI	Andrew P. Jonkis	1995	10,650
134 4/8	19 5/8	20 6/8	15 0/8	5	5	Jackson County	MO	Richard Kralicek	1995	10,650
134 4/8	24 2/8	24 4/8	17 2/8	6	5	Kent County	MI	John R. Scranton	1995	10,650
134 4/8	23 0/8	22 1/8	17 2/8	5	5	St. Croix County	WI	David J. Gazdik	1995	10,650
134 4/8	24 2/8	24 4/8	18 4/8	4	4	St. Joseph County	MI	Jeff Glaser	1995	10,650
134 4/8	22 6/8	21 7/8	17 3/8	5	7	Madison County	MT	James Nygaard	1996	10,650
134 4/8	21 0/8	21 3/8	17 2/8	5	5	La Salle County	IL	John Thomas	1996	10,650
134 4/8	21 7/8	23 3/8	16 6/8	5	5	Morris County	NJ	Craig L. Wilkie	1996	10,650
134 4/8	20 6/8	20 5/8	17 0/8	5	5	Ozaukee County	WI	Thomas E. Smetana	1996	10,650
134 4/8	23 7/8	23 5/8	18 4/8	4	4	Gallatin County	IL	Michael Robards	1996	10,650
134 4/8	24 5/8	24 5/8	19 6/8	4	5	Jackson County	OH	Barry W. Ickes	1996	10,650
134 4/8	22 2/8	21 4/8	16 6/8	7	6	Ashland County	WI	Randy D. Niewiadomski	1996	10,650
134 4/8	21 5/8	20 5/8	17 5/8	5	5	Saline County	IL	Bob Hoock	1996	10,650
134 4/8	23 2/8	23 1/8	18 4/8	5	5	Lunenburg County	NS	Nathan Hirtle	1997	10,650
134 4/8	23 2/8	23 2/8	20 0/8	4	4	Sangamon County	IL	William C. Sandidge	1997	10,650
134 4/8	22 4/8	24 3/8	17 6/8	4	4	Steuben County	NY	John R. Drost, Jr.	1997	10,650

WHITETAIL DEER (TYPICAL ANTLERS)

Minimum Score 125   Continued   429

SCORE	LENGTH OF MAIN BEAM R	LENGTH OF MAIN BEAM L	INSIDE SPREAD	NUMBER OF POINTS R	NUMBER OF POINTS L	AREA	STATE/PROVINCE	HUNTER'S NAME	DATE	RANK
134 4/8	24 2/8	23 6/8	18 2/8	4	5	Uvalde County	TX	Ray Lilley	1998	10,650
134 4/8	21 6/8	20 3/8	17 2/8	5	5	Chautauqua County	NY	James M. Hoffman	1998	10,650
134 3/8	23 4/8	22 1/8	17 1/8	4	5	Arkansas County	AR	Louis Rush	1959	10,742
134 3/8	20 5/8	20 5/8	17 3/8	5	5	Rice County	MN	Gary Roemhildt	1965	10,742
134 3/8	21 6/8	21 3/8	15 4/8	4	5	Cecil County	MD	Bernard Langhorne	1972	10,742
134 3/8	20 5/8	20 4/8	17 1/8	5	5	Powell County	MT	Paul E. Tadlock	1972	10,742
134 3/8	22 1/8	23 4/8	18 5/8	4	4	Tompkins County	NY	H. R. Swansbrough, Jr.	1977	10,742
134 3/8	24 2/8	24 1/8	22 6/8	5	5	Nicollet County	MN	John Seifert	1978	10,742
134 3/8	21 4/8	21 2/8	16 6/8	5	8	Phelps County	NE	Kirk Stroup	1981	10,742
134 3/8	20 6/8	20 0/8	15 1/8	5	5	Cumberland County	NJ	Bob Eisele	1981	10,742
134 3/8	22 7/8	22 0/8	17 6/8	5	4	Pike County	IL	Dan Wombles	1981	10,742
134 3/8	21 6/8	21 2/8	15 7/8	5	5	Pope County	AR	Danny Bennett	1981	10,742
134 3/8	23 4/8	23 7/8	18 5/8	6	3	Morrison County	MN	Arnie Borchert	1982	10,742
134 3/8	22 1/8	22 3/8	18 1/8	4	4	Texas County	OK	Curtis Clayton	1982	10,742
134 3/8	22 3/8	21 2/8	19 2/8	6	5	Chippewa County	MI	Joe Johnston	1983	10,742
134 3/8	23 4/8	22 4/8	18 5/8	4	4	Kingman County	KS	Ken Marsh	1984	10,742
134 3/8	22 7/8	22 3/8	14 4/8	6	5	Dawson County	MT	Alan H. Winkel	1984	10,742
134 3/8	25 2/8	25 3/8	18 3/8	4	4	Scioto County	OH	Ed Asbury	1984	10,742
134 3/8	24 5/8	24 7/8	16 0/8	5	6	Morrison County	MN	Gary Thomas	1985	10,742
134 3/8	21 2/8	22 1/8	18 0/8	7	6	Vermilion County	IL	Ken Gabehart	1986	10,742
134 3/8	24 2/8	24 7/8	16 0/8	5	5	Breckinridge County	KY	James R. Parks	1987	10,742
134 3/8	23 6/8	23 4/8	19 1/8	5	4	Montgomery County	AL	Foy H. Tatum	1987	10,742
134 3/8	22 2/8	22 3/8	16 1/8	4	4	Barbour County	AL	Harold Reynolds	1987	10,742
134 3/8	22 1/8	23 6/8	15 5/8	6	5	Kendall County	IL	Dean V. Ashton	1988	10,742
134 3/8	21 7/8	22 6/8	17 5/8	5	5	Pickaway County	OH	Tim Ritchie	1988	10,742
134 3/8	19 6/8	20 4/8	15 3/8	6	6	Florence County	WI	Chris H. Larson	1988	10,742
134 3/8	24 5/8	24 4/8	17 1/8	5	4	Washburn County	WI	Todd M. Skille	1988	10,742
134 3/8	22 1/8	22 5/8	16 4/8	4	6	Albert County	NBW	John Carty	1989	10,742
134 3/8	22 3/8	22 3/8	17 5/8	5	5	Kenosha County	WI	James D. Maricle	1989	10,742
134 3/8	25 4/8	25 3/8	20 5/8	5	5	Malden Twp.	ONT	Ed Faucher	1989	10,742
134 3/8	21 5/8	21 7/8	14 5/8	5	5	Panola County	TX	Twanda Paul Rozelle II	1990	10,742
134 3/8	20 7/8	20 2/8	14 7/8	5	5	Barron County	WI	Tony Chucka	1990	10,742
134 3/8	23 7/8	23 6/8	17 5/8	7	7	Crawford County	IL	Michael W. Elliott II	1990	10,742
134 3/8	23 6/8	24 0/8	16 5/8	4	4	Rock County	WI	Erik Hanson	1990	10,742
134 3/8	21 7/8	22 0/8	19 1/8	4	4	Knox County	IL	Michael J. McCall	1990	10,742
134 3/8	24 1/8	22 6/8	21 1/8	7	6	Linn County	IA	William Kula	1990	10,742
134 3/8	22 1/8	22 0/8	19 1/8	5	5	Perry County	IL	Wayne R. Hawkins	1990	10,742
134 3/8	21 5/8	21 1/8	15 7/8	6	5	Brown County	IL	John Knight	1991	10,742
134 3/8	24 1/8	22 3/8	17 7/8	4	4	Baltimore County	MD	Mike Kelly	1991	10,742
134 3/8	21 2/8	21 4/8	15 3/8	5	5	Kenedy County	TX	John W. Wallace	1992	10,742
134 3/8	23 7/8	23 1/8	19 7/8	7	7	Harrison County	OH	William G. Risher	1992	10,742
134 3/8	22 4/8	23 4/8	15 5/8	4	4	West Feliciana Parish	LA	David Fontenot	1993	10,742
134 3/8	21 6/8	21 3/8	17 1/8	5	5	Hopkins County	TX	Scott Moss	1993	10,742
134 3/8	23 5/8	22 2/8	19 3/8	6	4	Montgomery County	IL	James C. Moeller	1993	10,742
134 3/8	21 2/8	20 5/8	15 7/8	6	5	Burleigh County	ND	Jerry Speidel	1993	10,742
134 3/8	24 3/8	25 1/8	18 5/8	4	4	Green Lake County	WI	Mark J. Broder	1993	10,742
134 3/8	23 1/8	21 5/8	16 1/8	4	4	Cecil County	MD	Larry Wilson	1993	10,742
134 3/8	24 1/8	23 6/8	21 1/8	4	5	Westchester County	NY	Michael Chirico	1993	10,742
134 3/8	21 4/8	21 1/8	16 3/8	5	5	Bartholomew County	IN	Ronnie L. Fiesbeck	1993	10,742
134 3/8	21 3/8	21 6/8	14 3/8	5	6	Jasper County	IL	Ira May	1993	10,742
134 3/8	22 4/8	21 1/8	19 0/8	6	6	Dane County	WI	Rodney Krauth	1994	10,742
134 3/8	23 1/8	23 2/8	17 1/8	5	4	Winnebago County	IL	Mike Glavin	1994	10,742
134 3/8	20 6/8	21 0/8	14 3/8	6	5	St. Clair County	MI	Brian D. Girdley	1994	10,742
134 3/8	23 2/8	22 2/8	16 3/8	4	5	Rock County	WI	Daniel Sylvester	1994	10,742
134 3/8	23 1/8	23 2/8	17 2/8	6	5	Columbia County	WI	Frank Mittelstadt	1994	10,742
134 3/8	22 2/8	21 4/8	17 5/8	4	4	Coal County	OK	Steve Foster	1994	10,742
134 3/8	21 6/8	21 3/8	20 3/8	5	5	Maverick County	TX	Casey Harrison	1994	10,742
134 3/8	22 3/8	22 6/8	20 1/8	4	4	Ravalli County	MT	Gregg Welch	1995	10,742
134 3/8	20 5/8	20 3/8	22 3/8	5	5	Shackelford County	TX	James Marc Walraven	1995	10,742
134 3/8	22 3/8	23 6/8	18 1/8	5	5	Berks County	PA	Brian E. Klusewitz	1995	10,742
134 3/8	23 3/8	25 0/8	18 5/8	4	4	Ashland County	WI	Mitchell Mesko, Jr.	1995	10,742
134 3/8	20 1/8	20 1/8	17 1/8	5	5	Weld County	CO	Dale Elliott	1995	10,742
134 3/8	24 5/8	25 6/8	19 5/8	4	5	Bourbon County	KS	Doyle Slinkard	1995	10,742
134 3/8	20 7/8	21 3/8	15 3/8	6	6	Garden County	NE	Bob J. Kingsmill	1995	10,742
134 3/8	24 1/8	23 3/8	19 7/8	4	4	McHenry County	IL	Brent Smith	1995	10,742
134 3/8	20 7/8	20 2/8	15 1/8	5	5	Pike County	MO	Guy Young	1996	10,742
134 3/8	21 0/8	21 5/8	17 5/8	5	5	Marquette County	WI	Todd Zellmer	1996	10,742
134 3/8	21 5/8	20 2/8	21 3/8	5	5	Oregon County	MO	Scotty D. Simer	1996	10,742
134 3/8	22 0/8	22 2/8	19 5/8	4	6	Sauk County	WI	Steve Sprecher	1996	10,742
134 3/8	21 5/8	21 1/8	19 2/8	6	5	McLean County	IL	Dave M. Elliott	1996	10,742
134 3/8	21 1/8	21 5/8	18 1/8	5	5	Winona County	MN	Pete Reisdorf	1996	10,742
134 3/8	20 2/8	20 3/8	18 1/8	5	5	Missoula County	MT	Mark H. Dickhaut	1996	10,742
134 3/8	28 1/8	29 7/8	15 0/8	6	5	Chester County	PA	Steve Mihalcik	1996	10,742
134 3/8	23 0/8	24 1/8	18 2/8	6	4	Okfuskee County	OK	Brian Seaton	1996	10,742
134 3/8	24 1/8	24 4/8	20 4/8	4	4	Worcester County	MA	Bob Inangelo	1996	10,742
134 3/8	19 7/8	19 7/8	16 0/8	6	5	Burleigh County	ND	Terry Deeter	1996	10,742
134 3/8	23 5/8	22 4/8	15 6/8	4	6	Fillmore County	MN	Russell Schroeder	1997	10,742
134 3/8	23 1/8	23 1/8	15 7/8	4	5	Red Willow County	NE	Timothy J. Heckenlively	1997	10,742

WHITETAIL DEER (TYPICAL ANTLERS)

Minimum Score 125 — Continued

SCORE	LENGTH OF MAIN BEAM R	LENGTH OF MAIN BEAM L	INSIDE SPREAD	NUMBER OF POINTS R	NUMBER OF POINTS L	AREA	STATE/PROVINCE	HUNTER'S NAME	DATE	RANK
134 3/8	22 0/8	21 4/8	15 7/8	5	7	Columbia County	WI	Jeffrey T. Levey	1997	10,742
134 3/8	23 4/8	23 6/8	19 1/8	5	4	Forest County	WI	Randy Schultz	1997	10,742
134 3/8	21 7/8	21 2/8	15 3/8	5	5	Dunn County	WI	Jerold Olson	1997	10,742
134 3/8	23 0/8	22 4/8	18 1/8	6	4	Wyoming County	WV	Thomas Wiles	1997	10,742
134 3/8	26 2/8	26 3/8	20 1/8	5	4	Muscatine County	IA	John Russell	1997	10,742
134 3/8	22 5/8	21 4/8	19 6/8	6	7	La Salle County	IL	John Thomas	1998	10,742
134 2/8	21 0/8	21 2/8	16 4/8	5	5	Benton County	IA	Larry Walker	1961	10,824
134 2/8	22 2/8	21 4/8	16 0/8	5	5	Derby	IN	Jack E. Hungate	1963	10,824
134 2/8	21 4/8	22 7/8	18 0/8	4	4	Barton County	KS	Dr. Nicholas J. Gray	1973	10,824
134 2/8	24 2/8	23 4/8	20 4/8	5	5	McLean County	IL	Norman Price, Jr.	1973	10,824
134 2/8	23 4/8	22 1/8	21 0/8	5	7	Du Page County	IL	William M. Voight	1973	10,824
134 2/8	22 5/8	23 2/8	16 2/8	5	4	Burnett County	WI	Severin A. Wanous	1976	10,824
134 2/8	24 0/8	24 4/8	17 2/8	5	5	Fond du Lac County	WI	Doug Bilgo	1978	10,824
134 2/8	21 4/8	21 0/8	15 4/8	4	5	Morrison County	MN	Rodney Forbrook	1979	10,824
134 2/8	22 0/8	22 0/8	18 2/8	4	5	Spink County	SD	Douglas Price	1980	10,824
134 2/8	20 4/8	21 4/8	17 4/8	5	5	Muskingum County	OH	Allen R. Smith	1980	10,824
134 2/8	23 4/8	23 4/8	18 2/8	5	5	Adams County	IL	Ron Jackson	1981	10,824
134 2/8	22 7/8	23 4/8	16 4/8	4	4	Reno County	KS	Monte Long	1982	10,824
134 2/8	23 4/8	23 3/8	17 6/8	5	5	Johnson County	IA	Ken Sovers	1983	10,824
134 2/8	22 7/8	23 4/8	21 1/8	6	6	McLean County	ND	Rich Radke	1984	10,824
134 2/8	22 4/8	23 1/8	18 0/8	4	4	Sheboygan County	WI	Randy Kolpin	1984	10,824
134 2/8	20 5/8	20 0/8	18 4/8	5	5	Dodge County	MN	Chad A. Lenz	1984	10,824
134 2/8	22 4/8	22 3/8	17 6/8	5	5	Monroe County	WI	Steve Heintz	1985	10,824
134 2/8	22 7/8	21 7/8	18 2/8	4	5	Columbia County	WI	Brian P. Schepp	1985	10,824
134 2/8	22 7/8	22 1/8	15 4/8	4	4	Edwards County	TX	Steve Payne	1985	10,824
134 2/8	25 5/8	26 0/8	19 0/8	3	4	Barren County	KY	Wesley Bales	1985	10,824
134 2/8	24 1/8	22 4/8	16 2/8	4	5	Will County	IL	Hugh M. MacCracken	1986	10,824
134 2/8	23 4/8	24 3/8	14 6/8	4	4	St. Clair County	MI	Gerald Conrad	1986	10,824
134 2/8	22 0/8	21 7/8	16 4/8	5	5	Marinette County	WI	Gerald Valley, Jr.	1986	10,824
134 2/8	22 0/8	23 3/8	18 2/8	5	4	Kay County	OK	Jim Sheets	1986	10,824
134 2/8	23 3/8	21 6/8	17 2/8	5	5	Herkimer County	NY	Stanley D. Pomichter	1986	10,824
134 2/8	21 5/8	21 5/8	16 6/8	5	5	Flathead County	MT	Larry Hadley	1986	10,824
134 2/8	21 3/8	23 2/8	15 5/8	5	6	Douglas County	WI	Gary E. Braun	1987	10,824
134 2/8	21 5/8	21 1/8	16 6/8	5	5	Waukesha County	WI	Frank Turck, Jr.	1987	10,824
134 2/8	21 6/8	24 2/8	19 0/8	5	4	Westchester County	NY	Michael Wallace	1987	10,824
134 2/8	22 4/8	20 5/8	15 4/8	5	5	Hamilton County	OH	Ken Pfierman	1988	10,824
134 2/8	21 3/8	21 1/8	17 1/8	7	5	Chippewa County	WI	Rich Varsho	1988	10,824
134 2/8	26 5/8	26 4/8	21 2/8	3	3	Poinsett County	AR	Gary Flemon	1988	10,824
134 2/8	24 0/8	23 6/8	16 6/8	4	4	Kane County	IL	Tony Litts	1988	10,824
134 2/8	23 0/8	22 5/8	19 6/8	5	8	Oakland County	MI	Timothy Rock	1989	10,824
134 2/8	21 2/8	21 1/8	16 0/8	5	5	Logan County	KY	T. J. Faenza	1989	10,824
134 2/8	19 7/8	19 6/8	16 0/8	6	6	Greene County	IA	Glen Garnett	1989	10,824
134 2/8	21 3/8	22 3/8	16 6/8	6	5	Morrison County	MN	Dave Vomela	1989	10,824
134 2/8	20 3/8	20 3/8	16 6/8	5	4	Outagamie County	WI	Daryl Van Geffen	1989	10,824
134 2/8	23 1/8	22 1/8	19 2/8	4	4	Wabasha County	MN	Keith A. Ramthun	1990	10,824
134 2/8	19 4/8	20 2/8	16 4/8	5	5	Butler County	IA	Kent Karsjens	1990	10,824
134 2/8	22 6/8	23 5/8	16 6/8	6	8	Racine County	WI	Michael H. Poeschel	1990	10,824
134 2/8	19 5/8	20 6/8	16 2/8	4	4	Massac County	IL	Chris Sielbeck	1991	10,824
134 2/8	24 2/8	25 2/8	20 2/8	5	5	Genesee County	MI	Ned A. Gibson	1991	10,824
134 2/8	23 4/8	24 0/8	17 2/8	5	5	Athens County	OH	John P. Tolerton	1991	10,824
134 2/8	24 6/8	25 1/8	18 2/8	4	6	Montgomery County	IN	Chad Smith	1991	10,824
134 2/8	23 7/8	23 4/8	19 0/8	7	7	Monroe County	NY	Daniel C. Willard	1991	10,824
134 2/8	24 5/8	26 7/8	23 4/8	6	5	Knox County	KY	Dink Garland	1991	10,824
134 2/8	23 1/8	24 3/8	19 0/8	5	5	Waukesha County	WI	Dirk Stolz	1991	10,824
134 2/8	24 1/8	23 6/8	16 4/8	4	6	Genesee County	MI	Clifford R. Neville, Sr.	1991	10,824
134 2/8	23 6/8	23 4/8	17 5/8	6	5	Gull Lake	SAS	Mel Wiebe	1992	10,824
134 2/8	22 1/8	21 5/8	15 6/8	5	5	Rock Island County	IL	Jesse J. Crouch	1992	10,824
134 2/8	22 0/8	21 7/8	14 2/8	5	5	Columbia County	WI	Michael Reigstad	1992	10,824
134 2/8	20 4/8	22 0/8	15 4/8	5	5	Montgomery County	IL	Rick Laurent	1992	10,824
134 2/8	20 3/8	20 5/8	14 4/8	5	5	Olmsted County	MN	Gregory J. Pepin	1993	10,824
134 2/8	23 0/8	22 6/8	19 2/8	4	4	Winnebago County	WI	Darrell Tritt	1993	10,824
134 2/8	23 0/8	23 2/8	17 0/8	4	4	Pulaski County	IL	Keith Wilson	1993	10,824
134 2/8	24 7/8	23 7/8	17 4/8	7	5	Woodford County	IL	Donald E. Davis	1993	10,824
134 2/8	23 2/8	24 0/8	17 1/8	8	6	Stafford County	KS	Michael Layne	1993	10,824
134 2/8	20 7/8	23 1/8	19 2/8	5	4	Worcester County	MA	Thomas E. Whitaker	1993	10,824
134 2/8	21 7/8	21 7/8	16 0/8	5	5	Jackson County	AL	Benford Sanders	1994	10,824
134 2/8	23 1/8	25 4/8	23 4/8	4	5	Montgomery County	PA	Angus Brown	1994	10,824
134 2/8	22 3/8	22 4/8	18 7/8	6	5	White County	AR	Jamey Miller	1994	10,824
134 2/8	22 5/8	22 5/8	16 4/8	4	4	Morton County	ND	Todd Schaedler	1994	10,824
134 2/8	23 0/8	21 1/8	16 0/8	5	6	Pike County	IL	Donald J. Schreiber	1994	10,824
134 2/8	22 6/8	22 6/8	18 6/8	4	6	Douglas County	MN	Lance Norling	1995	10,824
134 2/8	22 4/8	22 4/8	19 0/8	4	5	Outagamie County	WI	Gene Katers	1995	10,824
134 2/8	23 0/8	22 2/8	16 4/8	4	4	Miami County	OH	Kevin House	1995	10,824
134 2/8	24 1/8	23 6/8	16 2/8	4	4	Chippewa County	WI	Ken Mullen	1995	10,824
134 2/8	22 2/8	21 6/8	16 0/8	5	5	Blue Earth County	MN	Karsten Severns	1995	10,824
134 2/8	21 7/8	21 7/8	16 0/8	6	5	Ohio County	IN	Robert Satchwill III	1996	10,824
134 2/8	23 3/8	23 2/8	17 0/8	5	4	Vilas County	WI	Reynold Schultz, Jr.	1996	10,824
134 2/8	21 1/8	21 7/8	17 4/8	4	4	Buffalo County	WI	Larry Seibel	1996	10,824

WHITETAIL DEER (TYPICAL ANTLERS)

Minimum Score 125   Continued

SCORE	LENGTH OF MAIN BEAM R	L	INSIDE SPREAD	NUMBER OF POINTS R	L	AREA	STATE/ PROVINCE	HUNTER'S NAME	DATE	RANK
134 2/8	23 0/8	24 4/8	20 1/8	5	5	Trempealeau County	WI	Gerald Straube	1996	10,824
134 2/8	25 3/8	24 7/8	15 4/8	4	5	Somerset County	NJ	Darek Wajda	1996	10,824
134 2/8	22 4/8	24 1/8	20 2/8	4	4	Coles County	IL	Cliff Campbell	1996	10,824
134 2/8	22 3/8	22 5/8	22 4/8	5	5	Mills County	IA	Tom Kelly	1996	10,824
134 2/8	24 5/8	23 1/8	17 2/8	4	4	Page County	VA	Paul Comer	1997	10,824
134 2/8	20 2/8	20 5/8	16 2/8	5	5	Winona County	MN	Jim Woods	1997	10,824
134 2/8	21 2/8	22 0/8	19 2/8	4	4	Cayuga County	NY	Paul W. Heath	1997	10,824
134 2/8	20 1/8	19 6/8	17 2/8	5	5	Jo Daviess County	IL	Mike Kane	1997	10,824
134 2/8	20 1/8	20 0/8	17 0/8	5	5	Forest County	WI	Richard G. Musselman	1997	10,824
134 1/8	23 2/8	23 3/8	20 1/8	5	5	Brown County	IN	Jason Thompson	1966	10,905
134 1/8	21 2/8	22 6/8	18 2/8	7	5	Vanderburgh County	IN	William H. Davis	1967	10,905
134 1/8	24 7/8	25 4/8	21 3/8	6	5	Morrison County	MN	Vincent Pajak	1973	10,905
134 1/8	24 3/8	23 6/8	20 2/8	4	5	Hopkins County	KY	James R. Williams	1978	10,905
134 1/8	19 6/8	19 7/8	16 2/8	7	7	Benton County	TN	Robert Blackstock	1978	10,905
134 1/8	24 6/8	22 7/8	17 3/8	5	5	Jones County	IA	Harold Erger	1979	10,905
134 1/8	22 4/8	22 7/8	16 3/8	4	4	Allen County	IN	Martin C. Yager	1979	10,905
134 1/8	23 0/8	21 0/8	16 3/8	4	4	Jackson County	MO	Marvin Thomey	1980	10,905
134 1/8	22 0/8	24 0/8	16 1/8	5	5	Day County	SD	Rick Stone	1981	10,905
134 1/8	23 4/8	22 2/8	19 1/8	5	5	Allamakee County	IA	Brian Carlson	1981	10,905
134 1/8	21 1/8	19 4/8	17 3/8	5	5	Genesee County	MI	Richard J. Parkhurst	1982	10,905
134 1/8	19 6/8	18 3/8	16 1/8	6	5	Washington County	WI	Christopher J. Dequardo	1982	10,905
134 1/8	22 2/8	22 0/8	17 4/8	6	7	Wabaunsee County	KS	Gary Hunsicker	1983	10,905
134 1/8	23 0/8	22 3/8	18 1/8	5	5	Westmoreland County	PA	Joseph Ringling	1985	10,905
134 1/8	22 3/8	17 3/8	15 3/8	8	5	Crawford County	WI	Randall Nash	1985	10,905
134 1/8	23 0/8	21 6/8	19 3/8	4	4	Perry County	IN	Junis S. Ingle	1985	10,905
134 1/8	22 6/8	23 6/8	16 7/8	4	4	Sussex County	NJ	Vincent Ridner	1985	10,905
134 1/8	24 0/8	23 0/8	18 5/8	5	6	Frederick County	MD	Melvin F. Keith, Jr.	1986	10,905
134 1/8	19 0/8	20 3/8	17 7/8	5	5	Carroll County	AR	Ronnie Smith	1986	10,905
134 1/8	21 6/8	21 0/8	15 3/8	5	5	Clinton County	MI	Jeffery A. Tolliver	1986	10,905
134 1/8	23 3/8	24 0/8	19 3/8	4	4	Poinsett County	AR	Jeff Vaughn	1986	10,905
134 1/8	25 4/8	26 2/8	19 3/8	4	4	Holmes County	OH	Richard A. Hawkins	1987	10,905
134 1/8	23 4/8	24 6/8	19 5/8	5	6	Pierce County	WI	Patrick McKenzie	1987	10,905
134 1/8	20 1/8	22 3/8	15 1/8	5	5	Buffalo County	WI	Marlin Mueller	1988	10,905
134 1/8	21 0/8	20 4/8	15 3/8	5	5	Marquette County	WI	William Steinfort	1988	10,905
134 1/8	23 6/8	23 6/8	20 1/8	4	6	Madison County	IA	Glenn D. Vondra	1988	10,905
134 1/8	23 1/8	23 4/8	17 3/8	5	5	Dodge County	MN	Robert Oldefendt	1989	10,905
134 1/8	23 2/8	23 3/8	18 5/8	4	4	Arkansas County	AR	Chuck Wallace	1989	10,905
134 1/8	22 0/8	22 0/8	16 0/8	7	5	Brooks County	TX	Mark Culver	1989	10,905
134 1/8	21 2/8	21 4/8	17 1/8	5	5	Broadwater County	MT	Barry Howard	1989	10,905
134 1/8	22 5/8	22 1/8	18 3/8	4	4	Sullivan County	IN	Ron Medley	1989	10,905
134 1/8	22 7/8	22 7/8	15 7/8	5	4	Hillsdale County	MI	John T. Glassburn	1989	10,905
134 1/8	20 0/8	20 0/8	15 5/8	5	5	Rock County	MN	David Paquette	1989	10,905
134 1/8	20 0/8	19 0/8	17 1/8	5	5	Pierce County	WI	Jeremy Shutz	1990	10,905
134 1/8	20 4/8	22 0/8	16 7/8	5	5	Parkland County	ALB	Christopher R. Green	1990	10,905
134 1/8	19 4/8	21 0/8	12 5/8	5	5	Franklin County	MO	Donald Hutchings	1991	10,905
134 1/8	22 1/8	22 5/8	18 1/8	4	4	Meade County	KY	William H. Biddle	1991	10,905
134 1/8	22 3/8	23 2/8	18 7/8	5	5	Lehigh County	PA	Ron Wentz, Jr.	1991	10,905
134 1/8	22 2/8	23 6/8	18 0/8	4	5	Watonwan County	MN	David G. Raney	1991	10,905
134 1/8	24 0/8	23 7/8	15 1/8	6	8	Linn County	KS	Gary Robertson	1991	10,905
134 1/8	21 2/8	21 3/8	12 6/8	8	7	Parker County	TX	Dustin Meaders	1991	10,905
134 1/8	23 2/8	23 6/8	18 3/8	4	4	Berkshire County	MA	Joseph Shaheen	1991	10,905
134 1/8	22 4/8	22 4/8	15 5/8	5	6	Franklin County	KS	Teryl Hrabe	1991	10,905
134 1/8	19 4/8	19 6/8	17 0/8	8	5	Kerr County	TX	Stephen W. Dean	1992	10,905
134 1/8	24 1/8	22 6/8	19 5/8	4	4	Cass County	IL	William Mayer	1992	10,905
134 1/8	21 6/8	19 2/8	17 3/8	5	5	Weyburn	SAS	Scott Brady	1992	10,905
134 1/8	24 0/8	23 4/8	19 3/8	5	4	Kandiyohi County	MN	Randy James Schoeneck	1992	10,905
134 1/8	20 0/8	20 2/8	16 6/8	5	7	Douglas County	NE	Brad Lewis	1992	10,905
134 1/8	24 0/8	22 7/8	16 7/8	5	6	Brown County	IL	Jerry D. Dale	1992	10,905
134 1/8	20 6/8	21 0/8	16 3/8	5	5	Seward County	KS	Travis Leonard	1992	10,905
134 1/8	22 7/8	23 7/8	17 5/8	4	4	St. Marys County	MD	Shawn M. Day	1993	10,905
134 1/8	19 5/8	21 2/8	16 1/8	5	5	Morrison County	MN	Craig L. Mohr	1993	10,905
134 1/8	20 7/8	21 2/8	16 1/8	5	5	Buffalo County	WI	Tony Snow	1993	10,905
134 1/8	21 6/8	22 3/8	15 1/8	5	5	Price County	WI	Craig B. Cummings	1993	10,905
134 1/8	24 6/8	24 2/8	20 3/8	5	4	Stark County	OH	John Spencer	1993	10,905
134 1/8	21 3/8	21 3/8	17 7/8	5	4	Delaware County	PA	David Burnshaw	1994	10,905
134 1/8	22 1/8	21 3/8	19 7/8	4	4	Screven County	GA	John J. Vickers	1994	10,905
134 1/8	20 6/8	21 1/8	16 3/8	5	5	Chase County	NE	Dennis Goodin	1994	10,905
134 1/8	22 6/8	23 0/8	20 1/8	4	5	Montgomery County	PA	Charlie Houck	1994	10,905
134 1/8	22 6/8	20 5/8	16 5/8	5	6	La Crosse County	WI	Lonnie Burkhardt	1994	10,905
134 1/8	23 3/8	23 5/8	15 3/8	4	5	Sangamon County	IL	Matthew W. Cloyd	1994	10,905
134 1/8	24 0/8	24 0/8	19 7/8	4	4	Will County	IL	Wilfredo Estremera	1994	10,905
134 1/8	23 2/8	23 2/8	20 5/8	4	4	Hamilton County	OH	Randy Cable	1994	10,905
134 1/8	23 4/8	23 2/8	17 6/8	6	6	Coles County	IL	Danny Terril	1994	10,905
134 1/8	22 6/8	23 7/8	19 3/8	4	4	Monmouth County	NJ	Richard Dorando	1995	10,905
134 1/8	21 0/8	21 3/8	15 0/8	6	6	Pulaski County	VA	Gary E. Carty	1995	10,905
134 1/8	22 0/8	22 6/8	15 7/8	5	6	Adams County	WI	Randy Williams	1995	10,905
134 1/8	21 6/8	22 6/8	16 7/8	4	4	Jefferson County	WI	Troy Wegner	1996	10,905
134 1/8	21 6/8	22 1/8	15 1/8	4	4	Frederick County	MD	Darrel L. Hall	1996	10,905

WHITETAIL DEER (TYPICAL ANTLERS)

Minimum Score 125 — Continued

SCORE	LENGTH OF R MAIN BEAM L		INSIDE SPREAD	NUMBER OF R POINTS L		AREA	STATE/ PROVINCE	HUNTER'S NAME	DATE	RANK
134 1/8	21 3/8	21 2/8	16 7/8	5	5	Buffalo County	WI	Gary Aron	1996	10,905
134 1/8	22 2/8	23 2/8	18 1/8	6	7	Greene County	OH	Joe L. Stewart	1997	10,905
134 1/8	21 3/8	20 4/8	15 2/8	5	6	Wabaunsee County	KS	Brad Porubsky	1997	10,905
134 1/8	21 3/8	20 2/8	14 7/8	5	5	Switzerland County	IN	Derek Fowler	1997	10,905
134 1/8	25 1/8	25 4/8	20 2/8	4	5	Pope County	IL	Ron Swanger	1997	10,905
134 1/8	23 1/8	22 2/8	16 5/8	4	5	Allamakee County	IA	Jim Kieler	1997	10,905
134 1/8	23 4/8	23 4/8	16 7/8	6	5	Holt County	MO	Rick Schenecker	1997	10,905
134 1/8	24 0/8	23 6/8	16 1/8	6	5	Mills County	IA	Steve Murphy	1997	10,905
134 1/8	21 0/8	21 1/8	18 1/8	5	5	Raleigh County	WV	Argle Cook	1997	10,905
134 1/8	21 5/8	21 7/8	15 5/8	4	4	Hardin County	KY	Tim Helm	1997	10,905
134 1/8	20 6/8	21 3/8	18 5/8	5	5	Beaver County	PA	David M. Moslen	1998	10,905
134 1/8	21 4/8	21 7/8	17 3/8	5	6	White Fox	SAS	Bruce Knapp	1998	10,905
134 0/8	23 7/8	23 7/8	19 0/8	4	5	Grundy County	IL	Henry F. Blaha	1977	10,986
134 0/8	23 1/8	22 6/8	15 6/8	7	6	Calhoun County	MI	James D. Warner	1979	10,986
134 0/8	23 4/8	24 1/8	17 6/8	6	5	St. Joseph County	MI	Randy A. Gordon	1981	10,986
134 0/8	23 6/8	22 7/8	20 4/8	5	6	Coshocton County	OH	William Randles	1981	10,986
134 0/8	23 6/8	25 2/8	17 6/8	4	4	Lawrence County	OH	Robert D. Wilson	1981	10,986
134 0/8	21 6/8	20 5/8	18 0/8	6	6	Nicollet County	MN	Karsten Severns	1982	10,986
134 0/8	21 1/8	21 1/8	17 2/8	5	5	Winnebago County	IL	Terry Hall	1982	10,986
134 0/8	22 2/8	21 7/8	20 0/8	5	4	Eau Claire County	WI	Donald E. Moss	1983	10,986
134 0/8	21 2/8	21 2/8	15 3/8	5	7	Reno County	KS	Norbert Bechtel	1983	10,986
134 0/8	22 5/8	22 1/8	16 6/8	5	5	Monroe County	WI	James Schwaegerl	1984	10,986
134 0/8	22 2/8	21 6/8	17 0/8	4	5	Miami County	KS	Jackie Bethel	1984	10,986
134 0/8	25 0/8	24 4/8	17 3/8	4	5	Fayette County	OH	Don M. Curtin	1984	10,986
134 0/8	19 5/8	20 2/8	16 6/8	6	6	Stephenson County	IL	Greg Deutsch	1984	10,986
134 0/8	23 3/8	24 0/8	18 6/8	4	4	Crawford County	IL	Robert Loveall	1985	10,986
134 0/8	22 1/8	22 0/8	17 4/8	4	4	Waukesha County	WI	James J. Mislang	1985	10,986
134 0/8	22 5/8	23 0/8	17 0/8	4	4	Washtenaw County	MI	James E. Bauer	1986	10,986
134 0/8	24 0/8	23 6/8	19 6/8	4	4	Jones County	MS	Samuel Husser	1986	10,986
134 0/8	20 0/8	20 4/8	13 4/8	5	5	Kenedy County	TX	David Almaraz	1986	10,986
134 0/8	21 4/8	22 6/8	16 0/8	5	5	Dane County	WI	Gordy M. Brings	1986	10,986
134 0/8	20 5/8	21 2/8	15 0/8	4	4	Morton County	ND	Doug Schlosser	1986	10,986
134 0/8	21 2/8	19 5/8	17 4/8	5	6	Shawnee County	KS	Tom Crites	1987	10,986
134 0/8	22 5/8	22 1/8	15 4/8	4	4	Boone County	MO	Curtis Thornhill	1987	10,986
134 0/8	22 0/8	22 6/8	18 4/8	5	4	Owen County	IN	Terry Brandenburg	1987	10,986
134 0/8	19 6/8	19 6/8	15 2/8	6	6	Butler County	KS	Mike Demel	1987	10,986
134 0/8	22 3/8	23 0/8	17 6/8	8	7	Seward County	NE	Pat Bogenreif	1988	10,986
134 0/8	22 3/8	21 4/8	17 2/8	5	4	Trempealeau County	WI	Laverne Dettinger	1988	10,986
134 0/8	24 4/8	24 1/8	17 6/8	6	5	Racine County	WI	Willie Montieth	1988	10,986
134 0/8	19 6/8	19 3/8	16 0/8	5	5	Saline County	MO	John F. Bacon	1988	10,986
134 0/8	20 1/8	20 0/8	15 6/8	5	6	Lake County	IL	John Roscop	1988	10,986
134 0/8	24 0/8	23 3/8	16 0/8	4	4	Mercer County	NJ	Wayne Kalinowski	1989	10,986
134 0/8	22 7/8	22 6/8	15 0/8	5	5	Fayette County	IL	Mike Cauble	1989	10,986
134 0/8	18 7/8	18 1/8	16 4/8	5	5	McHenry County	IL	William D. Weiss	1989	10,986
134 0/8	24 2/8	23 3/8	18 0/8	5	5	Wellington County	ONT	Jan Koszler	1989	10,986
134 0/8	22 7/8	22 7/8	18 6/8	6	5	Steuben County	NY	Paul Rowan	1989	10,986
134 0/8	22 3/8	21 7/8	15 2/8	5	5	Ravalli County	MT	Gary Lee Hall	1990	10,986
134 0/8	22 7/8	22 7/8	17 5/8	6	7	Frederick County	MD	Harry T. Lackey, Jr.	1990	10,986
134 0/8	22 3/8	22 1/8	17 6/8	5	5	Labette County	KS	Kevin Frogley	1990	10,986
134 0/8	22 3/8	23 1/8	21 2/8	4	4	Randolph County	IN	Don Fields	1990	10,986
134 0/8	23 4/8	23 1/8	16 5/8	6	6	Lawrence County	OH	Gerald W. Kouns	1990	10,986
134 0/8	21 3/8	23 1/8	16 6/8	6	6	Waupaca County	WI	Rod T. Gullixon	1990	10,986
134 0/8	23 7/8	23 4/8	19 1/8	6	10	Beltrami County	MN	Harold A. Borchers	1990	10,986
134 0/8	22 3/8	21 2/8	17 4/8	4	4	Harvey County	KS	Rick Dodd	1990	10,986
134 0/8	20 4/8	21 0/8	19 2/8	5	5	Marinette County	WI	Ryan J. Dorak	1991	10,986
134 0/8	23 7/8	23 3/8	16 4/8	6	5	Peoria County	IL	Don Harper	1991	10,986
134 0/8	23 1/8	24 0/8	16 0/8	4	5	Becker County	MN	Perry L. Bertek	1991	10,986
134 0/8	22 2/8	22 0/8	18 0/8	5	5	Madison County	NY	Llyod L. Weigel	1991	10,986
134 0/8	24 4/8	24 5/8	18 6/8	5	5	Sedgwick County	CO	John Graham	1991	10,986
134 0/8	24 0/8	23 1/8	16 6/8	5	5	Osage County	OK	Johnny Lamb	1991	10,986
134 0/8	21 4/8	21 4/8	16 4/8	4	4	Buffalo County	WI	Ralph Lyon	1992	10,986
134 0/8	21 2/8	22 7/8	16 0/8	5	5	Providence County	RI	Steven Santanelli	1992	10,986
134 0/8	22 4/8	22 1/8	16 2/8	5	5	Walworth County	WI	Pete Koerner	1992	10,986
134 0/8	22 5/8	22 0/8	15 6/8	4	5	Franklin County	KS	Timothy W. Berry	1992	10,986
134 0/8	26 7/8	26 2/8	19 6/8	4	4	Franklin County	MA	Hans Harris	1992	10,986
134 0/8	23 5/8	23 0/8	17 2/8	5	4	Dimmit County	TX	Hugh A. Fitzsimons III	1992	10,986
134 0/8	23 0/8	23 0/8	18 4/8	5	5	Bentley	ALB	Glen Pearson	1993	10,986
134 0/8	21 6/8	20 7/8	17 1/8	5	6	Scotland County	MO	Don Atterberry	1993	10,986
134 0/8	18 7/8	19 3/8	13 0/8	5	5	Portage County	WI	Shane R. Cyran	1993	10,986
134 0/8	21 6/8	22 6/8	19 2/8	5	4	Columbia County	WI	Derek W. Peetz	1993	10,986
134 0/8	20 5/8	19 6/8	15 3/8	6	5	Buffalo County	SD	Randy Knippling	1993	10,986
134 0/8	21 4/8	22 4/8	19 4/8	4	4	Genesee County	NY	Curt Miller	1993	10,986
134 0/8	24 5/8	23 1/8	18 1/8	4	9	Bond County	IL	Robert C. Lindley	1994	10,986
134 0/8	25 0/8	25 0/8	19 2/8	6	7	Franklin County	OH	Richard Critchfield	1994	10,986
134 0/8	21 6/8	21 2/8	18 4/8	4	4	Pottawattamie County	IA	Ron Rockwell	1994	10,986
134 0/8	22 7/8	21 5/8	22 6/8	5	5	Delaware County	OH	Brian A. Jenner	1994	10,986
134 0/8	21 2/8	21 3/8	14 4/8	5	5	EstEvan	SAS	Ken Chipley	1994	10,986
134 0/8	20 3/8	20 1/8	16 2/8	5	5	Rhein	SAS	Nelson Matechuk	1995	10,986

WHITETAIL DEER (TYPICAL ANTLERS)

Minimum Score 125 — Continued

SCORE	LENGTH OF MAIN BEAM R	LENGTH OF MAIN BEAM L	INSIDE SPREAD	NUMBER OF POINTS R	NUMBER OF POINTS L	AREA	STATE/PROVINCE	HUNTER'S NAME	DATE	RANK
134 0/8	24 2/8	22 3/8	17 2/8	4	5	Priddis	ALB	Lorne D. Rinkel	1995	10,986
134 0/8	22 7/8	22 3/8	15 6/8	5	5	Walworth County	SD	Dave D. Knecht	1995	10,986
134 0/8	22 6/8	20 3/8	16 1/8	7	6	Richland County	MT	R. Tim Reed	1995	10,986
134 0/8	21 3/8	21 5/8	16 4/8	5	4	Walsh County	ND	Brian Janikowski	1995	10,986
134 0/8	21 4/8	21 5/8	21 2/8	5	4	Putnam County	IL	David Sabotta	1995	10,986
134 0/8	22 4/8	21 3/8	16 2/8	6	5	Sheboygan County	WI	Martin Seering	1995	10,986
134 0/8	21 0/8	20 4/8	16 2/8	5	5	Montgomery County	IL	Bill Kroeger	1995	10,986
134 0/8	20 4/8	20 2/8	16 6/8	5	6	Stephenson County	IL	Shane B. Kempel	1995	10,986
134 0/8	22 6/8	23 3/8	18 6/8	7	7	Cedar County	IA	Douglas Behrle	1995	10,986
134 0/8	23 2/8	23 1/8	17 2/8	6	5	Webster County	IA	David Rial	1996	10,986
134 0/8	22 1/8	21 2/8	18 4/8	4	4	Van Buren County	IA	Vic Geibel	1996	10,986
134 0/8	22 4/8	22 6/8	19 2/8	6	5	Fond du Lac County	WI	Bryant L. Schumacher	1996	10,986
134 0/8	20 1/8	22 2/8	16 3/8	7	6	Delaware County	OK	John W. Sparkman	1997	10,986
134 0/8	20 2/8	20 3/8	14 6/8	5	5	Victoria County	TX	Trey Boatman	1997	10,986
134 0/8	24 3/8	23 7/8	23 7/8	5	5	Columbia County	WI	Scott N. Bartnick	1997	10,986
134 0/8	23 0/8	23 5/8	18 3/8	6	5	Westchester County	NY	Gus Congemi	1997	10,986
134 0/8	21 1/8	21 1/8	18 6/8	4	4	Potter County	PA	Richard L. Hribar	1997	10,986
134 0/8	23 7/8	23 4/8	20 4/8	5	4	Midland County	MI	Russell Lane Jones, Jr.	1997	10,986
134 0/8	22 0/8	21 7/8	19 0/8	4	4	Kent County	MI	Kenneth Engelsma	1997	10,986
134 0/8	22 2/8	22 1/8	16 2/8	5	5	Hamilton County	IL	Philip Smith	1998	10,986
133 7/8	22 7/8	23 0/8	20 5/8	6	7	Dodge County	MN	Myles Keller	1976	11,072
133 7/8	19 5/8	20 2/8	15 6/8	5	6	Newton County	IN	Howard Severs	1976	11,072
133 7/8	24 4/8	24 1/8	19 1/8	4	5	Barnstable County	MA	Randy Fisher	1977	11,072
133 7/8	23 5/8	22 1/8	18 1/8	4	4	Calhoun County	MI	Douglas Tasker	1978	11,072
133 7/8	20 2/8	20 2/8	16 7/8	5	4	Wabaunsee County	KS	Charles L. Bisnette	1979	11,072
133 7/8	22 1/8	21 7/8	21 1/8	4	4	Kalamazoo County	MI	Louis G. Sari	1979	11,072
133 7/8	19 7/8	20 2/8	16 5/8	6	7	Cortland County	NY	John S. Cutler	1982	11,072
133 7/8	20 4/8	19 6/8	14 5/8	5	6	Hennepin County	MN	Robert Boynton	1982	11,072
133 7/8	23 1/8	23 3/8	16 1/8	5	4	Knox County	IL	Dave Emken	1982	11,072
133 7/8	19 6/8	20 2/8	17 1/8	5	5	Wood County	WI	David J. Rademan	1983	11,072
133 7/8	20 4/8	20 1/8	17 6/8	6	5	Darke County	OH	Richard D. Baird	1983	11,072
133 7/8	22 3/8	22 1/8	18 5/8	4	4	Washington County	KS	Bill R. Mallean	1983	11,072
133 7/8	20 2/8	19 3/8	15 6/8	5	6	Brookings County	SD	William Gibbons	1983	11,072
133 7/8	24 6/8	25 5/8	18 3/8	4	4	Guernsey County	OH	Don Cady	1984	11,072
133 7/8	23 4/8	23 7/8	16 7/8	4	5	Dodge County	WI	Ricki Millard	1984	11,072
133 7/8	22 3/8	22 0/8	16 6/8	5	5	Brown County	IN	Ronald L. Gish	1984	11,072
133 7/8	22 1/8	21 4/8	19 5/8	5	5	Morrow County	OH	Mark D. Mann	1984	11,072
133 7/8	22 7/8	24 4/8	17 1/8	4	4	Jefferson County	WI	Gilbert Krueger	1985	11,072
133 7/8	23 7/8	24 6/8	21 3/8	5	5	Iroquois County	IL	Ray Savoie	1985	11,072
133 7/8	21 1/8	20 5/8	18 5/8	5	4	Stephenson County	IL	Steven Sager	1985	11,072
133 7/8	22 3/8	23 3/8	23 3/8	5	5	Green County	WI	Jeffrey D. Miller	1985	11,072
133 7/8	22 7/8	23 3/8	17 4/8	5	4	Hardin County	KY	Phillip Crady	1985	11,072
133 7/8	22 0/8	22 0/8	17 0/8	6	5	Barron County	WI	David Jansen	1986	11,072
133 7/8	23 3/8	23 1/8	16 5/8	5	5	Oconto County	WI	Daniel Bodart	1986	11,072
133 7/8	20 4/8	20 4/8	18 5/8	4	5	Clay County	MN	Craig Enervold	1987	11,072
133 7/8	21 7/8	21 3/8	15 3/8	4	5	Arenac County	MI	Kenneth C. Bender	1987	11,072
133 7/8	23 4/8	23 6/8	17 1/8	4	4	Rogers County	OK	Ernest Ross	1987	11,072
133 7/8	20 5/8	23 0/8	15 5/8	5	4	Boone County	MO	Tim Grace	1987	11,072
133 7/8	22 3/8	22 3/8	14 5/8	6	5	Pierce County	WI	Tony Snow	1987	11,072
133 7/8	22 1/8	20 2/8	17 0/8	5	7	Adams County	IL	George Kimbrell	1987	11,072
133 7/8	21 2/8	22 1/8	13 5/8	5	5	Osage County	OK	Lonny Bearden	1987	11,072
133 7/8	24 4/8	24 5/8	17 3/8	4	5	Logan County	OH	Alan Regier	1987	11,072
133 7/8	20 6/8	19 7/8	15 3/8	5	6	Miami County	KS	Dan Williams	1988	11,072
133 7/8	25 1/8	23 5/8	16 3/8	5	5	Chisago County	MN	Emil Folsom	1988	11,072
133 7/8	23 2/8	21 3/8	17 3/8	5	6	Bates County	MO	Mark J. Coster	1988	11,072
133 7/8	22 2/8	22 5/8	15 7/8	5	5	Polk County	MN	Darrell Ramsey	1989	11,072
133 7/8	23 2/8	23 4/8	18 3/8	4	4	Washington County	MN	Tim Kabrick	1989	11,072
133 7/8	23 0/8	22 4/8	16 7/8	4	4	Kalamazoo County	MI	Daniel Maurer	1989	11,072
133 7/8	22 4/8	22 2/8	15 0/8	6	6	Kenedy County	TX	Ron Serwa	1989	11,072
133 7/8	23 1/8	23 4/8	19 1/8	4	4	Livingston County	NY	David H. Kosowski	1989	11,072
133 7/8	24 0/8	22 7/8	18 5/8	4	4	Chippewa County	WI	Wayne Krejci	1989	11,072
133 7/8	20 1/8	20 5/8	15 7/8	6	5	Osage County	OK	Terry Mills	1989	11,072
133 7/8	23 1/8	23 1/8	19 3/8	4	4	Sawyer County	WI	Gary Haus	1990	11,072
133 7/8	20 4/8	21 6/8	18 1/8	5	5	Onondaga County	NY	Ron Daniels	1990	11,072
133 7/8	21 5/8	21 5/8	18 2/8	6	6	La Salle County	IL	Richard E. Bolden	1990	11,072
133 7/8	24 1/8	24 3/8	16 5/8	4	5	Lake County	IN	Bernie Pawlasek	1990	11,072
133 7/8	22 6/8	22 4/8	19 2/8	5	6	Salem County	NJ	Mark D. Olson	1990	11,072
133 7/8	26 5/8	26 4/8	21 7/8	5	7	Lake County	IL	Tom Kough	1990	11,072
133 7/8	21 2/8	22 0/8	16 2/8	5	6	Troup County	GA	Chris L. Wright	1991	11,072
133 7/8	24 4/8	24 2/8	19 5/8	5	4	Allegheny County	PA	Thomas W. Eiler	1991	11,072
133 7/8	22 0/8	22 4/8	17 3/8	5	5	Westchester County	NY	Steve Cristantiello	1991	11,072
133 7/8	22 4/8	22 7/8	17 7/8	5	6	Morrison County	MN	Joe Poirier	1991	11,072
133 7/8	22 7/8	23 3/8	16 1/8	5	5	Grant County	KY	Steve Rohling	1992	11,072
133 7/8	20 7/8	21 6/8	18 3/8	5	5	Sangamon County	IL	Donald Lowry	1992	11,072
133 7/8	22 4/8	23 6/8	17 5/8	6	5	Goodhue County	MN	Bill Prigge	1992	11,072
133 7/8	20 7/8	21 6/8	17 5/8	5	5	Chemung County	NY	Rickey A. Bartlett	1992	11,072
133 7/8	23 2/8	24 0/8	23 1/8	7	7	Blue Earth County	MN	Tom Rahn	1992	11,072
133 7/8	23 1/8	24 2/8	19 3/8	4	4	Alexander County	IL	Mark Elfrink	1992	11,072

WHITETAIL DEER (TYPICAL ANTLERS)

Minimum Score 125

SCORE	LENGTH OF MAIN BEAM R	LENGTH OF MAIN BEAM L	INSIDE SPREAD	NUMBER OF POINTS R	NUMBER OF POINTS L	AREA	STATE/PROVINCE	HUNTER'S NAME	DATE	RANK
133 7/8	24 1/8	24 2/8	17 1/8	5	4	Davis County	IA	Bruce Keller	1992	11,072
133 7/8	21 3/8	21 4/8	18 7/8	4	4	Hunterdon County	NJ	Michael S. Smith	1992	11,072
133 7/8	22 0/8	21 1/8	18 5/8	6	4	Macoupin County	IL	John Eldred	1992	11,072
133 7/8	22 0/8	20 6/8	17 1/8	5	5	Live Oak County	TX	Bret Walker	1992	11,072
133 7/8	21 4/8	21 4/8	18 1/8	4	4	Lake County	IL	David J. Tahaney	1993	11,072
133 7/8	22 4/8	22 5/8	17 5/8	5	5	Blue Earth County	MN	Jerry Ostgarden	1993	11,072
133 7/8	23 1/8	23 7/8	15 1/8	4	5	Du Page County	IL	Richard C. Klimes	1993	11,072
133 7/8	25 4/8	23 4/8	16 5/8	7	7	Dakota County	MN	Craig Adams	1993	11,072
133 7/8	22 3/8	22 3/8	19 3/8	4	5	Charles City County	VA	F. Scott Paschke	1994	11,072
133 7/8	23 7/8	21 7/8	15 5/8	4	5	Menard County	IL	John Grosboll	1994	11,072
133 7/8	20 7/8	22 4/8	17 0/8	8	8	Branch County	MI	Jay Larimer	1994	11,072
133 7/8	20 2/8	20 0/8	17 1/8	6	6	McMullen County	TX	Jerry B. Bogle	1995	11,072
133 7/8	22 2/8	22 7/8	17 5/8	5	5	Alpena County	MI	Terry I. Spigelmyre	1995	11,072
133 7/8	20 6/8	20 4/8	18 4/8	7	6	Hunterdon County	NJ	Robert G. Wachendorf	1995	11,072
133 7/8	22 5/8	23 2/8	18 5/8	4	4	Clarion County	PA	Stephen Ferris	1995	11,072
133 7/8	25 7/8	28 5/8	19 5/8	4	4	Miami County	OH	Richard M. Harvey, Sr.	1995	11,072
133 7/8	22 5/8	22 2/8	13 1/8	5	5	Saline County	IL	David Draves	1995	11,072
133 7/8	24 7/8	24 7/8	18 7/8	4	4	Gallia County	OH	Keith Caldwell	1995	11,072
133 7/8	24 2/8	23 5/8	16 5/8	5	5	Charles County	MD	Steven Martin, Jr.	1995	11,072
133 7/8	23 6/8	23 7/8	20 5/8	4	4	McDowell County	WV	Paul T. Perry, Jr.	1995	11,072
133 7/8	23 5/8	23 3/8	19 1/8	6	5	Bay County	MI	Dave Lee Donakowski	1996	11,072
133 7/8	24 0/8	23 6/8	18 3/8	4	4	Montgomery County	OH	John Kingery	1996	11,072
133 7/8	22 5/8	22 6/8	20 3/8	5	5	Berks County	PA	Leon H. Berndt, Jr.	1996	11,072
133 7/8	25 0/8	25 6/8	21 4/8	4	5	Chester County	PA	Craig Hacker	1996	11,072
133 7/8	21 6/8	21 3/8	17 2/8	5	6	Iowa County	WI	Leslie Ladd	1996	11,072
133 7/8	22 5/8	22 4/8	16 5/8	4	5	Essex	ONT	Charles Harb	1996	11,072
133 7/8	27 0/8	26 5/8	20 6/8	6	5	Scioto County	OH	Ryan Darnell	1997	11,072
133 7/8	20 7/8	20 6/8	12 7/8	5	5	Van Buren County	IA	Roger Holdenried	1997	11,072
133 7/8	20 6/8	21 0/8	15 4/8	6	5	Spink County	SD	Tom Wanttie	1997	11,072
133 7/8	21 3/8	21 5/8	17 2/8	4	5	Forest County	WI	Walter Freeman	1997	11,072
133 7/8	22 3/8	20 3/8	15 7/8	5	5	Monroe County	OH	Dean Gomish	1997	11,072
133 7/8	22 1/8	23 1/8	20 7/8	5	5	Winnebago County	IL	Dave Judy	1997	11,072
133 7/8	21 4/8	21 2/8	19 3/8	5	6	Harford County	MD	Richard C. Folino	1997	11,072
133 7/8	23 4/8	23 7/8	19 5/8	5	4	St. Louis County	MO	Richard Warden II	1997	11,072
133 6/8	22 6/8	24 7/8	17 2/8	5	4	Tama County	IA	Chad Sivertsen	1971	11,164
133 6/8	19 6/8	20 1/8	15 2/8	5	5	Stanley County	SD	Rick Ray	1972	11,164
133 6/8	24 2/8	25 2/8	19 7/8	4	6	McPherson County	KS	Mike Chambers	1975	11,164
133 6/8	22 5/8	21 5/8	17 4/8	4	4	St. Marys County	MD	Marvin T. Breeden	1979	11,164
133 6/8	19 5/8	21 5/8	15 6/8	5	5	Harrison County	WV	John Lowther	1982	11,164
133 6/8	22 4/8	22 4/8	17 1/8	6	5	Shawnee County	KS	Frank J. Delci, Jr.	1984	11,164
133 6/8	24 2/8	22 7/8	17 4/8	4	4	Rock County	WI	Gary Johnson	1985	11,164
133 6/8	23 0/8	23 6/8	18 6/8	4	5	Bon Homme County	SD	David "Bruce" Cull	1985	11,164
133 6/8	21 6/8	22 0/8	16 0/8	5	4	Oakland County	MI	Joseph Q. Quin	1986	11,164
133 6/8	22 0/8	21 2/8	15 6/8	6	7	Madison County	KY	Duff Wolfinbarger	1986	11,164
133 6/8	22 7/8	22 6/8	19 4/8	6	6	Canmore	ALB	Kenneth Baker	1986	11,164
133 6/8	22 5/8	22 6/8	17 2/8	5	5	Pottawatomie County	KS	Dennis Wilson	1986	11,164
133 6/8	23 0/8	22 6/8	18 2/8	6	4	Dodge County	WI	Steven H. Ohlemiller	1987	11,164
133 6/8	20 6/8	20 5/8	17 5/8	6	5	Delaware County	IA	John Dillon	1987	11,164
133 6/8	20 5/8	19 7/8	17 6/8	5	4	Jefferson County	IL	Terry Kash	1987	11,164
133 6/8	27 1/8	24 7/8	18 2/8	4	3	Clark County	IL	Gerald Shaffner	1987	11,164
133 6/8	22 4/8	23 1/8	14 3/8	6	5	Scott County	IL	Jack Wallis, Jr.	1988	11,164
133 6/8	24 0/8	22 5/8	18 5/8	4	5	Monroe County	NY	David E. Lang	1988	11,164
133 6/8	22 2/8	22 2/8	15 0/8	7	7	Okfuskee County	OK	Jake Crutchfield	1988	11,164
133 6/8	24 3/8	23 1/8	17 3/8	4	6	Story County	IA	Jon E. Von Feldt	1988	11,164
133 6/8	23 0/8	25 0/8	20 4/8	6	4	Jackson County	IN	Jack L. Young	1988	11,164
133 6/8	23 0/8	25 2/8	18 0/8	4	4	Dallas County	IA	Dan Pickell	1989	11,164
133 6/8	22 6/8	22 6/8	16 4/8	4	4	Albany County	NY	Louis Coluccio	1989	11,164
133 6/8	22 1/8	21 4/8	16 2/8	5	5	Sheboygan County	WI	Mark "Kissy" Kissinger	1989	11,164
133 6/8	24 6/8	24 1/8	18 7/8	5	5	Jo Daviess County	IL	Monte J. White	1990	11,164
133 6/8	22 0/8	22 0/8	16 0/8	5	5	Pepin County	WI	Donald W. Stewart	1990	11,164
133 6/8	24 1/8	23 4/8	20 6/8	4	5	Champaign County	IL	Bud Barnes	1990	11,164
133 6/8	20 2/8	21 3/8	16 4/8	5	5	Furnas County	NE	Kevin J. Bergstrom	1990	11,164
133 6/8	25 1/8	25 1/8	19 0/8	4	4	Irwin County	GA	J. Tony Coleman	1991	11,164
133 6/8	23 1/8	22 2/8	14 0/8	4	5	Jackson County	MO	George Fischer	1991	11,164
133 6/8	22 4/8	23 1/8	17 2/8	5	5	Tom Green County	TX	Ronnie Parsons	1991	11,164
133 6/8	21 1/8	21 5/8	19 6/8	4	4	Harford County	MD	Thomas Paulachok	1991	11,164
133 6/8	22 2/8	23 0/8	17 2/8	4	5	Wabash County	IN	Herbert Jr. Hall	1991	11,164
133 6/8	21 6/8	21 3/8	18 0/8	5	5	Oconto County	WI	Patrick J. Gauthier	1991	11,164
133 6/8	21 4/8	20 1/8	16 2/8	5	5	Clay County	MN	Max Fuxa	1991	11,164
133 6/8	21 1/8	21 1/8	17 3/8	6	6	Waukesha County	WI	Scott H. Van Lare	1991	11,164
133 6/8	25 6/8	26 2/8	16 6/8	8	7	Lake County	IL	Carl Pavlin	1991	11,164
133 6/8	21 7/8	20 4/8	19 2/8	5	5	La Porte County	IN	Ted J. Saliwanchik	1991	11,164
133 6/8	23 2/8	24 0/8	21 2/8	4	5	Effingham County	IL	Tony Hille	1991	11,164
133 6/8	24 3/8	24 6/8	18 4/8	4	5	Madison County	IL	Dennis Collman	1991	11,164
133 6/8	22 3/8	21 6/8	19 0/8	4	4	Shannon County	MO	Norman Yarber	1991	11,164
133 6/8	20 7/8	21 1/8	17 6/8	5	5	Humboldt County	IA	Jerry Lee	1991	11,164
133 6/8	19 7/8	20 6/8	18 6/8	5	7	Kiowa County	CO	Lynn Leonard	1991	11,164
133 6/8	26 4/8	23 7/8	21 6/8	6	6	Fairfax County	VA	Jeffrey S. Dambaugh	1991	11,164

Continued

WHITETAIL DEER (TYPICAL ANTLERS)

Minimum Score 125 Continued

SCORE	LENGTH OF MAIN BEAM R	LENGTH OF MAIN BEAM L	INSIDE SPREAD	NUMBER OF POINTS R	NUMBER OF POINTS L	AREA	STATE/PROVINCE	HUNTER'S NAME	DATE	RANK
133 6/8	22 3/8	21 1/8	17 6/8	5	4	Mercer County	PA	Kim E. Fors	1992	11,164
133 6/8	22 4/8	22 6/8	16 4/8	4	4	Litchfield County	CT	Steven K. Wilson	1992	11,164
133 6/8	23 2/8	23 6/8	16 2/8	6	5	Crockett County	TX	James Batchelor	1992	11,164
133 6/8	22 0/8	19 4/8	19 2/8	5	5	Cayuga County	NY	Richard "Snook" Murray	1992	11,164
133 6/8	20 7/8	21 2/8	18 0/8	5	5	Portage County	WI	Alan J. Thomas	1992	11,164
133 6/8	24 2/8	23 4/8	18 7/8	5	4	Clayton County	IA	Terry Krahn	1992	11,164
133 6/8	21 0/8	21 0/8	17 4/8	5	6	Marion County	IA	David Klobnak	1992	11,164
133 6/8	21 5/8	21 3/8	15 4/8	4	4	Edmonds County	SD	Jerry K. Leair	1992	11,164
133 6/8	23 2/8	24 0/8	20 1/8	5	5	Missoula County	MT	Steve Kamps	1992	11,164
133 6/8	22 4/8	22 0/8	15 6/8	5	5	Chippewa County	WI	Jeff A. Ginder	1993	11,164
133 6/8	21 4/8	22 4/8	17 4/8	5	5	Flathead County	MT	Ronny L. Nail	1993	11,164
133 6/8	21 5/8	21 4/8	13 2/8	5	5	Winneshiek County	IA	Michael McKim	1993	11,164
133 6/8	24 6/8	25 0/8	20 4/8	5	5	Lincoln County	MT	Butch Montagnino	1994	11,164
133 6/8	20 6/8	21 0/8	18 2/8	5	5	Iowa County	WI	Carey Bomkamp	1994	11,164
133 6/8	22 4/8	22 2/8	18 0/8	5	5	Reagan County	TX	Kenneth L. Zoller	1994	11,164
133 6/8	21 6/8	21 0/8	15 4/8	5	5	Shelby County	MO	Jeffrey Allen Bieniek	1994	11,164
133 6/8	23 3/8	22 4/8	16 2/8	4	4	Fairfield County	CT	Robert Padovani	1994	11,164
133 6/8	23 3/8	24 0/8	15 5/8	6	5	Jo Daviess County	IL	Jack Rife	1994	11,164
133 6/8	21 0/8	23 4/8	17 4/8	5	4	Dickinson County	IA	Darwin Goddard	1995	11,164
133 6/8	24 3/8	23 1/8	18 6/8	6	4	Ozaukee County	WI	Eric M. Poull	1995	11,164
133 6/8	21 2/8	20 3/8	16 0/8	5	5	McCulloch County	TX	Joe Dunn	1995	11,164
133 6/8	23 0/8	23 0/8	20 2/8	5	5	Wilkin County	MN	Tobbie Krueger	1995	11,164
133 6/8	22 4/8	22 3/8	15 6/8	5	5	Carter County	MO	Ronnie Peck	1996	11,164
133 6/8	22 3/8	22 5/8	15 6/8	5	5	Grant County	WI	Darin Schnepper	1996	11,164
133 6/8	24 0/8	24 6/8	19 6/8	4	4	Somerset County	NJ	John Puchalik	1996	11,164
133 6/8	21 5/8	21 5/8	17 6/8	4	4	Rock County	WI	Paul Henthorn	1996	11,164
133 6/8	22 0/8	21 6/8	14 2/8	5	5	Sumner County	KS	Jay Kerr	1996	11,164
133 6/8	18 4/8	18 7/8	13 6/8	7	6	Hillsdale County	MI	Michael J. Jarvis	1996	11,164
133 6/8	24 3/8	22 6/8	19 6/8	4	4	Portage County	OH	Donald Vargo	1996	11,164
133 6/8	22 7/8	23 2/8	15 5/8	4	5	Kent County	DE	Donald L. Wood	1996	11,164
133 6/8	21 3/8	21 0/8	20 6/8	5	4	Prince George County	VA	Raymond T. Collins, Jr.	1996	11,164
133 6/8	24 1/8	24 3/8	19 2/8	4	5	Clermont County	OH	Thomas M. Shiveley	1996	11,164
133 6/8	23 1/8	22 5/8	17 2/8	7	5	Butler County	KS	Mike Schweigert	1996	11,164
133 6/8	25 3/8	26 3/8	19 2/8	5	4	Delaware County	OH	Tracy W. Orsbon	1996	11,164
133 6/8	21 6/8	22 4/8	16 6/8	4	5	Jackson County	MI	Jerome Gulvas	1997	11,164
133 6/8	23 7/8	24 0/8	18 6/8	4	4	Monroe County	NY	Dominic Chirico	1997	11,164
133 6/8	22 4/8	22 4/8	15 0/8	5	4	Kaufman County	TX	William Nixon	1997	11,164
133 6/8	22 2/8	21 5/8	18 2/8	4	5	Marquette County	WI	Tim McFaul	1997	11,164
133 6/8	20 2/8	20 2/8	15 6/8	5	5	Macoupin County	IL	Jon Deneef	1997	11,164
133 6/8	22 1/8	23 1/8	17 0/8	4	4	Sauk County	WI	Richard A. Laabs	1997	11,164
133 6/8	23 3/8	23 3/8	21 2/8	4	5	Hampden County	MA	Richard Sorcinelli	1997	11,164
133 6/8	21 7/8	22 3/8	15 2/8	6	6	Macon County	MO	Dale Meyer	1997	11,164
133 6/8	21 1/8	22 0/8	18 6/8	4	4	Creek County	OK	Kevin Moore	1997	11,164
133 6/8	22 0/8	21 5/8	16 4/8	5	5	Suffolk County	NY	Jay Obermeyer	1997	11,164
133 6/8	22 7/8	21 5/8	15 2/8	6	6	Gove County	KS	Sheldon S. Showalter	1998	11,164
133 6/8	24 2/8	23 5/8	17 1/8	6	4	Vinton County	OH	Martin Larson	1998	11,164
133 6/8	22 7/8	22 5/8	18 7/8	4	5	Mercer County	PA	Diane Topper Knechtel	1998	11,164
133 5/8	23 3/8	23 2/8	17 1/8	4	4	Tripp County	SD	Larry Diehm	1965	11,255
133 5/8	19 6/8	19 4/8	16 5/8	5	5	Brookings County	SD	Rodney Foster	1967	11,255
133 5/8	26 6/8	25 7/8	19 3/8	3	4	Blue Earth County	MN	Dean Como	1973	11,255
133 5/8	22 3/8	21 5/8	14 7/8	5	6	Dorchester County	MD	Marlin L. Wolfe	1976	11,255
133 5/8	22 6/8	22 7/8	15 3/8	5	5	Murray County	MN	David D. Swanson	1979	11,255
133 5/8	24 0/8	23 7/8	16 7/8	4	4	Trempealeau County	WI	Robert J. Skroch	1979	11,255
133 5/8	21 6/8	21 7/8	17 2/8	5	6	Washington County	MN	Leonard Ellingson	1979	11,255
133 5/8	21 6/8	22 2/8	17 3/8	4	4	Republic County	KS	Curtis Klima	1979	11,255
133 5/8	22 6/8	23 3/8	16 5/8	7	8	Breckinridge County	KY	Aaron H. Pierce	1980	11,255
133 5/8	21 0/8	21 4/8	16 7/8	4	4	Norton County	KS	Robbie L. Madden	1980	11,255
133 5/8	24 1/8	24 7/8	19 5/8	4	4	Shelby County	IL	Walter Lash	1981	11,255
133 5/8	24 2/8	23 0/8	17 6/8	4	5	Lincoln County	SD	Robert Souter	1981	11,255
133 5/8	20 5/8	21 5/8	17 1/8	5	5	Sanders County	MT	Justin Hoy	1981	11,255
133 5/8	22 4/8	25 6/8	17 7/8	4	5	Dickinson County	IA	Rod M. Sheldon	1981	11,255
133 5/8	21 4/8	21 2/8	17 3/8	5	5	Buffalo County	WI	Tom Pehler	1983	11,255
133 5/8	22 5/8	22 2/8	16 5/8	5	6	Pittsburg County	OK	William A. Willis	1983	11,255
133 5/8	22 6/8	24 4/8	19 1/8	5	4	Strathcona	ALB	David Rose	1983	11,255
133 5/8	23 2/8	23 6/8	17 4/8	5	4	Winona County	MN	Dean K. Reidt	1984	11,255
133 5/8	23 3/8	24 1/8	19 7/8	5	4	St. Joseph County	MI	Timothy A. Balk	1984	11,255
133 5/8	21 4/8	23 1/8	17 5/8	5	5	Buffalo County	WI	Paul M Baures	1985	11,255
133 5/8	22 4/8	22 2/8	19 3/8	4	4	Dodge County	WI	Jim Gregory	1985	11,255
133 5/8	23 5/8	23 6/8	19 1/8	7	4	Rock County	MN	Al Kuehl	1985	11,255
133 5/8	20 7/8	21 1/8	17 2/8	5	4	Jefferson County	MT	Wayne Andersen	1986	11,255
133 5/8	22 2/8	22 3/8	18 7/8	4	4	Kanabec County	MN	Jim Kilpatrick	1986	11,255
133 5/8	21 5/8	22 1/8	17 1/8	5	5	Flathead County	MT	George Charles	1986	11,255
133 5/8	22 5/8	23 6/8	20 7/8	4	4	Holmes County	OH	William Boley, Jr.	1987	11,255
133 5/8	27 2/8	25 4/8	17 2/8	5	5	Campbell County	KY	Jim Young	1987	11,255
133 5/8	22 4/8	23 0/8	16 5/8	4	4	Dodge County	MN	John Fondell	1987	11,255
133 5/8	25 0/8	23 3/8	21 1/8	4	4	Jackson County	AL	Robert Downey	1987	11,255
133 5/8	21 7/8	22 1/8	17 3/8	5	4	Sheboygan County	WI	Glenn Luedtke	1987	11,255
133 5/8	22 0/8	22 4/8	17 2/8	6	6	Linn County	IA	Mike Halsor	1987	11,255

WHITETAIL DEER (TYPICAL ANTLERS)

Minimum Score 125   Continued

SCORE	LENGTH OF MAIN BEAM R	LENGTH OF MAIN BEAM L	INSIDE SPREAD	NUMBER OF POINTS R	NUMBER OF POINTS L	AREA	STATE/ PROVINCE	HUNTER'S NAME	DATE	RANK
133 5/8	24 4/8	24 4/8	17 5/8	4	4	Juneau County	WI	Karl Coyer	1987	11,255
133 5/8	22 0/8	22 3/8	18 5/8	4	4	Rock County	WI	Timothy Fett	1988	11,255
133 5/8	21 6/8	21 2/8	16 4/8	6	5	Green Lake	SAS	Pink Atkins	1988	11,255
133 5/8	24 1/8	24 3/8	18 3/8	5	5	Allamakee County	IA	James M. Vogel	1988	11,255
133 5/8	23 7/8	24 7/8	20 3/8	4	4	Sussex County	DE	Myles Bennett	1988	11,255
133 5/8	23 5/8	24 2/8	17 3/8	6	4	Pike County	IL	Randy Long	1989	11,255
133 5/8	21 4/8	21 4/8	13 6/8	6	5	Garfield County	MT	Mark Litke	1990	11,255
133 5/8	24 0/8	24 0/8	18 7/8	4	4	Crawford County	IL	Charlie Guyer	1990	11,255
133 5/8	22 3/8	22 0/8	20 6/8	8	5	Page County	IA	Chris Barton	1990	11,255
133 5/8	22 1/8	23 0/8	20 0/8	6	8	McHenry County	IL	Richard G. Hickey	1991	11,255
133 5/8	25 2/8	25 0/8	20 1/8	5	8	Grant County	WI	Charles P. Fralick	1991	11,255
133 5/8	24 3/8	23 7/8	18 7/8	5	5	Steuben County	NY	Cy R. Mowery	1991	11,255
133 5/8	19 5/8	20 3/8	14 7/8	5	5	Cass County	MI	Stanley Eugene Andersen	1991	11,255
133 5/8	24 0/8	26 0/8	21 7/8	3	5	Stearns County	MN	Steve Nelson	1991	11,255
133 5/8	22 5/8	22 2/8	17 3/8	5	5	Madison County	IL	Randall L. Perkins	1991	11,255
133 5/8	20 2/8	21 3/8	15 7/8	5	5	Kenedy County	TX	Ben B. Wallace	1991	11,255
133 5/8	23 1/8	21 3/8	17 5/8	5	5	Pierce County	WI	Alan Hines	1992	11,255
133 5/8	22 5/8	23 1/8	19 3/8	4	4	Dearborn County	IN	Matt Slayback	1992	11,255
133 5/8	19 3/8	20 3/8	15 0/8	5	5	Blue Earth County	MN	Darwin D. Arndt	1992	11,255
133 5/8	24 7/8	25 6/8	19 0/8	4	6	Huxbridge	ONT	Francis Ogden	1992	11,255
133 5/8	23 2/8	22 6/8	16 3/8	4	5	Morrison County	MN	Jason A. Vaaler	1992	11,255
133 5/8	24 2/8	22 1/8	18 3/8	5	5	Douglas County	WI	Chad Johnson	1992	11,255
133 5/8	20 3/8	20 7/8	19 3/8	5	4	Logan County	IL	Denis Kindred	1992	11,255
133 5/8	24 1/8	23 0/8	15 1/8	5	6	McHenry County	ND	Mike Lehmann	1993	11,255
133 5/8	21 4/8	21 4/8	15 6/8	6	6	Price County	WI	Greg Spacek	1993	11,255
133 5/8	23 0/8	23 0/8	17 7/8	4	4	Clark County	IL	Harold Funk	1993	11,255
133 5/8	20 2/8	22 0/8	19 7/8	5	5	Hennepin County	MN	Greg Wermerskirchen	1993	11,255
133 5/8	25 4/8	24 6/8	21 1/8	4	8	Washington County	KS	Randy Wilson	1993	11,255
133 5/8	20 4/8	21 1/8	16 3/8	5	5	Valley County	MT	Jim Miller	1993	11,255
133 5/8	22 3/8	22 3/8	17 1/8	6	5	Bent County	CO	Dusty Parr	1994	11,255
133 5/8	23 3/8	22 7/8	15 3/8	4	4	Dane County	WI	Dean Demrow	1994	11,255
133 5/8	23 3/8	23 7/8	19 7/8	5	5	Suffolk County	NY	Joseph Godsell	1994	11,255
133 5/8	21 5/8	21 5/8	21 6/8	5	5	Buffalo County	WI	Bob A. Brunkow	1994	11,255
133 5/8	22 2/8	22 2/8	19 5/8	5	5	Clay County	AR	Phillip Vanderpool	1994	11,255
133 5/8	21 0/8	23 7/8	18 1/8	5	5	Calvert County	MD	Kenneth R. Potter III	1994	11,255
133 5/8	22 5/8	22 7/8	17 1/8	4	4	Morris County	NJ	Russell Davidson	1994	11,255
133 5/8	20 2/8	21 4/8	16 1/8	5	5	Dimmit County	TX	Mark D. Roemer	1994	11,255
133 5/8	22 7/8	22 1/8	18 7/8	4	4	Stokes County	NC	Todd Rothrock	1995	11,255
133 5/8	22 6/8	23 7/8	14 3/8	4	4	Edgar County	IL	Mike Harris	1995	11,255
133 5/8	25 5/8	25 3/8	16 0/8	4	5	Buffalo County	WI	Jeff Owen	1995	11,255
133 5/8	22 4/8	22 0/8	16 1/8	5	7	Halifax County	VA	Randy D. Anderson	1995	11,255
133 5/8	24 4/8	20 0/8	19 3/8	4	4	Chautauqua County	NY	Gail Coan	1995	11,255
133 5/8	22 1/8	21 3/8	19 3/8	5	6	Hardin County	OH	Kyle J. Joseph	1995	11,255
133 5/8	18 2/8	18 6/8	12 5/8	5	5	McMullen County	TX	Roy Baird	1996	11,255
133 5/8	21 6/8	21 1/8	15 5/8	5	5	Sherburne County	MN	Brian J. Gradin	1996	11,255
133 5/8	22 5/8	22 1/8	18 3/8	5	4	Cass County	ND	Terry Freehauf	1996	11,255
133 5/8	21 3/8	22 0/8	17 1/8	5	5	Montgomery County	IA	Travis Paul	1996	11,255
133 5/8	21 0/8	20 3/8	16 5/8	5	5	Reagan County	TX	Jeff White	1997	11,255
133 5/8	22 2/8	28 2/8	19 6/8	4	5	Greene County	MO	Alan Fenimore	1997	11,255
133 5/8	22 7/8	22 7/8	19 3/8	4	6	Dane County	WI	John Bergeman	1997	11,255
133 5/8	20 3/8	20 5/8	16 5/8	5	5	Bon Homme County	SD	Greg Balvin	1997	11,255
133 5/8	22 2/8	21 0/8	16 3/8	6	4	Waukesha County	WI	Jim Suchocki	1997	11,255
133 5/8	20 2/8	20 2/8	15 7/8	4	4	Shelby County	KY	Robert P. Totten	1997	11,255
133 5/8	21 5/8	22 1/8	16 7/8	4	6	Bexar County	TX	Deno Poulos	1997	11,255
133 5/8	20 4/8	20 5/8	16 3/8	5	5	Sumter County	AL	Stan Naramore	1998	11,255
133 5/8	21 4/8	19 5/8	20 1/8	5	5	Big Horn County	WY	Mark Preston	1998	11,255
133 5/8	21 0/8	21 7/8	15 0/8	5	6	Adams County	IL	Nicholas Straniero	1998	11,255
133 4/8	22 2/8	22 0/8	17 2/8	5	5	Burleigh County	ND	Lyle F. Fischer	1956	11,343
133 4/8	23 5/8	23 1/8	19 5/8	4	4	Washington County	NE	John Johnson	1958	11,343
133 4/8	22 7/8	23 2/8	16 5/8	5	4	Hocking County	OH	Ted Schultz	1974	11,343
133 4/8	19 5/8	19 3/8	15 0/8	5	5	Sargent County	ND	Frank Pfeifer	1975	11,343
133 4/8	24 0/8	23 2/8	19 2/8	5	5	Charlotte County	VA	George A. Orme, Sr.	1976	11,343
133 4/8	22 3/8	22 6/8	17 0/8	4	4	Edmonton	ALB	Wilf Hunter	1978	11,343
133 4/8	20 3/8	21 5/8	16 0/8	4	5	Stanley County	SD	Patrick Hoing	1979	11,343
133 4/8	21 0/8	21 0/8	18 6/8	4	4	Jefferson County	WI	Larry Pohlman	1979	11,343
133 4/8	24 7/8	23 5/8	19 1/8	6	8	Pittsburg County	OK	Dwayne Durant	1981	11,343
133 4/8	23 7/8	24 6/8	18 6/8	4	4	Green Lake County	WI	Dan Walker	1982	11,343
133 4/8	21 1/8	20 7/8	16 5/8	5	7	Waupaca County	WI	Randy Hillskotter	1982	11,343
133 4/8	21 2/8	20 0/8	18 0/8	4	4	Franklin County	VA	Mike Weaver	1982	11,343
133 4/8	20 7/8	19 5/8	16 4/8	4	5	Portage County	WI	Tom Doyle	1983	11,343
133 4/8	25 5/8	24 2/8	19 2/8	5	4	Black Hawk County	IA	Jim Lee	1983	11,343
133 4/8	21 4/8	23 1/8	14 1/8	6	5	Door County	WI	Bill J. Peissig	1984	11,343
133 4/8	23 5/8	21 7/8	16 1/8	5	5	Roane County	TN	Ronald C. Cassell	1985	11,343
133 4/8	23 3/8	23 6/8	18 3/8	6	5	St. Croix County	WI	Tod Sturgul	1985	11,343
133 4/8	21 4/8	20 4/8	16 4/8	6	6	Marshall County	KS	Brian McNulty	1985	11,343
133 4/8	22 5/8	23 4/8	14 6/8	5	5	Dodge County	MN	Jimmie Hanna	1985	11,343
133 4/8	23 3/8	22 2/8	20 2/8	4	4	Morris County	NJ	Gary Schmitz	1986	11,343
133 4/8	21 4/8	20 7/8	16 5/8	6	5	Flathead County	MT	Dr. Bennie J. Rossetto	1987	11,343

WHITETAIL DEER (TYPICAL ANTLERS)

Minimum Score 125 — Continued

SCORE	LENGTH OF MAIN BEAM R	LENGTH OF MAIN BEAM L	INSIDE SPREAD	NUMBER OF POINTS R	NUMBER OF POINTS L	AREA	STATE/PROVINCE	HUNTER'S NAME	DATE	RANK
133 4/8	22 2/8	22 2/8	17 0/8	6	5	Dawson County	NE	Randy Ray Wilson	1988	11,343
133 4/8	24 4/8	23 6/8	17 4/8	4	5	Gull Lake	SAS	Robert D. Nye	1988	11,343
133 4/8	22 4/8	22 3/8	21 0/8	5	5	Bradford County	PA	Gary Dewey	1988	11,343
133 4/8	25 4/8	20 4/8	19 2/8	5	5	La Salle County	IL	Tom Sampson	1988	11,343
133 4/8	21 2/8	21 1/8	16 0/8	5	5	Kenosha County	WI	Gerald L. Johnson	1988	11,343
133 4/8	23 4/8	23 1/8	20 6/8	5	4	Polk County	WI	Gordon Bibeau	1988	11,343
133 4/8	23 6/8	23 5/8	16 4/8	6	6	Butler County	KY	Donald K. Russ	1989	11,343
133 4/8	21 7/8	21 6/8	16 4/8	5	5	Texas County	MO	Randy Nickels	1989	11,343
133 4/8	21 7/8	21 4/8	17 6/8	7	7	Tompkins County	NY	James S. Smiley, Sr.	1989	11,343
133 4/8	23 1/8	22 7/8	16 4/8	4	4	Allen County	KY	Ron Johnson	1989	11,343
133 4/8	20 6/8	21 3/8	16 4/8	5	5	Iron County	WI	Ron Leach	1989	11,343
133 4/8	22 0/8	22 0/8	16 4/8	4	5	Wayne County	MO	Donald P. Roper	1989	11,343
133 4/8	20 4/8	20 4/8	16 0/8	5	6	Waukesha County	WI	John A. Gilles	1989	11,343
133 4/8	23 6/8	23 3/8	19 2/8	5	6	Anne Arundel County	MD	Charles J. Pate, Sr.	1990	11,343
133 4/8	20 2/8	20 2/8	14 4/8	5	5	Ozark County	MO	Lane Crisp	1990	11,343
133 4/8	24 5/8	25 6/8	23 4/8	4	4	Kent County	RI	Frank E. Andrews, Sr.	1990	11,343
133 4/8	20 0/8	20 7/8	19 6/8	5	5	Florence County	WI	Scott R. Wilson	1990	11,343
133 4/8	23 2/8	23 4/8	18 6/8	4	4	DeKalb County	IL	Larry Scultz	1990	11,343
133 4/8	22 4/8	21 0/8	17 2/8	4	4	St. Landry Parish	LA	Charles R. Mistric	1991	11,343
133 4/8	21 6/8	21 4/8	15 3/8	5	6	Sheridan County	WY	Jeanette Neisess	1991	11,343
133 4/8	20 5/8	19 7/8	17 4/8	6	5	Randolph County	WV	Franklin E. Fortney	1991	11,343
133 4/8	23 4/8	23 0/8	15 7/8	5	6	Monroe County	OH	William K. Steed	1991	11,343
133 4/8	25 2/8	23 6/8	16 3/8	6	4	Clarke County	AL	D. Lee Guyton, Jr.	1991	11,343
133 4/8	23 1/8	23 6/8	16 4/8	5	4	Dubuque County	IA	Brian J. Krier	1991	11,343
133 4/8	21 1/8	20 7/8	19 0/8	4	4	Hillsdale County	MI	Ronald D. Truitt, Jr.	1991	11,343
133 4/8	21 4/8	22 6/8	16 2/8	5	5	Scott County	MN	Jason Sorenson	1991	11,343
133 4/8	20 6/8	20 5/8	17 0/8	4	4	Grand Forks County	ND	Eric J. Vein	1992	11,343
133 4/8	24 6/8	23 4/8	18 4/8	6	7	Frederick County	MD	George Dreyer	1992	11,343
133 4/8	23 2/8	22 7/8	17 6/8	5	6	Washington County	MN	Chris Ruemmele	1992	11,343
133 4/8	18 4/8	20 6/8	16 4/8	6	6	Allegheny County	PA	Mike Dowling	1992	11,343
133 4/8	20 5/8	22 1/8	18 5/8	8	8	Okfuskee County	OK	Jerry Nevels	1992	11,343
133 4/8	22 4/8	21 3/8	16 6/8	5	5	Stearns County	MN	Mike Betz	1993	11,343
133 4/8	23 2/8	23 4/8	17 0/8	7	7	Baraga County	MI	Kelly Hages	1993	11,343
133 4/8	22 4/8	22 3/8	17 6/8	4	4	Bureau County	IL	Quint P. Quiram	1993	11,343
133 4/8	19 7/8	21 3/8	16 4/8	5	5	Harding County	SD	Donald E. Miller	1993	11,343
133 4/8	23 6/8	23 4/8	16 0/8	6	4	Dakota County	MN	Frank O'Connor	1993	11,343
133 4/8	20 2/8	19 5/8	16 0/8	5	5	Randolph County	IL	Gene Jewell	1993	11,343
133 4/8	22 2/8	22 2/8	17 2/8	4	5	Warren County	VA	William Todd Cooper	1994	11,343
133 4/8	22 6/8	21 7/8	14 6/8	4	5	Jackson County	IL	Owen Keeton, Jr.	1994	11,343
133 4/8	21 3/8	22 3/8	18 0/8	6	6	Vinton County	OH	Robert R. Clark	1994	11,343
133 4/8	23 5/8	22 5/8	21 2/8	4	4	Refugio County	TX	Jack O. Hill	1994	11,343
133 4/8	24 5/8	23 2/8	16 7/8	7	6	Kane County	IL	Paula Blake	1995	11,343
133 4/8	23 0/8	22 7/8	17 4/8	4	5	Adams County	WI	Todd Boden	1995	11,343
133 4/8	22 0/8	21 7/8	19 5/8	4	5	Kerr County	TX	Frank Cavaretta, Jr.	1995	11,343
133 4/8	22 5/8	22 5/8	16 6/8	4	4	McHenry County	IL	Norman Pollock	1995	11,343
133 4/8	22 2/8	22 2/8	19 4/8	5	4	Wayne County	IN	Phil Engle	1995	11,343
133 4/8	23 2/8	24 1/8	18 2/8	4	5	Bayfield County	WI	Roy C. White	1995	11,343
133 4/8	22 6/8	22 2/8	17 4/8	4	4	Linn County	IA	Delbert Carmer	1995	11,343
133 4/8	22 7/8	23 1/8	18 0/8	4	4	Chester County	SC	Wayne Copeland	1995	11,343
133 4/8	23 4/8	23 7/8	19 2/8	4	5	Morris County	NJ	Dennis Hult	1995	11,343
133 4/8	24 4/8	24 6/8	20 6/8	4	4	Fairfield County	CT	Robert Lucas	1996	11,343
133 4/8	21 2/8	21 4/8	15 2/8	5	5	Bayfield County	WI	Craig Bichner	1996	11,343
133 4/8	21 7/8	22 7/8	16 2/8	5	4	Anne Arundel County	MD	Steve E. Willsey	1996	11,343
133 4/8	23 7/8	23 6/8	17 2/8	5	4	Oneida County	WI	Steven D. Glimm, Sr.	1996	11,343
133 4/8	22 4/8	21 6/8	17 6/8	4	4	Ross County	OH	Scott Rawlings	1996	11,343
133 4/8	21 5/8	20 4/8	19 2/8	4	5	Cerro Gordo County	IA	Dennis Neuberger	1996	11,343
133 4/8	21 5/8	21 7/8	18 0/8	5	4	Jefferson County	ID	Douglas S. Kauer	1996	11,343
133 4/8	21 7/8	21 7/8	16 0/8	4	4	Erath County	TX	Tom J. Brooks	1996	11,343
133 4/8	21 0/8	21 6/8	15 4/8	5	5	Looma	ALB	Glen Astle	1997	11,343
133 4/8	22 4/8	22 6/8	15 0/8	4	4	Benton County	TN	Daniel E. Cooper	1997	11,343
133 4/8	21 3/8	22 1/8	18 4/8	4	4	Somerset County	MD	Jerry Lee Pietroski, Sr.	1997	11,343
133 4/8	20 5/8	23 4/8	17 6/8	5	5	Saginaw County	MI	Scott D. Johnson	1997	11,343
133 4/8	21 3/8	20 3/8	15 4/8	6	5	Washburn County	WI	Gerald Rux	1997	11,343
133 4/8	23 2/8	22 3/8	18 4/8	5	4	Saline County	NE	Shane Smith	1997	11,343
133 4/8	24 0/8	22 2/8	17 6/8	4	5	Buffalo County	WI	Ronald A. Books	1997	11,343
133 4/8	24 0/8	26 2/8	17 4/8	4	4	Montgomery County	PA	Bob Kowalczyk	1997	11,343
133 4/8	22 4/8	21 4/8	16 0/8	4	5	Tama County	IA	Ronn Peters	1997	11,343
133 4/8	21 7/8	23 0/8	17 4/8	5	5	Calhoun County	IL	Ralph C. Becker	1997	11,343
133 4/8	23 2/8	22 2/8	16 4/8	4	4	Bartholomew County	IN	Matthew Artis	1997	11,343
133 4/8	21 1/8	21 6/8	15 4/8	5	5	Prince William County	VA	Michael Brown	1997	11,343
133 4/8	22 6/8	21 5/8	18 2/8	5	5	Coahoma County	MS	Wayne Strider, Jr.	1997	11,343
133 4/8	20 2/8	21 0/8	15 0/8	7	7	Brown County	WI	Dan Semrau	1997	11,343
133 3/8	21 0/8	21 2/8	19 6/8	5	4	Watonwan County	MN	Issac Davis	1962	11,436
133 3/8	24 7/8	24 1/8	23 1/8	6	6	Morrison County	MN	Frank Salisbury	1963	11,436
133 3/8	22 6/8	24 0/8	18 0/8	5	5	Dickinson County	IA	Keith F. Ellis	1973	11,436
133 3/8	21 0/8	21 3/8	17 1/8	6	6	Juneau County	WI	James M. Carriveau	1977	11,436
133 3/8	20 2/8	20 0/8	12 3/8	5	5	Pittsburg County	OK	Richard Gill	1977	11,436
133 3/8	24 5/8	24 2/8	16 2/8	6	6	Scott County	MO	Doug Jansen	1979	11,436

WHITETAIL DEER (TYPICAL ANTLERS)

Minimum Score 125 — Continued

SCORE	LENGTH OF MAIN BEAM R	LENGTH OF MAIN BEAM L	INSIDE SPREAD	NUMBER OF POINTS R	NUMBER OF POINTS L	AREA	STATE/ PROVINCE	HUNTER'S NAME	DATE	RANK
133 3/8	19 4/8	20 0/8	15 1/8	5	5	Arkansas County	AR	Dennis Chapman	1980	11,436
133 3/8	22 0/8	22 1/8	16 1/8	4	7	Stearns County	MN	Kevin Sabrowsky	1981	11,436
133 3/8	21 7/8	21 2/8	17 3/8	5	4	Columbia County	WI	Dennis Riggs	1983	11,436
133 3/8	23 5/8	22 3/8	16 7/8	4	4	McHenry County	IL	Randy Lehr	1984	11,436
133 3/8	21 3/8	20 7/8	16 5/8	6	4	Perry County	MO	Dale Korando	1985	11,436
133 3/8	21 6/8	21 6/8	17 5/8	5	5	Winona County	MN	Jim Reidt	1986	11,436
133 3/8	22 4/8	21 4/8	17 3/8	4	4	Fillmore County	MN	Gary Zahn	1986	11,436
133 3/8	22 0/8	21 4/8	17 0/8	7	5	Becker County	MN	David Dahring	1986	11,436
133 3/8	25 0/8	23 2/8	19 1/8	5	5	Jackson County	OH	Robert E. Thomas, Jr.	1986	11,436
133 3/8	22 4/8	22 2/8	15 7/8	6	4	Scott County	MN	Paul Welin	1987	11,436
133 3/8	24 3/8	22 6/8	16 3/8	4	4	Bandera County	TX	Richard M. Young, Jr.	1987	11,436
133 3/8	23 3/8	23 3/8	17 6/8	5	5	Pickaway County	OH	James McElhatton	1987	11,436
133 3/8	22 0/8	22 1/8	16 7/8	5	5	Winona County	MN	Arden M. Schock	1988	11,436
133 3/8	23 0/8	22 5/8	17 4/8	5	4	Rock County	WI	Jerry E. Shear	1988	11,436
133 3/8	21 5/8	20 6/8	18 3/8	4	5	Dodge County	MN	Clinton Wicks	1988	11,436
133 3/8	24 2/8	23 0/8	16 7/8	7	10	St. Clair County	IL	John Brown	1989	11,436
133 3/8	19 4/8	19 4/8	17 3/8	5	5	Harrison County	KY	Kevin Poe	1989	11,436
133 3/8	22 0/8	22 6/8	15 3/8	4	5	La Crosse County	WI	Tim Candahl	1989	11,436
133 3/8	20 2/8	20 4/8	16 5/8	5	5	Lucas County	IA	Bill Brown	1989	11,436
133 3/8	25 6/8	27 4/8	20 0/8	6	5	Hamilton County	TN	Robert L. Moon, Jr.	1989	11,436
133 3/8	23 1/8	22 5/8	20 0/8	4	6	Fulton County	IL	William T. Trainor, Jr.	1989	11,436
133 3/8	21 4/8	21 4/8	15 5/8	5	5	Columbia County	WA	Al Campbell	1990	11,436
133 3/8	22 5/8	21 5/8	17 3/8	5	5	McLean County	ND	Gary Berube	1990	11,436
133 3/8	22 4/8	22 0/8	16 6/8	5	6	Waukesha County	WI	Jim Schaefer	1990	11,436
133 3/8	23 5/8	21 4/8	16 5/8	5	4	Black Hawk County	IA	Jim Hinke	1990	11,436
133 3/8	20 0/8	20 2/8	18 3/8	5	5	Lincoln County	WI	David Van De Weerd	1990	11,436
133 3/8	21 2/8	20 0/8	16 4/8	5	7	La Porte County	IN	Bill Patton	1991	11,436
133 3/8	22 2/8	22 6/8	20 6/8	6	6	Clinton County	IA	Kenneth Hartmann	1991	11,436
133 3/8	22 5/8	22 2/8	18 7/8	4	4	Webster County	IA	Darle Myers	1991	11,436
133 3/8	23 0/8	23 1/8	17 1/8	4	4	Merrimack County	NH	Roger B. Letendre	1992	11,436
133 3/8	20 4/8	20 1/8	17 1/8	5	5	Duval County	TX	Billy R. Davis	1992	11,436
133 3/8	21 3/8	21 3/8	16 1/8	5	6	Washington County	MN	Rich Urbaniak	1992	11,436
133 3/8	22 3/8	22 0/8	15 1/8	6	6	Adams County	WI	Todd D. Stammen	1992	11,436
133 3/8	19 4/8	19 0/8	14 3/8	5	5	Chatham County	NC	John William Snead	1992	11,436
133 3/8	21 1/8	22 5/8	16 1/8	5	5	Osage County	OK	Scott Bennett	1992	11,436
133 3/8	22 2/8	21 6/8	15 7/8	5	6	Portage County	WI	Hubert R. Klesmith	1993	11,436
133 3/8	19 0/8	20 1/8	14 7/8	6	5	Waupaca County	WI	Rocky Warner	1993	11,436
133 3/8	22 2/8	22 6/8	16 5/8	5	5	Sutton	QUE	Alton Dunakin	1993	11,436
133 3/8	22 7/8	23 0/8	18 4/8	6	6	Johnston County	OK	Jim L. Jones	1993	11,436
133 3/8	20 3/8	20 3/8	15 1/8	5	5	Pine County	MN	John Adrian	1993	11,436
133 3/8	21 0/8	19 2/8	14 1/8	5	4	Haskell County	OK	Jerry C. Sturdy	1993	11,436
133 3/8	24 0/8	23 4/8	19 1/8	4	5	McDowell County	WV	Ray Burks	1993	11,436
133 3/8	21 7/8	21 7/8	17 5/8	6	5	Sumner County	KS	Douglas C. Cusick	1993	11,436
133 3/8	22 4/8	22 0/8	17 2/8	6	4	Brooks County	TX	Jimmy W. McBee	1993	11,436
133 3/8	25 0/8	24 7/8	20 1/8	4	4	Greene County	IL	Robert Neff	1994	11,436
133 3/8	22 4/8	22 3/8	15 3/8	5	6	Prairie County	AR	Chris Patton	1994	11,436
133 3/8	23 4/8	24 0/8	18 5/8	4	4	Washtenaw County	MI	Charles Larry Roehm	1994	11,436
133 3/8	23 0/8	22 4/8	15 1/8	4	4	Goodhue County	MN	John "Jack" Cordes	1994	11,436
133 3/8	22 1/8	23 6/8	16 7/8	4	5	Lake County	IL	Brian Fecteau	1994	11,436
133 3/8	22 5/8	22 5/8	18 5/8	4	4	Bucks County	PA	Ronald W. Krauss	1994	11,436
133 3/8	20 4/8	20 7/8	14 7/8	6	5	Pike County	IL	Sean Rider	1994	11,436
133 3/8	23 1/8	23 1/8	16 1/8	4	5	Washington County	MD	Donovan Fitz	1994	11,436
133 3/8	21 1/8	19 6/8	17 5/8	5	5	Payne County	OK	Vernon L. Dixon	1994	11,436
133 3/8	19 5/8	19 2/8	14 3/8	5	5	McMullen County	TX	Kathleen Ponders	1995	11,436
133 3/8	24 3/8	23 7/8	17 3/8	7	7	Hamilton County	OH	Bill Brinck	1995	11,436
133 3/8	24 1/8	24 2/8	14 3/8	4	4	Alachua County	FL	Craig C. Carpenter	1995	11,436
133 3/8	22 6/8	21 3/8	19 0/8	5	7	Washington County	OH	Rich Wynn	1995	11,436
133 3/8	22 3/8	22 1/8	15 3/8	4	4	Sauk County	WI	Keith Templin	1995	11,436
133 3/8	21 0/8	21 7/8	15 7/8	5	5	Saginaw County	MI	Thomas Amy	1995	11,436
133 3/8	22 6/8	21 1/8	14 7/8	6	5	Vermilion County	IL	William Cottrell	1995	11,436
133 3/8	20 6/8	20 0/8	18 3/8	6	5	Ravalli County	MT	Rob Bourne	1996	11,436
133 3/8	21 5/8	22 5/8	18 1/8	5	5	Jefferson County	WI	Troy A. Martinez	1996	11,436
133 3/8	21 3/8	21 7/8	21 3/8	4	4	Cortland County	NY	Chad Butts	1996	11,436
133 3/8	25 0/8	24 0/8	19 3/8	4	5	Jefferson County	WI	Karen Raasch	1996	11,436
133 3/8	22 0/8	21 3/8	13 7/8	5	5	Kane County	IL	Richard Hight	1996	11,436
133 3/8	26 0/8	25 0/8	20 0/8	4	6	Kane County	IL	Bill Yoakum	1996	11,436
133 3/8	22 1/8	22 3/8	16 1/8	5	5	Polk County	WI	David Lendosky	1997	11,436
133 3/8	21 5/8	23 2/8	15 7/8	4	4	Winona County	MN	Jim Panek	1997	11,436
133 3/8	24 1/8	24 4/8	19 3/8	4	4	Lawrence County	OH	John D. Davis	1997	11,436
133 3/8	20 6/8	21 5/8	17 5/8	4	4	Union County	SD	Bradley R. Bertrand	1998	11,436
133 3/8	20 2/8	19 4/8	16 1/8	5	5	Allegan County	MI	Dennis B. Dykhouse	1998	11,436
133 2/8	18 4/8	18 6/8	14 7/8	5	6	Mitchell County	IA	Omar A. Toye	1958	11,513
133 2/8	23 6/8	22 5/8	18 2/8	8	8	Olmsted County	MN	Roger E. Enderson	1961	11,513
133 2/8	23 6/8	23 6/8	18 5/8	4	4	Pittsburg County	OK	Fred Parkison	1968	11,513
133 2/8	21 1/8	20 7/8	18 2/8	5	5	Wabasha County	MN	Myles Keller	1977	11,513
133 2/8	22 1/8	22 5/8	16 0/8	8	7	Lafayette County	WI	Dave Carey	1979	11,513
133 2/8	19 0/8	19 1/8	16 4/8	5	5	Waushara County	WI	Kenneth A. Wollermann	1979	11,513
133 2/8	21 2/8	22 1/8	13 1/8	5	7	Portage County	WI	Alan Carter	1981	11,513

WHITETAIL DEER (TYPICAL ANTLERS)

Minimum Score 125

SCORE	LENGTH OF MAIN BEAM R	LENGTH OF MAIN BEAM L	INSIDE SPREAD	NUMBER OF POINTS R	NUMBER OF POINTS L	AREA	STATE/ PROVINCE	HUNTER'S NAME	DATE	RANK
133 2/8	20 2/8	20 3/8	15 0/8	5	5	St. Louis County	MN	Greg Opland	1981	11,513
133 2/8	24 7/8	24 6/8	20 2/8	4	3	Davis County	IA	Richard Squire	1981	11,513
133 2/8	20 4/8	20 4/8	20 0/8	4	5	Noble County	OH	ElRoy Kuhner	1982	11,513
133 2/8	24 1/8	23 2/8	17 0/8	6	7	Kingsbury County	SD	Stanley A. Rauch	1982	11,513
133 2/8	23 7/8	24 0/8	18 4/8	4	5	Shelby County	IL	Charles Martin, Jr.	1983	11,513
133 2/8	22 7/8	22 5/8	18 1/8	5	6	Harper County	KS	Steven R. Lowe	1983	11,513
133 2/8	23 4/8	25 4/8	19 1/8	6	6	Ford County	KS	Melvin Habiger	1983	11,513
133 2/8	23 3/8	23 2/8	20 6/8	4	4	Union County	IL	Brad Harris	1984	11,513
133 2/8	20 0/8	20 5/8	14 2/8	5	5	Madison County	AL	Tony Robinson	1985	11,513
133 2/8	22 4/8	22 2/8	19 5/8	5	6	Whiteside County	IL	Art Heinze	1985	11,513
133 2/8	22 7/8	24 0/8	16 6/8	6	7	Jersey County	IL	David F. Woolsey	1986	11,513
133 2/8	22 1/8	22 5/8	19 2/8	4	6	Morrison County	MN	Donald E. Trusty	1987	11,513
133 2/8	21 6/8	22 2/8	18 6/8	4	4	Forest County	WI	Rick H. Pendl	1988	11,513
133 2/8	24 6/8	23 3/8	19 3/8	8	6	Fulton County	IL	Patrick Cebuhar	1988	11,513
133 2/8	22 3/8	22 6/8	18 2/8	4	4	Hancock County	IL	William T. Kirby	1988	11,513
133 2/8	22 5/8	24 6/8	20 2/8	4	4	Pulaski County	GA	David Pounds	1988	11,513
133 2/8	22 5/8	22 6/8	16 2/8	5	5	Polk County	WI	Barry Wickstrom	1988	11,513
133 2/8	22 7/8	22 7/8	17 2/8	4	4	Buffalo County	WI	Dale Parker	1989	11,513
133 2/8	22 5/8	23 2/8	17 4/8	4	4	Keya Paha County	NE	Wesley Hitchcock	1989	11,513
133 2/8	21 3/8	21 6/8	15 0/8	5	5	Marinette County	WI	James L. Lesperance	1989	11,513
133 2/8	23 0/8	19 2/8	18 6/8	5	5	Adams County	IA	Dennis Haley	1989	11,513
133 2/8	24 4/8	23 6/8	18 0/8	5	5	Montgomery County	IL	Roy Alvin Burris	1989	11,513
133 2/8	21 5/8	23 3/8	19 0/8	4	5	Waukesha County	WI	Ralph Zalewski	1989	11,513
133 2/8	19 0/8	20 0/8	15 4/8	6	5	Brown County	SD	Bradley K. Larson	1989	11,513
133 2/8	22 3/8	23 3/8	20 0/8	4	5	Jefferson County	WI	Robert Green	1989	11,513
133 2/8	21 4/8	21 3/8	18 2/8	5	5	Rice County	KS	Hughlene Gillespie	1990	11,513
133 2/8	21 4/8	20 1/8	16 2/8	5	5	Pike County	IL	Chris Johnson	1990	11,513
133 2/8	22 4/8	22 4/8	19 2/8	6	4	Lake County	IL	Tom T. King	1990	11,513
133 2/8	24 4/8	22 4/8	15 4/8	5	5	Albany County	NY	Michael Rudolph	1990	11,513
133 2/8	23 2/8	22 2/8	16 4/8	5	7	Howard County	IA	Scott Runde	1990	11,513
133 2/8	23 7/8	23 5/8	14 1/8	5	5	Otoe County	NE	Larry Starner	1990	11,513
133 2/8	21 5/8	20 7/8	15 2/8	5	5	Dane County	WI	Steve Grabandt	1991	11,513
133 2/8	22 2/8	22 0/8	20 2/8	5	5	Warren County	GA	Ralph Owen	1991	11,513
133 2/8	24 5/8	24 4/8	19 1/8	7	5	Wagoner County	OK	Jon Brewer	1991	11,513
133 2/8	23 0/8	23 2/8	17 6/8	5	5	Winneshiek County	IA	Martin Andera	1991	11,513
133 2/8	24 0/8	23 4/8	18 4/8	5	6	Pike County	IL	Dale Carter	1991	11,513
133 2/8	23 6/8	22 6/8	16 4/8	6	5	Montgomery County	IA	Dick Paul	1991	11,513
133 2/8	21 2/8	21 7/8	15 6/8	6	6	Jo Daviess County	IL	Lynn Busch	1991	11,513
133 2/8	21 6/8	21 7/8	18 2/8	4	4	Seneca County	OH	Jill Mayes	1991	11,513
133 2/8	23 5/8	22 2/8	15 6/8	4	4	St. Marys County	MD	Keith Morgan	1992	11,513
133 2/8	21 3/8	21 2/8	18 6/8	5	4	Dane County	WI	Gene J. Loomis	1992	11,513
133 2/8	25 0/8	23 4/8	16 0/8	4	5	Preble County	OH	Gary Strawsburg	1992	11,513
133 2/8	21 5/8	21 4/8	19 0/8	5	4	Columbia County	WI	David L. Zitzner	1992	11,513
133 2/8	20 6/8	20 6/8	17 2/8	4	4	Walworth County	WI	Chuck Palmer	1992	11,513
133 2/8	25 2/8	23 2/8	20 4/8	4	5	Kane County	IL	Dean V. Ashton	1992	11,513
133 2/8	21 0/8	21 4/8	15 2/8	5	5	Will County	IL	David Bartlett	1992	11,513
133 2/8	19 6/8	21 6/8	19 2/8	5	6	Steele County	ND	David Brag	1993	11,513
133 2/8	22 2/8	20 4/8	17 4/8	4	4	Pickett County	TN	Robert E. Lee	1993	11,513
133 2/8	21 7/8	22 2/8	17 6/8	5	5	Izard County	AR	John M. Riggs	1993	11,513
133 2/8	23 6/8	22 0/8	18 6/8	5	6	Caledon	ONT	Carl Whittier	1993	11,513
133 2/8	20 7/8	20 3/8	17 4/8	5	5	Dodge County	WI	Ken Westphal	1993	11,513
133 2/8	20 3/8	22 0/8	18 2/8	4	4	Monroe County	OH	Brent D. Taylor	1993	11,513
133 2/8	23 1/8	24 2/8	20 3/8	6	5	Polk County	WI	Andrew Roger Lehman	1993	11,513
133 2/8	23 3/8	23 3/8	14 0/8	4	4	Jackson County	AL	Joey Arnold	1993	11,513
133 2/8	24 3/8	25 0/8	16 4/8	4	4	Holmes County	MS	Tony Johnson	1994	11,513
133 2/8	22 7/8	22 4/8	15 0/8	5	6	Marquette County	WI	Thomas M. Anacker	1994	11,513
133 2/8	23 1/8	21 6/8	16 6/8	5	5	Kenosha County	WI	Jerry Ewens	1994	11,513
133 2/8	22 1/8	21 6/8	17 4/8	4	4	Hand County	SD	Ed Werdel	1994	11,513
133 2/8	21 5/8	21 4/8	17 6/8	4	4	Stewart County	TN	Aaron Daniels	1994	11,513
133 2/8	21 6/8	22 3/8	15 0/8	5	6	Juneau County	WI	Steven S. Board	1994	11,513
133 2/8	20 5/8	19 7/8	15 4/8	5	4	Payne County	OK	Ronny Moody	1994	11,513
133 2/8	20 6/8	21 1/8	16 2/8	5	5	St. Clair County	MI	Donald R. Dewey	1994	11,513
133 2/8	22 5/8	23 2/8	17 0/8	5	4	Lee County	IA	Tim Garner	1994	11,513
133 2/8	21 7/8	23 2/8	18 2/8	5	5	Dane County	WI	John Beetham	1994	11,513
133 2/8	22 7/8	23 1/8	20 2/8	5	4	Union County	KY	Denver Wilson	1994	11,513
133 2/8	20 5/8	20 6/8	16 4/8	5	5	Burleigh County	ND	Elvin Agnew	1994	11,513
133 2/8	20 1/8	25 7/8	17 0/8	5	5	Shawnee County	KS	Greg Bax	1994	11,513
133 2/8	22 7/8	22 6/8	16 0/8	6	6	Brown County	SD	Lee Howell	1995	11,513
133 2/8	23 1/8	22 5/8	18 0/8	4	4	Dunn County	WI	Greg Reisimer	1995	11,513
133 2/8	22 7/8	23 3/8	20 2/8	5	5	Sarpy County	NE	Keith Southworth	1995	11,513
133 2/8	22 1/8	23 1/8	15 6/8	5	6	Greene County	OH	Rodney C. Bailey	1995	11,513
133 2/8	20 5/8	20 1/8	15 6/8	4	5	Muskegon County	MI	Tom Kelly	1995	11,513
133 2/8	20 1/8	22 2/8	15 4/8	4	4	Washington County	MN	Eric Lindberg	1995	11,513
133 2/8	22 3/8	23 5/8	17 2/8	4	7	Trempealeau County	WI	Joe Giemza	1995	11,513
133 2/8	20 1/8	20 0/8	16 4/8	4	5	McHenry County	IL	Al Waller	1995	11,513
133 2/8	21 7/8	21 1/8	14 6/8	5	7	Choctaw County	OK	Mark Holbrook	1995	11,513
133 2/8	22 5/8	23 2/8	16 6/8	4	5	Portage County	WI	James Scott Menadue	1995	11,513
133 2/8	22 6/8	23 4/8	16 2/8	8	9	Rusk County	WI	Thomas F. Tobias	1995	11,513

WHITETAIL DEER (TYPICAL ANTLERS)

Minimum Score 125 — Continued

SCORE	LENGTH OF MAIN BEAM R	LENGTH OF MAIN BEAM L	INSIDE SPREAD	NUMBER OF POINTS R	NUMBER OF POINTS L	AREA	STATE/ PROVINCE	HUNTER'S NAME	DATE	RANK
133 2/8	22 5/8	21 2/8	15 0/8	5	5	Concordia Parish	LA	Benny B. Burris, Jr.	1996	11,513
133 2/8	23 3/8	22 6/8	18 0/8	4	4	Washington County	MN	Todd Flod	1996	11,513
133 2/8	20 3/8	21 0/8	15 0/8	5	5	Gage County	NE	Brant Washburn	1996	11,513
133 2/8	19 7/8	20 4/8	14 6/8	5	6	Trempealeau County	WI	David N. Andersen	1996	11,513
133 2/8	21 7/8	19 6/8	16 0/8	5	5	Branch County	MI	Glenn M. Padmos	1996	11,513
133 2/8	22 4/8	23 2/8	20 6/8	6	5	Jo Daviess County	IL	Chris L. Schnitzler	1996	11,513
133 2/8	23 4/8	21 3/8	18 0/8	4	4	Dane County	WI	Jeffrey Zanow	1996	11,513
133 2/8	23 2/8	23 7/8	17 6/8	4	5	Oneida County	WI	Garth G. Mueller	1996	11,513
133 2/8	20 6/8	22 5/8	18 0/8	5	5	McMullen County	TX	George W. Semple	1996	11,513
133 2/8	22 2/8	22 0/8	15 4/8	4	4	Montgomery County	MD	Jeff Harrison	1996	11,513
133 2/8	23 1/8	25 4/8	19 4/8	5	5	Polk County	IA	Bill Summy	1997	11,513
133 2/8	21 6/8	22 0/8	19 0/8	4	4	Lake County	IL	Steve Andrews	1997	11,513
133 2/8	23 0/8	20 4/8	18 2/8	5	6	Furnas County	NE	Donnie Ray Brown	1997	11,513
133 2/8	21 4/8	21 4/8	16 2/8	4	4	Madison County	IA	Brad Cooper	1997	11,513
133 2/8	24 4/8	25 0/8	19 2/8	5	5	Calvert County	MD	Michael Wolfe	1997	11,513
133 2/8	22 7/8	22 1/8	16 2/8	6	5	Lyon County	KS	Johnny Drake	1997	11,513
133 2/8	25 0/8	24 0/8	24 0/8	5	5	Fairfield County	CT	Brian McCall	1997	11,513
133 2/8	22 3/8	20 6/8	14 2/8	5	6	Adams County	IL	Tim Walmsley	1997	11,513
133 2/8	23 5/8	22 4/8	18 1/8	6	6	Poinsett County	AR	Brian Emery	1997	11,513
133 2/8	21 3/8	21 4/8	17 4/8	4	4	Ralls County	MO	Terry Marshall	1998	11,513
133 2/8	22 5/8	22 2/8	20 4/8	5	6	Dunn County	WI	David T. Blanchard	1998	11,513
133 1/8	22 2/8	21 5/8	16 1/8	4	4	Roberts County	SD	Roland L. Hausmann	1964	11,619
133 1/8	24 5/8	23 7/8	20 1/8	4	4	Perry County	IL	Ron Lay	1974	11,619
133 1/8	20 5/8	20 5/8	17 2/8	6	6	Cowley County	KS	Dr. Phil L. Bradley	1975	11,619
133 1/8	23 2/8	25 2/8	16 3/8	5	5	Scott County	MN	George R. Arimond	1976	11,619
133 1/8	26 0/8	26 3/8	19 6/8	5	5	Litchfield County	CT	Phillip M. Demetri	1976	11,619
133 1/8	20 1/8	20 7/8	16 1/8	5	5	Monroe County	IN	Jeffrey S. Finley	1977	11,619
133 1/8	22 2/8	22 6/8	17 1/8	5	5	Jefferson County	WI	Dennis E. Dabel	1978	11,619
133 1/8	21 6/8	22 6/8	16 5/8	5	6	Hocking County	OH	Ted Schultz	1978	11,619
133 1/8	22 3/8	21 6/8	18 7/8	5	5	Muskingum County	OH	Randy Whitehair	1978	11,619
133 1/8	23 5/8	23 7/8	16 1/8	4	4	Pike County	MO	Jim Holdenried	1979	11,619
133 1/8	23 5/8	23 0/8	15 7/8	4	5	Sauk County	WI	Keith Peetz	1980	11,619
133 1/8	20 4/8	21 6/8	16 1/8	4	4	Bullitt County	KY	Dwight Hughes	1981	11,619
133 1/8	20 6/8	21 0/8	17 1/8	5	5	Walker County	GA	Richard Bradley	1981	11,619
133 1/8	21 3/8	21 5/8	17 1/8	6	6	Marion County	IL	Paul Duncan	1981	11,619
133 1/8	23 6/8	22 6/8	17 7/8	4	5	Morgan County	OH	Milan W. Boone	1981	11,619
133 1/8	21 3/8	20 5/8	15 3/8	5	5	Calvert County	MD	Al Sullivan	1982	11,619
133 1/8	22 2/8	22 4/8	17 7/8	4	4	Oakland County	MI	Gordon E. Bowser	1982	11,619
133 1/8	21 7/8	24 3/8	22 3/8	4	4	Geary County	KS	Mark Junghans	1982	11,619
133 1/8	19 6/8	19 6/8	16 2/8	6	5	Eau Claire County	WI	David Nelson	1984	11,619
133 1/8	22 4/8	25 4/8	21 1/8	4	5	Green County	WI	James K. Campbell	1984	11,619
133 1/8	22 7/8	24 0/8	17 4/8	7	4	Phillips County	KS	Michael Hoft	1984	11,619
133 1/8	21 6/8	23 6/8	18 1/8	5	6	Cascade County	MT	Tom Storm	1984	11,619
133 1/8	21 4/8	21 3/8	16 5/8	5	5	Leavenworth County	KS	John Garrison	1985	11,619
133 1/8	20 0/8	19 4/8	18 0/8	5	7	Clinton County	MI	Mark G. Rademacher	1986	11,619
133 1/8	23 1/8	23 2/8	18 3/8	4	5	Charlevoix County	MI	Norbert Scharenbroch	1986	11,619
133 1/8	24 3/8	24 3/8	19 1/8	5	4	Crawford County	KS	Fred Geier	1986	11,619
133 1/8	20 1/8	19 0/8	15 7/8	5	6	Douglas County	WI	Wallace K. Campbell	1986	11,619
133 1/8	21 3/8	23 4/8	17 3/8	4	4	Kenosha County	WI	Alan Weis	1986	11,619
133 1/8	25 1/8	24 2/8	18 3/8	5	5	Westchester County	NY	Anthony J. Capodicci	1986	11,619
133 1/8	21 1/8	20 3/8	13 7/8	5	5	Dallas County	MO	Thomas N. Crunkleton	1987	11,619
133 1/8	22 6/8	23 1/8	18 1/8	4	4	Hubbard County	MN	James Willet	1988	11,619
133 1/8	21 6/8	21 4/8	20 1/8	6	6	Chippewa County	WI	Daniel J. Sweeney	1988	11,619
133 1/8	25 2/8	24 5/8	16 7/8	5	5	Houston County	MN	Richard Gulbranson	1988	11,619
133 1/8	20 5/8	22 5/8	16 3/8	5	6	Woodbury County	IA	Tony Flesjer	1988	11,619
133 1/8	23 2/8	23 0/8	18 3/8	5	5	Pottawatomie County	KS	Michael Schirer	1988	11,619
133 1/8	24 0/8	24 4/8	15 5/8	5	5	Carroll County	MD	Merl T. Brilhart	1988	11,619
133 1/8	22 3/8	21 7/8	19 1/8	5	4	Wellington County	ONT	R. Brian Oates	1989	11,619
133 1/8	22 1/8	21 5/8	17 2/8	6	5	De Kalb County	MO	Jim W. Martin	1989	11,619
133 1/8	22 0/8	22 4/8	21 1/8	4	4	Reno County	KS	Edward Laverentz	1989	11,619
133 1/8	22 5/8	23 1/8	19 3/8	4	5	Marshall County	IL	Richard L. Johnson	1989	11,619
133 1/8	24 6/8	24 2/8	19 7/8	10	6	Jackson County	IL	Mark Guetersloh	1990	11,619
133 1/8	19 2/8	18 4/8	17 7/8	5	6	Crawford County	KS	Bryan E. Messmer	1990	11,619
133 1/8	21 4/8	21 6/8	16 5/8	5	6	Marinette County	WI	Richard Koss	1990	11,619
133 1/8	26 2/8	25 4/8	15 0/8	7	5	Northampton County	PA	Paul H. Beahn, Jr.	1990	11,619
133 1/8	23 0/8	22 4/8	17 3/8	4	4	Kent County	MI	Robert Groenke	1990	11,619
133 1/8	23 4/8	24 6/8	17 1/8	4	4	Pierce County	WI	Larry Hoyer	1990	11,619
133 1/8	21 3/8	22 1/8	16 1/8	5	5	Wayne County	MO	Donald Roper	1990	11,619
133 1/8	23 6/8	24 1/8	14 3/8	5	6	Price County	WI	Kevin W. Shibilski	1990	11,619
133 1/8	21 1/8	21 7/8	16 7/8	5	5	Clinton County	MI	Dan Bertalan	1990	11,619
133 1/8	22 1/8	22 4/8	18 1/8	5	5	Dodge County	WI	Jeff Pankow	1990	11,619
133 1/8	22 5/8	23 1/8	18 5/8	4	4	Medina County	OH	Tom Walker	1990	11,619
133 1/8	26 5/8	24 0/8	20 1/8	3	3	Anoka County	MN	William Lewno	1990	11,619
133 1/8	21 2/8	21 4/8	15 3/8	5	5	Des Moines County	IA	Kirk D. Wilson	1990	11,619
133 1/8	25 3/8	25 1/8	15 5/8	4	4	White County	AR	Kirk D. King	1990	11,619
133 1/8	21 4/8	21 4/8	16 3/8	5	5	Montgomery County	IN	Dan J. Truncone	1991	11,619
133 1/8	21 2/8	21 0/8	16 5/8	4	4	Shawano County	WI	Tim Klitzke	1991	11,619
133 1/8	23 5/8	22 1/8	16 3/8	5	5	Allegheny County	PA	James E. Lambert	1991	11,619

WHITETAIL DEER (TYPICAL ANTLERS)

Minimum Score 125 — Continued — 441

SCORE	LENGTH OF MAIN BEAM R	LENGTH OF MAIN BEAM L	INSIDE SPREAD	NUMBER OF POINTS R	NUMBER OF POINTS L	AREA	STATE/ PROVINCE	HUNTER'S NAME	DATE	RANK
133 1/8	20 2/8	19 7/8	15 1/8	5	5	Crawford County	PA	Gary L. Galford	1991	11,619
133 1/8	21 5/8	21 0/8	18 3/8	5	4	Defiance County	OH	Harold "Bill" Reynolds	1991	11,619
133 1/8	20 3/8	20 1/8	16 1/8	5	5	Rock Creek	BC	Ken A. Davidson	1991	11,619
133 1/8	23 0/8	22 4/8	20 3/8	5	5	Kingston	ONT	Randy J. Carlberg	1991	11,619
133 1/8	22 5/8	21 7/8	13 5/8	5	5	Bayfield County	WI	Terrence L. Peters	1991	11,619
133 1/8	22 5/8	20 7/8	16 3/8	5	5	Sumner County	KS	Stan Jones	1991	11,619
133 1/8	21 3/8	21 1/8	16 4/8	5	6	Florence County	WI	James Majewski	1992	11,619
133 1/8	19 4/8	19 6/8	15 5/8	5	5	Gloucester County	NJ	Wayne J. Gorrell	1992	11,619
133 1/8	22 1/8	22 6/8	19 0/8	5	6	Rusk County	WI	Kerry Wickersham	1992	11,619
133 1/8	23 1/8	21 5/8	16 5/8	5	4	Stony Plain	ALB	Dave Paplawski	1992	11,619
133 1/8	25 4/8	22 3/8	20 0/8	5	6	Jefferson County	OH	William J. Sich	1992	11,619
133 1/8	21 4/8	21 7/8	17 1/8	5	6	Jackson County	WI	Theodore H. Millot	1992	11,619
133 1/8	20 4/8	20 2/8	14 4/8	6	5	Franklin County	NE	Edward Andersen	1992	11,619
133 1/8	21 0/8	20 6/8	16 7/8	6	6	Charles County	MD	Donald Mazza	1992	11,619
133 1/8	23 1/8	23 4/8	18 3/8	4	4	Clark County	SD	Steven F. Reppe	1992	11,619
133 1/8	20 4/8	20 2/8	15 5/8	5	5	Jackson County	GA	Stanley C. Ogletree	1993	11,619
133 1/8	22 3/8	23 5/8	17 1/8	5	5	Armstrong County	PA	Scott Stitt	1993	11,619
133 1/8	21 0/8	22 0/8	16 3/8	5	4	Vermilion County	IL	Bruce Baker	1993	11,619
133 1/8	21 6/8	20 0/8	14 7/8	5	5	Buffalo County	WI	Thomas H. Schultz	1993	11,619
133 1/8	23 3/8	24 1/8	14 7/8	4	4	Uvalde County	TX	Mark Ezell	1993	11,619
133 1/8	18 7/8	18 4/8	14 5/8	6	6	Brown County	WI	Jeffrey G. Blake	1994	11,619
133 1/8	21 5/8	21 2/8	17 1/8	5	5	Juneau County	WI	Mark S. Presta	1994	11,619
133 1/8	21 4/8	21 4/8	13 7/8	5	5	Kenedy County	TX	Dr. Peeler G. Lacey, MD	1994	11,619
133 1/8	22 5/8	21 7/8	14 5/8	5	6	Sauk County	WI	Rick Kerska	1994	11,619
133 1/8	19 6/8	21 2/8	17 0/8	6	8	Luce County	MI	Robert Rekowski	1994	11,619
133 1/8	22 5/8	22 2/8	16 2/8	5	7	Ross County	OH	Steve Ray	1994	11,619
133 1/8	23 5/8	23 6/8	15 1/8	4	4	Geauga County	OH	Randal R. Hollis	1994	11,619
133 1/8	22 3/8	23 0/8	17 3/8	5	4	Sauk County	WI	Robert Forseth	1994	11,619
133 1/8	22 4/8	22 4/8	17 1/8	4	4	Ozaukee County	WI	Dan Lindloff	1994	11,619
133 1/8	21 7/8	22 0/8	17 3/8	4	4	Crawford County	MO	Billy Hunter	1994	11,619
133 1/8	18 6/8	19 0/8	15 3/8	5	5	Douglas County	WI	David D. Darwin	1994	11,619
133 1/8	23 1/8	23 4/8	15 5/8	5	5	Guilford County	NC	Clayton B. Denny	1995	11,619
133 1/8	21 5/8	22 3/8	16 5/8	4	4	Berks County	PA	Bob J. Fair	1995	11,619
133 1/8	23 6/8	24 5/8	17 1/8	4	5	Lawrence County	AR	Darrell Gann	1995	11,619
133 1/8	21 5/8	24 2/8	17 7/8	4	5	Stokes County	NC	Scott Posey	1995	11,619
133 1/8	22 4/8	22 5/8	16 3/8	4	4	Van Buren County	IA	John "Rosey" Roseland	1995	11,619
133 1/8	20 0/8	19 4/8	14 5/8	5	5	Parkland	ALB	Dale Johnson	1995	11,619
133 1/8	23 0/8	23 2/8	18 1/8	4	5	St. Croix County	WI	Banner E. Myer	1996	11,619
133 1/8	18 7/8	19 0/8	15 5/8	5	5	Duck Mtns.	MAN	Gregory W. Good	1996	11,619
133 1/8	21 5/8	20 5/8	14 1/8	5	5	Cole County	MO	Brent Berendzen	1996	11,619
133 1/8	21 2/8	20 3/8	17 1/8	4	4	San Saba County	TX	John Franklin Keith	1996	11,619
133 1/8	20 6/8	19 6/8	16 1/8	4	4	Dougherty County	GA	Russell Todd West	1996	11,619
133 1/8	23 0/8	23 3/8	17 1/8	4	5	Columbia County	WI	Andrew J. Cole	1997	11,619
133 1/8	25 3/8	23 7/8	16 3/8	5	4	Terrell County	GA	Robbie Sifford	1997	11,619
133 1/8	21 4/8	18 7/8	18 4/8	6	6	Cheyenne County	NE	Harry Needham	1997	11,619
133 1/8	21 0/8	21 0/8	15 7/8	5	7	Marquette County	WI	Douglas R. Parrott	1997	11,619
133 1/8	25 2/8	25 4/8	19 4/8	5	7	Will County	IL	Frank Cordes	1997	11,619
133 0/8	22 2/8	21 3/8	16 4/8	4	4	Luce County	MI	Rondell Bisbee	1953	11,723
133 0/8	24 0/8	24 1/8	17 6/8	4	4	Dunn County	WI	George Woodington	1969	11,723
133 0/8	19 0/8	19 3/8	16 6/8	5	5	Kingsbury County	SD	Arnold Aulner	1970	11,723
133 0/8	20 7/8	21 0/8	17 4/8	5	5	Litchfield County	CT	Dan Ferrara, Jr.	1976	11,723
133 0/8	24 6/8	24 6/8	25 4/8	3	3	Mercer County	OH	John Maury	1977	11,723
133 0/8	21 0/8	20 7/8	17 4/8	5	5	Somerset County	NJ	Dennis Bailey	1977	11,723
133 0/8	22 2/8	21 0/8	18 6/8	4	5	Jackson County	MI	Randy Childs	1977	11,723
133 0/8	23 5/8	22 1/8	17 4/8	5	6	Macon County	IL	Frank B. Graham	1977	11,723
133 0/8	23 3/8	23 1/8	19 4/8	5	7	Dawson County	MT	Bryant Shurtliff	1977	11,723
133 0/8	24 5/8	24 2/8	19 2/8	5	6	Huntingdon County	PA	John A. Williams	1978	11,723
133 0/8	23 2/8	22 6/8	18 4/8	4	4	Dane County	WI	Dean Cooper	1981	11,723
133 0/8	22 2/8	21 7/8	16 4/8	4	5	Geary County	KS	Mike Ehlebracht	1981	11,723
133 0/8	20 6/8	20 2/8	16 6/8	6	5	Burleigh County	ND	Donald Magstadt	1981	11,723
133 0/8	21 1/8	21 3/8	15 4/8	5	5	Montgomery County	MS	Harold L. Tutor	1981	11,723
133 0/8	22 7/8	22 6/8	15 6/8	4	5	Polk County	IA	Jeff Greider	1982	11,723
133 0/8	22 2/8	22 6/8	16 4/8	4	4	Jefferson County	OH	Edward D. Whitmore	1983	11,723
133 0/8	24 4/8	24 0/8	18 7/8	6	4	Pepin County	WI	Gerald Berg	1984	11,723
133 0/8	22 4/8	22 0/8	19 4/8	5	4	Middlesex County	ONT	Anna Burket	1985	11,723
133 0/8	24 0/8	23 0/8	18 7/8	5	6	Prince George County	VA	William Robert McCabe III	1986	11,723
133 0/8	23 0/8	21 7/8	16 4/8	4	4	Chautauqua County	NY	Ronald Olson	1986	11,723
133 0/8	22 7/8	23 0/8	16 6/8	4	4	Vermilion County	IL	Michael Lange	1986	11,723
133 0/8	27 2/8	28 3/8	16 1/8	6	6	Lawrence County	IL	Hugh Sexton	1986	11,723
133 0/8	22 6/8	23 3/8	15 6/8	5	5	Norman County	MN	Dick Stegeman	1987	11,723
133 0/8	23 5/8	23 7/8	20 6/8	4	4	Union County	KY	Dennis Helms	1987	11,723
133 0/8	24 0/8	24 1/8	18 0/8	5	4	Cass County	NE	Roger Buck	1987	11,723
133 0/8	23 5/8	23 4/8	14 5/8	4	5	Polk County	IA	Roy Mikesell	1987	11,723
133 0/8	22 4/8	22 4/8	16 2/8	6	5	McDowell County	WV	Douglas Abel	1987	11,723
133 0/8	23 4/8	22 2/8	18 0/8	4	4	Boone County	MO	Tommy Foster	1988	11,723
133 0/8	25 5/8	26 4/8	17 4/8	4	4	McHenry County	IL	William Adams	1988	11,723
133 0/8	22 3/8	22 4/8	17 0/8	5	6	Hampden County	MA	David Cox	1988	11,723
133 0/8	22 1/8	20 7/8	15 0/8	5	6	Geary County	KS	James L. Ullmer	1988	11,723

WHITETAIL DEER (TYPICAL ANTLERS)

Minimum Score 125

SCORE	LENGTH OF MAIN BEAM R	LENGTH OF MAIN BEAM L	INSIDE SPREAD	NUMBER OF POINTS R	NUMBER OF POINTS L	AREA	STATE/PROVINCE	HUNTER'S NAME	DATE	RANK
133 0/8	20 5/8	21 1/8	16 0/8	5	5	Prairie County	AR	Clay Bowie	1988	11,723
133 0/8	22 7/8	22 0/8	15 1/8	6	5	Lapeer County	MI	Thomas J. Baker	1989	11,723
133 0/8	22 0/8	22 6/8	18 6/8	5	5	Coles County	IL	Dave Miller	1989	11,723
133 0/8	24 0/8	23 4/8	15 1/8	6	6	Brooks County	TX	George W. Gallaspy	1990	11,723
133 0/8	22 3/8	23 1/8	17 6/8	5	5	Goliad County	TX	Roy M. Goodwin	1990	11,723
133 0/8	24 5/8	24 6/8	14 5/8	7	6	Scott County	KY	Gayle Humphrey	1990	11,723
133 0/8	23 1/8	23 2/8	15 7/8	4	6	Chickasaw County	IA	Robert F. Marion	1990	11,723
133 0/8	22 3/8	21 5/8	17 4/8	7	6	Greene County	MO	Clifford Kelley	1990	11,723
133 0/8	22 4/8	21 5/8	16 4/8	4	5	Rocky Mtn. House	ALB	Brian Sztym	1991	11,723
133 0/8	19 6/8	19 5/8	15 0/8	6	6	Alpena County	MI	David N. Robinette	1991	11,723
133 0/8	22 6/8	21 5/8	17 2/8	5	5	Columbia County	OH	Thomas K. Miller	1991	11,723
133 0/8	22 0/8	21 2/8	17 2/8	5	5	Rusk County	WI	Thomas Anders	1991	11,723
133 0/8	25 6/8	24 6/8	17 0/8	5	5	Darke County	OH	Rocky W. Stahl	1991	11,723
133 0/8	24 0/8	25 4/8	18 6/8	4	4	Jefferson County	WI	John E. Thurow	1992	11,723
133 0/8	22 5/8	21 4/8	16 4/8	5	5	Racine County	WI	Dan Seitz	1992	11,723
133 0/8	21 7/8	22 1/8	16 0/8	5	5	Douglas County	WI	Russell E. Harvey	1992	11,723
133 0/8	21 4/8	22 5/8	16 4/8	4	4	Jackson County	WV	Brent Sayre	1992	11,723
133 0/8	24 4/8	24 4/8	17 4/8	5	4	Pittsburg County	OK	K. E. Pennington	1992	11,723
133 0/8	23 6/8	24 0/8	15 0/8	4	4	Westchester County	NY	Don Hopko	1992	11,723
133 0/8	22 2/8	21 7/8	15 4/8	4	4	Rock County	WI	Thomas A. Keller	1992	11,723
133 0/8	22 4/8	22 6/8	17 2/8	4	5	Brown County	WI	Carl F. Vanderheyden	1992	11,723
133 0/8	21 7/8	21 5/8	18 0/8	5	5	Kalamazoo County	MI	Raymond S. Fleury	1993	11,723
133 0/8	22 1/8	22 2/8	17 2/8	4	4	Mayes County	OK	Lewis W. Coverdell	1993	11,723
133 0/8	21 4/8	22 3/8	16 2/8	5	7	Morgan County	KY	Bobby J. Adkins	1993	11,723
133 0/8	25 6/8	24 6/8	21 0/8	4	4	Washington County	MN	Mike Ostertag	1993	11,723
133 0/8	22 4/8	21 4/8	16 0/8	4	4	Calvert County	MD	Thomas B. Greenwell, Sr.	1993	11,723
133 0/8	21 2/8	20 6/8	17 5/8	5	5	Brown County	SD	Jason Braley	1993	11,723
133 0/8	23 4/8	22 3/8	18 5/8	8	6	Ida County	IA	Curtis L. Otto	1993	11,723
133 0/8	22 2/8	21 6/8	16 0/8	4	4	Oneida County	WI	Robert D. Walkowski	1994	11,723
133 0/8	21 2/8	21 5/8	17 2/8	5	5	Walworth County	WI	Charles Palmer	1994	11,723
133 0/8	21 7/8	21 4/8	16 4/8	5	6	Jefferson County	WI	Phil Eppler	1994	11,723
133 0/8	22 1/8	22 0/8	16 6/8	5	5	East Feliciana Parish	LA	Johnny Gibson	1994	11,723
133 0/8	22 7/8	22 2/8	18 4/8	6	7	Waukesha County	WI	John M. Miller	1994	11,723
133 0/8	22 1/8	22 7/8	17 4/8	6	5	Wayne County	KY	Randy Dodson	1994	11,723
133 0/8	21 3/8	20 6/8	16 4/8	5	5	Goliad County	TX	Ronald K. McConnell	1994	11,723
133 0/8	21 7/8	22 0/8	16 4/8	6	5	Columbia County	WI	Peter Schwoch	1994	11,723
133 0/8	18 1/8	17 4/8	15 0/8	5	5	Kane County	IL	George Moeller, Jr.	1994	11,723
133 0/8	23 0/8	21 3/8	17 0/8	5	5	McMullen County	TX	Daniel D. Countiss	1994	11,723
133 0/8	23 6/8	23 3/8	18 4/8	4	4	Shelby County	IL	James L. Harbert	1995	11,723
133 0/8	21 1/8	21 1/8	13 6/8	5	6	Crook County	WY	Troy Fisher	1995	11,723
133 0/8	21 0/8	20 6/8	14 6/8	7	5	Manitowoc County	WI	Randall L. Miller	1995	11,723
133 0/8	22 5/8	23 0/8	14 2/8	5	5	Montgomery County	KS	Barry E. Price	1995	11,723
133 0/8	22 0/8	21 2/8	16 0/8	5	5	Burnet County	TX	Ben Weagant	1995	11,723
133 0/8	20 5/8	22 1/8	20 7/8	5	4	Franklin County	IL	Virgil E. Losier	1995	11,723
133 0/8	20 0/8	20 7/8	16 2/8	5	5	Morris County	NJ	Hank Locker	1995	11,723
133 0/8	21 4/8	20 2/8	18 2/8	5	5	Oneida County	WI	Trygve Solberg	1995	11,723
133 0/8	25 3/8	23 5/8	19 0/8	6	8	Franklin County	IL	Melvin H. Jones	1995	11,723
133 0/8	21 7/8	22 2/8	16 6/8	5	4	Baraga County	MI	Bill Giddings	1995	11,723
133 0/8	19 4/8	20 0/8	18 0/8	5	5	Vilas County	WI	Phil Dreger	1995	11,723
133 0/8	22 2/8	20 7/8	17 4/8	5	5	Menifee County	KY	Kenneth R. Yarber	1996	11,723
133 0/8	24 4/8	25 4/8	15 2/8	4	4	Tazewell County	IL	Chad Hunziker	1996	11,723
133 0/8	22 4/8	22 3/8	16 2/8	6	5	Columbia County	WI	Kyle J. Ades	1996	11,723
133 0/8	22 5/8	21 4/8	20 2/8	5	5	Cattaraugus County	NY	Robert Songin	1996	11,723
133 0/8	23 3/8	22 5/8	17 0/8	5	5	Grant County	WI	Scott Dunn	1996	11,723
133 0/8	21 6/8	22 7/8	17 4/8	5	5	Winona County	MN	Bill Ware	1996	11,723
133 0/8	21 2/8	21 7/8	14 6/8	5	5	Westchester County	NY	Gus Congemi	1996	11,723
133 0/8	22 1/8	22 2/8	18 2/8	4	5	Wicomico County	MD	Paul Donalds	1996	11,723
133 0/8	23 7/8	24 3/8	14 5/8	5	4	St. Charles County	MO	Earl Beach	1996	11,723
133 0/8	19 4/8	18 5/8	19 4/8	5	5	Boone County	IL	Terry J. Smith	1996	11,723
133 0/8	22 1/8	22 5/8	17 4/8	5	5	Dakota County	MN	Lee S. Waltman	1996	11,723
133 0/8	20 1/8	21 7/8	17 0/8	5	5	Winona County	MN	John W. Zahrte	1996	11,723
133 0/8	20 7/8	22 6/8	17 3/8	5	7	Allamakee County	IA	Loren Miller	1996	11,723
133 0/8	22 5/8	22 1/8	18 6/8	4	5	Otter Tail County	MN	Josh Wilcox	1996	11,723
133 0/8	19 2/8	20 2/8	15 4/8	5	5	Sturgeon	ALB	Randy Tellier	1996	11,723
133 0/8	22 3/8	23 2/8	17 2/8	6	4	Jefferson County	IN	Bill Knoblock	1996	11,723
133 0/8	22 0/8	21 7/8	16 2/8	5	4	Rawlins County	KS	Bryant Shermoe	1996	11,723
133 0/8	23 7/8	23 3/8	19 1/8	7	4	Floyd County	IA	Tim Waid	1996	11,723
133 0/8	22 0/8	22 6/8	19 0/8	4	4	Suffolk County	NY	Neal Heaton	1996	11,723
133 0/8	21 5/8	20 7/8	13 3/8	7	7	La Crosse County	WI	Dave D. Konze	1996	11,723
133 0/8	23 4/8	23 2/8	19 6/8	4	5	Kalamazoo County	MI	Cameron R. Cudney	1996	11,723
133 0/8	22 1/8	21 6/8	18 2/8	5	4	Sawyer County	WI	Gary Haus	1996	11,723
133 0/8	23 7/8	23 0/8	18 2/8	4	4	La Crosse County	WI	Mark Francksen	1997	11,723
133 0/8	22 6/8	23 3/8	19 3/8	6	6	Grant County	WI	Rob Heise	1997	11,723
133 0/8	25 0/8	26 0/8	18 4/8	5	5	Barber County	KS	William Rule	1997	11,723
133 0/8	24 0/8	23 0/8	17 4/8	4	5	Portage County	WI	Jason L. Dombrowski	1997	11,723
133 0/8	22 3/8	20 7/8	16 7/8	6	5	Cameron County	TX	Michael E. Paul	1997	11,723
133 0/8	25 6/8	26 1/8	19 2/8	5	5	Granville County	NC	Richard A. Shorty	1997	11,723
133 0/8	21 6/8	22 4/8	19 0/8	4	5	Maverick County	TX	Spencer K. Gantt	1997	11,723

WHITETAIL DEER (TYPICAL ANTLERS)

Minimum Score 125 — Continued

SCORE	LENGTH OF MAIN BEAM R	LENGTH OF MAIN BEAM L	INSIDE SPREAD	NUMBER OF POINTS R	NUMBER OF POINTS L	AREA	STATE/PROVINCE	HUNTER'S NAME	DATE	RANK
132 7/8	21 0/8	21 0/8	15 3/8	5	7	Jefferson County	IN	Jerome Sexton	1962	11,832
132 7/8	20 0/8	18 6/8	15 5/8	5	6	Wilson County	KS	Warren Townsend	1970	11,832
132 7/8	24 4/8	20 6/8	20 2/8	7	7	Pine County	MN	Bob Sandwick	1973	11,832
132 7/8	20 0/8	20 6/8	14 6/8	5	6	Waushara County	WI	Gary Gundrum	1977	11,832
132 7/8	21 3/8	22 0/8	18 1/8	5	5	St. Croix County	WI	Randy St. Ores	1978	11,832
132 7/8	20 4/8	21 3/8	16 1/8	5	6	Wagoner County	OK	Sonny Charboneau	1978	11,832
132 7/8	20 3/8	21 0/8	14 5/8	5	5	Gallia County	OH	Gail C. Snyder	1980	11,832
132 7/8	21 2/8	21 4/8	16 3/8	6	6	Martin County	MN	James Zanke	1982	11,832
132 7/8	20 7/8	21 2/8	14 7/8	5	5	Warren County	MS	Ray Bufkin	1983	11,832
132 7/8	21 4/8	21 3/8	14 7/8	5	5	Anoka County	MN	John Cardinal	1983	11,832
132 7/8	21 2/8	22 6/8	17 5/8	4	4	Riley County	KS	Mike Huff	1983	11,832
132 7/8	23 4/8	23 2/8	17 3/8	5	5	Cherokee County	KS	Samuel F. Lancaster	1983	11,832
132 7/8	21 4/8	21 4/8	17 4/8	6	6	Sawyer County	WI	Ronald Lee Fischer	1983	11,832
132 7/8	24 3/8	22 6/8	14 1/8	5	4	Butler County	KS	David R. Rogers	1984	11,832
132 7/8	19 4/8	21 0/8	18 0/8	7	6	Alexander County	IL	Daniel Boyd	1985	11,832
132 7/8	20 2/8	20 3/8	17 7/8	5	6	Cowley County	KS	David M. Ross	1985	11,832
132 7/8	19 2/8	19 6/8	17 1/8	5	5	Mitchell County	KS	Connie Galliher	1986	11,832
132 7/8	18 1/8	21 4/8	19 7/8	5	4	Mason County	WV	Keith Donahue	1986	11,832
132 7/8	23 4/8	22 4/8	15 4/8	5	4	Greene County	MO	Jacob Estep	1986	11,832
132 7/8	20 2/8	21 4/8	15 7/8	5	5	Clearwater County	ID	Mark Neer	1986	11,832
132 7/8	23 0/8	24 2/8	18 5/8	4	4	Charles County	MD	Ralph L. Purcell, Jr.	1987	11,832
132 7/8	24 1/8	21 3/8	16 3/8	4	4	Gage County	NE	Gene Tupa	1987	11,832
132 7/8	23 0/8	23 3/8	18 6/8	6	7	Sauk County	WI	Richard J. Osgood	1987	11,832
132 7/8	24 0/8	23 4/8	14 1/8	4	4	Mercer County	NJ	James H. Swift, Jr.	1987	11,832
132 7/8	24 0/8	24 0/8	16 5/8	7	6	Butler County	KS	Denny Zimmerman	1988	11,832
132 7/8	21 7/8	22 6/8	17 5/8	4	5	Trempealeau County	WI	Dave Mikrut	1988	11,832
132 7/8	19 6/8	22 1/8	16 1/8	8	6	Henry County	VA	Mike Weaver	1988	11,832
132 7/8	20 6/8	21 0/8	17 7/8	4	4	Washtenaw County	MI	Chris Ehnis	1989	11,832
132 7/8	23 6/8	23 0/8	15 6/8	5	7	Jefferson County	WI	Peter Newcomb	1989	11,832
132 7/8	21 0/8	21 3/8	17 7/8	5	5	Fond du Lac County	WI	Steven J. Bethel	1989	11,832
132 7/8	22 1/8	21 7/8	14 2/8	5	6	Donalda	ALB	Garfield Vikse	1989	11,832
132 7/8	22 3/8	21 5/8	16 2/8	5	5	Jefferson County	MT	Sean S. Walp	1990	11,832
132 7/8	23 0/8	22 7/8	19 3/8	5	4	Livingston County	MI	Jean M. Musolf	1990	11,832
132 7/8	23 3/8	22 7/8	18 7/8	4	4	Latah County	ID	Roger A. Rea	1990	11,832
132 7/8	21 3/8	22 2/8	17 1/8	5	5	Burnett County	WI	Mikel Duncan	1991	11,832
132 7/8	20 3/8	20 5/8	14 3/8	4	4	Jackson County	IA	Nick Fondell	1991	11,832
132 7/8	23 5/8	24 3/8	20 2/8	4	6	Pendleton County	KY	Randy Sipple	1991	11,832
132 7/8	23 7/8	23 4/8	17 1/8	5	5	Pushmataha County	OK	Jason B. Manous	1991	11,832
132 7/8	26 2/8	27 5/8	19 1/8	6	6	De Soto County	MS	Chris Sanders	1991	11,832
132 7/8	22 2/8	21 2/8	19 4/8	6	5	Marshall County	IL	Mike Rinehart	1991	11,832
132 7/8	22 4/8	24 2/8	19 3/8	4	4	Union County	KY	Kenneth W. Sharp	1991	11,832
132 7/8	20 7/8	22 3/8	19 1/8	5	5	Trempealeau County	WI	Daniel R. Wall	1991	11,832
132 7/8	22 0/8	22 7/8	18 3/8	4	4	Williamson County	IL	Tony Kreke	1991	11,832
132 7/8	22 7/8	23 0/8	20 0/8	4	5	Suffolk County	NY	James Matuszewski	1991	11,832
132 7/8	22 4/8	22 6/8	15 6/8	5	4	Macoupin County	IL	Ron Stokes	1991	11,832
132 7/8	21 4/8	21 0/8	15 0/8	5	6	Bayfield County	WI	Steve M. Brilla	1992	11,832
132 7/8	22 4/8	22 5/8	19 7/8	5	6	Alexander County	IL	Craig Stoker	1992	11,832
132 7/8	21 4/8	21 6/8	17 5/8	5	5	Louisa County	IA	Robert G. McCulley	1992	11,832
132 7/8	20 3/8	20 5/8	14 5/8	6	5	La Salle County	TX	Roger Wintle	1992	11,832
132 7/8	23 6/8	23 6/8	17 1/8	4	4	Dodge County	MN	Mark D. Ray	1993	11,832
132 7/8	24 1/8	23 4/8	17 2/8	6	5	Monroe County	WI	Danny T. O'Gara	1993	11,832
132 7/8	21 0/8	20 0/8	15 7/8	5	5	Shawano County	WI	Kenneth R. Huebner	1993	11,832
132 7/8	22 6/8	21 2/8	15 5/8	4	5	Washington County	KS	Toby Bruna	1993	11,832
132 7/8	22 2/8	21 6/8	19 5/8	5	5	Marshall County	IN	Dave Haag	1994	11,832
132 7/8	21 5/8	21 2/8	14 7/8	5	5	Kalamazoo County	MI	Scott L. Bartholomew	1994	11,832
132 7/8	23 0/8	23 0/8	16 5/8	4	5	Stanley County	SD	Mark J. Anderson	1994	11,832
132 7/8	22 2/8	23 1/8	17 4/8	5	6	Jefferson County	WI	John Thielemann	1994	11,832
132 7/8	23 1/8	22 2/8	13 7/8	5	5	Green County	WI	David Schenk, Sr.	1994	11,832
132 7/8	20 7/8	20 4/8	18 3/8	5	5	Barron County	WI	Grant R. Gifford	1994	11,832
132 7/8	23 2/8	24 0/8	17 6/8	5	5	DeKalb County	IL	Dan Hardekopf	1994	11,832
132 7/8	20 7/8	21 6/8	16 3/8	7	6	Dane County	WI	Michael H. Jensen	1994	11,832
132 7/8	20 0/8	20 3/8	16 1/8	5	5	Belmont County	OH	Scott Dunfee	1994	11,832
132 7/8	22 3/8	22 4/8	17 1/8	4	4	Rock County	WI	Scott Tucker	1994	11,832
132 7/8	24 3/8	25 1/8	20 1/8	5	4	Mercer County	NJ	Jim McCloskey	1994	11,832
132 7/8	21 3/8	21 5/8	16 3/8	4	4	Polk County	MO	Jason Vestal	1995	11,832
132 7/8	19 2/8	19 5/8	13 5/8	5	5	Erath County	TX	Stephen Thornton	1995	11,832
132 7/8	24 5/8	24 4/8	17 5/8	5	4	Lincoln County	MO	Ronald D. Ragan	1995	11,832
132 7/8	21 7/8	21 6/8	17 7/8	5	7	Seward County	NE	Stan Luebbe	1995	11,832
132 7/8	21 4/8	21 6/8	15 5/8	5	5	Pepin County	WI	Richard L. Crabtree	1995	11,832
132 7/8	19 7/8	19 4/8	16 1/8	5	4	Grayson County	KY	Anthony W. Payton	1995	11,832
132 7/8	23 3/8	23 5/8	17 3/8	4	4	Oconto County	WI	Dan Moder	1995	11,832
132 7/8	23 1/8	23 1/8	17 3/8	5	5	Pike County	OH	Jim Borchelt	1995	11,832
132 7/8	22 7/8	22 7/8	14 5/8	5	5	Grenada County	MS	Bryan Harris	1995	11,832
132 7/8	24 1/8	24 4/8	21 3/8	4	4	Kalamazoo County	MI	Dan L. Willoughby	1995	11,832
132 7/8	25 6/8	24 6/8	18 5/8	5	4	Dodge County	WI	Mike Young	1995	11,832
132 7/8	23 5/8	24 0/8	18 5/8	4	5	Otsego County	NY	Al Cheney	1995	11,832
132 7/8	21 4/8	20 6/8	16 2/8	5	7	McLean County	IL	Bobby J. Evans, Jr.	1995	11,832
132 7/8	20 2/8	21 3/8	16 5/8	5	5	Lake County	IL	Theodore Hysell	1995	11,832

WHITETAIL DEER (TYPICAL ANTLERS)

Minimum Score 125

SCORE	LENGTH OF MAIN BEAM R	LENGTH OF MAIN BEAM L	INSIDE SPREAD	NUMBER OF POINTS R	NUMBER OF POINTS L	AREA	STATE/PROVINCE	HUNTER'S NAME	DATE	RANK
132 7/8	21 6/8	22 1/8	17 1/8	5	4	Laramie County	WY	Brian Rhead	1995	11,832
132 7/8	22 6/8	23 4/8	16 7/8	5	5	Eau Claire County	WI	Mike Rockow	1995	11,832
132 7/8	20 1/8	20 7/8	13 5/8	6	5	Kerr County	TX	Norman E. Hall	1995	11,832
132 7/8	23 1/8	22 1/8	17 5/8	5	4	Schleicher County	TX	Mike Morgan	1995	11,832
132 7/8	24 1/8	24 2/8	16 7/8	4	4	Fairfax County	VA	Roy Rasmussen	1996	11,832
132 7/8	20 5/8	21 1/8	18 5/8	4	5	Fillmore County	MN	Jim Duffy	1996	11,832
132 7/8	22 5/8	22 5/8	15 4/8	6	6	La Crosse County	WI	Tim Tisue	1996	11,832
132 7/8	25 6/8	23 6/8	19 3/8	4	4	Wyandot County	OH	Sean Welty	1997	11,832
132 7/8	24 4/8	25 4/8	19 1/8	5	4	Crawford County	PA	Tim Valencic, Jr.	1997	11,832
132 7/8	22 3/8	22 7/8	18 3/8	5	5	Polk County	WI	Rob Logghe	1997	11,832
132 7/8	21 3/8	21 2/8	16 1/8	5	5	Iowa County	WI	Randy Sporle	1997	11,832
132 7/8	22 4/8	22 1/8	16 3/8	5	5	Clark County	SD	Randy S. Bingner	1997	11,832
132 7/8	20 4/8	20 6/8	14 5/8	5	5	Bayfield County	WI	Duane Raspotnik	1997	11,832
132 7/8	20 4/8	21 7/8	14 1/8	5	4	Miller County	MO	Randy Williams	1997	11,832
132 7/8	22 6/8	22 7/8	17 3/8	4	4	Tazewell County	IL	Albert Hughes	1997	11,832
132 7/8	24 6/8	23 1/8	18 4/8	7	5	Lawrence County	IL	Russell Morris	1997	11,832
132 7/8	20 3/8	21 5/8	16 3/8	4	4	Henry County	IA	Bruce Barrie	1997	11,832
132 6/8	23 0/8	23 4/8	20 0/8	4	4	Summit County	OH	Dana C. Feather	1960	11,927
132 6/8	22 5/8	21 7/8	17 0/8	5	6	Waseca County	MN	Robert Barrie	1968	11,927
132 6/8	21 0/8	20 1/8	16 4/8	5	5	Worcester County	MD	Clifford A. Denney	1972	11,927
132 6/8	22 3/8	23 0/8	14 6/8	5	5	Jackson County	OH	Robert C. McGuire	1976	11,927
132 6/8	19 7/8	22 7/8	17 4/8	6	6	Union County	IL	Fred W. Achilles	1978	11,927
132 6/8	22 0/8	22 0/8	19 4/8	5	4	Waterloo County	ONT	Jim Scoggins	1979	11,927
132 6/8	22 2/8	22 0/8	14 6/8	4	5	Lancaster County	PA	Albert A. Swider	1980	11,927
132 6/8	21 2/8	23 1/8	20 6/8	7	6	Loup County	NE	Syl Glos	1981	11,927
132 6/8	21 3/8	21 1/8	17 4/8	4	4	Clinton County	IA	Kent Hoffmann	1982	11,927
132 6/8	19 6/8	20 2/8	16 0/8	5	5	Butler County	KS	Mark Scott	1983	11,927
132 6/8	21 7/8	22 4/8	17 0/8	4	4	Dawes County	NE	Darrell A. Bendel	1984	11,927
132 6/8	24 7/8	23 6/8	17 4/8	4	7	Carroll County	MO	Joe D. Earnest	1984	11,927
132 6/8	21 0/8	21 3/8	21 0/8	6	5	Lac qui Parle County	MN	Larry Angrimson	1984	11,927
132 6/8	20 2/8	22 2/8	19 2/8	5	4	Buffalo County	WI	Michael L Gates	1984	11,927
132 6/8	20 7/8	20 7/8	18 0/8	5	5	Cherry County	NE	Russell Burge	1984	11,927
132 6/8	23 4/8	23 1/8	16 4/8	4	4	Sawyer County	WI	Dave Phillips	1984	11,927
132 6/8	21 7/8	21 6/8	16 6/8	5	5	Linn County	IA	Jon Klein	1985	11,927
132 6/8	19 7/8	19 1/8	16 2/8	5	5	Mason County	TX	Thomas Joseph Hicks	1986	11,927
132 6/8	19 1/8	19 7/8	17 2/8	5	5	Oneida County	WI	Trygve Solberg	1986	11,927
132 6/8	19 5/8	20 2/8	17 0/8	5	5	Marshall County	WV	Dave Gibson	1986	11,927
132 6/8	23 4/8	24 2/8	16 4/8	4	4	Green County	WI	Mike Stone	1986	11,927
132 6/8	23 6/8	23 0/8	17 2/8	4	5	Vinton County	OH	Charles Barker, Jr.	1986	11,927
132 6/8	25 6/8	25 2/8	19 6/8	3	4	Troup County	GA	Kirby Fidler	1986	11,927
132 6/8	23 3/8	23 5/8	16 4/8	5	5	Pearl River County	MS	Chris Upton	1987	11,927
132 6/8	23 0/8	22 5/8	18 6/8	5	4	Peoria County	IL	Paul L. Gilles	1987	11,927
132 6/8	24 1/8	23 0/8	18 2/8	6	6	Stark County	OH	Robert L Knerr	1987	11,927
132 6/8	23 0/8	23 0/8	17 0/8	6	5	Woodward County	OK	Blake Cosper	1987	11,927
132 6/8	23 1/8	22 7/8	17 4/8	4	4	Isle of Wight County	VA	Robert Emory Caldwell	1988	11,927
132 6/8	22 3/8	23 5/8	17 0/8	4	5	Otsego County	MI	Keith Earl Randall	1988	11,927
132 6/8	22 0/8	21 0/8	18 4/8	4	4	Choctaw County	OK	Mark Holbrook	1988	11,927
132 6/8	23 3/8	24 5/8	17 2/8	5	4	Baltimore County	MD	Robert W. Brooks	1989	11,927
132 6/8	22 2/8	24 1/8	18 4/8	6	5	Jackson County	OH	Francis Keith Tomlinson	1989	11,927
132 6/8	25 2/8	26 2/8	20 0/8	7	7	Rock County	WI	Jerry Shear	1989	11,927
132 6/8	22 6/8	23 0/8	16 1/8	4	6	Forest County	WI	Norman C. Schmelling	1990	11,927
132 6/8	20 2/8	20 1/8	16 2/8	5	5	Columbia County	WI	Mark L. Preuss	1990	11,927
132 6/8	23 2/8	24 3/8	20 0/8	5	4	Clinton County	OH	Cliff Doyle	1990	11,927
132 6/8	21 5/8	22 0/8	18 0/8	4	4	Waupaca County	WI	Howard R. Becker	1990	11,927
132 6/8	23 6/8	24 6/8	16 5/8	7	7	Butler County	KS	Robert Van Deventer	1990	11,927
132 6/8	25 0/8	25 5/8	19 3/8	5	6	Albemarle County	VA	Larry Wayne Roberts	1990	11,927
132 6/8	20 6/8	23 3/8	16 6/8	5	6	Suffolk County	NY	Paul E. Jansen	1990	11,927
132 6/8	21 3/8	21 1/8	17 6/8	5	5	Jones County	IA	John Kertels	1990	11,927
132 6/8	20 7/8	20 4/8	17 0/8	5	5	Olmsted County	MN	Steven Tebay	1991	11,927
132 6/8	22 7/8	23 6/8	16 4/8	5	5	Cherokee County	KS	Danny Langerot, Jr.	1991	11,927
132 6/8	23 2/8	23 1/8	22 6/8	4	4	Hampden County	MA	Ian McLean	1991	11,927
132 6/8	19 6/8	20 4/8	16 4/8	5	5	Wood County	WV	Ron Schultz	1991	11,927
132 6/8	23 0/8	22 1/8	16 6/8	4	4	La Salle County	TX	Dennis Faulkenberry	1992	11,927
132 6/8	22 5/8	22 5/8	18 6/8	4	5	Hamilton County	IL	Chris Mitchell	1992	11,927
132 6/8	24 0/8	24 7/8	19 0/8	5	4	Washington County	NE	Andrew H. Long	1992	11,927
132 6/8	21 5/8	22 7/8	15 7/8	8	7	Lincoln County	SD	Bruce Mair	1992	11,927
132 6/8	24 6/8	23 6/8	20 5/8	5	5	Delaware County	IA	James R. Salow	1992	11,927
132 6/8	22 3/8	21 1/8	18 0/8	5	5	Jefferson County	WI	Matt Winn	1992	11,927
132 6/8	24 1/8	25 3/8	19 6/8	4	4	Winona County	MN	Joe Kaczorowski	1993	11,927
132 6/8	21 2/8	21 6/8	16 0/8	5	5	Vilas County	WI	Jeff Wendt	1993	11,927
132 6/8	22 6/8	21 5/8	16 2/8	4	4	Douglas County	WI	Brian K. Johnson	1993	11,927
132 6/8	21 4/8	21 6/8	16 2/8	5	5	Columbia County	WI	Gerald A. Francis	1993	11,927
132 6/8	23 7/8	24 0/8	19 0/8	5	5	Chester County	PA	Joseph D. Maddock	1993	11,927
132 6/8	22 0/8	22 3/8	14 1/8	5	6	Clark County	IL	Brad Wright	1993	11,927
132 6/8	22 5/8	22 6/8	17 0/8	4	4	Tazewell County	IL	Ruth Alt Turner	1993	11,927
132 6/8	20 7/8	20 7/8	15 6/8	5	5	Mower County	MN	John Mullen	1993	11,927
132 6/8	24 5/8	24 6/8	16 1/8	5	4	Boone County	MO	David Westmoreland	1993	11,927
132 6/8	24 2/8	23 2/8	21 0/8	4	4	Manitowoc County	WI	John M. Arkens	1994	11,927

WHITETAIL DEER (TYPICAL ANTLERS)

Minimum Score 125 — Continued

SCORE	LENGTH OF MAIN BEAM R	L	INSIDE SPREAD	NUMBER OF POINTS R	L	AREA	STATE/ PROVINCE	HUNTER'S NAME	DATE	RANK
132 6/8	23 3/8	23 0/8	19 1/8	5	6	Pepin County	WI	Richard Crabtree	1994	11,927
132 6/8	22 4/8	22 4/8	16 0/8	4	4	Montgomery County	MD	Terry J. Oldham, Jr.	1994	11,927
132 6/8	21 3/8	21 0/8	14 4/8	5	6	Trumbull County	OH	James A. Woodby, Jr.	1994	11,927
132 6/8	23 0/8	22 5/8	20 0/8	5	6	Iroquois County	IL	Terry L. Johnston	1994	11,927
132 6/8	23 2/8	22 6/8	19 2/8	4	4	Fairfield County	CT	Stephen T. Shay	1994	11,927
132 6/8	21 4/8	21 2/8	17 4/8	5	5	Hubbard County	MN	Neil Johnson	1994	11,927
132 6/8	21 4/8	21 5/8	15 4/8	5	5	La Salle County	TX	Mark Alexander	1994	11,927
132 6/8	22 6/8	22 6/8	17 6/8	5	5	Waushara County	WI	Todd Standke	1995	11,927
132 6/8	21 6/8	22 2/8	18 2/8	4	4	Dodge County	WI	John Steckling	1995	11,927
132 6/8	21 3/8	22 1/8	15 4/8	4	4	Madison County	GA	Johnny Dyer	1995	11,927
132 6/8	23 1/8	22 5/8	16 4/8	5	4	Douglas County	NE	Rod Sigel	1995	11,927
132 6/8	20 1/8	19 0/8	14 6/8	5	5	Pottawatomie County	KS	Gary Schwindt	1995	11,927
132 6/8	22 3/8	22 6/8	16 0/8	5	5	Hocking County	OH	William T. Peneston	1995	11,927
132 6/8	23 6/8	22 5/8	18 2/8	5	5	Clark County	WI	Bernell Lange	1996	11,927
132 6/8	22 5/8	22 2/8	15 2/8	4	4	Coshocton County	OH	Lee Cooper	1996	11,927
132 6/8	21 1/8	20 7/8	13 6/8	5	5	Waupaca County	WI	Todd Larsen	1996	11,927
132 6/8	20 3/8	20 0/8	15 6/8	6	5	Norman County	MN	Richard M. Sorensen	1997	11,927
132 6/8	21 5/8	21 6/8	16 0/8	4	4	Eau Claire County	WI	Paul C. Marten	1997	11,927
132 6/8	22 6/8	22 2/8	22 4/8	4	4	Hunterdon County	NJ	Gary A. Hubler	1997	11,927
132 6/8	21 0/8	20 1/8	15 6/8	5	5	Iowa County	WI	John R. Wood	1997	11,927
132 6/8	23 2/8	23 6/8	16 4/8	5	5	Richland County	WI	Michael J. Ray	1997	11,927
132 6/8	23 4/8	24 1/8	19 0/8	4	4	Tensas Parish	LA	Teddy Oliver	1998	11,927
132 6/8	19 7/8	19 7/8	15 2/8	5	5	Fond du Lac County	WI	Pat Engel	1998	11,927
132 6/8	24 6/8	23 7/8	19 2/8	6	5	Butler County	KY	Tommy Phelps	1998	11,927
132 6/8	25 4/8	23 0/8	19 4/8	5	4	Oakland County	MI	Matthew J. Jonik	1998	11,927
132 5/8	23 3/8	24 4/8	21 5/8	4	6	Tazewell County	IL	Don Lounsberry	1964	12,013
132 5/8	21 1/8	21 0/8	16 3/8	5	5	Irion County	TX	James E. Fox III	1977	12,013
132 5/8	24 2/8	23 0/8	19 2/8	6	6	Juneau County	WI	Michael Sigler	1978	12,013
132 5/8	23 1/8	22 5/8	18 5/8	4	5	Monmouth County	NJ	William Rusznak	1979	12,013
132 5/8	23 2/8	22 6/8	23 7/8	4	5	Burnett County	WI	James Larrabee	1980	12,013
132 5/8	19 4/8	20 0/8	16 1/8	6	6	Brookings County	SD	Timothy Modde	1981	12,013
132 5/8	23 4/8	24 1/8	18 1/8	4	4	Clearwater County	ID	Bob Proctor	1981	12,013
132 5/8	22 3/8	22 7/8	17 5/8	5	5	Furnas County	NE	Doug Huxoll	1982	12,013
132 5/8	22 3/8	22 1/8	14 2/8	5	4	Price County	WI	John D. Obadal	1983	12,013
132 5/8	20 4/8	20 0/8	16 1/8	5	5	West Baton Rouge Parrish	LA	Jim Thibodeaux	1984	12,013
132 5/8	21 5/8	21 2/8	17 1/8	5	5	Genesee County	MI	Jack Iman	1984	12,013
132 5/8	19 7/8	20 4/8	16 1/8	5	6	Morrison County	MN	John A. Pennoyer	1985	12,013
132 5/8	20 5/8	21 3/8	18 2/8	6	7	Buffalo County	WI	Glen Axness	1985	12,013
132 5/8	21 3/8	20 5/8	16 6/8	6	5	Goodhue County	MN	John "Jack" Cordes	1985	12,013
132 5/8	20 4/8	20 2/8	15 7/8	5	4	Iowa County	WI	Bill Snelgrove	1985	12,013
132 5/8	20 0/8	19 6/8	14 7/8	5	5	Goshen County	WY	Doug Starks	1986	12,013
132 5/8	19 6/8	20 6/8	14 7/8	6	6	Pittsburg County	OK	Ron Pennington	1986	12,013
132 5/8	21 2/8	21 2/8	15 1/8	5	5	Lewis & Clark County	MT	Sonny Templeton	1986	12,013
132 5/8	22 3/8	23 2/8	17 1/8	5	6	Meigs County	OH	William Charles Brewer	1986	12,013
132 5/8	24 1/8	23 1/8	15 1/8	4	4	Forest County	WI	Gary Maciolek	1987	12,013
132 5/8	21 7/8	22 4/8	15 7/8	5	5	Steele County	MN	Kyle N. Wolfe	1987	12,013
132 5/8	20 0/8	21 7/8	18 5/8	6	7	Montgomery County	IN	James Gates	1987	12,013
132 5/8	22 4/8	22 0/8	16 7/8	4	4	St. Clair County	MI	Jerry E. Korneffel	1987	12,013
132 5/8	21 5/8	21 3/8	19 1/8	4	4	Clinton County	IA	Gary G. Olson	1987	12,013
132 5/8	22 4/8	22 4/8	17 7/8	5	4	Saline County	KS	Doug Perrill	1987	12,013
132 5/8	20 0/8	20 0/8	15 3/8	6	5	Atascosa County	TX	Mike Palmer	1987	12,013
132 5/8	21 5/8	21 0/8	15 1/8	5	5	Sawyer County	WI	Rick Misfeldt	1989	12,013
132 5/8	21 5/8	20 2/8	17 3/8	4	4	Isanti County	MN	Mitch Reiners	1989	12,013
132 5/8	23 5/8	22 3/8	19 5/8	4	5	Trempealeau County	WI	Larry Tiedemann	1989	12,013
132 5/8	20 2/8	20 0/8	15 5/8	5	4	Montgomery County	IL	Joseph E. Carrilier	1989	12,013
132 5/8	22 1/8	21 1/8	16 7/8	4	4	Leelanau County	MI	William Ver Snyder	1990	12,013
132 5/8	22 0/8	24 4/8	17 3/8	5	5	Delaware County	OH	Brent Forman	1990	12,013
132 5/8	20 3/8	20 7/8	17 3/8	5	5	Brown County	IL	Tim Hasara	1990	12,013
132 5/8	24 1/8	24 2/8	20 1/8	6	4	Randolph County	IL	Scott Giovanetti	1990	12,013
132 5/8	21 2/8	19 5/8	15 0/8	5	6	Gallatin County	MT	Bob Morton	1991	12,013
132 5/8	22 3/8	22 1/8	18 5/8	6	4	Eau Claire County	WI	Jason Meyer	1991	12,013
132 5/8	24 2/8	22 6/8	17 5/8	5	5	Wyandotte County	KS	Tim K. Fowler	1991	12,013
132 5/8	19 5/8	21 5/8	17 4/8	5	6	Washburn County	WI	Jeff Tomesh	1991	12,013
132 5/8	21 2/8	21 4/8	14 3/8	5	5	Van Buren County	IA	Robin L. Geibel	1991	12,013
132 5/8	23 5/8	23 6/8	16 1/8	7	6	Buffalo County	WI	Brian Potter	1992	12,013
132 5/8	22 7/8	23 1/8	21 3/8	6	9	Guernsey County	OH	Michael J. Phillips	1992	12,013
132 5/8	23 2/8	23 5/8	16 7/8	4	4	Henry County	VA	Mike Weaver	1992	12,013
132 5/8	20 2/8	20 7/8	19 1/8	4	4	Racine County	WI	Michael A. Lietke	1992	12,013
132 5/8	22 3/8	23 2/8	16 1/8	4	5	Fayette County	IL	Jon Washburn	1992	12,013
132 5/8	22 2/8	23 1/8	15 2/8	6	7	Chippewa County	WI	Robert R. Povolo	1992	12,013
132 5/8	21 6/8	21 5/8	15 7/8	5	5	Burleigh County	ND	Don Bieber	1992	12,013
132 5/8	20 5/8	20 7/8	18 5/8	6	5	Morrison County	MN	Philip Trusty	1992	12,013
132 5/8	20 2/8	20 5/8	17 5/8	5	5	Marquette County	WI	Troy G. Engelman	1993	12,013
132 5/8	21 7/8	21 5/8	17 7/8	5	5	Du Page County	IL	Gerald Allison	1993	12,013
132 5/8	23 3/8	23 3/8	14 1/8	5	6	Dunn County	WI	Tim Taylor	1993	12,013
132 5/8	22 6/8	22 1/8	16 5/8	5	5	Wayne County	NY	Brett Stonewell	1993	12,013
132 5/8	22 6/8	23 1/8	18 3/8	5	6	Parkland	ALB	Craig Ostermayer	1993	12,013
132 5/8	25 3/8	24 6/8	17 1/8	5	4	Athens County	OH	Michael A. Rex	1993	12,013

WHITETAIL DEER (TYPICAL ANTLERS)

Minimum Score 125 — Continued

SCORE	LENGTH OF MAIN BEAM R	LENGTH OF MAIN BEAM L	INSIDE SPREAD	NUMBER OF POINTS R	NUMBER OF POINTS L	AREA	STATE/PROVINCE	HUNTER'S NAME	DATE	RANK
132 5/8	24 4/8	23 4/8	18 3/8	5	4	Cass County	MO	Jeremy Lemmer	1993	12,013
132 5/8	20 1/8	18 4/8	17 6/8	6	6	Union County	OR	Jerome Dean Norton	1994	12,013
132 5/8	23 1/8	23 6/8	18 7/8	4	5	Ogle County	IL	Peter LaRosa	1994	12,013
132 5/8	23 2/8	23 3/8	16 3/8	5	5	Geauga County	OH	George J. Lashley	1994	12,013
132 5/8	22 7/8	21 7/8	14 0/8	6	6	Dodge County	WI	Jeffery Fuerstenau	1994	12,013
132 5/8	20 2/8	19 1/8	15 3/8	5	7	Dodge County	WI	Thomas Filter	1994	12,013
132 5/8	23 6/8	25 4/8	18 5/8	4	5	Chester County	PA	Mark Moore	1994	12,013
132 5/8	21 4/8	22 3/8	20 7/8	5	5	Buffalo County	WI	Brian Stenseth	1994	12,013
132 5/8	22 2/8	22 7/8	18 3/8	4	4	Livingston County	MI	William W. Kidd, Jr.	1994	12,013
132 5/8	23 1/8	22 1/8	17 5/8	5	6	Lake County	IL	John S. Golladay	1994	12,013
132 5/8	22 5/8	21 3/8	17 1/8	4	4	Kent County	MD	Daniel D. Leonard	1995	12,013
132 5/8	21 0/8	21 1/8	16 4/8	7	6	Marquette County	WI	Jill Cain	1995	12,013
132 5/8	22 0/8	21 0/8	19 1/8	4	5	Bucks County	PA	David A. Cook	1995	12,013
132 5/8	22 1/8	22 4/8	18 5/8	5	5	La Crosse County	WI	Steven Froegel, Jr.	1995	12,013
132 5/8	21 2/8	22 0/8	17 5/8	5	5	Oceana County	MI	Allen F. Aerts	1995	12,013
132 5/8	21 0/8	21 7/8	15 5/8	6	5	Autauga County	AL	David Bufkin	1995	12,013
132 5/8	22 4/8	22 5/8	17 5/8	4	4	Shawnee County	KS	Chuck Kirmse	1995	12,013
132 5/8	23 7/8	23 4/8	16 5/8	6	5	Caldwell County	NC	Greg L. Simmons	1996	12,013
132 5/8	20 5/8	21 0/8	15 2/8	5	7	Ionia County	MI	Brian Keith Lake	1996	12,013
132 5/8	22 2/8	21 6/8	16 3/8	4	4	Appanoose County	IA	Karen Raasch	1996	12,013
132 5/8	21 7/8	21 6/8	16 5/8	7	5	Pawnee County	NE	Gary L. Brunberg	1996	12,013
132 5/8	20 4/8	20 2/8	16 3/8	4	4	Sarpy County	NE	Ed Smith	1996	12,013
132 5/8	23 7/8	24 7/8	19 1/8	4	4	Bartholomew County	IN	Bobby Glover	1996	12,013
132 5/8	23 0/8	23 7/8	19 5/8	5	5	Tioga County	NY	David Marsh	1996	12,013
132 5/8	22 3/8	23 4/8	17 3/8	5	5	Greene County	OH	John L. Kilian	1996	12,013
132 5/8	21 0/8	21 3/8	15 7/8	5	5	Henry County	TN	Lynn Hayes	1997	12,013
132 5/8	17 7/8	17 6/8	17 1/8	5	5	Langlade County	WI	Ronald J. Hintz	1997	12,013
132 5/8	22 5/8	21 5/8	17 3/8	5	5	Adams County	WI	Timothy J. Phalen	1997	12,013
132 5/8	20 0/8	20 3/8	17 1/8	5	5	Cuyahoga County	OH	Terry Skutt	1997	12,013
132 5/8	23 4/8	23 0/8	18 5/8	5	4	McDonald County	MO	Rick Mitchell	1997	12,013
132 5/8	21 5/8	21 5/8	15 7/8	4	4	Winneshiek County	IA	Bob Borowiak	1997	12,013
132 5/8	22 6/8	22 2/8	16 7/8	5	5	Ashland County	WI	Jim Zelhofer	1997	12,013
132 5/8	21 3/8	21 0/8	18 3/8	5	5	Marathon County	WI	Leonard Ziech	1998	12,013
132 5/8	23 0/8	24 4/8	18 5/8	7	6	Tompkins County	NY	Brian L. Marion	1998	12,013
132 5/8	23 3/8	22 4/8	16 7/8	4	5	Fremont County	IA	Thomas J. Hoffman	1998	12,013
132 4/8	23 4/8	23 0/8	16 3/8	6	5	Jackson County	WI	Howard Knockel	1957	12,101
132 4/8	25 4/8	26 0/8	21 0/8	4	4	Valley County	MT	Clare F. Mates	1961	12,101
132 4/8	21 5/8	21 7/8	15 6/8	4	4	Iowa County	IA	Mel Berstler	1965	12,101
132 4/8	21 6/8	21 6/8	16 0/8	5	5	Cowley County	KS	William L. Walker	1965	12,101
132 4/8	23 2/8	24 2/8	18 0/8	5	6	Morrison County	MN	Jerry James	1971	12,101
132 4/8	25 1/8	24 5/8	16 6/8	5	6	Sarpy County	NE	William R. Dengate	1972	12,101
132 4/8	24 6/8	23 7/8	18 3/8	5	5	Carbon County	PA	Frank Jackson	1972	12,101
132 4/8	24 5/8	24 6/8	17 3/8	7	5	Macon County	IL	Wayne Orrell	1976	12,101
132 4/8	23 2/8	23 1/8	15 2/8	5	5	Giles County	VA	Donald Lee Francis	1979	12,101
132 4/8	21 7/8	21 4/8	16 2/8	6	6	Tioga County	NY	Floyd Bowman, Jr.	1981	12,101
132 4/8	23 2/8	22 0/8	17 6/8	4	5	Medicine Hat	ALB	Warren McInenly	1981	12,101
132 4/8	26 0/8	26 6/8	16 6/8	6	6	Lake County	IL	Gary S. Rogers	1981	12,101
132 4/8	23 0/8	25 0/8	14 0/8	4	4	Lamar County	GA	David Brown	1982	12,101
132 4/8	19 3/8	18 5/8	16 2/8	5	5	Tuscola County	MI	Stanley N. Visniski	1982	12,101
132 4/8	20 0/8	20 3/8	17 4/8	4	4	Lyon County	MN	Bruce Londgren	1983	12,101
132 4/8	20 6/8	21 1/8	14 2/8	4	4	Live Oak County	TX	Rick Hayley	1983	12,101
132 4/8	22 3/8	22 2/8	17 0/8	4	4	Washington County	MD	Ronald D. Shank	1985	12,101
132 4/8	20 7/8	21 1/8	14 0/8	5	5	Iowa County	WI	Don Caron	1985	12,101
132 4/8	21 5/8	22 4/8	16 2/8	5	5	Washington County	WI	James O. Werner	1985	12,101
132 4/8	23 6/8	24 1/8	17 6/8	5	5	Barren County	KY	Jeff Scott	1985	12,101
132 4/8	22 1/8	21 6/8	16 6/8	5	6	Columbia County	WI	Wayne Woodstock	1985	12,101
132 4/8	22 7/8	22 1/8	15 2/8	4	5	La Crosse County	WI	Tom Blank	1986	12,101
132 4/8	21 1/8	20 7/8	19 2/8	4	4	Oconto County	WI	Duane Neumann	1986	12,101
132 4/8	22 3/8	22 4/8	16 4/8	5	4	Peoria County	IL	Dan Beaird	1986	12,101
132 4/8	22 0/8	22 2/8	17 7/8	7	8	Muscatine County	IA	Daryle Finley	1986	12,101
132 4/8	21 0/8	20 2/8	13 0/8	5	5	Atascosa County	TX	Joe Hernandez	1987	12,101
132 4/8	22 2/8	22 5/8	15 2/8	5	5	Eaton County	MI	Steven W. Kellogg	1987	12,101
132 4/8	21 5/8	22 0/8	17 0/8	4	4	Dodge County	WI	Joseph G. Tubbs	1987	12,101
132 4/8	22 1/8	22 7/8	15 7/8	4	5	Wyoming County	WV	Michael Prichard	1987	12,101
132 4/8	21 3/8	20 6/8	18 6/8	5	4	Delaware County	IA	Anthony Bass	1987	12,101
132 4/8	23 2/8	23 6/8	17 3/8	6	6	Morris County	NJ	John P. Sibilski	1987	12,101
132 4/8	20 7/8	20 2/8	17 2/8	5	5	Todd County	KY	David D. Haley	1988	12,101
132 4/8	22 6/8	23 0/8	18 0/8	4	4	Franklin County	OH	Tom Vernon	1988	12,101
132 4/8	22 6/8	21 1/8	16 4/8	6	5	Rockingham County	NC	Tim Myers	1988	12,101
132 4/8	19 4/8	20 0/8	17 2/8	5	5	Randolph County	IN	Don Fields	1988	12,101
132 4/8	21 1/8	20 2/8	15 4/8	4	4	Cass County	MI	Sylvester Ignowski	1988	12,101
132 4/8	18 5/8	18 7/8	15 0/8	5	5	Morton County	ND	Todd Schaedler	1988	12,101
132 4/8	22 0/8	22 2/8	17 0/8	5	4	Meagher County	MT	D. Mitch Kottas	1988	12,101
132 4/8	21 3/8	21 6/8	20 3/8	7	6	Will County	IL	Robert L. Bowermaster	1989	12,101
132 4/8	24 3/8	24 0/8	19 0/8	4	4	Sarpy County	NE	Michael S. Goodlander	1989	12,101
132 4/8	22 0/8	22 3/8	18 2/8	5	6	Lake County	IL	Mark M. Fugett	1989	12,101
132 4/8	23 6/8	24 5/8	15 4/8	5	5	Lincoln County	NE	Steve Stumbo	1989	12,101
132 4/8	24 6/8	23 0/8	20 4/8	4	3	Comanche County	KS	David Birmingham	1989	12,101

WHITETAIL DEER (TYPICAL ANTLERS)

Minimum Score 125 — Continued

SCORE	LENGTH OF MAIN BEAM R	L	INSIDE SPREAD	NUMBER OF POINTS R	L	AREA	STATE/ PROVINCE	HUNTER'S NAME	DATE	RANK
132 4/8	21 7/8	24 2/8	16 4/8	4	5	Bond County	IL	William A. Rench	1989	12,101
132 4/8	20 3/8	20 3/8	17 4/8	5	5	Stevens County	MN	Gary Joos	1989	12,101
132 4/8	21 2/8	21 3/8	16 0/8	5	5	Rusk County	WI	Edward H. Cichacki III	1990	12,101
132 4/8	20 7/8	21 1/8	17 0/8	5	5	Hardin County	IA	Dan Zoske	1990	12,101
132 4/8	20 2/8	21 0/8	15 0/8	5	5	Appanoose County	IA	Scott Rolffs	1990	12,101
132 4/8	24 5/8	25 1/8	20 0/8	5	4	Coles County	IL	Bret Patrick	1990	12,101
132 4/8	23 4/8	23 0/8	19 7/8	6	5	Grundy County	IL	Jay Truty	1990	12,101
132 4/8	21 4/8	23 0/8	15 6/8	6	6	Kleberg County	TX	Jarred W. Peeples	1990	12,101
132 4/8	23 7/8	24 4/8	17 0/8	4	4	Newton County	AR	Alex Billings	1991	12,101
132 4/8	18 3/8	18 1/8	13 4/8	6	5	Coke County	TX	Stanley Mayfield	1991	12,101
132 4/8	22 5/8	22 1/8	17 2/8	4	4	Walworth County	WI	Christopher Klein	1991	12,101
132 4/8	20 5/8	21 7/8	17 0/8	5	6	Jefferson County	IL	Matt Farabee	1991	12,101
132 4/8	22 1/8	21 6/8	16 2/8	5	4	Montgomery County	IN	Derrick W. Kidd	1991	12,101
132 4/8	23 1/8	23 4/8	17 2/8	4	5	Hancock County	OH	Steve Shilling	1991	12,101
132 4/8	22 2/8	23 4/8	18 4/8	5	5	Fillmore County	MN	Steve W. Utley	1991	12,101
132 4/8	22 4/8	22 1/8	18 2/8	4	4	Lee County	IL	Steve Cecchetti	1991	12,101
132 4/8	21 7/8	23 0/8	17 7/8	6	4	Kendall County	IL	David Musser	1991	12,101
132 4/8	22 0/8	21 2/8	16 6/8	4	4	Lake County	IN	Jack Jeralds	1992	12,101
132 4/8	22 1/8	21 7/8	22 0/8	5	5	Summerset County	NJ	Paul Fenwick	1992	12,101
132 4/8	23 5/8	22 7/8	15 7/8	5	7	Morrison County	MN	Jack Derks	1992	12,101
132 4/8	20 3/8	19 6/8	15 4/8	5	6	Walsh County	ND	Brian Janikowski	1992	12,101
132 4/8	22 1/8	21 7/8	22 0/8	5	5	Hunterdon County	NJ	Victor Gareoni	1992	12,101
132 4/8	21 5/8	21 6/8	13 5/8	6	7	Livingston County	MI	Ansel B. Flanery, Jr.	1992	12,101
132 4/8	25 4/8	25 5/8	16 1/8	7	7	Lake County	MN	Daniel H. Hall	1992	12,101
132 4/8	20 4/8	19 5/8	16 6/8	5	5	Paulding County	OH	Todd Jackson	1992	12,101
132 4/8	22 3/8	23 1/8	18 6/8	5	4	Wellington	ONT	Alex Morrison	1992	12,101
132 4/8	22 5/8	23 3/8	17 4/8	5	5	Kleberg County	TX	Gary A. Klingaman, Jr.	1992	12,101
132 4/8	23 3/8	23 3/8	19 4/8	4	5	Sherburne County	MN	Trent Midas	1993	12,101
132 4/8	22 0/8	22 3/8	17 4/8	4	5	Texas County	MO	Steve Williams	1993	12,101
132 4/8	22 0/8	21 4/8	15 3/8	6	9	Burleigh County	ND	Bill Fetsch	1993	12,101
132 4/8	21 3/8	23 5/8	18 2/8	7	4	Schuyler County	IL	John H. Johnston	1993	12,101
132 4/8	23 5/8	23 5/8	19 6/8	4	5	De Witt County	IL	Ken Mayer	1993	12,101
132 4/8	21 6/8	22 2/8	16 3/8	7	7	Chitek Lake	SAS	Garry Ard	1993	12,101
132 4/8	23 7/8	24 0/8	17 4/8	4	4	Montgomery County	IN	John Donald	1993	12,101
132 4/8	22 1/8	22 7/8	14 4/8	4	4	Yates County	NY	Warren Wood	1993	12,101
132 4/8	22 2/8	22 3/8	17 7/8	5	5	Osceola County	IA	Dan Lonneman	1993	12,101
132 4/8	21 6/8	22 2/8	16 0/8	5	5	Billings County	ND	Terry Buechler	1993	12,101
132 4/8	21 5/8	22 3/8	16 7/8	5	5	Licking County	OH	Dean Johnson, Sr.	1994	12,101
132 4/8	21 6/8	22 4/8	16 4/8	4	4	Polk County	WI	David Lendosky	1994	12,101
132 4/8	24 1/8	23 4/8	19 4/8	5	4	Kane County	IL	James Meyer	1994	12,101
132 4/8	21 4/8	21 5/8	17 4/8	4	5	Cass County	MI	Rick Anglemyer	1994	12,101
132 4/8	21 6/8	22 3/8	14 2/8	6	6	Slope County	ND	Steven B. Schroeder	1994	12,101
132 4/8	22 4/8	23 0/8	16 0/8	4	4	Cedar County	IA	Mark Schutt	1994	12,101
132 4/8	19 2/8	21 5/8	15 6/8	5	5	Kane County	IL	Robert M. Milcik	1995	12,101
132 4/8	24 5/8	23 3/8	18 2/8	5	5	Bullock County	AL	A. C. Marsh	1995	12,101
132 4/8	20 3/8	21 1/8	16 0/8	4	4	Kent County	MD	Jim Samis	1995	12,101
132 4/8	24 1/8	24 3/8	17 6/8	4	4	Somerset County	NJ	Dennis B. Shennard II	1995	12,101
132 4/8	22 5/8	20 7/8	14 4/8	5	5	Christian County	KY	Daniel Brown	1995	12,101
132 4/8	24 3/8	24 3/8	20 6/8	6	6	Buffalo County	WI	Jon Schutts	1995	12,101
132 4/8	20 0/8	19 5/8	19 2/8	6	5	Dane County	WI	Rollen J. Fries	1995	12,101
132 4/8	23 7/8	23 4/8	17 0/8	4	4	Prince Georges County	MD	Ronald A. Fimiani	1995	12,101
132 4/8	22 3/8	22 7/8	16 7/8	5	6	Armstrong County	PA	Mark R. Pennington	1996	12,101
132 4/8	21 0/8	20 5/8	16 6/8	5	5	Owen County	IN	David D. Bennett	1996	12,101
132 4/8	22 3/8	21 5/8	17 6/8	5	4	Parke County	IN	Mark Cuffle	1996	12,101
132 4/8	21 2/8	21 0/8	15 2/8	5	5	Grant County	WI	Jim A. Pitzer	1996	12,101
132 4/8	21 6/8	22 4/8	16 0/8	4	5	Saline County	AR	Mark Anthony	1996	12,101
132 4/8	19 4/8	20 4/8	19 0/8	5	4	Jefferson County	WI	Larry Braatz	1996	12,101
132 4/8	20 7/8	20 2/8	15 4/8	5	5	Cass County	MI	Mark Bell	1996	12,101
132 4/8	22 2/8	21 5/8	17 0/8	6	4	Van Buren County	IA	Keith Geibel	1996	12,101
132 4/8	19 0/8	18 3/8	14 0/8	5	5	Knox County	NE	Randy Olson	1997	12,101
132 4/8	20 5/8	21 2/8	17 2/8	4	4	Polk County	WI	Larry Loverude	1997	12,101
132 4/8	22 7/8	23 0/8	16 4/8	4	4	Frederick County	MD	Jeffrey Eyler	1997	12,101
132 4/8	21 7/8	22 0/8	17 0/8	5	4	Olmsted County	MN	Tim Vande Walker	1997	12,101
132 4/8	21 7/8	20 7/8	16 2/8	6	5	Genesee County	MI	Mitch Gray	1997	12,101
132 4/8	20 7/8	22 0/8	17 0/8	5	5	Sheboygan County	WI	James Overbeck	1997	12,101
132 4/8	20 6/8	20 5/8	15 3/8	5	6	Van Buren County	IA	Melvin T. Digman	1997	12,101
132 4/8	22 0/8	22 6/8	17 0/8	5	6	Berks County	PA	Clayton Smith	1997	12,101
132 4/8	21 7/8	21 5/8	16 6/8	6	6	Ingham County	MI	Greg S. Rupprecht	1997	12,101
132 4/8	21 4/8	22 4/8	17 4/8	5	6	Brown County	IL	Ricky Bishop	1997	12,101
132 4/8	23 0/8	21 6/8	17 5/8	5	6	La Salle County	IL	Todd J. Yeager	1997	12,101
132 4/8	24 4/8	24 1/8	19 3/8	6	5	Rock County	WI	Shawn Blaser	1997	12,101
132 4/8	20 0/8	20 0/8	17 7/8	6	5	Pike County	IL	Randy Helmkamp	1997	12,101
132 4/8	21 1/8	21 6/8	16 1/8	5	6	Winona County	MN	Bruce Williams	1997	12,101
132 4/8	20 3/8	20 7/8	22 2/8	4	5	Suffolk County	NY	Tim Connor	1997	12,101
132 4/8	21 7/8	21 7/8	18 0/8	6	5	Kenedy County	TX	Gary F. Bogner	1997	12,101
132 4/8	22 4/8	23 6/8	19 2/8	4	4	Green Lake County	WI	Jeff Balzer	1998	12,101
132 3/8	20 5/8	20 6/8	14 3/8	4	4	Buffalo County	NE	Al Dawson	1961	12,220
132 3/8	21 2/8	21 0/8	14 5/8	4	4	St. Joseph County	IN	Harry Ramsbey, Jr.	1963	12,220

WHITETAIL DEER (TYPICAL ANTLERS)

Minimum Score 125 — Continued

SCORE	LENGTH OF MAIN BEAM R	LENGTH OF MAIN BEAM L	INSIDE SPREAD	NUMBER OF POINTS R	NUMBER OF POINTS L	AREA	STATE/PROVINCE	HUNTER'S NAME	DATE	RANK
132 3/8	22 0/8	21 2/8	17 4/8	4	4	Morrison County	MN	Jay J. Jost	1968	12,220
132 3/8	21 6/8	22 6/8	18 7/8	5	6	Spink County	SD	Roger Michels	1968	12,220
132 3/8	22 6/8	21 7/8	15 3/8	4	4	Shawano County	WI	Gene M. Waite	1971	12,220
132 3/8	22 7/8	22 2/8	17 5/8	4	4	Sarpy County	NE	Doug Bowen	1974	12,220
132 3/8	25 4/8	24 3/8	19 3/8	7	7	Davis County	IA	Tommy Thompson	1975	12,220
132 3/8	22 6/8	24 1/8	15 7/8	5	4	Dunn County	WI	Loyd Donnelly	1980	12,220
132 3/8	22 0/8	21 7/8	15 5/8	5	4	Pine County	MN	Galen Miller	1982	12,220
132 3/8	25 3/8	25 1/8	19 2/8	8	5	Fulton County	IL	Ray Brown	1982	12,220
132 3/8	21 6/8	21 2/8	17 5/8	5	5	Kane County	IL	Gordon Sunderlage	1982	12,220
132 3/8	21 7/8	22 0/8	16 1/8	4	4	Greenwood County	SC	Warren Johnson	1985	12,220
132 3/8	21 4/8	21 2/8	13 6/8	5	5	Otter Tail County	MN	Kelly Shannon	1985	12,220
132 3/8	22 4/8	22 4/8	18 6/8	5	4	Kent County	MD	Michael A. Snyder	1985	12,220
132 3/8	21 6/8	22 2/8	14 5/8	4	4	Greene County	AL	Mike Wood	1986	12,220
132 3/8	20 4/8	19 5/8	14 3/8	5	5	Okmulgee County	OK	Howard D. Massie	1987	12,220
132 3/8	25 0/8	25 0/8	20 3/8	4	4	Allamakee County	IA	Jon Wolter	1987	12,220
132 3/8	21 6/8	21 4/8	19 4/8	5	6	Meigs County	OH	Steve Price	1987	12,220
132 3/8	25 4/8	25 1/8	19 3/8	4	4	Lake County	IL	Kevin Dahm	1987	12,220
132 3/8	20 3/8	20 6/8	17 0/8	5	7	Tripp County	SD	Byron E. Foreman	1988	12,220
132 3/8	20 4/8	19 7/8	14 1/8	5	5	Roberts County	SD	Ronald Backman	1988	12,220
132 3/8	24 1/8	24 4/8	17 5/8	3	4	Shawnee County	KS	Stuart Hazard	1988	12,220
132 3/8	22 4/8	23 3/8	15 3/8	5	5	Elmore County	AL	Rett Kelly	1988	12,220
132 3/8	23 2/8	21 4/8	18 3/8	4	8	Kane County	IL	John K. Zawaski	1989	12,220
132 3/8	22 4/8	21 5/8	14 7/8	6	5	Delta County	MI	William E. Heitman	1989	12,220
132 3/8	21 1/8	21 1/8	17 4/8	8	8	Creek County	OK	Joe Morgan	1989	12,220
132 3/8	21 2/8	21 1/8	16 5/8	4	4	Sangamon County	IL	Larry Skinner	1989	12,220
132 3/8	20 7/8	22 0/8	15 6/8	5	5	Marinette County	WI	Joseph J. Nushart	1990	12,220
132 3/8	21 5/8	21 6/8	15 1/8	4	4	Linn County	IA	John Aarni	1990	12,220
132 3/8	24 2/8	23 3/8	19 2/8	7	7	Baltimore County	MD	Shawn King	1990	12,220
132 3/8	19 2/8	18 7/8	18 1/8	5	5	Waukesha County	WI	Craig Pagenkopf	1990	12,220
132 3/8	24 6/8	25 0/8	20 5/8	4	4	Franklin County	MA	Richard Marcinowski	1990	12,220
132 3/8	23 3/8	23 7/8	18 2/8	9	6	Allamakee County	IA	Rodney Blake	1990	12,220
132 3/8	24 3/8	23 2/8	18 0/8	4	7	Wood County	OH	Othan E. Katakis	1990	12,220
132 3/8	21 5/8	22 7/8	17 7/8	5	7	Jo Daviess County	IL	Brian L. Randecker	1990	12,220
132 3/8	24 6/8	23 7/8	19 3/8	4	4	Madison County	MS	Stanley Coring	1990	12,220
132 3/8	24 6/8	24 0/8	16 5/8	3	5	De Witt County	IL	Thomas Wilson	1991	12,220
132 3/8	21 6/8	22 2/8	17 5/8	4	4	Iroquois County	IL	William Hendershott	1991	12,220
132 3/8	20 7/8	20 6/8	16 3/8	5	5	Patrick County	VA	David Mabe	1991	12,220
132 3/8	20 7/8	20 7/8	16 5/8	5	5	Lake County	IL	Greg Betlach	1991	12,220
132 3/8	25 4/8	26 3/8	25 5/8	3	3	Fairfax County	VA	Jeffrey A. Bieniek	1992	12,220
132 3/8	23 6/8	23 3/8	17 4/8	6	7	Buffalo County	WI	Ray Zastrow, Jr.	1992	12,220
132 3/8	23 2/8	23 4/8	17 3/8	4	4	Niagara County	NY	Rich Vanni	1992	12,220
132 3/8	22 6/8	23 0/8	16 3/8	6	4	Wilkin County	MN	Dave Balken	1992	12,220
132 3/8	22 6/8	22 6/8	16 5/8	5	5	Sibley County	MN	Ken Boehm	1992	12,220
132 3/8	22 2/8	22 0/8	20 1/8	4	5	Chautauqua County	NY	Rodney C. Smink	1992	12,220
132 3/8	23 1/8	23 3/8	17 1/8	4	4	Charles County	MD	Larry S. Murray	1992	12,220
132 3/8	20 4/8	21 5/8	16 1/8	5	5	Aroostook County	ME	Steve Emery	1993	12,220
132 3/8	25 4/8	22 4/8	19 5/8	5	5	Dawson County	NE	Larry Hermsmeyer	1993	12,220
132 3/8	24 0/8	22 6/8	16 7/8	4	4	Adams County	IL	Jon Wren	1993	12,220
132 3/8	23 2/8	23 5/8	19 5/8	4	4	Marinette County	WI	Ken Ganter	1993	12,220
132 3/8	24 5/8	23 2/8	17 3/8	4	4	Prince George County	VA	Joey J. Yemma	1993	12,220
132 3/8	20 4/8	21 5/8	17 6/8	5	7	Hardin County	KY	Danny Stevens	1993	12,220
132 3/8	23 6/8	23 5/8	16 0/8	6	5	Winneshiek County	IA	Steve Weber	1993	12,220
132 3/8	23 4/8	22 5/8	15 1/8	5	5	Scotland County	MO	Kevin Small	1993	12,220
132 3/8	24 0/8	25 2/8	17 6/8	5	4	Parke County	IN	Charles Paxton	1993	12,220
132 3/8	21 1/8	20 2/8	14 3/8	5	5	Kenedy County	TX	Ben B. Wallace	1993	12,220
132 3/8	22 1/8	23 1/8	18 1/8	4	4	Kandiyohi County	MN	Ron Welle	1994	12,220
132 3/8	18 6/8	19 4/8	13 7/8	5	5	Hunterdon County	NJ	Arnie Boccafogli	1994	12,220
132 3/8	21 1/8	20 7/8	15 1/8	5	5	Sheboygan County	WI	Charles W. Gahagan	1994	12,220
132 3/8	20 0/8	20 0/8	15 3/8	5	5	Buffalo County	WI	David W. Stuhr	1994	12,220
132 3/8	22 6/8	23 7/8	17 5/8	5	5	Pike County	IL	Douglas Wheelehon	1994	12,220
132 3/8	23 2/8	22 3/8	16 5/8	5	4	Monona County	IA	Todd Amenrud	1994	12,220
132 3/8	22 6/8	22 2/8	17 3/8	4	4	Jefferson County	ID	Douglas Kauer	1994	12,220
132 3/8	22 1/8	23 4/8	18 7/8	5	4	Lake County	IL	David Quist	1994	12,220
132 3/8	19 6/8	21 2/8	18 1/8	5	5	Arkansas County	AR	David E. Snowden, Jr.	1995	12,220
132 3/8	21 1/8	22 1/8	22 5/8	4	4	Wood County	WI	Pat L. Anderson	1995	12,220
132 3/8	22 3/8	22 4/8	19 1/8	4	4	Montgomery County	IL	Anthony Germanceri	1995	12,220
132 3/8	21 6/8	21 4/8	16 7/8	4	4	Vermillion County	IN	Todd Wickens	1995	12,220
132 3/8	26 7/8	27 4/8	21 3/8	8	6	Lake County	OH	Michael LaVan	1995	12,220
132 3/8	22 0/8	21 2/8	13 4/8	5	5	Seminole County	OK	Reggy Darbison	1995	12,220
132 3/8	20 7/8	22 3/8	16 7/8	6	6	Will County	IL	John Kamarauskas	1995	12,220
132 3/8	23 1/8	22 1/8	18 3/8	5	5	Fairfield County	CT	Dennis Mical	1995	12,220
132 3/8	22 5/8	22 6/8	15 5/8	4	5	Crook County	WY	Steven J. Huppert	1996	12,220
132 3/8	20 7/8	20 4/8	15 3/8	5	5	Powell County	MT	Dale Hyma	1996	12,220
132 3/8	20 1/8	20 4/8	16 5/8	5	5	Houston County	MN	Bob Borowiak	1996	12,220
132 3/8	22 2/8	22 7/8	19 6/8	5	4	Montgomery County	PA	Charles G. Falco	1996	12,220
132 3/8	21 4/8	21 5/8	15 6/8	11	6	Van Buren County	MI	Scott T. Spears	1996	12,220
132 3/8	24 7/8	25 4/8	15 5/8	4	4	Essex	ONT	Karl Bekaan	1996	12,220
132 3/8	24 1/8	25 0/8	15 5/8	4	5	Monona County	IA	Russell T. Reimer	1996	12,220

WHITETAIL DEER (TYPICAL ANTLERS)

Minimum Score 125 — Continued

SCORE	LENGTH OF MAIN BEAM R	L	INSIDE SPREAD	NUMBER OF POINTS R	L	AREA	STATE/ PROVINCE	HUNTER'S NAME	DATE	RANK
132 3/8	23 1/8	23 0/8	15 3/8	5	5	Roberts County	SD	James Michlitsch	1996	12,220
132 3/8	23 0/8	23 5/8	16 3/8	6	5	Dallas County	AL	Chris Mullinax	1997	12,220
132 3/8	24 6/8	24 0/8	16 3/8	5	4	Litchfield County	CT	Glen Costa	1997	12,220
132 3/8	22 2/8	21 6/8	14 5/8	5	5	Portage County	WI	Brian P. Kudronowicz	1997	12,220
132 3/8	22 1/8	22 3/8	14 5/8	5	4	Worsley	ALB	Les Baird	1997	12,220
132 3/8	23 0/8	22 5/8	17 5/8	4	5	Clayton County	IA	Jeffery D. Zelley	1997	12,220
132 3/8	21 0/8	21 1/8	17 7/8	6	5	Delaware County	IA	James Bailey	1997	12,220
132 3/8	21 6/8	22 7/8	17 4/8	7	6	Steuben County	NY	Rich Kauder	1997	12,220
132 3/8	21 2/8	20 2/8	17 1/8	4	4	Carroll County	KY	Greg Green	1997	12,220
132 3/8	22 7/8	22 5/8	17 3/8	5	5	Lincoln County	WI	Robert P. Agard	1997	12,220
132 3/8	22 7/8	22 3/8	18 5/8	5	4	Clark County	IL	Zack Irvin	1997	12,220
132 3/8	21 2/8	21 1/8	14 3/8	5	6	Concordia Parish	LA	Bill Dondero	1997	12,220
132 3/8	20 7/8	20 5/8	14 5/8	4	4	Williams County	ND	Richard Gustafson	1998	12,220
132 3/8	21 7/8	21 5/8	17 1/8	5	5	Kent County	MD	Troy Thomas	1998	12,220
132 3/8	23 6/8	25 1/8	20 3/8	4	4	Montgomery County	MD	Patrick Morningstar	1998	12,220
132 3/8	21 5/8	23 2/8	15 7/8	5	5	Tompkins County	NY	David C. Arsenault	1998	12,220
132 2/8	22 1/8	21 7/8	16 6/8	5	4	Waupaca County	WI	Al Wiltzius	1949	12,316
132 2/8	21 7/8	23 2/8	16 6/8	5	8	Cherokee County	IA	Darrell Magnussen	1962	12,316
132 2/8	22 0/8	22 4/8	19 2/8	4	4	Bullitt County	KY	Dell Pack	1962	12,316
132 2/8	21 4/8	23 5/8	20 4/8	4	5	Roberts County	SD	Clayton Forrette	1967	12,316
132 2/8	24 6/8	25 2/8	23 4/8	3	3	Stoddard County	MO	Ted Denkins	1971	12,316
132 2/8	21 3/8	21 7/8	16 4/8	4	4	Westmoreland County	PA	Robert C. Kichner	1971	12,316
132 2/8	24 3/8	23 6/8	17 4/8	4	4	Talbot County	MD	Walter Krom	1976	12,316
132 2/8	23 2/8	21 6/8	16 5/8	5	6	Clinton County	IL	James D. Rueter	1980	12,316
132 2/8	21 0/8	20 6/8	17 6/8	5	6	Perry County	IL	Bob Clark	1981	12,316
132 2/8	24 1/8	23 1/8	18 0/8	7	5	Brown County	SD	Jack Ness	1981	12,316
132 2/8	21 7/8	21 4/8	19 6/8	4	4	Vernon County	WI	Robert S. Navrestad	1982	12,316
132 2/8	21 5/8	22 5/8	16 1/8	6	5	Adams County	WI	David J. Niesen	1982	12,316
132 2/8	22 1/8	21 6/8	19 2/8	4	4	Carroll County	IL	Jeffrey Mathew	1983	12,316
132 2/8	23 6/8	22 0/8	15 1/8	4	5	Polk County	TX	James K. Hignett	1984	12,316
132 2/8	22 6/8	23 4/8	17 1/8	4	5	Phillips County	KS	Rick Chapin	1984	12,316
132 2/8	21 7/8	22 5/8	18 2/8	5	4	Montgomery County	PA	Ted Sherk	1985	12,316
132 2/8	21 2/8	21 5/8	15 4/8	5	5	Pepin County	WI	Bruce Hayden	1986	12,316
132 2/8	22 7/8	23 4/8	15 0/8	4	4	Jasper County	MS	Harmon Hill	1986	12,316
132 2/8	22 5/8	22 3/8	16 6/8	4	4	Champaign County	OH	Gene Watson	1986	12,316
132 2/8	21 6/8	22 4/8	16 4/8	6	7	Waushara County	WI	Lee D. Faust	1986	12,316
132 2/8	22 1/8	20 6/8	15 6/8	5	5	Waukesha County	WI	Dick Carlson	1986	12,316
132 2/8	23 4/8	22 4/8	18 0/8	4	5	Washington County	WI	Tony Snow	1986	12,316
132 2/8	23 1/8	23 2/8	16 7/8	6	4	Jackson County	WV	Charles E. Osborne, Jr.	1986	12,316
132 2/8	21 3/8	22 2/8	15 2/8	5	5	Troup County	GA	Tommy Roberts	1986	12,316
132 2/8	23 1/8	22 2/8	17 2/8	5	5	Otsego County	MI	Tom J. Holmes	1987	12,316
132 2/8	19 6/8	20 1/8	14 2/8	6	5	Pulaski County	KY	Casper Carroll Gibson	1987	12,316
132 2/8	22 4/8	21 4/8	18 1/8	4	5	Montgomery County	IL	Michael L. McCoy	1988	12,316
132 2/8	21 7/8	22 3/8	17 2/8	6	5	Vilas County	WI	Dan Vernetti	1988	12,316
132 2/8	21 3/8	22 3/8	13 7/8	7	5	Pawnee County	OK	Mark D. Riddle	1988	12,316
132 2/8	22 1/8	22 5/8	16 7/8	5	4	Tomahawk	ALB	David Cox	1989	12,316
132 2/8	20 6/8	22 1/8	17 2/8	5	5	Wilcox County	AL	Joe Headley	1989	12,316
132 2/8	23 7/8	24 7/8	17 2/8	6	7	Fulton County	OH	Mike Krasny	1989	12,316
132 2/8	24 2/8	24 1/8	17 0/8	4	4	Branch County	MI	Byron L. Harper	1989	12,316
132 2/8	21 4/8	20 6/8	15 4/8	4	5	Turner County	SD	Monte J. Waltner	1989	12,316
132 2/8	23 7/8	23 3/8	19 4/8	4	4	Jo Daviess County	IL	David J. Gerber	1989	12,316
132 2/8	22 5/8	24 0/8	21 0/8	4	5	Adolphustown	ONT	Mike Burriss	1989	12,316
132 2/8	22 0/8	21 6/8	16 0/8	5	5	Kenedy County	TX	B. J. McCord	1989	12,316
132 2/8	20 1/8	21 1/8	17 6/8	5	5	Rice County	MN	Richard Bohlmann	1990	12,316
132 2/8	22 6/8	22 7/8	18 3/8	5	5	Onondaga County	NY	James A. Terranova	1990	12,316
132 2/8	22 2/8	22 2/8	16 6/8	5	6	Le Sueur County	MN	Randy Mathwig	1990	12,316
132 2/8	21 2/8	20 5/8	15 4/8	5	5	Lowndes County	AL	Rett Kelly	1990	12,316
132 2/8	23 4/8	23 2/8	19 2/8	5	6	Stoddard County	MO	Lawson Metcalf	1990	12,316
132 2/8	19 0/8	19 1/8	16 2/8	6	5	Gregory County	SD	Daniel J. Roskos, Jr.	1991	12,316
132 2/8	22 6/8	22 6/8	14 6/8	5	5	Montgomery County	MD	Gregory J. Diatz	1991	12,316
132 2/8	21 2/8	19 5/8	15 4/8	5	4	Sauk County	WI	Dale Peat	1991	12,316
132 2/8	23 6/8	23 2/8	19 6/8	4	4	Hunterdon County	NJ	Joseph Guerino	1991	12,316
132 2/8	24 6/8	24 1/8	17 0/8	5	5	Buffalo County	WI	Daniel H. Folkedahl	1991	12,316
132 2/8	21 5/8	20 5/8	16 0/8	5	5	Parke County	IN	Philip A. Prock	1991	12,316
132 2/8	19 3/8	20 0/8	14 6/8	6	5	Comal County	TX	Deno Poulos	1991	12,316
132 2/8	22 7/8	24 1/8	18 6/8	5	4	Rush County	KS	George J. Seuser III	1991	12,316
132 2/8	19 5/8	20 4/8	17 0/8	5	5	Jasper County	IA	Craig Hoskins	1991	12,316
132 2/8	22 1/8	22 5/8	19 6/8	4	4	Will County	IL	Bret H. Roth	1992	12,316
132 2/8	20 3/8	21 0/8	15 6/8	5	5	Clark County	SD	Dale E. Springer	1992	12,316
132 2/8	21 4/8	22 1/8	15 4/8	5	5	Branch County	MI	Jeff V. Heckart	1992	12,316
132 2/8	22 0/8	20 7/8	18 2/8	5	4	Allegan County	MI	Mitch Wells	1992	12,316
132 2/8	23 7/8	23 7/8	16 6/8	5	5	Licking County	OH	Steve Bryan	1992	12,316
132 2/8	24 4/8	24 5/8	21 0/8	3	4	Berkshire County	MA	Steve Rivers	1992	12,316
132 2/8	22 0/8	22 0/8	17 4/8	5	5	Cheshire County	NH	Bruce E. Ward	1992	12,316
132 2/8	20 3/8	21 3/8	15 0/8	5	5	Winnebago County	IL	Greg L. Sill	1992	12,316
132 2/8	23 2/8	22 3/8	15 2/8	4	5	Erie County	PA	Ronald Hedlund	1993	12,316
132 2/8	22 3/8	23 3/8	19 2/8	4	4	Washington County	MS	Bobby R. Woods	1993	12,316
132 2/8	23 5/8	24 6/8	16 2/8	5	6	Talbot County	MD	Curtis C. Satchell	1993	12,316

WHITETAIL DEER (TYPICAL ANTLERS)

Minimum Score 125   Continued

SCORE	LENGTH OF MAIN BEAM R	L	INSIDE SPREAD	NUMBER OF POINTS R	L	AREA	STATE/ PROVINCE	HUNTER'S NAME	DATE	RANK
132 2/8	20 5/8	21 2/8	19 6/8	5	5	Dane County	WI	Tracy J. Thayer	1993	12,316
132 2/8	25 1/8	24 6/8	17 4/8	4	4	Shawano County	WI	Ross S. Berkhahn	1993	12,316
132 2/8	22 5/8	23 0/8	16 4/8	6	4	Macomb County	MI	Scott A. Stier	1993	12,316
132 2/8	23 3/8	24 3/8	16 6/8	4	4	Brown County	KS	Craig Gilbert	1993	12,316
132 2/8	21 5/8	22 0/8	18 6/8	5	5	Peoria County	IL	Larry Pollack	1993	12,316
132 2/8	22 2/8	22 6/8	19 3/8	4	6	Johnson County	IA	Gary E. Rohret	1993	12,316
132 2/8	22 2/8	22 6/8	18 4/8	4	4	Scott County	MO	William C. Nace	1993	12,316
132 2/8	22 2/8	22 2/8	17 6/8	4	4	Schuylkill County	PA	Clair Newswanger	1993	12,316
132 2/8	21 0/8	21 0/8	17 6/8	4	4	Burlington County	NJ	John A. Pullen, Jr.	1994	12,316
132 2/8	23 4/8	23 3/8	16 0/8	5	5	Sangamon County	IL	Bill Westlake	1994	12,316
132 2/8	22 0/8	22 6/8	17 6/8	5	4	Audrain County	MO	Kenny Jurgesmeyer	1994	12,316
132 2/8	24 5/8	24 0/8	17 0/8	5	4	Grand Traverse County	MI	Lew Farrell	1994	12,316
132 2/8	16 6/8	19 0/8	15 0/8	5	5	Kosciusko County	IN	Sam Whitaker	1994	12,316
132 2/8	21 1/8	21 1/8	16 2/8	6	9	Guthrie County	IA	Mike Erickson	1994	12,316
132 2/8	22 7/8	23 1/8	16 2/8	5	5	Marinette County	WI	Mike Burnside	1994	12,316
132 2/8	22 4/8	21 0/8	16 0/8	6	4	Buffalo County	WI	Kim M. Pronschinske	1994	12,316
132 2/8	22 4/8	21 7/8	18 4/8	5	5	Columbia County	WI	Dennis L. Simonson	1994	12,316
132 2/8	20 1/8	20 6/8	17 6/8	4	4	Pepin County	WI	Randy Gruber	1994	12,316
132 2/8	24 4/8	24 6/8	19 4/8	5	5	Rockingham County	NH	Robert V. Lang	1994	12,316
132 2/8	22 1/8	20 2/8	16 2/8	5	5	McLean County	ND	Harold Edwards	1994	12,316
132 2/8	21 4/8	22 6/8	19 0/8	5	5	McMullen County	TX	Daniel D. Countiss	1994	12,316
132 2/8	22 0/8	24 4/8	17 2/8	6	5	Lake County	IL	Don Tjader	1994	12,316
132 2/8	23 0/8	22 2/8	15 0/8	5	7	Osage County	OK	Bryan White	1995	12,316
132 2/8	23 5/8	23 5/8	17 4/8	4	4	Morrison County	MN	Paul E. Korn	1995	12,316
132 2/8	24 1/8	23 6/8	17 6/8	4	4	Green County	WI	Brandon J. Anderson	1995	12,316
132 2/8	21 2/8	21 4/8	16 4/8	5	5	Jackson County	WI	Travis L. Sorenson	1995	12,316
132 2/8	25 5/8	24 5/8	18 4/8	9	7	Warren County	IA	Tim Deskin	1995	12,316
132 2/8	21 2/8	21 2/8	14 1/8	6	5	Clay County	MO	Garrett Westfall	1995	12,316
132 2/8	22 7/8	22 6/8	17 4/8	5	4	Jefferson County	WI	Patrick Cherone	1996	12,316
132 2/8	22 2/8	22 0/8	16 4/8	4	4	St. Joseph County	MI	Jack F. Armstrong	1996	12,316
132 2/8	22 2/8	20 4/8	17 1/8	6	5	Fulton County	IL	Tim Wells	1996	12,316
132 2/8	23 4/8	23 6/8	16 4/8	4	4	Forest County	WI	Donald A. Rindahl	1996	12,316
132 2/8	23 5/8	24 0/8	18 4/8	5	4	Mindemoya	ONT	Chad Magoon	1996	12,316
132 2/8	20 0/8	20 2/8	15 4/8	5	5	Ravalli County	MT	Dale E. Dye	1996	12,316
132 2/8	21 6/8	22 4/8	17 0/8	5	5	Kewaunee County	WI	Bob Schmidt	1997	12,316
132 2/8	22 6/8	23 6/8	17 2/8	4	4	Shackelford County	TX	Rick Espino	1997	12,316
132 2/8	20 6/8	20 7/8	17 2/8	5	5	Rock County	WI	J. R. Crans	1997	12,316
132 2/8	22 7/8	22 3/8	21 2/8	4	4	Columbia County	WI	Dave Chappell	1997	12,316
132 2/8	22 2/8	21 3/8	16 4/8	5	4	Bourbon County	KS	Kevin Addington	1997	12,316
132 2/8	22 0/8	22 4/8	17 6/8	4	5	Hillsdale County	MI	William D. Griffiths	1997	12,316
132 2/8	21 6/8	21 4/8	17 0/8	4	5	Brown County	IL	Timothy I. Burkins	1997	12,316
132 2/8	19 7/8	19 6/8	13 2/8	6	5	Lincoln County	NE	Steven W. Stumbo	1997	12,316
132 2/8	22 0/8	22 2/8	14 4/8	4	4	Jim Hogg County	TX	Bob Gilbert	1997	12,316
132 2/8	24 1/8	18 1/8	16 3/8	5	6	Osborne County	KS	Gary L. Ozias	1997	12,316
132 2/8	20 6/8	21 4/8	15 0/8	5	6	Williams County	ND	Todd Erickson	1998	12,316
132 2/8	22 4/8	21 0/8	16 4/8	5	6	Ravalli County	MT	Edwin Russo	1998	12,316
132 2/8	22 5/8	22 0/8	19 7/8	6	6	Sangamon County	IL	Jim Davis	1998	12,316
132 1/8	18 1/8	19 7/8	18 3/8	5	5	Buffalo County	NE	Bill Orsborn	1962	12,425
132 1/8	20 3/8	20 0/8	17 1/8	5	5	Rice County	KS	Robert Lagree	1967	12,425
132 1/8	20 2/8	20 0/8	16 1/8	5	5	Kerr County	TX	Randolph Coleman	1972	12,425
132 1/8	22 4/8	24 1/8	16 3/8	4	5	Jasper County	IA	Paul Casper	1972	12,425
132 1/8	21 6/8	22 0/8	15 3/8	5	5	Pittsburg County	OK	Joe Admire	1975	12,425
132 1/8	21 5/8	21 5/8	17 7/8	5	5	Freeborn County	MN	Jerry Christenson	1977	12,425
132 1/8	20 5/8	20 2/8	16 5/8	6	5	Olmsted County	MN	Jerry V. Finley	1981	12,425
132 1/8	22 1/8	21 4/8	16 0/8	5	4	Black Hawk County	IA	Larry Graham	1981	12,425
132 1/8	19 6/8	20 0/8	16 4/8	6	5	Pepin County	WI	Terry A. G. Moline	1981	12,425
132 1/8	21 0/8	21 1/8	13 3/8	4	4	Cowley County	KS	Bill E. Wilson	1981	12,425
132 1/8	21 5/8	21 5/8	16 7/8	4	4	Mills County	TX	Tony Thomas	1982	12,425
132 1/8	22 0/8	20 7/8	15 5/8	5	5	Eau Claire County	WI	Thomas R. Budik	1982	12,425
132 1/8	24 1/8	24 1/8	18 7/8	4	4	Dunn County	WI	Richard O'Mara	1983	12,425
132 1/8	22 2/8	22 7/8	15 5/8	4	5	Walworth County	WI	Gifford Hisel	1984	12,425
132 1/8	22 5/8	24 4/8	17 7/8	4	5	McLean County	KY	Earl Smith	1985	12,425
132 1/8	23 3/8	23 4/8	19 0/8	5	4	Carroll County	MD	Herbert Eyler	1985	12,425
132 1/8	22 5/8	22 0/8	16 7/8	4	5	Sanilac County	MI	Randy Bernard Smith	1986	12,425
132 1/8	24 1/8	23 7/8	20 1/8	4	4	Chautauqua County	NY	Greg Buckley	1986	12,425
132 1/8	19 0/8	20 2/8	19 5/8	6	6	Morgan County	IL	Terry Joe Day	1987	12,425
132 1/8	22 6/8	22 6/8	17 1/8	4	4	Crawford County	PA	David H. Ingalls	1987	12,425
132 1/8	21 5/8	22 1/8	16 7/8	4	4	Waupaca County	WI	Pete Kallas	1987	12,425
132 1/8	22 1/8	22 2/8	16 3/8	4	4	Harvey County	KS	Dan Wilkerson	1987	12,425
132 1/8	20 1/8	20 7/8	14 3/8	5	5	Buffalo County	WI	David J. Gard	1987	12,425
132 1/8	25 0/8	23 4/8	20 3/8	4	5	Jackson County	IL	Tim Cobin	1987	12,425
132 1/8	22 5/8	21 5/8	19 1/8	4	5	Montgomery County	KS	John Battitori	1987	12,425
132 1/8	21 3/8	21 3/8	18 3/8	4	5	Portage County	WI	Bob Kitowski	1988	12,425
132 1/8	22 1/8	21 0/8	13 5/8	5	6	Barry County	MI	Brian Elliston	1988	12,425
132 1/8	23 2/8	21 2/8	16 3/8	5	4	Meigs County	OH	Jack Satterfield, Jr.	1988	12,425
132 1/8	22 5/8	22 1/8	23 2/8	4	4	Carroll County	MD	Dean Richardson	1988	12,425
132 1/8	22 7/8	23 0/8	20 5/8	4	4	St. Landry Parish	LA	Brent Fontenot	1989	12,425
132 1/8	24 2/8	23 6/8	17 2/8	5	6	Chatham County	NC	Tom McIntosh	1989	12,425

WHITETAIL DEER (TYPICAL ANTLERS)

Minimum Score 125   Continued 451

SCORE	LENGTH OF MAIN BEAM R	LENGTH OF MAIN BEAM L	INSIDE SPREAD	NUMBER OF POINTS R	NUMBER OF POINTS L	AREA	STATE/ PROVINCE	HUNTER'S NAME	DATE	RANK
132 1/8	22 0/8	22 1/8	17 1/8	4	6	Sibley County	MN	Robert M. Boettcher	1989	12,425
132 1/8	21 6/8	22 2/8	16 0/8	6	6	McHenry County	IL	Jim Neuses	1989	12,425
132 1/8	23 4/8	22 4/8	18 1/8	6	7	Kenosha County	WI	Myron L Hayes	1989	12,425
132 1/8	23 2/8	22 4/8	17 5/8	5	4	Woodbury County	IA	Michael W. McKenna	1989	12,425
132 1/8	21 0/8	23 0/8	18 5/8	4	4	Stokes County	NC	Roy R. Bullins	1989	12,425
132 1/8	23 6/8	21 4/8	14 1/8	5	5	Jefferson County	WI	Jeffrey Schemm	1989	12,425
132 1/8	22 1/8	22 4/8	16 3/8	4	4	Kankakee County	IL	Terry Marcukaitis	1989	12,425
132 1/8	24 1/8	24 0/8	17 7/8	6	6	McKenzie County	ND	Mark Stewart	1990	12,425
132 1/8	23 4/8	24 1/8	18 1/8	4	4	Forest County	WI	Steven C. Gevaert	1990	12,425
132 1/8	22 4/8	20 3/8	15 2/8	6	5	Norman County	MN	Rick Sorensen	1990	12,425
132 1/8	21 5/8	21 3/8	15 1/8	5	5	Dunn County	WI	Peter Moss	1990	12,425
132 1/8	20 0/8	21 6/8	19 1/8	6	5	Shannon County	MO	Bill Ipock	1990	12,425
132 1/8	25 3/8	21 6/8	19 5/8	4	4	De Witt County	IL	Kent Sharp	1990	12,425
132 1/8	23 4/8	23 1/8	16 7/8	4	4	Stoddard County	MO	Eddie McDowell	1990	12,425
132 1/8	23 0/8	24 2/8	18 5/8	4	4	Hennepin County	MN	Rick Simonson	1990	12,425
132 1/8	24 3/8	23 7/8	21 1/8	4	4	Lake County	IL	Curtis Adams	1990	12,425
132 1/8	22 4/8	22 7/8	20 1/8	4	4	Washington County	MS	Bobby R. Woods	1991	12,425
132 1/8	22 2/8	22 0/8	17 6/8	4	5	Dakota County	MN	Patrick Henderson	1991	12,425
132 1/8	23 1/8	24 0/8	17 3/8	5	5	Oklahoma County	OK	Darrell Edwin Fesler	1991	12,425
132 1/8	21 2/8	20 6/8	17 6/8	5	6	Pendleton County	WV	Junior Wimer	1991	12,425
132 1/8	22 7/8	24 7/8	18 7/8	4	5	Carroll County	MD	Don P. Powell	1992	12,425
132 1/8	21 4/8	20 6/8	17 7/8	5	5	Logan County	WV	Gregory M. Thompson	1992	12,425
132 1/8	20 6/8	21 0/8	19 0/8	5	4	Guthrie County	IA	Jeff Knights	1992	12,425
132 1/8	21 7/8	22 1/8	17 1/8	5	6	Jefferson County	MO	Richard Jensen	1992	12,425
132 1/8	21 4/8	21 3/8	14 7/8	5	5	Livingston County	MO	David Shada	1993	12,425
132 1/8	23 1/8	22 3/8	17 4/8	6	4	Henry County	IA	Eric Strothman	1993	12,425
132 1/8	21 5/8	21 1/8	17 3/8	4	5	Osceola County	IA	Daryl L. Tjaden	1993	12,425
132 1/8	22 6/8	20 6/8	16 7/8	4	4	Wood County	WI	Allan J. Bey	1993	12,425
132 1/8	21 1/8	20 5/8	20 1/8	5	5	Mercer County	PA	Wendell C. Thompson, Jr.	1994	12,425
132 1/8	23 0/8	22 5/8	18 0/8	5	7	Coshocton County	OH	Gene Mathias	1994	12,425
132 1/8	25 6/8	25 5/8	17 7/8	4	4	Vernon County	MO	Billy Luther	1994	12,425
132 1/8	21 7/8	21 5/8	18 3/8	5	5	Delaware County	IA	Greg Covington	1994	12,425
132 1/8	22 3/8	21 5/8	19 1/8	4	4	Clark County	WI	William R. Vyvan	1994	12,425
132 1/8	21 0/8	21 1/8	21 1/8	5	5	Morrison County	MN	Barry R. Aasen	1994	12,425
132 1/8	21 5/8	21 0/8	16 1/8	4	4	Greene County	IL	Terry Bowker	1994	12,425
132 1/8	24 1/8	24 4/8	22 3/8	4	5	Berks County	PA	Gary C. Wolf	1994	12,425
132 1/8	23 6/8	22 5/8	18 4/8	5	4	Kane County	IL	Boyd L. Gates	1994	12,425
132 1/8	23 6/8	22 4/8	17 5/8	5	5	Geauga County	OH	Daniel Hershberger	1994	12,425
132 1/8	22 6/8	21 6/8	16 5/8	5	6	Rock County	WI	Don Deegan	1994	12,425
132 1/8	21 3/8	21 2/8	15 5/8	5	5	Sebastian County	AR	Michael Johnson	1995	12,425
132 1/8	20 0/8	20 5/8	13 3/8	5	6	Pike County	MO	Aaron Houchins	1995	12,425
132 1/8	22 2/8	22 5/8	18 7/8	4	4	Laclede County	MO	Tony Jemes	1995	12,425
132 1/8	22 1/8	23 4/8	16 1/8	6	6	Jackson County	MI	Michael J. McMaster	1995	12,425
132 1/8	22 5/8	23 2/8	18 2/8	5	5	Butler County	KS	Larry Creel	1995	12,425
132 1/8	21 4/8	21 6/8	16 3/8	5	5	Washington County	WI	Brad Robbins	1995	12,425
132 1/8	24 4/8	25 2/8	18 5/8	4	5	Cheshire County	NH	Russell Salo	1996	12,425
132 1/8	23 6/8	23 0/8	18 2/8	5	6	Will County	IL	John Kamarauskas	1996	12,425
132 1/8	21 3/8	21 3/8	18 3/8	5	5	Kinney County	TX	Robert N. Neilson	1996	12,425
132 1/8	20 5/8	20 1/8	17 1/8	5	5	San Patricio County	TX	Joseph S. Nelson	1996	12,425
132 1/8	21 3/8	21 2/8	17 5/8	6	6	Wapello County	IA	Jeff Hopkins	1996	12,425
132 1/8	24 0/8	23 1/8	16 5/8	4	4	Custer County	NE	Robert Thompson	1996	12,425
132 1/8	20 7/8	20 1/8	17 2/8	6	6	Billings County	ND	Ryan Olsen	1997	12,425
132 1/8	22 1/8	21 5/8	14 5/8	4	5	Webster County	IA	Eric Aleksich	1997	12,425
132 1/8	21 5/8	21 2/8	16 5/8	4	4	Thomas County	NE	Gary M. Hornberger	1997	12,425
132 1/8	21 0/8	21 3/8	16 3/8	5	5	Dane County	WI	James C. Everson	1997	12,425
132 1/8	22 3/8	22 2/8	17 4/8	5	5	Allamakee County	IA	Don G. Bement	1997	12,425
132 1/8	23 0/8	23 0/8	20 3/8	5	4	Ashland County	WI	Ross A. Dreger	1997	12,425
132 1/8	20 1/8	19 7/8	16 5/8	5	6	Marquette County	WI	Curt Priem	1997	12,425
132 1/8	23 7/8	24 5/8	18 3/8	5	4	Athens County	OH	Roderick E. Nutter	1997	12,425
132 1/8	21 7/8	21 5/8	17 1/8	4	4	Linn County	IA	James L. Corkery	1997	12,425
132 1/8	20 4/8	20 4/8	17 5/8	4	5	Latah County	ID	Dana W. Daily	1998	12,425
132 1/8	22 3/8	22 5/8	16 3/8	4	4	St. Joseph County	IN	Michael L. Ritter	1998	12,425
132 0/8	21 4/8	21 2/8	18 2/8	4	4	Juneau County	WI	Arthur Witz	1966	12,518
132 0/8	22 5/8	22 2/8	18 6/8	5	5	Iowa County	IA	Larry King	1967	12,518
132 0/8	21 6/8	22 4/8	17 0/8	4	4	Harlan County	NE	Edward H. Backes	1969	12,518
132 0/8	20 0/8	20 5/8	14 6/8	4	4	Pittsburg County	OK	Fred Parkison	1969	12,518
132 0/8	21 4/8	21 1/8	16 4/8	6	5	Dunn County	WI	John R. Bilderback	1970	12,518
132 0/8	20 2/8	20 7/8	13 7/8	6	5	Burleigh County	ND	Scott Lang	1976	12,518
132 0/8	23 4/8	23 5/8	16 6/8	5	4	Wabasha County	MN	Myles Keller	1978	12,518
132 0/8	21 6/8	22 1/8	15 3/8	5	5	Monroe County	NY	Tyler D. Smith	1978	12,518
132 0/8	23 4/8	22 0/8	15 3/8	5	6	Portage County	WI	Michael K. Nuernberger	1979	12,518
132 0/8	20 6/8	21 3/8	18 5/8	5	5	Cambridge	ONT	Fred Law	1979	12,518
132 0/8	20 2/8	20 6/8	16 2/8	5	6	Pope County	MN	Wayne Charles	1980	12,518
132 0/8	21 4/8	21 1/8	15 6/8	5	5	Redwood County	MN	June E. Gilb	1980	12,518
132 0/8	20 0/8	21 6/8	14 0/8	5	4	Polk County	IA	Glenn D. Vondra	1980	12,518
132 0/8	22 4/8	22 4/8	17 2/8	5	4	Guernsey County	OH	Darwin D. JirLes	1981	12,518
132 0/8	21 6/8	21 5/8	16 1/8	6	5	Coweta County	GA	C. M. Edwards, Jr.	1982	12,518
132 0/8	22 6/8	23 4/8	17 2/8	4	4	Pierce County	WI	Mark Schafhauser	1982	12,518

WHITETAIL DEER (TYPICAL ANTLERS)

Minimum Score 125   Continued

SCORE	LENGTH OF R MAIN BEAM L		INSIDE SPREAD	NUMBER OF R POINTS L		AREA	STATE/ PROVINCE	HUNTER'S NAME	DATE	RANK
132 0/8	21 6/8	22 0/8	20 4/8	4	4	Lee County	IA	Randy Waschkat	1983	12,518
132 0/8	23 6/8	22 7/8	17 0/8	5	5	Dubuque County	IA	Richard P. Munz	1983	12,518
132 0/8	21 4/8	20 1/8	15 4/8	5	5	Shelby County	IL	Joe Thompson	1984	12,518
132 0/8	21 6/8	21 2/8	18 0/8	5	5	Buffalo County	WI	Robert L. Kampen	1984	12,518
132 0/8	21 6/8	22 3/8	20 6/8	5	5	Buffalo County	WI	Rex Secrist	1984	12,518
132 0/8	21 5/8	22 4/8	17 0/8	4	4	Winnebago County	IL	Glenn A. Johnson	1984	12,518
132 0/8	21 1/8	20 1/8	15 0/8	5	6	Marinette County	WI	John Katers	1985	12,518
132 0/8	23 4/8	24 4/8	17 2/8	4	5	Scott County	IA	Bob Hankins	1985	12,518
132 0/8	22 6/8	22 0/8	14 3/8	5	4	Humphreys County	TN	Tom Hutson	1986	12,518
132 0/8	22 2/8	22 1/8	16 6/8	4	5	Suffolk County	NY	Frederick Donarummo	1986	12,518
132 0/8	23 1/8	23 0/8	18 2/8	4	4	Edgar County	IL	Russell Guthrie	1987	12,518
132 0/8	20 5/8	21 4/8	14 0/8	5	5	Kenedy County	TX	Harold R. Arve, Jr.	1987	12,518
132 0/8	24 0/8	22 1/8	16 6/8	4	4	Door County	WI	Neil Groeschel	1987	12,518
132 0/8	23 5/8	24 0/8	18 2/8	4	4	De Kalb County	IN	Danny Lynn Helbert	1987	12,518
132 0/8	22 7/8	20 4/8	20 0/8	6	7	Morton County	ND	John Finck	1987	12,518
132 0/8	23 4/8	23 4/8	18 2/8	4	4	Guernsey County	OH	Dick Bayer	1987	12,518
132 0/8	21 1/8	21 6/8	17 2/8	8	8	Powder River County	MT	Mark L. Frank	1988	12,518
132 0/8	21 5/8	21 2/8	17 1/8	5	6	Rock County	WI	Dudley D. Rhoades	1988	12,518
132 0/8	22 4/8	21 1/8	15 4/8	5	6	Olmsted County	MN	Gary Kowalewski	1988	12,518
132 0/8	20 7/8	21 4/8	15 4/8	5	5	Hancock County	OH	Jill A. Smith	1988	12,518
132 0/8	21 0/8	21 1/8	16 2/8	4	4	Marquette County	WI	John Steckling	1988	12,518
132 0/8	20 3/8	20 3/8	15 0/8	5	5	Buffalo County	WI	Jeff Binger	1989	12,518
132 0/8	23 0/8	25 2/8	16 2/8	6	5	Newton County	AR	David Tomlinson	1989	12,518
132 0/8	21 3/8	22 4/8	17 6/8	5	4	Lafayette County	WI	Gregory S. Kuehne	1989	12,518
132 0/8	22 2/8	23 4/8	19 2/8	4	4	Berrien County	MI	Robert F. Svoboda, Jr.	1989	12,518
132 0/8	23 0/8	22 4/8	19 5/8	6	5	Mecklenburg County	VA	John W. McAden	1989	12,518
132 0/8	20 4/8	20 7/8	19 2/8	5	6	Winnebago County	IL	Derek Boeger	1989	12,518
132 0/8	21 2/8	21 5/8	16 4/8	5	5	Fayette County	IL	Richard L. Perry	1989	12,518
132 0/8	23 5/8	23 1/8	16 6/8	5	5	Brown County	OH	Mike Doyle	1989	12,518
132 0/8	20 1/8	20 7/8	17 6/8	4	4	Rockdale County	GA	Ricky L. Crumbley	1990	12,518
132 0/8	21 0/8	20 3/8	15 7/8	5	5	Mercer County	IL	Brad Peterson	1990	12,518
132 0/8	19 6/8	20 1/8	16 6/8	6	5	Clayton County	IA	Dan J. Nicks	1990	12,518
132 0/8	19 5/8	19 1/8	18 6/8	5	5	Douglas County	MN	Matt Perdue	1990	12,518
132 0/8	23 6/8	25 0/8	18 6/8	6	8	Twiggs County	GA	Stephen Cline Roberts, Jr.	1991	12,518
132 0/8	22 2/8	22 0/8	16 0/8	6	5	Madison County	MT	Michael Mitale	1991	12,518
132 0/8	22 6/8	23 4/8	19 2/8	4	4	McHenry County	IL	Richard Tudor	1991	12,518
132 0/8	24 2/8	24 6/8	18 2/8	6	4	Lake County	OH	Roger Lucas	1991	12,518
132 0/8	21 2/8	20 2/8	15 4/8	5	5	Jackson County	MI	Larry Kettinger	1991	12,518
132 0/8	23 4/8	23 4/8	17 6/8	7	5	Worcester County	MA	Peter R. Couillard	1991	12,518
132 0/8	20 6/8	20 5/8	17 6/8	5	5	Meeker County	MN	Chuck Schultz	1991	12,518
132 0/8	19 5/8	19 5/8	16 0/8	5	5	Valley County	MT	Dennis Sturgis, Jr.	1992	12,518
132 0/8	23 6/8	24 1/8	20 2/8	4	6	Orange County	IN	Troy Yeskie	1992	12,518
132 0/8	22 0/8	21 7/8	19 4/8	5	5	Fairfield County	CT	Jason Eriquez	1992	12,518
132 0/8	22 1/8	22 0/8	21 4/8	4	4	Clearfield County	PA	Rodney H. Boalich	1992	12,518
132 0/8	25 4/8	24 5/8	17 4/8	4	4	Montgomery County	VA	Quinter A. Cook	1992	12,518
132 0/8	20 3/8	23 6/8	18 2/8	4	4	Fairfield County	CT	Peter O. Ugosoli	1992	12,518
132 0/8	24 1/8	25 1/8	24 2/8	6	8	West Feliciana Parish	LA	Don Barge	1992	12,518
132 0/8	22 5/8	23 6/8	16 0/8	7	7	Armstrong County	PA	Everett Randall LeSueur	1992	12,518
132 0/8	20 6/8	21 5/8	18 2/8	5	5	Wayne County	NY	Steven M. LeRoy	1992	12,518
132 0/8	23 5/8	23 3/8	20 6/8	4	5	Barry County	MI	John D. Murray	1992	12,518
132 0/8	21 6/8	20 7/8	15 6/8	5	4	Stevens County	WA	MiLes Burmeister	1992	12,518
132 0/8	23 2/8	23 1/8	16 2/8	6	5	Berks County	PA	Alan C. Yost	1993	12,518
132 0/8	21 1/8	21 0/8	19 6/8	6	6	Woodford County	IL	Stan Bocian	1993	12,518
132 0/8	24 1/8	23 6/8	20 0/8	6	6	Montgomery County	OH	Robert E. Stephens	1993	12,518
132 0/8	22 6/8	23 3/8	17 4/8	5	4	Ross County	OH	Ronald P. Withrow	1993	12,518
132 0/8	23 7/8	23 3/8	17 4/8	4	5	Jackson County	IA	Tracy Templeton	1993	12,518
132 0/8	21 7/8	22 5/8	16 4/8	5	5	Dodge County	NE	Randy Morris	1993	12,518
132 0/8	22 0/8	22 5/8	18 5/8	6	4	Pike County	IL	Dan Perez	1993	12,518
132 0/8	21 3/8	21 5/8	16 2/8	5	5	Adams County	WI	Howard L. Edwards	1994	12,518
132 0/8	23 4/8	24 6/8	18 4/8	5	5	Portage County	OH	Ernest E. Woodby	1994	12,518
132 0/8	23 5/8	23 0/8	18 4/8	5	6	Rock County	WI	Thomas Robertson	1994	12,518
132 0/8	21 0/8	21 3/8	15 4/8	6	9	Livingston County	MI	Ronald J. Spitler	1994	12,518
132 0/8	26 1/8	25 6/8	20 1/8	7	7	Erie County	PA	Charles L. Hanson	1994	12,518
132 0/8	23 3/8	23 3/8	17 2/8	4	4	Athens County	OH	George T. Hoffman	1994	12,518
132 0/8	20 1/8	21 2/8	21 3/8	5	5	Manitowoc County	WI	Craig J. Neuser	1994	12,518
132 0/8	22 6/8	22 4/8	17 2/8	5	5	Randolph County	IL	Sam Eggemeyer	1994	12,518
132 0/8	22 3/8	22 1/8	19 4/8	4	4	Logan County	IL	Tim Heath	1994	12,518
132 0/8	22 4/8	21 5/8	17 1/8	6	5	Wayne County	WV	Larry Sword	1994	12,518
132 0/8	23 6/8	22 6/8	20 4/8	5	4	Montgomery County	MD	Richard C. Miller, Jr.	1994	12,518
132 0/8	21 1/8	21 3/8	17 1/8	5	5	Davis County	IA	Tracy Templeton	1994	12,518
132 0/8	24 7/8	25 4/8	19 2/8	4	4	Washington County	MS	Barry R. Briggs	1995	12,518
132 0/8	23 0/8	23 1/8	15 6/8	4	4	Claiborne County	MS	Woody Hanks	1995	12,518
132 0/8	22 7/8	23 2/8	14 2/8	5	6	St. Louis County	MO	Terry Comely	1995	12,518
132 0/8	22 6/8	23 4/8	18 2/8	4	4	Columbia County	WI	Aaron E. Soter	1995	12,518
132 0/8	21 4/8	21 5/8	18 7/8	5	4	Edgar County	IL	Brent Webster	1995	12,518
132 0/8	19 4/8	19 2/8	15 6/8	6	5	Erath County	TX	Tom Brooks	1995	12,518
132 0/8	22 7/8	22 6/8	18 2/8	4	4	Van Buren County	IA	Wayde Perry	1995	12,518
132 0/8	22 6/8	22 4/8	19 3/8	5	5	Branch County	MI	Wesley J. Weinberg	1996	12,518

WHITETAIL DEER (TYPICAL ANTLERS)

Minimum Score 125 — Continued

SCORE	LENGTH OF MAIN BEAM R	LENGTH OF MAIN BEAM L	INSIDE SPREAD	NUMBER OF POINTS R	NUMBER OF POINTS L	AREA	STATE/ PROVINCE	HUNTER'S NAME	DATE	RANK
132 0/8	20 2/8	20 1/8	16 4/8	4	7	Saline County	AR	John Bingham	1996	12,518
132 0/8	24 2/8	24 2/8	22 6/8	3	6	Green Lake County	WI	James J. Kuzmic	1996	12,518
132 0/8	22 4/8	22 3/8	19 0/8	5	4	Chester County	PA	John E. Griffy	1997	12,518
132 0/8	21 4/8	23 0/8	19 5/8	7	4	Dodge County	WI	Trevor Holzhueter	1997	12,518
132 0/8	25 4/8	24 5/8	19 6/8	5	4	Henderson County	TN	Walter Pope	1997	12,518
132 0/8	22 4/8	22 6/8	17 2/8	4	4	Buffalo County	WI	Allen Foegen	1997	12,518
132 0/8	22 1/8	21 7/8	15 4/8	5	5	Somerset County	PA	Timothy E. Kennell	1997	12,518
132 0/8	20 3/8	21 4/8	18 0/8	5	5	Blair County	PA	Brandon S. Rentz	1997	12,518
132 0/8	21 0/8	20 7/8	18 2/8	7	6	Manitowoc County	WI	Kenneth A. Woelfel	1997	12,518
132 0/8	21 6/8	21 5/8	15 7/8	5	5	Clarion County	PA	Patrick E. Shaffer	1997	12,518
132 0/8	19 4/8	19 4/8	18 6/8	5	5	Waukesha County	WI	Jerry Briski	1997	12,518
132 0/8	24 5/8	23 5/8	16 0/8	4	4	Buffalo County	WI	Dennis Buchholz	1997	12,518
132 0/8	19 2/8	19 7/8	17 0/8	5	5	Kenedy County	TX	Paul "Bear" Brewer	1997	12,518
132 0/8	19 3/8	20 2/8	15 4/8	8	5	Clay County	IN	Jesse Shattuck	1997	12,518
132 0/8	22 0/8	21 6/8	18 0/8	4	4	Westchester County	NY	Stephen L. Cook	1997	12,518
132 0/8	23 5/8	23 0/8	18 0/8	5	5	Cumberland County	NJ	Bob Eisele, Sr.	1998	12,518
131 7/8	22 0/8	22 7/8	22 2/8	6	4	Goodhue County	MN	James Jarvis	1964	12,628
131 7/8	22 0/8	23 1/8	15 1/8	4	5	Trempealeau County	WI	Clark Gallup	1967	12,628
131 7/8	21 1/8	22 1/8	17 5/8	4	4	Brown County	SD	Barry Smith	1967	12,628
131 7/8	20 3/8	20 6/8	14 6/8	6	6	Adams County	IL	David E. DeMoss	1970	12,628
131 7/8	22 2/8	21 1/8	20 5/8	4	5	Rock County	WI	Richard W. Pieterek	1972	12,628
131 7/8	21 3/8	20 4/8	15 7/8	6	5	Fulton County	AR	Larry Luther	1977	12,628
131 7/8	21 0/8	20 3/8	16 7/8	4	4	Washington County	KS	Bill R. Mallean	1977	12,628
131 7/8	21 3/8	21 2/8	19 7/8	5	4	Washtenaw County	MI	Philip J. Maly	1980	12,628
131 7/8	23 5/8	25 3/8	19 1/8	4	4	Logan County	OH	Thomas R. Weaver	1980	12,628
131 7/8	21 7/8	21 6/8	15 5/8	4	4	Russell County	KS	Joe Schulte	1982	12,628
131 7/8	22 3/8	23 4/8	16 1/8	5	5	Saline County	MO	Ed Coates	1983	12,628
131 7/8	21 3/8	21 5/8	17 1/8	4	4	Will County	IL	Mike Sheehan	1984	12,628
131 7/8	21 7/8	20 6/8	17 1/8	4	4	Lincoln County	KS	Robert Chitty	1985	12,628
131 7/8	22 3/8	20 6/8	16 1/8	5	5	Putnam County	OH	Randy Schroeder	1985	12,628
131 7/8	22 3/8	22 6/8	17 5/8	4	4	Douglas County	WI	Edward Flood	1985	12,628
131 7/8	19 6/8	20 5/8	15 1/8	5	5	Knox County	OH	Tom Bowman	1985	12,628
131 7/8	24 1/8	25 4/8	20 3/8	4	4	Westchester County	NY	Roger Jensen	1985	12,628
131 7/8	22 1/8	23 2/8	15 3/8	4	4	Garden County	NE	Reggie Spiegelberg	1985	12,628
131 7/8	21 3/8	21 2/8	25 2/8	5	4	Pratt County	KS	C. J. Eifert	1985	12,628
131 7/8	21 4/8	21 4/8	17 7/8	6	5	Morrison County	MN	Bruce A. Carlson	1986	12,628
131 7/8	21 2/8	20 6/8	16 5/8	6	5	Ripley County	IN	Clinton C. Miller	1986	12,628
131 7/8	23 1/8	22 6/8	15 5/8	4	4	Vernon County	WI	Dave Sarnowski	1986	12,628
131 7/8	22 1/8	22 2/8	16 7/8	7	5	Pittsburg County	OK	Charles Rake	1986	12,628
131 7/8	21 2/8	21 6/8	14 3/8	5	6	Johnson County	IN	Dan Craig	1987	12,628
131 7/8	20 1/8	22 0/8	19 1/8	4	5	Clark County	WI	John Schultz	1987	12,628
131 7/8	24 0/8	24 3/8	20 4/8	6	7	Harrison County	KY	Kendall Techau	1987	12,628
131 7/8	23 1/8	22 7/8	17 2/8	5	4	Madison County	MT	Doug Stonebraker	1988	12,628
131 7/8	20 1/8	20 4/8	17 5/8	6	5	Shelby County	MO	Gregory R. Troyer	1988	12,628
131 7/8	21 6/8	21 4/8	16 5/8	5	5	Buffalo County	WI	Bernard Becker	1988	12,628
131 7/8	21 1/8	21 7/8	17 3/8	4	5	Boone County	IL	Joseph C. Ware	1988	12,628
131 7/8	19 4/8	19 6/8	16 1/8	6	5	Hand County	SD	Terry Boomsma	1988	12,628
131 7/8	20 6/8	20 4/8	18 1/8	5	4	Buffalo County	WI	Roger Comero	1989	12,628
131 7/8	20 6/8	22 4/8	15 7/8	5	5	Crittenden County	KY	Mickey Tinsley	1989	12,628
131 7/8	24 2/8	25 1/8	19 3/8	4	5	Highland County	OH	Jeffrey A. Swerlein	1989	12,628
131 7/8	23 7/8	24 0/8	17 4/8	6	5	Morrison County	MN	Michael J. Randall	1989	12,628
131 7/8	20 5/8	19 3/8	17 4/8	7	5	Ramsey County	ND	Wayne Carlson	1989	12,628
131 7/8	20 5/8	22 3/8	16 3/8	4	5	Callaway County	MO	Ken Morse	1989	12,628
131 7/8	22 5/8	22 5/8	15 3/8	7	7	Cumberland County	IL	Jerome Light	1989	12,628
131 7/8	21 5/8	20 7/8	18 1/8	5	5	Ogle County	IL	Ted Hysell	1989	12,628
131 7/8	21 3/8	22 0/8	19 7/8	5	5	Winnebago County	IL	Joel Stiener	1989	12,628
131 7/8	21 0/8	20 0/8	16 3/8	5	5	Hennepin County	MN	Craig M. Johnson	1989	12,628
131 7/8	25 6/8	24 4/8	20 1/8	5	4	Shelby County	TN	Jim Baker	1990	12,628
131 7/8	20 3/8	21 0/8	16 5/8	5	6	Chariton County	MO	Donald W. Abeln	1990	12,628
131 7/8	20 5/8	21 4/8	18 5/8	6	5	Iron County	MO	Robert Eaves	1990	12,628
131 7/8	20 5/8	22 2/8	17 6/8	5	6	McLean County	KY	Hugh Dickens	1990	12,628
131 7/8	20 7/8	21 2/8	17 1/8	4	5	Allen County	OH	Mark A. Halker	1990	12,628
131 7/8	20 0/8	21 4/8	18 0/8	5	7	Hamilton County	IA	Larry Haren	1990	12,628
131 7/8	22 6/8	22 7/8	22 1/8	4	4	Bureau County	IL	Raymond Schindel	1990	12,628
131 7/8	23 2/8	22 2/8	20 1/8	5	4	Worcester County	MD	Mike Hill	1990	12,628
131 7/8	23 3/8	23 2/8	16 6/8	5	7	Anoka County	MN	Pat Ellias	1991	12,628
131 7/8	21 5/8	22 4/8	20 1/8	5	5	Starke County	IN	Scott Vieting	1991	12,628
131 7/8	20 5/8	20 4/8	15 5/8	5	5	Decatur County	IA	Ronald E. Tennant	1991	12,628
131 7/8	24 3/8	22 6/8	18 3/8	4	4	Winnebago County	IL	Jeff S. Olsen	1991	12,628
131 7/8	21 6/8	21 5/8	16 7/8	5	5	Wayne County	IL	Peewee Hall	1991	12,628
131 7/8	21 6/8	21 6/8	14 3/8	4	4	Cedar County	NE	David "Bruce" Cull	1992	12,628
131 7/8	21 5/8	21 3/8	19 4/8	6	7	Marion County	OH	Craig Ciola	1992	12,628
131 7/8	20 4/8	21 4/8	16 5/8	5	6	Wyandot County	OH	James Thiel	1992	12,628
131 7/8	22 1/8	20 4/8	14 3/8	4	5	Columbia County	WI	Douglas H. Williams	1992	12,628
131 7/8	20 7/8	20 6/8	16 1/8	5	5	Clay County	NE	Lonnie Goble	1992	12,628
131 7/8	23 1/8	21 1/8	15 1/8	5	5	Allen County	KS	Gary Greve	1992	12,628
131 7/8	23 1/8	24 2/8	20 6/8	7	6	Cecil County	MD	Ted McCracken	1992	12,628
131 7/8	21 3/8	21 6/8	17 5/8	5	5	Black Hawk County	IA	Jim Hinke	1992	12,628

WHITETAIL DEER (TYPICAL ANTLERS)

Minimum Score 125 — Continued

SCORE	LENGTH OF MAIN BEAM R	LENGTH OF MAIN BEAM L	INSIDE SPREAD	NUMBER OF POINTS R	NUMBER OF POINTS L	AREA	STATE/PROVINCE	HUNTER'S NAME	DATE	RANK
131 7/8	22 2/8	21 6/8	17 7/8	5	5	Rock County	WI	Bruce L. Douglas	1992	12,628
131 7/8	25 0/8	23 7/8	18 1/8	5	5	Cass County	MO	Tim Green	1993	12,628
131 7/8	23 4/8	23 3/8	17 1/8	5	4	Howard County	IN	James J. Daily	1993	12,628
131 7/8	22 0/8	21 3/8	14 5/8	4	4	Oconto County	WI	Douglas L. Van Lannen	1993	12,628
131 7/8	23 2/8	23 6/8	15 3/8	4	4	Pierce County	WI	Jim McCabe	1993	12,628
131 7/8	23 5/8	23 4/8	21 1/8	4	4	Will County	IL	Dennis Mazzorana	1993	12,628
131 7/8	19 1/8	19 6/8	15 3/8	5	5	Kent County	MI	Craig Kalman	1993	12,628
131 7/8	18 4/8	18 4/8	17 7/8	6	5	Rock County	WI	Todd Cleaton	1993	12,628
131 7/8	22 7/8	21 5/8	17 5/8	4	4	Madison County	AL	William Alan Glover	1993	12,628
131 7/8	20 0/8	21 2/8	16 5/8	4	4	Page County	IA	Chris Barton	1993	12,628
131 7/8	22 3/8	22 0/8	15 3/8	4	4	Stoddard County	MO	Allen Fry	1993	12,628
131 7/8	19 3/8	17 6/8	12 7/8	5	6	Stearns County	MN	Tom Klaverkamp	1994	12,628
131 7/8	18 6/8	20 5/8	15 2/8	6	6	Anderson County	KY	William L. Saunooke	1994	12,628
131 7/8	22 5/8	21 6/8	15 7/8	5	5	Rock County	WI	Jeffrey S. Moehrke	1994	12,628
131 7/8	21 0/8	21 3/8	16 7/8	5	5	La Crosse County	WI	Larry Felber	1994	12,628
131 7/8	22 5/8	21 7/8	18 3/8	5	4	Meigs County	OH	Rick Findley	1994	12,628
131 7/8	21 6/8	21 3/8	15 1/8	6	4	Hardin County	IA	Tom Marsteller	1994	12,628
131 7/8	23 3/8	23 4/8	18 5/8	5	5	Montgomery County	MD	Mark R. Davis	1994	12,628
131 7/8	23 6/8	23 2/8	16 1/8	4	5	Albany County	NY	Wayne Shrome	1994	12,628
131 7/8	20 1/8	20 1/8	13 0/8	5	6	Morgan County	MO	Charles H. Wells	1994	12,628
131 7/8	20 6/8	22 6/8	15 3/8	4	4	Madison Parish	LA	David Sheppert	1994	12,628
131 7/8	22 0/8	22 4/8	15 7/8	5	5	Harford County	MD	Russell A. Nichols	1995	12,628
131 7/8	22 0/8	21 4/8	20 5/8	4	4	Arkansas County	AR	Richard A. Fisher	1995	12,628
131 7/8	24 0/8	22 0/8	16 1/8	5	5	Calhoun County	MI	Michael L. Newhouse	1995	12,628
131 7/8	20 2/8	20 0/8	15 7/8	5	5	Worth County	IA	Kent Nitcher	1995	12,628
131 7/8	20 2/8	23 2/8	19 6/8	5	6	Meigs County	OH	Matt Wilson	1995	12,628
131 7/8	22 7/8	23 1/8	16 7/8	5	5	Yankton County	SD	Cory Schuster	1995	12,628
131 7/8	23 5/8	23 5/8	17 6/8	5	5	Monroe County	IA	Mike McDonald	1995	12,628
131 7/8	21 1/8	20 6/8	13 7/8	5	5	Trempealeau County	WI	Jerry Kramer	1995	12,628
131 7/8	20 1/8	20 2/8	14 5/8	5	5	Kenedy County	TX	Chad Clark	1995	12,628
131 7/8	21 6/8	21 6/8	15 7/8	5	5	Marquette County	WI	Kathy A. McReath	1996	12,628
131 7/8	22 5/8	22 5/8	15 4/8	5	6	Gallia County	OH	Dusty Hill	1996	12,628
131 7/8	22 1/8	21 5/8	16 3/8	4	4	Lee County	IA	Dan Moore	1996	12,628
131 7/8	23 3/8	22 1/8	16 3/8	5	5	Dane County	WI	Thomas Munz	1996	12,628
131 7/8	23 5/8	25 0/8	14 2/8	4	5	Queen Annes County	MD	Hugh A. McDonald	1996	12,628
131 7/8	22 4/8	22 6/8	19 1/8	5	5	Dane County	WI	Michael J. Krawczyk	1996	12,628
131 7/8	22 3/8	22 3/8	16 1/8	5	5	Shawano County	WI	Danny L. Schultz	1996	12,628
131 7/8	19 6/8	20 2/8	15 3/8	5	4	Washington County	KS	Toby M. Bruna	1996	12,628
131 7/8	21 5/8	20 4/8	16 7/8	5	5	Putnam County	MO	John Freihaut	1997	12,628
131 7/8	20 0/8	19 6/8	18 5/8	5	5	Houston County	MN	Bob Borowiak	1997	12,628
131 7/8	22 6/8	23 1/8	16 7/8	5	5	Grundy County	IL	Wayne W. Wagner	1997	12,628
131 7/8	22 0/8	21 7/8	15 7/8	5	4	Dane County	WI	Bob Dye	1997	12,628
131 7/8	21 0/8	21 1/8	15 5/8	7	6	Allegheny County	PA	Richard Kuortek	1997	12,628
131 7/8	22 6/8	22 3/8	16 5/8	7	6	Manitowoc County	WI	Thomas E. Zipperer	1997	12,628
131 7/8	24 1/8	23 0/8	19 1/8	4	4	Calhoun County	MI	Jim Ghesquire	1997	12,628
131 7/8	22 4/8	22 3/8	17 1/8	5	5	Ulster County	NY	Joe Marcinelli	1997	12,628
131 7/8	22 3/8	21 7/8	17 6/8	5	8	Ashland County	WI	Jeff L. Steede	1997	12,628
131 7/8	22 4/8	23 2/8	17 1/8	5	5	Arkansas County	AR	David E. Snowden, Jr.	1997	12,628
131 7/8	20 4/8	20 2/8	23 0/8	5	5	Jones County	IA	David E. Schenck, Jr.	1997	12,628
131 7/8	22 1/8	21 0/8	18 1/8	5	5	Clay County	NE	Charles A. Burr	1998	12,628
131 6/8	19 0/8	18 6/8	13 6/8	6	6	Norton County	KS	Harold Fisher	1966	12,740
131 6/8	22 3/8	22 1/8	17 2/8	4	5	Tuscarawas County	OH	Del Karnuth	1976	12,740
131 6/8	22 2/8	21 0/8	18 0/8	5	6	Kalamazoo County	MI	Richard Hettinga	1978	12,740
131 6/8	23 2/8	22 3/8	17 6/8	4	4	Randolph County	IL	Kevin Lucht	1981	12,740
131 6/8	20 1/8	19 2/8	15 6/8	5	5	Marquette County	WI	Steven McReath	1981	12,740
131 6/8	21 4/8	21 1/8	18 6/8	4	4	Hunterdon County	NJ	Chris Jensen	1982	12,740
131 6/8	24 3/8	24 3/8	17 4/8	4	4	Stearns County	MN	Mike Betz	1982	12,740
131 6/8	24 1/8	23 7/8	17 4/8	6	6	Brookings County	SD	Joseph M. Creager	1983	12,740
131 6/8	21 3/8	22 7/8	18 0/8	4	5	Walworth County	WI	Mike Jacobs	1983	12,740
131 6/8	19 3/8	21 0/8	18 0/8	10	8	Roscommon County	MI	David Lacey	1984	12,740
131 6/8	23 4/8	24 2/8	16 6/8	4	4	Saline County	NE	C. Michael Morrow	1984	12,740
131 6/8	24 0/8	24 1/8	17 6/8	4	5	Sawyer County	WI	Bob Swenson	1985	12,740
131 6/8	22 4/8	23 5/8	20 4/8	5	5	Fairfield County	CT	Willard T. Weeks	1986	12,740
131 6/8	23 1/8	22 0/8	17 0/8	5	5	Trempealeau County	WI	John McKeeth	1987	12,740
131 6/8	22 7/8	23 2/8	14 0/8	5	5	Jackson County	MI	William H. Leslie III	1987	12,740
131 6/8	22 2/8	21 6/8	16 4/8	5	5	Walworth County	WI	Jeff Schmalfeldt	1987	12,740
131 6/8	23 6/8	24 0/8	17 0/8	4	4	Eau Claire County	WI	Doug A. Larson	1987	12,740
131 6/8	21 5/8	22 3/8	16 4/8	4	4	St. Croix County	WI	Mark Randall	1987	12,740
131 6/8	22 4/8	21 3/8	17 0/8	4	4	McLean County	IL	Tilfred Eades	1987	12,740
131 6/8	22 2/8	22 1/8	19 6/8	5	5	Caroline County	MD	Garland L. Turner	1987	12,740
131 6/8	23 7/8	24 5/8	19 6/8	4	4	Pittsburg County	OK	Todd Tobey	1988	12,740
131 6/8	25 4/8	25 0/8	20 0/8	7	5	Bayfield County	WI	Paul M. Halverson	1988	12,740
131 6/8	22 7/8	22 7/8	19 2/8	4	4	Jackson County	OH	Terry S. Speakman	1988	12,740
131 6/8	18 0/8	18 0/8	14 0/8	5	5	Waukesha County	WI	Bob Koepp	1988	12,740
131 6/8	24 0/8	23 3/8	15 2/8	5	5	Randolph County	IL	Danny T. Wahl	1988	12,740
131 6/8	23 1/8	22 3/8	17 0/8	5	6	Winneshiek County	IA	Duane C. Baumler	1989	12,740
131 6/8	21 2/8	22 2/8	17 0/8	4	4	Spedden	ALB	Darryl Kublik	1989	12,740
131 6/8	18 7/8	19 4/8	17 0/8	5	5	Williams County	ND	Richard Liesener	1989	12,740

WHITETAIL DEER (TYPICAL ANTLERS)

Minimum Score 125 Continued

SCORE	LENGTH OF MAIN BEAM R	LENGTH OF MAIN BEAM L	INSIDE SPREAD	NUMBER OF POINTS R	NUMBER OF POINTS L	AREA	STATE/ PROVINCE	HUNTER'S NAME	DATE	RANK
131 6/8	21 0/8	21 0/8	16 0/8	4	4	Marathon County	WI	Bruce Stieber	1989	12,740
131 6/8	21 7/8	23 7/8	17 4/8	4	4	Wyandotte County	KS	Earl A. Cooksey	1989	12,740
131 6/8	22 7/8	23 5/8	17 4/8	5	5	Desha County	AR	Greg Sharp	1989	12,740
131 6/8	22 5/8	21 0/8	18 4/8	5	5	Saginaw County	MI	Bill H. Schack	1989	12,740
131 6/8	23 1/8	23 3/8	17 0/8	4	4	Floyd County	IA	Joel Gray	1990	12,740
131 6/8	22 2/8	23 0/8	16 5/8	4	5	Vernon County	WI	Mike Slivinski	1990	12,740
131 6/8	23 2/8	22 6/8	18 2/8	4	4	Hardin County	IL	Charles E. Spear	1990	12,740
131 6/8	20 1/8	21 3/8	14 6/8	5	6	Greene County	IN	James Tyree	1990	12,740
131 6/8	24 3/8	25 3/8	18 2/8	6	5	Dane County	WI	Kent Powell	1990	12,740
131 6/8	22 5/8	22 7/8	15 2/8	4	4	Seneca County	NY	Kenneth E. Briggs	1990	12,740
131 6/8	24 5/8	24 0/8	16 2/8	4	4	Albany County	NY	Mark Cintula	1990	12,740
131 6/8	24 6/8	24 1/8	18 6/8	4	4	McMullen County	TX	Guy Allcorn	1991	12,740
131 6/8	25 0/8	24 0/8	17 2/8	8	7	McPherson County	KS	Hal G. Krehbiel	1991	12,740
131 6/8	19 4/8	18 6/8	17 4/8	5	5	Woodward County	OK	Phil Lanier	1991	12,740
131 6/8	21 4/8	22 5/8	17 6/8	4	4	Parke County	IN	Wayne Loomis	1991	12,740
131 6/8	22 6/8	22 4/8	18 4/8	5	4	Kane County	IL	Dale Hoekstra	1991	12,740
131 6/8	21 2/8	23 2/8	13 4/8	4	4	Pottawatomie County	KS	Larry Carroll	1991	12,740
131 6/8	20 7/8	23 1/8	18 0/8	4	4	Isle of Wight County	VA	Raymond W. West	1991	12,740
131 6/8	21 5/8	21 5/8	18 0/8	4	4	Morrison County	MN	Russell Canfield	1992	12,740
131 6/8	25 1/8	24 0/8	22 5/8	4	5	Waukesha County	WI	Mike Denesha	1992	12,740
131 6/8	23 1/8	21 7/8	18 6/8	5	5	Greene County	MO	Keith Coons	1992	12,740
131 6/8	21 6/8	20 6/8	16 2/8	5	5	Iroquois County	IL	John A. Putnam	1992	12,740
131 6/8	21 5/8	20 6/8	16 2/8	5	5	Jackson County	OH	George W. Edmiston	1992	12,740
131 6/8	24 2/8	23 1/8	18 0/8	4	4	Irion County	TX	Steve Boster	1992	12,740
131 6/8	22 1/8	22 6/8	19 0/8	4	4	Knox County	NE	Duane Loecker	1992	12,740
131 6/8	22 5/8	23 0/8	18 4/8	4	4	Fond du Lac County	WI	John H. Gilgenbach	1993	12,740
131 6/8	21 6/8	22 1/8	17 4/8	4	4	Rusk County	WI	Randy Jochem	1993	12,740
131 6/8	23 3/8	22 7/8	15 5/8	5	5	Oconto County	WI	Jeffrey G. Blake	1993	12,740
131 6/8	20 7/8	20 2/8	15 0/8	5	5	Jefferson County	MS	Peter Dale	1993	12,740
131 6/8	20 2/8	20 3/8	18 0/8	6	6	Washburn County	WI	Keith Kardash	1993	12,740
131 6/8	23 6/8	23 5/8	18 2/8	5	6	Suffolk County	NY	John Espenkotter	1993	12,740
131 6/8	23 2/8	23 3/8	16 0/8	4	4	Buffalo County	WI	Timothy J. Sturz	1993	12,740
131 6/8	22 2/8	21 7/8	15 0/8	5	5	Shelby County	MO	Jack Davis	1993	12,740
131 6/8	22 3/8	22 2/8	16 4/8	4	4	Chippewa County	WI	Gary J. Yohnk	1993	12,740
131 6/8	19 7/8	19 5/8	13 4/8	5	5	Chickasaw County	IA	Dave Kerkove	1993	12,740
131 6/8	21 2/8	22 0/8	17 6/8	6	5	Jefferson County	PA	Doug Curran	1993	12,740
131 6/8	23 0/8	23 0/8	16 0/8	5	5	Eau Claire County	WI	Dave Strassman	1993	12,740
131 6/8	21 4/8	24 6/8	16 0/8	5	5	Middlesex County	MA	Mike Urban	1993	12,740
131 6/8	21 4/8	22 7/8	17 2/8	6	8	Polk County	MO	Larry Silver	1993	12,740
131 6/8	24 3/8	24 2/8	16 4/8	4	4	Juneau County	WI	Kevin Reynolds	1994	12,740
131 6/8	23 1/8	24 0/8	16 3/8	6	7	Columbia County	WI	Michael K. Paulcheck	1994	12,740
131 6/8	21 2/8	22 4/8	13 6/8	4	5	Clinton County	MO	David Eads	1994	12,740
131 6/8	23 0/8	23 0/8	16 6/8	4	6	Suffolk County	NY	Louie DiBiase	1994	12,740
131 6/8	20 2/8	20 6/8	17 4/8	5	5	Atlantic County	NJ	Wally Raciti	1995	12,740
131 6/8	22 1/8	21 6/8	16 0/8	5	5	Litchfield County	CT	Todd M. Carusillo	1995	12,740
131 6/8	22 3/8	22 7/8	17 0/8	4	4	Erath County	TX	Stephen Thornton	1995	12,740
131 6/8	22 1/8	23 3/8	15 2/8	5	5	Beadle County	SD	Fred Kober	1995	12,740
131 6/8	20 2/8	21 7/8	15 5/8	6	5	Tom Green County	TX	Ronnie Parsons	1995	12,740
131 6/8	20 0/8	21 2/8	17 0/8	4	4	Calhoun County	MI	Greg Parker	1995	12,740
131 6/8	23 0/8	23 7/8	17 0/8	5	4	Pickaway County	OH	Ed Flaherty	1995	12,740
131 6/8	22 0/8	22 0/8	17 7/8	5	7	Walworth County	WI	Larry L. Jones	1995	12,740
131 6/8	20 3/8	21 4/8	16 0/8	5	5	Waukesha County	WI	Dick Carlson	1995	12,740
131 6/8	24 5/8	24 4/8	18 6/8	5	5	Warren County	IA	Brad Curtis	1995	12,740
131 6/8	21 2/8	20 3/8	18 2/8	5	5	Beaver County	PA	Joel Chalupiak	1995	12,740
131 6/8	26 0/8	27 0/8	23 3/8	5	4	Marathon County	WI	Scott Redman	1995	12,740
131 6/8	23 0/8	22 5/8	19 6/8	4	4	Ontario County	NY	C. Gregory Harding	1995	12,740
131 6/8	23 4/8	22 6/8	16 0/8	4	4	Putnam County	NY	Samuel M. Slinskey III	1995	12,740
131 6/8	21 4/8	21 3/8	17 6/8	6	5	Buffalo County	WI	Nick T. Bray	1996	12,740
131 6/8	22 3/8	22 6/8	17 6/8	4	4	Ozaukee County	WI	Mark Woodward Nugent	1996	12,740
131 6/8	19 4/8	19 0/8	13 6/8	6	8	Appanoose County	IA	Robert Fuhrman	1996	12,740
131 6/8	25 0/8	22 2/8	19 4/8	5	6	La Salle County	IL	David Both	1996	12,740
131 6/8	22 0/8	22 2/8	16 0/8	5	5	Berrien County	MI	Daniel H. Frank	1996	12,740
131 6/8	22 3/8	22 5/8	16 1/8	5	5	Pike County	IL	Barry L. White	1996	12,740
131 6/8	21 4/8	20 4/8	21 7/8	5	5	Washington County	OH	Jeremiah Mohr	1996	12,740
131 6/8	21 6/8	22 2/8	15 6/8	5	5	Fairfax County	VA	Gary D. Knipling	1996	12,740
131 6/8	20 4/8	20 4/8	15 6/8	5	5	Pulaski County	MO	James Wells	1996	12,740
131 6/8	19 6/8	19 5/8	16 3/8	5	6	Rogers County	OK	Mark Grubbs	1996	12,740
131 6/8	21 2/8	22 2/8	15 4/8	5	5	Grant County	WI	Mark P. Whitish	1996	12,740
131 6/8	19 7/8	20 0/8	17 0/8	5	5	Peoria County	IL	Larry Oppe	1996	12,740
131 6/8	22 0/8	22 6/8	18 4/8	5	5	Sauk County	WI	Charles W. Arndt	1996	12,740
131 6/8	22 5/8	22 1/8	17 6/8	4	4	Cecil County	MD	John W. Guy	1996	12,740
131 6/8	20 5/8	20 4/8	15 4/8	4	4	Webster County	NE	Gary Reed	1996	12,740
131 6/8	21 7/8	21 5/8	16 2/8	4	5	Somerset County	PA	Bob Miller	1997	12,740
131 6/8	21 1/8	19 7/8	15 0/8	5	5	Winn Parish	LA	Robert McAllister	1997	12,740
131 6/8	22 4/8	21 5/8	18 2/8	4	4	Williamson County	IL	J. Scott Jinks	1997	12,740
131 6/8	21 5/8	21 2/8	16 6/8	6	6	Dane County	WI	Michael Affholder	1997	12,740
131 6/8	22 4/8	22 0/8	16 6/8	4	4	Idaho County	ID	Wade L. Carstens	1997	12,740
131 6/8	22 0/8	23 0/8	24 4/8	4	5	Henry County	IA	Kirt T. Snyder	1997	12,740

WHITETAIL DEER (TYPICAL ANTLERS)

Minimum Score 125 — Continued

SCORE	LENGTH OF MAIN BEAM R	LENGTH OF MAIN BEAM L	INSIDE SPREAD	NUMBER OF POINTS R	NUMBER OF POINTS L	AREA	STATE/PROVINCE	HUNTER'S NAME	DATE	RANK
131 6/8	23 4/8	24 0/8	16 5/8	5	5	Marion County	IA	Donald C. Clark	1997	12,740
131 6/8	25 7/8	25 3/8	20 1/8	6	4	Fulton County	IL	Gus Congemi	1997	12,740
131 6/8	20 7/8	21 0/8	14 6/8	5	5	Adair County	MO	Charles Zeman	1997	12,740
131 6/8	20 6/8	20 6/8	17 2/8	4	4	Chickasaw County	IA	Jess Ellingson	1998	12,740
131 6/8	24 0/8	24 2/8	17 6/8	4	4	Chester County	PA	Jack A. Horosky	1998	12,740
131 5/8	21 4/8	22 1/8	18 5/8	4	4	Forest County	WI	Max Wisnefske	1950	12,851
131 5/8	19 7/8	19 7/8	12 3/8	5	5	Jefferson County	IN	Ted Taylor	1959	12,851
131 5/8	23 4/8	22 5/8	14 1/8	4	5	Otter Tail County	MN	Gordon Swenson	1964	12,851
131 5/8	22 4/8	21 6/8	16 1/8	5	5	Hale County	AL	Bo Bonds	1976	12,851
131 5/8	23 4/8	25 0/8	18 4/8	5	5	Carroll County	OH	Charles B. Platt	1977	12,851
131 5/8	21 7/8	22 2/8	16 3/8	5	5	Washington County	WI	Steven L. Hoelz	1980	12,851
131 5/8	23 4/8	24 0/8	19 3/8	5	5	Marquette County	WI	Bryan Anderson	1982	12,851
131 5/8	23 7/8	22 4/8	16 7/8	6	7	Allen County	KS	Larry Robertson	1983	12,851
131 5/8	23 1/8	21 7/8	18 2/8	5	6	Kandiyohi County	MN	Mike Dallman	1983	12,851
131 5/8	19 5/8	20 2/8	17 3/8	5	5	Jefferson County	WI	Donald L. Zubke	1983	12,851
131 5/8	22 0/8	20 5/8	18 7/8	4	4	Gratiot County	MI	Robert Allen Mallory	1984	12,851
131 5/8	22 4/8	22 5/8	14 5/8	5	5	Fond du Lac County	WI	Daryl Zacharias	1985	12,851
131 5/8	20 4/8	19 2/8	15 1/8	5	7	Miller County	MO	John Ash	1985	12,851
131 5/8	24 3/8	23 3/8	20 0/8	5	8	Lake County	IL	Robert Norman Tropple	1985	12,851
131 5/8	25 1/8	25 2/8	16 7/8	4	4	Chatham County	NC	Jimmy Womble	1986	12,851
131 5/8	23 2/8	23 3/8	16 1/8	4	4	Manistee County	MI	Jerry L. Fink	1986	12,851
131 5/8	24 4/8	23 2/8	20 5/8	5	4	Morris County	NJ	Glenn Hullings	1986	12,851
131 5/8	20 5/8	20 4/8	15 7/8	4	5	Todd County	MN	Jim Friedrichs	1987	12,851
131 5/8	25 4/8	24 2/8	17 1/8	6	5	Woodbury County	IA	Lester J. Zahnley	1987	12,851
131 5/8	25 3/8	24 4/8	19 3/8	4	4	Preble County	OH	Stephen L. Parker	1987	12,851
131 5/8	23 0/8	23 0/8	17 3/8	6	7	Sawyer County	WI	Ron Miller	1987	12,851
131 5/8	20 4/8	21 4/8	17 1/8	5	9	Sheboygan County	WI	Keith D. Darling	1987	12,851
131 5/8	23 3/8	23 3/8	19 5/8	5	6	Pepin County	WI	Michael Schmidt	1988	12,851
131 5/8	20 5/8	21 1/8	14 5/8	5	6	Clay County	MN	Philip Reiling	1988	12,851
131 5/8	19 5/8	21 0/8	16 5/8	5	5	Cavalier County	ND	William Wightman	1988	12,851
131 5/8	22 6/8	23 2/8	18 0/8	5	5	Sherburne County	MN	Bill Cashman	1989	12,851
131 5/8	21 6/8	22 4/8	15 5/8	6	6	Fort Bend County	TX	Pat Byrne	1989	12,851
131 5/8	21 3/8	22 4/8	18 2/8	7	5	Pulaski County	IL	Bill Spaulding	1990	12,851
131 5/8	21 2/8	20 0/8	17 1/8	5	5	Hancock County	OH	Tom Phillips	1990	12,851
131 5/8	23 4/8	23 0/8	17 1/8	4	6	Suffolk County	NY	Leland Winslow	1990	12,851
131 5/8	23 3/8	21 4/8	17 0/8	5	4	Montgomery County	IN	John Donald	1991	12,851
131 5/8	21 1/8	20 4/8	18 2/8	6	7	Washburn County	WI	Steven J. Genson	1991	12,851
131 5/8	21 3/8	21 6/8	18 1/8	4	4	Forest County	WI	Flint Gilbert	1991	12,851
131 5/8	23 7/8	24 7/8	19 1/8	5	6	Jo Daviess County	IL	Ron Mann	1991	12,851
131 5/8	22 3/8	23 5/8	17 5/8	5	5	Buffalo County	WI	Jim Wondzell	1991	12,851
131 5/8	22 2/8	22 3/8	17 7/8	4	4	Henry County	VA	Mike Weaver	1991	12,851
131 5/8	21 3/8	21 0/8	16 3/8	5	6	Fremont County	IA	Dave Holt	1991	12,851
131 5/8	22 1/8	21 5/8	16 7/8	4	4	Henry County	IA	Todd Wibben	1991	12,851
131 5/8	23 0/8	23 5/8	19 0/8	6	5	Walworth County	WI	Allen Lehman	1991	12,851
131 5/8	23 5/8	23 1/8	16 5/8	5	5	Columbia County	WI	Bruce R. Walker	1992	12,851
131 5/8	20 0/8	20 1/8	19 2/8	5	4	Sauk County	WI	Elmer J. Ellis, Jr.	1992	12,851
131 5/8	21 5/8	21 7/8	17 1/8	5	4	Lawrence County	IN	Arter Thompson II	1992	12,851
131 5/8	20 4/8	21 4/8	17 7/8	5	5	St. Clair County	IL	Blake Alan Hoover	1992	12,851
131 5/8	21 5/8	21 6/8	17 7/8	6	6	Osage County	OK	Wayne Sanders	1993	12,851
131 5/8	20 4/8	20 1/8	15 5/8	4	4	Wabasha County	MN	Lee G. Partington	1993	12,851
131 5/8	21 6/8	22 4/8	17 1/8	4	4	Hennepin County	MN	Tom Wilson	1993	12,851
131 5/8	23 1/8	23 3/8	20 7/8	5	4	Allegany County	NY	Kenneth DeRitter	1993	12,851
131 5/8	19 4/8	20 0/8	13 0/8	6	5	Lyon County	KS	Aaron Lazzers	1993	12,851
131 5/8	21 6/8	21 6/8	21 3/8	5	5	Woodford County	IL	David L. Stine	1993	12,851
131 5/8	21 5/8	24 2/8	19 7/8	4	4	Montgomery County	AL	David J. Barrow	1994	12,851
131 5/8	21 0/8	21 3/8	16 3/8	6	6	Cayuga County	NY	Dave Suslik	1994	12,851
131 5/8	22 1/8	21 3/8	15 7/8	5	5	Belmont County	OH	Damon Detling	1994	12,851
131 5/8	22 0/8	22 5/8	17 7/8	4	4	Dekalb County	IL	Carl A. Kwak	1994	12,851
131 5/8	21 7/8	22 7/8	15 1/8	5	4	Issaquena County	MS	Allen McNight	1994	12,851
131 5/8	21 0/8	20 0/8	15 0/8	5	6	McMullen County	TX	Kathleen Ponders	1995	12,851
131 5/8	21 5/8	21 4/8	18 1/8	5	5	Cheshire County	NH	Michael Jarvis	1995	12,851
131 5/8	22 0/8	20 7/8	16 1/8	6	5	Alpena County	MI	Gerald R. Skupin	1995	12,851
131 5/8	24 0/8	23 7/8	16 1/8	5	4	Kittson County	MN	Tony R. Hoglo	1995	12,851
131 5/8	23 1/8	23 1/8	15 6/8	5	7	Grant County	WI	Randy Hochhausen	1995	12,851
131 5/8	21 6/8	21 6/8	15 5/8	5	5	Waushara County	WI	Brian J. Haase	1995	12,851
131 5/8	23 1/8	22 7/8	16 5/8	4	5	Atoka County	OK	Wesley H. Harden	1995	12,851
131 5/8	22 0/8	22 1/8	15 7/8	4	5	San Patricio County	TX	Billy Roy Leach	1995	12,851
131 5/8	21 1/8	20 7/8	14 7/8	5	5	Dekalb County	IL	Carl Kwak	1996	12,851
131 5/8	22 1/8	23 5/8	18 4/8	7	6	Will County	IL	Jim Esposito	1996	12,851
131 5/8	23 4/8	22 6/8	18 4/8	7	4	Adams County	IL	Dan Kramer	1996	12,851
131 5/8	20 6/8	21 3/8	17 7/8	4	4	Anoka County	MN	Cedric Williams IV	1996	12,851
131 5/8	21 0/8	21 2/8	17 1/8	5	5	Wood County	WI	Curtis J. Pelot	1996	12,851
131 5/8	24 1/8	24 3/8	20 4/8	6	5	Jackson County	IA	Daniel David Schuster	1996	12,851
131 5/8	22 4/8	23 2/8	16 5/8	5	4	Kewaunee County	WI	William J. Classon	1996	12,851
131 5/8	21 5/8	21 1/8	18 0/8	6	7	Kent County	MD	Tom Gustafson	1997	12,851
131 5/8	20 6/8	20 4/8	19 3/8	5	5	Peoria County	IL	Steven Janssen	1997	12,851
131 5/8	19 7/8	20 2/8	16 3/8	5	5	Vilas County	WI	Michael J. Tillmann	1997	12,851
131 5/8	19 1/8	20 2/8	18 3/8	5	5	Washington County	OH	John J. Hooper	1997	12,851

WHITETAIL DEER (TYPICAL ANTLERS)

Minimum Score 125 — Continued

SCORE	LENGTH OF MAIN BEAM R	LENGTH OF MAIN BEAM L	INSIDE SPREAD	NUMBER OF POINTS R	NUMBER OF POINTS L	AREA	STATE/PROVINCE	HUNTER'S NAME	DATE	RANK
131 5/8	25 0/8	25 3/8	16 7/8	4	4	Irion County	TX	Chuck A. Nelson	1997	12,851
131 5/8	20 5/8	21 4/8	17 5/8	4	4	Washington County	MN	James K. Rimer	1997	12,851
131 5/8	20 4/8	20 5/8	17 1/8	4	4	Camrose	ALB	Donald Dvoroznak	1998	12,851
131 5/8	22 6/8	23 2/8	19 3/8	6	4	Livingston County	NY	Eugene Stephens	1998	12,851
131 4/8	20 4/8	20 1/8	17 2/8	5	5	Benton County	IA	Wayne Keefer	1956	12,928
131 4/8	21 2/8	21 7/8	16 2/8	5	5	Johnson County	IN	James E. Thompson	1962	12,928
131 4/8	20 2/8	22 1/8	14 2/8	5	5	Price County	WI	Frank W. Taylor	1964	12,928
131 4/8	21 3/8	21 2/8	16 0/8	7	5	Roberts County	SD	Martin Carlson	1966	12,928
131 4/8	23 1/8	21 5/8	17 4/8	5	4	Calvert County	MD	William L. Neal	1970	12,928
131 4/8	20 7/8	22 5/8	18 3/8	5	5	Allamakee County	IA	Dayton Jones	1971	12,928
131 4/8	19 2/8	19 2/8	15 2/8	5	5	Sheboygan County	WI	Donald P. Feidmann	1974	12,928
131 4/8	23 3/8	23 4/8	16 4/8	4	4	Clinton County	IA	Gary Olson	1975	12,928
131 4/8	21 2/8	21 5/8	15 0/8	5	5	Newton County	IN	Ronnie Styck	1976	12,928
131 4/8	22 3/8	22 1/8	19 6/8	5	5	Fairfax County	VA	Dickie R. Powell	1979	12,928
131 4/8	21 2/8	21 5/8	15 0/8	5	5	Ward County	ND	Richard Huber	1980	12,928
131 4/8	24 2/8	22 6/8	16 6/8	4	4	Shelby County	OH	Wayne L. Goubeaux	1981	12,928
131 4/8	21 7/8	21 6/8	15 6/8	4	5	Christian County	IL	Dale W. Simmons	1982	12,928
131 4/8	21 6/8	21 1/8	16 6/8	5	4	Clay County	KS	Doug Adams	1982	12,928
131 4/8	21 6/8	21 0/8	15 2/8	5	5	Dawson County	MT	James C. Slaska	1984	12,928
131 4/8	23 3/8	23 6/8	19 5/8	7	5	Calhoun County	MI	Samuel E. Farrington	1984	12,928
131 4/8	20 2/8	21 5/8	17 6/8	4	4	Clay County	MN	Don Pake	1984	12,928
131 4/8	21 3/8	21 3/8	20 6/8	4	4	Montgomery County	IN	John R. Clark	1984	12,928
131 4/8	24 4/8	24 5/8	15 6/8	5	4	McNairy County	TN	Howard Russom	1984	12,928
131 4/8	21 4/8	23 1/8	19 0/8	6	5	Yuma County	CO	Greg Mekelburg	1985	12,928
131 4/8	22 6/8	21 4/8	14 6/8	5	5	Morrill County	NE	Kurt Gaertner	1985	12,928
131 4/8	22 3/8	22 5/8	17 6/8	4	5	Grant County	WI	Gary R. Bald	1985	12,928
131 4/8	20 5/8	20 1/8	15 4/8	5	5	Webster County	IA	Randy Bennett	1985	12,928
131 4/8	21 4/8	21 0/8	16 4/8	5	5	Swift County	MN	Gary Laughlin	1985	12,928
131 4/8	22 4/8	22 6/8	17 2/8	4	4	Dakota County	MN	Steve Dahnke	1986	12,928
131 4/8	21 4/8	23 0/8	18 4/8	4	4	Strathcona	ALB	John Visscher	1986	12,928
131 4/8	23 0/8	23 0/8	16 4/8	4	4	Edmunds County	SD	Jerry Leair	1986	12,928
131 4/8	23 0/8	25 2/8	14 0/8	5	5	Jackson County	WV	Michael B. Sankoff	1987	12,928
131 4/8	21 3/8	21 4/8	18 6/8	4	4	Knox County	IL	Bill T. Alton, Jr.	1987	12,928
131 4/8	26 6/8	26 3/8	18 4/8	4	5	Greenwood County	KS	Scott Moore	1987	12,928
131 4/8	22 7/8	22 4/8	23 6/8	5	5	Union County	IL	Steve Wilhite	1987	12,928
131 4/8	20 4/8	20 6/8	17 0/8	5	5	Lake County	IL	John F. Nobilio	1988	12,928
131 4/8	21 3/8	20 6/8	18 2/8	5	5	Lake County	IL	Carl Spaeth	1988	12,928
131 4/8	26 4/8	25 0/8	20 0/8	5	4	Douglas County	WI	Jim Webb	1988	12,928
131 4/8	23 5/8	24 2/8	19 1/8	5	7	Macoupin County	IL	Donald D. Snow, Sr.	1988	12,928
131 4/8	23 0/8	22 6/8	14 4/8	4	4	Sandusky County	OH	Greg S. Meek	1989	12,928
131 4/8	22 6/8	23 1/8	17 0/8	4	4	Newton County	TX	Mike Perdue	1989	12,928
131 4/8	22 0/8	23 4/8	20 2/8	4	4	Houston County	MN	Tony Rostad	1989	12,928
131 4/8	21 1/8	21 5/8	16 4/8	5	5	Buffalo County	WI	Mark Fetting	1989	12,928
131 4/8	22 2/8	23 1/8	17 4/8	4	5	Lapeer County	MI	Larry Rae Faught	1989	12,928
131 4/8	25 0/8	25 0/8	19 0/8	5	4	Hillsborough County	NH	Robert Dupuis	1990	12,928
131 4/8	23 3/8	23 2/8	17 4/8	4	4	Becker County	MN	Duane Hendrickson	1990	12,928
131 4/8	22 7/8	22 6/8	16 4/8	4	4	Taylor County	WI	Bryce Hinke	1990	12,928
131 4/8	21 2/8	20 3/8	17 2/8	5	5	Somerset County	NJ	Louis Mayersky	1990	12,928
131 4/8	21 4/8	21 2/8	15 6/8	4	5	Sawyer County	WI	Roger A. Niewiadomski	1990	12,928
131 4/8	20 2/8	23 0/8	17 2/8	6	5	Fairfield County	CT	Robert Padovani	1990	12,928
131 4/8	21 6/8	22 1/8	18 0/8	5	5	Dodge County	WI	Michael Vande Slunt	1990	12,928
131 4/8	22 4/8	22 0/8	16 6/8	5	6	Logan County	CO	Terry Weimer	1990	12,928
131 4/8	21 6/8	21 7/8	17 0/8	5	5	Morrison County	MN	Bob Deiley	1990	12,928
131 4/8	22 6/8	23 2/8	17 4/8	5	4	Suffolk County	NY	Richard Jensen	1990	12,928
131 4/8	21 2/8	20 7/8	18 5/8	5	7	Fillmore County	MN	David L. Carson	1991	12,928
131 4/8	22 0/8	22 4/8	19 0/8	4	5	Onondaga County	NY	Richard J. Canestrare	1991	12,928
131 4/8	22 0/8	21 6/8	15 7/8	5	4	Stevens County	WA	Steve Mitchell	1992	12,928
131 4/8	23 2/8	22 6/8	16 0/8	5	4	McHenry County	IL	Gary Reckers	1992	12,928
131 4/8	20 0/8	17 3/8	15 4/8	5	5	Nantucket County	MA	Lee A. Corkish	1992	12,928
131 4/8	21 7/8	22 1/8	18 4/8	5	5	Allamakee County	IA	Thomas W. Gavin	1992	12,928
131 4/8	23 7/8	24 3/8	18 4/8	4	4	Cattaraugus County	NY	Allen Ervin Westfall	1992	12,928
131 4/8	22 0/8	21 5/8	17 6/8	4	4	Randolph County	GA	Bob Lovett	1992	12,928
131 4/8	24 5/8	24 0/8	17 1/8	6	5	Trempealeau County	WI	James Burt	1993	12,928
131 4/8	23 5/8	24 4/8	16 2/8	6	7	Cass County	MI	Patrick G. Dowling	1993	12,928
131 4/8	23 6/8	23 2/8	16 6/8	5	4	La Crosse County	WI	Chris Tauscher	1993	12,928
131 4/8	19 3/8	21 2/8	18 2/8	6	5	St. Joseph County	IN	Joseph M. Sipocz	1993	12,928
131 4/8	23 7/8	24 7/8	16 5/8	6	6	Kent County	MD	Jim Samis	1993	12,928
131 4/8	22 3/8	22 4/8	16 4/8	4	4	Trempealeau County	WI	Steve Sobczak	1993	12,928
131 4/8	22 2/8	23 6/8	15 4/8	4	4	Johnson County	IA	Brian J. Bourgeois	1993	12,928
131 4/8	24 4/8	21 3/8	18 1/8	5	7	Van Buren County	IA	Elmer R. Luce, Jr.	1993	12,928
131 4/8	21 7/8	21 0/8	17 7/8	5	5	Allegheny County	PA	Francis Schlosser	1993	12,928
131 4/8	25 0/8	24 3/8	13 6/8	5	6	Moultrie County	IL	Steven K. Wood	1993	12,928
131 4/8	24 4/8	23 2/8	17 7/8	5	5	Franklin County	IN	Will McQueen	1993	12,928
131 4/8	21 7/8	21 6/8	15 5/8	4	5	Russell County	KS	Vickie L. Frost	1993	12,928
131 4/8	21 2/8	21 4/8	15 2/8	5	5	Dakota County	NE	Mike Cuka	1994	12,928
131 4/8	24 4/8	25 6/8	18 6/8	4	4	Middlesex County	CT	John P. Moriarty	1994	12,928
131 4/8	24 3/8	24 1/8	18 2/8	4	5	Monroe County	MO	Scott Minor	1994	12,928
131 4/8	23 0/8	22 7/8	17 2/8	4	5	Linn County	MO	Garrett Westfall	1994	12,928

WHITETAIL DEER (TYPICAL ANTLERS)

Minimum Score 125 — Continued

SCORE	LENGTH OF MAIN BEAM R	L	INSIDE SPREAD	NUMBER OF POINTS R	L	AREA	STATE/ PROVINCE	HUNTER'S NAME	DATE	RANK
131 4/8	23 2/8	22 4/8	16 4/8	6	5	Beltrami County	MN	Joseph W. Edlund	1994	12,928
131 4/8	20 1/8	21 3/8	16 0/8	6	5	Newton County	MO	Mike Goff	1994	12,928
131 4/8	23 3/8	22 6/8	17 6/8	4	4	Steuben County	IN	John Kabes	1994	12,928
131 4/8	20 7/8	20 3/8	15 4/8	5	5	Brown County	SD	Colin Hendry	1994	12,928
131 4/8	23 1/8	23 3/8	20 0/8	4	4	Prince Georges County	MD	Yates Clagett	1994	12,928
131 4/8	21 6/8	22 1/8	19 2/8	4	5	Waukesha County	WI	Kevin Watterson	1994	12,928
131 4/8	23 0/8	23 7/8	18 7/8	6	6	Dunn County	WI	Todd Kostman	1994	12,928
131 4/8	23 5/8	23 3/8	18 6/8	5	5	Wyoming County	WV	Gary Kirk II	1994	12,928
131 4/8	22 4/8	22 6/8	19 4/8	4	4	McHenry County	IL	Joe O'Malley	1994	12,928
131 4/8	21 2/8	23 0/8	19 0/8	4	4	Frederick County	MD	Richard W. Shaffer	1994	12,928
131 4/8	22 4/8	23 0/8	21 2/8	4	4	Berks County	PA	Terry A. Danenhower	1995	12,928
131 4/8	19 7/8	20 4/8	14 4/8	5	5	Crawford County	MO	Curtis Steinbach	1995	12,928
131 4/8	23 3/8	22 5/8	16 0/8	4	4	Jo Daviess County	IL	Rick Temperley	1995	12,928
131 4/8	21 7/8	20 0/8	15 2/8	5	5	Howard County	MD	Kenneth W. Nelson	1995	12,928
131 4/8	20 6/8	21 1/8	17 5/8	5	5	Ashland County	WI	Dwayne Watson	1995	12,928
131 4/8	21 7/8	20 6/8	15 4/8	5	6	Washtenaw County	MI	Keith Headley	1996	12,928
131 4/8	24 0/8	23 5/8	18 4/8	4	4	Buffalo County	WI	Eric Young	1996	12,928
131 4/8	23 3/8	23 0/8	18 2/8	5	6	Reno County	KS	Calvin Yoder	1996	12,928
131 4/8	22 2/8	22 0/8	19 0/8	5	5	Edmonton	ALB	Mike J. Krieg	1996	12,928
131 4/8	23 0/8	23 2/8	18 4/8	4	4	Adams County	MS	Ben McDonald	1997	12,928
131 4/8	20 7/8	20 5/8	18 0/8	4	5	Ogle County	IL	Ken J. Beach	1997	12,928
131 4/8	21 7/8	22 0/8	16 4/8	5	5	Dakota County	MN	Jeff Warren	1997	12,928
131 4/8	24 7/8	26 0/8	20 4/8	4	4	Warren County	IA	Howard Ratkovich	1997	12,928
131 4/8	23 4/8	24 2/8	18 4/8	4	5	Des Moines County	IA	Randy Gipple	1997	12,928
131 4/8	21 4/8	22 0/8	14 0/8	5	4	Sullivan County	MO	Michael Otto	1998	12,928
131 4/8	20 1/8	20 6/8	17 4/8	4	4	Buffalo County	WI	Daniel Hayden	1998	12,928
131 3/8	22 2/8	22 6/8	18 7/8	5	5	Beltrami County	MN	Charles R. Bowman	1961	13,028
131 3/8	21 7/8	21 6/8	17 7/8	4	4	Waushara County	WI	Reginald Vergin	1967	13,028
131 3/8	21 0/8	20 4/8	16 5/8	5	6	Delaware County	OH	Bobby Clenney	1975	13,028
131 3/8	21 3/8	21 4/8	18 3/8	4	5	Pope County	AR	Tom Quinton	1976	13,028
131 3/8	23 0/8	23 3/8	16 7/8	4	4	Trigg County	KY	Bruce E. Hollkamp	1978	13,028
131 3/8	22 2/8	20 5/8	13 6/8	5	5	Burleigh County	ND	Robert Baker	1980	13,028
131 3/8	21 7/8	21 1/8	15 4/8	5	4	Guernsey County	OH	Jim Conrad	1980	13,028
131 3/8	23 1/8	23 1/8	19 7/8	4	5	Morrison County	MN	Tim Deadrick	1981	13,028
131 3/8	21 1/8	21 1/8	17 1/8	5	5	Crawford County	WI	Michael G. O'Dair	1983	13,028
131 3/8	22 7/8	24 1/8	19 3/8	4	4	Dubuque County	IA	Michael W. Moore	1983	13,028
131 3/8	22 3/8	22 1/8	18 1/8	5	5	Marquette County	WI	Roger L. Abraham	1984	13,028
131 3/8	22 2/8	22 4/8	19 1/8	4	4	Roane County	TN	Doan Boling	1986	13,028
131 3/8	21 2/8	20 7/8	18 1/8	4	5	Racine County	WI	Steven Holterman	1986	13,028
131 3/8	21 4/8	22 4/8	17 1/8	4	5	Jefferson County	WI	Robert L. Cummings	1986	13,028
131 3/8	23 2/8	23 0/8	17 7/8	4	4	Jo Daviess County	IL	Bill Randecker	1986	13,028
131 3/8	21 5/8	22 1/8	17 7/8	5	5	Clark County	WI	Norbert Allan Lewis	1987	13,028
131 3/8	22 1/8	22 1/8	18 3/8	5	5	Dallas County	IA	William Chaplin	1987	13,028
131 3/8	22 1/8	22 2/8	16 3/8	5	5	Polk County	WI	Daniel Carlson	1987	13,028
131 3/8	22 5/8	24 3/8	17 4/8	6	6	Dane County	WI	Rollen "Bud" Fries	1987	13,028
131 3/8	23 5/8	24 4/8	16 5/8	5	4	Columbia County	WI	Mark L. Preuss	1987	13,028
131 3/8	20 4/8	21 5/8	15 1/8	5	6	Iron County	MI	Bernard Ohmer	1987	13,028
131 3/8	24 1/8	24 6/8	21 7/8	6	4	Door County	WI	Bruce H. Hartman	1987	13,028
131 3/8	22 0/8	23 1/8	15 2/8	7	7	Linn County	IA	John Dunham	1987	13,028
131 3/8	21 4/8	21 4/8	17 3/8	5	5	Lancaster County	PA	Henry O. Fromm	1988	13,028
131 3/8	21 0/8	21 6/8	18 3/8	6	5	Cass County	ND	John Baird	1988	13,028
131 3/8	20 3/8	20 0/8	16 5/8	6	7	Sherburne County	MN	Bryan J. Wieber	1988	13,028
131 3/8	21 2/8	20 1/8	15 7/8	5	6	Buffalo County	WI	John W. Zahrte	1988	13,028
131 3/8	23 3/8	23 1/8	17 1/8	5	5	Schuyler County	NY	Tim G. Carlton	1988	13,028
131 3/8	19 7/8	20 5/8	16 5/8	5	5	Francis	SAS	Ken Paslawski	1989	13,028
131 3/8	23 3/8	23 1/8	17 5/8	8	5	Colfax County	NE	Neil Chaudler	1989	13,028
131 3/8	23 0/8	23 0/8	17 5/8	4	4	Vermilion County	IL	Michael J. Howie	1989	13,028
131 3/8	22 7/8	22 5/8	21 1/8	4	4	Winneshiek County	IA	John Mullen	1989	13,028
131 3/8	21 6/8	22 2/8	19 1/8	4	5	Oakland County	MI	Gerald J. Pennington	1989	13,028
131 3/8	22 6/8	23 3/8	14 7/8	5	6	Hocking County	OH	Jim Bowman	1989	13,028
131 3/8	21 3/8	20 6/8	18 3/8	5	5	Champaign County	OH	E. Jeffrey Horne	1989	13,028
131 3/8	19 0/8	19 3/8	17 7/8	6	5	Warren County	KY	Tony Shoemake	1989	13,028
131 3/8	22 0/8	22 0/8	17 1/8	5	5	Lincoln County	SD	Chris A. Benson	1990	13,028
131 3/8	21 6/8	21 6/8	16 5/8	5	5	Carroll County	IL	Greg McGinnis	1990	13,028
131 3/8	21 0/8	20 4/8	16 3/8	4	5	Kemper County	MS	David L. Black	1990	13,028
131 3/8	20 2/8	20 2/8	18 3/8	4	5	Wayne County	MI	William Benedict	1990	13,028
131 3/8	22 2/8	23 4/8	18 0/8	5	5	Vernon County	MO	Mike Goucher	1990	13,028
131 3/8	23 3/8	22 7/8	18 3/8	5	5	Mills County	IA	Dave Messner	1990	13,028
131 3/8	20 6/8	22 2/8	16 1/8	4	4	Door County	WI	Wayne Lautenbach	1990	13,028
131 3/8	21 5/8	21 5/8	18 1/8	4	4	Huron County	OH	Michael Scheel	1990	13,028
131 3/8	21 6/8	22 5/8	18 7/8	4	4	Missoula County	MT	Christopher Blatt	1990	13,028
131 3/8	22 7/8	21 5/8	21 1/8	5	4	Warren County	IA	Brian Harrington	1991	13,028
131 3/8	22 0/8	21 4/8	17 1/8	5	4	St. Joseph County	IN	Rodney Reeder	1991	13,028
131 3/8	23 5/8	23 1/8	16 3/8	4	4	Claiborne County	MS	James R. House	1991	13,028
131 3/8	25 2/8	25 0/8	19 1/8	4	4	St. Clair County	MI	Michael Oakley	1992	13,028
131 3/8	19 2/8	22 0/8	16 5/8	6	6	Cuming County	NE	Ricky Heller	1992	13,028
131 3/8	19 4/8	20 3/8	16 1/8	5	5	Clayton County	IA	Joseph C. Hinderman	1992	13,028
131 3/8	21 6/8	21 1/8	18 3/8	5	5	Tom Green County	TX	Ronnie Parsons	1992	13,028

WHITETAIL DEER (TYPICAL ANTLERS)

Minimum Score 125 — Continued

SCORE	LENGTH OF MAIN BEAM R	LENGTH OF MAIN BEAM L	INSIDE SPREAD	NUMBER OF POINTS R	NUMBER OF POINTS L	AREA	STATE/PROVINCE	HUNTER'S NAME	DATE	RANK
131 3/8	25 1/8	23 5/8	19 3/8	5	4	Orange County	NY	Dennis Partridge	1993	13,028
131 3/8	22 3/8	21 1/8	16 1/8	5	5	McHenry County	IL	William D. Weiss	1993	13,028
131 3/8	24 4/8	22 3/8	21 0/8	5	6	Suffolk County	NY	Ken Homan	1993	13,028
131 3/8	24 0/8	24 5/8	19 3/8	4	4	Rock County	WI	Todd A. Clements	1993	13,028
131 3/8	25 6/8	22 5/8	15 5/8	5	6	Clark County	IL	Bobby Sharp	1993	13,028
131 3/8	25 2/8	26 4/8	23 1/8	4	3	Columbiana County	OH	Rex McCoy	1993	13,028
131 3/8	23 0/8	23 5/8	15 3/8	5	5	White County	IN	Steve Rider, Jr.	1993	13,028
131 3/8	19 7/8	19 7/8	15 5/8	5	5	Crook County	WY	Troy Leeb	1994	13,028
131 3/8	22 4/8	22 5/8	14 0/8	7	5	Benewah County	ID	J. D. Ragan	1994	13,028
131 3/8	20 2/8	21 0/8	18 3/8	5	6	Barron County	WI	Ron "Butch" Gowin	1994	13,028
131 3/8	23 3/8	23 2/8	16 3/8	4	4	Calhoun County	MI	Kenneth E. Bryan	1994	13,028
131 3/8	22 7/8	23 3/8	15 3/8	5	5	Chippewa County	WI	David I. Christie	1994	13,028
131 3/8	19 2/8	19 4/8	15 5/8	6	5	Day County	SD	Ricky Hanson	1994	13,028
131 3/8	22 2/8	22 4/8	17 7/8	4	4	McHenry County	IL	Ray Eisbrener	1994	13,028
131 3/8	23 2/8	23 5/8	17 7/8	4	6	Middlesex County	CT	Richard Rossi	1994	13,028
131 3/8	21 2/8	21 5/8	18 1/8	4	4	Westchester County	NY	Curt Jorgensen	1994	13,028
131 3/8	22 5/8	22 4/8	16 7/8	4	5	Buffalo County	NE	Rich Walters, Jr.	1994	13,028
131 3/8	22 4/8	21 7/8	16 5/8	5	5	La Salle County	TX	Andy Milam	1994	13,028
131 3/8	21 5/8	21 7/8	16 1/8	6	5	Fairfield County	OH	Eric Christopher McAfee	1994	13,028
131 3/8	23 1/8	21 7/8	15 7/8	5	5	Kerr County	TX	Dan Perez	1995	13,028
131 3/8	22 3/8	22 6/8	15 5/8	4	4	Allegany County	NY	Brian Campbell	1995	13,028
131 3/8	20 7/8	19 2/8	16 0/8	5	8	La Salle County	IL	John Thomas	1995	13,028
131 3/8	23 1/8	22 0/8	18 2/8	6	6	Schuyler County	IL	Joe O'Malley	1995	13,028
131 3/8	23 2/8	23 1/8	15 1/8	4	4	Albany County	NY	James Clyne	1995	13,028
131 3/8	22 4/8	22 5/8	18 7/8	6	5	Hancock County	WV	William Gary Rusinovich	1995	13,028
131 3/8	19 0/8	20 7/8	16 6/8	7	7	Kingman County	KS	Roger Rollmann	1995	13,028
131 3/8	21 4/8	21 7/8	16 6/8	5	5	Freeborn County	MN	Gordon Dale Sevley	1995	13,028
131 3/8	17 6/8	21 0/8	18 5/8	4	5	Kane County	IL	Michael D. Bryan	1996	13,028
131 3/8	22 7/8	22 5/8	17 1/8	4	4	Sauk County	WI	Donald Gieck	1996	13,028
131 3/8	18 6/8	22 5/8	15 3/8	5	4	Livingston County	MO	Mike Lollar	1996	13,028
131 3/8	24 4/8	25 1/8	17 1/8	5	4	Buffalo County	WI	Rick A. Olson	1996	13,028
131 3/8	21 6/8	21 0/8	18 1/8	5	5	Scioto County	OH	Randy S. Boggs	1996	13,028
131 3/8	23 1/8	22 4/8	15 7/8	5	4	Clayton County	GA	Chris Foster	1996	13,028
131 3/8	20 4/8	21 2/8	15 5/8	7	6	Harris County	GA	Larry E. Garner, Jr.	1996	13,028
131 3/8	19 6/8	18 5/8	16 1/8	6	5	Morrison County	MN	James J. Willard	1997	13,028
131 3/8	25 0/8	23 6/8	21 3/8	4	5	Pulaski County	MO	Trent Dismuke	1997	13,028
131 3/8	21 0/8	22 3/8	11 5/8	5	4	Kerr County	TX	Craig E. Stewart	1997	13,028
131 3/8	21 5/8	22 1/8	15 7/8	4	4	Linn County	KS	Gary E. Cox	1997	13,028
131 3/8	23 1/8	23 0/8	17 7/8	5	4	St. Marys County	MD	Ronald McKenzie	1997	13,028
131 2/8	19 2/8	19 4/8	17 0/8	5	5	Shawnee County	KS	Guy C. Michael	1968	13,119
131 2/8	20 3/8	19 4/8	14 6/8	5	5	Ripley County	IN	Robert Pitt	1969	13,119
131 2/8	24 5/8	22 5/8	16 0/8	4	5	Waushara County	WI	Randy Marks	1975	13,119
131 2/8	20 5/8	22 0/8	17 4/8	5	5	Scott County	KY	Jerry Peavler	1975	13,119
131 2/8	20 6/8	22 0/8	16 0/8	5	5	Clearwater County	ID	Edward L. Russell	1978	13,119
131 2/8	25 0/8	26 3/8	17 6/8	3	4	Scioto County	OH	Charles E. Stambaugh	1979	13,119
131 2/8	21 6/8	21 6/8	18 6/8	4	5	Claiborne County	MS	Mike Parker	1980	13,119
131 2/8	19 7/8	22 4/8	16 3/8	4	5	Osage County	MO	Rocky Pointer	1980	13,119
131 2/8	24 3/8	24 2/8	20 2/8	5	4	Boyle County	KY	Randy Webb	1980	13,119
131 2/8	22 0/8	22 0/8	17 2/8	4	5	Des Moines County	IA	Chuck Hawkins	1981	13,119
131 2/8	22 6/8	22 6/8	17 6/8	5	6	Carter County	MT	Jamie Byrne	1981	13,119
131 2/8	21 5/8	21 6/8	18 2/8	4	4	Scott County	IA	Robert D. Hankins	1983	13,119
131 2/8	22 0/8	22 1/8	19 0/8	4	5	Barren County	KY	Tony Deckard	1983	13,119
131 2/8	21 3/8	23 1/8	14 0/8	5	5	Edmonson County	KY	Joe Shereliff	1984	13,119
131 2/8	23 4/8	24 4/8	16 5/8	6	5	Allegany County	NY	Lawrence L Davis	1984	13,119
131 2/8	21 7/8	21 1/8	18 0/8	4	4	Ogle County	IL	Jerome F. Bruns	1984	13,119
131 2/8	21 6/8	21 2/8	14 0/8	6	5	Randolph County	IN	Ronald L. Arnold	1985	13,119
131 2/8	22 1/8	22 1/8	18 3/8	6	5	La Crosse County	WI	Don C. Polivoda	1986	13,119
131 2/8	23 6/8	24 4/8	20 6/8	9	7	Pittsburg County	OK	Neil Keyes	1986	13,119
131 2/8	22 6/8	22 3/8	17 2/8	4	4	Jo Daviess County	IL	Dave Martinek	1986	13,119
131 2/8	21 6/8	22 0/8	16 0/8	4	5	Greene County	IA	Darrel Mischke	1986	13,119
131 2/8	22 7/8	22 7/8	17 4/8	4	4	Westchester County	NY	Jim Cordeira	1986	13,119
131 2/8	22 5/8	23 6/8	15 6/8	6	5	Menard County	TX	Paul Garvin Beeson	1987	13,119
131 2/8	22 0/8	22 0/8	16 2/8	4	4	Washington County	MS	Bobby R. Woods	1987	13,119
131 2/8	20 0/8	22 2/8	21 4/8	3	3	Crawford County	IL	Billy Waddell	1987	13,119
131 2/8	23 3/8	21 1/8	16 4/8	4	4	McMullen County	TX	Pete Swenson	1987	13,119
131 2/8	21 4/8	21 0/8	17 2/8	4	4	Butler County	PA	James F. Govan	1988	13,119
131 2/8	21 6/8	22 0/8	18 0/8	4	4	Walworth County	WI	Dan Peters	1988	13,119
131 2/8	22 7/8	22 0/8	18 0/8	4	4	Washington County	MS	Bobby R. Woods	1988	13,119
131 2/8	23 7/8	22 4/8	17 6/8	6	5	Waukesha County	WI	Robert Bowe	1989	13,119
131 2/8	23 0/8	22 5/8	17 2/8	6	5	Charles County	MD	Scott Cutter	1989	13,119
131 2/8	23 6/8	24 1/8	20 4/8	4	4	Hampden County	MA	Michael P. Foote	1989	13,119
131 2/8	24 5/8	25 0/8	17 0/8	5	5	Vilas County	WI	Joseph Herzog	1990	13,119
131 2/8	22 3/8	21 6/8	16 4/8	4	4	Baraga County	MI	Fred W. Mikels	1990	13,119
131 2/8	22 3/8	22 5/8	16 6/8	5	5	Walworth County	WI	Russell Van Beek	1990	13,119
131 2/8	23 4/8	23 2/8	17 2/8	4	4	Livingston County	MI	Thomas R. Dorsey II	1990	13,119
131 2/8	22 3/8	22 4/8	18 4/8	5	5	Adams County	WI	Gerry L. Riddle	1990	13,119
131 2/8	22 4/8	23 0/8	14 6/8	5	5	Forest County	WI	Donald R. Welhouse	1990	13,119
131 2/8	20 6/8	20 6/8	14 7/8	5	6	Woodford County	IL	Ronald A. DeFreitas	1990	13,119

WHITETAIL DEER (TYPICAL ANTLERS)

Minimum Score 125 — Continued

SCORE	LENGTH OF MAIN BEAM R	LENGTH OF MAIN BEAM L	INSIDE SPREAD	NUMBER OF POINTS R	NUMBER OF POINTS L	AREA	STATE/PROVINCE	HUNTER'S NAME	DATE	RANK
131 2/8	19 1/8	20 1/8	17 2/8	5	5	Columbia County	WI	Bradd W. Price	1991	13,119
131 2/8	22 1/8	21 7/8	15 6/8	5	5	Forest County	WI	Thomas J. Wolf	1991	13,119
131 2/8	21 7/8	20 3/8	18 1/8	6	6	Union County	IL	Terry Wiseman, Jr.	1991	13,119
131 2/8	21 2/8	21 5/8	16 4/8	4	5	Williamson County	IL	Dale Reamy	1991	13,119
131 2/8	20 7/8	21 2/8	15 6/8	5	5	Langlade County	WI	Jerry Aulik	1991	13,119
131 2/8	20 0/8	19 2/8	15 0/8	6	6	Switzerland County	IN	Dave Wilder	1992	13,119
131 2/8	21 6/8	20 6/8	16 4/8	5	5	New Castle County	DE	Dave Christian	1992	13,119
131 2/8	22 5/8	21 6/8	16 2/8	6	5	Dixon County	NE	Lane L. Ostendorf	1992	13,119
131 2/8	21 4/8	21 1/8	16 2/8	5	5	Brown County	WI	Timothy J. Smith	1992	13,119
131 2/8	21 3/8	22 6/8	15 2/8	5	6	Door County	WI	Scott A. Weckler	1992	13,119
131 2/8	21 4/8	21 4/8	17 2/8	6	5	St. Joseph County	MI	Kirk Mason	1992	13,119
131 2/8	22 7/8	23 3/8	20 3/8	5	4	Geauga County	OH	James "Jim" Davis	1992	13,119
131 2/8	23 4/8	22 4/8	18 1/8	6	6	Appanoose County	IA	Scott Rolffs	1992	13,119
131 2/8	21 2/8	20 7/8	16 0/8	5	5	Dane County	WI	Kent Powell	1992	13,119
131 2/8	24 2/8	23 5/8	16 6/8	4	5	Prince Georges County	MD	Rob Clark	1992	13,119
131 2/8	24 3/8	24 3/8	16 4/8	5	5	Oconto County	WI	Terry Ullrich	1993	13,119
131 2/8	24 3/8	24 4/8	17 2/8	5	4	Pike County	IN	Jerrod Carlisle	1993	13,119
131 2/8	24 4/8	24 0/8	18 2/8	4	4	Alleghany County	VA	Shane M. McClung	1993	13,119
131 2/8	21 4/8	21 2/8	18 6/8	4	4	Manitowoc County	WI	Scott T. Habermann	1993	13,119
131 2/8	21 0/8	20 0/8	19 6/8	5	5	Marion County	OH	Mike Roshon	1993	13,119
131 2/8	21 0/8	24 2/8	18 4/8	4	5	Allamakee County	IA	Randy Petersburg	1993	13,119
131 2/8	20 1/8	21 0/8	15 0/8	4	5	Clark County	IL	Gerald Shaffner	1993	13,119
131 2/8	19 7/8	20 4/8	16 6/8	5	5	Fairfax County	VA	Robert P. Honus	1993	13,119
131 2/8	21 6/8	21 5/8	17 4/8	5	5	La Salle County	TX	Neal Bouldin	1994	13,119
131 2/8	23 1/8	20 1/8	20 0/8	5	5	Kandiyohi County	MN	Travis J. Boie	1994	13,119
131 2/8	22 6/8	22 6/8	18 0/8	4	4	Trempealeau County	WI	Shane Andre	1994	13,119
131 2/8	19 4/8	19 7/8	14 4/8	6	5	Crawford County	IL	John Hale	1994	13,119
131 2/8	20 5/8	20 6/8	16 4/8	5	5	Sauk County	WI	Jerald A. Leifer	1994	13,119
131 2/8	19 2/8	19 0/8	14 2/8	5	5	Sarpy County	NE	Dennis R. Schmidt	1994	13,119
131 2/8	22 5/8	23 0/8	17 6/8	6	6	Buffalo County	WI	Jim Wondzell	1994	13,119
131 2/8	21 4/8	21 6/8	18 1/8	6	5	McDowell County	WV	Roy S. Dyson	1994	13,119
131 2/8	23 2/8	22 1/8	15 2/8	5	5	Buffalo County	WI	Bill Spaeth	1994	13,119
131 2/8	22 0/8	21 3/8	16 2/8	6	6	Webb County	TX	Harry I. Bussa, Jr.	1994	13,119
131 2/8	24 6/8	23 5/8	19 2/8	4	4	Union County	IL	Ronald Ury	1994	13,119
131 2/8	20 5/8	19 5/8	17 0/8	5	5	Robertson County	KY	Kevin D. Anderson	1995	13,119
131 2/8	20 4/8	19 7/8	19 2/8	5	5	Ozaukee County	WI	Scott Chesak	1995	13,119
131 2/8	22 4/8	22 2/8	16 6/8	5	4	Todd County	MN	Wayne Dryburgh	1995	13,119
131 2/8	23 0/8	21 7/8	18 0/8	5	4	Barron County	WI	Matt Rappel	1995	13,119
131 2/8	25 1/8	24 2/8	18 2/8	6	6	Pike County	OH	David Langdon	1995	13,119
131 2/8	22 6/8	22 7/8	16 6/8	5	4	Trempealeau County	WI	Kathleen S. Harms	1995	13,119
131 2/8	26 4/8	26 4/8	22 4/8	7	4	Wayne County	IA	John Pherigo	1995	13,119
131 2/8	21 2/8	21 4/8	15 2/8	4	4	Lyon County	KS	Michael S. Esch	1995	13,119
131 2/8	21 3/8	20 6/8	16 0/8	5	5	Powhatan County	VA	Bruce E. Atkins	1996	13,119
131 2/8	23 4/8	23 6/8	14 6/8	4	5	Webster County	MS	Billy Neal Thrash	1996	13,119
131 2/8	22 6/8	23 4/8	20 0/8	4	5	Rockingham County	NH	Jeffrey Paradis	1996	13,119
131 2/8	24 2/8	24 2/8	16 6/8	4	4	Rockland County	NY	Jim Paglianti	1996	13,119
131 2/8	21 4/8	22 0/8	18 6/8	5	5	Outagamie County	WI	Randy Averbeck	1996	13,119
131 2/8	22 0/8	21 5/8	15 6/8	5	5	Washington County	MN	Sheldon Wendorf	1997	13,119
131 2/8	23 2/8	22 4/8	21 2/8	4	4	Dane County	WI	Kevin L. Ripp	1997	13,119
131 2/8	22 6/8	23 4/8	20 5/8	7	6	Green Lake County	WI	James L. Cluppert	1997	13,119
131 2/8	22 3/8	21 4/8	15 6/8	4	4	Cass County	MI	Butch Compoe	1997	13,119
131 2/8	22 2/8	23 2/8	19 2/8	4	4	Ramsey County	MN	Ron Carlson	1997	13,119
131 2/8	19 7/8	19 4/8	16 4/8	4	4	Pike County	MO	Thomas R. Jaeger	1997	13,119
131 2/8	23 6/8	22 4/8	18 0/8	4	4	Boone County	IA	Chris Doran	1997	13,119
131 2/8	21 4/8	21 3/8	17 0/8	4	4	Fulton County	IL	Russ Courter, Jr.	1997	13,119
131 2/8	22 3/8	24 4/8	20 3/8	7	6	Cass County	IL	Billy Bodford	1997	13,119
131 2/8	23 5/8	23 5/8	16 2/8	7	4	Delaware County	OH	Ronald E. Murphy	1997	13,119
131 2/8	22 7/8	22 4/8	16 2/8	4	5	Monroe County	MO	Jeffery B. O'Laughlin	1997	13,119
131 2/8	22 0/8	23 0/8	16 2/8	5	5	Kankakee County	IL	Don Blecha	1997	13,119
131 2/8	22 5/8	23 0/8	15 5/8	4	6	Monroe County	IA	Fred M. Blesener	1997	13,119
131 2/8	22 2/8	22 0/8	16 0/8	4	4	Davis County	IA	Tracy Templeton	1997	13,119
131 2/8	24 0/8	22 6/8	19 6/8	4	6	Montgomery County	MD	Charles Jones	1997	13,119
131 2/8	21 0/8	20 4/8	19 1/8	7	5	Macomb County	MI	Bryan K. Malone	1998	13,119
131 2/8	23 2/8	23 0/8	18 2/8	4	4	Goodhue County	MN	Bill Prigge	1998	13,119
131 1/8	22 3/8	22 1/8	20 1/8	4	5	Lafayette County	WI	Bob Wand	1971	13,222
131 1/8	25 2/8	25 6/8	18 7/8	4	5	Columbiana County	OH	Bill Henrich	1976	13,222
131 1/8	20 6/8	21 5/8	19 3/8	7	6	Neosho County	KS	Robert E. Willis	1979	13,222
131 1/8	23 1/8	21 7/8	19 1/8	4	4	Harford County	MD	Ronald D. Anderson	1980	13,222
131 1/8	22 7/8	22 7/8	17 7/8	4	4	Adams County	WI	Rich Varsho	1982	13,222
131 1/8	22 7/8	22 6/8	17 7/8	5	4	Jefferson County	WI	Scott Mill	1982	13,222
131 1/8	21 6/8	21 0/8	15 7/8	5	5	Frederick County	VA	Steven E Shoemaker	1983	13,222
131 1/8	22 2/8	22 4/8	17 1/8	4	4	Sedgwick County	KS	Delbert Antle	1983	13,222
131 1/8	24 7/8	23 7/8	18 3/8	5	6	Wright County	MN	John W. Horstman	1984	13,222
131 1/8	22 3/8	20 4/8	18 3/8	5	4	Washington County	KS	Bob Funke	1984	13,222
131 1/8	22 6/8	23 4/8	20 5/8	4	4	Suffolk County	NY	Conrad Grimm	1984	13,222

WHITETAIL DEER (TYPICAL ANTLERS)

Minimum Score 125 — Continued

SCORE	LENGTH OF MAIN BEAM R	LENGTH OF MAIN BEAM L	INSIDE SPREAD	NUMBER OF POINTS R	NUMBER OF POINTS L	AREA	STATE/PROVINCE	HUNTER'S NAME	DATE	RANK
131 1/8	21 4/8	21 5/8	16 7/8	5	4	Buffalo	ALB	Russell Thornberry	1985	13,222
131 1/8	25 0/8	24 0/8	17 3/8	4	5	Saline County	KS	David Keith Grittman	1985	13,222
131 1/8	23 2/8	23 3/8	20 0/8	4	5	Morris County	NJ	Donald Howering	1985	13,222
131 1/8	21 5/8	22 4/8	15 3/8	4	5	Outagamie County	WI	Dion R Heinemeyer	1985	13,222
131 1/8	24 1/8	23 4/8	18 3/8	4	4	Latah County	ID	Howard Holmes	1985	13,222
131 1/8	22 5/8	21 0/8	20 1/8	5	5	Brown County	SD	Mark Janco	1986	13,222
131 1/8	20 6/8	22 1/8	21 3/8	5	5	Montgomery County	IL	John Fleet	1987	13,222
131 1/8	22 5/8	21 5/8	19 4/8	5	6	Washington County	NE	H. Dan Thompson	1987	13,222
131 1/8	21 5/8	22 0/8	17 3/8	5	6	Chickasaw County	IA	David J. Kerkove	1987	13,222
131 1/8	21 5/8	21 0/8	18 3/8	4	4	Schuyler County	IL	Steve McCoy	1987	13,222
131 1/8	23 0/8	21 7/8	15 3/8	4	4	Tazewell County	IL	Robert J. Pratt	1987	13,222
131 1/8	23 2/8	22 5/8	15 3/8	6	4	Yell County	AR	Jackie Teel	1987	13,222
131 1/8	22 0/8	22 1/8	17 7/8	7	5	Graves County	KY	Darrell Forrester	1988	13,222
131 1/8	20 5/8	20 4/8	16 7/8	4	5	Bladen County	NC	Mike Wingenfeld	1988	13,222
131 1/8	19 3/8	19 6/8	15 7/8	5	5	Grand Traverse County	MI	Diane C. McPhall	1988	13,222
131 1/8	20 1/8	21 4/8	16 7/8	6	5	Oneida County	WI	Dennis Brock	1988	13,222
131 1/8	24 6/8	25 4/8	20 3/8	5	5	Morris County	NJ	Andy Zukowski	1988	13,222
131 1/8	23 7/8	23 3/8	20 1/8	5	4	Oakland County	MI	Mark DeGroat	1988	13,222
131 1/8	23 0/8	22 6/8	18 1/8	4	4	Ashland County	WI	Gary R. Jones	1988	13,222
131 1/8	21 0/8	21 2/8	16 3/8	5	5	Waukesha County	WI	Steven Schroeder	1988	13,222
131 1/8	24 4/8	24 0/8	16 7/8	5	6	Wapello County	IA	Doug Johnson	1989	13,222
131 1/8	23 0/8	22 6/8	16 5/8	5	4	Clinton County	IA	Stan Schmidt	1989	13,222
131 1/8	21 2/8	20 6/8	18 5/8	5	5	Lake County	IL	Ted Hysell	1990	13,222
131 1/8	18 6/8	19 4/8	13 5/8	5	5	Cape Girardeau County	MO	Randy Windeknecht	1990	13,222
131 1/8	21 1/8	20 3/8	15 3/8	5	5	Jasper County	IA	Gary D. Hobbs, Jr.	1990	13,222
131 1/8	23 1/8	22 0/8	17 3/8	4	4	Bay County	MI	Jim Barcia	1990	13,222
131 1/8	21 6/8	21 0/8	16 5/8	5	5	Branch County	MI	Robin M. Hutchison	1990	13,222
131 1/8	23 4/8	22 6/8	19 6/8	7	5	Franklin County	IA	Craig Eckhardt	1990	13,222
131 1/8	22 2/8	23 0/8	15 1/8	6	6	Jackson County	OH	James C. Ridge	1990	13,222
131 1/8	22 4/8	22 4/8	16 3/8	4	4	Clay County	MN	David Peckskamp	1990	13,222
131 1/8	20 3/8	20 7/8	17 3/8	5	5	Portage County	WI	Randy D. Niewiadomski	1991	13,222
131 1/8	22 3/8	21 6/8	15 1/8	4	4	Webb County	TX	Steve Leal	1991	13,222
131 1/8	23 3/8	22 7/8	16 5/8	4	4	Pike County	OH	Keith Howard	1991	13,222
131 1/8	21 2/8	21 5/8	18 7/8	5	5	Duval County	TX	Willie Esparza	1991	13,222
131 1/8	22 2/8	23 1/8	17 4/8	4	6	Allegheny County	PA	Troy Benson	1992	13,222
131 1/8	20 7/8	22 2/8	20 1/8	4	4	Kenedy County	TX	Danny R. Sefcik	1992	13,222
131 1/8	21 4/8	21 0/8	21 1/8	5	5	Ulster County	NY	William Wilhelm	1992	13,222
131 1/8	24 4/8	23 3/8	18 3/8	4	4	Johnson County	IL	Daryl Clark	1992	13,222
131 1/8	24 1/8	24 0/8	18 1/8	5	4	Trempealeau County	WI	Joseph J. Giemza	1992	13,222
131 1/8	22 6/8	21 6/8	19 3/8	4	4	Adams County	WI	Kenneth Roberts	1993	13,222
131 1/8	23 6/8	24 1/8	17 5/8	4	5	Jackson County	WI	Tom Yahnke	1993	13,222
131 1/8	21 6/8	21 3/8	17 7/8	5	6	Dodge County	WI	Darren Muche	1993	13,222
131 1/8	23 3/8	23 5/8	16 6/8	6	5	Howard County	MD	Daniel Peters	1993	13,222
131 1/8	19 7/8	22 2/8	14 1/8	5	5	Sanilac County	MI	Chuck Washe	1993	13,222
131 1/8	23 7/8	23 1/8	18 7/8	4	4	New Castle County	DE	Charles L. Messina	1993	13,222
131 1/8	21 4/8	21 0/8	16 3/8	5	5	Nicholas County	WV	Greg Dennison	1993	13,222
131 1/8	22 2/8	21 6/8	17 3/8	5	6	Monroe County	OH	Jack J. Szentmiklosi, Jr.	1993	13,222
131 1/8	21 6/8	22 0/8	18 7/8	4	4	Hughes County	OK	James F. Griffith	1993	13,222
131 1/8	21 3/8	22 5/8	18 3/8	5	6	Mills County	IA	Dave Messner	1993	13,222
131 1/8	23 4/8	23 4/8	16 5/8	4	5	Oakland County	MI	Carl E. Brown	1994	13,222
131 1/8	22 6/8	21 7/8	17 7/8	4	4	Olmsted County	MN	James A. Peterson	1994	13,222
131 1/8	23 6/8	22 6/8	18 7/8	4	4	Butler County	KS	Richard Krehbiel	1994	13,222
131 1/8	22 3/8	22 2/8	16 7/8	4	4	White County	AR	Raymond King	1994	13,222
131 1/8	23 2/8	22 2/8	20 1/8	5	4	Goodhue County	MN	Mark D. Ray	1994	13,222
131 1/8	20 6/8	20 1/8	17 3/8	6	6	Baldwin County	GA	Roy Nelson Sirmans	1994	13,222
131 1/8	21 4/8	22 2/8	16 5/8	5	5	Richland County	MT	Robert Granato	1994	13,222
131 1/8	22 2/8	20 7/8	18 1/8	5	5	Edmonton	ALB	Robert A. Mochilar	1994	13,222
131 1/8	22 3/8	22 1/8	17 3/8	5	5	Vernon County	WI	Joe Brye	1994	13,222
131 1/8	20 7/8	20 6/8	15 2/8	6	5	Ashland County	WI	Jeff Steede	1994	13,222
131 1/8	20 7/8	21 3/8	18 0/8	6	5	Darke County	OH	Bernard Grillot	1994	13,222
131 1/8	22 3/8	22 4/8	15 3/8	6	5	Ottawa County	MI	Robert Westhoff	1994	13,222
131 1/8	19 7/8	19 6/8	16 7/8	4	5	Johnson County	KS	Craig Rogers	1994	13,222
131 1/8	22 5/8	22 6/8	17 1/8	5	6	Woodbury County	IA	Mike Umbach	1994	13,222
131 1/8	20 0/8	21 2/8	16 1/8	5	5	Ravalli County	MT	Ned Coorough	1994	13,222
131 1/8	24 6/8	24 1/8	16 5/8	6	4	Dubuque County	IA	John Duggan	1994	13,222
131 1/8	23 2/8	22 0/8	15 1/8	4	4	Tolland County	CT	William E. Bugden, Jr.	1995	13,222
131 1/8	21 2/8	21 6/8	17 5/8	5	5	Sheboygan County	WI	Jim Klopf	1995	13,222
131 1/8	22 3/8	21 2/8	17 6/8	6	5	Marquette County	WI	Kevin L. Pelot	1995	13,222
131 1/8	21 5/8	21 2/8	16 1/8	6	5	Ohio County	KY	Leonard W. Worth	1995	13,222
131 1/8	22 1/8	22 3/8	16 2/8	6	5	Rock County	WI	John Bronson	1995	13,222
131 1/8	21 7/8	22 1/8	15 3/8	5	5	Luzerne County	PA	Earl A. Hess, Jr.	1995	13,222
131 1/8	23 3/8	22 7/8	18 4/8	4	5	Wright County	IA	Jim Costanzo	1995	13,222
131 1/8	18 1/8	22 4/8	16 5/8	4	5	Pike County	IL	R. L. Foster	1995	13,222
131 1/8	24 1/8	24 4/8	16 6/8	6	6	Logan County	WV	Bruce T. Copley	1995	13,222
131 1/8	22 1/8	23 4/8	17 4/8	6	8	Fremont County	IA	Dave Holt	1995	13,222
131 1/8	20 0/8	20 3/8	15 3/8	5	6	Grand Forks County	ND	Troy Uglem	1996	13,222
131 1/8	20 7/8	21 0/8	18 1/8	5	5	Livingston County	NY	Douglas Scott Charles	1996	13,222
131 1/8	24 5/8	23 5/8	16 7/8	4	4	Allegheny County	PA	Shawn P. Ferguson	1996	13,222

WHITETAIL DEER (TYPICAL ANTLERS)

Minimum Score 125 — Continued

SCORE	LENGTH OF MAIN BEAM R	LENGTH OF MAIN BEAM L	INSIDE SPREAD	NUMBER OF POINTS R	NUMBER OF POINTS L	AREA	STATE/PROVINCE	HUNTER'S NAME	DATE	RANK
131 1/8	23 0/8	22 5/8	19 5/8	5	5	Mills County	IA	Chris Cornish	1996	13,222
131 1/8	21 0/8	22 2/8	18 1/8	4	4	Hampden County	MA	Jeff Nadeau	1996	13,222
131 1/8	22 2/8	22 7/8	17 2/8	6	5	Linn County	IA	Harry Bruce Smith	1997	13,222
131 1/8	22 4/8	24 5/8	20 6/8	5	5	Rock County	WI	Kenneth L. Champion	1997	13,222
131 1/8	20 7/8	19 7/8	18 5/8	5	5	Kankakee County	IL	Don Blecha	1997	13,222
131 1/8	23 0/8	23 1/8	16 7/8	4	5	Williamson County	IL	Harlin D. Parnell	1997	13,222
131 1/8	19 5/8	19 5/8	15 5/8	5	5	Fergus County	MT	Jason W. Birdwell	1997	13,222
131 1/8	21 5/8	23 1/8	17 1/8	4	4	Cowley County	KS	Randy Ferman	1997	13,222
131 1/8	21 1/8	21 4/8	15 4/8	6	4	McHenry County	IL	Lonnie Millermon	1998	13,222
131 1/8	22 4/8	22 4/8	15 3/8	4	4	Belknap County	NH	David E. Gloddy	1998	13,222
131 1/8	21 6/8	21 2/8	17 5/8	5	5	Olmsted County	MN	Jeffrey W. Brobst	1998	13,222
131 1/8	20 0/8	21 4/8	16 3/8	6	6	Buffalo County	WI	Scott Bergner	1998	13,222
131 0/8	21 3/8	21 5/8	16 6/8	5	5	Flathead County	MT	Jack Whitney	1959	13,323
131 0/8	23 5/8	23 5/8	17 0/8	4	5	Scott County	IA	Ron Anderson	1966	13,323
131 0/8	21 7/8	22 0/8	14 6/8	4	4	Louisa County	IA	Larry King	1968	13,323
131 0/8	19 5/8	20 3/8	18 0/8	5	5	Sheboygan County	WI	Steve Rortvedt	1974	13,323
131 0/8	22 0/8	23 5/8	16 0/8	6	6	Union County	OH	Bill Steele	1974	13,323
131 0/8	21 7/8	21 4/8	16 2/8	4	5	Benton County	IA	Robert Kerkman	1975	13,323
131 0/8	21 3/8	21 0/8	17 0/8	5	5	Litchfield County	CT	Elmer L. Perry, Jr.	1978	13,323
131 0/8	23 7/8	26 1/8	12 2/8	6	6	Morrison County	MN	John Strait	1979	13,323
131 0/8	23 6/8	23 1/8	18 2/8	5	4	Butler County	PA	John E. Fry	1979	13,323
131 0/8	19 7/8	20 3/8	15 5/8	5	6	Richland County	MT	Verne L. Cashman	1980	13,323
131 0/8	20 7/8	20 3/8	15 4/8	4	5	Watonwan County	MN	George Nasman	1980	13,323
131 0/8	20 3/8	19 5/8	16 0/8	5	5	Burleigh County	ND	Jerry Schmitcke	1980	13,323
131 0/8	19 0/8	20 5/8	16 6/8	5	5	Manitowoc County	WI	Roger B. Schroeder	1981	13,323
131 0/8	22 6/8	22 0/8	17 0/8	5	5	Dane County	WI	Jeff Bauer	1981	13,323
131 0/8	22 3/8	22 4/8	17 6/8	4	4	Fulton County	PA	John A. Williams	1981	13,323
131 0/8	19 1/8	19 1/8	14 4/8	4	4	Codington County	SD	Gerald J. Comes	1981	13,323
131 0/8	22 6/8	22 5/8	18 2/8	5	5	Grundy County	IL	Michael Marchio	1981	13,323
131 0/8	18 4/8	19 3/8	17 4/8	5	5	Berkeley County	SC	Hugh Gaskins	1982	13,323
131 0/8	22 3/8	22 3/8	20 6/8	5	5	Menominee County	MI	Theodore R. Olsen	1982	13,323
131 0/8	20 0/8	20 4/8	15 4/8	5	5	Hamilton County	IN	Larry E. Eversole	1982	13,323
131 0/8	18 3/8	17 1/8	14 4/8	6	6	Will County	IL	Richard D. Tenute	1982	13,323
131 0/8	23 6/8	21 6/8	18 0/8	4	4	Shelby County	MO	Rodney Gander	1984	13,323
131 0/8	20 6/8	21 5/8	19 0/8	5	5	Crawford County	MO	Ray Morris	1984	13,323
131 0/8	23 4/8	22 0/8	18 0/8	4	4	Ottawa County	MI	Steve Lamberts	1985	13,323
131 0/8	21 3/8	21 2/8	15 0/8	5	6	Buffalo County	WI	Gary K. Robinson	1985	13,323
131 0/8	23 1/8	23 5/8	17 0/8	5	5	Chase County	KS	Jerry Keller	1985	13,323
131 0/8	21 3/8	21 0/8	19 0/8	5	5	Dodge County	WI	Mike O'Brien	1986	13,323
131 0/8	22 1/8	22 5/8	18 4/8	4	4	Henderson County	KY	Edward Wayne Wallace	1986	13,323
131 0/8	21 6/8	21 5/8	15 6/8	5	5	Lehigh County	PA	Daniel R. Bachman	1987	13,323
131 0/8	24 6/8	23 5/8	19 0/8	4	4	Gloucester County	NJ	Ken Klodnicki	1987	13,323
131 0/8	21 7/8	21 7/8	19 3/8	6	6	Bayfield County	WI	Margie Millhausen	1987	13,323
131 0/8	21 4/8	22 3/8	16 4/8	5	5	Chemung County	NY	Chuck L. Reynolds	1988	13,323
131 0/8	24 1/8	23 7/8	17 2/8	5	6	Ross County	OH	Tony L. Wheaton	1988	13,323
131 0/8	19 6/8	19 3/8	16 0/8	5	5	Saline County	MO	John F. Bacon	1988	13,323
131 0/8	21 2/8	20 4/8	14 6/8	5	4	Cavalier County	ND	James Sondeland	1988	13,323
131 0/8	23 1/8	24 6/8	18 6/8	4	4	Edmonson County	KY	Kevin T. Ray	1989	13,323
131 0/8	18 3/8	18 6/8	15 0/8	5	5	Winnebago County	IL	Robert W. Shallenberger, Sr.	1989	13,323
131 0/8	21 6/8	22 1/8	18 4/8	5	6	Fayette County	WV	Michael D. King	1989	13,323
131 0/8	21 3/8	20 4/8	15 2/8	4	4	Kane County	IL	John Kloeckner	1989	13,323
131 0/8	22 4/8	25 6/8	18 6/8	7	7	Logan County	OH	David L. Katterheinrich	1989	13,323
131 0/8	22 5/8	23 7/8	17 6/8	4	5	Chautauqua County	KS	Nels Hoadley	1989	13,323
131 0/8	23 0/8	21 2/8	16 4/8	4	4	Beltrami County	MN	Rick Mikesh	1990	13,323
131 0/8	22 4/8	23 6/8	15 4/8	7	7	Monroe County	IL	Kevin Alexander	1990	13,323
131 0/8	22 0/8	21 1/8	18 2/8	4	4	Franklin County	IA	Nancy L. Kramer	1990	13,323
131 0/8	22 0/8	23 2/8	15 3/8	5	6	Russell County	AL	Dr. Daniel Morgan	1990	13,323
131 0/8	20 6/8	20 3/8	14 4/8	6	7	Pittsburg County	OK	Christopher Wolf	1990	13,323
131 0/8	22 6/8	22 6/8	18 0/8	5	4	Washington County	WI	Jeffrey Lutz	1990	13,323
131 0/8	20 1/8	19 6/8	14 0/8	5	5	Lee County	IL	David L. Munch	1990	13,323
131 0/8	21 3/8	20 7/8	17 6/8	5	6	Putnam County	IL	Richard Kingsley	1990	13,323
131 0/8	22 0/8	22 3/8	17 1/8	5	5	Meade County	SD	Ray Glover	1990	13,323
131 0/8	19 7/8	20 1/8	15 4/8	5	5	Athens County	OH	John Edman	1991	13,323
131 0/8	20 5/8	21 0/8	16 4/8	5	4	Crawford County	IA	Steve Reetz	1991	13,323
131 0/8	22 3/8	22 3/8	15 2/8	4	4	Clarke County	IA	Don Mealey	1991	13,323
131 0/8	22 1/8	19 5/8	18 2/8	4	5	Chippewa County	WI	John Baker	1991	13,323
131 0/8	22 2/8	21 5/8	16 4/8	5	5	Trempealeau County	WI	Dennis R. Suchla	1992	13,323
131 0/8	21 2/8	21 3/8	19 2/8	4	4	Ashland County	WI	Jason Davis	1992	13,323
131 0/8	22 7/8	21 6/8	17 4/8	4	4	Atchison County	MO	Patrick L. Athen	1992	13,323
131 0/8	21 2/8	21 2/8	17 2/8	5	5	Washington County	MN	Steven A. Jansen	1992	13,323
131 0/8	21 3/8	20 7/8	14 0/8	4	4	Yankton County	SD	Jeff Koster	1992	13,323
131 0/8	22 0/8	22 3/8	17 6/8	5	5	Buffalo County	WI	Chad Nordman	1992	13,323
131 0/8	23 1/8	24 0/8	18 0/8	4	5	Sherburne County	MN	Lee A. Hennen	1992	13,323
131 0/8	23 0/8	23 6/8	15 4/8	6	6	Grundy County	IL	Jay Truty	1993	13,323
131 0/8	22 1/8	22 1/8	17 2/8	4	4	Anoka County	MN	Dean Michael Capra	1993	13,323
131 0/8	19 4/8	19 6/8	15 6/8	6	5	Maverick County	TX	Dennis Cooke	1993	13,323
131 0/8	20 3/8	20 4/8	16 1/8	7	5	Douglas County	WI	Michael R. Lawler	1993	13,323
131 0/8	20 7/8	21 5/8	18 4/8	4	4	Clark County	IL	Kevin Boyer	1993	13,323

WHITETAIL DEER (TYPICAL ANTLERS)

Minimum Score 125 — Continued

SCORE	LENGTH OF MAIN BEAM R	LENGTH OF MAIN BEAM L	INSIDE SPREAD	NUMBER OF POINTS R	NUMBER OF POINTS L	AREA	STATE/PROVINCE	HUNTER'S NAME	DATE	RANK
131 0/8	20 3/8	20 3/8	18 4/8	5	6	Defiance County	OH	Steve Anders	1993	13,323
131 0/8	19 5/8	18 7/8	15 4/8	5	5	St. Marys County	MD	John Burke	1993	13,323
131 0/8	21 6/8	21 2/8	18 0/8	4	4	Warren County	IA	Mike Schaefer	1993	13,323
131 0/8	21 5/8	21 2/8	18 2/8	5	5	Whiteside County	IL	Trent A. McKenna	1993	13,323
131 0/8	20 6/8	21 2/8	19 6/8	5	5	Peoria County	IL	Dewey B. DeWeese	1993	13,323
131 0/8	22 0/8	21 3/8	16 6/8	4	4	Sandusky County	OH	Robert Baumer	1993	13,323
131 0/8	24 2/8	25 2/8	16 0/8	4	4	Kent County	MD	Donald Travis	1993	13,323
131 0/8	21 1/8	21 4/8	17 4/8	4	4	Grant County	SD	Myles Keller	1993	13,323
131 0/8	23 0/8	23 0/8	15 6/8	4	4	Maury County	TN	James E. Reagan, Jr.	1994	13,323
131 0/8	23 4/8	23 4/8	14 6/8	5	5	Chatham County	GA	Ed Tillman	1994	13,323
131 0/8	23 3/8	24 0/8	17 4/8	5	4	Sauk County	WI	Brian D. Olson	1994	13,323
131 0/8	24 7/8	25 0/8	18 6/8	5	5	Geauga County	OH	Troy Lavo	1994	13,323
131 0/8	21 5/8	21 6/8	17 4/8	4	4	Schuyler County	NY	Benjamin E. Bond	1994	13,323
131 0/8	21 2/8	21 0/8	16 6/8	6	5	Macoupin County	IL	William R. March	1994	13,323
131 0/8	22 0/8	21 3/8	18 2/8	4	5	Lake County	IL	Jamie Boyd	1994	13,323
131 0/8	22 2/8	23 3/8	15 6/8	6	6	Will County	IL	Larry D. Grisham	1994	13,323
131 0/8	20 4/8	20 0/8	16 2/8	5	5	Sanborn County	SD	Thad Baysinger	1994	13,323
131 0/8	21 6/8	21 4/8	15 4/8	5	5	Sauk County	WI	Mark Knudson	1994	13,323
131 0/8	19 3/8	19 4/8	18 3/8	5	6	Kossuth County	IA	Kevin L. Peterson	1994	13,323
131 0/8	24 7/8	23 6/8	16 4/8	5	5	Tompkins County	NY	Jim Finnerty	1994	13,323
131 0/8	25 7/8	24 7/8	19 7/8	5	5	Clark County	IL	Gerald Shaffner	1994	13,323
131 0/8	22 0/8	23 1/8	19 2/8	4	4	Benton County	IA	Daniel Dunkel	1994	13,323
131 0/8	21 1/8	20 6/8	15 6/8	5	4	Madison County	IA	Jim Costanzo	1994	13,323
131 0/8	21 7/8	20 3/8	16 4/8	5	5	Price County	WI	Joey Alba	1994	13,323
131 0/8	23 7/8	24 4/8	19 4/8	4	4	Charles City County	VA	Jason Flippo	1995	13,323
131 0/8	22 5/8	25 0/8	18 4/8	4	5	Orange County	NY	Brian Brockett	1995	13,323
131 0/8	19 0/8	19 0/8	19 0/8	7	5	Hand County	SD	Kevin R. Hvam	1995	13,323
131 0/8	24 2/8	25 1/8	15 3/8	5	7	Boone County	WV	Tom Green	1995	13,323
131 0/8	20 5/8	21 4/8	16 0/8	5	5	Barton County	KS	Matt Schartz	1995	13,323
131 0/8	24 3/8	23 4/8	17 0/8	5	6	Delaware County	OH	Brent J. Smith	1995	13,323
131 0/8	19 2/8	18 7/8	16 0/8	5	5	Olmsted County	MN	Gary Cummings	1995	13,323
131 0/8	22 6/8	20 5/8	22 2/8	4	4	Champaign County	IL	Mike Walden	1995	13,323
131 0/8	19 6/8	19 5/8	18 2/8	5	5	Hays County	TX	Bobby J. Jones	1995	13,323
131 0/8	23 3/8	23 7/8	16 0/8	4	5	Freeborn County	MN	David L. Christenson	1995	13,323
131 0/8	22 0/8	22 2/8	17 1/8	6	6	Waukesha County	WI	Todd Krempasky	1995	13,323
131 0/8	22 0/8	21 7/8	16 0/8	4	4	Craig County	OK	Kelly Dougherty	1996	13,323
131 0/8	22 0/8	21 2/8	15 0/8	5	5	Floyd County	VA	Chris Blessing	1996	13,323
131 0/8	20 6/8	21 0/8	16 6/8	5	5	Newton County	MO	Bill E. Brewer	1996	13,323
131 0/8	21 7/8	21 3/8	16 6/8	4	5	Wood County	WV	James P. Lambert	1996	13,323
131 0/8	19 4/8	19 1/8	15 4/8	5	5	Van Buren County	IA	Kenneth G. Geibel	1996	13,323
131 0/8	23 3/8	23 2/8	17 2/8	4	4	Dodge County	WI	Steven R. Schramm	1996	13,323
131 0/8	22 4/8	22 0/8	20 4/8	5	5	Hidalgo	MEX	Alvaro Palazuelos	1997	13,323
131 0/8	19 5/8	20 2/8	14 1/8	7	5	Columbia County	WI	Patrick J. Holzem	1997	13,323
131 0/8	21 1/8	20 7/8	17 2/8	5	5	Branch County	MI	Bryan C. James	1997	13,323
131 0/8	22 2/8	21 1/8	15 4/8	4	6	Bredenbury	SAS	Richard Boscher	1997	13,323
131 0/8	21 1/8	20 5/8	15 1/8	5	5	St. Joseph County	IN	Mark D. Kajzer	1997	13,323
131 0/8	22 4/8	22 1/8	16 4/8	4	4	Allegany County	NY	John J. Jaroszewski	1997	13,323
131 0/8	20 2/8	20 4/8	17 2/8	5	5	Vermilion County	IL	Russell Guthrie	1997	13,323
131 0/8	21 5/8	20 2/8	20 4/8	6	5	Allegheny County	PA	Lawrence E. Pine	1997	13,323
131 0/8	23 5/8	22 0/8	16 2/8	5	5	Webster County	KY	Steve Melton	1997	13,323
131 0/8	25 2/8	24 7/8	20 4/8	6	8	McHenry County	IL	Kip V. Miller	1997	13,323
131 0/8	22 2/8	22 1/8	17 4/8	4	4	Walworth County	WI	Joseph Sterle	1997	13,323
131 0/8	23 3/8	23 0/8	18 6/8	4	4	Walworth County	WI	Shawn Barkas	1997	13,323
131 0/8	21 4/8	21 2/8	16 4/8	5	5	Waukesha County	WI	Rebecca L. Jackson	1997	13,323
131 0/8	22 4/8	22 2/8	14 0/8	5	4	La Salle Parish	LA	Charles Smith	1998	13,323
131 0/8	21 4/8	21 6/8	15 0/8	5	5	St. Charles County	MO	Paul Hubert	1998	13,323
130 7/8	22 3/8	23 0/8	14 1/8	4	5	Sarpy County	NE	Ronald Beranek	1966	13,445
130 7/8	21 6/8	23 1/8	15 4/8	6	5	Trempealeau County	WI	David Cater	1968	13,445
130 7/8	23 2/8	24 1/8	15 6/8	4	5	Clayton County	IA	Bryan Sears	1969	13,445
130 7/8	21 4/8	21 4/8	17 1/8	6	5	Trempealeau County	WI	Myles Keller	1975	13,445
130 7/8	20 0/8	19 0/8	17 0/8	6	5	Bedford County	VA	Bill Hurley	1977	13,445
130 7/8	23 6/8	24 4/8	16 3/8	5	4	Sangamon County	IL	Keith Stigleman	1979	13,445
130 7/8	24 6/8	24 4/8	17 5/8	5	5	Coshocton County	OH	Gary L. Fischer	1979	13,445
130 7/8	22 3/8	22 6/8	15 7/8	5	5	Mercer County	NJ	William P. Krueger	1979	13,445
130 7/8	22 2/8	21 5/8	16 5/8	5	4	Chickasaw County	IA	James Harris	1980	13,445
130 7/8	24 5/8	24 4/8	18 1/8	4	4	Saginaw County	MI	Tom Perrin	1980	13,445
130 7/8	23 1/8	22 5/8	16 5/8	5	4	Waukesha County	WI	Mark Heffner	1981	13,445
130 7/8	23 2/8	25 2/8	19 7/8	5	5	Licking County	OH	Thomas Hughes	1981	13,445
130 7/8	20 5/8	21 4/8	15 5/8	5	5	Fillmore County	MN	Dr. Eugene T. Altiere	1983	13,445
130 7/8	19 5/8	20 0/8	14 5/8	5	5	Camden County	MO	Mike Hutton	1983	13,445
130 7/8	22 3/8	22 6/8	21 2/8	7	7	Muscatine County	IA	Charles D. Linder	1984	13,445
130 7/8	22 0/8	21 7/8	16 5/8	5	5	Morrison County	MN	Jerry Perske	1984	13,445
130 7/8	22 3/8	23 0/8	16 5/8	5	5	Vermilion County	IL	Robert G. Downing	1985	13,445
130 7/8	22 6/8	22 3/8	15 7/8	4	5	Dodge County	WI	Franklin Koch	1986	13,445
130 7/8	20 7/8	21 0/8	15 5/8	4	4	Columbia County	WI	Michael J. Goza	1987	13,445
130 7/8	20 2/8	19 1/8	17 3/8	5	6	Clay County	MN	Kyle Bauman	1987	13,445
130 7/8	20 2/8	19 7/8	17 3/8	6	5	Flathead County	MT	Michael Arneson	1987	13,445
130 7/8	19 0/8	20 0/8	20 3/8	5	5	Butler County	KS	Charles A. Genter, Jr.	1987	13,445

WHITETAIL DEER (TYPICAL ANTLERS)

Minimum Score 125 | Continued | 465

SCORE	LENGTH OF MAIN BEAM R / L	INSIDE SPREAD	NUMBER OF POINTS R / L	AREA	STATE/PROVINCE	HUNTER'S NAME	DATE	RANK
130 7/8	22 6/8 / 22 4/8	20 3/8	4 / 4	Calhoun County	MI	Mary L. Aldrich	1987	13,445
130 7/8	23 6/8 / 24 0/8	20 3/8	5 / 5	Pike County	IL	Conel H. Rogers, Jr.	1987	13,445
130 7/8	19 6/8 / 20 4/8	15 3/8	6 / 7	Brown County	SD	Joseph J. Rieger	1987	13,445
130 7/8	24 2/8 / 23 2/8	19 7/8	3 / 4	Columbia County	WI	Norbert Wipperfurth	1988	13,445
130 7/8	22 1/8 / 22 1/8	17 3/8	5 / 5	Richland County	IL	Tony Harmon	1988	13,445
130 7/8	22 6/8 / 22 3/8	17 1/8	6 / 7	Berks County	PA	Vincent P Essig	1989	13,445
130 7/8	20 6/8 / 20 1/8	13 7/8	6 / 5	Sumner County	TN	Darrell C. Hamlett	1989	13,445
130 7/8	21 1/8 / 21 2/8	13 5/8	4 / 4	Jackson County	IL	Gerald L. Loepker	1989	13,445
130 7/8	22 1/8 / 22 5/8	18 5/8	6 / 4	Lake County	IL	Steven Derkson	1989	13,445
130 7/8	19 3/8 / 20 1/8	14 5/8	5 / 5	Ohio County	WV	Gene Petri	1990	13,445
130 7/8	23 0/8 / 24 1/8	18 3/8	5 / 4	Charles County	MD	James Jenkins	1990	13,445
130 7/8	24 6/8 / 23 1/8	14 4/8	5 / 6	Polk County	IA	Mitch Hosler	1990	13,445
130 7/8	21 7/8 / 22 7/8	16 1/8	5 / 5	Sutton County	TX	Monty Shropshire	1990	13,445
130 7/8	22 4/8 / 21 0/8	16 5/8	5 / 5	Tippecanoe County	IN	Mike Shumard	1991	13,445
130 7/8	21 6/8 / 21 6/8	15 3/8	4 / 5	Waupaca County	WI	Dan Herson	1991	13,445
130 7/8	21 4/8 / 21 5/8	17 5/8	4 / 4	Otter Tail County	MN	Joseph G. Reeve, DDS	1991	13,445
130 7/8	19 1/8 / 19 4/8	16 1/8	5 / 5	Coal County	OK	Gary Bruhwiler	1991	13,445
130 7/8	21 0/8 / 21 1/8	16 3/8	4 / 4	Shawano County	WI	Dan Buss	1992	13,445
130 7/8	20 5/8 / 21 2/8	20 1/8	4 / 4	St. Georges de	QUE	Antonio Incollingo	1992	13,445
130 7/8	23 1/8 / 23 0/8	18 1/8	4 / 4	Fairfax County	VA	Frank L. Carper	1992	13,445
130 7/8	21 6/8 / 21 7/8	17 5/8	4 / 4	Crawford County	WI	Ronald S. Pulcine	1992	13,445
130 7/8	21 3/8 / 21 7/8	16 3/8	4 / 4	Stafford County	KS	Calvin D. Blue	1992	13,445
130 7/8	20 3/8 / 20 1/8	19 3/8	4 / 5	Logan County	CO	Frank Piacentino	1992	13,445
130 7/8	22 4/8 / 23 2/8	16 3/8	5 / 5	Genesee County	MI	Alan DeBuck	1993	13,445
130 7/8	22 4/8 / 22 2/8	17 1/8	6 / 5	Stearns County	MN	Harvey Neubauer	1993	13,445
130 7/8	22 3/8 / 21 0/8	15 5/8	5 / 5	Green County	WI	Michael J. Moe	1993	13,445
130 7/8	22 4/8 / 23 1/8	17 3/8	5 / 4	Anoka County	MN	Joe Wickman	1993	13,445
130 7/8	23 5/8 / 22 6/8	17 7/8	7 / 7	Pike County	OH	Harry R. Fite	1993	13,445
130 7/8	20 3/8 / 20 3/8	14 1/8	5 / 5	Monroe County	WI	Steven D. Pfaff	1993	13,445
130 7/8	20 2/8 / 20 6/8	14 7/8	5 / 5	Grant County	WI	Errol Schluter	1993	13,445
130 7/8	21 2/8 / 21 4/8	16 5/8	4 / 5	Barton County	MO	Carroll M. Graham	1993	13,445
130 7/8	21 4/8 / 19 4/8	15 5/8	5 / 5	Hughes County	SD	Jeffrey Peters	1993	13,445
130 7/8	20 1/8 / 21 1/8	17 3/8	4 / 4	Webb County	TX	Andy Milam	1993	13,445
130 7/8	20 4/8 / 22 4/8	16 0/8	7 / 6	Goodhue County	MN	Richard W. Rolls	1994	13,445
130 7/8	20 4/8 / 20 6/8	18 3/8	5 / 5	Indiana County	PA	James R. Haugh	1994	13,445
130 7/8	21 3/8 / 20 7/8	16 5/8	5 / 5	Shawano County	WI	Todd M. Vandenberg	1994	13,445
130 7/8	20 5/8 / 20 2/8	15 7/8	5 / 5	Carroll County	IL	Roman Cirignani	1994	13,445
130 7/8	22 4/8 / 22 4/8	19 5/8	5 / 5	Buffalo County	WI	Gary Risen	1994	13,445
130 7/8	25 4/8 / 26 0/8	14 3/8	6 / 4	Lincoln County	ONT	Darren W. Wilson	1994	13,445
130 7/8	19 5/8 / 19 1/8	14 7/8	5 / 5	Iowa County	WI	Jeffery S. Grady	1995	13,445
130 7/8	21 5/8 / 21 6/8	19 1/8	4 / 4	Warren County	IN	Tim Ringle	1995	13,445
130 7/8	20 5/8 / 20 5/8	16 5/8	5 / 5	Kerr County	TX	Tim S. Breter	1995	13,445
130 7/8	18 1/8 / 18 6/8	13 5/8	5 / 5	Ellis County	TX	David Plumlee	1995	13,445
130 7/8	23 7/8 / 22 6/8	18 3/8	5 / 5	Dakota County	MN	Larry Cooke	1995	13,445
130 7/8	23 2/8 / 21 7/8	18 3/8	5 / 4	Fulton County	IL	Dave Voorhees	1995	13,445
130 7/8	21 6/8 / 22 3/8	17 3/8	5 / 5	Menard County	IL	George E. Hypke	1995	13,445
130 7/8	20 7/8 / 22 4/8	16 5/8	5 / 5	Calumet County	WI	Terry "Pune" Eickert	1995	13,445
130 7/8	22 4/8 / 22 0/8	18 0/8	5 / 7	Grant County	WI	James W. Udelhoven	1996	13,445
130 7/8	23 0/8 / 22 5/8	17 7/8	5 / 6	Dubuque County	IA	John E. Gau	1996	13,445
130 7/8	21 4/8 / 21 3/8	15 5/8	4 / 4	Laurens County	GA	Moody Oliver, Jr.	1996	13,445
130 7/8	24 1/8 / 23 4/8	19 3/8	4 / 3	Westchester County	NY	Santo Macri	1996	13,445
130 7/8	22 3/8 / 22 0/8	16 3/8	6 / 6	Menominee County	MI	Gene Thoney	1996	13,445
130 7/8	19 4/8 / 20 0/8	15 7/8	4 / 4	Yuma County	CO	Rocky Chisholm	1996	13,445
130 7/8	22 5/8 / 24 3/8	17 5/8	5 / 5	Dimmit County	TX	Chuck Adams	1997	13,445
130 7/8	20 4/8 / 21 1/8	11 7/8	5 / 5	Adair County	KY	Jerry Collins	1997	13,445
130 7/8	21 4/8 / 21 1/8	18 5/8	5 / 5	Kewaunee County	WI	Dan Heath	1997	13,445
130 7/8	21 5/8 / 21 6/8	15 6/8	4 / 6	Trempealeau County	WI	Robert Boos	1997	13,445
130 7/8	22 4/8 / 23 0/8	18 1/8	7 / 6	Leavenworth County	KS	Mark Germonprez	1997	13,445
130 7/8	22 4/8 / 22 6/8	17 1/8	5 / 4	Dane County	WI	Fred Andree	1997	13,445
130 7/8	20 5/8 / 19 1/8	16 1/8	5 / 5	Calhoun County	MI	Richard L. Grosteffon, Jr.	1997	13,445
130 7/8	23 2/8 / 22 5/8	19 1/8	4 / 5	Kleberg County	TX	Wayne Peeples	1997	13,445
130 7/8	20 1/8 / 19 7/8	15 3/8	6 / 5	Minnehaha County	SD	Chris A. Benson	1997	13,445
130 7/8	24 3/8 / 24 2/8	24 6/8	4 / 4	Prince Georges County	MD	Eugene W. McDonald	1997	13,445
130 7/8	20 3/8 / 22 3/8	17 0/8	6 / 5	Sarpy County	NE	Marcus O. Dryak	1998	13,445
130 7/8	19 0/8 / 18 2/8	16 1/8	5 / 5	Crawford County	PA	Daniel R. Kritikos	1998	13,445
130 7/8	20 4/8 / 20 4/8	16 3/8	5 / 5	Burleigh County	ND	Greg A. Ehli	1998	13,445
130 6/8	23 2/8 / 21 1/8	14 2/8	5 / 4	Dewey County	SD	Bill Dunn	1969	13,533
130 6/8	20 1/8 / 20 4/8	15 0/8	7 / 5	Rock County	WI	Mark Butzler	1978	13,533
130 6/8	22 1/8 / 21 7/8	17 6/8	4 / 5	Alfalfa County	OK	Hal Utsler	1980	13,533
130 6/8	21 0/8 / 21 0/8	16 0/8	5 / 4	Calhoun County	MI	Harold Vander Horst	1980	13,533
130 6/8	23 4/8 / 21 7/8	19 6/8	5 / 4	Washington County	MN	Joe Kohler	1981	13,533
130 6/8	22 7/8 / 22 3/8	18 4/8	4 / 4	Sullivan County	IN	Ron L. Buchanan	1982	13,533
130 6/8	22 1/8 / 23 0/8	19 4/8	4 / 4	Hayes County	NE	Randy Griffiths	1983	13,533
130 6/8	22 5/8 / 23 7/8	17 4/8	4 / 5	Shawano County	WI	Patrick G. Shulze	1984	13,533
130 6/8	21 4/8 / 21 7/8	17 0/8	4 / 5	Clarion County	PA	Gary Alan Bullers	1984	13,533
130 6/8	21 6/8 / 22 0/8	17 6/8	5 / 4	Stephenson County	IL	Eric Zimmerman	1984	13,533
130 6/8	23 4/8 / 23 4/8	14 6/8	4 / 4	Owen County	IN	Lanse C. Hale	1985	13,533
130 6/8	23 6/8 / 23 4/8	16 6/8	4 / 4	Jefferson County	WI	Ernie Turpin	1985	13,533

WHITETAIL DEER (TYPICAL ANTLERS)

Minimum Score 125 — Continued

SCORE	LENGTH OF MAIN BEAM R	LENGTH OF MAIN BEAM L	INSIDE SPREAD	NUMBER OF POINTS R	NUMBER OF POINTS L	AREA	STATE/ PROVINCE	HUNTER'S NAME	DATE	RANK
130 6/8	20 1/8	20 1/8	14 4/8	5	5	Ravalli County	MT	Terry See	1985	13,533
130 6/8	24 0/8	23 4/8	19 0/8	6	5	Burleigh County	ND	Todd Hecker	1986	13,533
130 6/8	22 7/8	22 7/8	18 2/8	4	4	Lincoln County	WI	Dick Yaeger	1986	13,533
130 6/8	21 0/8	20 6/8	18 2/8	5	5	Shawnee County	KS	Ed Stadler	1986	13,533
130 6/8	20 6/8	21 5/8	16 6/8	5	5	Lake County	IL	Donald W. Hansen, Jr.	1986	13,533
130 6/8	21 2/8	23 5/8	16 5/8	6	4	Vermilion County	IL	Kenneth Gabehart	1987	13,533
130 6/8	20 2/8	22 0/8	16 6/8	4	4	Fairfield County	OH	Gary Lockwood	1987	13,533
130 6/8	20 4/8	19 6/8	15 2/8	5	6	Clayton County	IA	Arlan E. Kickbush	1987	13,533
130 6/8	22 7/8	22 0/8	18 1/8	5	6	Bent County	CO	J. Keith Chastain	1987	13,533
130 6/8	22 3/8	22 3/8	15 6/8	4	4	Houston County	MN	Todd Grissman	1988	13,533
130 6/8	21 2/8	19 5/8	16 2/8	5	5	Jones County	IA	Brian A. Jacque	1988	13,533
130 6/8	21 3/8	21 4/8	16 6/8	5	6	Fairfield County	OH	Mark McCafferty	1988	13,533
130 6/8	24 4/8	24 0/8	18 2/8	4	4	Price County	WI	William Leonard	1989	13,533
130 6/8	19 4/8	19 0/8	16 3/8	5	7	Coryell County	TX	Andy Cloud	1989	13,533
130 6/8	24 7/8	24 0/8	21 0/8	3	3	Emmet County	IA	Mike G. Cornwell	1989	13,533
130 6/8	22 7/8	23 4/8	16 0/8	6	6	Essex County	NJ	Michael Nigro	1989	13,533
130 6/8	21 3/8	20 7/8	15 4/8	4	4	Ramsey County	ND	Dale Risinger	1989	13,533
130 6/8	20 4/8	19 4/8	15 4/8	5	5	Lee County	IA	Glenn Wagner	1989	13,533
130 6/8	22 3/8	20 7/8	15 6/8	4	4	Clinton County	OH	Kevin Lee Wilson	1989	13,533
130 6/8	24 1/8	22 5/8	17 4/8	3	4	Loudoun County	VA	Kenneth M. Fleming	1989	13,533
130 6/8	23 6/8	23 3/8	17 2/8	5	5	La Porte County	IN	Charles L. Allen	1989	13,533
130 6/8	24 4/8	23 7/8	19 3/8	7	7	Phelps County	MO	Derek Carroll	1990	13,533
130 6/8	23 0/8	22 5/8	17 6/8	5	7	Jefferson County	OH	Ron McFarland	1990	13,533
130 6/8	23 3/8	22 1/8	17 7/8	7	7	Buffalo County	WI	Bill Peterson	1990	13,533
130 6/8	24 4/8	23 4/8	16 2/8	4	6	Jefferson County	OH	Lawrence Roush	1990	13,533
130 6/8	21 1/8	22 1/8	15 4/8	5	5	Scott County	KY	Michael R. Duncan	1990	13,533
130 6/8	22 3/8	21 5/8	16 4/8	5	4	Dooly County	GA	Curtis Kitchens, Jr.	1990	13,533
130 6/8	26 1/8	24 2/8	19 0/8	5	6	Dearborn County	IN	David R. "Skeeter" McKain	1990	13,533
130 6/8	25 0/8	24 3/8	19 0/8	4	5	Lake County	IL	James D. Maricle II	1991	13,533
130 6/8	21 0/8	20 7/8	18 4/8	5	5	Copiah County	MS	Chris C. Toney	1991	13,533
130 6/8	21 6/8	22 4/8	15 0/8	4	6	Gasconade County	MO	Mark Witte	1991	13,533
130 6/8	20 5/8	20 7/8	14 0/8	5	5	Trempealeau County	WI	Ed Vallee	1991	13,533
130 6/8	21 6/8	22 0/8	15 2/8	4	4	Switzerland County	IN	Joe Ruffin	1991	13,533
130 6/8	22 0/8	22 0/8	18 0/8	5	4	Missoula County	MT	Monty Moravec	1991	13,533
130 6/8	24 2/8	25 4/8	20 0/8	4	4	Belknap County	NH	Mike Amaral	1992	13,533
130 6/8	21 1/8	20 1/8	15 2/8	4	4	Spalding County	GA	Robert W. Cheatham, Jr.	1992	13,533
130 6/8	21 0/8	20 0/8	17 2/8	5	5	Walworth County	SD	David Duane Knecht	1992	13,533
130 6/8	23 3/8	22 7/8	18 0/8	5	5	Clark County	SD	Scott Lindgren	1992	13,533
130 6/8	23 4/8	23 4/8	15 6/8	5	5	Appanoose County	IA	Rod Sale	1992	13,533
130 6/8	22 2/8	23 2/8	19 0/8	4	4	Rock County	MN	Darrell Huiskes	1992	13,533
130 6/8	22 3/8	21 5/8	20 0/8	5	4	Kenedy County	TX	George Sheffer	1993	13,533
130 6/8	23 5/8	24 1/8	18 2/8	6	5	Montgomery County	MD	Jeff Kelley	1993	13,533
130 6/8	20 6/8	21 4/8	15 6/8	5	5	Erin Township	ONT	Bill Break	1993	13,533
130 6/8	23 2/8	22 6/8	19 5/8	6	5	Big Stone County	MN	Andy McPherson	1993	13,533
130 6/8	21 4/8	21 5/8	15 6/8	5	4	Monroe County	WI	Robert J. Murphy	1993	13,533
130 6/8	23 4/8	23 5/8	17 6/8	6	4	Ashtabula County	OH	Charles A. Watts	1993	13,533
130 6/8	22 2/8	22 7/8	16 6/8	6	5	Vernon County	MO	Matthew A. Vesci	1993	13,533
130 6/8	22 0/8	22 1/8	17 6/8	5	4	St. Croix County	WI	Vincent W. Voeltz	1993	13,533
130 6/8	23 2/8	22 2/8	17 6/8	4	5	Berrien County	MI	Michael Benke	1993	13,533
130 6/8	22 1/8	22 2/8	16 4/8	4	5	Baltimore County	MD	Lee Haile	1993	13,533
130 6/8	20 5/8	19 7/8	15 6/8	5	5	Somerset County	PA	Timothy R. Sowers	1993	13,533
130 6/8	22 6/8	22 7/8	19 0/8	4	4	Peoria County	IL	Todd D. David	1993	13,533
130 6/8	21 6/8	21 5/8	16 4/8	4	5	Sawyer County	WI	Shannon Underwood	1994	13,533
130 6/8	22 7/8	23 3/8	15 4/8	4	5	Rusk County	WI	Benjamin A. Baker	1994	13,533
130 6/8	22 2/8	22 0/8	16 4/8	5	5	Jasper County	IL	Willie Runnels	1994	13,533
130 6/8	22 2/8	22 1/8	16 6/8	4	5	Waukesha County	WI	Richard B. Bell	1994	13,533
130 6/8	22 0/8	21 3/8	15 7/8	5	4	Osborne County	KS	Blake Grabast	1994	13,533
130 6/8	25 0/8	25 4/8	17 1/8	4	7	Wayne County	IL	Matt West	1994	13,533
130 6/8	20 6/8	21 5/8	14 4/8	5	5	Columbia County	WI	Richard C. Harris	1994	13,533
130 6/8	25 1/8	24 1/8	16 0/8	4	4	Gloucester County	NJ	Jonathan Luciano	1994	13,533
130 6/8	22 5/8	21 2/8	17 0/8	4	4	Lincoln County	SD	Leon R. Nyreen	1994	13,533
130 6/8	21 7/8	20 7/8	14 7/8	6	5	Racine County	WI	Dean R. Janke	1995	13,533
130 6/8	21 7/8	21 5/8	13 6/8	4	4	Jasper County	MO	Steve Ruzic	1995	13,533
130 6/8	22 0/8	22 2/8	14 0/8	4	4	Meigs County	OH	Marlin L. Wolfe	1995	13,533
130 6/8	19 4/8	19 4/8	14 4/8	5	5	Rock County	WI	Dickie Hitchcock	1995	13,533
130 6/8	23 3/8	22 2/8	16 0/8	4	4	La Salle County	IL	Donald Greathouse	1995	13,533
130 6/8	20 4/8	21 0/8	13 0/8	6	6	Pike County	IL	Dan Janes	1995	13,533
130 6/8	21 0/8	21 5/8	14 6/8	5	4	Crittenden County	KY	Jeffrey Wayne Humphrey	1995	13,533
130 6/8	23 0/8	21 6/8	19 2/8	5	4	La Salle County	IL	David P. Meyer	1995	13,533
130 6/8	22 2/8	21 3/8	16 4/8	5	5	Livingston County	IL	Mike Roberts	1995	13,533
130 6/8	21 7/8	21 0/8	18 4/8	4	4	Westchester County	NY	Robert Rea	1995	13,533
130 6/8	22 2/8	21 3/8	16 4/8	4	5	Allamakee County	IA	Joe Lieb	1995	13,533
130 6/8	19 4/8	20 0/8	16 0/8	5	6	Hunterdon County	NJ	Jeff Farr	1995	13,533
130 6/8	19 1/8	21 1/8	18 4/8	5	5	La Salle County	TX	Jimmy R. Glass	1995	13,533
130 6/8	20 6/8	19 6/8	16 2/8	4	5	Dane County	WI	Jeffrey R. DeLaura	1996	13,533
130 6/8	21 0/8	20 2/8	15 0/8	7	5	Washington County	FL	Ty Padgett	1996	13,533
130 6/8	20 0/8	20 2/8	15 4/8	5	5	Washington County	NE	Nick Hauge	1996	13,533
130 6/8	22 5/8	22 5/8	18 4/8	5	5	Grundy County	IL	Ernest J. Brown	1996	13,533

WHITETAIL DEER (TYPICAL ANTLERS)

Minimum Score 125   Continued

SCORE	LENGTH OF MAIN BEAM R	LENGTH OF MAIN BEAM L	INSIDE SPREAD	NUMBER OF POINTS R	NUMBER OF POINTS L	AREA	STATE/ PROVINCE	HUNTER'S NAME	DATE	RANK
130 6/8	21 4/8	21 6/8	17 0/8	4	5	Marion County	IA	Randy Des Camps	1996	13,533
130 6/8	20 6/8	20 6/8	12 6/8	5	5	Webb County	TX	Norman E. Speer	1996	13,533
130 6/8	20 5/8	20 4/8	16 2/8	4	5	Oklahoma County	OK	Lonnie L. Ferris	1996	13,533
130 6/8	20 2/8	20 5/8	17 2/8	5	4	Prairie County	AR	Donald R. Orr	1996	13,533
130 6/8	17 1/8	22 1/8	15 6/8	5	7	Sanford	MAN	Kim Meger	1996	13,533
130 6/8	22 1/8	22 2/8	14 6/8	5	4	Jefferson County	WI	Jeremy Clark	1997	13,533
130 6/8	24 2/8	23 5/8	18 5/8	7	4	Menard County	IL	Ron Wadsworth	1997	13,533
130 6/8	21 1/8	20 4/8	18 4/8	5	5	Missoula County	MT	Lloyd E. Acker	1997	13,533
130 6/8	24 3/8	24 6/8	21 2/8	4	3	La Crosse County	WI	Brad Bond	1997	13,533
130 6/8	23 5/8	23 2/8	17 6/8	5	5	Schuyler County	IL	Chad Ingles	1997	13,533
130 6/8	24 6/8	23 6/8	21 3/8	5	7	Sherburne County	MN	Garnet Howard Hommes	1997	13,533
130 6/8	23 5/8	24 0/8	16 2/8	5	4	Prince Georges County	MD	Donald Tompkins	1997	13,533
130 6/8	23 0/8	22 0/8	15 4/8	5	5	Lucas County	IA	Eric Adams	1997	13,533
130 6/8	18 1/8	18 0/8	15 3/8	6	7	Throckmorton County	TX	Daniel Kimmel	1997	13,533
130 6/8	20 6/8	18 7/8	15 2/8	5	5	Cobb County	GA	Russell DeJohn	1997	13,533
130 6/8	20 2/8	21 7/8	14 6/8	5	5	McMullen County	TX	Paul W. Moss	1997	13,533
130 6/8	21 6/8	22 2/8	18 4/8	4	4	Anoka County	MN	Mark Gibbs	1997	13,533
130 6/8	25 2/8	24 4/8	21 2/8	3	3	Chippewa County	WI	Joseph Bourget	1998	13,533
130 6/8	24 1/8	23 4/8	18 4/8	5	4	New Haven County	CT	John C. Murphy, Jr.	1998	13,533
130 5/8	23 4/8	21 4/8	18 1/8	4	5	Roberts County	SD	Franic W. Sherer, Jr.	1965	13,642
130 5/8	21 5/8	21 3/8	16 3/8	4	4	Tuscola County	MI	Gary A. Bower	1974	13,642
130 5/8	20 7/8	21 4/8	14 5/8	5	6	Marquette County	WI	Tom Murphy	1974	13,642
130 5/8	20 6/8	20 3/8	18 1/8	5	4	Fairfield County	CT	Mark Hensel	1979	13,642
130 5/8	25 3/8	25 2/8	18 2/8	6	7	Lucas County	OH	Patrick Miller	1979	13,642
130 5/8	19 4/8	19 4/8	17 6/8	5	6	Throckmorton County	TX	Steve Fikes	1980	13,642
130 5/8	20 4/8	21 0/8	15 1/8	5	5	Montgomery County	AL	Rett Kelly	1980	13,642
130 5/8	21 4/8	22 0/8	17 2/8	4	6	Knox County	IL	Fred Miller	1981	13,642
130 5/8	21 7/8	21 5/8	18 1/8	4	4	Darlingford	MAN	Robert Hunt	1982	13,642
130 5/8	24 2/8	24 3/8	18 7/8	4	4	Orange County	NY	David Babcock	1983	13,642
130 5/8	23 4/8	23 0/8	18 5/8	4	4	Chisago County	MN	James Swing	1983	13,642
130 5/8	21 4/8	21 7/8	16 3/8	4	4	Graham County	KS	Russell Hull	1983	13,642
130 5/8	22 2/8	21 5/8	15 5/8	5	5	Frontier County	NE	Steve Cole	1984	13,642
130 5/8	22 1/8	23 1/8	18 6/8	4	5	Sarpy County	NE	Don L. Harnish	1984	13,642
130 5/8	23 0/8	22 2/8	16 1/8	4	4	Westchester County	NY	Richard Manchur	1984	13,642
130 5/8	22 2/8	21 6/8	15 1/8	4	4	Kiowa County	KS	Karl Ballard	1984	13,642
130 5/8	20 0/8	20 4/8	19 2/8	4	5	Sussex County	DE	Allen Rogers	1986	13,642
130 5/8	22 0/8	22 2/8	18 3/8	4	4	Putnam County	NY	Alan Rossignol	1986	13,642
130 5/8	23 3/8	23 6/8	22 0/8	6	7	Lake County	IL	John Schnider, Jr.	1986	13,642
130 5/8	22 2/8	22 6/8	16 5/8	5	4	Rock County	WI	Greg Curl	1986	13,642
130 5/8	21 4/8	22 3/8	18 1/8	4	5	Clermont County	OH	Ken Hart	1987	13,642
130 5/8	20 0/8	21 2/8	13 3/8	6	5	Pike County	IL	Richard Dewey	1987	13,642
130 5/8	24 3/8	22 6/8	16 7/8	6	5	Copiah County	MS	Victor A. Youngblood	1988	13,642
130 5/8	22 1/8	21 1/8	16 7/8	5	5	Wood County	WI	Dale Kleifgen	1988	13,642
130 5/8	21 7/8	21 5/8	19 5/8	5	6	Caldwell County	KY	Boyd Smith	1988	13,642
130 5/8	21 7/8	21 4/8	14 5/8	6	5	Jackson County	WI	Ronald Aide	1988	13,642
130 5/8	22 2/8	23 5/8	18 1/8	4	4	Crawford County	IL	William David Johnson	1988	13,642
130 5/8	22 4/8	22 6/8	16 2/8	4	7	Becker County	MN	Gordon Retka	1989	13,642
130 5/8	21 0/8	20 1/8	14 5/8	4	5	Tama County	IA	Monte Read	1989	13,642
130 5/8	22 5/8	23 0/8	18 5/8	6	4	Price County	WI	Jerry J. Bedor	1989	13,642
130 5/8	21 6/8	21 2/8	18 0/8	4	5	Erie County	OH	Mark Costilow	1989	13,642
130 5/8	21 7/8	22 3/8	14 1/8	4	4	Walker County	TX	Jimmy Glass	1989	13,642
130 5/8	21 0/8	22 5/8	17 3/8	6	5	Bayfield County	WI	Jim Johnson	1989	13,642
130 5/8	23 2/8	24 1/8	18 5/8	4	4	Westchester County	NY	Gary Mammana	1989	13,642
130 5/8	23 0/8	23 5/8	16 6/8	5	4	Florence County	WI	John "Muzzy" Isajiw	1990	13,642
130 5/8	20 0/8	20 0/8	16 3/8	5	5	Wicomico County	MD	James J. Samis	1990	13,642
130 5/8	22 0/8	23 4/8	18 2/8	5	6	Leflore County	MS	Pittman Edwards	1990	13,642
130 5/8	22 1/8	23 4/8	18 3/8	4	5	Logan County	AR	T. L. Weir	1990	13,642
130 5/8	21 4/8	20 3/8	14 3/8	4	4	Ottoe County	NE	Raymond Bliss	1990	13,642
130 5/8	24 7/8	23 7/8	20 1/8	4	4	Delaware County	IA	Travis P. Heyer	1990	13,642
130 5/8	22 5/8	22 4/8	16 3/8	4	5	Yankton County	SD	Tom Sonichsen	1990	13,642
130 5/8	26 4/8	21 5/8	21 1/8	4	4	Mercer County	MO	Robert Trefz, Jr.	1990	13,642
130 5/8	21 6/8	22 2/8	19 0/8	6	5	Potter County	PA	Francis J. Simmitt	1991	13,642
130 5/8	21 7/8	22 1/8	17 7/8	4	4	Greene County	PA	Dominick Barbetta	1991	13,642
130 5/8	23 0/8	22 6/8	15 3/8	4	4	Vigo County	IN	Joseph Spurgeon	1991	13,642
130 5/8	20 7/8	21 0/8	14 5/8	5	5	Marathon County	WI	Floyd D. Matteson	1991	13,642
130 5/8	20 1/8	20 5/8	14 7/8	5	5	Adair County	MO	Kelvin Koger	1991	13,642
130 5/8	22 6/8	23 1/8	17 1/8	4	4	Berkshire County	MA	Andrew W. Stephenson	1991	13,642
130 5/8	20 6/8	22 3/8	15 1/8	5	5	Florence County	WI	Dan T. Leahy	1991	13,642
130 5/8	22 3/8	22 1/8	16 1/8	4	5	Wabaunsee County	KS	Kevin Townsend	1991	13,642
130 5/8	23 7/8	24 0/8	18 7/8	4	4	Jefferson County	OH	Michael O. Cottis	1991	13,642
130 5/8	23 0/8	23 2/8	19 7/8	5	4	Lincoln County	WI	Jeffrey H. Badeau	1992	13,642
130 5/8	23 1/8	22 5/8	18 3/8	4	4	Carroll County	MD	Tom W. Corbin	1992	13,642
130 5/8	19 5/8	20 2/8	15 3/8	5	5	Marshall County	OK	Kody Lockhart	1992	13,642
130 5/8	21 2/8	21 0/8	16 5/8	4	4	Richland County	ND	Larry Johnson	1992	13,642
130 5/8	23 0/8	22 3/8	23 2/8	5	7	Kerr County	TX	Chuck Adams	1992	13,642
130 5/8	20 2/8	20 1/8	14 1/8	5	5	Adams County	WI	Arthur L. Stormoen	1993	13,642
130 5/8	19 5/8	20 0/8	16 3/8	6	5	Trempealeau County	WI	Chad Losinski	1993	13,642
130 5/8	22 4/8	22 5/8	16 1/8	4	4	Bond County	IL	David Munie	1993	13,642

WHITETAIL DEER (TYPICAL ANTLERS)

Minimum Score 125 — Continued

SCORE	LENGTH OF MAIN BEAM R / L	INSIDE SPREAD	NUMBER OF POINTS R / L	AREA	STATE/ PROVINCE	HUNTER'S NAME	DATE	RANK
130 5/8	21 1/8 / 23 0/8	17 6/8	7 / 7	Hudson Bay	SAS	Ted K. Jaycox	1993	13,642
130 5/8	21 0/8 / 20 6/8	15 1/8	5 / 4	Burnett County	WI	Bob Thornley	1994	13,642
130 5/8	21 6/8 / 21 7/8	15 3/8	5 / 5	Rusk County	WI	Joshua Prohaska	1994	13,642
130 5/8	23 6/8 / 24 4/8	16 2/8	5 / 4	Vernon County	MO	Aaron M. Diehl	1994	13,642
130 5/8	24 4/8 / 23 6/8	16 1/8	4 / 4	Trempealeau County	WI	Daniel R. Wall	1994	13,642
130 5/8	23 1/8 / 22 3/8	17 6/8	5 / 4	Copiah County	MS	Garon LeBlanc	1994	13,642
130 5/8	23 7/8 / 20 7/8	15 1/8	7 / 6	Taylor County	IA	David L. Lundy	1994	13,642
130 5/8	20 5/8 / 20 4/8	13 7/8	5 / 5	Marathon County	WI	Duane L. Karau	1994	13,642
130 5/8	19 4/8 / 20 1/8	16 3/8	4 / 4	Valley County	MT	Ivan J. Muzljakovich	1994	13,642
130 5/8	22 0/8 / 22 4/8	15 1/8	5 / 5	Mercer County	OH	Nathan Wenning	1994	13,642
130 5/8	23 2/8 / 22 6/8	15 0/8	6 / 5	McPherson County	KS	Jack L. Nosecchi	1994	13,642
130 5/8	22 1/8 / 22 5/8	18 3/8	5 / 5	San Patricio County	TX	James Kerr Crain III	1994	13,642
130 5/8	22 7/8 / 22 5/8	17 1/8	4 / 4	Merrimack County	NH	Robert Dupuis	1994	13,642
130 5/8	22 1/8 / 21 5/8	17 1/8	4 / 4	Langlade County	WI	David A. Nelson	1994	13,642
130 5/8	21 7/8 / 22 2/8	18 7/8	4 / 4	Marathon County	WI	Randy Stank	1995	13,642
130 5/8	22 4/8 / 20 3/8	18 7/8	5 / 5	Orange County	NC	Jesse J. Mangol	1995	13,642
130 5/8	18 2/8 / 21 0/8	16 5/8	4 / 4	Whiteside County	IL	Abraham John Wuebben	1995	13,642
130 5/8	20 7/8 / 21 1/8	18 7/8	5 / 5	Washington County	MN	Mark P. Haan	1995	13,642
130 5/8	20 1/8 / 19 6/8	16 7/8	5 / 5	Waupaca County	WI	Rob Polley	1995	13,642
130 5/8	21 0/8 / 22 0/8	15 6/8	6 / 6	Labette County	KS	Victor L. Holloway	1995	13,642
130 5/8	22 1/8 / 23 2/8	16 1/8	4 / 5	Pike County	IL	Kevin Koch	1995	13,642
130 5/8	21 4/8 / 20 1/8	18 5/8	5 / 5	Waupaca County	WI	Dave Justmann	1995	13,642
130 5/8	21 5/8 / 22 3/8	17 3/8	5 / 5	Berks County	PA	Samuel C. Nunemaker	1995	13,642
130 5/8	22 1/8 / 23 2/8	18 7/8	5 / 4	Dane County	WI	Kurt Smith	1996	13,642
130 5/8	21 4/8 / 21 4/8	16 7/8	5 / 5	Appling County	GA	Michael Lewandowski	1996	13,642
130 5/8	24 7/8 / 24 3/8	19 3/8	4 / 4	Humphreys County	TN	Clarence R. Maness	1996	13,642
130 5/8	23 3/8 / 23 2/8	17 3/8	4 / 4	McHenry County	IL	Matt Schuster	1996	13,642
130 5/8	23 4/8 / 22 7/8	14 7/8	5 / 5	McHenry County	IL	Bill Kubik	1996	13,642
130 5/8	22 0/8 / 22 2/8	17 1/8	5 / 5	Morgan County	IN	Nathan K. Lowder	1996	13,642
130 5/8	23 7/8 / 23 1/8	18 3/8	5 / 5	Monroe County	WI	Chris R. Utke	1996	13,642
130 5/8	22 0/8 / 21 7/8	18 1/8	4 / 5	Sarpy County	NE	Tony Rono	1996	13,642
130 5/8	24 0/8 / 24 2/8	19 1/8	4 / 6	Kane County	IL	Bill Yoakum	1996	13,642
130 5/8	19 6/8 / 20 0/8	13 5/8	7 / 5	Kenedy County	TX	Roderick E. Nutter	1997	13,642
130 5/8	22 5/8 / 22 4/8	17 7/8	4 / 4	La Salle County	TX	Brad C. Bryant	1997	13,642
130 5/8	20 1/8 / 19 7/8	19 3/8	5 / 5	Sharp County	AR	Witt Stephens, Jr.	1997	13,642
130 5/8	21 6/8 / 21 7/8	20 1/8	5 / 5	Lincoln County	SD	Leon R. Nyreen	1997	13,642
130 5/8	22 6/8 / 21 2/8	16 7/8	4 / 4	Greene County	IN	Jerry E. Sturgeon	1997	13,642
130 5/8	24 4/8 / 24 4/8	15 7/8	4 / 5	Berkshire County	MA	Ray Gagnon	1997	13,642
130 5/8	23 7/8 / 24 3/8	17 6/8	5 / 4	Union County	SD	Craig A. Zoss	1997	13,642
130 5/8	21 7/8 / 21 2/8	17 5/8	5 / 5	Shawano County	WI	Boyd L. Dallmann	1997	13,642
130 5/8	21 6/8 / 21 2/8	15 7/8	5 / 6	Iowa County	WI	Bob Hopkins	1997	13,642
130 5/8	21 3/8 / 21 7/8	17 1/8	4 / 5	Centre County	PA	John D. Smith	1997	13,642
130 5/8	23 2/8 / 22 0/8	14 7/8	4 / 5	Crawford County	MO	Dennis Goldacker	1997	13,642
130 4/8	21 2/8 / 21 3/8	17 0/8	5 / 5	Allegan County	MI	Jack Yaeger	1942	13,744
130 4/8	21 0/8 / 20 4/8	18 2/8	5 / 5	Putnam County	WV	Dan Lloyd	1966	13,744
130 4/8	23 4/8 / 22 7/8	19 2/8	5 / 5	Berrien County	MI	Thomas L. Bommersbach	1978	13,744
130 4/8	23 3/8 / 21 1/8	17 6/8	5 / 5	Marquette County	WI	Gary J. Craig	1978	13,744
130 4/8	23 2/8 / 23 1/8	16 0/8	4 / 4	Harvey County	KS	Bob Stroble	1979	13,744
130 4/8	20 5/8 / 20 6/8	15 0/8	5 / 5	Louisa County	IA	Roger Gipple	1979	13,744
130 4/8	23 5/8 / 22 0/8	13 4/8	5 / 4	Cleveland County	OK	Tom Quinton	1979	13,744
130 4/8	23 5/8 / 22 7/8	18 2/8	6 / 5	Pittsburg County	OK	Bill Starry	1981	13,744
130 4/8	21 0/8 / 20 4/8	15 6/8	5 / 5	Clay County	NE	Rick Sadd	1981	13,744
130 4/8	21 5/8 / 22 2/8	14 6/8	5 / 5	Rusk County	TX	Dr. David Norman	1982	13,744
130 4/8	22 3/8 / 22 1/8	16 0/8	4 / 5	Riley County	KS	Dennis Peterson	1982	13,744
130 4/8	21 7/8 / 21 7/8	18 2/8	6 / 6	Knox County	OH	Mark E. Bretz	1983	13,744
130 4/8	22 4/8 / 22 2/8	17 0/8	4 / 4	Russell County	AL	Owen Veasey	1983	13,744
130 4/8	22 0/8 / 20 7/8	14 6/8	5 / 5	Wood County	WV	William G. Smith	1983	13,744
130 4/8	22 7/8 / 22 5/8	19 6/8	4 / 4	Hawkins County	TN	Johnny Ford	1985	13,744
130 4/8	22 6/8 / 22 7/8	17 2/8	4 / 4	Butler County	IA	Dave Bright	1985	13,744
130 4/8	20 2/8 / 20 2/8	16 3/8	7 / 5	Jefferson County	NE	Jerry W. Zabokrtsky	1985	13,744
130 4/8	23 5/8 / 23 3/8	18 0/8	4 / 4	Ionia County	MI	David L. Cooper	1986	13,744
130 4/8	21 2/8 / 21 0/8	17 1/8	6 / 5	Eaton County	MI	Westley J. Whitinger	1986	13,744
130 4/8	22 6/8 / 22 3/8	18 0/8	5 / 5	Passaic County	NJ	John G. Tucker	1987	13,744
130 4/8	21 2/8 / 21 6/8	18 0/8	8 / 6	Allen County	IN	Curtis P. Butler	1987	13,744
130 4/8	19 6/8 / 20 6/8	15 5/8	8 / 5	McHenry County	IL	Martin A. Pingel	1987	13,744
130 4/8	21 7/8 / 21 5/8	16 4/8	4 / 4	Okanogan County	WA	D. Kirk Sapp	1987	13,744
130 4/8	18 1/8 / 19 7/8	16 2/8	5 / 5	Bandera County	TX	Wayne Wilson	1988	13,744
130 4/8	22 4/8 / 23 5/8	13 7/8	5 / 5	Carroll County	OH	John M. Shockey	1988	13,744
130 4/8	22 2/8 / 22 6/8	18 4/8	4 / 4	Westchester County	NY	John Frevele	1988	13,744
130 4/8	21 0/8 / 21 2/8	16 2/8	4 / 4	Hocking County	OH	Martin R. Lohn	1988	13,744
130 4/8	21 6/8 / 21 0/8	15 7/8	4 / 5	Osage County	OK	Joe Admire	1988	13,744
130 4/8	22 5/8 / 21 4/8	16 6/8	4 / 4	Trempealeau County	WI	Richard J. Baures	1988	13,744
130 4/8	23 1/8 / 24 5/8	16 5/8	4 / 5	Kent County	MD	Ralph I Miller II	1989	13,744
130 4/8	22 4/8 / 23 5/8	19 4/8	5 / 5	Washington County	OH	Steven R. Davis	1989	13,744
130 4/8	21 7/8 / 22 5/8	17 6/8	4 / 4	Kent County	MI	Alan Ray Swendrowski	1989	13,744
130 4/8	22 0/8 / 21 4/8	14 5/8	12 / 8	Washington County	WI	Dave Klermund	1990	13,744
130 4/8	23 0/8 / 25 1/8	17 6/8	5 / 5	Crawford County	IL	Terry Sorgenfrey	1990	13,744
130 4/8	22 0/8 / 21 4/8	16 2/8	4 / 4	Waupaca County	WI	Randy Roland	1990	13,744

WHITETAIL DEER (TYPICAL ANTLERS)

Minimum Score 125

SCORE	LENGTH OF MAIN BEAM R	LENGTH OF MAIN BEAM L	INSIDE SPREAD	NUMBER OF POINTS R	NUMBER OF POINTS L	AREA	STATE/PROVINCE	HUNTER'S NAME	DATE	RANK
130 4/8	23 2/8	22 3/8	16 5/8	5	4	Rock County	MN	Al Kuehl	1990	13,744
130 4/8	21 0/8	20 7/8	18 7/8	6	6	Hughes County	OK	Tom Cartwright	1990	13,744
130 4/8	22 1/8	23 2/8	17 2/8	4	5	Logan County	WV	Kenneth Wilson	1990	13,744
130 4/8	23 5/8	22 2/8	18 1/8	5	6	Putnam County	IN	Gary Carmack	1990	13,744
130 4/8	20 6/8	22 3/8	16 0/8	6	6	Shawnee County	KS	Steve McPeek	1990	13,744
130 4/8	24 1/8	24 2/8	17 3/8	5	4	Westchester County	NY	Jerry Decarlo	1990	13,744
130 4/8	25 4/8	25 1/8	18 6/8	4	4	Madison County	IA	John Garrison	1990	13,744
130 4/8	23 6/8	23 0/8	17 4/8	4	4	Dunn County	WI	Dave Lieffort	1990	13,744
130 4/8	20 1/8	20 2/8	17 2/8	4	4	E. Feliciana Parish	LA	C. A. "Rick" Vallet	1990	13,744
130 4/8	23 2/8	23 7/8	21 4/8	4	5	Ramsey County	MN	Louie Peltier	1990	13,744
130 4/8	22 2/8	22 5/8	20 4/8	5	5	Dent County	MO	Jim Lewis	1990	13,744
130 4/8	20 7/8	19 6/8	16 4/8	7	6	Green County	WI	Tod A. Bean	1991	13,744
130 4/8	23 4/8	23 2/8	17 4/8	5	5	Alcona County	MI	Jim Thompson	1991	13,744
130 4/8	19 3/8	20 1/8	14 6/8	5	5	Pierce County	WI	Gary Seidling	1991	13,744
130 4/8	25 3/8	25 0/8	18 0/8	4	6	Woodford County	IL	Donald T. Bishop	1991	13,744
130 4/8	22 0/8	21 6/8	19 2/8	6	7	Missoula County	MT	Jim Bradford	1991	13,744
130 4/8	20 4/8	20 7/8	13 5/8	6	7	Chittick Lake	SAS	Clarence Bowers, Jr.	1991	13,744
130 4/8	23 3/8	25 0/8	16 6/8	4	4	Westchester County	NY	Thomas Iezzi	1991	13,744
130 4/8	21 0/8	20 7/8	15 7/8	4	5	Northumberland County	PA	Larry Young	1992	13,744
130 4/8	20 5/8	21 0/8	15 4/8	5	5	Jefferson County	WI	John Streich	1992	13,744
130 4/8	22 1/8	22 7/8	16 5/8	5	8	Harvey County	KS	Kyle Janzen	1992	13,744
130 4/8	24 5/8	24 3/8	16 4/8	4	4	Coahoma County	MS	Charles "Buck" Neely	1992	13,744
130 4/8	20 4/8	19 6/8	16 4/8	6	5	San Patricio County	TX	Domingo Lopez	1992	13,744
130 4/8	22 1/8	21 6/8	19 7/8	6	5	Columbia County	PA	Jim Pollard	1993	13,744
130 4/8	23 7/8	23 3/8	14 4/8	4	4	Newton County	MO	Timothy A. Bickett	1993	13,744
130 4/8	23 7/8	23 1/8	19 7/8	6	6	Buffalo County	WI	Mike Noll	1993	13,744
130 4/8	20 2/8	20 5/8	17 6/8	4	4	Chautauqua County	KS	Ben Pennington	1993	13,744
130 4/8	23 3/8	22 7/8	17 2/8	4	5	Essex County	NJ	Joe Good	1993	13,744
130 4/8	21 6/8	23 2/8	17 2/8	4	5	Anoka County	MN	Bob Ross	1993	13,744
130 4/8	21 4/8	21 3/8	19 0/8	4	4	La Salle County	TX	Jimmy R. Glass	1993	13,744
130 4/8	19 4/8	20 0/8	14 4/8	5	5	Buffalo County	WI	Mark Koger	1994	13,744
130 4/8	21 0/8	20 5/8	15 6/8	5	5	Switzerland County	IN	Herman C. Price, Jr.	1994	13,744
130 4/8	19 6/8	20 3/8	15 4/8	5	5	Jackson County	IN	Travis Sweany	1994	13,744
130 4/8	21 2/8	21 3/8	15 6/8	5	6	Franklin County	IN	Tony Willwerth	1994	13,744
130 4/8	19 2/8	19 6/8	13 5/8	6	6	Miller County	MO	Tony Luttrell	1994	13,744
130 4/8	23 5/8	23 1/8	18 4/8	4	4	Ashland County	WI	Daniel Bodinger	1994	13,744
130 4/8	21 7/8	21 7/8	14 4/8	4	4	Madison County	AR	Donald L. Randolph	1995	13,744
130 4/8	22 7/8	22 4/8	18 2/8	4	4	McDonald County	MO	Vernie Broyles	1995	13,744
130 4/8	22 5/8	23 3/8	14 2/8	6	6	Bedford County	VA	David H. Horne	1995	13,744
130 4/8	21 1/8	22 5/8	17 2/8	4	4	Hardin County	IL	Dennis A. Pop	1995	13,744
130 4/8	24 1/8	23 3/8	19 2/8	4	4	Fairfield County	CT	Fred DeFinis	1995	13,744
130 4/8	24 6/8	25 0/8	17 6/8	4	5	Hunterdon County	NJ	Gregory White	1995	13,744
130 4/8	20 3/8	22 6/8	20 0/8	5	5	Osage County	OK	Rick Gilley	1995	13,744
130 4/8	21 5/8	22 2/8	17 0/8	4	4	Clinton County	MI	Michelle Lynn Reynolds	1995	13,744
130 4/8	23 0/8	22 1/8	16 4/8	4	5	Jefferson County	IA	Steve Stoltz	1995	13,744
130 4/8	24 0/8	22 6/8	14 5/8	5	7	Uvalde County	TX	Monty McGrade	1995	13,744
130 4/8	22 5/8	21 7/8	18 2/8	5	5	Shannon County	MO	Garry Bland	1996	13,744
130 4/8	24 0/8	22 0/8	19 1/8	5	5	Gallatin County	MT	Bob Morton	1996	13,744
130 4/8	23 0/8	23 3/8	17 6/8	4	4	McLean County	IL	John Landrus	1996	13,744
130 4/8	24 1/8	23 4/8	18 6/8	4	4	Marquette County	WI	John W. Steuck	1996	13,744
130 4/8	20 2/8	20 1/8	15 2/8	5	5	Chippewa County	MI	Terry Lee Smith	1996	13,744
130 4/8	22 6/8	22 5/8	18 2/8	5	4	Barron County	WI	Ricky R. Church	1996	13,744
130 4/8	22 0/8	20 7/8	18 5/8	6	6	Lee County	IL	Craig B. Walter	1996	13,744
130 4/8	20 2/8	19 2/8	17 1/8	6	6	Putnam County	WV	Chad Napier	1996	13,744
130 4/8	24 1/8	23 7/8	20 2/8	4	5	Allamakee County	IA	Earl Lowell Goodman	1996	13,744
130 4/8	22 1/8	21 4/8	17 0/8	5	4	Clinton County	IL	Ryan Hummert	1996	13,744
130 4/8	22 4/8	23 4/8	20 5/8	5	5	Ozaukee County	WI	Ronald W. Frank	1996	13,744
130 4/8	20 6/8	20 1/8	16 0/8	5	5	Wapello County	IA	Arnold E. Vest	1997	13,744
130 4/8	22 0/8	21 4/8	16 4/8	4	4	Iowa County	WI	ArLen White	1997	13,744
130 4/8	20 5/8	20 5/8	17 5/8	7	6	Hennepin County	MN	Dennis Nelsen	1997	13,744
130 4/8	20 1/8	20 1/8	13 0/8	5	5	Issaquena County	MS	Richard Taylor	1997	13,744
130 4/8	21 6/8	22 4/8	20 0/8	5	4	Allegheny County	PA	John T. Bartram II	1997	13,744
130 4/8	23 0/8	23 3/8	17 2/8	4	4	Franklin County	PA	Justin Clark	1997	13,744
130 4/8	21 4/8	21 0/8	17 2/8	5	6	Dickinson County	IA	Richard E. Howard, Jr.	1997	13,744
130 4/8	19 4/8	19 5/8	16 6/8	5	5	Gage County	NE	Dale T. Thornburg	1997	13,744
130 4/8	23 3/8	23 3/8	19 4/8	5	4	Montcalm County	MI	Len Washburn	1998	13,744
130 4/8	21 1/8	20 4/8	16 0/8	5	5	Livingston County	NY	Robert T. Leslie	1998	13,744
130 4/8	23 5/8	23 6/8	17 4/8	5	5	Washington County	WI	James Van Beek	1998	13,744
130 3/8	21 2/8	20 6/8	14 1/8	5	5	Jefferson Prov. Grnds.	IN	Larry R. Smith	1966	13,847
130 3/8	18 6/8	17 3/8	15 4/8	5	6	Douglas County	NE	John Prentis	1978	13,847
130 3/8	20 1/8	20 4/8	15 3/8	6	5	Otter Tail County	MN	Dick Schmidt	1978	13,847
130 3/8	23 6/8	23 1/8	17 7/8	7	6	Adams County	IL	David Shupe	1981	13,847
130 3/8	20 2/8	20 4/8	17 7/8	5	5	Monroe County	WI	Tony P. Snow	1982	13,847
130 3/8	21 1/8	21 5/8	16 5/8	5	5	Polk County	WI	Russell Lee Johnson	1982	13,847
130 3/8	23 4/8	22 4/8	17 1/8	4	5	Garfield County	MT	Mitch Kottas	1983	13,847
130 3/8	21 5/8	21 1/8	13 5/8	5	6	Lawrence County	MO	Jim Botts	1983	13,847
130 3/8	21 2/8	21 7/8	16 7/8	4	4	Morrison County	MN	Arne Mickelberg	1983	13,847
130 3/8	22 0/8	22 0/8	18 3/8	9	8	Brown County	KS	Gerry Hertzel	1983	13,847

WHITETAIL DEER (TYPICAL ANTLERS)

Minimum Score 125 — Continued

SCORE	LENGTH OF MAIN BEAM R	LENGTH OF MAIN BEAM L	INSIDE SPREAD	NUMBER OF POINTS R	NUMBER OF POINTS L	AREA	STATE/ PROVINCE	HUNTER'S NAME	DATE	RANK
130 3/8	21 3/8	22 0/8	17 3/8	5	5	Ellsworth County	KS	Jeff Dohrman	1983	13,847
130 3/8	19 6/8	19 3/8	14 3/8	5	5	Buffalo County	WI	Roger Harm	1984	13,847
130 3/8	21 4/8	22 0/8	17 1/8	5	4	Allegheny County	PA	Richard J. Blauser	1984	13,847
130 3/8	22 5/8	22 2/8	15 1/8	5	5	Becker County	MN	David Schiller	1985	13,847
130 3/8	25 1/8	23 0/8	21 0/8	4	5	Buffalo County	WI	Jeff Joslin	1985	13,847
130 3/8	24 2/8	24 0/8	20 5/8	5	4	Middlesex County	CT	James Boczar	1985	13,847
130 3/8	21 7/8	21 6/8	16 5/8	4	4	Coles County	IL	John Gossett	1986	13,847
130 3/8	23 2/8	23 1/8	15 5/8	4	4	Sussex County	NJ	Andy Chappell	1986	13,847
130 3/8	21 2/8	22 0/8	16 3/8	5	5	Goodhue County	MN	Paul Hauck	1987	13,847
130 3/8	20 2/8	20 1/8	13 1/8	6	6	Ripley County	IN	Steve A. Allen	1987	13,847
130 3/8	21 4/8	22 6/8	20 2/8	7	5	Van Buren County	MI	Al Rybarski	1987	13,847
130 3/8	20 6/8	20 7/8	15 2/8	5	6	Crawford County	WI	Robert Hamann	1987	13,847
130 3/8	19 1/8	19 6/8	13 2/8	6	5	Buffalo County	WI	Jeff R. Owen	1987	13,847
130 3/8	22 3/8	22 1/8	15 4/8	6	5	Racine County	WI	Steve Holterman	1988	13,847
130 3/8	21 7/8	22 0/8	17 7/8	6	5	McHenry County	IL	Richard Sabat	1988	13,847
130 3/8	20 1/8	20 2/8	17 7/8	5	5	Brown County	SD	John Wanous	1988	13,847
130 3/8	21 7/8	23 4/8	19 5/8	5	5	Franklin County	KS	William A. Ferris	1988	13,847
130 3/8	22 2/8	22 2/8	15 1/8	4	5	Springbank Creek	ALB	David R Coupland	1989	13,847
130 3/8	20 3/8	21 5/8	15 3/8	5	5	Cherry County	NE	Randy D. Loken	1989	13,847
130 3/8	22 1/8	22 1/8	16 1/8	4	4	Mercer County	MO	Norman Folkerts	1989	13,847
130 3/8	23 0/8	22 0/8	16 5/8	5	4	Champaign County	IL	Kenny During	1989	13,847
130 3/8	25 3/8	24 1/8	18 1/8	4	4	Issaquena County	MS	Bobby R. Woods	1989	13,847
130 3/8	23 2/8	23 0/8	12 5/8	4	4	Coosa County	AL	Harry W. Strength	1989	13,847
130 3/8	22 4/8	23 2/8	22 7/8	6	4	Calgary	ALB	Richard Belbin	1990	13,847
130 3/8	21 0/8	21 1/8	14 5/8	6	6	Clay County	NE	Lonnie Goble	1990	13,847
130 3/8	23 6/8	25 1/8	16 2/8	4	5	Greene County	OH	Mike Walsh	1990	13,847
130 3/8	21 7/8	21 4/8	17 7/8	6	5	Wagoner County	OK	David M. Harris	1990	13,847
130 3/8	19 6/8	20 0/8	16 0/8	5	4	Dukes County	MA	David J. Medeiros	1990	13,847
130 3/8	24 6/8	24 2/8	20 7/8	4	4	Union County	IL	Eric P. Emmons	1990	13,847
130 3/8	23 4/8	22 7/8	18 3/8	4	5	Brooks County	TX	Larry Barton	1990	13,847
130 3/8	20 7/8	20 1/8	15 5/8	5	5	Chariton County	MO	Ben W. Gibson	1990	13,847
130 3/8	20 7/8	21 7/8	17 4/8	6	6	Belmont County	OH	Larry Michael	1991	13,847
130 3/8	22 3/8	22 0/8	16 1/8	4	5	St. Croix County	WI	Bruce Hatch	1991	13,847
130 3/8	21 5/8	21 5/8	18 1/8	5	6	Trempealeau County	WI	Brian Sylla	1991	13,847
130 3/8	24 6/8	24 6/8	16 2/8	6	4	Douglas County	NE	Brad Lewis	1991	13,847
130 3/8	23 7/8	24 0/8	19 4/8	4	5	King William County	VA	Marcel Joseph Lalik	1991	13,847
130 3/8	22 3/8	22 1/8	18 3/8	6	6	Howard County	MO	Ken Jones	1991	13,847
130 3/8	22 2/8	23 0/8	19 7/8	4	5	La Salle County	TX	Peter C. Swenson	1991	13,847
130 3/8	21 5/8	21 4/8	15 3/8	5	4	Steuben County	NY	Steven E. Dobles	1992	13,847
130 3/8	23 6/8	24 6/8	20 7/8	5	7	Will County	IL	Bernard Elwood	1992	13,847
130 3/8	21 0/8	21 0/8	16 4/8	6	5	Houston County	MN	Bill Schultz	1992	13,847
130 3/8	23 1/8	22 2/8	19 5/8	8	7	Brown County	IL	Richard L. Johnson	1992	13,847
130 3/8	23 1/8	23 1/8	17 7/8	6	7	Lapeer County	MI	Lawrence N. David	1992	13,847
130 3/8	21 2/8	20 3/8	15 3/8	5	5	Kane County	IL	Steven C. Ackmann	1992	13,847
130 3/8	25 6/8	22 6/8	22 3/8	4	4	Morgan County	AL	Darron Andrews	1992	13,847
130 3/8	19 6/8	21 5/8	16 2/8	5	6	Union County	IN	Fred C. "Ted" Stubbs	1993	13,847
130 3/8	21 5/8	20 7/8	17 7/8	4	4	Dunn County	WI	Roger Fillion	1993	13,847
130 3/8	20 6/8	18 7/8	14 7/8	5	5	Mayes County	OK	Kenny Eby	1993	13,847
130 3/8	24 1/8	24 0/8	19 7/8	4	4	Knox County	OH	John W. Hunt	1993	13,847
130 3/8	23 2/8	22 7/8	19 5/8	5	4	Somerset County	NJ	Jim Heron	1993	13,847
130 3/8	22 4/8	22 2/8	13 7/8	5	4	Chippewa County	WI	Cleo L. Hoel	1993	13,847
130 3/8	21 6/8	20 5/8	16 7/8	5	5	Clayton County	IA	Dennis M. Wemett	1993	13,847
130 3/8	21 7/8	21 7/8	14 1/8	6	7	Juneau County	WI	Nick Diciaula	1993	13,847
130 3/8	19 1/8	19 4/8	17 1/8	5	6	Butler County	OH	Michael Rumpler	1993	13,847
130 3/8	19 2/8	19 7/8	16 7/8	5	5	Barron County	WI	Roger Fagerlin	1993	13,847
130 3/8	20 4/8	21 0/8	16 5/8	5	5	Billings County	ND	Dan Erickstad	1993	13,847
130 3/8	21 7/8	22 3/8	17 5/8	4	4	Cavalier County	ND	Roger Furstenau	1994	13,847
130 3/8	25 6/8	25 2/8	20 3/8	4	4	Covington County	MS	Jim W. Rutland	1994	13,847
130 3/8	22 1/8	22 0/8	18 1/8	4	4	Oregon County	MO	Brian R. Whitus	1994	13,847
130 3/8	23 0/8	22 3/8	16 6/8	5	5	Oneida County	WI	Robert Wikel	1994	13,847
130 3/8	22 6/8	23 3/8	18 5/8	6	5	Cass County	MI	Armon Gipson	1994	13,847
130 3/8	23 4/8	24 0/8	21 7/8	5	6	Oklahoma County	OK	Dale Welchel	1994	13,847
130 3/8	21 1/8	21 4/8	19 5/8	4	4	Anoka County	MN	Steve Bruggeman	1994	13,847
130 3/8	22 5/8	22 2/8	14 5/8	4	5	Polk County	WI	David S. Thaemert	1994	13,847
130 3/8	22 5/8	21 5/8	19 2/8	5	5	Adams County	WI	Gary L. Birkholz	1995	13,847
130 3/8	23 1/8	22 0/8	16 1/8	4	5	Ontario County	NY	Ronald Van Harken	1995	13,847
130 3/8	23 6/8	23 4/8	16 5/8	5	4	Weld County	CO	Nathan L. Andersohn	1995	13,847
130 3/8	21 3/8	22 5/8	18 2/8	5	5	Buffalo County	WI	Larry W. Seibel	1995	13,847
130 3/8	20 4/8	22 6/8	17 5/8	5	5	Kosciusko County	IN	Steve Wright	1995	13,847
130 3/8	20 4/8	20 3/8	14 7/8	6	6	Nemaha County	NE	Danny E. Williams	1995	13,847
130 3/8	23 5/8	23 3/8	17 5/8	4	4	Middlesex County	MA	Jeff Smith	1995	13,847
130 3/8	21 7/8	21 4/8	19 1/8	4	4	Crittenden County	KY	Kelly E. Quertermous	1996	13,847
130 3/8	24 2/8	22 6/8	15 1/8	4	8	Greene County	MO	Rick Friend	1996	13,847
130 3/8	20 4/8	20 5/8	17 3/8	5	5	Lyon County	KS	Johnny Drake	1996	13,847
130 3/8	22 0/8	21 6/8	18 3/8	4	5	Livingston County	NY	Gerald Lynn, Jr.	1996	13,847
130 3/8	21 3/8	21 2/8	15 3/8	6	5	Scotland County	MO	Jim Pierceall	1996	13,847
130 3/8	20 6/8	22 2/8	19 5/8	4	4	Rock County	WI	Thomas McCulloch	1996	13,847
130 3/8	21 3/8	21 3/8	15 5/8	4	4	Knox County	IL	Greg Goodin	1996	13,847

WHITETAIL DEER (TYPICAL ANTLERS)

Minimum Score 125 — Continued

SCORE	LENGTH OF MAIN BEAM R	LENGTH OF MAIN BEAM L	INSIDE SPREAD	NUMBER OF POINTS R	NUMBER OF POINTS L	AREA	STATE/ PROVINCE	HUNTER'S NAME	DATE	RANK
130 3/8	23 4/8	23 0/8	20 1/8	4	4	Parkland	ALB	Daryl Harvie	1996	13,847
130 3/8	21 4/8	21 3/8	17 1/8	5	5	Fond du Lac County	WI	Charles Schimming	1997	13,847
130 3/8	19 2/8	19 3/8	15 1/8	5	5	Crook County	WY	Freddy King, Sr.	1997	13,847
130 3/8	23 2/8	22 2/8	18 1/8	5	5	Vernon County	WI	Joe Roberts	1997	13,847
130 3/8	21 4/8	22 6/8	19 3/8	5	5	Dakota County	MN	Dave Lofgren	1997	13,847
130 3/8	25 7/8	24 4/8	16 1/8	6	6	Ste. Genevieve County	MO	Peter C. McCaffrey	1997	13,847
130 3/8	23 1/8	22 0/8	15 4/8	5	4	Choctaw County	OK	Mark A. Holbrook	1997	13,847
130 3/8	20 2/8	19 7/8	16 0/8	6	5	Reno County	KS	Danny R. Gabbard, Sr.	1997	13,847
130 2/8	20 3/8	20 6/8	16 2/8	4	4	Yankton County	SD	Jack Begley	1959	13,943
130 2/8	26 7/8	26 3/8	17 3/8	8	6	Blue Earth County	MN	Ron Herz	1966	13,943
130 2/8	21 4/8	22 5/8	17 4/8	5	5	Montgomery County	AL	Charles D. Robinson	1976	13,943
130 2/8	16 0/8	20 3/8	18 6/8	6	6	Carroll County	IL	Arthur Heinze	1977	13,943
130 2/8	20 4/8	21 3/8	17 4/8	5	5	Pine County	MN	Ron Larsen	1978	13,943
130 2/8	21 5/8	21 7/8	15 0/8	6	5	Johnson County	IN	Ronnie L. Fiesbeck	1979	13,943
130 2/8	23 3/8	24 0/8	17 0/8	5	4	Washburn County	WI	William "Mike" Johnson	1980	13,943
130 2/8	20 3/8	20 7/8	13 4/8	4	5	Stanley County	SD	Richard Ray	1980	13,943
130 2/8	21 5/8	21 6/8	17 6/8	4	4	Saginaw County	MI	Charles R. Harper	1980	13,943
130 2/8	21 3/8	20 7/8	20 0/8	5	5	Allegheny County	PA	Thomas Fitz	1981	13,943
130 2/8	21 5/8	21 3/8	15 2/8	6	6	Grundy County	MO	John W. "Jack" Sherbo, Jr.	1982	13,943
130 2/8	21 1/8	21 5/8	14 4/8	6	6	Dane County	WI	Thomas B. Gannon	1982	13,943
130 2/8	22 0/8	21 2/8	19 5/8	7	5	St. Louis County	MO	Jack Repp	1982	13,943
130 2/8	22 0/8	21 0/8	20 2/8	5	6	Jefferson County	KS	Wayne Wenger	1983	13,943
130 2/8	22 1/8	23 1/8	20 2/8	4	5	Cheyenne County	NE	Marvin Clyncke	1983	13,943
130 2/8	21 7/8	22 0/8	16 0/8	6	7	Lincoln County	MO	Scott Gross	1983	13,943
130 2/8	21 1/8	21 6/8	16 0/8	4	4	Dodge County	WI	Steve Muche	1984	13,943
130 2/8	21 6/8	21 7/8	18 6/8	5	4	Jackson County	MI	Bruce A. Andrews	1984	13,943
130 2/8	21 7/8	21 2/8	16 4/8	5	6	Baltimore County	MD	Jay Holstein	1984	13,943
130 2/8	20 6/8	20 7/8	14 4/8	5	5	Clay County	MN	Randy Blankenship	1985	13,943
130 2/8	20 7/8	20 4/8	16 2/8	5	4	Shawnee County	KS	Randy Hildreth	1985	13,943
130 2/8	22 5/8	23 2/8	16 0/8	5	5	Licking County	OH	Glenn Dale Anderson	1986	13,943
130 2/8	23 3/8	23 0/8	14 7/8	5	7	St. Croix County	WI	Mike Cain	1986	13,943
130 2/8	20 7/8	20 4/8	15 3/8	4	6	Greenwood County	KS	Paul Edward Dean	1986	13,943
130 2/8	22 2/8	22 4/8	22 6/8	5	4	Lincoln County	OK	Ronnie J. Wolfe	1986	13,943
130 2/8	20 1/8	20 5/8	16 2/8	5	4	Clay County	IA	Gene A. Hall	1987	13,943
130 2/8	20 4/8	19 6/8	14 0/8	5	5	Wright County	MN	Brett Jarmuzek	1987	13,943
130 2/8	25 2/8	26 2/8	15 1/8	7	4	Saline County	MO	Mike Beach	1988	13,943
130 2/8	23 0/8	22 4/8	16 0/8	4	4	Sussex County	VA	Barry N. Hogge	1988	13,943
130 2/8	23 0/8	23 2/8	19 4/8	4	5	Fayette County	IA	Hugh Wright	1988	13,943
130 2/8	24 1/8	24 0/8	18 4/8	4	4	Forest County	WI	Jeff L. Steede	1988	13,943
130 2/8	21 6/8	21 2/8	20 0/8	4	5	Lincoln County	SD	John Lipetzky	1988	13,943
130 2/8	24 0/8	23 7/8	18 0/8	4	5	Columbia County	WI	Dennis L. Simonson	1988	13,943
130 2/8	24 1/8	23 4/8	16 0/8	6	4	Berkshire County	MA	Dale Martin	1988	13,943
130 2/8	22 4/8	22 7/8	18 0/8	4	4	Hardin County	KY	Donald J. Vittitow, Jr.	1988	13,943
130 2/8	21 5/8	20 4/8	14 4/8	5	7	St. Marys County	MD	Robert Garrett	1988	13,943
130 2/8	21 1/8	21 4/8	17 2/8	4	4	Lake County	IL	Carl Spaeth	1988	13,943
130 2/8	20 4/8	19 3/8	15 0/8	5	5	Osage County	OK	Dean Gratias	1989	13,943
130 2/8	20 4/8	20 2/8	13 6/8	4	4	Winneshiek County	IA	Kurt W. Stuebs	1989	13,943
130 2/8	21 5/8	22 1/8	18 6/8	5	5	Warren County	OH	Sam Y. Perone	1989	13,943
130 2/8	25 2/8	23 5/8	21 2/8	4	5	Jasper County	IL	Todd Hewing	1989	13,943
130 2/8	19 4/8	19 4/8	14 6/8	5	5	Menard County	IL	Dennis P. McCormick	1989	13,943
130 2/8	20 3/8	20 4/8	13 6/8	5	4	Traill County	ND	Tim Pederson	1990	13,943
130 2/8	21 7/8	22 6/8	17 0/8	4	4	Genesee County	MI	Billie R. Nash, Jr.	1991	13,943
130 2/8	20 5/8	21 4/8	14 2/8	6	6	Leflore County	MS	Brian Neely	1991	13,943
130 2/8	23 1/8	22 1/8	16 3/8	7	5	Jefferson County	OH	Kennith Mullins, Sr.	1991	13,943
130 2/8	23 0/8	22 1/8	17 2/8	5	5	New Haven County	CT	Gene J. Bialek	1991	13,943
130 2/8	23 7/8	24 2/8	16 2/8	5	4	Stafford County	VA	William E. Leege	1991	13,943
130 2/8	20 6/8	21 4/8	17 4/8	5	5	Barry County	MI	Steve G. Norris	1991	13,943
130 2/8	22 2/8	22 4/8	14 0/8	5	5	Oconto County	WI	Dennis R. Ullman	1991	13,943
130 2/8	22 4/8	23 4/8	18 3/8	5	5	Washington County	IN	Ben Willoughby	1991	13,943
130 2/8	20 5/8	22 3/8	18 0/8	4	5	Devon	ALB	Mike Mitchell	1991	13,943
130 2/8	22 2/8	22 1/8	15 5/8	5	6	Atascosa County	TX	R. G. Stein	1991	13,943
130 2/8	21 3/8	19 5/8	14 4/8	5	5	Todd County	KY	Larry Ross	1992	13,943
130 2/8	19 3/8	20 0/8	17 2/8	5	6	Pike County	IL	Tom Coakley	1992	13,943
130 2/8	20 0/8	23 2/8	17 2/8	5	5	Emmet County	MI	BLane Lagerman	1992	13,943
130 2/8	22 4/8	21 4/8	22 2/8	4	5	Stanstead	QUE	Gilles Beasse	1993	13,943
130 2/8	21 3/8	21 4/8	18 2/8	4	4	Ashland County	WI	Ryan Mesko	1993	13,943
130 2/8	24 2/8	22 4/8	16 0/8	4	4	Jefferson County	WI	Douglas Moyse	1993	13,943
130 2/8	21 4/8	21 7/8	17 1/8	5	4	Sumter County	AL	Gray Patrenos	1993	13,943
130 2/8	18 7/8	20 1/8	15 6/8	5	5	Grant County	NE	Douglas Brandt	1993	13,943
130 2/8	22 7/8	21 7/8	16 4/8	5	5	Taylor County	WI	Larry Kochendorfer	1993	13,943
130 2/8	22 1/8	22 2/8	16 0/8	5	5	Floyd County	IA	Justin Jung	1993	13,943
130 2/8	23 1/8	22 6/8	15 2/8	5	5	Meeker County	MN	Brent Swanson	1993	13,943
130 2/8	21 5/8	21 0/8	16 6/8	5	5	Kenedy County	TX	Chad Clark	1994	13,943
130 2/8	20 0/8	19 4/8	17 5/8	5	5	Polk County	WI	Wayne Logan	1994	13,943
130 2/8	19 7/8	19 5/8	16 4/8	5	5	Monroe County	PA	Gene Damron	1994	13,943
130 2/8	23 2/8	23 7/8	17 4/8	5	5	McMullen County	TX	Kathleen Ponders	1994	13,943
130 2/8	21 1/8	19 7/8	16 6/8	5	5	Webb County	TX	Norman E. Speer	1994	13,943
130 2/8	24 1/8	25 2/8	18 4/8	4	4	Cass County	IL	Donnie Sitterding	1994	13,943

WHITETAIL DEER (TYPICAL ANTLERS)

Minimum Score 125 — Continued

SCORE	LENGTH OF MAIN BEAM R	LENGTH OF MAIN BEAM L	INSIDE SPREAD	NUMBER OF POINTS R	NUMBER OF POINTS L	AREA	STATE/ PROVINCE	HUNTER'S NAME	DATE	RANK
130 2/8	20 2/8	20 4/8	15 4/8	5	5	Jackson County	IN	Tom Klakamp	1994	13,943
130 2/8	22 7/8	21 6/8	15 2/8	4	5	Vernon County	WI	John M. Rautiola	1994	13,943
130 2/8	22 5/8	21 5/8	18 2/8	5	10	Monroe County	NY	Dennis C. Briglin	1994	13,943
130 2/8	19 2/8	19 2/8	13 6/8	5	5	Polk County	WI	Lane M. Henck	1995	13,943
130 2/8	20 4/8	19 1/8	14 0/8	5	5	Dallas County	IA	Paul V. Strome III	1995	13,943
130 2/8	21 1/8	22 2/8	16 6/8	4	5	Steuben County	NY	Matthew L. Wagner	1995	13,943
130 2/8	22 4/8	22 4/8	16 7/8	7	7	Harlan County	KY	Kevin Jump	1995	13,943
130 2/8	22 2/8	21 7/8	16 0/8	5	5	Yates County	NY	Paul Durso	1995	13,943
130 2/8	21 6/8	21 6/8	17 4/8	4	4	Sheridan County	ND	David A. Alexander	1995	13,943
130 2/8	21 2/8	19 5/8	17 0/8	6	4	Douglas County	WI	Keith G. Olson	1995	13,943
130 2/8	21 6/8	20 0/8	15 0/8	5	5	Eau Claire County	WI	Wayne W. Price	1995	13,943
130 2/8	21 7/8	22 1/8	18 0/8	4	4	Montgomery County	PA	Ken Shemonski	1995	13,943
130 2/8	24 0/8	25 4/8	18 6/8	4	4	Scott County	IA	Jeffrey R. Coonts	1995	13,943
130 2/8	24 1/8	24 5/8	18 7/8	4	5	Westchester County	NY	Gary S. Gubinski	1995	13,943
130 2/8	22 4/8	22 4/8	15 4/8	6	4	White County	AR	Raymond King	1995	13,943
130 2/8	21 0/8	21 0/8	17 2/8	5	5	Montgomery County	MD	Frank H. Wilmot	1995	13,943
130 2/8	22 6/8	22 4/8	16 2/8	4	5	Rush County	IN	Brock Cross	1995	13,943
130 2/8	23 5/8	22 1/8	17 0/8	4	4	Waupaca County	WI	Roger A. Boushley	1996	13,943
130 2/8	23 5/8	23 6/8	14 6/8	4	4	Kent County	DE	Eric Miller	1996	13,943
130 2/8	22 1/8	22 7/8	16 1/8	6	5	Jay County	IN	Audie D. Burress	1996	13,943
130 2/8	22 1/8	22 3/8	16 4/8	5	7	Scotland County	MO	Chris Lippincott	1996	13,943
130 2/8	20 3/8	20 5/8	16 2/8	5	5	Ross County	OH	Matson Z. Smith	1996	13,943
130 2/8	20 3/8	20 2/8	16 2/8	5	5	Refusio County	TX	Ira L. Jones II	1996	13,943
130 2/8	20 4/8	20 5/8	16 0/8	5	5	Missoula County	MT	Fred Ehardt	1997	13,943
130 2/8	22 2/8	21 6/8	17 4/8	4	5	Fulton County	GA	Allen Marcus Hutcheson	1997	13,943
130 2/8	22 4/8	22 3/8	17 2/8	4	4	Price County	WI	Mike Couillard	1997	13,943
130 2/8	20 2/8	20 1/8	15 4/8	5	5	Trempealeau County	WI	Adam Schlesser	1997	13,943
130 2/8	22 2/8	22 1/8	15 4/8	4	4	Allegheny County	PA	Kevin Malley	1997	13,943
130 2/8	21 5/8	21 5/8	16 6/8	5	5	Outagamie County	WI	Peter D. Zuleger	1997	13,943
130 2/8	22 1/8	21 6/8	14 2/8	5	4	Jackson County	WI	Gary W. Thran	1997	13,943
130 2/8	21 1/8	21 1/8	17 4/8	4	4	Colfax County	NE	Nick Parry	1997	13,943
130 2/8	21 7/8	21 7/8	16 4/8	4	5	Van Buren County	MI	Avon Lee Arbo	1997	13,943
130 2/8	21 3/8	20 5/8	15 7/8	6	5	Sauk County	WI	Brian Frank	1997	13,943
130 2/8	21 7/8	22 2/8	15 4/8	4	4	Sauk County	WI	John H. Traxler	1997	13,943
130 2/8	20 0/8	20 1/8	16 6/8	5	5	Peoria County	IL	Troy Schlueter	1997	13,943
130 2/8	23 4/8	23 6/8	16 2/8	4	4	Coahoma County	MS	Brent Bass	1998	13,943
130 1/8	24 4/8	25 7/8	19 7/8	4	3	Waupaca County	WI	John Schoenike	1952	14,049
130 1/8	22 5/8	21 6/8	16 7/8	5	5	Oneida County	WI	Fred Felbab	1964	14,049
130 1/8	22 6/8	24 4/8	17 4/8	6	5	Morrison County	MN	Stephen L. Marklund	1964	14,049
130 1/8	22 6/8	24 0/8	18 2/8	6	5	Crow Wing County	MN	Robert Woods	1969	14,049
130 1/8	21 4/8	21 4/8	20 1/8	4	4	Garden County	NE	Larry Pierce	1976	14,049
130 1/8	20 4/8	21 4/8	13 7/8	5	5	Plymouth County	IA	Cash N. Howe	1978	14,049
130 1/8	25 2/8	25 4/8	16 0/8	5	5	Edwards County	KS	Matthew W. Schartz	1979	14,049
130 1/8	19 4/8	19 3/8	15 3/8	5	5	Warren County	MO	David A. Wilson	1980	14,049
130 1/8	23 0/8	21 7/8	17 7/8	4	4	Vernon County	WI	Michael R. Gregory	1981	14,049
130 1/8	20 4/8	20 3/8	16 3/8	4	4	Tazewell County	IL	Gary Joe Smith	1982	14,049
130 1/8	21 1/8	21 0/8	16 7/8	4	5	Perry County	OH	Michael W. Wintgens	1982	14,049
130 1/8	19 3/8	20 6/8	17 5/8	5	4	Muscatine County	IA	Brian Nebergall	1983	14,049
130 1/8	23 4/8	21 6/8	15 6/8	6	5	Clay County	MN	Joe Lahlum	1983	14,049
130 1/8	22 6/8	24 6/8	15 5/8	5	5	Door County	WI	Philip K. Riddle	1984	14,049
130 1/8	22 5/8	24 4/8	21 3/8	4	4	Hamilton County	IL	Richard Phelps	1984	14,049
130 1/8	22 5/8	22 5/8	19 1/8	4	5	Powell County	MT	Danny Moore	1984	14,049
130 1/8	23 1/8	22 3/8	18 5/8	4	4	Hardin County	OH	John B. Britton	1985	14,049
130 1/8	23 7/8	23 4/8	17 6/8	5	6	Montgomery County	MD	Donald Stancil Waters, Jr.	1985	14,049
130 1/8	23 0/8	22 6/8	16 3/8	4	5	Anderson County	TN	Harold D. Tackett	1985	14,049
130 1/8	24 4/8	23 0/8	16 1/8	5	5	Calhoun County	MI	David K. McWhorter	1985	14,049
130 1/8	24 2/8	23 2/8	20 1/8	4	4	Pepin County	WI	Michael J. Schmidt	1985	14,049
130 1/8	22 2/8	22 6/8	15 5/8	4	4	Clark County	KS	William A. Rule	1985	14,049
130 1/8	24 5/8	23 4/8	18 6/8	4	5	Dane County	WI	Thomas J. Sheahan	1986	14,049
130 1/8	21 7/8	21 1/8	17 4/8	5	6	Polk County	TX	O. H. Campbell, Jr.	1987	14,049
130 1/8	20 6/8	20 5/8	16 5/8	5	5	Price County	WI	Simon Britts	1987	14,049
130 1/8	21 0/8	21 3/8	15 7/8	5	5	Mason County	WV	Ed Jefferson	1987	14,049
130 1/8	19 5/8	20 0/8	17 3/8	5	5	Henderson County	IL	Timothy H. Allaman	1987	14,049
130 1/8	22 0/8	21 5/8	16 3/8	4	4	Holmes County	OH	Myron A. Hershberger	1987	14,049
130 1/8	18 2/8	19 4/8	16 1/8	5	5	Fayette County	PA	Scott Murray	1988	14,049
130 1/8	23 6/8	23 3/8	18 1/8	4	4	Gloucester County	NJ	William D. Latham, Jr.	1988	14,049
130 1/8	20 5/8	20 4/8	17 1/8	4	5	Price County	WI	Ralph Trzinski	1988	14,049
130 1/8	20 1/8	20 2/8	15 3/8	5	5	Clay County	MN	Brian Winter	1988	14,049
130 1/8	21 7/8	22 7/8	18 3/8	6	5	Hughes County	OK	Tom L. Cartwright	1989	14,049
130 1/8	23 1/8	22 4/8	18 1/8	5	4	Chariton County	MO	David L. Williams	1989	14,049
130 1/8	21 6/8	20 7/8	17 7/8	5	5	Kanawha County	WV	William H. Baldwin	1989	14,049
130 1/8	24 1/8	22 6/8	15 5/8	5	5	Brown County	MN	Gary Braun	1989	14,049
130 1/8	23 5/8	23 3/8	16 2/8	4	5	McMullen County	TX	W. Walker Lowry, Jr.	1989	14,049
130 1/8	20 4/8	20 4/8	17 5/8	4	4	Eau Claire County	WI	Steve Julson	1989	14,049
130 1/8	23 0/8	24 5/8	17 6/8	5	7	McDonough County	IL	Roger Wayne Jackson	1989	14,049
130 1/8	22 7/8	22 5/8	20 4/8	6	4	Albany County	NY	Skip Reilly	1989	14,049
130 1/8	23 4/8	22 3/8	18 6/8	6	5	Athens County	OH	Ron Tank, Jr.	1989	14,049
130 1/8	23 0/8	22 7/8	16 5/8	6	6	Bremer County	IA	Henry J. Rodrique	1989	14,049

WHITETAIL DEER (TYPICAL ANTLERS)

Minimum Score 125 — Continued

SCORE	LENGTH OF MAIN BEAM R	LENGTH OF MAIN BEAM L	INSIDE SPREAD	NUMBER OF POINTS R	NUMBER OF POINTS L	AREA	STATE/ PROVINCE	HUNTER'S NAME	DATE	RANK
130 1/8	22 2/8	23 2/8	15 1/8	5	5	Baldwin County	GA	Randy W. Wilson	1990	14,049
130 1/8	23 5/8	22 7/8	15 5/8	5	5	Morrison County	MN	Richard Jeska	1990	14,049
130 1/8	22 6/8	22 1/8	18 7/8	4	4	Dallas County	IA	John Flies	1990	14,049
130 1/8	21 1/8	20 6/8	18 3/8	5	5	Dodge County	WI	Randy Grulke	1990	14,049
130 1/8	22 3/8	21 2/8	16 2/8	4	6	Dane County	WI	John Schulz	1991	14,049
130 1/8	22 1/8	21 7/8	14 7/8	5	5	Webster County	MO	Link Stevens	1991	14,049
130 1/8	21 3/8	21 5/8	17 1/8	4	4	Elkhart County	IN	Leon R. Schwartz	1991	14,049
130 1/8	22 6/8	24 5/8	17 7/8	4	5	Macon County	IL	Dave Meyer	1991	14,049
130 1/8	23 1/8	21 4/8	15 3/8	6	6	Moultrie County	IL	Bruce Hill	1991	14,049
130 1/8	21 0/8	21 4/8	15 7/8	5	5	Grand Traverse County	MI	Bill Alpers	1991	14,049
130 1/8	18 7/8	20 2/8	14 5/8	5	5	La Porte County	IN	Louis Kuzdas	1992	14,049
130 1/8	21 1/8	19 3/8	19 1/8	5	5	Fillmore County	MN	Kevin Joyce	1992	14,049
130 1/8	22 4/8	22 3/8	16 7/8	5	5	Trempealeau County	WI	Dale Lyngen, Jr.	1992	14,049
130 1/8	21 3/8	21 3/8	15 1/8	4	4	Henry County	VA	Mike Weaver	1992	14,049
130 1/8	23 1/8	24 5/8	21 4/8	5	5	La Salle County	TX	David A. Henry	1992	14,049
130 1/8	19 2/8	18 0/8	13 1/8	5	5	Clay County	MS	Scott Hatcher	1992	14,049
130 1/8	22 4/8	21 3/8	16 7/8	5	5	Pepin County	WI	Jeff Gienau	1993	14,049
130 1/8	19 7/8	20 0/8	16 2/8	6	6	Kimble County	TX	Bobby E. Newmann	1993	14,049
130 1/8	21 5/8	21 4/8	17 3/8	6	5	La Salle County	IL	Albert W. Marshall	1993	14,049
130 1/8	22 7/8	22 2/8	18 3/8	4	6	Waupaca County	WI	Randy Roland	1993	14,049
130 1/8	23 7/8	23 4/8	20 5/8	4	4	Clayton County	IA	Robert Fink	1993	14,049
130 1/8	21 5/8	22 2/8	16 7/8	4	4	Randolph County	MO	Larry Threlkeld	1993	14,049
130 1/8	21 3/8	20 7/8	20 2/8	9	5	Henderson County	KY	Keith Conder	1993	14,049
130 1/8	23 3/8	23 2/8	15 6/8	6	4	Williams County	OH	Remont Scantlen	1993	14,049
130 1/8	21 3/8	21 3/8	17 3/8	4	4	Livingston County	IL	Dennis L. Griswold	1993	14,049
130 1/8	20 7/8	21 0/8	17 3/8	5	5	Waukesha County	WI	Leonard Brown	1993	14,049
130 1/8	23 6/8	23 3/8	16 7/8	5	4	Knox County	OH	Don Holbrook, Jr.	1993	14,049
130 1/8	21 1/8	21 2/8	16 1/8	4	4	Marshall County	MN	James B. Sondeland	1993	14,049
130 1/8	19 7/8	19 1/8	17 2/8	6	6	Benton County	IA	Francisco Ochoa-Estrada	1994	14,049
130 1/8	20 3/8	21 2/8	17 5/8	5	5	Lancaster County	PA	Curt Carter	1994	14,049
130 1/8	21 6/8	21 4/8	18 1/8	4	4	Portage County	OH	Buzzy Papalia	1994	14,049
130 1/8	20 3/8	21 2/8	16 5/8	5	5	Green Lake County	WI	Michael Otto	1994	14,049
130 1/8	22 0/8	23 0/8	17 3/8	5	4	Carroll County	MO	William P. Dickey	1994	14,049
130 1/8	20 7/8	15 1/8	17 1/8	5	6	Livingston County	IL	Kurt Hobart	1994	14,049
130 1/8	24 1/8	23 5/8	17 7/8	4	4	Knox County	IL	Dale T. Smith	1994	14,049
130 1/8	20 7/8	20 6/8	16 3/8	4	4	Brown County	IL	Freddy King, Jr.	1994	14,049
130 1/8	22 0/8	22 4/8	17 1/8	5	5	Waukesha County	WI	Brad Grober	1995	14,049
130 1/8	18 4/8	20 2/8	17 1/8	5	5	Monroe County	PA	Barry L. Shertzer	1995	14,049
130 1/8	21 3/8	21 5/8	14 1/8	7	6	Westchester County	NY	Stephen L. Cook	1995	14,049
130 1/8	23 0/8	22 3/8	16 1/8	4	4	Athens County	OH	Curtis R. Rutter	1995	14,049
130 1/8	22 1/8	21 0/8	17 1/8	5	5	Schleicher County	TX	Ray Scroggins	1995	14,049
130 1/8	20 3/8	20 2/8	19 3/8	5	5	Oakland County	MI	Richard Charles Foster	1996	14,049
130 1/8	22 2/8	23 3/8	19 0/8	5	5	Buffalo County	WI	Steve J. Borton	1996	14,049
130 1/8	21 3/8	20 7/8	18 3/8	6	6	Adams County	IN	Bradley J. Amstutz	1996	14,049
130 1/8	23 7/8	21 4/8	16 3/8	4	5	Darke County	OH	John Lonsinger	1996	14,049
130 1/8	22 6/8	22 3/8	17 5/8	4	4	Kenedy County	TX	Dennis Dunn	1996	14,049
130 1/8	21 2/8	22 5/8	18 1/8	4	4	Woodford County	IL	Michael H. Reatherford	1996	14,049
130 1/8	23 2/8	23 1/8	15 3/8	4	4	Westchester County	NY	William J. Evans	1996	14,049
130 1/8	21 2/8	20 5/8	16 3/8	5	5	Waukesha County	WI	Brian T. Linnan	1997	14,049
130 1/8	22 7/8	22 4/8	14 5/8	4	4	Waupaca County	WI	Mark H. Moen	1997	14,049
130 1/8	22 1/8	22 4/8	14 7/8	5	5	Waushara County	WI	David R. Eichinger	1997	14,049
130 1/8	23 1/8	22 7/8	13 3/8	4	6	Carroll County	MS	Sid Herring, Jr.	1997	14,049
130 1/8	20 2/8	21 1/8	13 5/8	5	5	Missoula County	MT	Lonnie H. Bray	1997	14,049
130 1/8	20 2/8	20 1/8	17 1/8	5	5	Throckmorton County	TX	Bruce Wayne Holt	1997	14,049
130 1/8	20 1/8	20 3/8	19 5/8	4	4	Queen Annes County	MD	Peter S. Jayne	1997	14,049
130 1/8	21 1/8	20 5/8	17 3/8	4	4	Tate County	MS	Readus Hudson III	1997	14,049
130 1/8	22 5/8	21 3/8	17 3/8	4	4	Vernon County	WI	Casey A. Blum	1997	14,049
130 1/8	22 0/8	20 5/8	16 7/8	5	5	Price County	WI	Jerry Gotz	1997	14,049
130 1/8	21 3/8	21 4/8	19 3/8	4	5	Hancock County	IL	Joe Taylor	1997	14,049
130 1/8	22 5/8	23 1/8	18 1/8	4	4	Burnett County	WI	Thomas L. Wasilensky	1997	14,049
130 1/8	21 7/8	20 3/8	15 7/8	4	4	Henry County	IL	Robert Aldred	1997	14,049
130 1/8	21 0/8	21 5/8	17 1/8	4	4	Jackson County	OH	Martin Larson	1997	14,049
130 1/8	23 2/8	22 5/8	15 2/8	4	6	Anoka County	MN	Robert G. Pillsbury	1997	14,049
130 1/8	20 4/8	20 4/8	16 7/8	5	5	Crawford County	WI	John Deiss	1997	14,049
130 1/8	23 1/8	22 2/8	20 1/8	5	4	Morris County	NJ	Stephen Olsson	1998	14,049
130 1/8	19 4/8	19 3/8	15 3/8	5	5	Crawford County	PA	Terry Groger, Sr.	1998	14,049
130 1/8	20 7/8	21 4/8	16 1/8	4	4	Thurston County	NE	Mike Lutt	1998	14,049
130 1/8	21 6/8	21 3/8	17 1/8	4	4	Buffalo County	WI	Richard E. Del Percio	1998	14,049
130 0/8	23 4/8	23 5/8	19 0/8	4	4	Wicomico County	MD	Donald J. Brown	1956	14,159
130 0/8	21 0/8	19 3/8	17 4/8	5	4	Roberts County	SD	Byron Siegel	1962	14,159
130 0/8	22 2/8	22 5/8	18 6/8	4	5	Berrien County	MI	Leon L. Williams	1965	14,159
130 0/8	20 2/8	20 6/8	15 0/8	5	5	Bucks County	PA	Don Fitting	1967	14,159
130 0/8	21 3/8	21 4/8	19 0/8	5	5	Vanderburgh County	IN	Scott E. Webster	1973	14,159
130 0/8	24 3/8	25 0/8	18 6/8	6	5	Pope County	AR	Douglas M. Atchley	1975	14,159
130 0/8	20 2/8	21 0/8	14 6/8	5	5	Stanly County	NC	Steve Efird	1978	14,159
130 0/8	22 4/8	22 2/8	19 0/8	4	4	Licking County	OH	James E. Sorg	1978	14,159
130 0/8	22 0/8	21 4/8	17 0/8	4	4	Will County	IL	Terry Marcukaitis	1979	14,159
130 0/8	23 2/8	24 2/8	18 0/8	4	4	Onondaga County	NY	Jack Sipfle	1980	14,159

WHITETAIL DEER (TYPICAL ANTLERS)

Minimum Score 125 — Continued

SCORE	LENGTH OF MAIN BEAM R / L	INSIDE SPREAD	NUMBER OF POINTS R / L	AREA	STATE/ PROVINCE	HUNTER'S NAME	DATE	RANK
130 0/8	21 7/8 / 21 2/8	16 1/8	6 / 6	Polk County	WI	Paul Petersen	1981	14,159
130 0/8	23 0/8 / 24 2/8	19 6/8	4 / 4	Westchester County	NY	Richard T. Burke	1982	14,159
130 0/8	23 4/8 / 23 3/8	15 4/8	5 / 5	McDonough County	IL	John E. Whalon	1982	14,159
130 0/8	24 1/8 / 23 6/8	13 6/8	5 / 4	Scott County	VA	Charles William Moore	1983	14,159
130 0/8	20 5/8 / 21 0/8	15 4/8	5 / 6	Fond du Lac County	WI	Tom Dickmann	1983	14,159
130 0/8	20 0/8 / 21 4/8	18 0/8	5 / 5	Kenosha County	WI	Ted Hysell	1983	14,159
130 0/8	25 1/8 / 25 2/8	17 6/8	6 / 7	Ottawa County	KS	Rod Ponton	1983	14,159
130 0/8	20 3/8 / 18 7/8	17 4/8	6 / 5	Perkins County	SD	H. Melvin Dutton	1983	14,159
130 0/8	22 7/8 / 21 6/8	18 0/8	6 / 7	Sauk County	WI	Duane Olson	1984	14,159
130 0/8	21 0/8 / 21 1/8	17 4/8	4 / 4	Rock County	WI	Dalee E. Applebee	1984	14,159
130 0/8	21 3/8 / 21 5/8	17 0/8	4 / 4	Marinette County	WI	Tom Hirte	1984	14,159
130 0/8	21 1/8 / 20 5/8	15 4/8	5 / 5	Shawnee County	KS	Roxie Kelly	1984	14,159
130 0/8	22 2/8 / 24 1/8	19 0/8	4 / 4	Orange County	NY	Richard F Kaufmann	1985	14,159
130 0/8	23 0/8 / 23 3/8	17 4/8	5 / 5	Minnehaha County	SD	Rick Rang	1985	14,159
130 0/8	19 2/8 / 21 7/8	16 0/8	4 / 5	Sarpy County	NE	Randy Stitt	1986	14,159
130 0/8	21 5/8 / 21 4/8	20 0/8	4 / 4	Roberts County	SD	Jeffery A. Nelson	1986	14,159
130 0/8	22 3/8 / 23 4/8	16 1/8	6 / 6	Charlevoix County	MI	Richard K. Arnold	1987	14,159
130 0/8	19 0/8 / 19 4/8	14 4/8	6 / 5	Clay County	MN	Phillip Reiling	1987	14,159
130 0/8	22 1/8 / 23 0/8	17 0/8	5 / 4	Dane County	WI	Gerald Westphal	1988	14,159
130 0/8	22 6/8 / 22 0/8	14 4/8	5 / 4	Pike County	OH	Larry Cornett	1988	14,159
130 0/8	20 5/8 / 20 2/8	15 6/8	5 / 5	Benzie County	MI	David Acha	1989	14,159
130 0/8	22 6/8 / 22 3/8	20 6/8	4 / 5	Wayne County	NY	Dallas Sumner	1989	14,159
130 0/8	22 0/8 / 23 2/8	19 0/8	4 / 4	Queensville	ONT	Paul Vaicunas	1989	14,159
130 0/8	21 6/8 / 21 2/8	16 2/8	6 / 6	Hampshire County	MA	Stephen E. Drumm	1989	14,159
130 0/8	21 5/8 / 21 3/8	17 6/8	4 / 4	Crawford County	IL	Bill Waddell	1989	14,159
130 0/8	24 3/8 / 24 6/8	18 6/8	4 / 4	Ulster County	NY	W. Thomas Tintle, Jr.	1989	14,159
130 0/8	19 7/8 / 20 0/8	16 2/8	5 / 5	Iron County	WI	Perry V. Elsemore	1990	14,159
130 0/8	22 2/8 / 22 5/8	18 6/8	5 / 4	Will County	IL	Scott A. Siuda	1990	14,159
130 0/8	21 2/8 / 21 1/8	17 0/8	5 / 5	Douglas County	WI	Ron Roen	1990	14,159
130 0/8	24 5/8 / 23 4/8	18 4/8	4 / 5	Custer County	NE	Rick Thaden	1991	14,159
130 0/8	20 5/8 / 21 4/8	17 4/8	5 / 5	Isanti County	MN	Rick Bryant	1991	14,159
130 0/8	19 2/8 / 19 5/8	15 4/8	5 / 5	Meeker County	MN	Lee R. Peterson	1991	14,159
130 0/8	23 3/8 / 22 7/8	16 6/8	4 / 4	Harvey County	KS	Ron Hershburger	1991	14,159
130 0/8	21 2/8 / 21 5/8	21 0/8	4 / 4	Saline County	MO	David L. Hedgpeth	1991	14,159
130 0/8	23 0/8 / 22 6/8	17 2/8	4 / 4	Jasper County	IL	Jim Hunsaker	1991	14,159
130 0/8	26 2/8 / 27 0/8	18 0/8	4 / 5	Logan County	CO	Pete Lauer	1991	14,159
130 0/8	21 2/8 / 22 2/8	20 2/8	6 / 6	McHenry County	IL	Bill G. Ehlers	1991	14,159
130 0/8	22 7/8 / 22 0/8	17 2/8	4 / 4	Muskegon County	MI	Dwayne Levandowski	1991	14,159
130 0/8	21 5/8 / 21 3/8	19 4/8	5 / 5	La Salle County	TX	Michael Corley	1991	14,159
130 0/8	22 1/8 / 21 6/8	19 6/8	5 / 5	Marshall County	IN	Ron Rhoads	1992	14,159
130 0/8	23 3/8 / 22 7/8	18 4/8	4 / 5	Cumberland County	ME	Nick Dimastrantonio	1992	14,159
130 0/8	23 6/8 / 23 6/8	19 6/8	4 / 4	Buffalo County	WI	Thad W. Henderson	1992	14,159
130 0/8	21 0/8 / 22 0/8	18 2/8	6 / 6	Van Buren County	IA	Tom Casey	1992	14,159
130 0/8	25 2/8 / 25 1/8	17 6/8	4 / 4	Berkshire County	MA	Gene Andrew	1992	14,159
130 0/8	21 7/8 / 22 1/8	16 6/8	4 / 4	Atchison County	MO	Chris Barton	1992	14,159
130 0/8	22 5/8 / 23 4/8	14 2/8	5 / 5	Lucas County	IA	Orval Bedell	1992	14,159
130 0/8	20 5/8 / 20 4/8	13 4/8	5 / 5	Edwards County	TX	Alan Reed	1992	14,159
130 0/8	20 6/8 / 19 5/8	17 5/8	6 / 5	Indiana County	PA	Loren J. Dudash	1993	14,159
130 0/8	21 0/8 / 22 3/8	16 6/8	7 / 5	Dodge County	WI	Brian Neitzel	1993	14,159
130 0/8	19 4/8 / 19 4/8	15 6/8	5 / 5	Pike County	IL	Michael St. John	1993	14,159
130 0/8	20 5/8 / 21 0/8	19 2/8	6 / 5	Dane County	WI	Carey J. Bomkamp	1993	14,159
130 0/8	22 5/8 / 22 0/8	13 2/8	6 / 5	Auglaize County	OH	Greg Brooks	1993	14,159
130 0/8	24 1/8 / 23 3/8	19 4/8	5 / 5	Onondaga County	NY	Dan Heaney	1993	14,159
130 0/8	19 7/8 / 20 0/8	16 2/8	5 / 5	Okotoks	ALB	Lindsey Paterson	1993	14,159
130 0/8	22 1/8 / 22 1/8	17 6/8	4 / 5	Kerr County	TX	Dan Perez	1993	14,159
130 0/8	20 6/8 / 20 7/8	17 0/8	5 / 5	Albany County	NY	Michael Mitale	1994	14,159
130 0/8	20 5/8 / 20 3/8	18 4/8	5 / 5	Barry County	MI	Jeffrey A. Rogers	1994	14,159
130 0/8	21 7/8 / 22 5/8	19 0/8	5 / 5	Cass County	IA	Kurt Steggall	1994	14,159
130 0/8	21 2/8 / 22 0/8	16 6/8	5 / 4	Washington County	WI	Russell A. Wegner	1994	14,159
130 0/8	20 4/8 / 19 6/8	14 0/8	4 / 5	Jackson County	WI	Kevin J. Kamrowski	1994	14,159
130 0/8	22 0/8 / 22 5/8	14 6/8	4 / 4	Lake County	IL	John K. Hunter	1994	14,159
130 0/8	25 2/8 / 25 2/8	19 0/8	5 / 4	Maverick County	TX	Richard McCarty	1994	14,159
130 0/8	22 1/8 / 22 2/8	16 2/8	5 / 5	New London County	CT	Brian Palmer	1995	14,159
130 0/8	21 4/8 / 21 0/8	15 0/8	5 / 5	Sherburne County	MN	Robert Christle	1995	14,159
130 0/8	20 7/8 / 22 3/8	17 0/8	5 / 6	Buffalo County	WI	William J. Kralewski	1995	14,159
130 0/8	23 2/8 / 23 0/8	18 4/8	4 / 4	Buffalo County	WI	Bob Tullius	1995	14,159
130 0/8	19 7/8 / 20 2/8	15 6/8	5 / 4	Pike County	IL	Richard Dewey	1995	14,159
130 0/8	23 0/8 / 23 7/8	23 0/8	5 / 5	Crawford County	WI	Michael G. O'Dair	1995	14,159
130 0/8	24 1/8 / 22 1/8	22 0/8	4 / 4	Carroll County	MD	James R. Aberts	1995	14,159
130 0/8	24 1/8 / 23 6/8	19 4/8	5 / 5	Richland County	WI	Robert A. Harper	1995	14,159
130 0/8	22 1/8 / 22 2/8	16 2/8	5 / 5	Montcalm County	MI	Steve Crooks	1995	14,159
130 0/8	24 4/8 / 22 7/8	22 6/8	6 / 4	Shelby County	IL	Daniel Doty	1995	14,159
130 0/8	23 4/8 / 22 6/8	17 7/8	5 / 5	Brown County	IL	Steve Capps	1995	14,159
130 0/8	23 5/8 / 23 6/8	16 6/8	4 / 5	Dorchester County	SC	Mike Coker	1996	14,159
130 0/8	19 7/8 / 20 2/8	13 1/8	5 / 6	Gallia County	OH	Mike Reynolds	1996	14,159
130 0/8	22 2/8 / 22 0/8	17 4/8	5 / 5	Marquette County	MI	Kevin T. Dewald	1996	14,159
130 0/8	22 5/8 / 23 4/8	20 0/8	5 / 6	Hamilton County	OH	Jay Knight	1996	14,159
130 0/8	19 7/8 / 19 7/8	14 2/8	7 / 5	Buffalo County	WI	David A. Linse	1996	14,159

WHITETAIL DEER (TYPICAL ANTLERS)

Minimum Score 125   Continued

SCORE	LENGTH OF MAIN BEAM R	LENGTH OF MAIN BEAM L	INSIDE SPREAD	NUMBER OF POINTS R	NUMBER OF POINTS L	AREA	STATE/PROVINCE	HUNTER'S NAME	DATE	RANK
130 0/8	20 1/8	20 4/8	13 4/8	6	5	White County	AR	Randy Nokes	1996	14,159
130 0/8	21 4/8	21 7/8	16 4/8	4	4	Fremont County	IA	Dave Holt	1996	14,159
130 0/8	24 3/8	22 7/8	20 0/8	5	6	Sawyer County	WI	Patrick Venzke	1996	14,159
130 0/8	21 7/8	22 2/8	16 0/8	4	4	Waupaca County	WI	Ron Diestler	1997	14,159
130 0/8	21 4/8	21 6/8	17 6/8	5	4	Vernon County	WI	Trevor Thurin	1997	14,159
130 0/8	21 7/8	21 0/8	21 6/8	5	5	Jackson County	WI	Jim Geraghty	1997	14,159
130 0/8	22 4/8	21 4/8	17 2/8	4	5	Cayuga County	NY	Paul R. Bovee	1997	14,159
130 0/8	22 3/8	21 4/8	18 6/8	4	4	Jackson County	MI	Brent L. Reed	1997	14,159
130 0/8	20 4/8	19 5/8	19 2/8	5	5	Waushara County	WI	Dave G. Chase	1997	14,159
130 0/8	21 7/8	23 4/8	18 2/8	4	4	Jefferson County	KS	Bud Artzer	1997	14,159
130 0/8	22 2/8	22 1/8	19 6/8	4	4	Fairfax County	VA	John A. Di Giulian	1997	14,159
130 0/8	22 4/8	23 3/8	14 4/8	6	4	Wilson County	KS	Troy A. Graziadei	1997	14,159
130 0/8	22 0/8	22 1/8	18 6/8	4	5	Live Oak County	TX	James D. Jones	1997	14,159
129 7/8	23 6/8	21 6/8	18 0/8	5	5	Winnebago County	IL	Leo M. Ruefer, Jr.	1958	14,260
129 7/8	21 7/8	22 0/8	16 5/8	4	4	Monroe County	WI	Jeff Skrade	1962	14,260
129 7/8	23 3/8	23 2/8	16 5/8	5	6	Allegan County	MI	Clayton Foster	1964	14,260
129 7/8	23 0/8	21 7/8	15 1/8	5	5	Jefferson County	KS	Delmar Tucking, Jr.	1966	14,260
129 7/8	22 3/8	22 6/8	20 7/8	4	4	Ashland County	WI	William Sutton	1968	14,260
129 7/8	19 7/8	19 3/8	20 2/8	5	5	Vilas County	WI	Art Heinze	1970	14,260
129 7/8	19 2/8	19 5/8	15 3/8	5	5	Columbia County	WI	Jay Rosendick	1970	14,260
129 7/8	22 4/8	21 7/8	17 1/8	4	4	Ogle County	IL	Henry E. Zimmerman	1970	14,260
129 7/8	20 3/8	20 6/8	15 5/8	6	5	Cottonwood County	MN	Gene Gustafson	1977	14,260
129 7/8	21 5/8	22 2/8	17 1/8	5	5	Sauk County	WI	Clair E. Keylock	1977	14,260
129 7/8	21 6/8	22 4/8	20 5/8	4	4	Tioga County	NY	Arthur Schumacher	1977	14,260
129 7/8	19 7/8	20 4/8	16 5/8	5	5	Adair County	IA	Wallace R. Waddell	1980	14,260
129 7/8	22 0/8	21 5/8	17 3/8	4	4	Hardin County	IA	Randall Martinson	1980	14,260
129 7/8	24 6/8	24 6/8	17 3/8	5	5	Oneida County	WI	Tom Knudsen	1981	14,260
129 7/8	20 6/8	21 1/8	18 7/8	6	6	Kingman County	KS	Kevin Wasson	1981	14,260
129 7/8	22 5/8	22 4/8	17 2/8	6	5	Berkeley County	SC	Hugh Gaskins	1983	14,260
129 7/8	20 5/8	20 7/8	16 1/8	4	5	Calumet County	WI	Bill Mertens	1983	14,260
129 7/8	21 5/8	21 2/8	15 7/8	5	5	Waupaca County	WI	William Millard	1984	14,260
129 7/8	21 2/8	22 7/8	17 1/8	4	4	Rock County	WI	Richard A. Viken	1984	14,260
129 7/8	20 6/8	20 4/8	14 7/8	4	5	Butler County	KS	Clifford Rogers	1984	14,260
129 7/8	20 6/8	21 1/8	14 5/8	6	5	De Kalb County	IN	Jay Vance	1987	14,260
129 7/8	21 4/8	21 3/8	17 1/8	6	6	Pepin County	WI	Shaughn Laehn	1987	14,260
129 7/8	22 4/8	23 0/8	17 1/8	5	5	Loudoun County	VA	Larry Bassett	1987	14,260
129 7/8	19 7/8	20 1/8	17 5/8	6	5	Washington County	MO	Jim Emily	1987	14,260
129 7/8	20 6/8	21 6/8	16 5/8	5	4	Walsh County	ND	Terry L. Lund	1988	14,260
129 7/8	25 6/8	25 4/8	15 5/8	4	5	Lamar County	GA	Joel Vaughn, Jr.	1989	14,260
129 7/8	20 1/8	20 3/8	17 1/8	5	5	Ravalli County	MT	Carol Karen Miller	1989	14,260
129 7/8	22 4/8	22 7/8	18 4/8	5	5	Winona County	MN	Douglas Kerska	1989	14,260
129 7/8	21 4/8	21 4/8	17 4/8	5	6	Allegheny County	PA	Rich Pavicic	1989	14,260
129 7/8	22 4/8	23 5/8	20 1/8	5	5	Franklin County	MA	John D. O'Brien, Jr.	1989	14,260
129 7/8	23 3/8	23 2/8	19 5/8	6	6	Burnett County	WI	Kent Bassett	1990	14,260
129 7/8	24 0/8	22 5/8	17 1/8	5	5	Camden County	MO	Scott Whitlock	1990	14,260
129 7/8	22 2/8	22 3/8	14 5/8	5	5	Waldo County	ME	Joseph L. Hall	1990	14,260
129 7/8	22 2/8	21 4/8	16 7/8	4	5	Chippewa County	WI	Jon D. Schroeder	1991	14,260
129 7/8	22 1/8	22 7/8	14 7/8	6	6	Scott County	MN	Lyle E. Krueger	1991	14,260
129 7/8	21 2/8	20 0/8	13 5/8	5	5	Douglas County	WI	Darren Lee	1991	14,260
129 7/8	22 0/8	21 1/8	14 5/8	5	4	Forest County	WI	Brent M. Kadubek	1991	14,260
129 7/8	21 0/8	21 6/8	15 4/8	6	5	Henry County	VA	Mike Weaver	1991	14,260
129 7/8	23 0/8	21 3/8	14 3/8	8	8	Cherokee County	OK	Norman Gale Culver	1991	14,260
129 7/8	21 5/8	21 0/8	16 1/8	5	6	Kanabec County	MN	Dale M. Anderson	1992	14,260
129 7/8	22 0/8	21 6/8	13 5/8	5	4	Vilas County	WI	Ronald F. Lax	1992	14,260
129 7/8	21 6/8	22 6/8	15 5/8	4	4	Union County	IL	Shannon Emmons	1992	14,260
129 7/8	21 5/8	21 7/8	14 3/8	5	6	Marathon County	WI	Edward Meis, Jr.	1992	14,260
129 7/8	25 7/8	25 2/8	19 1/8	5	4	Plymouth County	MA	Kevin DeMarco	1992	14,260
129 7/8	24 1/8	24 6/8	15 4/8	5	7	Bourbon County	KS	Tony Newman	1992	14,260
129 7/8	22 1/8	22 4/8	15 5/8	4	4	New Castle County	DE	John Walstrum, Jr.	1993	14,260
129 7/8	24 1/8	22 7/8	14 7/8	4	4	Worth County	GA	Ian Wolfgang Hindle	1993	14,260
129 7/8	21 2/8	21 3/8	15 7/8	4	4	Clinton County	MI	Eric Voisinet	1993	14,260
129 7/8	19 1/8	19 4/8	15 3/8	5	5	Marion County	WV	Mario Bombardiere	1993	14,260
129 7/8	21 6/8	21 4/8	17 3/8	5	5	Buffalo County	WI	Jeff Owens	1993	14,260
129 7/8	19 2/8	20 5/8	14 5/8	5	5	Boone County	MO	Todd Lowrey	1993	14,260
129 7/8	23 7/8	23 5/8	16 7/8	4	4	Moody County	SD	Robert A. Brown	1993	14,260
129 7/8	24 2/8	25 2/8	18 7/8	5	4	Guilford County	NC	Doug Clayton	1993	14,260
129 7/8	21 3/8	21 5/8	16 1/8	5	5	Washburn County	WI	John Weber	1993	14,260
129 7/8	23 3/8	22 7/8	20 5/8	5	5	La Salle County	IL	John P. Hartman	1993	14,260
129 7/8	22 4/8	22 1/8	17 7/8	5	5	Marathon County	WI	Paul D. Waliczek	1993	14,260
129 7/8	21 0/8	21 7/8	15 7/8	5	4	Whiteside County	IL	Clint Walker	1993	14,260
129 7/8	21 6/8	20 4/8	15 7/8	6	7	Lewis County	MO	Kevin Feldewerth	1993	14,260
129 7/8	24 0/8	23 2/8	19 3/8	5	5	San Patricio County	TX	Marty Luedke	1993	14,260
129 7/8	19 7/8	20 0/8	14 5/8	5	5	Williams County	ND	Milan R. Liesener	1994	14,260
129 7/8	20 3/8	20 6/8	14 3/8	5	5	Leduc	ALB	Steve MacKenzie	1994	14,260
129 7/8	21 1/8	21 3/8	17 5/8	4	5	Waukesha County	WI	Gary D. Naylor	1994	14,260
129 7/8	22 7/8	22 6/8	15 7/8	4	4	Hickory County	MO	Wayne Kautzky	1994	14,260
129 7/8	22 6/8	23 4/8	16 7/8	4	4	Montgomery County	VA	Edward Sowers	1994	14,260
129 7/8	18 1/8	18 0/8	16 2/8	5	6	Springbank	ALB	David R. Coupland	1994	14,260

WHITETAIL DEER (TYPICAL ANTLERS)

Minimum Score 125 Continued

SCORE	LENGTH OF MAIN BEAM R / L	INSIDE SPREAD	NUMBER OF POINTS R / L		AREA	STATE/ PROVINCE	HUNTER'S NAME	DATE	RANK
129 7/8	23 1/8	22 2/8	15 1/8	5	5	Berks County	PA	Tony Zawada	1995	14,260
129 7/8	21 3/8	21 4/8	17 7/8	5	5	St. Croix County	WI	Dan Cain	1995	14,260
129 7/8	21 1/8	19 5/8	18 3/8	5	5	Menard County	IL	John Grosboll	1995	14,260
129 7/8	19 7/8	20 1/8	14 3/8	4	4	Buffalo County	NE	Philip Badura	1995	14,260
129 7/8	22 5/8	20 6/8	22 7/8	5	5	Missoula County	MT	John D. Schindler	1995	14,260
129 7/8	24 2/8	22 2/8	18 3/8	5	4	Cross County	AR	Terry Padgett	1996	14,260
129 7/8	22 5/8	21 6/8	17 6/8	5	4	Marquette County	WI	Cary J. Rickmeyer	1996	14,260
129 7/8	20 6/8	20 5/8	16 5/8	5	6	Kalamazoo County	MI	Scott Lee Bartholomew	1996	14,260
129 7/8	21 4/8	21 0/8	20 7/8	5	5	Phelps County	MO	Tim Clynes	1996	14,260
129 7/8	20 0/8	20 0/8	14 7/8	6	6	Ray County	MO	Jon Krepps	1996	14,260
129 7/8	23 0/8	24 2/8	20 7/8	4	4	Dane County	WI	Gerald Jeranek	1996	14,260
129 7/8	22 0/8	21 5/8	17 5/8	5	5	Brown County	SD	Jesse Kurtenbach	1996	14,260
129 7/8	20 1/8	20 5/8	15 3/8	5	5	Sherburne County	MN	Michael J. Kunkel	1996	14,260
129 7/8	20 4/8	20 2/8	16 3/8	5	5	Cabell County	WV	Dino Corsetti	1996	14,260
129 7/8	21 3/8	20 7/8	17 0/8	6	4	Dekalb County	IL	Norman J. Rogers	1996	14,260
129 7/8	22 2/8	22 3/8	15 3/8	5	4	Madison County	NY	Barry Hutchinson	1997	14,260
129 7/8	20 4/8	21 2/8	16 4/8	6	7	Waukesha County	WI	Daniel Reddelien	1997	14,260
129 7/8	21 3/8	23 5/8	17 5/8	4	4	Bond County	IL	Larry Garmon	1997	14,260
129 7/8	24 0/8	23 0/8	19 0/8	4	6	Will County	IL	Mike O'Connor	1997	14,260
129 7/8	21 6/8	21 6/8	13 3/8	5	5	Buffalo County	WI	David A. O'Brien	1997	14,260
129 7/8	21 4/8	21 0/8	16 1/8	4	4	Sanilac County	MI	Eric R. Ehrlich	1997	14,260
129 7/8	22 2/8	21 6/8	14 5/8	5	5	Eaton County	MI	William D. Haney	1997	14,260
129 7/8	23 1/8	21 5/8	18 1/8	4	4	Lyon County	KS	Daniel Coffelt	1997	14,260
129 7/8	21 3/8	21 2/8	16 7/8	4	5	Lapeer County	MI	Steve M. Best	1997	14,260
129 7/8	21 3/8	21 4/8	13 5/8	4	4	Hancock County	IA	Ken Lonneman	1997	14,260
129 7/8	22 5/8	22 5/8	18 1/8	4	4	Hunterdon County	NJ	Daniel Sherwood	1997	14,260
129 7/8	23 5/8	23 2/8	16 7/8	5	5	Van Buren County	MI	Kevin Mann	1997	14,260
129 7/8	22 0/8	22 2/8	18 7/8	5	5	Kewaunee County	WI	Brian Lee Nemetz	1998	14,260
129 6/8	19 5/8	20 7/8	16 2/8	5	6	Adams County	IL	Mel Powell	1964	14,353
129 6/8	20 2/8	18 0/8	17 2/8	5	5	Johnson County	WY	Jim Bartz	1969	14,353
129 6/8	22 5/8	22 2/8	20 2/8	7	5	Morrison County	MN	Robert E. Nordstrom	1973	14,353
129 6/8	22 2/8	21 0/8	17 0/8	5	4	Lee County	IA	Jim Bohenkamp	1974	14,353
129 6/8	21 4/8	22 0/8	20 0/8	4	5	Washtenaw County	MI	Richard A. Hollo	1980	14,353
129 6/8	21 1/8	22 7/8	17 4/8	6	5	Prince Georges County	MD	Russell A. Nichols	1980	14,353
129 6/8	23 6/8	23 2/8	16 4/8	4	4	Lawrence County	OH	Ronald E. Clark	1981	14,353
129 6/8	24 2/8	23 0/8	15 7/8	6	5	Lawrence County	OH	Randy Gilmore	1982	14,353
129 6/8	22 1/8	22 1/8	15 6/8	4	4	Gallia County	OH	Jack Satterfield, Jr.	1982	14,353
129 6/8	22 5/8	23 1/8	16 6/8	4	4	Jo Daviess County	IL	Tom Smith	1982	14,353
129 6/8	20 5/8	22 2/8	19 0/8	4	4	Juneau County	WI	Larry Southworth	1983	14,353
129 6/8	21 4/8	22 1/8	15 4/8	5	5	Calhoun County	MI	Dick Coon	1983	14,353
129 6/8	18 6/8	18 5/8	21 2/8	7	5	Lake County	MI	James H. Wichman	1984	14,353
129 6/8	22 1/8	22 0/8	20 2/8	4	4	Will County	IL	Richard "Rick" Gagle	1984	14,353
129 6/8	22 3/8	22 0/8	15 2/8	5	5	Morrison County	MN	Richard W. Gamache	1984	14,353
129 6/8	22 1/8	21 1/8	17 2/8	5	5	Hunterdon County	NJ	Thaddeus A. Tykarsky III	1984	14,353
129 6/8	23 1/8	23 0/8	16 4/8	7	4	Grant County	WI	Jim Johnson	1985	14,353
129 6/8	20 2/8	20 5/8	14 4/8	5	5	White County	AR	Robbie Snowden	1986	14,353
129 6/8	24 7/8	23 0/8	16 6/8	5	5	Jefferson County	WI	David Springer, Jr.	1986	14,353
129 6/8	23 4/8	23 1/8	15 4/8	4	4	Scott County	KY	Michael R. Duncan	1986	14,353
129 6/8	22 5/8	23 0/8	19 2/8	5	5	Mercer County	NJ	Frank Prato	1986	14,353
129 6/8	22 0/8	21 6/8	17 0/8	4	4	Racine County	WI	Denis Sommers	1987	14,353
129 6/8	21 5/8	20 5/8	21 4/8	4	5	Calhoun County	MI	John P. Walters	1987	14,353
129 6/8	20 6/8	19 5/8	15 5/8	5	6	Kane County	IL	Thomas E. Prosser	1987	14,353
129 6/8	23 3/8	23 1/8	19 0/8	4	4	Wicomico County	MD	H. Noel Dykes, Jr.	1987	14,353
129 6/8	21 2/8	21 3/8	17 6/8	4	4	St. Charles County	MO	Larry Doe	1988	14,353
129 6/8	23 7/8	22 5/8	19 0/8	4	4	Howard County	MD	Leon Lantz II	1988	14,353
129 6/8	24 7/8	22 5/8	16 1/8	6	7	Ellsworth County	KS	Steven Siemsen	1988	14,353
129 6/8	20 4/8	20 6/8	17 0/8	5	4	Vermilion County	IL	Alan E. Cessna	1988	14,353
129 6/8	22 2/8	22 1/8	14 2/8	7	5	Taylor County	WI	Glen Ogle	1989	14,353
129 6/8	22 7/8	21 4/8	15 6/8	5	5	Kalamazoo County	MI	Mark Van Dalen	1989	14,353
129 6/8	23 1/8	22 2/8	19 4/8	5	5	Allegany County	MD	Gary Loar	1990	14,353
129 6/8	22 7/8	22 7/8	19 0/8	5	5	Tompkins County	NY	David E. Barnes	1990	14,353
129 6/8	21 3/8	20 6/8	17 0/8	5	5	Wayne County	NY	Rick Fox	1990	14,353
129 6/8	22 6/8	22 4/8	16 0/8	4	4	Douglas County	WI	Gary W. Holcombe	1990	14,353
129 6/8	24 0/8	22 1/8	14 2/8	4	4	Monona County	IA	Dennis Rush	1990	14,353
129 6/8	21 6/8	22 4/8	17 6/8	5	5	Powell County	MT	Roberta R. Culp	1990	14,353
129 6/8	22 7/8	25 2/8	20 1/8	4	5	Hardin County	KY	Donald J. Vittitow, Jr.	1991	14,353
129 6/8	21 6/8	21 2/8	17 6/8	4	4	Crawford County	MO	Monty R. Cooper	1991	14,353
129 6/8	21 0/8	20 2/8	16 0/8	5	5	Camden County	MO	Ronald J. Paskon	1991	14,353
129 6/8	20 5/8	21 1/8	18 3/8	5	6	Morgan County	IN	Joe Ferran	1991	14,353
129 6/8	21 7/8	23 3/8	18 0/8	4	4	Kent County	MD	Lewin S. Blackiston III	1991	14,353
129 6/8	20 2/8	19 6/8	17 0/8	5	7	La Salle County	IL	Michael Elbrecht	1991	14,353
129 6/8	21 3/8	20 4/8	18 6/8	4	4	Goliad County	TX	Gil Baumgarten	1991	14,353
129 6/8	20 5/8	21 1/8	15 4/8	6	5	Warren County	MS	Billy Bryant	1991	14,353
129 6/8	20 5/8	21 1/8	18 1/8	5	5	Henry County	VA	Mike Weaver	1991	14,353
129 6/8	23 0/8	22 6/8	14 6/8	4	4	Huron County	MI	Steven R. Verkerke	1992	14,353
129 6/8	22 3/8	23 6/8	18 0/8	5	5	Cookstown	ONT	Dan Hutchinson	1992	14,353
129 6/8	20 0/8	20 2/8	17 4/8	5	5	Dunn County	WI	Michael J. Shields	1992	14,353
129 6/8	20 3/8	20 4/8	15 4/8	5	5	Reagan County	TX	Ronald H. Ray	1992	14,353

WHITETAIL DEER (TYPICAL ANTLERS)

Minimum Score 125 — Continued

SCORE	LENGTH OF MAIN BEAM R	LENGTH OF MAIN BEAM L	INSIDE SPREAD	NUMBER OF POINTS R	NUMBER OF POINTS L	AREA	STATE/PROVINCE	HUNTER'S NAME	DATE	RANK
129 6/8	22 1/8	22 4/8	19 4/8	5	4	Suffolk County	NY	David Bunai	1992	14,353
129 6/8	19 2/8	20 2/8	13 6/8	5	5	Grant County	SD	Richard D. Schmidt	1993	14,353
129 6/8	19 2/8	17 6/8	15 4/8	5	5	Vernon County	WI	Robert S. Larson	1993	14,353
129 6/8	21 5/8	20 6/8	15 0/8	5	5	Maverick County	TX	Dennis Cooke	1993	14,353
129 6/8	22 3/8	23 0/8	17 5/8	5	4	Dunn County	WI	Curt Henderson	1993	14,353
129 6/8	23 6/8	24 2/8	15 4/8	5	4	Crow Wing County	MN	Andy Whitcomb	1993	14,353
129 6/8	22 7/8	21 7/8	17 0/8	4	4	Fairfax County	VA	S. Kirby Kerns	1993	14,353
129 6/8	19 6/8	20 0/8	15 6/8	5	5	Marinette County	WI	Neil Dretzka	1993	14,353
129 6/8	19 0/8	19 0/8	15 6/8	5	5	Peoria County	IL	Dennis D. Herold	1993	14,353
129 6/8	22 4/8	23 3/8	16 4/8	4	4	Licking County	OH	Thomas E. Lott	1993	14,353
129 6/8	21 6/8	19 4/8	15 6/8	6	6	Buffalo County	WI	Allen L. Covey	1993	14,353
129 6/8	19 2/8	20 0/8	16 2/8	5	4	Carroll County	MD	Carroll Thomas Roach	1993	14,353
129 6/8	22 4/8	22 5/8	16 1/8	6	4	Comanche County	KS	Ronnie Sawyers	1993	14,353
129 6/8	20 2/8	19 7/8	17 6/8	6	6	McClain County	OK	Jon Herd	1993	14,353
129 6/8	23 3/8	22 2/8	20 2/8	4	5	Prince Georges County	MD	Lance Canter	1994	14,353
129 6/8	21 0/8	21 1/8	16 2/8	4	4	McBride Lake	SAS	Robert Dyck	1994	14,353
129 6/8	21 7/8	23 5/8	15 2/8	5	6	Perry County	IL	Curtis Hutchings	1994	14,353
129 6/8	22 4/8	21 1/8	17 2/8	5	4	Woodford County	IL	Charles C. Colburn	1994	14,353
129 6/8	23 4/8	22 6/8	17 2/8	5	4	Grant County	WI	Jack L. Oostdik	1994	14,353
129 6/8	20 5/8	21 0/8	15 4/8	5	5	Adams County	IL	Jeff Fitts	1994	14,353
129 6/8	23 7/8	22 4/8	15 4/8	5	5	Decatur County	TN	David Wyatt	1995	14,353
129 6/8	21 7/8	22 0/8	18 0/8	4	4	Callaway County	MO	Chuck Hemmel	1995	14,353
129 6/8	22 2/8	22 2/8	17 2/8	5	4	La Crosse County	WI	Ronald E. Brown	1995	14,353
129 6/8	22 5/8	22 6/8	18 0/8	4	4	Morris County	NJ	John Mascellino, Jr.	1995	14,353
129 6/8	21 0/8	21 6/8	18 0/8	5	5	Letellier	MAN	Todd Amenrud	1995	14,353
129 6/8	20 2/8	20 6/8	14 2/8	5	5	Harris County	GA	Glenn Garner	1995	14,353
129 6/8	21 6/8	20 6/8	15 0/8	4	4	Sterling County	TX	Bud Dillard	1995	14,353
129 6/8	23 3/8	22 7/8	16 7/8	6	5	Bayfield County	WI	Bradley Kuhnert	1995	14,353
129 6/8	21 3/8	22 5/8	15 0/8	5	5	Lapeer County	MI	Thomas J. Baker	1995	14,353
129 6/8	22 5/8	21 7/8	14 5/8	5	6	Howard County	IA	Jess A. Ellingson	1995	14,353
129 6/8	21 2/8	19 7/8	19 2/8	4	6	Hamilton County	IL	Dennis Wheeler	1995	14,353
129 6/8	20 5/8	19 3/8	16 2/8	5	5	Spokane County	WA	Dennis Lee Truman	1996	14,353
129 6/8	21 3/8	21 0/8	20 5/8	5	5	Fillmore County	MN	Kirk Lee Ericson	1996	14,353
129 6/8	22 6/8	21 6/8	16 0/8	4	4	Sauk County	WI	Terry Woirol	1996	14,353
129 6/8	22 6/8	22 6/8	19 5/8	5	4	Carroll County	OH	Carl D. Leary	1996	14,353
129 6/8	21 6/8	23 0/8	17 0/8	5	5	Dane County	WI	Rick Waldschmidt	1996	14,353
129 6/8	21 6/8	22 2/8	16 2/8	5	5	Clark County	IL	Rex Kemper	1996	14,353
129 6/8	19 0/8	19 2/8	15 6/8	6	5	Cherry County	NE	Ted Ruffner	1996	14,353
129 6/8	21 7/8	21 4/8	17 0/8	6	5	Christian Valley	BC	Roy Gerrath	1996	14,353
129 6/8	19 4/8	20 1/8	16 0/8	5	5	Dodge County	MN	Lon E. Bleess	1996	14,353
129 6/8	19 6/8	20 2/8	16 0/8	6	5	Polk County	WI	Dawn A. Larson	1997	14,353
129 6/8	22 2/8	22 2/8	17 3/8	5	4	Pike County	IL	Tim Farniok	1997	14,353
129 6/8	21 0/8	21 7/8	18 2/8	5	6	Fond du Lac County	WI	Pat Engel	1997	14,353
129 6/8	20 1/8	21 1/8	17 0/8	5	5	Walworth County	WI	Randy Johnson	1997	14,353
129 6/8	22 6/8	22 5/8	19 6/8	6	6	Hampshire County	WV	Mark Payne	1997	14,353
129 6/8	21 0/8	23 4/8	19 6/8	4	4	Calloway County	KY	Alan Ray Jones	1997	14,353
129 5/8	23 2/8	24 0/8	17 6/8	4	4	Taylor County	WV	Jimmie R. Auvil	1959	14,449
129 5/8	22 5/8	22 1/8	20 1/8	5	5	Cowley County	KS	Charles O'Daniel	1966	14,449
129 5/8	22 3/8	22 4/8	17 5/8	4	5	Trigg County	KY	Ronald M. Goddard	1969	14,449
129 5/8	21 6/8	21 2/8	18 5/8	5	4	Waushara County	WI	Roger D. Johnson	1979	14,449
129 5/8	22 4/8	23 5/8	17 3/8	6	4	Ontario County	NY	Richard Rockefeller	1979	14,449
129 5/8	20 7/8	20 4/8	17 1/8	4	4	Fillmore County	MN	Robert Meyer	1981	14,449
129 5/8	23 0/8	23 2/8	19 5/8	4	5	Ontario County	NY	Ronald Molinari	1981	14,449
129 5/8	22 4/8	22 3/8	18 6/8	4	5	Lucas County	OH	James L. Davies	1982	14,449
129 5/8	20 6/8	19 2/8	13 7/8	5	5	Traill County	ND	Willis Mueller	1982	14,449
129 5/8	21 0/8	20 2/8	18 7/8	6	5	Scott County	KY	Ronnie Jacobs	1983	14,449
129 5/8	23 2/8	23 4/8	21 5/8	5	4	Dorchester County	MD	Thomas R. Pohuski	1984	14,449
129 5/8	23 4/8	23 4/8	15 1/8	4	4	Washington County	MN	Patrick F. Dolan	1984	14,449
129 5/8	24 4/8	26 0/8	16 5/8	4	4	Livingston County	NY	Christopher D. Walp	1985	14,449
129 5/8	20 6/8	21 4/8	19 0/8	6	4	Williams County	OH	Steven Reader	1985	14,449
129 5/8	22 6/8	20 3/8	17 6/8	4	6	Madison County	IL	Mark A. Thompson	1985	14,449
129 5/8	20 1/8	21 4/8	19 1/8	4	4	Henderson County	KY	Ken McKay	1986	14,449
129 5/8	22 3/8	21 5/8	17 1/8	5	4	Pike County	MO	Ray Hatfield	1986	14,449
129 5/8	23 0/8	22 3/8	19 1/8	4	4	Montgomery County	IN	Douglas P. Kellerman	1986	14,449
129 5/8	22 4/8	23 1/8	18 7/8	5	5	Mineral County	WV	Brad K. Gentzler	1986	14,449
129 5/8	21 6/8	22 0/8	16 3/8	5	5	Somerset County	NJ	Steven Niedzielski	1986	14,449
129 5/8	22 7/8	23 6/8	18 5/8	4	4	Somerset County	NJ	Steven J. Niedzielski	1987	14,449
129 5/8	23 1/8	23 0/8	18 3/8	5	5	Forest County	WI	Mark Schad	1987	14,449
129 5/8	21 3/8	21 1/8	15 7/8	5	4	Franklin Municipality	MAN	James Sondeland	1988	14,449
129 5/8	19 4/8	21 2/8	17 5/8	4	4	Schuyler County	IL	Charles W. Trone, Jr.	1988	14,449
129 5/8	18 3/8	16 4/8	17 5/8	5	5	Custer County	NE	James J. Spanel	1989	14,449
129 5/8	21 7/8	22 0/8	16 6/8	6	4	Northampton County	VA	Jeffre L. Jones	1989	14,449
129 5/8	23 1/8	22 4/8	16 7/8	5	5	Dane County	WI	Robert Bischel	1989	14,449
129 5/8	21 1/8	21 1/8	17 1/8	5	5	Dane County	WI	Paul T. Ovadal	1989	14,449
129 5/8	21 6/8	21 3/8	16 1/8	4	5	Kossuth County	IA	Kevin Peterson	1989	14,449
129 5/8	21 6/8	21 2/8	15 6/8	5	5	Callaway County	MO	Gene Nelson	1989	14,449
129 5/8	22 7/8	23 4/8	17 7/8	5	5	Duval County	TX	Shirley Oatman	1990	14,449
129 5/8	21 1/8	19 7/8	15 4/8	5	6	Graham County	KS	Gary Long	1990	14,449

WHITETAIL DEER (TYPICAL ANTLERS)

Minimum Score 125   Continued

SCORE	LENGTH OF MAIN BEAM R	LENGTH OF MAIN BEAM L	INSIDE SPREAD	NUMBER OF POINTS R	NUMBER OF POINTS L	AREA	STATE/ PROVINCE	HUNTER'S NAME	DATE	RANK
129 5/8	23 5/8	22 4/8	18 7/8	4	5	Prince William County	VA	Christopher Nichol	1990	14,449
129 5/8	21 1/8	20 5/8	17 2/8	7	5	St. Croix County	WI	Jerry Yaritz	1990	14,449
129 5/8	19 6/8	19 5/8	16 7/8	4	4	York County	NE	Marlin Seeman	1990	14,449
129 5/8	26 4/8	25 7/8	19 2/8	4	5	Union County	KY	Robert W. Ervin	1990	14,449
129 5/8	20 2/8	21 5/8	17 3/8	6	5	Dane County	WI	Randy Ree	1990	14,449
129 5/8	21 0/8	20 5/8	15 3/8	5	5	Geauga County	OH	Rudy M. Began	1990	14,449
129 5/8	22 7/8	22 2/8	19 7/8	6	4	Champaign County	OH	Tim Pond	1990	14,449
129 5/8	20 0/8	19 0/8	16 5/8	5	5	Houston County	TN	Bobby Bryant	1991	14,449
129 5/8	22 2/8	21 7/8	17 5/8	5	5	Lawrence County	IN	Arter Thompson II	1991	14,449
129 5/8	22 6/8	22 0/8	15 6/8	5	6	Perry County	AR	Allen Lovell	1991	14,449
129 5/8	21 7/8	22 3/8	17 3/8	5	5	Menard County	IL	Barry D. Sampson	1991	14,449
129 5/8	21 0/8	20 7/8	14 3/8	5	5	Washington County	IA	Kevin Langan	1991	14,449
129 5/8	21 5/8	21 4/8	16 1/8	5	6	Sauk County	WI	Gregory W. Stebler	1991	14,449
129 5/8	24 4/8	23 5/8	16 7/8	5	6	Washtenaw County	MI	Carl T. Ticknor	1991	14,449
129 5/8	19 7/8	18 6/8	14 7/8	8	6	Spokane County	WA	Nicholas Orth	1992	14,449
129 5/8	19 6/8	21 1/8	14 7/8	5	5	Edmonson County	KY	Marvin Pate	1992	14,449
129 5/8	22 2/8	21 7/8	15 5/8	6	7	Allegan County	MI	Ethan Belden	1992	14,449
129 5/8	23 0/8	22 2/8	15 7/8	5	4	La Porte County	IN	Paul Neidlinger	1992	14,449
129 5/8	21 5/8	21 5/8	16 5/8	4	4	Rusk County	WI	Randall Artrip	1992	14,449
129 5/8	20 0/8	20 2/8	20 3/8	6	5	Duval County	TX	Gilberto Guajardo, Jr.	1992	14,449
129 5/8	23 5/8	23 6/8	16 7/8	4	4	McMullen County	TX	Robert R. Corder IV	1992	14,449
129 5/8	22 7/8	22 6/8	18 5/8	4	4	Lincoln County	MT	Todd Lapka	1993	14,449
129 5/8	22 4/8	23 0/8	17 3/8	4	4	St. Joseph County	IN	William J. Hicks	1993	14,449
129 5/8	20 7/8	21 5/8	15 1/8	5	5	Houston County	MN	Chris Diersen	1993	14,449
129 5/8	24 1/8	23 2/8	19 3/8	4	4	Fulton County	IL	Tim Wells	1993	14,449
129 5/8	22 2/8	22 1/8	14 1/8	4	4	Franklin County	MO	Greg Reiker	1993	14,449
129 5/8	23 0/8	22 6/8	14 3/8	4	5	Greene County	MO	Richard Weaver	1993	14,449
129 5/8	21 0/8	21 7/8	16 7/8	4	4	Lenawee County	MI	Raymond B. Lubinski	1993	14,449
129 5/8	19 7/8	20 2/8	16 7/8	4	4	Christian County	IL	Lisa Sulcer	1993	14,449
129 5/8	20 0/8	20 2/8	17 5/8	4	4	Warren County	IA	Richard E. Stanton	1993	14,449
129 5/8	22 3/8	21 7/8	19 7/8	5	4	San Patricio County	TX	Bruce Barrie	1993	14,449
129 5/8	20 7/8	22 3/8	19 0/8	5	6	Jefferson County	WI	Gary Leverenz	1994	14,449
129 5/8	21 1/8	22 0/8	17 1/8	5	5	Bayfield County	WI	Bob Wiezorek	1994	14,449
129 5/8	22 0/8	21 2/8	16 5/8	4	5	Hendricks County	IN	Douglas Edwards	1994	14,449
129 5/8	20 7/8	21 2/8	16 1/8	5	5	Winneshiek County	IA	Gary Ludeking	1994	14,449
129 5/8	21 6/8	21 2/8	15 7/8	5	5	Clark County	WI	Steve Karner	1994	14,449
129 5/8	23 1/8	22 4/8	18 5/8	4	4	Van Buren County	MI	Rodney R. Doxtater	1994	14,449
129 5/8	23 7/8	21 1/8	20 1/8	4	4	Ouachita Parish	LA	Arvil Fowler	1995	14,449
129 5/8	22 3/8	22 3/8	16 6/8	5	5	Valley County	MT	Edwin Miller	1995	14,449
129 5/8	22 1/8	20 5/8	15 3/8	5	5	Jasper County	IL	Larry Hall	1995	14,449
129 5/8	20 2/8	22 0/8	18 5/8	5	6	Lawrence County	IL	Russell Morris	1995	14,449
129 5/8	22 1/8	23 1/8	15 1/8	4	4	Portage County	WI	Jonathan M. Lesniak	1995	14,449
129 5/8	21 2/8	21 5/8	16 7/8	5	5	Oconto County	WI	Randy Loberger	1995	14,449
129 5/8	20 3/8	20 5/8	18 3/8	5	5	Columbiana County	OH	James Lambert	1995	14,449
129 5/8	20 4/8	21 2/8	16 1/8	4	4	Langlade County	WI	Doug D. Samolinski	1995	14,449
129 5/8	19 5/8	20 0/8	14 7/8	6	6	Adair County	MO	Greg Eudaley	1995	14,449
129 5/8	23 3/8	23 3/8	17 1/8	4	4	St. Marys County	MD	Phillip Cartwright	1995	14,449
129 5/8	23 0/8	21 5/8	13 5/8	4	4	Cumberland County	NJ	Bob Eisele, Sr.	1995	14,449
129 5/8	21 5/8	21 6/8	18 1/8	6	5	Oakland County	MI	Michael J. DeWitt	1995	14,449
129 5/8	20 7/8	20 5/8	16 5/8	5	4	Frio County	TX	Johnny Haddad	1996	14,449
129 5/8	19 6/8	20 1/8	13 5/8	7	7	Sullivan County	IN	Lowell Blakley	1996	14,449
129 5/8	20 3/8	20 4/8	16 3/8	5	5	Williams County	ND	Ernie Leonard	1996	14,449
129 5/8	23 2/8	24 1/8	20 1/8	4	4	Mecklenburg County	NC	Paul Allan Palmer	1996	14,449
129 5/8	20 4/8	20 2/8	13 5/8	5	5	Dodge County	NE	Michael C. Diers	1996	14,449
129 5/8	20 2/8	20 5/8	17 1/8	5	5	Fulton County	IN	Tom C. Hunneshagen	1996	14,449
129 5/8	24 2/8	23 3/8	21 5/8	5	5	Broome County	NY	Stanley M. Myers	1996	14,449
129 5/8	22 2/8	22 2/8	17 7/8	5	5	Pike County	IL	Ivan J. Muzljakovich	1996	14,449
129 5/8	23 3/8	23 0/8	19 7/8	4	4	Laurens County	GA	Terry Garnto	1996	14,449
129 5/8	21 5/8	21 0/8	17 3/8	4	4	McHenry County	IL	Al Ortmann	1996	14,449
129 5/8	19 3/8	19 7/8	15 1/8	5	5	Pennington County	SD	Garold Shull	1996	14,449
129 5/8	22 4/8	22 5/8	15 3/8	6	6	Clark County	OH	Greg Thacker	1997	14,449
129 5/8	21 4/8	22 3/8	18 7/8	5	5	Buffalo County	WI	Tyler Bertel	1997	14,449
129 5/8	22 1/8	21 3/8	19 1/8	5	5	Marion County	IA	Gerald T. Dowell	1997	14,449
129 5/8	21 5/8	21 3/8	17 5/8	4	4	Manitowoc County	WI	Dan Kienbaum	1997	14,449
129 5/8	22 3/8	21 1/8	17 3/8	5	5	Columbia County	WI	Daniel J. Benson	1997	14,449
129 5/8	22 3/8	21 6/8	15 3/8	4	5	Weld County	CO	Eric Stern	1997	14,449
129 5/8	22 4/8	22 6/8	17 5/8	5	5	Morris County	NJ	Joe Russo	1997	14,449
129 5/8	19 2/8	19 0/8	14 1/8	4	4	Marathon County	WI	Randy Stank	1998	14,449
129 4/8	21 5/8	20 2/8	15 4/8	5	5	Sarpy County	NE	Russ Calloway	1962	14,549
129 4/8	22 4/8	21 7/8	17 6/8	5	5	Monroe County	GA	Robert S. Carey	1973	14,549
129 4/8	23 1/8	23 3/8	19 2/8	4	3	Green County	WI	Jerry Amundson	1976	14,549
129 4/8	23 4/8	22 0/8	15 4/8	5	5	Newton County	IN	Howard Culbertson	1976	14,549
129 4/8	20 2/8	20 4/8	16 5/8	5	5	Elk County	PA	Charles F. Eckl	1977	14,549
129 4/8	21 6/8	21 6/8	22 0/8	4	5	Puslinch Twp.	ONT	Larry Knarr	1980	14,549
129 4/8	22 2/8	22 1/8	16 4/8	4	5	Chippewa County	WI	John M. Hanzlik	1981	14,549
129 4/8	23 7/8	23 2/8	16 5/8	5	4	Lindsay	ONT	Ken Steele	1983	14,549
129 4/8	22 6/8	22 2/8	16 0/8	4	5	La Salle County	IL	Steve Wagner	1984	14,549
129 4/8	19 1/8	19 6/8	16 5/8	5	5	Juneau County	WI	Dean Tompkins	1984	14,549

WHITETAIL DEER (TYPICAL ANTLERS)

Minimum Score 125 — Continued

SCORE	LENGTH OF MAIN BEAM R	LENGTH OF MAIN BEAM L	INSIDE SPREAD	NUMBER OF POINTS R	NUMBER OF POINTS L	AREA	STATE/PROVINCE	HUNTER'S NAME	DATE	RANK
129 4/8	21 7/8	22 1/8	16 0/8	5	5	La Salle County	IL	John LiLes	1984	14,549
129 4/8	19 0/8	18 7/8	15 0/8	5	5	Marion County	TX	Woody L. Harmon	1985	14,549
129 4/8	22 6/8	23 7/8	18 2/8	5	5	Sherburne County	MN	Marvin Vogelgesang	1985	14,549
129 4/8	19 1/8	19 5/8	15 2/8	4	4	Pike County	IL	Lloyd Bateman	1985	14,549
129 4/8	19 6/8	21 5/8	14 2/8	5	5	Johnson County	MO	Scott Simmons	1986	14,549
129 4/8	23 5/8	23 2/8	19 0/8	4	5	Sheboygan County	WI	Paul Beimborn	1986	14,549
129 4/8	20 0/8	20 1/8	17 0/8	5	5	Dodge County	MN	Jay F. Deones	1986	14,549
129 4/8	21 1/8	21 4/8	16 2/8	5	5	Columbia County	WI	Mark Toso	1986	14,549
129 4/8	21 7/8	21 3/8	18 2/8	7	6	Lewis & Clark County	MT	Jim Ryan	1986	14,549
129 4/8	24 0/8	22 5/8	17 6/8	5	6	Fulton County	OH	Lonnie D. Blosser	1987	14,549
129 4/8	22 4/8	22 0/8	17 0/8	5	4	Randolph County	WV	Jesse Ramsey	1987	14,549
129 4/8	21 7/8	21 1/8	16 6/8	4	4	Walworth County	WI	David A. Bennett	1987	14,549
129 4/8	24 3/8	25 1/8	18 2/8	4	4	Greene County	OH	William T. Ashmore III	1987	14,549
129 4/8	21 1/8	21 3/8	17 4/8	4	4	Buffalo County	WI	Glen R. Axness	1987	14,549
129 4/8	23 2/8	23 5/8	15 2/8	5	6	Madison County	IL	Dennis Collman	1988	14,549
129 4/8	19 5/8	20 2/8	13 1/8	6	6	Lewis & Clark County	MT	Steven Leigh Jones	1988	14,549
129 4/8	20 0/8	19 6/8	14 4/8	5	5	Patrick County	VA	Mike Mitchell	1988	14,549
129 4/8	22 5/8	22 7/8	18 7/8	4	9	Cooke County	TX	David James Hoedebeck	1988	14,549
129 4/8	22 2/8	21 7/8	16 4/8	4	4	Lucas County	IA	Bill Brown	1988	14,549
129 4/8	22 5/8	23 1/8	21 0/8	5	5	Forest County	WI	Terry A. Kickbusch	1988	14,549
129 4/8	24 0/8	21 6/8	17 5/8	4	5	St. Croix County	WI	Randall Offner	1988	14,549
129 4/8	20 6/8	21 1/8	19 7/8	6	5	Parkland County	ALB	Sam Halabi	1988	14,549
129 4/8	22 6/8	21 7/8	14 2/8	6	4	Hudson Bay	SAS	Ron Tyacke	1989	14,549
129 4/8	22 6/8	23 6/8	16 4/8	5	5	Rock County	WI	Raymond Klug	1989	14,549
129 4/8	22 0/8	22 0/8	17 6/8	5	5	Jo Daviess County	IL	Mike Schubert	1989	14,549
129 4/8	20 2/8	20 0/8	14 6/8	5	5	Sedgwick County	KS	Louis Turner	1989	14,549
129 4/8	24 0/8	23 3/8	15 7/8	4	5	Suffolk County	VA	Scott W. Liebold	1989	14,549
129 4/8	22 0/8	21 0/8	15 4/8	5	6	Dodge County	WI	Dan Gourlie	1990	14,549
129 4/8	20 4/8	20 6/8	15 1/8	7	6	Franklin County	NE	Troy Patterson	1990	14,549
129 4/8	22 6/8	22 4/8	17 1/8	5	4	Weld County	CO	Doug Kayl	1990	14,549
129 4/8	22 7/8	23 0/8	17 6/8	4	4	Oneida County	WI	Tim Johnson	1990	14,549
129 4/8	22 3/8	23 4/8	15 4/8	6	6	Sullivan County	NH	Larry Dufresne	1991	14,549
129 4/8	21 4/8	21 6/8	16 6/8	5	4	Caswell County	NC	David E. Lancaster	1991	14,549
129 4/8	22 2/8	21 7/8	17 0/8	5	5	Gogebic County	MI	Douglas L. Below	1991	14,549
129 4/8	20 4/8	21 0/8	15 4/8	4	6	Coshocton County	OH	Gary Lynn Fischer	1991	14,549
129 4/8	22 3/8	22 7/8	17 0/8	4	5	Grant County	SD	Scott R. Miller	1991	14,549
129 4/8	21 4/8	20 3/8	19 4/8	5	5	Iron County	WI	D. J. Sulllvan	1991	14,549
129 4/8	22 2/8	22 2/8	15 2/8	5	5	Middlesex County	MA	Rick Knight	1991	14,549
129 4/8	22 5/8	21 0/8	18 0/8	5	5	Monroe County	IL	Randy Rettinghouse	1991	14,549
129 4/8	20 7/8	20 7/8	18 5/8	6	5	Missoula County	MT	Louis W. Bainbridge	1992	14,549
129 4/8	20 4/8	20 4/8	14 6/8	5	5	Newton County	MO	Bobby Warden	1992	14,549
129 4/8	21 4/8	22 2/8	15 4/8	5	5	Emanuel County	GA	James L. Brown, Jr.	1992	14,549
129 4/8	21 2/8	20 5/8	17 4/8	4	5	Hocking County	OH	Doug Moos	1992	14,549
129 4/8	23 4/8	23 3/8	18 6/8	4	4	Dane County	WI	David J. Stiklestad	1992	14,549
129 4/8	22 3/8	22 3/8	16 4/8	4	5	Worcester County	MA	Daniel A. Zanauskas	1992	14,549
129 4/8	22 4/8	22 4/8	17 2/8	4	4	Morris County	NJ	Steven J. Niedzielski	1992	14,549
129 4/8	24 1/8	24 1/8	20 4/8	4	4	Cheshire County	NH	Gregory G. Bath	1992	14,549
129 4/8	25 6/8	24 4/8	20 3/8	4	4	Morgan County	IL	Gary Tasker	1992	14,549
129 4/8	21 7/8	21 1/8	17 0/8	6	5	La Salle County	TX	Doug Corley	1992	14,549
129 4/8	25 4/8	24 4/8	17 2/8	6	4	Union County	IL	Tom Michael	1992	14,549
129 4/8	20 3/8	21 0/8	17 0/8	5	5	Black Hawk County	IA	Bill Kneeskern	1993	14,549
129 4/8	22 5/8	22 4/8	15 1/8	5	6	Edmonton	ALB	Andre Titley	1993	14,549
129 4/8	19 1/8	18 3/8	16 6/8	5	6	Will County	IL	Brian J. Smith	1993	14,549
129 4/8	20 1/8	20 1/8	13 6/8	6	6	Waushara County	WI	Chad Kropp	1993	14,549
129 4/8	19 4/8	19 5/8	15 0/8	5	5	St. Louis County	MO	Ben Kurtz	1993	14,549
129 4/8	21 3/8	21 7/8	16 2/8	4	4	Vermilion County	IL	Frank Christian, Jr.	1993	14,549
129 4/8	22 5/8	23 6/8	18 6/8	4	5	Polk County	WI	David Wald	1993	14,549
129 4/8	19 5/8	18 5/8	15 6/8	5	5	Lancaster County	NE	Gary Kurtzer	1993	14,549
129 4/8	22 3/8	21 6/8	16 2/8	5	5	Calhoun County	MI	James E. Rhoades	1993	14,549
129 4/8	20 0/8	21 3/8	15 0/8	5	5	Athens County	OH	Curtis R. Rutter	1993	14,549
129 4/8	18 2/8	20 4/8	13 4/8	5	5	Jefferson Davis County	MS	Clay Massey	1993	14,549
129 4/8	18 4/8	19 4/8	17 2/8	5	5	Hunterdon County	NJ	Jeff Farr	1994	14,549
129 4/8	20 7/8	21 2/8	14 6/8	5	4	Hillsdale County	MI	Gregory J. Raatz	1994	14,549
129 4/8	21 1/8	21 2/8	15 4/8	4	4	Lake County	IL	Steve Andrews	1994	14,549
129 4/8	20 3/8	19 5/8	16 2/8	5	5	Cayuga County	NY	Mark Reynolds	1994	14,549
129 4/8	21 7/8	21 2/8	16 0/8	5	6	Green County	WI	Forrest Ladwig	1994	14,549
129 4/8	22 0/8	24 6/8	17 6/8	6	7	Jackson County	OH	Larry J. Waugh	1994	14,549
129 4/8	25 5/8	25 1/8	19 5/8	6	6	Hamilton County	OH	Roger Perkins	1994	14,549
129 4/8	21 4/8	22 3/8	16 0/8	6	6	Jones County	IA	James Bailey	1994	14,549
129 4/8	19 1/8	17 7/8	14 2/8	5	5	Kerr County	TX	Ronald Ralston	1994	14,549
129 4/8	22 7/8	24 1/8	16 0/8	4	4	Jackson County	MI	Frederick E. Smith	1994	14,549
129 4/8	21 1/8	20 3/8	20 0/8	4	4	Weld County	CO	Alan Katchur	1994	14,549
129 4/8	22 3/8	22 3/8	14 6/8	5	4	Cowley County	KS	Dave Holt	1994	14,549
129 4/8	20 7/8	21 5/8	16 1/8	7	5	Wright County	MN	Bob Kuhlmann	1995	14,549
129 4/8	23 2/8	22 4/8	14 4/8	5	5	Carroll County	MD	Todd W. Pfoutz	1995	14,549
129 4/8	22 2/8	22 5/8	16 2/8	5	6	Fulton County	IN	Steven C. Bauer	1995	14,549
129 4/8	21 3/8	20 7/8	15 6/8	4	4	Greene County	IA	Dan Matthews	1995	14,549
129 4/8	18 4/8	19 0/8	16 4/8	5	5	Wood County	WV	Robert Cooper	1995	14,549

WHITETAIL DEER (TYPICAL ANTLERS)

Minimum Score 125   Continued

SCORE	LENGTH OF MAIN BEAM R	LENGTH OF MAIN BEAM L	INSIDE SPREAD	NUMBER OF POINTS R	NUMBER OF POINTS L	AREA	STATE/ PROVINCE	HUNTER'S NAME	DATE	RANK
129 4/8	21 7/8	20 3/8	16 2/8	4	4	Gallatin County	MT	James Martin Muzynoski	1995	14,549
129 4/8	21 5/8	21 7/8	18 6/8	5	5	Duval County	TX	Billy E. Corley	1995	14,549
129 4/8	19 7/8	20 0/8	15 0/8	5	4	Osage County	MO	Larry Groner	1996	14,549
129 4/8	25 1/8	23 6/8	16 6/8	7	6	Charles County	MD	Larry M. Chappelear	1996	14,549
129 4/8	20 4/8	20 5/8	15 6/8	4	4	Logan County	KS	Bryan Mulligan	1996	14,549
129 4/8	21 4/8	20 5/8	18 2/8	6	5	Iowa County	WI	Patrick Bushert	1996	14,549
129 4/8	22 2/8	22 2/8	16 2/8	5	4	Dane County	WI	Alan Motl	1996	14,549
129 4/8	21 1/8	22 4/8	17 6/8	4	4	Vernon County	WI	Paul Urbanek	1996	14,549
129 4/8	20 0/8	22 6/8	16 7/8	5	6	Calhoun County	MI	Jim McGovern	1996	14,549
129 4/8	22 2/8	21 6/8	20 4/8	4	4	Cuyahoga County	OH	Victor Jason	1996	14,549
129 4/8	22 4/8	22 7/8	16 3/8	4	5	Frederick County	MD	Brian L. Buckman	1997	14,549
129 4/8	19 6/8	21 0/8	14 2/8	5	5	Jefferson County	WI	Bob Johnson, Jr.	1997	14,549
129 4/8	22 2/8	23 1/8	17 4/8	5	4	Grenada County	MS	Richie Morgan	1997	14,549
129 4/8	23 0/8	22 4/8	17 3/8	5	4	Lake County	IL	Matt Porter	1997	14,549
129 4/8	23 2/8	22 7/8	19 0/8	4	4	Mercer County	NJ	John E. Martel	1997	14,549
129 4/8	21 1/8	22 0/8	16 2/8	6	6	Allegheny County	PA	Wallace E. Carr	1997	14,549
129 4/8	21 2/8	21 0/8	16 6/8	5	5	Webster County	WV	Robbie Floyd	1997	14,549
129 4/8	23 1/8	23 0/8	15 0/8	4	4	Warren County	IL	Lyle Hicks	1997	14,549
129 4/8	23 2/8	23 2/8	19 0/8	5	5	San Patricio County	TX	Joel I. Garcia	1997	14,549
129 4/8	22 7/8	22 4/8	16 3/8	5	5	Allamakee County	IA	Bill Saddler	1997	14,549
129 4/8	21 7/8	21 1/8	16 0/8	5	5	Walworth County	WI	Alvin Ortmann	1997	14,549
129 4/8	20 3/8	20 2/8	18 0/8	5	5	Vinton County	OH	Steven Shirkey	1997	14,549
129 4/8	21 1/8	24 0/8	18 0/8	4	5	Decatur County	KS	Scott Hargrove	1997	14,549
129 3/8	23 4/8	22 1/8	20 3/8	4	5	Bayfield County	WI	Kenneth R. Sweeny	1965	14,660
129 3/8	25 1/8	24 0/8	21 5/8	4	3	Des Moines County	IA	Jerry Snyder	1978	14,660
129 3/8	22 3/8	22 0/8	13 7/8	4	4	Waukesha County	WI	Gary S. Luedtke	1982	14,660
129 3/8	20 7/8	21 1/8	14 5/8	5	5	Monroe County	WI	Paul Moser	1983	14,660
129 3/8	20 6/8	20 7/8	20 2/8	7	9	White County	IN	Mark Mohler	1983	14,660
129 3/8	21 3/8	21 4/8	14 7/8	5	5	Carroll County	MD	Herbert Eyler	1984	14,660
129 3/8	20 4/8	20 4/8	15 4/8	6	5	Waupaca County	WI	Rick Lohff	1985	14,660
129 3/8	22 2/8	22 0/8	17 2/8	6	4	Door County	WI	Randy Berndt	1985	14,660
129 3/8	21 3/8	20 3/8	16 5/8	5	5	Albany County	NY	Frank Frederick	1986	14,660
129 3/8	21 5/8	21 3/8	16 1/8	4	4	Hunterdon County	NJ	John DeStefano	1986	14,660
129 3/8	20 4/8	20 3/8	16 7/8	4	4	Shawnee County	KS	Randy Hildreth	1986	14,660
129 3/8	19 6/8	21 2/8	15 1/8	4	5	Jersey County	IL	Howard Shaw	1987	14,660
129 3/8	21 0/8	21 0/8	15 3/8	6	5	Putnam County	MO	John Pherigo	1987	14,660
129 3/8	23 6/8	22 1/8	18 5/8	4	4	Baltimore County	MD	Bruce D. Hoover	1987	14,660
129 3/8	22 4/8	22 3/8	18 1/8	4	4	Montgomery County	IL	Mark Laurent	1987	14,660
129 3/8	21 7/8	22 2/8	16 0/8	4	5	Grant County	SD	Steven Karels	1988	14,660
129 3/8	20 1/8	21 0/8	16 5/8	5	5	Eaton County	MI	Randall W. Jecks	1988	14,660
129 3/8	22 0/8	21 7/8	20 3/8	4	5	McHenry County	IL	Gary Noe	1988	14,660
129 3/8	21 6/8	20 7/8	16 5/8	5	5	Missoula County	MT	Jeff Traska	1988	14,660
129 3/8	23 3/8	22 6/8	19 5/8	5	5	Buffalo County	WI	Dennis Palmer	1988	14,660
129 3/8	20 6/8	21 7/8	18 7/8	5	5	Sundre	NBW	Andrew Cariello, Jr.	1989	14,660
129 3/8	22 4/8	22 7/8	19 1/8	4	5	Fountain County	IN	Kenny Corey	1989	14,660
129 3/8	22 3/8	22 2/8	15 5/8	4	5	Waupaca County	WI	Kevin W. Hoffman	1989	14,660
129 3/8	20 6/8	20 6/8	13 5/8	5	5	Worth County	IA	Larry B. Porter	1989	14,660
129 3/8	20 4/8	21 7/8	15 5/8	5	5	Effingham County	IL	Dave Pontious	1989	14,660
129 3/8	24 7/8	23 0/8	17 1/8	7	5	Ionia County	MI	William D. Yoder	1989	14,660
129 3/8	23 2/8	22 5/8	16 7/8	5	4	Brown County	WI	Jeffrey G. Blake	1989	14,660
129 3/8	20 6/8	20 0/8	14 3/8	5	5	Rowan County	KY	Danny Mabry	1990	14,660
129 3/8	21 2/8	19 6/8	17 3/8	5	5	Morgan County	MO	David A. Haake	1990	14,660
129 3/8	22 7/8	20 4/8	18 3/8	4	5	Du Page County	IL	James J. Malek, Jr.	1990	14,660
129 3/8	26 4/8	25 4/8	18 5/8	3	3	Jefferson County	MO	Barry Geatley	1990	14,660
129 3/8	21 2/8	22 4/8	17 2/8	6	5	Tom Green County	TX	Jack Bains	1991	14,660
129 3/8	24 1/8	23 0/8	15 0/8	5	5	Ozark County	MO	Richard Eakins	1991	14,660
129 3/8	22 5/8	23 1/8	16 3/8	4	5	Green County	WI	David R. Covert	1991	14,660
129 3/8	22 1/8	21 6/8	18 1/8	5	5	Grant County	WI	Todd Blackbourn	1991	14,660
129 3/8	20 6/8	21 0/8	12 7/8	5	5	Passaic County	NJ	Dennis Sterzel	1991	14,660
129 3/8	23 0/8	24 1/8	15 5/8	4	5	Baltimore County	MD	Paul A. Waters	1991	14,660
129 3/8	22 0/8	22 4/8	15 3/8	5	5	Strathcona	ALB	Sheldon Fiske	1992	14,660
129 3/8	21 5/8	20 4/8	17 1/8	5	5	Sequoyah County	OK	Scott Hickman	1992	14,660
129 3/8	22 0/8	21 3/8	15 7/8	4	5	Chippewa County	WI	Lonnie Gray	1992	14,660
129 3/8	24 3/8	24 3/8	19 7/8	5	5	Cattaraugus County	NY	Dale Hebdon	1992	14,660
129 3/8	23 1/8	22 4/8	18 3/8	4	5	Fond du Lac County	WI	Kevin Beattie	1992	14,660
129 3/8	20 4/8	20 5/8	14 7/8	5	5	Fulton County	OH	John Wood	1992	14,660
129 3/8	21 2/8	21 1/8	17 5/8	5	5	Oktibbeha County	MS	Jeff Curtis	1992	14,660
129 3/8	24 6/8	23 7/8	19 1/8	4	4	Houston County	MN	Troy A. Maier	1992	14,660
129 3/8	22 0/8	22 5/8	12 5/8	5	5	Bay County	MI	Jim Knieper	1993	14,660
129 3/8	23 3/8	22 7/8	16 3/8	4	4	Forest County	WI	Darrow Bedor	1993	14,660
129 3/8	23 7/8	21 1/8	18 3/8	4	4	Allamakee County	IA	Cody Hawkins	1993	14,660
129 3/8	20 6/8	20 3/8	18 1/8	5	6	La Salle County	IL	Dave O'Dell	1993	14,660
129 3/8	24 1/8	23 2/8	17 3/8	4	4	Poinsett County	AR	Jimmy Linton	1993	14,660
129 3/8	22 5/8	22 3/8	17 5/8	4	4	Macomb County	MI	Dennis A. Schramm	1994	14,660
129 3/8	21 4/8	21 3/8	17 5/8	5	4	Tippecanoe County	IN	Mike Shumard	1994	14,660
129 3/8	22 5/8	23 7/8	20 1/8	4	5	Taylor County	WI	Bruce Fredrick	1994	14,660
129 3/8	23 5/8	22 6/8	21 1/8	4	4	Iowa County	WI	Denny Adler	1994	14,660
129 3/8	21 4/8	21 6/8	17 7/8	5	5	Broome County	NY	Gerry S. Ciotoli	1994	14,660

WHITETAIL DEER (TYPICAL ANTLERS)

Minimum Score 125 — Continued

SCORE	LENGTH OF R MAIN BEAM L		INSIDE SPREAD	NUMBER OF R POINTS L		AREA	STATE/ PROVINCE	HUNTER'S NAME	DATE	RANK
129 3/8	25 0/8	23 4/8	14 7/8	4	5	Douglas County	KS	Denzil Hackathorn	1994	14,660
129 3/8	22 3/8	22 1/8	14 1/8	5	4	East Carroll Parish	LA	Gregory Shullek	1994	14,660
129 3/8	20 7/8	20 7/8	16 0/8	6	5	Dimmit County	TX	Sonny Evans	1995	14,660
129 3/8	21 0/8	21 5/8	14 6/8	5	6	Goodhue County	MN	Dan Kelsey	1995	14,660
129 3/8	19 7/8	21 2/8	16 3/8	5	5	Lawrence County	OH	Rob Sturgill	1995	14,660
129 3/8	22 1/8	22 0/8	17 5/8	5	5	Kent County	MD	Jim Yeager	1995	14,660
129 3/8	21 0/8	22 1/8	16 5/8	5	4	Appanoose County	IA	Jay Smith	1995	14,660
129 3/8	24 7/8	22 2/8	16 1/8	6	6	Butler County	KS	Rod Hommertzheim	1995	14,660
129 3/8	19 6/8	19 2/8	16 0/8	6	5	Sutton County	TX	Dane Widner	1996	14,660
129 3/8	20 5/8	20 4/8	16 5/8	6	5	La Crosse County	WI	Steven W. Amann	1996	14,660
129 3/8	21 3/8	21 3/8	18 3/8	4	4	Buffalo County	WI	David J. Kamla	1996	14,660
129 3/8	22 0/8	22 2/8	17 5/8	5	5	Polk County	WI	Martin Eibs	1996	14,660
129 3/8	22 4/8	22 7/8	16 5/8	5	5	Taylor County	KY	Clay Hoskins	1996	14,660
129 3/8	23 7/8	23 3/8	16 7/8	4	4	Vernon County	WI	Michael S. McClurg	1996	14,660
129 3/8	20 1/8	20 5/8	17 3/8	5	4	Tompkins County	NY	Bruce Harris	1996	14,660
129 3/8	19 3/8	18 4/8	14 3/8	5	6	Clay County	NE	David J. Hamik	1996	14,660
129 3/8	22 0/8	20 7/8	14 5/8	4	4	Dimmit County	TX	Scott Yeomans	1996	14,660
129 3/8	20 6/8	21 0/8	17 1/8	5	5	Dimmit County	TX	Michael L. Sommer	1997	14,660
129 3/8	21 6/8	20 0/8	17 5/8	5	5	Colfax County	NE	Peter Jay Dart	1997	14,660
129 3/8	21 3/8	22 4/8	16 7/8	4	4	Kit Carson County	CO	Dave Mahler	1997	14,660
129 3/8	22 5/8	22 7/8	17 5/8	6	6	Trempealeau County	WI	Pat A. Lyga	1997	14,660
129 3/8	22 4/8	22 2/8	17 3/8	5	5	Langlade County	WI	Perry M. Miller	1997	14,660
129 3/8	22 0/8	22 4/8	18 3/8	6	6	Chase County	KS	Timothy Post	1997	14,660
129 3/8	23 1/8	22 7/8	16 3/8	4	6	Dooly County	GA	Eddie L. Biggers	1998	14,660
129 3/8	22 6/8	22 3/8	17 2/8	6	6	Oconto County	WI	John Englebert	1998	14,660
129 3/8	23 5/8	22 2/8	19 7/8	5	5	Clark County	IL	Howard Cutright	1998	14,660
129 3/8	20 6/8	20 6/8	20 1/8	5	4	Patrick County	VA	Tim Helbert	1998	14,660
129 2/8	19 2/8	20 1/8	16 5/8	7	6	Columbia County	WA	Al Farrell	1956	14,742
129 2/8	23 2/8	24 0/8	17 4/8	4	4	Juneau County	WI	Robert E. Schober	1977	14,742
129 2/8	21 7/8	21 4/8	16 2/8	5	5	Kendall County	IL	Fred W. Achilles	1979	14,742
129 2/8	22 3/8	23 4/8	16 6/8	4	4	Aitkin County	MN	Daniel L. Edelman	1982	14,742
129 2/8	20 3/8	20 4/8	17 4/8	5	5	Canmore	ALB	J. C. Mackid	1982	14,742
129 2/8	22 0/8	22 5/8	16 2/8	5	5	Muskingum County	OH	Dr. Jim Emerson	1982	14,742
129 2/8	20 6/8	21 6/8	17 2/8	4	4	Buffalo County	NE	Dan Johnson	1983	14,742
129 2/8	20 0/8	19 6/8	15 0/8	5	5	Portage County	WI	Jay W. Torkilsen	1984	14,742
129 2/8	19 4/8	19 2/8	14 4/8	5	5	Walsh	ALB	Reg Brooks	1984	14,742
129 2/8	24 1/8	23 0/8	15 0/8	5	4	Jasper County	IL	Guy Douglas Page	1984	14,742
129 2/8	20 7/8	21 3/8	18 6/8	5	5	Ross County	OH	Steven E Bower	1984	14,742
129 2/8	20 4/8	21 0/8	13 6/8	5	6	Pierce County	WI	William Kearns	1984	14,742
129 2/8	22 2/8	22 2/8	18 4/8	4	4	Calhoun County	MI	Jerry L. Teller	1984	14,742
129 2/8	21 6/8	22 1/8	16 6/8	4	4	Des Moines County	IA	Ray Waschkat	1984	14,742
129 2/8	20 1/8	19 7/8	18 4/8	5	5	Hillsdale County	MI	Garry Witfoth	1984	14,742
129 2/8	24 4/8	23 1/8	20 4/8	5	6	Columbiana County	OH	Robert Souders	1985	14,742
129 2/8	23 3/8	23 0/8	17 6/8	4	4	Hocking County	OH	Donald Webb	1985	14,742
129 2/8	20 5/8	21 7/8	16 0/8	4	4	Anderson County	KS	Jerry Howarter	1985	14,742
129 2/8	23 0/8	23 2/8	18 0/8	5	5	Waukesha County	WI	Gary Buck	1986	14,742
129 2/8	22 3/8	22 1/8	18 6/8	4	5	Lake County	IL	Eugene L. Miller	1987	14,742
129 2/8	20 5/8	20 5/8	15 4/8	5	5	Somerset County	NJ	Barry C. Ott	1987	14,742
129 2/8	22 6/8	20 2/8	18 4/8	4	4	Perry County	IL	Thomas R. Wilkens	1987	14,742
129 2/8	19 4/8	19 6/8	15 4/8	5	5	Custer County	SD	Stan Chiras	1988	14,742
129 2/8	23 3/8	23 1/8	16 1/8	4	5	Cedar County	MO	Ralph Burns	1988	14,742
129 2/8	21 6/8	21 5/8	15 0/8	5	5	Olmsted County	MN	Jim Leqve	1988	14,742
129 2/8	19 4/8	20 2/8	14 7/8	6	6	Kingfisher County	OK	Bruce Boyd	1988	14,742
129 2/8	18 7/8	19 4/8	18 0/8	6	5	Callahan County	TX	William B. Brown, Jr.	1989	14,742
129 2/8	22 5/8	22 5/8	17 4/8	4	4	La Salle County	IL	Jack Tabor	1989	14,742
129 2/8	22 2/8	23 1/8	17 4/8	5	5	Grant County	WI	Bob Bloom	1989	14,742
129 2/8	22 6/8	22 4/8	19 2/8	5	5	Gallatin County	IL	Mark Abell	1989	14,742
129 2/8	21 0/8	21 0/8	18 0/8	5	5	Sawyer County	WI	Michael Sawyer	1989	14,742
129 2/8	22 1/8	22 1/8	18 4/8	4	5	Kane County	IL	Charles E. Allen	1989	14,742
129 2/8	21 4/8	21 3/8	21 0/8	4	5	Calhoun County	MI	Douglas L. Rial	1989	14,742
129 2/8	20 0/8	22 0/8	16 2/8	5	4	Waukesha County	WI	Todd Meyers	1990	14,742
129 2/8	23 0/8	23 1/8	16 4/8	5	5	Price County	WI	Jerry J. Bedor	1990	14,742
129 2/8	22 2/8	22 7/8	17 2/8	4	4	Jackson County	IL	Richard Beckman	1990	14,742
129 2/8	22 0/8	21 6/8	16 6/8	4	4	Chautauqua County	KS	Bill Wilmeth	1990	14,742
129 2/8	19 7/8	20 1/8	14 6/8	4	5	Stony Plain	ALB	James W. Thomson	1990	14,742
129 2/8	20 5/8	20 2/8	17 2/8	5	5	Creek County	OK	Bill Morgan	1990	14,742
129 2/8	22 6/8	21 1/8	19 0/8	6	6	Richland County	ND	Andy Boyer	1991	14,742
129 2/8	19 2/8	19 5/8	13 0/8	5	5	Door County	WI	Steven R. Pluff	1991	14,742
129 2/8	19 6/8	19 5/8	14 6/8	5	5	Iron County	MI	Ted Sammond	1991	14,742
129 2/8	20 0/8	20 1/8	14 5/8	5	4	Marinette County	WI	Daniel C. Gibb	1991	14,742
129 2/8	21 4/8	21 7/8	16 6/8	6	5	Suffolk County	VA	Waverly E. White	1991	14,742
129 2/8	24 7/8	22 3/8	16 6/8	5	7	Kanabec County	MN	Roger A. Eggert	1991	14,742
129 2/8	22 1/8	23 0/8	18 2/8	4	4	Bayfield County	WI	Rick Tokarski	1992	14,742
129 2/8	21 3/8	20 2/8	16 3/8	4	6	Blue Earth County	MN	Greg Johnston	1992	14,742
129 2/8	22 5/8	20 6/8	16 0/8	5	5	Marshall County	IN	Ted Felgenhauer	1992	14,742
129 2/8	20 5/8	20 4/8	17 6/8	5	5	Christian County	KY	Brian M. Disterhaft	1992	14,742
129 2/8	23 1/8	22 3/8	15 0/8	5	4	Vermilion County	IL	Brody Prater	1992	14,742
129 2/8	20 5/8	20 2/8	19 1/8	5	6	Racine County	WI	Troy K. Peterson	1992	14,742

WHITETAIL DEER (TYPICAL ANTLERS)

Minimum Score 125   Continued

SCORE	LENGTH OF MAIN BEAM R	LENGTH OF MAIN BEAM L	INSIDE SPREAD	NUMBER OF POINTS R	NUMBER OF POINTS L	AREA	STATE/ PROVINCE	HUNTER'S NAME	DATE	RANK
129 2/8	21 6/8	22 2/8	18 6/8	4	5	Lake County	IL	Rick Bergstrom	1992	14,742
129 2/8	23 3/8	23 0/8	17 0/8	5	4	Oakland County	MI	Robert M. Rigney	1992	14,742
129 2/8	20 0/8	20 2/8	17 4/8	6	5	Polk County	WI	David J. Moris	1992	14,742
129 2/8	24 4/8	24 0/8	18 1/8	5	4	Lincoln County	MO	Danny Scoggins	1992	14,742
129 2/8	20 3/8	20 3/8	16 6/8	5	5	Harrison County	KY	Kevin Poe	1993	14,742
129 2/8	23 1/8	21 4/8	24 2/8	5	5	Taney County	MO	Larry Fry	1993	14,742
129 2/8	20 5/8	20 4/8	15 4/8	5	5	Columbia County	WI	Ronald W. Sopik	1993	14,742
129 2/8	20 2/8	20 5/8	18 7/8	6	4	Macon County	IL	Wayne A. Davenport	1993	14,742
129 2/8	21 3/8	21 6/8	15 4/8	4	4	Morrow County	OH	Vic Tumeo	1993	14,742
129 2/8	23 6/8	24 0/8	17 3/8	6	4	Jefferson County	OH	David S. Zack	1993	14,742
129 2/8	23 6/8	25 1/8	19 0/8	4	5	Geauga County	OH	Bill Svec	1993	14,742
129 2/8	21 7/8	21 0/8	16 2/8	6	7	Guthrie County	IA	Steven Duvall	1993	14,742
129 2/8	20 7/8	20 7/8	16 4/8	5	5	Flathead County	MT	Robert Morrow	1994	14,742
129 2/8	21 1/8	21 1/8	15 2/8	4	4	Benton County	MN	Gary Kampa	1994	14,742
129 2/8	17 0/8	18 1/8	18 2/8	6	6	Todd County	MN	Michael D. Roberts	1994	14,742
129 2/8	21 5/8	21 5/8	16 4/8	6	5	Humboldt County	IA	Tim Burres	1994	14,742
129 2/8	21 4/8	21 6/8	18 2/8	4	4	Westchester County	NY	Victor M. Mancini	1994	14,742
129 2/8	21 2/8	21 6/8	18 2/8	4	4	Fillmore County	MN	Daniel L. Nation	1994	14,742
129 2/8	21 3/8	21 5/8	16 6/8	5	5	Jones County	MS	Chris Holifield	1995	14,742
129 2/8	19 2/8	19 5/8	16 7/8	5	5	Estevan	SAS	Garry Leslie	1995	14,742
129 2/8	22 6/8	23 3/8	18 2/8	4	4	Montgomery County	MD	Jeffrey L. Harrison	1995	14,742
129 2/8	20 1/8	19 5/8	13 4/8	8	6	Bullitt County	KY	John E. Davis	1995	14,742
129 2/8	22 1/8	22 4/8	17 6/8	4	5	Clark County	SD	Scott Lindgren	1995	14,742
129 2/8	22 1/8	22 3/8	15 1/8	5	6	Pike County	IL	Robert Brush	1995	14,742
129 2/8	22 0/8	21 6/8	20 1/8	4	8	Benton County	IN	Richard D. Ellsworth, DDS	1995	14,742
129 2/8	20 2/8	20 3/8	18 0/8	4	4	Williamson County	IL	James W. Halley	1995	14,742
129 2/8	22 0/8	22 1/8	17 0/8	4	4	White County	AR	Jeff Webb	1995	14,742
129 2/8	20 1/8	20 1/8	15 6/8	4	4	Marshall County	IN	Teddy L. Bradley	1996	14,742
129 2/8	23 6/8	23 0/8	14 2/8	4	4	Morris County	NJ	Roger N. Busch	1996	14,742
129 2/8	21 6/8	21 0/8	16 6/8	4	4	Langlade County	WI	Kurt Krueger	1996	14,742
129 2/8	22 2/8	22 6/8	15 6/8	5	5	Bragg Creek	ALB	Paul Whitford	1996	14,742
129 2/8	23 5/8	23 3/8	18 2/8	5	4	Lake County	IN	Steven J. Natelborg	1996	14,742
129 2/8	19 5/8	20 4/8	19 0/8	6	5	Henry County	KY	Russell Gore	1996	14,742
129 2/8	21 3/8	22 1/8	16 7/8	5	5	Waupaca County	WI	Mark D. Pliska	1996	14,742
129 2/8	24 0/8	24 0/8	19 0/8	5	5	Webster County	IA	Randy Taylor	1996	14,742
129 2/8	22 6/8	22 2/8	15 4/8	5	4	Putnam County	OH	Ryan J. Annesser	1996	14,742
129 2/8	22 6/8	23 7/8	17 7/8	5	4	Rock County	MN	Jason Wessels	1996	14,742
129 2/8	20 4/8	20 4/8	15 7/8	6	6	Fergus County	MT	C. R. Wenger	1997	14,742
129 2/8	20 2/8	22 4/8	16 0/8	5	5	Harrison County	TX	J. Darren Turner	1997	14,742
129 2/8	21 5/8	21 7/8	16 4/8	4	4	Isabella County	MI	Garold J. Packer	1997	14,742
129 2/8	21 7/8	22 1/8	17 7/8	6	6	Darke County	OH	Nate Riffell	1997	14,742
129 2/8	18 6/8	21 2/8	19 7/8	6	5	Otsego County	NY	Mike Mattera	1997	14,742
129 2/8	24 5/8	25 3/8	16 6/8	3	4	York County	PA	Dan Sellers	1997	14,742
129 2/8	20 3/8	20 5/8	17 0/8	4	5	Lac qui Parle County	MN	Dan Scheeler	1997	14,742
129 2/8	21 3/8	22 0/8	18 6/8	5	4	Somerset County	NJ	Michael Bumback	1997	14,742
129 2/8	20 3/8	20 4/8	15 4/8	5	6	Pike County	IL	Michael C. Vaka	1997	14,742
129 2/8	20 4/8	21 4/8	15 4/8	5	5	Buffalo County	WI	John W. Zahrte	1997	14,742
129 2/8	22 5/8	21 4/8	17 4/8	4	4	Racine County	WI	James T. Bergles	1997	14,742
129 2/8	22 6/8	23 3/8	19 2/8	4	4	Litchfield County	CT	James Borg	1998	14,742
129 2/8	20 4/8	20 5/8	17 6/8	5	5	Jack County	TX	W. Shuford Davis	1998	14,742
129 1/8	22 4/8	21 4/8	17 5/8	5	5	Lee County	IA	Jim Bohenkamp	1973	14,843
129 1/8	20 6/8	21 6/8	16 5/8	5	5	Burnett County	WI	James G. Hurrle	1974	14,843
129 1/8	22 2/8	22 1/8	16 5/8	5	8	Wabasha County	MN	Richard H. McKnight	1975	14,843
129 1/8	22 0/8	22 4/8	15 5/8	6	6	Holt County	NE	Greg Wetthaufer	1980	14,843
129 1/8	22 2/8	22 1/8	17 7/8	5	5	Greene County	MS	Russell Herring	1980	14,843
129 1/8	22 1/8	22 0/8	15 7/8	4	4	Hancock County	OH	Kenneth E. Hornick	1980	14,843
129 1/8	19 2/8	20 0/8	15 3/8	5	5	Sheboygan County	WI	John Steinbruecker	1980	14,843
129 1/8	25 1/8	24 1/8	20 5/8	6	4	Houston County	MN	Gary Maier	1981	14,843
129 1/8	19 6/8	19 7/8	14 7/8	5	5	Clark County	SD	Bill Soyland	1981	14,843
129 1/8	21 5/8	21 7/8	17 1/8	4	5	Schuyler County	NY	Scott D. Bond	1982	14,843
129 1/8	21 6/8	21 0/8	17 5/8	4	4	Hughes County	SD	Alvin Truax	1984	14,843
129 1/8	19 5/8	19 4/8	14 7/8	5	5	Marathon County	WI	Richard J. Tokarski	1985	14,843
129 1/8	24 0/8	24 3/8	17 3/8	4	4	Jackson County	MI	Mark D. Bacon	1985	14,843
129 1/8	21 0/8	21 6/8	16 6/8	6	6	Walsh County	ND	Tobin L. Welch	1986	14,843
129 1/8	21 0/8	20 6/8	17 3/8	5	5	Wexford County	MI	Mike Goodrich	1986	14,843
129 1/8	22 1/8	22 4/8	17 5/8	6	5	Clark County	MO	Dennis Fish	1986	14,843
129 1/8	21 0/8	21 4/8	17 6/8	6	5	Bexar County	TX	Leonard E. Barbus	1986	14,843
129 1/8	20 2/8	19 5/8	14 7/8	5	5	Warren County	NJ	Theodore Barchowski, Jr.	1987	14,843
129 1/8	22 1/8	22 1/8	16 3/8	4	4	Ozaukee County	WI	Doug Hartwig	1987	14,843
129 1/8	24 6/8	25 1/8	16 5/8	6	5	Wayne County	MS	Robert Hall	1987	14,843
129 1/8	22 6/8	21 2/8	15 1/8	6	5	Anderson County	TN	Mack Hicks	1987	14,843
129 1/8	20 6/8	20 4/8	16 7/8	5	5	Shawano County	WI	Frank J. Kugel	1987	14,843
129 1/8	22 0/8	22 0/8	14 7/8	5	5	Des Moines County	IA	Kevin M. Peterson	1987	14,843
129 1/8	26 6/8	26 1/8	19 2/8	5	5	Gage County	NE	Russell Klein	1988	14,843
129 1/8	24 1/8	22 5/8	17 1/8	5	6	Columbia County	WI	Alva D. Fuller	1988	14,843
129 1/8	22 1/8	22 2/8	15 3/8	5	5	Litchfield County	CT	Paul Mirabelle	1988	14,843
129 1/8	22 4/8	22 5/8	19 3/8	5	4	McHenry County	IL	David A. Bennett	1988	14,843
129 1/8	21 0/8	21 6/8	16 1/8	5	6	Madison County	IA	Fred "Bud" Allen	1989	14,843

WHITETAIL DEER (TYPICAL ANTLERS)

Minimum Score 125 — Continued

SCORE	LENGTH OF R MAIN BEAM L		INSIDE SPREAD	NUMBER OF R POINTS L		AREA	STATE/ PROVINCE	HUNTER'S NAME	DATE	RANK
129 1/8	24 2/8	23 6/8	18 6/8	6	5	Ashland County	WI	Bill Plizka	1989	14,843
129 1/8	24 0/8	23 1/8	15 3/8	4	4	Ingham County	MI	Ted Harrison	1989	14,843
129 1/8	19 7/8	20 2/8	17 5/8	5	5	Barry County	MI	Kenneth W. Blauvelt	1989	14,843
129 1/8	20 1/8	20 2/8	16 2/8	6	7	Ohio County	WV	Gene Petri	1989	14,843
129 1/8	22 5/8	23 5/8	19 1/8	4	5	Westchester County	NY	Douglas Greenwich	1989	14,843
129 1/8	20 1/8	20 1/8	16 1/8	5	4	Morton County	ND	Leslie Ciavarella	1989	14,843
129 1/8	24 1/8	24 0/8	19 5/8	4	5	Allegheny County	PA	Lonnie R. Bowser	1990	14,843
129 1/8	23 5/8	22 6/8	17 7/8	4	5	Peoria County	IL	Frank R. Barnhart	1990	14,843
129 1/8	20 5/8	22 0/8	17 5/8	4	5	Menominee County	MI	Steve G. Drabick	1990	14,843
129 1/8	20 5/8	20 7/8	17 1/8	4	4	Warren County	NJ	Timothy Matthews	1990	14,843
129 1/8	22 2/8	22 3/8	18 6/8	4	5	Suffolk County	NY	Neal Heaton	1990	14,843
129 1/8	23 3/8	25 5/8	17 3/8	4	5	Sangamon County	IL	Dale Turley	1990	14,843
129 1/8	21 2/8	20 3/8	15 7/8	4	4	Cass County	NE	Steve Rueck	1991	14,843
129 1/8	24 0/8	24 2/8	16 5/8	5	4	Jackson County	OH	Edsel D. Duty	1991	14,843
129 1/8	22 6/8	22 4/8	15 7/8	4	5	Defiance County	OH	Don Willitzer	1991	14,843
129 1/8	21 2/8	20 0/8	16 3/8	5	6	Marathon County	WI	Terry E. Benzschawel	1991	14,843
129 1/8	21 6/8	21 5/8	18 3/8	5	5	Shawnee County	KS	Eldon Johnson	1991	14,843
129 1/8	21 4/8	21 1/8	17 7/8	4	4	Oakland County	MI	Perry S. Russo	1992	14,843
129 1/8	21 1/8	21 1/8	15 1/8	6	5	Rusk County	WI	Kim Mincoff	1992	14,843
129 1/8	20 5/8	20 4/8	16 6/8	6	7	Grundy County	IL	Randy Hooper	1992	14,843
129 1/8	22 1/8	23 2/8	17 0/8	5	4	Fairfield County	CT	Carl Ranieri	1992	14,843
129 1/8	22 3/8	23 1/8	20 5/8	4	5	Henry County	OH	Scott Helberg	1992	14,843
129 1/8	22 2/8	23 2/8	15 7/8	4	4	Vinton County	OH	Martin E. Cain	1993	14,843
129 1/8	19 1/8	19 3/8	14 7/8	6	5	Llano County	TX	Charles Wayne Grimes, Jr.	1993	14,843
129 1/8	22 5/8	22 7/8	18 4/8	5	5	Buffalo County	WI	Robert A. Oines	1993	14,843
129 1/8	19 6/8	19 4/8	15 0/8	7	7	San Patricio County	TX	William R. Roddy, Jr.	1993	14,843
129 1/8	20 1/8	20 6/8	15 7/8	4	4	Fillmore County	MN	Jon Hatleli	1993	14,843
129 1/8	21 2/8	21 4/8	17 1/8	5	4	Price County	WI	Jerry L. Heath	1993	14,843
129 1/8	23 2/8	23 7/8	18 3/8	4	5	Trempealeau County	WI	Mark Finner	1993	14,843
129 1/8	19 5/8	19 1/8	16 7/8	5	5	Marathon County	WI	Samuel V. Lockhart	1993	14,843
129 1/8	24 5/8	22 7/8	19 2/8	7	5	Marinette County	WI	Steve Campbell	1993	14,843
129 1/8	23 5/8	24 0/8	16 0/8	5	4	Knox County	IL	Dave EmKen	1993	14,843
129 1/8	23 3/8	22 2/8	17 5/8	4	4	Jefferson County	KY	William E. Morrow, Jr.	1994	14,843
129 1/8	20 0/8	20 2/8	18 7/8	5	5	Monroe County	PA	John Markowitz	1994	14,843
129 1/8	21 4/8	21 1/8	17 5/8	5	5	La Crosse County	WI	Ben J. Barrett	1994	14,843
129 1/8	22 1/8	20 3/8	13 4/8	5	6	Douglas County	KS	Ronnie D. Barnhardt	1994	14,843
129 1/8	21 4/8	22 2/8	20 7/8	4	4	Trempealeau County	WI	Pat Slaby	1994	14,843
129 1/8	24 1/8	23 6/8	20 1/8	4	4	Calhoun County	MI	Gy A. McGhee	1994	14,843
129 1/8	21 1/8	20 7/8	18 5/8	4	4	Fayette County	IL	Harold Warner	1994	14,843
129 1/8	23 1/8	22 5/8	14 5/8	4	4	Sarpy County	NE	Angelo Emmi, Jr.	1994	14,843
129 1/8	23 0/8	23 2/8	18 4/8	6	5	Scotland County	MO	Jim Ferry	1994	14,843
129 1/8	23 4/8	22 2/8	18 5/8	4	4	Delaware County	PA	Joseph D. Maddock	1994	14,843
129 1/8	21 7/8	21 0/8	17 5/8	5	5	Shelby County	MO	Chris Murphy	1994	14,843
129 1/8	22 7/8	23 4/8	16 0/8	6	5	Adams County	IL	Tim Walmsley	1994	14,843
129 1/8	20 1/8	20 2/8	15 7/8	6	6	Winona County	MN	Perry Erdahl	1995	14,843
129 1/8	22 2/8	22 7/8	17 2/8	4	5	Custer County	NE	James B. Meador	1995	14,843
129 1/8	24 0/8	23 1/8	16 3/8	4	4	McMullen County	TX	Joe G. Files	1995	14,843
129 1/8	23 2/8	23 0/8	16 5/8	4	4	Pottawattamie County	IA	Daniel F. Krettek	1996	14,843
129 1/8	24 2/8	23 7/8	15 3/8	4	6	Rockingham County	NC	Jr. Stratton	1996	14,843
129 1/8	23 0/8	23 4/8	16 7/8	4	4	Kleberg County	TX	John D. "Jack" Frost	1996	14,843
129 1/8	21 1/8	22 0/8	13 5/8	6	5	Jefferson County	MO	Steve Hohensee	1996	14,843
129 1/8	23 4/8	22 7/8	16 7/8	4	5	Buffalo County	WI	Dave Fredrickson	1996	14,843
129 1/8	23 4/8	22 7/8	20 1/8	7	4	Pike County	MO	Clayton Maxwell	1996	14,843
129 1/8	23 5/8	23 7/8	19 2/8	5	7	Washington County	KS	Ronald Montague	1996	14,843
129 1/8	22 1/8	21 2/8	16 3/8	5	5	Winneshiek County	IA	Gary Baumler	1996	14,843
129 1/8	22 3/8	22 4/8	17 7/8	4	4	Lake County	IL	Nick R. Heelein	1996	14,843
129 1/8	21 4/8	20 7/8	20 1/8	6	4	Brookings County	SD	Lonnie Henriksen	1996	14,843
129 1/8	22 4/8	19 2/8	16 5/8	5	4	McKenzie County	ND	Craig Richardson	1997	14,843
129 1/8	20 6/8	20 4/8	16 0/8	7	6	Dunn County	WI	Todd Danovsky	1997	14,843
129 1/8	23 0/8	21 1/8	20 7/8	4	5	Boone County	IL	Wilmer V. Garlick	1997	14,843
129 1/8	19 3/8	20 0/8	14 7/8	5	5	Renville County	MN	Dennis Bratsch	1997	14,843
129 1/8	23 4/8	24 6/8	22 3/8	4	4	Fairfax County	VA	Charlie Ugaz	1997	14,843
129 1/8	21 1/8	21 1/8	17 1/8	4	5	Hidalgo	MEX	Roberto Garza	1997	14,843
129 0/8	22 6/8	22 5/8	17 5/8	5	5	Adams County	IL	Roger W. Seehafer	1964	14,934
129 0/8	21 4/8	21 3/8	17 4/8	5	5	Monmouth County	NJ	Joseph N. Lazar	1967	14,934
129 0/8	23 4/8	24 0/8	19 6/8	5	4	Shawano County	WI	Merton Giessel	1970	14,934
129 0/8	19 6/8	20 6/8	19 0/8	4	4	Oneida County	WI	Gary Bohlman	1970	14,934
129 0/8	23 7/8	24 3/8	17 4/8	5	5	Erie County	OH	William G. Hlavin	1973	14,934
129 0/8	20 3/8	20 2/8	13 7/8	5	6	Ottawa County	KS	Martin Nunn	1976	14,934
129 0/8	20 6/8	21 2/8	15 5/8	6	6	Columbia County	WI	Greg Jacobson	1978	14,934
129 0/8	22 1/8	22 6/8	17 4/8	4	5	Mower County	MN	Jim Keim	1978	14,934
129 0/8	22 2/8	23 4/8	19 4/8	5	4	Trempealeau County	WI	Brian Skroch	1978	14,934
129 0/8	20 2/8	20 2/8	15 4/8	5	5	Washington County	WI	Francis N. Vande Boom	1978	14,934
129 0/8	20 3/8	20 4/8	19 0/8	4	4	Washington County	MS	Dan Hensley	1979	14,934
129 0/8	23 2/8	22 5/8	20 4/8	7	6	Carroll County	OH	Chuck Caldwell	1981	14,934
129 0/8	20 4/8	20 1/8	15 6/8	5	5	Columbia County	WI	Brent J. Nowak	1982	14,934
129 0/8	21 0/8	21 4/8	16 0/8	4	4	Wabaunsee County	KS	Tom Willard	1982	14,934
129 0/8	21 1/8	21 0/8	17 6/8	4	4	Grant County	WI	Wayne J. Droessler	1985	14,934

WHITETAIL DEER (TYPICAL ANTLERS)

Minimum Score 125 — Continued

SCORE	LENGTH OF MAIN BEAM R	LENGTH OF MAIN BEAM L	INSIDE SPREAD	NUMBER OF POINTS R	NUMBER OF POINTS L	AREA	STATE/ PROVINCE	HUNTER'S NAME	DATE	RANK
129 0/8	22 1/8	22 1/8	16 2/8	5	4	Cass County	ND	Ellery Kundert	1985	14,934
129 0/8	21 7/8	22 2/8	15 4/8	4	5	Iowa County	WI	Tim Palzkill	1985	14,934
129 0/8	22 2/8	22 7/8	17 2/8	4	4	Woodford County	IL	Bill Salsman	1985	14,934
129 0/8	21 2/8	21 3/8	16 2/8	6	6	Bremer County	IA	Martin Culpepper	1985	14,934
129 0/8	21 4/8	21 4/8	16 2/8	4	5	Pike County	MO	Richard Dewey	1985	14,934
129 0/8	20 0/8	20 4/8	16 5/8	6	6	Fond du Lac County	WI	Jeffrey D. Flitter	1986	14,934
129 0/8	23 0/8	22 5/8	16 2/8	8	5	La Crosse County	WI	Gary L. Maier	1986	14,934
129 0/8	22 1/8	22 2/8	16 4/8	5	5	Vernon County	WI	Bruce A. Gardner	1986	14,934
129 0/8	21 5/8	21 5/8	19 4/8	5	4	Suffolk County	NY	Joe Buscemi	1986	14,934
129 0/8	20 3/8	20 1/8	14 6/8	5	5	Morgan County	GA	Scot Rucker	1987	14,934
129 0/8	21 4/8	21 4/8	17 6/8	5	4	McHenry County	IL	David C. Novak	1987	14,934
129 0/8	22 3/8	21 1/8	16 6/8	5	5	Eau Claire County	WI	Anthony W. Olson	1988	14,934
129 0/8	21 0/8	22 0/8	16 2/8	6	7	Codington County	SD	Peter C. DeVille	1988	14,934
129 0/8	21 0/8	21 6/8	14 3/8	5	6	Tuscola County	MI	Dean Alan Broecker	1988	14,934
129 0/8	20 6/8	21 7/8	16 0/8	5	6	Daviess County	IN	Dennis R. Eger	1988	14,934
129 0/8	22 5/8	21 4/8	19 7/8	4	5	Jackson County	IL	Tim Cobin	1988	14,934
129 0/8	24 2/8	24 1/8	14 6/8	4	4	Wright County	MO	Buster Miller	1988	14,934
129 0/8	19 4/8	19 4/8	13 2/8	5	5	Wagoner County	OK	Lowell Due	1988	14,934
129 0/8	22 2/8	21 6/8	20 4/8	5	5	Llano County	TX	Bart J. Gillan III	1989	14,934
129 0/8	21 5/8	22 2/8	18 5/8	5	5	Douglas County	WI	Bruce Johnson	1989	14,934
129 0/8	20 6/8	20 7/8	16 4/8	5	5	Douglas County	MO	Matt Hensley	1989	14,934
129 0/8	21 4/8	21 4/8	17 2/8	4	4	Meigs County	OH	Jack Satterfield, Jr.	1989	14,934
129 0/8	22 1/8	21 1/8	14 0/8	5	4	Stearns County	MN	Paul Heinen	1990	14,934
129 0/8	21 2/8	21 4/8	17 0/8	4	5	Eels Lake	ONT	Ron McGarrity	1990	14,934
129 0/8	21 7/8	21 7/8	16 0/8	5	5	Allamakee County	IA	Paul "Buck" Farni, Jr.	1990	14,934
129 0/8	20 7/8	19 5/8	16 0/8	5	5	Jackson County	WV	Glenn Lacy	1990	14,934
129 0/8	22 5/8	23 2/8	18 2/8	4	4	Ohio County	KY	Henry Williams III	1990	14,934
129 0/8	23 5/8	22 7/8	18 0/8	5	5	E. Carroll Parish	LA	Mike Jones	1990	14,934
129 0/8	23 1/8	21 2/8	16 0/8	6	6	Montgomery County	TN	Adrien Boudin	1990	14,934
129 0/8	24 4/8	25 0/8	20 5/8	6	6	Edgar County	IL	Clark Piper	1990	14,934
129 0/8	24 4/8	23 3/8	17 4/8	5	5	Clinton County	OH	Brad Howard	1991	14,934
129 0/8	22 2/8	22 6/8	17 6/8	5	4	Bosque County	TX	Thomas Buxton	1991	14,934
129 0/8	21 4/8	21 6/8	16 2/8	4	4	Greene County	MO	Norm Nothnagel	1991	14,934
129 0/8	21 7/8	21 4/8	16 7/8	8	6	Crawford County	MO	Mike B. Jackson	1991	14,934
129 0/8	22 1/8	22 2/8	19 4/8	5	5	Price County	WI	Michael R. Lepak	1991	14,934
129 0/8	22 4/8	22 4/8	15 6/8	4	5	Kane County	IL	John Hoffman	1991	14,934
129 0/8	22 0/8	22 4/8	18 2/8	5	4	Westchester County	NY	Richard Semenza	1991	14,934
129 0/8	20 0/8	20 4/8	18 6/8	4	4	Buffalo County	WI	Robert Hohmann	1992	14,934
129 0/8	20 0/8	21 3/8	18 6/8	5	4	Monroe County	OH	Brian Goddard	1992	14,934
129 0/8	21 2/8	21 2/8	16 0/8	6	5	Scotland County	MO	John Mark James	1992	14,934
129 0/8	22 2/8	22 1/8	18 4/8	4	4	Buffalo County	WI	Mark Gerhard	1992	14,934
129 0/8	22 2/8	22 6/8	16 3/8	5	5	Delaware County	OH	Joe Murphy	1992	14,934
129 0/8	21 2/8	21 7/8	17 2/8	6	5	Dane County	WI	Scott Hassett	1992	14,934
129 0/8	18 1/8	18 3/8	15 4/8	4	5	McHenry County	IL	Steve Bauman	1992	14,934
129 0/8	23 5/8	24 5/8	17 6/8	4	4	Genesee County	MI	Gary A. Smith	1992	14,934
129 0/8	22 3/8	21 6/8	15 4/8	4	4	Kalamazoo County	MI	Edwin J. Noteboom	1993	14,934
129 0/8	19 5/8	19 6/8	17 2/8	5	5	De Kalb County	MO	Garry Pierson	1993	14,934
129 0/8	20 4/8	20 0/8	13 6/8	5	7	Todd County	MN	William H. Peterson	1993	14,934
129 0/8	20 5/8	21 3/8	17 0/8	4	4	Walworth County	WI	Jeffrey Lee Turbett	1993	14,934
129 0/8	21 4/8	22 0/8	17 4/8	5	9	Stephenson County	IL	David Miller	1993	14,934
129 0/8	22 6/8	23 0/8	18 6/8	5	4	Morrow County	OH	Harold G. West	1993	14,934
129 0/8	22 6/8	22 5/8	17 4/8	4	4	Kerr County	TX	Ronald G. Ralston	1993	14,934
129 0/8	22 7/8	21 4/8	18 0/8	4	5	Uvalde County	TX	Mark Ezell	1993	14,934
129 0/8	21 3/8	23 1/8	18 6/8	4	4	Dane County	WI	Gary Lehnherr	1994	14,934
129 0/8	20 3/8	20 4/8	15 2/8	5	5	Cattaraugus County	NY	Peter B. Cooney	1994	14,934
129 0/8	21 6/8	21 6/8	17 0/8	6	6	Bremer County	IA	Scott L. Knapp	1994	14,934
129 0/8	22 4/8	24 0/8	18 0/8	4	4	Tuscola County	MI	Gary William Maurer	1994	14,934
129 0/8	23 1/8	22 4/8	15 4/8	7	4	Ontario County	NY	David R. Gaston	1994	14,934
129 0/8	22 0/8	21 4/8	20 0/8	4	4	Houghton County	MI	Andre Soumis	1994	14,934
129 0/8	22 2/8	21 6/8	15 3/8	6	6	Pettis County	MO	Gale Logan	1994	14,934
129 0/8	24 4/8	24 1/8	17 7/8	5	5	Franklin County	MA	Michael J. Billiel	1994	14,934
129 0/8	20 2/8	19 4/8	16 4/8	5	5	Trempealeau County	WI	John Lewis Hestekin	1994	14,934
129 0/8	21 7/8	22 0/8	16 7/8	5	5	Olmsted County	MN	Jim Hanson	1994	14,934
129 0/8	21 1/8	21 2/8	14 6/8	7	8	Logan County	OK	Tom Quinton	1995	14,934
129 0/8	23 0/8	22 4/8	22 0/8	4	4	Lee County	IL	James Wentling	1995	14,934
129 0/8	22 1/8	20 7/8	16 4/8	7	5	Kalamazoo County	MI	Richard M. Bresson	1995	14,934
129 0/8	19 1/8	18 7/8	15 3/8	7	6	Platte County	MO	Darren Paden	1995	14,934
129 0/8	21 2/8	21 2/8	17 2/8	5	5	Waupaca County	WI	Ken R. Schampers	1995	14,934
129 0/8	21 4/8	22 4/8	18 2/8	4	5	Knox County	IL	Larry Hesterly	1995	14,934
129 0/8	20 6/8	20 7/8	13 4/8	4	5	Frio County	TX	Walter R. Copeland	1995	14,934
129 0/8	22 2/8	22 3/8	18 0/8	5	4	Brown County	SD	Ron Miller	1995	14,934
129 0/8	21 3/8	21 3/8	15 6/8	4	4	Uvalde County	TX	William Baker	1995	14,934
129 0/8	21 7/8	21 7/8	16 0/8	5	5	Monroe County	IA	Scott Perry	1995	14,934
129 0/8	22 4/8	22 0/8	16 6/8	4	4	Issaquena County	MS	Frank Greenlee	1995	14,934
129 0/8	25 1/8	25 0/8	19 0/8	5	5	Kenosha County	WI	Steve Clements	1995	14,934
129 0/8	21 5/8	21 3/8	17 6/8	4	4	Allegheny County	PA	Mark D. Benec	1996	14,934
129 0/8	18 4/8	18 4/8	16 0/8	5	5	Olmsted County	MN	Terry Reed	1996	14,934
129 0/8	20 0/8	20 5/8	14 6/8	4	5	McHenry County	ND	Aaron Faken	1996	14,934

WHITETAIL DEER (TYPICAL ANTLERS)

Minimum Score 125 — Continued

SCORE	LENGTH OF MAIN BEAM R	LENGTH OF MAIN BEAM L	INSIDE SPREAD	NUMBER OF POINTS R	NUMBER OF POINTS L	AREA	STATE/PROVINCE	HUNTER'S NAME	DATE	RANK
129 0/8	21 3/8	20 3/8	16 0/8	5	5	Stearns County	MN	Ron Bjorklund	1996	14,934
129 0/8	23 0/8	22 7/8	19 2/8	7	7	Trempealeau County	WI	Charles A. Gauger	1996	14,934
129 0/8	19 4/8	19 3/8	16 0/8	5	5	McKenzie County	ND	Michael Tofte	1996	14,934
129 0/8	23 1/8	22 0/8	20 4/8	5	4	Carroll County	MS	Gayle Reynolds	1996	14,934
129 0/8	20 4/8	20 2/8	16 6/8	5	5	Noble County	IN	Rick L. Zickafoose	1996	14,934
129 0/8	18 6/8	17 5/8	14 4/8	5	5	Linn County	MO	Marc Amer	1996	14,934
129 0/8	21 4/8	22 0/8	15 5/8	6	6	Kandiyohi County	MN	David Coahran	1996	14,934
129 0/8	22 7/8	24 1/8	14 2/8	4	5	Charlotte County	VA	Euell A. Lipscomb	1996	14,934
129 0/8	20 7/8	20 4/8	18 0/8	6	6	Hyde County	SD	Lucas Zemlicka	1996	14,934
129 0/8	26 2/8	26 7/8	20 0/8	5	4	Cuyahoga County	OH	Raymond William Videc, Jr.	1996	14,934
129 0/8	21 7/8	24 0/8	17 4/8	5	6	Harvey County	KS	John Wiebe	1996	14,934
129 0/8	23 4/8	25 3/8	17 6/8	4	5	Bullitt County	KY	Chris E. Couch	1997	14,934
129 0/8	22 6/8	21 2/8	18 6/8	4	4	Pierceland	SAS	Glenn Lau	1997	14,934
129 0/8	21 3/8	21 1/8	17 2/8	4	4	Dodge County	WI	Daniel Edwin Steele	1997	14,934
129 0/8	20 1/8	20 1/8	13 4/8	5	5	Callaway County	MO	Dennis Crane	1997	14,934
129 0/8	24 4/8	23 2/8	16 6/8	4	5	Dougherty County	GA	Michael Layfield	1997	14,934
129 0/8	20 3/8	20 6/8	17 0/8	5	5	Washington County	WI	William L. Lockwood	1997	14,934
129 0/8	22 5/8	22 4/8	18 6/8	4	4	Cayuga County	NY	Michael Pavlick, Sr.	1997	14,934
129 0/8	23 1/8	22 7/8	16 7/8	7	6	Pittsylvania County	VA	Ken Wood	1997	14,934
129 0/8	22 1/8	22 1/8	16 6/8	5	5	Putnam County	NY	Rodney Dow	1997	14,934
129 0/8	21 2/8	21 7/8	15 7/8	6	6	Green County	WI	Dave Covert	1997	14,934
129 0/8	20 6/8	23 0/8	20 6/8	4	4	Allegheny County	PA	Daniel Silsley	1997	14,934
129 0/8	20 5/8	20 3/8	18 3/8	6	6	Edmonton	ALB	Ryk Visscher	1997	14,934
129 0/8	23 4/8	23 2/8	15 2/8	4	4	Armstrong County	PA	Andrew Panchik	1998	14,934
128 7/8	19 1/8	20 6/8	13 7/8	5	5	Martin County	IN	J. Steve Albertson	1969	15,051
128 7/8	22 4/8	21 1/8	16 3/8	5	5	Grant County	WI	Kevin Freymiller	1975	15,051
128 7/8	22 6/8	22 3/8	15 2/8	5	5	Taylor County	WI	Eugene L. Racibowski	1976	15,051
128 7/8	21 0/8	20 1/8	18 1/8	5	4	Clark County	WI	Clarence J. Biddle	1977	15,051
128 7/8	23 3/8	23 1/8	15 4/8	4	4	Lake County	MN	Michael Seeber	1980	15,051
128 7/8	22 0/8	23 0/8	15 5/8	5	4	Erie County	NY	David J. Wetzler, Sr.	1980	15,051
128 7/8	24 1/8	25 3/8	21 6/8	7	6	Gentry County	MO	Bruce Shisler	1982	15,051
128 7/8	20 4/8	20 4/8	16 5/8	4	4	Blue Earth County	MN	Dean Como	1982	15,051
128 7/8	19 7/8	20 4/8	16 3/8	5	6	Richland County	MT	Dan Sturgis	1985	15,051
128 7/8	20 0/8	21 2/8	15 1/8	7	6	Washtenaw County	MI	Gerald Opsahl, Sr.	1985	15,051
128 7/8	22 7/8	23 3/8	19 6/8	5	6	Gallia County	OH	James E. Harris I	1986	15,051
128 7/8	22 2/8	22 3/8	17 7/8	5	4	Dubuque County	IA	Jeff Vogel	1986	15,051
128 7/8	20 0/8	21 4/8	19 1/8	4	4	Ramsey County	ND	Larry Kuntz	1986	15,051
128 7/8	21 1/8	22 2/8	18 3/8	4	5	Colfax County	NE	Dan Steiner	1987	15,051
128 7/8	20 6/8	21 1/8	17 7/8	5	7	Powell County	MT	Mark A. Balavender	1987	15,051
128 7/8	24 1/8	23 4/8	18 5/8	4	4	Union County	SC	Ronald Moon	1988	15,051
128 7/8	21 6/8	21 5/8	18 1/8	4	4	Morrison County	MN	David R. Wall	1988	15,051
128 7/8	21 6/8	22 1/8	19 3/8	4	4	Burnett County	WI	Michael D. Roberts	1988	15,051
128 7/8	20 0/8	22 6/8	16 5/8	4	4	McDowell County	WV	Ted Blankenship	1988	15,051
128 7/8	22 5/8	23 3/8	16 7/8	5	4	Franklin County	KS	Benjamin W. Braden	1989	15,051
128 7/8	20 5/8	21 0/8	17 7/8	4	4	Chisago County	MN	Michael R. Langin	1989	15,051
128 7/8	21 6/8	22 2/8	16 7/8	4	4	Ramsey County	ND	Charles McGarvey	1989	15,051
128 7/8	22 1/8	20 6/8	15 1/8	4	4	Trego County	KS	Fred Hunsicker	1989	15,051
128 7/8	23 7/8	23 1/8	16 0/8	5	5	Pike County	IL	Frank Dolbeare	1989	15,051
128 7/8	19 5/8	19 4/8	13 3/8	6	5	Lewis & Clark County	MT	William J. Tucker	1990	15,051
128 7/8	22 4/8	22 0/8	16 5/8	5	5	Delaware County	IA	Jeffrey J. Tobin	1990	15,051
128 7/8	20 0/8	21 1/8	20 1/8	5	5	Polk County	MN	Bart Ott	1991	15,051
128 7/8	23 7/8	22 3/8	17 5/8	6	5	Anoka County	MN	Greg Walter	1991	15,051
128 7/8	24 0/8	24 7/8	17 5/8	5	5	Chambers County	AL	Richard Williamson	1991	15,051
128 7/8	21 3/8	20 4/8	15 1/8	4	4	Cass County	IL	Mike Cox	1991	15,051
128 7/8	20 4/8	21 1/8	15 5/8	5	5	Boone County	IL	Jay Allen Ervin	1991	15,051
128 7/8	20 2/8	20 2/8	17 5/8	5	5	Iroquois County	IL	Steven K. Scharlach	1991	15,051
128 7/8	21 1/8	20 5/8	15 1/8	5	5	Livingston County	MI	Gerald Patrick Schleicher	1991	15,051
128 7/8	23 7/8	23 1/8	17 3/8	4	4	Grafton County	NH	Ronald W. Carpenter	1991	15,051
128 7/8	19 0/8	18 5/8	13 7/8	5	5	Chariton County	MO	Darrell Noth	1992	15,051
128 7/8	22 7/8	23 5/8	16 5/8	5	5	Carroll County	MS	Anthony W. Upchurch	1992	15,051
128 7/8	21 1/8	21 4/8	18 7/8	4	5	Carroll County	IL	Roman Cirignani	1992	15,051
128 7/8	22 2/8	21 6/8	16 7/8	4	5	Pulaski County	IL	Garrett Wilson	1992	15,051
128 7/8	23 7/8	23 7/8	18 2/8	5	7	Pottawattamie County	IA	Gary H. Matters	1992	15,051
128 7/8	19 6/8	18 2/8	15 1/8	4	4	Shawnee County	KS	David Diel	1992	15,051
128 7/8	23 6/8	22 6/8	19 7/8	4	5	Waukesha County	WI	Dennis Porter	1992	15,051
128 7/8	22 5/8	22 2/8	17 7/8	4	4	Sangamon County	IL	Don Casteel, Jr.	1993	15,051
128 7/8	23 0/8	23 1/8	20 3/8	4	4	Greene County	OH	John L. Kilian	1993	15,051
128 7/8	19 3/8	19 5/8	15 1/8	5	4	Manitowoc County	WI	Tom Bergner	1994	15,051
128 7/8	20 2/8	21 5/8	18 7/8	4	4	Saginaw County	MI	David G. Weber, Jr.	1994	15,051
128 7/8	20 2/8	21 4/8	15 2/8	5	6	Llano County	TX	Jerry Blankenship	1994	15,051
128 7/8	20 5/8	19 7/8	15 5/8	4	4	Polk County	WI	Keith Bastin	1994	15,051
128 7/8	21 2/8	21 2/8	15 5/8	6	6	Humboldt County	IA	Paul Detrick	1994	15,051
128 7/8	21 1/8	21 4/8	18 7/8	5	4	Waukesha County	WI	Tom Balestrieri	1994	15,051
128 7/8	21 3/8	23 1/8	15 5/8	5	5	Heard County	GA	Johnny Smith	1994	15,051
128 7/8	21 2/8	21 7/8	15 5/8	7	7	Anoka County	MN	Tom Evertz	1994	15,051
128 7/8	22 1/8	22 4/8	18 2/8	4	4	Westchester County	NY	Anthony Racanelli	1994	15,051
128 7/8	21 3/8	22 5/8	16 7/8	5	5	Jay County	IN	Emmitt Collett	1995	15,051
128 7/8	19 6/8	20 2/8	14 5/8	5	5	Sauk County	WI	Greg Schweppe	1995	15,051

485

WHITETAIL DEER (TYPICAL ANTLERS)

Minimum Score 125 — Continued

SCORE	LENGTH OF MAIN BEAM R / L	INSIDE SPREAD	NUMBER OF POINTS R / L	AREA	STATE/ PROVINCE	HUNTER'S NAME	DATE	RANK
128 7/8	20 4/8 / 19 4/8	14 5/8	5 / 5	Kenedy County	TX	Kenneth Sutton	1995	15,051
128 7/8	21 7/8 / 22 1/8	16 6/8	4 / 5	St. Louis County	MN	Frank Novak	1995	15,051
128 7/8	21 5/8 / 20 4/8	20 5/8	5 / 5	Lake County	IL	Mark A. Nelsen	1995	15,051
128 7/8	20 3/8 / 20 5/8	17 5/8	5 / 5	Berrien County	MI	Brett Marshall	1996	15,051
128 7/8	21 1/8 / 20 2/8	16 3/8	5 / 5	Athens County	OH	Daniel J. Chillinsky	1996	15,051
128 7/8	21 1/8 / 22 4/8	17 1/8	4 / 4	Sawyer County	WI	James T. Leahy	1996	15,051
128 7/8	22 1/8 / 21 4/8	15 5/8	4 / 5	Houston County	GA	Paul Brown	1996	15,051
128 7/8	21 4/8 / 21 5/8	17 3/8	6 / 5	Buffalo County	WI	Alan E. Schroeder	1996	15,051
128 7/8	22 1/8 / 21 3/8	15 7/8	5 / 5	Fairfax County	VA	Emory W. Swink III	1996	15,051
128 7/8	22 1/8 / 21 7/8	19 7/8	5 / 4	Nemaha County	NE	Robert Sailors	1996	15,051
128 7/8	23 7/8 / 23 2/8	19 6/8	5 / 6	Allen County	KY	Ronnie D. Wood	1997	15,051
128 7/8	24 5/8 / 25 2/8	22 7/8	4 / 4	Caledon	ONT	Jack Leggo	1997	15,051
128 7/8	20 2/8 / 20 6/8	14 3/8	5 / 5	Iowa County	WI	Troy K. Koelzer	1997	15,051
128 7/8	21 0/8 / 21 2/8	16 3/8	4 / 4	Marathon County	WI	Joshua R. Ostrowski	1997	15,051
128 7/8	23 1/8 / 22 5/8	18 5/8	4 / 4	Clay County	SD	Mark Tipton	1997	15,051
128 7/8	21 6/8 / 22 3/8	16 3/8	4 / 5	Decatur County	IA	Steve E. Snow	1997	15,051
128 7/8	21 4/8 / 22 0/8	15 5/8	4 / 5	Brown County	IL	William P. Sterling	1998	15,051
128 6/8	23 0/8 / 25 2/8	16 4/8	4 / 4	Buffalo County	NE	Bill Orsborn	1963	15,122
128 6/8	21 1/8 / 20 2/8	18 6/8	4 / 4	Johnson County	IA	Claire Doyle	1971	15,122
128 6/8	23 2/8 / 22 5/8	15 3/8	4 / 6	Lake County	IN	Bruce R. Prue	1977	15,122
128 6/8	19 4/8 / 20 0/8	18 2/8	6 / 5	Seward County	NE	Ronald G. Filip	1978	15,122
128 6/8	20 6/8 / 21 2/8	17 0/8	5 / 5	Brown County	SD	Jerome J. Lingor	1978	15,122
128 6/8	20 1/8 / 20 1/8	17 2/8	5 / 5	Adams County	OH	Larry David Adams	1981	15,122
128 6/8	25 5/8 / 25 6/8	18 1/8	5 / 6	Blount County	TN	David Dotson	1981	15,122
128 6/8	21 6/8 / 22 2/8	17 0/8	5 / 4	Riley County	KS	Dwayne Roepke	1981	15,122
128 6/8	22 0/8 / 22 2/8	16 6/8	4 / 4	Pierce County	WI	Joe Sukowatey	1981	15,122
128 6/8	23 3/8 / 23 6/8	17 6/8	4 / 5	Houston County	MN	James P. Finn	1982	15,122
128 6/8	21 4/8 / 21 4/8	17 0/8	5 / 5	Shelby County	IL	Larry E. Gibson	1982	15,122
128 6/8	22 6/8 / 21 0/8	17 4/8	5 / 5	Sangamon County	IL	James L. Aebel	1983	15,122
128 6/8	24 0/8 / 23 7/8	18 6/8	8 / 5	Buffalo County	WI	Michael Zastrow	1984	15,122
128 6/8	23 3/8 / 24 3/8	19 6/8	4 / 4	Dodge County	WI	Dale A. Hawkinson	1984	15,122
128 6/8	19 6/8 / 20 3/8	17 0/8	5 / 5	Robertson County	TN	Terry Louis Carter	1985	15,122
128 6/8	20 4/8 / 21 6/8	16 4/8	5 / 6	Waushara County	WI	David Polakowski	1985	15,122
128 6/8	22 1/8 / 20 3/8	19 0/8	5 / 6	Beaver County	PA	Mark Tallon	1985	15,122
128 6/8	18 4/8 / 20 5/8	17 0/8	4 / 4	Pittsburg County	OK	Edward P. Martin III	1985	15,122
128 6/8	24 1/8 / 25 5/8	18 1/8	5 / 4	Buffalo County	WI	Ed Brannen	1985	15,122
128 6/8	20 7/8 / 20 5/8	17 4/8	5 / 4	Adams County	WI	John Balaine	1986	15,122
128 6/8	20 7/8 / 19 6/8	16 2/8	5 / 5	Winona County	MN	John R. Micheel	1986	15,122
128 6/8	20 5/8 / 20 4/8	16 1/8	6 / 4	Stony Plain	ALB	Stan Chiras	1986	15,122
128 6/8	22 2/8 / 22 4/8	18 4/8	5 / 4	Hubbard County	MN	PascAl Perrin	1987	15,122
128 6/8	22 0/8 / 21 5/8	17 6/8	4 / 4	Newton County	MO	Brad Harris	1987	15,122
128 6/8	22 4/8 / 23 4/8	16 1/8	4 / 6	Logan County	IL	Gary W. Conrady	1987	15,122
128 6/8	22 5/8 / 23 5/8	16 6/8	4 / 4	Ripley County	IN	Terry G. Moore	1988	15,122
128 6/8	17 6/8 / 22 5/8	16 3/8	7 / 7	Williams County	OH	Charles Murray	1988	15,122
128 6/8	23 4/8 / 23 7/8	16 6/8	5 / 6	Anne Arundel County	MD	Mark D. Sanders	1988	15,122
128 6/8	20 5/8 / 24 4/8	20 6/8	4 / 4	Mercer County	NJ	Scott Lysenko	1988	15,122
128 6/8	19 4/8 / 18 7/8	15 0/8	5 / 5	Lynn County	TX	Al Kowalski	1988	15,122
128 6/8	22 3/8 / 23 2/8	17 6/8	4 / 4	Geary County	KS	Michael P. Boyer	1988	15,122
128 6/8	20 5/8 / 21 6/8	14 4/8	4 / 4	Iroquois County	IL	Warren Cary	1989	15,122
128 6/8	24 0/8 / 21 4/8	16 4/8	4 / 4	Medina County	TX	James Blocker, Jr.	1989	15,122
128 6/8	22 3/8 / 22 3/8	19 2/8	4 / 4	Stephenson County	IL	Jim Hastings	1989	15,122
128 6/8	21 3/8 / 21 1/8	17 6/8	4 / 4	Portage County	WI	Theodore Johnson	1989	15,122
128 6/8	26 5/8 / 25 4/8	21 4/8	3 / 5	St. Croix County	WI	Steve C. Ashley	1989	15,122
128 6/8	20 4/8 / 21 2/8	14 4/8	4 / 5	Barry County	MO	Robert Prisk	1989	15,122
128 6/8	24 2/8 / 24 2/8	19 0/8	4 / 4	Hampshire County	MA	John Higgins	1989	15,122
128 6/8	20 0/8 / 19 7/8	17 4/8	4 / 4	Cottonwood County	MN	Dennis Highby	1989	15,122
128 6/8	20 5/8 / 20 6/8	16 0/8	5 / 5	Juneau County	WI	Kurt R. Bassuener	1990	15,122
128 6/8	21 0/8 / 21 7/8	18 2/8	6 / 6	Brown County	IL	Jerry D. Dale	1990	15,122
128 6/8	22 2/8 / 23 0/8	18 0/8	4 / 4	Harvey County	KS	Danny Stahl	1990	15,122
128 6/8	19 4/8 / 19 5/8	15 6/8	5 / 6	Lincoln County	SD	Michael A. Deckert	1990	15,122
128 6/8	21 7/8 / 20 5/8	17 6/8	4 / 5	Peel	ONT	Carmen G. Bumbaca	1991	15,122
128 6/8	24 2/8 / 23 0/8	15 0/8	4 / 4	Greene County	PA	Dennis Blouir	1991	15,122
128 6/8	21 0/8 / 20 3/8	16 0/8	5 / 5	Hayes County	NE	William E. Wuerthele	1991	15,122
128 6/8	20 7/8 / 20 4/8	15 6/8	5 / 5	Freeborn County	MN	Darrell Loew	1991	15,122
128 6/8	20 5/8 / 21 0/8	15 5/8	6 / 6	Forest County	WI	Todd A. Kurszewski	1992	15,122
128 6/8	21 6/8 / 20 7/8	16 6/8	5 / 5	Vernon County	WI	Carl J. Knutson	1992	15,122
128 6/8	20 4/8 / 21 6/8	17 4/8	4 / 4	Buffalo County	WI	Jeff Owen	1992	15,122
128 6/8	19 2/8 / 21 4/8	18 3/8	6 / 5	Warren County	IA	Tom Steil	1992	15,122
128 6/8	23 1/8 / 24 1/8	15 0/8	5 / 5	Morrison County	MN	Roger W. Hansen	1992	15,122
128 6/8	21 0/8 / 21 2/8	15 0/8	6 / 5	Johnson County	IN	Mike Wilkinson	1992	15,122
128 6/8	21 4/8 / 22 1/8	18 3/8	6 / 4	Putnam County	IN	Monty Keyt	1992	15,122
128 6/8	21 3/8 / 21 7/8	16 5/8	5 / 6	Jefferson County	OH	Gregory A. Capers	1992	15,122
128 6/8	21 7/8 / 21 0/8	14 0/8	4 / 5	Crawford County	IA	Terry Pullen	1992	15,122
128 6/8	22 4/8 / 22 5/8	15 2/8	5 / 4	Stokes County	NC	Phillip D. Ring	1992	15,122
128 6/8	22 1/8 / 21 4/8	19 6/8	5 / 4	Limestone County	AL	Russell McMurry	1992	15,122
128 6/8	21 6/8 / 21 5/8	17 0/8	5 / 5	McMullen County	TX	Mark D. Kesteloot	1993	15,122
128 6/8	22 1/8 / 22 1/8	16 0/8	6 / 6	Buffalo County	WI	Terry C. Kuhnert	1993	15,122
128 6/8	21 5/8 / 21 4/8	14 4/8	4 / 4	Baraga County	MI	John A. Munn	1993	15,122

WHITETAIL DEER (TYPICAL ANTLERS)

Minimum Score 125   Continued

SCORE	LENGTH OF MAIN BEAM R	L	INSIDE SPREAD	NUMBER OF POINTS R	L	AREA	STATE/ PROVINCE	HUNTER'S NAME	DATE	RANK
128 6/8	22 4/8	22 1/8	16 4/8	5	4	Yankton County	SD	Les Marek	1993	15,122
128 6/8	21 2/8	21 1/8	14 4/8	4	4	Lunenburg County	VA	Thomas M. Hicks, Jr.	1993	15,122
128 6/8	22 2/8	22 0/8	17 0/8	4	5	McHenry County	IL	Alvin Ortmann	1993	15,122
128 6/8	20 1/8	21 2/8	15 6/8	5	5	Lincoln Parish	LA	Casey Ford	1994	15,122
128 6/8	26 1/8	23 0/8	19 2/8	5	5	Allegheny County	PA	William J. Ujhazy	1994	15,122
128 6/8	22 4/8	21 4/8	17 6/8	4	4	Union County	IL	Steve Torbet	1994	15,122
128 6/8	20 6/8	20 4/8	17 2/8	5	5	Adams County	WI	AdRyan Slaght	1994	15,122
128 6/8	22 0/8	22 6/8	20 0/8	4	5	Linn County	IA	Leo Matties	1994	15,122
128 6/8	20 5/8	21 6/8	13 7/8	6	6	Henderson County	TX	Doug McClung	1994	15,122
128 6/8	22 5/8	24 3/8	18 4/8	6	5	Columbia County	WI	Mike Guenther	1994	15,122
128 6/8	21 6/8	22 1/8	16 0/8	5	4	Trempealeau County	WI	Ross P. Lambert	1995	15,122
128 6/8	20 0/8	21 2/8	16 2/8	8	6	Roberts County	SD	Ronald L. Backman	1995	15,122
128 6/8	19 6/8	20 2/8	12 6/8	5	5	Fairfax County	VA	Emory W. Swink III	1995	15,122
128 6/8	22 0/8	20 3/8	17 6/8	5	5	Iowa County	WI	Kelvin W. Lancaster	1995	15,122
128 6/8	23 3/8	22 1/8	20 2/8	4	5	Claiborne County	MS	Paul Stokes	1995	15,122
128 6/8	21 5/8	21 6/8	19 2/8	6	9	Suffolk County	NY	Guy Lippo	1995	15,122
128 6/8	21 6/8	22 0/8	16 0/8	4	4	Marathon County	WI	Michael A. Reynolds	1996	15,122
128 6/8	19 5/8	19 7/8	17 6/8	5	5	Adams County	IL	Mark Green	1996	15,122
128 6/8	22 5/8	22 2/8	16 4/8	5	5	Marquette County	WI	Kenneth R. Bortz, Jr.	1996	15,122
128 6/8	21 3/8	20 7/8	15 6/8	5	5	Crawford County	WI	Douglas E. Mikkelson	1996	15,122
128 6/8	21 3/8	19 5/8	18 4/8	4	4	Washington County	PA	Timothy D. Miller	1996	15,122
128 6/8	22 2/8	21 3/8	16 4/8	4	5	Rock County	WI	Thomas Keller	1996	15,122
128 6/8	22 1/8	22 4/8	18 2/8	4	4	McHenry County	IL	Charles Simes	1996	15,122
128 6/8	21 0/8	21 4/8	15 6/8	5	5	Dimmit County	TX	Chuck Adams	1997	15,122
128 6/8	21 1/8	21 1/8	15 3/8	4	5	Buffalo County	WI	John Stewart	1997	15,122
128 6/8	21 6/8	22 1/8	18 4/8	4	4	Greene County	MO	Rick Cook	1997	15,122
128 6/8	26 5/8	25 3/8	21 4/8	6	8	St. Thomas	ONT	Greg Peters	1997	15,122
128 6/8	20 5/8	20 3/8	16 6/8	5	5	Claiborne County	MS	Cliff Covington	1997	15,122
128 6/8	21 3/8	21 5/8	16 2/8	5	4	Warren County	MS	Dale C. Claunch	1997	15,122
128 6/8	21 2/8	22 6/8	19 0/8	4	5	Allegheny County	PA	David T. Cunningham	1997	15,122
128 6/8	22 4/8	22 5/8	15 0/8	4	4	Sarpy County	NE	Tom Nauman	1997	15,122
128 6/8	24 4/8	23 4/8	14 4/8	4	6	Todd County	KY	William E. Page	1997	15,122
128 6/8	21 1/8	21 0/8	16 4/8	5	5	Fairfax County	VA	Roger Pearce	1997	15,122
128 6/8	20 6/8	20 5/8	18 0/8	4	4	Pike County	IL	Don Wood	1997	15,122
128 6/8	25 3/8	24 7/8	13 4/8	5	5	Monona County	IA	Steven Gray	1997	15,122
128 6/8	20 1/8	20 1/8	17 2/8	4	4	Crawford County	IL	Wayne H. Perrine	1997	15,122
128 6/8	19 1/8	18 6/8	15 4/8	5	6	Dakota County	MN	CameRon Leftwich	1997	15,122
128 6/8	22 4/8	22 2/8	17 4/8	5	5	Muskingum County	OH	Randy Scarlett	1997	15,122
128 6/8	23 1/8	22 7/8	15 7/8	4	5	Dallas County	AL	Leonard Bryant	1998	15,122
128 6/8	24 0/8	22 6/8	16 4/8	3	4	Waupaca County	WI	John H. Klinger	1998	15,122
128 6/8	21 5/8	21 2/8	16 6/8	4	4	Oconto County	WI	Craig Patz	1998	15,122
128 6/8	22 4/8	24 0/8	16 4/8	4	4	Jefferson County	WV	Daniel R. Staubs	1998	15,122
128 5/8	20 6/8	20 2/8	14 7/8	5	5	Mille Lacs County	MN	Milton J. Mattson	1952	15,225
128 5/8	14 7/8	26 2/8	20 5/8	5	5	Ford County	KS	Rod Lies	1966	15,225
128 5/8	18 1/8	18 5/8	15 3/8	5	5	Harford County	MD	Joseph Egner	1969	15,225
128 5/8	20 4/8	20 4/8	18 0/8	6	6	Lawrence County	SD	Ronald Hazledine	1969	15,225
128 5/8	21 6/8	22 0/8	17 5/8	4	4	Mercer County	IL	Kenneth E. Yeater	1971	15,225
128 5/8	21 3/8	21 0/8	18 5/8	5	5	Delaware County	IA	Jim L. Mahan	1974	15,225
128 5/8	22 2/8	22 4/8	15 7/8	5	5	Fond du Lac County	WI	Kevin Clark	1975	15,225
128 5/8	21 3/8	21 3/8	17 6/8	5	6	Whiteside County	IL	Art Heinze	1976	15,225
128 5/8	23 0/8	23 3/8	17 2/8	8	5	Kendall County	IL	David Martinek	1978	15,225
128 5/8	20 4/8	20 1/8	15 1/8	5	5	Ontario County	NY	William Danno	1980	15,225
128 5/8	21 0/8	20 7/8	14 5/8	5	5	Ionia County	MI	Ronald A. Denney	1980	15,225
128 5/8	23 4/8	24 0/8	19 0/8	6	6	Jackson County	WI	John D. Card	1981	15,225
128 5/8	22 2/8	21 5/8	16 7/8	5	5	Franklin County	MO	Lance Tyree	1982	15,225
128 5/8	21 5/8	23 0/8	17 1/8	8	6	Cedar County	NE	Charles Benertz	1982	15,225
128 5/8	22 6/8	23 4/8	19 6/8	5	6	Carroll County	IL	Art Heinze	1982	15,225
128 5/8	19 1/8	19 3/8	15 7/8	5	5	Juneau County	WI	Steve Baker	1982	15,225
128 5/8	20 1/8	20 2/8	17 1/8	5	5	Wetzel County	WV	Paul Pichardo	1983	15,225
128 5/8	22 1/8	21 4/8	17 7/8	4	4	Pike County	PA	Joseph V. Caccamo, Jr.	1984	15,225
128 5/8	21 6/8	22 7/8	16 3/8	5	4	Richland County	OH	Tod O. Duffner	1984	15,225
128 5/8	20 2/8	20 2/8	18 5/8	5	5	Kanabec County	MN	Milo L. Carlson	1985	15,225
128 5/8	22 1/8	22 1/8	14 5/8	5	5	Kenosha County	WI	Mike Mitten	1985	15,225
128 5/8	20 3/8	20 3/8	16 5/8	5	4	Iowa County	WI	Ralph J. Blum	1985	15,225
128 5/8	20 2/8	20 5/8	17 5/8	5	5	Kane County	IL	Roger Eberly	1985	15,225
128 5/8	22 5/8	22 5/8	19 0/8	6	4	Green County	WI	Michael G. Martin	1985	15,225
128 5/8	21 3/8	21 4/8	18 1/8	4	4	Suffolk County	NY	Richard Kent	1985	15,225
128 5/8	23 5/8	24 6/8	18 7/8	6	4	Kandiyohi County	MN	Timothy G. Caven	1986	15,225
128 5/8	19 4/8	19 7/8	14 7/8	5	5	Juneau County	WI	Scott Prucha	1986	15,225
128 5/8	22 0/8	21 6/8	15 5/8	4	5	Grant County	WI	Dean Lease	1986	15,225
128 5/8	21 3/8	22 0/8	18 1/8	4	4	Jackson County	OH	Terry S. Speakman	1986	15,225
128 5/8	18 7/8	19 1/8	15 4/8	6	5	Benton County	IA	Corby Miller	1986	15,225
128 5/8	22 0/8	21 7/8	17 3/8	5	5	Morris County	NJ	Larry Cacchio	1987	15,225
128 5/8	20 7/8	21 5/8	15 1/8	4	4	Jackson County	MN	Gary E. Anderson	1987	15,225
128 5/8	21 2/8	22 0/8	16 0/8	5	5	Iron County	MI	Ted Sammond	1988	15,225
128 5/8	22 4/8	21 0/8	14 7/8	5	4	Dickinson County	IA	Jeff Hiveley	1988	15,225
128 5/8	20 7/8	20 6/8	15 5/8	4	5	Anoka County	MN	Greg Seymour	1988	15,225
128 5/8	21 1/8	21 0/8	17 1/8	5	5	McHenry County	IL	John F. Schorsch, Jr.	1988	15,225

WHITETAIL DEER (TYPICAL ANTLERS)

Minimum Score 125 — Continued

SCORE	LENGTH OF MAIN BEAM R	LENGTH OF MAIN BEAM L	INSIDE SPREAD	NUMBER OF POINTS R	NUMBER OF POINTS L	AREA	STATE/PROVINCE	HUNTER'S NAME	DATE	RANK
128 5/8	20 2/8	19 1/8	14 1/8	4	7	Hall County	NE	Steve Cool	1989	15,225
128 5/8	21 1/8	21 0/8	16 5/8	5	5	Ashland County	WI	Maggie Falkenstein	1989	15,225
128 5/8	20 3/8	19 6/8	17 5/8	5	5	Chester County	PA	Robert L. Stephens, Jr.	1989	15,225
128 5/8	17 3/8	19 6/8	16 1/8	5	5	Clark County	WI	Richard Reddy	1989	15,225
128 5/8	20 2/8	21 3/8	18 6/8	5	5	Clark County	MO	Gary Twigg	1989	15,225
128 5/8	20 5/8	21 2/8	17 5/8	4	5	Washington County	IL	Edward Kurwicki	1990	15,225
128 5/8	20 3/8	21 1/8	15 5/8	5	5	Dodge County	WI	Rick Kluge	1990	15,225
128 5/8	20 5/8	20 3/8	18 3/8	5	5	Oakland County	MI	Keith Phillips	1990	15,225
128 5/8	23 1/8	22 2/8	17 7/8	6	5	Waukesha County	WI	Robert Rajnicek	1990	15,225
128 5/8	23 7/8	22 0/8	17 7/8	5	5	Van Buren County	IA	John "Rosey" Roseland	1990	15,225
128 5/8	22 5/8	22 2/8	19 1/8	5	4	Crow Wing County	MN	Glenn Johnson	1990	15,225
128 5/8	25 6/8	25 5/8	17 2/8	7	7	Goodhue County	MN	Bob Friedrick	1991	15,225
128 5/8	22 6/8	22 2/8	16 7/8	4	4	Jefferson County	WI	Steve Hein	1991	15,225
128 5/8	24 2/8	24 0/8	17 1/8	4	4	Oconto County	WI	Mitchell Meunier	1991	15,225
128 5/8	21 5/8	22 2/8	19 5/8	5	4	Jefferson County	OH	Gregg Platt	1991	15,225
128 5/8	22 0/8	21 0/8	15 7/8	5	5	Waukesha County	WI	Steve Hoelz	1991	15,225
128 5/8	21 4/8	21 4/8	11 5/8	5	6	Warren County	IA	Erv Wagner	1991	15,225
128 5/8	22 3/8	22 7/8	15 5/8	5	4	Iroquois County	IL	Chad McGinnis	1991	15,225
128 5/8	23 4/8	23 3/8	16 3/8	5	4	Lewis & Clark County	MT	Scott McGuire	1992	15,225
128 5/8	21 2/8	21 1/8	21 1/8	4	4	New Castle County	DE	Robert A. Clark	1992	15,225
128 5/8	21 2/8	22 0/8	16 3/8	4	4	Grant County	WI	Bob Bloom	1992	15,225
128 5/8	21 1/8	21 2/8	13 6/8	6	6	Monroe County	WI	Jerry C. Moser	1992	15,225
128 5/8	24 2/8	23 5/8	20 5/8	4	4	Dakota County	MN	Mike Sannan	1992	15,225
128 5/8	20 3/8	21 7/8	18 1/8	5	4	Goochland County	VA	Robert W. Overton III	1992	15,225
128 5/8	20 1/8	20 2/8	14 5/8	5	5	Wayne County	IL	Chris W. Moore	1992	15,225
128 5/8	20 5/8	20 2/8	19 1/8	5	5	Rockingham County	NH	George Trefethen	1992	15,225
128 5/8	20 4/8	20 2/8	15 5/8	5	5	Burnett County	WI	Tom D. Anderson	1993	15,225
128 5/8	20 2/8	19 5/8	16 1/8	6	7	Muskingum County	OH	Bob Staab	1993	15,225
128 5/8	23 2/8	23 1/8	15 7/8	4	4	Waukesha County	WI	Doug Wonoski	1993	15,225
128 5/8	24 1/8	25 4/8	18 1/8	5	4	Crawford County	IN	Mark A. Miller	1993	15,225
128 5/8	21 4/8	21 5/8	17 3/8	5	5	Hardin County	OH	Ray Davis	1993	15,225
128 5/8	21 3/8	20 5/8	13 3/8	5	5	Crittenden County	KY	Lynn Boone	1994	15,225
128 5/8	21 3/8	21 3/8	16 7/8	4	5	Westmoreland County	PA	Sean Rarrick	1994	15,225
128 5/8	21 0/8	23 3/8	15 5/8	5	5	White County	IN	Steve Rider, Jr.	1994	15,225
128 5/8	23 0/8	24 4/8	16 7/8	6	6	Cherokee County	OK	Edward Hatley	1994	15,225
128 5/8	22 5/8	20 6/8	16 5/8	4	4	Burnett County	WI	Joe Gohlike	1994	15,225
128 5/8	20 7/8	20 7/8	18 5/8	4	4	Menard County	IL	Ron Wadsworth	1994	15,225
128 5/8	21 6/8	22 0/8	16 0/8	5	6	Hocking County	OH	Tony Casagrande	1994	15,225
128 5/8	22 0/8	22 1/8	13 3/8	5	4	Menard County	TX	Billy J. Meeks	1994	15,225
128 5/8	22 6/8	23 4/8	18 3/8	6	5	Ontario County	NY	E. Michael Kosko	1994	15,225
128 5/8	23 0/8	25 2/8	19 5/8	4	4	Hennepin County	MN	Gerald P. Kieffer	1994	15,225
128 5/8	24 5/8	24 5/8	18 5/8	4	4	Vinton County	OH	Timothy E. Fleet	1994	15,225
128 5/8	21 5/8	20 4/8	15 5/8	6	6	Williams County	OH	Randy Smith	1994	15,225
128 5/8	22 6/8	22 5/8	16 1/8	4	4	Montgomery County	IL	Matthew J. Tallman	1994	15,225
128 5/8	22 0/8	21 0/8	15 1/8	5	5	Clayton County	IA	John P. DeLong	1995	15,225
128 5/8	22 6/8	21 5/8	17 7/8	5	5	Chatham County	NC	Farrell Ritter	1995	15,225
128 5/8	19 6/8	20 7/8	15 5/8	4	4	Robertson County	TN	Ed Anderson	1995	15,225
128 5/8	21 3/8	21 0/8	17 5/8	4	4	St. Charles County	MO	Scott Cowen	1995	15,225
128 5/8	17 6/8	18 5/8	15 4/8	6	6	Buffalo County	WI	Alan Oleson	1995	15,225
128 5/8	20 2/8	20 1/8	13 3/8	5	5	Adams County	IL	James Dodson, Jr.	1995	15,225
128 5/8	21 0/8	21 6/8	16 1/8	4	4	Pike County	IL	Eddie Claypool	1995	15,225
128 5/8	22 6/8	22 6/8	16 7/8	5	5	Portage County	WI	Gary J. Tuskowski	1995	15,225
128 5/8	22 0/8	22 0/8	16 2/8	6	5	Payne County	OK	James R. Weir	1995	15,225
128 5/8	22 5/8	24 5/8	18 7/8	4	4	Clay County	IA	Rick A. Petersen	1995	15,225
128 5/8	20 4/8	20 3/8	14 1/8	5	5	Maverick County	TX	Bill R. Gantt	1995	15,225
128 5/8	22 5/8	25 1/8	17 4/8	6	5	Flathead County	MT	Ronny L. Nail	1996	15,225
128 5/8	21 2/8	21 2/8	15 7/8	7	5	Dougherty County	GA	Gary A. Daniel	1996	15,225
128 5/8	19 2/8	20 2/8	19 7/8	5	6	Kankakee County	IL	Keith Horn	1996	15,225
128 5/8	19 4/8	19 7/8	15 5/8	5	5	Cascade County	MT	Ray Goff	1996	15,225
128 5/8	20 4/8	20 7/8	14 5/8	4	5	Ray County	MO	Christopher L. Lein	1996	15,225
128 5/8	23 1/8	23 7/8	16 3/8	4	4	Cecil County	MD	Michael Sadler	1997	15,225
128 5/8	21 0/8	22 7/8	18 3/8	4	4	Tuscaloosa County	AL	Will Tyner	1997	15,225
128 5/8	22 4/8	22 2/8	16 7/8	5	5	Carter County	MO	Jack E. Asbridge	1997	15,225
128 5/8	21 0/8	22 2/8	13 5/8	6	5	Wyandot County	OH	Roger A. Wentling	1997	15,225
128 5/8	20 3/8	20 5/8	14 2/8	6	5	Wilkinson County	MS	Patrick Kelleher	1997	15,225
128 5/8	21 1/8	20 5/8	17 3/8	4	4	Fillmore County	MN	Dean Irish	1998	15,225
128 4/8	25 0/8	23 7/8	17 0/8	4	4	Mozart	AR	Alfred Hirt	1959	15,327
128 4/8	20 4/8	21 0/8	17 7/8	7	5	Clay County	NE	Rollan Johnson	1961	15,327
128 4/8	21 1/8	21 2/8	15 0/8	5	4	Marion County	IA	Thomas Tucker	1968	15,327
128 4/8	20 0/8	21 2/8	16 7/8	6	7	McLeod County	MN	Merlin Eggersgluess	1971	15,327
128 4/8	21 6/8	22 3/8	16 6/8	5	5	Jones County	IA	Tom Postel	1971	15,327
128 4/8	22 3/8	23 2/8	17 5/8	5	6	Wright County	MN	Elwood Rokala	1971	15,327
128 4/8	22 6/8	23 0/8	23 7/8	4	4	Broad River	SC	John V. Orr	1973	15,327
128 4/8	20 1/8	20 2/8	15 2/8	5	5	Delaware County	OH	Denton O. Baumbarger	1973	15,327
128 4/8	25 4/8	23 0/8	15 1/8	5	6	Wapello County	IA	Rick Grooms	1974	15,327
128 4/8	23 1/8	22 0/8	19 0/8	4	4	Henry County	MO	Lavern Rucker	1974	15,327
128 4/8	19 5/8	20 3/8	15 4/8	5	5	Ozaukee County	WI	Ronald Mayer	1975	15,327
128 4/8	22 0/8	20 4/8	18 2/8	4	4	Rosebud County	MT	Bob Brill	1976	15,327

WHITETAIL DEER (TYPICAL ANTLERS)

Minimum Score 125 Continued 489

SCORE	LENGTH OF MAIN BEAM R	L	INSIDE SPREAD	NUMBER OF POINTS R	L	AREA	STATE/ PROVINCE	HUNTER'S NAME	DATE	RANK
128 4/8	19 2/8	19 5/8	15 0/8	5	5	Park County	MT	John Christiansen	1983	15,327
128 4/8	21 0/8	20 6/8	17 4/8	5	5	Kankakee County	IL	Wayne Webber	1983	15,327
128 4/8	22 6/8	22 4/8	14 6/8	6	7	Mississippi County	AR	Davy J. Shaw	1983	15,327
128 4/8	23 0/8	22 5/8	19 6/8	4	4	Delaware County	PA	Mark Gentry	1984	15,327
128 4/8	21 7/8	19 6/8	17 3/8	7	4	Griggs County	ND	Blaine Larson	1984	15,327
128 4/8	20 2/8	21 2/8	16 6/8	5	5	Grant County	WI	Jeffery Redfearn	1985	15,327
128 4/8	21 5/8	21 4/8	16 0/8	5	5	Kane County	IL	Jeff Stephens	1985	15,327
128 4/8	22 7/8	21 5/8	20 4/8	4	5	Platte County	WY	Jayde Allbright	1986	15,327
128 4/8	20 2/8	20 5/8	16 6/8	5	4	Sumner County	KS	Larry J. Pacey	1986	15,327
128 4/8	18 6/8	20 3/8	16 2/8	4	4	Plymouth County	IA	Donald F. Pankowski	1986	15,327
128 4/8	20 7/8	20 4/8	16 2/8	5	5	La Crosse County	WI	Gary Thomas Severson	1986	15,327
128 4/8	19 0/8	19 1/8	13 4/8	5	5	Eddy County	ND	Tim Finley	1987	15,327
128 4/8	21 4/8	21 0/8	14 6/8	5	5	Edmonson County	KY	Marvin Pate	1987	15,327
128 4/8	18 5/8	20 0/8	15 2/8	5	5	Porter County	IN	Thomas David Katona	1987	15,327
128 4/8	24 0/8	23 6/8	14 2/8	4	4	Jackson County	IN	Jeff Montgomery	1987	15,327
128 4/8	22 0/8	23 2/8	17 6/8	4	5	Somerset County	NJ	Brian Todaro	1987	15,327
128 4/8	23 4/8	22 6/8	17 0/8	5	4	Lawrence County	IL	Mike Forsythe	1987	15,327
128 4/8	20 5/8	20 5/8	16 4/8	5	5	Stearns County	MN	Roy Saari	1987	15,327
128 4/8	22 5/8	20 2/8	16 4/8	4	4	Boone County	IL	Ottie W. Rowe	1988	15,327
128 4/8	21 0/8	22 3/8	18 4/8	5	5	Indiana County	PA	Leonard Maday, Jr.	1988	15,327
128 4/8	20 3/8	20 1/8	16 4/8	6	5	Langlade County	WI	Scott A. McCann	1988	15,327
128 4/8	21 0/8	21 1/8	17 4/8	5	5	St. Joseph County	IN	Steve Sokol	1988	15,327
128 4/8	21 4/8	21 5/8	15 4/8	5	4	Oconto County	WI	Steven L. DeBauche	1988	15,327
128 4/8	23 1/8	23 2/8	18 0/8	5	5	Will County	IL	Henry John Christianson	1989	15,327
128 4/8	25 4/8	24 0/8	20 2/8	5	5	Jefferson County	OH	Jim Still	1989	15,327
128 4/8	21 0/8	21 0/8	19 0/8	5	5	Morgan County	OH	David G. Ferguson	1989	15,327
128 4/8	22 6/8	22 2/8	18 4/8	4	4	Wayne County	OH	Keith R. Dotterer	1990	15,327
128 4/8	23 3/8	23 5/8	21 0/8	5	4	Somerset County	NJ	Stephen Kotz	1990	15,327
128 4/8	21 2/8	21 3/8	15 4/8	4	4	Nacogdoches County	TX	Stephen Shinn	1990	15,327
128 4/8	24 3/8	24 0/8	19 6/8	4	5	Carroll County	MO	Charles Lichte III	1990	15,327
128 4/8	24 0/8	23 5/8	19 7/8	5	6	Cecil County	MD	James P. White II	1990	15,327
128 4/8	21 1/8	21 2/8	19 6/8	5	4	Wayne County	OH	Ronald Elliott	1990	15,327
128 4/8	22 2/8	24 1/8	17 4/8	4	5	Cochrane	ALB	Robin Ryan	1990	15,327
128 4/8	20 4/8	19 4/8	14 6/8	5	5	Atchison County	MO	Steve McManaman	1990	15,327
128 4/8	21 7/8	21 6/8	17 4/8	4	4	Sussex County	NJ	Michael Badami	1991	15,327
128 4/8	20 4/8	21 4/8	16 0/8	5	5	Somerset County	NJ	John F. Cleary	1991	15,327
128 4/8	23 3/8	23 5/8	17 4/8	5	5	Pierce County	WI	Dan Beyer	1991	15,327
128 4/8	22 7/8	23 4/8	18 3/8	6	6	Otter Tail County	MN	Marlin "Doc" Peach	1991	15,327
128 4/8	19 2/8	20 1/8	14 2/8	5	4	Johnson County	IA	Scott Ogden	1991	15,327
128 4/8	24 7/8	23 5/8	18 4/8	4	4	Gallia County	OH	Johnnie L. Metzger	1991	15,327
128 4/8	20 2/8	20 2/8	13 2/8	7	8	Waukesha County	WI	Ed Hamm	1992	15,327
128 4/8	20 6/8	21 3/8	15 2/8	5	5	Pike County	IL	William R. Graham	1992	15,327
128 4/8	20 2/8	23 0/8	17 0/8	5	5	Jackson County	MI	Steven R. Stilson	1992	15,327
128 4/8	22 2/8	21 7/8	15 1/8	5	7	Jefferson County	IL	George Bryant	1992	15,327
128 4/8	21 2/8	21 6/8	15 0/8	5	5	Goliad County	TX	Ronald K. McConnell	1992	15,327
128 4/8	20 0/8	20 1/8	17 3/8	8	8	Bonner County	ID	Glen Berry	1993	15,327
128 4/8	20 4/8	20 5/8	18 6/8	4	4	Davis County	IA	Larry D. Jones	1993	15,327
128 4/8	23 4/8	22 6/8	20 3/8	5	4	Hunterdon County	NJ	John D. Robachefski	1993	15,327
128 4/8	22 0/8	20 7/8	16 2/8	5	6	Osage County	OK	Joe Admire, Jr.	1993	15,327
128 4/8	21 5/8	20 5/8	15 6/8	7	5	Juneau County	WI	Bruce Boyum	1993	15,327
128 4/8	20 3/8	21 1/8	17 6/8	5	5	Jackson County	WI	Larry McDonald	1993	15,327
128 4/8	21 3/8	21 2/8	16 2/8	5	5	Ozaukee County	WI	Joe Seaman	1993	15,327
128 4/8	24 1/8	24 2/8	18 6/8	6	5	Winona County	MN	James J. Folcey	1993	15,327
128 4/8	22 6/8	22 1/8	21 0/8	5	5	Mercer County	NJ	Michael Papiez	1993	15,327
128 4/8	20 7/8	21 0/8	17 2/8	5	4	Muscatine County	IA	Todd A. Bermel	1993	15,327
128 4/8	21 0/8	21 4/8	17 4/8	4	4	Slope County	ND	Stan Godfrey	1993	15,327
128 4/8	25 0/8	22 7/8	20 0/8	5	5	Montgomery County	MD	Larry S. Heck	1993	15,327
128 4/8	24 6/8	23 5/8	14 6/8	4	4	Baltimore County	MD	Shane A. Fitzgerald	1994	15,327
128 4/8	23 0/8	22 7/8	17 4/8	5	4	Anson County	NC	William M. "Bill" Stroupe	1994	15,327
128 4/8	19 3/8	20 0/8	14 6/8	4	4	Shackelford County	TX	Ray MoraLes	1994	15,327
128 4/8	22 0/8	21 5/8	17 6/8	5	5	Llano County	TX	Marvin Human	1994	15,327
128 4/8	21 0/8	20 3/8	16 2/8	4	4	Polk County	TX	Russell D. Gordy	1994	15,327
128 4/8	22 3/8	23 2/8	17 6/8	5	5	Lehigh County	PA	Todd W. Rader	1994	15,327
128 4/8	21 7/8	21 7/8	19 6/8	4	5	La Porte County	IN	Henry C. Owens	1994	15,327
128 4/8	23 4/8	23 4/8	20 0/8	5	5	Madison County	IA	Gary D. Knoll	1994	15,327
128 4/8	20 5/8	19 3/8	16 0/8	5	6	McHenry County	IL	Lonnie Millerman	1994	15,327
128 4/8	21 0/8	21 1/8	17 2/8	5	5	Essex County	MA	Brad Fournier	1994	15,327
128 4/8	22 6/8	25 0/8	16 6/8	5	4	Montgomery County	MD	Roger Stewart	1994	15,327
128 4/8	23 3/8	23 2/8	18 6/8	4	4	Jackson County	MO	Doug Brown	1994	15,327
128 4/8	23 3/8	23 4/8	17 4/8	4	5	Chisago County	MN	Robert Krueger	1994	15,327
128 4/8	23 1/8	23 0/8	17 0/8	4	5	Shelby County	IN	Danny R. Johnson	1995	15,327
128 4/8	21 7/8	19 3/8	17 6/8	5	5	Sauk County	WI	Bill Seils	1995	15,327
128 4/8	22 7/8	23 1/8	17 1/8	6	6	Polk County	IA	Nicholas DeLouis	1995	15,327
128 4/8	26 2/8	25 1/8	19 6/8	4	4	Ripley County	IN	Samuel Durham	1995	15,327
128 4/8	20 3/8	22 1/8	17 4/8	4	5	Vinton County	OH	Burl Keesee	1995	15,327
128 4/8	18 6/8	20 5/8	16 0/8	5	5	Trempealeau County	WI	Duane Hoff	1995	15,327
128 4/8	21 4/8	21 6/8	18 2/8	4	5	Yates County	NY	Tom Taylor	1995	15,327
128 4/8	22 4/8	22 3/8	18 6/8	6	4	Barry County	MI	Ronald D. Watson	1996	15,327

WHITETAIL DEER (TYPICAL ANTLERS)

Minimum Score 125 — Continued

SCORE	LENGTH OF MAIN BEAM R	LENGTH OF MAIN BEAM L	INSIDE SPREAD	NUMBER OF POINTS R	NUMBER OF POINTS L	AREA	STATE/PROVINCE	HUNTER'S NAME	DATE	RANK
128 4/8	21 1/8	21 7/8	14 4/8	5	5	Clermont County	OH	Duane "Corky" Richardson	1996	15,327
128 4/8	21 1/8	23 1/8	15 6/8	5	6	Montgomery County	IA	Dick Paul	1996	15,327
128 4/8	22 1/8	22 7/8	18 2/8	5	6	Greene County	IL	Rick Kraut	1996	15,327
128 4/8	22 0/8	21 4/8	18 4/8	5	4	Iowa County	WI	Scott Kleppe	1997	15,327
128 4/8	20 7/8	20 2/8	15 6/8	5	5	Iowa County	WI	Russell Sharp	1997	15,327
128 4/8	22 6/8	22 6/8	15 6/8	5	5	Calhoun County	MI	George I. Swan, Jr.	1997	15,327
128 4/8	20 3/8	19 5/8	13 4/8	5	5	Carroll County	MS	Larry Wiggins, Jr.	1997	15,327
128 4/8	23 0/8	22 5/8	15 6/8	4	4	Adams County	WI	Tim Sherry	1997	15,327
128 4/8	21 1/8	22 0/8	15 6/8	5	4	Will County	IL	Herb Mathwig	1997	15,327
128 4/8	21 0/8	21 6/8	17 2/8	5	6	Cerro Gordo County	IA	Jim Fink	1997	15,327
128 4/8	21 1/8	20 3/8	15 0/8	5	5	Edmunds County	SD	Dave Knecht	1997	15,327
128 4/8	23 2/8	23 2/8	19 7/8	4	5	Clark County	OH	Mark A. Mabry	1997	15,327
128 4/8	21 3/8	20 4/8	15 6/8	5	5	Sauk County	WI	Harlen C. Olson	1997	15,327
128 4/8	22 6/8	22 7/8	19 5/8	5	4	Worcester County	MA	Dennis Vadenais	1997	15,327
128 4/8	24 3/8	24 3/8	16 3/8	4	4	Fairfield County	OH	Jim Henry	1997	15,327
128 4/8	21 5/8	21 6/8	17 0/8	5	5	Jackson County	WI	Michael K. Janicki, Sr.	1997	15,327
128 4/8	22 6/8	22 4/8	19 6/8	4	4	Knox County	IL	John Gilroy, Jr.	1997	15,327
128 4/8	21 2/8	21 0/8	20 0/8	4	4	Barron County	WI	Todd Larson	1998	15,327
128 3/8	23 3/8	23 0/8	20 3/8	4	5	Williamson County	IL	Don Walker	1959	15,435
128 3/8	23 4/8	23 2/8	17 3/8	6	7	Poncil	MT	Bob Samson	1962	15,435
128 3/8	19 1/8	19 6/8	15 2/8	6	4	Douglas County	NE	Cecil Smith	1962	15,435
128 3/8	20 6/8	20 5/8	14 1/8	5	4	Morrison County	MN	Ronald Thole	1964	15,435
128 3/8	19 6/8	19 7/8	16 7/8	6	5	Columbia County	WI	David D. Luetkens	1965	15,435
128 3/8	22 1/8	20 0/8	20 7/8	4	4	Brown County	SD	T. Michael Dunn	1966	15,435
128 3/8	21 0/8	22 1/8	18 5/8	5	5	Bartholomew County	IN	Harold Frye	1966	15,435
128 3/8	22 0/8	21 6/8	14 5/8	5	4	Allegany County	NY	Joseph Famiglietti	1972	15,435
128 3/8	23 4/8	23 3/8	19 5/8	4	4	Union County	IL	Randy Edmonds	1974	15,435
128 3/8	22 0/8	21 7/8	17 7/8	4	4	Switzerland County	IN	Samuel M. Durham	1979	15,435
128 3/8	20 4/8	22 1/8	15 1/8	5	5	Highland County	OH	Dean Herschede	1980	15,435
128 3/8	21 7/8	22 4/8	18 5/8	5	6	Menominee County	MI	James Saunoris	1980	15,435
128 3/8	21 4/8	21 2/8	16 5/8	5	5	Cameron County	TX	Jerry Spencer	1980	15,435
128 3/8	24 3/8	23 1/8	20 3/8	4	3	Tazewell County	IL	Jimmy C. Plemmons	1981	15,435
128 3/8	20 0/8	19 6/8	16 1/8	4	5	Henry County	KY	Donald Cornett	1982	15,435
128 3/8	19 0/8	17 1/8	14 4/8	6	6	Will County	IL	Richard D. Tenute	1982	15,435
128 3/8	22 5/8	22 1/8	16 1/8	6	5	Clark County	OH	Rick Rust	1983	15,435
128 3/8	23 6/8	23 3/8	20 1/8	4	4	Muskingum County	OH	Mike Spring	1983	15,435
128 3/8	20 7/8	21 3/8	17 1/8	5	4	Rock County	WI	Henry W. Holdorf, Jr.	1983	15,435
128 3/8	22 2/8	22 6/8	14 7/8	6	6	Clay County	SD	Marlowe Rames	1983	15,435
128 3/8	21 1/8	20 5/8	15 3/8	6	6	Anoka County	MN	John Cardinal	1984	15,435
128 3/8	23 7/8	22 5/8	20 1/8	4	4	Sheridan County	KS	Tom E. Bowman	1985	15,435
128 3/8	19 6/8	20 5/8	19 5/8	6	6	Kit Carson County	CO	Dave Holt	1985	15,435
128 3/8	20 6/8	20 7/8	17 0/8	6	4	Yuma County	CO	Bill Grammer	1986	15,435
128 3/8	23 1/8	23 1/8	17 5/8	5	4	Lawrence County	OH	Robert E. Burcham	1986	15,435
128 3/8	20 4/8	20 5/8	15 3/8	5	5	McLean County	ND	Lynn Wentz	1987	15,435
128 3/8	23 1/8	24 1/8	16 4/8	5	5	Dunn County	WI	Charles Storing	1987	15,435
128 3/8	21 7/8	22 0/8	15 7/8	5	5	Calumet County	WI	Ronald Campbell	1987	15,435
128 3/8	23 3/8	22 0/8	16 7/8	6	5	Forest County	WI	Darrow Bedor	1987	15,435
128 3/8	20 4/8	20 7/8	15 3/8	5	6	Lincoln County	NE	David J. Hinton	1987	15,435
128 3/8	23 3/8	23 5/8	17 7/8	5	4	Nuevo Leon	MEX	Paul H. Dickson	1988	15,435
128 3/8	20 2/8	20 2/8	17 5/8	5	7	Clay County	SD	Craig W. Myron	1988	15,435
128 3/8	22 5/8	22 4/8	17 5/8	4	4	Dane County	WI	Gene R. Herman	1988	15,435
128 3/8	24 5/8	24 6/8	19 3/8	4	4	Montgomery County	PA	Joseph D. Maddock	1988	15,435
128 3/8	20 1/8	20 2/8	16 1/8	4	5	Polk County	NE	Jim Czapla	1989	15,435
128 3/8	21 3/8	21 5/8	18 5/8	4	5	Warren County	OH	Dennis R. Gosney	1989	15,435
128 3/8	22 6/8	23 6/8	17 5/8	4	5	Monroe County	IA	Chris Keyes	1989	15,435
128 3/8	21 0/8	21 4/8	14 7/8	6	5	Tom Green County	TX	Mike Hegefeld	1989	15,435
128 3/8	20 3/8	20 0/8	18 7/8	5	5	Dawson Township	ONT	Tom Harper	1990	15,435
128 3/8	23 0/8	22 7/8	16 5/8	4	4	Marshall County	IL	Steve Boylan	1990	15,435
128 3/8	23 1/8	23 6/8	17 4/8	5	4	Montgomery County	IN	Stacy A. Hightower	1990	15,435
128 3/8	23 5/8	24 4/8	18 5/8	5	4	Vermillion County	IN	Brent Summerville	1990	15,435
128 3/8	24 5/8	22 2/8	17 1/8	4	4	Wayne County	NY	John W. Stringer	1990	15,435
128 3/8	21 6/8	21 1/8	18 3/8	4	4	Morris County	NJ	Michael F. De Pompe	1990	15,435
128 3/8	22 1/8	22 1/8	19 7/8	4	4	Hardin County	KY	Woody Noe	1990	15,435
128 3/8	21 6/8	21 1/8	17 5/8	6	5	Jackson County	IA	Joseph H. Krier	1990	15,435
128 3/8	21 5/8	20 2/8	15 1/8	5	5	McHenry County	IL	Michael F. Riske	1990	15,435
128 3/8	21 7/8	21 4/8	17 3/8	4	4	Warren County	IL	Tom Toops	1990	15,435
128 3/8	22 6/8	23 7/8	19 5/8	5	5	Warren County	OH	Danny J. Dykes	1990	15,435
128 3/8	21 6/8	22 4/8	15 3/8	4	4	La Salle County	TX	Dicky Newberry	1991	15,435
128 3/8	22 6/8	22 7/8	15 3/8	4	5	Eaton County	MI	Jeffrey J. Jolley	1991	15,435
128 3/8	22 2/8	20 6/8	15 3/8	4	5	Hickory County	MO	Billy Adams	1991	15,435
128 3/8	23 0/8	23 1/8	16 1/8	4	5	Ripley County	IN	Brian K. Hamer	1991	15,435
128 3/8	20 3/8	20 4/8	16 1/8	4	4	Glenboro	MAN	Robert R. Blain	1991	15,435
128 3/8	21 1/8	22 2/8	19 1/8	4	4	Marion County	SC	John S. Taylor, Jr.	1991	15,435
128 3/8	22 3/8	23 0/8	17 3/8	4	4	Vinton County	OH	Brian D. Ehrhart	1991	15,435
128 3/8	22 2/8	22 1/8	14 1/8	5	5	Douglas County	WI	Richard S. Gondik, Jr.	1991	15,435
128 3/8	22 5/8	22 0/8	17 7/8	6	5	Buffalo County	WI	Bryan A. Tamke	1991	15,435
128 3/8	21 1/8	21 0/8	13 7/8	5	5	Winneshiek County	IA	Joel Goodman	1991	15,435
128 3/8	24 2/8	23 5/8	18 5/8	5	6	Polk County	MN	James A. Strom	1991	15,435

WHITETAIL DEER (TYPICAL ANTLERS)

Minimum Score 125

SCORE	LENGTH OF MAIN BEAM R	LENGTH OF MAIN BEAM L	INSIDE SPREAD	NUMBER OF POINTS R	NUMBER OF POINTS L	AREA	STATE/PROVINCE	HUNTER'S NAME	DATE	RANK
128 3/8	22 0/8	20 6/8	15 0/8	5	5	Pike County	IL	Jim Pierceall	1991	15,435
128 3/8	19 6/8	19 7/8	15 5/8	5	5	Newton County	IN	Steve Narantic	1992	15,435
128 3/8	21 5/8	20 3/8	16 5/8	4	4	Winnebago County	IL	Scott A. Wenstrom	1992	15,435
128 3/8	20 3/8	20 2/8	15 4/8	6	6	Clark County	IL	Ronald E. Karst	1992	15,435
128 3/8	21 2/8	21 6/8	15 3/8	5	5	Uvalde County	TX	John Nelson	1993	15,435
128 3/8	22 3/8	21 7/8	17 1/8	5	4	Coles County	IL	Jon Willoughby	1993	15,435
128 3/8	22 4/8	23 0/8	19 5/8	4	4	Dawson County	MT	Mark Ascheman	1993	15,435
128 3/8	20 5/8	20 5/8	13 4/8	6	6	Warren County	NJ	Stephen DePerty	1993	15,435
128 3/8	20 6/8	20 7/8	14 1/8	5	5	Rockingham County	NC	Jerry Christopher Barnes	1993	15,435
128 3/8	21 5/8	20 1/8	17 3/8	5	4	Martin County	IN	Mark LueKen	1993	15,435
128 3/8	21 3/8	21 4/8	15 7/8	5	5	St. Croix County	WI	Paul E. Korn	1993	15,435
128 3/8	22 0/8	21 7/8	18 1/8	4	4	Macoupin County	IL	Anthony R. Bradley	1993	15,435
128 3/8	21 1/8	20 5/8	16 7/8	5	5	Queen Annes County	MD	John Farrow	1993	15,435
128 3/8	22 5/8	20 7/8	18 0/8	5	5	Seneca County	NY	Michael J. Welsh	1993	15,435
128 3/8	20 5/8	21 7/8	17 0/8	5	8	Buffalo County	WI	Pete J. Mancl	1994	15,435
128 3/8	21 6/8	20 5/8	17 5/8	5	5	Alleghany County	NC	Oscar Reeves	1994	15,435
128 3/8	20 2/8	21 0/8	15 7/8	5	5	Scott County	IA	Scott Templeton	1994	15,435
128 3/8	22 0/8	20 4/8	17 3/8	5	5	Jackson County	IL	Tim Cobin	1994	15,435
128 3/8	24 0/8	23 6/8	16 1/8	5	5	Baltimore County	MD	Gerald J. Boerner, Jr.	1994	15,435
128 3/8	22 1/8	22 3/8	19 1/8	4	5	Anoka County	MN	Mike Andrews	1994	15,435
128 3/8	21 1/8	20 5/8	16 7/8	5	5	New London County	CT	Benjamin O. Azeredo, Jr.	1995	15,435
128 3/8	24 3/8	23 5/8	16 7/8	5	5	Ontario County	NY	Michael R. Davis	1995	15,435
128 3/8	22 6/8	22 2/8	18 7/8	4	4	Allegheny County	PA	Glenn Rokicki	1995	15,435
128 3/8	22 1/8	23 4/8	18 4/8	5	4	Adams County	IN	Jeffery L. Gilbert	1995	15,435
128 3/8	22 6/8	22 5/8	20 1/8	5	4	Cass County	MI	Anthony L. Mudd	1995	15,435
128 3/8	19 6/8	20 7/8	16 7/8	5	5	Buffalo County	WI	Mike Wozney	1995	15,435
128 3/8	21 4/8	21 5/8	14 6/8	4	6	Darke County	OH	Steve Watercutter	1995	15,435
128 3/8	20 7/8	20 0/8	15 5/8	4	4	Coles County	IL	Randy Joe Miller	1995	15,435
128 3/8	20 6/8	21 1/8	16 1/8	5	5	Livingston County	MI	Bruce Baja	1995	15,435
128 3/8	22 1/8	22 4/8	16 4/8	5	6	Stark County	ND	Loren Adams	1996	15,435
128 3/8	20 4/8	20 3/8	16 3/8	5	5	Yuma County	CO	Scott Armitage	1996	15,435
128 3/8	21 7/8	22 2/8	15 1/8	4	4	Jackson County	IN	Tony Lambert	1996	15,435
128 3/8	22 7/8	21 1/8	16 3/8	8	6	Washington County	WI	Tim Monroe	1996	15,435
128 3/8	20 7/8	20 5/8	17 7/8	5	5	San Patricio County	TX	Wayne Ford	1996	15,435
128 3/8	22 0/8	21 2/8	15 5/8	5	6	Upton County	TX	Tommy Latham	1996	15,435
128 3/8	20 6/8	21 0/8	15 0/8	6	7	Dodge County	MN	Mike Walerak	1997	15,435
128 3/8	21 7/8	22 5/8	15 3/8	4	4	Mingo County	WV	Larry E. Maynard	1997	15,435
128 3/8	21 0/8	21 3/8	24 2/8	4	4	Dauphin County	PA	Ronald Bistline	1997	15,435
128 3/8	21 7/8	21 3/8	17 5/8	4	4	Buffalo County	WI	Peter Stanton	1997	15,435
128 3/8	20 7/8	21 3/8	18 0/8	6	6	Buffalo County	WI	Mark Giese	1997	15,435
128 3/8	22 7/8	23 7/8	16 5/8	4	4	Calhoun County	IL	Judy Kovar	1997	15,435
128 3/8	22 5/8	21 0/8	18 3/8	4	4	White County	IL	Donald H. Keck	1997	15,435
128 3/8	23 6/8	23 5/8	15 6/8	5	6	Montgomery County	MD	Jeffrey Harrison	1998	15,435
128 2/8	22 1/8	21 1/8	15 6/8	5	5	Franklin County	KS	Gary Hunsicker	1966	15,538
128 2/8	20 5/8	21 3/8	14 4/8	5	5	Waupaca County	WI	Dennis Arndt	1967	15,538
128 2/8	23 0/8	22 5/8	19 1/8	5	5	Lackawanna County	PA	Gary E. Schreck	1971	15,538
128 2/8	19 3/8	20 0/8	18 4/8	5	5	Pittsburg County	OK	Pack Giacomo	1972	15,538
128 2/8	22 2/8	22 3/8	17 0/8	4	4	Cherokee County	OK	Eddie Goss	1973	15,538
128 2/8	20 5/8	21 4/8	17 0/8	5	5	Buffalo County	NE	Lynn Bombeck	1974	15,538
128 2/8	23 1/8	22 7/8	20 3/8	4	5	Jefferson County	OH	Michael W. Brown	1976	15,538
128 2/8	21 0/8	21 3/8	17 2/8	4	5	Spokane County	WA	Michael A. Shane	1977	15,538
128 2/8	21 1/8	21 4/8	17 0/8	5	5	Green Lake County	WI	Albert G. Slife	1979	15,538
128 2/8	22 2/8	21 6/8	20 3/8	5	7	Iroquois County	IL	Jim Schroeder	1980	15,538
128 2/8	19 0/8	19 0/8	14 4/8	5	5	Walworth County	SD	Ronald Arbach	1980	15,538
128 2/8	19 0/8	19 1/8	14 4/8	5	5	Travis County	TX	Russell Schmidt	1982	15,538
128 2/8	20 4/8	19 6/8	17 6/8	6	5	Floyd County	IA	Johnny Nelson	1982	15,538
128 2/8	19 4/8	18 4/8	17 4/8	5	6	Dallas County	IA	Mike Inman	1982	15,538
128 2/8	21 7/8	22 4/8	16 6/8	4	4	Todd County	KY	Terry R. Baldwin	1983	15,538
128 2/8	22 5/8	22 3/8	17 4/8	3	5	Brown County	KS	Chuck McNally	1983	15,538
128 2/8	22 5/8	22 6/8	16 3/8	6	7	Juneau County	WI	Steve Hysell	1984	15,538
128 2/8	20 3/8	21 4/8	17 6/8	4	4	Nelson County	ND	Darren Asperheim	1985	15,538
128 2/8	22 1/8	22 0/8	17 2/8	6	6	Bleckley County	GA	Wallace Mullis	1985	15,538
128 2/8	20 4/8	20 0/8	16 4/8	5	5	Grant County	WI	Robert Govier	1985	15,538
128 2/8	21 2/8	19 6/8	17 6/8	4	4	Pottawatomie County	OK	Tom Larman	1986	15,538
128 2/8	21 7/8	21 1/8	16 6/8	4	4	Waupaca County	WI	John Harris	1987	15,538
128 2/8	21 7/8	22 4/8	19 1/8	5	6	Washington County	KS	Ronald Montague	1987	15,538
128 2/8	21 0/8	21 0/8	17 4/8	5	5	Jasper County	IA	Gordon L. Johnson	1987	15,538
128 2/8	23 2/8	23 3/8	20 4/8	4	5	Missoula County	MT	Greg L. Munther	1987	15,538
128 2/8	21 2/8	21 6/8	15 0/8	5	6	Haskell County	OK	Jerry C. Sturdy	1987	15,538
128 2/8	21 7/8	22 7/8	19 4/8	5	5	Graves County	KY	Robert Eubanks	1988	15,538
128 2/8	19 2/8	19 5/8	16 4/8	5	6	Lafayette County	WI	Robert Wedige	1988	15,538
128 2/8	21 4/8	21 1/8	16 6/8	4	4	Henry County	VA	Mike Weaver	1988	15,538
128 2/8	22 4/8	23 0/8	16 0/8	4	4	Oconto County	WI	David L. Follett	1988	15,538
128 2/8	22 6/8	23 0/8	21 0/8	4	5	Washtenaw County	MI	Donald L. Cox	1988	15,538
128 2/8	20 1/8	20 6/8	14 2/8	5	5	Dearborn County	IN	David R. "Skeeter" McKain	1989	15,538
128 2/8	21 2/8	21 7/8	14 1/8	6	7	Kay County	OK	Dean Gratias	1989	15,538
128 2/8	22 2/8	22 1/8	16 2/8	6	5	Montgomery County	IL	Rick L. Rork	1989	15,538
128 2/8	22 7/8	22 0/8	19 6/8	5	6	Yellow Medicine County	MN	Butch West	1989	15,538

WHITETAIL DEER (TYPICAL ANTLERS)

Minimum Score 125 — Continued

SCORE	LENGTH OF MAIN BEAM R	LENGTH OF MAIN BEAM L	INSIDE SPREAD	NUMBER OF POINTS R	NUMBER OF POINTS L	AREA	STATE/PROVINCE	HUNTER'S NAME	DATE	RANK
128 2/8	22 2/8	21 7/8	17 1/8	4	7	Price County	WI	John D. Haydock	1989	15,538
128 2/8	20 0/8	19 6/8	14 2/8	4	4	Ogle County	IL	Daniel M. Pierce	1989	15,538
128 2/8	24 1/8	23 3/8	16 6/8	4	4	Monroe County	NY	Wayne Meritt	1989	15,538
128 2/8	21 7/8	21 5/8	16 0/8	5	5	Buffalo County	WI	David W. Stuhr	1990	15,538
128 2/8	24 4/8	24 2/8	17 2/8	9	5	Ashland County	OH	Randy Beavers	1990	15,538
128 2/8	22 4/8	23 0/8	16 4/8	4	5	Erie County	NY	Michael R. Nowaczyk	1990	15,538
128 2/8	24 5/8	24 4/8	16 4/8	5	6	Holmes County	OH	Byron F. Burwell	1990	15,538
128 2/8	21 4/8	21 0/8	19 0/8	4	4	Langlade County	WI	Thomas Schuette	1990	15,538
128 2/8	23 1/8	24 0/8	16 6/8	4	4	Hardin County	OH	Kelly Jackson	1990	15,538
128 2/8	23 6/8	23 6/8	15 2/8	4	4	Chatham County	NC	Ricky Canoy	1991	15,538
128 2/8	20 0/8	20 5/8	15 5/8	7	6	Washington County	PA	Jason H. Snyder	1991	15,538
128 2/8	21 4/8	21 5/8	17 6/8	4	4	Jennings County	IN	Daniel E. Ramey	1991	15,538
128 2/8	22 1/8	22 1/8	15 0/8	4	4	Delaware County	OH	Steve Krakowka	1991	15,538
128 2/8	24 6/8	25 1/8	17 5/8	4	6	Somerset County	NJ	Steven J. Niedzielski	1991	15,538
128 2/8	22 1/8	21 6/8	17 3/8	6	5	Parke County	IN	Philip A. Prock	1991	15,538
128 2/8	25 5/8	26 2/8	16 2/8	6	4	Allamakee County	IA	Joe Lieb	1991	15,538
128 2/8	20 2/8	21 0/8	15 7/8	5	6	Muskingum County	OH	Jerry Johnson	1991	15,538
128 2/8	23 4/8	23 1/8	19 6/8	6	4	Boone County	IL	Wilmer V. Garlick	1991	15,538
128 2/8	21 4/8	21 3/8	17 6/8	4	4	Walworth County	WI	Todd Haefner	1992	15,538
128 2/8	22 2/8	22 1/8	16 2/8	5	5	Jo Daviess County	IL	Steve Cole	1992	15,538
128 2/8	19 5/8	19 3/8	16 2/8	5	5	Glascock County	GA	Jerry Myers	1992	15,538
128 2/8	21 7/8	21 7/8	17 0/8	5	5	Waupaca County	WI	Jeremy D. Gast	1992	15,538
128 2/8	20 5/8	20 6/8	16 2/8	7	5	Brown County	SD	Richard Sommers	1992	15,538
128 2/8	21 0/8	21 0/8	15 4/8	5	5	Shawano County	WI	David Schultz	1992	15,538
128 2/8	21 3/8	21 4/8	15 6/8	4	4	Florence County	WI	Dale T. Nixon	1992	15,538
128 2/8	23 1/8	23 3/8	17 6/8	5	4	Fulton County	IL	Donald T. Bishop	1992	15,538
128 2/8	25 2/8	23 3/8	21 0/8	6	5	Berkshire County	MA	Ronald Phillips	1992	15,538
128 2/8	22 5/8	22 6/8	17 6/8	4	5	La Salle County	TX	John W. Ellas	1992	15,538
128 2/8	23 3/8	23 3/8	19 6/8	5	4	La Grange County	IN	ArLen Hartman	1993	15,538
128 2/8	19 1/8	19 3/8	14 0/8	5	5	McKenzie County	ND	Perry Bertoni	1993	15,538
128 2/8	22 1/8	20 6/8	16 2/8	4	4	Meigs County	OH	Mike Bradley	1993	15,538
128 2/8	21 6/8	22 3/8	15 6/8	5	5	Hillsdale County	MI	Charles E. Clark	1993	15,538
128 2/8	22 1/8	21 6/8	18 3/8	6	5	Champaign County	OH	Kenny Pond	1993	15,538
128 2/8	18 1/8	21 1/8	16 2/8	5	5	Cedar County	NE	Scott Aase	1993	15,538
128 2/8	22 2/8	21 5/8	17 6/8	4	4	Rice County	KS	Gerald Aguilera	1993	15,538
128 2/8	20 1/8	22 0/8	19 1/8	6	4	Poinsett County	AR	Mike Gillis	1993	15,538
128 2/8	25 7/8	24 5/8	19 0/8	4	4	Washington County	MS	Danny Ray Sanders	1994	15,538
128 2/8	21 7/8	20 6/8	18 6/8	5	5	Allegheny County	PA	Richard Pontis	1994	15,538
128 2/8	23 0/8	22 4/8	16 0/8	5	5	Wyandot County	OH	James D. Herring	1994	15,538
128 2/8	21 1/8	22 7/8	18 7/8	5	4	Lake County	IL	Paul H. Woit	1994	15,538
128 2/8	24 2/8	22 5/8	19 5/8	5	5	Putnam County	MO	John Freihaut	1994	15,538
128 2/8	20 2/8	21 2/8	17 2/8	5	5	Rock County	WI	Shane Mussey	1994	15,538
128 2/8	22 0/8	21 5/8	16 0/8	5	5	Winneshiek County	IA	David G. Baumler	1994	15,538
128 2/8	19 5/8	20 4/8	19 0/8	5	5	Iroquois County	IL	Terry Doehring	1994	15,538
128 2/8	22 3/8	21 3/8	16 0/8	5	5	Marathon County	WI	Scott D. Geurink	1994	15,538
128 2/8	20 3/8	20 4/8	15 6/8	5	5	Douglas County	WI	Russ Sharpe	1994	15,538
128 2/8	22 2/8	23 4/8	17 4/8	6	7	Harrison County	OH	Ken Zitko	1994	15,538
128 2/8	20 7/8	21 1/8	17 0/8	6	6	Anoka County	MN	Tony Capra	1994	15,538
128 2/8	20 7/8	22 1/8	18 0/8	4	4	Howard County	MD	William Neal Eckenbarger	1995	15,538
128 2/8	21 0/8	20 6/8	16 0/8	5	5	Taylor County	TX	Lynn Ingalsbe	1995	15,538
128 2/8	22 4/8	22 2/8	18 4/8	5	4	Real County	TX	Daniel K. George	1995	15,538
128 2/8	20 2/8	21 2/8	16 4/8	5	5	Queen Annes County	MD	Edward D. Lockwood	1995	15,538
128 2/8	21 1/8	19 5/8	15 2/8	5	5	Harrison County	WV	Lawrence Yates	1995	15,538
128 2/8	22 5/8	21 1/8	18 2/8	5	4	Peoria County	IL	John Soehn	1995	15,538
128 2/8	21 5/8	21 6/8	19 2/8	4	5	Morgan County	CO	Pete Lauer, Jr.	1995	15,538
128 2/8	22 1/8	22 5/8	16 4/8	5	5	Adams County	WI	Jack Schuler	1996	15,538
128 2/8	21 2/8	21 2/8	16 6/8	4	5	Bosque County	TX	Tim White	1996	15,538
128 2/8	20 3/8	21 6/8	16 2/8	5	4	Brown County	WI	Mike Blohowiak	1996	15,538
128 2/8	22 6/8	22 3/8	15 4/8	4	4	Ashland County	WI	Keith A. Breunig	1996	15,538
128 2/8	21 0/8	21 1/8	19 4/8	4	4	Ozaukee County	WI	Ray Schultz	1996	15,538
128 2/8	23 3/8	23 5/8	18 2/8	6	5	Trempealeau County	WI	Jeff Larson	1996	15,538
128 2/8	20 7/8	20 4/8	16 4/8	5	5	Pike County	IL	Joel M. Riotto	1996	15,538
128 2/8	21 0/8	18 6/8	15 4/8	5	5	De Witt County	IL	Thomas R. Benedict	1996	15,538
128 2/8	24 3/8	27 4/8	21 6/8	5	6	Greene County	IL	Jay Edmiston	1996	15,538
128 2/8	19 6/8	19 3/8	17 1/8	5	5	Gove County	KS	Jared L. Ness	1996	15,538
128 2/8	20 4/8	21 0/8	17 6/8	5	6	Hamilton County	TX	Michael De Loach	1997	15,538
128 2/8	24 0/8	23 3/8	18 1/8	6	8	Fond du Lac County	WI	Wayne Freund	1997	15,538
128 2/8	21 2/8	20 4/8	18 4/8	5	5	Columbia County	WI	Dick Gjerde	1997	15,538
128 2/8	21 2/8	20 0/8	15 6/8	5	6	Pike County	IL	Leonard Goldstock	1997	15,538
128 2/8	21 2/8	20 1/8	14 0/8	4	5	Pike County	IL	Robert Sacher	1997	15,538
128 2/8	21 3/8	21 1/8	19 2/8	4	3	Polk County	WI	Derek Martin	1997	15,538
128 2/8	21 5/8	23 0/8	17 0/8	5	4	Fond du Lac County	WI	Brian Grade	1997	15,538
128 2/8	22 2/8	23 4/8	21 0/8	4	4	Middlesex County	NJ	Steven J. Pohling	1997	15,538
128 2/8	19 0/8	18 0/8	13 0/8	5	5	Medina County	TX	Kelly C. Parrino	1997	15,538
128 1/8	20 1/8	21 0/8	17 5/8	5	5	Dorchester County	MD	Powell D. Cook	1964	15,647
128 1/8	21 6/8	21 0/8	19 0/8	4	5	Adams County	IL	Clarence Grandt	1972	15,647
128 1/8	20 6/8	19 7/8	14 7/8	5	5	Ripley County	IN	Sam M. Durham	1978	15,647
128 1/8	21 1/8	22 2/8	17 0/8	5	4	Lafayette County	WI	W. Grinnell/G. Grinnell	1978	15,647

WHITETAIL DEER (TYPICAL ANTLERS)

Minimum Score 125 — Continued

SCORE	LENGTH OF MAIN BEAM R	LENGTH OF MAIN BEAM L	INSIDE SPREAD	NUMBER OF POINTS R	NUMBER OF POINTS L	AREA	STATE/PROVINCE	HUNTER'S NAME	DATE	RANK
128 1/8	22 6/8	24 0/8	15 1/8	4	4	Chilton County	AL	Dennis Burnett	1980	15,647
128 1/8	19 5/8	20 5/8	19 5/8	5	5	Sheboygan County	WI	Mark Kissinger	1980	15,647
128 1/8	21 4/8	23 3/8	20 3/8	5	4	Hastings	ONT	Ken McGarrity	1980	15,647
128 1/8	22 7/8	22 0/8	19 5/8	5	6	Kingman County	KS	Mark Renollet	1980	15,647
128 1/8	21 0/8	21 0/8	16 7/8	5	5	Miami County	OH	Kim V. Sevitts	1981	15,647
128 1/8	20 7/8	19 6/8	18 3/8	4	4	Jefferson County	IL	David R. Darnell	1981	15,647
128 1/8	22 7/8	21 7/8	20 1/8	4	4	Carter County	MO	Bill Howe	1981	15,647
128 1/8	22 1/8	20 0/8	17 0/8	5	6	Lake County	IL	Donald Schram	1981	15,647
128 1/8	21 4/8	22 0/8	17 4/8	4	5	Elgin	ONT	Peter Hartmann	1982	15,647
128 1/8	21 4/8	21 2/8	16 3/8	6	7	Winnebago County	IL	Robert W. Shallenberger, Sr.	1982	15,647
128 1/8	21 1/8	21 5/8	16 3/8	4	4	Calhoun County	MI	Clarence Bowers, Jr.	1982	15,647
128 1/8	22 1/8	22 1/8	18 3/8	5	5	Marquette County	WI	Newell Easley	1984	15,647
128 1/8	22 6/8	19 0/8	16 6/8	5	7	Rock County	WI	Rodger Veneman	1984	15,647
128 1/8	22 6/8	23 3/8	17 1/8	5	4	Brown County	SD	Ron Rockwell	1984	15,647
128 1/8	20 0/8	20 1/8	16 3/8	5	5	Mower County	MN	John S. Adams	1985	15,647
128 1/8	19 5/8	18 5/8	15 7/8	5	5	Robertson County	KY	Gary A. Linville	1985	15,647
128 1/8	21 5/8	21 2/8	18 5/8	4	4	Washington County	MS	Bobby Ray Woods	1985	15,647
128 1/8	23 1/8	22 7/8	16 1/8	5	4	Peoria County	IL	Dan P. Hollingsworth	1985	15,647
128 1/8	21 7/8	21 4/8	15 4/8	6	4	Dallas County	MO	Jay Strain	1985	15,647
128 1/8	22 4/8	22 3/8	18 5/8	5	5	Barry County	MI	Ron Rolfe	1985	15,647
128 1/8	23 0/8	22 6/8	16 1/8	4	4	Ripley County	IN	Thomas R. Martin	1986	15,647
128 1/8	22 4/8	22 2/8	16 3/8	5	5	Winona County	MN	Terry F. Banitt	1986	15,647
128 1/8	20 5/8	22 7/8	16 7/8	5	5	Effingham County	IL	Randy Hall	1987	15,647
128 1/8	22 2/8	21 5/8	18 5/8	5	5	St. Charles County	MO	Michael Vogt	1987	15,647
128 1/8	20 1/8	21 6/8	15 0/8	5	6	Gibson County	IN	Dean Monroe Deal	1987	15,647
128 1/8	22 0/8	22 4/8	18 2/8	4	6	Marquette County	MI	Loyal Norkett	1987	15,647
128 1/8	23 4/8	22 3/8	19 1/8	4	4	Monroe County	NY	Paul H. Beicke	1987	15,647
128 1/8	23 6/8	23 1/8	16 7/8	4	4	Jackson County	OH	Bob "Smokey" Lotts	1987	15,647
128 1/8	20 2/8	20 6/8	18 4/8	5	5	Crook County	WY	Wendell W. Koontz	1988	15,647
128 1/8	21 0/8	22 4/8	18 6/8	6	5	New Castle County	DE	Joseph J. Subolefsky	1988	15,647
128 1/8	21 1/8	20 2/8	16 5/8	4	5	Cheyenne County	KS	Kahle Helton	1988	15,647
128 1/8	23 0/8	22 1/8	17 7/8	5	4	Langlade County	WI	Bob Antoinewicz	1988	15,647
128 1/8	20 6/8	20 5/8	12 5/8	5	4	Adair County	MO	Joe Ed McCray	1988	15,647
128 1/8	20 4/8	20 4/8	15 4/8	6	5	Fergus County	MT	John "Rosey" Roseland	1988	15,647
128 1/8	20 1/8	20 3/8	16 5/8	5	5	Suffolk County	NY	Doug Brady	1988	15,647
128 1/8	21 6/8	21 7/8	17 1/8	5	6	Jones County	GA	Billy Ussery	1989	15,647
128 1/8	21 1/8	20 6/8	17 0/8	6	6	Winnebago County	IL	Richard C. McCormick	1989	15,647
128 1/8	20 5/8	20 4/8	14 5/8	5	5	Clinton County	IL	Glen F. Zurliene	1989	15,647
128 1/8	24 6/8	24 7/8	20 1/8	3	4	Hampden County	MA	Dick Scorzafava	1989	15,647
128 1/8	23 2/8	22 7/8	16 3/8	4	4	Page County	IA	Chris Barton	1989	15,647
128 1/8	23 3/8	20 1/8	18 0/8	6	5	Cass County	MO	Mike R. Wheeler	1989	15,647
128 1/8	20 6/8	22 0/8	14 6/8	4	6	Washburn County	WI	Andy Sirek	1990	15,647
128 1/8	20 2/8	21 0/8	13 7/8	5	5	Hancock County	OH	Steve Shilling	1990	15,647
128 1/8	21 7/8	22 5/8	17 5/8	4	4	Washburn County	WI	Ken Morse	1990	15,647
128 1/8	21 1/8	20 0/8	16 1/8	5	5	Marshall County	IL	Scott Sager	1990	15,647
128 1/8	24 2/8	23 7/8	15 3/8	4	4	Fairfield County	CT	Kerry Simard	1990	15,647
128 1/8	21 2/8	21 2/8	14 3/8	5	5	Calhoun County	IL	Randy Watters	1990	15,647
128 1/8	22 3/8	22 6/8	17 0/8	6	6	Macon County	IL	Jeff Slunder	1990	15,647
128 1/8	21 2/8	18 4/8	16 3/8	5	5	Queen Annes County	MD	Tim D. Rand	1991	15,647
128 1/8	19 5/8	19 5/8	14 7/8	5	5	Oakland County	MI	Kerry K. Kammer	1991	15,647
128 1/8	22 1/8	22 0/8	15 0/8	5	6	Greene County	PA	Ronald Virgili, Jr.	1991	15,647
128 1/8	23 1/8	22 3/8	17 1/8	4	4	Goliad County	TX	Edmond H. Fadal, Jr.	1991	15,647
128 1/8	22 7/8	21 7/8	15 5/8	5	4	Allegan County	MI	Roger Bronkhorst	1991	15,647
128 1/8	21 5/8	23 0/8	15 7/8	6	4	Chippewa County	WI	Mike Mason	1991	15,647
128 1/8	22 2/8	23 0/8	18 3/8	4	4	Burleigh County	ND	Jason Sjol	1991	15,647
128 1/8	19 7/8	18 7/8	15 1/8	5	5	Christian County	KY	Jerry D. Harmon	1991	15,647
128 1/8	22 6/8	23 1/8	17 1/8	5	4	Hamilton County	IA	Arlin Dickinson	1991	15,647
128 1/8	21 7/8	22 4/8	20 6/8	6	7	Knox County	OH	Jeffrey R. Kerr	1991	15,647
128 1/8	21 0/8	21 0/8	14 3/8	5	5	Poweshiek County	IA	Ed Stevens	1991	15,647
128 1/8	23 0/8	23 1/8	16 7/8	4	5	Walworth County	WI	Gergory G. Henan	1991	15,647
128 1/8	19 2/8	19 2/8	16 0/8	5	5	Hardin County	IA	Wayne Dewey	1991	15,647
128 1/8	20 0/8	20 3/8	14 1/8	5	5	Price County	WI	Ken Cork	1991	15,647
128 1/8	22 6/8	22 6/8	18 1/8	4	4	Greene County	OH	Douglas A. Skrlac	1992	15,647
128 1/8	19 7/8	19 5/8	14 3/8	5	5	Buffalo County	WI	Dave Blaschko	1992	15,647
128 1/8	19 1/8	19 2/8	15 3/8	5	7	Buffalo County	WI	Jeff Moore	1992	15,647
128 1/8	25 6/8	24 5/8	19 2/8	5	5	Scioto County	OH	Dwayne L. May	1992	15,647
128 1/8	21 4/8	20 7/8	14 5/8	4	4	Oakland County	MI	Ed L. Conrad	1992	15,647
128 1/8	21 5/8	22 4/8	16 7/8	5	5	Jewell County	KS	Emmitt Hamilton	1992	15,647
128 1/8	23 2/8	25 6/8	20 1/8	4	3	Clayton County	IA	Dave Cordes	1992	15,647
128 1/8	20 7/8	20 4/8	17 3/8	5	4	Barnes County	ND	Dennis Didier	1993	15,647
128 1/8	21 0/8	22 0/8	17 7/8	4	5	Allegan County	MI	Thomas Storr	1993	15,647
128 1/8	21 7/8	22 0/8	15 7/8	4	4	Jefferson County	WI	Thomas A. Anfang	1993	15,647
128 1/8	22 4/8	23 1/8	17 7/8	6	5	Christopher Lake	SAS	Les King	1993	15,647
128 1/8	23 4/8	23 1/8	16 3/8	4	5	Chester County	PA	Joseph A. Romeu	1993	15,647
128 1/8	24 2/8	22 5/8	19 6/8	4	5	Montgomery County	MD	Egon Tirbs III	1993	15,647
128 1/8	25 2/8	25 1/8	18 3/8	4	5	Buffalo County	WI	Dave J. Gatzlaff	1993	15,647
128 1/8	22 5/8	21 5/8	16 3/8	4	4	Montgomery County	AL	Frank E. McGough, Jr.	1993	15,647
128 1/8	20 7/8	20 6/8	16 3/8	5	5	Dekalb County	IL	Keith Adkins	1993	15,647

WHITETAIL DEER (TYPICAL ANTLERS)

Minimum Score 125 — Continued

SCORE	LENGTH OF MAIN BEAM R	LENGTH OF MAIN BEAM L	INSIDE SPREAD	NUMBER OF POINTS R	NUMBER OF POINTS L	AREA	STATE/PROVINCE	HUNTER'S NAME	DATE	RANK
128 1/8	23 2/8	22 6/8	17 1/8	4	4	Carroll County	MD	Michael Flaxcomb	1993	15,647
128 1/8	22 6/8	22 1/8	15 3/8	4	4	Madison County	IL	Kelly Harper	1993	15,647
128 1/8	21 6/8	21 0/8	15 7/8	4	5	Ravalli County	MT	Van E. Tamplin	1994	15,647
128 1/8	24 4/8	24 0/8	15 1/8	5	4	Rock County	WI	Gary Schiefelbien	1994	15,647
128 1/8	19 7/8	19 6/8	17 3/8	5	5	Ashland County	WI	Christopher J. Yaritz	1994	15,647
128 1/8	22 0/8	20 0/8	16 7/8	6	5	Delaware County	OH	David R. Ware	1994	15,647
128 1/8	19 4/8	20 0/8	13 7/8	5	5	Roscommon County	MI	Leland D. Skinner	1994	15,647
128 1/8	20 6/8	20 1/8	14 3/8	5	4	Ravalli County	MT	Joseph P. Smith, Jr.	1994	15,647
128 1/8	22 2/8	21 4/8	15 3/8	4	4	Calhoun County	MI	George I. Swan, Jr.	1994	15,647
128 1/8	21 4/8	21 3/8	17 5/8	5	5	Halifax County	VA	Billy Womack	1994	15,647
128 1/8	21 1/8	20 0/8	18 7/8	4	4	Richland County	WI	Steven W. Fuller	1994	15,647
128 1/8	21 4/8	21 7/8	16 5/8	4	4	Fayette County	IL	Christopher Guy/Steven Rose	1994	15,647
128 1/8	22 6/8	22 7/8	17 3/8	4	5	Morrison County	MN	Paul Vomela	1994	15,647
128 1/8	19 7/8	19 2/8	13 7/8	5	5	Macon County	IL	Dave Elliott	1994	15,647
128 1/8	19 6/8	20 1/8	16 1/8	7	6	Anoka County	MN	Jim Evertz	1994	15,647
128 1/8	20 5/8	21 6/8	17 5/8	5	5	Trempealeau County	WI	Charles A. Gauger	1994	15,647
128 1/8	23 4/8	24 1/8	15 7/8	5	5	Carroll County	AR	David Harp	1994	15,647
128 1/8	23 3/8	21 4/8	15 0/8	5	4	Sumner County	KS	Jerry Tooman	1994	15,647
128 1/8	22 3/8	22 0/8	17 7/8	5	5	Dimmit County	TX	Sonny Evans	1995	15,647
128 1/8	23 0/8	22 2/8	18 7/8	5	5	Montgomery County	PA	Nicholas Pupillo	1995	15,647
128 1/8	22 7/8	23 4/8	18 5/8	4	4	Anne Arundel County	MD	Carmen Cacioppo	1995	15,647
128 1/8	20 2/8	20 6/8	16 3/8	5	5	Wyoming County	WV	Walter Lane, Jr.	1995	15,647
128 1/8	22 3/8	22 1/8	15 7/8	4	4	Wyoming County	NY	Eric Burns	1995	15,647
128 1/8	21 2/8	21 2/8	16 1/8	5	5	Grant County	WI	Joe Udelhofen	1995	15,647
128 1/8	22 0/8	22 4/8	15 7/8	4	4	Oakland County	MI	Albert Thomas Perry	1995	15,647
128 1/8	23 3/8	23 7/8	21 5/8	5	4	Jackson County	IA	Ronald G. Hellweg	1995	15,647
128 1/8	22 2/8	22 2/8	18 1/8	5	5	E. Carroll Parish	LA	Calvin Hooker	1995	15,647
128 1/8	22 1/8	22 3/8	15 7/8	8	6	Osage County	MO	Dave Bartlett	1996	15,647
128 1/8	19 7/8	19 1/8	17 5/8	5	5	Darke County	OH	Dirk A. Lewis	1996	15,647
128 1/8	22 6/8	23 1/8	18 7/8	4	4	Buffalo County	WI	Gary Fleishauer	1996	15,647
128 1/8	20 6/8	21 3/8	14 7/8	6	5	Cherokee County	IA	Brad Husman	1996	15,647
128 1/8	23 3/8	23 3/8	16 2/8	5	6	Monona County	IA	Roger B. Reiling	1996	15,647
128 1/8	23 1/8	23 0/8	17 3/8	4	5	Harris County	GA	Larry E. Garner, Jr.	1996	15,647
128 1/8	18 4/8	18 0/8	14 5/8	5	5	Bartow County	GA	Roger Rittenhouse	1996	15,647
128 1/8	23 5/8	23 5/8	16 5/8	7	6	Morgan County	KY	James H. Standafer	1997	15,647
128 1/8	22 3/8	22 0/8	19 1/8	6	4	Shawano County	WI	Keane Lohmiller	1997	15,647
128 1/8	21 7/8	20 4/8	17 3/8	5	5	Marquette County	WI	James H. Poetter	1997	15,647
128 1/8	21 2/8	20 5/8	15 1/8	5	5	Olmsted County	MN	Donald F. Hanson	1997	15,647
128 1/8	20 6/8	21 0/8	16 1/8	4	4	Richmond County	GA	Dan Opalewski	1997	15,647
128 1/8	20 0/8	20 0/8	14 3/8	5	5	Richland County	WI	Max Goessel	1997	15,647
128 1/8	20 7/8	21 4/8	17 7/8	5	5	Wayne County	MS	Chad Stanley	1997	15,647
128 1/8	23 6/8	24 2/8	15 7/8	5	7	Iron County	MI	Daniel Brezinski	1997	15,647
128 1/8	21 2/8	21 6/8	17 3/8	4	4	Orange County	IN	David A. Hicks	1997	15,647
128 1/8	22 5/8	23 2/8	16 3/8	4	5	Osage County	OK	Bryan White	1997	15,647
128 1/8	21 1/8	21 6/8	14 7/8	4	4	Muskogee County	OK	Gary L. Peterson	1997	15,647
128 1/8	24 1/8	24 0/8	24 4/8	4	5	Lehigh County	PA	Mike Rieker	1997	15,647
128 1/8	20 7/8	21 1/8	15 5/8	5	4	Cowley County	KS	Dave Holt	1997	15,647
128 0/8	18 7/8	18 1/8	17 4/8	5	5	McLean County	ND	Bennie R. Maytum	1960	15,776
128 0/8	22 7/8	23 0/8	19 0/8	6	8	Sibley County	MN	Darwin Grack	1972	15,776
128 0/8	22 1/8	22 6/8	17 4/8	5	5	Pine County	MN	Larry Hochmayr	1973	15,776
128 0/8	22 3/8	21 2/8	17 0/8	4	4	Macon County	MO	Joe E. McCray	1973	15,776
128 0/8	23 2/8	23 0/8	18 2/8	5	5	Jasper County	IA	Paul Casper	1974	15,776
128 0/8	19 3/8	19 1/8	15 2/8	5	4	Clearwater County	MN	Warren Nelson	1975	15,776
128 0/8	23 0/8	22 6/8	16 6/8	4	4	Westchester County	NY	Theodore J. Korkidas	1978	15,776
128 0/8	21 5/8	20 5/8	16 0/8	4	4	Otter Tail County	MN	Scott M. Dirks	1978	15,776
128 0/8	19 6/8	21 0/8	15 5/8	5	6	Winona County	MN	Martin Szekeresh, Jr.	1978	15,776
128 0/8	18 7/8	17 6/8	15 2/8	5	6	Carroll County	IL	Art Heinze	1979	15,776
128 0/8	22 7/8	22 6/8	19 4/8	5	4	Manitowoc County	WI	Steve E. Nelson	1979	15,776
128 0/8	21 4/8	21 1/8	16 6/8	5	5	Harris County	GA	David M. Gallops	1980	15,776
128 0/8	20 1/8	19 5/8	18 6/8	4	4	Cumberland County	NJ	John J. Newton III	1980	15,776
128 0/8	21 5/8	21 7/8	17 6/8	4	5	Butler County	KS	Darrell Wolf	1980	15,776
128 0/8	21 1/8	21 6/8	18 0/8	6	8	Allegheny County	PA	Albert Polovich, Jr.	1981	15,776
128 0/8	21 2/8	21 1/8	16 4/8	5	6	La Salle County	IL	Richard Schupp	1983	15,776
128 0/8	20 6/8	20 0/8	18 6/8	5	5	St. Charles County	MO	Joseph L. Vincent	1983	15,776
128 0/8	22 1/8	22 0/8	15 2/8	5	5	Montgomery County	OH	Gary W. Roberson	1984	15,776
128 0/8	22 6/8	22 5/8	17 6/8	4	4	Effingham County	IL	Rick J. Hartke	1985	15,776
128 0/8	20 2/8	20 1/8	15 4/8	7	5	Pittsburg County	OK	Everett Laney	1985	15,776
128 0/8	21 2/8	21 4/8	16 4/8	5	4	Clark County	OH	Ronald Lockhart	1985	15,776
128 0/8	21 7/8	21 0/8	17 7/8	6	5	Rock County	WI	Jerry D. Amundson	1985	15,776
128 0/8	21 7/8	22 0/8	19 6/8	4	4	Licking County	OH	Randy D. Ricketts	1985	15,776
128 0/8	21 4/8	21 6/8	16 0/8	4	4	Louisa County	IA	Roger Gipple	1985	15,776
128 0/8	19 2/8	20 5/8	17 2/8	5	5	Green County	WI	David R. Covert	1986	15,776
128 0/8	21 0/8	21 4/8	15 2/8	5	5	Switzerland County	IN	James Holsapple	1986	15,776
128 0/8	20 1/8	19 3/8	16 6/8	4	4	Jefferson County	IL	Brian Scruggs	1986	15,776
128 0/8	21 5/8	22 0/8	18 0/8	4	4	Clark County	IL	Gerald Shaffner	1986	15,776
128 0/8	22 0/8	22 2/8	18 6/8	4	4	Washington County	MN	John Berglund	1987	15,776
128 0/8	22 7/8	22 1/8	16 0/8	4	4	Jo Daviess County	IL	Robert J. Chamberlain	1987	15,776
128 0/8	21 0/8	21 0/8	15 4/8	6	5	Dakota County	MN	Rick Nelson, Sr.	1987	15,776

WHITETAIL DEER (TYPICAL ANTLERS)

Minimum Score 125   Continued

SCORE	LENGTH OF MAIN BEAM R	LENGTH OF MAIN BEAM L	INSIDE SPREAD	NUMBER OF POINTS R	NUMBER OF POINTS L	AREA	STATE/ PROVINCE	HUNTER'S NAME	DATE	RANK
128 0/8	22 2/8	22 1/8	15 0/8	4	5	Buffalo County	WI	Randy Moy	1987	15,776
128 0/8	23 7/8	23 3/8	20 4/8	4	4	Sawyer County	WI	Eric Carlson	1988	15,776
128 0/8	19 6/8	19 4/8	16 4/8	4	4	Dubuque County	IA	Dwayne A. Murphy	1988	15,776
128 0/8	21 5/8	22 4/8	18 6/8	4	4	Oregon County	MO	Clifford Hayes	1988	15,776
128 0/8	22 6/8	22 0/8	16 4/8	4	4	Berkeley County	WV	Kenneth F. Moore	1988	15,776
128 0/8	22 3/8	22 6/8	21 5/8	5	4	Orleans County	NY	Warren L. Lewis	1988	15,776
128 0/8	20 6/8	22 7/8	18 2/8	4	5	Woodford County	IL	Dave Stine	1989	15,776
128 0/8	18 4/8	18 6/8	15 6/8	5	5	Throckmorton County	TX	Bruce Holt	1989	15,776
128 0/8	23 0/8	23 7/8	18 4/8	4	4	Baltimore County	MD	Mark Steven Petrucci	1989	15,776
128 0/8	20 2/8	21 1/8	17 6/8	6	5	Pepin County	WI	Richard Crabtree	1989	15,776
128 0/8	19 7/8	19 3/8	15 2/8	5	5	Hennepin County	MN	Dan Fellows	1989	15,776
128 0/8	22 3/8	22 3/8	18 6/8	4	5	Wayne County	OH	Tom P. Dotterer	1990	15,776
128 0/8	24 1/8	24 3/8	18 4/8	4	5	Coles County	IL	Rick Campbell	1990	15,776
128 0/8	24 2/8	25 0/8	18 0/8	5	5	Licking County	OH	Les Carver	1990	15,776
128 0/8	21 0/8	21 4/8	17 4/8	5	4	Columbia County	WI	Richard Schreiber	1990	15,776
128 0/8	21 4/8	22 4/8	15 6/8	4	4	Isle of Wight County	VA	Arthur Ray Phillips	1990	15,776
128 0/8	23 1/8	22 7/8	15 4/8	5	5	E. Carroll Parish	LA	Trip Hadad	1990	15,776
128 0/8	21 3/8	22 3/8	16 4/8	4	4	Morrow County	OH	Enoch Adkins, Jr.	1991	15,776
128 0/8	22 4/8	22 6/8	18 2/8	4	4	Frio County	TX	Terry Chambers	1991	15,776
128 0/8	20 2/8	20 1/8	13 4/8	5	6	Kleberg County	TX	Bradley Peltier	1991	15,776
128 0/8	20 0/8	20 5/8	17 4/8	4	4	Scott County	KY	Brad Redmon	1992	15,776
128 0/8	21 4/8	21 0/8	16 0/8	4	4	Cattaraugus County	NY	Richard Cooper	1992	15,776
128 0/8	20 4/8	20 4/8	15 6/8	5	5	Wood County	WV	Mark Daugherty	1992	15,776
128 0/8	25 4/8	23 5/8	18 0/8	4	5	Peoria County	IL	Dave Goodwin	1992	15,776
128 0/8	23 3/8	23 1/8	21 0/8	4	4	Kent County	MD	Jim Samis	1992	15,776
128 0/8	21 1/8	20 2/8	15 4/8	4	4	Lincoln County	WI	Steve Glimm	1992	15,776
128 0/8	22 0/8	22 0/8	17 4/8	4	5	Ozaukee County	WI	Jeff Wester	1993	15,776
128 0/8	21 2/8	20 6/8	15 6/8	4	4	Ogle County	IL	Eugene Syring	1993	15,776
128 0/8	22 0/8	21 7/8	17 4/8	5	5	Wayne County	KY	Paul Lowe	1993	15,776
128 0/8	19 3/8	18 2/8	17 4/8	5	5	San Patricio County	TX	Gilbert Guajardo, Jr.	1993	15,776
128 0/8	21 6/8	21 0/8	16 4/8	5	5	Polk County	WI	Thomas M. Frendt	1993	15,776
128 0/8	20 0/8	17 7/8	12 3/8	6	7	Brown County	IL	Bruce Cepicky	1993	15,776
128 0/8	21 7/8	21 0/8	14 6/8	4	4	Pulaski County	IL	Garrett Wilson	1993	15,776
128 0/8	21 6/8	22 3/8	15 6/8	4	5	Kingman County	KS	Scott Helmke	1993	15,776
128 0/8	23 1/8	23 1/8	18 6/8	4	5	Morrison County	MN	Ron W. Ekstrand	1994	15,776
128 0/8	20 0/8	20 1/8	19 2/8	5	5	Bayfield County	WI	Michael J. Fuss	1994	15,776
128 0/8	23 6/8	23 4/8	19 4/8	4	4	Charles City County	VA	Jerome O. Guyant	1994	15,776
128 0/8	24 5/8	24 1/8	17 0/8	5	5	Allen County	OH	Jon W. Mull	1994	15,776
128 0/8	21 0/8	21 3/8	16 6/8	5	5	Athens County	OH	Paul L. Kilzer	1994	15,776
128 0/8	20 4/8	20 3/8	16 6/8	6	5	Alger County	MI	Don C. Prater	1994	15,776
128 0/8	21 6/8	22 0/8	15 6/8	4	5	Grayson County	KY	Leonard W. Worth	1994	15,776
128 0/8	25 0/8	24 7/8	11 4/8	5	4	Montgomery County	MD	Charles E. Runion	1994	15,776
128 0/8	22 2/8	21 5/8	16 4/8	5	4	Suffolk County	NY	Neal Heaton	1994	15,776
128 0/8	19 3/8	22 5/8	16 6/8	6	5	Pierce County	WI	Pat McKenzie	1994	15,776
128 0/8	22 0/8	21 6/8	17 6/8	4	4	Monroe County	WI	Eric Ducklow	1995	15,776
128 0/8	21 0/8	20 6/8	17 4/8	5	5	Portage County	WI	Elliot Weisbrot	1995	15,776
128 0/8	22 2/8	21 5/8	17 5/8	4	6	Chippewa County	WI	Don Lunemann	1995	15,776
128 0/8	21 4/8	21 7/8	16 7/8	5	5	Winona County	MN	Larry Pflughoeft	1995	15,776
128 0/8	18 3/8	18 6/8	13 5/8	7	8	Irion County	TX	Ronnie L. Whitt	1995	15,776
128 0/8	22 5/8	21 6/8	20 4/8	4	4	Somerset County	NJ	Robert Staudt, Jr.	1995	15,776
128 0/8	20 3/8	20 4/8	17 1/8	7	5	Hancock County	OH	Michael Harris	1995	15,776
128 0/8	22 4/8	23 0/8	24 4/8	4	4	Wood County	WV	Roger Pape	1995	15,776
128 0/8	20 6/8	21 1/8	14 2/8	5	5	Upton County	TX	Dean Titsworth	1995	15,776
128 0/8	23 1/8	23 3/8	13 2/8	6	5	Fairfax County	VA	Byron E. Wates, Jr.	1995	15,776
128 0/8	19 0/8	19 0/8	17 0/8	5	5	Leavenworth County	KS	Roger Griffin	1995	15,776
128 0/8	20 5/8	21 5/8	17 4/8	4	4	Madison County	MS	Keith Courtney	1995	15,776
128 0/8	21 4/8	22 6/8	17 4/8	5	5	Jo Daviess County	IL	John G. Baunach	1995	15,776
128 0/8	23 5/8	23 7/8	18 0/8	4	5	Westchester County	NY	Tony Kissik	1995	15,776
128 0/8	22 3/8	21 7/8	17 6/8	5	5	Washington County	MN	William G. Greer	1996	15,776
128 0/8	22 2/8	22 0/8	17 2/8	4	4	Dane County	WI	Robert W. Erickson III	1996	15,776
128 0/8	21 2/8	21 0/8	12 4/8	4	5	Indiana County	PA	Jeff Harding	1996	15,776
128 0/8	21 2/8	21 2/8	17 0/8	4	4	Mills County	IA	Steve Martin	1996	15,776
128 0/8	19 5/8	18 4/8	17 4/8	5	5	Ravalli County	MT	Eric Treutel	1996	15,776
128 0/8	24 3/8	23 0/8	13 4/8	4	5	St. Louis County	MO	William Hill	1997	15,776
128 0/8	21 0/8	19 4/8	19 6/8	4	4	Shackelford County	TX	Mike Staton	1997	15,776
128 0/8	22 4/8	21 6/8	16 0/8	4	4	Carroll County	KY	Mark Lambert	1997	15,776
128 0/8	23 6/8	23 1/8	15 4/8	4	5	Chase County	NE	Brad Wheeler	1997	15,776
128 0/8	22 2/8	23 6/8	22 1/8	6	4	Carter County	MO	Rex Jones	1997	15,776
128 0/8	21 6/8	21 0/8	17 6/8	5	5	Westchester County	NY	David A. Lavelle	1997	15,776
128 0/8	22 0/8	21 5/8	17 2/8	5	5	Bayfield County	WI	Tom Vernau	1997	15,776
128 0/8	22 2/8	22 0/8	17 6/8	5	5	Jefferson County	WI	Joe Stacy	1997	15,776
128 0/8	23 2/8	22 4/8	17 6/8	7	7	Linn County	IA	John Huk	1997	15,776
128 0/8	22 5/8	23 1/8	16 2/8	4	4	Montgomery County	MD	Frederick T. Cissel	1997	15,776
128 0/8	19 6/8	19 6/8	15 7/8	5	6	Oconto County	WI	Jeffrey A. Magnin	1998	15,776
127 7/8	21 4/8	20 0/8	18 1/8	4	4	Monroe County	IN	Jerry L. Swafford	1968	15,881
127 7/8	21 5/8	21 2/8	15 5/8	6	6	Henderson County	IL	Randy Moore	1971	15,881
127 7/8	21 4/8	21 1/8	18 1/8	4	4	Fairfield County	OH	James Munyon	1971	15,881
127 7/8	19 2/8	20 3/8	15 7/8	6	5	Jones County	IA	Larry Stewart	1972	15,881

WHITETAIL DEER (TYPICAL ANTLERS)

Minimum Score 125 — Continued

SCORE	LENGTH OF MAIN BEAM R	LENGTH OF MAIN BEAM L	INSIDE SPREAD	NUMBER OF POINTS R	NUMBER OF POINTS L	AREA	STATE/PROVINCE	HUNTER'S NAME	DATE	RANK
127 7/8	20 3/8	20 2/8	18 5/8	4	4	Dawes County	NE	Roger Adamson	1975	15,881
127 7/8	23 5/8	24 5/8	16 7/8	5	6	Burleigh County	ND	Kevin Hertz	1980	15,881
127 7/8	22 7/8	23 1/8	17 1/8	5	5	Scott County	MN	Jim Manuel	1980	15,881
127 7/8	18 2/8	18 1/8	15 6/8	6	6	St. Croix County	WI	Larry Williamson	1981	15,881
127 7/8	22 1/8	22 0/8	18 1/8	6	5	Boyle County	KY	Carroll Williams	1981	15,881
127 7/8	21 7/8	20 4/8	17 7/8	5	5	Robertson County	TN	Walter C. Kirby	1983	15,881
127 7/8	21 1/8	21 4/8	16 7/8	4	4	Reno County	KS	Todd Murray	1983	15,881
127 7/8	20 4/8	21 0/8	15 3/8	5	5	Delta County	MI	Donald M. Seeley	1984	15,881
127 7/8	21 0/8	20 7/8	14 6/8	5	5	Genesee County	MI	Bob Bouck	1985	15,881
127 7/8	22 4/8	23 5/8	21 4/8	5	6	Lake County	IL	Edward H. Bellmore	1985	15,881
127 7/8	22 0/8	22 0/8	18 1/8	6	8	Nez Perce County	ID	Brad Johnson	1985	15,881
127 7/8	21 7/8	22 4/8	19 1/8	4	6	Marquette County	WI	James C. Lakin	1986	15,881
127 7/8	21 5/8	20 6/8	16 2/8	6	6	Clark County	IL	Tomas E. Rothrock	1986	15,881
127 7/8	23 1/8	22 6/8	18 1/8	5	4	Kane County	IL	Dennis Busto	1986	15,881
127 7/8	24 4/8	23 3/8	15 5/8	4	5	Green County	WI	Paul Ovadal	1987	15,881
127 7/8	19 7/8	20 1/8	20 3/8	5	5	Pontotoc County	OK	Joe David Abbott	1987	15,881
127 7/8	19 7/8	20 1/8	17 2/8	6	6	Portage County	WI	Gerald Pavelski	1987	15,881
127 7/8	20 4/8	21 2/8	17 0/8	6	6	Towner County	ND	Mike Haberstroh	1987	15,881
127 7/8	22 5/8	23 4/8	19 5/8	4	5	Saline County	NE	Larry E. Andelt	1987	15,881
127 7/8	21 4/8	20 1/8	15 3/8	6	8	Kenedy County	TX	Steven W. Vaughn	1988	15,881
127 7/8	23 3/8	22 5/8	16 4/8	6	4	Juneau County	WI	Merle D. Jensen	1988	15,881
127 7/8	23 1/8	23 1/8	19 0/8	5	4	Sawyer County	WI	Pat Stone	1988	15,881
127 7/8	21 0/8	20 4/8	13 1/8	5	5	Trumbull County	OH	Mark J. Drotar	1988	15,881
127 7/8	25 6/8	26 5/8	19 5/8	4	3	Fayette County	OH	Millard B. Stone, Jr.	1988	15,881
127 7/8	22 0/8	21 7/8	14 2/8	6	4	Putnam County	MO	Carl Robbins	1988	15,881
127 7/8	21 6/8	23 1/8	19 2/8	5	5	Mercer County	NJ	Keith Gadsby	1989	15,881
127 7/8	20 3/8	20 6/8	18 1/8	5	5	Crook County	WY	Steven F. Rogers	1989	15,881
127 7/8	23 6/8	23 2/8	16 1/8	4	4	Keokuk County	IA	Terry L. Bringman	1989	15,881
127 7/8	21 1/8	21 5/8	17 7/8	5	5	Genesee County	MI	Darrell S. King	1989	15,881
127 7/8	21 3/8	22 0/8	19 3/8	5	5	Woodford County	KY	James Humphrey	1989	15,881
127 7/8	20 6/8	21 3/8	19 7/8	5	4	Polk County	WI	Brian Estes	1989	15,881
127 7/8	22 4/8	23 2/8	15 6/8	5	6	Osage County	OK	Lester James Dibble	1989	15,881
127 7/8	21 5/8	20 6/8	18 2/8	5	8	Vermilion County	IL	David DeMoss	1989	15,881
127 7/8	21 7/8	21 5/8	17 1/8	5	5	Muskingum County	OH	Terry Romain	1989	15,881
127 7/8	22 5/8	22 2/8	17 7/8	4	4	Grundy County	IL	Rick Marks	1990	15,881
127 7/8	22 1/8	22 4/8	14 1/8	4	5	Buffalo County	WI	Fred Neitzel	1990	15,881
127 7/8	23 2/8	24 1/8	20 7/8	5	4	Putnam County	WV	Kevin Davis	1990	15,881
127 7/8	21 0/8	21 6/8	19 1/8	4	4	Henry County	VA	Mike Weaver	1990	15,881
127 7/8	22 7/8	23 0/8	19 7/8	5	4	Worth County	IA	Larry B. Porter	1990	15,881
127 7/8	24 2/8	26 0/8	19 2/8	4	5	Lincoln County	MO	Mark Peasel	1990	15,881
127 7/8	21 4/8	21 5/8	16 1/8	5	4	Ozark County	MO	Roger Patton	1990	15,881
127 7/8	19 5/8	20 4/8	14 5/8	5	5	Athens County	OH	Curtis D. Rutter	1990	15,881
127 7/8	20 7/8	21 3/8	18 0/8	5	6	Douglas County	WI	Steve Hedrington	1990	15,881
127 7/8	21 2/8	22 5/8	16 5/8	5	5	Fayette County	OH	George Massie	1990	15,881
127 7/8	24 2/8	23 2/8	19 7/8	4	5	Iowa County	IA	Rodney Smith	1990	15,881
127 7/8	19 0/8	22 2/8	15 3/8	4	5	Suffolk County	NY	William R. Simmons III	1990	15,881
127 7/8	20 0/8	22 0/8	17 6/8	4	4	Slope County	ND	William H. Guile	1990	15,881
127 7/8	24 4/8	23 5/8	19 5/8	5	5	Willacy County	TX	Al Kowalski	1990	15,881
127 7/8	21 0/8	22 2/8	15 7/8	4	5	McHenry County	IL	Edward C. Schultz	1990	15,881
127 7/8	22 2/8	21 3/8	19 1/8	5	5	Jasper County	MO	Frankie Reynolds	1990	15,881
127 7/8	22 1/8	22 0/8	16 3/8	5	5	Travis County	TX	Raymond G. McRae	1991	15,881
127 7/8	22 5/8	20 6/8	15 1/8	4	4	Newton County	MO	Craig Koelling	1991	15,881
127 7/8	23 0/8	24 2/8	16 5/8	4	5	Franklin County	MA	David M. Lauder	1991	15,881
127 7/8	21 6/8	23 1/8	15 4/8	6	5	Adams County	IL	Timothy Walmsley	1991	15,881
127 7/8	22 5/8	23 5/8	17 5/8	5	5	Onieda County	WI	Dan J. Blenker	1991	15,881
127 7/8	22 4/8	23 1/8	18 1/8	5	4	McHenry County	IL	Jeff Lunk	1991	15,881
127 7/8	21 0/8	21 4/8	13 7/8	6	5	Clayton County	IA	Paul "Buck" Farni, Jr.	1992	15,881
127 7/8	22 1/8	22 1/8	19 6/8	5	5	Carroll County	MS	David B. McElwrath	1992	15,881
127 7/8	23 7/8	24 2/8	20 5/8	4	4	Jackson County	OH	Richard E. Neal II	1992	15,881
127 7/8	22 0/8	21 6/8	15 3/8	4	4	Fayette County	AL	Frank Bagwell	1993	15,881
127 7/8	22 5/8	22 5/8	16 5/8	4	5	Kent County	DE	Lee Collins	1993	15,881
127 7/8	22 2/8	23 1/8	22 5/8	5	4	Northampton County	VA	Michael A. Lewis	1993	15,881
127 7/8	20 4/8	21 5/8	16 6/8	4	5	La Salle County	IN	Bill Ekhoff	1993	15,881
127 7/8	21 4/8	21 5/8	15 7/8	5	5	Westmoreland County	PA	David S. Shaffer	1993	15,881
127 7/8	21 3/8	21 0/8	16 7/8	5	5	Marinette County	WI	Robert "Lefty" Randerson	1993	15,881
127 7/8	23 3/8	23 3/8	19 1/8	4	5	Morgan County	CO	Mark Hansen	1993	15,881
127 7/8	24 3/8	23 4/8	19 5/8	4	4	Northumberland County	PA	Timothy W. Clark	1993	15,881
127 7/8	21 2/8	21 0/8	16 5/8	4	4	Carver County	MN	Robert J. Evans, Jr.	1993	15,881
127 7/8	21 7/8	22 1/8	15 1/8	4	4	Mason County	IL	Bruce W. Shallenberger	1994	15,881
127 7/8	20 4/8	20 6/8	15 5/8	5	6	Bartholomew County	IN	G. Douglas McPherson	1994	15,881
127 7/8	22 5/8	22 2/8	18 5/8	5	4	Sauk County	WI	Paul A. Huerth	1994	15,881
127 7/8	23 5/8	24 1/8	16 3/8	4	4	Fillmore County	MN	Russell Schroeder	1994	15,881
127 7/8	21 3/8	21 3/8	16 3/8	5	5	Fond du Lac County	WI	David B. Schry	1994	15,881
127 7/8	22 0/8	22 4/8	15 5/8	4	5	Nemaha County	KS	Matthew Roudybush	1994	15,881
127 7/8	22 1/8	22 2/8	16 5/8	4	4	Harrison County	MO	Stephen R. Witmer	1994	15,881
127 7/8	20 1/8	20 2/8	17 5/8	5	5	Belmont County	OH	Scott M. Ware	1994	15,881
127 7/8	21 1/8	21 6/8	16 5/8	4	4	Page County	IA	Chris Barton	1994	15,881
127 7/8	21 1/8	21 1/8	15 5/8	5	6	Wayne County	KY	Randall Ray Hall	1995	15,881

WHITETAIL DEER (TYPICAL ANTLERS)

Minimum Score 125 — Continued

SCORE	LENGTH OF MAIN BEAM R	L	INSIDE SPREAD	NUMBER OF POINTS R	L	AREA	STATE/PROVINCE	HUNTER'S NAME	DATE	RANK
127 7/8	23 0/8	22 6/8	16 0/8	5	6	Jefferson County	WI	Tim Frey	1995	15,881
127 7/8	21 1/8	20 5/8	15 3/8	4	5	Grant County	WI	Richard Weber	1995	15,881
127 7/8	21 7/8	22 5/8	17 7/8	4	4	Chester County	PA	Mickey D. Hendrickson	1995	15,881
127 7/8	21 2/8	21 7/8	20 1/8	4	4	Allegheny County	PA	Don King, Jr.	1995	15,881
127 7/8	23 2/8	23 5/8	17 3/8	4	7	Calhoun County	IL	Steve Donelson, Jr.	1995	15,881
127 7/8	20 0/8	19 7/8	14 5/8	5	5	Calgary	ALB	Archie Nesbitt	1995	15,881
127 7/8	21 3/8	21 1/8	18 1/8	4	4	Ashtabula County	OH	Tom Spencer, Sr.	1995	15,881
127 7/8	23 5/8	22 5/8	16 0/8	4	6	Scott County	IA	John Nupp	1996	15,881
127 7/8	20 7/8	21 2/8	15 3/8	5	5	Waukesha County	WI	Tim Bourdo	1996	15,881
127 7/8	21 6/8	21 2/8	16 1/8	5	4	Schuyler County	NY	Michael J. Clark	1996	15,881
127 7/8	22 1/8	20 0/8	16 7/8	4	4	Washington County	IA	Steven D. Pfaff	1996	15,881
127 7/8	21 6/8	22 6/8	15 1/8	4	5	Raleigh County	WV	Dana Dean	1996	15,881
127 7/8	22 0/8	22 0/8	15 7/8	4	4	Stanton County	NE	Matt Schuetz	1997	15,881
127 7/8	22 6/8	23 0/8	19 2/8	6	5	Dodge County	WI	James Checolinski	1997	15,881
127 7/8	22 5/8	22 6/8	15 1/8	7	7	Palo Pinto County	TX	Steve Hotchkiss	1997	15,881
127 7/8	21 6/8	21 4/8	16 5/8	5	5	Warren County	MS	Luke Parker	1997	15,881
127 7/8	19 6/8	20 6/8	17 6/8	6	5	Hampden County	MA	Mark Girhiny	1997	15,881
127 7/8	21 5/8	23 2/8	17 5/8	5	6	Cass County	NE	Roger E. Buck	1997	15,881
127 7/8	21 4/8	20 4/8	16 7/8	5	5	Buffalo County	WI	David Larson	1997	15,881
127 7/8	20 6/8	20 2/8	15 2/8	6	6	Hand County	SD	Anthony E. Rangel	1997	15,881
127 7/8	24 0/8	24 0/8	17 7/8	7	4	Buffalo County	WI	Donald R. Fox	1997	15,881
127 7/8	20 4/8	20 0/8	16 3/8	5	5	Decatur County	IA	David B. Green	1997	15,881
127 7/8	22 1/8	23 0/8	16 4/8	4	5	McHenry County	IL	Mike Chabalowski	1997	15,881
127 7/8	18 0/8	18 3/8	16 1/8	5	5	Otoe County	NE	Richard P. Flock	1998	15,881
127 7/8	24 7/8	24 3/8	16 2/8	6	6	Armstrong County	PA	Richard L. Seevers II	1998	15,881
127 6/8	21 3/8	22 2/8	16 2/8	4	4	Rice County	MN	David Knutson	1969	15,988
127 6/8	24 4/8	23 6/8	18 3/8	6	5	Muskingum County	OH	Charles F. Fineran	1974	15,988
127 6/8	20 0/8	19 3/8	17 0/8	4	4	Tucker County	WV	Larry A. Williams	1975	15,988
127 6/8	20 2/8	21 2/8	16 0/8	6	5	Rice County	MN	James Caron	1979	15,988
127 6/8	21 6/8	21 5/8	15 6/8	4	4	Ward County	ND	Larry Ziech	1979	15,988
127 6/8	23 2/8	23 6/8	18 1/8	5	5	Sumner County	KS	Mark Disney	1980	15,988
127 6/8	20 6/8	21 0/8	16 4/8	5	5	Marion County	KY	Hugh Glasscock	1980	15,988
127 6/8	21 7/8	21 7/8	17 6/8	5	5	Waupaca County	WI	Bryon Gyldenvand	1981	15,988
127 6/8	23 6/8	22 2/8	17 4/8	4	4	Hardin County	IA	Richard Pugh	1981	15,988
127 6/8	24 7/8	24 5/8	19 0/8	5	5	Clark County	SD	Jan Buri	1982	15,988
127 6/8	20 0/8	20 4/8	18 2/8	4	4	Yell County	AR	Keith L. Chronister	1982	15,988
127 6/8	24 2/8	23 1/8	20 0/8	4	4	Blue Earth County	MN	Bruce Barrie	1983	15,988
127 6/8	23 4/8	24 4/8	20 4/8	5	4	Waukesha County	WI	Max Mollgaard	1983	15,988
127 6/8	20 4/8	20 5/8	18 0/8	5	4	Monongalia County	WV	Marshall Ridenour	1984	15,988
127 6/8	22 1/8	21 6/8	16 6/8	4	4	Rogers County	OK	Tom Woosley	1984	15,988
127 6/8	22 1/8	21 5/8	17 0/8	4	5	St. Albert	ALB	Gary Kieser	1984	15,988
127 6/8	23 6/8	22 1/8	17 2/8	5	4	Darke County	OH	Bruce Knick	1985	15,988
127 6/8	20 4/8	20 6/8	15 4/8	4	5	Buffalo County	WI	David J. Gard	1985	15,988
127 6/8	23 6/8	23 1/8	20 4/8	3	3	Kearney County	NE	Larry Kuskie	1986	15,988
127 6/8	23 2/8	22 2/8	17 2/8	4	5	Trego County	KS	Brian Batman	1986	15,988
127 6/8	24 3/8	23 6/8	16 2/8	5	4	Guernsey County	OH	William E. Lee, Jr.	1986	15,988
127 6/8	20 1/8	20 6/8	13 4/8	5	5	Carroll County	IL	William Lilly	1986	15,988
127 6/8	24 3/8	24 0/8	18 1/8	5	5	St. Clair County	MO	Tim Donnelly	1987	15,988
127 6/8	22 2/8	20 7/8	17 4/8	5	5	Prince Georges County	MD	Kenny Walker	1987	15,988
127 6/8	23 7/8	24 0/8	16 6/8	4	4	Bent County	CO	Kurt W. Keskimaki	1987	15,988
127 6/8	23 4/8	23 1/8	17 0/8	6	5	Rockingham County	NH	George Denoncour	1988	15,988
127 6/8	20 2/8	20 5/8	18 0/8	5	6	Brooks County	TX	J. Dale Hale	1988	15,988
127 6/8	22 4/8	22 2/8	23 3/8	5	5	Green County	WI	Dan Cupp	1988	15,988
127 6/8	20 4/8	21 1/8	17 0/8	4	4	Lyon County	KS	Joe Buchtel	1988	15,988
127 6/8	22 7/8	22 6/8	18 6/8	4	4	Cedar County	IA	David Fleener	1988	15,988
127 6/8	22 4/8	22 4/8	16 6/8	4	4	Erie County	OH	Jeff Mallory	1988	15,988
127 6/8	20 6/8	19 7/8	18 6/8	5	4	Martin County	MN	Troy Kakeldey	1988	15,988
127 6/8	22 1/8	22 0/8	17 4/8	4	5	White County	AR	Freddy King, Jr.	1988	15,988
127 6/8	20 2/8	19 6/8	16 0/8	5	5	Teton County	MT	Brad Stewart	1989	15,988
127 6/8	23 2/8	23 1/8	17 1/8	6	4	Ingham County	MI	Michael A. Barnes	1989	15,988
127 6/8	22 5/8	21 4/8	14 6/8	5	4	Clarke County	GA	Walter P. Wood	1989	15,988
127 6/8	19 4/8	19 7/8	19 1/8	6	6	Bureau County	IL	Ronald Franklin	1989	15,988
127 6/8	24 7/8	24 6/8	17 3/8	6	6	Sullivan County	NH	Maurice Flinn	1989	15,988
127 6/8	20 6/8	21 2/8	17 2/8	5	6	Brooks County	TX	Thomas L. "Tag" Reed IV	1989	15,988
127 6/8	18 0/8	17 6/8	13 6/8	5	5	Allegan County	MI	Brian M. Nichols	1989	15,988
127 6/8	20 6/8	21 4/8	18 0/8	6	6	Reno County	KS	Monte Long	1989	15,988
127 6/8	19 7/8	19 6/8	16 0/8	5	5	Whitman County	WA	Pat McFadden	1990	15,988
127 6/8	20 2/8	20 5/8	16 0/8	5	5	Winston County	MS	Carl Mangrum, Jr.	1990	15,988
127 6/8	23 0/8	22 0/8	17 0/8	4	4	McKenzie County	ND	Steve Rehak	1990	15,988
127 6/8	21 5/8	21 5/8	17 6/8	5	4	Seneca County	OH	Michael E. Halbeisen	1990	15,988
127 6/8	19 7/8	20 1/8	15 0/8	5	6	Sheboygan County	WI	Troy Klein	1990	15,988
127 6/8	21 5/8	23 3/8	14 6/8	5	4	Waukesha County	WI	Ronald J. Mayer	1990	15,988
127 6/8	18 7/8	19 7/8	16 0/8	5	5	Harris County	GA	Gorman S. Riley	1990	15,988
127 6/8	22 0/8	21 6/8	17 4/8	4	4	Walworth County	WI	Michael Pautz	1990	15,988
127 6/8	23 6/8	22 5/8	17 4/8	5	5	Putnam County	OH	Ben Warnimont	1990	15,988
127 6/8	24 1/8	23 5/8	21 2/8	5	4	Desha County	AR	Allan Goodwin	1990	15,988
127 6/8	22 2/8	21 5/8	17 2/8	4	4	Phillips County	KS	Michael Sohm	1990	15,988
127 6/8	20 3/8	19 4/8	15 6/8	5	5	Dane County	WI	Stephen J. Field	1991	15,988

WHITETAIL DEER (TYPICAL ANTLERS)

Minimum Score 125 — Continued

SCORE	LENGTH OF MAIN BEAM R	LENGTH OF MAIN BEAM L	INSIDE SPREAD	NUMBER OF POINTS R	NUMBER OF POINTS L	AREA	STATE/PROVINCE	HUNTER'S NAME	DATE	RANK
127 6/8	21 0/8	21 2/8	17 0/8	5	4	Iron County	MI	Erick Friestrom	1991	15,988
127 6/8	22 4/8	22 1/8	21 4/8	4	6	Tulsa County	OK	Terry Buckner	1991	15,988
127 6/8	21 7/8	22 6/8	19 0/8	5	5	Marathon County	WI	Neil Daul	1991	15,988
127 6/8	21 1/8	22 0/8	17 0/8	4	4	Palo Alto County	IA	Roger V. Faulstick	1991	15,988
127 6/8	22 1/8	20 7/8	16 6/8	5	6	Oconto County	WI	Patrick J. Gauthier	1992	15,988
127 6/8	20 7/8	22 0/8	18 6/8	5	5	San Patricio County	TX	Audie W. Stephens	1992	15,988
127 6/8	20 0/8	19 7/8	15 2/8	6	5	Lawrence County	OH	Larry Marcum	1992	15,988
127 6/8	20 6/8	20 4/8	14 0/8	4	4	Pike County	MO	George Mehler	1992	15,988
127 6/8	20 4/8	21 4/8	16 4/8	4	4	Calhoun County	MI	Greg H. St. John	1992	15,988
127 6/8	21 6/8	21 6/8	17 2/8	4	4	Jo Daviess County	IL	Mark A. Risser	1992	15,988
127 6/8	21 0/8	20 7/8	16 0/8	4	4	Washington County	MN	Brian Helm	1992	15,988
127 6/8	22 2/8	23 2/8	18 6/8	5	4	Hughes County	SD	Douglas E. Hofer	1992	15,988
127 6/8	22 6/8	23 1/8	19 1/8	5	4	Westchester County	NY	Joe DeCarlo	1992	15,988
127 6/8	20 6/8	21 5/8	20 1/8	5	5	Oakland County	MI	Michael J. DeWitt	1992	15,988
127 6/8	21 6/8	22 4/8	18 0/8	5	5	Zavala County	TX	William Welton	1992	15,988
127 6/8	21 4/8	21 7/8	15 2/8	5	5	Clay County	NE	Gary Reed	1993	15,988
127 6/8	21 5/8	21 6/8	16 7/8	6	6	Dane County	WI	Norman C. Peterson	1993	15,988
127 6/8	21 5/8	21 4/8	16 0/8	6	6	Jefferson County	KS	Ronald D. Artzer	1993	15,988
127 6/8	21 1/8	21 0/8	16 4/8	5	5	Pierce County	WI	Rich J. Johnson	1993	15,988
127 6/8	18 7/8	22 5/8	18 1/8	5	4	Ford County	IL	Lloyd Kemnetz, Jr.	1993	15,988
127 6/8	24 3/8	23 6/8	18 4/8	4	4	Lee County	IL	Larry D. Nicklaus	1993	15,988
127 6/8	20 6/8	21 0/8	19 0/8	7	6	Gage County	NE	Steve Stedman	1993	15,988
127 6/8	21 5/8	19 6/8	17 0/8	5	4	Allegheny County	PA	Terry B. Lindenmuth	1993	15,988
127 6/8	22 0/8	22 3/8	17 4/8	6	5	Kit Carson County	CO	Bryant Shermoe	1993	15,988
127 6/8	23 4/8	24 6/8	17 2/8	4	4	Crow Wing County	MN	Patrick T. Erdrich	1993	15,988
127 6/8	23 3/8	22 0/8	18 6/8	4	4	Jefferson County	IL	Brad Kalmer	1993	15,988
127 6/8	24 1/8	24 5/8	19 2/8	6	7	Hennepin County	MN	Steven A. Hancock	1993	15,988
127 6/8	22 7/8	20 2/8	16 0/8	4	5	Valley County	MT	Nickie E. Roth	1993	15,988
127 6/8	19 5/8	19 4/8	14 6/8	5	5	Nuevo Laredo	MEX	Roy Marlow	1993	15,988
127 6/8	20 0/8	20 0/8	17 2/8	4	4	Portage County	WI	Jason L. Wisinski	1994	15,988
127 6/8	23 0/8	24 2/8	15 0/8	5	5	Anderson County	TN	Larry Herron	1994	15,988
127 6/8	22 4/8	22 0/8	16 0/8	5	5	Jo Daviess County	IL	Jeffery C. Ramthun	1994	15,988
127 6/8	20 6/8	20 2/8	16 4/8	5	5	Schenectady County	NY	Ron DeCocco	1994	15,988
127 6/8	20 6/8	19 5/8	16 2/8	5	7	Rush County	IN	Brock Cross	1994	15,988
127 6/8	21 2/8	21 6/8	17 6/8	5	4	Missoula County	MT	Tom J. Evans, Jr.	1994	15,988
127 6/8	21 3/8	22 2/8	15 0/8	4	5	Montgomery County	MD	Jeffrey L. Harrison	1995	15,988
127 6/8	19 3/8	19 6/8	14 5/8	5	7	Jefferson County	WI	Dean C. Evenson	1995	15,988
127 6/8	21 1/8	20 3/8	19 2/8	5	6	Pratt County	KS	Greg Windler	1995	15,988
127 6/8	20 5/8	21 6/8	18 0/8	5	5	Winnebago County	IL	Anthony Risney	1995	15,988
127 6/8	21 3/8	21 0/8	15 6/8	5	5	Douglas County	IL	Ricky L. Parker	1995	15,988
127 6/8	22 4/8	22 5/8	19 2/8	4	5	Bergen County	NJ	Kevin Garlasco	1995	15,988
127 6/8	22 6/8	22 7/8	16 5/8	6	6	St. Louis County	MN	Rob Nelson	1995	15,988
127 6/8	20 2/8	20 7/8	19 4/8	4	5	Pulaski County	IL	Gary Stearns	1996	15,988
127 6/8	20 7/8	21 1/8	17 4/8	5	5	Issaquena County	MS	James M. Barnett	1996	15,988
127 6/8	21 0/8	21 4/8	15 4/8	6	6	Daviess County	MO	Gary L. King	1996	15,988
127 6/8	25 2/8	26 1/8	20 4/8	3	4	Ashland County	OH	Jim Anderson	1996	15,988
127 6/8	24 0/8	24 0/8	16 6/8	6	5	Hillsborough County	NH	Alrick Hammar, Jr.	1996	15,988
127 6/8	17 6/8	18 0/8	16 4/8	5	5	Fulton County	GA	Edwin F. Adams	1996	15,988
127 6/8	21 2/8	20 7/8	17 0/8	5	4	Manitowoc County	WI	John Begotka	1996	15,988
127 6/8	22 3/8	22 0/8	19 0/8	5	5	Buffalo County	WI	Steven Schroeder	1996	15,988
127 6/8	27 0/8	26 7/8	21 6/8	4	6	Charles County	MD	Steven W. Bebow	1996	15,988
127 6/8	22 6/8	22 2/8	18 0/8	4	4	Kanawha County	WV	Randy Wills	1996	15,988
127 6/8	25 2/8	25 0/8	20 2/8	5	4	Hardin County	KY	Milton Hathcock, Jr.	1996	15,988
127 6/8	22 4/8	22 3/8	17 2/8	5	4	Charles County	MD	Bradley F. Herbert	1996	15,988
127 6/8	21 0/8	19 5/8	14 3/8	5	6	Yuma County	CO	Ronald L. King	1996	15,988
127 6/8	20 4/8	20 2/8	18 0/8	4	4	Creek County	OK	Bill Giacomo	1996	15,988
127 6/8	21 1/8	22 4/8	18 2/8	5	5	Kane County	IL	Janet Hight	1997	15,988
127 6/8	22 4/8	23 3/8	18 0/8	4	4	Chester County	PA	Victor Ferguson	1997	15,988
127 6/8	20 5/8	20 6/8	17 4/8	6	5	Kenosha County	WI	Gus Legler	1997	15,988
127 6/8	18 6/8	17 7/8	14 2/8	5	5	St. Croix County	WI	Pete Midthum	1997	15,988
127 6/8	21 1/8	21 4/8	18 4/8	4	4	Atascosa County	TX	Greg Messina	1997	15,988
127 6/8	21 5/8	20 3/8	16 4/8	4	4	Buffalo County	WI	Terrance R. Skebba	1997	15,988
127 6/8	21 4/8	20 6/8	17 6/8	6	5	Todd County	KY	George A. Addison, Jr.	1997	15,988
127 6/8	23 3/8	22 3/8	18 2/8	5	5	Washington County	MN	Gregory Videen	1997	15,988
127 6/8	21 1/8	21 4/8	16 4/8	4	4	Ingham County	MI	Victor Lee Domke	1997	15,988
127 6/8	23 6/8	23 1/8	17 6/8	5	6	Ontonagon County	MI	John A. Rutherford	1997	15,988
127 6/8	21 1/8	22 0/8	16 0/8	6	7	Sutton County	TX	Frank S. Noska IV	1997	15,988
127 6/8	18 7/8	19 2/8	14 2/8	6	5	Clarke County	IA	Tim Dumbeck	1997	15,988
127 6/8	19 4/8	20 2/8	17 6/8	5	5	Oneida County	WI	Shawn Tingley	1997	15,988
127 6/8	20 6/8	20 2/8	13 6/8	5	5	Dimmit County	TX	Gary F. Vaughn	1997	15,988
127 5/8	21 4/8	22 1/8	17 3/8	5	5	Monroe County	MO	C. R. Jackson	1962	16,111
127 5/8	22 3/8	22 3/8	16 5/8	6	5	Vilas County	WI	Carl R. Strauss	1968	16,111
127 5/8	21 2/8	21 0/8	18 3/8	5	5	Warren County	NJ	Jerry W. Kauffman	1972	16,111
127 5/8	22 0/8	22 6/8	14 7/8	4	4	Winnebago County	IA	Kenneth R. Coe, Jr.	1973	16,111
127 5/8	24 4/8	24 5/8	19 0/8	4	5	Wayne County	OH	Ronald Stine	1975	16,111
127 5/8	21 5/8	22 1/8	14 4/8	6	6	Sauk County	WI	Walter S. Jankowski	1976	16,111
127 5/8	21 0/8	21 3/8	16 5/8	4	4	Dickson County	TN	Andy Jackson	1976	16,111
127 5/8	23 2/8	22 4/8	16 1/8	5	5	Tuscarawas County	OH	Jon Scheetz	1976	16,111

WHITETAIL DEER (TYPICAL ANTLERS)

Minimum Score 125 — Continued

SCORE	LENGTH OF MAIN BEAM R	L	INSIDE SPREAD	NUMBER OF POINTS R	L	AREA	STATE/PROVINCE	HUNTER'S NAME	DATE	RANK
127 5/8	21 6/8	21 6/8	20 1/8	5	5	Rock County	WI	Jeffrey L. Kersten	1979	16,111
127 5/8	20 6/8	21 4/8	15 7/8	5	5	Clark County	WI	James Kleinschmidt	1979	16,111
127 5/8	22 5/8	21 3/8	14 7/8	5	5	Bell County	TX	Tim Wood	1980	16,111
127 5/8	21 7/8	22 4/8	18 5/8	5	5	Tuscarawas County	OH	John H. Raber	1981	16,111
127 5/8	19 6/8	19 4/8	17 7/8	5	5	Scott County	KY	Michael A. Fry	1982	16,111
127 5/8	24 2/8	25 1/8	14 5/8	4	4	Franklin County	KS	David R. Poore	1982	16,111
127 5/8	21 2/8	20 5/8	16 5/8	5	5	Polk County	WI	Tim Bump	1983	16,111
127 5/8	18 2/8	18 7/8	17 5/8	4	4	Sarpy County	NE	Ed Smith	1985	16,111
127 5/8	22 5/8	23 3/8	17 7/8	4	4	Roane County	TN	William A. "Bill" Simms	1985	16,111
127 5/8	20 5/8	18 7/8	16 6/8	6	6	Atchison County	MO	Tom Nauman	1985	16,111
127 5/8	21 3/8	23 5/8	14 5/8	5	5	Anoka County	MN	Robert G. Ross	1985	16,111
127 5/8	23 7/8	24 4/8	16 7/8	5	5	Licking County	OH	Michael Stumph	1985	16,111
127 5/8	21 2/8	20 7/8	16 7/8	7	8	Christian County	IL	Jeffrey S. Burdick	1985	16,111
127 5/8	21 0/8	21 2/8	20 1/8	5	5	Meigs County	OH	Eric A. Harris	1985	16,111
127 5/8	24 2/8	23 4/8	17 3/8	4	4	Kandiyohi County	MN	Mark Harder	1986	16,111
127 5/8	19 1/8	19 2/8	14 3/8	5	5	Newton County	MO	William V. Patterson	1986	16,111
127 5/8	24 2/8	23 5/8	15 6/8	5	7	Marshall County	IL	Howard P. Olson	1986	16,111
127 5/8	22 7/8	24 3/8	17 1/8	4	4	Pike County	OH	John Ribic	1986	16,111
127 5/8	21 6/8	21 6/8	15 6/8	6	4	Cavalier County	ND	Dayton H. Larson	1987	16,111
127 5/8	19 5/8	19 5/8	17 1/8	5	5	De Kalb County	MO	J. W. Martin	1987	16,111
127 5/8	20 1/8	19 6/8	16 1/8	5	5	Dodge County	WI	Joel F. Weber	1987	16,111
127 5/8	20 6/8	20 2/8	18 5/8	5	5	Price County	WI	David Baratka	1988	16,111
127 5/8	22 0/8	22 2/8	18 5/8	5	5	Ozaukee County	WI	William J. Ferguson	1988	16,111
127 5/8	23 5/8	23 1/8	16 1/8	5	4	Portage County	WI	Ronald S. Rosera	1989	16,111
127 5/8	21 6/8	22 3/8	16 7/8	5	4	Dane County	WI	Larry Sperry	1989	16,111
127 5/8	19 2/8	20 3/8	17 1/8	4	4	Cass County	MI	Richard N. Ayers	1989	16,111
127 5/8	21 0/8	22 0/8	16 4/8	6	5	Washington County	KS	Toby Bruna	1989	16,111
127 5/8	20 5/8	22 4/8	18 7/8	5	6	Fillmore County	MN	Duane C. Baumler	1990	16,111
127 5/8	23 6/8	21 7/8	16 7/8	4	4	Sheboygan County	WI	Jim Ziegler, Jr.	1990	16,111
127 5/8	21 2/8	20 3/8	15 3/8	5	5	Macon County	MO	Roger Rector	1990	16,111
127 5/8	22 6/8	22 2/8	19 7/8	4	4	Buffalo County	WI	Chris Klein	1990	16,111
127 5/8	22 7/8	22 5/8	14 3/8	5	5	Livingston County	MI	Michael L. Stefanka	1990	16,111
127 5/8	20 4/8	20 0/8	18 1/8	5	5	Plymouth County	IA	Bob D. Schlesser	1990	16,111
127 5/8	21 7/8	21 7/8	17 1/8	5	5	Sheboygan County	WI	James Drake	1990	16,111
127 5/8	23 0/8	22 6/8	15 7/8	5	7	Clarke County	IA	Don Mealey	1990	16,111
127 5/8	20 0/8	21 1/8	15 1/8	5	5	Lee County	IA	James D. Bohnenkamp	1990	16,111
127 5/8	20 0/8	19 4/8	15 5/8	5	5	Woodford County	KY	Tony Bobbitt	1991	16,111
127 5/8	20 0/8	20 4/8	13 3/8	5	5	Ray County	MO	Burt Pitchford	1991	16,111
127 5/8	22 3/8	22 3/8	15 5/8	5	5	Mason County	WV	Keith Reynolds	1991	16,111
127 5/8	22 6/8	22 1/8	16 3/8	4	4	Cook County	MN	Jeff Herrick	1991	16,111
127 5/8	21 0/8	21 3/8	15 1/8	5	5	Trempealeau County	WI	Rick Bryson	1991	16,111
127 5/8	20 2/8	22 1/8	14 5/8	5	4	Crawford County	IL	Dennis Sturgis, Jr.	1991	16,111
127 5/8	23 3/8	23 4/8	17 5/8	5	4	Montgomery County	MD	James C. Dalrymple, Jr.	1991	16,111
127 5/8	19 2/8	20 3/8	17 1/8	5	5	Sheboygan County	WI	George W. Klein	1991	16,111
127 5/8	23 2/8	23 2/8	19 5/8	4	4	Wabasha County	MN	Lee G. Partington	1992	16,111
127 5/8	21 2/8	24 4/8	18 7/8	5	4	Columbia County	PA	Randy Yasenchak	1992	16,111
127 5/8	22 4/8	22 3/8	17 1/8	5	4	Milwaukee County	WI	Steven B. Schroeder	1992	16,111
127 5/8	22 2/8	21 7/8	18 7/8	5	5	Washtenaw County	MI	Mike E. Smith	1992	16,111
127 5/8	20 2/8	21 1/8	15 4/8	6	5	Macon County	MO	Lary Close	1992	16,111
127 5/8	19 1/8	18 7/8	15 5/8	5	6	Clark County	WI	Earl Hubbard	1992	16,111
127 5/8	22 4/8	22 3/8	15 3/8	4	4	Kay County	OK	Brett Wittmer	1992	16,111
127 5/8	23 4/8	22 4/8	15 5/8	6	6	Desha County	AR	Steve Foyil	1992	16,111
127 5/8	19 6/8	20 6/8	13 1/8	5	7	Oklahoma County	OK	Billy W. McBride	1992	16,111
127 5/8	23 4/8	24 0/8	16 4/8	5	5	Wyoming County	WV	Harry G. Cooke, Jr.	1993	16,111
127 5/8	22 5/8	22 6/8	21 1/8	4	4	Mercer County	NJ	William K. Maul	1993	16,111
127 5/8	21 0/8	20 4/8	16 1/8	5	5	Steuben County	IN	Steve Schultz	1993	16,111
127 5/8	20 6/8	20 6/8	17 1/8	5	5	Iowa County	WI	Tim Tibbits	1993	16,111
127 5/8	21 3/8	21 2/8	15 5/8	5	5	Iowa County	WI	Dale J. Goytowski	1993	16,111
127 5/8	23 3/8	22 7/8	17 4/8	4	5	Muskingum County	OH	Vernon Sowers	1993	16,111
127 5/8	20 7/8	20 5/8	15 5/8	5	5	Brown County	SD	Donald D. Wolf	1993	16,111
127 5/8	18 7/8	20 5/8	16 5/8	4	4	Burlington County	NJ	Frank R. Buckman	1993	16,111
127 5/8	22 7/8	22 2/8	19 3/8	4	5	Monmouth County	NJ	Fred Deickmann	1993	16,111
127 5/8	21 6/8	22 6/8	17 3/8	4	4	Iowa County	WI	Jason Carden	1994	16,111
127 5/8	21 6/8	21 6/8	18 5/8	4	5	Douglas County	WI	Ron W. Ekstrand	1994	16,111
127 5/8	23 0/8	22 1/8	15 1/8	6	5	Sangamon County	IL	David Jostes	1994	16,111
127 5/8	22 4/8	23 5/8	18 5/8	4	4	Ashland County	WI	Ryan Miller	1994	16,111
127 5/8	23 2/8	23 0/8	19 1/8	4	4	Winnebago County	IL	Jon Sjostrom	1994	16,111
127 5/8	21 0/8	20 1/8	15 5/8	5	5	Winona County	MN	Jan Finley	1994	16,111
127 5/8	20 0/8	20 0/8	16 1/8	5	5	Broome County	NY	Bill Bunker	1994	16,111
127 5/8	19 6/8	18 5/8	14 5/8	5	5	Webster County	KY	Calvin L. Almond	1994	16,111
127 5/8	22 6/8	22 6/8	17 7/8	4	4	Wayne County	NY	Ronald O. Sochia	1994	16,111
127 5/8	21 5/8	20 6/8	18 5/8	4	5	Fairfield County	OH	Jonathan Kirk	1994	16,111
127 5/8	22 2/8	22 7/8	18 1/8	4	4	Waukesha County	WI	Robert J. Leader	1994	16,111
127 5/8	21 1/8	21 7/8	14 6/8	5	6	Macon County	GA	Dennis Wilson	1995	16,111
127 5/8	21 0/8	20 4/8	15 3/8	5	4	Langlade County	WI	Chris Johnson	1995	16,111
127 5/8	19 3/8	20 1/8	22 1/8	5	5	Frio County	TX	William H. Goodson	1995	16,111
127 5/8	19 5/8	19 1/8	14 7/8	5	5	Kenedy County	TX	Todd Beckham	1996	16,111
127 5/8	22 0/8	21 5/8	16 3/8	4	5	Sheboygan County	WI	Rich Kluth	1996	16,111

WHITETAIL DEER (TYPICAL ANTLERS)

Minimum Score 125

Continued

SCORE	LENGTH OF MAIN BEAM R	LENGTH OF MAIN BEAM L	INSIDE SPREAD	NUMBER OF POINTS R	NUMBER OF POINTS L	AREA	STATE/ PROVINCE	HUNTER'S NAME	DATE	RANK
127 5/8	21 6/8	22 3/8	14 5/8	4	4	Adams County	WI	David O. Schwark	1996	16,111
127 5/8	21 6/8	21 0/8	16 0/8	4	5	Portage County	WI	Michael D. Maslinski	1996	16,111
127 5/8	21 5/8	22 6/8	20 1/8	5	5	Ingham County	MI	Scott David Trelstad	1996	16,111
127 5/8	19 7/8	19 7/8	16 1/8	5	5	Kent County	MI	Gerald Meyerink	1996	16,111
127 5/8	22 3/8	21 3/8	17 1/8	4	4	Polk County	WI	Jerry Lunde	1996	16,111
127 5/8	22 3/8	20 6/8	15 0/8	5	5	Buffalo County	WI	David E. Diederich	1996	16,111
127 5/8	19 4/8	19 4/8	14 1/8	5	6	Polk County	WI	Shawn D. Johnson	1996	16,111
127 5/8	19 4/8	19 4/8	18 2/8	6	7	Des Moines County	IA	Michael C. Dysh	1996	16,111
127 5/8	22 4/8	22 6/8	19 1/8	4	4	Calgary	ALB	Mark Joseph Colosi	1996	16,111
127 5/8	22 2/8	20 2/8	20 0/8	4	7	Ogle County	IL	Dennis J. Rinaldo	1996	16,111
127 5/8	21 2/8	20 6/8	15 5/8	5	5	Franklin County	GA	Stuart Bowers	1996	16,111
127 5/8	20 7/8	20 4/8	17 1/8	4	4	Ravalli County	MT	Wayne Capp	1996	16,111
127 5/8	23 3/8	22 5/8	19 3/8	4	4	Renville County	ND	Jerick W. Hensen	1996	16,111
127 5/8	20 6/8	20 5/8	13 3/8	5	5	St. Tammany Parish	LA	Greg Jourdan	1996	16,111
127 5/8	23 1/8	23 1/8	18 3/8	4	4	Tazewell County	IL	William L. Short, Jr.	1997	16,111
127 5/8	21 5/8	21 5/8	14 5/8	4	4	Buchanan County	IA	Randy Reck	1997	16,111
127 5/8	21 0/8	21 5/8	16 7/8	5	5	Pulaski County	AR	Brian Kirkendoll	1997	16,111
127 5/8	21 6/8	21 2/8	16 3/8	4	4	Columbia County	WI	Kim S. Ades	1997	16,111
127 5/8	23 5/8	21 4/8	18 3/8	4	5	Marquette County	WI	Jason Reetz	1997	16,111
127 5/8	23 2/8	20 6/8	20 3/8	5	4	Cattaraugus County	NY	Matt W. Whitcher	1997	16,111
127 5/8	22 7/8	23 4/8	17 5/8	5	5	Irion County	TX	Kevin Kittrell	1997	16,111
127 5/8	21 6/8	21 7/8	16 1/8	5	5	Pottawattamie County	IA	Rodney Stahlnecker	1997	16,111
127 5/8	23 0/8	23 1/8	17 7/8	4	4	Lenawee County	MI	Mark DeWayne Harris	1997	16,111
127 5/8	20 3/8	22 1/8	15 7/8	5	4	Woodford County	IL	William T. Trainor	1998	16,111
127 4/8	20 5/8	20 5/8	16 2/8	5	5	Boone County	MO	Roger Soukup	1978	16,221
127 4/8	20 3/8	20 6/8	16 6/8	5	5	Wapello County	IA	Arnold E. Vest	1978	16,221
127 4/8	23 5/8	22 5/8	17 2/8	6	5	Muskingum County	OH	Mike Harris	1980	16,221
127 4/8	21 4/8	21 5/8	17 1/8	4	7	Trego County	KS	Ron Bain	1981	16,221
127 4/8	21 5/8	22 6/8	18 5/8	7	5	Des Moines County	IA	Jim Edwards	1982	16,221
127 4/8	19 4/8	18 5/8	16 4/8	5	5	Allen County	KS	Ivan Cooper	1983	16,221
127 4/8	21 3/8	22 4/8	17 0/8	4	4	Lake County	IL	Mike Mitten	1983	16,221
127 4/8	23 0/8	23 2/8	19 2/8	4	4	Van Buren County	MI	Ken Probst	1983	16,221
127 4/8	21 1/8	20 7/8	15 0/8	5	4	Nodaway County	MO	Jeff Davison	1983	16,221
127 4/8	19 6/8	20 0/8	16 6/8	5	5	Cherokee County	KS	Larry Thomas	1983	16,221
127 4/8	22 4/8	22 5/8	20 3/8	5	4	Nacogdoches County	TX	Harvy Hamby	1984	16,221
127 4/8	20 2/8	20 5/8	14 4/8	5	6	Crawford County	WI	Emil H. Loether, Jr.	1984	16,221
127 4/8	23 6/8	23 5/8	18 0/8	4	4	Lee County	IA	David D. Zaehringer	1984	16,221
127 4/8	21 1/8	19 7/8	17 0/8	4	4	Henderson County	KY	Wesley Campbell	1985	16,221
127 4/8	23 5/8	23 3/8	19 4/8	4	4	Somerset County	NJ	Steve Kotz	1985	16,221
127 4/8	21 2/8	21 6/8	15 4/8	5	4	Sawyer County	WI	Bernard A. Gaure	1985	16,221
127 4/8	22 2/8	21 5/8	15 2/8	6	6	Lake County	IL	David Mitten	1986	16,221
127 4/8	23 2/8	23 3/8	17 2/8	5	4	Waukesha County	WI	Ron Hill	1986	16,221
127 4/8	20 4/8	20 1/8	17 2/8	6	6	Hall County	NE	Ken Elshof	1986	16,221
127 4/8	21 0/8	21 0/8	15 4/8	5	5	Buffalo County	WI	Richard J. Conrad	1986	16,221
127 4/8	23 1/8	24 4/8	23 0/8	4	6	Athens County	OH	Keith E. Moody	1986	16,221
127 4/8	21 4/8	21 6/8	18 4/8	4	4	Delaware County	IA	John Dillon	1986	16,221
127 4/8	21 3/8	21 7/8	16 4/8	5	5	Dimmit County	TX	Brett Crawford	1987	16,221
127 4/8	22 2/8	21 6/8	15 0/8	5	4	Pittsburg County	OK	David L. Scott	1987	16,221
127 4/8	20 1/8	19 3/8	16 4/8	5	6	Cooper County	MO	Joe Stenger	1988	16,221
127 4/8	22 3/8	22 3/8	18 2/8	4	5	Somerset County	NJ	James C. Kelly	1988	16,221
127 4/8	20 6/8	23 2/8	20 4/8	4	5	Putnam County	MO	Floyd Innis	1988	16,221
127 4/8	20 2/8	20 7/8	14 2/8	5	5	Johnson County	IN	Frank Cross	1988	16,221
127 4/8	23 3/8	23 3/8	16 4/8	4	4	Lake County	IL	Gene NeSmith	1988	16,221
127 4/8	21 0/8	20 2/8	13 0/8	4	6	Nelson County	KY	Cliff Buzick	1988	16,221
127 4/8	20 0/8	21 1/8	15 0/8	5	5	Osage County	OK	Paul Robinson	1989	16,221
127 4/8	23 6/8	23 7/8	20 0/8	3	4	Fillmore County	MN	Duane C. Baumler	1989	16,221
127 4/8	19 3/8	19 2/8	14 0/8	5	5	Amite County	MS	Bob Miller	1989	16,221
127 4/8	23 3/8	23 7/8	23 0/8	4	4	Muhlenberg County	KY	Scott Harper	1989	16,221
127 4/8	21 6/8	21 4/8	17 0/8	4	5	Cayuga County	NY	Donald W. Dennis	1989	16,221
127 4/8	22 4/8	22 6/8	18 0/8	4	4	Green County	WI	David R. Covert	1989	16,221
127 4/8	21 6/8	21 4/8	15 4/8	4	5	Waushara County	WI	Andrew D. Sobieski	1989	16,221
127 4/8	22 4/8	22 6/8	18 0/8	4	4	La Salle County	IL	Bill Yessa	1989	16,221
127 4/8	22 0/8	20 6/8	18 2/8	4	4	Dodge County	MN	Steve Hughes	1989	16,221
127 4/8	20 3/8	20 4/8	15 6/8	5	5	Oneida County	WI	George Nowak	1989	16,221
127 4/8	20 5/8	21 2/8	14 5/8	6	4	Jefferson County	MT	George A. Vinal	1990	16,221
127 4/8	19 1/8	19 0/8	15 2/8	5	5	Hardin County	IA	William Stonebraker	1990	16,221
127 4/8	22 2/8	22 6/8	17 0/8	4	4	Cass County	MI	Daniel R. Horak	1990	16,221
127 4/8	22 1/8	20 1/8	14 4/8	6	8	Henry County	MO	Marvin Ferguson	1990	16,221
127 4/8	21 1/8	20 0/8	16 2/8	4	4	Houston County	TX	Jerry Pruitt, Jr.	1990	16,221
127 4/8	22 1/8	21 1/8	13 1/8	5	5	Genesee County	NY	Mike L. Martin	1990	16,221
127 4/8	20 2/8	20 0/8	12 4/8	6	7	Calumet County	WI	Tom Brink	1990	16,221
127 4/8	24 1/8	14 5/8	18 4/8	5	4	Vernon County	MO	Greg Harris	1990	16,221
127 4/8	21 1/8	21 0/8	15 0/8	4	4	Hamilton County	KS	Rick D. Bennett	1990	16,221
127 4/8	21 0/8	21 0/8	15 3/8	6	6	Washburn County	WI	Scott McFarren	1990	16,221
127 4/8	21 6/8	20 6/8	13 4/8	4	5	Genesee County	MI	Mark Joseph O'Brien	1991	16,221
127 4/8	19 7/8	19 7/8	17 4/8	5	5	Magrath	ALB	Cam Cook	1991	16,221
127 4/8	20 6/8	21 6/8	15 4/8	4	4	Livingston County	MI	James D. Duke	1991	16,221
127 4/8	21 6/8	21 0/8	17 0/8	4	5	Worth County	IA	Tom L. Vorland	1991	16,221

WHITETAIL DEER (TYPICAL ANTLERS)

Minimum Score 125 — Continued

SCORE	R MAIN BEAM L		INSIDE SPREAD	R POINTS L		AREA	STATE/ PROVINCE	HUNTER'S NAME	DATE	RANK
127 4/8	20 4/8	21 0/8	18 0/8	5	5	Freeborn County	MN	Marvin Thompson	1991	16,221
127 4/8	22 4/8	22 0/8	18 0/8	4	4	Ste. Genevieve County	MO	Alvin Donze, Jr.	1991	16,221
127 4/8	19 2/8	19 1/8	12 6/8	5	5	Switzerland County	IN	Dennis Hardesty	1991	16,221
127 4/8	20 6/8	20 6/8	15 3/8	5	6	Ravalli County	MT	Ned Coorough	1991	16,221
127 4/8	20 2/8	20 2/8	15 4/8	4	6	Forest County	WI	Ron Matzdorf	1991	16,221
127 4/8	19 1/8	19 3/8	14 2/8	6	5	Waupaca County	WI	Roland Myers	1992	16,221
127 4/8	22 3/8	21 4/8	17 2/8	4	4	Washington County	MN	Robert E. Nordstrom	1992	16,221
127 4/8	22 0/8	21 6/8	17 6/8	4	4	Polk County	WI	Bruce L. Palmsteen	1992	16,221
127 4/8	25 6/8	24 0/8	14 4/8	4	6	Clay County	NE	David J. Hamik	1992	16,221
127 4/8	24 3/8	21 4/8	20 6/8	4	6	Juneau County	WI	John A. Elsing	1992	16,221
127 4/8	22 2/8	22 1/8	17 2/8	4	4	Monroe County	IN	Charles Morries	1992	16,221
127 4/8	20 6/8	20 7/8	15 4/8	5	5	Chisago County	MN	Bill Cordell	1992	16,221
127 4/8	22 4/8	21 7/8	16 4/8	4	5	Kane County	IL	Dale Hoekstra	1992	16,221
127 4/8	20 0/8	20 4/8	20 4/8	4	4	Washington County	MD	Mark Jenkins	1992	16,221
127 4/8	22 4/8	22 4/8	15 6/8	4	5	Clark County	WI	Scott Zimmer	1992	16,221
127 4/8	21 4/8	21 6/8	17 2/8	4	4	Crittenden County	KY	Steve Glover	1992	16,221
127 4/8	21 7/8	21 4/8	14 6/8	6	4	Grant County	WI	Kevin R. Kelly	1993	16,221
127 4/8	23 4/8	22 7/8	17 0/8	6	6	Waupaca County	WI	Daniel W. Schultz	1993	16,221
127 4/8	19 5/8	19 4/8	17 2/8	4	5	Sebastian County	AR	John Scott	1993	16,221
127 4/8	21 4/8	20 6/8	17 6/8	6	6	Monona County	IA	Roger Reiling	1993	16,221
127 4/8	21 5/8	22 2/8	14 4/8	5	5	La Salle County	TX	Roger Wintle	1993	16,221
127 4/8	21 7/8	22 1/8	15 6/8	4	5	Belknap County	NH	James Henaghan	1994	16,221
127 4/8	22 1/8	21 2/8	18 2/8	5	5	Marathon County	WI	Jeff Firkus	1994	16,221
127 4/8	21 7/8	21 3/8	17 7/8	5	5	Huntington County	IN	Gregory A. Yahne	1994	16,221
127 4/8	22 0/8	22 2/8	17 2/8	4	4	Washington County	MN	Ray Durushia	1994	16,221
127 4/8	21 5/8	19 3/8	17 6/8	5	6	Hillsdale County	MI	Thomas R. Johnson	1994	16,221
127 4/8	22 4/8	23 1/8	18 5/8	4	5	Will County	IL	Tom Spence	1994	16,221
127 4/8	23 3/8	23 3/8	20 1/8	4	5	Bayfield County	WI	Brian L. Gerndt	1994	16,221
127 4/8	22 0/8	22 0/8	15 0/8	4	4	Crawford County	IL	Joe Patterson	1994	16,221
127 4/8	20 3/8	20 6/8	16 2/8	5	5	Sebastian County	AR	Mark Breashears	1994	16,221
127 4/8	22 6/8	22 1/8	14 2/8	5	4	Yancey County	NC	Nelson S. Burnette	1995	16,221
127 4/8	21 0/8	20 7/8	18 4/8	4	4	Carter County	MO	Lloyd G. Shelton	1995	16,221
127 4/8	21 2/8	20 6/8	20 4/8	4	4	Anderson County	TX	Bill Griswold	1995	16,221
127 4/8	23 0/8	23 3/8	18 4/8	4	4	Kent County	MI	William J. Fierens	1995	16,221
127 4/8	20 6/8	20 4/8	14 4/8	5	5	Sullivan County	IN	Mike Crist	1995	16,221
127 4/8	23 6/8	21 3/8	16 0/8	4	4	Greene County	IA	Dennis Matthews	1995	16,221
127 4/8	20 2/8	20 0/8	15 2/8	4	4	Tuscarawas County	OH	James C. Alexander, Jr.	1995	16,221
127 4/8	22 2/8	22 3/8	17 2/8	4	5	Kent County	MD	Bruce Fair	1995	16,221
127 4/8	22 1/8	22 2/8	16 2/8	5	5	Oakland County	MI	Brian McCarthy	1996	16,221
127 4/8	24 7/8	20 3/8	18 7/8	5	4	Seminole County	OK	Jason Ryan Miles	1996	16,221
127 4/8	20 2/8	19 2/8	19 6/8	6	5	San Patricio County	TX	Gary McKinny	1996	16,221
127 4/8	20 6/8	21 4/8	16 6/8	5	5	Columbia County	WI	Pete Schwoch	1996	16,221
127 4/8	25 4/8	25 0/8	14 4/8	3	4	Bristol County	MA	Brian Ramos	1996	16,221
127 4/8	21 3/8	20 5/8	14 6/8	5	4	Allamakee County	IA	Glenn Salow	1996	16,221
127 4/8	21 0/8	20 6/8	15 4/8	4	4	Woods County	OK	Kevin L. Dupus	1996	16,221
127 4/8	21 0/8	20 2/8	16 2/8	5	5	Edmunds County	SD	David D. Perrion	1996	16,221
127 4/8	22 0/8	22 4/8	17 2/8	5	5	Duval County	TX	Shirley Oatman	1997	16,221
127 4/8	20 4/8	19 6/8	14 7/8	4	4	Portage County	WI	Michael J. Somers	1997	16,221
127 4/8	23 3/8	24 5/8	19 0/8	6	5	Orange County	NC	David King, Jr.	1997	16,221
127 4/8	21 5/8	21 1/8	16 2/8	4	5	Cullman County	AL	Tim McKoy	1997	16,221
127 4/8	22 6/8	23 3/8	16 2/8	4	4	Dane County	WI	Mike Hughes	1997	16,221
127 4/8	20 7/8	19 1/8	16 2/8	5	5	Buffalo County	NE	Bruce L. Zeller	1997	16,221
127 4/8	20 2/8	19 3/8	16 0/8	5	5	Clark County	WI	James Boyer	1997	16,221
127 4/8	24 1/8	23 6/8	17 4/8	6	5	Jasper County	IA	Joe Carmichael	1997	16,221
127 4/8	20 4/8	20 6/8	18 6/8	5	5	Jones County	IA	Tracy Lee Meyers	1997	16,221
127 4/8	19 5/8	23 0/8	22 6/8	4	4	Dorchester County	MD	Philip Burch	1997	16,221
127 4/8	21 5/8	20 1/8	17 4/8	5	5	Harrison County	IA	Rodney Stahlnecker	1997	16,221
127 4/8	21 6/8	21 6/8	19 4/8	4	4	Walworth County	WI	Jeffrey G. Wiswell	1997	16,221
127 4/8	23 2/8	23 1/8	14 0/8	6	6	Haskell County	KS	Neal Heaton	1997	16,221
127 4/8	21 7/8	22 1/8	17 4/8	4	5	Jasper County	IA	Alan Good	1997	16,221
127 4/8	23 1/8	23 3/8	18 4/8	4	6	Will County	IL	David G. Whitehouse	1997	16,221
127 4/8	22 1/8	20 3/8	15 2/8	5	5	Elgin	ONT	Jeff Black	1997	16,221
127 4/8	21 3/8	22 4/8	20 0/8	4	4	La Crosse County	WI	Chris J. Houle	1997	16,221
127 4/8	19 7/8	20 0/8	16 5/8	5	6	Allen County	KY	Kevin Rippy	1998	16,221
127 4/8	19 5/8	21 5/8	16 6/8	5	5	Gallatin County	MT	Brian F. Koelzer	1998	16,221
127 4/8	23 0/8	21 3/8	16 6/8	4	4	Dodge County	NE	Nick Bilava	1998	16,221
127 3/8	22 0/8	22 1/8	17 3/8	4	4	Lee County	IA	Lewallen Foster	1972	16,341
127 3/8	19 5/8	19 7/8	17 1/8	6	5	Scott County	KY	John Farris	1977	16,341
127 3/8	20 1/8	20 4/8	16 7/8	4	5	Suffolk County	NY	William R. Quarltere	1979	16,341
127 3/8	21 6/8	21 1/8	15 6/8	5	5	Waupaca County	WI	Daniel E. Yaeger	1979	16,341
127 3/8	21 6/8	22 0/8	22 0/8	5	5	Cortland County	NY	John B. Andrews	1980	16,341
127 3/8	22 3/8	22 1/8	17 1/8	5	5	Washington County	KS	Bob Funke	1981	16,341
127 3/8	20 5/8	21 7/8	17 1/8	8	7	Sauk County	WI	Roger D. Vondrasek	1981	16,341
127 3/8	21 1/8	20 3/8	15 5/8	6	6	Miami County	KS	Tom Wiggin	1982	16,341
127 3/8	20 3/8	20 2/8	17 3/8	4	4	Neosho County	KS	John R. Blackburn	1983	16,341
127 3/8	23 6/8	23 0/8	18 1/8	4	4	Reno County	KS	Greig Sims	1983	16,341
127 3/8	20 0/8	20 0/8	17 7/8	5	5	Waldo County	ME	Debbie A. Small	1984	16,341
127 3/8	21 3/8	22 6/8	13 7/8	5	5	Columbia County	WI	Richard J. Sutter	1985	16,341

WHITETAIL DEER (TYPICAL ANTLERS)

Minimum Score 125

SCORE	LENGTH OF MAIN BEAM R	LENGTH OF MAIN BEAM L	INSIDE SPREAD	NUMBER OF POINTS R	NUMBER OF POINTS L	AREA	STATE/PROVINCE	HUNTER'S NAME	DATE	RANK
127 3/8	20 5/8	21 3/8	18 7/8	4	4	Outagamie County	WI	Robert Randerson	1985	16,341
127 3/8	22 2/8	23 0/8	15 7/8	4	4	La Salle County	IL	Rich Castelli	1986	16,341
127 3/8	18 7/8	18 6/8	17 2/8	5	6	Wallowa County	OR	Ken Purnell	1987	16,341
127 3/8	20 4/8	20 7/8	22 3/8	4	4	Carroll County	OH	John M Shockey	1987	16,341
127 3/8	21 3/8	22 2/8	17 2/8	5	6	Sauk County	WI	Mike Jensen	1987	16,341
127 3/8	20 2/8	22 0/8	16 3/8	4	4	Will County	IL	Mike Kluska	1987	16,341
127 3/8	23 4/8	23 1/8	18 1/8	4	4	Chippewa County	MI	Gary E. Messer	1987	16,341
127 3/8	22 5/8	22 2/8	16 5/8	4	4	Woodbury County	IA	Terry Lee Hansen	1988	16,341
127 3/8	22 3/8	20 4/8	17 1/8	7	5	Sauk County	WI	Garry D. Bunz	1988	16,341
127 3/8	22 7/8	22 7/8	15 7/8	5	4	Lawrence County	OH	Mike Dickess	1988	16,341
127 3/8	20 6/8	21 3/8	15 3/8	6	5	Chisago County	MN	Daniel Carlson	1988	16,341
127 3/8	21 2/8	20 0/8	18 1/8	4	4	Clay County	IA	Steve Stoermer	1988	16,341
127 3/8	20 1/8	20 4/8	15 1/8	4	4	Somerset County	MD	Donald H. Ennis	1988	16,341
127 3/8	21 1/8	21 2/8	17 4/8	7	5	McLean County	IL	Barbara Eades	1988	16,341
127 3/8	20 0/8	20 0/8	15 1/8	5	5	Forest County	WI	Chuck W. Wruck	1989	16,341
127 3/8	23 7/8	23 2/8	17 5/8	4	4	Buffalo County	WI	Greg Lorenz	1989	16,341
127 3/8	22 1/8	22 3/8	16 5/8	4	4	Kingman County	KS	Terry Morisse	1989	16,341
127 3/8	20 2/8	20 0/8	14 5/8	5	5	Brown County	WI	Don Maurer	1989	16,341
127 3/8	23 1/8	23 0/8	17 3/8	7	5	Clinton County	MI	Mark J. Morgan	1989	16,341
127 3/8	21 0/8	21 0/8	16 1/8	5	5	Chippewa County	WI	Steve R. Rank	1989	16,341
127 3/8	21 6/8	20 2/8	18 1/8	4	4	Caroline County	MD	Eric Wise	1989	16,341
127 3/8	21 2/8	20 4/8	17 6/8	5	5	Marathon County	WI	Barry Gertschen	1990	16,341
127 3/8	19 7/8	20 5/8	19 7/8	5	5	Ogle County	IL	Brent Rutherford	1990	16,341
127 3/8	22 6/8	22 1/8	18 5/8	4	4	Perry County	IL	Scott Rice	1990	16,341
127 3/8	23 4/8	24 1/8	19 3/8	5	4	Lee County	IL	Gordon Gableman	1990	16,341
127 3/8	21 7/8	22 0/8	18 4/8	4	6	Tulsa County	OK	Carl Chisom	1990	16,341
127 3/8	20 6/8	23 0/8	20 5/8	4	5	Berks County	PA	Richard S. Steiger	1991	16,341
127 3/8	22 2/8	22 6/8	16 5/8	4	5	Rusk County	WI	Roger Schumacher	1991	16,341
127 3/8	22 6/8	24 0/8	17 7/8	4	4	Talbot County	MD	Mark E. Laustsen	1991	16,341
127 3/8	22 6/8	23 0/8	14 1/8	4	4	Worcester County	MA	Jerry Ridley	1991	16,341
127 3/8	22 5/8	20 1/8	17 2/8	5	7	Andrew County	MO	Dan A. McLaughlin	1991	16,341
127 3/8	23 7/8	24 3/8	17 2/8	5	7	Champaign County	OH	Dan Short	1992	16,341
127 3/8	21 2/8	21 7/8	18 5/8	4	5	Buffalo County	WI	Jay J. Snopek	1992	16,341
127 3/8	19 4/8	18 7/8	15 3/8	5	5	Taylor County	WI	Steven L. Howe	1992	16,341
127 3/8	21 1/8	19 7/8	17 1/8	4	4	Parke County	IN	C. Wayne Loomis	1992	16,341
127 3/8	20 1/8	19 2/8	16 5/8	5	5	Price County	WI	Bill C. Getzloff	1992	16,341
127 3/8	23 1/8	20 6/8	16 1/8	4	4	Buffalo County	WI	Wayne Olson	1992	16,341
127 3/8	20 2/8	19 7/8	16 1/8	5	5	Oakland County	MI	Stephen Donald Austin	1992	16,341
127 3/8	20 0/8	20 4/8	17 0/8	6	5	Jackson County	IL	Bryan Campbell	1992	16,341
127 3/8	22 0/8	22 4/8	24 6/8	5	5	Ogle County	IL	Dean Kruger	1992	16,341
127 3/8	18 2/8	19 3/8	13 5/8	5	5	Morrison County	MN	James G. Anderson	1992	16,341
127 3/8	23 2/8	22 4/8	15 5/8	5	5	Boone County	IN	Larry A. Culley	1992	16,341
127 3/8	20 2/8	20 1/8	14 3/8	5	5	Faribault County	MN	Kevin Benson	1993	16,341
127 3/8	20 6/8	20 6/8	17 7/8	4	4	Bayfield County	WI	Mike Haroldson	1993	16,341
127 3/8	25 2/8	24 4/8	17 1/8	5	5	Hancock County	OH	Craig W. Sherman	1993	16,341
127 3/8	21 2/8	21 0/8	16 5/8	5	4	Shiawassee County	MI	Guy Jerome Ursery	1993	16,341
127 3/8	19 4/8	19 7/8	16 1/8	5	5	Granby River	BC	Eric Hoglund	1993	16,341
127 3/8	21 5/8	21 0/8	16 5/8	5	5	Steuben County	IN	Matthew C. Sommers	1994	16,341
127 3/8	22 1/8	22 1/8	18 1/8	4	4	Buffalo County	WI	Daniel Wenger	1994	16,341
127 3/8	21 1/8	21 2/8	16 3/8	5	5	Albany County	NY	Joe Vivenzio	1994	16,341
127 3/8	21 1/8	21 3/8	16 5/8	5	5	Ontario County	NY	Steve Posick	1994	16,341
127 3/8	22 1/8	21 6/8	16 3/8	4	4	Columbia County	WI	Shane D. Horton	1994	16,341
127 3/8	22 0/8	22 2/8	17 5/8	4	4	Huron County	MI	John A. McGrath	1994	16,341
127 3/8	22 2/8	22 3/8	15 5/8	6	5	Kalamazoo County	MI	Danne L. Willoughby	1994	16,341
127 3/8	20 2/8	20 6/8	19 5/8	5	4	Somerset County	NJ	Joseph Accardi, Jr.	1995	16,341
127 3/8	18 2/8	18 1/8	14 7/8	5	5	Frio County	TX	Andy Milam	1995	16,341
127 3/8	23 6/8	22 5/8	18 0/8	6	6	Buffalo County	WI	Ron Heidenreich	1995	16,341
127 3/8	21 0/8	19 6/8	18 1/8	4	5	Washington County	IA	Rick A. Albers	1995	16,341
127 3/8	22 3/8	22 5/8	18 5/8	4	4	Montgomery County	PA	Joseph E. DeAngelis	1995	16,341
127 3/8	21 1/8	20 5/8	14 3/8	4	5	Medina County	TX	Kip M. Melancon	1995	16,341
127 3/8	23 0/8	21 7/8	16 5/8	5	4	Pike County	IL	Robert Sacher	1995	16,341
127 3/8	22 1/8	21 1/8	15 3/8	4	5	Richland County	IL	Don Huskey	1995	16,341
127 3/8	18 7/8	19 4/8	16 5/8	4	4	Cook County	IL	LeRoy Peart	1995	16,341
127 3/8	19 5/8	19 2/8	14 1/8	5	5	La Salle County	TX	Billy Risseeuw	1995	16,341
127 3/8	19 6/8	21 2/8	18 0/8	6	4	Portage County	WI	Thomas J. Mocadlo, Jr.	1996	16,341
127 3/8	19 4/8	19 6/8	15 7/8	4	4	Jefferson County	WI	Thomas Underwood	1996	16,341
127 3/8	22 0/8	22 2/8	18 3/8	4	5	Pottawatomie County	KS	Michael Schirer	1996	16,341
127 3/8	22 6/8	22 2/8	17 2/8	6	4	Licking County	OH	Jose Luis Ortega	1996	16,341
127 3/8	20 2/8	20 5/8	15 3/8	4	5	Waushara County	WI	Tom Wilson	1997	16,341
127 3/8	21 2/8	21 4/8	17 5/8	5	5	Vernon County	WI	Dennis W. FLynn	1997	16,341
127 3/8	21 4/8	22 2/8	17 3/8	6	11	Washington County	IA	John H. Allard	1997	16,341
127 3/8	23 1/8	21 3/8	16 5/8	4	4	Buffalo County	WI	Steve D. Tenner	1997	16,341
127 3/8	23 3/8	24 6/8	16 1/8	6	5	Shelby County	IL	Mark K. Rothrock	1997	16,341
127 3/8	23 4/8	22 6/8	19 5/8	5	5	Schoharie County	NY	Todd Stoller	1997	16,341
127 2/8	22 2/8	23 1/8	16 2/8	5	5	Madison County	AR	Johnny Darris	1964	16,427
127 2/8	23 5/8	23 7/8	16 4/8	4	3	Lawrence County	IL	Steven R. Tice	1967	16,427
127 2/8	22 0/8	21 3/8	17 2/8	4	5	Champaign County	IL	Pete Shepley	1972	16,427
127 2/8	20 1/8	20 2/8	16 0/8	5	5	Ontario County	NY	Robert G. Achter	1973	16,427

WHITETAIL DEER (TYPICAL ANTLERS)

Minimum Score 125 Continued

SCORE	LENGTH OF R MAIN BEAM L		INSIDE SPREAD	NUMBER OF R POINTS L		AREA	STATE/ PROVINCE	HUNTER'S NAME	DATE	RANK
127 2/8	19 2/8	19 0/8	15 2/8	5	5	Blue Earth County	MN	Stanley R. Defries	1973	16,427
127 2/8	21 7/8	22 3/8	17 2/8	4	4	Latah County	ID	Mike VonLindern	1978	16,427
127 2/8	21 7/8	21 2/8	15 6/8	5	4	Jefferson County	IN	Robert Pitt	1978	16,427
127 2/8	23 6/8	22 4/8	20 2/8	4	4	Bayfield County	WI	Mark Milford	1980	16,427
127 2/8	22 4/8	21 6/8	16 4/8	4	5	Oconto County	WI	Don Fullerton	1982	16,427
127 2/8	23 3/8	21 3/8	20 3/8	5	5	Hunterdon County	NJ	Wayne Lisehora	1982	16,427
127 2/8	22 1/8	21 3/8	17 4/8	4	4	Stanley County	SD	Brad Taylor	1983	16,427
127 2/8	22 2/8	22 1/8	17 4/8	5	5	Sauk County	WI	James Byrnes	1983	16,427
127 2/8	23 1/8	24 0/8	19 4/8	6	9	Morrison County	MN	Ken Arnzen	1984	16,427
127 2/8	22 0/8	21 5/8	16 7/8	7	5	Christian County	IL	James Eck	1984	16,427
127 2/8	20 2/8	20 0/8	20 3/8	4	4	Towner County	ND	Trent Halberstroh	1984	16,427
127 2/8	22 6/8	23 2/8	14 6/8	4	4	Grant County	OK	Ronnie B Smart	1985	16,427
127 2/8	21 0/8	19 6/8	13 6/8	5	4	Marshall County	KS	Ray Aslin	1985	16,427
127 2/8	23 2/8	20 5/8	16 6/8	5	4	Clay County	KS	Jan Kissinger	1985	16,427
127 2/8	22 3/8	21 7/8	16 3/8	6	5	Powell County	MT	Sonny Templeton	1985	16,427
127 2/8	22 1/8	22 0/8	16 4/8	4	4	Dane County	WI	Perry R. Peterson	1986	16,427
127 2/8	20 5/8	20 6/8	13 6/8	4	4	McLean County	ND	Eugene Radke	1986	16,427
127 2/8	20 6/8	20 3/8	14 2/8	4	4	Keya Paha County	NE	Keith Nordeen	1986	16,427
127 2/8	24 0/8	23 4/8	16 4/8	5	5	Bertie County	NC	Roy Copeland	1986	16,427
127 2/8	19 0/8	16 4/8	17 4/8	5	5	Buffalo County	WI	Peter J. Mancl	1986	16,427
127 2/8	21 3/8	21 0/8	16 2/8	4	4	Pierce County	WI	Danny White	1986	16,427
127 2/8	22 0/8	22 0/8	17 0/8	5	5	Pittsburg County	OK	Mike Plunkett	1986	16,427
127 2/8	20 5/8	22 2/8	15 6/8	5	5	Calgary	ALB	Eric Soderberg	1986	16,427
127 2/8	20 6/8	20 6/8	15 2/8	5	4	Piatt County	IL	Eileen De Moss	1986	16,427
127 2/8	18 1/8	18 5/8	15 6/8	5	5	Botetourt County	VA	Charles E. Speck	1987	16,427
127 2/8	21 7/8	22 2/8	18 4/8	4	5	Peoria County	IL	Roger Arends	1987	16,427
127 2/8	21 2/8	21 3/8	16 6/8	4	4	Kent County	MI	Steve VanDerLaan	1987	16,427
127 2/8	22 3/8	21 4/8	18 0/8	4	5	Llano County	TX	Mark Warren	1988	16,427
127 2/8	20 2/8	20 5/8	15 0/8	4	4	Oklahoma County	OK	Bill F. Noble	1988	16,427
127 2/8	20 3/8	22 2/8	16 7/8	7	6	Cerro Gordo County	IA	Vern Schnoebelen	1988	16,427
127 2/8	23 0/8	21 6/8	18 6/8	6	4	Wayne County	NY	Jason S. Haas	1988	16,427
127 2/8	21 2/8	21 3/8	16 1/8	6	4	Cass County	MI	Michael L. Ritter	1988	16,427
127 2/8	21 1/8	21 0/8	17 4/8	4	4	Kane County	IL	Chuck Grant	1988	16,427
127 2/8	20 6/8	21 3/8	14 4/8	5	5	Otoe County	NE	Rick Lee Sedersten	1988	16,427
127 2/8	21 2/8	21 2/8	16 4/8	5	4	Barber County	KS	Bob Christensen	1988	16,427
127 2/8	18 6/8	18 7/8	17 2/8	6	6	Will County	IL	Tom S. Spence	1989	16,427
127 2/8	22 5/8	22 7/8	18 4/8	4	4	Jackson County	WI	Dave Arentz	1989	16,427
127 2/8	20 0/8	19 7/8	14 2/8	5	5	McPherson County	KS	Jimmy Dean Beard	1989	16,427
127 2/8	21 2/8	22 0/8	20 0/8	4	4	Prince Georges County	MD	Russell A. Nichols	1989	16,427
127 2/8	20 6/8	20 4/8	15 2/8	5	4	Butler County	KS	Dean Roedel, Jr.	1989	16,427
127 2/8	24 0/8	23 4/8	16 1/8	5	5	Henry County	KY	Kenneth R. Fante	1990	16,427
127 2/8	23 2/8	23 0/8	16 6/8	4	4	Clayton County	GA	Rodney Chris Bishop	1990	16,427
127 2/8	23 7/8	23 2/8	19 2/8	4	4	Trimble County	KY	Bill Drane	1990	16,427
127 2/8	19 7/8	19 1/8	12 4/8	6	5	Jefferson County	KS	Brian Artzer	1990	16,427
127 2/8	21 5/8	21 5/8	16 0/8	5	5	Trempealeau County	WI	Rusty Severson	1990	16,427
127 2/8	19 7/8	20 2/8	15 0/8	5	4	Wayne County	NY	Allan C. Tyo	1990	16,427
127 2/8	21 2/8	21 6/8	17 6/8	5	6	Athens County	OH	James S. Shipley	1990	16,427
127 2/8	23 0/8	22 5/8	19 0/8	4	5	Ellis County	OK	Bill Parry	1991	16,427
127 2/8	22 1/8	22 7/8	17 4/8	4	4	Wentworth	ONT	Kevin Parchem	1991	16,427
127 2/8	20 4/8	19 7/8	16 6/8	5	5	Washington County	PA	Bill B. Carden	1991	16,427
127 2/8	23 2/8	22 5/8	14 4/8	4	4	Highland County	OH	Martin Bullock	1991	16,427
127 2/8	20 3/8	21 3/8	14 6/8	5	7	Burleigh County	ND	Garett Strandemo	1991	16,427
127 2/8	22 2/8	21 7/8	19 2/8	4	4	Westchester County	NY	Steven Willard	1991	16,427
127 2/8	21 6/8	21 6/8	20 6/8	4	4	Logan County	IL	Steve Schilling	1991	16,427
127 2/8	22 6/8	23 0/8	23 0/8	5	5	Walworth County	WI	Jesse Adams, Jr.	1991	16,427
127 2/8	23 4/8	22 4/8	17 6/8	4	4	Wyandot County	OH	James D. Herring	1991	16,427
127 2/8	19 4/8	17 0/8	14 0/8	5	5	Waushara County	WI	Ron Inda	1992	16,427
127 2/8	21 3/8	21 6/8	16 2/8	4	4	Roscommon County	MI	Donald V. Hine	1992	16,427
127 2/8	21 3/8	19 1/8	16 4/8	5	5	Buffalo County	WI	Fred Neitzel	1992	16,427
127 2/8	19 7/8	22 1/8	19 2/8	6	6	Piatt County	IL	David James	1992	16,427
127 2/8	25 0/8	26 0/8	20 6/8	4	4	Peoria County	IL	Larry E. Pollack	1992	16,427
127 2/8	20 4/8	20 5/8	14 2/8	5	5	Webster County	KY	Robert George	1992	16,427
127 2/8	22 2/8	22 2/8	16 0/8	4	5	Harrison County	OH	Larry Holjencin	1992	16,427
127 2/8	23 1/8	22 5/8	16 5/8	4	6	Van Buren County	IA	John "Rosey" Roseland	1992	16,427
127 2/8	23 3/8	22 6/8	21 1/8	4	5	Hardin County	IL	Jeffrey L. Hall	1992	16,427
127 2/8	22 4/8	22 4/8	19 6/8	4	4	Montgomery County	KS	Sean Moody	1992	16,427
127 2/8	21 7/8	22 1/8	16 4/8	4	5	Washington County	IA	Mel Miller	1992	16,427
127 2/8	23 3/8	22 7/8	16 4/8	4	5	Caswell County	NC	Larry Wayne Pruitt, Jr.	1993	16,427
127 2/8	21 2/8	22 0/8	19 0/8	4	4	Harding County	SD	Kim R. Smith	1993	16,427
127 2/8	21 3/8	21 1/8	14 6/8	6	7	Osage County	OK	Joe Admire, Jr.	1993	16,427
127 2/8	21 5/8	22 1/8	18 2/8	4	4	Meeker County	MN	Drew Braseth	1993	16,427
127 2/8	23 5/8	23 3/8	19 7/8	6	7	Frio County	TX	Andy Milam	1993	16,427
127 2/8	22 0/8	22 3/8	14 0/8	5	5	Lincoln County	MO	Steve Hermann	1993	16,427
127 2/8	18 2/8	18 4/8	17 6/8	5	5	Goshen County	WY	Jeff Fitts	1993	16,427
127 2/8	20 6/8	21 7/8	17 6/8	5	5	La Salle County	TX	Neal Bouldin	1994	16,427
127 2/8	19 4/8	18 7/8	16 4/8	7	6	Fergus County	MT	Chris G. Sanford	1994	16,427
127 2/8	20 4/8	21 1/8	16 6/8	5	6	Iowa County	WI	Terry Yanske	1994	16,427
127 2/8	22 6/8	22 3/8	15 6/8	4	4	Columbia County	NY	Ed Van Nostrand, Sr.	1994	16,427

WHITETAIL DEER (TYPICAL ANTLERS)

Minimum Score 125 — Continued

SCORE	LENGTH OF MAIN BEAM R	LENGTH OF MAIN BEAM L	INSIDE SPREAD	NUMBER OF POINTS R	NUMBER OF POINTS L	AREA	STATE/PROVINCE	HUNTER'S NAME	DATE	RANK
127 2/8	21 4/8	21 5/8	18 2/8	10	7	Marquette County	WI	Mark O. Judas	1994	16,427
127 2/8	20 4/8	21 0/8	13 0/8	6	6	Lincoln County	NE	Ron Rockwell	1994	16,427
127 2/8	23 5/8	23 1/8	17 6/8	4	4	Bucks County	PA	Stephen C. Kremp	1994	16,427
127 2/8	20 1/8	19 6/8	18 2/8	5	5	Macon County	MO	Mike Cherner	1994	16,427
127 2/8	22 0/8	22 1/8	17 4/8	5	5	Eau Claire County	WI	Riley Fletchshock	1994	16,427
127 2/8	20 7/8	19 0/8	16 2/8	6	6	Nicholas County	KY	Tip Fryman	1994	16,427
127 2/8	21 2/8	22 0/8	18 6/8	5	5	Dane County	WI	K-Tal Johnson	1994	16,427
127 2/8	19 5/8	19 7/8	14 2/8	4	4	Valley County	MT	Todd W. Henck	1994	16,427
127 2/8	25 0/8	25 3/8	19 0/8	4	5	Clinton County	MO	Steve Chaney	1994	16,427
127 2/8	22 0/8	22 1/8	14 2/8	4	4	Scott County	KY	Robin A. Kern	1995	16,427
127 2/8	20 4/8	19 2/8	18 2/8	5	5	Shawano County	WI	James Lemke	1995	16,427
127 2/8	20 1/8	20 4/8	18 4/8	5	5	East Feliciana Parish	LA	Clint Michael Levert	1995	16,427
127 2/8	21 2/8	22 0/8	18 0/8	4	4	Osceola County	MI	Joseph Kovach	1995	16,427
127 2/8	22 0/8	21 4/8	19 2/8	5	5	Delaware County	OH	David D. Skutt	1995	16,427
127 2/8	25 1/8	24 0/8	17 6/8	4	4	Kenedy County	TX	Gary F. Bogner	1995	16,427
127 2/8	22 5/8	23 4/8	19 2/8	4	6	Gallia County	OH	Randy Epling	1995	16,427
127 2/8	22 0/8	21 3/8	18 0/8	7	5	Pike County	MO	Brad Hackett	1995	16,427
127 2/8	21 2/8	21 2/8	14 6/8	5	5	Jackson County	WI	Paul J. Tessmer	1995	16,427
127 2/8	21 2/8	21 5/8	17 6/8	7	5	Saline County	KS	Philip D. Baltazor	1995	16,427
127 2/8	20 1/8	20 4/8	17 4/8	6	5	Will County	IL	Kenneth A. Genovese	1995	16,427
127 2/8	21 6/8	21 7/8	14 0/8	4	4	Cass County	IA	Steve Mathias	1995	16,427
127 2/8	21 0/8	22 2/8	16 2/8	4	4	Pike County	IL	Joel P. Hunt	1996	16,427
127 2/8	19 4/8	19 0/8	12 7/8	7	6	Monroe County	IN	Kenny Webb	1996	16,427
127 2/8	22 5/8	22 3/8	20 4/8	4	4	Wayne County	NY	Ronald Pollay	1996	16,427
127 2/8	20 3/8	20 0/8	16 0/8	4	5	Fulton County	PA	Charles W. Rehor	1996	16,427
127 2/8	20 2/8	20 3/8	17 6/8	4	4	Washington County	KS	Stanley J. Brustowicz	1996	16,427
127 2/8	22 5/8	21 5/8	17 2/8	5	3	Houghton County	MI	Dan Infalt	1996	16,427
127 2/8	22 4/8	21 2/8	17 6/8	4	4	Jim Wells County	TX	Chuck McKinny	1997	16,427
127 2/8	20 2/8	20 6/8	16 0/8	4	4	Linn County	MO	Bill Rogers	1997	16,427
127 2/8	21 6/8	21 5/8	23 2/8	4	5	Erath County	TX	James Burns	1997	16,427
127 2/8	21 5/8	21 4/8	13 2/8	5	5	Montgomery County	PA	Bob Moody	1997	16,427
127 2/8	21 4/8	20 7/8	17 4/8	4	4	Iron County	WI	John Michalski	1997	16,427
127 2/8	21 0/8	20 1/8	17 2/8	4	5	Morgan County	IL	Philip K. Estell	1997	16,427
127 2/8	21 4/8	21 1/8	14 1/8	5	5	Columbia County	WI	Lane Furseth	1997	16,427
127 2/8	21 7/8	23 0/8	16 2/8	5	4	Washington County	WI	Tom Isaac	1997	16,427
127 2/8	21 0/8	21 4/8	16 4/8	4	4	Concho County	TX	Jeff Simmons	1997	16,427
127 2/8	21 2/8	23 0/8	15 6/8	4	6	Venango County	PA	James M. Varga	1997	16,427
127 2/8	22 2/8	21 6/8	17 0/8	4	5	Chautauqua County	KS	Jon R. Burgdorf	1997	16,427
127 2/8	23 1/8	22 4/8	17 7/8	5	4	Marshall County	AL	James R. "Bob" Taylor	1997	16,427
127 2/8	21 3/8	20 5/8	17 1/8	5	6	Morton County	ND	Dennis R. Erhardt	1998	16,427
127 2/8	21 2/8	21 0/8	15 0/8	4	4	Regina	SAS	Dean Koch	1998	16,427
127 2/8	20 3/8	21 1/8	15 4/8	5	6	Allegan County	MI	Daniel L. Reed	1998	16,427
127 1/8	19 5/8	20 5/8	15 1/8	4	4	Oneida County	WI	Fred Felbab	1961	16,551
127 1/8	21 0/8	20 4/8	18 3/8	6	5	Marion County	IA	Donald C. Clark	1970	16,551
127 1/8	18 0/8	20 5/8	15 5/8	5	5	Des Moines County	IA	Roy Veach	1970	16,551
127 1/8	23 0/8	23 0/8	16 7/8	4	4	Union County	IA	Richard Siddens	1971	16,551
127 1/8	22 7/8	21 6/8	16 5/8	5	5	Gratiot County	MI	Kim Hagerman	1979	16,551
127 1/8	20 6/8	21 4/8	16 5/8	4	4	Keith County	NE	Tom Tietz	1981	16,551
127 1/8	21 6/8	23 3/8	18 7/8	4	4	Massac County	IL	John Shelby	1981	16,551
127 1/8	19 4/8	20 2/8	16 3/8	5	6	Bon Homme County	SD	John P. Freidel	1982	16,551
127 1/8	20 3/8	19 1/8	16 5/8	5	5	Jefferson County	IL	Ed Knaus	1983	16,551
127 1/8	20 2/8	21 3/8	18 5/8	5	5	Leavenworth County	KS	Albert Lyle Karl	1983	16,551
127 1/8	21 3/8	21 4/8	17 0/8	5	5	Bullock County	AL	James D Sims	1984	16,551
127 1/8	21 6/8	21 7/8	15 3/8	5	5	Madison County	NY	Louis A Colasanti	1984	16,551
127 1/8	23 4/8	21 5/8	18 3/8	5	5	Wyandotte County	KS	Spencer G. Ishmael	1984	16,551
127 1/8	19 6/8	21 2/8	14 0/8	5	6	Scott County	MN	Ron Stier	1984	16,551
127 1/8	22 1/8	20 7/8	18 5/8	5	5	Somerset County	NJ	Joe Cotone	1985	16,551
127 1/8	23 1/8	24 1/8	19 0/8	8	6	Ogle County	IL	Bifford J. Wyatt	1985	16,551
127 1/8	22 6/8	23 4/8	16 3/8	5	4	Scott County	IA	Ronald L. Mott	1985	16,551
127 1/8	20 2/8	20 0/8	16 1/8	4	5	Cowley County	KS	Jack L. Dennett, Jr.	1986	16,551
127 1/8	23 0/8	22 5/8	18 4/8	6	4	Yuma County	CO	Tony Seahorn	1986	16,551
127 1/8	19 4/8	20 0/8	15 5/8	4	4	Forest County	WI	Ron Van Straten	1987	16,551
127 1/8	21 2/8	20 7/8	15 6/8	4	5	Licking County	OH	Michael J Boucher	1987	16,551
127 1/8	20 2/8	20 6/8	16 1/8	6	6	Huntington County	IN	Dennis I. Cottam	1987	16,551
127 1/8	23 1/8	24 2/8	20 0/8	5	4	Edgar County	IL	M. Mark Davis	1987	16,551
127 1/8	20 1/8	20 2/8	18 1/8	4	4	Lake County	IL	Dave Pederson	1987	16,551
127 1/8	20 5/8	19 7/8	16 6/8	6	5	Fulton County	IL	Jay D. Van Voorhis	1987	16,551
127 1/8	20 6/8	20 6/8	17 5/8	4	4	Franklin County	MA	Richard Scorzafava	1987	16,551
127 1/8	22 1/8	22 6/8	15 5/8	5	6	Angelina County	TX	Ben Bartlett	1987	16,551
127 1/8	21 7/8	22 4/8	16 1/8	4	4	Lake County	IL	Woody Scruggs	1988	16,551
127 1/8	21 6/8	20 6/8	17 3/8	4	4	Jo Daviess County	IL	Lewis Heidenreich	1988	16,551
127 1/8	21 5/8	21 6/8	18 3/8	4	4	Sussex County	DE	Rick Mazol	1989	16,551
127 1/8	22 3/8	22 3/8	20 5/8	4	4	Wyoming County	NY	Greg Hoffmeister	1989	16,551
127 1/8	22 2/8	21 5/8	17 2/8	5	4	Harlan County	NE	Paul Ekberg	1989	16,551
127 1/8	21 0/8	21 2/8	15 3/8	4	4	Washburn County	WI	Kevin P. Tripp	1990	16,551
127 1/8	20 7/8	21 4/8	18 0/8	5	6	Pike County	IL	Gary L. Goldasich	1990	16,551
127 1/8	21 7/8	21 7/8	15 3/8	4	5	Jasper County	TX	Kevin W. Walker, Sr.	1990	16,551
127 1/8	20 1/8	21 0/8	16 1/8	5	5	St. Joseph County	MI	Jeffery Daniel Stephens	1990	16,551

WHITETAIL DEER (TYPICAL ANTLERS)

Minimum Score 125

SCORE	LENGTH OF MAIN BEAM R L		INSIDE SPREAD	NUMBER OF POINTS R L		AREA	STATE/ PROVINCE	HUNTER'S NAME	DATE	RANK
127 1/8	21 7/8	23 2/8	18 0/8	5	6	Ashtabula County	OH	Paul Drotar	1990	16,551
127 1/8	18 5/8	18 6/8	11 7/8	5	5	Marathon County	WI	Tom R. Pankratz	1991	16,551
127 1/8	24 0/8	23 6/8	19 3/8	4	5	Edwards County	IL	Tim Brake	1991	16,551
127 1/8	24 1/8	23 7/8	18 0/8	5	4	Mercer County	NJ	Dennis Graber	1991	16,551
127 1/8	23 7/8	23 1/8	17 5/8	5	6	Armstrong County	PA	Michael Daquilante	1992	16,551
127 1/8	19 6/8	19 6/8	14 5/8	5	5	Pierce County	WI	Fred Hansen	1992	16,551
127 1/8	20 4/8	21 4/8	13 4/8	5	5	Knox County	IL	Larry Hesterly	1992	16,551
127 1/8	21 0/8	21 1/8	14 1/8	5	6	Douglas County	KS	Denzil Hackathorn	1992	16,551
127 1/8	21 4/8	21 5/8	17 1/8	4	4	Clarke County	IA	Don Mealey	1992	16,551
127 1/8	24 6/8	25 7/8	19 0/8	5	5	Buckingham County	VA	Steven W. Blosser	1992	16,551
127 1/8	21 1/8	21 1/8	14 7/8	5	5	McMullen County	TX	Richard Miller	1992	16,551
127 1/8	22 0/8	20 6/8	17 6/8	5	5	Kenedy County	TX	Gerry Olson	1993	16,551
127 1/8	20 3/8	20 1/8	16 1/8	5	5	Dodge County	WI	Rick Palmer	1993	16,551
127 1/8	22 1/8	21 4/8	16 1/8	5	5	Clermont County	OH	Larry W. Van	1993	16,551
127 1/8	21 3/8	21 0/8	16 7/8	5	4	Ralls County	MO	Michael Papka	1993	16,551
127 1/8	22 0/8	20 4/8	15 7/8	4	4	Roberts County	SD	James D. Backman	1993	16,551
127 1/8	23 2/8	23 1/8	19 1/8	4	5	Shelby County	KY	Steven D. Williams	1993	16,551
127 1/8	18 5/8	18 6/8	16 4/8	5	6	Medina County	TX	Jim Gresham	1993	16,551
127 1/8	22 5/8	21 4/8	16 3/8	5	5	Todd County	KY	Donald Bryant	1993	16,551
127 1/8	21 4/8	21 3/8	16 1/8	4	4	Warren County	PA	Timothy B. Giese	1993	16,551
127 1/8	20 0/8	20 0/8	16 7/8	5	5	Wapello County	IA	Rick Aalbers, Jr.	1993	16,551
127 1/8	21 0/8	21 1/8	15 5/8	5	5	Rogers County	OK	Bryce Collins	1993	16,551
127 1/8	20 5/8	22 2/8	16 7/8	5	5	Genesee County	NY	Alan W. Hayes	1993	16,551
127 1/8	19 1/8	19 0/8	18 1/8	5	5	Redwood County	MN	Todd Gilb	1993	16,551
127 1/8	22 5/8	23 4/8	16 1/8	6	4	Madison County	IA	Scott Creger	1993	16,551
127 1/8	20 6/8	21 0/8	15 5/8	4	4	Newton County	MO	Jamie Hatfield	1994	16,551
127 1/8	20 7/8	22 5/8	21 1/8	4	5	Kings County	NBW	Richard Hoar	1994	16,551
127 1/8	21 4/8	21 6/8	17 3/8	4	5	Clay County	IN	Ryan Albright	1994	16,551
127 1/8	20 1/8	20 5/8	16 1/8	5	5	Angelina County	TX	Jim E. Huggins	1994	16,551
127 1/8	20 3/8	21 4/8	16 7/8	5	5	Price County	WI	John W. Nyholm	1994	16,551
127 1/8	20 7/8	20 4/8	16 5/8	4	5	Pike County	IL	David B. Green	1994	16,551
127 1/8	20 3/8	19 7/8	14 3/8	5	5	Throckmorton County	TX	Bobby David Tipping	1994	16,551
127 1/8	21 0/8	21 1/8	14 5/8	5	5	Kleberg County	TX	Charles A. Clements	1994	16,551
127 1/8	22 3/8	22 5/8	16 4/8	5	4	Iron County	WI	Steven J. Krueger	1994	16,551
127 1/8	21 4/8	21 3/8	15 2/8	6	5	Randolph County	MO	Matthew Fleming	1995	16,551
127 1/8	23 0/8	23 0/8	15 3/8	4	4	Jackson County	KY	Vicki Spurlock	1995	16,551
127 1/8	21 4/8	21 5/8	16 3/8	5	5	Shawano County	WI	Paul J. Clark	1995	16,551
127 1/8	20 2/8	20 2/8	16 7/8	5	4	Buffalo County	WI	Greg Peterson	1995	16,551
127 1/8	19 6/8	21 4/8	16 5/8	5	5	Washington County	OH	Danny W. Grimm	1995	16,551
127 1/8	22 1/8	23 0/8	15 5/8	5	4	Fayette County	IA	Wayne S. Wise	1995	16,551
127 1/8	22 1/8	21 2/8	17 3/8	4	4	Sutton County	TX	Craig Horn	1995	16,551
127 1/8	23 0/8	23 4/8	18 1/8	5	5	Hardin County	TN	Tom Delaney	1996	16,551
127 1/8	19 6/8	19 6/8	19 3/8	5	6	Dane County	WI	Rock Taylor	1996	16,551
127 1/8	21 5/8	21 7/8	18 7/8	4	4	Warren County	NJ	Barry Meyers	1996	16,551
127 1/8	22 3/8	21 1/8	16 3/8	4	4	Wilcox County	AL	Mark Salter	1996	16,551
127 1/8	20 1/8	19 6/8	15 1/8	5	5	Montgomery County	MD	Richard L. Latimer, Jr.	1996	16,551
127 1/8	21 0/8	20 2/8	16 1/8	5	7	Allegheny County	PA	Wayne M. Bayer	1996	16,551
127 1/8	22 2/8	22 4/8	16 7/8	4	4	Sauk County	WI	John Belter	1996	16,551
127 1/8	22 2/8	21 1/8	14 2/8	7	7	Green Lake County	WI	Richard L. Shmauz	1996	16,551
127 1/8	24 3/8	23 6/8	19 7/8	4	4	Niagara County	NY	Bill Loeschke	1996	16,551
127 1/8	21 6/8	22 0/8	18 5/8	4	4	Mingo County	WV	Harrison Slone	1996	16,551
127 1/8	22 6/8	21 6/8	18 2/8	4	5	Bond County	IL	William T. Rench	1996	16,551
127 1/8	21 0/8	21 1/8	15 4/8	6	6	Granby River	BC	Glenn Dreger	1996	16,551
127 1/8	22 2/8	22 3/8	15 5/8	5	6	Warren County	MS	Randall R. Atchley	1996	16,551
127 1/8	22 3/8	22 2/8	17 4/8	8	6	Columbia County	WI	William P. Gentz	1997	16,551
127 1/8	22 3/8	22 4/8	14 7/8	5	6	Dearborn County	IN	Patrick Dean	1997	16,551
127 1/8	22 7/8	20 4/8	17 7/8	4	5	Goodhue County	MN	James Harrison	1997	16,551
127 1/8	18 1/8	18 7/8	19 0/8	5	4	Winnebago County	IL	Mark E. Lookingland	1997	16,551
127 1/8	20 2/8	20 2/8	14 0/8	5	6	Plymouth County	IA	Jeff Mandicino	1997	16,551
127 1/8	22 5/8	22 1/8	18 3/8	4	4	Springbank	ALB	Archie J. Nesbitt	1997	16,551
127 1/8	22 0/8	22 2/8	15 5/8	4	4	Ontario County	NY	David M. Pickering	1998	16,551
127 0/8	26 1/8	26 3/8	17 6/8	5	5	Boone County	KY	Steve ToLes	1976	16,648
127 0/8	19 6/8	18 3/8	17 6/8	6	6	Kossuth County	IA	Jerry L. Buscher	1977	16,648
127 0/8	20 3/8	20 3/8	15 6/8	6	6	Sauk County	WI	Adrian Julson	1979	16,648
127 0/8	23 5/8	23 3/8	19 0/8	5	4	Licking County	OH	Curtis W. Price	1979	16,648
127 0/8	20 0/8	20 7/8	18 2/8	5	5	Harris County	TX	Daniel Barnes	1980	16,648
127 0/8	22 4/8	21 4/8	15 4/8	5	6	Tuscarawas County	OH	David Pappas	1980	16,648
127 0/8	22 2/8	22 2/8	14 2/8	8	6	Kittson County	MN	John S. Ritter	1981	16,648
127 0/8	19 5/8	18 4/8	18 4/8	5	5	Graham County	KS	Russell Hull	1981	16,648
127 0/8	20 7/8	21 4/8	18 4/8	4	4	Miller County	MO	Gary Haupt	1982	16,648
127 0/8	21 1/8	20 3/8	14 6/8	5	5	Coahoma County	MS	Charles L. Campassi	1983	16,648
127 0/8	21 6/8	20 3/8	17 2/8	4	5	Dane County	WI	Charles F. Hilgendorf	1983	16,648
127 0/8	22 6/8	22 6/8	17 2/8	5	5	Spokane County	WA	William J. Lantiegne	1983	16,648
127 0/8	22 2/8	22 4/8	15 6/8	5	5	Sauk County	WI	Richard A. Galston	1984	16,648
127 0/8	23 1/8	23 1/8	16 5/8	4	5	Litchfield County	CT	Michael Cristillo	1984	16,648
127 0/8	19 6/8	18 3/8	16 6/8	5	5	Wayne County	NE	Mike Lutt	1984	16,648
127 0/8	19 6/8	19 3/8	16 4/8	5	5	Door County	WI	Wayne Lautenbach	1985	16,648
127 0/8	20 0/8	19 4/8	15 0/8	5	5	Audrain County	MO	Marty Bertels	1985	16,648

WHITETAIL DEER (TYPICAL ANTLERS)

Minimum Score 125 — Continued

SCORE	LENGTH OF MAIN BEAM R	LENGTH OF MAIN BEAM L	INSIDE SPREAD	NUMBER OF POINTS R	NUMBER OF POINTS L	AREA	STATE/ PROVINCE	HUNTER'S NAME	DATE	RANK
127 0/8	21 5/8	21 1/8	17 0/8	5	4	Powell County	MT	Sonny Templeton	1985	16,648
127 0/8	19 6/8	20 3/8	16 0/8	4	4	Dickinson County	KS	Bradley Wayne Whisler	1985	16,648
127 0/8	21 0/8	23 6/8	18 4/8	5	5	Lafayette County	WI	Jerod Ray	1985	16,648
127 0/8	19 1/8	20 4/8	15 6/8	4	4	Franklin County	OH	Craig A. Bonham	1985	16,648
127 0/8	23 7/8	24 3/8	16 0/8	4	5	Montgomery County	AL	David Barrow	1986	16,648
127 0/8	21 4/8	22 3/8	15 6/8	4	4	Marquette County	MI	Everett W. Shaw	1986	16,648
127 0/8	20 5/8	20 1/8	14 6/8	5	5	Big Stone County	MN	Pete Karels	1986	16,648
127 0/8	19 6/8	20 2/8	15 2/8	5	5	Portage County	WI	Brian Klesmith	1986	16,648
127 0/8	23 2/8	22 3/8	16 0/8	5	6	Ray County	MO	Kenneth Coats	1987	16,648
127 0/8	22 7/8	22 3/8	16 4/8	4	4	Dubuque County	IA	Kevin R. Schmitt	1987	16,648
127 0/8	22 3/8	22 2/8	15 2/8	4	4	Hitchcock County	NE	Dave Holt	1987	16,648
127 0/8	22 2/8	21 6/8	17 0/8	5	5	McNairy County	TN	Paul Steward	1988	16,648
127 0/8	21 3/8	20 5/8	15 6/8	5	5	Pulaski County	KY	Harold Allen	1988	16,648
127 0/8	20 2/8	20 5/8	17 4/8	5	5	Morrison County	MN	Vincent Meyer	1988	16,648
127 0/8	22 3/8	22 7/8	17 6/8	6	5	Greene County	IL	Gerald Isringhausen	1988	16,648
127 0/8	19 7/8	19 1/8	16 0/8	6	5	Nicollet County	MN	Ronny Cordes	1989	16,648
127 0/8	22 1/8	21 6/8	17 6/8	5	5	Atascosa County	TX	Mike Palmer	1989	16,648
127 0/8	17 2/8	17 5/8	15 4/8	5	5	Bexar County	TX	John W. Wallace	1989	16,648
127 0/8	19 7/8	19 7/8	15 4/8	5	5	Clay County	NE	David J. Hamik	1989	16,648
127 0/8	23 0/8	22 6/8	22 5/8	6	6	Will County	IL	Russell Robak	1989	16,648
127 0/8	22 5/8	22 2/8	18 0/8	4	4	Burleigh County	ND	Bill Helphrey	1989	16,648
127 0/8	20 5/8	20 4/8	19 0/8	5	5	De Witt County	IL	Sylvan Purcell	1989	16,648
127 0/8	21 6/8	21 3/8	16 6/8	4	4	New Castle County	DE	Joseph J. Subolesky	1990	16,648
127 0/8	22 2/8	21 0/8	17 3/8	6	4	Lawrence County	IL	Jeff Jones	1990	16,648
127 0/8	21 1/8	20 0/8	17 0/8	4	4	Portage County	WI	Jeffrey D. Carter	1990	16,648
127 0/8	23 0/8	22 2/8	13 6/8	5	6	Pawnee County	KS	Bob Faris	1990	16,648
127 0/8	21 4/8	21 5/8	16 4/8	5	4	McHenry County	IL	Matt N. Dieter	1991	16,648
127 0/8	22 0/8	21 7/8	15 1/8	7	5	St. Croix County	WI	Randal Ramberg	1991	16,648
127 0/8	20 1/8	20 2/8	14 6/8	5	5	Buffalo County	WI	Brian R. Potter	1991	16,648
127 0/8	22 6/8	22 0/8	18 4/8	5	5	Morris County	NJ	Andrew Murnock, Sr.	1991	16,648
127 0/8	23 1/8	23 6/8	16 7/8	5	4	Murray County	OK	Bobby Pope	1991	16,648
127 0/8	21 5/8	21 5/8	15 6/8	6	5	Yates County	NY	Mark R. Urban	1991	16,648
127 0/8	21 7/8	20 7/8	19 4/8	4	4	Monmouth County	NJ	Ivan Gottstein	1992	16,648
127 0/8	19 0/8	19 3/8	16 0/8	5	5	Washtenaw County	MI	James A. Diamantoni	1992	16,648
127 0/8	24 0/8	24 3/8	19 4/8	4	5	Genesee County	MI	Kurt A. Minto	1992	16,648
127 0/8	19 4/8	20 0/8	17 4/8	5	5	Meeker County	MN	Larry Krenik	1992	16,648
127 0/8	21 7/8	21 7/8	17 3/8	4	7	Buffalo County	WI	James A. Kamla	1992	16,648
127 0/8	21 1/8	20 6/8	13 2/8	5	5	Dodge County	WI	Mike Young	1992	16,648
127 0/8	22 4/8	21 0/8	17 4/8	4	4	Adams County	OH	Larry Napier	1992	16,648
127 0/8	21 4/8	21 4/8	17 0/8	4	4	Trempealeau County	WI	Eugene Klonecki	1992	16,648
127 0/8	22 0/8	22 0/8	15 6/8	5	5	Van Buren County	IA	Gerald A. Palmer	1992	16,648
127 0/8	20 7/8	20 6/8	18 4/8	5	5	Polk County	IA	Daryl Simmer	1992	16,648
127 0/8	19 5/8	19 5/8	16 6/8	5	5	Stanly County	NC	Kevin J. Efird	1993	16,648
127 0/8	22 1/8	22 3/8	19 6/8	4	4	Dubuque County	IA	Doug Westhoff	1993	16,648
127 0/8	20 6/8	20 6/8	18 4/8	5	5	Buffalo County	WI	Randy P. Secrist	1993	16,648
127 0/8	20 0/8	19 6/8	17 2/8	6	6	Lake County	IL	Riccardo A. Mazzanti	1993	16,648
127 0/8	23 2/8	22 0/8	14 0/8	4	4	Anne Arundel County	MD	Richard J. Folderauer, Jr.	1993	16,648
127 0/8	21 4/8	21 5/8	18 0/8	4	4	Motley County	TX	David Lynn Wigley	1993	16,648
127 0/8	20 5/8	20 5/8	16 6/8	5	5	Price County	WI	Tim Henderson	1994	16,648
127 0/8	19 4/8	20 0/8	14 6/8	6	5	Boone County	MO	Sylvester Walls	1994	16,648
127 0/8	24 6/8	24 4/8	16 5/8	4	5	Fond du Lac County	WI	Jim Schaub	1994	16,648
127 0/8	23 7/8	22 7/8	19 4/8	4	4	Somerset County	NJ	Scott Barrett	1994	16,648
127 0/8	22 6/8	23 1/8	16 4/8	4	4	Morgan County	IL	Robert DuRocher	1994	16,648
127 0/8	20 1/8	20 0/8	16 2/8	4	4	Anderson County	TX	Ray Loviette	1994	16,648
127 0/8	24 4/8	23 6/8	19 0/8	5	5	Wayne County	IL	Danny Barnfield	1994	16,648
127 0/8	23 1/8	22 1/8	17 0/8	4	4	Greene County	IN	James B. Landis	1994	16,648
127 0/8	20 4/8	20 1/8	19 0/8	5	5	Sheboygan County	WI	Doug Pilon	1994	16,648
127 0/8	21 3/8	21 1/8	20 4/8	5	5	San Patricio County	TX	Trent Hendrix	1994	16,648
127 0/8	24 0/8	24 2/8	19 6/8	4	4	Polk County	IA	John Flies	1994	16,648
127 0/8	24 1/8	22 7/8	17 7/8	4	5	Monroe County	MO	John Kevin Pelhank	1995	16,648
127 0/8	20 5/8	19 7/8	16 5/8	6	6	Ellis County	KS	Stanley M. Honas	1995	16,648
127 0/8	20 3/8	21 2/8	16 6/8	4	5	Carroll County	IL	Steven King	1995	16,648
127 0/8	20 0/8	20 6/8	17 2/8	4	4	Berks County	PA	Mark I. Lesher	1995	16,648
127 0/8	20 6/8	21 3/8	18 0/8	4	4	Chautauqua County	NY	Mark Irlbacher	1995	16,648
127 0/8	20 7/8	19 7/8	15 6/8	6	5	Kerr County	TX	Roy Raines	1995	16,648
127 0/8	18 4/8	18 6/8	15 2/8	6	6	Harris County	TX	Stan Gouger, Jr.	1995	16,648
127 0/8	20 4/8	20 7/8	16 6/8	5	5	Ozaukee County	WI	Ray Schultz	1995	16,648
127 0/8	21 3/8	21 5/8	17 2/8	4	5	Forest County	WI	Dennis Hoffman	1995	16,648
127 0/8	22 2/8	22 3/8	19 4/8	4	4	Washington County	MS	L. R. Westbrook	1996	16,648
127 0/8	23 3/8	23 4/8	20 0/8	4	5	Waukesha County	WI	John S. Ritter	1996	16,648
127 0/8	19 7/8	20 0/8	15 2/8	5	5	Owen County	IN	Robert L. May	1996	16,648
127 0/8	23 0/8	25 5/8	19 4/8	5	5	Harford County	MD	David Weber	1996	16,648
127 0/8	19 2/8	19 7/8	16 0/8	5	5	Fremont County	IA	James Beebe	1996	16,648
127 0/8	20 6/8	20 5/8	17 2/8	4	4	Jefferson County	KS	Shawn Harding	1996	16,648
127 0/8	20 1/8	21 1/8	15 7/8	5	5	Johnson County	IA	Brian J. Bourgeois	1996	16,648
127 0/8	22 1/8	23 1/8	17 2/8	4	5	Chester County	PA	Jeffrey Estock	1996	16,648
127 0/8	26 6/8	26 4/8	21 2/8	5	5	Fairfield County	OH	Michael Vaughn	1996	16,648
127 0/8	21 1/8	20 1/8	16 2/8	5	5	Greenwood County	KS	James L. Fowler	1996	16,648

WHITETAIL DEER (TYPICAL ANTLERS)

Minimum Score 125   Continued

SCORE	LENGTH OF MAIN BEAM R	LENGTH OF MAIN BEAM L	INSIDE SPREAD	NUMBER OF POINTS R	NUMBER OF POINTS L	AREA	STATE/ PROVINCE	HUNTER'S NAME	DATE	RANK
126 6/8	22 3/8	22 0/8	16 2/8	5	5	Warrick County	IN	Dale Rash	1989	16,862
126 6/8	20 4/8	20 5/8	17 4/8	4	5	Traill County	ND	James Strand	1990	16,862
126 6/8	19 5/8	20 6/8	13 6/8	5	5	Arenac County	MI	Anthony D. Windt	1990	16,862
126 6/8	21 6/8	21 5/8	15 0/8	5	5	Wayne County	MI	Paul Nash	1990	16,862
126 6/8	20 1/8	20 6/8	15 2/8	5	5	Flathead County	MT	Dennis Brieske	1990	16,862
126 6/8	19 2/8	20 5/8	16 2/8	6	5	Dane County	WI	Mike Crisman	1990	16,862
126 6/8	19 2/8	19 2/8	15 6/8	5	5	Dallas County	MO	Scott Hill	1990	16,862
126 6/8	23 6/8	24 0/8	15 4/8	5	4	Pierce County	WI	Erik Jensen	1990	16,862
126 6/8	25 1/8	24 6/8	17 3/8	5	3	Clark County	IL	Jim Baker	1990	16,862
126 6/8	19 5/8	20 4/8	15 1/8	5	6	Kossuth County	IA	Kevin L. Peterson	1990	16,862
126 6/8	22 3/8	23 3/8	17 6/8	4	5	Franklin County	MA	Timothy J. Wendell	1990	16,862
126 6/8	21 1/8	21 4/8	17 2/8	5	6	Chase County	KS	Larry Walker, Jr.	1991	16,862
126 6/8	21 5/8	22 6/8	14 4/8	5	5	Ashe County	NC	Roger L. Richardson	1991	16,862
126 6/8	19 4/8	20 4/8	15 2/8	6	6	Stillwater County	MT	Dr. Dale Schlehuber	1991	16,862
126 6/8	22 1/8	21 5/8	18 1/8	5	4	Tippecanoe County	IN	L. Paul Lewis	1991	16,862
126 6/8	22 0/8	22 2/8	18 2/8	5	5	Meade County	KS	Terry Cordes	1991	16,862
126 6/8	21 7/8	21 2/8	17 6/8	4	4	Price County	WI	Jerry J. Bedor	1991	16,862
126 6/8	22 2/8	22 4/8	18 4/8	4	4	Warren County	MS	Bob Lane	1991	16,862
126 6/8	18 6/8	18 7/8	14 6/8	5	5	Richland County	ND	Rob Punton	1992	16,862
126 6/8	20 5/8	21 0/8	15 4/8	4	4	Marinette County	WI	Scott J. Reindel	1992	16,862
126 6/8	21 6/8	22 4/8	14 6/8	5	4	Monroe County	NY	Lucas Hayes	1992	16,862
126 6/8	20 4/8	20 5/8	18 0/8	4	5	Suffolk County	NY	Neil Heaton	1992	16,862
126 6/8	24 2/8	24 5/8	17 6/8	3	3	Pointe Coupee Parish	LA	Michael T. McBride	1993	16,862
126 6/8	22 2/8	21 6/8	15 0/8	5	5	Fergus County	MT	Richard Dilling	1993	16,862
126 6/8	21 0/8	21 6/8	15 2/8	5	5	Madison County	MT	Mark Stonebraker	1993	16,862
126 6/8	21 3/8	20 0/8	17 3/8	5	5	Cass County	MI	Scott Edward Krueger	1993	16,862
126 6/8	20 4/8	20 0/8	17 4/8	4	4	McHenry County	IL	Robert J. Sarle	1993	16,862
126 6/8	22 1/8	22 2/8	16 4/8	5	5	Madison County	NY	Charles Pace	1993	16,862
126 6/8	22 2/8	21 0/8	15 2/8	4	6	Columbia County	WI	Allen Yaeger	1993	16,862
126 6/8	23 5/8	23 0/8	19 0/8	4	4	Fairfax County	VA	Robert P. Honus	1993	16,862
126 6/8	21 5/8	21 7/8	16 6/8	5	5	Wayne County	IA	John L. Pherigo	1994	16,862
126 6/8	19 6/8	20 3/8	15 2/8	5	5	Preble County	OH	Larry Hickman	1994	16,862
126 6/8	20 2/8	21 2/8	22 6/8	4	4	Hunterdon County	NJ	Bill Berner	1994	16,862
126 6/8	20 2/8	20 3/8	16 6/8	5	5	Dubuque County	IA	Bob Brosius	1994	16,862
126 6/8	21 4/8	21 6/8	16 4/8	6	5	Washington County	WI	Jeff Hager	1994	16,862
126 6/8	20 3/8	20 6/8	18 3/8	5	4	Sullivan County	IN	John Hale	1994	16,862
126 6/8	21 4/8	21 6/8	19 2/8	4	4	Stephenson County	IL	Josh Lipps	1994	16,862
126 6/8	21 0/8	21 1/8	21 0/8	5	4	Washington County	WI	Craig A. Mantz	1994	16,862
126 6/8	20 1/8	19 1/8	13 0/8	5	5	Washington County	TX	Wayne A. Naumann	1994	16,862
126 6/8	21 2/8	22 7/8	20 2/8	5	4	Columbia County	PA	Doyle L. Walters	1994	16,862
126 6/8	20 4/8	20 5/8	17 4/8	5	5	Rock County	MN	Jim Lorenzen	1994	16,862
126 6/8	21 6/8	22 4/8	17 2/8	6	5	Coleman County	TX	Ronald M. Ricks	1994	16,862
126 6/8	22 5/8	23 1/8	16 2/8	5	4	Fairfax County	VA	Patrick Michael Hayes, Jr.	1994	16,862
126 6/8	21 6/8	22 5/8	18 6/8	4	5	St. Marys County	MD	Howard Kimball	1995	16,862
126 6/8	20 7/8	21 0/8	18 2/8	5	6	Newton County	MO	James Crahan	1995	16,862
126 6/8	23 4/8	23 4/8	16 4/8	4	4	Mercer County	MO	Brenda Hudson	1995	16,862
126 6/8	23 1/8	21 7/8	16 6/8	4	4	Prince Georges County	MD	Roger Harris	1995	16,862
126 6/8	21 2/8	24 1/8	16 4/8	4	4	Walworth County	WI	Walter Anderson, Jr.	1995	16,862
126 6/8	22 0/8	21 6/8	16 2/8	5	5	Lapeer County	MI	Donald K. Kerby	1995	16,862
126 6/8	23 1/8	24 2/8	20 4/8	4	4	Montgomery County	PA	Joseph A. Rauch II	1995	16,862
126 6/8	22 0/8	22 1/8	18 0/8	4	4	Yates County	NY	Richard A. Sawyer	1995	16,862
126 6/8	21 5/8	21 2/8	16 0/8	4	4	Washington County	IA	Steve Baker	1995	16,862
126 6/8	18 3/8	19 5/8	13 6/8	5	5	Iroquois County	IL	Gary R. Roberge	1995	16,862
126 6/8	21 6/8	21 2/8	16 2/8	4	4	Edmonton	ALB	Robert A. Mochilar	1995	16,862
126 6/8	24 1/8	23 1/8	18 0/8	4	4	Hidalgo	MEX	Patricio Sada	1995	16,862
126 6/8	24 0/8	22 5/8	17 6/8	5	4	Lake County	IL	Carl Spaeth	1996	16,862
126 6/8	24 0/8	23 5/8	18 2/8	4	4	Garden County	NE	Dan Schmid	1996	16,862
126 6/8	21 5/8	22 0/8	17 2/8	5	5	Warren County	IA	Tim C. Deskin	1996	16,862
126 6/8	22 5/8	21 7/8	22 4/8	5	5	Somerset County	NJ	Timothy C. Groves	1996	16,862
126 6/8	22 3/8	22 4/8	14 0/8	5	4	Lyon County	KS	Norman L. Truelove	1996	16,862
126 6/8	20 4/8	20 1/8	16 2/8	6	5	Tuscola County	MI	Robert W. Badour, Sr.	1996	16,862
126 6/8	20 6/8	20 1/8	17 0/8	5	4	Jackson County	MO	Douglas Phillips	1996	16,862
126 6/8	24 2/8	24 2/8	17 1/8	7	6	Marion County	IN	Mark A. Jackson	1996	16,862
126 6/8	19 4/8	19 7/8	16 0/8	4	4	Marathon County	WI	Gary Olson	1996	16,862
126 6/8	22 2/8	22 2/8	16 2/8	4	4	Richland County	WI	Chris Duane Cina	1996	16,862
126 6/8	23 7/8	22 5/8	17 3/8	6	6	Keya Paha County	NE	Troy Olson	1997	16,862
126 6/8	20 1/8	20 7/8	17 1/8	7	6	Sauk County	WI	John R. Marquardt	1997	16,862
126 6/8	18 4/8	18 7/8	14 0/8	5	5	Shackelford County	TX	Ray Morales	1997	16,862
126 6/8	20 0/8	22 0/8	16 6/8	5	5	McHenry County	IL	Robert Tastsides	1997	16,862
126 6/8	21 4/8	21 7/8	18 5/8	5	6	Richland County	MT	Paul Meeks	1997	16,862
126 6/8	22 3/8	21 5/8	17 2/8	7	7	Northampton County	PA	David L. Hardcastle	1997	16,862
126 6/8	23 2/8	22 4/8	17 0/8	4	5	Sutton County	TX	Craig C. Horn	1997	16,862
126 6/8	22 5/8	21 4/8	16 0/8	4	4	Howard County	IA	John Koschmeder	1997	16,862
126 6/8	22 2/8	23 1/8	17 2/8	4	4	Ashland County	WI	Mitchell Mesko, Jr.	1997	16,862
126 6/8	21 1/8	20 0/8	18 2/8	4	4	Waupaca County	WI	David Schafhauser	1997	16,862
126 6/8	20 6/8	20 3/8	17 1/8	6	4	Hunterdon County	NJ	Jeff Farr	1998	16,862
126 6/8	19 3/8	19 4/8	16 4/8	5	5	Barren County	KY	Bennie Mutter	1998	16,862
126 6/8	23 3/8	23 5/8	21 6/8	4	4	Baltimore County	MD	Brody Atkinson	1998	16,862

WHITETAIL DEER (TYPICAL ANTLERS)

Minimum Score 125

SCORE	LENGTH OF MAIN BEAM R	LENGTH OF MAIN BEAM L	INSIDE SPREAD	NUMBER OF POINTS R	NUMBER OF POINTS L	AREA	STATE/PROVINCE	HUNTER'S NAME	DATE	RANK
126 5/8	22 4/8	22 0/8	21 5/8	4	4	Pine County	MN	Buck Doran	1945	16,977
126 5/8	22 5/8	23 0/8	19 0/8	5	5	Roberts County	SD	Roland L. Hausmann	1961	16,977
126 5/8	21 5/8	21 3/8	19 3/8	4	4	Johnson County	IN	Roger E. Harvey	1975	16,977
126 5/8	23 4/8	25 0/8	19 7/8	6	6	Wellington County	ONT	James A. Reid	1976	16,977
126 5/8	21 4/8	21 6/8	17 2/8	7	7	Jackson County	MI	Gary A. Dawson	1980	16,977
126 5/8	21 0/8	19 7/8	16 5/8	4	4	Greene County	AL	Alvin Pearson	1980	16,977
126 5/8	19 7/8	19 3/8	14 1/8	5	4	Owen County	IN	Bill G. Tanner	1980	16,977
126 5/8	23 6/8	24 7/8	17 3/8	5	4	Jackson County	MN	Kerry Ella	1981	16,977
126 5/8	19 5/8	20 4/8	16 3/8	5	5	Waupaca County	WI	Mark Jahr	1981	16,977
126 5/8	20 7/8	22 6/8	16 1/8	4	4	Jefferson County	ID	Roger W. Atwood	1982	16,977
126 5/8	18 2/8	18 2/8	12 7/8	6	5	Johnson County	WY	Jerry N. Blossom	1983	16,977
126 5/8	21 2/8	21 7/8	14 3/8	4	4	Boone County	IA	Tim Marshall	1983	16,977
126 5/8	21 5/8	21 3/8	16 6/8	6	6	Lake County	IL	Mark Fugett	1984	16,977
126 5/8	23 0/8	22 7/8	15 3/8	5	5	Bedford County	VA	Russell A. Barton	1985	16,977
126 5/8	22 3/8	21 0/8	16 1/8	5	5	Jefferson County	KS	Brian Artzer	1986	16,977
126 5/8	22 2/8	22 4/8	18 5/8	5	4	Grand Traverse County	MI	Daniel D. Morrison	1986	16,977
126 5/8	21 7/8	23 0/8	17 5/8	4	4	Lafayette County	WI	Mike Traub	1986	16,977
126 5/8	21 4/8	21 2/8	15 5/8	5	5	Switzerland County	IN	Edwin L. McDaniel	1986	16,977
126 5/8	21 2/8	20 7/8	19 5/8	5	4	Roberts County	SD	Paul Sand	1986	16,977
126 5/8	22 1/8	22 2/8	18 5/8	4	4	Warren County	NJ	Dennis Stankovitz	1987	16,977
126 5/8	19 6/8	19 6/8	16 3/8	5	5	Uvalde County	TX	William E. Legg	1987	16,977
126 5/8	19 4/8	19 6/8	16 0/8	6	5	Jefferson County	NE	Kevin Wagner	1988	16,977
126 5/8	22 2/8	21 6/8	18 2/8	7	4	Columbia County	WI	Robert L. Lex	1988	16,977
126 5/8	22 0/8	22 5/8	17 4/8	6	6	Marshall County	IN	Richard Flory	1988	16,977
126 5/8	19 3/8	20 3/8	14 5/8	5	5	Grant County	OK	Jim Sheets	1988	16,977
126 5/8	23 1/8	22 6/8	18 4/8	4	6	Crawford County	IL	Bill Waddell	1988	16,977
126 5/8	22 2/8	21 1/8	15 1/8	4	4	Forest County	WI	Ralph L. Horsens	1989	16,977
126 5/8	23 0/8	23 2/8	15 3/8	4	4	Terrell County	GA	Bob Miles	1989	16,977
126 5/8	18 5/8	19 1/8	17 3/8	7	6	Thomas County	NE	Dan Neal	1989	16,977
126 5/8	20 0/8	20 0/8	14 1/8	5	5	Russell County	AL	James Vernon Adcock	1989	16,977
126 5/8	21 6/8	21 2/8	16 6/8	5	5	Jackson County	WV	Joseph H. Bigley	1989	16,977
126 5/8	20 5/8	21 0/8	14 5/8	4	4	Eau Claire County	WI	Robert Nelson	1989	16,977
126 5/8	26 0/8	26 1/8	20 7/8	3	4	Fairfax County	VA	William D. Puso	1989	16,977
126 5/8	23 4/8	22 6/8	16 5/8	4	8	Warren County	IA	Lanny Caligiuri	1989	16,977
126 5/8	22 1/8	23 0/8	18 5/8	4	6	McLean County	IL	Kenneth Kolakowski	1989	16,977
126 5/8	20 0/8	20 0/8	16 1/8	4	4	Camden County	MO	Josh Bills	1990	16,977
126 5/8	19 3/8	18 3/8	15 5/8	5	5	Grand Forks County	ND	Kirke Henry	1990	16,977
126 5/8	21 4/8	21 7/8	16 5/8	4	4	Dukes County	MA	Paul C. Jackson, Sr.	1990	16,977
126 5/8	21 5/8	21 0/8	16 1/8	4	5	Carroll County	IL	John L. Ashby	1990	16,977
126 5/8	20 5/8	20 3/8	14 3/8	4	5	Pender County	NC	Randy Carroll	1991	16,977
126 5/8	19 2/8	19 2/8	14 3/8	5	5	Nemaha County	KS	D. Jay Hartter	1991	16,977
126 5/8	21 3/8	19 7/8	15 3/8	4	4	Chautauqua County	NY	Peter Smith, Jr.	1991	16,977
126 5/8	20 4/8	19 3/8	16 7/8	5	5	Walworth County	WI	Mark Luther	1991	16,977
126 5/8	23 2/8	24 4/8	20 7/8	6	4	Fayette County	IL	DeWayne E. Maples	1991	16,977
126 5/8	21 4/8	21 6/8	16 2/8	6	6	Dodge County	WI	Brian Zubke	1991	16,977
126 5/8	20 7/8	20 6/8	18 5/8	4	4	Forest County	WI	Paul M. Senso	1992	16,977
126 5/8	22 1/8	21 6/8	15 4/8	6	5	Winnebago County	WI	Darrell Tritt	1992	16,977
126 5/8	24 2/8	24 1/8	20 5/8	4	4	Westchester County	NY	James Williams	1992	16,977
126 5/8	23 1/8	22 5/8	15 7/8	6	6	Noble County	OH	Kenneth McHaffie	1992	16,977
126 5/8	23 0/8	21 1/8	19 3/8	7	7	Muskingum County	OH	Russ L. Coen	1992	16,977
126 5/8	21 4/8	21 3/8	18 3/8	5	5	Sauk County	WI	James E. Riphon	1993	16,977
126 5/8	20 6/8	20 4/8	15 1/8	5	5	Jennings County	IN	Kevin D. Hall	1993	16,977
126 5/8	22 2/8	21 7/8	18 5/8	4	4	Scott County	IL	Gene Meier	1993	16,977
126 5/8	22 4/8	21 7/8	16 3/8	5	8	De Kalb County	GA	William C. Abernethy	1993	16,977
126 5/8	23 1/8	22 3/8	14 1/8	5	5	Peoria County	IL	Chad Breedlove	1994	16,977
126 5/8	22 4/8	22 6/8	22 3/8	4	4	Montgomery County	MD	Frederick T. Cissel	1994	16,977
126 5/8	20 5/8	20 5/8	15 5/8	7	5	Ferry County	WA	Jerry Solie	1994	16,977
126 5/8	21 7/8	25 1/8	18 3/8	5	5	Brown County	OH	Brian H. Baer	1994	16,977
126 5/8	24 2/8	25 7/8	19 7/8	5	5	Lake County	OH	Robin T. Wilson	1994	16,977
126 5/8	21 5/8	21 7/8	16 5/8	5	5	Litchfield County	CT	Paul Massai	1994	16,977
126 5/8	21 2/8	20 6/8	15 3/8	5	5	Caldwell Parish	LA	Billy Thomas	1995	16,977
126 5/8	20 6/8	20 1/8	18 5/8	5	4	Buffalo County	WI	Curt Rotering	1995	16,977
126 5/8	21 6/8	21 4/8	17 3/8	5	5	Sauk County	WI	Andrew M. Mistele	1995	16,977
126 5/8	20 5/8	21 2/8	15 7/8	5	5	McMullen County	TX	Kevin Hilbig	1995	16,977
126 5/8	19 7/8	19 4/8	13 3/8	5	5	Tom Green County	TX	Jack Bains	1995	16,977
126 5/8	21 2/8	21 2/8	15 0/8	6	5	Henry County	IA	Bruce Krause	1995	16,977
126 5/8	22 3/8	23 6/8	22 1/8	4	5	Franklin County	OH	Steve Byerly	1995	16,977
126 5/8	23 5/8	22 6/8	18 5/8	5	4	Dane County	WI	Randy Wileman	1995	16,977
126 5/8	20 6/8	19 3/8	15 7/8	6	5	Lake County	IL	Steven Hysell	1996	16,977
126 5/8	22 2/8	22 4/8	17 7/8	5	4	Ravalli County	MT	Wayne Capp	1996	16,977
126 5/8	21 6/8	21 0/8	15 1/8	5	5	Iron County	WI	Dan Pribek	1996	16,977
126 5/8	20 1/8	20 1/8	15 5/8	7	6	Gallatin County	MT	James Martin Muzynoski	1997	16,977
126 5/8	22 1/8	21 6/8	17 1/8	5	4	Major County	OK	Robin Mackie	1997	16,977
126 5/8	25 3/8	23 2/8	15 7/8	7	5	Hamilton County	OH	David Hill	1997	16,977
126 5/8	22 4/8	21 7/8	15 7/8	5	5	Irion County	TX	David L. Duncan	1997	16,977
126 5/8	20 7/8	23 4/8	18 2/8	4	6	Fillmore County	MN	Rick Lutz	1997	16,977
126 5/8	20 0/8	19 4/8	14 1/8	5	5	Butler County	KS	David Kuttler	1997	16,977
126 5/8	23 0/8	23 3/8	19 2/8	4	5	York County	PA	Brian McFarland	1997	16,977

Continued

WHITETAIL DEER (TYPICAL ANTLERS)

Minimum Score 125

SCORE	LENGTH OF MAIN BEAM R	LENGTH OF MAIN BEAM L	INSIDE SPREAD	NUMBER OF POINTS R	NUMBER OF POINTS L	AREA	STATE/PROVINCE	HUNTER'S NAME	DATE	RANK
126 5/8	20 5/8	21 5/8	17 7/8	6	5	Edwards County	TX	Chaise A. Flippo	1997	16,977
126 5/8	22 4/8	22 4/8	16 0/8	5	7	Dubuque County	IA	Terry J. Meyer	1997	16,977
126 5/8	21 5/8	21 4/8	17 7/8	4	4	Jackson County	IL	Tim Cobin	1997	16,977
126 4/8	20 4/8	21 2/8	18 6/8	5	5	Warren County	PA	Fred Massa	1967	17,058
126 4/8	21 2/8	21 3/8	15 2/8	4	4	Chester County	PA	Joseph R. Yannelli	1967	17,058
126 4/8	19 7/8	19 6/8	16 4/8	5	5	Owen County	IN	G. Fred Asbell	1971	17,058
126 4/8	22 4/8	21 6/8	17 4/8	4	4	Waupaca County	WI	Arlin Kersten, Jr.	1971	17,058
126 4/8	22 1/8	22 0/8	18 2/8	5	4	Cayuga County	NY	John Pardee	1971	17,058
126 4/8	21 2/8	21 3/8	12 4/8	4	4	Bayfield County	WI	Del Zwiefelhofer	1972	17,058
126 4/8	24 6/8	25 0/8	17 0/8	5	5	Portage County	OH	Burt Thompson, Jr.	1976	17,058
126 4/8	23 4/8	24 2/8	17 6/8	4	4	Westchester County	NY	Richard T. Burke	1977	17,058
126 4/8	22 3/8	20 7/8	15 6/8	4	4	Phillips County	KS	Orville D. Blubaugh	1977	17,058
126 4/8	21 1/8	21 5/8	17 6/8	4	4	Macon County	MO	Bruce Hamel	1979	17,058
126 4/8	20 4/8	20 3/8	16 2/8	5	5	Harford County	MD	Donald P. Conley	1980	17,058
126 4/8	21 6/8	22 3/8	18 4/8	4	4	Cameron County	TX	Louis Skrobarczyk, Jr.	1981	17,058
126 4/8	21 7/8	21 0/8	16 0/8	4	5	Edmonton	ALB	Al Schulz	1981	17,058
126 4/8	20 4/8	19 6/8	13 2/8	5	5	Olmsted County	MN	Tom Lofgren	1983	17,058
126 4/8	20 6/8	21 1/8	15 2/8	4	4	Dane County	WI	Victor H. Mittelstaedt	1983	17,058
126 4/8	19 4/8	21 4/8	20 4/8	5	5	Schuyler County	NY	Richard Murphy	1983	17,058
126 4/8	21 0/8	21 3/8	15 6/8	5	5	Kent County	MD	Raymond A. Boley	1984	17,058
126 4/8	21 6/8	21 6/8	15 4/8	5	5	Somerset County	NJ	Ronald L. Taylor, Sr.	1985	17,058
126 4/8	20 0/8	20 3/8	17 4/8	5	4	Marshall County	IN	Gene E. Smith	1985	17,058
126 4/8	20 1/8	20 1/8	17 2/8	6	5	Hancock County	WV	Mark G. Konchar	1985	17,058
126 4/8	23 4/8	21 2/8	17 5/8	6	5	Menard County	IL	Donald Alwerdt	1985	17,058
126 4/8	21 6/8	21 0/8	17 6/8	5	6	Muskingum County	OH	Allen Randal Smith	1985	17,058
126 4/8	19 6/8	20 2/8	13 6/8	5	5	Dallas County	IA	Glenn D. Vondra	1985	17,058
126 4/8	22 1/8	21 1/8	17 4/8	6	6	Ionia County	MI	Todd E. Peacock	1986	17,058
126 4/8	23 7/8	22 6/8	17 2/8	5	4	Eaton County	MI	Curtis Bumbalough	1986	17,058
126 4/8	20 5/8	21 1/8	17 4/8	7	6	Ozaukee County	WI	Jack T. Klotz	1986	17,058
126 4/8	21 3/8	21 4/8	17 2/8	6	4	Ford County	KS	James A. Konda	1986	17,058
126 4/8	21 0/8	20 3/8	16 0/8	5	5	Marinette County	WI	Paul Becker	1986	17,058
126 4/8	24 2/8	21 7/8	17 0/8	6	5	Ohio County	WV	Robert B. Ewing	1986	17,058
126 4/8	25 7/8	26 7/8	18 7/8	5	5	Hamilton County	IA	Larry Haren	1987	17,058
126 4/8	20 0/8	19 7/8	16 0/8	4	4	Allegan County	MI	Mark A. Dykstra	1988	17,058
126 4/8	21 7/8	23 0/8	18 0/8	4	5	Cayuga County	NY	John E. Ryan, Jr.	1988	17,058
126 4/8	20 4/8	20 0/8	17 6/8	4	4	Henderson County	KY	Edward Wayne Wallace	1988	17,058
126 4/8	22 6/8	22 7/8	18 2/8	4	5	Union County	KY	Chad Robison	1988	17,058
126 4/8	21 4/8	21 7/8	16 6/8	6	4	Saginaw County	MI	Dave L. Tanney	1988	17,058
126 4/8	23 7/8	22 6/8	18 0/8	4	5	Douglas County	NE	Dave Simon	1988	17,058
126 4/8	20 1/8	21 2/8	17 4/8	5	4	Bucks County	PA	Jerome F. Robideau	1989	17,058
126 4/8	20 3/8	20 4/8	17 0/8	4	5	Dane County	WI	Gerald Westphal	1989	17,058
126 4/8	20 3/8	19 6/8	15 4/8	5	5	Maries County	MO	Tracy L. Crider	1989	17,058
126 4/8	22 3/8	22 6/8	15 0/8	6	4	Marinette County	WI	Mike R. Collette	1989	17,058
126 4/8	21 2/8	21 2/8	12 0/8	5	5	Boone County	KY	Stan Clore	1989	17,058
126 4/8	22 2/8	20 7/8	16 2/8	5	5	Price County	WI	Wayne J. Steiner	1989	17,058
126 4/8	19 4/8	18 7/8	18 2/8	4	4	Benton County	MO	Rex M. Suiter	1989	17,058
126 4/8	22 4/8	22 7/8	16 6/8	7	8	Dukes County	MA	Jason A. Ben David	1989	17,058
126 4/8	19 7/8	20 7/8	17 4/8	5	5	Boone County	IA	Chris Doran	1989	17,058
126 4/8	21 4/8	21 2/8	17 0/8	5	4	Northampton County	PA	David Lichtenwalner	1990	17,058
126 4/8	23 2/8	24 0/8	14 6/8	5	6	Saline County	NE	Roger D. Hanneman	1990	17,058
126 4/8	17 0/8	22 0/8	20 6/8	4	4	Kalamazoo County	MI	Larry A. Bussema	1990	17,058
126 4/8	20 0/8	18 5/8	15 4/8	5	5	Cass County	MO	David Johnson	1990	17,058
126 4/8	22 7/8	22 1/8	16 4/8	4	5	St. Croix County	WI	Mike Mattis	1990	17,058
126 4/8	20 4/8	21 4/8	15 1/8	4	5	Saline County	KS	Philip D. Baltazor	1990	17,058
126 4/8	20 5/8	20 2/8	16 2/8	4	4	Marion County	IA	Kyle Goodwin	1990	17,058
126 4/8	23 5/8	22 4/8	16 2/8	4	3	Washington County	IA	Brent J. Graber	1990	17,058
126 4/8	21 1/8	22 2/8	19 6/8	4	4	Kleberg County	TX	Jarred W. Peeples	1991	17,058
126 4/8	20 6/8	21 1/8	11 3/8	6	5	Hardeman County	TN	Paul Blankenship	1991	17,058
126 4/8	21 1/8	22 5/8	16 0/8	4	4	Callaway County	MO	Dennis Crane	1991	17,058
126 4/8	19 4/8	20 3/8	15 2/8	5	5	Pittsburg County	OK	Kevin Stone	1991	17,058
126 4/8	23 3/8	21 5/8	17 2/8	5	4	Missoula County	MT	Tim Hunt	1991	17,058
126 4/8	20 5/8	21 0/8	18 2/8	5	5	Harris County	TX	Daniel K. Barnes	1991	17,058
126 4/8	22 5/8	22 3/8	15 2/8	5	5	Lincoln County	WI	Jerry W. Badeau	1991	17,058
126 4/8	20 3/8	19 5/8	17 0/8	4	4	Langlade County	WI	Douglas L. Below	1992	17,058
126 4/8	20 6/8	20 4/8	16 2/8	4	4	Sawyer County	WI	David A Canfield	1992	17,058
126 4/8	22 4/8	22 2/8	15 6/8	4	4	Waukesha County	WI	Bruce L. Leben	1992	17,058
126 4/8	21 1/8	20 7/8	16 6/8	5	4	Menard County	IL	Larry Rebbe, Jr.	1992	17,058
126 4/8	21 5/8	22 4/8	18 0/8	6	4	Morgan County	CO	Fred Espinoza	1992	17,058
126 4/8	23 4/8	23 1/8	17 1/8	4	5	Evangeline Parish	LA	Prentiss Perkins	1992	17,058
126 4/8	22 0/8	21 0/8	13 0/8	6	5	Oglethorpe County	GA	Stuart Bowers	1992	17,058
126 4/8	22 7/8	22 3/8	18 2/8	5	5	Brown County	IL	Gary Grant	1992	17,058
126 4/8	24 3/8	24 6/8	18 2/8	5	4	Franklin County	KS	Gary Shields	1993	17,058
126 4/8	21 5/8	20 6/8	17 6/8	4	5	Dane County	WI	Steven M. Olson	1993	17,058
126 4/8	22 4/8	22 1/8	15 6/8	5	5	Washtenaw County	MI	Douglas W. Rampy	1993	17,058
126 4/8	19 4/8	19 4/8	14 4/8	6	5	Lincoln County	NE	Jeff Thomas	1993	17,058
126 4/8	22 3/8	22 2/8	17 4/8	4	4	Allegheny County	PA	Tom Lodovico	1993	17,058
126 4/8	20 2/8	20 5/8	18 0/8	4	4	Waushara County	WI	William Steinfort	1993	17,058
126 4/8	22 6/8	22 5/8	17 0/8	4	4	Putnam County	MO	Jeffrey Latimer	1993	17,058

WHITETAIL DEER (TYPICAL ANTLERS)

Minimum Score 125 — Continued

SCORE	LENGTH OF MAIN BEAM R	L	INSIDE SPREAD	NUMBER OF POINTS R	L	AREA	STATE/PROVINCE	HUNTER'S NAME	DATE	RANK
126 4/8	19 0/8	19 1/8	14 6/8	5	5	Waushara County	WI	James Love	1993	17,058
126 4/8	21 6/8	22 2/8	15 0/8	4	5	Crawford County	PA	Barry L. Ebright	1993	17,058
126 4/8	19 4/8	20 0/8	15 6/8	6	5	Fairfield County	OH	Mike Wotring	1993	17,058
126 4/8	23 1/8	22 7/8	17 6/8	6	4	Madison County	FL	Lee Sisson	1994	17,058
126 4/8	20 5/8	21 3/8	16 0/8	4	4	Valley County	MT	Rob Crawford	1994	17,058
126 4/8	24 1/8	24 1/8	17 0/8	5	4	Pottawatomie County	KS	Gerry L. Dickinson	1994	17,058
126 4/8	20 7/8	21 1/8	16 0/8	5	5	Livingston County	NY	Michael Cornwell	1994	17,058
126 4/8	23 3/8	23 6/8	17 0/8	4	4	Cass County	MI	James E. Akey	1994	17,058
126 4/8	21 3/8	21 6/8	16 6/8	4	4	Pulaski County	IL	Paul Landewee	1994	17,058
126 4/8	21 5/8	21 4/8	15 2/8	4	5	Wapello County	IA	Dennis Bradley	1994	17,058
126 4/8	21 5/8	21 3/8	14 4/8	5	4	Pike County	IL	Kurt Edward Meyers	1994	17,058
126 4/8	20 4/8	18 5/8	18 6/8	5	5	Dunn County	WI	Roland W. Palmer	1994	17,058
126 4/8	22 4/8	22 1/8	15 4/8	6	4	Jackson County	WI	Glenn Wood	1994	17,058
126 4/8	20 5/8	20 6/8	17 0/8	5	5	Morgan County	OH	Lynn A. Weingart	1994	17,058
126 4/8	22 0/8	21 1/8	16 4/8	5	4	Livingston County	NY	W. Alec Martusewicz	1994	17,058
126 4/8	22 7/8	21 7/8	16 3/8	6	7	Slope County	ND	Jim Kokott	1994	17,058
126 4/8	20 3/8	19 7/8	17 0/8	6	5	Sanders County	MT	Greg L. Munther	1995	17,058
126 4/8	21 0/8	21 2/8	18 0/8	5	5	Holt County	NE	Terry Schaaf	1995	17,058
126 4/8	18 7/8	18 7/8	16 2/8	6	6	McCulloch County	TX	L. Eric Hoskins	1995	17,058
126 4/8	20 2/8	21 1/8	14 6/8	5	5	Blue Earth County	MN	Fred White	1995	17,058
126 4/8	22 1/8	21 2/8	16 4/8	4	4	Daviess County	KY	Keith Conder	1995	17,058
126 4/8	21 6/8	21 5/8	14 6/8	4	4	Cherokee County	OK	Todd McKinney	1995	17,058
126 4/8	22 5/8	22 2/8	15 2/8	4	4	Eau Claire County	WI	Dennis Etlicher	1995	17,058
126 4/8	21 1/8	21 3/8	18 2/8	4	4	Dimmit County	TX	Sonny Evans	1995	17,058
126 4/8	22 0/8	23 0/8	15 1/8	4	6	Lake County	MN	Randy Bowe	1995	17,058
126 4/8	19 1/8	17 6/8	15 1/8	5	6	Washington County	WI	Brian Strachota	1995	17,058
126 4/8	20 2/8	20 5/8	18 6/8	5	5	Pike County	IL	Durrell G. Miller	1995	17,058
126 4/8	21 2/8	20 7/8	15 4/8	4	4	Franklin County	VA	Mike Weaver	1995	17,058
126 4/8	22 3/8	22 5/8	18 0/8	6	6	McHenry County	IL	Brent Smith	1995	17,058
126 4/8	22 0/8	23 0/8	20 0/8	4	5	Webb County	TX	Harry "Hank" I. Bussa, Jr.	1996	17,058
126 4/8	23 2/8	22 4/8	18 2/8	6	4	Roanoke County	VA	Leonard E. Goldstock	1996	17,058
126 4/8	21 6/8	23 0/8	18 6/8	4	4	Grant County	KY	Mark Meadows	1996	17,058
126 4/8	21 4/8	21 2/8	14 4/8	5	5	Clay County	MO	Mike Cherner	1996	17,058
126 4/8	23 3/8	23 5/8	22 2/8	5	5	Ross County	OH	Terry L. Bridenbaugh, Jr.	1996	17,058
126 4/8	24 0/8	24 2/8	17 2/8	5	5	Warren County	OH	Bruce Gregory Allen	1996	17,058
126 4/8	25 1/8	25 0/8	18 4/8	4	4	Anne Arundel County	MD	Mark D. Sanders	1996	17,058
126 4/8	23 5/8	23 6/8	21 0/8	4	4	McHenry County	IL	Mike Stanonik	1997	17,058
126 4/8	21 4/8	20 0/8	15 2/8	4	5	Livingston County	MI	Donald J. Egbert	1997	17,058
126 4/8	19 5/8	20 4/8	15 4/8	6	5	Blackfalds	ALB	Colin Campbell	1997	17,058
126 4/8	21 5/8	21 0/8	16 6/8	5	5	Iowa County	WI	Tracy Johnson	1997	17,058
126 4/8	22 2/8	22 1/8	15 0/8	5	4	Osage County	OK	Jim Bunnell	1997	17,058
126 4/8	21 0/8	20 4/8	16 6/8	5	5	Calhoun County	MI	Joseph W. Michilizzi	1997	17,058
126 4/8	21 6/8	18 5/8	17 3/8	7	7	Monona County	IA	Ken Holtz	1997	17,058
126 4/8	21 5/8	21 4/8	13 6/8	5	5	Jefferson County	ID	Doug Kauer	1997	17,058
126 4/8	22 5/8	22 5/8	16 6/8	4	4	Zavala County	TX	Joseph D. Krout III	1998	17,058
126 4/8	22 5/8	21 5/8	15 6/8	5	4	Griggs County	ND	Darren Fougner	1998	17,058
126 4/8	21 0/8	20 6/8	18 4/8	4	5	Flathead County	MT	John Bartlett	1998	17,058
126 4/8	22 3/8	22 2/8	17 2/8	5	5	Allegheny County	PA	Jerry Horn	1998	17,058
126 3/8	22 6/8	21 3/8	15 5/8	4	4	Lac qui Parle County	MN	Elmer Hubbs	1965	17,181
126 3/8	23 1/8	23 3/8	17 5/8	4	4	Sussex County	NJ	Jim Ott	1972	17,181
126 3/8	21 5/8	20 2/8	17 0/8	5	6	Gallatin County	KY	Robert L. Hegge, Jr.	1973	17,181
126 3/8	22 4/8	22 4/8	16 3/8	5	5	Eau Claire County	WI	Steven P. Gilbertson	1977	17,181
126 3/8	21 0/8	21 5/8	17 7/8	7	6	Clark County	KS	William Rule	1978	17,181
126 3/8	25 3/8	25 0/8	18 4/8	5	5	Morris County	NJ	Kurt Carlson	1982	17,181
126 3/8	23 3/8	22 4/8	15 3/8	4	4	Cayuga County	NY	John Pardee	1982	17,181
126 3/8	20 0/8	20 5/8	14 1/8	5	5	Shoshone County	ID	Richard J. O'Grady	1983	17,181
126 3/8	23 4/8	23 4/8	21 7/8	5	5	Green County	WI	Doug Cupp	1983	17,181
126 3/8	22 4/8	23 4/8	16 5/8	5	5	Sheboygan County	WI	Ronald Cook	1983	17,181
126 3/8	19 3/8	19 4/8	15 5/8	4	4	Polk County	WI	Allen Lunde	1984	17,181
126 3/8	22 3/8	21 4/8	18 2/8	6	6	Rock County	WI	John Van Altena	1984	17,181
126 3/8	21 2/8	21 1/8	14 6/8	6	6	Washington County	KS	Stan Brustowicz	1984	17,181
126 3/8	21 4/8	20 0/8	16 7/8	5	5	Dodge County	WI	Carl Schuett	1985	17,181
126 3/8	21 7/8	20 4/8	16 3/8	4	4	Waukesha County	WI	Dale J. Henderson	1985	17,181
126 3/8	20 2/8	18 2/8	16 1/8	4	5	Gregory County	SD	Dennis Lengkeek	1986	17,181
126 3/8	21 7/8	22 3/8	16 4/8	5	5	Brooke County	WV	Don Weekley	1986	17,181
126 3/8	21 1/8	21 3/8	17 4/8	8	5	Stephenson County	IL	Donald Miller	1986	17,181
126 3/8	19 7/8	20 4/8	15 5/8	4	4	Dodge County	GA	C. W. Wright	1987	17,181
126 3/8	22 7/8	23 4/8	18 7/8	4	4	Bay County	MI	Andrew F. Zawacki	1987	17,181
126 3/8	21 1/8	22 1/8	15 7/8	4	4	Frederick County	MD	Jeffrey S. Clark	1987	17,181
126 3/8	24 6/8	24 3/8	20 4/8	8	6	Reno County	KS	Bob Williams	1987	17,181
126 3/8	24 0/8	22 4/8	18 0/8	6	6	Union County	IL	Sam Shafer	1987	17,181
126 3/8	21 3/8	21 5/8	20 7/8	6	5	Washington County	MN	David L. Hart	1988	17,181
126 3/8	22 0/8	22 2/8	17 1/8	5	5	Hardin County	TN	Tom Oaks	1988	17,181
126 3/8	21 1/8	19 7/8	14 6/8	5	4	Pike County	IL	Emmett D. Carter	1988	17,181
126 3/8	22 2/8	22 2/8	16 5/8	5	5	Blue Earth County	MN	Dave Schultz	1988	17,181
126 3/8	22 2/8	22 2/8	20 5/8	4	4	Clay County	KY	Clarence Douglas Cupp	1988	17,181
126 3/8	23 1/8	21 4/8	18 7/8	4	4	Chase County	KS	Lee Ayres	1988	17,181
126 3/8	24 4/8	23 6/8	19 3/8	3	3	Perry County	IL	Terrence E. Dierkes	1988	17,181

WHITETAIL DEER (TYPICAL ANTLERS)

Minimum Score 125 — Continued

SCORE	LENGTH OF MAIN BEAM R	LENGTH OF MAIN BEAM L	INSIDE SPREAD	NUMBER OF POINTS R	NUMBER OF POINTS L	AREA	STATE/PROVINCE	HUNTER'S NAME	DATE	RANK
126 3/8	22 2/8	22 1/8	16 7/8	6	6	Kenedy County	TX	Romulo Rangel, Jr.	1989	17,181
126 3/8	22 6/8	22 1/8	15 7/8	4	4	Webster County	IA	Curtis Martens	1989	17,181
126 3/8	23 0/8	22 4/8	17 7/8	4	5	Linn County	IA	Jim Maxson	1989	17,181
126 3/8	20 4/8	19 4/8	18 7/8	4	5	Washington County	MS	Bobby R. Woods	1990	17,181
126 3/8	19 2/8	21 0/8	19 1/8	5	5	Price County	WI	Timothy Welch	1990	17,181
126 3/8	20 7/8	21 1/8	14 7/8	6	5	Chippewa County	WI	Mark Nelson	1990	17,181
126 3/8	23 2/8	21 7/8	17 0/8	6	7	Dodge County	MN	Ed Pitzenberger	1990	17,181
126 3/8	20 1/8	20 7/8	15 2/8	6	5	Goodhue County	MN	John "Jack" Cordes	1990	17,181
126 3/8	23 3/8	22 2/8	18 0/8	5	4	Montgomery County	MD	Frank H. Wilmot	1990	17,181
126 3/8	21 6/8	21 1/8	15 2/8	5	6	Johnson County	IA	Lowell Miller	1991	17,181
126 3/8	21 3/8	22 1/8	16 7/8	5	6	Malahide Township	ONT	Tim Rochette	1991	17,181
126 3/8	20 0/8	20 3/8	16 1/8	5	5	Logan County	OK	Eric D. Wynn	1991	17,181
126 3/8	22 1/8	20 6/8	14 5/8	4	5	Butler County	KS	Gary Talkington	1991	17,181
126 3/8	21 5/8	21 6/8	16 1/8	4	4	Lake County	IN	Thomas A. Cope	1991	17,181
126 3/8	21 6/8	19 5/8	16 5/8	5	5	Polk County	WI	Gene Hill	1991	17,181
126 3/8	21 6/8	22 1/8	16 3/8	5	5	Burleigh County	ND	Eric L. Martel	1991	17,181
126 3/8	22 3/8	19 4/8	17 7/8	5	4	Champaign County	OH	Thomas J. Flohre	1991	17,181
126 3/8	20 6/8	20 6/8	16 3/8	4	4	Mahnomen County	MN	Wendell Paulson	1992	17,181
126 3/8	20 7/8	21 4/8	17 7/8	6	6	York County	PA	Roy T. Weaver	1992	17,181
126 3/8	22 4/8	22 6/8	19 3/8	5	4	Washington County	GA	Nick Daniel	1992	17,181
126 3/8	21 2/8	21 4/8	18 3/8	5	4	Adams County	IL	Ron Hemken	1992	17,181
126 3/8	21 2/8	21 4/8	16 6/8	5	5	Stark County	OH	Charles M. Martin	1992	17,181
126 3/8	21 4/8	22 7/8	15 7/8	4	4	Tom Green County	TX	Jack Bains	1992	17,181
126 3/8	22 3/8	22 3/8	14 7/8	4	4	Marion County	IA	Keith Davis	1992	17,181
126 3/8	22 2/8	21 5/8	16 4/8	6	6	Billings County	ND	Corey Hugelen	1993	17,181
126 3/8	21 4/8	21 5/8	15 5/8	4	4	Logan County	CO	Kent Sump	1993	17,181
126 3/8	20 3/8	20 1/8	14 1/8	5	5	Boone County	MO	Ralph W. Olinger	1993	17,181
126 3/8	24 2/8	24 4/8	17 7/8	5	4	Johnson County	IN	Larry J. Kinser	1993	17,181
126 3/8	22 4/8	22 2/8	18 3/8	4	5	Langlade County	WI	Todd M. Hartman	1993	17,181
126 3/8	17 7/8	18 1/8	14 7/8	5	5	Uvalde County	TX	Monty McGrade	1994	17,181
126 3/8	21 3/8	20 3/8	14 7/8	4	5	Lewis County	KY	Joseph H. Pflum	1994	17,181
126 3/8	22 6/8	22 1/8	20 1/8	4	4	Tolland County	CT	Lionel Lavallee	1994	17,181
126 3/8	19 1/8	19 3/8	16 7/8	5	5	Columbia County	WI	Greg Klawes	1994	17,181
126 3/8	21 2/8	22 2/8	17 1/8	4	4	Dubuque County	IA	Steve M. Seipp	1994	17,181
126 3/8	19 0/8	19 5/8	16 5/8	6	6	Van Buren County	IA	Timothy M. Boyer	1994	17,181
126 3/8	22 5/8	23 1/8	20 2/8	5	4	Pike County	IL	Gregory S. Guerrieri	1994	17,181
126 3/8	21 4/8	19 7/8	15 1/8	5	4	Edgar County	IL	Dennis A. Duzan	1994	17,181
126 3/8	22 6/8	22 6/8	18 5/8	5	4	Montgomery County	PA	Richard B. Driscoll	1994	17,181
126 3/8	20 1/8	20 5/8	20 1/8	4	4	Barrow County	GA	Cory Thompson	1995	17,181
126 3/8	20 5/8	21 0/8	15 4/8	7	7	Fond du Lac County	WI	Ralph Jaber	1995	17,181
126 3/8	20 6/8	21 0/8	16 7/8	4	4	Douglas County	WI	Scott Jones	1995	17,181
126 3/8	23 1/8	21 2/8	19 0/8	8	5	Tompkins County	NY	Jared S. Prentiss	1995	17,181
126 3/8	22 1/8	21 7/8	13 5/8	5	5	Lancaster County	PA	Jeff Williams	1995	17,181
126 3/8	20 7/8	21 5/8	16 5/8	4	4	Boone County	MO	Robert Hagans	1995	17,181
126 3/8	19 7/8	18 3/8	15 7/8	5	5	Saginaw County	MI	John Knieper	1995	17,181
126 3/8	22 2/8	22 1/8	16 1/8	5	5	Pulaski County	IN	Jim Govert	1995	17,181
126 3/8	22 3/8	21 7/8	17 1/8	4	5	Montgomery County	AL	David J. Barrow	1995	17,181
126 3/8	21 7/8	21 6/8	14 3/8	5	5	Mills County	IA	Jim Wilshire	1996	17,181
126 3/8	20 6/8	20 6/8	15 5/8	5	5	York County	PA	Wayne D. Heidlebaugh	1996	17,181
126 3/8	22 3/8	22 2/8	18 7/8	4	5	Stanley County	SD	Gene Hove	1996	17,181
126 3/8	21 6/8	23 4/8	15 5/8	6	5	Jackson County	WI	Dale Boehnen	1996	17,181
126 3/8	21 7/8	21 7/8	17 1/8	4	4	Tazewell County	IL	Jerry Manning	1996	17,181
126 3/8	22 0/8	21 2/8	17 1/8	4	5	Lincoln County	WI	Rich Ashbrenner	1996	17,181
126 3/8	22 7/8	20 5/8	17 7/8	4	4	Chester County	PA	Harry Hatzipavlides	1996	17,181
126 3/8	22 0/8	21 6/8	17 5/8	4	5	Grant County	WI	Brian Sherman	1996	17,181
126 3/8	20 7/8	20 6/8	17 7/8	4	4	Iowa County	WI	Dean Jorgenson	1996	17,181
126 3/8	19 0/8	19 2/8	14 3/8	5	7	Johnson County	NE	Brian Brinkman	1996	17,181
126 3/8	20 1/8	20 5/8	16 7/8	5	5	Douglas County	WI	Duane A. Fonger	1996	17,181
126 3/8	22 0/8	22 5/8	19 3/8	4	4	Carroll County	MD	Tom Blizzard	1997	17,181
126 3/8	18 4/8	17 5/8	13 0/8	6	5	Wharton County	TX	Taylor Radley	1997	17,181
126 3/8	21 1/8	21 3/8	17 3/8	5	4	Calhoun County	MI	Greg J. Slone	1997	17,181
126 3/8	21 1/8	20 3/8	15 7/8	5	5	Winona County	MN	Gary Bauer	1997	17,181
126 3/8	21 7/8	21 3/8	18 7/8	5	5	Sauk County	WI	Reed Horton	1997	17,181
126 3/8	25 4/8	24 7/8	17 2/8	5	6	Barbour County	AL	Chad Baxter	1997	17,181
126 3/8	20 1/8	21 0/8	14 2/8	6	5	Winona County	MN	Bill Ware	1997	17,181
126 3/8	23 4/8	23 0/8	19 5/8	4	4	Vigo County	IN	Rocky May	1997	17,181
126 3/8	24 2/8	25 0/8	20 1/8	4	5	Macoupin County	IL	Dave Burcham	1997	17,181
126 3/8	21 0/8	22 1/8	16 7/8	4	4	Bayfield County	WI	David Conklin	1997	17,181
126 3/8	20 4/8	20 1/8	15 2/8	8	7	Olmsted County	MN	James L. Kobriger	1998	17,181
126 2/8	22 7/8	22 0/8	17 2/8	5	5	Lee County	IL	Edmund R. Braun	1959	17,280
126 2/8	22 0/8	20 6/8	17 6/8	4	4	Johnson County	IA	Paul F. Spicer	1963	17,280
126 2/8	20 0/8	19 3/8	16 0/8	4	4	Harding County	SD	Gerald Swayze	1965	17,280
126 2/8	21 3/8	21 4/8	15 4/8	4	4	Morrison County	MN	Frank Hogan	1967	17,280
126 2/8	20 6/8	20 2/8	15 6/8	5	5	Adams County	IL	Adrian K. Smith	1967	17,280
126 2/8	21 4/8	21 4/8	16 2/8	4	4	Ford County	KS	Bob Stephenson	1967	17,280
126 2/8	20 1/8	20 7/8	14 4/8	5	5	Platte County	NE	Keith Bruhn	1968	17,280
126 2/8	23 7/8	23 5/8	17 3/8	5	4	Marathon County	WI	Dan Niehaus	1968	17,280
126 2/8	24 1/8	23 7/8	14 6/8	4	4	Winneshiek County	IA	Marc Headington	1971	17,280

WHITETAIL DEER (TYPICAL ANTLERS)

Minimum Score 125

SCORE	LENGTH OF MAIN BEAM R	LENGTH OF MAIN BEAM L	INSIDE SPREAD	NUMBER OF POINTS R	NUMBER OF POINTS L	AREA	STATE/ PROVINCE	HUNTER'S NAME	DATE	RANK
126 2/8	21 0/8	20 7/8	16 0/8	5	5	Carroll County	IL	Art Heinze	1972	17,280
126 2/8	22 1/8	21 5/8	16 0/8	5	5	Dade County	MO	Charles A. Myers	1975	17,280
126 2/8	20 0/8	20 0/8	14 6/8	5	5	Washington County	OH	Joe D. Schofield	1977	17,280
126 2/8	20 7/8	21 4/8	16 0/8	5	5	Dodge County	WI	Keith Peterson	1977	17,280
126 2/8	18 0/8	18 5/8	15 0/8	5	5	Wood County	WI	David Kievet	1978	17,280
126 2/8	20 6/8	20 5/8	13 5/8	6	6	Stevens County	WA	David B. Muffly	1978	17,280
126 2/8	21 4/8	21 7/8	17 2/8	5	5	Waupaca County	WI	Daniel E. Yaeger	1978	17,280
126 2/8	22 2/8	22 4/8	16 4/8	4	3	Franklin County	OH	Steven H. Byerly	1979	17,280
126 2/8	20 0/8	20 3/8	16 2/8	4	4	Greenwood County	SC	E. Dale Carwile	1980	17,280
126 2/8	22 5/8	21 6/8	17 2/8	6	5	Livingston County	MO	Myles Keller	1980	17,280
126 2/8	24 0/8	24 4/8	19 0/8	4	4	Autauga County	AL	George Poston, Jr.	1981	17,280
126 2/8	21 5/8	22 4/8	16 4/8	9	4	Jefferson County	NE	Bob Funke	1981	17,280
126 2/8	21 5/8	20 7/8	20 2/8	4	5	Lyon County	MN	Wayne Kumm	1981	17,280
126 2/8	22 2/8	22 2/8	17 2/8	4	6	Kearny County	KS	David Meyers	1981	17,280
126 2/8	21 2/8	21 2/8	15 2/8	4	5	Meigs County	OH	Charles H. Murray	1982	17,280
126 2/8	22 1/8	22 2/8	15 4/8	5	5	Live Oak County	TX	Rick Hayley	1983	17,280
126 2/8	23 1/8	23 0/8	20 3/8	6	6	Marquette County	WI	Stewart McReath	1983	17,280
126 2/8	22 2/8	21 2/8	17 2/8	5	5	Venango County	PA	Jeffrey S. Morrison	1983	17,280
126 2/8	22 6/8	22 5/8	13 4/8	5	6	Preble County	OH	Roger D. Dolph	1983	17,280
126 2/8	21 0/8	21 1/8	17 4/8	4	4	Lake County	IL	Henry J. Schwarz	1983	17,280
126 2/8	19 2/8	20 5/8	17 6/8	6	5	Clay County	MN	Steve Steinhoff	1983	17,280
126 2/8	22 6/8	22 1/8	14 4/8	4	5	Dane County	WI	Dennis L. Stiklestad	1983	17,280
126 2/8	19 6/8	19 6/8	13 4/8	6	6	Montcalm County	MI	Steve A. Alexander	1984	17,280
126 2/8	21 0/8	20 0/8	12 6/8	5	5	Augusta County	VA	Nicholas C. Taylor	1984	17,280
126 2/8	19 0/8	20 0/8	18 0/8	5	5	Athens County	OH	Craig Littler	1984	17,280
126 2/8	20 3/8	19 6/8	14 4/8	5	5	McKenzie County	ND	Tim Finley	1985	17,280
126 2/8	18 4/8	19 6/8	15 2/8	4	4	Pulaski County	IN	Tony Bean	1985	17,280
126 2/8	22 2/8	21 2/8	17 2/8	4	5	Pittsburg County	OK	Jim Stith	1985	17,280
126 2/8	22 0/8	22 4/8	15 4/8	5	6	Boone County	MO	Tommy Foster	1985	17,280
126 2/8	22 5/8	22 3/8	16 2/8	4	4	Langlade County	WI	Douglas L. Below	1986	17,280
126 2/8	20 2/8	20 0/8	15 2/8	5	5	Meeker County	MN	Brent Swanson	1986	17,280
126 2/8	24 0/8	23 5/8	17 4/8	9	5	Sullivan County	TN	Austin Morrison	1986	17,280
126 2/8	21 1/8	21 1/8	15 2/8	5	5	Sawyer County	WI	Ralph Isham	1986	17,280
126 2/8	21 4/8	20 1/8	16 6/8	5	5	Pushmataha County	OK	Jan R. Coleman	1987	17,280
126 2/8	23 0/8	22 5/8	15 4/8	5	5	Darke County	OH	Matt Arnold	1987	17,280
126 2/8	19 7/8	20 4/8	18 5/8	6	7	Ogle County	IL	Gary Shaw	1987	17,280
126 2/8	23 6/8	23 3/8	16 5/8	4	6	Iroquois County	IL	Bill Price	1987	17,280
126 2/8	24 0/8	24 2/8	16 1/8	6	4	Kent County	MD	Tony M. Panaro	1988	17,280
126 2/8	20 4/8	21 1/8	18 4/8	4	5	Dunn County	WI	George Woodington	1988	17,280
126 2/8	23 1/8	23 4/8	17 4/8	4	6	Buffalo County	WI	Gunner J. Hagen	1988	17,280
126 2/8	20 4/8	20 2/8	18 0/8	4	4	Le Sueur County	MN	Randy Mathwig	1989	17,280
126 2/8	21 6/8	21 4/8	15 6/8	4	4	Passaic County	NJ	Michael Stabile	1989	17,280
126 2/8	20 0/8	20 0/8	13 6/8	4	4	Codington County	SD	Tim Chandler	1989	17,280
126 2/8	22 3/8	22 0/8	17 0/8	5	5	Wood County	WI	Paul S. Esser	1989	17,280
126 2/8	21 0/8	20 4/8	17 2/8	4	4	Guernsey County	OH	Edward E. Vasko	1989	17,280
126 2/8	22 1/8	23 0/8	18 4/8	7	6	Butler County	KS	Larry Yarbrough	1989	17,280
126 2/8	22 6/8	23 4/8	15 2/8	4	4	Clark County	IL	Charles E. Guyer	1989	17,280
126 2/8	23 7/8	17 2/8	15 4/8	4	4	Woodford County	IL	Lyle E. Stine	1989	17,280
126 2/8	19 7/8	21 3/8	17 0/8	5	4	Macomb County	MI	Barry Martin	1990	17,280
126 2/8	21 3/8	21 6/8	17 6/8	4	4	Guernsey County	OH	Daniel L. Kerns	1990	17,280
126 2/8	21 5/8	22 1/8	16 4/8	4	4	Allegheny County	PA	Jared Roscart	1991	17,280
126 2/8	22 5/8	22 2/8	17 6/8	4	4	Ashland County	WI	Ryan S. Mesko	1991	17,280
126 2/8	22 5/8	22 4/8	18 6/8	4	4	Marathon County	WI	Randy L. Feltz	1991	17,280
126 2/8	21 0/8	21 2/8	16 2/8	5	5	Creek County	OK	Shane Murphy	1991	17,280
126 2/8	21 0/8	22 7/8	18 0/8	5	5	Kleberg County	TX	Dr. Terry W. Brandt	1991	17,280
126 2/8	18 5/8	21 4/8	17 0/8	5	7	McHenry County	IL	Chuck Chism	1992	17,280
126 2/8	21 6/8	21 6/8	18 0/8	4	4	Howard County	MD	Jeffrey D. Carlson	1992	17,280
126 2/8	22 4/8	22 6/8	16 4/8	5	6	Waukesha County	WI	Donn Koglin	1992	17,280
126 2/8	21 2/8	21 2/8	15 6/8	5	5	Burnett County	WI	Stan Falkenhagen	1992	17,280
126 2/8	21 0/8	21 4/8	17 2/8	4	4	Erie County	NY	Michael Weber	1993	17,280
126 2/8	20 4/8	20 7/8	15 6/8	4	4	Dane County	WI	Tracy S. Retallick	1993	17,280
126 2/8	23 7/8	23 3/8	19 2/8	4	4	Rusk County	WI	Richard G. Schafer	1993	17,280
126 2/8	21 5/8	21 7/8	15 0/8	5	4	Miami County	KS	Randy Stoughton	1993	17,280
126 2/8	22 1/8	21 1/8	17 4/8	4	4	Madison County	IA	Merle Allen	1993	17,280
126 2/8	18 7/8	18 5/8	16 0/8	5	5	Iowa County	WI	Raube R. Pann	1993	17,280
126 2/8	20 5/8	19 1/8	17 4/8	6	5	St. Croix County	WI	Marv Raska	1993	17,280
126 2/8	23 3/8	22 4/8	14 6/8	4	4	Hendricks County	IN	Jerry Skinner	1993	17,280
126 2/8	21 2/8	22 1/8	18 6/8	4	4	Bureau County	IL	Jeff A. Lucas	1993	17,280
126 2/8	22 4/8	23 5/8	17 1/8	6	4	Geauga County	OH	Jason A. Petrovic	1993	17,280
126 2/8	19 2/8	18 5/8	16 0/8	5	5	Olmsted County	MN	Mark R. Batterson	1993	17,280
126 2/8	22 1/8	22 3/8	18 4/8	5	6	Ozaukee County	WI	Bob Bach	1994	17,280
126 2/8	22 1/8	21 6/8	16 6/8	4	4	Kerr County	TX	Vincent Grasso	1994	17,280
126 2/8	20 6/8	21 3/8	17 5/8	4	6	Kent County	MI	Robert J. Alt	1994	17,280
126 2/8	20 1/8	19 5/8	16 4/8	4	5	Fairfield County	OH	Charles D. Humphreys	1994	17,280
126 2/8	21 6/8	21 6/8	17 2/8	4	4	Polk County	WI	Dan L. Kelley	1994	17,280
126 2/8	21 7/8	21 6/8	17 6/8	5	4	Iron County	WI	Dave Matis	1994	17,280
126 2/8	23 0/8	22 4/8	22 1/8	5	5	Hunterdon County	NJ	John A. Lupi	1994	17,280
126 2/8	21 4/8	21 3/8	15 0/8	5	5	Mercer County	IL	Daniel R. Bergen	1994	17,280

Continued

WHITETAIL DEER (TYPICAL ANTLERS)

Minimum Score 125 — Continued

SCORE	LENGTH OF MAIN BEAM R	LENGTH OF MAIN BEAM L	INSIDE SPREAD	NUMBER OF POINTS R	NUMBER OF POINTS L	AREA	STATE/ PROVINCE	HUNTER'S NAME	DATE	RANK
126 2/8	20 0/8	20 1/8	16 6/8	6	7	Chester County	PA	Steve A. Mack, Jr.	1994	17,280
126 2/8	21 4/8	21 6/8	15 0/8	4	4	Bladen County	NC	Bobby Richardson	1994	17,280
126 2/8	21 7/8	21 5/8	17 4/8	4	4	Pike County	IL	Jay Verzuh	1994	17,280
126 2/8	21 6/8	22 4/8	18 0/8	5	5	McHenry County	IL	Charles Weech	1994	17,280
126 2/8	20 7/8	20 3/8	16 4/8	5	5	Refusio County	TX	Ira L. Jones II	1994	17,280
126 2/8	20 3/8	19 7/8	15 6/8	5	5	Monmouth County	NJ	Joseph Rada	1995	17,280
126 2/8	19 0/8	19 4/8	15 4/8	5	5	Adams County	WI	Howard L. Chilewski	1995	17,280
126 2/8	19 6/8	20 2/8	16 2/8	5	5	St. Croix County	WI	Bruce D. Gehrman	1995	17,280
126 2/8	22 4/8	22 7/8	14 0/8	7	4	Crawford County	PA	Mark D. Rogan	1995	17,280
126 2/8	22 4/8	22 3/8	16 3/8	6	5	Waukesha County	WI	John Riehle	1995	17,280
126 2/8	23 6/8	21 7/8	16 6/8	4	5	Jersey County	IL	Bart Shaw	1995	17,280
126 2/8	20 4/8	22 6/8	17 6/8	4	4	Dekalb County	IL	Glenn Gustafson	1995	17,280
126 2/8	17 3/8	18 1/8	16 6/8	5	5	Allegany County	NY	Michael Judd	1995	17,280
126 2/8	19 5/8	18 7/8	16 4/8	5	5	Refugio County	TX	Gary Hayek	1995	17,280
126 2/8	23 7/8	23 3/8	18 0/8	5	5	Cayuga County	NY	David S. Suslik	1996	17,280
126 2/8	22 2/8	23 0/8	18 0/8	5	4	Winona County	MN	Lance Johnson	1996	17,280
126 2/8	21 3/8	21 0/8	16 6/8	5	5	Buffalo County	WI	Stuart Hagen	1996	17,280
126 2/8	21 0/8	21 0/8	17 2/8	5	6	Buffalo County	WI	Don Linse	1996	17,280
126 2/8	20 4/8	20 0/8	15 4/8	4	4	Keya Paha County	NE	Terry N. Marcukaitis	1996	17,280
126 2/8	20 2/8	20 2/8	15 0/8	4	4	Gallatin County	IL	Donald L. Smith	1996	17,280
126 2/8	19 5/8	19 5/8	15 4/8	5	5	McMullen County	TX	David E. Gillioz	1996	17,280
126 2/8	22 0/8	20 6/8	17 6/8	5	4	Dodge County	MN	Steve E. Snow	1997	17,280
126 2/8	21 0/8	22 4/8	16 2/8	6	5	Hopkins County	KY	Larry Rhoden	1997	17,280
126 2/8	20 2/8	20 1/8	15 0/8	5	5	Buffalo County	WI	Jeremy L. Pank	1997	17,280
126 2/8	18 6/8	19 4/8	19 2/8	5	5	Manitowoc County	WI	Dan Biely	1997	17,280
126 2/8	22 1/8	21 2/8	15 4/8	4	6	Screven County	GA	Thad Beckum	1997	17,280
126 2/8	22 2/8	22 4/8	17 6/8	4	5	Black Hawk County	IA	Bradley Heath	1997	17,280
126 2/8	20 6/8	20 3/8	14 0/8	5	5	Iowa County	WI	R. Lowell Davis	1997	17,280
126 2/8	23 2/8	22 4/8	18 4/8	4	4	Franklin County	PA	Mike Jones	1997	17,280
126 2/8	21 2/8	21 0/8	16 2/8	5	6	Union County	IL	Mark A. Gregorich	1997	17,280
126 2/8	19 6/8	21 4/8	15 6/8	4	4	Rogers County	OK	Chris Sinor	1997	17,280
126 2/8	21 2/8	20 6/8	15 6/8	5	5	Clark County	WI	Bruce Vandeberg	1997	17,280
126 2/8	21 0/8	22 1/8	14 6/8	4	4	Jo Daviess County	IL	Mike Henkelman	1997	17,280
126 2/8	22 4/8	23 2/8	16 6/8	5	5	Geauga County	OH	Gregory A. Anderson	1997	17,280
126 2/8	22 2/8	21 7/8	17 4/8	6	4	Fairfield County	OH	Larry Farmer, Jr.	1997	17,280
126 2/8	23 6/8	23 5/8	16 2/8	4	4	Mercer County	OH	Don Kahlig	1997	17,280
126 2/8	20 5/8	20 7/8	17 0/8	5	5	Pike County	IL	Dan Perez	1997	17,280
126 2/8	22 4/8	22 6/8	18 4/8	5	4	Westchester County	NY	Craig Breighner	1997	17,280
126 2/8	19 6/8	20 5/8	17 2/8	6	5	Washington County	MS	Tony Arnold	1998	17,280
126 2/8	20 2/8	19 4/8	15 4/8	5	4	Waushara County	WI	Patrick M. Goss	1998	17,280
126 1/8	25 2/8	24 5/8	18 5/8	4	4	York County	PA	Gregory E. Smith	1969	17,407
126 1/8	22 1/8	21 7/8	16 5/8	5	4	Monmouth County	NJ	Charles C. Lasala	1970	17,407
126 1/8	20 4/8	18 6/8	18 1/8	4	4	Pope County	IL	Murray Schuhart	1972	17,407
126 1/8	21 4/8	21 4/8	16 3/8	4	5	Lincoln County	SD	Stephen K. Sona	1975	17,407
126 1/8	21 3/8	20 5/8	14 4/8	5	4	Oconto County	WI	Rick Moudry	1977	17,407
126 1/8	22 0/8	21 1/8	17 1/8	5	5	Gladwin County	MI	Dave Longstreth	1980	17,407
126 1/8	18 1/8	18 7/8	15 3/8	5	5	Brown County	SD	Charles Fulker	1980	17,407
126 1/8	23 4/8	22 3/8	16 6/8	6	5	Rice County	MN	Jeff Purdie	1981	17,407
126 1/8	21 4/8	21 5/8	17 1/8	5	5	Richland County	WI	David P. Berns	1982	17,407
126 1/8	20 2/8	20 2/8	15 7/8	4	4	Pulaski County	KY	Johnny Farmer	1983	17,407
126 1/8	20 4/8	21 2/8	14 4/8	5	6	Lyon County	KY	Bobby G. "Butch" McCarley	1983	17,407
126 1/8	22 1/8	21 5/8	18 7/8	4	4	Lamoure County	ND	Rodney W. Peterson	1985	17,407
126 1/8	23 2/8	21 5/8	15 7/8	4	4	Iowa County	WI	Jamie Gottschall	1986	17,407
126 1/8	23 5/8	23 4/8	16 7/8	4	6	Waukesha County	WI	Bob Blunck	1986	17,407
126 1/8	23 2/8	23 3/8	17 7/8	4	4	Frederick County	MD	Kenneth R. Peomroy	1986	17,407
126 1/8	19 7/8	19 3/8	13 7/8	5	5	Mobile County	AL	Scott Jordon	1987	17,407
126 1/8	20 0/8	20 1/8	16 2/8	6	6	Pittsburg County	OK	Wanda Larimer	1987	17,407
126 1/8	23 6/8	22 6/8	19 4/8	6	7	Dane County	WI	Dale H. Anderson	1987	17,407
126 1/8	22 5/8	21 6/8	15 7/8	4	4	Highland County	OH	Dan Sowders	1987	17,407
126 1/8	22 4/8	20 0/8	16 0/8	5	6	Hocking County	OH	Greg Sutton	1987	17,407
126 1/8	21 2/8	21 5/8	15 5/8	4	4	New Castle County	DE	Joseph J. Subolefsky	1988	17,407
126 1/8	20 2/8	19 4/8	13 1/8	5	6	Adams County	WI	Jim Haslow	1988	17,407
126 1/8	22 6/8	19 2/8	21 7/8	4	4	Harford County	MD	Mike Kelly	1988	17,407
126 1/8	22 7/8	23 6/8	17 2/8	4	7	Monmouth County	NJ	Bob Sacher	1988	17,407
126 1/8	21 7/8	23 1/8	18 3/8	4	5	Calhoun County	MI	Ron Allen	1989	17,407
126 1/8	20 7/8	20 2/8	16 7/8	5	5	Jefferson County	IN	Rodney W. Stratton	1989	17,407
126 1/8	24 1/8	23 6/8	19 1/8	7	6	Lake County	IN	Doyle Niemeyer	1989	17,407
126 1/8	20 3/8	20 4/8	14 3/8	6	6	Ralls County	MO	Larry David	1989	17,407
126 1/8	19 6/8	19 5/8	15 7/8	5	5	Llano County	TX	Kip Reagor	1989	17,407
126 1/8	22 4/8	22 0/8	16 1/8	6	7	Putnam County	OH	Isidore Schnipke	1989	17,407
126 1/8	23 2/8	23 2/8	18 7/8	4	3	Bollinger County	MO	Jesse Whittley, Jr.	1989	17,407
126 1/8	21 1/8	21 5/8	16 3/8	4	4	Knox County	MO	Mike Siebeneck	1990	17,407
126 1/8	21 0/8	19 2/8	16 7/8	5	5	La Salle County	TX	Dennis C. Faulkenberry	1990	17,407
126 1/8	21 2/8	21 7/8	16 7/8	4	4	Marathon County	WI	Randy Feltz	1990	17,407
126 1/8	20 1/8	20 6/8	15 3/8	6	6	Somerset County	NJ	Robert Staudt, Jr.	1990	17,407
126 1/8	19 7/8	20 5/8	20 6/8	4	5	Macon County	AL	George P. Mann	1990	17,407
126 1/8	20 5/8	20 6/8	19 5/8	5	5	Craig County	OK	Eddie Claypool	1990	17,407
126 1/8	21 2/8	21 3/8	17 3/8	4	4	Dunn County	WI	Paul C. Becker	1991	17,407

WHITETAIL DEER (TYPICAL ANTLERS)

Minimum Score 125 — Continued

SCORE	LENGTH OF MAIN BEAM R	L	INSIDE SPREAD	NUMBER OF POINTS R	L	AREA	STATE/ PROVINCE	HUNTER'S NAME	DATE	RANK
126 1/8	21 3/8	22 5/8	16 7/8	4	4	Monongalia County	WV	Dave McLaughlin	1991	17,407
126 1/8	20 7/8	22 2/8	17 1/8	5	5	Granville County	NC	Ricky Lewis Keller	1991	17,407
126 1/8	20 2/8	20 5/8	18 1/8	5	5	Douglas County	WI	Steve Wittke	1991	17,407
126 1/8	20 3/8	21 6/8	17 3/8	5	5	St. Clair County	IL	Gregory F. Elceser	1991	17,407
126 1/8	21 3/8	21 3/8	16 3/8	4	4	Tuscaloosa County	AL	Larry E. Lee	1991	17,407
126 1/8	21 0/8	20 7/8	16 7/8	4	4	Granville County	NC	David W. Jernigan	1992	17,407
126 1/8	20 5/8	20 1/8	16 7/8	4	4	Price County	WI	Robert J. Hornenberger	1992	17,407
126 1/8	23 5/8	24 4/8	21 3/8	4	5	Rock County	WI	Robert J. Coleman	1992	17,407
126 1/8	23 6/8	21 3/8	17 5/8	5	5	Angelina County	TX	Danny L. Havard	1992	17,407
126 1/8	19 3/8	20 1/8	15 7/8	5	5	Washington County	MN	Konrad Koosmann	1992	17,407
126 1/8	23 4/8	23 5/8	18 4/8	7	5	Morrison County	MN	Walt Anderson	1992	17,407
126 1/8	23 7/8	23 4/8	16 0/8	6	5	Lake County	IL	Mark Nelsen	1992	17,407
126 1/8	20 3/8	20 5/8	18 3/8	5	5	St. Croix County	WI	Paul E. Korn	1992	17,407
126 1/8	22 2/8	22 2/8	15 0/8	5	8	Washington County	WI	Conrad Hannula	1992	17,407
126 1/8	21 7/8	23 4/8	14 5/8	4	4	Alexander County	IL	Larry McHughs	1992	17,407
126 1/8	21 0/8	21 7/8	18 1/8	4	5	Ferry County	WA	Steve Winter	1992	17,407
126 1/8	22 3/8	21 7/8	16 1/8	4	4	Rock County	WI	Gregg C. Sutherland	1992	17,407
126 1/8	22 3/8	23 4/8	17 7/8	4	4	Westchester County	NY	Don Connolly	1992	17,407
126 1/8	18 5/8	19 5/8	17 5/8	5	6	Grant County	WI	Steven Dobson	1993	17,407
126 1/8	22 6/8	23 2/8	16 7/8	5	4	Fulton County	GA	James Parivechio III	1993	17,407
126 1/8	22 5/8	23 2/8	15 5/8	5	4	Kalamazoo County	MI	Ken K. Springsteen	1993	17,407
126 1/8	20 5/8	20 5/8	17 3/8	4	4	Dane County	WI	Wayne A. Aeschlimann	1993	17,407
126 1/8	23 1/8	22 6/8	16 0/8	6	4	Lake County	IL	Tim J. Stevens	1993	17,407
126 1/8	22 0/8	22 1/8	18 7/8	4	4	Forest County	WI	Paul Bowers	1993	17,407
126 1/8	21 6/8	21 2/8	20 3/8	5	4	Columbia County	WI	Steven F. Heiling	1993	17,407
126 1/8	21 0/8	21 5/8	17 1/8	4	4	Labette County	KS	Kent Schenker	1993	17,407
126 1/8	22 4/8	22 1/8	17 7/8	5	4	Hardin County	KY	Ricky K. Taylor	1993	17,407
126 1/8	19 4/8	19 1/8	15 5/8	5	5	Racine County	WI	Matt Luxem	1993	17,407
126 1/8	22 0/8	21 3/8	17 5/8	4	4	Monmouth County	NJ	Harold J. Smith	1993	17,407
126 1/8	23 0/8	23 4/8	20 4/8	5	4	Mason County	IL	John R. Troxell	1993	17,407
126 1/8	21 7/8	21 0/8	18 5/8	4	4	Jasper County	IN	Kevin Terpstra	1993	17,407
126 1/8	22 0/8	22 4/8	18 5/8	4	4	Hunterdon County	NJ	Peter Grimard	1993	17,407
126 1/8	21 0/8	20 2/8	15 3/8	5	5	Jefferson County	TX	William H. Goodson	1993	17,407
126 1/8	20 3/8	19 3/8	14 7/8	7	7	Sedgwick County	KS	Jon Burgdorf	1994	17,407
126 1/8	20 0/8	19 6/8	15 7/8	5	4	Reagan County	TX	Roy M. Proctor	1994	17,407
126 1/8	22 0/8	21 3/8	15 3/8	5	4	Lee County	IA	Dan Glasgow, Sr.	1994	17,407
126 1/8	21 6/8	21 1/8	16 5/8	5	4	Rusk County	WI	Marc LeClair	1994	17,407
126 1/8	21 7/8	20 5/8	14 5/8	6	5	Jefferson County	WI	Wally Steinke	1994	17,407
126 1/8	19 1/8	18 5/8	13 1/8	5	5	Codington County	SD	LeAllen Endres	1994	17,407
126 1/8	20 6/8	21 1/8	17 1/8	5	5	Adams County	IL	Brian Schenck	1994	17,407
126 1/8	20 2/8	20 6/8	17 7/8	5	5	La Salle County	TX	Gary R. Vaughn	1994	17,407
126 1/8	23 0/8	23 6/8	16 5/8	4	4	Somerset County	NJ	Steven J. Niedzielski	1994	17,407
126 1/8	19 1/8	19 2/8	17 3/8	5	5	Taylor County	TX	Max Paddock	1995	17,407
126 1/8	19 2/8	18 4/8	17 5/8	5	5	Kenedy County	TX	M. R. James	1995	17,407
126 1/8	22 2/8	22 1/8	18 3/8	4	4	Brown County	IL	Freddy King, Jr.	1995	17,407
126 1/8	21 3/8	21 3/8	15 3/8	5	5	Fulton County	GA	Lee E. Johnson	1995	17,407
126 1/8	23 0/8	22 6/8	16 4/8	4	5	Monroe County	NY	Don Eichas	1995	17,407
126 1/8	18 4/8	19 6/8	15 5/8	5	5	Brown County	IL	Sylvan Purcell	1995	17,407
126 1/8	22 7/8	22 6/8	19 1/8	4	4	Warren County	MS	Luke Parker	1995	17,407
126 1/8	21 1/8	21 4/8	16 7/8	5	4	Bourbon County	KS	Larry H. Walden	1995	17,407
126 1/8	26 1/8	25 7/8	18 3/8	3	3	Dakota County	MN	Len Barnhill	1995	17,407
126 1/8	20 3/8	21 3/8	17 3/8	5	5	Fillmore County	MN	Alan Joswick	1996	17,407
126 1/8	20 7/8	21 1/8	16 3/8	5	5	Oakland County	MI	Michael J. DeWitt	1996	17,407
126 1/8	21 6/8	22 6/8	16 0/8	6	5	Bourbon County	KS	Kevin G. Asbury	1996	17,407
126 1/8	24 6/8	24 3/8	17 5/8	4	5	Franklin County	MA	David M. Underwood	1996	17,407
126 1/8	21 7/8	22 5/8	14 1/8	5	5	Lapeer County	MI	Ken Vanniman	1996	17,407
126 1/8	22 1/8	22 1/8	15 3/8	4	5	Shelby County	MO	Kyle Manning	1996	17,407
126 1/8	22 2/8	22 3/8	15 7/8	5	5	McMullen County	TX	Art Haws	1996	17,407
126 1/8	20 4/8	19 1/8	14 3/8	5	5	Kandiyohi County	MN	Ron Welle	1997	17,407
126 1/8	19 6/8	20 6/8	16 1/8	4	5	Clare County	MI	Chuck Duzan	1997	17,407
126 1/8	20 7/8	20 6/8	14 7/8	5	5	St. Marys County	MD	Phillip Cartwright	1997	17,407
126 1/8	20 3/8	21 0/8	16 7/8	4	5	Richland County	WI	Jerome "Mac" McKenzie	1997	17,407
126 1/8	21 4/8	21 4/8	15 7/8	5	5	Polk County	IA	Steve Quenette	1997	17,407
126 1/8	22 1/8	21 7/8	17 5/8	4	4	Pike County	IL	Jason Cummings	1997	17,407
126 1/8	19 5/8	18 6/8	15 3/8	5	5	Calhoun County	MI	Peter R. Grevers	1997	17,407
126 1/8	23 0/8	22 3/8	18 1/8	4	5	Kent County	MI	Joseph R. Garvon	1997	17,407
126 1/8	21 2/8	23 3/8	18 7/8	5	4	Lake County	IL	Jeffrey D. Miller	1997	17,407
126 1/8	24 1/8	22 6/8	22 3/8	4	4	Washington County	MS	Joe Hubbard, Jr.	1998	17,407
126 1/8	20 7/8	20 5/8	16 1/8	5	5	Albany County	WY	Willard Woods	1998	17,407
126 1/8	22 0/8	22 0/8	16 4/8	4	6	Fulton County	IN	Steven C. Bauer	1998	17,407
126 1/8	22 6/8	21 1/8	14 3/8	5	5	Beaver County	PA	Keith Furness	1998	17,407
126 0/8	20 3/8	20 3/8	14 0/8	4	4	Cherry County	NE	Dean Bergman	1975	17,516
126 0/8	22 1/8	20 4/8	16 2/8	5	4	McMinn County	TN	Wesley B. Snyder	1975	17,516
126 0/8	18 4/8	17 5/8	13 6/8	5	5	Delaware County	NY	Alan Beyer	1976	17,516
126 0/8	20 4/8	21 6/8	17 0/8	4	4	Dunn County	WI	Richard Paul	1977	17,516
126 0/8	20 2/8	18 6/8	15 0/8	4	4	Polk County	IA	Ervin Wagner	1978	17,516
126 0/8	20 0/8	20 3/8	16 0/8	5	5	Oneida County	WI	Gerald Bonfigt	1980	17,516
126 0/8	18 3/8	18 4/8	15 4/8	5	5	Bexar County	TX	James R. Carter	1980	17,516

WHITETAIL DEER (TYPICAL ANTLERS)

Minimum Score 125   Continued

SCORE	LENGTH OF MAIN BEAM R	LENGTH OF MAIN BEAM L	INSIDE SPREAD	NUMBER OF POINTS R	NUMBER OF POINTS L	AREA	STATE/ PROVINCE	HUNTER'S NAME	DATE	RANK
126 0/8	20 4/8	20 4/8	15 4/8	4	5	Iron County	MI	Bill Paiter, Sr.	1980	17,516
126 0/8	20 0/8	20 4/8	13 6/8	4	4	Kandiyohi County	MN	Dwayne B. Power	1980	17,516
126 0/8	22 1/8	22 6/8	19 0/8	4	4	Westchester County	NY	Thomas Ippolito	1981	17,516
126 0/8	19 5/8	19 7/8	15 4/8	4	4	Des Moines County	IA	Doris Hawkins	1981	17,516
126 0/8	19 4/8	18 1/8	14 3/8	5	6	Calhoun County	MI	Jerry L. Boggess, Jr.	1981	17,516
126 0/8	22 2/8	23 2/8	16 2/8	5	4	Washington County	OH	James D. Boyce	1981	17,516
126 0/8	21 4/8	19 6/8	16 4/8	4	4	Reno County	KS	Otto Henning	1982	17,516
126 0/8	20 4/8	21 0/8	15 4/8	5	6	Cayuga County	NY	Arthur Quadrini	1982	17,516
126 0/8	20 4/8	21 5/8	19 5/8	4	6	Burleigh County	ND	Scott Fairman	1982	17,516
126 0/8	20 0/8	20 2/8	18 6/8	4	5	Jo Daviess County	IL	Jerry Smith	1982	17,516
126 0/8	20 7/8	21 3/8	16 6/8	4	6	Brookings County	SD	Michael Kjellsen	1982	17,516
126 0/8	20 2/8	19 3/8	13 7/8	6	6	Buffalo County	NE	Richard D. Lange	1983	17,516
126 0/8	19 4/8	20 0/8	16 2/8	5	4	Watonwan County	MN	Rory Jensen	1983	17,516
126 0/8	20 0/8	20 0/8	13 2/8	5	5	Jefferson County	IN	Dwight Webb	1983	17,516
126 0/8	21 0/8	20 4/8	15 2/8	5	5	Dallas County	IA	John S. Winslow	1983	17,516
126 0/8	20 6/8	20 6/8	16 4/8	4	4	Dawson County	NE	Randy Wilson	1983	17,516
126 0/8	21 5/8	21 6/8	16 6/8	4	4	St. Louis County	MO	Huston Martin	1983	17,516
126 0/8	22 4/8	20 7/8	15 6/8	5	4	Iowa County	WI	Mark E. Bennett	1984	17,516
126 0/8	20 1/8	20 2/8	14 4/8	5	6	Des Moines County	IA	Duane R. Mabry	1984	17,516
126 0/8	24 3/8	23 4/8	16 0/8	3	4	Bissett Creek	BC	Mark Siegmueller	1984	17,516
126 0/8	22 2/8	22 7/8	19 4/8	4	4	Mackinac County	MI	Kirk A. Radtke	1984	17,516
126 0/8	20 0/8	20 3/8	16 0/8	6	6	Pittsburg County	OK	Rocky Williams	1985	17,516
126 0/8	20 2/8	19 7/8	16 6/8	5	5	Monroe County	NY	Gregrey Madison	1985	17,516
126 0/8	21 5/8	22 4/8	16 6/8	5	4	Stearns County	MN	Rick Kantor	1985	17,516
126 0/8	19 3/8	19 1/8	13 5/8	6	5	Sauk County	WI	Arend Harms	1985	17,516
126 0/8	22 4/8	22 4/8	17 1/8	4	5	Westchester County	NY	Louis J. Miceli III	1985	17,516
126 0/8	23 3/8	22 3/8	16 0/8	5	5	Outagamie County	WI	Chad Buss	1986	17,516
126 0/8	22 1/8	21 4/8	17 2/8	5	5	Polk County	WI	Dan Johnson	1986	17,516
126 0/8	24 0/8	24 4/8	16 2/8	6	4	Van Buren County	IA	Don Kieler	1986	17,516
126 0/8	21 6/8	21 6/8	18 2/8	6	6	Douglas County	NE	Bryce Lambley	1987	17,516
126 0/8	22 4/8	21 5/8	17 2/8	4	4	Isanti County	MN	John Armstrong	1987	17,516
126 0/8	23 7/8	23 2/8	19 2/8	4	5	Shawano County	WI	Scott Solomon	1987	17,516
126 0/8	22 6/8	22 5/8	15 4/8	4	4	Tuscaloosa County	AL	Elbert J. Buckelew	1987	17,516
126 0/8	22 7/8	23 5/8	21 2/8	4	4	Lawrence County	AR	Dwight Milgrim	1987	17,516
126 0/8	22 3/8	20 0/8	15 7/8	4	6	Marshall County	IN	David Wagoner	1988	17,516
126 0/8	21 2/8	20 6/8	16 2/8	4	4	Sussex County	NJ	Alex Wiecek	1988	17,516
126 0/8	20 0/8	20 4/8	17 0/8	4	5	Newton County	IN	James Gates	1988	17,516
126 0/8	20 4/8	20 4/8	16 2/8	4	5	Hubbard County	MN	Kelly Craft	1988	17,516
126 0/8	20 3/8	20 3/8	16 6/8	5	5	Mille Lacs County	MN	Daniel Newcombe	1988	17,516
126 0/8	22 5/8	20 6/8	16 6/8	4	5	Edgar County	IL	Jerry R. David	1988	17,516
126 0/8	22 5/8	22 5/8	16 2/8	4	5	Jackson County	MO	Steve Gowen	1988	17,516
126 0/8	23 6/8	24 1/8	19 5/8	5	5	New Haven County	CT	Lawrence St.John	1989	17,516
126 0/8	22 3/8	21 7/8	20 7/8	6	5	Hunterdon County	NJ	Gary W. Dudbridge	1989	17,516
126 0/8	20 3/8	21 7/8	17 0/8	4	4	Waupaca County	WI	Daniel D. Bestul	1989	17,516
126 0/8	21 3/8	21 6/8	18 2/8	4	4	Missoula County	MT	Myron Holland	1989	17,516
126 0/8	19 3/8	20 1/8	14 2/8	4	4	Fox Valley	SAS	Richard G. Paice	1990	17,516
126 0/8	22 4/8	22 5/8	17 2/8	4	4	Henrico County	VA	Robert A. Brooke	1990	17,516
126 0/8	20 0/8	20 5/8	18 4/8	5	5	Scott County	IA	Richard D. Bergert	1990	17,516
126 0/8	20 7/8	20 6/8	15 0/8	4	4	Russell County	KS	Mark J. Ferrero	1990	17,516
126 0/8	25 6/8	24 0/8	20 4/8	5	5	Westchester County	NY	Ralph Maietta	1990	17,516
126 0/8	21 3/8	21 7/8	19 1/8	6	7	Milwaukee County	WI	Tony Snow	1991	17,516
126 0/8	16 1/8	17 6/8	17 7/8	5	5	Haskell County	OK	James Woods	1991	17,516
126 0/8	20 6/8	19 6/8	16 0/8	4	4	Williamson County	IL	Jeff Bundren	1991	17,516
126 0/8	22 6/8	22 6/8	18 5/8	6	4	Iron County	WI	Perry V. Elsemore	1991	17,516
126 0/8	22 1/8	23 1/8	18 4/8	4	5	St. Joseph County	IN	Shane Hansen	1991	17,516
126 0/8	22 1/8	21 6/8	17 6/8	4	4	Hardin County	IL	Thomas R. Grabowski	1991	17,516
126 0/8	22 6/8	21 4/8	16 4/8	4	4	Monroe County	MO	Coy C. Dollens	1991	17,516
126 0/8	21 2/8	19 6/8	17 0/8	5	5	Winona County	MN	Jeffrey R. Keogh	1991	17,516
126 0/8	20 6/8	20 6/8	18 0/8	5	5	Shackelford County	TX	Mike Staton	1992	17,516
126 0/8	21 5/8	21 1/8	14 0/8	5	6	Waupaca County	WI	Ken R. Schampers	1992	17,516
126 0/8	22 0/8	21 5/8	16 4/8	4	4	Chippewa County	WI	Jeffery Allen Ginder	1992	17,516
126 0/8	18 6/8	18 5/8	17 4/8	5	5	Vilas County	WI	Lance E. Gudmundson	1992	17,516
126 0/8	21 4/8	22 0/8	19 2/8	4	4	Jo Daviess County	IL	Jack T. Wolf	1992	17,516
126 0/8	19 1/8	19 1/8	16 6/8	5	5	Frio County	TX	Leonard B. Wood, Jr.	1992	17,516
126 0/8	25 7/8	24 3/8	19 0/8	3	4	Bath	ONT	Kevin McLaughlin	1992	17,516
126 0/8	19 1/8	20 0/8	15 2/8	4	4	McMullen County	TX	Ryan Guyote	1993	17,516
126 0/8	20 2/8	20 7/8	17 7/8	5	6	Vermilion County	IL	Jim Richards	1993	17,516
126 0/8	21 1/8	19 7/8	17 6/8	5	5	Hudson Bay	SAS	William R. Vyvan	1993	17,516
126 0/8	20 6/8	21 2/8	17 6/8	5	5	Buffalo County	WI	Mark Butzler	1993	17,516
126 0/8	21 1/8	22 4/8	18 6/8	4	4	Louisa County	VA	Edward W. Fielder	1993	17,516
126 0/8	22 7/8	21 2/8	16 3/8	5	4	Menard County	IL	Ron Wadsworth	1993	17,516
126 0/8	21 3/8	21 4/8	16 0/8	4	4	Dane County	WI	Dale Zweifel	1993	17,516
126 0/8	20 2/8	20 0/8	17 3/8	6	5	Cecil County	MD	Alex Kish	1993	17,516
126 0/8	21 0/8	21 3/8	14 6/8	4	4	Winnebago County	WI	Timothy S. Meilahn	1993	17,516
126 0/8	22 1/8	22 3/8	18 6/8	4	4	Vilas County	WI	Robert D. Valliere	1993	17,516
126 0/8	24 6/8	24 1/8	18 1/8	7	5	Mason County	WV	Norman Campbell	1993	17,516
126 0/8	21 4/8	21 3/8	16 2/8	6	5	Hughes County	SD	John Simpson	1993	17,516
126 0/8	21 6/8	22 3/8	14 4/8	4	5	Marquette County	WI	Rick Grams	1994	17,516

WHITETAIL DEER (TYPICAL ANTLERS)

Minimum Score 125 — Continued

SCORE	R MAIN BEAM L		INSIDE SPREAD	R POINTS L		AREA	STATE/PROVINCE	HUNTER'S NAME	DATE	RANK
126 0/8	21 7/8	21 6/8	16 2/8	5	5	Dodge County	WI	Jerry Punzel	1994	17,516
126 0/8	21 1/8	21 5/8	16 3/8	4	5	St. Croix County	WI	Jerry Rose, Jr.	1994	17,516
126 0/8	23 0/8	23 4/8	16 6/8	4	4	Guilford County	NC	Steve L. Yarborough	1994	17,516
126 0/8	21 6/8	22 4/8	18 2/8	4	4	Buffalo County	WI	Michael Szymanski	1994	17,516
126 0/8	23 7/8	24 0/8	19 2/8	4	5	Kalamazoo County	MI	Chris R. Kallgren	1994	17,516
126 0/8	22 0/8	23 0/8	17 6/8	5	5	Montgomery County	MD	William S. Nalley	1994	17,516
126 0/8	21 2/8	21 2/8	14 6/8	5	5	Rock County	WI	Jim Strunz	1994	17,516
126 0/8	22 4/8	24 4/8	20 0/8	5	4	Baltimore County	MD	Charles Farinetti, Jr.	1994	17,516
126 0/8	22 7/8	21 6/8	18 4/8	4	4	Brown County	IL	David Roate	1994	17,516
126 0/8	21 7/8	19 3/8	14 6/8	5	5	Vinton County	OH	Clark Miller	1994	17,516
126 0/8	21 6/8	21 2/8	15 0/8	4	4	Van Buren County	IA	Robin L. Geibel	1994	17,516
126 0/8	21 6/8	22 2/8	15 6/8	4	5	Allen County	OH	Ed Wieging	1994	17,516
126 0/8	20 0/8	21 3/8	14 6/8	4	4	Washington County	MS	Odis Hill, Jr.	1995	17,516
126 0/8	20 2/8	20 2/8	16 0/8	5	5	Kerr County	TX	Brandon Ray	1995	17,516
126 0/8	20 0/8	20 6/8	18 0/8	5	5	Wirt County	WV	Michael Shrader	1995	17,516
126 0/8	23 0/8	23 2/8	17 6/8	4	4	Waupaca County	WI	Dennis Zietlow	1995	17,516
126 0/8	19 0/8	18 6/8	15 1/8	6	6	Kenedy County	TX	Gary F. Bogner	1995	17,516
126 0/8	21 5/8	20 7/8	18 0/8	4	4	Montgomery County	PA	Paul Warren	1995	17,516
126 0/8	22 6/8	23 4/8	17 2/8	4	5	De Witt County	IL	Scott O. Adreon	1995	17,516
126 0/8	23 5/8	24 0/8	18 4/8	4	4	Morris County	NJ	Gary Hult	1995	17,516
126 0/8	21 1/8	22 1/8	17 1/8	5	4	Franklin County	IA	Willie Knipfel	1995	17,516
126 0/8	22 0/8	23 5/8	19 0/8	4	4	Howard County	IA	Jeff Myron	1995	17,516
126 0/8	21 4/8	21 4/8	16 0/8	5	5	McMullen County	TX	Ed Endsley	1995	17,516
126 0/8	20 3/8	21 7/8	15 2/8	4	4	Warren County	IA	David Wolfkill	1995	17,516
126 0/8	24 1/8	22 6/8	15 2/8	7	5	Kleberg County	TX	Robert Nichols	1995	17,516
126 0/8	20 3/8	20 6/8	16 2/8	5	4	Kleberg County	TX	Roderick E. Nutter	1996	17,516
126 0/8	20 3/8	20 2/8	14 6/8	4	4	Cheshire County	NH	Bradford A. Bardwell	1996	17,516
126 0/8	21 4/8	22 0/8	18 4/8	5	5	Barry County	MI	Timothy R. Power	1996	17,516
126 0/8	22 0/8	21 6/8	15 4/8	4	4	New Castle County	DE	Timothy Leonard Wildermuth	1996	17,516
126 0/8	22 4/8	22 6/8	17 0/8	6	6	Osage County	OK	Bryan White	1996	17,516
126 0/8	19 2/8	19 2/8	16 1/8	6	5	Carroll County	IN	Brian K. Kirts	1996	17,516
126 0/8	23 2/8	20 6/8	16 2/8	4	4	Kent County	MD	Danny Dulin	1996	17,516
126 0/8	19 5/8	19 5/8	14 6/8	5	5	Paulding County	GA	Lawrence R. Thrash, Jr.	1996	17,516
126 0/8	21 7/8	23 0/8	16 2/8	5	4	Sussex County	NJ	Robert Conner, Jr.	1996	17,516
126 0/8	20 1/8	21 2/8	18 2/8	4	4	Davis County	IA	Gary Wissmueller	1996	17,516
126 0/8	23 2/8	22 4/8	17 4/8	4	4	Ellsworth County	KS	Jackie D. Robison	1996	17,516
126 0/8	21 5/8	23 0/8	14 2/8	4	5	Jennings County	IN	Curtis Haines	1996	17,516
126 0/8	21 0/8	22 0/8	16 3/8	5	5	Brown County	WI	Robert J. Zepnick	1997	17,516
126 0/8	22 3/8	21 7/8	20 0/8	4	4	Delaware County	PA	Thomas Gartland	1997	17,516
126 0/8	20 2/8	19 6/8	17 6/8	4	4	Eau Claire County	WI	Tom Kloss	1997	17,516
126 0/8	21 4/8	21 2/8	17 6/8	4	4	Roscommon County	MI	Richard J. Bonk	1997	17,516
126 0/8	21 5/8	21 3/8	16 4/8	5	4	Oconto County	WI	Rich Rosio	1997	17,516
126 0/8	20 2/8	21 0/8	17 4/8	5	4	Fond du Lac County	WI	Tim Lamonska	1997	17,516
126 0/8	23 1/8	23 3/8	20 5/8	5	6	Brown County	OH	Kendall Techau	1997	17,516
126 0/8	23 1/8	23 1/8	18 6/8	4	4	Mercer County	NJ	Eric N. Papiez	1997	17,516
126 0/8	23 6/8	24 7/8	21 1/8	6	3	Des Moines County	IA	Roy Patterson	1997	17,516
126 0/8	23 0/8	23 3/8	20 0/8	4	5	Sterling County	TX	Dennis Downing	1998	17,516
125 7/8	20 0/8	20 0/8	14 5/8	5	5	Oconto County	WI	Chuck Matyska	1972	17,648
125 7/8	22 7/8	22 5/8	15 3/8	4	4	Pope County	AR	William E. Campbell	1974	17,648
125 7/8	22 4/8	23 0/8	15 1/8	4	4	Fayette County	IL	Edward G. Myers	1975	17,648
125 7/8	20 6/8	22 7/8	15 5/8	5	5	Butler County	PA	John Schmiedlin	1976	17,648
125 7/8	20 2/8	20 2/8	15 1/8	5	5	Waupaca County	WI	Thomas E. Labisch	1976	17,648
125 7/8	20 0/8	20 2/8	16 2/8	5	6	Greene County	IN	Jim Cunningham	1977	17,648
125 7/8	21 5/8	22 0/8	15 1/8	4	4	Douglas County	MN	Dan Zinda	1977	17,648
125 7/8	20 4/8	20 4/8	17 7/8	4	4	Sebastian County	AR	Robert Wilkinson	1979	17,648
125 7/8	24 0/8	22 4/8	14 5/8	7	6	Jones County	GA	William R. Shaw	1979	17,648
125 7/8	23 4/8	22 5/8	15 7/8	5	4	Boone County	IA	Max Brower	1980	17,648
125 7/8	22 2/8	21 7/8	20 1/8	6	4	Ionia County	MI	David Seidelman	1980	17,648
125 7/8	20 4/8	20 7/8	15 1/8	4	4	Lewis & Clark County	MT	Tom Storm	1981	17,648
125 7/8	21 7/8	21 7/8	16 1/8	5	5	Dakota County	MN	John M. Lippka	1982	17,648
125 7/8	21 0/8	21 0/8	16 3/8	5	4	Lake County	IL	Russell F. Orr	1982	17,648
125 7/8	23 0/8	21 7/8	15 5/8	4	4	Sauk County	WI	Dan Cupp	1982	17,648
125 7/8	20 7/8	20 7/8	17 7/8	4	4	Marion County	IL	Lavon Doremire, Sr.	1983	17,648
125 7/8	21 7/8	22 2/8	18 4/8	4	5	Westchester County	NY	John Cucinella	1983	17,648
125 7/8	20 2/8	20 0/8	15 1/8	5	6	Ferry County	WA	Robert McIntosh	1983	17,648
125 7/8	20 4/8	21 1/8	17 1/8	5	5	Des Moines County	IA	Mark Sivill	1984	17,648
125 7/8	19 4/8	18 7/8	14 7/8	5	5	Dodge County	WI	James G. Schoebeck	1984	17,648
125 7/8	22 4/8	23 6/8	18 0/8	4	4	Sumner County	KS	Warren C. Townsend	1985	17,648
125 7/8	20 1/8	19 2/8	15 3/8	5	5	Green County	WI	David R. Covert	1985	17,648
125 7/8	20 4/8	18 4/8	15 5/8	5	5	Johnson County	WY	Jimmy Womble	1986	17,648
125 7/8	22 1/8	22 1/8	18 1/8	4	4	Middlesex County	NJ	William J. Matuchek	1987	17,648
125 7/8	19 6/8	18 6/8	15 7/8	5	4	Pope County	MN	Dennis Linde	1987	17,648
125 7/8	22 1/8	22 5/8	17 3/8	4	4	Oneida County	WI	Mike Buksyk	1988	17,648
125 7/8	21 7/8	21 7/8	20 4/8	4	5	Isabella County	MI	Roger L. Roberson	1988	17,648
125 7/8	20 0/8	19 7/8	16 5/8	4	5	Jo Daviess County	IL	Thomas J. Hoffman	1988	17,648
125 7/8	20 5/8	21 5/8	17 1/8	4	4	Hutchinson County	SD	Terry Waltner	1988	17,648
125 7/8	22 7/8	22 1/8	15 4/8	5	6	St. Croix County	WI	Jack Rasmussen	1989	17,648
125 7/8	19 1/8	19 1/8	16 3/8	5	5	Morris County	NJ	Tony Salernitano	1989	17,648

WHITETAIL DEER (TYPICAL ANTLERS)

Minimum Score 125 — Continued

SCORE	LENGTH OF MAIN BEAM R	LENGTH OF MAIN BEAM L	INSIDE SPREAD	NUMBER OF POINTS R	NUMBER OF POINTS L	AREA	STATE/ PROVINCE	HUNTER'S NAME	DATE	RANK
125 7/8	21 5/8	22 0/8	16 5/8	5	5	Rockingham County	NH	Mark A. George	1989	17,648
125 7/8	20 2/8	20 4/8	17 5/8	5	5	Ohio County	WV	Matt Farabee	1989	17,648
125 7/8	20 7/8	20 5/8	17 3/8	4	4	St. Charles County	MO	Terry Schulte	1989	17,648
125 7/8	21 6/8	20 7/8	19 1/8	5	5	Todd County	KY	Donald Wayne Bryant	1989	17,648
125 7/8	18 5/8	19 1/8	14 5/8	5	5	Luzerne County	PA	Dennis Beck	1990	17,648
125 7/8	21 1/8	20 3/8	17 3/8	5	5	Shelby County	KY	Kenneth E. Ferrell	1990	17,648
125 7/8	20 4/8	19 4/8	17 0/8	5	4	Cherry County	NE	Ken Colburn	1990	17,648
125 7/8	23 3/8	22 7/8	17 7/8	4	4	Kettle River	BC	Ken Davidson	1990	17,648
125 7/8	21 1/8	20 5/8	17 5/8	4	4	Union County	KY	Calvin L. Almond	1990	17,648
125 7/8	19 5/8	19 6/8	18 1/8	5	4	Crook County	WY	Susan Syvertson	1991	17,648
125 7/8	23 1/8	20 6/8	17 1/8	4	4	Chisago County	MN	Dave Condon	1991	17,648
125 7/8	20 5/8	21 2/8	16 1/8	4	4	St. Croix County	WI	Dennis J. Armbruster	1991	17,648
125 7/8	22 1/8	22 2/8	16 3/8	4	4	Jefferson County	OH	Genevieve K. Rogers	1991	17,648
125 7/8	21 4/8	22 1/8	20 5/8	4	4	Wabash County	IL	Mike Beesley	1991	17,648
125 7/8	23 2/8	18 6/8	15 5/8	6	4	Hamilton County	IA	Larry Haren	1991	17,648
125 7/8	24 1/8	24 4/8	16 2/8	5	4	Stephenson County	IL	Scott Davis	1991	17,648
125 7/8	21 2/8	21 6/8	16 5/8	4	4	Sussex County	NJ	Robert Ernst	1992	17,648
125 7/8	22 0/8	22 5/8	16 7/8	4	5	Lake County	IL	John Roscop	1992	17,648
125 7/8	21 7/8	21 7/8	16 5/8	5	5	Nicholas County	WV	William L. Atkins	1992	17,648
125 7/8	20 2/8	20 0/8	15 2/8	6	6	Marshall County	IN	Jim Phend	1992	17,648
125 7/8	22 0/8	21 3/8	16 7/8	4	4	Sussex County	NJ	John Wallace	1992	17,648
125 7/8	20 0/8	21 0/8	16 5/8	5	5	Parke County	IN	Charles Paxton	1992	17,648
125 7/8	20 0/8	20 3/8	13 7/8	4	4	Calumet County	WI	Mary Jane Klotz	1992	17,648
125 7/8	21 3/8	21 5/8	16 4/8	4	5	Ulster County	NY	Dean Martin	1992	17,648
125 7/8	21 5/8	22 3/8	22 6/8	4	4	Perry County	OH	Bill Bixler	1992	17,648
125 7/8	24 3/8	24 3/8	18 6/8	6	5	McLean County	IL	Donald Raymer	1992	17,648
125 7/8	20 3/8	21 5/8	18 5/8	4	4	Bayfield County	WI	William L. Butterworth	1993	17,648
125 7/8	21 2/8	19 2/8	15 5/8	5	5	Waupaca County	WI	Pete Gerndt	1993	17,648
125 7/8	22 3/8	23 4/8	20 4/8	5	5	Pike County	IL	Eddie Claypool	1993	17,648
125 7/8	21 4/8	21 7/8	17 3/8	4	4	Suffolk County	NY	Timothy Howell	1993	17,648
125 7/8	19 5/8	18 4/8	13 5/8	5	5	Okotoks	ALB	David W. Scott	1993	17,648
125 7/8	19 7/8	20 2/8	17 2/8	6	4	Le Sueur County	MN	Keith Westphal	1993	17,648
125 7/8	20 7/8	20 7/8	18 3/8	4	4	Tensas Parish	LA	John D. McAdams III	1993	17,648
125 7/8	21 2/8	22 2/8	16 7/8	4	4	Jefferson County	WI	Edward L. Anfang	1994	17,648
125 7/8	19 4/8	19 5/8	17 1/8	4	4	Stephenson County	IL	David L. Miller	1994	17,648
125 7/8	22 4/8	22 7/8	19 5/8	4	4	Rock County	WI	Jill Pohlman	1994	17,648
125 7/8	24 3/8	23 5/8	16 7/8	4	4	Worcester County	MA	Wayne A. Andrews	1994	17,648
125 7/8	20 5/8	22 1/8	16 1/8	4	4	Hardin County	KY	Arnold Campbell	1994	17,648
125 7/8	20 6/8	20 7/8	17 7/8	5	5	Sawyer County	WI	Craig Cooper	1994	17,648
125 7/8	22 1/8	21 5/8	16 3/8	5	5	Chisago County	MN	Russell Goudge	1995	17,648
125 7/8	21 6/8	22 0/8	14 7/8	4	4	Mercer County	WV	Brian Janutolo	1995	17,648
125 7/8	21 5/8	22 3/8	20 1/8	5	5	Waukesha County	WI	James Jorgenson	1995	17,648
125 7/8	19 2/8	19 0/8	15 7/8	4	5	Gage County	NE	Jerry N. Roever	1995	17,648
125 7/8	22 4/8	22 5/8	19 5/8	4	4	Westchester County	NY	Randy Pearson	1995	17,648
125 7/8	24 4/8	22 4/8	16 3/8	4	4	Schuyler County	IL	Chad Ingles	1995	17,648
125 7/8	21 6/8	22 2/8	17 7/8	4	5	Pike County	IL	Don P. Roper	1995	17,648
125 7/8	20 0/8	22 1/8	17 1/8	4	4	McDowell County	WV	Kevin P. Kelley	1995	17,648
125 7/8	20 0/8	21 0/8	17 7/8	4	4	Dodge County	MN	Bradley Blanchard	1995	17,648
125 7/8	21 4/8	22 0/8	17 3/8	5	4	Hocking County	OH	Douglas E. Reed, Jr.	1996	17,648
125 7/8	21 2/8	23 2/8	18 5/8	5	6	Lake County	IL	Kevin Dahm	1996	17,648
125 7/8	20 1/8	19 3/8	19 3/8	5	5	Polk County	WI	Steven R. Haas	1996	17,648
125 7/8	24 2/8	23 6/8	19 1/8	4	4	Monroe County	IA	Bill Kirkpatrick	1996	17,648
125 7/8	22 5/8	22 0/8	17 3/8	4	4	Washington County	MN	John Evangelist	1996	17,648
125 7/8	19 0/8	20 1/8	16 5/8	5	5	Marshall County	IN	John W. Pierce	1996	17,648
125 7/8	22 0/8	22 1/8	17 3/8	4	4	Okanogan County	WA	Dan L. Sapp	1997	17,648
125 7/8	18 1/8	18 5/8	16 6/8	6	5	Madison County	MT	J. Dudley Ottley	1997	17,648
125 7/8	20 2/8	21 0/8	15 7/8	4	4	Ozaukee County	WI	Eric Lehner	1997	17,648
125 7/8	23 2/8	23 2/8	19 2/8	5	4	Kent County	MI	Glenn R. Elliott	1997	17,648
125 7/8	22 2/8	22 6/8	16 5/8	5	5	Hunterdon County	NJ	Francis P. Paciullo	1997	17,648
125 7/8	24 0/8	23 6/8	17 2/8	5	6	Putnam County	MO	Patrick M. O'Reilly	1997	17,648
125 7/8	21 0/8	20 7/8	18 5/8	5	5	Williams County	OH	Roger Lloyd	1997	17,648
125 7/8	22 7/8	21 5/8	16 4/8	5	4	Langlade County	WI	Chad Baerwald	1997	17,648
125 7/8	20 2/8	19 5/8	17 5/8	4	4	Fond du Lac County	WI	Mike D. Schaefer	1997	17,648
125 7/8	22 5/8	23 4/8	21 1/8	4	4	Madison County	IL	Leroy Q. Daiber	1997	17,648
125 6/8	23 0/8	23 4/8	19 2/8	4	4	Bath County	VA	W. C. Bedall, Jr.	1958	17,743
125 6/8	19 5/8	19 3/8	16 2/8	5	5	Wood County	WI	Dennis Palmer	1967	17,743
125 6/8	21 4/8	21 5/8	18 6/8	4	4	Martin County	MN	Robert Barnett	1970	17,743
125 6/8	20 0/8	21 6/8	20 1/8	6	4	Palo Alto County	IA	Earl J. Gustafson	1971	17,743
125 6/8	22 0/8	22 4/8	16 4/8	4	4	Muskingum County	OH	Jim L. Lewis	1976	17,743
125 6/8	20 6/8	20 5/8	14 0/8	5	5	Buffalo County	WI	Rudy Klink	1981	17,743
125 6/8	20 4/8	20 2/8	17 0/8	5	5	Douglas County	MN	Jerry D. Kuhlman	1981	17,743
125 6/8	19 4/8	20 4/8	18 0/8	5	5	Miami County	KS	Gary L. Robertson	1982	17,743
125 6/8	20 2/8	21 2/8	18 2/8	4	5	Sauk County	WI	Hank Lee	1982	17,743
125 6/8	22 6/8	22 2/8	15 4/8	4	4	Sedgwick County	KS	Jim Nicholson	1983	17,743
125 6/8	21 1/8	21 2/8	17 5/8	6	6	Licking County	OH	Roy L Wilson, Jr.	1984	17,743
125 6/8	21 3/8	21 5/8	15 2/8	5	5	Montgomery County	KS	Grady Jabben	1985	17,743
125 6/8	19 7/8	22 0/8	19 2/8	5	6	Cedar County	MO	Terry Myers	1985	17,743
125 6/8	21 5/8	21 5/8	14 4/8	5	4	Vernon County	WI	Thomas Erie	1985	17,743

WHITETAIL DEER (TYPICAL ANTLERS)

Minimum Score 125   Continued

SCORE	LENGTH OF MAIN BEAM R	LENGTH OF MAIN BEAM L	INSIDE SPREAD	NUMBER OF POINTS R	NUMBER OF POINTS L	AREA	STATE/ PROVINCE	HUNTER'S NAME	DATE	RANK
125 6/8	20 2/8	20 4/8	15 2/8	4	4	Branch County	MI	Douglas L. Curey	1985	17,743
125 6/8	18 1/8	18 1/8	14 2/8	5	5	Cerro Gordo County	IA	Eric Coe	1985	17,743
125 6/8	21 6/8	22 0/8	17 4/8	4	4	Buffalo County	WI	Richard A. Viken	1985	17,743
125 6/8	22 2/8	21 4/8	16 4/8	4	4	Green County	WI	Evan Steinhorst	1986	17,743
125 6/8	21 1/8	22 0/8	17 2/8	4	4	Mason County	WV	John C. Cochran	1986	17,743
125 6/8	25 2/8	25 3/8	21 0/8	4	4	Westchester County	NY	Carl Ranieri	1986	17,743
125 6/8	22 0/8	21 7/8	19 4/8	5	4	Jackson County	OH	Mike Parrish	1986	17,743
125 6/8	20 4/8	19 6/8	16 6/8	5	5	Coahoma County	MS	Allen Rauch	1987	17,743
125 6/8	22 1/8	20 6/8	17 2/8	4	5	Grundy County	IL	Ernest J. Brown	1987	17,743
125 6/8	20 2/8	21 0/8	17 6/8	4	5	St. Charles County	MO	Dennis Orf	1987	17,743
125 6/8	22 4/8	23 0/8	16 5/8	5	6	Wyandot County	OH	James D. Herring	1987	17,743
125 6/8	23 4/8	25 3/8	20 2/8	4	4	Henry County	IA	Carolyn Prottsman	1987	17,743
125 6/8	19 1/8	21 1/8	16 6/8	5	5	Parke County	IN	Phillip E. Walker	1988	17,743
125 6/8	22 1/8	21 3/8	17 2/8	7	6	Marquette County	WI	Russell N. Reetz	1988	17,743
125 6/8	21 6/8	22 7/8	17 0/8	4	4	Kankakee County	IL	Doug Stam	1988	17,743
125 6/8	21 5/8	20 2/8	18 0/8	4	4	Boone County	MO	David Westmoreland	1988	17,743
125 6/8	20 0/8	19 7/8	14 2/8	4	4	Morgan County	IL	Dennis Heitz	1988	17,743
125 6/8	21 6/8	21 3/8	17 6/8	4	4	Rutherford County	TN	Randall Richardson	1989	17,743
125 6/8	22 4/8	22 7/8	16 6/8	5	5	Orleans County	VT	Jim LeBlanc	1989	17,743
125 6/8	23 6/8	24 3/8	15 5/8	6	5	Hillsdale County	MI	Bert Wilson	1989	17,743
125 6/8	20 7/8	22 7/8	18 6/8	5	4	Lake County	IL	Robert H. Fugett	1989	17,743
125 6/8	20 4/8	20 6/8	14 4/8	5	4	Kane County	IL	Alan S. Runde	1989	17,743
125 6/8	22 3/8	19 2/8	20 2/8	4	4	Winnebago County	WI	Donald Werner	1989	17,743
125 6/8	21 7/8	21 6/8	16 0/8	4	4	Creek County	OK	James L. Fowler	1989	17,743
125 6/8	21 5/8	21 1/8	18 2/8	5	4	Mower County	MN	Joseph Landherr	1989	17,743
125 6/8	19 0/8	18 6/8	18 0/8	5	4	Greenlake	SAS	Pink Atkins	1989	17,743
125 6/8	22 4/8	21 3/8	20 6/8	5	4	Jefferson County	MS	George L. Pink II	1990	17,743
125 6/8	21 6/8	22 3/8	16 6/8	5	5	Wayne County	IL	Peewee Hall	1990	17,743
125 6/8	21 5/8	22 1/8	18 0/8	4	4	Jackson County	OH	Gary Turner	1990	17,743
125 6/8	22 2/8	22 6/8	20 0/8	4	4	Edgar County	IL	Russell O. Weir	1990	17,743
125 6/8	21 3/8	22 0/8	16 6/8	4	5	Morrison County	MN	Mike Hiltner	1990	17,743
125 6/8	23 0/8	22 1/8	18 2/8	4	5	Sawyer County	WI	Nick V. Loshuk	1991	17,743
125 6/8	21 1/8	22 1/8	15 6/8	5	5	Onieda County	WI	Mike Novak	1991	17,743
125 6/8	20 2/8	20 0/8	16 2/8	5	5	Reagan County	TX	James E. Borron	1991	17,743
125 6/8	20 2/8	19 7/8	17 0/8	5	5	Morrison County	MN	James Bittner	1991	17,743
125 6/8	19 7/8	19 0/8	16 0/8	5	4	Washington County	MN	Wayne Edgerton	1991	17,743
125 6/8	21 3/8	20 5/8	18 1/8	6	4	Iron County	WI	Mark D. Levra	1991	17,743
125 6/8	21 6/8	21 4/8	18 0/8	4	5	Dane County	WI	Mark Hirssig	1991	17,743
125 6/8	22 6/8	21 1/8	19 0/8	5	7	Adams County	IL	Bill Swift, Jr.	1991	17,743
125 6/8	18 0/8	18 0/8	16 6/8	5	5	Appanoose County	IA	Scott Rolffs	1991	17,743
125 6/8	20 7/8	21 4/8	19 0/8	5	5	Crook County	WY	Michael La Van	1992	17,743
125 6/8	22 0/8	21 3/8	17 0/8	4	5	Buffalo County	WI	Michael R. Schamaum	1992	17,743
125 6/8	20 2/8	23 5/8	17 2/8	5	5	Monroe County	WI	Daniel S. Hendricks	1992	17,743
125 6/8	22 6/8	23 7/8	18 6/8	4	4	Hardy County	WV	Charles E. Southerly	1992	17,743
125 6/8	19 3/8	19 4/8	15 0/8	5	6	Douglas County	MN	Rudy Vrana	1992	17,743
125 6/8	19 7/8	21 2/8	16 3/8	5	6	Scott County	MN	Billy Muelken	1992	17,743
125 6/8	20 3/8	21 1/8	17 0/8	5	5	Douglas County	WI	Todd D. Sorenson	1992	17,743
125 6/8	21 7/8	21 7/8	17 5/8	4	5	Winnebago County	IL	Ron DeMus	1992	17,743
125 6/8	21 1/8	20 0/8	15 2/8	4	4	Lawrence County	OH	John Fields	1992	17,743
125 6/8	22 0/8	22 0/8	15 0/8	4	5	Mercer County	IL	Russell W. Courter, Jr.	1992	17,743
125 6/8	20 4/8	20 1/8	16 2/8	5	5	Linn County	IA	Chris Swanke	1992	17,743
125 6/8	22 3/8	23 2/8	16 5/8	5	5	Jones County	IA	Kevin Prull	1992	17,743
125 6/8	20 3/8	20 7/8	17 2/8	5	5	Washington County	MN	Ronald Krienke	1993	17,743
125 6/8	20 1/8	19 5/8	16 6/8	5	4	Steele County	MN	Jane L. Wagner	1993	17,743
125 6/8	23 0/8	23 4/8	19 2/8	5	4	Kendall County	IL	Ray Muellner	1993	17,743
125 6/8	21 2/8	20 7/8	17 2/8	5	5	Osage County	MO	Elston Neuner	1993	17,743
125 6/8	24 3/8	22 6/8	18 0/8	4	4	Prince Georges County	MD	James E. Burton	1993	17,743
125 6/8	20 3/8	20 3/8	16 3/8	6	5	Winona County	MN	Jan Finley	1993	17,743
125 6/8	23 2/8	22 1/8	14 1/8	6	6	St. Joseph County	IN	Paul Papczynski	1993	17,743
125 6/8	18 5/8	21 0/8	16 6/8	5	5	Bartholomew County	IN	Jack W. Dunn	1993	17,743
125 6/8	21 4/8	21 7/8	17 2/8	4	4	Goliad County	TX	Jerry Smith	1993	17,743
125 6/8	20 1/8	20 3/8	14 6/8	5	5	Cabell County	WV	Raymond Kingery	1993	17,743
125 6/8	22 2/8	22 3/8	15 6/8	4	5	Marquette County	WI	Greg Sidoff	1994	17,743
125 6/8	21 4/8	21 3/8	13 0/8	5	5	Decatur County	GA	Gene Smith	1994	17,743
125 6/8	22 0/8	20 3/8	16 4/8	4	4	Kane County	IL	Dean V. Ashton	1994	17,743
125 6/8	24 0/8	23 1/8	18 4/8	5	5	Chautauqua County	NY	Peter Smith, Jr.	1994	17,743
125 6/8	20 4/8	21 6/8	17 0/8	5	5	Anoka County	MN	Tony Zimmerman	1994	17,743
125 6/8	21 5/8	19 0/8	13 6/8	4	6	Appanoose County	IA	Scott Rolffs	1994	17,743
125 6/8	23 1/8	22 7/8	20 4/8	4	4	Berkshire County	MA	Shawn Walker	1994	17,743
125 6/8	23 0/8	23 4/8	18 6/8	6	5	Westchester County	NY	Benjamin L. Thompson	1994	17,743
125 6/8	21 1/8	21 3/8	16 2/8	4	4	Pierce County	WI	David Hovel	1994	17,743
125 6/8	22 2/8	21 6/8	19 5/8	6	5	Muskegon County	MI	Victor Nelson	1994	17,743
125 6/8	23 1/8	23 1/8	20 6/8	4	6	Trempealeau County	WI	Allan D. Stuhr	1994	17,743
125 6/8	22 2/8	22 2/8	17 4/8	5	4	Warren County	IA	Robert J. McClemons	1994	17,743
125 6/8	21 4/8	21 5/8	17 6/8	5	5	Carroll County	OH	Randy S. Collins	1994	17,743
125 6/8	21 5/8	21 7/8	17 6/8	4	4	Montgomery County	PA	Anthony Joseph Giordano	1995	17,743
125 6/8	20 4/8	19 7/8	18 2/8	5	4	Jim Wells County	TX	Paul W. Liberato	1995	17,743
125 6/8	18 7/8	18 4/8	15 0/8	4	4	Clandonald	ALB	Vern Goad	1995	17,743

WHITETAIL DEER (TYPICAL ANTLERS)

Minimum Score 125

Continued

SCORE	LENGTH OF MAIN BEAM R L		INSIDE SPREAD	NUMBER OF POINTS R L		AREA	STATE/ PROVINCE	HUNTER'S NAME	DATE	RANK
125 6/8	23 0/8	22 7/8	19 4/8	5	4	Roseau County	MN	Fred H. Streiff	1995	17,743
125 6/8	20 7/8	20 5/8	16 0/8	5	5	Schuyler County	IL	Paul Behrens	1995	17,743
125 6/8	21 7/8	21 3/8	16 0/8	5	5	Branch County	MI	Craig A. Gallup	1995	17,743
125 6/8	21 1/8	21 5/8	16 4/8	5	6	Houghton County	MI	Mary Jo McGinnis	1995	17,743
125 6/8	23 3/8	22 4/8	17 7/8	4	5	Edgar County	IL	Troy A. Lewis	1995	17,743
125 6/8	17 7/8	18 3/8	15 4/8	5	5	Lake County	IN	James C. Gates	1995	17,743
125 6/8	22 4/8	21 3/8	15 2/8	5	5	Logan County	CO	Wayne Depperschmidt	1995	17,743
125 6/8	18 4/8	19 0/8	16 0/8	5	5	Will County	IL	Gary Tyranski	1995	17,743
125 6/8	19 2/8	19 5/8	15 0/8	5	5	San Patricio County	TX	Frank Cavaretta, Jr.	1995	17,743
125 6/8	18 6/8	19 3/8	12 6/8	5	5	La Salle County	TX	John W. Ellas	1996	17,743
125 6/8	21 7/8	21 2/8	15 6/8	4	4	Powell County	MT	Donald S. Dvoroznak	1996	17,743
125 6/8	20 1/8	20 4/8	16 4/8	4	4	Winona County	MN	Jan Finley	1996	17,743
125 6/8	18 6/8	19 2/8	14 6/8	5	5	Stephenson County	IL	Ron Kaderly	1996	17,743
125 6/8	22 7/8	20 3/8	16 6/8	5	6	Mason County	IL	Jeff Heilman	1996	17,743
125 6/8	22 1/8	22 5/8	19 0/8	4	4	Westchester County	NY	Doug Erickson	1996	17,743
125 6/8	22 2/8	21 6/8	17 2/8	4	4	Morgan County	IL	John M. Conklin	1996	17,743
125 6/8	22 3/8	19 6/8	14 4/8	5	5	Webb County	TX	Troy Hardesty	1996	17,743
125 6/8	22 5/8	22 2/8	16 0/8	5	5	Fulton County	GA	Terry Allen	1996	17,743
125 6/8	19 2/8	20 3/8	15 4/8	5	5	Linn County	KS	Scott H. Woods	1996	17,743
125 6/8	21 3/8	20 7/8	18 2/8	5	5	Ashland County	WI	Joe Bradle	1996	17,743
125 6/8	21 5/8	21 2/8	16 6/8	5	6	Polk County	MO	Page Jones	1997	17,743
125 6/8	22 0/8	21 3/8	17 2/8	5	5	Sauk County	WI	Todd R. Peper	1997	17,743
125 6/8	21 0/8	20 2/8	18 2/8	4	4	Calhoun County	MI	John H. McManus	1997	17,743
125 6/8	21 7/8	20 6/8	14 2/8	4	5	Logan County	OK	Danny H. Heskett	1997	17,743
125 6/8	21 1/8	20 4/8	17 2/8	5	4	Piatt County	IL	Jody M. Schenkel	1997	17,743
125 6/8	23 1/8	22 4/8	16 4/8	5	4	Waupaca County	WI	Robert L. Pagel, Jr.	1997	17,743
125 6/8	23 7/8	22 2/8	18 7/8	6	6	La Porte County	IN	Bruce A. Young, Jr.	1997	17,743
125 6/8	20 2/8	21 4/8	19 0/8	5	5	Van Buren County	MI	James Dale	1997	17,743
125 6/8	20 0/8	20 5/8	17 0/8	6	5	St. Louis County	MO	David Shelton	1997	17,743
125 6/8	19 4/8	19 2/8	15 2/8	6	5	Chester County	PA	George Paul Charles	1997	17,743
125 5/8	21 4/8	21 3/8	18 3/8	4	4	Brown County	SD	Leo J. Weber	1965	17,865
125 5/8	21 5/8	21 4/8	17 5/8	4	4	Lyman County	SD	Dennis Lien	1966	17,865
125 5/8	19 2/8	19 3/8	16 3/8	5	5	Sauk County	WI	Andre J. Jestafie	1968	17,865
125 5/8	22 1/8	25 0/8	20 1/8	5	6	Meade County	KS	Kent Davis	1971	17,865
125 5/8	19 7/8	18 7/8	15 5/8	5	5	Jo Daviess County	IL	Tom Spraetz	1976	17,865
125 5/8	21 5/8	21 4/8	16 5/8	5	5	Kent County	MD	Harry A. Weishaar	1977	17,865
125 5/8	24 6/8	24 2/8	15 5/8	4	4	Fairfield County	SC	Danny Duncan	1978	17,865
125 5/8	22 6/8	22 6/8	14 0/8	6	6	Ripley County	IN	Richard Gambrel	1979	17,865
125 5/8	22 4/8	22 0/8	17 5/8	4	4	Keokuk County	IA	Roger E. Claypool	1980	17,865
125 5/8	23 1/8	23 7/8	14 7/8	5	5	Alpena County	MI	Cameron Cogsdill	1981	17,865
125 5/8	21 1/8	21 2/8	17 5/8	4	4	Green Lake County	WI	Raymond E. Golomski	1981	17,865
125 5/8	19 7/8	19 3/8	16 1/8	6	6	Jackson County	MN	Rodney Borer	1982	17,865
125 5/8	21 2/8	21 1/8	18 7/8	4	4	Clermont County	OH	Claud F. Combs	1982	17,865
125 5/8	19 3/8	18 5/8	14 3/8	5	6	Washington County	OH	Ronald G. Boone	1982	17,865
125 5/8	23 3/8	22 7/8	15 3/8	5	5	Vernon County	MO	Roger L. Hensley	1982	17,865
125 5/8	21 0/8	20 7/8	16 1/8	4	4	Ozaukee County	WI	Thomas G. Bloomingdale	1983	17,865
125 5/8	21 5/8	21 1/8	17 3/8	4	4	Will County	IL	Angelo L. Chirban	1983	17,865
125 5/8	21 6/8	21 6/8	17 5/8	4	4	Cherokee County	OK	Jon C. Rogers	1983	17,865
125 5/8	20 2/8	20 2/8	14 3/8	5	5	Oliver County	ND	Al Zeller	1984	17,865
125 5/8	22 6/8	22 3/8	19 3/8	4	5	Lycoming County	PA	Gary A Pennycoff	1985	17,865
125 5/8	22 0/8	22 1/8	15 3/8	4	4	Polk County	WI	Jon Leisch	1986	17,865
125 5/8	24 7/8	23 7/8	21 4/8	5	5	Jackson County	IL	Charles Barwick	1986	17,865
125 5/8	21 4/8	21 6/8	17 5/8	4	4	McDowell County	WV	Jerry Carroll	1986	17,865
125 5/8	18 4/8	19 4/8	14 7/8	7	5	Uvalde County	TX	Mark Ezell	1987	17,865
125 5/8	20 6/8	20 5/8	14 3/8	5	5	Menominee County	MI	Robert Brittson	1987	17,865
125 5/8	24 1/8	22 5/8	14 7/8	5	4	Bradford County	PA	Kyle Dewey	1987	17,865
125 5/8	20 0/8	20 2/8	18 1/8	5	5	Trigg County	KY	Ricky Boatright	1987	17,865
125 5/8	21 6/8	21 3/8	16 7/8	5	7	Knox County	IL	Bill Crowden	1987	17,865
125 5/8	21 1/8	21 5/8	17 5/8	5	5	Frontier County	NE	Steven P. Salmieri	1987	17,865
125 5/8	22 7/8	21 7/8	17 1/8	4	4	Starke County	IN	Paul W. Arndt	1987	17,865
125 5/8	21 3/8	20 3/8	17 1/8	5	5	Lawrence County	MO	David L. Lundy	1988	17,865
125 5/8	20 5/8	20 4/8	17 5/8	5	4	Jefferson County	WI	Bob Chaveriat	1988	17,865
125 5/8	22 3/8	21 6/8	19 4/8	6	4	Faribault County	MN	Bob Prange	1988	17,865
125 5/8	20 4/8	22 0/8	17 0/8	6	6	Logan County	IL	Gary W. Conrady	1988	17,865
125 5/8	23 2/8	23 2/8	18 1/8	5	6	Jefferson County	OH	Kevin Sokolowski	1988	17,865
125 5/8	21 3/8	22 3/8	16 7/8	4	4	Richland County	IL	Billy Joe Hicks	1988	17,865
125 5/8	19 6/8	20 2/8	14 5/8	5	5	Woodbury County	IA	Todd Carr	1988	17,865
125 5/8	19 0/8	18 6/8	15 5/8	5	5	Prairie County	AR	Scotty Burch	1988	17,865
125 5/8	23 2/8	23 0/8	18 3/8	4	4	Lyon County	KS	Gary Atchison	1988	17,865
125 5/8	21 2/8	21 5/8	19 1/8	5	5	Jefferson County	OH	William Gary Rusinovich	1989	17,865
125 5/8	23 2/8	22 5/8	18 5/8	5	4	La Salle County	IL	John Thomas	1989	17,865
125 5/8	24 1/8	25 0/8	18 3/8	3	3	Calhoun County	MI	Ron Allen	1989	17,865
125 5/8	21 0/8	21 3/8	17 7/8	7	6	Pittsylvania County	VA	Robbie Lee Bryant	1989	17,865
125 5/8	21 3/8	22 2/8	17 5/8	5	4	Wayne County	MO	Don Reynolds	1989	17,865
125 5/8	19 4/8	19 0/8	15 7/8	5	5	Uvalde County	TX	Mark Ezell	1989	17,865
125 5/8	22 2/8	21 6/8	14 3/8	4	4	Heard County	GA	Robert M. Foran	1990	17,865
125 5/8	21 2/8	20 3/8	16 3/8	4	4	Perry County	IN	Thomas L. Goeppner	1990	17,865
125 5/8	20 4/8	20 6/8	17 3/8	5	5	Bent County	CO	Chris Anderson	1990	17,865

WHITETAIL DEER (TYPICAL ANTLERS)

Minimum Score 125 — Continued

SCORE	LENGTH OF MAIN BEAM R	L	INSIDE SPREAD	NUMBER OF POINTS R	L	AREA	STATE/ PROVINCE	HUNTER'S NAME	DATE	RANK
125 5/8	19 5/8	20 5/8	15 5/8	5	5	Arenac County	MI	Patrick D. York	1990	17,865
125 5/8	23 1/8	23 1/8	17 5/8	4	5	Morris County	NJ	Russ Davidson	1990	17,865
125 5/8	21 6/8	21 5/8	18 3/8	4	4	Whiteside County	IL	Art Heinze	1990	17,865
125 5/8	23 2/8	23 2/8	16 1/8	4	5	Hancock County	OH	Robert E. Ebert	1990	17,865
125 5/8	23 1/8	22 1/8	17 3/8	4	6	Ballard County	KY	AlBert Hargis	1991	17,865
125 5/8	22 6/8	22 7/8	18 1/8	5	4	Jenkins County	GA	Frank J. Nelson, Jr.	1991	17,865
125 5/8	21 5/8	20 5/8	21 5/8	5	4	Mercer County	NJ	Richard Deveney	1991	17,865
125 5/8	17 4/8	20 6/8	15 5/8	5	6	Crawford County	IL	Billy J. Waddell	1991	17,865
125 5/8	24 3/8	24 2/8	17 1/8	3	5	Schoharie County	NY	Chris Aernecke	1991	17,865
125 5/8	20 0/8	19 6/8	18 5/8	5	5	Lake County	IL	Ron Miller	1991	17,865
125 5/8	22 4/8	21 1/8	16 1/8	5	6	Whiteside County	IL	Clint Walker	1991	17,865
125 5/8	22 1/8	22 1/8	16 7/8	4	4	Oswego County	NY	Ellis B. Barber	1991	17,865
125 5/8	19 6/8	19 3/8	16 2/8	5	5	Polk County	WI	Dan L. Kelley	1991	17,865
125 5/8	21 4/8	22 5/8	18 1/8	5	5	Spencer County	IN	Larry Beeler	1992	17,865
125 5/8	23 5/8	23 2/8	18 7/8	5	8	Prince Edward County	VA	Jeff Brubaker	1992	17,865
125 5/8	19 4/8	21 0/8	20 3/8	6	5	Goodhue County	MN	Scott Hayes	1992	17,865
125 5/8	21 4/8	21 4/8	17 3/8	6	6	Walworth County	WI	Daniel A. McLean	1992	17,865
125 5/8	23 1/8	21 2/8	16 3/8	4	4	Jefferson County	OH	James R. Howell	1992	17,865
125 5/8	19 4/8	21 1/8	13 5/8	5	5	Caswell County	NC	Tim Myers	1992	17,865
125 5/8	23 0/8	22 7/8	19 3/8	5	5	Fountain County	IN	Jeff Frazier	1992	17,865
125 5/8	22 7/8	22 5/8	16 5/8	4	4	Fairfield County	CT	Brian McCall	1992	17,865
125 5/8	19 5/8	20 2/8	16 3/8	5	5	Florence County	WI	Jack VandenHeuvel	1992	17,865
125 5/8	22 0/8	21 5/8	18 6/8	5	6	Butler County	PA	Keith Lark	1993	17,865
125 5/8	21 5/8	21 4/8	15 5/8	5	5	Dane County	WI	Dave Dilley	1993	17,865
125 5/8	20 6/8	21 4/8	16 5/8	4	4	Branch County	MI	Mark Cosby	1993	17,865
125 5/8	21 6/8	21 6/8	17 1/8	4	4	Nacogdoches County	TX	Donald McMillan	1993	17,865
125 5/8	21 0/8	20 5/8	17 1/8	5	5	Portage County	WI	Mark A. Gawlik	1993	17,865
125 5/8	24 0/8	23 5/8	17 2/8	6	6	Sanilac County	MI	James C. Whitehead	1993	17,865
125 5/8	22 3/8	22 7/8	15 4/8	6	5	Clay County	MO	Joel Kimrey	1993	17,865
125 5/8	23 2/8	22 2/8	17 7/8	4	4	Franklin County	PA	Wayne Brensinger	1994	17,865
125 5/8	23 2/8	21 3/8	14 5/8	5	5	Montour County	PA	Jason Michael	1994	17,865
125 5/8	20 1/8	20 5/8	16 5/8	5	5	Calhoun County	MI	Bart D. Mauk	1994	17,865
125 5/8	21 6/8	21 7/8	15 2/8	5	4	Erath County	TX	Kevin Mitchell	1994	17,865
125 5/8	22 6/8	22 4/8	16 3/8	4	4	Knox County	IL	Kevin Phillips	1994	17,865
125 5/8	20 1/8	19 6/8	16 0/8	6	5	Cass County	MO	David M. Golden	1994	17,865
125 5/8	22 0/8	23 3/8	17 3/8	4	4	Allen County	OH	Rick Phillips	1994	17,865
125 5/8	21 7/8	22 0/8	16 7/8	5	5	Suffolk County	NY	Ben Brinkmann	1994	17,865
125 5/8	22 4/8	21 6/8	14 3/8	6	6	Allegheny County	PA	Michael D. Bain	1994	17,865
125 5/8	18 4/8	18 4/8	16 5/8	5	6	Greene County	IA	Dan Matthews	1994	17,865
125 5/8	20 3/8	19 7/8	13 1/8	5	5	Monroe County	WI	Dave G. Carr	1994	17,865
125 5/8	23 7/8	23 5/8	17 1/8	5	4	Monroe County	NY	Craig A. Rusin	1994	17,865
125 5/8	23 1/8	22 1/8	17 7/8	4	4	Morrow County	OH	Phil Caudill	1994	17,865
125 5/8	21 6/8	21 3/8	17 3/8	4	5	Fairfield County	CT	Dennis Mical	1994	17,865
125 5/8	20 6/8	20 3/8	15 3/8	4	4	Polk County	MN	Greg Ranz	1994	17,865
125 5/8	21 1/8	21 2/8	16 5/8	5	5	Sebastian County	AR	Joe Manes	1995	17,865
125 5/8	22 7/8	22 2/8	17 5/8	4	4	Mercer County	IL	Thomas Kevin Peck	1995	17,865
125 5/8	20 6/8	22 0/8	18 5/8	4	4	Vilas County	WI	Dale Mayo	1995	17,865
125 5/8	21 5/8	22 0/8	16 1/8	5	5	Jefferson County	IA	Robin Geibel	1995	17,865
125 5/8	23 5/8	21 6/8	20 5/8	4	4	Pike County	KY	Nicholas Todd Cantrell	1995	17,865
125 5/8	18 6/8	19 4/8	15 5/8	6	5	Redwood County	MN	Troy Pabst	1995	17,865
125 5/8	19 7/8	20 7/8	15 3/8	4	4	Prowers County	CO	David L. Skiff	1995	17,865
125 5/8	19 6/8	19 0/8	15 3/8	5	5	Jackson County	WI	Rick Boullion	1995	17,865
125 5/8	19 6/8	19 4/8	14 7/8	5	5	Lamar County	GA	Mike Dyal	1996	17,865
125 5/8	21 7/8	21 4/8	17 3/8	4	4	Washington County	MN	Joe Thill	1996	17,865
125 5/8	20 6/8	21 2/8	18 1/8	4	4	Sauk County	WI	Randy McGrath	1996	17,865
125 5/8	24 1/8	23 5/8	17 7/8	4	5	Buffalo County	WI	Brett "Hubbs" Hubbartt	1996	17,865
125 5/8	22 0/8	21 7/8	17 1/8	4	4	Morris County	NJ	Frank DiGrazia	1996	17,865
125 5/8	23 4/8	22 7/8	18 7/8	4	4	Jackson County	OH	Martin Larson	1996	17,865
125 5/8	22 1/8	21 0/8	16 1/8	5	5	Washington County	RI	Kenneth W. Gordon	1996	17,865
125 5/8	20 0/8	25 2/8	16 4/8	5	8	De Kalb County	GA	Michael Burchik	1996	17,865
125 5/8	23 1/8	22 1/8	16 5/8	4	5	Dallas County	IA	Russ Clarken	1996	17,865
125 5/8	21 3/8	23 6/8	17 3/8	4	4	Maverick County	TX	Dennis J. Marbach	1996	17,865
125 5/8	18 7/8	19 6/8	15 3/8	5	5	Camrose	ALB	Andrew Gerber	1997	17,865
125 5/8	19 5/8	20 2/8	15 6/8	6	7	Tom Green County	TX	Ronnie Parsons	1997	17,865
125 5/8	21 4/8	21 6/8	16 1/8	6	5	Jo Daviess County	IL	Gerald J. Smith	1997	17,865
125 5/8	22 1/8	22 2/8	18 3/8	4	4	Hopkins County	KY	Tracy Daves	1997	17,865
125 5/8	19 2/8	19 2/8	17 7/8	5	4	Buffalo County	WI	Michael J. Kaufmann	1997	17,865
125 5/8	17 6/8	17 3/8	11 3/8	5	5	Pierce County	WI	Dennis G. Hughes	1997	17,865
125 5/8	20 0/8	21 6/8	17 3/8	4	4	Bayfield County	WI	Dan Scholl	1997	17,865
125 5/8	20 6/8	20 4/8	16 3/8	4	4	Dane County	WI	Jim Licht	1997	17,865
125 5/8	21 5/8	20 6/8	18 3/8	4	4	White County	IL	Greg Scheer	1997	17,865
125 5/8	19 5/8	20 4/8	15 3/8	4	6	Macoupin County	IL	Kevin Underwood	1997	17,865
125 5/8	20 7/8	20 3/8	18 1/8	5	4	Marathon County	WI	Paul Gustafson	1997	17,865
125 4/8	24 7/8	21 6/8	17 2/8	4	4	Marion County	IA	Thomas Tucker	1962	17,986
125 4/8	20 4/8	20 7/8	19 0/8	4	4	Clark County	MO	Allen L. Courtney	1971	17,986
125 4/8	20 2/8	21 3/8	16 6/8	5	5	Otter Tail County	MN	Terry Tamke	1971	17,986
125 4/8	20 7/8	21 0/8	16 0/8	4	5	Meeker County	MN	Chuck Schultz	1978	17,986
125 4/8	22 6/8	22 7/8	15 1/8	4	5	Williams County	OH	Norman J. Spindler	1979	17,986

WHITETAIL DEER (TYPICAL ANTLERS)

Minimum Score 125 — Continued

SCORE	LENGTH OF MAIN BEAM R	LENGTH OF MAIN BEAM L	INSIDE SPREAD	NUMBER OF POINTS R	NUMBER OF POINTS L	AREA	STATE/PROVINCE	HUNTER'S NAME	DATE	RANK
125 4/8	19 7/8	20 1/8	15 2/8	4	5	Rice County	KS	Daniel G. Willems	1979	17,986
125 4/8	20 1/8	20 2/8	17 1/8	5	4	Bearspaw Dam	ALB	David R. Coupland	1979	17,986
125 4/8	21 4/8	21 6/8	14 2/8	5	4	Worcester County	MA	David M. Peters	1980	17,986
125 4/8	23 0/8	24 1/8	17 4/8	5	4	Murray County	MN	Kerry Ella	1981	17,986
125 4/8	20 5/8	20 3/8	17 4/8	5	5	Union County	KY	Brad Tucker	1982	17,986
125 4/8	21 3/8	21 5/8	12 6/8	5	5	Oktibbeha County	MS	Stennis Jones	1983	17,986
125 4/8	21 7/8	22 5/8	14 2/8	4	4	Knox County	OH	Tom Kayser	1984	17,986
125 4/8	20 3/8	19 3/8	14 0/8	6	5	Trempealeau County	WI	Chris Fechner	1985	17,986
125 4/8	21 1/8	21 2/8	15 6/8	4	4	Vernon County	WI	Michael Lang	1985	17,986
125 4/8	21 4/8	22 6/8	15 6/8	4	4	Greene County	AR	Danny J. Walker	1985	17,986
125 4/8	16 4/8	22 0/8	16 4/8	5	4	Monona County	IA	Larry Couron	1985	17,986
125 4/8	21 7/8	21 7/8	19 4/8	5	4	Warren County	IL	Bob Rawlings	1985	17,986
125 4/8	21 4/8	22 0/8	16 6/8	4	4	Buffalo County	WI	Brian P. Bork	1986	17,986
125 4/8	22 5/8	21 5/8	18 4/8	4	4	Delaware County	OH	William D. Merdeath	1986	17,986
125 4/8	18 6/8	19 6/8	16 4/8	5	4	Des Moines County	IA	Randy R. Mack	1986	17,986
125 4/8	24 4/8	17 4/8	17 2/8	4	5	Gibson County	IN	Darvin Hulfachor	1986	17,986
125 4/8	21 4/8	20 4/8	17 3/8	7	7	Lawrence County	MS	Robert L. George	1987	17,986
125 4/8	21 2/8	22 1/8	17 2/8	4	5	Iron County	MI	John Ohmer	1987	17,986
125 4/8	21 4/8	21 3/8	18 0/8	4	4	Washtenaw County	MI	Charles E. Benedict	1987	17,986
125 4/8	23 2/8	23 0/8	20 2/8	4	4	Washtenaw County	MI	Robert Lee Smith, Jr.	1987	17,986
125 4/8	19 1/8	19 3/8	14 1/8	5	5	Crook County	WY	Scotty Powell	1988	17,986
125 4/8	23 1/8	23 6/8	18 0/8	4	6	Monroe County	WI	Lesley Strunk	1988	17,986
125 4/8	21 1/8	20 2/8	14 0/8	4	4	Jasper County	IA	James L. Seieroe	1988	17,986
125 4/8	20 1/8	20 4/8	15 2/8	4	4	Weld County	CO	Doug Kayl	1988	17,986
125 4/8	22 2/8	21 5/8	15 7/8	9	6	Carver County	MN	Paul Welin	1988	17,986
125 4/8	22 3/8	22 6/8	17 6/8	5	5	McKenzie County	ND	Kelly Evanson	1988	17,986
125 4/8	22 4/8	22 1/8	19 4/8	4	5	Sauk County	WI	Michael J. McGann	1989	17,986
125 4/8	24 6/8	24 7/8	17 4/8	5	4	Montgomery County	PA	Martin R. Graner	1989	17,986
125 4/8	19 6/8	20 3/8	16 5/8	5	5	Carbon County	PA	Salvatore Sorace	1989	17,986
125 4/8	19 5/8	19 6/8	13 7/8	4	6	Cedar County	NE	Kevin Schmidt	1989	17,986
125 4/8	21 6/8	20 1/8	17 0/8	5	6	Pottawattamie County	IA	Jim W. Zientek	1989	17,986
125 4/8	19 0/8	19 3/8	15 0/8	5	5	Brown County	IL	Barry Rich	1989	17,986
125 4/8	21 4/8	23 0/8	15 2/8	5	4	Lake County	IL	Lynn Anderson	1989	17,986
125 4/8	21 2/8	22 1/8	17 1/8	6	4	Monmouth County	NJ	Matthew McGowan	1989	17,986
125 4/8	24 3/8	24 1/8	15 4/8	4	4	Washington County	RI	Kenneth W. Gordon	1989	17,986
125 4/8	21 2/8	21 3/8	16 2/8	5	5	Webb County	TX	Cliff Barnett	1990	17,986
125 4/8	22 4/8	22 3/8	16 6/8	4	4	Atascosa County	TX	Marc Knight	1990	17,986
125 4/8	18 3/8	19 0/8	15 4/8	4	4	Houston County	MN	Bob Augedahl	1990	17,986
125 4/8	23 0/8	23 2/8	15 4/8	4	4	Ste. Genevieve County	MO	Thomas Layton	1990	17,986
125 4/8	21 4/8	21 0/8	15 4/8	6	5	Sanford	MAN	Martin Lavoie	1990	17,986
125 4/8	21 5/8	21 4/8	16 0/8	5	4	Peoria County	IL	Joe Rahn	1990	17,986
125 4/8	22 5/8	21 7/8	21 0/8	4	4	Powell County	MT	Daniel K. Kuehn	1991	17,986
125 4/8	19 5/8	19 5/8	14 6/8	5	5	Meagher County	MT	D. Mitch Kottas	1991	17,986
125 4/8	21 7/8	21 3/8	18 4/8	5	5	La Salle County	TX	Gary Pitts	1991	17,986
125 4/8	22 1/8	22 0/8	19 6/8	4	4	Crawford County	PA	Bob Dunton	1991	17,986
125 4/8	23 4/8	22 5/8	17 2/8	4	4	Ross County	OH	Mark E. Rickey	1991	17,986
125 4/8	21 5/8	21 0/8	18 4/8	4	5	Hardin County	IA	William J. Stonebraker	1991	17,986
125 4/8	21 0/8	21 6/8	18 0/8	5	4	Camden County	NJ	Richard C. Jones	1991	17,986
125 4/8	21 2/8	22 3/8	15 6/8	5	5	Houston County	MN	Mike Schweisthal	1992	17,986
125 4/8	23 2/8	23 2/8	14 4/8	4	4	Litchfield County	CT	Steve Sears	1992	17,986
125 4/8	25 0/8	23 6/8	17 2/8	6	5	St. Helena Parish	LA	Brent Stevens	1992	17,986
125 4/8	21 1/8	23 2/8	16 0/8	4	4	Knox County	KY	David Disney	1992	17,986
125 4/8	19 6/8	19 7/8	15 2/8	5	6	Otsego County	MI	Jerome H. Lubbers	1992	17,986
125 4/8	20 3/8	21 2/8	15 2/8	5	4	Chippewa County	WI	William L. Stobb	1992	17,986
125 4/8	21 6/8	21 4/8	19 6/8	4	4	Racine County	WI	Greg Hanson	1992	17,986
125 4/8	22 0/8	23 6/8	19 2/8	4	4	Meigs County	OH	Ron Plemmons, Jr.	1992	17,986
125 4/8	22 2/8	21 1/8	16 0/8	5	5	East Feliciana Parish	LA	Charles Denstorff	1993	17,986
125 4/8	21 4/8	19 6/8	16 4/8	4	4	Livingston County	MI	Keith Headley	1993	17,986
125 4/8	21 4/8	21 2/8	16 4/8	6	4	Brown County	IL	Jeff Darr	1993	17,986
125 4/8	19 6/8	19 6/8	14 2/8	5	6	Crittenden County	KY	William Roy Barrett	1993	17,986
125 4/8	21 4/8	21 4/8	15 4/8	4	5	St. Clair County	MI	Chet Chamberlin	1993	17,986
125 4/8	23 5/8	22 6/8	15 6/8	4	5	Williamson County	IL	Fred Lawrence	1993	17,986
125 4/8	23 0/8	22 4/8	21 6/8	4	4	Livingston County	NY	Greg Bendzus, Sr.	1993	17,986
125 4/8	20 3/8	20 2/8	13 4/8	6	5	Pierce County	WI	Wade Sotona	1993	17,986
125 4/8	23 3/8	22 7/8	16 0/8	5	5	Albany County	NY	Joe Reagan	1993	17,986
125 4/8	25 0/8	24 4/8	17 7/8	6	6	Okanogan County	WA	Kevin P. Skirko	1994	17,986
125 4/8	21 1/8	21 2/8	17 6/8	4	4	Shelby County	TN	Keith Giffin	1994	17,986
125 4/8	23 3/8	23 0/8	19 2/8	4	4	Trempealeau County	WI	John Franson	1994	17,986
125 4/8	20 6/8	20 0/8	14 0/8	4	4	Washtenaw County	MI	Matthew Callahan	1994	17,986
125 4/8	22 2/8	21 3/8	16 6/8	5	5	Washburn County	WI	Mike Schwartz	1994	17,986
125 4/8	18 5/8	18 2/8	16 0/8	5	5	Beaver County	PA	Jeff Lopes	1994	17,986
125 4/8	21 5/8	22 3/8	16 6/8	4	4	Guernsey County	OH	Doug Woods	1994	17,986
125 4/8	22 6/8	20 0/8	18 0/8	4	5	Peoria County	IL	John Soehn	1994	17,986
125 4/8	20 1/8	21 0/8	14 2/8	5	5	La Salle County	TX	James O. Weison	1994	17,986
125 4/8	19 1/8	19 0/8	16 0/8	4	4	Henry County	VA	Mike Weaver	1994	17,986
125 4/8	22 6/8	22 5/8	18 0/8	4	5	Tippecanoe County	IN	Brian Kirts	1994	17,986
125 4/8	21 7/8	21 3/8	20 0/8	4	4	Cochrane	ALB	Tom Foss	1994	17,986
125 4/8	23 5/8	23 3/8	15 6/8	4	4	Marinette County	WI	Gary M. Hawley	1994	17,986

WHITETAIL DEER (TYPICAL ANTLERS)

Minimum Score 125   Continued

SCORE	LENGTH OF MAIN BEAM R	LENGTH OF MAIN BEAM L	INSIDE SPREAD	NUMBER OF POINTS R	NUMBER OF POINTS L	AREA	STATE/ PROVINCE	HUNTER'S NAME	DATE	RANK
125 4/8	23 0/8	22 4/8	17 4/8	4	6	Dallas County	AL	Phillip Knight	1994	17,986
125 4/8	21 6/8	21 1/8	15 2/8	4	4	Hale County	AL	Danny Moore	1995	17,986
125 4/8	19 2/8	19 0/8	15 0/8	5	6	Refugio County	TX	Danny R. Boswell	1995	17,986
125 4/8	24 2/8	23 5/8	17 0/8	5	4	Pepin County	WI	Allen Brantner	1995	17,986
125 4/8	20 3/8	20 5/8	14 6/8	5	5	Davis County	IA	Mark P. Wagner	1995	17,986
125 4/8	21 5/8	20 5/8	16 2/8	4	4	Hennepin County	MN	Jeffrey W. Braa	1995	17,986
125 4/8	21 2/8	21 3/8	20 6/8	4	4	Woodford County	IL	Bobby J. Evans, Sr.	1995	17,986
125 4/8	22 2/8	20 7/8	15 6/8	4	4	McHenry County	IL	Brad Wiehr	1995	17,986
125 4/8	18 5/8	19 6/8	15 6/8	5	4	Dekalb County	IL	John Zawaski	1995	17,986
125 4/8	18 3/8	18 1/8	13 1/8	7	5	Page County	IA	Chris Barton	1995	17,986
125 4/8	20 2/8	21 1/8	14 4/8	5	5	Idaho County	ID	Cory Schmid	1995	17,986
125 4/8	22 7/8	22 5/8	17 4/8	4	4	Refugio County	TX	Jeff Watson	1995	17,986
125 4/8	22 2/8	21 5/8	17 4/8	4	5	Douglas County	WI	Kenneth C. Fedyn	1996	17,986
125 4/8	21 5/8	21 1/8	16 0/8	7	6	Franklin County	OH	William E. Albright	1996	17,986
125 4/8	22 6/8	22 0/8	17 2/8	4	5	Ramsey County	MN	Don Buckentin	1996	17,986
125 4/8	20 2/8	20 7/8	20 2/8	4	4	Stokes County	NC	Tony Ray Mabe	1996	17,986
125 4/8	21 6/8	21 2/8	17 2/8	4	4	Schuyler County	MO	Derek McMurry	1996	17,986
125 4/8	20 1/8	18 4/8	17 7/8	7	5	Hamilton County	FL	Erich M. Sulllvan	1996	17,986
125 4/8	21 6/8	21 5/8	16 6/8	5	5	Columbia County	WI	Larry Lee Prochnow	1996	17,986
125 4/8	20 6/8	20 2/8	15 2/8	5	6	Barry County	MI	Owen L. Reigler, Jr.	1996	17,986
125 4/8	19 6/8	19 5/8	17 0/8	5	5	Crawford County	PA	Edward J. Haregsin	1996	17,986
125 4/8	21 1/8	21 0/8	15 6/8	5	5	Forest County	WI	Chris Dombrowski	1996	17,986
125 4/8	20 6/8	21 0/8	17 4/8	5	5	Somerset County	PA	Mark Klonicke	1996	17,986
125 4/8	21 3/8	20 4/8	16 4/8	4	5	Meigs County	OH	Tim Smith	1996	17,986
125 4/8	19 3/8	18 5/8	14 6/8	6	5	Kenedy County	TX	Rich Kimball	1996	17,986
125 4/8	17 5/8	18 2/8	14 2/8	5	5	Valley County	MT	Dan Frank	1997	17,986
125 4/8	20 2/8	19 4/8	16 2/8	5	5	St. Clair County	MI	Robert Watson	1997	17,986
125 4/8	22 6/8	23 0/8	17 4/8	5	5	Fayette County	PA	Anthony M. Ryan	1997	17,986
125 4/8	23 2/8	23 2/8	16 0/8	4	4	Bedford County	VA	Doug Saunders	1997	17,986
125 4/8	20 0/8	19 7/8	16 0/8	5	4	Yates County	NY	Jeffrey R. Englin	1997	17,986
125 4/8	21 0/8	19 3/8	19 2/8	5	4	Washtenaw County	MI	James A. Rapchick	1997	17,986
125 4/8	23 1/8	23 1/8	18 4/8	5	4	Waupaca County	WI	Joel Dobberpuhl	1997	17,986
125 4/8	22 7/8	22 0/8	16 2/8	7	5	Fayette County	IL	Barry Reynolds	1997	17,986
125 4/8	20 0/8	19 4/8	17 2/8	5	5	Boone County	WV	Tom Green	1997	17,986
125 4/8	20 0/8	19 4/8	17 2/8	5	5	Boone County	WV	Tom Green	1997	17,986
125 4/8	21 0/8	19 6/8	13 6/8	5	5	Jasper County	MS	George Kylan Love	1998	17,986
125 4/8	22 5/8	22 3/8	16 6/8	5	4	Portage County	WI	Vincent E. Fellers	1998	17,986
125 3/8	20 5/8	21 4/8	16 5/8	5	4	Stephenson County	IL	Vaughn Zimmerman	1969	18,106
125 3/8	24 0/8	24 6/8	17 3/8	4	5	Wabasha County	MN	David Mohler	1971	18,106
125 3/8	20 7/8	20 3/8	15 3/8	4	4	Newport News County	VA	Dr. Glenn A. Parker	1972	18,106
125 3/8	21 7/8	22 6/8	16 3/8	4	5	Warren County	IA	Michael Woolman	1974	18,106
125 3/8	22 6/8	23 4/8	18 4/8	7	6	Pawnee County	KS	Don Jensen	1977	18,106
125 3/8	19 2/8	19 7/8	14 1/8	5	5	Jasper County	IN	Frank Benka	1978	18,106
125 3/8	22 2/8	23 6/8	16 3/8	4	4	Louisa County	IA	Lee Cassabaum	1979	18,106
125 3/8	22 0/8	22 2/8	15 5/8	4	4	Saginaw County	MI	James L. Bassett	1980	18,106
125 3/8	20 5/8	21 7/8	18 1/8	4	4	Neosho County	KS	Damie Coomes	1982	18,106
125 3/8	20 1/8	20 1/8	14 7/8	5	5	Dorchester County	MD	Jim Roy	1983	18,106
125 3/8	20 4/8	20 1/8	17 7/8	4	5	Hardin County	IA	Bill Stonebraker	1983	18,106
125 3/8	19 4/8	20 1/8	15 7/8	5	5	Watson	SAS	Wayne Dickson	1983	18,106
125 3/8	20 7/8	20 1/8	15 5/8	5	5	Suffolk County	NY	Anthony Bernard	1983	18,106
125 3/8	21 3/8	21 2/8	18 1/8	4	4	Oconto County	WI	Bob Richardson, Jr.	1984	18,106
125 3/8	22 4/8	22 0/8	18 5/8	5	5	Scott County	MN	Bruce Kramer	1984	18,106
125 3/8	18 7/8	18 4/8	15 3/8	5	5	Wellington County	ONT	Fred Law	1984	18,106
125 3/8	21 4/8	20 6/8	15 7/8	5	5	Cheboygan County	MI	Steven Schrauben	1984	18,106
125 3/8	22 1/8	21 5/8	18 1/8	4	4	Washington County	WI	Gordon Bell	1985	18,106
125 3/8	22 6/8	21 5/8	14 3/8	4	4	Somerset County	ME	Alfred Corson	1985	18,106
125 3/8	22 0/8	22 3/8	18 0/8	4	6	Morrison County	MN	Mike Mitten	1985	18,106
125 3/8	18 6/8	18 7/8	16 3/8	5	5	Ramsey County	ND	Charles McGarvey	1985	18,106
125 3/8	21 4/8	22 4/8	16 3/8	4	5	Iowa County	WI	Don Schuld	1985	18,106
125 3/8	23 1/8	21 5/8	13 6/8	5	4	St. Charles County	MO	Edgar Ralph Welch	1985	18,106
125 3/8	21 2/8	23 1/8	20 5/8	5	5	Augusta County	VA	Mark D. Huffman	1986	18,106
125 3/8	24 1/8	24 3/8	16 7/8	4	4	Bond County	IL	Bob Goestenkors	1986	18,106
125 3/8	24 3/8	22 4/8	18 3/8	5	5	Caroline County	MD	Eric Wise	1986	18,106
125 3/8	20 5/8	21 6/8	18 5/8	4	4	Sawyer County	WI	Mike Fawley	1987	18,106
125 3/8	21 1/8	20 3/8	15 3/8	5	5	Waukesha County	WI	Daniel Buchta	1987	18,106
125 3/8	20 1/8	20 1/8	15 1/8	4	4	Fayette County	IL	Terry Jackson	1987	18,106
125 3/8	24 4/8	22 5/8	20 3/8	5	4	Vermilion County	IL	Allen Walker	1987	18,106
125 3/8	19 7/8	20 3/8	14 7/8	4	4	Campbell County	TN	Truman E. Wilson	1987	18,106
125 3/8	21 3/8	21 5/8	16 7/8	4	5	Carroll County	MD	Dana P. Calhoun	1987	18,106
125 3/8	20 0/8	20 2/8	15 7/8	5	5	Muskingum County	OH	G. Vernon Sowers	1987	18,106
125 3/8	20 2/8	20 7/8	18 3/8	6	5	Dorchester County	MD	Mark Alan Gadow	1987	18,106
125 3/8	21 7/8	22 0/8	17 6/8	6	5	Polk County	WI	Mark Gustafson	1988	18,106
125 3/8	19 0/8	18 7/8	15 5/8	5	5	Jefferson County	KS	Mike Campbell	1988	18,106
125 3/8	21 3/8	21 3/8	13 6/8	5	6	Jefferson County	WI	Jeffrey T. Engel	1988	18,106
125 3/8	23 5/8	23 2/8	18 3/8	4	4	Buffalo County	WI	Randy A. Harms	1988	18,106
125 3/8	20 7/8	20 7/8	17 1/8	5	5	Dunn County	WI	LeRoy Leftwich	1988	18,106
125 3/8	21 4/8	20 7/8	16 3/8	5	5	Kewaunee County	WI	David D. Zima	1988	18,106
125 3/8	20 5/8	21 4/8	12 3/8	5	5	Coles County	IL	Robert A. Bryant	1988	18,106

WHITETAIL DEER (TYPICAL ANTLERS)

Minimum Score 125

SCORE	LENGTH OF MAIN BEAM R	LENGTH OF MAIN BEAM L	INSIDE SPREAD	NUMBER OF POINTS R	NUMBER OF POINTS L	AREA	STATE/PROVINCE	HUNTER'S NAME	DATE	RANK
125 3/8	22 1/8	22 2/8	16 1/8	4	4	St. Croix County	WI	Glenn D. Khalar	1988	18,106
125 3/8	19 7/8	20 1/8	14 7/8	4	5	Marquette County	WI	Tim Butula	1988	18,106
125 3/8	20 3/8	18 6/8	14 3/8	5	6	Shelby County	IL	Tim J. Dow	1989	18,106
125 3/8	20 4/8	19 6/8	13 7/8	5	5	Chippewa County	WI	Jon Oemig	1989	18,106
125 3/8	20 6/8	21 4/8	17 2/8	6	4	Douglas County	WI	David P. Lindelof	1989	18,106
125 3/8	21 2/8	21 0/8	17 3/8	5	5	Logan County	IL	Eldon R. Broster	1989	18,106
125 3/8	21 2/8	24 7/8	18 5/8	4	4	Cross County	AR	Chris Vanaman	1989	18,106
125 3/8	21 6/8	21 4/8	16 1/8	5	5	Wood County	WI	Steve Peterson	1990	18,106
125 3/8	21 3/8	21 3/8	16 1/8	5	5	Richland County	WI	Dean A. Jewell	1990	18,106
125 3/8	19 2/8	18 7/8	17 2/8	5	6	Osage County	OK	Terry Brady	1990	18,106
125 3/8	21 2/8	20 4/8	17 3/8	5	5	Anoka County	MN	Wayne A. Nicholson	1990	18,106
125 3/8	19 6/8	20 0/8	13 7/8	6	6	Orange County	NY	Ben Risley	1990	18,106
125 3/8	23 3/8	23 4/8	18 3/8	4	4	Delaware County	PA	Jay P. Kelly	1990	18,106
125 3/8	21 3/8	22 2/8	14 6/8	5	5	Flathead County	MT	Gordon L. Lewis	1991	18,106
125 3/8	21 1/8	21 1/8	17 1/8	5	5	Swift County	MN	Jan Rangens	1991	18,106
125 3/8	22 2/8	21 1/8	16 1/8	5	4	Hall County	GA	Tim Butler	1991	18,106
125 3/8	20 4/8	20 4/8	16 3/8	4	5	Polk County	MN	Greg Ranz	1991	18,106
125 3/8	20 1/8	20 2/8	14 3/8	5	5	Bartow County	GA	Christopher C. King	1991	18,106
125 3/8	21 2/8	21 0/8	15 3/8	4	4	Marion County	KS	Galen Chizek	1991	18,106
125 3/8	22 6/8	23 3/8	15 7/8	6	4	Vigo County	IN	Billy Wright	1991	18,106
125 3/8	22 7/8	22 3/8	19 1/8	4	3	Lawrence County	IN	Larry Deaton	1991	18,106
125 3/8	19 6/8	19 7/8	16 1/8	5	5	Van Buren County	MI	Martin L. Price	1991	18,106
125 3/8	18 6/8	18 1/8	13 5/8	5	6	Sawyer County	WI	James C. Snortum	1991	18,106
125 3/8	23 5/8	24 4/8	16 1/8	7	6	Sullivan County	MO	Darren Stephenson	1991	18,106
125 3/8	20 0/8	20 4/8	13 1/8	5	5	Perry County	OH	Gary J. Boley	1991	18,106
125 3/8	23 6/8	22 4/8	16 3/8	6	4	St. Clair County	MI	Kurt M. Zurawski	1991	18,106
125 3/8	20 6/8	20 4/8	15 3/8	5	5	Warren County	IA	Dan Thomlinson	1991	18,106
125 3/8	20 5/8	20 6/8	17 7/8	4	4	Marathon County	WI	Larry A. Karlmann	1992	18,106
125 3/8	23 3/8	23 4/8	16 3/8	4	4	Sawyer County	WI	Daniel Kolberg	1992	18,106
125 3/8	23 1/8	22 4/8	17 6/8	6	6	Green County	WI	Abby C. Rensberry	1992	18,106
125 3/8	21 3/8	22 1/8	17 6/8	7	5	Winnebago County	IL	Loyd Sandidge	1992	18,106
125 3/8	21 6/8	22 0/8	18 5/8	4	4	Bureau County	IL	Greg Bowers	1992	18,106
125 3/8	20 1/8	20 0/8	16 7/8	4	4	Muskingum County	OH	Tom Krahe	1992	18,106
125 3/8	21 6/8	21 4/8	13 5/8	4	4	Stearns County	MN	Brian Kelzenberg	1993	18,106
125 3/8	20 7/8	22 6/8	19 3/8	4	4	Kane County	IL	Earl Sirchia	1993	18,106
125 3/8	23 0/8	23 7/8	17 5/8	5	4	Wyandot County	OH	James D. Herring	1993	18,106
125 3/8	21 5/8	22 3/8	19 7/8	4	4	Monmouth County	NJ	Joseph E. Tilton	1993	18,106
125 3/8	24 4/8	23 2/8	18 4/8	5	5	Howard County	IN	William Troy Williams	1993	18,106
125 3/8	21 7/8	22 4/8	16 5/8	6	6	Kay County	OK	Jason Rhodes	1993	18,106
125 3/8	21 2/8	24 0/8	17 1/8	3	4	Letellier	MAN	John Haspel	1993	18,106
125 3/8	20 6/8	21 5/8	17 3/8	5	5	Jefferson County	OH	Forrest Wietfeld	1994	18,106
125 3/8	18 5/8	18 3/8	16 1/8	5	5	Osceola County	MI	Dennis L. Lucas	1994	18,106
125 3/8	19 6/8	19 3/8	15 6/8	4	4	Iowa County	WI	Tom Philipps	1994	18,106
125 3/8	22 4/8	22 4/8	18 5/8	4	4	Cook County	IL	Timothy L. Harkness	1994	18,106
125 3/8	23 4/8	23 3/8	16 5/8	6	5	McClain County	OK	Ross M. Puckett	1994	18,106
125 3/8	22 4/8	21 3/8	14 4/8	5	6	Clermont County	OH	Tim Carter	1994	18,106
125 3/8	21 6/8	21 5/8	16 3/8	4	4	Johnson County	IL	Mike Daniel	1994	18,106
125 3/8	20 4/8	21 0/8	16 5/8	5	5	Winnebago County	IL	Steve Gorman	1994	18,106
125 3/8	21 4/8	21 6/8	17 1/8	4	4	Albany County	NY	Matt Pigliavento	1994	18,106
125 3/8	21 5/8	21 4/8	16 6/8	5	5	Ohio County	KY	Ricky Phelps	1995	18,106
125 3/8	21 5/8	21 0/8	17 1/8	5	6	Muskingum County	OH	Clint Frame	1995	18,106
125 3/8	20 0/8	19 4/8	14 7/8	4	6	Giles County	TN	Steve W. Tyler	1995	18,106
125 3/8	21 1/8	22 3/8	18 1/8	5	6	Barry County	MO	David Counts	1995	18,106
125 3/8	23 3/8	23 0/8	16 5/8	5	4	La Crosse County	WI	Joe Brye	1995	18,106
125 3/8	22 0/8	21 6/8	16 5/8	5	5	Valley County	MT	Richard Penn	1995	18,106
125 3/8	20 4/8	22 6/8	16 1/8	8	6	Guernsey County	OH	James E. McMasters	1995	18,106
125 3/8	23 2/8	22 4/8	20 3/8	5	5	Osage County	OK	Todd McClintock	1995	18,106
125 3/8	21 3/8	21 7/8	15 7/8	4	4	Vilas County	WI	Ken Alft	1996	18,106
125 3/8	23 7/8	22 6/8	21 3/8	4	4	Dekalb County	IL	Jeffrey B. Johnson	1996	18,106
125 3/8	22 0/8	23 5/8	16 1/8	5	5	Genesee County	MI	Joe Polidan	1996	18,106
125 3/8	22 2/8	22 4/8	17 6/8	5	5	Jackson County	WI	David Loschko	1996	18,106
125 3/8	22 4/8	21 7/8	18 4/8	5	4	Suffolk County	NY	Timothy McCarthy	1996	18,106
125 3/8	21 7/8	21 0/8	15 3/8	5	5	Dane County	WI	Gary Lehnherr	1996	18,106
125 3/8	19 7/8	20 0/8	18 1/8	5	5	Canadian County	OK	Jerry Stover	1996	18,106
125 3/8	21 7/8	22 6/8	15 5/8	5	5	Miami County	OH	Rick Busse	1996	18,106
125 3/8	21 1/8	20 3/8	17 1/8	5	4	Wood County	TX	Paul R. Bovee	1996	18,106
125 3/8	21 0/8	22 3/8	18 5/8	4	5	Dodge County	MN	Allen Iverson	1996	18,106
125 3/8	19 5/8	19 6/8	14 7/8	5	5	Dakota County	NE	Gordon L. Hegge	1997	18,106
125 3/8	21 1/8	21 1/8	17 4/8	7	7	Allegheny County	PA	Jim L. Lamont	1997	18,106
125 3/8	22 3/8	22 3/8	16 7/8	5	5	Morrison County	MN	Kevin R. Yineman	1997	18,106
125 3/8	22 1/8	21 4/8	17 7/8	4	4	Green County	WI	Daryl Thompson	1997	18,106
125 3/8	20 0/8	20 4/8	17 5/8	5	5	Linn County	IA	George Roland	1997	18,106
125 3/8	21 1/8	21 4/8	16 7/8	4	4	Clermont County	OH	Will Mullis	1997	18,106
125 3/8	21 1/8	21 4/8	17 7/8	4	4	Jackson County	MI	Jon A. Colby	1997	18,106
125 3/8	19 3/8	19 2/8	15 1/8	5	5	Monroe County	IA	Bill Kirkpatrick	1997	18,106
125 3/8	19 7/8	19 7/8	15 3/8	5	6	Webb County	TX	Harry I. Bussa, Jr.	1997	18,106
125 3/8	19 6/8	19 6/8	15 1/8	5	5	Irion County	TX	Terry Tadsen	1997	18,106
125 3/8	22 6/8	23 3/8	15 3/8	5	5	Webb County	TX	Jim Dougherty	1997	18,106

WHITETAIL DEER (TYPICAL ANTLERS)

Minimum Score 125
Continued

SCORE	LENGTH OF R MAIN BEAM L		INSIDE SPREAD	NUMBER OF R POINTS L		AREA	STATE/ PROVINCE	HUNTER'S NAME	DATE	RANK
125 3/8	19 5/8	19 3/8	17 1/8	6	6	Adair County	MO	Charles Zeman	1997	18,106
125 3/8	22 0/8	21 6/8	14 1/8	6	5	Pamlico County	NC	Merrill Kahl	1998	18,106
125 2/8	19 3/8	20 0/8	15 0/8	4	4	Missaukee County	MI	Eugene D. Garris, DDS	1966	18,227
125 2/8	26 5/8	25 2/8	22 2/8	4	3	Fulton County	IL	Arnold C. Hegele	1967	18,227
125 2/8	20 6/8	20 7/8	15 6/8	4	4	Sussex County	NJ	Tom Barber	1973	18,227
125 2/8	22 6/8	22 2/8	17 2/8	4	3	Washington County	IA	Danny B. Jirsa	1974	18,227
125 2/8	21 5/8	21 4/8	17 6/8	5	4	Columbia County	WI	Gary Cahoon	1977	18,227
125 2/8	22 2/8	24 7/8	17 6/8	4	4	Guernsey County	OH	Butch Todd	1977	18,227
125 2/8	21 7/8	21 7/8	16 2/8	4	4	Jackson County	MI	Bernard Stachowicz	1979	18,227
125 2/8	23 2/8	24 6/8	19 2/8	4	4	Baltimore County	MD	Robert E. Arndt	1980	18,227
125 2/8	22 3/8	21 6/8	18 6/8	5	6	Goodhue County	MN	John "Jack" Cordes	1981	18,227
125 2/8	18 6/8	18 1/8	13 6/8	5	5	Boone County	MO	Jeff Jennings	1981	18,227
125 2/8	23 2/8	22 6/8	16 2/8	4	4	Trempealeau County	WI	Fred Obgartel	1982	18,227
125 2/8	21 6/8	22 4/8	15 0/8	4	4	Shawano County	WI	David J. Gard	1983	18,227
125 2/8	20 6/8	21 4/8	15 2/8	5	5	Calvert County	MD	Gary Fillmann	1983	18,227
125 2/8	20 0/8	21 0/8	17 6/8	6	5	Cherokee County	KS	Sam F. Lancaster	1984	18,227
125 2/8	19 3/8	19 0/8	14 0/8	4	4	Kiowa County	KS	Susan Manwarren	1984	18,227
125 2/8	24 1/8	23 4/8	17 4/8	4	4	Blue Earth County	MN	Ray Smothers	1985	18,227
125 2/8	21 0/8	21 4/8	19 4/8	8	8	Des Moines County	IA	Rod Waschkat	1985	18,227
125 2/8	24 0/8	23 0/8	17 0/8	4	5	Harford County	MD	Warren J. Barth	1986	18,227
125 2/8	21 1/8	21 1/8	16 3/8	6	5	Mingo County	WV	Danny Thompson	1986	18,227
125 2/8	22 2/8	22 6/8	18 5/8	6	6	Suffolk County	NY	Lee James Garrant	1986	18,227
125 2/8	21 5/8	20 6/8	17 4/8	4	4	Butler County	KS	Ray Manfull	1986	18,227
125 2/8	24 0/8	23 2/8	20 7/8	5	4	Suffolk County	NY	Steve Schoen	1986	18,227
125 2/8	21 6/8	21 3/8	19 0/8	4	4	Dubuque County	IA	Andy Chase	1986	18,227
125 2/8	21 5/8	20 5/8	19 7/8	5	6	Buffalo County	WI	Wayne Olson	1986	18,227
125 2/8	20 1/8	21 2/8	18 2/8	5	5	Sabine County	TX	Russell C. Lantier	1986	18,227
125 2/8	21 5/8	21 3/8	14 6/8	4	4	Otoe County	NE	Richard R. Pope	1987	18,227
125 2/8	21 1/8	21 0/8	18 6/8	4	4	Morris County	NJ	Gene Rurka	1987	18,227
125 2/8	22 0/8	23 0/8	17 0/8	4	4	Adams County	WI	Randall Ebbe	1987	18,227
125 2/8	20 6/8	21 3/8	16 4/8	5	5	La Grange County	IN	David Sauders	1987	18,227
125 2/8	22 3/8	21 5/8	17 6/8	4	4	Cayuga County	NY	Brian Fenner	1987	18,227
125 2/8	22 1/8	22 4/8	18 6/8	4	4	Langlade County	WI	Andrae D'Acquisto	1987	18,227
125 2/8	21 1/8	20 7/8	16 6/8	4	4	Litchfield County	CT	John Swiklas	1987	18,227
125 2/8	21 3/8	20 2/8	16 2/8	5	5	Washington County	PA	Victor J. Columbus	1988	18,227
125 2/8	20 4/8	21 0/8	15 0/8	5	5	Dunn County	WI	Mike J. Kurschner	1988	18,227
125 2/8	20 6/8	20 2/8	16 6/8	5	5	Kent County	MD	Randy L. Heim	1988	18,227
125 2/8	24 2/8	24 4/8	17 5/8	6	5	Dane County	WI	Todd P. Schultz	1988	18,227
125 2/8	22 0/8	22 6/8	16 6/8	4	5	Jackson County	IN	Jeffrey J. Hurd	1988	18,227
125 2/8	19 7/8	19 2/8	19 2/8	4	4	Washington County	MS	Bobby R. Woods	1989	18,227
125 2/8	23 6/8	23 5/8	12 4/8	4	5	Sequatchie County	TN	Robert L. Moon, Jr.	1989	18,227
125 2/8	20 5/8	21 4/8	14 6/8	6	5	Hardin County	KY	Jimmie Williams	1989	18,227
125 2/8	21 5/8	20 5/8	18 0/8	4	4	Sussex County	DE	Jeff Minor	1989	18,227
125 2/8	21 7/8	22 7/8	14 2/8	8	5	Greene County	AR	Andy Vangilder	1989	18,227
125 2/8	21 3/8	21 1/8	16 6/8	4	4	Johnson County	IA	Jim Bohnenkamp	1989	18,227
125 2/8	21 6/8	22 6/8	13 4/8	5	5	Wilcox County	AL	Billy Perryman	1989	18,227
125 2/8	18 4/8	19 7/8	13 4/8	6	6	Duval County	TX	Dean Oatman	1989	18,227
125 2/8	22 3/8	21 2/8	17 0/8	4	4	Washington County	WI	Mark Reinert	1990	18,227
125 2/8	18 5/8	18 4/8	15 6/8	5	5	Big Stone County	MN	Steven Butzke	1990	18,227
125 2/8	20 0/8	20 3/8	17 5/8	7	5	Waupaca County	WI	Dan Herson	1990	18,227
125 2/8	23 0/8	23 0/8	18 0/8	4	4	Bucks County	PA	Chuck Metz	1990	18,227
125 2/8	22 1/8	22 2/8	17 6/8	4	6	Antrim County	MI	Mike Losee	1990	18,227
125 2/8	20 7/8	20 5/8	16 4/8	5	5	Pike County	OH	Robert Irwin Bazell	1990	18,227
125 2/8	23 4/8	24 5/8	17 0/8	4	4	Isle of Wight County	VA	Mark W. Trybe	1990	18,227
125 2/8	20 1/8	20 7/8	15 4/8	5	5	Osage County	OK	Jeff Fitts	1990	18,227
125 2/8	24 7/8	23 2/8	19 2/8	4	4	Fremont County	IA	John W. Nebel	1990	18,227
125 2/8	21 3/8	21 1/8	19 2/8	4	4	Will County	IL	Robert L. Kamenjarin	1990	18,227
125 2/8	22 1/8	21 7/8	14 2/8	5	5	Atascosa County	TX	Mike Palmer	1990	18,227
125 2/8	22 2/8	21 6/8	15 5/8	6	5	Delaware County	OH	Dave Ware	1990	18,227
125 2/8	20 4/8	20 4/8	15 4/8	5	5	Adams County	OH	Larry D. Napier	1991	18,227
125 2/8	20 5/8	20 2/8	12 4/8	6	6	St. Marys County	MD	Dale K. Hubbartt	1991	18,227
125 2/8	19 0/8	18 6/8	14 6/8	7	6	Clarion County	PA	V. Craig Hagan	1991	18,227
125 2/8	21 5/8	21 4/8	16 4/8	4	4	Burnett County	WI	Larry M. Looman	1991	18,227
125 2/8	21 4/8	21 5/8	16 4/8	5	4	Pike County	IL	Dan Perez	1991	18,227
125 2/8	20 0/8	19 4/8	16 4/8	5	5	Webb County	TX	Stephen McCarty	1992	18,227
125 2/8	22 4/8	23 0/8	17 0/8	5	4	Lapeer County	MI	Toby Parker	1992	18,227
125 2/8	20 0/8	20 1/8	15 4/8	4	4	Morris County	NJ	Tom Conlon	1992	18,227
125 2/8	22 1/8	21 4/8	17 2/8	4	6	St. Clair County	MI	Rich Papineau	1992	18,227
125 2/8	22 5/8	22 7/8	18 1/8	8	5	Douglas County	WI	Donald Ray Piper	1992	18,227
125 2/8	20 7/8	21 1/8	16 4/8	5	6	Cold Lake	ALB	Eric Rauhanen	1992	18,227
125 2/8	20 7/8	20 4/8	15 4/8	4	4	Shelby County	AL	Greg Kadlick	1992	18,227
125 2/8	19 7/8	20 5/8	14 2/8	5	6	Goliad County	TX	Steven J. Waible	1992	18,227
125 2/8	20 7/8	19 2/8	19 0/8	5	5	Waukesha County	WI	Jim Suchocki	1992	18,227
125 2/8	22 1/8	21 4/8	16 0/8	4	4	McMullen County	TX	Bill Crome, Jr.	1993	18,227
125 2/8	19 7/8	20 0/8	15 1/8	7	7	St. Joseph County	IN	Michael L. Ritter	1993	18,227
125 2/8	20 3/8	21 0/8	18 1/8	5	5	Traverse County	MN	Brad G. Raguse	1993	18,227
125 2/8	22 6/8	22 5/8	16 0/8	4	4	Rockland County	NY	Peter Graziosi	1993	18,227
125 2/8	22 3/8	22 4/8	14 4/8	5	7	Louisa County	IA	Jay Beenblossom	1993	18,227

WHITETAIL DEER (TYPICAL ANTLERS)

Minimum Score 125 — Continued

SCORE	LENGTH OF MAIN BEAM R	LENGTH OF MAIN BEAM L	INSIDE SPREAD	NUMBER OF POINTS R	NUMBER OF POINTS L	AREA	STATE/ PROVINCE	HUNTER'S NAME	DATE	RANK
125 2/8	22 4/8	23 5/8	16 4/8	4	4	Blue Earth County	MN	Jeff Berndt	1993	18,227
125 2/8	21 4/8	22 3/8	16 6/8	4	4	Crawford County	IL	Charlie Guyer	1993	18,227
125 2/8	21 3/8	21 2/8	18 4/8	6	5	Christina Lake	BC	R. E. Bogstie	1993	18,227
125 2/8	22 1/8	22 4/8	16 7/8	5	5	Boone County	MO	Kenny Graham	1993	18,227
125 2/8	21 2/8	21 5/8	17 4/8	5	5	Morton County	ND	Bruce A. Schultz	1994	18,227
125 2/8	18 7/8	19 6/8	16 2/8	6	5	Latimer County	OK	George Lancaster	1994	18,227
125 2/8	23 2/8	23 2/8	17 4/8	4	5	Dane County	WI	Robert W. Erickson III	1994	18,227
125 2/8	19 7/8	19 3/8	14 4/8	6	5	Newaygo County	MI	Gerald C. Inman	1994	18,227
125 2/8	22 5/8	21 2/8	17 0/8	5	5	Pulaski County	IL	Doug Jansen	1994	18,227
125 2/8	21 3/8	20 6/8	16 0/8	5	5	Sedgwick County	CO	Larry Welchlen	1994	18,227
125 2/8	23 3/8	20 1/8	19 1/8	4	7	Montgomery County	IL	Randy Keiser	1994	18,227
125 2/8	21 3/8	21 1/8	15 0/8	4	4	Fulton County	GA	Kirk Hopkins	1994	18,227
125 2/8	24 7/8	26 5/8	16 2/8	5	4	Logan County	IL	Michael Krasinski	1994	18,227
125 2/8	21 5/8	22 4/8	19 4/8	4	4	Newaygo County	MI	Ed Mascarenas	1994	18,227
125 2/8	18 6/8	20 7/8	15 2/8	4	4	Putnam County	IL	Eric Jeppson	1994	18,227
125 2/8	18 6/8	18 7/8	15 6/8	6	5	Warren County	NJ	Michael Ridner	1994	18,227
125 2/8	23 2/8	23 1/8	15 6/8	5	4	East Carroll Parish	LA	Frank Greenlee	1995	18,227
125 2/8	21 5/8	22 0/8	16 6/8	4	4	Waushara County	WI	Jeffrey A. Vandenberg	1995	18,227
125 2/8	24 6/8	24 7/8	16 2/8	3	4	Marion County	IL	Rich Neff, Jr.	1995	18,227
125 2/8	20 6/8	21 3/8	15 2/8	4	4	Carroll County	OH	Damon Moran	1995	18,227
125 2/8	20 5/8	20 6/8	18 6/8	4	5	Queens County	NBW	Mike Bowling	1995	18,227
125 2/8	23 2/8	21 6/8	13 2/8	4	4	Harrison County	KY	Charles Stroub	1995	18,227
125 2/8	22 4/8	22 4/8	16 2/8	4	5	St. Mary Parish	LA	Willie Blanchard	1995	18,227
125 2/8	19 6/8	19 0/8	16 2/8	6	6	Brown County	NE	Joel Klammer	1995	18,227
125 2/8	21 3/8	21 0/8	17 0/8	4	4	Walworth County	WI	Richard Martin	1995	18,227
125 2/8	21 2/8	19 7/8	16 4/8	5	5	Marathon County	WI	Richard Andres	1995	18,227
125 2/8	21 6/8	21 6/8	15 2/8	6	5	Logan County	IL	Eldon R. Broster	1995	18,227
125 2/8	18 4/8	19 2/8	17 2/8	4	4	Washburn County	WI	Rollin J. Swanson	1995	18,227
125 2/8	20 7/8	20 0/8	18 0/8	5	5	Bayfield County	WI	Larry A. Taylor	1995	18,227
125 2/8	21 4/8	22 7/8	18 4/8	4	4	Ida County	IA	Dan D. Soellner	1995	18,227
125 2/8	18 7/8	19 5/8	16 6/8	4	4	Washington County	OH	Robert Earl Sands	1995	18,227
125 2/8	22 1/8	22 2/8	19 2/8	5	4	Kenedy County	TX	Rick Daab	1995	18,227
125 2/8	19 6/8	20 1/8	16 4/8	4	4	Richland County	MT	Brad Hayward	1996	18,227
125 2/8	20 6/8	21 0/8	14 4/8	5	4	Kent County	MD	Robert H. Bramble, Jr.	1996	18,227
125 2/8	19 4/8	19 1/8	15 6/8	5	5	Dodge County	WI	John R. Puetz	1996	18,227
125 2/8	19 4/8	19 0/8	17 7/8	7	5	Genesee County	NY	Jim Sullivan	1996	18,227
125 2/8	20 6/8	21 3/8	14 6/8	4	4	Mason County	WV	Rodney A. Weaver	1996	18,227
125 2/8	21 5/8	22 1/8	15 6/8	4	4	Calvert County	MD	Steve E. Willsey	1996	18,227
125 2/8	21 7/8	23 0/8	19 6/8	4	4	Delaware County	IA	Daniel G. Putz	1996	18,227
125 2/8	22 2/8	22 2/8	18 0/8	4	4	Ottawa County	MI	Michael P. Postema	1996	18,227
125 2/8	20 2/8	20 6/8	14 6/8	5	5	Hillsdale County	MI	Dale E. Buehrer	1996	18,227
125 2/8	24 1/8	22 7/8	18 3/8	5	5	Calvert County	MD	Sherri Fillmann	1996	18,227
125 2/8	20 3/8	20 3/8	17 2/8	5	5	Cattaraugus County	NY	Mike Furman	1996	18,227
125 2/8	20 5/8	21 4/8	17 4/8	5	5	Bureau County	IL	Robert Michel	1996	18,227
125 2/8	22 5/8	21 4/8	18 6/8	5	5	Buffalo County	WI	Gunnar J. Hagen	1997	18,227
125 2/8	19 7/8	19 6/8	16 4/8	5	5	Braxton County	WV	Brian Given	1997	18,227
125 2/8	21 0/8	21 2/8	17 0/8	5	4	Cass County	IL	Billy Bodford	1997	18,227
125 2/8	25 6/8	25 2/8	21 0/8	4	4	Chester County	PA	R. Douglas Horrocks	1997	18,227
125 2/8	21 6/8	21 6/8	15 3/8	4	5	Jackson County	IA	Thomas L. Decker	1997	18,227
125 2/8	21 1/8	19 5/8	16 1/8	4	6	Sanilac County	MI	Randy B. Smith	1997	18,227
125 2/8	21 0/8	20 2/8	15 4/8	4	4	Sauk County	WI	Jeff Wiedel	1997	18,227
125 2/8	22 4/8	22 0/8	18 6/8	4	4	Appanoose County	IA	Tom Pedley	1997	18,227
125 2/8	18 6/8	18 1/8	15 1/8	6	5	McClain County	OK	Craig Pullen	1997	18,227
125 2/8	24 6/8	24 6/8	24 6/8	4	7	Sangamon County	IL	William C. Sandidge	1997	18,227
125 2/8	21 3/8	21 2/8	15 4/8	4	4	Jackson County	WI	Eric R. Frazee	1997	18,227
125 2/8	20 6/8	21 1/8	16 6/8	5	4	Decatur County	IA	Dave Sabrowsky	1997	18,227
125 2/8	22 5/8	23 3/8	16 0/8	4	4	Middlesex County	NJ	Peter Wojciechowski	1997	18,227
125 2/8	24 6/8	24 3/8	22 5/8	4	7	Bourbon County	KS	Doyle Slinkard	1997	18,227
125 2/8	21 3/8	21 2/8	17 0/8	5	4	Cass County	MI	John W. Isabel	1997	18,227
125 2/8	20 1/8	20 1/8	14 2/8	4	5	Shackelford County	TX	Dale E. Harkins	1997	18,227
125 2/8	21 0/8	20 6/8	15 7/8	5	7	Kenedy County	TX	Thomas J. Hoffman	1998	18,227
125 1/8	19 1/8	19 7/8	14 7/8	5	5	Ozaukee County	WI	Don Schwerin	1966	18,364
125 1/8	20 7/8	20 6/8	15 3/8	4	4	Graham County	KS	Russell Hull	1975	18,364
125 1/8	22 3/8	23 5/8	20 0/8	5	5	Vermilion County	IL	Mel Mueller	1976	18,364
125 1/8	18 3/8	19 0/8	15 1/8	5	5	Ogle County	IL	Gary Shaw	1979	18,364
125 1/8	21 1/8	20 7/8	13 5/8	5	5	Muskogee County	OK	Don Anderson	1979	18,364
125 1/8	22 3/8	22 5/8	18 7/8	4	5	Cortland County	NY	Ted W. Renninger	1981	18,364
125 1/8	19 4/8	19 4/8	18 5/8	6	5	Manitowoc County	WI	Peter J. Ording	1982	18,364
125 1/8	20 0/8	21 0/8	14 1/8	6	5	Adair County	MO	Terry Findling	1982	18,364
125 1/8	21 7/8	22 0/8	17 5/8	5	4	Morrison County	MN	Gordie Rieber	1982	18,364
125 1/8	19 7/8	20 1/8	18 6/8	6	7	Des Moines County	IA	David R. Bessine	1983	18,364
125 1/8	20 7/8	20 0/8	17 1/8	5	5	Brown County	SD	Jim C. Hill	1983	18,364
125 1/8	22 1/8	22 3/8	18 3/8	5	7	Codington County	SD	Brad Bach	1983	18,364
125 1/8	22 3/8	22 1/8	17 5/8	4	4	Hillsdale County	MI	Andy Keefe	1983	18,364
125 1/8	19 3/8	19 6/8	17 1/8	5	5	Waupaca County	WI	Peter J. Burton	1984	18,364
125 1/8	20 2/8	21 2/8	16 3/8	4	4	De Witt County	IL	Thomas E. Wilson	1984	18,364
125 1/8	18 6/8	19 6/8	15 0/8	5	6	Valley County	MT	Leith S Wimmer	1984	18,364
125 1/8	20 1/8	21 0/8	16 1/8	5	5	Lapeer County	MI	Daniel Kavalunas	1984	18,364

WHITETAIL DEER (TYPICAL ANTLERS)

Minimum Score 125 — Continued

SCORE	LENGTH OF MAIN BEAM R	LENGTH OF MAIN BEAM L	INSIDE SPREAD	NUMBER OF POINTS R	NUMBER OF POINTS L	AREA	STATE/ PROVINCE	HUNTER'S NAME	DATE	RANK
125 1/8	21 1/8	21 4/8	16 7/8	4	5	Forest County	WI	Joseph P. Weber	1984	18,364
125 1/8	22 4/8	23 0/8	19 3/8	4	5	Winnebago County	IL	Richard Amundson	1985	18,364
125 1/8	21 3/8	20 7/8	16 3/8	4	4	Clayton County	IA	Duane F. Kennicker	1985	18,364
125 1/8	21 7/8	21 2/8	16 5/8	4	5	Allamakee County	IA	Joe Lieb	1985	18,364
125 1/8	21 0/8	21 3/8	19 3/8	5	5	Washington County	WI	Judy Staedler	1986	18,364
125 1/8	22 4/8	21 3/8	16 3/8	4	4	Westmoreland County	PA	Robert L. Waddell	1986	18,364
125 1/8	20 4/8	20 5/8	14 7/8	5	4	Clinton County	MI	Dan Bertalan	1986	18,364
125 1/8	19 2/8	19 5/8	14 7/8	5	5	Dakota County	MN	Arthur Ellsworth	1987	18,364
125 1/8	22 4/8	23 0/8	17 3/8	4	5	Webb County	TX	Frank Ramirez	1987	18,364
125 1/8	23 1/8	23 7/8	16 7/8	5	5	Coweta County	GA	Jerry M. Kirby, Jr.	1987	18,364
125 1/8	21 7/8	21 1/8	18 7/8	5	5	Mason County	WV	George A. Kearns	1987	18,364
125 1/8	18 3/8	18 2/8	14 7/8	5	5	Linn County	MO	Roy A. Simpson	1987	18,364
125 1/8	22 6/8	22 2/8	16 7/8	4	4	Waushara County	WI	Rodney L. Hering	1988	18,364
125 1/8	21 0/8	20 7/8	16 1/8	5	4	Hunterdon County	NJ	Michael P. Wanat	1988	18,364
125 1/8	20 0/8	20 1/8	15 3/8	5	5	Iron County	MI	Steven P. Sendek	1988	18,364
125 1/8	22 4/8	22 7/8	17 2/8	5	6	Morgan County	MO	Steve Rollins	1988	18,364
125 1/8	22 7/8	21 2/8	16 1/8	4	6	Coffey County	KS	Glen Neilson	1988	18,364
125 1/8	20 4/8	20 3/8	16 7/8	5	7	Strathcona	ALB	Corey Rasmussen	1988	18,364
125 1/8	21 2/8	21 3/8	20 1/8	4	4	Muskegon County	MI	Arthur Langlois	1989	18,364
125 1/8	20 1/8	20 0/8	18 3/8	5	4	Burleigh County	ND	Mark Froelich	1989	18,364
125 1/8	20 3/8	20 7/8	16 7/8	4	4	Sangamon County	IL	Steve Tice	1989	18,364
125 1/8	21 6/8	22 2/8	15 5/8	4	4	Wheeler County	GA	Terry Fountain	1989	18,364
125 1/8	22 4/8	21 0/8	17 3/8	4	4	Spencer County	IN	Russ Meyer	1989	18,364
125 1/8	23 3/8	23 3/8	16 1/8	4	4	Morgan County	MO	Steve Rollins	1989	18,364
125 1/8	21 1/8	21 2/8	16 5/8	4	4	Sanilac County	MI	Randolph J. Hempton	1989	18,364
125 1/8	21 1/8	19 7/8	15 5/8	5	5	Parke County	IN	Chuck Peters	1990	18,364
125 1/8	23 6/8	21 3/8	17 7/8	4	5	Jackson County	MO	Ernie Bigler	1990	18,364
125 1/8	19 4/8	19 4/8	13 7/8	6	5	Pulaski County	KY	Rick Mounce	1990	18,364
125 1/8	23 0/8	22 3/8	16 3/8	5	4	Sullivan County	IN	John D. Thomas	1990	18,364
125 1/8	22 5/8	22 2/8	17 3/8	4	5	Oneida County	WI	Michael Schreiner	1990	18,364
125 1/8	21 1/8	21 4/8	16 1/8	4	4	Hand County	SD	Bob Templeton	1990	18,364
125 1/8	23 1/8	22 7/8	16 5/8	4	5	Pierce County	WI	Ron Zaudke	1990	18,364
125 1/8	21 7/8	23 0/8	14 7/8	5	5	Plymouth County	IA	Bill Conlon	1990	18,364
125 1/8	23 4/8	24 3/8	18 1/8	4	4	Camden County	NJ	Richard C. Jones	1990	18,364
125 1/8	19 1/8	19 1/8	15 3/8	5	5	Allamakee County	IA	Robert L. Kampen	1990	18,364
125 1/8	21 3/8	20 7/8	17 7/8	4	4	Licking County	OH	Robert H. Wise	1990	18,364
125 1/8	21 5/8	20 6/8	16 5/8	4	6	Fillmore County	MN	Wayne Volkart	1991	18,364
125 1/8	23 0/8	22 7/8	17 0/8	4	5	Jackson County	IA	Warren F. Amling	1991	18,364
125 1/8	19 3/8	18 7/8	15 5/8	6	5	Wright County	IA	Scott Smith	1991	18,364
125 1/8	20 2/8	20 1/8	17 1/8	5	5	Carver County	MN	Anthony Noor	1991	18,364
125 1/8	20 7/8	20 3/8	16 1/8	4	4	Carroll County	IL	Paul Shipman	1991	18,364
125 1/8	20 0/8	18 3/8	14 1/8	6	5	Oneida County	WI	Robert Wikel	1991	18,364
125 1/8	20 4/8	19 6/8	15 3/8	5	5	Bates County	MO	Tony A. Davis	1991	18,364
125 1/8	18 5/8	19 1/8	15 6/8	7	5	Spruce Grove	ALB	James Thomson	1991	18,364
125 1/8	21 6/8	22 3/8	16 3/8	4	4	Montgomery County	MD	Jake Smith	1992	18,364
125 1/8	25 1/8	23 7/8	19 7/8	4	4	Wake County	NC	Robert Thomas Hodge	1992	18,364
125 1/8	20 1/8	20 2/8	15 2/8	6	6	Crawford County	IA	John Shumate	1992	18,364
125 1/8	21 2/8	21 1/8	14 1/8	4	4	Darke County	OH	Dave Shellhaas	1992	18,364
125 1/8	21 2/8	21 6/8	17 7/8	5	4	Westchester County	NY	Douglas Greenwich	1992	18,364
125 1/8	22 4/8	22 0/8	19 5/8	4	4	Missaukee County	MI	Jeff Steffey	1992	18,364
125 1/8	23 1/8	23 2/8	20 1/8	8	5	Woodbury County	IA	Bill Haase	1992	18,364
125 1/8	20 6/8	20 5/8	14 5/8	5	5	Franklin County	OH	Jim Montrose	1992	18,364
125 1/8	20 4/8	22 2/8	16 4/8	5	5	Kane County	IL	Thomas M. Toenies	1992	18,364
125 1/8	20 7/8	20 6/8	14 5/8	4	4	Henry County	IA	Eric Strothman	1992	18,364
125 1/8	22 2/8	20 7/8	18 5/8	5	6	Suffolk County	NY	Stephen Haufsk	1992	18,364
125 1/8	19 3/8	19 5/8	18 1/8	5	5	Latah County	ID	Roger Stewart	1992	18,364
125 1/8	20 0/8	20 4/8	16 1/8	6	5	Beadle County	SD	Fred Kober	1992	18,364
125 1/8	21 3/8	21 6/8	19 1/8	6	5	Kenedy County	TX	John W. Wallace	1993	18,364
125 1/8	21 3/8	20 4/8	15 3/8	5	5	Hubbard County	MN	Bernard Hasse	1993	18,364
125 1/8	23 0/8	23 2/8	15 7/8	5	5	Portage County	WI	Wallace J. Zywicki	1993	18,364
125 1/8	20 2/8	19 2/8	17 3/8	5	5	Allegheny County	PA	Michael A. Dowling	1993	18,364
125 1/8	20 5/8	20 3/8	16 5/8	5	5	Trempealeau County	WI	Keith Johnson	1993	18,364
125 1/8	22 2/8	24 2/8	17 5/8	6	5	Meade County	KS	Terry E. Cordes	1993	18,364
125 1/8	20 2/8	20 5/8	17 6/8	4	5	Allamakee County	IA	Gary Grotegut	1993	18,364
125 1/8	21 5/8	21 5/8	18 3/8	4	5	St. Croix County	WI	Mike Norelius	1993	18,364
125 1/8	23 7/8	24 1/8	19 3/8	4	4	Sussex County	NJ	Dennis E. Williams	1993	18,364
125 1/8	22 4/8	22 0/8	17 7/8	4	4	Sauk County	WI	John H. Groth	1993	18,364
125 1/8	18 2/8	18 1/8	14 7/8	5	5	Flathead County	MT	John Voelker	1994	18,364
125 1/8	21 0/8	20 6/8	14 3/8	5	5	Washington County	MN	Robert D. Clendenon	1994	18,364
125 1/8	23 1/8	22 3/8	20 1/8	4	4	Elkhart County	IN	David Yoder	1994	18,364
125 1/8	23 1/8	23 4/8	16 2/8	6	5	Washington County	MO	David Schmidt	1994	18,364
125 1/8	20 1/8	19 5/8	15 1/8	5	5	St. Mary Parish	LA	Eric Alleman	1994	18,364
125 1/8	23 0/8	24 0/8	15 7/8	4	4	Waukesha County	WI	Dan Infalt	1994	18,364
125 1/8	23 2/8	24 1/8	14 7/8	5	5	Waukesha County	WI	Jonathan Kizivat	1994	18,364
125 1/8	19 3/8	19 0/8	13 7/8	5	5	Buffalo County	WI	Bob Kostecki	1994	18,364
125 1/8	23 1/8	23 3/8	16 1/8	4	4	Garrett County	MD	Gary Richardson	1994	18,364
125 1/8	23 5/8	22 7/8	17 5/8	4	4	Randolph County	GA	Bob Lovett	1994	18,364
125 1/8	22 1/8	22 5/8	16 1/8	5	4	Bullock County	AL	Robert "Grub" Matthews	1994	18,364

WHITETAIL DEER (TYPICAL ANTLERS)

Minimum Score 125   Continued

SCORE	LENGTH OF MAIN BEAM R	LENGTH OF MAIN BEAM L	INSIDE SPREAD	NUMBER OF POINTS R	NUMBER OF POINTS L	AREA	STATE/ PROVINCE	HUNTER'S NAME	DATE	RANK
125 1/8	21 1/8	21 4/8	14 5/8	4	6	Jefferson County	KS	Stuart Hazard	1994	18,364
125 1/8	18 4/8	18 2/8	14 1/8	5	5	Valley County	MT	Ralph Dowgin III	1995	18,364
125 1/8	18 2/8	20 2/8	18 1/8	5	4	Richland County	MT	Bryant Shermoe	1995	18,364
125 1/8	24 6/8	24 2/8	25 0/8	5	8	Anoka County	MN	Cedric Williams IV	1995	18,364
125 1/8	22 0/8	21 1/8	16 2/8	6	6	Iowa County	WI	Mark DeSmet	1995	18,364
125 1/8	23 1/8	22 5/8	16 1/8	4	4	Waukesha County	WI	Jason Collins	1995	18,364
125 1/8	18 7/8	19 4/8	14 5/8	5	5	Hand County	SD	Chad Resel	1995	18,364
125 1/8	24 0/8	24 5/8	19 3/8	5	6	Christian County	KY	Jason Scruggs	1995	18,364
125 1/8	22 7/8	22 3/8	16 3/8	5	4	Pawnee County	OK	Roger Cunningham	1995	18,364
125 1/8	21 2/8	20 4/8	15 1/8	4	4	Chautauqua County	NY	Ronald Olson	1995	18,364
125 1/8	20 7/8	21 0/8	16 3/8	4	4	Gloucester County	NJ	Jonathan Luciano	1995	18,364
125 1/8	22 7/8	21 2/8	17 1/8	4	8	La Salle County	IL	Kevin E. Freese	1995	18,364
125 1/8	22 7/8	22 4/8	17 1/8	4	4	Clay County	WV	Gregory Todd Osborne	1995	18,364
125 1/8	22 5/8	23 5/8	16 4/8	6	4	Muskingum County	OH	Dan Jennings	1995	18,364
125 1/8	18 5/8	19 2/8	16 3/8	6	6	St. Croix County	WI	Dave Iverson	1995	18,364
125 1/8	21 0/8	21 7/8	17 1/8	6	5	Washington County	KS	Gary L. Tubbs	1995	18,364
125 1/8	19 3/8	19 6/8	15 1/8	5	5	Schoolcraft County	MI	Russell Jackson, Jr.	1995	18,364
125 1/8	25 5/8	25 7/8	16 6/8	4	4	Clark County	IL	Gerald "Gabe" Shaffner	1995	18,364
125 1/8	20 0/8	21 4/8	15 5/8	5	5	St. Joseph County	IN	Michael L. Ritter	1995	18,364
125 1/8	24 0/8	21 0/8	16 5/8	5	5	Jackson County	MO	Mark Vestal	1995	18,364
125 1/8	22 0/8	21 7/8	16 3/8	5	5	Winneshiek County	IA	Chad R. Wagner	1995	18,364
125 1/8	19 1/8	19 0/8	15 5/8	5	5	Maverick County	TX	Anthony Heye	1995	18,364
125 1/8	22 6/8	21 0/8	12 5/8	4	5	Randolph County	MO	Mike Gittemeier	1995	18,364
125 1/8	21 1/8	22 2/8	16 1/8	7	4	Christian County	IL	Jacky Chandler	1996	18,364
125 1/8	22 1/8	23 4/8	17 1/8	6	4	Allegan County	MI	Daniel L. Reed	1996	18,364
125 1/8	20 6/8	22 0/8	18 7/8	5	4	Mifflin County	PA	Matthew J. Byler	1996	18,364
125 1/8	20 7/8	21 2/8	17 5/8	4	4	Juneau County	WI	Steven Loew	1996	18,364
125 1/8	23 4/8	24 1/8	21 3/8	3	3	Elkhart County	IN	James Evans	1996	18,364
125 1/8	21 2/8	21 3/8	15 3/8	5	5	Monroe County	NY	Donald Brongo	1996	18,364
125 1/8	18 0/8	19 0/8	17 5/8	5	5	St. Croix County	WI	Tony Rizzo	1996	18,364
125 1/8	22 6/8	22 5/8	16 7/8	4	4	Westchester County	NY	David Bilotti	1996	18,364
125 1/8	21 1/8	21 1/8	16 5/8	5	4	Marion County	KS	Travis R. Sargent	1996	18,364
125 1/8	21 3/8	21 0/8	17 7/8	4	4	Kent County	MD	James A. Warwick, Sr.	1996	18,364
125 1/8	19 4/8	19 5/8	15 5/8	5	5	Christian County	MO	David Hodges	1997	18,364
125 1/8	20 4/8	20 1/8	17 3/8	4	5	Iowa County	WI	Gary A. Johnson	1997	18,364
125 1/8	21 0/8	20 5/8	16 5/8	4	4	Langlade County	WI	James Spurgeon	1997	18,364
125 1/8	21 6/8	21 7/8	15 3/8	4	5	Clay County	MO	Will Moffet	1997	18,364
125 1/8	22 1/8	22 3/8	19 1/8	4	4	Walworth County	WI	Brian Turnbull	1997	18,364
125 1/8	24 1/8	23 0/8	16 3/8	5	5	Jones County	IA	Jerry Casey	1997	18,364
125 1/8	23 0/8	22 4/8	16 3/8	4	4	Appanoose County	IA	Lee Jernigan	1997	18,364
125 1/8	21 3/8	21 7/8	16 5/8	5	4	Pepin County	WI	Gordon Weiss	1997	18,364
125 1/8	21 2/8	19 6/8	15 7/8	4	5	Pike County	IL	Stephen J. Micio	1997	18,364
125 1/8	22 7/8	22 2/8	19 4/8	5	4	Sawyer County	WI	Kevin T. Bugel	1997	18,364
125 1/8	22 0/8	22 0/8	14 7/8	5	4	Erie County	NY	Peter H. Burns	1997	18,364
125 1/8	20 7/8	21 6/8	15 4/8	4	5	La Crosse County	WI	Chad S. Blank	1997	18,364
125 1/8	21 1/8	20 6/8	14 7/8	5	5	Delaware County	OH	Dave Orndorf	1997	18,364
125 1/8	20 2/8	20 2/8	17 3/8	4	5	Woodbury County	IA	Gregg Mathistad	1997	18,364
125 1/8	19 0/8	19 0/8	15 7/8	5	5	New Castle County	DE	Dave Christian	1998	18,364
125 1/8	20 0/8	20 6/8	14 1/8	5	5	Outagamie County	WI	Brandon Conrad	1998	18,364
125 1/8	22 6/8	22 4/8	17 7/8	5	4	Manitowoc County	WI	George Luckow	1998	18,364
125 1/8	22 2/8	22 6/8	17 1/8	5	6	Lapeer County	MI	Donald Paul Bridgeman	1998	18,364
125 0/8	20 6/8	20 6/8	16 6/8	5	5	Sheboygan County	WI	Earl Uhl	1962	18,510
125 0/8	22 4/8	23 0/8	15 4/8	5	5	Hughes County	SD	Robert A. Clough	1967	18,510
125 0/8	20 5/8	20 5/8	17 2/8	4	4	Livingston County	NY	Robert A. Carone	1969	18,510
125 0/8	22 0/8	22 0/8	17 4/8	6	6	Dodge County	WI	Charles E. Songstad	1970	18,510
125 0/8	24 2/8	24 4/8	17 5/8	8	4	Pope County	AR	Tom Quinton	1977	18,510
125 0/8	20 5/8	20 6/8	18 2/8	4	4	Freeborn County	MN	Jerry Christenson	1980	18,510
125 0/8	23 0/8	21 6/8	17 0/8	4	4	Switzerland County	IN	Barry Scott	1981	18,510
125 0/8	19 1/8	20 0/8	16 6/8	5	5	Indiana County	PA	Stephen C. Shesko	1981	18,510
125 0/8	21 3/8	20 4/8	16 0/8	5	5	Ontario County	NY	Jim Wicks	1982	18,510
125 0/8	23 0/8	22 7/8	16 2/8	5	4	Yates County	NY	Ed O'Dell	1982	18,510
125 0/8	21 6/8	21 7/8	15 2/8	4	5	Somerset County	NJ	Thomas Takacs	1982	18,510
125 0/8	20 4/8	21 0/8	16 2/8	5	5	Bexar County	TX	John E. West	1982	18,510
125 0/8	23 0/8	23 3/8	21 4/8	4	4	Seneca County	NY	Richard Williamson	1982	18,510
125 0/8	19 6/8	19 4/8	15 2/8	7	6	Richland County	MT	Bill Cundiff	1984	18,510
125 0/8	20 5/8	20 0/8	17 6/8	4	4	Alfalfa County	OK	Paul E. Keck	1984	18,510
125 0/8	20 0/8	20 0/8	17 4/8	4	4	Sauk County	WI	Robert E. McKenna	1984	18,510
125 0/8	22 2/8	21 2/8	17 0/8	4	4	Price County	WI	Dennis W. Steinberger	1984	18,510
125 0/8	17 7/8	19 1/8	14 6/8	6	5	Dane County	WI	Keith Peterson	1984	18,510
125 0/8	20 2/8	21 2/8	19 6/8	5	4	Kane County	IL	Tom Cousland	1984	18,510
125 0/8	21 4/8	21 4/8	15 4/8	5	5	Crow Wing County	MN	Richard Stokke	1985	18,510
125 0/8	22 5/8	22 7/8	18 4/8	7	4	Burleigh County	ND	Dave Feist	1985	18,510
125 0/8	19 4/8	21 1/8	18 0/8	4	5	Orange County	NY	Richard Powles	1985	18,510
125 0/8	21 0/8	21 4/8	14 6/8	5	5	Monroe County	WI	Jeffery S. Oler	1985	18,510
125 0/8	21 4/8	20 5/8	13 6/8	5	5	Roane County	WV	Richard Prine	1986	18,510
125 0/8	22 1/8	22 1/8	17 0/8	5	4	Tama County	IA	Dick Baker	1986	18,510
125 0/8	21 6/8	22 0/8	15 7/8	5	5	Westchester County	NY	Robert Frees	1986	18,510
125 0/8	20 1/8	21 0/8	17 0/8	5	4	Freeborn County	MN	Steven R. Olson	1987	18,510

WHITETAIL DEER (TYPICAL ANTLERS)

Minimum Score 125 — Continued

SCORE	LENGTH OF MAIN BEAM R	LENGTH OF MAIN BEAM L	INSIDE SPREAD	NUMBER OF POINTS R	NUMBER OF POINTS L	AREA	STATE/PROVINCE	HUNTER'S NAME	DATE	RANK
125 0/8	22 5/8	22 6/8	15 6/8	4	4	St. Clair County	MO	Rickey D. Adams	1987	18,510
125 0/8	21 2/8	21 3/8	16 4/8	5	4	Oneida County	WI	John P. Butler	1987	18,510
125 0/8	20 0/8	20 4/8	14 0/8	4	4	Winona County	MN	John W. Zahrte	1988	18,510
125 0/8	18 2/8	18 6/8	16 6/8	4	4	Norman County	MN	Cordell Willison	1988	18,510
125 0/8	20 2/8	20 1/8	20 2/8	4	4	Gloucester County	NJ	Tom Weise	1988	18,510
125 0/8	21 1/8	21 1/8	17 4/8	4	4	Licking County	OH	Randy D. Ricketts	1988	18,510
125 0/8	21 0/8	21 1/8	18 2/8	4	4	Pecos County	TX	Joe Christman	1989	18,510
125 0/8	21 4/8	21 3/8	18 4/8	4	4	Susquehanna County	PA	Norris Cobb	1989	18,510
125 0/8	21 3/8	21 1/8	15 0/8	5	5	La Salle County	IL	John P. Hartman	1989	18,510
125 0/8	22 5/8	23 0/8	18 0/8	4	4	Westchester County	NY	Art Tatavitto	1989	18,510
125 0/8	24 3/8	23 2/8	21 1/8	5	4	Jackson County	IA	Larry Nemmers	1989	18,510
125 0/8	20 3/8	20 0/8	17 2/8	4	4	Clark County	IL	Robin L. Geibel	1989	18,510
125 0/8	21 3/8	21 4/8	16 2/8	4	4	Powell County	MT	Therman Madeira	1989	18,510
125 0/8	19 0/8	19 1/8	13 6/8	5	6	Sebastian County	AR	Frank Theising	1989	18,510
125 0/8	24 3/8	19 7/8	16 1/8	6	6	Racine County	WI	Brad M. Antoniak	1989	18,510
125 0/8	22 1/8	22 1/8	18 2/8	4	4	Dodge County	WI	Timothy J. Minnema	1990	18,510
125 0/8	22 5/8	21 4/8	15 3/8	5	5	Manitowoc County	WI	Kevin A. Young	1990	18,510
125 0/8	23 2/8	23 5/8	22 2/8	3	4	Ogle County	IL	Mark E. Guffey	1990	18,510
125 0/8	20 6/8	21 7/8	19 2/8	5	4	Caroline County	MD	Eric Wise	1990	18,510
125 0/8	23 2/8	24 3/8	17 4/8	4	5	Ductchess County	NY	Tom Pampalone	1990	18,510
125 0/8	19 0/8	20 7/8	17 6/8	4	4	Richland County	WI	Terry L. Laufenberg	1990	18,510
125 0/8	18 3/8	18 4/8	16 2/8	4	4	Natrona County	WY	Dave McCoy	1991	18,510
125 0/8	20 7/8	20 5/8	17 2/8	5	5	Burnett County	WI	John Lindstrom	1991	18,510
125 0/8	21 0/8	21 0/8	15 6/8	5	5	Adair County	MO	Tony L. Jones	1991	18,510
125 0/8	20 5/8	19 6/8	16 4/8	5	5	Portage County	WI	Pete J. Klismith	1991	18,510
125 0/8	19 0/8	19 2/8	14 6/8	4	5	Morgan County	IL	John Conklin	1991	18,510
125 0/8	22 7/8	22 4/8	20 3/8	5	5	Ferry County	WA	Allen Payne	1991	18,510
125 0/8	21 1/8	20 4/8	16 4/8	5	5	Windham County	CT	Myron Wojnilo	1991	18,510
125 0/8	20 6/8	21 7/8	17 3/8	5	6	Brown County	IL	Robert Cunningham	1992	18,510
125 0/8	20 1/8	23 1/8	16 7/8	6	6	Branch County	MI	Tony Rakoske	1992	18,510
125 0/8	21 4/8	20 4/8	18 4/8	4	4	McHenry County	IL	Eugene W. Hurley	1992	18,510
125 0/8	22 0/8	21 1/8	16 4/8	5	4	Oklahoma County	OK	Steven Lemons	1992	18,510
125 0/8	20 0/8	21 6/8	17 1/8	7	8	Brule County	SD	Alan Summerville	1992	18,510
125 0/8	23 5/8	23 2/8	16 2/8	4	4	Prince Georges County	MD	Lance Canter	1993	18,510
125 0/8	20 3/8	20 7/8	14 4/8	5	4	Peoria County	IL	Donald Russell	1993	18,510
125 0/8	21 3/8	21 7/8	17 0/8	5	6	Oconto County	WI	Scott Roskom	1993	18,510
125 0/8	19 0/8	18 6/8	17 2/8	5	5	Frio County	TX	Walter R. Copeland	1993	18,510
125 0/8	21 2/8	22 2/8	15 4/8	4	4	Livingston County	IL	Mark A. Harder	1993	18,510
125 0/8	22 1/8	21 0/8	16 4/8	5	4	Shelby County	KY	Robert P. Totten	1993	18,510
125 0/8	21 5/8	20 7/8	16 4/8	6	5	Pettis County	MO	David Harms	1993	18,510
125 0/8	20 7/8	21 1/8	17 2/8	5	4	Cass County	ND	Joe Lahlum	1993	18,510
125 0/8	19 7/8	20 5/8	16 0/8	5	4	Washington County	NE	Dave Hauge	1993	18,510
125 0/8	20 1/8	20 6/8	18 0/8	5	5	Worcester County	MA	Bruce C. Kirk	1993	18,510
125 0/8	19 2/8	19 5/8	17 0/8	4	4	Washington County	MN	Steven A. Jansen	1993	18,510
125 0/8	22 4/8	21 4/8	13 6/8	5	5	Howard County	MD	Daniel R. Peters	1994	18,510
125 0/8	20 3/8	20 6/8	16 0/8	4	4	Milwaukee County	WI	Brad M. Antoniak	1994	18,510
125 0/8	20 4/8	21 1/8	16 6/8	5	5	Latimer County	OK	Scott Davis	1994	18,510
125 0/8	20 3/8	20 1/8	15 6/8	5	5	Trempealeau County	WI	Danny D. Kampa	1994	18,510
125 0/8	21 2/8	21 2/8	18 0/8	4	4	Livingston County	MI	Michael D. Duggan	1994	18,510
125 0/8	20 4/8	20 0/8	18 2/8	4	4	Putnam County	IL	Gene Dixon	1994	18,510
125 0/8	23 1/8	22 5/8	17 4/8	4	4	Dunn County	WI	Mark Pilgrim	1994	18,510
125 0/8	19 7/8	20 1/8	14 6/8	5	5	Waupaca County	WI	Matt Wilson	1994	18,510
125 0/8	21 6/8	21 6/8	18 4/8	4	4	Cecil County	MD	Stephen M. Weaver	1994	18,510
125 0/8	21 5/8	21 6/8	18 6/8	5	4	St. Charles County	MO	Rick Clynes	1994	18,510
125 0/8	21 2/8	22 2/8	16 2/8	4	5	St. Louis County	MO	Chris Murphy	1994	18,510
125 0/8	21 1/8	20 7/8	17 2/8	4	4	Jackson County	AL	Johnny M. Johnson	1994	18,510
125 0/8	22 4/8	21 4/8	17 4/8	4	4	Burlington County	NJ	Bradley E. Heffley	1995	18,510
125 0/8	21 3/8	21 2/8	19 0/8	4	4	Kane County	IL	David Duncan	1995	18,510
125 0/8	21 2/8	21 1/8	15 2/8	4	4	Adams County	IL	Steve A. Allen	1995	18,510
125 0/8	21 6/8	21 4/8	17 4/8	4	4	Price County	WI	Chuck Pasewald	1995	18,510
125 0/8	20 3/8	20 4/8	17 0/8	5	5	Putnam County	MO	Scott Whitlock	1995	18,510
125 0/8	20 1/8	19 6/8	16 4/8	4	4	Kerr County	TX	Glenn Hurst	1995	18,510
125 0/8	21 2/8	21 6/8	19 2/8	5	4	Christian County	IL	Timothy S. Barton	1995	18,510
125 0/8	19 6/8	19 2/8	15 4/8	5	5	Pike County	IL	Dr. Hans H. Stuting	1995	18,510
125 0/8	19 2/8	19 2/8	17 4/8	5	5	Hunterdon County	NJ	Bucky Angle	1995	18,510
125 0/8	19 4/8	19 3/8	16 6/8	5	5	Logan County	CO	Michael Stanley	1995	18,510
125 0/8	21 0/8	20 5/8	17 6/8	4	4	Anoka County	MN	Blair Rawlings	1996	18,510
125 0/8	21 6/8	21 5/8	15 2/8	4	4	Ramsey County	MN	Rick Lutz	1996	18,510
125 0/8	20 1/8	21 4/8	16 6/8	4	4	Hunterdon County	NJ	John Tagliareni	1996	18,510
125 0/8	20 3/8	20 0/8	16 2/8	5	5	De Witt County	IL	Ken Giunta	1996	18,510
125 0/8	20 2/8	20 0/8	17 6/8	5	4	Walsh County	ND	Gary Foltz	1996	18,510
125 0/8	23 6/8	23 6/8	21 0/8	4	4	Delaware County	PA	Peter Cipolla	1996	18,510
125 0/8	21 3/8	21 6/8	19 5/8	4	4	Buffalo County	WI	Dave Brion	1996	18,510
125 0/8	18 6/8	19 7/8	13 4/8	5	4	Richland County	MT	David Samuel	1996	18,510
125 0/8	22 2/8	21 5/8	16 4/8	4	5	Iron County	WI	Paul Larson	1996	18,510
125 0/8	23 7/8	23 5/8	18 0/8	5	7	Henry County	IA	Chris E. Barr	1996	18,510
125 0/8	22 2/8	22 4/8	16 0/8	5	5	Jackson County	WI	Bruce Barrett	1996	18,510
125 0/8	18 2/8	20 0/8	19 6/8	5	4	Eaton County	MI	Bob Burns	1996	18,510

WHITETAIL DEER (TYPICAL ANTLERS)

Minimum Score 125 — Continued

SCORE	LENGTH OF MAIN BEAM R	L	INSIDE SPREAD	NUMBER OF POINTS R	L	AREA	STATE/PROVINCE	HUNTER'S NAME	DATE	RANK
125 0/8	20 1/8	17 6/8	16 0/8	5	5	Allamakee County	IA	Joe Saddler	1996	18,510
125 0/8	22 2/8	22 1/8	15 6/8	4	5	Keokuk County	IA	Josh R.W. Martin	1996	18,510
125 0/8	20 1/8	20 7/8	16 0/8	5	5	Vernon County	WI	Chad C. Maas	1996	18,510
125 0/8	20 6/8	20 4/8	13 4/8	4	4	Peoria County	IL	David B. Voorhees	1997	18,510
125 0/8	21 5/8	21 1/8	17 0/8	5	4	La Crosse County	WI	Troy A. Maier	1997	18,510
125 0/8	21 4/8	22 0/8	19 2/8	5	4	Onondaga County	NY	John Guzelak	1997	18,510
125 0/8	21 7/8	22 2/8	18 6/8	4	4	Licking County	OH	Kurt Zurawski	1997	18,510
125 0/8	20 6/8	20 6/8	13 6/8	5	5	Stevens County	WA	J. Rand Lothspeich	1997	18,510
125 0/8	20 1/8	20 3/8	15 0/8	6	5	Price County	WI	Brent Zierer	1998	18,510
125 0/8	22 3/8	21 7/8	19 3/8	4	5	Olmsted County	MN	Gary H. Wobig	1998	18,510
125 0/8	20 7/8	21 4/8	18 2/8	4	5	Shackelford County	TX	Mike Staton	1998	18,510

WHITETAIL DEER (TYPICAL VELVET ANTLERS)

Minimum Score 125

SCORE	LENGTH OF MAIN BEAM R	L	INSIDE SPREAD	NUMBER OF POINTS R	L	AREA	STATE/PROVINCE	HUNTER'S NAME	DATE	RANK
168 4/8	26 3/8	26 4/8	21 0/8	5	5	Granville County	NC	David W. Jernigan	1992	*
160 7/8	21 6/8	20 7/8	13 7/8	5	6	Shackelford County	TX	K. C. Jones	1998	*
160 1/8	24 5/8	25 3/8	20 2/8	5	6	Ferry County	WA	Shaun L. Henderson	1996	*
157 3/8	25 1/8	24 6/8	18 7/8	5	6	Pulaski County	GA	James Ellis	1997	*
156 2/8	21 5/8	22 0/8	17 4/8	5	5	Perry County	IL	Roger D. Pyron	1984	*
154 4/8	25 6/8	24 4/8	20 0/8	6	8	Kent County	DE	Milton Karbaum, Jr.	1990	*
153 5/8	24 6/8	24 5/8	17 1/8	5	5	Menominee County	WI	Al Crowe	1994	*
152 0/8	25 1/8	25 3/8	21 2/8	4	4	Goodhue County	MN	Rex Novek	1995	*
150 5/8	23 0/8	21 5/8	16 4/8	5	7	Parkland	ALB	Gunther Tondeleir	1997	*
148 1/8	23 6/8	23 3/8	18 5/8	4	4	Renville County	ND	Tom J. Burns	1995	*
146 5/8	22 5/8	22 4/8	17 1/8	6	5	Slope County	ND	Todd Seymanski	1992	*
145 0/8	22 0/8	22 6/8	17 2/8	6	6	Grant County	WI	Kerry Pospichal	1995	*
144 6/8	22 6/8	23 2/8	17 6/8	5	5	Perry County	AL	Vaughn P. Rives	1996	*
144 0/8	24 2/8	24 0/8	19 0/8	4	4	Tay River	ALB	Chad Lenz	1988	*
143 1/8	24 5/8	24 2/8	18 4/8	6	7	Converse County	WY	Rick L. Morley	1996	*
137 7/8	22 6/8	22 6/8	15 6/8	6	7	Spokane County	WA	Nicholas Orth	1997	*
137 3/8	21 5/8	23 5/8	15 3/8	4	4	Ravalli County	MT	Dave Bourne	1996	*
137 1/8	23 1/8	22 7/8	17 7/8	5	5	Boundary County	ID	Walter Dinning	1994	*
136 4/8	21 3/8	22 5/8	14 6/8	4	5	Sanders County	MT	Greg L. Munther	1990	*
136 4/8	21 4/8	21 2/8	16 7/8	5	6	St-Lazare	MAN	Justin Simard	1996	*
135 7/8	22 0/8	21 2/8	16 0/8	5	5	Meagher County	MT	D. Mitch Kottas	1989	*
133 6/8	20 7/8	20 2/8	15 4/8	5	5	Lamar County	MS	Mark Weldon Smith	1993	*
133 2/8	21 6/8	21 2/8	14 2/8	4	4	Ravalli County	MT	Lyle S. Bainbridge	1993	*
131 2/8	22 5/8	23 0/8	16 1/8	6	5	Kandiyohi County	MN	Brian J. Mathiason	1995	*
129 2/8	22 1/8	22 4/8	15 6/8	5	5	Burleigh County	ND	Ben Buntrock	1996	*
129 1/8	21 2/8	21 7/8	21 6/8	6	5	Kent County	DE	Dale H. Sipple	1984	*
128 0/8	20 6/8	19 5/8	11 6/8	5	5	Musselshell County	MT	Shawn Lar	1994	*
127 2/8	18 7/8	18 4/8	14 3/8	7	6	Shoshone County	ID	Roy A. Clanton	1991	*
125 7/8	18 6/8	19 6/8	16 5/8	5	5	Spokane County	WA	Nicholas Orth	1996	*
125 6/8	18 7/8	18 1/8	12 0/8	5	5	McKenzie County	ND	Richard Gustafson	1997	*
125 5/8	22 1/8	22 1/8	15 3/8	4	5	McLean County	KY	Earl R. Smith	1988	*
125 4/8	23 0/8	22 1/8	15 0/8	5	5	Sand Creek	BC	George Terpsma	1998	*
125 3/8	20 4/8	22 5/8	19 3/8	4	6	New Castle County	DE	John M. Hodgson	1998	*
125 0/8	21 3/8	21 6/8	15 6/8	5	5	New Castle County	DE	Anton S. Burr	1992	*
125 0/8	23 1/8	24 5/8	14 5/8	5	4	Prince Georges County	MD	John Bosley	1998	*

* *Velvet entries will be listed in only one record book.*

World Record Whitetail Deer (Non-Typical Antlers)
Score: 279 7/8
Hall County, Nebraska - 1962
Hunter: Del Austin

WHITETAIL DEER (NON-TYPICAL ANTLERS)

Minimum Score 155

Odocoileus virginianus and certain related subspecies

SCORE	LENGTH OF MAIN BEAM R	LENGTH OF MAIN BEAM L	INSIDE SPREAD	NUMBER OF POINTS R	NUMBER OF POINTS L	AREA	STATE/PROVINCE	HUNTER'S NAME	DATE	RANK
279 7/8	27 7/8	28 1/8	21 3/8	21	18	Hall County	NE	Del Austin	1962	1
257 0/8	27 1/8	25 7/8	18 6/8	12	11	Reno County	KS	Kenneth B. Fowler	1988	2
250 6/8	29 4/8	26 7/8	24 0/8	12	12	Miami County	KS	Kenneth R. Cartwright	1994	3
249 6/8	28 0/8	27 7/8	20 2/8	8	10	Greenwood County	KS	Clifford Pickell	1968	4
246 3/8	27 7/8	26 1/8	29 3/8	9	14	Anderson County	KS	Richard Stahl	1992	5
245 5/8	29 4/8	29 3/8	20 3/8	16	15	Vermilion County	IL	Robert E. Chestnut	1981	6
245 4/8	28 5/8	28 4/8	19 1/8	18	12	Chase County	KS	Douglas A. Siebert	1988	7
241 2/8	25 4/8	26 3/8	18 2/8	19	20	Cochrane	ALB	Dean Dwernuchuk	1984	8
240 0/8	28 5/8	27 5/8	17 0/8	10	11	Allen County	KS	Douglas Whitcomb	1987	9
238 6/8	22 6/8	22 2/8	18 3/8	18	15	Mahoning County	OH	Ronald K. Osborne	1986	10
238 0/8	23 7/8	26 1/8	17 5/8	10	11	Meade County	KS	Kevin Wright	1994	11
237 5/8	22 4/8	25 4/8	16 5/8	13	12	Wilson County	KS	Gilbert Boss	1986	12
234 1/8	26 1/8	26 4/8	21 1/8	11	14	Hamilton County	IL	Mark A. Potts	1995	13
234 1/8	29 6/8	29 2/8	19 7/8	13	10	Lewis County	KY	Joey Smith	1997	13
233 7/8	28 4/8	27 1/8	22 0/8	17	16	Greenwood County	KS	Randy Young	1989	15
232 7/8	26 0/8	25 3/8	20 6/8	12	10	Kiowa County	KS	Royce E. Frazier	1987	16
231 7/8	25 5/8	26 1/8	18 1/8	9	12	Windham County	CT	Paul Seremet	1994	17
231 7/8	27 0/8	26 3/8	24 7/8	11	10	Dallas County	IA	Russ Clarken	1994	17
231 5/8	28 1/8	26 5/8	19 2/8	11	11	Dane County	WI	Dennis Shanks	1979	19
231 4/8	26 0/8	25 6/8	18 3/8	11	10	Iroquois County	IL	Sam G. Townsend	1986	20
231 0/8	25 2/8	26 2/8	22 4/8	16	12	Phillips County	KS	Virgil Henry	1987	21
230 6/8	26 1/8	27 6/8	19 5/8	11	11	Peoria County	IL	Tophil L. Simon	1984	22
229 7/8	25 2/8	25 6/8	19 1/8	12	15	Yuma County	CO	David "Jake" Powell	1986	23
229 5/8	26 5/8	26 7/8	18 6/8	10	11	Madison County	IA	Mike Hobart	1993	24
229 4/8	27 5/8	26 2/8	21 3/8	13	9	Polk County	IA	Terry M. Long	1995	25
229 0/8	27 1/8	27 4/8	16 2/8	8	9	Lake County	IL	Rodney Rasmussen	1995	26
227 6/8	25 5/8	25 4/8	20 6/8	13	20	Fulton County	IL	Richard Keener	1977	27
227 0/8	29 4/8	30 1/8	26 3/8	11	11	Dominion City	MAN	Terry S. Pearse	1994	28
227 0/8	29 4/8	30 4/8	23 1/8	10	11	Decatur County	IA	Jack Jr. Schuler, Jr.	1995	28
225 1/8	29 4/8	28 4/8	23 1/8	9	12	Walworth County	WI	F. Dan Dinelli	1992	30
224 3/8	28 5/8	27 1/8	23 0/8	9	10	Stevens County	WA	J. C. Baker	1987	31
224 0/8	23 1/8	21 6/8	17 3/8	13	14	La Salle County	IL	Ronald R. Lahman, Sr.	1989	32
222 7/8	27 5/8	28 1/8	18 6/8	9	7	Coles County	IL	Kim L. Boes	1989	33
222 5/8	27 3/8	27 0/8	20 0/8	10	12	Todd County	MN	Gary Martin	1992	34
222 1/8	26 5/8	25 6/8	17 5/8	15	12	Hancock County	IA	J. M. Monson	1977	35
222 0/8	26 2/8	25 7/8	20 6/8	8	8	Marion County	KS	Claude Allen	1989	36
222 0/8	24 3/8	24 4/8	20 1/8	14	11	Riley County	KS	Larry Fronce	1997	36
221 2/8	27 3/8	25 6/8	31 4/8	11	13	Logan County	IL	Donald D. Stiner	1993	38
221 0/8	25 7/8	29 0/8	17 0/8	12	9	Warren County	IN	Robert C. Philips, Jr.	1993	39
220 7/8	26 1/8	25 1/8	25 2/8	9	11	Gove County	KS	Mike Shull	1986	40
220 7/8	17 1/8	27 6/8	16 5/8	15	11	Scotland County	MO	Glen Young	1996	40
220 6/8	24 6/8	25 2/8	17 6/8	18	16	Rock Island County	IL	John L. Angel	1979	42
220 3/8	25 3/8	24 5/8	18 3/8	13	9	Riley County	KS	Melvin D. Padgett	1989	43
219 3/8	28 1/8	27 5/8	20 5/8	12	17	Webster County	IA	David Propst	1987	44
219 0/8	27 3/8	27 0/8	17 6/8	8	11	Morrison County	MN	Michael R. Langin	1992	45
218 1/8	26 2/8	25 6/8	17 3/8	10	9	Clay County	IA	Blaine R. Salzkorn	1970	46
217 5/8	24 5/8	23 0/8	19 7/8	14	9	Morrison County	MN	Allan D. Yager	1993	47
216 6/8	25 0/8	25 0/8	18 0/8	13	14	Menard County	IL	Randy Boyle	1995	48
215 6/8	27 4/8	28 7/8	18 6/8	11	14	Meeker County	MN	Steve Turck	1982	49
215 5/8	24 2/8	27 0/8	22 2/8	11	7	Wayne County	IA	Chris Hackney	1983	50
215 0/8	30 3/8	30 0/8	22 7/8	10	8	Allen County	KS	Jim Baker	1992	51
214 5/8	29 7/8	28 2/8	20 4/8	14	8	Fulton County	IL	Tim Wells	1994	52
214 4/8	20 5/8	20 6/8	15 7/8	16	15	Parker County	TX	George C. Courtney	1991	53
214 4/8	23 4/8	20 7/8	28 6/8	15	12	De Witt County	IL	Kelly Riggs	1996	53
214 2/8	23 7/8	26 6/8	15 6/8	13	9	Lyon County	KS	Gary Dall, Jr.	1992	55
214 2/8	27 1/8	27 1/8	20 6/8	6	9	Buffalo County	WI	Paul R. Borowick	1996	55
213 7/8	25 6/8	27 5/8	20 7/8	7	9	Pope County	IL	Jason B. Potts	1995	57
213 5/8	24 7/8	25 6/8	19 7/8	12	13	Ogle County	IL	Jerome F. Bruns	1994	58
212 5/8	23 5/8	25 5/8	20 1/8	8	7	Allamakee County	IA	George A. Smith	1991	59
212 3/8	23 4/8	23 3/8	19 1/8	11	9	Martin County	IN	David D. Foote	1988	60
212 3/8	28 0/8	27 6/8	22 2/8	10	9	Thurston County	NE	Ronald E. Kelly	1995	60
212 2/8	27 3/8	26 3/8	18 2/8	15	6	Williams County	OH	Michael A. Bowling	1993	62
212 0/8	26 0/8	24 5/8	17 7/8	12	7	Barber County	KS	Dennis L. Rule	1992	63
211 0/8	27 0/8	26 4/8	19 3/8	9	10	Lenawee County	MI	Paul Kintner	1996	64
210 7/8	23 1/8	23 2/8	18 6/8	9	9	Teton County	MT	Todd Jensen	1986	65
210 6/8	25 5/8	24 5/8	19 4/8	9	8	Marion County	KS	Bruce Schroeder	1985	66
210 5/8	25 7/8	27 1/8	20 3/8	7	7	Waukesha County	WI	Gerald J. Roethle, Jr.	1991	67
210 5/8	26 6/8	27 2/8	22 1/8	9	8	Ogle County	IL	Dan Pierce	1994	67
210 3/8	27 2/8	28 4/8	19 1/8	12	6	Lac qui Parle County	MN	Steven J. Karels	1974	69
210 0/8	22 0/8	24 0/8	13 5/8	10	8	Jefferson County	IA	Jared Rebling	1998	70
209 7/8	30 0/8	30 0/8	22 3/8	10	12	Richardson County	NE	Albert W. Montgomery	1989	71
209 6/8	25 4/8	25 0/8	19 5/8	14	18	Pulaski County	KY	Alan Sidwell	1988	72
209 6/8	26 5/8	27 5/8	20 7/8	9	8	Sangamon County	IL	Mark A. Rademaker	1994	72
209 3/8	24 6/8	26 6/8	20 1/8	10	9	Racine County	WI	Lon Swatek	1994	74
209 2/8	26 5/8	27 6/8	21 4/8	10	10	McPherson County	KS	Lonnie Ensminger	1968	75
209 2/8	25 6/8	22 2/8	20 4/8	9	11	De Witt County	IL	Ron L. Willmore	1997	75
209 1/8	23 4/8	22 7/8	17 3/8	10	12	Riley County	KS	Jerry McIntyre	1994	77
208 5/8	26 2/8	26 4/8	22 3/8	9	9	Buffalo County	NE	Carl Clements	1985	78

WHITETAIL DEER (NON-TYPICAL ANTLERS)

Minimum Score 155 — Continued

SCORE	LENGTH OF MAIN BEAM R	LENGTH OF MAIN BEAM L	INSIDE SPREAD	NUMBER OF POINTS R	NUMBER OF POINTS L	AREA	STATE/PROVINCE	HUNTER'S NAME	DATE	RANK
208 1/8	26 6/8	26 5/8	18 3/8	11	9	Brown County	IL	Mark V. Piazza	1989	79
208 0/8	23 5/8	24 2/8	16 0/8	11	11	Marshall County	KS	Tim Wanklyn	1994	80
207 7/8	28 3/8	27 5/8	19 0/8	8	10	Otter Tail County	MN	Patrick Millard	1986	81
207 1/8	24 3/8	25 6/8	18 6/8	9	10	Macoupin County	IL	Kurt A. Bohl	1996	82
207 1/8	29 3/8	28 4/8	25 4/8	8	7	Page County	IA	Jeremy Williams	1997	82
207 0/8	27 7/8	28 1/8	17 7/8	9	11	Noble County	IN	Joesph A. Fulford	1987	84
206 7/8	27 2/8	24 3/8	20 6/8	8	8	Smoky River	ALB	Kirby Smith	1991	85
206 7/8	30 5/8	29 3/8	21 6/8	8	9	McPherson County	KS	Dennis G. Bordner	1994	85
206 7/8	26 3/8	25 0/8	17 2/8	11	8	Hamilton County	OH	Mickey E. Lotz	1995	85
206 6/8	26 7/8	27 0/8	20 1/8	7	10	Buffalo County	WI	Monte R. Nichols	1996	88
206 2/8	26 2/8	25 2/8	21 1/8	10	8	Monona County	IA	Robert J. Humpal	1994	89
206 0/8	22 3/8	24 1/8	17 4/8	9	11	Saunders County	NE	Nordean E. Bade	1964	90
205 7/8	21 5/8	23 3/8	19 4/8	9	14	Valley County	MT	Richard Blank	1995	91
205 7/8	25 0/8	25 6/8	21 6/8	8	9	Greene County	IL	Ronald R. Okonek	1998	91
205 6/8	25 7/8	25 4/8	21 3/8	14	9	Cottonwood County	MN	Larry Gravely	1975	93
205 4/8	27 0/8	26 7/8	24 6/8	7	9	Seward County	KS	Lynn Leonard	1988	94
205 3/8	25 1/8	24 0/8	15 0/8	8	12	Beltrami County	MN	Matt Stone	1990	95
205 1/8	28 7/8	29 0/8	24 1/8	9	8	Erie County	NY	Mark Surdi	1996	96
205 0/8	25 4/8	25 4/8	18 7/8	12	10	Marathon County	WI	Joshua J. Erdman	1994	97
204 1/8	26 5/8	26 2/8	22 0/8	7	9	Dubuque County	IA	Joe Rettenmeier	1987	98
204 0/8	27 1/8	25 2/8	16 6/8	14	12	Webster County	MS	Denver Eshee	1996	99
204 0/8	26 2/8	26 4/8	22 6/8	12	8	Warren County	IA	Jack J. Schuler, Jr.	1997	99
203 7/8	25 7/8	25 1/8	20 2/8	11	9	Union County	OR	Joe Mengore	1982	101
203 6/8	23 6/8	24 6/8	19 6/8	10	8	Washtenaw County	MI	Ronald "Rick" Chabot	1996	102
203 5/8	25 1/8	25 1/8	17 5/8	9	11	Warren County	IA	Ted Miller	1986	103
203 4/8	26 6/8	27 6/8	17 0/8	7	13	Dodge County	MN	Lawrence Sowieja	1955	104
203 3/8	25 0/8	24 2/8	19 0/8	10	13	Marquette County	WI	Joseph E. Bell	1969	105
203 3/8	24 3/8	24 5/8	20 5/8	10	9	Adams County	IL	Elroy Little	1981	105
203 3/8	24 3/8	25 3/8	20 4/8	12	10	Lehigh County	PA	Craig E. Krisher	1988	105
203 2/8	26 0/8	27 2/8	21 5/8	12	13	Decatur County	IA	Kenneth R. Jones	1995	108
203 0/8	25 0/8	25 4/8	19 3/8	12	10	Geauga County	OH	Rudy Grecar	1969	109
203 0/8	25 6/8	26 2/8	21 2/8	7	10	Du Page County	IL	Kevin J. Moran	1995	109
202 7/8	25 3/8	26 7/8	20 1/8	11	12	Decatur County	IA	Kevin J. Anderson	1992	111
202 7/8	27 2/8	28 3/8	22 6/8	10	8	Brown County	IL	Slyvan Purcell, Jr.	1992	111
202 2/8	23 3/8	25 6/8	19 6/8	12	9	Clay County	SD	Patrick Hudson	1969	113
202 0/8	29 0/8	27 1/8	22 6/8	9	8	Clark County	KS	Dennis Rule	1982	114
201 6/8	27 2/8	27 4/8	20 1/8	10	10	Fulton County	IL	Darren Gardner	1994	115
201 5/8	24 2/8	24 6/8	16 6/8	15	9	Kane County	IL	Keith Kampert	1991	116
201 5/8	25 6/8	26 2/8	19 7/8	13	8	Sheboygan County	WI	Darren Winter	1995	116
201 4/8	23 3/8	22 6/8	25 5/8	10	10	Rock Island County	IL	Jeff Maier	1989	118
201 3/8	24 4/8	25 3/8	20 2/8	14	12	Grayson County	TX	Donnie M. Brewer	1995	119
201 2/8	23 7/8	24 5/8	20 0/8	13	8	Stearns County	MN	Richard D. Berens	1991	120
201 2/8	25 6/8	24 1/8	21 2/8	9	9	Garden County	NE	Gayle Verbeck	1995	120
201 1/8	28 0/8	27 2/8	20 6/8	8	10	Carroll County	IL	Mel Landwehr	1991	122
200 7/8	25 3/8	25 1/8	20 0/8	10	12	Morgan County	KY	Greg Powers	1989	123
200 7/8	28 2/8	28 1/8	18 7/8	6	9	Washington County	KS	Ronald Montague	1990	123
200 5/8	25 1/8	27 0/8	18 7/8	7	7	Clayton County	IA	Dorrance Arnold	1977	125
200 5/8	26 2/8	25 2/8	18 3/8	8	9	Madison County	IA	Steve Marsh	1994	125
200 5/8	23 4/8	24 1/8	18 4/8	11	8	Grayson County	TX	Forrest L. Robertson	1995	125
200 4/8	25 4/8	22 5/8	18 4/8	7	9	Macon County	MO	Brad Hudelson	1982	128
200 3/8	25 6/8	25 7/8	20 3/8	8	8	Branch County	MI	Mitchell S. Brock	1995	129
200 2/8	26 2/8	25 1/8	20 3/8	11	7	Will County	IL	Tom Gawczynski	1993	130
200 1/8	28 5/8	27 0/8	19 3/8	12	7	Ogle County	IL	Theodore H. Hysell	1993	131
200 1/8	26 4/8	24 3/8	20 4/8	12	10	Riley County	KS	Bryan Glaser	1997	131
199 6/8	28 3/8	28 4/8	18 2/8	8	16	Jackson County	MO	Jack Hollingsworth	1989	133
199 6/8	24 2/8	26 2/8	20 2/8	11	9	Crawford County	WI	John M. Kane	1996	133
199 4/8	24 6/8	24 3/8	19 4/8	10	9	Jackson County	IN	J. Anthony Ray	1992	135
199 3/8	24 3/8	23 4/8	22 2/8	12	11	Atchison County	KS	Kirby A. Clifton	1973	136
199 3/8	24 3/8	23 1/8	17 6/8	8	8	Comanche County	KS	Phillip L. Kirkland	1981	136
199 0/8	29 6/8	28 4/8	20 0/8	8	10	Lake County	IL	Steven Hysell	1994	138
199 0/8	27 7/8	27 2/8	18 4/8	7	7	Macoupin County	IL	Jon DeNeef	1995	138
198 7/8	27 0/8	26 7/8	17 7/8	11	13	Logan County	KY	Oscar Howard	1989	140
198 6/8	22 5/8	24 5/8	15 0/8	11	11	Peoria County	IL	Roger Woodcock	1989	141
198 6/8	23 7/8	25 4/8	19 6/8	10	7	Randolph County	IL	John Brown	1992	141
198 5/8	26 2/8	25 0/8	22 6/8	5	5	Douglas County	NE	Ivan Mascher	1961	143
198 5/8	27 2/8	29 5/8	19 4/8	6	9	Montgomery County	IL	Earl W. Law, Jr.	1989	143
198 3/8	24 3/8	24 3/8	20 7/8	10	10	Lyon County	MN	Edward Matthys	1966	145
198 3/8	27 2/8	26 6/8	18 6/8	10	7	Reno County	KS	Greig Sims	1987	145
198 3/8	23 6/8	23 3/8	19 7/8	9	7	Pottawattamie County	IA	Rodney P. Stahlnecker	1991	145
198 2/8	25 7/8	27 2/8	19 5/8	7	9	Fulton County	IL	Mike Massingale	1991	148
198 1/8	27 0/8	26 3/8	20 2/8	10	7	Hocking County	OH	Hugh Cox	1964	149
197 7/8	22 2/8	23 0/8	19 2/8	8	12	Latah County	ID	Dean Weyen	1992	150
197 7/8	25 2/8	25 2/8	20 0/8	12	11	Richardson County	NE	Bob Campbell	1996	150
197 6/8	23 6/8	22 4/8	17 4/8	8	11	Pratt County	KS	Mike Patton	1987	152
197 5/8	25 2/8	25 2/8	18 7/8	10	10	Preble County	OH	Mike McCabe	1995	153
197 4/8	25 0/8	23 7/8	22 2/8	7	7	Johnson County	IA	Dennis R. Ballard	1971	154
197 4/8	25 3/8	26 3/8	16 7/8	6	8	Lyon County	KS	John R. Clifton	1984	154
197 3/8	27 3/8	26 3/8	20 4/8	8	9	Faribault County	MN	Randy Lee Sandt	1982	156

WHITETAIL DEER (NON-TYPICAL ANTLERS)

Minimum Score 155   Continued

SCORE	LENGTH OF R MAIN BEAM L		INSIDE SPREAD	NUMBER OF R POINTS L		AREA	STATE/ PROVINCE	HUNTER'S NAME	DATE	RANK
197 3/8	23 7/8	21 7/8	24 0/8	7	10	Gallia County	OH	Jim W. Brumfield	1992	156
197 3/8	24 3/8	24 4/8	20 1/8	8	7	Clark County	SD	Steve Frank	1995	156
197 2/8	27 3/8	27 6/8	19 1/8	9	10	Nemaha County	KS	D. Jay Hartter	1990	159
197 1/8	26 4/8	24 2/8	18 5/8	9	12	Linn County	IA	Marsha Fairbanks	1974	160
197 1/8	26 1/8	26 3/8	17 3/8	8	7	Jackson County	MO	Jim Martin	1984	160
197 1/8	16 4/8	18 3/8	18 0/8	10	10	Bullock County	AL	Ronnie Everett	1990	160
197 1/8	24 0/8	25 2/8	17 5/8	7	7	Bourbon County	KS	David Cox	1997	160
197 0/8	26 1/8	26 4/8	21 5/8	8	9	Marshall County	IL	Larry Rowe	1975	164
197 0/8	21 1/8	22 2/8	21 0/8	9	7	Woodford County	KY	Daniel E. Jackson II	1994	164
196 7/8	30 1/8	26 5/8	21 0/8	9	7	Lake County	IL	Kory Lang	1991	166
196 7/8	25 1/8	25 1/8	18 5/8	11	11	Jackson County	MI	Herbert C. Miller, Jr.	1993	166
196 7/8	21 6/8	25 5/8	17 6/8	8	10	Linn County	IA	James L. Newman	1996	166
196 7/8	28 0/8	28 2/8	22 0/8	7	11	Winneshiek County	IA	David G. Baumler	1997	166
196 6/8	24 5/8	25 1/8	23 6/8	6	8	Lawrence County	IN	John E. Johnson	1987	170
196 2/8	24 7/8	24 6/8	18 4/8	8	7	Louisa County	IA	Tony Thomas	1995	171
196 1/8	27 5/8	26 2/8	20 2/8	7	8	Edgar County	IL	Jerry R. David	1988	172
196 0/8	26 6/8	23 3/8	15 5/8	9	9	Cumberland County	IL	Jeff Light	1997	173
195 6/8	27 1/8	26 6/8	21 5/8	7	6	Dubuque County	IA	Jim H. Dougherty	1985	174
195 5/8	28 6/8	28 2/8	20 2/8	9	10	Martin County	MN	Ben Johnson	1973	175
195 5/8	24 1/8	24 2/8	19 0/8	9	7	Waushara County	WI	Randy Chamberlain	1984	175
195 5/8	27 3/8	27 3/8	19 7/8	9	10	Allamakee County	IA	Gary L. Mezera	1994	175
195 5/8	24 1/8	23 5/8	21 7/8	12	11	Livingston County	MI	Patrick Harris	1995	175
195 4/8	27 2/8	28 1/8	18 2/8	9	7	Putnam County	IN	Chris M. Tanner	1982	179
195 4/8	25 2/8	26 2/8	19 7/8	6	7	Crawford County	IA	Larry Sparks	1985	179
195 4/8	21 4/8	23 4/8	15 2/8	11	8	Jessamine County	KY	Tony W. Drury	1991	179
195 4/8	25 6/8	24 0/8	15 3/8	11	9	Allegan County	MI	Jason A. Newman	1994	179
195 4/8	26 3/8	27 3/8	18 1/8	8	10	Morris County	KS	Craig Johnson	1994	179
195 3/8	22 2/8	19 5/8	16 1/8	15	11	Pope County	IL	Dennis Boaz	1993	184
195 3/8	26 4/8	27 5/8	21 0/8	8	8	Dallas County	IA	Darrell Langworthy	1997	184
195 2/8	24 7/8	25 5/8	20 0/8	8	9	Dakota County	MN	Mark LeMay	1993	186
195 1/8	27 0/8	25 7/8	15 5/8	9	9	Cecil County	MD	Chuck Crouse	1995	187
195 1/8	27 5/8	29 0/8	21 5/8	6	4	Clinton County	IA	Steve Wagner	1995	187
195 0/8	26 6/8	25 0/8	16 3/8	9	13	Juneau County	WI	Maurice Sterba	1955	189
195 0/8	27 4/8	27 7/8	20 2/8	9	10	Jersey County	IL	Glenn Wilson	1994	189
195 0/8	25 6/8	27 2/8	20 1/8	11	9	Westmoreland County	PA	Eugene W. Livingston	1995	189
195 0/8	25 4/8	26 1/8	22 0/8	8	9	McLean County	IL	Frank Bartels	1996	189
195 0/8	27 3/8	27 0/8	18 5/8	7	9	Guthrie County	IA	Chad Laabs	1996	189
194 7/8	27 7/8	26 1/8	19 0/8	11	10	Warren County	MO	Dennis Jones	1982	194
194 5/8	26 3/8	24 7/8	20 7/8	7	8	Guernsey County	OH	Dick Bayer	1985	195
194 5/8	26 2/8	24 0/8	23 7/8	6	7	Lake County	IL	Paul H. Woit	1991	195
194 4/8	28 1/8	26 2/8	18 4/8	8	7	Miami County	KS	Alfred E. Smith	1990	197
194 4/8	26 7/8	27 0/8	24 2/8	9	8	Polk County	IA	Paul Beesley	1990	197
194 3/8	27 5/8	28 0/8	22 4/8	7	7	Fulton County	IL	Dwayne Etter	1994	199
194 2/8	27 1/8	26 0/8	23 5/8	9	6	Pike County	MO	William E. Knowles	1980	200
194 2/8	24 3/8	23 6/8	14 1/8	12	10	Pulaski County	VA	Roger N. White	1996	200
194 1/8	25 7/8	25 4/8	20 2/8	9	8	Jackson County	KS	Fred Dunn	1996	202
194 0/8	24 5/8	24 4/8	18 5/8	9	11	Cass County	NE	Sean Platt	1996	203
193 7/8	25 1/8	27 2/8	18 0/8	11	11	Blaine County	MT	Gene Wensel	1981	204
193 7/8	27 6/8	26 3/8	21 1/8	9	9	Eau Claire County	WI	Greg Miller	1990	204
193 6/8	29 6/8	28 0/8	20 2/8	9	9	Lake County	IN	Walter Sobczak	1979	206
193 4/8	26 1/8	27 4/8	18 5/8	9	8	Clarke County	IA	Don Mealey	1993	207
193 4/8	28 0/8	27 7/8	21 2/8	11	8	Parke County	IN	James H. Griggs	1996	207
193 3/8	24 3/8	25 3/8	19 3/8	16	9	Roanoke County	VA	Randy Brookshier	1983	209
193 2/8	25 0/8	24 3/8	19 6/8	8	7	Pottawatomie County	KS	Dale R. Larson	1997	210
193 2/8	25 2/8	23 6/8	18 5/8	7	8	Fulton County	IL	James Crane	1997	210
193 0/8	27 4/8	27 1/8	19 7/8	8	7	Lake County	IL	Steven Derkson	1989	212
192 7/8	20 6/8	19 5/8	14 3/8	9	11	Charles County	MD	Fred Hoffman	1991	213
192 6/8	27 0/8	27 7/8	21 7/8	8	6	Washington County	KS	Jim Snyder	1986	214
192 6/8	27 3/8	26 2/8	17 7/8	9	7	Vermilion County	IL	Ed Gudgel	1988	214
192 6/8	24 1/8	23 4/8	18 5/8	10	9	Clay County	IN	Gordon Eldridge	1994	214
192 6/8	26 4/8	25 7/8	17 1/8	10	8	Nemaha County	KS	Tyran L. Hartter	1996	214
192 6/8	24 2/8	23 0/8	17 2/8	6	11	Anderson County	KS	Raymond Yoder	1997	214
192 5/8	25 0/8	27 0/8	22 1/8	6	8	Republic County	KS	Don Dejmal	1983	219
192 5/8	27 5/8	27 5/8	20 7/8	9	8	Putnam County	MO	Timothy W. Murchison	1995	219
192 4/8	21 4/8	20 5/8	15 4/8	11	10	Redwood County	MN	Mark A. Steinle	1973	221
192 4/8	25 5/8	25 1/8	22 2/8	9	8	Edmonton	ALB	Jon Okonek	1997	221
192 3/8	25 4/8	25 6/8	20 1/8	9	7	Pickaway County	OH	Gerald E. Dunn	1992	223
192 3/8	25 2/8	27 4/8	22 3/8	10	6	Edgar County	IL	Brad Davis	1996	223
192 3/8	25 6/8	25 7/8	21 7/8	7	6	Warren County	IA	Randy Messer	1997	223
192 2/8	25 1/8	27 0/8	20 5/8	6	9	Jasper County	IL	Dan Flach	1994	226
192 1/8	24 3/8	21 1/8	17 3/8	11	10	Gray County	KS	Randall Koehn	1985	227
192 1/8	28 2/8	27 0/8	19 5/8	10	9	Brown County	OH	Paul R. Durbin	1992	227
192 1/8	25 1/8	26 1/8	18 0/8	7	7	Somerset County	MD	Archie East	1993	227
192 0/8	26 2/8	25 6/8	25 6/8	7	10	Day County	SD	Doug Rumpca	1985	230
191 7/8	21 3/8	21 4/8	15 4/8	9	9	Du Page County	IL	Pete Heliotis	1986	231
191 6/8	23 2/8	20 7/8	16 5/8	6	15	Murray County	MN	Delbert Peck	1956	232
191 6/8	28 5/8	28 6/8	16 4/8	7	6	Preble County	OH	Claude Adkins	1989	232
191 6/8	25 0/8	24 7/8	18 2/8	9	11	Dodge County	MN	Corey Chick	1997	232

535

WHITETAIL DEER (NON-TYPICAL ANTLERS)

Minimum Score 155   Continued

SCORE	LENGTH OF MAIN BEAM R	LENGTH OF MAIN BEAM L	INSIDE SPREAD	NUMBER OF POINTS R	NUMBER OF POINTS L	AREA	STATE/PROVINCE	HUNTER'S NAME	DATE	RANK
191 5/8	27 1/8	25 7/8	18 2/8	8	8	Riley County	KS	Larry Larson	1994	235
191 4/8	23 3/8	25 1/8	18 3/8	10	7	Tippecanoe County	IN	Jim Foster	1993	236
191 3/8	22 1/8	22 5/8	20 1/8	9	9	St. Joseph County	IN	Daniel T. Karaszewski	1979	237
191 2/8	25 7/8	25 0/8	22 3/8	8	9	Westchester County	NY	Nick Rigano	1987	238
191 2/8	27 2/8	27 1/8	18 5/8	7	9	Pike County	IL	Timothy M. Fulmer	1991	238
191 2/8	25 0/8	25 5/8	20 6/8	8	7	Pottawattamie County	IA	Buddy Simons	1997	238
191 1/8	26 2/8	26 2/8	21 0/8	7	6	Crawford County	OH	Michael B. Hoffman	1988	241
191 1/8	21 5/8	21 5/8	15 2/8	10	11	St. Louis County	MO	Gene Werges	1996	241
191 0/8	23 5/8	24 1/8	20 6/8	13	11	Pope County	MN	Ron Johnson	1985	243
191 0/8	25 5/8	26 1/8	21 2/8	6	9	Greenwood County	KS	Don Copley	1992	243
190 7/8	25 0/8	18 4/8	15 1/8	11	13	Douglas County	KS	Leon J. Bidinger	1983	245
190 7/8	25 4/8	25 0/8	20 6/8	8	7	Nemaha County	KS	Larry Burdiek	1995	245
190 6/8	24 6/8	25 7/8	19 4/8	12	11	Lake County	IL	Donald Linnean	1992	247
190 5/8	23 5/8	22 3/8	21 1/8	13	11	Lee County	IA	Tim Digman	1981	248
190 5/8	21 2/8	21 1/8	14 2/8	11	11	Johnston County	OK	Kevin Lovett	1993	248
190 4/8	29 2/8	28 0/8	18 6/8	8	8	Licking County	OH	John McGee	1982	250
190 4/8	22 4/8	25 3/8	16 3/8	11	7	Lake County	IL	Kirk J. Preti	1989	250
190 4/8	25 6/8	24 7/8	22 3/8	7	6	Douglas County	MN	Rodney McClellan	1992	250
190 4/8	25 5/8	25 6/8	20 2/8	9	9	Dane County	WI	Dean Goecks	1995	250
190 3/8	25 4/8	24 1/8	16 5/8	9	9	Saginaw County	MI	Robert T. Morey	1975	254
190 2/8	20 0/8	23 4/8	19 7/8	8	9	Isanti County	MN	Johnny J. Williams	1982	255
190 2/8	27 5/8	29 0/8	20 2/8	12	8	Montgomery County	PA	David S. Krempasky	1985	255
190 1/8	28 4/8	25 6/8	21 3/8	8	7	Cook County	IL	Rusy Mitcheff III	1995	257
190 0/8	24 3/8	24 6/8	18 0/8	8	8	Douglas County	KS	Dan Norris	1977	258
190 0/8	24 4/8	25 2/8	19 1/8	7	8	McHenry County	IL	Edward Schultz	1984	258
190 0/8	27 0/8	25 7/8	18 6/8	9	6	Tippecanoe County	IN	Mitchell R. Tuinstra	1994	258
190 0/8	26 1/8	26 2/8	26 4/8	7	8	Pottawatomie County	KS	Dale R. Larson	1996	258
189 7/8	26 1/8	26 3/8	24 3/8	7	7	Logan County	OH	Larry Pooler	1989	262
189 7/8	26 1/8	25 0/8	18 2/8	10	11	Benton County	MO	Steve Nichols	1996	262
189 6/8	24 4/8	23 0/8	16 3/8	9	7	Chisago County	MN	Reinhold L. Lind	1956	264
189 6/8	25 4/8	25 3/8	18 3/8	10	9	Jefferson County	OH	Ed Gates	1993	264
189 5/8	21 1/8	22 4/8	15 5/8	14	10	Stearns County	MN	Nathan Batzel	1991	266
189 5/8	25 4/8	17 6/8	18 1/8	9	6	Monroe County	IA	Tom O'Brien	1994	266
189 4/8	23 7/8	23 6/8	17 2/8	7	9	Cass County	IL	Ronald L. McClure	1994	268
189 4/8	23 4/8	24 2/8	19 5/8	10	9	Houston County	MN	Chad Burroughs	1996	268
189 2/8	21 4/8	23 1/8	21 3/8	10	8	Clayton County	IA	Jim Monat	1981	270
189 2/8	23 1/8	23 0/8	20 0/8	6	7	Buffalo County	WI	Roger Comero	1987	270
189 1/8	21 5/8	24 2/8	17 3/8	13	7	Graham County	KS	Don Berry	1970	272
189 1/8	23 5/8	25 0/8	19 4/8	8	6	McDowell County	WV	Lonnie Wolfe	1991	272
189 1/8	24 4/8	22 1/8	16 6/8	11	8	Hodgeman County	KS	Gary Tenbrink	1997	272
189 1/8	24 7/8	24 3/8	18 6/8	7	10	Harrison County	IA	Lane Ostendorf	1997	272
189 1/8	24 4/8	25 4/8	18 0/8	10	10	St. Clair County	MO	Lavern Rucker	1997	272
189 0/8	22 4/8	21 7/8	22 4/8	10	9	Scott County	MN	Chris Rivers	1987	277
189 0/8	25 3/8	25 3/8	20 0/8	7	8	Grant County	WI	Chad Tracy	1995	277
188 7/8	27 4/8	28 1/8	18 3/8	11	9	Marinette County	WI	James Spielvogel	1981	279
188 7/8	26 5/8	27 1/8	17 6/8	8	8	Preble County	OH	Jim Lipps	1994	279
188 7/8	23 7/8	23 7/8	21 7/8	8	6	Harper County	KS	Kevin Albright	1994	279
188 7/8	27 6/8	27 2/8	19 5/8	9	11	Mercer County	IL	Dana Pace, Jr.	1997	279
188 6/8	23 5/8	22 6/8	19 1/8	8	10	Adair County	MO	David C. Reid	1991	283
188 5/8	27 3/8	27 0/8	18 6/8	7	5	Ross County	OH	Dan Seymour	1987	284
188 4/8	28 0/8	27 5/8	21 0/8	8	8	Edgar County	IL	Bruce Huey Lankster	1992	285
188 3/8	24 0/8	24 4/8	18 4/8	9	7	Benton County	IA	Lyle Miller	1977	286
188 3/8	26 0/8	26 7/8	19 0/8	6	9	Rock County	WI	Steven J. Shull	1988	286
188 3/8	25 3/8	27 3/8	20 3/8	10	7	Washington County	KS	William B. Wilgers	1994	286
188 3/8	25 2/8	24 1/8	16 4/8	12	8	Payne County	OK	Robert L. Lochmiller	1995	286
188 1/8	26 5/8	26 0/8	19 4/8	7	10	Barnes County	ND	William Cruff	1961	290
188 1/8	26 3/8	26 0/8	19 5/8	10	7	Dane County	WI	Bill Needham	1983	290
188 0/8	23 2/8	22 3/8	17 3/8	8	8	La Salle County	IL	Gary Tabor	1983	292
188 0/8	24 5/8	25 5/8	16 2/8	8	11	Buffalo County	WI	Russell G. Goldsmith	1991	292
187 7/8	24 4/8	24 7/8	20 3/8	8	8	Shiawassee County	MI	Joseph S. Lunkas	1978	294
187 7/8	25 3/8	24 6/8	19 1/8	7	9	Sedgwick County	KS	Phil Mohr	1992	294
187 7/8	28 2/8	27 4/8	22 0/8	8	9	Chisago County	MN	Chris Johnson	1998	294
187 6/8	22 7/8	25 0/8	19 1/8	7	7	Hitchcock County	NE	Tom Chance	1986	297
187 6/8	23 1/8	24 0/8	16 7/8	10	7	Bent County	CO	Chris Malden	1991	297
187 6/8	27 0/8	27 1/8	25 0/8	6	7	Peoria County	IL	Christopher J. Karl	1997	297
187 6/8	25 6/8	25 5/8	18 5/8	7	8	Gage County	NE	Terry Charf	1997	297
187 5/8	27 6/8	25 2/8	18 0/8	8	6	Monroe County	IA	Cecil Dicks	1961	301
187 5/8	26 0/8	26 0/8	17 4/8	11	9	Washburn County	WI	Russell Worman	1988	301
187 5/8	24 6/8	24 5/8	15 7/8	9	7	Barrhead	ALB	J. J. Handel	1993	301
187 3/8	23 2/8	23 1/8	17 1/8	11	10	Vernon County	WI	Darrell A. Bendel	1986	304
187 3/8	26 3/8	25 5/8	20 4/8	6	6	Vermilion County	IL	Ronald D. Nunn	1996	304
187 3/8	30 0/8	23 1/8	19 2/8	9	8	Adams County	OH	Pete Detro	1997	304
187 2/8	25 3/8	23 6/8	21 0/8	7	9	Morrill County	NE	Glenn Schmidt	1975	307
187 2/8	27 1/8	26 1/8	16 6/8	7	7	Waupaca County	WI	Timothy J. Dercks	1991	307
187 1/8	22 5/8	23 3/8	14 2/8	9	9	Palo Pinto County	TX	Scott Layne	1994	309
187 1/8	25 2/8	24 6/8	16 1/8	9	7	Clark County	IL	Myron S. Johnson	1995	309
187 0/8	27 5/8	28 5/8	21 2/8	8	10	Clayton County	IA	Rick Felder	1994	311
187 0/8	24 4/8	24 1/8	17 7/8	9	9	Buffalo County	WI	Travis L. Althoff	1995	311

WHITETAIL DEER (NON-TYPICAL ANTLERS)

Minimum Score 155   Continued

SCORE	LENGTH OF MAIN BEAM R	LENGTH OF MAIN BEAM L	INSIDE SPREAD	NUMBER OF POINTS R	NUMBER OF POINTS L	AREA	STATE/PROVINCE	HUNTER'S NAME	DATE	RANK
186 6/8	24 2/8	25 1/8	19 3/8	9	10	Traverse County	MN	Roland L. Hausmann	1964	313
186 6/8	24 6/8	23 6/8	18 3/8	10	10	Mackinac County	MI	Steve Gorsuch	1989	313
186 6/8	25 3/8	25 5/8	17 6/8	8	6	Coles County	IL	Philip H. Blaase	1994	313
186 5/8	25 3/8	25 0/8	20 7/8	7	9	Scotland County	MO	Charles Lee Smith	1984	316
186 5/8	25 7/8	24 5/8	18 2/8	6	6	Stafford County	KS	Robert G. Williams	1997	316
186 3/8	22 0/8	23 4/8	20 0/8	9	8	Perry County	IL	Scott Kreger	1996	318
186 3/8	27 2/8	25 6/8	18 2/8	10	10	Kiowa County	KS	George Martinez	1996	318
186 3/8	27 6/8	27 6/8	21 7/8	6	7	La Salle County	IL	Kevin Gibson	1997	318
186 2/8	23 1/8	22 5/8	18 6/8	9	9	Otter Tail County	MN	D. F. Vraspir	1959	321
186 1/8	25 3/8	26 2/8	18 0/8	8	9	Lake County	IL	Alan F. Benson	1990	322
186 1/8	23 0/8	24 4/8	17 7/8	8	9	Lyon County	KS	Edward Bess	1991	322
186 1/8	24 0/8	23 7/8	16 2/8	11	10	Stevens County	WA	John Wantulok	1992	322
186 1/8	25 6/8	25 6/8	18 7/8	7	10	St. Joseph County	IN	Mike Ritter, Jr.	1992	322
186 0/8	25 6/8	22 4/8	23 6/8	8	9	Jefferson County	KS	Bob George	1991	326
186 0/8	25 0/8	24 4/8	16 4/8	10	7	Washington County	AR	Gary Powell	1994	326
186 0/8	26 7/8	25 6/8	17 5/8	8	8	Indiana County	PA	Frank R. Lecorchick	1996	326
185 7/8	24 7/8	22 2/8	18 0/8	6	10	Jones County	GA	Wallace Reeves, Jr.	1973	329
185 7/8	25 6/8	27 6/8	21 2/8	8	11	Cass County	MO	Mike Wheeler	1989	329
185 7/8	26 3/8	28 0/8	18 3/8	8	6	Todd County	KY	Alan Mansfield	1998	329
185 6/8	26 1/8	26 0/8	25 0/8	7	6	Christian County	IL	Donald D. Stiner	1990	332
185 5/8	27 0/8	25 3/8	18 6/8	11	12	Anderson County	KS	Wayne Hanna	1991	333
185 4/8	29 2/8	28 0/8	22 1/8	8	8	Pickaway County	OH	Jerry R. Forson	1979	334
185 4/8	22 6/8	23 6/8	18 6/8	7	6	Grant County	WI	Jeff Hochhausen	1994	334
185 4/8	24 7/8	24 6/8	19 0/8	6	8	Grand Forks County	ND	Tom Lunski	1994	334
185 4/8	26 4/8	26 5/8	20 3/8	8	9	Jefferson County	KS	Mark Dennis	1994	334
185 4/8	28 2/8	27 2/8	19 2/8	10	6	Greene County	IA	Dennis Matthews	1994	334
185 3/8	27 6/8	27 4/8	23 5/8	8	8	Allamakee County	IA	LeRoy B. Spiker	1968	339
185 3/8	27 3/8	26 7/8	20 7/8	6	6	Rice County	MN	Wayne Jahnke	1975	339
185 3/8	27 2/8	27 3/8	20 4/8	8	10	Lyon County	KS	Jim Black	1991	339
185 3/8	25 6/8	26 0/8	20 4/8	8	7	Wayne County	IL	Randy Sawyer	1991	339
185 3/8	26 2/8	26 5/8	21 1/8	7	6	Beaumont	ALB	Glen Pettinger	1997	339
185 2/8	26 1/8	25 0/8	16 6/8	9	8	Sedgwick County	KS	Alfred Weaver	1965	344
185 2/8	23 6/8	24 3/8	19 2/8	9	6	Winneshiek County	IA	Steve Herold	1994	344
185 2/8	23 5/8	23 6/8	23 1/8	9	8	Pickaway County	OH	Rob McCarley	1994	344
185 2/8	25 0/8	25 0/8	17 3/8	8	9	Buffalo County	WI	Gale Zich	1995	344
185 2/8	25 6/8	25 6/8	20 5/8	9	8	Suffolk County	NY	Paul Davidson	1996	344
185 1/8	27 3/8	26 7/8	18 0/8	9	9	Lewis County	KY	Jeremie Lee Bretz	1992	349
185 1/8	23 5/8	23 1/8	20 7/8	7	8	Calhoun County	IL	Mike Bucher	1995	349
184 7/8	25 0/8	25 4/8	25 2/8	7	9	Monona County	IA	Patrick Salmen	1989	351
184 7/8	26 2/8	24 4/8	18 6/8	10	7	St. Agathe	MAN	Maurice A. Trudeau	1995	351
184 7/8	24 0/8	23 4/8	19 5/8	7	7	New Haven County	CT	Alan P. Tracy	1995	351
184 6/8	30 4/8	28 0/8	22 2/8	8	7	Scioto County	OH	Ryan Darnell	1990	354
184 6/8	22 6/8	23 6/8	19 0/8	9	6	Nemaha County	KS	Monty G. Noland	1996	354
184 6/8	19 1/8	22 1/8	15 1/8	13	11	Jasper County	IN	Mike T. Stowers	1996	354
184 5/8	26 1/8	24 7/8	20 4/8	10	11	Vinton County	OH	Dan Davis	1985	357
184 5/8	24 1/8	23 5/8	18 6/8	9	9	Waushara County	WI	Jeffrey Van Zeeland	1995	357
184 5/8	28 1/8	27 7/8	19 2/8	9	7	Cass County	IL	Gary Holbrook	1996	357
184 4/8	26 3/8	26 6/8	23 0/8	8	6	Washington County	MN	Ron Schleusner	1994	360
184 4/8	23 2/8	23 4/8	18 4/8	7	7	Cerro Gordo County	IA	Ed Adamski	1997	360
184 3/8	22 7/8	22 6/8	17 6/8	8	11	Texas County	OK	William E. Miller	1983	362
184 3/8	23 2/8	23 3/8	21 5/8	10	8	Black Hawk County	IA	Paul Hughson	1985	362
184 3/8	26 5/8	26 6/8	18 2/8	7	7	McLean County	IL	Michael F. Bily	1997	362
184 2/8	25 2/8	24 5/8	19 0/8	9	9	Linn County	KS	Mike R. Wheeler	1994	365
184 2/8	28 6/8	30 7/8	23 7/8	5	9	Hamilton County	OH	Dan Misali	1997	365
184 2/8	26 5/8	27 0/8	20 5/8	5	6	Washington County	NE	Russ Campbell	1997	365
184 1/8	25 1/8	26 3/8	21 3/8	7	6	St. Charles County	MO	Larry D. Stelzer	1962	368
184 1/8	24 3/8	26 5/8	19 1/8	8	9	Waushara County	WI	Dwight A. Olson	1979	368
184 1/8	22 0/8	22 7/8	17 0/8	7	10	Jasper County	IA	Dan Ingle	1993	368
184 1/8	28 7/8	26 5/8	21 3/8	7	7	Pulaski County	IL	Donny Drew	1993	368
184 1/8	24 0/8	25 1/8	21 0/8	7	6	Prince Georges County	MD	Clarence Parsons	1996	368
184 0/8	22 5/8	22 7/8	16 7/8	7	8	Buffalo County	WI	Jeff Owen	1996	373
183 7/8	19 3/8	22 0/8	15 4/8	9	9	Williamson County	IL	Lowell D. Mausey	1992	374
183 7/8	24 7/8	24 2/8	18 4/8	8	9	Cross County	AR	Randal Harris	1993	374
183 7/8	24 2/8	26 1/8	13 6/8	8	9	Brown County	WI	Jeff Gajeski	1996	374
183 7/8	26 2/8	27 0/8	18 4/8	7	6	Edwards County	IL	Gary Gifford	1997	374
183 6/8	25 3/8	25 4/8	18 2/8	7	10	Lake County	MN	Christopher Harristhal	1990	378
183 5/8	25 1/8	25 0/8	17 7/8	10	10	Lincoln County	SD	Mervin Sterk	1985	379
183 5/8	28 0/8	28 0/8	21 5/8	6	6	Polk County	IA	Chris Olson	1993	379
183 5/8	26 0/8	25 3/8	21 2/8	10	8	Polk County	WI	Ron R. Fehlen	1995	379
183 5/8	24 0/8	24 0/8	18 1/8	6	10	Douglas County	WI	Frank Fudally	1997	379
183 5/8	26 5/8	26 2/8	19 4/8	8	7	Sherburne County	MN	Greg Newhouse	1997	379
183 4/8	26 2/8	24 7/8	18 1/8	10	8	Stark County	OH	Richard M. Cratty	1993	384
183 4/8	22 6/8	22 7/8	17 0/8	9	8	Benton County	IA	Matt Wildman	1996	384
183 3/8	24 3/8	25 2/8	19 0/8	11	10	Morrison County	MN	Ralph Hakel	1974	386
183 3/8	24 4/8	25 5/8	16 5/8	8	9	Fillmore County	MN	Michael M. Gehrking	1985	386
183 2/8	27 3/8	24 5/8	21 7/8	6	9	Holt County	NE	Lyle Ruff	1967	388
183 2/8	28 4/8	26 6/8	16 4/8	10	9	Christian County	MO	Roger J. Newell	1984	388
183 2/8	27 4/8	26 4/8	20 7/8	7	7	Riley County	KS	Larry Larson	1985	388

537

WHITETAIL DEER (NON-TYPICAL ANTLERS)

Minimum Score 155

SCORE	LENGTH OF MAIN BEAM R	LENGTH OF MAIN BEAM L	INSIDE SPREAD	NUMBER OF POINTS R	NUMBER OF POINTS L	AREA	STATE/PROVINCE	HUNTER'S NAME	DATE	RANK
183 2/8	24 0/8	25 3/8	20 3/8	10	8	Washburn County	WI	Jerry J. Genson	1989	388
182 7/8	24 2/8	25 5/8	19 2/8	9	7	Arkansas County	AR	Tommy Horton	1972	392
182 7/8	24 3/8	25 2/8	18 0/8	11	5	Olmsted County	MN	Dan Matheson	1973	392
182 7/8	24 4/8	25 0/8	20 5/8	6	8	Dane County	WI	Clayton Bodoh, Jr.	1997	392
182 6/8	26 1/8	28 7/8	21 1/8	8	8	Jefferson County	NE	Robert W. Peperkorn	1997	395
182 5/8	23 7/8	23 6/8	18 4/8	8	8	Osage County	MO	Ronnie Lee Tyree	1995	396
182 5/8	25 6/8	24 2/8	19 0/8	5	6	Washington County	KS	Scott A. Wilkens	1997	396
182 4/8	19 5/8	26 7/8	17 2/8	11	11	Will County	IL	Richard Heintz	1971	398
182 4/8	25 7/8	25 5/8	19 0/8	9	9	Macoupin County	IL	John Tevini	1991	398
182 4/8	24 3/8	23 5/8	18 3/8	6	8	Wapello County	IA	Arnold E. Vest	1993	398
182 4/8	26 6/8	26 7/8	18 1/8	10	9	Walton County	GA	Michael Thomas	1996	398
182 3/8	29 3/8	27 7/8	20 5/8	6	8	Goodhue County	MN	Jim Danielson	1984	402
182 3/8	25 5/8	25 5/8	19 5/8	6	8	Warren County	IN	Gregory S. Zak	1990	402
182 3/8	24 6/8	25 4/8	20 6/8	8	6	Pike County	IL	William R. Graham	1997	402
182 2/8	27 2/8	26 2/8	18 1/8	11	7	Pike County	IL	Dennis Kendall	1990	405
182 2/8	24 2/8	24 6/8	18 0/8	9	10	Macoupin County	IL	Les Rhodes	1994	405
182 2/8	26 5/8	26 6/8	22 2/8	8	8	Waukesha County	WI	J. Bradley Bence	1995	405
182 2/8	21 4/8	22 3/8	15 5/8	8	7	Logan County	IL	Rick Redfairn	1995	405
182 2/8	26 5/8	26 3/8	20 3/8	7	9	Pike County	IL	Paul Schmidt	1997	405
182 1/8	22 4/8	22 4/8	17 1/8	10	9	Brown County	KS	Bill Butrick	1985	410
182 0/8	24 3/8	24 5/8	17 1/8	6	7	Albemarle County	VA	Richard A. Shifflett	1989	411
182 0/8	25 2/8	25 1/8	15 6/8	7	9	Sawyer County	WI	Joel McVinnie	1995	411
181 7/8	24 4/8	24 4/8	18 6/8	7	10	Marion County	IA	Roger DeMoss	1990	413
181 7/8	24 0/8	23 6/8	18 6/8	9	8	El Paso County	CO	Kyle Schomaker	1992	413
181 7/8	24 3/8	26 4/8	18 4/8	8	6	Whiteside County	IL	Kyle A. Kennedy	1996	413
181 7/8	26 6/8	26 4/8	19 2/8	8	7	Chester County	PA	Robert E. Ferguson, Jr.	1998	413
181 6/8	23 2/8	22 6/8	20 1/8	8	7	Adams County	IL	Festal McCarty	1967	417
181 6/8	25 4/8	25 0/8	18 1/8	7	11	Kiowa County	KS	Royce E. Frazier	1985	417
181 6/8	24 1/8	23 1/8	17 7/8	8	10	Cross County	AR	Britt Johnson	1995	417
181 6/8	22 2/8	22 7/8	21 4/8	9	7	St. Charles County	MO	Tony Oxford	1995	417
181 6/8	24 3/8	24 5/8	17 4/8	7	9	Kane County	IL	Ed Saloga	1996	417
181 6/8	23 0/8	23 1/8	16 4/8	6	9	Macoupin County	IL	Kurt A. Bohl	1997	417
181 6/8	25 6/8	27 2/8	16 1/8	7	8	Johnson County	IA	Craig Goetz	1997	417
181 5/8	21 3/8	23 5/8	19 7/8	9	8	Bureau County	IL	Louis J. Guerrini	1990	424
181 5/8	25 5/8	26 7/8	18 6/8	9	8	Pike County	IL	Steven R. Tice	1991	424
181 5/8	24 5/8	25 5/8	20 5/8	7	6	Okanagon	BC	Richard Kirkvold	1994	424
181 4/8	26 1/8	26 0/8	21 0/8	10	9	Morrison County	MN	Peter De Chaine	1984	427
181 4/8	25 6/8	26 0/8	19 7/8	9	8	Wyoming County	WV	Bobby Smith	1985	427
181 4/8	20 6/8	23 0/8	19 1/8	8	14	Edgar County	IL	Dennis Gosnell	1991	427
181 4/8	22 1/8	22 4/8	17 4/8	7	6	Howard County	IA	Rod Ellingson	1993	427
181 4/8	24 0/8	26 4/8	19 2/8	7	6	Alexander County	IL	Terry L. Kepley	1996	427
181 3/8	28 0/8	28 0/8	20 5/8	11	6	Hardin County	IA	Howard Nelson	1963	432
181 3/8	26 2/8	24 3/8	16 6/8	9	8	Sawyer County	WI	Bill "Red" Gilbert	1989	432
181 3/8	27 6/8	23 2/8	18 7/8	8	6	Muskingum County	OH	Donnie Ledbetter	1996	432
181 3/8	24 0/8	26 6/8	15 1/8	13	8	Crawford County	IL	Robert Loveall	1996	432
181 2/8	22 1/8	24 5/8	19 0/8	12	8	Desha County	AR	John T. Greer	1962	436
181 2/8	26 1/8	25 4/8	25 0/8	12	9	Darke County	OH	Dean P. Neff	1979	436
181 2/8	24 5/8	22 3/8	20 6/8	9	7	Clark County	IA	Larry Bear	1991	436
181 2/8	27 3/8	27 0/8	22 3/8	8	7	Madison County	IL	Michael N. Doles	1994	436
181 1/8	24 1/8	24 1/8	17 6/8	9	6	Coles County	IL	Gerald L. Davis	1973	440
181 1/8	24 2/8	25 5/8	17 7/8	7	8	Tazewell County	IL	Gerald Sweckard	1994	440
181 1/8	24 7/8	23 4/8	18 1/8	11	8	Warren County	OH	Bobby Clark	1995	440
181 1/8	23 6/8	25 6/8	18 3/8	6	9	Randolph County	MO	Donnie Lee Palmatory	1996	440
181 0/8	24 6/8	25 4/8	19 6/8	11	8	Knox County	OH	Don Quick	1984	444
181 0/8	23 7/8	23 5/8	19 1/8	12	9	Pittsburg County	OK	Harold Jones	1986	444
181 0/8	23 4/8	24 1/8	17 2/8	8	9	Clark County	IL	Harold A. Funk	1991	444
181 0/8	25 0/8	23 3/8	18 3/8	8	7	Holt County	MO	Jim Zawodny	1992	444
181 0/8	28 3/8	26 3/8	18 4/8	11	8	Massac County	IL	Gilbert McNichols	1995	444
181 0/8	25 5/8	25 2/8	18 0/8	7	7	Houston County	MN	Tom Murray	1997	444
180 7/8	28 2/8	24 2/8	21 6/8	10	9	Hamilton County	OH	David Beard	1994	450
180 6/8	22 3/8	24 1/8	17 3/8	8	7	Pope County	AR	Johnny Reed	1983	451
180 6/8	23 4/8	23 6/8	16 6/8	6	9	Lee County	IA	Matthew A. Trexel	1994	451
180 5/8	28 5/8	28 6/8	24 5/8	7	7	Preble County	OH	James R. Whittaker	1978	453
180 5/8	27 5/8	26 3/8	21 1/8	9	6	Linn County	IA	Craig Shepard	1980	453
180 5/8	27 0/8	28 0/8	18 6/8	6	9	Delaware County	OH	John P. Stark	1994	453
180 5/8	24 1/8	23 5/8	16 2/8	11	11	Cherokee County	KS	Gene R. Hamilton	1996	453
180 4/8	23 0/8	23 0/8	16 3/8	7	8	Teton County	MT	James Dean	1981	457
180 4/8	26 7/8	27 3/8	21 1/8	7	6	Buffalo County	WI	John L. Smith	1988	457
180 4/8	24 7/8	25 4/8	21 2/8	8	6	Butler County	KS	John Parsons	1989	457
180 4/8	23 6/8	24 2/8	15 2/8	10	7	Osage County	OK	James H. Farmer	1991	457
180 4/8	24 6/8	24 7/8	19 1/8	8	7	Jewell County	KS	Bruce Meyer	1991	457
180 4/8	25 7/8	26 1/8	17 6/8	10	8	Price County	WI	John Michalski	1991	457
180 4/8	25 4/8	26 1/8	17 5/8	8	7	Gage County	NE	Gary L. Stohs	1994	457
180 3/8	23 5/8	23 5/8	16 1/8	9	11	Edgar County	IL	Timothy W. Kirby	1993	464
180 3/8	24 2/8	24 6/8	17 4/8	8	6	Monroe County	WI	Craig C. Tormoen	1996	464
180 3/8	27 0/8	28 1/8	18 5/8	5	5	Knox County	IL	Bryan E. DeJaynes	1997	464
180 2/8	25 4/8	25 3/8	18 7/8	10	8	Woodford County	KY	Gary Hatton	1993	467
180 2/8	26 1/8	25 4/8	20 5/8	6	7	Kleberg County	TX	Mike Lemker	1995	467

WHITETAIL DEER (NON-TYPICAL ANTLERS)

Minimum Score 155 — Continued

SCORE	LENGTH OF MAIN BEAM R	LENGTH OF MAIN BEAM L	INSIDE SPREAD	NUMBER OF POINTS R	NUMBER OF POINTS L	AREA	STATE/ PROVINCE	HUNTER'S NAME	DATE	RANK
180 1/8	24 2/8	23 4/8	18 5/8	10	8	Winnebago County	IA	Jim Orthel	1983	469
180 1/8	26 5/8	26 6/8	20 0/8	8	8	McLean County	IL	Tim Kaufman	1995	469
180 1/8	24 6/8	24 5/8	18 5/8	7	9	Cook County	IL	Roger Kleinfelder	1996	469
180 1/8	23 6/8	24 7/8	19 6/8	8	7	Mercer County	MO	John D. Green	1996	469
180 1/8	26 0/8	27 2/8	22 2/8	7	9	Ogle County	IL	John Kaltenbach	1997	469
180 1/8	25 5/8	24 2/8	17 5/8	8	9	Buffalo County	WI	Paul B. Doenier	1998	469
180 0/8	26 4/8	25 1/8	19 6/8	6	6	Buchanan County	IA	Robert R. Parker	1996	475
180 0/8	23 7/8	24 3/8	20 5/8	7	6	Saline County	KS	Jack Goates	1997	475
179 7/8	26 4/8	26 5/8	23 1/8	7	7	Cass County	IL	Jeffrey A. Williams	1995	477
179 7/8	24 0/8	24 6/8	19 7/8	7	6	Washington County	MN	Mike Haines	1996	477
179 6/8	24 4/8	24 2/8	21 0/8	7	8	Creek County	OK	Marion Lewis	1975	479
179 6/8	24 7/8	25 7/8	22 0/8	6	7	Hamilton County	OH	Lawrence Ashbrook	1981	479
179 6/8	25 1/8	22 5/8	17 4/8	8	11	Licking County	OH	Tony Johnson	1992	479
179 6/8	23 4/8	24 2/8	17 4/8	7	8	Sauk County	WI	Reg Acker	1994	479
179 5/8	24 4/8	25 6/8	19 5/8	9	11	Fillmore County	MN	Wayne Pfremmer	1972	483
179 5/8	29 4/8	25 7/8	20 1/8	5	8	Dane County	WI	Kip Kalscheur	1989	483
179 5/8	23 7/8	25 0/8	19 7/8	8	7	Allegheny County	PA	Anthony Vecenie, Jr.	1995	483
179 5/8	24 0/8	23 7/8	16 3/8	10	7	Pottawattamie County	IA	Murray Stewart	1996	483
179 4/8	26 3/8	26 1/8	20 1/8	7	7	Sawyer County	WI	Wesley A. Marcsis	1996	487
179 4/8	28 7/8	27 6/8	22 0/8	9	9	Des Moines County	IA	Mark Thomson	1996	487
179 3/8	26 3/8	26 4/8	19 5/8	6	6	Cass County	IL	Craig Myers	1994	489
179 2/8	25 4/8	23 4/8	23 0/8	12	7	Marion County	IA	Roger DeMoss	1982	490
179 2/8	24 7/8	25 7/8	21 5/8	8	7	Chippewa County	WI	Kip Knez	1986	490
179 2/8	21 6/8	23 2/8	14 0/8	8	13	Sangamon County	IL	Guy R. Hinrichs	1993	490
179 2/8	21 1/8	19 3/8	15 7/8	8	9	Oneida County	WI	Kathy Fancher	1993	490
179 1/8	26 0/8	26 3/8	20 1/8	6	8	Will County	IL	Michael Suggs	1990	494
179 0/8	24 0/8	23 5/8	20 0/8	6	7	Bearspaw	ALB	Rick Eliuk	1994	495
179 0/8	23 7/8	24 3/8	17 6/8	8	6	Anoka County	MN	Jeff Schultz	1995	495
178 7/8	21 7/8	24 1/8	16 0/8	8	7	Big Stone County	MN	Jerry Lundgren	1992	497
178 7/8	26 1/8	25 3/8	20 0/8	9	7	Warren County	IA	Larry Hyler	1993	497
178 7/8	27 4/8	26 4/8	23 6/8	9	10	Bayfield County	WI	Max Karl	1994	497
178 6/8	21 2/8	25 3/8	20 5/8	9	8	Lincoln County	SD	H. L. Tuggle	1975	500
178 6/8	22 2/8	23 1/8	13 4/8	10	9	Madison County	IL	Michael B. Fenton	1984	500
178 6/8	24 2/8	25 5/8	18 2/8	10	6	Clark County	OH	Jerry B. Sowards	1994	500
178 6/8	23 0/8	22 3/8	19 1/8	8	10	Pike County	IL	Blake McCann	1995	500
178 5/8	24 5/8	25 3/8	16 0/8	8	7	Clay County	IN	Jim Tracy	1989	504
178 5/8	24 4/8	23 6/8	17 6/8	6	9	Ozaukee County	WI	Robert A. Wallock	1989	504
178 5/8	25 0/8	26 3/8	17 3/8	10	9	Ozaukee County	WI	Gerald Berres	1991	504
178 4/8	22 1/8	23 6/8	17 0/8	12	11	Keokuk County	IA	Ron Turner	1983	507
178 4/8	26 2/8	25 2/8	18 2/8	8	6	St. Croix County	WI	James Walsh	1988	507
178 4/8	26 0/8	20 3/8	16 3/8	8	11	Tama County	IA	Duane Bossman	1997	507
178 3/8	23 3/8	22 7/8	19 6/8	8	8	Traverse County	MN	Roland L. Hausmann	1953	510
178 3/8	25 1/8	24 4/8	19 6/8	8	10	Mineral County	MT	Gene Wensel	1981	510
178 3/8	22 6/8	24 7/8	17 0/8	11	10	Finney County	KS	Randy Miller	1984	510
178 3/8	25 6/8	24 6/8	21 6/8	7	7	Jefferson County	IL	Bill Kesler	1992	510
178 1/8	24 7/8	25 4/8	19 0/8	11	9	Montgomery County	OH	Jack B. Odum	1990	514
178 1/8	22 7/8	21 3/8	15 0/8	9	10	Douglas County	WI	Greg A. Kaczmarski	1994	514
178 0/8	24 1/8	25 4/8	19 0/8	8	6	Jefferson County	WI	Mike Leslie	1988	516
178 0/8	24 7/8	25 3/8	14 0/8	9	8	Kenedy County	TX	Miguel Mireles	1991	516
178 0/8	25 7/8	25 3/8	18 7/8	9	7	Jefferson County	KY	Arson Thornsbury, Sr.	1992	516
178 0/8	25 6/8	24 2/8	18 3/8	7	9	Morgan County	CO	Douglas Nagle	1994	516
178 0/8	25 6/8	28 1/8	21 3/8	6	7	Pottawattamie County	IA	Mike Feeney	1995	516
177 7/8	28 2/8	27 0/8	18 3/8	6	6	Ross County	OH	Robert L. Elliott	1981	521
177 7/8	26 5/8	25 2/8	18 2/8	8	7	Pottawatomie County	KS	Loyd C. Flowers	1983	521
177 7/8	26 3/8	27 4/8	23 0/8	8	5	Shelby County	IL	Joe E. Carnahan, Jr.	1996	521
177 6/8	21 4/8	22 2/8	18 1/8	10	9	Pope County	MN	Roger Tollefson	1977	524
177 6/8	23 0/8	21 2/8	16 0/8	6	13	Delaware County	OH	Ronald Eugene Murphy	1983	524
177 6/8	22 0/8	22 4/8	20 4/8	9	8	Des Moines County	IA	Dave Bremhorst	1994	524
177 6/8	20 7/8	20 3/8	18 1/8	10	11	St. Louis County	MO	Keith Gunn	1994	524
177 6/8	24 0/8	23 4/8	18 0/8	7	7	St. Croix County	WI	Charles T. Hutera	1997	524
177 5/8	24 4/8	23 6/8	21 0/8	8	9	Menard County	IL	Donald Alwerdt	1993	529
177 4/8	23 4/8	22 6/8	18 1/8	7	8	Flathead County	MT	Jerry Karsky	1972	530
177 4/8	26 1/8	25 2/8	18 7/8	8	6	Butler County	OH	Michael Rumpler	1994	530
177 4/8	19 6/8	22 0/8	15 6/8	14	7	Beaumont	ALB	Jake Goodwin	1998	530
177 3/8	25 2/8	22 7/8	16 1/8	15	19	Pike County	IL	Daniel Doran	1992	533
177 3/8	23 2/8	24 2/8	18 4/8	10	10	Marengo County	AL	David Darnell	1997	533
177 1/8	23 0/8	22 6/8	18 6/8	7	12	Pope County	MN	Doyle Anderson	1988	535
177 1/8	25 0/8	27 1/8	19 6/8	8	9	Delaware County	OH	Jeff Miller	1993	535
177 0/8	25 2/8	25 6/8	18 6/8	7	9	Rock County	WI	Kirk C. Douglas	1987	537
177 0/8	24 3/8	22 6/8	17 0/8	7	9	Boone County	IA	Robert J. Van Roekel	1989	537
177 0/8	24 0/8	24 3/8	16 0/8	7	7	Olmsted County	MN	Leo Kuisle	1991	537
176 7/8	24 2/8	23 7/8	20 7/8	8	8	Suffolk County	NY	James Matuszewski	1994	540
176 6/8	28 4/8	28 2/8	19 4/8	8	9	Dodge County	WI	Erwin C. Koehler	1957	541
176 6/8	29 0/8	26 3/8	22 3/8	7	5	Allamakee County	IA	Jim Dyer	1993	541
176 5/8	22 2/8	21 3/8	16 4/8	10	7	Day County	SD	Lonnie L. Heuer	1987	543
176 5/8	24 1/8	24 0/8	19 4/8	8	8	Polk County	WI	Jesse Tonn	1991	543
176 5/8	25 1/8	24 6/8	18 7/8	6	9	Pickaway County	OH	Jerry L. Rhoades	1992	543
176 4/8	23 2/8	21 7/8	17 1/8	9	8	Macon County	IL	Dave Elliot	1997	546

WHITETAIL DEER (NON-TYPICAL ANTLERS)

Minimum Score 155 Continued

SCORE	LENGTH OF MAIN BEAM R	LENGTH OF MAIN BEAM L	INSIDE SPREAD	NUMBER OF POINTS R	NUMBER OF POINTS L	AREA	STATE/ PROVINCE	HUNTER'S NAME	DATE	RANK
176 3/8	24 6/8	25 4/8	20 3/8	8	8	Greene County	OH	Leroy M. Thompson	1982	547
176 2/8	22 2/8	22 5/8	15 2/8	7	8	Winnebago County	WI	Todd A. Pitsch	1994	548
176 1/8	22 0/8	23 3/8	21 4/8	7	6	Brandon	MAN	Larry J. Pollock	1980	549
176 1/8	27 0/8	27 6/8	20 4/8	4	7	Pike County	OH	Jim Widdig	1997	549
176 1/8	22 2/8	25 4/8	17 4/8	10	8	Marshall County	IL	William J. Starry	1997	549
176 0/8	22 6/8	22 3/8	21 7/8	6	7	Todd County	MN	Richard L. Boelter	1993	552
176 0/8	26 0/8	27 1/8	24 4/8	9	9	Linn County	KS	Tipton Cook	1993	552
176 0/8	23 2/8	24 2/8	20 1/8	8	9	Dekalb County	IL	Kevin M. Grivetti	1995	552
175 7/8	27 4/8	28 1/8	23 3/8	8	7	Guernsey County	OH	Jack L. Milligan	1971	555
175 7/8	24 3/8	25 1/8	17 4/8	9	8	Freeborn County	MN	Douglas Swank	1979	555
175 7/8	23 3/8	22 2/8	17 1/8	7	7	Clark County	IL	Alan Lee	1995	555
175 6/8	22 4/8	22 2/8	19 2/8	5	7	Rush County	IN	Kent D. Clark	1991	558
175 6/8	25 1/8	24 7/8	17 5/8	9	9	Sangamon County	IL	Brian Bergmann	1994	558
175 6/8	25 7/8	25 5/8	19 2/8	10	5	Orange County	IN	Mark Verble	1995	558
175 6/8	26 3/8	25 7/8	21 6/8	6	8	Fond du Lac County	WI	Willard Nolan	1997	558
175 4/8	22 4/8	22 7/8	19 2/8	10	10	Woodbury County	IA	Everett Gothier	1962	562
175 4/8	28 4/8	27 5/8	20 6/8	7	7	Belmont County	OH	Dan Clutter	1985	562
175 4/8	26 6/8	25 4/8	23 2/8	13	7	Fairfield County	OH	Ron Perdew	1992	562
175 3/8	24 5/8	23 7/8	20 1/8	8	7	Grant County	MN	Lee Offerdahl	1972	565
175 3/8	26 2/8	25 3/8	14 4/8	8	11	Buffalo County	WI	Timothy L. Brommer	1984	565
175 3/8	23 4/8	24 3/8	19 6/8	7	9	Salem County	NJ	Richard Wendt	1985	565
175 3/8	25 4/8	23 2/8	16 5/8	8	8	Hennepin County	MN	Robert R. Herman	1993	565
175 3/8	24 6/8	23 5/8	19 7/8	6	8	Schoolcraft County	MI	Jim Hedglen	1995	565
175 3/8	24 2/8	23 3/8	18 4/8	6	6	Elk County	KS	Gary Fritzler	1997	565
175 2/8	26 1/8	26 0/8	17 1/8	9	7	McHenry County	IL	Richard G. Hickey	1988	571
175 2/8	20 0/8	21 6/8	21 1/8	9	9	Jackson County	MI	Scott A. Weaver	1996	571
175 2/8	28 3/8	28 0/8	22 1/8	5	8	Howard County	MD	Robert W. Evans	1998	571
175 1/8	26 4/8	25 1/8	20 0/8	6	7	Dubuque County	IA	Gregory Klein	1983	574
175 1/8	24 4/8	23 3/8	17 2/8	9	10	Cherokee County	KS	Darren Collins	1988	574
175 1/8	25 7/8	25 2/8	18 3/8	6	8	Franklin County	KS	Dennis N. Ballweg	1988	574
175 1/8	24 6/8	24 5/8	18 6/8	7	9	Wayne County	MO	Jesse Whittley, Jr.	1988	574
175 1/8	25 6/8	26 5/8	19 0/8	6	6	Chase County	KS	Greg Windler	1988	574
175 1/8	23 3/8	15 6/8	23 1/8	9	9	Clinton County	IA	Mark Schutt	1993	574
175 1/8	23 7/8	23 2/8	16 4/8	7	8	Roseau County	MN	Ernest Janousek	1994	574
175 1/8	24 3/8	25 6/8	18 4/8	13	9	Jersey County	IL	Terry Dale	1994	574
175 1/8	24 4/8	26 3/8	16 3/8	9	6	Dane County	WI	Kevin Tennant	1998	574
175 0/8	26 2/8	28 3/8	21 2/8	5	6	Jersey County	IL	Judy Kovar	1988	583
175 0/8	23 2/8	23 5/8	18 4/8	7	6	Pottawatomie County	KS	Tod Edwin Anthony	1993	583
175 0/8	21 3/8	21 3/8	14 2/8	8	7	Roane County	WV	Carroll Rogers	1994	583
174 7/8	26 6/8	25 3/8	19 7/8	9	9	Waseca County	MN	Robert Barrie	1974	586
174 7/8	25 5/8	27 3/8	19 2/8	10	6	Des Moines County	IA	Tom Lappe	1985	586
174 7/8	23 7/8	22 1/8	16 4/8	7	11	Branch County	MI	Roy D. Grigsby	1994	586
174 7/8	22 5/8	22 5/8	20 0/8	6	7	Goliad County	TX	Mark Thompson	1995	586
174 6/8	22 2/8	21 5/8	19 0/8	7	7	Columbia County	WI	Robert L. Lex	1992	590
174 6/8	22 0/8	22 2/8	18 2/8	13	9	Carroll County	MO	Danny Davies	1994	590
174 6/8	24 0/8	23 3/8	21 0/8	7	8	Pulaski County	VA	Gary Blackwell	1997	590
174 6/8	25 6/8	26 3/8	20 4/8	6	6	Menard County	IL	Ron Wadsworth	1998	590
174 5/8	23 3/8	21 6/8	16 0/8	9	9	Harvey County	KS	Richard Krehbiel	1995	594
174 4/8	24 0/8	25 4/8	22 5/8	5	6	Otter Tail County	MN	Don Oelschlager	1976	595
174 4/8	22 1/8	22 3/8	16 4/8	8	8	Benson County	ND	Curtis A. Ehnert	1977	595
174 4/8	21 1/8	21 0/8	17 2/8	8	9	Brown County	IL	Angela Vogel	1988	595
174 3/8	26 0/8	25 7/8	18 2/8	9	7	Vinton County	OH	Jack McConnell	1982	598
174 3/8	28 4/8	28 3/8	22 2/8	6	8	Winnebago County	IL	Dave Fisher	1986	598
174 3/8	22 1/8	21 7/8	18 2/8	8	9	Marshall County	MN	Barry Liimatainen	1993	598
174 3/8	25 4/8	24 3/8	16 1/8	9	7	Sauk County	WI	John Skau, Jr.	1995	598
174 3/8	29 0/8	28 1/8	22 6/8	7	5	Scott County	MN	Joshua Gross	1996	598
174 2/8	26 6/8	25 1/8	19 7/8	9	6	Clay County	IA	Darrell Magnussen	1962	603
174 2/8	22 3/8	24 0/8	16 0/8	10	9	Rawlins County	KS	Curtis Walston	1991	603
174 2/8	22 3/8	22 4/8	16 1/8	6	7	Greene County	MO	Norm Nothnagel	1993	603
174 1/8	26 1/8	25 7/8	26 2/8	7	8	Charles County	MD	Robert H. Jones, Sr.	1971	606
174 1/8	25 5/8	27 1/8	18 4/8	9	6	Henderson County	IL	Ron De May	1997	606
174 1/8	24 6/8	24 4/8	16 6/8	6	7	Collingsworth County	TX	Brad Casal	1997	606
174 1/8	22 4/8	22 3/8	19 1/8	8	7	Franklin County	KY	Michael Riddle	1998	606
174 0/8	26 0/8	27 6/8	26 6/8	7	6	Delaware County	OH	Michael H. Seamster	1983	610
174 0/8	22 7/8	21 3/8	20 2/8	7	7	Coles County	IL	Fred Hartbank	1994	610
174 0/8	26 0/8	26 6/8	18 4/8	8	6	E. Carroll Parish	LA	Gary D. Carr	1996	610
173 7/8	27 5/8	26 0/8	18 0/8	10	7	Marshall County	KS	Michael J. Krogman	1984	613
173 7/8	24 4/8	23 3/8	19 7/8	7	7	Anne Arundel County	MD	David R. McMullen, Sr.	1992	613
173 7/8	24 6/8	25 0/8	17 3/8	9	7	Morrison County	MN	Mike Sannan	1993	613
173 7/8	22 6/8	22 5/8	19 1/8	9	9	Dane County	WI	Eric L. Hamele	1993	613
173 7/8	25 0/8	25 2/8	20 3/8	7	7	Richland County	WI	Mathew D. Omernik	1994	613
173 6/8	25 4/8	25 2/8	22 0/8	8	9	Spink County	SD	Milton Haag	1959	618
173 6/8	19 3/8	19 5/8	17 1/8	9	9	Douglas County	MN	John Duberowski	1980	618
173 6/8	25 3/8	24 5/8	17 6/8	7	7	Cass County	MI	James Akey	1995	618
173 6/8	26 4/8	20 7/8	21 6/8	11	11	Norton County	KS	Jeff Dold	1997	618
173 5/8	25 4/8	24 3/8	18 1/8	7	6	Gray County	KS	Allen D. Bailey	1982	622
173 5/8	22 7/8	23 2/8	18 4/8	8	6	Pepin County	WI	Don Linse	1988	622
173 5/8	23 1/8	22 3/8	17 2/8	11	7	St. Louis County	MO	Michael M. Branson	1989	622

WHITETAIL DEER (NON-TYPICAL ANTLERS)

Minimum Score 155   Continued

SCORE	LENGTH OF MAIN BEAM R	LENGTH OF MAIN BEAM L	INSIDE SPREAD	NUMBER OF POINTS R	NUMBER OF POINTS L	AREA	STATE/PROVINCE	HUNTER'S NAME	DATE	RANK
173 5/8	29 1/8	28 4/8	17 4/8	11	9	Chippewa County	WI	George A. Olson	1991	622
173 5/8	26 7/8	27 1/8	18 7/8	7	7	Pope County	IL	Doug Casey	1995	622
173 5/8	22 5/8	24 4/8	17 7/8	8	8	Christian County	IL	Dave L. Gross	1996	622
173 4/8	24 7/8	25 5/8	21 6/8	6	6	Barton County	KS	Norman Kimber	1967	628
173 4/8	22 4/8	23 7/8	14 1/8	6	8	Trumbull County	OH	Peter Bradley	1969	628
173 4/8	26 1/8	21 7/8	16 7/8	7	10	Renville County	MN	Larry Godejahn	1973	628
173 4/8	25 1/8	25 4/8	17 6/8	7	8	Scott County	KY	Joey Lusby	1995	628
173 4/8	24 3/8	23 6/8	16 1/8	10	6	Cass County	MO	Jerrol Walton	1996	628
173 4/8	27 2/8	25 6/8	19 6/8	6	5	Walworth County	WI	Charles G. Palmer	1996	628
173 4/8	23 0/8	23 3/8	18 1/8	6	8	Pike County	IL	Shawn Baker	1997	628
173 3/8	26 4/8	26 2/8	19 5/8	8	7	Pike County	IL	Ronnie Bauer	1988	635
173 3/8	24 4/8	24 4/8	20 5/8	6	8	Dekalb County	IL	Tom Kane	1995	635
173 3/8	25 3/8	25 5/8	19 2/8	8	7	Dane County	WI	David D. Hilgers	1997	635
173 3/8	26 2/8	26 1/8	20 6/8	9	7	Prince Georges County	MD	Phil Harris	1997	635
173 2/8	27 4/8	27 0/8	20 6/8	7	9	Ross County	OH	Glen A. Cummings	1991	639
173 2/8	25 2/8	25 4/8	20 1/8	6	7	Jefferson County	IA	James Steele	1992	639
173 2/8	24 4/8	24 6/8	14 7/8	6	10	Marion County	KY	J. W. Witt	1993	639
173 2/8	20 4/8	21 0/8	18 5/8	8	8	Brown County	SD	Barry J. Smith	1995	639
173 2/8	24 0/8	23 4/8	17 7/8	6	6	Lyon County	IA	Michael Judas	1996	639
173 1/8	24 6/8	24 6/8	18 1/8	8	9	Lee County	IA	Dan Enger	1992	644
173 1/8	23 4/8	22 5/8	16 6/8	8	8	Waukesha County	WI	David J. Timm	1994	644
173 0/8	22 4/8	21 5/8	16 6/8	7	8	Lincoln County	KS	Scott Kingery	1988	646
173 0/8	24 0/8	24 2/8	17 6/8	6	9	Champaign County	IL	Greg Burr	1994	646
173 0/8	22 7/8	23 4/8	18 0/8	9	10	Boyd County	NE	Lora Cline	1997	646
172 7/8	24 0/8	21 4/8	14 4/8	10	10	McIntosh County	OK	Clark Utley	1976	649
172 7/8	23 6/8	24 1/8	16 7/8	9	9	Morrison County	MN	Harlan Grams	1988	649
172 7/8	22 5/8	23 7/8	19 3/8	8	8	Sedgwick County	KS	Cary Renner	1989	649
172 7/8	23 3/8	24 2/8	19 2/8	6	10	Barton County	KS	Alan D. Bullard	1994	649
172 7/8	26 1/8	25 0/8	21 4/8	6	7	Zavala County	TX	Joe Little	1997	649
172 6/8	22 2/8	22 6/8	16 2/8	9	11	Washburn County	WI	Clint Atkinson	1986	654
172 5/8	24 2/8	25 2/8	17 6/8	11	7	Trumbull County	OH	Dick Keagy	1989	655
172 5/8	26 3/8	24 7/8	17 2/8	8	9	Brown County	SD	Craig Papke	1995	655
172 4/8	18 0/8	25 2/8	19 0/8	14	7	Marshall County	MN	James C. Pederson	1992	657
172 3/8	23 6/8	23 0/8	18 4/8	7	8	Mississippi County	AR	Dennis Perkins	1990	658
172 3/8	23 2/8	24 5/8	18 6/8	9	5	Chariton County	MO	Dennis W. Meyers	1991	658
172 2/8	24 5/8	23 6/8	15 4/8	9	10	Calhoun County	MI	Roger W. Hanselman	1989	660
172 2/8	22 3/8	23 5/8	18 2/8	7	7	Cadogan	ALB	Howard Schreiber	1991	660
172 2/8	25 0/8	25 2/8	25 6/8	9	8	Cass County	MO	Jerrol Walton	1992	660
172 2/8	27 0/8	25 0/8	21 3/8	7	9	Henderson County	IL	Darren E. Blakley	1993	660
172 2/8	26 0/8	26 0/8	17 6/8	8	8	Tazewell County	VA	Michael L. Sawyers	1995	660
172 1/8	22 6/8	23 2/8	24 7/8	8	7	Green County	WI	Dean Dilly	1974	665
172 1/8	25 0/8	25 4/8	18 0/8	9	7	Chippewa County	MN	Sheldon Holzheimer	1993	665
172 1/8	23 5/8	23 2/8	19 4/8	6	7	Kanawha County	WV	Billy Lamb	1995	665
172 0/8	24 4/8	25 4/8	17 4/8	7	7	Warren County	IA	Dennis R. Jacobe	1988	668
172 0/8	23 5/8	23 5/8	17 2/8	5	8	Onaway	ALB	Edward Toelken	1994	668
172 0/8	21 5/8	22 2/8	18 2/8	11	10	Charles County	MD	Harold J. Welch	1997	668
171 7/8	22 4/8	22 3/8	19 6/8	11	9	Will County	IL	James Giese	1987	671
171 7/8	22 7/8	23 7/8	19 2/8	8	8	Calgary	ALB	James Sheret	1990	671
171 7/8	23 4/8	23 6/8	19 7/8	8	9	Brown County	MN	Chad Freiderick	1995	671
171 7/8	24 0/8	23 6/8	18 4/8	9	11	Pike County	OH	Marcus Hoholick	1997	671
171 6/8	22 3/8	21 5/8	20 5/8	8	9	Dubuque County	IA	Dick Theis	1975	675
171 6/8	26 0/8	26 7/8	19 6/8	9	7	Vermilion County	IL	Gene Maier	1984	675
171 6/8	23 7/8	18 3/8	18 0/8	7	10	Leavenworth County	KS	Albert Lyle Karl	1987	675
171 6/8	23 0/8	23 5/8	15 6/8	7	7	Montgomery County	TN	Dennis Morris	1991	675
171 6/8	25 7/8	25 5/8	18 6/8	9	8	McLean County	IL	Kenneth Kolakowski	1993	675
171 6/8	25 0/8	25 1/8	21 2/8	4	7	Sangamon County	IL	Robert Churchill	1995	675
171 6/8	21 3/8	21 1/8	17 5/8	8	6	McHenry County	IL	Frank Oakley	1997	675
171 5/8	22 7/8	24 1/8	16 4/8	7	7	Wapello County	IA	Rex Jones	1983	682
171 5/8	26 1/8	21 4/8	24 0/8	6	8	Iroquois County	IL	Frank Snow	1987	682
171 5/8	24 0/8	23 0/8	19 2/8	6	9	Muskingum County	OH	Dan Jennings	1991	682
171 4/8	24 5/8	24 5/8	19 1/8	7	7	Butler County	KS	Jeff Stevens	1982	685
171 4/8	23 2/8	24 3/8	17 7/8	9	8	Monona County	IA	Kevin M. Rittenhouse	1994	685
171 3/8	20 4/8	23 7/8	19 4/8	8	10	Logan County	OK	Billy Wayne McBride	1989	687
171 3/8	18 2/8	18 3/8	11 4/8	9	9	Chariton County	MO	Jeff Brand	1991	687
171 3/8	24 1/8	21 7/8	19 5/8	6	8	Kane County	IL	Matthew Peterson	1991	687
171 3/8	26 0/8	25 0/8	17 3/8	7	5	Delaware County	IA	Parker Fransen	1997	687
171 2/8	27 0/8	27 0/8	18 5/8	4	5	Van Buren County	MI	David Anderson	1979	691
171 2/8	23 5/8	24 7/8	14 4/8	6	6	Scotts Bluff County	NE	Doug Hauser	1984	691
171 2/8	25 4/8	25 4/8	17 3/8	7	6	Trempealeau County	WI	Steven W. Franck	1995	691
171 2/8	25 2/8	25 3/8	18 5/8	6	9	Ozaukee County	WI	Jamie Langerman	1998	691
171 1/8	23 4/8	24 0/8	20 2/8	8	6	Jackson County	MI	Shawn R. Surque	1985	695
171 1/8	25 4/8	25 4/8	18 6/8	6	8	Birds Hill	MAN	Daniel Kowalchuk	1991	695
171 1/8	26 7/8	26 0/8	19 7/8	7	8	Coffey County	KS	Kevin Parks	1992	695
171 1/8	23 0/8	24 2/8	16 1/8	10	8	Bayfield County	WI	Eric Carlson	1995	695
171 0/8	24 0/8	24 4/8	18 1/8	7	7	Dodge County	WI	Dallas Johnson	1955	699
171 0/8	26 3/8	22 6/8	22 4/8	4	10	Lee County	IA	Gary Frost	1967	699
171 0/8	25 7/8	26 0/8	26 0/8	6	5	Clark County	KS	William A. Rule	1993	699
170 7/8	24 5/8	25 2/8	15 3/8	6	6	Redwood County	MN	Todd G. Gilb	1982	702

WHITETAIL DEER (NON-TYPICAL ANTLERS)

Minimum Score 155

SCORE	LENGTH OF MAIN BEAM R	LENGTH OF MAIN BEAM L	INSIDE SPREAD	NUMBER OF POINTS R	NUMBER OF POINTS L	AREA	STATE/PROVINCE	HUNTER'S NAME	DATE	RANK
170 7/8	21 6/8	23 2/8	14 6/8	10	12	Kleberg County	TX	Bradley Peltier	1989	702
170 7/8	23 6/8	24 1/8	16 5/8	9	9	Cook County	IL	Kenneth S. Koeneman	1997	702
170 6/8	24 3/8	23 6/8	17 2/8	9	8	Nobles County	MN	David Janssen	1973	705
170 6/8	23 7/8	23 6/8	18 2/8	6	12	Washtenaw County	MI	Dennis D. Clarke	1989	705
170 6/8	22 0/8	20 7/8	14 5/8	9	7	Anoka County	MN	Wayne Nicholson	1991	705
170 6/8	23 5/8	22 6/8	16 4/8	10	8	St. Charles County	MO	Jack A. Jones	1992	705
170 6/8	27 5/8	26 0/8	20 2/8	5	5	Dakota County	MN	Craig Adams	1994	705
170 6/8	22 2/8	22 7/8	17 2/8	8	7	Adams County	IL	Steve M. Giesing	1995	705
170 6/8	25 1/8	25 2/8	19 0/8	7	6	Linn County	IA	James L. Corkery	1996	705
170 6/8	26 0/8	25 1/8	25 5/8	7	11	Henderson County	IL	Terry L. Cook	1997	705
170 5/8	18 1/8	26 2/8	21 7/8	10	6	Oklahoma County	OK	Tim R. Reid	1990	713
170 5/8	24 4/8	24 4/8	22 0/8	6	6	Wallowa County	OR	Marte Scheuffele	1994	713
170 5/8	22 6/8	24 6/8	19 0/8	8	6	Fulton County	IL	Mike Foster	1994	713
170 5/8	25 4/8	22 7/8	17 4/8	6	9	Warren County	IA	David Wolfkill	1994	713
170 5/8	26 2/8	25 3/8	19 2/8	8	6	Winnebago County	IA	Terry L. Hammond	1995	713
170 5/8	27 1/8	26 2/8	21 1/8	6	4	Dane County	WI	Keith Green	1996	713
170 4/8	26 3/8	26 1/8	20 5/8	7	7	Tazewell County	IL	Bret Hamilton	1982	719
170 4/8	25 6/8	25 6/8	19 2/8	7	6	Sauk County	WI	Del R. Hisel	1994	719
170 4/8	27 7/8	26 4/8	17 7/8	8	5	Guthrie County	IA	Larry Bryan	1995	719
170 3/8	24 1/8	22 7/8	21 1/8	6	8	Fairfield County	OH	Brian Morrison	1987	722
170 3/8	24 1/8	22 7/8	21 1/8	6	8	Fairfield County	OH	Brian Morrison	1987	722
170 3/8	22 6/8	23 5/8	17 2/8	7	9	Logan County	NE	John Croghan	1994	722
170 3/8	23 4/8	23 4/8	21 6/8	8	8	Webster County	IA	Edward E. Ulicki	1996	722
170 2/8	24 7/8	25 5/8	17 6/8	11	9	Callaway County	MO	Larry Murphy	1988	726
170 2/8	26 4/8	26 2/8	18 7/8	7	6	Stephenson County	IL	James Heiler	1988	726
170 2/8	22 1/8	23 6/8	19 0/8	7	9	Warren County	IA	Grant A. Poindexter	1991	726
170 1/8	24 1/8	22 3/8	17 6/8	7	9	Lyon County	KS	Russell Reed	1986	729
170 1/8	22 6/8	23 0/8	17 2/8	9	8	Cowley County	KS	Aaron Chaplin	1990	729
170 1/8	21 1/8	22 0/8	16 1/8	7	8	Grayson County	TX	Freddie Gowin	1992	729
170 1/8	23 0/8	24 3/8	17 7/8	10	11	Washington County	KS	Bruce A. Eickmann	1994	729
170 1/8	22 4/8	25 2/8	19 3/8	8	7	Trempealeau County	WI	Don Baardseth	1997	729
170 1/8	25 0/8	24 0/8	21 2/8	8	7	Logan County	IL	Doug Knox	1997	729
170 0/8	25 1/8	21 6/8	19 5/8	9	12	Van Buren County	IA	Gary W. Schutt	1987	735
170 0/8	23 5/8	23 1/8	18 5/8	4	11	Lawrence County	IL	Steven M. Blinn	1995	735
169 7/8	25 2/8	23 4/8	21 3/8	10	12	Marion County	IA	Gerald T. Dowell	1994	737
169 7/8	25 2/8	26 4/8	21 6/8	5	7	Will County	IL	Dwane G. Young	1995	737
169 7/8	24 3/8	24 3/8	18 6/8	9	7	Dodge County	NE	Erik Palle	1997	737
169 6/8	24 4/8	25 1/8	17 7/8	6	6	Carter County	KY	Timothy Carter	1974	740
169 5/8	26 5/8	27 6/8	22 0/8	7	7	Dodge County	MN	Lawrence Sowieja	1973	741
169 5/8	22 7/8	20 4/8	20 0/8	7	7	Pike County	MO	Marlin E. Foree	1988	741
169 4/8	25 5/8	24 2/8	23 0/8	6	8	Branch County	MI	Roy D. Grigsby	1988	743
169 4/8	25 2/8	25 4/8	21 0/8	6	7	Price County	WI	James E. Johnson	1990	743
169 4/8	21 4/8	21 3/8	14 0/8	8	8	Adams County	IL	Sal Carlomagno	1996	743
169 3/8	25 6/8	25 0/8	18 6/8	8	6	Emmet County	IA	Paul Love	1992	746
169 2/8	23 4/8	23 7/8	18 5/8	6	8	Rice County	MN	Vernon J. Kleve	1972	747
169 2/8	25 4/8	26 4/8	19 4/8	7	8	Schuyler County	IL	Robert J. Logsdon	1981	747
169 2/8	23 2/8	23 6/8	17 4/8	7	8	Washington County	WI	Tony Snow	1991	747
169 2/8	24 0/8	23 4/8	18 4/8	6	7	La Crosse County	WI	Ronald E. Anderson	1995	747
169 2/8	22 1/8	22 6/8	17 1/8	8	9	Saginaw County	MI	Dawn M. Adlen	1998	747
169 1/8	22 2/8	22 2/8	15 5/8	9	10	Lincoln County	NE	Michael Scott Chase	1994	752
169 0/8	23 5/8	22 6/8	22 6/8	11	9	Suffolk County	NY	John Bennett	1991	753
169 0/8	23 4/8	22 1/8	16 4/8	6	6	Vilas County	WI	Dan Herson	1992	753
168 7/8	22 4/8	21 6/8	19 4/8	7	8	Meeker County	MN	Ralph Hakel	1964	755
168 7/8	25 5/8	23 5/8	19 7/8	6	8	Otoe County	NE	Roberto Z. Duran	1990	755
168 7/8	26 7/8	26 3/8	19 5/8	7	6	Dane County	WI	Craig Lunaas	1997	755
168 6/8	24 1/8	25 1/8	20 3/8	9	8	Olmsted County	MN	Jeff Meyer	1974	758
168 6/8	21 3/8	21 2/8	15 3/8	11	9	Alfalfa County	OK	William D. Yirka	1991	758
168 6/8	25 2/8	25 1/8	16 6/8	8	6	La Salle County	IL	David J. Kinczewski	1995	758
168 6/8	26 2/8	26 1/8	19 2/8	6	9	Elgin	ONT	Steve Marcinkiewicz	1995	758
168 5/8	21 0/8	19 4/8	13 7/8	7	7	Lyon County	KS	Russell Reed	1984	762
168 5/8	23 6/8	23 6/8	17 5/8	7	10	Waukesha County	WI	Jeff Stanton	1991	762
168 5/8	27 6/8	26 4/8	19 5/8	7	7	Prince Georges County	MD	Mark Andrew DeVaughn	1997	762
168 4/8	24 5/8	23 5/8	16 1/8	5	7	Stearns County	MN	Robert Opatz	1987	765
168 4/8	24 4/8	24 4/8	18 1/8	7	6	Fulton County	IN	Dennis L. Kamp	1988	765
168 4/8	19 7/8	21 1/8	13 0/8	8	6	Pend Oreille County	WA	Aaron Coleman	1991	765
168 3/8	23 1/8	22 7/8	18 7/8	6	8	Jefferson County	IN	Michael Abston	1987	768
168 3/8	22 2/8	22 0/8	15 7/8	8	7	Winona County	MN	Dan Hengel	1992	768
168 3/8	25 1/8	25 4/8	15 1/8	7	7	Knox County	IL	Frank Thomas Cain	1994	768
168 3/8	25 4/8	26 6/8	20 0/8	6	6	Lee County	IL	Gordon Gabelmann	1995	768
168 3/8	24 2/8	24 4/8	20 6/8	6	7	Morgan County	IL	Roger Hedgpeth	1997	768
168 2/8	20 6/8	19 7/8	23 1/8	7	8	Washington County	OH	Mike Ferrell	1982	773
168 2/8	25 6/8	26 4/8	18 5/8	5	9	Madison County	IA	Sam Greer	1995	773
168 2/8	22 6/8	22 4/8	16 5/8	7	8	Burleigh County	ND	Jeff Schulz	1996	773
168 2/8	20 6/8	22 0/8	17 1/8	8	8	Winneshiek County	IA	Bob Le Cocq	1997	773
168 1/8	22 3/8	23 0/8	18 3/8	6	7	Ozaukee County	WI	Joe Spata	1991	777
168 1/8	23 6/8	24 1/8	18 3/8	7	8	Cedar County	IA	Dan Burnette	1997	777
168 1/8	19 4/8	20 7/8	19 7/8	10	7	Houston County	MN	Donald Woodhouse	1998	777
168 0/8	21 3/8	21 2/8	15 6/8	7	9	Martin County	MN	Charles Sutphin	1974	780

WHITETAIL DEER (NON-TYPICAL ANTLERS)

Minimum Score 155   Continued

SCORE	LENGTH OF MAIN BEAM R	LENGTH OF MAIN BEAM L	INSIDE SPREAD	NUMBER OF POINTS R	NUMBER OF POINTS L	AREA	STATE/PROVINCE	HUNTER'S NAME	DATE	RANK
168 0/8	23 6/8	23 5/8	18 0/8	8	6	Jackson County	OH	Larry Carter	1996	780
167 7/8	23 4/8	26 6/8	20 1/8	8	5	Trempealeau County	WI	Tom Reedy	1984	782
167 7/8	22 2/8	22 2/8	19 7/8	6	8	Cypress River	MAN	Harvey Gagne	1987	782
167 7/8	27 6/8	26 1/8	18 2/8	5	6	Greenwood County	KS	Danny Linnebur	1991	782
167 7/8	22 4/8	21 7/8	20 4/8	7	9	Oldham County	KY	Michael G. Jeffries	1993	782
167 7/8	22 4/8	23 0/8	17 6/8	9	9	Ferry County	WA	Tim Jerald	1994	782
167 7/8	25 0/8	25 2/8	20 4/8	7	7	St. Clair County	IL	Bryan J. Apostol	1995	782
167 6/8	24 3/8	24 3/8	19 7/8	9	7	Scott County	IA	Gordon Vrana	1967	788
167 6/8	21 7/8	23 3/8	14 5/8	8	8	Barton County	KS	Lance Hockett	1990	788
167 6/8	26 1/8	26 4/8	18 5/8	10	6	Calhoun County	MI	Joseph D. Tallent	1995	788
167 6/8	22 2/8	22 7/8	15 1/8	7	8	Bremer County	IA	Larry Burman	1997	788
167 5/8	23 7/8	21 0/8	19 4/8	5	8	Frederick County	MD	Kenneth T. Ward	1991	792
167 5/8	26 1/8	25 1/8	21 1/8	8	8	Harrison County	IA	Curt Van Lith	1992	792
167 5/8	27 3/8	26 6/8	21 3/8	6	9	Washington County	KS	Bob Funke	1997	792
167 5/8	23 5/8	23 3/8	20 6/8	9	8	Johnson County	IA	Mike Borwig	1997	792
167 4/8	24 1/8	23 6/8	16 0/8	9	10	Iroquois County	IL	Al Weissbohn	1986	796
167 4/8	22 1/8	22 7/8	16 5/8	8	8	Olmsted County	MN	Jay R. Flicker	1997	796
167 3/8	23 5/8	24 4/8	18 7/8	6	9	Vigo County	IN	Darren Scott	1994	798
167 2/8	24 0/8	24 3/8	17 1/8	7	6	Sauk County	WI	Charles Davenport	1969	799
167 2/8	24 5/8	26 1/8	20 3/8	9	6	Lee County	IL	Glenn L. Whitehouse	1994	799
167 2/8	23 0/8	22 4/8	17 3/8	6	6	Buffalo County	WI	Steven B. Schroeder	1998	799
167 1/8	23 1/8	22 0/8	21 6/8	7	9	Floyd County	IA	Patrick E. Barrett	1990	802
167 1/8	23 4/8	23 4/8	18 4/8	8	10	Licking County	OH	Mike Stevens	1994	802
167 1/8	20 5/8	19 6/8	14 5/8	6	7	Hillsdale County	MI	Michael Leshkevich	1994	802
167 0/8	22 2/8	22 1/8	18 3/8	8	5	Wright County	IA	Robert Filbrandt	1974	805
167 0/8	24 7/8	24 0/8	19 0/8	7	9	Pawnee County	NE	Ed Baburek	1987	805
167 0/8	21 3/8	22 0/8	14 4/8	5	6	Jackson County	WI	Craig R. Johnson	1993	805
167 0/8	23 6/8	23 7/8	18 1/8	8	6	Juneau County	WI	Darren M. Green, Sr.	1994	805
167 0/8	21 5/8	24 2/8	18 1/8	7	6	Amherst County	VA	Anthony Olswfski	1996	805
166 7/8	25 3/8	25 6/8	18 2/8	6	6	Hubbard County	MN	Jack Smythe	1973	810
166 6/8	25 1/8	24 5/8	17 7/8	7	7	Kenedy County	TX	Steve Ray Dollar	1990	811
166 5/8	28 3/8	26 6/8	15 2/8	8	9	Shelby County	IA	Billy Custer	1968	812
166 5/8	22 7/8	21 7/8	20 5/8	7	7	Wabaunsee County	KS	Charles Bisnette	1991	812
166 4/8	22 0/8	23 3/8	14 5/8	9	5	Midland County	MI	Michael D. Pretzer	1987	814
166 3/8	24 5/8	24 5/8	16 2/8	6	6	Brown County	SD	Frank Bauer	1974	815
166 3/8	21 6/8	20 3/8	17 3/8	7	7	Okotoks	ALB	Darren Dale	1980	815
166 3/8	21 7/8	24 5/8	18 4/8	9	7	Seminole County	OK	Aliene Turner	1994	815
166 2/8	23 3/8	23 2/8	18 0/8	7	9	Linn County	IA	Guy D. Williams, Jr.	1986	818
166 2/8	27 0/8	25 3/8	21 3/8	6	10	Cecil County	MD	John E. Kostic	1991	818
166 2/8	22 6/8	22 4/8	19 4/8	9	8	Washington County	WI	William R. Mahnke	1995	818
166 1/8	22 5/8	23 1/8	17 3/8	7	7	Reagan County	TX	James E. Borron	1997	821
166 1/8	24 7/8	23 6/8	16 1/8	9	10	Suffolk County	NY	Anthony Alesi	1997	821
166 0/8	23 0/8	27 0/8	20 1/8	8	7	Ross County	OH	Randy Johnson	1981	823
166 0/8	21 5/8	20 2/8	15 3/8	8	8	Pope County	AR	Donald Alan Barnett	1983	823
166 0/8	24 4/8	22 5/8	18 1/8	7	8	Talbot County	MD	Ritchy Eason	1987	823
166 0/8	25 5/8	26 1/8	18 4/8	8	8	Winnebago County	IA	Greg Beaver	1996	823
166 0/8	25 2/8	24 7/8	17 3/8	10	6	Clinton County	MO	Chris Thomas	1996	823
166 0/8	25 6/8	26 2/8	18 3/8	6	8	Madison County	IA	Gary Knoll	1997	823
166 0/8	26 3/8	26 3/8	19 7/8	6	9	Mills County	IA	Allen Bruce	1997	823
165 7/8	24 2/8	22 2/8	17 3/8	6	6	Arkansas County	AR	Bruce Wiggins	1959	830
165 7/8	21 1/8	25 6/8	19 3/8	8	8	Gallatin County	KY	John C. Vetter	1977	830
165 7/8	23 0/8	22 7/8	19 4/8	6	8	Brown County	IL	Angela Vogel	1983	830
165 7/8	25 4/8	25 1/8	16 3/8	6	8	Carroll County	MD	John F. Brunnett	1986	830
165 7/8	20 3/8	21 6/8	14 5/8	8	9	Sedgwick County	KS	Gary Raney	1988	830
165 7/8	24 0/8	23 6/8	16 4/8	9	6	Hardin County	KY	Dale Roberson	1995	830
165 7/8	23 3/8	23 0/8	17 4/8	5	8	Pike County	MO	Paul Wickerham	1997	830
165 6/8	23 0/8	25 0/8	19 5/8	8	6	Bureau County	IL	Timothy J. Ellis	1992	837
165 6/8	19 0/8	26 6/8	20 0/8	6	5	Pope County	IL	Jeff Richardson	1993	837
165 6/8	23 1/8	23 4/8	18 2/8	7	6	Vermilion County	IL	John D. Brassard, Sr.	1995	837
165 6/8	25 3/8	23 5/8	17 0/8	9	6	Morris County	NJ	Russell Davidson	1995	837
165 6/8	23 5/8	22 0/8	16 1/8	6	7	Polk County	IA	Todd Doering	1996	837
165 5/8	25 0/8	24 5/8	20 4/8	11	8	Washington County	MS	James Goss, Jr.	1987	842
165 5/8	22 3/8	21 5/8	18 6/8	8	7	Delaware County	OH	Brent Forman	1992	842
165 5/8	23 6/8	24 4/8	13 5/8	9	7	Clark County	IL	Michael L. Ealy	1994	842
165 5/8	24 6/8	25 5/8	18 7/8	9	9	Outagamie County	WI	Mark Lamers	1995	842
165 5/8	22 7/8	22 5/8	19 2/8	6	8	Waupaca County	WI	Charlie Diestler	1997	842
165 5/8	25 2/8	24 6/8	18 7/8	5	7	White Fox	SAS	Edward Toelken	1998	842
165 4/8	23 5/8	22 2/8	16 2/8	5	8	Boundary County	ID	Gary Stueve	1991	848
165 4/8	25 3/8	26 5/8	19 4/8	6	6	Lake County	IL	Daniel H. Goff	1995	848
165 4/8	23 0/8	24 0/8	17 6/8	6	6	Stevens County	WA	Glen Berry	1995	848
165 4/8	23 6/8	23 0/8	18 0/8	7	8	Dodge County	WI	Mike Pawelka	1996	848
165 2/8	20 3/8	21 0/8	15 2/8	8	10	Lee County	IA	Gary Frost	1991	852
165 2/8	25 0/8	24 7/8	21 0/8	6	6	McHenry County	IL	William Weiss	1996	852
165 2/8	23 6/8	23 0/8	18 6/8	6	6	Washington County	WI	Mike Reckner	1996	852
165 1/8	21 1/8	23 4/8	17 0/8	7	8	Creek County	OK	Gary Roberson	1991	855
165 1/8	24 4/8	23 6/8	20 3/8	9	7	Brooks County	GA	Charles E. Mullins	1992	855
165 1/8	21 4/8	23 0/8	20 3/8	7	6	Suffolk County	NY	Jim Matuszewski	1992	855
165 1/8	22 4/8	23 0/8	18 5/8	11	8	Summit County	OH	Robert M. Wysocki	1993	855

WHITETAIL DEER (NON-TYPICAL ANTLERS)

Minimum Score 155

SCORE	LENGTH OF MAIN BEAM R	LENGTH OF MAIN BEAM L	INSIDE SPREAD	NUMBER OF POINTS R	NUMBER OF POINTS L	AREA	STATE/PROVINCE	HUNTER'S NAME	DATE	RANK
165 1/8	21 4/8	20 3/8	16 4/8	8	10	Grant County	WI	Eugene Willkomm	1994	855
165 1/8	25 1/8	24 2/8	19 0/8	8	6	Vermilion County	IL	Jim Melton	1997	855
165 1/8	23 6/8	23 6/8	15 6/8	7	5	Hendricks County	IN	Scott L. First	1997	855
165 0/8	24 3/8	24 3/8	19 0/8	9	9	Columbia County	WI	Daniel L. Golz	1987	862
165 0/8	22 3/8	22 1/8	15 0/8	7	8	Wabaunsee County	KS	Ron Phillips	1991	862
165 0/8	23 3/8	23 7/8	17 7/8	7	5	Buffalo County	WI	Thomas H. Schultz	1994	862
165 0/8	22 7/8	23 0/8	14 6/8	6	7	Madison County	TX	Robert G. Skinner	1995	862
164 7/8	20 1/8	22 4/8	16 4/8	7	6	Murray County	MN	Lanny Engler	1975	866
164 7/8	23 2/8	23 7/8	17 2/8	9	8	Beltrami County	MN	Kelly O'Brien	1986	866
164 7/8	20 1/8	20 4/8	19 3/8	6	9	Bentley	ALB	Gary Bruns	1990	866
164 7/8	22 3/8	22 2/8	17 2/8	9	9	Plymouth County	IA	Dale E. Brock	1990	866
164 6/8	18 0/8	20 4/8	16 1/8	9	9	Chippewa County	MN	Steven P. Ellingson	1975	870
164 6/8	21 4/8	20 3/8	17 4/8	7	10	Will County	IL	Gene R. Francisco	1988	870
164 6/8	18 3/8	22 4/8	18 3/8	12	8	Piatt County	IL	Boomer Dolbert	1990	870
164 5/8	23 5/8	22 0/8	18 6/8	6	8	Fulton County	IL	Jeff Parsons	1992	873
164 5/8	20 0/8	18 5/8	15 6/8	9	8	Fremont County	IA	Phillip M. Revering	1995	873
164 5/8	20 1/8	20 5/8	15 6/8	7	7	Waukesha County	WI	Richard A. Riehle, Jr.	1995	873
164 5/8	23 4/8	23 0/8	16 4/8	8	5	Columbia County	WI	Mark Preuss	1997	873
164 5/8	23 4/8	23 5/8	14 1/8	8	8	Columbia County	WI	Kim D. Standke	1997	873
164 4/8	23 4/8	23 4/8	19 0/8	7	10	Iowa County	IA	Bob Moenk	1994	878
164 4/8	25 5/8	25 2/8	19 6/8	8	7	Harrison County	MO	Richard Pemberton	1996	878
164 3/8	24 1/8	22 5/8	17 2/8	7	6	Lake County	IL	Steven Hysell	1995	880
164 2/8	22 1/8	23 4/8	14 2/8	10	6	Rush County	KS	Shawn McHaley	1988	881
164 2/8	26 2/8	25 5/8	19 7/8	4	7	Lawrence County	OH	Pete G. McCloud	1990	881
164 2/8	24 3/8	25 3/8	18 0/8	8	7	Laclede County	MO	Jerry Goans	1996	881
164 2/8	26 2/8	25 1/8	19 5/8	6	7	Ross County	OH	Daniel Rawlings	1997	881
164 1/8	23 5/8	22 1/8	18 5/8	9	8	Winona County	MN	Charles W. Benson	1974	885
164 1/8	23 4/8	23 6/8	20 5/8	5	6	Seward County	KS	Lynn Leonard	1984	885
164 1/8	28 0/8	27 2/8	20 4/8	5	6	Christian County	KY	Thomas A. Patterson	1989	885
164 1/8	20 6/8	22 3/8	16 3/8	7	9	Meeker County	MN	Mike Rollinger	1989	885
164 1/8	27 0/8	26 5/8	18 4/8	8	13	Wyandot County	OH	James D. Herring	1995	885
164 0/8	20 6/8	21 7/8	15 0/8	7	7	Guthrie County	IA	Dick Rote	1980	890
164 0/8	27 0/8	27 3/8	23 3/8	5	5	Fairfax County	VA	Larry C. Sherertz	1987	890
164 0/8	22 0/8	22 3/8	17 6/8	6	6	Lake County	IL	Ted Hysell	1990	890
164 0/8	23 6/8	23 4/8	16 0/8	7	7	Randolph County	IL	Scott Oathout	1991	890
164 0/8	23 6/8	23 0/8	17 6/8	5	6	Coshocton County	OH	Lee Cooper	1993	890
164 0/8	21 6/8	21 3/8	15 7/8	7	9	Boone County	IN	Gary R. Barb	1995	890
164 0/8	23 2/8	23 0/8	19 2/8	8	7	Pike County	IL	Ben Beine	1996	890
163 7/8	27 1/8	25 1/8	20 5/8	6	6	Dickinson County	IA	Eldon L. Kraninger	1969	897
163 6/8	22 0/8	20 6/8	18 7/8	8	7	Kenedy County	TX	Miguel Mireles	1987	898
163 6/8	24 2/8	23 4/8	18 5/8	6	7	Buffalo County	WI	Dave Fredrickson	1994	898
163 5/8	23 4/8	20 7/8	17 6/8	7	8	Pepin County	WI	Mike J. Breitung	1988	900
163 4/8	25 1/8	25 1/8	18 1/8	6	5	Hancock County	ME	Daniel D. Hardy	1990	901
163 3/8	21 2/8	23 5/8	15 5/8	9	5	Wapello County	IA	Rick Grooms	1990	902
163 3/8	19 4/8	20 4/8	18 5/8	6	7	Kane County	IL	Paul Neidhardt	1992	902
163 3/8	24 4/8	24 1/8	21 2/8	7	8	Will County	IL	Alton Miller	1994	902
163 3/8	23 3/8	21 2/8	21 6/8	7	10	Hancock County	WV	William Gary Rusinovich	1995	902
163 2/8	22 7/8	23 5/8	17 2/8	7	9	Elkhart County	IN	Karl E. Miller	1997	906
163 1/8	21 6/8	22 0/8	16 7/8	7	7	Cherry County	NE	Walter Cady	1975	907
163 1/8	20 5/8	20 2/8	17 1/8	7	7	Burke County	GA	John A. "Andy" Tisdale	1989	907
163 1/8	21 5/8	22 4/8	18 7/8	8	7	Sac County	IA	Lee C. Green	1991	907
163 1/8	24 5/8	24 7/8	17 3/8	6	5	Walworth County	WI	Steven Johnson	1994	907
163 1/8	22 4/8	24 2/8	15 7/8	8	7	Prince Georges County	MD	Paul Brocht	1995	907
163 1/8	25 6/8	25 7/8	17 2/8	6	7	Clarke County	IA	Mike Veigulis	1996	907
163 1/8	24 7/8	24 5/8	17 7/8	8	6	Chautauqua County	KS	Steve Stoltz	1996	907
163 0/8	20 6/8	21 1/8	17 0/8	10	11	Caddo County	OK	Donald Boling	1975	914
163 0/8	25 5/8	24 6/8	16 6/8	5	6	Richland County	WI	Katherine A. Ellenbolt	1994	914
162 7/8	20 5/8	20 4/8	17 3/8	7	8	Walsh County	ND	Randy Schuster	1985	916
162 6/8	23 4/8	24 3/8	22 4/8	9	7	Webb County	TX	James Richter, Jr.	1977	917
162 6/8	26 7/8	26 3/8	20 0/8	6	9	Crawford County	IL	Charlie Guyer	1987	917
162 6/8	23 2/8	22 4/8	11 3/8	7	6	Franklin County	OH	Randy Kelley	1991	917
162 6/8	23 2/8	19 3/8	19 3/8	6	8	Buffalo County	WI	Dave Parker	1994	917
162 6/8	23 2/8	23 6/8	15 4/8	7	7	Crook County	WY	Heron H. Head	1995	917
162 6/8	23 1/8	23 1/8	18 5/8	6	9	Suffolk County	NY	Robert Lee III	1996	917
162 5/8	25 2/8	24 1/8	19 1/8	7	5	Burnett County	WI	Scott L. Treague	1989	923
162 5/8	22 1/8	22 1/8	18 7/8	7	8	Columbia County	PA	Paul Weisser, Jr.	1989	923
162 5/8	25 0/8	22 7/8	16 3/8	6	9	Iroquois County	IL	James Albricht	1991	923
162 5/8	24 4/8	21 7/8	16 4/8	6	9	Coshocton County	OH	Bill Randles	1995	923
162 5/8	19 2/8	22 2/8	20 1/8	8	6	Calvert County	MD	Troy T. Naylor	1996	923
162 5/8	23 1/8	25 0/8	17 0/8	8	8	Hardin County	IA	Chad D. Hagen	1997	923
162 4/8	25 7/8	26 5/8	18 3/8	6	9	Houston County	MN	Russell Craig Kruse	1991	929
162 4/8	24 2/8	25 5/8	15 5/8	7	5	Jasper County	MO	Douglas H. Roberts	1991	929
162 4/8	23 7/8	23 5/8	16 7/8	7	6	Clayton County	IA	Mark M. Muir	1992	929
162 4/8	23 0/8	23 4/8	19 6/8	10	7	Taylor County	WI	Tony Caramanidis	1995	929
162 3/8	22 0/8	22 7/8	19 0/8	6	6	Cold Lake	ALB	Eric Rauhanen	1994	933
162 2/8	24 6/8	25 0/8	20 7/8	6	7	Elma	MAN	Wendell Schatkowsky	1990	934
162 2/8	22 1/8	23 0/8	17 7/8	6	6	Pike County	IL	Robert Sacher	1994	934
162 1/8	25 4/8	23 6/8	18 2/8	7	11	Jackson County	IA	Larry R. Zirkelbach	1990	936

WHITETAIL DEER (NON-TYPICAL ANTLERS)

Minimum Score 155 — Continued

SCORE	R MAIN BEAM L		INSIDE SPREAD	R POINTS L		AREA	STATE/PROVINCE	HUNTER'S NAME	DATE	RANK
162 1/8	22 2/8	21 7/8	20 1/8	8	8	Chippewa County	WI	Jeffrey T. Miller	1995	936
162 1/8	22 0/8	21 7/8	18 7/8	8	11	Portage County	WI	Timothy J. Kitowski	1997	936
162 0/8	23 4/8	24 6/8	16 6/8	8	8	Coshocton County	OH	Richard Morgan	1987	939
162 0/8	25 3/8	25 0/8	17 7/8	7	7	Montgomery County	IA	Dick R. Paul	1990	939
162 0/8	22 3/8	22 2/8	16 7/8	7	6	Becker County	MN	Ronald Hendrickson	1993	939
162 0/8	23 5/8	24 7/8	20 5/8	5	10	Ontario County	NY	Lee Beaton	1995	939
162 0/8	26 0/8	25 3/8	18 0/8	6	6	Muskingum County	OH	Arnold Schlater	1995	939
161 7/8	24 7/8	25 5/8	22 0/8	7	9	Cascade County	MT	Kits Smith	1980	944
161 7/8	24 4/8	28 4/8	17 3/8	6	11	Warren County	IA	Bob R. Branchcomb	1988	944
161 7/8	21 7/8	22 6/8	16 2/8	8	7	Gorlitz	SAS	Greg Landstad	1994	944
161 7/8	23 0/8	22 5/8	17 4/8	6	9	Kenosha County	WI	Kevin Meyers	1994	944
161 7/8	21 2/8	23 4/8	19 6/8	9	8	Ogle County	IL	Marvin E. Stewart	1997	944
161 7/8	26 3/8	26 2/8	15 7/8	8	5	Kingman County	KS	George Schuttler	1998	944
161 6/8	22 7/8	23 3/8	20 3/8	7	9	Vernon County	WI	Jeff M. Fish	1992	950
161 6/8	22 0/8	22 2/8	16 1/8	7	8	St. Marys County	MD	Richard Gooding	1996	950
161 5/8	21 6/8	21 0/8	15 6/8	8	9	White Fox	SAS	Edward Toelken	1995	952
161 5/8	21 3/8	22 5/8	19 5/8	6	8	Winneshiek County	IA	Marvin Folstad	1997	952
161 4/8	22 3/8	23 4/8	15 4/8	9	9	Butler County	KS	Dave Rogers	1989	954
161 4/8	23 1/8	24 0/8	16 2/8	7	6	Woodbury County	IA	Matt Van Meter	1995	954
161 3/8	23 5/8	22 2/8	18 0/8	5	7	Tippecanoe County	IN	Brian Blankenship	1994	956
161 3/8	25 4/8	26 3/8	17 3/8	7	6	Mason County	KY	Brian P. Maynard	1995	956
161 2/8	25 2/8	28 4/8	20 1/8	5	9	Des Moines County	IA	Whitey Johnson	1987	958
161 1/8	22 2/8	24 4/8	17 3/8	9	8	Marshall County	MN	Richard Hoff	1983	959
161 1/8	22 4/8	23 3/8	21 7/8	8	7	Sauk County	WI	Pat Reed	1993	959
161 1/8	23 0/8	23 0/8	17 5/8	7	7	Elkhart County	IN	David G. Sanders	1995	959
161 0/8	22 6/8	23 4/8	21 2/8	7	6	Douglas County	NE	Ivan Mascher	1969	962
161 0/8	24 4/8	23 3/8	17 6/8	5	8	Johnson County	NE	Stan Pfingsten	1988	962
161 0/8	20 3/8	21 1/8	15 4/8	6	7	Kleberg County	TX	Jarred W. Peeples	1993	962
161 0/8	22 2/8	22 3/8	13 3/8	7	7	Dane County	WI	William "Bruce" Webb	1995	962
161 0/8	24 5/8	24 4/8	28 3/8	5	6	Will County	IL	Brian Kirkpatrick	1996	962
161 0/8	21 4/8	21 0/8	17 4/8	7	8	Dakota County	MN	Glen J. Tischler	1997	962
160 7/8	22 6/8	23 4/8	19 4/8	7	6	Saginaw County	MI	Marty Massa	1986	968
160 7/8	23 5/8	26 7/8	17 3/8	8	8	Roane County	TN	Rodney Maynard	1986	968
160 7/8	23 0/8	23 0/8	16 1/8	7	5	Jefferson County	WI	Robert G. Magnussen	1996	968
160 6/8	20 4/8	21 4/8	18 4/8	7	5	Bremer County	IA	Steven Sims	1983	971
160 6/8	25 4/8	23 4/8	17 0/8	8	8	Columbiana County	OH	David Tice	1987	971
160 6/8	24 6/8	25 2/8	18 1/8	6	6	Neosho County	KS	William E. Louvier	1992	971
160 6/8	25 6/8	24 1/8	17 6/8	6	7	Nemaha County	KS	Mike Hiltibrand	1993	971
160 5/8	19 6/8	21 6/8	17 0/8	11	9	Adams County	IL	Ray Gedaminski	1967	975
160 5/8	22 2/8	23 4/8	18 4/8	5	9	Rice County	KS	Carl Gillespie	1990	975
160 5/8	21 5/8	22 5/8	18 3/8	7	6	Dane County	WI	Roger Taylor	1995	975
160 5/8	25 0/8	24 1/8	18 3/8	7	7	St. Joseph County	IN	Al Lusk	1997	975
160 4/8	22 1/8	24 7/8	21 6/8	8	10	McDonough County	IL	David S. Irwin	1987	979
160 3/8	23 1/8	23 1/8	16 1/8	8	13	Winnebago County	WI	John M. Duchatschek	1980	980
160 3/8	22 0/8	23 5/8	16 7/8	7	7	Jackson County	MO	Wendell Hood	1991	980
160 3/8	21 7/8	21 5/8	16 7/8	8	6	Brown County	IL	Steven B. Schroeder	1994	980
160 3/8	23 2/8	24 0/8	17 1/8	7	6	Kenedy County	TX	Rich Kimball	1996	980
160 2/8	23 1/8	23 1/8	15 3/8	6	7	Lawrence County	IL	Mike Deckard	1978	984
160 2/8	21 3/8	21 3/8	15 7/8	7	6	Scott County	IA	Jeffrey R. Coonts	1989	984
160 2/8	21 4/8	23 4/8	17 4/8	7	9	Waukesha County	WI	Kyle Kaltz	1994	984
160 1/8	19 7/8	23 0/8	19 1/8	8	6	Kenedy County	TX	Johnnie R. Walters	1994	987
160 0/8	27 4/8	26 6/8	18 0/8	7	6	Gallatin County	KY	William J. Epeards	1980	988
160 0/8	19 0/8	20 2/8	17 2/8	7	9	Rockingham County	NC	Michael R. Chrismon	1987	988
160 0/8	23 6/8	23 5/8	22 1/8	7	8	Dekalb County	IL	Jeffery M. Peterson	1993	988
160 0/8	21 1/8	23 3/8	18 5/8	6	7	Cedar County	IA	Jack J. Sines	1994	988
160 0/8	23 1/8	23 0/8	22 3/8	8	11	Edgar County	IL	Russell Guthrie	1995	988
160 0/8	23 5/8	23 0/8	15 5/8	9	6	Harper County	KS	Darren Boden	1997	988
159 7/8	22 1/8	24 4/8	19 2/8	9	8	Edmonton	ALB	Brian Bruce	1981	994
159 7/8	23 2/8	24 1/8	18 2/8	5	6	Huron County	OH	Donald W. Howard	1984	994
159 7/8	21 4/8	20 2/8	16 2/8	6	6	Huron County	OH	John R. Gockstetter	1984	994
159 7/8	23 2/8	23 1/8	17 4/8	6	7	Columbia County	WI	Neil D. Miller	1995	994
159 7/8	25 5/8	25 3/8	22 7/8	8	7	Polk County	IA	Reenie Doornenbal	1996	994
159 6/8	21 6/8	26 5/8	15 6/8	10	7	Greene County	AR	Randy Ladd	1985	999
159 6/8	20 5/8	21 5/8	17 0/8	11	8	Dane County	WI	Karl J. Ketelboeter	1993	999
159 6/8	22 7/8	21 5/8	16 7/8	7	7	Cass County	NE	Duane Denton	1995	999
159 4/8	20 7/8	20 5/8	15 4/8	6	8	McPherson County	KS	Kenneth L. Vogts	1979	1,002
159 4/8	23 3/8	25 4/8	17 5/8	7	6	Davis County	IA	Douglas E. Miller	1997	1,002
159 3/8	25 2/8	25 3/8	16 1/8	10	6	Vernon County	WI	Daniel F. Malin	1986	1,004
159 3/8	22 6/8	22 2/8	18 5/8	7	8	Brown County	IL	Angela Vogel	1987	1,004
159 3/8	23 1/8	23 0/8	15 3/8	6	7	Cherokee County	OK	Jeff Matlock	1995	1,004
159 3/8	23 3/8	25 3/8	19 7/8	5	9	Edgar County	IL	William M. Liffick	1996	1,004
159 2/8	21 3/8	20 3/8	16 2/8	7	10	Knox County	OH	Dennis Campbell	1992	1,008
159 2/8	22 1/8	21 7/8	15 4/8	7	8	Kenedy County	TX	Grayson Lacey	1993	1,008
159 2/8	23 0/8	22 5/8	17 3/8	7	9	Buffalo County	WI	Daniel G. Motszko	1994	1,008
159 2/8	22 6/8	23 2/8	19 2/8	8	5	Clarke County	IA	Don Mealey	1994	1,008
159 2/8	23 3/8	23 3/8	18 2/8	7	6	Outagamie County	WI	Randy Lemke	1995	1,008
159 2/8	23 1/8	24 1/8	21 3/8	7	6	Bedford County	VA	John P. Dowdy	1995	1,008
159 1/8	21 5/8	21 6/8	13 3/8	8	10	Scott County	KY	Vic Morrison	1972	1,014

WHITETAIL DEER (NON-TYPICAL ANTLERS)

Minimum Score 155

SCORE	LENGTH OF MAIN BEAM R	LENGTH OF MAIN BEAM L	INSIDE SPREAD	NUMBER OF POINTS R	NUMBER OF POINTS L	AREA	STATE/PROVINCE	HUNTER'S NAME	DATE	RANK
159 1/8	21 0/8	21 3/8	16 6/8	6	9	Columbia County	WI	Scott M. Hazard	1980	1,014
159 1/8	22 3/8	21 4/8	14 2/8	6	8	Price County	WI	Ernie P. Jablonsky, Jr.	1995	1,014
159 1/8	22 2/8	21 5/8	21 3/8	5	11	Garvin County	OK	Lindell R. Armstrong	1995	1,014
159 0/8	24 0/8	24 4/8	17 3/8	7	5	Lake County	IL	Robert H. Fugett	1976	1,018
159 0/8	22 5/8	21 5/8	21 1/8	6	8	Sullivan County	IN	Steve Hobbs	1980	1,018
159 0/8	22 6/8	23 6/8	17 7/8	7	6	Winnebago County	IL	Gordon Bates	1994	1,018
159 0/8	18 4/8	19 2/8	14 6/8	7	8	Lafayette County	WI	Richard Ames	1997	1,018
158 7/8	27 1/8	25 1/8	22 7/8	5	6	Buffalo County	WI	Ted Bauer	1984	1,022
158 7/8	25 4/8	25 1/8	15 4/8	7	7	Washtenaw County	MI	Larry R. Lange	1984	1,022
158 7/8	25 5/8	25 3/8	16 5/8	7	7	Monroe County	IL	Wayne Doerr	1987	1,022
158 7/8	24 4/8	24 5/8	21 3/8	8	6	Clark County	IL	Eric Montgomery	1994	1,022
158 7/8	23 5/8	22 7/8	19 4/8	6	5	Haskell County	KS	Neal Heaton	1996	1,022
158 6/8	25 0/8	25 1/8	20 4/8	8	6	Osborne County	KS	Robert Grabast	1981	1,027
158 6/8	23 2/8	21 2/8	17 7/8	7	7	Jo Daviess County	IL	Gerald J. Dupasquier	1987	1,027
158 6/8	25 0/8	26 1/8	20 0/8	9	4	Licking County	OH	Scott Popplewell	1997	1,027
158 5/8	21 2/8	21 1/8	14 5/8	6	7	Sullivan County	IN	John P. Hale	1986	1,030
158 5/8	23 6/8	24 0/8	16 1/8	7	8	Elk County	KS	Jason Beem	1995	1,030
158 5/8	22 6/8	22 0/8	15 5/8	5	6	Brown County	SD	Eric J. Voss	1995	1,030
158 5/8	18 6/8	24 2/8	14 4/8	9	10	Carroll County	OH	Martin V. Joliat	1996	1,030
158 5/8	22 1/8	22 3/8	18 3/8	7	7	Peoria County	IL	Ross A. Edwards	1997	1,030
158 4/8	22 6/8	24 1/8	19 4/8	7	4	Winona County	MN	Randy Supalla	1985	1,035
158 4/8	23 6/8	22 6/8	16 4/8	7	7	Winnebago County	WI	Michael S. Henschel	1993	1,035
158 4/8	25 7/8	23 4/8	15 2/8	7	9	Bent County	CO	Bob Renner	1995	1,035
158 4/8	25 2/8	26 2/8	19 6/8	7	7	Ross County	OH	Terry Bridenbaugh	1998	1,035
158 3/8	24 7/8	24 0/8	16 2/8	8	6	Morrison County	MN	Duane Rodine	1987	1,039
158 2/8	23 0/8	23 1/8	21 0/8	7	6	La Salle County	IL	John Thomas	1988	1,040
158 2/8	21 1/8	21 4/8	16 6/8	8	6	Greene County	PA	Donald Angott	1998	1,040
158 1/8	19 2/8	21 0/8	17 1/8	6	8	Jackson County	MI	Kim H. Whittman	1982	1,042
158 1/8	22 0/8	20 4/8	14 5/8	6	7	Hughes County	OK	Trent Hodgins	1993	1,042
158 0/8	24 3/8	23 4/8	18 2/8	6	6	Peoria County	IL	E. Scott Phillips	1994	1,044
158 0/8	20 7/8	22 0/8	17 4/8	8	11	Gwinnett County	GA	Stephen Patrick Finn	1995	1,044
158 0/8	23 6/8	24 1/8	22 4/8	7	5	Suffolk County	NY	Paul Sharpe	1995	1,044
158 0/8	23 5/8	21 7/8	15 3/8	7	7	Greene County	OH	Neil D. Preibisch	1996	1,044
158 0/8	20 4/8	19 6/8	15 1/8	6	6	Thurston County	NE	Kelly S. Buske	1997	1,044
158 0/8	25 3/8	23 7/8	16 0/8	7	7	Waukesha County	WI	James Rossi	1997	1,044
157 7/8	22 6/8	23 2/8	16 7/8	10	8	Dane County	WI	Donald W. Pache	1982	1,050
157 7/8	25 1/8	21 4/8	18 0/8	8	5	Macoupin County	IL	Floyd Wiltshire	1987	1,050
157 7/8	24 5/8	24 6/8	21 2/8	5	6	Suffolk County	NY	Glen Thorne	1996	1,050
157 7/8	21 7/8	22 6/8	18 2/8	7	8	Montgomery County	IL	Toby Hicks	1997	1,050
157 6/8	23 7/8	22 7/8	17 4/8	7	7	Lincoln County	SD	Mac Butler	1987	1,054
157 6/8	21 6/8	21 4/8	17 0/8	8	7	Saunders County	NE	Joseph S. Loomis	1993	1,054
157 6/8	23 1/8	22 4/8	19 5/8	7	7	Oneida County	WI	Randy W. Michael	1993	1,054
157 6/8	21 6/8	21 7/8	18 4/8	5	6	Jackson County	MO	Jeff Stahl	1994	1,054
157 6/8	21 0/8	22 1/8	16 2/8	10	9	Morris County	KS	Shawn Younts	1996	1,054
157 5/8	25 3/8	25 1/8	17 5/8	8	8	Black Hawk County	IA	Darrell Zacharias	1976	1,059
157 5/8	21 5/8	21 6/8	13 4/8	8	9	Menard County	IL	Barry D. Sampson	1992	1,059
157 5/8	21 0/8	21 4/8	16 1/8	6	9	Adams County	WI	Tim Hickey	1995	1,059
157 3/8	20 3/8	24 2/8	18 1/8	7	6	Guernsey County	OH	Robert T. Fedorke, Jr.	1993	1,062
157 3/8	23 0/8	24 2/8	17 2/8	7	7	Green Lake County	WI	Rodney R. Sommer	1998	1,062
157 2/8	22 4/8	19 6/8	22 4/8	6	6	Crawford County	IA	Scott Pelino	1990	1,064
157 2/8	23 4/8	25 3/8	19 1/8	8	7	Montgomery County	IL	Charles O. Herman III	1991	1,064
157 2/8	26 6/8	26 6/8	18 1/8	6	7	Raleigh County	WV	Jackie Davis	1997	1,064
157 1/8	23 1/8	22 7/8	16 4/8	8	6	Rock County	WI	Daniel T. Steinke	1982	1,067
156 7/8	23 2/8	22 2/8	16 2/8	8	9	Suffolk County	NY	Neal Heaton	1994	1,068
156 7/8	22 6/8	22 1/8	18 1/8	6	6	Menard County	IL	Ron Wadsworth	1996	1,068
156 7/8	25 4/8	22 6/8	23 4/8	5	6	Lake County	IL	Kris Wilson	1997	1,068
156 6/8	26 7/8	24 7/8	18 4/8	9	7	Prince Georges County	MD	Anthony C. Malpasso	1979	1,071
156 6/8	23 4/8	23 4/8	16 5/8	8	5	Buffalo County	WI	Pat Slaby	1986	1,071
156 6/8	22 1/8	22 2/8	18 1/8	8	9	Jackson County	MO	Daniel L. Johnson	1986	1,071
156 6/8	21 6/8	21 2/8	16 6/8	7	7	Green Lake County	WI	Douglas L. Jenkins	1995	1,071
156 5/8	23 7/8	24 3/8	20 1/8	8	7	Highland County	OH	Samuel D. Chinn	1993	1,075
156 5/8	19 4/8	21 2/8	13 7/8	9	7	Lake County	IL	Aaron J. Jecevicus	1994	1,075
156 5/8	25 2/8	25 1/8	13 6/8	6	4	Greenwood County	KS	Mike Holland	1996	1,075
156 4/8	24 6/8	23 3/8	20 2/8	7	9	Winnebago County	IL	Jim Dorney	1975	1,078
156 4/8	21 2/8	22 0/8	18 1/8	7	6	Monroe County	NY	David Stymus	1991	1,078
156 4/8	19 5/8	21 3/8	16 2/8	6	8	Clay County	MN	Joe Lahlum	1991	1,078
156 4/8	19 2/8	18 7/8	15 0/8	8	6	Valley County	MT	Michael J. Sandy	1992	1,078
156 4/8	23 4/8	25 2/8	19 7/8	5	5	Sedgwick County	KS	Louis E. Turner	1994	1,078
156 3/8	21 6/8	21 2/8	20 2/8	7	6	Washington County	KS	Doug Kruse	1993	1,083
156 3/8	21 4/8	21 4/8	21 1/8	9	8	Suffolk County	NY	James Matuszewski	1995	1,083
156 3/8	24 6/8	24 3/8	18 1/8	5	5	Jefferson County	WI	Robert Simoneau	1998	1,083
156 2/8	23 2/8	20 0/8	16 4/8	8	5	Holt County	NE	Darrell Clyde	1963	1,086
156 2/8	21 5/8	22 4/8	17 2/8	7	5	Meriwether County	GA	William Clark Brown	1990	1,086
156 2/8	20 1/8	20 6/8	16 4/8	8	6	Buffalo County	WI	Randy C. Reidt	1993	1,086
156 2/8	26 7/8	26 4/8	20 4/8	6	6	Delaware County	IA	Dean Dempster	1995	1,086
156 2/8	24 1/8	24 5/8	18 4/8	8	4	Dubuque County	IA	Michael D. Wolter	1995	1,086
156 1/8	24 4/8	27 7/8	23 3/8	8	9	Cottonwood County	MN	Joe Earl	1959	1,091
156 1/8	24 5/8	25 5/8	20 3/8	5	5	Lake County	IL	Mike Mitten	1984	1,091

WHITETAIL DEER (NON-TYPICAL ANTLERS)

Minimum Score 155 — Continued

SCORE	LENGTH OF MAIN BEAM R	LENGTH OF MAIN BEAM L	INSIDE SPREAD	NUMBER OF POINTS R	NUMBER OF POINTS L	AREA	STATE/PROVINCE	HUNTER'S NAME	DATE	RANK
156 1/8	23 4/8	23 0/8	20 6/8	6	7	Walworth County	WI	Al Lehman	1988	1,091
156 0/8	25 3/8	24 0/8	15 7/8	8	6	Stewart County	TN	Ronald M. Widner	1974	1,094
156 0/8	21 0/8	22 0/8	18 5/8	7	7	Lake County	SD	Lonnie Iverson	1987	1,094
156 0/8	24 4/8	23 4/8	15 6/8	8	6	Poinsett County	AR	Wallace G. Perkins	1994	1,094
156 0/8	22 6/8	23 2/8	16 1/8	6	6	Uvalde County	TX	John T. Halbert	1997	1,094
156 0/8	24 5/8	24 1/8	17 0/8	10	7	Cass County	MI	Wilbur Seager, Jr.	1997	1,094
155 7/8	27 4/8	27 0/8	21 4/8	6	6	Bureau County	IL	Lester Behrends	1992	1,099
155 7/8	22 0/8	23 2/8	15 5/8	7	7	Pulaski County	KY	Billy Taylor	1994	1,099
155 6/8	23 2/8	23 7/8	20 2/8	6	6	Sedgwick County	KS	Keith Jopp	1987	1,101
155 6/8	22 0/8	22 3/8	15 5/8	8	7	Cadogan	ALB	Vernon C. Smedley	1994	1,101
155 6/8	22 4/8	21 2/8	16 0/8	7	6	Jo Daviess County	IL	Tim Koester	1997	1,101
155 6/8	23 1/8	21 2/8	19 2/8	4	8	Monroe County	OH	Dave Gomish	1997	1,101
155 5/8	25 3/8	24 1/8	18 6/8	6	5	Chickasaw County	IA	David J. Kerkove	1995	1,105
155 5/8	20 4/8	18 7/8	16 4/8	8	10	Ravalli County	MT	James A. Schott	1996	1,105
155 5/8	22 2/8	22 3/8	19 0/8	6	6	Waukesha County	WI	James A. Hitchcock	1997	1,105
155 4/8	25 1/8	25 1/8	16 3/8	9	9	Pottawatomie County	KS	Richard L. Ruetti	1970	1,108
155 4/8	23 0/8	21 0/8	19 4/8	6	8	Douglas County	MN	Al Ratajesak	1986	1,108
155 4/8	21 5/8	23 0/8	17 3/8	6	6	Fayette County	IA	James E. Smith	1991	1,108
155 4/8	23 6/8	23 2/8	22 0/8	6	6	Logan County	WV	Raymond Snyder	1995	1,108
155 3/8	21 2/8	21 3/8	16 5/8	12	8	Winona County	MN	John W. Zahrte	1974	1,112
155 3/8	24 2/8	23 6/8	17 6/8	7	8	Morton County	ND	Dennis Simenson	1981	1,112
155 3/8	22 0/8	22 4/8	15 2/8	6	6	Vigo County	IN	Lowell Leturgez	1991	1,112
155 3/8	23 2/8	23 5/8	16 7/8	7	5	Warren County	OH	Sam Y. Perone	1993	1,112
155 3/8	20 6/8	19 0/8	12 5/8	7	8	Shawnee County	KS	Richard Hochanadel	1993	1,112
155 2/8	23 3/8	23 7/8	18 6/8	7	7	Missoula County	MT	Dino Fanelli	1994	1,117
155 2/8	22 0/8	22 4/8	17 0/8	9	7	Washington County	OH	Tulsa Lee Green	1995	1,117
155 2/8	22 3/8	22 6/8	20 0/8	5	8	Rogers County	OK	Brian J. Potter	1998	1,117
155 1/8	25 5/8	22 5/8	20 3/8	4	6	Jo Daviess County	IL	James Boop	1991	1,120
155 1/8	26 2/8	24 2/8	21 3/8	7	4	Ashtabula County	OH	James D. Bunce, Jr.	1994	1,120
155 1/8	22 6/8	22 1/8	15 1/8	6	7	Buffalo County	WI	Tony Heil	1995	1,120
155 1/8	20 4/8	21 2/8	16 6/8	6	7	Rock County	WI	Terry Saunders	1997	1,120
155 0/8	24 4/8	23 7/8	17 2/8	8	5	McCreary County	KY	Eddie Howard	1985	1,124
155 0/8	23 5/8	23 4/8	16 5/8	7	8	Buffalo County	WI	Robert P. Jansen	1994	1,124
155 0/8	24 2/8	24 0/8	22 4/8	6	6	Delaware County	OH	Maurice Rice	1994	1,124
155 0/8	26 0/8	25 6/8	14 4/8	6	4	Winona County	MN	David R. Olson	1995	1,124
155 0/8	25 1/8	24 3/8	16 0/8	5	7	Waukesha County	WI	Dan Bauman	1996	1,124
154 7/8	22 0/8	21 2/8	15 1/8	7	7	Lake County	IL	Mark Mitten	1993	1,129
154 0/8	22 2/8	23 4/8	17 6/8	7	7	Montgomery County	IL	Mark A. Laurent	1992	1,130
153 0/8	24 5/8	22 6/8	22 2/8	7	5	Fawcett	ALB	Helgie Eymundson	1992	1,131
153 0/8	23 3/8	23 0/8	17 3/8	7	5	Wabaunsee County	KS	Ronald Arand	1993	1,132
152 2/8	20 1/8	19 5/8	14 3/8	7	8	Sheridan County	MT	Dr. Robert Kane	1994	1,133
151 6/8	24 6/8	25 2/8	14 3/8	7	7	Washington County	IA	Larry Blum	1989	1,134
151 5/8	23 4/8	24 0/8	17 7/8	11	11	Butler County	KS	Rick Kirk	1991	1,135
151 5/8	23 7/8	23 6/8	13 7/8	9	10	Hennepin County	MN	Kieth Stephas	1992	1,135
151 5/8	24 7/8	24 0/8	19 6/8	6	5	Gallia County	OH	Ron Greathouse	1993	1,135
150 3/8	22 5/8	23 2/8	17 0/8	8	6	Kalamazoo County	MI	John V. Menzor	1993	1,138
150 1/8	23 3/8	24 1/8	17 6/8	7	8	Crawford County	IL	Billy J. Waddell	1994	1,139

WHITETAIL DEER (NON-TYPICAL VELVET ANTLERS)

Minimum Score 155

SCORE	LENGTH OF MAIN BEAM R	LENGTH OF MAIN BEAM L	INSIDE SPREAD	NUMBER OF POINTS R	NUMBER OF POINTS L	AREA	STATE/PROVINCE	HUNTER'S NAME	DATE	RANK
197 4/8	20 7/8	21 3/8	17 4/8	9	12	Birchbark Lake	SAS	Edward H. Kowal	1996	*
177 2/8	18 1/8	17 0/8	13 2/8	13	18	Hardin County	IA	Keith Robison	1997	*
170 0/8	22 4/8	23 4/8	18 0/8	7	6	Okanogan County	WA	Kirk Sapp	1998	*

* *Velvet entries will be listed in only one record book.*

World Record Roosevelt "Olympic" Elk
Score: 367 3/8
Tillamook County, Oregon - 1985
Hunter: Dale Baumgarter/Ken Sisco

ROOSEVELT "OLYMPIC" ELK

Minimum Score 225

Cervus elaphus roosevelti

SCORE	LENGTH OF MAIN BEAM R	L	INSIDE SPREAD	NUMBER OF POINTS R	L	AREA	STATE/PROVINCE	HUNTER'S NAME	DATE	RANK
367 3/8	43 5/8	45 6/8	40 0/8	7	8	Tillamook County	OR	D. Baumgartner / K. Sisco	1985	1
353 3/8	51 6/8	53 1/8	38 2/8	7	7	Columbia County	OR	Ken R. Adamson	1985	2
343 6/8	54 7/8	56 0/8	39 5/8	7	7	Curry County	OR	Kendal Smith	1986	3
343 3/8	51 4/8	52 3/8	31 5/8	7	7	Clatsop County	OR	Jim Pekola	1995	4
343 2/8	48 4/8	49 5/8	38 6/8	8	7	Lewis County	WA	Keith Heldreth	1988	5
339 6/8	47 4/8	48 1/8	35 6/8	7	7	Union Bay	BC	Thomas J. Hoffman	1995	6
331 4/8	47 2/8	44 1/8	39 2/8	7	9	Washer Creek	BC	Archie J. Nesbitt	1997	7
326 2/8	47 3/8	48 0/8	34 1/8	7	7	Clatsop County	OR	Marte Scheuffele	1981	8
324 4/8	45 3/8	44 6/8	44 6/8	7	7	Jefferson County	WA	Larry Haddock	1988	9
318 6/8	45 7/8	44 5/8	37 0/8	6	6	Jefferson County	WA	David J. Miller	1986	10
318 5/8	50 2/8	53 1/8	41 0/8	6	7	Douglas County	OR	Shane Kronberger	1996	11
318 4/8	51 1/8	48 0/8	38 5/8	6	7	Vancouver Island	BC	Ed Kellow	1993	12
315 6/8	48 5/8	46 2/8	31 4/8	6	6	Lewis County	WA	Marte Scheuffele	1990	13
315 2/8	41 6/8	43 0/8	39 6/8	7	7	Columbia County	OR	David Evenson	1998	14
312 4/8	42 1/8	41 3/8	48 0/8	7	7	Columbia County	OR	Marte Scheuffele	1976	15
312 4/8	52 1/8	49 5/8	36 2/8	6	6	Coos County	OR	Robert Dean Dunson	1982	15
312 1/8	48 5/8	46 5/8	34 3/8	6	7	Clallam County	WA	Michael L. Fisher	1993	17
309 6/8	48 6/8	48 0/8	38 2/8	6	7	Clallam County	WA	Jon Blank	1997	18
309 1/8	47 3/8	40 6/8	40 7/8	7	7	Jefferson County	WA	Walter L. Campbell	1987	19
309 0/8	47 2/8	48 2/8	38 6/8	7	6	Douglas County	OR	Bert Petit	1984	20
308 1/8	48 4/8	48 4/8	42 3/8	6	7	Coos County	OR	Dean Dunson	1986	21
307 3/8	51 4/8	51 0/8	41 2/8	6	8	Jefferson County	WA	David Sanford	1997	22
306 6/8	50 2/8	50 4/8	38 6/8	6	6	Polk County	OR	James Wallen	1980	23
306 2/8	48 5/8	48 3/8	38 2/8	6	6	Jefferson County	WA	Chong Pak	1992	24
306 1/8	49 2/8	45 4/8	40 4/8	7	6	Jefferson County	WA	Monte Dahlstrom	1987	25
304 4/8	44 2/8	42 0/8	47 2/8	6	6	Grays Harbor County	WA	Jim Pekola	1992	26
303 1/8	47 1/8	45 1/8	39 0/8	6	6	Jefferson County	WA	Ray Capp	1997	27
302 3/8	43 4/8	45 2/8	39 0/8	7	6	Jefferson County	WA	Jim Pekola	1994	28
301 0/8	45 0/8	47 3/8	37 1/8	8	8	Washington County	OR	Jon King	1987	29
301 0/8	47 0/8	46 6/8	42 7/8	6	6	Jefferson County	WA	Russ Poppe	1994	29
300 5/8	48 7/8	47 1/8	42 0/8	6	6	Curry County	OR	Allen Boice	1998	31
300 3/8	48 2/8	50 7/8	36 1/8	5	6	Washington County	OR	Marte Scheuffele	1975	32
299 6/8	46 4/8	43 2/8	36 3/8	8	7	Columbia County	OR	Kelley Lungberg	1993	33
298 7/8	46 3/8	46 5/8	41 6/8	6	6	Jefferson County	WA	Wayne McReynolds	1990	34
298 6/8	48 3/8	49 3/8	33 6/8	5	6	Lane County	OR	Joe Waite	1981	35
298 6/8	45 5/8	45 2/8	32 0/8	6	7	Jefferson County	WA	Robert C. Allan	1993	35
298 0/8	44 3/8	46 7/8	38 6/8	8	8	Washington County	OR	Ron Adamson	1992	37
297 3/8	41 5/8	41 1/8	38 1/8	6	6	Jefferson County	WA	Doug Smith	1989	38
297 2/8	46 0/8	45 7/8	42 7/8	6	6	Clallam County	WA	Arnold LaGambina	1988	39
296 6/8	40 3/8	41 2/8	39 3/8	6	7	Clatsop County	OR	Edwin J. Thompson	1987	40
296 6/8	43 0/8	43 5/8	41 4/8	6	6	Jefferson County	WA	Kurt Goesch	1989	40
296 4/8	46 6/8	47 0/8	41 3/8	7	7	Pacific County	WA	Jess Martin, Jr.	1971	42
295 6/8	43 2/8	43 3/8	41 1/8	6	7	Clatsop County	OR	Brian Stanley	1992	43
295 0/8	45 6/8	45 4/8	39 0/8	8	7	Columbia County	OR	Smokey Crews	1987	44
294 7/8	46 7/8	49 0/8	41 6/8	6	6	Jefferson County	WA	Bob Rosie	1990	45
294 7/8	48 3/8	48 5/8	38 6/8	6	6	Benton County	OR	Corey Putney	1992	45
294 0/8	44 2/8	46 0/8	41 2/8	6	6	Jefferson County	WA	Sam Windle	1993	47
293 6/8	50 3/8	47 5/8	37 6/8	5	6	Jefferson County	WA	Ronald E. Ihrig	1984	48
293 6/8	42 7/8	46 4/8	34 3/8	9	7	Yamhill County	OR	Dean A. McMullen	1993	48
293 6/8	46 2/8	47 1/8	39 5/8	6	6	Lincoln County	OR	Ted Gibson	1996	48
292 1/8	42 3/8	44 0/8	40 0/8	6	6	Lane County	OR	Thomas A. Whitaker	1988	51
291 4/8	41 0/8	43 1/8	33 5/8	6	7	Pacific County	WA	Dan Free	1983	52
291 2/8	41 1/8	42 1/8	41 4/8	6	6	Clallam County	WA	Russ Spaulding	1985	53
291 1/8	42 3/8	44 1/8	40 0/8	6	7	Curry County	OR	James Atherton	1985	54
291 0/8	42 1/8	42 1/8	37 0/8	7	7	Lincoln County	OR	Terry W. Smith	1997	55
290 2/8	45 2/8	45 6/8	37 6/8	5	5	Jefferson County	WA	Jim Pekola	1993	56
289 2/8	44 7/8	44 4/8	34 6/8	6	6	Clatsop County	OR	Marte Scheuffele	1978	57
289 2/8	44 7/8	44 7/8	32 4/8	6	5	Pacific County	WA	Dan Free	1980	57
285 1/8	47 3/8	48 1/8	37 1/8	6	6	Clackamas County	OR	Randy W. Kubitz	1986	59
284 0/8	42 1/8	43 3/8	40 0/8	8	7	Jefferson County	WA	Daniel J. Siegner	1991	60
283 5/8	47 4/8	48 0/8	40 7/8	6	6	Jefferson County	WA	Robert J. Rosie	1990	61
283 3/8	46 0/8	42 7/8	29 7/8	6	5	Skamania County	WA	Jerry L. Carter	1973	62
283 3/8	46 0/8	47 1/8	30 5/8	6	6	Polk County	OR	Terry W. Smith	1991	62
283 3/8	43 0/8	41 7/8	44 0/8	6	6	Jefferson County	WA	Paul Szumlanski	1991	62
283 2/8	45 3/8	45 3/8	34 4/8	6	6	Pacific County	WA	Jerry Webster	1979	65
283 2/8	43 4/8	41 1/8	38 6/8	6	7	Clallam County	WA	Wayne Haag	1982	65
282 6/8	42 6/8	45 2/8	38 6/8	6	6	Jefferson County	WA	Gary M. Douthit	1986	67
282 4/8	44 6/8	44 1/8	38 7/8	7	6	Afognak Island	AK	Edward L. Russell	1980	68
282 0/8	45 0/8	43 6/8	42 0/8	6	6	Jefferson County	WA	Dave Robertson	1970	69
282 0/8	45 2/8	44 7/8	35 6/8	7	7	Jefferson County	WA	Michael C. Giardino	1992	69
281 1/8	44 3/8	44 7/8	33 6/8	6	8	Lincoln County	OR	Kevin Dean Zook	1996	71
281 0/8	41 6/8	40 7/8	34 4/8	6	6	Jefferson County	WA	Talmadge Dobbs	1989	72
281 0/8	46 4/8	47 1/8	31 1/8	6	6	Yamhill County	OR	Dale R. Thornton	1997	72
280 6/8	45 6/8	44 1/8	38 1/8	6	6	Jefferson County	WA	Donald N. Morey	1978	74
280 4/8	43 2/8	43 0/8	33 0/8	6	6	Lane County	OR	Jeff Sindt	1982	75
280 2/8	42 0/8	43 0/8	39 2/8	6	5	Jefferson County	WA	Wayne McReynolds	1984	76
279 7/8	47 4/8	47 2/8	37 2/8	5	6	Grays Harbor County	WA	G. A. "Toby" Hart	1986	77
279 7/8	44 1/8	46 6/8	34 6/8	5	6	Jefferson County	WA	Jim Pekola	1990	77

ROOSEVELT "OLYMPIC" ELK

Minimum Score 225 — Continued

SCORE	LENGTH OF MAIN BEAM R	LENGTH OF MAIN BEAM L	INSIDE SPREAD	NUMBER OF POINTS R	NUMBER OF POINTS L	AREA	STATE/PROVINCE	HUNTER'S NAME	DATE	RANK
277 4/8	41 1/8	40 0/8	43 0/8	6	6	Jefferson County	WA	Robert C. Allan	1996	79
276 7/8	45 5/8	44 1/8	35 5/8	5	5	Tillamook County	OR	Steve Weeks	1994	80
276 6/8	40 4/8	40 1/8	39 7/8	6	6	Clallam County	WA	Clyde E. Graham	1985	81
276 5/8	41 3/8	41 6/8	36 6/8	6	5	Jefferson County	WA	Kevin Barber	1995	82
275 5/8	48 4/8	45 1/8	38 3/8	5	6	Jefferson County	WA	Jerry Childs	1991	83
275 3/8	37 0/8	37 4/8	36 1/8	7	7	Tillamook County	OR	Alan Richardson	1980	84
275 2/8	41 2/8	38 3/8	36 0/8	7	8	Jefferson County	WA	Jon E. Nelson	1986	85
274 6/8	42 3/8	44 0/8	39 4/8	5	5	Columbia County	OR	Steve Cox	1989	86
274 2/8	48 4/8	47 7/8	36 6/8	5	5	Grays Harbor County	WA	Jim Pekola	1995	87
273 7/8	42 4/8	42 4/8	32 5/8	7	7	Jefferson County	WA	Dave Dasher	1989	88
273 4/8	44 6/8	45 1/8	38 3/8	6	6	Pacific County	WA	Glen Watland	1980	89
273 4/8	42 1/8	42 4/8	35 6/8	6	7	Jefferson County	WA	George Walker	1994	89
273 0/8	44 2/8	44 0/8	35 0/8	5	5	Jefferson County	WA	Ken Chamberlin	1987	91
272 7/8	39 6/8	38 5/8	37 4/8	6	7	Clatsop County	OR	Lester "Skip" Croft, Jr.	1993	92
272 5/8	46 4/8	45	36 1/8	5	5	Jefferson County	WA	Bryan Mittge	1986	93
272 2/8	42 6/8	44 6/8	39 5/8	7	6	Polk County	OR	Tom Krauthoefer	1994	94
272 1/8	39 4/8	40 6/8	33 5/8	5	5	Wahkiakum County	WA	Russ Poppe	1982	95
271 4/8	41 3/8	42 0/8	37 2/8	6	6	Douglas County	OR	Kenneth A. French	1995	96
271 3/8	44 3/8	44 3/8	38 0/8	6	5	Grays Harbor County	WA	Scott Bergen	1985	97
271 2/8	40 2/8	40 2/8	33 4/8	6	6	Cowlitz County	WA	Kelly King	1991	98
271 1/8	46 0/8	45 3/8	33 3/8	6	6	Afognak Island	AK	David Harper	1970	99
270 3/8	38 2/8	39 5/8	36 4/8	8	6	Clatsop County	OR	James L. Friesz	1981	100
270 3/8	40 5/8	42 4/8	37 4/8	6	6	Grays Harbor County	WA	Brian Mitchell	1990	100
270 2/8	44 6/8	44 1/8	44 4/8	4	5	Grays Harbor County	WA	Bill Brown	1959	102
270 2/8	43 2/8	44 2/8	40 3/8	6	5	Jefferson County	WA	Patrick Stoddard	1993	102
270 0/8	41 1/8	42 1/8	36 0/8	5	5	Clallam County	WA	Arne Swanson	1990	104
269 7/8	36 7/8	37 1/8	33 7/8	6	6	Jefferson County	WA	Jim Pekola	1988	105
269 5/8	45 2/8	46 0/8	33 7/8	6	6	Lewis County	WA	Marte Scheuffele	1996	106
269 4/8	39 3/8	40 6/8	39 0/8	5	5	Clallam County	WA	George McDonald	1985	107
269 2/8	45 6/8	45 0/8	33 1/8	6	6	Jefferson County	WA	Ray Capp	1987	108
269 2/8	43 4/8	43 4/8	31 3/8	6	6	Tillamook County	OR	Daniel A. Fleming	1995	108
269 1/8	40 5/8	41 5/8	35 3/8	6	6	Clatsop County	OR	David M. Jones	1982	110
268 7/8	40 5/8	41 1/8	34 1/8	5	7	Coos County	OR	Thomas E. Tipton	1986	111
268 2/8	43 7/8	43 7/8	41 0/8	5	5	Grays Harbor County	WA	Terry Plato	1984	112
268 1/8	38 0/8	39 2/8	37 3/8	6	6	Clatsop County	OR	Ed Beisley	1967	113
267 7/8	44 7/8	44 1/8	33 6/8	6	5	Jefferson County	WA	L. Scot Jenkins	1998	114
267 4/8	38 5/8	36 1/8	35 2/8	8	7	Lincoln County	OR	Timothy J. Edwards	1996	115
267 3/8	37 0/8	36 3/8	34 3/8	6	6	Clatsop County	OR	Douglas W. Hamilton	1982	116
267 2/8	43 3/8	42 4/8	40 2/8	5	5	Jefferson County	WA	Dave Mirka	1987	117
266 5/8	37 3/8	38 1/8	35 5/8	5	5	Clallam County	WA	George McDonald	1989	118
266 5/8	41 7/8	40 6/8	39 3/8	6	5	Conuma Valley	BC	Lance Grubisich	1997	118
266 3/8	46 3/8	41 6/8	45 0/8	5	6	Grays Harbor County	WA	Mark R. Nieznalski	1984	120
266 2/8	42 2/8	45 7/8	32 3/8	6	6	Columbia County	OR	Kent Moeller	1995	121
265 6/8	39 7/8	40 0/8	35 6/8	5	5	Clallam County	WA	George McDonald	1990	122
265 3/8	39 3/8	37 4/8	44 5/8	5	5	Clallam County	WA	Ray Capp	1989	123
264 5/8	38 2/8	36 1/8	33 1/8	5	5	Douglas County	OR	Steve Simpson	1993	124
264 2/8	38 0/8	42 2/8	37 2/8	6	6	Vancouver Island	BC	Gary F. Bogner	1993	125
263 5/8	42 5/8	42 1/8	34 4/8	6	6	Lincoln County	OR	Malcam Moberly	1988	126
263 3/8	41 2/8	42 6/8	29 1/8	6	6	Lane County	OR	Max Lee	1980	127
263 1/8	36 3/8	36 2/8	36 6/8	6	7	Douglas County	OR	Robert J. Huselton	1998	128
262 7/8	40 1/8	40 0/8	34 0/8	6	6	Coos County	OR	Larry Frost	1985	129
262 7/8	44 5/8	45 0/8	32 3/8	6	6	Clatsop County	OR	James A. Davis, Jr.	1997	129
262 2/8	45 4/8	45 5/8	28 6/8	6	6	Douglas County	OR	Dennis Olson	1984	131
262 2/8	38 2/8	38 3/8	33 2/8	5	5	Grays Harbor County	WA	Jim Pekola	1997	131
262 0/8	39 6/8	40 2/8	41 0/8	5	5	Coos County	OR	Tom Tipton	1991	133
261 6/8	43 0/8	43 3/8	38 3/8	6	6	Jefferson County	WA	Robert C. Allan	1988	134
261 5/8	40 7/8	41 2/8	38 7/8	5	5	Jefferson County	WA	Mark J. Tupper	1986	135
261 5/8	40 0/8	40 2/8	36 3/8	6	6	Clatsop County	OR	William H. Stevens	1991	135
261 4/8	41 1/8	41 3/8	36 1/8	6	6	Columbia County	OR	Dale Buxton	1995	137
261 1/8	45 5/8	44 7/8	38 5/8	6	5	Clatsop County	OR	Marte Scheuffele	1989	138
261 1/8	46 2/8	45 6/8	38 0/8	6	5	Tillamook County	OR	Scott McKibbin	1995	138
260 5/8	41 2/8	40 0/8	37 4/8	6	7	Jefferson County	WA	Gaillard R. Graham	1990	140
260 4/8	41 4/8	41 1/8	34 4/8	6	5	Douglas County	OR	J. B. Hollander	1984	141
260 3/8	45 0/8	44 2/8	35 1/8	6	5	Benton County	OR	Timothy Pearson	1989	142
260 0/8	40 1/8	38 6/8	38 7/8	6	6	Columbia County	OR	Smokey Crews	1988	143
259 6/8	43 1/8	42 1/8	37 6/8	6	6	Columbia County	OR	Don Malloy	1988	144
259 2/8	42 3/8	42 4/8	37 0/8	5	5	Coos County	OR	James M. Speelman	1974	145
259 1/8	42 1/8	40 2/8	34 2/8	6	6	Clallam County	WA	Frank LaGambina	1980	146
258 5/8	40 3/8	38 4/8	32 6/8	7	7	Columbia County	OR	Larry W. Fox	1987	147
258 5/8	40 3/8	38 2/8	31 6/8	6	6	Lane County	OR	Todd L. Wilkinson	1996	147
257 6/8	37 7/8	38 4/8	33 0/8	6	6	Clatsop County	OR	Gerald T. Bogh	1993	149
257 1/8	40 4/8	40 0/8	43 1/8	6	6	Columbia County	OR	Randy Jennings	1985	150
256 3/8	44 5/8	45 3/8	30 4/8	6	6	Polk County	OR	Gregg Allen Youngerman	1996	151
255 5/8	36 7/8	36 7/8	38 2/8	7	6	Tillamook County	OR	Parry M. Hurliman	1994	152
255 2/8	41 4/8	42 3/8	38 6/8	5	5	Jefferson County	WA	Daniel Siegner	1993	153

ROOSEVELT "OLYMPIC" ELK

Minimum Score 225 — Continued

SCORE	LENGTH OF MAIN BEAM R	LENGTH OF MAIN BEAM L	INSIDE SPREAD	NUMBER OF POINTS R	NUMBER OF POINTS L	AREA	STATE/PROVINCE	HUNTER'S NAME	DATE	RANK
253 7/8	45 2/8	43 5/8	29 5/8	5	7	Yamhill County	OR	Jerry S. Bailey	1986	154
253 4/8	39 3/8	39 2/8	28 6/8	7	7	Coos County	OR	Craig Matson	1980	155
253 1/8	43 1/8	42 0/8	33 6/8	5	6	Pacific County	WA	Bill Egner	1977	156
253 0/8	35 1/8	36 4/8	36 1/8	6	5	Clatsop County	OR	John C. Bernards	1985	157
253 0/8	39 6/8	38 1/8	31 0/8	6	6	Clatsop County	OR	Bob Bingham	1994	157
252 7/8	40 7/8	42 1/8	31 3/8	6	6	Pacific County	WA	John Wall	1979	159
251 5/8	41 4/8	36 2/8	40 6/8	6	6	Jefferson County	WA	Sanford Windle	1972	160
251 2/8	39 1/8	40 4/8	33 2/8	6	6	Jefferson County	WA	Bill Pudell	1982	161
251 1/8	37 2/8	35 2/8	35 0/8	6	6	Coos County	OR	Robon Evans	1993	162
250 7/8	38 7/8	39 4/8	34 7/8	6	6	Polk County	OR	Terry W. Smith	1996	163
250 4/8	35 6/8	35 5/8	30 0/8	6	7	Clatsop County	OR	Jim Pekola	1997	164
249 5/8	43 2/8	44 6/8	30 3/8	6	6	Tillamook County	OR	Steve Pieren	1982	165
249 4/8	45 3/8	45 7/8	32 6/8	6	6	Polk County	OR	Kevin Dean Zook	1992	166
249 3/8	41 1/8	39 3/8	32 4/8	6	6	Clatsop County	OR	Charles Lee Smith	1990	167
248 4/8	40 0/8	39 3/8	43 1/8	5	5	Jefferson County	WA	Chris Krueger	1987	168
248 4/8	41 7/8	43 4/8	32 2/8	7	5	Jefferson County	WA	Mike Sturman	1991	168
248 3/8	39 1/8	40 2/8	35 3/8	5	5	Jefferson County	WA	Larry Haddock	1987	170
248 2/8	42 6/8	43 0/8	40 2/8	5	5	Jefferson County	WA	Robert J. Rosie	1992	171
247 6/8	34 4/8	36 6/8	37 1/8	5	5	Grays Harbor County	WA	Wayne McReynolds	1981	172
247 6/8	45 2/8	44 2/8	38 7/8	6	5	Coos County	OR	Mark E. Cox	1990	172
247 0/8	39 6/8	38 4/8	39 6/8	5	5	Olympic Peninsula	WA	Lloyd Beebe	1951	174
246 6/8	39 5/8	37 3/8	34 0/8	6	6	Jefferson County	WA	Eugene Wells	1960	175
245 1/8	38 3/8	37 5/8	34 7/8	7	5	Columbia County	OR	Leroy E. Lewis	1989	176
244 4/8	36 5/8	36 2/8	35 7/8	7	7	Clallam County	WA	Arnold La Gambina	1989	177
243 6/8	43 4/8	41 4/8	33 0/8	5	5	Clallam County	WA	Glenn St. Charles	1952	178
243 6/8	34 2/8	33 3/8	34 2/8	6	6	Lincoln County	OR	Randy Smith II	1998	178
243 0/8	45 0/8	44 0/8	40 2/8	5	5	Jefferson County	WA	James M. Stark	1977	180
242 3/8	34 5/8	33 0/8	38 7/8	7	7	Douglas County	OR	Chad T. Montgomery	1993	181
241 6/8	39 7/8	39 1/8	34 6/8	6	5	Clatsop County	OR	David Lawrence	1982	182
241 6/8	39 7/8	38 2/8	39 4/8	5	5	Clallam County	WA	Arnold LaGambina	1986	182
241 5/8	37 1/8	37 1/8	36 1/8	5	5	Washington County	OR	Douglas Rick Clark	1991	184
241 2/8	36 0/8	36 2/8	27 3/8	6	7	Clatsop County	OR	Robert G. Mucken	1989	185
240 7/8	36 7/8	36 3/8	36 6/8	5	6	Douglas County	OR	Richard J. Huselton	1992	186
238 6/8	36 5/8	37 6/8	38 0/8	5	6	Grays Harbor County	WA	Richard Mazzei	1984	187
238 6/8	40 3/8	39 3/8	32 4/8	6	6	Lincoln County	OR	Warren Lynch	1986	187
238 5/8	40 3/8	40 0/8	38 3/8	5	5	Benton County	OR	Donald E. Zuhlke	1989	189
238 2/8	46 2/8	45 1/8	39 6/8	5	4	Pacific County	WA	John R. Martin	1978	190
238 2/8	39 4/8	37 3/8	37 0/8	5	5	Grays Harbor County	WA	Jack McDougall	1986	190
238 0/8	39 7/8	40 4/8	34 2/8	5	5	Jefferson County	WA	Larry Jensen	1985	192
238 0/8	40 0/8	39 7/8	34 6/8	5	6	Lincoln County	OR	Travis L. Robison	1998	192
237 6/8	36 0/8	36 6/8	33 4/8	7	6	Lincoln County	OR	Teddy Kosydar	1989	194
237 2/8	32 4/8	33 1/8	36 2/8	6	6	Clatsop County	OR	Robert J. Wilkie	1984	195
236 6/8	39 0/8	37 3/8	31 3/8	6	6	Jefferson County	WA	Mathew Hayvaz	1984	196
236 6/8	39 5/8	41 5/8	30 7/8	6	6	Lane County	OR	Steven T. Jones	1994	196
236 3/8	36 0/8	34 4/8	27 7/8	5	6	Coos County	OR	James T. Russ	1997	198
236 1/8	37 1/8	38 4/8	32 6/8	6	5	Washington County	OR	Joe Rutledge	1993	199
235 7/8	37 1/8	37 0/8	35 4/8	6	6	Polk County	OR	Joseph K. Saboe	1990	200
235 2/8	38 0/8	39 1/8	34 0/8	5	5	Tillamook County	OR	Smokey Crews	1983	201
235 2/8	37 4/8	38 5/8	33 7/8	5	6	Clallam County	WA	Daniel Siegner	1986	201
235 0/8	39 1/8	39 2/8	31 2/8	6	5	Josephine County	OR	Joel Robertson	1982	203
235 0/8	36 2/8	34 1/8	38 0/8	6	6	Tillamook County	OR	Parry M. Hurliman	1995	203
234 4/8	36 6/8	34 7/8	34 6/8	5	6	Coos County	OR	Bruce B. Stamp	1993	205
234 2/8	39 5/8	38 4/8	33 6/8	5	5	Clallam County	WA	Dean R. Swerin	1985	206
233 4/8	40 2/8	40 6/8	28 6/8	5	5	Grays Harbor County	WA	John J. Durst	1987	207
233 4/8	36 1/8	37 4/8	33 0/8	6	5	Tillamook County	OR	Joe Hulburt	1992	207
233 1/8	41 4/8	40 3/8	30 0/8	5	6	Curry County	OR	Kendal Smith	1982	209
233 0/8	35 6/8	37 1/8	28 0/8	5	5	Pacific County	WA	Parry Bagley	1991	210
232 1/8	40 4/8	41 3/8	33 5/8	5	5	Columbia County	OR	Mitch Elliott	1993	211
231 7/8	35 5/8	37 4/8	32 3/8	5	5	Clallam County	WA	Frank LaGambina	1979	212
231 5/8	40 3/8	39 4/8	40 7/8	5	5	Grays Harbor County	WA	Todd Plato	1992	213
231 4/8	33 4/8	37 4/8	30 2/8	6	5	Grays Harbor County	WA	Jim Pekola	1996	214
231 3/8	35 3/8	33 5/8	30 6/8	6	6	Washington County	OR	Gregory D. Lueptow	1990	215
231 1/8	37 3/8	38 0/8	29 7/8	5	5	Yamhill County	OR	Curtis C. Altman	1983	216
231 0/8	34 2/8	34 6/8	40 0/8	5	6	Clatsop County	OR	Ronald Ray Noel	1989	217
230 6/8	35 2/8	34 4/8	32 2/8	5	5	Clallam County	WA	Wayne Haag	1980	218
230 2/8	38 5/8	36 4/8	38 0/8	5	5	Coos County	OR	Thomas Tipton	1984	219
230 1/8	39 5/8	39 6/8	24 6/8	6	7	Douglas County	OR	Lee R. Hutsell	1996	220
230 0/8	35 6/8	34 7/8	34 0/8	6	6	Yamhill County	OR	Doug Bain	1994	221
229 0/8	44 3/8	44 3/8	35 6/8	5	4	Clallam County	WA	Pete J. Germeau	1982	222
228 1/8	36 7/8	34 7/8	34 1/8	5	5	Columbia County	OR	Mitch Elliott	1987	223
228 0/8	36 2/8	36 0/8	32 1/8	6	6	Curry County	OR	Ken French	1988	224
227 5/8	40 3/8	38 1/8	34 2/8	6	7	Clatsop County	OR	Ray C Nelson	1985	225
227 5/8	41 3/8	38 6/8	34 5/8	5	4	Clallam County	WA	Arnold LaGambina	1987	225
227 2/8	37 5/8	40 4/8	29 4/8	5	6	Benton County	OR	Felix Alan Lafond	1986	227
227 1/8	36 2/8	31 0/8	29 5/8	5	7	Clatsop County	OR	Randy Jennings	1980	228

ROOSEVELT "OLYMPIC" ELK

Minimum Score 225 — Continued

SCORE	LENGTH OF MAIN BEAM R	LENGTH OF MAIN BEAM L	INSIDE SPREAD	NUMBER OF POINTS R	NUMBER OF POINTS L	AREA	STATE/PROVINCE	HUNTER'S NAME	DATE	RANK
227 1/8	42 1/8	40 6/8	28 3/8	6	5	Clatsop County	OR	David Braem	1982	228
227 0/8	38 1/8	36 3/8	35 1/8	6	6	Lincoln County	OR	Richard Smith	1989	230
227 0/8	37 4/8	37 4/8	30 5/8	5	6	Clatsop County	OR	Roy R. Stevens	1992	230
226 3/8	42 0/8	40 6/8	26 5/8	5	5	Clatsop County	OR	Jim Pekola	1993	232
226 1/8	39 1/8	38 5/8	29 5/8	5	5	Yamhill County	OR	Patrick L. McGanty	1993	233
225 4/8	37 0/8	35 6/8	35 2/8	5	5	Jefferson County	WA	Rodger Squirrel	1984	234
225 3/8	33 0/8	32 7/8	33 3/8	6	7	Polk County	OR	Gary Freuler	1988	235

World Record Yellowstone "American" Elk (Typical Antlers)
Score: 404 0/8
Coconino County, Arizona - 1992
Hunter: William Wright

YELLOWSTONE "AMERICAN" ELK (TYPICAL ANTLERS)

Minimum Score 260

Cervus elaphus nelsoni and certain related subspecies

SCORE	LENGTH OF R MAIN BEAM L		INSIDE SPREAD	NUMBER OF R POINTS L		AREA	STATE/ PROVINCE	HUNTER'S NAME	DATE	RANK
404 0/8	56 4/8	57 1/8	44 0/8	7	7	Coconino County	AZ	William Wright	1992	1
400 4/8	58 0/8	60 4/8	43 0/8	6	6	Coconino County	AZ	Larry C. Fischer	1998	2
398 3/8	60 3/8	65 4/8	50 5/8	7	8	Navajo County	AZ	Marvin W. Wuertz	1993	3
395 0/8	56 4/8	54 3/8	39 4/8	7	6	Childs Lake	MAN	Irvin Funk	1998	4
393 2/8	57 6/8	57 6/8	43 7/8	7	7	Coconino County	AZ	Chad J. Connor	1995	5
393 1/8	61 5/8	63 0/8	43 7/8	7	9	Montrose County	CO	Wayne Bradley	1986	6
391 4/8	55 4/8	56 4/8	43 3/8	6	6	Catron County	NM	Bob Miller	1997	7
390 7/8	55 3/8	55 1/8	36 5/8	6	6	Duck Mtns.	MAN	Melvin J. Podaima	1991	8
390 7/8	57 5/8	60 2/8	42 7/8	9	8	Grant County	NM	David L. Morgan	1992	8
389 2/8	63 6/8	63 0/8	42 1/8	7	7	Coconino County	AZ	Jay Elmer	1980	10
389 1/8	59 7/8	58 5/8	41 6/8	8	7	Catron County	NM	Kim E. Womer	1998	11
388 1/8	54 4/8	54 6/8	40 3/8	6	7	Meagher County	MT	D. "Mitch" Kottas	1994	12
388 0/8	54 6/8	54 0/8	41 6/8	7	6	Beaver County	UT	Daniel Carter	1998	13
387 3/8	54 7/8	57 6/8	51 5/8	6	7	Catron County	NM	Brad Miller	1995	14
386 5/8	53 5/8	53 6/8	41 2/8	8	7	Madison County	MT	Allan Mintken	1986	15
386 4/8	56 4/8	55 0/8	51 4/8	7	6	Larimer County	CO	David McCormick	1997	16
386 0/8	61 2/8	59 6/8	37 2/8	8	8	Coconino County	AZ	Randy Elmer	1988	17
385 6/8	55 3/8	55 6/8	50 0/8	7	7	Beaverhead County	MT	Ray Ford	1998	18
385 2/8	55 5/8	56 5/8	40 4/8	6	6	Catron County	NM	Tracy G. Hardy	1993	19
384 6/8	55 2/8	53 4/8	44 2/8	6	7	Coconino County	AZ	Jay Elmer	1979	20
384 4/8	53 4/8	54 6/8	45 4/8	7	7	Meagher County	MT	David Snyder	1981	21
384 2/8	58 0/8	58 0/8	43 0/8	6	6	Catron County	NM	Robert John Seeds	1996	22
384 1/8	57 6/8	62 6/8	47 7/8	6	7	Coconino County	AZ	Mike Taylor	1985	23
384 1/8	50 5/8	50 4/8	41 1/8	6	6	Coconino County	AZ	Dave Pierce	1997	23
383 4/8	56 7/8	55 5/8	38 6/8	7	6	Coconino County	AZ	Gilbert Romero	1992	25
383 3/8	65 0/8	61 7/8	48 5/8	6	6	Catron County	NM	Rudy O. Duran	1988	26
382 6/8	58 7/8	56 4/8	40 6/8	7	7	Coconino County	AZ	Patrick J. Loescher	1997	27
382 2/8	60 0/8	60 0/8	47 2/8	6	6	Coconino County	AZ	Don R. Newton, Jr.	1985	28
382 2/8	51 7/8	52 5/8	39 6/8	7	6	Fergus County	MT	LeRoy Sabe	1996	28
381 3/8	56 4/8	56 6/8	34 7/8	6	6	Catron County	NM	Gary Jamieson	1993	30
380 6/8	56 7/8	55 5/8	48 0/8	6	7	Socorro County	NM	Michael S. Weldon	1992	31
380 6/8	57 0/8	54 3/8	47 2/8	7	7	Coconino County	AZ	John C. McClendon	1995	31
380 5/8	56 0/8	56 0/8	43 0/8	8	8	Apache County	AZ	Mike Aleff	1995	33
380 3/8	53 4/8	53 2/8	51 7/8	7	7	Rich County	UT	Fahy S. Robinson, Jr.	1988	34
380 3/8	56 3/8	58 0/8	44 1/8	7	6	Catron County	NM	Don Parks, Jr.	1988	34
380 2/8	56 2/8	54 1/8	45 0/8	7	6	Coconino County	AZ	Doug Kittredge	1975	36
380 2/8	53 3/8	53 0/8	39 2/8	6	6	Sierra County	NM	John Harris	1998	36
380 1/8	55 3/8	56 2/8	40 5/8	7	7	Coconino County	AZ	Paul R. Titus	1995	38
379 6/8	57 7/8	56 5/8	47 6/8	6	6	Coconino County	AZ	Gregory K. Scott	1986	39
379 3/8	53 4/8	56 0/8	42 7/8	7	8	Coconino County	AZ	Jeff Elmer	1984	40
379 3/8	55 6/8	56 5/8	36 3/8	6	7	Catron County	NM	Mark Nelson	1995	40
379 2/8	54 5/8	53 5/8	41 2/8	6	6	Millard County	UT	Timothy D. Park	1996	42
378 7/8	52 2/8	52 2/8	45 7/8	7	6	Coconino County	AZ	James G. Wells	1995	43
378 6/8	57 4/8	57 7/8	39 0/8	9	8	Shoshone County	ID	Steven W. Mullin	1981	44
378 5/8	60 4/8	59 3/8	41 7/8	6	6	Coconino County	AZ	Robb G. Evans	1997	45
377 7/8	56 6/8	53 3/8	39 7/8	6	6	Coconino County	AZ	Dennis Lee Manuell	1997	46
377 0/8	59 2/8	57 1/8	39 4/8	6	6	Coconino County	AZ	Jack Frazier	1981	47
377 0/8	56 1/8	51 1/8	40 3/8	7	8	Coconino County	AZ	Larry Thomas	1985	47
376 6/8	47 2/8	50 3/8	39 2/8	6	7	Adams County	ID	Jack D. Sheppard	1966	49
376 3/8	60 1/8	59 1/8	40 3/8	6	7	Catron County	NM	Wayne K. Curtis	1986	50
376 1/8	48 1/8	47 7/8	52 6/8	6	7	Johnson County	WY	Tom Roush	1993	51
375 5/8	55 7/8	54 1/8	37 7/8	6	6	Catron County	NM	Steve Ortiz	1992	52
375 5/8	47 1/8	51 1/8	47 7/8	6	6	Socorro County	NM	David R. Aikin	1993	52
375 2/8	56 0/8	55 0/8	38 0/8	6	6	Converse County	WY	Don Stewart	1981	54
375 1/8	53 5/8	55 7/8	46 7/8	6	6	Jackson County	CO	Vincent Kvidera	1976	55
375 0/8	52 3/8	53 7/8	39 1/8	6	7	Sierra County	NM	Jim Wagner	1986	56
375 0/8	55 6/8	53 1/8	41 2/8	6	6	Catron County	NM	Ed Sautier	1991	56
375 0/8	57 7/8	57 5/8	49 4/8	6	6	Coconino County	AZ	Arthur Ortiz	1993	56
375 0/8	59 4/8	58 0/8	42 0/8	8	7	Cibola County	NM	Archie J. Nesbitt	1997	56
374 7/8	52 2/8	50 7/8	44 0/8	8	6	Catron County	NM	David A. Hughes	1996	60
374 3/8	53 5/8	53 7/8	41 1/8	6	6	Grant County	NM	Jesse O. Ogas	1990	61
374 1/8	57 6/8	51 2/8	48 0/8	7	9	Catron County	NM	Martin D. Huggins	1992	62
373 1/8	57 5/8	57 6/8	41 5/8	6	6	Crook County	OR	Jeffrey E. Hale	1988	63
373 1/8	49 1/8	48 4/8	41 7/8	7	6	Albany County	WY	Wes Walton	1990	63
372 3/8	50 7/8	49 1/8	39 7/8	6	6	Minitonas	MAN	Brian Brownlie	1989	65
372 0/8	52 2/8	52 2/8	44 0/8	7	6	Lincoln County	MT	Jerry Regh	1986	66
371 7/8	52 3/8	53 0/8	46 5/8	6	6	Mineral County	MT	Scott J. Stern	1983	67
371 7/8	59 3/8	57 2/8	42 7/8	6	6	Coconino County	AZ	George Flournoy	1986	67
371 2/8	55 1/8	53 7/8	42 2/8	6	6	Skamania County	WA	Kevin Schmid	1990	69
371 0/8	58 6/8	60 0/8	39 2/8	6	6	Coconino County	AZ	Judson J. Brown, Jr.	1993	70
371 0/8	47 1/8	49 2/8	50 0/8	6	7	Campbell County	WY	Kurt A. Bohl	1996	70
370 7/8	56 0/8	58 0/8	42 5/8	6	6	Coconino County	AZ	Mike Moulton	1987	72
370 5/8	49 5/8	49 5/8	38 1/8	6	6	Spruce Woods	MAN	Peter Sawatzky	1992	73
370 5/8	54 3/8	54 0/8	37 3/8	6	6	Catron County	NM	Dan Evans	1997	73
370 3/8	56 3/8	56 3/8	42 3/8	6	6	Sheridan County	WY	Ron Johnson	1991	75
370 3/8	60 7/8	59 0/8	43 5/8	7	7	Coconino County	AZ	Michael S. Weldon	1992	75
370 3/8	56 7/8	56 2/8	33 6/8	7	6	Madison County	MT	Lee Poole	1992	75
370 1/8	51 5/8	50 7/8	41 5/8	6	6	Petroleum County	MT	G. L. 'Buck' Damone	1985	78

YELLOWSTONE "AMERICAN" ELK (TYPICAL ANTLERS)

Minimum Score 260 — Continued

SCORE	LENGTH OF MAIN BEAM R	LENGTH OF MAIN BEAM L	INSIDE SPREAD	NUMBER OF POINTS R	NUMBER OF POINTS L	AREA	STATE/ PROVINCE	HUNTER'S NAME	DATE	RANK
370 0/8	52 0/8	51 1/8	40 0/8	6	6	Catron County	NM	Len Abernathy	1994	79
370 0/8	52 2/8	52 5/8	49 0/8	6	7	Catron County	NM	Marty Reddell	1996	79
369 6/8	54 6/8	53 0/8	47 6/8	6	6	Greenlee County	AZ	Clifford White	1986	81
369 5/8	59 7/8	58 6/8	44 7/8	6	6	Coconino County	AZ	Jeff Schorey	1992	82
369 4/8	53 2/8	51 2/8	39 4/8	7	7	Bonner County	ID	Steve Noort	1986	83
369 4/8	53 0/8	53 0/8	42 4/8	6	7	Catron County	NM	Frank A. Hayes	1986	83
369 4/8	53 0/8	56 6/8	43 7/8	7	7	Sheridan County	WY	Mike Barrett	1998	83
369 2/8	51 0/8	55 4/8	48 4/8	6	6	Madison County	MT	Jeff Engler	1977	86
369 0/8	57 2/8	56 4/8	38 2/8	7	6	Coconino County	AZ	Tom Hinson	1987	87
368 7/8	54 1/8	56 3/8	43 4/8	6	7	Sweet Grass County	MT	Frank Frampton	1995	88
368 6/8	52 1/8	51 0/8	39 6/8	6	6	Coconino County	AZ	John V. Beaufeaux	1990	89
368 6/8	57 1/8	56 0/8	47 0/8	6	6	Cibola County	NM	Archie J. Nesbitt	1998	89
368 2/8	53 0/8	53 1/8	40 2/8	7	7	Kittitas County	WA	Robert Carl Sater	1987	91
368 0/8	52 7/8	52 3/8	44 4/8	6	6	Grant County	OR	Greg E. Willmore	1988	92
367 7/8	58 7/8	53 2/8	43 3/8	7	6	Coconino County	AZ	Gary Hanson	1993	93
367 7/8	55 3/8	55 4/8	39 5/8	6	6	Catron County	NM	Patrick L. McMaster	1995	93
367 6/8	50 7/8	51 0/8	36 2/8	6	6	Teton County	MT	Gene Ward	1994	95
367 3/8	47 7/8	49 3/8	45 1/8	8	7	Larimer County	CO	H. Troxell/B. Alexander	1970	96
367 3/8	54 1/8	51 7/8	43 2/8	8	8	Gila County	AZ	Patrick Kirby	1992	96
367 2/8	55 4/8	57 7/8	46 0/8	6	6	Lemhi County	ID	Ben Fahnholz	1982	98
367 2/8	55 4/8	54 3/8	42 4/8	6	6	Rio Arriba County	NM	David O. Conrad	1990	98
366 7/8	53 2/8	52 1/8	40 4/8	7	7	Mineral County	MT	Gerry Lamarre	1977	100
366 5/8	53 0/8	53 2/8	45 3/8	7	7	Shoshone County	ID	D. A. Johnson	1962	101
366 5/8	46 1/8	47 1/8	35 6/8	6	7	Phillips County	MT	Ronnie Molstad	1983	101
366 5/8	50 4/8	52 4/8	45 5/8	6	6	Valencia County	NM	Dean Dunaway	1991	101
366 4/8	49 7/8	55 1/8	39 6/8	6	6	Duck Mtns.	MAN	Brian W. Brownlie	1992	104
366 4/8	52 3/8	53 4/8	43 2/8	7	7	Coconino County	AZ	Lloyd H. Farr	1994	104
366 3/8	52 5/8	50 7/8	41 7/8	6	6	Fergus County	MT	J. Douglas Krings	1980	106
366 3/8	55 5/8	57 6/8	40 5/8	6	6	Catron County	NM	J. W. Young	1990	106
366 2/8	54 4/8	51 1/8	45 6/8	6	6	Catron County	NM	Michael C. Dean	1994	108
366 1/8	52 3/8	51 0/8	43 7/8	6	6	Berland River	ALB	Brad Sidebottom	1986	109
366 1/8	55 5/8	55 4/8	45 7/8	7	7	Catron County	NM	Danny Ray	1992	109
366 1/8	53 1/8	51 5/8	39 6/8	6	7	Catron County	NM	Stephen L. Penrod	1994	109
365 5/8	52 4/8	50 1/8	38 7/8	6	6	Rio Blanco County	CO	Jay Verzuh	1995	112
365 1/8	51 4/8	51 2/8	38 5/8	7	7	Sandoval County	NM	John C. McClendon	1985	113
365 0/8	60 6/8	61 4/8	50 2/8	7	7	Fergus County	MT	John Jeide	1983	114
364 6/8	50 3/8	46 2/8	39 2/8	6	6	Grant County	OR	William C. Sanowski	1976	115
364 5/8	50 7/8	50 0/8	39 3/8	6	6	Rossburn	MAN	Fred Hay	1993	116
364 3/8	57 2/8	51 6/8	37 3/8	8	7	Kootenai County	ID	Curtis Yanzick	1990	117
364 1/8	54 4/8	56 5/8	46 3/8	6	6	Catron County	NM	Lee Hetrick	1991	118
364 0/8	52 7/8	52 7/8	40 4/8	6	7	Catron County	NM	Paul J. Butler	1988	119
363 7/8	50 5/8	47 0/8	41 4/8	7	8	Converse County	WY	David P. Lindman	1986	120
363 5/8	56 3/8	54 7/8	43 1/8	6	6	Graham County	AZ	Steve M. Titla	1988	121
363 5/8	56 5/8	59 6/8	42 5/8	6	6	Catron County	NM	W. Glenn Wood, Jr.	1992	121
363 5/8	50 6/8	52 5/8	38 4/8	8	7	Catron County	NM	Paul D. Payne II	1994	121
363 2/8	50 5/8	51 2/8	37 0/8	6	6	Coconino County	AZ	Robert E. Reed	1994	124
363 1/8	56 0/8	57 7/8	43 1/8	7	6	Catron County	NM	Jimmy Kruckenberg	1994	125
363 0/8	57 1/8	58 0/8	42 0/8	6	6	Coconino County	AZ	Dan Heasley	1995	126
362 6/8	50 5/8	53 2/8	37 4/8	6	7	Catron County	NM	Ray Cloud	1993	127
362 2/8	50 2/8	49 4/8	46 2/8	7	7	Jackson County	CO	Alfred H. O'Brien	1972	128
362 0/8	48 4/8	53 5/8	42 4/8	6	7	Coconino County	AZ	Frank Robert Ortiz	1993	129
361 5/8	52 0/8	57 4/8	45 3/8	7	6	Catron County	NM	Robert A. Oines	1997	130
361 5/8	52 2/8	52 7/8	38 7/8	6	6	Musselshell County	MT	Poncho McCoy	1997	130
361 4/8	51 5/8	54 0/8	48 0/8	6	6	Fergus County	MT	D. Mitch Kottas	1992	132
361 3/8	54 3/8	51 0/8	47 3/8	6	6	Coconino County	AZ	Dean Dunaway	1990	133
361 2/8	58 4/8	56 4/8	37 0/8	6	6	Coconino County	AZ	Tom Phelps	1986	134
361 0/8	54 0/8	55 0/8	44 4/8	6	6	Coconino County	AZ	Laura Wuertz	1986	135
361 0/8	51 7/8	49 2/8	34 6/8	7	6	Gila County	AZ	Dick Gephard	1990	135
360 7/8	54 7/8	56 1/8	41 7/8	7	6	Lemhi County	ID	Tony Latham	1983	137
360 7/8	52 1/8	52 1/8	37 5/8	6	6	White Pine County	NV	Darcy Tate	1993	137
360 7/8	52 0/8	51 0/8	46 1/8	6	6	Catron County	NM	Mark Jacobson	1997	137
360 6/8	51 1/8	49 7/8	37 0/8	6	6	Petroleum County	MT	Kerby A. Durbin	1987	140
360 4/8	61 7/8	57 3/8	43 5/8	8	7	White Pine County	NV	Thomas Enewold	1990	141
360 4/8	54 2/8	54 4/8	42 6/8	8	7	Catron County	NM	Blaine Underwood	1991	141
360 4/8	55 7/8	56 3/8	40 2/8	7	7	Albany County	WY	Kevin Christopherson	1996	141
360 3/8	57 5/8	53 2/8	48 7/8	7	6	Socorro County	NM	James A. Trujillo	1987	144
360 3/8	46 0/8	47 3/8	39 1/8	6	6	Catron County	NM	Glenn W. Isler	1994	144
360 2/8	54 5/8	55 0/8	46 4/8	8	6	Clark County	ID	Tim Thomas	1996	146
360 1/8	49 3/8	49 3/8	37 5/8	6	6	Sandoval County	NM	Robert Seeds	1995	147
360 0/8	47 1/8	44 4/8	42 4/8	7	6	Las Animas County	CO	Rob Lucero	1992	148
359 6/8	54 1/8	55 2/8	38 6/8	7	7	Catron County	NM	George Pieros, Jr.	1994	149
359 5/8	50 4/8	52 0/8	47 1/8	6	6	Pierce County	WA	Doug Nearhood	1985	150
359 5/8	50 5/8	42 5/8	36 1/8	6	6	Powder River County	MT	Randy Trucano	1994	150
359 5/8	51 5/8	50 1/8	42 3/8	6	6	Edgerton	ALB	Archie Day	1997	150
359 3/8	48 1/8	49 2/8	48 1/8	6	6	Mesa County	CO	David W. Christopherson	1978	153
359 2/8	51 0/8	52 5/8	42 0/8	6	9	Coconino County	AZ	Robert Cecrle	1972	154
359 2/8	58 2/8	56 7/8	42 0/8	6	6	Coconino County	AZ	Jim David	1974	154
359 2/8	56 3/8	53 7/8	40 0/8	7	6	Greenlee County	AZ	N. Richard McMullan	1992	154

YELLOWSTONE "AMERICAN" ELK (TYPICAL ANTLERS)

Minimum Score 260

Continued

SCORE	LENGTH OF MAIN BEAM R	LENGTH OF MAIN BEAM L	INSIDE SPREAD	NUMBER OF POINTS R	NUMBER OF POINTS L	AREA	STATE/ PROVINCE	HUNTER'S NAME	DATE	RANK
359 2/8	50 6/8	52 7/8	42 2/8	6	6	Morgan County	UT	Hugh H. Hogle	1993	154
359 2/8	53 4/8	54 1/8	50 0/8	7	6	Garfield County	UT	Kurt Gale	1997	154
359 1/8	54 4/8	54 0/8	41 7/8	6	6	Grant County	OR	Marte Scheuffele	1983	159
359 1/8	49 0/8	52 4/8	36 0/8	7	6	Coconino County	AZ	Frank J. Mayorga	1987	159
359 0/8	56 4/8	57 2/8	36 4/8	6	6	Coconino County	AZ	Michael J. Proulx	1986	161
359 0/8	50 4/8	50 0/8	47 6/8	7	6	Baca County	CO	Randy Bacon/Rich Pianalto	1994	161
359 0/8	55 0/8	53 5/8	43 0/8	6	6	Park County	WY	Bob Whisonant	1998	161
359 0/8	54 2/8	51 4/8	46 0/8	6	6	Coconino County	AZ	Michael L. Wolfe	1998	161
358 7/8	55 5/8	54 5/8	40 7/8	6	6	Coconino County	AZ	Gary Bills	1986	165
358 6/8	51 7/8	55 0/8	47 6/8	6	6	Sheridan County	WY	Mike Barrett	1986	166
358 5/8	53 0/8	49 7/8	38 3/8	6	6	Cibola County	NM	Moises Perea	1980	167
358 5/8	48 6/8	48 5/8	47 1/8	6	6	Coconino County	AZ	Tom Crabill	1998	167
358 4/8	58 1/8	57 4/8	40 2/8	6	6	Sierra County	NM	Steve J. Koscher	1993	169
358 4/8	52 3/8	52 0/8	39 0/8	7	7	Cibola County	NM	Thomas R. Grabowski	1997	169
358 4/8	52 5/8	54 6/8	37 3/8	7	6	Greenlee County	AZ	Bill Madison	1997	169
358 3/8	52 3/8	52 5/8	39 5/8	6	6	Sanders County	MT	Eugene Roesler	1986	172
358 3/8	55 6/8	55 6/8	31 5/8	6	6	Catron County	NM	Steve D. Lozano	1992	172
358 2/8	54 1/8	51 4/8	47 0/8	6	6	Crook County	OR	Oliver Weger	1983	174
358 2/8	58 6/8	54 3/8	42 0/8	6	6	Catron County	NM	David G. Anderson	1993	174
358 1/8	56 2/8	60 2/8	42 7/8	6	6	Catron County	NM	Robert E. Duke	1991	176
358 0/8	52 3/8	54 3/8	40 4/8	6	8	Grant County	NM	David O. Smith	1997	177
357 7/8	54 2/8	54 6/8	45 1/8	7	7	Coconino County	AZ	Mark Clammer	1987	178
357 7/8	54 6/8	57 1/8	45 5/8	6	6	Albany County	WY	Richard L. Andre	1990	178
357 7/8	54 0/8	53 3/8	42 7/8	6	6	Catron County	NM	Mike Moore	1990	178
357 7/8	54 1/8	50 7/8	37 7/8	6	6	Sierra County	NM	David Swisher	1992	178
357 6/8	50 2/8	50 6/8	40 4/8	6	6	Park County	CO	Donald R. Looper	1975	182
357 6/8	53 4/8	56 3/8	46 4/8	6	6	Apache County	AZ	John B. Bowman	1991	182
357 4/8	52 5/8	55 0/8	37 6/8	7	6	Fergus County	MT	Michael B. Hedrick	1981	184
357 4/8	52 1/8	52 5/8	46 6/8	7	7	Bonneville County	ID	Gregg Allen Youngerman	1996	184
357 3/8	56 2/8	49 2/8	37 1/8	6	6	Meagher County	MT	David G. Snyder	1978	186
357 3/8	50 4/8	50 4/8	34 5/8	6	6	Swan River	MAN	Kelly Shykitka	1986	186
357 3/8	55 6/8	54 0/8	37 7/8	6	6	Moffat County	CO	Kurt W. Keskimaki	1987	186
357 3/8	55 0/8	53 7/8	41 5/8	7	6	Missoula County	MT	Andrew J. Kelly	1990	186
357 3/8	54 4/8	53 1/8	42 5/8	7	7	Catron County	NM	Linda Strong	1994	186
357 0/8	54 2/8	56 0/8	41 0/8	6	6	Caribou County	ID	Howard E. Johnson	1968	191
357 0/8	56 5/8	56 7/8	46 6/8	6	6	Gila County	AZ	David L. Crockett	1973	191
357 0/8	53 5/8	53 6/8	43 2/8	6	7	Strawberry Lake	CO	Frank Fraser	1977	191
356 7/8	54 1/8	53 6/8	53 7/8	6	7	Park County	MT	Charles Alkire	1964	194
356 7/8	49 6/8	51 0/8	46 3/8	7	6	Flathead County	MT	Terry Krogstad	1984	194
356 6/8	51 0/8	50 2/8	41 2/8	6	6	Grant County	OR	James M. Carter	1988	196
356 6/8	52 5/8	52 2/8	40 6/8	6	6	Coconino County	AZ	Ralph E. Anderson	1993	196
356 6/8	49 7/8	50 6/8	39 0/8	7	7	Catron County	NM	Bear Brewer	1995	196
356 6/8	52 2/8	51 0/8	42 0/8	7	7	Catron County	NM	Kyle M. Meintzer	1998	196
356 4/8	57 3/8	53 1/8	46 4/8	6	6	Catron County	NM	Bill Elmer	1986	200
356 4/8	54 5/8	56 0/8	40 2/8	6	6	Coconino County	AZ	Blaine "Bub" Mathews	1990	200
356 3/8	52 4/8	48 6/8	36 1/8	6	7	Fergus County	MT	Leonard L. Weeks	1984	202
356 1/8	54 3/8	53 0/8	39 3/8	6	8	Catron County	NM	Edward Eskew	1990	203
356 0/8	52 1/8	50 1/8	36 4/8	7	6	Linn County	OR	David E. Renoud	1983	204
356 0/8	61 2/8	60 2/8	51 0/8	6	6	Coconino County	AZ	Kent G. Frei	1990	204
356 0/8	56 2/8	59 0/8	40 0/8	7	6	Coconino County	AZ	John Mertz	1995	204
355 6/8	53 6/8	58 2/8	34 2/8	6	6	Larimer County	CO	Shawn Greathouse	1993	207
355 5/8	49 7/8	46 7/8	41 0/8	8	8	Catron County	NM	Doug Aikin	1987	208
355 5/8	53 5/8	55 3/8	47 3/8	6	6	Cibola County	NM	Steven M. Prince	1997	208
355 4/8	54 7/8	56 5/8	42 6/8	6	6	Beaverhead County	MT	Robert B. McKay	1973	210
355 4/8	52 4/8	50 5/8	45 4/8	6	6	Catron County	NM	Phil Kirkland	1991	210
355 4/8	53 1/8	52 1/8	40 4/8	6	6	Musselshell County	MT	Joseph Karls	1996	210
355 3/8	48 7/8	48 6/8	40 3/8	6	6	Jumping Pound Creek	ALB	Archie J. Nesbitt	1997	213
355 3/8	48 1/8	49 5/8	38 3/8	6	6	Summit County	UT	Bridger Bolinder	1998	213
355 2/8	52 1/8	51 5/8	35 2/8	6	6	Otero County	NM	Jimmy King	1989	215
355 2/8	50 3/8	57 1/8	37 0/8	6	6	Rio Arriba County	NM	Nelson Martinez, Jr.	1997	215
355 1/8	50 6/8	50 2/8	35 1/8	6	6	Fergus County	MT	Rusten L. Barnes	1995	217
355 0/8	50 1/8	50 1/8	38 0/8	6	6	Shoshone County	ID	Vern Clay/Ed Oliver	1978	218
355 0/8	53 6/8	53 7/8	45 2/8	6	6	Park County	CO	Mark Martin	1996	218
354 7/8	51 4/8	51 0/8	41 6/8	6	6	Greenlee County	AZ	David Dickson	1986	220
354 7/8	56 3/8	56 4/8	43 5/8	6	6	Coconino County	AZ	Noel Harris	1991	220
354 7/8	48 6/8	48 2/8	43 1/8	7	7	Wheeler County	OR	Dan R. Kinder	1996	220
354 6/8	54 0/8	53 7/8	36 6/8	6	6	Valley County	MT	Kenneth R. Johnson	1986	223
354 6/8	56 5/8	56 4/8	44 3/8	7	8	Custer County	ID	Wayne VanVechten	1987	223
354 5/8	55 6/8	56 6/8	37 7/8	6	6	Catron County	NM	Duane "Corky" Richardson	1991	225
354 4/8	49 1/8	50 4/8	38 6/8	6	6	Coconino County	AZ	Ron Scherer	1980	226
354 4/8	53 6/8	53 2/8	42 6/8	6	6	Navajo County	AZ	Erik M. Thorsrud	1994	226
354 4/8	55 3/8	58 3/8	40 0/8	6	6	Coconino County	AZ	James Peoble	1998	226
354 3/8	56 0/8	55 3/8	39 1/8	6	7	Converse County	WY	Edward Coy	1972	229
354 3/8	53 2/8	58 3/8	46 1/8	6	6	Coconino County	AZ	James M. Frey	1980	229
354 3/8	52 5/8	52 7/8	45 1/8	6	6	Valley County	MT	Gregg Pauley	1985	229
354 3/8	51 3/8	53 1/8	39 7/8	6	6	Lincoln County	MT	Keith Krumbeck	1986	229
354 2/8	48 0/8	44 2/8	50 4/8	6	6	Morgan County	UT	Dennis Shirley	1987	233
354 2/8	52 3/8	51 4/8	42 0/8	6	6	Catron County	NM	E. Lance Whary	1997	233

YELLOWSTONE "AMERICAN" ELK (TYPICAL ANTLERS)

Minimum Score 260 — Continued

SCORE	LENGTH OF MAIN BEAM R	L	INSIDE SPREAD	NUMBER OF POINTS R	L	AREA	STATE/ PROVINCE	HUNTER'S NAME	DATE	RANK
354 0/8	60 4/8	61 2/8	34 4/8	7	6	Coconino County	AZ	Jack Cahill	1982	235
354 0/8	53 0/8	51 1/8	41 0/8	6	6	Duck Mtns.	MAN	Bob Ginther	1992	235
353 7/8	54 0/8	54 2/8	40 7/8	6	7	Catron County	NM	Joe Pruett	1998	237
353 6/8	53 5/8	50 2/8	44 2/8	6	6	Coconino County	AZ	Rodney Robinson	1987	238
353 6/8	53 4/8	55 5/8	44 2/8	7	6	Catron County	NM	C. H. Anderson	1992	238
353 5/8	50 5/8	51 0/8	40 5/8	6	6	Sheridan County	WY	Ron Johnson	1990	240
353 5/8	47 4/8	51 2/8	41 7/8	6	7	Catron County	NM	Fred M. Fox	1995	240
353 4/8	54 3/8	54 3/8	43 0/8	6	6	Flathead County	MT	Cory Lamb	1989	242
353 3/8	56 6/8	56 0/8	34 5/8	6	6	Otero County	NM	Bill Stage	1993	243
353 1/8	59 6/8	60 4/8	40 1/8	7	6	Coconino County	AZ	Richard S. Jones	1991	244
353 1/8	48 0/8	50 2/8	41 1/8	6	8	Converse County	WY	Glen Mark Gates	1991	244
353 0/8	50 4/8	49 6/8	43 2/8	6	6	Coconino County	AZ	Richard M. Larsen	1980	246
353 0/8	47 2/8	46 1/8	38 0/8	6	7	Grant County	OR	Kenneth Mills	1983	246
353 0/8	53 3/8	53 1/8	46 2/8	6	6	Coconino County	AZ	Bob Dawson	1992	246
352 7/8	54 4/8	53 4/8	42 0/8	6	7	Teton County	MT	Jack Howard	1972	249
352 7/8	51 6/8	52 1/8	41 7/8	6	6	Sandoval County	NM	John W. Rose	1981	249
352 6/8	53 4/8	50 5/8	40 6/8	6	6	Catron County	NM	Francis D. Elias	1993	251
352 5/8	50 1/8	50 0/8	37 5/8	6	6	Woody Ridge	AZ	Oscar Dale Porter	1982	252
352 4/8	54 2/8	52 1/8	37 2/8	6	6	Coconino County	AZ	John F. Gurasich	1988	253
352 1/8	53 2/8	53 1/8	36 3/8	6	6	Petroleum County	MT	Gorm Scarpholt	1987	254
352 1/8	54 1/8	54 0/8	47 1/8	7	6	Catron County	NM	James F. Welles	1993	254
352 1/8	51 1/8	53 1/8	41 3/8	6	6	Conejos County	CO	Mike Crites	1998	254
352 0/8	51 4/8	53 0/8	38 5/8	6	7	Coconino County	AZ	Bill Elmer	1981	257
352 0/8	51 3/8	51 2/8	43 6/8	6	6	Powell County	MT	Philip L. Karper	1987	257
352 0/8	49 4/8	51 0/8	44 3/8	8	7	Catron County	NM	Tom Hoffman	1991	257
352 0/8	51 4/8	51 4/8	44 4/8	6	6	Kootenai County	ID	Mark Gerber	1997	257
351 7/8	50 6/8	50 2/8	40 4/8	7	6	Crook County	OR	Curtis Demaris	1983	261
351 7/8	46 4/8	46 4/8	39 5/8	7	7	Park County	MT	Randy F. Petrich	1991	261
351 7/8	54 2/8	54 5/8	39 7/8	8	8	Catron County	NM	George T. Basabilvazo	1998	261
351 4/8	51 7/8	51 2/8	39 4/8	7	7	Coconino County	AZ	Marvin L. Slaughter	1979	264
351 4/8	50 6/8	49 7/8	40 0/8	6	6	Grant County	OR	Curtis Demaris	1980	264
351 4/8	56 5/8	56 0/8	46 4/8	6	6	Coconino County	AZ	John F. Gurasich	1986	264
351 4/8	43 7/8	45 3/8	40 0/8	6	6	Lincoln County	NM	Terry Arnim	1986	264
351 3/8	49 6/8	54 2/8	48 2/8	8	7	Grant County	OR	Bob Lindsay	1981	268
351 3/8	50 3/8	50 4/8	39 1/8	6	6	Millarville	ALB	Barry Pocha	1991	268
351 3/8	53 6/8	55 0/8	40 3/8	6	6	Greenlee County	AZ	Dennis Jensen	1991	268
351 3/8	56 0/8	57 4/8	44 3/8	7	7	Ferry County	WA	Brett Black	1997	268
351 2/8	55 6/8	53 5/8	41 6/8	6	6	Coconino County	AZ	Jay Elmer	1977	272
351 2/8	51 5/8	50 3/8	34 0/8	7	7	Missoula County	MT	James P. Loughran	1986	272
351 2/8	52 1/8	49 1/8	40 4/8	6	6	Morgan County	UT	Dr. Peter E. Paulos	1994	272
351 2/8	48 5/8	50 4/8	37 6/8	6	6	Socorro County	NM	Doug Aikin	1995	272
351 2/8	47 4/8	51 6/8	45 0/8	7	6	Wasco County	OR	Sheldon D. Ayres	1995	272
351 1/8	54 0/8	52 3/8	40 3/8	6	6	Lincoln County	NM	Frank Scott	1989	277
351 0/8	54 6/8	51 3/8	36 0/8	6	6	Greenlee County	AZ	Jim Coleman	1987	278
351 0/8	51 7/8	51 6/8	38 2/8	6	6	Canmore	ALB	Gunter Lemke	1987	278
351 0/8	51 4/8	50 7/8	42 0/8	7	6	Coconino County	AZ	Robert Bejarano	1998	278
350 6/8	53 5/8	53 0/8	40 2/8	6	6	Sheridan County	WY	Kurt M. Baughman	1980	281
350 6/8	48 7/8	49 6/8	37 2/8	6	6	Catron County	NM	Al Hankins	1998	281
350 5/8	49 7/8	49 5/8	40 6/8	7	6	Catron County	NM	Cary Cuba	1987	283
350 5/8	53 4/8	52 6/8	39 3/8	6	6	Catron County	NM	Billy R. Leach	1992	283
350 3/8	48 7/8	48 5/8	41 7/8	8	7	Fergus County	MT	G. L. 'Buck' Damone	1981	285
350 3/8	53 5/8	53 7/8	41 1/8	6	6	Catron County	NM	George Richardson	1993	285
350 2/8	51 6/8	48 7/8	40 2/8	6	6	Routt County	CO	Mark L. Houslet	1977	287
350 2/8	53 4/8	53 1/8	41 2/8	6	6	Sandoval County	NM	Jose Montalvo	1981	287
350 2/8	54 1/8	53 3/8	39 2/8	6	6	Catron County	NM	Bobby Elkins	1993	287
350 1/8	50 2/8	52 5/8	37 7/8	6	6	Cibola County	NM	Ted Shinn	1987	290
350 1/8	54 7/8	52 5/8	44 7/8	6	7	Summit County	CO	Jeffrey J. Granowsky	1987	290
350 1/8	52 2/8	52 1/8	37 1/8	6	6	Petroleum County	MT	Dennis Bergan	1994	290
350 1/8	54 7/8	53 4/8	34 5/8	6	6	Navajo County	AZ	Don Parks, Jr.	1995	290
350 0/8	53 1/8	51 5/8	38 6/8	6	6	Sandoval County	NM	Tom David	1984	294
350 0/8	51 6/8	50 2/8	33 6/8	6	6	Catron County	NM	Philip G. McClelland	1988	294
350 0/8	51 6/8	53 6/8	41 4/8	6	6	Catron County	NM	Eddie Claypool	1990	294
349 7/8	50 1/8	51 1/8	48 5/8	6	6	Crook County	OR	Dale Shiery	1984	297
349 7/8	43 6/8	46 0/8	38 1/8	6	6	Catron County	NM	Kenny T. Rhodes	1991	297
349 6/8	53 0/8	52 6/8	41 6/8	6	6	Wheeler County	OR	Dale Shiery	1983	299
349 6/8	57 4/8	56 4/8	40 4/8	6	7	Coconino County	AZ	Gary A. Linendoll	1991	299
349 6/8	53 6/8	55 0/8	39 6/8	6	6	Idaho County	ID	Louis Wasniewski	1996	299
349 5/8	46 0/8	44 4/8	37 1/8	6	6	Huerfano County	CO	Richard L. Doman	1972	302
349 5/8	51 4/8	52 2/8	40 4/8	8	7	Coconino County	AZ	Cindi J. Richardson	1991	302
349 5/8	50 5/8	49 7/8	33 7/8	6	7	Taos County	NM	Michael R. Deschamps	1992	302
349 5/8	52 1/8	51 4/8	40 4/8	6	7	Albany County	WY	Mark Adamson	1998	302
349 4/8	58 0/8	58 6/8	43 6/8	7	6	Idaho County	ID	Jim Robbins	1996	306
349 4/8	53 2/8	53 3/8	36 5/8	6	8	Catron County	NM	Paul R. Bovee	1997	306
349 3/8	52 2/8	51 7/8	36 7/8	6	6	Fergus County	MT	Charles R. Bowman	1966	308
349 3/8	50 4/8	45 2/8	46 1/8	6	6	Park County	CO	Gary Jones	1984	308
349 3/8	53 3/8	54 6/8	43 1/8	6	6	Apache County	AZ	David Sullivan	1986	308
349 2/8	50 6/8	51 0/8	39 4/8	7	6	Clackamas County	OR	Paul Smith	1984	311
349 2/8	53 0/8	54 0/8	35 0/8	6	7	Albany County	WY	Mark Stiller	1993	311

YELLOWSTONE "AMERICAN" ELK (TYPICAL ANTLERS)

Minimum Score 260

Continued

SCORE	LENGTH OF MAIN BEAM R	LENGTH OF MAIN BEAM L	INSIDE SPREAD	NUMBER OF POINTS R	NUMBER OF POINTS L	AREA	STATE/ PROVINCE	HUNTER'S NAME	DATE	RANK
349 2/8	54 1/8	51 3/8	35 6/8	7	7	Sierra County	NM	Joe H. Campbell	1994	311
349 1/8	56 4/8	60 2/8	45 3/8	6	7	Coconino County	AZ	Alan R. Miller	1975	314
349 1/8	59 4/8	58 6/8	45 5/8	6	6	San Miguel County	NM	James L. Maves	1991	314
349 0/8	51 1/8	47 6/8	39 2/8	6	6	Los Alamos County	NM	Chuck Adams	1982	316
349 0/8	59 7/8	59 6/8	46 0/8	7	6	Catron County	NM	William C. Davis	1993	316
349 0/8	52 5/8	51 6/8	47 6/8	6	6	Coconino County	AZ	Claud F. Adams	1994	316
349 0/8	51 0/8	51 2/8	38 5/8	7	8	Catron County	NM	David L. Workman	1997	316
348 6/8	50 1/8	50 2/8	37 0/8	6	6	Phillips County	MT	Ron Bachmeier	1990	320
348 6/8	52 1/8	53 0/8	42 0/8	6	6	Apache County	AZ	Mace D. Cochran	1995	320
348 5/8	52 2/8	53 5/8	46 3/8	6	6	Caribou County	ID	Kenneth P. Kelley	1991	322
348 5/8	50 4/8	49 0/8	36 5/8	7	6	Grand County	CO	Gary Williamson	1994	322
348 4/8	55 0/8	55 0/8	43 6/8	6	6	Coconino County	AZ	Bob Jensen	1981	324
348 4/8	45 3/8	44 6/8	41 6/8	6	6	Bonneville County	ID	Ronald L. Mueller	1982	324
348 3/8	50 0/8	51 7/8	34 4/8	7	7	Pierce County	WA	John Lyday	1984	326
348 3/8	50 3/8	48 1/8	37 3/8	6	6	Duchesne County	UT	Victor J. Fossat	1995	326
348 2/8	30 7/8	47 3/8	34 4/8	6	7	Rio Blanco County	CO	Clark Gallup	1976	328
348 2/8	50 0/8	50 4/8	41 6/8	6	7	Carbon County	UT	Rick G. Huempfner	1989	328
348 2/8	47 7/8	48 2/8	39 2/8	6	6	Sanders County	MT	Glen Haas	1991	328
348 0/8	53 4/8	53 6/8	43 6/8	6	6	Sheridan County	WY	Mark S. Hutchins	1992	331
348 0/8	50 7/8	48 5/8	41 1/8	7	8	Adams County	ID	Darwin DeCroo	1996	331
347 7/8	49 2/8	47 2/8	36 5/8	6	6	Swan River	MAN	Carl Robblee	1988	333
347 6/8	51 4/8	47 6/8	38 0/8	6	6	Valley County	MT	Greg Zahn	1981	334
347 6/8	49 6/8	52 1/8	38 6/8	6	6	Phillips County	MT	Craig Hall	1986	334
347 5/8	54 4/8	54 1/8	41 3/8	6	6	Coconino County	AZ	Allen L. King II	1992	336
347 4/8	50 2/8	49 5/8	45 6/8	7	6	Fremont County	ID	Bob Baird	1961	337
347 4/8	48 2/8	48 5/8	38 0/8	6	6	Fergus County	MT	Mark DeBoo	1988	337
347 2/8	46 2/8	51 0/8	41 0/8	6	6	Socorro County	NM	Donald H. Paul	1992	339
347 2/8	50 3/8	50 5/8	38 4/8	7	7	Navajo County	AZ	Henry Roberts	1994	339
347 2/8	58 0/8	56 7/8	43 6/8	6	6	Catron County	NM	Hector Aguirre	1998	339
347 1/8	54 1/8	53 2/8	37 3/8	6	6	Clackamas County	OR	Bill Lancaster	1986	342
347 0/8	49 1/8	51 2/8	36 0/8	7	8	Apache County	AZ	Jesus T. Guerena	1988	343
346 7/8	54 1/8	51 4/8	35 5/8	7	7	Lake County	MT	Scott Ganz	1984	344
346 7/8	50 7/8	51 7/8	37 5/8	6	6	Mora County	NM	James L. Romero	1987	344
346 7/8	50 5/8	48 3/8	36 3/8	6	6	Fergus County	MT	D. Mitch Kottas	1998	344
346 7/8	53 4/8	54 6/8	42 5/8	7	6	Sheridan County	WY	Daniel K. Doke	1998	344
346 7/8	51 2/8	50 7/8	39 3/8	7	7	Fergus County	MT	Brad Tank	1998	344
346 6/8	44 2/8	45 4/8	41 0/8	6	6	Bighorn Mountain	WY	John Yeager	1980	349
346 5/8	52 6/8	53 6/8	44 5/8	7	6	San Miguel County	NM	Frank C. Sciorilli	1977	350
346 4/8	51 4/8	51 1/8	42 5/8	7	6	Coconino County	AZ	Brett Kendall	1990	351
346 4/8	54 2/8	54 1/8	40 2/8	6	6	Catron County	NM	Michael J. Nielsen	1994	351
346 4/8	60 2/8	60 0/8	40 2/8	6	6	Sierra County	NM	Deone Johnson	1997	351
346 1/8	50 7/8	50 0/8	40 7/8	7	8	White Pine County	NV	James R. Puryear	1988	354
346 1/8	56 2/8	51 3/8	39 5/8	7	6	Catron County	NM	Teddy Orr	1992	354
346 1/8	50 2/8	50 3/8	41 3/8	6	7	Linn County	OR	Jeff Baker	1995	354
346 0/8	49 5/8	45 2/8	35 4/8	6	6	Coconino County	AZ	Chris Kengla	1993	357
345 7/8	52 5/8	52 0/8	41 5/8	7	6	Blaine County	ID	Danny F. Watson	1977	358
345 7/8	47 6/8	47 4/8	36 1/8	6	7	White Pine County	NV	Gregg Tanner	1989	358
345 7/8	59 1/8	57 4/8	35 5/8	6	6	Catron County	NM	A. E. McCaskill	1991	358
345 7/8	52 6/8	52 2/8	42 3/8	6	6	Phillips County	MT	Michael J. McFate	1992	358
345 7/8	48 2/8	48 5/8	42 7/8	6	6	Catron County	NM	Ricky Adams	1996	358
345 7/8	51 1/8	50 4/8	51 6/8	6	6	Albany County	WY	Aaron G. Madsen	1998	358
345 6/8	54 0/8	55 6/8	40 0/8	6	6	Graham County	AZ	Steve M. Titla	1987	364
345 6/8	51 5/8	54 2/8	36 4/8	6	6	Summit County	UT	Monty Dyke	1992	364
345 6/8	52 6/8	52 6/8	43 0/8	6	6	Lemhi County	ID	Elmer Hamilton	1995	364
345 5/8	50 3/8	51 0/8	36 7/8	6	6	Socorro County	NM	Frederick V. Brown	1995	367
345 5/8	54 6/8	54 1/8	38 7/8	6	6	Catron County	NM	Elmer R. Luce, Jr.	1995	367
345 5/8	53 7/8	54 6/8	30 7/8	7	7	Coconino County	AZ	Stephen Frost	1998	367
345 4/8	52 1/8	52 3/8	37 4/8	7	7	Ravalli County	MT	Howard Nichols	1983	370
345 2/8	54 3/8	53 4/8	41 4/8	7	6	Coconino County	AZ	Jim P. Harris	1995	371
345 1/8	49 2/8	51 7/8	43 7/8	6	6	Catron County	NM	Ron Adam	1987	372
345 0/8	52 3/8	55 0/8	37 4/8	6	7	Archuleta County	CO	Val M. Koeberlein	1989	373
344 6/8	53 6/8	55 0/8	41 0/8	8	7	Coconino County	AZ	Les Shelton	1979	374
344 6/8	50 7/8	49 3/8	38 6/8	7	7	Coconino County	AZ	Mark R. Harvey	1986	374
344 6/8	53 4/8	52 7/8	34 0/8	7	7	King County	WA	Robin F. Buck	1989	374
344 5/8	53 4/8	53 3/8	37 1/8	7	7	Mohave County	AZ	Jim Machac	1998	377
344 3/8	52 0/8	52 6/8	45 1/8	6	6	Lincoln County	MT	Lance Sink	1984	378
344 3/8	50 0/8	49 7/8	36 3/8	7	7	Petroleum County	MT	Dennis R. Thompson	1985	378
344 3/8	50 4/8	54 7/8	40 7/8	6	6	Catron County	NM	Christopher D. Walp	1992	378
344 3/8	51 6/8	46 0/8	42 5/8	6	6	Moffat County	CO	Dean Carey	1996	378
344 2/8	49 0/8	48 4/8	38 2/8	6	6	Ravalli County	MT	Steven Welty	1987	382
344 2/8	52 1/8	50 6/8	39 4/8	6	6	Catron County	NM	J. B. Lemon	1995	382
344 1/8	49 0/8	50 6/8	36 5/8	6	6	Mesa County	CO	Dick Steele	1994	384
344 0/8	49 7/8	52 7/8	41 4/8	6	7	Catron County	NM	Wayne Ludington	1985	385
343 7/8	49 0/8	49 4/8	42 3/8	6	6	Union County	OR	Craig Gorham	1983	386
343 7/8	50 7/8	50 2/8	36 5/8	6	6	Grant County	NM	Randall Madding	1991	386
343 7/8	52 0/8	51 2/8	41 5/8	6	6	Catron County	NM	Tim Friday	1995	386
343 6/8	45 6/8	46 2/8	45 2/8	6	6	Catron County	NM	Russell Gash	1990	389
343 6/8	50 2/8	48 4/8	41 6/8	6	7	Cascade County	MT	Leighton Dresch	1996	389

YELLOWSTONE "AMERICAN" ELK (TYPICAL ANTLERS)

Minimum Score 260   Continued

SCORE	LENGTH OF MAIN BEAM R	LENGTH OF MAIN BEAM L	INSIDE SPREAD	NUMBER OF POINTS R	NUMBER OF POINTS L	AREA	STATE/PROVINCE	HUNTER'S NAME	DATE	RANK
343 6/8	54 6/8	55 4/8	38 2/8	6	6	Coconino County	AZ	Daniel P. Cartwright	1997	389
343 5/8	52 4/8	55 3/8	38 7/8	6	7	Coconino County	AZ	J. R. Wilhelmy	1976	392
343 5/8	48 5/8	53 0/8	39 3/8	6	6	Catron County	NM	Ralph "Abe" Meline	1992	392
343 5/8	55 3/8	57 7/8	37 1/8	6	7	Grant County	NM	Toby B. Rascon	1993	392
343 5/8	43 0/8	42 3/8	32 3/8	8	8	Lewis & Clark County	MT	Dennis Perkins	1993	392
343 5/8	54 4/8	53 6/8	33 7/8	6	6	Navajo County	AZ	Randy Ulmer	1995	392
343 5/8	50 4/8	52 4/8	41 7/8	6	6	Lemhi County	ID	Gabriel R. Gibbons	1998	392
343 4/8	49 2/8	46 6/8	49 5/8	6	6	Grand County	CO	Leon Lambert	1981	398
343 4/8	49 2/8	47 0/8	37 6/8	6	6	Lemhi County	ID	Roger Brockhoff	1985	398
343 4/8	51 4/8	52 1/8	38 4/8	6	7	Socorro County	NM	Richard Dewey	1986	398
343 4/8	53 7/8	52 4/8	44 6/8	6	6	Sierra County	NM	Robert A. Maurin III	1992	398
343 3/8	58 5/8	59 5/8	40 7/8	6	7	Mesa County	CO	Don Boyles	1990	402
343 3/8	48 3/8	46 7/8	39 7/8	7	7	Sublette County	WY	John C. Prince	1994	402
343 2/8	52 2/8	51 2/8	40 0/8	6	6	Idaho County	ID	Mike Schlegel	1978	404
343 2/8	51 7/8	52 7/8	42 3/8	7	7	Morgan County	UT	Warren Strickland	1993	404
343 2/8	49 2/8	46 1/8	40 2/8	8	6	Yellowstone County	MT	Richard D. Cunningham	1997	404
343 2/8	56 6/8	55 6/8	53 2/8	7	6	Beaver County	UT	Kasey Willden	1998	404
343 1/8	50 3/8	54 3/8	42 5/8	7	6	Coconino County	AZ	Jeff Currey	1997	408
343 0/8	54 4/8	52 7/8	38 2/8	6	6	Fergus County	MT	Doug Sereday	1993	409
343 0/8	55 0/8	50 2/8	43 6/8	8	9	Coconino County	AZ	Tom Jensen	1994	409
343 0/8	57 2/8	52 0/8	42 0/8	6	6	Socorro County	NM	Anthony J. Turrietta	1995	409
342 7/8	54 3/8	54 3/8	42 2/8	8	8	Grand County	CO	G. Fred Asbell	1980	412
342 7/8	56 3/8	56 1/8	43 0/8	7	6	Catron County	NM	Bill Elmer	1991	412
342 7/8	54 6/8	56 3/8	44 1/8	6	6	Coconino County	AZ	Rusty K. Kappel	1992	412
342 7/8	56 4/8	56 5/8	37 7/8	6	6	Petroleum County	MT	James C. Miller	1998	412
342 7/8	52 2/8	52 2/8	49 5/8	6	6	Coconino County	AZ	Brian Bejarano	1998	412
342 6/8	48 6/8	49 4/8	46 0/8	5	6	Catron County	NM	Carlton Armstrong	1990	417
342 6/8	51 4/8	52 6/8	41 4/8	6	6	Catron County	NM	Glenn W. Isler	1992	417
342 6/8	50 6/8	50 4/8	40 4/8	6	6	Colfax County	NM	Robert Torstenson	1995	417
342 5/8	48 4/8	46 6/8	38 3/8	6	6	Routt County	CO	Brad Jones	1987	420
342 5/8	53 2/8	49 4/8	36 1/8	6	6	Coconino County	AZ	Victor Lee	1991	420
342 4/8	55 4/8	55 0/8	42 0/8	6	6	Morgan County	UT	Hugh H. Hogle	1990	422
342 4/8	50 0/8	49 3/8	37 3/8	7	7	Archuleta County	CO	M. R. James	1996	422
342 4/8	50 5/8	50 7/8	35 2/8	6	6	Catron County	NM	Gary Wisdom	1997	422
342 3/8	54 7/8	53 7/8	42 5/8	6	6	Flathead County	MT	Eric Schmidt	1994	425
342 3/8	46 1/8	46 0/8	48 3/8	7	7	Garfield County	MT	Steve Rehak	1998	425
342 2/8	49 7/8	49 2/8	37 2/8	6	6	Grant County	NM	Larry M. Sellers	1985	427
342 2/8	49 2/8	48 4/8	35 1/8	6	7	Uintah County	UT	Charles "Smiley" Denver	1988	427
342 2/8	49 6/8	48 4/8	35 6/8	8	7	Coconino County	AZ	Gary Steinmann	1991	427
342 2/8	56 6/8	56 4/8	35 4/8	7	7	Catron County	NM	David H. Boland	1992	427
342 2/8	50 6/8	50 4/8	40 6/8	6	6	Petroleum County	MT	Michael R. Johnson	1994	427
342 2/8	49 6/8	51 5/8	40 4/8	6	6	Fergus County	MT	John Kryfka	1998	427
342 1/8	52 3/8	52 4/8	45 1/8	6	6	Routt County	CO	Jerry A. Krueger	1981	433
342 1/8	53 7/8	50 4/8	34 7/8	6	7	Jackson County	OR	J. T. Tepper	1986	433
342 1/8	47 0/8	48 6/8	34 5/8	6	6	Coconino County	AZ	Lynn M. Johnson	1994	433
342 1/8	49 5/8	48 4/8	41 3/8	6	6	Coconino County	AZ	George Richardson	1995	433
342 0/8	58 6/8	59 0/8	46 6/8	6	6	Cibola County	NM	Dois R. Chesshir	1986	437
342 0/8	56 1/8	55 7/8	40 0/8	7	7	Socorro County	NM	Tom Alvin	1992	437
342 0/8	52 4/8	54 5/8	40 6/8	6	8	Socorro County	NM	Randall C. Barnes	1996	437
342 0/8	48 6/8	49 1/8	35 4/8	6	6	Mineral County	CO	Kenneth L. Ryan	1996	437
341 7/8	49 5/8	50 2/8	37 4/8	7	8	Fergus County	MT	Keith Meckling	1992	441
341 7/8	50 6/8	50 6/8	44 1/8	6	6	Umatilla County	OR	Don Sturm	1997	441
341 6/8	54 7/8	53 1/8	44 2/8	6	6	Greenlee County	AZ	Pete Shepley	1983	443
341 6/8	55 3/8	53 3/8	45 6/8	6	6	Garfield County	CO	Gary Frauenkron	1983	443
341 6/8	55 3/8	55 0/8	33 5/8	7	6	Catron County	NM	Mike Hillis	1988	443
341 6/8	51 4/8	50 1/8	38 3/8	7	6	Grant County	NM	Dick Stoll	1989	443
341 6/8	50 3/8	52 0/8	48 0/8	6	6	Kittitas County	WA	Cindy Coker	1993	443
341 6/8	49 1/8	48 7/8	39 4/8	6	6	Socorro County	NM	Don Carpenter	1998	443
341 5/8	54 4/8	56 2/8	44 3/8	6	6	Socorro County	NM	Ross Johnson	1982	449
341 5/8	54 1/8	52 2/8	45 1/8	6	6	Garfield County	MT	Darryl Turner	1985	449
341 5/8	47 0/8	47 2/8	39 3/8	6	6	Clackamas County	OR	Paul Smith	1987	449
341 5/8	48 7/8	46 5/8	33 7/8	6	6	Navajo County	AZ	Leon W. Smith	1989	449
341 5/8	51 0/8	51 2/8	36 5/8	6	6	Petroleum County	MT	Randy Jonjak	1992	449
341 4/8	45 6/8	47 5/8	37 4/8	6	6	Las Animas County	CO	Douglas F. Murray	1974	454
341 4/8	53 4/8	54 6/8	36 6/8	6	6	Pitkin County	CO	Nelson Harrington	1977	454
341 4/8	50 5/8	48 5/8	39 4/8	6	6	Adams County	ID	Emery Meeks	1982	454
341 4/8	52 3/8	51 7/8	46 0/8	7	7	Routt County	CO	Todd Bandemer	1991	454
341 4/8	51 6/8	52 0/8	31 2/8	6	6	Jefferson County	CO	Mickey Wirth	1992	454
341 3/8	47 7/8	48 1/8	44 5/8	6	6	Chaffee County	CO	Tom E. Bowman	1979	459
341 3/8	54 0/8	52 3/8	37 7/8	9	7	Missoula County	MT	Ted Miller	1984	459
341 3/8	54 1/8	51 6/8	42 3/8	6	6	McKinley County	NM	Glenn W. Isler	1988	459
341 3/8	49 7/8	50 4/8	46 2/8	7	6	Canmore	ALB	Lee Oshust	1989	459
341 3/8	55 6/8	53 4/8	35 3/8	7	7	Klickitat County	WA	Bill "Razz" Philley, Jr.	1991	459
341 3/8	51 0/8	48 4/8	38 7/8	6	6	Catron County	NM	Robert A. Williams	1993	459
341 2/8	53 0/8	54 6/8	44 6/8	6	7	Coconino County	AZ	Dean Dunaway	1991	465
341 2/8	51 7/8	51 0/8	38 4/8	7	7	Umatilla County	OR	Tim Guild	1996	465
341 0/8	54 2/8	54 1/8	40 6/8	6	6	Catron County	NM	Ronnie Coburn	1986	467
341 0/8	53 0/8	53 0/8	42 6/8	6	6	Custer County	ID	John R. Sample	1986	467

YELLOWSTONE "AMERICAN" ELK (TYPICAL ANTLERS)

Minimum Score 260

Continued

SCORE	LENGTH OF R MAIN BEAM L		INSIDE SPREAD	NUMBER OF R POINTS L		AREA	STATE/ PROVINCE	HUNTER'S NAME	DATE	RANK
341 0/8	55 5/8	54 4/8	40 4/8	6	6	White Pine County	NV	Justin T. Williams	1994	467
340 7/8	48 1/8	47 4/8	37 5/8	6	6	Carbon County	WY	Roger Swensen	1977	470
340 7/8	56 3/8	56 4/8	39 5/8	7	7	Yakima County	WA	Randy Kaech	1986	470
340 7/8	54 7/8	52 7/8	40 0/8	6	7	Coconino County	AZ	Kevin B. Call	1994	470
340 7/8	46 2/8	42 3/8	41 3/8	6	6	Washakie County	WY	Scott Long	1997	470
340 7/8	50 4/8	50 1/8	49 1/8	6	7	Boise County	ID	Kenneth Hyde	1998	470
340 6/8	56 6/8	59 5/8	33 6/8	6	6	Coconino County	AZ	Earnest E. Milton	1976	475
340 6/8	54 0/8	51 7/8	41 2/8	7	6	Petroleum County	MT	John 'Rosey' Roseland	1983	475
340 6/8	46 0/8	46 4/8	40 2/8	6	6	Granite County	MT	Tom Adams	1991	475
340 6/8	48 2/8	46 4/8	40 2/8	6	6	Larimer County	CO	Arnold Hale	1992	475
340 6/8	52 5/8	52 0/8	46 2/8	6	6	Lemhi County	ID	David Tande	1994	475
340 6/8	51 6/8	49 6/8	35 2/8	6	6	Coconino County	AZ	John D. Audsley	1997	475
340 5/8	47 3/8	48 6/8	33 1/8	6	6	Nordegg	ALB	Thaddaus Fenske	1978	481
340 5/8	54 5/8	53 2/8	39 1/8	6	6	Coconino County	AZ	Gregory S. Wood	1990	481
340 5/8	52 4/8	54 6/8	41 3/8	6	6	Sierra County	NM	Dr. Hamid Massiha	1991	481
340 5/8	54 2/8	53 7/8	40 7/8	6	7	Coconino County	AZ	Paul Hicks	1991	481
340 5/8	58 3/8	55 5/8	42 4/8	6	7	Catron County	NM	Walter Palmer	1994	481
340 5/8	51 2/8	52 1/8	38 4/8	7	7	Shoshone County	ID	Matt Capka	1998	481
340 4/8	51 5/8	49 1/8	41 2/8	6	6	Sanders County	MT	Walt Borgmann	1983	487
340 4/8	51 0/8	52 4/8	42 0/8	6	7	Catron County	NM	Brice McWethy	1985	487
340 4/8	50 6/8	50 5/8	39 2/8	6	7	Sierra County	NM	Tony L. Jones	1988	487
340 4/8	53 2/8	54 6/8	44 6/8	6	6	Morgan County	UT	Patrick Hogle	1994	487
340 3/8	51 0/8	51 1/8	38 1/8	6	6	Crook County	OR	Curtis Edwards	1989	491
340 3/8	51 1/8	48 4/8	33 5/8	7	6	Catron County	NM	Manuel Baeza	1998	491
340 2/8	53 3/8	54 2/8	40 4/8	6	6	Missoula County	MT	David M. Anderson	1978	493
340 2/8	50 4/8	51 3/8	36 7/8	7	6	Socorro County	NM	Randy B. Furr	1983	493
340 2/8	54 4/8	56 4/8	43 2/8	6	7	Catron County	NM	John Fehrenbacher	1986	493
340 2/8	50 6/8	50 7/8	37 4/8	6	6	Lincoln County	NM	Tony L. Najar	1993	493
340 2/8	51 1/8	50 7/8	45 4/8	6	6	Hudson Bay	SAS	Kenneth Baker	1994	493
340 2/8	55 4/8	57 1/8	38 2/8	6	6	Coconino County	AZ	Duane A. Wilson, Jr.	1994	493
340 2/8	54 5/8	55 6/8	41 2/8	6	6	Flathead County	MT	Erik Wenum	1994	493
340 2/8	52 2/8	52 6/8	46 7/8	6	6	Coconino County	AZ	Richard H. Wetnight	1984	500
340 1/8	52 1/8	50 5/8	43 7/8	6	6	Judith Basin County	MT	Jeffrey M. Smith	1998	500
340 0/8	49 2/8	50 7/8	37 4/8	7	7	Flathead County	MT	Henry Herman	1984	502
339 7/8	52 6/8	53 3/8	38 1/8	6	6	Yavapai County	AZ	Gene Barcak	1991	503
339 6/8	47 7/8	46 7/8	41 4/8	6	6	Lewis & Clark County	MT	Doug J. Powell	1983	504
339 6/8	51 4/8	51 4/8	46 4/8	6	6	Otero County	NM	Bonnie A. Allen	1987	504
339 6/8	50 5/8	50 6/8	42 6/8	6	6	Beaver County	UT	Calvin Dalke	1995	504
339 6/8	51 6/8	52 1/8	35 0/8	6	6	Niton Junction	ALB	Ron Sargent	1996	504
339 5/8	51 6/8	53 5/8	47 1/8	6	6	Coconino County	AZ	Bruce D. Ludeke	1977	508
339 5/8	45 2/8	43 3/8	44 7/8	6	7	Bighorn Mtns.	WY	Edward F. Hanlon	1979	508
339 5/8	45 4/8	45 6/8	39 1/8	6	6	Sanders County	MT	Robert A. Sieloff	1994	508
339 4/8	49 0/8	48 7/8	38 0/8	7	7	Grant County	OR	Dan Dorn	1986	511
339 4/8	51 3/8	50 5/8	39 2/8	6	6	Mineral County	MT	Tom Porter	1986	511
339 4/8	51 0/8	51 2/8	38 0/8	6	7	Colfax County	NM	Christopher Green	1990	511
339 3/8	48 4/8	49 5/8	42 1/8	6	6	Cibola County	NM	Delbert Mariano	1980	514
339 3/8	47 4/8	44 7/8	43 6/8	6	7	Petroleum County	MT	Steven A. Barstow	1989	514
339 2/8	51 7/8	51 0/8	40 6/8	7	6	Fremont County	ID	Gary Skoy	1981	516
339 1/8	50 5/8	49 5/8	42 6/8	6	7	Coconino County	AZ	Stretch Penberthy	1987	517
339 1/8	56 0/8	52 7/8	39 3/8	6	6	Sublette County	WY	Tony Burchett	1988	517
339 1/8	52 2/8	52 2/8	42 1/8	6	8	Grant County	OR	Brad Miller	1988	517
339 1/8	47 5/8	46 3/8	40 3/8	9	8	Catron County	NM	Danny V. Bennett	1990	517
339 1/8	44 1/8	44 4/8	34 1/8	7	7	Bonner County	ID	H. Dale Stone	1990	517
339 1/8	54 4/8	54 4/8	48 1/8	6	6	Navajo County	AZ	Larry D. Jones	1993	517
339 1/8	51 0/8	54 3/8	39 7/8	6	6	Coconino County	AZ	William C. Bolt, Jr.	1995	517
339 1/8	50 1/8	50 2/8	42 7/8	6	7	Millarville	ALB	Stuart Sinclair-Smith	1995	517
339 1/8	54 6/8	52 6/8	40 1/8	6	6	Catron County	NM	Kim E. Womer	1997	517
339 0/8	50 6/8	51 2/8	45 4/8	6	6	Powell County	MT	Kenneth M. Darr	1996	526
339 0/8	49 0/8	50 1/8	44 0/8	6	6	Catron County	NM	Gerard Pugliese	1997	526
338 6/8	45 6/8	45 6/8	43 0/8	6	7	Greenlee County	AZ	Jed Dahar	1989	528
338 6/8	47 4/8	45 6/8	44 0/8	7	6	Beaverhead County	MT	Gene Loder	1991	528
338 6/8	51 6/8	50 5/8	40 6/8	7	7	Grant County	NM	Lance Maloney	1997	528
338 6/8	49 7/8	48 4/8	38 4/8	6	6	Coconino County	AZ	Frank T. Sandstedt	1997	528
338 5/8	50 4/8	53 4/8	42 1/8	6	6	Rio Arriba County	NM	Lee Braudt	1983	532
338 5/8	49 2/8	48 4/8	36 5/8	6	6	Lincoln County	WY	Doug Jenkins	1986	532
338 5/8	53 7/8	55 0/8	39 3/8	5	6	Fremont County	ID	James R. Foote	1995	532
338 5/8	50 7/8	49 5/8	42 3/8	6	7	Lemhi County	ID	Robert Reed	1996	532
338 5/8	55 2/8	55 5/8	34 7/8	6	7	Idaho County	ID	Robert Maves	1998	532
338 4/8	49 2/8	49 6/8	29 0/8	6	6	Catron County	NM	Eugene Arndt	1993	537
338 4/8	50 4/8	50 4/8	41 6/8	6	6	Smoky River	ALB	Norris Bates	1995	537
338 3/8	55 5/8	54 0/8	36 7/8	6	6	Sheridan County	WY	Mike Barrett	1981	539
338 3/8	51 3/8	52 5/8	35 5/8	8	7	Coconino County	AZ	Mike Uebel	1998	539
338 2/8	48 1/8	52 2/8	38 3/8	7	7	Garfield County	MT	Richard R. Chamberlin	1989	541
338 2/8	47 7/8	47 4/8	36 2/8	7	6	Catron County	NM	Nick Arnett	1990	541
338 2/8	49 0/8	51 0/8	39 6/8	6	6	Deer Lodge County	MT	Stephen Herrera	1990	541
338 2/8	49 7/8	50 2/8	36 6/8	7	7	Natrona County	WY	Kevin Christopherson	1997	541
338 2/8	51 1/8	48 2/8	41 6/8	6	6	Sanders County	MT	Darrell "Speed" Tessier	1998	541
338 1/8	50 4/8	50 5/8	37 1/8	7	7	Lincoln County	NM	Kurt Hollis	1987	546

YELLOWSTONE "AMERICAN" ELK (TYPICAL ANTLERS)

Minimum Score 260 — Continued

SCORE	LENGTH OF MAIN BEAM R	L	INSIDE SPREAD	NUMBER OF POINTS R	L	AREA	STATE/ PROVINCE	HUNTER'S NAME	DATE	RANK
338 1/8	47 0/8	50 7/8	39 3/8	5	6	Lincoln County	WY	Gary L. Sims	1991	546
338 0/8	47 4/8	46 6/8	45 5/8	7	6	Caribou County	ID	Jim L. Fowler	1987	548
338 0/8	53 5/8	54 7/8	41 6/8	6	7	Catron County	NM	James Baumgardner	1990	548
338 0/8	51 4/8	52 5/8	41 0/8	6	6	Coconino County	AZ	Mike Leach	1991	548
338 0/8	44 7/8	46 1/8	35 3/8	8	8	Apache County	AZ	Frank P. Martinez	1992	548
338 0/8	55 4/8	53 3/8	40 0/8	6	6	Mesa County	CO	David G. Anderson	1994	548
337 6/8	45 0/8	46 0/8	37 4/8	6	7	Boulder County	CO	Roger Schuett	1977	553
337 6/8	55 2/8	55 2/8	45 6/8	5	5	Socorro County	NM	Wesley Henderson	1986	553
337 6/8	51 1/8	50 3/8	38 4/8	7	6	Coconino County	AZ	Robert Dishmon	1991	553
337 6/8	47 6/8	49 0/8	42 0/8	7	6	Washakie County	WY	Roger Peabody	1991	553
337 6/8	48 2/8	47 4/8	43 2/8	6	6	Otero County	NM	Allen Dalton	1991	553
337 5/8	49 1/8	49 6/8	39 1/8	6	6	Granite County	MT	George E. Wood	1978	558
337 5/8	52 1/8	52 6/8	37 3/8	6	6	Missoula County	MT	Mel Nyman, Jr.	1983	558
337 5/8	49 3/8	51 4/8	36 1/8	6	6	Coconino County	AZ	Danny Eloy Martinez	1985	558
337 5/8	53 2/8	53 3/8	39 7/8	6	6	Grant County	OR	Marte Scheuffele	1992	558
337 4/8	52 3/8	54 5/8	41 4/8	7	6	Coconino County	AZ	Alan Blanchard	1972	562
337 4/8	63 6/8	62 3/8	42 0/8	6	6	Coconino County	AZ	Gregory B. Minton	1992	562
337 4/8	51 6/8	52 0/8	56 0/8	6	6	Converse County	WY	Mike Hammond	1998	562
337 3/8	53 0/8	49 2/8	42 1/8	6	5	Mesa County	CO	Mike Flores	1970	565
337 3/8	46 4/8	45 7/8	34 5/8	6	7	Rio Blanco County	CO	Jay Verzuh	1990	565
337 3/8	55 2/8	50 0/8	35 5/8	6	6	Coconino County	AZ	Cindi Richardson	1995	565
337 2/8	48 2/8	49 4/8	41 6/8	6	8	Beaverhead County	MT	Theodore T. Ralls, Sr.	1990	568
337 2/8	50 4/8	53 3/8	44 4/8	6	6	Coconino County	AZ	Henry L. Roberts	1990	568
337 2/8	51 5/8	53 2/8	48 4/8	6	6	Lincoln County	NM	Wayne McMakin	1992	568
337 1/8	51 3/8	50 0/8	37 1/8	6	6	Catron County	NM	Larry Evanson	1992	571
337 1/8	51 7/8	51 2/8	42 1/8	6	6	Mesa County	CO	Don Boyles	1993	571
337 1/8	51 4/8	50 0/8	37 7/8	7	6	Catron County	NM	Bill L. Marek	1998	571
337 0/8	52 4/8	51 4/8	38 2/8	6	6	Socorro County	NM	Ron White	1976	574
337 0/8	57 6/8	57 6/8	36 2/8	7	7	Lewis County	WA	Terry LaFrance	1984	574
337 0/8	49 2/8	49 4/8	39 4/8	6	6	Idaho County	ID	Roger O. Wyant	1987	574
337 0/8	50 3/8	50 3/8	41 6/8	6	6	Albany County	WY	Gordon Wigdahl	1997	574
336 7/8	49 3/8	48 0/8	43 1/8	7	7	Apache County	AZ	Eric Penrod	1982	578
336 7/8	53 1/8	53 1/8	37 5/8	6	6	Missoula County	MT	Pao K. Moua	1996	578
336 6/8	50 7/8	51 3/8	34 6/8	6	7	Uintah County	UT	Everett Burson	1981	580
336 6/8	53 5/8	53 3/8	39 4/8	6	6	Taos County	NM	Jeff Lampe	1992	580
336 6/8	53 5/8	51 0/8	32 6/8	6	6	Catron County	NM	Glen P. Gerhart	1992	580
336 6/8	48 1/8	48 6/8	50 4/8	6	6	Beaverhead County	MT	Corey W. Murray	1993	580
336 6/8	50 3/8	50 1/8	39 2/8	6	6	Park County	WY	William Manske	1994	580
336 6/8	46 6/8	48 6/8	41 6/8	6	7	Fremont County	ID	Kendon H. Jensen	1998	580
336 5/8	46 7/8	48 2/8	36 1/8	6	6	Lincoln County	WY	Len Merritt	1994	586
336 5/8	53 5/8	52 7/8	47 3/8	5	6	Socorro County	NM	Dr. Mark J. Yurchisin	1998	586
336 4/8	56 2/8	55 6/8	36 6/8	6	7	Coconino County	AZ	David M. Geiger	1990	588
336 4/8	50 7/8	50 1/8	41 4/8	7	6	Meagher County	MT	George O. Johnson	1991	588
336 4/8	51 2/8	48 7/8	43 7/8	7	6	Big Horn County	WY	Lance Crawford	1992	588
336 4/8	49 0/8	49 2/8	37 0/8	7	7	White Pine County	NV	Robert McDonald	1993	588
336 4/8	51 3/8	49 0/8	40 0/8	6	6	Beaverhead County	MT	Lee Murphree	1994	588
336 4/8	53 1/8	52 0/8	37 2/8	6	6	Catron County	NM	Delbert Capps	1995	588
336 3/8	47 7/8	48 2/8	34 1/8	6	6	Meagher County	MT	Ronald K. Granneman	1973	594
336 3/8	56 0/8	54 5/8	41 3/8	6	6	Custer County	ID	Gregg Welch	1984	594
336 2/8	52 4/8	50 6/8	33 2/8	6	6	Lewis & Clark County	MT	Ronald K. Granneman	1979	596
336 2/8	52 4/8	51 5/8	40 2/8	6	6	Coconino County	AZ	Jeremy Harness	1993	596
336 2/8	55 5/8	56 5/8	42 2/8	6	6	Catron County	NM	Mike H. Farwell	1994	596
336 2/8	51 6/8	51 7/8	38 0/8	7	6	Malheur County	OR	Raymond R. Kappell	1994	596
336 1/8	54 6/8	52 1/8	40 2/8	7	6	Catron County	NM	R. Grant Clawson	1986	600
336 1/8	48 0/8	48 2/8	34 6/8	7	7	Fergus County	MT	Randall L. Zeman	1991	600
336 1/8	48 4/8	47 2/8	41 1/8	6	6	Archuleta County	CO	Lester Hawkins, Jr.	1998	600
336 0/8	50 0/8	50 1/8	42 4/8	6	6	Granite County	MT	Tom Storm	1982	603
336 0/8	50 3/8	50 6/8	40 4/8	5	7	White Pine County	NV	Don Snodgrass	1989	603
336 0/8	51 2/8	52 5/8	47 0/8	6	6	Coconino County	AZ	Darell Lee Christensen	1997	603
336 0/8	55 3/8	56 6/8	33 0/8	6	6	White Pine County	NV	John David Stanley, Jr.	1997	603
335 6/8	53 4/8	53 1/8	37 6/8	7	8	Phillips County	MT	John 'Rosey' Roseland	1977	607
335 6/8	51 2/8	53 6/8	39 2/8	6	6	Shoshone County	ID	Ernest W. Clanton	1983	607
335 6/8	51 3/8	51 6/8	40 0/8	8	7	Fergus County	MT	Larry L. Schweitzer	1985	607
335 6/8	49 1/8	50 0/8	41 6/8	6	6	Spray Lakes	ALB	Danny Moore	1987	607
335 6/8	53 2/8	53 0/8	51 4/8	6	6	Catron County	NM	Scot P. McClelland	1988	607
335 6/8	51 2/8	49 4/8	41 4/8	7	6	Coconino County	AZ	James Whitaker	1989	607
335 6/8	53 4/8	52 3/8	41 2/8	6	7	Powell County	MT	Theodore J. Poper	1991	607
335 5/8	52 6/8	50 7/8	43 3/8	6	6	Catron County	NM	Barrett L. Lemmon	1991	614
335 5/8	43 5/8	46 4/8	38 3/8	8	7	Phillips County	MT	David E. Snowden, Jr.	1995	614
335 5/8	52 0/8	51 4/8	40 1/8	6	6	Larimer County	CO	Jim Botner	1996	614
335 5/8	45 5/8	46 6/8	35 3/8	6	6	Phillips County	MT	Dan VanderPloeg	1996	614
335 4/8	47 4/8	48 6/8	49 0/8	6	6	Clearwater County	ID	Robert J. Kreisher	1958	618
335 4/8	52 0/8	52 6/8	45 4/8	7	7	Skamania County	WA	Ted Jaycox	1985	618
335 2/8	52 1/8	51 4/8	37 4/8	6	6	Millard County	UT	Raymond M. Loveless	1993	620
335 1/8	46 4/8	46 2/8	38 1/8	6	6	Camas County	ID	Derek Trent	1991	621
335 1/8	51 6/8	50 7/8	40 3/8	6	6	Coconino County	AZ	David J. Martin	1992	621
335 1/8	50 6/8	51 5/8	40 3/8	6	6	Phillips County	MT	Tom S. Crabill	1992	621
335 0/8	50 7/8	50 5/8	40 0/8	6	6	Caribou County	ID	Charles Humphreys	1977	624

561

YELLOWSTONE "AMERICAN" ELK (TYPICAL ANTLERS)

Minimum Score 260   Continued

SCORE	LENGTH OF MAIN BEAM R	LENGTH OF MAIN BEAM L	INSIDE SPREAD	NUMBER OF POINTS R	NUMBER OF POINTS L	AREA	STATE/PROVINCE	HUNTER'S NAME	DATE	RANK
335 0/8	53 3/8	52 0/8	39 4/8	6	6	Sanders County	MT	Gil Gilbertson	1984	624
335 0/8	51 0/8	53 0/8	40 2/8	7	7	Grant County	NM	Johnny W. Morris	1991	624
335 0/8	50 6/8	49 1/8	34 2/8	8	7	Petroleum County	MT	Craig Wagner	1992	624
335 0/8	48 0/8	48 3/8	38 4/8	7	7	Harney County	OR	Joel R. Griffin	1993	624
335 0/8	49 5/8	48 3/8	35 2/8	7	6	Grant County	OR	Charlie A. Gannon	1996	624
335 0/8	53 0/8	54 4/8	39 3/8	6	7	Catron County	NM	Dyrk Eddie	1996	624
335 0/8	50 3/8	48 5/8	37 2/8	6	6	Catron County	NM	Tony Cutbirth	1998	624
334 6/8	51 4/8	51 7/8	44 6/8	6	6	Summit County	CO	Michael Beckwith	1976	632
334 6/8	52 0/8	52 2/8	43 0/8	6	6	Custer County	ID	Hal J. Dillashaw	1991	632
334 6/8	54 3/8	52 4/8	36 0/8	6	7	White Pine County	NV	Gene A. Jones	1992	632
334 6/8	49 4/8	49 7/8	44 2/8	6	6	Catron County	NM	Richard Gage	1996	632
334 6/8	51 4/8	50 7/8	43 0/8	6	7	White Pine County	NV	Richard Sandoz	1998	632
334 5/8	50 0/8	49 5/8	34 1/8	7	7	Garfield County	CO	Darren Mack	1989	637
334 5/8	50 3/8	49 1/8	38 5/8	6	6	Navajo County	AZ	Tod Thornton	1994	637
334 5/8	53 1/8	51 2/8	33 0/8	6	8	Petroleum County	MT	Mutt Wilson	1995	637
334 4/8	49 7/8	48 5/8	46 4/8	6	6	Gunnison County	CO	Roy M. Goodwin	1988	640
334 3/8	53 3/8	52 5/8	38 5/8	6	6	Coconino County	AZ	Stephen Jon McGaughey	1988	641
334 3/8	54 4/8	54 1/8	40 3/8	6	6	Catron County	NM	Dave Holt	1995	641
334 3/8	49 0/8	50 0/8	37 7/8	6	6	Socorro County	NM	Ron Madsen	1996	641
334 2/8	52 5/8	49 0/8	38 4/8	6	6	Sweetwater County	WY	Lawrence Branson	1984	644
334 2/8	47 7/8	46 4/8	44 0/8	6	6	Albany County	WY	Thomas Bradach	1988	644
334 2/8	50 3/8	49 7/8	32 6/8	6	6	White Pine County	NV	Richard A. Hanson	1992	644
334 2/8	50 2/8	51 2/8	40 4/8	6	6	Petroleum County	MT	Michael Thomas	1995	644
334 1/8	48 3/8	51 0/8	39 5/8	6	6	Madison County	MT	John Aalto	1979	648
334 1/8	46 2/8	49 2/8	43 5/8	6	6	Boulder County	CO	Billy E. Corley	1991	648
334 1/8	54 2/8	54 2/8	40 7/8	6	6	Madison County	MT	Bruce A. Traucht	1992	648
334 1/8	52 5/8	50 2/8	42 3/8	7	6	Fremont County	ID	Cecil F. Crow	1994	648
334 1/8	49 6/8	50 2/8	40 3/8	6	6	Catron County	NM	James A. Trujillo	1995	648
334 1/8	44 7/8	44 7/8	37 5/8	7	6	Valhalla Centre	ALB	Roger D. VanEerden	1996	648
334 0/8	45 5/8	47 6/8	41 2/8	7	6	Boulder County	CO	Gus Roe	1984	654
334 0/8	50 2/8	50 4/8	43 4/8	6	6	Pennington County	SD	Stuart A. Jacobsen	1996	654
333 7/8	51 6/8	49 0/8	34 6/8	7	7	Fergus County	MT	Edwin Evans	1983	656
333 6/8	49 4/8	49 4/8	45 0/8	6	6	Baker County	OR	Russell B. Jones	1946	657
333 6/8	53 4/8	52 2/8	44 2/8	7	6	Sheridan County	WY	Chuck McKenzie	1976	657
333 6/8	46 5/8	47 1/8	38 6/8	6	6	Otero County	NM	Richard D. Burton	1997	657
333 4/8	47 2/8	47 0/8	35 0/8	6	6	Waterton Park	ALB	Barry Linklater	1987	660
333 4/8	49 1/8	48 0/8	39 6/8	7	7	Canmore	ALB	Jordon Ohrn	1988	660
333 3/8	45 6/8	47 4/8	39 7/8	6	6	Catron County	NM	Gary A Littauer	1984	662
333 3/8	46 0/8	46 0/8	34 3/8	7	6	Union County	OR	Mark Simmons	1985	662
333 3/8	54 7/8	55 3/8	43 2/8	6	7	Canmore	ALB	Brian Francis	1986	662
333 3/8	50 6/8	50 6/8	43 7/8	6	7	Wheatland County	MT	Tim Klosterman	1996	662
333 3/8	49 0/8	49 0/8	41 1/8	6	6	Beaverhead County	MT	Colleen Rose	1996	662
333 3/8	49 0/8	55 4/8	41 5/8	6	6	Albany County	WY	Don Maston	1997	662
333 3/8	51 4/8	53 4/8	39 1/8	6	6	Apache County	AZ	Shane Howard	1997	662
333 2/8	47 0/8	48 4/8	39 4/8	6	6	Jefferson County	CO	Jerry Gruenberg	1988	669
333 2/8	52 6/8	54 0/8	38 0/8	7	6	Teton County	WY	Jerry W. Lashuay	1988	669
333 2/8	47 1/8	46 5/8	41 4/8	6	6	Carbon County	UT	Tom Paluso	1989	669
333 2/8	50 0/8	50 2/8	37 6/8	6	6	Catron County	NM	Bill Powell	1991	669
333 2/8	48 5/8	49 1/8	35 0/8	6	7	Ravalli County	MT	Ray Joy	1993	669
333 1/8	41 3/8	46 2/8	41 3/8	6	6	Grand County	CO	Dennis Wehling	1981	674
333 1/8	49 0/8	49 0/8	40 3/8	6	6	Natrona County	WY	Mike Urlacher	1993	674
333 1/8	51 0/8	50 1/8	43 5/8	6	6	Judith Basin County	MT	Jerry Tabacco	1996	674
333 0/8	45 7/8	47 1/8	37 0/8	6	6	Catron County	NM	J. B. Lemon	1993	677
333 0/8	56 3/8	53 7/8	31 0/8	7	7	Coconino County	AZ	Stephen C. Christensen	1997	677
333 0/8	52 1/8	50 2/8	41 4/8	6	6	Catron County	NM	Bill Brown	1997	677
333 0/8	53 3/8	48 5/8	44 5/8	7	7	Coconino County	AZ	John Kovac	1997	677
332 7/8	48 4/8	49 3/8	41 3/8	7	7	Grant County	OR	Neil Hinton	1985	681
332 7/8	52 1/8	49 6/8	36 1/8	6	6	Phillips County	MT	Todd A. Erickson	1989	681
332 7/8	51 3/8	53 7/8	40 1/8	6	6	Catron County	NM	Marvin H. Walter	1992	681
332 7/8	48 1/8	47 3/8	41 7/8	7	7	Valley County	ID	Tracy Hunt	1992	681
332 7/8	55 0/8	53 6/8	43 7/8	6	6	Catron County	NM	Kevin L. Reid	1998	681
332 6/8	53 7/8	51 6/8	43 2/8	6	6	Albany County	WY	Pat McAteer	1981	686
332 6/8	52 0/8	49 2/8	37 0/8	6	6	Catron County	NM	John Howard	1984	686
332 6/8	51 1/8	51 7/8	32 0/8	7	6	King County	WA	Curtis H. Fowler	1987	686
332 6/8	51 6/8	50 4/8	40 4/8	6	6	Carbon County	UT	Dan Summers	1989	686
332 5/8	50 7/8	49 7/8	45 3/8	6	6	Teton County	MT	Wayne Lawrence	1995	690
332 5/8	48 6/8	47 0/8	34 5/8	6	6	Lincoln County	NV	Larry Pabst	1997	690
332 4/8	54 4/8	53 2/8	41 6/8	7	7	Apache County	AZ	Steve Schaufer	1989	692
332 4/8	47 2/8	47 0/8	45 1/8	6	7	Coconino County	AZ	Gregory B. Minton	1991	692
332 3/8	54 4/8	52 0/8	33 7/8	7	6	Apache County	AZ	Charles G. Dawe	1986	694
332 3/8	49 4/8	49 4/8	42 7/8	6	6	Coconino County	AZ	Jerry Vogel	1990	694
332 1/8	53 4/8	54 6/8	36 7/8	6	6	Coconino County	AZ	James R. Moore	1980	696
332 1/8	47 0/8	50 4/8	40 1/8	6	6	Sublette County	WY	Danny E. Williams	1995	696
332 1/8	47 2/8	46 6/8	31 7/8	6	6	Jumping Pound Creek	ALB	Archie Nesbitt	1996	696
332 0/8	49 2/8	50 5/8	38 2/8	7	7	Caribou County	ID	Joseph M. Hulse	1967	699
332 0/8	52 0/8	51 6/8	42 0/8	7	6	Clearwater County	ID	Don West	1983	699
332 0/8	51 3/8	50 6/8	37 2/8	6	6	Custer County	ID	Delos G. Robinson	1987	699
332 0/8	49 5/8	49 0/8	37 0/8	6	6	Catron County	NM	Christopher Green	1990	699

YELLOWSTONE "AMERICAN" ELK (TYPICAL ANTLERS)

Minimum Score 260

SCORE	LENGTH OF MAIN BEAM R	LENGTH OF MAIN BEAM L	INSIDE SPREAD	NUMBER OF POINTS R	NUMBER OF POINTS L	AREA	STATE/PROVINCE	HUNTER'S NAME	DATE	RANK
332 0/8	47 1/8	46 1/8	38 4/8	6	6	Clearwater County	ID	Richard L. Sandusky	1990	699
332 0/8	52 3/8	50 0/8	56 1/8	6	7	Coconino County	AZ	Andrew L. Grannan	1991	699
332 0/8	50 3/8	49 6/8	37 2/8	6	6	Grant County	OR	Robert Reed	1992	699
332 0/8	50 2/8	48 3/8	39 4/8	6	6	Catron County	NM	Carl McGlothlin	1994	699
332 0/8	51 7/8	51 6/8	37 6/8	6	6	Taos County	NM	Steve R. Rivera	1994	699
332 0/8	48 2/8	51 5/8	48 7/8	7	6	Catron County	NM	William E. Fleshman	1995	699
331 7/8	53 3/8	50 4/8	36 7/8	6	7	Los Alamos County	NM	Robert Barrie	1986	709
331 7/8	50 0/8	50 5/8	41 3/8	6	6	Catron County	NM	Thomas Blaeser	1991	709
331 7/8	45 2/8	45 0/8	31 4/8	6	6	Catron County	NM	Carl D. Bradford	1993	709
331 7/8	53 7/8	52 1/8	43 7/8	6	6	Ravalli County	MT	Eddie Polich	1994	709
331 6/8	48 0/8	49 6/8	45 7/8	7	6	Canmore	ALB	Ken Madsen	1985	713
331 6/8	48 0/8	50 4/8	37 2/8	6	6	Catron County	NM	Randall S. Madding	1988	713
331 6/8	49 4/8	50 2/8	37 2/8	6	6	Jefferson County	OR	Gary Naugher	1996	713
331 6/8	54 0/8	54 3/8	42 0/8	6	6	Garfield County	MT	Dave Gins	1997	713
331 5/8	51 3/8	48 6/8	43 7/8	6	6	Sublette County	WY	Rod Knight	1983	717
331 5/8	49 0/8	47 4/8	41 5/8	6	6	Fremont County	ID	Rick Harris	1986	717
331 5/8	48 0/8	46 5/8	35 1/8	6	7	Flathead County	MT	David L. Thompson	1991	717
331 5/8	51 2/8	50 4/8	39 5/8	6	6	Custer County	ID	Garry L. Bolinder	1993	717
331 5/8	49 1/8	49 0/8	41 1/8	6	6	Petroleum County	MT	Chuck Adams	1994	717
331 5/8	50 0/8	47 5/8	45 1/8	6	7	Park County	WY	Dan Hart	1998	717
331 4/8	47 1/8	48 5/8	40 6/8	6	6	Shoshone County	ID	John C. Dawson II	1990	723
331 4/8	53 0/8	54 7/8	42 6/8	7	6	Coconino County	AZ	Mike Norman Oliver	1990	723
331 4/8	54 0/8	53 5/8	39 4/8	6	6	Boulder County	CO	Ron Readmond	1991	723
331 4/8	51 2/8	49 3/8	38 4/8	7	8	Coconino County	AZ	Kevin Forsman	1992	723
331 4/8	49 7/8	50 6/8	39 0/8	6	6	Beaverhead County	MT	Gerald DeBoar	1992	723
331 4/8	50 3/8	50 6/8	41 0/8	6	6	Navajo County	AZ	Randy L. Hill	1995	723
331 4/8	51 5/8	50 0/8	40 3/8	7	7	Beaverhead County	MT	Jeremy Liedtka	1996	723
331 4/8	51 1/8	50 4/8	37 4/8	6	6	Judith Basin County	MT	Kelly Norskog	1997	723
331 3/8	55 6/8	54 1/8	40 7/8	6	6	Lemhi County	ID	James A. Spinti	1994	731
331 3/8	52 0/8	51 4/8	41 1/8	6	7	King County	WA	David Wayne Bentley	1995	731
331 3/8	50 2/8	52 0/8	44 3/8	6	6	Madison County	MT	Kurt D. Rued	1997	731
331 3/8	43 7/8	46 0/8	41 5/8	6	6	Catron County	NM	Steve Murphy	1998	731
331 2/8	52 3/8	47 4/8	43 0/8	7	6	Catron County	NM	Monte Green	1993	735
331 1/8	48 3/8	48 1/8	38 3/8	6	6	Sheridan County	WY	Mike Barrett	1984	736
331 1/8	46 7/8	47 0/8	40 5/8	6	6	Apache County	AZ	Blaine C. Mullenaux	1993	736
331 1/8	46 4/8	45 7/8	39 1/8	6	6	Pitkin County	CO	James L. Behn	1997	736
331 1/8	52 1/8	49 0/8	41 7/8	6	6	Park County	WY	Vince Philipps	1998	736
331 0/8	51 5/8	52 5/8	45 2/8	7	6	Sublette County	WY	Clair Adams	1987	740
331 0/8	50 6/8	49 6/8	40 2/8	6	6	Catron County	NM	Randal E. Probst	1993	740
330 7/8	53 5/8	50 4/8	39 5/8	6	6	Coconino County	AZ	Jeff W. Elmer	1985	742
330 7/8	50 2/8	50 0/8	41 1/8	6	6	Catron County	NM	J. D. Mills	1988	742
330 7/8	52 1/8	51 6/8	38 7/8	7	7	Coconino County	AZ	Douglas W. Koepsel	1992	742
330 6/8	47 0/8	46 3/8	37 4/8	6	6	Jackson County	CO	Marshall F. Whitsel, Jr.	1996	745
330 5/8	49 1/8	51 5/8	38 1/8	6	6	Otero County	NM	Timothy K. Richards	1992	746
330 5/8	52 4/8	54 4/8	35 7/8	6	6	Catron County	NM	Eugene Smith	1993	746
330 5/8	52 0/8	51 3/8	37 1/8	6	6	White Pine County	NV	Patty Cornejo	1994	746
330 5/8	49 7/8	50 2/8	40 5/8	6	6	Union County	OR	Steven Wayne Brooks	1997	746
330 4/8	44 6/8	46 4/8	38 1/8	6	6	Latah County	ID	John K. Pell	1964	750
330 4/8	54 7/8	54 3/8	34 0/8	7	6	Shoshone County	ID	Kelly Thompson	1986	750
330 4/8	55 3/8	55 4/8	38 0/8	6	6	Coconino County	AZ	Larry Moore	1991	750
330 3/8	50 6/8	49 1/8	38 5/8	6	6	Madison County	MT	Tom Koelzer	1975	753
330 3/8	53 6/8	52 1/8	39 5/8	8	10	Coconino County	AZ	James L. Ludrigson	1985	753
330 3/8	48 6/8	48 5/8	38 7/8	6	6	Grant County	NM	Jack W. Hooper	1989	753
330 3/8	53 1/8	54 3/8	38 5/8	7	6	Coconino County	AZ	Dave Pierce, Jr.	1993	753
330 3/8	50 3/8	50 1/8	37 1/8	7	6	Catron County	NM	Eddie Claypool	1997	753
330 3/8	56 3/8	53 6/8	46 7/8	6	5	Catron County	NM	Tim Canalito	1998	753
330 3/8	47 3/8	50 1/8	34 3/8	6	6	Eagle Lake	SAS	Floyd Forster	1998	753
330 1/8	50 1/8	50 0/8	42 7/8	6	6	Grant County	OR	James M. Carter	1986	760
330 1/8	46 5/8	47 4/8	43 7/8	6	6	Larimer County	CO	Danny M. Holt	1996	760
330 1/8	48 0/8	46 7/8	35 6/8	8	7	Bonneville County	ID	Myron T. Custer	1997	760
330 0/8	53 2/8	53 5/8	45 0/8	6	6	Socorro County	NM	Ron White	1977	763
330 0/8	48 7/8	49 0/8	37 0/8	7	7	Sanders County	MT	Steve Larson	1981	763
330 0/8	52 7/8	50 4/8	33 4/8	6	6	Petroleum County	MT	John Fleharty	1985	763
330 0/8	46 7/8	49 7/8	43 6/8	6	6	Albany County	WY	Paul Ayotte	1985	763
330 0/8	52 5/8	52 6/8	41 2/8	6	6	Catron County	NM	Russell Arndt	1998	763
329 7/8	46 1/8	45 1/8	36 7/8	6	6	Eagle County	CO	Jeffrey A. Duckworth	1981	768
329 7/8	51 4/8	48 6/8	39 3/8	6	6	Powell County	MT	Marlon J. Clapham	1986	768
329 7/8	47 2/8	49 2/8	34 3/8	6	6	Crook County	OR	Terry Luther	1991	768
329 7/8	50 3/8	49 1/8	37 5/8	7	7	Catron County	NM	Donald M. Graves	1991	768
329 7/8	47 4/8	46 5/8	33 1/8	6	6	Phillips County	MT	Rick Miller	1992	768
329 7/8	47 4/8	49 4/8	39 5/8	6	7	Shoshone County	ID	Kenny M. Nelson	1996	768
329 6/8	49 1/8	49 0/8	37 4/8	6	6	Rio Blanco County	CO	Myles Keller	1974	774
329 6/8	48 1/8	47 6/8	38 0/8	6	6	Coconino County	AZ	Mike Moulton	1983	774
329 6/8	53 0/8	51 0/8	34 4/8	6	6	Phillips County	MT	Gregg Pauley	1987	774
329 6/8	44 0/8	47 0/8	36 6/8	6	6	Catron County	NM	Eddie Claypool	1991	774
329 6/8	57 2/8	58 0/8	50 0/8	6	6	Cibola County	NM	Johnny M. Perea	1991	774
329 6/8	54 1/8	54 2/8	49 0/8	6	6	Larimer County	CO	Billy E. Corley	1993	774
329 5/8	42 1/8	44 7/8	34 2/8	6	7	Adams County	ID	Curtis Lemon	1978	780

YELLOWSTONE "AMERICAN" ELK (TYPICAL ANTLERS)

Minimum Score 260

Continued

SCORE	LENGTH OF MAIN BEAM R	LENGTH OF MAIN BEAM L	INSIDE SPREAD	NUMBER OF POINTS R	NUMBER OF POINTS L	AREA	STATE/PROVINCE	HUNTER'S NAME	DATE	RANK
329 5/8	54 6/8	52 7/8	40 5/8	6	7	Silver Bow County	MT	William E. Bullock	1981	780
329 5/8	52 1/8	49 0/8	40 1/8	7	6	Washington County	ID	Kevin Tams	1994	780
329 4/8	47 4/8	47 3/8	43 2/8	6	6	Custer County	ID	Gary Kimball	1979	783
329 4/8	48 2/8	48 4/8	35 2/8	6	6	Catron County	NM	Donald W. Duewall	1982	783
329 4/8	49 2/8	51 4/8	45 0/8	6	8	Phillips County	MT	Dennis R. King	1989	783
329 4/8	47 2/8	48 2/8	38 2/8	6	6	Coconino County	AZ	Lynn M. Johnson	1995	783
329 4/8	51 5/8	52 1/8	39 6/8	6	6	Beaverhead County	MT	Todd P. Green	1998	783
329 3/8	55 4/8	51 1/8	37 2/8	7	6	Catron County	NM	James Scarbrough	1986	788
329 3/8	50 0/8	49 7/8	39 1/8	6	6	Gallatin County	MT	Mark Hanshue	1987	788
329 3/8	52 7/8	53 1/8	37 2/8	6	7	Lincoln County	NM	Henry Vega	1988	788
329 2/8	52 3/8	52 4/8	44 4/8	6	6	Valley County	ID	B. C. Cunningham	1969	791
329 2/8	50 1/8	52 4/8	35 6/8	6	6	Valley County	MT	Thomas L. Solem	1981	791
329 2/8	48 6/8	51 1/8	38 2/8	7	6	Bonneville County	ID	Paul H. Laver	1981	791
329 2/8	50 0/8	53 2/8	38 2/8	7	6	Sanders County	MT	Glenn Nerby	1991	791
329 1/8	47 7/8	49 4/8	40 1/8	6	6	Adams County	ID	Curt Lemmons	1965	795
329 1/8	51 5/8	53 7/8	44 3/8	7	7	Moffat County	CO	Glenn W. Pritchard	1972	795
329 1/8	44 6/8	44 2/8	37 0/8	6	6	Rio Blanco County	CO	Harold Boyack	1976	795
329 1/8	45 4/8	46 1/8	39 7/8	6	6	Mineral County	MT	Gary A. Hudson	1988	795
329 1/8	54 6/8	53 5/8	40 1/8	6	6	Erickson	MAN	Kim Meger	1996	795
329 1/8	51 4/8	50 3/8	37 7/8	6	7	Judith Basin County	MT	Shawn P. Price	1997	795
329 1/8	53 5/8	54 0/8	39 4/8	7	6	Clark County	NV	Ron Reed	1997	795
329 1/8	53 1/8	54 4/8	40 5/8	6	6	Ouray County	CO	Mike Masker	1997	795
329 1/8	52 4/8	53 6/8	44 7/8	6	6	Sevier County	UT	Steve Ulibarri	1998	795
329 0/8	56 0/8	54 3/8	40 2/8	8	6	Yakima County	WA	Jerry Harris	1963	804
329 0/8	48 1/8	48 1/8	38 6/8	6	7	Sanders County	MT	Fred Mensik	1983	804
329 0/8	49 3/8	48 5/8	37 2/8	6	6	Garfield County	CO	Vance A. Fairhurst	1993	804
329 0/8	50 5/8	54 0/8	39 4/8	6	6	Catron County	NM	Joseph A. Lorenz	1995	804
328 7/8	47 5/8	50 4/8	43 5/8	6	7	Catron County	NM	Gil Holland	1995	808
328 6/8	48 5/8	49 0/8	43 6/8	6	6	Crook County	OR	Gary Kiepert	1983	809
328 6/8	46 1/8	47 1/8	38 6/8	6	6	Colfax County	NM	Robert Torstenson	1996	809
328 5/8	52 7/8	54 0/8	34 3/8	7	7	Catron County	NM	George F. Corriher	1991	811
328 4/8	50 1/8	47 6/8	39 0/8	6	6	Sanders County	MT	Kenneth B. Neubauer	1983	812
328 4/8	49 5/8	50 0/8	47 0/8	6	6	Rio Arriba County	NM	Schuyler B. Marshall	1994	812
328 4/8	55 2/8	52 3/8	35 0/8	6	6	Apache County	AZ	Bryan R. Yorksmith	1997	812
328 4/8	55 7/8	53 7/8	45 2/8	6	6	Catron County	NM	John W. Ellas	1998	812
328 3/8	47 6/8	48 3/8	40 1/8	7	8	Kittitas County	WA	Gary W. Fletcher	1993	816
328 3/8	54 5/8	55 7/8	29 1/8	7	7	Coconino County	AZ	Cary Jellison	1995	816
328 3/8	48 0/8	50 0/8	37 1/8	6	6	Lemhi County	ID	Mike Dunn	1996	816
328 3/8	47 4/8	48 7/8	39 7/8	7	6	Umatilla County	OR	Chris Neufeld	1997	816
328 2/8	48 4/8	49 4/8	40 4/8	6	7	Crook County	OR	Scott Reed	1984	820
328 2/8	52 3/8	50 6/8	43 4/8	6	6	Adams County	ID	Ted Cutler/Craig Keyser	1985	820
328 2/8	52 0/8	52 6/8	37 2/8	6	6	Coconino County	AZ	Richard D. Tone	1989	820
328 2/8	50 7/8	53 2/8	44 2/8	6	6	Union County	OR	Steven Nichols	1996	820
328 1/8	44 7/8	44 3/8	41 3/8	6	6	Lewis County	WA	Larry F. Smith	1986	824
328 1/8	45 6/8	47 6/8	37 1/8	6	7	Albany County	WY	Brian L. Biel	1986	824
328 1/8	46 7/8	46 3/8	40 5/8	7	6	Catron County	NM	William Holdman	1993	824
328 0/8	54 1/8	51 3/8	40 0/8	6	7	Coconino County	AZ	James L. Hyde	1977	827
328 0/8	44 2/8	44 3/8	39 6/8	6	6	Larimer County	CO	J. G. Hamblet, Jr.	1979	827
328 0/8	50 6/8	52 0/8	39 6/8	6	7	Coconino County	AZ	Clay Stazenski	1991	827
328 0/8	50 7/8	50 4/8	45 6/8	6	6	Madison County	MT	Joseph K. Stokes	1993	827
327 7/8	48 1/8	46 2/8	46 3/8	6	6	Lewis & Clark County	MT	Darrell J. Archey	1984	831
327 7/8	48 0/8	48 4/8	43 5/8	5	6	Cochrane	ALB	Rod Newsham	1986	831
327 7/8	46 1/8	47 2/8	36 5/8	6	6	Coconino County	AZ	Drazen Baricevic	1996	831
327 6/8	51 6/8	53 1/8	36 2/8	6	6	Coconino County	AZ	Jim Parker	1989	834
327 6/8	50 7/8	52 6/8	40 0/8	6	6	Mesa County	CO	Brian Karsten	1991	834
327 6/8	50 5/8	51 5/8	38 6/8	7	6	Gallatin County	MT	Scott L. Koelzer	1993	834
327 6/8	49 0/8	47 7/8	47 4/8	6	6	Lemhi County	ID	Robert A. Johnson	1998	834
327 5/8	48 5/8	49 4/8	38 3/8	6	6	Lincoln County	WY	Kirby Booth	1990	838
327 5/8	49 3/8	49 4/8	37 1/8	6	6	Lincoln County	WY	Brett R. Ure	1995	838
327 5/8	50 7/8	52 0/8	44 1/8	6	6	Coconino County	AZ	Patrick F. Connelly	1995	838
327 5/8	53 0/8	53 2/8	39 1/8	6	6	Lemhi County	ID	Mike Virgin	1996	838
327 4/8	48 4/8	46 6/8	43 6/8	6	6	Beaverhead County	MT	Dave Knudsen	1974	842
327 4/8	49 4/8	47 4/8	40 4/8	6	6	Lewis & Clark County	MT	Richard J. Kornick	1980	842
327 4/8	49 6/8	48 0/8	39 0/8	6	6	Beaverhead County	MT	Roy F. Bach	1984	842
327 4/8	51 7/8	48 2/8	34 6/8	6	7	Mesa County	CO	Dr. John R. Thodos	1987	842
327 4/8	49 5/8	48 5/8	37 6/8	6	6	Yakima County	WA	Jim Rathbun	1989	842
327 3/8	47 4/8	47 0/8	34 3/8	7	7	Coconino County	AZ	Richard D. Tone	1991	847
327 3/8	49 6/8	48 2/8	41 5/8	6	6	Phillips County	MT	Ervin Langseth	1992	847
327 2/8	49 5/8	50 6/8	36 2/8	6	6	Clackamas County	OR	Jeff Youngberg	1993	849
327 2/8	49 5/8	49 1/8	35 0/8	6	6	Boulder County	CO	Steve Nichols	1996	849
327 1/8	50 3/8	48 2/8	43 3/8	6	6	Park County	MT	Dale Alt	1968	851
327 0/8	50 6/8	51 7/8	40 4/8	6	6	Clearwater County	ID	C. Randall Byers	1976	852
327 0/8	48 0/8	48 2/8	39 6/8	6	6	Catron County	NM	David Chavez	1981	852
327 0/8	50 0/8	50 2/8	36 0/8	6	7	Rossburn	MAN	Glen J. White	1986	852
327 0/8	48 7/8	47 0/8	37 4/8	7	6	Sandoval County	NM	Freddie Barber	1989	852
327 0/8	44 7/8	44 1/8	33 2/8	6	6	Meagher County	MT	Robert L. Crafts	1991	852
327 0/8	47 7/8	47 2/8	39 2/8	6	6	Park County	MT	Richard Backes	1996	852
326 7/8	48 6/8	47 4/8	38 1/8	6	6	Custer County	CO	Rohn L. Garnhart	1990	858

YELLOWSTONE "AMERICAN" ELK (TYPICAL ANTLERS)

Minimum Score 260   Continued

SCORE	LENGTH OF MAIN BEAM R	LENGTH OF MAIN BEAM L	INSIDE SPREAD	NUMBER OF POINTS R	NUMBER OF POINTS L	AREA	STATE/ PROVINCE	HUNTER'S NAME	DATE	RANK
326 7/8	55 4/8	57 3/8	40 5/8	6	6	Grant County	NM	Toby B. Rascon	1995	858
326 7/8	47 0/8	47 6/8	40 1/8	6	6	Petroleum County	MT	Dennis Trapp	1997	858
326 6/8	48 5/8	50 3/8	43 0/8	7	6	Bighorn Mtns.	WY	Rick Mitchell	1981	861
326 6/8	50 4/8	47 4/8	48 2/8	6	7	Larimer County	CO	Tom Duncan	1983	861
326 6/8	46 6/8	46 4/8	39 4/8	6	6	Colfax County	NM	John L. Chapman	1984	861
326 6/8	52 1/8	51 5/8	35 6/8	6	6	Rio Arriba County	NM	Vincent R. Vicenti	1989	861
326 6/8	50 6/8	53 0/8	34 1/8	9	6	Catron County	NM	Ron Rhodes	1993	861
326 6/8	51 2/8	51 6/8	45 2/8	6	6	Blaine County	ID	John Wells	1995	861
326 5/8	52 1/8	53 5/8	42 1/8	6	7	Coconino County	AZ	Larry Glasson	1975	867
326 5/8	48 3/8	50 3/8	40 7/8	6	6	Clackamas County	OR	William E. Lancaster	1987	867
326 5/8	47 2/8	47 3/8	39 1/8	6	6	Wallowa County	OR	Dusty Powers	1988	867
326 5/8	48 6/8	46 3/8	43 7/8	6	6	King County	WA	Eric Johnson	1993	867
326 4/8	51 5/8	51 0/8	37 6/8	6	6	King County	WA	Leonard L Stolen	1984	871
326 4/8	53 1/8	52 1/8	36 0/8	6	6	Coconino County	AZ	John Coffman	1990	871
326 4/8	56 1/8	51 5/8	38 0/8	7	6	Fergus County	MT	Ronald Nelson	1992	871
326 3/8	51 3/8	51 1/8	47 1/8	5	6	Socorro County	NM	Billy R. Spears	1976	874
326 3/8	55 0/8	55 4/8	39 3/8	6	6	Flathead County	MT	Phil Von Bargen	1976	874
326 3/8	51 1/8	52 6/8	41 1/8	6	6	Otero County	NM	Donald E. Westerbur	1994	874
326 3/8	49 4/8	51 3/8	36 5/8	6	6	Custer County	ID	Tony Jerulle	1995	874
326 2/8	48 3/8	53 3/8	38 0/8	7	7	Carbon County	UT	Scott Wilkins	1989	878
326 2/8	46 5/8	48 3/8	35 2/8	6	6	Fergus County	MT	Michael F. Otto	1997	878
326 1/8	44 6/8	46 6/8	35 5/8	6	6	Lemhi County	ID	Ray Torrey	1967	880
326 1/8	54 2/8	54 5/8	37 5/8	6	6	Grand County	CO	Paul Adams	1977	880
326 1/8	49 5/8	48 6/8	34 1/8	6	7	Converse County	WY	Kevin Conway	1992	880
326 1/8	49 7/8	51 7/8	43 1/8	6	6	Idaho County	ID	Ron Perry	1997	880
326 0/8	51 1/8	50 6/8	46 2/8	7	6	Boulder County	CO	Duke Prentup	1977	884
326 0/8	51 4/8	51 3/8	38 4/8	6	6	Beaverhead County	MT	Scott P. Swan	1978	884
326 0/8	49 3/8	47 4/8	36 4/8	6	6	Catron County	NM	Randall Cooley	1984	884
326 0/8	53 1/8	49 2/8	39 6/8	6	6	Socorro County	NM	Ray Hatfield	1984	884
326 0/8	46 2/8	46 7/8	36 6/8	6	6	Lemhi County	ID	John Bennett	1992	884
326 0/8	51 0/8	52 2/8	36 4/8	7	6	Custer County	ID	Judd Mackintosh	1994	884
326 0/8	50 4/8	50 4/8	45 0/8	6	6	Catron County	NM	Dean G. Martin	1996	884
326 0/8	53 2/8	50 7/8	39 6/8	6	6	Pembina River	ALB	Kevin Nicol	1996	884
325 7/8	50 7/8	47 1/8	35 4/8	7	7	Idaho County	ID	Robert C. Mitchell	1978	892
325 7/8	45 3/8	45 1/8	34 5/8	6	6	Canmore	ALB	Douglas A. Parker	1984	892
325 7/8	46 6/8	47 4/8	36 5/8	6	6	Catron County	NM	James Willard	1997	892
325 7/8	52 4/8	50 3/8	39 3/8	6	6	Hinton	ALB	Jason Spenst	1997	892
325 6/8	49 1/8	51 5/8	43 6/8	6	6	Beaverhead County	MT	Bob Helming	1980	896
325 6/8	46 7/8	46 5/8	40 0/8	6	6	Marion County	OR	Ron Bergeron	1983	896
325 6/8	47 4/8	45 4/8	40 2/8	6	6	Otero County	NM	Jessie Cheramie	1993	896
325 6/8	45 7/8	47 2/8	39 2/8	6	6	Caribou County	ID	William Trainor, Jr.	1995	896
325 6/8	53 1/8	53 2/8	41 2/8	6	6	Catron County	NM	Patrick Kirby	1995	896
325 6/8	49 2/8	51 4/8	41 0/8	6	6	Platte County	WY	Pat Souza	1996	896
325 6/8	50 2/8	48 1/8	36 0/8	6	6	Catron County	NM	Zeb Kern	1998	896
325 5/8	43 6/8	45 0/8	39 1/8	7	7	Beaverhead County	MT	Danny Moore	1983	903
325 5/8	51 2/8	52 3/8	41 5/8	6	6	Wheeler County	OR	Robert V. Martin	1986	903
325 5/8	51 2/8	50 2/8	37 5/8	6	6	Deschutes County	OR	Royce D. Nelson	1992	903
325 5/8	51 0/8	49 2/8	38 1/8	7	6	Washakie County	WY	Alan Grzybowski	1997	903
325 4/8	49 6/8	50 3/8	40 4/8	6	6	Montrose County	CO	Carol Cassidy	1973	907
325 4/8	45 4/8	45 5/8	38 6/8	6	6	Larimer County	CO	Arnold Hale	1989	907
325 4/8	48 1/8	51 2/8	38 0/8	6	6	Catron County	NM	Steve Van Zile	1991	907
325 4/8	48 4/8	49 6/8	42 0/8	6	6	Fremont County	WY	Rene Suda	1995	907
325 4/8	51 5/8	50 4/8	36 0/8	6	6	Sagauche County	CO	Tony Heil	1998	907
325 3/8	47 3/8	45 2/8	33 3/8	7	6	Benewah County	ID	Tim Chandler	1984	912
325 3/8	51 0/8	51 4/8	40 3/8	6	7	Coconino County	AZ	Les Shelton	1989	912
325 3/8	50 2/8	51 5/8	40 7/8	6	6	Coconino County	AZ	Gary D. Bills	1991	912
325 3/8	51 0/8	51 2/8	41 5/8	6	6	Apache County	AZ	Igor E. Ivanoff	1992	912
325 2/8	49 0/8	49 0/8	36 6/8	6	6	Caribou County	ID	Doug Foss	1986	916
325 2/8	49 1/8	49 3/8	39 6/8	6	6	Lemhi County	ID	Mike Benton	1989	916
325 2/8	50 3/8	49 2/8	42 6/8	6	7	Coconino County	AZ	Jerry L. Stewart	1992	916
325 2/8	48 1/8	46 5/8	36 6/8	6	6	Gilpin County	CO	Joseph W. Mourray	1996	916
325 1/8	48 3/8	49 3/8	39 5/8	6	6	Lincoln County	NM	John D. Fitzgibbon	1991	920
325 1/8	49 4/8	49 0/8	44 3/8	6	6	Caribou County	ID	Dennis Nelson	1994	920
325 1/8	52 6/8	51 5/8	40 5/8	6	6	Apache County	AZ	R. Christopher Ellis	1997	920
325 1/8	50 5/8	51 4/8	40 3/8	7	6	Umatilla County	OR	Merritt E. Tuttle	1998	920
325 0/8	47 1/8	47 3/8	35 6/8	7	7	Silver Bow County	MT	Bob Gossack	1977	924
325 0/8	52 4/8	49 5/8	39 4/8	6	6	Catron County	NM	Courtney King	1985	924
325 0/8	44 7/8	51 0/8	45 2/8	6	6	Catron County	NM	Steve McCoy	1988	924
325 0/8	49 7/8	51 1/8	41 0/8	7	7	Rio Arriba County	NM	Gene White	1990	924
325 0/8	50 4/8	50 5/8	46 0/8	6	6	Valley County	ID	Will Grasmick	1998	924
324 7/8	52 4/8	47 1/8	36 7/8	6	6	Coconino County	AZ	William V. West	1995	929
324 6/8	47 1/8	46 2/8	42 0/8	7	6	Coconino County	AZ	William S. Acheson	1979	930
324 6/8	45 7/8	45 2/8	37 0/8	6	6	Beaverhead County	MT	Tyler Robinson	1983	930
324 6/8	46 4/8	46 0/8	42 0/8	6	6	Flathead County	MT	James Norvell	1995	930
324 5/8	46 0/8	47 4/8	32 1/8	6	8	Moffat County	CO	Glenn W. Pritchard	1986	933
324 4/8	49 3/8	48 7/8	40 6/8	6	6	Grant County	OR	Chuck Boatman	1982	934
324 4/8	48 3/8	49 2/8	34 6/8	6	6	Petroleum County	MT	Gary Damuth	1986	934
324 4/8	50 1/8	50 2/8	46 7/8	7	8	Musselshell County	MT	Ted Steinke	1988	934

YELLOWSTONE "AMERICAN" ELK (TYPICAL ANTLERS)

Minimum Score 260

SCORE	LENGTH OF MAIN BEAM R	LENGTH OF MAIN BEAM L	INSIDE SPREAD	NUMBER OF POINTS R	NUMBER OF POINTS L	AREA	STATE/PROVINCE	HUNTER'S NAME	DATE	RANK
324 4/8	50 6/8	50 3/8	34 0/8	7	7	Catron County	NM	Richard V. Gray	1998	934
324 3/8	53 2/8	54 7/8	33 7/8	7	6	Summit County	CO	Gordon R. Horn	1986	938
324 2/8	47 5/8	47 4/8	31 0/8	6	6	Hodgson	MAN	Barry Bird	1982	939
324 2/8	52 0/8	51 1/8	37 5/8	6	7	Catron County	NM	Thomas Drumme	1990	939
324 2/8	46 5/8	49 2/8	43 6/8	5	5	Socorro County	NM	Daniel T. Webb	1996	939
324 2/8	45 2/8	45 5/8	40 4/8	6	7	Wallowa County	OR	Ron Williams	1996	939
324 1/8	47 7/8	48 6/8	46 7/8	6	7	Rio Arriba County	NM	Richard Manwell	1986	943
324 1/8	54 2/8	53 3/8	44 1/8	6	7	Apache County	AZ	Rick Mazol	1989	943
324 1/8	53 5/8	55 5/8	34 0/8	6	6	Coconino County	AZ	Phillip C. Dalrymple	1990	943
324 1/8	47 5/8	48 6/8	43 1/8	7	7	Shoshone County	ID	Jerry D. Ely	1991	943
324 1/8	53 1/8	52 2/8	32 7/8	6	7	Sanders County	MT	John Boger	1992	943
324 1/8	46 4/8	44 7/8	35 7/8	6	7	Harney County	OR	Jeff Nichols	1994	943
324 1/8	48 0/8	49 2/8	40 1/8	6	6	Jackson County	CO	Tom G. Kelley	1998	943
324 0/8	45 2/8	44 4/8	46 1/8	6	7	Madison County	MT	Alan Noack	1991	950
324 0/8	52 0/8	50 0/8	41 4/8	7	6	Catron County	NM	Dave Scott	1991	950
324 0/8	51 5/8	51 5/8	36 4/8	6	6	Catron County	NM	John Ruppert	1994	950
323 7/8	48 7/8	47 2/8	37 1/8	6	6	Granite County	MT	Clint Carlson	1983	953
323 7/8	50 7/8	52 0/8	43 3/8	6	6	Coconino County	AZ	John Stigsell	1987	953
323 7/8	45 1/8	46 2/8	37 3/8	6	6	Phillips County	MT	Todd A. Erickson	1991	953
323 7/8	53 6/8	51 3/8	39 3/8	7	7	Coconino County	AZ	Joseph O. Fogleman	1992	953
323 7/8	53 6/8	53 1/8	37 5/8	6	6	Sierra County	NM	Dennis D. Johnson	1998	953
323 6/8	48 2/8	51 1/8	43 6/8	6	6	Valley County	ID	Rodney Bremer	1983	958
323 6/8	51 0/8	49 6/8	38 2/8	6	7	Sandoval County	NM	Johnny Zoetjes	1996	958
323 5/8	46 6/8	46 3/8	40 3/8	7	6	Teton County	MT	Ron Granneman	1978	960
323 5/8	47 4/8	48 7/8	35 5/8	6	7	Custer County	ID	John R. Sample	1983	960
323 5/8	52 0/8	53 7/8	42 4/8	6	8	Cascade County	MT	Bill Tesinsky	1983	960
323 5/8	48 0/8	47 6/8	36 7/8	6	6	Taos County	NM	Jeffrey D. Butts	1987	960
323 5/8	50 5/8	51 1/8	37 3/8	7	7	Flathead County	MT	John Hale	1990	960
323 5/8	47 1/8	47 7/8	34 5/8	6	6	Taos County	NM	Chris T. Sanner	1991	960
323 5/8	49 6/8	49 5/8	35 3/8	6	6	Catron County	NM	John Sielicki	1993	960
323 5/8	54 7/8	53 3/8	34 5/8	6	6	Sevier County	UT	David Hughes	1995	960
323 5/8	47 1/8	44 4/8	36 7/8	6	6	Navajo County	AZ	Gayland Jones	1995	960
323 5/8	50 3/8	49 5/8	35 4/8	6	7	Mesa County	CO	James Snortum	1996	960
323 5/8	45 6/8	47 2/8	38 1/8	6	6	Skamania County	WA	Cory Schmid	1998	960
323 4/8	40 7/8	41 2/8	35 6/8	6	6	Phillips County	MT	Buzz Beto	1983	971
323 4/8	49 4/8	48 6/8	37 6/8	6	6	Missoula County	MT	John W. Zahrte	1987	971
323 4/8	51 5/8	52 0/8	35 0/8	6	6	Spirit River	ALB	Gerald Desjardins	1990	971
323 4/8	44 2/8	47 3/8	37 2/8	6	6	Catron County	NM	Abe Dimas	1992	971
323 4/8	50 4/8	53 4/8	43 4/8	5	6	Socorro County	NM	Tom Alvin	1996	971
323 3/8	50 6/8	50 1/8	37 7/8	7	6	Gallatin County	MT	Rick Jones	1977	976
323 3/8	50 1/8	51 1/8	38 3/8	6	6	Catron County	NM	Roy L. Hall	1991	976
323 3/8	52 0/8	51 7/8	40 1/8	6	6	Archuleta County	CO	Matthew T. Old	1994	976
323 3/8	52 3/8	52 1/8	38 5/8	7	7	Fergus County	MT	Tod Rector	1998	976
323 2/8	55 7/8	53 5/8	44 2/8	6	6	Grant County	OR	Andy Day	1982	980
323 2/8	46 7/8	46 4/8	38 7/8	7	8	Catron County	NM	Thomas R. Sansom	1984	980
323 2/8	50 6/8	49 0/8	40 2/8	6	6	Adams County	ID	Stacy V. LaFay	1993	980
323 2/8	51 2/8	50 5/8	41 2/8	6	6	Rio Arriba County	NM	Allen J. Martinez	1996	980
323 1/8	49 6/8	49 5/8	42 3/8	6	6	Blaine County	ID	Larry Whittaker	1988	984
323 1/8	50 6/8	51 0/8	36 5/8	6	6	Flathead County	MT	Don Mills	1992	984
323 1/8	50 3/8	46 7/8	35 3/8	6	6	Catron County	NM	David A. Chester	1997	984
323 0/8	52 5/8	50 1/8	39 0/8	6	6	Blaine County	ID	Ted Chu	1977	987
323 0/8	54 7/8	50 0/8	45 5/8	6	7	Gallatin County	MT	Tim Wells	1983	987
323 0/8	47 4/8	48 3/8	40 0/8	6	6	Grand County	CO	Russell Gross	1985	987
323 0/8	50 4/8	51 0/8	40 0/8	6	6	White Pine County	NV	Paul D. Patterson	1987	987
323 0/8	50 7/8	51 4/8	39 2/8	6	6	Morgan County	UT	Hugh H. Hogle	1991	987
323 0/8	51 3/8	50 3/8	43 4/8	6	6	Nye County	NV	Ken Longballa	1993	987
323 0/8	54 3/8	51 0/8	40 4/8	6	6	Coconino County	AZ	Glen D. Whited	1993	987
323 0/8	47 4/8	48 2/8	30 0/8	6	6	Meagher County	MT	D. (Mitch) Kottas	1993	987
323 0/8	51 0/8	48 0/8	35 4/8	6	6	Beaverhead County	MT	Shaun P. Twardoski	1995	987
323 0/8	47 0/8	47 2/8	34 2/8	6	6	Adams County	ID	Michael A. Bledsoe	1995	987
323 0/8	43 3/8	43 3/8	37 2/8	6	6	Las Animas County	CO	Steve Barnhill	1996	987
322 7/8	50 6/8	51 0/8	44 3/8	6	7	Phillips County	MT	Ray Hoveskeland	1967	998
322 7/8	48 5/8	46 5/8	36 5/8	6	6	Deer Lodge County	MT	Eddie McGreevey	1977	998
322 7/8	51 3/8	52 2/8	41 4/8	7	7	Coconino County	AZ	Darrell Christensen	1979	998
322 7/8	47 4/8	47 5/8	36 1/8	6	6	Canmore	ALB	David R. Coupland	1982	998
322 7/8	48 6/8	50 4/8	38 7/8	7	6	Coconino County	AZ	Dave Holt	1994	998
322 6/8	49 2/8	48 5/8	36 4/8	6	6	Rio Arriba County	NM	Santos E. Corriz	1982	1,003
322 6/8	46 6/8	46 1/8	44 0/8	7	5	McKinley County	NM	Dennis L. Stettler	1995	1,003
322 6/8	46 4/8	44 5/8	47 7/8	6	6	Jefferson County	MT	Chet Graham	1997	1,003
322 6/8	44 5/8	46 6/8	37 0/8	6	6	Clark County	ID	Brad Foster	1998	1,003
322 5/8	49 4/8	47 1/8	37 7/8	6	6	Taos County	NM	Jason Kent	1991	1,007
322 4/8	51 3/8	48 7/8	40 0/8	6	7	Lewis & Clark County	MT	Jerry Biresch	1970	1,008
322 4/8	48 5/8	49 1/8	36 4/8	6	6	Sublette County	WY	Charles T. Moore II	1988	1,008
322 4/8	46 6/8	48 2/8	41 2/8	6	6	Coconino County	AZ	Lee J. Sorcinelli	1997	1,008
322 3/8	46 7/8	44 2/8	40 1/8	6	6	Coconino County	AZ	Salvatore J. Carlomagno	1991	1,011
322 3/8	51 2/8	48 2/8	38 3/8	6	8	Catron County	NM	Stoney Jeff Black	1993	1,011
322 3/8	51 0/8	51 4/8	41 7/8	6	6	Beaverhead County	MT	Russell Swindall	1996	1,011
322 2/8	51 5/8	53 1/8	33 0/8	6	6	Colfax County	NM	Tom L. Handy	1986	1,014

Continued

YELLOWSTONE "AMERICAN" ELK (TYPICAL ANTLERS)

Minimum Score 260   Continued

SCORE	LENGTH OF MAIN BEAM R	L	INSIDE SPREAD	NUMBER OF POINTS R	L	AREA	STATE/ PROVINCE	HUNTER'S NAME	DATE	RANK
322 2/8	52 4/8	49 7/8	38 2/8	6	6	Catron County	NM	Sam Chavez	1990	1,014
322 2/8	47 5/8	46 4/8	41 2/8	6	6	Catron County	NM	Gino Giannetti	1993	1,014
322 2/8	50 0/8	49 4/8	37 4/8	6	6	Albany County	WY	Scott Woolsey	1997	1,014
322 1/8	50 4/8	50 6/8	37 3/8	6	6	Coconino County	AZ	John F. Schultz	1978	1,018
322 1/8	50 5/8	50 4/8	37 3/8	6	6	Powell County	MT	Gene Coughlin	1982	1,018
322 1/8	45 6/8	44 3/8	34 3/8	7	8	Fergus County	MT	Ben Starburg	1985	1,018
322 1/8	47 0/8	47 2/8	40 3/8	6	6	Beaverhead County	MT	Ric Twardoski	1987	1,018
322 1/8	47 5/8	49 5/8	43 3/8	7	7	Coconino County	AZ	Roger O. Iveson	1990	1,018
322 1/8	53 1/8	51 5/8	42 2/8	6	8	Rio Arriba County	NM	Michael Herrera	1991	1,018
322 1/8	49 7/8	50 5/8	37 3/8	6	6	Coconino County	AZ	David L. Schwartz, Sr.	1992	1,018
322 0/8	50 3/8	50 6/8	36 2/8	7	8	Coconino County	AZ	Dick Hensley	1979	1,025
322 0/8	46 3/8	48 0/8	36 2/8	6	6	Sandoval County	NM	John McClendon	1983	1,025
322 0/8	52 6/8	53 0/8	35 0/8	6	6	Moffat County	CO	Guy Love	1984	1,025
322 0/8	47 2/8	49 0/8	40 6/8	6	6	Pierce County	WA	Dale Kistenmacher	1985	1,025
322 0/8	48 4/8	49 0/8	34 4/8	6	7	Boggy Creek	MAN	Tom Nebbs	1986	1,025
322 0/8	52 6/8	53 1/8	41 2/8	6	7	Caribou County	ID	Brian D. Bailey	1991	1,025
322 0/8	50 3/8	50 0/8	41 6/8	6	6	Coconino County	AZ	Daniel P. Cartwright	1995	1,025
322 0/8	53 5/8	52 7/8	40 2/8	6	6	Wallowa County	OR	Jared C. Rogers	1996	1,025
322 0/8	52 2/8	52 7/8	36 0/8	6	7	Navajo County	AZ	Wayne Riley	1997	1,025
322 0/8	46 0/8	46 1/8	34 4/8	6	6	Umatilla County	OR	Doug A. Holland	1997	1,025
321 7/8	47 7/8	43 6/8	41 7/8	6	6	Taos County	NM	Dr. Dean A. Henbest	1971	1,035
321 7/8	49 3/8	53 2/8	34 1/8	6	6	Coconino County	AZ	Mike Burm	1981	1,035
321 7/8	51 0/8	50 5/8	37 7/8	6	6	Teller County	CO	Harry Rathke	1983	1,035
321 7/8	47 2/8	49 1/8	36 5/8	6	6	Flathead County	MT	Pat Fleming	1992	1,035
321 6/8	50 6/8	52 5/8	38 6/8	6	6	Fergus County	MT	Jake Damone	1991	1,039
321 6/8	49 1/8	47 7/8	40 2/8	6	7	Grant County	OR	Randy Walz	1995	1,039
321 6/8	49 2/8	49 4/8	40 4/8	6	6	Fergus County	MT	Rolly Nelson	1998	1,039
321 6/8	52 5/8	50 5/8	36 2/8	6	6	Catron County	NM	Donnie Sultan	1998	1,039
321 4/8	45 2/8	56 2/8	39 2/8	5	6	Apache County	AZ	John D. 'Jack' Frost	1986	1,043
321 4/8	48 4/8	48 3/8	40 0/8	6	6	Petroleum County	MT	David Mitchell	1994	1,043
321 4/8	48 6/8	49 0/8	38 4/8	7	7	Petroleum County	MT	Jay Kintzing	1995	1,043
321 3/8	45 6/8	45 6/8	43 3/8	6	6	Gallatin County	MT	Ed Tertelgte	1975	1,046
321 3/8	44 2/8	46 6/8	44 5/8	6	6	Sibbald Flats	ALB	Archie J. Nesbitt	1998	1,046
321 2/8	46 1/8	48 4/8	40 0/8	6	6	Larimer County	CO	Tom Tietz	1981	1,048
321 2/8	50 6/8	50 5/8	35 6/8	6	6	Elmore County	ID	Robert M. Egusquiza	1991	1,048
321 2/8	53 1/8	53 5/8	41 6/8	6	7	Camas County	ID	Steve Wiedmeier	1992	1,048
321 2/8	46 7/8	46 2/8	35 6/8	6	6	Gallatin County	MT	Lee Poole	1998	1,048
321 1/8	48 6/8	50 6/8	38 1/8	6	6	Lincoln County	NM	Jay H. Henley, Sr.	1985	1,052
321 1/8	43 0/8	45 3/8	36 1/8	8	8	Idaho County	ID	Randy J. Demro	1989	1,052
321 1/8	46 3/8	46 7/8	34 3/8	6	6	Pierce County	WA	Joe H. Frields	1990	1,052
321 1/8	49 6/8	51 0/8	38 3/8	6	6	Park County	MT	Brian D. Stoner	1994	1,052
321 1/8	48 6/8	48 0/8	40 1/8	6	6	Gallatin County	MT	Robert Louis Bratton	1996	1,052
321 0/8	46 4/8	46 7/8	46 4/8	7	6	Lincoln County	MT	Steve A. Kluver	1986	1,057
321 0/8	51 7/8	49 4/8	42 4/8	6	6	Shoshone County	ID	Chax Peterson	1991	1,057
321 0/8	50 2/8	50 6/8	41 2/8	6	6	Carbon County	WY	Keith Hansen	1994	1,057
320 7/8	49 2/8	52 0/8	45 5/8	6	6	Jefferson County	OR	Steve C. Yeoman	1991	1,060
320 7/8	54 5/8	49 5/8	39 1/8	6	6	Catron County	NM	Robert L. Bryant	1993	1,060
320 7/8	50 0/8	49 4/8	41 5/8	6	6	Teton County	WY	Donald R. Hoard	1994	1,060
320 7/8	51 6/8	51 2/8	41 1/8	6	6	Crook County	OR	Bob Hayes	1995	1,060
320 6/8	56 2/8	55 4/8	41 2/8	5	6	Coconino County	AZ	Michael P. Hendrix	1995	1,064
320 6/8	49 6/8	48 7/8	35 4/8	6	6	Grant County	OR	Larry L. Wagoner	1995	1,064
320 6/8	53 0/8	53 0/8	43 4/8	6	6	Sheridan County	WY	Duane E. McClure, Jr.	1997	1,064
320 5/8	46 3/8	46 4/8	38 3/8	6	6	Phillips County	MT	Richard R. Gardner	1992	1,067
320 5/8	48 5/8	47 5/8	38 7/8	7	7	Madison County	MT	Richard King	1993	1,067
320 5/8	47 1/8	46 0/8	37 1/8	7	6	Fergus County	MT	Eric C. Abbott	1995	1,067
320 5/8	44 5/8	47 1/8	42 3/8	6	6	Rich County	UT	Edwin L. DeYoung	1998	1,067
320 4/8	53 2/8	51 4/8	42 2/8	6	6	Catron County	NM	Ray Francingues III	1996	1,071
320 4/8	52 0/8	49 4/8	36 0/8	6	6	Mesa County	CO	Jeffery Lynn Birchfield	1997	1,071
320 4/8	50 1/8	51 2/8	38 6/8	6	7	Catron County	NM	Dale Jenkins	1998	1,071
320 3/8	46 1/8	46 6/8	39 3/8	6	6	Rio Grande County	CO	Bing Kemp	1966	1,074
320 3/8	49 3/8	50 7/8	36 5/8	7	6	Catron County	NM	Randall S. Madding	1986	1,074
320 2/8	52 0/8	50 6/8	36 0/8	6	6	Meagher County	MT	Ted Hysell	1983	1,076
320 2/8	49 4/8	49 6/8	47 6/8	6	6	Shoshone County	ID	Tom J. O'Grady	1986	1,076
320 2/8	45 1/8	44 2/8	30 6/8	6	6	Garfield County	CO	Jason Adamson	1990	1,076
320 2/8	47 6/8	45 5/8	44 6/8	6	6	Beaverhead County	MT	Raymond Cote	1991	1,076
320 2/8	48 2/8	50 5/8	38 3/8	7	6	Catron County	NM	Dean Dunaway	1993	1,076
320 2/8	46 4/8	44 3/8	44 6/8	7	6	Shoshone County	ID	Ron Long	1996	1,076
320 2/8	45 2/8	45 7/8	37 0/8	6	6	Conejos County	CO	Mike Crites	1997	1,076
320 2/8	49 2/8	49 2/8	38 2/8	6	6	Albany County	WY	Richard A. Strickland	1998	1,076
320 1/8	46 2/8	47 7/8	41 3/8	6	6	Madison County	MT	Lee J. Poole	1976	1,084
320 1/8	48 6/8	48 7/8	38 7/8	6	6	Fergus County	MT	J. Douglas Krings	1979	1,084
320 1/8	48 1/8	45 1/8	44 3/8	6	7	Albany County	WY	Doug Pope	1979	1,084
320 1/8	50 1/8	48 4/8	37 1/8	6	6	Lemhi County	ID	Joe Fraser	1980	1,084
320 1/8	52 6/8	51 1/8	41 1/8	6	6	Yellowstone County	MT	Robert M. Labert	1986	1,084
320 1/8	50 5/8	49 1/8	46 7/8	6	6	Cibola County	NM	Howard Schreiber	1992	1,084
320 1/8	52 6/8	53 7/8	39 2/8	6	6	Catron County	NM	Bruce Fair	1995	1,084
320 1/8	53 3/8	53 5/8	41 7/8	6	6	Harney County	OR	William "Bill" L. Sherrill	1997	1,084
320 0/8	50 6/8	53 1/8	39 6/8	6	6	Mineral County	MT	Michael Ruhkala	1980	1,092

YELLOWSTONE "AMERICAN" ELK (TYPICAL ANTLERS)

Minimum Score 260

Continued

SCORE	LENGTH OF MAIN BEAM R	LENGTH OF MAIN BEAM L	INSIDE SPREAD	NUMBER OF POINTS R	NUMBER OF POINTS L	AREA	STATE/PROVINCE	HUNTER'S NAME	DATE	RANK
320 0/8	51 4/8	50 5/8	36 6/8	6	6	Huerfano County	CO	Mike Culwell	1984	1,092
320 0/8	48 7/8	48 1/8	41 0/8	7	6	Grant County	OR	James M. Carter	1985	1,092
320 0/8	48 1/8	50 0/8	37 0/8	6	6	Catron County	NM	Henry Montoya	1992	1,092
320 0/8	49 6/8	48 2/8	35 0/8	6	6	Fergus County	MT	Rick A. Martin	1993	1,092
320 0/8	51 1/8	50 4/8	34 2/8	7	7	Coconino County	AZ	Jim Van Lieu	1996	1,092
319 7/8	51 7/8	50 2/8	38 1/8	7	8	Socorro County	NM	David Ryles	1977	1,098
319 7/8	51 7/8	52 2/8	40 5/8	6	6	Hinton	ALB	Blair D. Crites	1979	1,098
319 7/8	46 3/8	47 6/8	39 7/8	7	6	Otero County	NM	Simon L. Gomez	1986	1,098
319 7/8	51 6/8	52 2/8	44 3/8	7	6	Fergus County	MT	Richard Dilling	1993	1,098
319 7/8	48 7/8	47 6/8	42 3/8	6	5	Garfield County	CO	Paul J. Chackan	1997	1,098
319 7/8	46 3/8	45 7/8	30 7/8	6	6	Jefferson County	CO	Ed Kuehster	1998	1,098
319 6/8	46 3/8	44 7/8	34 0/8	6	7	Larimer County	CO	Jeremy Oberlander	1995	1,104
319 5/8	48 3/8	50 7/8	39 0/8	7	6	Catron County	NM	Roy L. Walk	1993	1,105
319 5/8	45 3/8	47 0/8	36 5/8	6	6	Morgan County	UT	James A. Martin, MD	1996	1,105
319 5/8	47 6/8	47 3/8	38 5/8	6	6	Edgerton	ALB	Trevor Thorpe	1997	1,105
319 4/8	48 4/8	49 0/8	40 2/8	6	6	Pitkin County	CO	Bob Gulman	1975	1,108
319 4/8	49 5/8	49 6/8	36 4/8	7	6	Clearwater County	ID	Audie Powers	1979	1,108
319 4/8	50 6/8	52 0/8	41 2/8	6	6	Caribou County	ID	Mark Hill	1980	1,108
319 3/8	44 2/8	43 2/8	35 4/8	7	7	Crook County	OR	Jeff Carver	1985	1,111
319 3/8	52 6/8	54 1/8	42 5/8	6	6	Catron County	NM	Travis Gillentine	1987	1,111
319 3/8	47 5/8	47 1/8	37 1/8	6	6	Fergus County	MT	Edwin Evans	1990	1,111
319 3/8	47 3/8	48 2/8	39 7/8	6	6	Sublette County	WY	Douglas Weir/ Glenn Socia	1990	1,111
319 2/8	45 2/8	46 1/8	35 0/8	6	6	Morgan County	UT	C. Keith Maynes	1987	1,115
319 2/8	48 6/8	50 0/8	36 0/8	6	6	Granite County	MT	Bob Clouse	1991	1,115
319 1/8	45 2/8	45 0/8	36 3/8	7	7	Rio Arriba County	NM	Dr. O. D. Brown	1986	1,117
319 1/8	52 1/8	50 5/8	37 1/8	7	6	Fremont County	ID	Steve W. Sherick	1994	1,117
319 1/8	49 1/8	51 5/8	40 3/8	6	6	Coconino County	AZ	Tom Pasley	1995	1,117
319 0/8	48 7/8	53 2/8	39 6/8	5	6	Catron County	NM	Eddie Howard	1983	1,120
319 0/8	53 3/8	55 0/8	35 4/8	6	6	McKinley County	NM	David M. Richards	1993	1,120
319 0/8	49 7/8	49 3/8	44 6/8	7	6	Clearwater County	ID	Burgess Blevins	1993	1,120
319 0/8	47 2/8	47 1/8	35 6/8	6	6	Kakwa River	ALB	Paul L. Holtz	1996	1,120
318 7/8	45 6/8	45 4/8	37 1/8	7	6	Fergus County	MT	Donald R. Hecht	1984	1,124
318 7/8	48 0/8	49 6/8	41 5/8	6	6	Carbon County	UT	Sam Raby	1989	1,124
318 7/8	48 4/8	49 4/8	34 1/8	6	6	Coconino County	AZ	Eugene E. Hafen	1990	1,124
318 7/8	46 0/8	46 2/8	43 5/8	7	7	Lemhi County	ID	Jim Pekola	1994	1,124
318 7/8	43 3/8	43 4/8	36 5/8	7	7	Lincoln County	MT	Terry V. Crooks	1997	1,124
318 6/8	48 5/8	48 1/8	42 2/8	6	7	Larimer County	CO	Tony Seahorn	1972	1,129
318 6/8	52 1/8	51 1/8	39 2/8	7	6	Niobrara County	WY	Donald L. Smith	1973	1,129
318 6/8	50 1/8	53 6/8	45 0/8	7	6	Coconino County	AZ	Tom Dalrymple	1980	1,129
318 6/8	47 4/8	47 4/8	39 4/8	6	6	Sanders County	MT	Wayne L. Haines	1982	1,129
318 6/8	44 3/8	44 2/8	35 2/8	6	6	Bow Valley	ALB	Pat Leiser	1986	1,129
318 6/8	48 6/8	46 2/8	31 2/8	6	6	Morgan County	UT	Hugh H. Hogle	1988	1,129
318 6/8	46 6/8	47 5/8	43 2/8	6	6	Converse County	WY	Chris D. Yeoman	1990	1,129
318 6/8	54 7/8	53 3/8	37 6/8	6	6	Coconino County	AZ	Eldon L. Helm	1995	1,129
318 5/8	44 4/8	44 0/8	34 6/8	6	6	Mineral County	CO	David Powell	1969	1,137
318 5/8	54 0/8	55 7/8	39 7/8	6	6	Beaverhead County	MT	Greg L. Munther	1981	1,137
318 5/8	49 3/8	49 7/8	37 7/8	6	6	Missoula County	MT	J. Scott Graham	1982	1,137
318 5/8	47 7/8	49 6/8	43 1/8	6	6	Lincoln County	WY	Randy Ulmer	1990	1,137
318 5/8	46 7/8	46 7/8	44 3/8	6	7	Sweetwater County	WY	Mark Hamilton	1990	1,137
318 5/8	49 0/8	50 3/8	43 3/8	6	6	Morgan County	UT	Bob Frank	1991	1,137
318 4/8	43 7/8	42 6/8	39 4/8	6	6	Bighorn Mountains	WY	Ron Johnson	1975	1,143
318 4/8	51 1/8	49 4/8	43 0/8	6	6	Shoshone County	ID	Michael R. Whaley	1989	1,143
318 4/8	46 4/8	48 2/8	47 0/8	6	6	Apache County	AZ	Dave Mortimer	1989	1,143
318 4/8	42 2/8	45 5/8	40 0/8	7	6	Catron County	NM	Tracy G. Hardy	1992	1,143
318 4/8	51 4/8	50 6/8	38 4/8	7	7	Flathead County	MT	Jeffrey M. Benda	1992	1,143
318 4/8	44 3/8	44 1/8	35 6/8	6	6	Park County	WY	Paul Bormes	1993	1,143
318 4/8	45 2/8	44 6/8	41 2/8	6	6	Saguache County	CO	Charlie VanTreese	1996	1,143
318 4/8	46 5/8	48 5/8	37 0/8	6	6	Grant County	NM	D. Kyle Brown	1996	1,143
318 4/8	52 3/8	54 2/8	38 0/8	6	6	Fergus County	MT	Jeffrey M. Stockhill	1997	1,143
318 3/8	51 4/8	49 7/8	33 3/8	6	6	Mineral County	MT	Farrell Cooper	1975	1,152
318 3/8	52 4/8	51 5/8	41 0/8	7	6	Deer Lodge County	MT	Dennis Neitzke	1980	1,152
318 3/8	48 1/8	48 1/8	36 5/8	6	6	Sierra County	NM	Jim Ryan	1988	1,152
318 3/8	51 0/8	51 6/8	34 3/8	6	6	Catron County	NM	Dr. Dale Mansfield	1992	1,152
318 2/8	45 1/8	45 4/8	36 0/8	6	6	Gunnison County	CO	Brian Newton	1989	1,156
318 2/8	53 0/8	52 4/8	41 0/8	6	6	Catron County	NM	Ray Francingues III	1992	1,156
318 2/8	45 7/8	46 1/8	38 4/8	6	6	Fergus County	MT	Bob Allen	1992	1,156
318 2/8	49 4/8	48 4/8	34 0/8	6	6	Beaverhead County	MT	Skip G. Mathewson	1994	1,156
318 2/8	51 0/8	50 0/8	34 4/8	6	6	Lemhi County	ID	John David Stuart	1997	1,156
318 2/8	48 2/8	45 7/8	38 6/8	6	6	Sheridan County	WY	Shane J. Shannon	1998	1,156
318 2/8	42 2/8	41 0/8	38 4/8	7	6	Rimbey	ALB	Bruno Greco	1998	1,156
318 1/8	48 4/8	47 0/8	34 2/8	7	7	Ravalli County	MT	Rick Twardoski	1984	1,163
318 1/8	49 3/8	47 1/8	36 7/8	6	6	Uintah County	UT	Everett Burson	1986	1,163
318 1/8	48 7/8	51 2/8	41 1/8	6	6	Catron County	NM	Delbert Holley	1987	1,163
318 1/8	50 0/8	52 2/8	35 7/8	7	8	Baker County	OR	John Buck	1987	1,163
318 1/8	52 7/8	52 4/8	36 3/8	6	6	Fergus County	MT	John Benes	1992	1,163
318 1/8	49 1/8	48 4/8	38 3/8	6	6	Rio Arriba County	NM	Jerry R. McManus, Jr.	1994	1,163
318 1/8	46 6/8	46 3/8	34 5/8	6	6	Fergus County	MT	James Sproul	1996	1,163
318 1/8	47 5/8	48 0/8	36 4/8	6	7	Petroleum County	MT	Chris Sanford	1997	1,163

YELLOWSTONE "AMERICAN" ELK (TYPICAL ANTLERS)

Minimum Score 260 — Continued

SCORE	LENGTH OF MAIN BEAM R	LENGTH OF MAIN BEAM L	INSIDE SPREAD	NUMBER OF POINTS R	NUMBER OF POINTS L	AREA	STATE/PROVINCE	HUNTER'S NAME	DATE	RANK
318 0/8	45 6/8	45 2/8	44 4/8	7	8	Bighorn Mtns.	WY	Henry 'Hank' Frey	1977	1,171
318 0/8	45 6/8	48 4/8	46 6/8	6	6	Carbon County	WY	James Blocker	1980	1,171
318 0/8	50 1/8	48 6/8	34 6/8	7	6	Fergus County	MT	Don Davidson	1995	1,171
317 7/8	45 6/8	45 4/8	45 1/8	6	6	Teton County	MT	Ronald K. Granneman	1974	1,174
317 7/8	47 6/8	43 3/8	38 5/8	6	6	Park County	WY	Wesley D. Engleman	1983	1,174
317 7/8	53 0/8	53 7/8	42 5/8	6	6	Flathead County	MT	James Norvell	1986	1,174
317 7/8	46 2/8	45 4/8	44 1/8	6	6	Clackamas County	OR	Gerald L. Egbert	1987	1,174
317 7/8	50 6/8	50 1/8	35 5/8	6	6	White Pine County	NV	Michael Scott Laity	1989	1,174
317 7/8	44 6/8	45 6/8	34 7/8	6	6	Fergus County	MT	James Schneider	1993	1,174
317 6/8	47 3/8	48 0/8	44 6/8	6	6	Valley County	ID	William R. "Steve" Stephenson	1988	1,180
317 6/8	55 2/8	55 2/8	41 0/8	6	7	Coconino County	AZ	Pete Foti	1990	1,180
317 6/8	44 3/8	44 1/8	35 4/8	6	6	Lincoln County	MT	Ron Halvorson	1991	1,180
317 6/8	44 1/8	44 5/8	35 6/8	6	6	Albany County	WY	Kenneth T. Tingo	1997	1,180
317 5/8	47 6/8	47 7/8	42 3/8	6	6	Lemhi County	ID	Lewis Zane Abbott	1981	1,184
317 5/8	56 6/8	55 5/8	35 3/8	6	6	Grant County	NM	Jimmy Head	1988	1,184
317 5/8	48 3/8	45 4/8	42 1/8	6	6	Pincher Creek	ALB	John Jacoby	1989	1,184
317 5/8	49 6/8	49 5/8	40 5/8	6	6	Beaverhead County	MT	Jim Muzynoski	1990	1,184
317 5/8	43 0/8	43 0/8	37 5/8	6	6	Jackson County	CO	Hal Rogers	1991	1,184
317 5/8	55 7/8	52 1/8	43 1/8	7	7	Grant County	OR	Larry McWilliams	1991	1,184
317 5/8	50 0/8	49 3/8	36 1/8	6	6	Coconino County	AZ	Randy S. Wagner	1992	1,184
317 5/8	55 0/8	52 3/8	48 1/8	5	5	McKinley County	NM	Ken Coleman	1997	1,184
317 4/8	52 0/8	52 3/8	40 2/8	6	6	Custer County	ID	Ed McIntosh	1989	1,192
317 4/8	52 4/8	53 0/8	38 4/8	5	6	Catron County	NM	C. Eric Wickman	1995	1,192
317 4/8	49 1/8	47 5/8	39 0/8	6	6	Park County	CO	Mark DeFurio	1996	1,192
317 4/8	49 7/8	49 1/8	42 0/8	7	6	Blaine County	ID	David Doxey	1997	1,192
317 4/8	49 5/8	51 2/8	35 0/8	6	6	Coconino County	AZ	Gerald Wachob	1997	1,192
317 3/8	49 0/8	48 3/8	40 7/8	6	6	Fremont County	ID	Donald M. Sherick	1982	1,197
317 3/8	45 1/8	47 1/8	36 4/8	7	7	Boundary County	ID	Walt Dinning	1987	1,197
317 3/8	51 3/8	50 0/8	37 1/8	6	6	Coconino County	AZ	Jim Norris	1991	1,197
317 3/8	47 1/8	48 1/8	44 6/8	9	6	Fergus County	MT	Jess Knerr	1992	1,197
317 2/8	51 4/8	52 6/8	36 4/8	6	6	Coconino County	AZ	Blaine "Bub" Mathews	1991	1,201
317 2/8	53 2/8	53 1/8	35 0/8	6	6	Coconino County	AZ	Michael Ellena	1992	1,201
317 2/8	47 7/8	47 7/8	40 2/8	5	5	Pennington County	SD	Dan Hotchkiss	1992	1,201
317 2/8	51 4/8	50 4/8	42 2/8	6	6	Petroleum County	MT	Bryant Shermoe	1992	1,201
317 2/8	47 4/8	47 7/8	48 1/8	7	7	Coconino County	AZ	Brian Beamer	1997	1,201
317 1/8	49 0/8	47 0/8	39 7/8	6	6	Catron County	NM	Eddie Claypool	1989	1,206
317 1/8	49 1/8	47 7/8	35 5/8	6	6	Catron County	NM	Robert Haymaker	1990	1,206
317 1/8	47 5/8	47 0/8	47 7/8	6	6	Catron County	NM	Rick L. Chukas	1990	1,206
317 1/8	47 2/8	47 5/8	39 5/8	6	6	Colfax County	NM	Mike Wiley	1990	1,206
317 1/8	49 1/8	53 0/8	38 7/8	6	7	Coconino County	AZ	Bill Grahlherr	1991	1,206
317 1/8	46 6/8	48 0/8	36 7/8	6	6	Wallowa County	OR	Russ Hultberg	1996	1,206
317 1/8	47 6/8	48 2/8	40 1/8	6	6	Valley County	MT	D. J. Elletson	1996	1,206
317 1/8	51 0/8	48 7/8	36 7/8	6	6	Sandoval County	NM	Mark D. Bauder	1998	1,206
317 0/8	46 5/8	47 0/8	42 2/8	6	7	Apache County	AZ	Robert H. Warren	1975	1,214
317 0/8	51 3/8	51 7/8	39 4/8	6	6	Rio Arriba County	NM	Alfred Vigil	1984	1,214
317 0/8	48 4/8	43 3/8	41 4/8	6	6	Mineral County	MT	S. Howie Henrikson	1987	1,214
317 0/8	49 3/8	51 1/8	37 0/8	6	6	Catron County	NM	Lars E. Winquist	1991	1,214
316 7/8	52 7/8	51 6/8	41 5/8	6	6	Converse County	WY	Troy Wickman	1993	1,218
316 6/8	49 3/8	49 7/8	35 6/8	6	6	Lodgepole	ALB	Lynn M. Kasper	1991	1,219
316 6/8	47 6/8	48 5/8	35 2/8	6	6	Coconino County	AZ	Joseph O. Fogleman	1991	1,219
316 6/8	46 7/8	48 2/8	39 0/8	6	6	Otero County	NM	Marvin Samford, Jr.	1993	1,219
316 6/8	50 5/8	49 5/8	45 4/8	6	6	Catron County	NM	Bill Shaw	1993	1,219
316 6/8	49 1/8	50 3/8	37 2/8	6	6	Valley County	MT	Larry Ochsner	1993	1,219
316 6/8	52 0/8	51 1/8	39 0/8	6	6	Musselshell County	MT	Chuck Adams	1998	1,219
316 5/8	46 1/8	49 3/8	37 5/8	6	7	Morrow County	OR	Bob Lindsay	1989	1,225
316 5/8	48 7/8	46 5/8	39 7/8	7	7	Coconino County	AZ	John Gurasich	1989	1,225
316 5/8	54 4/8	53 4/8	41 0/8	7	6	Garfield County	MT	David Cochell	1997	1,225
316 4/8	49 2/8	48 5/8	39 4/8	6	6	Grant County	OR	A. Corey Heath	1984	1,228
316 4/8	54 0/8	56 6/8	40 2/8	7	6	Kootenai County	ID	Theodore Costo	1991	1,228
316 4/8	49 3/8	53 5/8	38 6/8	6	6	Catron County	NM	John Sielicki	1994	1,228
316 3/8	51 0/8	51 0/8	40 5/8	6	6	Missoula County	MT	Ben L. Jennings	1984	1,231
316 3/8	52 3/8	51 1/8	38 5/8	6	6	Lewis County	WA	Leonard L. Stolen	1986	1,231
316 3/8	50 1/8	48 4/8	39 1/8	6	6	Coconino County	AZ	Joseph D. Ehmann	1992	1,231
316 3/8	50 6/8	48 5/8	37 7/8	6	6	Yavapai County	AZ	Jack Seckington	1994	1,231
316 3/8	46 0/8	45 6/8	36 7/8	6	6	Catron County	NM	Cindi Richardson	1996	1,231
316 3/8	53 0/8	52 6/8	40 0/8	6	6	McKinley County	NM	Stephen M. Milano	1997	1,231
316 3/8	49 4/8	48 7/8	36 7/8	6	6	Coconino County	AZ	Troy A. Graziadei	1998	1,231
316 2/8	48 2/8	48 2/8	34 6/8	7	7	Coconino County	AZ	William M. Lanese	1981	1,238
316 2/8	49 5/8	49 1/8	39 4/8	6	6	Canmore	ALB	Glenn Derovin	1990	1,238
316 2/8	52 7/8	51 3/8	42 6/8	6	6	Shoshone County	ID	Randy Lee Collecchi	1995	1,238
316 2/8	49 4/8	48 1/8	38 6/8	6	6	Coconino County	AZ	Darr Colburn	1995	1,238
316 2/8	43 4/8	44 0/8	40 0/8	6	5	Eureka County	NV	Ken Mallory	1996	1,238
316 2/8	50 3/8	48 1/8	36 6/8	6	6	Lewis & Clark County	MT	Dave Jaraczeski	1997	1,238
316 1/8	54 0/8	51 0/8	37 7/8	6	6	Valley County	MT	Dan Sturgis	1981	1,244
316 1/8	44 1/8	47 4/8	39 3/8	6	6	Rio Blanco County	CO	Darrell S. Jones	1987	1,244
316 1/8	48 1/8	48 6/8	43 1/8	6	6	Fergus County	MT	Joe Rud	1995	1,244
316 0/8	48 4/8	46 0/8	52 7/8	7	6	Deer Lodge County	MT	Bob Gossack	1976	1,247
316 0/8	46 4/8	48 2/8	40 0/8	6	6	Archuleta County	CO	Loren Hofeldt	1981	1,247

YELLOWSTONE "AMERICAN" ELK (TYPICAL ANTLERS)

Minimum Score 260 — Continued

SCORE	LENGTH OF R MAIN BEAM	L	INSIDE SPREAD	NUMBER OF R POINTS	L	AREA	STATE/ PROVINCE	HUNTER'S NAME	DATE	RANK
316 0/8	54 3/8	52 1/8	38 0/8	6	6	Sweet Grass County	MT	Marlin F. Dunlap	1983	1,247
316 0/8	45 1/8	43 7/8	43 2/8	6	6	Rich County	UT	Robert G. Petersen	1988	1,247
316 0/8	48 3/8	49 0/8	39 4/8	7	7	Apache County	AZ	Melvin E. Norris	1989	1,247
316 0/8	44 0/8	45 4/8	36 0/8	6	6	Coconino County	AZ	Earnest D. Stanley	1991	1,247
316 0/8	45 6/8	48 0/8	35 0/8	6	6	Lincoln County	NV	Kevin Paintner	1995	1,247
316 0/8	50 5/8	48 7/8	38 2/8	6	6	Colfax County	NM	Gudrun M. Richardson	1996	1,247
316 0/8	48 7/8	50 4/8	35 4/8	6	6	Lemhi County	ID	Gary Triplett	1997	1,247
316 0/8	49 2/8	46 5/8	39 0/8	6	6	Park County	WY	John Morlang	1998	1,247
315 7/8	51 2/8	51 4/8	43 3/8	6	6	Wasco County	OR	Ivan Duncan	1982	1,257
315 7/8	51 7/8	51 0/8	34 5/8	6	6	Sheridan County	WY	Dan Doke	1990	1,257
315 7/8	54 1/8	54 0/8	51 1/8	6	6	Cibola County	NM	Wayne A. Nicholson	1994	1,257
315 7/8	49 4/8	49 0/8	42 5/8	6	6	Coconino County	AZ	John Strippelman	1995	1,257
315 6/8	47 7/8	48 5/8	38 0/8	6	6	Nez Perce County	ID	Alfred J. Gemrich	1984	1,261
315 6/8	48 4/8	47 2/8	34 2/8	6	6	Converse County	WY	Arthur Rubel	1987	1,261
315 6/8	49 1/8	50 5/8	41 4/8	7	8	Converse County	WY	Frank Moore	1989	1,261
315 6/8	40 0/8	47 7/8	42 4/8	6	6	Caribou County	ID	Coby Tigert	1990	1,261
315 6/8	49 6/8	56 0/8	31 6/8	6	6	Catron County	NM	John S. Patterson	1992	1,261
315 6/8	46 6/8	48 4/8	32 4/8	6	6	Catron County	NM	Jorge Garcia-Segovia	1992	1,261
315 6/8	50 1/8	50 7/8	41 0/8	7	7	Larimer County	CO	Anthony Artessa	1995	1,261
315 6/8	48 4/8	45 7/8	41 6/8	6	6	Sierra County	NM	Deone Johnson	1998	1,261
315 5/8	48 6/8	47 6/8	36 3/8	6	6	Gallatin National Forest	MT	Rocky Miller	1981	1,269
315 5/8	47 0/8	46 3/8	45 1/8	6	6	Lemhi County	ID	Jeffrey T. Shaffer	1990	1,269
315 5/8	55 2/8	54 1/8	39 4/8	8	6	Coconino County	AZ	David C. Fretz	1992	1,269
315 4/8	51 7/8	49 0/8	42 6/8	6	6	Wallowa County	OR	Dr. Russell A. Colgan	1976	1,272
315 4/8	45 2/8	46 3/8	44 4/8	7	6	Harney County	OR	"Ray" L. D. Reimers	1989	1,272
315 4/8	48 2/8	48 2/8	34 2/8	7	6	Coconino County	AZ	Gregg Thurston	1994	1,272
315 3/8	53 0/8	50 7/8	37 3/8	6	6	Clear Creek County	CO	Gary Christoffersen	1982	1,275
315 3/8	51 3/8	50 4/8	37 3/8	6	6	Judith Basin County	MT	David Decker	1992	1,275
315 3/8	51 3/8	51 4/8	39 3/8	6	6	Coconino County	AZ	Jim Wheeler	1997	1,275
315 2/8	51 0/8	51 1/8	41 2/8	6	6	Teton County	MT	Ronald K. Granneman	1976	1,278
315 2/8	50 4/8	52 0/8	40 2/8	6	6	Clark County	ID	Ken Vander Linden	1986	1,278
315 2/8	46 6/8	45 6/8	41 4/8	6	6	Canmore	ALB	Dennis Francis	1986	1,278
315 2/8	45 7/8	45 6/8	40 0/8	5	6	Custer County	ID	Edward Allen Mack	1987	1,278
315 2/8	45 0/8	44 3/8	33 6/8	6	6	Catron County	NM	Christopher D. Walp	1994	1,278
315 1/8	42 4/8	43 4/8	38 3/8	6	6	Grant County	OR	Rod Curtis	1988	1,283
315 1/8	50 0/8	47 1/8	43 1/8	6	6	Bear Lake County	ID	Jerry B. Tueller	1991	1,283
315 1/8	47 1/8	48 2/8	37 3/8	6	6	Butte County	ID	Kirk W. Reese	1995	1,283
315 1/8	46 4/8	43 5/8	39 1/8	6	6	Phillips County	MT	Joey Ardrey	1996	1,283
315 1/8	49 3/8	48 2/8	35 7/8	6	6	Montrose County	CO	Stanley Van	1997	1,283
315 0/8	52 3/8	50 0/8	38 6/8	6	6	Grant County	OR	Bryan Kue	1994	1,288
315 0/8	50 0/8	48 7/8	38 6/8	6	6	Apache County	AZ	Larry R. Marin	1997	1,288
314 7/8	51 5/8	48 5/8	38 3/8	6	6	Catron County	NM	Dale R. Larson	1996	1,290
314 6/8	50 0/8	51 3/8	40 0/8	6	6	Catron County	NM	Wayne K. Curtis	1984	1,291
314 6/8	46 7/8	45 6/8	42 2/8	6	6	Catron County	NM	Dennis Curtis	1986	1,291
314 6/8	48 3/8	48 1/8	31 0/8	6	6	Mesa County	CO	Parker Leon	1989	1,291
314 6/8	44 4/8	46 0/8	34 6/8	6	7	Catron County	NM	Marvis Meyer	1992	1,291
314 6/8	45 1/8	46 5/8	36 2/8	6	6	Lemhi County	ID	Shawn M. West	1997	1,291
314 5/8	50 6/8	52 7/8	35 3/8	7	7	Hinsdale County	CO	Leon Shreve, Jr.	1995	1,296
314 5/8	52 7/8	53 0/8	39 3/8	6	5	Coconino County	AZ	John D. Beers	1997	1,296
314 4/8	48 0/8	48 2/8	39 4/8	6	6	Caribou County	ID	Alan E. Christiansen	1982	1,298
314 4/8	47 7/8	47 6/8	36 0/8	6	6	Moffat County	CO	Dave Holt	1985	1,298
314 4/8	47 0/8	48 5/8	35 6/8	6	6	Big Horn County	WY	Steve Schulz	1998	1,298
314 3/8	48 4/8	46 1/8	41 3/8	6	6	Caribou County	ID	Bruce N. Moss	1980	1,301
314 3/8	48 4/8	52 3/8	35 3/8	6	6	Grant County	NM	Ronald L. Pack, Sr.	1988	1,301
314 3/8	45 5/8	45 4/8	42 3/8	6	6	Catron County	NM	Bruce Carlisle	1989	1,301
314 2/8	48 6/8	45 3/8	47 0/8	6	6	Coconino County	AZ	Michael Faherty	1986	1,304
314 2/8	44 6/8	44 4/8	36 6/8	6	6	Coconino County	AZ	Ron Kirk	1989	1,304
314 2/8	50 2/8	51 2/8	35 6/8	6	6	Uintah County	UT	J. Brad Denver	1995	1,304
314 2/8	50 5/8	51 7/8	36 6/8	6	6	Gilpin County	CO	John Arnesen	1997	1,304
314 1/8	51 0/8	51 2/8	41 5/8	6	6	Gallatin County	MT	C. W. Smith	1974	1,308
314 1/8	49 1/8	49 7/8	35 1/8	6	6	Custer County	ID	Ken Mallory	1994	1,308
314 0/8	47 7/8	48 2/8	44 0/8	6	6	Fremont County	ID	Tom Savage	1981	1,310
314 0/8	46 1/8	45 6/8	36 4/8	6	7	Phillips County	MT	Mark D. Hughes	1982	1,310
314 0/8	50 3/8	50 1/8	40 4/8	6	6	Catron County	NM	Randall F. Cooley	1983	1,310
314 0/8	54 3/8	54 4/8	37 0/8	6	5	Coconino County	AZ	James R. Dreves	1985	1,310
314 0/8	45 6/8	46 4/8	42 4/8	7	7	Big Horn County	WY	Mike Belcourt	1986	1,310
314 0/8	49 5/8	49 2/8	42 6/8	6	6	Flathead County	MT	Jim Hawkins	1986	1,310
314 0/8	44 4/8	44 4/8	35 2/8	6	6	Lemhi County	ID	Frank L. Dumbeck	1991	1,310
314 0/8	45 2/8	46 0/8	47 5/8	6	6	Fremont County	ID	Donald M. Sherick	1995	1,310
314 0/8	47 4/8	48 4/8	32 2/8	6	6	Catron County	NM	Gregory G. Clark	1996	1,310
314 0/8	47 5/8	47 1/8	37 4/8	6	6	Montrose County	CO	Jim Holdenried	1996	1,310
313 7/8	47 5/8	44 7/8	33 3/8	7	7	Porcupine Hills	ALB	John Archibald	1980	1,320
313 7/8	49 2/8	47 3/8	44 2/8	7	6	Coconino County	AZ	Don R. Newton	1980	1,320
313 7/8	44 4/8	44 3/8	34 1/8	6	6	Apache County	AZ	Doug Kleck	1986	1,320
313 7/8	49 0/8	52 5/8	41 5/8	6	6	Rich County	UT	C. Keith Maynes	1990	1,320
313 7/8	49 6/8	51 1/8	46 1/8	6	6	Johnson County	WY	Gary D. Hughes	1992	1,320
313 7/8	49 4/8	45 7/8	34 1/8	7	7	Albany County	WY	Bill Gorman	1992	1,320
313 7/8	52 4/8	48 6/8	35 1/8	6	6	Idaho County	ID	Mike Estrada	1996	1,320

YELLOWSTONE "AMERICAN" ELK (TYPICAL ANTLERS)

Minimum Score 260

SCORE	LENGTH OF MAIN BEAM R	LENGTH OF MAIN BEAM L	INSIDE SPREAD	NUMBER OF POINTS R	NUMBER OF POINTS L	AREA	STATE/ PROVINCE	HUNTER'S NAME	DATE	RANK
313 7/8	44 3/8	44 5/8	35 1/8	6	6	Fergus County	MT	Josef K. Rud	1996	1,320
313 7/8	45 2/8	45 2/8	38 1/8	7	7	Catron County	NM	Jimmy W. Stafford	1998	1,320
313 6/8	47 7/8	47 7/8	36 2/8	6	6	Otero County	NM	Lynn Saxon	1987	1,329
313 6/8	44 4/8	45 2/8	48 0/8	6	5	Moffat County	CO	Mike Wallers	1991	1,329
313 6/8	51 1/8	50 7/8	42 4/8	7	7	Sublette County	WY	Ron Couture	1993	1,329
313 6/8	46 3/8	48 4/8	33 4/8	7	6	Washington County	ID	Jorden Doggett	1997	1,329
313 5/8	53 3/8	53 2/8	31 4/8	6	7	Coconino County	AZ	Michael John Bylina	1988	1,333
313 5/8	47 5/8	46 7/8	37 1/8	6	6	Valley County	ID	Kevin Primrose	1996	1,333
313 5/8	52 3/8	50 3/8	38 7/8	6	6	Sweetwater County	WY	Patrick J. Malone	1997	1,333
313 4/8	45 0/8	43 4/8	41 4/8	6	6	Jefferson County	CO	Charles Cater	1976	1,336
313 4/8	50 5/8	51 0/8	43 4/8	6	6	Grant County	OR	Andy Day	1980	1,336
313 4/8	51 2/8	52 4/8	45 2/8	6	6	Catron County	NM	Mike Moore	1988	1,336
313 4/8	47 6/8	46 1/8	40 6/8	6	6	Coconino County	AZ	Troy Dagenhart	1995	1,336
313 4/8	44 4/8	45 2/8	40 4/8	6	6	Albany County	WY	Mark E. Adamson	1997	1,336
313 3/8	42 7/8	42 4/8	34 1/8	6	6	Apache County	AZ	Ronald Mellick	1990	1,341
313 3/8	47 2/8	47 2/8	37 5/8	6	7	Harney County	OR	Robert M. Choate	1990	1,341
313 3/8	55 5/8	54 2/8	36 3/8	6	6	Rio Arriba County	NM	Eudane Vicenti	1995	1,341
313 3/8	49 2/8	48 6/8	35 5/8	6	6	Rio Arriba County	NM	Eudane Vicenti	1997	1,341
313 3/8	45 6/8	44 1/8	32 1/8	6	6	Garfield County	MT	Ron Borgeson	1997	1,341
313 2/8	49 2/8	46 0/8	44 2/8	6	6	Albany County	WY	Jerry Bowen	1979	1,346
313 2/8	43 4/8	44 1/8	30 4/8	7	7	Park County	MT	Robert Wennerstrom	1985	1,346
313 2/8	51 2/8	51 2/8	39 6/8	6	6	Bonneville County	ID	Ron Mueller	1986	1,346
313 2/8	51 4/8	50 7/8	45 4/8	6	6	Idaho County	ID	William E. Dean	1994	1,346
313 2/8	48 2/8	47 4/8	39 6/8	6	5	Coconino County	AZ	Todd Smith	1994	1,346
313 2/8	47 1/8	46 5/8	39 0/8	7	6	Lincoln County	MT	Tony Bierwagen	1996	1,346
313 2/8	48 3/8	49 4/8	37 0/8	6	6	Archuleta County	CO	Jerome C. Haverda	1997	1,346
313 2/8	55 0/8	50 6/8	41 0/8	6	6	Carbon County	WY	Sonny Jaramillo	1998	1,346
313 1/8	46 1/8	49 3/8	34 0/8	8	7	Chaffee County	CO	Rick D. Montgomery	1986	1,354
313 1/8	49 5/8	49 1/8	42 4/8	7	6	Glacier County	MT	Rick R. Winkowitsch	1989	1,354
313 1/8	51 2/8	50 6/8	35 3/8	6	6	Albany County	WY	Mark Stiller	1992	1,354
313 1/8	47 6/8	48 7/8	38 7/8	6	6	Shoshone County	ID	David Keith Robertson	1992	1,354
313 1/8	49 3/8	49 6/8	34 3/8	6	6	Beaverhead County	MT	Michael John Smith	1994	1,354
313 1/8	52 0/8	49 5/8	36 3/8	6	6	Albany County	WY	Jerry Bowen	1995	1,354
313 1/8	43 6/8	42 5/8	32 7/8	6	6	Sublette County	WY	Tony Crnkovich	1996	1,354
313 0/8	48 4/8	47 3/8	46 2/8	6	6	Park County	MT	Charles Milner	1973	1,361
313 0/8	48 3/8	47 3/8	31 4/8	6	6	Catron County	NM	Steven J. Vittetow	1987	1,361
313 0/8	56 5/8	55 4/8	39 4/8	6	6	Coconino County	AZ	Vince Dimiceli	1989	1,361
313 0/8	47 2/8	46 2/8	35 6/8	7	6	Greenlee County	AZ	Charles Steven Williams	1990	1,361
313 0/8	49 5/8	50 1/8	35 6/8	7	6	Sierra County	NM	Gerald Lambert Lopez	1991	1,361
313 0/8	46 2/8	46 2/8	39 2/8	6	7	Sanders County	MT	Doug Van Tassell	1995	1,361
313 0/8	50 1/8	50 5/8	40 0/8	6	6	Judith Basin County	MT	Kelly Norskog	1996	1,361
313 0/8	53 3/8	52 6/8	39 4/8	5	6	Blaine County	ID	Tom Daquino	1996	1,361
313 0/8	47 5/8	46 7/8	42 0/8	6	6	Blaine County	ID	M. Wayne Carey	1997	1,361
312 7/8	46 7/8	50 1/8	43 7/8	6	6	Shoshone County	ID	Harry Barker	1962	1,370
312 7/8	49 6/8	50 0/8	41 6/8	6	7	Catron County	NM	Lee Braudt	1988	1,370
312 7/8	45 7/8	46 1/8	31 5/8	7	7	Alder Flats	ALB	John Miller	1990	1,370
312 7/8	44 4/8	45 3/8	38 7/8	6	6	Valley County	MT	Kenneth Smoker, Jr.	1990	1,370
312 7/8	50 0/8	52 4/8	36 7/8	6	6	Moffat County	CO	Glenn W. Pritchard	1991	1,370
312 7/8	50 1/8	50 2/8	37 1/8	6	6	Catron County	NM	Randall S. Ulmer	1991	1,370
312 7/8	47 6/8	49 1/8	32 3/8	7	7	Catron County	NM	Robin Klemme	1997	1,370
312 7/8	44 5/8	46 7/8	36 3/8	6	6	Greenlee County	AZ	Mark A. Vallejo	1998	1,370
312 6/8	44 3/8	46 1/8	33 4/8	7	6	Clearwater County	ID	Doyle Anderegg	1975	1,378
312 6/8	55 2/8	54 0/8	40 4/8	5	5	Cibola County	NM	Mark Webber	1982	1,378
312 6/8	53 3/8	53 6/8	39 4/8	6	6	Greenlee County	AZ	Dick Hall	1986	1,378
312 5/8	47 0/8	47 3/8	39 5/8	6	6	Caribou County	ID	Dean Humphreys	1962	1,381
312 5/8	50 4/8	54 4/8	41 7/8	6	6	Fremont County	ID	Blair R. Jones	1987	1,381
312 5/8	46 7/8	47 6/8	32 3/8	6	6	Park County	CO	William Elfland	1991	1,381
312 4/8	51 0/8	51 6/8	42 3/8	9	7	Sanders County	MT	Ron Halvorson	1980	1,384
312 4/8	46 4/8	49 5/8	40 2/8	6	6	Clearwater County	ID	Steven E. Baxter	1984	1,384
312 4/8	48 6/8	46 6/8	37 2/8	6	6	Coconino County	AZ	Tony W. Zimbaro	1989	1,384
312 4/8	51 6/8	51 4/8	38 6/8	7	6	Grant County	OR	James M. Carter	1991	1,384
312 4/8	53 3/8	51 6/8	35 5/8	6	7	Catron County	NM	Johnny C. Parsons	1992	1,384
312 4/8	49 4/8	48 3/8	35 0/8	7	6	Phillips County	MT	Jerry Parsons	1995	1,384
312 4/8	46 7/8	47 6/8	39 2/8	6	6	Big Horn County	WY	Steve Schulz	1997	1,384
312 3/8	53 5/8	52 0/8	36 1/8	6	6	Socorro County	NM	James C. Hayes	1992	1,391
312 2/8	46 4/8	48 4/8	49 2/8	7	7	Ravalli County	MT	Dick Robertson	1973	1,392
312 2/8	44 6/8	44 7/8	38 2/8	6	6	Eagle County	CO	Gary D. Allen	1974	1,392
312 2/8	48 1/8	48 4/8	36 4/8	6	6	Larimer County	CO	Steve Stumbo	1975	1,392
312 2/8	50 0/8	49 0/8	35 5/8	7	8	Butte County	ID	Floyd L. Collins, Jr.	1982	1,392
312 2/8	46 4/8	46 2/8	35 0/8	6	7	Catron County	NM	Billy E. Gourley	1984	1,392
312 1/8	45 5/8	45 3/8	33 3/8	6	6	Garfield County	UT	Russell Peterson	1984	1,397
312 1/8	45 2/8	44 4/8	35 3/8	6	6	Catron County	NM	Randy Williams	1985	1,397
312 1/8	50 2/8	50 4/8	34 7/8	6	6	Lemhi County	ID	Mike S. Szekely	1986	1,397
312 1/8	48 4/8	47 6/8	36 1/8	6	6	Musselshell County	MT	Bill Krenz	1992	1,397
312 1/8	45 5/8	46 3/8	42 1/8	6	6	Catron County	NM	James D. Powless	1996	1,397
312 0/8	48 2/8	48 6/8	37 7/8	6	6	Montrose County	CO	Stanley R. Godfrey	1978	1,402
312 0/8	49 7/8	49 7/8	39 0/8	6	6	Rio Blanco County	CO	John Richardson	1990	1,402
312 0/8	49 0/8	48 6/8	36 6/8	6	7	Clackamas County	OR	Jeromy F. Adamson	1992	1,402

YELLOWSTONE "AMERICAN" ELK (TYPICAL ANTLERS)

Minimum Score 260

Continued

SCORE	LENGTH OF R MAIN BEAM L		INSIDE SPREAD	NUMBER OF R POINTS L		AREA	STATE/ PROVINCE	HUNTER'S NAME	DATE	RANK
312 0/8	45 3/8	46 7/8	38 1/8	8	6	Navajo County	AZ	David A. Niemann	1994	1,402
312 0/8	41 7/8	43 1/8	34 4/8	6	6	Otero County	NM	Mark S. Hahn	1997	1,402
312 0/8	51 3/8	51 6/8	45 2/8	6	6	Larimer County	CO	Steven W. Stumbo	1997	1,402
311 7/8	46 0/8	44 5/8	32 3/8	6	6	Albany County	WY	Paul Jakovac	1994	1,408
311 7/8	46 4/8	48 0/8	34 1/8	6	6	Socorro County	NM	J. Dale Hale	1996	1,408
311 6/8	47 6/8	47 1/8	37 6/8	6	8	Lewis & Clark County	MT	Douglas L. Conrady	1980	1,410
311 6/8	51 5/8	52 1/8	38 4/8	6	6	Deschutes County	OR	Gary Scroggins	1988	1,410
311 6/8	49 7/8	48 6/8	35 2/8	6	6	White Pine County	NV	Sherri Pinnock	1993	1,410
311 6/8	50 2/8	48 5/8	41 2/8	6	6	Beaverhead County	MT	Pete Zemljak	1995	1,410
311 6/8	52 7/8	51 5/8	42 4/8	6	6	Butte County	ID	John Whipple	1996	1,410
311 6/8	46 4/8	48 1/8	39 4/8	6	6	Petroleum County	MT	Jerry Wandler	1998	1,410
311 5/8	47 0/8	48 7/8	35 1/8	7	7	Larimer County	CO	Roger J. Kabage	1992	1,416
311 5/8	48 0/8	48 4/8	34 1/8	6	6	Catron County	NM	George D. Cain	1993	1,416
311 5/8	46 2/8	47 4/8	33 5/8	6	6	Park County	WY	Langdon G. Smith, Jr.	1994	1,416
311 4/8	52 3/8	51 6/8	39 4/8	6	6	Coconino County	AZ	Richard Foss	1977	1,419
311 4/8	48 7/8	45 7/8	37 2/8	6	6	Bonneville County	ID	Gene H. Dressen	1978	1,419
311 4/8	46 2/8	45 6/8	38 0/8	6	6	Rio Blanco County	CO	Jack Lambert	1980	1,419
311 4/8	55 6/8	54 4/8	37 4/8	6	6	Archuleta County	CO	Tim Chavez	1983	1,419
311 4/8	44 6/8	44 2/8	37 2/8	6	6	Cypress River	MAN	Perry Fleet	1986	1,419
311 4/8	48 2/8	48 1/8	38 4/8	6	6	Idaho County	ID	Stan Myers	1988	1,419
311 4/8	48 0/8	49 2/8	34 4/8	6	6	Greenlee County	AZ	Carl L. Plasterer	1990	1,419
311 4/8	51 0/8	50 7/8	41 0/8	7	7	Coconino County	AZ	John Mullins	1994	1,419
311 4/8	48 0/8	47 7/8	38 4/8	6	6	Coconino County	AZ	Daniel Tone	1998	1,419
311 3/8	48 4/8	46 5/8	37 3/8	7	7	Sanders County	MT	Rus Willis	1981	1,428
311 3/8	49 3/8	48 6/8	39 7/8	6	6	Coconino County	AZ	Greg Winn	1991	1,428
311 3/8	48 2/8	47 5/8	44 3/8	6	8	Catron County	NM	Duane "Corky" Richardson	1992	1,428
311 2/8	44 5/8	46 2/8	33 6/8	6	6	Park County	CO	Lynn Campbell	1981	1,431
311 2/8	48 3/8	48 5/8	37 0/8	6	6	Clackamas County	OR	Bill Hensley	1984	1,431
311 2/8	47 7/8	49 3/8	32 2/8	6	7	Madison County	MT	Jacob Baine	1991	1,431
311 2/8	50 0/8	49 1/8	35 0/8	6	6	Socorro County	NM	Frank Sanders	1991	1,431
311 2/8	49 3/8	49 1/8	34 6/8	6	6	Mesa County	CO	David Parker Leon	1996	1,431
311 2/8	43 1/8	42 6/8	36 0/8	7	8	Lemhi County	ID	Thomas E. Lingenfelter	1998	1,431
311 2/8	48 1/8	45 6/8	41 6/8	6	7	Harney County	OR	Marte Scheuffele	1998	1,431
311 1/8	51 2/8	50 0/8	40 7/8	6	6	Ravalli County	MT	Gary J. Hartman	1989	1,438
311 1/8	48 6/8	47 6/8	34 5/8	6	6	Flathead County	MT	Ron Krueger	1989	1,438
311 1/8	42 2/8	44 3/8	42 1/8	6	6	Coconino County	AZ	Todd Walsh	1994	1,438
311 0/8	51 6/8	50 0/8	41 6/8	6	6	Teton County	WY	Fred Bear	1953	1,441
311 0/8	51 1/8	49 5/8	47 2/8	8	6	Larimer County	CO	H. Mike Palmer	1983	1,441
311 0/8	47 3/8	47 4/8	43 6/8	6	6	Beaverhead County	MT	Jerry Strodtman	1985	1,441
311 0/8	46 0/8	46 0/8	41 0/8	6	6	Mineral County	MT	Robert F. Erickson	1988	1,441
311 0/8	49 1/8	49 0/8	38 2/8	6	6	Sanders County	MT	Rick Dieterich	1990	1,441
311 0/8	46 3/8	48 2/8	41 6/8	6	6	Coconino County	AZ	Eddy Broderick	1992	1,441
311 0/8	48 3/8	46 0/8	37 6/8	6	6	Phillips County	MT	William K. Stephens	1995	1,441
311 0/8	48 7/8	48 1/8	44 4/8	7	6	Valley County	ID	Timothy Hill	1998	1,441
310 7/8	55 2/8	53 6/8	53 1/8	6	6	Pitkin County	CO	Bob Gulman	1973	1,449
310 7/8	45 6/8	45 0/8	36 3/8	6	6	Flathead County	MT	Scott Halama	1986	1,449
310 7/8	48 4/8	47 1/8	36 5/8	6	6	Uintah County	UT	J. Brad Denver	1994	1,449
310 7/8	43 7/8	43 2/8	35 1/8	6	6	Catron County	NM	Keith Vanderburg	1996	1,449
310 6/8	49 5/8	51 2/8	43 4/8	6	6	Lemhi County	ID	Joe Hollifield	1977	1,453
310 6/8	45 5/8	46 2/8	35 0/8	7	8	Fergus County	MT	Steven J. Nelson	1977	1,453
310 6/8	45 6/8	47 0/8	36 2/8	6	7	Ravalli County	MT	Alan Lear	1988	1,453
310 6/8	44 6/8	42 2/8	39 6/8	6	6	Fergus County	MT	Billy E. Martin	1993	1,453
310 6/8	48 4/8	48 4/8	37 2/8	6	6	Flathead County	MT	Justin D. Lasater	1995	1,453
310 6/8	43 6/8	44 3/8	34 4/8	7	7	Fergus County	MT	Scott Abrams	1995	1,453
310 5/8	51 3/8	51 2/8	38 3/8	6	6	Little Belt Mtns.	MT	Jim Ekness	1978	1,459
310 5/8	47 1/8	44 6/8	39 3/8	7	6	Coconino County	AZ	Rick Brewer	1984	1,459
310 5/8	49 5/8	50 7/8	49 5/8	5	6	Granite County	MT	Shaun Twardoski	1992	1,459
310 5/8	55 2/8	53 2/8	42 1/8	6	6	Coconino County	AZ	Gary S. Kessinger	1992	1,459
310 5/8	50 2/8	50 2/8	37 3/8	6	6	Yellowstone County	MT	Monte Meredith	1997	1,459
310 5/8	47 0/8	46 4/8	40 1/8	6	6	Adams County	ID	Daniel Wisner	1997	1,459
310 4/8	49 0/8	49 0/8	43 6/8	6	6	La Plata County	CO	Tom Price	1967	1,465
310 4/8	43 2/8	43 6/8	38 2/8	6	6	Baker County	OR	Billy J. Cruise	1970	1,465
310 4/8	46 7/8	46 6/8	37 4/8	6	6	Clearwater County	ID	Rory Roby	1981	1,465
310 4/8	46 1/8	46 3/8	41 0/8	6	6	Valley County	ID	Ron Phillips	1983	1,465
310 4/8	53 3/8	51 1/8	37 0/8	6	6	Converse County	WY	Dennis Spawn	1986	1,465
310 4/8	52 2/8	51 2/8	33 2/8	6	7	Apache County	AZ	Steve McInelly	1986	1,465
310 4/8	45 2/8	45 7/8	42 6/8	6	6	Grant County	OR	Dean P. Pasche	1990	1,465
310 3/8	49 0/8	51 0/8	39 2/8	8	6	Caribou County	ID	Patrick G. Selfridge	1980	1,472
310 3/8	43 7/8	46 0/8	36 1/8	6	6	Santa Fe County	NM	Bennie "Buddy" Rhodes, Jr.	1990	1,472
310 3/8	55 0/8	48 7/8	37 4/8	7	9	Catron County	NM	Steven J. Niedzielski	1993	1,472
310 3/8	53 5/8	52 7/8	42 1/8	6	6	Larimer County	CO	Michael Raymer	1993	1,472
310 3/8	48 4/8	47 4/8	42 5/8	6	6	Boise County	ID	Neil J. Russell	1994	1,472
310 3/8	49 7/8	50 1/8	35 7/8	6	6	Coconino County	AZ	James Dale Casady	1996	1,472
310 2/8	49 4/8	50 0/8	30 0/8	6	6	Phillips County	MT	Daniel Tollefson	1981	1,478
310 2/8	45 0/8	45 4/8	33 4/8	6	6	Canmore	ALB	Cam Wilson	1984	1,478
310 2/8	48 2/8	49 2/8	34 6/8	6	6	Coconino County	AZ	Russ Warner	1984	1,478
310 2/8	45 1/8	43 4/8	39 0/8	6	6	Gallatin County	MT	David Burtch	1986	1,478
310 2/8	45 3/8	47 6/8	46 6/8	6	6	Coconino County	AZ	Alan H. Timonen	1992	1,478

YELLOWSTONE "AMERICAN" ELK (TYPICAL ANTLERS)

Minimum Score 260   Continued

SCORE	LENGTH OF MAIN BEAM R	LENGTH OF MAIN BEAM L	INSIDE SPREAD	NUMBER OF POINTS R	NUMBER OF POINTS L	AREA	STATE/ PROVINCE	HUNTER'S NAME	DATE	RANK
310 2/8	45 7/8	45 7/8	35 2/8	6	6	Phillips County	MT	David L. Skiff	1996	1,478
310 1/8	50 3/8	50 4/8	48 3/8	8	5	Idaho County	ID	Roy S. Lathen	1988	1,484
310 1/8	51 4/8	52 7/8	40 3/8	5	5	Rio Arriba County	NM	Isaac Julian, Sr.	1989	1,484
310 0/8	51 2/8	50 3/8	38 0/8	6	6	Ravalli County	MT	Bob Sappenfield	1978	1,486
310 0/8	46 5/8	49 1/8	37 2/8	5	6	Grant County	OR	Andy Day	1987	1,486
310 0/8	47 1/8	48 7/8	33 2/8	6	8	Clearwater County	ID	Jim Lashly	1990	1,486
310 0/8	48 6/8	48 7/8	44 2/8	6	7	Grant County	OR	Darin C. Jenison	1992	1,486
310 0/8	47 4/8	49 6/8	40 0/8	6	6	Coconino County	AZ	Rodman Ward	1993	1,486
309 7/8	47 2/8	47 3/8	37 3/8	6	7	Baker County	OR	James D. Ward	1983	1,491
309 7/8	47 0/8	44 7/8	42 1/8	7	7	Creston	BC	Derek Vance	1993	1,491
309 7/8	48 5/8	49 7/8	38 1/8	7	6	Lemhi County	ID	Dick McKeown	1996	1,491
309 7/8	48 0/8	48 3/8	36 3/8	6	6	Fremont County	WY	Larry Orr	1996	1,491
309 6/8	43 1/8	43 4/8	35 0/8	6	6	Routt County	CO	Steve Gorr	1971	1,495
309 6/8	50 6/8	51 0/8	40 0/8	7	6	Sanders County	MT	Brad Borden	1984	1,495
309 6/8	48 6/8	50 6/8	43 2/8	6	6	Coconino County	AZ	Robert L. Smith	1986	1,495
309 6/8	48 3/8	46 5/8	37 0/8	6	6	Park County	MT	Steve Kamps	1987	1,495
309 6/8	46 2/8	49 2/8	42 3/8	7	6	Yavapai County	AZ	Mark A. Rucker	1991	1,495
309 6/8	46 7/8	45 7/8	43 0/8	6	6	Dolores County	CO	Rev Charles Brannon	1992	1,495
309 6/8	43 7/8	43 4/8	37 4/8	7	6	Las Animas County	CO	Sal Petrolino	1998	1,495
309 5/8	51 0/8	50 6/8	39 7/8	6	6	Flathead County	MT	Paul Roney	1976	1,502
309 5/8	46 2/8	44 7/8	37 1/8	6	6	Lincoln County	MT	Mike Billingsley	1990	1,502
309 5/8	50 0/8	47 1/8	36 1/8	6	6	Garfield County	CO	Andy Jeanjaquet	1994	1,502
309 5/8	47 1/8	47 5/8	35 7/8	6	6	Coconino County	AZ	Daniel Omner Ward	1997	1,502
309 4/8	44 3/8	44 5/8	30 0/8	6	6	Valley County	MT	Charles Seiler	1976	1,506
309 4/8	42 6/8	41 7/8	32 6/8	6	6	Lincoln County	MT	Lee S. Lampton	1992	1,506
309 4/8	52 3/8	53 4/8	39 6/8	6	6	Catron County	NM	Bill Horvath	1997	1,506
309 3/8	47 0/8	47 4/8	35 7/8	6	6	Granite County	MT	Dwayne Garner	1985	1,509
309 3/8	44 0/8	42 4/8	41 1/8	7	6	Crook County	OR	Hank Baxter	1996	1,509
309 3/8	49 6/8	50 0/8	40 7/8	6	6	Socorro County	NM	Jimmy Donahoo	1996	1,509
309 2/8	51 1/8	51 2/8	38 6/8	7	7	Garfield County	CO	Harry Earl Temple	1960	1,512
309 2/8	44 6/8	47 4/8	44 4/8	5	6	Fremont County	ID	Larry Bauer	1960	1,512
309 2/8	45 0/8	45 7/8	34 4/8	6	6	Union County	OR	Ron Angell	1981	1,512
309 2/8	48 0/8	47 6/8	42 2/8	6	6	Sheridan County	WY	George Rogers	1988	1,512
309 2/8	48 2/8	47 4/8	41 4/8	6	6	Uintah County	UT	Justin Arrowchis	1990	1,512
309 2/8	45 0/8	44 4/8	44 2/8	5	6	Rio Arriba County	NM	Dr. Leo A. Lucas	1990	1,512
309 2/8	44 0/8	43 0/8	39 2/8	6	6	Phillips County	MT	Randy S. Bowler	1994	1,512
309 2/8	48 0/8	47 4/8	35 4/8	6	7	Union County	OR	Robert H. Deibel	1994	1,512
309 2/8	49 7/8	50 4/8	45 4/8	6	6	Coconino County	AZ	Henry Robert Garcia, Sr.	1995	1,512
309 2/8	48 6/8	47 0/8	40 2/8	6	6	Socorro County	NM	Richard Berger	1996	1,512
309 2/8	43 5/8	44 6/8	40 5/8	9	7	Park County	MT	Paul Meyers	1997	1,512
309 1/8	44 4/8	46 4/8	34 5/8	6	6	Coconino County	AZ	Les Butters	1981	1,523
309 1/8	48 0/8	46 6/8	39 7/8	6	6	Missoula County	MT	Chad Spicknall	1984	1,523
309 1/8	49 5/8	50 0/8	37 5/8	6	6	Mora County	NM	Randy Ries	1990	1,523
309 1/8	45 6/8	45 5/8	37 1/8	6	6	Toad River	BC	Peter Swenson	1991	1,523
309 1/8	48 6/8	50 0/8	41 1/8	6	6	Sandoval County	NM	Chuck Adams	1991	1,523
309 1/8	50 5/8	48 2/8	42 1/8	6	6	Coconino County	AZ	John Woodruff	1992	1,523
309 1/8	48 0/8	45 4/8	37 1/8	6	6	Fergus County	MT	Donny Roy	1996	1,523
309 0/8	46 3/8	45 5/8	38 6/8	6	6	Boise County	ID	Steve Groff	1989	1,530
309 0/8	47 3/8	48 6/8	38 6/8	6	6	Archuleta County	CO	Darla Bramwell	1997	1,530
309 0/8	43 3/8	42 6/8	39 6/8	7	7	Coconino County	AZ	Richard D. Tone	1998	1,530
308 7/8	47 4/8	47 4/8	37 7/8	6	7	Wallowa County	OR	Greg Bogh	1997	1,533
308 6/8	44 6/8	45 0/8	36 6/8	7	6	Lincoln County	MT	Steve Kluver	1987	1,534
308 5/8	47 5/8	46 3/8	40 1/8	7	6	Wasco County	OR	Gary Paugh	1984	1,535
308 5/8	50 2/8	51 2/8	37 5/8	6	6	Taos County	NM	Nicholas J Rowley	1985	1,535
308 4/8	47 7/8	47 7/8	41 2/8	7	6	Socorro County	NM	Jack W. Bruton	1985	1,537
308 4/8	48 0/8	48 2/8	39 0/8	6	6	Catron County	NM	Bob A. Gourley	1986	1,537
308 4/8	45 1/8	47 4/8	40 4/8	6	6	Elmore County	ID	Matt March, Jr.	1987	1,537
308 4/8	47 6/8	46 6/8	37 7/8	7	7	Elmore County	ID	Anthony L. Mudd	1992	1,537
308 4/8	45 3/8	44 6/8	37 2/8	6	6	Custer County	ID	Clayton Nielson	1995	1,537
308 4/8	50 2/8	51 1/8	41 0/8	6	6	Lincoln County	MT	Brian Wilkins	1995	1,537
308 3/8	49 0/8	50 4/8	38 5/8	7	6	Idaho County	ID	Bill G. Davis	1989	1,543
308 3/8	48 3/8	47 3/8	37 1/8	6	6	Lincoln County	MT	John C. McDivitt	1992	1,543
308 3/8	49 5/8	48 4/8	33 3/8	7	7	Missoula County	MT	Joseph J. Simone, Jr.	1992	1,543
308 3/8	46 1/8	37 4/8	34 1/8	6	6	Petroleum County	MT	Rob Miller	1997	1,543
308 2/8	42 4/8	44 0/8	42 4/8	6	6	Kane County	UT	Ron Simmers	1991	1,547
308 2/8	44 4/8	44 4/8	38 4/8	6	6	Lincoln County	WY	Tom A. Daughetee	1991	1,547
308 2/8	51 2/8	50 3/8	43 0/8	6	7	Rich County	UT	Hugh H. Hogle	1992	1,547
308 2/8	46 6/8	47 1/8	37 4/8	6	6	Jefferson County	OR	Jay T. Roth	1997	1,547
308 1/8	51 1/8	50 6/8	42 7/8	6	5	Crook County	OR	Jim Hodson	1983	1,551
308 1/8	48 3/8	49 4/8	39 1/8	6	6	Coconino County	AZ	Richard D. Tone	1987	1,551
308 1/8	49 3/8	49 7/8	40 1/8	6	7	Missoula County	MT	Kevin P. Grenier	1990	1,551
308 1/8	48 0/8	47 7/8	42 4/8	6	7	Sevier County	UT	Jim Madsen	1996	1,551
308 0/8	43 4/8	48 0/8	32 6/8	6	6	Shoshone County	ID	Randy Hammond	1983	1,555
307 7/8	46 5/8	46 3/8	37 5/8	6	6	Ravalli County	MT	Ray Tlamka	1984	1,556
307 7/8	47 3/8	48 6/8	36 3/8	6	5	Baca County	CO	Max Crocker	1989	1,556
307 7/8	47 4/8	46 4/8	43 1/8	6	6	Carbon County	WY	Brenda Sapp	1998	1,556
307 6/8	47 0/8	47 1/8	40 2/8	6	6	Valley County	ID	Neil Thagard	1991	1,559
307 6/8	49 0/8	51 4/8	35 4/8	6	6	Graham County	AZ	Steven Monroe	1992	1,559

YELLOWSTONE "AMERICAN" ELK (TYPICAL ANTLERS)

Minimum Score 260

Continued

SCORE	LENGTH OF MAIN BEAM R	LENGTH OF MAIN BEAM L	INSIDE SPREAD	NUMBER OF POINTS R	NUMBER OF POINTS L	AREA	STATE/ PROVINCE	HUNTER'S NAME	DATE	RANK
307 6/8	44 7/8	46 2/8	49 2/8	6	6	Madison County	MT	Everett W. Ayers, Sr.	1992	1,559
307 6/8	45 5/8	45 1/8	41 4/8	6	6	Fergus County	MT	Jerry Knerr	1993	1,559
307 6/8	46 4/8	43 7/8	35 0/8	6	6	San Juan County	NM	Terry L. Lewis	1994	1,559
307 5/8	48 5/8	50 3/8	35 1/8	6	6	San Juan County	UT	Christopher M. Beck	1997	1,564
307 4/8	45 5/8	42 7/8	37 4/8	7	7	Huerfano County	CO	Wilbur F. Lay, Jr.	1974	1,565
307 4/8	47 7/8	48 0/8	40 4/8	5	6	Caribou County	ID	Charlie Humphreys	1979	1,565
307 4/8	54 6/8	54 6/8	46 3/8	7	7	Apache County	AZ	Tom David	1985	1,565
307 4/8	44 0/8	43 7/8	40 4/8	6	5	Gallatin County	MT	Don Syvrud	1985	1,565
307 4/8	46 7/8	47 1/8	37 2/8	6	6	Teller County	CO	James M. Strampe	1985	1,565
307 4/8	44 4/8	43 7/8	33 6/8	6	6	Valley County	ID	Brian Hunter Heck	1990	1,565
307 4/8	47 1/8	48 0/8	34 4/8	6	6	Beaverhead County	MT	Gary Dudden	1991	1,565
307 4/8	51 2/8	49 6/8	37 6/8	6	6	Archuleta County	CO	Lester D. Hawkins, Jr.	1992	1,565
307 3/8	46 2/8	36 4/8	33 3/8	6	6	Garfield County	MT	Jerry L. Molstad	1986	1,573
307 3/8	48 2/8	47 4/8	36 1/8	6	6	Lemhi County	ID	George C. Engelhardt	1988	1,573
307 3/8	46 5/8	47 0/8	37 7/8	7	6	Greenlee County	AZ	Clifford White	1989	1,573
307 3/8	42 4/8	43 3/8	51 7/8	7	7	Park County	CO	Marko Green	1989	1,573
307 3/8	50 4/8	47 4/8	34 7/8	6	6	Coconino County	AZ	Jim Beaumier	1992	1,573
307 3/8	43 3/8	43 5/8	40 5/8	6	6	Delta County	CO	Cliff Beaver	1995	1,573
307 2/8	49 5/8	50 4/8	35 6/8	6	6	Coconino County	AZ	Larry Hines	1981	1,579
307 2/8	48 6/8	46 1/8	35 1/8	7	7	Bonner County	ID	Brian T. Farley	1982	1,579
307 2/8	52 5/8	47 0/8	38 1/8	7	8	Idaho County	ID	John Moehrle	1987	1,579
307 2/8	44 6/8	46 0/8	38 2/8	6	6	Grand County	CO	Gary W. Billiet	1993	1,579
307 2/8	50 2/8	49 4/8	34 7/8	6	7	Phillips County	MT	David T. Borek	1997	1,579
307 1/8	54 4/8	52 4/8	40 3/8	6	6	Park County	MT	David Thiry	1981	1,584
307 1/8	47 0/8	47 5/8	43 1/8	6	6	Grant County	OR	George Schiedler	1983	1,584
307 1/8	50 4/8	51 0/8	42 3/8	6	6	Park County	MT	Robert Ward	1983	1,584
307 1/8	47 1/8	46 6/8	33 3/8	6	6	Navajo County	AZ	Warren A. Adams	1992	1,584
307 1/8	48 5/8	45 4/8	33 1/8	6	6	Missoula County	MT	Tou Lee	1992	1,584
307 1/8	47 5/8	49 6/8	40 7/8	6	6	Coconino County	AZ	Duane "Corky" Richardson	1995	1,584
307 1/8	54 2/8	54 5/8	35 5/8	6	6	Jefferson County	CO	Bill Ramsey	1997	1,584
307 1/8	45 0/8	47 4/8	46 7/8	6	6	Grant County	OR	Jon Simonson	1997	1,584
307 1/8	47 4/8	47 4/8	36 1/8	6	7	Wainwright	ALB	Dale Johnson	1998	1,584
307 0/8	51 5/8	50 2/8	35 6/8	6	6	Judith Basin County	MT	Mark A. Petroni	1982	1,593
307 0/8	49 3/8	50 6/8	37 0/8	6	6	Apache County	AZ	Melvin Edward Norris	1986	1,593
307 0/8	53 1/8	52 0/8	38 6/8	6	7	Clearwater County	ID	Ralph L. Albright	1986	1,593
307 0/8	48 6/8	48 0/8	36 2/8	6	6	Sheridan County	WY	Jerome D. Larson	1997	1,593
306 7/8	46 0/8	44 0/8	42 5/8	6	6	Sandoval County	NM	Rett Kelly	1991	1,597
306 7/8	41 2/8	42 5/8	41 1/8	6	6	Boundary County	ID	Roger N. Myers	1994	1,597
306 7/8	43 7/8	44 4/8	40 7/8	7	7	Grant County	NM	James Schulz	1997	1,597
306 7/8	49 3/8	49 1/8	41 3/8	6	7	Custer County	ID	Patrick Corcoran	1997	1,597
306 7/8	44 6/8	46 6/8	31 1/8	6	6	Shoshone County	ID	Edward J. Wagner	1998	1,597
306 6/8	50 5/8	43 7/8	35 6/8	6	6	Coconino County	AZ	Philip M. Rippey	1988	1,602
306 6/8	44 7/8	46 0/8	30 2/8	8	6	Fergus County	MT	Roland E. Sanford, Jr.	1988	1,602
306 6/8	43 0/8	42 5/8	32 4/8	6	6	Sanders County	MT	Jeffrey M. Myny	1991	1,602
306 6/8	50 2/8	50 2/8	35 6/8	6	6	Millard County	UT	Ross J. Madsen	1993	1,602
306 6/8	43 3/8	45 4/8	34 6/8	6	6	Johnson County	WY	Brett Burditt	1994	1,602
306 6/8	39 7/8	40 7/8	35 2/8	6	6	Crook County	OR	Jeff Wingert	1996	1,602
306 6/8	50 3/8	49 3/8	37 6/8	6	7	Pueblo County	CO	James L. Smith	1996	1,602
306 5/8	50 2/8	49 1/8	39 7/8	5	5	Granite County	MT	J. Greg Jones	1983	1,609
306 5/8	47 5/8	46 4/8	31 7/8	7	6	White Pine County	NV	Jerry A. Manges	1992	1,609
306 5/8	47 5/8	47 3/8	37 5/8	8	6	Mora County	NM	Kenneth Morga	1993	1,609
306 5/8	47 4/8	46 5/8	33 7/8	7	7	Phillips County	MT	Bob H. Paine	1994	1,609
306 5/8	49 6/8	49 2/8	38 7/8	6	6	Judith Basin County	MT	Brandon Johns	1997	1,609
306 5/8	45 6/8	45 7/8	37 1/8	6	6	Larimer County	CO	Mike Kelly	1998	1,609
306 4/8	42 7/8	43 2/8	43 4/8	5	5	Lemhi County	ID	A. Laverne Hokanson	1974	1,615
306 4/8	43 4/8	44 5/8	40 0/8	6	6	Clearwater County	ID	Kim J. Vander Sys	1977	1,615
306 4/8	46 4/8	47 2/8	37 4/8	6	6	Blaine County	ID	Tom Goicoechea	1982	1,615
306 4/8	45 6/8	46 3/8	33 6/8	6	6	Valley County	ID	Bob Shaw	1991	1,615
306 4/8	51 2/8	49 4/8	43 2/8	6	6	McKinley County	NM	Ben W. Gibson	1992	1,615
306 4/8	47 4/8	45 2/8	40 4/8	6	6	Crook County	OR	Jack Robertson	1992	1,615
306 3/8	48 4/8	48 5/8	40 6/8	7	6	Summit County	UT	Clifton B. Johnson	1978	1,621
306 3/8	45 3/8	47 1/8	32 7/8	6	6	Catron County	NM	Jim R. Wood	1992	1,621
306 2/8	49 3/8	48 3/8	40 2/8	6	6	Garfield County	UT	Bruce E. Carlisle	1985	1,623
306 2/8	46 2/8	45 7/8	37 3/8	7	6	Catron County	NM	Sonny Turner	1991	1,623
306 2/8	45 2/8	43 1/8	41 6/8	6	6	Garfield County	WA	Lee Campbell	1997	1,623
306 1/8	48 6/8	46 0/8	34 1/8	6	7	Beaverhead County	MT	Kenneth M. Carlson	1983	1,626
306 1/8	49 5/8	47 2/8	39 5/8	6	6	Catron County	NM	Martin Plugge	1991	1,626
306 1/8	52 0/8	52 0/8	34 5/8	6	6	Sheridan County	WY	Ron Johnson	1993	1,626
306 1/8	48 0/8	47 4/8	32 5/8	6	6	Sublette County	WY	Casey Saxton	1997	1,626
306 0/8	45 0/8	44 3/8	36 6/8	6	6	Eagle County	CO	Walt Williams	1979	1,630
306 0/8	49 2/8	48 7/8	34 2/8	6	6	Catron County	NM	William C. Davis	1986	1,630
306 0/8	53 2/8	53 2/8	39 4/8	6	6	Ravalli County	MT	Dave L. Fretz	1987	1,630
306 0/8	48 7/8	48 1/8	39 3/8	7	6	Phillips County	MT	Dave Farnsworth	1991	1,630
306 0/8	49 5/8	50 0/8	35 1/8	6	7	Mora County	NM	Larry A. Claar	1993	1,630
306 0/8	44 3/8	44 2/8	39 0/8	7	7	Garfield County	MT	Darren J. Moulthrop	1995	1,630
305 7/8	46 5/8	46 6/8	37 7/8	6	6	Grant County	OR	Gregory Stathos	1987	1,636
305 7/8	46 0/8	46 2/8	39 1/8	7	6	Sheridan County	WY	Randy Lee Reece	1990	1,636
305 7/8	49 3/8	51 2/8	41 7/8	5	6	Catron County	NM	Jerry Romero	1993	1,636

YELLOWSTONE "AMERICAN" ELK (TYPICAL ANTLERS)

Minimum Score 260

SCORE	LENGTH OF MAIN BEAM R	LENGTH OF MAIN BEAM L	INSIDE SPREAD	NUMBER OF POINTS R	NUMBER OF POINTS L	AREA	STATE/ PROVINCE	HUNTER'S NAME	DATE	RANK
305 7/8	48 1/8	39 6/8	36 3/8	6	6	Lincoln County	NM	Harold Dean Britt	1996	1,636
305 7/8	48 5/8	48 5/8	37 0/8	7	7	Grant County	NM	Paul R. Bovee	1996	1,636
305 6/8	46 7/8	47 7/8	34 0/8	6	6	Larimer County	CO	Steve Stumbo	1980	1,641
305 6/8	45 2/8	46 4/8	38 4/8	6	6	Kootenai County	ID	Brent K. Jacobson	1982	1,641
305 6/8	47 6/8	47 2/8	33 4/8	6	6	Catron County	NM	Randall S. Madding	1984	1,641
305 6/8	40 1/8	42 0/8	36 4/8	7	6	Gilpin County	CO	Dennis Myer	1985	1,641
305 6/8	44 5/8	46 1/8	38 2/8	6	6	Lincoln County	WY	Steven J. Vanlerberghe	1987	1,641
305 6/8	52 7/8	52 7/8	37 0/8	5	5	Catron County	NM	Russell Hull	1989	1,641
305 6/8	37 1/8	44 0/8	37 2/8	6	6	Santa Fe County	NM	Anthony J. Turrietta	1993	1,641
305 6/8	46 3/8	46 3/8	33 4/8	6	7	Phillips County	MT	John R. Koschmeder	1994	1,641
305 6/8	44 3/8	45 7/8	40 0/8	7	6	Sanders County	MT	Stephen E. Quinn	1995	1,641
305 6/8	46 5/8	46 1/8	47 5/8	6	7	Ravalli County	MT	Bill Sullivan	1995	1,641
305 5/8	48 6/8	49 6/8	36 3/8	6	6	Archuleta County	CO	Lester Hawkins, Jr.	1989	1,651
305 5/8	43 7/8	45 3/8	33 5/8	6	6	Catron County	NM	M. Richard Warner	1993	1,651
305 5/8	46 1/8	46 5/8	38 5/8	6	6	Rio Arriba County	NM	James C. Slack	1994	1,651
305 5/8	49 6/8	47 4/8	36 1/8	6	6	Jefferson County	CO	Brad Lenz	1997	1,651
305 4/8	46 7/8	47 5/8	43 6/8	5	6	Clackamas County	OR	Bill Lancaster	1981	1,655
305 4/8	47 4/8	47 5/8	40 2/8	6	6	Catron County	NM	Stan Rauch	1985	1,655
305 4/8	50 1/8	52 1/8	40 4/8	7	6	Mesa County	CO	Don Boyles	1987	1,655
305 4/8	48 0/8	48 6/8	37 2/8	6	6	Coconino County	AZ	Wayne Miller	1988	1,655
305 4/8	44 1/8	48 4/8	41 0/8	5	6	Morgan County	UT	Tim J. Misewicz	1995	1,655
305 4/8	47 2/8	47 2/8	40 6/8	7	7	Catron County	NM	David Rodriguez	1995	1,655
305 4/8	52 0/8	48 6/8	44 5/8	7	7	Fremont County	ID	Brad Foster	1996	1,655
305 4/8	46 4/8	47 6/8	41 2/8	5	5	Catron County	NM	E. Lance Whary	1996	1,655
305 3/8	47 3/8	43 6/8	34 7/8	6	6	Caribou County	ID	Russ W. Arman	1992	1,663
305 3/8	44 5/8	46 2/8	38 5/8	6	6	Morgan County	UT	Poncho McCoy	1993	1,663
305 3/8	47 4/8	48 0/8	29 3/8	6	7	Mohave County	AZ	Deb Fuller	1993	1,663
305 3/8	55 2/8	54 4/8	31 5/8	6	6	Greenlee County	AZ	Kevin H. Johnson	1993	1,663
305 3/8	48 5/8	48 4/8	34 1/8	6	6	Yavapai County	AZ	Robert W. Ledbetter	1993	1,663
305 3/8	49 3/8	48 3/8	46 3/8	7	7	Coconino County	AZ	Eddy Broderick	1995	1,663
305 3/8	45 2/8	45 0/8	35 1/8	7	6	Beaverhead County	MT	Danny Moore	1997	1,663
305 3/8	51 3/8	50 4/8	40 1/8	6	6	Archuleta County	CO	Drew McCartney	1997	1,663
305 2/8	50 2/8	51 2/8	39 4/8	6	6	Larimer County	CO	Craig Nelson	1968	1,671
305 2/8	48 7/8	48 6/8	38 0/8	6	6	Catron County	NM	Glen L. Dillehay	1984	1,671
305 2/8	47 0/8	45 2/8	38 1/8	7	6	Lincoln County	NM	Henry Vega	1987	1,671
305 2/8	49 4/8	48 5/8	36 0/8	6	6	Lincoln County	NM	Johnny King	1988	1,671
305 2/8	48 6/8	49 5/8	40 2/8	6	6	Grant County	OR	Randy Burgess	1990	1,671
305 2/8	47 6/8	46 5/8	33 5/8	7	6	Granite County	MT	Jeremy J. Sandoz	1992	1,671
305 2/8	46 6/8	46 3/8	37 0/8	6	6	Beaverhead County	MT	Gene Loder	1993	1,671
305 2/8	51 6/8	51 7/8	40 2/8	6	6	Madison County	MT	David K. Naibert, Jr.	1993	1,671
305 2/8	47 5/8	46 7/8	33 6/8	6	6	Garfield County	WA	Dan Spanner	1993	1,671
305 2/8	50 0/8	49 3/8	39 6/8	5	6	Skamania County	WA	Bob Morehouse	1993	1,671
305 2/8	47 1/8	46 5/8	33 3/8	8	7	Shoshone County	ID	David B. Cobb	1994	1,671
305 2/8	48 3/8	48 2/8	37 2/8	7	6	Beaverhead County	MT	Mike Davis	1995	1,671
305 2/8	52 5/8	51 7/8	32 4/8	6	6	Coconino County	AZ	Bret Lee Meacham	1995	1,671
305 2/8	46 0/8	46 1/8	36 4/8	6	6	Petroleum County	MT	Chuck Adams	1996	1,671
305 2/8	44 5/8	44 5/8	39 6/8	6	6	Ravalli County	MT	John Sain	1998	1,671
305 1/8	45 1/8	45 5/8	38 4/8	7	7	Fergus County	MT	Gary O. Stewart	1986	1,686
305 1/8	47 1/8	45 1/8	34 3/8	6	6	Meagher County	MT	Jim Bouchard	1995	1,686
305 1/8	46 7/8	47 2/8	33 3/8	6	7	North Saskatchewan River	ALB	Darrin Petrie	1997	1,686
305 0/8	44 6/8	43 5/8	37 6/8	6	6	Morgan County	UT	Hugh Hogle	1987	1,689
305 0/8	47 4/8	47 1/8	36 4/8	6	6	Mountain View	ALB	Randy Bernier	1994	1,689
305 0/8	44 4/8	45 0/8	47 3/8	5	6	Catron County	NM	Leonard Scarborough	1994	1,689
305 0/8	44 2/8	43 4/8	38 6/8	6	6	Sweetwater County	WY	Michael D. Haden	1995	1,689
305 0/8	46 5/8	46 2/8	40 0/8	6	6	Greenlee County	AZ	Tim Wells	1995	1,689
304 7/8	47 4/8	47 2/8	37 1/8	7	7	Garfield County	MT	Todd O. Kletke	1995	1,694
304 6/8	42 4/8	45 0/8	45 6/8	6	6	Coconino County	AZ	Art Potter	1976	1,695
304 6/8	49 6/8	50 2/8	43 2/8	7	6	Coconino County	AZ	Jerry Carpenter	1979	1,695
304 6/8	46 4/8	46 7/8	37 6/8	6	6	Madison County	MT	Fred B. McCullar	1993	1,695
304 5/8	51 1/8	49 6/8	37 5/8	6	6	Catron County	NM	A. Jerry McBride	1991	1,698
304 5/8	46 0/8	49 6/8	27 1/8	6	7	Park County	WY	Marion O. DeBusk	1992	1,698
304 5/8	46 2/8	46 1/8	39 1/8	6	6	Uintah County	UT	Jim Arrant	1994	1,698
304 5/8	47 2/8	49 0/8	37 3/8	7	6	Fergus County	MT	Michael R. Hassinger	1995	1,698
304 4/8	46 7/8	45 4/8	45 2/8	6	6	Grant County	OR	Clayton Severin	1982	1,702
304 4/8	52 1/8	52 7/8	39 4/8	6	6	Catron County	NM	Robert W. Chilcutt	1986	1,702
304 4/8	45 7/8	45 7/8	35 0/8	6	6	Missoula County	MT	Byron Schurg	1989	1,702
304 4/8	48 7/8	46 0/8	35 0/8	6	6	Coconino County	AZ	David Rabellino	1995	1,702
304 4/8	47 1/8	45 5/8	35 6/8	6	5	Petroleum County	MT	Chuck Adams	1995	1,702
304 3/8	50 6/8	48 1/8	44 1/8	6	6	McKinley County	NM	Rick Collard	1987	1,707
304 2/8	46 6/8	49 0/8	36 4/8	6	6	Flathead County	MT	Steven C. Street	1980	1,708
304 2/8	49 5/8	49 6/8	34 4/8	6	6	Sanders County	MT	Ray J. Baenen	1982	1,708
304 2/8	48 2/8	47 3/8	40 6/8	6	6	Cibola County	NM	Jim Pepper	1983	1,708
304 2/8	45 2/8	45 5/8	33 4/8	6	6	Douglas County	CO	James Phelps	1990	1,708
304 2/8	49 7/8	49 6/8	34 2/8	6	5	Routt County	CO	Craig Greenheck	1990	1,708
304 2/8	45 1/8	43 5/8	35 0/8	6	6	Otero County	NM	James E. Borron	1990	1,708
304 2/8	55 2/8	53 3/8	32 4/8	6	6	Greenlee County	AZ	Lonnie R. Lashley	1991	1,708
304 2/8	45 4/8	42 0/8	35 2/8	6	6	Mesa County	CO	Baree Weber	1995	1,708
304 2/8	47 1/8	45 1/8	34 4/8	6	6	Petroleum County	MT	George Klaysmat	1996	1,708

YELLOWSTONE "AMERICAN" ELK (TYPICAL ANTLERS)

Minimum Score 260   Continued

SCORE	LENGTH OF R MAIN BEAM L		INSIDE SPREAD	NUMBER OF R POINTS L		AREA	STATE/ PROVINCE	HUNTER'S NAME	DATE	RANK
304 2/8	47 4/8	50 4/8	37 0/8	6	6	Cibola County	NM	Mark Siedschlag	1998	1,708
304 2/8	50 1/8	49 4/8	34 2/8	6	6	Catron County	NM	Richard Van Valkenburg	1998	1,708
304 2/8	51 4/8	49 6/8	37 6/8	6	6	Grant County	OR	Randy Carter	1998	1,708
304 2/8	48 5/8	48 5/8	31 0/8	6	6	Harney County	OR	Jason L. Radinovich	1998	1,708
304 1/8	46 6/8	47 0/8	42 7/8	6	6	Coconino County	AZ	Dyrk Eddie	1994	1,721
304 1/8	50 7/8	49 7/8	37 3/8	6	6	San Juan County	UT	Shad D. Schmidt	1996	1,721
304 0/8	47 5/8	46 6/8	39 6/8	6	6	Grant County	OR	James E. Hodson	1981	1,723
304 0/8	50 1/8	48 4/8	37 0/8	5	5	Park County	CO	Ronald King	1981	1,723
304 0/8	49 3/8	53 4/8	44 2/8	6	6	Cibola County	NM	Wayne L. Mathews	1986	1,723
304 0/8	48 5/8	48 7/8	37 2/8	6	6	Chouteau County	MT	K. C. Palagi	1986	1,723
304 0/8	43 5/8	42 5/8	32 4/8	6	6	Harney County	OR	Patrick E. Wheeler	1993	1,723
304 0/8	50 6/8	52 5/8	36 2/8	6	6	Grant County	NM	Marlin A. Olson	1995	1,723
304 0/8	45 2/8	44 3/8	32 6/8	6	6	Lemhi County	ID	Dan Laboone	1996	1,723
303 7/8	48 6/8	46 0/8	41 7/8	6	6	Pitkin County	CO	Joseph Mendozza	1980	1,730
303 7/8	43 3/8	43 4/8	41 3/8	6	6	Fergus County	MT	Carson J. Rife	1984	1,730
303 7/8	46 3/8	44 4/8	37 5/8	6	6	Flathead County	MT	Doug Bronson	1987	1,730
303 7/8	42 4/8	44 7/8	41 1/8	6	8	Apache County	AZ	Jim Scholes	1991	1,730
303 7/8	46 1/8	39 6/8	37 1/8	6	6	Shoshone County	ID	Richard Enck	1995	1,730
303 6/8	46 2/8	47 7/8	36 2/8	6	6	Eagle County	CO	Tim W. Hulce	1981	1,735
303 6/8	44 6/8	44 4/8	38 2/8	6	6	Benewah County	ID	Eugene Lewis	1989	1,735
303 6/8	46 0/8	44 4/8	36 0/8	6	6	Coconino County	AZ	David S. Stone	1990	1,735
303 6/8	47 2/8	47 4/8	36 6/8	6	6	Linn County	OR	Jeff Baker	1997	1,735
303 6/8	47 0/8	38 7/8	40 2/8	7	7	Carbon County	WY	Sherrod W. France	1997	1,735
303 6/8	44 5/8	44 2/8	41 0/8	6	6	Montrose County	CO	Dennis E. Lerum	1997	1,735
303 5/8	51 7/8	51 0/8	36 3/8	6	6	Grant County	OR	James M. Carter	1987	1,741
303 5/8	52 1/8	54 2/8	39 3/8	7	6	Pierce County	WA	Joe Harrison Frields	1987	1,741
303 5/8	49 3/8	48 2/8	35 2/8	6	6	Sandoval County	NM	Gerald Schullo	1988	1,741
303 5/8	49 7/8	49 5/8	38 1/8	6	6	Catron County	NM	A. Jerry McBride	1988	1,741
303 4/8	49 1/8	42 1/8	41 0/8	6	6	Grand County	CO	Jim Cleland	1977	1,745
303 4/8	44 6/8	45 3/8	36 2/8	6	6	Sierra County	NM	Chuck Wagner	1986	1,745
303 4/8	48 0/8	47 4/8	38 4/8	6	6	Sheridan County	WY	Dan G. Powers	1991	1,745
303 4/8	44 2/8	43 4/8	43 6/8	6	6	Idaho County	ID	Glen Burney	1991	1,745
303 4/8	48 5/8	48 7/8	39 6/8	6	6	Coconino County	AZ	Patrick Fillman	1991	1,745
303 4/8	43 5/8	43 5/8	40 0/8	6	6	Rio Arriba County	NM	Gene Bishop	1992	1,745
303 4/8	45 0/8	45 4/8	41 1/8	6	7	Park County	WY	John Kilgore	1994	1,745
303 4/8	46 5/8	46 0/8	40 6/8	6	6	Broadwater County	MT	James Gelhaus	1994	1,745
303 4/8	48 3/8	47 4/8	39 2/8	6	6	Catron County	NM	Kenneth M. Thompson	1998	1,745
303 3/8	44 0/8	43 0/8	42 7/8	5	6	Adams County	ID	Rick Mason	1984	1,754
303 3/8	45 4/8	45 4/8	42 2/8	6	7	Park County	MT	Bryon D. Long	1989	1,754
303 3/8	47 1/8	48 1/8	38 5/8	6	6	Flathead County	MT	Kenneth M. Sharp	1992	1,754
303 3/8	45 4/8	45 4/8	37 5/8	7	6	Platte County	WY	Willard Woods	1994	1,754
303 3/8	46 3/8	45 5/8	34 5/8	6	6	Rio Arriba County	NM	Eugene R. Lujan	1995	1,754
303 3/8	47 0/8	46 1/8	38 5/8	6	6	Ravalli County	MT	David Bradt	1995	1,754
303 3/8	50 5/8	50 5/8	38 1/8	6	6	Canmore	ALB	J. Raymond Temchuk	1996	1,754
303 2/8	47 4/8	45 6/8	38 4/8	6	6	Garfield County	CO	Alan Harbin	1980	1,761
303 2/8	47 1/8	47 0/8	35 4/8	6	6	Park County	WY	James Dinkins	1983	1,761
303 2/8	49 0/8	50 4/8	34 2/8	6	7	Grant County	OR	James M. Carter	1989	1,761
303 2/8	46 6/8	46 0/8	38 0/8	6	8	Millard County	UT	Bryon M. Griffiths	1990	1,761
303 2/8	56 7/8	51 5/8	42 4/8	6	6	Custer County	ID	John W. Heimes	1991	1,761
303 2/8	47 4/8	48 0/8	35 4/8	6	6	Greenlee County	AZ	Tim E. Downs	1991	1,761
303 2/8	45 4/8	44 2/8	31 6/8	6	6	Catron County	NM	Joseph A. Lorenz	1992	1,761
303 2/8	46 0/8	48 1/8	35 2/8	6	6	Catron County	NM	Ron Madsen	1992	1,761
303 2/8	50 0/8	49 7/8	42 2/8	6	6	Catron County	NM	Jerry A. Davis	1997	1,761
303 1/8	45 7/8	46 7/8	35 7/8	6	6	Jackson County	OR	Armone FouLon	1990	1,770
303 1/8	49 4/8	50 3/8	33 1/8	6	7	Navajo County	AZ	Randy Ulmer	1993	1,770
303 1/8	44 4/8	44 0/8	41 1/8	6	6	Fremont County	ID	Brett Ball	1993	1,770
303 0/8	48 7/8	47 6/8	41 0/8	5	6	Las Animas County	CO	David L. Brady	1983	1,773
303 0/8	48 0/8	50 7/8	35 2/8	6	6	Fergus County	MT	Mark Robbins	1990	1,773
303 0/8	48 2/8	50 1/8	37 6/8	8	9	Catron County	NM	L. David Hubler, MD	1990	1,773
302 7/8	44 6/8	45 6/8	38 5/8	6	6	Swan River	MT	Joe Lawrence	1969	1,776
302 7/8	46 0/8	44 5/8	39 5/8	6	6	Beaverhead County	MT	John L. Palmer, Sr.	1985	1,776
302 7/8	43 3/8	45 0/8	41 7/8	7	6	Grant County	OR	Jim Richardson	1990	1,776
302 7/8	41 1/8	41 6/8	41 5/8	6	6	Valley County	ID	Gary Christensen	1997	1,776
302 7/8	45 1/8	46 7/8	47 4/8	6	6	Harney County	OR	Jerry Mills	1997	1,776
302 7/8	45 2/8	45 7/8	31 5/8	6	6	Navajo County	AZ	Michael Hunter McCarey	1997	1,776
302 6/8	49 4/8	47 4/8	43 0/8	5	6	Apache County	AZ	Gary Preston	1981	1,782
302 6/8	49 1/8	47 0/8	34 0/8	7	7	Converse County	WY	Fred Romero	1992	1,782
302 6/8	52 2/8	50 6/8	41 6/8	6	6	Catron County	NM	Stephen Herrera	1994	1,782
302 6/8	46 6/8	45 3/8	41 3/8	6	7	Catron County	NM	Lawrence B. Dickson, Jr.	1994	1,782
302 6/8	42 3/8	47 2/8	43 0/8	6	6	Coconino County	AZ	Roy R. Clark	1994	1,782
302 5/8	45 0/8	46 0/8	42 3/8	6	6	Clear Creek County	CO	Billy E. Corley	1987	1,787
302 5/8	49 2/8	48 7/8	38 7/8	6	6	Beaverhead County	MT	Jack Brilz	1990	1,787
302 5/8	39 2/8	41 3/8	40 3/8	6	6	Socorro County	NM	Tom Alvin	1991	1,787
302 5/8	48 2/8	48 1/8	38 3/8	6	6	Lemhi County	ID	Tim Thomas	1993	1,787
302 5/8	46 7/8	47 4/8	35 1/8	6	7	Shoshone County	ID	Erin Sacksteder	1996	1,787
302 5/8	46 4/8	45 4/8	35 3/8	6	6	Idaho County	ID	Scott Hurd	1997	1,787
302 4/8	47 7/8	47 2/8	38 5/8	6	6	Eagle County	CO	Roger Rothhaar	1974	1,793
302 4/8	46 4/8	46 2/8	37 0/8	6	6	Beaverhead County	MT	Dennis Rehse	1982	1,793

YELLOWSTONE "AMERICAN" ELK (TYPICAL ANTLERS)

Minimum Score 260 — Continued

SCORE	LENGTH OF MAIN BEAM R	LENGTH OF MAIN BEAM L	INSIDE SPREAD	NUMBER OF POINTS R	NUMBER OF POINTS L	AREA	STATE/ PROVINCE	HUNTER'S NAME	DATE	RANK
302 4/8	50 3/8	48 5/8	38 4/8	6	5	Johnson County	WY	Zachary A. Rust	1993	1,793
302 4/8	47 4/8	50 1/8	39 6/8	7	6	Sublette County	WY	Bill Pickett	1994	1,793
302 4/8	45 6/8	44 4/8	36 6/8	5	5	Adams County	ID	Wayne Crownover	1997	1,793
302 4/8	51 3/8	49 0/8	35 7/8	7	7	Catron County	NM	Gary Swinson	1998	1,793
302 3/8	44 0/8	45 0/8	35 3/8	6	6	Routt County	CO	Mike Newman	1989	1,799
302 3/8	49 2/8	44 3/8	30 7/8	6	6	Coconino County	AZ	Jeffery Duane Hines	1992	1,799
302 3/8	49 7/8	49 4/8	34 7/8	6	6	Coconino County	AZ	Michael Campbell	1992	1,799
302 3/8	44 1/8	45 4/8	39 1/8	5	5	Catron County	NM	Wayne "Audie" Gowens	1996	1,799
302 3/8	46 4/8	45 4/8	38 3/8	7	6	Rio Grande County	CO	Stephen Teague	1997	1,799
302 3/8	53 6/8	52 0/8	41 4/8	6	7	Idaho County	ID	Lonnie L. Jenkins	1998	1,799
302 2/8	48 7/8	48 7/8	39 0/8	6	6	Grant County	OR	Randy Bonner	1983	1,805
302 2/8	53 3/8	50 3/8	39 6/8	6	6	Coconino County	AZ	G. Henry Strohm	1986	1,805
302 2/8	45 6/8	45 4/8	36 6/8	7	7	Cascade County	MT	Jay Sherley	1993	1,805
302 2/8	49 6/8	48 2/8	35 4/8	6	6	Catron County	NM	Richard V. Gray	1994	1,805
302 2/8	49 3/8	49 4/8	38 0/8	7	6	Catron County	NM	Jeffrey Tate	1994	1,805
302 2/8	48 1/8	46 7/8	43 4/8	6	7	Park County	WY	Brian L. Wagner	1994	1,805
302 2/8	46 6/8	46 0/8	36 4/8	6	6	Fremont County	WY	Joel Nirider	1996	1,805
302 2/8	42 5/8	44 2/8	36 2/8	6	6	Petroleum County	MT	Gerry Brusletten	1998	1,805
302 2/8	45 6/8	45 3/8	43 4/8	6	6	Park County	WY	Robert C. Gregory, DVM	1998	1,805
302 1/8	51 1/8	49 4/8	37 7/8	6	6	Canmore	ALB	David R. Coupland	1984	1,814
302 1/8	44 1/8	44 1/8	35 1/8	6	6	Greenlee County	AZ	Timothy Hall	1985	1,814
302 1/8	48 1/8	46 7/8	37 3/8	6	6	Valley County	ID	Michael S. Moore	1987	1,814
302 1/8	51 2/8	51 3/8	39 5/8	8	6	Catron County	NM	Jay J. Sopiwnik	1988	1,814
302 1/8	46 6/8	47 0/8	40 1/8	6	7	Beaverhead County	MT	Fred C. Church	1991	1,814
302 1/8	44 5/8	44 7/8	42 1/8	6	6	Routt County	CO	Tim Oestmann	1992	1,814
302 1/8	45 7/8	47 4/8	38 1/8	6	6	Okotoks	ALB	Brent Brown	1994	1,814
302 1/8	48 1/8	50 2/8	26 2/8	7	7	Catron County	NM	Duane "Corky" Richardson	1995	1,814
302 1/8	40 2/8	40 3/8	38 5/8	6	6	Big Horn County	WY	Mark Masamori	1996	1,814
302 0/8	45 0/8	46 6/8	40 0/8	6	6	Archuleta County	CO	Billy Ellis	1977	1,823
302 0/8	50 4/8	49 6/8	38 6/8	6	6	Eagle County	CO	John Schell	1980	1,823
302 0/8	42 3/8	41 6/8	31 0/8	6	6	Routt County	CO	Kevin Stailey	1981	1,823
302 0/8	47 6/8	48 0/8	35 4/8	6	7	Missoula County	MT	Richard W. Talbert	1986	1,823
302 0/8	44 0/8	43 7/8	37 4/8	6	6	Fremont County	WY	Edward A. Dykstra	1988	1,823
302 0/8	44 6/8	45 2/8	34 0/8	6	6	Lemhi County	ID	Buster Williams	1990	1,823
302 0/8	51 3/8	53 0/8	36 6/8	6	6	Taos County	NM	Jeffrey D. Butts	1995	1,823
302 0/8	47 0/8	47 7/8	36 6/8	5	5	Laramie County	WY	Robert Allen Robbins	1996	1,823
301 7/8	44 2/8	44 2/8	38 3/8	6	6	Larimer County	CO	Adrian H. Farmer, Jr.	1984	1,831
301 7/8	53 3/8	54 4/8	38 1/8	6	6	Coconino County	AZ	Michael N. Miller	1998	1,831
301 6/8	47 2/8	46 2/8	36 0/8	6	6	Missoula County	MT	Guy Leibenguth	1976	1,833
301 6/8	40 6/8	40 5/8	33 6/8	6	6	Yakima County	WA	James Garner	1989	1,833
301 6/8	55 7/8	55 2/8	41 0/8	6	6	Millard County	UT	Chad J. Hall	1995	1,833
301 5/8	44 1/8	42 2/8	39 2/8	7	7	Ravalli County	MT	Dick Kerr	1977	1,836
301 5/8	44 0/8	41 2/8	31 5/8	7	6	Grant County	NM	Raymond Albertina	1991	1,836
301 5/8	49 2/8	50 1/8	38 7/8	6	7	Ravalli County	MT	Ned Coorough	1992	1,836
301 5/8	47 3/8	45 2/8	42 5/8	6	6	Coconino County	AZ	Ron Eckerman	1995	1,836
301 5/8	46 4/8	47 3/8	36 7/8	6	6	Rich County	UT	Glen O. Hallows	1996	1,836
301 5/8	46 2/8	47 4/8	40 6/8	7	8	Kootenai County	ID	D. V. Moyer	1996	1,836
301 5/8	50 0/8	50 0/8	39 5/8	5	6	Bonner County	ID	Ron Britton	1997	1,836
301 5/8	55 6/8	52 3/8	42 7/8	6	6	Socorro County	NM	Vernon C. Smedley	1997	1,836
301 5/8	47 7/8	48 7/8	37 5/8	6	6	Sierra County	NM	Dave Holt	1998	1,836
301 4/8	45 1/8	44 6/8	37 0/8	6	6	Lewis & Clark County	MT	Doug Conrady	1979	1,845
301 4/8	47 3/8	44 5/8	41 1/8	6	7	Park County	MT	Donald Lee Ferguson	1988	1,845
301 4/8	45 5/8	44 2/8	42 0/8	6	6	Madison County	MT	Vaughn Ballard	1989	1,845
301 4/8	43 3/8	42 4/8	33 1/8	6	9	Wallowa County	OR	Tim Andrew Collins	1990	1,845
301 4/8	46 0/8	47 0/8	40 2/8	6	6	McKinley County	NM	Ben Gibson	1991	1,845
301 3/8	47 1/8	48 4/8	35 5/8	5	6	Catron County	NM	Timothy C. Junior	1992	1,850
301 3/8	46 2/8	45 2/8	40 1/8	6	6	Clearwater County	ID	David Thorkildsen	1996	1,850
301 2/8	47 6/8	47 5/8	39 4/8	6	6	Catron County	NM	Dale Mansfield	1995	1,852
301 2/8	50 2/8	49 4/8	38 4/8	6	6	Narraway River	ALB	Rick Martin	1996	1,852
301 2/8	52 0/8	53 0/8	37 3/8	6	6	McKinley County	NM	Billy Gordon	1997	1,852
301 1/8	45 0/8	41 2/8	38 4/8	7	6	Teton County	WY	Craig Sorenson	1979	1,855
301 1/8	43 7/8	44 1/8	32 1/8	6	6	Clearwater County	ID	Jim Walters	1981	1,855
301 1/8	47 3/8	45 7/8	37 7/8	6	6	Lincoln County	MT	Paul Buti	1984	1,855
301 1/8	46 6/8	47 7/8	36 3/8	6	6	Larimer County	CO	Randy A. Reeves	1993	1,855
301 0/8	46 2/8	49 6/8	38 4/8	5	6	Sandoval County	NM	Fred J. McDonald	1985	1,859
301 0/8	48 7/8	48 3/8	36 6/8	6	6	Coconino County	AZ	Roy E. Grace	1993	1,859
300 7/8	45 6/8	44 5/8	39 1/8	6	5	Teton County	MT	Bill Schenck	1979	1,861
300 7/8	48 6/8	51 6/8	34 3/8	6	6	Converse County	WY	Kevin Christopherson	1995	1,861
300 7/8	42 1/8	43 2/8	33 5/8	6	7	Park County	CO	Mark Martin	1995	1,861
300 7/8	44 2/8	45 3/8	45 6/8	6	6	Boise County	ID	Jason L. Angell	1996	1,861
300 7/8	46 4/8	49 5/8	34 1/8	6	6	Rio Blanco County	CO	Jim Dougherty	1996	1,861
300 7/8	50 0/8	50 6/8	35 3/8	6	6	Garfield County	MT	D. Mitch Kottas	1997	1,861
300 6/8	42 1/8	43 7/8	36 4/8	6	6	Sheridan County	WY	Kerry Struckman	1992	1,867
300 6/8	47 6/8	48 5/8	35 1/8	8	8	Bonneville County	ID	Danel R. Thomas	1996	1,867
300 6/8	49 1/8	48 0/8	36 0/8	6	6	Blaine County	ID	Tim W. Chadwick	1997	1,867
300 6/8	42 7/8	42 2/8	35 4/8	6	6	Cutbank River	ALB	Brent Watson	1998	1,867
300 5/8	44 3/8	44 5/8	44 6/8	6	6	Beaverhead County	MT	Monty Moravec	1989	1,871
300 5/8	46 3/8	44 0/8	33 3/8	7	6	Benewah County	ID	Joel L. Emerson	1991	1,871

YELLOWSTONE "AMERICAN" ELK (TYPICAL ANTLERS)

Minimum Score 260

Continued

SCORE	LENGTH OF MAIN BEAM R	LENGTH OF MAIN BEAM L	INSIDE SPREAD	NUMBER OF POINTS R	NUMBER OF POINTS L	AREA	STATE/PROVINCE	HUNTER'S NAME	DATE	RANK
300 5/8	46 0/8	46 6/8	38 1/8	6	6	Lemhi County	ID	Brad White	1996	1,871
300 4/8	42 2/8	44 4/8	38 6/8	6	6	Boundary County	ID	John Thomas	1992	1,874
300 4/8	44 1/8	47 1/8	43 4/8	6	6	Lewis & Clark County	MT	Dr. David Baldridge	1993	1,874
300 4/8	45 3/8	45 4/8	38 6/8	6	6	Lincoln County	MT	Ron Halvorson	1994	1,874
300 4/8	45 7/8	45 2/8	36 4/8	6	6	Boise County	ID	Ralph L. Albright	1995	1,874
300 4/8	50 1/8	49 2/8	43 6/8	6	7	Sublette County	WY	Raymond Kennedy	1996	1,874
300 4/8	47 6/8	47 5/8	47 0/8	6	6	Fremont County	WY	David Stepp	1997	1,874
300 3/8	41 5/8	40 0/8	36 1/8	6	6	Fergus County	MT	Randy Cook	1981	1,880
300 3/8	46 5/8	44 5/8	44 0/8	7	7	Marion County	OR	Ron Bergeron	1986	1,880
300 3/8	47 3/8	48 4/8	30 5/8	6	6	Madison County	MT	Gary Moris	1992	1,880
300 3/8	47 4/8	45 3/8	37 3/8	6	6	Dolores County	CO	Todd Giles	1992	1,880
300 3/8	45 7/8	45 3/8	40 3/8	6	6	Madison County	MT	Lee Poole	1993	1,880
300 3/8	51 0/8	50 0/8	40 5/8	6	6	La Plata County	CO	Walter G. Sievers	1994	1,880
300 3/8	44 7/8	45 1/8	29 3/8	6	7	Phillips County	MT	Stephen T. Musser	1995	1,880
300 2/8	46 2/8	45 3/8	41 0/8	6	6	McKinley County	NM	Mark Sauters	1987	1,887
300 2/8	45 7/8	46 6/8	38 2/8	5	6	Coconino County	AZ	Bradley Mitchell Irish	1990	1,887
300 2/8	41 0/8	41 2/8	38 2/8	6	6	Petroleum County	MT	Ron Kukus	1991	1,887
300 2/8	49 4/8	47 6/8	33 4/8	6	6	Garfield County	CO	Judson Smith	1997	1,887
300 1/8	45 4/8	47 4/8	39 7/8	6	6	San Miguel County	NM	Lawrence Stiscak	1977	1,891
300 1/8	46 3/8	44 2/8	35 7/8	6	6	Clearwater County	ID	Danny Moore	1985	1,891
300 1/8	46 3/8	44 7/8	36 1/8	6	6	Sandoval County	NM	Bob Young	1990	1,891
300 1/8	43 3/8	44 6/8	38 3/8	6	6	La Plata County	CO	Bob E. Wren	1992	1,891
300 1/8	44 6/8	44 5/8	41 3/8	6	6	Fremont County	ID	James K. Nash	1996	1,891
300 1/8	49 5/8	51 3/8	36 7/8	6	6	Socorro County	NM	Marvin H. Walter	1997	1,891
300 0/8	43 0/8	44 2/8	43 2/8	6	6	Albany County	WY	Jerry Bowen	1980	1,897
300 0/8	45 2/8	44 5/8	47 3/8	6	6	Beaverhead County	MT	Greg L. Munther	1980	1,897
300 0/8	39 5/8	42 0/8	37 4/8	7	6	Coconino County	AZ	Mike Kentera	1985	1,897
300 0/8	47 4/8	46 0/8	40 0/8	6	6	Missoula County	MT	Anthony K Nease	1985	1,897
300 0/8	48 5/8	48 4/8	38 4/8	6	6	Adams County	ID	Robert Dowen	1985	1,897
300 0/8	41 4/8	42 6/8	34 6/8	6	6	Catron County	NM	Ned Smith	1991	1,897
300 0/8	45 4/8	46 7/8	38 1/8	6	7	Catron County	NM	Rafael Espino	1994	1,897
300 0/8	52 0/8	50 6/8	35 2/8	6	6	Lemhi County	ID	Kody L. Harrison	1995	1,897
300 0/8	43 4/8	44 2/8	33 2/8	6	6	Natrona County	WY	Keith Frick	1995	1,897
300 0/8	45 4/8	44 7/8	35 2/8	7	6	Union County	OR	Randy Carter	1997	1,897
299 7/8	51 0/8	54 0/8	41 0/8	6	7	Fergus County	MT	Charles R. Bowman	1966	1,907
299 7/8	44 4/8	44 0/8	36 3/8	5	5	Routt County	CO	Mark Wuerthele	1987	1,907
299 7/8	47 4/8	43 6/8	36 3/8	5	6	Rio Blanco County	CO	Mike Zech	1995	1,907
299 7/8	44 7/8	45 3/8	41 5/8	6	7	Beaverhead County	MT	Larry Gerlach	1995	1,907
299 7/8	49 1/8	47 3/8	35 7/8	6	6	Catron County	NM	Sam Y. Perone	1998	1,907
299 6/8	50 6/8	48 1/8	37 0/8	6	6	Albany County	WY	Jerry Bowen	1982	1,912
299 6/8	41 4/8	42 1/8	37 0/8	6	6	Shoshone County	ID	Glen Berry	1987	1,912
299 6/8	53 2/8	53 7/8	44 6/8	6	6	Coconino County	AZ	Michael L. Campbell	1987	1,912
299 6/8	50 4/8	49 2/8	35 6/8	6	6	Flathead County	MT	Ken White	1989	1,912
299 6/8	43 1/8	44 6/8	37 0/8	6	6	Caribou County	ID	Steven J. Slaton	1994	1,912
299 6/8	44 6/8	46 1/8	32 6/8	6	6	Lemhi County	ID	John McCarthy	1996	1,912
299 6/8	49 0/8	49 3/8	34 2/8	6	6	Custer County	ID	Robin Glantz	1997	1,912
299 5/8	48 0/8	48 6/8	34 1/8	5	6	Taos County	NM	Bubba Finstad	1987	1,919
299 5/8	45 2/8	44 7/8	43 5/8	6	7	Klamath County	OR	Ron Botsford	1991	1,919
299 5/8	48 2/8	49 2/8	32 1/8	6	6	Mohave County	AZ	Greg Carmichael	1992	1,919
299 5/8	50 5/8	50 3/8	40 2/8	7	6	King County	WA	David C. Andress	1993	1,919
299 5/8	46 2/8	47 7/8	37 1/8	7	7	Dolores County	CO	Gaylen Schaugaard	1995	1,919
299 4/8	44 2/8	45 7/8	34 0/8	6	6	White Pine County	NV	Audrey Hanson	1998	1,924
299 3/8	45 2/8	46 2/8	38 3/8	6	6	Gunnison County	CO	Gene Chastain	1985	1,925
299 3/8	42 1/8	42 3/8	42 4/8	6	8	Coconino County	AZ	Tony W. Zimbaro	1992	1,925
299 3/8	51 3/8	54 0/8	38 3/8	6	6	Harney County	OR	Patrick E. Wheeler	1995	1,925
299 3/8	43 7/8	43 7/8	36 7/8	6	6	Routt County	CO	Steve B. Cooper	1997	1,925
299 2/8	47 2/8	46 1/8	34 4/8	6	6	Caribou County	ID	Tex Wolfley	1979	1,929
299 2/8	51 4/8	49 7/8	37 2/8	6	6	Coconino County	AZ	Larry VanLiew	1983	1,929
299 2/8	46 4/8	43 3/8	32 2/8	6	7	Idaho County	ID	Neal Forrester	1989	1,929
299 2/8	47 6/8	48 1/8	39 0/8	6	6	Custer County	ID	Robert Ward	1995	1,929
299 2/8	46 7/8	46 3/8	34 4/8	6	5	McKinley County	NM	Ronald Hanna	1997	1,929
299 1/8	44 2/8	41 2/8	32 5/8	6	6	Lincoln County	WY	Richard Peart	1980	1,934
299 1/8	47 0/8	48 1/8	39 5/8	6	6	Madison County	MT	Royce A. Carroll	1988	1,934
299 1/8	51 4/8	50 0/8	38 6/8	7	8	Catron County	NM	Thomas Merritt	1990	1,934
299 1/8	45 2/8	47 6/8	34 1/8	6	7	Catron County	NM	Jules Pacheco	1990	1,934
299 1/8	47 3/8	48 3/8	34 1/8	6	7	Caribou County	ID	Steven Boothe	1992	1,934
299 1/8	46 5/8	45 2/8	36 2/8	7	7	Boundary County	ID	Roger N. Myers	1992	1,934
299 1/8	48 2/8	49 7/8	41 7/8	6	7	Sandoval County	NM	Melvin Sloan	1992	1,934
299 1/8	45 6/8	46 6/8	39 4/8	7	8	Lemhi County	ID	David Tande	1993	1,934
299 1/8	51 4/8	50 6/8	37 3/8	6	6	Petroleum County	MT	Mark Hegge	1996	1,934
299 0/8	42 3/8	43 1/8	33 0/8	6	6	Mineral County	CO	Gary Oden	1976	1,943
299 0/8	45 5/8	46 4/8	37 2/8	6	6	Powell County	MT	Paul Brunner	1979	1,943
299 0/8	46 1/8	47 3/8	42 0/8	6	6	Park County	MT	Joe Skaggs	1988	1,943
299 0/8	45 0/8	46 3/8	40 4/8	6	6	Clearwater County	ID	James L. Tucker	1992	1,943
299 0/8	49 2/8	51 2/8	39 4/8	6	6	Klamath County	OR	Gene Hamilton	1997	1,943
299 0/8	44 5/8	46 4/8	31 7/8	8	7	Phillips County	MT	Layton W. Foltyn	1997	1,943
299 0/8	44 6/8	44 0/8	35 0/8	6	6	Petroleum County	MT	Eddie McGreevey	1998	1,943
298 7/8	45 5/8	46 1/8	39 7/8	6	6	Jefferson County	CO	Jerry Grueneberg	1989	1,950

YELLOWSTONE "AMERICAN" ELK (TYPICAL ANTLERS)

Minimum Score 260   Continued

SCORE	LENGTH OF MAIN BEAM R	LENGTH OF MAIN BEAM L	INSIDE SPREAD	NUMBER OF POINTS R	NUMBER OF POINTS L	AREA	STATE/ PROVINCE	HUNTER'S NAME	DATE	RANK
298 7/8	45 5/8	46 4/8	35 3/8	6	6	Coconino County	AZ	Craig Dunlap	1993	1,950
298 7/8	52 6/8	50 3/8	36 1/8	6	6	Platte County	WY	Jeff Murray	1994	1,950
298 7/8	51 5/8	51 4/8	35 5/8	6	6	Coconino County	AZ	Phil Villamor	1997	1,950
298 7/8	49 3/8	49 2/8	36 1/8	6	6	Catron County	NM	Lynn Saxon	1998	1,950
298 6/8	46 3/8	46 3/8	31 5/8	6	7	Mineral County	MT	James Kingsley	1983	1,955
298 6/8	44 2/8	45 5/8	38 0/8	6	6	Gallatin County	MT	Steven P Hopkins	1984	1,955
298 6/8	50 6/8	52 4/8	37 2/8	6	6	Catron County	NM	Wayne Keehart	1986	1,955
298 6/8	48 1/8	48 4/8	33 0/8	6	6	Sheridan County	WY	Robert H. Bookman	1992	1,955
298 6/8	49 5/8	48 0/8	35 6/8	6	6	Missoula County	MT	Lykou Lee	1995	1,955
298 6/8	48 4/8	48 4/8	37 0/8	6	6	Archuleta County	CO	John M. Pringle	1996	1,955
298 5/8	55 0/8	56 5/8	38 3/8	5	6	Coconino County	AZ	Kevin Cox	1979	1,961
298 5/8	46 0/8	47 5/8	41 7/8	6	6	Coconino County	AZ	Pete Shepley	1986	1,961
298 5/8	43 3/8	40 0/8	48 6/8	6	6	Gem County	ID	Ron Williams	1988	1,961
298 5/8	42 2/8	42 5/8	44 5/8	6	6	Sandoval County	NM	Robert Woeck	1991	1,961
298 5/8	45 3/8	44 2/8	40 1/8	6	7	Catron County	NM	Sam Thompson	1992	1,961
298 5/8	49 0/8	48 7/8	33 1/8	7	6	Colfax County	NM	Kim Sevitts	1995	1,961
298 5/8	53 2/8	51 5/8	38 3/8	6	6	Mesa County	CO	Jimmy Wayne Birchfield	1996	1,961
298 4/8	44 5/8	46 1/8	42 6/8	6	7	Coconino County	AZ	Les Shelton	1991	1,968
298 4/8	48 4/8	46 6/8	36 6/8	6	6	Catron County	NM	Steve Mastagni	1992	1,968
298 4/8	47 7/8	48 7/8	42 5/8	7	6	Coconino County	AZ	Tony Leverty	1992	1,968
298 4/8	49 4/8	49 2/8	32 0/8	8	5	Sheridan County	WY	Paul Schaumburg	1994	1,968
298 4/8	56 2/8	52 0/8	36 4/8	6	6	Sweetwater County	WY	Gordon M. Tattersall	1995	1,968
298 4/8	45 1/8	44 5/8	34 5/8	7	6	Caribou County	ID	Daniel J. Pritzl	1997	1,968
298 4/8	52 6/8	52 2/8	34 2/8	7	8	Converse County	WY	Frank N. Moore	1997	1,968
298 4/8	46 7/8	44 4/8	36 4/8	6	6	Moffat County	CO	Gary Kohler	1998	1,968
298 3/8	44 0/8	45 6/8	49 4/8	7	7	Navajo County	AZ	Stan Hacker	1993	1,976
298 3/8	43 1/8	45 0/8	31 1/8	6	6	Phillips County	MT	Larry I. Nordlund	1993	1,976
298 2/8	48 6/8	46 6/8	35 6/8	6	6	Fremont County	ID	Tad Parke	1994	1,978
298 2/8	48 1/8	48 3/8	40 4/8	6	6	Catron County	NM	Quentin Fisher	1994	1,978
298 1/8	49 7/8	48 0/8	33 1/8	6	6	Park County	WY	Bruce K. Fauskee	1986	1,980
298 1/8	46 2/8	47 1/8	33 3/8	6	6	Iron County	UT	Brad Robinson	1992	1,980
298 1/8	46 6/8	48 2/8	40 7/8	8	6	Mora County	NM	Kenneth J. Morga	1995	1,980
298 1/8	48 2/8	48 1/8	36 7/8	6	6	Catron County	NM	Dale Hoekstra	1995	1,980
298 0/8	45 6/8	46 4/8	37 0/8	6	6	Caribou County	ID	Dean Monson	1982	1,984
298 0/8	48 6/8	47 2/8	38 6/8	6	6	Delta County	CO	Todd B. Roberts	1992	1,984
298 0/8	40 0/8	41 2/8	42 0/8	6	6	Yakima County	WA	Troy Goben	1992	1,984
298 0/8	49 5/8	49 0/8	35 4/8	6	6	Grant County	OR	Scott H. Stewart	1998	1,984
297 7/8	44 5/8	46 7/8	31 1/8	7	8	Coconino County	AZ	Mark Vancas	1980	1,988
297 7/8	46 4/8	47 0/8	33 5/8	6	6	Lincoln County	MT	Darryl Lien	1985	1,988
297 7/8	45 4/8	44 2/8	37 7/8	6	7	Clear Creek County	CO	Paul Ray	1988	1,988
297 7/8	46 3/8	45 0/8	37 5/8	6	6	Catron County	NM	Gale A. Hedges	1989	1,988
297 7/8	44 6/8	40 6/8	40 4/8	6	7	Idaho County	ID	Kenneth Kirkeby	1994	1,988
297 7/8	45 1/8	47 4/8	40 5/8	5	6	Otero County	NM	Tony Heil	1995	1,988
297 7/8	43 4/8	42 0/8	39 2/8	7	7	Sanders County	MT	Tony Bierwagen	1995	1,988
297 7/8	43 7/8	44 5/8	39 3/8	6	6	Coconino County	AZ	Jeff Persenaire	1996	1,988
297 6/8	46 4/8	46 5/8	41 4/8	6	6	Boulder County	CO	Steve Gorr	1969	1,996
297 6/8	48 6/8	50 0/8	38 6/8	6	7	Caribou County	ID	Doug Cushman, Jr.	1981	1,996
297 6/8	45 6/8	43 6/8	37 6/8	6	6	Apache County	AZ	Donata P. Montgomery	1990	1,996
297 5/8	45 4/8	44 2/8	37 5/8	6	6	Caribou County	ID	Tom M. Carter	1990	1,999
297 5/8	46 2/8	47 5/8	34 5/8	6	6	Coconino County	AZ	Wayne A. Nicholson	1997	1,999
297 4/8	45 1/8	41 6/8	43 0/8	6	7	King County	WA	Larry L. Sheward	1984	2,001
297 4/8	47 2/8	48 6/8	39 2/8	6	7	Lewis & Clark County	MT	Mike McDaniel	1992	2,001
297 4/8	41 3/8	42 2/8	34 6/8	6	7	Huerfano County	CO	Esco R. Billings III	1992	2,001
297 4/8	44 5/8	46 1/8	29 2/8	6	7	Catron County	NM	Robert Lepard	1997	2,001
297 4/8	47 3/8	48 7/8	35 0/8	6	6	Coconino County	AZ	Bob Kyhn	1997	2,001
297 3/8	46 1/8	45 2/8	42 3/8	5	7	Fremont County	ID	Thomas W. Savage	1982	2,006
297 3/8	50 2/8	53 2/8	39 7/8	6	6	Taos County	NM	Randal Church	1989	2,006
297 3/8	48 3/8	47 5/8	37 3/8	6	7	Moffat County	CO	Glenn Pritchard	1990	2,006
297 3/8	46 5/8	47 0/8	35 5/8	6	6	Wheeler County	OR	James Deyo	1998	2,006
297 2/8	50 0/8	47 5/8	30 6/8	6	6	Grant County	OR	Joe Copeland	1986	2,010
297 2/8	47 2/8	49 4/8	50 6/8	6	7	Musselshell County	MT	John A. Dallas	1995	2,010
297 2/8	43 2/8	47 0/8	43 4/8	6	5	Caribou County	ID	Rick Dunn	1996	2,010
297 2/8	44 0/8	45 4/8	40 6/8	6	6	Meade County	SD	Brynolf Wanhanen	1996	2,010
297 1/8	46 1/8	44 2/8	42 3/8	6	8	Missoula County	MT	David E. Torrey, Jr.	1977	2,014
297 1/8	46 0/8	48 0/8	40 6/8	7	8	Coconino County	AZ	Dave Baker	1979	2,014
297 1/8	43 0/8	42 3/8	39 3/8	6	6	Wainwright	ALB	Norman Hookes	1982	2,014
297 1/8	45 0/8	45 3/8	38 3/8	6	6	Granite County	MT	Ralph W. Phillips	1992	2,014
297 1/8	49 0/8	45 7/8	41 7/8	6	6	Bear Lake County	ID	Randy K. Guinn	1993	2,014
297 1/8	43 7/8	43 7/8	38 3/8	5	6	Fergus County	MT	Edwin Evans	1995	2,014
297 1/8	44 7/8	44 7/8	46 6/8	6	6	Beaverhead County	MT	Greg L. Munther	1996	2,014
297 0/8	46 4/8	46 0/8	36 2/8	6	6	Wallowa County	OR	Martha J Soeth	1985	2,021
297 0/8	44 4/8	44 3/8	34 0/8	6	6	Rich County	UT	Hugh H. Hogle	1986	2,021
297 0/8	41 6/8	46 5/8	37 2/8	6	6	Rio Arriba County	NM	Patrick Smith	1988	2,021
297 0/8	43 2/8	42 0/8	36 2/8	6	6	Coconino County	AZ	Gary Linendoll	1990	2,021
297 0/8	50 1/8	45 3/8	43 2/8	7	6	Park County	WY	John Morlang	1993	2,021
297 0/8	44 6/8	42 0/8	34 6/8	6	6	Catron County	NM	Walter Troy Slape	1993	2,021
297 0/8	51 7/8	51 3/8	38 2/8	6	6	Sanders County	MT	Thomas B. Cramer III	1993	2,021
297 0/8	41 7/8	42 7/8	40 6/8	6	6	Big Horn County	WY	Jerome Larson	1993	2,021

YELLOWSTONE "AMERICAN" ELK (TYPICAL ANTLERS)

Minimum Score 260

Continued

SCORE	LENGTH OF MAIN BEAM R	LENGTH OF MAIN BEAM L	INSIDE SPREAD	NUMBER OF POINTS R	NUMBER OF POINTS L	AREA	STATE/PROVINCE	HUNTER'S NAME	DATE	RANK
297 0/8	47 0/8	43 4/8	31 0/8	6	6	Socorro County	NM	Edward C. Robinson	1998	2,021
296 7/8	45 2/8	45 4/8	43 3/8	6	6	Lemhi County	ID	Jim Frazier	1995	2,030
296 7/8	46 4/8	46 4/8	36 3/8	6	6	Lemhi County	ID	DelRay Layton	1996	2,030
296 7/8	44 7/8	44 3/8	38 5/8	6	6	Catron County	NM	Chris L. Skinner	1998	2,030
296 6/8	47 4/8	46 4/8	35 6/8	6	6	Idaho County	ID	Gerald B. Jameson	1987	2,033
296 6/8	50 7/8	51 6/8	40 6/8	6	6	Coconino County	AZ	Jerry W. Lilly	1992	2,033
296 6/8	46 0/8	42 6/8	42 0/8	6	6	Shoshone County	ID	Dan Payne	1994	2,033
296 6/8	44 3/8	47 0/8	41 4/8	5	5	Greenlee County	AZ	Ben Montgomery	1994	2,033
296 5/8	46 6/8	44 6/8	32 6/8	6	7	Kakwa River	ALB	Wilf Lehners	1990	2,037
296 5/8	48 2/8	52 1/8	44 7/8	6	7	Greenlee County	AZ	Bill Golden	1992	2,037
296 5/8	46 0/8	45 1/8	33 5/8	6	6	Moffat County	CO	Jim Willems	1994	2,037
296 5/8	42 2/8	43 0/8	35 7/8	6	6	Montrose County	CO	Jim Holdenried	1997	2,037
296 5/8	50 6/8	52 0/8	35 3/8	8	7	Catron County	NM	Christopher D. Matthews	1998	2,037
296 4/8	45 1/8	46 7/8	35 4/8	6	6	Catron County	NM	Randall N. Bostick	1988	2,042
296 4/8	42 5/8	40 7/8	35 6/8	6	6	Park County	WY	John R. Buche	1989	2,042
296 4/8	42 1/8	41 6/8	37 2/8	6	6	Phillips County	MT	Mike Crites	1993	2,042
296 4/8	46 5/8	46 0/8	31 2/8	6	6	Harney County	OR	Wayne Rogers	1994	2,042
296 4/8	51 4/8	52 4/8	40 4/8	6	6	Archuleta County	CO	William D. Burch, DDS	1997	2,042
296 4/8	50 1/8	50 5/8	35 2/8	6	6	Sweet Grass County	MT	Fred Holbert	1997	2,042
296 4/8	44 7/8	46 0/8	32 6/8	5	5	Big Horn County	MT	Richard Cunningham	1998	2,042
296 3/8	40 5/8	40 4/8	32 7/8	6	6	Teton County	MT	Myron E. Moore	1976	2,049
296 3/8	41 7/8	44 2/8	39 3/8	6	6	Idaho County	ID	Jerry Vega	1985	2,049
296 3/8	39 3/8	39 1/8	42 7/8	6	6	Sheridan County	WY	Richard M. Young, Jr.	1988	2,049
296 3/8	41 3/8	44 3/8	35 5/8	6	6	Socorro County	NM	Thomas J. Leach	1997	2,049
296 2/8	45 7/8	44 6/8	37 0/8	6	7	Clackamas County	OR	Bill Lancaster	1984	2,053
296 2/8	44 6/8	44 2/8	36 0/8	6	6	Crook County	OR	Rod Curtis	1984	2,053
296 2/8	48 7/8	45 4/8	37 6/8	6	6	Moffat County	CO	Robert L Syvertson, Jr.	1984	2,053
296 2/8	48 4/8	48 0/8	40 2/8	6	6	Catron County	NM	Pete Raynor	1989	2,053
296 2/8	49 2/8	49 1/8	35 2/8	6	6	Canal Flats	BC	Glenn Dreger	1990	2,053
296 2/8	49 4/8	48 1/8	37 2/8	7	6	Coconino County	AZ	Charles Urban	1992	2,053
296 2/8	40 7/8	43 1/8	34 4/8	6	6	Catron County	NM	Jim Eppler	1994	2,053
296 2/8	46 3/8	45 7/8	39 1/8	6	8	Baca County	CO	Robert D. Downs	1995	2,053
296 2/8	46 6/8	46 4/8	41 6/8	6	6	Caribou County	ID	Todd R. Burgin	1997	2,053
296 2/8	48 5/8	48 4/8	33 0/8	6	6	Gila County	AZ	Brett W. Bostian	1997	2,053
296 2/8	44 1/8	42 6/8	24 0/8	7	7	Phillips County	MT	Mike Liane	1998	2,053
296 1/8	43 2/8	45 3/8	43 1/8	6	6	Sheridan County	WY	Mike Barrett	1982	2,064
296 1/8	44 3/8	44 3/8	32 1/8	6	6	Wolverine Creek	ALB	Dave Bathke	1990	2,064
296 1/8	46 4/8	45 2/8	40 1/8	6	6	Valley County	ID	Jeff D. Dursteler	1997	2,064
296 0/8	44 2/8	45 0/8	39 4/8	6	6	Gallatin County	MT	Bob Savage	1968	2,067
296 0/8	48 7/8	46 6/8	37 6/8	6	6	Bighorn Mtns.	WY	Dean Fudge	1979	2,067
296 0/8	40 7/8	41 7/8	28 4/8	8	6	Spruce Woods	MAN	Brian Morash	1981	2,067
296 0/8	44 5/8	44 0/8	33 4/8	6	6	Flathead County	MT	Mark Fopp	1987	2,067
296 0/8	48 7/8	50 6/8	40 2/8	6	5	Lemhi County	ID	David C. Manca	1991	2,067
296 0/8	47 2/8	52 0/8	41 4/8	5	6	Phillips County	MT	Ronald S. Kline	1991	2,067
296 0/8	45 6/8	45 6/8	38 6/8	6	6	Montrose County	CO	Bobby David Tipping	1992	2,067
296 0/8	50 0/8	48 5/8	35 0/8	6	6	Albany County	WY	Merle Vowers	1995	2,067
296 0/8	48 7/8	49 1/8	39 2/8	6	6	Ravalli County	MT	Evelio Elledias, Jr.	1996	2,067
296 0/8	46 1/8	46 6/8	33 2/8	6	6	Lincoln County	NM	Harold Dean Britt	1998	2,067
296 0/8	43 2/8	43 3/8	30 6/8	6	6	Coconino County	AZ	Will Pick	1998	2,067
295 7/8	42 5/8	40 5/8	38 2/8	6	7	Larimer County	CO	Ben Alexander	1972	2,078
295 7/8	44 4/8	43 7/8	38 1/8	6	7	Madison County	MT	Kevin Fogal	1985	2,078
295 7/8	46 7/8	48 2/8	33 5/8	6	6	Union County	OR	Andy Mickelson	1994	2,078
295 6/8	49 6/8	50 0/8	38 4/8	6	6	Bonneville County	ID	Jim Cox	1976	2,081
295 6/8	43 7/8	44 6/8	32 6/8	6	6	Powell County	MT	Bryan C. Anderson	1985	2,081
295 6/8	42 0/8	46 0/8	40 2/8	6	6	Boulder County	CO	Jerry Bryan	1986	2,081
295 6/8	45 5/8	45 3/8	41 0/8	6	6	Gallatin County	MT	H. C. Tysinger, Jr.	1986	2,081
295 6/8	43 2/8	44 5/8	38 0/8	6	6	Mesa County	CO	James Stover	1992	2,081
295 6/8	44 1/8	42 4/8	35 4/8	7	7	Granite County	MT	Chris Pileski	1996	2,081
295 6/8	47 0/8	48 5/8	37 4/8	6	6	Sheridan County	WY	Dave Moss	1997	2,081
295 4/8	48 0/8	47 1/8	37 0/8	6	6	Custer County	ID	A. Lynn Burton	1982	2,088
295 4/8	46 4/8	45 3/8	42 0/8	6	6	Clearwater County	ID	Jerry Weverka	1988	2,088
295 4/8	46 1/8	45 0/8	39 4/8	6	6	Clackamas County	OR	David L. Winters	1989	2,088
295 4/8	47 6/8	47 5/8	37 0/8	6	6	Colfax County	NM	Charles H. Morrisette, Jr.	1992	2,088
295 4/8	50 1/8	50 3/8	33 2/8	6	6	Navajo County	AZ	Joe D. Insall	1993	2,088
295 4/8	45 5/8	46 2/8	34 0/8	6	6	Navajo County	AZ	Stephen Hoblick	1998	2,088
295 3/8	45 2/8	43 6/8	37 1/8	6	6	Catron County	NM	Ricardo Unzueta	1992	2,094
295 3/8	44 3/8	43 0/8	36 5/8	8	6	Weber County	UT	David R. Drysdale/K. Taylor	1992	2,094
295 3/8	47 5/8	47 7/8	33 7/8	6	6	Socorro County	NM	Doug Aikin	1992	2,094
295 3/8	46 4/8	47 5/8	38 7/8	7	7	Mineral County	MT	Denny Morkert	1992	2,094
295 3/8	50 0/8	48 7/8	39 1/8	6	6	Phillips County	MT	Lynn Paris	1995	2,094
295 2/8	45 0/8	46 0/8	38 4/8	6	6	Lincoln County	NM	Bart J. Gillan III	1984	2,099
295 2/8	51 3/8	51 3/8	37 0/8	7	6	Kittitas County	WA	Kirk Cresto	1984	2,099
295 2/8	48 4/8	48 4/8	40 6/8	6	6	Catron County	NM	Gary Burnett	1986	2,099
295 2/8	43 4/8	48 4/8	39 6/8	6	5	Catron County	NM	Spencer O. Moore III	1986	2,099
295 2/8	42 5/8	42 0/8	41 4/8	6	6	Clearwater County	ID	Rudy Marmelo, Jr.	1988	2,099
295 2/8	44 4/8	44 1/8	51 1/8	6	6	Pueblo County	CO	Steve Willsey	1991	2,099
295 2/8	45 3/8	44 6/8	38 2/8	7	6	Sanders County	MT	Barry L. Dore	1995	2,099
295 1/8	43 1/8	42 0/8	39 1/8	6	6	Gallatin County	MT	Tom L. Miller	1986	2,106

YELLOWSTONE "AMERICAN" ELK (TYPICAL ANTLERS)

Minimum Score 260   Continued

SCORE	LENGTH OF R MAIN BEAM L		INSIDE SPREAD	NUMBER OF R POINTS L		AREA	STATE/ PROVINCE	HUNTER'S NAME	DATE	RANK
295 1/8	42 4/8	44 0/8	36 3/8	6	6	Sublette County	WY	Ronald A. Noble	1989	2,106
295 1/8	48 0/8	49 4/8	38 2/8	6	6	Catron County	NM	Craig Chilson	1994	2,106
295 1/8	47 0/8	46 2/8	38 1/8	6	7	Garfield County	MT	Steve Kreitinger	1997	2,106
295 1/8	44 4/8	44 4/8	32 7/8	6	6	Phillips County	MT	Mark Meyer	1997	2,106
295 1/8	49 4/8	48 5/8	30 5/8	6	6	Las Animas County	CO	Robert Hicks	1998	2,106
295 0/8	51 2/8	49 7/8	38 5/8	7	6	Crook County	OR	Michael Hawkins	1983	2,112
295 0/8	43 7/8	42 7/8	36 6/8	6	6	Catron County	NM	Loyd Street	1988	2,112
295 0/8	46 5/8	46 6/8	32 2/8	6	6	Greenlee County	AZ	Robert Cisneros	1991	2,112
295 0/8	46 4/8	47 6/8	37 2/8	6	6	Lincoln County	WY	Dale Williams	1992	2,112
295 0/8	47 2/8	46 0/8	39 4/8	6	6	Park County	MT	Steve Kamps	1993	2,112
295 0/8	45 6/8	45 0/8	35 6/8	5	5	Otero County	NM	Gary Garcia	1996	2,112
294 7/8	42 1/8	41 0/8	46 3/8	6	6	Catron County	NM	John McClendon	1987	2,118
294 7/8	48 4/8	44 5/8	44 3/8	6	6	Coconino County	AZ	Michael Weldon	1988	2,118
294 7/8	41 1/8	40 6/8	38 7/8	6	6	Priddis Creek	ALB	Roger Meyer	1991	2,118
294 7/8	48 6/8	48 6/8	37 3/8	6	6	Coconino County	AZ	Ralph B. Harris	1991	2,118
294 6/8	47 1/8	48 2/8	35 2/8	6	7	Crook County	OR	John F. Nelson	1994	2,122
294 6/8	46 7/8	48 5/8	37 2/8	6	6	Archuleta County	CO	Wayne Peeples	1997	2,122
294 6/8	42 4/8	42 4/8	35 6/8	6	6	Lemhi County	ID	Richard F. Skinner	1998	2,122
294 6/8	42 7/8	43 6/8	41 2/8	6	6	Gallatin County	MT	Vince Galli	1998	2,122
294 5/8	41 2/8	39 7/8	38 7/8	6	6	Fremont County	CO	William Bowlby	1984	2,126
294 5/8	52 3/8	49 0/8	38 7/8	5	6	Sanders County	MT	Ralph W. Flockerzi	1987	2,126
294 5/8	50 0/8	47 2/8	35 5/8	6	6	Sandoval County	NM	Robert K. Woeck	1992	2,126
294 4/8	46 0/8	45 2/8	40 2/8	6	6	Deer Lodge County	MT	Dale J. Goytowski	1986	2,129
294 4/8	48 3/8	50 0/8	46 4/8	6	6	McKinley County	NM	Eugene Duran	1987	2,129
294 4/8	45 2/8	47 1/8	32 4/8	6	6	Coconino County	AZ	Jesse Smith	1988	2,129
294 4/8	45 2/8	41 5/8	41 6/8	6	7	Grant County	OR	James M. Carter	1990	2,129
294 4/8	46 4/8	45 6/8	39 0/8	6	6	Shoshone County	ID	David V. Wait	1992	2,129
294 4/8	46 1/8	44 7/8	38 6/8	6	6	Otero County	NM	Lewis Green	1998	2,129
294 3/8	45 0/8	48 4/8	37 1/8	5	7	Saguache County	CO	David A. Larson	1978	2,135
294 3/8	45 1/8	46 0/8	35 1/8	6	6	Socorro County	NM	Eddie Claypool	1988	2,135
294 3/8	45 7/8	44 1/8	44 7/8	6	6	Granite County	MT	Scott A. Breum	1992	2,135
294 3/8	43 2/8	44 1/8	36 7/8	6	6	Lincoln County	WY	Steven B. Julander	1992	2,135
294 3/8	47 6/8	46 1/8	43 5/8	6	6	Coconino County	AZ	George J. Alvarez	1996	2,135
294 2/8	50 2/8	45 6/8	37 0/8	7	6	La Plata County	CO	J. Barry Dyar	1983	2,140
294 2/8	43 5/8	45 4/8	40 2/8	7	6	Apache County	AZ	Fred Clifford	1985	2,140
294 2/8	42 5/8	46 2/8	42 0/8	6	6	Catron County	NM	Billy Barber	1986	2,140
294 2/8	43 7/8	40 7/8	35 2/8	6	6	Otero County	NM	Bruce Bonnet	1990	2,140
294 2/8	48 4/8	48 2/8	38 1/8	7	6	Grand County	CO	Mike Brown	1992	2,140
294 2/8	48 7/8	48 3/8	36 0/8	6	6	Coconino County	AZ	Randy McKusick	1993	2,140
294 2/8	46 6/8	46 6/8	33 0/8	6	6	Fergus County	MT	Douglas C. McWilliams	1994	2,140
294 2/8	49 2/8	45 6/8	44 1/8	8	5	Rio Blanco County	CO	Larry McCarty	1994	2,140
294 1/8	41 6/8	42 3/8	39 3/8	6	6	Lincoln County	WY	Bill Swett	1997	2,148
294 0/8	41 1/8	42 5/8	33 0/8	6	6	Clearwater County	ID	Don Kubasch	1981	2,149
294 0/8	44 7/8	44 5/8	31 4/8	6	6	Big Horn County	WY	Dave Moss	1988	2,149
293 7/8	46 3/8	48 0/8	40 5/8	6	6	Gunnison County	CO	Robert C. Goodman	1974	2,151
293 7/8	42 6/8	44 4/8	34 5/8	6	5	Graham County	AZ	Clifford White	1982	2,151
293 7/8	50 4/8	47 5/8	33 5/8	6	6	Phillips County	MT	Mike Mjelstad	1987	2,151
293 7/8	45 5/8	45 4/8	39 5/8	5	5	Idaho County	ID	Michael J. Collins	1990	2,151
293 7/8	48 0/8	48 6/8	37 3/8	6	6	Custer County	ID	Tom Szurgot	1990	2,151
293 7/8	48 3/8	48 3/8	33 3/8	6	6	Missoula County	MT	Pao K. Moua	1990	2,151
293 7/8	40 0/8	51 6/8	30 1/8	6	6	Sierra County	NM	Don Draper	1993	2,151
293 7/8	43 2/8	43 3/8	35 5/8	6	6	Valencia County	NM	A. M. Oakes, Jr.	1993	2,151
293 7/8	42 6/8	41 7/8	41 5/8	7	7	Crook County	OR	Randy Baker	1998	2,151
293 6/8	47 0/8	45 4/8	37 0/8	6	6	Archuleta County	CO	Eddie Claypool	1985	2,160
293 6/8	43 1/8	46 0/8	46 6/8	6	6	Lemhi County	ID	Ben L. Fahnholz	1987	2,160
293 6/8	49 3/8	48 0/8	38 6/8	6	6	Sheridan County	WY	Gary T. Laya	1988	2,160
293 6/8	50 4/8	52 2/8	31 0/8	6	6	Rio Arriba County	NM	Paul Locey	1990	2,160
293 6/8	48 3/8	47 0/8	45 0/8	6	7	Grant County	OR	Tim L. Hayward	1991	2,160
293 6/8	42 2/8	43 0/8	42 0/8	6	6	Pitkin County	CO	Norman Shawn Hopkins	1992	2,160
293 6/8	45 1/8	46 1/8	42 2/8	6	6	Judith Basin County	MT	Ken Schmidt	1993	2,160
293 5/8	42 6/8	43 3/8	39 7/8	6	6	West	MT	Raymond Alt	1962	2,167
293 5/8	46 2/8	47 7/8	38 5/8	6	6	Larimer County	CO	Wayne R. Haas	1996	2,167
293 5/8	49 4/8	46 6/8	40 1/8	6	7	Taos County	NM	Matthew Howard	1998	2,167
293 4/8	49 5/8	50 2/8	42 2/8	6	5	Sheridan County	WY	Mike Barrett	1980	2,170
293 4/8	47 4/8	46 6/8	34 6/8	6	6	Beaverhead County	MT	Dennis Rehse	1981	2,170
293 4/8	50 0/8	46 4/8	33 6/8	6	6	Catron County	NM	Bob Gourley	1984	2,170
293 4/8	44 1/8	44 0/8	37 4/8	6	6	Idaho County	ID	Gary Knoles	1993	2,170
293 4/8	45 3/8	44 7/8	38 2/8	5	5	Grand County	CO	Carlis Stephens	1996	2,170
293 3/8	46 0/8	45 5/8	37 5/8	6	6	Boise County	ID	David Hale	1983	2,175
293 3/8	46 0/8	45 5/8	30 5/8	6	7	Lemhi County	ID	William C. Shuster	1986	2,175
293 3/8	46 6/8	47 4/8	32 5/8	6	6	Gallatin County	MT	Michael Groulx	1990	2,175
293 3/8	45 1/8	43 0/8	40 1/8	5	6	Morgan County	UT	Poncho McCoy	1992	2,175
293 3/8	46 6/8	46 5/8	36 5/8	6	6	Lewis County	WA	Scott Murray	1992	2,175
293 2/8	47 2/8	47 6/8	39 2/8	6	6	Musselshell County	MT	Dan Acord	1986	2,180
293 2/8	42 6/8	42 6/8	32 4/8	6	6	Flathead County	MT	Larry O. Hadley	1987	2,180
293 2/8	46 6/8	46 6/8	35 6/8	6	6	Navajo County	AZ	Corky Richardson	1990	2,180
293 2/8	47 7/8	47 7/8	36 6/8	6	6	Los Alamos County	NM	Jeffrey M. Bradley	1992	2,180
293 2/8	46 6/8	47 6/8	35 0/8	6	6	Platte County	WY	Willard Woods	1993	2,180

YELLOWSTONE "AMERICAN" ELK (TYPICAL ANTLERS)

Minimum Score 260

Continued

SCORE	LENGTH OF MAIN BEAM R	LENGTH OF MAIN BEAM L	INSIDE SPREAD	NUMBER OF POINTS R	NUMBER OF POINTS L	AREA	STATE/ PROVINCE	HUNTER'S NAME	DATE	RANK
293 2/8	54 5/8	53 6/8	40 0/8	6	8	Chouteau County	MT	Gus Smith	1995	2,180
293 2/8	48 5/8	49 1/8	35 6/8	6	6	Carbon County	WY	Larry J. Thoney	1997	2,180
293 1/8	44 6/8	39 1/8	32 1/8	6	6	Clearwater County	ID	T. LeRoy West	1981	2,187
293 1/8	42 6/8	39 6/8	35 1/8	6	6	Catron County	NM	Butch Allen	1990	2,187
293 1/8	47 1/8	45 6/8	45 0/8	6	7	Rio Blanco County	CO	Mike Wallers	1993	2,187
293 0/8	49 0/8	48 4/8	32 4/8	6	6	Beaverhead County	MT	Martin L. Sapp	1988	2,190
293 0/8	42 7/8	44 2/8	40 4/8	6	6	Sandoval County	NM	John Clarence Rector	1990	2,190
293 0/8	42 6/8	45 4/8	40 2/8	8	7	Wallowa County	OR	Dwight Huffman	1990	2,190
293 0/8	44 0/8	44 1/8	38 6/8	6	6	Catron County	NM	Leonard Rohlik	1991	2,190
293 0/8	47 6/8	44 3/8	43 4/8	6	6	Otero County	NM	Jim Howard	1997	2,190
292 7/8	48 0/8	52 4/8	38 5/8	6	6	Sweet Grass County	MT	Dr. Dale Schlehuber	1986	2,195
292 7/8	46 7/8	46 4/8	40 5/8	6	6	Lincoln County	MT	Dan Bundrock	1989	2,195
292 7/8	41 4/8	41 3/8	38 5/8	6	6	Boulder County	CO	Ron Readmond	1990	2,195
292 7/8	45 5/8	44 1/8	36 1/8	6	6	Petroleum County	MT	Don Davidson	1992	2,195
292 6/8	42 3/8	44 5/8	34 0/8	6	6	Chouteau County	MT	Tom Brady	1987	2,199
292 6/8	44 5/8	45 4/8	36 2/8	6	6	Carbon County	UT	David J. Hansen	1993	2,199
292 6/8	46 4/8	47 6/8	35 0/8	6	6	Jackson County	CO	William R. Aycock	1995	2,199
292 6/8	43 0/8	43 4/8	40 0/8	6	6	Catron County	NM	Mike Holland	1996	2,199
292 6/8	41 6/8	41 3/8	34 0/8	6	6	Cascade County	MT	Edward Keltgen	1997	2,199
292 5/8	43 6/8	42 1/8	34 1/8	7	6	Rio Blanco County	CO	James Raetz	1976	2,204
292 5/8	45 2/8	42 6/8	35 1/8	6	6	Catron County	NM	John Stanley	1987	2,204
292 5/8	41 1/8	41 1/8	33 5/8	6	6	Albany County	WY	Michael Lancaster	1990	2,204
292 5/8	39 2/8	38 5/8	39 7/8	6	7	Colfax County	NM	Dave Holt	1990	2,204
292 5/8	44 0/8	44 6/8	38 1/8	6	6	Larimer County	CO	Todd K. Johnson	1993	2,204
292 5/8	44 7/8	43 7/8	36 7/8	6	6	Crook County	OR	Jason Simpson	1995	2,204
292 5/8	43 5/8	46 7/8	37 5/8	6	6	Coconino County	AZ	Stephen Herrera	1997	2,204
292 4/8	48 0/8	50 4/8	33 4/8	6	6	Sanders County	MT	Doug Gunderson	1978	2,211
292 4/8	43 0/8	43 6/8	40 2/8	6	6	Jackson County	CO	Daniel H. Chaney	1981	2,211
292 4/8	43 1/8	42 1/8	30 0/8	6	6	Strathcona	ALB	Jack Kempf	1984	2,211
292 4/8	46 6/8	46 2/8	34 4/8	6	6	Grant County	OR	Terry J. Caster	1990	2,211
292 4/8	42 4/8	42 0/8	37 0/8	6	6	Morgan County	UT	Brad T. Francis	1991	2,211
292 4/8	46 4/8	47 4/8	38 4/8	5	6	Mesa County	CO	Victor Zugibe	1995	2,211
292 3/8	44 6/8	40 4/8	35 1/8	6	6	Idaho County	ID	Robert C. Mitchell	1979	2,217
292 3/8	44 6/8	44 2/8	36 3/8	6	6	Ravalli County	MT	Paul Hamilton	1984	2,217
292 3/8	44 3/8	43 0/8	40 1/8	6	6	Ravalli County	MT	Pao K. Moua	1998	2,217
292 2/8	41 2/8	44 4/8	39 6/8	6	6	Idaho County	ID	Richard C. Nichols	1975	2,220
292 2/8	47 5/8	46 1/8	31 4/8	6	6	Mineral County	MT	Kenneth D. Verley	1981	2,220
292 2/8	45 2/8	49 1/8	33 4/8	6	6	Grant County	OR	Robert R. Gedlick	1983	2,220
292 2/8	42 5/8	41 3/8	35 2/8	6	6	Clark County	ID	Billy Burbank III	1988	2,220
292 2/8	47 5/8	50 0/8	35 2/8	6	7	Missoula County	MT	Jeffrey G. Winter	1993	2,220
292 2/8	43 5/8	42 4/8	34 0/8	6	6	Sheridan County	WY	Mike Barrett	1996	2,220
292 2/8	48 5/8	46 0/8	37 0/8	5	5	Nose Mtn.	ALB	Les Baird	1997	2,220
292 2/8	48 5/8	47 1/8	36 6/8	6	6	Sevier County	UT	Darren Peterson	1997	2,220
292 2/8	46 6/8	46 0/8	43 4/8	6	6	Blaine County	ID	Jim Wentworth	1998	2,220
292 1/8	44 7/8	47 0/8	34 3/8	6	6	Powell County	MT	Richard W. Malone	1976	2,229
292 1/8	47 5/8	47 0/8	46 7/8	6	6	Coconino County	AZ	Bryant McGee	1980	2,229
292 1/8	49 4/8	48 2/8	39 5/8	6	6	Custer County	ID	James Schrader	1991	2,229
292 1/8	40 3/8	38 4/8	41 4/8	6	6	Park County	WY	Scott Moore	1991	2,229
292 1/8	44 4/8	48 4/8	43 3/8	6	6	Socorro County	NM	Manfred Quentel	1996	2,229
292 1/8	46 4/8	44 4/8	37 3/8	6	6	Otero County	NM	Brad A. King	1997	2,229
292 0/8	36 2/8	37 6/8	33 4/8	6	6	Lincoln County	NM	Terence A. Wahlgren	1985	2,235
292 0/8	46 0/8	45 0/8	34 0/8	6	6	Catron County	NM	Brad Blanchard	1989	2,235
292 0/8	43 7/8	43 0/8	36 2/8	6	7	Uintah County	UT	Smiley Arrowchis	1989	2,235
292 0/8	44 6/8	44 6/8	39 0/8	6	6	Coconino County	AZ	Mark J. Dominguez	1991	2,235
292 0/8	48 1/8	49 2/8	36 6/8	6	6	Apache County	AZ	Aaron J. Scott	1994	2,235
292 0/8	44 1/8	44 5/8	36 0/8	6	6	Park County	WY	Beau Beck	1998	2,235
291 7/8	45 7/8	45 0/8	46 2/8	6	6	Coconino County	AZ	Dick & Gary Mendenhall	1974	2,241
291 7/8	45 5/8	45 2/8	38 5/8	6	6	Chaffee County	CO	Douglas E. Wilson	1982	2,241
291 7/8	52 7/8	51 5/8	46 1/8	5	6	King County	WA	Ty Martin	1984	2,241
291 7/8	44 2/8	44 0/8	35 7/8	6	6	Saguache County	CO	Dario J. Archuleta	1991	2,241
291 7/8	46 6/8	43 2/8	39 1/8	5	5	Fremont County	WY	Nelson Scherrer	1991	2,241
291 7/8	44 6/8	46 0/8	35 4/8	7	6	Coconino County	AZ	Roy Jimenez	1994	2,241
291 7/8	49 0/8	48 1/8	37 5/8	6	6	Malheur County	OR	Landel M. McBride	1995	2,241
291 7/8	39 6/8	44 1/8	34 1/8	8	6	NoJack	ALB	Calvin Briggs	1998	2,241
291 6/8	45 2/8	45 5/8	41 0/8	6	6	Summit County	CO	Howard Moser	1972	2,249
291 6/8	45 4/8	45 1/8	40 0/8	6	6	Gem County	ID	Larry Holmquist	1986	2,249
291 6/8	47 0/8	47 1/8	31 4/8	6	6	Wapiti River	ALB	Ted Brown	1993	2,249
291 6/8	49 6/8	49 2/8	32 4/8	6	6	Lane County	OR	James Phelps	1994	2,249
291 5/8	53 2/8	54 6/8	34 7/8	7	7	Coconino County	AZ	Bruce Ludeke	1989	2,253
291 5/8	43 1/8	44 3/8	36 1/8	6	6	Catron County	NM	Timothy J. Duffney	1993	2,253
291 5/8	45 0/8	47 4/8	34 3/8	6	6	Columbia County	WA	James Stenersen	1995	2,253
291 5/8	44 5/8	46 2/8	33 7/8	6	6	Shoshone County	ID	Linda Leake	1996	2,253
291 5/8	50 3/8	51 6/8	34 4/8	6	6	Beaverhead County	MT	Jerry T. Arch	1996	2,253
291 5/8	41 3/8	46 7/8	39 3/8	6	6	Grant County	OR	A. Duane Drewett	1997	2,253
291 4/8	45 4/8	43 7/8	38 4/8	6	6	Dolores County	CO	William W. Gurley	1977	2,259
291 4/8	42 2/8	43 4/8	35 2/8	7	6	Garfield County	MT	Gaylord Johnson	1983	2,259
291 4/8	44 2/8	44 6/8	34 4/8	6	6	Sanders County	MT	Matthew J. Dorenkamper	1992	2,259
291 4/8	44 0/8	42 5/8	31 4/8	6	6	Routt County	CO	Mark Upson	1994	2,259

YELLOWSTONE "AMERICAN" ELK (TYPICAL ANTLERS)

Minimum Score 260   Continued

SCORE	LENGTH OF MAIN BEAM R	LENGTH OF MAIN BEAM L	INSIDE SPREAD	NUMBER OF POINTS R	NUMBER OF POINTS L	AREA	STATE/ PROVINCE	HUNTER'S NAME	DATE	RANK
291 4/8	46 7/8	45 3/8	36 4/8	6	6	Catron County	NM	Chris Skinner	1997	2,259
291 3/8	44 6/8	46 1/8	42 1/8	6	5	Idaho County	ID	Dr. Brian M. Howard	1987	2,264
291 3/8	45 4/8	46 2/8	36 3/8	7	6	Grant County	OR	Terry Harling	1994	2,264
291 3/8	40 2/8	40 2/8	37 1/8	6	6	Caribou County	ID	Darryl D. Lamoreaux	1997	2,264
291 2/8	44 1/8	48 1/8	27 0/8	6	6	Phillips County	MT	Scott L. Augustine	1980	2,267
291 2/8	47 5/8	45 0/8	36 6/8	6	6	Albany County	WY	Oliver P. Williamson	1982	2,267
291 2/8	43 7/8	44 6/8	46 5/8	6	7	Clearwater County	ID	Scott Rabe	1984	2,267
291 2/8	43 6/8	46 7/8	31 4/8	7	6	Gilpin County	CO	Lee L. Florian	1986	2,267
291 2/8	52 1/8	51 4/8	35 4/8	6	6	Clearwater County	ID	Jim Horneck	1987	2,267
291 2/8	42 4/8	41 6/8	34 4/8	6	6	Lincoln County	WY	George Walker	1993	2,267
291 2/8	45 0/8	47 2/8	36 2/8	6	6	Fremont County	WY	Dale D. Gettel	1993	2,267
291 2/8	48 1/8	48 0/8	36 2/8	8	6	Musselshell County	MT	Shawn Lar	1996	2,267
291 2/8	46 4/8	45 2/8	37 4/8	5	6	Otero County	NM	Richard D. Burton	1998	2,267
291 1/8	43 4/8	41 6/8	35 3/8	7	6	Coconino County	AZ	Tom Jensen	1989	2,276
291 1/8	48 1/8	47 6/8	39 5/8	6	6	Grant County	OR	Dennis McClelland	1991	2,276
291 1/8	46 7/8	47 2/8	30 5/8	6	6	Montrose County	CO	Lannie Ellis	1991	2,276
291 1/8	46 6/8	46 7/8	36 3/8	6	6	Fremont County	CO	Michael Miller	1998	2,276
291 0/8	48 4/8	49 4/8	40 4/8	6	6	Custer County	CO	Douglas R. Jones	1970	2,280
291 0/8	50 2/8	49 1/8	35 0/8	6	6	Elmore County	ID	Gary Briggs	1986	2,280
291 0/8	47 2/8	47 0/8	38 4/8	6	5	Skamania County	WA	Terry Kern	1987	2,280
291 0/8	44 2/8	41 4/8	37 0/8	6	6	Park County	WY	Paul W. McClelland, Jr.	1995	2,280
291 0/8	49 6/8	49 7/8	33 6/8	6	6	Garfield County	MT	Bryant Shermoe	1995	2,280
291 0/8	46 0/8	48 6/8	38 4/8	6	6	Shoshone County	ID	Neil Kimberling	1996	2,280
290 7/8	44 6/8	42 6/8	38 5/8	6	6	Ravalli County	MT	Sheldon M. Jones	1991	2,286
290 7/8	49 5/8	45 7/8	35 5/8	6	6	Converse County	WY	John Fanto	1995	2,286
290 7/8	45 6/8	44 0/8	32 7/8	6	6	Archuleta County	CO	Johnnie R. Walters	1997	2,286
290 6/8	42 4/8	43 0/8	35 6/8	6	6	Park County	WY	William P. Mastrangel	1955	2,289
290 6/8	42 6/8	43 6/8	36 2/8	5	5	Larimer County	CO	Tom Tietz	1979	2,289
290 6/8	41 5/8	41 3/8	38 0/8	6	6	Rio Arriba County	NM	Craig Barrows	1990	2,289
290 6/8	46 2/8	46 5/8	38 6/8	6	7	Coconino County	AZ	Duane "Corky" Richardson	1991	2,289
290 6/8	42 4/8	43 6/8	38 2/8	6	6	Madison County	MT	Randy Brown	1991	2,289
290 6/8	46 3/8	43 4/8	35 2/8	6	6	Otero County	NM	Ronnie L. Elswick	1994	2,289
290 5/8	45 2/8	46 6/8	36 7/8	8	8	Greenlee County	AZ	Sonny Turner	1986	2,295
290 5/8	51 7/8	50 0/8	30 3/8	6	7	Coconino County	AZ	John Alfred Musgrove	1989	2,295
290 5/8	41 2/8	41 4/8	35 4/8	7	6	Larimer County	CO	Steve W. Stumbo	1995	2,295
290 5/8	51 5/8	52 4/8	37 7/8	6	6	Moffat County	CO	Rob Syvertson	1995	2,295
290 5/8	44 5/8	45 1/8	37 5/8	6	6	Lemhi County	ID	Kevin L. Kenney	1996	2,295
290 5/8	45 5/8	47 1/8	31 3/8	6	6	Mineral County	MT	William B. Ross	1996	2,295
290 5/8	46 5/8	46 5/8	38 1/8	6	6	Granite County	MT	Frank H. Wilmot	1996	2,295
290 4/8	48 3/8	51 3/8	34 2/8	5	6	Garfield County	CO	John W. Ellas	1998	2,302
290 3/8	49 4/8	48 7/8	36 7/8	6	6	Custer County	ID	Tom Jarvis	1984	2,303
290 3/8	49 2/8	49 2/8	39 5/8	6	6	Sublette County	WY	Joey Gomes	1989	2,303
290 3/8	46 6/8	45 0/8	32 1/8	6	6	Idaho County	ID	Stanley L. Rider	1993	2,303
290 3/8	42 6/8	41 6/8	31 5/8	6	6	Catron County	NM	Jim Talak	1994	2,303
290 3/8	48 6/8	51 2/8	34 5/8	6	7	Coconino County	AZ	Randy H. Sifford	1996	2,303
290 2/8	45 7/8	46 4/8	41 4/8	6	6	Gunnison County	CO	Jack Allen Rasmusson	1982	2,308
290 2/8	42 6/8	44 5/8	40 0/8	6	6	Granite County	MT	Dennis Neitzke	1985	2,308
290 2/8	42 1/8	40 3/8	34 6/8	6	6	Gallatin County	MT	Chris Cey	1991	2,308
290 2/8	50 5/8	53 4/8	42 4/8	5	6	Cibola County	NM	Brandon Wynn	1992	2,308
290 2/8	43 4/8	46 0/8	42 6/8	6	6	Jefferson County	CO	Gene Swanson	1992	2,308
290 1/8	45 6/8	44 7/8	38 3/8	6	6	Grant County	OR	James M. Carter	1984	2,313
290 1/8	49 4/8	49 4/8	40 7/8	6	6	McKinley County	NM	Larry Dwyer	1989	2,313
290 1/8	43 0/8	45 6/8	40 1/8	6	6	Colfax County	NM	Robert Torstenson	1997	2,313
290 0/8	47 2/8	46 4/8	39 0/8	6	6	Phillips County	MT	Cecil I. Tharp	1978	2,316
290 0/8	41 6/8	43 5/8	43 5/8	6	7	Canmore	ALB	David R. Coupland	1980	2,316
290 0/8	45 7/8	42 4/8	35 6/8	6	6	Shoshone County	ID	Larry Rose	1988	2,316
290 0/8	47 7/8	44 0/8	34 7/8	7	6	Sandoval County	NM	Robert L. Pagel	1989	2,316
289 7/8	43 0/8	41 0/8	40 3/8	6	6	Boulder County	CO	John Powell	1983	2,320
289 7/8	47 7/8	47 4/8	36 5/8	6	6	Missoula County	MT	Bill Spicknall	1984	2,320
289 7/8	41 5/8	46 3/8	40 3/8	6	6	Mesa County	CO	George P. Sofronas	1986	2,320
289 7/8	44 6/8	45 0/8	39 3/8	6	6	Sandoval County	NM	William F. Gorman	1996	2,320
289 7/8	42 1/8	43 6/8	40 5/8	6	6	Adams County	ID	Greg Richardson	1997	2,320
289 7/8	44 3/8	41 0/8	28 7/8	6	6	Caribou County	ID	Anthony Robinson	1997	2,320
289 6/8	45 3/8	45 0/8	35 6/8	6	6	Ravalli County	MT	Dan Smith	1980	2,326
289 6/8	42 3/8	41 6/8	33 0/8	5	6	Rich County	UT	Raymond E. Goff	1989	2,326
289 6/8	45 4/8	45 6/8	42 6/8	6	6	Los Alamos County	NM	Bruce Barrie	1989	2,326
289 6/8	46 3/8	46 4/8	36 2/8	6	6	Coconino County	AZ	Tom H. Sissom	1995	2,326
289 6/8	42 7/8	41 2/8	36 2/8	7	7	Cowlitz County	WA	Larry Bryan Skaar	1997	2,326
289 5/8	42 2/8	42 2/8	38 3/8	6	6	Ravalli County	MT	Michael S. Mitchell	1985	2,331
289 4/8	48 0/8	50 3/8	33 2/8	6	6	Clearwater County	ID	LeRoy West	1983	2,332
289 4/8	48 0/8	46 4/8	41 0/8	6	6	Coconino County	AZ	Fred Searle	1985	2,332
289 4/8	44 5/8	42 0/8	39 2/8	7	7	Grant County	OR	Ray Martin	1988	2,332
289 4/8	45 5/8	43 6/8	38 2/8	6	5	Ravalli County	MT	Shaun Twardoski	1993	2,332
289 4/8	44 4/8	44 3/8	38 0/8	6	6	Flathead County	MT	Douglas E. Skoczek	1995	2,332
289 4/8	48 0/8	47 0/8	40 0/8	8	6	Coconino County	AZ	Steve Christensen	1996	2,332
289 4/8	41 7/8	42 3/8	40 4/8	6	6	Grant County	OR	Kevin P. Scanlan	1997	2,332
289 3/8	43 1/8	43 4/8	38 7/8	5	5	Lewis County	WA	Douglas H. Brandt	1986	2,339
289 3/8	40 4/8	42 0/8	37 3/8	6	7	Valley County	MT	Erik E. Scarpholt	1986	2,339

YELLOWSTONE "AMERICAN" ELK (TYPICAL ANTLERS)

Minimum Score 260

Continued

SCORE	LENGTH OF MAIN BEAM R L		INSIDE SPREAD	NUMBER OF POINTS R L		AREA	STATE/ PROVINCE	HUNTER'S NAME	DATE	RANK
289 3/8	41 7/8	44 5/8	38 7/8	6	6	Hinsdale County	CO	Kevin W. Bauman	1989	2,339
289 3/8	46 1/8	46 1/8	44 1/8	6	6	Sandoval County	NM	Randy Erickson	1992	2,339
289 3/8	44 1/8	44 0/8	35 5/8	6	6	Larimer County	CO	Gary Greathouse	1993	2,339
289 3/8	41 6/8	44 5/8	39 7/8	6	6	Lincoln County	WY	Lyle S. Bainbridge	1994	2,339
289 2/8	43 7/8	45 3/8	33 0/8	6	6	Converse County	WY	Darin L. Geringer	1989	2,345
289 2/8	48 0/8	50 0/8	34 2/8	6	6	Sandoval County	NM	Danny Lee Reed	1989	2,345
289 2/8	49 2/8	48 0/8	41 4/8	6	6	Pitkin County	CO	James L. Behn	1990	2,345
289 2/8	54 7/8	55 4/8	38 0/8	7	7	Grant County	NM	Adam Jimenez, Jr.	1991	2,345
289 2/8	39 0/8	41 2/8	37 0/8	6	6	Clark County	ID	John C. Miller	1994	2,345
289 2/8	43 6/8	43 4/8	39 2/8	6	6	Clark County	ID	Tony L. Rossi	1995	2,345
289 2/8	46 1/8	46 0/8	46 0/8	5	5	Elmore County	ID	George T. Peter, Jr.	1995	2,345
289 2/8	43 7/8	46 1/8	34 2/8	6	6	Ravalli County	MT	Ric Twardoski	1996	2,345
289 1/8	46 0/8	46 1/8	35 1/8	6	6	Catron County	NM	Paul D. Payne	1986	2,353
289 1/8	46 5/8	45 7/8	38 3/8	6	6	Flathead County	MT	Bill Love	1987	2,353
289 1/8	43 4/8	48 1/8	35 7/8	6	6	Lemhi County	ID	Danny Moore	1988	2,353
289 1/8	45 4/8	47 0/8	37 5/8	6	6	Johnson County	WY	Donald Janoff, DDS	1993	2,353
289 1/8	47 7/8	49 3/8	36 6/8	7	7	Catron County	NM	Chris Trujillo	1995	2,353
289 1/8	45 7/8	43 7/8	32 1/8	6	6	Teller County	CO	Ron Largent	1996	2,353
289 1/8	44 3/8	44 5/8	38 3/8	6	6	Idaho County	ID	Mike Marano	1996	2,353
289 0/8	51 6/8	50 0/8	38 6/8	6	6	Socorro County	NM	Will Eckelhoff	1991	2,360
289 0/8	48 1/8	47 7/8	33 6/8	7	7	Flathead County	MT	Mason Gray Riley II	1995	2,360
289 0/8	41 0/8	40 6/8	35 6/8	6	6	Baker County	OR	Francis Tyler	1997	2,360
288 7/8	47 6/8	46 3/8	38 1/8	6	6	Linn County	OR	Richard D. Howell	1986	2,363
288 7/8	44 6/8	45 4/8	38 6/8	6	7	Ravalli County	MT	David Harris Stalling	1992	2,363
288 7/8	44 6/8	43 6/8	33 7/8	6	6	Coconino County	AZ	Dale Milton	1994	2,363
288 7/8	48 6/8	49 4/8	42 5/8	6	6	Granite County	MT	Randy L. Cloak	1996	2,363
288 6/8	53 1/8	52 5/8	34 2/8	5	6	Lane County	OR	Ken Abraham	1986	2,367
288 6/8	43 3/8	44 0/8	31 2/8	6	6	Teton County	MT	Brad Stewart	1992	2,367
288 6/8	50 3/8	49 6/8	31 2/8	6	6	Umatilla County	OR	Mike Billman	1998	2,367
288 5/8	46 5/8	44 6/8	39 1/8	6	6	Rio Arriba County	NM	Keith Cheatham	1988	2,370
288 5/8	43 0/8	45 4/8	37 5/8	6	6	Adams County	ID	Randal R. Siemens	1990	2,370
288 5/8	49 6/8	48 5/8	38 3/8	6	6	Sierra County	NM	Bill Elmer	1990	2,370
288 5/8	47 3/8	44 2/8	35 3/8	6	6	Coconino County	AZ	David C. Fretz	1991	2,370
288 5/8	47 5/8	46 6/8	42 0/8	7	6	Sierra County	NM	Olaf R. Lundquist	1995	2,370
288 4/8	50 2/8	49 2/8	34 4/8	6	6	Lemhi County	ID	Ben L. Fahnholz	1984	2,375
288 4/8	44 5/8	48 3/8	39 4/8	5	6	San Miguel County	NM	Robert B. Lewis	1987	2,375
288 4/8	40 6/8	41 5/8	38 6/8	6	6	Sandoval County	NM	Peter C. Swenson	1990	2,375
288 4/8	44 0/8	45 0/8	44 0/8	6	6	Klickitat County	WA	Tom Gaul	1991	2,375
288 4/8	47 6/8	49 3/8	40 4/8	6	6	Rio Arriba County	NM	Scott Miller	1992	2,375
288 4/8	47 5/8	46 5/8	36 0/8	6	7	Fergus County	MT	Josef Rud	1993	2,375
288 3/8	43 2/8	44 5/8	34 7/8	6	6	Marion County	OR	Daniel Smith	1989	2,381
288 3/8	46 5/8	46 5/8	34 1/8	6	6	Park County	WY	Michael Turner	1993	2,381
288 3/8	42 6/8	44 5/8	37 7/8	6	6	Navajo County	AZ	Kevin D. Hatfield	1993	2,381
288 3/8	48 4/8	46 7/8	38 1/8	6	6	Baker County	OR	David J. Freske	1994	2,381
288 3/8	39 2/8	40 2/8	38 5/8	6	6	Sandoval County	NM	Michael G. Morton	1996	2,381
288 3/8	44 7/8	45 5/8	42 5/8	6	6	Shoshone County	ID	Tony A. Hartman	1998	2,381
288 2/8	50 6/8	48 3/8	39 2/8	6	6	Lincoln County	MT	Robert L. Burk	1976	2,387
288 2/8	46 2/8	45 0/8	39 6/8	6	6	Lemhi County	ID	John A. McCarthy	1984	2,387
288 2/8	44 5/8	44 1/8	32 7/8	7	6	Greenlee County	AZ	John C. Jackson	1987	2,387
288 2/8	48 0/8	48 2/8	30 6/8	6	6	Madison County	MT	Ben Manor	1990	2,387
288 2/8	45 2/8	45 6/8	35 4/8	6	6	Apache County	AZ	James L. Crampton	1992	2,387
288 2/8	45 7/8	46 0/8	43 4/8	6	5	Beaverhead County	MT	Danny Moore	1995	2,387
288 2/8	44 0/8	42 6/8	35 6/8	6	6	Garfield County	MT	Bryant Shermoe	1996	2,387
288 2/8	44 1/8	44 0/8	33 0/8	6	6	Idaho County	ID	Stanley L. Rider	1997	2,387
288 2/8	46 0/8	45 7/8	36 4/8	6	6	Phillips County	MT	Joe K. Aldworth	1998	2,387
288 1/8	48 4/8	48 7/8	37 5/8	7	6	Fergus County	MT	Craig Leslie Osborne	1993	2,396
288 1/8	50 2/8	48 4/8	35 7/8	6	6	Catron County	NM	David LeClaire	1995	2,396
288 1/8	41 5/8	43 1/8	39 7/8	6	6	Valley County	ID	Andy D. Anderson	1996	2,396
288 1/8	47 4/8	44 2/8	32 1/8	6	6	Socorro County	NM	Marvin H. Walter	1996	2,396
288 1/8	43 3/8	40 3/8	46 2/8	5	5	Custer County	ID	Daryl Pilarski	1997	2,396
288 0/8	46 4/8	44 4/8	35 0/8	6	6	Albany County	WY	Dan Kolb	1981	2,401
288 0/8	49 2/8	47 7/8	36 0/8	5	6	Carbon County	UT	David A. Justmann	1989	2,401
288 0/8	44 3/8	45 6/8	44 0/8	6	6	Yakima County	WA	Gaylen Bierman	1990	2,401
288 0/8	46 2/8	47 3/8	36 6/8	6	6	Coconino County	AZ	Randall Madding	1992	2,401
288 0/8	40 0/8	41 0/8	34 4/8	6	6	Fergus County	MT	Kelly Norskog	1993	2,401
288 0/8	39 3/8	39 3/8	31 2/8	6	6	Clark County	ID	Brian McIlnay	1994	2,401
287 7/8	38 1/8	38 4/8	34 7/8	6	6	Garfield County	CO	Michael J. Reid	1981	2,407
287 7/8	47 1/8	48 1/8	38 7/8	6	6	Granite County	MT	Stephen F. Culp	1991	2,407
287 7/8	44 7/8	44 7/8	33 3/8	6	6	Park County	WY	Robert J. Horner	1992	2,407
287 7/8	41 5/8	44 4/8	34 6/8	7	6	Fergus County	MT	Mike T. Dellwo	1994	2,407
287 6/8	44 0/8	44 0/8	35 4/8	6	6	Idaho County	ID	Ronald Ward	1984	2,411
287 6/8	38 7/8	38 7/8	30 2/8	6	6	Cypress Hills	ALB	Clayton Knutson	1993	2,411
287 5/8	50 4/8	48 5/8	38 1/8	6	7	Park County	MT	George Kamps	1987	2,413
287 5/8	42 5/8	43 0/8	34 3/8	6	6	Catron County	NM	Danny Burgess	1994	2,413
287 5/8	42 0/8	45 1/8	37 3/8	6	6	Greenlee County	AZ	Steve Rainey	1995	2,413
287 5/8	45 6/8	46 5/8	42 3/8	7	6	Lemhi County	ID	Bob Johnson	1996	2,413
287 5/8	40 7/8	40 3/8	37 1/8	6	6	Las Animas County	CO	Lannie B. Philley	1997	2,413
287 5/8	46 0/8	46 1/8	35 3/8	6	6	Linn County	OR	Todd A. Walsh	1998	2,413

YELLOWSTONE "AMERICAN" ELK (TYPICAL ANTLERS)

Minimum Score 260 — Continued

SCORE	LENGTH OF MAIN BEAM R	LENGTH OF MAIN BEAM L	INSIDE SPREAD	NUMBER OF POINTS R	NUMBER OF POINTS L	AREA	STATE/PROVINCE	HUNTER'S NAME	DATE	RANK
287 5/8	45 5/8	43 4/8	32 5/8	6	6	Valley County	ID	Dennis Crew	1998	2,413
287 4/8	44 4/8	45 0/8	38 2/8	6	6	Adams County	ID	Gary Kinney	1986	2,420
287 4/8	45 2/8	44 0/8	39 0/8	6	6	Baker County	OR	Larry D. Jones	1987	2,420
287 4/8	43 1/8	41 6/8	36 1/8	6	7	Morgan County	UT	Hal Stauff	1987	2,420
287 4/8	45 4/8	44 5/8	35 6/8	6	6	Phillips County	MT	William P. Kirkman	1987	2,420
287 4/8	42 0/8	41 0/8	37 2/8	6	6	Phillips County	MT	Kenneth E. Ruzicka	1988	2,420
287 4/8	46 2/8	46 2/8	39 0/8	7	7	Rio Grande County	CO	Chris Hale	1997	2,420
287 4/8	43 6/8	49 1/8	34 4/8	6	6	Coconino County	AZ	Glen Dillehay	1997	2,420
287 3/8	45 2/8	43 2/8	29 3/8	6	7	Bighorn Mtns.	WY	Don Dvoroznak	1977	2,427
287 3/8	49 7/8	50 4/8	35 4/8	6	7	Coconino County	AZ	William P. Pate	1979	2,427
287 3/8	51 3/8	50 0/8	44 1/8	6	7	Beaverhead County	MT	Ronnie Everett	1982	2,427
287 3/8	50 7/8	50 1/8	39 3/8	6	6	Lane County	OR	Charles M. Reich	1991	2,427
287 3/8	50 2/8	50 6/8	37 3/8	6	6	Coconino County	AZ	Steven G. Rickner	1993	2,427
287 3/8	43 5/8	43 5/8	37 3/8	6	6	Otero County	NM	Terry Morrow	1995	2,427
287 3/8	47 7/8	47 1/8	34 5/8	6	6	Rio Arriba County	NM	Dr. Gary E. Palmer, D.C.	1997	2,427
287 3/8	40 7/8	39 3/8	43 7/8	6	6	Albany County	WY	Jerry Bowen	1998	2,427
287 2/8	41 4/8	41 4/8	29 2/8	6	6	San Isabel National Forest	CO	Richard L. Doman	1977	2,435
287 2/8	50 0/8	50 6/8	35 4/8	6	6	Grand County	CO	Robert Pitt	1978	2,435
287 2/8	42 6/8	41 6/8	32 0/8	6	6	Flathead County	MT	Rod Hickle	1982	2,435
287 2/8	45 6/8	46 7/8	35 6/8	6	6	Sublette County	WY	Ron A. Noble	1987	2,435
287 2/8	40 0/8	41 6/8	36 4/8	7	6	Larimer County	CO	Brent Byram	1989	2,435
287 2/8	46 4/8	46 5/8	32 4/8	5	6	Catron County	NM	Glenn Isler	1991	2,435
287 2/8	42 0/8	41 2/8	38 0/8	6	6	La Plata County	CO	Brook Jobes	1991	2,435
287 2/8	41 6/8	43 6/8	38 6/8	6	6	San Juan County	CO	William J. Farrell	1991	2,435
287 2/8	44 1/8	45 6/8	34 0/8	6	6	Sandoval County	NM	Joe H. Campbell	1992	2,435
287 2/8	43 2/8	43 2/8	36 1/8	7	6	Shoshone County	ID	Charles Gerhard	1992	2,435
287 2/8	42 3/8	43 0/8	33 2/8	6	7	Canmore	ALB	John Visscher	1995	2,435
287 1/8	46 0/8	45 6/8	37 3/8	6	7	Valley County	ID	L. Lombard/C. Rukkala	1980	2,446
287 1/8	44 1/8	44 0/8	32 7/8	6	6	Apache County	AZ	John A. Holcomb	1981	2,446
287 1/8	44 7/8	43 6/8	37 3/8	7	7	Sheridan County	WY	Richard Miller	1987	2,446
287 1/8	48 0/8	49 5/8	37 5/8	6	6	Washakie County	WY	Terry Kuhnert	1991	2,446
287 1/8	44 1/8	44 3/8	41 1/8	6	6	Uinta County	WY	Jason Rooney	1992	2,446
287 1/8	45 4/8	50 1/8	30 5/8	5	7	Coconino County	AZ	Jack W. Starnes	1993	2,446
287 1/8	44 3/8	45 0/8	37 3/8	6	6	Little Elbow River	ALB	Roger E. Meyer	1996	2,446
287 0/8	46 2/8	47 2/8	42 6/8	6	5	Three Sisters Mtn.	ALB	David R. Coupland	1986	2,453
286 7/8	42 4/8	42 0/8	40 5/8	6	6	Lewis & Clark County	MT	Stephen Tylinski	1979	2,454
286 7/8	48 2/8	46 4/8	36 7/8	6	6	Valley County	MT	Jim Seiler	1986	2,454
286 7/8	43 0/8	42 6/8	39 1/8	6	7	Fergus County	MT	Robert L. Little, Jr.	1989	2,454
286 7/8	49 2/8	48 0/8	33 7/8	7	6	Coconino County	AZ	Van Clark	1989	2,454
286 7/8	45 2/8	46 1/8	31 5/8	5	5	Park County	MT	George Kamps	1991	2,454
286 7/8	41 4/8	42 1/8	32 3/8	6	6	Rio Blanco County	CO	Roxie Kelly	1994	2,454
286 7/8	52 1/8	49 1/8	37 5/8	6	6	Catron County	NM	Ted Winchester	1995	2,454
286 7/8	48 5/8	48 2/8	35 5/8	6	6	Petroleum County	MT	Lee Moore	1996	2,454
286 6/8	46 5/8	47 0/8	36 2/8	6	6	Valley County	ID	Phil VonBargen	1982	2,462
286 6/8	49 7/8	47 2/8	35 2/8	6	6	Sandoval County	NM	Wilbern Glenn Hitt	1985	2,462
286 6/8	43 7/8	45 4/8	38 2/8	6	6	Mesa County	CO	Brad R. Davidson	1988	2,462
286 6/8	44 0/8	44 6/8	32 4/8	6	5	Petroleum County	MT	Scott Ballem	1992	2,462
286 6/8	45 3/8	43 3/8	35 0/8	6	6	Adams County	ID	Paul Kinberg	1996	2,462
286 6/8	47 3/8	44 2/8	34 0/8	6	6	Crook County	OR	Seth R. Michel	1997	2,462
286 5/8	42 1/8	42 0/8	39 3/8	6	6	Gallatin County	MT	Arnold Marolf	1977	2,468
286 5/8	43 4/8	42 4/8	39 5/8	6	6	Routt County	CO	Floyd Montgomery	1994	2,468
286 5/8	46 4/8	45 4/8	33 1/8	6	6	Otero County	NM	Todd Tschirhart	1996	2,468
286 4/8	43 1/8	44 1/8	39 4/8	6	6	Shoshone County	ID	Donald A. Young	1979	2,471
286 4/8	41 4/8	43 6/8	39 4/8	6	6	Clackamas County	OR	Larry D. Jones	1983	2,471
286 4/8	49 0/8	52 2/8	30 6/8	6	6	Coconino County	AZ	Bob Dooley	1984	2,471
286 4/8	44 0/8	44 2/8	36 0/8	6	6	Morgan County	UT	Robert G. Petersen	1987	2,471
286 4/8	40 5/8	40 5/8	35 6/8	6	6	Ravalli County	MT	Rod Osburn	1989	2,471
286 4/8	47 2/8	46 6/8	34 2/8	6	6	Boise County	ID	Todd Kane	1990	2,471
286 4/8	47 0/8	46 7/8	40 4/8	6	6	Phillips County	MT	Mark Meyer	1994	2,471
286 4/8	43 7/8	45 0/8	36 2/8	6	6	Idaho County	ID	David P. Lewis	1997	2,471
286 3/8	42 2/8	41 7/8	38 7/8	6	6	Rio Arriba County	NM	Jim Dougherty	1989	2,479
286 3/8	46 5/8	46 3/8	39 1/8	6	6	San Miguel County	NM	Jerry Hands	1996	2,479
286 3/8	44 1/8	44 5/8	35 3/8	6	6	Wheeler County	OR	Mark Winslow	1998	2,479
286 2/8	44 6/8	47 6/8	43 6/8	6	6	Uintah County	UT	Larry L. Parker	1990	2,482
286 2/8	44 6/8	44 2/8	38 0/8	6	6	La Plata County	CO	David A. Crom	1991	2,482
286 2/8	48 2/8	51 5/8	40 4/8	6	6	Rio Arriba County	NM	Eudane Vicenti	1993	2,482
286 2/8	45 3/8	46 2/8	34 6/8	7	6	Umatilla County	OR	Kurt Rosenberg	1994	2,482
286 2/8	44 4/8	49 0/8	36 0/8	6	6	Coconino County	AZ	Michael Harrell	1994	2,482
286 2/8	49 5/8	50 2/8	34 6/8	6	7	Crook County	OR	Eric Shawn Haney	1995	2,482
286 2/8	49 3/8	48 5/8	32 0/8	6	6	Johnson County	WY	Charles H. Sagner	1998	2,482
286 1/8	44 6/8	44 6/8	41 7/8	6	6	Mineral County	MT	Ken Drake	1981	2,489
286 1/8	46 6/8	49 5/8	38 3/8	6	6	Yakima County	WA	Raymond Gimlin	1984	2,489
286 1/8	41 7/8	41 5/8	40 0/8	6	7	Beaverhead County	MT	Shaun Twardoski	1987	2,489
286 1/8	48 2/8	49 4/8	33 1/8	6	6	Catron County	NM	Michael Travis	1992	2,489
286 1/8	47 2/8	46 0/8	37 3/8	6	6	Custer County	ID	Clayton L. Nielson	1996	2,489
286 1/8	42 4/8	42 4/8	38 4/8	6	7	Cypress Hills	ALB	Gary Weiss	1997	2,489
286 0/8	45 3/8	45 0/8	35 2/8	6	6	Lemhi County	ID	Steve Vetrhus	1990	2,495
286 0/8	45 6/8	45 5/8	31 6/8	6	6	Fergus County	MT	Tom Madden	1991	2,495

YELLOWSTONE "AMERICAN" ELK (TYPICAL ANTLERS)

Minimum Score 260 — Continued

SCORE	LENGTH OF MAIN BEAM R	LENGTH OF MAIN BEAM L	INSIDE SPREAD	NUMBER OF POINTS R	NUMBER OF POINTS L	AREA	STATE/PROVINCE	HUNTER'S NAME	DATE	RANK
286 0/8	43 0/8	42 0/8	44 2/8	6	6	Catron County	NM	Ken C. Taylor	1995	2,495
286 0/8	43 1/8	44 2/8	40 0/8	7	6	Fremont County	WY	Dwight Sempert	1996	2,495
285 7/8	45 7/8	46 0/8	42 3/8	6	6	Beaverhead County	MT	Lawrence J. Young	1996	2,499
285 6/8	46 1/8	47 4/8	30 6/8	6	6	Blaine County	ID	Andy Moore	1985	2,500
285 6/8	41 4/8	41 3/8	41 0/8	6	6	Crook County	OR	Scott Stomps	1988	2,500
285 6/8	40 0/8	39 5/8	35 2/8	5	5	Morgan County	UT	Rick C. Wilson	1996	2,500
285 6/8	40 4/8	42 2/8	32 4/8	7	6	Fergus County	MT	Donny Roy	1998	2,500
285 5/8	47 3/8	48 2/8	45 3/8	6	6	Lemhi County	ID	Dennis DesJardins	1969	2,504
285 5/8	42 7/8	39 5/8	44 3/8	6	6	Lemhi County	ID	Larry Cross	1981	2,504
285 5/8	45 3/8	45 1/8	37 3/8	6	7	Missoula County	MT	Paul Pasquariello	1982	2,504
285 5/8	44 4/8	43 6/8	34 3/8	6	6	Taos County	NM	Randal Church	1987	2,504
285 5/8	45 6/8	46 4/8	41 5/8	6	6	Coconino County	AZ	Robert V. Ruiz	1988	2,504
285 5/8	42 1/8	41 1/8	38 3/8	6	6	Larimer County	CO	George Banderia	1989	2,504
285 4/8	42 2/8	38 1/8	40 4/8	6	5	Catron County	NM	Eddie Collins	1986	2,510
285 4/8	43 6/8	44 4/8	41 2/8	6	6	Beaverhead County	MT	Mike Davis	1989	2,510
285 4/8	42 6/8	43 5/8	36 0/8	7	6	Catron County	NM	Les Norman	1990	2,510
285 4/8	46 1/8	39 5/8	40 4/8	7	6	Socorro County	NM	Gilbert Apodaca	1990	2,510
285 4/8	49 4/8	48 4/8	36 4/8	6	5	Coconino County	AZ	Harold L. Gibbons	1992	2,510
285 4/8	43 7/8	43 3/8	36 4/8	6	6	Jackson County	OR	Mike Kaiser	1993	2,510
285 4/8	43 4/8	44 4/8	31 2/8	6	6	Musselshell County	MT	Chris A. Hipple	1996	2,510
285 4/8	41 7/8	41 0/8	31 4/8	6	7	King County	WA	John R. Olson	1997	2,510
285 4/8	54 0/8	54 2/8	41 2/8	6	6	Musselshell County	MT	David W. Smith	1997	2,510
285 3/8	45 4/8	45 7/8	36 1/8	6	6	Umatilla County	OR	Bob Burggraff	1982	2,519
285 3/8	46 5/8	38 4/8	32 5/8	6	6	Caribou County	ID	Craig Hill	1988	2,519
285 3/8	46 3/8	45 5/8	37 1/8	6	6	Mineral County	CO	Douglas A. Ducote, Jr.	1990	2,519
285 3/8	43 2/8	45 4/8	35 5/8	6	6	Grant County	OR	Dean Pasche	1991	2,519
285 3/8	42 3/8	43 0/8	34 1/8	6	6	Lemhi County	ID	Bob Johnson	1997	2,519
285 3/8	45 6/8	46 0/8	31 2/8	7	7	Catron County	NM	William N. Thompson	1997	2,519
285 2/8	43 2/8	41 5/8	52 0/8	6	6	Albany County	WY	Douglas Cringan	1991	2,525
285 2/8	46 0/8	45 7/8	31 0/8	6	6	Caribou County	ID	John C. Miller	1991	2,525
285 2/8	46 6/8	47 5/8	42 2/8	6	6	Madison County	MT	Marvin J. Holt	1996	2,525
285 1/8	44 6/8	46 0/8	45 4/8	7	6	Sanders County	MT	Conrad Anderson	1983	2,528
285 1/8	46 6/8	46 7/8	34 3/8	6	5	Gallatin County	MT	Mark Heckel	1993	2,528
285 1/8	43 3/8	45 0/8	33 7/8	6	6	Missoula County	MT	Kirt Alan Tanner	1995	2,528
285 0/8	45 4/8	45 2/8	33 4/8	6	6	Fergus County	MT	James Southworth	1980	2,531
285 0/8	40 3/8	44 6/8	33 4/8	6	6	Umatilla County	OR	Ray A. Warren	1982	2,531
285 0/8	47 7/8	47 4/8	37 2/8	5	6	Sandoval County	NM	Robert L. Pagel	1987	2,531
285 0/8	51 3/8	49 7/8	33 0/8	6	6	Besa River	BC	Chris Barker	1993	2,531
285 0/8	42 2/8	43 3/8	42 4/8	5	5	Catron County	NM	Charles G. Collier, Jr.	1996	2,531
285 0/8	49 0/8	47 1/8	40 6/8	6	6	Johnson County	WY	Warren March, Jr.	1998	2,531
284 7/8	44 2/8	44 7/8	35 7/8	6	6	Lewis & Clark County	MT	Ron Granneman	1977	2,537
284 7/8	43 3/8	42 4/8	44 1/8	6	6	Malheur County	OR	Kent Kemble	1982	2,537
284 7/8	43 0/8	44 1/8	35 1/8	6	7	Catron County	NM	Dean Hamilton	1986	2,537
284 7/8	44 2/8	43 4/8	32 3/8	6	6	Sanders County	MT	Jim Regh, Jr.	1986	2,537
284 7/8	49 4/8	48 0/8	34 3/8	6	6	Judith Basin County	MT	Fred Reed	1995	2,537
284 7/8	44 5/8	44 0/8	41 3/8	6	6	Summit County	UT	Michael V. Arrant	1996	2,537
284 6/8	47 5/8	47 7/8	37 4/8	6	6	Marion County	OR	Jack Smith	1984	2,543
284 6/8	46 4/8	45 4/8	39 6/8	6	5	Coconino County	AZ	Dan Howe	1990	2,543
284 6/8	43 2/8	43 6/8	43 0/8	6	6	Socorro County	NM	Kenneth M. Thompson	1991	2,543
284 6/8	45 0/8	45 0/8	38 6/8	6	6	Grand County	CO	Carlis Stephens	1993	2,543
284 6/8	46 1/8	47 1/8	41 4/8	6	5	Rio Arriba County	NM	Kermit Evans	1993	2,543
284 5/8	44 0/8	45 0/8	33 7/8	5	7	Eagle County	CO	Stan Hunt	1981	2,548
284 5/8	41 1/8	40 6/8	37 3/8	6	6	Fergus County	MT	Frank R. Thompson	1991	2,548
284 5/8	42 0/8	40 2/8	37 7/8	6	6	Boundary County	ID	Steve Kamps	1994	2,548
284 5/8	49 6/8	48 0/8	36 1/8	6	6	Beaverhead County	MT	E. Lance Whary	1995	2,548
284 4/8	46 4/8	40 0/8	40 2/8	6	7	Gallatin National Forest	MT	Dennis Fishbaugher	1981	2,552
284 4/8	38 0/8	40 0/8	38 4/8	6	6	Garfield County	CO	Bruce Easterly	1985	2,552
284 4/8	47 6/8	50 0/8	36 6/8	6	6	Sheridan County	WY	Dave Moss	1995	2,552
284 4/8	44 7/8	44 3/8	38 2/8	6	6	King County	WA	Robert Wilber	1996	2,552
284 3/8	44 1/8	43 6/8	46 4/8	7	6	Clearwater County	ID	Neil Hinton	1983	2,556
284 3/8	44 0/8	41 2/8	35 7/8	6	6	Sierra County	NM	Gerald Lambert Lopez	1990	2,556
284 3/8	46 3/8	47 4/8	33 3/8	7	6	Coconino County	AZ	George Toot, Jr.	1990	2,556
284 3/8	46 7/8	45 0/8	36 5/8	6	6	Petroleum County	MT	Dale Herritz	1993	2,556
284 2/8	45 3/8	45 3/8	41 6/8	6	6	Mineral County	MT	Dwayne Garner	1982	2,560
284 2/8	47 7/8	46 3/8	34 4/8	6	6	Apache County	AZ	Ronald King	1985	2,560
284 2/8	49 3/8	48 0/8	37 2/8	6	6	Coconino County	AZ	John Toot	1990	2,560
284 2/8	48 3/8	47 6/8	37 0/8	6	6	Moffat County	CO	Frank Harper	1995	2,560
284 1/8	50 4/8	49 3/8	37 7/8	5	6	Clear Creek County	CO	Gary Christoffersen	1980	2,564
284 1/8	44 1/8	43 1/8	31 1/8	6	6	Sandoval County	NM	Steve Alderete	1986	2,564
284 1/8	48 2/8	47 2/8	34 5/8	7	6	Apache County	AZ	David N. Brilhart	1989	2,564
284 1/8	44 5/8	44 4/8	37 1/8	7	6	Fergus County	MT	Tom Madden	1990	2,564
284 1/8	50 0/8	44 7/8	45 3/8	7	7	Catron County	NM	Wayne W. Franzen	1992	2,564
284 1/8	47 7/8	45 2/8	32 7/8	6	6	Coconino County	AZ	Gerardo Saldivar	1995	2,564
284 0/8	49 4/8	46 7/8	42 2/8	6	6	Grant County	OR	Robert Gedlick	1981	2,570
284 0/8	41 3/8	43 6/8	39 4/8	6	7	Clearwater County	ID	Steve Richards	1986	2,570
284 0/8	49 6/8	48 4/8	37 2/8	6	6	Colfax County	NM	John L. Chapman	1989	2,570
284 0/8	45 7/8	48 4/8	34 6/8	6	6	Phillips County	MT	Henry J. Mischel	1990	2,570
284 0/8	46 5/8	45 6/8	33 7/8	7	6	Missoula County	MT	James W. Kelly	1994	2,570

YELLOWSTONE "AMERICAN" ELK (TYPICAL ANTLERS)

Minimum Score 260   Continued

SCORE	LENGTH OF MAIN BEAM R	LENGTH OF MAIN BEAM L	INSIDE SPREAD	NUMBER OF POINTS R	NUMBER OF POINTS L	AREA	STATE/PROVINCE	HUNTER'S NAME	DATE	RANK
284 0/8	43 0/8	43 5/8	39 6/8	6	6	Rio Blanco County	CO	Steve N. Wilson	1995	2,570
284 0/8	41 7/8	42 2/8	38 2/8	6	6	Catron County	NM	Doug Turner	1995	2,570
284 0/8	41 1/8	40 4/8	40 4/8	6	6	Coconino County	AZ	Chad Loy	1997	2,570
284 0/8	46 5/8	45 4/8	39 0/8	6	6	Idaho County	ID	Kenneth C. Prince	1998	2,570
283 7/8	47 5/8	47 2/8	33 3/8	6	6	Phillips County	MT	Doug Quilling	1979	2,579
283 7/8	42 6/8	43 5/8	33 5/8	6	6	Adams County	ID	Richard Fletcher	1987	2,579
283 7/8	44 2/8	45 0/8	31 7/8	6	6	Harney County	OR	Craig D. Hawkins	1991	2,579
283 7/8	49 3/8	49 2/8	43 7/8	6	7	Shoshone County	ID	Dennis Doyle	1993	2,579
283 7/8	45 1/8	44 0/8	33 5/8	6	6	Catron County	NM	William E. Fleshman	1996	2,579
283 7/8	42 0/8	42 2/8	41 7/8	6	6	Fremont County	WY	Dana Richardson	1996	2,579
283 7/8	48 5/8	48 7/8	36 1/8	7	7	Lemhi County	ID	Dave Batterton	1997	2,579
283 7/8	45 6/8	44 2/8	32 3/8	6	6	Gallatin County	MT	Kurt D. Rued	1998	2,579
283 7/8	43 5/8	43 6/8	33 7/8	6	6	Catron County	NM	Robert Duke	1998	2,579
283 6/8	46 0/8	45 4/8	40 6/8	6	6	Conejos County	CO	Arthur M. Davis	1974	2,588
283 6/8	47 3/8	49 0/8	36 6/8	6	6	Custer County	ID	Donald Johnson	1986	2,588
283 6/8	43 6/8	43 1/8	44 2/8	6	6	Mesa County	CO	Lawrence Clark	1987	2,588
283 6/8	46 2/8	45 1/8	39 0/8	6	6	Eagle County	CO	Keith Scheitzer	1990	2,588
283 6/8	48 2/8	48 6/8	35 4/8	6	6	Deschutes County	OR	Royce D. Nelson	1994	2,588
283 5/8	46 6/8	45 6/8	33 7/8	6	6	Hinsdale County	CO	Dennis Pistole	1990	2,593
283 4/8	40 3/8	40 2/8	39 6/8	6	6	Apache County	AZ	Sonny Turner	1985	2,594
283 4/8	49 1/8	47 7/8	39 2/8	6	6	Rio Arriba County	NM	Ray Milligan	1987	2,594
283 4/8	46 6/8	44 7/8	35 2/8	6	6	Park County	MT	Jon Okonek	1990	2,594
283 4/8	55 1/8	51 2/8	36 4/8	4	6	Gallatin County	MT	Rourk Price	1994	2,594
283 4/8	43 4/8	43 5/8	43 0/8	6	6	Douglas County	OR	Kevin Pearce	1997	2,594
283 3/8	42 0/8	44 4/8	31 7/8	6	6	Routt County	CO	Kevin Cole	1990	2,599
283 3/8	44 1/8	44 4/8	31 5/8	7	6	Routt County	CO	Randy Kendrick	1996	2,599
283 2/8	44 6/8	40 5/8	32 6/8	6	6	Clearwater County	ID	Jay Deones	1983	2,601
283 2/8	44 6/8	46 0/8	45 4/8	7	6	Lincoln County	NM	Steve Morgan	1986	2,601
283 2/8	37 4/8	38 0/8	43 2/8	6	6	Sandoval County	NM	Gary F. Bogner	1994	2,601
283 2/8	45 2/8	42 4/8	42 4/8	6	5	Mineral County	MT	William E. Sansom	1995	2,601
283 2/8	46 2/8	44 0/8	42 2/8	7	6	Douglas County	OR	Tobin J. Howell	1998	2,601
283 1/8	50 3/8	48 1/8	31 6/8	6	7	Bighorn Mtns.	WY	David Shoop	1979	2,606
283 1/8	41 2/8	40 6/8	38 7/8	6	7	Bergen	ALB	Sandy Watt	1991	2,606
283 1/8	41 6/8	40 7/8	32 1/8	7	7	Lincoln County	MT	Scott Westlund	1994	2,606
283 1/8	43 6/8	42 7/8	35 7/8	6	6	Sheridan County	WY	Dale Stahl	1995	2,606
283 1/8	44 3/8	46 6/8	38 1/8	6	6	Catron County	NM	Gary Rowles	1995	2,606
283 1/8	43 2/8	42 5/8	36 2/8	7	6	Catron County	NM	Gary D. Martinez	1996	2,606
283 0/8	42 7/8	44 5/8	41 0/8	6	6	Baker County	OR	Don Rajnus	1962	2,612
283 0/8	45 1/8	47 5/8	43 2/8	6	6	Grand County	CO	G. Fred Asbell	1973	2,612
283 0/8	48 4/8	46 4/8	36 2/8	6	6	Crook County	OR	Rick V. Herbst	1985	2,612
283 0/8	43 6/8	44 3/8	33 0/8	6	6	La Plata County	CO	David R. Hall	1985	2,612
283 0/8	42 2/8	43 3/8	35 5/8	7	6	Bear Lake County	ID	Barry James Shelton	1989	2,612
283 0/8	39 4/8	39 3/8	34 0/8	6	6	Fergus County	MT	Matthew McWilliams	1994	2,612
283 0/8	43 2/8	44 2/8	33 0/8	6	6	Catron County	NM	Rick L. Morley	1997	2,612
282 7/8	41 7/8	41 4/8	38 7/8	6	6	Wallowa County	OR	Steven R. Zollman	1986	2,619
282 7/8	47 3/8	47 4/8	37 7/8	7	6	Albany County	WY	Doug Cringan	1993	2,619
282 7/8	40 0/8	40 1/8	43 5/8	6	6	Pueblo County	CO	Steven Belport	1996	2,619
282 7/8	48 7/8	49 1/8	44 1/8	5	5	Apache County	AZ	Donald W. Williams	1996	2,619
282 6/8	39 7/8	40 2/8	42 3/8	6	6	Gallatin County	MT	Gregg L. Welch	1982	2,623
282 6/8	46 4/8	47 3/8	31 0/8	6	6	Colfax County	NM	Melvin Sloan	1990	2,623
282 6/8	45 4/8	45 1/8	31 4/8	6	6	Larimer County	CO	Thomas Langer	1991	2,623
282 6/8	39 3/8	42 7/8	35 6/8	6	6	Jumping Pound Creek	ALB	Archie Nesbitt	1992	2,623
282 6/8	50 7/8	49 5/8	33 6/8	7	6	Coconino County	AZ	Sheffield Jordan	1995	2,623
282 6/8	41 6/8	42 0/8	34 6/8	6	6	Beaverhead County	MT	Gary Dudden	1996	2,623
282 6/8	44 3/8	44 0/8	36 0/8	6	6	Otero County	NM	James T. Summers	1996	2,623
282 6/8	45 7/8	44 6/8	37 2/8	6	6	Petroleum County	MT	Chuck Adams	1997	2,623
282 5/8	50 0/8	47 2/8	42 1/8	7	6	Gallatin County	MT	Scott L. Koelzer	1979	2,631
282 5/8	47 1/8	44 7/8	39 7/8	6	6	Meagher County	MT	Pete Ecker	1980	2,631
282 5/8	39 2/8	43 7/8	33 3/8	5	6	Valley County	ID	Dennis Gratton	1983	2,631
282 5/8	42 6/8	43 0/8	42 7/8	6	6	Dolores County	CO	Mike Zion	1985	2,631
282 5/8	41 2/8	41 6/8	35 5/8	6	6	Mesa County	CO	Jeffrey Price	1989	2,631
282 5/8	47 0/8	43 4/8	24 3/8	6	6	Sheridan County	WY	Mike Barrett	1990	2,631
282 5/8	44 4/8	48 1/8	33 0/8	7	7	Catron County	NM	Bill Harmon	1992	2,631
282 5/8	42 7/8	40 3/8	35 7/8	6	6	Sanders County	MT	John H. Reynolds	1994	2,631
282 5/8	45 2/8	43 2/8	29 2/8	7	5	Catron County	NM	Mike W. Leonard	1995	2,631
282 4/8	32 6/8	39 2/8	36 6/8	6	6	Judith Basin County	MT	Jerome R. Parsons	1981	2,640
282 4/8	46 0/8	45 7/8	42 4/8	7	6	Custer County	ID	Joel C. Lenz	1986	2,640
282 4/8	40 7/8	40 7/8	37 0/8	6	6	Lemhi County	ID	Dan Hooper	1996	2,640
282 4/8	39 0/8	41 4/8	37 0/8	6	6	Granite County	MT	Gene Meisner	1997	2,640
282 3/8	44 2/8	41 0/8	38 1/8	6	6	Larimer County	CO	Dale E. Wenger	1981	2,644
282 3/8	44 6/8	46 2/8	34 3/8	7	6	Catron County	NM	Todd Zeuske	1987	2,644
282 3/8	44 4/8	44 4/8	35 1/8	6	6	Clearwater County	ID	Jerry Long	1994	2,644
282 3/8	41 7/8	42 5/8	39 5/8	6	6	Pierce County	WA	Mike Rumpza	1996	2,644
282 3/8	44 4/8	43 3/8	35 5/8	6	6	Moffat County	CO	Gary Hinaman	1998	2,644
282 3/8	42 4/8	44 4/8	33 3/8	6	6	Ravalli County	MT	Cory Johnson	1998	2,644
282 2/8	42 6/8	43 1/8	39 2/8	6	6	Wallowa County	OR	Neil Summers	1986	2,650
282 2/8	44 6/8	43 3/8	30 6/8	6	6	Harney County	OR	Steven J. Christensen	1990	2,650
282 2/8	39 4/8	38 4/8	34 6/8	6	6	Routt County	CO	Marion A. Heintz	1991	2,650

YELLOWSTONE "AMERICAN" ELK (TYPICAL ANTLERS)

Minimum Score 260

Continued

SCORE	LENGTH OF MAIN BEAM R	LENGTH OF MAIN BEAM L	INSIDE SPREAD	NUMBER OF POINTS R	NUMBER OF POINTS L	AREA	STATE/PROVINCE	HUNTER'S NAME	DATE	RANK
282 2/8	38 6/8	39 4/8	38 2/8	6	6	Petroleum County	MT	John Wooldridge	1996	2,650
282 1/8	45 4/8	44 7/8	44 7/8	5	6	Wallowa County	OR	Dale F. Story	1967	2,654
282 1/8	43 7/8	43 4/8	33 3/8	6	6	Teton County	MT	James Dean	1977	2,654
282 1/8	43 3/8	44 2/8	32 3/8	6	6	Sheridan County	WY	Mike Barrett	1983	2,654
282 1/8	40 7/8	41 6/8	40 5/8	7	6	Monterey County	CA	Chuck Adams	1990	2,654
282 1/8	45 4/8	42 5/8	35 1/8	6	6	Coconino County	AZ	Ronald G. Scherer	1990	2,654
282 1/8	43 6/8	41 0/8	32 5/8	6	6	Coconino County	AZ	Brett W. Bostian	1993	2,654
282 1/8	41 6/8	42 4/8	36 5/8	6	6	Valley County	ID	Darren W. Robbins	1993	2,654
282 1/8	45 2/8	47 3/8	37 1/8	6	6	Cibola County	NM	Robert H. Ennis	1995	2,654
282 0/8	53 7/8	53 5/8	34 0/8	6	6	Moffat County	CO	Clark Stokes	1985	2,662
282 0/8	44 0/8	45 0/8	37 0/8	6	6	Otero County	NM	John Bowman	1991	2,662
282 0/8	41 5/8	41 5/8	32 2/8	6	6	Lincoln County	NM	Gary E. Wright	1995	2,662
281 7/8	49 3/8	48 7/8	33 5/8	6	6	Costilla County	CO	Nathan Jones	1995	2,665
281 7/8	49 1/8	48 5/8	30 3/8	6	6	Coconino County	AZ	Steve Thurmon	1995	2,665
281 7/8	42 1/8	40 0/8	34 1/8	6	6	Catron County	NM	Daniel J. Loucks	1996	2,665
281 7/8	49 1/8	49 3/8	38 4/8	7	6	Coconino County	AZ	Eric Loeffler	1998	2,665
281 6/8	38 4/8	39 3/8	32 5/8	7	6	Powell County	MT	James L. Tillotson	1980	2,669
281 6/8	40 7/8	42 2/8	42 5/8	6	6	Missoula County	MT	Charles E. Hansen	1982	2,669
281 6/8	41 7/8	42 4/8	37 0/8	7	7	Lincoln County	MT	Mark Wachsman	1982	2,669
281 6/8	43 4/8	45 0/8	38 6/8	6	6	Custer County	ID	Vito Palazzolo	1983	2,669
281 6/8	43 7/8	44 3/8	36 0/8	6	6	Mesa County	CO	Don Boyles	1986	2,669
281 6/8	48 2/8	47 4/8	38 0/8	6	5	Greenlee County	AZ	Joseph Barry	1986	2,669
281 6/8	46 0/8	46 4/8	38 4/8	6	7	San Miguel County	CO	Tony Thomas	1988	2,669
281 6/8	35 3/8	48 0/8	41 5/8	5	7	Mesa County	CO	Don Boyles	1989	2,669
281 6/8	45 3/8	42 3/8	39 5/8	7	6	Wheeler County	OR	Roetta Williams	1990	2,669
281 5/8	44 6/8	45 6/8	39 3/8	6	6	Phillips County	MT	Robert Monhollon	1986	2,678
281 5/8	50 3/8	49 7/8	44 1/8	5	6	Latah County	ID	Mark Gottschalk	1992	2,678
281 5/8	42 4/8	42 0/8	36 1/8	6	6	Mesa County	CO	Ron M. O'Dell	1995	2,678
281 4/8	43 1/8	42 4/8	36 0/8	6	6	Sandoval County	NM	Robert L. Pagel	1988	2,681
281 4/8	47 4/8	48 3/8	40 0/8	6	6	Catron County	NM	Randy Lockhart	1991	2,681
281 4/8	48 6/8	49 6/8	30 0/8	6	6	Colfax County	NM	Howard L. Samit	1991	2,681
281 4/8	47 7/8	48 0/8	34 2/8	6	6	Crook County	OR	Hank Baxter	1998	2,681
281 3/8	45 1/8	45 4/8	36 3/8	6	6	Coconino County	AZ	Judy Shelton	1991	2,685
281 3/8	37 5/8	37 0/8	36 1/8	6	6	Gunnison County	CO	Doug McCauley	1992	2,685
281 3/8	42 1/8	41 1/8	37 5/8	6	6	Madison County	MT	Kurt D. Rued	1996	2,685
281 3/8	47 3/8	48 1/8	33 1/8	6	6	Coconino County	AZ	Donald C. Azlin	1997	2,685
281 3/8	45 1/8	45 5/8	31 3/8	6	6	Harney County	OR	Bob Daniels	1997	2,685
281 2/8	43 4/8	44 4/8	35 2/8	6	6	Powell County	MT	John Bottman	1986	2,690
281 2/8	47 5/8	46 4/8	34 6/8	6	6	Sublette County	WY	Shawn Witte	1993	2,690
281 2/8	41 6/8	41 3/8	34 0/8	6	6	Montezuma County	CO	Darrell Knierihm	1997	2,690
281 1/8	42 4/8	44 1/8	35 6/8	6	6	Larimer County	CO	Gary Galloway	1984	2,693
281 1/8	44 0/8	44 7/8	39 3/8	6	6	Shoshone County	ID	Dean C. Weyen	1988	2,693
281 1/8	41 3/8	42 4/8	37 5/8	7	7	Fergus County	MT	Tom Madden	1989	2,693
281 1/8	45 6/8	43 2/8	41 1/8	5	6	Malheur County	OR	Dennis H. Slagle	1992	2,693
281 1/8	44 4/8	45 0/8	36 3/8	6	6	Coconino County	AZ	Ron Warring	1994	2,693
281 0/8	43 2/8	43 4/8	38 0/8	6	6	Lemhi County	ID	A. Marc Whisler	1980	2,698
281 0/8	47 0/8	45 5/8	37 0/8	6	6	Baker County	OR	Robert L. Unruh	1982	2,698
281 0/8	44 4/8	49 0/8	36 6/8	6	6	Moffat County	CO	Lonny Vanatta	1984	2,698
281 0/8	42 6/8	42 1/8	34 2/8	6	6	Sublette County	WY	George E. Hall	1984	2,698
281 0/8	42 5/8	41 3/8	39 2/8	6	6	Lemhi County	ID	William Bullock, Sr.	1984	2,698
281 0/8	51 3/8	52 1/8	37 0/8	5	6	Apache County	AZ	Kendall R. Adair	1991	2,698
281 0/8	39 1/8	41 1/8	41 0/8	6	6	Lincoln County	WY	Tim Isaacson	1995	2,698
281 0/8	47 1/8	45 3/8	32 0/8	6	6	Clark County	NV	Dan Klebenow	1995	2,698
281 0/8	45 7/8	48 0/8	36 4/8	6	6	Catron County	NM	Steve Garner	1996	2,698
281 0/8	50 2/8	48 2/8	44 6/8	5	6	Custer County	ID	Lucien Rouse	1998	2,698
280 7/8	43 1/8	42 3/8	32 7/8	6	6	Johnson County	WY	Paul S. Warren	1979	2,708
280 7/8	45 7/8	41 0/8	38 1/8	6	6	Jefferson County	CO	David A. Graham	1991	2,708
280 7/8	42 7/8	43 1/8	33 3/8	6	6	Shoshone County	ID	Harold L. Sterner, Jr.	1991	2,708
280 7/8	46 3/8	44 0/8	34 3/8	6	6	Lemhi County	ID	M. G. Reynolds	1992	2,708
280 7/8	50 5/8	50 2/8	45 3/8	5	6	Apache County	AZ	Fred Clifford	1995	2,708
280 7/8	44 6/8	45 2/8	31 7/8	6	6	Pierce County	WA	William H. Wakeley	1997	2,708
280 6/8	48 5/8	47 0/8	38 2/8	6	6	Summit County	UT	John B. Rice, Jr.	1986	2,714
280 6/8	44 6/8	44 1/8	35 6/8	6	6	Yakima County	WA	Kevin Spencer	1989	2,714
280 6/8	40 7/8	45 4/8	43 4/8	6	6	Socorro County	NM	Eugene Flick	1994	2,714
280 6/8	42 4/8	42 6/8	36 2/8	6	6	Idaho County	ID	C. R. Wenger	1998	2,714
280 5/8	44 2/8	41 4/8	39 3/8	6	6	Coconino County	AZ	Randall S. MacMillan	1990	2,718
280 5/8	42 0/8	40 4/8	33 7/8	7	7	Rocky Mountain House	ALB	Terry Brew	1991	2,718
280 5/8	44 5/8	44 7/8	36 3/8	7	6	Catron County	NM	Eddie Claypool	1992	2,718
280 5/8	43 3/8	42 5/8	42 7/8	6	6	Bear Lake County	ID	Bryce W. Crane	1998	2,718
280 4/8	46 3/8	44 6/8	34 2/8	6	6	Boise County	ID	Robert D. Dowen	1991	2,722
280 4/8	44 5/8	43 4/8	35 6/8	6	6	Catron County	NM	Bob "Jake" Jacobsen	1992	2,722
280 4/8	41 4/8	43 0/8	30 2/8	6	6	Phillips County	MT	Jim Edmundson	1994	2,722
280 3/8	49 7/8	49 1/8	37 5/8	5	5	Rocky Mtn. House	ALB	Eugene Lopushinsky	1981	2,725
280 3/8	47 0/8	46 2/8	36 3/8	6	6	Clearwater County	ID	Tony Hyde	1986	2,725
280 3/8	50 4/8	53 5/8	37 7/8	6	6	Coconino County	AZ	David H. Scott	1995	2,725
280 2/8	39 2/8	37 3/8	33 6/8	6	5	Routt County	CO	D. F. Holt	1981	2,728
280 2/8	42 4/8	42 1/8	34 2/8	6	6	Beaverhead County	MT	Danny Moore	1987	2,728
280 2/8	44 5/8	43 2/8	36 2/8	6	6	La Plata County	CO	Jeff Tusing	1996	2,728

YELLOWSTONE "AMERICAN" ELK (TYPICAL ANTLERS)

Minimum Score 260 — Continued

SCORE	LENGTH OF MAIN BEAM R	LENGTH OF MAIN BEAM L	INSIDE SPREAD	NUMBER OF POINTS R	NUMBER OF POINTS L	AREA	STATE/ PROVINCE	HUNTER'S NAME	DATE	RANK
280 2/8	44 4/8	43 6/8	36 6/8	6	6	Valley County	ID	Shane D. Miller	1998	2,728
280 1/8	44 0/8	40 2/8	38 7/8	6	7	Coconino County	AZ	Scott Kellner	1983	2,732
280 1/8	39 3/8	40 0/8	29 7/8	6	6	Phillips County	MT	Thomas R. Herman	1987	2,732
280 1/8	51 4/8	48 0/8	40 5/8	6	6	Coconino County	AZ	Todd Hinkins	1989	2,732
280 1/8	44 5/8	39 0/8	34 0/8	6	7	Sanders County	MT	Gerry Mercer	1992	2,732
280 1/8	46 2/8	46 3/8	40 1/8	6	6	Wasco County	OR	Ben Munoz	1994	2,732
280 1/8	47 5/8	50 1/8	29 5/8	6	6	Coconino County	AZ	Darren Edward Burke	1998	2,732
280 1/8	48 0/8	46 1/8	42 3/8	6	6	Baker County	OR	Tana Thompson	1998	2,732
280 0/8	45 4/8	45 3/8	33 6/8	6	6	Rio Blanco County	CO	Rolland M. Esterline	1969	2,739
280 0/8	47 3/8	45 5/8	32 5/8	6	7	Judith Basin County	MT	Ronald Ozbun	1987	2,739
280 0/8	45 6/8	45 0/8	27 4/8	6	6	King County	WA	George Dan Feighner	1987	2,739
280 0/8	43 0/8	42 6/8	41 4/8	6	6	Washington County	ID	Randy Wilkins	1989	2,739
280 0/8	45 7/8	46 4/8	35 0/8	6	6	Park County	WY	David C. Ruhl	1992	2,739
280 0/8	47 7/8	49 7/8	35 6/8	6	6	Catron County	NM	Glen L. Dillehay	1993	2,739
279 7/8	43 6/8	44 0/8	40 2/8	7	6	Valley County	ID	Kenneth A Hyde	1983	2,745
279 7/8	40 1/8	37 6/8	32 6/8	7	9	Umatilla County	OR	Kurt Rosenberg	1995	2,745
279 6/8	45 7/8	44 2/8	33 0/8	6	6	Valley County	ID	Phil Barton	1989	2,747
279 6/8	44 6/8	43 2/8	34 0/8	6	6	Catron County	NM	Abe Dimas, Jr.	1993	2,747
279 6/8	40 6/8	40 3/8	40 0/8	5	5	Colfax County	NM	David C. Lighty	1996	2,747
279 6/8	43 6/8	42 7/8	39 0/8	6	6	Archuleta County	CO	Dr. Vernon Ray	1996	2,747
279 6/8	44 1/8	44 1/8	31 6/8	6	6	Valley County	MT	Christian Duane Gartner	1997	2,747
279 6/8	43 7/8	44 0/8	41 0/8	6	6	Blaine County	ID	Don Torbert, Sr.	1998	2,747
279 5/8	41 2/8	42 5/8	41 1/8	6	6	Sheridan County	WY	Mike Barrett	1987	2,753
279 5/8	43 4/8	45 6/8	33 7/8	6	6	Catron County	NM	John Wirth, Jr.	1991	2,753
279 5/8	41 5/8	41 5/8	39 5/8	6	6	Sublette County	WY	Dale L. White	1995	2,753
279 5/8	43 1/8	43 0/8	38 1/8	6	6	Fremont County	WY	Dean P. Simmons	1996	2,753
279 5/8	46 5/8	45 6/8	42 7/8	6	6	Custer County	ID	Lars L. Colberg	1998	2,753
279 4/8	41 2/8	39 0/8	33 0/8	6	6	Wallowa County	OR	James R. Brackenbury	1970	2,758
279 4/8	46 5/8	45 0/8	40 4/8	6	5	Idaho County	ID	Richard C. Nichols	1973	2,758
279 4/8	41 6/8	40 6/8	33 2/8	6	6	Clearwater County	ID	John Burns, Sr.	1982	2,758
279 4/8	41 7/8	41 5/8	38 0/8	5	5	Duck Mtns.	MAN	Harvey Gagne	1995	2,758
279 4/8	40 6/8	41 5/8	37 0/8	6	6	Petroleum County	MT	Carlton DeFoor	1997	2,758
279 3/8	45 6/8	45 1/8	39 1/8	6	6	Phillips County	MT	Dave Zimmer	1983	2,763
279 2/8	45 2/8	46 0/8	34 0/8	6	6	Clearwater County	ID	Don West	1981	2,764
279 2/8	48 7/8	46 5/8	33 6/8	6	5	Clear Creek County	CO	Ken Shelton	1986	2,764
279 2/8	46 2/8	45 6/8	28 4/8	6	6	Phillips County	MT	Bill Rackley	1986	2,764
279 2/8	42 1/8	46 5/8	29 2/8	6	7	Missoula County	MT	Jim B. Bradford	1987	2,764
279 2/8	42 1/8	40 7/8	31 6/8	6	6	Grant County	NM	David H. Walske	1991	2,764
279 2/8	41 3/8	43 0/8	38 0/8	5	5	Custer County	ID	Bruce Miller	1994	2,764
279 1/8	45 2/8	44 6/8	35 5/8	6	6	Coconino County	AZ	Todd B. Rice	1990	2,770
279 1/8	48 2/8	45 2/8	45 5/8	5	6	Elko County	NV	Jerry Vega	1998	2,770
279 0/8	44 6/8	44 5/8	32 4/8	7	6	Las Animas County	CO	Ray Ramirez	1976	2,772
279 0/8	41 1/8	39 5/8	36 6/8	6	6	Caribou County	ID	Randy J. Stephens	1979	2,772
279 0/8	43 2/8	40 6/8	40 4/8	6	6	Cascade County	MT	Rick Holzheimer	1991	2,772
279 0/8	47 1/8	46 0/8	35 4/8	6	6	Coconino County	AZ	Russ Pearson	1991	2,772
279 0/8	45 4/8	44 0/8	40 6/8	6	6	Granite County	MT	Garret Decker	1991	2,772
279 0/8	44 3/8	44 7/8	38 5/8	7	7	Custer County	ID	Jeff A. Buck	1993	2,772
279 0/8	42 6/8	43 6/8	37 4/8	6	6	Sheridan County	WY	Mike Barrett	1994	2,772
279 0/8	44 3/8	43 4/8	44 2/8	5	6	Park County	MT	George Kamps	1996	2,772
279 0/8	46 6/8	46 1/8	31 4/8	6	6	Wallowa County	OR	Cameron R. Hanes	1997	2,772
279 0/8	42 4/8	45 1/8	33 2/8	8	7	Catron County	NM	Richard L. Peterson, Jr.	1997	2,772
279 0/8	43 4/8	43 4/8	41 5/8	7	6	Valley County	ID	Frank B. Gettig	1998	2,772
278 7/8	45 7/8	45 6/8	33 3/8	6	6	Apache County	AZ	Marvin W. Wuertz	1989	2,783
278 7/8	42 5/8	40 1/8	44 7/8	5	6	Los Alamos County	NM	Stevan R. Weekly	1997	2,783
278 7/8	48 7/8	46 5/8	34 5/8	6	7	Petroleum County	MT	Scott J. Strese	1997	2,783
278 6/8	43 5/8	43 7/8	35 2/8	6	6	Cascade County	MT	Norman T. Frusti	1979	2,786
278 6/8	42 3/8	39 0/8	36 4/8	6	6	Park County	MT	George Kamps	1984	2,786
278 6/8	44 0/8	44 6/8	33 2/8	6	6	Sevier County	UT	Dall Dimick	1987	2,786
278 6/8	40 4/8	43 0/8	35 0/8	6	6	Grant County	OR	Dennis Marshall	1989	2,786
278 6/8	46 7/8	45 3/8	38 2/8	6	6	Clearwater County	ID	Bryan Ohlms	1990	2,786
278 6/8	38 6/8	39 4/8	35 2/8	7	7	Phillips County	MT	Lee D. Laeupple	1992	2,786
278 5/8	46 0/8	46 5/8	34 7/8	6	6	Rio Arriba County	NM	Michael J. Cullen	1987	2,792
278 5/8	45 4/8	50 5/8	42 5/8	6	6	Sierra County	NM	David Swisher	1991	2,792
278 5/8	46 0/8	44 1/8	36 3/8	6	6	Idaho County	ID	Greg Walter	1995	2,792
278 4/8	45 4/8	43 4/8	31 4/8	6	6	Cascade County	MT	David Holloway	1983	2,795
278 4/8	42 5/8	42 0/8	38 6/8	6	6	Socorro County	NM	Randall McAfee	1989	2,795
278 4/8	51 2/8	51 1/8	32 4/8	6	7	Navajo County	AZ	William R. "Randy" Vaughn	1990	2,795
278 4/8	46 3/8	45 5/8	33 0/8	6	6	Valley County	MT	Myran Gartner	1991	2,795
278 4/8	44 5/8	41 5/8	35 0/8	6	6	Catron County	NM	David L. Willis	1992	2,795
278 4/8	43 2/8	44 2/8	33 4/8	6	6	Rio Arriba County	NM	Alfred Vigil	1993	2,795
278 4/8	48 7/8	49 3/8	38 0/8	6	6	Missoula County	MT	Andrew J. Kelly	1993	2,795
278 4/8	43 6/8	44 1/8	32 0/8	6	6	Grant County	OR	Robert J. Schriever	1997	2,795
278 4/8	43 0/8	41 3/8	36 2/8	6	6	Baker County	OR	Mike Raney	1998	2,795
278 3/8	48 7/8	44 0/8	35 7/8	6	6	Madison County	MT	Jerome E. Skinner, Jr.	1992	2,804
278 3/8	51 0/8	51 0/8	39 3/8	6	6	Moffat County	CO	Paul E. Miller	1994	2,804
278 3/8	41 7/8	44 3/8	30 1/8	6	6	Phillips County	MT	Darwin J. Roberts	1998	2,804
278 2/8	46 5/8	46 0/8	33 0/8	6	6	Blaine County	ID	Larry R. Newton	1993	2,807
278 2/8	42 6/8	42 3/8	39 6/8	6	6	Camas County	ID	Russell R. Scharman	1996	2,807

YELLOWSTONE "AMERICAN" ELK (TYPICAL ANTLERS)

Minimum Score 260

Continued

SCORE	LENGTH OF MAIN BEAM R	LENGTH OF MAIN BEAM L	INSIDE SPREAD	NUMBER OF POINTS R	NUMBER OF POINTS L	AREA	STATE/PROVINCE	HUNTER'S NAME	DATE	RANK
278 2/8	41 5/8	41 6/8	40 4/8	6	6	Mora County	NM	Mike Landmesser	1997	2,807
278 2/8	40 4/8	39 4/8	36 0/8	6	6	Idaho County	ID	Mike Nowaczyk	1998	2,807
278 1/8	42 3/8	43 0/8	38 3/8	6	6	Ravalli County	MT	Michael J. Nielsen	1992	2,811
278 1/8	44 7/8	44 2/8	39 5/8	6	6	Beaverhead County	MT	Danny L. Moore	1993	2,811
278 1/8	42 4/8	42 2/8	32 1/8	6	6	Coconino County	AZ	Robert J. "Bob" Cates	1996	2,811
278 0/8	48 2/8	44 3/8	47 0/8	6	6	Lincoln County	MT	Bud Journey	1978	2,814
278 0/8	41 2/8	43 1/8	37 2/8	6	6	Grant County	OR	Clayton Severin	1984	2,814
278 0/8	46 1/8	46 5/8	37 4/8	5	6	Rio Arriba County	NM	Fred Vigil	1994	2,814
278 0/8	45 3/8	45 6/8	37 6/8	6	6	Coconino County	AZ	Ricardo Saldivar	1994	2,814
278 0/8	46 2/8	49 1/8	35 2/8	6	6	Grant County	NM	Scott Maloney	1996	2,814
278 0/8	47 3/8	46 3/8	36 4/8	6	6	McKinley County	NM	Jim Gresham	1996	2,814
277 7/8	42 2/8	41 7/8	36 3/8	6	6	Beaverhead County	MT	Gary Palmer	1990	2,820
277 7/8	45 5/8	45 4/8	36 7/8	6	6	Caribou County	ID	Tyler Martinsen	1994	2,820
277 6/8	39 0/8	38 6/8	37 0/8	7	7	High River	ALB	Andrew Schrock	1987	2,822
277 6/8	47 2/8	47 6/8	34 4/8	6	6	Big Horn County	WY	Robert Partridge	1992	2,822
277 6/8	48 0/8	45 5/8	33 4/8	7	6	Fremont County	WY	Guy LeMonnier, Jr.	1993	2,822
277 6/8	45 7/8	46 7/8	39 6/8	6	6	Catron County	NM	Jeff Persenaire	1998	2,822
277 5/8	47 1/8	45 6/8	38 1/8	6	6	Sandoval County	NM	David V. Collis	1983	2,826
277 5/8	45 7/8	44 4/8	33 5/8	6	7	Catron County	NM	Donny Guest	1992	2,826
277 5/8	44 1/8	44 0/8	30 1/8	6	6	Archuleta County	CO	Ed DeYoung	1995	2,826
277 4/8	45 2/8	47 4/8	38 0/8	6	6	La Plata County	CO	Andy White	1980	2,829
277 4/8	43 4/8	45 2/8	37 0/8	6	6	Larimer County	CO	Bruce Bowman	1985	2,829
277 4/8	44 3/8	43 3/8	30 0/8	7	7	Caribou County	ID	Royce Brown	1986	2,829
277 4/8	42 4/8	41 1/8	36 4/8	6	6	Clearwater County	ID	Fred Gill	1994	2,829
277 4/8	43 0/8	41 3/8	34 6/8	6	6	Lawrence County	SD	Larry J. Hannan	1996	2,829
277 4/8	43 3/8	46 1/8	38 6/8	6	6	Fremont County	ID	Wayne M. Jensen	1998	2,829
277 3/8	37 7/8	39 2/8	37 3/8	6	6	Greenlee County	AZ	Clifford White	1984	2,835
277 3/8	42 1/8	43 0/8	38 1/8	6	6	Larimer County	CO	Forrest McMichael	1987	2,835
277 3/8	44 0/8	44 5/8	33 2/8	7	6	Lodgepole	ALB	Marvin Dusterhoft	1990	2,835
277 3/8	39 5/8	39 5/8	40 3/8	6	6	Shoshone County	ID	Russell A. Keaton	1993	2,835
277 3/8	43 7/8	43 0/8	33 7/8	6	6	Fremont County	WY	Kyle H. Frandsen	1994	2,835
277 3/8	43 4/8	42 0/8	39 1/8	6	6	Catron County	NM	Frank S. Noska IV	1998	2,835
277 2/8	47 0/8	47 3/8	40 2/8	6	6	Bonneville County	ID	Jerry Clark	1979	2,841
277 2/8	41 1/8	39 7/8	40 2/8	6	7	Fergus County	MT	Ray Lundin	1982	2,841
277 2/8	38 6/8	38 6/8	38 2/8	6	6	Colfax County	NM	Kenny Brice Poulson	1988	2,841
277 2/8	39 4/8	37 3/8	34 0/8	5	6	Clearwater County	ID	Thomas Storr	1989	2,841
277 2/8	42 4/8	43 3/8	37 0/8	6	6	Granite County	MT	Christian L. Frank	1992	2,841
277 2/8	43 5/8	44 6/8	31 2/8	6	6	Coconino County	AZ	Gregg Tanner	1994	2,841
277 2/8	41 2/8	42 7/8	34 0/8	6	6	Phillips County	MT	Casey Lyle Prell	1998	2,841
277 1/8	41 7/8	39 3/8	42 5/8	6	6	Clearwater County	ID	Jon Skinner	1988	2,848
277 1/8	48 4/8	48 6/8	37 7/8	6	6	Valley County	ID	Brian Holbrook	1993	2,848
277 1/8	44 1/8	42 1/8	34 5/8	6	6	Columbia County	WA	Shane Broeske	1997	2,848
277 1/8	46 0/8	43 3/8	34 5/8	6	6	Valley County	ID	Erik I. Jacobs	1998	2,848
277 1/8	39 5/8	40 6/8	39 5/8	6	6	Fremont County	ID	Merrill Huntsman	1998	2,848
277 0/8	43 0/8	43 0/8	31 6/8	6	6	Grant County	OR	Andy Day	1981	2,853
277 0/8	40 4/8	40 3/8	32 0/8	6	6	Cascade County	MT	David Yaeger	1983	2,853
277 0/8	39 0/8	40 3/8	35 4/8	6	6	Flathead County	MT	Jerry L. Wootan	1984	2,853
277 0/8	43 1/8	42 4/8	36 0/8	6	6	Sanders County	MT	Chuck Adams	1985	2,853
277 0/8	45 6/8	46 4/8	44 4/8	5	5	Coconino County	AZ	Steve Neuberger	1993	2,853
277 0/8	40 3/8	40 1/8	39 4/8	6	6	Pierce County	WA	Joe Lilley	1994	2,853
277 0/8	47 0/8	47 0/8	39 6/8	6	6	Custer County	ID	Shawn Perry	1996	2,853
277 0/8	43 3/8	42 6/8	30 4/8	6	6	Catron County	NM	Thomas Guetzke	1998	2,853
276 7/8	46 4/8	46 1/8	38 1/8	6	7	Pitkin County	CO	Byron S. Donahue	1981	2,861
276 7/8	47 6/8	47 2/8	26 5/8	7	6	Rio Arriba County	NM	Michael G. Fierro	1982	2,861
276 7/8	42 2/8	41 3/8	37 1/8	6	6	Benewah County	ID	Greg DesLaurier	1984	2,861
276 7/8	46 1/8	45 4/8	33 5/8	6	6	Grant County	OR	Gary Nyden	1984	2,861
276 7/8	49 0/8	46 4/8	33 5/8	6	6	Idaho County	ID	Charles Edward Steve	1995	2,861
276 6/8	45 0/8	44 1/8	34 4/8	6	6	Lincoln County	MT	Jerry Brown	1982	2,866
276 6/8	45 2/8	45 0/8	36 2/8	6	6	Taos County	NM	Calvin Farner	1986	2,866
276 6/8	42 0/8	45 0/8	35 0/8	6	6	Carbon County	UT	Kenneth D. Evans	1989	2,866
276 6/8	40 7/8	38 0/8	31 4/8	6	6	Larimer County	CO	Todd Johnson	1990	2,866
276 6/8	44 5/8	45 3/8	32 4/8	6	6	Archuleta County	CO	Don Myers	1995	2,866
276 6/8	42 6/8	43 4/8	29 6/8	6	6	Colfax County	NM	Jack Dell	1996	2,866
276 6/8	41 2/8	45 5/8	39 4/8	6	6	Skamania County	WA	Melody R. Newman	1998	2,866
276 5/8	45 7/8	45 1/8	32 5/8	6	6	Belmont Creek	MT	Max G. Bauer, Jr.	1980	2,873
276 5/8	46 6/8	45 5/8	35 1/8	6	6	Teton County	MT	William McRae	1982	2,873
276 5/8	44 4/8	43 4/8	36 5/8	6	6	Bear Lake County	ID	Troy Hymas	1984	2,873
276 5/8	39 6/8	37 2/8	31 3/8	6	6	Custer County	ID	Donald Brydon	1994	2,873
276 5/8	43 0/8	41 7/8	34 5/8	6	6	Beaverhead County	MT	Mark J. Sherick	1994	2,873
276 5/8	43 7/8	46 2/8	31 1/8	6	6	Catron County	NM	Neal Childers	1998	2,873
276 4/8	41 1/8	40 2/8	35 0/8	6	6	Rio Blanco County	CO	Tom O. Milligan	1976	2,879
276 4/8	42 3/8	42 2/8	34 0/8	6	6	Gallatin County	MT	George Kamps	1981	2,879
276 4/8	46 6/8	50 1/8	38 4/8	6	5	Clearwater County	ID	Marvin J. Gerking	1983	2,879
276 4/8	43 0/8	42 4/8	33 0/8	6	6	Shoshone County	ID	Stephen P. Rapier	1983	2,879
276 4/8	47 2/8	44 3/8	36 0/8	6	6	Navajo County	AZ	Randy L. Hill	1991	2,879
276 4/8	39 1/8	37 5/8	36 2/8	6	6	Morgan County	UT	Rob Helfrich	1992	2,879
276 4/8	44 5/8	41 3/8	36 6/8	7	6	Marion County	OR	Jack T. Hinkle	1994	2,879
276 4/8	45 0/8	45 4/8	34 4/8	6	6	Jackson County	CO	Tom Kelley	1995	2,879

YELLOWSTONE "AMERICAN" ELK (TYPICAL ANTLERS)

Minimum Score 260 — Continued

SCORE	LENGTH OF MAIN BEAM R	LENGTH OF MAIN BEAM L	INSIDE SPREAD	NUMBER OF POINTS R	NUMBER OF POINTS L	AREA	STATE/ PROVINCE	HUNTER'S NAME	DATE	RANK
276 4/8	44 2/8	44 5/8	36 0/8	6	6	Park County	WY	Paul Pearson	1996	2,879
276 4/8	45 6/8	46 2/8	33 6/8	6	6	Flathead County	MT	Stephan Secrest	1997	2,879
276 3/8	45 6/8	47 2/8	33 1/8	5	5	McKinley County	NM	Shawn R. Bloom	1993	2,889
276 2/8	50 4/8	44 2/8	40 6/8	6	7	Fremont County	ID	Rene' Harrop	1981	2,890
276 2/8	43 5/8	44 2/8	38 4/8	5	6	Sandoval County	NM	Rett Kelly	1987	2,890
276 2/8	45 6/8	45 7/8	35 5/8	6	5	Park County	WY	Mike Hamra	1993	2,890
276 2/8	41 2/8	41 1/8	33 2/8	6	7	Archuleta County	CO	Bruce Morris	1995	2,890
276 2/8	46 4/8	47 2/8	31 2/8	6	6	Coconino County	AZ	Bob Dawson	1995	2,890
276 2/8	43 5/8	46 0/8	37 0/8	6	6	Coconino County	AZ	Kimball Taylor	1998	2,890
276 1/8	42 3/8	38 7/8	41 7/8	6	6	Saguache County	CO	Jerry Woodland	1977	2,896
276 1/8	44 4/8	45 7/8	33 1/8	7	6	Caribou County	ID	Irv Wanlass	1981	2,896
276 1/8	47 2/8	47 6/8	39 3/8	6	7	Greenlee County	AZ	Joel W. Hampton	1993	2,896
276 0/8	42 2/8	44 6/8	33 4/8	6	6	Teller County	CO	Dr. David B. Johnson	1983	2,899
276 0/8	42 5/8	42 6/8	33 2/8	6	6	Morgan County	UT	Hugh H. Hogle	1989	2,899
276 0/8	41 7/8	41 0/8	30 6/8	6	6	Lincoln County	WY	Rodney L. Dehart	1991	2,899
276 0/8	40 4/8	41 1/8	32 4/8	6	6	Routt County	CO	Charles DeLong	1991	2,899
276 0/8	45 6/8	45 6/8	38 3/8	6	5	Sheridan County	WY	Fred P. Rybarz, Sr.	1993	2,899
276 0/8	39 4/8	39 7/8	31 7/8	7	6	Archuleta County	CO	Dr. Robert Speegle	1993	2,899
276 0/8	42 1/8	42 4/8	44 6/8	5	5	Catron County	NM	Kenny E. Leo	1994	2,899
275 7/8	47 1/8	46 5/8	39 1/8	6	6	Madison County	MT	Edward Wright	1990	2,906
275 6/8	45 6/8	44 2/8	34 0/8	6	6	Valley County	ID	David G. Nagelmann	1986	2,907
275 6/8	48 4/8	48 3/8	36 4/8	6	7	Teton County	MT	Keith Aune	1988	2,907
275 6/8	44 7/8	43 5/8	30 4/8	6	6	Idaho County	ID	Jerry Vega	1989	2,907
275 6/8	49 2/8	50 4/8	36 2/8	6	5	Phillips County	MT	Mark L. Meyer	1993	2,907
275 6/8	40 6/8	42 2/8	36 6/8	6	6	Catron County	NM	John D. Lowe	1995	2,907
275 6/8	42 7/8	40 1/8	37 2/8	6	6	Lemhi County	ID	Paul Gritton	1998	2,907
275 6/8	44 5/8	44 4/8	38 4/8	6	6	Lawrence County	SD	Scott Guffey	1998	2,907
275 5/8	42 1/8	43 6/8	38 7/8	6	6	Ravalli County	MT	Rod Osburn	1980	2,914
275 5/8	45 4/8	44 4/8	34 7/8	6	6	Moffat County	CO	Glenn Pritchard	1988	2,914
275 5/8	46 2/8	45 1/8	35 1/8	6	6	Sheridan County	WY	Ron Niziolek	1990	2,914
275 5/8	46 4/8	44 2/8	33 1/8	6	6	Coconino County	AZ	Allen Farnsworth	1990	2,914
275 4/8	35 6/8	40 2/8	33 6/8	6	6	Valley County	MT	Andy Hicks	1983	2,918
275 4/8	48 5/8	48 7/8	34 2/8	6	6	Clackamas County	OR	Rip H. Caswell	1986	2,918
275 4/8	43 6/8	42 4/8	33 2/8	6	6	Catron County	NM	James E. Willard	1994	2,918
275 4/8	40 7/8	38 4/8	39 2/8	6	7	Catron County	NM	Bob Bruss	1994	2,918
275 3/8	47 0/8	46 5/8	34 1/8	5	6	Carbon County	WY	James T. Luxem	1992	2,922
275 3/8	44 2/8	46 4/8	30 1/8	5	6	Rich County	UT	Rick Wilson	1993	2,922
275 2/8	44 0/8	44 3/8	30 6/8	6	6	Missoula County	MT	John A. Reiter	1990	2,924
275 2/8	43 5/8	44 5/8	37 6/8	6	6	Grant County	OR	Tim Hall	1990	2,924
275 2/8	50 3/8	49 5/8	40 0/8	6	6	Wheeler County	OR	Anthony DiMaggio	1995	2,924
275 2/8	41 6/8	42 3/8	35 6/8	6	6	Clearwater County	ID	Mark E. Kuechenmeister	1996	2,924
275 2/8	40 7/8	43 1/8	28 0/8	6	6	Colfax County	NM	Ralph E. Johnson, Jr.	1997	2,924
275 2/8	40 7/8	41 0/8	40 6/8	6	6	Petroleum County	MT	Thomas J. Madden	1998	2,924
275 1/8	42 6/8	39 6/8	39 7/8	6	6	Bonner County	ID	Ren Hone	1980	2,930
275 1/8	46 6/8	44 6/8	28 7/8	6	6	Idaho County	ID	Hollis Sapp, Jr.	1986	2,930
275 1/8	44 4/8	45 6/8	34 7/8	6	6	Jefferson County	MT	Ron Scharf	1986	2,930
275 1/8	38 1/8	39 1/8	35 6/8	6	7	San Juan County	NM	Gerry J. Johnson	1988	2,930
275 1/8	45 5/8	44 2/8	28 1/8	6	6	Rio Arriba County	NM	Terry Karl	1989	2,930
275 1/8	46 0/8	47 0/8	39 5/8	5	6	Socorro County	NM	Randall C. Barnes	1990	2,930
275 1/8	42 6/8	43 1/8	39 1/8	7	6	Jackson County	CO	Kevin Primrose	1992	2,930
275 1/8	44 4/8	45 2/8	41 5/8	6	6	Wallowa County	OR	Sam Shuh	1992	2,930
275 0/8	43 1/8	44 6/8	33 0/8	7	6	Garfield County	MT	Frank Kasten	1982	2,938
275 0/8	45 1/8	42 3/8	33 4/8	6	6	Conejos County	CO	Dewey Brown	1982	2,938
275 0/8	45 3/8	45 5/8	38 3/8	6	7	Madison County	ID	Shayne L. Ard	1982	2,938
275 0/8	45 2/8	44 6/8	36 6/8	6	6	Missoula County	MT	Terry See	1985	2,938
275 0/8	44 4/8	42 2/8	36 0/8	6	6	Eagle County	CO	Kevin Scott	1994	2,938
275 0/8	44 0/8	44 6/8	32 0/8	6	6	Pennington County	SD	Dave Hicks	1997	2,938
275 0/8	41 6/8	40 6/8	32 6/8	6	6	Routt County	CO	Keith A. Trout	1998	2,938
274 7/8	43 5/8	43 4/8	37 1/8	6	6	Flathead County	MT	Dean F. Cole	1985	2,945
274 7/8	43 7/8	42 7/8	35 5/8	6	6	Fremont County	ID	Shawn Allgood	1995	2,945
274 7/8	45 4/8	43 2/8	36 7/8	5	5	Coconino County	AZ	Tony Opheim	1995	2,945
274 7/8	48 7/8	49 3/8	36 7/8	6	6	Catron County	NM	William B. Crum, Jr.	1996	2,945
274 7/8	44 2/8	45 3/8	32 1/8	6	6	Eagle County	CO	Mark Martin	1997	2,945
274 6/8	42 4/8	41 1/8	29 7/8	7	7	Rimbey	ALB	Clifford Hill	1984	2,950
274 6/8	44 0/8	39 6/8	41 4/8	5	5	Navajo County	AZ	Troy Eiffert	1988	2,950
274 6/8	44 0/8	44 3/8	32 4/8	6	6	Union County	OR	Gene Macomb	1990	2,950
274 6/8	35 0/8	42 2/8	35 2/8	5	6	Larimer County	CO	Troy Freed	1993	2,950
274 6/8	39 3/8	35 7/8	33 0/8	6	6	Morgan County	UT	Poncho McCoy	1996	2,950
274 5/8	39 6/8	40 1/8	35 7/8	6	6	Coconino County	AZ	Paul E. Wells	1992	2,955
274 5/8	44 1/8	43 3/8	36 1/8	6	6	Mesa County	CO	Ron Stanley	1993	2,955
274 5/8	39 6/8	38 6/8	37 7/8	6	6	Jackson County	CO	John Fuller	1994	2,955
274 5/8	51 6/8	52 7/8	38 7/8	6	6	Coconino County	AZ	James E. Richards III	1995	2,955
274 5/8	45 0/8	44 0/8	40 3/8	6	5	Yavapai County	AZ	Danny Womack	1996	2,955
274 4/8	44 1/8	43 5/8	37 2/8	5	5	Sandoval County	NM	Dave McInroy	1988	2,960
274 4/8	46 1/8	51 3/8	34 0/8	6	6	Stevens County	WA	Dusty N. Rieckers	1992	2,960
274 3/8	41 3/8	42 0/8	31 1/8	6	6	Saguache County	CO	Jerry Woodland	1973	2,962
274 3/8	47 1/8	44 7/8	28 7/8	6	6	Cabinet County	MT	Gayle A. Voisine	1992	2,962
274 3/8	43 3/8	44 2/8	38 7/8	7	6	Apache County	AZ	Michael W. Goodyear	1992	2,962

YELLOWSTONE "AMERICAN" ELK (TYPICAL ANTLERS)

Minimum Score 260 Continued

SCORE	LENGTH OF MAIN BEAM R	LENGTH OF MAIN BEAM L	INSIDE SPREAD	NUMBER OF POINTS R	NUMBER OF POINTS L	AREA	STATE/PROVINCE	HUNTER'S NAME	DATE	RANK
274 3/8	45 4/8	45 0/8	36 3/8	6	6	El Paso County	CO	William R. Hull	1997	2,962
274 2/8	42 4/8	42 3/8	40 0/8	6	6	Fremont County	ID	Clarence A. Frickey	1981	2,966
274 2/8	46 4/8	46 6/8	35 6/8	6	6	Blaine County	ID	Larry Newton	1987	2,966
274 2/8	50 3/8	53 6/8	40 4/8	6	5	McKinley County	NM	Malcolm D. Snyder	1991	2,966
274 2/8	45 6/8	43 3/8	35 0/8	6	6	Phillips County	MT	Mark L. Meyer	1992	2,966
274 2/8	48 0/8	49 2/8	37 6/8	7	6	Garfield County	CO	Bruce Hendy	1995	2,966
274 2/8	44 6/8	44 2/8	33 2/8	6	6	Larimer County	CO	William E. Peck, Jr.	1997	2,966
274 1/8	42 2/8	43 7/8	38 0/8	7	6	Gallatin County	MT	David F. Gibson	1974	2,972
274 1/8	48 3/8	48 3/8	34 5/8	6	6	Converse County	WY	Jeffrey Rieker	1979	2,972
274 1/8	49 5/8	41 3/8	31 3/8	6	5	Dunn County	ND	Craig Richardson	1989	2,972
274 1/8	46 1/8	46 3/8	34 1/8	6	7	Catron County	NM	Tommy C. Jones	1992	2,972
274 1/8	41 5/8	43 4/8	36 3/8	6	6	Clearwater County	ID	Carl F. Conklin	1993	2,972
274 1/8	44 5/8	44 7/8	36 3/8	6	6	Custer County	CO	Mark Wuerthele	1995	2,972
274 1/8	38 7/8	39 7/8	46 4/8	6	6	Park County	WY	Larry Hicks	1997	2,972
274 1/8	43 5/8	42 6/8	39 1/8	6	6	Rio Blanco County	CO	Troy Johnson	1998	2,972
274 0/8	43 3/8	43 4/8	31 2/8	6	6	Clearwater County	ID	Jay Deones	1984	2,980
274 0/8	43 0/8	41 4/8	36 0/8	6	6	Grant County	OR	Robert D. Coffey	1986	2,980
274 0/8	41 3/8	41 6/8	31 2/8	7	6	Delta County	CO	Ronnie Steve Hall	1992	2,980
274 0/8	38 4/8	38 3/8	37 2/8	6	6	Colfax County	NM	Howard Gallegos	1993	2,980
274 0/8	49 4/8	48 0/8	33 6/8	6	6	Gallatin County	MT	Gordon Strachan II	1994	2,980
274 0/8	44 0/8	43 5/8	34 6/8	6	6	Missoula County	MT	Tou Lee	1996	2,980
273 7/8	45 7/8	45 1/8	36 5/8	6	6	Custer County	ID	Scott A. Wondergem	1993	2,986
273 7/8	42 1/8	41 4/8	36 7/8	6	6	Linn County	OR	Ben McKillop	1994	2,986
273 7/8	46 2/8	47 2/8	37 3/8	6	6	Routt County	CO	Joe Wilhelm	1995	2,986
273 7/8	43 4/8	43 1/8	31 7/8	6	6	Colfax County	NM	Jack Dell	1997	2,986
273 6/8	48 4/8	49 0/8	33 6/8	6	6	Lemhi County	ID	Greg Munther	1963	2,990
273 6/8	42 1/8	43 3/8	33 0/8	6	6	Broadwater County	MT	Don Lovely	1978	2,990
273 6/8	39 3/8	37 6/8	37 6/8	6	6	Grant County	OR	John Bridgewater	1983	2,990
273 6/8	44 5/8	43 6/8	40 6/8	6	6	Valley County	ID	Tom Scoggin	1990	2,990
273 6/8	47 5/8	46 5/8	32 6/8	6	6	Sandoval County	NM	Robert K. Woeck	1993	2,990
273 6/8	44 6/8	42 7/8	36 0/8	6	6	Coconino County	AZ	Daniel P. Spatchek	1994	2,990
273 6/8	45 3/8	46 7/8	34 0/8	6	6	Coconino County	AZ	Dawn J. Butterfield	1998	2,990
273 5/8	48 0/8	47 6/8	40 5/8	6	7	Sublette County	WY	Lyndon W. Henri	1987	2,997
273 5/8	44 6/8	43 1/8	29 5/8	6	6	Beaverhead County	MT	Danny Moore	1988	2,997
273 5/8	41 4/8	39 5/8	35 2/8	6	7	Shoshone County	ID	Orrin R. Cox	1995	2,997
273 5/8	41 3/8	44 0/8	38 1/8	6	6	Larimer County	CO	Chris F. Seiler	1997	2,997
273 4/8	43 1/8	43 3/8	32 6/8	6	6	Archuleta County	CO	J.D. "Chip" Davis, Jr.	1990	3,001
273 4/8	44 4/8	42 6/8	31 1/8	8	7	Douglas County	OR	Ken French	1990	3,001
273 4/8	36 1/8	38 0/8	38 2/8	6	6	Mesa County	CO	John J. Ferrara	1990	3,001
273 4/8	41 1/8	42 6/8	39 0/8	6	6	Fremont County	WY	Ken Davis	1991	3,001
273 3/8	44 4/8	44 2/8	35 3/8	6	7	Sanders County	MT	Douglas Weber	1992	3,005
273 3/8	43 1/8	42 6/8	38 5/8	6	5	Grant County	NM	Patrick Sughroue	1996	3,005
273 3/8	43 4/8	43 5/8	29 3/8	6	6	Ravalli County	MT	Gary Palmer	1998	3,005
273 2/8	46 5/8	47 5/8	31 6/8	6	6	Phillips County	MT	Buddy Lundstrom	1981	3,008
273 2/8	45 5/8	44 3/8	37 6/8	6	6	Coconino County	AZ	Tony W. Zimbaro	1986	3,008
273 2/8	35 1/8	34 4/8	34 4/8	6	6	Elmore County	ID	George Law	1988	3,008
273 2/8	40 0/8	37 3/8	39 4/8	6	6	Custer County	ID	Jerry L. Bowhay	1990	3,008
273 2/8	47 3/8	44 0/8	35 0/8	6	6	Sandoval County	NM	Steve E. Lynch	1991	3,008
273 2/8	44 4/8	43 3/8	32 6/8	6	6	Lane County	OR	Rick Willhite	1992	3,008
273 2/8	42 4/8	44 3/8	36 2/8	6	6	Lemhi County	ID	Robert Merrill	1995	3,008
273 1/8	42 3/8	41 7/8	39 3/8	6	6	Mora County	NM	Michael J. Maes	1986	3,015
273 1/8	48 1/8	48 6/8	31 3/8	6	6	Duchesne County	UT	Bob Dawson	1990	3,015
273 0/8	42 2/8	42 1/8	32 6/8	6	6	Sandoval County	NM	George Bennett, Jr.	1984	3,017
273 0/8	41 1/8	40 7/8	37 2/8	6	6	Grant County	OR	Coby Moulton	1987	3,017
273 0/8	48 1/8	46 0/8	34 4/8	6	6	Custer County	ID	Randy Guinn	1987	3,017
273 0/8	47 0/8	46 2/8	37 2/8	6	6	Teton County	MT	Jerry Bianchi	1988	3,017
273 0/8	40 0/8	40 2/8	37 1/8	7	6	Apache County	AZ	John F. Richards	1990	3,017
273 0/8	47 3/8	44 7/8	36 6/8	6	5	Coconino County	AZ	Wiley Burnett	1990	3,017
273 0/8	44 6/8	42 2/8	36 0/8	6	6	Carbon County	WY	Rodney C. Hill	1990	3,017
273 0/8	41 7/8	42 4/8	31 0/8	6	6	Red Deer Lake	ALB	Dennis Smith	1992	3,017
273 0/8	44 3/8	44 6/8	36 2/8	6	6	Jackson County	CO	Hal Rogers	1994	3,017
273 0/8	41 3/8	42 3/8	31 4/8	6	6	Gallatin County	MT	Jerry Karsky	1998	3,017
272 7/8	39 6/8	40 0/8	37 7/8	6	6	Clackamas County	OR	Ed Bensel	1959	3,027
272 7/8	37 1/8	37 1/8	36 0/8	6	6	Rio Blanco County	CO	Dr. Charles Leidheiser	1973	3,027
272 7/8	44 7/8	44 2/8	41 5/8	5	6	Sanders County	MT	Donald R. Read	1991	3,027
272 7/8	42 7/8	42 6/8	30 7/8	6	6	Carbon County	WY	Steven Perkins	1995	3,027
272 7/8	40 7/8	41 2/8	37 3/8	6	6	Coconino County	AZ	Barry Louis Defer	1995	3,027
272 6/8	51 6/8	48 3/8	31 6/8	7	6	Beaverhead County	MT	Ms. Charlie I. White	1988	3,032
272 6/8	47 0/8	44 6/8	38 0/8	6	6	Catron County	NM	Rick Mann	1991	3,032
272 6/8	41 2/8	42 1/8	39 2/8	6	6	Gallatin County	MT	Eddie Claypool	1996	3,032
272 6/8	44 0/8	41 1/8	32 2/8	6	6	Madison County	MT	Erik Hoar	1998	3,032
272 5/8	44 7/8	42 1/8	36 3/8	6	6	Pitkin County	CO	Robert F. Cutting	1975	3,036
272 5/8	44 0/8	45 1/8	35 7/8	6	6	Baker County	OR	Lloyd V. Christensen	1987	3,036
272 5/8	44 4/8	44 7/8	35 1/8	6	6	Sublette County	WY	John B. Rice, Jr.	1990	3,036
272 5/8	40 5/8	39 4/8	42 5/8	6	6	Greenlee County	AZ	Craig Marietta	1990	3,036
272 5/8	42 7/8	42 4/8	32 5/8	6	5	Coconino County	AZ	Michael Fabritz	1995	3,036
272 5/8	45 0/8	47 6/8	33 3/8	6	6	Clark County	ID	Brian S. McIlnay	1998	3,036
272 4/8	42 5/8	43 7/8	35 6/8	6	6	Grant County	OR	Dean P. Pasche	1981	3,042

YELLOWSTONE "AMERICAN" ELK (TYPICAL ANTLERS)

Minimum Score 260 — Continued

SCORE	LENGTH OF MAIN BEAM R	LENGTH OF MAIN BEAM L	INSIDE SPREAD	NUMBER OF POINTS R	NUMBER OF POINTS L	AREA	STATE/PROVINCE	HUNTER'S NAME	DATE	RANK
272 4/8	42 7/8	41 5/8	33 4/8	6	6	Lincoln County	WY	Peggy Barcak	1987	3,042
272 4/8	40 6/8	39 6/8	36 4/8	6	7	Lincoln County	WY	David McKae	1987	3,042
272 4/8	39 4/8	39 3/8	38 2/8	7	6	Sibbald Flats	ALB	Archie Nesbitt	1989	3,042
272 4/8	40 2/8	41 5/8	40 0/8	6	6	Lincoln County	WY	James J. Doherty, Jr.	1996	3,042
272 4/8	40 6/8	39 3/8	36 4/8	6	6	Garfield County	CO	Frank Spartano	1996	3,042
272 4/8	39 1/8	40 3/8	37 0/8	6	6	Lemhi County	ID	Tom Heltemes	1997	3,042
272 3/8	41 7/8	39 5/8	35 3/8	6	6	Skagit County	WA	Steve Gorr	1982	3,049
272 3/8	38 0/8	39 6/8	38 5/8	7	6	Teller County	CO	Rick K. Campbell	1987	3,049
272 3/8	44 1/8	42 3/8	40 1/8	6	6	Harney County	OR	Doug Foster	1989	3,049
272 3/8	37 2/8	38 5/8	38 6/8	6	6	Catron County	NM	James F. Welles	1991	3,049
272 3/8	42 5/8	42 5/8	36 5/8	6	5	Mist Creek	ALB	Shawn D. Hillstead	1996	3,049
272 3/8	38 6/8	41 6/8	35 7/8	6	6	Otero County	NM	Tex Welch	1997	3,049
272 3/8	40 4/8	43 5/8	35 7/8	7	6	Pima County	AZ	Jeff Newbold	1997	3,049
272 2/8	38 6/8	39 4/8	34 4/8	6	6	Idaho County	ID	Stanley D. Miles	1976	3,056
272 2/8	48 0/8	46 5/8	37 2/8	5	5	Saguache County	CO	Kenneth A. Wollermann	1986	3,056
272 2/8	45 2/8	39 3/8	39 6/8	6	5	Morgan County	UT	Don Keady	1992	3,056
272 2/8	45 6/8	44 0/8	34 4/8	6	6	Valley County	MT	Dan E. Sturgis	1995	3,056
272 2/8	47 0/8	47 7/8	37 2/8	5	6	Clear Creek County	CO	Clint E. O'Hotto	1997	3,056
272 1/8	43 0/8	41 0/8	33 5/8	6	6	Garfield County	CO	Kevin L. Sheets	1998	3,061
272 0/8	43 7/8	44 4/8	38 0/8	6	6	Saguache County	CO	Buster Mize	1968	3,062
272 0/8	45 5/8	45 0/8	37 4/8	6	6	Idaho County	ID	Donald M. Martin	1978	3,062
272 0/8	44 2/8	43 4/8	37 6/8	6	6	Clear Creek County	CO	Matt Burrows	1994	3,062
271 7/8	47 4/8	49 1/8	32 5/8	6	6	Chelan County	WA	Claude E. Gates	1973	3,065
271 7/8	40 7/8	38 7/8	31 3/8	6	6	Lincoln County	WY	Doug Plumstead	1995	3,065
271 6/8	46 4/8	46 5/8	33 6/8	6	6	Sheridan County	WY	Mike Barrett	1985	3,067
271 6/8	41 7/8	43 7/8	32 6/8	6	6	Catron County	NM	Mark D. Barboa	1990	3,067
271 6/8	41 1/8	40 7/8	38 0/8	6	6	Phillips County	MT	Kevin Bertsch	1992	3,067
271 6/8	39 6/8	42 1/8	40 2/8	6	6	Sheridan County	WY	Ron Apel	1996	3,067
271 6/8	41 3/8	40 4/8	33 2/8	6	6	Adams County	ID	Larry Hoff	1998	3,067
271 5/8	43 1/8	43 6/8	36 1/8	5	6	Park County	MT	Dennis Vance	1975	3,072
271 5/8	38 5/8	39 5/8	36 1/8	6	6	Larimer County	CO	Kenneth D. Allen	1981	3,072
271 5/8	43 5/8	44 4/8	32 7/8	6	6	Lewis County	WA	Keith Heldreth	1985	3,072
271 5/8	38 6/8	41 2/8	40 5/8	6	6	Natrona County	WY	Brian L. Wagner	1996	3,072
271 5/8	44 6/8	44 6/8	38 3/8	6	6	Lemhi County	ID	Mike Studt	1997	3,072
271 4/8	38 4/8	40 6/8	34 2/8	6	6	Mud Creek	ID	Jr. Barnett	1977	3,077
271 4/8	44 4/8	45 6/8	43 0/8	6	5	Caribou County	ID	Preston Phelps	1980	3,077
271 4/8	46 3/8	47 2/8	36 2/8	6	6	Sweetwater County	WY	Vaughn Cross	1981	3,077
271 4/8	45 2/8	46 3/8	36 0/8	6	5	Flathead County	MT	Rick Meyer	1987	3,077
271 4/8	38 5/8	38 7/8	37 4/8	7	7	King County	WA	G. Dan Feighner	1989	3,077
271 4/8	42 5/8	41 0/8	29 0/8	6	8	Shoshone County	ID	Roy A. Clanton	1992	3,077
271 4/8	41 5/8	41 6/8	34 4/8	6	6	Beaverhead County	MT	Gary Lampkins	1997	3,077
271 4/8	46 2/8	47 3/8	35 0/8	6	5	Cibola County	NM	Kirby Hunter Wynn	1997	3,077
271 3/8	42 7/8	42 5/8	39 7/8	6	6	Rio Arriba County	NM	Bryan Adair	1984	3,085
271 3/8	40 4/8	41 3/8	36 3/8	7	6	Idaho County	ID	Dan Hollibush	1994	3,085
271 3/8	44 5/8	46 3/8	38 6/8	7	6	Coconino County	AZ	Wayne Smith	1997	3,085
271 2/8	44 2/8	45 7/8	27 0/8	6	6	Gunnison County	CO	Jeff Helming	1984	3,088
271 2/8	39 5/8	39 5/8	32 2/8	6	6	Rio Arriba County	NM	Lee Braudt	1985	3,088
271 2/8	42 1/8	43 4/8	39 4/8	6	5	Grant County	OR	Don D. Litts	1986	3,088
271 2/8	41 0/8	39 3/8	34 4/8	7	7	Rio Arriba County	NM	Greg Harmsen	1986	3,088
271 2/8	38 6/8	38 3/8	39 5/8	6	6	Sanders County	MT	Z. Kent Sullivan	1988	3,088
271 2/8	38 6/8	40 6/8	39 6/8	6	6	Lemhi County	ID	Glen Berry	1989	3,088
271 2/8	39 6/8	39 1/8	34 4/8	6	6	Socorro County	NM	Ted A. Shinn	1990	3,088
271 2/8	44 4/8	46 1/8	32 0/8	6	6	Sandoval County	NM	Robert L. Pagel	1990	3,088
271 2/8	51 5/8	45 5/8	34 2/8	6	5	Otero County	NM	Rocky Abney	1991	3,088
271 2/8	45 4/8	46 3/8	35 6/8	5	6	Grand County	CO	Dave Rayfield	1992	3,088
271 2/8	40 1/8	40 5/8	37 6/8	6	6	Lemhi County	ID	Michael Studt	1998	3,088
271 1/8	45 1/8	45 6/8	31 3/8	6	6	Rio Arriba County	NM	James A. Waters	1988	3,099
271 1/8	43 3/8	43 4/8	38 3/8	6	6	Lemhi County	ID	David A. Bronson	1991	3,099
271 1/8	49 3/8	48 6/8	35 1/8	6	6	Rio Arriba County	NM	Owen Phone	1994	3,099
271 1/8	40 1/8	39 5/8	36 1/8	6	6	Las Animas County	CO	Paul Strong	1996	3,099
271 1/8	41 6/8	41 6/8	39 3/8	5	5	McKinley County	NM	David Westmoreland	1996	3,099
271 0/8	48 0/8	47 7/8	34 2/8	6	5	Park County	CO	Victor B. Hines	1981	3,104
271 0/8	41 2/8	41 3/8	33 4/8	6	6	Routt County	CO	Starlene Clayson	1991	3,104
271 0/8	40 6/8	41 0/8	33 0/8	6	6	Las Animas County	CO	Jason Crockett Pettigrew	1992	3,104
271 0/8	36 7/8	41 2/8	43 0/8	5	6	Coconino County	AZ	Louie S. Herrera	1993	3,104
271 0/8	46 2/8	48 5/8	35 6/8	6	6	Archuleta County	CO	Jose A. Morales	1995	3,104
271 0/8	48 5/8	57 1/8	45 4/8	5	5	Catron County	NM	Bob "Jake" Jacobsen	1995	3,104
271 0/8	43 6/8	45 5/8	31 2/8	6	5	Navajo County	AZ	Brian Goble	1998	3,104
270 7/8	38 5/8	38 4/8	34 5/8	6	6	Gallatin National Forest	MT	Steve D. Wing	1979	3,111
270 7/8	37 1/8	42 6/8	31 3/8	6	6	Morgan County	UT	Hugh H. Hogle	1983	3,111
270 7/8	40 5/8	38 5/8	38 5/8	5	6	King County	WA	Ken Gettman	1987	3,111
270 7/8	42 4/8	43 5/8	30 3/8	6	6	Petroleum County	MT	Bryant Shermoe	1989	3,111
270 7/8	42 0/8	41 5/8	35 3/8	6	6	Natrona County	WY	Jeff Kovalick	1990	3,111
270 7/8	42 0/8	43 7/8	32 3/8	6	6	Shoshone County	ID	Glen Berry	1990	3,111
270 7/8	43 1/8	41 6/8	32 3/8	6	6	Mineral County	CO	Larry M. Moore	1996	3,111
270 7/8	42 1/8	40 4/8	39 3/8	6	6	Caribou County	ID	Mark L. Olson	1997	3,111
270 6/8	44 3/8	45 0/8	35 0/8	6	6	Custer County	ID	Scott Mackintosh	1994	3,119
270 6/8	46 0/8	45 7/8	37 6/8	6	6	Beaverhead County	MT	Fred C. Church	1996	3,119

YELLOWSTONE "AMERICAN" ELK (TYPICAL ANTLERS)

Minimum Score 260 — Continued

SCORE	LENGTH OF MAIN BEAM R	LENGTH OF MAIN BEAM L	INSIDE SPREAD	NUMBER OF POINTS R	NUMBER OF POINTS L	AREA	STATE/PROVINCE	HUNTER'S NAME	DATE	RANK
270 5/8	38 1/8	39 2/8	36 3/8	6	6	Routt County	CO	Jake Hoeschler	1977	3,121
270 5/8	45 7/8	45 5/8	35 5/8	6	6	Granite County	MT	Michael J. Nielsen	1988	3,121
270 5/8	45 3/8	45 3/8	38 1/8	6	6	Judith Basin County	MT	Jeff Jackson	1995	3,121
270 5/8	42 1/8	42 2/8	36 7/8	6	6	Park County	WY	Winston G. Irvin, Jr.	1995	3,121
270 4/8	50 5/8	48 6/8	42 0/8	5	5	King County	WA	Jon Fuller	1985	3,125
270 4/8	44 1/8	45 3/8	35 4/8	6	6	Rio Blanco County	CO	Perry Smith	1989	3,125
270 4/8	42 5/8	41 0/8	30 4/8	6	6	Clearwater County	ID	Bob Moenk	1992	3,125
270 4/8	46 2/8	48 1/8	35 2/8	6	6	Ouray County	CO	Joseph Testerman	1993	3,125
270 4/8	41 3/8	43 0/8	31 6/8	5	6	Sheridan County	WY	Ron Niziolek	1995	3,125
270 4/8	42 7/8	42 6/8	37 0/8	6	6	Blaine County	ID	Aaron J. Fortune	1996	3,125
270 3/8	40 6/8	40 4/8	36 5/8	6	6	Ravalli County	MT	Wayne Buhler	1982	3,131
270 3/8	46 0/8	46 4/8	36 7/8	6	6	Grant County	OR	Dennis G. Marshall	1986	3,131
270 3/8	43 5/8	42 6/8	34 7/8	6	6	Catron County	NM	Bill Clink	1989	3,131
270 3/8	47 4/8	46 0/8	30 1/8	6	6	Rio Arriba County	NM	C. Randall Byers	1994	3,131
270 2/8	42 6/8	41 6/8	36 2/8	6	6	Montezuma County	CO	Dwight V. English	1976	3,135
270 2/8	38 6/8	37 0/8	32 2/8	6	6	Blaine County	ID	John Turner	1977	3,135
270 2/8	42 7/8	44 4/8	43 6/8	5	6	Shoshone County	ID	Roy Meyer	1979	3,135
270 2/8	41 0/8	40 4/8	35 4/8	5	6	Simonette River	ALB	Gerald Rogers	1990	3,135
270 2/8	41 6/8	43 2/8	39 4/8	6	6	Coconino County	AZ	James Dale Casady	1993	3,135
270 1/8	38 1/8	39 1/8	35 5/8	6	6	Powell County	MT	E. Kits Smith	1976	3,140
270 1/8	36 3/8	36 7/8	42 0/8	6	6	Albany County	WY	Jerry Bowen	1984	3,140
270 1/8	41 2/8	42 5/8	28 5/8	6	6	Petroleum County	MT	Ken Rustad	1991	3,140
270 1/8	42 7/8	43 1/8	36 1/8	6	5	Catron County	NM	George Morris	1991	3,140
270 1/8	43 6/8	43 6/8	27 7/8	6	6	Conejos County	CO	Jack A. Gardner	1991	3,140
270 1/8	41 0/8	42 6/8	36 5/8	6	6	Big Horn County	WY	Dave Moss	1992	3,140
270 1/8	42 7/8	40 4/8	43 6/8	6	6	Wasco County	OR	Jeffrey M. Kortge	1995	3,140
270 0/8	45 6/8	46 5/8	31 2/8	6	6	Coconino County	AZ	James H. Hansen	1981	3,147
270 0/8	48 6/8	47 5/8	32 4/8	6	6	Coconino County	AZ	Wade L. Carstens	1983	3,147
270 0/8	46 0/8	48 5/8	41 5/8	6	5	Umatilla County	OR	Steven Hemrich	1994	3,147
270 0/8	41 1/8	40 4/8	32 4/8	6	6	Custer County	SD	Jon D. Heck	1998	3,147
269 7/8	38 2/8	36 6/8	28 1/8	6	6	Bear Lake County	ID	Dennis Burdick	1969	3,151
269 7/8	45 4/8	45 4/8	38 5/8	6	5	Park County	MT	Jay Bosma	1984	3,151
269 7/8	36 2/8	39 4/8	33 3/8	5	6	Rio Blanco County	CO	Brad Murray	1990	3,151
269 7/8	43 3/8	39 0/8	37 4/8	6	7	Daggett County	UT	Michiel D. Watts	1991	3,151
269 6/8	47 4/8	47 5/8	46 2/8	6	5	Idaho County	ID	Edward Keeton	1985	3,155
269 6/8	44 4/8	46 5/8	36 4/8	6	6	Malheur County	OR	Jim Hodson	1986	3,155
269 6/8	38 4/8	39 4/8	32 4/8	6	6	Ravalli County	MT	Mark Hoselton	1987	3,155
269 6/8	43 1/8	45 3/8	35 6/8	6	6	Archuleta County	CO	Floyd Earl Fralish	1990	3,155
269 6/8	40 4/8	38 0/8	41 0/8	6	6	Fremont County	WY	Justin Dvergsdal	1996	3,155
269 6/8	39 0/8	38 2/8	37 0/8	6	6	Lemhi County	ID	James R. Giovanelli	1997	3,155
269 6/8	46 1/8	44 0/8	37 6/8	6	6	Granite County	MT	Mark S. Golder	1997	3,155
269 6/8	44 5/8	44 7/8	31 0/8	6	6	Shoshone County	ID	Linda Leake	1998	3,155
269 5/8	41 6/8	42 3/8	35 5/8	6	6	Bonneville County	ID	Mike Taylor	1980	3,163
269 5/8	42 0/8	41 1/8	36 1/8	6	6	Caribou County	ID	Chet Hopkins	1985	3,163
269 5/8	44 4/8	44 1/8	33 1/8	6	6	Park County	MT	George Kamps	1986	3,163
269 4/8	42 7/8	42 4/8	35 6/8	6	7	Pinal County	AZ	Larry P. Matthews	1985	3,166
269 4/8	45 1/8	45 0/8	40 3/8	7	5	Custer County	ID	Bryan R. Sword	1988	3,166
269 4/8	44 4/8	44 2/8	33 7/8	6	7	Huerfano County	CO	Danny Ray	1992	3,166
269 4/8	41 6/8	41 7/8	30 3/8	7	6	Powell County	MT	Douglas J. Peters	1996	3,166
269 3/8	46 1/8	47 2/8	36 5/8	5	6	Cibola County	NM	Deryl Moore	1986	3,170
269 2/8	44 0/8	43 2/8	34 2/8	6	6	Grant County	NM	Joe F. Apodaca	1990	3,171
269 2/8	42 1/8	44 5/8	39 2/8	6	6	Catron County	NM	Gerry W. Carstens	1995	3,171
269 2/8	42 2/8	43 3/8	38 6/8	7	7	Larimer County	CO	Gary Kelley	1996	3,171
269 1/8	41 7/8	42 5/8	34 1/8	6	6	Archuleta County	CO	George Eubank	1989	3,174
269 1/8	42 1/8	42 0/8	33 1/8	6	6	Rio Arriba County	NM	Robert Nichols	1993	3,174
269 1/8	41 4/8	42 2/8	37 5/8	6	6	Hinsdale County	CO	Arland N. Rininger	1994	3,174
269 0/8	48 5/8	44 6/8	39 6/8	5	6	Bighorn Mtns.	WY	Dennis A. Phaneuf	1980	3,177
269 0/8	41 3/8	40 5/8	35 6/8	6	6	Idaho County	ID	Larry A. Youngdell	1980	3,177
269 0/8	39 2/8	40 6/8	37 2/8	6	6	Lewis & Clark County	MT	Steven E. Miller	1982	3,177
269 0/8	42 7/8	41 1/8	33 4/8	6	6	Converse County	WY	Jim Young	1982	3,177
269 0/8	35 5/8	35 5/8	33 2/8	6	6	Park County	CO	Jarold Allen Shriver	1988	3,177
269 0/8	39 2/8	38 2/8	39 0/8	7	6	Boise County	ID	Jeffrey S. Stevens	1988	3,177
269 0/8	41 6/8	45 0/8	33 2/8	6	6	Teton County	MT	Don Davidson	1990	3,177
269 0/8	44 4/8	45 4/8	37 6/8	6	7	Lane County	OR	Jeff Bell	1998	3,177
268 7/8	44 0/8	43 4/8	34 7/8	6	6	Judith Basin County	MT	Dan Hassel	1985	3,185
268 7/8	41 6/8	42 2/8	34 3/8	6	6	Sanders County	MT	Craig R. Johnson	1986	3,185
268 7/8	41 0/8	41 0/8	36 7/8	6	6	Grand County	CO	Neal Morse	1995	3,185
268 7/8	40 6/8	39 0/8	36 5/8	7	6	Gallatin County	MT	Kelly D. Johnson	1995	3,185
268 7/8	45 0/8	40 4/8	40 1/8	6	5	Catron County	NM	Sam Sowders	1996	3,185
268 6/8	41 3/8	42 5/8	39 4/8	6	6	Park County	CO	Wayne Helming	1983	3,190
268 6/8	44 7/8	43 4/8	35 0/8	6	7	Huerfano County	CO	Lee Moore	1985	3,190
268 6/8	48 2/8	47 7/8	34 0/8	6	6	Ouray County	CO	Keith Peeples	1990	3,190
268 6/8	43 5/8	44 6/8	31 4/8	6	7	San Miguel County	CO	Jeff Keehfuss	1995	3,190
268 6/8	41 5/8	43 2/8	31 0/8	6	5	Mesa County	CO	Bob Boarman	1996	3,190
268 5/8	41 7/8	43 1/8	32 2/8	6	6	Hinsdale County	CO	Billy R. Spears	1973	3,195
268 5/8	39 1/8	40 4/8	38 3/8	6	6	Catron County	NM	Scott Miltenberger	1990	3,195
268 5/8	46 2/8	43 3/8	30 1/8	6	6	Coconino County	AZ	Paul M. Rogers	1991	3,195
268 5/8	39 7/8	38 6/8	38 0/8	7	5	Lincoln County	MT	Jerry Brown	1996	3,195

YELLOWSTONE "AMERICAN" ELK (TYPICAL ANTLERS)

Minimum Score 260 Continued

SCORE	LENGTH OF MAIN BEAM R	L	INSIDE SPREAD	NUMBER OF POINTS R	L	AREA	STATE/PROVINCE	HUNTER'S NAME	DATE	RANK
268 5/8	43 3/8	42 6/8	32 6/8	6	6	Custer County	ID	Jeff A. Buck	1998	3,195
268 4/8	43 6/8	43 4/8	32 4/8	5	6	Coconino County	AZ	Charles R. Haverin	1984	3,200
268 4/8	49 1/8	48 4/8	33 2/8	5	5	Sandoval County	NM	Roby Grossheim	1988	3,200
268 4/8	46 2/8	46 0/8	36 0/8	5	5	Shoshone County	ID	Steven Rinaldi	1991	3,200
268 4/8	41 4/8	42 0/8	32 4/8	6	6	Lemhi County	ID	Kevin Walsh	1995	3,200
268 4/8	46 4/8	46 6/8	29 2/8	6	5	Catron County	NM	Mark A. Lutz	1997	3,200
268 3/8	41 1/8	40 4/8	29 5/8	6	6	Harney County	OR	Robert M. Choate	1996	3,205
268 2/8	45 6/8	42 6/8	35 2/8	6	6	Navajo County	AZ	Julius Fortuna	1983	3,206
268 1/8	39 0/8	40 3/8	30 0/8	7	6	Lincoln County	WY	Troy Miller	1973	3,207
268 1/8	45 2/8	46 0/8	36 5/8	5	6	Gallatin County	MT	William L. Anderson	1982	3,207
268 1/8	44 3/8	44 5/8	34 1/8	6	6	Silver Bow County	MT	Andrew Kuchtyn	1982	3,207
268 1/8	44 4/8	44 2/8	35 1/8	6	6	Grant County	OR	Gary Persinger	1983	3,207
268 1/8	42 5/8	41 0/8	33 7/8	6	6	Caribou County	ID	Max F. Park	1990	3,207
268 1/8	39 6/8	39 0/8	31 1/8	6	6	Mesa County	CO	Rich Grannis	1993	3,207
268 1/8	43 3/8	42 2/8	44 1/8	5	5	Idaho County	ID	Richard J. McEwen	1996	3,207
268 0/8	42 3/8	40 5/8	32 6/8	6	5	Baker County	OR	Les Thoreby	1963	3,214
268 0/8	41 7/8	42 2/8	33 3/8	7	6	Idaho County	ID	Richard C. Nichols	1974	3,214
268 0/8	41 0/8	40 7/8	35 2/8	6	6	Colfax County	NM	Peter J. Santi	1991	3,214
268 0/8	42 0/8	43 3/8	34 6/8	6	6	Gallatin County	MT	Matt Rognlie	1998	3,214
267 7/8	45 2/8	43 5/8	41 3/8	6	6	Valley County	ID	Jack St. Germain	1981	3,218
267 7/8	44 2/8	43 6/8	32 7/8	6	6	Los Alamos County	NM	Doug Aikin	1983	3,218
267 7/8	41 4/8	42 0/8	29 4/8	7	6	Phillips County	MT	Dr. Richard L. Lopez	1987	3,218
267 7/8	46 5/8	44 7/8	47 7/8	6	5	Coconino County	AZ	Kenneth Wilson	1989	3,218
267 7/8	40 3/8	39 0/8	41 0/8	6	6	Silver Bow County	MT	Steve Petroni	1990	3,218
267 6/8	43 3/8	47 0/8	39 6/8	6	6	Caribou County	ID	Jerry Baird	1976	3,223
267 6/8	47 3/8	46 2/8	33 2/8	5	5	Rich County	UT	C. Keith Maynes	1989	3,223
267 6/8	40 1/8	39 4/8	31 4/8	7	7	Catron County	NM	Ronald R. Johnson	1990	3,223
267 6/8	46 0/8	45 2/8	41 2/8	6	6	Coconino County	AZ	Denzil Hackathorn	1993	3,223
267 6/8	48 1/8	46 1/8	36 2/8	6	6	Moffat County	CO	Michael Hackett	1995	3,223
267 6/8	42 5/8	44 2/8	38 2/8	6	6	Hinsdale County	CO	William D. Seaman, Jr.	1998	3,223
267 6/8	41 6/8	41 2/8	37 0/8	5	5	Otero County	NM	Terry N. Morrow	1998	3,223
267 5/8	42 2/8	42 4/8	33 3/8	6	6	Larimer County	CO	Dennis Worrell	1979	3,230
267 5/8	40 0/8	39 6/8	33 7/8	6	6	Chaffee County	CO	Bruce Long	1985	3,230
267 5/8	35 4/8	36 1/8	39 6/8	6	6	Wallowa County	OR	Peter E. Palmer	1989	3,230
267 5/8	47 5/8	46 2/8	33 5/8	8	6	Coconino County	AZ	Steven Takajo	1992	3,230
267 5/8	42 2/8	42 2/8	37 1/8	6	6	Meagher County	MT	James F. Wright	1994	3,230
267 4/8	42 2/8	44 4/8	31 6/8	6	6	Gallatin County	MT	Jim Wondzell	1990	3,235
267 4/8	42 7/8	52 1/8	36 2/8	5	6	Mesa County	CO	Don Boyles	1991	3,235
267 4/8	43 7/8	43 4/8	41 3/8	5	6	Grant County	OR	Jerry W. Simmons	1992	3,235
267 4/8	44 2/8	47 5/8	40 4/8	7	6	Archuleta County	CO	Eddie Claypool	1995	3,235
267 4/8	41 4/8	39 4/8	32 4/8	6	6	Butte County	ID	Brent L. McMillan	1996	3,235
267 4/8	42 3/8	41 5/8	35 4/8	6	6	Catron County	NM	John H. Trewern	1997	3,235
267 4/8	40 7/8	38 6/8	31 6/8	6	6	Routt County	CO	Thomas E. Garrett	1998	3,235
267 3/8	40 4/8	39 3/8	30 3/8	6	6	Ravalli County	MT	Harold Wilson	1977	3,242
267 3/8	38 2/8	47 4/8	33 1/8	5	6	Coconino County	AZ	John C. McClendon	1980	3,242
267 3/8	43 6/8	45 6/8	35 5/8	6	6	Linn County	OR	Michael Hawkins	1982	3,242
267 3/8	40 6/8	42 3/8	36 7/8	5	7	Greenlee County	AZ	Robert B. Miller	1992	3,242
267 2/8	44 4/8	47 4/8	35 2/8	5	5	Grand County	CO	David C. Goble	1994	3,246
267 2/8	40 6/8	40 0/8	29 4/8	6	6	Pennington County	SD	Delana D. Nelson	1994	3,246
267 2/8	46 3/8	48 2/8	34 4/8	6	5	Shoshone County	ID	Ernest W. Clanton	1995	3,246
267 1/8	42 3/8	42 4/8	33 3/8	6	6	Beaverhead County	MT	Neal Davis	1987	3,249
267 1/8	39 4/8	40 4/8	38 3/8	6	6	Albany County	WY	Jerry Bowen	1988	3,249
267 1/8	41 2/8	42 3/8	36 1/8	6	6	Lincoln County	NM	Gregory A. Lompart	1993	3,249
267 1/8	42 7/8	42 6/8	30 3/8	6	6	Archuleta County	CO	Richard Robbins	1994	3,249
267 1/8	46 3/8	44 4/8	36 6/8	6	6	Petroleum County	MT	Dustin B. Sturm	1997	3,249
267 0/8	43 2/8	37 7/8	36 1/8	7	6	Teton County	WY	James Yager	1990	3,254
267 0/8	42 2/8	39 3/8	31 0/8	6	6	Coconino County	AZ	Russell C. Horst	1992	3,254
267 0/8	39 6/8	38 5/8	37 2/8	6	6	Garfield County	MT	Jeff Fisher	1995	3,254
267 0/8	45 3/8	45 0/8	36 0/8	6	6	Adams County	ID	Smokey Crews	1997	3,254
266 7/8	36 2/8	39 7/8	40 0/8	6	6	Carbon County	WY	Merle M. Vowers	1992	3,258
266 6/8	41 0/8	40 4/8	32 6/8	6	6	Lemhi County	ID	Scott Spaeth	1978	3,259
266 6/8	45 5/8	43 2/8	37 4/8	6	6	Apache County	AZ	Tom David	1980	3,259
266 6/8	43 7/8	44 6/8	39 2/8	6	6	Caribou County	ID	Max Park	1981	3,259
266 6/8	42 5/8	42 7/8	29 0/8	6	6	Rio Blanco County	CO	Bill McMahan	1989	3,259
266 6/8	41 6/8	41 6/8	33 1/8	6	7	Catron County	NM	Jack Dykstra	1991	3,259
266 6/8	42 3/8	41 4/8	32 7/8	7	9	Big Horn County	WY	Scott White	1993	3,259
266 6/8	49 1/8	50 3/8	40 2/8	6	6	Missoula County	MT	Lucas Osellame	1994	3,259
266 6/8	44 7/8	44 0/8	34 6/8	6	6	Fremont County	WY	Matthew L. Wheeler	1997	3,259
266 5/8	42 1/8	43 7/8	29 5/8	6	6	Chaffee County	CO	Frank A. Morminello	1977	3,267
266 5/8	48 1/8	45 0/8	42 5/8	6	6	Caribou County	ID	Max Park	1982	3,267
266 5/8	43 2/8	43 2/8	31 7/8	6	6	Phillips County	MT	Steve Baeth	1985	3,267
266 5/8	47 0/8	43 2/8	29 7/8	6	5	White Pine County	NV	Gary Wright	1989	3,267
266 5/8	42 7/8	40 7/8	39 5/8	6	6	Sandoval County	NM	Peter F. Woeck II	1991	3,267
266 5/8	44 6/8	42 0/8	36 5/8	6	6	Routt County	CO	Craig Thrasher	1991	3,267
266 5/8	41 2/8	41 5/8	33 3/8	6	6	Mesa County	CO	Jimmy Wayne Birchfield	1991	3,267
266 5/8	47 0/8	42 5/8	33 7/8	6	6	Jefferson County	OR	David G. Sonnenburg	1994	3,267
266 5/8	46 4/8	44 4/8	32 1/8	6	6	Ravalli County	MT	Russell Byrne	1997	3,267
266 5/8	39 2/8	37 7/8	35 7/8	5	5	Custer County	ID	Michael Scott Park	1998	3,267

YELLOWSTONE "AMERICAN" ELK (TYPICAL ANTLERS)

Minimum Score 260   Continued

SCORE	LENGTH OF MAIN BEAM R	LENGTH OF MAIN BEAM L	INSIDE SPREAD	NUMBER OF POINTS R	NUMBER OF POINTS L	AREA	STATE/ PROVINCE	HUNTER'S NAME	DATE	RANK
266 5/8	46 0/8	43 3/8	36 5/8	6	6	Crook County	OR	Robert A. Rosales	1998	3,267
266 4/8	36 7/8	37 0/8	30 4/8	6	6	Lewis & Clark County	MT	Laurence F. Crim	1977	3,278
266 4/8	41 7/8	43 1/8	35 2/8	6	6	Gem County	ID	Randy L. Wilkins	1985	3,278
266 4/8	41 5/8	42 2/8	39 4/8	6	6	Missoula County	MT	Steve Byerly	1988	3,278
266 4/8	44 6/8	49 6/8	35 0/8	6	6	Coconino County	AZ	Rick Betten	1992	3,278
266 4/8	42 3/8	42 6/8	41 0/8	7	7	Rio Arriba County	NM	Dave Conrad	1992	3,278
266 4/8	40 0/8	41 1/8	41 0/8	6	5	Lane County	OR	Michael Kreiling	1992	3,278
266 4/8	46 0/8	43 0/8	38 4/8	6	5	Coconino County	AZ	Michael Chamberlain	1992	3,278
266 4/8	44 1/8	43 0/8	37 4/8	6	6	Lemhi County	ID	Frederick J. Gimbel	1993	3,278
266 4/8	44 4/8	42 6/8	30 4/8	6	6	Los Alamos County	NM	M. R. James	1994	3,278
266 4/8	46 3/8	47 0/8	34 4/8	6	5	Boundary County	ID	Roger N. Myers	1995	3,278
266 4/8	44 3/8	46 7/8	38 2/8	6	6	Rio Arriba County	NM	Mark Patrick Seraly, MD	1995	3,278
266 4/8	46 2/8	44 2/8	30 0/8	6	6	Yavapai County	AZ	Chance H. Cheatham	1997	3,278
266 3/8	45 1/8	45 3/8	31 7/8	6	6	Archuleta County	CO	Mark Lowery	1989	3,290
266 3/8	42 2/8	42 6/8	31 7/8	5	6	Sandoval County	NM	Greg Strait	1989	3,290
266 3/8	41 1/8	43 1/8	36 3/8	5	6	Teller County	CO	James Wolfe	1990	3,290
266 2/8	47 3/8	45 6/8	36 4/8	5	6	La Plata County	CO	Charlie Chrane	1977	3,293
266 2/8	45 7/8	46 6/8	41 2/8	6	6	McKinley County	NM	Robert Stearns	1987	3,293
266 2/8	39 4/8	40 6/8	30 6/8	6	6	Fremont County	ID	Gary Detwiler	1995	3,293
266 2/8	40 4/8	40 2/8	30 4/8	6	6	Muskwa River	BC	Jim Nowakowski	1995	3,293
266 2/8	39 1/8	38 4/8	31 2/8	6	6	Colfax County	NM	Pete Pieper	1997	3,293
266 2/8	44 6/8	47 0/8	36 6/8	6	6	Wallowa County	OR	Steven M. Stoneking	1997	3,293
266 1/8	42 6/8	43 6/8	32 3/8	6	6	Skamania County	WA	James S. Newman	1986	3,299
266 1/8	41 2/8	42 1/8	36 5/8	6	6	Idaho County	ID	Charles E. Groft	1988	3,299
266 1/8	45 6/8	47 0/8	34 7/8	6	6	Otero County	NM	Bruce Barrie	1998	3,299
266 0/8	47 1/8	45 7/8	38 6/8	6	6	Sandoval County	NM	Lloyd Baird	1984	3,302
266 0/8	48 5/8	47 5/8	31 0/8	5	6	Douglas County	CO	James Robert Phelps	1986	3,302
266 0/8	38 4/8	39 6/8	34 2/8	6	6	Sublette County	WY	Michael D. Haden	1992	3,302
266 0/8	40 2/8	39 5/8	39 4/8	6	5	McKinley County	NM	Neil J. Patrone	1998	3,302
266 0/8	38 4/8	40 4/8	29 1/8	6	7	Valley County	MT	Charles J. Schultz	1998	3,302
265 7/8	40 1/8	40 5/8	36 5/8	6	7	San Miguel County	CO	Bubba Schmidt	1988	3,307
265 7/8	42 4/8	45 0/8	37 7/8	6	6	Coconino County	AZ	Prentiss Chanceller	1988	3,307
265 7/8	43 7/8	47 0/8	30 7/8	6	6	Coconino County	AZ	Cy Hershey	1990	3,307
265 7/8	39 5/8	38 4/8	43 5/8	6	6	Elkford	BC	Dale Webber	1997	3,307
265 6/8	41 2/8	40 6/8	36 0/8	6	6	Wallowa County	OR	Grainger Hunt	1987	3,311
265 6/8	39 2/8	40 6/8	32 2/8	6	6	Madison County	MT	Richard Ballard	1987	3,311
265 6/8	40 4/8	39 6/8	40 2/8	6	6	Sheridan County	WY	Skip Reilly	1988	3,311
265 6/8	49 4/8	50 3/8	40 4/8	5	5	Boise County	ID	John E. Smith	1988	3,311
265 6/8	39 2/8	39 0/8	28 2/8	6	6	Lincoln County	WY	Donlee L. Jackson	1990	3,311
265 6/8	39 2/8	40 6/8	39 0/8	6	5	Coconino County	AZ	John Brooks	1996	3,311
265 5/8	41 6/8	42 1/8	40 1/8	5	6	Rio Blanco County	CO	Jerry Bowen	1974	3,317
265 5/8	37 2/8	38 4/8	29 1/8	6	6	Shoshone County	ID	Jeff Jackson	1987	3,317
265 5/8	44 0/8	44 6/8	31 1/8	6	6	Huerfano County	CO	Steve Jeans	1988	3,317
265 5/8	43 4/8	43 4/8	33 3/8	5	5	Mineral County	CO	Greg Ogle	1988	3,317
265 5/8	44 4/8	43 2/8	39 3/8	6	6	Wallowa County	OR	Rick Turner	1990	3,317
265 5/8	45 4/8	44 6/8	29 1/8	6	6	Columbia County	WA	Jess Mings	1992	3,317
265 5/8	42 4/8	42 2/8	35 5/8	6	7	Teton County	ID	Shane Albertson	1997	3,317
265 4/8	43 2/8	42 7/8	32 6/8	6	6	Delta County	CO	Emil C. Frein	1973	3,324
265 4/8	49 4/8	45 5/8	31 6/8	6	6	Dolores County	CO	Scott Roberts	1975	3,324
265 4/8	37 6/8	35 3/8	39 5/8	6	6	Catron County	NM	John D. Smith	1989	3,324
265 4/8	43 6/8	43 2/8	38 6/8	5	5	Jumping Pound Creek	ALB	Archie Nesbitt	1993	3,324
265 4/8	45 4/8	44 1/8	31 2/8	6	6	Meagher County	MT	Theodore H. Hysell	1994	3,324
265 4/8	46 0/8	47 0/8	36 2/8	6	6	Ouray County	CO	Michael D. Riley	1994	3,324
265 4/8	44 3/8	44 1/8	33 4/8	6	6	Rio Arriba County	NM	Brian T. Christman	1995	3,324
265 3/8	39 7/8	38 5/8	34 3/8	6	6	Mineral County	CO	Will Pick	1993	3,331
265 1/8	41 2/8	39 2/8	29 1/8	6	7	Mineral County	CO	Rod Wintz	1968	3,332
265 1/8	44 2/8	43 5/8	31 3/8	6	6	Huerfano County	CO	Duane Raspotnik	1989	3,332
265 1/8	40 4/8	40 6/8	39 1/8	5	6	Catron County	NM	Jeffrey Aycock	1990	3,332
265 1/8	42 4/8	44 4/8	28 5/8	6	6	Navajo County	AZ	Steve Johnston	1991	3,332
265 1/8	45 0/8	42 7/8	34 5/8	6	6	Caribou County	ID	Richard Fletcher	1991	3,332
265 1/8	46 3/8	45 5/8	36 1/8	6	6	Boise County	ID	Jeffrey Stevens	1993	3,332
265 1/8	35 6/8	40 3/8	44 0/8	7	6	Catron County	NM	Matt Burrows	1994	3,332
265 1/8	38 6/8	38 7/8	38 1/8	6	6	Eagle County	CO	Randy Chastain	1996	3,332
265 0/8	44 5/8	43 2/8	30 0/8	6	6	Kittitas County	WA	Eric Seim	1991	3,340
265 0/8	43 0/8	42 1/8	34 4/8	6	6	Petroleum County	MT	Mark Rigotti	1992	3,340
264 7/8	42 5/8	45 5/8	33 1/8	6	6	Coconino County	AZ	Dennis Newman	1973	3,342
264 7/8	39 1/8	42 2/8	33 5/8	6	6	Huerfano County	CO	Michael J. Eutsler	1986	3,342
264 7/8	40 0/8	38 2/8	39 7/8	6	6	Union County	OR	Ellis E. Speer	1986	3,342
264 7/8	42 6/8	42 0/8	35 5/8	5	6	Sandoval County	NM	Pat Lovato	1993	3,342
264 7/8	45 0/8	45 3/8	36 3/8	5	6	Garfield County	MT	Richard Hjort	1993	3,342
264 6/8	38 5/8	37 4/8	32 6/8	6	6	Teton County	WY	Paul Birkholz	1966	3,347
264 6/8	41 4/8	40 5/8	35 4/8	6	6	Pitkin County	CO	Donald Hanford	1981	3,347
264 6/8	43 0/8	44 1/8	36 0/8	5	5	Meagher County	MT	Gary H. Thompson	1981	3,347
264 6/8	41 3/8	41 0/8	36 4/8	6	6	Meagher County	MT	Gene Clark	1982	3,347
264 6/8	39 3/8	39 2/8	32 6/8	6	6	Duchesne County	UT	Russel McClellan	1994	3,347
264 6/8	44 1/8	44 2/8	39 2/8	6	5	Lemhi County	ID	John Hanowski	1995	3,347
264 4/8	44 6/8	45 7/8	34 4/8	7	7	Boise County	ID	Robert Hiller	1969	3,353
264 4/8	38 6/8	39 2/8	33 6/8	6	6	Jefferson County	CO	Darrell Kitzman	1986	3,353

YELLOWSTONE "AMERICAN" ELK (TYPICAL ANTLERS)

Minimum Score 260 — Continued

SCORE	LENGTH OF MAIN BEAM R	LENGTH OF MAIN BEAM L	INSIDE SPREAD	NUMBER OF POINTS R	NUMBER OF POINTS L	AREA	STATE/PROVINCE	HUNTER'S NAME	DATE	RANK
264 4/8	46 3/8	49 6/8	39 2/8	6	6	Sierra County	NM	Guy D. Pointer	1988	3,353
264 4/8	42 3/8	42 1/8	37 0/8	6	6	Lincoln County	NM	Jim Tyler	1988	3,353
264 4/8	42 4/8	43 7/8	36 4/8	5	6	Catron County	NM	Adam Jimenez, Jr.	1989	3,353
264 4/8	42 4/8	42 3/8	30 2/8	6	6	Saguache County	CO	Arthur D. Johnson	1991	3,353
264 4/8	42 7/8	41 6/8	37 6/8	6	6	Powell County	MT	Dan J. Burns	1995	3,353
264 3/8	44 2/8	44 4/8	30 7/8	6	6	Coconino County	AZ	Joel R. Youngblood III	1990	3,360
264 3/8	39 4/8	40 1/8	33 5/8	6	6	Huerfano County	CO	Esco R. Billings, III	1991	3,360
264 3/8	40 7/8	41 0/8	38 1/8	6	6	Meagher County	MT	Donovan A. Khalar	1995	3,360
264 2/8	41 5/8	43 5/8	27 6/8	6	6	Coconino County	AZ	Randy Breland	1984	3,363
264 2/8	39 7/8	39 3/8	39 6/8	5	5	Catron County	NM	Adam Jimenez Jr.	1986	3,363
264 2/8	43 5/8	43 4/8	38 6/8	6	5	Gunnison County	CO	Mark Asplund	1987	3,363
264 2/8	39 6/8	40 1/8	27 2/8	6	6	Sheridan County	WY	Richard E. Jones	1992	3,363
264 2/8	47 1/8	44 4/8	32 2/8	6	6	Ravalli County	MT	Scott Wilke	1994	3,363
264 1/8	40 4/8	39 0/8	39 7/8	5	5	Larimer County	CO	Eric Peterson	1982	3,368
264 1/8	39 7/8	38 7/8	31 3/8	6	6	Taos County	NM	Ronald Corvin	1990	3,368
264 1/8	41 3/8	41 3/8	36 1/8	6	6	Valencia County	NM	Chett Britton	1994	3,368
264 0/8	40 1/8	40 5/8	37 0/8	6	6	Valley County	ID	Brian Crook	1989	3,371
264 0/8	49 1/8	48 6/8	37 6/8	6	6	Montrose County	CO	Gary Chambliss	1995	3,371
264 0/8	36 4/8	36 0/8	39 6/8	5	5	Catron County	NM	Vicki L. Leonard	1996	3,371
263 7/8	46 4/8	46 7/8	39 7/8	6	5	Boise County	ID	Jack Brennan	1964	3,374
263 7/8	41 2/8	40 4/8	35 1/8	6	6	Valley County	MT	Myron Gartner	1976	3,374
263 6/8	38 3/8	38 6/8	36 0/8	6	6	Sandoval County	NM	Michael G. Morton	1995	3,376
263 6/8	38 4/8	36 1/8	35 2/8	6	6	Meagher County	MT	John Roberts	1995	3,376
263 6/8	40 5/8	41 6/8	38 2/8	6	6	Larimer County	CO	Ron Wahl	1998	3,376
263 5/8	40 5/8	39 6/8	34 3/8	6	6	Ouray County	CO	Doug McCauley	1982	3,379
263 5/8	35 2/8	37 7/8	32 1/8	6	6	Petroleum County	MT	Greg Deutsch	1993	3,379
263 5/8	39 7/8	39 3/8	33 0/8	7	6	Mesa County	CO	Mark Crain	1997	3,379
263 4/8	41 5/8	41 4/8	37 4/8	6	6	Caribou County	ID	Wade Dursteler	1988	3,382
263 4/8	42 2/8	43 0/8	37 2/8	6	6	Lemhi County	ID	Rob Valnoski	1994	3,382
263 4/8	39 6/8	42 1/8	29 4/8	6	6	Lemhi County	ID	Gary R. Heward	1997	3,382
263 3/8	38 7/8	38 4/8	33 5/8	6	6	Idaho County	ID	John C. Mitchell	1985	3,385
263 3/8	40 1/8	39 2/8	38 2/8	6	7	Larimer County	CO	B.D. Ramsey	1988	3,385
263 3/8	51 3/8	49 3/8	36 4/8	6	6	Rio Blanco County	CO	Brad Murray	1992	3,385
263 3/8	42 0/8	40 1/8	33 5/8	6	6	Beaverhead County	MT	Steve Rigby	1996	3,385
263 2/8	40 7/8	43 1/8	32 5/8	6	7	Coconino County	AZ	Michael H. Bingham	1982	3,389
263 2/8	45 3/8	43 5/8	34 2/8	6	6	Gallatin County	MT	Bob Fromme	1983	3,389
263 2/8	43 7/8	43 6/8	35 4/8	6	6	Fremont County	WY	Guy LeMonnier, Jr.	1989	3,389
263 2/8	39 2/8	40 7/8	36 0/8	6	6	Ouray County	CO	Dexter G. Efird	1990	3,389
263 2/8	39 4/8	40 4/8	28 2/8	7	7	Petroleum County	MT	Ken Rustad	1990	3,389
263 2/8	38 3/8	41 6/8	35 6/8	6	6	Pitkin County	CO	Rocky Dan Tschappat	1994	3,389
263 2/8	42 2/8	42 0/8	35 4/8	6	6	Fremont County	ID	Chad Berry	1995	3,389
263 2/8	37 5/8	37 3/8	36 2/8	6	6	Huerfano County	CO	Jack L. Sciacca	1996	3,389
263 2/8	47 0/8	45 5/8	36 0/8	6	6	Smoky River	ALB	Kirby Smith	1996	3,389
263 1/8	43 5/8	42 6/8	35 5/8	6	5	Lewis County	WA	Keith Heldreth	1984	3,398
263 1/8	44 6/8	42 6/8	36 3/8	6	6	Socorro County	NM	Joe Caskey	1986	3,398
263 1/8	44 2/8	46 0/8	30 3/8	7	7	Blaine County	ID	James B. Thompson	1992	3,398
263 0/8	41 0/8	41 3/8	36 2/8	6	6	Clear Creek County	CO	Don Bording	1982	3,401
263 0/8	41 7/8	42 6/8	35 2/8	6	6	Los Alamos County	NM	Doug Aikin	1984	3,401
263 0/8	38 7/8	39 4/8	38 6/8	6	6	Grant County	OR	Phillip Koep	1991	3,401
263 0/8	42 2/8	43 7/8	33 4/8	5	6	Silver Bow County	MT	Victor Romano	1992	3,401
263 0/8	45 2/8	42 2/8	37 0/8	5	5	Hinsdale County	CO	Mark J. Wollert	1995	3,401
263 0/8	41 3/8	44 2/8	30 4/8	6	6	Catron County	NM	Mike W. Leonard	1996	3,401
262 7/8	37 7/8	36 7/8	34 3/8	6	6	Garfield County	CO	Clifford White	1977	3,407
262 7/8	43 4/8	44 1/8	36 5/8	7	6	Coconino County	AZ	Dr. Van Bennett	1985	3,407
262 6/8	40 5/8	42 1/8	31 6/8	6	6	Archuleta County	CO	David W. Cather	1984	3,409
262 6/8	39 5/8	41 2/8	37 6/8	6	6	Lemhi County	ID	Thomas N. Thiel	1996	3,409
262 6/8	42 4/8	41 1/8	39 4/8	6	6	Caribou County	ID	William T. Trainor	1997	3,409
262 5/8	39 5/8	39 4/8	36 7/8	6	6	Pierce County	WA	David T. Robertson	1985	3,412
262 5/8	41 5/8	39 3/8	34 7/8	6	6	Custer County	ID	Brent McBride	1987	3,412
262 5/8	47 5/8	46 0/8	30 1/8	6	6	Routt County	CO	John Pershing Lundberg	1990	3,412
262 4/8	39 4/8	40 0/8	31 6/8	6	7	Coconino County	AZ	Donald L. Kennedy	1977	3,415
262 4/8	42 6/8	43 4/8	38 4/8	6	6	Flathead County	MT	Chester Fessum	1983	3,415
262 4/8	42 7/8	43 2/8	30 2/8	5	6	Pierce County	WA	Andy Bales	1989	3,415
262 4/8	40 5/8	41 1/8	39 6/8	6	6	Montezuma County	CO	Ron Laird	1991	3,415
262 4/8	38 4/8	38 0/8	39 0/8	6	6	Chaffee County	CO	Joel D. Morgan	1991	3,415
262 4/8	40 3/8	42 4/8	38 2/8	6	7	Catron County	NM	Zeb Kern	1997	3,415
262 3/8	46 1/8	44 5/8	32 6/8	7	6	Rio Arriba County	NM	Ronnie Williams	1986	3,421
262 3/8	43 3/8	43 3/8	32 0/8	7	6	Kakwa River	ALB	Wilf Lehners	1991	3,421
262 3/8	43 0/8	42 0/8	34 7/8	6	5	Clearwater County	ID	Mark E. Kuechenmeister	1994	3,421
262 3/8	39 1/8	39 1/8	35 5/8	6	6	Fergus County	MT	Gary "Grizz" Hoffer	1995	3,421
262 2/8	45 0/8	45 3/8	32 6/8	5	5	Grand County	CO	G. Fred Asbell	1979	3,425
262 2/8	41 4/8	40 2/8	37 0/8	5	5	Crook County	OR	Terry A. Luther	1981	3,425
262 2/8	46 1/8	43 5/8	38 4/8	6	6	Saguache County	CO	Burton R. Thompson, Jr.	1995	3,425
262 2/8	46 1/8	47 6/8	38 6/8	6	6	Coconino County	AZ	Donald A. Karcher	1995	3,425
262 2/8	38 6/8	39 2/8	41 1/8	6	6	Douglas County	CO	Michael Manning	1997	3,425
262 1/8	43 7/8	44 2/8	31 7/8	6	6	Blaine County	ID	Bruce Anderson	1996	3,430
262 0/8	43 4/8	43 6/8	35 4/8	6	6	Chaffee County	CO	Ray Nelson	1981	3,431
262 0/8	42 4/8	42 1/8	37 4/8	6	6	Deer Lodge County	MT	Todd R. Zeuske	1982	3,431

YELLOWSTONE "AMERICAN" ELK (TYPICAL ANTLERS)

Minimum Score 260

Continued

SCORE	LENGTH OF R MAIN BEAM L		INSIDE SPREAD	NUMBER OF R POINTS L		AREA	STATE/ PROVINCE	HUNTER'S NAME	DATE	RANK
262 0/8	38 5/8	41 4/8	34 2/8	6	6	Catron County	NM	Bob "Jake" Jacobsen	1993	3,431
262 0/8	38 2/8	39 0/8	29 6/8	6	6	Montrose County	CO	Ted Winchester	1993	3,431
262 0/8	44 4/8	42 5/8	38 6/8	6	6	Catron County	NM	Robert J. Martin	1996	3,431
262 0/8	43 6/8	42 7/8	31 2/8	6	6	Montrose County	CO	Steven M. Grantham	1997	3,431
261 7/8	36 6/8	41 3/8	34 7/8	6	6	Coconino County	AZ	Charles Stevenson	1980	3,437
261 7/8	41 1/8	41 0/8	35 7/8	6	6	Clearwater County	ID	Jim Prudhomme	1990	3,437
261 7/8	42 5/8	41 3/8	34 3/8	6	6	Montezuma County	CO	Gene Benavidez	1998	3,437
261 6/8	38 0/8	40 0/8	37 6/8	6	5	Taos County	NM	Dr. D. A. Henbest	1972	3,440
261 6/8	39 4/8	40 2/8	32 4/8	6	6	Delta County	CO	John C. Lamont	1989	3,440
261 6/8	44 6/8	44 0/8	36 0/8	7	6	Coconino County	AZ	Gary Hanson	1992	3,440
261 6/8	47 6/8	46 5/8	32 4/8	6	5	Albany County	WY	Doug Cringan	1992	3,440
261 6/8	40 4/8	41 4/8	45 4/8	6	6	Coconino County	AZ	Robert F. Plew	1994	3,440
261 6/8	36 3/8	40 2/8	33 6/8	6	6	Otero County	NM	Ronald Friesner	1995	3,440
261 5/8	40 0/8	37 2/8	33 5/8	6	6	Rio Blanco County	CO	H. V. McFarland, Jr.	1974	3,446
261 5/8	37 1/8	36 1/8	37 6/8	6	6	Flathead County	MT	Dr. Brad Black	1981	3,446
261 5/8	35 6/8	35 4/8	34 5/8	6	6	Fremont County	ID	Todd J. Frickey	1987	3,446
261 5/8	43 1/8	43 2/8	37 5/8	5	6	Garfield County	CO	Francis J. Dehner	1989	3,446
261 5/8	39 1/8	40 2/8	34 1/8	6	6	Beaverhead County	MT	Eduard Hale	1990	3,446
261 5/8	36 5/8	35 0/8	36 6/8	6	6	Missoula County	MT	Vinnie Pisani	1993	3,446
261 5/8	39 0/8	41 1/8	38 6/8	6	6	Comanche County	OK	Richard J. Warren	1993	3,446
261 5/8	43 7/8	44 0/8	36 1/8	6	6	Archuleta County	CO	Keith Sherrill	1997	3,446
261 5/8	37 4/8	36 6/8	32 5/8	6	6	Rio Blanco County	CO	Jimmy N. Brown	1998	3,446
261 4/8	43 0/8	43 2/8	35 0/8	6	6	Caribou County	ID	Randy K. Guinn	1986	3,455
261 4/8	42 0/8	39 3/8	31 6/8	6	6	Madison County	MT	Robert J. Kleinhans	1992	3,455
261 3/8	41 6/8	41 3/8	31 1/8	6	6	Fremont County	ID	Gary Owens	1980	3,457
261 3/8	39 0/8	40 1/8	34 7/8	6	6	Gallatin County	MT	Paul D. Amdahl	1993	3,457
261 3/8	38 6/8	38 7/8	31 1/8	6	6	Lincoln County	WY	Gerald Henrickson	1994	3,457
261 3/8	42 0/8	42 6/8	40 1/8	5	5	Wallowa County	OR	Sidney R. Marks	1996	3,457
261 3/8	43 5/8	43 6/8	35 7/8	6	6	Valley County	ID	Alan R. Bentley	1997	3,457
261 2/8	42 5/8	42 4/8	31 0/8	5	5	Rio Arriba County	NM	Donald N. Lehman	1983	3,462
261 2/8	42 4/8	41 3/8	33 4/8	6	6	Costilla County	CO	Timothy L. Walters	1985	3,462
261 2/8	44 6/8	44 1/8	34 0/8	5	5	Cibola County	NM	Duane T. Corley	1986	3,462
261 2/8	46 2/8	44 3/8	37 6/8	6	6	Sheridan County	WY	Mike Barrett	1988	3,462
261 2/8	41 4/8	41 4/8	29 0/8	6	6	Colfax County	NM	Ronald Ralston	1994	3,462
261 1/8	37 7/8	36 2/8	37 7/8	6	6	Jackson County	CO	Knut A. Paulsen	1975	3,467
261 1/8	44 1/8	43 1/8	36 7/8	6	7	Caribou County	ID	Richard T. Vance	1975	3,467
261 1/8	41 1/8	42 6/8	35 5/8	6	6	Clearwater County	ID	Steve Eiede	1988	3,467
261 1/8	41 5/8	40 6/8	40 2/8	6	7	Lewis & Clark County	MT	Sonny Templeton	1991	3,467
261 0/8	46 6/8	45 6/8	32 4/8	6	5	Saguache County	CO	Irene M. Blaskowski	1990	3,471
261 0/8	46 0/8	45 1/8	36 2/8	6	6	Clearwater County	ID	Don Leedham	1991	3,471
261 0/8	44 2/8	42 6/8	38 6/8	5	5	Sublette County	WY	Kim A. Glasgow	1991	3,471
261 0/8	47 7/8	40 6/8	37 1/8	7	6	Taos County	NM	David Muzny	1994	3,471
261 0/8	37 0/8	37 2/8	35 0/8	6	6	Tuchodi River	BC	Scott Ebert	1994	3,471
260 7/8	37 6/8	37 6/8	34 3/8	6	6	Grant County	OR	Colby Moulton	1986	3,476
260 7/8	41 7/8	42 0/8	38 7/8	6	6	Pitkin County	CO	Jim Plett	1987	3,476
260 7/8	41 2/8	41 1/8	31 3/8	6	6	Madison County	MT	Chester Graham	1992	3,476
260 7/8	38 0/8	38 1/8	42 5/8	6	6	San Miguel County	CO	Wayne Carlton	1993	3,476
260 7/8	44 3/8	45 0/8	35 1/8	6	6	Dolores County	CO	Scott Hawthorne	1994	3,476
260 7/8	36 7/8	37 7/8	38 3/8	7	8	Franklin County	ID	James R. Keller	1995	3,476
260 7/8	40 2/8	39 6/8	35 1/8	5	5	Grant County	NM	Harold L. Sides	1996	3,476
260 6/8	40 4/8	44 6/8	30 2/8	7	7	Coconino County	AZ	James Casady	1978	3,483
260 6/8	38 0/8	37 3/8	34 0/8	6	6	Converse County	WY	Russell Burghard	1983	3,483
260 6/8	38 0/8	37 5/8	34 2/8	6	6	Clearwater County	ID	Chuck Lynde	1988	3,483
260 6/8	40 2/8	40 2/8	35 6/8	6	6	Beaverhead County	MT	Marvin Hearon	1992	3,483
260 6/8	42 7/8	41 6/8	33 6/8	6	6	Gallatin County	MT	Edd L. Clack	1993	3,483
260 6/8	42 7/8	43 1/8	36 4/8	5	5	Lewis & Clark County	MT	James Gravatt	1993	3,483
260 6/8	48 2/8	48 0/8	39 4/8	5	6	Linn County	OR	Joe Etter II	1994	3,483
260 6/8	40 7/8	39 7/8	36 4/8	6	6	Park County	MT	Barry S. Schultz	1994	3,483
260 6/8	47 2/8	45 4/8	32 2/8	5	6	Archuleta County	CO	Darla Bramwell	1996	3,483
260 6/8	43 6/8	41 4/8	36 6/8	6	6	Rio Arriba County	NM	Bob Hubbard	1997	3,483
260 5/8	40 4/8	42 0/8	34 7/8	6	6	Kimberley	BC	Rick Hammond	1986	3,493
260 5/8	38 1/8	38 4/8	38 1/8	6	6	Catron County	NM	Michael J. Bradeen	1990	3,493
260 5/8	40 6/8	40 4/8	34 3/8	6	6	Mineral County	MT	Chris W. Dix	1992	3,493
260 5/8	36 2/8	37 2/8	34 0/8	7	7	Phillips County	MT	Mark Meyer	1995	3,493
260 5/8	45 0/8	44 2/8	36 1/8	6	6	Catron County	NM	David M. Bufkin	1996	3,493
260 4/8	40 4/8	40 7/8	38 0/8	6	6	Blaine County	ID	Wesley Moore	1986	3,498
260 4/8	40 6/8	40 1/8	34 0/8	6	7	Fergus County	MT	Jerry Knerr	1987	3,498
260 4/8	40 2/8	37 4/8	34 0/8	6	6	Elmore County	ID	Roger W. Atwood	1988	3,498
260 4/8	46 2/8	44 7/8	34 5/8	6	7	Montrose County	CO	David Henkie	1989	3,498
260 4/8	38 6/8	38 5/8	33 6/8	6	6	Catron County	NM	Jerry G. Roberts	1992	3,498
260 4/8	40 6/8	44 4/8	32 4/8	6	6	Coconino County	AZ	Patrick Donald Dufek	1992	3,498
260 4/8	43 1/8	43 1/8	36 2/8	5	6	Sandoval County	NM	Mitchell Lee Chapman	1993	3,498
260 4/8	37 2/8	38 5/8	35 4/8	6	5	Catron County	NM	Charlie Schlosser	1998	3,498
260 3/8	38 4/8	38 7/8	30 7/8	6	6	Madison County	ID	Paul L. Beesley	1979	3,506
260 3/8	42 2/8	41 5/8	32 2/8	6	6	Archuleta County	CO	Lester D. Hawkins, Jr.	1988	3,506
260 3/8	37 5/8	40 0/8	37 7/8	6	6	Lewis & Clark County	MT	Jeff Jackson	1992	3,506
260 3/8	42 0/8	40 5/8	39 1/8	6	6	Carbon County	UT	Kit Critchlow	1993	3,506
260 3/8	42 5/8	47 6/8	36 0/8	8	6	Coconino County	AZ	Tony W. Zimbaro	1993	3,506

YELLOWSTONE "AMERICAN" ELK (TYPICAL ANTLERS)

Minimum Score 260

SCORE	LENGTH OF R MAIN BEAM L		INSIDE SPREAD	NUMBER OF R POINTS L		AREA	STATE/ PROVINCE	HUNTER'S NAME	DATE	RANK
260 3/8	46 2/8	46 3/8	33 3/8	6	5	Grant County	OR	Jerry W. Simmons	1995	3,506
260 3/8	37 4/8	39 4/8	35 3/8	6	6	Catron County	NM	Kenneth Brongo	1998	3,506
260 2/8	41 2/8	41 4/8	37 0/8	6	6	Pitkin County	CO	Wayne MacDonnell	1987	3,513
260 2/8	37 0/8	38 0/8	35 0/8	6	6	Rio Blanco County	CO	Charles R. Clark	1991	3,513
260 2/8	39 5/8	40 5/8	38 6/8	6	7	San Luis Obispo County	CA	Gary F. Bogner	1997	3,513
260 2/8	46 1/8	46 2/8	35 4/8	5	6	Cibola County	NM	Reid S. Christopher, M.D.	1997	3,513
260 1/8	44 1/8	43 2/8	37 5/8	6	6	Catron County	NM	Bob "Jake" Jacobsen	1989	3,517
260 1/8	41 0/8	44 3/8	36 3/8	5	5	Catron County	NM	Jim Eppler	1990	3,517
260 1/8	39 7/8	38 4/8	33 3/8	6	6	Fisher Creek	ALB	Rick Lepp	1991	3,517
260 1/8	42 4/8	44 1/8	35 5/8	5	5	Idaho County	ID	Steven L. DeBauche	1992	3,517
260 1/8	47 1/8	46 2/8	35 6/8	5	7	Meagher County	MT	Robert Davison	1996	3,517
260 1/8	39 3/8	39 3/8	34 7/8	6	7	Pembina County	ND	George E. Walker III	1997	3,517
260 1/8	39 2/8	39 6/8	34 5/8	6	6	Valley County	MT	Dan Sturgis	1998	3,517
260 0/8	36 4/8	36 4/8	39 5/8	6	6	Grand County	CO	Kevin O'Connell	1981	3,524
260 0/8	44 7/8	44 3/8	35 4/8	6	6	Catron County	NM	Duane "Corky" Richardson	1996	3,524
260 0/8	38 7/8	39 3/8	38 4/8	5	6	Carbon County	UT	James L. Stowe	1998	3,524

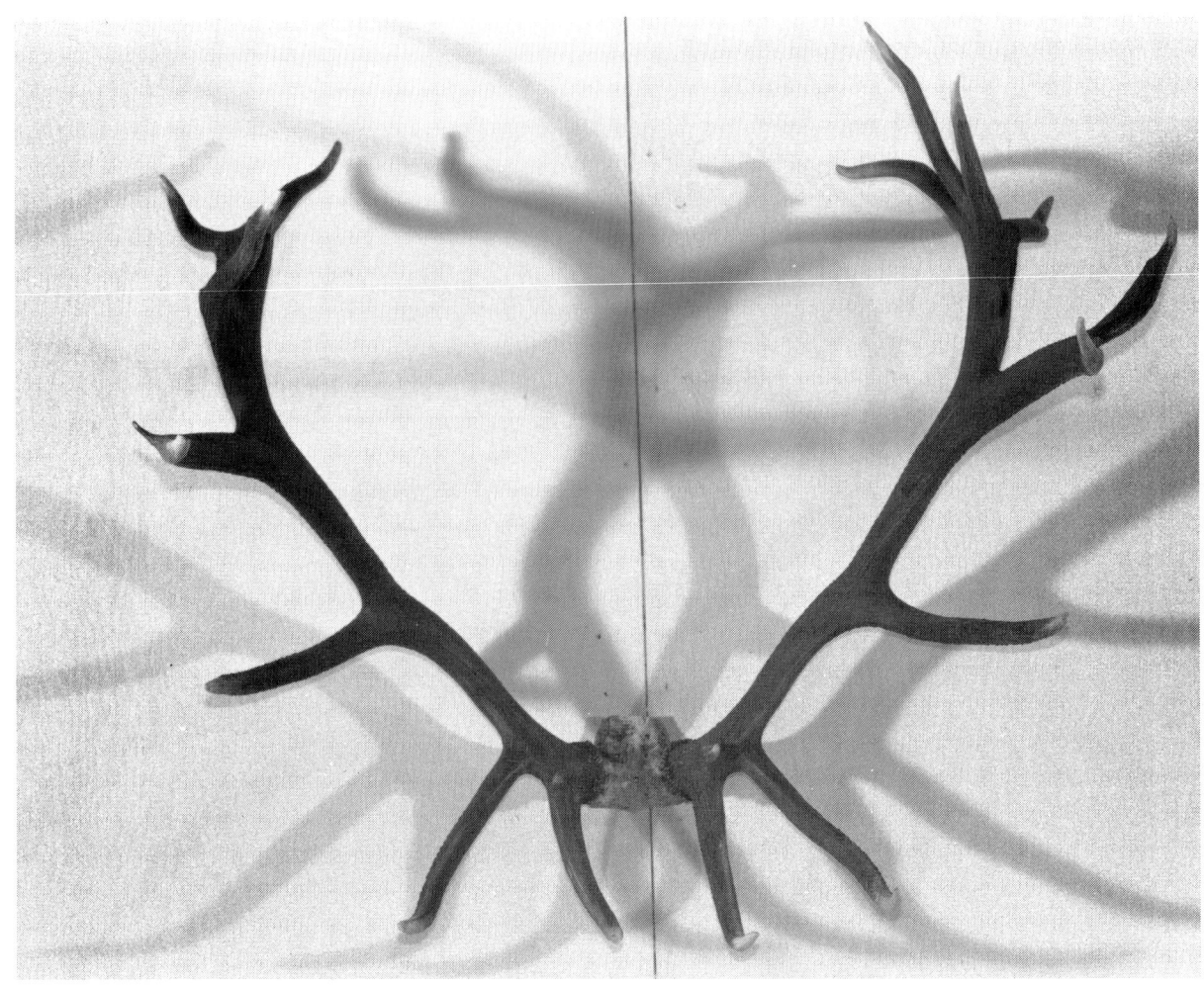

World Record Yellowstone "American" Elk (Non-Typical Antlers)
Score: 419 5/8
Coconino County, Arizona - 1985
Hunter: James L. Ludvigson

YELLOWSTONE "AMERICAN" ELK (NON-TYPICAL ANTLERS)

Minimum Score 335 *Cervus elaphus nelsoni* and certain related subspecies

SCORE	LENGTH OF R MAIN BEAM L		INSIDE SPREAD	NUMBER OF R POINTS L		AREA	STATE/ PROVINCE	HUNTER'S NAME	DATE	RANK
419 5/8	53 1/8	51 6/8	39 4/8	8	10	Coconino County	AZ	James L. Ludvigson	1985	1
417 0/8	56 0/8	56 1/8	51 7/8	8	7	Coconino County	AZ	Brady J. Dupke	1993	2
409 0/8	54 7/8	53 5/8	40 4/8	8	7	Lincoln County	MT	Terry V. Crooks	1996	3
403 0/8	49 0/8	50 2/8	39 0/8	8	9	Powell County	MT	Donald Roberson	1987	4
398 1/8	53 4/8	52 2/8	42 5/8	8	8	White Pine County	NV	Brian Harwood	1998	5
391 7/8	40 5/8	40 1/8	34 3/8	13	11	Camp Hughs	MAN	Brent Maxwell	1991	6
391 4/8	50 1/8	53 4/8	35 1/8	9	7	Garfield County	MT	D. Mitch Kottas	1995	7
389 5/8	52 4/8	54 0/8	35 6/8	7	7	Douglas County	CO	Mark Martin	1998	8
387 4/8	53 0/8	52 5/8	38 4/8	6	9	Lincoln County	NV	Cory Lytle	1998	9
387 2/8	48 6/8	48 3/8	37 3/8	7	7	Catron County	NM	Robert J. Brooks	1992	10
381 7/8	54 2/8	54 1/8	42 2/8	7	7	Coconino County	AZ	Dick Kirby	1992	11
381 7/8	53 6/8	54 1/8	44 5/8	8	8	Catron County	NM	Anthony J. Berardis, Jr.	1997	11
381 3/8	52 7/8	51 5/8	41 5/8	7	8	Coconino County	AZ	David A. Niemann	1990	13
380 6/8	51 0/8	51 0/8	39 7/8	8	6	Catron County	NM	Mike Garretson	1996	14
380 3/8	54 2/8	54 5/8	43 1/8	8	7	Socorro County	NM	George Rude	1994	15
377 3/8	50 7/8	51 1/8	32 6/8	9	8	Huerfano County	CO	Brett Wyka	1996	16
376 0/8	48 0/8	49 3/8	57 1/8	7	7	Catron County	NM	Shaun D. Finch	1995	17
373 2/8	47 1/8	47 6/8	41 2/8	7	8	Lincoln County	MT	Larry M. Monroe	1992	18
373 0/8	53 5/8	52 7/8	43 5/8	6	8	Navajo County	AZ	Randy Ulmer	1994	19
371 1/8	53 0/8	49 5/8	48 0/8	7	9	Sierra County	NM	Kevin L. Keyes	1989	20
371 1/8	50 0/8	49 2/8	42 5/8	7	7	Catron County	NM	Eddie Collins	1991	20

YELLOWSTONE "AMERICAN" ELK (NON-TYPICAL ANTLERS)

Minimum Score 335

SCORE	LENGTH OF R MAIN BEAM L		INSIDE SPREAD	NUMBER OF R POINTS L		AREA	STATE/ PROVINCE	HUNTER'S NAME	DATE	RANK
371 0/8	48 1/8	50 4/8	48 5/8	7	6	Mora County	NM	George P. Mann	1990	22
370 7/8	51 6/8	52 6/8	40 6/8	8	8	Millard County	UT	Jeff Mitchell	1997	23
370 3/8	53 0/8	54 0/8	47 3/8	8	9	Gila County	AZ	John Bush	1989	24
369 4/8	51 6/8	53 7/8	44 4/8	7	7	Otero County	NM	Leland Wood	1997	25
368 3/8	54 1/8	56 4/8	39 7/8	8	6	Custer County	ID	Scott Griggs	1992	26
368 2/8	49 3/8	48 3/8	37 7/8	7	8	Catron County	NM	Craig J. Cooper	1997	27
367 7/8	53 1/8	53 0/8	41 3/8	7	10	Catron County	NM	Steve Mathis	1997	28
367 0/8	55 6/8	55 1/8	38 5/8	7	7	Catron County	NM	Shayne Franzoy	1994	29
366 1/8	46 2/8	45 4/8	44 1/8	6	7	Catron County	NM	Craig C. Sanchez	1997	30
365 0/8	44 3/8	44 0/8	41 6/8	7	8	Lincoln County	NM	Kurt Hollis	1992	31
364 6/8	54 7/8	53 1/8	42 5/8	6	7	Fergus County	MT	Jerry Knerr	1997	32
364 4/8	53 1/8	53 5/8	36 0/8	8	8	Coconino County	AZ	David Ferrario	1994	33
364 3/8	50 1/8	50 0/8	29 2/8	6	8	Catron County	NM	Wayne K. Curtis	1988	34
363 6/8	49 4/8	52 0/8	41 7/8	8	8	Coconino County	AZ	Dean Dunaway	1993	35
363 6/8	54 6/8	52 6/8	38 7/8	8	8	Navajo County	AZ	Chad Jasperson	1997	35
362 0/8	46 1/8	47 5/8	33 0/8	7	7	Catron County	NM	Dave Holt	1997	37
361 3/8	45 6/8	45 1/8	39 5/8	8	8	Nez Perce County	ID	Randy Hollibaugh	1989	38
361 3/8	47 1/8	48 3/8	35 4/8	8	7	Apache County	AZ	Tom Ensman	1995	38
361 0/8	48 6/8	47 2/8	41 2/8	8	7	Flathead County	MT	Chester G. Fossum, Jr.	1992	40
359 3/8	51 1/8	44 4/8	37 2/8	8	7	Catron County	NM	Ronald M. Gerdes	1992	41
356 1/8	55 5/8	49 7/8	35 2/8	8	7	Greenlee County	AZ	Robert M. Dryden	1995	42
355 6/8	47 2/8	46 1/8	39 0/8	7	8	Umatilla County	OR	Guy P. Hurlbert	1998	43
353 5/8	50 0/8	48 4/8	37 4/8	7	6	Coconino County	AZ	Russell Richardson	1995	44
350 4/8	48 1/8	49 0/8	31 3/8	6	7	Socorro County	NM	Marvin H. Walter	1998	45
350 0/8	40 3/8	39 0/8	40 2/8	7	7	Meagher County	MT	Steven W. Prunty	1996	46
349 2/8	45 4/8	45 0/8	42 1/8	7	8	Garfield County	MT	D. Mitch Kottas	1996	47
347 3/8	53 1/8	53 4/8	42 5/8	7	8	Fergus County	MT	John Fleharty	1992	48
346 2/8	48 7/8	49 4/8	39 3/8	7	6	Shoshone County	ID	Dan Payne	1995	49
345 7/8	47 2/8	47 5/8	50 4/8	8	9	Valley County	ID	Julian Salutregui	1998	50
345 4/8	48 0/8	49 4/8	31 6/8	7	7	Coconino County	AZ	Barry Stonehouse	1992	51
345 1/8	44 2/8	45 2/8	46 6/8	8	8	Catron County	NM	Jerry Leair	1998	52
345 0/8	48 4/8	51 0/8	30 4/8	7	8	Grant County	NM	Charles T. Wood	1998	53
344 5/8	42 0/8	41 7/8	34 6/8	7	10	Catron County	NM	Glenn Isler	1993	54
344 3/8	51 2/8	48 1/8	33 7/8	8	7	Elko County	NV	Kent Arrien	1996	55
342 7/8	52 7/8	51 4/8	38 7/8	7	7	Greenlee County	AZ	Bill Golden	1990	56
340 4/8	49 7/8	50 6/8	36 6/8	7	7	Navajo County	AZ	Stan H. Hacker	1996	57
340 1/8	53 2/8	53 2/8	41 6/8	7	8	Valley County	ID	Curt Giese	1998	58
335 6/8	43 5/8	40 4/8	42 4/8	9	8	Solano County	CA	Audrey Goodnight	1990	59
335 5/8	45 5/8	42 6/8	40 0/8	8	7	Catron County	NM	Paul T. Horne	1990	60
335 4/8	46 1/8	48 0/8	34 0/8	8	8	Moffat County	CO	Tom Walker	1996	61

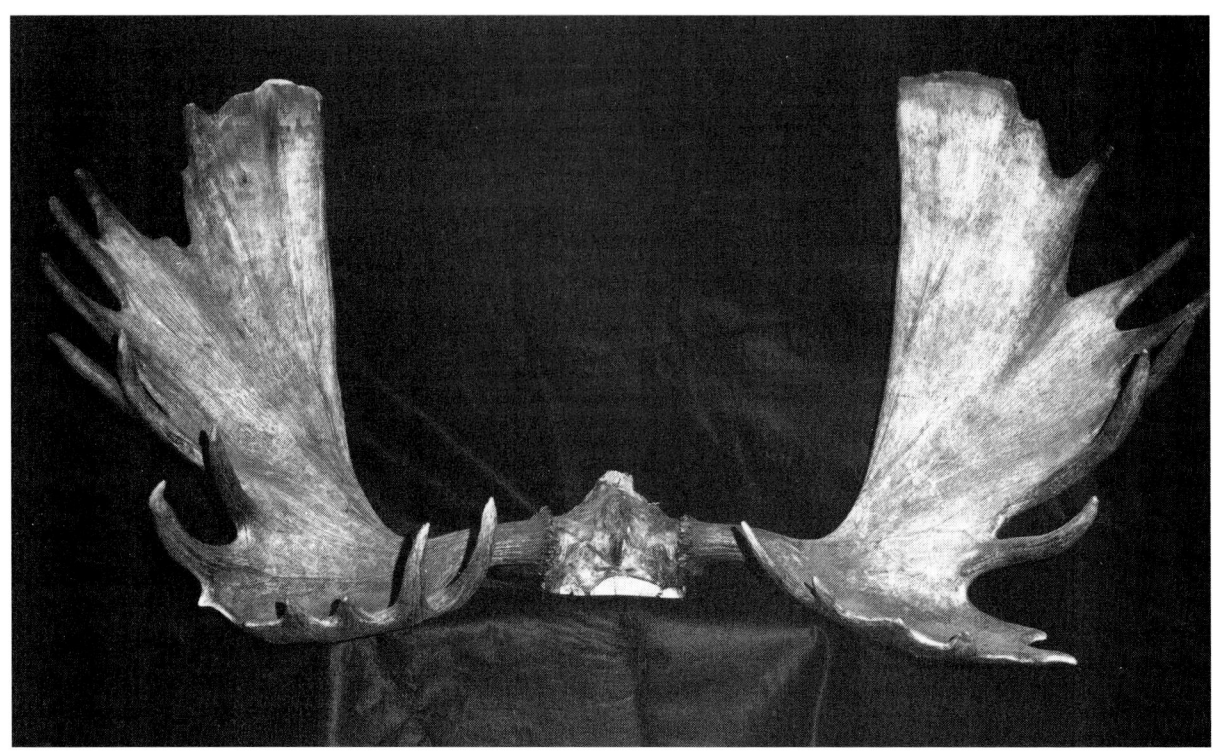

World Record Alaska-Yukon Moose
Score: 248 0/8
Bear Creek, Alaska - 1973
Hunter: Dr. Michael L. Cusack

ALASKA-YUKON MOOSE

Minimum Score 170

Alces alces gigas

SCORE	GREATEST SPREAD	WIDTH OF PALM R	WIDTH OF PALM L	NUMBER OF POINTS R	NUMBER OF POINTS L	AREA	STATE/ PROVINCE	HUNTER'S NAME	DATE	RANK
248 0/8	74 0/8	18 6/8	19 2/8	11	11	Bear Creek	AK	Dr. Michael L. Cusack	1973	1
240 4/8	70 6/8	16 2/8	15 6/8	12	12	Galena	AK	Sam Smith	1995	2
227 7/8	68 3/8	18 2/8	16 3/8	14	13	Earn Lake	YUK	Ted Brown	1995	3
227 6/8	60 0/8	17 1/8	16 1/8	13	12	Koyukuk River	AK	Larry Oppe	1998	4
224 3/8	59 5/8	17 0/8	16 4/8	15	13	Lake Iliamna	AK	George Faerber	1974	5
224 2/8	67 4/8	19 0/8	14 5/8	10	12	Mosquito Flats	AK	William C. Shuster	1998	6
224 0/8	65 4/8	15 0/8	14 2/8	12	12	Lake Iliamna	AK	Zane Streater	1995	7
224 0/8	65 0/8	15 0/8	14 1/8	12	13	Dulbi River	AK	Rick Boullion	1995	7
223 7/8	73 7/8	14 2/8	16 0/8	12	11	Kugruk River	AK	Rocky Tope	1978	9
223 2/8	68 0/8	14 3/8	16 2/8	11	14	Innoko River	AK	Roger Stewart	1993	10
223 1/8	62 5/8	13 3/8	14 2/8	11	11	Sugarloaf Mtn.	AK	James C. Walters	1990	11
222 1/8	67 1/8	20 0/8	15 4/8	13	12	Lower Susitna	AK	Steve McCalmant	1981	12
221 6/8	64 2/8	16 0/8	16 0/8	9	9	Moose John River	AK	Michael S. Pasztor	1993	13
221 6/8	60 2/8	16 1/8	14 7/8	14	17	Mac Millan River	YUK	Dr. Warren Strickland	1998	13
221 4/8	64 2/8	15 5/8	15 2/8	11	12	Koyukuk River	AK	Windell Arnold	1995	15
220 3/8	57 3/8	16 0/8	16 2/8	12	11	Little Delta River	AK	William Wright	1959	16
219 7/8	65 5/8	14 4/8	14 5/8	16	14	Hart River	YUK	Kim S. Hussong	1994	17
219 0/8	61 0/8	14 4/8	8 0/8	13	12	Kichatna River	AK	Ronald N. Kolpin	1974	18
218 2/8	69 0/8	15 7/8	17 4/8	10	8	Galena	AK	Lon E. Lauber	1993	19
217 4/8	71 2/8	13 2/8	12 6/8	10	12	Ugashik River	AK	Gary Hoffer	1986	20
217 4/8	63 6/8	18 4/8	18 3/8	14	11	Grayling Creek	AK	Carl Spaeth	1995	20
217 3/8	64 1/8	17 0/8	15 0/8	14	15	Moose John River	AK	Mike Parsons	1991	22
216 4/8	57 6/8	16 1/8	18 1/8	13	13	Jim River	AK	James A. Todhunter	1996	23
216 1/8	57 1/8	16 7/8	16 1/8	11	12	Cheeneetnuk River	AK	Rocky D. Tschappat	1995	24
215 7/8	63 3/8	13 2/8	12 1/8	15	14	Koyukuk River	AK	Rickie D. Snell	1990	25
215 4/8	68 0/8	14 0/8	19 2/8	12	10	Cinder River	AK	D. Kevin Moore, DDS	1997	26
215 3/8	71 7/8	13 5/8	12 7/8	11	11	Boston Creek	AK	Charles Harrison	1992	27
215 0/8	56 2/8	14 0/8	13 2/8	13	17	Koyukuk River	AK	Patricio Sada	1998	28
214 4/8	63 4/8	15 2/8	17 2/8	8	11	Mac Millan River	YUK	Robert W. Harris	1996	29
214 2/8	57 2/8	14 5/8	17 2/8	11	16	Cheeneetnuk River	AK	Dean Layman	1988	30
213 3/8	70 5/8	15 7/8	14 1/8	7	8	Two Peat Mtn.	YUK	Mark Zimmerman	1998	31

ALASKA-YUKON MOOSE

Minimum Score 170 — Continued — 603

SCORE	GREATEST SPREAD	WIDTH OF PALM R	WIDTH OF PALM L	NUMBER OF POINTS R	NUMBER OF POINTS L	AREA	STATE/ PROVINCE	HUNTER'S NAME	DATE	RANK
213 2/8	62 4/8	18 4/8	15 6/8	9	10	Rainy Pass	AK	Rick Tollison	1978	32
213 1/8	59 7/8	17 3/8	18 1/8	13	12	Mulchatna River	AK	Peter Weatherford	1988	33
213 0/8	55 6/8	14 0/8	14 3/8	13	13	Kobuk River	AK	Joe Ellsworth	1998	34
212 7/8	65 7/8	13 0/8	17 6/8	9	10	Mulchatna River	AK	Jay Massey	1973	35
212 7/8	65 5/8	12 4/8	15 5/8	12	14	Tetlin River	AK	Mike Kistler	1997	35
212 5/8	69 3/8	11 5/8	13 3/8	12	13	Keni	AK	Charles Palmer	1993	37
212 2/8	62 6/8	14 2/8	15 0/8	12	13	Koyukuk River	AK	Joe Caswell	1991	38
212 1/8	58 3/8	15 0/8	14 6/8	16	15	Brooks Range	AK	Roger Stewart	1985	39
212 1/8	60 1/8	14 1/8	15 2/8	12	13	Mac Millan River	YUK	Jerry Seyller	1998	39
211 2/8	66 6/8	15 0/8	14 4/8	9	9	Anchorage	AK	Dr. Rex Hancock	1961	41
211 2/8	66 6/8	21 3/8	16 0/8	7	9	Meshik River	AK	Art Kragness	1970	41
211 1/8	55 1/8	16 2/8	13 0/8	11	10	Mac Millan River	YUK	David Emken	1994	43
211 0/8	59 4/8	12 0/8	13 0/8	14	13	Galena	AK	John C. Fisher	1996	44
210 6/8	60 0/8	12 7/8	13 1/8	13	13	New Stuyahok	AK	Thomas Clevenger	1988	45
210 6/8	64 6/8	15 3/8	12 6/8	13	11	Mystery Creek	AK	Kevin M. Krause	1997	45
210 5/8	60 1/8	15 0/8	15 6/8	13	10	Kichatna River	AK	Frank Leonardo	1996	47
210 5/8	61 3/8	15 3/8	15 3/8	10	11	Mac Millan River	YUK	Don Lind	1998	47
210 1/8	64 5/8	14 1/8	13 6/8	8	9	Nabesna	AK	Bill Ellis	1965	49
209 7/8	60 5/8	13 2/8	11 3/8	14	14	Koyukuk River	AK	Gerald Weeks	1990	50
209 6/8	69 0/8	13 0/8	14 4/8	9	9	Port Heiden	AK	Margaret Cooley	1966	51
209 4/8	59 4/8	11 1/8	12 5/8	11	11	Healy	AK	Jack P. Lohrenz	1996	52
209 3/8	63 3/8	15 3/8	14 3/8	11	13	Mac Millan River	YUK	David Harris	1995	53
209 1/8	62 7/8	14 6/8	19 4/8	8	9	Susitna River	AK	John D. 'Jack' Frost	1981	54
209 1/8	64 7/8	15 0/8	16 0/8	9	10	Tagagawik River	AK	Bill Grahlherr	1984	54
209 1/8	63 1/8	15 0/8	14 1/8	13	13	Mac Millan River	YUK	David Baldwin	1989	54
208 6/8	63 0/8	13 3/8	13 7/8	9	9	Galena	AK	James McCloskey	1988	57
208 6/8	64 2/8	11 4/8	12 6/8	11	14	Koyukuk River	AK	David Emken	1998	57
208 4/8	65 2/8	14 2/8	13 3/8	12	12	Kemuk Mtn.	AK	L. Grant Foster	1997	59
208 1/8	59 7/8	13 5/8	15 2/8	13	13	Brooks Range	AK	Ted Grover	1985	60
208 0/8	65 4/8	13 0/8	12 0/8	9	7	Alaska Peninsula	AK	Jack Niles	1970	61
207 5/8	59 1/8	14 3/8	14 2/8	14	15	Coleen River	AK	Lyle Willmarth	1990	62
207 2/8	60 2/8	12 1/8	16 6/8	10	10	Yenlo Mtns.	AK	John F. Sumrall	1979	63
206 5/8	62 1/8	12 2/8	13 2/8	12	13	Kotzebue	AK	Bruce A. Moe	1980	64
206 3/8	69 3/8	12 0/8	9 4/8	7	9	Alaska Peninsula	AK	Dr. Charles R. Leidheiser	1974	65
206 2/8	59 4/8	12 5/8	15 2/8	15	14	Kuparuk River	AK	Kurt Lepping	1987	66
206 2/8	50 6/8	16 5/8	16 2/8	13	17	Mac Millan River	YUK	T. Sanford Roberts	1990	66
206 0/8	65 0/8	12 1/8	14 0/8	12	11	Chulitna River	AK	Rodney Bremer	1988	68
206 0/8	57 6/8	13 2/8	16 7/8	15	10	Grayling Creek	AK	Karl R. Spaeth	1997	68
205 7/8	55 1/8	13 1/8	14 0/8	12	10	Innoko River	AK	Jack Smythe	1974	70
205 6/8	70 0/8	15 7/8	13 3/8	9	9	Alaska Peninsula	AK	Dr. Howard Schneider	1982	71
205 6/8	67 6/8	11 6/8	12 0/8	12	9	Kuskokwim River	AK	Jimmy Harkins	1986	71
205 4/8	57 6/8	13 4/8	13 3/8	11	13	Horsetrail Lake	AK	Donald Poole	1979	73
205 2/8	64 0/8	14 0/8	12 7/8	8	12	Alaska Peninsula	AK	Donald B. McIntosh	1969	74
205 1/8	57 7/8	14 2/8	12 4/8	15	13	Telaquana	AK	Mike Mitten	1988	75
205 1/8	63 3/8	15 1/8	14 3/8	13	14	Mac Millan River	YUK	David M. Richards	1996	75
204 7/8	60 3/8	14 5/8	15 6/8	10	11	Paxon	AK	Alan Perry	1972	77
204 7/8	68 3/8	14 7/8	14 6/8	7	11	Black Lake	AK	Stanley Winslow	1973	77
204 7/8	58 1/8	15 1/8	15 4/8	12	11	Jim River	AK	Eldon Holm	1990	77
204 4/8	58 0/8	12 6/8	13 0/8	11	11	Chilikadrotna River	AK	Peter Thomas Weatherford	1987	80
204 2/8	61 4/8	13 4/8	12 5/8	10	11	Fairbanks	AK	Keith Jensen	1986	81
204 2/8	56 6/8	14 1/8	14 3/8	14	12	Deer Hunting Slough	AK	Ted K. Jaycox	1995	81
204 1/8	57 3/8	14 1/8	15 5/8	15	10	Cooper Creek	AK	Joe W. Harrison	1993	83
203 6/8	66 0/8	11 5/8	12 7/8	13	11	Port Heiden	AK	Jim Dougherty	1968	84
203 3/8	66 7/8	11 0/8	11 7/8	13	12	Seven Mile Lake	AK	Dr. William J. Young, Jr.	1980	85
203 3/8	66 5/8	15 2/8	17 5/8	11	13	Dulbi River	AK	Kenneth E. Gordon	1998	85
202 7/8	58 1/8	12 6/8	13 4/8	15	13	Earn Lake	YUK	Dr. R. D. Keeler	1986	87
202 7/8	66 3/8	13 2/8	12 4/8	8	14	Susitna River	AK	David Bieganski	1997	87
202 4/8	49 6/8	14 2/8	14 4/8	10	12	Brooks Range	AK	Brent Chapman	1978	89
202 4/8	58 2/8	15 2/8	14 1/8	13	12	Chulitna River	AK	Rickie D. Snell	1982	89
202 2/8	62 6/8	12 5/8	13 4/8	9	10	Toolik River	AK	George P. Mann	1987	91
202 0/8	63 1/8	14 2/8	13 5/8	10	8	Moose John River	AK	Kent Brigham	1985	92
202 0/8	63 0/8	13 0/8	12 0/8	15	14	Big Bend	AK	Roger O. Wyant	1992	92
202 0/8	61 2/8	12 2/8	13 2/8	13	13	Yukon River	AK	Tom Skripps	1994	92
201 6/8	59 0/8	11 7/8	13 0/8	13	12	Brooks Range	AK	Mike Rosetti	1985	95
201 2/8	62 4/8	14 1/8	13 2/8	10	10	Rackla Lake	YUK	Paul Hight	1991	96
201 2/8	63 6/8	14 7/8	14 7/8	14	13	Brooks Range	AK	James L. Behn	1991	96
200 7/8	58 5/8	12 5/8	15 0/8	13	13	Wrangell Mtns.	AK	Robert Warpack	1988	98
200 3/8	61 1/8	13 3/8	13 7/8	10	11	Chanuk Creek	AK	Roger O. Wyant	1989	99
200 2/8	64 2/8	14 4/8	14 0/8	10	11	Dog Salmon River	AK	Robert C. Keadle	1972	100
200 2/8	62 2/8	13 1/8	12 7/8	12	12	King Salmon	AK	Ken Slaght	1982	100
200 2/8	60 4/8	13 6/8	11 0/8	12	12	Skentna River	AK	David Bailey	1983	100
200 0/8	65 2/8	12 2/8	15 1/8	9	12	Galena	AK	Sam Smith	1993	103
199 6/8	52 0/8	12 5/8	12 2/8	10	11	Timberline Lk. Kenai	AK	Dewayne Benton	1984	104
199 5/8	61 3/8	15 2/8	14 2/8	13	14	Koyukuk Basin	AK	Dan Waelbrock	1989	105
199 5/8	59 0/8	12 6/8	12 2/8	13	11	Kalzas Lake	YUK	Robert Krasinski	1996	105
199 3/8	56 1/8	11 2/8	11 2/8	9	9	Nelchina	AK	Henry Wichers	1962	107
199 2/8	58 6/8	14 4/8	14 7/8	12	10	Koyukuk River	AK	Joe Caswell	1990	108
198 7/8	63 7/8	11 1/8	13 0/8	8	10	Gulkana Basin	AK	Thomas L. A. Pucci	1970	109

ALASKA-YUKON MOOSE

Minimum Score 170

SCORE	GREATEST SPREAD	WIDTH OF PALM R	L	NUMBER OF POINTS R	L	AREA	STATE/ PROVINCE	HUNTER'S NAME	DATE	RANK
198 7/8	64 1/8	15 3/8	15 6/8	7	8	Tag River	AK	Thomas E. Rothrock	1991	109
198 4/8	60 2/8	16 0/8	15 4/8	9	10	Arctic Wildlife Refuge	AK	William Gardner Rowell	1981	111
198 2/8	52 2/8	17 0/8	13 4/8	8	10	Nenana River	AK	Dr. Harley Scholz	1973	112
198 1/8	63 5/8	11 3/8	11 6/8	10	12	Rainy Pass	AK	Dr. Henry C. McDonald	1970	113
198 1/8	53 5/8	14 3/8	15 2/8	12	9	Grayling Creek	AK	James C. Carlson	1995	113
197 6/8	64 0/8	11 4/8	11 2/8	12	11	King Salmon	AK	Gary L. Petty	1976	115
197 6/8	63 2/8	13 2/8	12 1/8	8	9	Susitna	AK	Mark S Bode	1989	115
197 6/8	54 4/8	15 4/8	13 4/8	6	8	Mac Millan River	YUK	Alan Schroeder	1995	115
197 5/8	59 5/8	12 7/8	12 5/8	9	9	Galena	AK	George Ollert	1988	118
197 4/8	65 4/8	13 0/8	14 5/8	6	9	Ugashik River	AK	Robert Borland	1972	119
197 4/8	61 4/8	10 6/8	12 1/8	8	11	Ugashik Lake	AK	John Wallace	1974	119
197 4/8	59 2/8	11 4/8	15 2/8	12	12	Chulitna River	AK	Rickie D. Snell	1983	119
197 2/8	64 2/8	12 3/8	14 4/8	8	8	Sugar Loaf Mtns.	AK	Jeffrey S. Stevens	1988	122
197 1/8	62 1/8	14 4/8	11 1/8	12	10	Susitna River	AK	Jake Sonnentag	1969	123
197 1/8	59 3/8	19 1/8	13 5/8	11	8	Mac Millan River	YUK	Bob Fromme	1991	123
197 0/8	62 6/8	12 0/8	12 3/8	8	11	King Salmon	AK	Brian L. Heise	1977	125
197 0/8	64 0/8	16 2/8	15 4/8	11	7	Deer Hunting Slough	AK	Ronnie Everett	1995	125
196 6/8	63 6/8	13 2/8	16 4/8	6	6	Alaska Peninsula	AK	Phillip Durr	1969	127
196 5/8	58 3/8	15 2/8	14 1/8	9	10	Kaktovik	AK	Judy Grooms	1987	128
196 4/8	63 0/8	11 1/8	11 1/8	10	10	Chilikadrotna River	AK	Patrick J. Lefemine	1991	129
196 4/8	55 0/8	13 1/8	14 1/8	10	11	Koyukuk River	AK	Mike Misch	1994	129
196 2/8	58 0/8	11 0/8	11 5/8	8	9	Mulchatna River	AK	Kurt M. Zurawski	1989	131
195 7/8	55 5/8	13 3/8	12 2/8	13	14	June Lake	NWT	Chuck Adams	1993	132
195 6/8	55 2/8	10 1/8	11 3/8	13	11	Koyukuk River	AK	Mark Hanson	1990	133
195 6/8	56 6/8	11 4/8	11 6/8	14	14	Kuskokwim River	AK	Brian Brockette	1996	133
195 5/8	52 5/8	11 4/8	11 0/8	12	12	Fairbanks	AK	Rocky Chisholm	1988	135
195 4/8	55 6/8	12 6/8	13 6/8	10	10	Bonnet Plume Lake	YUK	Billy Ellis	1981	136
195 1/8	53 5/8	14 2/8	13 2/8	10	9	Artic Red River	NWT	Raymond E. Stongle	1995	137
195 0/8	68 2/8	14 0/8	12 6/8	7	7	Lake Iliamna	AK	Rex William Maurer	1987	138
194 7/8	53 1/8	11 7/8	12 4/8	13	14	Tustumena Lake	AK	Lavern Davidhizar	1980	139
194 6/8	56 6/8	12 2/8	12 3/8	9	9	Juniper Creek	AK	David L. Stull	1991	140
194 4/8	64 0/8	17 5/8	15 3/8	11	7	Alaska Peninsula	AK	Jim Dougherty	1962	141
194 3/8	57 5/8	11 4/8	15 5/8	11	12	Mystery Creek	AK	Joe Kelly	1989	142
194 2/8	61 6/8	12 7/8	13 7/8	7	12	Koyukuk River	AK	Thomas J. Hentrick	1984	143
194 0/8	58 6/8	13 6/8	12 2/8	8	9	Lake Clark	AK	Dr. Gary G. Sauer	1987	144
194 0/8	59 6/8	11 4/8	12 2/8	12	13	Kotzebue	AK	Mark D. Mishinski	1990	144
193 5/8	60 3/8	10 7/8	12 5/8	8	9	Beluga Mtn.	AK	Dennis A. Lundine	1984	146
193 4/8	57 0/8	14 4/8	14 2/8	10	10	Pilot Point	AK	Lucien Rouse	1997	147
193 3/8	53 7/8	11 6/8	11 6/8	10	10	Kenai Peninsula	AK	Robert LaFollette	1962	148
193 0/8	52 6/8	13 5/8	12 3/8	8	10	Kateel River	AK	Dennis Tol	1987	149
193 0/8	53 2/8	12 2/8	12 4/8	10	12	Galena	AK	Greg Campbell	1996	149
192 7/8	56 3/8	13 7/8	12 7/8	9	10	Little Tok River	AK	Dennis L. Lattery	1977	151
192 6/8	57 0/8	11 6/8	11 7/8	12	13	Old Steese Hwy.	AK	Michael R. Chadwick	1994	152
192 5/8	55 1/8	10 5/8	12 5/8	11	13	Wrangell Mtns.	AK	Loren Willey	1973	153
192 4/8	60 6/8	14 2/8	12 4/8	7	9	Kluane Lake	YUK	Eugene A. Tieman	1973	154
192 4/8	51 0/8	10 6/8	9 2/8	14	12	Fort Richardson	AK	Donald D. Roberts	1984	154
192 4/8	61 4/8	11 3/8	12 0/8	8	10	Kuparuk River	AK	Robert Barrie	1987	154
192 3/8	55 7/8	11 6/8	12 0/8	11	11	Eklutna Lake	AK	Ron C. Harvey	1989	157
192 3/8	60 5/8	15 6/8	12 2/8	12	10	Wood River	AK	David A. Van Dyke	1996	157
192 1/8	51 3/8	12 0/8	13 0/8	12	12	Koyukuk River	AK	Jeffery R. Barnett	1997	159
192 0/8	52 6/8	14 2/8	16 2/8	8	10	Clarence Lake	AK	John Schoenike	1966	160
192 0/8	69 6/8	10 6/8	13 4/8	7	9	Wood River	AK	Doug Strecker	1981	160
192 0/8	56 4/8	14 0/8	13 3/8	8	9	Koyukuk River	AK	Joe Caswell	1989	160
192 0/8	56 6/8	14 4/8	11 1/8	11	12	Kilik River	AK	John S. Borg	1991	160
192 0/8	59 6/8	11 6/8	12 6/8	9	9	Mac Millan River	YUK	Rick Morley	1993	160
191 7/8	57 7/8	16 3/8	14 7/8	8	10	Rainy Pass	AK	Rick Tollison	1977	165
191 7/8	67 7/8	10 5/8	10 4/8	8	7	Fish Creek	AK	Richard D. Clemons	1998	165
191 6/8	54 6/8	12 3/8	12 2/8	9	12	Brooks Range	AK	Joseph Stanevich	1986	167
191 5/8	59 5/8	11 6/8	12 5/8	11	12	Mac Millan River	YUK	Mike Craig	1996	168
191 3/8	57 3/8	14 0/8	14 5/8	8	11	Whitefish Lake	AK	Jim Hoss	1975	169
191 3/8	61 1/8	16 4/8	11 7/8	10	9	Koyukuk River	AK	Gary Olsen	1992	169
191 1/8	58 5/8	13 2/8	14 2/8	11	9	Galena	AK	Frank Prata	1988	171
190 7/8	59 1/8	11 4/8	10 4/8	8	10	Innoko River	AK	Samuel D. Adams	1997	172
190 7/8	56 7/8	14 0/8	13 7/8	8	11	Farewell Station	AK	Jim Horneck	1998	172
190 6/8	52 4/8	11 3/8	10 3/8	10	11	Ugashik Lake	AK	Dr. William Schultz	1987	174
190 5/8	57 3/8	8 4/8	9 2/8	11	10	Kotzebue	AK	Raymond Lengyel	1990	175
190 5/8	60 3/8	13 1/8	12 7/8	12	13	Kotzebue	AK	Larry Welchlen	1995	175
190 4/8	63 6/8	11 0/8	11 1/8	7	7	Mother Goose Lake	AK	Cecil Jarvis	1987	177
190 3/8	57 3/8	13 0/8	13 0/8	12	12	Teslin Lake	YUK	Paul Schafer	1977	178
190 3/8	62 3/8	13 6/8	15 1/8	11	12	Derby Creek	AK	Greg Kempf	1991	178
190 2/8	58 4/8	14 0/8	13 2/8	9	14	Yentna River	AK	Dan Hollingsworth	1978	180
190 2/8	57 0/8	11 6/8	13 2/8	13	12	Anchorage	AK	Paul Persano	1981	180
190 2/8	53 2/8	13 5/8	14 5/8	8	11	Moose John River	AK	Monty Moravec	1992	180
190 1/8	60 5/8	11 2/8	10 6/8	10	12	Alaska Peninsula	AK	Rick W. Simpson	1979	183
190 0/8	57 4/8	12 4/8	15 1/8	11	11	Lime Village	AK	Jerad Dittrich	1976	184
190 0/8	56 6/8	12 2/8	11 7/8	9	13	Mackenzie Mtns.	NWT	Robert A. Hermann	1992	184
189 6/8	51 4/8	15 1/8	15 0/8	9	12	Imuruk Basin	AK	Roger O. Wyant	1993	186
189 6/8	57 2/8	15 4/8	13 4/8	4	9	Iliamna	AK	Thomas R. Grabowski	1994	186

ALASKA-YUKON MOOSE

Minimum Score 170 — Continued

SCORE	GREATEST SPREAD	WIDTH OF PALM R	L	NUMBER OF POINTS R	L	AREA	STATE/ PROVINCE	HUNTER'S NAME	DATE	RANK
189 4/8	53 2/8	11 1/8	9 4/8	8	7	Stony River	AK	Douglas P. Reichel	1993	188
189 2/8	61 0/8	12 0/8	10 5/8	10	10	Kateel River	AK	Jack Boullion	1995	189
189 1/8	57 1/8	11 0/8	8 5/8	11	12	Wood River	AK	David Van Dyke	1994	190
189 0/8	53 6/8	13 1/8	13 1/8	9	13	Alaska Peninsula	AK	Richard T. Vance	1972	191
189 0/8	55 0/8	13 0/8	14 2/8	11	11	Latna River	AK	Ed Wentzler	1995	191
188 7/8	57 7/8	11 1/8	12 5/8	13	10	Sagavanirktok River	AK	Robert G. Chouinard	1980	193
188 7/8	59 1/8	14 3/8	14 3/8	10	9	Cantwell	AK	John W. Williams	1983	193
188 5/8	60 3/8	12 5/8	13 6/8	8	7	Lake Clark	AK	David Westmoreland	1995	195
188 4/8	63 0/8	11 5/8	12 3/8	8	8	Kenai Peninsula	AK	Dale L. Lofstedt	1969	196
188 4/8	55 6/8	12 5/8	12 2/8	10	11	Koidern Mtn.	YUK	D. Kirk Brown, MD	1997	196
188 2/8	61 2/8	12 3/8	11 0/8	10	9	Upper Dog Salmon River	AK	Robert T. Morgan	1983	198
188 1/8	53 7/8	12 5/8	13 2/8	11	13	Alaska Range	AK	Richard Moran	1991	199
188 1/8	55 5/8	13 0/8	12 1/8	10	10	Kichatna River	AK	Douglas W. Hill	1994	199
187 7/8	67 7/8	11 4/8	13 4/8	10	11	Jim River	AK	Ernie Dempsey	1981	201
187 7/8	48 1/8	14 4/8	14 4/8	10	13	Watson Lake	YUK	Pete Shepley	1985	201
187 7/8	56 5/8	13 1/8	13 0/8	8	9	Koyukuk River	AK	Mike O'Connor	1996	201
187 5/8	60 5/8	12 5/8	11 6/8	12	12	Innoko River	AK	Ron Madsen	1989	204
187 4/8	60 4/8	13 6/8	12 0/8	9	13	Koyuk River	AK	V. Randy Liljenquist	1994	205
187 3/8	56 3/8	12 1/8	12 4/8	9	10	Stony River	AK	Bob Ameen	1993	206
186 6/8	62 0/8	12 1/8	12 2/8	7	6	Ugashik Lake	AK	Richard King	1988	207
186 6/8	56 6/8	12 1/8	12 5/8	12	12	Tsiu River	AK	Dean F. Stebner	1997	207
186 5/8	53 1/8	12 0/8	12 7/8	10	10	Squirrel River	AK	Randy Martin	1992	209
186 4/8	50 4/8	12 5/8	13 7/8	13	13	Fox Mtn.	YUK	Steve Crooks	1991	210
186 4/8	52 4/8	11 7/8	13 4/8	11	12	Dennison River	AK	Bronk Jorgensen	1993	210
186 3/8	52 5/8	13 5/8	14 0/8	10	11	Middle Fork	AK	Glen Williams	1969	212
186 3/8	50 7/8	12 4/8	12 7/8	11	12	Hess River	YUK	Russell Thornberry	1987	212
186 3/8	56 7/8	11 1/8	11 3/8	10	10	Mackenzie Mtns.	NWT	Chuck Adams	1990	212
186 2/8	56 2/8	11 2/8	12 4/8	8	8	Cook Inlet	AK	George Moerlein	1961	215
186 2/8	62 6/8	13 2/8	12 2/8	9	9	Kejulik River	AK	John Crump	1981	215
186 1/8	61 5/8	10 6/8	10 7/8	10	9	Cinder River	AK	Glenn Hisey	1976	217
186 1/8	56 5/8	13 1/8	13 2/8	12	12	Salcha River	AK	Chris Sanford	1996	217
185 7/8	56 5/8	11 2/8	10 7/8	8	9	Susitna Valley	AK	Dan J. Tobin	1984	219
185 7/8	55 1/8	12 2/8	11 0/8	11	11	Kanuti River	AK	Scott R. Nordin	1989	219
185 5/8	56 3/8	14 0/8	14 3/8	7	6	Cantwell	AK	John Eilertson	1983	221
185 4/8	56 4/8	12 0/8	9 4/8	12	11	Fort Richardson	AK	David Dodds	1991	222
185 3/8	57 5/8	10 0/8	9 6/8	10	11	King Salmon	AK	Paul Persano	1982	223
185 0/8	56 0/8	10 6/8	11 6/8	10	11	Squirrel River	AK	James Borron	1992	224
184 7/8	59 7/8	13 1/8	11 5/8	12	10	Susitna Valley	AK	Dan J. Tobin	1988	225
184 6/8	55 6/8	11 3/8	12 4/8	5	10	Cinder River	AK	Francis Hosch	1965	226
184 6/8	59 4/8	15 4/8	13 3/8	7	8	Anaktuvak Pass	AK	Rod Van DeGraaf	1990	226
184 6/8	57 0/8	11 6/8	14 4/8	10	12	Yentna River	AK	Herman J. Griese	1997	226
184 4/8	55 0/8	12 1/8	12 0/8	10	9	Port Heiden	AK	Frank 'Rit' Heller	1974	229
184 4/8	59 6/8	12 0/8	12 2/8	9	15	Eklutna Lake	AK	Steve J. Latz	1986	229
184 3/8	53 5/8	9 4/8	13 4/8	12	13	Palmer	AK	A. H. Stange, Jr.	1962	231
184 3/8	63 3/8	12 4/8	11 0/8	12	8	Mishik River	AK	George Wright	1969	231
184 3/8	56 5/8	12 5/8	14 1/8	11	10	Mac Millan River	YUK	Larry Oppe	1994	231
184 2/8	67 4/8	12 4/8	12 7/8	5	11	Nushagak River	AK	David C. Ferrario	1997	234
184 1/8	59 7/8	11 1/8	13 0/8	10	10	Brooks Range	AK	Kent Devine	1988	235
184 1/8	50 3/8	9 3/8	12 0/8	11	12	Swift River	AK	J. Dale Hale	1993	235
184 1/8	55 3/8	13 3/8	12 3/8	8	9	Fort Richardson	AK	Daniel S. Osborn	1995	235
184 0/8	59 6/8	11 0/8	10 6/8	6	7	Whitefish Lake	AK	George A. Mohr	1982	238
183 6/8	50 4/8	12 5/8	12 1/8	8	8	Nabesna	AK	George Moerlein	1962	239
183 3/8	53 5/8	12 5/8	12 5/8	10	9	Nahanni Butte	NWT	Roy M. Goodwin	1990	240
183 2/8	53 4/8	11 4/8	11 7/8	7	7	Brooks Range	AK	Matt Jones	1990	241
183 0/8	54 6/8	11 1/8	11 2/8	10	10	Alaska Peninsula	AK	Jerry Putnam	1973	242
183 0/8	61 0/8	10 1/8	11 1/8	7	7	Kelly River	AK	Doug Burgard	1994	242
182 7/8	55 1/8	11 0/8	12 0/8	11	11	Eklutna Lake	AK	K. Edward Atwood	1986	244
182 7/8	52 1/8	12 3/8	11 7/8	8	10	Ivishak River	AK	Ed Strayhorn	1987	244
182 7/8	55 1/8	12 0/8	11 2/8	11	13	Pat Creek	AK	Kelly Collins	1998	244
182 6/8	55 0/8	13 3/8	13 2/8	11	11	Nowetta River	AK	Alan Winger	1988	247
182 6/8	52 4/8	10 4/8	9 0/8	11	11	Kahiltna River	AK	Ronald R. Hull	1998	247
182 5/8	57 5/8	11 2/8	16 1/8	10	9	Little Delta River	AK	Keith R. Clemmons	1957	249
182 5/8	54 5/8	13 5/8	13 2/8	9	8	Juniper River	AK	Dennis Faulkenberry	1986	249
182 5/8	59 5/8	12 5/8	15 0/8	5	12	Koyukuk River	AK	Troy A. Graziadei	1993	249
182 5/8	56 7/8	13 1/8	13 2/8	7	10	Koyukuk River	AK	Jeff Barnett	1993	249
182 4/8	56 0/8	12 0/8	12 0/8	6	7	Fort Richardson	AK	Mark Wojtalik	1988	253
182 3/8	50 5/8	13 2/8	12 5/8	13	13	Witna River	AK	Stan Parkerson	1993	254
182 3/8	54 1/8	12 1/8	11 6/8	10	7	Talkeetna River	AK	Rick Hayley	1997	254
182 2/8	57 4/8	12 2/8	12 6/8	7	8	Nome	AK	Erv Plotz	1979	256
182 2/8	57 4/8	11 5/8	10 5/8	12	12	Innoko River	AK	Jim Fitzgerald	1993	256
182 1/8	56 5/8	9 7/8	12 0/8	7	9	Toolik River	AK	Reggie Spiegelberg	1986	258
182 1/8	56 5/8	9 7/8	11 1/8	12	12	Colville River	AK	Kurt Lepping	1990	258
182 1/8	54 7/8	12 6/8	12 5/8	7	8	Wrench Creek	AK	Kirk Westervelt	1993	258
182 0/8	59 0/8	12 0/8	11 4/8	10	10	Slope Mtn.	AK	Roger Wheelock	1980	261
181 7/8	56 1/8	13 0/8	14 0/8	7	7	Arctic Wildlife Refuge	AK	Thomas J. Hoffman	1996	262
181 6/8	56 0/8	11 4/8	12 6/8	10	12	Moose Creek	AK	Bill Brown	1991	263
181 5/8	53 5/8	12 6/8	12 4/8	11	14	Koyukuk River	AK	Greg L. Munther	1995	264
181 4/8	57 2/8	14 3/8	16 6/8	7	9	Port Heiden	AK	Bill L. Carlos	1970	265

ALASKA-YUKON MOOSE

Minimum Score 170 — Continued

SCORE	GREATEST SPREAD	WIDTH OF PALM R	L	NUMBER OF POINTS R	L	AREA	STATE/ PROVINCE	HUNTER'S NAME	DATE	RANK
181 4/8	55 4/8	12 4/8	12 6/8	6	10	Ft. Yukon	AK	Ron Rockwell	1985	265
181 3/8	58 3/8	11 4/8	12 1/8	8	8	Nicuhuna Lake	AK	Benny R. Reed	1993	267
181 3/8	56 5/8	9 6/8	10 0/8	13	10	White River	YUK	Ray F. Daniels	1994	267
181 1/8	57 7/8	9 7/8	10 0/8	10	11	Ugashik Lake	AK	Scott Showalter	1972	269
181 1/8	54 1/8	8 6/8	10 2/8	8	10	King Salmon	AK	Joe Fogleman	1982	269
181 0/8	56 6/8	13 3/8	12 3/8	7	6	Colville River	AK	Kurt Lepping	1986	271
180 7/8	54 1/8	10 6/8	10 3/8	9	11	Earn Lake	YUK	Glen R. Cousins	1978	272
180 7/8	48 7/8	12 6/8	12 3/8	10	11	Coal River	YUK	M. Richard Warner	1996	272
180 5/8	51 3/8	11 1/8	11 2/8	8	9	Port Heiden	AK	Art Heinze	1973	274
180 4/8	57 6/8	12 7/8	11 3/8	10	8	Middle Fork	AK	Norm Goodwin	1969	275
180 4/8	52 0/8	15 1/8	15 3/8	8	10	Sheenjek River	AK	David W. Doran	1992	275
180 2/8	61 4/8	11 6/8	10 2/8	7	10	Alaska Peninsula	AK	Keith Pilz	1976	277
180 2/8	53 6/8	11 0/8	12 1/8	8	10	Lake Clark	AK	Paul L. Fischer	1988	277
179 7/8	56 1/8	11 3/8	11 2/8	9	9	Sugar Loaf Mtn.	AK	James White	1988	279
179 7/8	46 3/8	10 5/8	10 5/8	8	9	Noatak River	AK	Rob Swanson	1995	279
179 6/8	59 2/8	9 3/8	12 3/8	8	7	Susitna River	AK	Robert Pitt	1968	281
179 6/8	54 2/8	14 3/8	12 6/8	9	9	Tag River	AK	Scott Privette	1986	281
179 6/8	54 6/8	13 2/8	11 0/8	10	10	Wrangell Mtns.	AK	Bret T. Walker	1991	281
179 5/8	53 3/8	11 0/8	11 2/8	11	12	Berry Creek	AK	Larry Jones	1962	284
179 5/8	53 1/8	9 4/8	13 3/8	10	13	Kenai Peninsula	AK	George Moerlein	1969	284
179 4/8	48 2/8	11 0/8	11 2/8	12	12	Kotzebue	AK	Stephen Kotz	1990	286
179 4/8	59 0/8	11 4/8	16 4/8	6	6	Mac Millan River	YUK	Ed DeYoung	1993	286
179 3/8	56 3/8	9 7/8	9 6/8	8	9	Stony River	AK	Bob Ameen	1986	288
179 3/8	47 1/8	12 4/8	14 0/8	11	12	Coal River	YUK	Gip Friesen	1996	288
179 2/8	57 0/8	11 4/8	11 6/8	8	10	Brooks Range	AK	Kurt W. Keskimaki	1989	290
179 1/8	55 7/8	13 1/8	12 0/8	6	7	Fort Yukon	AK	Barry J. Smith	1985	291
179 0/8	53 0/8	13 6/8	13 3/8	8	10	Ft. Richardson	AK	Earl G. Brown	1984	292
178 6/8	49 2/8	13 0/8	12 3/8	10	11	Earn Lake	YUK	Greg Wadsworth	1995	293
178 5/8	52 5/8	10 5/8	11 3/8	12	12	Koyukuk River	AK	Steven M. Stroka	1991	294
178 4/8	55 4/8	13 0/8	11 5/8	10	9	Kuskokwim River	AK	Bill Stonebraker	1980	295
178 4/8	53 2/8	12 7/8	11 0/8	11	13	Koyukuk River	AK	Mark Reyher	1997	295
178 3/8	53 7/8	9 6/8	7 2/8	13	9	Tustumena Lake	AK	Lowell Thomas	1973	297
178 2/8	52 2/8	11 0/8	10 3/8	8	10	Mac Millan River	YUK	Mike Lutt	1994	298
178 1/8	59 1/8	10 1/8	9 5/8	9	7	Cheeneetnuk River	AK	H. R. 'Rusty' Neely	1982	299
177 5/8	58 1/8	13 2/8	12 5/8	7	8	Babble River	AK	Rick Karbowski	1995	300
177 4/8	57 0/8	11 2/8	9 5/8	8	7	American River	AK	Paul Van Dongen	1995	301
177 3/8	61 1/8	10 4/8	10 5/8	6	12	Iliamna	AK	Thad Barnes	1989	302
177 3/8	58 7/8	11 0/8	11 4/8	11	12	Galena	AK	Larry Spiva	1992	302
177 2/8	51 6/8	12 4/8	12 0/8	9	9	Kenai Peninsula	AK	Alan Perry	1971	304
177 2/8	55 0/8	13 7/8	12 1/8	7	12	Whitehorse	YUK	Scott Koelzer	1977	304
177 2/8	60 0/8	10 1/8	10 0/8	8	7	Juniper River	AK	Boyd Holley	1986	304
177 2/8	61 0/8	11 0/8	14 7/8	9	13	Noatak River	AK	Guy M. Leibenguth	1995	304
177 1/8	53 7/8	12 3/8	15 0/8	10	11	Fox Mtn.	YUK	Todd R. Zeuske	1995	308
177 1/8	52 1/8	11 4/8	11 6/8	11	10	Nowitna River	AK	David C. Manca	1998	308
177 0/8	62 0/8	9 0/8	9 2/8	5	7	Port Heiden	AK	James R. Scott	1966	310
176 6/8	56 6/8	10 4/8	11 4/8	11	11	Brooks Range	AK	Steve Weekly	1990	311
176 5/8	57 3/8	10 1/8	11 0/8	11	10	Crow Pass	AK	Michael J. Schneider	1982	312
176 4/8	50 0/8	11 6/8	9 3/8	11	8	Jim River	AK	Patrick A. Campanella	1997	313
176 2/8	54 0/8	10 2/8	10 1/8	11	8	Chugiak	AK	Jerry D. Fletcher	1990	314
176 2/8	55 4/8	9 3/8	9 7/8	9	8	Eklutna Lake	AK	Thomas J. Rutz	1991	314
176 2/8	48 0/8	11 3/8	11 2/8	10	12	Kuskokwim River	AK	Terry Hanson	1996	314
176 1/8	56 3/8	10 7/8	11 3/8	7	9	Innoko River	AK	John McCullough	1998	317
175 6/8	48 2/8	10 0/8	9 0/8	11	11	Anvil Mtns.	YUK	James V. Barwick	1994	318
175 4/8	60 4/8	11 6/8	10 0/8	7	8	Susitna River	AK	David A. Drover	1971	319
175 4/8	50 6/8	11 4/8	11 3/8	9	9	Kuparuk River	AK	Bill Krenz	1984	319
175 3/8	46 3/8	11 3/8	13 1/8	11	15	Kaktovik	AK	Grant Poindexter	1987	321
175 2/8	56 6/8	11 7/8	11 1/8	4	5	Brooks Range	AK	Thomas T. King	1989	322
175 1/8	51 3/8	11 2/8	12 1/8	9	10	Healy	AK	Vic Killian	1991	323
174 6/8	58 6/8	8 0/8	9 6/8	8	8	McCarty Creek	AK	Stanley J. Rogers, Jr.	1972	324
174 5/8	58 1/8	13 3/8	12 3/8	8	8	Koyukuk River	AK	Gerald L. Weeks	1991	325
174 4/8	57 5/8	12 5/8	12 0/8	13	8	Tustumena Lake	AK	Gary Wall	1974	326
174 3/8	52 1/8	11 3/8	12 3/8	9	10	Koyukuk River	AK	Roger Stewart	1982	326
174 3/8	53 5/8	11 0/8	10 1/8	8	8	Wrench Creek	AK	Alan Harris	1993	326
174 2/8	54 6/8	10 0/8	10 0/8	12	9	Delta River	AK	Dr. R. Congdon	1960	329
174 2/8	58 0/8	11 3/8	11 6/8	11	9	Kejulik River	AK	Mike Hedrick	1984	329
174 2/8	56 2/8	9 0/8	9 0/8	9	9	Stony River	AK	Bob Ameen	1991	329
174 2/8	54 0/8	8 0/8	10 1/8	11	9	Lake Telequana	AK	Greg S. Fields	1992	329
174 1/8	57 3/8	11 6/8	11 0/8	6	10	Kelly River	AK	Richard L. Westervelt	1994	333
173 6/8	49 0/8	9 2/8	10 7/8	10	11	Chistochina River	AK	Larry L. Schweitzer	1982	334
173 6/8	53 6/8	10 6/8	10 4/8	7	6	Colville River	AK	Bob Gulman	1984	334
173 5/8	57 5/8	12 5/8	11 4/8	12	10	Northway	AK	Chuck Adams	1978	336
173 5/8	55 1/8	12 7/8	12 4/8	8	8	Juniper River	AK	Dr. F. D. Elias	1986	336
173 4/8	54 4/8	11 6/8	9 4/8	10	8	Elmendorf AFB	AK	Sidney Parris	1997	338
173 0/8	50 4/8	10 1/8	10 4/8	12	12	Koyukuk River	AK	William E. Lee	1984	339
173 0/8	58 2/8	11 2/8	10 4/8	11	10	Koksitna Drainage	AK	Ron Hopkins	1987	339
172 6/8	49 3/8	14 0/8	12 6/8	12	12	Coldfoot	AK	Danny F. Watson	1988	341
172 5/8	47 1/8	11 0/8	12 0/8	7	7	Brooks Range	AK	John Ribic	1983	342
172 1/8	55 1/8	12 4/8	10 3/8	11	9	Stony River	AK	Bob Ameen	1992	343

ALASKA-YUKON MOOSE

Minimum Score 170

SCORE	GREATEST SPREAD	R	WIDTH OF PALM	L	R	NUMBER OF POINTS	L	AREA	STATE/ PROVINCE	HUNTER'S NAME	DATE	RANK
172 0/8	54 3/8	12 4/8		13 5/8	6		9	Iliamna	AK	Jim Jensen	1994	344
171 7/8	60 5/8	9 2/8		7 5/8	13		10	Brooks Range	AK	Bruce R. Schoeneweis	1989	345
171 5/8	57 3/8	10 6/8		9 0/8	13		7	Hayes Creek	AK	Keith R. Clemmons	1962	346
171 4/8	49 4/8	10 2/8		10 6/8	12		9	Delta River	AK	Richard R. Cooper	1959	347
171 4/8	57 0/8	10 2/8		10 0/8	10		12	Fish Creek	AK	Doug Keller	1990	347
171 2/8	59 0/8	12 0/8		10 1/8	11		9	Big River Flats	AK	Lonnie Rumley	1988	349
171 2/8	58 6/8	10 2/8		13 2/8	6		9	Rohn Roadhouse	AK	Fred Eichler	1994	349
171 2/8	52 2/8	7 6/8		10 2/8	8		10	Earn Lake	YUK	Wayne Greene	1996	349
171 1/8	53 3/8	10 4/8		10 2/8	10		12	Tillei Lake	YUK	Roger M. Tyler	1989	352
171 1/8	50 1/8	14 3/8		13 7/8	6		8	Alaska Peninsula	AK	Jack Dykstra	1993	352
171 0/8	48 2/8	12 0/8		11 4/8	7		8	Brooks Range	AK	Edward Keltgen	1986	354
171 0/8	45 2/8	11 1/8		8 4/8	8		7	Bonnet Plume Lake	YUK	Stan Rauch	1989	354
170 7/8	58 1/8	12 0/8		10 6/8	8		5	Port Heiden	AK	John E. Lawson	1970	356
170 7/8	48 5/8	11 0/8		9 2/8	9		10	King Salmon River	AK	Bob Sweisthal	1986	356
170 7/8	62 7/8	10 1/8		11 4/8	6		9	Ugashik Lake	AK	Dennis Statham	1989	356
170 6/8	56 0/8	10 0/8		12 1/8	9		8	Ugashik Lake	AK	Dr. Von A. Mitton	1978	359
170 6/8	44 6/8	12 3/8		12 3/8	12		10	Moose John River	AK	Mike Pasztor	1996	359
170 4/8	52 6/8	12 1/8		11 4/8	10		9	Unit 13D	AK	Dayle Paulson	1969	361
170 1/8	50 1/8	10 3/8		11 2/8	9		9	Fort Richardson	AK	Harry Gordon Evans	1989	362
170 0/8	58 2/8	12 2/8		11 5/8	9		10	Zone 4	YUK	Keith Baker	1988	363
170 0/8	48 2/8	13 0/8		11 5/8	15		13	Tsiu River	AK	Gary F. Bogner	1998	363

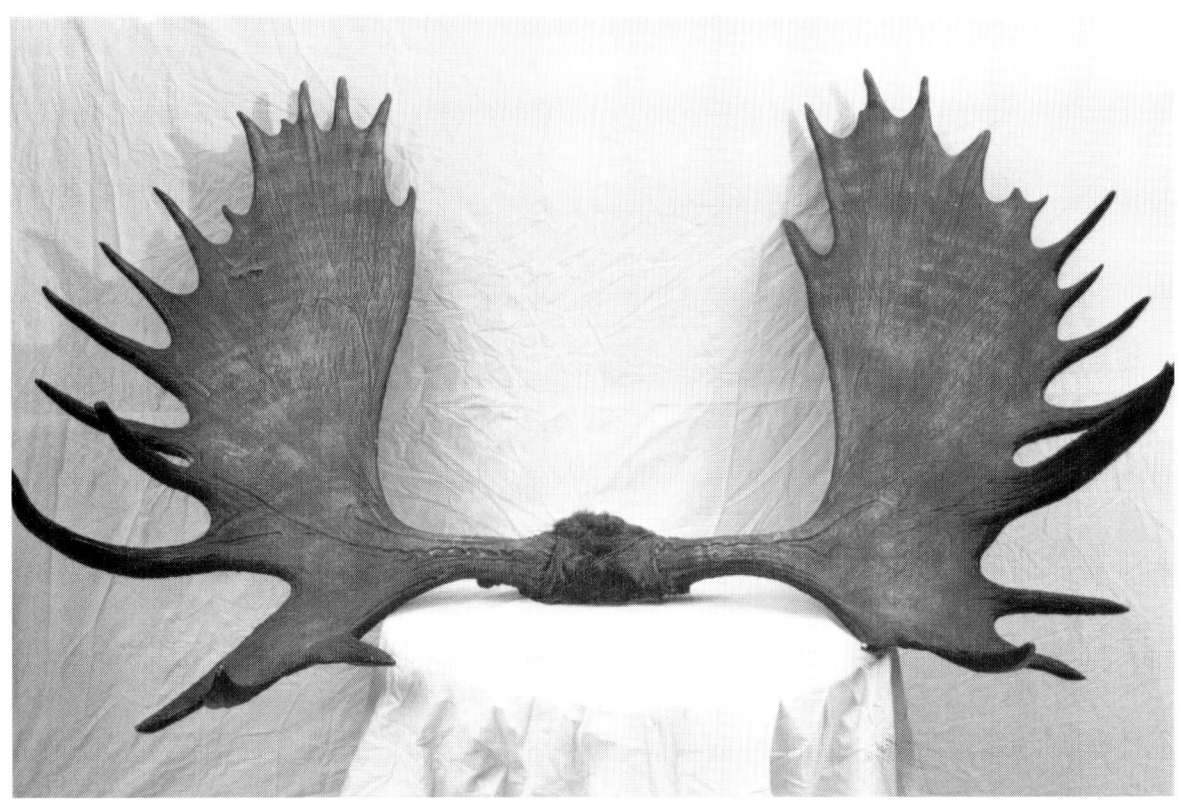

World Record Canada Moose
Score: 222 1/8
Cap Chat, Quebec - 1988
Hunter: Charles Roy

CANADA MOOSE

Minimum Score 135

Alces alces americana and *Alces alces andersoni*

SCORE	GREATEST SPREAD	R	WIDTH OF PALM	L	R	NUMBER OF POINTS	L	AREA	STATE/ PROVINCE	HUNTER'S NAME	DATE	RANK
222 1/8	66 1/8	16 1/8		14 7/8	16		15	Cap-Chat	QUE	Charles Roy	1988	1
217 2/8	56 0/8	14 4/8		14 6/8	12		11	Birch Mtn.	ALB	Fredrick J. Gimbel	1994	2
214 3/8	55 7/8	14 1/8		14 4/8	16		17	Chevis Creek	BC	Wayne Carlton	1988	3
201 4/8	55 2/8	12 4/8		11 4/8	12		12	Mt. Lady Laurier	BC	Peter Halbig	1968	4
201 2/8	60 4/8	11 1/8		11 1/8	12		11	Hutt Twp.	ONT	Fred Robinson	1986	5
199 3/8	55 7/8	15 0/8		14 5/8	8		11	Turtle Mtn.	MAN	Jan Collins	1994	6
199 0/8	56 0/8	12 6/8		14 5/8	11		11	Redwillow River	BC	Steven W. Hiebert	1992	7
199 0/8	57 4/8	14 0/8		13 2/8	10		10	Teslin River	BC	Scott L. Koelzer	1996	7
198 6/8	56 6/8	16 3/8		16 7/8	15		13	Toad River	BC	Dirk V. Lawyer	1984	9
197 0/8	58 6/8	16 4/8		13 5/8	9		7	Cold Fish Lake	BC	Steve Gorr	1975	10
196 7/8	52 3/8	17 3/8		14 6/8	16		15	Dryden	ONT	Murray Macquarrie	1990	11
196 6/8	48 6/8	16 4/8		15 2/8	12		13	Besa River	BC	Edward Flowerdew	1976	12
196 2/8	59 5/8	14 4/8		13 7/8	10		13	Skeena	BC	Larry Garoutte	1972	13
196 2/8	53 6/8	12 3/8		15 4/8	13		12	Nacht Creek	BC	Scott L. Koelzer	1991	13
195 4/8	59 2/8	13 2/8		13 6/8	12		17	Teslin Lake	BC	Kent Michie	1993	15
194 6/8	61 0/8	12 4/8		11 2/8	11		11	Lake LeRoy	BC	Lee Poole	1998	16
194 4/8	55 6/8	13 4/8		14 2/8	11		13	Thunder Bay	ONT	Bob Toderash	1987	17
193 6/8	56 2/8	17 2/8		15 4/8	10		13	Heiss Lake	ONT	Bob Toderash	1993	18
192 7/8	55 3/8	14 4/8		15 6/8	12		13	Algoma	ONT	Larry Pilon	1989	19
192 6/8	56 6/8	11 5/8		10 5/8	12		13	Cassiar Mtns.	BC	Thomas B. Frye	1978	20
192 3/8	61 1/8	12 3/8		13 6/8	7		8	Thunder Bay	ONT	Ron Mahler	1992	21
191 6/8	53 6/8	12 2/8		12 0/8	8		8	Lake Discella	BC	Sid Morrison	1995	22
191 2/8	51 4/8	13 0/8		12 6/8	12		14	Duck Mtn.	MAN	M. Dale Robins	1992	23
191 0/8	67 0/8	12 7/8		12 0/8	10		12	Dease Lake	BC	Adrian Erickson	1989	24
190 2/8	55 2/8	15 4/8		16 0/8	9		6	Lake Nipigon	ONT	Ohne Raasch	1991	25
190 2/8	49 6/8	12 5/8		11 6/8	10		11	Fouch Lake	ONT	Camille Hache	1995	25
190 1/8	53 5/8	13 1/8		13 2/8	11		9	Ignace	ONT	Michael Barkac	1993	27
190 0/8	60 4/8	14 1/8		12 6/8	13		12	Nakina River	BC	Ricardo L. Garza	1997	28
189 3/8	60 3/8	13 2/8		11 2/8	12		11	Sultan	ONT	Michael Wiseman	1989	29
189 2/8	52 4/8	13 6/8		13 2/8	11		12	McNalley Lake	ALB	DeWayne Mullins	1995	30

CANADA MOOSE

Minimum Score 135   Continued   609

SCORE	GREATEST SPREAD	WIDTH OF PALM R	WIDTH OF PALM L	NUMBER OF POINTS R	NUMBER OF POINTS L	AREA	STATE/ PROVINCE	HUNTER'S NAME	DATE	RANK
188 7/8	47 3/8	15 3/8	12 6/8	11	14	Stikine River	BC	Will Pick	1997	31
188 6/8	53 4/8	11 2/8	11 6/8	11	11	Devon	ONT	Lorne Davis	1993	32
188 5/8	52 5/8	10 0/8	10 6/8	8	8	Sultan	ONT	Mike R. Nowaczyk	1986	33
188 0/8	57 0/8	12 3/8	13 2/8	12	10	Thunder Bay	ONT	David Nuttall	1993	34
187 5/8	57 0/8	13 3/8	12 1/8	11	13	Turnagin River	BC	Glenn Hisey	1978	35
187 3/8	50 7/8	11 1/8	11 7/8	11	13	Muskwa River	BC	Kevin J. Kansky	1997	36
187 0/8	50 6/8	12 6/8	11 5/8	13	13	Dibble Lake	ONT	Bruce Zuehlke	1992	37
187 0/8	54 0/8	13 6/8	11 4/8	10	9	Ear Falls	ONT	Robert Scott Ellery	1995	37
187 0/8	49 2/8	13 4/8	13 5/8	11	8	Kechika River	BC	Scott Neil	1998	37
186 7/8	57 1/8	13 2/8	13 1/8	8	12	Klastline River	BC	Gregory White	1992	40
186 3/8	53 7/8	12 7/8	12 6/8	12	12	Wawa	ONT	William D. Brooks	1994	41
186 3/8	48 7/8	12 1/8	12 0/8	13	13	Turnagin River	BC	Scott Ebert	1995	41
186 2/8	54 0/8	11 2/8	11 2/8	10	11	Ash Mtn.	BC	Pink Atkins	1984	43
186 1/8	53 1/8	14 1/8	13 2/8	11	12	Pitman Lake	BC	Kevin Schmid	1990	44
186 0/8	62 0/8	10 5/8	10 4/8	10	13	St. Gilles	QUE	Michel Aubert	1986	45
186 0/8	53 0/8	10 5/8	9 5/8	14	13	Ardrossan	ALB	Brian Burrows	1994	45
185 3/8	54 3/8	11 4/8	11 3/8	13	11	Mossy River	SAS	Jerome J. Huseby	1966	47
185 2/8	53 0/8	10 5/8	11 6/8	12	11	Buffalo Creek	ALB	Philip Ramish	1998	48
184 7/8	58 7/8	11 3/8	11 4/8	9	9	Goat Creek	BC	Atley Lovelace	1974	49
184 7/8	57 3/8	11 0/8	11 0/8	10	11	Trapper Lake	BC	David E. Stepp	1998	49
184 6/8	55 7/8	11 7/8	11 5/8	13	8	Blanchard Creek	BC	Ron Johnson	1974	51
184 2/8	49 0/8	12 5/8	13 2/8	11	11	St. Gilles	QUE	Michel Aubert	1985	52
183 4/8	60 6/8	10 4/8	11 5/8	10	9	Terminus Valley	BC	Paul P. Schafer	1975	53
182 7/8	52 5/8	13 6/8	12 2/8	11	6	Christian Falls	BC	Mike Ryan	1990	54
182 7/8	50 7/8	13 2/8	16 2/8	10	9	Upsala	ONT	Mark Berringer	1992	54
182 4/8	58 4/8	14 6/8	14 3/8	8	9	East Hereford	QUE	Daniel Fecteau	1990	56
182 1/8	50 5/8	11 2/8	11 1/8	10	10	Stanley Creek	BC	Donald L. Pahl	1973	57
181 4/8	54 2/8	11 5/8	10 6/8	12	11	Muncho Lake	BC	Gary Martin	1995	58
181 1/8	51 5/8	12 0/8	11 5/8	12	13	Halfway River	BC	Duane L. Scroggins	1977	59
181 1/8	47 5/8	14 3/8	17 7/8	11	13	Lake Nipigon	ONT	Raymond J. Seguin	1994	59
181 0/8	56 6/8	14 6/8	12 6/8	11	11	Ear Falls	ONT	Dell Mercey	1995	61
180 3/8	54 7/8	11 7/8	11 0/8	8	9	Cristina Falls	BC	Fred Ray Woods	1994	62
180 2/8	44 6/8	12 4/8	11 4/8	13	14	Lake Lac Seul	ONT	Josef K. Rud	1989	63
180 2/8	46 6/8	13 4/8	11 4/8	13	10	Steamboat Mtn.	BC	Wayne Norris	1994	63
180 1/8	47 3/8	11 6/8	11 1/8	12	13	Unit 23	ONT	Paul F. J. Petrie	1985	65
180 0/8	55 4/8	12 0/8	13 0/8	9	10	Algoma	ONT	Larry Pilon	1988	66
179 6/8	50 6/8	11 5/8	13 2/8	11	12	Dease Lake	BC	Robert G. Petersen	1985	67
179 6/8	59 2/8	9 3/8	11 7/8	9	12	Penobscot County	ME	Scott E. Phillips	1998	67
179 1/8	56 3/8	11 0/8	10 0/8	11	9	Atikokan	ONT	Russ Martin	1987	69
179 0/8	47 2/8	14 5/8	14 2/8	12	12	Alliance	ALB	Chad O'Hagan	1996	70
178 5/8	51 2/8	11 1/8	12 6/8	10	10	Kechika River	BC	Scott L. Koelzer	1976	71
178 5/8	57 5/8	12 3/8	11 6/8	8	11	Kawdy Plateau	BC	Gary F. Bogner	1996	71
178 5/8	46 3/8	12 3/8	11 6/8	13	14	Muskwa River	BC	Jim Boyer	1997	71
178 4/8	50 4/8	11 6/8	12 6/8	8	7	Worsley	ALB	Mike Scott	1993	74
178 0/8	46 6/8	11 2/8	11 1/8	10	12	Ketchika Valley	BC	Edd Clack	1991	75
177 2/8	52 2/8	10 7/8	9 0/8	10	8	Thrimble Lake	BC	Chester Schardt	1966	76
177 2/8	43 6/8	14 6/8	14 2/8	14	15	Herod	ONT	Bill McQuillen	1995	76
177 1/8	56 7/8	12 7/8	12 4/8	7	8	Heyson Twp.	ONT	R. S. Illingworth	1986	78
177 1/8	53 7/8	10 5/8	10 0/8	10	10	Ignace	ONT	Roland Matte	1996	78
176 6/8	52 0/8	12 5/8	12 2/8	9	13	Majuba Lake	BC	Glenn Dreger	1990	80
176 5/8	51 5/8	10 4/8	10 0/8	11	11	Mine Centre	ONT	Charles Harb	1997	81
176 4/8	58 4/8	11 6/8	11 4/8	8	6	McNalley Lake	ALB	Judd Cooney	1993	82
176 4/8	54 0/8	11 1/8	11 7/8	10	12	Algoma	ONT	Larry Pilon	1996	82
176 3/8	47 7/8	11 2/8	10 4/8	10	10	Algoma	ONT	Edward Broderick	1989	84
176 3/8	52 1/8	12 0/8	11 4/8	8	8	Ignace	ONT	Bruce R.S. Turner	1996	84
176 2/8	57 6/8	9 4/8	10 4/8	9	9	Fallon Twp.	ONT	Frank J. Julling	1987	86
176 1/8	48 3/8	11 2/8	12 1/8	11	13	Hyland Lake	BC	Randall S. Smith	1998	87
176 0/8	55 2/8	13 6/8	14 2/8	9	14	Long Range Mtns.	NFL	Waldemar D. Maya	1965	88
176 0/8	58 2/8	9 5/8	9 0/8	9	9	Algoma	ONT	Larry Pilon	1987	88
175 6/8	59 4/8	12 7/8	14 4/8	4	5	Kenora	ONT	Franlin Mullen	1992	90
175 4/8	50 6/8	11 2/8	9 6/8	10	10	Moose Lake	BC	Dan Martin	1986	91
175 3/8	51 7/8	11 4/8	11 7/8	8	9	Dease Lake	BC	Bill Coburn	1979	92
175 1/8	47 5/8	10 4/8	11 4/8	11	13	Lake Nipigon	ONT	Raymond J. Seguin	1986	93
175 1/8	50 3/8	12 0/8	11 6/8	10	11	Northern Light Lake	ONT	Ian Robinson	1991	93
175 0/8	52 0/8	10 1/8	10 7/8	10	9	Central	BC	Ronald Lauretti	1973	95
175 0/8	53 4/8	10 4/8	12 0/8	8	10	Kechika River	BC	Paul F. Schafer	1974	95
175 0/8	50 6/8	13 6/8	14 1/8	12	10	Hyland Lake	BC	Gene A. Welle	1997	95
174 6/8	54 6/8	13 4/8	9 4/8	11	11	Algoma	ONT	Larry Pilon	1990	98
174 5/8	50 5/8	11 3/8	10 7/8	12	11	McConnell Range	BC	Dave Young	1976	99
174 4/8	42 2/8	11 4/8	11 1/8	10	9	Sikanni Chief River	BC	Bob W. Ehle	1996	100
174 3/8	56 1/8	13 0/8	10 2/8	10	7	Algoma District	ONT	Paul Kovich	1981	101
174 2/8	51 4/8	12 1/8	12 2/8	9	8	Atikokan	ONT	David Williams	1992	102
174 0/8	48 2/8	10 7/8	11 0/8	12	11	Taku Plateau	BC	Walter J. Palmer	1995	103
173 5/8	52 1/8	9 4/8	11 1/8	10	10	Lake Lac Seul	ONT	Josef K. Rud	1990	104
173 4/8	50 6/8	11 6/8	14 5/8	12	12	Rainy River	ONT	Robert White	1998	105
173 2/8	52 6/8	10 6/8	12 3/8	12	10	Red Deer Lake	ALB	Terry Lane	1988	106
173 2/8	55 2/8	11 3/8	9 4/8	10	8	Churchill River	MAN	Kirk Wermager	1997	106

CANADA MOOSE

Minimum Score 135 — Continued

SCORE	GREATEST SPREAD	WIDTH OF PALM R	L	NUMBER OF POINTS R	L	AREA	STATE/ PROVINCE	HUNTER'S NAME	DATE	RANK
173 0/8	56 6/8	9 4/8	10 5/8	9	8	Somerset County	ME	Richard Bjornson	1996	108
172 4/8	53 0/8	9 0/8	10 4/8	11	12	Besa River	BC	Mark H. Freeman	1979	109
172 4/8	59 2/8	10 4/8	9 4/8	11	9	Piscataquis County	ME	Frank White	1989	109
172 2/8	61 4/8	10 2/8	9 5/8	9	8	Lake County	MN	Chuck Schultz	1987	111
172 2/8	57 4/8	10 2/8	11 3/8	8	11	Thurston Lake	ALB	Garry G. Schalla	1997	111
172 0/8	50 6/8	11 4/8	11 7/8	10	10	Thutade Lake	BC	Larry Nirk	1975	113
172 0/8	53 0/8	11 2/8	10 2/8	9	7	Timmins	ONT	Carl Doerner	1976	113
172 0/8	48 6/8	11 4/8	11 3/8	11	10	Magone Township	ONT	John L. Burket	1986	113
172 0/8	50 0/8	12 2/8	10 7/8	11	9	Ignace	ONT	Paul A. Strong	1993	113
171 6/8	48 4/8	10 4/8	12 2/8	12	11	S. Branch	NFL	Paul Erdbrink	1966	117
171 5/8	44 1/8	15 5/8	13 1/8	13	11	Cape Anquille Mtns.	NFL	Terrance Estes	1966	118
171 4/8	50 6/8	10 5/8	10 4/8	7	9	Algoma	ONT	David Reinke	1991	119
171 2/8	53 2/8	12 6/8	12 6/8	9	13	Atikokan	ONT	Mark C. Johnson	1987	120
171 0/8	53 4/8	8 3/8	8 5/8	9	8	Gaspe'	QUE	Claude St'Amour	1989	121
170 7/8	49 3/8	10 2/8	10 6/8	9	9	Graham River	BC	Dr. James Shubert	1979	122
170 6/8	55 4/8	12 2/8	11 2/8	8	11	Perrault Falls	ONT	Terry A. Zarr	1993	123
170 6/8	51 4/8	10 6/8	11 7/8	10	10	Kingman	ALB	Brian Green	1996	123
170 4/8	44 4/8	10 7/8	12 4/8	13	12	Quibell	ONT	Fred Bear	1945	125
170 2/8	52 0/8	11 3/8	10 0/8	7	10	Tua Lake	BC	Jeff Koelzer	1991	126
170 0/8	55 2/8	13 0/8	12 3/8	8	7	Aroostook County	ME	Cory Mattson	1996	127
169 3/8	48 5/8	11 1/8	12 0/8	8	10	Geraldton	ONT	Cello Milani	1996	128
169 2/8	50 0/8	11 4/8	11 4/8	11	10	Somerset County	ME	Diane Brochu/Brian Brochu	1994	129
169 1/8	50 7/8	12 5/8	12 2/8	9	11	Stikine River	BC	Dave Brousseau	1979	130
168 5/8	54 7/8	14 2/8	11 3/8	11	10	Terrace Bay	ONT	Otto Ten Hoeve	1996	131
168 1/8	45 7/8	12 5/8	11 1/8	13	10	Fort St. John	BC	Duane Hicks	1981	132
168 1/8	48 1/8	11 1/8	11 6/8	5	6	Stone Lake	ONT	D. E. "Babe" Winkelman	1991	132
168 1/8	44 7/8	9 5/8	10 6/8	12	9	Nose Mtn.	ALB	Ted Brown	1998	132
168 0/8	46 4/8	10 3/8	11 0/8	11	12	Kechika River	BC	Dave Seidelman	1989	135
168 0/8	52 4/8	12 5/8	12 1/8	10	12	Nipigon	ONT	Charles Steven DeLeeuw	1990	135
167 6/8	50 6/8	10 2/8	11 0/8	6	6	Chevis Creek	BC	Wayne Carlton	1989	137
167 3/8	49 3/8	13 5/8	13 0/8	11	8	Thunder Bay	ONT	Rob Remus	1994	138
167 0/8	58 4/8	10 7/8	10 7/8	11	11	Argenteuil	QUE	Richard K. Clark	1983	139
166 7/8	51 1/8	12 2/8	11 4/8	10	10	Stikine River	BC	Scott Golike	1998	140
166 6/8	48 4/8	9 4/8	9 4/8	9	10	Nipisi Lake	ALB	Lee Hamilton	1991	141
166 6/8	54 2/8	11 0/8	9 5/8	7	11	Dease Lake	BC	Don Davidson	1993	141
166 6/8	49 6/8	10 6/8	10 5/8	10	11	Disella Lake	BC	John D. "Jack" Frost	1996	141
166 6/8	45 2/8	11 2/8	9 5/8	11	12	Athabasca	ALB	Thomas C. Johnson	1998	141
166 4/8	46 4/8	12 0/8	12 0/8	12	10	Atikokan	ONT	David Wolf	1995	145
166 4/8	52 2/8	10 2/8	11 1/8	9	9	Leland Lake	ALB	Richard Orich/Ken Madsen	1995	145
166 0/8	54 6/8	8 0/8	8 4/8	8	8	Lake Nipigon	ONT	Raymond J. Seguin	1991	147
165 6/8	40 4/8	10 6/8	11 0/8	11	10	Buckinghorse Lake	BC	Lloyd Benedict	1993	148
165 2/8	50 0/8	14 0/8	12 5/8	5	7	Cottonwood River	BC	Scott L. Koelzer	1995	149
164 4/8	46 4/8	10 6/8	10 3/8	10	9	Woman River	ONT	Jim C. Dehoey	1991	150
164 4/8	48 4/8	9 4/8	9 4/8	10	9	Sikanni Chief River	BC	Joel M. Riotto	1998	150
164 3/8	47 7/8	10 2/8	10 3/8	9	12	Fort St. John	BC	Chuck Adams	1976	152
164 1/8	49 3/8	12 5/8	11 2/8	12	10	Tweedsmuir Pk.	BC	Glenn St. Charles	1954	153
164 0/8	48 4/8	12 6/8	11 6/8	7	9	Atlin	BC	Thomas J. Hoffman	1997	154
163 7/8	49 7/8	9 6/8	11 4/8	8	10	Ignace	ONT	Wayne Yocum, Jr.	1996	155
163 6/8	47 6/8	10 4/8	10 2/8	11	9	Pink Mtn.	BC	Gerald R. Dishion	1987	156
163 5/8	47 7/8	11 7/8	12 3/8	8	9	Wegg	ONT	Scott Pelino	1991	157
163 3/8	45 1/8	11 1/8	10 2/8	10	10	McKeough Township	ONT	Larry Pilon	1991	158
163 3/8	50 1/8	9 2/8	9 1/8	10	9	Wawa	ONT	William D. Brooks	1994	158
163 3/8	53 3/8	11 2/8	10 2/8	10	8	Ignace	ONT	Paul Strong	1996	158
163 2/8	45 2/8	9 4/8	10 2/8	10	9	Cassiar Mtns.	BC	Harold Boyack	1978	161
163 1/8	50 3/8	10 6/8	10 4/8	9	9	Edmonton	ALB	Pat Marek	1989	162
163 1/8	52 1/8	9 3/8	10 0/8	13	9	Okotoks	ALB	Stuart Sinclair-Smith	1996	162
163 1/8	51 7/8	11 3/8	12 3/8	8	8	Cook County	MN	Kirk D. Grupa	1997	162
163 0/8	50 4/8	10 1/8	11 2/8	6	6	Nakanok Lake	BC	Phil Forte	1984	165
163 0/8	54 6/8	9 0/8	8 0/8	10	8	Algoma	ONT	Larry Pilon	1986	165
163 0/8	54 0/8	9 1/8	9 0/8	8	8	Sudbury	ONT	Vite Chomicki	1986	165
163 0/8	51 6/8	12 1/8	12 6/8	7	10	Turtle Mtn.	MAN	Daryl Fisher	1987	165
162 6/8	47 0/8	10 5/8	11 2/8	6	7	Kenora	ONT	John P. Hartman	1991	169
162 4/8	48 0/8	9 0/8	9 0/8	10	11	Kapuskasing	ONT	Ron Alguire	1963	170
162 4/8	50 0/8	8 2/8	8 0/8	10	13	Andrew Lake	ALB	Warren Witherspoon	1994	170
162 2/8	50 0/8	12 7/8	11 5/8	9	8	Nakina Lake	BC	Dee C. Steinheiser	1986	172
162 2/8	44 6/8	10 6/8	11 1/8	9	11	Dryden	ONT	Ronald Hintz/Gary Hintz	1995	172
162 1/8	48 3/8	11 6/8	11 6/8	11	8	Cook County	MN	Terry Krahn	1994	174
162 1/8	49 7/8	10 4/8	10 6/8	10	11	Hearst	ONT	Jim Jones	1997	174
161 6/8	48 0/8	11 6/8	11 6/8	8	10	Somerset County	ME	George A. Vinal	1994	176
161 6/8	39 4/8	9 4/8	9 1/8	8	9	Clear Hills	ALB	Geordie Lund	1996	176
161 5/8	51 1/8	10 0/8	10 4/8	10	10	Ramsey County	ND	Boone Liane	1998	178
161 4/8	50 0/8	6 4/8	9 5/8	7	7	Tatla Lake	BC	Bill Nickerson	1985	179
161 3/8	49 1/8	10 0/8	9 2/8	8	8	Dease Lake	BC	Gene Welle	1995	180
161 3/8	47 3/8	13 6/8	11 4/8	9	6	Mine Centre	ONT	Norman R. Drefcinski	1996	180
161 2/8	46 6/8	10 0/8	10 1/8	9	9	Schalze River	BC	Dale Snyder	1983	182
161 2/8	40 2/8	10 0/8	9 2/8	11	10	Nakina Lake	BC	Dean Stebner	1988	182
161 1/8	45 5/8	10 5/8	11 6/8	11	11	Lloyds River	NFL	Harold A. Hill	1966	184

CANADA MOOSE

Minimum Score 135

SCORE	GREATEST SPREAD	WIDTH OF PALM R	WIDTH OF PALM L	NUMBER OF POINTS R	NUMBER OF POINTS L	AREA	STATE/PROVINCE	HUNTER'S NAME	DATE	RANK
161 0/8	47 4/8	9 3/8	10 1/8	10	10	Toad River	BC	Archie Nesbitt	1994	185
160 7/8	51 1/8	9 3/8	9 0/8	8	8	Metagama	ONT	Kerry Koning/Andy Weisgerber	1994	186
160 4/8	46 0/8	10 4/8	10 4/8	10	9	Muskwa River	BC	W. Jay Boynton III	1970	187
160 4/8	41 0/8	13 1/8	11 7/8	8	9	Cook County	MN	Kevin Walsh	1993	187
160 1/8	50 7/8	10 0/8	9 5/8	9	8	Toad River	BC	Jerry Leair	1986	189
160 1/8	43 5/8	10 0/8	11 6/8	6	7	Lilly Lake	ONT	Fern Duquette	1996	189
160 0/8	49 2/8	10 0/8	9 6/8	8	9	Matane	QUE	Claude St' Amour	1990	191
160 0/8	47 0/8	11 4/8	11 7/8	10	9	Machion	ONT	Michael J. Goza	1991	191
159 5/8	49 5/8	15 2/8	12 2/8	6	6	Moose Lake	BC	Michael Delfino, Sr.	1988	193
159 3/8	53 5/8	9 4/8	6 5/8	8	8	Josephburg	ALB	Doug Long	1996	194
159 1/8	51 7/8	9 5/8	8 7/8	9	8	Gogama	ONT	Jack Richard	1984	195
158 7/8	50 7/8	12 1/8	11 7/8	13	11	Kirkland Lake	ONT	Luther Gordon	1963	196
158 6/8	50 4/8	12 0/8	12 1/8	8	10	Dryden	ONT	Dean J. Smaney	1990	197
158 6/8	48 6/8	8 5/8	9 0/8	8	8	Odin Lake	ONT	Bob Page	1996	197
158 5/8	47 1/8	8 4/8	9 7/8	10	9	Hillsport	ONT	Mark Stephenson	1996	199
158 4/8	46 2/8	12 4/8	11 7/8	7	8	Millarville	ALB	Stuart Sinclair-Smith	1993	200
158 0/8	49 0/8	8 0/8	8 5/8	7	8	Williams Lake	BC	Gary Swan	1968	201
158 0/8	47 6/8	10 2/8	9 7/8	11	13	Strathcona	ALB	Darrell Stiles	1985	201
157 6/8	47 4/8	10 4/8	9 5/8	7	8	Thunder Bay	ONT	Bill Stringer	1991	203
157 6/8	46 6/8	9 4/8	8 4/8	10	10	Mossy River	SAS	John Ross	1997	203
157 6/8	46 2/8	9 5/8	8 3/8	10	8	Clear Hills	ALB	Les Baird	1998	203
157 5/8	47 5/8	10 4/8	10 7/8	9	11	Bottineau County	ND	Curtis Michaelson	1994	206
157 4/8	46 0/8	11 4/8	10 7/8	9	10	Rocky Mtn. House	ALB	Dennis Meyer	1988	207
157 3/8	47 3/8	11 6/8	9 2/8	11	9	St. Louis County	MN	Gus Maxfield	1987	208
157 3/8	45 7/8	9 6/8	10 7/8	8	10	Perrault Falls	ONT	Scott A. Cisewski	1997	208
157 1/8	46 7/8	11 2/8	12 5/8	9	11	Ear Falls	ONT	Chad Crowley	1995	210
156 4/8	48 2/8	10 6/8	9 0/8	8	11	Tsayta Lake	BC	Bob Duncan	1986	211
156 4/8	50 2/8	9 7/8	9 6/8	4	4	Phair Lake	ONT	Teijo Villa	1987	211
156 4/8	50 6/8	8 4/8	9 5/8	5	6	Kluachesi Lake	BC	Jerry R. Stutt	1987	211
156 4/8	42 0/8	9 3/8	10 0/8	11	10	Westward Ho	ALB	Danny Moore	1993	211
156 2/8	42 0/8	9 6/8	9 5/8	9	9	AK Hwy. Milepost 163	BC	John Zahrte	1978	215
156 2/8	49 0/8	10 3/8	10 4/8	7	8	Canton De Kondiaronk	QUE	Wayne J. Martin	1991	215
156 1/8	46 1/8	10 1/8	9 2/8	10	10	Muskwa River	BC	Steve D. Munier	1995	217
155 6/8	48 6/8	9 5/8	8 7/8	7	9	Maniwaki	QUE	Jay Pitha	1983	218
155 6/8	46 2/8	10 5/8	10 5/8	9	9	Sioux Lookout	ONT	Ross Lehne	1994	218
155 3/8	34 2/8	8 0/8	10 0/8	8	10	Smithers	BC	Chris Vanderhorst	1974	220
155 3/8	48 7/8	8 7/8	9 2/8	9	11	Kapuskasing	ONT	Tom Nowakowski	1980	220
155 2/8	44 0/8	8 2/8	8 2/8	8	6	Algoma	ONT	Dan Bertalan	1991	222
155 1/8	51 5/8	10 3/8	10 4/8	8	9	Algoma District	ONT	Carol Wert	1963	223
155 1/8	52 3/8	9 0/8	9 0/8	7	9	LeLuv Township	ONT	David Lawson	1994	223
154 7/8	49 7/8	10 3/8	11 4/8	8	11	Saddler Pond	NFL	Paul Locey	1982	225
154 7/8	44 3/8	9 5/8	9 4/8	9	9	Duffield Creek	BC	Wayne Johnson	1990	225
154 4/8	48 6/8	12 1/8	11 4/8	10	9	Turtle Mtn.	MAN	Jack Barrows	1992	227
154 1/8	44 3/8	9 7/8	9 7/8	8	11	Thutade Lake	BC	Donald N. Lehman	1973	228
154 0/8	49 2/8	10 0/8	10 3/8	9	8	Jackfish Creek	ONT	Darryl Miller	1987	229
154 0/8	46 4/8	9 1/8	9 1/8	9	8	Phillips Lake	ONT	Mark D. Stephenson	1992	229
153 5/8	45 3/8	10 6/8	11 2/8	7	12	Lloyds River	NFL	Harold A. Hill	1964	231
153 4/8	45 2/8	9 0/8	7 2/8	8	8		QUE	Bruce R. Wilson	1983	232
152 7/8	42 7/8	9 1/8	9 7/8	10	10	Zone 1	NFL	Harold A. Hill	1961	233
152 7/8	47 1/8	8 4/8	10 1/8	8	8	Trout Lake	ONT	Mike Brees	1998	233
152 6/8	45 2/8	10 0/8	9 4/8	6	6	Tetsa River	BC	Mark Calkins	1993	235
152 6/8	42 0/8	10 7/8	11 1/8	10	10	Lake County	MN	Cody Lane Detzel	1994	235
152 4/8	49 0/8	8 0/8	8 3/8	6	6	Gilbault Creek	BC	David V. Collis	1977	237
152 4/8	54 2/8	7 7/8	8 1/8	9	8	McKeough Township	ONT	Larry Pilon	1992	237
152 4/8	52 4/8	9 4/8	12 4/8	6	13	Wawa	ONT	William D. Brooks	1996	237
152 2/8	49 6/8	11 2/8	10 6/8	5	6	Nakina Lake	BC	Guy Anttila	1982	240
152 1/8	48 7/8	8 3/8	10 0/8	9	11	Thutade Lake	BC	Rodney Lee Wilt	1991	241
152 1/8	47 1/8	9 3/8	9 2/8	7	9	Atikokan	ONT	David Wolf	1993	241
152 0/8	49 2/8	10 7/8	9 7/8	8	6	Devon Twsp.	ONT	Lorne Davis	1991	243
152 0/8	45 6/8	9 0/8	8 4/8	8	8	Nakina	ONT	Richard Denes	1997	243
151 6/8	47 6/8	11 5/8	9 6/8	9	10		NFL	Bill Hirst	1960	245
151 6/8	44 0/8	10 6/8	9 4/8	9	9	Duti Lake	BC	Walter J. Sawicki	1972	245
151 5/8	53 3/8	8 7/8	9 6/8	8	6	Stikine River	BC	James A. Farnsworth	1973	247
151 4/8	51 4/8	9 2/8	9 2/8	7	12	Muncho Lake	BC	Chad Lenz	1994	248
151 2/8	42 2/8	8 2/8	9 4/8	9	9	Josephburg	ALB	Darwin Hunter	1990	249
150 7/8	43 7/8	8 1/8	8 2/8	8	9	Gander River	NFL	David Lamoreaux	1997	250
150 6/8	43 4/8	11 0/8	10 2/8	9	5	Serpentine River	NFL	John Wietecha	1997	251
150 4/8	41 0/8	10 4/8	11 2/8	10	7	Red Lake	ONT	Joseph B. Burgess	1993	252
150 2/8	42 2/8	9 1/8	8 4/8	9	11	Dumbell Lake	ONT	Gregory D. Keeton	1998	253
150 1/8	48 3/8	8 2/8	10 4/8	8	10	Thunder Bay	ONT	Carl Whittier	1990	254
150 1/8	47 7/8	7 6/8	7 5/8	9	7	Fort McMurray	ALB	Bruce Hendy	1992	254
150 0/8	45 6/8	9 6/8	9 0/8	8	7	Atikokan	ONT	Albert Clement	1991	256
149 6/8	46 2/8	8 5/8	9 3/8	7	7	Little Johnny Lake	BC	Larry D. Jones	1988	257
149 6/8	46 6/8	10 0/8	10 7/8	8	9	Gaspie Peninsula	QUE	Cecil A. Stanley	1997	257
149 5/8	52 1/8	11 5/8	11 0/8	9	9	Manitouwadge	ONT	David W. Sturrus	1992	259
149 2/8	44 2/8	9 4/8	9 4/8	9	9	Muskwa River	BC	Evan Steinhorst	1995	260
148 6/8	43 6/8	9 3/8	8 1/8	9	9	Edmonton	ALB	Doug Long	1995	261

CANADA MOOSE

Minimum Score 135

SCORE	GREATEST SPREAD	WIDTH OF PALM R	L	NUMBER OF POINTS R	L	AREA	STATE/ PROVINCE	HUNTER'S NAME	DATE	RANK
148 6/8	41 6/8	10 0/8	10 6/8	7	9	Highland Lake	BC	Renee Welle	1996	261
148 3/8	42 1/8	9 2/8	9 2/8	10	10	S. Branch	NFL	W. P. Hirst	1964	263
148 2/8	40 4/8	9 7/8	9 7/8	10	8	Hearst	ONT	Jim Jones, Jr.	1996	264
148 0/8	47 6/8	9 0/8	9 1/8	9	11	Spray Lakes	ALB	Yves Blanchette	1991	265
148 0/8	48 0/8	10 4/8	10 2/8	3	7	Coos County	NH	Stephen C. Van Hoose	1997	265
147 6/8	49 6/8	9 7/8	10 6/8	10	9	Millarville	ALB	Blaine Southgate	1997	267
147 2/8	48 2/8	8 2/8	7 4/8	9	8	Kenora	ONT	John P. Hartman	1990	268
146 6/8	39 4/8	8 1/8	9 5/8	8	10	King George IV Lake	NFL	Bill Hirst	1966	269
146 5/8	45 5/8	11 2/8	11 6/8	10	12	Prophet River	BC	Brian P. Williams	1994	270
146 3/8	45 3/8	9 2/8	10 2/8	6	9	Ardrossan	ALB	John Visscher	1987	271
146 3/8	45 7/8	8 4/8	10 2/8	8	9	Caramat	ONT	L. Reed Breight	1988	271
146 1/8	42 5/8	8 5/8	8 2/8	10	9	Toad River	BC	Glen Berry	1991	273
146 0/8	46 0/8	8 4/8	8 0/8	9	8	Tarnezell Lake	BC	Dr. Rex Hancock	1960	274
146 0/8	40 2/8	7 5/8	8 4/8	9	9	Algoma	ONT	Mauri Uusitalo	1993	274
145 7/8	47 5/8	8 5/8	10 0/8	6	6	Kitchener Lake	BC	Randy E. Doyle	1979	276
145 7/8	45 1/8	8 6/8	7 3/8	9	10	Atikokan	ONT	Loran M. Marceau	1993	276
145 6/8	47 4/8	8 3/8	8 4/8	8	8	Princess Lake	NFL	John Iannuzzo	1967	278
145 5/8	41 1/8	9 2/8	7 6/8	8	8	Ft. McMurray	ALB	Jim Miller, Jr.	1993	279
145 4/8	45 4/8	9 1/8	8 3/8	9	8	Tatlatui Lake	BC	G. Fred Asbell	1975	280
145 3/8	48 5/8	9 0/8	8 6/8	9	9	Duck Mtns.	MAN	Richard Hay	1986	281
145 2/8	45 0/8	10 0/8	9 4/8	10	8	Morton	MAN	Dennis Olischefski	1988	282
145 2/8	45 6/8	10 1/8	12 4/8	7	11	Lewisporte	NFL	Francis Ogden	1995	282
145 1/8	46 3/8	12 4/8	9 5/8	7	8	Trapnarrows Lake	ONT	John A. Schmidt	1985	284
145 1/8	45 1/8	8 4/8	10 2/8	5	7	Muskwa Valley	BC	K-Tal Johnson	1995	284
144 6/8	41 6/8	9 4/8	11 0/8	9	11	Dease Lake	BC	Dave Ramsay	1981	286
144 6/8	46 2/8	7 3/8	8 7/8	6	8	Newbrook	ALB	Ernest Larocque	1997	286
144 6/8	49 6/8	11 0/8	8 2/8	8	9	Fraserdale	ONT	A. Michael Matala, Jr.	1997	286
144 3/8	48 3/8	8 4/8	10 5/8	6	9	Vermilion Bay	ONT	Robert Scott Ellery	1994	289
144 2/8	50 0/8	8 5/8	10 3/8	8	9	Raith	ONT	Gerald D. Young	1983	290
144 1/8	44 3/8	8 0/8	7 0/8	7	6	Charlotte Lake	BC	Stanley D. Moore	1996	291
144 1/8	42 5/8	9 2/8	9 3/8	8	8	Trout River	ONT	James C. Gates	1998	291
144 0/8	47 2/8	10 1/8	10 0/8	8	9	Besa River	BC	Chris Barker	1991	293
143 6/8	44 0/8	10 0/8	11 1/8	7	6	Lake Nipigon	ONT	Ohne Raasch	1992	294
143 1/8	44 3/8	9 0/8	8 3/8	9	9	Algoma	ONT	Larry Pilon	1985	295
142 4/8	47 0/8	10 2/8	7 7/8	7	9	Myrnam	ALB	Orest Popil	1995	296
142 3/8	42 5/8	8 6/8	8 1/8	8	8	Hurdman Lake	QUE	Bill Dunn	1987	297
142 2/8	42 2/8	10 3/8	9 2/8	8	8	Lake Discella	BC	Ken Grosslight	1995	298
142 0/8	49 4/8	8 4/8	8 6/8	9	8	Zec St. Patrice	QUE	Henry P. Bouchard	1993	299
141 7/8	43 5/8	9 2/8	9 5/8	10	9	Spruce View	ALB	Glen Cunningham	1998	300
141 6/8	41 2/8	11 4/8	9 5/8	6	9	Sheba Township	ONT	Jerry Boudreault	1987	301
141 4/8	44 0/8	8 3/8	8 3/8	7	6	Keily Creek	BC	Tom Vanasche	1998	302
141 4/8	49 0/8	6 0/8	6 4/8	7	8	Pakwash Lake	ONT	John Flies	1998	302
141 3/8	44 5/8	12 1/8	13 0/8	6	4	Penobscot County	ME	Gregory A. Bonecutter, Sr.	1991	304
141 2/8	42 6/8	8 2/8	8 5/8	7	10	Lamont	ALB	William Como	1996	305
141 2/8	44 4/8	9 0/8	9 1/8	8	9	Numakoos Lake	MAN	Leonard G. Ahlen	1998	305
141 1/8	45 5/8	10 4/8	8 4/8	9	8	Thunder Bay	ONT	Greg Peters	1994	307
140 7/8	43 1/8	9 0/8	9 0/8	6	6	Strathcona	ALB	Pat Marek	1985	308
140 2/8	48 2/8	7 0/8	7 2/8	7	7	Princess Lake	NFL	John Musacchia	1966	309
140 0/8	39 0/8	9 3/8	9 6/8	8	9	Sturgeon Lake	ONT	Terry Hanson	1990	310
139 7/8	40 5/8	8 2/8	9 0/8	10	10	Edmonton	ALB	Wes Pietz	1991	311
139 7/8	38 3/8	10 2/8	10 5/8	10	9	Saskatoon Mtn.	ALB	Wilf Lehners	1995	311
139 5/8	40 7/8	8 0/8	9 0/8	8	8	Fort St. John	BC	Michael R. Traub	1981	313
139 4/8	38 0/8	8 5/8	7 4/8	8	9	Edmonton	ALB	Kevin Jeffrey	1991	314
139 1/8	49 5/8	6 3/8	4 7/8	6	6	Aroostook County	ME	William G. Miller II	1994	315
139 1/8	45 7/8	9 0/8	7 7/8	8	8	Smithers	BC	Joseph M. Clevinger	1997	315
138 7/8	48 1/8	8 1/8	7 6/8	8	9	Lodgepole	ALB	Randy Ewen	1997	317
138 2/8	44 4/8	9 0/8	9 0/8	7	9	Chapleau	ONT	Gary Riedke	1992	318
138 0/8	34 4/8	11 2/8	10 5/8	8	10	St. George Lake	NFL	Bill Carlos	1968	319
137 7/8	41 5/8	8 1/8	10 6/8	7	8	Princess Lake	NFL	Ken Rapp	1966	320
137 6/8	48 0/8	7 0/8	7 4/8	8	7	Algoma	ONT	Edward K. Broderick	1987	321
137 6/8	42 0/8	12 5/8	10 3/8	6	7	Rolette County	ND	Robert J. Benth	1991	321
137 6/8	42 6/8	8 4/8	10 3/8	5	7	Belby Pond	NFL	Michael J. Kennedy	1997	321
137 5/8	44 7/8	7 7/8	7 0/8	8	9	Thutade Lake	BC	Kim S Ades	1984	324
137 1/8	44 7/8	8 0/8	8 4/8	9	9	Gowganda	ONT	James Kelley	1993	325
136 6/8	54 0/8	10 0/8	12 6/8	3	5	Dryden	ONT	Mark Mussey	1996	326
136 5/8	41 7/8	8 7/8	10 4/8	9	8	Pants Lake	BC	William Bos	1994	327
136 2/8	46 4/8	7 2/8	7 4/8	6	6	Aroostook County	ME	Dennis M. Hayden	1993	328
136 1/8	39 3/8	8 2/8	9 4/8	6	9	Buchans Plateau	NFL	Lesley Bartus	1998	329
135 7/8	43 3/8	7 4/8	7 2/8	7	6	Sangudo	ALB	Allan C. Doell	1983	330
135 6/8	40 2/8	8 7/8	8 5/8	6	7	Blue Bell Mtn.	BC	Dr. Chuck Leidheiser	1996	331
135 6/8	41 4/8	7 5/8	9 4/8	8	10	Bottineau County	ND	Dale Mowder	1997	331
135 6/8	44 6/8	8 4/8	9 7/8	8	6	Cynthia	ALB	Randy Tellier	1998	331
135 4/8	47 2/8	8 3/8	9 0/8	4	7	Sheerway Lake	QUE	Richard A. Sawyer	1985	334
135 4/8	47 0/8	8 2/8	6 4/8	9	6	Kananaskis	ALB	John Visscher	1992	334
135 4/8	46 2/8	9 1/8	7 6/8	8	7	South Flanders	ONT	Corey Hayes	1996	334
135 3/8	49 5/8	6 7/8	8 0/8	6	7	Bighill Creek	ALB	Rick Lepp	1996	337
135 2/8	41 2/8	11 0/8	12 3/8	9	4	Boissevain	MAN	Hellar Nakonechny	1987	338

World Record Shiras "Wyoming" Moose
Score: 185 6/8
Sheridan County, Wyoming - 1987
Hunter: Richard E. Jones

SHIRAS "WYOMING" MOOSE

Minimum Score 125

Alces alces shirasi

SCORE	GREATEST SPREAD	WIDTH OF PALM R	L	NUMBER OF POINTS R	L	AREA	STATE/ PROVINCE	HUNTER'S NAME	DATE	RANK
185 6/8	54 0/8	9 3/8	8 4/8	8	11	Sheridan County	WY	Richard E. Jones	1987	1
185 5/8	50 1/8	13 1/8	12 4/8	11	11	Big Horn County	WY	John Harvey	1996	2
180 3/8	48 1/8	10 4/8	11 0/8	10	10	Fremont County	ID	Kenneth K. Fordyce	1983	3
177 5/8	43 3/8	11 5/8	10 0/8	10	12	Madison County	ID	Gerald Madsen	1998	4
177 1/8	43 1/8	15 6/8	13 3/8	13	14	Bingham County	ID	David Cederberg	1995	5
174 7/8	45 1/8	11 5/8	13 5/8	15	13	Caribou County	ID	James Keller	1992	6
174 3/8	48 1/8	13 0/8	15 2/8	14	12	Bonneville County	ID	David C. Cole	1987	7
174 2/8	55 2/8	11 4/8	9 5/8	11	11	Idaho County	ID	Larry Hoff	1991	8
173 6/8	47 4/8	9 2/8	8 3/8	12	13	Teton County	ID	Van W. Shotzman	1988	9
172 0/8	46 6/8	10 4/8	10 0/8	12	11	Madison County	ID	Trent Wood	1983	10
170 2/8	47 2/8	8 6/8	11 4/8	9	10	Madison County	ID	Ron Stacey	1988	11
169 7/8	51 5/8	12 3/8	8 6/8	13	11	Sheridan County	WY	James L. Nealey	1990	12
169 2/8	53 0/8	10 7/8	11 7/8	9	12	Park County	MT	Sam A. Terakedis	1995	13
167 7/8	46 3/8	12 1/8	13 0/8	11	7	Teton County	WY	Jon S. Fossel	1998	14
166 5/8	50 1/8	10 1/8	11 0/8	11	10	Madison County	ID	Dale Johnson	1987	15
166 4/8	45 4/8	10 6/8	13 2/8	9	11	Sheridan County	WY	Don Groskopf	1986	16
166 3/8	44 5/8	9 2/8	12 2/8	9	14	Sheridan County	WY	Rob Marosok	1993	17
166 1/8	53 3/8	10 1/8	10 6/8	10	11	Madison County	ID	Roger K. Wood	1995	18
165 5/8	47 7/8	10 1/8	8 7/8	11	11	Gallatin County	MT	Albert D. Williams	1986	19

SHIRAS "WYOMING" MOOSE

Minimum Score 125

Continued

SCORE	GREATEST SPREAD	WIDTH OF PALM R	L	NUMBER OF POINTS R	L	AREA	STATE/PROVINCE	HUNTER'S NAME	DATE	RANK
165 4/8	47 4/8	10 4/8	10 4/8	9	8	Utah County	UT	Chad J. Hall	1997	20
164 7/8	49 3/8	8 6/8	9 6/8	9	10	Idaho County	ID	Oliver E. Robinett	1980	21
164 3/8	48 5/8	10 3/8	13 0/8	10	11	Cache County	UT	Bob "Jake" Jacobsen	1994	22
164 1/8	41 3/8	13 4/8	13 2/8	14	12	Gallatin County	MT	Larry Schweitzer	1984	23
164 1/8	55 3/8	7 2/8	9 0/8	9	9	Teton County	WY	Rick Parish	1996	23
163 7/8	53 5/8	9 2/8	8 2/8	10	8	Lincoln County	WY	Brad Hugh Jacobs	1990	25
163 6/8	44 6/8	13 1/8	13 4/8	12	10	Lincoln County	WY	Walter Walbridge	1980	26
163 3/8	44 7/8	9 6/8	11 4/8	12	12	Morgan County	UT	Archie Nesbitt	1987	27
163 1/8	48 1/8	11 3/8	10 6/8	11	11	Weber County	UT	Randy K. Allen	1992	28
162 3/8	48 1/8	12 1/8	10 2/8	11	11	Teton County	ID	Howard W. Beins	1994	29
162 1/8	50 5/8	11 3/8	10 7/8	11	10	Gallatin County	MT	Jerry D. Johnson	1994	30
162 0/8	51 4/8	8 3/8	9 4/8	8	11	Sheridan County	WY	Dan Hart	1996	31
161 7/8	50 7/8	10 1/8	10 1/8	8	9	Jackson County	CO	Kirt Krieger	1992	32
161 6/8	47 0/8	11 3/8	11 0/8	9	10	Sheridan County	WY	John D. "Jack" Frost	1988	33
160 6/8	51 6/8	9 3/8	8 0/8	10	8	Bonneville County	ID	Marty George	1986	34
160 4/8	47 0/8	9 3/8	10 0/8	12	9	Weber County	UT	Hugh H. Hogle	1989	35
160 4/8	50 4/8	11 0/8	9 5/8	10	10	Jackson County	CO	Ron Madsen	1996	35
159 6/8	43 0/8	15 4/8	12 0/8	6	7	Teton County	WY	Daniel B. White	1978	37
159 6/8	45 6/8	9 0/8	9 3/8	11	11	Sweetwater County	WY	Mike Deaton	1992	37
159 1/8	49 5/8	12 7/8	10 7/8	8	10	Gallatin County	MT	Keith Wheat	1960	39
159 0/8	48 0/8	9 4/8	9 5/8	10	8	Sheridan County	WY	Bradley Carl Wichman	1990	40
158 6/8	50 2/8	10 6/8	11 0/8	11	11	Lincoln County	WY	Mike Smith	1976	41
158 4/8	51 0/8	7 4/8	10 5/8	8	10	Ravalli County	MT	Stan Billingsley	1998	42
158 3/8	44 3/8	10 4/8	10 2/8	12	13	Sublette County	WY	Steve Gosar	1996	43
158 1/8	45 5/8	9 1/8	10 5/8	10	10	Wasatch County	UT	Todd Lemley	1992	44
157 1/8	45 3/8	11 6/8	12 1/8	8	8	Bighorn Mtns.	WY	Jeffrey L. Welsh	1980	45
155 5/8	47 5/8	10 1/8	10 0/8	9	9	Lemhi County	ID	Bob Johnson	1991	46
155 5/8	45 5/8	12 4/8	10 6/8	12	9	Bannock County	ID	Geoff Hogander	1997	46
154 6/8	45 4/8	11 0/8	10 5/8	10	8	Sheridan County	WY	Jerry Bailey	1992	48
154 5/8	44 1/8	12 1/8	7 6/8	10	13	Caribou County	ID	James F. Dougherty	1992	49
154 4/8	41 4/8	10 0/8	10 6/8	9	9	Cache County	UT	Kirk Peterson	1992	50
154 3/8	45 7/8	9 6/8	10 0/8	10	9	Gallatin County	MT	Greg Flaherty	1998	51
154 0/8	49 4/8	9 1/8	8 7/8	8	9	Flathead County	MT	C. P. Mendenhall	1960	52
154 0/8	45 2/8	9 2/8	9 2/8	10	11	Caribou County	ID	Brett Dee Hymas	1986	52
153 7/8	43 5/8	8 0/8	9 4/8	7	8	Clearwater County	ID	Ray Matson	1993	54
153 6/8	42 0/8	11 7/8	11 0/8	13	11	Bonneville County	ID	Lonnie Pickens	1988	55
153 5/8	48 3/8	7 7/8	10 4/8	9	11	Teton County	WY	M. R. James	1992	56
153 4/8	45 4/8	10 0/8	12 6/8	9	11	Deer Lodge County	MT	Terry L. Button	1986	57
153 4/8	45 0/8	8 7/8	8 7/8	8	8	Jackson County	CO	Scott Koester	1996	57
153 1/8	45 7/8	10 5/8	12 4/8	8	8	Sheridan County	WY	William Ludwig	1994	59
152 7/8	46 5/8	10 6/8	9 5/8	10	9	Lincoln County	WY	Franklin H Sheets	1989	60
152 4/8	39 6/8	13 2/8	12 2/8	9	10	Sweetwater County	WY	Patti Pollard	1990	61
151 6/8	43 4/8	10 3/8	8 2/8	12	6	Morgan County	UT	Len Cardinale	1987	62
151 6/8	46 0/8	10 5/8	10 4/8	10	9	Lincoln County	WY	Kenneth M. Thompson	1997	62
151 5/8	40 5/8	8 5/8	8 5/8	10	9	Sanders County	MT	Jim Ryan	1989	64
151 3/8	47 1/8	12 4/8	10 4/8	12	9	Rich County	UT	Mike Poynor	1990	65
151 2/8	44 0/8	9 2/8	9 0/8	9	8	Johnson County	WY	Nicolette Hanson	1998	66
151 0/8	49 4/8	10 4/8	10 1/8	8	8	Bonneville County	ID	Alan L. Hall	1998	67
150 7/8	42 3/8	10 7/8	9 7/8	10	10	Clark County	ID	Joseph E. Packer	1981	68
150 6/8	39 4/8	9 4/8	11 2/8	9	11	Sublette County	WY	Bryan Radakovich	1990	69
150 4/8	48 6/8	9 3/8	8 7/8	9	10	Rich County	UT	Blake Poppleton	1987	70
150 4/8	49 4/8	8 4/8	8 3/8	7	8	Sheridan County	WY	Darrell Cook	1991	70
150 4/8	42 6/8	9 7/8	11 0/8	9	10	Bonneville County	ID	Dr. Tom W. Dorrell, Jr.	1996	70
149 2/8	37 4/8	9 2/8	10 2/8	9	11	Park County	WY	Marion J. De Busk	1994	73
149 2/8	41 4/8	8 6/8	9 3/8	9	8	Lincoln County	WY	Dustin C. Hays	1998	73
149 1/8	46 1/8	9 2/8	10 0/8	8	10	Clark County	ID	Spence Settles	1990	75
149 1/8	49 7/8	9 6/8	9 4/8	7	7	Lincoln County	WY	Ken Hoehn	1994	75
148 3/8	49 3/8	7 6/8	7 2/8	6	6	Lincoln County	MT	Jeffrey A. Hintz	1998	77
148 2/8	43 0/8	9 7/8	10 2/8	7	10	Sublette County	WY	Carol Niziolek	1996	78
147 7/8	47 5/8	8 7/8	9 1/8	11	7	Weber County	UT	Michael L. Pope	1997	79
147 6/8	46 4/8	10 0/8	10 2/8	8	9	Uinta County	WY	Vernon M. Poynor	1989	80
147 5/8	45 3/8	9 4/8	9 0/8	7	9	Bonneville County	ID	Steven R. Eldredge	1993	81
147 4/8	41 2/8	10 0/8	11 3/8	8	10	Sublette County	WY	Michael Beckwith	1985	82
147 4/8	41 0/8	8 4/8	11 4/8	9	10	Jackson County	CO	Dan Pfannenstiel	1993	82
147 3/8	47 7/8	10 7/8	9 1/8	10	8	Salt Lake County	UT	R. Todd Inman	1997	84
147 2/8	41 6/8	10 6/8	10 2/8	5	8	Madison County	ID	Randy Lee Davison	1987	85
147 2/8	42 4/8	7 7/8	8 3/8	7	9	Sheridan County	WY	Larry Katz	1992	85
147 1/8	43 5/8	7 5/8	8 3/8	8	9	Summit County	UT	Jerry Cross	1979	87
147 1/8	46 3/8	10 1/8	9 6/8	10	9	Lincoln County	WY	Gary Gale	1988	87
147 0/8	45 0/8	11 3/8	9 6/8	9	8	Teton County	WY	Jerry Bowen	1982	89
147 0/8	46 2/8	6 1/8	11 1/8	8	13	Weber County	UT	Matthew G. Hogle	1990	89
146 4/8	44 4/8	7 3/8	7 5/8	6	6	Park County	MT	Randy Cook	1982	91
146 4/8	42 4/8	11 0/8	9 2/8	10	6	Spokane County	WA	Lance B. Cussons	1991	91
146 3/8	45 1/8	9 1/8	9 1/8	8	7	Sheridan County	WY	Cecil Benner	1990	93
146 3/8	43 1/8	10 5/8	10 0/8	10	11	Jackson County	CO	Dave Hughes	1993	93
146 1/8	40 5/8	10 4/8	8 4/8	9	9	Sheridan County	WY	Dan Barngrover	1989	95
145 5/8	52 1/8	7 2/8	7 6/8	6	6	Flathead County	MT	Paul Albertoni	1996	96
145 4/8	41 2/8	10 5/8	10 3/8	7	6	Meagher County	MT	Kenny Roy	1997	97

SHIRAS "WYOMING" MOOSE

Minimum Score 125

SCORE	GREATEST SPREAD	WIDTH OF PALM R	L	NUMBER OF POINTS R	L	AREA	STATE/ PROVINCE	HUNTER'S NAME	DATE	RANK
145 1/8	45 1/8	9 4/8	8 2/8	5	6	Beaverhead County	MT	Greg L. Munther	1982	98
144 6/8	56 0/8	5 5/8	7 4/8	6	8	Summit County	UT	Ryan R. Anderson	1993	99
144 6/8	34 2/8	11 2/8	11 6/8	7	8	Sublette County	WY	Bill G. Davis	1994	99
144 4/8	43 0/8	11 0/8	10 7/8	9	8	Sublette County	WY	Boyd Andersen	1988	101
144 3/8	47 5/8	8 5/8	10 4/8	9	8	Weber County	UT	Chuck Adams	1987	102
143 6/8	38 4/8	10 0/8	8 2/8	8	8	Bonneville County	ID	Chris R. Tripp	1994	103
143 3/8	43 7/8	10 2/8	10 2/8	10	10	Silver Bow County	MT	J. Ray Haffey	1994	104
143 2/8	47 6/8	9 3/8	10 0/8	9	7	Idaho County	ID	Stanley Leake	1979	105
143 0/8	47 6/8	13 3/8	8 4/8	9	8	Clark County	ID	Alton Howell	1987	106
143 0/8	47 0/8	8 7/8	8 2/8	7	7	Sheridan County	WY	Ronald Jay Buisman	1996	106
142 6/8	40 6/8	9 4/8	9 4/8	8	7	Gallatin County	MT	Stuart J. Georgitis	1986	108
142 6/8	39 0/8	9 3/8	9 6/8	10	12	Uinta County	WY	Kevin Earl	1996	108
142 5/8	39 5/8	10 2/8	11 0/8	9	10	Lincoln County	WY	Clayton "Karl" Knudsen	1992	110
142 3/8	45 3/8	8 4/8	10 4/8	9	10	Weber County	UT	Ken C. Taylor	1995	111
142 2/8	46 4/8	9 0/8	10 3/8	10	8	Hot Springs County	WY	William L. Robing	1997	112
142 0/8	43 2/8	8 4/8	8 3/8	9	9	Sheridan County	WY	Thomas Ostrander	1995	113
141 5/8	46 7/8	11 1/8	9 0/8	4	4	Fremont County	WY	Craig J. Engelhard	1996	114
141 4/8	40 4/8	12 2/8	11 1/8	9	9	Lincoln County	WY	Von K. Merritt	1992	115
141 2/8	44 2/8	9 3/8	9 6/8	7	9	Caribou County	ID	Steve Chikato	1992	116
141 1/8	40 5/8	11 5/8	10 5/8	8	9	Granite County	MT	Robert G. Felts	1996	117
141 0/8	41 1/8	9 5/8	9 4/8	8	7	Lincoln County	WY	V. Kay Bangerter	1978	118
140 6/8	42 6/8	10 1/8	11 0/8	11	6	Sublette County	WY	Jerry Harding	1993	119
140 4/8	44 2/8	11 5/8	12 3/8	8	5	Morgan County	UT	Bruce Carlisle	1988	120
140 3/8	46 3/8	9 3/8	10 5/8	9	10	Lincoln County	WY	Charles W. Gilgore	1992	121
140 2/8	42 2/8	10 5/8	10 6/8	9	6	Lincoln County	WY	Keith Dana	1977	122
139 7/8	42 5/8	9 5/8	9 7/8	10	11	Bear Lake County	ID	Robby Taylor	1996	123
139 3/8	42 1/8	8 4/8	7 6/8	5	7	Idaho County	ID	Ray Torrey	1968	124
139 0/8	46 4/8	7 4/8	7 7/8	8	8	Sheridan County	WY	Tom Hlinka	1986	125
139 0/8	42 2/8	9 0/8	9 6/8	9	11	Weber County	UT	Mike Steckel	1991	125
138 4/8	40 6/8	11 4/8	13 2/8	6	7	Teton County	WY	Jerry A. Bodar	1990	127
138 4/8	41 0/8	8 3/8	8 6/8	10	11	Teton County	WY	Gary F. Bogner	1994	127
138 2/8	42 0/8	9 6/8	7 6/8	9	7	Lincoln County	MT	Thomas A. DeShazer	1965	129
137 7/8	47 1/8	9 2/8	11 3/8	7	9	Sublette County	WY	R. H. Siegert	1969	130
137 7/8	49 5/8	7 1/8	6 5/8	8	7	Madison County	ID	Paul Beesley	1993	130
137 6/8	43 0/8	7 2/8	7 3/8	9	10	Park County	WY	Chuck Hassler	1995	132
137 2/8	42 4/8	10 4/8	9 0/8	8	11	Lincoln County	WY	Robert K. Robinson	1978	133
136 7/8	42 1/8	6 5/8	9 6/8	8	10	Cache County	UT	Larry Cross	1986	134
136 7/8	43 1/8	6 3/8	5 5/8	7	8	Clark County	ID	Gayland Gilson	1987	134
136 1/8	46 3/8	11 4/8	7 7/8	8	7	Sheridan County	WY	Mike Traub	1993	136
136 0/8	43 2/8	8 6/8	8 2/8	7	7	Sublette County	WY	August S. Gray	1991	137
135 7/8	44 7/8	8 4/8	7 3/8	7	8	Park County	WY	Mike Yonker	1987	138
135 3/8	46 1/8	9 4/8	8 4/8	8	8	Sublette County	WY	Dave Funderburk	1978	139
135 3/8	42 7/8	8 4/8	9 2/8	6	6	Idaho County	ID	Ronald Smith	1986	139
135 2/8	40 2/8	8 4/8	10 4/8	9	8	Fremont County	ID	Shayne Ard	1998	141
135 0/8	43 2/8	8 2/8	9 0/8	8	7	Teton County	WY	Greg Perkins	1997	142
134 7/8	40 5/8	8 0/8	10 2/8	6	8	Lincoln County	MT	Jerry Brown	1982	143
134 4/8	38 6/8	8 1/8	7 5/8	8	9	Lincoln County	MT	Don Davidson	1989	144
133 6/8	43 0/8	9 3/8	6 7/8	8	8	Teton County	WY	Dr. Joel J. Bickler	1996	145
133 5/8	44 3/8	8 0/8	9 1/8	7	7	Sheridan County	WY	Duff De Lon	1989	146
133 3/8	45 5/8	10 3/8	7 5/8	9	7	Lincoln County	WY	Mike Johnston	1988	147
133 1/8	40 7/8	8 2/8	9 1/8	8	8	Jackson County	CO	Mike Brezonick	1993	148
133 0/8	41 6/8	8 6/8	7 4/8	10	9	Teton County	WY	Bob Dawson	1988	149
132 7/8	43 3/8	8 4/8	9 3/8	8	6	Weber County	UT	Brian Ferebee	1998	150
132 2/8	37 6/8	10 3/8	10 6/8	11	9	Lincoln County	WY	Dennis L. Shirley	1988	151
132 1/8	42 1/8	8 5/8	9 1/8	8	8	Lincoln County	WY	Lee Challinor	1982	152
132 1/8	38 3/8	7 5/8	11 5/8	8	9	Lincoln County	WY	Bennett L. McMillian	1997	152
132 1/8	43 1/8	8 2/8	10 0/8	9	10	Weber County	UT	Craig P. Mitton	1998	152
131 6/8	44 0/8	7 6/8	7 7/8	7	7	Lincoln County	WY	Kevin Jackson	1980	155
131 6/8	40 4/8	8 6/8	10 3/8	9	9	Morgan County	UT	Larry Mathis	1989	155
131 6/8	42 0/8	8 1/8	8 5/8	4	7	Sheridan County	WY	Daniel Henthorn	1995	155
131 6/8	45 0/8	8 5/8	6 0/8	7	7	Caribou County	ID	Mark L. Mansfield	1995	155
131 5/8	34 7/8	11 0/8	11 1/8	4	4	Madison County	ID	William E. Dean	1996	159
131 4/8	47 0/8	8 1/8	8 7/8	7	7	Gallatin County	MT	Scott L. Koelzer	1992	160
131 3/8	43 5/8	8 5/8	8 3/8	7	8	Sublette County	WY	Kenneth R. Keierleber	1992	161
131 2/8	34 4/8	10 6/8	11 0/8	8	8	Bonneville County	ID	Edward Keller	1986	162
131 2/8	43 6/8	9 5/8	7 7/8	9	8	Uinta County	WY	Larry Lee Francis, Jr.	1991	162
130 7/8	39 5/8	8 6/8	9 1/8	9	8	Lincoln County	WY	Dave Cordes	1982	164
130 6/8	46 2/8	7 2/8	7 5/8	6	6	Lincoln County	WY	Ken Allen	1986	165
130 6/8	37 4/8	10 2/8	13 6/8	9	10	Lincoln County	WY	Brian L. Wagner	1987	165
130 5/8	38 3/8	8 4/8	8 3/8	7	11	Park County	WY	Greg Deatsman	1985	167
130 5/8	36 7/8	7 4/8	9 3/8	8	7	Beaverhead County	MT	Robert Rooney	1991	167
129 7/8	39 1/8	8 2/8	10 2/8	9	11	Lincoln County	WY	Bob Tynsky	1987	169
129 7/8	37 1/8	7 0/8	9 7/8	7	9	Sheridan County	WY	Michael L. Graham	1988	169
129 7/8	38 7/8	8 0/8	8 6/8	7	7	Sublette County	WY	Kevin Cross	1989	169
129 6/8	38 6/8	10 1/8	9 0/8	7	7	Sublette County	WY	Tim Thompson	1998	172
129 5/8	44 5/8	9 0/8	8 5/8	7	7	Weber County	UT	Jamie Roper	1991	173
129 3/8	42 7/8	7 6/8	9 0/8	7	9	Lincoln County	MT	Jerry Brown	1990	174
129 3/8	40 5/8	9 2/8	8 0/8	9	9	Lincoln County	MT	Kevin Hadley	1997	174

SHIRAS "WYOMING" MOOSE

Minimum Score 125

Continued

SCORE	GREATEST SPREAD	WIDTH OF PALM R	L	NUMBER OF POINTS R	L	AREA	STATE/ PROVINCE	HUNTER'S NAME	DATE	RANK
129 2/8	37 2/8	8 6/8	8 5/8	8	8	Sublette County	WY	Jerrold M. Judkins	1979	176
129 0/8	39 4/8	7 4/8	8 0/8	9	8	Flathead County	MT	Dyrk Eddie	1991	177
129 0/8	45 0/8	8 4/8	6 6/8	7	8	Morgan County	UT	Robert G. Petersen	1992	177
128 4/8	40 0/8	13 0/8	8 4/8	7	9	Sheridan County	WY	Robert R. Long	1994	179
128 1/8	40 5/8	6 4/8	6 0/8	6	6	Teton County	WY	Keith Frick	1984	180
128 0/8	39 0/8	7 6/8	9 4/8	6	8	Fremont County	WY	Gary M. Oksuita	1997	181
128 0/8	40 6/8	8 3/8	9 6/8	6	11	Sublette County	WY	Donald J. Propson	1997	181
127 4/8	35 0/8	9 6/8	12 0/8	8	8	Lincoln County	WY	Al Bitker	1982	183
127 4/8	36 6/8	7 0/8	7 4/8	7	7	Idaho County	ID	Brad Johnson	1985	183
127 3/8	42 5/8	8 2/8	8 2/8	6	9	Fremont County	WY	Richard J. Tokarski	1997	185
127 2/8	41 2/8	6 4/8	6 4/8	9	8	Missoula County	MT	Richard Schaub	1997	186
126 7/8	44 7/8	5 2/8	6 2/8	6	8	Summit County	UT	Kenneth D. Evans	1996	187
126 2/8	43 4/8	8 6/8	9 1/8	7	7	Idaho County	ID	Robert Jackson	1990	188
125 5/8	49 3/8	8 2/8	7 7/8	8	7	Weber County	UT	Clark Stokes	1986	189
125 4/8	39 4/8	9 4/8	9 4/8	8	8	Lemhi County	ID	Lewis Zane Abbott	1992	190
125 4/8	41 2/8	7 7/8	6 0/8	10	7	Duchesne County	UT	Jonny C. Parsons	1994	190
125 0/8	34 6/8	9 5/8	8 6/8	9	9	Morgan County	UT	C. Danny Butler	1991	192
125 0/8	37 6/8	7 3/8	9 1/8	8	9	Weber County	UT	Frank L. Fackovec	1993	192
124 6/8	40 2/8	10 1/8	10 1/8	5	3	Lincoln County	WY	David H. Boland	1977	194
124 2/8	41 2/8	6 7/8	6 7/8	6	7	Lincoln County	WY	Doug Stults	1994	195
124 1/8	37 7/8	6 7/8	7 5/8	6	7	Bonneville County	ID	Wayne Jones	1991	196
124 0/8	40 4/8	7 4/8	8 4/8	8	6	Fremont County	WY	John Applegate	1977	197
123 7/8	43 3/8	6 3/8	8 0/8	8	8	Uinta County	WY	Pep Brinkerhoff	1986	198
123 5/8	40 7/8	9 0/8	7 6/8	7	6	Clearwater County	ID	Ron Long	1996	199
123 5/8	39 5/8	9 4/8	9 2/8	5	7	Lincoln County	MT	Gregory B. McPhillips	1998	199
123 4/8	39 6/8	6 4/8	8 3/8	6	7	Madison County	MT	Erwin Clark	1992	201
123 4/8	34 6/8	9 0/8	8 6/8	9	9	Weber County	UT	Dave Justmann	1992	201
123 4/8	38 4/8	7 7/8	7 5/8	8	8	Summit County	UT	Stuart James Walker	1994	201
123 2/8	37 6/8	8 5/8	7 4/8	9	7	Rich County	UT	Richard Ballard	1987	204
123 2/8	35 0/8	8 2/8	8 7/8	9	8	Lincoln County	WY	Ronald D. Halvorson	1988	204
123 1/8	35 7/8	7 6/8	8 0/8	7	8	Weber County	UT	Randall S. Ulmer	1991	206
122 5/8	39 1/8	6 6/8	9 2/8	6	9	Powell County	MT	Dave Brummond	1997	207
122 4/8	36 6/8	8 2/8	7 3/8	7	7	Morgan County	UT	Robert K. Paulson	1987	208
122 3/8	38 1/8	7 4/8	6 4/8	6	8	Park County	MT	Steve Kamps	1996	209
122 2/8	41 4/8	7 5/8	8 3/8	7	8	Sublette County	WY	Larry Honeycutt	1990	210
122 0/8	40 6/8	9 0/8	8 6/8	7	7	Caribou County	ID	Blair W. Lewis	1995	211
121 7/8	44 3/8	8 4/8	7 0/8	8	8	Caribou County	ID	Rick Bergholm	1993	212
121 4/8	44 2/8	9 4/8	7 5/8	8	5	Lincoln County	WY	Craig P. Mitton	1987	213
121 2/8	39 6/8	7 3/8	7 2/8	9	6	Sublette County	WY	Vern A. Butler	1973	214
121 2/8	37 6/8	6 6/8	6 2/8	7	7	Beaverhead County	MT	Mike Nieskens	1996	214
121 1/8	44 7/8	6 4/8	6 7/8	7	6	Cache County	UT	Bret F. Davis	1996	216
121 0/8	39 2/8	7 3/8	8 1/8	8	8	Jackson County	CO	Lee Kline	1994	217
121 0/8	36 0/8	6 7/8	6 0/8	7	7	Morgan County	UT	Thomas J. Hoffman	1996	217
120 7/8	42 5/8	6 7/8	7 2/8	5	5	Sublette County	WY	Wade L. Carstens	1982	219
120 6/8	34 6/8	9 2/8	9 4/8	9	8	Caribou County	ID	Chad Doell	1992	220
120 0/8	49 4/8	3 7/8	5 6/8	5	7	Sublette County	WY	Dick Mauch	1959	221
119 7/8	37 1/8	8 2/8	7 7/8	9	7	Teton County	WY	Todd Zeuske	1989	222
119 6/8	35 4/8	9 6/8	9 6/8	7	8	Weber County	UT	Kenny E. Leo	1993	223
119 5/8	40 3/8	6 4/8	9 0/8	6	6	Franklin County	ID	Benton Christensen	1995	224
119 4/8	40 4/8	7 3/8	7 4/8	4	4	Idaho County	ID	David Wilken	1986	225
119 2/8	39 0/8	7 1/8	7 4/8	8	7	Sheridan County	WY	James T. Dawson	1987	226
119 2/8	42 0/8	6 2/8	9 2/8	7	6	Fremont County	WY	Craig Overman	1996	226
119 0/8	35 4/8	7 0/8	8 6/8	8	9	La Barge	WY	Glen Talbott	1980	228
119 0/8	37 0/8	7 2/8	7 2/8	7	7	Summit County	UT	Charles R. Justmann	1989	228
118 6/8	37 0/8	8 7/8	7 3/8	8	8	Park County	WY	Raymond E. Questiaux	1991	230
118 6/8	41 4/8	7 3/8	7 5/8	7	7	Sublette County	WY	Casey Blum	1991	230
118 4/8	40 2/8	6 2/8	6 4/8	7	7	Teton County	WY	Richard Lopez	1988	232
117 5/8	38 5/8	7 5/8	7 1/8	7	6	Uinta County	WY	David Kaden	1982	233
117 5/8	44 3/8	12 0/8	9 2/8	11	3	Cache County	UT	Mark Wright	1985	233
117 5/8	34 1/8	9 4/8	7 6/8	7	7	Caribou County	ID	Randy K. Vranes	1991	233
117 3/8	40 7/8	6 6/8	6 4/8	6	6	Summit County	UT	Mike Christiansen	1988	236
117 1/8	41 1/8	6 0/8	8 0/8	5	7	Daggett County	UT	Scott K. Moulton	1993	237
117 1/8	35 1/8	7 7/8	7 7/8	8	9	Jackson County	CO	Douglas P. Dodson	1996	237
117 0/8	40 6/8	6 0/8	8 0/8	7	10	Teton County	WY	Larry Dickerson	1991	239
116 7/8	45 1/8	6 0/8	6 0/8	5	5	Jagg Creek	WY	Robert W. Steller	1975	240
116 6/8	42 0/8	8 1/8	7 2/8	6	6	Lincoln County	WY	Kirt Prestwich	1986	241
116 5/8	33 5/8	8 6/8	6 6/8	7	7	Sublette County	WY	Terry Brown	1989	242
116 2/8	41 4/8	8 6/8	9 6/8	5	4	Lincoln County	MT	Lee Lampton	1982	243
116 2/8	40 6/8	7 7/8	6 7/8	8	7	Weber County	UT	Todd Hinkins	1990	243
116 2/8	43 0/8	7 5/8	8 6/8	2	6	Jackson County	CO	John L. Gardner	1992	243
116 0/8	33 0/8	8 3/8	7 6/8	8	7	Lincoln County	WY	Glenn Hisey	1982	246
116 0/8	36 4/8	7 0/8	7 0/8	8	8	Lincoln County	WY	Jack M. Conner	1988	246
115 5/8	36 1/8	8 6/8	7 5/8	8	8	Lincoln County	WY	Cathy Lee Jordan	1983	248
115 5/8	42 7/8	5 5/8	5 6/8	7	6	Duchesne County	UT	Sam Nesi	1987	248
115 1/8	41 1/8	7 7/8	6 3/8	9	4	Sheridan County	WY	Bradley T. Miller	1991	250
115 0/8	36 2/8	7 3/8	7 2/8	7	7	Idaho County	ID	Tom Fliss	1987	251
115 0/8	36 2/8	9 5/8	7 6/8	8	7	Teton County	WY	Carl Gramlich	1996	251
115 0/8	43 0/8	9 1/8	6 4/8	5	5	Lincoln County	MT	Don Davidson	1997	251

SHIRAS "WYOMING" MOOSE (VELVET ANTLERS)

Minimum Score 125

SCORE	GREATEST SPREAD	R	WIDTH OF PALM	L	R	NUMBER OF POINTS	L	AREA	STATE/ PROVINCE	HUNTER'S NAME	DATE	RANK
175 2/8	46 4/8	10 7/8		11 2/8	11		12	Teton County	WY	Monty M. Baldwin	1998	*
139 5/8	37 3/8	10 2/8		11 0/8	10		7	Uinta County	WY	Lee P. Quillinan	1996	*
126 2/8	43 6/8	7 2/8		6 4/8	5		7	Lincoln County	WY	Jeff J. Connors	1995	*

* *Velvet entries will be listed in only one record book.*

World Record Muskox (Tie)
Score: 127 2/8
Coppermine, Northwest Territories - 1996
Hunter: Bob Black

World Record Muskox (Tie)
Score: 127 2/8
Coppermine, Northwest Territories - 1998
Hunter: William L. Cox

MUSKOX

Minimum Score 90 — *Ovibos moschatus* and certain related subspecies

SCORE	LENGTH OF HORN R	L	WIDTH OF BOSS R	L	GREATEST SPREAD	AREA	STATE/PROVINCE	HUNTER'S NAME	DATE	RANK
127 2/8	30 1/8	30 1/8	10 1/8	10 2/8	31 0/8	Coppermine	NWT	Bob Black	1996	1
127 2/8	29 0/8	29 0/8	11 4/8	11 5/8	29 3/8	Coppermine	NWT	William L. Cox	1998	1
126 4/8	29 3/8	29 3/8	11 1/8	11 2/8	28 4/8	Coppermine	NWT	Fred P. Gonzales	1996	3
121 6/8	27 6/8	29 0/8	11 1/8	11 0/8	28 4/8	Coppermine	NWT	Jay Clayson	1995	4
121 0/8	29 1/8	28 2/8	10 3/8	10 2/8	29 4/8	Coppermine	NWT	Raymond Young	1996	5
118 6/8	29 0/8	27 2/8	10 6/8	11 0/8	28 2/8	Coppermine	NWT	David A. Bower	1995	6
117 6/8	27 4/8	27 0/8	10 2/8	10 2/8	28 3/8	Coppermine	NWT	Robert Edward Speegle, MD	1997	7
115 4/8	27 2/8	29 7/8	10 4/8	10 2/8	27 6/8	Coppermine	NWT	David G. Anderson	1996	8
115 2/8	27 0/8	28 0/8	9 3/8	9 4/8	24 4/8	Horton River	NWT	John R. Wilson	1996	9
114 2/8	29 1/8	28 0/8	9 0/8	9 3/8	28 7/8	Ellice River	NWT	Steve Munier	1988	10
114 0/8	27 4/8	27 6/8	9 0/8	8 7/8	30 6/8	Perry Island	NWT	J. T. Smith	1988	11
113 2/8	25 2/8	25 6/8	9 5/8	9 5/8	28 1/8	Kent Peninsula	NWT	Archie Nesbitt	1989	12
113 0/8	27 1/8	28 3/8	9 5/8	9 4/8	27 7/8	Anderson River	NWT	Jack Leggo	1995	13
112 2/8	27 7/8	27 3/8	9 1/8	9 1/8	27 4/8	Rendez-vous Lake	NWT	Mike E. Kuglitsch	1994	14
112 0/8	24 3/8	23 7/8	10 0/8	10 0/8	25 3/8	Banks Island	NWT	Bill Lancaster	1995	15
111 4/8	26 3/8	26 0/8	9 5/8	9 5/8	25 5/8	Banks Island	NWT	David V. Collis	1985	16
111 0/8	26 1/8	26 6/8	8 6/8	8 6/8	26 4/8	Rendez-vous Lake	NWT	Mike Morgan	1995	17
110 6/8	27 1/8	27 2/8	8 5/8	8 4/8	26 3/8	Nunivak Island	AK	Todd A. Sneesby	1988	18
110 6/8	26 6/8	26 0/8	8 7/8	8 7/8	28 5/8	McLoughlin River	NWT	Archie J. Nesbitt	1990	18
110 4/8	27 0/8	27 3/8	9 2/8	9 3/8	26 1/8	Banks Island	NWT	Robert L. Jacobsen	1987	20
110 2/8	26 1/8	26 7/8	10 0/8	9 5/8	28 2/8	Rendez-vous Lake	NWT	Craig Adams	1995	21
110 2/8	27 2/8	26 0/8	8 5/8	8 5/8	28 0/8	Nuluk River	AK	Al Grierson	1998	21
110 0/8	28 0/8	27 2/8	8 3/8	8 5/8	26 7/8	Nunivak Island	AK	Richard Moran	1988	23
109 4/8	26 2/8	26 5/8	9 5/8	9 5/8	26 7/8	Banks Island	NWT	Roger Anderson	1986	24
109 4/8	26 1/8	26 0/8	9 4/8	9 5/8	25 5/8	Banks Island	NWT	Larry Hoff	1986	24
109 4/8	25 6/8	25 6/8	9 7/8	9 6/8	25 5/8	Banks Island	NWT	Jim Ryan	1989	24
109 2/8	26 3/8	27 2/8	9 0/8	8 5/8	26 7/8	Nunivak Island	AK	Craig Scarbrough	1988	27
109 2/8	25 4/8	25 4/8	9 2/8	9 2/8	25 6/8	Victoria Island	NWT	Larry Barton	1991	27
108 4/8	26 3/8	28 2/8	9 5/8	9 6/8	27 0/8	Paulatuk	NWT	Ron Kolpin	1981	29
108 2/8	26 4/8	26 6/8	8 7/8	8 2/8	24 5/8	Bluenose Lake	NWT	George P. Mann	1990	30
108 2/8	26 6/8	28 5/8	8 6/8	8 2/8	26 4/8	Nelson Island	AK	Dexter Lemon	1994	30
108 0/8	27 5/8	28 5/8	8 4/8	8 4/8	25 4/8	Nelson Island	AK	Dexter Lemon	1986	32
108 0/8	26 0/8	25 3/8	9 3/8	9 4/8	26 1/8	Perry Island	NWT	Theodore Dzienis	1986	32
108 0/8	26 0/8	26 0/8	9 2/8	9 3/8	25 2/8	Sachs Harbor	NWT	K-Tal Johnson	1997	32
107 6/8	25 1/8	27 3/8	9 6/8	9 5/8	27 3/8	Banks Island	NWT	Rusty Neely	1987	35
107 6/8	25 1/8	25 5/8	8 7/8	9 0/8	25 3/8	Coppermine	NWT	Glenn Thurman	1993	35
107 6/8	25 1/8	25 3/8	8 3/8	8 2/8	26 0/8	Nuluk River	AK	Al Grierson	1997	35
107 4/8	26 3/8	26 0/8	9 5/8	10 0/8	25 7/8	Banks Island	NWT	John McAteer	1986	38
107 4/8	25 0/8	25 1/8	8 1/8	8 1/8	26 3/8	Nunivak Island	AK	Timothy A. Gleason	1992	38
107 4/8	26 2/8	25 5/8	8 3/8	8 4/8	27 1/8	Nunivak Island	AK	Merle R. Frank	1997	38
107 2/8	24 6/8	25 3/8	10 0/8	10 1/8	26 7/8	Victoria Island	NWT	Ray Keenan	1987	41
107 2/8	26 2/8	26 4/8	9 0/8	9 1/8	24 6/8	Banks Island	NWT	Karen K. Jacobsen	1987	41
107 2/8	26 2/8	26 6/8	9 0/8	9 1/8	27 0/8	Victoria Island	NWT	Johnnie R. Walters	1993	41
107 2/8	25 6/8	27 3/8	9 7/8	9 6/8	26 6/8	Bay Chimo	NWT	Dyrk Eddie	1998	41
107 0/8	28 2/8	26 3/8	9 3/8	9 4/8	26 7/8	Banks Island	NWT	Dennis Kamstra	1987	45
106 6/8	25 5/8	26 2/8	8 5/8	9 0/8	27 6/8	Banks Island	NWT	Billy Ellis	1982	46
106 6/8	25 5/8	25 6/8	8 6/8	8 2/8	27 6/8	Nelson Island	AK	Dexter Lemon	1985	46
106 6/8	28 6/8	27 3/8	8 5/8	8 4/8	28 1/8	Nunivak Island	AK	Ernest J. Emmi	1991	46
106 6/8	26 0/8	27 3/8	9 5/8	9 5/8	27 3/8	Banks Island	NWT	Jim Gall	1995	46
106 6/8	25 6/8	25 1/8	9 3/8	9 2/8	26 7/8	Beyaingayolehok Lake	NWT	Dave Justmann	1997	46
106 4/8	24 3/8	24 5/8	8 3/8	8 4/8	27 3/8	Nunivak Island	AK	Joseph O. Fogleman	1976	51
106 4/8	26 7/8	27 3/8	8 0/8	8 0/8	27 4/8	Nunivak Island	AK	John D. 'Jack' Frost	1986	51
106 4/8	26 5/8	27 2/8	8 5/8	8 3/8	26 2/8	Nelson Island	AK	Dexter Lemon	1990	51
106 4/8	25 7/8	25 3/8	9 2/8	9 3/8	25 1/8	Paulatuk	NWT	Tom Taylor	1994	51
106 2/8	25 4/8	25 5/8	8 2/8	8 2/8	27 5/8	Kaktovik	AK	Herman Griese	1984	55
106 2/8	26 4/8	25 7/8	7 6/8	8 1/8	27 6/8	Perry River	NWT	Jack Downing	1988	55
105 6/8	25 1/8	25 1/8	9 2/8	9 2/8	26 0/8	Banks Island	NWT	Kirk Westervelt	1986	57
105 6/8	24 2/8	25 1/8	9 1/8	9 1/8	27 2/8	Coppermines	NWT	Leo F. Neuls	1991	57
105 4/8	26 0/8	25 2/8	8 7/8	8 5/8	28 5/8	Perry Island	NWT	Ronald E. Sanders	1988	59
105 4/8	25 5/8	24 2/8	9 0/8	9 0/8	26 5/8	Sachs Harbor	NWT	David G. Sonnenburg	1994	59
105 2/8	25 6/8	26 2/8	8 6/8	9 2/8	27 4/8	Victoria Island	NWT	Len Cardinale	1987	61
105 0/8	25 1/8	26 4/8	8 7/8	8 6/8	26 2/8	Kaktovik	AK	Bill Petrovish	1984	62
105 0/8	27 2/8	26 4/8	8 2/8	9 0/8	28 0/8	Nunivak Island	AK	Harvey A. Kolberg	1991	62
104 6/8	24 5/8	25 0/8	9 4/8	9 2/8	25 0/8	Banks Island	NWT	Susan D. Sherer	1986	64
104 6/8	24 6/8	24 1/8	8 2/8	8 4/8	27 3/8	Combo Lake	NWT	Nathan L. Andersohn	1997	64
104 4/8	27 2/8	25 4/8	9 2/8	9 2/8	27 2/8	Banks Island	NWT	Dr. Howard Schneider	1985	66
104 4/8	25 4/8	25 2/8	9 0/8	9 1/8	25 4/8	Banks Island	NWT	Ronald L. Sherer	1986	66
104 4/8	24 6/8	25 0/8	9 2/8	9 2/8	26 0/8	Banks Island	NWT	Richard L. Westervelt	1986	66
104 4/8	25 1/8	26 1/8	9 5/8	9 2/8	25 7/8	West Victoria Island	NWT	John Janelli	1987	66
104 4/8	24 1/8	24 2/8	9 3/8	9 3/8	26 4/8	Banks Island	NWT	James R. Gabrick	1997	66
104 0/8	24 3/8	24 6/8	9 6/8	9 5/8	24 4/8	Banks Island	NWT	Larry Hoff	1986	71
104 0/8	24 6/8	25 4/8	8 4/8	8 3/8	26 6/8	Perry River	NWT	Bruce R. Schoeneweis	1990	71
104 0/8	25 3/8	24 5/8	9 5/8	9 5/8	25 5/8	Holman	NWT	Ryk Visscher	1998	71
103 6/8	26 0/8	26 4/8	8 1/8	8 1/8	27 3/8	Nunivak Island	AK	Carl E. Brent	1993	74
103 4/8	27 0/8	27 0/8	8 1/8	8 2/8	25 5/8	Paulatuk	NWT	Erv Plotz	1980	75
103 2/8	26 6/8	26 0/8	9 1/8	9 0/8	25 0/8	Holman	NWT	Scott Trelstad	1997	75
103 0/8	22 6/8	23 5/8	8 5/8	8 4/8	26 7/8	Nunivak Island	AK	P.J. Londo	1977	77
103 0/8	25 1/8	24 7/8	9 1/8	9 1/8	24 7/8	Holman	NWT	Ronald Regan	1992	77

MUSKOX

Minimum Score 90 — Continued

SCORE	LENGTH OF HORN R	LENGTH OF HORN L	WIDTH OF BOSS R	WIDTH OF BOSS L	GREATEST SPREAD	AREA	STATE/PROVINCE	HUNTER'S NAME	DATE	RANK
102 6/8	25 0/8	27 0/8	8 7/8	8 3/8	29 0/8	Nunivak Island	AK	Jim Voeller	1978	79
102 6/8	24 4/8	24 6/8	9 3/8	9 2/8	26 0/8	Banks Island	NWT	Frank C. Eifert	1987	79
102 6/8	25 0/8	23 7/8	9 3/8	9 1/8	27 5/8	Victoria Island	NWT	Jerry R. Westcott	1997	79
102 4/8	25 4/8	27 1/8	8 7/8	9 0/8	25 0/8	Holman Bay	NWT	Benny White	1992	82
102 4/8	25 2/8	26 1/8	9 1/8	8 6/8	25 5/8	Nunivak Island	AK	David A. Widby	1993	82
102 4/8	25 1/8	25 5/8	9 3/8	9 3/8	24 7/8	Holman	NWT	Warren Witherspoon	1997	82
102 2/8	24 4/8	25 0/8	8 5/8	8 6/8	26 5/8	Nunivak Island	AK	Raymond C. Bahma, Jr.	1994	85
101 6/8	24 3/8	24 5/8	7 7/8	7 7/8	27 3/8	Nunivak Island	AK	Tim Moerlein	1990	86
101 6/8	23 7/8	24 0/8	8 1/8	8 0/8	26 2/8	Nunivak Island	AK	Rick D. Snell	1994	86
101 6/8	25 4/8	24 6/8	8 2/8	8 1/8	23 7/8	Banks Island	NWT	James R. Gabrick	1997	86
101 4/8	24 6/8	25 2/8	8 6/8	8 6/8	27 6/8	Nunivak Island	AK	David A. Widby	1983	89
101 4/8	26 4/8	25 1/8	8 3/8	8 6/8	26 3/8	Nunivak Island	AK	Lon E. Lauber	1991	89
101 4/8	24 4/8	24 4/8	8 3/8	8 3/8	25 3/8	Nunivak Island	AK	Larry Daly	1994	89
101 4/8	25 3/8	26 2/8	9 2/8	9 6/8	24 5/8	Holman Island	NWT	Anthony "Del" Delmastro	1995	89
101 4/8	23 0/8	22 5/8	8 4/8	8 3/8	25 3/8	Banks Island	NWT	Dean Grommet	1995	89
101 2/8	24 4/8	25 2/8	9 4/8	9 3/8	26 0/8	Banks Island	NWT	James C. Hicks	1995	94
101 2/8	25 4/8	24 6/8	9 0/8	8 5/8	24 6/8	Ellice River	NWT	Ralph F. Merkley	1995	94
101 2/8	24 1/8	24 5/8	9 1/8	9 0/8	22 7/8	Holman Island	NWT	Anthony "Del" Delmastro	1995	94
101 0/8	25 1/8	25 0/8	8 0/8	8 2/8	26 2/8	Nunivak Island	AK	Edward L. Russell	1984	97
101 0/8	24 7/8	26 4/8	8 0/8	8 2/8	26 0/8	Nunivak Island	AK	Michael J. Lettis	1989	97
101 0/8	23 6/8	22 7/8	8 7/8	9 2/8	33 1/8	Banks Island	NWT	Jim Gall	1997	97
100 6/8	24 1/8	25 1/8	7 7/8	7 7/8	24 1/8	Nunivak Island	AK	Dr. Von A. Mitton	1978	100
100 6/8	24 1/8	25 0/8	8 6/8	8 6/8	26 3/8	Victoria Island	NWT	David Richey	1988	100
100 6/8	26 4/8	25 2/8	8 3/8	8 3/8	25 7/8	Nunivak Island	AK	Maxallen D. Jackson	1991	100
100 4/8	25 2/8	26 2/8	7 7/8	7 6/8	28 1/8	Nunivak Island	AK	Bruce J. Werba	1977	103
100 4/8	24 5/8	26 4/8	10 2/8	10 1/8	27 2/8	Banks Island	NWT	Dr. Howard Schneider	1985	103
100 4/8	24 1/8	24 7/8	9 2/8	8 7/8	26 0/8	Nunivak Island	AK	Rick Schikora	1993	103
100 4/8	24 3/8	24 3/8	8 5/8	8 3/8	27 4/8	Nunivak Island	AK	Ron C. Harvey	1994	103
100 4/8	25 4/8	26 2/8	8 2/8	8 3/8	27 1/8	Nunivak Island	AK	Kurt M. Burroughs	1995	103
100 2/8	24 5/8	25 5/8	8 3/8	7 7/8	24 0/8	Nunivak Island	AK	Curt Lynn	1984	108
100 2/8	25 3/8	24 4/8	8 2/8	8 3/8	27 3/8	Nunivak Island	AK	Rex Wright	1992	108
100 2/8	25 2/8	25 0/8	8 4/8	8 4/8	25 0/8	Victoria Island	NWT	Mark Buehrer	1997	108
100 2/8	25 3/8	25 7/8	8 3/8	8 0/8	23 0/8	Combo Lake	NWT	Thomas J. Hoffman	1997	108
100 0/8	25 0/8	26 4/8	8 4/8	8 3/8	25 1/8	Nunivak Island	AK	Max C. Lyon, Jr.	1991	112
100 0/8	24 4/8	26 3/8	8 7/8	8 7/8	27 1/8	Paulatuk	NWT	Roy Goodwin	1994	112
100 0/8	24 5/8	25 6/8	7 6/8	7 7/8	27 4/8	Nunivak Island	AK	Ted Nugent	1996	112
99 6/8	24 0/8	23 6/8	8 5/8	8 2/8	26 0/8	Nunivak Island	AK	David A. Widby	1996	115
99 4/8	24 6/8	22 7/8	9 3/8	9 0/8	25 1/8	Cambridge Bay	NWT	Ricardo Longoria	1998	116
99 2/8	25 4/8	25 6/8	8 5/8	8 5/8	25 3/8	Banks Island	NWT	Jim Gall	1995	117
99 2/8	25 2/8	25 2/8	8 6/8	8 4/8	22 1/8	Holman	NWT	Tom Nelson	1997	117
99 2/8	24 7/8	23 3/8	8 3/8	8 4/8	24 7/8	Paulatuk	NWT	Tom Foss	1997	117
98 6/8	23 6/8	24 6/8	9 2/8	9 0/8	25 7/8	Holman Island	NWT	Wayne E. Meyers	1994	120
98 6/8	25 3/8	26 4/8	8 1/8	7 5/8	25 7/8	Nunivak Island	AK	Gary R. Crawford	1998	120
98 6/8	24 2/8	25 3/8	8 6/8	8 4/8	24 1/8	Holman	NWT	Larry Streiff	1998	120
98 4/8	23 4/8	24 2/8	9 0/8	8 5/8	25 7/8	Sachs Harbor	NWT	Dwight Pfeiffer	1989	123
98 4/8	23 5/8	24 1/8	8 0/8	8 0/8	25 0/8	Holman	NWT	Duane Hicks	1997	123
98 2/8	23 5/8	24 1/8	7 3/8	7 5/8	28 3/8	Nunivak Island	AK	Tony Russ	1990	125
98 2/8	25 1/8	24 4/8	8 6/8	8 6/8	26 3/8	Victoria Island	NWT	Ronald Sallman	1993	125
98 0/8	23 7/8	23 4/8	8 5/8	8 7/8	24 4/8	Banks Island	PROVINCE	Scott Zoellick	1995	127
97 2/8	24 3/8	25 2/8	8 5/8	8 5/8	24 7/8	Sachs Harbor	NWT	George Engelhardt	1995	128
97 0/8	24 4/8	24 1/8	8 3/8	8 4/8	28 0/8	Nunivak Island	AK	Michael J. Schneider	1983	129
97 0/8	23 7/8	25 2/8	9 3/8	9 2/8	25 3/8	Banks Island	NWT	Michael Teff	1997	129
96 6/8	22 5/8	24 0/8	8 2/8	8 0/8	26 2/8	Nunivak Island	AK	Bob Hammond	1988	131
96 6/8	24 2/8	25 3/8	8 4/8	8 3/8	28 3/8	Nunivak Island	AK	Matt Jones	1992	131
96 6/8	24 4/8	26 2/8	8 2/8	8 2/8	24 3/8	Nunivak Island	AK	Paul Ritz	1997	131
96 4/8	25 1/8	24 1/8	8 0/8	8 2/8	26 0/8	Victoria Island	NWT	Charles G. Schibler	1992	134
96 2/8	23 1/8	25 1/8	9 0/8	9 0/8	25 4/8	Victoria Island	NWT	Martin Glover	1997	135
95 6/8	25 0/8	23 2/8	8 7/8	9 1/8	25 0/8	Sachs Harbor	NWT	K-Tal Johnson	1997	136
95 4/8	21 0/8	20 6/8	8 0/8	8 2/8	26 2/8	Nunivak Island	AK	Dick Gulman	1978	137
95 4/8	26 6/8	24 7/8	8 0/8	8 2/8	27 6/8	Nunivak Island	AK	Ken Vorisek	1995	137
95 4/8	23 7/8	23 5/8	8 7/8	8 6/8	24 2/8	Sachs Harbor	NWT	Alan E. Schroeder	1998	137
94 6/8	25 0/8	23 2/8	8 3/8	8 3/8	25 6/8	Nunivak Island	AK	Jeff Eichholz	1997	140
94 4/8	24 5/8	23 6/8	6 6/8	6 6/8	26 7/8	Nunivak Island	AK	C. Vernon Humble	1976	141
94 4/8	21 0/8	22 7/8	9 2/8	9 2/8	25 1/8	South Gjoa Haven	NWT	Gary Bogner	1991	141
94 2/8	23 2/8	24 3/8	8 6/8	8 3/8	24 3/8	Victoria Island	NWT	Rick Kroll	1993	143
94 0/8	23 4/8	23 2/8	6 0/8	6 0/8	25 4/8	Paulatuk	NWT	Doug Burgard	1995	144
94 0/8	22 0/8	22 7/8	8 6/8	8 7/8	23 2/8	Caperon Lake	NWT	L. Scot Jenkins	1996	144
94 0/8	24 0/8	23 4/8	8 5/8	8 2/8	27 7/8	Victoria Island	NWT	Mark Connor	1997	144
93 6/8	23 0/8	22 5/8	7 6/8	8 4/8	24 6/8	Grise Fiord	NWT	Joseph Testerman	1993	147
93 4/8	24 5/8	24 2/8	7 5/8	7 2/8	20 1/8	Paulatuk	NWT	Tom Foss	1997	148
92 4/8	23 1/8	23 4/8	8 4/8	8 5/8	23 0/8	Cambridge Bay	NWT	Dale Slama	1993	149

World Record Pronghorn
Score: 91 4/8
Yavapai County, Arizona - 1995
Hunter: Marvin N. Zieser

PRONGHORN

Minimum Score 67 — *Autilocapra americana americana* and related subspecies

SCORE	LENGTH OF HORN R	L	CIRCUMFERENCE OF BASE R	L	INSIDE SPREAD	AREA	STATE/PROVINCE	HUNTER'S NAME	DATE	RANK
91 4/8	16 7/8	17 0/8	6 6/8	6 6/8	6 6/8	Yavapai County	AZ	Marvin N. Zieser	1995	1
90 6/8	17 0/8	17 0/8	7 0/8	6 7/8	9 3/8	Coconino County	AZ	Les Shelton	1998	2
90 0/8	16 3/8	17 3/8	7 1/8	7 2/8	11 4/8	Lake County	OR	Roger W. Clarno	1993	3
89 6/8	17 0/8	16 7/8	6 3/8	6 3/8	9 1/8	Yavapai County	AZ	Kevin Robinson	1996	4
88 6/8	15 6/8	15 7/8	7 2/8	7 0/8	14 2/8	Grant County	ND	Archie Malm	1958	5
87 0/8	16 6/8	16 5/8	6 3/8	6 4/8	12 4/8	Yavapai County	AZ	Garnet Kingsland	1995	6
86 6/8	16 0/8	15 7/8	6 6/8	6 6/8	8 6/8	Maple Creek	SAS	Jerry Bien	1990	7
86 2/8	18 3/8	18 4/8	6 3/8	6 2/8	12 4/8	Yavapai County	AZ	Perry Schaal	1994	8
85 6/8	16 2/8	15 4/8	6 6/8	6 7/8	13 2/8	Coconino County	AZ	Kevin Rector	1996	9
85 2/8	16 1/8	16 4/8	6 5/8	6 5/8	13 1/8	Carbon County	WY	Lonny Curtis	1990	10
85 2/8	16 4/8	16 3/8	6 4/8	6 4/8	10 0/8	Coconino County	AZ	Les R. Shelton	1995	10
85 0/8	17 2/8	17 1/8	6 4/8	6 4/8	10 3/8	Moffat County	CO	Judd Cooney	1983	12
85 0/8	16 7/8	16 6/8	6 1/8	6 1/8	10 1/8	Malheur County	OR	Kenneth L. Barstad	1994	12
85 0/8	16 1/8	16 1/8	7 1/8	7 1/8	13 0/8	Natrona County	WY	Mark B. Steffen	1997	12
84 6/8	16 2/8	16 6/8	6 6/8	6 6/8	8 0/8	Otero County	CO	Larry C. Hansen	1992	15
84 4/8	17 0/8	16 7/8	6 4/8	6 4/8	11 4/8	White Pine County	NV	Harold R. "Bud" Kirk	1988	16
84 4/8	15 2/8	16 2/8	7 1/8	7 0/8	12 0/8	Catron County	NM	Martin Silva	1997	16
84 2/8	16 0/8	15 6/8	6 3/8	6 3/8	10 0/8	Garfield County	MT	Ron J. Hoaglund	1989	18
84 2/8	15 7/8	15 7/8	7 1/8	7 0/8	9 3/8	Sweetwater County	WY	Kurt D. Olson	1990	18
84 2/8	16 3/8	16 2/8	6 4/8	6 2/8	13 4/8	Goshen County	WY	Gary Korell	1992	18

PRONGHORN

Minimum Score 67

SCORE	LENGTH OF HORN R	L	CIRCUMFERENCE OF BASE R	L	INSIDE SPREAD	AREA	STATE/ PROVINCE	HUNTER'S NAME	DATE	RANK
84 2/8	15 2/8	15 3/8	7 4/8	7 5/8	11 6/8	Sweetwater County	WY	Jared Mason	1995	18
84 0/8	16 2/8	15 5/8	6 7/8	6 7/8	11 6/8	Perkins County	SD	Spike Jorgensen	1964	22
84 0/8	16 6/8	16 3/8	6 4/8	6 4/8	11 0/8	Catron County	NM	Perry Harper	1991	22
84 0/8	17 1/8	17 1/8	6 5/8	6 5/8	10 6/8	Campbell County	WY	Loy Dean Peters	1992	22
84 0/8	16 0/8	16 1/8	6 7/8	6 5/8	14 1/8	Youngstown	ALB	Kevin D. Parker	1994	22
84 0/8	15 7/8	16 4/8	6 7/8	7 0/8	11 6/8	Socorro County	NM	Patrick Snyder	1996	22
84 0/8	15 2/8	15 3/8	6 7/8	6 6/8	10 2/8	Yavapai County	AZ	Perry Schaal	1996	22
83 6/8	15 4/8	15 2/8	7 3/8	7 3/8	15 2/8	Washoe County	NV	Fred Church	1978	28
83 6/8	15 2/8	15 6/8	6 3/8	6 4/8	11 6/8	Nye County	NV	Rich Sauer	1985	28
83 6/8	16 3/8	16 3/8	7 0/8	7 1/8	10 2/8	Harney County	OR	John S. Hansen	1990	28
83 6/8	15 7/8	15 7/8	6 3/8	6 2/8	11 5/8	Yavapai County	AZ	Roland J. Chooljian	1991	28
83 6/8	17 0/8	17 0/8	6 3/8	6 2/8	8 4/8	Sioux County	NE	Daniel F. Hejl	1991	28
83 6/8	15 2/8	15 3/8	6 4/8	6 4/8	9 6/8	Catron County	NM	Dave Fulson	1994	28
83 6/8	15 4/8	16 0/8	6 1/8	6 2/8	13 7/8	Coconino County	AZ	Steven Winiecki	1995	28
83 4/8	16 1/8	16 1/8	6 2/8	6 1/8	10 7/8	Yavapai County	AZ	Richard S. Jones	1987	35
83 4/8	15 2/8	15 2/8	6 7/8	6 7/8	9 3/8	Campbell County	WY	James N. Monat	1990	35
83 4/8	15 4/8	15 4/8	6 6/8	6 7/8	9 2/8	Moffat County	CO	L. Dale Adkins	1992	35
83 4/8	14 5/8	15 0/8	7 0/8	7 0/8	9 4/8	Sweetwater County	WY	Keith Dana	1994	35
83 4/8	15 1/8	15 0/8	7 7/8	7 6/8	11 7/8	Emery County	UT	Rick Stockburger	1997	35
83 2/8	15 3/8	15 7/8	6 6/8	6 5/8	8 5/8	Natrona County	WY	Gary L. Miller	1990	40
83 2/8	16 4/8	16 3/8	6 3/8	6 2/8	9 1/8	Catron County	NM	James F. Welles	1991	40
83 2/8	17 1/8	16 4/8	6 6/8	6 6/8	10 6/8	Baca County	CO	Earl Leon Hollenback	1993	40
83 0/8	17 0/8	17 0/8	6 0/8	6 0/8	12 3/8	Eddy County	NM	Jim Stell	1984	43
83 0/8	16 6/8	16 6/8	6 1/8	6 0/8	13 6/8	Coconino County	AZ	William P Pate	1985	43
83 0/8	16 4/8	16 4/8	6 5/8	6 4/8	15 7/8	Moffat County	CO	Mike Wallers	1989	43
83 0/8	15 6/8	15 5/8	7 2/8	6 7/8	14 5/8	Washoe County	NV	Daniel R. Brown	1990	43
82 6/8	16 4/8	16 3/8	6 2/8	6 3/8	8 5/8	Sublette County	WY	Michael D. Towne	1987	47
82 6/8	16 1/8	15 5/8	6 6/8	6 4/8	12 6/8	Coconino County	AZ	Kenneth C. Fulk	1988	47
82 6/8	16 2/8	16 1/8	6 5/8	6 4/8	9 0/8	Juab County	UT	David B. Nielsen	1992	47
82 6/8	16 2/8	16 1/8	6 5/8	6 6/8	12 0/8	Yavapai County	AZ	Larry Kindred	1994	47
82 6/8	16 0/8	16 1/8	6 3/8	6 2/8	8 5/8	Yavapai County	AZ	Paul S. Keltner	1997	47
82 4/8	15 1/8	16 0/8	6 5/8	6 3/8	6 3/8	McLean County	ND	Edward J. Weigel	1966	52
82 4/8	17 1/8	15 4/8	6 4/8	6 4/8	8 5/8	Yavapai County	AZ	Chris Skoczylas	1988	52
82 4/8	15 6/8	15 6/8	6 2/8	6 4/8	9 2/8	Graham County	AZ	Daniel C Hicks	1989	52
82 4/8	16 7/8	16 5/8	6 3/8	6 2/8	17 0/8	Luna County	NM	Ed Lowry	1990	52
82 4/8	14 2/8	14 1/8	7 0/8	6 7/8	10 1/8	Elko County	NV	Paul M. Adams	1994	52
82 4/8	17 1/8	17 4/8	6 4/8	6 5/8	16 6/8	Coconino County	AZ	Ken Patrick	1996	52
82 4/8	16 3/8	16 4/8	6 1/8	6 1/8	8 2/8	Santa Cruz County	AZ	Stan Haag	1996	52
82 4/8	15 2/8	15 1/8	6 6/8	6 6/8	10 6/8	Moffat County	CO	Kim Steven Hussong	1996	52
82 4/8	17 1/8	17 1/8	6 0/8	6 0/8	8 2/8	Yavapai County	AZ	Mike Brogdon	1997	52
82 4/8	14 7/8	14 6/8	6 7/8	6 7/8	7 2/8	Campbell County	WY	Richard E. LaCrone	1998	52
82 2/8	15 7/8	15 6/8	7 0/8	6 6/8	12 1/8	Elko County	NV	Monte D. Fuller	1987	62
82 2/8	16 5/8	16 1/8	6 3/8	6 4/8	14 1/8	Dunn County	ND	Peter Braun	1990	62
82 2/8	14 6/8	14 5/8	6 5/8	6 4/8	8 0/8	Washoe County	NV	Mark Mannens	1994	62
82 2/8	15 5/8	16 0/8	6 3/8	6 4/8	13 2/8	Catron County	NM	Jimmy Cotant	1995	62
82 2/8	16 0/8	16 0/8	6 6/8	6 5/8	10 1/8	Fergus County	MT	Brad Burney	1998	62
82 0/8	17 4/8	18 2/8	6 6/8	6 2/8	15 6/8	Guadalupe County	NM	C. E. Foster, Jr.	1961	67
82 0/8	16 3/8	16 2/8	6 3/8	6 4/8	9 6/8	Coconino County	AZ	Fred W. Fernow, Jr.	1981	67
82 0/8	16 4/8	17 0/8	7 0/8	7 0/8	14 4/8	Billings County	ND	Kenneth E. Ruzicka	1987	67
82 0/8	16 0/8	16 0/8	6 3/8	6 2/8	15 0/8	Coconino County	AZ	Mike Kentera	1988	67
82 0/8	16 4/8	16 3/8	6 3/8	6 3/8	13 0/8	Cochise County	AZ	Dan Larkin	1992	67
82 0/8	14 6/8	14 6/8	6 2/8	6 2/8	6 3/8	Navajo County	AZ	Shane Koury	1993	67
82 0/8	15 0/8	15 1/8	6 3/8	6 3/8	12 5/8	Las Animas County	CO	Gary L. Cleaver	1994	67
82 0/8	16 1/8	16 5/8	6 3/8	6 3/8	8 7/8	Moffat County	CO	Marv Clyncke	1998	67
82 0/8	16 3/8	16 3/8	6 6/8	6 5/8	9 5/8	Socorro County	NM	Alan W. Krause	1998	67
81 6/8	15 0/8	15 3/8	6 4/8	6 4/8	11 0/8	Coconino County	AZ	Noel Harris	1988	76
81 4/8	15 4/8	15 1/8	7 0/8	6 7/8	13 1/8	Washoe County	NV	Owen K. Mercer, Jr.	1981	77
81 4/8	16 3/8	16 6/8	6 2/8	5 7/8	13 6/8	Yellowstone County	MT	Robert M. Labert	1984	77
81 4/8	16 4/8	16 4/8	6 6/8	6 6/8	17 2/8	Jackson County	CO	Steve Jackson	1985	77
81 4/8	16 5/8	16 5/8	6 2/8	6 2/8	11 3/8	Yavapai County	AZ	James C. Roth	1990	77
81 4/8	15 2/8	15 3/8	6 5/8	6 4/8	10 6/8	Lake County	OR	Jeff Eder	1990	77
81 4/8	13 7/8	14 0/8	7 1/8	7 0/8	12 3/8	Natrona County	WY	Brian L. Wagner	1991	77
81 4/8	16 3/8	16 3/8	6 1/8	6 1/8	8 7/8	Lea County	NM	Mike Cowger	1992	77
81 4/8	16 2/8	15 4/8	5 7/8	6 1/8	12 4/8	Custer County	ID	Rick Day	1996	77
81 4/8	17 4/8	17 2/8	6 0/8	6 2/8	10 0/8	Coconino County	AZ	Patrick Loescher	1997	77
81 2/8	15 4/8	15 3/8	7 1/8	7 1/8	6 6/8	Sweetwater County	WY	Clifford Rockhold	1985	86
81 2/8	16 2/8	16 3/8	6 1/8	5 7/8	17 3/8	Coconino County	AZ	Les Shelton	1985	86
81 2/8	15 2/8	15 1/8	6 2/8	6 3/8	10 4/8	Sublette County	WY	Ronald J. Clark	1986	86
81 2/8	15 5/8	15 4/8	6 7/8	6 6/8	10 0/8	Jefferson County	ID	Scott Griggs	1987	86
81 2/8	17 0/8	17 1/8	6 3/8	6 2/8	22 2/8	Yavapai County	AZ	Rick Anderson	1987	86
81 2/8	15 7/8	15 2/8	6 2/8	6 1/8	11 7/8	Yavapai County	AZ	Marty Cowie	1988	86
81 2/8	14 6/8	15 0/8	6 5/8	6 5/8	7 4/8	Etzikom	ALB	Rick Livingston	1988	86
81 2/8	16 2/8	16 4/8	6 5/8	6 5/8	13 1/8	Coconino County	AZ	Bob Gourley	1990	86
81 2/8	16 0/8	15 5/8	6 7/8	6 5/8	10 6/8	Catron County	NM	Jim Machac	1992	86
81 2/8	15 7/8	15 7/8	6 3/8	6 1/8	13 1/8	Coconino County	AZ	Glenn David Myrick	1992	86
81 2/8	16 2/8	16 5/8	6 2/8	6 1/8	10 1/8	Fergus County	MT	Jess Knerr	1993	86
81 2/8	15 3/8	15 4/8	6 4/8	6 5/8	8 0/8	Natrona County	WY	Wayne E. Brensinger	1995	86
81 2/8	16 4/8	16 2/8	6 2/8	6 2/8	12 4/8	Millard County	UT	Bob J. McGill	1996	86

PRONGHORN

Minimum Score 67 — Continued

SCORE	LENGTH OF HORN R	LENGTH OF HORN L	CIRCUMFERENCE OF BASE R	CIRCUMFERENCE OF BASE L	INSIDE SPREAD	AREA	STATE/ PROVINCE	HUNTER'S NAME	DATE	RANK
81 2/8	16 7/8	16 7/8	6 2/8	6 2/8	11 6/8	Washoe County	NV	Patrick F. Ryle	1997	86
81 2/8	15 4/8	15 4/8	6 7/8	6 6/8	10 0/8	Big Horn County	WY	Brian P. Voss	1998	86
81 0/8	15 7/8	15 6/8	6 7/8	6 6/8	10 7/8	McLean County	ND	James Lahman	1971	101
81 0/8	15 3/8	15 4/8	7 0/8	6 6/8	12 0/8	Ormsby	WY	Richard L. Huber	1978	101
81 0/8	15 4/8	15 4/8	6 6/8	6 6/8	11 6/8	Elko County	NV	Darcy W. Tate	1979	101
81 0/8	14 6/8	16 4/8	6 3/8	6 4/8	10 0/8	Coconino County	AZ	Jim Scott	1984	101
81 0/8	15 5/8	16 6/8	6 3/8	6 3/8	9 2/8	Yavapai County	AZ	Dan Robbins	1986	101
81 0/8	15 2/8	15 1/8	6 4/8	6 4/8	8 3/8	Lassen County	CA	Brian McCoslin	1990	101
81 0/8	16 4/8	16 3/8	6 3/8	6 4/8	8 5/8	Coconino County	AZ	John Lund	1990	101
81 0/8	15 7/8	15 4/8	6 3/8	6 3/8	9 6/8	Orion	ALB	Dan Kilborn	1990	101
81 0/8	16 7/8	17 1/8	6 2/8	6 1/8	6 4/8	Yavapai County	AZ	Walter J. Kellner, Jr.	1991	101
81 0/8	14 6/8	14 6/8	6 4/8	6 6/8	10 5/8	Humboldt County	NV	Scott Tilzey	1992	101
81 0/8	15 1/8	15 1/8	6 3/8	6 4/8	8 0/8	Yavapai County	AZ	Ben Gibson	1992	101
81 0/8	15 7/8	14 4/8	6 1/8	5 7/8	8 4/8	Hartley County	TX	Todd Hodnett	1992	101
81 0/8	14 2/8	13 7/8	7 2/8	7 2/8	13 3/8	Larimer County	CO	Allen Muirhead	1993	101
81 0/8	16 1/8	15 7/8	6 2/8	6 2/8	10 6/8	Yavapai County	AZ	Gene Lucas	1994	101
81 0/8	15 4/8	15 4/8	6 2/8	6 1/8	10 7/8	Saguache County	CO	Thomas Torrez	1996	101
80 6/8	15 5/8	15 5/8	6 3/8	6 2/8	11 6/8	Lincoln County	NM	Robert W. Davis	1959	116
80 6/8	16 0/8	15 4/8	5 7/8	5 7/8	10 1/8	Converse County	WY	Greg Winters	1989	116
80 6/8	16 0/8	16 0/8	6 1/8	6 2/8	8 4/8	Harney County	OR	Russell Jacobs	1990	116
80 6/8	14 2/8	14 3/8	6 7/8	6 7/8	8 2/8	Albany County	WY	John Buxton	1990	116
80 6/8	15 6/8	15 6/8	7 0/8	7 1/8	10 3/8	Washoe County	NV	Dave Holt	1992	116
80 6/8	16 2/8	15 7/8	6 0/8	6 2/8	6 4/8	Dawes County	NE	Ron Amack	1992	116
80 6/8	15 0/8	15 1/8	6 6/8	6 6/8	12 2/8	Rosebud County	MT	Mike Cummings	1992	116
80 6/8	16 0/8	16 1/8	6 4/8	6 4/8	11 6/8	Thomas County	NE	Andrew L. Glidden	1993	116
80 6/8	14 4/8	14 3/8	6 6/8	6 6/8	11 1/8	Deuel County	NE	Ev Tarrell	1993	116
80 6/8	16 6/8	16 6/8	6 1/8	6 1/8	10 0/8	Yavapai County	AZ	Henry Robert Garcia, Sr.	1994	116
80 6/8	15 3/8	15 6/8	7 4/8	7 3/8	9 4/8	Lake County	OR	Brian Day	1994	116
80 6/8	15 1/8	15 1/8	6 6/8	6 6/8	9 0/8	Big Horn County	WY	Tim Kindred	1998	116
80 4/8	16 5/8	17 0/8	5 5/8	5 6/8	10 3/8	Humboldt County	NV	Shane E. Evans	1984	128
80 4/8	15 0/8	15 0/8	6 4/8	6 4/8	9 7/8	Sweetwater County	WY	Christopher J. Cordes	1986	128
80 4/8	16 3/8	16 0/8	6 3/8	6 2/8	9 0/8	Sweetwater County	WY	Gene McFadden	1987	128
80 4/8	15 3/8	15 3/8	6 6/8	6 6/8	9 2/8	Owyhee County	ID	Shane Gehring	1991	128
80 4/8	16 0/8	15 4/8	7 0/8	7 0/8	8 5/8	Dawes County	NE	Roger Westemeier	1992	128
80 4/8	16 6/8	16 4/8	6 1/8	6 0/8	12 2/8	Yavapai County	AZ	Marvin N. Zieser	1993	128
80 4/8	15 2/8	15 0/8	6 6/8	6 6/8	7 7/8	Yuma County	CO	Randy Wilkins	1993	128
80 4/8	15 6/8	15 6/8	6 1/8	6 0/8	11 6/8	Wallace County	KS	Danny Pfaff	1996	128
80 2/8	14 5/8	14 5/8	7 1/8	7 3/8	8 6/8	Natrona County	WY	Dr. J. A. Martin	1964	136
80 2/8	14 1/8	13 7/8	7 3/8	7 3/8	10 6/8	Butte County	ID	Danny Owens	1974	136
80 2/8	15 4/8	15 3/8	6 6/8	6 6/8	8 7/8	Modoc County	CA	Ed Dowling	1982	136
80 2/8	14 5/8	14 7/8	6 6/8	6 7/8	10 4/8	Yuma County	CO	Mark Sievers	1982	136
80 2/8	15 7/8	15 6/8	6 4/8	6 4/8	8 4/8	Yavapai County	AZ	Jim Machac	1988	136
80 2/8	15 7/8	15 7/8	6 6/8	6 4/8	13 0/8	Natrona County	WY	Brian L. Wagner	1989	136
80 2/8	16 3/8	14 4/8	6 4/8	6 4/8	11 3/8	Lassen County	CA	Greg Morris	1990	136
80 2/8	15 4/8	15 5/8	6 6/8	6 6/8	11 0/8	Mora County	NM	George P. Mann	1991	136
80 2/8	15 2/8	14 7/8	6 4/8	6 4/8	10 4/8	Rio Blanco County	CO	Don Collier	1993	136
80 2/8	15 6/8	15 7/8	6 6/8	6 6/8	11 2/8	Rio Blanco County	CO	Gary L. Hinaman	1993	136
80 2/8	13 4/8	13 6/8	6 4/8	6 2/8	12 0/8	Coconino County	AZ	Chris Tabor	1994	136
80 2/8	13 5/8	13 5/8	6 3/8	6 3/8	8 0/8	Dundy County	NE	Matt Gideon	1995	136
80 2/8	17 0/8	17 3/8	6 3/8	6 1/8	13 0/8	Campbell County	WY	David Westmoreland	1995	136
80 2/8	15 3/8	15 2/8	6 3/8	6 4/8	9 3/8	Humboldt County	NV	Ivan Brown	1998	136
80 2/8	15 5/8	15 6/8	6 2/8	6 1/8	9 4/8	Yavapai County	AZ	David A. Niemann	1998	136
80 0/8	16 6/8	16 5/8	6 1/8	6 1/8	13 6/8	Albany County	WY	Dave A. Current	1969	151
80 0/8	16 0/8	15 7/8	6 2/8	6 2/8	10 7/8	Washoe County	NV	Kevin S. Wheeler	1983	151
80 0/8	16 4/8	16 2/8	6 4/8	6 4/8	13 0/8	McKinley County	NM	Steve Yearout	1985	151
80 0/8	15 6/8	15 6/8	6 0/8	6 2/8	8 5/8	Coconino County	AZ	Jim Felt	1987	151
80 0/8	15 7/8	16 4/8	6 5/8	6 4/8	14 0/8	Coconino County	AZ	David Bushell	1988	151
80 0/8	16 1/8	15 5/8	6 4/8	6 3/8	9 7/8	Rosebud County	MT	Everett M. Morris	1988	151
80 0/8	14 6/8	15 0/8	7 0/8	7 0/8	8 5/8	Humboldt County	NV	James Puryear	1990	151
80 0/8	14 7/8	14 7/8	6 5/8	6 4/8	13 0/8	Cibola County	NM	Shaun Finch	1990	151
80 0/8	16 3/8	16 3/8	6 1/8	6 1/8	11 0/8	McKenzie County	ND	Travis Wollan	1990	151
80 0/8	15 0/8	14 4/8	6 4/8	6 5/8	6 6/8	Moffat County	CO	Breck Johnson	1992	151
80 0/8	15 0/8	15 3/8	6 5/8	6 4/8	11 2/8	Natrona County	WY	Jeff Laub	1992	151
80 0/8	14 6/8	14 6/8	6 4/8	6 6/8	12 3/8	Converse County	WY	Kevin Louis Stier	1992	151
80 0/8	16 4/8	16 4/8	6 1/8	6 0/8	11 4/8	Millard County	UT	John Tuttle	1995	151
80 0/8	15 4/8	15 3/8	6 5/8	6 4/8	7 6/8	Weld County	CO	Rick Parish	1995	151
80 0/8	15 4/8	16 0/8	6 3/8	6 2/8	10 2/8	Sweetwater County	WY	Ken McFarland	1998	151
79 6/8	15 4/8	14 6/8	7 1/8	7 3/8	9 3/8	Mellette County	SD	John Anderson	1970	166
79 6/8	15 4/8	15 4/8	6 0/8	6 0/8	10 5/8	Washoe County	NV	Mike J. Ellena	1983	166
79 6/8	13 7/8	13 6/8	6 5/8	6 4/8	11 5/8	Modoc County	CA	Dave Masamori	1990	166
79 6/8	15 2/8	15 3/8	6 4/8	6 4/8	12 2/8	Converse County	WY	Roger J. Reynolds	1990	166
79 6/8	16 0/8	15 7/8	6 1/8	6 1/8	14 4/8	McKenzie County	ND	Kevin Caroline	1990	166
79 6/8	15 4/8	15 3/8	6 4/8	6 4/8	11 0/8	Sweetwater County	WY	Keith Dana	1991	166
79 6/8	16 0/8	15 6/8	6 4/8	6 4/8	11 4/8	Dunn County	ND	Vance Vaagen	1991	166
79 6/8	15 7/8	16 0/8	6 6/8	6 4/8	17 1/8	Washoe County	NV	James P. Mason	1992	166
79 6/8	15 3/8	15 2/8	6 5/8	6 5/8	13 5/8	Yavapai County	AZ	Patrick Kirby	1992	166
79 6/8	15 5/8	15 6/8	6 3/8	6 3/8	10 0/8	Weld County	CO	Erik J. Smith	1993	166
79 6/8	15 5/8	15 5/8	6 7/8	6 5/8	9 4/8	Rosebud County	MT	Jeff Mitchell	1993	166

PRONGHORN

Minimum Score 67 — Continued

SCORE	LENGTH OF HORN R	LENGTH OF HORN L	CIRCUMFERENCE OF BASE R	CIRCUMFERENCE OF BASE L	INSIDE SPREAD	AREA	STATE/PROVINCE	HUNTER'S NAME	DATE	RANK
79 6/8	16 2/8	15 7/8	6 2/8	6 1/8	12 0/8	Campbell County	WY	Brian Tweeden	1993	166
79 6/8	15 6/8	15 6/8	6 3/8	6 2/8	13 4/8	Coconino County	AZ	Robert Y. Childers	1995	166
79 6/8	14 7/8	14 4/8	6 0/8	5 7/8	12 1/8	Yavapai County	AZ	John Bute	1996	166
79 6/8	16 4/8	16 2/8	6 2/8	6 1/8	11 2/8	Yavapai County	AZ	Jacob M. Underwood	1998	166
79 4/8	14 3/8	14 4/8	5 7/8	5 6/8	11 6/8	Mountrail County	ND	Bill Kurry	1976	181
79 4/8	16 4/8	16 0/8	6 3/8	6 4/8	9 0/8	Klamath County	OR	Harold Benson	1977	181
79 4/8	14 4/8	14 4/8	6 3/8	6 3/8	7 5/8	Converse County	WY	Russ Guerndt, Jr.	1985	181
79 4/8	14 1/8	14 0/8	7 2/8	7 2/8	9 2/8	Carbon County	WY	Michael L. Cone	1986	181
79 4/8	15 1/8	15 0/8	6 1/8	6 2/8	12 5/8	Dundy County	NE	Bradley Wiese	1987	181
79 4/8	16 0/8	16 0/8	6 2/8	6 2/8	13 3/8	Dunn County	ND	Terry Buechler	1990	181
79 4/8	15 5/8	15 5/8	6 1/8	6 2/8	10 6/8	Juab County	UT	Julie Robertson	1992	181
79 4/8	15 0/8	15 6/8	6 3/8	6 7/8	10 5/8	Socorro County	NM	Gerald Chavez	1993	181
79 4/8	15 3/8	15 3/8	6 6/8	6 6/8	10 6/8	Uintah County	UT	David A. Young	1993	181
79 4/8	16 0/8	16 2/8	6 0/8	6 0/8	11 4/8	Washoe County	NV	Lee McKenzie	1995	181
79 2/8	14 3/8	14 5/8	6 4/8	6 2/8	9 2/8	Musselshell County	MT	Jon Kowalski	1982	191
79 2/8	15 5/8	15 3/8	6 6/8	6 4/8	9 4/8	Moffat County	CO	Alan Martellaro	1986	191
79 2/8	15 5/8	15 4/8	6 5/8	6 4/8	10 6/8	Washoe County	NV	Kenneth J. Wilkinson	1987	191
79 2/8	15 2/8	15 0/8	6 2/8	6 1/8	8 4/8	Lincoln County	WY	LeRoy Moulding	1987	191
79 2/8	16 1/8	15 5/8	6 2/8	6 1/8	13 6/8	Eddy County	NM	Carl D. Bradford	1987	191
79 2/8	15 0/8	15 4/8	6 5/8	6 5/8	10 4/8	Sublette County	WY	Steven Hill	1990	191
79 2/8	15 3/8	15 2/8	6 6/8	6 6/8	10 7/8	Colfax County	NM	Delbert T. Vigil	1991	191
79 2/8	16 1/8	16 3/8	6 3/8	6 3/8	12 5/8	Washoe County	NV	A. H. "Wilk" Wilkerson	1992	191
79 2/8	15 3/8	15 4/8	6 7/8	7 0/8	11 2/8	Weld County	CO	Kevin Waller	1992	191
79 2/8	16 3/8	15 7/8	6 2/8	6 4/8	11 1/8	Lincoln County	WY	C. R. (Bob) Bolton	1992	191
79 2/8	14 1/8	13 7/8	6 6/8	6 7/8	8 6/8	Moffat County	CO	Steven Vittetow	1992	191
79 2/8	13 5/8	13 6/8	7 0/8	6 5/8	11 0/8	Twin Falls County	ID	Brent L. Compton	1992	191
79 2/8	13 6/8	14 0/8	7 1/8	7 2/8	10 4/8	Moffat County	CO	Mike Kiser	1997	191
79 2/8	14 6/8	14 6/8	6 2/8	6 2/8	11 6/8	Lincoln County	NM	Robert John Seeds	1997	191
79 2/8	15 1/8	15 3/8	6 7/8	6 6/8	14 4/8	Weld County	CO	Neil Chandler	1998	191
79 0/8	15 0/8	15 3/8	6 3/8	6 3/8	11 5/8	Washoe County	NV	Tom Thompson	1979	206
79 0/8	15 7/8	15 6/8	6 2/8	6 2/8	12 6/8	Carbon County	WY	Michael Ambur	1982	206
79 0/8	14 4/8	14 6/8	6 6/8	6 6/8	15 3/8	Moffat County	CO	Steven J. Lepic	1983	206
79 0/8	14 7/8	15 0/8	6 3/8	6 2/8	8 5/8	Carbon County	WY	Kim Cooper	1983	206
79 0/8	14 6/8	14 5/8	7 2/8	7 3/8	7 0/8	Sweetwater County	WY	Steve Rueck	1985	206
79 0/8	14 1/8	14 4/8	6 3/8	6 2/8	11 5/8	Millard County	UT	Keith Dana	1988	206
79 0/8	14 6/8	15 0/8	6 5/8	6 4/8	9 4/8	Sweetwater County	WY	Gerry Wolfe	1988	206
79 0/8	15 7/8	15 7/8	6 0/8	6 1/8	9 4/8	Harney County	OR	Jim Nielsen	1990	206
79 0/8	15 0/8	15 0/8	7 4/8	7 3/8	11 2/8	Campbell County	WY	Mike "Pie" Piaskowski	1990	206
79 0/8	16 4/8	17 1/8	6 1/8	6 0/8	8 7/8	Yavapai County	AZ	T. J. Baehre	1991	206
79 0/8	15 0/8	13 6/8	6 6/8	7 1/8	12 2/8	Bennett County	SD	Wayne Johnson	1991	206
79 0/8	14 6/8	14 7/8	6 2/8	6 3/8	10 7/8	Luna County	NM	Ray Trejo	1993	206
79 0/8	15 5/8	15 2/8	6 3/8	6 3/8	9 2/8	Quay County	NM	Kenneth McKinney	1993	206
79 0/8	15 2/8	15 1/8	6 2/8	6 1/8	12 7/8	Clark County	ID	Fred H. Hanks	1994	206
79 0/8	15 1/8	15 1/8	6 7/8	6 7/8	11 3/8	Weld County	CO	Fred Eichler	1995	206
79 0/8	15 1/8	15 2/8	6 5/8	6 5/8	15 2/8	Colfax County	NM	Stephen Nilsen	1995	206
79 0/8	14 7/8	14 7/8	6 6/8	6 5/8	10 3/8	Campbell County	WY	Ronald T. Morgan	1995	206
79 0/8	15 1/8	15 0/8	6 2/8	6 2/8	9 6/8	Saguache County	CO	Alan R. Palmer	1995	206
78 6/8	16 5/8	16 2/8	6 4/8	6 2/8	7 4/8	Sweetwater County	WY	Mike Holmes	1982	224
78 6/8	14 2/8	14 4/8	7 1/8	7 1/8	12 2/8	Johnson County	WY	Steve Winkey	1982	224
78 6/8	16 1/8	16 3/8	6 3/8	6 3/8	15 4/8	Clark County	ID	Dennis R Marshall	1985	224
78 6/8	15 5/8	15 7/8	6 2/8	6 2/8	9 7/8	Converse County	WY	Tom Glendinning	1988	224
78 6/8	15 6/8	15 7/8	6 2/8	6 1/8	10 1/8	Catron County	NM	Steve Frazier	1991	224
78 6/8	13 4/8	14 0/8	7 0/8	6 7/8	10 5/8	Natrona County	WY	Timothy D. Baer	1991	224
78 6/8	15 7/8	15 7/8	6 2/8	6 1/8	11 0/8	Hudspeth County	TX	Craig B. Baird	1991	224
78 6/8	15 5/8	16 0/8	6 2/8	6 2/8	12 5/8	Humboldt County	NV	Carl W. Rose	1992	224
78 6/8	14 0/8	14 0/8	6 4/8	6 4/8	9 3/8	Sweetwater County	WY	Mark L. Preston	1992	224
78 6/8	14 5/8	14 6/8	6 3/8	6 3/8	10 2/8	Sweetwater County	WY	Mike Barrett	1992	224
78 6/8	15 3/8	15 6/8	6 3/8	6 2/8	10 0/8	McKenzie County	ND	Travis Wollan	1992	224
78 6/8	16 0/8	15 4/8	6 1/8	6 0/8	9 4/8	Wallace County	KS	Loren Goss	1993	224
78 6/8	13 4/8	13 6/8	6 6/8	6 6/8	8 4/8	Sublette County	WY	Stephen Kotz	1994	224
78 6/8	15 5/8	15 2/8	6 2/8	6 3/8	8 3/8	Campbell County	WY	Danny D. Brown	1995	224
78 6/8	14 0/8	14 5/8	6 4/8	6 4/8	11 2/8	Yavapai County	AZ	George A. Ovalle	1995	224
78 6/8	15 2/8	15 2/8	6 3/8	6 3/8	11 2/8	Nye County	NV	Todd Bresemann	1996	224
78 6/8	14 0/8	14 1/8	6 5/8	6 3/8	10 0/8	Elko County	NV	Beau M. Nyrehn	1998	224
78 6/8	15 1/8	17 7/8	6 1/8	6 2/8	8 7/8	Socorro County	NM	Elton Warriner	1998	224
78 4/8	16 0/8	15 7/8	6 0/8	6 2/8	11 4/8	Chaves County	NM	Dr. D. A. Henbest	1957	242
78 4/8	15 1/8	14 7/8	6 5/8	6 5/8	10 0/8	Mountrail County	ND	Bennie J. Burtts	1967	242
78 4/8	14 4/8	14 1/8	6 3/8	6 2/8	10 6/8	Klamath County	OR	Paul D. Lewis	1976	242
78 4/8	13 7/8	14 0/8	6 4/8	6 2/8	8 2/8	Moffat County	CO	Mike Brezonick	1986	242
78 4/8	15 7/8	16 0/8	6 0/8	6 1/8	13 2/8	Coconino County	AZ	Randy McKusick	1988	242
78 4/8	14 1/8	14 6/8	7 0/8	7 1/8	10 2/8	Big Horn County	MT	Ron Johnson	1988	242
78 4/8	15 2/8	15 1/8	6 2/8	6 2/8	9 1/8	Lassen County	CA	Eddie L. Boyd	1989	242
78 4/8	15 0/8	15 2/8	6 3/8	6 2/8	11 0/8	Sweetwater County	WY	Kenneth Stinchcomb	1989	242
78 4/8	14 3/8	14 3/8	7 0/8	6 6/8	7 6/8	Sweetwater County	WY	Mark L. Preston	1989	242
78 4/8	15 3/8	15 0/8	6 2/8	6 4/8	10 3/8	Catron County	NM	Wade Finch	1990	242
78 4/8	16 2/8	16 3/8	5 6/8	5 6/8	14 5/8	Lea County	NM	Jim King	1990	242
78 4/8	15 3/8	15 1/8	6 4/8	6 4/8	9 5/8	Petroleum County	MT	Clark Jenner	1990	242
78 4/8	14 2/8	14 4/8	6 1/8	6 0/8	10 2/8	Medicine Hat	ALB	Dale Fournier	1990	242

PRONGHORN

Minimum Score 67 — Continued — 625

SCORE	LENGTH OF HORN R	L	CIRCUMFERENCE OF BASE R	L	INSIDE SPREAD	AREA	STATE/PROVINCE	HUNTER'S NAME	DATE	RANK
78 4/8	14 5/8	14 5/8	7 1/8	7 3/8	11 0/8	Klamath County	OR	Chuck Woolley	1991	242
78 4/8	15 0/8	14 7/8	6 2/8	6 2/8	10 0/8	Millard County	UT	Nathan Lucas	1992	242
78 4/8	17 6/8	18 0/8	6 2/8	6 3/8	6 6/8	Las Animas County	CO	Darren Peacock	1992	242
78 4/8	13 7/8	13 7/8	6 7/8	7 0/8	10 1/8	Converse County	WY	Ronald D. Stoynoff	1992	242
78 4/8	15 4/8	15 4/8	6 3/8	6 3/8	14 6/8	Converse County	WY	Gary Lynn Fischer	1993	242
78 4/8	16 2/8	16 2/8	6 1/8	6 1/8	15 1/8	Moffat County	CO	Tim R. Hamilton	1993	242
78 4/8	15 0/8	15 0/8	5 4/8	5 4/8	9 6/8	Grant County	NM	Art Ramirez	1994	242
78 4/8	14 1/8	14 4/8	6 2/8	6 1/8	9 6/8	Custer County	SD	Jon Hardesty	1994	242
78 4/8	15 0/8	14 7/8	6 7/8	6 6/8	9 3/8	Albany County	WY	Todd Fugate	1995	242
78 4/8	15 3/8	15 6/8	6 3/8	6 2/8	14 0/8	Colfax County	NM	James F. Welles	1995	242
78 4/8	15 1/8	14 7/8	6 3/8	6 3/8	11 6/8	Carbon County	WY	Peeler G. Lacey, MD	1995	242
78 4/8	15 4/8	15 7/8	6 1/8	6 2/8	11 2/8	Socorro County	NM	William Schultz	1996	242
78 4/8	15 6/8	15 6/8	6 0/8	6 0/8	8 7/8	Socorro County	NM	Archie J. Nesbitt	1997	242
78 2/8	17 3/8	17 1/8	5 5/8	5 6/8	14 6/8	Guadalupe County	NM	James L. Henry	1961	268
78 2/8	15 2/8	15 0/8	6 2/8	6 2/8	10 6/8	Wheatland County	MT	Phil Reno	1981	268
78 2/8	16 1/8	16 1/8	6 2/8	6 1/8	6 2/8	Moffat County	CO	Dan Liccardi	1982	268
78 2/8	15 2/8	15 7/8	5 7/8	5 7/8	7 3/8	Moffat County	CO	Ralph L. Albright	1985	268
78 2/8	14 3/8	14 4/8	6 1/8	6 1/8	11 3/8	Cochise County	AZ	Michael John Bylina	1985	268
78 2/8	13 7/8	14 0/8	6 2/8	6 2/8	12 6/8	Sweetwater County	WY	Tom Domson	1986	268
78 2/8	15 7/8	15 7/8	5 7/8	5 6/8	12 2/8	Washoe County	NV	Robert Jenney	1988	268
78 2/8	16 0/8	16 4/8	6 1/8	6 1/8	5 0/8	Klamath County	OR	Chuck Warner	1989	268
78 2/8	16 1/8	15 7/8	6 2/8	6 2/8	13 1/8	Coconino County	AZ	Randy McKusick	1989	268
78 2/8	15 0/8	15 2/8	6 0/8	6 0/8	10 2/8	Socorro County	NM	Glenn W. Isler	1990	268
78 2/8	14 0/8	14 1/8	6 2/8	6 1/8	9 0/8	Socorro County	NM	Mike Van Wormer	1990	268
78 2/8	13 6/8	13 7/8	6 5/8	6 4/8	8 7/8	Natrona County	WY	Jack Conner	1990	268
78 2/8	16 2/8	15 2/8	6 7/8	6 6/8	11 0/8	Sweetwater County	WY	Mark Olson	1991	268
78 2/8	15 6/8	15 5/8	5 7/8	6 0/8	13 5/8	Wayne County	UT	Shane Daley	1991	268
78 2/8	15 0/8	15 3/8	6 7/8	6 7/8	9 2/8	Natrona County	WY	Rene Suda	1991	268
78 2/8	15 0/8	15 3/8	6 1/8	6 0/8	11 2/8	Yavapai County	AZ	Van M. Clark	1992	268
78 2/8	15 1/8	15 2/8	6 3/8	6 3/8	10 2/8	Converse County	WY	Kevin W. Schmieg	1992	268
78 2/8	16 7/8	16 4/8	6 5/8	6 5/8	9 1/8	Box Butte County	NE	Michael L. Dietrich	1993	268
78 2/8	16 2/8	16 0/8	6 2/8	6 3/8	6 7/8	Rio Grande County	CO	Todd R. Slade	1995	268
78 2/8	15 2/8	15 2/8	6 3/8	6 3/8	10 0/8	Yavapai County	AZ	Kendall R. Adair	1995	268
78 2/8	14 5/8	14 4/8	6 0/8	6 0/8	11 0/8	Natrona County	WY	Don Meyer	1996	268
78 2/8	14 5/8	14 4/8	6 3/8	6 3/8	8 4/8	Twin Falls County	ID	Louis W. Wasniewski	1997	268
78 2/8	13 0/8	13 1/8	7 1/8	7 4/8	9 5/8	Moffat County	CO	David L. Skiff	1997	268
78 2/8	14 4/8	16 3/8	6 2/8	6 3/8	9 2/8	Socorro County	NM	David A. Little	1998	268
78 0/8	15 5/8	15 1/8	6 2/8	6 2/8	18 2/8	Sweetwater County	WY	Don Dvoroznak	1976	292
78 0/8	15 0/8	14 7/8	6 3/8	6 2/8	11 5/8	Lemhi County	ID	Eugene J. Ottonello	1980	292
78 0/8	15 1/8	15 2/8	6 2/8	6 1/8	11 3/8	Stanley County	SD	Rick Ray	1980	292
78 0/8	15 3/8	15 2/8	6 7/8	6 4/8	13 7/8	Moffat County	CO	Tony Seahorn	1980	292
78 0/8	14 4/8	14 5/8	5 7/8	6 0/8	12 4/8	Stanley County	SD	George Hipple	1982	292
78 0/8	14 7/8	14 4/8	6 5/8	6 3/8	7 5/8	Fremont County	WY	Joe E. Nelson	1983	292
78 0/8	16 0/8	16 0/8	6 0/8	6 0/8	12 2/8	Washoe County	NV	Gregg Tanner	1986	292
78 0/8	14 1/8	14 2/8	6 5/8	6 5/8	13 2/8	Moffat County	CO	Calvin Farner	1986	292
78 0/8	14 5/8	14 4/8	5 6/8	6 0/8	10 1/8	Coconino County	AZ	Les Shelton	1990	292
78 0/8	14 6/8	14 1/8	6 7/8	7 1/8	11 6/8	Lincoln County	WY	Marlin Batista	1991	292
78 0/8	15 4/8	15 3/8	6 1/8	6 1/8	12 3/8	Saguache County	CO	Dan Bertalan	1991	292
78 0/8	14 3/8	14 4/8	6 3/8	6 3/8	14 3/8	Campbell County	WY	Mark A. Hoffman	1992	292
78 0/8	13 7/8	15 3/8	6 7/8	6 6/8	11 6/8	Yavapai County	AZ	Rick Kimball	1994	292
78 0/8	14 4/8	14 5/8	6 3/8	6 3/8	8 3/8	Converse County	WY	Rick L. Morley	1995	292
78 0/8	14 7/8	15 0/8	7 0/8	7 0/8	12 4/8	Baker County	OR	Michael D. Towne	1997	292
78 0/8	14 6/8	14 6/8	6 1/8	6 0/8	8 6/8	Lassen County	CA	Ray Bailey	1997	292
78 0/8	15 0/8	15 0/8	6 4/8	6 4/8	9 6/8	Moffat County	CO	Bob Black	1997	292
78 0/8	13 2/8	13 2/8	6 6/8	6 6/8	10 3/8	Big Horn County	WY	Charlotte Moss	1998	292
77 6/8	15 4/8	15 4/8	6 2/8	6 1/8	11 5/8	McKinley County	NM	Lee Burnett	1975	310
77 6/8	15 7/8	15 0/8	6 0/8	5 6/8	10 4/8	Lincoln County	CO	Steve Winkelman	1978	310
77 6/8	14 3/8	14 1/8	6 5/8	6 5/8	6 0/8	Moffat County	CO	Phil Hughes	1983	310
77 6/8	14 5/8	15 0/8	6 4/8	6 5/8	9 0/8	Converse County	WY	Ed Toelken	1988	310
77 6/8	14 0/8	14 0/8	7 0/8	6 5/8	12 1/8	Navajo County	AZ	Pat Nichols	1989	310
77 6/8	15 6/8	15 6/8	5 7/8	5 6/8	13 2/8	Powder River County	MT	Bob Carlson	1989	310
77 6/8	14 1/8	14 5/8	7 1/8	7 1/8	12 5/8	Musselshell County	MT	Wayne Muth	1990	310
77 6/8	14 7/8	14 7/8	6 1/8	6 1/8	10 2/8	Williams County	ND	Jeff Syverson	1990	310
77 6/8	13 1/8	13 4/8	6 6/8	6 7/8	7 5/8	Big Horn County	WY	Terry A. Long	1990	310
77 6/8	15 0/8	15 0/8	6 2/8	6 1/8	8 5/8	Fremont County	WY	Gary Laya	1991	310
77 6/8	15 7/8	15 6/8	6 2/8	6 2/8	12 7/8	Harney County	OR	Michael J. Kaiser	1991	310
77 6/8	14 7/8	14 6/8	5 7/8	5 6/8	11 6/8	Millard County	UT	Jeanie Clements	1992	310
77 6/8	14 7/8	15 0/8	6 1/8	6 1/8	10 7/8	Millard County	UT	Dave Scott	1992	310
77 6/8	14 0/8	14 0/8	6 5/8	6 3/8	9 0/8	Hot Springs County	WY	Larry Dickerson	1992	310
77 6/8	14 3/8	15 0/8	6 4/8	6 3/8	8 2/8	McKenzie County	ND	Don G. Scofield	1992	310
77 6/8	14 6/8	14 3/8	6 2/8	6 2/8	13 3/8	Yavapai County	AZ	Josiah Scott	1994	310
77 6/8	14 3/8	14 4/8	6 1/8	6 1/8	9 7/8	Billings County	ND	Jeff Lafferre	1994	310
77 6/8	15 2/8	15 3/8	5 7/8	5 7/8	13 2/8	Medicine Hat	ALB	Paul Unger	1994	310
77 6/8	15 7/8	14 7/8	5 6/8	5 6/8	7 5/8	Hudspeth County	TX	Ernest M. Elbert, Jr.	1994	310
77 6/8	14 7/8	14 7/8	6 3/8	6 3/8	12 7/8	Rio Blanco County	CO	Ray Richardson	1997	310
77 6/8	14 7/8	15 2/8	6 5/8	6 5/8	10 7/8	Golden Valley County	MT	John Ohmer	1997	310
77 6/8	14 1/8	14 2/8	6 5/8	6 5/8	10 1/8	Harding County	SD	Henry Loving	1997	310
77 6/8	16 0/8	16 2/8	5 6/8	5 6/8	10 0/8	Yavapai County	AZ	Gregg Murray	1998	310

PRONGHORN

Minimum Score 67 — Continued

SCORE	LENGTH OF HORN R	L	CIRCUMFERENCE OF BASE R	L	INSIDE SPREAD	AREA	STATE/ PROVINCE	HUNTER'S NAME	DATE	RANK
77 4/8	15 1/8	15 1/8	6 0/8	6 0/8	8 3/8	Washoe County	NV	Christian J. Coleman	1979	333
77 4/8	15 1/8	15 1/8	6 1/8	6 2/8	13 6/8	Butte County	ID	Ron Johnson	1979	333
77 4/8	15 7/8	16 1/8	5 7/8	5 7/8	12 0/8	Carbon County	WY	Doug Cringan	1983	333
77 4/8	14 7/8	14 5/8	6 1/8	6 2/8	9 2/8	Graham County	AZ	Scott Kellner	1984	333
77 4/8	16 0/8	16 0/8	6 4/8	6 2/8	12 5/8	Washoe County	NV	James Mason	1985	333
77 4/8	14 0/8	14 4/8	6 2/8	6 2/8	11 5/8	Sweetwater County	WY	Dean Simmons	1987	333
77 4/8	15 4/8	15 1/8	6 1/8	6 1/8	12 4/8	McKenzie County	ND	Scott Borchert	1987	333
77 4/8	14 5/8	14 5/8	6 4/8	6 3/8	8 1/8	Moffat County	CO	Robert W. Wilkerson	1988	333
77 4/8	16 6/8	16 0/8	6 2/8	6 3/8	13 1/8	Yavapai County	AZ	Jay Dee Shaw	1988	333
77 4/8	14 7/8	14 7/8	6 2/8	6 2/8	10 6/8	Golden Valley County	ND	Terry Buechler	1988	333
77 4/8	15 4/8	15 2/8	6 4/8	6 3/8	9 6/8	Yavapai County	AZ	Robert M. Dryden	1989	333
77 4/8	14 3/8	14 4/8	6 3/8	6 3/8	15 0/8	Campbell County	WY	Michael H. Albers	1989	333
77 4/8	16 0/8	16 5/8	6 0/8	6 0/8	10 1/8	Sioux County	NE	Lane Ostendorf	1990	333
77 4/8	14 7/8	14 6/8	6 4/8	6 4/8	8 7/8	Moffat County	CO	Tim Atwater	1991	333
77 4/8	16 2/8	15 4/8	6 3/8	6 3/8	9 2/8	Fremont County	WY	Gary L. Hinaman	1992	333
77 4/8	14 7/8	15 4/8	6 3/8	6 3/8	10 6/8	Duchesne County	UT	Cindy Labrum	1992	333
77 4/8	15 6/8	15 6/8	6 1/8	6 0/8	14 1/8	Lincoln County	WY	Allen D. Sellers	1992	333
77 4/8	16 4/8	15 5/8	6 3/8	6 1/8	10 0/8	Carbon County	WY	Zack Koch	1993	333
77 4/8	13 7/8	14 1/8	6 5/8	6 5/8	12 6/8	Lake County	OR	Raymon L. Johnson	1993	333
77 4/8	14 0/8	14 2/8	6 3/8	6 2/8	10 5/8	Chaves County	NM	Brandon Griffith	1994	333
77 4/8	15 1/8	15 2/8	6 0/8	6 1/8	9 4/8	Lincoln County	WY	Rocky Rollins	1994	333
77 4/8	13 7/8	13 7/8	7 1/8	7 0/8	10 6/8	Moffat County	CO	Michael Schirer	1995	333
77 4/8	14 5/8	14 4/8	6 2/8	6 2/8	8 7/8	Malheur County	OR	Ken Barstad	1995	333
77 4/8	15 2/8	15 1/8	6 2/8	6 2/8	11 6/8	Lincoln County	NM	Rick Pope	1996	333
77 4/8	15 3/8	14 0/8	6 3/8	6 3/8	11 4/8	Yavapai County	AZ	Daniel A. Kasprzyk	1996	333
77 4/8	14 6/8	14 4/8	6 6/8	6 6/8	12 0/8	Big Horn County	WY	Tim Kindred	1996	333
77 4/8	14 3/8	14 3/8	6 5/8	6 5/8	10 7/8	Rosebud County	MT	David William Bieber	1997	333
77 2/8	16 3/8	16 4/8	6 0/8	6 0/8	10 0/8	Lincoln County	NM	Charles L. Hughes	1960	360
77 2/8	15 0/8	15 1/8	5 7/8	5 7/8	9 0/8	Treasure County	MT	Tom Grunhuvd	1975	360
77 2/8	14 6/8	15 1/8	6 2/8	6 0/8	12 1/8	Sweetwater County	WY	William Dolenc	1978	360
77 2/8	15 4/8	15 2/8	6 1/8	5 1/8	10 4/8	Yavapai County	AZ	Tim Pender	1978	360
77 2/8	15 1/8	15 1/8	6 5/8	6 3/8	8 7/8	Moffat County	CO	Tom States	1981	360
77 2/8	15 6/8	15 4/8	6 1/8	6 0/8	14 4/8	Moffat County	CO	Mike Brust	1982	360
77 2/8	14 0/8	14 2/8	6 7/8	6 6/8	14 0/8	Sweetwater County	WY	David L. Price	1983	360
77 2/8	14 4/8	14 3/8	6 0/8	6 0/8	8 7/8	Mesa County	CO	Bob Black	1983	360
77 2/8	16 3/8	16 3/8	6 3/8	6 3/8	14 1/8	Bowman County	ND	Donald C. Hestekin	1983	360
77 2/8	14 4/8	14 4/8	6 3/8	6 1/8	10 6/8	Custer County	MT	Joe Good	1984	360
77 2/8	14 0/8	14 0/8	6 0/8	6 0/8	14 6/8	Garfield County	MT	Paul Schafer	1984	360
77 2/8	14 5/8	14 5/8	6 1/8	6 1/8	10 3/8	Moffat County	CO	David Gunning	1987	360
77 2/8	15 5/8	15 3/8	6 2/8	6 1/8	9 3/8	Rosebud County	MT	Dr. Dale Schlehuber	1987	360
77 2/8	15 0/8	15 2/8	6 1/8	6 1/8	11 1/8	Rosebud County	MT	Gene Welle	1988	360
77 2/8	16 0/8	16 4/8	5 5/8	5 5/8	7 7/8	Humboldt County	NV	Clayton Keister	1989	360
77 2/8	15 7/8	16 0/8	6 2/8	6 1/8	8 6/8	Natrona County	WY	Kenneth D. Sundquist	1989	360
77 2/8	15 0/8	15 0/8	6 2/8	6 3/8	10 7/8	Golden Valley County	ND	Terry Buechler	1989	360
77 2/8	14 0/8	14 0/8	6 6/8	6 5/8	10 6/8	Lassen County	CA	Danny Westerberg	1990	360
77 2/8	15 1/8	15 1/8	5 6/8	5 5/8	8 6/8	Harney County	OR	Donald R. Paulsen	1990	360
77 2/8	15 6/8	15 0/8	6 3/8	6 2/8	10 4/8	Yavapai County	AZ	James N. Schmidt	1991	360
77 2/8	14 2/8	14 2/8	6 1/8	6 0/8	10 2/8	Harney County	OR	Ralph Burt	1991	360
77 2/8	14 5/8	14 5/8	7 2/8	7 2/8	10 3/8	Radville	SAS	Ken Paslawski	1991	360
77 2/8	14 2/8	14 2/8	6 5/8	6 6/8	11 3/8	Sweetwater County	WY	Brad Hugh Jacobs	1992	360
77 2/8	15 2/8	14 7/8	6 1/8	6 1/8	9 4/8	Uintah County	UT	Daniel B. Hammons	1993	360
77 2/8	14 3/8	14 3/8	6 2/8	6 1/8	9 6/8	Powder River County	MT	John Martinson	1993	360
77 2/8	15 2/8	15 2/8	6 5/8	6 4/8	10 2/8	Sweetwater County	WY	Mike Barrett	1994	360
77 2/8	12 2/8	12 5/8	6 5/8	6 4/8	8 2/8	Box Elder County	UT	Verl Hanchett	1994	360
77 2/8	13 7/8	14 0/8	6 2/8	6 3/8	10 7/8	Custer County	ID	Jim Marek	1994	360
77 2/8	15 3/8	15 1/8	6 2/8	6 3/8	13 0/8	Converse County	WY	Dan Schneewind	1994	360
77 2/8	15 2/8	15 3/8	6 2/8	6 2/8	12 0/8	Coconino County	AZ	Bob Kyhn	1995	360
77 0/8	15 4/8	15 4/8	5 5/8	5 5/8	16 7/8	Dunn County	ND	Allan Lynch	1975	390
77 0/8	14 1/8	15 2/8	6 2/8	6 0/8	9 4/8	Billings County	ND	Jonathan Zieman	1984	390
77 0/8	14 4/8	14 5/8	6 2/8	6 1/8	11 1/8	Rosebud County	MT	Steve Cutright	1987	390
77 0/8	15 2/8	15 1/8	6 0/8	6 0/8	10 5/8	Garfield County	MT	Daryl P. Hinther	1987	390
77 0/8	14 7/8	14 7/8	6 0/8	6 1/8	7 3/8	Sweetwater County	WY	Rod Schmidt	1988	390
77 0/8	15 2/8	15 0/8	6 1/8	6 2/8	8 5/8	Moffat County	CO	Louis Dodaro	1988	390
77 0/8	14 0/8	14 0/8	6 3/8	6 2/8	11 0/8	Cochise County	AZ	Brian Davis	1988	390
77 0/8	14 4/8	15 1/8	5 7/8	5 7/8	11 3/8	Park County	WY	Rocky Deromedi	1988	390
77 0/8	14 2/8	14 3/8	5 7/8	5 7/8	8 0/8	Bare Creek	ALB	Paul Ronald Goodberry	1988	390
77 0/8	15 1/8	14 6/8	5 7/8	5 6/8	11 4/8	Washoe County	NV	Jeffrey L. Dodge	1990	390
77 0/8	14 2/8	14 2/8	6 0/8	6 1/8	10 1/8	Mesa County	CO	Darren K. Peacock	1990	390
77 0/8	15 6/8	15 4/8	6 1/8	6 1/8	16 4/8	Coconino County	AZ	Kevin Shackleford	1990	390
77 0/8	14 7/8	15 2/8	6 0/8	5 7/8	10 6/8	Millard County	UT	Vee F. Hanks	1990	390
77 0/8	14 7/8	14 4/8	6 3/8	6 3/8	8 4/8	Humboldt County	NV	Mike Fillmore	1992	390
77 0/8	14 7/8	14 4/8	6 0/8	5 7/8	7 4/8	Carbon County	WY	Scott Penman	1992	390
77 0/8	15 0/8	14 7/8	6 2/8	6 2/8	9 3/8	Carbon County	WY	Rod Schmidt	1992	390
77 0/8	15 1/8	15 5/8	6 4/8	6 2/8	10 1/8	Box Butte County	NE	Tim Christophersen	1992	390
77 0/8	15 4/8	15 5/8	6 2/8	6 1/8	9 6/8	Hudspeth County	TX	William R. Fair	1992	390
77 0/8	16 1/8	16 4/8	5 4/8	5 5/8	10 4/8	Socorro County	NM	Ronald C. Zengerly	1993	390
77 0/8	14 2/8	14 2/8	6 1/8	6 0/8	12 2/8	Converse County	WY	John S. Miller	1993	390
77 0/8	14 3/8	14 6/8	6 1/8	6 4/8	7 7/8	Washoe County	NV	Randy Tognoni	1994	390

PRONGHORN

Minimum Score 67 — Continued

SCORE	LENGTH OF HORN R	L	CIRCUMFERENCE OF BASE R	L	INSIDE SPREAD	AREA	STATE/PROVINCE	HUNTER'S NAME	DATE	RANK
77 0/8	15 0/8	15 2/8	5 7/8	5 6/8	11 1/8	Millard County	UT	Don Bates	1995	390
77 0/8	14 7/8	15 1/8	6 1/8	6 1/8	10 3/8	Larimer County	CO	Fred M. Velasquez	1995	390
77 0/8	14 4/8	14 4/8	5 6/8	5 6/8	9 5/8	Catron County	NM	Carl D. Bradford	1995	390
77 0/8	15 0/8	15 1/8	6 6/8	6 6/8	10 4/8	Campbell County	WY	Mark D. Sesvold	1995	390
77 0/8	13 7/8	14 0/8	6 6/8	6 4/8	8 7/8	Millard County	UT	Cory S. Christensen	1996	390
76 6/8	14 1/8	14 5/8	6 2/8	6 2/8	14 2/8	Fremont County	WY	Jim Puthoff	1969	416
76 6/8	14 6/8	14 6/8	6 3/8	6 3/8	10 5/8	Fremont County	WY	Ron D. Evitt	1982	416
76 6/8	14 2/8	14 2/8	6 1/8	6 0/8	12 4/8	Campbell County	WY	Tony Janssen	1984	416
76 6/8	14 6/8	14 6/8	6 1/8	6 1/8	8 6/8	Converse County	WY	Vito Palazzolo	1984	416
76 6/8	15 5/8	15 7/8	5 7/8	5 7/8	10 2/8	Butte County	ID	Champ Church	1986	416
76 6/8	14 0/8	13 6/8	5 5/8	5 6/8	13 4/8	San Miguel County	CO	Stuart Howard	1986	416
76 6/8	16 7/8	17 1/8	5 7/8	6 0/8	10 6/8	Humboldt County	NV	Lance R. Wodke	1987	416
76 6/8	15 0/8	15 0/8	6 1/8	6 0/8	10 3/8	Dunn County	ND	Ron Bachmeier	1987	416
76 6/8	15 5/8	15 5/8	6 3/8	6 4/8	9 2/8	Fremont County	WY	Dan Chappell	1990	416
76 6/8	14 1/8	14 0/8	7 0/8	6 7/8	14 1/8	Natrona County	WY	Brian L. Wagner	1990	416
76 6/8	14 3/8	13 6/8	6 0/8	6 1/8	13 7/8	Jackson County	CO	Dominic Florian	1990	416
76 6/8	16 2/8	15 7/8	5 7/8	5 7/8	10 7/8	Santa Cruz County	AZ	Jerry A. Clarno	1990	416
76 6/8	15 1/8	15 1/8	6 2/8	6 1/8	8 2/8	Moffat County	CO	Roderick E. Nutter	1991	416
76 6/8	13 5/8	14 1/8	6 5/8	6 5/8	8 3/8	Natrona County	WY	Gary L. Miller	1991	416
76 6/8	14 5/8	15 2/8	6 0/8	6 0/8	10 4/8	Carbon County	WY	Marc D. HalLowell	1991	416
76 6/8	15 1/8	15 1/8	6 5/8	6 4/8	11 7/8	Grant County	NM	John Trewern	1992	416
76 6/8	15 6/8	15 6/8	5 5/8	5 5/8	12 3/8	Park County	CO	William E. Karnish, Jr.	1992	416
76 6/8	14 0/8	14 0/8	6 4/8	6 3/8	9 4/8	Moffat County	CO	Doy K. Curtis	1993	416
76 6/8	12 4/8	12 2/8	6 7/8	6 6/8	9 1/8	Moffat County	CO	James L. Tatro	1993	416
76 6/8	14 3/8	14 3/8	5 7/8	5 7/8	6 7/8	Converse County	WY	James C. Gates	1993	416
76 6/8	15 6/8	15 4/8	5 4/8	5 6/8	11 0/8	Washoe County	NV	Ed Madsen	1994	416
76 6/8	15 3/8	15 0/8	6 2/8	6 4/8	7 4/8	Twin Falls County	ID	Cory Brodine	1994	416
76 6/8	15 4/8	14 3/8	7 0/8	6 7/8	10 2/8	Weld County	CO	Alan J. Douthit	1995	416
76 6/8	14 4/8	14 7/8	6 3/8	6 1/8	14 4/8	Jackson County	CO	Matt Archuleta	1996	416
76 6/8	16 2/8	16 0/8	6 5/8	6 5/8	7 2/8	Socorro County	NM	Doug Aikin	1996	416
76 6/8	14 3/8	14 6/8	6 5/8	6 3/8	10 1/8	Campbell County	WY	Dennis D. Klemick	1996	416
76 6/8	14 5/8	14 6/8	6 7/8	6 6/8	11 4/8	Elmore County	ID	Steven B. Alderman	1996	416
76 4/8	14 5/8	14 6/8	5 6/8	5 7/8	10 3/8	Lemhi County	ID	Roger W. Atwood	1977	443
76 4/8	14 6/8	14 6/8	6 1/8	6 1/8	12 3/8	Custer County	ID	Juilan Salutregui	1983	443
76 4/8	14 1/8	14 1/8	6 0/8	6 0/8	7 4/8	Converse County	WY	Scott Ames	1983	443
76 4/8	16 0/8	15 7/8	6 2/8	6 2/8	9 2/8	McKinley County	NM	Patrick J. Sharp	1984	443
76 4/8	15 1/8	14 6/8	6 0/8	6 0/8	11 3/8	Carter County	MT	Jamie Byrne	1984	443
76 4/8	13 6/8	13 6/8	6 6/8	6 6/8	10 3/8	Carbon County	WY	Jerry DeCroo	1985	443
76 4/8	15 2/8	15 2/8	6 1/8	6 1/8	12 1/8	Washoe County	NV	Ken Tavener	1986	443
76 4/8	15 4/8	15 4/8	6 2/8	6 3/8	12 6/8	Coconino County	AZ	Gary D. Davis	1986	443
76 4/8	15 2/8	15 3/8	6 0/8	6 0/8	8 1/8	Clark County	SD	Scott Lindgren	1988	443
76 4/8	13 2/8	12 7/8	6 0/8	6 0/8	11 3/8	Sceptre	SAS	Ron Todd	1988	443
76 4/8	16 0/8	16 1/8	6 1/8	6 0/8	14 4/8	Humboldt County	NV	Dwight Schuh	1989	443
76 4/8	14 1/8	13 7/8	6 3/8	6 7/8	9 5/8	Coconino County	AZ	Dennis Pugh	1990	443
76 4/8	14 2/8	14 7/8	6 1/8	6 2/8	13 5/8	Yavapai County	AZ	Josiah Scott	1990	443
76 4/8	14 2/8	14 4/8	5 7/8	6 0/8	10 2/8	Carter County	MT	Donald Travis	1990	443
76 4/8	15 1/8	15 0/8	6 1/8	6 1/8	10 4/8	Fergus County	MT	Dwight Martin	1990	443
76 4/8	15 5/8	15 5/8	6 0/8	6 0/8	8 2/8	Beaverhead County	MT	Neil L. Jacobson	1990	443
76 4/8	15 0/8	15 1/8	6 4/8	6 3/8	11 7/8	Thomas County	NE	Andrew L. Glidden	1990	443
76 4/8	15 4/8	15 4/8	6 0/8	5 7/8	11 0/8	Delta County	CO	Donald E. Liddell	1991	443
76 4/8	14 3/8	14 3/8	6 4/8	6 3/8	11 5/8	Sweetwater County	WY	Randy Downs	1991	443
76 4/8	14 7/8	14 7/8	6 1/8	6 1/8	11 6/8	Fremont County	WY	Gary Laya	1992	443
76 4/8	13 5/8	13 3/8	5 7/8	5 7/8	9 0/8	Converse County	WY	G. Allen Sink	1992	443
76 4/8	14 1/8	14 1/8	6 3/8	6 3/8	10 6/8	Humboldt County	NV	Kyle Swanson	1993	443
76 4/8	15 3/8	15 1/8	5 7/8	5 7/8	15 6/8	Yavapai County	AZ	Patrick M. Kirby	1993	443
76 4/8	14 5/8	14 6/8	6 3/8	6 1/8	8 6/8	Stanley County	SD	Chris Hipple	1993	443
76 4/8	14 0/8	13 6/8	6 2/8	6 0/8	7 6/8	Converse County	WY	Dan Baker	1993	443
76 4/8	14 2/8	14 4/8	6 6/8	6 2/8	10 2/8	Wallace County	KS	Kent Hensley	1993	443
76 4/8	15 3/8	15 5/8	5 6/8	5 6/8	13 2/8	Socorro County	NM	Glenn W. Isler	1994	443
76 4/8	14 5/8	14 3/8	6 6/8	6 6/8	10 6/8	Meagher County	MT	D. "Mitch" Kottas	1994	443
76 4/8	14 0/8	14 1/8	6 3/8	6 3/8	8 2/8	Albany County	WY	Leonard Sheaffer	1994	443
76 4/8	15 4/8	15 1/8	6 1/8	6 2/8	8 7/8	Coconino County	AZ	David Shiflet	1994	443
76 4/8	15 0/8	14 5/8	6 1/8	6 1/8	10 5/8	Larimer County	CO	Mark N. Johnson	1995	443
76 4/8	13 3/8	13 3/8	6 5/8	6 5/8	12 5/8	Big Horn County	WY	Dan Moss	1995	443
76 4/8	15 2/8	14 7/8	6 2/8	6 0/8	8 7/8	Bernalillo County	NM	Brian D. Shaw	1995	443
76 4/8	13 5/8	13 5/8	6 5/8	6 6/8	13 1/8	Colfax County	NM	Patrick Lovato	1995	443
76 4/8	14 3/8	14 0/8	5 7/8	5 7/8	10 4/8	Jackson County	CO	Bruce Ayers	1995	443
76 4/8	15 6/8	16 0/8	6 0/8	5 7/8	9 6/8	Rosebud County	MT	Jack Ferguson	1996	443
76 4/8	14 6/8	15 0/8	6 2/8	6 2/8	10 3/8	Roosevelt County	NM	Justin Jackson	1997	443
76 4/8	15 6/8	15 3/8	5 6/8	6 0/8	8 0/8	Moffat County	CO	Robert G. Ronsse	1997	443
76 4/8	15 3/8	15 3/8	5 7/8	5 7/8	11 7/8	Catron County	NM	William King	1998	443
76 4/8	15 0/8	14 7/8	6 5/8	6 5/8	10 2/8	Weld County	CO	Cindy Rothrock	1998	443
76 2/8	14 5/8	14 1/8	6 1/8	6 1/8	10 3/8	Citten	ND	Richard R. Chandler	1972	483
76 2/8	14 1/8	14 2/8	6 4/8	6 2/8	10 6/8	Converse County	WY	Jack Cassidy	1980	483
76 2/8	13 6/8	14 1/8	6 2/8	6 2/8	8 5/8	Converse County	WY	Chris Cassidy	1980	483
76 2/8	14 7/8	14 6/8	5 5/8	5 6/8	8 6/8	Blaine County	ID	Champ Church	1980	483
76 2/8	16 3/8	16 1/8	6 0/8	6 1/8	8 5/8	Weston County	WY	David M. Nahrgang	1980	483
76 2/8	16 0/8	15 6/8	5 7/8	6 1/8	11 4/8	Converse County	WY	Jack M. Conner	1981	483

PRONGHORN

Minimum Score 67 — Continued

SCORE	LENGTH OF HORN R	L	CIRCUMFERENCE OF BASE R	L	INSIDE SPREAD	AREA	STATE/PROVINCE	HUNTER'S NAME	DATE	RANK
76 2/8	14 3/8	14 3/8	5 6/8	5 7/8	9 2/8	Converse County	WY	Robert R. Vance	1981	483
76 2/8	14 6/8	14 6/8	6 3/8	6 3/8	11 1/8	Moffat County	CO	James Bowerman	1982	483
76 2/8	14 4/8	14 5/8	6 2/8	6 2/8	10 5/8	Sweetwater County	WY	Darrell H. Nations	1982	483
76 2/8	14 4/8	14 5/8	6 0/8	6 0/8	10 2/8	Taos County	NM	Galen G. Roumpf	1983	483
76 2/8	13 4/8	13 7/8	6 4/8	6 2/8	10 6/8	Wallace County	KS	Steve Rugg	1983	483
76 2/8	14 6/8	14 7/8	6 5/8	6 3/8	7 7/8	Sweetwater County	WY	Steve L. Rueck	1984	483
76 2/8	14 6/8	14 7/8	5 7/8	5 6/8	10 6/8	Eddy County	NM	Derek A. Tierney	1986	483
76 2/8	14 0/8	13 6/8	6 2/8	6 1/8	9 1/8	Converse County	WY	David Kugler	1987	483
76 2/8	15 2/8	15 2/8	6 4/8	6 4/8	10 4/8	Hettinger County	ND	Bill Clink	1988	483
76 2/8	14 3/8	14 7/8	6 5/8	6 4/8	11 2/8	Bowman County	ND	Craig Egeland	1988	483
76 2/8	15 2/8	15 2/8	5 7/8	5 7/8	11 3/8	Empress	ALB	Kenneth John Akkermans	1988	483
76 2/8	16 0/8	16 3/8	5 7/8	5 7/8	12 1/8	Lassen County	CA	Gary Bagnaschi	1989	483
76 2/8	15 0/8	15 0/8	5 7/8	5 7/8	11 1/8	Moffat County	CO	Robert M. Fromme	1990	483
76 2/8	13 4/8	13 6/8	7 3/8	7 2/8	9 3/8	Mountrail County	ND	Lonny G. Waggoner	1990	483
76 2/8	15 0/8	15 0/8	6 2/8	6 3/8	13 4/8	Harney County	OR	Trevin Webster	1990	483
76 2/8	15 2/8	15 1/8	6 0/8	6 0/8	9 5/8	Catron County	NM	Cary Cuba	1991	483
76 2/8	15 0/8	15 0/8	6 3/8	6 2/8	10 1/8	Sweetwater County	WY	William Metz	1991	483
76 2/8	13 5/8	13 5/8	6 5/8	6 5/8	8 4/8	Converse County	WY	William L. Randles	1991	483
76 2/8	14 7/8	14 4/8	6 1/8	6 2/8	9 2/8	Johnson County	WY	Joseph L. Ravis	1991	483
76 2/8	15 0/8	14 6/8	6 4/8	6 3/8	10 4/8	Box Butte County	NE	Myron R. Drumheller	1991	483
76 2/8	16 5/8	16 5/8	6 3/8	6 1/8	14 2/8	Lake County	OR	Robert Gentry	1992	483
76 2/8	15 0/8	15 1/8	6 2/8	6 2/8	9 3/8	Saguache County	CO	Gary W. Bohochik	1992	483
76 2/8	14 6/8	15 0/8	6 3/8	6 2/8	11 3/8	Weld County	CO	Mike Brooks	1994	483
76 2/8	15 6/8	15 4/8	6 1/8	6 1/8	10 1/8	Rio Blanco County	CO	Dave Holt	1994	483
76 2/8	15 6/8	14 5/8	6 3/8	6 2/8	9 4/8	Yavapai County	AZ	Henry Redondo Garcia	1994	483
76 2/8	14 6/8	14 4/8	6 0/8	6 1/8	9 6/8	Jackson County	CO	Bob Sanders	1994	483
76 2/8	16 1/8	16 4/8	5 5/8	5 5/8	8 0/8	White Pine County	NV	Denis Joiner	1995	483
76 2/8	15 3/8	15 2/8	6 2/8	6 2/8	11 7/8	Coconino County	AZ	Michael L. Campbell	1995	483
76 2/8	14 6/8	14 5/8	5 6/8	5 6/8	10 3/8	Petroleum County	MT	Craig Richardson	1995	483
76 2/8	15 5/8	16 2/8	6 1/8	6 0/8	11 7/8	Medicine Hat	ALB	Jim Osinchuk	1995	483
76 2/8	14 6/8	14 7/8	6 2/8	6 1/8	7 6/8	Platte County	WY	Derek Long II	1998	483
76 0/8	15 0/8	14 7/8	6 0/8	6 0/8	14 6/8	Mountrail County	ND	Wayne A. Metcalf	1972	520
76 0/8	14 5/8	14 5/8	6 2/8	6 4/8	13 4/8	Clark County	ID	Kerry Hillman	1977	520
76 0/8	14 7/8	14 3/8	5 6/8	6 1/8	10 0/8	Sweetwater County	WY	John Grady Lee	1983	520
76 0/8	14 2/8	14 2/8	6 1/8	6 1/8	9 3/8	Converse County	WY	Richard Rabe, Jr.	1985	520
76 0/8	14 4/8	14 3/8	6 0/8	6 1/8	9 7/8	Nye County	NV	Paul Campos	1988	520
76 0/8	14 0/8	14 1/8	6 0/8	6 0/8	8 7/8	Yavapai County	AZ	T. J. Baehre	1989	520
76 0/8	14 6/8	14 7/8	6 4/8	6 5/8	19 1/8	Colfax County	NM	Ron Serwa	1990	520
76 0/8	14 6/8	14 3/8	6 5/8	6 4/8	10 4/8	Sweetwater County	WY	Lori Kay Stinchcomb	1990	520
76 0/8	14 2/8	13 6/8	6 3/8	6 3/8	11 2/8	Campbell County	WY	James K. Keim	1990	520
76 0/8	15 4/8	15 2/8	6 0/8	5 7/8	12 2/8	Quay County	NM	Tommy C. Jones	1991	520
76 0/8	15 4/8	15 5/8	6 3/8	6 2/8	8 7/8	Milk River	ALB	Daniel Harder	1991	520
76 0/8	15 5/8	16 0/8	6 1/8	5 7/8	10 5/8	Sublette County	WY	Roger O. Wyant	1991	520
76 0/8	15 2/8	15 2/8	6 0/8	6 0/8	12 1/8	Morton County	ND	Gary Hanson	1991	520
76 0/8	14 2/8	14 1/8	6 3/8	6 2/8	9 5/8	Campbell County	WY	Doy K. Curtis	1991	520
76 0/8	15 4/8	15 6/8	5 4/8	5 3/8	13 7/8	Lake County	OR	Donald R. Pritchett	1992	520
76 0/8	13 5/8	13 5/8	6 5/8	6 4/8	9 6/8	Sweetwater County	WY	Justin Miller	1992	520
76 0/8	13 6/8	13 5/8	6 5/8	6 5/8	10 1/8	Converse County	WY	Melvin Wells	1992	520
76 0/8	15 0/8	15 1/8	5 7/8	5 4/8	9 7/8	Sioux County	NE	Jack F. Buckley	1992	520
76 0/8	14 3/8	14 4/8	6 0/8	6 0/8	8 2/8	Lincoln County	NV	Gary F. Bogner	1993	520
76 0/8	14 6/8	14 5/8	6 3/8	6 3/8	10 1/8	Moffat County	CO	David Buell	1993	520
76 0/8	13 5/8	13 3/8	6 4/8	6 2/8	8 3/8	Jefferson County	OR	Clinton J. Hall	1993	520
76 0/8	13 4/8	13 4/8	7 0/8	6 7/8	14 2/8	Big Horn County	WY	Jason Doumitt	1994	520
76 0/8	15 1/8	15 2/8	6 3/8	6 1/8	8 6/8	Natrona County	WY	Bradley Chamberlain	1996	520
76 0/8	15 6/8	15 4/8	5 6/8	5 5/8	11 1/8	Toole County	MT	Keith Miller	1996	520
76 0/8	13 1/8	13 0/8	6 4/8	6 5/8	9 3/8	Platte County	WY	Jerry Bowen	1996	520
76 0/8	15 0/8	15 0/8	6 1/8	6 0/8	12 7/8	Catron County	NM	Frank Argo	1997	520
76 0/8	13 7/8	14 0/8	6 4/8	6 5/8	11 1/8	Natrona County	WY	Richard Manchur	1997	520
76 0/8	14 6/8	14 5/8	6 5/8	6 4/8	10 4/8	Rosebud County	MT	Chuck Adams	1997	520
75 6/8	14 0/8	14 0/8	6 1/8	6 1/8	12 4/8	Sweetwater County	WY	Gene McFadden	1982	548
75 6/8	14 4/8	14 6/8	6 1/8	6 1/8	10 0/8	Natrona County	WY	Jack M. Conner	1982	548
75 6/8	15 2/8	14 6/8	5 7/8	5 7/8	11 1/8	Moffat County	CO	Judd Cooney	1982	548
75 6/8	15 1/8	15 1/8	6 2/8	6 2/8	10 3/8	Converse County	WY	Lonny G. Herrick	1983	548
75 6/8	15 0/8	15 0/8	5 7/8	5 6/8	14 2/8	Sweetwater County	WY	Marty Martin	1986	548
75 6/8	14 1/8	14 0/8	6 2/8	6 2/8	10 4/8	Moffat County	CO	Tom Foss	1987	548
75 6/8	14 2/8	15 2/8	6 6/8	6 6/8	15 2/8	Moffat County	CO	Randy Major/Frank Major	1988	548
75 6/8	13 5/8	14 0/8	6 4/8	6 3/8	6 3/8	Carbon County	WY	David Wiltse	1988	548
75 6/8	15 0/8	15 1/8	5 5/8	5 5/8	9 1/8	Sublette County	WY	Ronell Skinner	1988	548
75 6/8	13 5/8	13 5/8	6 0/8	6 1/8	11 7/8	Coconino County	AZ	Noel Harris	1989	548
75 6/8	14 6/8	14 5/8	6 0/8	5 7/8	9 2/8	Moffat County	CO	Joseph Schwartz	1990	548
75 6/8	15 6/8	15 2/8	6 0/8	5 6/8	10 4/8	Elko County	NV	Paul J. Vietti	1990	548
75 6/8	14 2/8	14 3/8	5 6/8	6 1/8	6 5/8	Carbon County	WY	Clarence E. Faber	1990	548
75 6/8	13 6/8	13 3/8	6 1/8	6 0/8	12 4/8	Sublette County	WY	Mike Lamade	1990	548
75 6/8	15 1/8	15 2/8	5 7/8	5 7/8	9 4/8	Millard County	UT	Dennis L. Shirley	1990	548
75 6/8	15 2/8	15 3/8	6 1/8	6 1/8	12 4/8	Harney County	OR	Gary Nyden	1990	548
75 6/8	12 6/8	12 5/8	6 3/8	6 6/8	7 6/8	Harney County	OR	Eugene F. Martin	1990	548
75 6/8	13 6/8	13 7/8	6 3/8	6 4/8	10 4/8	Converse County	WY	Wayne Sanders	1990	548
75 6/8	14 6/8	15 1/8	5 6/8	5 6/8	8 1/8	Lemhi County	ID	Ben Fahnholz	1991	548

PRONGHORN

Minimum Score 67 — Continued

SCORE	LENGTH OF HORN R	LENGTH OF HORN L	CIRCUMFERENCE OF BASE R	CIRCUMFERENCE OF BASE L	INSIDE SPREAD	AREA	STATE/ PROVINCE	HUNTER'S NAME	DATE	RANK
75 6/8	15 1/8	15 3/8	6 0/8	6 0/8	10 7/8	Yavapai County	AZ	Paul Fritzinger	1991	548
75 6/8	15 4/8	15 4/8	5 7/8	5 6/8	10 1/8	Socorro County	NM	Mike Van Wormer	1992	548
75 6/8	15 7/8	16 2/8	6 0/8	6 0/8	6 2/8	Carbon County	WY	Jeff Martin	1992	548
75 6/8	14 0/8	13 7/8	6 6/8	6 5/8	10 4/8	Jenner	ALB	Carter Calliou	1992	548
75 6/8	14 3/8	14 3/8	6 4/8	6 3/8	9 5/8	Fremont County	WY	Gary L. Hinaman	1993	548
75 6/8	14 3/8	14 5/8	6 3/8	6 4/8	10 5/8	Hot Springs County	WY	Greg Lompart	1993	548
75 6/8	14 7/8	14 7/8	6 2/8	6 3/8	11 0/8	Cheyenne County	NE	Matt Highby	1994	548
75 6/8	14 7/8	15 2/8	6 4/8	6 4/8	8 5/8	Lake County	OR	Glen Bridgmon	1994	548
75 6/8	14 6/8	14 3/8	6 2/8	6 2/8	11 0/8	Yavapai County	AZ	Herb Fisher	1995	548
75 6/8	13 7/8	14 4/8	6 3/8	6 3/8	12 0/8	Campbell County	WY	Dave Hinton	1995	548
75 6/8	13 3/8	13 3/8	6 5/8	6 4/8	8 2/8	Sweetwater County	WY	Roger Wintle	1996	548
75 6/8	14 4/8	14 6/8	5 6/8	6 0/8	14 3/8	Weld County	CO	Kaylan Shaffer	1996	548
75 6/8	13 1/8	13 2/8	6 4/8	6 6/8	7 4/8	Moffat County	CO	Timothy J. Schneider	1997	548
75 6/8	14 6/8	14 5/8	5 4/8	5 4/8	8 2/8	Converse County	WY	Tim Connaughty	1997	548
75 6/8	14 6/8	14 5/8	6 2/8	6 2/8	9 5/8	Campbell County	WY	Jim Dunigan	1998	548
75 4/8	12 1/8	12 2/8	5 7/8	6 0/8	8 2/8	Campbell County	WY	Dr. R. F. Helzerman	1960	582
75 4/8	17 2/8	16 4/8	6 0/8	5 6/8	15 0/8	Guadalupe County	NM	M. K. Vance	1962	582
75 4/8	14 7/8	14 7/8	6 0/8	6 0/8	12 0/8	Williams County	ND	Terry L. Halgrimson	1970	582
75 4/8	14 3/8	14 2/8	6 0/8	6 2/8	12 6/8	McLean County	ND	Don Sorge	1970	582
75 4/8	13 3/8	13 4/8	6 6/8	6 7/8	11 6/8	Ormsby	WY	Richard L. Huber	1979	582
75 4/8	15 3/8	15 2/8	5 6/8	5 6/8	12 5/8	Fergus County	MT	Don Davidson	1981	582
75 4/8	14 5/8	14 7/8	6 2/8	6 2/8	9 6/8	Klamath County	OR	Larry E. Jones	1982	582
75 4/8	16 0/8	16 0/8	6 0/8	5 7/8	11 0/8	Moffat County	CO	John R. Morris II	1983	582
75 4/8	14 4/8	14 4/8	6 4/8	6 4/8	11 6/8	Coconino County	AZ	Gary Warnica	1983	582
75 4/8	14 0/8	14 0/8	6 2/8	6 2/8	10 0/8	Powder River County	MT	Raleigh D. Buckmaster	1983	582
75 4/8	16 2/8	16 2/8	6 0/8	6 0/8	12 0/8	Coconino County	AZ	Harry M. Weeks	1984	582
75 4/8	14 4/8	14 0/8	6 4/8	6 4/8	12 1/8	Weld County	CO	Lorn Barnica	1984	582
75 4/8	14 6/8	14 6/8	6 0/8	6 0/8	11 1/8	Lassen County	CA	Pete Becker	1985	582
75 4/8	15 1/8	15 2/8	6 0/8	5 7/8	9 3/8	Meagher County	MT	Don Babcock	1986	582
75 4/8	15 0/8	14 4/8	5 6/8	5 7/8	6 7/8	Washoe County	NV	Conrad Stitser	1987	582
75 4/8	14 3/8	14 5/8	5 5/8	5 7/8	12 0/8	Coconino County	AZ	Bill Kerr	1987	582
75 4/8	14 7/8	14 6/8	6 1/8	6 2/8	10 3/8	Cochise County	AZ	Jerry Clarno	1987	582
75 4/8	14 0/8	14 1/8	6 6/8	6 4/8	8 1/8	Moffat County	CO	Tracy L. Gulliksen	1987	582
75 4/8	15 6/8	15 3/8	6 1/8	6 2/8	12 3/8	Humboldt County	NV	G. Todd Brooks	1988	582
75 4/8	15 3/8	15 1/8	6 7/8	6 7/8	7 4/8	Custer County	ID	Matt March	1990	582
75 4/8	13 6/8	13 6/8	6 0/8	6 0/8	10 0/8	Coconino County	AZ	Rick Betten	1991	582
75 4/8	14 4/8	14 0/8	6 0/8	6 0/8	12 7/8	Campbell County	WY	Gene Bremmer	1991	582
75 4/8	14 5/8	14 5/8	6 0/8	6 0/8	10 5/8	Sweetwater County	WY	Harvey L. Dalton	1992	582
75 4/8	14 1/8	14 1/8	6 2/8	6 1/8	10 1/8	Yavapai County	AZ	Jeffrey W. Adams	1992	582
75 4/8	14 2/8	14 2/8	5 7/8	5 6/8	10 2/8	Stanley County	SD	Robert G. Barden	1992	582
75 4/8	13 6/8	13 6/8	6 5/8	6 3/8	9 6/8	Carbon County	WY	Larry Cross	1992	582
75 4/8	14 5/8	14 5/8	5 5/8	5 5/8	8 4/8	Catron County	NM	Carl D. Bradford	1993	582
75 4/8	12 6/8	12 6/8	6 7/8	6 6/8	9 7/8	Box Elder County	UT	Wayne Payne	1993	582
75 4/8	15 6/8	15 6/8	6 1/8	6 1/8	11 6/8	Chaves County	NM	Matt Hentrick	1994	582
75 4/8	15 3/8	15 2/8	5 7/8	6 0/8	10 7/8	Owyhee County	ID	Neil Thagard	1995	582
75 4/8	14 5/8	15 1/8	5 6/8	5 5/8	11 1/8	Moffat County	CO	Jordan T. Smith	1995	582
75 4/8	14 7/8	15 1/8	6 3/8	6 3/8	9 2/8	Colfax County	NM	Robert L. Pagel, Sr.	1995	582
75 4/8	15 6/8	15 6/8	6 0/8	6 0/8	7 3/8	Yavapai County	AZ	James C. Roth	1995	582
75 4/8	15 1/8	15 2/8	6 1/8	6 0/8	14 7/8	Owyhee County	ID	Gary Angell	1996	582
75 4/8	14 3/8	14 0/8	5 7/8	5 7/8	11 0/8	Yavapai County	AZ	Erik Pedersen	1996	582
75 4/8	14 5/8	15 1/8	6 0/8	6 0/8	9 3/8	Sheridan County	WY	Jack Hayes	1996	582
75 4/8	14 4/8	14 3/8	6 1/8	6 2/8	11 5/8	Saguache County	CO	Robert E. Schwanke	1997	582
75 4/8	14 3/8	14 4/8	6 2/8	6 2/8	10 7/8	Moffat County	CO	Tim Cuthriell	1997	582
75 4/8	14 2/8	14 2/8	6 1/8	6 1/8	12 7/8	Powder River County	MT	Bob Yeakel	1997	582
75 4/8	15 4/8	15 4/8	5 7/8	5 7/8	9 6/8	Elko County	NV	Phil Kendall	1998	582
75 4/8	14 2/8	14 2/8	6 0/8	5 6/8	7 4/8	Albany County	WY	Jerry Bowen	1998	582
75 2/8	15 4/8	15 3/8	5 7/8	5 7/8	8 6/8	Burke County	ND	Richard R. Chandler	1971	623
75 2/8	16 1/8	16 6/8	5 6/8	5 5/8	11 2/8	Klamath County	OR	Steve H. Bell	1973	623
75 2/8	14 3/8	14 5/8	6 3/8	6 4/8	9 2/8	Carbon County	WY	Duane Caudle	1980	623
75 2/8	14 5/8	14 5/8	6 2/8	6 2/8	10 2/8	Musselshell County	MT	John Crump	1980	623
75 2/8	13 0/8	13 0/8	7 0/8	7 1/8	10 6/8	Sweetwater County	WY	Charlene Shaw	1985	623
75 2/8	15 0/8	14 4/8	7 0/8	6 6/8	9 2/8	Sweetwater County	WY	Marlene Bowen	1986	623
75 2/8	14 0/8	14 5/8	6 0/8	6 0/8	12 0/8	Coconino County	AZ	David L. Wolf	1986	623
75 2/8	13 7/8	14 0/8	6 5/8	6 4/8	12 5/8	Dunn County	ND	Jeff J. Kostelecky	1987	623
75 2/8	14 1/8	14 0/8	6 2/8	6 2/8	8 5/8	Lea County	NM	Lynn Sims	1987	623
75 2/8	13 7/8	13 6/8	6 4/8	6 5/8	11 2/8	Coconino County	AZ	Johnny Rooker	1988	623
75 2/8	15 6/8	16 0/8	6 3/8	6 2/8	10 7/8	Phillips County	MT	Don Andrews	1988	623
75 2/8	14 4/8	14 4/8	6 3/8	6 3/8	12 3/8	Presidio County	TX	Tommy Culbertson	1988	623
75 2/8	15 0/8	14 5/8	6 2/8	6 3/8	8 7/8	Sweetwater County	WY	Norman Bradley	1989	623
75 2/8	13 7/8	14 0/8	6 0/8	5 7/8	7 1/8	Moffat County	CO	Rickey Phillips	1989	623
75 2/8	13 7/8	14 0/8	6 1/8	6 2/8	12 5/8	Sweetwater County	WY	Harv Dalton	1989	623
75 2/8	15 3/8	15 4/8	5 6/8	5 6/8	11 3/8	Eddy County	NM	Dennis L. Howell	1989	623
75 2/8	14 4/8	14 5/8	6 1/8	6 2/8	9 0/8	Washoe County	NV	Cory Pengelly	1990	623
75 2/8	14 2/8	14 1/8	6 2/8	6 2/8	7 3/8	Sweetwater County	WY	Edward Ferebee	1990	623
75 2/8	15 7/8	15 4/8	5 5/8	5 5/8	6 5/8	Sweetwater County	WY	Ron Serwa	1990	623
75 2/8	14 4/8	14 5/8	6 1/8	6 0/8	12 2/8	Moffat County	CO	Ronald King	1990	623
75 2/8	15 4/8	16 1/8	5 7/8	5 5/8	9 1/8	Harney County	OR	Stanley Miles	1990	623
75 2/8	14 3/8	14 1/8	5 6/8	5 6/8	9 0/8	Billings County	ND	Mark Sowieja	1990	623

PRONGHORN

Minimum Score 67

SCORE	LENGTH OF HORN R	L	CIRCUMFERENCE OF BASE R	L	INSIDE SPREAD	AREA	STATE/ PROVINCE	HUNTER'S NAME	DATE	RANK
75 2/8	14 2/8	14 0/8	6 1/8	6 3/8	9 3/8	Wallace County	KS	Daniel P. Carmen	1990	623
75 2/8	14 3/8	14 4/8	6 3/8	6 3/8	14 4/8	Moffat County	CO	Bud Boker	1991	623
75 2/8	14 3/8	14 3/8	6 1/8	6 0/8	11 3/8	Carbon County	WY	Greg Bonetti	1991	623
75 2/8	13 2/8	13 4/8	6 5/8	6 4/8	12 0/8	Garfield County	MT	Kim Tatman	1991	623
75 2/8	15 1/8	15 0/8	6 6/8	6 5/8	11 1/8	Sioux County	NE	Steve Woitaszewski	1991	623
75 2/8	14 6/8	14 5/8	5 6/8	5 6/8	10 2/8	Catron County	NM	Patrick Kirk	1992	623
75 2/8	13 5/8	13 7/8	6 7/8	6 6/8	8 0/8	Twin Falls County	ID	Gary Painter	1992	623
75 2/8	13 7/8	15 0/8	6 2/8	6 2/8	10 1/8	Yavapai County	AZ	Roland J. Chooljian	1992	623
75 2/8	15 6/8	14 4/8	6 0/8	6 0/8	9 7/8	Yavapai County	AZ	Don Parks, Jr.	1992	623
75 2/8	14 0/8	14 0/8	5 6/8	5 7/8	8 4/8	Yavapai County	AZ	Keith A. Robinson	1993	623
75 2/8	15 0/8	14 7/8	5 4/8	5 4/8	11 3/8	Juab County	UT	Bruce Carlisle	1993	623
75 2/8	13 7/8	14 0/8	6 0/8	6 0/8	9 4/8	Clark County	SD	Jared Mason	1993	623
75 2/8	13 2/8	13 2/8	7 0/8	6 4/8	11 1/8	Campbell County	WY	Michael J. Kennedy	1993	623
75 2/8	13 5/8	13 7/8	6 0/8	6 0/8	8 0/8	Platte County	WY	John M. Dobish	1993	623
75 2/8	13 3/8	13 4/8	6 0/8	6 1/8	10 6/8	Converse County	WY	Ralph Inverso	1993	623
75 2/8	15 4/8	16 2/8	6 0/8	6 0/8	8 5/8	Sioux County	NE	John J. Schaffer	1993	623
75 2/8	13 6/8	13 7/8	6 4/8	6 6/8	10 1/8	Rio Blanco County	CO	Richard Muller	1994	623
75 2/8	14 7/8	14 5/8	6 0/8	5 7/8	8 5/8	Jenner	ALB	Tim Sailer	1994	623
75 2/8	14 4/8	15 2/8	6 0/8	6 2/8	8 2/8	Hot Springs County	WY	Dale "Chuck" Cornella	1994	623
75 2/8	13 3/8	13 2/8	6 4/8	6 3/8	9 3/8	Big Horn County	WY	Charlotte Moss	1995	623
75 2/8	15 3/8	15 4/8	6 0/8	6 0/8	12 4/8	Juab County	UT	Paul R. Quayle	1995	623
75 2/8	13 4/8	13 4/8	6 5/8	6 5/8	8 1/8	Weld County	CO	David L. Skiff	1995	623
75 2/8	15 1/8	15 2/8	6 1/8	6 1/8	11 1/8	Rosebud County	MT	Charles E. Speck	1995	623
75 2/8	14 3/8	14 3/8	6 0/8	5 5/8	10 5/8	Millard County	UT	Brandon Snell	1996	623
75 2/8	13 4/8	13 2/8	6 3/8	6 2/8	6 3/8	Haakon County	SD	Aaron Doolittle	1997	623
75 2/8	13 6/8	13 2/8	6 3/8	6 3/8	11 4/8	Sweetwater County	WY	Vic R. Dana	1998	623
75 0/8	14 2/8	14 2/8	6 3/8	6 1/8	10 2/8	Butte County	ID	Ross M. Conlin	1971	671
75 0/8	14 0/8	13 6/8	7 4/8	7 4/8	11 6/8	Sheridan County	ND	Dave Baumiller	1973	671
75 0/8	13 4/8	13 5/8	6 5/8	6 3/8	10 2/8	Campbell County	WY	Mick Larson	1975	671
75 0/8	13 6/8	14 0/8	6 2/8	6 2/8	8 6/8	Bairoil	WY	Mike Ward	1976	671
75 0/8	14 5/8	14 4/8	6 2/8	6 1/8	8 7/8	Humboldt County	NV	Robert Mathews	1977	671
75 0/8	14 2/8	14 1/8	6 3/8	6 3/8	10 1/8	Bairoil	WY	Earl Frye	1980	671
75 0/8	14 0/8	14 0/8	5 5/8	5 6/8	9 7/8	Moffat County	CO	Ronald C. Halpin	1980	671
75 0/8	14 0/8	14 0/8	6 1/8	6 0/8	12 6/8	Wheatland County	MT	Phil Reno	1980	671
75 0/8	13 5/8	14 6/8	6 0/8	6 0/8	13 0/8	Moffat County	CO	Carl Smith	1981	671
75 0/8	15 0/8	14 7/8	6 2/8	6 2/8	9 0/8	Natrona County	WY	Richard A. Schreiber	1982	671
75 0/8	14 5/8	14 5/8	6 0/8	6 0/8	12 1/8	Meagher County	MT	Gene Clark	1984	671
75 0/8	15 5/8	15 3/8	6 0/8	6 0/8	11 6/8	Coconino County	AZ	Jim Scott	1986	671
75 0/8	14 4/8	14 4/8	5 5/8	5 5/8	10 4/8	Converse County	WY	William G. Mason	1986	671
75 0/8	14 4/8	14 4/8	5 6/8	5 6/8	13 5/8	Sweetwater County	WY	Steve Bellis	1988	671
75 0/8	14 6/8	14 6/8	5 6/8	5 6/8	11 2/8	Pueblo County	CO	Freeman Howard	1989	671
75 0/8	14 3/8	14 4/8	6 1/8	6 2/8	9 2/8	Custer County	MT	Marty Penrod	1989	671
75 0/8	12 0/8	12 1/8	6 2/8	6 2/8	9 4/8	Campbell County	WY	Richard Reeb	1990	671
75 0/8	14 4/8	13 6/8	6 0/8	6 0/8	11 2/8	Grant County	NM	Brandon Jones	1991	671
75 0/8	13 6/8	13 5/8	6 2/8	6 1/8	11 7/8	Carbon County	WY	Heather E. Haines	1991	671
75 0/8	13 7/8	13 7/8	6 4/8	6 5/8	12 7/8	Carbon County	WY	Kenneth J. Kahler	1991	671
75 0/8	14 5/8	14 5/8	6 2/8	6 4/8	9 2/8	Fremont County	WY	Joel Nirider	1991	671
75 0/8	13 5/8	13 7/8	6 1/8	6 2/8	12 2/8	Mercer County	ND	Leland A. Mehlhoff	1991	671
75 0/8	15 3/8	15 3/8	5 3/8	5 2/8	9 0/8	Converse County	WY	Robert Brenneman	1991	671
75 0/8	14 1/8	13 7/8	6 3/8	6 3/8	8 6/8	Sweetwater County	WY	James B. White	1992	671
75 0/8	14 3/8	14 3/8	6 1/8	6 1/8	10 2/8	Sweetwater County	WY	Donald Ace Morgan	1992	671
75 0/8	15 0/8	15 0/8	6 2/8	6 1/8	8 3/8	Butte County	ID	L. D. Green	1992	671
75 0/8	15 3/8	15 4/8	6 1/8	6 0/8	9 6/8	Millard County	UT	Terry Costa	1992	671
75 0/8	13 6/8	14 0/8	6 1/8	6 1/8	9 0/8	Sweetwater County	WY	Jonathan M. Kautt	1992	671
75 0/8	13 6/8	14 3/8	6 7/8	7 1/8	12 4/8	Moffat County	CO	Glenn W. Pritchard	1992	671
75 0/8	14 4/8	14 2/8	6 3/8	6 3/8	9 5/8	Moffat County	CO	Jim Leqve	1993	671
75 0/8	15 1/8	15 5/8	6 0/8	5 6/8	11 5/8	Washoe County	NV	Gilbert Hernandez	1993	671
75 0/8	13 6/8	13 1/8	6 1/8	6 1/8	11 2/8	Weld County	CO	B. Duane Kropf	1993	671
75 0/8	14 6/8	14 6/8	6 2/8	6 1/8	7 5/8	Natrona County	WY	Brian L. Wagner	1993	671
75 0/8	15 0/8	14 6/8	6 3/8	6 2/8	9 1/8	Yavapai County	AZ	Steve Rawlins	1993	671
75 0/8	15 2/8	15 2/8	6 2/8	6 2/8	11 6/8	Manyberries	ALB	Doug Erickson	1993	671
75 0/8	15 4/8	15 2/8	6 0/8	6 0/8	9 3/8	Yellowstone County	MT	Gary R. Petty	1993	671
75 0/8	14 4/8	15 1/8	5 6/8	6 0/8	10 1/8	San Miguel County	NM	Marty Martinez	1994	671
75 0/8	12 6/8	13 2/8	6 4/8	6 4/8	12 1/8	Graham County	AZ	John C. Rhodes	1994	671
75 0/8	14 4/8	14 6/8	5 7/8	5 7/8	16 1/8	Harney County	OR	John Jaques	1994	671
75 0/8	13 5/8	13 6/8	7 2/8	7 0/8	10 0/8	Mankota	SAS	Kelly Johnson	1994	671
75 0/8	14 5/8	14 7/8	6 1/8	6 1/8	10 1/8	Hanna	ALB	Glen Hutton	1994	671
75 0/8	14 1/8	14 4/8	5 7/8	5 7/8	6 5/8	Campbell County	WY	Bruce Witte	1994	671
75 0/8	13 7/8	13 4/8	6 0/8	5 7/8	10 3/8	Hudspeth County	TX	Paul Thurman	1994	671
75 0/8	14 2/8	14 2/8	7 0/8	7 0/8	13 1/8	Weld County	CO	Stuart Stevens	1995	671
75 0/8	15 5/8	15 2/8	6 2/8	6 4/8	6 4/8	Custer County	ID	George Versis	1995	671
75 0/8	14 4/8	14 3/8	6 5/8	6 3/8	10 4/8	Buffalo County	SD	Ed Werdel	1995	671
75 0/8	12 4/8	12 4/8	6 5/8	6 5/8	8 6/8	Hot Springs County	WY	Micheal H. Eastman	1995	671
75 0/8	14 3/8	14 2/8	6 4/8	6 4/8	8 7/8	Moffat County	CO	Paul M. Martin	1996	671
75 0/8	14 4/8	14 6/8	6 3/8	6 1/8	9 6/8	Yavapai County	AZ	Archie J. Nesbitt	1997	671
75 0/8	14 2/8	14 2/8	6 0/8	5 7/8	11 5/8	Carbon County	UT	McCade Mascaro	1997	671
75 0/8	14 0/8	13 7/8	6 5/8	6 5/8	8 6/8	Toole County	MT	Keith Miller	1997	671
75 0/8	14 0/8	14 0/8	6 1/8	6 0/8	11 7/8	Big Horn County	WY	Dave Moss	1998	671

PRONGHORN

Minimum Score 67 — Continued

SCORE	LENGTH OF HORN R	L	CIRCUMFERENCE OF BASE R	L	INSIDE SPREAD	AREA	STATE/ PROVINCE	HUNTER'S NAME	DATE	RANK
75 0/8	16 5/8	16 2/8	5 4/8	5 4/8	9 0/8	Lemhi County	ID	Scott Bridges	1998	671
74 6/8	14 3/8	14 3/8	5 5/8	5 5/8	9 5/8	Lemhi County	ID	Kent Merrill	1979	724
74 6/8	13 5/8	13 2/8	7 4/8	7 5/8	11 2/8	Converse County	WY	George A. Zanoni	1980	724
74 6/8	14 4/8	14 5/8	6 3/8	6 1/8	7 0/8	Converse County	WY	Norm Goodwin	1981	724
74 6/8	14 3/8	14 5/8	5 6/8	5 6/8	10 1/8	Fremont County	WY	James R. Mecca	1981	724
74 6/8	14 2/8	14 2/8	6 1/8	6 1/8	9 1/8	Sweetwater County	WY	Pete J Cintorino	1982	724
74 6/8	14 7/8	14 1/8	6 2/8	6 1/8	12 1/8	Moffat County	CO	Richard K. Hess	1982	724
74 6/8	14 1/8	14 1/8	6 0/8	5 7/8	5 7/8	Converse County	WY	Thomas Fleming	1982	724
74 6/8	14 4/8	14 5/8	6 0/8	6 1/8	9 6/8	Converse County	WY	Steve Gorr	1982	724
74 6/8	13 7/8	14 0/8	5 7/8	6 1/8	12 4/8	Carbon County	WY	Len Cardinale	1982	724
74 6/8	14 3/8	14 3/8	6 2/8	6 2/8	8 6/8	Sweetwater County	WY	Mike Denney	1982	724
74 6/8	14 7/8	14 7/8	6 0/8	6 0/8	8 7/8	Humboldt County	NV	Ken Mallory	1983	724
74 6/8	14 0/8	14 1/8	6 0/8	5 7/8	10 3/8	Moffat County	CO	Wallace Hobby	1983	724
74 6/8	14 5/8	14 6/8	6 2/8	6 2/8	9 7/8	Campbell County	WY	Arthur Geltz	1984	724
74 6/8	14 4/8	14 4/8	6 2/8	6 2/8	10 3/8	Moffat County	CO	Susan Bingham Syvertson	1985	724
74 6/8	15 3/8	15 4/8	5 7/8	5 6/8	8 0/8	Fremont County	WY	Joe E. Nelson	1985	724
74 6/8	14 1/8	14 0/8	6 1/8	6 0/8	7 3/8	Sweetwater County	WY	Dennis L. Shirley	1986	724
74 6/8	14 2/8	14 1/8	6 4/8	6 3/8	9 6/8	Sweetwater County	WY	Michael Chaffin	1986	724
74 6/8	14 3/8	14 7/8	6 1/8	6 0/8	10 5/8	Carbon County	WY	Robert L. Hudman	1988	724
74 6/8	14 5/8	14 6/8	5 7/8	5 7/8	10 7/8	Billings County	ND	Pam Baird	1988	724
74 6/8	14 3/8	14 3/8	5 7/8	5 7/8	8 3/8	Converse County	WY	James Erickson	1988	724
74 6/8	13 4/8	13 3/8	6 3/8	6 3/8	11 0/8	Humboldt County	NV	David Stoker	1991	724
74 6/8	14 3/8	14 5/8	6 1/8	6 1/8	11 7/8	Perkins County	SD	Darin Allen Manthie	1991	724
74 6/8	14 7/8	14 6/8	5 7/8	6 0/8	7 2/8	Washoe County	NV	Jim Bradley	1992	724
74 6/8	15 2/8	14 7/8	5 7/8	5 7/8	7 4/8	Washoe County	NV	Charlie Powning	1992	724
74 6/8	14 6/8	14 5/8	6 2/8	6 1/8	10 6/8	Sweetwater County	WY	Dwight Brown, Jr.	1992	724
74 6/8	13 7/8	14 0/8	6 6/8	6 6/8	7 7/8	Sweetwater County	WY	Robert G. Petersen	1992	724
74 6/8	13 4/8	13 2/8	6 6/8	7 0/8	8 7/8	Natrona County	WY	Russ Weakland	1992	724
74 6/8	13 4/8	13 4/8	5 7/8	6 0/8	8 0/8	Converse County	WY	Russell A. Nichols	1992	724
74 6/8	14 6/8	14 5/8	5 7/8	5 7/8	11 1/8	Natrona County	WY	Elmer R. Luce, Jr.	1992	724
74 6/8	14 6/8	14 7/8	6 1/8	6 1/8	6 1/8	Lemhi County	ID	Pat McFadden	1993	724
74 6/8	14 2/8	14 5/8	6 1/8	6 2/8	11 4/8	Johnson County	WY	James E. Taylor	1993	724
74 6/8	14 3/8	14 1/8	6 2/8	6 2/8	12 2/8	Twin Falls County	ID	John Stevens	1994	724
74 6/8	15 1/8	15 4/8	6 0/8	6 1/8	10 3/8	Fergus County	MT	Jerry Knerr	1994	724
74 6/8	14 4/8	13 6/8	6 3/8	6 2/8	9 2/8	Rosebud County	MT	Kyle Zimmerman	1994	724
74 6/8	14 5/8	14 6/8	5 6/8	5 6/8	9 4/8	Owyhee County	ID	Mark K. Rackowitz	1994	724
74 6/8	14 6/8	14 3/8	6 0/8	5 7/8	7 6/8	Broadwater County	MT	Neil Larson	1994	724
74 6/8	14 7/8	14 7/8	6 0/8	6 1/8	12 5/8	Colfax County	NM	Pat Lovato	1995	724
74 6/8	14 4/8	14 5/8	6 0/8	6 0/8	12 6/8	Mercer County	ND	Jim Helling	1995	724
74 6/8	13 4/8	13 3/8	6 2/8	6 0/8	8 2/8	Lincoln County	NV	Michael Zech	1996	724
74 6/8	13 1/8	13 4/8	6 5/8	6 3/8	7 5/8	Weld County	CO	Guy Pierce	1996	724
74 6/8	13 5/8	13 7/8	6 4/8	6 4/8	8 5/8	Campbell County	WY	Dennis W. Klemick	1996	724
74 6/8	14 3/8	14 0/8	6 6/8	6 4/8	12 2/8	Weld County	CO	Guy Pierce	1997	724
74 6/8	14 1/8	14 6/8	6 0/8	6 0/8	10 0/8	Moffat County	CO	Steven R. Hickok	1997	724
74 6/8	13 4/8	13 4/8	6 2/8	6 1/8	11 6/8	Malheur County	OR	Ricky D. Stratton	1997	724
74 6/8	14 5/8	14 6/8	6 4/8	6 4/8	12 1/8	Moffat County	CO	Jerry Douthit	1997	724
74 6/8	14 1/8	14 2/8	6 2/8	6 2/8	8 5/8	Sweetwater County	WY	Paul R. Quayle	1997	724
74 6/8	16 4/8	15 7/8	5 3/8	5 2/8	7 1/8	Yavapai County	AZ	Bruce Felker	1997	724
74 6/8	14 3/8	14 1/8	6 4/8	6 3/8	5 5/8	Carbon County	WY	Steve Torok	1998	724
74 6/8	14 1/8	13 6/8	6 1/8	6 1/8	10 4/8	Musselshell County	MT	Paul S. Black	1998	724
74 6/8	15 1/8	15 3/8	5 4/8	5 4/8	10 4/8	Campbell County	WY	Kenneth Morga	1998	724
74 4/8	14 6/8	14 4/8	6 2/8	6 2/8	12 3/8	Campbell County	WY	William P. Mastrangel	1957	774
74 4/8	15 3/8	15 3/8	6 3/8	6 2/8	11 2/8	Lincoln County	NM	Harvey May	1960	774
74 4/8	14 2/8	14 0/8	6 0/8	6 1/8	12 0/8	Ward County	ND	Bennie Burtts	1964	774
74 4/8	14 1/8	14 0/8	6 6/8	6 5/8	8 7/8	Wheeler County	NE	Lynn M. Briggs	1965	774
74 4/8	13 4/8	13 6/8	7 1/8	7 2/8	8 5/8	Sioux County	NE	Bill Carlos	1969	774
74 4/8	14 0/8	14 2/8	6 4/8	6 4/8	11 5/8	Lyman County	SD	Loran Hills	1970	774
74 4/8	15 4/8	15 2/8	5 6/8	5 6/8	9 7/8	Sweetwater County	WY	Clifford White	1977	774
74 4/8	14 4/8	14 4/8	6 0/8	5 6/8	7 2/8	Logan County	KS	Calvin Henry	1980	774
74 4/8	13 3/8	13 3/8	6 1/8	6 0/8	9 0/8	Moffat County	CO	George Griffiths	1981	774
74 4/8	14 2/8	14 2/8	6 4/8	6 4/8	10 0/8	Baca County	CO	Bill McEndree	1982	774
74 4/8	12 5/8	12 7/8	6 4/8	6 4/8	10 5/8	Arapahoe County	CO	Sid Strzok	1982	774
74 4/8	13 1/8	13 2/8	6 4/8	6 6/8	12 2/8	Pinal County	AZ	Marte Scheuffele	1983	774
74 4/8	13 5/8	13 2/8	6 3/8	6 3/8	12 1/8	Moffat County	CO	Dale Drilling	1985	774
74 4/8	14 1/8	14 5/8	6 1/8	6 2/8	14 4/8	Modoc County	CA	George Taylor	1985	774
74 4/8	14 1/8	13 7/8	5 0/8	5 0/8	9 4/8	Converse County	WY	Ronald M. Cook	1985	774
74 4/8	13 3/8	13 3/8	6 5/8	6 5/8	10 0/8	Sweetwater County	WY	Bill Clink	1986	774
74 4/8	13 3/8	13 3/8	6 4/8	6 4/8	7 4/8	Sweetwater County	WY	Glenn Hisey	1986	774
74 4/8	14 3/8	12 7/8	6 4/8	6 4/8	10 2/8	Carbon County	UT	Don R. Logston	1986	774
74 4/8	14 2/8	14 4/8	6 4/8	6 3/8	15 7/8	Rosebud County	MT	Wayne Pearson	1986	774
74 4/8	15 3/8	15 4/8	6 0/8	6 0/8	8 4/8	Washoe County	NV	Timothy P. Wooley	1987	774
74 4/8	14 4/8	14 4/8	6 0/8	6 0/8	10 2/8	Natrona County	WY	James R. McCain	1988	774
74 4/8	14 4/8	14 4/8	6 4/8	6 3/8	8 6/8	Moffat County	CO	Doy K. Curtis	1988	774
74 4/8	15 0/8	14 6/8	5 7/8	5 7/8	6 5/8	Nye County	NV	Jim Loncar	1989	774
74 4/8	14 0/8	13 7/8	5 7/8	5 7/8	8 1/8	Tooele County	UT	Paul H. Laver	1989	774
74 4/8	14 4/8	15 1/8	6 1/8	6 1/8	14 1/8	Washoe County	NV	Darrel Reed	1990	774
74 4/8	13 5/8	14 0/8	6 7/8	6 7/8	11 4/8	Washoe County	NV	Rick Lund	1990	774
74 4/8	14 2/8	14 1/8	5 7/8	6 0/8	8 1/8	Carbon County	WY	Dennis Bader	1990	774

631

PRONGHORN

Minimum Score 67 — Continued

SCORE	LENGTH OF HORN R	L	CIRCUMFERENCE OF BASE R	L	INSIDE SPREAD	AREA	STATE/PROVINCE	HUNTER'S NAME	DATE	RANK
74 4/8	13 4/8	13 3/8	6 2/8	6 1/8	10 4/8	Yavapai County	AZ	Van Clark	1990	774
74 4/8	15 1/8	15 1/8	5 5/8	5 5/8	13 3/8	Millard County	UT	Tom Stephenson	1991	774
74 4/8	14 1/8	14 3/8	6 2/8	6 2/8	6 7/8	Rosebud County	MT	Rick Miller	1991	774
74 4/8	14 2/8	14 2/8	6 2/8	6 2/8	14 5/8	Toole County	MT	Ryan Winkowitsch	1991	774
74 4/8	13 5/8	13 3/8	6 7/8	6 2/8	9 0/8	Butte County	SD	Gary English	1992	774
74 4/8	13 3/8	13 3/8	6 6/8	6 7/8	10 3/8	Uinta County	WY	Clifford Rockhold	1992	774
74 4/8	15 0/8	15 2/8	6 0/8	6 0/8	10 4/8	Carbon County	WY	Robert E. Bergquist	1992	774
74 4/8	15 0/8	15 0/8	6 0/8	6 1/8	12 3/8	Converse County	WY	A. M. Oakes, Jr.	1992	774
74 4/8	14 2/8	14 0/8	6 3/8	6 3/8	9 7/8	Kimball County	NE	Kevin Matthews	1993	774
74 4/8	14 1/8	14 3/8	6 2/8	6 2/8	8 3/8	Carbon County	WY	Willis Duhon	1993	774
74 4/8	15 7/8	15 4/8	5 5/8	5 4/8	11 0/8	Hudspeth County	TX	Randy Martin	1993	774
74 4/8	14 6/8	13 7/8	6 4/8	6 4/8	18 1/8	Yavapai County	AZ	Patrick Kirby	1994	774
74 4/8	14 4/8	14 4/8	6 2/8	6 2/8	7 6/8	Grand County	UT	MeLinda Schmidt	1994	774
74 4/8	13 3/8	13 3/8	6 1/8	6 0/8	9 5/8	Campbell County	WY	Lee Seeley	1994	774
74 4/8	13 7/8	13 5/8	6 1/8	6 1/8	9 1/8	Moffat County	CO	Michael L. Cone	1995	774
74 4/8	14 6/8	14 7/8	5 6/8	5 6/8	11 0/8	Golden Valley County	ND	Terry Buechler	1995	774
74 4/8	13 7/8	14 0/8	6 2/8	6 1/8	9 7/8	Petroleum County	MT	Mark D. Hughes	1995	774
74 4/8	14 3/8	14 2/8	6 7/8	6 4/8	10 4/8	Huerfano County	CO	George S. Smith III	1995	774
74 4/8	14 2/8	14 0/8	6 1/8	6 1/8	8 1/8	Natrona County	WY	Dale A. Storey	1995	774
74 4/8	14 6/8	14 3/8	6 1/8	6 1/8	12 4/8	Sweetwater County	WY	Paul D. Kauchich	1996	774
74 4/8	13 2/8	13 2/8	6 4/8	6 4/8	9 0/8	Weld County	CO	Neil Chandler	1997	774
74 2/8	13 4/8	13 7/8	5 5/8	5 5/8	8 1/8	Sweet Grass County	MT	Charles Alkire	1964	822
74 2/8	14 5/8	14 6/8	6 3/8	6 2/8	10 3/8	Sioux County	NE	Wayne Scherbarth	1969	822
74 2/8	14 1/8	14 0/8	6 0/8	6 0/8	9 2/8	Moffat County	CO	Bret Thomas Atkins	1981	822
74 2/8	13 2/8	13 2/8	6 7/8	6 7/8	10 2/8	Converse County	WY	Arnie Roytek	1981	822
74 2/8	14 0/8	14 0/8	6 1/8	6 1/8	11 4/8	Carbon County	WY	Scott A. Smith	1981	822
74 2/8	14 6/8	14 4/8	6 0/8	6 1/8	14 7/8	Moffat County	CO	Dennis Heitz	1982	822
74 2/8	14 2/8	14 2/8	5 3/8	5 3/8	8 5/8	Moffat County	CO	Rich Padula	1982	822
74 2/8	13 1/8	13 0/8	6 2/8	6 2/8	7 6/8	Sweetwater County	WY	Keith Dana	1983	822
74 2/8	14 6/8	14 7/8	6 0/8	5 7/8	9 1/8	Graham County	AZ	Jeran E Montierth	1983	822
74 2/8	14 4/8	14 3/8	5 7/8	5 7/8	9 5/8	Union County	NM	Keith Cheatham	1983	822
74 2/8	13 3/8	13 5/8	6 1/8	6 0/8	11 7/8	Converse County	WY	John Ellas	1983	822
74 2/8	12 6/8	14 4/8	6 4/8	6 4/8	12 7/8	Crook County	OR	Garry Rodakowski	1986	822
74 2/8	13 4/8	13 4/8	6 1/8	6 0/8	12 2/8	Moffat County	CO	Tim Decker	1987	822
74 2/8	14 6/8	14 7/8	6 0/8	6 0/8	13 1/8	Sweetwater County	WY	Marty Talbott	1987	822
74 2/8	14 5/8	14 4/8	5 6/8	5 7/8	10 0/8	Cochise County	AZ	Jim Tomlin	1987	822
74 2/8	15 4/8	15 6/8	5 7/8	5 7/8	10 4/8	Eddy County	NM	Jimmy King	1987	822
74 2/8	15 3/8	15 4/8	6 5/8	6 6/8	13 0/8	Rosebud County	MT	Ricky L. Miller	1987	822
74 2/8	13 4/8	13 5/8	6 4/8	6 4/8	9 0/8	Sweetwater County	WY	Brenda Hatcher	1988	822
74 2/8	15 4/8	14 7/8	6 1/8	6 3/8	13 0/8	Natrona County	WY	George A. Fenton	1988	822
74 2/8	14 4/8	14 7/8	6 0/8	6 0/8	9 3/8	Natrona County	WY	Gerry C. Stinski	1988	822
74 2/8	13 5/8	13 5/8	5 7/8	5 6/8	8 3/8	Coconino County	AZ	Jim Wheeler	1989	822
74 2/8	13 6/8	13 6/8	6 1/8	6 1/8	11 0/8	Sweetwater County	WY	Quince Hale	1989	822
74 2/8	14 4/8	14 6/8	6 2/8	6 0/8	11 2/8	Washoe County	NV	Robert D. Jeffers	1990	822
74 2/8	14 6/8	15 0/8	5 6/8	5 5/8	9 2/8	Laramie County	WY	Steve Bellis	1990	822
74 2/8	14 4/8	14 6/8	6 2/8	6 3/8	8 7/8	Rich County	UT	Patrick Hogle	1990	822
74 2/8	15 0/8	15 0/8	6 0/8	6 0/8	10 0/8	Billings County	ND	Todd Winczewski	1990	822
74 2/8	15 0/8	15 0/8	5 7/8	5 6/8	7 7/8	Natrona County	WY	Paul A. Anderson	1990	822
74 2/8	14 0/8	13 5/8	6 3/8	6 3/8	7 6/8	Rich County	UT	Robert G. Petersen	1990	822
74 2/8	12 7/8	12 7/8	6 0/8	6 0/8	12 2/8	Johnson County	WY	Gerald V. Shields	1990	822
74 2/8	14 4/8	14 3/8	5 4/8	5 4/8	8 5/8	Carter County	MT	Jamie Byrne	1990	822
74 2/8	14 2/8	14 5/8	6 2/8	6 0/8	8 2/8	Moffat County	CO	John L. Gardner	1991	822
74 2/8	14 0/8	14 0/8	6 2/8	6 3/8	10 0/8	Moffat County	CO	Michael Dziekan	1991	822
74 2/8	14 1/8	13 6/8	6 3/8	6 3/8	11 6/8	Moffat County	CO	Cary Laman	1991	822
74 2/8	13 7/8	14 0/8	6 4/8	6 2/8	8 2/8	Carbon County	WY	Daniel H. House, Jr.	1991	822
74 2/8	14 0/8	14 1/8	6 2/8	6 2/8	11 0/8	Moffat County	CO	Bruno Ammann	1991	822
74 2/8	14 2/8	14 2/8	5 5/8	5 5/8	9 5/8	Converse County	WY	Gene Mathias	1991	822
74 2/8	15 1/8	15 4/8	5 6/8	5 6/8	16 1/8	Hettinger County	ND	Scott Wiseman	1991	822
74 2/8	15 0/8	14 7/8	5 6/8	5 6/8	7 3/8	Natrona County	WY	Ronald Dean Nelson	1991	822
74 2/8	13 3/8	13 2/8	6 3/8	6 3/8	9 7/8	Laramie County	WY	Jim Krawczyk	1992	822
74 2/8	14 2/8	14 3/8	6 7/8	6 6/8	10 0/8	Natrona County	WY	Gary Morse	1992	822
74 2/8	13 1/8	13 1/8	6 5/8	6 4/8	9 3/8	Weld County	CO	Michael J. McArtor	1992	822
74 2/8	15 3/8	15 3/8	5 3/8	5 2/8	10 0/8	Socorro County	NM	John J. Hayes	1993	822
74 2/8	14 2/8	14 3/8	5 7/8	5 6/8	13 1/8	Moffat County	CO	K-Tal G. Johnson	1993	822
74 2/8	15 0/8	15 1/8	6 0/8	6 3/8	12 2/8	Owyhee County	ID	Jay D. King	1993	822
74 2/8	14 2/8	13 6/8	5 6/8	5 6/8	10 2/8	Nemiscam	ALB	Murray T. Campbell	1993	822
74 2/8	13 2/8	13 3/8	6 0/8	6 0/8	9 0/8	Box Butte County	NE	Richard E. Placzek	1994	822
74 2/8	13 6/8	13 6/8	6 3/8	6 3/8	8 5/8	Campbell County	WY	Dave Justmann	1994	822
74 2/8	14 1/8	14 2/8	5 7/8	5 6/8	10 1/8	Owyhee County	ID	Jason L. Angell	1996	822
74 2/8	16 0/8	16 2/8	5 0/8	4 6/8	8 3/8	Yavapai County	AZ	Mickey Clancy	1996	822
74 2/8	14 0/8	14 2/8	6 4/8	6 4/8	9 5/8	Moffat County	CO	Casey Oliver	1996	822
74 2/8	12 1/8	12 3/8	6 4/8	6 5/8	12 5/8	Lyman County	SD	Kirk C. Graham	1996	822
74 2/8	14 0/8	14 2/8	6 3/8	6 2/8	9 0/8	Moffat County	CO	David L. Butler	1996	822
74 2/8	14 5/8	14 6/8	5 6/8	5 7/8	10 5/8	Lake County	OR	Marte Scheuffele	1996	822
74 2/8	14 1/8	14 3/8	6 1/8	6 1/8	9 0/8	Moffat County	CO	Scott George	1996	822
74 2/8	15 3/8	15 3/8	5 4/8	5 4/8	10 5/8	Pima County	AZ	Michael John Bylina	1997	822
74 2/8	14 6/8	14 7/8	6 0/8	6 0/8	7 7/8	Natrona County	WY	Joel Goodman	1997	822
74 2/8	14 3/8	14 4/8	6 3/8	6 2/8	10 3/8	Albany County	WY	Mark J. Anderson	1998	822

PRONGHORN

Minimum Score 67 — Continued

SCORE	LENGTH OF HORN R	L	CIRCUMFERENCE OF BASE R	L	INSIDE SPREAD	AREA	STATE/ PROVINCE	HUNTER'S NAME	DATE	RANK
74 2/8	14 1/8	14 0/8	5 7/8	5 7/8	12 2/8	Grant County	NM	John H. Trewern	1998	822
74 2/8	13 7/8	14 0/8	5 6/8	5 6/8	8 7/8	Malheur County	OR	Rick Martin	1998	822
74 0/8	14 1/8	13 7/8	6 2/8	6 2/8	9 5/8	Carbon County	WY	James N. Willcox	1977	881
74 0/8	15 2/8	15 5/8	6 2/8	6 3/8	11 4/8	McKinley County	NM	Alfred J. Herrera	1979	881
74 0/8	14 3/8	14 0/8	6 3/8	6 1/8	11 3/8	Jefferson County	ID	Earl Peterson	1980	881
74 0/8	15 0/8	15 1/8	5 5/8	5 5/8	10 5/8	Wallace County	KS	Mike Gilbert	1980	881
74 0/8	16 0/8	15 4/8	5 6/8	5 4/8	8 6/8	Converse County	WY	Frank Moore	1981	881
74 0/8	13 7/8	13 7/8	6 1/8	6 2/8	10 1/8	Moffat County	CO	Randy Sanburg	1981	881
74 0/8	14 5/8	14 4/8	6 4/8	6 2/8	8 6/8	Valley County	MT	Tom Devlin	1984	881
74 0/8	13 4/8	13 3/8	5 7/8	5 6/8	10 4/8	Sweetwater County	WY	Herb Voyles	1985	881
74 0/8	15 1/8	14 6/8	6 1/8	6 1/8	8 4/8	Moffat County	CO	John Cottrell	1986	881
74 0/8	14 1/8	14 0/8	6 4/8	6 4/8	11 7/8	Billings County	ND	Greg Schafer	1986	881
74 0/8	14 2/8	14 3/8	6 2/8	6 0/8	8 7/8	Klamath County	OR	Randall T. Drabandt	1987	881
74 0/8	14 3/8	14 1/8	6 0/8	5 7/8	8 3/8	Moffat County	CO	Bob Bain	1987	881
74 0/8	15 1/8	15 3/8	6 2/8	6 2/8	10 6/8	Sweetwater County	WY	Jackie Simmons	1988	881
74 0/8	14 0/8	13 6/8	5 6/8	5 5/8	11 3/8	Millard County	UT	John G. Homatas	1988	881
74 0/8	15 0/8	14 4/8	6 4/8	6 4/8	8 7/8	Sweetwater County	WY	Norman Lee Bradley	1990	881
74 0/8	14 1/8	13 5/8	6 6/8	6 4/8	12 1/8	Carbon County	WY	Rod Schmidt	1990	881
74 0/8	15 0/8	14 5/8	5 3/8	5 3/8	8 3/8	Moffat County	CO	Glenn Pritchard	1990	881
74 0/8	14 2/8	14 7/8	5 7/8	5 5/8	8 0/8	Carter County	MT	Mark Frank	1990	881
74 0/8	13 1/8	13 2/8	6 4/8	6 3/8	8 5/8	County of 40 Mile	ALB	Brent Van Maarion	1990	881
74 0/8	14 1/8	14 1/8	6 3/8	6 2/8	12 3/8	Sierra County	NM	Peter La Scala	1991	881
74 0/8	14 5/8	14 7/8	6 5/8	6 5/8	9 5/8	Morgan County	UT	Dallas Smith	1991	881
74 0/8	13 1/8	13 4/8	6 5/8	6 4/8	9 3/8	Niobrara County	WY	Tom J. Bruegger	1991	881
74 0/8	13 4/8	13 4/8	6 1/8	6 1/8	7 2/8	Millard County	UT	Craig Bonham	1992	881
74 0/8	14 3/8	13 6/8	6 1/8	6 2/8	10 7/8	Lake County	OR	Rick Breckel	1992	881
74 0/8	14 2/8	14 0/8	6 2/8	6 1/8	10 2/8	Johnson County	WY	Gary L. Miller	1992	881
74 0/8	14 1/8	14 3/8	5 7/8	5 7/8	11 1/8	Converse County	WY	Louis Cinquegrano	1992	881
74 0/8	13 3/8	13 3/8	6 5/8	6 4/8	10 2/8	Sioux County	NE	Roger Dekok	1993	881
74 0/8	14 7/8	15 1/8	5 7/8	5 6/8	9 5/8	Sweetwater County	WY	Bill Clink	1993	881
74 0/8	13 4/8	13 4/8	6 3/8	6 4/8	9 6/8	Johnson County	WY	Gary G. Olson	1993	881
74 0/8	13 6/8	14 0/8	5 7/8	5 7/8	9 1/8	Uintah County	UT	Ron Williams	1994	881
74 0/8	12 6/8	13 0/8	6 6/8	6 6/8	10 2/8	Wallace County	KS	Dale R. Larson	1994	881
74 0/8	13 4/8	13 4/8	6 6/8	6 5/8	7 6/8	Converse County	WY	David L. Miller	1994	881
74 0/8	13 4/8	13 7/8	5 7/8	5 6/8	13 6/8	Converse County	WY	John S. Miller	1994	881
74 0/8	15 4/8	15 6/8	5 5/8	5 5/8	9 7/8	Lincoln County	NM	Ed Whitten	1995	881
74 0/8	15 0/8	14 5/8	6 0/8	6 0/8	13 1/8	Lemhi County	ID	Ben Fahnholz	1995	881
74 0/8	14 0/8	14 3/8	6 0/8	5 7/8	12 0/8	Campbell County	WY	Ryan J. Dorak	1995	881
74 0/8	13 4/8	13 4/8	6 4/8	6 4/8	10 5/8	Moffat County	CO	Jim Halbritter	1996	881
74 0/8	13 2/8	13 3/8	6 1/8	6 0/8	5 6/8	Moffat County	CO	E. Damon Handley	1996	881
74 0/8	15 5/8	15 2/8	5 6/8	5 6/8	8 2/8	Colfax County	NM	Robert L. Pagel, Jr.	1996	881
74 0/8	14 4/8	14 6/8	5 7/8	6 0/8	10 6/8	Moffat County	CO	Dan Hedgecoke	1996	881
74 0/8	13 4/8	15 1/8	6 0/8	6 0/8	11 0/8	Coconino County	AZ	Mark Purcell	1996	881
74 0/8	14 2/8	14 1/8	5 7/8	5 7/8	9 0/8	Natrona County	WY	Richard Manchur	1996	881
74 0/8	13 3/8	13 3/8	7 1/8	7 1/8	11 5/8	Natrona County	WY	Todd C. Braschler	1996	881
74 0/8	13 0/8	13 3/8	6 4/8	6 3/8	10 7/8	Moffat County	CO	Chuck Adams	1997	881
74 0/8	14 5/8	14 0/8	6 1/8	6 1/8	14 6/8	Lea County	NM	John A. Barnes	1997	881
74 0/8	15 4/8	15 3/8	5 7/8	5 6/8	8 4/8	Yavapai County	AZ	Michael Aleff	1997	881
74 0/8	14 6/8	15 4/8	5 7/8	5 7/8	10 1/8	Campbell County	WY	Michael King	1997	881
73 6/8	14 0/8	14 0/8	6 1/8	6 2/8	13 7/8	Williams County	ND	Robert Halseth	1967	928
73 6/8	14 2/8	14 0/8	6 2/8	6 2/8	10 4/8	Sweetwater County	WY	Dan Winder	1973	928
73 6/8	13 4/8	13 3/8	5 6/8	5 6/8	10 5/8	Sweetwater County	WY	Ellen Lewis	1978	928
73 6/8	14 4/8	15 0/8	6 0/8	6 0/8	10 0/8	Sweetwater County	WY	Clifford White	1978	928
73 6/8	14 2/8	14 1/8	6 1/8	6 0/8	7 7/8	Converse County	WY	Charles Stephens	1980	928
73 6/8	14 2/8	14 1/8	6 5/8	6 4/8	8 5/8	Converse County	WY	Don Schram	1982	928
73 6/8	14 4/8	14 7/8	6 0/8	5 7/8	9 3/8	Sweetwater County	WY	Larry J. Aksamit	1983	928
73 6/8	13 4/8	13 4/8	6 2/8	6 2/8	12 2/8	Carbon County	WY	Willis P. Duhon, Jr.	1983	928
73 6/8	13 3/8	13 4/8	6 3/8	6 1/8	10 1/8	Natrona County	WY	John Priday	1983	928
73 6/8	12 7/8	12 7/8	7 0/8	6 7/8	10 7/8	Natrona County	WY	Pat McAteer	1984	928
73 6/8	14 7/8	15 0/8	5 6/8	5 6/8	14 0/8	Custer County	MT	Marty PenRod	1984	928
73 6/8	15 1/8	15 0/8	5 7/8	5 7/8	10 3/8	Moffat County	CO	Lonny Vanatta	1985	928
73 6/8	14 6/8	14 4/8	6 0/8	6 0/8	10 6/8	Moffat County	CO	Kurt Keskimaki	1986	928
73 6/8	13 3/8	13 6/8	6 0/8	6 1/8	8 5/8	Sweetwater County	WY	Ryan Roark	1986	928
73 6/8	14 1/8	13 6/8	6 3/8	6 3/8	10 7/8	McKinley County	NM	Terry L. Sanders	1986	928
73 6/8	14 3/8	14 2/8	6 2/8	6 3/8	8 6/8	Lemhi County	ID	Ben Fahnholz	1987	928
73 6/8	15 4/8	15 1/8	6 0/8	6 1/8	11 1/8	Divide County	ND	Kenneth Engelhart	1987	928
73 6/8	14 2/8	14 1/8	6 1/8	6 1/8	10 6/8	Campbell County	WY	Tamas M. Raday	1988	928
73 6/8	14 7/8	14 6/8	6 2/8	6 2/8	10 4/8	Converse County	WY	Bruce Warburg	1988	928
73 6/8	13 7/8	13 6/8	6 0/8	6 1/8	9 6/8	Campbell County	WY	Nick Hengel	1988	928
73 6/8	14 2/8	14 2/8	5 7/8	5 6/8	11 6/8	Moffat County	CO	Ron Rockwell	1988	928
73 6/8	13 7/8	13 7/8	6 0/8	6 0/8	11 4/8	Converse County	WY	Gary De Smidt	1988	928
73 6/8	14 5/8	15 0/8	6 0/8	6 0/8	11 0/8	Carbon County	WY	Rod Schmidt	1989	928
73 6/8	14 3/8	14 2/8	6 2/8	6 2/8	8 1/8	Washoe County	NV	Gregory G. Koehl	1990	928
73 6/8	14 3/8	14 4/8	6 4/8	6 4/8	8 0/8	Natrona County	WY	Ron Niziolek	1990	928
73 6/8	13 6/8	14 1/8	6 2/8	6 0/8	10 3/8	Moffat County	CO	Ron Serwa	1990	928
73 6/8	14 2/8	14 4/8	5 7/8	5 6/8	9 4/8	Cascade County	MT	Dan Holskey	1990	928
73 6/8	14 1/8	14 1/8	5 6/8	5 7/8	10 3/8	Moffat County	CO	Robert L. Syvertson, Jr.	1991	928
73 6/8	13 7/8	13 7/8	6 2/8	6 1/8	9 3/8	Las Animas County	CO	J. Austin Warfield	1991	928

PRONGHORN

Minimum Score 67

SCORE	LENGTH OF HORN R / L		CIRCUMFERENCE OF BASE R / L		INSIDE SPREAD	AREA	STATE/PROVINCE	HUNTER'S NAME	DATE	RANK
73 6/8	14 7/8	14 5/8	5 5/8	5 5/8	11 2/8	Campbell County	WY	Russ Miller	1991	928
73 6/8	14 1/8	14 1/8	6 1/8	6 0/8	13 2/8	Harney County	OR	Donald R. Paulsen	1991	928
73 6/8	13 7/8	13 7/8	6 1/8	6 1/8	10 7/8	Converse County	WY	Jerry Worley	1991	928
73 6/8	14 6/8	15 0/8	6 1/8	5 7/8	8 1/8	Madison County	MT	Doug Stonebraker	1991	928
73 6/8	14 3/8	14 3/8	5 6/8	5 4/8	10 2/8	Campbell County	WY	Bruce Hudalla	1991	928
73 6/8	15 4/8	15 2/8	5 5/8	5 6/8	8 7/8	Rosebud County	MT	Michael J. Kemp	1991	928
73 6/8	13 4/8	13 4/8	6 1/8	6 1/8	9 0/8	Sheridan County	WY	Gerhard Eimer	1991	928
73 6/8	14 1/8	14 0/8	6 1/8	6 1/8	9 6/8	Uinta County	WY	Joseph D. Maddock	1992	928
73 6/8	14 2/8	13 7/8	6 4/8	6 2/8	7 7/8	Manyberries	ALB	Dale Farn	1992	928
73 6/8	14 6/8	15 4/8	6 4/8	6 4/8	14 4/8	Yavapai County	AZ	Curtis Gregory	1993	928
73 6/8	13 6/8	13 7/8	6 1/8	6 1/8	12 7/8	Jackson County	CO	Richard Bellows	1993	928
73 6/8	13 0/8	13 0/8	6 0/8	6 0/8	10 3/8	Cypress	ALB	Dan David	1993	928
73 6/8	13 5/8	13 2/8	6 2/8	6 3/8	10 3/8	Sweetwater County	WY	Renee A. Dana	1994	928
73 6/8	14 5/8	14 5/8	6 1/8	6 1/8	9 3/8	Custer County	ID	David A. Faike	1994	928
73 6/8	14 0/8	14 0/8	6 4/8	6 3/8	9 4/8	Crook County	WY	Mike Galles	1994	928
73 6/8	15 6/8	15 7/8	5 5/8	5 4/8	12 2/8	Harding County	SD	Al Kuntz	1994	928
73 6/8	14 3/8	14 1/8	5 7/8	5 6/8	10 0/8	Carbon County	WY	Larry Cross	1995	928
73 6/8	13 7/8	13 7/8	6 1/8	6 1/8	12 2/8	Weld County	CO	Jim Tatro	1995	928
73 6/8	15 3/8	15 0/8	5 5/8	5 4/8	7 3/8	Jenner	ALB	Melvin Barr	1995	928
73 6/8	14 5/8	14 5/8	6 3/8	6 1/8	10 0/8	Platte County	WY	Dennis Crew	1995	928
73 6/8	13 7/8	13 4/8	5 6/8	5 6/8	10 6/8	White Pine County	NV	Robert McDonald	1996	928
73 6/8	14 4/8	14 4/8	6 0/8	6 0/8	9 2/8	Elko County	NV	Chief Nutting	1996	928
73 6/8	13 4/8	13 2/8	6 3/8	6 2/8	11 2/8	Moffat County	CO	Jeff LaBaw	1996	928
73 6/8	14 1/8	13 7/8	5 5/8	5 5/8	8 7/8	Converse County	WY	Jeff Haltom	1996	928
73 6/8	13 2/8	13 2/8	5 7/8	5 7/8	7 6/8	Moffat County	CO	Warren Strickland	1997	928
73 6/8	14 4/8	14 5/8	5 6/8	5 4/8	8 6/8	Uintah County	UT	Jerry Dee Slaugh	1998	928
73 6/8	15 0/8	14 6/8	6 5/8	6 2/8	11 7/8	Natrona County	WY	Beth Nelson	1998	928
73 6/8	14 3/8	14 4/8	6 0/8	6 0/8	10 6/8	Weld County	CO	Wesley Peterson	1998	928
73 4/8	15 4/8	15 1/8	5 6/8	5 7/8	8 3/8	Moffat County	CO	Henry Wichers	1957	985
73 4/8	16 0/8	16 4/8	5 6/8	5 6/8	15 6/8	Guadalupe County	NM	Jack McCaw	1961	985
73 4/8	15 7/8	16 0/8	5 7/8	5 6/8	10 5/8	Coconino County	AZ	Charles Meriwether	1968	985
73 4/8	13 0/8	12 5/8	6 1/8	6 2/8	9 4/8	Carbon County	WY	John Marolt III	1971	985
73 4/8	13 0/8	12 6/8	6 1/8	6 6/8	10 7/8	McLean County	ND	Roy O. Yunker	1971	985
73 4/8	13 2/8	13 2/8	6 7/8	6 6/8	10 0/8	Moffat County	CO	Curtis Lynn	1972	985
73 4/8	15 4/8	15 4/8	5 3/8	5 3/8	12 4/8	Natrona County	WY	Mel Johnson	1981	985
73 4/8	14 4/8	14 6/8	6 3/8	6 3/8	8 3/8	Natrona County	WY	Kim S. Ades	1982	985
73 4/8	13 0/8	13 4/8	6 3/8	6 3/8	10 6/8	Sublette County	WY	Terry Reach	1982	985
73 4/8	15 0/8	15 2/8	5 6/8	5 7/8	8 4/8	Val Marie	SAS	Allan Sykes	1982	985
73 4/8	15 4/8	15 4/8	6 0/8	6 1/8	13 2/8	Fremont County	WY	Dan Lookingbill	1983	985
73 4/8	13 7/8	14 1/8	6 2/8	6 3/8	8 6/8	Sweetwater County	WY	Jim Dougherty	1983	985
73 4/8	14 0/8	13 7/8	6 3/8	6 2/8	9 6/8	Weston County	WY	Dick Kinder	1983	985
73 4/8	15 2/8	15 3/8	5 3/8	5 3/8	9 4/8	Prowers County	CO	Lloyd M. Brown	1984	985
73 4/8	15 1/8	15 0/8	5 4/8	5 4/8	9 0/8	Coconino County	AZ	Richard Ball	1985	985
73 4/8	13 7/8	14 2/8	6 1/8	6 0/8	9 7/8	Converse County	WY	Leland E. Scott	1985	985
73 4/8	15 2/8	15 4/8	5 4/8	5 3/8	12 6/8	Lassen County	CA	Richard K. Hoppis	1986	985
73 4/8	14 7/8	14 4/8	6 2/8	6 3/8	12 4/8	Garfield County	MT	John Fleharty	1986	985
73 4/8	14 1/8	14 5/8	6 2/8	6 1/8	7 7/8	Moffat County	CO	Roger Gipple	1986	985
73 4/8	13 6/8	14 2/8	6 0/8	6 0/8	8 3/8	Carbon County	WY	Rod Schmidt	1987	985
73 4/8	14 2/8	14 6/8	6 0/8	6 0/8	7 3/8	Jefferson County	ID	Lonnie Gilson	1988	985
73 4/8	14 4/8	14 1/8	6 1/8	6 0/8	9 1/8	Fremont County	WY	Jim Thieme	1988	985
73 4/8	15 0/8	14 7/8	6 5/8	6 5/8	7 4/8	Campbell County	WY	Jim Keim	1988	985
73 4/8	13 6/8	13 5/8	6 0/8	5 7/8	9 2/8	Carbon County	WY	Larry N. Perkins	1990	985
73 4/8	14 2/8	14 1/8	6 1/8	6 1/8	8 1/8	Moffat County	CO	Michael LaVan	1990	985
73 4/8	15 0/8	14 5/8	6 4/8	6 4/8	10 4/8	Millard County	UT	Robert Quayle	1990	985
73 4/8	14 6/8	14 6/8	6 2/8	6 1/8	13 3/8	White Pine County	NV	Patrick Fillman	1991	985
73 4/8	12 5/8	12 6/8	6 7/8	6 7/8	8 1/8	Campbell County	WY	Elroy Thorson	1991	985
73 4/8	13 1/8	13 4/8	6 0/8	6 2/8	12 0/8	Dunn County	ND	Keith Kaste	1991	985
73 4/8	15 4/8	15 4/8	6 0/8	5 7/8	14 2/8	Harney County	OR	Charles L. Boatman	1991	985
73 4/8	14 6/8	14 6/8	5 6/8	5 6/8	12 5/8	Harney County	OR	Roger Bersin	1991	985
73 4/8	14 2/8	14 2/8	6 0/8	5 7/8	7 5/8	Platte County	WY	John Stienmetz	1991	985
73 4/8	15 2/8	15 3/8	6 0/8	6 0/8	15 7/8	Washoe County	NV	Gregg Tanner	1992	985
73 4/8	15 7/8	15 6/8	5 6/8	5 6/8	12 1/8	Mora County	NM	Doug Aikin	1992	985
73 4/8	14 3/8	14 3/8	6 4/8	6 4/8	7 6/8	Washoe County	NV	Trinidad Guillen	1992	985
73 4/8	13 6/8	13 5/8	6 0/8	6 0/8	12 6/8	Grant County	NM	Senovid Perea	1992	985
73 4/8	13 6/8	13 7/8	6 3/8	6 3/8	8 7/8	Lincoln County	WY	Darrell Hansen	1992	985
73 4/8	15 0/8	15 0/8	5 4/8	5 3/8	10 7/8	Millard County	UT	Steven Jackson	1992	985
73 4/8	13 2/8	13 6/8	5 7/8	6 0/8	9 1/8	Malheur County	OR	Fredrick Johnson	1992	985
73 4/8	13 2/8	13 2/8	6 1/8	6 1/8	9 1/8	Natrona County	WY	Gregory A. Lompart	1992	985
73 4/8	14 3/8	14 2/8	5 7/8	6 2/8	8 3/8	Fremont County	WY	Gerald S. O'Dean	1992	985
73 4/8	13 4/8	14 4/8	6 0/8	6 0/8	8 6/8	Campbell County	WY	Phillip M. Revering	1992	985
73 4/8	14 6/8	14 5/8	6 0/8	5 5/8	10 0/8	Moffat County	CO	Scott Nelson	1993	985
73 4/8	13 1/8	13 4/8	6 7/8	6 7/8	10 2/8	Moffat County	CO	Rett Kelly	1993	985
73 4/8	14 1/8	14 0/8	6 2/8	6 1/8	11 1/8	Rosebud County	MT	Val Dierks	1993	985
73 4/8	15 6/8	16 0/8	6 1/8	6 2/8	10 6/8	Wallace County	KS	Russell Hull	1993	985
73 4/8	14 7/8	12 0/8	7 0/8	6 6/8	7 4/8	Rich County	UT	Hugh H. Hogle	1993	985
73 4/8	14 3/8	15 1/8	6 2/8	6 0/8	10 6/8	Klamath County	OR	Patrick E. Wheeler	1994	985
73 4/8	14 7/8	15 3/8	6 2/8	6 1/8	9 2/8	Weld County	CO	David L. Skiff	1994	985
73 4/8	13 7/8	13 4/8	6 2/8	6 2/8	7 1/8	Converse County	WY	Bock Low	1994	985

PRONGHORN

Minimum Score 67 — Continued

SCORE	LENGTH OF HORN R	L	CIRCUMFERENCE OF BASE R	L	INSIDE SPREAD	AREA	STATE/ PROVINCE	HUNTER'S NAME	DATE	RANK
73 4/8	14 2/8	14 3/8	6 3/8	6 2/8	7 5/8	Clark County	ID	Max Heberling	1995	985
73 4/8	14 5/8	14 5/8	6 0/8	6 0/8	12 0/8	Sweetwater County	WY	Ken Lumpkin	1996	985
73 4/8	14 0/8	13 5/8	6 2/8	6 3/8	10 6/8	Moffat County	CO	Gary Stampka	1996	985
73 4/8	14 1/8	13 7/8	6 3/8	6 3/8	8 5/8	Big Horn County	WY	Rob J. Westby	1996	985
73 4/8	15 2/8	15 1/8	6 0/8	6 0/8	8 6/8	Moffat County	CO	Dave Accashian	1997	985
73 4/8	14 1/8	14 1/8	5 7/8	5 7/8	11 1/8	Grand County	UT	Timothy D. Park	1997	985
73 4/8	14 4/8	14 0/8	5 7/8	5 6/8	10 3/8	Lake County	OR	Donald W. Smith	1997	985
73 4/8	13 4/8	13 4/8	6 1/8	6 1/8	11 5/8	Weld County	CO	Dennis Conran	1997	985
73 4/8	14 1/8	14 0/8	7 2/8	7 0/8	10 7/8	Sweetwater County	WY	Clifford W. Rockhold	1998	985
73 4/8	14 3/8	13 4/8	6 2/8	5 6/8	9 0/8	Campbell County	WY	Curtis C. Stull	1998	985
73 4/8	13 5/8	13 5/8	6 4/8	6 5/8	11 7/8	Converse County	WY	Jason Abel	1998	985
73 2/8	13 0/8	13 1/8	6 6/8	6 4/8	11 3/8	Fremont County	WY	Chuck Kroll	1952	1,046
73 2/8	11 3/8	11 7/8	6 3/8	6 3/8	11 1/8	Carter County	MT	Benny F. Padden	1960	1,046
73 2/8	14 2/8	14 2/8	5 2/8	5 2/8	7 5/8	Fergus County	MT	Wayne Miller	1962	1,046
73 2/8	14 6/8	14 3/8	6 0/8	6 0/8	9 2/8	Garfield County	MT	Paul Brunner	1976	1,046
73 2/8	13 5/8	13 3/8	6 2/8	6 1/8	9 5/8	Converse County	WY	Abe White	1980	1,046
73 2/8	15 2/8	15 2/8	5 5/8	5 5/8	8 3/8	Sweetwater County	WY	Randy Gamble	1982	1,046
73 2/8	15 2/8	15 0/8	5 4/8	5 5/8	9 4/8	Santa Cruz County	AZ	Tracy G. Hardy	1982	1,046
73 2/8	13 3/8	13 5/8	6 2/8	6 2/8	13 3/8	Fremont County	WY	Bill Lookingbill	1982	1,046
73 2/8	13 6/8	13 3/8	6 0/8	6 0/8	12 5/8	Musselshell County	MT	Daniel A. Nielsen	1982	1,046
73 2/8	11 5/8	11 5/8	7 3/8	7 1/8	7 3/8	Siskiyou County	CA	Mike Domeyer	1982	1,046
73 2/8	13 6/8	13 5/8	6 0/8	5 7/8	9 6/8	Natrona County	WY	James I. Shipley, Jr.	1982	1,046
73 2/8	12 7/8	13 2/8	5 7/8	6 0/8	11 0/8	Moffat County	CO	Jack Cassidy	1983	1,046
73 2/8	13 2/8	13 3/8	6 3/8	6 2/8	9 3/8	Moffat County	CO	John W. Rose	1983	1,046
73 2/8	14 2/8	14 4/8	6 1/8	6 1/8	12 1/8	Moffat County	CO	Paul Locey	1983	1,046
73 2/8	15 4/8	17 0/8	6 1/8	6 0/8	9 6/8	Coconino County	AZ	Randy Fix	1983	1,046
73 2/8	13 4/8	14 0/8	5 7/8	6 1/8	10 4/8	Moffat County	CO	Charles B. Lanzarone	1983	1,046
73 2/8	13 7/8	14 0/8	6 2/8	6 2/8	13 4/8	Fremont County	WY	John Priday	1984	1,046
73 2/8	14 4/8	14 3/8	6 4/8	6 3/8	8 7/8	Converse County	WY	Lee Jernigan	1984	1,046
73 2/8	14 2/8	14 4/8	6 1/8	6 1/8	10 0/8	Rosebud County	MT	Greg Munther	1986	1,046
73 2/8	13 4/8	13 6/8	6 3/8	6 3/8	12 2/8	Moffat County	CO	Evans V. Brewster	1986	1,046
73 2/8	14 5/8	15 0/8	6 1/8	6 0/8	15 1/8	Sweetwater County	WY	Harvey L. Dalton	1988	1,046
73 2/8	14 3/8	14 3/8	5 7/8	5 7/8	8 2/8	Converse County	WY	Ron Rockwell	1988	1,046
73 2/8	14 3/8	15 0/8	5 7/8	5 7/8	10 5/8	Washoe County	NV	Larry Burchard	1990	1,046
73 2/8	14 4/8	14 2/8	6 2/8	6 1/8	7 7/8	Abbey	SAS	Clarence Hughes	1990	1,046
73 2/8	14 6/8	14 4/8	6 1/8	6 0/8	11 7/8	Fergus County	MT	Jess Knerr	1990	1,046
73 2/8	13 1/8	13 2/8	6 1/8	6 0/8	9 7/8	Mountrail County	ND	Don Scofield	1990	1,046
73 2/8	13 2/8	13 5/8	6 2/8	6 2/8	10 5/8	Campbell County	WY	Russell Guerndt	1990	1,046
73 2/8	14 4/8	14 3/8	5 6/8	5 6/8	10 3/8	Buffalo	ALB	Roger Meyer	1990	1,046
73 2/8	13 3/8	12 7/8	6 2/8	6 1/8	9 3/8	Musselshell County	MT	Michael James Songer	1990	1,046
73 2/8	14 0/8	13 7/8	6 0/8	5 7/8	11 1/8	Sweetwater County	WY	Norman Lee Bradley	1991	1,046
73 2/8	13 0/8	13 0/8	7 2/8	6 6/8	9 1/8	Converse County	WY	Russ Weakland	1991	1,046
73 2/8	15 1/8	15 2/8	5 7/8	5 7/8	11 4/8	McKenzie County	ND	John H. Holt	1991	1,046
73 2/8	14 4/8	14 6/8	5 6/8	5 7/8	10 2/8	Val Marie	SAS	Steve Von Hagen	1991	1,046
73 2/8	15 3/8	15 1/8	5 7/8	5 6/8	11 6/8	Musselshell County	MT	Keith W. Hice	1991	1,046
73 2/8	13 1/8	13 0/8	6 4/8	6 5/8	11 3/8	Sweetwater County	WY	Jeff Castagna	1992	1,046
73 2/8	13 6/8	13 6/8	6 1/8	6 1/8	12 0/8	Sweetwater County	WY	Fred R. Trujillo	1992	1,046
73 2/8	14 7/8	14 2/8	5 7/8	5 7/8	8 0/8	Moffat County	CO	Anthony Harrison	1992	1,046
73 2/8	15 2/8	15 1/8	6 4/8	6 4/8	7 1/8	Butte County	ID	Troy Dale Green	1992	1,046
73 2/8	13 7/8	14 0/8	6 1/8	6 1/8	11 3/8	Sweetwater County	WY	Richard L. Gasser	1992	1,046
73 2/8	14 0/8	14 4/8	6 4/8	6 4/8	9 6/8	Laramie County	WY	Larry C. Bramich, Jr.	1992	1,046
73 2/8	14 7/8	15 0/8	6 0/8	5 6/8	11 7/8	Jerome County	ID	John Wells	1992	1,046
73 2/8	16 0/8	15 5/8	5 7/8	5 7/8	10 4/8	Sioux County	NE	Orville J. DeVoss	1992	1,046
73 2/8	13 1/8	13 0/8	6 2/8	6 2/8	9 4/8	Rosebud County	MT	Michael J. Kemp	1992	1,046
73 2/8	15 0/8	15 1/8	5 7/8	5 7/8	8 3/8	Converse County	WY	Donna M. Johnson	1992	1,046
73 2/8	13 6/8	13 6/8	6 0/8	5 7/8	8 5/8	Moffat County	CO	Kenneth M. Appelgren	1993	1,046
73 2/8	15 0/8	15 2/8	5 4/8	5 4/8	13 7/8	Eddy County	NM	Adam T. Wortley	1993	1,046
73 2/8	12 7/8	13 0/8	6 2/8	6 2/8	11 2/8	Converse County	WY	Stephen C. Kremp	1993	1,046
73 2/8	14 2/8	14 5/8	6 1/8	6 1/8	10 0/8	Converse County	WY	Mark Zastrow	1993	1,046
73 2/8	14 2/8	14 2/8	6 0/8	5 7/8	11 2/8	Jenner	ALB	Kevin Stewart	1993	1,046
73 2/8	13 4/8	13 2/8	6 3/8	6 3/8	10 0/8	Butte County	ID	Troy Green	1994	1,046
73 2/8	14 4/8	14 2/8	5 6/8	5 6/8	12 0/8	Coconino County	AZ	Paul T. Carter	1994	1,046
73 2/8	14 2/8	14 2/8	6 0/8	6 0/8	9 2/8	Lake County	OR	Mike Jackson	1994	1,046
73 2/8	14 5/8	14 4/8	6 0/8	6 0/8	8 4/8	Campbell County	WY	Richard Lee Collins	1994	1,046
73 2/8	15 4/8	14 7/8	6 1/8	6 1/8	11 2/8	Lake County	OR	Jeffrey A. Eder	1994	1,046
73 2/8	14 2/8	14 1/8	5 7/8	5 7/8	10 3/8	Converse County	WY	Herbert F. Mielke	1994	1,046
73 2/8	13 7/8	14 4/8	6 3/8	6 2/8	9 2/8	Jenner	ALB	Kevin Stewart	1994	1,046
73 2/8	14 3/8	14 2/8	6 0/8	6 2/8	11 1/8	Deuel County	NE	Everett Tarrell	1994	1,046
73 2/8	13 6/8	13 5/8	6 0/8	6 2/8	11 6/8	Beaverhead County	MT	Justin B. Quilling	1994	1,046
73 2/8	14 1/8	13 6/8	6 2/8	6 1/8	7 4/8	Rio Blanco County	CO	Wade Shults	1995	1,046
73 2/8	13 4/8	13 5/8	6 1/8	6 2/8	7 3/8	Twin Falls County	ID	Darrell Nunez	1995	1,046
73 2/8	13 5/8	13 7/8	6 0/8	5 6/8	9 7/8	Fergus County	MT	Chris Sanford	1995	1,046
73 2/8	13 6/8	14 0/8	6 1/8	5 6/8	8 0/8	Campbell County	WY	Derek J. Green	1995	1,046
73 2/8	14 5/8	15 1/8	5 7/8	6 0/8	7 5/8	Sheridan County	WY	Thomas Ostrander	1995	1,046
73 2/8	14 6/8	13 7/8	6 1/8	6 0/8	12 4/8	Carter County	MT	Scott Garner	1995	1,046
73 2/8	14 1/8	13 5/8	6 1/8	6 0/8	7 6/8	Converse County	WY	Don Miller	1995	1,046
73 2/8	14 0/8	13 7/8	6 1/8	6 2/8	10 2/8	Moffat County	CO	Bud Boker	1996	1,046
73 2/8	14 7/8	15 0/8	5 5/8	5 6/8	12 1/8	Gunnison County	CO	George H. Bock	1996	1,046

PRONGHORN

Minimum Score 67 — Continued

SCORE	LENGTH OF HORN R / L		CIRCUMFERENCE OF BASE R / L		INSIDE SPREAD	AREA	STATE/ PROVINCE	HUNTER'S NAME	DATE	RANK
73 2/8	13 6/8	13 7/8	6 7/8	6 5/8	9 7/8	Converse County	WY	Ralph M. Inverso	1996	1,046
73 2/8	13 5/8	13 6/8	6 1/8	5 7/8	10 0/8	Moffat County	CO	Bob Gulliksen	1997	1,046
73 2/8	14 5/8	15 0/8	6 3/8	6 3/8	10 1/8	Moffat County	CO	Ron Lightley	1997	1,046
73 2/8	13 5/8	13 3/8	6 4/8	6 4/8	12 3/8	Weld County	CO	Lynn Reese	1997	1,046
73 2/8	14 3/8	14 1/8	6 3/8	6 2/8	12 1/8	Campbell County	WY	John A. Meyen	1997	1,046
73 2/8	16 0/8	15 1/8	6 0/8	5 6/8	9 0/8	Yavapai County	AZ	Nathan Shane Garcia	1998	1,046
73 2/8	14 4/8	14 3/8	6 3/8	6 2/8	13 3/8	Brown County	NE	Wade Luther	1998	1,046
73 2/8	14 5/8	15 0/8	6 1/8	6 0/8	10 7/8	El Paso County	CO	Gene Pask	1998	1,046
73 0/8	13 5/8	13 5/8	5 3/8	5 3/8	9 6/8	Harding County	SD	Ted G. Carter	1961	1,121
73 0/8	12 7/8	12 6/8	6 2/8	6 3/8	11 7/8	Stark County	ND	Ronald D. Hauck	1970	1,121
73 0/8	15 1/8	14 6/8	6 1/8	6 1/8	7 1/8	Converse County	WY	Ed Coy	1976	1,121
73 0/8	14 0/8	14 2/8	5 4/8	5 4/8	11 6/8	Moffat County	CO	Fred Cornish	1980	1,121
73 0/8	14 4/8	13 5/8	6 0/8	5 7/8	8 4/8	Klamath County	OR	Tom Tipton	1981	1,121
73 0/8	13 7/8	13 7/8	6 3/8	6 2/8	11 0/8	Rosebud County	MT	Dan Helm	1982	1,121
73 0/8	14 1/8	13 2/8	6 5/8	6 5/8	9 1/8	Sioux County	NE	Dick Kohles	1983	1,121
73 0/8	13 5/8	13 7/8	5 6/8	5 6/8	7 6/8	Converse County	WY	Edward Oswald	1983	1,121
73 0/8	13 4/8	13 4/8	6 1/8	6 0/8	11 2/8	Sweetwater County	WY	Marty Stubstad	1985	1,121
73 0/8	14 1/8	13 7/8	5 5/8	5 5/8	9 6/8	Yavapai County	AZ	Christopher R. Jackson	1985	1,121
73 0/8	14 7/8	12 6/8	6 0/8	10 1/8	9 1/8	Coconino County	AZ	Todd Rice	1987	1,121
73 0/8	15 3/8	15 2/8	5 4/8	5 4/8	8 2/8	Blaine County	ID	Bruce McStay	1988	1,121
73 0/8	13 2/8	13 4/8	6 4/8	6 2/8	10 6/8	Moffat County	CO	Garret Decker	1988	1,121
73 0/8	16 0/8	16 0/8	5 3/8	5 5/8	12 0/8	Coconino County	AZ	Gary Steinmann	1988	1,121
73 0/8	15 0/8	15 2/8	5 4/8	5 4/8	11 2/8	Converse County	WY	James Gates	1988	1,121
73 0/8	14 1/8	14 2/8	6 0/8	6 0/8	10 6/8	Sargent County	ND	Dennis Wheeler	1988	1,121
73 0/8	14 2/8	14 4/8	6 1/8	5 5/8	11 7/8	Washoe County	NV	Daryl Salley	1989	1,121
73 0/8	13 5/8	13 7/8	5 7/8	5 7/8	8 6/8	Moffat County	CO	James Phelps	1989	1,121
73 0/8	14 0/8	13 6/8	6 1/8	6 1/8	8 1/8	Sweetwater County	WY	David Urasky	1989	1,121
73 0/8	15 0/8	15 1/8	5 6/8	5 6/8	12 0/8	Sublette County	WY	David Seaver	1989	1,121
73 0/8	14 6/8	14 1/8	6 0/8	6 2/8	10 5/8	Sioux County	NE	David Clancy	1989	1,121
73 0/8	15 4/8	15 0/8	5 5/8	5 5/8	14 7/8	Washoe County	NV	Jeffrey M. Kovac	1990	1,121
73 0/8	13 3/8	13 5/8	6 4/8	6 5/8	9 5/8	Fremont County	WY	Gary Laya	1990	1,121
73 0/8	13 1/8	13 3/8	5 7/8	6 1/8	8 2/8	Millard County	UT	Michael Pietropaolo	1990	1,121
73 0/8	13 5/8	13 4/8	5 6/8	5 6/8	7 1/8	Lake County	OR	Rodney W. Ferry	1990	1,121
73 0/8	14 0/8	13 5/8	5 7/8	5 7/8	7 6/8	Natrona County	WY	Greg Downs	1990	1,121
73 0/8	14 1/8	14 4/8	6 2/8	6 2/8	13 4/8	Lassen County	CA	Stan Xavier	1991	1,121
73 0/8	15 2/8	15 1/8	6 0/8	6 0/8	9 2/8	Rich County	UT	Hugh H. Hogle	1991	1,121
73 0/8	13 0/8	13 0/8	6 2/8	6 2/8	8 6/8	Converse County	WY	Wayne Nicholson	1991	1,121
73 0/8	15 0/8	15 1/8	5 7/8	5 6/8	7 2/8	Sioux County	NE	Dave Wray	1991	1,121
73 0/8	14 1/8	14 2/8	6 6/8	6 5/8	8 1/8	Owyhee County	ID	Sam Wells	1992	1,121
73 0/8	14 6/8	14 4/8	6 4/8	6 4/8	6 5/8	Twin Falls County	ID	Derek Trent	1992	1,121
73 0/8	13 4/8	13 4/8	6 5/8	6 6/8	11 2/8	Sweetwater County	WY	Neil E. Hanson	1992	1,121
73 0/8	15 2/8	15 0/8	5 5/8	5 5/8	11 3/8	Converse County	WY	Florentino G. Escobedo	1992	1,121
73 0/8	13 4/8	13 2/8	6 2/8	6 3/8	9 3/8	Converse County	WY	Jon Brockfeld	1992	1,121
73 0/8	13 1/8	13 2/8	6 1/8	6 1/8	8 0/8	Carbon County	WY	Joe Parziale	1993	1,121
73 0/8	14 1/8	14 1/8	6 2/8	6 0/8	12 6/8	Sweetwater County	WY	Mike Barrett	1993	1,121
73 0/8	13 7/8	13 7/8	5 6/8	5 6/8	11 1/8	Billings County	ND	Ron Feland	1993	1,121
73 0/8	15 6/8	13 5/8	5 7/8	5 7/8	12 6/8	Hudspeth County	TX	Craig Baird	1993	1,121
73 0/8	14 1/8	14 1/8	5 6/8	5 7/8	9 2/8	Klamath County	OR	Jason Townsend	1994	1,121
73 0/8	13 3/8	13 3/8	6 4/8	6 4/8	8 7/8	Converse County	WY	George A. Zanoni	1994	1,121
73 0/8	13 7/8	14 1/8	5 6/8	5 6/8	8 2/8	Medicine Hat	ALB	David W. Stuhr	1994	1,121
73 0/8	14 7/8	13 4/8	6 4/8	6 4/8	7 6/8	Campbell County	WY	Kathy M. Patrone	1994	1,121
73 0/8	13 1/8	13 4/8	6 1/8	6 0/8	9 6/8	Moffat County	CO	Bob Hoaglin, Jr.	1995	1,121
73 0/8	14 4/8	14 3/8	5 6/8	5 6/8	10 1/8	Albany County	WY	Stuart Hazard	1995	1,121
73 0/8	13 4/8	13 4/8	6 6/8	6 5/8	12 4/8	Converse County	WY	Frank S. Noska IV	1995	1,121
73 0/8	13 4/8	13 0/8	5 7/8	6 0/8	9 2/8	Wallace County	KS	Kent Hensley	1995	1,121
73 0/8	13 6/8	13 6/8	6 1/8	6 1/8	9 2/8	Lincoln County	WY	Doug Jenkins	1996	1,121
73 0/8	14 2/8	14 4/8	6 0/8	6 0/8	12 4/8	Coconino County	AZ	Glen Whited	1996	1,121
73 0/8	14 3/8	14 2/8	6 0/8	6 0/8	9 6/8	Natrona County	WY	Brian L. Wagner	1996	1,121
73 0/8	14 1/8	14 3/8	6 4/8	6 3/8	9 6/8	Campbell County	WY	Dan W. Collins	1996	1,121
73 0/8	13 7/8	14 1/8	6 0/8	6 0/8	10 1/8	Dunn County	ND	Troy A. Morris	1996	1,121
73 0/8	15 1/8	15 0/8	6 0/8	6 0/8	9 1/8	Socorro County	NM	Lucas Robbins	1997	1,121
73 0/8	13 2/8	13 2/8	6 5/8	6 3/8	10 5/8	Saguache County	CO	Alan R. Palmer	1997	1,121
73 0/8	13 6/8	13 7/8	6 2/8	6 1/8	11 3/8	Beaverhead County	MT	Colleen Rose	1998	1,121
72 6/8	14 3/8	14 2/8	6 0/8	6 0/8	8 0/8	Washoe County	NV	Lawrence Heward	1973	1,176
72 6/8	12 1/8	12 1/8	6 6/8	6 6/8	10 6/8	Natrona County	WY	Dennis Spawn	1974	1,176
72 6/8	15 1/8	14 6/8	5 6/8	5 7/8	9 2/8	Carbon County	WY	I. C. Benjamin	1976	1,176
72 6/8	14 0/8	14 1/8	5 6/8	5 7/8	10 7/8	Washoe County	NV	Ritchard E. Golden	1977	1,176
72 6/8	12 1/8	11 6/8	6 7/8	6 7/8	9 1/8	Moffat County	CO	Dwight D. Greenwell	1980	1,176
72 6/8	13 2/8	13 2/8	6 2/8	6 3/8	12 4/8	Moffat County	CO	Albert Ahlrich	1981	1,176
72 6/8	14 0/8	14 0/8	5 6/8	5 6/8	14 6/8	Converse County	WY	Jack Cassidy	1981	1,176
72 6/8	13 5/8	13 2/8	5 6/8	5 4/8	7 1/8	Moffat County	CO	Lyle Willmarth	1981	1,176
72 6/8	14 5/8	14 5/8	5 7/8	5 5/8	8 0/8	Washoe County	NV	Gary Furman	1982	1,176
72 6/8	13 3/8	13 4/8	6 3/8	6 2/8	11 3/8	Moffat County	CO	Thomas H. States	1982	1,176
72 6/8	13 4/8	13 6/8	5 7/8	5 7/8	9 5/8	Hettinger County	ND	Jeff Watne	1983	1,176
72 6/8	14 0/8	13 6/8	6 0/8	6 0/8	7 0/8	Moffat County	CO	Jim Dougherty	1983	1,176
72 6/8	14 0/8	14 0/8	6 2/8	6 1/8	9 0/8	Converse County	WY	Willis Chapman	1983	1,176
72 6/8	14 6/8	15 1/8	5 6/8	5 6/8	9 0/8	Duchesne County	UT	Delos W. 'Sonny' Kempton	1984	1,176
72 6/8	14 0/8	14 1/8	5 7/8	5 7/8	7 1/8	Natrona County	WY	Dorian Gilbert	1985	1,176

PRONGHORN

Minimum Score 67

SCORE	LENGTH OF HORN R / L		CIRCUMFERENCE OF BASE R / L		INSIDE SPREAD	AREA	STATE/ PROVINCE	HUNTER'S NAME	DATE	RANK
72 6/8	13 7/8	13 7/8	5 7/8	6 0/8	13 5/8	Yavapai County	AZ	Richard S. Jones	1985	1,176
72 6/8	13 6/8	13 7/8	6 1/8	6 0/8	11 7/8	Washington County	CO	Randy Fassler	1986	1,176
72 6/8	14 1/8	14 2/8	6 4/8	6 3/8	10 5/8	Fergus County	MT	Daniel R. Vogl	1986	1,176
72 6/8	12 7/8	12 7/8	6 1/8	6 0/8	10 1/8	Coconino County	AZ	Phillip K. Hugh	1987	1,176
72 6/8	14 0/8	14 0/8	5 4/8	5 3/8	8 4/8	Wheatland County	MT	Bob Radocy	1988	1,176
72 6/8	15 0/8	15 0/8	5 7/8	5 6/8	9 2/8	Mountrail County	ND	Todd Boechler	1988	1,176
72 6/8	14 4/8	15 3/8	6 0/8	6 0/8	10 3/8	Sublette County	WY	Steven Hill	1989	1,176
72 6/8	14 5/8	14 2/8	6 0/8	6 0/8	8 3/8	Meagher County	MT	D. Mitch Kottas	1989	1,176
72 6/8	13 7/8	13 7/8	5 7/8	5 6/8	11 0/8	Moffat County	CO	Ralph Compton	1990	1,176
72 6/8	12 3/8	12 4/8	5 6/8	5 6/8	11 3/8	Moffat County	CO	Gary Biles	1990	1,176
72 6/8	14 4/8	14 0/8	6 0/8	6 0/8	9 2/8	Moffat County	CO	Dave Palonis	1990	1,176
72 6/8	13 2/8	13 3/8	6 0/8	6 0/8	13 0/8	Moffat County	CO	Pat Grogan	1990	1,176
72 6/8	13 7/8	14 0/8	6 0/8	6 1/8	11 7/8	Moffat County	CO	Ron Rockwell	1990	1,176
72 6/8	14 3/8	14 3/8	5 7/8	5 6/8	6 2/8	Campbell County	WY	Gary DeSmidt	1990	1,176
72 6/8	13 3/8	13 3/8	6 2/8	6 1/8	12 4/8	Sweet Grass County	MT	Dr. Dale Schlehuber	1990	1,176
72 6/8	14 0/8	13 3/8	5 7/8	5 6/8	9 2/8	Natrona County	WY	Kim Cooper	1990	1,176
72 6/8	15 3/8	15 2/8	5 6/8	5 6/8	11 6/8	Elko County	NV	Jimmie Rebich	1991	1,176
72 6/8	15 1/8	15 0/8	5 5/8	5 4/8	13 1/8	Box Elder County	UT	Henry O. Davies	1991	1,176
72 6/8	14 0/8	13 6/8	6 0/8	5 7/8	8 7/8	Campbell County	WY	Mark Yelken	1991	1,176
72 6/8	13 6/8	13 6/8	6 0/8	6 0/8	8 0/8	Sheridan County	WY	Michael Briganti	1991	1,176
72 6/8	14 0/8	14 4/8	6 2/8	6 3/8	8 7/8	Beaverhead County	MT	Neal Davis	1991	1,176
72 6/8	14 2/8	14 3/8	6 6/8	6 5/8	7 5/8	Crook County	WY	John A. Bogucki	1991	1,176
72 6/8	14 0/8	14 0/8	5 7/8	6 0/8	9 7/8	Humboldt County	NV	Tim Iveson	1992	1,176
72 6/8	13 3/8	13 0/8	6 1/8	6 0/8	11 2/8	Sweetwater County	WY	Clayton "Karl" Knudsen	1992	1,176
72 6/8	13 2/8	13 1/8	6 5/8	6 7/8	13 0/8	Laramie County	WY	Wayne Mackey	1992	1,176
72 6/8	13 5/8	13 6/8	5 6/8	5 6/8	9 6/8	Crook County	WY	Chuck Mead	1992	1,176
72 6/8	13 7/8	13 3/8	5 7/8	5 6/8	10 6/8	Weld County	CO	James L. Tatro	1992	1,176
72 6/8	12 5/8	12 4/8	5 7/8	5 6/8	8 7/8	Converse County	WY	Donald Paul Charpentier	1992	1,176
72 6/8	14 3/8	14 5/8	5 5/8	5 5/8	8 1/8	Fall River County	SD	Bill Lynch	1992	1,176
72 6/8	13 4/8	13 5/8	6 0/8	6 1/8	11 5/8	Converse County	WY	John W. Flies	1992	1,176
72 6/8	13 6/8	13 6/8	6 2/8	6 1/8	8 6/8	Rosebud County	MT	Walter J. Palmer	1992	1,176
72 6/8	13 2/8	13 2/8	6 6/8	6 6/8	11 1/8	Slope County	ND	Rick A. Schaeffer	1992	1,176
72 6/8	14 3/8	14 4/8	6 2/8	6 2/8	8 6/8	Albany County	WY	Jack Satterfield, Jr.	1992	1,176
72 6/8	14 3/8	14 6/8	5 6/8	5 6/8	9 5/8	Yellowstone County	MT	Tom Wulfekuhle	1992	1,176
72 6/8	12 2/8	13 0/8	6 7/8	6 7/8	8 1/8	Campbell County	WY	Suzy Smith	1992	1,176
72 6/8	13 0/8	12 4/8	6 6/8	6 6/8	8 4/8	Fremont County	WY	Chris Ruys	1993	1,176
72 6/8	13 2/8	13 1/8	6 3/8	6 3/8	10 4/8	Campbell County	WY	John S. Shields	1993	1,176
72 6/8	15 3/8	15 7/8	5 6/8	5 6/8	8 6/8	Estevan	SAS	Garry Leslie	1993	1,176
72 6/8	14 2/8	14 2/8	6 3/8	6 2/8	8 7/8	Albany County	WY	Ron Books, Sr.	1994	1,176
72 6/8	13 0/8	13 0/8	6 5/8	6 6/8	10 3/8	Moffat County	CO	Jasen Decker	1994	1,176
72 6/8	13 0/8	13 1/8	6 4/8	6 3/8	10 1/8	Moffat County	CO	Eugene Ray, Sr.	1994	1,176
72 6/8	13 6/8	13 7/8	6 0/8	6 0/8	11 2/8	Moffat County	CO	Joel A. Anderson	1994	1,176
72 6/8	15 4/8	15 2/8	5 4/8	5 4/8	14 0/8	Chaves County	NM	John B. Bright	1994	1,176
72 6/8	13 7/8	14 0/8	6 2/8	6 1/8	10 3/8	Campbell County	WY	Grant Telleri	1994	1,176
72 6/8	13 3/8	13 3/8	6 1/8	6 1/8	11 5/8	Powder River County	MT	Don G. Scofield	1994	1,176
72 6/8	13 3/8	13 5/8	5 5/8	5 6/8	8 1/8	Converse County	WY	Kevin Schmieg	1994	1,176
72 6/8	12 5/8	12 6/8	6 2/8	6 0/8	11 4/8	Cheyenne County	NE	Michael McCallister	1994	1,176
72 6/8	14 4/8	14 5/8	5 7/8	5 7/8	7 6/8	Rio Arriba County	NM	Len Cardinale	1995	1,176
72 6/8	14 6/8	14 6/8	5 4/8	5 5/8	10 3/8	Platte County	WY	Tim Millikin	1995	1,176
72 6/8	13 3/8	13 3/8	5 7/8	6 0/8	11 6/8	Moffat County	CO	Dean Gribble	1997	1,176
72 6/8	15 0/8	15 2/8	5 4/8	5 2/8	10 5/8	Chaves County	NM	Douglas R. Johnson	1997	1,176
72 6/8	14 0/8	14 2/8	6 3/8	6 1/8	8 2/8	Moffat County	CO	Brad Herman	1997	1,176
72 6/8	14 1/8	14 2/8	6 2/8	6 1/8	10 1/8	Yavapai County	AZ	Dan Kasprzyk	1997	1,176
72 6/8	13 5/8	14 0/8	6 1/8	6 1/8	14 4/8	Navajo County	AZ	William C. Bolt, Jr.	1997	1,176
72 6/8	13 3/8	13 6/8	6 3/8	6 0/8	12 4/8	Converse County	WY	Douglas Edward Colle	1997	1,176
72 6/8	13 4/8	13 2/8	5 7/8	5 7/8	9 7/8	Moffat County	CO	Brad Suitts	1997	1,176
72 6/8	13 2/8	13 4/8	5 6/8	5 5/8	9 7/8	Malheur County	OR	Randy Ashcraft	1997	1,176
72 6/8	14 6/8	14 5/8	5 7/8	6 0/8	8 6/8	Crook County	WY	Terry Gordon	1997	1,176
72 6/8	12 4/8	12 4/8	6 3/8	6 2/8	7 7/8	Big Horn County	WY	Don Davidson, Jr.	1998	1,176
72 6/8	12 4/8	12 3/8	6 1/8	6 1/8	7 5/8	Grand County	UT	Cori L. McClellan	1998	1,176
72 6/8	14 2/8	14 3/8	6 3/8	6 2/8	11 1/8	Petroleum County	MT	Mark D. Hughes	1998	1,176
72 4/8	13 6/8	13 5/8	7 0/8	7 3/8	9 4/8	Meade County	SD	Wallace C. Neville	1977	1,252
72 4/8	14 3/8	14 2/8	6 0/8	6 0/8	8 4/8	Jefferson County	ID	Kenny Peterson	1980	1,252
72 4/8	15 4/8	15 4/8	5 5/8	5 2/8	9 0/8	Converse County	WY	Joseph F. Scheuerman	1982	1,252
72 4/8	13 6/8	13 3/8	5 7/8	5 7/8	8 1/8	Natrona County	WY	Gilbert Clement	1983	1,252
72 4/8	13 7/8	13 6/8	5 5/8	5 4/8	10 4/8	Carbon County	WY	Jerome Deaven	1983	1,252
72 4/8	13 2/8	13 3/8	6 4/8	6 4/8	11 5/8	Natrona County	WY	Tony Lanzarone	1983	1,252
72 4/8	13 7/8	14 0/8	5 7/8	5 6/8	8 3/8	Converse County	WY	Lee Jernigan	1983	1,252
72 4/8	13 1/8	13 1/8	6 0/8	5 7/8	8 2/8	Moffat County	CO	Holt Dougherty	1984	1,252
72 4/8	15 2/8	14 0/8	6 1/8	6 1/8	11 3/8	Modoc County	CA	Tim Sayer	1986	1,252
72 4/8	14 6/8	14 3/8	5 7/8	5 7/8	8 2/8	Sweetwater County	WY	Kirby Warnock	1986	1,252
72 4/8	12 7/8	12 3/8	6 4/8	6 2/8	10 5/8	Lemhi County	ID	Matt March, Jr.	1986	1,252
72 4/8	13 3/8	13 3/8	6 2/8	6 0/8	9 3/8	Fremont County	WY	John Lemke	1986	1,252
72 4/8	13 5/8	13 5/8	6 3/8	6 2/8	7 5/8	Moffat County	CO	Terry Weimer	1987	1,252
72 4/8	13 7/8	13 7/8	6 2/8	6 1/8	9 4/8	Moffat County	CO	Judd Cooney	1987	1,252
72 4/8	13 6/8	13 4/8	5 7/8	5 7/8	9 5/8	Sweetwater County	WY	Stan Godfrey	1987	1,252
72 4/8	14 3/8	14 6/8	5 7/8	6 1/8	12 6/8	Petroleum County	MT	D. Mitch Kottas	1987	1,252
72 4/8	14 1/8	13 1/8	6 3/8	6 3/8	6 3/8	Rosebud County	MT	Vic Riggs	1987	1,252

PRONGHORN

Minimum Score 67 — Continued

SCORE	LENGTH OF HORN R / L	CIRCUMFERENCE OF BASE R / L	INSIDE SPREAD	AREA	STATE/PROVINCE	HUNTER'S NAME	DATE	RANK
72 4/8	14 3/8 / 14 0/8	5 3/8 / 5 7/8	16 0/8	Clark County	ID	Shane Bird	1988	1,252
72 4/8	15 6/8 / 15 4/8	6 2/8 / 6 1/8	15 6/8	Converse County	WY	Frank Moore	1988	1,252
72 4/8	13 4/8 / 13 2/8	5 5/8 / 5 4/8	7 4/8	Navajo County	AZ	Mike D. Meyer	1989	1,252
72 4/8	14 6/8 / 14 6/8	6 1/8 / 6 1/8	10 0/8	Stewart Valley	SAS	Sean Ferguson	1989	1,252
72 4/8	14 3/8 / 14 1/8	5 3/8 / 5 3/8	9 6/8	Yavapai County	AZ	Daniel J. Hellman	1989	1,252
72 4/8	14 6/8 / 14 5/8	5 3/8 / 5 3/8	12 5/8	Las Animas County	CO	Bill Swift	1989	1,252
72 4/8	15 5/8 / 15 3/8	5 5/8 / 5 5/8	8 6/8	Natrona County	WY	Michael Ryan	1989	1,252
72 4/8	14 0/8 / 13 6/8	5 7/8 / 5 6/8	11 0/8	Sweetwater County	WY	Bryan Radakovich	1990	1,252
72 4/8	14 1/8 / 13 3/8	6 4/8 / 6 3/8	10 7/8	Sweetwater County	WY	Ted Williams	1990	1,252
72 4/8	14 4/8 / 13 4/8	5 6/8 / 5 5/8	10 2/8	Natrona County	WY	John Comstock, Jr.	1990	1,252
72 4/8	14 0/8 / 14 1/8	5 7/8 / 6 0/8	5 5/8	Washoe County	NV	Terrie Powning	1991	1,252
72 4/8	13 5/8 / 14 2/8	6 3/8 / 6 3/8	12 2/8	Sweetwater County	WY	George R. Koebel	1991	1,252
72 4/8	13 1/8 / 12 7/8	5 6/8 / 5 6/8	9 4/8	Weld County	CO	Bruce Butterworth	1991	1,252
72 4/8	14 2/8 / 14 0/8	5 7/8 / 5 7/8	11 4/8	Campbell County	WY	Jim Reints	1991	1,252
72 4/8	14 0/8 / 14 2/8	6 0/8 / 5 7/8	10 1/8	Natrona County	WY	Gerald Gay	1991	1,252
72 4/8	13 7/8 / 14 1/8	5 2/8 / 5 3/8	8 4/8	Converse County	WY	Bruce R. Schoeneweis	1991	1,252
72 4/8	15 0/8 / 15 0/8	5 3/8 / 5 2/8	6 5/8	Converse County	WY	Kenneth D. Musgrove	1991	1,252
72 4/8	14 3/8 / 14 3/8	5 7/8 / 5 6/8	9 4/8	Sioux County	NE	Steve Leichleiter	1991	1,252
72 4/8	14 5/8 / 15 0/8	5 7/8 / 5 7/8	10 0/8	Rosebud County	MT	Gene A. Welle	1991	1,252
72 4/8	14 0/8 / 14 4/8	5 5/8 / 5 6/8	10 6/8	Stark County	ND	Randy A. Heitz	1991	1,252
72 4/8	12 6/8 / 12 7/8	6 2/8 / 6 4/8	9 3/8	Sioux County	NE	Lyle Prell	1991	1,252
72 4/8	13 3/8 / 12 6/8	6 7/8 / 6 7/8	11 5/8	Rich County	UT	Hal Stauff	1991	1,252
72 4/8	14 1/8 / 13 7/8	5 7/8 / 5 7/8	14 7/8	Humboldt County	NV	Tony Reinolds	1992	1,252
72 4/8	13 7/8 / 13 7/8	5 5/8 / 5 5/8	9 3/8	Elko County	NV	Jeremy Loncar	1992	1,252
72 4/8	13 2/8 / 13 0/8	6 3/8 / 6 2/8	10 0/8	Weld County	CO	Scott Butterworth	1992	1,252
72 4/8	13 3/8 / 13 3/8	6 7/8 / 6 5/8	9 6/8	Twin Falls County	ID	Ron Klimes	1992	1,252
72 4/8	13 4/8 / 13 3/8	6 3/8 / 6 2/8	7 6/8	Moffat County	CO	Chuck Adams	1993	1,252
72 4/8	12 6/8 / 13 0/8	5 7/8 / 6 0/8	7 6/8	Box Elder County	UT	Scott Payne	1993	1,252
72 4/8	15 2/8 / 14 7/8	6 1/8 / 6 0/8	8 6/8	Coconino County	AZ	Dan Turner	1993	1,252
72 4/8	13 4/8 / 13 6/8	6 3/8 / 6 4/8	9 0/8	Hot Springs County	WY	Richard Wormington	1993	1,252
72 4/8	14 4/8 / 14 5/8	6 0/8 / 6 0/8	8 1/8	Johnson County	WY	Charles H. Sagner	1993	1,252
72 4/8	13 3/8 / 13 3/8	6 0/8 / 6 0/8	9 2/8	Moffat County	CO	Roger Stewart	1994	1,252
72 4/8	14 1/8 / 14 1/8	6 2/8 / 6 1/8	9 5/8	Jackson County	CO	Paul Martin	1994	1,252
72 4/8	13 0/8 / 13 0/8	6 2/8 / 6 0/8	10 3/8	Campbell County	WY	Ritch A. Stolpe	1994	1,252
72 4/8	14 3/8 / 14 3/8	5 5/8 / 5 5/8	10 0/8	Converse County	WY	Dale A. Storey	1994	1,252
72 4/8	14 2/8 / 14 2/8	6 2/8 / 6 2/8	10 5/8	Laramie County	WY	Dave Gregory	1994	1,252
72 4/8	13 2/8 / 13 1/8	6 3/8 / 6 2/8	11 2/8	Sweetwater County	WY	Roger Wintle	1995	1,252
72 4/8	14 1/8 / 14 0/8	5 2/8 / 5 2/8	11 2/8	Socorro County	NM	Joel R. Mills	1995	1,252
72 4/8	13 1/8 / 13 2/8	6 5/8 / 6 3/8	9 4/8	Lincoln County	WY	Scott Hesterly	1995	1,252
72 4/8	14 0/8 / 14 2/8	5 4/8 / 5 5/8	6 7/8	Lake County	OR	Troy Garrison	1995	1,252
72 4/8	13 7/8 / 14 0/8	6 0/8 / 5 7/8	11 0/8	Moffat County	CO	Richard A. Smith	1996	1,252
72 4/8	14 2/8 / 14 1/8	5 5/8 / 5 5/8	12 1/8	Grand County	UT	Mark Sheets	1996	1,252
72 4/8	14 4/8 / 14 4/8	6 0/8 / 5 7/8	9 3/8	Moffat County	CO	Rocky Tschappat	1996	1,252
72 4/8	14 2/8 / 13 4/8	6 2/8 / 6 2/8	12 6/8	Rosebud County	MT	Kevin Brewer	1996	1,252
72 4/8	13 1/8 / 13 1/8	6 4/8 / 6 3/8	8 6/8	Moffat County	CO	Clifford R. Neville, Sr.	1997	1,252
72 4/8	14 2/8 / 14 2/8	6 2/8 / 6 1/8	10 0/8	Yavapai County	AZ	Dawn J. Butterfield	1997	1,252
72 4/8	13 7/8 / 13 6/8	6 2/8 / 6 2/8	9 2/8	Rosebud County	MT	Craig Richardson	1998	1,252
72 2/8	13 5/8 / 13 5/8	6 2/8 / 6 1/8	11 1/8	Carbon County	WY	William Scoggin	1953	1,316
72 2/8	14 0/8 / 14 0/8	6 0/8 / 5 7/8	10 4/8	Campbell County	WY	K. K. Knickerbocker	1954	1,316
72 2/8	13 1/8 / 13 2/8	6 1/8 / 6 1/8	7 3/8	Campbell County	WY	Carol Wert	1966	1,316
72 2/8	13 4/8 / 13 5/8	5 7/8 / 5 7/8	10 5/8	Carbon County	WY	Harold Boyack	1972	1,316
72 2/8	15 1/8 / 14 7/8	5 5/8 / 5 4/8	8 6/8	Meade County	SD	John S. Anderson	1973	1,316
72 2/8	14 3/8 / 14 3/8	6 0/8 / 5 7/8	9 5/8	Valley County	MT	Wayne Anderson	1975	1,316
72 2/8	14 1/8 / 14 0/8	6 2/8 / 6 3/8	8 5/8	Moffat County	CO	Glenn Pritchard	1977	1,316
72 2/8	13 7/8 / 13 6/8	6 1/8 / 5 7/8	8 0/8	Carbon County	WY	Arthur Heinze	1977	1,316
72 2/8	13 7/8 / 13 6/8	6 0/8 / 6 0/8	7 2/8	Butte County	ID	Dennis A. Gratton	1978	1,316
72 2/8	14 3/8 / 14 4/8	6 1/8 / 6 0/8	12 3/8	Moffat County	CO	Glenn Pritchard	1979	1,316
72 2/8	14 3/8 / 14 6/8	5 4/8 / 5 4/8	13 0/8	Coconino County	AZ	Terry E. Hansen	1981	1,316
72 2/8	17 0/8 / 15 5/8	5 4/8 / 5 5/8	9 0/8	Klamath County	OR	Richard Howell	1981	1,316
72 2/8	11 3/8 / 11 3/8	6 3/8 / 6 3/8	10 4/8	Humboldt County	NV	Verlyn Owens	1981	1,316
72 2/8	13 3/8 / 13 2/8	6 1/8 / 6 1/8	7 3/8	Moffat County	CO	Wayne A. Jensen	1982	1,316
72 2/8	13 0/8 / 12 7/8	6 1/8 / 6 1/8	6 6/8	Converse County	WY	Thomas Brannagan	1982	1,316
72 2/8	14 4/8 / 14 5/8	6 0/8 / 6 2/8	6 6/8	Carbon County	WY	Kim Cooper	1982	1,316
72 2/8	14 0/8 / 13 7/8	6 0/8 / 6 0/8	7 6/8	Morgan County	CO	Barry Smith	1983	1,316
72 2/8	13 5/8 / 13 4/8	5 6/8 / 5 6/8	8 2/8	Moffat County	CO	Dan Liccardi	1983	1,316
72 2/8	12 7/8 / 12 7/8	6 3/8 / 6 1/8	8 0/8	Converse County	WY	Tim Cassidy	1983	1,316
72 2/8	13 2/8 / 13 6/8	6 0/8 / 5 7/8	10 5/8	Carbon County	WY	Paul Persano	1983	1,316
72 2/8	13 1/8 / 13 2/8	6 1/8 / 6 2/8	10 3/8	Carbon County	WY	Larry Hayes	1983	1,316
72 2/8	13 6/8 / 13 4/8	6 4/8 / 6 4/8	14 2/8	Converse County	WY	James B. Evans, Jr.	1983	1,316
72 2/8	13 5/8 / 13 7/8	5 6/8 / 5 5/8	11 5/8	Valley County	MT	David Tofte	1983	1,316
72 2/8	13 0/8 / 13 0/8	6 1/8 / 6 2/8	9 3/8	Carbon County	WY	Robert L. Hudman	1984	1,316
72 2/8	14 7/8 / 15 0/8	6 0/8 / 5 7/8	14 1/8	Campbell County	WY	Mike Ballard	1985	1,316
72 2/8	15 2/8 / 15 0/8	6 0/8 / 6 1/8	16 3/8	Modoc County	CA	Richard Wormington	1986	1,316
72 2/8	14 3/8 / 14 1/8	6 4/8 / 6 1/8	10 4/8	Lemhi County	ID	Peter Cintorino	1986	1,316
72 2/8	13 4/8 / 13 4/8	6 1/8 / 6 2/8	10 5/8	Natrona County	WY	J. Bruce Ashcroft	1986	1,316
72 2/8	14 0/8 / 14 0/8	5 7/8 / 6 0/8	11 1/8	Sweetwater County	WY	Dale Hill	1987	1,316
72 2/8	13 0/8 / 13 2/8	6 3/8 / 6 3/8	8 7/8	Jackson County	CO	Bruce Ayers	1987	1,316
72 2/8	15 0/8 / 14 6/8	5 4/8 / 5 4/8	8 2/8	Sweetwater County	WY	Michael Chaffin	1987	1,316

PRONGHORN

Minimum Score 67 — Continued

SCORE	LENGTH OF HORN R	L	CIRCUMFERENCE OF BASE R	L	INSIDE SPREAD	AREA	STATE/ PROVINCE	HUNTER'S NAME	DATE	RANK
72 2/8	13 1/8	13 2/8	6 0/8	6 0/8	11 0/8	Carter County	MT	Robert Keith Hacker	1987	1,316
72 2/8	14 4/8	14 0/8	6 0/8	6 2/8	12 4/8	Moffat County	CO	Richard King	1987	1,316
72 2/8	14 0/8	14 0/8	5 6/8	5 4/8	11 1/8	Carbon County	WY	Paul M. Kniss	1988	1,316
72 2/8	12 5/8	12 7/8	6 3/8	6 3/8	12 2/8	Fremont County	WY	Kevin Anderson	1989	1,316
72 2/8	14 3/8	14 3/8	5 5/8	5 3/8	14 2/8	Yavapai County	AZ	Richard Anderson	1989	1,316
72 2/8	14 4/8	14 6/8	5 2/8	5 2/8	7 5/8	Rio Grande County	CO	James A. Phillips	1989	1,316
72 2/8	13 7/8	13 6/8	6 3/8	6 4/8	8 4/8	Moffat County	CO	Scott A. Wilson	1990	1,316
72 2/8	14 3/8	13 6/8	6 0/8	6 0/8	8 6/8	Billings County	ND	William R. Metzger	1990	1,316
72 2/8	13 2/8	13 6/8	6 7/8	6 4/8	14 5/8	Converse County	WY	Tommy L. Mackey	1990	1,316
72 2/8	15 4/8	16 0/8	6 1/8	6 0/8	16 3/8	Washoe County	NV	Gene A. Jones	1991	1,316
72 2/8	13 3/8	13 6/8	6 0/8	5 7/8	11 4/8	Catron County	NM	Clifford Armstrong	1991	1,316
72 2/8	14 0/8	13 7/8	6 4/8	6 2/8	9 5/8	Fremont County	WY	Troy Stone	1991	1,316
72 2/8	15 0/8	15 3/8	5 5/8	5 6/8	9 5/8	Fox Valley	SAS	Floyd Forster	1991	1,316
72 2/8	14 2/8	14 2/8	5 7/8	5 6/8	7 1/8	Converse County	WY	Kevin Stier	1991	1,316
72 2/8	14 3/8	14 3/8	5 6/8	5 7/8	11 0/8	Rosebud County	MT	Robert L. Fraley	1991	1,316
72 2/8	13 4/8	13 5/8	6 3/8	6 5/8	11 0/8	Moffat County	CO	Wayne Depperschmidt	1992	1,316
72 2/8	14 2/8	14 0/8	6 4/8	6 3/8	10 3/8	Moffat County	CO	J. Keith Chastain	1992	1,316
72 2/8	13 2/8	13 2/8	6 3/8	6 1/8	8 2/8	Moffat County	CO	Janet George	1992	1,316
72 2/8	13 4/8	13 3/8	6 3/8	6 3/8	13 7/8	Manyberries	ALB	Terry Ermel	1992	1,316
72 2/8	15 2/8	15 4/8	5 7/8	5 4/8	11 3/8	Hill County	MT	Lon Waid	1992	1,316
72 2/8	14 6/8	14 7/8	5 6/8	5 6/8	10 0/8	Campbell County	WY	David Vomela	1992	1,316
72 2/8	13 1/8	12 4/8	6 0/8	5 7/8	12 1/8	Garfield County	MT	Christopher Downs	1992	1,316
72 2/8	14 0/8	14 1/8	5 2/8	5 2/8	11 6/8	Chaves County	NM	Bill Daniel	1993	1,316
72 2/8	14 1/8	14 2/8	5 4/8	5 4/8	10 6/8	Moffat County	CO	Steve Murphy	1993	1,316
72 2/8	13 0/8	13 3/8	6 3/8	6 2/8	11 2/8	Box Elder County	UT	Brett Payne	1993	1,316
72 2/8	14 1/8	14 2/8	5 4/8	5 5/8	9 3/8	Wayne County	UT	Johnny C. Parsons	1993	1,316
72 2/8	13 5/8	13 7/8	5 7/8	5 7/8	15 1/8	Sublette County	WY	T. J. Dupee	1993	1,316
72 2/8	13 0/8	13 0/8	6 0/8	6 0/8	12 3/8	Garfield County	MT	L. "Andy" Anderson	1993	1,316
72 2/8	15 1/8	14 7/8	5 7/8	5 7/8	10 2/8	Hudspeth County	TX	Bruce Baird	1993	1,316
72 2/8	13 7/8	14 0/8	6 0/8	5 7/8	10 0/8	Sweetwater County	WY	Shaneon Lance	1994	1,316
72 2/8	14 0/8	14 1/8	6 0/8	6 1/8	11 6/8	Carbon County	UT	Kooper Pierce	1994	1,316
72 2/8	13 4/8	13 3/8	5 5/8	5 5/8	8 5/8	Butte County	ID	L. D. Green	1994	1,316
72 2/8	14 4/8	14 6/8	5 6/8	5 5/8	8 3/8	Millard County	UT	Jeremy Harness	1994	1,316
72 2/8	13 4/8	13 3/8	5 7/8	5 7/8	12 0/8	Campbell County	WY	Jim Hengel	1994	1,316
72 2/8	14 3/8	14 4/8	5 5/8	5 4/8	12 1/8	Hilda	ALB	Steve MacKenzie	1994	1,316
72 2/8	14 0/8	14 0/8	5 7/8	5 7/8	9 5/8	Phillips County	MT	Brad Walker	1994	1,316
72 2/8	15 4/8	15 7/8	5 4/8	5 4/8	10 2/8	Nye County	NV	James F. Watson	1995	1,316
72 2/8	13 5/8	14 3/8	6 2/8	6 2/8	12 3/8	Modoc County	CA	Gerald W. Smith	1995	1,316
72 2/8	14 6/8	14 4/8	5 6/8	5 6/8	7 4/8	Rio Grande County	CO	David R. Hall	1995	1,316
72 2/8	13 1/8	13 1/8	5 6/8	6 0/8	8 7/8	Weld County	CO	Jason Rhodes	1995	1,316
72 2/8	15 0/8	15 0/8	5 7/8	5 7/8	10 3/8	Larimer County	CO	Mark A. Germonprez	1995	1,316
72 2/8	13 4/8	13 1/8	6 0/8	6 0/8	9 7/8	Moffat County	CO	Jim Brewer	1995	1,316
72 2/8	13 4/8	13 6/8	6 2/8	6 2/8	13 0/8	Converse County	WY	Ralph Inverso	1995	1,316
72 2/8	15 0/8	15 0/8	5 6/8	5 6/8	9 6/8	Navajo County	AZ	Amy Holladay	1995	1,316
72 2/8	13 2/8	13 3/8	6 3/8	6 3/8	8 6/8	Campbell County	WY	Jeffrey A. Hoover	1995	1,316
72 2/8	15 0/8	14 6/8	6 0/8	6 0/8	9 5/8	Duchesne County	UT	William T. Burbridge	1996	1,316
72 2/8	14 1/8	14 1/8	5 6/8	5 6/8	9 5/8	Millard County	UT	David Anderson	1996	1,316
72 2/8	13 3/8	13 0/8	6 0/8	6 0/8	8 5/8	Converse County	WY	Tim Angelo	1996	1,316
72 2/8	12 6/8	12 4/8	5 7/8	5 6/8	9 0/8	Converse County	WY	Marlin Stapleton, Jr.	1996	1,316
72 2/8	13 2/8	13 2/8	5 7/8	5 7/8	8 6/8	Rosebud County	MT	Richard M. Penn	1996	1,316
72 2/8	14 7/8	14 4/8	6 2/8	6 2/8	10 0/8	Sierra County	NM	Audie F. Click	1997	1,316
72 2/8	14 1/8	14 1/8	5 7/8	5 7/8	8 7/8	Weld County	CO	Rodney E. Perrine	1997	1,316
72 2/8	13 1/8	13 1/8	6 3/8	6 1/8	11 1/8	Moffat County	CO	Mark C. Gardner	1998	1,316
72 2/8	13 0/8	13 0/8	7 0/8	7 0/8	10 7/8	Custer County	MT	Lyle R. Prell	1998	1,316
72 2/8	13 6/8	13 7/8	5 6/8	5 5/8	8 1/8	Valley County	MT	Scott Lysenko	1998	1,316
70 0/8	13 4/8	13 5/8	5 6/8	5 7/8	9 4/8	Perkins County	SD	Ben Clark	1974	1,402
70 0/8	13 3/8	13 3/8	5 6/8	6 0/8	11 2/8	Sioux County	NE	Richard Koons	1974	1,402
70 0/8	12 7/8	12 4/8	6 7/8	6 7/8	10 1/8	Bennett County	SD	Donald Pierce	1978	1,402
70 0/8	13 3/8	13 1/8	5 7/8	5 7/8	10 5/8	Butte County	ID	Mike Ellis	1980	1,402
70 0/8	14 1/8	14 3/8	5 7/8	5 6/8	14 5/8	Custer County	ID	Gene Nelson	1981	1,402
70 0/8	13 3/8	13 2/8	6 1/8	5 7/8	6 2/8	Klamath County	OR	Harold McCraven	1981	1,402
70 0/8	13 3/8	13 1/8	6 0/8	6 0/8	11 0/8	Natrona County	WY	E. W. Onken	1981	1,402
70 0/8	13 3/8	13 3/8	5 7/8	5 7/8	10 4/8	Moffat County	CO	Gary Smith	1981	1,402
70 0/8	13 4/8	14 0/8	6 3/8	6 3/8	9 3/8	Carbon County	WY	Charles A. Vande Hei	1982	1,402
70 0/8	13 7/8	14 1/8	5 6/8	5 7/8	11 2/8	Carbon County	WY	Michael Beckwith	1982	1,402
70 0/8	14 3/8	14 2/8	5 5/8	5 5/8	8 6/8	Moffat County	CO	Augie Nicolas	1983	1,402
70 0/8	13 1/8	13 1/8	6 1/8	6 1/8	8 2/8	Converse County	WY	Tom Flemming	1983	1,402
70 0/8	14 1/8	13 6/8	5 7/8	5 6/8	12 3/8	McCone County	MT	Gary Rueh	1983	1,402
70 0/8	14 2/8	14 1/8	5 6/8	5 7/8	10 2/8	Carter County	MT	Dean Irwin	1983	1,402
70 0/8	14 6/8	14 6/8	5 3/8	5 3/8	10 6/8	Tide Lake	ALB	Adrian Erickson	1983	1,402
70 0/8	14 3/8	14 6/8	5 5/8	5 5/8	10 4/8	Washoe County	NV	C. J. Coleman	1984	1,402
70 0/8	13 2/8	13 1/8	6 0/8	6 0/8	8 7/8	Moffat County	CO	Lynn Pariso	1985	1,402
70 0/8	13 6/8	13 3/8	6 2/8	6 2/8	8 1/8	Carbon County	UT	Kenny E. Leo	1986	1,402
70 0/8	14 5/8	15 0/8	5 5/8	5 5/8	11 6/8	Moffat County	CO	Roger Gipple	1987	1,402
70 0/8	13 4/8	13 2/8	6 4/8	6 3/8	11 4/8	Box Elder County	UT	Gary E. Craner	1987	1,402
70 0/8	13 6/8	13 5/8	6 0/8	6 1/8	13 5/8	Rosebud County	MT	Dr. Kevin Brewer	1987	1,402
70 0/8	14 2/8	14 3/8	5 6/8	5 6/8	7 2/8	Humboldt County	NV	Carl J. Corey	1988	1,402
70 0/8	14 2/8	14 3/8	5 6/8	5 7/8	12 1/8	Moffat County	CO	Tom Bartholomew	1988	1,402

PRONGHORN

Minimum Score 67

SCORE	LENGTH OF HORN R / L		CIRCUMFERENCE OF BASE R / L		INSIDE SPREAD	AREA	STATE/ PROVINCE	HUNTER'S NAME	DATE	RANK
72 0/8	13 2/8	13 0/8	6 1/8	6 2/8	8 6/8	Carbon County	WY	Darrus D. Martin	1988	1,402
72 0/8	13 7/8	13 7/8	5 2/8	5 2/8	9 2/8	Moffat County	CO	M. R. James	1988	1,402
72 0/8	13 2/8	13 4/8	6 0/8	6 0/8	10 1/8	Grant County	ND	Mark Bogert	1988	1,402
72 0/8	12 5/8	12 5/8	5 7/8	5 7/8	10 6/8	Wallace County	KS	Roger Potter	1988	1,402
72 0/8	13 0/8	12 7/8	6 2/8	6 2/8	10 0/8	Klamath County	OR	Bob Baley	1989	1,402
72 0/8	14 0/8	13 7/8	6 1/8	6 1/8	9 5/8	Campbell County	WY	Dave Vomela	1989	1,402
72 0/8	13 7/8	13 7/8	5 4/8	5 4/8	8 2/8	Carbon County	WY	Raymond R. Robison	1989	1,402
72 0/8	13 5/8	13 4/8	6 1/8	6 2/8	7 6/8	Uinta County	WY	Drew Dockstader	1989	1,402
72 0/8	13 7/8	13 3/8	6 3/8	6 0/8	9 6/8	Uinta County	WY	Scott Dockstader	1989	1,402
72 0/8	14 4/8	14 3/8	5 7/8	6 0/8	9 1/8	Moffat County	CO	Keith Hensel	1989	1,402
72 0/8	12 1/8	12 2/8	6 4/8	6 3/8	8 6/8	Carbon County	WY	Dean Stebner	1990	1,402
72 0/8	12 7/8	12 7/8	6 2/8	6 0/8	10 6/8	Converse County	WY	Kelvin W. Lancaster	1990	1,402
72 0/8	12 5/8	13 0/8	7 0/8	7 0/8	11 4/8	Rosebud County	MT	Gary C. Wolf	1990	1,402
72 0/8	14 0/8	14 0/8	5 3/8	5 3/8	11 4/8	Converse County	WY	Roy W. Mackey	1990	1,402
72 0/8	14 7/8	14 5/8	5 6/8	5 6/8	9 6/8	Elko County	NV	Jimmy Cooney	1991	1,402
72 0/8	13 2/8	13 2/8	5 6/8	6 0/8	8 6/8	Park County	WY	Craig Childress	1991	1,402
72 0/8	13 7/8	13 7/8	5 7/8	5 6/8	9 5/8	Sweetwater County	WY	R. E. "Bud" Watson	1991	1,402
72 0/8	13 7/8	13 7/8	5 5/8	5 5/8	11 4/8	Navajo County	AZ	Charles P. Cooley	1991	1,402
72 0/8	13 7/8	13 7/8	5 7/8	5 6/8	14 6/8	Crook County	OR	Clint Hall	1991	1,402
72 0/8	13 1/8	12 7/8	6 0/8	6 0/8	11 1/8	Laramie County	WY	Gary W. Brimm	1991	1,402
72 0/8	12 6/8	12 5/8	6 3/8	6 2/8	8 6/8	Wallace County	KS	Darren Collins	1991	1,402
72 0/8	14 3/8	14 2/8	6 0/8	6 0/8	8 2/8	Sioux County	NE	Gaylen Rogers	1991	1,402
72 0/8	13 3/8	13 4/8	6 0/8	6 0/8	12 4/8	Washoe County	NV	Gary Wright	1992	1,402
72 0/8	13 1/8	13 6/8	6 0/8	6 0/8	9 6/8	Union County	NM	Dave Conrad	1992	1,402
72 0/8	13 4/8	13 7/8	5 6/8	5 6/8	9 3/8	Saguache County	CO	Mark Wuerthele	1992	1,402
72 0/8	13 4/8	13 6/8	6 5/8	6 4/8	11 6/8	Sioux County	NE	Jim Ritz	1992	1,402
72 0/8	14 4/8	14 3/8	6 1/8	6 1/8	10 4/8	Converse County	WY	Richard Wheeler	1992	1,402
72 0/8	13 3/8	12 6/8	6 2/8	6 1/8	15 4/8	Albany County	WY	Vince DiMiceli	1992	1,402
72 0/8	14 0/8	13 6/8	6 0/8	6 0/8	11 6/8	Moffat County	CO	Eugene Ray, Sr.	1993	1,402
72 0/8	14 1/8	14 1/8	6 0/8	6 0/8	12 5/8	Sweetwater County	WY	Tim Isaacson	1993	1,402
72 0/8	14 0/8	14 2/8	5 2/8	5 2/8	7 7/8	Coconino County	AZ	Tom Alvin	1993	1,402
72 0/8	13 5/8	13 7/8	6 2/8	6 2/8	13 2/8	Moffat County	CO	Bruce A. Hatch	1993	1,402
72 0/8	14 4/8	14 5/8	6 3/8	6 2/8	20 3/8	Harney County	OR	Joel Modey	1993	1,402
72 0/8	13 6/8	14 1/8	6 0/8	6 0/8	10 6/8	Rosebud County	MT	Jerry W. Crow	1993	1,402
72 0/8	13 2/8	13 0/8	6 6/8	6 6/8	11 6/8	Converse County	WY	Dave Canfield	1993	1,402
72 0/8	12 7/8	13 2/8	5 7/8	5 7/8	9 3/8	Sweetwater County	WY	Dave Holt	1994	1,402
72 0/8	14 7/8	14 5/8	6 0/8	6 2/8	11 2/8	Washoe County	NV	Elizabeth F. Wright	1994	1,402
72 0/8	14 7/8	15 0/8	5 5/8	5 7/8	9 1/0	Owyhee County	ID	Jason Angell	1994	1,402
72 0/8	14 2/8	13 6/8	6 1/8	6 1/8	10 4/8	Campbell County	WY	Kevin Brady	1994	1,402
72 0/8	14 3/8	14 3/8	5 6/8	5 4/8	13 4/8	Moffat County	CO	John M. Pollock	1994	1,402
72 0/8	13 6/8	13 5/8	6 2/8	6 2/8	8 6/8	Harding County	SD	Kim R. Smith	1994	1,402
72 0/8	14 0/8	13 5/8	6 3/8	6 3/8	9 4/8	Buffalo	ALB	Darryl Kublik	1994	1,402
72 0/8	13 5/8	13 3/8	6 4/8	6 3/8	11 1/8	Converse County	WY	Steve Thomas, Jr.	1995	1,402
72 0/8	14 3/8	14 4/8	5 4/8	5 4/8	7 7/8	Oyen	ALB	Gary Gillett	1995	1,402
72 0/8	13 2/8	13 4/8	6 3/8	6 3/8	10 3/8	Moffat County	CO	Calvin P. Miller, Jr.	1995	1,402
72 0/8	15 4/8	15 3/8	5 6/8	5 6/8	12 7/8	Campbell County	WY	Donald Fauth	1995	1,402
72 0/8	14 6/8	14 2/8	6 1/8	6 1/8	14 0/8	Johnson County	WY	Charles H. Sagner	1995	1,402
72 0/8	14 2/8	14 3/8	6 0/8	5 7/8	10 6/8	Hudspeth County	TX	Ernest M. Elbert	1995	1,402
72 0/8	14 1/8	14 2/8	6 2/8	6 2/8	9 0/8	Moffat County	CO	Jim Leqve	1996	1,402
72 0/8	13 7/8	14 2/8	5 5/8	5 6/8	11 6/8	Rio Grande County	CO	Douglas C. Cotten	1996	1,402
72 0/8	15 1/8	14 6/8	5 5/8	5 5/8	11 1/8	Converse County	WY	David L. MacDonald	1996	1,402
72 0/8	14 1/8	14 0/8	6 0/8	5 7/8	10 3/8	Weld County	CO	Matt Dickerson	1997	1,402
72 0/8	13 0/8	12 7/8	6 1/8	6 1/8	7 5/8	Jerome County	ID	Scott L. Allen	1997	1,402
72 0/8	13 4/8	13 3/8	6 1/8	6 1/8	9 4/8	Campbell County	WY	John Fleharty	1997	1,402
72 0/8	14 1/8	14 0/8	5 6/8	5 5/8	9 6/8	Uintah County	UT	Mark E. Callahan	1997	1,402
72 0/8	14 1/8	14 3/8	6 2/8	6 1/8	12 1/8	Converse County	WY	Ron Riel	1997	1,402
72 0/8	14 0/8	14 2/8	5 7/8	5 6/8	8 0/8	Sierra County	NM	V. Randy Liljenquist	1998	1,402
72 0/8	13 7/8	14 1/8	6 3/8	6 5/8	10 5/8	Logan County	NE	Drew Armstrong	1998	1,402
72 0/8	13 5/8	13 6/8	6 1/8	6 1/8	7 1/8	Jackson County	CO	Paul M. Martin	1998	1,402
71 6/8	14 2/8	14 1/8	5 6/8	5 7/8	10 5/8	Klamath County	OR	Jerry Phillips	1977	1,484
71 6/8	13 5/8	13 3/8	6 1/8	6 0/8	11 0/8	Natrona County	WY	George Kegler	1980	1,484
71 6/8	14 2/8	14 5/8	5 6/8	5 6/8	10 6/8	Converse County	WY	Ron Spratling	1981	1,484
71 6/8	13 0/8	13 0/8	5 5/8	5 4/8	8 7/8	Bowman County	ND	Donald C. Hestekin	1982	1,484
71 6/8	13 1/8	13 1/8	5 4/8	5 4/8	10 6/8	Converse County	WY	Robert R. Vance	1982	1,484
71 6/8	13 5/8	14 4/8	5 7/8	5 6/8	10 2/8	Carbon County	WY	Don Carter	1983	1,484
71 6/8	12 5/8	12 7/8	6 3/8	6 1/8	6 6/8	Converse County	WY	Jim Nielsen	1983	1,484
71 6/8	14 3/8	14 5/8	5 7/8	5 7/8	11 6/8	Fremont County	WY	Jim Walters	1983	1,484
71 6/8	14 6/8	14 6/8	5 7/8	5 7/8	10 5/8	Powder River County	MT	Ron Thompson	1983	1,484
71 6/8	13 7/8	14 0/8	6 1/8	6 0/8	7 3/8	Converse County	WY	Bill Welker	1984	1,484
71 6/8	14 5/8	14 1/8	6 2/8	6 1/8	7 4/8	Campbell County	WY	Mike Ingold	1985	1,484
71 6/8	13 6/8	13 4/8	6 3/8	6 2/8	9 1/8	Sweetwater County	WY	James E. Summerall	1986	1,484
71 6/8	13 4/8	13 6/8	5 5/8	5 4/8	10 4/8	Moffat County	CO	Denny Williamson	1987	1,484
71 6/8	14 0/8	13 7/8	5 3/8	5 4/8	8 7/8	Natrona County	WY	Scott Privette	1987	1,484
71 6/8	13 6/8	14 0/8	5 6/8	5 6/8	12 3/8	Rosebud County	MT	Daniel Hudek	1987	1,484
71 6/8	13 5/8	14 0/8	6 0/8	6 0/8	8 2/8	Converse County	WY	Frank Moore	1987	1,484
71 6/8	13 0/8	13 0/8	6 0/8	6 0/8	14 1/8	Natrona County	WY	Kim Cooper	1987	1,484
71 6/8	13 3/8	13 0/8	5 7/8	5 7/8	6 5/8	Lassen County	CA	Tom Devlin	1988	1,484
71 6/8	13 0/8	12 7/8	6 3/8	6 4/8	13 5/8	Carbon County	WY	Randy Long	1988	1,484

PRONGHORN

Minimum Score 67 — Continued

SCORE	LENGTH OF HORN R	L	CIRCUMFERENCE OF BASE R	L	INSIDE SPREAD	AREA	STATE/PROVINCE	HUNTER'S NAME	DATE	RANK
71 6/8	14 0/8	14 2/8	5 5/8	5 6/8	10 2/8	Moffat County	CO	David Greenwalt	1988	1,484
71 6/8	12 1/8	13 7/8	6 0/8	6 0/8	9 5/8	Las Animas County	CO	Bill Swift	1988	1,484
71 6/8	13 4/8	13 4/8	6 1/8	6 0/8	10 4/8	Cutbank Creek	ALB	Darrell Peters	1988	1,484
71 6/8	14 4/8	13 6/8	5 4/8	5 7/8	11 1/8	Moffat County	CO	David Travaglio	1989	1,484
71 6/8	14 6/8	14 5/8	6 1/8	6 0/8	9 4/8	Campbell County	WY	Donald J. Ridgley	1989	1,484
71 6/8	16 0/8	16 2/8	6 1/8	6 0/8	10 6/8	Bowman County	ND	Gene D. Davis	1989	1,484
71 6/8	13 0/8	12 3/8	6 3/8	6 2/8	8 3/8	Rosebud County	MT	Kent Kaufman	1989	1,484
71 6/8	14 5/8	14 4/8	5 6/8	5 5/8	9 5/8	Washoe County	NV	George F. Howard	1990	1,484
71 6/8	13 6/8	14 1/8	6 1/8	6 1/8	9 4/8	Carbon County	WY	Sam Amberson	1990	1,484
71 6/8	14 2/8	14 6/8	5 5/8	5 4/8	11 3/8	Lincoln County	WY	Jeff Blain	1990	1,484
71 6/8	13 5/8	13 6/8	5 6/8	5 5/8	8 4/8	Rosebud County	MT	Jesse Meyer	1990	1,484
71 6/8	15 5/8	15 7/8	5 1/8	5 2/8	7 4/8	Golden Valley County	ND	Wayne Streitz	1990	1,484
71 6/8	14 2/8	14 3/8	6 0/8	6 0/8	8 6/8	Fergus County	MT	Ronald Eugene Sanford, Jr.	1990	1,484
71 6/8	14 0/8	13 6/8	5 3/8	5 4/8	10 0/8	Converse County	WY	Tom Mulchay	1990	1,484
71 6/8	14 6/8	14 4/8	5 4/8	5 4/8	12 3/8	Orion	ALB	Gunter Lemke	1990	1,484
71 6/8	15 1/8	15 0/8	6 0/8	6 0/8	11 0/8	Hudspeth County	TX	James E. Borron	1990	1,484
71 6/8	14 3/8	14 3/8	5 5/8	5 5/8	8 0/8	Weld County	CO	Michael J. McArtor	1991	1,484
71 6/8	13 6/8	13 7/8	6 3/8	6 3/8	11 2/8	Moffat County	CO	R. Tim Reed	1991	1,484
71 6/8	13 4/8	13 4/8	5 7/8	5 7/8	9 6/8	Yavapai County	AZ	James Monroe Haines	1991	1,484
71 6/8	13 5/8	13 4/8	6 3/8	6 4/8	8 2/8	Custer County	ID	Matt March	1991	1,484
71 6/8	14 1/8	13 5/8	6 3/8	6 3/8	10 7/8	Rich County	UT	Peter E. Paulds, Jr.	1991	1,484
71 6/8	14 2/8	14 0/8	6 2/8	6 1/8	12 1/8	Converse County	WY	Jack Schatz	1991	1,484
71 6/8	14 6/8	14 4/8	5 4/8	5 3/8	10 3/8	Platte County	WY	Jack Baltz	1991	1,484
71 6/8	13 3/8	13 7/8	6 0/8	6 0/8	8 0/8	Campbell County	WY	Dr. Robert Edward Speegle	1991	1,484
71 6/8	14 4/8	14 0/8	6 0/8	5 7/8	8 5/8	Sweetwater County	WY	Jed R. Ashworth	1992	1,484
71 6/8	14 2/8	14 3/8	5 7/8	5 6/8	8 5/8	Union County	NM	Jeff Fitts	1992	1,484
71 6/8	14 7/8	14 0/8	6 3/8	6 1/8	12 4/8	Lincoln County	WY	Lance Brown	1992	1,484
71 6/8	13 2/8	13 1/8	6 4/8	6 1/8	12 2/8	Moffat County	CO	Bruce Eggenberger	1992	1,484
71 6/8	14 0/8	13 7/8	5 6/8	5 7/8	8 7/8	Rich County	UT	Guy G. Fitzgerald	1992	1,484
71 6/8	13 7/8	14 0/8	5 7/8	6 0/8	10 6/8	Moffat County	CO	Dave Parri	1992	1,484
71 6/8	13 3/8	13 0/8	5 4/8	5 7/8	12 6/8	Sublette County	WY	Phil N. Skinner	1992	1,484
71 6/8	12 2/8	12 1/8	6 0/8	6 0/8	8 2/8	Converse County	WY	Joe Cronin	1992	1,484
71 6/8	13 5/8	13 7/8	6 3/8	6 3/8	8 6/8	Natrona County	WY	Ed Gawel	1992	1,484
71 6/8	14 1/8	14 1/8	5 7/8	5 7/8	11 0/8	Buffalo	ALB	Dewain Ollenberger	1992	1,484
71 6/8	13 2/8	13 0/8	5 7/8	5 6/8	11 1/8	Moffat County	CO	Kevin C. Massaro	1992	1,484
71 6/8	14 4/8	14 1/8	5 7/8	5 6/8	10 0/8	Converse County	WY	Michael L. Hoft	1992	1,484
71 6/8	12 7/8	13 2/8	6 2/8	6 1/8	4 7/8	Kimball County	NE	James J. Beebe	1992	1,484
71 6/8	13 0/8	12 4/8	6 2/8	6 2/8	12 0/8	Slope County	ND	Robert R. Parker	1992	1,484
71 6/8	13 5/8	13 5/8	6 2/8	6 1/8	9 3/8	Billings County	ND	Les Tomanek	1992	1,484
71 6/8	13 4/8	13 3/8	7 0/8	6 4/8	12 4/8	Campbell County	WY	Paul Vomela	1992	1,484
71 6/8	13 7/8	14 1/8	6 2/8	6 0/8	11 3/8	Natrona County	WY	Mike Mikalowsky	1992	1,484
71 6/8	15 2/8	15 2/8	5 4/8	5 5/8	9 5/8	Jeff Davis County	TX	Wayne North	1992	1,484
71 6/8	14 2/8	13 7/8	5 3/8	5 3/8	8 2/8	Mohave County	AZ	Dave Fuller	1993	1,484
71 6/8	14 2/8	14 5/8	6 2/8	6 2/8	11 0/8	White Pine County	NV	Jerry A. Davis	1993	1,484
71 6/8	13 7/8	15 2/8	5 7/8	6 0/8	7 6/8	Dawes County	NE	Francis Ohlsen	1993	1,484
71 6/8	14 7/8	14 5/8	5 4/8	5 4/8	11 1/8	Hays	ALB	Steen Sorensen	1993	1,484
71 6/8	14 2/8	14 2/8	6 2/8	5 7/8	13 3/8	McKenzie County	ND	David Tofte	1993	1,484
71 6/8	14 1/8	13 4/8	5 5/8	5 6/8	10 6/8	Dundy County	NE	Clint Burrell	1993	1,484
71 6/8	13 6/8	13 1/8	6 2/8	6 2/8	9 1/8	Harding County	SD	Lonnie G. Tschumper	1993	1,484
71 6/8	13 2/8	13 2/8	5 7/8	5 7/8	11 4/8	Duchesne County	UT	Dennis L. Shirley	1994	1,484
71 6/8	14 3/8	14 4/8	6 0/8	6 1/8	8 6/8	Ada County	ID	Robert Dowen	1994	1,484
71 6/8	13 7/8	13 7/8	6 3/8	6 3/8	7 5/8	Converse County	WY	Ralph Inverso	1994	1,484
71 6/8	13 4/8	13 4/8	6 0/8	6 0/8	9 3/8	Slope County	ND	Neil D. Mellesmoen	1994	1,484
71 6/8	12 7/8	13 0/8	6 4/8	6 6/8	12 2/8	Lake County	OR	Rodney W. Ferry	1994	1,484
71 6/8	13 7/8	13 5/8	6 0/8	6 1/8	10 4/8	Converse County	WY	David Miller	1995	1,484
71 6/8	15 2/8	15 5/8	5 5/8	5 4/8	7 0/8	Hudspeth County	TX	Bruce Baird	1995	1,484
71 6/8	15 0/8	14 7/8	5 5/8	5 5/8	8 2/8	Beaver County	UT	Allan Mayer	1996	1,484
71 6/8	14 3/8	14 2/8	6 3/8	6 1/8	10 4/8	Carbon County	UT	Brent Oman	1996	1,484
71 6/8	14 4/8	14 6/8	5 2/8	5 1/8	10 1/8	Lincoln County	NM	Ron Randle	1996	1,484
71 6/8	12 7/8	13 2/8	6 1/8	6 0/8	9 7/8	Rosebud County	MT	Gene A. Welle	1996	1,484
71 6/8	13 7/8	14 1/8	6 2/8	6 2/8	8 4/8	Billings County	ND	Gary Wiley	1996	1,484
71 6/8	13 4/8	13 0/8	7 0/8	6 7/8	10 3/8	Weld County	CO	Kevin Ayers	1997	1,484
71 6/8	14 1/8	14 0/8	5 7/8	5 7/8	10 0/8	Powder River County	MT	Dave R. Christofferson	1997	1,484
71 6/8	13 3/8	13 5/8	6 2/8	6 1/8	10 7/8	Tooele County	UT	Ryan Isaacson	1998	1,484
71 6/8	14 3/8	14 4/8	5 6/8	5 6/8	8 6/8	Weld County	CO	Rodney E. Perrine	1998	1,484
71 4/8	13 6/8	13 4/8	6 4/8	6 2/8	10 0/8	Carbon County	WY	Bill Scoggin	1957	1,568
71 4/8	14 7/8	14 7/8	6 0/8	6 2/8	13 5/8	Moffat County	CO	Henry Wichers	1959	1,568
71 4/8	13 4/8	13 3/8	6 0/8	6 0/8	8 2/8	Tripp County	SD	Dan Smith	1965	1,568
71 4/8	14 2/8	14 0/8	5 4/8	5 4/8	9 6/8	Carbon County	WY	Jerry Bowen	1976	1,568
71 4/8	14 1/8	14 0/8	6 2/8	6 3/8	9 1/8	Sweetwater County	WY	Val Jones	1978	1,568
71 4/8	14 4/8	14 4/8	5 6/8	5 5/8	9 7/8	Albany County	WY	Tom Tietz	1978	1,568
71 4/8	12 6/8	12 6/8	5 6/8	5 6/8	8 2/8	Carbon County	WY	Ronald J. Wedge	1978	1,568
71 4/8	13 0/8	13 0/8	6 0/8	5 6/8	9 3/8	Converse County	WY	Mike Burley	1980	1,568
71 4/8	12 4/8	12 1/8	6 4/8	6 3/8	9 7/8	Carbon County	WY	Bruce Butkiewicz	1980	1,568
71 4/8	13 1/8	13 6/8	6 1/8	6 2/8	11 4/8	Yavapai County	AZ	Peter C. Knagge	1980	1,568
71 4/8	13 6/8	13 6/8	6 0/8	6 0/8	6 6/8	Sheridan County	WY	David Shoop	1980	1,568
71 4/8	12 6/8	12 5/8	5 7/8	5 6/8	10 0/8	Natrona County	WY	David Manthei	1981	1,568
71 4/8	12 7/8	12 4/8	6 7/8	6 4/8	12 7/8	Carbon County	WY	Dennis Crank	1982	1,568

PRONGHORN

Minimum Score 67 — Continued

SCORE	LENGTH OF HORN R	L	CIRCUMFERENCE OF BASE R	L	INSIDE SPREAD	AREA	STATE/ PROVINCE	HUNTER'S NAME	DATE	RANK
71 4/8	15 0/8	15 0/8	5 7/8	5 6/8	10 6/8	Perkins County	SD	H. Melvin Dutton	1982	1,568
71 4/8	13 0/8	13 0/8	5 6/8	5 7/8	9 4/8	Delta County	CO	Doug McCauley	1983	1,568
71 4/8	13 3/8	13 4/8	6 2/8	6 1/8	9 2/8	Carbon County	WY	Bob Moore	1983	1,568
71 4/8	12 6/8	13 0/8	6 0/8	6 1/8	10 0/8	Perkins County	SD	H. Melvin Dutton	1983	1,568
71 4/8	14 0/8	14 1/8	6 1/8	6 1/8	6 5/8	Grand Forks	ALB	Ian Sangster	1983	1,568
71 4/8	13 2/8	13 1/8	6 2/8	6 1/8	7 5/8	Converse County	WY	George Hecker	1984	1,568
71 4/8	12 0/8	14 3/8	6 3/8	6 2/8	8 1/8	Petroleum County	MT	Ben Maughan	1984	1,568
71 4/8	15 3/8	15 2/8	5 7/8	6 0/8	15 2/8	Moffat County	CO	Richard King	1985	1,568
71 4/8	13 7/8	13 6/8	6 0/8	5 7/8	9 3/8	Beaverhead County	MT	Ron Oswald	1985	1,568
71 4/8	14 6/8	14 3/8	5 5/8	5 5/8	12 1/8	Humboldt County	NV	Martin J. Larraneta, Jr.	1986	1,568
71 4/8	13 0/8	13 0/8	6 2/8	6 0/8	9 1/8	Moffat County	CO	Terry Weimer	1986	1,568
71 4/8	14 0/8	14 2/8	5 5/8	5 6/8	9 5/8	Sublette County	WY	Jim Carr	1986	1,568
71 4/8	13 6/8	14 0/8	6 0/8	5 7/8	11 0/8	Converse County	WY	Scott Wilke	1986	1,568
71 4/8	14 2/8	14 1/8	6 1/8	5 7/8	8 7/8	Mountrail County	ND	Todd W. Boechler	1986	1,568
71 4/8	14 1/8	14 6/8	5 6/8	5 5/8	8 4/8	Coconino County	AZ	Tim Edwards	1987	1,568
71 4/8	14 1/8	13 7/8	5 7/8	6 0/8	11 6/8	Moffat County	CO	Mike Ottenbacher	1987	1,568
71 4/8	12 1/8	12 1/8	6 0/8	6 1/8	9 1/8	Sublette County	WY	GayLynn Turner	1988	1,568
71 4/8	14 2/8	14 4/8	6 1/8	6 0/8	10 4/8	Moffat County	CO	Robert A. Hermann	1988	1,568
71 4/8	13 6/8	13 6/8	6 0/8	6 0/8	10 7/8	Buffalo	ALB	Stuart Sinclair-Smith	1988	1,568
71 4/8	13 5/8	13 6/8	6 1/8	6 0/8	9 6/8	Moffat County	CO	Michael Magana	1989	1,568
71 4/8	12 4/8	12 7/8	6 1/8	6 2/8	9 7/8	Moffat County	CO	James VanAlstine	1989	1,568
71 4/8	13 4/8	13 4/8	6 0/8	5 7/8	9 0/8	Billings County	ND	MicheAl Ness	1989	1,568
71 4/8	13 2/8	14 4/8	5 7/8	5 6/8	10 2/8	Yavapai County	AZ	Richard M Compau	1989	1,568
71 4/8	14 4/8	14 1/8	5 5/8	5 4/8	11 5/8	Foremost	ALB	Kelly Kerner	1989	1,568
71 4/8	14 7/8	13 4/8	5 7/8	5 6/8	11 0/8	Jackson County	CO	Lance Barnica	1990	1,568
71 4/8	14 3/8	13 4/8	5 7/8	5 7/8	9 5/8	Dunn County	ND	Rick Stein	1990	1,568
71 4/8	13 3/8	13 4/8	6 1/8	6 2/8	9 5/8	Twin Falls County	ID	John Stevens	1991	1,568
71 4/8	13 1/8	13 4/8	6 2/8	6 2/8	12 7/8	Owyhee County	ID	Steve Stephenson	1991	1,568
71 4/8	13 7/8	14 0/8	6 0/8	6 0/8	8 6/8	Converse County	WY	Charles R. Cramer	1991	1,568
71 4/8	13 6/8	14 0/8	6 1/8	6 1/8	9 0/8	Campbell County	WY	Wayne Jossart	1991	1,568
71 4/8	13 5/8	13 4/8	6 4/8	6 4/8	11 5/8	Converse County	WY	Steve Gorr	1991	1,568
71 4/8	13 2/8	13 1/8	6 0/8	6 3/8	14 6/8	Fremont County	WY	Glen L. Mahlum	1991	1,568
71 4/8	13 7/8	14 1/8	5 6/8	5 7/8	10 0/8	Lake County	OR	Phillip L. Severson	1992	1,568
71 4/8	14 6/8	14 2/8	5 7/8	5 1/8	9 0/8	Klamath County	OR	Frank Sanders	1992	1,568
71 4/8	13 5/8	13 3/8	6 3/8	6 2/8	6 2/8	Moffat County	CO	Mark D. Thomson	1992	1,568
71 4/8	13 3/8	13 0/8	6 2/8	6 2/8	9 6/8	Carbon County	WY	Jim Kurth	1992	1,568
71 4/8	14 3/8	14 6/8	5 6/8	5 5/8	12 5/8	County of 40 Mile	ALB	Murray T. Campbell	1992	1,568
71 4/8	14 1/8	14 3/8	5 6/8	5 7/8	6 7/8	Sweetwater County	WY	Thad W. Sullivan	1993	1,568
71 4/8	13 5/8	13 4/8	6 0/8	6 0/8	9 6/8	Moffat County	CO	Cynthia Dziekan	1993	1,568
71 4/8	13 7/8	14 2/8	5 5/8	5 7/8	9 2/8	Moffat County	CO	Bob Nelson	1993	1,568
71 4/8	14 0/8	13 7/8	6 1/8	6 1/8	10 5/8	Millard County	UT	Jerry A. Davis	1993	1,568
71 4/8	13 4/8	13 1/8	6 1/8	6 1/8	10 5/8	Weld County	CO	Wes Lowrie	1993	1,568
71 4/8	13 7/8	13 7/8	6 0/8	5 7/8	8 3/8	Lewis & Clark County	MT	Al Schellinger	1993	1,568
71 4/8	13 2/8	13 1/8	5 5/8	5 4/8	12 2/8	Empress	ALB	Michael E. Kessler	1993	1,568
71 4/8	13 0/8	13 6/8	6 1/8	5 7/8	10 5/8	Sweetwater County	WY	Billy Tillotson	1994	1,568
71 4/8	13 0/8	12 3/8	5 7/8	5 7/8	10 0/8	Platte County	WY	Tom Pindell	1994	1,568
71 4/8	13 6/8	14 1/8	6 4/8	6 2/8	9 0/8	Saguache County	CO	Thomas J. Torrez	1994	1,568
71 4/8	13 2/8	13 4/8	5 6/8	5 7/8	11 4/8	Custer County	ID	Matt March	1994	1,568
71 4/8	14 7/8	15 0/8	5 6/8	5 4/8	10 0/8	Weld County	CO	Michael J. McArtor	1994	1,568
71 4/8	12 4/8	12 4/8	6 1/8	6 1/8	12 2/8	Larimer County	CO	Fred Eichler	1994	1,568
71 4/8	13 0/8	14 1/8	5 6/8	5 7/8	9 3/8	Moffat County	CO	Kurt W. Keskimaki	1994	1,568
71 4/8	13 5/8	13 3/8	6 0/8	6 0/8	8 4/8	Converse County	WY	Lou Edelis	1994	1,568
71 4/8	14 1/8	13 5/8	5 5/8	5 5/8	9 5/8	Natrona County	WY	Bruce R. Linke	1994	1,568
71 4/8	13 2/8	13 3/8	6 5/8	6 3/8	10 5/8	Niobrara County	WY	Robert B. Otto	1994	1,568
71 4/8	13 2/8	13 1/8	5 7/8	5 7/8	9 7/8	Converse County	WY	Trish D'Agostino	1994	1,568
71 4/8	13 7/8	14 4/8	6 7/8	6 4/8	10 3/8	Campbell County	WY	Roy M. Wible, Jr.	1994	1,568
71 4/8	14 1/8	14 4/8	5 7/8	5 6/8	10 6/8	Carter County	MT	Marty Adams	1994	1,568
71 4/8	14 0/8	13 7/8	6 1/8	5 7/8	10 2/8	Big Horn County	WY	Don R. Gifford	1994	1,568
71 4/8	13 2/8	13 2/8	5 5/8	5 5/8	9 5/8	Johnson County	WY	Rick T. Wardle	1994	1,568
71 4/8	14 3/8	14 5/8	6 0/8	6 1/8	8 1/8	Moffat County	CO	Doug Weimer	1995	1,568
71 4/8	13 3/8	13 4/8	6 2/8	6 3/8	13 2/8	Moffat County	CO	Dennis Hollenbeck	1995	1,568
71 4/8	15 3/8	15 5/8	5 5/8	5 4/8	8 0/8	Park County	WY	Brad McMillin	1995	1,568
71 4/8	13 7/8	14 0/8	6 1/8	6 0/8	8 6/8	Moffat County	CO	John Gross	1995	1,568
71 4/8	12 7/8	12 7/8	6 0/8	6 0/8	8 3/8	Weld County	CO	Jim Smith	1995	1,568
71 4/8	14 1/8	14 6/8	5 5/8	5 4/8	10 3/8	Carbon County	WY	Mark Nessman	1995	1,568
71 4/8	13 4/8	13 4/8	6 0/8	6 0/8	11 5/8	Harding County	SD	Marty Adams	1995	1,568
71 4/8	13 1/8	12 7/8	7 0/8	6 7/8	12 5/8	Moffat County	CO	Toxey Haas	1996	1,568
71 4/8	14 2/8	14 4/8	6 0/8	6 1/8	12 3/8	Weld County	CO	Mark Johnson	1996	1,568
71 4/8	14 0/8	14 2/8	5 7/8	5 6/8	11 5/8	Moffat County	CO	Tim L. Decker	1996	1,568
71 4/8	13 6/8	13 6/8	6 1/8	6 1/8	8 3/8	Sweetwater County	WY	Craig Germond	1996	1,568
71 4/8	12 5/8	12 4/8	6 1/8	6 1/8	7 6/8	Weld County	CO	Michael Radford	1996	1,568
71 4/8	13 5/8	14 0/8	6 2/8	6 0/8	10 2/8	Weld County	CO	Thomas Allen	1996	1,568
71 4/8	12 2/8	12 2/8	5 6/8	5 6/8	10 2/8	Coconino County	AZ	Michael L. Powers	1996	1,568
71 4/8	13 7/8	13 5/8	5 6/8	5 6/8	9 7/8	McKenzie County	ND	Don G. Scofield	1996	1,568
71 4/8	12 6/8	13 1/8	5 5/8	5 4/8	10 2/8	Gunnison County	CO	Chester J. Thompson	1996	1,568
71 4/8	13 4/8	13 6/8	5 5/8	5 3/8	10 4/8	Rosebud County	MT	Kerry Keller	1996	1,568
71 4/8	14 4/8	14 3/8	6 1/8	6 1/8	7 6/8	Humboldt County	NV	Cody K. Brinkerhoff	1997	1,568
71 4/8	14 0/8	14 0/8	6 1/8	5 7/8	9 3/8	Saguache County	CO	John Borge	1997	1,568

PRONGHORN

Minimum Score 67

SCORE	LENGTH OF HORN R / L	CIRCUMFERENCE OF BASE R / L	INSIDE SPREAD	AREA	STATE/ PROVINCE	HUNTER'S NAME	DATE	RANK
71 4/8	13 2/8 13 1/8	6 2/8 6 3/8	7 0/8	Rosebud County	MT	Joe Lasch	1997	1,568
71 4/8	14 0/8 14 1/8	5 4/8 5 5/8	8 3/8	Grand County	UT	Kurt Wood	1998	1,568
71 4/8	14 0/8 13 7/8	6 1/8 6 0/8	7 6/8	Converse County	WY	Bernard R. Belaire, Jr.	1998	1,568
71 4/8	13 4/8 13 4/8	5 7/8 5 7/8	10 3/8	Medicine Hat	ALB	Mark E. Titus	1998	1,568
71 4/8	14 2/8 13 5/8	6 0/8 5 7/8	9 7/8	Converse County	WY	David H. Boland	1998	1,568
71 2/8	14 4/8 14 2/8	5 7/8 5 7/8	8 1/8	Musselshell County	MT	A. A. Anderson	1960	1,664
71 2/8	14 3/8 14 5/8	5 4/8 5 4/8	13 1/8	Perkins County	SD	Elwood Patterson	1961	1,664
71 2/8	15 0/8 15 3/8	5 3/8 5 2/8	9 7/8	Natrona County	WY	Doug Pope	1976	1,664
71 2/8	14 5/8 14 7/8	5 2/8 5 2/8	12 0/8	McLean County	ND	Leo N. Patch	1977	1,664
71 2/8	12 7/8 12 6/8	5 7/8 5 7/8	9 1/8	Converse County	WY	G. Merrill Jones	1980	1,664
71 2/8	14 2/8 14 4/8	6 1/8 6 2/8	8 3/8	Sweetwater County	WY	Terry Walbridge	1980	1,664
71 2/8	13 3/8 13 3/8	5 5/8 5 6/8	8 3/8	Natrona County	WY	Hayden Allen, Jr.	1981	1,664
71 2/8	13 4/8 13 1/8	6 2/8 6 2/8	8 4/8	Sweetwater County	WY	Lyle R. Prell	1981	1,664
71 2/8	12 3/8 12 3/8	6 4/8 6 5/8	9 6/8	Sargent County	ND	Terry Hopewell	1982	1,664
71 2/8	13 4/8 13 5/8	6 0/8 5 5/8	12 0/8	Natrona County	WY	Rick Landeis	1983	1,664
71 2/8	13 0/8 13 2/8	6 2/8 6 2/8	10 7/8	Converse County	WY	Jack M. Conner	1983	1,664
71 2/8	15 0/8 15 1/8	5 7/8 5 6/8	8 4/8	Washoe County	NV	Robert L. Brooks, Jr.	1984	1,664
71 2/8	12 2/8 12 1/8	6 0/8 6 0/8	9 5/8	Converse County	WY	Jack M. Conner	1984	1,664
71 2/8	14 4/8 14 6/8	6 1/8 5 6/8	8 0/8	Powder River County	MT	Steve Kramer	1984	1,664
71 2/8	13 1/8 12 6/8	5 6/8 6 2/8	11 6/8	Johnson County	WY	Glenn Tappen	1984	1,664
71 2/8	14 3/8 13 2/8	6 0/8 5 7/8	11 6/8	Hot Springs County	WY	Mike Conner	1985	1,664
71 2/8	13 4/8 13 4/8	6 1/8 6 0/8	11 6/8	Natrona County	WY	Kelley Swift	1985	1,664
71 2/8	13 3/8 13 4/8	6 2/8 6 2/8	8 7/8	Sweetwater County	WY	David S. Petrie	1987	1,664
71 2/8	14 3/8 14 4/8	5 7/8 5 7/8	11 2/8	Tide Lake	ALB	Archie Nesbitt	1987	1,664
71 2/8	13 2/8 13 1/8	6 4/8 6 3/8	11 3/8	Moffat County	CO	Randy Lamdin	1988	1,664
71 2/8	13 0/8 13 1/8	5 1/8 5 1/8	11 2/8	White Pine County	NV	Steven P. Newberger	1988	1,664
71 2/8	13 4/8 13 5/8	6 1/8 6 0/8	8 6/8	Moffat County	CO	Daniel L. Tekavec	1988	1,664
71 2/8	14 2/8 14 2/8	6 1/8 6 1/8	10 0/8	Converse County	WY	David L. Mosher	1988	1,664
71 2/8	13 4/8 13 3/8	5 5/8 5 7/8	11 6/8	Modoc County	CA	Gary M. Gentile	1988	1,664
71 2/8	13 2/8 12 6/8	6 2/8 6 2/8	9 6/8	Lassen County	CA	John Diedrich	1988	1,664
71 2/8	12 7/8 12 7/8	6 2/8 6 1/8	11 2/8	Natrona County	WY	Michael Ryan	1988	1,664
71 2/8	13 6/8 13 2/8	5 7/8 5 7/8	9 7/8	Carbon County	WY	Willis Duhon	1989	1,664
71 2/8	13 3/8 12 6/8	6 1/8 6 0/8	8 1/8	Converse County	WY	Edward W. Vetter	1989	1,664
71 2/8	12 7/8 13 0/8	6 0/8 6 0/8	9 6/8	Harding County	SD	Daniel Dietrich	1989	1,664
71 2/8	13 1/8 13 2/8	5 4/8 5 3/8	9 6/8	Socorro County	NM	Jose Romero	1990	1,664
71 2/8	13 6/8 13 6/8	6 2/8 6 2/8	6 2/8	Moffat County	CO	Michael P. McCarty	1990	1,664
71 2/8	13 4/8 13 3/8	6 3/8 6 2/8	9 5/8	Uinta County	WY	Earl Sutherland	1990	1,664
71 2/8	14 4/8 13 6/8	5 7/8 5 5/8	8 0/8	Greenlee County	AZ	Tracy G. Hardy	1990	1,664
71 2/8	13 4/8 13 1/8	6 2/8 6 2/8	7 6/8	Johnson County	WY	Joe Coleman	1990	1,664
71 2/8	13 0/8 13 0/8	6 3/8 6 3/8	12 2/8	Forty Mile County	ALB	Darrell Hougen	1990	1,664
71 2/8	12 7/8 13 2/8	6 0/8 5 7/8	10 7/8	Converse County	WY	Dave Vander Vorst	1990	1,664
71 2/8	13 5/8 13 1/8	6 0/8 6 1/8	9 2/8	Harding County	SD	Jamie Byrne	1990	1,664
71 2/8	14 6/8 14 0/8	6 4/8 6 4/8	12 2/8	Washoe County	NV	David Niehaus	1991	1,664
71 2/8	14 1/8 14 4/8	5 5/8 5 6/8	6 5/8	Sweetwater County	WY	Larry Dickerson	1991	1,664
71 2/8	13 4/8 13 6/8	6 5/8 6 5/8	10 3/8	Converse County	WY	Steve Duranso	1991	1,664
71 2/8	13 2/8 13 1/8	6 4/8 6 2/8	7 3/8	Rosebud County	MT	Everett M. Morris	1991	1,664
71 2/8	14 1/8 14 1/8	5 7/8 5 6/8	9 1/8	Moffat County	CO	Ken Assmus	1992	1,664
71 2/8	14 1/8 13 7/8	5 4/8 5 4/8	9 6/8	Millard County	UT	Jim Fowler	1992	1,664
71 2/8	13 6/8 13 5/8	5 7/8 6 0/8	8 3/8	Sweetwater County	WY	Brian Kerr	1992	1,664
71 2/8	14 1/8 14 4/8	6 0/8 5 7/8	5 1/8	Twin Falls County	ID	Vincent Trent	1992	1,664
71 2/8	13 1/8 13 4/8	6 4/8 6 3/8	11 0/8	Sioux County	NE	Tommy M. Brown	1992	1,664
71 2/8	14 2/8 14 3/8	5 5/8 5 6/8	8 3/8	Billings County	ND	Jeff Dudgeon	1992	1,664
71 2/8	12 1/8 12 3/8	6 2/8 6 1/8	9 2/8	Converse County	WY	Steve Williams	1992	1,664
71 2/8	13 3/8 13 2/8	6 0/8 6 0/8	8 6/8	Campbell County	WY	Bob Pozner	1992	1,664
71 2/8	13 3/8 13 3/8	6 2/8 6 1/8	10 1/8	Converse County	WY	Richard Pippenger	1992	1,664
71 2/8	13 6/8 13 5/8	6 0/8 6 0/8	11 6/8	Bowman County	ND	LeAnn Buchholz	1992	1,664
71 2/8	14 3/8 14 1/8	6 1/8 5 7/8	6 4/8	Campbell County	WY	Chad S. Blank	1992	1,664
71 2/8	13 7/8 14 0/8	5 7/8 5 7/8	13 2/8	Campbell County	WY	Doy K. Curtis	1992	1,664
71 2/8	12 6/8 13 0/8	5 6/8 5 6/8	9 1/8	Moffat County	CO	Scott George	1993	1,664
71 2/8	14 0/8 14 0/8	6 3/8 6 1/8	9 6/8	Moffat County	CO	Robert E. Kearney	1994	1,664
71 2/8	12 5/8 12 6/8	6 1/8 6 1/8	10 0/8	Campbell County	WY	James D. Bradley	1994	1,664
71 2/8	13 3/8 13 4/8	6 0/8 6 0/8	12 6/8	Campbell County	WY	Matt Manske	1994	1,664
71 2/8	14 0/8 14 0/8	5 6/8 5 6/8	12 2/8	Yellowstone County	MT	Thomas J. Madden	1994	1,664
71 2/8	13 4/8 13 5/8	6 2/8 6 1/8	12 1/8	Moffat County	CO	John Giordano	1995	1,664
71 2/8	13 2/8 13 2/8	6 3/8 6 2/8	9 6/8	Sweetwater County	WY	Susan K. Barrett	1995	1,664
71 2/8	12 5/8 12 1/8	6 1/8 6 1/8	11 2/8	Tooele County	UT	E. Kip Fowler	1995	1,664
71 2/8	13 1/8 13 4/8	6 0/8 6 0/8	12 5/8	Converse County	WY	Terry R. Cassatt	1995	1,664
71 2/8	14 7/8 14 5/8	5 5/8 5 5/8	9 6/8	Campbell County	WY	Randy Kerian	1995	1,664
71 2/8	14 2/8 14 5/8	5 6/8 5 6/8	9 0/8	Campbell County	WY	Dean Revering	1995	1,664
71 2/8	14 0/8 13 6/8	5 4/8 5 5/8	7 3/8	Sioux County	NE	Clarence L. Poteet	1995	1,664
71 2/8	11 7/8 11 7/8	6 6/8 6 5/8	8 0/8	Moffat County	CO	Chuck Adams	1996	1,664
71 2/8	14 0/8 14 0/8	6 2/8 6 1/8	11 3/8	Humboldt County	NV	Robert Gillespie	1996	1,664
71 2/8	14 3/8 14 3/8	5 7/8 5 7/8	12 7/8	Juab County	UT	Kirk W. Reese	1996	1,664
71 2/8	13 5/8 13 5/8	5 7/8 6 0/8	10 2/8	Colfax County	NM	Patrick Lovato	1996	1,664
71 2/8	13 4/8 13 6/8	5 5/8 5 4/8	11 3/8	Moffat County	CO	Steve E. Sheehy	1996	1,664
71 2/8	14 6/8 14 6/8	5 4/8 5 3/8	11 4/8	McKenzie County	ND	Brad Blanchard	1996	1,664
71 2/8	13 3/8 13 3/8	6 3/8 6 2/8	12 5/8	Weld County	CO	Robert J. Vescio	1997	1,664
71 2/8	13 2/8 13 0/8	6 4/8 6 4/8	8 0/8	Weld County	CO	Paul R. Cox	1997	1,664

PRONGHORN

Minimum Score 67 — Continued

SCORE	LENGTH OF HORN R	L	CIRCUMFERENCE OF BASE R	L	INSIDE SPREAD	AREA	STATE/ PROVINCE	HUNTER'S NAME	DATE	RANK
71 2/8	14 1/8	14 2/8	6 0/8	6 0/8	14 1/8	Garfield County	MT	Sonny Templeton	1997	1,664
71 2/8	14 5/8	14 3/8	6 0/8	5 6/8	13 2/8	Harding County	SD	Jerome O. Guyant	1997	1,664
71 2/8	12 5/8	12 7/8	5 6/8	5 6/8	9 4/8	Saguache County	CO	Paul Keys	1998	1,664
71 2/8	14 2/8	14 3/8	5 6/8	5 3/8	10 2/8	Larimer County	CO	Timothy N. Gardner	1998	1,664
71 2/8	14 2/8	14 2/8	5 5/8	5 6/8	14 0/8	Rosebud County	MT	Keith M. Ross	1998	1,664
71 2/8	13 6/8	13 6/8	6 1/8	5 7/8	11 3/8	Fergus County	MT	Donny Roy	1998	1,664
71 0/8	14 0/8	13 6/8	6 2/8	5 7/8	10 4/8	Sioux County	NE	Roger F. Rehborg	1975	1,743
71 0/8	12 7/8	12 7/8	6 1/8	6 1/8	12 6/8	Washoe County	NV	Roger Iveson	1980	1,743
71 0/8	14 0/8	14 1/8	5 6/8	5 7/8	8 3/8	Converse County	WY	Eugene Smith, Jr.	1980	1,743
71 0/8	13 2/8	13 0/8	6 0/8	6 0/8	11 5/8	Converse County	WY	Mike Butler	1981	1,743
71 0/8	13 7/8	13 5/8	6 0/8	6 0/8	7 3/8	Sweetwater County	WY	Vaughn Cross	1981	1,743
71 0/8	14 1/8	14 1/8	5 7/8	5 7/8	13 2/8	Moffat County	CO	Scott Kelley	1981	1,743
71 0/8	14 7/8	14 7/8	5 6/8	5 6/8	8 1/8	Modoc County	CA	Jeff Scheetz	1982	1,743
71 0/8	13 5/8	13 4/8	5 6/8	5 6/8	8 4/8	Converse County	WY	Ted J. Jaycox	1982	1,743
71 0/8	14 4/8	14 5/8	5 5/8	5 4/8	9 3/8	McKenzie County	ND	Mark D. Hughes	1982	1,743
71 0/8	13 0/8	13 0/8	6 0/8	5 7/8	14 0/8	Carbon County	WY	Ron Stacey	1983	1,743
71 0/8	13 1/8	13 4/8	6 4/8	6 4/8	9 6/8	Moffat County	CO	Lance Cussons	1983	1,743
71 0/8	13 3/8	13 3/8	5 7/8	5 7/8	8 1/8	Natrona County	WY	Wade L. Carstens	1983	1,743
71 0/8	14 0/8	14 1/8	6 0/8	6 0/8	9 1/8	Garfield County	MT	Bruce W. Blauvelt	1983	1,743
71 0/8	13 6/8	13 4/8	5 6/8	5 6/8	10 4/8	White Pine County	NV	Simo O. Ahlgren	1984	1,743
71 0/8	14 4/8	14 2/8	5 6/8	5 6/8	9 2/8	Sweetwater County	WY	Earl Kennedy	1986	1,743
71 0/8	13 4/8	13 3/8	6 1/8	6 0/8	8 0/8	Stark County	ND	Daniel W. Johnson	1987	1,743
71 0/8	14 5/8	14 7/8	5 2/8	5 2/8	9 6/8	Moffat County	CO	Bruce HalLowell	1988	1,743
71 0/8	14 5/8	14 6/8	5 7/8	5 7/8	10 2/8	Millard County	UT	Len Cardinale	1988	1,743
71 0/8	13 2/8	13 3/8	5 6/8	5 6/8	9 3/8	Converse County	WY	Ron Foote	1988	1,743
71 0/8	14 0/8	13 5/8	5 6/8	5 6/8	13 1/8	Converse County	WY	Roy G. Burton	1988	1,743
71 0/8	14 2/8	14 2/8	5 1/8	5 1/8	17 5/8	Taos County	NM	Daniel Allred	1989	1,743
71 0/8	13 5/8	13 4/8	6 4/8	6 2/8	10 2/8	Natrona County	WY	Rickey E. Morse	1989	1,743
71 0/8	15 0/8	14 5/8	5 5/8	5 6/8	8 6/8	Musselshell County	MT	Darren Parker	1989	1,743
71 0/8	14 3/8	14 3/8	5 7/8	5 6/8	11 2/8	Valley County	MT	Ty Milne	1989	1,743
71 0/8	13 1/8	13 1/8	6 4/8	6 2/8	12 1/8	Modoc County	CA	Darrel Sudduth	1990	1,743
71 0/8	13 2/8	13 2/8	5 4/8	5 5/8	9 5/8	Moffat County	CO	Dennis Newton	1990	1,743
71 0/8	15 3/8	15 0/8	5 5/8	5 5/8	9 2/8	Converse County	WY	Paul Sieg	1990	1,743
71 0/8	13 7/8	13 5/8	6 0/8	6 0/8	7 0/8	Converse County	WY	Jeff Fitts	1991	1,743
71 0/8	13 7/8	14 0/8	5 6/8	5 5/8	11 5/8	Rosebud County	MT	Anthony Hess	1991	1,743
71 0/8	12 7/8	12 7/8	6 2/8	6 1/8	11 3/8	Converse County	WY	J. Todd Payne	1991	1,743
71 0/8	13 7/8	13 5/8	5 7/8	6 0/8	10 2/8	Buffalo	ALB	Andy P. Charchun	1991	1,743
71 0/8	13 6/8	13 7/8	5 6/8	5 6/8	9 7/8	Garfield County	MT	Randal R. Mayes	1991	1,743
71 0/8	14 2/8	14 2/8	5 7/8	5 5/8	12 6/8	Converse County	WY	Barry J. Smith	1991	1,743
71 0/8	13 0/8	13 2/8	6 2/8	6 2/8	11 6/8	Sweetwater County	WY	John Cheese	1992	1,743
71 0/8	12 6/8	13 2/8	6 1/8	6 1/8	8 3/8	Moffat County	CO	Marvin Weible	1992	1,743
71 0/8	13 0/8	13 2/8	6 4/8	6 2/8	11 1/8	Fremont County	WY	Tim Downs	1992	1,743
71 0/8	13 1/8	13 0/8	6 0/8	6 0/8	6 6/8	Converse County	WY	Mark Graham	1992	1,743
71 0/8	14 4/8	14 4/8	6 0/8	6 1/8	9 3/8	Malheur County	OR	Rick Martin	1992	1,743
71 0/8	13 7/8	14 2/8	5 5/8	5 4/8	9 1/8	Converse County	WY	Jerry Rush	1992	1,743
71 0/8	12 7/8	14 0/8	6 1/8	6 1/8	8 4/8	Rosebud County	MT	Donald Kemkes	1992	1,743
71 0/8	12 4/8	12 2/8	6 6/8	6 4/8	12 3/8	Meade County	SD	LeRoy Capp	1992	1,743
71 0/8	14 0/8	13 7/8	6 3/8	6 1/8	10 3/8	Goshen County	WY	Jerry Harding	1992	1,743
71 0/8	14 0/8	14 0/8	5 5/8	5 5/8	9 1/8	Campbell County	WY	Tim Stahman	1992	1,743
71 0/8	14 2/8	14 2/8	5 5/8	5 6/8	7 4/8	Sheridan County	WY	Billy S. Huff	1992	1,743
71 0/8	13 4/8	13 0/8	6 1/8	6 2/8	15 0/8	Grand County	UT	Shad D. Schmidt	1993	1,743
71 0/8	13 7/8	13 7/8	5 5/8	5 5/8	9 2/8	Socorro County	NM	Abe Dimas, Jr.	1993	1,743
71 0/8	12 7/8	12 2/8	5 7/8	6 0/8	8 2/8	Moffat County	CO	Blazer McClure	1993	1,743
71 0/8	14 1/8	14 3/8	5 6/8	5 6/8	11 5/8	Platte County	WY	Jeffery Allen Roback	1993	1,743
71 0/8	14 5/8	14 3/8	5 6/8	5 6/8	9 5/8	Dawes County	NE	Duane Loecker	1993	1,743
71 0/8	14 0/8	14 1/8	6 0/8	5 7/8	4 6/8	Harding County	SD	Nick Larsen	1993	1,743
71 0/8	12 6/8	13 2/8	6 2/8	6 1/8	12 7/8	Sweetwater County	WY	Tim Isaacson	1994	1,743
71 0/8	13 5/8	13 0/8	6 3/8	6 2/8	11 4/8	Moffat County	CO	Troy Cunningham	1994	1,743
71 0/8	14 2/8	14 2/8	5 4/8	5 5/8	9 0/8	Moffat County	CO	Matt Burrows	1994	1,743
71 0/8	12 7/8	12 7/8	6 2/8	6 2/8	8 6/8	Campbell County	WY	Gary English	1994	1,743
71 0/8	13 6/8	14 0/8	5 6/8	5 6/8	8 0/8	Hays	ALB	Larry Knibbs/Doug Messenger	1994	1,743
71 0/8	12 5/8	12 5/8	6 4/8	6 3/8	11 1/8	Moffat County	CO	Rocky Drake	1995	1,743
71 0/8	13 1/8	13 2/8	6 3/8	6 2/8	7 1/8	Humboldt County	NV	Archie Nesbitt	1995	1,743
71 0/8	14 6/8	14 5/8	6 0/8	6 0/8	7 2/8	Albany County	WY	Jon Deeter	1995	1,743
71 0/8	15 1/8	14 6/8	5 6/8	5 6/8	9 6/8	Weld County	CO	Dave Mahler	1995	1,743
71 0/8	14 2/8	14 2/8	6 1/8	6 0/8	6 2/8	Fergus County	MT	D. Mitch Kottas	1995	1,743
71 0/8	14 1/8	14 4/8	5 6/8	5 4/8	7 6/8	Nye County	NV	Gary Zupanic	1996	1,743
71 0/8	13 6/8	13 0/8	6 0/8	6 0/8	13 6/8	Moffat County	CO	Ron Miller	1996	1,743
71 0/8	14 3/8	14 3/8	6 1/8	5 7/8	14 3/8	Lincoln County	NM	Gregory L. Gray	1996	1,743
71 0/8	14 6/8	14 5/8	5 6/8	5 5/8	12 5/8	Sweetwater County	WY	Robert S. Jones	1996	1,743
71 0/8	14 0/8	13 6/8	5 4/8	5 4/8	10 0/8	Campbell County	WY	Todd Galbreath	1997	1,743
71 0/8	13 1/8	13 0/8	6 0/8	5 7/8	8 6/8	Moffat County	CO	Dale R. Petefish	1998	1,743
71 0/8	14 6/8	15 1/8	5 6/8	5 7/8	12 2/8	Sweetwater County	WY	Mike Barrett	1998	1,743
71 0/8	14 0/8	13 2/8	6 0/8	6 1/8	7 4/8	Powder River County	MT	Don G. Scofield	1998	1,743
70 6/8	14 7/8	15 2/8	5 5/8	5 4/8	10 3/8	Washoe County	NV	Frank M. Davis	1967	1,811
70 6/8	13 2/8	13 2/8	6 3/8	6 2/8	9 6/8	Washoe County	NV	Gordon A. Nicholson	1972	1,811
70 6/8	12 5/8	12 4/8	5 5/8	5 4/8	9 0/8	Natrona County	WY	Bernard R. Giacoletto	1973	1,811
70 6/8	14 1/8	14 3/8	5 6/8	5 7/8	15 6/8	Deschutes County	OR	William E. Lancaster	1973	1,811

PRONGHORN

Minimum Score 67

SCORE	LENGTH OF HORN R / L		CIRCUMFERENCE OF BASE R / L		INSIDE SPREAD	AREA	STATE/PROVINCE	HUNTER'S NAME	DATE	RANK
70 6/8	11 2/8	11 2/8	6 0/8	6 0/8	10 1/8	Natrona County	WY	Jerry Zanandrea	1976	1,811
70 6/8	13 4/8	13 6/8	5 7/8	5 6/8	9 7/8	Lemhi County	ID	Alan Monroe	1979	1,811
70 6/8	13 0/8	13 3/8	5 6/8	5 5/8	7 4/8	Stanley County	SD	Rick Ray	1979	1,811
70 6/8	13 6/8	14 0/8	5 4/8	5 3/8	12 1/8	Converse County	WY	Russell Hull	1980	1,811
70 6/8	14 0/8	14 0/8	5 4/8	5 4/8	12 6/8	Converse County	WY	Frank Moore	1980	1,811
70 6/8	13 3/8	13 5/8	6 0/8	6 0/8	13 7/8	Sweetwater County	WY	Victor Organ	1980	1,811
70 6/8	14 3/8	14 1/8	5 4/8	5 3/8	12 5/8	Tillard Ranch	WY	Charles A. Myers	1981	1,811
70 6/8	13 4/8	13 4/8	6 2/8	6 2/8	10 1/8	Moffat County	CO	Mike Miller	1981	1,811
70 6/8	15 0/8	15 1/8	5 5/8	5 4/8	10 4/8	Klamath County	OR	Paul D. Lewis	1982	1,811
70 6/8	12 5/8	12 5/8	5 7/8	5 7/8	9 4/8	Converse County	WY	Steve Woodman	1982	1,811
70 6/8	13 7/8	13 7/8	6 0/8	6 1/8	10 4/8	Butte County	ID	Larry A. Wilde	1983	1,811
70 6/8	13 5/8	13 3/8	5 6/8	5 6/8	9 4/8	Converse County	WY	Dan Naccarto	1983	1,811
70 6/8	13 1/8	13 1/8	6 0/8	5 6/8	11 1/8	Natrona County	WY	Don Wilson	1983	1,811
70 6/8	12 4/8	13 0/8	6 4/8	6 3/8	14 1/8	Powder River County	MT	Daryl E. Jennings	1983	1,811
70 6/8	16 2/8	15 4/8	5 1/8	5 1/8	9 6/8	Golden Valley County	ND	Thomas S. Lunski	1983	1,811
70 6/8	13 7/8	13 7/8	5 3/8	5 2/8	9 3/8	Moffat County	CO	Darryl Quidort	1984	1,811
70 6/8	15 1/8	14 6/8	6 1/8	6 0/8	12 7/8	Lassen County	CA	Wayne Goodrich	1985	1,811
70 6/8	12 6/8	14 3/8	5 7/8	5 6/8	11 3/8	Slope County	ND	Todd Seymanski	1985	1,811
70 6/8	14 3/8	14 2/8	5 7/8	5 6/8	11 1/8	Sweetwater County	WY	Craig Boheler	1986	1,811
70 6/8	13 0/8	13 3/8	6 3/8	6 1/8	10 2/8	Jefferson County	ID	Tony Hyde	1986	1,811
70 6/8	14 0/8	13 6/8	5 7/8	5 7/8	7 0/8	Moffat County	CO	Mike Ottenbacher	1986	1,811
70 6/8	13 1/8	13 4/8	6 2/8	6 0/8	11 0/8	Rosebud County	MT	Gary Olsen	1986	1,811
70 6/8	13 0/8	12 6/8	6 4/8	6 4/8	10 0/8	Billings County	ND	Ron Tudahl	1987	1,811
70 6/8	13 0/8	12 6/8	6 4/8	6 3/8	12 2/8	Moffat County	CO	Steven Wilson	1988	1,811
70 6/8	14 2/8	14 2/8	5 4/8	5 3/8	7 4/8	Slope County	ND	Scott Bradac	1988	1,811
70 6/8	14 0/8	14 0/8	5 5/8	5 5/8	11 0/8	Converse County	WY	David M. Ackland, Jr.	1988	1,811
70 6/8	13 7/8	13 7/8	5 5/8	5 4/8	7 1/8	Converse County	WY	Kevin "Krauty" Krautkramer	1988	1,811
70 6/8	12 6/8	12 6/8	6 3/8	6 1/8	8 4/8	Campbell County	WY	Bob Austin	1988	1,811
70 6/8	14 0/8	13 6/8	5 7/8	5 6/8	10 5/8	Moffat County	CO	Wayne Depperschmidt	1989	1,811
70 6/8	13 2/8	13 1/8	5 5/8	5 4/8	9 7/8	Millard County	UT	David B. Nielsen	1989	1,811
70 6/8	13 1/8	13 1/8	6 2/8	6 1/8	7 3/8	Billings County	ND	Al Zeller	1989	1,811
70 6/8	14 0/8	13 4/8	5 6/8	5 6/8	10 4/8	Moffat County	CO	Dan Gillenwater	1989	1,811
70 6/8	13 3/8	13 4/8	6 3/8	6 3/8	8 6/8	Moffat County	CO	Mike Boland	1989	1,811
70 6/8	12 7/8	13 6/8	5 7/8	5 6/8	11 1/8	Hughes County	SD	Lyle Goodall	1989	1,811
70 6/8	12 2/8	12 4/8	6 2/8	6 4/8	10 2/8	Garfield County	MT	Bob Morton	1989	1,811
70 6/8	14 0/8	14 0/8	6 0/8	6 0/8	7 7/8	Uinta County	WY	Douglas Shelby	1990	1,811
70 6/8	14 2/8	14 2/8	5 7/8	5 7/8	8 4/8	Moffat County	CO	Marvin Cochran	1990	1,811
70 6/8	13 4/8	13 4/8	5 7/8	6 0/8	7 6/8	Moffat County	CO	Dennis Modlin	1990	1,811
70 6/8	12 5/8	13 2/8	6 3/8	6 3/8	9 7/8	Natrona County	WY	Edward J. Brennan	1990	1,811
70 6/8	14 1/8	14 1/8	5 6/8	5 6/8	10 0/8	Modoc County	CA	John Garr	1991	1,811
70 6/8	14 2/8	14 4/8	6 1/8	6 1/8	12 7/8	Meade County	SD	Dan Limmer	1991	1,811
70 6/8	13 2/8	13 3/8	6 1/8	6 1/8	11 2/8	White Pine County	NV	Brett North	1992	1,811
70 6/8	13 6/8	13 4/8	5 7/8	5 7/8	6 6/8	Owyhee County	ID	Brian Hunter Heck	1992	1,811
70 6/8	13 6/8	14 0/8	6 2/8	6 1/8	12 4/8	Carbon County	WY	Boyd Burbank	1992	1,811
70 6/8	12 3/8	12 3/8	6 0/8	6 0/8	9 2/8	Converse County	WY	Justin Wells	1992	1,811
70 6/8	14 3/8	14 1/8	5 6/8	5 6/8	11 0/8	Converse County	WY	John North	1992	1,811
70 6/8	12 4/8	12 3/8	5 6/8	5 6/8	7 6/8	Billings County	ND	Jeff Hapala	1992	1,811
70 6/8	13 2/8	13 4/8	5 6/8	5 6/8	11 1/8	Converse County	WY	Gary Boldt	1992	1,811
70 6/8	13 7/8	13 7/8	5 7/8	6 0/8	8 5/8	Fergus County	MT	Kelly Norskog	1992	1,811
70 6/8	15 0/8	14 6/8	5 3/8	5 5/8	18 3/8	McHenry County	ND	Paul Klimpel	1992	1,811
70 6/8	13 2/8	13 1/8	5 6/8	5 5/8	9 5/8	Harding County	SD	John Simpson	1992	1,811
70 6/8	14 1/8	14 0/8	6 0/8	6 0/8	10 7/8	Sioux County	NE	Walter Wright	1992	1,811
70 6/8	13 6/8	13 4/8	6 4/8	6 2/8	11 3/8	Chaves County	NM	Joseph Strasser, Jr.	1993	1,811
70 6/8	14 5/8	14 2/8	5 7/8	5 5/8	12 1/8	Fremont County	WY	Bradley T. Miller	1994	1,811
70 6/8	13 6/8	13 5/8	5 5/8	5 4/8	11 2/8	Millard County	UT	Troy Ross	1994	1,811
70 6/8	13 4/8	13 6/8	5 6/8	5 6/8	8 4/8	Owyhee County	ID	Jeff L. Varner	1994	1,811
70 6/8	13 6/8	13 4/8	5 5/8	5 5/8	13 2/8	Washington County	CO	Guy Pierce	1994	1,811
70 6/8	13 3/8	13 5/8	6 3/8	6 2/8	10 3/8	Sweetwater County	WY	Mark L. Preston	1994	1,811
70 6/8	12 6/8	12 6/8	6 1/8	6 1/8	10 6/8	Weld County	CO	James L. Tatro	1994	1,811
70 6/8	14 6/8	14 6/8	5 3/8	5 2/8	9 6/8	Manyberries	ALB	Eric Rauhanen	1994	1,811
70 6/8	13 0/8	13 1/8	6 3/8	6 4/8	9 2/8	Kimball County	NE	Brian Ray Pierce	1994	1,811
70 6/8	13 7/8	13 5/8	6 3/8	6 2/8	6 1/8	Campbell County	WY	Mike Reardon	1994	1,811
70 6/8	13 4/8	13 7/8	5 3/8	5 4/8	9 7/8	Lincoln County	NM	Curtis D. O'Brien	1994	1,811
70 6/8	12 4/8	12 5/8	5 6/8	5 6/8	9 2/8	Wallace County	KS	Daniel P. Carmen	1994	1,811
70 6/8	15 1/8	15 0/8	5 2/8	5 2/8	10 7/8	Union County	NM	Paul Rigsby	1995	1,811
70 6/8	12 7/8	12 6/8	6 1/8	6 2/8	10 7/8	Converse County	WY	Mike Castleberry	1995	1,811
70 6/8	13 5/8	13 5/8	5 6/8	5 7/8	8 7/8	Campbell County	WY	Anna Nyreen	1995	1,811
70 6/8	14 3/8	14 1/8	5 7/8	5 5/8	10 6/8	Garfield County	MT	Sonny Templeton	1995	1,811
70 6/8	12 3/8	12 1/8	6 2/8	6 4/8	10 4/8	Converse County	WY	Greg Peters	1995	1,811
70 6/8	14 0/8	13 7/8	5 4/8	5 6/8	7 1/8	Carbon County	UT	Frank Anderson	1996	1,811
70 6/8	14 6/8	14 0/8	6 2/8	6 4/8	10 5/8	Lincoln County	NM	Mariano Taglialegami	1996	1,811
70 6/8	13 2/8	13 2/8	6 0/8	5 6/8	9 6/8	Natrona County	WY	Jerry D. Porter	1996	1,811
70 6/8	13 4/8	13 6/8	5 7/8	5 6/8	7 0/8	Converse County	WY	Frank S. Noska IV	1996	1,811
70 6/8	13 0/8	13 0/8	6 0/8	5 6/8	9 2/8	Converse County	WY	Paul Maples	1996	1,811
70 6/8	14 1/8	14 5/8	6 1/8	6 0/8	9 2/8	Converse County	WY	George Postma	1996	1,811
70 6/8	12 5/8	12 7/8	5 3/8	5 3/8	9 3/8	Rosebud County	MT	Mark R. Sherman	1996	1,811
70 6/8	13 6/8	13 2/8	6 0/8	6 1/8	10 1/8	Fergus County	MT	Gary Wiley	1996	1,811
70 6/8	14 2/8	14 4/8	6 1/8	6 2/8	10 1/8	Campbell County	WY	Kevin A. LaRoche	1997	1,811

PRONGHORN

Minimum Score 67 — Continued

SCORE	LENGTH OF HORN R / L	CIRCUMFERENCE OF BASE R / L	INSIDE SPREAD	AREA	STATE/ PROVINCE	HUNTER'S NAME	DATE	RANK
70 6/8	12 7/8 12 2/8	6 3/8 6 3/8	10 6/8	Johnson County	WY	Ronald E. Witwer	1997	1,811
70 6/8	14 6/8 14 5/8	5 6/8 5 5/8	7 2/8	Lander County	NV	Jason R. New	1998	1,811
70 6/8	13 0/8 13 1/8	6 1/8 6 1/8	10 2/8	Owyhee County	ID	Steve Wiedmeier	1998	1,811
70 6/8	13 7/8 14 0/8	5 5/8 5 6/8	11 0/8	Tooele County	UT	Chad J. Hall	1998	1,811
70 6/8	14 1/8 14 3/8	5 3/8 5 2/8	8 7/8	Larimer County	CO	Richard E. DeLia	1998	1,811
70 6/8	13 4/8 14 0/8	6 1/8 6 0/8	12 5/8	Rosebud County	MT	Jason Flaherty	1998	1,811
70 4/8	14 1/8 14 2/8	5 6/8 5 5/8	13 6/8	Custer County	MT	Bob Torgerson	1964	1,899
70 4/8	12 3/8 12 3/8	5 7/8 5 6/8	7 5/8	Ward County	ND	Bob Torgerson	1964	1,899
70 4/8	12 5/8 12 4/8	6 0/8 6 0/8	10 5/8	Sweetwater County	WY	Vern A. Butler	1973	1,899
70 4/8	14 2/8 14 1/8	5 5/8 5 4/8	8 2/8	Fall River County	SD	Noel Feather, Jr.	1975	1,899
70 4/8	13 0/8 13 0/8	6 4/8 6 4/8	9 3/8	Clark County	ID	Larry Cross	1977	1,899
70 4/8	14 5/8 14 0/8	6 4/8 6 1/8	9 6/8	Meade County	SD	Floyd McElroy	1977	1,899
70 4/8	13 6/8 13 4/8	6 1/8 6 1/8	11 6/8	Grant County	NE	Albert Kant	1978	1,899
70 4/8	13 2/8 13 1/8	5 4/8 5 3/8	7 5/8	Clark County	ID	Ron Johnson	1980	1,899
70 4/8	13 0/8 13 1/8	6 1/8 6 1/8	9 1/8	Area 55	WY	Walter Walbridge	1980	1,899
70 4/8	13 4/8 13 6/8	5 7/8 5 7/8	11 4/8	Converse County	WY	James D. Miller	1981	1,899
70 4/8	13 7/8 13 4/8	6 1/8 6 0/8	14 1/8	Moffat County	CO	Gene Moore	1981	1,899
70 4/8	15 0/8 15 0/8	5 3/8 5 3/8	8 7/8	Perkins County	SD	John Pollreisz	1981	1,899
70 4/8	13 7/8 13 5/8	5 6/8 5 6/8	9 1/8	Natrona County	WY	Gordon W. Stone	1981	1,899
70 4/8	13 3/8 13 0/8	6 1/8 6 1/8	9 3/8	Hughes County	SD	Darrel L. Reinke	1982	1,899
70 4/8	14 2/8 14 3/8	5 5/8 5 5/8	8 6/8	Natrona County	WY	Ray Smith	1982	1,899
70 4/8	12 4/8 13 1/8	6 3/8 6 3/8	8 6/8	Moffat County	CO	Janet Schreur	1983	1,899
70 4/8	13 5/8 13 5/8	5 6/8 5 7/8	7 7/8	Converse County	WY	Al Sullivan	1983	1,899
70 4/8	13 1/8 13 1/8	6 2/8 6 0/8	10 4/8	Converse County	WY	Rick Poe	1983	1,899
70 4/8	12 7/8 13 1/8	5 6/8 5 6/8	8 3/8	Moffat County	CO	Gary McCain	1983	1,899
70 4/8	13 4/8 13 4/8	5 7/8 5 6/8	8 2/8	Converse County	WY	Rick Walker	1983	1,899
70 4/8	13 1/8 13 0/8	5 7/8 6 0/8	8 3/8	Moffat County	CO	H. R. 'Rusty' Neely	1984	1,899
70 4/8	13 2/8 13 3/8	6 0/8 6 0/8	8 3/8	Converse County	WY	Anthony Ruggeri	1984	1,899
70 4/8	12 4/8 13 0/8	6 4/8 6 4/8	11 1/8	Converse County	WY	Robin Klemme	1984	1,899
70 4/8	12 1/8 12 3/8	6 0/8 6 0/8	10 6/8	Converse County	WY	John M. McAteer	1984	1,899
70 4/8	13 5/8 13 4/8	6 0/8 6 0/8	10 0/8	Campbell County	WY	Tony Snow	1984	1,899
70 4/8	13 2/8 13 2/8	6 1/8 6 1/8	11 6/8	Modoc County	CA	Robert L. Smith	1986	1,899
70 4/8	15 1/8 15 7/8	5 6/8 5 5/8	15 0/8	Lassen County	CA	Tom Gordon	1986	1,899
70 4/8	14 3/8 13 0/8	5 7/8 5 7/8	11 3/8	San Miguel County	CO	Bill Wilson	1986	1,899
70 4/8	13 5/8 13 6/8	5 3/8 5 3/8	11 6/8	Moffat County	CO	Glenn Pritchard	1986	1,899
70 4/8	13 1/8 13 2/8	6 0/8 6 0/8	8 3/8	Brewster County	TX	Michael M. Reamy	1986	1,899
70 4/8	13 2/8 12 7/8	6 5/8 6 4/8	9 2/8	Sweetwater County	WY	Brenda Hatcher	1987	1,899
70 4/8	13 3/8 13 2/8	6 4/8 6 4/8	9 7/8	Converse County	WY	Eric Wayne Noble	1987	1,899
70 4/8	13 7/8 13 6/8	5 6/8 5 4/8	11 1/8	Presidio County	TX	K. D. Sandifer	1987	1,899
70 4/8	14 7/8 15 0/8	5 3/8 5 3/8	12 5/8	Sweetwater County	WY	Don Waechtler	1988	1,899
70 4/8	13 2/8 13 2/8	6 0/8 6 0/8	11 0/8	Campbell County	WY	Gary D. Johansen	1988	1,899
70 4/8	13 6/8 13 1/8	5 6/8 6 1/8	6 7/8	Humboldt County	NV	Dr. John F. Lohse	1989	1,899
70 4/8	13 6/8 14 0/8	5 7/8 6 0/8	10 4/8	Washoe County	NV	David A. Heffner	1989	1,899
70 4/8	13 2/8 13 3/8	6 3/8 6 3/8	8 5/8	Carbon County	WY	Robert R. Sherman	1989	1,899
70 4/8	13 6/8 13 6/8	5 7/8 5 7/8	9 3/8	Millard County	UT	Stan Xavier	1989	1,899
70 4/8	14 1/8 14 1/8	5 6/8 5 6/8	13 6/8	Hot Springs County	WY	Jim Fraizer	1989	1,899
70 4/8	13 2/8 13 4/8	6 4/8 6 5/8	11 4/8	Converse County	WY	Clem Grimaldi	1989	1,899
70 4/8	13 2/8 12 7/8	6 0/8 6 0/8	7 6/8	Natrona County	WY	Ohne Raasch	1989	1,899
70 4/8	14 6/8 14 7/8	5 4/8 5 4/8	7 4/8	Bowman County	ND	Nolan A. Johnson	1989	1,899
70 4/8	13 0/8 13 2/8	6 1/8 6 0/8	8 2/8	Moffat County	CO	Steve Overstreet	1990	1,899
70 4/8	13 7/8 13 7/8	5 6/8 5 6/8	12 2/8	Moffat County	CO	Jeff Knights	1990	1,899
70 4/8	13 4/8 13 0/8	6 0/8 6 0/8	8 6/8	Uinta County	WY	Kyle D. Hansen	1990	1,899
70 4/8	12 7/8 12 7/8	6 4/8 6 4/8	8 7/8	Natrona County	WY	Kevin Davis	1990	1,899
70 4/8	14 3/8 14 3/8	6 0/8 6 0/8	11 5/8	Douglas County	NV	Mark Custis	1991	1,899
70 4/8	13 1/8 12 7/8	5 6/8 5 7/8	6 3/8	Moffat County	CO	Kurt W. Keskimaki	1991	1,899
70 4/8	13 5/8 13 5/8	5 7/8 5 6/8	12 2/8	Park County	WY	Charles R. Durm	1991	1,899
70 4/8	14 1/8 14 0/8	5 4/8 5 2/8	14 0/8	Divide County	ND	Robert M. Brunner	1991	1,899
70 4/8	12 4/8 12 4/8	5 6/8 5 7/8	8 7/8	Golden Valley County	ND	Terry Buechler	1991	1,899
70 4/8	14 0/8 13 4/8	6 0/8 6 0/8	12 0/8	Lincoln County	WY	John E. Alexander	1992	1,899
70 4/8	14 3/8 14 3/8	5 5/8 5 6/8	6 4/8	Moffat County	CO	Ken Hoehn	1992	1,899
70 4/8	12 4/8 12 6/8	6 2/8 6 3/8	9 5/8	Fremont County	WY	Lyle R. Prell	1992	1,899
70 4/8	13 6/8 13 6/8	5 5/8 5 4/8	8 4/8	Converse County	WY	Robert Radford	1992	1,899
70 4/8	13 7/8 14 2/8	6 1/8 6 0/8	11 5/8	Campbell County	WY	Karl Schilling	1992	1,899
70 4/8	13 5/8 13 6/8	6 0/8 6 0/8	9 3/8	Fergus County	MT	Jerry Knerr	1992	1,899
70 4/8	14 3/8 14 3/8	5 3/8 5 3/8	14 1/8	McKenzie County	ND	Vernon D. Hahn	1992	1,899
70 4/8	12 6/8 13 1/8	6 5/8 6 3/8	16 2/8	Natrona County	WY	Brian L. Wagner	1992	1,899
70 4/8	15 2/8 15 2/8	5 3/8 5 3/8	13 7/8	Owyhee County	ID	Terry Bennett	1993	1,899
70 4/8	13 4/8 13 4/8	6 1/8 6 2/8	10 6/8	Garfield County	MT	Mike Coleman	1993	1,899
70 4/8	13 0/8 13 0/8	6 2/8 6 1/8	8 1/8	Moffat County	CO	Elmer R. Luce, Jr.	1993	1,899
70 4/8	13 2/8 13 3/8	6 0/8 6 0/8	11 5/8	Moffat County	CO	Jay Dart	1994	1,899
70 4/8	13 4/8 13 5/8	5 5/8 5 6/8	9 6/8	McCone County	MT	Dan Sturgis	1994	1,899
70 4/8	13 4/8 13 4/8	5 4/8 5 4/8	10 4/8	Campbell County	WY	Bruce Hudalla	1994	1,899
70 4/8	14 3/8 14 5/8	5 6/8 5 6/8	7 5/8	Thomas County	NE	Phil Chvala	1994	1,899
70 4/8	14 0/8 13 6/8	5 6/8 6 0/8	9 2/8	Elko County	NV	John R. Sneed	1995	1,899
70 4/8	15 1/8 15 2/8	5 3/8 5 3/8	11 6/8	Socorro County	NM	Ray A. Krause	1995	1,899
70 4/8	13 6/8 13 5/8	5 3/8 5 4/8	6 4/8	Saguache County	CO	Burton R. Thompson, Jr.	1995	1,899
70 4/8	14 0/8 13 4/8	5 6/8 5 5/8	9 6/8	Saguache County	CO	Ted McMillion	1995	1,899
70 4/8	13 6/8 14 0/8	5 4/8 5 3/8	10 4/8	Big Horn County	WY	Jerome D. Larson	1996	1,899

PRONGHORN

Minimum Score 67
Continued

SCORE	LENGTH OF HORN R / L		CIRCUMFERENCE OF BASE R / L		INSIDE SPREAD	AREA	STATE/ PROVINCE	HUNTER'S NAME	DATE	RANK
70 4/8	13 4/8	13 6/8	5 6/8	5 5/8	9 6/8	Moffat County	CO	Marvin Reichenau	1996	1,899
70 4/8	12 7/8	12 6/8	6 2/8	6 2/8	8 3/8	Campbell County	WY	Clayton E. Klingensmith	1996	1,899
70 4/8	13 2/8	13 3/8	5 6/8	5 6/8	8 2/8	Converse County	WY	Scott Hallock	1996	1,899
70 4/8	13 6/8	13 3/8	6 0/8	5 7/8	12 0/8	Natrona County	WY	Wayne H. Andersen	1996	1,899
70 4/8	14 0/8	13 6/8	5 6/8	5 5/8	8 6/8	Converse County	WY	Paul J. Herrera	1996	1,899
70 4/8	14 2/8	13 7/8	5 5/8	5 5/8	6 7/8	Weston County	WY	Joseph B. Hines	1996	1,899
70 4/8	13 2/8	13 1/8	5 6/8	5 6/8	11 3/8	Converse County	WY	Byron LaFollette	1996	1,899
70 4/8	13 0/8	13 3/8	5 6/8	5 5/8	8 5/8	Carbon County	UT	Kyle Fox	1997	1,899
70 4/8	14 4/8	14 7/8	5 7/8	5 7/8	7 7/8	Weld County	CO	Fred Johnson	1997	1,899
70 4/8	15 0/8	14 7/8	5 3/8	5 3/8	8 0/8	Big Horn County	MT	Jason Watson	1997	1,899
70 4/8	14 0/8	14 0/8	5 6/8	5 6/8	7 6/8	Converse County	WY	Jim G. Winjum	1998	1,899
70 4/8	13 2/8	12 7/8	6 0/8	6 0/8	9 5/8	Larimer County	CO	Mark E. Gonyo	1998	1,899
70 4/8	12 4/8	12 4/8	6 4/8	6 1/8	9 2/8	Converse County	WY	Patrick Sullivan	1998	1,899
70 4/8	13 6/8	13 6/8	5 4/8	5 4/8	7 3/8	Natrona County	WY	Alfred J. Gemrich	1998	1,899
70 2/8	15 2/8	15 4/8	5 4/8	5 3/8	11 5/8	Natrona County	WY	Larry J. Colombo	1970	1,985
70 2/8	12 7/8	12 7/8	6 1/8	6 1/8	12 5/8	Converse County	WY	Edward Coy	1972	1,985
70 2/8	14 0/8	14 0/8	5 6/8	5 6/8	13 7/8	Butte County	ID	Dale Dunn	1973	1,985
70 2/8	12 6/8	13 0/8	6 3/8	6 3/8	9 0/8	Dawes County	NE	Bruce Troester	1973	1,985
70 2/8	12 2/8	12 2/8	5 5/8	5 5/8	9 2/8	Saguache County	CO	Sandra Scheid	1975	1,985
70 2/8	13 2/8	13 4/8	5 6/8	5 6/8	11 0/8	Saguache County	CO	Tom Tietz	1977	1,985
70 2/8	13 6/8	13 6/8	6 6/8	6 4/8	10 6/8	Sweetwater County	WY	Vaughn Cross	1980	1,985
70 2/8	14 2/8	11 7/8	6 1/8	6 1/8	10 0/8	Converse County	WY	Anthony Wells	1980	1,985
70 2/8	13 7/8	13 5/8	6 0/8	6 0/8	9 3/8	Moffat County	CO	Dave Skiff	1981	1,985
70 2/8	13 1/8	13 2/8	6 2/8	6 1/8	8 1/8	Natrona County	WY	Jim Plemmons	1981	1,985
70 2/8	14 2/8	14 3/8	5 5/8	5 5/8	9 6/8	Lassen County	CA	B. Jensen/F. Searle	1981	1,985
70 2/8	12 6/8	12 7/8	6 0/8	5 7/8	9 6/8	Carbon County	WY	George Raab	1982	1,985
70 2/8	14 0/8	14 0/8	5 7/8	5 6/8	10 2/8	Converse County	WY	Brad Johnson	1982	1,985
70 2/8	13 6/8	14 1/8	6 1/8	6 0/8	12 2/8	Natrona County	WY	Tim Sturm	1982	1,985
70 2/8	12 4/8	12 4/8	5 5/8	5 7/8	10 6/8	Moffat County	CO	Wendy Decker	1983	1,985
70 2/8	12 2/8	12 2/8	6 0/8	6 0/8	10 3/8	Converse County	WY	Ron Montross	1983	1,985
70 2/8	13 0/8	13 4/8	5 6/8	5 7/8	10 6/8	Moffat County	CO	Rick Kralicek	1983	1,985
70 2/8	13 4/8	13 6/8	5 7/8	5 5/8	9 7/8	Sweetwater County	WY	Judd Cooney	1983	1,985
70 2/8	13 2/8	13 5/8	5 5/8	5 5/8	10 6/8	Converse County	WY	Rocky Chisholm	1983	1,985
70 2/8	13 0/8	13 0/8	5 6/8	5 6/8	11 6/8	Sweetwater County	WY	Michael R. Westvang	1984	1,985
70 2/8	12 6/8	13 2/8	5 7/8	5 7/8	11 1/8	Carbon County	WY	Ken Bean	1984	1,985
70 2/8	13 5/8	13 6/8	6 1/8	5 7/8	10 3/8	McCone County	MT	Frank Kasten III	1984	1,985
70 2/8	13 0/8	12 6/8	6 0/8	6 0/8	12 1/8	Sweetwater County	WY	David Wells	1985	1,985
70 2/8	13 0/8	12 7/8	6 2/8	6 2/8	9 3/8	Converse County	WY	Theodore C. Dzienis	1985	1,985
70 2/8	13 6/8	14 1/8	6 1/8	6 1/8	8 7/8	Powder River County	MT	Stephen J. Jaworski	1985	1,985
70 2/8	15 0/8	14 7/8	5 1/8	5 1/8	9 6/8	Las Animas County	CO	Bill Swift	1985	1,985
70 2/8	13 5/8	13 4/8	5 6/8	5 7/8	8 6/8	Sweetwater County	WY	Darren L. Shirley	1986	1,985
70 2/8	13 5/8	13 5/8	6 0/8	6 1/8	8 0/8	Billings County	ND	Randy Bakken	1986	1,985
70 2/8	13 3/8	13 3/8	5 6/8	5 5/8	9 2/8	Carbon County	WY	Duane Hicks	1987	1,985
70 2/8	13 2/8	13 3/8	6 0/8	5 7/8	9 5/8	Converse County	WY	James H. Miller	1987	1,985
70 2/8	13 4/8	14 0/8	6 0/8	6 2/8	10 2/8	Lincoln County	NV	Michael W. Zech	1987	1,985
70 2/8	14 6/8	14 2/8	5 5/8	5 6/8	9 2/8	Humboldt County	NV	Clayton J. Larsen	1988	1,985
70 2/8	13 2/8	14 0/8	5 7/8	5 7/8	15 1/8	Moffat County	CO	Kurt W. Keskimaki	1988	1,985
70 2/8	12 5/8	12 7/8	5 7/8	5 7/8	14 6/8	Moffat County	CO	Sam Godfrey	1988	1,985
70 2/8	13 4/8	13 5/8	6 0/8	5 7/8	11 0/8	Moffat County	CO	Jim Tatro	1988	1,985
70 2/8	13 4/8	12 6/8	5 7/8	5 6/8	11 2/8	Slope County	ND	Todd Seymanski	1988	1,985
70 2/8	14 2/8	14 2/8	5 6/8	5 6/8	8 5/8	Converse County	WY	M. R. James	1988	1,985
70 2/8	14 1/8	14 0/8	5 5/8	5 4/8	10 4/8	Chouteau County	MT	Jack A. Clouse	1988	1,985
70 2/8	14 0/8	13 6/8	6 0/8	6 0/8	9 1/8	Converse County	WY	Joel M. Riotto	1989	1,985
70 2/8	14 7/8	14 7/8	5 4/8	5 3/8	16 2/8	Converse County	WY	Fred Wallace	1989	1,985
70 2/8	13 1/8	13 2/8	6 0/8	5 7/8	10 7/8	Carbon County	WY	Donald P. Peel	1989	1,985
70 2/8	14 1/8	14 1/8	5 4/8	5 4/8	11 3/8	Petroleum County	MT	Clark Jenner	1989	1,985
70 2/8	14 5/8	15 1/8	5 4/8	5 3/8	7 7/8	Klamath County	OR	Randy Carter	1990	1,985
70 2/8	12 4/8	12 5/8	6 0/8	6 0/8	9 4/8	McKenzie County	ND	Alan Smith	1990	1,985
70 2/8	12 1/8	12 0/8	6 1/8	6 1/8	7 6/8	Campbell County	WY	Craig Boheler	1990	1,985
70 2/8	14 0/8	13 7/8	5 6/8	5 5/8	10 2/8	Carbon County	WY	Tim Cuthriell	1991	1,985
70 2/8	13 4/8	13 2/8	6 0/8	6 2/8	11 3/8	Uinta County	WY	Kevin D. Hatfield	1991	1,985
70 2/8	12 4/8	12 4/8	6 2/8	6 0/8	7 5/8	Sweetwater County	WY	Carl G. Esterly	1991	1,985
70 2/8	14 0/8	13 6/8	5 5/8	5 5/8	8 0/8	Powder River County	MT	Don Scofield	1991	1,985
70 2/8	14 2/8	14 0/8	5 5/8	5 4/8	12 0/8	Coconino County	AZ	Kevin Robinson	1991	1,985
70 2/8	12 5/8	13 1/8	6 2/8	6 2/8	10 5/8	Sublette County	WY	Stephen Kotz	1991	1,985
70 2/8	14 6/8	15 2/8	5 5/8	5 4/8	8 3/8	Converse County	WY	Charles Peters	1991	1,985
70 2/8	14 6/8	14 3/8	6 0/8	5 6/8	10 3/8	Converse County	WY	Roger Brittain	1991	1,985
70 2/8	13 0/8	12 6/8	5 7/8	6 0/8	7 6/8	Niobrara County	WY	Thomas D. Mackowski	1991	1,985
70 2/8	13 4/8	13 2/8	6 0/8	5 7/8	14 1/8	Daggett County	UT	Steve Dailey	1991	1,985
70 2/8	13 6/8	14 2/8	5 7/8	5 6/8	10 0/8	Campbell County	WY	Al Ratajesak	1991	1,985
70 2/8	13 2/8	13 1/8	6 1/8	6 1/8	8 2/8	Converse County	WY	Michael E. Zimmerman	1991	1,985
70 2/8	12 5/8	12 7/8	6 3/8	6 3/8	9 0/8	Converse County	WY	Myron Jochmann	1991	1,985
70 2/8	14 7/8	14 4/8	5 6/8	5 6/8	9 6/8	Sioux County	NE	Steve Neujahr	1991	1,985
70 2/8	15 1/8	14 2/8	5 6/8	5 6/8	11 1/8	McKenzie County	ND	Travis Wollan	1991	1,985
70 2/8	13 1/8	13 0/8	5 7/8	5 6/8	11 4/8	San Miguel County	NM	Leon M. Reed	1992	1,985
70 2/8	14 6/8	15 0/8	5 5/8	5 5/8	8 1/8	Twin Falls County	ID	John Stevens	1992	1,985
70 2/8	13 7/8	14 2/8	5 7/8	5 5/8	7 6/8	Moffat County	CO	Conrad Anderson	1992	1,985
70 2/8	12 2/8	12 6/8	6 0/8	6 1/8	10 1/8	Moffat County	CO	Gerald Dowell	1992	1,985

PRONGHORN

Minimum Score 67 — Continued

SCORE	LENGTH OF HORN R	L	CIRCUMFERENCE OF BASE R	L	INSIDE SPREAD	AREA	STATE/ PROVINCE	HUNTER'S NAME	DATE	RANK
70 2/8	13 2/8	13 0/8	6 2/8	6 1/8	9 5/8	San Juan County	UT	Ronald Kirk	1992	1,985
70 2/8	13 5/8	13 3/8	5 7/8	5 7/8	9 6/8	Converse County	WY	Michael J. Whitish	1992	1,985
70 2/8	13 4/8	13 5/8	5 7/8	5 7/8	8 5/8	Uinta County	WY	Layne Foxley	1992	1,985
70 2/8	13 5/8	14 1/8	5 6/8	5 6/8	9 2/8	Lincoln County	WY	Rocky Rollins	1992	1,985
70 2/8	13 5/8	13 6/8	6 1/8	6 1/8	9 2/8	Natrona County	WY	David L. Willis	1992	1,985
70 2/8	15 5/8	15 4/8	5 2/8	5 3/8	10 5/8	Perkins County	SD	James J. Willard	1992	1,985
70 2/8	13 5/8	13 6/8	5 3/8	5 3/8	9 3/8	Cheyenne County	NE	David Trump	1992	1,985
70 2/8	13 7/8	13 6/8	5 7/8	5 7/8	8 3/8	Colfax County	NM	Mike F. Mallory	1993	1,985
70 2/8	15 1/8	14 7/8	5 6/8	5 5/8	11 7/8	Yavapai County	AZ	Mark Ovitt	1993	1,985
70 2/8	13 5/8	13 6/8	6 0/8	5 7/8	8 4/8	Natrona County	WY	George Hendon	1993	1,985
70 2/8	14 3/8	14 2/8	5 5/8	5 4/8	10 1/8	Moffat County	CO	Jim Leqve	1994	1,985
70 2/8	13 2/8	13 2/8	6 0/8	6 1/8	8 1/8	Moffat County	CO	Chuck Adams	1994	1,985
70 2/8	13 5/8	13 4/8	5 2/8	5 2/8	10 5/8	Millard County	UT	Kevin Higley	1994	1,985
70 2/8	13 2/8	13 1/8	5 7/8	6 0/8	9 6/8	Moffat County	CO	Rudy Meyers	1994	1,985
70 2/8	13 5/8	13 2/8	5 4/8	5 5/8	12 1/8	Sweetwater County	WY	Bryce E. Carley	1994	1,985
70 2/8	13 0/8	13 0/8	5 7/8	5 7/8	7 4/8	Chaffee County	CO	Tim Cuthriell	1994	1,985
70 2/8	14 1/8	14 1/8	6 2/8	6 1/8	9 4/8	Valley County	MT	Val Dierks	1994	1,985
70 2/8	14 0/8	14 1/8	5 5/8	5 4/8	11 4/8	Platte County	WY	Jeffrey Colman	1994	1,985
70 2/8	14 7/8	13 4/8	6 0/8	5 7/8	6 2/8	Campbell County	WY	Craig Martin	1994	1,985
70 2/8	14 0/8	13 7/8	5 6/8	5 5/8	10 3/8	Johnson County	WY	Charlie H. Sagner	1994	1,985
70 2/8	12 4/8	12 5/8	5 6/8	5 6/8	9 3/8	Campbell County	WY	Steve Huppert	1994	1,985
70 2/8	13 6/8	13 7/8	6 0/8	5 7/8	11 5/8	Moffat County	CO	Michael Ingold	1995	1,985
70 2/8	14 2/8	14 2/8	5 5/8	5 5/8	11 0/8	Klamath County	OR	Dennis Dahlgren	1995	1,985
70 2/8	13 2/8	13 4/8	6 0/8	6 2/8	12 0/8	Moffat County	CO	Ken Hoehn	1995	1,985
70 2/8	14 2/8	14 0/8	5 7/8	5 6/8	10 5/8	Moffat County	CO	Mark Montgomery	1995	1,985
70 2/8	13 1/8	13 0/8	5 6/8	5 7/8	9 6/8	Guadalupe County	NM	Brandon Ray	1995	1,985
70 2/8	14 1/8	13 7/8	5 7/8	5 7/8	10 1/8	Rosebud County	MT	David Burrows	1995	1,985
70 2/8	13 3/8	13 6/8	6 1/8	6 2/8	10 2/8	Powder River County	MT	Don G. Scofield	1995	1,985
70 2/8	13 7/8	13 7/8	5 7/8	5 5/8	12 5/8	Campbell County	WY	Wright W. Allen	1995	1,985
70 2/8	13 3/8	13 2/8	6 3/8	6 0/8	8 3/8	Moffat County	CO	Connie Renfro	1996	1,985
70 2/8	13 2/8	13 3/8	5 6/8	5 5/8	8 1/8	Yavapai County	AZ	Henry Robert Garcia, Sr.	1996	1,985
70 2/8	13 7/8	14 0/8	5 5/8	5 6/8	9 3/8	Campbell County	WY	Tim Kanapeckas	1996	1,985
70 2/8	13 3/8	13 4/8	6 0/8	5 7/8	11 2/8	Campbell County	WY	Terry L. Wright	1996	1,985
70 2/8	14 6/8	14 7/8	5 7/8	5 6/8	9 0/8	Estevan	SAS	Allen Johnson	1996	1,985
70 2/8	13 1/8	13 1/8	6 0/8	5 6/8	9 6/8	Twin Falls County	ID	Darrell Nunez	1997	1,985
70 2/8	14 4/8	14 2/8	5 4/8	5 7/8	9 2/8	Saguache County	CO	Steven J. Vittetow	1998	1,985
70 2/8	13 6/8	13 5/8	5 6/8	5 5/8	7 4/8	Millard County	UT	Jim Madsen	1998	1,985
70 2/8	14 2/8	12 5/8	6 7/8	6 6/8	11 6/8	Converse County	WY	Larry Comer	1998	1,985
70 0/8	13 1/8	13 1/8	6 1/8	6 1/8	13 1/8	Butte County	SD	Wayne Wanhanen	1961	2,087
70 0/8	13 6/8	13 7/8	5 6/8	5 6/8	11 4/8	Garfield County	MT	Paul M. Ramsey	1963	2,087
70 0/8	14 0/8	14 0/8	5 3/8	5 3/8	9 5/8	Harding County	SD	Ira Hilburn	1964	2,087
70 0/8	13 1/8	13 4/8	5 6/8	5 6/8	9 0/8	Morton County	ND	Paul R. Shannon	1971	2,087
70 0/8	13 4/8	13 2/8	6 1/8	6 0/8	12 5/8	Pennington County	SD	Thomas Huitfeldt	1974	2,087
70 0/8	13 1/8	13 2/8	5 7/8	5 6/8	8 2/8	Dawes County	NE	Allan Mintken	1974	2,087
70 0/8	13 4/8	13 7/8	5 4/8	5 5/8	9 0/8	Rio Grande County	CO	Arthur M. Davis	1975	2,087
70 0/8	14 5/8	14 6/8	5 6/8	5 5/8	7 1/8	Humboldt County	NV	Wally Lopey	1981	2,087
70 0/8	12 5/8	12 3/8	5 4/8	5 4/8	7 5/8	Moffat County	CO	Charles A. Nicholas	1981	2,087
70 0/8	13 7/8	13 6/8	5 5/8	5 5/8	12 5/8	Sweetwater County	WY	Gerri Risley	1981	2,087
70 0/8	13 2/8	13 2/8	6 0/8	5 7/8	10 5/8	Natrona County	WY	Mark A. Smith	1981	2,087
70 0/8	13 6/8	13 6/8	5 4/8	5 4/8	8 7/8	White Pine County	NV	Richard Fillman	1982	2,087
70 0/8	13 0/8	13 0/8	5 7/8	5 6/8	12 4/8	Converse County	WY	Steven A. Wolff	1982	2,087
70 0/8	13 6/8	14 1/8	5 7/8	5 7/8	8 1/8	Carbon County	WY	Ron Breitsprecher	1982	2,087
70 0/8	13 7/8	13 6/8	5 4/8	5 5/8	10 3/8	Sargent County	ND	Terry Freehauf	1983	2,087
70 0/8	13 1/8	13 1/8	5 7/8	5 6/8	9 4/8	Converse County	WY	Dean Taylor	1983	2,087
70 0/8	13 5/8	13 5/8	5 7/8	5 5/8	9 2/8	Perkins County	SD	Jeffery Rieker	1983	2,087
70 0/8	13 3/8	12 5/8	6 1/8	6 1/8	8 0/8	Rosebud County	MT	Daniel A. Nielsen	1983	2,087
70 0/8	13 2/8	13 2/8	6 0/8	6 0/8	7 2/8	Custer County	ID	Brad Chilton	1984	2,087
70 0/8	14 5/8	14 0/8	5 5/8	5 6/8	5 7/8	Moffat County	CO	Dale Drilling	1984	2,087
70 0/8	13 4/8	13 4/8	5 5/8	5 4/8	9 4/8	Moffat County	CO	Todd Clyncke	1984	2,087
70 0/8	12 4/8	12 4/8	5 7/8	5 7/8	8 3/8	Converse County	WY	Bill Doemland	1984	2,087
70 0/8	13 4/8	13 4/8	5 4/8	5 3/8	11 6/8	Slope County	ND	Gene D. Davis	1984	2,087
70 0/8	12 0/8	12 0/8	6 1/8	6 0/8	7 4/8	Elko County	NV	Ted Simpson	1985	2,087
70 0/8	13 3/8	13 0/8	6 1/8	6 0/8	8 6/8	Converse County	WY	David Stuhr	1985	2,087
70 0/8	13 0/8	12 7/8	5 4/8	5 3/8	10 1/8	Converse County	WY	Dean Herschede	1985	2,087
70 0/8	13 2/8	13 4/8	6 0/8	6 0/8	9 7/8	Carter County	MT	James Jessen	1985	2,087
70 0/8	14 6/8	15 0/8	5 5/8	5 5/8	14 5/8	Carbon County	WY	David Pawlicki	1986	2,087
70 0/8	13 1/8	13 1/8	5 6/8	5 6/8	7 6/8	Converse County	WY	John Unser	1986	2,087
70 0/8	13 2/8	13 1/8	6 2/8	6 2/8	9 6/8	Moffat County	CO	John Hunter	1987	2,087
70 0/8	13 3/8	13 7/8	6 1/8	6 1/8	9 0/8	Converse County	WY	Bruce Warberg	1987	2,087
70 0/8	14 2/8	14 0/8	5 3/8	5 3/8	9 4/8	Moffat County	CO	Roger Gipple	1988	2,087
70 0/8	14 4/8	14 0/8	5 4/8	5 2/8	9 4/8	Converse County	WY	George A. Zanoni	1988	2,087
70 0/8	14 3/8	14 3/8	5 3/8	5 1/8	11 2/8	Moffat County	CO	Glenn Pritchard	1988	2,087
70 0/8	13 5/8	13 6/8	5 6/8	5 6/8	11 3/8	Dunn County	ND	Rick Regeth	1988	2,087
70 0/8	13 6/8	14 4/8	5 7/8	5 6/8	8 2/8	Sweetwater County	WY	Dennis L. Shirley	1989	2,087
70 0/8	15 3/8	14 6/8	5 7/8	5 5/8	8 6/8	Custer County	ID	Matt March, Jr.	1989	2,087
70 0/8	13 2/8	13 7/8	5 6/8	5 6/8	7 7/8	Sweetwater County	WY	Larry Norris	1989	2,087
70 0/8	12 2/8	12 5/8	5 7/8	6 0/8	9 3/8	Moffat County	CO	Bob Solimena	1989	2,087
70 0/8	13 6/8	13 7/8	5 6/8	5 4/8	8 4/8	McKenzie County	ND	Michael Lee	1989	2,087

PRONGHORN

Minimum Score 67 — Continued

SCORE	LENGTH OF HORN R	L	CIRCUMFERENCE OF BASE R	L	INSIDE SPREAD	AREA	STATE/PROVINCE	HUNTER'S NAME	DATE	RANK
70 0/8	12 5/8	12 2/8	5 6/8	5 6/8	11 5/8	Rosebud County	MT	Shawn A. Wahl	1989	2,087
70 0/8	13 1/8	13 0/8	6 3/8	6 3/8	11 0/8	Harney County	OR	Raymon L. Johnson	1990	2,087
70 0/8	13 0/8	13 0/8	6 2/8	6 2/8	10 1/8	Modoc County	CA	Monty Clemmer	1991	2,087
70 0/8	13 3/8	13 4/8	5 5/8	5 4/8	8 6/8	Butte County	SD	Bryce Lambley	1991	2,087
70 0/8	12 6/8	12 6/8	6 2/8	6 4/8	9 1/8	Campbell County	WY	Robert A. Carman	1991	2,087
70 0/8	12 1/8	12 3/8	6 1/8	6 2/8	10 4/8	Campbell County	WY	Gary R. Shields	1991	2,087
70 0/8	13 7/8	14 1/8	5 7/8	5 7/8	12 0/8	Harney County	OR	Dwight Griffin	1991	2,087
70 0/8	11 7/8	12 0/8	6 1/8	6 0/8	9 6/8	Powder River County	MT	Ronald J. Watt	1991	2,087
70 0/8	14 2/8	14 2/8	5 5/8	5 4/8	11 3/8	Millard County	UT	Steven Bowen Plett	1992	2,087
70 0/8	13 5/8	13 3/8	5 6/8	5 6/8	7 7/8	Moffat County	CO	Ren A. Leitner	1992	2,087
70 0/8	14 6/8	15 1/8	5 5/8	5 4/8	7 6/8	Moffat County	CO	Steve Barnhill	1992	2,087
70 0/8	12 6/8	12 3/8	6 0/8	6 1/8	8 0/8	Millard County	UT	Clark A. Moss	1992	2,087
70 0/8	13 6/8	13 4/8	5 3/8	5 3/8	9 5/8	Yavapai County	AZ	Rick Peebles	1992	2,087
70 0/8	13 6/8	13 5/8	5 7/8	5 6/8	11 6/8	Converse County	WY	Trent Findley	1992	2,087
70 0/8	13 7/8	14 1/8	5 5/8	5 6/8	9 0/8	Magrath	ALB	Cameron Cook	1992	2,087
70 0/8	13 4/8	13 4/8	6 0/8	6 0/8	11 4/8	Box Elder County	UT	Andrew Parker	1992	2,087
70 0/8	12 5/8	13 0/8	6 2/8	6 2/8	10 5/8	Carbon County	WY	J. David Cole	1993	2,087
70 0/8	13 5/8	13 4/8	6 4/8	6 3/8	13 2/8	Union County	NM	Wayne A. Naumann	1993	2,087
70 0/8	14 2/8	13 5/8	5 6/8	5 6/8	11 3/8	Torrance County	NM	Dennis A. Muirhead	1993	2,087
70 0/8	14 1/8	14 0/8	5 5/8	6 0/8	10 4/8	Carbon County	WY	Jeffrey Mueller	1994	2,087
70 0/8	14 0/8	13 3/8	6 3/8	6 2/8	10 6/8	Sweetwater County	WY	Reggie Alcorn	1994	2,087
70 0/8	15 0/8	14 5/8	5 6/8	5 5/8	8 4/8	Converse County	WY	D. Michael Taylor	1994	2,087
70 0/8	14 1/8	14 4/8	5 7/8	5 6/8	8 6/8	Niobrara County	WY	Floyd L. Foslien	1994	2,087
70 0/8	13 2/8	13 5/8	5 7/8	5 7/8	9 2/8	McKenzie County	ND	Randy Kjorstad	1994	2,087
70 0/8	14 2/8	14 2/8	5 6/8	5 6/8	8 4/8	Custer County	MT	Kenneth M. Backes	1994	2,087
70 0/8	13 6/8	14 0/8	5 5/8	5 5/8	9 1/8	Platte County	WY	Erich Bernd Scheinpflug	1994	2,087
70 0/8	14 0/8	14 0/8	5 5/8	5 5/8	15 5/8	Campbell County	WY	Troy Pickett	1994	2,087
70 0/8	13 3/8	13 4/8	6 1/8	6 1/8	10 5/8	Sioux County	NE	Michael Judas	1994	2,087
70 0/8	13 5/8	13 5/8	5 3/8	5 3/8	11 6/8	Moffat County	CO	Chuck Adams	1995	2,087
70 0/8	14 0/8	14 0/8	5 3/8	5 4/8	7 3/8	Moffat County	CO	David Parri	1995	2,087
70 0/8	13 7/8	13 7/8	5 5/8	5 6/8	10 0/8	Campbell County	WY	Ramon Neil Bell	1995	2,087
70 0/8	12 3/8	12 7/8	6 7/8	6 7/8	9 5/8	Converse County	WY	LeRoy Bassett	1995	2,087
70 0/8	13 3/8	13 7/8	5 4/8	5 4/8	8 5/8	Converse County	WY	H. Dewey Thompson	1995	2,087
70 0/8	13 6/8	13 6/8	5 2/8	5 2/8	8 4/8	Moffat County	CO	Thane Anderson	1995	2,087
70 0/8	13 4/8	13 2/8	5 6/8	5 6/8	12 3/8	Harding County	SD	Jeff Poppenga	1995	2,087
70 0/8	13 1/8	13 3/8	6 0/8	5 7/8	8 6/8	Converse County	WY	Gregory White	1995	2,087
70 0/8	14 1/8	14 1/8	5 5/8	5 5/8	8 4/8	Wayne County	UT	Thomas R. Hudson	1996	2,087
70 0/8	14 0/8	13 5/8	6 5/8	6 5/8	12 3/8	Sweetwater County	WY	Clifford W. Rockhold	1996	2,087
70 0/8	13 6/8	13 6/8	6 0/8	6 0/8	9 4/8	Moffat County	CO	Wally Schaub	1996	2,087
70 0/8	15 1/8	14 4/8	5 7/8	4 7/8	9 4/8	Curry County	NM	Jason Evans	1997	2,087
70 0/8	13 7/8	12 5/8	6 0/8	5 6/8	10 4/8	Campbell County	WY	Patrick Cahill	1997	2,087
70 0/8	13 4/8	13 1/8	5 4/8	5 3/8	9 2/8	Wayne County	UT	Robert A. Patey	1998	2,087
70 0/8	14 5/8	14 4/8	5 6/8	5 5/8	10 5/8	Carter County	MT	Willie Hettinger	1998	2,087
69 6/8	12 6/8	12 6/8	6 6/8	6 6/8	11 4/8	Custer County	ID	Dr. Richard Hagerman	1966	2,170
69 6/8	13 4/8	13 4/8	6 2/8	6 2/8	10 5/8	Carbon County	WY	Maurice Savora	1972	2,170
69 6/8	13 6/8	13 5/8	5 6/8	5 6/8	9 0/8	Ormsby	WY	Edward Pitchkites	1973	2,170
69 6/8	14 6/8	14 6/8	5 2/8	5 2/8	10 2/8	Perkins County	SD	Marvin R. Bohnet	1974	2,170
69 6/8	14 4/8	14 5/8	5 2/8	5 4/8	10 0/8	Meade County	SD	David Martin	1976	2,170
69 6/8	14 0/8	14 2/8	5 2/8	5 0/8	9 0/8	Sublette County	WY	John Kelly	1977	2,170
69 6/8	13 0/8	12 5/8	5 6/8	5 7/8	9 5/8	Carbon County	WY	John L. Craig	1978	2,170
69 6/8	14 5/8	14 5/8	5 3/8	5 3/8	13 4/8	Coconino County	AZ	Robin Underdown	1978	2,170
69 6/8	13 0/8	12 7/8	6 0/8	6 0/8	8 6/8	Arapahoe County	CO	Wayne E. Watson, Sr.	1979	2,170
69 6/8	13 2/8	13 2/8	5 4/8	5 4/8	10 0/8	Arapahoe County	CO	Steve Cosper	1980	2,170
69 6/8	13 3/8	13 5/8	5 1/8	5 1/8	10 4/8	Converse County	WY	Rickey Melde	1981	2,170
69 6/8	13 5/8	13 6/8	5 7/8	5 6/8	9 0/8	Converse County	WY	Jeff Reynolds	1982	2,170
69 6/8	13 6/8	13 7/8	5 6/8	5 5/8	9 7/8	Moffat County	CO	Albert Ahlrich	1982	2,170
69 6/8	14 0/8	13 5/8	6 2/8	6 2/8	8 4/8	Siskiyou County	CA	Scott Walker	1983	2,170
69 6/8	13 6/8	13 6/8	5 4/8	5 3/8	8 4/8	Moffat County	CO	Gary Decker	1983	2,170
69 6/8	13 2/8	12 6/8	5 4/8	5 3/8	10 7/8	Moffat County	CO	Richard Gearhart	1983	2,170
69 6/8	11 7/8	11 6/8	6 2/8	6 2/8	9 4/8	Moffat County	CO	Cathy Lee Jordon	1983	2,170
69 6/8	13 4/8	13 1/8	6 2/8	6 2/8	9 7/8	Moffat County	CO	Galen J. Wertz	1983	2,170
69 6/8	14 0/8	13 2/8	5 6/8	5 6/8	10 0/8	Converse County	WY	Jeff Davis	1983	2,170
69 6/8	13 5/8	13 6/8	6 0/8	6 0/8	15 4/8	Sweetwater County	WY	Bill Clink	1985	2,170
69 6/8	13 1/8	13 2/8	5 7/8	5 7/8	10 3/8	Sweetwater County	WY	Michael Chaffin	1985	2,170
69 6/8	14 6/8	15 0/8	5 7/8	6 0/8	13 6/8	Modoc County	CA	Bill Golden	1985	2,170
69 6/8	14 0/8	14 0/8	5 5/8	5 4/8	10 6/8	Powder River County	MT	David Fitton	1985	2,170
69 6/8	13 2/8	13 0/8	5 7/8	6 0/8	10 4/8	Moffat County	CO	Howard Tieden	1986	2,170
69 6/8	13 5/8	13 6/8	5 6/8	5 6/8	10 0/8	McCone County	MT	Mitch Kottas	1986	2,170
69 6/8	12 3/8	12 3/8	5 5/8	5 6/8	8 0/8	Rio Arriba County	NM	Derek Tierney	1987	2,170
69 6/8	12 6/8	12 6/8	6 3/8	6 4/8	10 5/8	Moffat County	CO	Dale Elliott	1987	2,170
69 6/8	13 5/8	13 5/8	6 0/8	6 1/8	13 1/8	Fremont County	WY	Keith L. Frick	1987	2,170
69 6/8	14 7/8	14 6/8	6 0/8	5 7/8	9 5/8	McKinley County	NM	Travis Taylor	1987	2,170
69 6/8	13 1/8	14 4/8	6 1/8	6 2/8	14 5/8	Moffat County	CO	Wendy Decker	1988	2,170
69 6/8	13 6/8	13 4/8	5 3/8	5 3/8	9 2/8	Moffat County	CO	Alvin Tieden	1988	2,170
69 6/8	14 2/8	14 1/8	5 2/8	5 3/8	10 1/8	Converse County	WY	Carolyn S. Zanoni	1988	2,170
69 6/8	13 7/8	14 0/8	5 7/8	5 6/8	13 6/8	Manyberries	ALB	Randy Bernier	1989	2,170
69 6/8	13 3/8	13 4/8	5 1/8	5 1/8	9 4/8	Brewster County	TX	Thomas J. Buxton	1989	2,170
69 6/8	13 6/8	13 6/8	6 1/8	6 1/8	10 4/8	Niobrara County	WY	Jim Jepson	1990	2,170

PRONGHORN

Minimum Score 67 — Continued

SCORE	LENGTH OF HORN R	L	CIRCUMFERENCE OF BASE R	L	INSIDE SPREAD	AREA	STATE/ PROVINCE	HUNTER'S NAME	DATE	RANK
69 6/8	13 6/8	13 6/8	6 0/8	5 7/8	8 0/8	Campbell County	WY	Mark E. Heberlein	1990	2,170
69 6/8	14 1/8	14 4/8	5 6/8	5 4/8	13 7/8	Fergus County	MT	Kelly Norskog	1990	2,170
69 6/8	15 1/8	15 1/8	5 4/8	5 4/8	10 3/8	Valencia County	NM	Frank Montano	1991	2,170
69 6/8	12 5/8	12 6/8	5 5/8	5 6/8	7 0/8	Blaine County	ID	John Wells	1991	2,170
69 6/8	13 2/8	13 2/8	6 0/8	5 7/8	9 1/8	Natrona County	WY	David J. Steger	1991	2,170
69 6/8	13 5/8	13 4/8	6 0/8	6 0/8	8 4/8	Malheur County	OR	Fredrick J. Johnson	1991	2,170
69 6/8	13 2/8	13 2/8	6 1/8	6 0/8	11 2/8	Larimer County	CO	Randy Brian Snyder	1991	2,170
69 6/8	13 5/8	13 6/8	5 7/8	5 7/8	12 5/8	Converse County	WY	Shirley Jochmann	1991	2,170
69 6/8	13 7/8	14 0/8	5 6/8	5 6/8	10 1/8	Garfield County	MT	Peter J. Mancl	1991	2,170
69 6/8	14 0/8	13 4/8	5 6/8	5 6/8	9 4/8	Beaverhead County	MT	Jim Muzynoski	1991	2,170
69 6/8	13 0/8	13 0/8	6 0/8	6 0/8	7 2/8	Bowman County	ND	Jim Hicks	1991	2,170
69 6/8	12 2/8	12 2/8	6 1/8	6 0/8	9 0/8	Carbon County	WY	Mark Wardlaw	1992	2,170
69 6/8	13 6/8	13 3/8	5 6/8	5 5/8	10 0/8	Sweetwater County	WY	Andrew Tkach	1992	2,170
69 6/8	12 1/8	12 4/8	6 1/8	6 1/8	7 3/8	Converse County	WY	Troy McGinnis	1992	2,170
69 6/8	13 2/8	13 3/8	5 4/8	5 5/8	9 7/8	Billings County	ND	Richard C. Lautenschlager	1992	2,170
69 6/8	13 4/8	13 4/8	5 6/8	5 6/8	10 7/8	Crook County	WY	Robert Michelena	1992	2,170
69 6/8	13 1/8	13 2/8	5 4/8	5 3/8	9 7/8	Moffat County	CO	Jon P. Hollabaugh	1993	2,170
69 6/8	13 0/8	12 4/8	5 6/8	5 6/8	9 6/8	Moffat County	CO	Gary L. Biles	1993	2,170
69 6/8	13 6/8	13 6/8	5 4/8	5 6/8	11 6/8	Moffat County	CO	Chad Johnson	1993	2,170
69 6/8	12 7/8	12 7/8	6 1/8	6 1/8	8 4/8	Moffat County	CO	Karl Randolph	1993	2,170
69 6/8	13 4/8	13 1/8	6 1/8	6 0/8	11 3/8	Bowman County	ND	Michael Whiteside	1993	2,170
69 6/8	14 6/8	13 2/8	5 5/8	5 6/8	10 5/8	Bowman County	ND	Dan Thiel	1993	2,170
69 6/8	15 0/8	15 4/8	5 6/8	5 6/8	9 1/8	Stanley County	SD	Robert G. Barden	1993	2,170
69 6/8	14 6/8	14 6/8	5 6/8	5 6/8	13 1/8	Lake County	OR	Donald R. Pritchett	1993	2,170
69 6/8	12 1/8	12 5/8	6 3/8	6 2/8	10 5/8	Coconino County	AZ	Ernie Martinez	1994	2,170
69 6/8	13 4/8	13 2/8	5 5/8	5 5/8	11 2/8	Yavapai County	AZ	Allen King II	1994	2,170
69 6/8	14 1/8	13 6/8	5 5/8	5 5/8	11 2/8	Campbell County	WY	Thomas E. Lawrence	1994	2,170
69 6/8	14 0/8	14 0/8	5 5/8	5 3/8	13 6/8	Converse County	WY	Phil Perry	1994	2,170
69 6/8	13 5/8	13 4/8	6 0/8	5 7/8	10 2/8	Converse County	WY	Ronald D. Stoynoff	1994	2,170
69 6/8	13 3/8	13 4/8	5 5/8	5 5/8	10 4/8	Campbell County	WY	James C. Campbell, Jr.	1994	2,170
69 6/8	14 4/8	14 2/8	5 1/8	5 1/8	8 1/8	Keya Paha County	NE	Clay Beck	1994	2,170
69 6/8	13 1/8	13 1/8	6 4/8	6 3/8	10 4/8	Converse County	WY	Harold Osborne	1994	2,170
69 6/8	13 3/8	13 5/8	5 6/8	5 6/8	10 0/8	Campbell County	WY	Jerry Bodar	1994	2,170
69 6/8	12 7/8	13 0/8	5 4/8	5 5/8	8 6/8	Park County	MT	George Kamps	1994	2,170
69 6/8	12 4/8	12 2/8	6 2/8	6 0/8	8 6/8	Moffat County	CO	Vince Migliorato	1995	2,170
69 6/8	12 7/8	12 5/8	6 2/8	6 2/8	9 0/8	Converse County	WY	Ray Maudsley	1995	2,170
69 6/8	13 7/8	13 5/8	5 7/8	5 7/8	6 7/8	Yavapai County	AZ	Ron Eckerman	1995	2,170
69 6/8	14 2/8	13 1/8	6 1/8	6 3/8	9 6/8	Moffat County	CO	Bill McDonald	1995	2,170
69 6/8	13 4/8	13 4/8	5 5/8	5 5/8	7 2/8	Moffat County	CO	Kevin Bertsch	1995	2,170
69 6/8	13 7/8	13 7/8	5 4/8	5 4/8	10 3/8	Beaverhead County	MT	Raymond L. Gross	1995	2,170
69 6/8	14 2/8	14 2/8	5 4/8	5 5/8	9 2/8	Klamath County	OR	Michael W. Schulte	1996	2,170
69 6/8	12 4/8	12 5/8	6 0/8	6 1/8	8 6/8	Weld County	CO	Ed Fanchin	1996	2,170
69 6/8	13 5/8	13 3/8	5 4/8	5 4/8	9 6/8	Clark County	ID	Max Heberling	1996	2,170
69 6/8	12 6/8	12 6/8	5 5/8	5 4/8	13 6/8	Natrona County	WY	James Mathias	1996	2,170
69 6/8	14 2/8	14 0/8	5 6/8	5 6/8	8 7/8	Weld County	CO	Philip Wray	1996	2,170
69 6/8	13 2/8	13 5/8	5 6/8	5 5/8	7 4/8	Bowman County	ND	Jon Brewer	1996	2,170
69 6/8	12 0/8	13 5/8	6 0/8	5 7/8	10 7/8	Sweetwater County	WY	Mark Preston	1997	2,170
69 6/8	12 6/8	12 5/8	5 5/8	5 7/8	8 1/8	Clark County	ID	Thomas Thiel	1997	2,170
69 6/8	14 0/8	13 3/8	5 6/8	5 6/8	8 0/8	Big Horn County	WY	Jerome D. Larson	1997	2,170
69 6/8	11 7/8	12 1/8	5 6/8	5 5/8	10 4/8	Converse County	WY	Eddie Wynne	1997	2,170
69 6/8	13 3/8	13 3/8	5 7/8	5 7/8	9 3/8	Powder River County	MT	Lesley Strunk	1997	2,170
69 6/8	12 3/8	12 5/8	6 5/8	6 2/8	11 1/8	Campbell County	WY	Tom Stapf	1997	2,170
69 6/8	13 0/8	12 6/8	5 7/8	5 7/8	10 0/8	Moffat County	CO	Mike Dziekan	1998	2,170
69 6/8	12 4/8	12 5/8	5 7/8	5 7/8	10 3/8	Converse County	WY	Clark M. Vickers	1998	2,170
69 4/8	15 0/8	13 6/8	5 4/8	5 4/8	5 6/8	Rosebud County	MT	Glenn Gibson	1958	2,259
69 4/8	14 4/8	14 2/8	5 2/8	5 2/8	10 6/8	Grant County	NM	Harold W. Groves	1960	2,259
69 4/8	14 4/8	14 2/8	5 5/8	5 4/8	9 4/8	Washoe County	NV	Kenneth D. Allen	1972	2,259
69 4/8	13 2/8	13 0/8	6 0/8	6 0/8	10 6/8	Natrona County	WY	John Benetti	1973	2,259
69 4/8	13 6/8	14 0/8	5 5/8	5 3/8	9 6/8	Washoe County	NV	Jack S. McCracken	1973	2,259
69 4/8	12 0/8	12 4/8	6 0/8	6 1/8	9 1/8	Meade County	SD	Lelan L. Anderson	1974	2,259
69 4/8	14 3/8	14 4/8	5 5/8	5 3/8	8 4/8	Park County	CO	Ed Zehner	1974	2,259
69 4/8	12 6/8	12 3/8	5 7/8	6 0/8	9 4/8	Lemhi County	ID	Randy J. Stephens	1980	2,259
69 4/8	13 0/8	13 0/8	5 5/8	5 5/8	9 5/8	Jefferson County	ID	Ron Stacey	1981	2,259
69 4/8	12 7/8	12 7/8	6 0/8	6 0/8	9 5/8	Moffat County	CO	Martin James Murrish	1981	2,259
69 4/8	13 6/8	13 4/8	6 5/8	6 6/8	11 0/8	Carbon County	WY	Mike C. Montgomery	1981	2,259
69 4/8	11 5/8	11 6/8	6 4/8	6 4/8	10 5/8	Converse County	WY	Ben Munoz	1981	2,259
69 4/8	13 5/8	14 3/8	6 1/8	5 7/8	11 5/8	Converse County	WY	Dr. James R. Scott	1981	2,259
69 4/8	12 6/8	12 7/8	5 7/8	5 7/8	9 5/8	Bowman County	ND	Ron Cizek	1982	2,259
69 4/8	14 1/8	14 2/8	5 4/8	5 3/8	6 5/8	Converse County	WY	Ronnie Everett	1982	2,259
69 4/8	13 4/8	13 7/8	5 4/8	5 4/8	8 1/8	Moffat County	CO	Rich Humpal	1982	2,259
69 4/8	12 2/8	11 7/8	6 0/8	6 0/8	8 0/8	Beaver County	UT	Joey Leko	1982	2,259
69 4/8	14 0/8	14 0/8	5 6/8	5 5/8	9 6/8	Sweetwater County	WY	Ronnie Williams	1982	2,259
69 4/8	14 0/8	13 7/8	5 2/8	5 3/8	6 1/8	Converse County	WY	Jim Wilbur	1983	2,259
69 4/8	13 4/8	12 4/8	6 1/8	6 1/8	10 5/8	Natrona County	WY	Paul Persano	1984	2,259
69 4/8	12 7/8	13 1/8	5 2/8	5 2/8	7 3/8	Moffat County	CO	Roy V. Roig	1984	2,259
69 4/8	14 1/8	14 2/8	6 0/8	5 7/8	15 0/8	Fergus County	MT	James W. Southworth	1984	2,259
69 4/8	13 6/8	14 7/8	5 7/8	5 7/8	11 6/8	Sweetwater County	WY	Glenn Hisey	1985	2,259
69 4/8	12 6/8	12 5/8	6 0/8	6 1/8	7 3/8	Sweetwater County	WY	Rod Knight	1985	2,259

PRONGHORN

Minimum Score 67   Continued   651

SCORE	LENGTH OF HORN R	L	CIRCUMFERENCE OF BASE R	L	INSIDE SPREAD	AREA	STATE/PROVINCE	HUNTER'S NAME	DATE	RANK
69 4/8	13 5/8	13 2/8	5 2/8	5 2/8	8 3/8	Converse County	WY	Samuel M. Durham	1985	2,259
69 4/8	13 3/8	13 0/8	5 6/8	5 6/8	13 2/8	Billings County	ND	Pat Caroline	1985	2,259
69 4/8	12 5/8	12 5/8	5 6/8	5 6/8	8 3/8	Uintah County	UT	Rob Johnston	1986	2,259
69 4/8	13 2/8	13 2/8	5 6/8	5 5/8	8 6/8	Sublette County	WY	John Cheese	1987	2,259
69 4/8	13 7/8	13 6/8	5 2/8	5 2/8	10 2/8	Musselshell County	MT	Jeff Matson	1987	2,259
69 4/8	13 2/8	13 2/8	5 7/8	5 6/8	11 4/8	Converse County	WY	John A. Driver	1987	2,259
69 4/8	14 2/8	14 1/8	6 0/8	5 7/8	10 6/8	Carbon County	WY	Steven Perkins	1988	2,259
69 4/8	12 7/8	12 6/8	6 4/8	6 2/8	6 0/8	Moffat County	CO	Dale Drilling	1988	2,259
69 4/8	13 3/8	13 3/8	6 3/8	6 2/8	9 0/8	McKinley County	NM	Gary Isom	1988	2,259
69 4/8	14 1/8	14 1/8	5 1/8	5 1/8	8 4/8	Moffat County	CO	Ron Scherer	1988	2,259
69 4/8	13 3/8	13 5/8	6 0/8	5 7/8	8 6/8	Natrona County	WY	Shawn Kinker	1988	2,259
69 4/8	13 2/8	13 5/8	5 6/8	5 6/8	11 2/8	Carbon County	WY	Lonny Curtis	1988	2,259
69 4/8	12 5/8	12 7/8	6 0/8	5 7/8	11 0/8	Albany County	WY	William Zahradka	1988	2,259
69 4/8	14 7/8	14 4/8	6 2/8	6 2/8	14 1/8	Campbell County	WY	Curt Christensen	1988	2,259
69 4/8	13 4/8	13 0/8	6 3/8	6 2/8	10 6/8	Crook County	WY	David Hinton	1988	2,259
69 4/8	13 0/8	13 0/8	6 2/8	6 1/8	8 4/8	Converse County	WY	Kevin Stier	1988	2,259
69 4/8	12 2/8	12 1/8	6 5/8	6 4/8	11 6/8	Natrona County	WY	Steve Turck	1988	2,259
69 4/8	14 2/8	14 4/8	5 7/8	5 7/8	10 1/8	Buffalo	ALB	Larry Flaata	1988	2,259
69 4/8	13 0/8	12 5/8	5 2/8	5 1/8	9 4/8	Weld County	CO	Larry Ford	1989	2,259
69 4/8	13 0/8	13 0/8	5 7/8	5 6/8	11 3/8	Rosebud County	MT	Gene Welle	1989	2,259
69 4/8	14 2/8	13 7/8	5 5/8	5 5/8	9 2/8	Lassen County	CA	Guy Rozar	1990	2,259
69 4/8	12 0/8	11 7/8	6 3/8	6 3/8	10 6/8	Fremont County	WY	David J. Steger	1990	2,259
69 4/8	13 4/8	13 2/8	5 6/8	5 5/8	10 4/8	Moffat County	CO	Eugene Ray, Sr.	1990	2,259
69 4/8	12 6/8	13 6/8	6 0/8	6 1/8	13 5/8	Moffat County	CO	Reggie Spiegelberg	1990	2,259
69 4/8	13 7/8	13 7/8	5 3/8	5 4/8	11 7/8	Lake County	OR	Buck Windom	1990	2,259
69 4/8	12 3/8	12 2/8	6 0/8	6 1/8	9 7/8	Ward County	ND	Glen R. Hauf	1990	2,259
69 4/8	13 0/8	13 1/8	6 0/8	6 1/8	12 2/8	Fremont County	WY	G. R. Pool	1991	2,259
69 4/8	13 3/8	13 5/8	6 0/8	6 0/8	15 2/8	Harney County	OR	Barry Haney	1991	2,259
69 4/8	14 1/8	14 2/8	5 2/8	5 2/8	9 7/8	Billings County	ND	Harold Hugelen	1991	2,259
69 4/8	13 6/8	13 5/8	5 5/8	5 5/8	9 4/8	Lincoln County	WY	Bob Grace	1992	2,259
69 4/8	13 0/8	13 1/8	6 0/8	6 0/8	11 2/8	Converse County	WY	Jeff Glaser	1992	2,259
69 4/8	12 3/8	12 2/8	6 2/8	6 2/8	8 0/8	Campbell County	WY	Mark D. Christopherson	1992	2,259
69 4/8	12 4/8	12 3/8	6 2/8	6 4/8	9 4/8	Carbon County	WY	Roy F. Meyer, Jr.	1992	2,259
69 4/8	13 1/8	13 3/8	6 0/8	6 0/8	7 5/8	Converse County	WY	Lou Edelis	1992	2,259
69 4/8	14 5/8	14 2/8	5 6/8	5 5/8	7 1/8	Powder River County	MT	James Larry Wilson	1992	2,259
69 4/8	13 3/8	13 2/8	5 7/8	5 6/8	11 3/8	Converse County	WY	Rodney L. Hamann	1992	2,259
69 4/8	14 2/8	14 1/8	5 5/8	5 5/8	10 7/8	Converse County	WY	Jim Schmidt	1992	2,259
69 4/8	13 2/8	13 0/8	5 5/8	5 6/8	10 1/8	Deuel County	NE	Ev Tarrell	1992	2,259
69 4/8	12 5/8	12 5/8	6 4/8	6 4/8	8 5/8	Moffat County	CO	Herbert M. Groetsch	1993	2,259
69 4/8	13 5/8	13 5/8	6 0/8	6 0/8	10 1/8	Moffat County	CO	Jared Mason	1993	2,259
69 4/8	13 4/8	13 5/8	6 1/8	6 0/8	15 4/8	Natrona County	WY	Jim Gaffney	1993	2,259
69 4/8	13 5/8	13 5/8	6 0/8	6 0/8	9 5/8	Owyhee County	ID	Ron Stockdale	1993	2,259
69 4/8	12 2/8	12 2/8	6 0/8	6 0/8	10 6/8	Natrona County	WY	Guy Young	1993	2,259
69 4/8	13 0/8	13 1/8	5 7/8	6 0/8	9 1/8	McKenzie County	ND	John Schaffer	1993	2,259
69 4/8	13 1/8	12 3/8	6 2/8	6 2/8	10 5/8	Meagher County	MT	D. (Mitch) Kottas	1993	2,259
69 4/8	13 4/8	13 4/8	5 6/8	5 6/8	10 2/8	Carter County	MT	Marty Adams	1993	2,259
69 4/8	13 5/8	13 4/8	5 6/8	5 7/8	10 6/8	Elko County	NV	Bob Sneed	1994	2,259
69 4/8	13 2/8	13 0/8	5 4/8	5 4/8	9 6/8	Weld County	CO	Douglas P. Douthit	1994	2,259
69 4/8	13 0/8	13 0/8	6 0/8	6 0/8	8 3/8	Moffat County	CO	Billy Tillotson	1994	2,259
69 4/8	15 7/8	15 7/8	5 2/8	5 2/8	10 1/8	Lea County	NM	Richard Lynn Morris	1994	2,259
69 4/8	13 2/8	13 4/8	5 6/8	5 6/8	10 0/8	Larimer County	CO	Shawn Greathouse	1994	2,259
69 4/8	11 5/8	12 3/8	5 7/8	5 7/8	9 4/8	Moffat County	CO	Mitch Arnold	1994	2,259
69 4/8	13 5/8	13 6/8	6 0/8	5 7/8	13 5/8	Yavapai County	AZ	Patricia M. Goetzenberger	1994	2,259
69 4/8	13 7/8	13 6/8	5 3/8	5 3/8	8 7/8	Moffat County	CO	Todd J. Rider	1994	2,259
69 4/8	14 2/8	14 2/8	5 4/8	5 5/8	11 2/8	Moffat County	CO	Reggie Spiegelberg	1994	2,259
69 4/8	14 0/8	14 1/8	5 5/8	5 7/8	8 6/8	Blaine County	ID	John Wells	1995	2,259
69 4/8	13 5/8	13 3/8	5 7/8	5 7/8	10 0/8	Powder River County	MT	Charles M. Fogarty	1995	2,259
69 4/8	14 5/8	14 5/8	5 1/8	5 1/8	9 3/8	Carter County	MT	Marty Adams	1995	2,259
69 4/8	13 1/8	13 3/8	5 1/8	5 2/8	12 2/8	Carbon County	WY	Kevin Anderson	1996	2,259
69 4/8	12 7/8	12 7/8	6 1/8	5 7/8	13 0/8	Carbon County	WY	Jim Schmid	1996	2,259
69 4/8	12 4/8	12 6/8	6 2/8	6 1/8	10 0/8	Harding County	SD	Mark Connor	1996	2,259
69 4/8	13 1/8	13 2/8	6 1/8	6 1/8	11 5/8	Powder River County	MT	Richard Driscoll	1996	2,259
69 4/8	14 2/8	14 2/8	5 6/8	5 4/8	9 3/8	Converse County	WY	Michael D. Hansen	1997	2,259
69 4/8	13 7/8	13 5/8	6 0/8	5 7/8	8 6/8	Fergus County	MT	Herbert Chavez	1997	2,259
69 4/8	12 0/8	12 1/8	6 2/8	6 1/8	11 6/8	Weld County	CO	Jon Meyer	1998	2,259
69 4/8	14 2/8	13 7/8	5 5/8	5 4/8	7 5/8	Clark County	ID	Thomas Thiel	1998	2,259
69 2/8	14 2/8	13 7/8	5 4/8	5 4/8	11 6/8	Custer County	ID	Jack Edwards	1960	2,349
69 2/8	13 5/8	13 4/8	5 3/8	5 2/8	6 2/8	Haakon County	SD	Floyd Hauk	1966	2,349
69 2/8	12 3/8	12 1/8	5 5/8	5 6/8	8 0/8	Converse County	WY	Bill Martin	1976	2,349
69 2/8	12 7/8	12 7/8	5 3/8	5 5/8	11 7/8	Converse County	WY	Dr. James L. Emerson	1980	2,349
69 2/8	12 4/8	12 1/8	6 0/8	6 0/8	9 5/8	Morgan County	CO	Filiberto Lopez	1980	2,349
69 2/8	11 6/8	13 5/8	6 1/8	6 1/8	8 6/8	Custer County	ID	Dick Fleming	1981	2,349
69 2/8	13 2/8	14 0/8	5 5/8	5 5/8	11 0/8	Converse County	WY	Gene A. Esch	1981	2,349
69 2/8	13 1/8	13 3/8	5 4/8	5 4/8	7 7/8	Butte County	ID	Garry Gunderson	1981	2,349
69 2/8	12 4/8	13 0/8	5 7/8	5 5/8	11 5/8	Moffat County	CO	Jim Jarvis	1981	2,349
69 2/8	14 3/8	13 7/8	5 7/8	5 6/8	10 4/8	Valencia County	NM	Reggie Spiegelberg	1981	2,349
69 2/8	12 7/8	13 0/8	5 7/8	5 5/8	11 0/8	Sweetwater County	WY	Dean Kendall	1982	2,349
69 2/8	13 2/8	13 6/8	6 2/8	6 2/8	9 5/8	Albany County	WY	Peter Vasek	1982	2,349

PRONGHORN

SCORE	LENGTH OF HORN R	L	CIRCUMFERENCE OF BASE R	L	INSIDE SPREAD	AREA	STATE/ PROVINCE	HUNTER'S NAME	DATE	RANK
69 2/8	12 7/8	13 1/8	5 5/8	5 4/8	8 4/8	Moffat County	CO	Ross Dieffenbaucher	1982	2,349
69 2/8	12 7/8	12 5/8	4 7/8	4 7/8	14 1/8	Moffat County	CO	Keith R. Hardy	1983	2,349
69 2/8	14 3/8	14 0/8	5 7/8	5 7/8	8 0/8	Moffat County	CO	Les Smith	1983	2,349
69 2/8	14 2/8	13 7/8	6 0/8	6 0/8	8 1/8	Natrona County	WY	Joe M. Skipp	1983	2,349
69 2/8	12 7/8	12 4/8	5 7/8	5 6/8	9 3/8	Converse County	WY	Bruce H. Sabaini	1983	2,349
69 2/8	13 7/8	13 4/8	5 4/8	5 4/8	10 6/8	White Pine County	NV	Patrick Fillman	1984	2,349
69 2/8	14 4/8	14 6/8	5 6/8	5 2/8	10 6/8	Converse County	WY	Donald Jackson	1984	2,349
69 2/8	13 3/8	13 1/8	5 6/8	5 6/8	10 5/8	Converse County	WY	Bob Frank	1984	2,349
69 2/8	13 3/8	12 4/8	6 1/8	6 1/8	12 0/8	McKenzie County	ND	Bill Zahradka	1984	2,349
69 2/8	13 2/8	13 2/8	5 7/8	5 7/8	10 5/8	Carbon County	WY	Steve Bolan	1985	2,349
69 2/8	12 6/8	12 4/8	6 5/8	6 4/8	9 0/8	Moffat County	CO	Casey Veach	1985	2,349
69 2/8	13 0/8	12 7/8	5 6/8	5 4/8	11 2/8	Yavapai County	AZ	Tony W. Zimbaro	1985	2,349
69 2/8	12 1/8	12 0/8	5 7/8	5 7/8	8 4/8	Converse County	WY	Larry L. Fies	1985	2,349
69 2/8	12 5/8	12 7/8	6 1/8	6 0/8	11 1/8	Moffat County	CO	Lynn Ingalsbe	1986	2,349
69 2/8	13 4/8	13 4/8	6 0/8	6 0/8	9 4/8	Moffat County	CO	Gil Gilbertson	1986	2,349
69 2/8	13 4/8	13 3/8	5 5/8	5 5/8	10 4/8	Converse County	WY	Don Schram	1986	2,349
69 2/8	13 4/8	13 5/8	5 5/8	5 5/8	8 3/8	Presidio County	TX	Larry Zimmerman	1986	2,349
69 2/8	13 6/8	14 1/8	6 0/8	5 6/8	9 7/8	Jefferson County	OR	Karen J. Demaris	1987	2,349
69 2/8	13 3/8	13 3/8	5 2/8	5 1/8	9 1/8	Natrona County	WY	Mike Mitten	1987	2,349
69 2/8	13 0/8	13 0/8	5 5/8	5 6/8	11 5/8	Campbell County	WY	Rick Mowles	1987	2,349
69 2/8	13 5/8	12 6/8	5 5/8	5 6/8	10 2/8	Presidio County	TX	Jack F. Demetruk	1987	2,349
69 2/8	12 1/8	12 0/8	5 7/8	5 7/8	8 3/8	Moffat County	CO	John Wagner	1988	2,349
69 2/8	14 4/8	14 3/8	5 6/8	5 6/8	12 6/8	Modoc County	CA	Bill C. Osborne	1988	2,349
69 2/8	14 2/8	13 7/8	5 2/8	5 1/8	10 5/8	Pima County	AZ	Barry Sopher	1988	2,349
69 2/8	13 4/8	13 3/8	5 6/8	5 6/8	8 6/8	Hot Springs County	WY	Dan Wood	1988	2,349
69 2/8	13 3/8	13 3/8	5 6/8	5 5/8	10 0/8	Converse County	WY	Denny Raper	1988	2,349
69 2/8	14 5/8	15 0/8	6 4/8	6 1/8	12 2/8	Sweetwater County	WY	Mike Barrett	1989	2,349
69 2/8	13 7/8	13 6/8	5 7/8	5 7/8	9 3/8	Mountrail County	ND	Brian C. Johnson	1989	2,349
69 2/8	13 3/8	13 0/8	5 5/8	5 5/8	9 7/8	Buffalo	ALB	Steve Mackenzie	1989	2,349
69 2/8	12 0/8	12 2/8	6 2/8	6 2/8	12 1/8	Carbon County	WY	Jeffrey Mueller	1990	2,349
69 2/8	14 4/8	14 4/8	5 7/8	6 0/8	7 2/8	Harding County	SD	Dean Wagner	1990	2,349
69 2/8	13 6/8	13 2/8	5 7/8	5 7/8	13 4/8	Coconino County	AZ	Charles Steven Williams	1990	2,349
69 2/8	11 3/8	11 3/8	6 1/8	6 2/8	6 7/8	Natrona County	WY	Robert E. Ebert	1990	2,349
69 2/8	12 5/8	12 2/8	6 0/8	6 0/8	8 6/8	Converse County	WY	Robert Frank	1990	2,349
69 2/8	13 4/8	13 1/8	5 7/8	6 0/8	11 4/8	Powder River County	MT	John Witschen	1990	2,349
69 2/8	13 0/8	13 1/8	5 5/8	5 5/8	11 2/8	Billings County	ND	Gary W. Heidecker	1990	2,349
69 2/8	13 5/8	13 3/8	6 2/8	6 2/8	12 6/8	Fremont County	WY	Dave Holt	1991	2,349
69 2/0	13 2/8	13 0/8	5 5/8	5 5/8	9 1/8	Natrona County	WY	Carson V. Brown II	1991	2,349
69 2/8	13 1/8	13 3/8	5 6/8	5 5/8	10 4/8	Campbell County	WY	John Shields	1991	2,349
69 2/8	12 0/8	12 0/8	6 0/8	5 6/8	9 2/8	McKenzie County	ND	Benjamin Stewart	1991	2,349
69 2/8	14 1/8	13 6/8	6 2/8	6 0/8	10 2/8	Converse County	WY	John Flies	1991	2,349
69 2/8	11 6/8	11 6/8	6 1/8	6 0/8	11 0/8	Campbell County	WY	Ron Ralston	1991	2,349
69 2/8	14 1/8	14 1/8	6 0/8	5 7/8	7 2/8	Converse County	WY	Wayne Radley	1991	2,349
69 2/8	11 7/8	12 0/8	6 1/8	6 1/8	10 2/8	Moffat County	CO	Don Sousa	1992	2,349
69 2/8	14 2/8	14 0/8	5 4/8	5 4/8	11 2/8	Catron County	NM	Glenn W. Isler	1992	2,349
69 2/8	14 0/8	14 1/8	5 7/8	6 1/8	8 2/8	Lassen County	CA	Randy Jarvis	1992	2,349
69 2/8	13 0/8	12 3/8	6 2/8	6 0/8	7 5/8	Uinta County	WY	George Fabian	1992	2,349
69 2/8	12 4/8	12 7/8	6 3/8	6 4/8	9 4/8	Sweetwater County	WY	Mark Grace	1992	2,349
69 2/8	12 7/8	13 1/8	6 6/8	6 6/8	13 2/8	Sweetwater County	WY	Bill Clink	1992	2,349
69 2/8	14 6/8	14 3/8	5 4/8	5 4/8	8 2/8	Hettinger County	ND	Scott Wiseman	1992	2,349
69 2/8	13 2/8	13 3/8	5 4/8	5 5/8	9 0/8	Lincoln County	WY	Raul "Randy" Quayle	1992	2,349
69 2/8	13 7/8	13 7/8	5 3/8	5 3/8	8 5/8	Sweetwater County	WY	Justin J. Shirley	1993	2,349
69 2/8	12 3/8	12 3/8	6 1/8	6 1/8	10 7/8	Rosebud County	MT	Kyle R. Zimmerman	1993	2,349
69 2/8	13 4/8	13 5/8	6 0/8	5 7/8	10 7/8	Park County	WY	Ron Niziolek	1993	2,349
69 2/8	12 7/8	13 0/8	6 0/8	5 7/8	8 0/8	Campbell County	WY	Norm Dustin	1993	2,349
69 2/8	13 4/8	13 4/8	5 6/8	5 7/8	11 3/8	Natrona County	WY	Greg Morse	1993	2,349
69 2/8	13 6/8	13 5/8	5 5/8	5 4/8	11 7/8	Sweetwater County	WY	Craig Boheler	1994	2,349
69 2/8	14 4/8	14 4/8	5 3/8	5 4/8	7 2/8	Uinta County	WY	Franklin W. Sheets	1994	2,349
69 2/8	14 4/8	14 4/8	5 6/8	5 7/8	12 2/8	Owyhee County	ID	Neil Thagard	1994	2,349
69 2/8	13 0/8	12 6/8	6 1/8	6 0/8	9 1/8	Park County	WY	Tonja L. Schmidt	1994	2,349
69 2/8	13 1/8	13 1/8	6 1/8	6 0/8	10 7/8	Moffat County	CO	Lonny Vanatta	1994	2,349
69 2/8	13 7/8	13 7/8	5 2/8	5 2/8	12 7/8	Billings County	ND	Douglas A. Baumiller	1994	2,349
69 2/8	14 2/8	13 7/8	5 5/8	5 5/8	10 2/8	Campbell County	WY	Charles Suchy	1994	2,349
69 2/8	13 6/8	13 5/8	5 5/8	5 5/8	10 2/8	Johnson County	WY	Ellis Wall	1994	2,349
69 2/8	13 1/8	13 1/8	6 2/8	6 2/8	8 1/8	Converse County	WY	Richard Cochran	1994	2,349
69 2/8	13 6/8	13 3/8	6 3/8	6 2/8	7 4/8	Fergus County	MT	James A. Schneider	1994	2,349
69 2/8	12 4/8	12 4/8	6 2/8	6 1/8	10 2/8	Youngstown	ALB	Gary Gillett	1994	2,349
69 2/8	14 0/8	13 7/8	6 2/8	6 2/8	6 6/8	McKenzie County	ND	John Schaffer	1994	2,349
69 2/8	14 1/8	14 1/8	5 4/8	5 4/8	10 3/8	Campbell County	WY	Ken A. Rimer	1994	2,349
69 2/8	13 1/8	12 3/8	6 2/8	6 3/8	9 2/8	Converse County	WY	Joel T. Oxley	1995	2,349
69 2/8	14 5/8	14 6/8	5 1/8	5 2/8	9 4/8	Washoe County	NV	Alan Harris	1995	2,349
69 2/8	12 6/8	12 6/8	6 0/8	6 0/8	10 0/8	Natrona County	WY	Dave Moritzen	1995	2,349
69 2/8	12 6/8	13 4/8	5 6/8	5 5/8	6 1/8	Apache County	AZ	Fred Clifford	1995	2,349
69 2/8	13 7/8	14 3/8	5 7/8	9 1/8	7 2/8	Converse County	WY	Luigi Puglia	1995	2,349
69 2/8	14 6/8	14 5/8	5 1/8	5 1/8	9 1/8	Rosebud County	MT	John Richardson	1995	2,349
69 2/8	13 0/8	12 4/8	6 0/8	6 0/8	7 7/8	Campbell County	WY	Paul E. Korn	1995	2,349
69 2/8	12 4/8	12 7/8	5 7/8	5 7/8	8 6/8	Converse County	WY	Robert L. Pagel, Jr.	1996	2,349

PRONGHORN

Minimum Score 67 — Continued

SCORE	LENGTH OF HORN R	L	CIRCUMFERENCE OF BASE R	L	INSIDE SPREAD	AREA	STATE/PROVINCE	HUNTER'S NAME	DATE	RANK
69 2/8	12 6/8	12 4/8	5 6/8	5 5/8	12 5/8	Converse County	WY	Derl Phelps	1996	2,349
69 2/8	13 1/8	13 1/8	5 6/8	6 0/8	11 7/8	Converse County	WY	Todd Smith	1996	2,349
69 2/8	14 2/8	14 1/8	5 5/8	5 4/8	11 0/8	Manyberries	ALB	George W. Schoonover III	1996	2,349
69 2/8	12 3/8	12 2/8	6 1/8	6 0/8	11 3/8	Perkins County	SD	Troy Hanson	1996	2,349
69 2/8	13 6/8	13 5/8	5 4/8	5 4/8	10 4/8	Weld County	CO	Shane E. Cole	1997	2,349
69 2/8	12 6/8	12 7/8	6 0/8	6 0/8	9 0/8	Converse County	WY	Randon Earl Saunoris	1997	2,349
69 2/8	13 2/8	13 4/8	5 7/8	6 1/8	11 2/8	Converse County	WY	Jerry Ellingson	1997	2,349
69 2/8	13 1/8	13 2/8	5 7/8	5 6/8	9 0/8	Johnson County	WY	James Bornman	1997	2,349
69 2/8	11 5/8	11 4/8	6 3/8	6 3/8	11 2/8	Converse County	WY	Frank S. Noska IV	1997	2,349
69 2/8	14 2/8	13 5/8	5 4/8	5 4/8	9 5/8	Sweetwater County	WY	Larry Cross	1997	2,349
69 2/8	12 6/8	12 6/8	6 1/8	5 7/8	8 5/8	Moffat County	CO	Linda Strong	1998	2,349
69 2/8	12 7/8	13 6/8	5 7/8	5 6/8	9 1/8	Millard County	UT	Jess J. Jacobson	1998	2,349
69 2/8	14 4/8	14 2/8	5 4/8	5 5/8	14 2/8	Converse County	WY	John D. Edman	1998	2,349
69 2/8	13 2/8	13 2/8	5 7/8	5 6/8	9 7/8	McKenzie County	ND	John Paul Schaffer	1998	2,349
69 0/8	12 7/8	13 0/8	5 6/8	5 7/8	8 4/8	Fall River County	SD	Francis R. Tovar	1968	2,453
69 0/8	14 0/8	14 2/8	5 2/8	5 3/8	9 1/8	Mercer County	ND	John J. Willoughby	1977	2,453
69 0/8	13 4/8	13 2/8	5 6/8	5 5/8	8 3/8	Butte County	ID	Larry Roberts	1979	2,453
69 0/8	14 1/8	13 7/8	5 4/8	5 3/8	10 0/8	Carbon County	WY	Grant Poindexter	1980	2,453
69 0/8	14 0/8	14 2/8	5 7/8	5 6/8	8 0/8	Converse County	WY	Don Clark	1981	2,453
69 0/8	13 2/8	13 3/8	5 6/8	5 5/8	11 0/8	Converse County	WY	George Place	1981	2,453
69 0/8	12 5/8	12 4/8	5 6/8	5 6/8	9 5/8	Fremont County	WY	A. E. 'Butch' Whelchel	1981	2,453
69 0/8	12 6/8	12 6/8	5 6/8	5 6/8	12 5/8	Converse County	WY	Jeff Wright	1981	2,453
69 0/8	13 5/8	13 6/8	5 7/8	6 0/8	11 6/8	Washoe County	NV	Dr. Ronald H. Thole	1982	2,453
69 0/8	13 0/8	12 6/8	6 0/8	6 0/8	7 0/8	Park County	CO	Greg Brown	1983	2,453
69 0/8	12 4/8	12 4/8	6 0/8	6 1/8	9 4/8	Moffat County	CO	Burton Arbogast	1983	2,453
69 0/8	13 2/8	13 3/8	5 6/8	5 6/8	11 4/8	Moffat County	CO	Mike Wallers	1983	2,453
69 0/8	13 4/8	13 4/8	6 0/8	6 1/8	10 3/8	Converse County	WY	Michael Nimmer	1983	2,453
69 0/8	13 0/8	13 1/8	6 1/8	6 1/8	9 2/8	Converse County	WY	Lloyd E. Musser	1983	2,453
69 0/8	13 4/8	12 7/8	5 7/8	5 6/8	9 2/8	Converse County	WY	James R. Dreves	1983	2,453
69 0/8	14 1/8	14 0/8	5 4/8	5 4/8	10 1/8	Johnson County	WY	Steve Nolte	1984	2,453
69 0/8	12 7/8	12 5/8	6 0/8	6 1/8	11 2/8	Converse County	WY	Janice Peterman	1984	2,453
69 0/8	13 2/8	13 3/8	5 6/8	5 7/8	13 3/8	Converse County	WY	John L Kosharek	1985	2,453
69 0/8	12 7/8	12 6/8	6 0/8	5 7/8	9 3/8	Campbell County	WY	Bill Heinike	1985	2,453
69 0/8	13 1/8	13 2/8	5 5/8	5 6/8	12 4/8	Carbon County	WY	Richard L. Westervelt	1987	2,453
69 0/8	12 2/8	13 3/8	5 5/8	5 5/8	10 2/8	Moffat County	CO	Harry Torkilson	1987	2,453
69 0/8	14 0/8	14 0/8	5 3/8	5 4/8	7 1/8	Natrona County	WY	Ricky A. Wall	1987	2,453
69 0/8	12 4/8	12 4/8	6 0/8	6 0/8	8 4/8	Moffat County	CO	Brent Newton	1988	2,453
69 0/8	13 2/8	13 2/8	5 6/8	5 6/8	9 4/8	Campbell County	WY	Dennis Klemick	1988	2,453
69 0/8	13 0/8	13 0/8	6 1/8	6 0/8	9 6/8	Converse County	WY	Michael E. Rice	1988	2,453
69 0/8	13 1/8	13 3/8	5 7/8	6 0/8	8 7/8	Converse County	WY	Steve VanZile	1988	2,453
69 0/8	12 7/8	12 7/8	5 7/8	5 6/8	8 5/8	Sweetwater County	WY	Robert G. Petersen	1989	2,453
69 0/8	13 0/8	12 7/8	6 0/8	5 5/8	10 6/8	Modoc County	CA	Cheryl Vermilion	1989	2,453
69 0/8	14 5/8	14 5/8	5 4/8	5 4/8	9 4/8	Converse County	WY	Brian Bass	1989	2,453
69 0/8	12 5/8	14 3/8	5 6/8	5 5/8	8 5/8	Navajo County	AZ	Ron Nichols	1989	2,453
69 0/8	13 4/8	13 5/8	5 3/8	5 3/8	9 0/8	Converse County	WY	Robert Moon	1989	2,453
69 0/8	12 7/8	12 5/8	5 6/8	5 6/8	9 0/8	Albany County	WY	Gene Welle	1989	2,453
69 0/8	14 0/8	13 6/8	5 4/8	5 4/8	12 0/8	Campbell County	WY	Tippy Clark	1989	2,453
69 0/8	13 2/8	13 2/8	5 7/8	5 7/8	10 3/8	White Pine County	NV	David Brown	1990	2,453
69 0/8	13 3/8	13 1/8	5 4/8	5 3/8	9 1/8	Moffat County	CO	John Morris	1990	2,453
69 0/8	13 7/8	14 0/8	5 7/8	5 7/8	7 4/8	Campbell County	WY	Elroy Thorson	1990	2,453
69 0/8	14 1/8	14 3/8	5 6/8	5 6/8	10 5/8	Moffat County	CO	Rett Kelly	1990	2,453
69 0/8	12 6/8	12 5/8	6 0/8	6 0/8	7 2/8	Converse County	WY	Stan Rauch	1990	2,453
69 0/8	13 5/8	13 3/8	6 0/8	6 0/8	11 1/8	Natrona County	WY	Tony Zirkelbach	1990	2,453
69 0/8	13 2/8	13 3/8	5 5/8	5 6/8	11 3/8	Jenner	ALB	Dale Johnson	1990	2,453
69 0/8	14 3/8	14 0/8	6 2/8	5 7/8	11 4/8	Wallace County	KS	Mike Jenkins	1990	2,453
69 0/8	13 1/8	13 2/8	5 6/8	5 4/8	13 6/8	Manyberries	ALB	Ken Maier	1990	2,453
69 0/8	13 5/8	13 2/8	5 4/8	5 5/8	11 7/8	Carbon County	WY	Karl Knudsen	1991	2,453
69 0/8	12 5/8	12 6/8	5 5/8	5 6/8	10 1/8	Sweetwater County	WY	Patricia C. Sands	1991	2,453
69 0/8	13 3/8	13 2/8	6 0/8	6 0/8	10 4/8	Modoc County	CA	Dave S. Semple	1991	2,453
69 0/8	14 4/8	13 0/8	5 4/8	5 4/8	9 3/8	Natrona County	WY	Gregory L. Reed	1991	2,453
69 0/8	12 6/8	13 0/8	5 6/8	5 7/8	11 3/8	Converse County	WY	Ed Toelken	1991	2,453
69 0/8	13 6/8	14 0/8	5 6/8	5 6/8	9 7/8	Bowman County	ND	Mark Froelich	1991	2,453
69 0/8	13 6/8	14 1/8	6 1/8	6 2/8	13 5/8	Buffalo County	SD	Darrell Hahn	1991	2,453
69 0/8	13 7/8	13 4/8	5 4/8	5 3/8	12 2/8	Sioux County	NE	Roger Dekok	1991	2,453
69 0/8	13 6/8	13 6/8	5 3/8	5 4/8	7 1/8	Meagher County	MT	D. Mitch Kottas	1991	2,453
69 0/8	14 4/8	14 2/8	5 5/8	5 5/8	9 1/8	Petroleum County	MT	Mark D. Hughes	1991	2,453
69 0/8	14 4/8	15 6/8	5 2/8	5 1/8	9 1/8	Hudspeth County	TX	Kenneth L. Zoller	1991	2,453
69 0/8	12 4/8	12 3/8	5 7/8	5 7/8	9 4/8	Bowman County	ND	Dale J. Neva	1991	2,453
69 0/8	12 2/8	12 4/8	6 1/8	6 1/8	9 4/8	Butte County	ID	David Wayne Ary	1992	2,453
69 0/8	12 3/8	12 3/8	6 3/8	6 2/8	6 2/8	Campbell County	WY	Barb Kleve	1992	2,453
69 0/8	13 4/8	13 6/8	5 4/8	5 4/8	9 7/8	Converse County	WY	Larry M. Peterson	1992	2,453
69 0/8	13 0/8	13 1/8	6 0/8	6 0/8	9 4/8	Albany County	WY	Roger Sheaffer	1992	2,453
69 0/8	12 7/8	13 5/8	6 5/8	6 5/8	8 0/8	Campbell County	WY	Jack Savini	1992	2,453
69 0/8	13 5/8	13 5/8	5 4/8	5 4/8	10 0/8	Perkins County	SD	Fred Kober	1992	2,453
69 0/8	13 6/8	13 6/8	5 3/8	5 3/8	11 3/8	Weston County	WY	Roland Weeg	1992	2,453
69 0/8	13 5/8	13 7/8	5 5/8	5 5/8	10 7/8	Petroleum County	MT	Mark D. Hughes	1992	2,453
69 0/8	13 2/8	13 3/8	5 3/8	5 2/8	8 7/8	Saguache County	CO	Bennie Koch, Jr.	1993	2,453
69 0/8	14 0/8	14 0/8	5 6/8	5 5/8	9 6/8	Custer County	ID	Chris J. Crisler	1993	2,453

PRONGHORN

Minimum Score 67 — Continued

SCORE	LENGTH OF HORN R	L	CIRCUMFERENCE OF BASE R	L	INSIDE SPREAD	AREA	STATE/ PROVINCE	HUNTER'S NAME	DATE	RANK
69 0/8	12 2/8	12 1/8	6 2/8	6 0/8	11 4/8	Moffat County	CO	Glen Hotchkiss	1993	2,453
69 0/8	13 5/8	13 7/8	6 1/8	6 1/8	8 5/8	Carbon County	WY	Stephen Wilcoxson	1993	2,453
69 0/8	13 2/8	13 1/8	5 4/8	5 3/8	8 6/8	Campbell County	WY	Dale Miller	1993	2,453
69 0/8	13 5/8	13 3/8	6 0/8	6 0/8	9 1/8	Natrona County	WY	Richard J. Yates	1993	2,453
69 0/8	12 0/8	12 0/8	6 0/8	6 0/8	12 1/8	Converse County	WY	G. William Buxton	1993	2,453
69 0/8	14 4/8	14 3/8	5 4/8	5 4/8	8 5/8	Medicine Hat	ALB	Glen Garton	1993	2,453
69 0/8	13 2/8	13 2/8	6 0/8	6 0/8	9 6/8	Moffat County	CO	Raymond L. Lunnon	1993	2,453
69 0/8	15 0/8	15 0/8	5 6/8	5 6/8	13 0/8	Youngstown	ALB	Dominic Barbario	1993	2,453
69 0/8	13 2/8	12 6/8	5 6/8	5 6/8	6 5/8	Sweetwater County	WY	Douglas E. Walton	1994	2,453
69 0/8	12 7/8	13 0/8	6 0/8	6 0/8	7 7/8	Moffat County	CO	Jim Shanks	1994	2,453
69 0/8	13 3/8	13 4/8	5 6/8	5 6/8	14 3/8	Rio Blanco County	CO	John R. Cabot	1994	2,453
69 0/8	12 6/8	12 6/8	6 1/8	6 2/8	9 4/8	Sublette County	WY	Guy L. Williamson	1994	2,453
69 0/8	12 3/8	12 5/8	6 0/8	6 1/8	9 5/8	Campbell County	WY	Walter Phillips	1994	2,453
69 0/8	13 2/8	13 4/8	6 1/8	5 6/8	8 1/8	Johnson County	WY	Don Mealey	1994	2,453
69 0/8	14 2/8	14 0/8	5 6/8	5 6/8	11 6/8	Saguache County	CO	Jason Embry	1994	2,453
69 0/8	13 0/8	13 0/8	5 6/8	5 6/8	9 1/8	Sioux County	NE	Steven L. Anderson	1994	2,453
69 0/8	12 7/8	13 0/8	5 6/8	5 6/8	10 5/8	Park County	WY	Timothy J. Aydt	1994	2,453
69 0/8	12 7/8	12 7/8	5 7/8	5 7/8	11 5/8	Millard County	UT	Shane T. Newman	1995	2,453
69 0/8	12 7/8	12 6/8	6 2/8	6 3/8	9 4/8	Moffat County	CO	Dave Culter	1995	2,453
69 0/8	12 7/8	12 5/8	5 7/8	6 0/8	12 2/8	Big Horn County	WY	Dave Moss	1995	2,453
69 0/8	13 4/8	13 4/8	5 4/8	5 4/8	7 5/8	Rosebud County	MT	Kent Kaufman	1995	2,453
69 0/8	13 5/8	13 7/8	5 5/8	5 5/8	9 5/8	Campbell County	WY	Curt Rotering	1995	2,453
69 0/8	13 4/8	13 3/8	6 1/8	6 0/8	9 1/8	Dundy County	NE	Sara Gideon	1995	2,453
69 0/8	12 3/8	12 4/8	5 7/8	5 7/8	8 7/8	Weld County	CO	Scott Cumings	1996	2,453
69 0/8	14 4/8	14 0/8	6 0/8	5 6/8	11 7/8	Colfax County	NM	David R. Aikin	1996	2,453
69 0/8	12 6/8	12 5/8	7 1/8	7 1/8	9 1/8	Moffat County	CO	Byron Dean	1996	2,453
69 0/8	14 3/8	14 0/8	5 6/8	5 6/8	8 4/8	El Paso County	CO	Jeff Elem	1996	2,453
69 0/8	13 7/8	13 6/8	5 4/8	5 4/8	9 2/8	Socorro County	NM	Alan W. Krause	1997	2,453
69 0/8	14 1/8	14 4/8	6 4/8	6 2/8	10 5/8	Sweetwater County	WY	George Fabian	1997	2,453
69 0/8	15 3/8	15 1/8	5 0/8	5 1/8	6 4/8	Moffat County	CO	LeRoy A. Brincks	1997	2,453
69 0/8	13 0/8	13 1/8	6 3/8	5 7/8	8 5/8	Campbell County	WY	Chris Gates	1997	2,453
69 0/8	14 3/8	14 4/8	5 5/8	5 5/8	8 3/8	Converse County	WY	K-Tal Johnson	1997	2,453
69 0/8	13 7/8	14 1/8	6 0/8	5 6/8	10 6/8	Park County	MT	David Smith	1998	2,453
69 0/8	13 3/8	13 3/8	5 4/8	5 5/8	11 4/8	Carter County	MT	Shane W. Helmich	1998	2,453
68 6/8	14 7/8	14 7/8	5 4/8	5 4/8	12 0/8	Sweetwater County	WY	Dr. Fred Mack	1960	2,551
68 6/8	13 7/8	14 2/8	5 6/8	5 4/8	7 7/8	Haakon County	SD	William Nankivel	1970	2,551
68 6/8	13 2/8	13 4/8	6 1/8	6 1/8	7 4/8	Gallatin County	MT	Robert Savage	1971	2,551
68 6/8	12 3/8	12 4/8	6 4/8	6 2/8	11 0/8	Sweetwater County	WY	Keith Dana	1978	2,551
68 6/8	13 6/8	13 5/8	5 3/8	5 5/8	9 0/8	Park County	MT	George Kamps	1980	2,551
68 6/8	13 0/8	12 7/8	5 7/8	5 4/8	9 0/8	Natrona County	WY	Jim L. McCrory	1981	2,551
68 6/8	12 4/8	12 4/8	5 5/8	5 4/8	7 3/8	Converse County	WY	Donald Schram	1981	2,551
68 6/8	13 0/8	13 2/8	5 7/8	5 7/8	11 6/8	Weld County	CO	Ron Montross	1983	2,551
68 6/8	12 4/8	12 0/8	6 4/8	6 3/8	9 4/8	Crook County	WY	Jim P Hallock	1983	2,551
68 6/8	13 4/8	13 3/8	5 5/8	5 5/8	7 6/8	Converse County	WY	Gary Duncan	1983	2,551
68 6/8	13 3/8	13 5/8	5 1/8	5 1/8	12 2/8	Garfield County	MT	Darwin Frison	1983	2,551
68 6/8	14 0/8	14 0/8	5 3/8	5 2/8	10 6/8	Moffat County	CO	Gary Fritzler	1984	2,551
68 6/8	12 4/8	12 5/8	6 0/8	6 3/8	9 1/8	McKinley County	NM	John W. Rose	1984	2,551
68 6/8	14 3/8	14 3/8	5 4/8	5 4/8	9 4/8	Butte County	SD	Reginald E. Faber, Jr.	1984	2,551
68 6/8	12 6/8	12 4/8	6 0/8	5 7/8	8 2/8	Converse County	WY	Eric Bruce	1984	2,551
68 6/8	13 4/8	14 0/8	5 6/8	5 4/8	11 1/8	Washoe County	NV	Gary Zunino	1985	2,551
68 6/8	13 7/8	13 1/8	6 2/8	6 2/8	11 2/8	Sweetwater County	WY	W.R. "Tony" Dukes	1985	2,551
68 6/8	14 0/8	13 6/8	6 3/8	6 2/8	14 6/8	Converse County	WY	Frank Moore	1985	2,551
68 6/8	13 0/8	12 7/8	5 5/8	5 4/8	5 3/8	Sweetwater County	WY	Gary Belvoir	1986	2,551
68 6/8	13 7/8	14 2/8	5 5/8	5 5/8	11 6/8	Washoe County	NV	Gilbert Hernandez	1987	2,551
68 6/8	13 2/8	12 6/8	5 6/8	5 4/8	8 1/8	Custer County	ID	Brian Hunter Heck	1987	2,551
68 6/8	13 2/8	13 4/8	6 5/8	6 4/8	6 1/8	Garfield County	CO	Rory Robie	1987	2,551
68 6/8	12 6/8	12 6/8	6 4/8	6 3/8	11 3/8	Moffat County	CO	Tommy M. Brown	1987	2,551
68 6/8	12 5/8	12 5/8	5 7/8	5 6/8	12 7/8	Sweetwater County	WY	David Breakfield	1987	2,551
68 6/8	12 4/8	12 5/8	5 5/8	5 5/8	10 2/8	Converse County	WY	David L. Lundy	1987	2,551
68 6/8	13 7/8	13 5/8	6 1/8	6 0/8	9 3/8	Beaverhead County	MT	Mervin Johnston	1987	2,551
68 6/8	13 4/8	13 7/8	5 6/8	5 5/8	9 6/8	Buffalo	ALB	Lou Carrier	1987	2,551
68 6/8	12 5/8	12 5/8	6 4/8	6 3/8	16 4/8	Washoe County	NV	Robert Reed	1988	2,551
68 6/8	13 5/8	14 0/8	5 5/8	5 4/8	10 1/8	Buffalo	ALB	Orest Popil	1988	2,551
68 6/8	12 7/8	12 6/8	5 5/8	5 4/8	9 3/8	Medicine Hat	ALB	Owen Telke	1988	2,551
68 6/8	13 1/8	13 2/8	5 5/8	5 5/8	11 0/8	Sublette County	WY	Peter L. Bucklin	1989	2,551
68 6/8	13 0/8	12 6/8	5 7/8	6 0/8	11 3/8	Yavapai County	AZ	Charles P. Cooley	1989	2,551
68 6/8	13 7/8	13 5/8	5 5/8	5 7/8	10 3/8	McCone County	MT	JaRon Schillinger	1989	2,551
68 6/8	13 6/8	14 0/8	5 6/8	5 7/8	10 7/8	Jenner	ALB	Brian J. Ward	1989	2,551
68 6/8	14 0/8	14 2/8	6 4/8	6 2/8	10 5/8	Phillips County	MT	Mike Dunwell	1989	2,551
68 6/8	13 4/8	13 0/8	5 6/8	5 5/8	13 4/8	Wallace County	KS	Larry Buchholz	1989	2,551
68 6/8	13 2/8	13 1/8	5 4/8	5 5/8	7 2/8	Natrona County	WY	R. Ray Wix	1990	2,551
68 6/8	12 4/8	12 3/8	5 5/8	5 5/8	13 0/8	Natrona County	WY	James V. Siebels	1990	2,551
68 6/8	13 1/8	13 2/8	5 3/8	5 4/8	9 6/8	Campbell County	WY	Randy Cook	1990	2,551
68 6/8	12 3/8	12 2/8	6 1/8	6 1/8	9 2/8	Hyde County	SD	Robert Moriarty	1990	2,551
68 6/8	14 5/8	14 3/8	5 3/8	5 4/8	9 7/8	Washoe County	NV	Richard Oliver	1991	2,551
68 6/8	12 0/8	11 5/8	6 6/8	6 6/8	10 4/8	Converse County	WY	Bob Arne	1991	2,551
68 6/8	13 1/8	13 0/8	5 7/8	5 7/8	9 1/8	Converse County	WY	Phil Perry	1991	2,551
68 6/8	13 0/8	13 0/8	6 3/8	6 2/8	7 3/8	Campbell County	WY	Allan White	1991	2,551

PRONGHORN

Minimum Score 67 — Continued — 655

SCORE	LENGTH OF HORN R	L	CIRCUMFERENCE OF BASE R	L	INSIDE SPREAD	AREA	STATE/PROVINCE	HUNTER'S NAME	DATE	RANK
68 6/8	13 4/8	13 3/8	5 5/8	5 4/8	10 5/8	Campbell County	WY	Dan M. Mooney	1991	2,551
68 6/8	12 2/8	12 4/8	5 6/8	5 6/8	11 0/8	Rosebud County	MT	Craig Gerber	1991	2,551
68 6/8	13 3/8	13 7/8	6 0/8	6 1/8	11 2/8	Fergus County	MT	Chris G. Sanford	1991	2,551
68 6/8	13 6/8	13 5/8	5 6/8	5 5/8	8 0/8	Washoe County	NV	Anthony L. Mudd	1992	2,551
68 6/8	13 0/8	12 7/8	6 1/8	6 1/8	8 6/8	Humboldt County	NV	Erik L. Self	1992	2,551
68 6/8	14 0/8	13 7/8	6 0/8	5 5/8	9 4/8	Sweetwater County	WY	Jeffrey J. Petersen	1992	2,551
68 6/8	13 1/8	13 0/8	5 1/8	5 1/8	8 1/8	Moffat County	CO	David Joyce	1992	2,551
68 6/8	12 7/8	12 6/8	6 1/8	6 0/8	9 1/8	Carbon County	WY	Mark Alan Bartkoski	1992	2,551
68 6/8	13 2/8	13 2/8	5 6/8	5 6/8	8 7/8	Campbell County	WY	Darryl Winslow	1992	2,551
68 6/8	12 5/8	12 3/8	6 0/8	5 7/8	7 1/8	Manyberries	ALB	John Visscher	1992	2,551
68 6/8	13 4/8	13 2/8	5 3/8	5 4/8	10 0/8	Fremont County	WY	Ronald Lane Turner	1992	2,551
68 6/8	12 5/8	12 4/8	5 4/8	5 5/8	12 3/8	Coconino County	AZ	John J. Anderson	1993	2,551
68 6/8	13 1/8	13 4/8	5 4/8	5 4/8	9 6/8	Apache County	AZ	Fred Clifford	1993	2,551
68 6/8	13 0/8	12 7/8	5 2/8	5 3/8	6 7/8	Beaverhead County	MT	Troy Bungay	1993	2,551
68 6/8	15 0/8	14 6/8	5 5/8	5 6/8	10 3/8	Owyhee County	ID	Tony E. Hyde	1993	2,551
68 6/8	14 4/8	14 3/8	5 0/8	5 0/8	10 0/8	Manyberries	ALB	Ryk Visscher	1993	2,551
68 6/8	13 6/8	13 1/8	6 2/8	6 2/8	11 2/8	Sweetwater County	WY	Robert G. Petersen	1993	2,551
68 6/8	13 3/8	13 5/8	6 2/8	6 0/8	13 6/8	Washoe County	NV	Edwin A. Charkowicz	1994	2,551
68 6/8	12 4/8	12 5/8	6 2/8	6 1/8	13 1/8	Box Elder County	UT	Brian Ray Spencer	1994	2,551
68 6/8	14 4/8	14 2/8	5 4/8	5 4/8	8 3/8	Moffat County	CO	J. Keith Chastain	1994	2,551
68 6/8	12 6/8	12 4/8	5 7/8	6 0/8	8 7/8	Crook County	WY	Aaron Hickman	1994	2,551
68 6/8	13 3/8	13 3/8	5 2/8	5 2/8	8 0/8	Converse County	WY	Timothy Otis	1994	2,551
68 6/8	13 1/8	12 7/8	6 3/8	6 1/8	9 4/8	Converse County	WY	Carlos D. Landers, Jr.	1994	2,551
68 6/8	13 7/8	14 1/8	6 0/8	5 6/8	13 4/8	Converse County	WY	Tim Schneewind	1994	2,551
68 6/8	13 5/8	14 5/8	5 6/8	5 5/8	12 4/8	Lassen County	CA	Dominic H. Choi	1995	2,551
68 6/8	14 0/8	12 6/8	5 3/8	5 3/8	11 6/8	Grand County	UT	Kevin L. Sheets	1995	2,551
68 6/8	13 4/8	13 6/8	5 3/8	5 3/8	10 7/8	Coconino County	AZ	Phillip C. Dalrymple	1995	2,551
68 6/8	11 4/8	11 4/8	6 4/8	6 6/8	11 6/8	Yavapai County	AZ	Don Parks, Jr.	1995	2,551
68 6/8	13 4/8	13 3/8	5 4/8	5 4/8	6 4/8	Campbell County	WY	Steve Upton	1995	2,551
68 6/8	13 5/8	13 6/8	5 6/8	5 6/8	9 4/8	Campbell County	WY	Gary English	1995	2,551
68 6/8	12 3/8	12 3/8	5 5/8	5 5/8	7 6/8	Juab County	UT	Rebecca J. Simpson	1996	2,551
68 6/8	13 1/8	13 0/8	6 0/8	6 0/8	5 6/8	Weld County	CO	Dave Holt	1996	2,551
68 6/8	13 0/8	13 0/8	5 5/8	5 6/8	9 1/8	Harding County	SD	Garland Holley	1996	2,551
68 6/8	13 3/8	13 4/8	6 0/8	6 1/8	9 3/8	Clark County	ID	Marc R. Beesley	1996	2,551
68 6/8	13 1/8	13 2/8	5 6/8	5 6/8	8 5/8	Owyhee County	ID	Michael S. Moore	1996	2,551
68 6/8	12 5/8	13 2/8	5 4/8	5 4/8	10 0/8	Natrona County	WY	Ray Wix	1996	2,551
68 6/8	13 2/8	13 0/8	5 4/8	5 4/8	9 5/8	Converse County	WY	David W. Wagner	1996	2,551
68 6/8	13 3/8	13 5/8	5 4/8	5 5/8	8 5/8	Converse County	WY	William G. Mason	1996	2,551
68 6/8	12 7/8	13 0/8	6 1/8	6 1/8	10 4/8	Rosebud County	MT	R. Gerald Ebert	1996	2,551
68 6/8	14 2/8	14 2/8	5 2/8	5 1/8	10 4/8	Weston County	WY	Warren DeSmidt	1996	2,551
68 6/8	13 2/8	13 4/8	5 6/8	5 6/8	12 4/8	Hays	ALB	Larry Knibbs	1996	2,551
68 6/8	13 2/8	15 0/8	5 6/8	5 6/8	14 1/8	Johnson County	WY	Charles H. Sagner	1996	2,551
68 6/8	13 1/8	13 1/8	5 5/8	5 5/8	8 1/8	Fall River County	SD	Gary DeJong	1996	2,551
68 6/8	13 1/8	13 3/8	6 1/8	6 2/8	11 0/8	Twin Falls County	ID	Randal Scott O'Melia	1997	2,551
68 6/8	12 6/8	12 3/8	6 0/8	6 0/8	8 3/8	Campbell County	WY	Glenn Wotring	1998	2,551
68 6/8	14 2/8	14 0/8	5 2/8	5 2/8	8 7/8	Albany County	WY	Roger M. Tyler	1998	2,551
68 6/8	12 6/8	12 7/8	5 7/8	5 7/8	10 2/8	Fergus County	MT	Chris Sanford	1998	2,551
68 4/8	13 4/8	13 0/8	5 4/8	5 5/8	8 6/8	Tripp County	SD	Spike Jorgensen	1965	2,642
68 4/8	14 1/8	14 1/8	5 2/8	5 1/8	12 3/8	Lincoln County	NM	James H. Simmons	1966	2,642
68 4/8	12 6/8	12 2/8	6 5/8	6 5/8	12 1/8	McLean County	ND	Tom O'Connell	1970	2,642
68 4/8	13 2/8	13 2/8	5 5/8	5 5/8	13 3/8	Carbon County	WY	Robert Pitt	1974	2,642
68 4/8	14 1/8	14 0/8	5 4/8	5 2/8	10 5/8	Johnson County	WY	David Collis	1975	2,642
68 4/8	12 6/8	12 7/8	6 0/8	6 0/8	9 4/8	Billings County	ND	Dean Nevland	1975	2,642
68 4/8	12 6/8	12 4/8	5 6/8	5 7/8	9 3/8	Converse County	WY	Ron Carpenter	1976	2,642
68 4/8	13 0/8	12 7/8	5 5/8	6 0/8	8 3/8	Lincoln County	WY	Preston C. Phelps	1977	2,642
68 4/8	13 7/8	13 4/8	5 6/8	5 5/8	13 1/8	Logan County	CO	Tony Seahorn	1978	2,642
68 4/8	13 7/8	14 0/8	6 0/8	5 7/8	12 4/8	McKinley County	NM	James M. Finn	1979	2,642
68 4/8	14 1/8	14 1/8	5 4/8	5 5/8	10 5/8	Butte County	ID	Clifton Robinson	1979	2,642
68 4/8	13 3/8	13 2/8	5 5/8	5 5/8	13 0/8	Carbon County	WY	Dale Gauthier	1980	2,642
68 4/8	13 0/8	12 5/8	5 7/8	5 7/8	10 3/8	Moffat County	CO	Ron Bolinger	1981	2,642
68 4/8	13 6/8	13 5/8	5 0/8	5 0/8	8 4/8	Natrona County	WY	Dan Skolaski	1981	2,642
68 4/8	13 5/8	13 4/8	5 4/8	5 3/8	12 1/8	Converse County	WY	Richard Stokke	1981	2,642
68 4/8	12 6/8	13 3/8	5 7/8	6 0/8	9 1/8	Converse County	WY	Charles O. Boggs	1982	2,642
68 4/8	14 1/8	13 7/8	5 5/8	5 6/8	8 6/8	Eddy County	NM	Jim Stell	1982	2,642
68 4/8	13 6/8	14 0/8	5 4/8	5 5/8	13 2/8	Converse County	WY	Harold Leslie	1982	2,642
68 4/8	13 4/8	13 5/8	5 3/8	5 3/8	13 3/8	Converse County	WY	Kent Brigham	1982	2,642
68 4/8	12 4/8	13 0/8	6 3/8	6 1/8	8 6/8	Carbon County	WY	Willis Duhon	1982	2,642
68 4/8	12 7/8	13 0/8	6 0/8	6 0/8	9 6/8	Natrona County	WY	Roger Smith	1982	2,642
68 4/8	12 3/8	12 1/8	6 2/8	6 3/8	10 3/8	Natrona County	WY	Steve Turck	1982	2,642
68 4/8	12 7/8	12 7/8	5 5/8	5 4/8	10 6/8	Moffat County	CO	Len Cardinale	1983	2,642
68 4/8	13 4/8	13 4/8	5 2/8	5 1/8	10 5/8	Sweetwater County	WY	Dean Dolenc	1983	2,642
68 4/8	13 3/8	13 6/8	5 5/8	5 4/8	7 2/8	Sioux County	NE	Chuck Starr	1983	2,642
68 4/8	13 6/8	13 6/8	5 2/8	5 3/8	7 6/8	Logan County	KS	Lynn Freese	1984	2,642
68 4/8	13 6/8	13 6/8	5 6/8	5 4/8	11 2/8	Converse County	WY	Marty Horn	1984	2,642
68 4/8	13 6/8	14 5/8	5 4/8	5 4/8	11 2/8	Converse County	WY	Joe Guth	1984	2,642
68 4/8	12 2/8	12 3/8	6 0/8	6 0/8	10 7/8	Campbell County	WY	John 'Jack' Cordes	1984	2,642
68 4/8	12 0/8	12 0/8	5 5/8	5 5/8	8 2/8	Moffat County	CO	Robert Syvertson, Sr.	1985	2,642
68 4/8	13 6/8	13 6/8	5 7/8	5 7/8	11 5/8	Coconino County	AZ	Jesse E. Smith	1985	2,642

PRONGHORN

SCORE	LENGTH OF HORN R	L	CIRCUMFERENCE OF BASE R	L	INSIDE SPREAD	AREA	STATE/ PROVINCE	HUNTER'S NAME	DATE	RANK
68 4/8	12 0/8	11 5/8	5 5/8	5 5/8	9 6/8	Converse County	WY	Steve Woodman	1985	2,642
68 4/8	12 3/8	12 5/8	5 6/8	5 7/8	10 5/8	Campbell County	WY	Thomas R. Dvorak	1985	2,642
68 4/8	13 4/8	13 2/8	5 4/8	5 4/8	9 4/8	WMU 151	ALB	Allen Avery	1985	2,642
68 4/8	13 0/8	13 0/8	5 6/8	5 7/8	10 7/8	Campbell County	WY	Donald Ace Morgan	1986	2,642
68 4/8	12 0/8	12 4/8	5 7/8	5 7/8	9 0/8	Billings County	ND	Rick Froehlich	1986	2,642
68 4/8	12 4/8	12 2/8	5 6/8	5 5/8	9 0/8	Moffat County	CO	Mike Callaway	1987	2,642
68 4/8	13 3/8	12 7/8	5 7/8	5 4/8	9 4/8	Slope County	ND	Terry Buechler	1987	2,642
68 4/8	13 1/8	13 2/8	5 3/8	5 3/8	11 6/8	Moffat County	CO	Tim Cuthriell	1988	2,642
68 4/8	14 1/8	14 1/8	5 7/8	5 7/8	11 2/8	Carbon County	WY	Raymond R. Robison	1988	2,642
68 4/8	13 0/8	13 0/8	5 4/8	5 4/8	6 2/8	Moffat County	CO	Steve Barnhill	1988	2,642
68 4/8	13 5/8	13 6/8	5 5/8	5 5/8	11 1/8	Converse County	WY	Mick Cochrane	1988	2,642
68 4/8	13 4/8	13 6/8	6 0/8	6 0/8	10 4/8	Campbell County	WY	Al Haugestuen	1988	2,642
68 4/8	13 1/8	13 1/8	5 5/8	5 5/8	11 6/8	Klamath County	OR	Steve Tandy	1989	2,642
68 4/8	11 7/8	11 7/8	5 6/8	5 6/8	9 3/8	Billings County	ND	Harold Hugelen	1989	2,642
68 4/8	14 2/8	14 3/8	5 5/8	5 5/8	9 6/8	Buffalo	ALB	Glenn Moir	1989	2,642
68 4/8	13 4/8	13 2/8	5 6/8	5 4/8	10 0/8	Washoe County	NV	Linda Manion	1990	2,642
68 4/8	13 2/8	13 1/8	5 6/8	5 6/8	9 4/8	Moffat County	CO	Cheryl Ray	1990	2,642
68 4/8	14 4/8	13 6/8	5 6/8	5 6/8	16 5/8	Millard County	UT	Bob McGill, Jr.	1990	2,642
68 4/8	12 0/8	12 0/8	6 1/8	6 0/8	12 6/8	Weld County	CO	Kenneth W. Ayers	1991	2,642
68 4/8	12 3/8	12 0/8	6 1/8	5 5/8	7 5/8	Moffat County	CO	Mark Petersen	1991	2,642
68 4/8	13 2/8	13 0/8	5 4/8	5 3/8	13 1/8	Campbell County	WY	Marlene Odahlen-Hinz	1991	2,642
68 4/8	13 2/8	13 7/8	5 3/8	5 4/8	9 4/8	Converse County	WY	Dean K. Reidt	1991	2,642
68 4/8	13 2/8	13 1/8	6 1/8	6 1/8	11 0/8	Campbell County	WY	James W. Torseth	1991	2,642
68 4/8	11 7/8	11 7/8	6 2/8	6 0/8	8 2/8	Campbell County	WY	Jon Lammle	1991	2,642
68 4/8	13 4/8	13 2/8	5 6/8	5 4/8	8 5/8	Custer County	ID	John R. Sample	1991	2,642
68 4/8	13 7/8	14 0/8	5 6/8	5 4/8	9 0/8	Petroleum County	MT	Theodore J. Poper	1991	2,642
68 4/8	13 1/8	13 2/8	6 1/8	5 6/8	11 4/8	Converse County	WY	Michael L. Hoft	1991	2,642
68 4/8	13 0/8	12 1/8	5 7/8	5 7/8	7 6/8	Musselshell County	MT	Scott A. Silverness	1991	2,642
68 4/8	12 6/8	12 7/8	5 6/8	6 0/8	7 4/8	Moffat County	CO	Tim Dehn	1992	2,642
68 4/8	13 4/8	13 7/8	5 7/8	6 0/8	7 1/8	Converse County	WY	Mark Whitish	1992	2,642
68 4/8	13 1/8	13 1/8	6 2/8	6 2/8	13 1/8	Converse County	WY	Rick Hartley	1992	2,642
68 4/8	13 0/8	13 0/8	5 7/8	5 6/8	9 5/8	Johnson County	WY	Mike Neilson	1992	2,642
68 4/8	12 7/8	12 7/8	6 0/8	5 7/8	7 5/8	Hand County	SD	Jeff Poppenga	1992	2,642
68 4/8	12 6/8	12 7/8	6 1/8	5 7/8	8 3/8	Beaverhead County	MT	Terry Barkell	1992	2,642
68 4/8	14 2/8	13 7/8	5 4/8	5 4/8	10 2/8	Johnson County	WY	Charles Sagner	1992	2,642
68 4/8	13 6/8	13 5/8	6 0/8	5 6/8	7 5/8	Sioux County	NE	Ken Roth	1993	2,642
68 4/8	12 7/8	12 7/8	5 5/8	5 5/8	9 4/8	Campbell County	WY	Dave Hinton	1993	2,642
68 4/8	12 0/8	12 2/8	6 1/8	5 6/8	10 2/8	Converse County	WY	Delbert Bybee	1993	2,642
68 4/8	13 2/8	13 2/8	5 6/8	5 6/8	9 5/8	Natrona County	WY	Kenneth M. Friess	1993	2,642
68 4/8	13 6/8	14 4/8	6 1/8	6 2/8	13 3/8	Phillips County	MT	Darvin Henry	1993	2,642
68 4/8	13 7/8	14 0/8	5 4/8	5 4/8	12 6/8	McKenzie County	ND	Steve Rehak	1993	2,642
68 4/8	14 2/8	14 1/8	6 1/8	6 1/8	9 2/8	Sweet Grass County	MT	Scott R. Barefoot	1993	2,642
68 4/8	13 4/8	13 4/8	6 1/8	5 7/8	8 6/8	Manyberries	ALB	Jeff Davies	1993	2,642
68 4/8	13 1/8	12 7/8	6 4/8	6 5/8	11 1/8	Sioux County	NE	Clarence Poteet	1993	2,642
68 4/8	13 1/8	13 2/8	5 6/8	5 6/8	9 6/8	Fremont County	WY	Kevin Maynard	1994	2,642
68 4/8	13 2/8	13 2/8	5 6/8	5 5/8	8 0/8	Campbell County	WY	Jim Keim	1994	2,642
68 4/8	12 4/8	12 4/8	6 5/8	6 4/8	9 0/8	Crook County	WY	Dean C. Henke	1994	2,642
68 4/8	12 5/8	12 4/8	5 6/8	5 6/8	9 4/8	Moffat County	CO	Joseph Miguel	1995	2,642
68 4/8	13 6/8	13 4/8	6 0/8	5 7/8	14 1/8	Moffat County	CO	Chris Reilly	1995	2,642
68 4/8	14 3/8	14 4/8	5 2/8	5 0/8	10 2/8	Campbell County	WY	Danny J. Brown	1995	2,642
68 4/8	13 5/8	13 3/8	5 6/8	5 6/8	10 3/8	Converse County	WY	Robert L. Pagel, Jr.	1995	2,642
68 4/8	12 7/8	12 3/8	6 7/8	6 6/8	11 2/8	Moffat County	CO	Dennis D. Johnson	1996	2,642
68 4/8	13 4/8	13 2/8	5 4/8	5 4/8	12 7/8	Weld County	CO	Randy Wampler	1996	2,642
68 4/8	12 7/8	12 7/8	5 5/8	5 5/8	9 3/8	Converse County	WY	Brian Goble	1996	2,642
68 4/8	12 6/8	12 2/8	6 0/8	6 0/8	11 0/8	Campbell County	WY	Richard E. LaCrone	1996	2,642
68 4/8	12 7/8	12 6/8	6 0/8	6 0/8	9 6/8	Converse County	WY	V. Gene Mathias	1996	2,642
68 4/8	13 0/8	13 0/8	5 6/8	5 5/8	8 2/8	Magrath	ALB	Cameron Cook	1996	2,642
68 4/8	14 0/8	13 7/8	5 6/8	5 7/8	13 1/8	Chouteau County	MT	Jim Wright	1996	2,642
68 4/8	13 5/8	13 3/8	5 2/8	5 2/8	9 0/8	Guadalupe County	NM	Brandon Ray	1997	2,642
68 4/8	13 1/8	13 2/8	5 7/8	6 0/8	11 3/8	Albany County	WY	Marlene Bowen	1997	2,642
68 4/8	14 5/8	14 4/8	5 2/8	5 1/8	7 4/8	Johnson County	WY	Paul R. Chaffee	1997	2,642
68 4/8	13 7/8	13 0/8	5 5/8	5 5/8	7 4/8	Moffat County	CO	Charlie Colby	1997	2,642
68 4/8	11 4/8	12 0/8	7 0/8	6 6/8	8 1/8	Moffat County	CO	Dewayne Mullins	1998	2,642
68 4/8	12 3/8	12 6/8	5 7/8	5 7/8	6 2/8	Weld County	CO	Pat Sauvageau	1998	2,642
68 4/8	12 6/8	12 6/8	5 6/8	5 5/8	10 4/8	Duchesne County	UT	Brian Ferebee	1998	2,642
68 4/8	12 7/8	12 7/8	5 6/8	5 7/8	10 1/8	Custer County	MT	Casey Lyle Prell	1998	2,642
68 4/8	13 2/8	13 1/8	5 0/8	4 7/8	8 0/8	Johnson County	WY	Donald Wayne Smith	1998	2,642
68 2/8	12 4/8	12 4/8	6 2/8	6 0/8	11 6/8	Moffat County	CO	Burl Duckworth	1958	2,740
68 2/8	12 6/8	12 6/8	5 7/8	5 5/8	10 5/8	Harding County	SD	Chet Wohlhueter	1963	2,740
68 2/8	13 5/8	13 3/8	5 3/8	5 2/8	8 7/8	Morton County	ND	Fred F. Heer	1973	2,740
68 2/8	13 2/8	13 2/8	5 6/8	6 0/8	9 1/8	Sweetwater County	WY	Charles Bartlett	1978	2,740
68 2/8	13 0/8	12 5/8	5 6/8	5 5/8	8 1/8	Thomas County	NE	Harold L. Bowman	1978	2,740
68 2/8	13 1/8	13 1/8	5 3/8	5 2/8	9 5/8	Saguache County	CO	Doy K. Curtis	1978	2,740
68 2/8	13 6/8	14 2/8	5 5/8	5 4/8	7 2/8	Lemhi County	ID	Richard Dewey	1978	2,740
68 2/8	12 4/8	12 5/8	6 2/8	6 3/8	11 4/8	Fremont County	WY	Bob Freese	1978	2,740
68 2/8	13 5/8	13 2/8	5 4/8	5 4/8	8 4/8	Fremont County	WY	Will Yeates	1978	2,740
68 2/8	12 1/8	11 7/8	5 6/8	5 7/8	8 0/8	Lemhi County	ID	Larry Cross	1979	2,740
68 2/8	14 1/8	13 7/8	5 5/8	6 0/8	7 5/8	Coconino County	AZ	Jim Ellis	1979	2,740

PRONGHORN

Minimum Score 67 — Continued

SCORE	LENGTH OF HORN R	L	CIRCUMFERENCE OF BASE R	L	INSIDE SPREAD	AREA	STATE/ PROVINCE	HUNTER'S NAME	DATE	RANK
68 2/8	13 6/8	13 7/8	6 2/8	6 2/8	8 6/8	Sweetwater County	WY	Dean Kendall	1980	2,740
68 2/8	12 6/8	12 6/8	6 0/8	6 1/8	7 3/8	Sweetwater County	WY	Ed Budge	1981	2,740
68 2/8	13 0/8	13 0/8	6 0/8	5 5/8	9 0/8	Natrona County	WY	William E. Ehrman	1981	2,740
68 2/8	12 3/8	12 4/8	5 6/8	5 6/8	8 0/8	Moffat County	CO	Barry J. Smith	1981	2,740
68 2/8	13 0/8	13 0/8	5 7/8	5 6/8	6 7/8	Natrona County	WY	Rodger Warwick	1981	2,740
68 2/8	12 6/8	12 6/8	5 4/8	5 5/8	10 0/8	Natrona County	WY	R. G. Williams	1981	2,740
68 2/8	12 0/8	12 2/8	5 6/8	5 6/8	8 0/8	Converse County	WY	Butch Crawford	1982	2,740
68 2/8	14 1/8	13 7/8	5 4/8	5 4/8	13 1/8	Converse County	WY	Donald Schram	1982	2,740
68 2/8	11 7/8	12 1/8	6 1/8	6 1/8	9 3/8	White Pine County	NV	Tony S. Whitten	1983	2,740
68 2/8	14 6/8	14 6/8	5 2/8	5 1/8	10 6/8	Saguache County	CO	Steve Van Treese	1983	2,740
68 2/8	12 7/8	12 6/8	5 4/8	5 4/8	9 4/8	Sublette County	WY	Terry Wright	1983	2,740
68 2/8	13 3/8	13 1/8	5 4/8	5 4/8	11 1/8	Weld County	CO	Dennis Schweitzer	1983	2,740
68 2/8	13 5/8	13 5/8	5 4/8	5 4/8	10 4/8	Bingham County	ID	Doug Foss	1983	2,740
68 2/8	13 1/8	12 7/8	5 7/8	5 6/8	11 7/8	Wallace County	KS	Darren Collins	1983	2,740
68 2/8	13 5/8	13 1/8	5 3/8	5 3/8	10 3/8	Hughes County	SD	Darrel L. Reinke	1984	2,740
68 2/8	13 1/8	13 3/8	5 6/8	5 6/8	11 3/8	Carbon County	WY	Ron Breitsprecher	1984	2,740
68 2/8	14 3/8	14 6/8	6 1/8	5 7/8	11 1/8	Fremont County	WY	Thomas E. Axthelm	1984	2,740
68 2/8	12 2/8	13 2/8	5 3/8	5 4/8	6 7/8	Converse County	WY	Al Sullivan	1984	2,740
68 2/8	12 4/8	12 7/8	6 3/8	6 2/8	8 6/8	Natrona County	WY	Ray L. Harbin	1985	2,740
68 2/8	14 0/8	13 6/8	5 4/8	5 4/8	10 5/8	Carter County	MT	Juanita Byrne	1985	2,740
68 2/8	12 3/8	12 6/8	5 4/8	5 7/8	9 2/8	White Pine County	NV	Carlos Hernandez	1987	2,740
68 2/8	13 1/8	13 2/8	5 7/8	5 7/8	8 4/8	Jenner	ALB	Jack Kempf	1987	2,740
68 2/8	13 3/8	13 4/8	5 4/8	5 4/8	10 3/8	Dawson County	MT	Dave Athas	1987	2,740
68 2/8	14 0/8	14 0/8	5 4/8	5 4/8	12 1/8	Sweetwater County	WY	Marvin L. Temme	1988	2,740
68 2/8	13 5/8	13 7/8	5 5/8	5 5/8	9 3/8	Meagher County	MT	Gene Clark	1988	2,740
68 2/8	13 3/8	13 4/8	6 0/8	5 6/8	6 7/8	Converse County	WY	Morris Karski	1989	2,740
68 2/8	12 7/8	12 7/8	5 5/8	5 6/8	14 5/8	McKenzie County	ND	Wayne R. Streitz	1989	2,740
68 2/8	13 2/8	13 2/8	5 4/8	5 4/8	9 6/8	Park County	MT	Steve Kamps	1989	2,740
68 2/8	12 5/8	13 0/8	5 3/8	5 3/8	8 0/8	Morton County	ND	Mike Fischer	1989	2,740
68 2/8	14 2/8	14 5/8	5 6/8	5 6/8	13 0/8	Garfield County	MT	Ken Davidson	1989	2,740
68 2/8	12 5/8	13 1/8	5 7/8	5 5/8	11 7/8	Campbell County	WY	Allen Jackson	1989	2,740
68 2/8	11 2/8	11 1/8	6 0/8	6 1/8	11 2/8	Moffat County	CO	Richard C. Green	1990	2,740
68 2/8	13 2/8	13 4/8	5 3/8	5 2/8	8 5/8	Moffat County	CO	Lonny Vanatta	1990	2,740
68 2/8	13 3/8	13 2/8	5 4/8	5 3/8	9 0/8	Carter County	MT	Lewis E. Hartenstine	1990	2,740
68 2/8	11 3/8	11 4/8	5 6/8	5 6/8	8 6/8	Cypress	ALB	Dan David	1990	2,740
68 2/8	11 7/8	12 2/8	6 0/8	5 6/8	9 1/8	Converse County	WY	Len Elie	1990	2,740
68 2/8	13 3/8	13 4/8	5 5/8	5 4/8	13 4/8	Campbell County	WY	Troy C. Christensen	1991	2,740
68 2/8	13 7/8	14 1/8	5 6/8	5 5/8	11 7/8	Slope County	ND	Gene D. Davis	1991	2,740
68 2/8	13 2/8	13 2/8	5 4/8	5 4/8	8 1/8	Converse County	WY	John S. Lewis III	1991	2,740
68 2/8	12 4/8	12 3/8	5 6/8	5 6/8	8 7/8	Campbell County	WY	Dave Vomela	1991	2,740
68 2/8	13 4/8	13 2/8	5 6/8	5 6/8	17 0/8	Slope County	ND	Rydell Becker	1991	2,740
68 2/8	13 6/8	14 1/8	5 7/8	5 6/8	13 5/8	Campbell County	WY	Ken Rimer	1991	2,740
68 2/8	13 0/8	12 6/8	5 7/8	6 0/8	9 2/8	Moffat County	CO	Kenneth Thompson	1992	2,740
68 2/8	13 0/8	12 7/8	6 1/8	6 0/8	9 1/8	Moffat County	CO	Jeffrey C. Fretz	1992	2,740
68 2/8	13 3/8	12 3/8	6 2/8	6 0/8	11 2/8	Union County	NM	James David Vinson	1992	2,740
68 2/8	13 5/8	13 7/8	6 2/8	6 2/8	12 2/8	Sweetwater County	WY	Daryl Burttschell	1992	2,740
68 2/8	13 5/8	13 2/8	5 5/8	5 4/8	11 0/8	Campbell County	WY	Vernon Kleve	1992	2,740
68 2/8	13 2/8	12 6/8	5 6/8	5 7/8	12 1/8	Converse County	WY	Johnnie R. Walters	1992	2,740
68 2/8	13 0/8	13 0/8	6 1/8	6 0/8	10 0/8	Dunn County	ND	Larry Olheiser	1992	2,740
68 2/8	12 4/8	13 1/8	6 0/8	5 7/8	9 1/8	Manyberries	ALB	Gary Goulet	1992	2,740
68 2/8	13 2/8	13 2/8	5 6/8	5 5/8	8 0/8	Fremont County	WY	Reggie Scheierman	1992	2,740
68 2/8	13 4/8	13 3/8	5 7/8	5 6/8	12 4/8	MD Cypress	ALB	David Moore	1992	2,740
68 2/8	14 2/8	14 1/8	5 3/8	5 3/8	11 2/8	Washoe County	NV	Richard A. Hanson	1993	2,740
68 2/8	13 5/8	13 4/8	5 4/8	5 4/8	7 6/8	Moffat County	CO	Kurt W. Keskimaki	1993	2,740
68 2/8	14 4/8	14 4/8	5 2/8	5 3/8	15 3/8	De Baca County	NM	Danny Griffith	1993	2,740
68 2/8	13 2/8	12 7/8	5 7/8	5 6/8	7 7/8	Sweetwater County	WY	Terry Story	1993	2,740
68 2/8	13 4/8	13 2/8	5 2/8	5 3/8	8 5/8	Converse County	WY	Robert Fulton	1993	2,740
68 2/8	13 4/8	13 5/8	5 3/8	5 2/8	7 7/8	Converse County	WY	Ken Mamazzo	1993	2,740
68 2/8	12 5/8	13 1/8	5 4/8	5 7/8	10 0/8	Cheyenne County	NE	Michael McCallister	1993	2,740
68 2/8	13 1/8	13 1/8	5 5/8	5 5/8	10 0/8	Corson County	SD	Fred Kober	1993	2,740
68 2/8	13 7/8	13 6/8	5 3/8	5 2/8	10 0/8	Humboldt County	NV	Katherine Lee Fillmore	1994	2,740
68 2/8	13 2/8	13 0/8	5 6/8	5 6/8	10 1/8	Sweetwater County	WY	James B. White	1994	2,740
68 2/8	14 2/8	14 1/8	6 0/8	6 0/8	13 2/8	Humboldt County	NV	Robert L. Brooks	1994	2,740
68 2/8	13 5/8	14 1/8	5 4/8	5 4/8	9 5/8	Moffat County	CO	Robert Goodnight	1994	2,740
68 2/8	14 1/8	14 0/8	5 3/8	5 4/8	10 0/8	Washoe County	NV	Clayton D. Johnson	1994	2,740
68 2/8	13 3/8	13 2/8	5 4/8	5 2/8	9 4/8	Millard County	UT	Carl R. Gramlich	1994	2,740
68 2/8	13 2/8	13 5/8	5 7/8	5 7/8	11 1/8	Sweetwater County	WY	Darin L. Howe	1994	2,740
68 2/8	13 0/8	13 3/8	5 4/8	5 5/8	9 3/8	Fremont County	WY	Ken Maynard	1994	2,740
68 2/8	13 6/8	13 7/8	5 7/8	6 0/8	11 2/8	Millard County	UT	David Edwards	1994	2,740
68 2/8	12 0/8	12 6/8	6 2/8	6 2/8	8 7/8	Crook County	WY	Dean Ransbottom	1994	2,740
68 2/8	13 0/8	12 7/8	6 0/8	6 0/8	12 7/8	Lake County	OR	Mark Penninger	1994	2,740
68 2/8	13 2/8	13 6/8	5 4/8	5 7/8	10 7/8	Sheridan County	WY	Steve Boster	1994	2,740
68 2/8	13 6/8	14 1/8	5 6/8	5 5/8	8 2/8	Petroleum County	MT	Craig Richardson	1994	2,740
68 2/8	12 7/8	12 4/8	6 4/8	6 4/8	9 2/8	Converse County	WY	Robert K. Woeck	1994	2,740
68 2/8	13 4/8	13 5/8	5 4/8	5 4/8	9 2/8	Niobrara County	WY	Gene H. Anderson	1994	2,740
68 2/8	13 7/8	14 0/8	5 4/8	5 3/8	11 6/8	Sweetwater County	WY	Craig Boheler	1995	2,740
68 2/8	13 4/8	13 3/8	5 3/8	5 3/8	9 6/8	Moffat County	CO	Juanita Brewer	1995	2,740
68 2/8	13 4/8	13 4/8	5 6/8	5 4/8	7 2/8	Campbell County	WY	Gordon L. Doyle	1995	2,740

PRONGHORN

Minimum Score 67 — Continued

SCORE	LENGTH OF HORN R	L	CIRCUMFERENCE OF BASE R	L	INSIDE SPREAD	AREA	STATE/ PROVINCE	HUNTER'S NAME	DATE	RANK
68 2/8	11 5/8	11 4/8	6 4/8	6 5/8	8 5/8	Big Horn County	WY	Jerome D. Larson	1995	2,740
68 2/8	13 4/8	13 4/8	6 0/8	5 7/8	10 6/8	Billings County	ND	Irvin E. Prough	1995	2,740
68 2/8	13 4/8	13 5/8	6 1/8	6 1/8	8 7/8	Converse County	WY	Steve Thomas, Sr.	1995	2,740
68 2/8	12 6/8	13 1/8	5 6/8	5 6/8	11 3/8	Custer County	MT	James Bornman	1995	2,740
68 2/8	13 6/8	13 6/8	6 1/8	5 7/8	10 5/8	Custer County	MT	Don Jones	1995	2,740
68 2/8	12 4/8	12 4/8	5 5/8	5 5/8	9 3/8	Campbell County	WY	Gene Faul	1995	2,740
68 2/8	14 2/8	14 6/8	5 4/8	5 3/8	8 1/8	Montrose County	CO	Dave Emken	1995	2,740
68 2/8	13 7/8	14 0/8	5 4/8	5 3/8	12 2/8	Powder River County	MT	Richard Driscoll	1995	2,740
68 2/8	13 6/8	13 6/8	5 3/8	5 3/8	13 6/8	Guadalupe County	NM	Brandon Ray	1996	2,740
68 2/8	12 3/8	12 4/8	6 0/8	6 0/8	8 4/8	Moffat County	CO	Eric A. Sawyer	1996	2,740
68 2/8	12 1/8	12 0/8	5 6/8	5 6/8	7 7/8	Converse County	WY	Mark Kronyak	1996	2,740
68 2/8	12 3/8	12 6/8	6 1/8	6 0/8	6 7/8	Powder River County	MT	Lindsey M. Manca	1996	2,740
68 2/8	14 2/8	14 0/8	5 3/8	5 3/8	7 6/8	Hays	ALB	Steve MacKenzie	1996	2,740
68 2/8	13 2/8	13 0/8	5 4/8	5 4/8	8 5/8	Custer County	SD	Jim DeRungs	1996	2,740
68 2/8	14 0/8	13 4/8	5 4/8	5 4/8	12 2/8	Garfield County	MT	D. Mitch Kottas	1996	2,740
68 2/8	14 0/8	14 0/8	5 7/8	5 7/8	6 4/8	Moffat County	CO	Kevin L. Reid	1997	2,740
68 2/8	14 3/8	14 3/8	5 2/8	5 3/8	6 3/8	Tooele County	UT	Gilbert Hernandez	1997	2,740
68 2/8	14 5/8	14 2/8	5 5/8	5 4/8	11 3/8	Campbell County	WY	James M. Augustine	1997	2,740
68 2/8	12 3/8	12 2/8	5 7/8	5 2/8	6 6/8	Powder River County	MT	Scott Miller	1997	2,740
68 2/8	12 7/8	12 3/8	5 5/8	5 4/8	8 2/8	Manyberries	ALB	Bob Barden	1997	2,740
68 2/8	12 7/8	12 7/8	5 7/8	5 7/8	9 7/8	Weld County	CO	Barry J. Smith	1998	2,740
68 2/8	12 5/8	12 4/8	6 0/8	6 0/8	8 6/8	Converse County	WY	Bernard Robert Belaire III	1998	2,740
68 2/8	12 6/8	12 2/8	6 0/8	5 7/8	9 4/8	Converse County	WY	Michael Travis	1998	2,740
68 2/8	12 4/8	13 5/8	6 2/8	6 1/8	14 2/8	Converse County	WY	Len Butler	1998	2,740
68 2/8	14 0/8	14 0/8	5 3/8	5 4/8	9 4/8	Orion	ALB	Lorne D. Rinkel	1998	2,740
68 2/8	14 0/8	13 5/8	5 2/8	5 2/8	9 7/8	Albany County	WY	Lance Tyler	1998	2,740
68 2/8	14 2/8	13 4/8	6 2/8	6 1/8	12 7/8	Campbell County	WY	Anthony G. Sexe	1998	2,740
68 0/8	14 1/8	13 0/8	5 4/8	5 6/8	7 7/8	Campbell County	WY	Reinhold L. Lind	1961	2,856
68 0/8	13 4/8	13 4/8	5 4/8	5 4/8	7 5/8	Carbon County	WY	Bill Cunningham	1963	2,856
68 0/8	14 0/8	13 6/8	5 2/8	5 3/8	8 0/8	Morton County	ND	Roy D. Russell, Jr.	1967	2,856
68 0/8	11 4/8	11 3/8	5 7/8	5 6/8	7 3/8	Burke County	ND	Allen L. Nelson	1974	2,856
68 0/8	13 0/8	13 0/8	5 7/8	5 7/8	9 6/8	Saguache County	CO	David Scheid	1974	2,856
68 0/8	12 4/8	12 5/8	5 6/8	5 5/8	10 6/8	Custer County	ID	Gary Schaffner	1975	2,856
68 0/8	13 0/8	13 3/8	5 5/8	5 4/8	9 7/8	Clark County	ID	Ron Parish	1977	2,856
68 0/8	13 5/8	13 3/8	5 6/8	5 6/8	10 3/8	Humboldt County	NV	Vic Christison	1978	2,856
68 0/8	13 2/8	12 7/8	6 1/8	6 0/8	10 1/8	Sweetwater County	WY	Jack Riddle	1979	2,856
68 0/8	12 2/8	12 4/8	5 6/8	5 5/8	8 4/8	Natrona County	WY	Todd James	1980	2,856
68 0/8	13 6/8	12 3/8	5 6/8	5 5/8	7 2/8	Moffat County	CO	Judd Cooney	1981	2,856
68 0/8	13 3/8	13 5/8	5 4/8	5 4/8	8 2/8	Butte County	SD	James S. Nelson IV	1981	2,856
68 0/8	13 3/8	14 3/8	5 3/8	5 5/8	15 4/8	Campbell County	WY	Joseph Strasser, Jr.	1981	2,856
68 0/8	14 1/8	14 1/8	5 4/8	5 1/8	6 7/8	Lassen County	CA	Junior Morris	1982	2,856
68 0/8	13 4/8	13 6/8	5 6/8	5 5/8	13 4/8	Sweetwater County	WY	Sy Gilliland	1982	2,856
68 0/8	13 2/8	13 3/8	5 5/8	5 4/8	11 0/8	Fremont County	WY	Everett A. Boss	1982	2,856
68 0/8	12 4/8	12 3/8	6 0/8	5 7/8	14 4/8	Yavapai County	AZ	Jeff W. Elmer	1982	2,856
68 0/8	13 2/8	13 2/8	5 7/8	5 6/8	10 1/8	Converse County	WY	Bill Frodl	1982	2,856
68 0/8	12 2/8	12 7/8	5 7/8	6 0/8	6 7/8	Natrona County	WY	E. Michael Onken	1983	2,856
68 0/8	13 1/8	13 1/8	5 6/8	5 5/8	9 0/8	Converse County	WY	William Kobart	1983	2,856
68 0/8	13 0/8	13 2/8	5 6/8	5 5/8	10 1/8	Ziebach County	SD	Jim Glines	1983	2,856
68 0/8	13 6/8	13 7/8	5 5/8	5 5/8	12 2/8	Converse County	WY	David P. Lindman	1983	2,856
68 0/8	13 1/8	13 2/8	5 7/8	5 6/8	7 5/8	Albany County	WY	Adrian H. Farmer, Jr.	1983	2,856
68 0/8	14 0/8	14 1/8	5 2/8	5 4/8	12 4/8	Coconino County	AZ	Dean Zuern	1984	2,856
68 0/8	12 6/8	12 0/8	6 0/8	5 7/8	10 1/8	Converse County	WY	Michael Murphy	1984	2,856
68 0/8	13 4/8	13 5/8	5 6/8	5 5/8	8 6/8	Sweetwater County	WY	Robert L Kampen	1985	2,856
68 0/8	13 3/8	13 4/8	5 1/8	5 2/8	6 5/8	Natrona County	WY	Joe Brant	1985	2,856
68 0/8	13 0/8	13 1/8	5 7/8	5 7/8	9 4/8	Natrona County	WY	Dave James	1985	2,856
68 0/8	12 3/8	12 5/8	5 4/8	5 4/8	11 5/8	Natrona County	WY	David Bouchard	1985	2,856
68 0/8	12 3/8	12 4/8	6 2/8	6 2/8	9 0/8	Converse County	WY	Mark Slaughter	1986	2,856
68 0/8	12 5/8	12 7/8	6 1/8	5 6/8	13 5/8	Converse County	WY	John May	1986	2,856
68 0/8	13 0/8	13 1/8	6 0/8	6 1/8	9 4/8	Keya Paha County	NE	Rory Swim	1987	2,856
68 0/8	13 5/8	13 2/8	5 5/8	5 6/8	8 5/8	Converse County	WY	Jimmy R. Speer	1987	2,856
68 0/8	12 6/8	12 6/8	6 1/8	6 1/8	8 6/8	Converse County	WY	Dan Bertalan	1987	2,856
68 0/8	13 7/8	13 6/8	5 5/8	5 3/8	11 0/8	Washoe County	NV	Bill Fuller	1988	2,856
68 0/8	13 7/8	13 7/8	5 5/8	5 4/8	10 3/8	Butte County	ID	Andy Moore	1988	2,856
68 0/8	13 3/8	13 3/8	5 5/8	5 4/8	14 6/8	Moffat County	CO	Stan Manuel	1988	2,856
68 0/8	12 6/8	12 7/8	5 7/8	5 7/8	8 5/8	Moffat County	CO	Randy Gipple	1988	2,856
68 0/8	12 6/8	12 7/8	5 6/8	5 5/8	9 5/8	Natrona County	WY	Nolan C. Fowles	1988	2,856
68 0/8	13 1/8	13 2/8	5 3/8	5 3/8	9 1/8	Moffat County	CO	Rich McNutt	1988	2,856
68 0/8	13 4/8	13 6/8	5 4/8	5 4/8	10 3/8	Moffat County	CO	Dennis Wehling	1989	2,856
68 0/8	12 7/8	12 7/8	5 6/8	5 5/8	9 2/8	Garfield County	MT	Bruce Balerud	1989	2,856
68 0/8	12 4/8	12 2/8	6 4/8	6 2/8	8 2/8	Campbell County	WY	Thomas J. Buchner	1989	2,856
68 0/8	12 1/8	12 3/8	5 2/8	5 4/8	11 0/8	Sargent County	ND	Richard G. Olson	1989	2,856
68 0/8	15 4/8	15 3/8	4 7/8	4 7/8	8 4/8	Powder River County	MT	John A. Stuver	1989	2,856
68 0/8	12 3/8	12 3/8	5 6/8	5 6/8	10 2/8	Moffat County	CO	Mike Lamade	1990	2,856
68 0/8	12 6/8	12 4/8	5 6/8	5 6/8	8 1/8	Moffat County	CO	John Brassard	1990	2,856
68 0/8	12 5/8	12 6/8	5 7/8	5 6/8	7 0/8	Delta County	CO	James C. Lake	1990	2,856
68 0/8	13 5/8	14 0/8	5 4/8	5 5/8	7 5/8	Johnson County	WY	L. Dan Neebe	1990	2,856
68 0/8	12 4/8	12 5/8	5 6/8	6 0/8	6 7/8	Converse County	WY	Paul J. Ganzen	1990	2,856
68 0/8	13 2/8	12 7/8	6 3/8	6 3/8	14 0/8	Natrona County	WY	Kurt W. Keskimaki	1990	2,856

PRONGHORN

Minimum Score 67 — Continued

SCORE	LENGTH OF HORN R	L	CIRCUMFERENCE OF BASE R	L	INSIDE SPREAD	AREA	STATE/ PROVINCE	HUNTER'S NAME	DATE	RANK
68 0/8	13 3/8	13 3/8	5 6/8	5 6/8	10 3/8	Chouteau County	MT	K. C. Palagi	1990	2,856
68 0/8	13 2/8	12 7/8	5 6/8	5 7/8	7 6/8	Campbell County	WY	Timothy Hammes	1990	2,856
68 0/8	12 3/8	11 5/8	5 6/8	5 6/8	8 3/8	Slope County	ND	Dennis Moritz	1990	2,856
68 0/8	12 3/8	12 5/8	6 0/8	6 0/8	9 1/8	Moffat County	CO	Ronald Dinger	1991	2,856
68 0/8	12 5/8	12 5/8	5 5/8	5 5/8	11 2/8	Fremont County	WY	Jerry A. Bodar	1991	2,856
68 0/8	11 2/8	11 0/8	5 6/8	5 6/8	10 1/8	Natrona County	WY	Scott D. Baer	1991	2,856
68 0/8	13 0/8	13 7/8	5 4/8	5 5/8	8 5/8	Thomas County	NE	Matt Gideon	1991	2,856
68 0/8	12 0/8	12 1/8	6 5/8	6 4/8	10 3/8	Converse County	WY	Derek Goto	1991	2,856
68 0/8	13 5/8	13 2/8	5 7/8	5 6/8	10 1/8	Sheridan County	WY	Marty Krohn	1991	2,856
68 0/8	13 3/8	13 5/8	5 6/8	5 6/8	8 4/8	Bowman County	ND	Kendall Bauer	1991	2,856
68 0/8	13 1/8	13 0/8	6 0/8	5 6/8	9 3/8	Sioux County	NE	Alton Schroeder	1991	2,856
68 0/8	13 7/8	14 0/8	5 5/8	5 5/8	7 1/8	Ward County	ND	Russel Jon Hardy	1991	2,856
68 0/8	12 4/8	12 2/8	6 2/8	6 3/8	9 2/8	Converse County	WY	Jeff Reynolds	1991	2,856
68 0/8	13 6/8	13 7/8	5 6/8	5 6/8	9 0/8	Washoe County	NV	David Schopper	1992	2,856
68 0/8	13 4/8	13 4/8	5 7/8	6 0/8	9 5/8	Carbon County	WY	Steven R. Hohensee	1992	2,856
68 0/8	12 6/8	12 6/8	6 0/8	5 7/8	11 6/8	Campbell County	WY	Randy Hill	1992	2,856
68 0/8	13 2/8	13 3/8	5 7/8	5 7/8	9 7/8	Owyhee County	ID	DeLoy Desaro	1992	2,856
68 0/8	12 5/8	12 6/8	5 6/8	5 6/8	9 0/8	Campbell County	WY	Kurt Outcelt	1992	2,856
68 0/8	11 4/8	11 4/8	5 7/8	5 6/8	9 2/8	Campbell County	WY	Philip G. Bauer	1992	2,856
68 0/8	13 6/8	13 2/8	5 6/8	6 0/8	9 6/8	Campbell County	WY	Ken Rimer	1992	2,856
68 0/8	12 3/8	12 3/8	6 0/8	5 6/8	10 5/8	Moffat County	CO	Thomas L. "Tag" Reed	1993	2,856
68 0/8	13 5/8	13 4/8	5 5/8	5 4/8	8 6/8	Wayne County	UT	Jonathan D. Pemberton	1993	2,856
68 0/8	13 3/8	13 3/8	6 0/8	6 1/8	8 0/8	Moffat County	CO	Jerome R. Mann	1993	2,856
68 0/8	14 4/8	14 4/8	6 2/8	6 2/8	12 5/8	Manyberries	ALB	Gary Gillett	1993	2,856
68 0/8	13 4/8	13 6/8	5 1/8	5 0/8	12 1/8	Manyberries	ALB	Jeff Knowlton	1993	2,856
68 0/8	14 4/8	14 3/8	5 3/8	5 2/8	10 5/8	Owyhee County	ID	Gary Angell	1993	2,856
68 0/8	12 6/8	12 5/8	6 1/8	6 1/8	12 3/8	Albany County	WY	Ron Books, Jr.	1994	2,856
68 0/8	13 1/8	13 2/8	5 4/8	5 4/8	8 0/8	Albany County	WY	Orvie Linsin	1994	2,856
68 0/8	12 6/8	12 7/8	5 7/8	6 0/8	9 5/8	Carbon County	WY	Steve J. Turner	1994	2,856
68 0/8	13 0/8	12 7/8	5 6/8	5 6/8	10 3/8	Wayne County	UT	Steven W. Mitchell	1994	2,856
68 0/8	13 7/8	13 3/8	5 5/8	5 4/8	8 3/8	Iron County	UT	Wade Ovard	1994	2,856
68 0/8	13 7/8	13 7/8	5 2/8	5 3/8	9 6/8	Converse County	WY	Mark Hockenberry	1994	2,856
68 0/8	13 4/8	13 3/8	5 2/8	5 1/8	8 6/8	Converse County	WY	Robert J. Manske	1994	2,856
68 0/8	13 6/8	14 0/8	5 3/8	5 2/8	10 0/8	Rosebud County	MT	Mark Buehrer	1994	2,856
68 0/8	13 2/8	12 6/8	5 6/8	6 0/8	12 0/8	Carbon County	WY	Guy Young	1994	2,856
68 0/8	12 2/8	12 2/8	5 4/8	5 4/8	11 6/8	Hanna	ALB	Troy Dzioba	1994	2,856
68 0/8	12 0/8	14 0/8	6 2/8	6 2/8	15 5/8	Meagher County	MT	John Fleharty	1994	2,856
68 0/8	14 2/8	14 0/8	5 3/8	5 4/8	11 5/8	Lincoln County	NM	Ryan Turner	1995	2,856
68 0/8	12 7/8	13 0/8	5 7/8	5 5/8	11 3/8	Brown County	NE	Rich Walters, Jr.	1995	2,856
68 0/8	13 0/8	13 2/8	6 2/8	6 2/8	10 6/8	Sweetwater County	WY	Raymond Kennedy	1996	2,856
68 0/8	13 4/8	13 4/8	5 2/8	5 2/8	12 4/8	Lincoln County	NM	Janet Leigh Taylor	1996	2,856
68 0/8	13 3/8	13 2/8	5 3/8	5 4/8	11 5/8	Owyhee County	ID	Anthony L. Mudd	1996	2,856
68 0/8	12 5/8	12 5/8	5 7/8	5 7/8	11 1/8	Campbell County	WY	Ritch A. Stolpe	1996	2,856
68 0/8	13 4/8	13 4/8	5 6/8	5 5/8	11 2/8	Chouteau County	MT	Gus Smith	1996	2,856
68 0/8	13 4/8	13 3/8	5 3/8	5 2/8	7 2/8	Logan County	KS	Walt Lovins	1996	2,856
68 0/8	13 3/8	13 6/8	5 5/8	5 5/8	6 5/8	Campbell County	WY	Chris Wichman	1997	2,856
68 0/8	12 6/8	13 0/8	5 4/8	5 2/8	5 6/8	Moffat County	CO	Dale Selby	1998	2,856
68 0/8	13 2/8	13 2/8	6 2/8	6 1/8	12 4/8	Sweetwater County	WY	Susan K. Barrett	1998	2,856
68 0/8	14 6/8	14 3/8	5 2/8	5 3/8	6 6/8	Owyhee County	ID	John F. Burke	1998	2,856
68 0/8	12 4/8	13 5/8	5 4/8	5 4/8	11 0/8	Moffat County	CO	Dawn Vallee	1998	2,856
68 0/8	13 0/8	13 0/8	5 5/8	5 6/8	7 5/8	Campbell County	WY	Wright Allen	1998	2,856
68 0/8	12 6/8	12 6/8	6 0/8	6 0/8	11 0/8	Park County	WY	Gary Shinn	1998	2,856
68 0/8	12 6/8	12 4/8	6 0/8	6 0/8	11 0/8	Garfield County	MT	Kenneth E. Fischer	1998	2,856
68 0/8	13 4/8	13 3/8	6 1/8	5 7/8	8 0/8	Fergus County	MT	D. Mitch Kottas	1998	2,856
67 6/8	12 3/8	12 4/8	5 6/8	5 5/8	9 0/8	McHenry County	ND	Darryl Ablestad	1967	2,961
67 6/8	12 6/8	12 4/8	6 2/8	6 0/8	11 3/8	McHenry County	ND	Jim Budeau	1968	2,961
67 6/8	13 4/8	13 4/8	5 5/8	5 5/8	11 2/8	Logan County	CO	Loren Johnston	1968	2,961
67 6/8	13 3/8	13 2/8	5 2/8	5 5/8	10 1/8	Fremont County	WY	Doris Clark	1970	2,961
67 6/8	14 0/8	13 1/8	5 0/8	5 0/8	13 4/8	Butte County	ID	Craig L. Hansen	1974	2,961
67 6/8	12 4/8	12 6/8	5 5/8	5 5/8	11 1/8	Carbon County	WY	James Beeson	1976	2,961
67 6/8	14 0/8	14 0/8	5 2/8	5 2/8	11 1/8	Park County	WY	Fred W. Achilles	1978	2,961
67 6/8	13 7/8	13 6/8	5 2/8	5 2/8	8 5/8	Moffat County	CO	Dave Skiff	1980	2,961
67 6/8	11 2/8	11 2/8	5 6/8	5 5/8	8 1/8	Converse County	WY	Ron Carpenter	1980	2,961
67 6/8	11 6/8	11 7/8	5 6/8	5 5/8	8 6/8	Carbon County	WY	Bob Funke	1980	2,961
67 6/8	13 1/8	13 2/8	5 4/8	5 2/8	9 7/8	Sweetwater County	WY	Jerry Giovannoni	1980	2,961
67 6/8	13 0/8	13 1/8	5 2/8	5 4/8	13 3/8	Natrona County	WY	Clifford G. James	1980	2,961
67 6/8	13 6/8	13 2/8	5 6/8	5 6/8	11 4/8	Natrona County	WY	David Stejskal	1980	2,961
67 6/8	13 5/8	12 6/8	5 5/8	5 4/8	10 4/8	Custer County	ID	Gerard J. Krauth	1981	2,961
67 6/8	13 7/8	13 6/8	5 6/8	5 5/8	9 2/8	Rio Arriba County	NM	Jose R. Montalvo	1982	2,961
67 6/8	13 4/8	13 6/8	5 4/8	5 4/8	11 7/8	Moffat County	CO	Robert L. Kinser	1982	2,961
67 6/8	14 5/8	14 1/8	4 6/8	4 7/8	9 7/8	Carbon County	WY	Bill Nation	1982	2,961
67 6/8	13 5/8	13 5/8	5 3/8	5 2/8	8 0/8	Beaverhead County	MT	L. C. Trimber	1982	2,961
67 6/8	12 2/8	12 1/8	5 7/8	5 7/8	11 4/8	Moffat County	CO	Mike Ward	1982	2,961
67 6/8	12 2/8	12 6/8	5 4/8	5 4/8	11 7/8	Converse County	WY	Joe Ed McCray	1982	2,961
67 6/8	12 3/8	13 1/8	5 2/8	5 2/8	12 2/8	Larimer County	CO	William Shuster	1983	2,961
67 6/8	13 3/8	13 3/8	5 4/8	5 3/8	8 7/8	Converse County	WY	Roger Schmitt	1983	2,961
67 6/8	14 0/8	13 6/8	5 3/8	5 2/8	9 5/8	Las Animas County	CO	Edward F. Bryan, Jr.	1983	2,961
67 6/8	14 2/8	14 3/8	5 7/8	6 0/8	11 1/8	Hettinger County	ND	Mike Schiwal	1984	2,961

PRONGHORN

Minimum Score 67

SCORE	LENGTH OF HORN R	L	CIRCUMFERENCE OF BASE R	L	INSIDE SPREAD	AREA	STATE/ PROVINCE	HUNTER'S NAME	DATE	RANK
67 6/8	13 0/8	13 0/8	5 6/8	5 6/8	11 5/8	Natrona County	WY	Kirk H. Soulliere	1985	2,961
67 6/8	12 6/8	12 4/8	6 0/8	5 7/8	14 3/8	Carbon County	WY	Willis Duhon	1985	2,961
67 6/8	14 4/8	14 4/8	5 3/8	5 2/8	8 0/8	Carbon County	WY	Bob Boyle	1985	2,961
67 6/8	11 5/8	11 5/8	6 5/8	6 3/8	15 3/8	McKinley County	NM	Robert Allen Stearns	1985	2,961
67 6/8	12 6/8	12 6/8	6 1/8	6 1/8	7 6/8	Sweetwater County	WY	Dean Lawver	1986	2,961
67 6/8	13 4/8	13 5/8	6 2/8	6 0/8	9 6/8	Mountrail County	ND	Kevin Ohlhauser	1986	2,961
67 6/8	13 3/8	13 4/8	5 4/8	5 5/8	6 4/8	Tom Green County	TX	Terry Turney	1986	2,961
67 6/8	12 1/8	12 2/8	6 2/8	6 2/8	11 6/8	Converse County	WY	Martin Scott Campbell	1987	2,961
67 6/8	13 3/8	13 2/8	5 6/8	5 6/8	10 5/8	Sublette County	WY	Randy Tolman	1987	2,961
67 6/8	13 0/8	13 0/8	5 5/8	5 4/8	7 6/8	Medicine Hat	ALB	James Pike	1987	2,961
67 6/8	13 6/8	13 2/8	5 4/8	5 5/8	9 1/8	Moffat County	CO	Carol Ashurst	1988	2,961
67 6/8	12 3/8	12 4/8	5 6/8	5 6/8	12 2/8	Converse County	WY	Larry Crouch	1988	2,961
67 6/8	14 1/8	13 7/8	5 4/8	5 3/8	14 5/8	Suffield	ALB	Jay Brown	1988	2,961
67 6/8	12 4/8	12 4/8	5 4/8	5 4/8	9 5/8	Sweetwater County	WY	Mark Perqande	1989	2,961
67 6/8	13 5/8	14 0/8	5 2/8	5 3/8	9 3/8	Campbell County	WY	Robert F. Synder	1989	2,961
67 6/8	12 7/8	13 3/8	6 4/8	5 4/8	8 6/8	Campbell County	WY	Charles Smith	1989	2,961
67 6/8	12 6/8	13 1/8	5 6/8	5 5/8	7 1/8	Converse County	WY	Brian Bass	1990	2,961
67 6/8	13 3/8	13 2/8	5 7/8	5 6/8	15 0/8	Platte County	WY	Derek Long	1990	2,961
67 6/8	12 7/8	13 2/8	5 4/8	5 3/8	10 5/8	Hudspeth County	TX	Melvin Sloan	1990	2,961
67 6/8	14 0/8	14 5/8	5 6/8	5 5/8	10 1/8	Natrona County	WY	Michael Running	1991	2,961
67 6/8	13 1/8	12 0/8	5 6/8	5 5/8	9 0/8	Yavapai County	AZ	Gary French	1991	2,961
67 6/8	12 6/8	12 6/8	5 7/8	5 6/8	9 2/8	Campbell County	WY	Joe Gohres	1991	2,961
67 6/8	13 3/8	13 0/8	5 5/8	5 5/8	10 4/8	Converse County	WY	James C. Gates	1991	2,961
67 6/8	13 2/8	13 0/8	5 7/8	6 0/8	11 0/8	Grant County	ND	Troy Hanson	1991	2,961
67 6/8	12 4/8	12 6/8	5 7/8	5 7/8	8 7/8	Perkins County	SD	James S. Bidwell	1991	2,961
67 6/8	13 4/8	13 2/8	5 4/8	5 4/8	6 1/8	Beaverhead County	MT	Curtis A. Green	1991	2,961
67 6/8	12 4/8	13 0/8	6 2/8	6 2/8	11 4/8	Harding County	SD	Jeff Poppenga	1991	2,961
67 6/8	12 5/8	12 5/8	6 1/8	6 0/8	8 1/8	Colfax County	NM	Dave W. Wright	1992	2,961
67 6/8	13 7/8	13 6/8	5 5/8	5 6/8	6 4/8	Owyhee County	ID	David R. Heck	1992	2,961
67 6/8	13 0/8	13 0/8	5 7/8	5 5/8	12 4/8	Converse County	WY	Carolyn Siebrasse Zanoni	1992	2,961
67 6/8	13 2/8	13 4/8	5 6/8	5 6/8	9 1/8	Slope County	ND	Gene Davis	1992	2,961
67 6/8	12 2/8	12 2/8	6 0/8	6 0/8	11 1/8	Johnson County	WY	Thomas J. Mihutz	1992	2,961
67 6/8	12 5/8	12 3/8	5 7/8	5 7/8	9 3/8	Natrona County	WY	Kim Cooper	1992	2,961
67 6/8	13 1/8	13 1/8	6 0/8	6 0/8	9 2/8	Bowman County	ND	Gene Welle	1992	2,961
67 6/8	13 5/8	13 7/8	5 4/8	5 5/8	9 3/8	Campbell County	WY	Michael J. Stuefen	1992	2,961
67 6/8	13 1/8	12 6/8	5 5/8	5 5/8	11 7/8	Natrona County	WY	Mark Tanner	1992	2,961
67 6/8	13 3/8	13 5/8	5 7/8	5 6/8	5 6/8	Sioux County	NE	Ron Suponchick	1992	2,961
67 6/8	12 7/8	12 2/8	6 0/8	5 7/8	9 2/8	Moffat County	CO	Jerry Mason	1993	2,961
67 6/8	12 5/8	12 5/8	5 6/8	5 6/8	8 1/8	Moffat County	CO	Rick A. Albers	1993	2,961
67 6/8	12 4/8	12 3/8	6 0/8	6 0/8	8 4/8	Box Elder County	UT	David M. Schopper	1993	2,961
67 6/8	13 3/8	13 3/8	5 6/8	5 5/8	6 7/8	Moffat County	CO	Brad Herman	1994	2,961
67 6/8	14 2/8	13 7/8	5 5/8	5 4/8	8 4/8	Clark County	ID	Max Heberling	1994	2,961
67 6/8	12 5/8	12 4/8	5 7/8	6 0/8	12 1/8	Weld County	CO	Kirk Hiller	1994	2,961
67 6/8	13 3/8	13 3/8	5 6/8	5 6/8	13 5/8	Campbell County	WY	Jeff Helmers	1994	2,961
67 6/8	14 2/8	13 4/8	5 6/8	5 5/8	7 6/8	McKenzie County	ND	Don G. Scofield	1994	2,961
67 6/8	12 3/8	12 3/8	5 6/8	5 6/8	11 4/8	Converse County	WY	Roger W. Hansen	1994	2,961
67 6/8	12 6/8	12 5/8	5 5/8	5 4/8	7 6/8	Converse County	WY	Dr. Andy Jones	1994	2,961
67 6/8	12 4/8	12 2/8	5 6/8	5 6/8	10 6/8	Moffat County	CO	Nathan Andersohn	1994	2,961
67 6/8	11 6/8	11 5/8	5 7/8	5 7/8	6 5/8	Stanley County	SD	Mike Moody	1994	2,961
67 6/8	13 3/8	13 3/8	5 3/8	5 3/8	11 0/8	Campbell County	WY	Bob Pozner	1994	2,961
67 6/8	13 7/8	13 7/8	5 4/8	5 3/8	8 2/8	Juab County	UT	Rick Searle	1995	2,961
67 6/8	12 4/8	11 2/8	6 0/8	5 7/8	8 1/8	Converse County	WY	John S. Lewis III	1995	2,961
67 6/8	12 7/8	12 7/8	6 2/8	6 2/8	11 6/8	Rosebud County	MT	Gene Welle	1995	2,961
67 6/8	14 7/8	15 3/8	5 4/8	5 4/8	8 5/8	Owyhee County	ID	Ron Sherer	1995	2,961
67 6/8	13 2/8	13 1/8	6 0/8	6 1/8	12 2/8	Carbon County	WY	Guy Hinrichs	1995	2,961
67 6/8	13 1/8	12 6/8	6 0/8	5 7/8	8 0/8	Crook County	WY	Roger D. Smith	1995	2,961
67 6/8	12 7/8	13 2/8	5 6/8	5 5/8	11 7/8	Rosebud County	MT	Gregory G. Henan	1995	2,961
67 6/8	12 5/8	12 6/8	5 5/8	5 5/8	8 4/8	McLean County	ND	Todd Weisenburger	1995	2,961
67 6/8	12 6/8	13 0/8	6 1/8	6 0/8	7 7/8	Converse County	WY	Myron E. Jochmann	1995	2,961
67 6/8	12 1/8	12 2/8	5 5/8	6 0/8	10 4/8	Rosebud County	MT	Bill Dollar	1995	2,961
67 6/8	14 5/8	14 3/8	5 5/8	5 5/8	8 4/8	White Pine County	NV	William C. Brewer	1996	2,961
67 6/8	14 6/8	14 6/8	5 2/8	5 3/8	7 0/8	Millard County	UT	Valene Tuttle	1996	2,961
67 6/8	13 2/8	13 4/8	5 5/8	5 4/8	11 6/8	Moffat County	CO	Ken Custer	1996	2,961
67 6/8	13 4/8	13 5/8	5 7/8	6 0/8	8 2/8	Campbell County	WY	Tom Blank	1996	2,961
67 6/8	12 2/8	12 4/8	6 2/8	6 1/8	10 5/8	Crook County	OR	Clinton J. Hall	1996	2,961
67 6/8	14 0/8	13 3/8	5 4/8	5 5/8	8 1/8	Harding County	SD	Karen DeRungs	1996	2,961
67 6/8	12 2/8	12 0/8	6 2/8	6 1/8	9 2/8	Converse County	WY	James Gabrick	1997	2,961
67 6/8	14 2/8	14 4/8	5 2/8	5 3/8	8 0/8	Campbell County	WY	Richard E. LaCrone	1997	2,961
67 6/8	12 7/8	13 4/8	6 2/8	6 0/8	13 0/8	Musselshell County	MT	Bob L. Walker	1997	2,961
67 6/8	12 5/8	12 4/8	5 5/8	5 6/8	10 7/8	Moffat County	CO	Chuck Adams	1998	2,961
67 6/8	12 5/8	12 5/8	5 5/8	5 3/8	8 0/8	Moffat County	CO	Destiny Schoon	1998	2,961
67 6/8	13 6/8	13 5/8	5 5/8	5 4/8	10 4/8	Fergus County	MT	Don E. Kottas	1998	2,961
67 6/8	13 3/8	13 4/8	6 1/8	5 7/8	10 4/8	Converse County	WY	Toby Hershey	1998	2,961
67 6/8	13 0/8	13 0/8	5 6/8	5 5/8	6 7/8	Hays	ALB	Marty Belisle	1998	2,961
67 6/8	13 2/8	13 4/8	5 5/8	5 4/8	12 0/8	Wallace County	KS	Doug Duncan	1998	2,961
67 6/8	13 6/8	13 6/8	5 4/8	5 4/8	11 0/8	Milk River	ALB	Bruce LeBen	1998	2,961
67 6/8	14 7/8	14 3/8	5 5/8	5 5/8	9 1/8	Rosebud County	MT	William E. Lee, Jr.	1998	2,961
67 4/8	13 4/8	13 5/8	5 3/8	5 2/8	13 3/8	Cherry County	NE	Marlin Wells	1967	3,062

PRONGHORN

Minimum Score 67 — Continued — 661

SCORE	LENGTH OF HORN R / L	CIRCUMFERENCE OF BASE R / L	INSIDE SPREAD	AREA	STATE/ PROVINCE	HUNTER'S NAME	DATE	RANK
67 4/8	13 7/8 13 7/8	5 3/8 5 2/8	10 1/8	Oregon Basin	WY	John Pruszyski	1973	3,062
67 4/8	13 3/8 13 2/8	5 4/8 5 4/8	9 0/8	Meade County	SD	Jim Bohls	1974	3,062
67 4/8	14 2/8 14 0/8	5 2/8 5 1/8	8 5/8	Jackson County	CO	Robert Souza	1974	3,062
67 4/8	13 1/8 13 2/8	5 7/8 5 5/8	13 3/8	Carbon County	WY	Steve Stumbo	1975	3,062
67 4/8	12 4/8 12 5/8	5 4/8 5 4/8	11 6/8	Converse County	WY	Bob Jensen	1976	3,062
67 4/8	13 6/8 13 4/8	5 6/8 5 4/8	11 7/8	Natrona County	WY	Steve Turck	1976	3,062
67 4/8	13 1/8 13 5/8	5 4/8 5 4/8	8 2/8	Converse County	WY	James E. Boland	1979	3,062
67 4/8	12 6/8 12 5/8	5 6/8 5 6/8	10 0/8	Converse County	WY	Bruce Sanders	1980	3,062
67 4/8	12 5/8 12 0/8	6 1/8 5 6/8	9 1/8	Moffat County	CO	Robert L. Wright	1981	3,062
67 4/8	13 5/8 13 4/8	5 4/8 5 4/8	10 1/8	Converse County	WY	Ron Breitsprecher	1981	3,062
67 4/8	14 1/8 13 0/8	5 6/8 5 6/8	10 2/8	Lemhi County	ID	Daniel A. Davis	1981	3,062
67 4/8	14 2/8 14 4/8	5 4/8 5 3/8	7 4/8	Carbon County	WY	Mike Fortman	1982	3,062
67 4/8	11 6/8 12 6/8	5 5/8 5 4/8	8 1/8	Moffat County	CO	Ken Keller	1983	3,062
67 4/8	13 0/8 13 2/8	5 3/8 5 3/8	6 5/8	Custer County	CO	Rohn L. Garnhart	1983	3,062
67 4/8	12 3/8 12 4/8	5 4/8 5 4/8	9 1/8	Converse County	WY	Roberta Byerly	1983	3,062
67 4/8	13 0/8 13 1/8	5 6/8 5 5/8	9 0/8	Converse County	WY	Jon Arneson	1983	3,062
67 4/8	14 1/8 14 0/8	5 4/8 5 4/8	9 7/8	Converse County	WY	Gary Hunsicker	1983	3,062
67 4/8	12 4/8 12 6/8	6 3/8 6 1/8	8 4/8	Converse County	WY	Jim Hodson	1984	3,062
67 4/8	12 3/8 12 4/8	6 0/8 5 7/8	9 0/8	Sweetwater County	WY	Craig Richardson	1984	3,062
67 4/8	13 0/8 12 6/8	5 6/8 5 6/8	11 0/8	Bowman County	ND	Mark Delong	1984	3,062
67 4/8	13 4/8 13 3/8	5 4/8 5 4/8	10 3/8	Campbell County	WY	Rick Gilley	1984	3,062
67 4/8	13 2/8 13 5/8	5 4/8 5 2/8	11 3/8	Johnson County	WY	Edward Carmichael	1984	3,062
67 4/8	13 4/8 13 4/8	5 4/8 5 4/8	12 0/8	Phillips County	MT	Ken Ruzicka	1984	3,062
67 4/8	13 1/8 13 1/8	5 6/8 5 6/8	9 2/8	Sweetwater County	WY	Kevin J. Slovak	1985	3,062
67 4/8	13 0/8 13 0/8	6 2/8 6 3/8	9 4/8	Billings County	ND	Ronald M. Bachmeier	1985	3,062
67 4/8	13 0/8 12 7/8	5 3/8 5 3/8	8 3/8	Converse County	WY	Len Cardinale	1985	3,062
67 4/8	12 7/8 12 6/8	5 3/8 5 2/8	9 0/8	Converse County	WY	Burt Thompson, Jr.	1985	3,062
67 4/8	12 3/8 12 7/8	5 5/8 5 5/8	9 6/8	Converse County	WY	Thomas Vitale	1985	3,062
67 4/8	12 1/8 12 0/8	5 7/8 6 0/8	9 2/8	Sweetwater County	WY	Chris Switzer	1986	3,062
67 4/8	13 7/8 12 7/8	5 6/8 5 6/8	8 3/8	McKenzie County	ND	David Tofte	1986	3,062
67 4/8	11 3/8 11 3/8	6 3/8 6 2/8	9 0/8	Lemhi County	ID	C. Richard Wenger	1987	3,062
67 4/8	12 5/8 12 5/8	5 5/8 5 5/8	8 6/8	Billings County	ND	Ivan Bachamp	1987	3,062
67 4/8	11 7/8 11 7/8	5 6/8 5 6/8	10 0/8	Daggett County	UT	L. Scot Jenkins	1987	3,062
67 4/8	12 4/8 12 4/8	5 7/8 5 7/8	9 7/8	Yellowstone County	MT	Jack S. Esterly, Jr.	1987	3,062
67 4/8	13 3/8 13 2/8	5 2/8 5 2/8	8 4/8	Moffat County	CO	E. Damon Handley	1988	3,062
67 4/8	12 6/8 12 6/8	5 5/8 5 5/8	10 4/8	Natrona County	WY	Paul Jayson	1988	3,062
67 4/8	12 2/8 12 2/8	5 6/8 5 7/8	7 5/8	Converse County	WY	J. G. "Rusty" Watson	1988	3,062
67 4/8	10 7/8 11 2/8	6 1/8 6 0/8	8 0/8	Converse County	WY	Rick Simonson	1988	3,062
67 4/8	12 2/8 12 2/8	5 1/8 5 2/8	8 2/8	Weston County	WY	Keith Gould	1988	3,062
67 4/8	13 4/8 12 1/8	5 6/8 5 6/8	8 3/8	Moffat County	CO	Todd Weiszbrod	1989	3,062
67 4/8	12 3/8 12 2/8	5 5/8 5 6/8	10 5/8	Moffat County	CO	James "Boomer" Hayden	1989	3,062
67 4/8	13 4/8 13 0/8	5 4/8 5 4/8	9 6/8	Otero County	CO	Tim Wells	1990	3,062
67 4/8	12 0/8 12 0/8	5 5/8 5 4/8	8 6/8	Moffat County	CO	James A. Davison	1990	3,062
67 4/8	12 7/8 12 7/8	5 6/8 5 5/8	7 7/8	Chaffee County	CO	Joel Morgan	1990	3,062
67 4/8	13 3/8 13 3/8	5 4/8 5 3/8	12 0/8	Clark County	ID	Tom Thiel	1990	3,062
67 4/8	12 7/8 14 2/8	6 0/8 6 0/8	10 4/8	Lake County	OR	Rick D. Breckel	1990	3,062
67 4/8	14 0/8 13 7/8	5 5/8 5 5/8	8 1/8	Walsh	ALB	David R. Coupland	1990	3,062
67 4/8	12 3/8 12 4/8	6 0/8 6 0/8	12 1/8	Rosebud County	MT	Scott Propst	1990	3,062
67 4/8	13 2/8 13 0/8	6 1/8 5 7/8	9 2/8	Johnson County	WY	Brian R. Potter	1990	3,062
67 4/8	13 2/8 13 0/8	5 3/8 5 2/8	6 4/8	Outram	SAS	Garry Leslie	1990	3,062
67 4/8	12 4/8 12 4/8	6 0/8 5 7/8	8 0/8	Converse County	WY	Greg McTee	1990	3,062
67 4/8	13 5/8 13 6/8	5 4/8 5 4/8	12 2/8	Meagher County	MT	D. Mitch Kottas	1990	3,062
67 4/8	13 1/8 12 7/8	5 7/8 5 7/8	11 7/8	Hemaruka	ALB	Larry McNalley	1990	3,062
67 4/8	12 5/8 12 3/8	6 3/8 5 6/8	7 4/8	Natrona County	WY	Mark D. Christopherson	1991	3,062
67 4/8	13 6/8 12 4/8	5 5/8 5 4/8	9 4/8	Malheur County	OR	Dave Seida	1991	3,062
67 4/8	12 5/8 12 2/8	6 0/8 5 7/8	12 1/8	Fremont County	WY	Lyle Prell	1991	3,062
67 4/8	14 1/8 13 3/8	5 3/8 5 4/8	11 2/8	Campbell County	WY	Edwin John Durushia	1991	3,062
67 4/8	13 6/8 13 3/8	6 0/8 6 0/8	10 2/8	Rosebud County	MT	Danny L. Parrott	1991	3,062
67 4/8	13 5/8 13 2/8	5 7/8 5 7/8	12 1/8	Madison County	MT	Jim Powell	1991	3,062
67 4/8	13 4/8 13 4/8	5 4/8 5 4/8	8 2/8	Harding County	SD	John R. Simpson	1991	3,062
67 4/8	12 4/8 13 0/8	6 0/8 6 0/8	8 1/8	Converse County	WY	Peter F. Woech	1991	3,062
67 4/8	12 5/8 13 0/8	6 1/8 6 1/8	9 0/8	Weld County	CO	Michael J. McArtor	1992	3,062
67 4/8	13 6/8 14 0/8	5 4/8 5 4/8	13 4/8	Owyhee County	ID	Frank Sanders	1992	3,062
67 4/8	13 0/8 13 3/8	5 6/8 5 4/8	12 2/8	Owyhee County	ID	Jay D. King	1992	3,062
67 4/8	12 4/8 12 3/8	5 5/8 5 6/8	9 6/8	Converse County	WY	Ron Bernash	1992	3,062
67 4/8	13 5/8 13 4/8	5 4/8 5 4/8	12 0/8	Dunn County	ND	Jay Gunwall	1992	3,062
67 4/8	12 3/8 12 4/8	5 6/8 5 6/8	9 0/8	Converse County	WY	Pat Forliti	1992	3,062
67 4/8	13 5/8 13 7/8	5 2/8 5 3/8	12 0/8	Campbell County	WY	John W. Hampton	1992	3,062
67 4/8	12 7/8 12 5/8	6 2/8 6 0/8	8 3/8	Sioux County	NE	Dave Tunink	1992	3,062
67 4/8	13 1/8 13 5/8	6 1/8 6 1/8	10 6/8	Carbon County	WY	Norman Wolfe	1992	3,062
67 4/8	13 5/8 14 0/8	5 3/8 5 2/8	9 7/8	Socorro County	NM	Thomas Vieth	1993	3,062
67 4/8	13 1/8 13 1/8	6 0/8 6 0/8	8 5/8	Johnson County	WY	Charles B. Cureton	1993	3,062
67 4/8	13 0/8 12 6/8	5 6/8 5 5/8	9 7/8	Moffat County	CO	Thomas P. Bartholomew	1994	3,062
67 4/8	12 7/8 12 6/8	5 2/8 5 1/8	9 0/8	Wayne County	UT	Mike S. Mitchell	1994	3,062
67 4/8	13 3/8 13 3/8	5 6/8 5 5/8	11 3/8	Park County	WY	Charlotte Moss	1994	3,062
67 4/8	13 4/8 13 3/8	5 7/8 5 5/8	9 0/8	Owyhee County	ID	Terry L. Bennett	1994	3,062
67 4/8	13 0/8 13 1/8	5 2/8 5 2/8	8 2/8	Carbon County	UT	Cory D. Oaks	1994	3,062
67 4/8	13 2/8 13 3/8	5 4/8 5 4/8	7 7/8	Converse County	WY	Dave Canfield	1994	3,062

PRONGHORN

Minimum Score 67

SCORE	LENGTH OF HORN R	L	CIRCUMFERENCE OF BASE R	L	INSIDE SPREAD	AREA	STATE/ PROVINCE	HUNTER'S NAME	DATE	RANK
67 4/8	11 6/8	12 6/8	6 0/8	5 7/8	9 3/8	Converse County	WY	Gary M. Gmeiner	1994	3,062
67 4/8	11 7/8	12 0/8	5 6/8	5 7/8	13 2/8	Moffat County	CO	Dave Greenwalt	1994	3,062
67 4/8	13 0/8	12 6/8	5 4/8	5 5/8	9 0/8	Bowman County	ND	Ray Hajek	1994	3,062
67 4/8	12 6/8	12 2/8	5 6/8	5 6/8	12 5/8	Converse County	WY	Jerry Nichols	1994	3,062
67 4/8	12 6/8	12 6/8	5 4/8	5 4/8	7 2/8	Musselshell County	MT	Dan Ermatinger	1994	3,062
67 4/8	13 4/8	14 4/8	5 6/8	5 6/8	10 2/8	McKenzie County	ND	Pat Weigel	1994	3,062
67 4/8	12 4/8	12 0/8	5 6/8	5 6/8	10 2/8	Campbell County	WY	Roger Peabody	1994	3,062
67 4/8	12 5/8	13 0/8	5 5/8	5 6/8	10 5/8	Manyberries	ALB	Henry E. Moore, Jr.	1994	3,062
67 4/8	13 0/8	11 6/8	5 5/8	5 5/8	11 2/8	Milk River	ALB	Ted Brown	1994	3,062
67 4/8	14 1/8	13 3/8	5 5/8	5 5/8	13 0/8	Moffat County	CO	Max Thomas	1995	3,062
67 4/8	12 3/8	12 1/8	6 0/8	5 7/8	11 1/8	Coconino County	AZ	Andrew L. Grannan	1995	3,062
67 4/8	11 6/8	11 4/8	6 6/8	6 4/8	11 6/8	Converse County	WY	G. Lowe Morrison	1995	3,062
67 4/8	13 5/8	13 5/8	5 5/8	5 5/8	5 7/8	Converse County	WY	Dan Weiss	1995	3,062
67 4/8	14 0/8	13 5/8	5 6/8	5 5/8	6 5/8	Converse County	WY	Joe Krejci	1995	3,062
67 4/8	14 4/8	14 4/8	5 5/8	5 5/8	9 5/8	Cheyenne County	NE	Everett A. Tarrell	1995	3,062
67 4/8	12 6/8	12 4/8	5 4/8	5 5/8	11 3/8	Harney County	OR	Dave Creekmore	1996	3,062
67 4/8	14 4/8	14 2/8	5 2/8	5 2/8	11 0/8	Wallace County	KS	David R. Rogers	1996	3,062
67 4/8	12 4/8	12 3/8	5 7/8	5 7/8	12 1/8	Moffat County	CO	Justin Bliss	1997	3,062
67 4/8	13 5/8	13 2/8	5 5/8	5 6/8	10 2/8	Sweetwater County	WY	Gary Brewer	1997	3,062
67 4/8	12 5/8	12 6/8	5 4/8	5 1/8	8 4/8	Campbell County	WY	Craig Olthoff	1997	3,062
67 4/8	11 6/8	11 7/8	6 1/8	6 0/8	10 4/8	Weld County	CO	Justin Wenthe	1998	3,062
67 2/8	12 1/8	12 1/8	6 0/8	5 5/8	11 6/8	Carbon County	WY	Dennis Behn	1974	3,162
67 2/8	12 7/8	13 0/8	5 2/8	5 2/8	6 4/8	Musselshell County	MT	Scott L. Koelzer	1976	3,162
67 2/8	13 7/8	14 0/8	5 4/8	5 4/8	9 2/8	Campbell County	WY	Larry Tiner	1978	3,162
67 2/8	13 0/8	13 0/8	5 3/8	5 3/8	14 3/8	Natrona County	WY	Dennis Keyser	1978	3,162
67 2/8	12 6/8	13 1/8	5 7/8	5 7/8	9 5/8	Sweetwater County	WY	Blair Smith	1978	3,162
67 2/8	11 5/8	11 5/8	5 0/8	5 0/8	9 2/8	Converse County	WY	Eugene Smith, Jr.	1979	3,162
67 2/8	13 1/8	13 0/8	5 4/8	5 5/8	9 2/8	Converse County	WY	Ronald J. Collier	1980	3,162
67 2/8	13 5/8	13 1/8	5 5/8	5 5/8	10 3/8	Humboldt County	NV	Jeff Purcell	1980	3,162
67 2/8	13 3/8	13 4/8	5 5/8	5 4/8	10 2/8	Converse County	WY	John Zawaski	1980	3,162
67 2/8	12 6/8	12 6/8	5 3/8	5 3/8	12 3/8	Converse County	WY	Al Gross	1981	3,162
67 2/8	13 7/8	13 7/8	5 4/8	5 4/8	11 2/8	Converse County	WY	Wayne W. Wagner	1981	3,162
67 2/8	13 1/8	13 2/8	5 2/8	5 1/8	9 4/8	Pueblo County	CO	Mitchell McMahon	1982	3,162
67 2/8	14 1/8	12 7/8	5 4/8	5 4/8	10 6/8	Moffat County	CO	Steven Neal	1982	3,162
67 2/8	13 4/8	13 4/8	5 4/8	5 3/8	8 2/8	Wallace County	KS	Steve Rugg	1982	3,162
67 2/8	11 6/8	11 5/8	6 0/8	6 0/8	12 6/8	Sioux County	NE	Melvin L. Rein	1982	3,162
67 2/8	13 6/8	12 3/8	6 1/8	6 1/8	9 6/8	White Pine County	NV	Larry T. Gilbertson	1983	3,162
67 2/8	11 7/8	12 0/8	5 7/8	5 7/8	9 4/8	Bowman County	ND	Greg Braun	1983	3,162
67 2/8	14 3/8	14 2/8	5 4/8	5 4/8	12 0/8	Perkins County	SD	Vilas Schoenfelder	1983	3,162
67 2/8	13 0/8	12 4/8	6 0/8	5 6/8	7 3/8	Converse County	WY	Larry Crooks	1983	3,162
67 2/8	13 1/8	12 7/8	5 5/8	5 6/8	11 5/8	Converse County	WY	Gary Holtz	1983	3,162
67 2/8	12 5/8	12 3/8	5 3/8	5 4/8	11 7/8	Meade County	SD	Steve D. Krier	1983	3,162
67 2/8	13 0/8	13 0/8	5 5/8	5 5/8	8 1/8	Hettinger County	ND	Brian Scherr	1983	3,162
67 2/8	12 0/8	12 2/8	5 7/8	6 1/8	7 3/8	Campbell County	WY	William Heineke	1984	3,162
67 2/8	13 1/8	13 1/8	4 5/8	4 7/8	11 7/8	Moffat County	CO	Glenn Pritchard	1984	3,162
67 2/8	12 0/8	12 1/8	5 6/8	5 5/8	7 7/8	Converse County	WY	Ron Rockwell	1984	3,162
67 2/8	12 4/8	12 3/8	6 0/8	6 0/8	12 0/8	Sweetwater County	WY	John Cheese	1985	3,162
67 2/8	13 2/8	13 2/8	5 4/8	5 2/8	7 2/8	Moffat County	CO	John E. Axelson	1985	3,162
67 2/8	13 3/8	12 6/8	5 4/8	5 4/8	7 6/8	Moffat County	CO	Kurt Keskimaki	1985	3,162
67 2/8	12 4/8	12 4/8	5 6/8	5 6/8	8 3/8	Moffat County	CO	James A. Davison	1985	3,162
67 2/8	13 1/8	12 7/8	5 7/8	5 6/8	9 3/8	Carbon County	WY	Richard L. Westervelt	1985	3,162
67 2/8	13 7/8	13 7/8	5 6/8	5 5/8	11 1/8	Converse County	WY	David Jerome	1985	3,162
67 2/8	12 5/8	12 5/8	5 3/8	5 3/8	9 0/8	Converse County	WY	William Doemland	1985	3,162
67 2/8	13 2/8	13 2/8	5 1/8	5 1/8	8 4/8	Campbell County	WY	Richard Andre	1985	3,162
67 2/8	13 2/8	13 1/8	5 7/8	5 6/8	11 0/8	Converse County	WY	Craig James Stransky	1985	3,162
67 2/8	12 4/8	12 3/8	6 0/8	5 7/8	10 1/8	Valley County	MT	Bryan Erickson	1986	3,162
67 2/8	12 7/8	12 7/8	6 0/8	5 6/8	8 5/8	Converse County	WY	Gregory White	1986	3,162
67 2/8	12 4/8	12 2/8	6 2/8	6 2/8	10 0/8	Converse County	WY	Richard Crawford	1986	3,162
67 2/8	13 6/8	13 7/8	4 7/8	5 0/8	9 3/8	Chouteau County	MT	Wayne Arnold	1986	3,162
67 2/8	11 3/8	12 4/8	5 6/8	5 6/8	9 2/8	Blaine County	ID	Wesley Moore	1988	3,162
67 2/8	12 4/8	12 7/8	5 4/8	5 4/8	9 5/8	Bingham County	ID	Reggie N. Scheierman	1988	3,162
67 2/8	11 4/8	11 6/8	6 1/8	6 0/8	7 6/8	McKenzie County	ND	Bill Kelly	1988	3,162
67 2/8	13 0/8	12 7/8	5 5/8	5 5/8	7 1/8	Converse County	WY	Carmine Agostine	1988	3,162
67 2/8	13 2/8	13 1/8	5 7/8	6 0/8	10 6/8	Petroleum County	MT	Leamon D. Ferrell	1988	3,162
67 2/8	12 4/8	12 6/8	5 7/8	5 6/8	9 5/8	Moffat County	CO	Barry Rich	1989	3,162
67 2/8	12 2/8	12 5/8	5 4/8	5 3/8	8 7/8	Converse County	WY	Jason W. Zebrowski	1989	3,162
67 2/8	13 1/8	13 4/8	5 6/8	5 5/8	7 2/8	Campbell County	WY	Robin D. Johnson	1989	3,162
67 2/8	11 1/8	11 3/8	6 2/8	6 1/8	10 1/8	Custer County	MT	Mark L. Frank	1989	3,162
67 2/8	13 2/8	13 2/8	5 6/8	5 6/8	10 1/8	Billings County	ND	Jeff Brigham	1989	3,162
67 2/8	13 2/8	13 0/8	5 3/8	5 3/8	9 3/8	Converse County	WY	David A. Widby	1990	3,162
67 2/8	12 7/8	13 2/8	6 0/8	5 7/8	10 4/8	Harney County	OR	Richard Wright	1990	3,162
67 2/8	12 2/8	12 5/8	5 5/8	5 4/8	11 0/8	Sweetwater County	WY	Dave Holt	1990	3,162
67 2/8	13 2/8	13 1/8	5 3/8	5 5/8	9 6/8	Sheridan County	WY	Tom Hlinka	1990	3,162
67 2/8	13 3/8	13 3/8	5 6/8	5 4/8	8 5/8	Wallace County	KS	Roger Potter	1990	3,162
67 2/8	13 5/8	13 5/8	5 6/8	5 4/8	9 0/8	Harding County	SD	Marty Adams	1990	3,162
67 2/8	12 7/8	13 1/8	5 7/8	5 6/8	7 1/8	Owyhee County	ID	Jesse M. Frandsen	1991	3,162
67 2/8	12 5/8	12 4/8	5 5/8	5 5/8	9 4/8	Sweetwater County	WY	Mark Petersen	1991	3,162
67 2/8	12 0/8	12 7/8	6 2/8	6 1/8	7 6/8	Converse County	WY	Ed Defibaugh	1991	3,162

PRONGHORN

Minimum Score 67 — Continued

SCORE	LENGTH OF HORN R	L	CIRCUMFERENCE OF BASE R	L	INSIDE SPREAD	AREA	STATE/ PROVINCE	HUNTER'S NAME	DATE	RANK
67 2/8	13 3/8	13 3/8	5 6/8	5 6/8	9 2/8	Campbell County	WY	William J. McGrath	1991	3,162
67 2/8	11 5/8	11 7/8	5 7/8	5 6/8	8 7/8	McKenzie County	ND	Mark D. Hughes	1991	3,162
67 2/8	13 5/8	13 5/8	6 1/8	6 1/8	7 7/8	Corson County	SD	Fred Kober	1991	3,162
67 2/8	13 2/8	13 1/8	5 6/8	5 5/8	11 0/8	Campbell County	WY	Tom Griffin	1991	3,162
67 2/8	13 0/8	13 1/8	6 2/8	6 2/8	12 2/8	Carbon County	WY	Levi Nelson	1991	3,162
67 2/8	12 4/8	12 6/8	5 6/8	5 6/8	7 0/8	Butte County	SD	Larry Kracht	1991	3,162
67 2/8	13 0/8	13 1/8	5 7/8	6 0/8	9 3/8	Sierra County	NM	Daryl Tow	1992	3,162
67 2/8	13 4/8	13 2/8	5 5/8	5 5/8	9 7/8	Moffat County	CO	Garry Woodman	1992	3,162
67 2/8	14 1/8	13 6/8	6 0/8	5 7/8	14 4/8	Sweetwater County	WY	Ronda Williams	1992	3,162
67 2/8	13 2/8	13 3/8	5 7/8	5 6/8	10 6/8	Moffat County	CO	Rett Kelly	1992	3,162
67 2/8	12 3/8	12 1/8	5 6/8	5 6/8	7 2/8	Converse County	WY	Gene Mathias	1992	3,162
67 2/8	13 3/8	13 3/8	5 2/8	5 2/8	12 1/8	Bowman County	ND	David Brag	1992	3,162
67 2/8	12 0/8	12 0/8	6 0/8	6 0/8	10 4/8	Moffat County	CO	Kenneth L. Shelton	1992	3,162
67 2/8	13 4/8	13 4/8	5 5/8	5 5/8	8 2/8	Fox Valley	SAS	Floyd Forster	1992	3,162
67 2/8	13 1/8	13 3/8	5 0/8	5 0/8	11 2/8	Converse County	WY	Scott McCormack	1992	3,162
67 2/8	13 3/8	12 6/8	6 2/8	6 1/8	6 6/8	Rosebud County	MT	John W. Offord	1992	3,162
67 2/8	14 1/8	14 2/8	5 5/8	5 6/8	9 3/8	Yavapai County	AZ	Brian K. Tinker	1993	3,162
67 2/8	14 0/8	14 2/8	5 3/8	5 3/8	13 1/8	Sweet Grass County	MT	John M. Rigney	1993	3,162
67 2/8	13 0/8	13 0/8	6 4/8	6 4/8	11 4/8	Converse County	WY	Donald Miller	1993	3,162
67 2/8	13 0/8	13 2/8	5 6/8	5 6/8	7 3/8	Campbell County	WY	Tom Gleason	1993	3,162
67 2/8	12 2/8	12 3/8	5 7/8	5 7/8	9 4/8	Yavapai County	AZ	Van M. Clark, Jr.	1994	3,162
67 2/8	14 5/8	14 2/8	5 4/8	5 4/8	10 5/8	Buffalo	ALB	Larry Flaata	1994	3,162
67 2/8	12 5/8	12 5/8	5 5/8	5 4/8	11 5/8	Campbell County	WY	Bob Atwood	1994	3,162
67 2/8	11 6/8	11 6/8	5 7/8	5 6/8	7 5/8	Moffat County	CO	Peter F. Woeck	1995	3,162
67 2/8	14 1/8	13 5/8	5 1/8	5 2/8	7 6/8	Natrona County	WY	Rodney L. Dehart	1995	3,162
67 2/8	12 1/8	12 2/8	6 1/8	6 1/8	10 5/8	Moffat County	CO	Mike Boland	1995	3,162
67 2/8	13 3/8	13 2/8	5 4/8	5 4/8	10 6/8	Dunn County	ND	Mike Morris	1995	3,162
67 2/8	13 3/8	13 5/8	5 4/8	5 3/8	12 3/8	Converse County	WY	Dr. Eugene T. Altiere	1995	3,162
67 2/8	13 2/8	12 6/8	5 5/8	5 4/8	12 6/8	Converse County	WY	Chuck Kronenwetter	1995	3,162
67 2/8	12 4/8	12 2/8	5 7/8	6 0/8	10 1/8	Aden	ALB	Douglas W. Cannons	1995	3,162
67 2/8	14 0/8	14 1/8	5 3/8	5 3/8	11 1/8	Harding County	SD	Scott Ketchmark	1995	3,162
67 2/8	14 2/8	14 0/8	4 6/8	4 6/8	10 5/8	Yavapai County	AZ	Robert B. Buchanan	1996	3,162
67 2/8	12 3/8	13 6/8	5 7/8	6 0/8	7 6/8	Moffat County	CO	Rod Lampe	1996	3,162
67 2/8	13 0/8	13 0/8	5 6/8	5 6/8	11 0/8	Harding County	SD	Renee Welle	1996	3,162
67 2/8	12 0/8	12 1/8	6 4/8	6 4/8	10 3/8	Converse County	WY	George A. Zanoni	1996	3,162
67 2/8	13 7/8	13 7/8	5 4/8	5 4/8	12 6/8	Converse County	WY	Anthony "Del" DelMastro	1996	3,162
67 2/8	12 7/8	14 4/8	5 6/8	5 7/8	11 1/8	Campbell County	WY	Gary English	1997	3,162
67 2/8	12 5/8	12 2/8	6 7/8	7 0/8	12 0/8	Converse County	WY	Pam Hamilton	1998	3,162
67 2/8	13 1/8	13 1/8	5 1/8	5 1/8	10 5/8	Weld County	CO	Bob Chapman	1998	3,162
67 0/8	12 7/8	12 7/8	5 6/8	5 4/8	10 2/8	Butte County	SD	David Lind	1961	3,258
67 0/8	13 0/8	13 2/8	5 5/8	5 5/8	10 6/8	McLean County	ND	Harold Janssen	1971	3,258
67 0/8	13 0/8	12 4/8	6 0/8	6 0/8	10 4/8	Campbell County	WY	Gerald L. Egbert	1975	3,258
67 0/8	11 0/8	11 0/8	6 6/8	6 4/8	8 3/8	Converse County	WY	Eddie Hayden	1978	3,258
67 0/8	12 6/8	12 4/8	6 1/8	6 0/8	11 2/8	Converse County	WY	Kenneth L. Stoneburner	1978	3,258
67 0/8	12 7/8	12 7/8	5 5/8	5 5/8	7 2/8	Converse County	WY	Alton Gross	1980	3,258
67 0/8	11 5/8	11 5/8	6 0/8	6 0/8	9 0/8	Weld County	CO	Dennis Schweitzer	1980	3,258
67 0/8	12 3/8	12 2/8	5 5/8	5 6/8	8 7/8	Sheridan County	WY	Travis Adsit	1981	3,258
67 0/8	12 6/8	13 0/8	5 5/8	5 6/8	10 7/8	Natrona County	WY	Robert Arvey	1981	3,258
67 0/8	11 6/8	11 6/8	5 6/8	5 6/8	9 1/8	Converse County	WY	Richard Smith	1981	3,258
67 0/8	13 7/8	14 0/8	5 7/8	5 7/8	10 5/8	Converse County	WY	Robert A. Christensen	1982	3,258
67 0/8	12 2/8	12 1/8	5 6/8	5 6/8	9 3/8	Converse County	WY	Howard Holmes	1982	3,258
67 0/8	13 7/8	14 1/8	5 2/8	5 2/8	10 7/8	Lassen County	CA	Don Rossiter	1983	3,258
67 0/8	15 0/8	14 7/8	5 2/8	5 2/8	11 2/8	Yavapai County	AZ	Michael John Bylina	1983	3,258
67 0/8	12 2/8	12 4/8	7 0/8	7 0/8	9 7/8	Converse County	WY	Eric Ames	1983	3,258
67 0/8	13 5/8	14 0/8	5 3/8	5 3/8	11 3/8	Natrona County	WY	Charles Lanzarone	1983	3,258
67 0/8	12 7/8	12 5/8	5 6/8	5 5/8	11 0/8	Broadwater County	MT	Bob A. Closson	1983	3,258
67 0/8	12 5/8	12 5/8	5 3/8	5 1/8	10 6/8	Converse County	WY	Thomas L. Hughes	1983	3,258
67 0/8	12 3/8	12 3/8	5 5/8	5 5/8	8 4/8	Carbon County	WY	Raymond R. Robison	1984	3,258
67 0/8	12 5/8	12 4/8	5 5/8	5 4/8	10 3/8	Custer County	ID	Matt March, Jr.	1984	3,258
67 0/8	13 4/8	13 3/8	5 2/8	5 3/8	11 2/8	Sweetwater County	WY	Cliff Wiseman	1985	3,258
67 0/8	13 1/8	12 7/8	5 4/8	5 4/8	7 6/8	Sweetwater County	WY	Chuck Ashton	1985	3,258
67 0/8	12 5/8	12 5/8	5 4/8	5 3/8	9 2/8	Modoc County	CA	Anthony R. Dipino	1986	3,258
67 0/8	13 6/8	14 0/8	5 4/8	5 4/8	9 5/8	Carbon County	WY	Rod Schmidt	1986	3,258
67 0/8	12 4/8	12 3/8	6 2/8	6 2/8	7 7/8	Campbell County	WY	Keith Olson	1986	3,258
67 0/8	13 5/8	13 3/8	6 0/8	6 1/8	10 6/8	Mountrail County	ND	Charles Lerohl	1986	3,258
67 0/8	13 5/8	13 5/8	5 4/8	5 3/8	10 7/8	Modoc County	CA	Rick Holbrook	1987	3,258
67 0/8	12 4/8	12 2/8	6 0/8	6 0/8	11 4/8	Moffat County	CO	Grant Adkisson	1987	3,258
67 0/8	13 4/8	14 0/8	5 5/8	5 4/8	9 2/8	Uinta County	WY	Dave Murray	1987	3,258
67 0/8	13 4/8	13 7/8	5 1/8	5 2/8	6 7/8	Natrona County	WY	Doug Anderson	1987	3,258
67 0/8	13 0/8	12 6/8	6 0/8	6 0/8	11 5/8	Converse County	WY	Jack C. Staley, Jr.	1987	3,258
67 0/8	12 5/8	12 5/8	5 4/8	5 4/8	12 2/8	Fergus County	MT	Jess Knerr	1987	3,258
67 0/8	13 1/8	12 6/8	5 6/8	5 6/8	7 6/8	Moffat County	CO	James Libra	1988	3,258
67 0/8	13 4/8	13 4/8	5 5/8	5 4/8	9 2/8	Moffat County	CO	Terry Weimer	1988	3,258
67 0/8	13 2/8	13 3/8	5 6/8	5 5/8	11 1/8	Butte County	ID	Edward F. Keeton	1988	3,258
67 0/8	12 4/8	12 5/8	5 5/8	5 4/8	10 1/8	Natrona County	WY	Charles Lanzarone	1988	3,258
67 0/8	14 2/8	14 4/8	5 2/8	5 1/8	6 5/8	Converse County	WY	Jay Deones	1988	3,258
67 0/8	13 4/8	13 3/8	5 6/8	5 6/8	10 7/8	Rio Grande County	CO	Arthur G. Garcia	1988	3,258
67 0/8	13 5/8	13 4/8	5 5/8	5 6/8	8 5/8	Eddy County	NM	Jess Stuart	1988	3,258

PRONGHORN

Minimum Score 67 — Continued

SCORE	LENGTH OF HORN R	L	CIRCUMFERENCE OF BASE R	L	INSIDE SPREAD	AREA	STATE/ PROVINCE	HUNTER'S NAME	DATE	RANK
67 0/8	13 4/8	13 6/8	5 7/8	6 0/8	11 4/8	Sublette County	WY	Tony Litts	1989	3,258
67 0/8	13 4/8	13 0/8	5 2/8	5 2/8	8 5/8	Richland County	MT	Douglas A. Lang	1989	3,258
67 0/8	12 6/8	12 7/8	5 5/8	5 5/8	10 4/8	Moffat County	CO	Dennis M. Hayden	1989	3,258
67 0/8	12 3/8	11 7/8	6 3/8	6 4/8	11 4/8	Converse County	WY	James C. Gates	1989	3,258
67 0/8	12 2/8	12 4/8	5 6/8	5 6/8	8 5/8	Garfield County	MT	Glen Prestegaard	1989	3,258
67 0/8	12 2/8	12 2/8	6 0/8	6 0/8	10 4/8	Converse County	WY	Arthur Wirsing, Jr.	1989	3,258
67 0/8	12 5/8	12 6/8	6 0/8	6 0/8	8 2/8	Moffat County	CO	Chuck Leidheiser	1990	3,258
67 0/8	13 7/8	13 7/8	5 4/8	5 3/8	10 7/8	Moffat County	CO	Bob Radocy	1990	3,258
67 0/8	11 5/8	12 5/8	5 5/8	5 7/8	10 3/8	Sweetwater County	WY	Kurt Zurawski	1990	3,258
67 0/8	14 7/8	14 4/8	5 7/8	5 6/8	10 7/8	Rich County	UT	Robert K. Paulson	1990	3,258
67 0/8	13 1/8	13 1/8	5 5/8	5 4/8	12 2/8	Fox Valley	SAS	Floyd Forster	1990	3,258
67 0/8	12 3/8	12 3/8	6 0/8	5 7/8	8 1/8	McKenzie County	ND	Terry Sivertson	1990	3,258
67 0/8	13 1/8	13 1/8	5 4/8	5 3/8	11 0/8	Rosebud County	MT	Sherrill McNalley	1990	3,258
67 0/8	12 2/8	12 1/8	6 1/8	6 1/8	8 7/8	Converse County	WY	Gerry Smarelli	1990	3,258
67 0/8	12 6/8	13 4/8	5 7/8	5 6/8	11 2/8	McKenzie County	ND	Burnell Sammons	1990	3,258
67 0/8	13 5/8	14 6/8	4 7/8	5 0/8	11 2/8	Hudspeth County	TX	Ernest M. Elbert, Jr.	1990	3,258
67 0/8	13 3/8	13 2/8	5 4/8	5 2/8	11 3/8	Harding County	SD	William J. Bushong	1991	3,258
67 0/8	13 4/8	13 1/8	6 0/8	5 7/8	12 5/8	Owyhee County	ID	Terry Bennett	1991	3,258
67 0/8	13 2/8	13 0/8	5 6/8	5 6/8	9 6/8	Natrona County	WY	Eugene Damron	1991	3,258
67 0/8	13 0/8	13 0/8	6 1/8	5 7/8	9 6/8	Converse County	WY	Gary M. Funk	1991	3,258
67 0/8	12 0/8	12 1/8	6 0/8	6 0/8	9 4/8	Campbell County	WY	Jerry Hinz	1991	3,258
67 0/8	14 2/8	15 0/8	5 3/8	5 2/8	7 7/8	Converse County	WY	Kathy Strecker	1991	3,258
67 0/8	11 2/8	12 1/8	5 7/8	6 0/8	9 2/8	Natrona County	WY	Jeffrey Johnson	1991	3,258
67 0/8	13 6/8	14 0/8	5 3/8	5 2/8	9 3/8	Converse County	WY	Lou Edelis	1991	3,258
67 0/8	13 4/8	13 3/8	5 5/8	5 5/8	10 4/8	Dawes County	NE	Scott Binderup	1991	3,258
67 0/8	12 7/8	12 5/8	5 5/8	5 5/8	9 0/8	Converse County	WY	Michael J. Kennedy	1991	3,258
67 0/8	13 6/8	14 0/8	5 4/8	5 5/8	8 7/8	Colfax County	NM	Dr. David E. Samuel	1992	3,258
67 0/8	12 4/8	13 0/8	5 5/8	5 4/8	9 0/8	Moffat County	CO	Richard Davis	1992	3,258
67 0/8	12 6/8	12 4/8	6 1/8	6 2/8	11 6/8	Carbon County	WY	Willis Duhon	1992	3,258
67 0/8	12 0/8	12 1/8	6 3/8	6 3/8	9 5/8	Carbon County	WY	Steve Hinton	1992	3,258
67 0/8	12 5/8	12 5/8	5 3/8	5 2/8	9 1/8	Bowman County	ND	Darren Martel	1992	3,258
67 0/8	13 0/8	13 1/8	5 4/8	5 4/8	11 3/8	Garfield County	MT	Rick Stinson	1992	3,258
67 0/8	12 4/8	13 0/8	6 1/8	6 0/8	9 1/8	Converse County	WY	Robert K. Woeck	1992	3,258
67 0/8	13 6/8	13 7/8	5 7/8	6 0/8	10 1/8	Madison County	MT	Mark Stonebraker	1992	3,258
67 0/8	13 6/8	13 7/8	5 6/8	5 6/8	8 7/8	Moffat County	CO	Kevin Reed	1993	3,258
67 0/8	13 4/8	13 5/8	5 3/8	5 3/8	12 5/8	Yavapai County	AZ	Steve Parizek	1993	3,258
67 0/8	13 0/8	12 6/8	5 6/8	5 5/8	/ 6/8	Carbon County	WY	GayLynn Turner	1003	3,258
67 0/8	13 4/8	13 6/8	5 4/8	5 4/8	12 0/8	Mohave County	AZ	Jerry Zitterkopf	1993	3,258
67 0/8	12 7/8	13 0/8	5 4/8	5 4/8	11 6/8	Converse County	WY	Dane Clark	1993	3,258
67 0/8	12 3/8	12 4/8	6 0/8	5 6/8	9 2/8	Sheridan County	WY	Gregory J. Woodhouse	1993	3,258
67 0/8	12 5/8	13 0/8	5 7/8	5 7/8	10 1/8	Sioux County	NE	Rob Thompson	1994	3,258
67 0/8	11 7/8	12 0/8	5 4/8	5 4/8	8 5/8	Moffat County	CO	C. Ron Cannon, MD	1994	3,258
67 0/8	12 6/8	12 6/8	5 0/8	5 0/8	9 0/8	Saguache County	CO	Jerry Berry	1994	3,258
67 0/8	12 2/8	12 1/8	5 6/8	5 7/8	9 1/8	Converse County	WY	Michael T. Wheeler	1994	3,258
67 0/8	14 0/8	13 4/8	5 0/8	5 0/8	9 6/8	Sweetwater County	WY	Max Reagin, Jr.	1994	3,258
67 0/8	13 1/8	13 4/8	5 3/8	5 4/8	10 1/8	Bowman County	ND	David Janssen	1994	3,258
67 0/8	13 3/8	12 4/8	5 7/8	5 6/8	8 0/8	Rosebud County	MT	George E. Wood	1994	3,258
67 0/8	12 5/8	13 2/8	5 6/8	5 6/8	9 1/8	Converse County	WY	Chris Wotrang	1994	3,258
67 0/8	13 0/8	12 6/8	6 0/8	6 0/8	11 5/8	Wallace County	KS	Deanna L. Carmen	1994	3,258
67 0/8	12 2/8	12 3/8	5 3/8	5 4/8	12 5/8	Wallace County	KS	Roger Potter	1994	3,258
67 0/8	12 6/8	12 7/8	5 3/8	5 4/8	8 3/8	Converse County	WY	Dennis Roberts	1994	3,258
67 0/8	14 2/8	14 7/8	5 1/8	5 0/8	11 0/8	Rosebud County	MT	Edd Clack	1994	3,258
67 0/8	11 5/8	12 6/8	7 0/8	6 4/8	8 3/8	Moffat County	CO	Dennis N. Ballweg	1995	3,258
67 0/8	12 2/8	12 6/8	5 7/8	6 1/8	10 7/8	Moffat County	CO	Bill Plowman	1995	3,258
67 0/8	13 3/8	12 6/8	5 7/8	5 6/8	9 2/8	Converse County	WY	William R. Vyvyan	1995	3,258
67 0/8	12 3/8	12 4/8	5 4/8	5 4/8	9 4/8	Converse County	WY	David W. Wagner	1995	3,258
67 0/8	14 3/8	14 1/8	5 1/8	5 1/8	10 1/8	Phillips County	MT	Bob L. Walker	1995	3,258
67 0/8	13 6/8	14 1/8	5 5/8	5 5/8	7 4/8	Campbell County	WY	Anthony Lopez	1995	3,258
67 0/8	12 6/8	12 7/8	6 2/8	6 2/8	11 5/8	Musselshell County	MT	Anthony Wagner	1995	3,258
67 0/8	13 2/8	13 2/8	5 5/8	5 4/8	10 0/8	Moffat County	CO	Gary Biles	1996	3,258
67 0/8	11 2/8	11 0/8	6 3/8	6 2/8	10 7/8	Albany County	WY	Joseph Osvath	1996	3,258
67 0/8	13 3/8	13 2/8	5 6/8	5 6/8	10 5/8	Moffat County	CO	Todd Szmania	1996	3,258
67 0/8	13 1/8	12 6/8	6 0/8	6 0/8	10 3/8	Natrona County	WY	David M. Krampitz	1996	3,258
67 0/8	12 6/8	12 6/8	6 0/8	5 7/8	7 7/8	Moffat County	CO	Willy Colby	1996	3,258
67 0/8	12 6/8	12 7/8	5 5/8	5 5/8	7 7/8	Sioux County	NE	Clarence Poteet	1996	3,258
67 0/8	12 5/8	12 3/8	5 7/8	5 4/8	8 7/8	White Pine County	NV	Larry Pabst	1997	3,258
67 0/8	13 6/8	13 5/8	5 5/8	5 2/8	9 4/8	Moffat County	CO	Jon P. Miller	1997	3,258
67 0/8	12 4/8	13 4/8	5 6/8	5 4/8	11 5/8	Moffat County	CO	Mike Delamater	1997	3,258
67 0/8	14 1/8	14 0/8	5 2/8	5 2/8	8 4/8	Campbell County	WY	Charles W. Drexler, Sr.	1997	3,258
67 0/8	13 1/8	13 6/8	5 5/8	5 5/8	11 6/8	Lake County	OR	Jeffrey A. Eder	1997	3,258
67 0/8	12 0/8	11 6/8	6 2/8	6 2/8	9 4/8	Converse County	WY	Bernard R. Belaire, Jr.	1997	3,258
67 0/8	15 0/8	14 6/8	5 2/8	5 2/8	9 1/8	Butte County	ID	Mikeal A. Carter	1998	3,258
67 0/8	12 5/8	12 6/8	5 2/8	5 1/8	7 6/8	Converse County	WY	Timothy Angelo	1998	3,258
67 0/8	14 2/8	14 1/8	5 1/8	5 0/8	10 7/8	Campbell County	WY	Jay Hill	1998	3,258
66 6/8	14 4/8	14 2/8	5 3/8	5 4/8	13 5/8	Converse County	WY	Roland Gravenkemper	1955	3,371
66 6/8	13 3/8	13 1/8	5 7/8	5 7/8	8 4/8	Campbell County	WY	Pete Erickson	1967	3,371
66 6/8	12 4/8	12 4/8	5 6/8	5 6/8	10 3/8	Butte County	SD	Dr. William L. Lee	1974	3,371
66 6/8	12 6/8	12 6/8	5 6/8	5 5/8	10 0/8	Butte County	SD	Charles C. Tippton, Jr.	1974	3,371

PRONGHORN

Minimum Score 67 — Continued

SCORE	LENGTH OF HORN R	L	CIRCUMFERENCE OF BASE R	L	INSIDE SPREAD	AREA	STATE/PROVINCE	HUNTER'S NAME	DATE	RANK
66 6/8	14 1/8	13 2/8	5 5/8	5 4/8	10 6/8	Wallace County	KS	David Stevenson	1975	3,371
66 6/8	12 7/8	12 7/8	5 4/8	5 4/8	9 4/8	Natrona County	WY	Mel Johnson	1978	3,371
66 6/8	13 1/8	13 0/8	5 4/8	5 2/8	11 6/8	Johnson County	WY	Frederick A. Suran	1978	3,371
66 6/8	11 6/8	11 3/8	5 4/8	5 3/8	9 6/8	Carbon County	WY	Ed Downard	1980	3,371
66 6/8	12 5/8	12 7/8	5 6/8	5 6/8	8 0/8	Natrona County	WY	James R. Kilgore	1980	3,371
66 6/8	12 2/8	12 2/8	5 7/8	5 7/8	7 4/8	Converse County	WY	Carl W. Van Ryswyk	1980	3,371
66 6/8	12 5/8	13 0/8	5 7/8	5 6/8	13 3/8	Natrona County	WY	Richard Iverson	1981	3,371
66 6/8	13 0/8	13 0/8	5 3/8	5 4/8	7 4/8	Moffat County	CO	Tim Chastain	1981	3,371
66 6/8	13 0/8	13 0/8	5 7/8	5 6/8	7 7/8	Blaine County	ID	Champ Church	1981	3,371
66 6/8	13 3/8	14 3/8	5 3/8	5 3/8	11 4/8	Natrona County	WY	Dean Hamilton	1981	3,371
66 6/8	14 0/8	11 3/8	5 2/8	5 2/8	10 7/8	Converse County	WY	Lee Jernigan	1981	3,371
66 6/8	11 6/8	11 4/8	5 5/8	5 5/8	12 6/8	Converse County	WY	Tom Kayser	1981	3,371
66 6/8	11 7/8	11 5/8	5 5/8	5 6/8	9 0/8	Converse County	WY	Charlie Kroll	1981	3,371
66 6/8	12 2/8	12 3/8	5 7/8	5 6/8	8 0/8	Clark County	ID	Richard K. Russell	1981	3,371
66 6/8	12 1/8	12 0/8	5 4/8	5 5/8	10 4/8	Converse County	WY	John S. Shields	1983	3,371
66 6/8	14 1/8	14 2/8	5 1/8	5 0/8	12 2/8	Moffat County	CO	Rick Stockburger	1983	3,371
66 6/8	13 1/8	13 2/8	5 3/8	5 4/8	9 2/8	Converse County	WY	Gene Gilmer	1983	3,371
66 6/8	12 6/8	12 7/8	5 5/8	5 5/8	11 7/8	Converse County	WY	Spencer Wilker	1983	3,371
66 6/8	13 2/8	12 6/8	5 7/8	5 6/8	9 2/8	Converse County	WY	Randy Dittmer	1984	3,371
66 6/8	13 7/8	14 0/8	5 6/8	5 6/8	12 7/8	McKenzie County	ND	Mitch Griebel	1984	3,371
66 6/8	12 7/8	12 5/8	6 2/8	5 7/8	11 4/8	Campbell County	WY	Robert Finelli	1984	3,371
66 6/8	14 4/8	14 0/8	5 2/8	5 3/8	10 1/8	Rio Arriba County	NM	Michael M. Hawkes	1985	3,371
66 6/8	12 5/8	12 6/8	6 0/8	5 6/8	10 7/8	Converse County	WY	Jack Leggo	1985	3,371
66 6/8	12 4/8	12 7/8	5 4/8	5 4/8	9 4/8	Carbon County	WY	Kim Cooper	1985	3,371
66 6/8	12 7/8	12 7/8	5 5/8	5 5/8	10 4/8	Natrona County	WY	Rickey E. Morse	1986	3,371
66 6/8	12 4/8	12 6/8	5 6/8	5 5/8	9 4/8	Fergus County	MT	Charles B. Vogl	1986	3,371
66 6/8	13 7/8	13 1/8	5 4/8	5 4/8	11 5/8	Petroleum County	MT	Stan Colton	1986	3,371
66 6/8	12 2/8	12 5/8	5 6/8	5 4/8	7 4/8	Sweetwater County	WY	Winston Parkinson	1987	3,371
66 6/8	12 4/8	12 6/8	6 0/8	5 7/8	9 5/8	Laramie County	WY	Robert S. Simms, Jr.	1987	3,371
66 6/8	13 0/8	12 5/8	5 6/8	5 6/8	9 0/8	Petroleum County	MT	Mark D. Hughes	1987	3,371
66 6/8	13 0/8	12 7/8	5 3/8	5 3/8	12 5/8	Tide Lake	ALB	Archie Nesbitt	1988	3,371
66 6/8	13 1/8	12 4/8	5 1/8	5 1/8	10 0/8	Carbon County	WY	Ray Dierking	1989	3,371
66 6/8	12 3/8	12 1/8	5 7/8	5 7/8	9 6/8	Moffat County	CO	Bruno Ammann	1989	3,371
66 6/8	13 4/8	13 4/8	5 3/8	5 3/8	7 0/8	Campbell County	WY	Gary D. Johansen	1989	3,371
66 6/8	12 1/8	12 6/8	6 4/8	6 3/8	11 3/8	Sioux County	NE	Victor Reese	1989	3,371
66 6/8	12 6/8	12 5/8	6 1/8	6 1/8	8 2/8	Ward County	ND	Russel Goodwin	1989	3,371
66 6/8	13 3/8	13 0/8	5 4/8	5 4/8	9 6/8	Buffalo	ALB	Larry Mandseth	1989	3,371
66 6/8	12 7/8	12 7/8	5 4/8	5 3/8	11 1/8	Meagher County	MT	Gene Clark	1989	3,371
66 6/8	12 7/8	13 0/8	5 4/8	5 4/8	7 6/8	Washoe County	NV	Scott Jones	1990	3,371
66 6/8	12 7/8	12 5/8	5 3/8	5 4/8	8 4/8	Moffat County	CO	Roy M. Goodwin	1990	3,371
66 6/8	13 4/8	13 4/8	6 1/8	6 0/8	14 2/8	Corson County	SD	Bill Soyland	1990	3,371
66 6/8	12 1/8	12 4/8	5 7/8	5 7/8	9 3/8	Natrona County	WY	Douglas R. Hahn	1990	3,371
66 6/8	12 5/8	12 1/8	6 2/8	6 1/8	9 0/8	Natrona County	WY	Nelson Beane	1990	3,371
66 6/8	13 3/8	13 5/8	5 2/8	5 2/8	9 6/8	Harney County	OR	Joel Modey	1990	3,371
66 6/8	13 5/8	13 7/8	5 6/8	5 4/8	9 6/8	McKenzie County	ND	Cecil I. Tharp	1990	3,371
66 6/8	13 2/8	13 4/8	5 4/8	5 4/8	11 6/8	Rosebud County	MT	Harvey McNalley	1990	3,371
66 6/8	12 1/8	13 0/8	5 3/8	5 3/8	7 6/8	Catron County	NM	Rick Forrest	1991	3,371
66 6/8	14 3/8	13 4/8	5 0/8	5 0/8	11 4/8	Tooele County	UT	Michael Tim McIntyre	1991	3,371
66 6/8	13 1/8	13 2/8	5 2/8	5 3/8	10 0/8	Coconino County	AZ	Duane "Corky" Richardson	1991	3,371
66 6/8	13 4/8	13 4/8	5 6/8	5 6/8	8 4/8	Bowman County	ND	Sheldon D. Snyder	1991	3,371
66 6/8	12 5/8	11 6/8	6 0/8	6 1/8	10 7/8	Campbell County	WY	John Tregembo	1991	3,371
66 6/8	13 2/8	13 4/8	5 4/8	5 4/8	13 1/8	Sioux County	NE	Tom Tobiasson	1991	3,371
66 6/8	12 6/8	12 6/8	5 5/8	5 5/8	8 4/8	Golden Valley County	ND	Les Tomanek	1991	3,371
66 6/8	13 3/8	13 3/8	5 4/8	5 2/8	10 0/8	Lewis & Clark County	MT	Mike Saulter	1991	3,371
66 6/8	13 0/8	13 0/8	5 4/8	5 3/8	8 5/8	Fremont County	WY	Jerry Bodar	1992	3,371
66 6/8	13 4/8	13 6/8	5 1/8	5 1/8	8 5/8	Saguache County	CO	Ronnie Ellington	1992	3,371
66 6/8	13 3/8	13 7/8	5 1/8	5 1/8	7 3/8	Owyhee County	ID	Tony E. Hyde	1992	3,371
66 6/8	13 6/8	13 5/8	5 1/8	5 3/8	7 3/8	Pima County	AZ	Robert Forrest	1992	3,371
66 6/8	13 0/8	13 2/8	5 6/8	5 6/8	9 6/8	Sioux County	NE	Ivan Buss	1992	3,371
66 6/8	13 3/8	13 5/8	5 4/8	5 5/8	12 2/8	Owyhee County	ID	Bryce Moore	1992	3,371
66 6/8	14 0/8	14 1/8	5 4/8	5 5/8	10 3/8	Fremont County	WY	Ron Niziolek	1992	3,371
66 6/8	11 4/8	11 7/8	6 0/8	6 0/8	10 4/8	Malheur County	OR	Phillip T. Staton	1992	3,371
66 6/8	13 5/8	13 4/8	5 6/8	5 6/8	10 1/8	Butte County	SD	Mike R. Erickson	1992	3,371
66 6/8	13 1/8	13 6/8	6 1/8	6 0/8	8 0/8	Saguache County	CO	Bob Rogers	1992	3,371
66 6/8	11 6/8	11 6/8	6 0/8	6 0/8	8 6/8	Natrona County	WY	Joseph A. Romeu	1992	3,371
66 6/8	11 6/8	11 6/8	6 3/8	6 2/8	6 6/8	Campbell County	WY	Gary Wobig	1992	3,371
66 6/8	13 0/8	12 4/8	5 4/8	5 4/8	8 3/8	Jeff Davis County	TX	Joe Coody	1992	3,371
66 6/8	12 6/8	11 7/8	6 0/8	6 0/8	9 4/8	Moffat County	CO	Bernard Paul	1993	3,371
66 6/8	13 7/8	13 6/8	5 3/8	5 3/8	11 3/8	Natrona County	WY	Jerry E. Burt	1993	3,371
66 6/8	11 6/8	11 5/8	6 4/8	6 0/8	7 1/8	Fremont County	WY	Norb Mullaney	1993	3,371
66 6/8	12 2/8	12 2/8	5 5/8	5 5/8	9 6/8	Butte County	SD	Guy Tillett	1993	3,371
66 6/8	12 7/8	13 0/8	5 4/8	5 3/8	9 3/8	Natrona County	WY	Suzanne E. Gay	1993	3,371
66 6/8	12 1/8	12 1/8	5 5/8	5 5/8	9 7/8	Moffat County	CO	James R. Bland	1994	3,371
66 6/8	13 1/8	13 2/8	5 5/8	5 5/8	10 3/8	Powder River County	MT	Theodore A. Adams	1994	3,371
66 6/8	12 4/8	12 3/8	5 7/8	5 7/8	10 2/8	Rosebud County	MT	Paul Bridenbaugh	1994	3,371
66 6/8	13 6/8	13 4/8	5 1/8	5 1/8	5 7/8	Converse County	WY	B. J. Higley	1994	3,371
66 6/8	12 5/8	12 4/8	5 7/8	5 6/8	10 5/8	Campbell County	WY	David Westmoreland	1994	3,371
66 6/8	12 1/8	12 3/8	5 6/8	5 6/8	8 4/8	Converse County	WY	Greg Webster	1994	3,371

PRONGHORN

Minimum Score 67 — Continued

SCORE	LENGTH OF HORN R / L		CIRCUMFERENCE OF BASE R / L		INSIDE SPREAD	AREA	STATE/ PROVINCE	HUNTER'S NAME	DATE	RANK
66 6/8	12 0/8	11 5/8	5 6/8	5 7/8	7 4/8	Sioux County	NE	Steve Leichleiter	1994	3,371
66 6/8	12 2/8	12 1/8	6 0/8	5 7/8	7 5/8	Campbell County	WY	William Joel Cotter	1994	3,371
66 6/8	12 6/8	12 3/8	5 5/8	5 4/8	11 4/8	Campbell County	WY	Tim D. Baer	1994	3,371
66 6/8	12 7/8	12 5/8	6 0/8	6 1/8	10 2/8	Washoe County	NV	Kenneth J. Wilkinson	1995	3,371
66 6/8	11 2/8	11 5/8	6 6/8	7 0/8	9 7/8	Converse County	WY	Derl Phelps	1995	3,371
66 6/8	13 2/8	13 0/8	6 1/8	6 0/8	7 6/8	Rosebud County	MT	Robert W. McCarley	1995	3,371
66 6/8	12 5/8	12 6/8	5 7/8	5 6/8	7 7/8	Meade County	SD	Mark Wonders	1995	3,371
66 6/8	13 5/8	13 2/8	5 4/8	5 2/8	11 7/8	Weld County	CO	William Sherrard	1996	3,371
66 6/8	14 2/8	14 1/8	5 2/8	5 2/8	8 0/8	Moffat County	CO	T. J. Thrasher	1996	3,371
66 6/8	13 4/8	13 2/8	5 3/8	5 5/8	9 3/8	El Paso County	CO	Victor Walth	1996	3,371
66 6/8	12 1/8	12 2/8	5 6/8	5 6/8	10 5/8	Campbell County	WY	Wade W. Clark, Jr.	1996	3,371
66 6/8	13 0/8	13 0/8	5 6/8	5 6/8	11 7/8	Campbell County	WY	Gary English	1996	3,371
66 6/8	13 2/8	13 0/8	5 4/8	5 3/8	11 3/8	Moffat County	CO	Tim Cuthriell	1996	3,371
66 6/8	13 3/8	13 1/8	6 4/8	6 1/8	9 2/8	Campbell County	WY	David Westmoreland	1996	3,371
66 6/8	13 0/8	13 1/8	5 4/8	5 4/8	8 3/8	Weston County	WY	Steven Butzke	1996	3,371
66 6/8	13 0/8	12 7/8	5 7/8	5 7/8	10 7/8	Harding County	SD	Jerome O. Guyant	1996	3,371
66 6/8	12 7/8	12 5/8	5 5/8	5 6/8	9 6/8	Socorro County	NM	Ray A. Krause	1997	3,371
66 6/8	13 0/8	13 0/8	5 6/8	5 5/8	8 3/8	Campbell County	WY	Robert "Bob" Pierson	1998	3,371
66 6/8	11 7/8	12 0/8	6 0/8	5 6/8	13 5/8	Moffat County	CO	Rick Duggan	1998	3,371
66 6/8	12 5/8	12 5/8	5 4/8	5 4/8	11 6/8	Campbell County	WY	Glenn Klingensmith, Jr.	1998	3,371
66 4/8	12 0/8	12 0/8	5 5/8	5 4/8	12 0/8	Fremont County	WY	Fred Bear	1955	3,473
66 4/8	13 6/8	13 4/8	5 4/8	5 4/8	11 2/8	Guadalupe County	NM	Paul Link	1962	3,473
66 4/8	12 6/8	12 2/8	6 0/8	6 0/8	8 2/8	Stark County	ND	Dennis A. Schneider	1965	3,473
66 4/8	13 4/8	13 7/8	5 4/8	5 4/8	6 5/8	Harding County	SD	Richard Bolyard	1974	3,473
66 4/8	11 2/8	11 6/8	7 0/8	6 5/8	12 4/8	Natrona County	WY	Bill Emery	1974	3,473
66 4/8	13 4/8	13 7/8	5 4/8	5 4/8	8 6/8	Valley County	MT	Tom Solem	1979	3,473
66 4/8	12 4/8	12 7/8	5 4/8	5 4/8	8 4/8	Dawes County	NE	Jerry Dennis	1980	3,473
66 4/8	13 0/8	13 0/8	5 6/8	5 4/8	9 0/8	Converse County	WY	Ronald J. Collier	1981	3,473
66 4/8	13 4/8	13 3/8	5 6/8	6 0/8	9 5/8	Fremont County	WY	Everett A. Boss	1981	3,473
66 4/8	13 0/8	13 0/8	5 6/8	5 5/8	7 2/8	Converse County	WY	Andy Tkach	1981	3,473
66 4/8	12 3/8	12 3/8	5 4/8	5 4/8	12 2/8	Moffat County	CO	Bill Yessa	1981	3,473
66 4/8	13 1/8	11 7/8	5 7/8	5 7/8	9 0/8	Siskiyou County	CA	Doug Walker	1982	3,473
66 4/8	12 4/8	12 7/8	5 7/8	5 6/8	10 0/8	Power County	ID	Robert Bennett	1982	3,473
66 4/8	13 6/8	14 1/8	6 2/8	6 4/8	13 3/8	Bowman County	ND	Curt Wells	1982	3,473
66 4/8	12 6/8	12 7/8	5 4/8	5 4/8	7 4/8	Moffat County	CO	Dennis J. Erkinger	1982	3,473
66 4/8	13 1/8	13 1/8	5 5/8	5 5/8	12 6/8	McCone County	MT	Dan Sturgis	1982	3,473
66 4/8	12 4/8	13 1/8	5 6/8	5 4/8	11 1/8	Moffat County	CO	Chris Cassidy	1983	3,473
66 4/8	12 3/8	12 4/8	6 1/8	5 7/8	12 4/0	Moffat County	CO	Toni R. Roberts	1983	3,473
66 4/8	13 0/8	12 6/8	5 6/8	5 6/8	8 4/8	Converse County	WY	Steve Byerly	1983	3,473
66 4/8	12 1/8	12 1/8	5 7/8	5 4/8	9 1/8	Natrona County	WY	Arthur S. Wert	1983	3,473
66 4/8	12 5/8	12 3/8	5 6/8	5 4/8	8 1/8	McKenzie County	ND	James R. Greutman	1983	3,473
66 4/8	13 0/8	12 6/8	5 7/8	5 6/8	13 1/8	Coconino County	AZ	Scott Kellner	1983	3,473
66 4/8	12 5/8	12 4/8	6 0/8	6 0/8	10 1/8	Carbon County	WY	James D. Davis	1983	3,473
66 4/8	12 5/8	12 5/8	5 7/8	5 4/8	9 2/8	Converse County	WY	Gary White	1983	3,473
66 4/8	11 7/8	12 0/8	5 5/8	5 5/8	6 5/8	Moffat County	CO	Tim Decker	1984	3,473
66 4/8	12 6/8	13 0/8	5 3/8	5 6/8	9 5/8	Carbon County	WY	Paul Kniss	1984	3,473
66 4/8	12 2/8	12 3/8	5 7/8	5 6/8	12 1/8	Campbell County	WY	Mark S. Presta	1984	3,473
66 4/8	13 1/8	13 2/8	5 3/8	5 3/8	12 2/8	Converse County	WY	Charles E Gose	1984	3,473
66 4/8	12 6/8	12 6/8	5 6/8	5 3/8	10 1/8	Johnson County	WY	Jerry Leair	1984	3,473
66 4/8	13 3/8	13 4/8	5 2/8	5 2/8	10 0/8	Moffat County	CO	Reina Kemp	1985	3,473
66 4/8	12 7/8	13 4/8	5 4/8	5 3/8	10 0/8	Tooele County	UT	Scott Anderson	1985	3,473
66 4/8	11 7/8	11 6/8	5 5/8	5 5/8	9 7/8	Musselshell County	MT	Brian Acton	1985	3,473
66 4/8	12 0/8	12 2/8	5 2/8	5 2/8	9 2/8	Yellowstone County	MT	Jim Forwood	1986	3,473
66 4/8	12 7/8	12 3/8	5 6/8	5 5/8	10 3/8	Stark County	ND	Howard Sharp	1987	3,473
66 4/8	12 7/8	12 7/8	5 6/8	5 6/8	8 0/8	Campbell County	WY	Nick Hengel	1987	3,473
66 4/8	11 3/8	12 6/8	6 0/8	5 7/8	9 4/8	Jefferson County	ID	Richard Beesley	1988	3,473
66 4/8	12 3/8	12 3/8	6 0/8	6 0/8	8 2/8	Moffat County	CO	Barry J. Smith	1988	3,473
66 4/8	13 0/8	13 1/8	5 5/8	5 6/8	8 4/8	Converse County	WY	Paul Mehnert	1988	3,473
66 4/8	11 5/8	11 4/8	5 4/8	5 3/8	10 0/8	Power County	ID	Frank W. Sparkman	1988	3,473
66 4/8	13 0/8	13 0/8	5 4/8	5 3/8	9 2/8	Garfield County	MT	Bill Helphrey	1988	3,473
66 4/8	12 7/8	12 7/8	5 4/8	5 4/8	12 1/8	Converse County	WY	Harold Osborne	1988	3,473
66 4/8	12 4/8	12 5/8	5 5/8	5 3/8	8 6/8	Natrona County	WY	Mike Kistler	1989	3,473
66 4/8	13 1/8	13 1/8	5 4/8	5 4/8	10 2/8	Manyberries	ALB	John Visscher	1989	3,473
66 4/8	12 5/8	10 6/8	6 2/8	6 1/8	10 0/8	Campbell County	WY	Larry Honeycutt	1989	3,473
66 4/8	12 2/8	12 7/8	5 5/8	5 5/8	11 1/8	Las Animas County	CO	William D. Yirka	1990	3,473
66 4/8	12 0/8	11 7/8	5 4/8	5 4/8	8 1/8	Sweetwater County	WY	Ronald E. Hergott	1990	3,473
66 4/8	13 4/8	12 0/8	6 2/8	6 0/8	11 4/8	Rosebud County	MT	Robert Bartlett	1990	3,473
66 4/8	13 6/8	13 5/8	5 2/8	5 0/8	10 3/8	Morton County	ND	Mark W. Bogert	1990	3,473
66 4/8	12 4/8	12 4/8	6 1/8	6 0/8	6 7/8	Lincoln County	WY	Mark Grace	1991	3,473
66 4/8	12 5/8	11 7/8	5 7/8	5 6/8	12 4/8	Moffat County	CO	Cecil D. Richburg	1991	3,473
66 4/8	13 6/8	13 7/8	5 0/8	5 1/8	7 6/8	Converse County	WY	Matt Curry	1991	3,473
66 4/8	13 6/8	13 7/8	5 4/8	5 3/8	7 2/8	Beaverhead County	MT	Terry Barkel	1991	3,473
66 4/8	12 3/8	12 5/8	6 4/8	6 4/8	8 4/8	Sioux County	NE	Mike Morrow	1991	3,473
66 4/8	13 0/8	13 1/8	5 4/8	5 3/8	8 6/8	Converse County	WY	Richard Peloquin	1991	3,473
66 4/8	11 6/8	11 4/8	5 3/8	5 2/8	13 2/8	Deuel County	NE	Ev Tarrell	1991	3,473
66 4/8	13 4/8	12 6/8	5 4/8	5 4/8	10 4/8	Klamath County	OR	Robert N. Titus	1992	3,473
66 4/8	12 5/8	12 5/8	5 5/8	5 4/8	8 4/8	Meade County	SD	Casey A. Weisser	1992	3,473
66 4/8	13 2/8	13 1/8	5 6/8	5 5/8	5 6/8	Uinta County	WY	Carol Ann Fitzgerald	1992	3,473

PRONGHORN

Minimum Score 67 — Continued

SCORE	LENGTH OF HORN R	L	CIRCUMFERENCE OF BASE R	L	INSIDE SPREAD	AREA	STATE/PROVINCE	HUNTER'S NAME	DATE	RANK
66 4/8	12 7/8	13 1/8	5 6/8	5 6/8	10 0/8	Maple Creek	SAS	Dwayne Onofriechuck	1992	3,473
66 4/8	13 1/8	13 1/8	5 5/8	5 4/8	13 0/8	Walsh	ALB	Norm Lacroix	1992	3,473
66 4/8	12 4/8	12 6/8	6 3/8	6 3/8	9 4/8	Carbon County	WY	Barry J. Horton	1992	3,473
66 4/8	12 3/8	12 4/8	5 6/8	5 6/8	9 2/8	Stanley County	SD	Dan Dietrich	1992	3,473
66 4/8	11 7/8	12 3/8	6 1/8	6 4/8	9 2/8	Moffat County	CO	Brad Mason	1993	3,473
66 4/8	13 6/8	13 2/8	5 4/8	5 4/8	7 2/8	Moffat County	CO	Wesley W. Hester III	1993	3,473
66 4/8	13 3/8	13 5/8	6 3/8	6 4/8	11 3/8	Larimer County	CO	Rex A. Adams	1993	3,473
66 4/8	12 3/8	12 4/8	5 6/8	5 6/8	9 6/8	Converse County	WY	Todd A. Doering	1993	3,473
66 4/8	13 0/8	12 6/8	5 4/8	5 6/8	9 1/8	Converse County	WY	B. J. Higley	1993	3,473
66 4/8	14 0/8	13 6/8	5 3/8	5 2/8	11 7/8	Campbell County	WY	Doy K. Curtis	1993	3,473
66 4/8	12 2/8	12 2/8	5 5/8	5 5/8	5 3/8	Moffat County	CO	J. Ken Martin	1994	3,473
66 4/8	13 7/8	14 3/8	5 4/8	5 1/8	12 1/8	Weld County	CO	Steve Hohensee	1994	3,473
66 4/8	12 4/8	12 6/8	6 0/8	6 2/8	6 5/8	Union County	NM	Paul W. Liberato	1994	3,473
66 4/8	11 7/8	11 7/8	5 6/8	5 6/8	8 4/8	Carbon County	WY	Gene Melby	1994	3,473
66 4/8	12 6/8	12 6/8	5 6/8	5 6/8	7 1/8	Moffat County	CO	Dave Spacek	1994	3,473
66 4/8	13 4/8	13 2/8	5 4/8	5 2/8	9 3/8	Natrona County	WY	Gary D. Wear	1994	3,473
66 4/8	12 4/8	12 4/8	5 2/8	5 2/8	10 2/8	Campbell County	WY	Ralph Prestidge	1994	3,473
66 4/8	12 4/8	12 2/8	6 1/8	6 0/8	9 3/8	Campbell County	WY	Todd Amenrud	1994	3,473
66 4/8	12 6/8	12 2/8	5 3/8	5 4/8	10 3/8	Converse County	WY	James Wotrang	1994	3,473
66 4/8	12 1/8	12 0/8	5 6/8	5 6/8	8 0/8	Campbell County	WY	Frank English	1994	3,473
66 4/8	13 7/8	13 5/8	6 1/8	6 0/8	12 2/8	Fergus County	MT	Chris G. Sanford	1994	3,473
66 4/8	13 5/8	13 3/8	5 4/8	5 5/8	10 7/8	Lincoln County	WY	Larry Hesterly	1995	3,473
66 4/8	13 0/8	12 6/8	5 4/8	5 4/8	8 6/8	Converse County	WY	Jerry Worley	1995	3,473
66 4/8	11 7/8	12 1/8	5 5/8	5 4/8	11 3/8	Billings County	ND	Corey Hugelen	1995	3,473
66 4/8	13 2/8	13 0/8	5 5/8	5 4/8	7 6/8	Converse County	WY	Stephen J. Surber	1995	3,473
66 4/8	13 3/8	13 2/8	5 6/8	5 5/8	10 5/8	Garfield County	MT	Kenneth Dale Wiers	1995	3,473
66 4/8	12 6/8	12 6/8	5 6/8	5 5/8	8 6/8	Converse County	WY	Vernon Sowers	1996	3,473
66 4/8	13 0/8	12 6/8	5 5/8	5 6/8	7 1/8	Weld County	CO	Neil Chandler	1996	3,473
66 4/8	14 4/8	14 2/8	5 0/8	5 1/8	11 5/8	Rosebud County	MT	Robert E. Ebert	1996	3,473
66 4/8	11 7/8	12 0/8	5 5/8	5 4/8	9 6/8	Campbell County	WY	Jeff Bassindale	1996	3,473
66 4/8	13 2/8	13 6/8	5 7/8	5 5/8	6 7/8	Rio Grande County	CO	Russell E. "Rusty" Hinger	1997	3,473
66 4/8	13 1/8	13 0/8	5 4/8	5 4/8	10 2/8	Lincoln County	WY	Marcel Bergeron	1997	3,473
66 4/8	13 5/8	13 6/8	5 2/8	5 3/8	10 2/8	Thomas County	NE	Gary Zimmerer	1997	3,473
66 4/8	11 5/8	11 5/8	6 1/8	6 1/8	10 7/8	Campbell County	WY	Rick East	1997	3,473
66 4/8	12 7/8	13 2/8	5 5/8	5 3/8	8 3/8	Campbell County	WY	Bruce Hudalla	1997	3,473
66 4/8	12 7/8	12 7/8	5 6/8	5 4/8	10 4/8	Converse County	WY	Craig Holcomb	1997	3,473
66 4/8	13 3/8	13 2/8	5 4/8	5 4/8	11 4/8	Golden Valley County	ND	Jon P. Smythe	1997	3,473
66 4/8	12 6/8	13 0/8	5 5/8	5 5/8	7 4/8	Musselshell County	MT	Steven B. Schroeder	1997	3,473
66 4/8	13 6/8	13 5/8	5 4/8	5 5/8	14 3/8	Broadwater County	MT	Jim Winjum	1997	3,473
66 4/8	12 4/8	12 1/8	5 7/8	5 6/8	11 6/8	Moffat County	CO	Larry Lucero	1998	3,473
66 4/8	13 3/8	13 1/8	5 5/8	5 6/8	8 7/8	Converse County	WY	Gary Rodocker	1998	3,473
66 4/8	12 2/8	12 4/8	5 4/8	5 5/8	7 3/8	Campbell County	WY	Shirley Allen	1998	3,473
66 2/8	12 7/8	13 0/8	5 3/8	5 3/8	8 7/8	McLean County	ND	Robert Freeberg	1967	3,573
66 2/8	12 5/8	12 6/8	5 5/8	5 4/8	9 2/8	Carbon County	WY	Steve Gorr	1971	3,573
66 2/8	12 1/8	12 1/8	6 3/8	6 4/8	11 5/8	Converse County	WY	Denny Behn	1979	3,573
66 2/8	13 3/8	13 2/8	5 6/8	5 4/8	11 1/8	Natrona County	WY	Don Schram	1980	3,573
66 2/8	11 4/8	11 4/8	5 6/8	5 6/8	8 3/8	Natrona County	WY	Billy Ellis	1981	3,573
66 2/8	12 4/8	12 5/8	5 7/8	5 5/8	9 0/8	Campbell County	WY	William F. Heineke	1981	3,573
66 2/8	13 0/8	12 7/8	5 5/8	5 4/8	8 7/8	Campbell County	WY	Pat Mitchell	1981	3,573
66 2/8	12 5/8	12 4/8	5 5/8	5 5/8	10 1/8	Lincoln County	WY	Lonnie Smith	1981	3,573
66 2/8	11 6/8	12 1/8	5 7/8	5 6/8	8 4/8	Moffat County	CO	Earl Stout	1981	3,573
66 2/8	11 7/8	12 0/8	5 5/8	5 5/8	10 7/8	Moffat County	CO	Warren P. Uhl	1981	3,573
66 2/8	11 4/8	11 4/8	6 7/8	6 6/8	7 7/8	Converse County	WY	Albert R. Taylor	1982	3,573
66 2/8	12 4/8	12 4/8	5 7/8	6 0/8	9 2/8	Bowman County	ND	Dean Albertson	1982	3,573
66 2/8	11 3/8	11 4/8	5 6/8	5 6/8	8 4/8	Converse County	WY	David Hell	1982	3,573
66 2/8	13 1/8	12 7/8	5 5/8	5 4/8	9 7/8	Meagher County	MT	D. Mitch Kottas	1982	3,573
66 2/8	12 6/8	13 1/8	5 5/8	5 6/8	9 1/8	Lemhi County	ID	Richard C. Nichols	1982	3,573
66 2/8	10 7/8	11 0/8	6 3/8	6 2/8	8 6/8	Moffat County	CO	Ray Ryan	1983	3,573
66 2/8	13 6/8	13 4/8	5 5/8	5 5/8	8 1/8	Weston County	WY	Pat Graham	1983	3,573
66 2/8	12 6/8	12 4/8	5 5/8	5 3/8	10 0/8	Converse County	WY	Michael Arneson	1983	3,573
66 2/8	12 6/8	12 7/8	5 4/8	5 2/8	13 5/8	Converse County	WY	Melvin R. Wells	1983	3,573
66 2/8	12 3/8	12 3/8	5 4/8	5 4/8	8 5/8	Campbell County	WY	Joseph Strasser, Jr.	1984	3,573
66 2/8	12 3/8	13 0/8	5 4/8	5 4/8	8 3/8	Crook County	WY	Terry Walton	1984	3,573
66 2/8	13 3/8	13 3/8	5 4/8	5 4/8	10 2/8	Washoe County	NV	Ralph L Albright	1985	3,573
66 2/8	13 0/8	12 4/8	5 5/8	5 5/8	11 5/8	Fremont County	WY	David Dickson	1985	3,573
66 2/8	13 0/8	13 0/8	5 5/8	5 6/8	9 3/8	Moffat County	CO	Randy Lamdin	1986	3,573
66 2/8	12 0/8	12 1/8	5 5/8	5 5/8	9 7/8	Converse County	WY	John Rook	1986	3,573
66 2/8	12 4/8	12 6/8	5 6/8	5 6/8	11 0/8	Box Elder County	UT	Bob Richardson	1986	3,573
66 2/8	12 3/8	11 6/8	6 0/8	5 6/8	10 2/8	Valley County	MT	Gerald Polesky	1986	3,573
66 2/8	12 6/8	13 4/8	5 6/8	5 5/8	10 3/8	Grand Forks	ALB	Paul Deme	1986	3,573
66 2/8	14 0/8	14 4/8	5 3/8	5 4/8	11 0/8	Converse County	WY	Roger L. Hensley	1987	3,573
66 2/8	12 4/8	12 3/8	5 6/8	5 4/8	9 4/8	Converse County	WY	Gary Lee Gregg	1987	3,573
66 2/8	13 4/8	13 4/8	5 4/8	5 3/8	9 6/8	Converse County	WY	Michael Murphy	1987	3,573
66 2/8	12 5/8	12 6/8	5 5/8	5 5/8	8 7/8	Albany County	WY	James Rapp	1988	3,573
66 2/8	12 2/8	12 0/8	5 6/8	5 5/8	8 4/8	Moffat County	CO	Michael L. Callaway	1988	3,573
66 2/8	12 5/8	13 3/8	5 5/8	5 4/8	11 4/8	Daggett County	UT	Steve Dailey	1988	3,573
66 2/8	14 1/8	14 1/8	4 7/8	5 0/8	8 2/8	Humboldt County	NV	Mike Williams	1989	3,573
66 2/8	11 7/8	12 0/8	6 2/8	6 2/8	8 5/8	Converse County	WY	James W. Casto, Jr.	1989	3,573

PRONGHORN

SCORE	LENGTH OF HORN R	L	CIRCUMFERENCE OF BASE R	L	INSIDE SPREAD	AREA	STATE/PROVINCE	HUNTER'S NAME	DATE	RANK
66 2/8	14 1/8	13 5/8	5 4/8	5 4/8	10 7/8	Rosebud County	MT	Keith D. Kemkes	1989	3,573
66 2/8	12 2/8	12 4/8	5 1/8	5 1/8	10 1/8	Converse County	WY	James Bragg	1989	3,573
66 2/8	12 6/8	12 6/8	5 1/8	5 1/8	4 6/8	Converse County	WY	Jack Dellger	1989	3,573
66 2/8	13 3/8	13 2/8	5 6/8	5 5/8	10 2/8	Sweetwater County	WY	Donald R. Williamson	1989	3,573
66 2/8	13 0/8	13 4/8	5 3/8	5 2/8	6 1/8	Sweetwater County	WY	Steve Brockmann	1990	3,573
66 2/8	12 5/8	13 1/8	5 7/8	5 6/8	9 3/8	Custer County	ID	Doug Burkman	1990	3,573
66 2/8	13 4/8	13 5/8	5 0/8	5 1/8	10 4/8	Harney County	OR	Don R. Davidson	1990	3,573
66 2/8	12 2/8	12 2/8	5 4/8	5 4/8	9 3/8	Weston County	WY	James P. Landwehr	1990	3,573
66 2/8	13 0/8	13 1/8	5 4/8	5 4/8	7 1/8	Powder River County	MT	John McCarthy	1990	3,573
66 2/8	13 1/8	13 3/8	5 7/8	5 6/8	8 6/8	Moffat County	CO	Blake Hortenstine	1991	3,573
66 2/8	12 7/8	12 4/8	5 2/8	5 3/8	9 0/8	Uintah County	UT	F. Jeffrey Peterson	1991	3,573
66 2/8	12 0/8	12 2/8	5 2/8	5 2/8	7 7/8	Converse County	WY	Russell A. Nichols	1991	3,573
66 2/8	14 5/8	14 5/8	5 2/8	5 1/8	8 3/8	Converse County	WY	James Saunoris	1991	3,573
66 2/8	13 0/8	13 0/8	5 6/8	5 7/8	12 5/8	Converse County	WY	Jerome D. Larson	1991	3,573
66 2/8	13 0/8	12 6/8	5 6/8	5 6/8	10 4/8	Petroleum County	MT	Debbie Jenner	1991	3,573
66 2/8	11 6/8	12 0/8	6 1/8	6 4/8	11 7/8	Rosebud County	MT	Mark A. Schwartznau	1991	3,573
66 2/8	12 4/8	12 1/8	5 5/8	5 5/8	9 3/8	Converse County	WY	Russ Tye	1991	3,573
66 2/8	13 5/8	13 4/8	5 6/8	5 5/8	9 6/8	Sioux County	NE	Orville J. DeVoss	1991	3,573
66 2/8	12 6/8	12 7/8	6 0/8	6 1/8	11 2/8	Powder River County	MT	Edwin John Durushia	1991	3,573
66 2/8	12 2/8	12 2/8	5 5/8	5 5/8	8 5/8	Moffat County	CO	Betty Gulman	1992	3,573
66 2/8	12 5/8	12 5/8	5 2/8	5 2/8	8 7/8	Moffat County	CO	Joe Prueher	1992	3,573
66 2/8	12 3/8	12 5/8	6 1/8	6 0/8	9 3/8	Crook County	WY	Dean A. Ransbottom	1992	3,573
66 2/8	11 7/8	11 7/8	6 0/8	6 2/8	11 0/8	Natrona County	WY	R. L. Erdmann	1992	3,573
66 2/8	12 3/8	12 0/8	5 7/8	5 7/8	9 5/8	Campbell County	WY	Janet J. Wilk	1992	3,573
66 2/8	13 2/8	13 1/8	5 5/8	5 3/8	9 2/8	Natrona County	WY	Robert Stone	1992	3,573
66 2/8	13 7/8	12 5/8	5 7/8	5 6/8	11 0/8	Sioux County	NE	Andrew Bjorson	1992	3,573
66 2/8	12 0/8	12 0/8	6 0/8	6 0/8	9 0/8	Klamath County	OR	Bryan Martin	1993	3,573
66 2/8	12 6/8	12 7/8	5 7/8	5 6/8	12 4/8	Rosebud County	MT	Chris Appert	1993	3,573
66 2/8	12 5/8	12 5/8	5 4/8	5 3/8	10 1/8	Rosebud County	MT	Michael J. Kemp	1993	3,573
66 2/8	13 4/8	13 7/8	6 0/8	5 7/8	9 4/8	Rosebud County	MT	Bill Lilly	1993	3,573
66 2/8	12 0/8	12 0/8	5 7/8	5 7/8	12 2/8	Moffat County	CO	David M. Richards	1994	3,573
66 2/8	13 4/8	13 2/8	5 4/8	5 4/8	9 7/8	Mora County	NM	Louis Gallegos	1994	3,573
66 2/8	12 6/8	12 1/8	5 6/8	5 5/8	12 7/8	Catron County	NM	John Shaffer, Jr.	1994	3,573
66 2/8	12 2/8	13 5/8	5 4/8	5 4/8	13 5/8	Converse County	WY	Robert G. Fulton	1994	3,573
66 2/8	12 1/8	12 0/8	5 5/8	5 5/8	11 7/8	Converse County	WY	William Moore	1994	3,573
66 2/8	13 6/8	13 6/8	5 4/8	5 3/8	11 3/8	Harding County	SD	Bill Bushong	1994	3,573
66 2/8	13 3/8	13 1/8	5 5/8	5 4/8	10 4/8	Harding County	SD	Tony Waltner	1994	3,573
66 2/8	14 2/8	14 1/8	5 1/8	5 2/8	11 1/8	Bowman County	ND	Gene Davis	1994	3,573
66 2/8	13 2/8	13 2/8	6 3/8	6 1/8	8 5/8	Harding County	SD	Lonnie Tschumper	1994	3,573
66 2/8	11 6/8	11 6/8	5 7/8	5 7/8	12 1/8	Campbell County	WY	K. Edward Atwood	1994	3,573
66 2/8	12 1/8	12 1/8	5 4/8	5 6/8	10 4/8	Campbell County	WY	Thomas L. Oldfather	1994	3,573
66 2/8	13 2/8	13 3/8	5 5/8	5 5/8	8 7/8	Owyhee County	ID	John F. Burke	1995	3,573
66 2/8	12 4/8	12 4/8	5 4/8	5 5/8	8 2/8	Converse County	WY	Roger Little	1995	3,573
66 2/8	12 3/8	12 3/8	5 5/8	5 4/8	8 1/8	Moffat County	CO	Ken Shelton	1995	3,573
66 2/8	13 5/8	14 0/8	5 6/8	5 5/8	8 2/8	Converse County	WY	David A. Swain	1995	3,573
66 2/8	12 6/8	12 5/8	5 4/8	5 4/8	8 7/8	Converse County	WY	Brad Kohlhof	1995	3,573
66 2/8	12 6/8	12 5/8	5 7/8	6 0/8	9 1/8	Campbell County	WY	Tim Burres	1995	3,573
66 2/8	12 6/8	13 1/8	5 5/8	5 5/8	11 1/8	Slope County	ND	Tom Griffin	1995	3,573
66 2/8	13 3/8	13 4/8	5 4/8	5 3/8	11 3/8	Juab County	UT	Craig P. Mitton	1996	3,573
66 2/8	13 2/8	13 4/8	5 4/8	5 4/8	12 1/8	Uintah County	UT	Patricia F. Joyner	1996	3,573
66 2/8	13 0/8	12 4/8	6 3/8	6 1/8	8 4/8	Sweetwater County	WY	George Fabian	1996	3,573
66 2/8	12 2/8	12 6/8	5 7/8	5 5/8	8 0/8	Natrona County	WY	Alan M. McGraw	1996	3,573
66 2/8	12 3/8	12 3/8	6 1/8	6 1/8	7 3/8	Campbell County	WY	Clinton Fox	1996	3,573
66 2/8	12 3/8	12 6/8	5 4/8	5 4/8	12 6/8	Converse County	WY	Joe Cronin	1996	3,573
66 2/8	12 7/8	13 0/8	5 4/8	5 4/8	7 6/8	Campbell County	WY	Todd Amenrud	1996	3,573
66 2/8	12 4/8	12 1/8	5 5/8	5 4/8	9 6/8	Converse County	WY	J. Thomas Edman	1996	3,573
66 2/8	12 1/8	11 7/8	5 6/8	5 6/8	8 5/8	Campbell County	WY	Blair Kleeberger	1996	3,573
66 2/8	13 0/8	13 0/8	5 5/8	5 5/8	7 5/8	Converse County	WY	Ronald A. Worden	1996	3,573
66 2/8	12 6/8	12 6/8	5 4/8	5 4/8	7 6/8	Converse County	WY	Gerald Gwaltney	1996	3,573
66 2/8	13 1/8	13 1/8	5 6/8	5 6/8	15 4/8	Converse County	WY	Bill Uleano	1996	3,573
66 2/8	13 2/8	13 1/8	5 3/8	5 2/8	9 4/8	Beaverhead County	MT	Steve Rigby	1996	3,573
66 2/8	11 5/8	13 4/8	6 1/8	5 6/8	7 3/8	Moffat County	CO	Roy E. Pepple	1997	3,573
66 2/8	13 0/8	12 5/8	5 4/8	5 4/8	12 0/8	Moffat County	CO	William T. Bos	1997	3,573
66 2/8	12 7/8	12 2/8	5 7/8	6 1/8	6 2/8	Converse County	WY	Timothy L. Ross	1997	3,573
66 2/8	12 2/8	12 1/8	5 4/8	5 6/8	10 4/8	Natrona County	WY	Keith Mark	1997	3,573
66 2/8	12 2/8	14 0/8	6 0/8	5 7/8	11 4/8	Fergus County	MT	D. Mitch Kottas	1997	3,573
66 2/8	12 0/8	12 6/8	6 3/8	6 2/8	8 3/8	Jackson County	CO	Donny Snell	1998	3,573
66 2/8	12 0/8	11 6/8	6 1/8	6 1/8	10 5/8	Johnson County	WY	Kenneth A. Gher	1998	3,573
66 0/8	12 0/8	12 0/8	5 5/8	5 4/8	11 1/8	Rock County	NE	Mac Forbes	1967	3,677
66 0/8	10 6/8	10 4/8	5 6/8	5 7/8	11 3/8	Pennington County	SD	Dean Nevland	1970	3,677
66 0/8	13 4/8	13 6/8	5 0/8	5 0/8	13 7/8	Haakon County	SD	Ward McCaughey	1971	3,677
66 0/8	12 5/8	12 5/8	6 1/8	5 6/8	8 2/8	Sublette County	WY	Frank D. Prentup	1976	3,677
66 0/8	12 7/8	12 7/8	5 2/8	5 2/8	9 0/8	Stewart Valley	SAS	Daniel N. Rayner	1976	3,677
66 0/8	12 6/8	12 6/8	6 0/8	6 1/8	11 6/8	Mountrail County	ND	Wade F. Williamson	1976	3,677
66 0/8	14 4/8	14 3/8	5 5/8	5 3/8	7 6/8	Butte County	ID	Richard B. Harvey	1978	3,677
66 0/8	13 0/8	12 4/8	5 7/8	5 6/8	8 3/8	Converse County	WY	Pat Walker	1978	3,677
66 0/8	12 0/8	11 7/8	6 1/8	5 7/8	8 5/8	Natrona County	WY	Daniel Carlson	1980	3,677
66 0/8	10 6/8	11 0/8	5 5/8	5 6/8	7 1/8	Stanley County	SD	Brian Fox	1980	3,677

PRONGHORN

Minimum Score 67 — Continued

SCORE	LENGTH OF HORN R	L	CIRCUMFERENCE OF BASE R	L	INSIDE SPREAD	AREA	STATE/PROVINCE	HUNTER'S NAME	DATE	RANK
66 0/8	11 4/8	12 0/8	5 7/8	5 7/8	8 4/8	Moffat County	CO	William T. Shoemaker	1980	3,677
66 0/8	13 0/8	13 2/8	5 3/8	5 3/8	11 6/8	Johnson County	WY	Denny Ennis	1981	3,677
66 0/8	11 4/8	11 4/8	5 5/8	5 4/8	7 4/8	Converse County	WY	Ronald Grzybowski	1981	3,677
66 0/8	13 0/8	13 3/8	5 2/8	5 1/8	9 5/8	Natrona County	WY	Dan Kolb	1981	3,677
66 0/8	11 0/8	10 2/8	5 4/8	5 3/8	7 7/8	Moffat County	CO	Gail Martin	1981	3,677
66 0/8	12 3/8	12 2/8	6 0/8	6 2/8	8 7/8	Lassen County	CA	Ronald R. Mayfield	1981	3,677
66 0/8	12 4/8	11 5/8	5 4/8	5 3/8	8 7/8	Weld County	CO	Mike Nobe	1982	3,677
66 0/8	13 1/8	13 1/8	5 4/8	5 3/8	11 1/8	Lemhi County	ID	Ben Fahnholz	1983	3,677
66 0/8	13 4/8	13 5/8	5 7/8	5 6/8	12 2/8	Carbon County	WY	Jim Hodson	1983	3,677
66 0/8	13 0/8	13 1/8	5 0/8	5 0/8	9 4/8	Moffat County	CO	Jerry Lotspeich	1983	3,677
66 0/8	13 2/8	12 4/8	5 5/8	5 5/8	10 3/8	Converse County	WY	David S. Bunce	1983	3,677
66 0/8	12 7/8	12 5/8	5 5/8	5 4/8	6 6/8	Converse County	WY	Roger Wintle	1983	3,677
66 0/8	13 1/8	13 2/8	5 2/8	5 4/8	11 2/8	Converse County	WY	David Baldwin	1983	3,677
66 0/8	11 5/8	11 6/8	6 0/8	6 0/8	11 1/8	Converse County	WY	Reggie Spiegelberg	1983	3,677
66 0/8	12 5/8	12 5/8	5 2/8	5 6/8	11 2/8	Converse County	WY	Jon Thomas	1983	3,677
66 0/8	12 5/8	13 0/8	5 4/8	5 4/8	7 0/8	Washoe County	NV	Randall T. Harris	1984	3,677
66 0/8	11 6/8	11 0/8	6 0/8	5 7/8	9 1/8	Converse County	WY	Jeff Wagstaff	1984	3,677
66 0/8	13 5/8	13 4/8	5 2/8	5 1/8	11 6/8	Carbon County	WY	Kirk Westervelt	1985	3,677
66 0/8	12 5/8	12 6/8	5 2/8	5 3/8	9 6/8	Garfield County	MT	T. Anthony Brock	1985	3,677
66 0/8	13 2/8	13 4/8	5 2/8	5 0/8	10 4/8	Perkins County	SD	Michael P. Brust	1985	3,677
66 0/8	13 0/8	13 0/8	6 0/8	6 0/8	10 3/8	Crook County	WY	Pink Atkins	1985	3,677
66 0/8	12 3/8	12 4/8	5 2/8	5 2/8	9 4/8	Slope County	ND	Tim Belland	1985	3,677
66 0/8	12 4/8	12 4/8	5 7/8	5 6/8	10 2/8	Sweetwater County	WY	Harv Dalton	1986	3,677
66 0/8	13 4/8	13 4/8	5 3/8	5 2/8	10 2/8	Converse County	WY	Larry Hesterly	1986	3,677
66 0/8	12 6/8	12 6/8	5 7/8	5 7/8	6 1/8	Moffat County	CO	John Lupi	1987	3,677
66 0/8	12 0/8	12 0/8	5 7/8	5 7/8	9 2/8	Moffat County	CO	Bob Rennels	1987	3,677
66 0/8	13 2/8	13 2/8	5 2/8	5 2/8	10 1/8	Carbon County	WY	Kirk Westervelt	1987	3,677
66 0/8	12 1/8	12 2/8	5 6/8	5 5/8	13 0/8	Moffat County	CO	Pat Grogan	1987	3,677
66 0/8	12 6/8	12 2/8	5 4/8	5 4/8	11 3/8	Custer County	ID	Paul A. Dupuis	1987	3,677
66 0/8	11 6/8	12 1/8	6 0/8	5 7/8	8 7/8	Moffat County	CO	Randy Lamdin	1987	3,677
66 0/8	13 2/8	13 4/8	5 1/8	5 1/8	8 2/8	Clark County	ID	Max Lewis	1988	3,677
66 0/8	12 5/8	12 5/8	5 4/8	5 3/8	8 7/8	Sweetwater County	WY	Scott Sanders	1988	3,677
66 0/8	13 1/8	13 1/8	5 5/8	5 6/8	8 3/8	Washoe County	NV	Dr. Lawrence L. Heward	1988	3,677
66 0/8	13 2/8	13 1/8	5 0/8	5 2/8	5 4/8	Converse County	WY	Harold M. Burton	1988	3,677
66 0/8	12 2/8	12 2/8	5 4/8	5 4/8	7 4/8	Converse County	WY	Donald L. Nelson	1988	3,677
66 0/8	10 3/8	15 0/8	7 4/8	7 0/8	14 0/8	Rosebud County	MT	Gail Martin	1988	3,677
66 0/8	12 3/8	12 2/8	5 6/8	5 6/8	11 0/8	Sweetwater County	WY	Craig Boheler	1989	3,677
66 0/8	12 0/8	12 2/8	6 3/8	6 3/8	9 4/8	McKenzie County	ND	Don G. Scofield	1989	3,677
66 0/8	12 7/8	13 4/8	5 4/8	5 4/8	11 5/8	Bowman County	ND	Kendell Bauer	1989	3,677
66 0/8	11 0/8	11 5/8	6 1/8	6 0/8	10 7/8	Converse County	WY	Richard Gustafson	1989	3,677
66 0/8	11 5/8	11 5/8	5 7/8	5 7/8	7 2/8	Blaine County	ID	Brian Hunter Heck	1990	3,677
66 0/8	14 2/8	13 2/8	5 6/8	5 5/8	7 1/8	Carbon County	WY	Jim Finn	1990	3,677
66 0/8	12 5/8	12 4/8	5 5/8	5 4/8	10 6/8	Moffat County	CO	Joe Vincent	1990	3,677
66 0/8	13 3/8	13 0/8	5 6/8	5 6/8	7 0/8	Custer County	SD	Craig Fuhrmann	1990	3,677
66 0/8	12 2/8	12 6/8	5 3/8	5 3/8	9 4/8	Weston County	WY	Greg Seymour	1990	3,677
66 0/8	13 2/8	13 2/8	5 4/8	5 3/8	11 0/8	Campbell County	WY	Richard F. Nelson	1991	3,677
66 0/8	12 7/8	12 7/8	5 7/8	5 6/8	12 1/8	Harding County	SD	Chad Barth	1991	3,677
66 0/8	13 2/8	13 2/8	5 7/8	5 5/8	10 5/8	Weston County	WY	Mark R. Batterson	1991	3,677
66 0/8	11 4/8	11 3/8	5 6/8	5 6/8	9 6/8	Converse County	WY	John E. Wencley	1991	3,677
66 0/8	13 7/8	14 0/8	5 6/8	5 5/8	10 6/8	Rich County	UT	Carol B. Hogle	1992	3,677
66 0/8	13 6/8	13 3/8	6 0/8	6 2/8	9 2/8	Custer County	ID	Matt March	1992	3,677
66 0/8	12 3/8	12 5/8	5 5/8	5 4/8	10 1/8	Converse County	WY	Ronald Mifflin	1992	3,677
66 0/8	13 0/8	12 3/8	5 4/8	5 4/8	9 2/8	Converse County	WY	Kevin Ball	1992	3,677
66 0/8	13 0/8	12 1/8	6 0/8	6 0/8	11 4/8	Moffat County	CO	Brian Karsten	1993	3,677
66 0/8	12 1/8	12 1/8	5 7/8	5 6/8	8 3/8	Natrona County	WY	Elmer R. Luce, Jr.	1993	3,677
66 0/8	12 4/8	12 5/8	6 0/8	6 0/8	8 5/8	Campbell County	WY	John Haspel	1993	3,677
66 0/8	13 1/8	13 0/8	5 4/8	5 3/8	10 4/8	Campbell County	WY	Robert Bettenhausen	1994	3,677
66 0/8	13 3/8	13 4/8	5 5/8	5 4/8	10 2/8	Converse County	WY	Jerry M. Gmeiner	1994	3,677
66 0/8	12 6/8	13 0/8	6 0/8	6 0/8	10 7/8	Harding County	SD	Terry Kuhnert	1994	3,677
66 0/8	12 2/8	12 1/8	6 0/8	6 0/8	13 3/8	Meagher County	MT	John D. Wells	1994	3,677
66 0/8	12 2/8	12 2/8	5 5/8	5 6/8	11 3/8	Millard County	UT	Don R. Gifford	1995	3,677
66 0/8	12 4/8	12 2/8	5 5/8	5 4/8	8 0/8	Clark County	ID	Mark J. Sherick	1995	3,677
66 0/8	13 1/8	13 1/8	5 5/8	5 5/8	9 4/8	Sioux County	NE	Neil Chandler	1995	3,677
66 0/8	12 4/8	12 3/8	5 5/8	5 5/8	7 4/8	Eagle Butte	ALB	David R. Coupland	1995	3,677
66 0/8	12 4/8	12 6/8	5 3/8	5 3/8	12 2/8	Manyberries	ALB	Michael R. Deschamps	1995	3,677
66 0/8	13 7/8	13 4/8	5 6/8	5 5/8	12 0/8	Perkins County	SD	Jeff Holmin	1995	3,677
66 0/8	11 2/8	11 2/8	5 5/8	5 5/8	10 2/8	Converse County	WY	Anthony R. Eck	1995	3,677
66 0/8	12 7/8	12 5/8	5 2/8	5 2/8	10 7/8	Elko County	NV	Ben French	1996	3,677
66 0/8	12 1/8	12 0/8	5 7/8	5 7/8	9 0/8	Moffat County	CO	Dallas Smith	1996	3,677
66 0/8	11 4/8	11 5/8	5 6/8	5 6/8	9 7/8	Moffat County	CO	Ted N. McMillion	1996	3,677
66 0/8	12 6/8	12 6/8	5 4/8	5 4/8	9 4/8	Moffat County	CO	Robert M. Benton	1996	3,677
66 0/8	13 1/8	13 2/8	5 5/8	5 5/8	10 7/8	Rosebud County	MT	Don Conrad	1996	3,677
66 0/8	12 7/8	12 7/8	5 6/8	5 6/8	12 5/8	Converse County	WY	Carmen Cucuzza	1996	3,677
66 0/8	12 6/8	12 4/8	5 6/8	5 4/8	12 1/8	Natrona County	WY	Doug Meyer	1996	3,677
66 0/8	11 5/8	11 6/8	6 0/8	6 0/8	11 0/8	Moffat County	CO	Brian Laleme	1997	3,677
66 0/8	12 2/8	12 4/8	5 2/8	5 0/8	10 5/8	Converse County	WY	Bernard F. Balon	1997	3,677
66 0/8	12 7/8	12 0/8	5 4/8	5 4/8	9 0/8	Hutchinson County	TX	Brandon Ray	1997	3,677
66 0/8	13 6/8	12 6/8	5 6/8	5 6/8	8 7/8	Weld County	CO	Thomas E. Rothrock	1998	3,677

PRONGHORN

Minimum Score 67 — Continued

SCORE	LENGTH OF HORN R	L	CIRCUMFERENCE OF BASE R	L	INSIDE SPREAD	AREA	STATE/PROVINCE	HUNTER'S NAME	DATE	RANK
66 0/8	13 4/8	13 2/8	5 1/8	5 1/8	7 2/8	Wayne County	UT	Bryant Buttars	1998	3,677
66 0/8	14 3/8	14 2/8	5 3/8	5 4/8	10 3/8	Moffat County	CO	Jack L. "Jackson" Ward	1998	3,677
66 0/8	12 6/8	12 3/8	5 5/8	5 5/8	7 4/8	Converse County	WY	Theodore Guinn	1998	3,677
66 0/8	13 2/8	13 5/8	5 3/8	5 4/8	8 2/8	Campbell County	WY	Angela K. Walk	1998	3,677
66 0/8	13 0/8	12 4/8	5 4/8	5 4/8	9 4/8	Garfield County	MT	Sonny Templeton	1998	3,677
66 0/8	12 1/8	12 2/8	5 5/8	5 6/8	9 2/8	McKenzie County	ND	Mike Pavek	1998	3,677
65 6/8	13 2/8	13 5/8	5 1/8	5 1/8	10 6/8	Lincoln County	NM	Frank W. Evans	1960	3,771
65 6/8	13 0/8	13 0/8	5 4/8	5 3/8	6 7/8	Rock County	NE	Del Austin	1964	3,771
65 6/8	13 1/8	13 1/8	6 1/8	5 5/8	11 2/8	Campbell County	WY	Russell Wright	1966	3,771
65 6/8	12 5/8	12 2/8	5 6/8	5 7/8	11 0/8	Perkins County	SD	Gerald Bentson	1968	3,771
65 6/8	11 4/8	11 7/8	5 3/8	5 4/8	9 2/8	McCone County	MT	Charles M. Carlson	1970	3,771
65 6/8	11 7/8	12 2/8	6 0/8	5 7/8	12 6/8	Natrona County	WY	Greg L. Pope	1979	3,771
65 6/8	12 4/8	12 3/8	5 6/8	5 6/8	10 1/8	Carter County	MT	John Fleharty	1981	3,771
65 6/8	12 2/8	12 6/8	5 7/8	5 6/8	4 7/8	Yavapai County	AZ	Oscar Dale Porter	1981	3,771
65 6/8	12 1/8	12 0/8	6 1/8	6 0/8	8 3/8	Weld County	CO	Larry Gann	1981	3,771
65 6/8	13 5/8	13 1/8	5 2/8	5 3/8	15 1/8	Converse County	WY	Michael Smith	1981	3,771
65 6/8	11 6/8	11 6/8	8 2/8	8 2/8	10 7/8	Moffat County	CO	Ray Ryan	1982	3,771
65 6/8	13 4/8	13 2/8	5 5/8	5 4/8	8 5/8	Campbell County	WY	Robert Erickson	1982	3,771
65 6/8	12 4/8	12 4/8	5 4/8	5 4/8	11 4/8	Converse County	WY	Steven A. Janik	1982	3,771
65 6/8	12 6/8	12 6/8	5 4/8	5 4/8	12 1/8	Clark County	ID	Ron Stacey	1982	3,771
65 6/8	12 6/8	12 4/8	5 6/8	5 7/8	8 6/8	Johnson County	WY	James Kaszynski	1982	3,771
65 6/8	13 0/8	12 6/8	5 7/8	6 0/8	11 7/8	Converse County	WY	Steve Miller	1982	3,771
65 6/8	13 2/8	13 1/8	5 2/8	5 1/8	7 2/8	Converse County	WY	Larry Noland	1982	3,771
65 6/8	13 7/8	14 0/8	5 2/8	5 2/8	11 4/8	Sweetwater County	WY	Matt March, Jr.	1983	3,771
65 6/8	13 2/8	12 7/8	5 4/8	5 2/8	8 0/8	Lemhi County	ID	Larry Cross	1983	3,771
65 6/8	12 6/8	13 0/8	5 2/8	5 5/8	7 2/8	Carbon County	WY	Mike Schuchard	1983	3,771
65 6/8	14 6/8	14 4/8	5 1/8	5 1/8	9 7/8	Natrona County	WY	William W. Onken	1983	3,771
65 6/8	12 3/8	12 3/8	5 2/8	5 1/8	7 0/8	Campbell County	WY	Jeff Deline	1983	3,771
65 6/8	12 5/8	12 3/8	5 1/8	5 2/8	9 7/8	Converse County	WY	Robert M. Sweisthal, Jr.	1983	3,771
65 6/8	11 6/8	12 2/8	5 4/8	5 4/8	9 0/8	Converse County	WY	Joe Trinceri	1983	3,771
65 6/8	11 7/8	11 7/8	5 5/8	5 6/8	10 4/8	Sioux County	NE	Kevin Langan	1983	3,771
65 6/8	12 1/8	12 1/8	5 5/8	5 5/8	10 3/8	Moffat County	CO	Stephen Mikkelsen	1984	3,771
65 6/8	12 5/8	12 5/8	5 3/8	5 2/8	6 7/8	Converse County	WY	R. Tim Reed	1984	3,771
65 6/8	12 5/8	12 2/8	5 6/8	5 3/8	8 0/8	Weston County	WY	Gary D. Johansen	1984	3,771
65 6/8	13 2/8	13 2/8	5 2/8	5 2/8	10 4/8	Converse County	WY	Gene A. Welle	1984	3,771
65 6/8	12 2/8	13 3/8	5 7/8	5 7/8	6 7/8	Moffat County	CO	Gary Spangenberg	1985	3,771
65 6/8	12 2/8	12 0/8	5 5/8	5 4/8	8 7/8	Natrona County	WY	Kurt Keskimaki	1985	3,771
65 6/8	13 2/8	13 3/8	5 2/8	5 2/8	9 5/8	Pinal County	AZ	Marte Scheuffele	1985	3,771
65 6/8	11 3/8	11 3/8	6 0/8	6 0/8	8 6/8	Converse County	WY	Dick Gambrel	1985	3,771
65 6/8	12 2/8	12 4/8	5 5/8	5 5/8	10 0/8	Converse County	WY	Mark Folk	1985	3,771
65 6/8	12 4/8	13 0/8	5 4/8	5 4/8	8 3/8	Campbell County	WY	Tony Snow	1985	3,771
65 6/8	11 5/8	11 6/8	5 6/8	5 6/8	7 0/8	Yuma County	CO	Larry Bishop	1986	3,771
65 6/8	13 2/8	13 6/8	5 2/8	5 2/8	9 1/8	Mercer County	ND	Howell J. Flowers	1986	3,771
65 6/8	12 6/8	12 5/8	5 4/8	5 5/8	8 5/8	Carbon County	WY	Larry Hayes	1986	3,771
65 6/8	13 2/8	13 0/8	4 6/8	4 7/8	11 4/8	Presidio County	TX	Kenny N. Heath	1986	3,771
65 6/8	13 0/8	13 3/8	5 4/8	5 2/8	7 3/8	Moffat County	CO	Douglas Burton	1987	3,771
65 6/8	12 4/8	12 4/8	5 6/8	5 6/8	9 2/8	Moffat County	CO	Ed Vallee	1987	3,771
65 6/8	14 2/8	13 4/8	5 2/8	5 3/8	11 4/8	Campbell County	WY	Jim Keim	1987	3,771
65 6/8	13 5/8	13 2/8	5 6/8	5 6/8	6 7/8	Sweetwater County	WY	Christopher J. Cordes	1988	3,771
65 6/8	12 0/8	11 5/8	5 4/8	5 4/8	6 3/8	Moffat County	CO	Bob Dawson	1988	3,771
65 6/8	12 6/8	13 2/8	5 4/8	5 4/8	6 7/8	Moffat County	CO	Neal Kelly	1988	3,771
65 6/8	12 4/8	12 3/8	4 7/8	5 0/8	6 6/8	Converse County	WY	James Lawless Sullivan	1988	3,771
65 6/8	13 2/8	13 0/8	5 4/8	5 4/8	12 2/8	Converse County	WY	David L. Fuller	1988	3,771
65 6/8	11 3/8	11 3/8	5 6/8	5 7/8	10 4/8	Converse County	WY	Melvin Wells	1988	3,771
65 6/8	12 4/8	12 5/8	5 7/8	6 0/8	9 2/8	Converse County	WY	Tom Siebeneck	1988	3,771
65 6/8	14 1/8	14 1/8	5 2/8	5 2/8	11 1/8	McCone County	MT	Dan Sturgis	1988	3,771
65 6/8	12 6/8	11 6/8	5 6/8	5 7/8	7 4/8	Converse County	WY	Chad Rabe	1988	3,771
65 6/8	13 0/8	13 0/8	5 3/8	5 3/8	8 6/8	Campbell County	WY	Daniel "Boone" Bell	1989	3,771
65 6/8	11 1/8	11 5/8	5 5/8	5 4/8	9 6/8	Campbell County	WY	Jeffrey W. Murray	1989	3,771
65 6/8	13 0/8	13 0/8	5 3/8	5 2/8	7 7/8	Natrona County	WY	Gary L. Morse	1989	3,771
65 6/8	12 1/8	11 7/8	5 5/8	5 5/8	7 5/8	Converse County	WY	Donald Travis	1989	3,771
65 6/8	12 0/8	12 0/8	5 7/8	5 7/8	8 7/8	Campbell County	WY	Dave Grabow	1989	3,771
65 6/8	12 4/8	12 3/8	5 2/8	5 4/8	8 1/8	Moffat County	CO	John Weiss	1990	3,771
65 6/8	12 6/8	12 7/8	5 4/8	5 5/8	9 0/8	Sweetwater County	WY	Ken Maynard	1990	3,771
65 6/8	11 6/8	11 3/8	6 0/8	5 7/8	11 7/8	Converse County	WY	Darwood J. "Doug" Anderson	1990	3,771
65 6/8	13 6/8	13 5/8	5 2/8	5 3/8	7 4/8	Lemhi County	ID	Stanley Leake	1990	3,771
65 6/8	13 3/8	13 2/8	5 1/8	5 0/8	6 7/8	Converse County	WY	Rich Fait	1990	3,771
65 6/8	12 7/8	12 6/8	5 2/8	5 1/8	11 7/8	Moffat County	CO	Thomas P. Bartholomew	1991	3,771
65 6/8	13 5/8	13 4/8	5 3/8	5 2/8	9 7/8	Custer County	ID	Robert D. Dowen	1991	3,771
65 6/8	12 7/8	12 7/8	5 6/8	5 6/8	6 1/8	Converse County	WY	Larry C. Osborne	1991	3,771
65 7/8	12 6/8	12 1/8	5 5/8	5 6/8	8 5/8	Converse County	WY	Dale Shove	1991	3,771
65 6/8	11 5/8	11 7/8	5 7/8	5 6/8	10 4/8	Natrona County	WY	Mark Owsley	1991	3,771
65 6/8	11 5/8	12 1/8	5 5/8	5 4/8	9 0/8	Moffat County	CO	Dennis Hayden	1992	3,771
65 6/8	13 3/8	13 7/8	5 3/8	5 3/8	11 7/8	Tooele County	UT	Dean Leland Smith	1992	3,771
65 6/8	12 2/8	12 2/8	5 7/8	5 7/8	13 0/8	Moffat County	CO	Bob Nelson	1992	3,771
65 6/8	12 2/8	12 3/8	5 5/8	5 4/8	8 7/8	Park County	WY	Chip Moller	1992	3,771
65 6/8	13 7/8	12 7/8	5 4/8	5 4/8	9 4/8	Natrona County	WY	Dan L. Moultrie	1992	3,771
65 6/8	12 7/8	12 6/8	5 3/8	5 2/8	8 7/8	McKenzie County	ND	Mark D. Hughes	1992	3,771

PRONGHORN

Minimum Score 67 — Continued

SCORE	LENGTH OF HORN R	L	CIRCUMFERENCE OF BASE R	L	INSIDE SPREAD	AREA	STATE/PROVINCE	HUNTER'S NAME	DATE	RANK
65 6/8	12 5/8	12 1/8	6 3/8	6 3/8	9 5/8	Lake County	OR	Walter L. Aldridge	1992	3,771
65 6/8	12 4/8	12 5/8	5 4/8	5 4/8	7 7/8	Converse County	WY	Wayne A. Grasseth	1992	3,771
65 6/8	13 6/8	13 5/8	5 4/8	5 2/8	10 7/8	Moffat County	CO	Kevin Synder	1992	3,771
65 6/8	13 1/8	13 1/8	5 4/8	5 5/8	9 6/8	Powder River County	MT	Raymond J. Bendici	1992	3,771
65 6/8	13 6/8	14 0/8	5 6/8	5 6/8	11 6/8	Sioux County	NE	Chris Vinton	1992	3,771
65 6/8	13 6/8	14 4/8	5 7/8	5 7/8	8 6/8	Thomas County	NE	Phil Chvala	1992	3,771
65 6/8	13 3/8	13 6/8	5 4/8	5 4/8	14 0/8	Moffat County	CO	Lonny Vanatta	1993	3,771
65 6/8	13 4/8	13 2/8	5 1/8	4 7/8	14 4/8	Eddy County	NM	Michael Scott McDaniel	1993	3,771
65 6/8	13 0/8	13 0/8	5 4/8	5 3/8	11 5/8	Chaves County	NM	Joe T. Moore	1993	3,771
65 6/8	12 5/8	12 3/8	5 6/8	5 4/8	9 7/8	Park County	WY	Marion O. DeBusk	1993	3,771
65 6/8	12 1/8	12 1/8	5 5/8	5 5/8	7 1/8	Converse County	WY	Mike Iuzzolino	1993	3,771
65 6/8	13 0/8	13 0/8	5 3/8	5 2/8	10 7/8	Converse County	WY	Peter F. Woeck	1993	3,771
65 6/8	12 3/8	12 3/8	5 3/8	5 3/8	12 3/8	Jeff Davis County	TX	Joe Coody	1993	3,771
65 6/8	12 4/8	12 6/8	5 3/8	5 4/8	11 0/8	Hot Springs County	WY	Larry Dickerson	1993	3,771
65 6/8	12 4/8	12 6/8	5 5/8	5 6/8	11 4/8	Lassen County	CA	Brad Langslet	1994	3,771
65 6/8	12 6/8	12 5/8	5 5/8	5 5/8	10 7/8	Moffat County	CO	Cary Laman	1994	3,771
65 6/8	12 5/8	12 3/8	5 4/8	5 4/8	9 1/8	Moffat County	CO	Lonnie Morton	1994	3,771
65 6/8	13 3/8	13 1/8	5 5/8	5 4/8	9 3/8	Converse County	WY	Carol Ann Mauch	1994	3,771
65 6/8	11 5/8	11 7/8	5 7/8	5 6/8	11 5/8	Billings County	ND	Ryan Hugelen	1994	3,771
65 6/8	13 2/8	13 4/8	5 5/8	5 6/8	13 5/8	Park County	WY	Matt Buche	1994	3,771
65 6/8	13 4/8	13 2/8	5 3/8	5 2/8	11 0/8	Musselshell County	MT	Paul A. Connelly	1994	3,771
65 6/8	11 5/8	13 4/8	5 6/8	5 6/8	13 2/8	Culberson County	TX	Gary J. Oden	1994	3,771
65 6/8	12 1/8	12 1/8	6 7/8	6 7/8	8 6/8	Converse County	WY	Sandra A. LaPlatney	1994	3,771
65 6/8	12 1/8	12 1/8	6 1/8	6 0/8	12 6/8	Moffat County	CO	Alfred J. Gemrich	1995	3,771
65 6/8	12 7/8	12 4/8	5 7/8	5 4/8	6 0/8	Moffat County	CO	Wayne Deppperschmidt	1995	3,771
65 6/8	12 5/8	12 1/8	6 2/8	6 1/8	9 3/8	Campbell County	WY	Ellis Wall	1995	3,771
65 6/8	10 7/8	12 1/8	6 2/8	6 3/8	11 3/8	Converse County	WY	Todd A. Doering	1995	3,771
65 6/8	13 0/8	13 0/8	5 4/8	5 4/8	11 7/8	Campbell County	WY	Steven Tebay	1995	3,771
65 6/8	12 4/8	12 5/8	5 2/8	5 2/8	6 7/8	Campbell County	WY	Louis J. Lorenzo	1995	3,771
65 6/8	13 6/8	13 5/8	5 4/8	5 4/8	10 7/8	Moffat County	CO	Tim Atwater	1996	3,771
65 6/8	11 5/8	11 6/8	5 4/8	5 4/8	8 5/8	Sweetwater County	WY	Scott Moon	1996	3,771
65 6/8	13 4/8	13 5/8	5 3/8	5 3/8	9 4/8	Converse County	WY	Joe Cronin	1996	3,771
65 6/8	13 1/8	12 6/8	5 4/8	5 5/8	10 6/8	Converse County	WY	Gary Kautz	1996	3,771
65 6/8	13 6/8	13 6/8	5 5/8	5 6/8	8 2/8	Moffat County	CO	Jim Leqve	1997	3,771
65 6/8	13 2/8	13 5/8	5 4/8	5 3/8	9 4/8	Klamath County	OR	Erik Halverson	1997	3,771
65 6/8	13 5/8	13 2/8	5 6/8	5 4/8	11 5/8	Campbell County	WY	Michael Darling	1997	3,771
65 6/8	12 4/8	12 3/8	6 0/8	5 6/8	10 7/8	Converse County	WY	Tamra Dawn Belaire	1997	3,771
65 6/8	12 7/8	13 0/8	5 5/8	5 5/8	8 4/8	Fergus County	MT	Josef Rud	1997	3,771
65 6/8	13 4/8	13 4/8	5 2/8	5 3/8	8 5/8	Moffat County	CO	Scot L. Hamilton	1998	3,771
65 6/8	12 4/8	12 7/8	6 0/8	5 6/8	11 4/8	Campbell County	WY	Dennis Kelly	1998	3,771
65 6/8	12 7/8	12 5/8	5 3/8	5 2/8	8 3/8	Campbell County	WY	Brian O'Connor	1998	3,771
65 6/8	12 4/8	12 3/8	5 6/8	5 6/8	9 7/8	Converse County	WY	Donald L. Sagner	1998	3,771
65 6/8	12 2/8	12 2/8	6 0/8	6 0/8	8 4/8	Campbell County	WY	Ritch A. Stolpe	1998	3,771
65 6/8	11 2/8	11 3/8	5 7/8	5 7/8	9 0/8	Weld County	CO	Ron "Ham" E. Perrine, Jr.	1998	3,771
65 4/8	12 0/8	12 0/8	5 4/8	5 4/8	8 4/8	Butte County	SD	Alden Hobbs	1958	3,887
65 4/8	12 3/8	12 2/8	5 5/8	5 4/8	7 0/8	Natrona County	WY	Clarence J. Grandt	1973	3,887
65 4/8	11 6/8	11 6/8	5 7/8	5 6/8	11 0/8	Natrona County	WY	Pat Inman	1973	3,887
65 4/8	12 2/8	12 2/8	5 5/8	5 4/8	9 6/8	Carbon County	WY	G. Fred Asbell	1974	3,887
65 4/8	12 0/8	11 7/8	5 4/8	5 0/8	9 1/8	Johnson County	WY	Charles Jahnke	1979	3,887
65 4/8	12 1/8	12 1/8	5 3/8	5 2/8	9 4/8	Converse County	WY	Robert V. Anderson	1981	3,887
65 4/8	13 5/8	13 1/8	5 2/8	5 2/8	11 3/8	Natrona County	WY	Jack H. Williams	1981	3,887
65 4/8	10 3/8	11 2/8	5 5/8	5 4/8	11 3/8	Moffat County	CO	Harry Campagnola	1982	3,887
65 4/8	13 2/8	12 2/8	5 6/8	5 7/8	8 7/8	Johnson County	WY	Fred Thanel	1982	3,887
65 4/8	12 7/8	13 1/8	5 0/8	5 0/8	6 6/8	Converse County	WY	Terry Wobig	1983	3,887
65 4/8	12 6/8	12 6/8	5 1/8	5 1/8	8 3/8	Custer County	ID	Dwight Rollins	1984	3,887
65 4/8	13 4/8	13 3/8	5 5/8	5 5/8	9 2/8	White Pine County	NV	Bob Price	1984	3,887
65 4/8	12 1/8	12 2/8	5 4/8	5 3/8	9 7/8	Converse County	WY	Don Schram	1984	3,887
65 4/8	13 3/8	13 4/8	5 2/8	5 3/8	6 7/8	Natrona County	WY	Gregory R. Bonetti	1984	3,887
65 4/8	11 7/8	11 4/8	5 7/8	5 6/8	9 5/8	Converse County	WY	Ron Hopkins	1984	3,887
65 4/8	12 5/8	12 4/8	5 7/8	5 6/8	8 5/8	Moffat County	CO	Win Knechtel	1985	3,887
65 4/8	12 0/8	12 0/8	6 0/8	6 0/8	8 5/8	Moffat County	CO	Randy Lamdin	1985	3,887
65 4/8	12 7/8	13 1/8	5 0/8	5 0/8	11 1/8	Converse County	WY	Daniel R Sowders	1985	3,887
65 4/8	13 0/8	13 0/8	5 0/8	5 1/8	8 2/8	Converse County	WY	Gerry Rubalcaba	1985	3,887
65 4/8	12 5/8	12 3/8	5 4/8	5 4/8	12 0/8	Glasscock County	TX	Courtney King	1985	3,887
65 4/8	11 6/8	12 4/8	5 2/8	5 3/8	11 2/8	Hettinger County	ND	Bill Clink	1986	3,887
65 4/8	13 1/8	13 1/8	5 6/8	5 6/8	11 2/8	Campbell County	WY	Dan R. Kohl	1986	3,887
65 4/8	12 0/8	12 2/8	5 3/8	5 3/8	9 0/8	Converse County	WY	James S. Saunoris	1986	3,887
65 4/8	12 5/8	12 2/8	5 6/8	5 7/8	9 1/8	McKenzie County	ND	Mark D. Hughes	1987	3,887
65 4/8	12 2/8	12 4/8	5 7/8	5 6/8	7 4/8	Converse County	WY	George Ollert	1987	3,887
65 4/8	12 5/8	12 5/8	5 2/8	5 2/8	12 0/8	Natrona County	WY	Robert L. Perkins	1987	3,887
65 4/8	12 1/8	12 1/8	5 3/8	5 4/8	9 4/8	Carbon County	WY	Steve J. Turner	1988	3,887
65 4/8	14 1/8	13 7/8	5 1/8	5 2/8	8 3/8	Converse County	WY	Leonard Kohan	1988	3,887
65 4/8	13 1/8	12 7/8	5 3/8	5 3/8	8 2/8	Converse County	WY	Tom Prosser	1988	3,887
65 4/8	13 2/8	13 2/8	5 2/8	5 3/8	6 2/8	Converse County	WY	Randy E. Doyle	1988	3,887
65 4/8	13 1/8	13 4/8	5 5/8	5 4/8	12 3/8	Millard County	UT	Bob Spina	1989	3,887
65 4/8	12 3/8	12 1/8	5 0/8	5 0/8	12 1/8	Campbell County	WY	Jay Riewestahl	1989	3,887
65 4/8	12 3/8	12 2/8	5 4/8	5 4/8	8 5/8	Moffat County	CO	Fred Richter	1990	3,887
65 4/8	13 7/8	14 0/8	5 3/8	5 3/8	6 7/8	Converse County	WY	Ron Voigt	1990	3,887

PRONGHORN

Minimum Score 67 — Continued

SCORE	LENGTH OF HORN R	L	CIRCUMFERENCE OF BASE R	L	INSIDE SPREAD	AREA	STATE/PROVINCE	HUNTER'S NAME	DATE	RANK
65 4/8	13 0/8	12 0/8	5 4/8	5 3/8	9 6/8	Washoe County	NV	Audrey Hanson	1991	3,887
65 4/8	12 6/8	13 2/8	5 2/8	5 2/8	10 2/8	Washoe County	NV	Michael Bradeen	1991	3,887
65 4/8	13 0/8	12 7/8	6 0/8	5 7/8	17 0/8	Weld County	CO	Wesley Lowrie	1991	3,887
65 4/8	12 4/8	12 4/8	5 3/8	5 3/8	7 7/8	Sioux County	NE	Neil R. Blohm	1991	3,887
65 4/8	12 3/8	12 3/8	6 0/8	6 3/8	9 5/8	Campbell County	WY	Thomas Hlinka	1991	3,887
65 4/8	13 4/8	13 5/8	5 3/8	5 4/8	8 1/8	Sioux County	NE	Tom Rutt	1991	3,887
65 4/8	13 6/8	14 0/8	5 3/8	5 1/8	10 2/8	Sioux County	NE	Ivan Buss	1991	3,887
65 4/8	13 1/8	13 2/8	5 0/8	5 0/8	10 3/8	Modoc County	CA	Wayne Piersol	1992	3,887
65 4/8	13 4/8	13 1/8	5 0/8	5 0/8	10 2/8	Coconino County	AZ	George R. Richardson	1992	3,887
65 4/8	12 6/8	12 3/8	5 2/8	5 2/8	12 3/8	Converse County	WY	Patricia Stewart	1992	3,887
65 4/8	12 0/8	12 0/8	5 3/8	5 3/8	8 0/8	Converse County	WY	Mark Jones	1992	3,887
65 4/8	12 6/8	12 5/8	5 4/8	5 4/8	9 6/8	Harding County	SD	Gene M. Hove	1992	3,887
65 4/8	13 2/8	13 2/8	5 7/8	5 5/8	11 0/8	Harding County	SD	Marty Adams	1992	3,887
65 4/8	12 4/8	12 4/8	5 7/8	5 6/8	12 1/8	Chaves County	NM	Andy Morley	1993	3,887
65 4/8	12 7/8	12 7/8	5 3/8	5 2/8	9 0/8	Juab County	UT	Karl Hirst	1993	3,887
65 4/8	11 6/8	12 0/8	6 2/8	6 1/8	6 6/8	Natrona County	WY	James R. Crane	1993	3,887
65 4/8	13 0/8	13 0/8	5 4/8	5 4/8	11 0/8	Harding County	SD	Mike Anderson	1993	3,887
65 4/8	12 7/8	12 7/8	5 4/8	5 4/8	9 4/8	Campbell County	WY	David A. Widby	1993	3,887
65 4/8	12 7/8	12 7/8	5 5/8	5 4/8	12 0/8	Garfield County	MT	Richard Hjort	1993	3,887
65 4/8	13 1/8	13 0/8	5 6/8	5 5/8	9 7/8	Natrona County	WY	Gary W. Denny	1994	3,887
65 4/8	12 0/8	12 2/8	6 0/8	6 0/8	12 4/8	Campbell County	WY	Randy Ross	1994	3,887
65 4/8	12 6/8	12 6/8	5 6/8	5 5/8	10 2/8	McKenzie County	ND	Dave Stanley	1994	3,887
65 4/8	12 4/8	12 4/8	5 4/8	5 6/8	10 1/8	Campbell County	WY	John Skau, Jr.	1994	3,887
65 4/8	12 0/8	12 0/8	6 0/8	6 0/8	8 4/8	Wallace County	KS	Robert Faris II	1994	3,887
65 4/8	11 4/8	11 5/8	5 7/8	5 5/8	10 3/8	Modoc County	CA	Danny Meeker	1995	3,887
65 4/8	11 7/8	12 0/8	5 6/8	5 6/8	7 5/8	Converse County	WY	Gary L. Wilford	1995	3,887
65 4/8	11 6/8	11 5/8	6 0/8	5 7/8	10 1/8	Modoc County	CA	Michael Flores	1996	3,887
65 4/8	12 7/8	12 6/8	5 3/8	5 3/8	8 4/8	Colfax County	NM	Charlie Schlosser	1996	3,887
65 4/8	12 6/8	13 0/8	5 3/8	5 2/8	10 6/8	Medicine Hat	ALB	John Carber, Jr.	1996	3,887
65 4/8	12 3/8	12 4/8	5 3/8	5 3/8	6 1/8	Converse County	WY	Larry Oltman	1996	3,887
65 4/8	13 3/8	13 0/8	5 2/8	5 2/8	10 6/8	Hooker County	NE	Kirk L. Stieb	1996	3,887
65 4/8	13 5/8	13 6/8	5 2/8	5 1/8	7 2/8	Hays	ALB	Shelley Bahr	1996	3,887
65 4/8	12 7/8	12 5/8	5 1/8	5 2/8	6 4/8	Sioux County	NE	Robert Thompson	1996	3,887
65 4/8	13 4/8	13 2/8	5 3/8	5 3/8	7 6/8	Brown County	NE	David J. Theis	1996	3,887
65 4/8	12 7/8	13 1/8	5 7/8	5 7/8	7 7/8	Moffat County	CO	Joel A. Druley	1997	3,887
65 4/8	11 7/8	11 5/8	5 4/8	5 4/8	10 1/8	Otero County	CO	Bill Hull	1997	3,887
65 4/8	13 2/8	12 7/8	5 5/8	5 5/8	12 5/8	Moffat County	CO	Tavis Rogers	1997	3,887
65 4/8	13 6/8	13 5/8	5 1/8	5 0/8	9 7/8	McKenzie County	ND	John Paul Schaffer	1997	3,887
65 4/8	12 2/8	12 3/8	5 6/8	5 5/8	9 6/8	Rosebud County	MT	R. Gerald Ebert	1997	3,887
65 4/8	12 4/8	12 4/8	5 3/8	5 3/8	10 1/8	Medicine Hat	ALB	John Carber, Jr.	1997	3,887
65 4/8	11 7/8	11 5/8	5 5/8	5 5/8	9 2/8	Saguache County	CO	Mathew Blazis	1998	3,887
65 4/8	13 6/8	13 2/8	5 3/8	5 4/8	13 0/8	Grand Forks	ALB	Bill Riel	1998	3,887
65 4/8	12 0/8	12 0/8	5 4/8	5 4/8	9 0/8	Converse County	WY	Peter Ripp	1998	3,887
65 4/8	13 1/8	13 1/8	5 2/8	5 3/8	8 4/8	Converse County	WY	Lon Scott	1998	3,887
65 2/8	11 6/8	12 3/8	6 0/8	5 7/8	10 1/8	Moffat County	CO	Henry Wichers	1958	3,965
65 2/8	12 0/8	11 7/8	6 2/8	6 2/8	10 3/8	Clark County	ID	Larry Cross	1978	3,965
65 2/8	13 4/8	13 3/8	4 7/8	4 7/8	11 0/8	Natrona County	WY	Mark Smith	1978	3,965
65 2/8	14 6/8	13 6/8	5 4/8	5 4/8	9 2/8	Johnson County	WY	D. Collis/R. Smith	1979	3,965
65 2/8	12 4/8	11 7/8	6 0/8	5 5/8	11 3/8	Petroleum County	MT	Danny Moore	1980	3,965
65 2/8	13 0/8	13 1/8	5 5/8	5 3/8	12 1/8	Converse County	WY	Robert King	1980	3,965
65 2/8	13 0/8	13 0/8	5 2/8	5 2/8	9 4/8	Converse County	WY	Jim Keim	1981	3,965
65 2/8	13 3/8	13 4/8	5 6/8	5 6/8	10 7/8	Converse County	WY	William Pyle	1981	3,965
65 2/8	12 2/8	12 6/8	5 4/8	5 4/8	9 5/8	Converse County	WY	Hank Sisil	1981	3,965
65 2/8	12 4/8	12 1/8	5 5/8	5 5/8	8 3/8	Valley County	MT	Leith S. Wimmer	1982	3,965
65 2/8	14 1/8	14 0/8	4 7/8	4 5/8	8 7/8	Fergus County	MT	Don Davidson	1982	3,965
65 2/8	13 1/8	13 3/8	5 4/8	5 3/8	10 2/8	Converse County	WY	Richard C. Martell	1982	3,965
65 2/8	11 2/8	11 2/8	6 1/8	6 1/8	9 2/8	Lemhi County	ID	Blair G. Fisher	1982	3,965
65 2/8	12 1/8	12 0/8	6 0/8	5 7/8	9 6/8	Butte County	ID	Doug Ramsey	1983	3,965
65 2/8	12 0/8	12 1/8	5 6/8	5 6/8	10 5/8	Natrona County	WY	Vincent Cina	1983	3,965
65 2/8	12 4/8	12 3/8	5 5/8	5 3/8	10 2/8	Moffat County	CO	Gene E. Smith	1983	3,965
65 2/8	11 2/8	11 1/8	5 6/8	5 6/8	9 1/8	Converse County	WY	Ken Horton	1983	3,965
65 2/8	12 5/8	12 3/8	6 0/8	6 0/8	10 4/8	Sweetwater County	WY	Bryan Radakovich	1984	3,965
65 2/8	12 0/8	12 3/8	5 2/8	5 2/8	8 5/8	Lemhi County	ID	Larry Cross	1984	3,965
65 2/8	11 2/8	11 4/8	5 7/8	5 6/8	9 4/8	Carbon County	WY	Dick Bean	1984	3,965
65 2/8	12 7/8	13 2/8	6 0/8	6 1/8	8 6/8	Sweetwater County	WY	Evan Bellville	1986	3,965
65 2/8	12 1/8	12 0/8	5 4/8	5 4/8	9 3/8	Clark County	ID	Jay Parke	1987	3,965
65 2/8	12 1/8	12 1/8	5 4/8	5 4/8	8 7/8	Santa Cruz County	AZ	Dallas Smith	1987	3,965
65 2/8	12 3/8	12 0/8	5 3/8	5 3/8	11 4/8	Coconino County	AZ	Dan Robbins	1987	3,965
65 2/8	13 0/8	12 6/8	5 4/8	5 3/8	8 7/8	Converse County	WY	George A. Zanoni	1987	3,965
65 2/8	11 2/8	11 4/8	6 2/8	6 2/8	10 1/8	Crook County	WY	Robert Thompson	1987	3,965
65 2/8	13 1/8	12 7/8	5 3/8	5 3/8	9 5/8	Natrona County	WY	Paul A. Anderson	1989	3,965
65 2/8	11 4/8	11 4/8	6 1/8	6 0/8	9 5/8	Moffat County	CO	Ron Jarvis	1990	3,965
65 2/8	12 3/8	12 5/8	5 4/8	5 3/8	8 3/8	Sioux County	NE	Gary L. Mason	1990	3,965
65 2/8	13 0/8	12 7/8	5 3/8	5 2/8	11 5/8	Empress	ALB	David E. Powell	1990	3,965
65 2/8	12 4/8	12 3/8	5 6/8	5 6/8	10 0/8	Rosebud County	MT	Tim Finley	1990	3,965
65 2/8	13 1/8	12 2/8	5 5/8	5 5/8	8 4/8	Albany County	WY	Larry Dickerson	1991	3,965
65 2/8	13 2/8	12 7/8	5 5/8	5 4/8	9 5/8	Campbell County	WY	Alan Solley	1991	3,965
65 2/8	12 6/8	12 6/8	5 4/8	5 3/8	7 7/8	McKenzie County	ND	Joel Beck	1991	3,965

PRONGHORN

Minimum Score 67 — Continued

SCORE	LENGTH OF HORN R L		CIRCUMFERENCE OF BASE R L		INSIDE SPREAD	AREA	STATE/ PROVINCE	HUNTER'S NAME	DATE	RANK
65 2/8	12 2/8	12 2/8	5 4/8	5 4/8	11 2/8	Converse County	WY	Robert Webster	1991	3,965
65 2/8	13 3/8	12 5/8	5 4/8	5 5/8	7 3/8	Washoe County	NV	Allen Davis	1992	3,965
65 2/8	11 1/8	11 0/8	5 7/8	5 6/8	9 0/8	Sweetwater County	WY	Craig Boheler	1992	3,965
65 2/8	13 5/8	13 2/8	6 0/8	5 4/8	11 6/8	Clark County	ID	Mark Sherick	1992	3,965
65 2/8	13 1/8	11 7/8	5 7/8	5 7/8	9 6/8	Moffat County	CO	J. Philip Coulson	1992	3,965
65 2/8	12 4/8	12 1/8	5 6/8	5 6/8	8 7/8	Converse County	WY	Ken Gettman	1992	3,965
65 2/8	11 7/8	12 1/8	5 6/8	5 6/8	10 4/8	Sioux County	NE	Rick Thaden	1992	3,965
65 2/8	13 1/8	13 5/8	6 0/8	5 6/8	5 4/8	Sweetwater County	WY	James B. White	1993	3,965
65 2/8	13 0/8	13 0/8	5 4/8	5 6/8	6 7/8	Millard County	UT	Clark A. Moss	1993	3,965
65 2/8	13 1/8	13 2/8	5 3/8	5 2/8	9 1/8	Moffat County	CO	Bill Cox	1993	3,965
65 2/8	11 5/8	12 0/8	6 2/8	6 0/8	8 4/8	Converse County	WY	Gene Mathias	1993	3,965
65 2/8	12 2/8	12 0/8	5 4/8	5 5/8	9 1/8	Campbell County	WY	Richard Penkalski	1993	3,965
65 2/8	13 2/8	13 1/8	5 3/8	5 4/8	9 1/8	Slope County	ND	Robert Lund	1993	3,965
65 2/8	13 1/8	12 7/8	5 2/8	5 2/8	10 7/8	Arapahoe County	CO	Ken Borucki	1993	3,965
65 2/8	12 2/8	12 2/8	5 4/8	5 4/8	10 5/8	Lyman County	SD	Steven Rossow	1993	3,965
65 2/8	12 7/8	13 0/8	5 2/8	5 2/8	7 4/8	Thomas County	NE	Brian L. Klatt	1994	3,965
65 2/8	12 5/8	12 3/8	5 5/8	5 6/8	11 2/8	Park County	WY	Don Davidson	1994	3,965
65 2/8	13 0/8	13 2/8	5 0/8	5 2/8	11 2/8	Converse County	WY	Greg Kempf	1994	3,965
65 2/8	12 4/8	12 4/8	5 4/8	5 4/8	16 0/8	Converse County	WY	William G. Mason	1994	3,965
65 2/8	12 5/8	12 5/8	5 5/8	5 5/8	8 5/8	Manyberries	ALB	Michael R. Deschamps	1994	3,965
65 2/8	12 6/8	12 3/8	5 6/8	5 6/8	9 6/8	Converse County	WY	Peter F. Woeck	1994	3,965
65 2/8	12 2/8	12 3/8	5 7/8	5 6/8	11 7/8	Buffalo	ALB	Glenn E. Moir	1994	3,965
65 2/8	13 1/8	13 5/8	5 3/8	5 3/8	11 1/8	Campbell County	WY	Leon R. Nyreen	1995	3,965
65 2/8	12 0/8	12 1/8	6 0/8	5 7/8	8 6/8	Converse County	WY	Jim Young	1995	3,965
65 2/8	12 5/8	13 2/8	5 6/8	6 0/8	11 0/8	Klamath County	OR	Bill Martin	1995	3,965
65 2/8	13 4/8	13 4/8	5 0/8	5 1/8	10 7/8	Garfield County	MT	Roger Stewart	1995	3,965
65 2/8	13 2/8	13 4/8	5 4/8	5 2/8	10 7/8	Hays	ALB	Raymond Bahr	1995	3,965
65 2/8	12 7/8	12 3/8	5 5/8	5 5/8	9 1/8	Converse County	WY	Marlin Stapleton, Jr.	1995	3,965
65 2/8	13 1/8	13 2/8	5 4/8	5 4/8	10 4/8	Fergus County	MT	Donny Roy	1995	3,965
65 2/8	12 0/8	12 1/8	5 7/8	5 7/8	10 4/8	Carbon County	WY	Justin Bliss	1996	3,965
65 2/8	13 3/8	13 2/8	5 2/8	5 1/8	13 2/8	Campbell County	WY	Kevin J. Klemick	1996	3,965
65 2/8	11 6/8	11 3/8	6 3/8	6 2/8	11 5/8	Campbell County	WY	Timothy E. Louis	1996	3,965
65 2/8	12 2/8	12 2/8	5 6/8	5 6/8	11 1/8	Converse County	WY	John Tillotson	1996	3,965
65 2/8	12 5/8	12 6/8	5 6/8	5 4/8	11 7/8	Campbell County	WY	Duane P. Domaszek	1996	3,965
65 2/8	12 0/8	12 0/8	5 4/8	5 3/8	7 1/8	Converse County	WY	Joe Maciejewski	1996	3,965
65 2/8	12 7/8	12 6/8	5 3/8	5 5/8	11 7/8	Roberts County	TX	Steve Purviance	1996	3,965
65 2/8	13 0/8	12 6/8	5 3/8	5 2/8	5 5/8	Butte County	ID	Bryce DeForest	1997	3,965
65 2/8	12 5/8	12 5/8	5 6/8	5 6/8	8 0/8	Carter County	MT	Marty Adams	1997	3,965
65 2/8	12 5/8	12 6/8	5 6/8	5 4/8	8 7/8	Moffat County	CO	Cindy Dziekan	1998	3,965
65 2/8	12 5/8	12 6/8	5 5/8	5 5/8	13 5/8	McKenzie County	ND	Don G. Scofield	1998	3,965
65 0/8	13 2/8	13 3/8	5 0/8	4 7/8	10 2/8	Lincoln County	NM	Ben Evans	1962	4,039
65 0/8	12 6/8	12 6/8	5 2/8	5 3/8	12 6/8	McLean County	ND	John Zahrte	1974	4,039
65 0/8	13 5/8	13 3/8	4 7/8	5 0/8	14 2/8	Carbon County	WY	David T. Funderburk	1978	4,039
65 0/8	12 4/8	12 2/8	5 4/8	6 1/8	8 3/8	Albany County	WY	Robert Gorge	1979	4,039
65 0/8	12 6/8	12 6/8	5 6/8	5 5/8	12 5/8	Converse County	WY	Joseph Hopwood	1980	4,039
65 0/8	12 2/8	12 2/8	5 6/8	5 6/8	10 0/8	Moffat County	CO	Lyle Willmarth	1980	4,039
65 0/8	11 2/8	11 2/8	6 2/8	6 1/8	7 7/8	Converse County	WY	David E. Smith	1982	4,039
65 0/8	13 0/8	12 4/8	5 6/8	5 5/8	14 1/8	Converse County	WY	Gene Solyntjes	1982	4,039
65 0/8	12 3/8	12 3/8	5 7/8	6 0/8	9 3/8	Converse County	WY	Mark R. Mussey	1982	4,039
65 0/8	13 2/8	13 0/8	5 5/8	5 4/8	9 5/8	Bowel Tower	ALB	Chris Kearing	1982	4,039
65 0/8	11 7/8	12 2/8	5 6/8	5 6/8	10 3/8	Converse County	WY	Darrell A. Bendel	1982	4,039
65 0/8	13 4/8	13 0/8	5 3/8	5 3/8	8 6/8	Converse County	WY	Kathy Kelly	1982	4,039
65 0/8	12 4/8	12 6/8	5 2/8	5 2/8	10 6/8	Albany County	WY	Claude Oppegard	1982	4,039
65 0/8	13 0/8	13 1/8	5 4/8	5 2/8	9 4/8	Sweetwater County	WY	Joe Dombovy	1983	4,039
65 0/8	12 0/8	12 2/8	5 4/8	5 2/8	10 7/8	Carbon County	WY	Steven Bins	1983	4,039
65 0/8	12 4/8	12 1/8	5 3/8	5 2/8	11 4/8	Carbon County	WY	Dan McPherson	1983	4,039
65 0/8	12 5/8	12 4/8	5 3/8	5 2/8	7 1/8	Slope County	ND	Ed Steidler	1983	4,039
65 0/8	12 0/8	12 0/8	6 0/8	6 0/8	11 4/8	Converse County	WY	Gary R. Shields	1983	4,039
65 0/8	12 1/8	12 2/8	5 6/8	5 6/8	8 2/8	Moffat County	CO	Reggie Spiegelberg	1983	4,039
65 0/8	13 4/8	14 0/8	5 6/8	5 4/8	10 0/8	Sweetwater County	WY	Kevin Jackson	1983	4,039
65 0/8	12 3/8	12 3/8	5 2/8	5 2/8	11 6/8	Cochise County	AZ	Dennis R Ward	1984	4,039
65 0/8	11 7/8	11 6/8	5 3/8	5 3/8	8 7/8	Garfield County	MT	Loren Blossom	1984	4,039
65 0/8	13 7/8	14 2/8	5 0/8	5 1/8	10 4/8	Rosebud County	MT	Daniel A. Nielson	1984	4,039
65 0/8	11 6/8	12 1/8	6 1/8	5 7/8	11 2/8	Carbon County	WY	James Smith	1985	4,039
65 0/8	13 3/8	13 5/8	5 4/8	5 4/8	9 0/8	McHenry County	ND	Kevin Ohlhauser	1985	4,039
65 0/8	12 0/8	12 2/8	6 1/8	6 0/8	9 0/8	Grassy Lake	ALB	Sam Kadoyama	1985	4,039
65 0/8	12 0/8	11 5/8	5 4/8	5 4/8	10 7/8	Converse County	WY	B. J. Higley, Sr.	1986	4,039
65 0/8	14 6/8	14 1/8	6 2/8	6 0/8	13 4/8	Petroleum County	MT	Brad Borden	1986	4,039
65 0/8	12 3/8	12 0/8	5 0/8	5 2/8	8 7/8	Moffat County	CO	Robert Gulliksen	1987	4,039
65 0/8	11 7/8	11 7/8	5 6/8	5 6/8	9 3/8	Natrona County	WY	Louis Strahler	1987	4,039
65 0/8	11 3/8	11 5/8	6 1/8	6 1/8	12 2/8	Harney County	OR	Stanley Miles	1988	4,039
65 0/8	12 1/8	12 1/8	5 6/8	5 6/8	10 3/8	Converse County	WY	Gary L. Fischer	1988	4,039
65 0/8	12 2/8	12 2/8	5 3/8	5 3/8	8 1/8	Converse County	WY	Dean K. Reidt	1988	4,039
65 0/8	13 3/8	13 4/8	5 4/8	5 3/8	9 4/8	Malheur County	OR	Charles R. Bagent	1988	4,039
65 0/8	11 3/8	11 3/8	6 1/8	6 2/8	11 0/8	Moffat County	CO	Cecil O. Richburg	1988	4,039
65 0/8	11 3/8	11 2/8	5 6/8	5 7/8	11 2/8	Fall River County	SD	Bill Lynch	1988	4,039
65 0/8	13 3/8	13 4/8	5 1/8	5 2/8	9 4/8	Dunn County	ND	Don Paul	1988	4,039
65 0/8	13 0/8	12 5/8	5 5/8	5 4/8	8 1/8	Crook County	WY	John Papenfuss	1989	4,039

PRONGHORN

Minimum Score 67 — Continued

SCORE	LENGTH OF HORN R	L	CIRCUMFERENCE OF BASE R	L	INSIDE SPREAD	AREA	STATE/ PROVINCE	HUNTER'S NAME	DATE	RANK
65 0/8	11 6/8	12 0/8	5 6/8	5 6/8	8 2/8	Carbon County	WY	Cecilia M. Watts	1990	4,039
65 0/8	12 1/8	11 6/8	5 6/8	5 6/8	8 4/8	Wildhorse	ALB	Dave Gerber	1990	4,039
65 0/8	11 7/8	11 7/8	6 0/8	6 0/8	11 0/8	Moffat County	CO	Kenneth Thompson	1991	4,039
65 0/8	12 6/8	12 4/8	5 5/8	5 4/8	8 6/8	Natrona County	WY	Jerry E. Burt	1991	4,039
65 0/8	13 2/8	13 1/8	5 1/8	5 1/8	9 3/8	Lincoln County	WY	Bob Grace	1991	4,039
65 0/8	12 7/8	12 6/8	5 4/8	5 2/8	10 1/8	Campbell County	WY	Robert A. Deems	1991	4,039
65 0/8	12 3/8	12 4/8	5 5/8	5 5/8	8 1/8	Converse County	WY	Walter H. Kennedy	1991	4,039
65 0/8	12 0/8	12 1/8	5 0/8	5 0/8	10 6/8	Converse County	WY	Larry L. Haines	1991	4,039
65 0/8	12 5/8	12 6/8	5 2/8	5 1/8	9 0/8	Big Horn County	MT	Terry Selph	1991	4,039
65 0/8	12 0/8	12 2/8	5 4/8	5 4/8	9 5/8	Converse County	WY	Gary R. Trumpy	1991	4,039
65 0/8	11 7/8	11 5/8	6 2/8	6 0/8	9 3/8	Campbell County	WY	Steve Ashley	1991	4,039
65 0/8	12 2/8	11 7/8	5 5/8	5 4/8	12 1/8	Yavapai County	AZ	Ted Spradling	1992	4,039
65 0/8	12 3/8	12 2/8	5 6/8	5 5/8	12 2/8	Rosebud County	MT	Everett "Eb" Morris	1992	4,039
65 0/8	12 3/8	12 6/8	5 7/8	5 6/8	10 3/8	Sweetwater County	WY	Jeff Vance	1993	4,039
65 0/8	13 0/8	13 2/8	5 0/8	5 1/8	17 1/8	Quay County	NM	J. B. Lemon	1993	4,039
65 0/8	13 2/8	13 3/8	5 2/8	5 1/8	8 2/8	Campbell County	WY	Lee J. Keim	1993	4,039
65 0/8	12 4/8	12 3/8	5 2/8	5 2/8	9 3/8	Campbell County	WY	Bob Mattlin	1993	4,039
65 0/8	13 1/8	13 0/8	5 5/8	5 4/8	7 0/8	San Juan County	UT	Gary A. Clum	1993	4,039
65 0/8	13 3/8	13 4/8	5 4/8	5 4/8	10 3/8	Milk River	ALB	Gary Erickson	1993	4,039
65 0/8	13 1/8	13 4/8	5 1/8	5 0/8	6 5/8	Millard County	UT	Kenneth J. Wilkinson	1994	4,039
65 0/8	12 4/8	12 4/8	5 3/8	5 2/8	8 6/8	Rosebud County	MT	Gene A. Welle	1994	4,039
65 0/8	11 6/8	11 7/8	5 4/8	5 3/8	5 7/8	Converse County	WY	Richard A. Stark	1994	4,039
65 0/8	11 7/8	12 3/8	5 5/8	5 5/8	9 2/8	Moffat County	CO	David R. Gerhardt	1994	4,039
65 0/8	13 2/8	13 1/8	5 6/8	5 6/8	9 5/8	Calgary	ALB	Dr. Mark Calkins	1994	4,039
65 0/8	13 5/8	13 7/8	5 2/8	5 1/8	8 2/8	Johnson County	WY	Luther L. Lightcap	1994	4,039
65 0/8	11 4/8	11 6/8	5 7/8	5 7/8	10 0/8	Santa Fe County	NM	Mark E. Chavez	1995	4,039
65 0/8	11 7/8	12 0/8	5 7/8	5 7/8	9 1/8	Moffat County	CO	John E. Axelson	1995	4,039
65 0/8	12 1/8	12 3/8	5 5/8	5 6/8	8 5/8	Converse County	WY	Bill Ware	1995	4,039
65 0/8	12 4/8	12 4/8	5 2/8	5 4/8	11 1/8	Campbell County	WY	David C. Lane	1995	4,039
65 0/8	11 3/8	12 3/8	5 7/8	5 7/8	10 1/8	Campbell County	WY	Donald J. Kane	1995	4,039
65 0/8	12 2/8	12 3/8	5 4/8	5 4/8	9 4/8	Natrona County	WY	James Lenker	1996	4,039
65 0/8	13 2/8	13 4/8	4 4/8	4 5/8	8 1/8	Weld County	CO	Brian Paxton	1996	4,039
65 0/8	12 1/8	11 6/8	5 3/8	5 4/8	7 4/8	Campbell County	WY	Fred M. Blesener	1996	4,039
65 0/8	11 5/8	11 6/8	5 5/8	5 6/8	7 2/8	Converse County	WY	Joe Cucuzza	1996	4,039
65 0/8	12 3/8	12 4/8	5 4/8	5 3/8	10 0/8	Harding County	SD	Neil Brand	1996	4,039
65 0/8	13 1/8	13 1/8	5 1/8	5 1/8	7 5/8	Meade County	SD	Edward R. Wilkerson	1996	4,039
65 0/8	12 3/8	12 6/8	5 7/8	5 6/8	10 6/8	Campbell County	WY	Gary Foltz	1996	4,039
65 0/8	12 0/8	12 0/8	6 2/8	6 3/8	10 0/8	Moffat County	CO	Dewayne Mullins	1997	4,039
65 0/8	12 1/8	12 2/8	5 4/8	5 2/8	11 3/8	Converse County	WY	Jim Winjum	1997	4,039
65 0/8	12 6/8	12 1/8	5 5/8	5 5/8	11 4/8	Converse County	WY	Tom Carpenter	1997	4,039
65 0/8	13 0/8	13 0/8	5 4/8	5 3/8	8 7/8	Campbell County	WY	David W. Korver	1997	4,039
65 0/8	12 4/8	12 5/8	5 7/8	5 6/8	9 1/8	Medicine Hat	ALB	John Carber	1997	4,039
65 0/8	12 3/8	12 2/8	5 6/8	5 6/8	11 0/8	Fergus County	MT	Chris Sanford	1997	4,039
65 0/8	12 7/8	12 7/8	5 1/8	5 4/8	8 5/8	Beaverhead County	MT	Raymond Gross	1997	4,039
65 0/8	13 4/8	13 3/8	5 0/8	5 2/8	12 4/8	Moffat County	CO	Raymond F. Dupuis, Jr.	1998	4,039
65 0/8	12 3/8	12 3/8	5 6/8	5 5/8	11 5/8	Converse County	WY	Frank S. Noska IV	1998	4,039
64 6/8	12 5/8	12 6/8	5 3/8	5 2/8	9 4/8	Perkins County	SD	Richard Bolyard	1975	4,123
64 6/8	12 5/8	12 7/8	5 2/8	5 3/8	7 7/8	Area 34	WY	John Dykes	1975	4,123
64 6/8	11 3/8	11 4/8	5 5/8	5 6/8	8 7/8	Johnson County	WY	James E. Taylor	1975	4,123
64 6/8	12 3/8	12 4/8	5 3/8	5 2/8	12 2/8	Lemhi County	ID	Dale Johnson	1977	4,123
64 6/8	11 6/8	11 6/8	6 0/8	6 1/8	7 3/8	Natrona County	WY	James E. Hodson	1979	4,123
64 6/8	12 0/8	11 6/8	5 7/8	5 7/8	6 6/8	Sweetwater County	WY	Silas Risely	1980	4,123
64 6/8	10 5/8	10 5/8	5 5/8	5 6/8	8 0/8	Converse County	WY	Papa Al Walther	1980	4,123
64 6/8	12 0/8	12 3/8	5 5/8	5 4/8	13 6/8	Sweetwater County	WY	Mike Gallo	1981	4,123
64 6/8	12 2/8	12 5/8	5 5/8	5 6/8	8 1/8	Converse County	WY	James H. Cox	1981	4,123
64 6/8	12 3/8	12 2/8	5 4/8	5 4/8	11 5/8	Converse County	WY	James K. Keim	1982	4,123
64 6/8	12 3/8	12 5/8	5 4/8	5 4/8	9 2/8	Converse County	WY	A. M. Oakes, Jr.	1982	4,123
64 6/8	12 1/8	11 4/8	5 3/8	5 3/8	10 3/8	Sweetwater County	WY	Bryan Radakovich	1982	4,123
64 6/8	12 6/8	13 1/8	5 0/8	5 2/8	10 5/8	Butte County	ID	William A. Burns	1983	4,123
64 6/8	12 0/8	11 6/8	6 0/8	5 6/8	10 0/8	Carbon County	WY	Paul Bowers	1983	4,123
64 6/8	13 4/8	13 5/8	5 0/8	5 0/8	8 4/8	Converse County	WY	Robert D Hankins	1984	4,123
64 6/8	13 1/8	13 0/8	5 6/8	5 4/8	13 0/8	Converse County	WY	Steve Woodman	1984	4,123
64 6/8	12 2/8	12 3/8	5 2/8	5 2/8	8 5/8	Johnson County	WY	Cecil Benner	1984	4,123
64 6/8	11 5/8	12 0/8	5 5/8	5 5/8	11 0/8	Converse County	WY	Rocky Chisholm	1984	4,123
64 6/8	11 1/8	11 2/8	6 0/8	6 0/8	8 5/8	Converse County	WY	Roy Goodwin	1984	4,123
64 6/8	12 2/8	12 5/8	5 3/8	5 2/8	8 3/8	Converse County	WY	John W. Dillon	1984	4,123
64 6/8	12 0/8	11 7/8	5 5/8	5 5/8	9 6/8	White Pine County	NV	Eugene W McNutt	1985	4,123
64 6/8	12 7/8	13 0/8	4 7/8	4 6/8	9 3/8	Moffat County	CO	Gary Oden	1985	4,123
64 6/8	10 6/8	10 7/8	5 7/8	5 7/8	11 3/8	Dunn County	ND	Scott Lang	1985	4,123
64 6/8	12 1/8	12 1/8	5 3/8	5 2/8	9 5/8	Converse County	WY	Leonard J. Emmen	1985	4,123
64 6/8	11 7/8	11 7/8	5 7/8	5 6/8	8 5/8	Weston County	WY	Loren J. Liedl	1985	4,123
64 6/8	11 4/8	11 3/8	5 7/8	5 7/8	8 0/8	Converse County	WY	John M. Negley	1985	4,123
64 6/8	12 5/8	12 5/8	5 2/8	5 2/8	11 4/8	Converse County	WY	Rodney D. Johnson	1985	4,123
64 6/8	12 4/8	12 5/8	5 5/8	5 4/8	11 3/8	Rosebud County	MT	Greg L. Munther	1985	4,123
64 6/8	11 7/8	11 7/8	5 7/8	5 6/8	9 0/8	Garfield County	MT	John Fleharty	1985	4,123
64 6/8	12 0/8	12 1/8	5 3/8	5 3/8	7 3/8	Billings County	ND	Howard Sharp	1985	4,123
64 6/8	13 3/8	13 4/8	5 4/8	5 2/8	9 2/8	Converse County	WY	Floyd Horton	1986	4,123
64 6/8	12 4/8	12 4/8	5 4/8	5 4/8	9 4/8	Sweetwater County	WY	Ron Books	1987	4,123

PRONGHORN

Minimum Score 67 — Continued

SCORE	LENGTH OF HORN R	L	CIRCUMFERENCE OF BASE R	L	INSIDE SPREAD	AREA	STATE/ PROVINCE	HUNTER'S NAME	DATE	RANK
64 6/8	11 6/8	11 2/8	6 2/8	6 3/8	11 2/8	Natrona County	WY	Richard Tudor	1987	4,123
64 6/8	11 5/8	11 4/8	5 5/8	5 5/8	11 1/8	Presidio County	TX	Gary J. Oden	1987	4,123
64 6/8	13 2/8	13 2/8	5 2/8	5 2/8	6 7/8	Blaine County	ID	Danny Moore	1988	4,123
64 6/8	11 4/8	11 3/8	5 7/8	5 7/8	9 3/8	Moffat County	CO	Mark Balavender	1988	4,123
64 6/8	12 4/8	12 5/8	5 1/8	5 1/8	7 0/8	Converse County	WY	Matt Curry	1988	4,123
64 6/8	12 5/8	12 4/8	5 3/8	5 3/8	3 4/8	Converse County	WY	William L. Ewald	1988	4,123
64 6/8	12 0/8	12 1/8	5 3/8	5 1/8	9 4/8	Converse County	WY	Ronald E. Marion	1988	4,123
64 6/8	12 6/8	13 2/8	5 4/8	5 2/8	11 1/8	Uintah County	UT	Everett Burson	1988	4,123
64 6/8	11 4/8	11 4/8	5 4/8	5 4/8	9 6/8	Converse County	WY	Ronald Zajac	1988	4,123
64 6/8	12 5/8	12 7/8	5 4/8	5 5/8	9 2/8	Jenner	ALB	Neil Ostermayer	1988	4,123
64 6/8	12 2/8	13 4/8	5 2/8	5 2/8	11 1/8	Sublette County	WY	Dr. David Samuel	1989	4,123
64 6/8	13 4/8	14 0/8	5 5/8	5 4/8	9 6/8	Harney County	OR	Gregory R. Cole	1989	4,123
64 6/8	12 6/8	12 6/8	5 2/8	5 3/8	8 2/8	Natrona County	WY	Jerry Novak	1989	4,123
64 6/8	12 2/8	12 3/8	5 2/8	5 1/8	9 1/8	Rosebud County	MT	Donald A. Kemkes	1989	4,123
64 6/8	11 6/8	11 7/8	5 7/8	5 7/8	8 7/8	Campbell County	WY	Terry Williams	1989	4,123
64 6/8	13 3/8	14 5/8	5 1/8	5 1/8	11 0/8	Slope County	ND	Tim Belland	1989	4,123
64 6/8	10 3/8	11 1/8	5 7/8	5 7/8	7 4/8	Converse County	WY	Dennis C. Faulkenberry	1990	4,123
64 6/8	11 4/8	11 7/8	5 7/8	5 7/8	10 0/8	Converse County	WY	William L. Doolittle	1990	4,123
64 6/8	12 4/8	12 2/8	5 2/8	5 3/8	11 2/8	Converse County	WY	Tony Naismith	1990	4,123
64 6/8	11 7/8	11 6/8	5 1/8	5 2/8	10 3/8	Jackson County	SD	Barry W. Scholes	1991	4,123
64 6/8	12 4/8	12 5/8	5 1/8	5 0/8	10 5/8	Morton County	ND	John Finck	1991	4,123
64 6/8	12 0/8	11 6/8	5 2/8	5 2/8	8 6/8	Converse County	WY	Larry Sylvester	1991	4,123
64 6/8	13 0/8	13 0/8	5 0/8	5 1/8	10 7/8	Converse County	WY	Jerome A. Wallenfang, Jr.	1991	4,123
64 6/8	12 6/8	12 7/8	5 1/8	5 0/8	8 3/8	Converse County	WY	Norman Roy	1991	4,123
64 6/8	13 3/8	13 1/8	4 7/8	4 7/8	11 7/8	Tide Lake	ALB	Kevin Stewart	1991	4,123
64 6/8	13 6/8	12 5/8	5 6/8	5 5/8	8 6/8	Harding County	SD	Marty Adams	1991	4,123
64 6/8	12 1/8	12 2/8	5 4/8	5 4/8	8 1/8	Petroleum County	MT	Richard Gensch	1991	4,123
64 6/8	12 5/8	12 6/8	5 6/8	5 6/8	8 6/8	Butte County	SD	Jim Thompson	1992	4,123
64 6/8	12 0/8	12 1/8	5 4/8	5 4/8	6 6/8	Converse County	WY	Alex McClelland	1992	4,123
64 6/8	12 2/8	14 1/8	5 4/8	5 7/8	7 6/8	Lake County	OR	Rodney W. Ferry	1992	4,123
64 6/8	13 4/8	12 4/8	5 2/8	5 2/8	13 6/8	Converse County	WY	John Leo Hojan	1992	4,123
64 6/8	13 1/8	12 2/8	5 6/8	5 5/8	11 5/8	Buffalo	ALB	Darryl Kublik	1992	4,123
64 6/8	11 7/8	11 5/8	5 3/8	5 3/8	8 5/8	Sheridan County	WY	David L. Tullock	1992	4,123
64 6/8	11 5/8	11 7/8	5 6/8	5 5/8	10 2/8	Moffat County	CO	Lonnie Morton	1993	4,123
64 6/8	12 4/8	12 1/8	5 5/8	5 6/8	10 0/8	Park County	WY	Timothy J. Aydt	1993	4,123
64 6/8	12 0/8	11 7/8	6 0/8	6 0/8	7 7/8	Campbell County	WY	Edward D. Dougherty	1993	4,123
64 6/8	11 2/8	11 2/8	6 1/8	6 1/8	9 1/8	Converse County	WY	Gregory Hise	1993	4,123
64 6/8	12 3/8	12 7/8	5 3/8	5 3/8	9 2/8	Natrona County	WY	Gary L. Morse	1993	4,123
64 6/8	12 1/8	12 1/8	5 6/8	5 6/8	9 5/8	Campbell County	WY	Bradley Revering	1993	4,123
64 6/8	13 4/8	13 3/8	5 3/8	5 2/8	9 4/8	Campbell County	WY	Brian Olson	1993	4,123
64 6/8	12 2/8	12 2/8	6 1/8	6 1/8	8 3/8	Moffat County	CO	Wyatt C. Watson	1994	4,123
64 6/8	13 2/8	12 6/8	5 7/8	6 0/8	6 2/8	Lemhi County	ID	James G. Bedsole IV	1994	4,123
64 6/8	13 3/8	13 4/8	5 0/8	4 7/8	9 5/8	Millard County	UT	Bruce Whiting	1994	4,123
64 6/8	11 7/8	11 5/8	5 5/8	6 1/8	7 7/8	Converse County	WY	Carolyn Siebrasse Zanoni	1994	4,123
64 6/8	12 7/8	12 4/8	5 0/8	4 7/8	8 5/8	Converse County	WY	Paul "Buck" Farni, Jr.	1994	4,123
64 6/8	12 4/8	12 7/8	5 3/8	5 2/8	11 3/8	McKenzie County	ND	Ron Lee	1994	4,123
64 6/8	13 1/8	13 3/8	5 3/8	5 4/8	10 1/8	Converse County	WY	Robert Fox	1994	4,123
64 6/8	12 4/8	12 5/8	5 4/8	5 3/8	9 1/8	Meade County	SD	Branden Dornquast	1994	4,123
64 6/8	12 3/8	12 2/8	5 6/8	5 6/8	9 5/8	Moffat County	CO	Richard A. Smith	1995	4,123
64 6/8	13 1/8	13 3/8	5 1/8	5 1/8	13 5/8	Fremont County	WY	Tom DeKing	1995	4,123
64 6/8	12 7/8	12 7/8	5 5/8	5 5/8	6 3/8	Campbell County	WY	Brent Van Vonderen	1995	4,123
64 6/8	13 0/8	13 0/8	5 0/8	5 2/8	10 1/8	Park County	WY	Skip Holmes	1995	4,123
64 6/8	12 0/8	11 0/8	6 0/8	5 7/8	10 4/8	Moffat County	CO	Chad E. Nelson	1996	4,123
64 6/8	12 1/8	11 6/8	5 6/8	5 7/8	8 5/8	Converse County	WY	Morris O. Pearson	1996	4,123
64 6/8	13 1/8	13 5/8	5 6/8	5 4/8	15 4/8	Rosebud County	MT	Jason R. Osting	1996	4,123
64 6/8	12 6/8	12 5/8	5 5/8	5 4/8	7 7/8	Foremost	ALB	David Chorkwa	1996	4,123
64 6/8	12 6/8	12 5/8	5 3/8	5 4/8	10 1/8	Natrona County	WY	Dale R. Finkbeiner	1997	4,123
64 6/8	13 1/8	12 7/8	5 0/8	5 1/8	8 5/8	Garfield County	MT	Roger Stewart	1997	4,123
64 6/8	13 0/8	13 4/8	5 4/8	5 2/8	9 5/8	Campbell County	WY	Lisa Meyen	1997	4,123
64 6/8	12 6/8	12 4/8	5 3/8	5 2/8	11 0/8	Moffat County	CO	Dick Steele, DVM	1998	4,123
64 6/8	11 7/8	12 0/8	5 3/8	5 3/8	8 7/8	Converse County	WY	Daniel D. Leonard	1998	4,123
64 6/8	13 3/8	13 2/8	5 4/8	5 4/8	9 7/8	Carter County	MT	Patricia K. Helmich	1998	4,123
64 4/8	12 2/8	11 5/8	5 5/8	5 5/8	7 2/8	Harding County	SD	Floyd Hauk	1959	4,217
64 4/8	12 1/8	12 0/8	4 7/8	4 7/8	9 3/8	Stanley County	SD	Ned E. Fogle	1965	4,217
64 4/8	10 7/8	10 7/8	6 2/8	6 2/8	9 2/8	Cherry County	NE	Jack Joseph	1970	4,217
64 4/8	13 3/8	13 4/8	5 4/8	5 4/8	9 6/8	Mineral County	NV	Gordon Diehl	1974	4,217
64 4/8	11 2/8	12 0/8	5 5/8	5 2/8	7 2/8	Carbon County	WY	Art Heinze	1976	4,217
64 4/8	13 4/8	13 1/8	5 0/8	5 0/8	12 2/8	Washoe County	NV	Roger O. Iveson	1979	4,217
64 4/8	12 7/8	12 3/8	5 1/8	5 1/8	6 0/8	Jefferson County	ID	Doug M. Chase	1980	4,217
64 4/8	12 1/8	12 0/8	5 3/8	5 2/8	7 5/8	Converse County	WY	John D. Davis	1980	4,217
64 4/8	11 6/8	11 2/8	6 0/8	5 6/8	8 7/8	Jones County	SD	Kenneth Kuchta	1980	4,217
64 4/8	13 1/8	13 0/8	5 2/8	5 0/8	9 1/8	Natrona County	WY	Carl W. Waggle	1981	4,217
64 4/8	12 4/8	12 4/8	5 2/8	5 2/8	13 3/8	Moffat County	CO	Harvey Grady	1981	4,217
64 4/8	13 0/8	12 7/8	5 2/8	5 2/8	10 2/8	Natrona County	WY	Harry A. Ulrich	1981	4,217
64 4/8	12 6/8	13 0/8	5 2/8	5 1/8	8 3/8	Converse County	WY	Bob Whitton	1981	4,217
64 4/8	12 3/8	12 0/8	5 5/8	5 4/8	10 0/8	Moffat County	CO	Mary Ann Madrigal	1982	4,217
64 4/8	13 3/8	12 6/8	5 6/8	5 6/8	10 6/8	Klamath County	OR	Richard D. Howell	1982	4,217
64 4/8	12 1/8	12 4/8	5 7/8	6 0/8	9 3/8	Natrona County	WY	Joseph Guerra	1982	4,217

PRONGHORN

Minimum Score 67

SCORE	LENGTH OF HORN R / L		CIRCUMFERENCE OF BASE R / L		INSIDE SPREAD	AREA	STATE/ PROVINCE	HUNTER'S NAME	DATE	RANK
64 4/8	11 5/8	11 5/8	5 5/8	5 5/8	6 6/8	Converse County	WY	Larry Lendman	1982	4,217
64 4/8	10 5/8	11 2/8	6 1/8	6 2/8	7 5/8	Wallace County	KS	Doug Wilson	1982	4,217
64 4/8	12 1/8	12 3/8	5 5/8	5 4/8	6 3/8	Harding County	SD	Chuck Bame	1983	4,217
64 4/8	11 7/8	11 6/8	4 7/8	4 7/8	8 5/8	Butler	WY	Timmy Glass	1983	4,217
64 4/8	13 3/8	13 2/8	5 4/8	5 2/8	5 4/8	Converse County	WY	Dave Skiff	1983	4,217
64 4/8	12 1/8	12 2/8	5 7/8	5 7/8	10 3/8	Converse County	WY	Randy Rhoads	1984	4,217
64 4/8	12 5/8	12 4/8	5 5/8	5 4/8	7 6/8	Converse County	WY	Steve D. Munier	1984	4,217
64 4/8	12 4/8	12 6/8	5 7/8	5 6/8	8 4/8	Converse County	WY	Wayne Miller	1984	4,217
64 4/8	12 4/8	12 6/8	5 2/8	5 2/8	7 0/8	Washoe County	NV	Michael Davis	1985	4,217
64 4/8	12 0/8	11 5/8	5 4/8	5 4/8	9 0/8	Hettinger County	ND	William D. Helphrey	1986	4,217
64 4/8	11 5/8	11 5/8	5 6/8	5 5/8	8 7/8	Ward County	ND	Michael Dene Karna	1986	4,217
64 4/8	12 5/8	12 4/8	5 0/8	4 6/8	7 0/8	Moffat County	CO	Doug Beck	1987	4,217
64 4/8	13 2/8	13 3/8	5 0/8	5 0/8	8 5/8	Natrona County	WY	Michael G. McCarthy	1987	4,217
64 4/8	11 4/8	11 5/8	5 5/8	5 4/8	10 2/8	Moffat County	CO	Jack Van Vianen	1988	4,217
64 4/8	13 6/8	13 5/8	5 1/8	5 1/8	5 4/8	Butte County	ID	Clifton Robinson	1988	4,217
64 4/8	11 5/8	11 3/8	5 5/8	5 5/8	8 2/8	Converse County	WY	Steve Williams	1988	4,217
64 4/8	13 0/8	13 1/8	5 3/8	5 2/8	7 6/8	Converse County	WY	Gretchen Burton	1988	4,217
64 4/8	12 5/8	12 3/8	5 2/8	5 1/8	9 7/8	Campbell County	WY	Eric Wayne Noble	1988	4,217
64 4/8	13 4/8	13 4/8	5 2/8	5 4/8	9 4/8	Musselshell County	MT	Carl E. Nelsen	1988	4,217
64 4/8	12 1/8	12 0/8	6 0/8	5 5/8	7 5/8	Moffat County	CO	Thomas J. Hoffman	1989	4,217
64 4/8	13 2/8	13 0/8	5 3/8	5 3/8	10 2/8	Sweetwater County	WY	Len Cardinale	1989	4,217
64 4/8	12 6/8	12 6/8	5 7/8	5 5/8	11 7/8	Natrona County	WY	Larry Crouch	1989	4,217
64 4/8	11 6/8	12 0/8	5 4/8	5 3/8	11 3/8	Tompkins	SAS	Clarence R. Hughes	1989	4,217
64 4/8	12 4/8	12 6/8	5 5/8	5 3/8	8 3/8	Moffat County	CO	Mark Livingston	1990	4,217
64 4/8	13 6/8	13 6/8	5 2/8	5 0/8	9 6/8	Moffat County	CO	Mike Knight	1990	4,217
64 4/8	13 0/8	13 2/8	5 6/8	5 4/8	13 1/8	Fremont County	WY	Stanley Bocian	1990	4,217
64 4/8	12 5/8	12 7/8	5 4/8	5 2/8	8 5/8	Sioux County	NE	James D. Bourn	1990	4,217
64 4/8	13 1/8	13 0/8	5 4/8	5 2/8	11 1/8	Converse County	WY	Robert Oxley	1990	4,217
64 4/8	12 2/8	12 2/8	5 1/8	5 0/8	7 2/8	Laramie County	WY	Craig Boheler	1991	4,217
64 4/8	12 5/8	12 3/8	4 7/8	4 6/8	10 7/8	Converse County	WY	David DiPaolo	1991	4,217
64 4/8	11 4/8	11 4/8	5 4/8	5 4/8	6 6/8	Weston County	WY	Chuck Mead	1991	4,217
64 4/8	13 0/8	13 4/8	5 1/8	5 1/8	9 0/8	Bowman County	ND	Dennis Moritz	1991	4,217
64 4/8	11 4/8	11 4/8	5 6/8	5 7/8	9 2/8	Converse County	WY	William Siebeneck	1991	4,217
64 4/8	13 5/8	11 5/8	5 6/8	5 5/8	7 7/8	Malheur County	OR	Glenn W. Abbott	1992	4,217
64 4/8	12 1/8	11 7/8	5 5/8	5 4/8	10 5/8	Moffat County	CO	Joe Testerman	1992	4,217
64 4/8	11 7/8	11 5/8	5 5/8	5 4/8	9 3/8	Harding County	SD	Robert L. Karlen, Jr.	1992	4,217
64 4/8	12 7/8	12 6/8	5 5/8	5 4/8	8 4/8	Phillips County	MT	Kevin Bertsch	1992	4,217
64 4/8	11 7/8	12 1/8	5 6/8	5 4/8	11 2/8	Converse County	WY	Lee J. Keim	1992	4,217
64 4/8	10 6/8	12 1/8	5 7/8	5 7/8	6 5/8	Tide Lake	ALB	Hubertus W. Ten Pierik	1992	4,217
64 4/8	12 1/8	12 3/8	5 6/8	5 6/8	11 2/8	Stark County	ND	Mark Carter	1992	4,217
64 4/8	12 3/8	13 0/8	6 1/8	5 7/8	10 5/8	Moffat County	CO	Allan White	1993	4,217
64 4/8	12 6/8	12 5/8	5 3/8	5 3/8	8 7/8	Albany County	WY	Jim Shanks	1993	4,217
64 4/8	12 6/8	12 7/8	5 3/8	5 1/8	11 1/8	Fremont County	WY	Dave Holt	1993	4,217
64 4/8	12 2/8	12 4/8	5 6/8	5 5/8	12 3/8	Yavapai County	AZ	Don Parks, Jr.	1993	4,217
64 4/8	12 5/8	12 6/8	5 4/8	5 4/8	9 4/8	Converse County	WY	M. R. James	1993	4,217
64 4/8	13 0/8	13 3/8	5 6/8	5 6/8	10 2/8	Converse County	WY	Myron E. Jochmann	1993	4,217
64 4/8	11 7/8	12 0/8	5 1/8	5 2/8	10 7/8	Sweetwater County	WY	Vic White	1994	4,217
64 4/8	11 2/8	10 7/8	5 7/8	6 0/8	8 5/8	Carbon County	WY	Les Malsch	1994	4,217
64 4/8	12 0/8	12 3/8	5 5/8	5 5/8	9 3/8	McKenzie County	ND	Duwayne Larson	1994	4,217
64 4/8	12 3/8	12 7/8	5 1/8	5 1/8	7 1/8	Converse County	WY	Richard L. Mauch	1994	4,217
64 4/8	13 0/8	13 0/8	5 2/8	5 2/8	7 2/8	Harding County	SD	Kenny Kuchta	1994	4,217
64 4/8	14 2/8	13 6/8	5 6/8	5 5/8	8 6/8	Sioux County	ND	John Helmers	1994	4,217
64 4/8	12 2/8	12 2/8	5 4/8	5 4/8	8 5/8	Moffat County	CO	Paul Bohochik	1995	4,217
64 4/8	11 6/8	11 5/8	5 6/8	5 5/8	10 0/8	Campbell County	WY	Jim Kocik	1995	4,217
64 4/8	14 0/8	13 7/8	5 0/8	4 7/8	9 1/8	Crook County	WY	Chuck Mead	1995	4,217
64 4/8	12 2/8	12 3/8	6 1/8	6 0/8	11 1/8	Converse County	WY	Steve Tice	1995	4,217
64 4/8	11 7/8	12 0/8	5 7/8	6 0/8	11 2/8	Stillwater County	MT	Mike W. Schlegel	1995	4,217
64 4/8	12 2/8	12 5/8	5 5/8	5 5/8	13 2/8	Moffat County	CO	Jeff Puls	1996	4,217
64 4/8	13 3/8	12 4/8	5 1/8	5 0/8	9 6/8	Rosebud County	MT	Kent Kaufman	1996	4,217
64 4/8	12 6/8	12 7/8	5 2/8	5 2/8	8 6/8	Converse County	WY	Dewey Thompson	1996	4,217
64 4/8	12 4/8	12 3/8	5 2/8	5 2/8	9 4/8	Rosebud County	MT	Craig Richardson	1996	4,217
64 4/8	12 5/8	12 7/8	5 4/8	5 3/8	9 7/8	Rosebud County	MT	Ryan Brewer	1996	4,217
64 4/8	13 0/8	12 3/8	5 3/8	5 4/8	8 4/8	Moffat County	CO	Richard Gamache, Jr.	1997	4,217
64 4/8	11 4/8	11 3/8	6 0/8	6 0/8	9 4/8	Rio Grande County	CO	Thadius Countess	1997	4,217
64 4/8	12 2/8	12 2/8	5 2/8	5 4/8	9 5/8	Converse County	WY	Mark Kronyak	1997	4,217
64 4/8	13 2/8	12 7/8	5 3/8	5 3/8	8 3/8	Klamath County	OR	Bernie Weisgerber	1998	4,217
64 4/8	12 0/8	12 3/8	5 6/8	5 3/8	10 6/8	Saguache County	CO	Mark Blazis	1998	4,217
64 4/8	12 2/8	12 2/8	5 6/8	5 5/8	11 2/8	Converse County	WY	Steven Ripp	1998	4,217
64 2/8	12 0/8	12 2/8	5 6/8	5 7/8	10 6/8	Harding County	SD	Rodney Foster	1965	4,301
64 2/8	11 5/8	12 2/8	5 4/8	5 3/8	9 3/8	Butte County	SD	Donald V. Friberg	1968	4,301
64 2/8	12 4/8	12 5/8	5 2/8	5 3/8	9 0/8	Stanley County	SD	George Hipple	1971	4,301
64 2/8	12 0/8	11 7/8	6 1/8	5 7/8	7 0/8	Ormsby	WY	Frank C. Rathje	1973	4,301
64 2/8	12 7/8	12 6/8	5 7/8	5 4/8	10 6/8	Perkins County	SD	Greg Larsen	1977	4,301
64 2/8	12 1/8	13 3/8	5 3/8	5 3/8	10 3/8	Natrona County	WY	Richard Aylward	1980	4,301
64 2/8	11 2/8	10 7/8	5 4/8	5 4/8	9 7/8	Moffat County	CO	Jeff Ollinger	1980	4,301
64 2/8	12 2/8	12 3/8	5 4/8	5 7/8	10 4/8	Converse County	WY	David E. Smith	1980	4,301
64 2/8	12 3/8	12 4/8	5 6/8	5 6/8	10 6/8	Carbon County	WY	Ervin Wagner	1980	4,301
64 2/8	12 6/8	12 6/8	5 4/8	5 3/8	8 6/8	Park County	WY	John Sides	1981	4,301

PRONGHORN

SCORE	LENGTH OF HORN R	L	CIRCUMFERENCE OF BASE R	L	INSIDE SPREAD	AREA	STATE/ PROVINCE	HUNTER'S NAME	DATE	RANK
64 2/8	11 7/8	11 6/8	5 7/8	5 7/8	10 7/8	Custer County	ID	Robert J. Mayton	1981	4,301
64 2/8	12 0/8	11 7/8	5 0/8	5 1/8	6 3/8	Moffat County	CO	Dave Ellis	1982	4,301
64 2/8	11 6/8	11 7/8	5 4/8	5 5/8	9 1/8	Natrona County	WY	Douglas R. Parrott	1982	4,301
64 2/8	12 2/8	11 7/8	5 4/8	5 3/8	11 0/8	Moffat County	CO	George T. Kili	1982	4,301
64 2/8	13 1/8	12 0/8	5 4/8	5 4/8	11 1/8	Moffat County	CO	Gregory White	1982	4,301
64 2/8	12 4/8	12 4/8	5 4/8	5 4/8	9 3/8	Jefferson County	ID	C. Eugene Jordan	1983	4,301
64 2/8	12 7/8	12 6/8	5 5/8	5 4/8	7 2/8	Converse County	WY	David Arndt	1983	4,301
64 2/8	12 6/8	12 2/8	5 3/8	5 3/8	8 5/8	Sublette County	WY	Dennis L. Shirley	1983	4,301
64 2/8	11 6/8	11 6/8	5 2/8	5 2/8	11 3/8	Moffat County	CO	Dan Liccardi	1984	4,301
64 2/8	12 4/8	12 5/8	5 2/8	5 2/8	9 0/8	Converse County	WY	Donald W Malina	1984	4,301
64 2/8	11 2/8	10 7/8	5 6/8	5 4/8	10 6/8	Converse County	WY	Jason S. Miller	1984	4,301
64 2/8	12 1/8	12 2/8	5 5/8	5 4/8	6 7/8	Phillips County	MT	Dyrk Eddie	1984	4,301
64 2/8	13 0/8	13 0/8	5 2/8	5 2/8	11 2/8	Converse County	WY	Bill Sande	1984	4,301
64 2/8	14 0/8	14 3/8	4 6/8	4 6/8	12 0/8	Eddy County	NM	Noble Sinclair	1984	4,301
64 2/8	12 5/8	12 6/8	5 4/8	5 4/8	11 4/8	Sweetwater County	WY	Craig Boheler	1985	4,301
64 2/8	12 4/8	13 0/8	5 3/8	5 2/8	6 6/8	Converse County	WY	Dennis Dunn	1985	4,301
64 2/8	12 4/8	12 4/8	5 0/8	4 6/8	6 6/8	Converse County	WY	Mark Labarbera	1985	4,301
64 2/8	11 7/8	12 1/8	5 3/8	5 2/8	8 3/8	Campbell County	WY	Richard Sapp	1985	4,301
64 2/8	13 1/8	13 1/8	5 4/8	5 3/8	12 5/8	Custer County	MT	James R. Thibault	1985	4,301
64 2/8	11 7/8	12 3/8	5 4/8	5 4/8	9 7/8	Converse County	WY	Floyd Rettler	1985	4,301
64 2/8	12 2/8	11 6/8	5 7/8	5 7/8	9 3/8	Stark County	ND	Scott Borchert	1986	4,301
64 2/8	12 0/8	12 2/8	5 6/8	6 0/8	11 2/8	Moffat County	CO	Fred Wallace	1987	4,301
64 2/8	13 2/8	13 4/8	5 2/8	5 2/8	9 3/8	McKenzie County	ND	Brent Perdue	1987	4,301
64 2/8	12 4/8	12 7/8	6 4/8	6 2/8	10 6/8	Billings County	ND	Robert Shannon	1987	4,301
64 2/8	11 1/8	11 0/8	5 6/8	5 6/8	9 4/8	Moffat County	CO	Steven Tisdale	1988	4,301
64 2/8	13 4/8	13 6/8	5 4/8	5 3/8	10 0/8	Carbon County	WY	Dave Gerhardt	1988	4,301
64 2/8	12 7/8	13 2/8	5 0/8	4 7/8	9 2/8	Moffat County	CO	John Axelson	1988	4,301
64 2/8	12 5/8	12 6/8	5 5/8	5 6/8	8 6/8	Converse County	WY	Marcel Kulas	1988	4,301
64 2/8	12 4/8	12 4/8	5 1/8	5 1/8	10 7/8	Moffat County	CO	Gary Fischer	1989	4,301
64 2/8	13 6/8	13 5/8	5 4/8	5 3/8	9 5/8	Rosebud County	MT	Steve Anderson	1989	4,301
64 2/8	12 6/8	12 6/8	5 2/8	5 1/8	8 3/8	Sheridan County	WY	Benjamin A. Dorward	1989	4,301
64 2/8	13 0/8	12 7/8	5 2/8	5 2/8	9 6/8	Moffat County	CO	Roy "Butch" Goodwin, Jr.	1990	4,301
64 2/8	12 3/8	12 2/8	5 3/8	5 4/8	8 6/8	Natrona County	WY	Roger L. Hendricks	1990	4,301
64 2/8	13 6/8	13 4/8	5 2/8	5 1/8	10 2/8	Sheridan County	WY	Grant A. Poindexter	1990	4,301
64 2/8	12 4/8	12 4/8	5 0/8	5 0/8	6 7/8	Powder River County	MT	Edwin John Durushia	1990	4,301
64 2/8	11 6/8	11 6/8	6 0/8	6 1/8	9 6/8	Powder River County	MT	Rick Simonson	1990	4,301
64 2/8	11 6/8	11 6/8	5 6/8	5 7/8	9 0/8	Bowman County	ND	Gene Welle	1991	4,301
64 2/8	13 0/8	12 7/8	5 1/8	5 2/8	10 3/8	Campbell County	WY	Larry Streiff	1991	4,301
64 2/8	11 0/8	11 2/8	6 0/8	6 0/8	7 5/8	Johnson County	WY	Robert M. Larson	1991	4,301
64 2/8	13 1/8	13 3/8	5 0/8	5 1/8	7 7/8	Washoe County	NV	Bill G. Davis	1992	4,301
64 2/8	13 2/8	13 0/8	5 2/8	5 2/8	12 3/8	Washoe County	NV	Bob Laylon	1992	4,301
64 2/8	13 5/8	12 5/8	5 5/8	5 4/8	12 0/8	Quay County	NM	Tommy C. Jones	1992	4,301
64 2/8	12 6/8	12 6/8	5 1/8	5 1/8	9 1/8	Moffat County	CO	Charlie Hanawalt	1992	4,301
64 2/8	12 3/8	13 6/8	5 5/8	5 4/8	13 6/8	Converse County	WY	Anthony DiChiara	1992	4,301
64 2/8	12 6/8	12 4/8	5 2/8	5 2/8	12 4/8	Grant County	NM	Ruben Chavira	1992	4,301
64 2/8	12 4/8	12 5/8	5 4/8	5 4/8	7 4/8	Converse County	WY	Scott Norton	1992	4,301
64 2/8	12 2/8	12 2/8	5 3/8	5 3/8	9 4/8	McKenzie County	ND	Mike Hauser	1992	4,301
64 2/8	12 6/8	12 6/8	5 5/8	5 4/8	11 5/8	Campbell County	WY	Lois J. O'Brien	1992	4,301
64 2/8	12 7/8	12 3/8	5 2/8	5 1/8	7 7/8	Sioux County	NE	Lane L. Ostendorf	1992	4,301
64 2/8	13 0/8	13 2/8	5 1/8	5 1/8	10 2/8	Chaves County	NM	Michael R. Perry	1993	4,301
64 2/8	13 4/8	13 7/8	5 0/8	5 0/8	8 7/8	Otero County	CO	Tim Wells	1993	4,301
64 2/8	11 1/8	12 0/8	6 0/8	6 0/8	10 6/8	Weld County	CO	Tim Bradley	1993	4,301
64 2/8	14 1/8	14 2/8	5 3/8	5 3/8	8 6/8	Campbell County	WY	Todd Amenrud	1993	4,301
64 2/8	13 0/8	12 4/8	5 2/8	5 2/8	10 6/8	Wallace County	KS	Darrell Allen	1993	4,301
64 2/8	12 2/8	12 6/8	5 4/8	5 3/8	9 5/8	Meagher County	MT	John Fleharty	1993	4,301
64 2/8	11 7/8	12 0/8	6 0/8	5 7/8	7 6/8	Sweet Grass County	MT	Andrew J. Kelly	1993	4,301
64 2/8	11 3/8	11 0/8	6 0/8	6 1/8	8 5/8	Sweetwater County	WY	George Fabian	1994	4,301
64 2/8	12 0/8	11 5/8	6 0/8	6 0/8	8 4/8	Moffat County	CO	Durand D. Dickman	1994	4,301
64 2/8	12 2/8	12 2/8	5 5/8	5 4/8	8 5/8	Rosebud County	MT	Mike Mrdjenovich	1994	4,301
64 2/8	12 3/8	12 3/8	5 3/8	5 3/8	12 2/8	Bowman County	ND	Gene A. Welle	1994	4,301
64 2/8	13 2/8	13 6/8	5 4/8	5 5/8	17 5/8	Campbell County	WY	Carl Pugliese	1994	4,301
64 2/8	12 1/8	12 0/8	5 2/8	5 1/8	9 0/8	Petroleum County	MT	Mark D. Hughes	1994	4,301
64 2/8	12 7/8	12 2/8	5 6/8	5 6/8	11 5/8	Del Bonita	ALB	Brent Watson	1994	4,301
64 2/8	12 5/8	12 4/8	5 2/8	5 3/8	11 1/8	Converse County	WY	Ken Mamazzo	1994	4,301
64 2/8	12 4/8	12 4/8	5 4/8	5 4/8	9 6/8	Big Horn County	MT	Jim Wilkins	1994	4,301
64 2/8	12 5/8	12 5/8	5 4/8	5 3/8	11 3/8	Moffat County	CO	Tammarie Smith	1995	4,301
64 2/8	12 0/8	11 7/8	5 3/8	5 3/8	8 7/8	Converse County	WY	Frank Williams	1995	4,301
64 2/8	13 0/8	12 5/8	5 0/8	5 0/8	10 5/8	Rosebud County	MT	Scott J. Winkle	1995	4,301
64 2/8	12 2/8	11 5/8	5 1/8	5 1/8	11 4/8	Campbell County	WY	Page A. Eldridge	1995	4,301
64 2/8	11 0/8	11 3/8	6 0/8	5 7/8	8 7/8	Chaffee County	CO	Joel Morgan	1995	4,301
64 2/8	12 6/8	12 7/8	5 2/8	5 2/8	9 3/8	Owyhee County	ID	Brian A. Ferebee	1996	4,301
64 2/8	11 3/8	12 1/8	5 3/8	5 3/8	11 4/8	Saguache County	CO	Carole R. Borg	1996	4,301
64 2/8	12 2/8	12 7/8	5 3/8	5 2/8	10 2/8	Moffat County	CO	William R. McClure	1996	4,301
64 2/8	13 4/8	13 0/8	5 2/8	5 2/8	7 1/8	Converse County	WY	Michael Stys	1996	4,301
64 2/8	12 4/8	12 5/8	5 6/8	5 6/8	9 4/8	Bowman County	ND	Renee Welle	1996	4,301
64 2/8	12 5/8	12 7/8	5 2/8	5 3/8	10 7/8	Converse County	WY	Edd Woslum	1996	4,301
64 2/8	12 5/8	12 4/8	5 4/8	5 3/8	7 1/8	Keya Paha County	NE	Russ Wentworth	1996	4,301
64 2/8	11 3/8	11 2/8	5 6/8	5 6/8	5 6/8	Moffat County	CO	Bryan Holley	1997	4,301

PRONGHORN

Minimum Score 67 | Continued

SCORE	LENGTH OF HORN R	L	CIRCUMFERENCE OF BASE R	L	INSIDE SPREAD	AREA	STATE/ PROVINCE	HUNTER'S NAME	DATE	RANK
64 2/8	12 2/8	12 2/8	5 3/8	5 3/8	7 7/8	Converse County	WY	Steven VanZandt	1997	4,301
64 2/8	12 2/8	12 4/8	5 4/8	5 4/8	9 0/8	Rosebud County	MT	Brian Helzer	1997	4,301
64 2/8	13 0/8	13 0/8	5 3/8	5 3/8	12 0/8	Sierra County	NM	Matthew Liljenquist	1998	4,301
64 2/8	12 3/8	12 2/8	5 4/8	5 3/8	10 3/8	Moffat County	CO	Tom Weaver	1998	4,301
64 2/8	12 5/8	12 6/8	5 3/8	5 3/8	8 3/8	Campbell County	WY	Dan Boss	1998	4,301
64 0/8	12 4/8	12 4/8	5 0/8	5 0/8	8 6/8	Campbell County	WY	Carol Wert	1964	4,394
64 0/8	12 6/8	12 5/8	5 2/8	5 2/8	8 6/8	Lincoln County	NM	Harold Groves	1966	4,394
64 0/8	12 6/8	12 6/8	5 3/8	5 4/8	7 1/8	Natrona County	WY	Bernard Giacoletto	1970	4,394
64 0/8	12 1/8	12 1/8	6 1/8	6 0/8	11 3/8	Natrona County	WY	Mike Massa	1971	4,394
64 0/8	12 7/8	12 7/8	5 1/8	5 2/8	9 0/8	Sioux County	NE	Clyde M. Storie	1971	4,394
64 0/8	11 6/8	12 4/8	5 5/8	5 5/8	11 7/8	Harding County	SD	Roger Moul	1972	4,394
64 0/8	13 2/8	13 3/8	5 3/8	5 2/8	12 4/8	Harding County	SD	DeWayne Yantes	1973	4,394
64 0/8	11 3/8	11 3/8	5 3/8	5 5/8	11 4/8	Converse County	WY	Mike Lifford	1981	4,394
64 0/8	11 7/8	12 0/8	5 6/8	5 6/8	11 4/8	Moffat County	CO	Dennis Behn	1981	4,394
64 0/8	12 1/8	12 2/8	5 5/8	5 6/8	8 0/8	Sweetwater County	WY	Mark Chapman	1981	4,394
64 0/8	13 0/8	13 1/8	5 1/8	5 1/8	10 7/8	Converse County	WY	Todd Schulz	1981	4,394
64 0/8	12 0/8	12 1/8	5 4/8	5 6/8	7 2/8	Natrona County	WY	Jim Smith	1982	4,394
64 0/8	12 3/8	12 0/8	5 3/8	5 3/8	10 3/8	Carbon County	WY	Ron Stacey	1982	4,394
64 0/8	12 2/8	11 7/8	5 4/8	5 3/8	10 3/8	Converse County	WY	Richard Samson	1983	4,394
64 0/8	12 3/8	12 2/8	5 2/8	5 3/8	9 1/8	McCone County	MT	Mike Elsbernd	1983	4,394
64 0/8	11 7/8	13 1/8	5 6/8	5 4/8	10 6/8	Niobrara County	WY	Elgie D. Rewey	1983	4,394
64 0/8	12 3/8	12 5/8	5 4/8	5 4/8	14 0/8	Carbon County	WY	Kim S. Brockhoff	1984	4,394
64 0/8	12 5/8	12 5/8	5 4/8	5 4/8	12 2/8	Converse County	WY	Dicky Newberry	1984	4,394
64 0/8	12 4/8	12 5/8	5 1/8	5 1/8	9 4/8	Corson County	SD	Richard D. Hansen	1984	4,394
64 0/8	12 7/8	12 0/8	5 6/8	5 5/8	8 1/8	Campbell County	WY	Frank S McClain	1984	4,394
64 0/8	12 2/8	12 0/8	5 4/8	5 3/8	9 1/8	White Pine County	NV	David W Taylor	1985	4,394
64 0/8	12 6/8	12 6/8	5 1/8	5 0/8	8 1/8	Converse County	WY	Randy Johnson	1985	4,394
64 0/8	12 2/8	12 2/8	5 5/8	5 6/8	8 3/8	Natrona County	WY	Gary C. Cargill	1985	4,394
64 0/8	11 7/8	12 1/8	5 5/8	5 6/8	8 7/8	Ward County	ND	Michael Dene Karna	1985	4,394
64 0/8	13 0/8	13 5/8	5 4/8	5 3/8	9 4/8	Washoe County	NV	David Powning	1986	4,394
64 0/8	11 7/8	12 1/8	5 4/8	5 5/8	11 2/8	Converse County	WY	Bill Doemland	1986	4,394
64 0/8	12 3/8	12 0/8	5 5/8	5 5/8	11 0/8	Moffat County	CO	Dennis J. Modlin	1987	4,394
64 0/8	13 3/8	13 2/8	5 4/8	5 1/8	11 0/8	Natrona County	WY	Gary L. Morse	1987	4,394
64 0/8	12 4/8	12 6/8	5 2/8	5 2/8	7 6/8	Moffat County	CO	Rex Blackwell	1988	4,394
64 0/8	13 2/8	13 3/8	4 7/8	4 7/8	7 0/8	Sublette County	WY	Earl Butts	1988	4,394
64 0/8	11 5/8	11 0/8	5 7/8	5 7/8	10 1/8	Campbell County	WY	Randy Deones	1988	4,394
64 0/8	11 7/8	11 7/8	5 5/8	5 4/8	11 5/8	Converse County	WY	Brad Holm	1988	4,394
64 0/8	12 2/8	12 1/8	5 5/8	5 4/8	10 4/8	Converse County	WY	Tom Nelson	1988	4,394
64 0/8	13 4/8	13 4/8	5 4/8	5 4/8	9 6/8	Converse County	WY	William Chaplin	1988	4,394
64 0/8	11 3/8	11 6/8	5 2/8	5 2/8	11 2/8	Johnson County	WY	Mike Renn II	1988	4,394
64 0/8	12 7/8	12 3/8	5 1/8	5 1/8	11 3/8	Rosebud County	MT	Ed Morris	1989	4,394
64 0/8	12 3/8	12 3/8	5 5/8	5 4/8	9 0/8	Morgan County	CO	Tim Bradley	1989	4,394
64 0/8	13 7/8	13 7/8	5 2/8	5 3/8	7 2/8	Converse County	WY	Randy Doyle	1989	4,394
64 0/8	12 4/8	12 4/8	5 6/8	5 5/8	10 7/8	Manyberries	ALB	Dale Peters	1989	4,394
64 0/8	13 0/8	12 3/8	5 3/8	5 3/8	7 0/8	McKenzie County	ND	Joe Hoffart	1989	4,394
64 0/8	12 2/8	12 3/8	5 2/8	5 1/8	9 6/8	Park County	CO	Daniel J. Lee	1990	4,394
64 0/8	13 2/8	13 3/8	5 4/8	5 5/8	8 3/8	Billings County	ND	John Serna	1990	4,394
64 0/8	13 2/8	13 4/8	5 4/8	5 4/8	10 0/8	Converse County	WY	Dick H. Fischer	1990	4,394
64 0/8	11 6/8	11 5/8	5 3/8	5 3/8	9 1/8	Campbell County	WY	Sheldon Showalter	1990	4,394
64 0/8	12 1/8	12 2/8	5 3/8	5 4/8	8 5/8	Campbell County	WY	Dave Vomela	1990	4,394
64 0/8	13 7/8	12 3/8	5 6/8	5 5/8	7 6/8	Converse County	WY	Mark Graham	1990	4,394
64 0/8	12 1/8	12 4/8	5 3/8	5 4/8	7 7/8	Converse County	WY	James Gorczynski	1990	4,394
64 0/8	11 5/8	11 4/8	6 1/8	6 2/8	8 7/8	Natrona County	WY	Russell A. Nichols	1990	4,394
64 0/8	12 0/8	12 0/8	6 0/8	5 7/8	11 1/8	Campbell County	WY	John Keenan	1990	4,394
64 0/8	11 6/8	13 5/8	5 6/8	5 5/8	5 3/8	Sioux County	NE	Richard W. Waller	1990	4,394
64 0/8	12 2/8	12 4/8	5 4/8	5 5/8	8 2/8	Sioux County	NE	Michael A. Ellingson	1990	4,394
64 0/8	12 4/8	12 4/8	6 0/8	5 6/8	9 6/8	Elko County	NV	Kurt W. Carpenter	1991	4,394
64 0/8	12 6/8	13 1/8	5 5/8	5 4/8	8 6/8	Campbell County	WY	Randy Springborn	1991	4,394
64 0/8	12 3/8	12 1/8	5 3/8	5 4/8	6 2/8	Converse County	WY	Donald L. Mott	1991	4,394
64 0/8	12 5/8	12 5/8	5 2/8	5 2/8	11 6/8	Converse County	WY	H. B. (Pat) Clark	1991	4,394
64 0/8	13 3/8	13 4/8	5 1/8	5 2/8	7 2/8	Bowman County	ND	Owen L. Wentz	1991	4,394
64 0/8	12 2/8	12 1/8	5 4/8	5 4/8	10 6/8	Converse County	WY	Rodney L. Eckberg	1991	4,394
64 0/8	12 1/8	12 1/8	5 3/8	5 2/8	6 6/8	Sioux County	NE	Ron Suponchick	1991	4,394
64 0/8	12 0/8	11 7/8	5 4/8	5 4/8	10 0/8	Moffat County	CO	John C. (Jack) Culpepper III	1992	4,394
64 0/8	11 4/8	11 3/8	5 4/8	5 5/8	8 1/8	Moffat County	CO	Dennis E. Lerum	1992	4,394
64 0/8	12 7/8	13 0/8	5 2/8	5 2/8	5 3/8	Moffat County	CO	Mike Boland	1992	4,394
64 0/8	13 5/8	13 2/8	5 4/8	5 3/8	8 7/8	Campbell County	WY	Richard Schmidt	1992	4,394
64 0/8	11 6/8	11 5/8	6 0/8	5 6/8	8 7/8	Converse County	WY	Richard Anderson	1992	4,394
64 0/8	12 1/8	12 4/8	5 3/8	5 3/8	10 3/8	Converse County	WY	Aaron Hartley	1992	4,394
64 0/8	13 3/8	13 5/8	5 4/8	5 4/8	10 0/8	Bowman County	ND	Renee Welle	1992	4,394
64 0/8	12 3/8	12 1/8	5 7/8	5 6/8	9 3/8	Carbon County	WY	John B. Bowman	1992	4,394
64 0/8	12 4/8	12 6/8	5 5/8	5 4/8	9 5/8	Rosebud County	MT	Rick Miller	1992	4,394
64 0/8	13 2/8	13 3/8	5 1/8	5 1/8	6 5/8	Moffat County	CO	Brandon Ray	1993	4,394
64 0/8	12 4/8	12 4/8	5 1/8	5 1/8	8 0/8	Saguache County	CO	Paul A. Bohochik	1993	4,394
64 0/8	11 7/8	11 6/8	5 6/8	5 6/8	6 7/8	Weld County	CO	Tim Carlson	1993	4,394
64 0/8	13 1/8	13 1/8	5 3/8	5 3/8	10 1/8	Yavapai County	AZ	Brian D. Bilyeu	1993	4,394
64 0/8	12 2/8	12 3/8	5 1/8	5 2/8	9 0/8	Converse County	WY	John E. Wencley	1993	4,394
64 0/8	11 6/8	11 6/8	6 1/8	6 0/8	8 7/8	Campbell County	WY	Charles Bailey	1993	4,394

PRONGHORN

Minimum Score 67   Continued

SCORE	LENGTH OF HORN R	L	CIRCUMFERENCE OF BASE R	L	INSIDE SPREAD	AREA	STATE/ PROVINCE	HUNTER'S NAME	DATE	RANK
64 0/8	13 0/8	12 2/8	5 4/8	5 4/8	9 2/8	Sheridan County	WY	Charles Petersen	1993	4,394
64 0/8	11 7/8	11 7/8	5 4/8	5 3/8	10 3/8	Sweet Grass County	MT	Lee W. Miller	1993	4,394
64 0/8	12 2/8	12 2/8	5 3/8	5 2/8	11 0/8	Converse County	WY	Frank S. Noska IV	1994	4,394
64 0/8	12 2/8	12 3/8	5 1/8	5 4/8	7 4/8	Platte County	WY	Gregory White	1994	4,394
64 0/8	12 7/8	13 0/8	5 2/8	5 2/8	8 5/8	Campbell County	WY	Dean K. Eriksen	1994	4,394
64 0/8	12 1/8	12 2/8	5 3/8	5 3/8	8 4/8	Musselshell County	MT	Don Davidson	1994	4,394
64 0/8	12 0/8	12 3/8	5 5/8	5 5/8	9 1/8	Converse County	WY	Robert "Grub" Matthews	1994	4,394
64 0/8	12 0/8	12 0/8	5 4/8	5 4/8	7 3/8	Blindloss	ALB	Peter Dohrs	1994	4,394
64 0/8	13 2/8	12 4/8	5 4/8	5 3/8	11 1/8	Campbell County	WY	Mark S. Petrucci	1994	4,394
64 0/8	13 0/8	12 6/8	5 2/8	5 1/8	10 3/8	Fergus County	MT	Edwin Evans	1994	4,394
64 0/8	12 7/8	12 5/8	5 2/8	5 2/8	10 1/8	Campbell County	WY	Glenn Hermeier	1994	4,394
64 0/8	12 4/8	12 4/8	5 3/8	5 3/8	10 4/8	Sioux County	NE	Wade Luther	1994	4,394
64 0/8	13 4/8	13 0/8	5 2/8	5 2/8	6 6/8	Campbell County	WY	John Mullen	1995	4,394
64 0/8	12 4/8	12 3/8	5 4/8	5 3/8	9 5/8	Converse County	WY	Robert Harris	1995	4,394
64 0/8	12 6/8	12 6/8	5 2/8	5 1/8	9 5/8	Moffat County	CO	Joel D. Morgan	1996	4,394
64 0/8	12 3/8	12 3/8	5 4/8	5 4/8	9 5/8	Converse County	WY	Thomas Ray Gross	1996	4,394
64 0/8	10 5/8	11 7/8	6 2/8	6 2/8	8 5/8	Natrona County	WY	Richard P. Stroud	1996	4,394
64 0/8	12 5/8	12 4/8	5 4/8	5 4/8	8 5/8	Campbell County	WY	Robert Filbrandt	1996	4,394
64 0/8	12 5/8	12 3/8	5 5/8	5 4/8	9 1/8	Manyberries	ALB	George W. Schoonover, Jr.	1996	4,394
64 0/8	12 3/8	12 3/8	6 1/8	6 0/8	12 2/8	Wheatland County	MT	Jim Winjum	1996	4,394
64 0/8	13 2/8	13 0/8	5 4/8	5 3/8	6 4/8	Campbell County	WY	Barry J. Horton	1996	4,394
64 0/8	12 2/8	11 6/8	5 5/8	5 4/8	6 6/8	Converse County	WY	Rick L. Morley	1997	4,394
64 0/8	12 4/8	12 0/8	5 3/8	5 2/8	6 4/8	Moffat County	CO	Stan Neighbors	1998	4,394

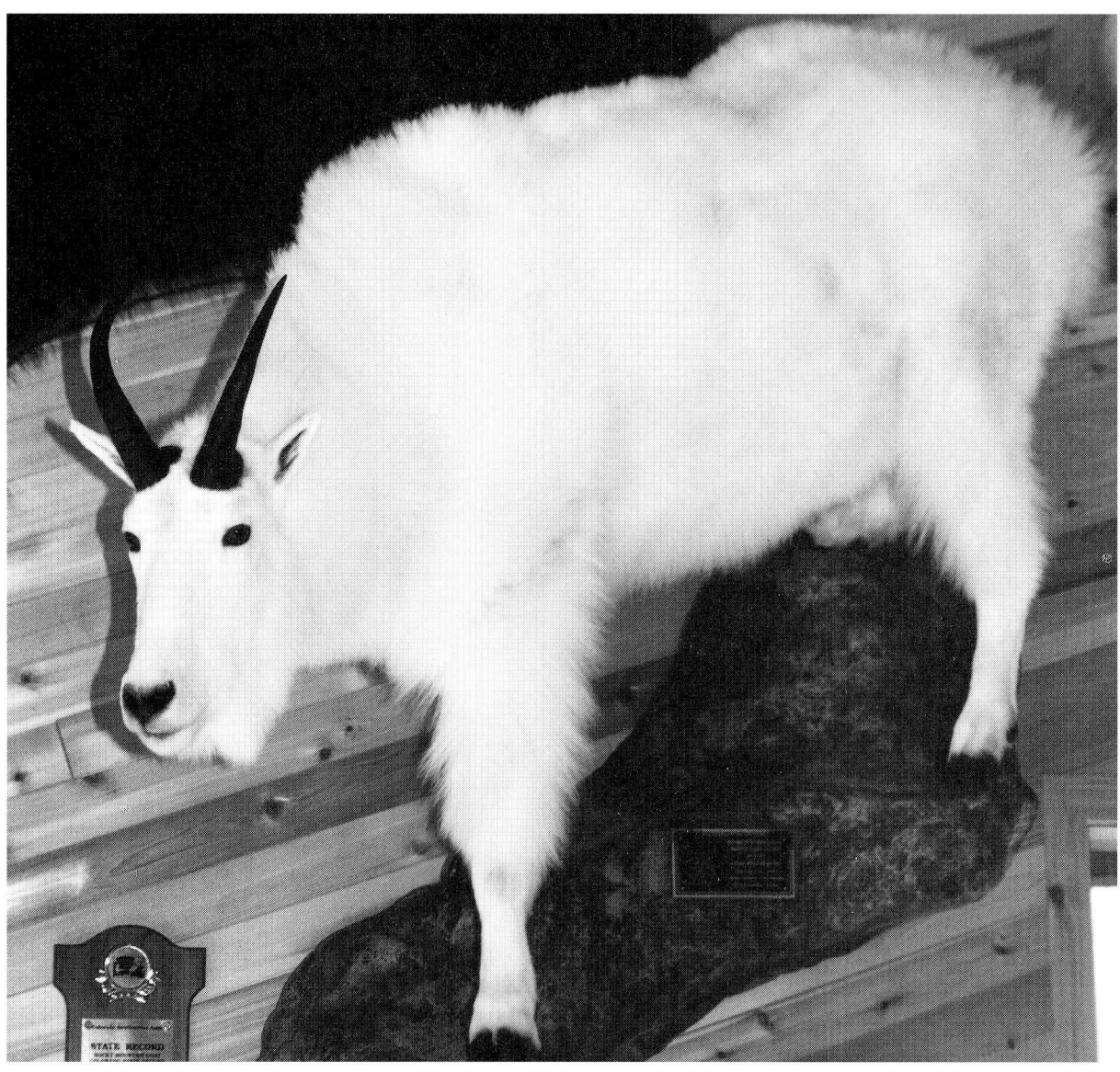

World Record Rocky Mountain Goat
Score: 52 4/8
Park County, Colorado - 1988
Hunter: Lyle K. Willmarth

ROCKY MOUNTAIN GOAT

Minimum Score 40

Oreamnos americanus americanus and related subspecies

SCORE	LENGTH OF HORN R	L	CIRCUMFERENCE OF BASE R	L	GREATEST SPREAD	SEX	AREA	STATE/ PROVINCE	HUNTER'S NAME	DATE	RANK
52 4/8	11 3/8	11 2/8	5 7/8	5 7/8	8 1/8	M	Park County	CO	Lyle K. Willmarth	1988	1
52 0/8	10 2/8	10 2/8	5 5/8	5 6/8	8 2/8	M	Atlin	BC	Mike Jennett	1994	2
51 4/8	10 5/8	10 2/8	5 6/8	5 5/8	7 4/8	M	Wrangell	AK	C. Wayne Treadway	1988	3
51 4/8	10 2/8	10 2/8	5 5/8	5 5/8	8 2/8	M	Nanika Lake	BC	Reg Meisner	1995	3
51 4/8	9 3/8	9 1/8	6 0/8	6 1/8	8 0/8	M	Kispiox Mtn.	BC	Duncan Henderson	1998	3
51 2/8	9 7/8	10 0/8	6 1/8	6 1/8	7 5/8	M	Nahlin Mtn.	BC	Dan Brockman	1995	6
51 0/8	9 6/8	9 6/8	5 7/8	6 0/8	7 4/8	M	Terrace	BC	Dave Ramsay	1982	7
50 6/8	9 6/8	9 5/8	5 7/8	5 6/8	7 0/8	M	Bella Coola	BC	Randy Svisdahl	1995	8
50 2/8	10 7/8	10 6/8	5 3/8	5 3/8	5 6/8	M	Ketchikan	AK	Kurt Kuehl	1989	9
50 0/8	10 2/8	10 1/8	5 7/8	5 6/8	5 4/8	M	Kittitas County	WA	Bob Haugen	1971	10
50 0/8	10 5/8	10 2/8	5 5/8	5 5/8	7 0/8	M	Snohomish County	WA	Edward M. Beitner	1984	10
50 0/8	10 2/8	10 2/8	5 4/8	5 4/8	6 3/8	M	Wrangell	AK	Bob Fromme	1987	10
50 0/8	10 2/8	10 2/8	5 4/8	5 5/8	10 2/8	M	Klastline River	BC	Gregory White	1992	10
49 6/8	9 1/8	9 1/8	5 6/8	5 6/8	7 6/8	M	Tesla Lake	BC	Peter Halbig	1970	14
49 6/8	9 5/8	9 6/8	5 5/8	5 5/8	6 2/8	M	Gallatin County	MT	Clark Kelly III	1990	14

ROCKY MOUNTAIN GOAT

Minimum Score 40 — Continued — 681

SCORE	LENGTH OF HORN R	L	CIRCUMFERENCE OF BASE R	L	GREATEST SPREAD	SEX	AREA	STATE/PROVINCE	HUNTER'S NAME	DATE	RANK
49 4/8	10 0/8	10 0/8	5 4/8	5 4/8	6 1/8	M	Custer County	SD	William G. Chipman	1991	16
49 4/8	9 2/8	9 4/8	6 1/8	6 2/8	5 2/8	M	Pierce County	WA	Kirby Warner	1995	16
49 2/8	9 7/8	9 6/8	5 5/8	5 4/8	7 6/8	M	King County	WA	Jerry Solie	1978	18
49 2/8	10 4/8	10 5/8	5 2/8	5 3/8	7 1/8	M	Snohomish County	WA	Jonathon L. Bogle	1987	18
49 2/8	9 3/8	9 4/8	5 6/8	5 6/8	7 1/8	M	Taku River	BC	Jerry Davis	1991	18
49 2/8	9 4/8	9 3/8	5 6/8	5 6/8	6 6/8	M	Utah County	UT	Dennis L. Dobson	1992	18
49 2/8	10 3/8	10 1/8	5 3/8	5 3/8	6 7/8	M	Clear Creek County	CO	Gayle Lippold	1994	18
49 0/8	9 5/8	9 4/8	5 1/8	5 0/8	7 6/8	M	Whatcom County	WA	Courtney Salmonsen	1974	23
49 0/8	9 1/8	9 1/8	5 6/8	5 5/8	7 0/8	M	Snohomish County	WA	Dick Smethurst	1975	23
49 0/8	9 0/8	9 0/8	5 6/8	5 6/8	6 7/8	M	Bennett Lake	BC	Jack Stephen	1982	23
49 0/8	10 2/8	10 3/8	5 3/8	5 3/8	6 0/8	M	Cleveland Peninsula	AK	Kurt Kuehl	1990	23
49 0/8	10 3/8	10 3/8	5 4/8	5 4/8	6 2/8	M	Nakusp	BC	Harvey J. Surina	1992	23
49 0/8	10 2/8	10 1/8	5 4/8	5 4/8	6 5/8	M	Snootli Creek	BC	Randy Svisdahl	1996	23
48 6/8	10 0/8	9 4/8	5 5/8	5 5/8	7 6/8	M	Hedley	BC	Ernest Popoff	1981	29
48 6/8	9 2/8	9 4/8	5 4/8	5 4/8	8 6/8	M	Atlin	BC	Thomas J. Hoffman	1997	29
48 4/8	9 5/8	9 5/8	5 5/8	5 5/8	7 3/8	M	Clallam County	WA	Dr. Charles F. Raab	1967	31
48 4/8	9 1/8	9 1/8	5 5/8	5 5/8	5 6/8	M	Terrace	BC	Dave Ramsay	1979	31
48 2/8	9 3/8	9 4/8	5 6/8	5 5/8	6 6/8	M	Seebe	ALB	Chris Kroll	1962	33
48 2/8	9 3/8	9 2/8	5 6/8	5 5/8	7 2/8	M	Crown Mtn.	AK	Harold W. Jacobson	1973	33
48 2/8	9 7/8	9 2/8	5 7/8	5 7/8	6 4/8	M	Chaffee County	CO	Marvin Clyncke	1978	33
48 2/8	9 1/8	8 7/8	5 4/8	5 4/8	5 3/8	M	Kittitas County	WA	Jim Pavack	1983	33
48 2/8	9 3/8	9 3/8	5 4/8	5 4/8	6 6/8	M	Kittitas County	WA	L. T. Spring	1986	33
48 2/8	9 3/8	9 2/8	5 3/8	5 4/8	7 0/8	M	Telegraph Creek	BC	Al Schroeder	1987	33
48 2/8	9 5/8	9 5/8	5 6/8	5 6/8	7 2/8	M	Jefferson County	WA	G. A. "Toby" Hart	1987	33
48 2/8	9 4/8	9 4/8	5 5/8	5 4/8	6 0/8	M	Natlude Lake	BC	Darrell Yetter	1988	33
48 2/8	9 7/8	9 7/8	5 0/8	5 1/8	6 1/8	M	Snohomish County	WA	Mathew Hayvaz	1991	33
48 2/8	9 5/8	9 4/8	5 6/8	5 6/8	6 6/8	M	Kodiak Island	AK	Lon E. Lauber	1996	33
48 0/8	9 4/8	9 7/8	5 5/8	5 5/8	7 4/8	M	Kitchener Lake	BC	Walt Sawicki	1975	43
48 0/8	9 6/8	10 0/8	5 5/8	5 5/8	6 2/8	M	Firesteel River	BC	John H. Kaykendall	1978	43
48 0/8	9 5/8	9 5/8	5 2/8	5 4/8	5 4/8	M	Snohomish County	WA	Gerry J. Lamarre	1978	43
48 0/8	9 3/8	9 3/8	5 3/8	5 2/8	6 7/8	M	Snohomish County	WA	Greg A. McTee	1986	43
48 0/8	9 4/8	9 4/8	5 3/8	5 4/8	6 7/8	M	Blunt Mtn.	BC	Kurt Saffarek	1994	43
48 0/8	9 4/8	9 3/8	5 3/8	5 3/8	6 0/8	M	Lyell Creek	BC	Ron Books	1994	43
47 6/8	9 2/8	9 2/8	5 5/8	5 4/8	7 0/8	M	Terminus Mtn.	BC	Paul P. Schafer	1975	49
47 6/8	9 5/8	9 3/8	5 5/8	5 6/8	6 4/8	M	Thuodadi Lake	BC	Phil Bauer	1978	49
47 6/8	9 5/8	9 7/8	5 3/8	5 3/8	6 6/8	M	Clallam County	WA	Wayne Haag	1979	49
47 6/8	9 3/8	9 3/8	5 4/8	5 4/8	7 3/8	M	Bonneville County	ID	Darrus D. Martin	1985	49
47 6/8	9 4/8	9 2/8	5 4/8	5 4/8	5 7/8	M	Snohomish County	WA	Colin McRae	1991	49
47 6/8	9 3/8	9 3/8	5 4/8	5 4/8	6 7/8	M	Jefferson County	WA	Donald Phipps	1992	49
47 6/8	9 3/8	9 3/8	5 4/8	5 4/8	7 4/8	M	Hope	AK	Demitrios N. Deoudes	1992	49
47 6/8	9 1/8	9 2/8	5 5/8	5 5/8	6 7/8	M	Utah County	UT	David H. Beratto	1993	49
47 4/8	9 4/8	9 4/8	5 4/8	5 4/8	5 6/8	M	Jefferson County	WA	Bob Dierick	1976	57
47 4/8	9 6/8	9 6/8	5 3/8	5 3/8	7 1/8	M	Stalk Lake	BC	Chester J. Thompson	1977	57
47 4/8	9 5/8	9 3/8	5 4/8	5 4/8	6 2/8	M	Gallatin County	MT	Mark Ness	1984	57
47 4/8	9 7/8	9 5/8	5 1/8	5 1/8	6 7/8	M	Skagit County	WA	Steve Kempf	1987	57
47 4/8	9 3/8	9 3/8	5 3/8	5 3/8	7 4/8	M	Spencer Glacier	AK	Lon Lauber	1989	57
47 4/8	9 4/8	9 4/8	5 2/8	5 2/8	6 7/8	M	Dease Lake	BC	Don Davidson	1993	57
47 4/8	9 4/8	10 0/8	5 3/8	5 3/8	6 7/8	M	Taku River	BC	Joseph A. Romeu	1994	57
47 4/8	9 2/8	9 6/8	5 6/8	5 5/8	12 3/8	M	Wright Peaks	AK	Larry Daly	1995	57
47 4/8	9 0/8	9 1/8	5 4/8	5 4/8	7 0/8	M	Utah County	UT	Dallas Smith	1995	57
47 2/8	9 4/8	9 3/8	5 3/8	5 4/8	6 2/8	M	Kennedy Springs	MT	Don Leondorf	1964	66
47 2/8	8 6/8	8 7/8	5 3/8	5 4/8	6 2/8	M	Kittitas County	WA	Arnold L. Deckwa	1969	66
47 2/8	9 2/8	9 2/8	6 2/8	6 2/8	7 5/8	M	Kenai Peninsula	AK	John Moline	1971	66
47 2/8	9 5/8	9 5/8	5 2/8	5 2/8	7 0/8	M	Alsek River	AK	F. Wyatt Cook	1976	66
47 2/8	9 1/8	9 2/8	5 4/8	5 4/8	6 6/8	M	Cassier Inlet	BC	Peter L. Halbig	1984	66
47 2/8	8 7/8	9 0/8	5 4/8	5 4/8	6 4/8	M	Clear Creek County	CO	Don Stiles	1984	66
47 2/8	9 4/8	9 5/8	5 3/8	5 3/8	6 2/8	M	Lewis & Clark County	MT	Doug Getz	1985	66
47 2/8	10 0/8	9 5/8	5 1/8	5 1/8	7 2/8	M	Ravalli County	MT	Ray Tlamka	1985	66
47 2/8	9 2/8	9 2/8	5 2/8	5 3/8	5 5/8	M	Mitchell Mtn.	BC	Vincent Pisani	1986	66
47 2/8	9 7/8	10 0/8	5 2/8	5 2/8	6 3/8	M	Clear Creek County	CO	Richard A. Devrous, Jr.	1990	66
47 2/8	10 1/8	9 7/8	5 2/8	5 2/8	6 6/8	M	Ravalli County	MT	Shaun Twardoski	1992	66
47 2/8	9 1/8	9 2/8	5 3/8	5 4/8	6 2/8	M	Bella Coola	BC	Lawrence Michalchuk	1993	66
47 2/8	9 5/8	9 4/8	5 2/8	5 2/8	5 5/8	M	Chilkat River	AK	Bart W. Colledge	1993	66
47 2/8	9 1/8	9 4/8	5 4/8	5 4/8	7 5/8	M	Dall Lake	BC	Bob "Jake" Jacobsen	1994	66
47 2/8	10 1/8	10 0/8	5 1/8	5 1/8	6 5/8	M	Clearwater County	ID	Paul N. Rogers	1995	66
47 2/8	6 0/8	6 5/8	5 6/8	5 6/8	7 1/8	M	Atlin	BC	E. Lance Whary	1998	66
47 0/8	9 3/8	9 3/8	5 3/8	5 4/8	7 2/8	M	Olympic Peninsula	WA	William V. Mishler	1968	82
47 0/8	9 1/8	9 1/8	5 2/8	5 2/8	5 6/8	M	Lemhi County	ID	Eugene E. Farmer	1972	82
47 0/8	9 1/8	9 1/8	5 5/8	5 5/8	6 4/8	M	Mason County	WA	Bob Brandfas	1976	82
47 0/8	9 3/8	9 0/8	5 5/8	5 5/8	6 6/8	M	Kenai Mtn.	AK	Rick Tollison	1978	82
47 0/8	9 2/8	9 3/8	5 5/8	5 4/8	6 0/8	M	Chaffee County	CO	Calvin Farner	1981	82
47 0/8	10 1/8	10 1/8	5 1/8	5 1/8	6 5/8	M	La Plata County	CO	Mark Wuerthele	1987	82
47 0/8	9 1/8	9 2/8	5 3/8	5 3/8	6 1/8	M	Smithers	BC	Philip Stegenga	1995	82
47 0/8	8 6/8	8 6/8	5 4/8	5 4/8	6 6/8	M	Blunt Mtn.	BC	DeWayne Mullins	1997	82
46 6/8	9 2/8	9 2/8	5 3/8	5 2/8	6 1/8	M	Haines	AK	Lowell Marylin	1962	90
46 6/8	9 3/8	9 3/8	5 2/8	5 2/8	7 0/8	M	Cordova	AK	Dwane J. Sykes	1973	90
46 6/8	9 2/8	9 3/8	5 4/8	5 4/8	6 2/8	M	Clallam County	WA	Dean Cook	1978	90
46 6/8	9 0/8	9 0/8	5 3/8	5 2/8	6 3/8	M	Stalk Lakes	BC	Walt Krom	1979	90

ROCKY MOUNTAIN GOAT

Minimum Score 40 — Continued

SCORE	LENGTH OF HORN R	LENGTH OF HORN L	CIRCUMFERENCE OF BASE R	CIRCUMFERENCE OF BASE L	GREATEST SPREAD	SEX	AREA	STATE/PROVINCE	HUNTER'S NAME	DATE	RANK
46 6/8	8 2/8	9 5/8	5 6/8	5 6/8	6 3/8	M	Kittitas County	WA	Robert J. Fischer	1981	90
46 6/8	10 0/8	10 1/8	5 3/8	5 4/8	6 0/8	M	Clearwater County	ID	Timothy A. Hyde	1986	90
46 6/8	9 2/8	9 0/8	5 3/8	5 3/8	6 6/8	M	Babine Range	BC	Don St. Jean	1987	90
46 6/8	9 7/8	9 4/8	5 2/8	5 2/8	6 4/8	M	Bonneville County	ID	Coby Tigert	1989	90
46 6/8	8 3/8	8 4/8	5 3/8	5 3/8	6 4/8	M	Todagin Mtn.	BC	Len Cardinale	1990	90
46 6/8	9 0/8	8 7/8	6 0/8	6 0/8	7 1/8	M	San Juan County	CO	Steven J. Vittetow	1993	90
46 6/8	9 2/8	9 2/8	5 3/8	5 4/8	6 3/8	M	Salt Lake County	UT	Patrick G. Hogle	1995	90
46 6/8	8 6/8	9 0/8	5 3/8	5 4/8	7 0/8	M	Atlin	BC	Tim R. Dawson	1998	90
46 6/8	9 3/8	9 2/8	5 4/8	5 4/8	6 0/8	M	Chaffee County	CO	Esco Billings III	1998	90
46 4/8	9 1/8	8 7/8	5 3/8	5 3/8	7 1/8	M	Clallam County	WA	Thos. J. Smith	1969	103
46 4/8	9 6/8	9 0/8	5 4/8	5 4/8	7 2/8	M	Day Harbor	AK	William L. Ruby	1970	103
46 4/8	10 0/8	9 7/8	5 2/8	5 1/8	7 4/8	M	Thuodadi Lake	BC	Gary Petee	1979	103
46 4/8	9 3/8	9 4/8	5 2/8	5 3/8	6 6/8	M	Olympic Peninsula	WA	Gerald Egbert	1980	103
46 4/8	10 2/8	10 2/8	5 0/8	5 0/8	6 3/8	M	Sheslay River	BC	Marte Scheuffele	1983	103
46 4/8	9 2/8	9 1/8	5 4/8	5 4/8	5 6/8	M	Chaffee County	CO	Ken McIntosh	1983	103
46 4/8	9 1/8	9 0/8	5 4/8	5 4/8	6 7/8	M	Jefferson County	WA	Greg Tedlund	1986	103
46 4/8	8 3/8	8 2/8	5 5/8	5 5/8	6 0/8	M	Chaffee County	CO	Todd Clyncke	1987	103
46 4/8	8 4/8	9 6/8	5 5/8	5 4/8	7 6/8	M	Chouteau County	MT	Robert Lucas	1988	103
46 4/8	9 0/8	8 7/8	5 5/8	5 5/8	6 0/8	M	Kodiak Island	AK	Roger Stewart	1989	103
46 4/8	8 6/8	8 6/8	5 3/8	5 3/8	6 6/8	M	Atlin	BC	Gary M. Martin	1990	103
46 4/8	9 0/8	9 0/8	5 2/8	5 2/8	5 5/8	M	Bella Coola	BC	Barry McCay	1990	103
46 4/8	8 4/8	9 3/8	5 5/8	5 6/8	7 1/8	M	Moose Pass	AK	Craig Scarbrough	1990	103
46 4/8	8 5/8	8 6/8	5 3/8	5 4/8	7 2/8	M	Kodiak Island	AK	Lon E. Lauber	1992	103
46 4/8	9 0/8	8 7/8	5 2/8	5 2/8	5 2/8	M	Telegraph Creek	BC	Lou Kindred	1993	103
46 4/8	9 1/8	9 3/8	5 1/8	5 1/8	6 0/8	M	Taku Plateau	BC	Walter J. Palmer	1995	103
46 4/8	9 0/8	9 2/8	5 5/8	5 5/8	6 2/8	M	Chaffee County	CO	John R. Olson	1996	103
46 2/8	9 2/8	9 5/8	5 2/8	5 3/8	6 5/8	M	Lewis & Clark County	MT	W. J. Fuller	1958	120
46 2/8	9 1/8	9 1/8	5 2/8	5 3/8	6 2/8	M	Lemhi County	ID	Ray Torrey	1967	120
46 2/8	9 4/8	9 3/8	5 1/8	5 1/8	5 5/8	M	Kittitas County	WA	Keith E. Anyan	1978	120
46 2/8	8 7/8	8 6/8	5 3/8	5 3/8	6 3/8	M	Terrace	BC	Bill Coburn	1979	120
46 2/8	9 3/8	9 3/8	4 4/8	4 5/8	6 3/8	M	Snohomish County	WA	Fred Collins	1980	120
46 2/8	9 1/8	9 0/8	5 3/8	5 3/8	6 3/8	M	Smithers	BC	Robert M. Fromme	1990	120
46 2/8	9 1/8	8 7/8	5 3/8	5 3/8	6 5/8	M	Clear Creek County	CO	Kurt W. Keskimaki	1991	120
46 2/8	8 3/8	9 2/8	5 4/8	5 4/8	7 1/8	M	Kodiak Island	AK	Mark A. Pfost	1992	120
46 2/8	9 1/8	9 2/8	5 3/8	5 3/8	6 6/8	M	Kodiak Island	AK	Troy A. Graziadei	1993	120
46 0/8	9 3/8	9 4/8	5 2/8	5 2/8	6 6/8	M	Whidbey Bay	AK	George Moerlein	1964	129
46 0/8	8 5/8	8 5/8	5 0/8	5 0/8	6 2/8	M	Boise County	ID	Jerry E. Burt	1971	129
46 0/8	8 7/8	9 0/8	5 4/8	5 4/8	7 6/8	M	Kenai Peninsula	AK	Roger D. Morris	1971	129
46 0/8	9 1/8	9 3/8	5 1/8	5 1/8	6 2/8	M	Clear Creek County	CO	Kurt Keskimaki	1979	129
46 0/8	8 7/8	9 0/8	5 4/8	5 4/8	6 5/8	M	Kechika Range	BC	Roger Stewart	1980	129
46 0/8	9 2/8	9 2/8	5 2/8	5 2/8	6 6/8	M	Clear Creek County	CO	David Skiff	1981	129
46 0/8	9 3/8	9 3/8	5 2/8	5 1/8	5 7/8	M	Chouteau County	MT	Kay Davidson	1984	129
46 0/8	9 0/8	9 0/8	5 2/8	5 1/8	6 5/8	M	Kenai Peninsula	AK	Robert D. Warpack	1985	129
46 0/8	9 1/8	9 1/8	5 1/8	5 2/8	8 2/8	M	Spencer Glacier	AK	Matt Jones	1990	129
46 0/8	9 1/8	9 2/8	5 3/8	5 3/8	7 0/8	M	Jefferson County	WA	David K. Olson	1991	129
46 0/8	9 0/8	8 7/8	5 2/8	5 2/8	6 5/8	M	Kenai Peninsula	AK	John Sarvis	1993	129
46 0/8	8 2/8	8 1/8	5 4/8	5 3/8	6 2/8	M	Dease River	BC	Dale Selby	1995	129
46 0/8	9 1/8	9 2/8	5 1/8	5 1/8	7 2/8	M	Knik Glacier	AK	Stephen Kotz	1996	129
46 0/8	11 1/8	10 7/8	4 5/8	4 5/8	8 4/8	F	Fremont County	ID	Del Morton	1996	129
46 0/8	9 1/8	9 0/8	5 1/8	5 2/8	5 6/8	M	Chaffee County	CO	Joe B. Farmer	1997	129
45 6/8	8 5/8	8 5/8	5 3/8	5 2/8	7 3/8	M	Skagway	AK	Rick Furniss	1972	144
45 6/8	8 5/8	8 5/8	5 2/8	5 2/8	6 4/8	M	Jefferson County	WA	John Lund	1978	144
45 6/8	9 0/8	8 7/8	5 1/8	5 1/8	5 4/8	M	Stalk Lakes	BC	John Stadler	1980	144
45 6/8	8 6/8	9 0/8	5 1/8	5 2/8	6 7/8	M	Cordova	AK	Gary A. Twigg	1980	144
45 6/8	9 1/8	9 1/8	5 2/8	5 2/8	6 0/8	M	Duti Lake	BC	Wm. "Bill" MacCarty III	1981	144
45 6/8	9 3/8	9 4/8	5 2/8	5 2/8	5 3/8	M	Mount Jeldness	BC	Gerald Bond	1982	144
45 6/8	8 7/8	9 1/8	5 3/8	5 3/8	7 0/8	M	Todagin Mtn.	BC	Reggie Spiegelberg	1984	144
45 6/8	9 6/8	9 6/8	5 0/8	5 1/8	6 2/8	M	Clearwater County	ID	Mike VonLindern	1984	144
45 6/8	8 4/8	8 7/8	5 3/8	5 3/8	7 6/8	M	Atlin	BC	Harrison O'Conner	1985	144
45 6/8	9 0/8	8 5/8	5 1/8	5 0/8	7 0/8	M	Snohomish County	WA	Norman Ward	1987	144
45 6/8	8 7/8	8 6/8	5 2/8	5 1/8	6 2/8	M	Kittitas County	WA	William R. Kinnan	1991	144
45 6/8	8 6/8	8 7/8	5 2/8	5 2/8	6 4/8	M	Snohomish County	WA	Stuart L. Keck	1994	144
45 6/8	8 5/8	8 4/8	5 3/8	5 2/8	7 5/8	M	Knik Glacier	AK	Braun Kopsack	1994	144
45 6/8	8 7/8	8 7/8	5 2/8	5 2/8	6 2/8	M	Valdez	AK	Jerry Vega	1997	144
45 4/8	9 2/8	9 3/8	5 3/8	5 3/8	6 0/8	M	Lemhi County	ID	A. LaVerne Hokanson	1968	158
45 4/8	8 7/8	8 7/8	5 2/8	5 1/8	8 1/8	M	Kenai Peninsula	AK	Dean Lust	1969	158
45 4/8	8 7/8	8 6/8	5 2/8	5 2/8	6 6/8	M	McCarthy Glacier	AK	John F. Sumrall	1974	158
45 4/8	9 0/8	8 7/8	5 2/8	5 2/8	6 0/8	M	Bonner County	ID	Dean A. Cox	1979	158
45 4/8	8 7/8	9 0/8	5 2/8	5 3/8	6 2/8	M	Kenai Peninsula	AK	Chris Kempf	1981	158
45 4/8	9 3/8	9 2/8	5 1/8	5 2/8	6 3/8	M	Jefferson County	WA	Gary R. Fountain	1987	158
45 4/8	8 7/8	8 6/8	5 2/8	5 2/8	6 4/8	M	Wrangell	AK	David Schuelke	1988	158
45 4/8	8 4/8	8 4/8	5 2/8	5 2/8	5 5/8	M	Snohomish County	WA	Timothy T. Neal	1988	158
45 4/8	9 4/8	9 3/8	5 2/8	5 2/8	6 1/8	M	Chaffee County	CO	Troy Cunningham	1993	158
45 4/8	9 3/8	9 1/8	5 2/8	5 2/8	6 4/8	M	Gunnison County	CO	Robert L. Syvertson, Jr.	1993	158
45 4/8	9 1/8	9 1/8	5 1/8	5 1/8	6 1/8	M	Clear Creek County	CO	Otho Hobbs	1995	158
45 4/8	9 0/8	9 0/8	5 1/8	5 1/8	6 0/8	M	Keremeos	BC	Gary F. Bogner	1995	158
45 4/8	8 6/8	9 1/8	5 4/8	5 4/8	5 4/8	M	La Plata County	CO	Robert D. Crask	1997	158
45 4/8	9 4/8	9 5/8	5 2/8	5 1/8	7 0/8	M	Pop Lake	BC	Kevin L. Reid	1998	158

ROCKY MOUNTAIN GOAT

Minimum Score 40 — Continued

SCORE	LENGTH OF HORN R	L	CIRCUMFERENCE OF BASE R	L	GREATEST SPREAD	SEX	AREA	STATE/PROVINCE	HUNTER'S NAME	DATE	RANK
45 4/8	9 0/8	9 0/8	5 1/8	5 1/8	6 3/8	M	Clear Creek County	CO	Larry O. Baker	1998	158
45 2/8	8 6/8	8 7/8	5 5/8	5 4/8	7 4/8	M	Telegraph Creek	BC	Troy M. Miller	1968	173
45 2/8	9 3/8	9 0/8	5 2/8	5 2/8	6 5/8	M	Kenai Mtn.	AK	Robert Borland	1970	173
45 2/8	9 5/8	9 4/8	5 0/8	5 0/8	7 1/8	M	Lemhi County	ID	D. Kittredge/R. Torrey	1973	173
45 2/8	8 3/8	8 5/8	5 1/8	5 2/8	6 2/8	M	Kechika River	BC	Paul Brunner	1974	173
45 2/8	8 5/8	8 5/8	5 3/8	5 3/8	5 3/8	M	Kittitas County	WA	Jim Novak	1974	173
45 2/8	8 6/8	8 7/8	5 2/8	5 4/8	6 2/8	M	Jefferson County	WA	Larry Ramsey	1978	173
45 2/8	9 4/8	10 1/8	5 0/8	5 0/8	7 6/8	M	Valdez	AK	Kevin Chelf	1984	173
45 2/8	9 1/8	9 3/8	5 0/8	5 0/8	5 5/8	M	Snohomish County	WA	Douglas H. Brandt	1988	173
45 2/8	8 7/8	8 7/8	5 3/8	5 2/8	7 0/8	M	Valdez	AK	Rickie D. Snell	1990	173
45 2/8	9 2/8	9 1/8	5 2/8	5 2/8	6 1/8	M	Clark County	ID	Kenneth Ruzicka	1994	173
45 2/8	8 7/8	8 5/8	5 4/8	5 4/8	7 2/8	M	Eagle County	CO	Connie Renfro	1995	173
45 2/8	9 0/8	9 3/8	5 3/8	5 3/8	6 2/8	M	Gunnison County	CO	K. Craig Vaughn	1995	173
45 0/8	9 3/8	9 1/8	5 3/8	5 3/8	5 5/8	M	Flathead County	MT	Jack Whitney	1962	185
45 0/8	9 0/8	9 1/8	5 0/8	5 0/8	6 3/8	M	Boise County	ID	Bradley H. Jolley	1972	185
45 0/8	9 4/8	9 3/8	5 0/8	5 0/8	7 1/8	M	Lemhi County	ID	G. Yasuda/R. White	1973	185
45 0/8	8 7/8	8 7/8	4 7/8	5 0/8	5 6/8	M	Jefferson County	WA	Edward H. Boyle	1974	185
45 0/8	9 2/8	9 6/8	5 2/8	5 2/8	7 2/8	M	Lemhi County	ID	Donald J. Keady	1976	185
45 0/8	8 6/8	9 0/8	5 2/8	5 2/8	6 4/8	M	Kenai Peninsula	AK	Eugene Smith, Jr.	1976	185
45 0/8	8 2/8	8 2/8	5 4/8	5 3/8	5 3/8	M	Big Sheep Creek	BC	Gerald Bond	1981	185
45 0/8	9 2/8	9 1/8	5 2/8	5 2/8	6 1/8	M	English Bay	AK	Maxallen D. Jackson	1982	185
45 0/8	8 1/8	8 2/8	5 2/8	5 2/8	6 4/8	M	Moricetown	BC	Don St. Jean	1985	185
45 0/8	9 2/8	9 2/8	5 2/8	5 2/8	5 5/8	M	La Plata County	CO	Jeffrey Yehl	1986	185
45 0/8	8 7/8	8 7/8	5 3/8	5 2/8	5 6/8	M	Kodiak Island	AK	Patricia Stewart	1989	185
45 0/8	9 1/8	9 2/8	5 2/8	5 2/8	6 3/8	M	Park County	WY	Jon E. Umphlett	1990	185
45 0/8	9 0/8	8 7/8	5 2/8	5 2/8	6 6/8	M	Bonneville County	ID	Randy K. Vranes	1990	185
45 0/8	9 5/8	9 4/8	4 7/8	4 7/8	6 2/8	M	Clear Creek County	CO	Sherwin Van Kooten	1990	185
45 0/8	9 1/8	9 1/8	5 2/8	5 2/8	6 6/8	M	Blaine County	ID	James Deitrick	1991	185
45 0/8	10 4/8	10 3/8	4 4/8	4 5/8	10 1/8	F	Bonneville County	ID	Mike Yantis	1992	185
45 0/8	9 1/8	9 0/8	5 2/8	5 3/8	5 7/8	M	San Juan County	CO	Valerie A. Gardner	1993	185
45 0/8	8 7/8	8 7/8	5 2/8	5 1/8	5 6/8	M	Kemano	BC	Randy McGregor	1995	185
44 6/8	8 6/8	8 5/8	5 1/8	5 1/8	0/8	M	Kittitas County	WA	Les Turner	1967	203
44 6/8	8 4/8	8 4/8	5 2/8	5 2/8	4 7/8	M	Snohomish County	WA	Kelly King	1977	203
44 6/8	8 7/8	8 6/8	5 1/8	5 1/8	6 1/8	M	Fox River	AK	John F. Sumrall	1977	203
44 6/8	8 7/8	8 6/8	5 2/8	5 3/8	6 7/8	M	Park County	WY	Scott Steere	1982	203
44 6/8	9 1/8	9 1/8	5 1/8	5 1/8	6 6/8	M	Valdez	AK	Rick D. Snell	1991	203
44 6/8	8 7/8	9 0/8	5 1/8	5 1/8	6 5/8	M	Pierce County	WA	Stan Nelson	1993	203
44 6/8	8 4/8	8 5/8	5 2/8	5 3/8	6 0/8	M	Madison County	MT	Dan Johnerson	1993	203
44 6/8	8 0/8	9 0/8	5 3/8	5 4/8	7 1/8	M	Clear Creek County	CO	Bob Chapman	1995	203
44 6/8	9 6/8	9 5/8	5 0/8	5 0/8	6 0/8	M	Elk Valley	BC	Dale Webber	1995	203
44 6/8	8 5/8	8 5/8	5 0/8	4 7/8	6 5/8	M	Carbon County	MT	Bradley S. Warren	1996	203
44 4/8	9 7/8	9 7/8	4 3/8	4 3/8	8 5/8	F	Cold Fish Lake	BC	K. K. Knickerbocker	1957	213
44 4/8	8 7/8	9 0/8	5 1/8	5 1/8	6 4/8	M	Kenai Peninsula	AK	Larry Jones	1969	213
44 4/8	8 5/8	8 5/8	5 1/8	5 2/8	6 1/8	M	Kittitas County	WA	David L. Smartt	1972	213
44 4/8	8 6/8	8 5/8	5 1/8	5 1/8	6 6/8	M	Stalk Lakes	BC	Richard J. Crowder	1977	213
44 4/8	10 1/8	10 2/8	4 4/8	4 4/8	8 5/8	F	Stock Creek	BC	Jay Deones	1978	213
44 4/8	9 0/8	9 0/8	4 7/8	4 7/8	6 6/8	M	Murky Lake	BC	Chuck Adams	1979	213
44 4/8	8 1/8	8 2/8	5 2/8	5 1/8	5 7/8	M	Jefferson County	WA	David P. Sanford	1981	213
44 4/8	9 2/8	9 2/8	5 2/8	5 2/8	5 5/8	M	Idaho County	ID	Darrell Howard	1982	213
44 4/8	10 2/8	10 1/8	4 3/8	4 3/8	7 6/8	F	Thatade Lake	BC	Jerry Baek	1984	213
44 4/8	9 2/8	9 3/8	4 6/8	4 5/8	7 7/8	M	Chugach Mtns.	AK	Darryl Quidort	1985	213
44 4/8	9 0/8	9 1/8	5 0/8	5 0/8	6 2/8	M	Atlin	BC	Tom Tietz	1985	213
44 4/8	8 5/8	8 5/8	5 1/8	5 1/8	6 4/8	M	Chugach Mtns.	AK	Gary White	1986	213
44 4/8	9 1/8	9 2/8	5 0/8	5 0/8	5 7/8	M	Chaffee County	CO	Tim Cuthriell	1987	213
44 4/8	9 0/8	8 5/8	5 0/8	5 0/8	6 5/8	M	Mason County	WA	Dan Howell	1987	213
44 4/8	9 2/8	8 6/8	5 3/8	5 3/8	5 6/8	M	Custer County	SD	Vilas Schoenfelder	1988	213
44 4/8	8 6/8	8 5/8	5 1/8	5 1/8	5 3/8	M	Todagin Mtn.	BC	Craig Reichmuth	1989	213
44 4/8	8 5/8	8 5/8	5 2/8	5 2/8	6 7/8	M	Hyland Lake	YUK	Gregory White	1989	213
44 4/8	9 0/8	9 0/8	5 0/8	5 1/8	5 4/8	M	Kittitas County	WA	Jim Charlton	1989	213
44 4/8	9 2/8	9 4/8	5 0/8	5 0/8	6 7/8	M	Madison County	MT	Steve Rhodes	1989	213
44 4/8	9 2/8	9 1/8	4 7/8	4 7/8	6 6/8	M	Summit County	CO	Steve Fausel	1990	213
44 4/8	8 7/8	8 5/8	5 2/8	5 2/8	5 7/8	M	Custer County	SD	R. Craig Oberle	1990	213
44 4/8	9 0/8	8 7/8	5 2/8	5 1/8	7 0/8	M	Jefferson County	WA	Steve Brown	1990	213
44 4/8	8 5/8	8 6/8	5 2/8	5 2/8	6 1/8	M	Kodiak Island	AK	Larry Spiva	1992	213
44 4/8	8 0/8	9 0/8	5 5/8	5 5/8	6 3/8	M	Carbon County	MT	Chris G. Sanford	1992	213
44 4/8	8 5/8	9 0/8	5 2/8	5 2/8	6 3/8	M	Mason County	WA	Scott A. Nixon	1993	213
44 4/8	8 6/8	8 5/8	5 1/8	5 1/8	5 5/8	M	Clear Creek County	CO	Barry J. Smith	1994	213
44 4/8	9 0/8	9 0/8	5 1/8	5 1/8	7 0/8	M	Clear Creek County	CO	E. Damon Handley	1997	213
44 4/8	8 6/8	8 6/8	5 1/8	5 1/8	6 3/8	M	Clear Creek County	CO	Steve Smith	1997	213
44 2/8	8 5/8	8 5/8	5 1/8	5 0/8	5 6/8	M	Kenai Lake	AK	James R. Carr	1973	241
44 2/8	8 6/8	9 0/8	5 1/8	5 1/8	6 5/8	M	Cold Fish Lake	BC	Dennis Behn	1975	241
44 2/8	7 7/8	7 6/8	5 1/8	5 2/8	5 2/8	M	King County	WA	Ronald A. Carpenter	1977	241
44 2/8	8 3/8	8 6/8	5 1/8	5 1/8	7 0/8	M	Todagin Lake	BC	Stanley D. Moore	1978	241
44 2/8	9 0/8	8 7/8	5 1/8	5 2/8	6 7/8	M	Custer County	SD	Kent D. Keenlyne	1981	241
44 2/8	8 0/8	8 0/8	5 5/8	5 4/8	6 2/8	M	Tutachi Lake	BC	Ray Keenan	1987	241
44 2/8	9 2/8	9 2/8	5 0/8	5 0/8	6 1/8	M	Gallatin County	MT	Phil Auble	1987	241
44 2/8	9 2/8	9 4/8	5 0/8	5 0/8	6 2/8	M	Clear Creek County	CO	Elmer R. Luce, Jr.	1990	241
44 2/8	8 6/8	8 6/8	5 0/8	5 0/8	7 1/8	M	Day Harbor	AK	Braun Kopsack	1992	241

ROCKY MOUNTAIN GOAT

Minimum Score 40 — Continued

SCORE	LENGTH OF HORN R	L	CIRCUMFERENCE OF BASE R	L	GREATEST SPREAD	SEX	AREA	STATE/PROVINCE	HUNTER'S NAME	DATE	RANK
44 2/8	8 6/8	9 0/8	5 1/8	5 1/8	7 3/8	M	Wrangell Mtns.	AK	Dr. John Ribic	1992	241
44 2/8	8 4/8	8 3/8	5 1/8	5 1/8	5 6/8	M	Chilkat River	AK	Eric Colledge	1993	241
44 2/8	9 0/8	9 1/8	5 2/8	5 2/8	6 5/8	M	La Plata County	CO	Brian Myers	1996	241
44 2/8	6 7/8	8 1/8	5 5/8	5 5/8	5 6/8	M	King County	WA	Daniel A. Whitmus	1996	241
44 0/8	7 4/8	9 0/8	5 4/8	5 4/8	6 0/8	M	Clallam County	WA	Virgil T. Cole, Jr.	1973	254
44 0/8	8 5/8	8 4/8	5 0/8	5 0/8	5 3/8	M	Chelan County	WA	Steve Gorr	1975	254
44 0/8	8 4/8	8 3/8	4 6/8	4 6/8	4 0/8	M	Snohomish County	WA	Steve Gorr	1978	254
44 0/8	8 6/8	8 6/8	5 1/8	5 1/8	5 2/8	M	Clear Creek County	CO	Lee Kline	1978	254
44 0/8	9 3/8	9 4/8	4 6/8	4 6/8	6 4/8	M	Valley County	ID	Jack Barrett	1980	254
44 0/8	7 6/8	7 7/8	5 3/8	5 3/8	5 6/8	M	Duti Lake	BC	Mike Morgan	1981	254
44 0/8	8 5/8	8 6/8	5 2/8	5 1/8	5 7/8	M	Idaho County	ID	Randy Ulmer	1982	254
44 0/8	9 0/8	9 2/8	5 0/8	5 0/8	6 6/8	M	Lake Tatlatui	BC	Rick Gilley	1983	254
44 0/8	9 6/8	6 3/8	5 7/8	5 7/8	7 5/8	M	Kenai Peninsula	AK	Michael R. Traub	1983	254
44 0/8	9 1/8	8 7/8	5 3/8	5 2/8	5 6/8	M	Lincoln County	MT	Jerry Brown	1983	254
44 0/8	8 4/8	8 3/8	4 7/8	4 7/8	6 5/8	M	Cordova	AK	James A. Davison	1985	254
44 0/8	8 7/8	8 7/8	5 1/8	5 1/8	6 6/8	M	Clark County	ID	Brent Poulter	1985	254
44 0/8	8 7/8	9 0/8	4 7/8	4 7/8	5 7/8	M	Snohomish County	WA	Stan Hansen	1985	254
44 0/8	8 4/8	9 1/8	5 1/8	5 1/8	5 7/8	M	Snohomish County	WA	Mark Knaus	1987	254
44 0/8	8 5/8	8 6/8	5 0/8	5 0/8	5 4/8	M	Bella Coola	BC	Randy Svisdahl	1991	254
44 0/8	9 1/8	9 2/8	4 6/8	4 7/8	5 6/8	M	Madison County	MT	James "Buck" MacLaurin	1994	254
44 0/8	9 0/8	9 1/8	4 7/8	5 0/8	6 0/8	M	Chaffee County	CO	Mark Montgomery	1994	254
44 0/8	9 2/8	9 2/8	4 6/8	4 6/8	6 5/8	M	Park County	WY	Terry Fieseler	1996	254
44 0/8	9 0/8	9 0/8	5 0/8	5 0/8	6 0/8	M	Clear Creek County	CO	Rick Duggan	1997	254
43 6/8	8 4/8	8 4/8	5 1/8	5 0/8	5 4/8	M	Kittitas County	WA	Joe Walker	1967	273
43 6/8	9 3/8	9 4/8	4 6/8	4 4/8	7 3/8	F	Duti River	BC	Walter J. Sawicki	1976	273
43 6/8	8 2/8	8 3/8	5 1/8	5 2/8	6 3/8	M	Park County	WY	Pat McAteer	1979	273
43 6/8	8 7/8	8 7/8	5 0/8	5 0/8	6 7/8	M	Bonner County	ID	Howard W. Holmes	1983	273
43 6/8	8 5/8	8 6/8	5 1/8	5 1/8	5 3/8	M	Chaffee County	CO	Doug Beck	1988	273
43 6/8	8 4/8	8 4/8	4 6/8	4 6/8	5 7/8	M	Kittitas County	WA	Greg "WildHorse" Willette	1989	273
43 6/8	9 0/8	9 3/8	5 0/8	5 0/8	7 1/8	M	Sulpher Creek	BC	Anthony P. Zielinski	1992	273
43 6/8	8 4/8	8 4/8	5 0/8	5 0/8	6 5/8	M	Head Keily Creek	BC	Bruce R. Schoeneweis	1997	273
43 4/8	8 7/8	8 7/8	4 7/8	4 7/8	6 0/8	M	Lake County	MT	Jack J. Whitney	1969	281
43 4/8	8 7/8	9 1/8	5 1/8	5 1/8	5 1/8	M	Lemhi County	ID	Joe Becker	1977	281
43 4/8	8 7/8	8 6/8	5 0/8	5 0/8	5 1/8	M	Kittitas County	WA	Glen Berry	1979	281
43 4/8	8 0/8	8 2/8	5 0/8	5 0/8	6 5/8	M	Ice Mtn.	BC	Larry Streiff	1979	281
43 4/8	8 5/8	8 5/8	4 7/8	4 7/8	6 2/8	M	Kitchener Lake	BC	James Saunoris	1983	281
43 4/8	8 3/8	8 5/8	5 1/8	5 2/8	5 6/8	M	Chaffee County	CO	Dan Eastin	1983	281
43 4/8	8 6/8	8 6/8	5 1/8	5 1/8	5 6/8	M	Chaffee County	CO	Don Bording	1983	281
43 4/8	9 1/8	9 2/8	4 4/8	4 4/8	7 0/8	F	Inklin River	BC	Dee C. Steinheiser	1986	281
43 4/8	9 0/8	8 7/8	4 7/8	4 7/8	6 1/8	M	Clear Creek County	CO	Daniel L. Tekavec	1986	281
43 4/8	8 2/8	8 4/8	5 0/8	5 0/8	5 5/8	M	Bella Coola	BC	Randy Svisdahl	1988	281
43 4/8	10 4/8	10 1/8	4 3/8	4 3/8	6 2/8	F	Clear Creek County	CO	Donald Ace Morgan	1989	281
43 4/8	9 6/8	9 6/8	4 4/8	4 3/8	7 6/8	F	Ealue Lake	BC	Dave Hannas	1990	281
43 4/8	8 3/8	8 3/8	5 2/8	5 2/8	5 6/8	M	Park County	MT	Steve Kamps	1991	281
43 4/8	8 7/8	9 2/8	5 0/8	5 1/8	6 3/8	M	Summit County	CO	Linda Strong	1994	281
43 4/8	8 6/8	8 4/8	5 0/8	5 0/8	6 2/8	M	Lemhi County	ID	Ben Fahnholz	1996	281
43 2/8	10 0/8	10 0/8	4 2/8	4 2/8	8 0/8	F	Tutaday Lake	BC	Larry Alma	1982	296
43 2/8	8 4/8	8 3/8	5 0/8	5 0/8	7 4/8	M	Telegraph Creek	BC	Jamie Byrne	1990	296
43 2/8	9 0/8	9 0/8	5 1/8	5 0/8	5 4/8	M	Ewilka Peak	BC	Larry D. Jones	1990	296
43 2/8	8 6/8	8 6/8	5 0/8	5 0/8	6 1/8	M	Chaffee County	CO	Shawn Kingery	1997	296
43 0/8	10 5/8	8 7/8	5 1/8	5 1/8	4 6/8	M		BC	Vic Clarkson	1960	300
43 0/8	10 0/8	10 0/8	4 4/8	4 4/8	6 2/8	F	Kittitas County	WA	Richard L. Thrasher	1968	300
43 0/8	10 1/8	10 2/8	3 7/8	3 7/8	8 0/8	F	Haines	AK	Roger O. Iveson	1972	300
43 0/8	8 7/8	8 2/8	5 0/8	5 0/8	7 3/8	M	Lemhi County	ID	Gregory D. Dodson	1977	300
43 0/8	9 0/8	9 0/8	5 1/8	5 1/8	5 2/8	M	Lemhi County	ID	Larry Nirk	1977	300
43 0/8	8 4/8	8 5/8	4 7/8	4 7/8	6 5/8	M	Mason County	WA	Andrew E. Appleby	1982	300
43 0/8	9 3/8	9 4/8	4 5/8	4 5/8	5 5/8	M	Custer County	ID	Larry A. Wilde	1983	300
43 0/8	8 0/8	8 1/8	5 0/8	5 1/8	6 6/8	M	Kittitas County	WA	Lance B. Cussons	1986	300
43 0/8	9 0/8	8 6/8	5 1/8	5 0/8	5 5/8	M	Keele River	NWT	Jim Ryan	1990	300
43 0/8	8 3/8	8 4/8	5 0/8	5 0/8	5 5/8	M	Border Lake	BC	Dean Stebner	1990	300
43 0/8	8 2/8	8 2/8	4 7/8	4 7/8	4 0/8	M	Pierce County	WA	Howard L. Harding	1990	300
43 0/8	8 1/8	8 1/8	5 1/8	5 1/8	5 4/8	M	Kittitas County	WA	John R. Sample	1991	300
43 0/8	8 2/8	8 4/8	5 1/8	5 1/8	4 4/8	M	Pierce County	WA	John DeWeber	1993	300
43 0/8	8 5/8	8 6/8	5 0/8	5 0/8	5 6/8	M	Gunnison County	CO	Kenneth Shelton	1994	300
43 0/8	8 7/8	8 7/8	4 7/8	5 0/8	5 1/8	M	Custer County	ID	Doug Hawker	1994	300
42 6/8	9 7/8	9 7/8	4 3/8	4 3/8	7 6/8	F	Lake County	MT	Jack Whitney	1965	315
42 6/8	8 2/8	8 7/8	5 0/8	5 0/8	6 0/8	M	Chaffee County	CO	Chuck Hutton	1979	315
42 6/8	9 0/8	7 3/8	5 5/8	5 4/8	6 3/8	M	Chaffee County	CO	Duke Prentup	1979	315
42 6/8	9 7/8	9 7/8	4 0/8	4 0/8	9 2/8	F	Knik Glacier	AK	Gary G. Wall	1985	315
42 6/8	8 4/8	8 5/8	4 7/8	4 7/8	6 2/8	M	Jefferson County	WA	Kevin Boyle	1986	315
42 6/8	9 4/8	9 3/8	4 3/8	4 3/8	6 7/8	F	Park County	CO	Corey Clyncke	1989	315
42 6/8	8 5/8	8 5/8	5 0/8	5 0/8	6 7/8	M	Jefferson County	WA	Gary Worth	1989	315
42 6/8	8 6/8	8 6/8	5 0/8	5 0/8	5 3/8	M	Ravalli County	MT	Dwight Schuh	1990	315
42 6/8	8 4/8	8 0/8	5 1/8	5 1/8	6 2/8	M	Summit County	CO	Stan Rauch	1994	315
42 6/8	7 7/8	8 2/8	5 2/8	5 2/8	6 0/8	M	Powell County	MT	Bruce Davidson	1994	315
42 6/8	8 3/8	8 3/8	4 6/8	4 6/8	5 4/8	M	Blaine County	ID	Thomas Daquino	1998	315
42 4/8	8 4/8	9 0/8	5 2/8	5 1/8	5 0/8	M	Chelan County	WA	G. H. Malinoski	1964	326
42 4/8	8 5/8	8 6/8	4 7/8	4 6/8	4 4/8	M	Goat Area 12	WA	James F. Miller	1977	326

ROCKY MOUNTAIN GOAT

Minimum Score 40

SCORE	LENGTH OF HORN R	L	CIRCUMFERENCE OF BASE R	L	GREATEST SPREAD	SEX	AREA	STATE/ PROVINCE	HUNTER'S NAME	DATE	RANK
42 4/8	8 5/8	8 6/8	4 6/8	4 6/8	5 4/8	M	Custer County	ID	Jim Wilson	1989	326
42 4/8	8 7/8	8 6/8	5 0/8	4 7/8	4 7/8	M	Custer County	ID	Kirk Westervelt	1989	326
42 4/8	8 7/8	9 2/8	5 0/8	4 7/8	6 7/8	M	Custer County	ID	David R. Anderson	1991	326
42 4/8	8 6/8	7 5/8	5 2/8	5 2/8	7 1/8	M	Park County	WY	Rob Marosok	1992	326
42 4/8	8 4/8	7 5/8	5 3/8	5 3/8	5 7/8	M	San Juan County	CO	Dennis L. Howell	1992	326
42 4/8	8 3/8	8 3/8	4 6/8	4 7/8	5 3/8	M	Howser Creek	BC	Alan Bressanutti	1992	326
42 2/8	7 6/8	8 2/8	5 0/8	5 0/8	5 4/8	M	Kleena Kleene	BC	William P. Mastrangel	1956	334
42 2/8	8 5/8	9 0/8	4 7/8	5 0/8	5 7/8	M	Terminus Mtn.	BC	Paul P. Schafer	1976	334
42 2/8	10 3/8	10 4/8	4 0/8	4 0/8	9 2/8	F	Kenai Peninsula	AK	Gilbert M. W. Smith	1976	334
42 2/8	8 3/8	8 5/8	4 7/8	5 0/8	5 2/8	M	Snohomish County	WA	Eric A. Olson	1979	334
42 2/8	8 1/8	8 1/8	5 1/8	5 0/8	5 1/8	M	Snohomish County	WA	Thomas E. Tipton	1985	334
42 2/8	9 0/8	9 0/8	4 3/8	4 3/8	7 3/8	F	Inklin River	BC	Dean Stebner	1987	334
42 2/8	8 1/8	8 1/8	4 7/8	4 7/8	7 2/8	M	Turnagain Pass	AK	Craig E. Scarbrough	1988	334
42 2/8	7 6/8	7 6/8	5 1/8	5 0/8	5 3/8	M	Snohomish County	WA	Jim Cowgill	1988	334
42 2/8	8 4/8	8 4/8	4 7/8	4 6/8	5 6/8	M	Park County	CO	Marvin Clyncke	1989	334
42 2/8	8 3/8	8 2/8	4 7/8	5 0/8	6 3/8	M	Eastman Mtn.	BC	Ron Serwa	1990	334
42 2/8	7 4/8	8 1/8	5 0/8	5 0/8	5 2/8	M	Bralorne	BC	Larry Anderson	1992	334
42 2/8	8 0/8	8 0/8	5 2/8	5 0/8	5 7/8	M	Pierce County	WA	Steve Felbinger	1994	334
42 2/8	9 0/8	7 7/8	5 1/8	5 0/8	6 4/8	M	Madison County	MT	Rob Sturtz	1994	334
42 2/8	8 4/8	8 3/8	4 7/8	4 7/8	5 5/8	M	Custer County	ID	Doug Ramsey	1996	334
42 0/8	7 2/8	8 2/8	5 1/8	5 1/8	7 0/8	M	Taylor Lake	BC	Bill Brown	1957	348
42 0/8	8 4/8	8 5/8	5 0/8	5 0/8	5 7/8	F	Swan Range	MT	Jack Whitney	1960	348
42 0/8	8 4/8	8 4/8	4 5/8	4 5/8	6 1/8	M	Lemhi County	ID	Frank N. Hough	1968	348
42 0/8	8 4/8	8 5/8	4 6/8	4 6/8	5 3/8	M	Lewis & Clark County	MT	Don Davidson	1978	348
42 0/8	9 4/8	9 4/8	4 0/8	4 0/8	6 1/8	F	Snohomish County	WA	Joseph R. St. Charles	1980	348
42 0/8	9 6/8	9 6/8	4 2/8	4 2/8	6 3/8	F	Chouteau County	MT	Terry Albrecht	1981	348
42 0/8	9 3/8	9 1/8	4 3/8	4 3/8	4 6/8	F	Lewis County	WA	James Garner	1982	348
42 0/8	9 3/8	9 4/8	4 0/8	4 1/8	7 3/8	F	Todagin Mtns.	BC	Neil Summers	1985	348
42 0/8	8 5/8	8 7/8	5 0/8	4 7/8	6 2/8	M	Ware	BC	Tim Good	1986	348
42 0/8	8 3/8	8 2/8	4 7/8	5 0/8	5 4/8	M	Ravalli County	MT	Jon Cusker	1987	348
42 0/8	8 1/8	8 3/8	4 7/8	4 7/8	6 5/8	M	Park County	CO	Doug Rininger	1990	348
42 0/8	8 2/8	8 2/8	5 0/8	5 0/8	5 5/8	M	Beaverhead County	MT	Bryant Shermoe	1995	348
42 0/8	9 0/8	9 1/8	4 2/8	4 2/8	6 4/8	F	Okanogan County	WA	T. J. Conrads	1995	348
42 0/8	8 5/8	8 4/8	5 1/8	5 0/8	5 4/8	M	Chaffee County	CO	Dean Aggson	1998	348
41 6/8	8 1/8	8 0/8	4 7/8	4 7/8	6 3/8	F	Lord River	BC	Dr. R. Congdon	1958	362
41 6/8	8 1/8	8 1/8	4 7/8	4 6/8	5 6/8	M	Beaverhead County	MT	Mike Bartz	1976	362
41 6/8	9 1/8	9 1/8	4 3/8	4 3/8	5 3/8	F	Snohomish County	WA	Scott McDermott	1980	362
41 6/8	9 4/8	9 4/8	4 2/8	4 1/8	6 2/8	F	Snohomish County	WA	Steve Novy	1981	362
41 6/8	8 2/8	8 2/8	4 6/8	4 6/8	5 6/8	M	Jefferson County	WA	Richard Van Calcar	1983	362
41 6/8	7 6/8	7 5/8	4 7/8	4 7/8	5 5/8	M	Lawson Lake	BC	David Baldwin	1984	362
41 6/8	7 3/8	7 6/8	5 1/8	5 1/8	5 0/8	M	Snohomish County	WA	Jack Williams	1984	362
41 6/8	8 3/8	8 3/8	4 7/8	4 7/8	5 3/8	M	Jefferson County	WA	Steve Wyman	1984	362
41 6/8	8 6/8	8 7/8	4 6/8	4 7/8	5 5/8	M	La Plata County	CO	Sid Strzok	1986	362
41 6/8	8 3/8	8 3/8	4 7/8	4 6/8	6 2/8	M	Clear Creek County	CO	Tony Snow	1988	362
41 6/8	8 3/8	8 2/8	4 7/8	4 7/8	5 0/8	M	Chaffee County	CO	Doug Aiken	1992	362
41 6/8	8 0/8	8 7/8	5 0/8	5 0/8	5 7/8	M	Chaffee County	CO	Ron Sniff	1992	362
41 6/8	9 7/8	9 7/8	4 1/8	4 1/8	5 3/8	F	Madison County	MT	Kris Thorson	1992	362
41 6/8	8 0/8	8 3/8	4 6/8	4 6/8	6 3/8	M	Heart Mtn.	BC	Tim Walters	1993	362
41 6/8	8 2/8	8 2/8	4 7/8	4 7/8	5 0/8	M	La Plata County	CO	Chad R. Bedell	1993	362
41 6/8	8 6/8	8 4/8	5 0/8	4 7/8	5 4/8	M	Gunnison County	CO	Duwayne Langseth	1996	362
41 6/8	8 2/8	8 3/8	4 7/8	5 0/8	5 6/8	M	Clear Creek County	CO	Kevin Bertsch	1998	362
41 6/8	7 5/8	8 0/8	5 2/8	5 2/8	5 3/8	M	Park County	MT	Sean Shea	1998	362
41 4/8	10 2/8	10 2/8	4 0/8	4 0/8	10 1/8	F	Takia River	BC	William L. Sullivan	1966	380
41 4/8	8 1/8	8 1/8	4 6/8	4 7/8	5 4/8	M	Summit County	CO	Wayne Depperschmidt	1979	380
41 4/8	9 5/8	9 6/8	3 6/8	3 5/8	7 2/8	F	Snohomish County	WA	Steve Wait	1981	380
41 4/8	9 3/8	9 1/8	4 1/8	4 1/8	7 1/8	F	Whatcom County	WA	Adam Redford	1981	380
41 4/8	9 4/8	9 4/8	4 2/8	4 2/8	10 0/8	F	Atlin Lake	BC	Ty Harpain	1989	380
41 4/8	8 2/8	8 2/8	4 7/8	5 0/8	6 0/8	M	La Plata County	CO	Dale Struble	1990	380
41 4/8	8 4/8	8 5/8	4 4/8	4 5/8	7 5/8	M	Prince William Sound	AK	John D. "Jack" Frost	1990	380
41 4/8	7 5/8	8 2/8	5 1/8	5 1/8	5 6/8	M	Clear Creek County	CO	Lonny Vanatta	1992	380
41 4/8	8 3/8	8 4/8	4 7/8	4 7/8	6 1/8	M	Clear Creek County	CO	Larry Bishop	1994	380
41 4/8	9 2/8	8 5/8	4 2/8	4 2/8	6 4/8	F	Chouteau County	MT	Donny Roy	1994	380
41 4/8	8 2/8	8 2/8	4 6/8	4 6/8	6 3/8	M	Island Lake	BC	Kevin D. Hatfield	1996	380
41 4/8	8 6/8	8 5/8	4 6/8	4 6/8	6 1/8	M	La Plata County	CO	Kurt C. Hall	1997	380
41 2/8	9 7/8	9 6/8	4 2/8	4 2/8	6 4/8	F	Crazy Mtns.	MT	Glenn Gibson	1957	392
41 2/8	8 3/8	8 3/8	4 3/8	4 3/8	5 1/8	F	Kittitas County	WA	Dennis Dunn	1973	392
41 2/8	8 3/8	8 2/8	4 6/8	4 6/8	5 3/8	M	Teton County	MT	Edwin Evans	1983	392
41 2/8	9 2/8	9 2/8	4 2/8	4 2/8	6 1/8	F	Rusty Creek	BC	Ronald Montross	1984	392
41 2/8	8 2/8	8 2/8	4 7/8	4 6/8	6 0/8	M	Pierce County	WA	Dale Holpainen	1986	392
41 2/8	9 3/8	9 3/8	3 7/8	3 7/8	8 1/8	F	Chugach Mtns.	AK	Richard Moran	1988	392
41 2/8	7 7/8	7 7/8	4 7/8	4 7/8	5 3/8	M	Snohomish County	WA	Dale Drilling	1988	392
41 2/8	8 4/8	8 4/8	4 6/8	4 5/8	6 0/8	M	Chaffee County	CO	Larick Spencer	1990	392
41 2/8	8 2/8	8 2/8	4 6/8	4 6/8	7 0/8	M	Otter Tail Creek	BC	Vaughn D. Ballard	1991	392
41 2/8	8 7/8	8 7/8	4 6/8	4 6/8	5 5/8	M	Chaffee County	CO	David C. Dahl	1992	392
41 2/8	8 3/8	8 3/8	4 6/8	4 6/8	5 6/8	M	Summit County	CO	Dominic Florian	1992	392
41 2/8	7 6/8	8 0/8	4 6/8	4 7/8	5 6/8	M	Bralorne	BC	Larry Anderson	1993	392
41 2/8	8 3/8	8 3/8	4 5/8	4 5/8	5 3/8	M	Custer County	ID	Jim Schrader	1996	392
41 0/8	8 6/8	8 5/8	4 2/8	4 2/8	7 0/8	M	Penticton	BC	Bill Brown	1958	405

ROCKY MOUNTAIN GOAT

Minimum Score 40 — Continued

SCORE	LENGTH OF HORN R	L	CIRCUMFERENCE OF BASE R	L	GREATEST SPREAD	SEX	AREA	STATE/PROVINCE	HUNTER'S NAME	DATE	RANK
41 0/8	8 7/8	9 0/8	4 4/8	4 4/8	5 5/8	F	Snohomish County	WA	Bud Peck	1960	405
41 0/8	10 0/8	10 0/8	3 6/8	3 7/8	6 2/8	F	Holly Creek	BC	Jim Jackson	1964	405
41 0/8	9 2/8	9 3/8	3 7/8	3 7/8	10 0/8	F	Valdez	AK	Jim Jarvis	1979	405
41 0/8	8 7/8	9 0/8	4 0/8	3 7/8	5 7/8	F	Snohomish County	WA	Mark S. Jacobs	1980	405
41 0/8	8 1/8	8 1/8	4 6/8	4 6/8	5 7/8	M	Clallam County	WA	Russ Spaulding	1981	405
41 0/8	8 1/8	7 4/8	4 7/8	4 7/8	6 4/8	M	Bennett Lake	BC	Dave Richardson	1982	405
41 0/8	9 1/8	9 1/8	4 0/8	4 0/8	6 1/8	F	Snohomish County	WA	Richard Kobel	1984	405
41 0/8	7 7/8	8 0/8	4 6/8	4 6/8	4 6/8	F	Bonner County	ID	Linda Leake	1984	405
41 0/8	9 0/8	9 2/8	4 2/8	4 3/8	4 4/8	F	Snohomish County	WA	Smokey Crews	1985	405
41 0/8	8 3/8	8 2/8	4 5/8	4 5/8	6 1/8	M	Park County	CO	Scott George	1990	405
41 0/8	9 5/8	9 3/8	4 2/8	4 2/8	6 4/8	F	Clear Creek County	CO	John Borlang	1991	405
41 0/8	7 2/8	7 2/8	5 0/8	5 0/8	5 2/8	M	Lake George	AK	Thomas A. Chadwick	1993	405
41 0/8	8 7/8	8 7/8	4 3/8	4 4/8	5 2/8	F	Cranbrook	BC	Stan Godfrey	1993	405
41 0/8	9 4/8	9 6/8	4 0/8	4 0/8	7 0/8	F	Beaverhead County	MT	Danny Moore	1996	405
40 6/8	8 3/8	8 3/8	4 6/8	4 6/8	5 2/8	M	Boise County	ID	Ronald L. Sherer	1970	420
40 6/8	7 3/8	7 2/8	4 7/8	4 6/8	6 1/8	M	Kitchener Lake	BC	Walt Krom	1971	420
40 6/8	8 0/8	7 7/8	4 5/8	4 5/8	6 0/8	M	Kenai Lake	AK	Dennis Lattery	1973	420
40 6/8	8 6/8	8 5/8	4 6/8	4 6/8	5 5/8	M	Park County	WY	Jeff Umphlett	1979	420
40 6/8	9 1/8	9 1/8	4 1/8	4 1/8	5 4/8	F	Kittitas County	WA	Roger Pitman	1980	420
40 6/8	9 0/8	9 0/8	4 3/8	4 4/8	6 2/8	F	San Juan County	CO	Bill McEwen	1984	420
40 6/8	9 2/8	9 1/8	4 1/8	4 1/8	5 6/8	F	Kittitas County	WA	L. James Bailey	1984	420
40 6/8	8 1/8	8 5/8	4 4/8	4 5/8	6 3/8	M	Clallam County	WA	Dave Kanters	1988	420
40 6/8	9 0/8	8 7/8	4 2/8	4 2/8	6 6/8	F	Mt. Hunter	BC	Dennis Kamstra	1990	420
40 6/8	9 2/8	9 3/8	4 1/8	4 1/8	5 5/8	F	Clear Creek County	CO	Dave Culter	1990	420
40 6/8	8 2/8	8 2/8	4 6/8	4 7/8	5 2/8	M	Golden	BC	Jeffrey W. Murray	1992	420
40 6/8	8 4/8	8 6/8	4 4/8	4 4/8	6 3/8	M	Custer County	ID	Bruce Meyer	1993	420
40 6/8	7 7/8	7 7/8	4 6/8	4 7/8	6 5/8	M	Frog River	BC	David F. Perkin	1994	420
40 6/8	8 5/8	7 7/8	4 6/8	4 7/8	5 5/8	M	Custer County	ID	Don Glenn, Jr.	1994	420
40 6/8	9 5/8	10 0/8	3 6/8	3 7/8	6 1/8	F	Findlay Creek	BC	M. Rodney Denton	1995	420
40 6/8	9 0/8	8 0/8	4 6/8	4 6/8	6 0/8	M	Beaverhead County	MT	Poncho McCoy	1996	420
40 6/8	8 0/8	8 0/8	4 6/8	4 6/8	5 2/8	M	Madison County	MT	Eric Huff	1996	420
40 4/8	9 0/8	8 3/8	4 1/8	4 1/8	7 5/8	F	Little Johnstone Bay	AK	Ray Uhl	1965	437
40 4/8	8 7/8	8 6/8	4 1/8	4 1/8	6 4/8	F	Smithers	BC	Chris Vanderhorst	1974	437
40 4/8	9 4/8	9 5/8	3 7/8	4 0/8	10 3/8	F	Kenai Mtn.	AK	David E. Smith	1976	437
40 4/8	8 6/8	8 4/8	4 2/8	4 2/8	4 7/8	F	Kittitas County	WA	Kirk Cresto	1981	437
40 4/8	7 3/8	8 4/8	5 0/8	5 0/8	6 6/8	M	Cordova	AK	Ray Ryan	1986	437
40 4/8	6 6/8	8 7/8	5 3/8	5 2/8	6 7/8	M	La Plata County	CO	John Gardner	1986	437
40 4/8	8 1/8	8 1/8	4 5/8	4 5/8	4 7/8	M	Snohomish County	WA	Gregg Welch	1987	437
40 4/8	8 4/8	8 4/8	4 2/8	4 2/8	6 7/8	F	Clear Creek County	CO	Reggie Spiegelberg	1991	437
40 2/8	7 6/8	7 3/8	4 5/8	4 5/8	5 5/8	M	Boise County	ID	Jack Arbaugh	1975	445
40 2/8	8 5/8	8 4/8	4 0/8	4 0/8	5 7/8	F	Kittitas County	WA	Bob McClure	1977	445
40 2/8	7 2/8	7 2/8	4 5/8	4 5/8	5 3/8	M	Tustemena Glacier	AK	Lloyd M. Minerich	1988	445
40 2/8	9 0/8	8 7/8	4 1/8	4 1/8	6 0/8	F	Clear Creek County	CO	Wes Heiland	1991	445
40 2/8	8 0/8	8 1/8	4 5/8	4 5/8	5 6/8	M	Clear Creek County	CO	Thomas J. Hoffman	1991	445
40 2/8	8 5/8	8 7/8	4 1/8	4 1/8	5 7/8	F	Revelstoke	BC	Rick A. Albers	1995	445
40 2/8	7 4/8	8 7/8	4 6/8	4 7/8	7 0/8	M	Gallatin County	MT	Jerry Karsky	1995	445
40 2/8	6 7/8	8 0/8	4 7/8	5 0/8	7 0/8	M	Firvale	BC	Rick Paquette	1998	445
40 0/8	8 7/8	8 7/8	4 2/8	4 2/8	6 6/8	F	Chaffee County	CO	Wayne Spencer	1973	453
40 0/8	8 3/8	8 2/8	4 5/8	4 6/8	6 1/8	M	Lemhi County	ID	Marvin Tye	1973	453
40 0/8	8 3/8	8 3/8	4 1/8	4 1/8	5 1/8	F	Snohomish County	WA	Albert A. Rinaldi, Jr.	1974	453
40 0/8	7 5/8	7 5/8	4 6/8	4 6/8	5 0/8	M	Cordova	AK	Ray P. Noregaard	1975	453
40 0/8	9 1/8	9 1/8	4 1/8	4 1/8	6 7/8	F	Kitchener Lake	BC	John Dmytryka	1976	453
40 0/8	9 4/8	9 2/8	4 2/8	4 1/8	7 5/8	F	Cimari Valley	ID	Robert Frank	1976	453
40 0/8	8 3/8	8 2/8	4 5/8	4 5/8	4 7/8	M	Lemhi County	ID	H. R. 'Rusty' Neely	1976	453
40 0/8	8 5/8	8 5/8	4 3/8	4 2/8	6 1/8	F	Summit County	CO	Michael Beckwith	1978	453
40 0/8	8 7/8	8 5/8	4 1/8	4 1/8	5 5/8	F	Kittitas County	WA	Wilton Viall	1984	453
40 0/8	9 3/8	9 2/8	4 1/8	4 1/8	6 0/8	F	La Plata County	CO	Daniel Willems	1988	453
40 0/8	9 0/8	8 7/8	4 1/8	4 2/8	6 4/8	F	Bonneville County	ID	Tab R. Mendenhall	1989	453
40 0/8	7 5/8	7 6/8	4 6/8	4 6/8	6 3/8	M	Clear Creek County	CO	Monty Ace Morgan	1990	453
40 0/8	8 7/8	9 0/8	3 6/8	3 6/8	7 0/8	F	Kynck Inlet	BC	Steve Schmid	1990	453
40 0/8	8 7/8	9 2/8	4 1/8	4 1/8	6 4/8	F	La Plata County	CO	Tony Casagrande	1992	453
40 0/8	7 4/8	7 4/8	4 6/8	4 6/8	5 5/8	M	Salt Lake County	UT	Gary Brewer	1992	453
40 0/8	7 0/8	6 0/8	4 7/8	4 7/8	5 3/8	M	Custer County	ID	Duane Zemliska	1992	453
40 0/8	8 4/8	8 3/8	4 4/8	4 4/8	5 0/8	M	Flathead County	MT	Eric Kress	1993	453
40 0/8	8 0/8	8 0/8	4 6/8	4 5/8	5 5/8	M	Quarry Creek	BC	Archie J. Nesbitt	1997	453

World Record Bighorn Sheep
Score: 191 3/8
El Paso County, Colorado - 1983
Hunter: Gene Moore

BIGHORN SHEEP

Minimum Score 140 *Ovis canadensis canadensis* and certain related subspecies

SCORE	LENGTH OF R HORN L		CIRCUMFERENCE R OF BASE L		GREATEST SPREAD	AREA	STATE/ PROVINCE	HUNTER'S NAME	DATE	RANK
191 3/8	42 3/8	42 2/8	15 5/8	15 4/8	24 0/8	El Paso County	CO	Gene Moore	1983	1
190 6/8	40 0/8	40 0/8	15 6/8	15 6/8	23 0/8	Gregg Creek	ALB	Bob "Yukon" Huebschwerlen	1998	2
190 2/8	39 4/8	39 4/8	16 4/8	16 3/8	20 4/8	Canmore	ALB	Brian Eloschuk	1982	3
189 2/8	36 5/8	37 1/8	15 6/8	15 6/8	26 2/8	Fergus County	MT	George Harms	1998	4
186 1/8	38 2/8	37 1/8	15 5/8	15 3/8	20 7/8	Canmore	ALB	Cornel Yarmoloy	1982	5
184 6/8	39 1/8	37 5/8	16 5/8	16 5/8	20 2/8	Ravalli County	MT	Bill A. Richichi	1996	6
184 1/8	38 4/8	38 7/8	15 5/8	15 5/8	21 1/8	Pigeon Mtn.	ALB	Guy Woods	1985	7
184 0/8	39 1/8	37 7/8	15 3/8	15 1/8	20 2/8	Canmore	ALB	Al Schroeder	1989	8
183 7/8	38 3/8	38 6/8	15 4/8	15 5/8	24 5/8	Deer Lodge County	MT	Jerry Parsons	1986	9
183 7/8	36 6/8	37 1/8	15 0/8	15 0/8	22 0/8	Clear Creek County	CO	Ray Alt	1988	9
183 4/8	40 3/8	41 1/8	15 5/8	15 6/8	23 3/8	Lincoln County	MT	Paul Schafer	1983	11
183 4/8	38 4/8	39 0/8	16 1/8	16 0/8	19 6/8	Ravalli County	MT	Jim Chinn	1986	11
183 2/8	40 4/8	39 2/8	14 7/8	14 7/8	21 6/8	El Paso County	CO	Bob Renner	1979	13
183 2/8	37 4/8	36 2/8	16 3/8	16 3/8	24 1/8	Larimer County	CO	Jim Black	1992	13
182 7/8	38 2/8	38 5/8	15 3/8	15 3/8	22 6/8	El Paso County	CO	Fred Church	1989	15
182 0/8	39 6/8	39 6/8	15 0/8	15 0/8	22 4/8	Sanders County	MT	John T. Beyer	1990	16
181 5/8	38 1/8	34 4/8	16 2/8	16 2/8	23 0/8	Canmore	ALB	Paul Inzanti	1984	17
181 1/8	38 1/8	39 0/8	14 3/8	14 3/8	21 6/8	Clear Creek County	CO	Gary Renfro	1982	18
180 7/8	37 3/8	38 4/8	15 4/8	15 4/8	22 1/8	Granite County	MT	Alden Gregory Beard	1992	19

BIGHORN SHEEP

Minimum Score 140   Continued

SCORE	LENGTH OF HORN R / L		CIRCUMFERENCE OF BASE R / L		GREATEST SPREAD	AREA	STATE/ PROVINCE	HUNTER'S NAME	DATE	RANK
180 3/8	37 6/8	36 5/8	15 2/8	15 2/8	19 5/8	San Miguel County	NM	Ronald D. Rod	1992	20
180 1/8	37 4/8	37 3/8	15 2/8	15 2/8	22 7/8	Clear Creek County	CO	Charles W. Hanawalt	1990	21
180 1/8	40 5/8	39 2/8	15 5/8	15 5/8	23 7/8	Blaine County	MT	Mike Montgomery	1995	21
179 7/8	35 7/8	34 2/8	15 4/8	15 2/8	21 4/8	Huerfano County	CO	Dennis Gardner	1996	23
179 6/8	38 6/8	38 6/8	15 2/8	15 4/8	21 0/8	Exshaw Creek	ALB	Kenneth F. Bills	1993	24
179 5/8	39 4/8	38 3/8	14 4/8	14 2/8	22 1/8	El Paso County	CO	Doy K. Curtis	1977	25
179 3/8	38 1/8	37 4/8	15 7/8	15 7/8	21 0/8	Mineral County	MT	Craig Thomas	1985	26
179 2/8	37 6/8	37 4/8	14 4/8	14 3/8	21 6/8	El Paso County	CO	Thomas H. States	1982	27
178 6/8	35 2/8	35 0/8	16 3/8	16 3/8	19 6/8	Mt. Livingston	ALB	Jim Smetaniuk	1982	28
178 5/8	38 4/8	37 5/8	15 4/8	15 3/8	23 0/8	Park County	MT	Mike Mahlman	1983	29
178 0/8	36 3/8	35 3/8	15 5/8	16 0/8	19 7/8	Greenlee County	AZ	Jim Machac	1994	30
177 7/8	34 6/8	34 1/8	16 2/8	16 4/8	22 0/8	Fergus County	MT	Rob Lucas	1988	31
177 6/8	34 6/8	36 0/8	15 6/8	15 6/8	25 1/8	El Paso County	CO	John Diedrich	1990	32
177 2/8	32 5/8	34 3/8	15 3/8	15 3/8	22 3/8	Larimer County	CO	Mark Montgomery	1992	33
177 2/8	39 3/8	37 1/8	14 4/8	14 4/8	23 2/8	Granite County	MT	Neil L. Jacobson	1998	33
177 0/8	36 6/8	35 4/8	15 3/8	15 3/8	20 0/8	Powell County	MT	Jerry D. McPherson	1998	35
176 7/8	38 3/8	36 2/8	14 4/8	14 6/8	21 3/8	El Paso County	CO	Brian Nicely	1996	36
176 3/8	37 3/8	39 0/8	14 6/8	14 4/8	22 0/8	Sweet Grass County	MT	Ray Alt	1968	37
176 2/8	37 2/8	38 0/8	14 4/8	14 3/8	22 1/8	Clear Creek County	CO	Dominic Florian	1989	38
176 1/8	35 3/8	37 4/8	15 4/8	15 3/8	24 4/8	El Paso County	CO	Tony Seahorn	1977	39
176 1/8	39 4/8	38 1/8	14 7/8	15 2/8	22 2/8	Phillips County	MT	Ty Milne	1991	39
176 1/8	38 0/8	39 7/8	15 0/8	15 1/8	19 6/8	Rio Arriba County	NM	Kevin L. Reid	1994	39
176 1/8	37 1/8	37 0/8	15 1/8	15 1/8	19 6/8	Nordegg	ALB	Scott Cragg	1994	39
176 0/8	35 2/8	36 2/8	15 2/8	15 2/8	23 5/8	El Paso County	CO	Gary Eastwood	1982	43
175 2/8	35 2/8	33 0/8	15 4/8	15 2/8	25 2/8	Lake County	OR	Stephen Herrera	1989	44
175 1/8	39 5/8	39 6/8	15 2/8	15 2/8	19 4/8	Canmore	ALB	Dave Addie	1985	45
174 7/8	40 3/8	34 4/8	14 3/8	14 3/8	24 0/8	El Paso County	CO	Robert Reed	1993	46
174 2/8	35 6/8	36 0/8	14 2/8	14 2/8	19 6/8	Saguache County	CO	David "Jake" Powell	1995	47
174 1/8	38 1/8	37 6/8	15 1/8	15 2/8	21 5/8	Canmore	ALB	Todd Zeuske	1993	48
174 1/8	35 4/8	35 3/8	15 7/8	15 7/8	22 0/8	Clear Creek County	CO	Larry C. Baker	1998	48
174 0/8	35 2/8	35 4/8	16 0/8	16 2/8	21 3/8	Wind Ridge	ALB	Dirk Kieft	1984	50
173 7/8	35 1/8	37 0/8	15 1/8	15 3/8	20 7/8	Sanders County	MT	Bart Schleyer	1987	51
173 7/8	37 1/8	37 4/8	14 6/8	14 6/8	21 7/8	Clear Creek County	CO	Dan Teets	1998	51
173 6/8	32 6/8	34 0/8	16 1/8	16 1/8	19 1/8	Canmore	ALB	Michael Ukrainetz	1983	53
173 6/8	39 0/8	35 0/8	14 4/8	14 4/8	20 0/8	Fergus County	MT	Charles Hueth	1996	53
173 5/8	34 4/8	35 5/8	14 4/8	14 3/8	21 7/8	Clear Creek County	CO	Ronald Rockwell	1995	55
173 4/8	38 0/8	38 0/8	15 0/8	15 0/8	23 5/8	Cougar Canyon	ALB	Curt Lynn	1983	56
172 7/8	36 0/8	35 5/8	13 6/8	13 7/8	21 4/8	Boulder County	CO	Scott George	1995	57
172 6/8	35 6/8	36 4/8	14 3/8	14 3/8	22 0/8	El Paso County	CO	Duane Imhoff	1982	58
172 2/8	34 2/8	36 0/8	14 6/8	14 6/8	20 4/8	Nordegg	ALB	Gerard Stark	1994	59
172 1/8	35 7/8	35 0/8	14 4/8	14 4/8	21 4/8	Clear Creek County	CO	Jim Fitzgerald	1998	60
171 7/8	38 3/8	35 2/8	14 5/8	14 5/8	22 0/8	Canmore	ALB	Chuck Adams	1985	61
171 7/8	37 1/8	37 2/8	15 4/8	15 3/8	22 2/8	Canmore	ALB	Merlyn Howg	1990	61
171 6/8	34 6/8	33 4/8	15 3/8	15 2/8	21 4/8	Clear Creek County	CO	Lonny Vanatta	1988	63
171 5/8	35 4/8	34 5/8	15 3/8	15 3/8	21 4/8	Granite County	MT	Marlon Clapham	1994	64
170 7/8	37 2/8	37 1/8	14 6/8	14 6/8	21 1/8	Mora County	NM	Dave McInroy	1991	65
170 7/8	34 2/8	37 5/8	14 1/8	14 2/8	21 2/8	Greenlee County	AZ	Patrick Kirby	1996	65
170 5/8	33 3/8	33 4/8	14 1/8	14 1/8	21 0/8	Clear Creek County	CO	Robert L Syvertson,Jr	1989	67
170 5/8	36 1/8	37 2/8	14 3/8	14 4/8	21 5/8	Beaverhead County	MT	Jerry Allen	1991	67
170 0/8	35 6/8	36 2/8	14 2/8	14 3/8	22 2/8	Clear Creek County	CO	Troy Cunningham	1988	69
169 7/8	32 2/8	38 3/8	14 5/8	14 7/8	22 4/8	Fergus County	MT	Terry L. Selph	1990	70
169 6/8	35 2/8	34 4/8	14 4/8	14 4/8	23 0/8	Clear Creek County	CO	Janet George	1989	71
169 2/8	33 2/8	33 6/8	14 5/8	14 6/8	21 4/8	Clear Creek County	CO	Barry J. Smith	1992	72
169 0/8	33 2/8	35 2/8	14 3/8	14 2/8	20 2/8	Cougar Canyon	ALB	Paul Schwengler	1980	73
169 0/8	34 0/8	35 2/8	15 6/8	15 7/8	21 6/8	Canmore	ALB	Dave Gerber	1989	73
169 0/8	36 2/8	36 6/8	14 0/8	14 0/8	22 0/8	Las Animas County	CO	Lonny Stuht	1994	73
168 7/8	37 0/8	36 1/8	16 0/8	16 1/8	29 4/8	Chouteau County	MT	Mark L. Gilkey	1990	76
168 6/8	34 7/8	34 3/8	14 2/8	14 2/8	20 0/8	Larimer County	CO	Richard Marshburn	1995	77
168 1/8	32 2/8	32 7/8	15 0/8	14 7/8	20 5/8	Saguache County	CO	Simon Aragi	1990	78
168 0/8	33 6/8	33 6/8	15 1/8	15 0/8	20 6/8	Custer County	CO	Jennings Cress	1977	79
167 6/8	36 3/8	36 1/8	14 6/8	14 6/8	21 1/8	N. Saskatchewan River	ALB	Larry Jones	1962	80
167 6/8	34 4/8	35 0/8	15 4/8	15 4/8	22 2/8	Sanders County	MT	Robert L. Borden	1983	80
167 6/8	32 3/8	35 1/8	14 7/8	15 0/8	20 0/8	Canmore	ALB	Ken Madsen	1984	80
167 6/8	35 1/8	32 3/8	14 4/8	14 4/8	20 5/8	Idaho County	ID	Bill Fisk	1991	80
167 4/8	31 4/8	32 0/8	15 4/8	15 3/8	22 2/8	Clear Creek County	CO	Reggie Spiegelberg	1988	84
167 3/8	33 4/8	35 3/8	15 2/8	15 2/8	21 6/8	Canmore	ALB	Gregory Koehl	1989	85
167 2/8	36 1/8	32 5/8	15 3/8	15 4/8	23 3/8	Greenlee County	AZ	John C. McClendon	1992	86
167 2/8	33 0/8	34 4/8	14 1/8	14 1/8	23 3/8	Fergus County	MT	Jim G. Winjum	1998	86
167 1/8	34 1/8	34 4/8	14 2/8	14 5/8	22 4/8	Lincoln County	MT	Ron Bain	1974	88
167 1/8	38 5/8	32 4/8	15 4/8	15 6/8	19 0/8	Blaine County	MT	Ed Evans	1990	88
166 7/8	31 4/8	34 7/8	14 7/8	14 6/8	21 5/8	Clear Creek County	CO	Thomas J. Hoffman	1986	90
166 5/8	33 5/8	33 6/8	15 4/8	15 4/8	21 6/8	Canmore	ALB	Mike Traub	1988	91
166 2/8	32 6/8	36 2/8	14 6/8	14 6/8	20 7/8	County of Bighorn	ALB	Jeff B. Davis	1991	92
166 2/8	33 0/8	31 4/8	14 0/8	14 0/8	21 0/8	Clear Creek County	CO	Ken Hoffmeyer	1997	92
166 1/8	33 3/8	33 2/8	15 2/8	15 2/8	21 7/8	Idaho County	ID	Michael Schnider	1994	94
166 1/8	34 6/8	34 1/8	14 0/8	14 1/8	19 6/8	Saguache County	CO	Jeff Puls	1997	94
166 0/8	33 2/8	32 2/8	14 7/8	14 7/8	19 7/8	Jefferson County	CO	Robert Sorrell	1977	96
165 7/8	36 1/8	37 0/8	13 4/8	13 3/8	19 3/8	Kananaskis	ALB	Richard G. Perrett	1980	97

BIGHORN SHEEP

Minimum Score 140 — Continued

SCORE	LENGTH OF HORN R	L	CIRCUMFERENCE OF BASE R	L	GREATEST SPREAD	AREA	STATE/ PROVINCE	HUNTER'S NAME	DATE	RANK
165 6/8	35 2/8	34 0/8	14 2/8	14 2/8	22 2/8	Clear Creek County	CO	Lee Beckwith	1994	98
165 5/8	31 4/8	36 1/8	14 6/8	14 6/8	21 4/8	Clear Creek County	CO	Kurt Keskimaki	1984	99
165 5/8	35 6/8	32 5/8	14 6/8	14 7/8	20 2/8	Canmore	ALB	Jay A. Brown	1996	99
165 3/8	33 7/8	34 4/8	13 7/8	13 6/8	19 4/8	Saguache County	CO	Tom Sieverding	1987	101
164 7/8	38 0/8	37 3/8	14 3/8	14 4/8	20 1/8	Yakima County	WA	Albert Rinaldi, Jr.	1973	102
164 6/8	32 4/8	34 0/8	14 1/8	13 7/8	22 5/8	Saguache County	CO	Rick Duggan	1995	103
164 5/8	32 3/8	32 6/8	15 6/8	15 6/8	21 7/8	Larimer County	CO	Dennis Campbell	1989	104
164 4/8	35 6/8	37 6/8	13 4/8	13 5/8	24 5/8	Columbia County	WA	Jack Sandvig	1981	105
164 4/8	33 0/8	33 6/8	15 0/8	15 0/8	20 6/8	Teller County	CO	Michael K. Ward	1993	105
164 2/8	34 4/8	33 6/8	14 6/8	14 6/8	20 4/8	Clear Creek County	CO	Matt Burrows	1996	107
163 7/8	34 3/8	32 4/8	14 7/8	14 7/8	22 6/8	Teller County	CO	Dale Struble	1987	108
163 7/8	32 7/8	35 6/8	13 5/8	13 6/8	23 6/8	Lake County	OR	Robert T. Arnott	1992	108
163 7/8	32 5/8	32 2/8	15 5/8	15 5/8	20 7/8	Teller County	CO	William Elfland	1994	108
163 6/8	35 3/8	35 3/8	15 2/8	15 3/8	23 1/8	Lincoln County	MT	Paul Brunner	1983	111
163 5/8	32 0/8	30 3/8	14 3/8	14 3/8	21 2/8	Clear Creek County	CO	Jim Lake	1990	112
163 5/8	31 2/8	31 1/8	15 6/8	15 6/8	21 0/8	Las Animas County	CO	Carroll Holl	1995	112
163 5/8	34 3/8	34 2/8	15 6/8	15 6/8	20 1/8	Idaho County	ID	Mark Moeller	1996	112
163 4/8	31 7/8	30 5/8	14 1/8	14 0/8	19 1/8	Saguache County	CO	David Hall	1990	115
163 4/8	35 3/8	33 7/8	15 4/8	15 5/8	19 7/8	Canmore	ALB	Ryk Visscher	1992	115
163 3/8	34 1/8	34 4/8	15 6/8	15 7/8	20 6/8	Canmore	ALB	John Visscher	1986	117
163 2/8	34 6/8	34 0/8	15 5/8	15 5/8	22 3/8	Fremont County	WY	Randy Nelson	1984	118
163 2/8	37 2/8	32 0/8	14 2/8	14 1/8	20 4/8	Canmore	ALB	Rodney E. Carley	1994	118
163 1/8	33 4/8	33 1/8	14 7/8	14 7/8	23 0/8	Chaffee County	CO	Roger Stewart	1976	120
163 1/8	34 0/8	34 3/8	14 1/8	14 2/8	21 4/8	Larimer County	CO	Hal Rogers	1992	120
163 0/8	36 3/8	36 3/8	13 7/8	13 7/8	22 0/8	Lake County	MT	Steve Gorr	1973	122
162 7/8	32 4/8	32 7/8	14 2/8	14 2/8	22 2/8	Clear Creek County	CO	Lyle Willmarth	1982	123
162 7/8	33 3/8	34 2/8	14 7/8	15 0/8	22 3/8	Canmore	ALB	Thomas J. Hoffman	1985	123
162 5/8	33 4/8	34 1/8	14 7/8	15 0/8	21 5/8	Canmore	ALB	Jordon Ohrn	1988	125
162 5/8	33 5/8	32 4/8	15 4/8	15 2/8	19 1/8	Huerfano County	CO	Nathan Goudeau	1995	125
162 3/8	31 6/8	33 5/8	13 6/8	13 7/8	19 7/8	Greenlee County	AZ	James Bradley Miller	1990	127
162 2/8	37 6/8	34 6/8	13 7/8	14 0/8	23 0/8	Lemhi County	ID	Arne Vetrhus	1988	128
162 1/8	30 6/8	33 5/8	15 0/8	15 1/8	23 7/8	Park County	CO	Wayne Depperschmidt	1977	129
162 1/8	31 6/8	31 5/8	14 4/8	14 4/8	22 0/8	Clear Creek County	CO	Linda Strong	1990	129
162 0/8	34 1/8	33 1/8	13 4/8	13 4/8	20 1/8	Park County	WY	Tom Stoffel, Jr.	1990	131
161 7/8	36 0/8	35 3/8	14 0/8	14 0/8	20 3/8	Canmore	ALB	Chris Kempf	1986	132
161 5/8	33 6/8	32 5/8	13 0/8	13 0/8	18 0/8	Canmore	ALB	Ron Layden	1991	133
161 1/8	33 4/8	33 5/8	15 6/8	15 5/8	20 4/8	Custer County	MT	Joe Frazier	1984	134
161 0/8	36 3/8	33 7/8	13 7/8	13 7/8	24 4/8	Kittitas County	WA	Rick Kobel	1985	135
160 5/8	31 1/8	32 6/8	14 3/8	14 3/8	21 1/8	Fremont County	WY	Daniel S. Fritz	1982	136
160 5/8	35 7/8	34 6/8	14 5/8	14 2/8	21 6/8	Canmore	ALB	John D. "Jack" Frost	1984	136
160 5/8	35 5/8	33 4/8	14 2/8	14 1/8	20 6/8	Catron County	NM	Barry Dyar	1986	136
160 5/8	33 0/8	32 3/8	14 0/8	14 0/8	21 2/8	Clear Creek County	CO	John F. Barnard	1997	136
160 4/8	33 6/8	29 0/8	15 6/8	15 7/8	21 3/8	Grand County	UT	Maury Butterfield	1996	140
160 3/8	34 2/8	33 3/8	14 6/8	15 0/8	23 2/8	Canmore	ALB	Ralph L. Albright	1993	141
160 3/8	33 4/8	33 1/8	14 4/8	14 5/8	24 3/8	Owyhee County	ID	Mike J. McCollum	1995	141
160 2/8	30 0/8	30 0/8	14 7/8	14 6/8	17 7/8	Saguache County	CO	Jim Ryan	1988	143
160 2/8	31 6/8	32 2/8	13 6/8	14 0/8	19 0/8	Saguache County	CO	Tim Cuthriell	1991	143
160 2/8	36 0/8	32 2/8	14 0/8	14 1/8	22 2/8	Canmore	ALB	Doug Doram	1996	143
160 1/8	33 0/8	33 1/8	15 2/8	15 0/8	19 7/8	Canmore	ALB	Jordon Ohrn	1991	146
160 0/8	27 2/8	28 6/8	15 0/8	15 0/8	21 2/8	Pueblo County	CO	Joe Lupini	1993	147
159 6/8	36 4/8	32 2/8	14 4/8	14 4/8	20 1/8	Idaho County	ID	David J. Bailey	1993	148
159 5/8	31 3/8	32 0/8	14 6/8	14 7/8	19 7/8	Eagle County	CO	Wally Schaub	1997	149
159 3/8	31 4/8	34 5/8	15 0/8	15 0/8	19 1/8	Canmore	ALB	David R. Coupland	1982	150
159 0/8	30 7/8	31 5/8	15 2/8	15 2/8	23 6/8	Park County	CO	Glen Frank	1996	151
158 5/8	30 1/8	30 0/8	15 4/8	15 3/8	21 5/8	Park County	CO	Marvin Clyncke	1977	152
158 4/8	30 3/8	28 7/8	15 0/8	15 0/8	21 6/8	Rio Grande County	CO	Claude Bellefeuille	1997	153
158 3/8	30 2/8	27 3/8	14 4/8	14 4/8	20 4/8	Fremont County	CO	John Quick	1974	154
158 3/8	31 7/8	31 0/8	14 4/8	14 2/8	24 2/8	Lake County	CO	Wayne Lucero	1981	154
158 3/8	34 4/8	34 5/8	15 0/8	15 0/8	21 1/8	Park County	WY	Terry Constable	1988	154
158 3/8	32 3/8	32 6/8	15 5/8	15 4/8	21 4/8	Saguache County	CO	John L. Gardner	1990	154
158 2/8	30 6/8	35 4/8	15 2/8	15 2/8	19 5/8	Canmore	ALB	Jim Wondzell	1992	158
158 0/8	32 6/8	37 0/8	14 0/8	14 1/8	19 6/8	Canmore	ALB	Jeff Gaudry	1981	159
158 0/8	33 4/8	33 2/8	13 7/8	13 7/8	19 4/8	Exshaw	ALB	Alfred E. Baldwin	1992	159
158 0/8	32 4/8	31 2/8	14 4/8	14 4/8	20 2/8	Fremont County	WY	Dyrk Eddie	1996	159
157 5/8	32 0/8	29 5/8	14 4/8	14 4/8	21 1/8	Larimer County	CO	Glen Vlass	1991	162
157 5/8	29 4/8	30 5/8	15 2/8	15 0/8	21 7/8	Park County	CO	M. R. James	1996	162
157 2/8	33 0/8	31 0/8	13 3/8	13 2/8	19 0/8	Fremont County	CO	Steve Gorr	1973	164
156 7/8	32 5/8	32 4/8	13 4/8	13 4/8	19 4/8	Fergus County	MT	Jay Almas	1988	165
156 5/8	31 1/8	34 2/8	14 5/8	14 5/8	23 4/8	El Paso County	CO	Barry J. Smith	1983	166
156 4/8	32 4/8	32 0/8	12 7/8	12 7/8	19 5/8	Saguache County	CO	John Duggan	1995	167
156 2/8	35 2/8	35 0/8	14 0/8	14 0/8	20 3/8	Exshaw Creek	ALB	Dennis Dunn	1994	168
156 2/8	32 4/8	32 4/8	15 0/8	15 2/8	19 6/8	Las Animas County	CO	Pat Powell	1997	168
156 1/8	32 4/8	29 7/8	13 4/8	13 4/8	22 4/8	Harney County	OR	James Schrader	1987	170
156 1/8	29 4/8	32 7/8	14 0/8	14 1/8	19 5/8	Park County	WY	Terry Sieveke	1991	170
155 6/8	33 6/8	33 2/8	13 0/8	13 0/8	17 1/8	Canmore	ALB	William O. Dudley	1985	172
155 4/8	31 0/8	34 4/8	14 2/8	14 2/8	21 0/8	Canmore	ALB	Barry Dyar	1985	173
155 4/8	33 3/8	33 7/8	14 2/8	14 2/8	21 6/8	Larimer County	CO	Dale Elliott	1994	173
155 2/8	30 0/8	30 6/8	14 5/8	14 5/8	21 3/8	Clear Creek County	CO	Garret Decker	1990	175

BIGHORN SHEEP

Minimum Score 140 — Continued

SCORE	LENGTH OF HORN R	L	CIRCUMFERENCE OF BASE R	L	GREATEST SPREAD	AREA	STATE/PROVINCE	HUNTER'S NAME	DATE	RANK
154 7/8	32 0/8	31 7/8	15 0/8	15 0/8	21 1/8	El Paso County	CO	Lee Kline	1976	176
154 6/8	31 2/8	35 6/8	13 2/8	13 2/8	21 4/8	San Miguel County	NM	Rick Otero	1991	177
154 4/8	31 7/8	32 7/8	13 5/8	13 6/8	19 0/8	Kittitas County	WA	Rick Vandergiessen	1984	178
154 4/8	30 6/8	31 2/8	14 6/8	14 6/8	20 5/8	Chaffee County	CO	Ray Nelson	1986	178
154 3/8	34 5/8	34 4/8	15 0/8	14 6/8	25 0/8	Sanders County	MT	John Voelker	1980	180
154 0/8	33 4/8	32 0/8	14 3/8	14 5/8	20 1/8	Jefferson County	CO	Dennis Behn	1974	181
154 0/8	29 4/8	30 4/8	14 2/8	14 4/8	20 7/8	Clear Creek County	CO	Kevin D. Hatfield	1993	181
154 0/8	32 3/8	33 5/8	14 5/8	14 4/8	22 2/8	Catron County	NM	Gina Chavez	1994	181
154 0/8	30 6/8	29 2/8	15 4/8	15 7/8	20 3/8	Teller County	CO	Shawn Kingery	1996	181
153 4/8	29 2/8	30 0/8	13 0/8	13 0/8	19 4/8	Clear Creek County	CO	Jeff Lampe	1994	185
153 2/8	28 7/8	26 7/8	14 6/8	15 0/8	20 0/8	Saguache County	CO	Steve Van Treese	1982	186
153 2/8	31 7/8	29 3/8	15 0/8	14 7/8	19 0/8	Park County	WY	William J. Gartland	1982	186
153 2/8	33 1/8	30 7/8	14 6/8	14 7/8	17 2/8	Canmore	ALB	Derrick Spracklin	1991	186
153 2/8	33 6/8	33 2/8	14 1/8	14 0/8	19 6/8	Las Animas County	CO	James R. Phelps	1996	186
153 0/8	31 4/8	30 6/8	14 0/8	13 3/8	22 4/8	Saguache County	CO	Larick F. Spencer	1996	190
152 2/8	31 6/8	32 2/8	14 5/8	14 5/8	19 3/8	Canmore	ALB	Jay Brown	1991	191
151 4/8	33 0/8	29 0/8	14 2/8	14 3/8	16 4/8	Canmore	ALB	V. Randy Liljenquist	1995	192
151 2/8	31 5/8	30 7/8	14 4/8	14 3/8	19 0/8	Canmore	ALB	Dave Browne	1992	193
151 2/8	29 2/8	30 6/8	13 4/8	13 3/8	20 5/8	Alamosa County	CO	Alan R. Palmer	1994	193
151 1/8	31 3/8	31 4/8	15 1/8	15 2/8	21 2/8	Cougar Creek	ALB	Archie Nesbitt	1983	195
151 1/8	30 4/8	31 7/8	13 5/8	13 6/8	19 4/8	Cougar Creek	ALB	Tim R. Dawson	1997	195
151 0/8	34 6/8	33 0/8	13 6/8	13 6/8	22 1/8	Park County	WY	Larry L. Schweitzer	1984	197
150 6/8	29 2/8	29 4/8	14 6/8	14 6/8	19 3/8	Saguache County	CO	David 'Jake' Powell	1985	198
150 6/8	30 1/8	31 1/8	13 6/8	13 7/8	21 5/8	Lemhi County	ID	Scott Woodland	1988	198
150 6/8	30 4/8	30 4/8	13 5/8	13 7/8	22 7/8	Owyhee County	ID	Stan Godfrey	1992	198
150 4/8	29 5/8	29 7/8	15 0/8	14 6/8	20 6/8	Park County	WY	James R. Dreves	1988	201
150 3/8	31 3/8	33 2/8	13 4/8	13 4/8	18 6/8	Kittitas County	WA	Duane Fink	1984	202
150 1/8	28 4/8	29 3/8	15 4/8	15 3/8	18 0/8	Clear Creek County	CO	Calvin Farner	1990	203
149 4/8	31 2/8	29 2/8	15 0/8	14 7/8	19 3/8	Canmore	ALB	Larry Vayro	1989	204
149 4/8	28 6/8	29 4/8	15 1/8	15 0/8	20 0/8	Fremont County	CO	David E. Smith	1996	204
149 3/8	30 0/8	26 5/8	13 6/8	13 6/8	24 6/8	Lake County	OR	Don Rajnus	1982	206
149 3/8	32 0/8	29 7/8	15 2/8	15 2/8	18 0/8	Canmore	ALB	Warren Witherspoon	1986	206
149 2/8	30 0/8	28 6/8	15 0/8	14 7/8	20 3/8	El Paso County	CO	Mark Heiland	1989	208
149 2/8	30 0/8	31 0/8	13 6/8	13 6/8	19 4/8	Clear Creek County	CO	Michael Dziekan	1994	208
148 7/8	29 1/8	31 6/8	14 4/8	14 5/8	20 5/8	Canmore	ALB	Kent Hillard	1990	210
148 4/8	28 2/8	29 0/8	14 2/8	14 3/8	20 4/8	Teller County	CO	Joel D. Morgan	1995	211
148 2/8	30 6/8	29 6/8	14 5/8	14 5/8	21 4/8	Park County	CO	Roland D. Cameron	1979	212
147 6/8	30 0/8	29 2/8	15 5/8	15 5/8	20 1/8	El Paso County	CO	Glenn R. Kuklick	1988	213
147 4/8	27 6/8	24 2/8	15 6/8	15 7/8	20 2/8	Saguache County	CO	Charles Grumley	1988	214
147 3/8	30 3/8	31 4/8	14 2/8	14 2/8	17 7/8	Canmore	ALB	Don Ferguson	1981	215
147 2/8	30 2/8	32 0/8	14 3/8	13 7/8	20 3/8	Eagle County	CO	Joe Theaman	1989	216
147 2/8	28 7/8	34 1/8	13 3/8	13 3/8	23 4/8	Park County	WY	Jamie Byrne	1991	216
147 1/8	29 7/8	30 0/8	13 6/8	13 7/8	19 6/8	Lake County	CO	G. Fred Asbell	1979	218
147 0/8	30 6/8	30 0/8	13 3/8	13 3/8	21 3/8	El Paso County	CO	Sherman Spoelstra	1983	219
145 5/8	29 4/8	30 3/8	13 2/8	13 2/8	19 3/8	Canmore	ALB	Oran Hirsch	1979	220
145 5/8	30 1/8	29 6/8	15 2/8	15 3/8	18 4/8	Lemhi County	ID	Dale Johnson	1985	220
145 1/8	29 3/8	30 6/8	14 6/8	14 4/8	20 5/8	Trout Creek	ALB	Chad Lenz	1992	222
144 6/8	33 0/8	29 4/8	13 5/8	13 4/8	20 0/8	Canmore	ALB	Bennett L. McMillian	1993	223
144 5/8	29 3/8	29 0/8	14 5/8	14 4/8	20 4/8	Clear Creek County	CO	Rob Firth	1988	224
144 1/8	30 0/8	26 7/8	15 2/8	15 1/8	24 4/8	Chaffee County	CO	Dwight Schuh	1993	225
143 5/8	28 2/8	28 1/8	13 4/8	13 4/8	20 6/8	Clear Creek County	CO	Otho Hobbs	1991	226
143 4/8	32 0/8	32 0/8	14 0/8	14 1/8	18 0/8	Couger Creek	ALB	Will Pick	1993	227
142 6/8	26 1/8	28 7/8	14 0/8	14 0/8	19 2/8	Teller County	CO	Steve Barnhill	1990	228
142 0/8	30 7/8	30 7/8	13 2/8	13 2/8	21 0/8	Clear Creek County	CO	Jeff Reynolds	1989	229
142 0/8	28 2/8	28 4/8	13 6/8	13 5/8	19 2/8	Park County	CO	Dave Reichley	1998	229
141 6/8	25 6/8	27 4/8	14 4/8	14 7/8	19 2/8	Chaffee County	CO	Ron Breitsprecher	1978	231
141 5/8	31 0/8	30 5/8	13 3/8	12 7/8	18 6/8	Park County	WY	Kurt H. Eisenach	1988	232
141 4/8	29 1/8	27 3/8	13 3/8	13 3/8	21 0/8	Adams County	CO	Jim Usrey	1976	233
141 2/8	30 7/8	29 1/8	12 6/8	12 5/8	18 6/8	Chaffee County	CO	Tom Tietz	1984	234
141 2/8	25 4/8	27 6/8	13 4/8	13 6/8	17 3/8	Saguache County	CO	Dennis L. Howell	1993	234
141 1/8	29 5/8	29 6/8	14 3/8	14 5/8	18 4/8	Chelan County	WA	Greg Winters	1992	236
141 1/8	25 5/8	27 6/8	14 5/8	14 4/8	20 1/8	Pueblo County	CO	Gary Bohochik	1994	236
141 1/8	26 7/8	26 6/8	14 6/8	14 5/8	19 5/8	Saguache County	CO	John L. Gardner	1998	236
141 0/8	27 4/8	28 2/8	13 5/8	13 6/8	21 0/8	Park County	CO	Dan Tekavec	1980	239
141 0/8	28 0/8	28 0/8	14 1/8	14 1/8	19 2/8	Fremont County	WY	Jerry W. Mathewes	1983	239
140 7/8	27 6/8	33 3/8	14 1/8	14 0/8	19 6/8	Kittitas County	WA	Stan Hansen	1984	241
140 6/8	28 6/8	28 6/8	14 1/8	14 1/8	19 1/8	Valley County	ID	Michael Schlegel	1987	242
140 4/8	29 6/8	30 2/8	14 1/8	14 1/8	21 5/8	Canmore	ALB	Bruce R. Schoeneweis	1992	242
140 3/8	27 1/8	30 2/8	14 0/8	14 0/8	19 3/8	Clear Creek County	CO	Paul Navarre	1997	244
140 0/8	30 5/8	27 7/8	13 4/8	13 5/8	23 6/8	Kittitas County	WA	Martin Sapp	1990	245

World Record Dall Sheep
Score: 171 0/8
Chugach Mountains, Alaska - 1988
Hunter: Tony Russ

DALL SHEEP

Minimum Score 120

Ovis dalli dalli and *Ovis dalli kenaiensis*

SCORE	LENGTH OF R HORN L		CIRCUMFERENCE R OF BASE L		GREATEST SPREAD	AREA	STATE/ PROVINCE	HUNTER'S NAME	DATE	RANK
171 0/8	42 1/8	42 5/8	14 2/8	13 6/8	22 6/8	Chugach Mtns.	AK	Tony Russ	1988	1
168 6/8	39 4/8	42 2/8	13 0/8	13 0/8	23 5/8	Tok	AK	John Sarvis	1998	2
166 4/8	41 1/8	40 7/8	13 3/8	13 3/8	26 2/8	East Fork	AK	Braun Kopsack	1990	3
165 3/8	37 1/8	37 4/8	13 6/8	14 0/8	21 7/8	Eklutna	AK	James D. Eskelson	1998	4
165 1/8	39 0/8	40 3/8	13 2/8	13 2/8	22 0/8	Talkeetna Mtns.	AK	Braun Kopsack	1997	5
164 5/8	40 6/8	41 3/8	13 3/8	13 5/8	28 4/8	Nahanni Butte	NWT	Gary Laya	1986	6
162 3/8	38 7/8	39 0/8	12 4/8	12 4/8	22 6/8	Delta River	AK	Dr. Russell Congdon	1960	7
162 2/8	38 6/8	39 0/8	13 3/8	13 4/8	23 0/8	Chugach Mtns.	AK	Braun Kopsack	1996	8
162 0/8	38 6/8	37 0/8	13 4/8	13 7/8	22 3/8	Chugach Mtns.	AK	Richard Moran	1991	9
161 5/8	41 2/8	40 3/8	13 0/8	13 0/8	24 3/8	Liard Range	NWT	Pete Iacavazzi	1994	10
161 3/8	37 1/8	39 0/8	13 5/8	13 4/8	25 0/8	Talkeetna Mtns.	AK	Braun Kopsack	1992	11

DALL SHEEP

Minimum Score 120 — Continued

SCORE	LENGTH OF HORN R	L	CIRCUMFERENCE OF BASE R	L	GREATEST SPREAD	AREA	STATE/PROVINCE	HUNTER'S NAME	DATE	RANK
160 6/8	39 6/8	37 6/8	13 2/8	13 2/8	22 7/8	Nahanni Butte	NWT	Lonny Vanatta	1986	12
160 4/8	39 2/8	40 2/8	13 7/8	13 4/8	23 5/8	Nahanni Butte	NWT	Joseph D. Maddock	1989	13
160 2/8	39 2/8	42 4/8	12 5/8	12 3/8	22 3/8	Post River	AK	Duke Prentup	1997	14
159 2/8	40 1/8	40 5/8	12 6/8	12 5/8	26 3/8	Mackenzie Mtns.	NWT	Jerry Bowen	1990	15
158 2/8	38 0/8	38 0/8	13 4/8	13 0/0	27 2/8	Knik River	AK	Tony Huss	1989	16
158 1/8	39 5/8	36 2/8	12 7/8	12 6/8	20 4/8	Tanana Hills	AK	Richard Swisher	1995	17
157 6/8	38 3/8	39 7/8	12 2/8	12 2/8	26 6/8	Brooks Range	AK	Kurt Lepping	1988	18
157 5/8	37 4/8	38 1/8	13 2/8	13 2/8	24 6/8	Eklutna Lake	AK	Tony Russ	1997	19
157 4/8	38 6/8	38 6/8	12 7/8	12 7/8	24 2/8	Eagle River	AK	David Litchfield	1988	20
157 2/8	34 3/8	37 3/8	13 0/8	13 0/8	23 7/8	Chugach Mtns.	AK	Jim Young	1996	21
157 1/8	39 1/8	40 2/8	12 3/8	12 3/8	24 3/8	Nahanni Butte	NWT	Tom Tietz	1987	22
157 1/8	38 0/8	35 1/8	13 0/8	13 1/8	22 0/8	Chugach Mtns.	AK	Calvin W. Hall	1991	22
157 0/8	35 4/8	35 4/8	13 6/8	14 0/8	21 2/8	Chitina Glacier	AK	Roger Morris	1973	24
156 6/8	38 3/8	38 5/8	12 5/8	12 5/8	24 1/8	Talkeetna Mtns.	AK	Braun Kopsack	1994	25
155 6/8	33 0/8	36 6/8	13 4/8	13 4/8	27 3/8	Eklutna Glacier	AK	Tom Kron	1998	26
155 5/8	36 3/8	35 0/8	12 6/8	12 6/8	19 5/8	Mackenzie Mtns.	NWT	Bob Renner	1983	27
155 1/8	37 1/8	37 2/8	13 4/8	13 4/8	25 7/8	Rams Head Mtn.	NWT	Ron Breitsprecher	1981	28
155 1/8	36 6/8	35 7/8	13 2/8	13 2/8	19 5/8	Liard Range	NWT	John E. Haefeli	1988	28
155 1/8	39 2/8	37 7/8	12 6/8	12 6/8	25 5/8	East Fork	AK	Braun Kopsack	1989	28
155 1/8	40 4/8	37 3/8	12 5/8	12 5/8	25 5/8	Alaska Range	AK	Ed Hull	1990	28
155 0/8	36 6/8	36 6/8	13 5/8	13 4/8	23 7/8	Nahanni Butte	NWT	Tom Vanasche	1994	32
154 7/8	35 2/8	34 7/8	14 1/8	14 1/8	21 4/8	Mackenzie Mtns.	NWT	Mike Barrett	1983	33
154 7/8	37 3/8	36 6/8	12 6/8	12 6/8	22 3/8	Kenai Mtns.	AK	Lon E. Lauber	1992	33
154 6/8	35 6/8	37 2/8	13 0/8	13 2/8	20 6/8	Chugach Mtns.	AK	Rick Tollison	1979	35
154 6/8	33 2/8	38 2/8	13 4/8	13 4/8	25 3/8	Brooks Range	AK	Kurt Lepping	1987	35
154 4/8	38 0/8	34 6/8	13 1/8	13 2/8	21 6/8	Chugach Mtns.	AK	Mike Traub	1998	37
154 3/8	37 7/8	36 6/8	13 2/8	13 2/8	24 7/8	Brooks Range	AK	John Sarvis	1995	38
153 5/8	35 1/8	36 6/8	13 3/8	13 3/8	21 6/8	Nahanni Butte	NWT	E. Damon Handley	1989	39
153 3/8	37 5/8	37 4/8	13 1/8	13 1/8	26 4/8	Divide Lake	NWT	Stanley Walchuk, Jr.	1984	40
153 3/8	36 5/8	36 4/8	13 3/8	13 3/8	23 5/8	Chugach Mtns.	AK	Nathan Callis	1986	40
153 2/8	37 6/8	33 0/8	13 2/8	13 2/8	20 4/8	Rams Head Mtn.	NWT	Dennis Schweitzer	1981	42
153 2/8	36 6/8	37 0/8	13 0/8	13 0/8	24 5/8	Keele River	NWT	Ron Serwa	1988	42
153 1/8	37 2/8	37 1/8	13 0/8	13 0/8	24 6/8	Nahanni Buttes	NWT	Gary F. Bogner	1995	44
152 7/8	39 0/8	38 7/8	13 3/8	13 4/8	28 3/8	Nahanni Butte	NWT	Monty Moravec	1993	45
152 7/8	36 1/8	36 0/8	13 3/8	13 5/8	21 2/8	Kosina Creek	AK	George E. Mann	1996	45
152 6/8	37 1/8	36 5/8	13 1/8	13 1/8	30 0/8	Wrangell Mtns	AK	Ray Torrey	1973	47
152 5/8	38 6/8	39 3/8	12 3/8	12 4/8	31 2/8	Keele River	NWT	Thomas J. Hoffman	1986	48
152 4/8	33 0/8	34 0/8	12 6/8	12 6/8	18 5/8	Mackenzie Mtns.	NWT	Al Reay	1982	49
152 2/8	37 0/8	36 2/8	12 5/8	12 5/8	23 4/8	Kuskokwim Mtn.	AK	Kenneth R. Wallenberg	1978	50
152 0/8	37 0/8	37 0/8	12 4/8	12 4/8	27 4/8	Wrangell Mtns.	AK	Dr. Rex Hancock	1962	51
152 0/8	31 3/8	34 3/8	12 4/8	12 7/8	20 6/8	Brooks Range	AK	Calvin Farner	1988	51
152 0/8	35 6/8	35 4/8	13 4/8	13 4/8	26 1/8	Boulder Creek	AK	Rick D. Snell	1993	51
151 6/8	35 7/8	35 1/8	13 5/8	13 5/8	28 0/8	Chugach Mtns.	AK	John D. 'Jack' Frost	1984	54
151 6/8	40 1/8	35 7/8	12 3/8	12 4/8	23 1/8	Matanuska River	AK	Tony Russ	1990	54
151 5/8	37 4/8	38 1/8	12 7/8	12 6/8	22 5/8	Keele River	NWT	Thomas J. Hoffman	1998	56
151 3/8	37 6/8	36 3/8	12 5/8	12 5/8	22 3/8	Keele River	NWT	Will Pick	1998	57
151 2/8	36 6/8	36 6/8	12 6/8	12 6/8	26 4/8	Johnson River	AK	Larry Jones	1963	58
151 2/8	36 4/8	36 4/8	13 7/8	13 6/8	23 4/8	Tonsona Creek	AK	Bruce Stephens	1974	58
151 2/8	35 5/8	36 1/8	13 2/8	13 0/8	25 0/8	Rainy Pass	AK	Roger Stewart	1978	58
151 1/8	37 3/8	38 6/8	12 3/8	12 4/8	25 3/8	Keele River	NWT	Chuck Adams	1995	61
151 0/8	35 4/8	34 4/8	13 3/8	13 5/8	27 3/8	Mackenzie Mtns.	NWT	Mike Barrett	1986	62
150 7/8	34 1/8	34 6/8	13 5/8	13 5/8	21 2/8	Chugach Mtns.	AK	David A. Widby	1997	63
150 5/8	36 0/8	36 1/8	13 1/8	13 2/8	22 7/8	Liard Range	NWT	Harry Walker	1995	64
150 3/8	36 1/8	36 2/8	12 4/8	12 5/8	24 2/8	Mountain River	NWT	George Flournoy	1985	65
150 2/8	37 5/8	33 3/8	12 4/8	12 2/8	19 7/8	Brooks Range	AK	James A. Baker	1971	66
150 1/8	37 4/8	37 1/8	12 3/8	12 3/8	18 6/8	Mackenzie Mtns.	NWT	Robert L. Kampen	1988	67
149 6/8	40 0/8	34 2/8	12 3/8	12 3/8	22 4/8	Keele River	NWT	Jim Ryan	1990	68
149 3/8	37 1/8	34 4/8	13 2/8	13 2/8	25 7/8	Wrangell Mtns.	AK	J. Barry Dyar	1984	69
149 2/8	36 1/8	35 7/8	13 1/8	13 1/8	25 0/8	Keele River	NWT	V. Randy Liljenquist	1997	70
149 1/8	34 1/8	34 4/8	13 4/8	13 5/8	21 3/8	Eklutna Lake	AK	Steven J. Latz	1988	71
149 0/8	34 7/8	35 3/8	13 3/8	13 3/8	23 3/8	Keele River	NWT	Thomas J. Hoffman	1985	72
149 0/8	37 4/8	37 0/8	12 0/8	11 6/8	22 1/8	Nahanni Butte	NWT	Robert Pyne	1989	72
148 7/8	36 0/8	36 1/8	13 1/8	13 1/8	26 2/8	Tok	AK	Lon E. Lauber	1996	74
148 6/8	37 6/8	38 0/8	12 2/8	12 2/8	22 5/8	Nahanni Butte	NWT	Bill Grammer	1986	75
148 6/8	35 1/8	38 5/8	12 1/8	12 1/8	22 0/8	Nahanni Butte	NWT	Gary M. Martin	1992	75
148 4/8	35 7/8	35 3/8	13 2/8	13 2/8	26 6/8	Brooks Range	AK	Randy Butler	1979	77
148 4/8	31 4/8	35 4/8	13 6/8	13 6/8	25 0/8	Mackenzie Mtns.	NWT	Dyrk Eddie	1986	77
148 3/8	33 4/8	35 1/8	13 3/8	13 3/8	24 2/8	Atigun Pass	AK	Maxallen D. Jackson	1984	79
148 2/8	37 2/8	35 6/8	13 2/8	12 6/8	19 6/8	Chugach Mtns.	AK	Roy Ruiz	1997	80
148 0/8	38 3/8	35 5/8	12 6/8	12 7/8	28 1/8	Delta	AK	Mike Hedrick	1988	81
148 0/8	33 0/8	36 4/8	13 2/8	13 1/8	19 2/8	Chugach Mtns.	AK	Stephen Kotz	1995	81
147 6/8	35 1/8	35 1/8	12 4/8	12 6/8	19 7/8	Tlogotsho Range	NWT	Archie Nesbitt	1986	83
147 6/8	35 0/8	35 0/8	13 2/8	13 3/8	24 0/8	Chugach Mtns.	AK	Richard Moran/Lon Lauber	1989	83
147 5/8	35 0/8	35 3/8	12 6/8	12 7/8	22 5/8	Dadina Glacier	AK	Roger O. Wyant	1990	85
147 5/8	31 0/8	33 5/8	12 4/8	12 3/8	17 7/8	Jackfish Mtn.	NWT	Daniel C. Hurd	1996	85
147 4/8	34 6/8	35 4/8	12 0/8	12 0/8	21 5/8	Mackenzie Mtns.	NWT	Paul Brunner	1982	87
147 3/8	34 4/8	35 1/8	13 0/8	13 0/8	20 0/8	DeLong Mtns.	AK	Carl E. Brent	1991	88
147 2/8	35 2/8	35 4/8	12 5/8	12 5/8	25 2/8	Mackenzie Mtns.	NWT	Janice J. Traub	1987	89

DALL SHEEP

Minimum Score 120 — Continued

SCORE	LENGTH OF HORN R	L	CIRCUMFERENCE OF BASE R	L	GREATEST SPREAD	AREA	STATE/ PROVINCE	HUNTER'S NAME	DATE	RANK
147 2/8	35 5/8	35 1/8	12 2/8	12 2/8	22 6/8	Eklutna Lake	AK	John McCullough	1988	89
147 2/8	32 3/8	32 3/8	12 6/8	12 7/8	20 4/8	Talkeetna Mtns.	AK	Jeffrey S. Stevens	1997	89
147 1/8	35 5/8	32 2/8	12 0/8	12 0/8	20 3/8	Chugach Mtns.	AK	Lon E. Lauber	1990	92
147 0/8	36 0/8	36 2/8	12 4/8	12 4/8	25 1/8	Nahanni Butte	NWT	Jim Arnold	1988	93
147 0/8	34 7/8	35 1/8	13 0/8	12 7/8	21 7/8	Chugach Mtns.	AK	Tony Russ	1992	93
146 6/8	35 0/8	34 4/8	12 2/8	12 3/8	23 5/8	Liard Range	NWT	Dennis Dunn	1984	95
146 6/8	30 7/8	33 5/8	12 2/8	12 4/8	19 2/8	Post River	AK	James R. Gabrick	1998	95
146 5/8	36 3/8	35 0/8	11 6/8	11 5/8	21 0/8	Liard Range	NWT	Ron Rockwell	1983	97
146 4/8	33 4/8	34 2/8	12 0/8	12 2/8	25 7/8	Delta River	AK	Elisha Gray	1958	98
146 4/8	34 1/8	33 5/8	12 5/8	12 5/8	23 4/8	Jones Creek	BC	Randy De Biasio	1994	98
146 4/8	33 2/8	33 6/8	13 3/8	13 3/8	19 3/8	Chugach Mtns.	AK	Bob Ameen	1997	98
146 3/8	34 7/8	35 0/8	12 3/8	12 3/8	19 6/8	Kotaneellee Range	NWT	James A. Schneider	1997	101
146 2/8	33 4/8	32 6/8	11 5/8	11 4/8	17 6/8	Nahanni Butte	NWT	Barry J. Smith	1989	102
145 6/8	29 0/8	36 6/8	12 5/8	12 6/8	24 1/8	Brooks Range	AK	Maxallen D. Jackson	1989	103
145 4/8	33 1/8	37 7/8	11 6/8	11 6/8	21 2/8	Brooks Range	AK	John D. 'Jack' Frost	1982	104
145 2/8	35 1/8	35 5/8	12 3/8	12 4/8	25 5/8	Talkeetna Mtns.	AK	Jay Deones	1980	105
145 2/8	36 2/8	36 2/8	12 0/8	12 1/8	23 0/8	Liard Mtns.	NWT	Steve Weekly	1998	105
145 1/8	32 2/8	33 1/8	13 4/8	13 7/8	23 5/8	Wood River	AK	Art Young	1923	107
145 1/8	34 5/8	35 0/8	13 2/8	13 2/8	25 5/8	DoDo Mtn.	NWT	Tom D. Slusser	1990	107
145 0/8	33 5/8	33 5/8	13 0/8	13 0/8	25 5/8	Mt. Ibex	YUK	Martin Hanson	1957	109
145 0/8	33 4/8	35 6/8	12 2/8	12 2/8	23 0/8	Liard Range	NWT	Mike Ukrainetz	1995	109
144 5/8	34 5/8	35 2/8	13 0/8	13 0/8	23 1/8	Mt. Hayes	AK	Keith R. Clemmons	1962	111
144 2/8	33 1/8	33 3/8	12 5/8	12 4/8	21 6/8	Liard Range	NWT	Richard W. Sage	1986	112
144 2/8	33 7/8	33 7/8	12 6/8	13 0/8	24 0/8	Yellow Jacket Pass	AK	G. Fred Asbell	1993	112
144 1/8	33 3/8	36 4/8	12 3/8	13 0/8	25 4/8	Delta Management	AK	John W. Williams	1978	114
143 6/8	35 0/8	35 2/8	13 0/8	12 7/8	25 0/8	Chistochina River	AK	Capt. Leonard Mackler	1977	115
143 4/8	35 0/8	34 2/8	12 5/8	12 6/8	22 4/8	Nahanni Butte	NWT	Dirk Lawyer	1985	116
143 3/8	35 0/8	34 5/8	12 0/8	12 2/8	19 4/8	Endicott Mtns.	AK	Dwane J. Sykes	1968	117
143 3/8	31 3/8	42 0/8	13 0/8	13 0/8	25 5/8	Talkeetna Mtns.	AK	Braun Kopsack	1995	117
143 2/8	31 0/8	35 2/8	12 4/8	12 4/8	23 6/8	Mackenzie Mtns.	NWT	Paul Schafer	1983	119
143 1/8	32 0/8	32 5/8	13 3/8	13 3/8	21 4/8	Chugach Mtns.	AK	Glenn R. L. Schmidt	1977	120
143 0/8	36 0/8	34 6/8	11 4/8	11 4/8	21 2/8	Nahanni Butte	NWT	Lee Veldhouse	1983	121
143 0/8	35 2/8	31 4/8	12 3/8	12 4/8	23 1/8	Nahanni Butte	NWT	T. Sanford Roberts	1993	121
142 2/8	33 4/8	36 2/8	11 5/8	11 5/8	24 3/8	Post River	AK	Rick Tollison	1978	123
142 2/8	33 1/8	33 1/8	12 4/8	12 5/8	27 4/8	Brooks Range	AK	Larry E. Townsend	1991	123
142 1/8	35 7/8	35 6/8	11 6/8	11 6/8	23 7/8	Nahanni Butte	NWT	Todd Szmania	1995	125
142 1/8	32 6/8	34 1/8	13 0/8	13 0/8	26 3/8	Grey Ridge	YUK	Patrick D. Quinn	1997	125
142 0/8	28 1/8	33 5/8	12 1/8	12 0/8	22 1/8	Atigun Pass	AK	Maxallen D. Jackson	1980	127
141 6/8	32 0/8	32 4/8	12 0/8	12 1/8	20 2/8	Mackenzie Mtns.	NWT	Reggie Spiegelberg	1982	128
141 5/8	31 7/8	32 0/8	13 0/8	13 0/8	26 2/8	Mackenzie Mtns.	NWT	Chuck Adams	1985	129
141 0/8	35 6/8	36 6/8	11 5/8	11 5/8	22 0/8	Ptarmigan Pass	AK	Ralph Ertz	1977	130
141 0/8	31 4/8	31 6/8	13 6/8	13 6/8	20 2/8	Eklutna Lake	AK	Craig Scarbrough	1989	130
140 7/8	33 3/8	34 2/8	13 0/8	13 0/8	23 3/8	Wrangell Mtns.	AK	Mike Renfro	1987	132
140 5/8	32 4/8	31 5/8	12 4/8	12 4/8	23 7/8	Liard River	NWT	Greg Munther	1984	133
140 1/8	34 3/8	34 4/8	11 7/8	11 7/8	20 4/8	Nahanni Butte	NWT	Fred C. Church	1990	134
140 0/8	35 2/8	34 4/8	11 5/8	11 4/8	25 4/8	Tlogotcho Plateau	NWT	Bruce R. Schoeneweis	1996	135
140 0/8	31 4/8	36 0/8	12 4/8	12 4/8	22 4/8	Yerrick Creek	AK	Garry A. Thoms	1998	135
139 6/8	33 1/8	33 3/8	12 5/8	12 5/8	17 7/8	Chugach Mtns.	AK	John Sarvis	1988	137
139 6/8	33 7/8	33 5/8	12 5/8	12 6/8	25 3/8	Wrangell Mtns.	AK	Bret T. Walker	1991	137
139 4/8	33 0/8	33 2/8	12 3/8	12 3/8	21 7/8	Chugach Mtns.	AK	Tom S. Lenort	1990	139
139 1/8	34 2/8	34 7/8	12 3/8	12 3/8	27 7/8	Tok	AK	Gardner Rowell	1991	140
139 0/8	37 2/8	32 6/8	11 7/8	12 0/8	26 4/8	Talkeetna Mtns.	AK	Rusty Hayes	1975	141
138 6/8	31 4/8	32 4/8	11 4/8	11 4/8	21 3/8	Brooks Range	AK	Dewayne J. Benton	1987	142
138 4/8	32 6/8	34 0/8	12 6/8	12 5/8	22 6/8	Chitina	AK	Robert Ewers	1972	143
138 1/8	33 5/8	33 4/8	12 0/8	12 0/8	19 7/8	Nahanni Butte	NWT	Robert Edward Speegle, MD	1997	144
138 0/8	29 3/8	35 5/8	12 4/8	12 4/8	26 7/8	Hula Hula River	AK	Paul Persano	1985	145
137 5/8	30 4/8	30 5/8	12 1/8	12 1/8	21 4/8	Canning River	AK	Garry A. Thoms	1989	146
137 4/8	31 2/8	31 2/8	13 2/8	13 3/8	18 5/8	Mackenzie Mtns.	NWT	William R. VyVyan	1990	147
137 2/8	34 2/8	32 0/8	11 2/8	11 1/8	21 1/8	Liard Range	NWT	Tom Taylor	1992	148
137 0/8	33 2/8	34 4/8	12 1/8	12 1/8	24 6/8	Talkeetna Mtns.	AK	Braun Kopsack	1987	149
137 0/8	33 4/8	33 4/8	12 0/8	12 0/8	18 6/8	N. Liards Mtns.	NWT	Nathan Andersohn	1994	149
136 5/8	30 0/8	31 1/8	12 1/8	12 1/8	23 2/8	Brooks Range	AK	Jim Ryan	1986	151
136 0/8	32 2/8	32 2/8	12 1/8	12 1/8	23 7/8	Brooks Range	AK	Ken Vorisek	1990	152
135 7/8	33 0/8	32 3/8	11 3/8	11 3/8	22 4/8	Nahanni Buttes	NWT	Wayne A. Nicholson	1997	153
135 3/8	34 5/8	34 6/8	11 2/8	11 3/8	22 0/8	Nahanni Butte	NWT	Will Pick	1994	154
135 1/8	34 0/8	33 5/8	11 4/8	11 4/8	23 0/8	Alaska Range	AK	Richard Moran	1988	155
135 1/8	31 1/8	30 6/8	12 5/8	12 7/8	20 1/8	Chugach Mtns.	AK	Grant Arii	1994	155
135 0/8	31 2/8	31 2/8	12 0/8	11 7/8	23 6/8	Liard Range	NWT	Mark Checki	1988	157
134 6/8	33 4/8	33 2/8	11 3/8	11 3/8	21 7/8	Nahanni Butte	NWT	Linda Strong	1987	158
134 5/8	32 1/8	33 0/8	11 2/8	11 2/8	20 6/8	Nahanni Butte	NWT	Jerry Leair	1990	159
133 2/8	32 0/8	31 6/8	11 7/8	11 6/8	21 2/8	Nabesna River	AK	George A. Moerlein	1983	160
133 2/8	30 0/8	31 0/8	11 2/8	11 3/8	24 2/8	Mackenzie Mtns.	NWT	Dean Stebner	1989	160
133 1/8	31 5/8	31 6/8	11 6/8	11 6/8	25 6/8	Liard Range	NWT	Tony Casagrande	1996	162
133 0/8	30 6/8	30 4/8	12 4/8	12 5/8	27 1/8	Wrangell Mtns.	AK	George A. Moerlein	1971	163
132 7/8	32 0/8	32 1/8	11 6/8	11 6/8	21 0/8	Mackenzie Mtns.	NWT	Stan Godfrey	1988	164
132 6/8	30 2/8	30 4/8	12 5/8	12 5/8	18 2/8	Brooks Range	AK	Robert Warpack	1986	165
132 2/8	30 6/8	30 5/8	11 7/8	11 5/8	20 6/8	Nahanni Butte	NWT	Steve Byerly	1996	166
131 6/8	31 5/8	31 1/8	12 5/8	12 5/8	17 6/8	Wrangell Mtns.	AK	John Sarvis	1985	167

DALL SHEEP

Minimum Score 120

SCORE	LENGTH OF HORN R	L	CIRCUMFERENCE OF BASE R	L	GREATEST SPREAD	AREA	STATE/PROVINCE	HUNTER'S NAME	DATE	RANK
131 4/8	30 7/8	31 7/8	11 3/8	11 1/8	21 4/8	Nahanni Butte	NWT	Ralph L. Albright	1990	168
130 7/8	32 6/8	28 5/8	12 4/8	12 4/8	20 6/8	Talkeetna Mtns.	AK	John L. Wozniak	1984	169
130 0/8	30 2/8	30 6/8	11 4/8	11 4/8	20 6/8	Liard Range	NWT	John Borlang	1986	170
129 6/8	31 2/8	31 6/8	11 1/8	11 0/8	21 2/8	Liard Range	NWT	Rick Duggan	1998	171
128 5/8	31 2/8	31 3/8	11 1/8	11 3/8	20 5/8	Liard Range	NWT	Mark Buehrer/Mike Grue	1998	172
128 3/8	30 0/8	30 7/8	12 1/8	12 1/8	20 4/8	Liard Range	NWT	Jim Wondzell	1994	173
128 0/8	31 2/8	31 4/8	11 2/8	11 3/8	24 0/8	Wrangell	AK	Gilbert M. W. Smith	1977	174
127 0/8	29 7/8	29 3/8	11 2/8	11 1/8	21 2/8	Sheep Creek	AK	Ray Uhl, Jr.	1968	175
125 7/8	31 6/8	31 3/8	10 4/8	10 4/8	21 1/8	Alaska Range	AK	Larry Jones	1969	176
125 0/8	29 1/8	29 1/8	11 2/8	11 2/8	17 4/8	Liard Range	NWT	Todd Henck	1988	177
124 0/8	30 1/8	30 5/8	11 2/8	11 0/8	17 5/8	Kuskokwin River	AK	Marvin Clyncke	1997	178
123 3/8	30 1/8	30 0/8	11 0/8	11 0/8	24 2/8	Kongakut River	AK	Stan Parkerson	1984	179
121 6/8	30 4/8	30 4/8	10 2/8	10 2/8	22 6/8	Alaska Range	AK	Lon E. Lauber	1988	180
121 4/8	27 6/8	28 0/8	11 2/8	11 2/8	19 7/8	Nahanni Butte	NWT	Neil Thagard	1997	181
121 1/8	27 3/8	28 2/8	10 7/8	10 6/8	21 4/8	Brooks Range	AK	Thomas Chadwick	1984	182
120 5/8	29 1/8	29 4/8	11 4/8	11 5/8	21 0/8	Atigun Pass	AK	Steve Herrera	1991	183

World Record Desert Bighorn Sheep
Score: 176 7/8
Pima County, Arizona - 1990
Hunter: Mark D. Morris

DESERT BIGHORN SHEEP

Minimum Score 140 *Ovis canadensis nelsoni* and certain related subspecies

SCORE	LENGTH OF R HORN L		CIRCUMFERENCE R OF BASE L		GREATEST SPREAD	AREA	STATE/ PROVINCE	HUNTER'S NAME	DATE	RANK
176 7/8	36 3/8	35 2/8	15 2/8	15 1/8	19 6/8	Pima County	AZ	Mark D. Morris	1990	1
175 0/8	35 5/8	36 5/8	14 7/8	14 7/8	22 5/8	Graham County	AZ	Jim Ryan	1989	2
167 1/8	34 5/8	34 2/8	14 7/8	14 7/8	23 5/8	Maricopa County	AZ	Peter C. Knagge	1985	3
166 6/8	28 6/8	34 4/8	14 5/8	14 5/8	21 7/8	San Bernardino County	CA	Jim Ryan	1988	4
166 2/8	36 1/8	36 5/8	14 2/8	14 2/8	22 2/8	Graham County	AZ	Max T. Hinton	1987	5
164 2/8	32 4/8	31 6/8	15 3/8	15 3/8	21 1/8	Maricopa County	AZ	Chuck Meacham	1984	6
163 4/8	33 5/8	33 1/8	14 7/8	14 5/8	23 3/8	Mohave County	AZ	Gary Steinmann	1986	7
163 2/8	34 0/8	33 0/8	15 0/8	15 1/8	19 6/8	Sonora	MEX	Gary F. Bogner	1993	8
163 1/8	34 6/8	35 5/8	15 4/8	15 4/8	22 3/8	Clark County	NV	Fred Church	1984	9
162 1/8	34 2/8	33 3/8	14 3/8	14 2/8	20 2/8	Mohave County	AZ	Darell Lee Christensen	1987	10
160 3/8	31 5/8	32 2/8	14 4/8	14 4/8	23 2/8	Nye County	NV	Gary N. Smith	1993	11

DESERT BIGHORN SHEEP

Minimum Score 140

SCORE	LENGTH OF HORN R / L		CIRCUMFERENCE OF BASE R / L		GREATEST SPREAD	AREA	STATE/ PROVINCE	HUNTER'S NAME	DATE	RANK
159 4/8	32 6/8	32 2/8	14 7/8	14 7/8	21 4/8	Sonora	MEX	Thomas J. Hoffman	1989	12
157 5/8	32 3/8	33 4/8	13 1/8	13 2/8	21 7/8	Yuma County	AZ	Barry Sopher	1985	13
157 3/8	30 4/8	31 5/8	14 2/8	14 2/8	22 3/8	Lincoln County	NV	James R. Puryear	1984	14
156 3/8	32 7/8	31 4/8	14 3/8	14 6/8	26 2/8	Nye County	NV	Jerry Vega	1987	15
156 2/8	33 4/8	34 0/8	13 7/8	13 7/8	29 0/8	Mineral County	NV	Bob Sneed	1996	16
155 7/8	30 5/8	30 2/8	14 4/8	14 4/8	25 7/8	Nye County	NV	David Powning	1984	17
155 5/8	31 6/8	33 7/8	15 1/8	15 2/8	20 0/8	Sonora	MEX	Thomas J. Hoffman	1985	18
154 1/8	30 5/8	31 2/8	14 0/8	14 1/8	22 7/8	Nye County	NV	Richard J. Panelli	1985	19
154 0/8	31 6/8	30 0/8	13 5/8	13 7/8	22 7/8	Mohave County	AZ	Ward Villamor	1989	20
153 7/8	31 2/8	31 3/8	15 2/8	15 4/8	19 6/8	Maricopa County	AZ	Brad L. Siefarth	1979	21
153 6/8	34 0/8	31 6/8	13 5/8	12 5/8	19 2/8	Yuma County	AZ	Jeffery Stevens	1990	22
153 3/8	31 3/8	30 6/8	13 5/8	13 5/8	22 2/8	Mohave County	AZ	Kevin Robinson	1996	23
152 1/8	30 0/8	30 3/8	14 7/8	14 5/8	19 1/8	Mohave County	AZ	Pete Shepley	1986	24
151 6/8	29 0/8	30 6/8	14 2/8	14 2/8	22 6/8	Nye County	NV	David Snyder	1994	25
151 3/8	32 3/8	34 6/8	12 6/8	12 1/8	21 2/8	Clark County	NV	Gilbert Hernandez	1985	26
151 0/8	32 4/8	31 4/8	14 1/8	13 4/8	21 5/8	Imperial County	CA	John P. Rake	1996	27
149 7/8	28 0/8	29 7/8	14 4/8	14 1/8	19 7/8	Imperial County	CA	Greg Silva	1995	28
148 7/8	31 4/8	30 5/8	14 4/8	14 3/8	27 2/8	Mohave County	AZ	Randy Ulmer	1991	29
146 0/8	28 6/8	28 6/8	13 0/8	13 3/8	19 4/8	Yuma County	AZ	Mark F. Vancas	1990	30
145 4/8	29 2/8	32 2/8	14 1/8	14 2/8	24 0/8	Mohave County	AZ	Cindi Richardson	1992	31
145 1/8	28 6/8	28 3/8	13 7/8	13 7/8	20 4/8	Lincoln County	NV	San Stiver	1980	32
144 4/8	31 3/8	29 3/8	12 0/8	12 1/8	20 0/8	Clark County	NV	Ken Tavener	1996	33
142 6/8	26 1/8	26 5/8	12 5/8	12 5/8	21 5/8	Lincoln County	NV	Kurt W. Keskimaki	1991	34
142 3/8	28 7/8	28 4/8	14 4/8	14 3/8	22 5/8	Mohave County	AZ	Keith A. Robinson	1993	35
142 0/8	28 4/8	28 6/8	13 6/8	13 6/8	18 0/8	Clark County	NV	Ralph L. Albright	1995	36
141 2/8	27 0/8	29 2/8	13 2/8	13 2/8	19 0/8	Mohave County	AZ	Chuck Adams	1986	37

Continued

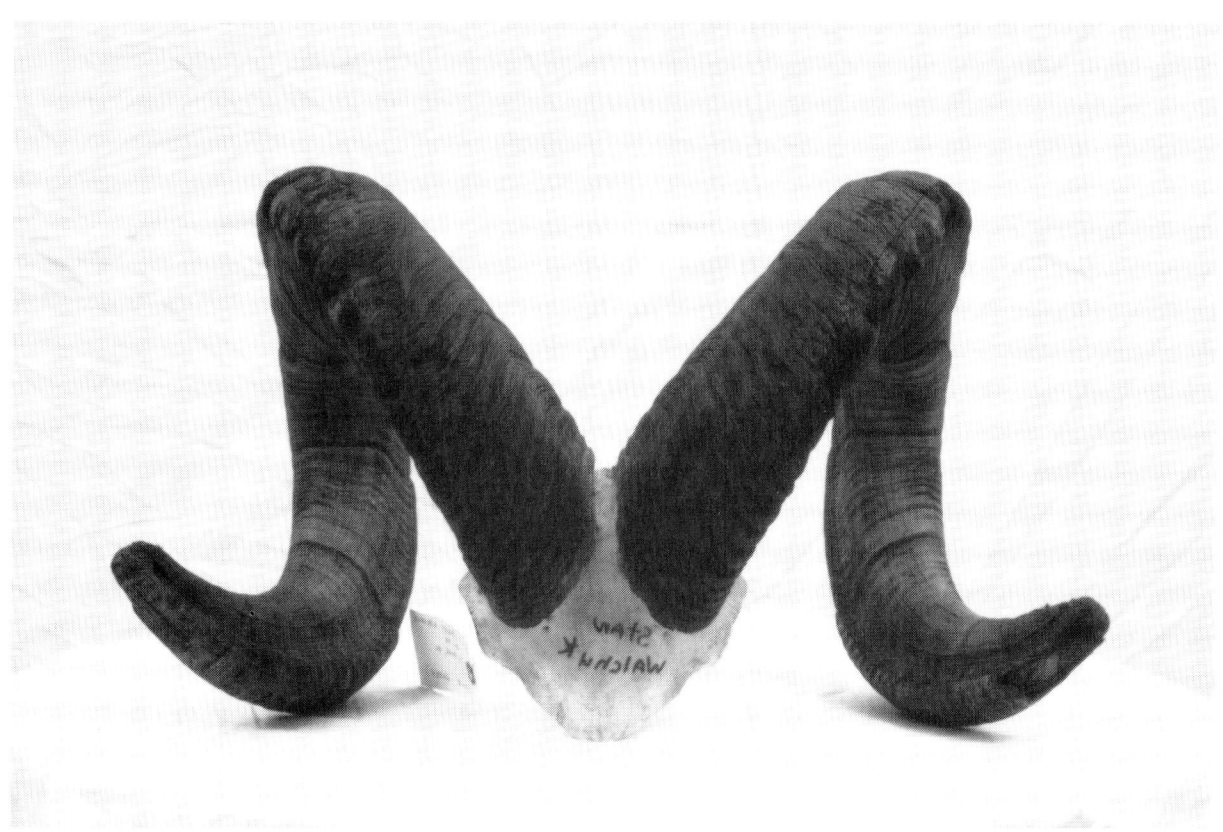

World Record Stone Sheep
Score: 174 2/8
Tetsa River, British Columbia - 1992
Hunter: Stanley Walchuk, Jr.

STONE SHEEP

Minimum Score 120

Ovis dalli stonei

SCORE	LENGTH OF R HORN L		CIRCUMFERENCE R OF BASE L		GREATEST SPREAD	AREA	STATE/ PROVINCE	HUNTER'S NAME	DATE	RANK
174 2/8	41 1/8	42 1/8	12 4/8	12 4/8	22 0/8	Tetsa River	BC	Stanley Walchuk, Jr.	1992	1
174 0/8	41 5/8	39 5/8	14 5/8	14 7/8	25 0/8	Gathto Creek	BC	Dyrk Eddie	1997	2
170 2/8	41 6/8	42 0/8	14 1/8	14 1/8	27 2/8	Blue Lake	BC	Ralph L. Albright	1995	3
168 0/8	41 2/8	41 6/8	13 6/8	13 3/8	25 0/8	Todagin Mtn.	BC	Peter T. Woloshyn	1994	4
167 6/8	38 2/8	38 4/8	14 3/8	14 1/8	26 6/8	Gathto Creek	BC	Jim Boyer	1994	5
165 3/8	39 5/8	41 6/8	13 0/8	13 1/8	23 4/8	Mac Millan River	YUK	Lonny Vanatta	1989	6
163 1/8	39 2/8	35 5/8	14 0/8	14 0/8	22 4/8	Racing River	BC	Archie Nesbitt	1989	7
162 6/8	38 6/8	38 4/8	14 3/8	14 2/8	22 1/8	Toad River	BC	Fred C. Church	1993	8
162 5/8	34 5/8	35 2/8	14 2/8	14 4/8	21 2/8	Muskwa River	BC	Thomas J. Hoffman	1987	9
161 0/8	34 0/8	37 4/8	14 1/8	14 1/8	23 4/8	Ram Creek	BC	Al Baldwin	1997	10
160 1/8	38 7/8	38 2/8	13 0/8	13 0/8	26 2/8	Todagin Mtn.	BC	Bob Renner	1987	11
160 0/8	39 2/8	38 6/8	13 0/8	13 0/8	26 1/8	Todagin Mtn.	BC	Ken Scheer	1990	12
159 0/8	38 3/8	37 3/8	13 1/8	13 1/8	16 3/8	Gathto Creek	BC	Teijo Villa	1998	13
158 4/8	36 0/8	39 2/8	12 5/8	12 6/8	22 0/8	Ram Mtn.	BC	Mike Traub	1991	14
158 2/8	37 6/8	38 0/8	13 4/8	13 4/8	23 6/8	Todagin Mtn.	BC	Randy De Biasio	1992	15
158 1/8	40 4/8	38 3/8	12 4/8	13 1/8	27 0/8	Cold Fish Lake	BC	Fred Bear	1957	16
157 6/8	35 2/8	38 6/8	12 5/8	12 5/8	23 1/8	Todagin Lake	BC	Mickey McDonald	1991	17
157 4/8	37 5/8	37 3/8	13 3/8	13 3/8	25 0/8	Todagin Mtn.	BC	Bruce Ambler	1991	18
157 2/8	32 2/8	34 6/8	14 2/8	14 1/8	25 3/8	Lower Besa River	BC	Gary F. Bogner	1998	19
157 1/8	36 2/8	35 5/8	13 4/8	13 4/8	21 0/8	Trygue Lake	BC	Walt Krom	1979	20
156 7/8	37 2/8	37 7/8	13 4/8	13 5/8	25 6/8	Todagin Mtn.	BC	Len Cardinale	1990	21
156 1/8	37 1/8	39 0/8	13 0/8	13 2/8	24 0/8	Mount Armstrong	YUK	J. Bradley Thurston	1987	22
156 0/8	38 3/8	37 5/8	13 0/8	12 7/8	27 4/8	Todagin Mtn.	BC	Lee Veldhouse	1984	23
155 5/8	35 5/8	38 2/8	13 0/8	13 1/8	24 6/8	Bonnet Plume Range	YUK	Tim Good	1995	24
155 3/8	36 3/8	35 2/8	13 2/8	13 2/8	19 3/8	Muncho Lake	BC	Gary Martin	1994	25
155 2/8	38 1/8	37 1/8	13 1/8	13 2/8	26 6/8	Todagin Mtn.	BC	Reggie Spiegelberg	1984	26
155 1/8	36 6/8	36 3/8	13 2/8	13 2/8	21 6/8	Telegraph Creek	BC	Jamie Byrne	1990	27

STONE SHEEP

Minimum Score 120

SCORE	LENGTH OF HORN R / L		CIRCUMFERENCE OF BASE R / L		GREATEST SPREAD	AREA	STATE/PROVINCE	HUNTER'S NAME	DATE	RANK
155 1/8	35 0/8	36 3/8	13 7/8	14 0/8	19 6/8	Gathto Creek	BC	Bert Nadeau	1998	27
154 3/8	35 6/8	36 3/8	13 2/8	13 3/8	25 3/8	Todagin Creek Mtn.	BC	Roy Lynch	1983	29
154 2/8	38 0/8	34 4/8	12 7/8	12 7/8	21 3/8	Todagin Mtn.	BC	Stanley R. Godfrey	1991	30
154 1/8	35 7/8	34 6/8	13 3/8	13 3/8	23 5/8	Cassiar Mtns.	BC	Calvin Farner	1986	31
154 1/8	36 7/8	36 4/8	13 0/8	13 0/8	23 6/8	Todagin Mtn.	BC	Dennis Palmer	1991	31
154 0/8	36 3/8	36 5/8	12 7/8	13 0/8	24 5/8	Todagin Mtn.	BC	A. E. "Gene" Tisdale	1994	33
153 7/8	36 3/8	34 6/8	13 1/8	13 0/8	24 6/8	Cassiar Mtns.	BC	Marvin Clyncke	1994	34
153 5/8	38 0/8	39 2/8	14 0/8	14 0/8	24 1/8	Kechika River	BC	Paul Brunner	1974	35
153 1/8	36 1/8	34 2/8	13 6/8	13 6/8	20 6/8	Kechika River	BC	John D. 'Jack' Frost	1985	36
153 0/8	37 2/8	36 2/8	13 3/8	13 3/8	25 5/8	Pelly Mtns.	YUK	Todd R. Zeuske	1997	37
152 3/8	30 6/8	37 5/8	13 4/8	13 4/8	24 2/8	Tucho Lake	BC	Chuck Adams	1985	38
152 2/8	37 1/8	36 3/8	13 2/8	13 1/8	20 5/8	Todagin Mtn.	BC	Richard Paquette	1994	39
151 4/8	33 2/8	33 0/8	13 2/8	13 2/8	20 3/8	Racing River	BC	Pete Shepley	1985	40
151 4/8	38 5/8	37 7/8	12 3/8	12 3/8	22 7/8	Mac Millan River	YUK	Bob Fromme	1991	40
151 2/8	35 7/8	34 7/8	13 3/8	13 3/8	24 1/8	Todagin Mtn.	BC	Craig Kohorst	1991	42
151 1/8	36 3/8	36 6/8	12 7/8	13 1/8	25 2/8	Todagin Mtn.	BC	Rob Frew	1993	43
150 7/8	35 4/8	36 1/8	13 2/8	13 2/8	22 7/8	Todagin Creek	BC	Rick Paquette	1990	44
150 3/8	36 1/8	33 2/8	13 3/8	13 1/8	19 6/8	Toad River	BC	Jim Ryan	1987	45
150 3/8	28 0/8	36 5/8	13 4/8	13 3/8	23 6/8	Todagin Mtn.	BC	Bill Nickerson	1987	45
149 1/8	35 4/8	35 3/8	13 2/8	13 1/8	21 6/8	Terminus Mtn.	BC	Paul P. Schafer	1975	47
148 3/8	34 0/8	35 7/8	13 0/8	13 1/8	28 0/8	Todagin Mtn.	BC	Al Klopfenstein	1977	48
148 1/8	36 3/8	33 6/8	12 4/8	14 0/8	21 5/8	Tetachi Lake	BC	Robert Pyne	1987	49
147 7/8	35 7/8	30 0/8	13 3/8	13 3/8	28 0/8	Tatogga Lake	BC	Eric Hoglund	1979	50
147 6/8	33 4/8	35 0/8	12 5/8	12 5/8	19 7/8	Todagin Mtn.	BC	James R. Gabrick	1996	51
147 4/8	34 4/8	35 0/8	13 2/8	13 4/8	20 0/8	Stikine River	BC	Will Pick	1995	52
146 6/8	33 7/8	33 5/8	12 6/8	13 1/8	21 2/8	Todagin Mtn.	BC	Lawrence Michalchuk	1994	53
146 4/8	35 5/8	35 3/8	13 0/8	13 3/8	27 1/8	Atlin	BC	Tom Tietz	1985	54
145 7/8	34 4/8	34 7/8	13 0/8	13 0/8	22 1/8	Todagin Mtn.	BC	Lee Kline	1983	55
145 7/8	34 0/8	34 1/8	13 0/8	13 0/8	22 4/8	Todagin Mtn.	BC	Vinnie Pisani	1995	55
145 6/8	33 1/8	33 7/8	12 5/8	12 5/8	21 4/8	Todagin Lake	BC	Thomas J. Hoffman	1985	57
145 6/8	33 7/8	33 5/8	12 6/8	12 6/8	18 6/8	Todagin Mtn.	BC	Alan Bressanutti	1992	57
144 5/8	37 3/8	33 4/8	12 1/8	12 1/8	23 4/8	Cassiar Mtns.	BC	V. Randy Liljenquist	1996	59
143 5/8	33 0/8	34 5/8	12 3/8	12 4/8	19 0/8	Christian Falls	BC	Jim Ryan	1990	60
143 5/8	33 2/8	33 3/8	12 7/8	12 7/8	21 1/8	Crehan Creek	BC	Chris Barker	1997	60
142 2/8	33 6/8	34 2/8	12 2/8	12 1/8	22 1/8	Todagin Mtn.	BC	David Hooper	1977	62
140 5/8	35 0/8	34 7/8	12 1/8	12 0/8	23 3/8	Turnagin River	BC	Maxallen D. Jackson	1984	63
140 4/8	32 5/8	32 7/8	12 5/8	12 7/8	21 4/8	Todagin Creek Mtn.	BC	Dennis McCarthy	1983	64
136 6/8	31 6/8	29 4/8	12 4/8	12 4/8	21 0/8	Tucho Lake	BC	Jim Wondzell	1998	65
132 3/8	30 6/8	30 5/8	12 6/8	12 5/8	21 1/8	Anvil Mtn.	YUK	Kurt H. Eisenach	1994	66
126 4/8	27 3/8	31 1/8	11 6/8	11 6/8	19 2/8	Todagin Mtn.	BC	Don St. Jean	1987	67
120 5/8	20 2/8	33 5/8	13 1/8	13 0/8	16 4/8	Stikine River	BC	Will Pick	1997	68

Pope and Young President G. Fred Asbell

APPENDIX

BOWHUNTER'S BIG GAME RECORDS
A PROGRAM OF
POPE AND YOUNG CLUB

Under the heading of North American Big Game are included the following with the minimum point score requirements (Boone & Crockett/Pope & Young scoring system) effective January 1, 1995.

To be eligible for entry into the Pope and Young Records and awards, the trophy must equal or exceed the score listed on the Minimum List and must have been taken by the individual or persons who are entering it, entirely by means of the Bow and Arrow under the Club's Rules of Fair Chase. A Trophy Award Certificate will be issued to each qualifying entry.

Cougar taken in any area where a bounty provision of any type is allowed are not eligible for entry in Pope and Young Club Records.

Southern Boundary of North America to be defined as the Southern Boundary of Mexico.

MINIMUM POINT SCORE REQUIREMENTS

Alaska Brown Bear 20
Black Bear 18
Grizzly Bear 19
Polar Bear 20
Bison 100
* Barren Ground Caribou 325
* Central Canada Barren Ground Caribou 300
* Mountain Caribou 300
* Quebec-Labrador Caribou 325
* Woodland Caribou 220
Cougar 13 8/16
* Columbian Blacktail Deer 90
* Columbian Blacktail Deer, Non-Typical 125
* Sitka Blacktail Deer 75
* Coues' Deer, Typical 65
* Coues' Deer, Non-Typical 95
* Mule Deer, Typical 145

* Mule Deer, Non-Typical. 170
* Whitetail Deer, Typical 125
* Whitetail Deer, Non-Typical 155
* Roosevelt's (Olympic) Elk. 225
* Yellowstone (Wapiti) Elk 260
* Yellowstone Elk, Non-Typical.. 335
Rocky Mountain Goat. 40
* Alaska-Yukon Moose 170
* Canada Moose 135
* Shiras' Moose. 125
Muskox. 90
Pronghorn 67
Bighorn Sheep .140
Dall's (White) Sheep 120
Desert Bighorn Sheep 140
Stone's Sheep. 120

* Velvet entries are accepted in these categories, the above minimums apply.

Revised January, 1999

HOW TO
ENTER A TROPHY

FOR AN ANIMAL to qualify for entry into the Pope and Young Club's records, it must equal or exceed established minimum score requirements and must have been legally taken by a bowhunter under the rules detailed on the Fair Chase Affidavit.

Successful hunters need not be members of the Pope and Young Club to enter their trophies. The Club's records are open to any bowhunter who has legally taken an eligible North American big game animal.

Each trophy must be scored by an official measurer of either the Pope and Young or Boone and Crockett Club. Before any trophy can be officially measured, 60 days must have passed since the date of kill. During this entire "drying period," the trophy should be stored at room temperature without any modifications and without the attachment of any items designed to prevent normal drying. All successful bowhunters must complete and submit a scoring form and a signed Fair Chase Affidavit.

Each record book entry must be accompanied by a minimum of three photos showing the left side, right side, and frontal view. If possible, a site-of-kill photo showing the entire animal should be provided. Color or black and white prints, including clear Polaroid shots, are acceptable; however, color transparencies may not be submitted.

At the present time an entry fee of $25.00 (U.S. Funds) is required for each trophy being submitted for record book entry. Personal checks or money orders, payable to the Pope and Young Club, are acceptable. Volunteer measurers do not receive a fee for scoring the trophy animal.

To obtain the name, address, and telephone number of the nearest official measurer, any bowhunter may write or call:

Pope and Young Club
P. O. Box 548
Chatfield, MN 55923
(507) 867-4144

POPE & YOUNG CLUB
NORTH AMERICAN BIG GAME TROPHY SCORING FORM
BOWHUNTING
BIG GAME RECORDS

BEAR

KIND OF BEAR _____

SEX _____

	SEE OTHER SIDE FOR INSTRUCTIONS		Measurements
A.	Greatest Length Without Lower Jaw	(Measured in Sixteenths)	
B.	Greatest Width	(Measured in Sixteenths)	
	TOTAL AND FINAL SCORE		

Exact locality where killed _____ (County) _____ (State) _____

Date killed _____ By whom killed _____

Present owner _____ Phone ( ) _____

Address _____

Guide's Name and Address _____

REMARKS (Mention any abnormalities) _____

Were dogs used in conjunction with the pursuit and harvest of this animal? YES _____ NO _____

If yes, the following statements apply:
1. I was present on the hunt at the time the dogs were released to pursue this animal.
2. If electric collars were attached to any of the dogs, <u>at no time</u> from the beginning of the chase until the harvest of this animal were receivers used in the pursuit and harvest.

If you answered yes and if conditions #1 or #2 do not apply, please explain on separate sheet.

_____ _____
(HUNTERS SIGNATURE) DATE

• •

I certify that I have measured the above trophy on _____ 19 ____

at (address) _____ City _____

State _____ Zip Code _____ and that these measurements and data are, to the best

of my knowledge and belief, made in accordance with the instructions given.

Witness: _____ Signature _____
(To Measurer's Signature)   Pope & Young Club Official Measurer

MEASURER (Print) _____
ADDRESS _____
CITY _____ STATE _____ ZIP _____

INSTRUCTIONS

All measurements must be made with a flexible steel tape to the nearest one-sixteenth of an inch.

Official measurements cannot be taken for at least sixty days after the animal was killed. Photographs of right side, left side, and front of skull are required.

A. Greatest Length is measured between perpendiculars to the long axis of the skull WITHOUT the lower jaw and EXLUDING malformations. (Normal teeth are included.)

B. Greatest Width is measured between perpendiculars at right angles to the long axis.

All adhering flesh, membrane and cartilage must be completely removed before official measurements are taken.

Photographs: All entries **must** include photographs of the trophy. A right side, left side and front view photograph is required for all skulls. A photograph of the entire animal, preferably at the site of kill, is requested if at all possible. The front view is best taken from above at a 45° angle.

Drying Period: To be eligible for entry in the Pope & Young Records, a trophy must first have been stored under normal room temperature and humidity for at least 60 days after date of kill. No trophy will be considered which has in any way been altered from its natural state.

<u>All flesh and membrane **must** be completely removed from skull prior to measuring.</u>

IF DOGS ARE USED, THE HUNTER MUST BE PRESENT AT THE TIME THE DOGS ARE RELEASED

THIS SCORING FORM MUST BE ACCOMPANIED BY A SIGNED POPE & YOUNG FAIR CHASE AFFIDAVIT, 3 PHOTOS OF SKULL, AND A RECORDING FEE OF $25.00

Copyright 1988 Boone & Crockett Club
(Written Request for Privilege of Complete Reproduction is Required)

POPE & YOUNG CLUB
NORTH AMERICAN BIG GAME TROPHY SCORING FORM
BOWHUNTING

BISON

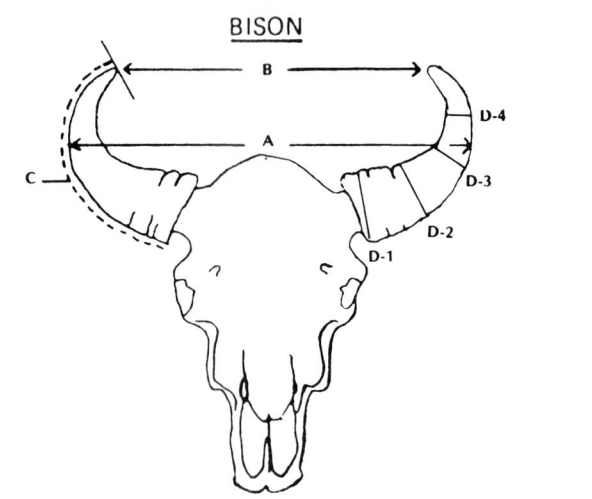

SEX _____

SEE OTHER SIDE FOR INSTRUCTIONS		Supplementary Data	Column 1 Right Horn	Column 2 Left Horn	Column 3 Difference
A	Greatest Spread				
B	Tip to Tip Spread				
C	Length of Horn				
D-1	Circumference of Base				
D-2	Circumference at First Quarter (this measurement taken at _____ inches from base)				
D-3	Circumference at Second Quarter (this measurement taken at _____ inches from base)				
D-4	Circumference at Third Quarter (this measurement taken at _____ inches from base)				
TOTALS					

ADD	Column 1		Location where killed (County) (State)
	Column 2		Date killed By whom killed
TOTAL			Present owner Phone ( )
SUBTRACT Column 3			Address
FINAL SCORE			Guide's Name and Address
			Remarks: (Mention any abnormalities)

I certify that I have measured the above trophy on _____ 19 _____
at (address) _____ City _____
State _____ Zip Code _____ and that these measurements and data are, to the best of my knowledge and belief, made in accordance with the instructions given.
Witness: _____   Signature _____
(To Measurer's Signature)
Pope & Young Club Official Measurer

MEASURER (Print) _____

ADDRESS _____

CITY   STATE   ZIP

INSTRUCTIONS

Measurements must be made with a flexible steel tape to the nearest one-eighth of an inch. To simplify addition, please enter fractional figures in **eighths.** Official measurements cannot be taken for at least sixty days after the day the animal was killed. **Please submit photographs [see below].**

A. **Greatest Spread** is measured between perpendiculars at right angles to the center line of the skull.

B. **Tip to Tip Spread** is measured between tips of horns.

C. **Length of Horn** is measured from lowest point on under side over outer curve to a point in line with tip. Use a straight edge, perpendicular to horn axis, to end the measurement, if necessary.

D-1 **Circumferernce of Base** is measured at right angles to axis of horn. **DO NOT** follow irregular edge of horn. The line of measurement must be entirely on horn material, not the jagged edge often noted. Circumference measurements must be taken with a steel tape.

D-2-3-4 Divide measurement C of **LONGER** horn by four, mark **BOTH** horns at these quarters even though other horn is shorter, and measure circumference at these marks. Mark quarters by starting from base only.

Photographs: All entries must include photographs of the trophy. A right side, left side and front view photograph is required of the horns. A photograph of the entire animal, preferably at the site of kill, is requested if at all possible.

Drying Period: To be eligible for entry in the Pope & Young Records, a trophy must first have been stored under normal room temperature and humidity for at least 60 days after date of kill. No trophy will be considered which has in any way been altered from its natural state.

THIS SCORING FORM MUST BE ACCOMPANIED BY A SIGNED POPE & YOUNG FAIR CHASE AFFIDAVIT, 3 PHOTOS OF HORNS, AND A RECORDING FEE OF $25.00.

Copyright 1981 by Boone and Crockett Club
(Written request for privilege of complete reproduction is required)

POPE AND YOUNG CLUB
NORTH AMERICAN BIG GAME TROPHY SCORING FORM

BIG GAME RECORDS

CARIBOU

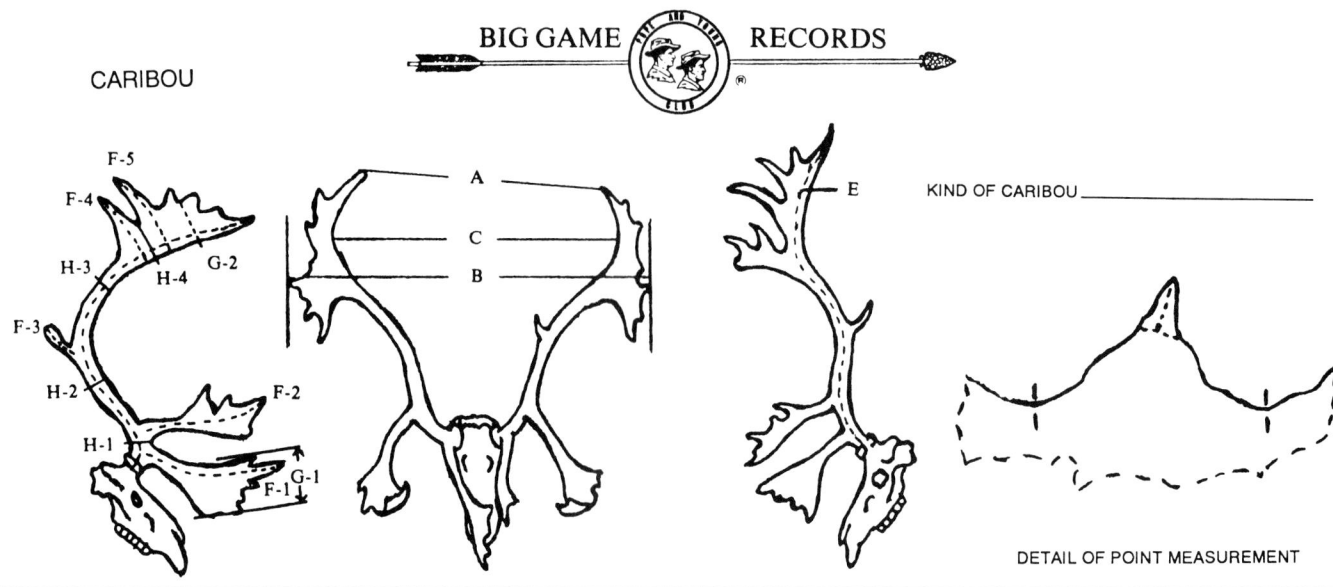

KIND OF CARIBOU _____

DETAIL OF POINT MEASUREMENT

SEE OTHER SIDE FOR INSTRUCTIONS		Supplementary Data	Column 1 Spread Credit	Column 2 Right Antler	Column 3 Left Antler	Column 4 Difference
A.	Tip to Tip Spread					
B.	Greatest Spread					
C.	Inside Spread of MAIN BEAMS	Spread credit may equal but not exceed length of longer antler				
D.	Number of Points on Each Antler excluding brows					
	Number of Points on Each Brow					
E.	Length of Main Beam					
F-1	Length of Brow Palm or First Point					
F-2	Length of Bez or Second Point					
F-3	Length of Rear Point, if present					
F-4	Length of Second Longest Top Point					
F-5	Length of Longest Top Point					
G-1	Width of Brow Palm					
G-2	Width of Top Palm					
H-1	Circumference at Smallest Place Between Brow and Bez Points					
H-2	Circumference at Smallest Place Between Bez and Rear Points, if present					
H-3	Circumference at Smallest Place Before First Top Point					
H-4	Circumference at Smallest Place Between Two Longest Top Palm Points					
	TOTALS					

ADD	Column 1		Exact locality where killed	
	Column 2		Date killed	By whom killed
	Column 3		Present owner	Phone ( )
	Total		Address	
	SUBTRACT Column 4		Guide's Name and Address	
	FINAL SCORE		Remarks: (Mention any abnormalities)	

I certify that I have measured the above trophy on_____19_____
at (address)_____City_____
State_____Zip Code_____and that these measurements and data are, to the
best of my knowledge and belief, made in accordance with the instructions given.

Witness:_____ Signature _____
           (To measurer's signature)   Pope & Young Club Official Measurer

_____
MEASURER   (Print)

_____
ADDRESS

_____
CITY   STATE   ZIP

INSTRUCTIONS

Measurements must be made with a flexible steel tape or steel cable to the nearest one-eighth of an inch. To simplify addition, please enter fractional figures in eighths. Official measurements cannot be taken for at least sixty days after the animal was killed. Please submit photographs (see below).

A. Tip to Tip Spread is measured between tips of Main Beams.

B. Greatest Spread is measured between perpendiculars at right angles to the center line of the skull at widest part whether across main beams or points.

C. Inside Spread of Main Beams is measured at right angles to the center line of the skull at the widest point between main beams. Enter this measurement again in "Spread Credit" column if it is less than or equal to the length of longer antler; if longer, enter longer antler length for Spread Credit.

D. Number of points on each antler. To be counted a point, a projection must be at least one-half inch long and this length must exceed the breadth at the point of measurement. The length may be measured to any location - at least one-half inch from the tip - at which the length of the point exceeds its breadth. Beam tip is counted as a point but not measured as a point. There are no "abnormal" points on caribou.

E. Length of Main Beam is measured from lowest outside edge of burr over outer curve to the most distant point of what is, or appears to be, the main beam. The point of beginning is that point on the burr where the center line along the outer curve of the beam intersects the burr.

F-1-2-3. Length of Points. The lengths of these points are measured from nearest edge of beam on the shortest line over outer curve to tip. To determine nearest edge (top edge) of beam, lay the tape along the outer curve of the beam so that the top edge of the tape coincides with the tip edge of the beam on both sides of the point. Draw line along top edge of tape. This line will be base line from which point is measured.

F-4-5. The length of these points are measured from the tip of the point to the top of the beam, then at right angle to the LOWER EDGE of beam. The second longest Top Point **cannot** be a point branch of the Longest Top Point.

G-1. Width of Brow is measured in a straight line from top edge to lower edge, as illustrated, with measurement line at a right angle to main axis of brow.

G-2. Width of Top Palm is measured from midpoint of lower rear edge of main beam to midpoint of a dip between points, at widest part of palm. The line of measurement begins and ends at mid-points of palm edges, which gives credit for palm thickness.

H-1-2-3-4. Circumferences - If rear point is missing, take H-2 and H-3 measurements at smallest place between bez and first top point. A steel tape must be used to take circumference measurements (a cable cannot be used for these measurements).

Photographs: All entries must include photographs of the trophy. A right side, left side and front view photograph will be required for all antlers. A photograph of the entire animal is requested if at all possible.

Drying Period: To be eligible for entry in the Pope & Young Records, a trophy must first have been stored under normal room temperature and humidity for at least 60 consecutive days. No trophy will be considered which has in any way been altered from its natural state.

THIS SCORING FORM MUST BE ACCOMPANIED BY A SIGNED POPE & YOUNG FAIR CHASE AFFIDAVIT, 3 PHOTOS OF ANTLERS, AND A RECORDING FEE OF $25.00.

Copyright 1981 by Boone and Crockett Club
(Written request for privilege of complete reproduction is required)

POPE & YOUNG CLUB
NORTH AMERICAN BIG GAME TROPHY SCORING FORM
BOWHUNTING

COUGAR   SEX _____

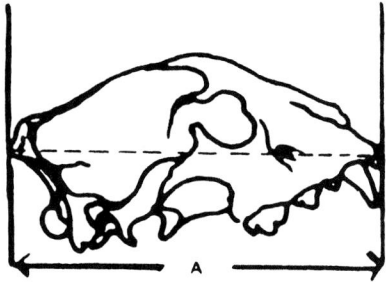   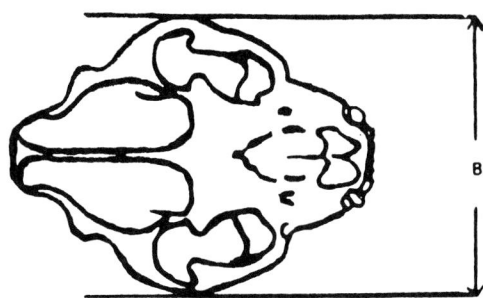

SEE OTHER SIDE FOR INSTRUCTIONS		Measurements
A. Greatest Length Without Lower Jaw	(Measured in Sixteenths)	
B. Greatest Width	(Measured in Sixteenths)	
TOTAL AND FINAL SCORE		

Exact locality where killed _____ (County) _____ (State) _____

Date killed _____ By whom killed _____

Present owner _____ Phone ( )

Address _____

Guide's Name and Address _____

REMARKS (Mention any abnormalities) _____

Were dogs used in conjunction with the pursuit and harvest of this animal?   YES _____ NO _____

If yes, the following statements apply:
1. I was present on the hunt at the time the dogs were released to pursue this animal.
2. If electric collars were attached to any of the dogs, <u>at no time</u> from the beginning of the chase until the harvest of this animal were receivers used in the pursuit and harvest.

If you answered yes and if conditions #1 or #2 do not apply, please explain on separate sheet.

_____   _____
(HUNTERS SIGNATURE)   DATE

• •

I certify that I have measured the above trophy on _____ 19_____

at (address) _____ City _____

State _____ Zip Code _____ and that these measurements and data are, to the best of my knowledge and belief, made in accordance with the instructions given.

Witness: _____ Signature _____
(To Measurer's Signature)   Pope & Young Club Official Measurer

MEASURER (Print) _____
ADDRESS _____
CITY _____ STATE _____ ZIP _____

INSTRUCTIONS

All measurements must be made with a flexible steel tape to the nearest one-sixteenth of an inch.

Official measurements cannot be taken for at least sixty days after the animal was killed. Photographs of right side, left side, and front of skull are required.

A. Greatest Length is measured between perpendiculars to the long axis of the skull WITHOUT the lower jaw and EXLUDING malformations. (Normal teeth are included.)

B. Greatest Width is measured between perpendiculars at right angles to the long axis.

All adhering flesh, membrane and cartilage must be completely removed before official measurements are taken.

Photographs: All entries **must** include photographs of the trophy. A right side, left side and front view photograph is required for all skulls. A photograph of the entire animal, preferably at the site of kill, is requested if at all possible. The front view is best taken from above at a 45° angle.

Drying Period: To be eligible for entry in the Pope & Young Records, a trophy must first have been stored under normal room temperature and humidity for at least 60 days after date of kill. No trophy will be considered which has in any way been altered from its natural state.

All flesh and membrane **must** be completely removed from skull prior to measuring.

IF DOGS ARE USED, THE HUNTER MUST BE PRESENT AT THE TIME THE DOGS ARE RELEASED

THIS SCORING FORM MUST BE ACCOMPANIED BY A SIGNED POPE & YOUNG FAIR CHASE AFFIDAVIT, 3 PHOTOS OF SKULL, AND A RECORDING FEE OF $25.00

Copyright 1988 Boone & Crockett Club
(Written Request for Privilege of Complete Reproduction is Required)

POPE & YOUNG CLUB
NORTH AMERICAN BIG GAME TROPHY SCORING FORM
BOWHUNTING

BIG GAME   RECORDS

KIND OF DEER _____

TYPICAL MULE AND BLACKTAIL DEER

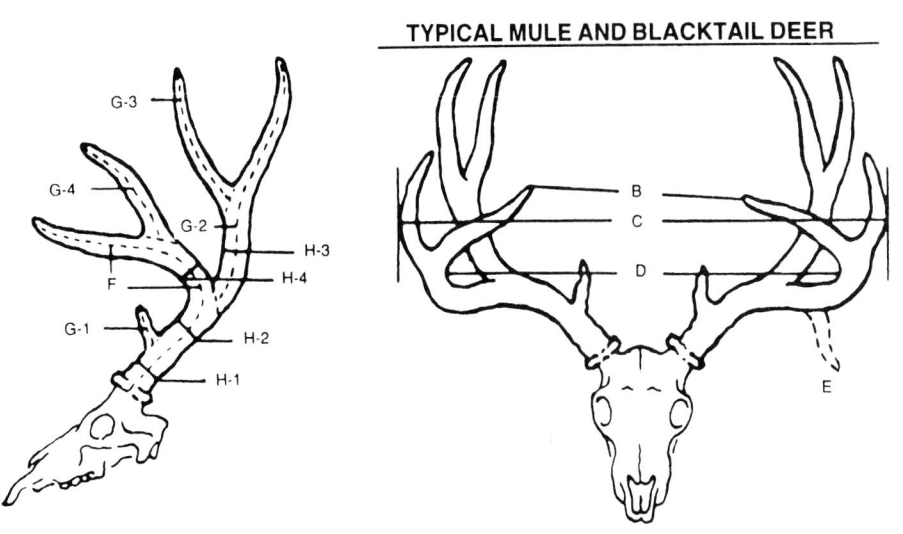

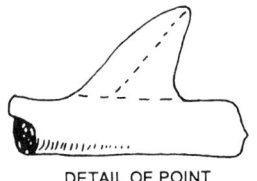

DETAIL OF POINT MEASUREMENT

Abnormal Points	
Right	Left
Total To E	

	SEE OTHER SIDE FOR INSTRUCTIONS		Supplementary Data		Column 1	Column 2	Column 3	Column 4
			R	L	Spread Credit	Right Antler	Left Antler	Difference
A.	Number of Points on Each Antler							
B.	Tip to Tip Spread							
C.	Greatest Spread							
D.	Inside Spread of MAIN BEAMS		Spread credit may equal but not exceed length of longer antler					
E.	Total of Lengths of all Abnormal Points							
F.	Length of Main Beam							
G-1	Length of First Point, if present							
G-2	Length of Second Point							
G-3	Length of Third Point							
G-4	Length of Fourth Point, if present							
H-1	Circumference at Smallest Place Between Burr and First Point							
H-2	Circumference at Smallest Place Between First and Second Points							
H-3	Circumference at Smallest Place Between Main and Second Points							
H-4	Circumference at Smallest Place between Second and Fourth Points							
TOTALS								

	Column 1		Exact locality where killed	(County)	(State)
ADD	Column 2		Date killed	By whom killed	
	Column 3		Present owner	Phone ( )	
	Total		Address		
SUBTRACT Column 4			Guide's name and Complete Address		
FINAL SCORE			Remarks: (Mention any abnormalities)		

I certify that I have measured the above trophy on _____ 19_____
at (address)_____ City _____
State_____ Zip Code _____ and that these measurements and data are, to the best of my knowledge and belief, made in accordance with the instructions given.
Witness: _____ Signature _____
                (To Measurer's Signature)   Pope & Young Club Official Measurer

_____
MEASURER (Print)

_____
ADDRESS

_____
CITY   STATE   ZIP

INSTRUCTIONS

Measurements must be made with a flexible steel tape or steel cable to the nearest one-eighth of an inch. To simplify addition, please enter fractional figures in **eighths**. Official measurements cannot be taken for at least sixty days after the animal was killed. **Please submit photographs (see below).**

A. Number of Points on each antler. To be counted a point, a projection must be at least one inch long AND at some location, at least one inch from the tip, the length of the projection must exceed its width. **Beam tip is counted as a point but not measured as a point.**

B. Tip to Tip Spread is measured between tips of main beams.

C. Greatest Spread is measured between perpendiculars at right angles to the center line of the skull at widest part whether across main beams or points.

D. Inside Spread on Main Beam is measured at right angles to the center line of the skull at widest point between main beams. Enter this measurement again in "Spread Credit" column if it is less than or equal to the length of longer antler: if longer, enter longer antler length for spread credit.

E. Total of Length of all Abnormal Points. Abnormal points are generally considered to be those non-typical in shape or location. Sketch all abnormal points on antler illustration (front of form) showing location and approximate size. Measure in usual manner and enter in appropriate blanks.

F. Length of Main Beam is measured from lowest outside edge of burr over outer curve to the most distant point of the main beam. The point of beginning is that point on the burr where the center line along the outer curve of the beam intersects the burr.

G. 1-2-3-4. Length of Normal Points. Normal points are the brow (or first) and the upper and lower forks as shown in illustration. They are measured from nearest edge of beam over outer curve to tip. To determine nearest edge (top edge) of beam, lay the tape along the outer curve of the beam so that the top edge of the tape coincides with the top edge of the beam on both sides of the point. Draw line along top of tape. This line will be base line from which point is measured.

H-1-2-3-4. Circumferences. If first point is missing, take H-1 and H-2 at smallest place between burr and second point. If third point is missing, take H-3 halfway between the base and tip of second point. If the fourth is missing, take H-4 halfway between the second point and tip of main beam. Circumference measurements must be taken with a steel tape (a cable cannot be used for these measurements).

Photographs: All entries must include photographs of the trophy. A right side, left side and front view photograph is required for all antlers. A photograph of the entire animal is requested if at all possible.

Drying Period: To be eligible for entry in the Pope & Young Records, a trophy must first have been stored under normal room temperature and humidity for at least 60 days. No trophy will be considered which has in any way been altered from its natural state.

**THIS SCORING FORM MUST BE ACCOMPANIED BY A SIGNED
POPE & YOUNG FAIR CHASE AFFIDAVIT, 3 PHOTOS OF ANTLERS, AND
A RECORDING FEE OF $25.00.**

**Copyright 1981 by Boone and Crockett Club
(Written request for privilege of complete reproduction is required)**

POPE & YOUNG CLUB
NORTH AMERICAN BIG GAME TROPHY SCORING FORM
BOWHUNTING
BIG GAME RECORDS

NON-TYPICAL MULE DEER

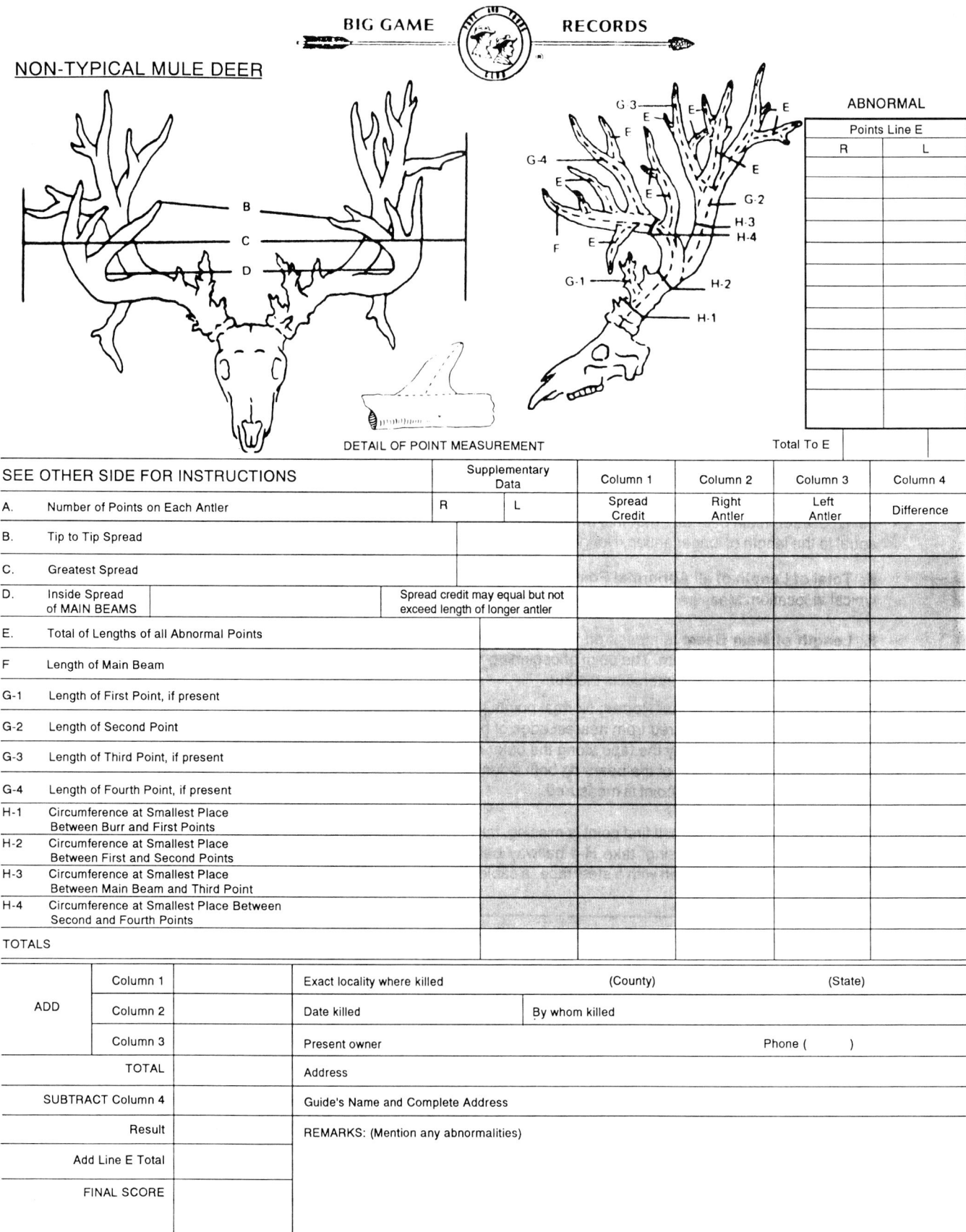

DETAIL OF POINT MEASUREMENT

ABNORMAL	
Points Line E	
R	L
Total To E	

SEE OTHER SIDE FOR INSTRUCTIONS	Supplementary Data		Column 1	Column 2	Column 3	Column 4
	R	L	Spread Credit	Right Antler	Left Antler	Difference
A. Number of Points on Each Antler						
B. Tip to Tip Spread						
C. Greatest Spread						
D. Inside Spread of MAIN BEAMS	Spread credit may equal but not exceed length of longer antler					
E. Total of Lengths of all Abnormal Points						
F Length of Main Beam						
G-1 Length of First Point, if present						
G-2 Length of Second Point						
G-3 Length of Third Point, if present						
G-4 Length of Fourth Point, if present						
H-1 Circumference at Smallest Place Between Burr and First Points						
H-2 Circumference at Smallest Place Between First and Second Points						
H-3 Circumference at Smallest Place Between Main Beam and Third Point						
H-4 Circumference at Smallest Place Between Second and Fourth Points						
TOTALS						

ADD	Column 1		Exact locality where killed (County) (State)
	Column 2		Date killed By whom killed
	Column 3		Present owner Phone ( )
TOTAL			Address
SUBTRACT Column 4			Guide's Name and Complete Address
Result			REMARKS: (Mention any abnormalities)
Add Line E Total			
FINAL SCORE			

I certify that I have measured the above trophy on _____ 19_____
at (address) _____ City _____
State _____ Zip Code _____ and that these measurements and data are, to the best
of my knowledge and belief, made in accordance with the instructions given.
Witness: _____ Signature _____
              (To Measurer's Signature)   Pope & Young Club Official Measurer

---
MEASURER (Print)

ADDRESS

CITY   STATE   ZIP

INSTRUCTIONS

Measurements must be made with a flexible steel tape or steel cable to the nearest one-eighth of an inch. To simplify addition, please enter fractional figures in **eighths**. Official measurements cannot be taken for at least sixty days after the day the animal was killed. **Please submit photographs [see below].**

A. Number of Points on each antler. To be counted a point, a projection must be at least one inch long AND at some location, at least one inch from the tip, the length of the projection must exceed its width. **Beam tip is counted as a point but not measured as a point.**

B. Tip to Tip Spread is measured between tips of main beams.

C. Greatest Spread is measured between perpendiculars at right angles to the center line of the skull at widest part whether across main beams or points.

D. Inside Spread on Main Beam is measured at right angles to the center line of the skull at widest point between main beams. Enter this measurement again in "Spread Credit" column if it is less than or equal to the length of longer antler; if longer, enter longer antler length for spread credit.

E. Total of Length of all Abnormal Points. Abnormal points are generally considered to be those non-typical in location. Measure in usual manner and enter in appropriate blanks.

F. Length of Main Beam is measured from lowest outside edge of burr over outer curve to the most distant point of the main beam. The point of beginning is that point on the burr where the center line along the outer curve of the beam intersects the burr.

G-1-2-3-4. Length of Normal Points. Normal points project from the top of the main beam as shown in illustration. They are measured from nearest edge of beam over outer curve to tip. To determine nearest edge (top edge) of beam, lay the tape along the outer curve of the beam so that the top edge of the tape coincides with the top edge of the beam on both sides of the point. Draw line along top of tape. This line will be base line from which point is measured.

H-1-2-3-4. Circumferences. If first point is missing, take H-1 and H-2 at smallest place between burr and second point. If G-4 is missing, take H-4 halfway between G-3 and tip of main beam. Circumference measurements must be taken with a steel tape (a cable cannot be used for these measurements).

Photographs: All entries must include photographs of the trophy. A right side, left side and front view photograph is required for all antlers. A photograph of the entire animal, preferably at the site of kill, is requested if at all possible.

Drying Period: To be eligible for entry in the Pope & Young Records, a trophy must first have been stored under normal room temperature and humidity for at least 60 days after date of kill. No trophy will be considered which has in any way been altered from its natural state.

THIS SCORING FORM MUST BE ACCOMPANIED BY A SIGNED
POPE & YOUNG FAIR CHASE AFFIDAVIT, 3 PHOTOS OF ANTLERS, AND A
RECORDING FEE OF $25.00.

Copyright 1981 by Boone and Crockett Club
(Written request for privilege of complete reproduction is required)

POPE & YOUNG CLUB
NORTH AMERICAN BIG GAME TROPHY SCORING FORM
BOWHUNTING

KIND OF DEER _____

TYPICAL
WHITETAIL AND COUES DEER

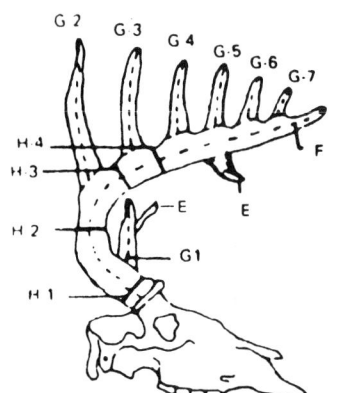

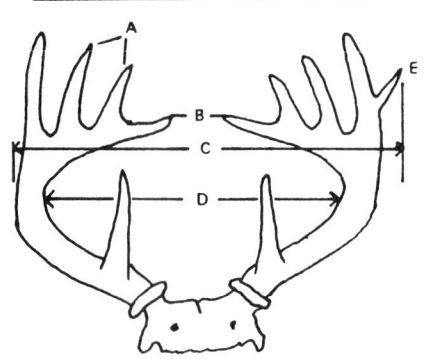

DETAIL OF POINT MEASUREMENT

Abnormal Points	
Right	Left
Total To E	

	SEE OTHER SIDE FOR INSTRUCTIONS	Supplementary Data		Column 1	Column 2	Column 3	Column 4
		R	L	Spread Credit	Right Antler	Left Antler	Difference
A.	Number of Points on Each Antler						
B.	Tip to Tip Spread						
C.	Greatest Spread						
D.	Inside Spread of MAIN BEAMS	Spread credit may equal but not exceed length of longer antler					
E.	Total of Lengths of all Abnormal Points						
F.	Length of Main Beam						
G-1	Length of First Point, if present						
G-2	Length of Second Point						
G-3	Length of Third Point						
G-4	Length of Fourth Point, if present						
G-5	Length of Fifth Point, if present						
G-6	Length of Sixth Point, if present						
G-7	Length of Seventh Point, if present						
H-1	Circumference at Smallest Place Between Burr and First Point						
H-2	Circumference at Smallest Place Between First and Second Points						
H-3	Circumference at Smallest Place Between Second and Third Points						
H-4	Circumference at Smallest Place between Third and Fourth Points Or half way between Third point and Beam Tip if Fourth Point is missing						
TOTALS							

ADD	Column 1		Location of kill		(County)	(State)
	Column 2		Date killed	By whom killed		
	Column 3		Present owner		Phone ( )	
	Total		Address			
SUBTRACT Column 4			Guide's name and Complete Address			
FINAL SCORE			Remarks: (Mention any abnormalities)			

I certify that I have measured the above trophy on_____ 19_____
at (address)_____ City_____
State_____ Zip Code_____ and that these measurements and data are, to the best of my knowledge and belief, made in accordance with the instructions given.
Witness:_____ Signature_____
             (To Measurer's Signature)
                                              Pope & Young Club Official Measurer

_____
MEASURER (Print)
_____
ADDRESS
_____
CITY   STATE   ZIP

INSTRUCTIONS

Measurements must be made with a flexible steel tape or steel cable to the nearest one-eighth of an inch. To simplify addition, please enter fractional figures in **eighths**. Official measurements cannot be taken for at least sixty days after the day the animal was killed. **Please submit photographs (see below).**

A. Number of Points on each antler. To be counted a point, a projection must be at least one inch long AND at some location at least one inch from the tip, the length of the projection must exceed its width. **Beam tip is counted as a point but not measured as a point.**

B. Tip to Tip Spread is measured between tips of main beams.

C. Greatest Spread is measured between perpendiculars at right angles to the center line of the skull at widest part whether across main beams or points.

D. Inside Spread on Main Beam is measured at right angles to the center line of the skull at widest point between main beams. Enter this measurement again in "Spread Credit" column if it is less than or equal to the length of longer antler; if longer, enter longer antler length for spread credit.

E. Total of Length of all Abnormal Points. Abnormal points are generally considered to be those non-typical in location. Sketch all abnormal points on antler illustration (front of form) showing location and approximate size. Measure in usual manner and enter in appropriate blanks.

F. Length of Main Beam is measured from lowest outside edge of burr over outer curve to the most distant point of the main beam. The point of beginning is that point on the burr where the center line along the outer curve of the beam intersects the burr.

G-1-2-3-4-5-6-7. Length of Normal Points. Normal points project from the top of the main beam as shown in illustration. They are measured from nearest edge of beam over outer curve to tip. To determine nearest edge (top edge) of beam, lay the tape along the outer curve of the beam so that the top edge of the tape coincides with the top edge of the beam on both sides of the point. Draw line along top of tape. This line will be base line from which point is measured.

H-1-2-3-4. Circumferences. If first point is missing, take H-1 and H-2 at smallest place between burr and second point. If G-4 is missing, take H-4 halfway between G-3 and tip of main beam. Circumference measurements must be taken with a steel tape (a cable cannot be used for these measurements).

Photographs: All entries must include photographs of the trophy. A right side, left side and front view photograph is required for all antlers. A photograph of the entire animal, preferably at the site of kill, is requested if at all possible.

Drying Period: To be eligible for entry in the Pope & Young Records, a trophy must first have been stored under normal room temperature and humidity for at least 60 days after date of kill. No trophy will be considered which has in any way been altered from its natural state.

THIS SCORING FORM MUST BE ACCOMPANIED BY A SIGNED POPE & YOUNG FAIR CHASE AFFIDAVIT, 3 PHOTOS OF ANTLERS, AND A RECORDING FEE OF $25.00.

Copyright 1988 by Boone and Crockett Club
(Written request for privilege of complete reproduction is required)

POPE & YOUNG CLUB
NORTH AMERICAN BIG GAME TROPHY SCORING FORM
BOWHUNTING
BIG GAME RECORDS

KIND OF DEER _____

NON-TYPICAL WHITETAIL AND COUES' DEER

ABNORMAL

Points Line E	
R	L

Total To E

DETAIL OF POINT MEASUREMENT

	SEE OTHER SIDE FOR INSTRUCTIONS	Supplementary Data		Column 1	Column 2	Column 3	Column 4
		R	L	Spread Credit	Right Antler	Left Antler	Difference
A.	Number of Points on Each Antler						
B.	Tip to Tip Spread						
C.	Greatest Spread						
D.	Inside Spread of MAIN BEAMS	Spread credit may equal but not exceed length of longer antler					
E.	Total of Lengths of all Abnormal Points						
F	Length of Main Beam						
G-1	Length of First Point, if present						
G-2	Length of Second Point						
G-3	Length of Third Point						
G-4	Length of Fourth Point, if present						
G-5	Length of Fifth Point, if present						
G-6	Length of Sixth Point, if present						
G-7	Length of Seventh Point, if present						
H-1	Circumference at Smallest Place Between Burr and First Points						
H-2	Circumference at Smallest Place Between First and Second Points						
H-3	Circumference at Smallest Place Between Second and Third Points						
H-4	Circumference at Smallest Place Between Third and Fourth Points or half way between Third Point and Beam Tip if Fourth Point is missing						
TOTALS							

	ADD	Column 1	
		Column 2	
		Column 3	
	TOTAL		
	SUBTRACT Column 4		
	Result		
	Add Line E Total		
	FINAL SCORE		

Exact locality where killed _____ (County) _____ (State)

Date killed _____ By whom killed _____

Present owner _____ Phone ( )

Address _____

Guide's Name and Complete Address _____

REMARKS: (Mention any abnormalities)

I certify that I have measured the above trophy on _____ 19_____
at (address)_____ City _____
State_____ Zip Code _____ and that these measurements and data are, to the best of my knowledge and belief, made in accordance with the instructions given.
Witness: _____ Signature_____
(To Measurer's Signature) Pope & Young Club Official Measurer

MEASURER (Print) _____

ADDRESS _____

CITY _____ STATE _____ ZIP _____

INSTRUCTIONS

Measurements must be made with a flexible steel tape or steel cable to the nearest one-eighth of an inch. To simplify addition, please enter fractional figures in **eighths**. Official measurements cannot be taken for at least sixty days after the day the animal was killed. **Please submit photographs (see below).**

A. Number of Points on each antler. To be counted a point, a projection must be at least one inch long AND at some location, at least one inch from the tip, the length of the projection must exceed its width. **Beam tip is counted as a point but not measured as a point.**

B. Tip to Tip Spread is measured between tips of main beams.

C. Greatest Spread is measured between perpendiculars at right angles to the center line of the skull at widest part whether across main beams or points.

D. Inside Spread on Main Beam is measured at right angles to the center line of the skull at widest point between main beams. Enter this measurement again in "Spread Credit" column if it is less than or equal to the length of longer antler: if longer, enter longer antler length for spread credit.

E. Total of Length of all Abnormal Points. Abnormal points are generally considered to be those non-typical in location. Measure in usual manner and enter in appropriate blanks.

F. Length of Main Beam is measured from lowest outside edge of burr over outer curve to the distant point of the main beam. The point of beginning is that point on the burr where the center line along the outer curve of the beam intersects the burr.

G. 1-2-3-4-5-6-7. Length of Normal Points. Normal points project from the top of the main beam as shown in illustration. They are measured from nearest edge of beam over outer curve to tip. To determine nearest edge (top edge) of beam, lay the tape along the outer curve of the beam so that the top edge of the tape coincides with the top edge of the beam on both sides of the point. Draw line along top of tape. This line will be base line from which point is measured.

H-1-2-3-4. Circumferences. If first point is missing, take H-1 and H-2 at smallest place between burr and second point. If G-4 is missing, take H-4 halfway between G-3 and tip of main beam. Circumference measurements must be taken with a steel tape (a cable cannot be used for these measurements).

Photographs: All entries must include photographs of the trophy. A right side, left side and front view photograph is required for all antlers. A photograph of the entire animal, preferably at the side of kill, is requested if al all possible.

Drying Period: To be eligible for entry in the Pope & Young Records, a trophy must first have been stored under normal room temperature and humidity for at least 60 days after date of kill. No trophy will be considered wihich has in any way been altered from its natural state.

THIS SCORING FORM MUST BE ACCOMPANIED BY A SIGNED POPE & YOUNG FAIR CHASE AFFIDAVIT, 3 PHOTOS OF ANTLERS, AND A RECORDING FEE OF $25.00.

Copyright 1981 by Boone and Crockett Club
(Written request for privilege of complete reproduction is required)

POPE & YOUNG CLUB
NORTH AMERICAN BIG GAME TROPHY SCORING FORM
BOWHUNTING BIG GAME RECORDS

ROOSEVELT'S ELK

Crown Points	
Right	Left
Total	

Abnormal Points	
Right	Left
Total To E	

	SEE OTHER SIDE FOR INSTRUCTIONS	Supplementary Data		Column 1	Column 2	Column 3	Column 4
		R	L	Spread Credit	Right Antler	Left Antler	Difference
A.	Number of Points on Each Antler						
B.	Tip to Tip Spread						
C.	Greatest Spread						
D.	Inside Spread of MAIN BEAMS	Spread credit may equal but not exceed length of longer antler					
E.	Total of Lengths of all Abnormal Points						
F.	Length of Main Beam						
G-1	Length of First Point, if present						
G-2	Length of Second Point						
G-3	Length of Third Point						
G-4	Length of Fourth (Royal) Point						
G-5	Length of Fifth Point, if present						
G-6	Length of Sixth Point, if present						
G-7	Length of Seventh Point, if present						
H-1	Circumference at Smallest Place Between First and Second Point						
H-2	Circumference at Smallest Place Between Second and Third Points						
H-3	Circumference at Smallest Place Between Third and Fourth Points						
H-4	Circumference at Smallest Place Between Fourth and Fifth Points						
TOTALS							

ADD	Column 1	
	Column 2	
	Column 3	
Total		
SUBTRACT Column 4		
Result		
Add Crown Point Total		
Final Score		

Exact locality where killed _____ (County) _____ (State)

Date killed _____ By whom killed _____

Present owner _____ Phone ( )

Address _____

Guide's name and Address _____

REMARKS: (Mention any abnormalities)

I certify that I have measured the above trophy on _____ 19_____
at (address)_____ City _____
State_____ Zip Code_____ and that these measurements and data are, to the best of my knowledge and belief, made in accordance with the instructions given.
Witness:_____ Signature_____
       (To Measurer's Signature)   Pope & Young Club Official Measurer

_____
MEASURER (Print)
_____
ADDRESS
_____
CITY   STATE   ZIP

INSTRUCTIONS

Measurements must be made with a flexible steel tape or steel cable to the nearest one-eighth of an inch. To simplify addition, please enter fractional figures in **eighths**. Official measurements cannot be taken for at least sixty days after the day the animal was killed. **Please submit photographs (see below).**

A. Number of Points on each antler. To be counted a point, a projection must be at least one inch long AND at some location, at least one inch from the tip, the length of the projection must exceed its width. **Beam tip is counted as a point but not measured as a point.**

B. Tip to Tip Spread is measured between tips of main beams.

C. Greatest Spread is measured between perpendiculars at right angles to the center line of the skull at widest part whether across main beams or points.

D. Inside Spread of Main Beam is measured at right angles to the center line of the skull at widest point between main beams. Enter this measurement again in "Spread Credit" column if it is less than or equal to the length of longer antler; if longer, enter longer antler length for spread credit.

E. Total of Length of all Abnormal Points. Abnormal points are generally considered to be those non-typical in location on or below G-3. Sketch all abnormal points on antler illustration (front of form) showing location and approximate size. Measure in usual manner and enter in appropriate blanks.

Total Length of Crown Points. Crown points are any points projecting from the main beam or from another point on or above G-4 that are **NOT** typical in shape and location. Sketch these points on the form, enter their individual lengths in the crown point box. Then transfer the total to the score as provided.

F. Length of Main Beam is measured from lowest outside edge of burr over outer curve to the most distant point of the main beam. The point of beginning is that point on the burr where the center line along the outer curve of the beam intersects the burr.

G-1-2-3-4-5-6-7. Length of Normal Points. Normal points project from the top or front of the main beam in the general pattern illustrated. They are measured from the nearest edge of main beam over outer curve to tip. Record point length in appropriate blanks.

H-1-2-3. Circumference. If first point is missing, take H-1 and H-2 at smallest place between burr and second point. A steel tape must be used to take circumference measurements (a cable can not be used for these measurements).

H-4 Circumference. Take H-4 between G-4 and what appears to be the typical G-5 point. The H-4 score should not be unduely influenced by the presence of crown points. If the typical G-5 point is missing, take H-4 halfway between G-4 and beam tip.

Photographs: All entries must include photographs of the trophy. A right side, left side and front view photograph is required for all antlers. A photograph of the entire animal, preferably at the site of kill, is requested if at all possible.

Drying Period: To be eligible for entry in the Pope & Young Records, a trophy must first have been stored under normal room temperature and humidity for at least 60 days after date of kill. No trophy will be considered which has in any way been altered from its natural state.

THIS SCORING FORM MUST BE ACCOMPANIED BY A SIGNED POPE & YOUNG FAIR CHASE AFFIDAVIT, 3 PHOTOS OF ANTLERS, AND A RECORDING FEE OF $25.00.

Copyright 1988 by Boone and Crockett Club
(Written request for privilege of complete reproduction is required)

POPE & YOUNG CLUB
NORTH AMERICAN BIG GAME TROPHY SCORING FORM
BOWHUNTING

YELLOWSTONE ELK

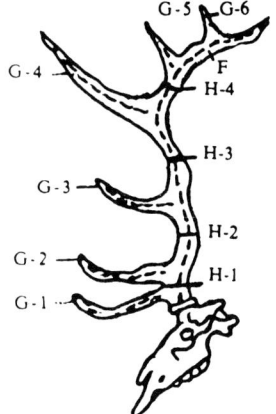

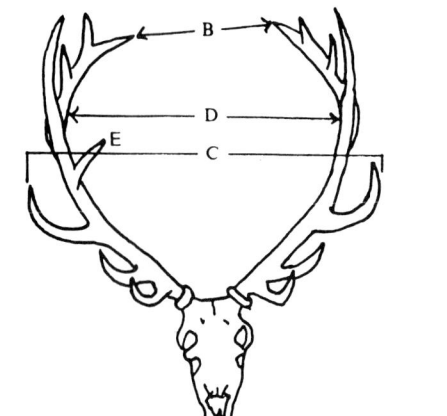

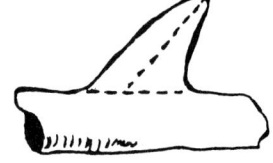

DETAIL OF POINT MEASUREMENT

Abnormal Points	
Right	Left
Total To E	

SEE OTHER SIDE FOR INSTRUCTIONS		Supplementary Data		Column 1	Column 2	Column 3	Column 4
		R	L	Spread Credit	Right Antler	Left Antler	Difference
A.	Number of Points on Each Antler						
B.	Tip to Tip Spread						
C.	Greatest Spread						
D.	Inside Spread of MAIN BEAMS	Spread credit may equal but not exceed length of longer antler					
E.	Total of Lengths of all Abnormal Points						
F.	Length of Main Beam						
G-1	Length of First Point						
G-2	Length of Second Point						
G-3	Length of Third Point						
G-4	Length of Fourth Point						
G-5	Length of Fifth Point, if present						
G-6	Length of Sixth Point, if present						
G-7	Length of Seventh Point, if present						
H-1	Circumference at Smallest Place Between First and Second Points						
H-2	Circumference at Smallest Place Between Second and Third Points						
H-3	Circumference at Smallest Place Between Third and Fourth Points						
H-4	Circumference at Smallest Place Between Fourth and Fifth Points						
TOTALS							

	Column 1		Exact locality where killed	(County)	(State)
ADD	Column 2		Date killed	By whom killed	
	Column 3		Present owner	Phone ( )	
	Total		Address		
SUBTRACT Column 4			Guide's Name and Complete Address		
FINAL SCORE			Remarks: (Mention any abnormalities)		

I certify that I have measured the above trophy on _____ 19_____
at (address)_____ City _____
State_____ Zip Code _____ and that these measurements and data are, to the best
of my knowledge and belief, made in accordance with the instructions given.
Witness: _____ Signature_____
(To Measurer's Signature)   Pope & Young Club Official Measurer

_____
MEASURER (Print)

_____
ADDRESS

_____
CITY   STATE   ZIP

INSTRUCTIONS

Measurements must be made with a flexible steel tape or steel cable to the nearest one-eighth of an inch. To simplify addition, please enter fractional figures in **eighths**. Official measurements cannot be taken for at least sixty days after the day the animal was killed. **Please submit photographs (see below).**

A. Number of Points on each antler. To be counted a point, a projection must be at least one inch long AND at some location, at least one inch from the tip, the length of the projection must exceed its width. **Beam tip is counted as a point but not measured as a point.**

B. Tip to Tip Spread is measured between tips of main beams.

C. Greatest Spread is measured between perpendiculars at right angles to the center line of the skull at widest part whether across main beams or points.

D. Inside Spread on Main Beam is measured at right angles to the center line of the skull at widest point between main beams. Enter this measurement again in "Spread Credit" column if it is less than or equal to the length of longer antler: if longer, enter longer antler length for spread credit.

E. Total of Length of all Abnormal Points. Abnormal points are generally considered to be those non-typical in location. Sketch abnormal points on antler illustration (front of form) showing location and approximate size. Measure in usual manner and enter in appropriate blanks.

F. Length of Main Beam is measured from lowest outside edge of burr over outer curve to the distant point of the main beam. The point of beginning is that point on the burr where the center line along the outer curve of the beam intersects the burr.

G. 1-2-3-4-5-6-7. Length of Normal Points. Normal points project from the top or front of the main beam as shown in illustration. They are measured from nearest edge of beam over outer curve to tip. To determine nearest edge (top edge) of beam, lay the tape along the outer curve of the beam so that the top edge of the tape coincides with the top edge of the beam on both sides of the point. Draw line along top of tape. This line will be base line from which point is measured.

H-1-2-3-4. Circumferences. If first point is missing, take H-1 at smallest place between burr and second point. If G-5 is missing, take H-4 halfway between G-4 and beam tip. A steel tape must be used to take circumference measurements (a cable cannot be used for these measurements).

Photographs: All entries must include photographs of the trophy. A right side, left side and front view photograph is required for all antlers. A photograph of the entire animal, preferably at the site of kill, is requested if at all possible.

Drying Period: To be eligible for entry in the Pope & Young Records, a trophy must first have been stored under normal room temperature and humidity for at least 60 days after date of kill. No trophy will be considered which has in any way been altered from its natural state.

THIS SCORING FORM MUST BE ACCOMPANIED BY A SIGNED POPE & YOUNG FAIR CHASE AFFIDAVIT, 3 PHOTOS OF ANTLERS, AND A RECORDING FEE OF $25.00.

Copyright 1988 by Boone and Crockett Club
(Written request for privilege of complete reproduction is required)

POPE & YOUNG CLUB
NORTH AMERICAN BIG GAME TROPHY SCORING FORM
BOWHUNTING
BIG GAME RECORDS

NON-TYPICAL YELLOWSTONE ELK

DETAIL OF POINT MEASUREMENT

ABNORMAL

Points Line E	
R	L

Total To E

SEE OTHER SIDE FOR INSTRUCTIONS		Supplementary Data		Column 1	Column 2	Column 3	Column 4
		R	L	Spread Credit	Right Antler	Left Antler	Difference
A.	Number of Points on Each Antler						
B.	Tip to Tip Spread						
C.	Greatest Spread						
D.	Inside Spread of MAIN BEAMS		Spread credit may equal but not exceed length of longer antler				
E.	Total of Lengths of all Abnormal Points						
F.	Length of Main Beam						
G-1	Length of First Point						
G-2	Length of Second Point						
G-3	Length of Third Point						
G-4	Length of Fourth Point						
G-5	Length of Fifth Point, if present						
G-6	Length of Sixth Point, if present						
G-7	Length of Seventh Point, if present						
H-1	Circumference at Smallest Place Between First and Second Points						
H-2	Circumference at Smallest Place Between Second and Third Points						
H-3	Circumference at Smallest Place Between Third and Fourth Points						
H-4	Circumference at Smallest Place Between Fourth and Fifth Points						
TOTALS							

ADD	Column 1	
	Column 2	
	Column 3	
TOTAL		
SUBTRACT Column 4		
Result		
Add Line E Total		
FINAL SCORE		

Exact locality where killed _____ (County) _____ (State)

Date killed _____ By whom killed _____

Present owner _____ Phone ( )

Address _____

Guide's Name and Complete Address _____

REMARKS: (Mention any abnormalities)

I certify that I have measured the above trophy on _____ 19_____
at (address) _____ City _____
State _____ Zip Code _____ and that these measurements and data are, to the best
of my knowledge and belief, made in accordance with the instructions given.
Witness: _____ Signature _____
           (To Measurer's Signature)   Pope & Young Club Official Measurer

MEASURER (Print) _____

ADDRESS _____

CITY _____ STATE _____ ZIP _____

INSTRUCTIONS

Measurements must be made with a flexible steel tape or steel cable to the nearest one-eighth of an inch. To simplify addition, please enter fractional figures in **eighths**. Official measurements cannot be taken for at least sixty days after the day the animal was killed. **Please submit photographs [see below].**

A. Number of Points on each antler. To be counted a point, a projection must be at least one inch long AND at some location, at least one inch from the tip, the length of the projection must exceed its width. **Beam tip is counted as a point but not measured as a point.**

B. Tip to Tip Spread is measured between tips of main beams.

C. Greatest Spread is measured between perpendiculars at right angles to the center line of the skull at widest part whether across main beams or points.

D. Inside Spread on Main Beam is measured at right angles to the center line of the skull at widest point between main beams. Enter this measurement again in "Spread Credit" column if it is less than or equal to the length of longer antler; if longer, enter longer antler length for spread credit.

E. Total of Length of all Abnormal Points. Abnormal points are generally considered to be those non-typical in location. Measure in usual manner and enter in appropriate blanks.

F. Length of Main Beam is measured from lowest outside edge of burr over outer curve to the distant point of the main beam. The point of beginning is that point on the burr where the center line along the outer curve of the beam intersects the burr.

G-1-2-3-4-5-6-7. Length of Normal Points. Normal points project from the top or front of the main beam as shown in illustration. They are measured from nearest edge of beam over outer curve to tip. To determine nearest edge (top edge) of beam, lay the tape along the outer curve of the beam so that the top edge of the tape coincides with the top edge of the beam on both sides of the point. Draw line along top of tape. This line will be base line from which point is measured.

H-1-2-3-4. Circumferences. If first point is missing, take H-1 at smallest place between burr and second point. If G-5 is missing, take H-4 halfway between G-4 and beam tip. A steel tape must be used to take circumference measurements (a cable cannot be used for these measurements).

    Photographs: All entries must include photographs of the trophy. A right side, left side and front view photograph is required for all antlers. A photograph of the entire animal, preferably at the site of kill, is requested if at all possible.

    Drying Period: To be eligible for entry in the Pope & Young Records, a trophy must first have been stored under normal room temperature and humidity for at least 60 days after date of kill. No trophy will be considered which has in any way been altered from its natural state.

**THIS SCORING FORM MUST BE ACCOMPANIED BY A SIGNED
POPE & YOUNG FAIR CHASE AFFIDAVIT, 3 PHOTOS OF ANTLERS, AND A
RECORDING FEE OF $25.00.**

Copyright 1988 by Boone and Crockett Club
(Written request for privilege of complete reproduction is required)

POPE & YOUNG CLUB
NORTH AMERICAN BIG GAME TROPHY SCORING FORM
BOWHUNTING

MOOSE

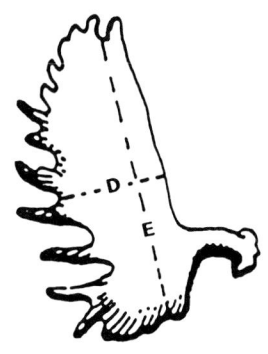

UNDER SURFACE OF ANTLER

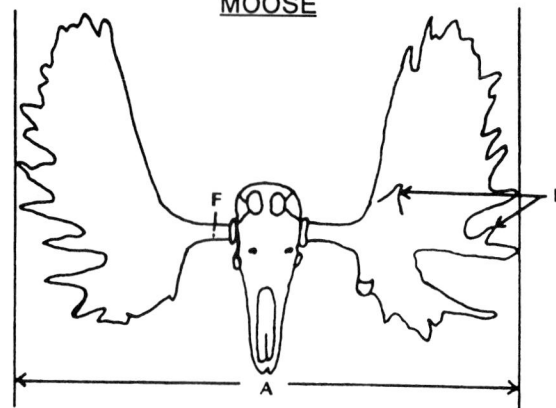

KIND OF MOOSE _____

DETAIL OF POINT MEASUREMENT

SEE OTHER SIDE FOR INSTRUCTIONS

		Column 1	Column 2	Column 3	Column 4
			Right Antler	Left Antler	Difference
A.	Greatest Spread				
B.	Number of Abnormal Points on Both Antlers		■	■	
C.	Number of Normal Points	■			
D.	Width of Palm	■			
E.	Length of Palm including Brow Palm	■			
F.	Circumference of Beam at Smallest Place	■			
TOTALS					

ADD	Column 1	
	Column 2	
	Column 3	
TOTAL		
SUBTRACT Column 4		
FINAL SCORE		

Exact locality where killed _____ (County) _____ (State)

Date killed _____ By whom killed _____

Present owner _____ Phone ( )

Address _____

Guide's Name and Address _____

REMARKS: (Mention any abnormalities) _____

I certify that I have measured the above trophy on _____ 19 _____
at (address) _____ City _____
State _____ Zip Code _____ and that these measurements and data are, to the best
of my knowledge and belief, made in accordance with the instructions given.
Witness: _____ Signature _____
(To Measurer's Signature)

Pope & Young Club Official Measurer

MEASURER (Print) _____

ADDRESS _____

CITY _____ STATE _____ ZIP _____

INSTRUCTIONS

Measurements must be made with a flexible steel tape or steel cable to the nearest one-eighth of an inch. To simplify addition, please enter fractional figures in **eighths.** Official measurements cannot be taken for at least sixty days after the day the animal was killed. **Please submit photographs [see below].**

A. Greatest Spread is measured between perpendiculars in a straight line at a right angle to the center line of the skull.

B. Number of Abnormal Points on Both Antlers - Abnormal points are those originating from normal points or from the upper or lower palm surface, or from the inner edge of palm (see illustration). Abnormal points must be at least one inch long, with length exceeding width at one inch or more of length.

C. Number of Normal Points - Normal points originate from the outer edge of palm. To be counted a point, a projection must be at least one inch long, with the length exceeding width at one inch or more of length.

D. Width of Palm is taken in contact with the under surface of palm, at a right angle to the length of palm measurement line. The line of measurement should begin and end at the midpoint of the palm edge, which give credit for the desirable character of palm thickness.

E. Length of Palm including Brow Palm is taken in contact with the surface along the under side of the palm, **parallel** to the inner edge, from dips between points at the top to dips between points (if present) at the bottom. If a bay is present, measure across the open bay if the proper line of measurement **parallel to inner edge,** follows this path. The line of measurement should begin and end at the midpoint of the palm edge, which give credit for the desirable character of palm thickness.

F. Circumference of Beam at smallest place is taken as illustrated.

Photographs: All entries must include photographs of the trophy. A right side, left side and front view photograph is required of the antlers. A photograph of the entire animal, preferably at the site of kill, is requested if at all possible.

Drying Period: To be eligible for entry in the Pope & Young Records, a trophy must first have been stored under normal room temperature and humidity for at least 60 days after date of kill. No trophy will be considered which has in any way been altered from its natural state.

THIS SCORING FORM MUST BE ACCOMPANIED BY A SIGNED POPE & YOUNG FAIR CHASE AFFIDAVIT, 3 PHOTOS OF ANTLERS, AND A RECORDING FEE OF $25.00.

Copyright 1981 by Boone and Crockett Club
(Written request for privilege of complete reproduction is required)

POPE & YOUNG CLUB
NORTH AMERICAN BIG GAME TROPHY SCORING FORM
BOWHUNTING

MUSKOX

SEX _____

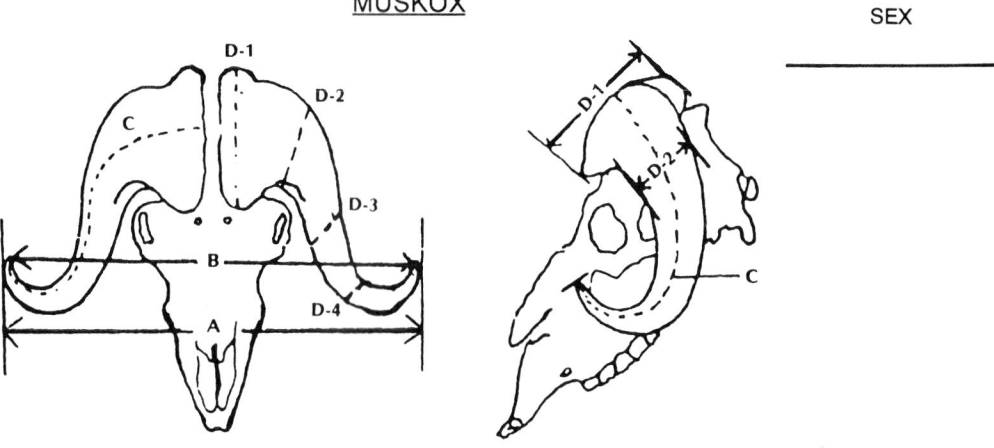

SEE OTHER SIDE FOR INSTRUCTIONS		Supplementary Data	Column 1	Column 2	Column 3
A.	Greatest Spread		Right Horn	Left Horn	Difference
B.	Tip to Tip Spread				
C.	Length of Horn				
D-1	Width of Boss				
D-2	Width at First Quarter	(this measurement taken at _____ inches from base)			
D-3	Circumference at Second Quarter	(this measurement taken at _____ inches from base)			
D-4	Circumference at Third Quarter	(this measurement taken at _____ inches from base)			
TOTALS					

ADD	Column 1		Exact locality where killed (County) (State)
	Column 2		Date killed _____ By whom killed _____
TOTAL			Present owner _____ Phone ( )
SUBTRACT Column 3			Address
FINAL SCORE			Guide's Name and Address
			REMARKS: (Mention any abnormalities)

I certify that I have measured the above trophy on _____ 19____
at (address) _____ City _____
State _____ Zip Code _____ and that these measurements and data are, to the best
of my knowledge and belief, made in accordance with the instructions given.
Witness: _____ Signature _____
(To Measurer's Signature)
Pope & Young Club Official Measurer

_____
MEASURER (Print)
_____
ADDRESS
_____
CITY   STATE   ZIP

INSTRUCTIONS

Measurements must be made with a flexible steel tape or steel cable, and adjustable calipers to the nearest one-eight of an inch. To simplify addition, please enter fractional figures in **eighths**. Official measurements cannot be taken for at least sixty days after the animal was killed. **Please submit photographs (see below).**

A. Greatest Spread is measured between perpendiculars at right angles to the center line of the skull.

B. Tip to Tip Spread is measured between tips of horns.

C. Length of Horn is measured along center of upper horn surface, staying within curve of horn as illustrated, to a point in line with tip. Attempt to free the connective tissue between the horns at the center of the boss to determine the lowest point of horn material on each side, near the top center of the skull. Hook the tape under the lowest point of the horn and measure the length of horn, with the measurement line maintained in the center of the upper surface of horn following the converging lines to the horn tip.

D-1 Width of Boss is measured with calipers at greatest width of base, with measurement line forming a right angle with horn axis. It is often helpful to measure D-1 before c, marking the midpoint of the boss as the correct path of C.

D-2-3-4 Divide measurement C of **LONGER** horn by four. Starting at base, mark **BOTH** horns at these quarters (even though other horn is shorter). Then, using calipers, measure width of the horn at D-2, making sure the measurement is perpendicular to the surface of horn excluding boss material. Circumferences are then measured at D-3 and D-4, with measurements being taken at right angles to horn axis.

Photographs: All entries must include photographs of the trophy. A right side, left side and front view photograph is required of the horns. A photograph of the entire animal, preferable at the site of kill, is requested if at all possible.

Drying Period: To be eligible for entry in the Pope & Young Records, a trophy must first have been stored under normal room temperature and humidity for at least 60 days after date of kill. No trophy will be considered which has in any way been altered from its natural state.

THIS SCORING FORM MUST BE ACCOMPANIED BY A SIGNED POPE & YOUNG FAIR CHASE AFFIDAVIT, 3 PHOTOS OF HORNS, AND A RECORDING FEE OF $25.00.

Copyright 1981 by Boone and Crockett Club
(Written request for privilege of complete reproduction is required)

POPE & YOUNG CLUB
NORTH AMERICAN BIG GAME TROPHY SCORING FORM
BOWHUNTING BIG GAME RECORDS

PRONGHORN

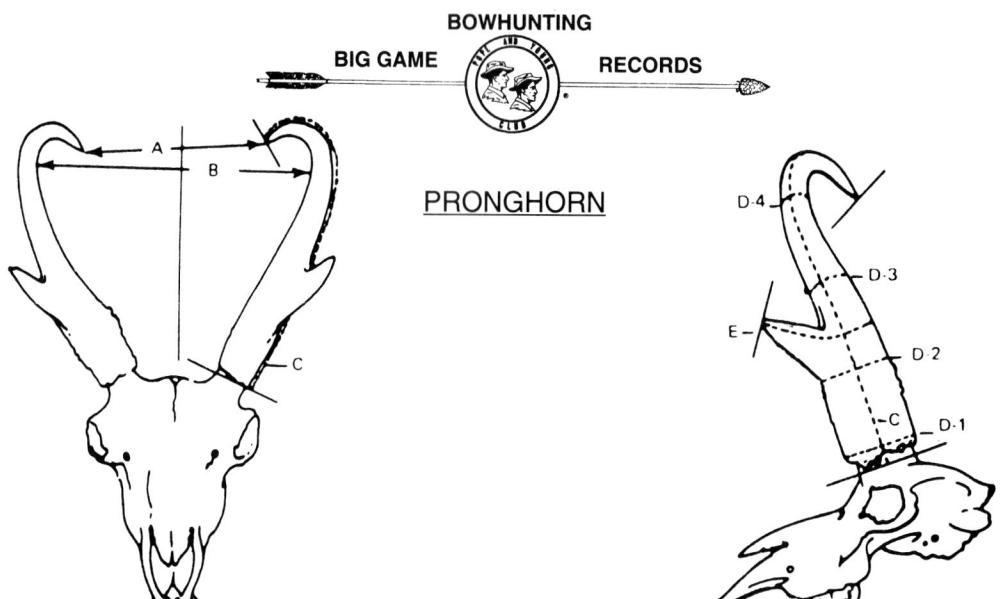

SEE OTHER SIDE FOR INSTRUCTIONS	Supplementary Data	Column 1 Right Horn	Column 2 Left Horn	Column 3 Difference
A. Tip to Tip Spread				
B. Inside Spread of Main Beams				
C. Length of Horn				
D-1 Circumference of Base				
D-2 Circumference at First Quarter (this measurement taken at _____ inches from base)				
D-3 Circumference at Second Quarter (this measurement taken at _____ inches from base)				
D-4 Circumference at Third Quarter (this measurement taken at _____ inches from base)				
E. Length of Prong				
TOTALS				

ADD	Column 1		Location where killed	(County)	(State)
	Column 2		Date killed	By whom killed	
TOTAL			Present owner		Phone ( )
SUBTRACT Column 3			Address		
FINAL SCORE			Guide's name and Complete Address		
			REMARKS: (mention any abnormalities)		

I certify that I have measured the above trophy on _____ 19 ___
at (address) _____ City _____
State _____ Zip Code _____ and that these measurements and data are, to the best of my knowledge and belief, made in accordance with the instructions given.
Witness: _____ Signature _____
(To Measurer's Signature) Pope & Young Official Measurer

MEASURER (Print) _____

ADDRESS _____

CITY   STATE   ZIP

INSTRUCTIONS

Measurements must be made with a flexible steel tape to the nearest one-eighth of an inch. To simplify addition, please enter fractional figured in **Eighths.** Official measurements cannot be taken for at least sixty days after the day the animal was killed. **Please submit photographs (see below)**

A. Tip to Tip Spread measured between tip of horns.

B. Inside Spread of Main Beams measured at right angles to the center line of the skull at widest point between main beams.

C. Length of horn is measured on the outside curve, so the line taken will vary with different heads, depending on the direction of the curvature. Measure along the center of the outer curve from tip of horn to a point in line with the lowest edge of the base.

D-1 Measure around base of horn at right angles to long axis. Tape must be in contact with the lowest circumference of the horn in which there are no serrations.

D-2-3-4. Divide measurement of LONGER horn by four: **measuring from the base,** mark BOTH horns at these quarters even though one horn is shorter and measure circumferences at these marks. Note D-3 **must** be taken above the prong. If D-3 falls on or below the prong then take this measurement immediately **above** the prong. Should D-2 land on the swelling of the prong, take D-2 measurement **immediately below** swelling of prong. If adjustments are made for swelling of prong on D-2 or D-3 measurement, note these adjustments in "REMARKS" section. Circumference measurements must be taken with a steel tape (a cable cannot be used for these measurements).

E. Length of Prong - Measure from the tip of the prong along the upper edge of the outer side to the horn; thence, around the horn to a point at the rear of the horn where a straight edge across the back of both horns touches the horn. This measurement around the horn from the base of the prong should be taken at right angles to the long axis of the horn.

Photographs: All entries must include photographs of the trophy. A right side, left side and front view photograph is required of the horns. A photograph of the entire animal, preferably at the site of kill, is requested if at all possible.

Drying Period: To be eligible for entry in the Pope & Young Records, a trophy must first have been stored under normal room temperature and humidity for at least 60 days after date of kill. No trophy will be considered which has in any way been altered from its natural state.

THIS SCORING FORM MUST BE ACCOMPANIED BY A SIGNED POPE & YOUNG FAIR CHASE AFFIDAVIT, 3 PHOTOS OF HORNS, AND A RECORDING FEE OF $25.00.

Copyright 1988 by Boone and Crockett Club
(Written request for privilege of complete reproduction is required)

POPE & YOUNG CLUB
NORTH AMERICAN BIG GAME TROPHY SCORING FORM
BOWHUNTING
BIG GAME RECORDS

ROCKY MOUNTAIN GOAT

SEX _____

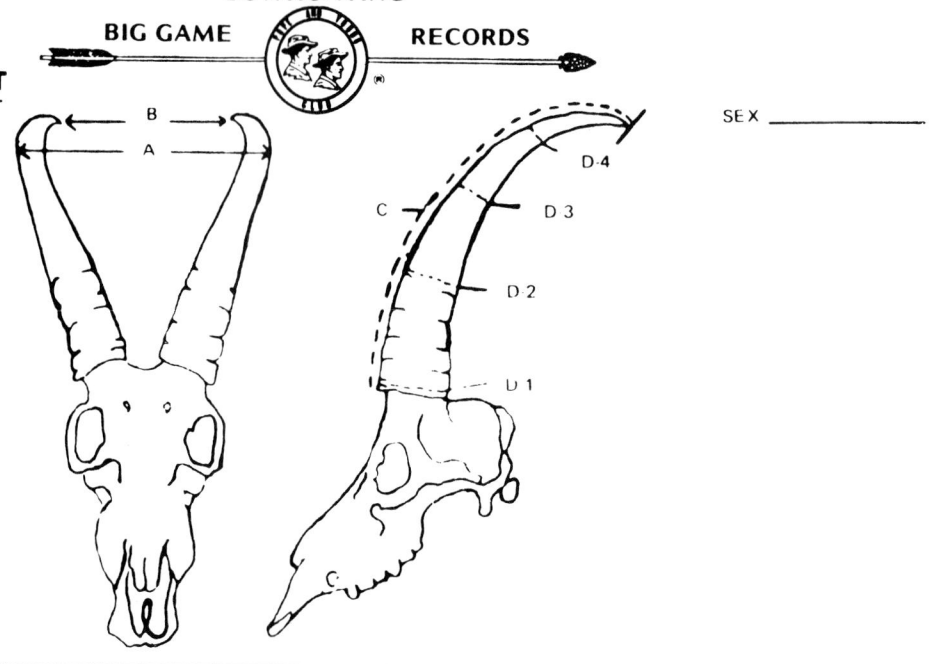

SEE OTHER SIDE FOR INSTRUCTIONS		Supplementary Data	Column 1 Right Horn	Column 2 Left Horn	Column 3 Difference
A.	Greatest Spread				
B.	Tip to Tip Spread				
C.	Length of Horn				
D-1.	Circumference of Base				
D-2.	Circumference at First Quarter (this measurement taken at _____ inches from base)				
D-3.	Circumference at Second Quarter (this measurement taken at _____ inches from base)				
D-4.	Circumference at Third Quarter (this measurement taken at _____ inches from base)				
TOTALS					

ADD	Column 1		Exact locality where killed (County) (State)
	Column 2		Date killed / By whom killed
TOTAL			Present owner / Phone ( )
SUBTRACT Column 3			Address
FINAL SCORE			Guide's Name and Address
			REMARKS (Mention any abnormalities)

I certify that I have measured the above trophy on _____ 19_____
at (address)_____ City _____
State _____ Zip Code _____ and that these measurements and data are, to the best of my knowledge and belief, made in accordance with the instructions given.

Witness:_____ Signature_____
(To Measurer's Signature)   Pope & Young Club Official Measurer

MEASURER (Print) _____

ADDRESS _____

CITY   STATE   ZIP

INSTRUCTIONS

Measurements must be made with a flexible steel tape to the nearest one-eighth of an inch. To simplify addition, please enter fractional figures in **eighths**. Official measurements cannot be taken for at least sixty days after the day the animal was killed. **Please submit photographs (see below).**

A. **Greatest Spread** is measured between perpendiculars at right angles to the center line of the skull.

B. **Tip to Tip Spread** is measured between tips of horns.

C. **Length of Horn** is measured from lowest point in front over outer curve to a point in line with tip.

D-1. **Circumference of Base** is measured at right angles to axis of horn. **DO NOT** FOLLOW IRREGULAR EDGE OF HORN. Circumference measurements must be taken with a steel tape.

D-1-2-3-4. Divide measurement C of LONGER horn by four, mark **BOTH** horns at these quarters even though other horn is shorter, and measure circumference at these marks. Mark quarters by starting from base only. Circumference measurements must be taken with a steel tape.

Photographs: All entries must include photographs of the trophy. A right side, left side and front view photograph is required of the horns. A photograph of the entire animal, preferably at the site of kill, is requested if at all possible.

Drying Period: To be eligible for entry in the Pope & Young Records, a trophy must first have been stored under normal room temperature and humidity for at least 60 days after date of kill. No trophy will be considered which has in any way been altered from its natural state.

THIS SCORING FORM MUST BE ACCOMPANIED BY A SIGNED POPE & YOUNG FAIR CHASE AFFIDAVIT, 3 PHOTOS OF HORNS, AND A RECORDING FEE OF $25.00.

Copyright 1988 by Boone and Crockett Club
(Written request for privilege of complete reproduction is required)

POPE & YOUNG CLUB
NORTH AMERICAN BIG GAME TROPHY SCORING FORM
BOWHUNTING

SHEEP

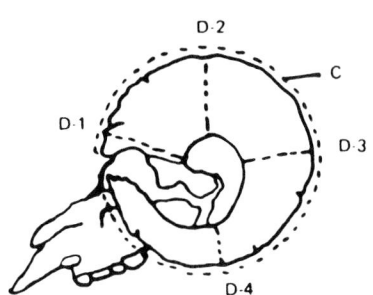
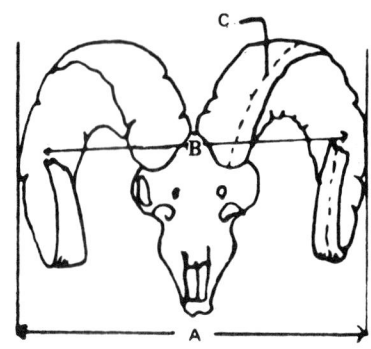

KIND OF SHEEP
_____

MEASURE TO A POINT IN LINE WITH TIP OF HORN

SEE OTHER SIDE FOR INSTRUCTIONS		Supplementary Data	Column 1 Right Horn	Column 2 Left Horn	Column 3 Difference
A.	Greatest Spread (Is often Tip to Tip Spread)				
B.	Tip to Tip Spread (If Greatest Spread, Enter again here)				
C.	Length of Horn				
D-1.	Circumference of Base				
D-2.	Circumference at First Quarter (this measurement taken at _____ inches from base)				
D-3.	Circumference at Second Quarter (this measurement taken at _____ inches from base)				
D-4.	Circumference at Third Quarter (this measurement taken at _____ inches from base)				
TOTALS					

ADD	Column 1		Exact locality where killed (County) (State)
	Column 2		Date killed / By whom killed
	TOTAL		Present owner / Phone ( )
SUBTRACT Column 3			Address
FINAL SCORE			Guide's Name and Address
			REMARKS (Mention any abnormalities)

I certify that I have measured the above trophy on _____ 19____
at (address) _____ City _____
State _____ Zip Code _____ and that these measurements and data are, to the best of my knowledge and belief, made in accordance with the instructions given.
Witness: _____ Signature _____
(To Measurer's Signature)   Pope & Young Club Official Measurer

MEASURER (Print) _____
ADDRESS _____
CITY   STATE   ZIP

INSTRUCTIONS

Measurements must be made with a flexible steel tape to the nearest one-eighth of an inch. To simplify addition, please enter fractional figures in **eighths.** Official measurements cannot be taken for at least sixty days after the day the animal was killed. **Please submit photographs [see below].**

A. Greatest Spread is measured between perpendiculars at right angles to the center line of the skull.

B. Tip to Tip Spread is measured between tips of horns.

C. Length of Horn measured from lowest point in front on outer curve to a point in line with tip. **DO NOT** press tape into depressions. The low point of the outer curve of the horn is considered to be the low point of the frontal portion of the horn, situated above and slightly medial to the eye socket, (not on the outside edge of the horn). Use a straight edge, perpendicular to horn axis, to end measurement on "broomed" horns.

D-1 Circumferrence of Base measured at right angles to axis of horn. **DO NOT** follow irregular edge of horn. The line of measurement must be entirely on horn material, not the jagged edge often noted.

D-2-3-4 Divide measurement C of **LONGER** horn by four, mark **BOTH** horns at these quarters even though other horn is shorter, and measure circumferences at these marks. Mark quarters by starting from base only.

Photographs: All entries must include photographs of the trophy. A right side, left side and front view photograph is required of the horns. A photograph of the entire animal, preferably at the site of kill, is requested if at all possible.

Drying Period: To be eligible for entry in the Pope & Young Records, a trophy must first have been stored under normal room temperature and humidity for at least 60 days after date of kill. No trophy will be considered which has in any way been altered from its natural state.

THIS SCORING FORM MUST BE ACCOMPANIED BY A SIGNED POPE & YOUNG FAIR CHASE AFFIDAVIT, 3 PHOTOS OF HORNS, AND A RECORDING FEE OF $25.00.

Copyright 1981 by Boone and Crockett Club
(Written request for privilege of complete reproduction is required)

BOWHUNTING

BIG GAME

RECORDS

POPE & YOUNG CLUB
P.O. BOX 548
CHATFIELD, MN 55923

FAIR CHASE AFFIDAVIT

To be entered into the Pope & Young Club Records, the animal must meet the minimum scoring requirements, and must be taken in complete compliance with the controlling game laws and the Rules of Fair Chase. The term "Fair Chase" shall not include the taking of animals under the following conditions:

1. Helpless in a trap, deep snow or water, or on ice.
2. From any power vehicle or power boat.
3. While confined behind fences as on game farms, etc.
4. By "Jacklighting" or shining at night.
5. By the use of any tranquilizers or poisons.
6. By the use of any power vehicles or power boat for herding or driving animals, including use of aircraft to land alongside or to communicate with or direct a hunter on the ground.
7. By the use of electronic devices for attracting, locating or pursuing game, or guiding the hunter to such game, or by the use of a bow or arrow to which any electronic device is attached.
8. Any other condition considered by the Board of Directors as unsportsmanlike.

SPECIAL NOTE: For the purpose of the Pope & Young Club, a bow shall be defined as a longbow, recurve bow or compound bow that is hand-held and hand-drawn, and that has no mechanical device to enable the hunter to lock the bow at full or partial draw. Other than energy stored by the drawn bow, no device to propel the arrow will be permitted. A letoff of sixty-five (65) percent on a compound bow is the maximum allowed.

SEARCH & RECOVERY: Was the animal recovered on the same day as hit? YES ☐ NO* ☐
(check one)

* If "NO", give **COMPLETE DETAILS** of recovery on back, [COMMENTS], or on a separate sheet.

Falsification of the Fair Chase Affidavit is grounds for dismissal from the Pope & Young Club. Falsification will cause the entry to be rejected, no future entries accepted and all past entries dropped from the Pope & Young Club records for the individual falsifying the affidavit. In addition to the requirements of this affidavit, by submitting this entry the applicant agrees that the sole decision of acceptance of this entry belongs to the Board of Directors and its discretionary decision is in all respects final.

I, _____ attest that my _____
         (print)   (species)

was taken entirely by the means of BOW & ARROW, and in complete compliance with the controlling game laws and the rules of Fair Chase.

WE THE UNDERSIGNED, DECLARE THAT THE FOREGOING STATEMENTS ARE TRUE TO THE BEST OF OUR KNOWLEDGE AND BELIEF:

_____   _____
           Hunter's Signature   Date

_____   _____
Witness to verification of bow kill,   Signature of witness   (please print name)
(Does not have to be Eye Witness)

_____   _____   _____   _____   _____
       Address of witness   City   State   Zip   Phone No.

THIS FORM MUST BE COMPLETELY FILLED OUT!
REVISED MARCH, 1989

Please complete the following form as it relates to the harvest of this trophy. This information is used by the Pope & Young Club to provide an overall view of the nature of hunts for the various North American big game animals for which we maintain records.

1. SPECIES _____ **SEX** _____

2. HUNTER INFORMATION: Age _____ Sex _____ Years of bowhunting experience _____

3. HUNT INFORMATION: Guide ☐ ☐   Date of Kill _____ , _____ , _____
                                     yes   no   month   day   year

    WEATHER CONDITIONS AT TIME OF KILL: Clear ☐   Cloudy ☐   Rain ☐   Snow ☐   Other _____
    Time _____ a.m. p.m. Temperature _____

4. DISTANCE OF SHOT: (if more than one shot, write distance of each arrow in appropriate box)
#1. _____ yds. #2. _____ yds. #3. _____ yds. #4. _____ yds.

For the next two questions, place an X in the space corresponding to each arrow, e.g. if arrow #1 and #3 were both broadside, record your entry as follows:
                                                        Broadside
                                 EXAMPLE   ☒ ☐ ☒ ☐
                                                            1   2   3   4

ANGLE OF THE SHOT:

Broadside	Rear Quartering	Front Quartering	Rear	Front	Above
☐ ☐ ☐ ☐	☐ ☐ ☐ ☐	☐ ☐ ☐ ☐	☐ ☐ ☐ ☐	☐ ☐ ☐ ☐	☐ ☐ ☐ ☐
1 2 3 4	1 2 3 4	1 2 3 4	1 2 3 4	1 2 3 4	1 2 3 4

WHERE ARROW STRUCK ANIMAL:

Chest	Paunch	Rump	Leg	Head	Other _____
☐ ☐ ☐ ☐	☐ ☐ ☐ ☐	☐ ☐ ☐ ☐	☐ ☐ ☐ ☐	☐ ☐ ☐ ☐	☐ ☐ ☐ ☐
1 2 3 4	1 2 3 4	1 2 3 4	1 2 3 4	1 2 3 4	1 2 3 4

5. STYLE OF HUNTING: Bait ☐   Stalk ☐   Still ☐   Tree Stand ☐   Ground Blind ☐   Calling ☐   Dogs ☐
    (Stalk - spotting animal first then moving in: Still - locating animal by moving)

6. NUMBER OF MEMBERS IN YOUR HUNTING PARTY WHEN ANIMAL WAS HARVESTED _____

7. NUMBER OF DAYS HUNTING DURING THE SEASON FOR THIS SPECIES _____

8. NUMBER OF ARROWS SHOT DURING THE SEASON AT THIS SPECIES _____

9. NUMBER OF ANIMALS OF THIS SPECIES SEEN DURING THE SEASON _____

10. TYPE OF BOW: Longbow ☐   Recurve ☐   Compound ☐   Draw Weight _____ lbs.

    IF COMPOUND BOW: % Letoff _____

    TYPE OF QUIVER: Hip ☐   Back ☐   Bow ☐   Other (specify) _____ **Quiver size** (number of arrows) _____

    TYPE OF BROADHEAD: Fixed blade (no insert) ☐   Fixed blade (with insert) ☐   Replaceable Blade ☐
    Other _____ Number of blades _____

    TYPE OF ARROWS: Wood ☐   Carbon ☐   Aluminum ☐   Other (specify) _____ Length _____

11. COMMENTS:

PAST AND PRESENT CLUB OFFICERS

President
Glenn St. Charles — December 1967 - August 1972
Larry Bamford — August 1972 - August 1975
George Morelein — August 1975 - April 1976
Jim Dougherty — April 1976 - April 1984
G. Fred Asbell — April 1984 -

First Vice President
Fred Bear — December 1967 - August 1970
Larry Bamford — August 1970 - August 1972
Norm Goodwin — August 1972 - August 1974
George Morelein — August 1974 - August 1975
None — August 1975 - April 1976
John Culpepper — April 1976 - April 1978
Paul Shannon — April 1978 - April 1980
Charlie Kroll — April 1980 - April 1984
Marvin Clyncke — April 1984 - April 1988
Rick Grooms — April 1988 - April 1989
M. R. James — April 1990 -

Second Vice President
Dr. Dean Henbest — December 1967 - August 1970
Dr. Rex Hancock — August 1970 - August 1972
George Morelein — August 1972 - August 1974
Norm Goodwin — August 1974 - April 1976
Doug Kittredge — April 1976 - April 1978
Charlie Kroll — April 1978 - April 1980
Paul Shannon — April 1980 - April 1982
Scott Showalter — April 1982 - April 1984
Note: This Club office was eliminated by a vote of the membership, effective April 1984.

Third/Second Vice President
Charles A. Young — January 1970 - April 1980
Frank "Duke" Prentup — April 1980 - April 1982

Rick Grooms — April 1982 - April 1988
Glenn Hisey — April 1988 - April 1990
Naomi Torrey-Simmons — April 1990 - April 1992
Stan Rauch — April 1992 -
Note: With the elimination of the original Second Vice President Club office in 1984, the Third Vice President's office representing the Associate membership was renamed Second Vice President.

Executive Secretary
Charlie Kroll — December 1967 - April 1969
Jim Dougherty — December 1969 - July 1970
Dick Mauch — July 1970 - August 1972
Doug Walker — August 1972 - April 1974
Scott Showalter — April 1974 - January 1975
Carl M. Hulbert — January 1975 - June 1976
Naomi Torrey-Simmons — July 1976 - September 1989
Glenn Hisey — September 1989 -

Treasurer
Carl M. Hulbert — December 1967 - June 1976
Naomi Torrey-Simmons — July 1976 - May 1987
Donald Ace Morgan — May 1987 -

Directors
Richard Cooley — December 1967 - August 1970
Doug Walker — December 1967 - August 1970
G. H. Malinoski — December 1967 - August 1972
George Morelein — December 1967 - August 1972 & April 1984 - March 1992
Fred Bear — August 1970 - April 1978
Peter Halbig — August 1970 - August 1974
Dick Mauch — August 1972 - August 1976
Wayne Trimm — August 1972 - April 1976
Dr. Lowell Eddy — August 1974 - April 1976
Ray Torrey — April 1976 - October 1983
Marvin Clyncke — April 1976 - April 1984
Len Cardinale — April 1976 - April 1978
G. Fred Asbell — April 1978 - April 1984
Frank "Rit" Heller — April 1978 - April 1990
Scott Showalter — April 1984 - April 1988 & April 1990 - April 1994
Art Kragness — April 1984 - April 1986
M. R. James — April 1986 - April 1990
Ron Sherer — April 1988 -
Bill Krenz — April 1990 - April 1994
Larry Streiff — April 1992 - April 1996
Dr. C. Randall Byers — April 1994 - April 1998
David Coupland — April 1994 -
Billy Ellis III — April 1996 -
Roger Atwood — April 1998 -

Past President Directors
Glenn St. Charles — August 1972 - April 1975
George Morelein — April 1976 - April 1984
Jim Dougherty — April 1984 -

Records Committee Chairman
Glenn St. Charles — January 1961 - February 1968
Dick Mauch — February 1968 - August 1972
Doug Walker — August 1972 - April 1974
Scott Showalter — April 1974 - December 1980
Ray Torrey — January 1981 - October 1983
Dr. C. Randall Byers — November 1983 - April 1994
Larry Streiff — April 1994 - April 1998
Dr. C. Randall Byers — April 1998 -

Membership Chairman
Dr. Dean Henbest — December 1967 - May 1969
Larry Bamford — May 1969 - September 1972
Scott Showalter — September 1972 - January 1975
Harv Ebers — January 1975 -

Conservation Committee Chairman
Dr. Lowell Eddy — February 1975 - April 1976
Wayne Trimm — February 1975 - April 1976
Charlie Kroll — March 1977 - April 1989
Dr. David Samuel — April 1989 -

Current Club officers include (seated, left to right) Dr. Don Morgan, G. Fred Asbell, Ron Sherer, Dr. Randy Byers, Jim Dougherty and M. R. James; (standing, from left), Dave Coupland, Dr. Dave Samuel, Stan Rauch, Roger Atwood, Harv Ebers, Billy Ellis III, and Glenn Hisey.

THE ISHI AWARDS

THE ISHI AWARD is the highest honor that can be bestowed by the Pope and Young Club. It is presented only when a truly outstanding North American big game animal is deemed worthy of special recognition. Nominations are made and votes are cast by the Board of Directors. Only one Ishi Award may be presented during any biennial recording period. Following are the Pope and Young Ishi Award winners honored to date:

Non-Typical Whitetail Deer — 279 7/8
4th Recording Period (1963-1964)
Taken in Nebraska by Del Austin (1962)

Typical Whitetail Deer — 204 4/8
6th Recording Period (1967-1968)
Taken in Illinois by Mel Johnson (1965)

Bighorn Sheep — 176 3/8
7th Recording Period (1969-1970)
Taken in Montana by Ray Alt (1968)

Barren Ground Caribou — 446 6/8
8th Recording Period (1971-1972)
Taken in Alaska by Art Kragness (1970)

Alaska-Yukon Moose — 248 0/8
9th Recording Period (1973-1974)
Taken in Alaska by Dr. Michael Cusak (1973)

Columbian Blacktail Deer — 172 2/8
11th Recording Period (1977-1978)
Taken in Oregon by B. G. Shurtleff (1969)

Black Bear — 22 4/16
12th Recording Period (1979-1980)
Taken in Colorado by Ray Cox (1978)

Cougar — 15 11/16
13th Recording Period (1981-1982)
Taken in Idaho by Jerry James (1982)

Typical Mule Deer — 203 1/8
14th Recording Period (1983-1984)
Taken in Colorado by Bill Barcus (1979)

Dall Sheep — 164 5/8
15th Recording Period (1985-1986)
Taken in the Northwest Territories by Gary Laya (1986)

Non-Typical Yellowstone Elk — 419 5/8
16th Recording Period (1987-1988)
Taken in Arizona by James L. Ludvigson (1985)

Non-Typical Blacktail Deer — 194 4/8
17th Recording Period (1989-1990)
Taken in Oregon by James Decker (1988)

Canada Moose — 222 1/8
18th Recording Period (1991-1992)
Taken in Quebec by Charles Roy (1988)

Pronghorn Antelope — 90 0/8
19th Recording Period (1993-1994)
Taken in Oregon by Roger W. Clarno (1993)

DEPARTMENTS OF FISH & GAME

United States

Alabama Division of Fish & Game
64 N. Union St.
Montgomery, AL 36130
(334) 242-3848

Arizona Game & Fish Department
2221 W. Greenway Rd.
Phoenix, AZ 85023-4399
(602) 942-3000

California Department of Fish & Game
1416 Ninth St.
Sacramento, CA 95814
(916) 653-7203

**Connecticut Department of
Environmental Protection**
79 Elm St.
Wildlife Division
Hartford, CT 06106-5127
(860) 424-3105

**Florida Game & Freshwater Fish
Commission**
620 S. Meridian St.
Tallahassee, FL 32399-1600
(904) 488-3831

Alaska Department of Fish & Game
P. O. Box 25526
Juneau, AK 99802-5526
(907) 465-4190

Arkansas Game & Fish Commission
2 Natural Resources Dr.
Little Rock, AR 72205
(501) 223-6359

Colorado Division of Wildlife
6060 Broadway
Denver, CO 80216
(303) 297-1192

Delaware Division of Fish & Wildlife
89 Kings Highway
P. O. Box 1401
Dover, DE 19903
(302) 739-5297

Georgia Wildlife Resources Division
270 US Highway 278 SE
Social Circle, GA 30279
(770) 918-6404

Hawaii Division of Forestry & Wildlife
1151 Punchbowl St., Rm. 325
Honolulu, HI 96813
(808) 587-0166

Illinois Department of Natural Resources
524 S. 2nd St.
Springfield, IL 62704
(217) 785-0970

Iowa Department of Natural Resources
Wallace State Office Building
9th & Grand Ave.
Des Moines, IA 50319
(515) 281-8681

Kentucky Department of Fish & Wildlife
1 Game Farm Road
Frankfort, KY 40601
(502) 564-4406

**Maine Department of Inland Fisheries
& Wildlife**
41 State House Station
284 State St.
Augusta, ME 04333
(207) 287-8000

**Massachusetts Department of
Fisheries & Wildlife**
Route 135
Westboro, MA 01581
(508) 792-7270

**Minnesota Department of Natural
Resources**
Division of Fish & Wildlife
500 Lafayette Rd.
St. Paul, MN 55155-4007
(612) 296-6157

Missouri Department of Conservation
2910 W. Truman Rd.
P. O. Box 180
Jefferson City, MO 65102
(573) 751-4115

Nebraska Game & Parks Commission
2200 N. 33rd
Lincoln, NE 68503
(402) 471-0641

Idaho Fish & Game Department
600 S. Walnut, Box 25
Boise, ID 83707
(208) 334-3700

Indiana Division of Fish & Wildlife
402 W. Washington St., Rm. W160
Indianapolis, IN 46204
(317) 233-4976

Kansas Department of Fish & Wildlife
512 SE 25th Ave.
Pratt, KS 67124
(316) 672-5911

Louisiana Department of Wildlife & Fisheries
P. O. Box 98000
Baton Rouge, LA 70898-9000
(504) 756-2346

**Maryland Department of Fisheries
& Wildlife**
Wildlife Division
580 Taylor Ave.
Annapolis, MD 21401
(410) 974-3195

**Michigan Department of Natural
Resources, Wildlife Division**
P. O. Box 30444
Lansing, MI 48909
(517) 373-1263

**Mississippi Department of Wildlife,
Fisheries & Parks**
P. O. Box 451
Jackson, MS 39205-0451
(601) 362-9212

**Montana Department of Fish,
Wildlife & Parks**
P. O. Box 200701
Helena, MT 59620-0701
(406) 444-2535

Nevada Department of Wildlife
P. O. Box 10678
Reno, NV 89520
(702) 688-1500

New Hampshire Fish & Game Department
2 Hazen Dr.
Concord, NH 03301
(603) 271-2461

New Mexico Game & Fish Department
P. O. Box 25112
Santa Fe, NM 87504
(505) 827-7911

North Carolina Wildlife Resources Commission
512 N. Salisbury St.
Raleigh, NC 27604-1188
(919) 733-7291

Ohio Division of Wildlife
1840 Belcher Dr.
Columbus, OH 43224
(614) 265-6300

Oregon Department of Fish & Wildlife Conservation
P. O. Box 59
Portland, OR 97207
(503) 872-5260

Rhode Island Division of Fish & Wildlife
P. O. Box 218
West Kingston, RI 02892
(401) 781-0281

South Dakota Game, Fish & Parks
445 E. Capitol
Pierre, SD 57501
(605) 394-2391

Texas Parks & Wildlife Department
4200 Smith School Rd.
Austin, TX 78744
(512) 389-4800 or 1-800-792-1112, Ext. 51

Vermont Fish & Wildlife Department
103 S. Main St.
Waterbury, VT 05671
(802) 241-3700

New Jersey Division of Fish, Game & Wildlife
501 E. State St.
P. O. Box 400
Trenton, NJ 08625
(609) 292-2965

New York Department of Environment Conservation
50 Wolf Rd., Rm. 111
Albany, NY 12233-4790
(518) 457-3730

North Dakota State Game & Fish Commission
100 N. Bismarck Expressway
Bismarck, ND 58505-5095
(701) 328-6320

Oklahoma Department of Wildlife Conservation
Game Division
P. O. Box 53465
Oklahoma City, OK 73152
(405) 521-2739

Pennsylvania Game Commission
2001 Elmerton Ave.
Harrisburg, PA 17110-9797
(717) 787-5529

South Carolina Department of Natural Resources
P. O. Box 167
Columbia, SC 29202
(803) 734-3898

Tennessee Wildlife Resources Agency
P. O. Box 40747
Nashville, TN 37204
(615) 781-6500

Utah Department of Natural Resources, Wildlife Division
1594 W. North Temple
Salt Lake City, UT 84114-6301
(801) 538-4700

Virginia Department of Game & Inland Fisheries
4010 S. Broad St.
P. O. Box 11104
Richmond, VA 23230
(804) 367-1000

Washington Department of Fish & Wildlife
600 Capitol Way N.
Olympia, WA 98501
(360) 902-2200

Wisconsin Department of Natural Resources
P. O. Box 7921
Madison, WI 53707
(608) 266-2621

West Virginia Department of Natural Resources
1900 Kanawha Blvd. East
Charleston, WV 25305
(304) 558-2771

Wyoming Game & Fish Department
5400 Bishop Blvd.
Cheyenne, WY 82006
(307) 777-4600

Canada

Alberta Wildlife Management Division
Main Floor, North Tower
Petroleum Plaza
9945 108th St.
Edmonton, Alberta T5K 2G6
(403) 427-2079

Manitoba Department of Natural Resources
200 Saulteaux Crescent, Box 24
Winnipeg, Manitoba R3J 3W3
(204) 945-6784

Newfoundland Department of Forest Resources & Agrifoods
Wildlife Division
Bldg. #810 Pleasantville
P. O. Box 8700
St. Johns, Newfoundland A1B 4J6
(709) 729-2630

Nova Scotia Department of Natural Resources
136 Exhibition St.
Kentville, Nova Scotia B4N 4E5
(902) 679-6091

Prince Edward Island Fish & Wildlife Division
P. O. Box 2000
Charlottetown, Prince Edward Island C1A 7N8
(902) 368-4683

Saskatchewan Parks & Renewable Resources
Wildlife Branch
3211 Albert St., Rm. 436
Regina, Saskatchewan S4S 5W6
(306) 787-3017

British Columbia Ministry of the Environment, Lands & Parks
Wildlife Branch
780 Blanshard St.
Victoria, British Columbia V8V 1X5
(250) 387-9793

New Brunswick Department of Natural Resources
Fish & Wildlife Branch
P. O. Box 6000
Fredricton, New Brunswick E3B 5H1
(506) 453-2440

Northwest Territories Resources, Wildlife & Economic Development
P. O. Box 2668
Yellowknife, Northwest Territories X1A 2P9
(403) 873-7184

Ontario Ministry of Natural Resources
Wildlife Branch
300 Water St.
Peterboro, Ontario K9J 8M5
(416) 314-2000

Quebec Department of Recreation
Fish & Wildlife Division
150 Rene Levesque E. 4th Floor
Quebec City, Quebec G1R 5V7
(418) 643-3127

Yukon Department of Renewable Resources
Wildlife Branch
P. O. Box 2703
Whitehorse, Yukon Territory Y1A 2C6
(403) 667-5221

POPE & YOUNG CLUB
OFFICIAL MEASURERS

United States

ALABAMA
Jeff Baker, Daleville
Spencer Bonjean, Leeds
Randall Bush, McCalla
Dennis Campbell, Birmingham
Ronnie M. Cornhill, Hartselle
Garry Lee Frost, Glencoe
Keith Guyse, Elmore
Dr. G. Merrill Jones, Huntsville
Edward Jones, Tanner
Rett Kelly, Wetumpka
Bruce Lundy, Robertsdale
Larry J. Manning, Adamsville
Butch Parker, Thomasville
Gardner Rowell, Tuscaloosa
T. H. Tanner, Semmes
Dana Watkins, Opelika
Paul L. Watkins, Columbiana

ALASKA
Carl E. Brent, Wasilla
Steve Brockmann, Ketchikan
Ron Deis, Anchorage
Wayne DiSarro, Wasilla
Ralph Ertz, Anchorage
Dennis Goldbach, Fairbanks
Doug Larsen, Juneau
Dennis L. Lattery, Eagle River
George Moerlein, Anchorage
Stan Parkerson, Fairbanks
Edward L. Russell, Anchorage
David Widby, Anchorage

ARIZONA
Marty Allred, Safford
G. Steven Blackett, Mesa
Rodger L. Bruce, Phoenix
Jerry A. Clarno, Tucson
Michael C. Cupell, Phoenix
Thomas Dalrymple, Tucson
Peter D. Dufek, Tucson
Chris J. Dunn, Cornville
Jimmie Engelmann, Tucson
Kirk Kelso, Oro Valley
Chuck Meacham, Tucson
James C. Scott, Tucson
Richard D. Tone, Gilbert
David L. Wolf, Flagstaff
Bryan Yorksmith, Pinetop

ARKANSAS
Cliff Beaver, Compton
Michael E. Cartwright, Calico Rock
James M. DeSpain, Manila
Dan Doughty, Magnolia
J. David Ensminger, Little Rock
Jack Johnson, Rogers
Joseph W. Moody, Lonoke
Carl Turpin, Clarksville
Craig Uyeda, Conway

CALIFORNIA
Stuart Bosch, Lodi
Michael J. Bradeen, Grass Valley
Rocky Chisholm, Placentia
South Cox, Garberville
Ronald Crouch, Visalia
Ed Fanchin, Lake Matthews

Pual Farina, Santa Clara
Robert Frost, Lincoln
Patrick J. Gilligan, Hillsborough
Gary Hoffer, Madera
Guy Hooper, Eureka
Ronald Hopkins, Corona
Ron Jarvis, Stockton
Dennis Kelly, Granite Bay
Jef Lindenmayer, El Cajon
Jerry Maytum, Palmdale
Gary R. McCain, Bakersfield
Rick Pollard, Redding
Robert Solimena, Concord
Darrel Sudduth, Manteca
David J. Tande, Redding
Steve Thurmon, Auburn
Gary J. Torre, Stockton
Naomi Torrey-Simmons,
  Grizzly Flats
Doug Walker, Squaw Valley
Clifford White, Paradise
Rodney York, North Fork

COLORADO
Grant Adkisson, Canon City
Frank Alameno, Rifle
Bob Black, Whitewater
Gary W. Bohochik, Salida
Todd A. Brickel, Colorado Springs
Hal Burdick, Colorado Springs
Marvin Clyncke, Boulder
Judd Cooney, Pagosa Springs
James M. Finn, Bayfield
John L. Gardner, Durango
W. E. (Bill) Goosman, Meeker

Scott Hargrove, Crested Butte
Dave F. Holt, Lakewood
Lee Kline, Loveland
Bill Krenz, Colorado Springs
Bryon D. Long, Dolores
Bill Marchand, Grand Junction
Doug McCauley, Olathe
Michael B. Moline, Broomfield
A. M. (Mike) Oakes, Jr., Highlands Ranch
John R. Olson, Alamosa
Glenn W. Pritchard, Craig
Ronald Rockwell, Aurora
Barry J. Smith, Hot Sulphur Springs
Ronald E. Sniff, Pueblo
Dennis Stawsky, Thornton
Gregg Stults, Wray
Leo R. Sauzo II, Commerce City
Mark D. Thomson, Thornton
Jay Verzuh, Grand Junction
Don Waechtler, Glenwood Springs
Ed Wiseman, Moffat

CONNECTICUT
Christian D. Chaffin, Newtown
David Allan Sanford, West Redding
Bernard Sippin, Monroe
Edward R. Thompson, Jr., Ashford

DELAWARE
William L. Jones, Magnolia
Thaddeus M. Wishowsky, Wilmington

FLORIDA
Timothy A. Breault, Tallahassee
Cal Clevenger, Pensacola
Ronnie Everett, Gainesville
Donald Lee Francis, Quincy
William Frankenberger, Gainesville
Robert D. Hancock, Jr., Chuluota
Stanley Kirkland, Lynn Haven
Phil Palmer, Havana
Al Youman, Ocala

GEORGIA
David M. Carlock, Gainesville
William L. Cooper, Tifton
Oscar Dewberry, Bainbridge
Dave Grabow, Kennesaw
R. Larry Marchinton, Athens
J. Scott McDonald, Fort Valley
Bob Monroe, Darien
Reggie Thackston, Forsyth
David Waldrop, Hamilton

HAWAII
W. T. Yoshimoto, Honolulu

IDAHO
John E. Anderson, Boise
Steven Michael Anderson, Pocatello
Roger Atwood, Rexburg
C. Randall Byers, Moscow
Bruce Carlisle, Idaho Falls
Philip W. Cooper, Coeur d' Alene
Larry Cross, Preston
Larry Hlavaty, Soda Springs
Stanley Leake, Bayview
Michael Lewis, Twin Falls
Matt March, Jr., Eagle
Harvey J. (Jack) McNeel, Coeur d' Alene
Gary R. (Sam) McNeill, Lewiston
Kenneth R. Perry, Pocatello
Kenneth E. Ruzicka, Boise
Michael Schlegel, McCall
Ronald Sherer, Eagle
Tad Sherman, Garden City
Randy Stephens, Soda Springs
Roger Stewart, Post Falls
William Vanderhoef, Boise
C. R. Wenger, Salmon

ILLINOIS
Fred Achilles, Oswego
Rick A. Albers, Algonquin
Jim Berry, Litchfield
Thomas J. Beissel, Sterling
John D. Brassard, Milford
Patrick Cebuhar, Cuba
Richard Dewey, Pleasant Hill
Richard D. Ellington, Martinsville
Robert Erb, Rockford
Bert W. Everett, Jr., Hillsboro
Jared K. Garver, Jonesboro
Robert A. Gorge, Elk Grove Village
Keith J. Graham, Carlinville
Larry D. Grant, Godfrey
Thomas A. Grover, Rushville
Edward E. Hendricks, Mt. Sterling
Loran Hoffman, Dongola
Melvin Johnson, Metamora
Mike Kistler, Brownstown
John H. Kube, Petersburg
Gerald D. Lively, Jr., Odin
Thomas Micetich, Olney
Skip Moore, Newton
K. David Neal, Paris
Gregory A. Nixon, Quincy
Larry J. Oppe, Hanna City
Mark E. Pittman, Danville
William T. Rench, Greenville
Jack Rife, Lena
Gary S. Rogers, Palatine
Glen C. Sanderson, Champaign
Brian D. Scarnegie, Island Lake
Carl H. Spaeth, Zion
Dr. John R. Thodos, Palatine
Steven R. Tice, Springfield
Timothy D. Walmsley, Fowler
Kevin Edward Weeks, Grafton
Gary L. Wilford, Westville
Ronald L. Willmore, Decatur
Steven Wolff, Crete
George Zanoni, Westchester

INDIANA
G. Fred Asbell, Petersburg
Alan Baxter, Bloomington
H. Neil Becker, Clarks Hill
John Bogucki, North Liberty
Danny M. Bost, Portland
Jon L. Bronnenberg, Warren
Don Castrup, Newburgh
Donald L. Clark, Angola
Jeffrey A. Cumberworth, Holton
Philip Hawkins, Franklin
Brad Herndon, Brownstown
Gene Hopkins, Columbus
David M. Jackson, Rising Sun
Arthur Kragness, Schererville
Mike E. Neilson, Danville
Gregory Raatz, Fremont
Thomas Rothrock, Terre Haute
Duyane E. Tucker, Indianapolis

IOWA
Duane C. Baumler, Decorah
Bill Black, Wapello
Larry J. Briney, Cedar Rapids
William H. Bunger, Boone
Douglas Clayton, Council Bluffs
Robert Dolan, Independence
Paul "Buck" Farni, Jr., Durango
Robert Filbrandt, Dows
Kevin Freymiller, Des Moines
Leonard C. Grimes, Pella
Guy H. Hempey, Sioux City
Kenneth P. Herring, Earlham
Joel Hoenk, Spirit Lake
Ronald G. Howing, Wallingford
Jeffrey A. Japsen, Burlington
Steve Manary, Solon
Michael W. McKenna, Salix
Randy G. McPherren, Unionville
Don Mealey, Norwalk
Joseph Meder, Solon
Loren D. Miller, Lansing
Bob Moenk, Cedar Rapids
Thomas Oldfather, Elk Run Heights
Donald G. Pfeiffer, Washington
Dr. David Schrody, Clinton
Richard J. Tebbs, Fort Madison
Randy K. Templeton, Blue Grass
Thomas L. Tucker, Knoxville
Ervin Wagner, Des Moines
LaVerne E. Woock, Waterloo

KANSAS
Clavin Baumgarten, Olathe
Tommie A. Berger, Sylvan Grove
Tom E. Bowman, Wakefield
Lloyd B. Fox, Emporia
Michael Gilbert, Garden City
Blake Grabast, Osborne
Wally Hayward, Jr., Kansas City
Bill D. Hlavachick, Pratt
Leonard Hopper, Colby
Gary Hunsicker, Topeka

Connie Larson, Olsburg
Dale R. Larson, Olsburg
Lynn Leonard, Sublette
Ronald Little, Dodge City
Stan R. Mangas, Onaga
Michael McFadden, Lawrence
Tom Mosher, Emporia
Todd Murray, Buhler
David Rogers, El Dorado
Keith Sexson, Pratt
Scott Showalter, Garden City
Michael Sohm, Great Bend
Dr. Mark B. Steffen, Hutchinson
Odie Sudbeck, Seneca
Tom Swan, Mound City
Charles Swank, Great Bend
Marvin D. Whitehead, Fredonia
Daniel Willems, Windom
Greg L. Wright, Wichita

KENTUCKY
Roy Wayne Biddle, Falmouth
Joseph Bland, Simpsonville
Karl W. Brantley, Marion
Eugene Culver, New Haven
Robert A. Dale, Mt. Sterling
Roy A. Grimes, Lawreneburg
Gregory Ison, Cornettsville
Stephen T. McMillen,
    Stephensport
Kenny Morphew, Beaver Dam
John Phillips, Williamstown
Michael L. Roberts, Bagdad
Larry Ross, Elkton
Chris Sielbeck, Goshen
Dale Weddle, Nancy
Charles Wilkins, La Center

LOUISIANA
Kenneth E. Dyess, Monroe
Marty Edmunds, Ruston
Joe Herring, Baton Rouge
Jefferson Jackson, Lafayette
Robert Kimble, Minden
David W. Moreland, Baton Rouge
Tommy L. Ramage, Bastrop
Kerney Sonnier, Opelousas
Reggie Wycoff, Ferriday

MAINE
Don Cote, Eustis
Terrence H. Estes, Winslow
Harvey L. Libby, Gorham
Edgar Simonton, Union
Al Wentworth, Dover-Foxcroft

MARYLAND
Robert A. Beyer, Mt. Airy
Lance Dale Canter, Aquasco
August S. Gray, Hampstead
Dr. Hillard J. Hayzlett, Hagerstown
Frederick H. Horn, Baltimore
Walter E. Johnson, Poolesville
Steven W. Keithley, Dunkirk

Larry C. Reese, Centreville
Al Sullivan, Dunkirk
Michael E. Travis, Rock Hall
Paul Wigfield, Salisbury

MASSACHUSETTS
Richard Christoforo, Revere
Roy Goodwin, Upton
Walter L. Hingley, East
    Bridgewater
Richard N. Kimball, Belchertown
Richard LaBlue, Adams
David J. Lamoreaux, South Barre
John W. Rovedo, Jr., Bellingham
Richard Scorzafava, Granville

MICHIGAN
Wayne H. Andersen, Ludington
Gary J. Bandrow, Sterling Heights
Gary C. Berger, Houghton Lake
Clarence Bowers, Jr., Albion
Cameron Cogsdill,
    Commerce Twp.
James Dean, Williamsburg
Ned E. Fogle, Lansing
James H. Hammill, Crystal Falls
LeRoy L. Hansen, Greenville
Larry D. Hayes, Hastings
Leland Holbrook, Boyne Falls
James E. Johnson, Midland
Raymond J. Kastura, Freeland
M. Dan LaRose, Northville
Jack R. Menges, Three Rivers
Ron Morgan, Ada
Thomas A. O'Brien, Dryden
John Robert Ohmer, Yale
Paul Ranft, Niles
David L. Roose, Cadillac
Reg Smith, Whitehall
Harry W. (Pete) Squibb,
    Potterville
Joseph L. Vincent, Fenton
David J. Wellman, Bark River
John E. Wencley, Metamora
Glenn Williams, Dearborn

MINNESOTA
Dr. Eugene Altiere, Duluth
Darwin Arndt, Madelia
Chuck Bailey, Ottertail
Robert Berggren, Forest Lake
David H. Boland, Chatfield
David Brandenburger, Dayton
Patrick R. Cahill, Isanti
Ron Carlson, Mahtomedi
Christopher J. Cordes, Kenyon
Ronald D. Court, Rice
Rodney L. Dehart,
    International Falls
David B. Dickey, Aitkin
Keith David Edberg, Cannon Falls
James "Mike" Eidson, Owatonna
Adam Flod, Marine
Kevin Paul Fredrickson, Champlin

James Gorden, Deer River
Glenn Hisey, Chatfield
Kevin Hisey, Chatfield
Douglas E. Huderle, East
    Grand Forks
Floyd B. Johnson, Alvarado
Scott B. Johnson, Hoyt Lakes
Willie Johnson, Oslo
Ronald Kienholz, Dilworth
Joseph Landherr, Rose Creek
Sharon Larsen, St. Paul
Michael E. McDonald, Baxter
Thomas E. Miller, Kilkenny
Robin L. Naplin, Park Rapids
Cary Olson, Williams
Dennis L. Patrick, Palisade
Craig R. Pierce, Lewiston
Bob Sandwick, Janesville
Cecil M. Smith, Chaska
Doug B. Strecker, Coon Rapids
Larry Streiff, Rochester
Dean Westby, Mounds View

MISSISSIPPI
Randy Breland, Hollandale
Larry Castle, Kilmichael
Dan Cotton, Macon
Harry Daniels, Carthage
J. Dale Hale, Isola
Don Lewis, Brookhaven
Jim McCrory, Greenwood
Corey Neill, Carrollton
Robert G. Skinner, Wiggins
Bobby J. Wilson, Smithville

MISSOURI
Jerry Abernathy, Bland
Marc J. Bowen, Blue Springs
Doug Campbell, Stockton
John Detjen, Frankford
R. Dale Dortch, Ozark
Ronnie Gadberry, St. Mary
Brett Gray, Clinton
Heath Halley, Milan
Steven A. Hardy, New London
Dennis Harper, Gladstone
Roger Hensley, Nevada
James Holdenried, Jr., Oakville
Dan P. Hollingsworth,
    Jefferson City
Dan Janes, Hannibal
Daniel L. Johnson, Blue Springs
Bill Kohne, Sullivan
Martin Marks, Meadville
James W. Martin, Weatherby
Joe Ed McCray, Fulton
Anthony Mihalevich, Kirksville
Steve Moody, Mansfield
James E. Mraz, Fenton
Chris M. Murphy, Chesterfield
Charles A. Myers, Greenfield
David Nance, Grandin
Chris Patton, Maryville
Wayne Porath, Columbia

Dale H. Ream, Jr., Unionville
Joe Ream, Unionville
Donald P. Roper, Farmington
Carl Schwarz, St. Louis
Lee Smith, Trenton
Gerald W. Webber, Unionville
Jerry M. Worley, Lamar

MONTANA
Jerry Brown, Libby
Ben R. Cook, Rexford
G. L. "Buck" Damone, Lewistown
Neal Davis, Dillon
Mark George DeLong, Billings
Robert DesJardins, Great Falls
Frank H. Dodge, Jr., Hamilton
Bryan Jay Erickson, Glasgow
John Fleharty, Lewistown
Dwayne C. Garner, Missoula
Dr. Nicholas J. Gray, Whitefish
Bernie Hildebrand, Miles City
M. R. James, Whitefish
Larry Jensen, Lewistown
Lorraine Karwaski, Helena
Fred J. King, Bozeman
Scott Koelzer, West Yellowstone
Vern Lindquist, Glendive
Bill Matteson, Fort Peck
John Morris II, Bozeman
Lyle R. Prell, Forsyth
Stan Rauch, Victor
Jeff M. Reiter, Miles City
Jack Reneau, Missoula
Roger L. Selner, Livingston
David W. Sorensen, Harlowton
Brad Stewart, Billings
Graham S. Taylor, Great Falls
Chris Tonkinson, Missoula
Thomas F. Wagner, Bozeman
Lewis Yearout, Great Falls

NEBRASKA
Samuel D. Cowan III, Beatrice
Thomas E. Day, Republican City
Ray Dierking, Broken Bow
Michael J. Dudzinski, Elkhorn
Ken Elshof, Grand Island
Bradley S. English, Grand Island
Daniel E. Evasco, Oshkosh
Donald Goracke, Burr
Denny C. Graham, Holdrege
Lee B. Hansen, Superior
Jerry R. Kelly, Omaha
Ricky Krueger, West Point
Richard Mauch, Bassett
Donald Ace Morgan, Kearney
Russell A. Mort, Nebraska City
George Nason, North Platte
James H. Newman, Fremont
Richard E. Placzek, McCook
Dan Rochford, North Platte
Randy G. Stutheit, Lincoln
Harvey Suetsugu, Alliance
Bruce D. Trindle, Norfolk

Kurt C. VerCauteren, Lincoln
William L. Vodehnal, Bassett
Bradley L. Wiese, Benkelman
Steve Woitaszewski, Lincoln

NEVADA
Louis Victor Clark, Verdi
Chris J. Coleman, Carson City
Gilbert Hernandez, Elko
Robert A. McDonald, Las Vegas
Anthony L. "Tony" Mudd, Reno
Paul Podborny, Ely
David Snyder, Las Vegas
Dennis Spawn, Las Vegas
Gregg Tanner, Fallon
Mike Wickersham, Las Vegas

NEW HAMPSHIRE
Roscoe Blaisdell, Raymond
Brian R. Brochu, Rochester
William Earle, Portsmouth
Brian J. Emerson, Groveton
Reginald Moore, Keene

NEW JERSEY
Emanuele J. Barone, Kinnelon
David Burke, Egg Harbor
Leonard Cardinale, Belleville
David Chanda, Trenton
John Janelli, Union City
Cindy Kuenstner, Trenton
Robert C. Lund, Belvidere
James McCloskey, Jr., Lawrenceville
Ronald S. Newman, Stanton
Susan Predl, Hampton
Fred Snyder, Woodbury

NEW MEXICO
Douglas J. Aikin, Los Alamos
David Collis, San Ysidro
Tom David, Albuquerque
Dan P. Fleming, Bosque Farms
Fred Fox, Silver City
Volney W. Howard, Jr., Las Cruces
Ronald W. Madsen, Albuquerque
Ray Milligan, Chama
Terry Sanders, Albuquerque
Lynn Saxon, Hobbs
Roger Schoolcraft, Tularosa
C. Bob Stevens, Farmington
George L. Taulman, Taos
Eudane Vicenti, Dulce
Tom J. Watts, Dulce
James S. Willems, Farmington

NEW YORK
David F. Baldwin, Patchogue
Charles G. Banks, Jr., Katonah
John W. Borlang, Hudson Falls
Alfred D. Cheney, Gloversville
Merritt C. Compton, Trumansburg
Stephen L. Cook, Sr., Ossining
Brian Dam, Vernon
James W. Dowd, Oriskany Falls

Bob Estes, Caledonia
Nelson Harrington, Delmar
Donald W. Hunt, Nichols
Collins F. Kellogg, Sr., Croghan
Richard Kent, Farmingville
Peter M. Labushesky,
    North Tonawanda
Phil Liddle, Schoharie
James Matuszewski, Flanders
John McAteer, Dix Hills
James Pasco, Oswego
Roger D. Smith, Naples
Robert Songin, Rochester
Peter N. Synyard, Farmington
Jon P. Thomas, Staten Island
Robert L. Turk, Silver Creek
Victor Zarnock, Pearl River

NORTH CAROLINA
Denton O. Baumbarger,
    Burlington
Ramon N. Bell, Stokesdale
Richard W. Burnette,
    Hendersonville
Donald H. Cockman, Robbins
Michael Louis DeAngury,
    Charlotte
Jim Edwards, Colerain
Gary W. Evers, Pleasant Garden
Bernard J. Garcarz, Hendersonville
Harlan T. Hall, Burlington
Donald A. Hayes, State Road
J. Scott Osborne, Sanford
Michael H. Seamster, Providence
David Eugene Stepp,
    Hendersonville
Benny R. Wilhelm, Statesville

NORTH DAKOTA
Timothy Belland, Mapleton
Warren O. Buss, Fargo
Dane K. Eider, Bismarck
Tim Finley, Oberon
Scott M. Lang, Bismarck
James V. McKenzie, Mandan
Wayne Muth, Mandan
John Plesuk, Minot
Craig Richardson, Williston
Paul R. Shannon, Bismarck
Cecil I. Tharp, Williston
Lee M. Wahlund, Carrington

OHIO
Scott T. Bare, Zanesville
George W. Bauer, West Union
Mark Buehrer, Leipsic
Randall J. Clark, Covington
Barry Cooper, Galena
David M. Couch, Okeana
Lloyd Culbertson, Athens
Roger Davis, Newbury
Mike Dickess, Ironton
Jack E. Henderson, Barnesville
Tom Hentrick, Kettering

Thomas L. Hughes, Chillicothe
William E. Lee, Jr., Dayton
Charles M. Martin, Massillon
Michael D. McQuigg,
   Fredericktown
Gerald E. Meyer, Millfield
Mike Moutoux, Stone Creek
John Myers, Toledo
David Orndorf, Sunbury
Jeff Parks, Greenville
Randy Oliver Pepper,
   North Canton
Ronald Perrine, Sr., Xenia
Ron Riel, Mt. Vernon
Jack Satterfield, Jr., Pomeroy
Mike Serio, Cincinnati
Randall C. Smith, Harrod
Ralph C. Stephen, Canton
Elbert Butch Todd, Cambridge
Don Weisenbarger, Troy
James R. Williamson,
   East Springfield

OKLAHOMA
Jontie W. Aldrich, Coweta
Deveral Bridges, Chandler
Kevin Cackler, Grove
Dennis Campbell, Ponca City
Sonny Charboneau, Wagoner
Tracy L. Daniel, Ponca City
Jim Dougherty, Tulsa
James Edwards, Stonewall
Jeff B. Fitts, Claremore
Dennis Geary, Ardmore
Richard J. Hoar, Broken Arrow
David Jilge, Prague
Arlen Lipper, Midwest City
Kevin Lyon, Edmond
Steven A. Schmid, Tulsa
Michael G. Shaw, Oklahoma City
Rod W. Smith, Lawton

OREGON
Glenn W. Abbott, Sandy
Robert J. Bouret, Portland
Eldon "Buck" Buckner, Baker City
David W. Doran, Bend
Curt Harrison, Fossil
Dr. Stephen Herrera, Sutherlin
Larry D. Jones, Springfield
Gary Madison, Prineville
Gary Maytum, Yamhill
Steven A. Mazzola, Grants Pass
Robert Merrill, Bend
Stanley D. Miles, Corvallis
George R. Mitchell, Bend
Don Poole, Redmond
Donald Rajnus, Malin
Charles Sarrett, LaGrande
Eugene Smith, Jr., Joseph
John E. Stone, Lebanon

PENNSYLVANIA
Thomas P. Bartholomew,
   Greenville
Rodney T. Bear, Beaver
George H. Block, Eighty Four
Glenn L. Bowers, Dillsburg
Timothy O. Bowers, Dillsburg
Edward T. Clark, Austin
Ed Defibaugh, Venus
Phillip Durr, McKees Rocks
Carl Graybill, Jr., Harrisburg
Darrell W. Grove, Norwood
Frank "Rit" Heller, Reading
Mark Hockenberry, Meadville
Dr. Steven Homyack, Jr., Robesonia
Dennis E. Jones, Ligonier
Perry G. Klein, Ridgway
Charles Kohler, Butler
Daniel J. Lalli, Erie
Rick A. Latshaw, Somerset
Ronald G. Lowe, Strasburg
Gregory B. McPhillips, Pennsburg
Barry K. Moore, Blandon
William P. Nordby, Rural Valley
Mark Parker, Selinsgrove
Dennis Scicchitano, Locust Gap
Jacob F. Serfass, Jr., Thornhurst
Curt Slopey, West Grove
Thomas Slusser, Bloomsburg
Richard C. Strayer,
   McConnellsburg
Daniel R. Strickland, Towanda
James B. Walter, Jr., Pittsburgh
Ronald A. Worden, Shinglehouse

RHODE ISLAND
Ernest A. LaFazia, Chepachet

SOUTH CAROLINA
David Baumann, Bonneau
Robert W. Gooding, Greenwood
William E. Mahan, Bonneau
Derrell A. Shipes, Columbia

SOUTH DAKOTA
Paul A. Anderson, Crooks
Kevin Bertsch, St. Lawrence
Robert A. Fraser, Brandon
Larry F. Fredrickson, Chamberlain
A. Dean Gretschmann, Pierre
Eldon Hagen, Sioux Falls
Danny Havens, Spearfish
Roger Heupel, Bath
Daniel L. Jass, Rapid City
Thomas Kuck, Aberdeen
Craig R. Oberle, Mellette
Ron Pesek, Yankton
Arthur H. Richardson, Custer
Paul Sieg, Watertown

TENNESSEE
Buddy Adkisson, Talbott
Norman B. Bates,
   Thompson Station
Terry Ray Chapman, Memphis
Clarence D. Coffey, Crossville
Joseph C. Coleman, Jackson
Tom Grimsley, Jackson
Larry C. Marcum, Nashville
Thomas Pinkston, Cordova
James A. Reed, Tullahoma
Robert D. Ripley, Talbott

TEXAS
Gilbert T. Adams, Beaumont
Kenneth W. Baker, Vernon
Viron Barbay, Milam
Ben Bartlett, Lufkin
Earle Bateman III, Fischer
Dale N. Bigger, Humble
James E. Borron, Midland
Ty S. Brumfield, Sulphur Springs
Owen P. "Trey" Carpenter III,
   Burnet
Joseph W. Carroll, Katy
Tommy L. Caruthers, Sr., Denton
Curtis S. Chastain, Fort Worth
Randolph Coleman, San Antonio
Ronald J. Collier, Austin
Gary Damuth, Brady
J. Paul Ellis, Round Rock
Edwin J. Foreman, Orangefield
Jeffrey L. Foster, Georgetown
Earl Griffith, Marble Falls
Mickey W. Hellickson, Kingsville
Barry Hurtt, Farmers Branch
Douglas R. Johnson, Lubbock
Denzil Jones, Springtown
Billy R. Leach, Texas City
James R. Lewis, Cedar Hill
T. A. Low IV, Brenham
Ron McCoy, Harwood
Clyde Miller, Corpus Christi
James H. Miller, Canadian
Michael Morris, Del Rio
Michael W. Murphey, Deer Park
Tony Naismith, Livingston
Curtis D. O'Brien, Madisonville
Dean Oatman, Adkins
Robert L. Oliver, Abilene
Ronnie Parsons, Lubbock
Mike Pillow, Angleton
Brent Pool, Pflugerville
Mike Ramage, Spur
Randal A. Reeves, Spring
Ray Roussett, Jr., Tomball
A. C. "Bubba" Smith, San Antonio
Don Sherpy, Dallas
Garth Stokes, Texarkana
Ed Strayhorn, Austin
Robert D. Sweisthal, Spring
Kyle Wells, Iowa Park
Dane Widner, Odessa
Ken Witt, Burleson

UTAH
Dave Baierline, West Valley
William Bradwisch, Farmington

Donald E. Campbell,
    Pleasant Grove
Todd Scott Hinkins, Orangeville
Kenny Leo, Price
Jerry Mason, Brigham City
David B. Nielsen, American Fork
Robert S. Price, St. George
Brad W. Robinson, Koosharem
Dennis L. Shirley, Elk Ridge

VERMONT
Ron Boucher, Wallingford

VIRGINIA
Robert Byrne, Haymarket
Max Carpenter, Dayton
Gary E. Carty, Bristol
Clay Harrison, Great Falls
W. Matt Knox, Forest
Dr. William MacCarty III,
    South Boston
Robert H. Mayer, Petersburg
William Harold Nesbitt,
    Woodbridge
Don Alan Quackenbush,
    Harrisonburg
Dennis F. Scott, Hopewell
C. D. Tarter, Wytheville

WASHINGTON
Robert "Red" Buchholz,
    Mt. Vernon
Larry R. Carey, Spokane
Brooks Carmichael, Poulsbo
Kevin Charles Conners, Roy
Timothy J. Conrads, Vashon
John O. "Buzzi" Cook III,
    North Bend
Dean H. Cook, Jr., Naches
Lance B. Cussons, Yakima
Jack Davis, Mt. Vernon
Donne Durst, Port Orchard
John Durst, Port Orchard
G. L. "Jerry" Egbert, Vancouver
Rick Kobel, Enumclaw
Henry T. Kohler, Spokane
Kevin C. Krause, Port Orchard
Larry C. Lack, Port Angeles
Charles Lynde, Ridgefield
Gail Martin, Walla Walla
Dr. Robert A. Maves, Twisp
Greg McTee, Snohomish
Charles B. Smith, Kettle Falls
Russ Spaulding, Auburn
Glenn St. Charles, Seattle
Jay St. Charles, Des Moines
Robert Trask, Silverdale
George Tsukamoto, Olympia
Wayne Van Zwoll, Bridgeport
Tim J. Wiggins, Auburn

WEST VIRGINIA
Craig J. Acheson, Morgantown
Thomas Allen, Elkins

Larry A. Berry, Beckley
Greg Bonecutter, Sr., Letart
Kevin M. Bowles, Rock Cave
Michael Burks, Bluefield
Tom Dotson, Point Pleasant
James H. Durst, Henderson
John D. Edman, Washington
James Evans, Fairmont
Jim Farren, Charleston
Allan C. Glasscock, Petersburg
James Hill, Parkersburg
Ray W. Knotts, French Creek
Larry W. McCarty, Apple Grove

WISCONSIN
Steven Ashley, Hudson
Patrick Barwick, West Allis
Dave Bathke, Franklin
Michael Beaufeaux, Rhinelander
Thomas Bloomingdale, Hartford
Richard A. Case, Ontario
Jack Cook, Mondovi
Craig Cousins, Milltown
Christopher W. Fechner, La Crosse
Caren Fish, Pepin
Steven Fish, Pepin
Donnie Fisher, Eastman
Robert C. Fitzsimons, Dodgeville
Clark Gallup, La Crosse
Thomas M. Gehl, Racine
Stan Godfrey, Whitewater
Donald W. Goers, Shawano
Bill Grosskreutz, Greenbush
Roger W. Hansen, South Range
Larrie Hazen, Mt. Hope
Jim Hjort, Eau Claire
J. Robert Hults, Hartford
Lester Jass, Merrillan
K-Tal Johnson, Janesville
Michael J. Kaufmann, Birnamwood
Arlyn E. Loomans, Rhinelander
Kris D. Nelson, Medford
Jim Nowakowski, Marinette
David A. O'Brien, Dresser
Thomas A. Orlikowski,
    Stevens Point
Paul F. Ostrum, Hayward
Robert L. Pagel, Mequon
Ken J. Rimer, Hudson
John Romans, New Berlin
Curtis J. Rotering, Waumandee
Richard Schimenti, Kenosha
Richard Schreiber, Portage
Steve Sirianni, Wausau
Richard Strait, Siren
Debra L. Tegels, Hayward
Brian Tessmann, Waukesha
Walter White, Cable
Stan Zirbel, Greenleaf

WYOMING
Chuck Anderson, Jr., Laramie
Mike Barrett, Dayton
Shawn R. Bayless, Lander

Jon Bloom, Green River
Jerry R. Bowen, Wheatland
Gary Cole, Newcastle
Lonny L. Curtis, Baggs
Keith Dana, Rock Springs
Vic Dana, Rock Springs
Robert H. Hanson, Wapiti
David J. Hinton, Sheridan
G. Richard "Dick" Keeney, Casper
Dick Mankin, Gillette
Pat McAteer, Casper
Ron Niziolek, Cody
David A. Pawlicki, Cheyenne
Ronell Skinner, Bedford
Rene Suda, Dubois
George K. Warner, Sheridan
James Willcox, Rawlins

Canada

ALBERTA
Sylvester Baier, Camrose
David R. Coupland, Calgary
Albert England, Lloydminster
Brian Fode, Foremost
John M. (Jack) Graham,
　Edmonton
Duane Hicks, Tofield
Gunter Lemke, Calgary
Duane Nelson, Glenwood
David Paplawski, St. Albert
Dave Richardson, Calgary
Brian A. Rudyk, Athabasca
Steve K. Swinhoe, Ft. McMurray
Ryk Visscher, Edmonton
Brent Watson, Grande Prairie

BRITISH COLUMBIA
Brian Churchill, Fort St. John
Douglas Clinkenbeard, Smithers
Bill Dear, Nelson
Scott Ebert, Fort St. John
Robert Frew, Fruitvale
Peter Halbig, Chilliwack
Larry Henriet, Sparwood
Dr. William G. Hills, Cranbrook
Wilfred Klingsat, West Vancouver
Peter Martinson, Terrace
R. J. (Bob) Petrie, Kamloops
Laurie Riedel, Williams Lake
Kenneth W. Scheer, Abbotsford
Paul Stone, Grand Forks
Ed Swanson, Cranbrook
Allan Tew, 150 Mile House

MANITOBA
Delmar E. Bamford, Birtle
Vince Crichton, Winnipeg
Geordie Daneliuk, Russell
Mike Dudar, Ethelbert
L. Greg Fehr, Gladstone
Jerry C. Hayduk, West St. Paul
Rick Hogg, Rosser
Scott Homan, Brandon
Ron Kehler, St. Francois Xavier
Russell K. Mehling, Steinbach
Shelley Mehling, Steinbach
Brad Minshull, Pierson
Jamie Poole, McAuley
Gil Rodger, Brandon
R. Mark Routledge, Kenton
J. Rudy Truman, Winnipeg

NEW BRUNSWICK
Mike A. Bowling, Saint John
Danny C. Mott, Saint John

NEWFOUNDLAND
W. Charles Banfield, Deer Lake
Gerard R. Beaulieu, Deer Lake
Laurance A. Smith, Stephenville

NORTHWEST TERRITORIES
Warren St. Germaine, Yellowknife

NOVA SCOTIA
Daniel G. Caldwell, Windsor
Allan J. Gallant, Middle Sackville

ONTARIO
David T. Beaudry, Ear Falls
Carl Doerner, Waterloo
Roland Hasner, Sudbury
John W. Horner, Gloucester
Dennis Laporte, Belle River
Fred Law, Cambridge
Jack Leggo, Inglewood
Don J. McVittie, Huntsville
R. Brian Oates, Erin
Greg Peters, London
Richard M. Poulin, Nepean
Fred Robinson, Bonfield
Ian Robinson, Thunder Bay

QUEBEC
Alex Davidson, Sawyerville
Michel Jerome, La Sarre
Ken H. Taylor, Rouyn-Noranda

SASKATCHEWAN
Robert Allemand, Shaunavon
Allan Brehaut, Wawota
Bill Deyo, Moose Jaw
Chad Fink, Assiniboia
Dennis John Francais, Nipawin
Howard Hanson, Mankota
Murray Allan Hanson, Watrous
Allan Hill, Moose Jaw
Allan J. Holtvogt, Annaheim
John Kuzma, Norquay
Wayne Leonhardt, Saskatoon
Glenn M. Loffler, Glenavon
Joyce E. Lorenz, Raymore
Archie Lovelace, Pilot Butte
Frank Mosley, Estevan
Brett E. Seidle, Medstead

Europe
Pascal Perrin, Paris

Mexico
Jose C. Trevino, Chihuahua